Serving collectors since 1863

1987
Specialized Catalogue of United States Stamps

SIXTY-FIFTH EDITION

**CONFEDERATE STATES
CANAL ZONE — DANISH WEST INDIES
GUAM — HAWAII — UNITED NATIONS
UNITED STATES ADMINISTRATION:
Cuba - Puerto Rico - Philippines - Ryukyu Islands
Marshall Islands - Micronesia - Palau**

PRESIDENT	Wayne Lawrence
EXECUTIVE VP/PUBLISHER	Charles M. Pritchett
EDITORIAL DIRECTOR	Richard L. Sine
EDITOR	William W. Cummings
ASSISTANT EDITOR	Elaine Cummings
PRICING EDITOR	Martin J. Frankevicz
NEW ISSUES EDITOR	Robin A. Denaro
EDITORIAL ASSISTANTS	Joyce A. Cecil
	Julie A. Sharp
ASSOCIATE EDITOR	Irving Koslow
ART/PRODUCTION DIRECTOR	Edward Heys
DIRECTOR OF MARKETING & SALES	Stuart J. Morrissey
ADVERTISING MANAGER	David Lodge
PROMOTIONAL MANAGER	Craig A. McIntyre

Copyright© 1986 by

Scott Publishing Co.

911 Vandemark Road, Sidney, Ohio 45365
A division of AMOS PRESS INC., publishers of *Linn's Stamp News, Coin World, Cars & Parts* magazine and *The Sidney Daily News.*

TABLE OF CONTENTS

INDEX	5
Domestic Letter Rates	6
Special Notice	13
Acknowledgments	14
Information for Collectors	15
Territorial and Statehood Dates	39
IDENTIFIER	41
Commemorative Index	79
UNITED STATES	83
Confederate States	770
United Nations	916
Number Changes	979

Copyright Notice

The contents of this book, are owned exclusively by Scott Publishing Co. and all rights thereto are reserved under the Pan American and Universal Copyright Conventions.

Copyright© 1986 by Scott Publishing Co., Sidney, OH. Printed in U.S.A.

COPYRIGHT NOTE
Permission is hereby given for the use of material in this book and covered by copyright if:
  (a) The material is used in advertising matter, circulars or price lists for the purpose of offering stamps for sale or purchase at the prices listed therein; and
  (b) Such use is incidental to the business of buying and selling stamps and is limited in scope and length, i.e., it does not cover a substantial portion of the total number of stamps issued by any country or of any special category of stamps of any country; and
  (c) Such material is not used as part of any catalogue, stamp album or computerized or other system based upon the Scott catalogue numbers, or in any updated valuations of stamps not offerd for sale or purchase; and
  (d) Such use is not competitive with the business of the copyright owner.
  Any use of the material in this book which does not satisfy all the foregoing conditions is forbidden in any form unless permission in each instance is given in writing by the copyright owner.

Trademark Notice

The terms SCOTT, SCOTT'S, SCOTT CATALOGUE NUMBERING SYSTEM, SCOTT CATALOGUE NUMBER, SCOTT NUMBER and abbreviations thereof, are trademarks of Scott Publishing Co., used to identify its publications and its copyrighted system for identifying and classifying postage stamps for dealers and collectors. These trademarks are to be used only with the prior consent of Scott Publishing Co.

No part of this work may be reproduced in any form or by any means, electronic or mechanical, including photocopying, without permission in writing from Scott Publishing Co.

Please Note

Effective as of 1978, designs of all United States stamps are copyrighted.

Scott Catalogues accept all advertisements in good faith, but does not endorse or assume any responsibility for the contents of advertisements.

ISBN: 0-89487-083-1   Library of Congress Card No. 2-3301

HS & C

A NAME YOU CAN TRUST

- SELLING QUALITY MATERIAL
- BUYING at top prices for collections, accumulations, estates & inventories
- INVESTMENT COUNSELING, Pension plans
- PUBLIC AUCTIONS
- APPRAISALS
- RETAIL STORE
- NUMISMATIC MATERIAL

FOR ADDITIONAL INFORMATION SEE OUR BUSINESS REPLY CARD
IN THE BACK OF THIS CATALOGUE.

HOURS
Open Tuesday through Saturday 10 AM to 6 PM
Closed Sunday and Monday

HUNTINGTON STAMP & COIN

1060 E. Jericho Tpke., Huntington, N.Y. 11743
(516) 421-5230

Outside N.Y. Call Toll-free 800-645-5441

WE ARE BUYING!!

We at *REGAL STAMP COMPANY*, are Buying everything in stamps and are paying *TOP* market prices in order to obtain any better stamp collections, accumulations and estates. We will buy whatever you have - *ANY COUNTRY! ANY QUANTITY!* From an individual Rarity or Specialized collection, to a Worldwide collection or dealer stock. Large quantities, Investment holdings, or promotional items are especially needed! **WE ALSO BUY ALL COIN COLLECTIONS AND ESTATES**

You name it, we are interested! Call us *NOW!* TOLL FREE AT 1-800-772-0054 to discuss what you have for sale. We will travel immediately to view and purchase large collections or even give you a free estimate of what we can pay, over the phone! Not bad, a *FREE* appraisal over the telephone!

You may then ship your stamps directly to us by registered mail (if bulky use United Parcel Service) for our immediate top cash offer - subject, of course, to your approval. Years of *COURTEOUS* service and *TOP* prices, guarantees your complete *SATISFACTION!*

CALL TODAY — TOLL FREE

1-800-772-0054
In New York State Call 1-212-689-1919

When you talk to *REGAL*, you are dealing with a company with an international reputation for fairness. You will join the many satisfied collectors and dealers who have sold to us in the past, and who continue to do so. We are members of every major society, including the A.S.D.A., I.F.S.D.A., A.P.S., S.O.P., P.F., A.R.A. just to name a few.

We are located in the heart of New York City, (not a post office box in a small town) so you know who you are dealing with. We look forward to hearing from you soon!

Regal Stamp Company   Date_____

379 Fifth Avenue - New York, NY 10016

- ☐ I am interested in selling my individual stamps or collections. Please have one of your buyers contact me.
  I estimate their value to be $_____
- ☐ I am a collector, dealer or investor and would like to receive your monthly listings, including your wholesale specials.
- ☐ I am interested in buying Rare stamps for an investment. I would like more information on how I can start a rare stamp portfolio. (Minimum $5,000.)

Name_____

Address_____

City_____ State _____ Zip _____

Telephone (_____)_____

REGAL STAMP COMPANY

"America's Leading Cash Buyers!"

Phone Toll Free 1-800-772-0054 in N.Y. State call 1-212-689-1919

379 Fifth Avenue   New York, NY 10016

INDEX

The capital letters in parentheses and below "Revenues" are used with the catalogue numbers to indicate the different classifications.

Air Post Envelopes & Letter Sheets (UC)	596
Air Post Postal Cards (UXC)	629
Air Post Semi-Official Stamp (CLI)	389
Air Post Special Delivery (CE)	389
Air Post Stamps (C)	373
Air Post Stamps — Quantities Issued	490
Booklet Panes, Booklets	442
Canal Zone	799
Carrier's Stamps (LO, LB)	491
Certified Mail Stamps (FA)	394
Christmas Seals (WX)	758
Commemorative Panels	734
Commemorative Stamps — Index	79
Commemorative Stamps — Quantities Issued	486
Confederate States General Issues	789
Confederate States Postmasters' Provisionals	770
Cuba	825
Danish West Indies	831
Die and Plate Proofs (-P)	702
Encased Postage Stamps	745
Envelopes and Wrappers (U, W)	553
Envelope watermarks	554, 586
First Day Covers — Air Post	440
First Day Covers — Postage	422
Guam	835
Hawaii	837
Imperforate Coil Stamps (-S, -E)	485
International Reply Coupons	750
Local Stamps (L, LU)	497
Local Handstamped Covers	534
Marshall Islands	844
Micronesia	848
Newspapers and Periodicals (PR)	411
Offices in China (K)	399
Official Envelopes (UO)	603
Official Postal Card (UZ)	632
Official Stamps (O)	400
Palau	851
Parcel Post Due Stamps (JQ)	421
Parcel Post Stamps (Q)	418
Philippines	857
Postage	89
Postage Currency	749
Postage Due Stamps (J)	395
Postal Cards (UX)	609
Postal Cards, Paid Reply (UY)	625
Postal Insurance Labels (QI)	420
Postal Note Stamps (PN)	417
Postal Savings Mail (O)	409
Postal Savings Stamps (PS)	741
Postal Savings Envelopes (UO)	607
Postmasters General	40
Postmasters' Provisionals (X, XU)	83
Post Office Seals (OX)	752
Proofs (-P)	702
Puerto Rico	880
Registration (F)	394
Ryukyu Islands	884
R Revenues, General and Documentary	633
RB " Proprietary	652
RC " Future Delivery	654
RD " Stock Transfer	655
RE " Cordials and Wines	660
RE " Puerto Rico, Rectified Spirits	882
RF " Playing Cards	668
RFV " Playing Cards, Virgin Isls.	665
RG " Silver Tax	665
RH " Cigarette Tubes	666
RI " Potato Tax	667
RJ " Tobacco Sales Tax	667
RJA " Narcotic Tax	667
RK " Consular Service Fee	669
RL " Customs Fee	670
RM " Embossed Revenue Stamped Paper	670
RN " Revenue Stamped Paper	677
RO " Private Die Match	682
RP " Private Die Canned Fruit	685
RS " Private Die Medicine	685
RT " Private Die Perfumery	690
RU " Private Die Playing Cards	691
RV " Motor Vehicle Use	692
RVB " Boating	691
RW " Hunting Permit	695
RX " Distilled Spirits Excise Tax	700
RY " Firearms	701
RZ " Rectification Tax	701
'R.F.' Overprints (CM)	390
'R.F.' Stamped Envelopes (UCM)	390
Sanitary Fair Stamps (WV)	550
Savings Stamps (S)	742
Shanghai (Offices in China) (K)	399
Souvenir Cards	730
Special Delivery (E)	391
Special Handling (QE)	420
Specimen (-S)	735
Telegraph Stamps (T)	540
Trial Color Proofs (-TC)	718
Treasury Savings Stamps (TS)	744
United Nations	916
Vending and Affixing Machine Perforations	478
War Savings Stamps (WS)	743

DOMESTIC LETTER RATES

Effective Date	Prepaid	Collect
1845, July 1		
Reduction from 6c to 25c range on single-sheet letters.		
Under 300 miles, per ½ oz.	5c	5c
Over 300 miles, per ½ oz.	10c	10c
Drop letters	2c	
1847-1848		
East, to or from Havana (Cuba) per ¼ oz.	12½c	12½c
East, to or from Chagres (Panama) per ½ oz.	20c	20c
East, to or from Panama, across Isthmus, per ½ oz.	30c	30c
To or from Astoria (Ore.) or Pacific Coast, per ½ oz.	40c	40c
Along Pacific Coast, per ½ oz.	12½c	12½c
1847, July 1		
Unsealed circulars 1 oz. or less	3c	
1851, July 1		
Elimination of rates of 1847-1848 listed above		
Up to 3,000 miles, per ½ oz.	3c	5c
Over 3,000 miles, per ½ oz.	6c	10c
Drop letters	1c	
Unsealed circulars		
1 oz. or less up to 500 miles	1c	
Over 500 miles to 1,500 miles	2c	
Over 1,500 miles to 2,500 miles	3c	
Over 2,500 miles to 3,500 miles	4c	
Over 3,500 miles	5c	
1852, Sept. 30		
Unsealed circulars		
3 oz. or less anywhere in U. S.	1c	
Each additional ounce	1c	
(Double charge if collect.)		
1855, April 1		
Prepayment made compulsory.		
Not over 3,000 miles, per ½ oz.	3c	
Over 3,000 miles, per ½ oz.	10c	
Drop letters	1c	
1863, July 1		
Distance differential eliminated.		
All parts of United States, per ½ oz.	3c	

Effective Date	Prepaid
1883, Oct. 1	
Letter rate reduced one-third.	
All parts of United States, per ½ oz.	2c
1885, July 1	
Weight increased to 1 oz.	
All parts of United States, per 1 oz.	2c
1896, Oct. 1	
Rural Free Delivery started.	
1917, Nov. 2	
War emergency.	
All parts of United States, per 1 oz.	3c
1919, July 1	
Restoration of pre-war rate.	
All parts of United States, per 1 oz.	2c
1932, July 6	
Rise due to depression.	
All parts of United States, per 1 oz.	3c
1958, Aug. 1	
All parts of United States, per 1 oz.	4c
1963, Jan. 7	
All parts of United States, per 1 oz.	5c
1968, Jan. 7	
All parts of United States, per 1 oz.	6c
1971, May 16	
All parts of United States, per 1 oz.	8c
1974, Mar. 2	
All parts of United States, per 1 oz.	10c
1975, Dec. 31	
All parts of United States, 1st oz.	13c
1978, May 29	
All parts of United States, 1st oz.	15c
1981, Mar. 22	
All parts of United States, 1st oz.	18c
1981, Nov. 1	
All parts of United States, 1st oz.	20c
1985, Feb. 17	
All parts of United States, 1st oz.	22c

United States Commemorative Album Pages

The Album you can keep up-to-date with year after year after year

Incomparable? Exceptional? Extraordinary? Yes, these and other superlatives have been used by collectors over the years to describe America's favorite White Ace: The popular album for U.S. Commemoratives.

Featuring illustrated frames for singles of all commemoratives since the 1893 Columbians, this sectional album also has background stories that place the stamps in their historic perspective. And to highlight the stamps, there's a distinctively designed border with the multicolored pictorial illuminations that have become a White Ace trademark. But there's more to this White Ace than meets the eye, for the heavy album page card stock is acid-free, your assurance of long-lasting freshness. and the looseleaf style provides flexiblility, so the album, can grow with your collection. What's more, with annual suplements it always will be up-to-date.

Choose this White Ace album for your U.S. Commemorative singles (or one of its commpanion albums for blocks or plate blocks). You will be opting for America's superlative stamp album.

COLORFUL...HISTORICAL...SECTIONAL

WHITE ACE COMMEMORATIVE ALBUM PRICES	
SINGLE PAGES (1893-1939) Part One	$9.25
SINGLE PAGES (1940-1949) Part Two	7.15
SINGLE PAGES (1950-1970) Part Three	17.25
SINGLE PAGES (1971-1979) Part Four	16.25
SINGLE PAGES (1980-1985) Part Five	16.25
Matching Border Blank-Pack of 15	3.35
Gold-stamped Deluxe Binder	10.50
Binder Dustcase	6.75
Commemorative album pages are available for blocks and plate blocks. Ask for complete list.	

ON MAIL ORDERS . . . please add $1.50 for packing
(Canada and Foreign According to Weight)

White Ace

AVAILABLE AT YOUR FAVORITE STAMP SHOP OR DIRECT

THE WASHINGTON PRESS
PUBLISHERS FLORHAM PARK, NEW JERSEY 07932

Why are ScottMounts Superior?

Because...

- They're completely interchangeable with Showgard® mounts, come with 10% more mounts to the package.
- They're made of two welded sheets of 100 percent inert polystyrol foil.
- They're center-split across the back for easy insertion of your stamps.
- The Black-backed mounts are totally opaque for perfect stamp framing.
- Crystal clear mount faces eliminate distracting distortions.
- Double layers of gum assure stay-put bonding, yet they're easily peeled off.
- They come packed in their own reuseable storage trays.
- To get your **FREE SAMPLE PACKAGE** of ScottMounts, circle reader service card number 100.

Available from your local dealer or direct from Scott.

SCOTT® P.O. Box 828
Sidney, OH 45365

1987 our 69th year

STAMPS WANTED

WE URGENTLY NEED ADDITIONAL MATERIAL

For Purchase or Auction Consignment

We sell over 150,000 auction lots annually and are in constant need of new material and are prepared and readily willing to pay accordingly.

If you are contemplating selling your stamp holdings, please WRITE or CALL collect. Before inviting strangers into your home, we would like you to get to know us, so on receipt of your communication we will send you a company prospectus with background information, financial status and unsolicited recommendations from individuals who have dealt with us in the past.

(Dealers please note: If you are offered properties that you are not interested in acquiring, WE DO PAY a 10% commission on all referrals!)

J. & H. STOLOW, INC.

989 Avenue of the Americas, New York, NY 10018
Telephone: (212) 594-1144

Stolow's has purchased outright, at the top market price, with immediate cash payment, more than $100,000,000 worth of fine stamps. Our needs are unlimited. Fair treatment is always assured.

You will also find it pays to deal directly with the firm first in stamps by all standard authorities.

"Dealers in Fine Quality Stamps"
UNITED STATES
AND WORLDWIDE

BUYING AND SELLING

EXPERT APPRAISALS

Independent Appraisals For: Individuals, Groups, Attorneys, Insurance Companies, Estates & Trusts, Commercial Banks, State & Federal Courts, Internal Revenue Service, U.S. Customs Service, U.S. Small Business Admin., Disabled Am. Veterans. Call for further information.

PHONE 304-623-4100
WEST VIRGINIA PHILATELIC CLASSICS
"Established 1971. Over $10,000,000 in current assets"

Store Address: Galleria Mini-Mall 348 West Main Street, Clarksburg, WV

Mail Address: P.O. Box 283, Clarksburg, WV 26302-0283 USA

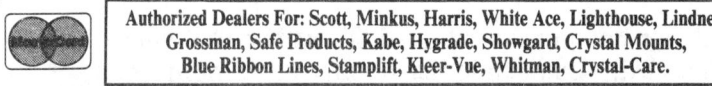
Authorized Dealers For: Scott, Minkus, Harris, White Ace, Lighthouse, Lindner. Grossman, Safe Products, Kabe, Hygrade, Showgard, Crystal Mounts, Blue Ribbon Lines, Stamplift, Kleer-Vue, Whitman, Crystal-Care.

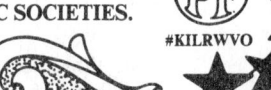
Appraisals Ph. 304-623-5526. Retail Store 304-623-4100.
MEMBER OF MOST MAJOR PHILATELIC SOCIETIES.

#139539 #KILRWVO

People Who Need To Know Real Stamp Prices Read Stamp Auction News.

- In-Depth Coverage Of The Stamp Auction World
- Reports On Thousands Of Realized Prices Monthly
- Provides Information Vital To Success when You Buy And Sell At Auction
- Now New and Improved

Subscribe Now
To the monthly magazine reporting real stamp prices
One Year $29.00
CLIP AND MAIL TODAY

STAMP AUCTION NEWS
P.O. BOX 13449 DEPT. S
HOUSTON, TX 77219-3449

☐ YES, I would like to subscribe to **STAMP AUCTION NEWS** for one year.

☐ U.S., Canada & Mexico ($29/yr.) ☐ Europe & Asia ($55/yr.)
(By Air Mail)

I will pay as indicated below:
☐ Check Enclosed   ☐ MasterCard   ☐ Visa

Full Card No. ☐☐☐☐☐☐☐☐☐☐☐☐☐☐☐☐
Expires _____/_____

NAME _____
ADDRESS _____
CITY_____ STATE_____ ZIP_____
SIGNATURE_____
Signature Required for Charge Orders

Scott Album Supplement Schedule

January
U.S. Commemorative
  Plate Blocks
Regular & Air Plate Blocks
U.N. Singles & Postal
  Stationery
U.N. Imprint Blocks
National Hingeless

March
Austria
France
Germany

April
Great Britain
British Europe
Channel Islands
Ireland
Monaco & Fr. Andorra
Korea
Israel Singles
Israel Tabs

May
Switzerland
Liechtenstein
Greece
Scandinavia &
  Finland

June
Japan
Portugal
Spain & Sp. Andorra
Italy
San Marino
Vatican City

July
Belgium
Netherlands
Luxembourg
U.S.S.R.
Czechoslovakia
Poland
Hungary

August
Australia & Dep.
New Zealand
New Zealand Dep.
Mexico
Br. America Vol. 1
Br. America Vol. 2

November
National
Minuteman
American
Canada
Master Canada
International

December
U.S. Booklet Panes
U.S. Commemorative
  Singles
U.S. Blocks of 4
U.S. Postal Stationery
U.S. Postal Cards

Scott Publishing Company
P.O. Box 828
Sidney, OH 45365

All supplements are available from your local dealer or direct from Scott.

SPECIAL NOTICES

LISTINGS

This Catalogue lists the various groups of United States stamps in specialized detail. The form of listing is similar to that used in Scott's Standard Postage Stamp Catalogue. Example:

United States

230   A71   1c   deep blue............**30.00**   25

The number (230) in the first column is the index or identification number. The letter-number combination (A71) indicates the design and refers to the illustration having this (A71) designation. Next comes the denomination (1c), followed by the color (deep blue). The prices are in two columns at the right, the first **30.00** being that of an uncanceled stamp, and the second (25) of a canceled one.

When a stamp is printed in black on colored paper, the color of the paper alone is given in italics.

With stamps printed in two or more colors, the color given first is that of the frame or outer parts of the design, starting at the upper left corner. The colors that follow are those of the vignette or inner parts of the design.

PRICING LIMITATIONS

Each price appearing in this catalogue represents an estimate by Scott Publishing Co. of the current value basis for a specimen of that single stamp (or, where noted, set of stamps) of the condition noted in the first section of this explanation, offered by a retail stamp dealer to a collector. Because this catalogue is issued only once each year, it is impossible for it to reflect the price fluctuations that may occur over the short term. What should remain constant, however, is the relative price (value) of items over the long term.

These prices are not intended to reflect "wholesale" transactions, i.e., between dealers or a collector selling to a dealer. Many factors may affect the differential between an individual price shown in these pages and the actual price of a transaction: individual bargaining, the effect of dealer mark-up and profit margins, condition of the item in question, changes in popularity of the item, temporary change in supply of the item, local custom, unusual postal markings on a used example of the item, unexpected political situations within the country of issue, newly discovered philatelic or other information, or changes in the relative value of that nation's currency against the U.S. dollar.

As a point of philatelic economic fact, the lower the price shown for an item in this catalogue, the greater the percentage of that price which is attributed to dealer mark-up and profit margin. Thus, packets of 1,000 different stamps — all of which have a catalogue price of at least 5 cents — normally sell for considerably less than $50!

Scott Publishing Co. endeavors to obtain more than one judgment of the prices and to incorporate in its pricing the various price factors listed above. There can be no assurance, however, that all of the prices listed are accurate estimates of prices which would be paid in actual transactions. Some of the items listed have not been publicly traded recently. The pricing, therefore, is based on the editors' estimates of the probable prices which the stamp would command if it were offered individually for sale to a collector.

Users of this Catalogue should not enter into any transaction solely in reliance on the prices, valuations, or stamp availability information set forth the Catalogue. Persons wishing to further establish the value of a particular stamp or other material may wish to consult with recognized stamp experts (collector or dealer) and review current information or recent developments which would affect stamp prices.

Scott Publishing Co. assumes no obligation to revise the prices during the distribution period of this Catalogue or to advise users of other factors, such as stamp availability, political and economic conditions, or collecting preferences, all of which may have an immediate positive or negative impact on prices. The publisher endeavors to balance these factors with its general understanding of stamp pricing considerations to avoid unnecessary fluctuations in the prices included in this Catalogue.

It should be noted that persons relied upon for pricing information also may deal in stamps and/or may maintain substantial personal stamp collections. They may buy, sell, and deal in stamps for their own account and for the account of others and therefore may have both a direct and indirect interest in the price of the stamps. In some cases, the references to prices may reflect valuations of their personal holdings for stamps in which they deal for themselves and others.

UNDERSTANDING PRICING NOTATIONS

The absence of a price does not necessarily indicate that the stamp is scarce or rare. In the United States listings, a dash in the price column means that the stamp is known in a stated form or variety, but that information is lacking or insufficient for pricing.

The minimum price of a stamp is fixed at 5 cents to cover a dealer's labor and service cost of purchasing that stamp at wholesale and preparing it for resale. As noted above, the sum of these list prices does not properly represent the "value" of a packet of unsorted or unmounted stamps sold in bulk which generally consists of only the lesser valued stamps.

Prices in the "unused" column are for stamps that have been hinged for United States items through 1960. Prices for unused stamps after that date are for unhinged examples. Where prices for a used example of a stamp is considerably higher than for the unused stamp, the price applies to a stamp showing a distinct contemporary postmark of origin.

EXAMINATION

Scott Publishing Co. cannot undertake to pass upon genuineness or condition of stamps, to appraise or identify. For expertizing, the company refers collectors to the several committees which do this work. These include the American Philatelic Expertization Service, P.O. Box 8000, State College, Pa. 16801, and the Philatelic Foundation Expert Committee, 270 Madison Ave., New York, N.Y. 10016.

COVERS

Prices paid for stamps on original covers vary greatly in accordance with condition, appearance, cancellation or postmark and usage. Prices given are for the commonest form with stamps in fine condition "tied on" by the cancellation. A stamp is said to be "tied" to an envelope or card when the cancellation or postmark falls on both the stamp and envelope or card. Letters addressed to foreign countries showing unusual rates and transit markings are much in demand and often bring large premiums.

Prices are for covers bearing a single copy of the stamp referred to used during the period when the stamp was on sale at post offices. If the postage rate was higher than the denomination of the stamp, then the stamp must represent the highest denomination possible to use in making up this rate. As a general rule the stamp must be "tied" to the cover. Exceptions include some of the early local adhesives for which canceling was not customary.

Prices for patriotic covers of the Civil War period (bearing pictorial designs of a patriotic nature) are for the commonest designs. Over 11,000 varieties of designs are known.

CANCELLATIONS

As a complete treatment of this subject is impossible in a catalogue of this limited size, only postal markings of **meaning** or of color are recorded, while those owing their origin to **fancy** are disregarded. The former were necessary for the proper functioning of the Postal Service; the latter were the result of the whim of some postal official. Many of these odd designs, however, command high prices dependent on their scarcity and clearness of impression.

Though there are many types of most of the cancellations that are listed, only one of each is illustrated. The prices quoted are for the commonest type of each.

Prices for cancellation varieties are for specimens off cover. If on cover, the distinctive cancellation must be on the stamp in order to merit catalogue valuation. However, postmarks that denote origin or a service (as distinct from cancelling a stamp) merit catalogue valuation when on a cover apart from the stamp, provided the stamp is otherwise tied to the cover by a cancellation.

One type of "Paid" cancellation used in Boston, and pictured under Postal Markings—Examples, is common and prices are for types other than this.

ACKNOWLEDGMENT

The Editors extend sincere thanks to all those who have helped, by giving their time and knowledge, in the annual task of revising this Catalogue in line with the goal of a complete, accurate United States philatelic handbook.

Among the organizations that have helped are:
American Air Mail Society, 102 Arbor Road, Cinnaminson, NJ 08077
American First Day Cover Society, Sol Koved, 14 Samoset Rd., Cranford, NJ 07016
American Philatelic Society, P.O. Box 8000, State College, PA 16803
American Revenue Association, Bruce Miller, Sec'y, 701 S. First Ave., Suite 332, Arcadia, CA 91006
Bureau Issues Association, 4630 Greylock St., Boulder, CO 80301
Canal Zone Study Group, Alfred R. Bew, Sec'y., 29 S. South Carolina Ave., Atlantic City, NJ 08401
Confederate Stamp Alliance, Brian M. Green, c/o Philatelic Foundation, 270 Madison Ave., New York, NY 10016
Essay-Proof Society, Kenneth Minuse, Sec'y., 1236 Grand Concourse, Bronx, NY 10456
Philatelic Foundation, 270 Madison AVe., New York, NY 10016
Precancel Stamp Society, 12045 Hickory Hills Court, Oakton, VA 22124
Ryukyu Philatelic Specialist Society, Ltd., Dr. A. L-F, Askins, P.O. Box 4092, Berkeley, CA 94704
United Postal Stationery Society, P.O. Box 48, Redlands, CA 92373
U.S. Philatelic Classics Society, Robert R. Hegland, P.O. Box 1011, Falls Church, VA 22041
U.S. Possessions Philatelic Society, Kenneth M. Koller, Sec'y., 217 Tyler Ave., Cuyahoga Falls, OH 44221

Individuals who have generously given their help include:
Charles Andrews, Arthur L-F, Askins, Philip T. Basner, Brian M. Bleckwenn, John R. Boker, Jr., Vernon E. Bressler, George W. Brett, William T. Crowe, Falk Finkelburg, Morton P. Goldfarb, Brian M. Green, Calvet M. Hahn, John Hain, John B. Head, Cordell Hoffer, Eric Jackson, Mrs. Alvin F. Kantor, Warren Kaplan, Lewis S. Kaufman, Thomas C. Kingsley, Victor B. Krievins, Joseph E. Landry, Jr., Walter J. Mader III, Robert L. Markovits, Adam Perkal, Gilbert N. Plass, Henrik Pollak, William N. Salomon, Henry B. Scheuer, Jacques C. Schiff, Jr., Richard Schwartz, Rick Schwartz, Robert A. Siegel, Edward Siskin, Sherwood Springer, Samuel S. Smith, Berb Taub and Al Zimmerman.

The editors also thank the United States Postal Service and the Bureau of Engraving and Printing.

INFORMATION FOR COLLECTORS

For the sake of clarity this section is separated into two main divisions, as follows:

1—A general index to philatelic terms (which immediately follows), and

2—An explanation of the terms themselves grouped under subjects in the following order:
Plate
Printing
Paper
Perforations
Luminescence
Postal Markings

The general index lists all terms with explanation or designates proper subject under which the explanation may be found.

INDEX OF
INFORMATION FOR COLLECTORS

Arrows ....See Plate Markings
Bisect

 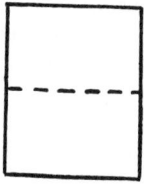 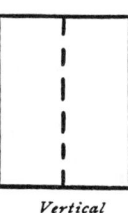

Diagonal   Horizontal   Vertical

Stamps cut in half so that each portion prepaid postage, used in emergencies where no stamps of the lower denomination were available. These may be diagonal, horizontal or vertical. Example: No. 2a. Listings are for bisects on full covers. Those on piece or part of a cover sell for considerably less.

Blocks ....See Plate
Booklet Panes ....See Plate
Booklets ....See Plate
Booklets, A. E. F.....................See Plate

Bureau Prints
A term applied to stamps printed by the Bureau of Engraving and Printing at Washington, D. C., or the precancellations applied by this Bureau. See: Precancellations.

Cancellations ....See Postal Markings
Cancellations, Examples of........See Postal Markings
Cancellations, New York City Foreign Mail
..................................See Postal Markings
Cancellations, Patent ....See Postal Markings
Cancellations, Supplementary Mail.See Postal Markings
Carrier Postmark ....See Postal Markings
Center Line Blocks........................See Plate
Coarse Perforation ....See Perforations
Coils ....See Plate
Coil Waste ....See Plate
Color Trials ....See Printing

Commemorative Stamps.
Special issues which commemorate some anniversary or event of local, national or international importance, or which honor some person. Usually such stamps are used for a limited period concurrently with the ordinary series.

Examples: Nos. 230–245, 620–621, 946, 1266, C68, U218–U221, UC25, R733.

Compound Perforation ....See Perforations
Corner Blocks ....See Plate
Cracked Plate ....See Plate
Crystallization Cracks ....See Plate
Curvature Cracks ....See Plate

Cut Square
An envelope stamp cut rectangularly from the envelope.

Diagonal Half ....See Bisect
Die ....See Plate
Double Impression .... See Printing
Double Paper ....See Paper
Double Perforation ....See Perforations
Double Transfer ....See Plate
Dry Printings...............See note after No. 1029

Electric Eye ....See Perforations
Embossed Printing ....See Printing
End Roller Grills ....See Paper
Engraving ....See Printing

Error
A stamp is called an error when it differs from the normal variety by some mistake or omission in the inscription, color, paper, impression, watermark or perforation.

Essay ....See Printing

Fine Perforation ....See Perforations

First Day Cover
A philatelic term to designate the use of a certain stamp (on cover) on the first day of sale at a place officially designated for such sale and so postmarked.

Flat Plate Printing......................See Printing
Flat Press Printing......................See Printing

Giori Press..............................See Printing
Gridiron Cancellation ....See Postal Markings
Grills ....See Paper
Grill with Points Up......................See Paper
Gripper Cracks ....See Plate
Guide Dots ....See Plate
Guide Lines ....See Plate Markings
Guide Line Blocks ....See Plate
Gum Breaker Ridges
Colorless marks across the backs of some rotary press stamps, impressed during manufacture to prevent curling. A dozen varieties of "gum breaks" exist.

Gutter ....See Plate Markings

Hidden Plate Number ....See Plate
Horizontal Half ....See Bisect

Imperforate ....See Perforations
Imprint ....See Plate Markings
Imprint Blocks ....See Plate
India Paper ....See Paper
Intaglio ....See Printing
Inverted Center ....See Printing

Joint Line Pair...............................See Plate

INFORMATION FOR COLLECTORS

Laid Paper ....See Paper
Line Engraved ....See Printing
Line Pair ....See Plate
Lithography ....See Printing
Luminescent Coating..............See Luminescence

Manila Paper ....See Paper
Margin ....See Plate Markings
Margin Blocks ....See Plate
Margin Block with Arrow.................See Plate
Margin Block with Imprint...............See Plate
Margin Block with Plate # ....See Plate
Multicolored Stamps ....See Printing

Offset Printing ....See Printing
Original Gum
 A stamp is described as "O.G." if it has the original gum as applied when printed. Some are issued without gum, as Nos. 730, 731, 735, 752, etc.; government reproductions, as Nos. 3 and 4, and official reprints.

Overprint ....See Printing
Pair Imperf. Between............See Perforations
Pane ....See Plate
Part Perforate ....See Perforations
Paste-up ....See Plate
Paste-up Pair ....See Plate
Patriotic Covers
 Envelopes of the Civil War period showing patriotic designs or inscriptions.

Pelure Paper ....See Paper
Phosphor Tagged ....See Luminescence
Plate, 400-Subject ....See Plate
Plate Arrangement ....See Plate
Plate Flaws ....See Plate
Plates for Stamp Booklets.............See Plate
Plates for Coil Stamps................See Plate
Plate Markings ....See Plate
Plate Numbers ....See Plate
Postal Markings, History of......See Postal Markings
Postmarks ....See Postal Markings
Printing, Kinds of...................See Printing
Printed on Both Sides...............See Printing
Proofs ....See Printing
Propaganda Covers
 Envelopes carrying inscriptions pertaining to Cheaper Postage, Temperance, Anti-Slavery, etc.

Railroad Postmarks ....See Postal Markings
Receiving Mark ....See Postal Markings
Recut ....See Plate
Recutting ....See Plate
Re-engraved ....See Plate
Re-entry ....See Plate
Registry Markings ....See Plate Markings
Reissues ....See Printing
Relief ....See Plate
Reprints ....See Printing
Retouch ....See Plate
Rosette Crack ....See Printing
Rotary Press Printings ....See Printing
Rotary Press Double Paper...........See Paper
Rough Perforation..............See Perforations
Rouletting ....See Perforation

Se-tenant
 Joined together. Applies to pairs or larger multiples embracing stamps of different denomination, design, surcharge or overprint. Examples: Nos. 1421a and 1451a.

Sheet ....See Plate
Shifted Transfer ....See Plate
Ship Postmarks ....See Postal Markings
Short Transfer ....See Plate
Silk Paper ....See Paper
Specialization
 Term usually applied to the study and collection of the stamps of any special issue or group as distinguished from collecting along general lines.

Special Printings ....See Printing
Split Grill ....See Paper
Stampless Covers
 Prior to the issuance of United States Government adhesive postage stamps, and for some time thereafter, letters were mailed "collect" or postage was prepaid in cash. In such instances the covers often bear, in addition to the town postmark, a notation such as "Paid", "Paid 10", etc. The tyro is apt to confuse these stampless covers with the rare postmasters' provisionals issued prior to government stamps.
 While many of these covers have no great commercial value, they are of historical value to collectors interested in the postal history and operations of the United States Post Office Department.

Stars ....See Plate Markings
Stitch Watermark ....See Paper
Strip
 A number of unsevered stamps forming a vertical or horizontal row.

Surface Printing ....See Printing
Surcharges ....See Printing

Tête bêche
 A French term applied to stamps printed upside down in relation to one another. This is usually due to accidental insertion of one or more clichés in a stamp plate wrong way up, or by wrong transfers. Tête bêche stamps must be collected in pairs; when separated the stamps show no peculiarity.

Tied On ....See Postal Markings
Transfer ....See Plate
Transfer Roll ....See Plate
Triple Transfer ....See Plate

Type
 1. The catalogue illustration of the stamp design. The Kennedy memorial stamp is type A678. 2. One of two or more forms of the design, differing in one or more details. The corner triangles of Nos. 248–252 are illustrated and listed in Types I, II and III.

Typeset ....See Printing
Typeset Stamps....................See Printing
Typography ....See Printing

Vertical Half ....See Bisect

Watermarks ....See Paper
Wet Printings.............See note after No. 1029
Wove Paper ....See Paper

INFORMATION FOR COLLECTORS

PLATE—LINE ENGRAVING (INTAGLIO). THE PROCESS.

Die

Transfer Roll

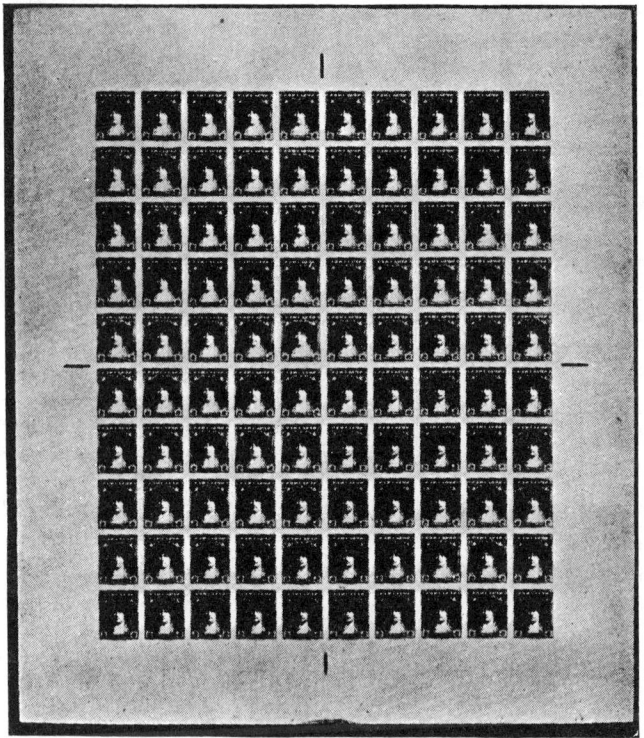

Plate

Die. Making the "die" is the initial operation. The "die" is a small flat piece of soft steel on which the subject (design) is recess engraved in reverse. Dies are usually of a "single subject" type; but dies exist with "multiple subjects" of the same design, or different designs. After the engraving is completed, the "die" is hardened to withstand the stress of subsequent operations.

Transfer Roll. The next operation is the making of the "transfer roll" which, as its name implies, is the medium used to transfer the subject from the "die" to the "plate". A blank roll of soft steel, mounted on a mandrel, is placed under the bearers of a "transfer press", so as to allow it to roll freely on its axis. The hardened "die" is placed on the bed of the press and the face of the roll is brought to bear on the "die" under pressure. The bed is then rocked back and forth under increasing pressure until the soft steel of the roll is forced into every line of the "die". The resulting impression on the roll is known as a "relief" or a "relief transfer." Several "reliefs" are usually rocked in on each roll. After the required "reliefs" have been made, the roll is hardened.

Relief. A "relief" is the normal reproduction of the design on the "die" in reverse. A "defective relief", caused by a minute piece of foreign material lodging on the "die", may occur during the "rocking in" process, or from other causes. Imperfections in the steel of the transfer roll may also result in a breaking away of parts of the design; if the damaged relief is continued in use, it will transfer a repeating defect to the plate. Also, reliefs are sometimes deliberately altered. "Broken relief" and "altered relief" are terms used to designate these changed conditions.

Plate. A flat piece of soft steel replaces the "die" on the bed of the transfer press and one of the "reliefs" on the transfer roll is brought to bear on it. The position on the plate is determined by "position dots", which have been lightly marked on the plate in advance. After the position of the "relief" is determined, pressure is brought to bear and, by following the same method used in the making of the transfer roll, a "transfer" is entered, which reproduces in reverse every detail of the design of the "relief". As many "transfers" are entered on the plate as there are to be subjects.

After the required "transfers" have been entered, the position dots, layout dots and lines, scratches, etc., are generally burnished out; and any required "guide lines", "plate numbers" or other marginal markings are added. A proof impression is then taken and if "certified" (approved), the plate is machined for fitting to the press, hardened and sent to the plate vault as being ready for use.

Rotary press plates, after being certified, require additional machining. They are curved to fit the press cylinder and "gripper slots" are cut into the back of each plate to receive the "grippers", which hold the plate securely in the press, after which the plate is hardened.

The practice of chromium plating the steel plates began in 1927. It reduces wear and secures increased production, as the plates may be replated many times.

Transfer. An impression entered on the plate by the transfer roll. A "relief transfer" is also made when entering the design of the die on the transfer roll.

Double Transfer. A term used to describe the condition of a "transfer" on a plate that shows evidences of a duplication of all, or a portion of the design. It is usually the result of the changing of the registration between the "relief" and the "plate", during the rolling in of the original entry. It is sometimes necessary to remove the original "transfer" from a plate and enter the "relief" a second time, when the finished re-transfer shows indications of the original "transfer", due to incomplete erasure, the result is also a "double transfer".

Triple Transfer. Similar to a "double transfer" but showing evidences of a third entry or two duplications.

Re-entry. When executing a "re-entry", the transfer roll is reapplied to the plate at some time after it has been put to press. Thus, worn-out designs may be resharpened by carefully re-entering the transfer roll. If not very carefully entered, the registration will not be true and a "double transfer" will result. With the protective qualities of "chromium plating", it is no longer necessary to resharpen the plate. In fact, after a plate has been curved for the rotary press, it is impossible to make a re-entry.

Shifted Transfer (Shift). In transferring, the metal displaced on the plate by the entry of the ridges, constituting the design on the transfer roll, is forced ahead of the roll, as well as pressed out at the sides.

The amount of displaced metal increases with the depth of the entry, but when the depth is increased evenly, the design will be uniformly entered. Most of the displaced metal is pressed ahead of the roll. If too much pressure is exerted on any "pass" (rocking), the impression of the previous partial entry may be floated (pushed) ahead of the roll and thus cause a duplication of the final design, appearing as an increased width of frame lines or a doubling of the lines.

The ridges of the displaced metal are flattened out by hammering or rolling the back of the plate along the space occupied by the subject margins.

Short Transfer. It sometimes happens that the transfer roll is not rocked its entire length in the entering of a transfer on a plate, with the result that the finished transfer fails to show the complete design. This is known as a "short transfer." Type III of the one cent issue of 1851-56 is a good example.

Re-engraved. A term used in connection with "line engraving". Either the die that has been used to make a plate or the plate itself may have its "temper" drawn (softened) and be re-cut. The resulting impressions from such re-engraved die or plate may differ very slightly from the original issue, and are known as "re-engraved".

Recut. A "recut" is line strengthening or altering by use of an engraving tool on unhardened plates.

Retouching. A "retouch" is line strengthening or altering by means of etching.

PLATE—Arrangement

Arrangement. The first engraved plates used to produce United States postage stamps in 1847 contained 200 subjects. The number of subjects to a plate varied between 100 and 300 until the issue of 1890, when the 400-subject plate was first laid down. Since that time, this size of plate has been used for a majority of the regular postal issues. Exceptions to this practice exist and will be found listed under the headings of the various issues in the catalogue.

INFORMATION FOR COLLECTORS

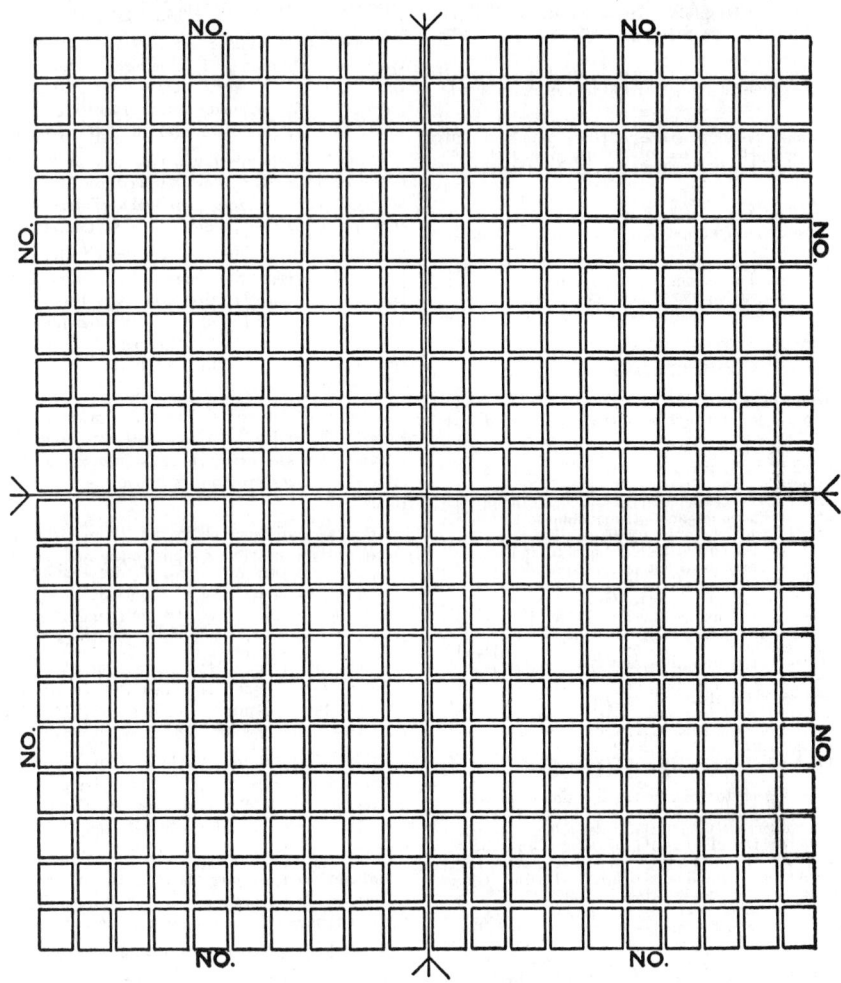

A typical 400-subject plate of 1922.

Plate Markings. The illustration above shows a typical 400-subject flat plate of the 1922 issue with markings as found on this type of plate. Other layouts and markings will be described further on in the text.

Sheet. In single color printings, the complete impression from a plate is termed a sheet. A sheet of multicolored stamps (two or more colors) may come from a single impression of a plate (many Giori-type press printings from 1957) or from as many impressions from separate plates as there are inks used for the particular stamp. Combination process printings may use both methods of multicolor production: Giori-type intaglio with offset lithography or with photogravure.

The Huck multicolor press (the "nine-color press") uses plates of different format (40, 80 or 72 subjects). The sheet it produces has 200 subjects for normal-size commemoratives or 400 subjects for ordinary-size stamps, similar to the regular products of other presses.

Pane. A pane is a part of the original sheet as it is issued for sale at post offices. A pane may be the same as an entire sheet where the plate is small, or it may be a half, or a quarter, or some other regular fraction of a sheet where the plate is large. The illustration shows the layout of a 400-subject sheet from a flat plate which for issuance would have been divided along the intersecting guide lines into four panes of 100.

Panes are classified in normal reading position according to their location on the printed sheet by being designated "U.L." (Upper Left), "U.R." (Upper Right), "L.L." (Lower Left) and "L.R." (Lower Right). Where only two panes appear on a sheet, they are designated "R" (Right), "L" (Left) or "T" (Top), "B" (Bottom), depending on whether the sheet is divided vertically or horizontally.

To fix the location of a particular stamp on any pane, the pane is held with the subjects in the normal position and a number is given to each stamp starting with the first stamp in the upper left corner and proceeding horizontally to the right, then starting on the second row at the left and across to the right, and so on to the last stamp in the lower right corner. (For a discussion on applying this system of designation to the product of the Huck multicolor press, see article "Position Description for Stamps Printed on the 9-color Huck Press," by George W. Brett, The United States Specialist, July, 1974, v. 45, p. 306.)

It is important to remember that in describing the location of a stamp on a sheet prior to 1894, the practice is to give the stamp number first, then the pane position and finally the plate number: "1 R XXII", as on No. 160. Beginning with the 1894 issue and on all later issues, the method used is to give the plate number first, then the position of the pane and finally the number of the stamp: "16807 L.L. 48", as on No. 619; or "2138 L. 2", as on No. 323.

Plates For Stamp Booklets. These are illustrated and fully described under "Booklet Panes." See Index.

Booklets. These are stamps issued in small booklets for the convenience of users. They are sold by the Post Office at a small premium.

Booklet Panes. Small panes especially printed and cut to be sold in booklets. Panes are straight-edged on bottom and both sides, but perforated between the stamps.

Booklets, A. E. F. Prepared principally for the use of the U. S. Army in France, during World War I. Issued in 1c and 2c denominations with 30 stamps to a pane (10 × 3), bound at right or left. As soon as Gen. John J. Pershing's organization reached France, soldiers' mail was sent free by the use of franked envelopes. Stamps were required during the war for the civilian personnel, also for registry mail, parcel post and other divisions of the postal service. See Nos. 498f, 499f.

COIL STAMPS

Originally in 1908-09 coils were made in two sizes, 500 or 1,000 stamps, arranged endways or sideways and issued with or without perforations.

Stamps issued in rolls for use in affixing or vending machines were made first by private companies and later by the Bureau of Engraving and Printing. Originally it was customary for the Post Office Department to sell, to the private vending machine companies and others, imperforate sheets of stamps printed from the ordinary 400-subject flat plates. These sheets were then pasted together end-to-end or side-to-side by the purchaser and cut into rolls as desired, the perforations being applied to suit the requirements of the individual machines. Such "Private Perforations" are listed under "Vending and Affixing Machine Perforations." See Index.

Later the Bureau produced coils by the same method, also in sizes of 500 or 1,000 stamps, arranged endways or sideways and issued with or without perforations.

With the introduction of the Stickney rotary press, curved plates made for use on these presses were put into use at the Bureau, and the sale of imperforate sheets was discontinued. This marked the end of the "Private Perforations." Rotary press coils have been made in sizes of 100, 500, 1,000 and 3,000 stamps.

Paste-up. Term used to describe the junction of two *flat-plate* printings joined by pasting the edge of one sheet onto the edge of another sheet to make coils. The two-stamp specimen to show this joining would be a "paste-up pair."

Line Pair. Pair of flat-plate-printed coil stamps with *printed* line between. This line is identical with the "Guide Line" in sheets. See "Plate Markings."

Joint Line. The edges of two curved plates do not meet exactly on the press, and the small space between them takes ink and prints a line. A pair of *rotary-press-printed* stamps with such a line between is called a "joint line pair."

Splice. Term used to describe the junction of two *rotary-press* printings joined by butting the ends of the continuous-printed web together and pasting a strip of perforated translucent paper on the back of the junction. The two-stamp specimen to show this would be a "spliced pair."

A splice might be made for repair of a single coil which broke, but was most often made to join two continuous-printed webs to make up a desired count. To facilitate counting, the two parts joined were usually broken at their joint lines and these lines placed together at the butt joint.

Hidden Plate Number. A plate number may be found entire on a coil made from flat plates, but is usually hidden by a part of the next sheet which had been lapped over it.

Plate Number. On a rotary-press coil the top or bottom part of a plate number may show. The number was entered on the plate so as to be cut off when the web was sliced into coils, and could be found only when the web was sliced off center.

Every rotary coil plate number was adjacent to a joint line, so both features could occur together in one strip. Logic would call for breaking the coil into strips so that the favored feature, either the line or the plate number, would be at mid-strip.

Coil Waste. Certain stamps issued in perforated sheets which were prepared from short lengths left over at the end of a run of printing stamps to be made into coils. Sometimes the salvaged sections were those which had been laid aside for mutilation because of some defect. As the paper had been moistened during printing, it sometimes stretched slightly, providing added printing surface at the end of a run. Sheets of 70, 100 and 170 have been seen. See Nos. 538-541, 544-546, 578-579, 594-595.

PLATE MARKINGS

Guide Lines. Horizontal or vertical colored lines between the stamps, and extending wholly or partially across the sheet are "guide lines." They serve as guides for the operators of perforating machines, or to indicate the line of separation of the sheet into panes.

A block of stamps divided by any of the guide lines is known as a "Line" or "Guide Line Block", while the block of stamps from the exact center of the sheet, showing the crossed guide lines, is a "Center Line Block."

Gutters. Ordinarily when guide lines are used to divide the sheet into panes, the spaces between the panes are not greater than the space between any other of the stamps on the sheet. On some plates, however, a wide space or "Gutter" is left between the panes, and on such plates the "guide lines" usually do not appear.

A block of stamps showing this wide space running between is called a "Gutter Block", and a block of stamps from the exact center of the sheet showing the two wide spaces crossing is known as a "Center Gutter Block".

Arrows. On issues between 1870 and 1894 guide lines were not usually used, but marginal arrow shaped markings, known as "arrows", were substituted, and served the same purpose as the guide lines. Since 1894, guide lines with arrows at both ends have been the standard practice on flat plate printings.

A marginal block of four stamps showing the "arrow" centered at one edge is called a "Margin Block with Arrow", but the number of stamps in the block need not necessarily be limited to four.

Registry Markings. Various shaped marks used as an aid in properly registering the frame and vignette impressions of bicolored stamps. In the catalogue listing, a "registry marking" is referred to as an "arrow marker".

Imprint. An oblong rectangular design containing the name of the producer of the stamps, appearing on the sheet margin adjoining the plate number.

A block of stamps with the sheet margin attached, bearing the "imprint," is known as an "Imprint Block." Imprints were usually collected in blocks of six, or of sufficient length to include the entire imprint. In 1894-95 the fashion was to collect imprints in strips of three and these have been noted in the catalogue.

The imprint and plate number are found in eight types, illustrated after Nos. 245 and E3. Example: "T V" means Type V.

Plate Numbers. Serial numbers assigned to plates, appearing on one or more margins of the sheet or pane to identify the plate.

Flat Press Plate Numbers are usually collected in a marginal block of six stamps with the plate number centered in the margin.

Rotary Press Plate Numbers are collected in a corner margin block large enough to show the plate number(s) and its position along the margin. Most regular issues have a single plate number at the corner of the sheet, and for these a block of four suffices. During 1933-39 some plates had the number opposite the third stamp (up or down) from the corner of the sheet and for these the number is customarily collected in a corner block of no less than eight stamps. Multicolored stamps may have more than one plate number in the sheet margin and the "plate block" may then be expanded to suit the collector's desire.

Plate numbers take a further designation from the position on the sheet in which they appear, thus there would be U.L. (Upper Left), etc.

INFORMATION FOR COLLECTORS

Stars. "Stars" on the flat plates were used to indicate a change from the previous spacing of the stamps, and were used as a check on the assignment of the printed sheets to a perforating machine of the proper setting. Stars appear on certain rotary plates used for printing stamps for coils, appearing adjacent to the plate joint line and above stamp No. 1 on the 170-subject plates, and to the left of stamp No. 141 on the 150-subject plates.

"A". See definition for flat plate "stars".

"C.S." and "C". Indicate that the plate is made of "Chrome Steel".

"F". Used to indicate the plate is ready for hardening. This appears only on flat plates and generally precedes the upper right plate number.

"EI". Signifies "Electrolytic Iron" and is used to designate plates made by the electrolytic process.

"Top". A marking on the top sheet margin of printings from both plates of certain bicolored issues and used to check printings for "inverts". Beginning with the 6¢ bicolored airmail issue of 1938, bicolored crosses also appear as an additional check.

"Coil Stamps". Appearing on the side sheet margins to designate plates used in the production of endwise coils.

"S 20", "S 30", "S 40". Marginal markings appearing on certain 150 and 170-subject rotary press plates to designate experimental variations in the depth and character of the frame lines to overcome excess inking. "S 30" was adopted as the standard. Blocks showing these markings are designated as "Margin Block with S 20", etc., in the catalogue.

Initials. Initials in sheet margins were used to identify individuals in the Bureau who participated in the production or use of the plates.

Gutter Dashes. On the first 400-subject rotary plates, 3/16 inch horizontal dashes appear in the gutter between the 10th and 11th vertical rows of stamps. This arrangement was superseded by dashes 3/16 inch long at the extreme ends of the vertical and horizontal gutters, and ¼ inch cross at the central gutter intersection. This latter arrangement continued until replaced by the scanning marks on the Electric Eye plates. See Electric Eye.

Margin. The border outside the printed design of a stamp, or the similar border of a sheet of stamps. A block of stamps from the top, side or bottom of a sheet or pane to which is attached the margin is known as a "Margin Block". A block of stamps from the corner of a sheet with full margins attached to two adjoining sides is known as a "Corner Block".

Note. In the foregoing, it is indicated that a certain number of stamps make up an Arrow or Plate Number Block. Naturally any block of stamps, no matter how large or small, which had an arrow or a plate number on its margin would be designated by that name. But the usual practice is to collect flat Plate Numbers in margin blocks of 6, and Arrow Blocks in margin blocks of 4. Plate Number Blocks from rotary press printings are generally collected in blocks of 4 as the plate number usually appears beside the stamp at any of the four corners of the sheet. Also, particularly in bi-colored stamps, an Arrow Block is not separated from a Plate Number Block. Thus the two together form a block of 8 or 10 as the case might be.

PRINTING

Methods Used. The methods employed in producing United States stamps include all three basic forms of printing: "Intaglio", "Lithography" and "Typography".

Recess or Intaglio-Engraved. In this process the ink is received and held in lines depressed below the surface of the plate, and in printing from these plates the damp paper is forced down into the depressed lines and picks up the ink. In consequence the lines on the face of the stamp are slightly raised and when seen from the back of the stamp are slightly depressed. When the ornamental work is engraved by a machine, it is called "engine turned" or lathe work engraving. A good example of lathe work background is the 3c of 1861.

Engraved stamps were printed only with flat plates until 1915 when Rotary Press Printing was introduced. "Wet" and "Dry" printings are explained in the note after No. 1029. The **Giori** press, used to print certain U.S. stamps since 1957 (see No. 1094, the 4c Flag issue), applies two or three different colored inks simultaneously.

The **Huck Multicolor** press, put into service at the Bureau of Engraving and Printing in 1968, was first used to produce the 1968 Christmas stamp (No. 1363) and the 6c Flag coil (No. 1338A). Developed by the Bureau's technical staff and the firm of graphic arts engineers whose name it bears, the Huck Multicolor prints, phosphor tags, gums and perforates stamps in a continuous operation, doing the printing in as many as nine colors. Fed by paper from a roll, the Huck Multicolor uses many recess-engraved plates of smaller size than any used previously for U.S. stamp printing. Its product has certain characteristics which other U.S. stamps do not have. Post office panes of No. 1363, for example, show seven or eight plate numbers in the margins.

Photogravure. In this rapid process of reproduction, the design is usually photographed through an extremely fine screen lined in minute quadrille. This breaks up the reproduction into tiny dots. These dots are etched into the plate and the depressions thus formed hold the ink, which is lifted out by the paper when it is pressed against the plate.

For U.S. stamps, photogravure first appeared in 1967 with the Eakins 5c, No. 1335. The early photogravure stamps were printed in the plants of outside contractors until the Bureau obtained the multicolor Andreotti press in 1971. The earliest "Andreotti" stamp is No. 1426, the Missouri Statehood 8c. Color control bars, dashes or dots are printed on the margin of one pane in each "Andreotti" sheet of 200, 160 or 128. These are generally collected in blocks of 20 or 16 (two full rows of one pane) which include the full complement of plate numbers, Mr. Zip and the Zip and Mail Early slogans.

Details on the Combination Press follow No. 1703.

Lithography. A common and the cheapest process for printing stamps. In this method the design is drawn by hand or transferred from an original engraving to the surface of a lithographic stone or metal plate in greasy ink. The stone or plate is wet with an acid fluid, which causes it to repel the printing ink except on the greasy lines of the design. A fine lithographic print closely resembles an engraving, but the lines are not raised on the face or depressed on the back, and there is usually a duller appearance in the lithograph than in the engraving.

Offset Printing or **Offset Lithography** is a modern development of the lithographic process. Anything that will print—type, woodcuts, photoengravings, plates engraved or etched in intaglio, halftone plates, linoleum blocks, lithographic stones or plates, photogravure plates, rubber stamps, etc., may be used. Greasy ink is applied to the dampened plate or form and an impression made on a rubber blanket. Paper is immediately pressed against the blanket, which transfers the ink.

INFORMATION FOR COLLECTORS

Because of its greater flexibility, offset printing has largely displaced lithography. Since the processes and results obtained are similar, stamps printed by either of these two methods are designated "lithographed."

The first application was in printing Post Office seals, probably using stone printing bases. Offset lithography was used for the 1914 documentary revenues, Nos. R195-R216. Postage stamps followed in 1918-20 (Nos. 525-536) because of wartime ink, plate and manpower shortages in connection with the regular line-intaglio production.

The next use of offset lithography for postage stamps was in 1964 with the Homemakers 5c, No. 1253, in combination with line-intaglio. Many similar issues followed, including the Bicentennial souvenir sheets of 1976, Nos. 1686-1689, which were all offset-litho. The process serves best for soft backgrounds and tonal effects.

Typography. The exact reverse of engraved plate printing. In this process the parts of the design which are to show in color are left at the original level of the plate and the spaces between are cut away. The ink is applied to the raised lines on the plate and the pressure of printing forces these lines, more or less, into the paper, impressing the colored lines of the face of the stamp and slightly raising them on the back of the stamp. In practice a large number of electrotypes of the original are made and assembled together into a plate with the requisite number of designs for printing a sheet of stamps. Stamps printed by this process show great uniformity, and the process is cheaper than intaglio printing.

The first American stamp use of typography or letterpress under national authority was the 1846 "2" surcharge on the United States City Despatch Post 3c, Carrier stamp No. 6LB7. The next time was for the 1865 Newspaper and Periodical stamp issue which for security reasons combined the techniques of machine engraving, colorless embossing and typography, creating an unusual first.

Most U.S. stamp typography consists of overprints such as those for Canal Zone, the Molly Pitcher 2c, the Kansas-Nebraska controls, precancels and specimens.

Embossed (Relief) Printing. A method in which the design is sunk in the metal of the die and the printing is done against a yielding platen, such as leather or linoleum, which is forced up into the depression of the die, thus forming the design on the paper in relief. Embossing may be done without color, or with part color and part colorless, as the U. S. stamped envelopes.

PRINTING—TERMS USED

Multicolored Stamps. Until 1957 when the Giori press was introduced, producing stamps in two or more colors with a single press run, bicolored stamps were printed on a flat bed press in two runs. Example: the Norse-American issue of 1925 (Nos. 620-621). In the flat press bicolors, if the sheet were fed to the press on the second run in reversed position, the part printed in the second color would be upside down, producing Inverted Centers, such as No. C3a. Many bicolored and multicolored stamps show varying degrees of poor alignment of the colors. Such varieties are not listed.

Bureau Prints. (Precancels) Stamps having cancellations applied before the stamps are sold to the public holding permits for their purchase. The cancellations are printed on the stamps during the process of manufacture by the Bureau of Engraving and Printing, and consist of the name of the city and state where the stamps are to be used. "City type" precancels have the cancellations printed on them before sale but the printing differs in type from the "Bureau Prints" and is done locally.

Color Trials. These are printings in various colors made to facilitate selection of color for the issued stamps.

Double Impression. A second impression of a stamp over the original impression. It should not be confused with a "double transfer" which is a plate imperfection and does not show a doubling of the entire design. A double impression shows every line clearly doubled. See: "Printed on Both Sides".

Essay. A design submitted in stamp form but not necessarily accepted for issuance. Printings in various colors other than the issued stamp are known as "Color Trials". See: "Color Trials".

Inverted Center. A stamp with the center printed upside down in relation to the rest of the design. See: "Multicolored Stamps".

Flat Plate Printing. See: "Flat Press Printing".

Flat Press Printing. Stamp printed on the ordinary flat-bed press, as distinguished from rotary press printing. See: "Plate".

Overprint. Any word, inscription or device printed across the face of a stamp to alter its use or locality, or to serve a special purpose. An example of the last is No. 646, which is No. 634 overprinted "Molly Pitcher" as a memorial to the Revolutionary War heroine. See: "Surcharge".

Printed On Both Sides. Occasionally a sheet of stamps already printed will, through error, be turned over and passed through the press a second time, thus creating the rare "printed on both sides" variety. This is often confused with an offset which occurs when sheets of stamps are stacked while the ink is still wet. There is, however, an outstanding difference: the "printed on both sides" variety shows a positive design (all inscriptions reading correctly) on both sides of the paper. An "offset" shows a reverse impression on the back of the stamp, that is, all wording, etc., reading backwards. See: "Double Impression".

Proofs. Trial printings of a stamp made from the original die or the finished plate.

Reissues. An official printing of a stamp, or stamps, that has been discontinued. This term is usually applied to fresh printings of such stamps, which can be distinguished in some way from those of the original issue. While reissues are usually intended for regular usage, there are exceptions, as Nos. 40, etc., 102, etc., reissued during the Centennial Exposition for stamp collectors. See: "Reprints", "Special Printings".

Reprints. Impressions from the original plates, blocks or stones, from which the original stamps were printed, taken after the issuance of the stamps to post offices had ceased and their postal use had been voided. See: "Reissues", "Special Printings".

Reproductions. Stamps made from a new plate to imitate the original issue. See Nos. 3-4. See "Souvenir Cards" section of this Catalogue.

INFORMATION FOR COLLECTORS

Rotary Press Printings. These are stamps which have been printed on a rotary type press from curved plates as compared to stamps printed from flat plates on a flat bed press. Rotary press stamps are longer or wider than the same stamps printed from flat plates. All rotary press printings through 1953, except coil waste end (such as No. 538), exist with horizontal "Gum Breaker Ridges" varying from 1 to 4 a stamp. See: "Plate".

Special Printings. Stamps of current design reissued, as during the Centennial Exposition of 1876. Examples: Nos. 167-177, 752-771. See "Reissues"; "Reprints".

Surcharge. An overprint which alters or restates the face value or denomination of the stamp to which it was applied (as No. K1, where U. S. stamps were surcharged for Offices in China). Many "surcharges" are typeset. See: "Overprint": "Typeset".

Typeset. Made from movable type.

Typeset Stamps. Printed from ordinary printer's type. Sometimes electrotype or stereotype plates are made, but as such stamps are usually printed only in small quantities for temporary use, movable type is often used for the purpose. This method of printing is apt to show lack of uniformity and broken type.

PRINTING—COMMON FLAWS

Cracked Plate. A term to describe stamps which show evidences that the plate, from which they were printed, was cracked.

Plate cracks come from various causes, each resulting in a different formation of the crack and its intensity. Cracks similar to the above illustration are quite common in the older issues and are largely due to too-quick immersion in the cooling bath when being tempered. These cracks are known as crystallization cracks. A jagged line running generally in one direction and most often in the gutter between stamps is due to the stress of the steel during the rolling in or transferring process.

In curved plates (rotary) there are two types of cracks. One is the bending or curving crack, which is quite marked and always runs in the direction in which the plate is curved.

The illustration shows the second type, which is the "Gripper Crack" and is caused by the cracking of the plate over the slots cut in the under side of the plate, which receive the "grippers" that fasten the plate to the press. These occur only on curved plates. They are to be found in the row of stamps adjoining the plate joint, and appear on the printed impression as light irregular colored lines, usually parallel to the plate joint line.

Rosette Crack. A cluster of fine cracks radiating from a central point in irregular lines. Usually caused by the plate receiving a blow.

Scratched Plate. Caused by foreign matter scratching the plate. These are usually too minor to mention. See: "Gouge".

Gouge. Exceptionally heavy, usually short scratch. May be caused by a tool falling on the plate.

Surface Stains. Irregular circular marks resembling the outline of a pond on a map. Authorities differ as to the cause and they are too minor to list.

PAPER

Paper consists of vegetable fibers, linen, cotton, straw, wood and certain grasses, which, after being pulped and bleached, are spread evenly and thinly, by hand or machinery first upon a wire cloth. The resultant film consolidates into a wet web of pulp, which being passed to felt cloths and through other processes becomes a sheet of paper. This is then finished and cut into sheets for printing. Any coloring is added to the pulp mixture before it is run on the wire cloths.

Paper falls broadly into two divisions: "wove" and "laid". The difference in the appearance is caused by the wire cloth upon which the pulp is first formed.

Wove. In "wove" paper the wire cloth is of an even and closely woven nature, producing a sheet of uniform texture throughout, showing no light or dark figures when held to the light.

Laid. If the wire cloth is formed of closely spaced parallel wires crossed at much wider intervals by cross wires, the resultant paper will show alternate light and dark lines, and is called "laid" paper. The distances apart and the thickness of the lines vary but on any one piece of paper they are all alike.

Paper is also distinguished as thick or thin, hard or soft, and by its color, as bluish, yellowish, greenish, etc.

Pelure. Pelure paper is a very thin, semi-transparent paper, which may be either wove or laid.

Bluish. The 1909 bluish paper was made with 35 per cent rag stock instead of all wood pulp. The bluish color goes through the paper, showing clearly on back and face.

Manila. Manila paper is a coarse paper formerly made of Manila hemp fiber. Since about 1890, so-called "Manila" paper has been manufactured entirely from wood fiber. It is used for cheaper grades of envelopes and newspaper wrappers. It is usually a natural light brown, and sometimes color is added, as in the United States "amber Manila" envelopes. It may be wove or laid.

Silk. Silk paper in philately is of two kinds: first, that in which one or more threads of silk, embedded in the substance of the paper, extend across the stamp. In the catalogues this style of paper is usually designated as "with silk threads". Many United States revenues are on paper which has short silk fibers strewn over it and impressed into it during manufacture. This is the second style and is called simply "silk paper".

Ribbed. Paper which shows fine parallel ridges on one or both sides of a stamp.

India. India paper is a soft, silky appearing wove paper, usually used for proof impressions.

Double Paper. Double paper, as patented by Charles F. Steel, consisted of two layers, a thin surface paper and a thicker backing paper. The paper was supposed to be an absolute safeguard against cleaning, for any attempt to remove the cancellation would result in the destruction of the upper layer. The Continental Bank Note Co. experimented with this paper in the course of printing Nos. 156-165.

China Clay Paper. See note above No. 331.

Fluorescent or Bright Paper. See **Luminescence**.

ROTARY PRESS DOUBLE PAPER

Rotary Press printings are occasionally found printed on a double sheet of paper. The web of paper used on these presses must be continuous. Therefore any break in the process of manufacture must be lapped **and pasted. This overlapping portion, when printed upon,** is known as a "Double Paper" variety. Recently the lapped ends are joined with transparent adhesive tape. In one instance known, two splices had been made, thus giving three thicknesses of paper. Double paper varieties were first listed because of their novelty and scarcity. These listings are now discontinued as all Rotary Press stamps may exist on double paper. Interest has lessened due to increasing finds.

PAPER—WATERMARKS

Closely allied to the paper, as they are usually formed in the process of manufacturing the paper. Watermarks of the United States consist of the letters "USPS" (No. 264, etc.); "USPOD" (No. UX1, etc.); seal of the U. S. (No. OX11, etc.) "USIR" (No. RF3, etc.), and are composed of double-lined and single-lined letters. They are formed of wire or cut from metal and soldered to the frame on which the pulp is caught or to a roll under which it is passed. The action of these is similar to the wires causing the "laid" lines, the designs making thin places in the paper which show by transmitting light. The best method to detect them is to lay the stamp face down on a tray with a black background and immerse in benzine, which brings up the watermark in dark lines against a lighter background. (Note: This method of detecting watermarks is dangerous for certain foreign stamps printed with inks that run when immersed in benzine.)

All watermarks listed in the Standard Postage Stamp Catalogue are numbered for convenience of identification. The numbers 190 and 191, designating watermarks pertaining to the United States, Canal Zone, Cuba, Guam, Philippines and Puerto Rico, are retained to facilitate cross reference with that catalogue.

Wmk. 191

PERIOD OF USE

Postage 1895-1910
Revenue ....none

In the 1895-98 issues, the paper was used so that the watermark letters read horizontally (USPS) on some impressions and vertically on other impressions.

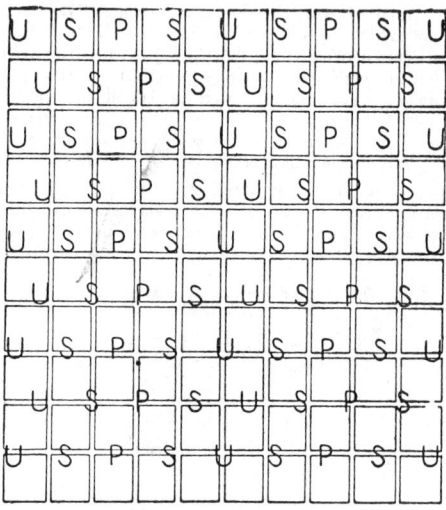

Wmk. 190

PERIOD OF USE

Postage........................1910-1916
Revenue...........................1914

INFORMATION FOR COLLECTORS

USIR
Wmk. 191R
PERIOD OF USE

Postage (unintentionally)
....1895 (271a, 272a), 1951 (832b)
Revenue..............1878 to 1958

Paper watermarked USPOD was used for Postal Cards from 1873 to 1875. For watermarks on stamped envelope paper, see Envelope Section.

Watermarks may be found normal, reversed, inverted, inverted reversed and sideways, as seen from the back of the stamp.

Stitch Watermark. A type of watermark consisting of a row of short parallel lines. This is caused by the stitches, which join the ends of the band on which the paper pulp is first formed. "Stitch watermarks" have been found on a great many issues and may exist on all.

PAPER—GRILLS

Grill. The grill (sometimes called embossing) consists of small square pyramids in parallel rows impressed or embossed on the stamp, with the object to break the fibers of the paper so that the cancellation ink would soak in and make washing for re-use impossible. Grill impressions, when viewed from the face of the stamp may be either "points up" or "points down". Used on U. S. stamps Nos. 79-101, 112-122, 134-144, 156-165, 178-179.

Regular Grill   Continuous Marginal Grill   Split Grill

Continuous Marginal Grill. Includes continuous rows of grill points impressed by the untrimmed parts of the ends of the grill rollers, noted as "end roller grill" on the 1870 and 1873 issues, and those grills which came from a continuous band lengthwise of the roller.

Split Grill. Describes a stamp showing portions of two or more grills, caused by a sheet being fed under the grill roller "off center".

Rotary Grills. The grilled appearance occasionally found on rotary press printings is unintentionally produced by a knurled roller during the perforating process.

PERFORATIONS

Perforation. The chief style of separation of stamps, and the one which today is in almost universal use, is called "perforating". By this process the paper between the stamps is cut away in a line of holes, usually round, leaving little bridges of paper between the stamps to hold them together until they are to be separated. These little bridges are called the teeth of the perforation, and of course project from the stamp when it is torn from the sheet. As the gauge of the perforation is often a guide to the date of issue of the stamp, it is necessary to measure them and describe them by a gauge number. Thus we say a stamp is perforated 12 or 13½. This does not mean that there are 12 or 13½ perforations on the side or end of the stamp, but that 12 or 13½ perforations can be counted in the space of two centimeters. This space has been arbitrarily adopted by collectors the world over as the length in which perforation shall be measured, and the number of perforations in two centimeters is called the gauge of that perforation. Thus a stamp perforated 12 would have perforations so spaced that twelve of them would measure two centimeters. United States stamps from 1861 to 1912 were perforated 12, and give readily obtainable material for testing the above rule.

Perforation Gauge. Gauge for measuring perforations as above.

Fine Perforation. Perforation with small holes and teeth close together.

Coarse Perforation. Perforation with large holes and teeth far apart.

Rough Perforation. Holes not clean cut, but jagged.

Compound Perforation. Where perforations at the top and bottom differ from the perforations at the sides. In describing "compound perforations" the gauge of the top is given first, then the sides. Some stamps are found where one side will differ from the other three, and in this case the reading will be the top first, then the right side, then the bottom and the left side last.

Double Perforations. Often found on early U. S. revenue stamps and occasionally on regular postage issues, double perforations are applied in error. They do not generally command a premium over catalogue prices of properly perforated stamps. These are not to be confused with a variety found on occasional rotary press printings where stamps adjacent to the center gutters will show the entire width of the gutter and a line of perforations on the far end of the gutter. These are caused by the sheet having been cut when off center and they are called "Gutter Snipes". They command a small premium.

INFORMATION FOR COLLECTORS

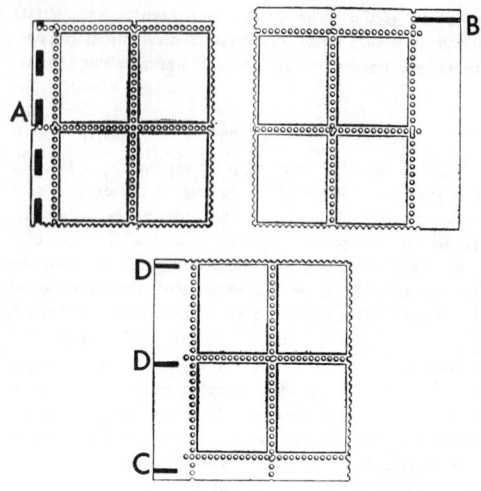

ELECTRIC EYE

An electronically controlled mechanical device acting as a guide in the operation of the perforating machine. Positive identification of stamps perforated by the "electric eye" process may be made by means of the distinctive marks in the gutters and margins of the full sheets on the printed web of paper. The original marks consisted of a series of heavy dashes dividing the vertical sheet gutter between the left and right panes (illustration "A"), together with a single line ("Margin Line," illustration "B"), in the right sheet margin at the end of the horizontal sheet gutter between the upper and lower panes. They were first used in 1933 on 400-subject plates for stamp No. 634, which was distributed to post offices in 1935 (special plates Nos. 21149-50; 21367-68). On these plates the plate numbers were placed opposite the ends of the third row of stamps from the top or bottom of the full sheets.

In later experiments the margin line was broken up into closely spaced thin vertical lines. Then it was again returned to its original form but somewhat narrower.

In 1939 the Bureau installed a new perforating machine which required a different layout to operate the centering mechanism. The vertical dashes remained the same but the margin line was removed from the right sheet margin and a corresponding line ("Gutter Bar," illustration "C"), was placed in the left sheet margin at the end of the horizontal sheet gutter. Additional horizontal lines ("Frame Bars," illustration "D"), were added in the left sheet margin opposite the top frame line of the adjacent stamp design of all horizontal rows except the upper horizontal row of each left pane, where the frame bar is omitted. The plate numbers were moved back to their normal positions adjoining the corner stamps. Plates for the two types of machines could not be interchanged.

Later in 1939 a "convertible" plate was employed. This consisted of a combination of the two previous layouts, the current one with the addition of a margin line (B) in its former position in the right sheet margin, thus making the perforation possible on either machine.

Originally laid out as 400-subject plates, electric eye plates were later used for 200-subject horizontal format and 200-subject vertical format (Commemorative, Special Delivery and Air Mail issues), 280-subject ("Famous Americans," "Edison" and "Carver" issues) and 180 and 360-subject plates (booklet panes of the "ordinary," "air mail," "postal savings" and "war savings" issues). At present, all rotary press plates receive the "electric eye" marks with the exception of the 150 and 170-subject plates used for the printing of coil stamps.

In laying out the plates for the 400-subject and 200-subject horizontal format issues, the marks retained the same relative positions to the stamp designs. This was changed, however, in entering the designs for the stamps on the 200-subject vertical format and 280-subject issues, in that the stamp designs were turned 90 degrees, that is, the designs were entered on the plates with the longer dimension horizontal. Although the electric eye marks were entered on the plates in the usual positions, on the printed sheets they appear as though shifted 90 degrees when the stamps are held in the customary upright position. Thus, a "horizontal" mark on a 400-subject or 200-subject horizontal format sheet would become a "vertical" mark on a 200-subject vertical format or 280-subject sheet. This situation has caused confusion among collectors and dealers in determining a definite description of the various marks. The designation of the position of the plate numbers also has not been uniform for the "turned" designs.

To solve this "confusion," the Bureau Issues Association adopted a standardized terminology of all the marks appearing on the "electric eye" sheets, "Dashes" (A), "Margin Line" (B), "Gutter Bar" (C) and "Frame Bars" (D), whereby each type of mark may be readily identified without referring to its plate number position. The "plate number" designation of the panes will continue to be established by holding the pane of stamps with the designs in an upright position; the corner of the pane on which the plate number appears will determine whether the pane is "upper left" (UL), "upper right" (UR), "lower left" (LL), or "lower right" (LR).

Scott Publishing Co. will use these terms in its catalogues, wherever necessary.

Imperforate. Stamps without perforations, rouletting or other forms of separation between them.

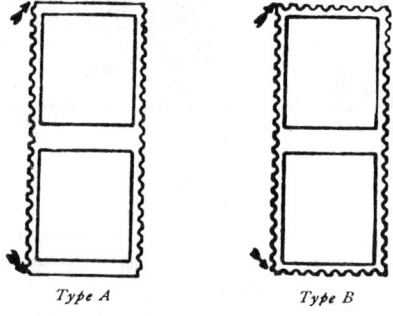

Type A   *Type B*

Part-Perforate. Stamps with perforations on the two opposite sides, the other two sides remaining imperforate.

INFORMATION FOR COLLECTORS

Vertical Pair Imperforate Horizontally. (Type A) This indicates that the pair is fully perforated vertically but is imperforate horizontally.

Horizontal Pair Imperforate Vertically. (Type A) This indicates that the pair is fully perforated horizontally but is imperforate vertically.

Vertical Pair Imperforate Between. (Type B) This indicates that the vertical pair is fully perforated at the top, sides and bottom but is imperforate between the stamps.

Horizontal Pair Imperforate Between. (Type B) This indicates that the horizontal pair is fully perforated at the top, sides and bottom but is imperforate between the stamps.

Of the above types A and B, type A is the commoner. Examples: U. S. Revenue stamps, 1862, etc. An example of a vertical pair type B is No. 499c.

Rouletting. Short consecutive cuts in the paper to facilitate separation of the stamps, made with a toothed wheel or disc.

LUMINESCENCE

Kinds of Luminescence. Fluorescence and phosphorescence, two different luminescent qualities, are found in U.S. postage stamps and postal stationery. While all luminescent stamps glow when exposed to shortwave ultraviolet (UV) light, only those with phosphorescent properties display brief afterglow when the UV light source is turned off.

Fluorescent or 'Hi-bright' Papers. The Bureau of Engraving and Printing, accepting stamp paper without regard to fluorescent properties, unknowingly used a mix of infinitely varying amounts of fluorescent optical brighteners added during the papermaking process. In March, 1964, to preserve uniformity of product and as a safeguard for an emerging but still incomplete plan for nationwide use of luminescent stamps, purchasing specifications were amended to limit the use of fluorescent paper brighteners. The amended specification permitted paper with *some* brightener content, but excluded brilliantly glowing papers known in trade jargon as "Hi-bright." Stamps printed on such papers emit a distinctive, intense whitish-violet glow when viewed with either long or shortwave UV. In following years stamps were produced on papers with lower levels of fluorescence permitted by amended specifications.

Tagged Stamps. The Post Office Department field-tested automated mail-handling equipment to face, cancel and sort mail at rates up to 30,000 pieces an hour, by sensing UV-light-activated afterglow from phosphorescent substances. For the first tests at Dayton, Ohio, started after Aug. 1, 1963, 8c carmine airmail stamps (No. C64a) were overprinted (tagged) with a so-called "nearly invisible" calcium-silicate compound which phosphoresces orange-red when exposed to shortwave UV. A facer-canceler, with modifications that included a rapidly cycling on-off UV light, activated the phosphor-tagged airmail stamps and extracted envelopes bearing them from the regular flow of mail.

While the airmail extraction test was still in progress, the entire printing of the City Mail Delivery commemorative (No. 1238) was ordered tagged with a yellow-green glowing zinc-orthosilicate compound intended for use with the automated recognition circuits to be tested with surface transported letter mail. After the first day ceremonies Oct. 26, 1963, at Washington, it was learned the stamps had been tagged to publicize the innovative tests by coupling tagging with stamps memorializing "100 years of postal progress" and to provide the first national distribution of tagged stamps for collectors. Between Oct. 28 and Nov. 2, to broaden the scope of the test in the Dayton area, the 4c and 5c denominations of the regular issue (Nos. 1036b, 1213b, 1213c and 1229a) were issued with the same green glowing compound applied in an experimental tagging format.

By June, 1964, testing had proven sufficiently effective for the Post Office Department to order all 8c airmail adhesive stamps phosphor-tagged for general distribution. By January, 1966, all airmail stamps regardless of denomination were ordered tagged. Meanwhile, from 1963 through 1965, limited quantities of the Christmas issues (Nos. 1240a, 1254a–1257a and 1276a) were tagged for use in the continuing test in the Dayton area.

On May 19, 1966, the use of phosphor-tagged stamps was expanded to the Cincinnati Postal Region which then included offices in Ohio, Kentucky and Indiana. During the last half of 1966, primarily to meet the postal needs of that region, phosphor-tagged issues were authorized to include additional denominations of regular issues, some postal stationery, and about 12 percent of each commemorative issue starting with the National Park Service 5c (No. 1314a) and continuing through the Mary Cassatt 5c (No. 1322a). After Jan. 1, 1967, most regular values through the 16c, all commemoratives, and additional items of postal stationery were ordered tagged.

However, adhesive stamps precanceled by the Bureau of Engraving and Printing were not tagged, except No. 1394, 1596, 1608 and 1610. Since there was no need to cancel mail with these stamps and since precancel permit holders post such mail already faced, postal officials by-passed facer-canceler operations and avoided the cost of tagging.

Phosphorescent overprints when newly issued are practically invisible in ordinary light, but after aging three to five years the tagging discolors and appears tawny or toasted. When viewed with UV there is little change in the hue of either orange-red or yellow-green emitted light. Even though observable discoloration exists, the presence or absence of tagging is best determined by examination with UV light.

Bar tagging, instead of the usual overall phosphorescent overprint, was used for some stamps starting with No. 1468, the Andreotti-printed Mail Order Business 8c.

Band tagging, a bar extending across two or more stamps, was first used for Nos. 1489–1498.

Most of the luminescent issues of 1967–70 exist with the luminescent coating unintentionally omitted. This group includes Nos. 1323–1338, 1339, 1342–1356, 1358, 1360, 1365–1370, 1372–1374. Earlier omissions of luminescence include Nos. 1238, 1278, 1281, 1298, 1305.

In some postal stationery, such as Nos. U551, UC40, UX48a and UX55, the luminescent element is in the ink with which the stamp design is printed.

The luminescent varieties of stamped envelopes Nos. U550 and UC37 were made by applying a vertical phosphorescent bar or panel at left of stamp. On No. UC42, this "glow-bar" passes through the tri-globe design.

Caution. Users of UV light should avoid prolonged exposure which can burn the eyes. Sunglasses or prescription eyeglasses, tinted or plain, screen the rays and provide protection.

POSTAL MARKINGS

Postal markings are those marks placed by the post office of this or other countries on the stamp or cover or both, which indicate mailing place of a letter, date, rate, route, accounting between post offices, etc.

In addition to the basic town markings there are many varieties of *supplemental markings*. These include *rate marks*, *route marks*, *obliterators*, special *dating markings* usually found on advertised or dead letter covers, transportation markings (rail, steam, ship, airmail, etc), and services markings (advertised, forwarded, missent, second delivery, mail route, too late, charged, paid box, due, returned for postage, soldier's letter, held for postage, short paid, unpaid, not paid, paid, free, dead letter office, etc.)

In what is now the United States, these markings originated in the Colonial period when manuscript postal markings were first introduced under the Ordinance of Dec. 10, 1672, of New York which established an inland postal system between the colonies. A "Post Payd" is found on the first letter ever sent under this system, on Jan. 22, 1673. Manuscript postal markings continued in use right on through the pre-stamp period and can still be found on some letters in the present era.

Handstamp postal markings were introduced at New York in 1756 when a post office packet service was established between Falmouth, England, and New York. The marking was a two-line straightline reading NEW/YORK. Similar markings were later introduced at other towns such as ANNA/POLIS (by 1766), CHARLES/TOWN (by 1770), PHILA/DELPHIA (by 1766), HART/FORD (by 1766), etc., while other offices received a single-line marking: BOSTON (by 1769), ALBANY (by 1773), PENSACOLA (by 1772), SAVANNA (by 1765), BALTIMORE (by 1772), WMSBURG (by 1770).

Some of these early letters also bear a circular date stamp containing the month in abbreviated form as "IV" (June) or "IY" (July) and the date in a 14-17mm circle. Known from at least nine towns, these are called "Franklin marks," after Benjamin Franklin, then Deputy Postmaster General for the English Crown, or "American Bishopmarks" to distinguish them from the Bishopmark used in England, which has a center line.

During 1774-1775, an American "provisional" postal system was set up in opposition to that of the English Crown. Both manuscript and handstamp markings have been attributed to it by various students. This system was taken over by Congress on July 26, 1775, and the same markings were continued in use. The earliest reported Congressional marks are a manuscript "Camb Au 8" and a blue-green straightline "NEW*YORK*AU:24". Postal markings are known throughout the Revolution, including English occupation markings, and most are manuscript.

In the post-war Confederation period, handstamped circular markings were introduced at Charleston, S.C. (1778-1780), and later at New London, Conn. (1793). However, straightlines and manuscripts dominated until oval markings became widespread around 1800, with circles becoming the predominant marking shortly thereafter.

Handstamp rate markings are known as early as the pennyweight markings of Albany in 1789. They become more common in the 1830's, and almost standard by the "5" and "10" cent rate period which began July 1, 1845. This is also when envelopes began replacing folded lettersheets (before that date, envelopes were charged with an extra rate of postage). These "5", "10", and the succeeding "3", "6", "5", and "10" rates of 1851-56, were common on domestic mail until prepayment became compulsory on all but drop or local letters on April 1, 1855, and on foreign mail until about 1875.

Only 1.3% of all letters posted between 1847 and 1852 bore stamps. This proportion increased to 25% in 1852, 32% in 1853, 34% in 1854, 40% in 1855 and 64% in 1856. The attic searcher or collector who has never seen a prestamp or "stampless" cover obviously would be wrong to assume that one was a great rarity, although some are highly prized. Most, however, are more common than the stamps of the period.

While the government began issuing handstamps as early as 1799, and obliterators in 1847, many postmasters were required or permitted to purchase their own canceling devices or to use pen strokes. Pen cancellations continued to be common in the smaller offices into the 1880's. Because of collector prejudice against pen-canceled stamps, many have ended up being "cleaned." These are sold either as unused or with a different, faked cancellation to cover the evidence of cleaning. Ultraviolet light will usually reveal traces of the original pen marking.

From around 1850 until 1900 many postmasters used obliterators cut from wood or cork. Many bear fanciful designs such as bees, bears, chickens, locks, eagles, Masonic symbols, flags, numerals, etc. Some of the designs symbolized the town of origin. These are not listed in this catalogue as they owe their origin to the whim of some individual rather than a requirement of the postal regulations. Many command high prices and are eagerly sought by collectors. This has led to extensive forgery of such markings so that collectors are well advised to check them carefully.

Rapid machine cancellations were introduced at Boston in 1880-90 and later spread across the country. Each of the various canceling machine types has identifiable characteristics and collectors do form collections of them. One subspecialty is that of flag cancellations. While handstamp flag designs are known earlier, the first machine flag cancellation was that of Boston in November-December 1894.

Specialists have noted that different canceling inks are used at different times, depending partly on the type of canceling device used. Rubber handstamps, prohibited in 1893 although used for parcel post and precanceling after that date, require a different type of ink from the boxwood or type-metal cancelers of the classic period, while a still different ink is used for the steel devices of the machine cancels.

Registry of letters was first authorized in the Dutch colony of New Netherland on overseas mail. Records of valuable letters were kept by postmasters throughout the stampless period while an "R" marking was introduced at Philadelphia in 1845 for "recorded" mail. Cincinnati also had such a "recorded" system. The first appearance of the word "registered" appears on mail in November, 1847, in manuscript, and in handstamp in May, 1850. However, the official registration system for U.S. mail did not begin until July 1, 1855.

In recent years the handstamped and machine types of cancellations have been standardized by the Post Office Department and supplied to the various post offices.

Postmarks. Markings to indicate the office of origin, or manner of the postal conveyance. Generally speaking the postmark refers to the post office of origin, but sometimes there are also receiving postmarks of the post office of destination or of transit. Other post office markings include: Advertised, Forwarded, Mail Route, Missent, Paid, Not Paid, Second Delivery, Too Late, etc., etc. Postmarks often serve also to cancel postage stamps with or without additional obliterating cancels.

Cancellations. A cancellation is a postal marking which cancels the stamp, making its further use impossible. As used in the listings in this Catalogue, cancellations include both postmarks used as cancellations, and obliterations intended primarily to cancel (or "kill") the stamp.

Carrier Postmarks. These usually show the words "Carrier", "City Delivery" or "U. S. P. O. Dispatch". (See illustration under Cancellations.) They were applied

INFORMATION FOR COLLECTORS

to letters to indicate the delivery of mail by U. S. Government carriers. These markings should not be confused with those of Local Posts or other private mail services which used postmarks of their own. Free delivery of city mail by carriers was begun on July 1, 1863.

Free. Handstamp generally used on free, franked mail. Occasionally seen on early adhesives of the U. S. used as a cancelling device.

Railroad Postmarks. Usually handstamps, used to postmark unpouched mail received by Route Agents of the Post Office Department traveling on trains on railway mail routes. The route name in an agent's postmark often was similar to the name of the railroad or included the terminals of the route. The earliest known use of the word "Railroad" as a postmark is 1838. Route Agents gradually became R.P.O. clerks and some continued to use their handstamps after the Route Agent service ceased June 30, 1882. The railroad postmarks of the 1850 period and later usually carried the name of the railroad.

A sub-group of railroad postmarks comprises those applied in the early days by railroad station agents, using the railroad's ticket dating handstamp as a postmark. Sometimes the station agent was also the postmaster.

In 1864, the Post Office Department equipped cars for the general distribution of mails between Chicago and Clinton, Iowa.

Modern railroad marks such as "R.P.O." (Railway Post Office) indicate transportation by railroad cars on designated routes and distribution of mail in transit. "R. M. S." (Railway Mail Service) is a mark indicating transportation by railroad, and includes Railway Post Office, Terminal Railway Post Office, Transfer Office, Closed Mail Service, Air Mail Field and Highway Post Office.

Effective Nov. 1, 1949, the Railway Mail Service (RMS) was merged with others of like nature under the new consolidated title, Postal Transportation Service (PTS).

The modern and current "Railway marks" are quite common and are not the types referred to under cancellations as listed in the catalogue.

Way Markings. Way letters are those received by a mail-carrier on his way between post offices and delivered at the first post office he reached. The postmaster ascertained where the carrier received them and charged, in his post-bills, the postage from those places to destination. He wrote "Way" against those charges in his bills and also wrote or stamped "Way" upon each letter. If the letter were exempt from postage, it should have been marked "Free."

"Mail-carrier" in the foregoing paragraph refers to any carrier under contract to carry U. S. mails: a stage line, a horseback rider, or a steamboat or railroad that did not have a route agent on board. Only unpouched mail (not previously placed in a post office) was eligible for a Way fee of 1 cent. The postmaster paid this fee to the carrier, if demanded, for the carrier's extra work of bringing the letter individually to the post office. For a limited time at certain post offices, the Way fee was added to the regular postage. This explains the use of a numeral with "Way."

Packet Markings. Packet markings listed in this catalogue are those applied on a boat traveling on inland or coastal waterways. This group does not include mail to foreign countries that contains the words "British Packet," "American Packet," etc., or their abbreviations (Br. Pkt., etc.); these are U. S. foreign-mail exchange-office markings.

Listed packet markings are in two groups: (1) Waterways route-agent markings which denote service exactly the same as that of railroad route-agent markings except that the route agent traveled on a boat instead of a train. (2) Name-of-boat markings placed on the cover to advertise the boat or, as some believe, to expedite payment of Way and Steam fees at the post office where such letters entered the U. S. mails.

Occasionally waterways route-agent markings included the name of a boat, or "S.B.," "STEAMBOAT," "STEAM," or merely a route number. Such supplemental designations do not alter the character of the markings as route-agent markings.

U. S. Express Mail Postmarks. In pre-stamp days these represented either an extra-fast mail service or mail given into the care of an express-mail messenger who also carried out-of-mail express packages, permitted as a practical means of competing with package express companies that also carried mail in competition with U. S. mails. Several of these early postmarks were later used by U. S. mail route agents on the New York-Boston and New York-Albany runs, or by U. S. steamboat letter carriers on the coastal run between Boston and St. John, N.B.

Steamboat or Steam Markings. Except the circular markings reading "Maysville Ky. Steam" and "Terre Haute Stb." and the rectangular "Troy & New York Steam Boat," these markings contain only the word "STEAMBOAT" or "STEAM," with or without a rating numeral. They represent service exactly similar to that of Way markings, except that the carrier was an inland or coastal steamer that had no contract to carry U. S. mails. Such boats, however, were required by law to carry to the nearest post office any mail given them at landings. The boat owner was paid a 2-cent fee for each letter so delivered, except on Lake Erie where the fee was 1 cent. At some post offices in the early days the Steamboat fee was added to regular postage. In 1861 the 2-cent fee was again added to the postage, and in 1863 double postage was charged.

Ship Postmarks. Postal markings indicating arrival on a private ship (one not under contract to carry mails). This marking was applied to letters delivered by such ships to the post office at their port of entry as required by law, for which they received a fee and the letters were taxed with a specified fee for the service in place of the ordinary open postage.

The use of U. S. postage stamps on ship letters is unusual, except for letters from Hawaii, because the U. S. inland postage on ship letters from a foreign point did not need to be prepaid. "U. S. SHIP" is a special marking applied to mail posted on naval vessels, especially in the Civil War period.

Steamship Postmarks. These are akin to Ship postmarks but they appear to have been used mostly on mail from Caribbean or Pacific ports to New Orleans or Atlantic ports carried on steamships having a U. S. mail contract. An associated numeral usually designates the through rate from where the letter was received by the ship to its inland destination.

Receiving Mark. Impression placed on the back of envelopes by the receiving office to indicate name of office and date of arrival. Also known as "backstamp". Generally discontinued about 1913, but was employed for a time on airmail service until it was found the practice slowed up the service. Now used on Registry and Special Delivery mail.

Miscellaneous Route Markings. Wordings associated with the previously described markings include Bay Route, River Mail, Steamer, Mail Route, etc. Classification of the marking is ordinarily evident from usage, or it can be identified from publications on postal markings.

U. S. Foreign-Mail Exchange-Office Markings. These serve to meet the accounting requirements of the various mail treaties before the Universal Postal Union was established. The markings usually designate the exchange office or the carrier (British Packet, Bremen Packet, American Packet, etc.). Sometimes they are a restatement of the through rate, or a numeral designating the amount credited or debited to the foreign country as a means of allocating the respective parts of the total postage, according to conditions of route, method of transit, weight, etc.

Gridiron Cancellations. Commonest types of cancellations on early U. S. stamps. Consist of circles enclosing parallel lines. There are, however, many varieties of grid cancellations, especially the New York square grid.

Paid Markings. Generally consist of the word "PAID," sometimes within a frame, indicating regular postage prepaid by the sender of a letter. They are found as separate handstamps, within town or city postmarks, and as a part of obliterating cancels. In each case the "paid" marking may be used with or without an accompanying or combined rate numeral indication.

Precancels. Stamps having the cancellation applied before the article is presented for mailing. The purpose is to reduce handling and speed up the mails. A permit is required for use by the public except for special cases such as the experiments using Nos. 1384a and 1414–1418a for Christmas mail. Normally the precanceling is done with devices not used for ordinary postal service. Most precancellations consist of the city and state names between two lines or bars.

Precancels are divided into two groups: "locals" and "Bureaus." Locals are printed, usually from 100-subject plates, or handstamped at the office using the stamps by means of a 10 or 25-subject device having a rubber, metal or vinyl surface. Most locals are made with devices furnished by the Postal Service, but a number have been made with devices created in the city using them. Early locals include the printed "PAID" or "paid" on Nos. 7 and 9, the "CUMBERLAND, ME." on Nos. 24-26 and the Glen Allen, Va., stars.

Many styles of precancellation are known. Over 600,000 different precancels exist from more than 20,000 post offices in the United States.

The Bureaus, or Bureau Prints, are precancels printed by the Bureau of Engraving and Printing. They originated in 1916 when postal officials were seeking ways to reduce costs as well as increase the legibility of the overprint. They tried applying the precancellation at the Bureau during the production of the stamps which resulted in the "experimentals." These 16 denominations, including two dues, were issued for Augusta, Me. (1 value), Springfield, Mass. (14 values), and New Orleans (6 values) in quantities ranging from 4,000,000 down to 10,000. Electrotype plates mounted on a flat bed press were used to print the precancellations.

Regular production of Bureau Prints began on May 2, 1923, with No. 581 precanceled New York, N.Y. All regular Bureaus until 1954 were produced by the Stickney rotary press, whereby the stamps, immediately after printing, pass under the precancelling plates. Then the roll is gummed, perforated and cut into sheets or coils. Since 1954 a variety of printing methods have been used.

Tied On. A stamp is "tied on" when the cancellation (or postmark) extends from the stamp to the envelope.

DAVID G. PHILLIPS CO., INC.

AUCTIONEER AND DEALER
FINE U.S. COVERS & POSTAL HISTORY
Current Lists Available Upon Request.

*Publisher of American Stampless Cover Catalog
and American Illustrated Cover Catalog*

 P.O. Box 611388, North Miami, Florida 33161-1388
Phone (305) 895-0470

INFORMATION FOR COLLECTORS

POSTAL MARKINGS—Examples of Cancellations

The Common Boston Paid Cancellation
(See note in Special Notices)

Numerals

Prices are for rating marks such as those illustrated.
Later types of numerals In grids, targets. etc. are common.

FREE
"Free"

PAID
" Paid "

PAID ALL
" Paid All "

STEAMBOAT
"Steamboat"

SHIP
"Ship"

STEAM
"Steam"

"Way"

Steamship

Steamboat
(Route agent marking)

Packet Boat
(Name-of-boat marking)

Railroad
(Route agent marking)

Packet Boat
(Name-of-boat marking)

U. S. Express Mail
(Route agent marking)

Packet Boat
(Name-of-boat marking)

INFORMATION FOR COLLECTORS

U. S. Exchange-Office
(In red on letter to Germany
via Prussian Closed Mail,
via British Packet.
Credits 7 cents to Prussia.)

Express Company

Carrier

Canadian

U. S. Postmark
used in China

Army Field Post

U. S. Postmark
used in Japan

Town

Fort

Year dated

Vera Cruz, Mexico, 1914

Exposition Station.
Used while exposition is open.
Many styles.

Exposition advertising.
Used before exposition opens.
Many styles.

POSTAL MARKINGS—New York City Foreign Mail

A group of design cancellations used during the period from 1871 to 1877 in New York City on outgoing foreign mail only. This group of handstamps totals about 100 different fancy stars, geometric designs, wheels, conventionalized flowers, etc., the majority within a circle 26-29mm. in diameter. Examples follow.

POSTAL MARKINGS—Patent Defacing Cancellations

When adhesive stamps came into general use, the Post Office Department made constant efforts to find a type of cancellation which would make the re-use of the stamp impossible. Many patents were granted to inventors and some of the cancellations (killers) came into more or less general use. Some of them appear in combination with the town postmarks.

About 125 different types are known on the stamp issues up to about 1887. Their principal use and greatest variety occur on Nos. 65, 147, 158, 183 and 184.

Generally speaking, Patent Cancellations fall into three groups:

1. Small pins or punches which pierce the paper or depress it sufficiently to break the fiber.
2. Sharp blades or other devices for cutting the paper.
3. Rotation of a portion of the canceller so that part of the paper is scraped away.

Four are illustrated below.

1
Dot punches through paper.

2
Blades cut the paper.

2.
Small circle cuts the paper.

3.
Scraped in the shaded circle.

POSTAL MARKINGS—Supplementary Mail

Supplementary Mail markings designate the special P.O. service of dispatching mail after the regular mail closed. Two kinds of supplementary mail were available:

1. Foreign mail. For New York the Postmaster General established in 1853 a fee of double the regular rate. This paid for getting the mail aboard ship after the regular mail closing and before sailing time. The service continued until 1939. Postmark types A, D, E, F and G were used.

In several other ports similar service was provided without special postmarks. Honolulu used a "Late Fee" handstamp.

2. Domestic mail. For Chicago the extra fee entitled a letter to catch the late East-bound train. Postmark types B and C were used. No foreign destination was implied.

Similar service without "Supplementary" in the postmark was apparently available in Philadelphia and possible elsewhere.

Type A

Type D

Type E

Type F
Combination Handstamp
(Also comes with numeral "1")

C

Type G
(Also with other numerals)

Type B

Type C

INFORMATION FOR COLLECTORS

WORLD WAR I SOLDIERS' LETTERS.

At the time the United States declared war against Germany on April 6, 1917, a postal regulation existed to the effect that letters could be sent without prepayment of postage by soldiers, sailors and marines to places in the United States when endorsed "Soldier's letter," etc., and countersigned by an officer, and only the single rate collected from the recipient (Sec. 406 P.L.R. May 4, 1914). Few of the enlisted men, however, took advantage of this privilege in sending letters while in the United States and practically all letters sent by soldiers from some 200 World War I military post offices (Fig. A) in the United States bear regular postage stamps.

Fig. A

Soon after the arrival of the first units of the American Expeditionary Force in France this regulation was modified to include letters which, although not endorsed, bore the postmark of the United States Army Postal Service (Postal Guide, August, 1917). The War Revenue Act of Congress of October 3, 1917 (section 1100), provided free postage for soldiers, sailors and marines assigned to duty overseas.

Therefore, letters from members of the A.E.F. sent before October, 1917, without postage stamps were properly chargeable with postage due, while those sent after that time went through post free.

This provision of free postage did not ordinarily apply to civilians permitted to accompany the army, such as welfare workers, Post Office Department representatives, war correspondents and others; neither did it apply to the registration fee on soldiers' letters nor to parcel post matter. It was necessary to pay such postage by means of postage stamps.

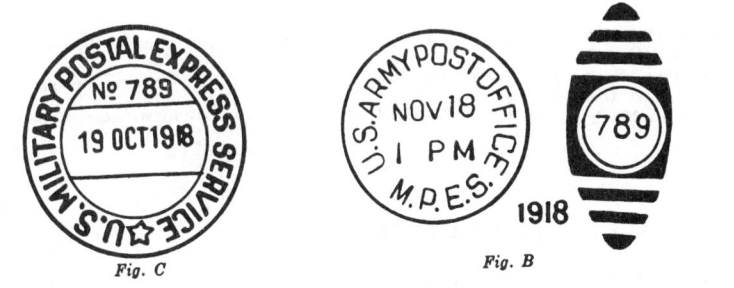

Fig. C   Fig. B   Fig. D

United States Army post offices, (Fig. B), known as A.P.O.'s were established in France, the earliest being that at St. Nazaire on July 10, 1917. The A.P.O.'s were at first operated by the Post Office Department, but in May, 1918, Military Postal Express Service was established (Fig. C) and the army took over their operation. Later the name was changed to Postal Express Service (Fig. D).

Army post offices were given code numbers, and were at first numbered from No. 1 (St. Nazaire) to No. 18 (Saumur). In December, 1917, they were renumbered 701, 702, etc., and some 169 A.P.O.'s were established on the Western Front, including offices in Italy, Belgium, Netherlands, Luxembourg and Germany after the Armistice. Most of the A.P.O.'s were located at fixed places, but "mobile" post offices were assigned to divisions, army corps and armies and were moved from place to place. Many A.P.O.'s had stations or branches, some of which used postmarks with different code numbers from those assigned to the main office.

INFORMATION FOR COLLECTORS

Fig. F

Fig. E

Fig. G

Until July, 1919, all A.E.F. mail was censored, and letters will be found with "company" censor marks (Fig. E) as well as "regimental" censor marks (Fig. F). Distinctive censor marks were used at the base censor's office in Paris (Fig. G).

An interesting variety of subsidiary markings will be found on soldiers' letters, typical items being: ADDRESSEE RETURNED TO U.S.A., CANNOT BE FOUND, DECEASED - VERIFIED, NO RECORD, SOLDIER'S MAIL, and UNIT RETURNED TO U. S.

Many styles of stationery were used, mainly those furnished by welfare organizations. Only a few envelopes of a pictorial nature were used; but a considerable variety of patriotic and pictorial post cards may be obtained, in addition to officially printed form post cards.

Fig. H

Fig. I

A postal agency was in operation in Siberia from 1918 to 1920 and distinctive postmarks (Fig. H) and censor marks were used there. A few American soldiers were sent to North Russia, and postmarks used there were those of the British Expeditionary Force's North Russia postal service (Fig. I).

World War I postmarks have been classified by collectors, and the "American Classification System" prepared by the War Cover Club is in general use by collectors of these items.

WORLD WAR II

Commencing in January, 1941, U. S. post offices were established in Newfoundland, Bermuda and other naval bases acquired as a result of the exchange of destroyers with Great Britain. The names of the bases were at first included in the postmark, later A.P.O. code numbers were adopted, in a similar manner to those used during World War I. Towards the middle of 1942 the A.P.O. numbers were cut out of the postmark so that nothing appears to indicate the A.P.O. at which a letter was mailed, although the already established practice was continued of the writer giving his A.P.O. number in the return address. Early in 1943, A.P.O. numbers were replaced in the postmarking stamps at many military post offices.

More than 1,000 different A.P.O. numbers were used. At least 90 types of postmarks exist, of which 45 are handstamped and 40 machine-struck.

Men in the armed services, both at home and abroad, were given the franking privilege early in April, 1942, the frank consisting of the written word "Free" in the upper right corner of the envelope.

A wide variety of censor marks was used, differing radically in design from those used during World War I.

POSTAL MARKINGS—Bureau Precancels

| AUGUSTA MAINE | NEW ORLEANS LA. | SPRINGFIELD MASS. |

Experimentals

| PERU IND. | LANSING MICH. | SAINT LOUIS MO. | New Orleans La. | San Francisco Calif. |

PORTLAND ME.

| LAKEWOOD N. J. | KANSAS CITY MO. |

| POUGHKEEPSIE N. Y. | LONG ISLAND CITY, N. Y. | CORPUS CHRISTI TEXAS | ATLANTA GEORGIA | ATLANTA GA. |

| PEORIA IL | CINCINNATI OH |

POSTAL MARKINGS—Local Precancels

QUINCY ILLINOIS	FITCHBURG MASS.	LOS ANGELES CALIF.	Fergus Falls Minn.
COVINGTON KY.	REDWOOD CITY CALIF.	BELMONT CALIF.	ELGIN ILLINOIS

Electroplates

Ashland Wis.	PALMYRA N. Y.	Northhampton MASS.	DES PLAINES ILL.
RICHMOND VA.	BROOKFIELD ILLINOIS	PAONIA COLO.	GOSHEN IND
TOWER CITY N. DAK.	NEW BRUNSWICK N. J.	ORLANDO, FLA.	RICHTON PARK ILL.
MULINO, OREG.	PINE HILL N.Y.	FARRELL, PA	SACRAMENTO CA

Handstamps

TERRITORIAL AND STATEHOOD DATES

	Territorial Date	Statehood Date	
Alabama	Aug. 15, 1817	Dec. 14, 1819	Territory by Act of March 3, 1817, effective Aug. 15, 1817.
Alaska	Oct. 18, 1867	Jan. 3, 1959	A District from Oct. 18, 1867, until it became an Organized Territory Aug. 24, 1912.
Arizona	Feb. 24, 1863	Feb. 14, 1912	This region was sometimes called Arizona before 1863 though still in the Territory of New Mexico.
Arkansas	July 5, 1819*	June 15, 1836	The Territory was larger than the State. The left-over area to the west after statehood had post offices which continued for some years to use an Arkansas abbreviation in the postmarks though really in the "Indian Country."
California		Sept. 9, 1850	Ceded by Mexico by the Guadalupe-Hidalgo Treaty, concluded Feb. 2, 1848 and proclaimed July 4, 1848. From then until statehood, California had first a military government until Dec. 20, 1849 and then a local civil government. It never had a territorial form of government.
Colorado	Feb. 28, 1861	Aug. 1, 1876	
Dakota	March 2, 1861	Nov. 2, 1889	Became two states—North and South Dakota.
Deseret	March 5, 1849		March 5, 1849 Brigham Young created the unofficial territory of Deseret. In spite of the fact that Utah Territory was created Sept. 9, 1850, Deseret continued to exist unofficially in what is now Utah for several years, at least as late as 1862.
Frankland or Franklin			This unofficial state was formed in Aug. 1784 in the northeast corner of what is now Tennessee, and the government existed until 1788. In reality it was part of North Carolina.
Florida	March 30, 1822	March 3, 1845	
Hawaii	Aug. 12, 1898	Aug. 21, 1959	The territorial date given is that of the formal transfer to the United States, with Sanford B. Dole as first Governor.
Idaho	March 3, 1863	July 3, 1890	
Illinois	March 2, 1809*	Dec. 3, 1818	
Indiana	July 5, 1800*	Dec. 11, 1816	There was a residue of Indiana Territory which continued to exist under that name from Dec. 11, 1816 until Dec. 3, 1818 when it was attached to Michigan Territory.
Indian Territory		Nov. 16, 1907	In the region first called the "Indian Country," established June 30, 1834. Never had a territorial form of government. Finally, with Oklahoma Territory, became the State of Oklahoma, Nov. 16, 1907.
Iowa	July 4, 1838	Dec. 28, 1846	
Jefferson	Oct. 24, 1859		An unofficial territory from Oct. 24, 1859 to Feb. 28, 1861. In reality it included parts of Kansas, Nebraska, Utah and New Mexico Territories, about 30% being in each of the first three and 10% in New Mexico. The settled portion was mostly in Kansas Territory until Jan. 29, 1861 when the State of Kansas was formed from the eastern part of Kansas Territory. From this date the heart of "Jefferson" was in unorganized territory until Feb. 28, 1861, when it became the Territory of Colorado.
Kansas	May 30, 1854	Jan. 29, 1861	
Kentucky		June 1, 1792	Never a territory. Was part of Virginia until statehood.
District of Louisiana	Oct. 1, 1804		An enormous region—all of the Louisiana Purchase except the Territory of Orleans. Created by Act of March 26, 1804, effective Oct. 1, 1804 and attached for administrative purposes to the Territory of Indiana.
Territory of Louisiana	July 4, 1805		By Act of March 3, 1805, effective July 4, 1805, the District of Louisiana became the Territory of Louisiana.
District of Maine		March 16, 1820	What is now the State of Maine was before statehood called the District of Maine and belonged to Massachusetts.
Michigan	July 1, 1805	Jan. 26, 1837	
Minnesota	March 3, 1849	May 11, 1858	
Mississippi	May 7, 1798	Dec. 10, 1817	Territory by Act of April 7, 1798, effective May 7, 1798.

TERRITORIAL AND STATEHOOD DATES

	Territorial Date	Statehood Date	
Missouri	Dec. 7, 1812	Aug. 10, 1821	The State was much smaller than the Territory. The area to the west and northwest of the State, which had been in the Territory, was commonly known as the "Missouri Country" until May 30, 1854 and certain of the post offices in this area show a Missouri abbreviation in the postmark.
Montana	May 26, 1864	Nov. 8, 1889	
Nebraska	May 30, 1854	March 1, 1867	
Nevada	March 2, 1861	Oct. 31, 1864	
New Mexico	Dec. 13, 1850	Jan. 6, 1912	
North Dakota		Nov. 2, 1889	Had been part of the Territory of Dakota.
Northwest Territory	July 13, 1787		Ceased to exist March 1, 1803 when Ohio became a state. The date given is in dispute, Nov. 29, 1802 often being accepted.
Ohio		March 1, 1803	Had been part of Northwest Territory until statehood.
Oklahoma	May 2, 1890	Nov. 16, 1907	The State was formed from Oklahoma Territory and Indian Territory.
Oregon	Aug. 14, 1848	Feb. 14, 1859	
Orleans	Oct. 1, 1804		A Territory by Act of March 26, 1804, effective Oct. 1, 1804. Became with certain boundary changes, the State of Louisiana, April 30, 1812.
South Dakota		Nov. 2, 1889	Had been part of Dakota Territory.
Southwest Territory			Became the State of Tennessee, with minor boundary changes, June 1 1796.
Tennessee		June 1, 1796	Had been Southwest Territory before statehood.
Texas		Dec. 29, 1845	Had been an independent Republic before statehood.
Utah	Sept. 9, 1850	Jan. 4, 1896	
Vermont		March 4, 1791	Until statehood, had been a region claimed by both New York and New Hampshire.
Washington	March 2, 1853	Nov. 11, 1889	
West Virginia		June 20, 1863	Had been part of Virginia until statehood.
Wisconsin	July 4, 1836	May 29, 1848	The State was smaller than the Territory, and the left-over area continued to be called the Territory of Wisconsin until March 3, 1849.
Wyoming	July 29, 1868	July 10, 1890	

* The dates followed by an asterisk are one day later than those generally accepted. The reason is that the Act states, with Arkansas for example, "from and after July 4." While it was undoubtedly the intention of Congress to create Arkansas as a Territory on July 4, the United States Supreme Court decided that "from and after July 4," for instance, meant "July 5." Territorial and statehood data compiled by Dr. Carroll Chase and Richard McP. Cabeen.

POSTMASTERS GENERAL OF THE UNITED STATES

1775 Benjamin Franklin, Pa., July 26.
1776 Richard Bache, Pa., Nov. 7.
1782 Ebenezer Hazard, N. Y., Jan. 28.
1789 Samuel Osgood, Mass., Sept. 26.
1791 Timothy Pickering, Pa., Aug. 12.
1795 Joseph Habersham, Ga., Feb. 25.
1801 Gideon Granger, Conn., Nov. 28.
1814 Return J. Meigs, Jr., Ohio, Apr. 11.
1823 John McLean, Ohio, July 1.
1829 William T. Barry, Ky., Apr. 6.
1835 Amos Kendall, Ky., May 1.
1840 John M. Niles, Conn., May 26.
1841 Francis Granger, N. Y., Mar. 8.
1841 Charles A. Wickliffe, Ky., Oct. 13.
1845 Cave Johnson, Tenn., Mar. 7.
1849 Jacob Collamer, Vt., Mar. 8.
1850 Nathan K. Hall, N. Y., July 23.
1852 Samuel D. Hubbard, Conn., Sept. 14.
1853 James Campbell, Pa., Mar. 8

1857 Aaron V. Brown, Tenn., Mar. 7.
1859 Joseph Holt, Ky., Mar. 14.
1861 Horatio King, Maine, Feb. 12.
1861 Montgomery Blair, D. C., Mar. 9.
1864 William Dennison, Ohio, Oct. 1.
1866 Alexander W. Randall, Wis., July 25.
1869 John A. J. Creswell, Md., Mar. 6.
1874 Jas. W. Marshall, N. J., July 7.
1874 Marshall Jewell, Conn., Sept. 1.
1876 James N. Tyner, Ind., July 13.
1877 David McK. Key, Tenn., Mar. 13.
1880 Horace Maynard, Tenn., Aug. 25.
1881 Thomas L. James, N. Y., Mar. 8.
1882 Timothy O. Howe, Wis., Jan. 5.
1883 Walter Q. Gresham, Ind., Apr. 11.
1884 Frank Hatton, Iowa, Oct. 14.
1885 Wm. F. Vilas, Wis., Mar. 7.
1888 Don M. Dickinson, Mich., Jan. 17.
1889 John Wanamaker, Pa., Mar. 6.
1893 Wilson S. Bissell, N. Y., Mar. 7.
1895 William L. Wilson, W. Va., Apr. 4.
1897 James A. Gary, Md., Mar. 6.
1898 Charles Emory Smith, Pa., Apr. 22.

1902 Henry C. Payne, Wis., Jan. 15.
1904 Robert J. Wynne, Pa., Oct. 10.
1905 Geo. B. Cortelyou, N. Y., Mar. 7.
1907 Geo. von L. Meyer, Mass., Mar. 4.
1909 Frank H. Hitchcock, Mass., Mar. 6.
1913 Albert S. Burleson, Tex., Mar. 5.
1921 Will H. Hays, Ind., Mar. 5.
1922 Hubert Work, Colo., Mar. 4.
1923 Harry S. New, Ind., Mar. 4.
1929 Walter F. Brown, Ohio, Mar. 6.
1933 James A. Farley, N. Y., Mar. 4.
1940 Frank C. Walker, Pa., Sept. 11.
1945 Robert E. Hannegan, Mo., July 1.
1947 Jesse M. Donaldson, Ill., Dec. 16.
1953 Arthur E. Summerfield, Mich., Jan. 21.
1961 J. Edward Day, Calif., Jan. 21.
1963 John A. Gronouski, Wis., Sept. 30.
1965 Lawrence F. O'Brien, Mass., Nov. 3.
1968 W. Marvin Watson, Tex., Apr. 26.
1969 Winton M. Blount, Ala., Jan. 22.

U.S. Postal Service

1971 Elmer T. Klassen, Mass., Dec. 7.
1975 Benjamin Bailar, Md., Feb. 15
1978 William F. Bolger, Conn., Mar. 1.
1985 Paul N. Carlin, Calif., Jan. 1

IDENTIFIER
of
Definitive Issues
Arranged by Type Numbers

ISSUES of 1847-75

Imperforate and Unwatermarked

Design Number			Scott Number
A1	5c	red brown	1
A1	5c	dark brown	1a
A1	5c	orange brown	1b
A1	5c	red orange	1c
A1	5c	blue (reproduction)	**948a**
A3	5c	red brown (reproduction)	3
A2	10c	black	2
	10c	brown orange (reproduction)	**948b**
A4	10c	black (reproduction)	4

A1 Benjamin Franklin

Reproduction

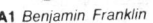

5c On the originals the left side of the white shirt frill touches the oval on a level with the top of the "F" of "Five". On the reproductions it touches the oval about on a level with the top of the figure "5"

ISSUE of 1851-75

A2 George Washington.

Reproduction

Original

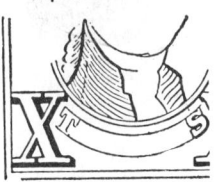

Reproduction

10c. On the originals line of coat (A) points to "T" of TEN and (B) it points between "T" and "S" of CENTS.

On the reproductions line of coat (A) points to right tip of 'X" and line of coat (B) points to center of "S."

On the reproductions the eyes have a sleepy look, the line of the mouth is straighter, and in the curl of the hair near the left cheek is a strong black dot, while the originals have only a faint one.

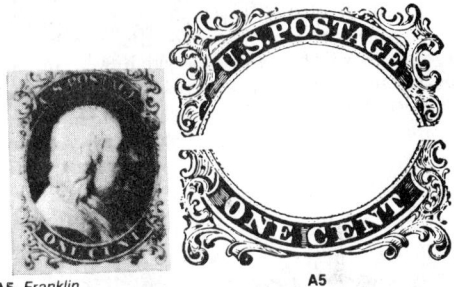

A5 Franklin   **A5**

Type I. Has a curved line outside the labels with "U. S. Postage" and "One Cent". The scrolls below the lower label are turned under, forming little balls. The scrolls and outer line at top are complete.

A6

Type Ia. Same as I at bottom but top ornaments and outer line at top are partly cut away.

Type Ib. Same as I but balls below the bottom label are not so clear. The plume-like scrolls at bottom are not complete.

A7

Type II. The little balls of the bottom scrolls and the bottoms of the lower plume ornaments are missing. The side ornaments are complete.

A8

Type III. The top and bottom curved lines outside the labels are broken in the middle. The side ornaments are complete.

Type IIIa. Similar to III with the outer line broken at top or bottom but not both. Type IIIa from Plate IV generally shows signs of plate erasure between the horizontal rows. Those from Plate IE show only a slight break in the line at top or bottom.

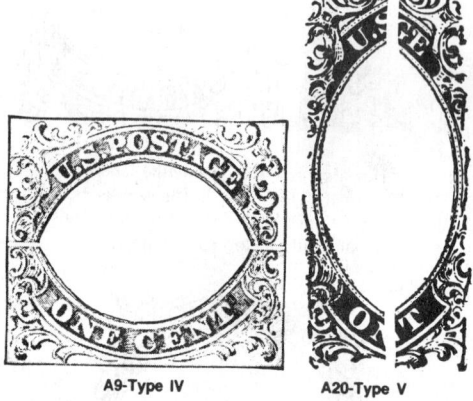

A9-Type IV   A20-Type V

Type IV. Similar to II, but with the curved lines outside the labels recut at top or bottom or both.

The seven types listed account for most of the varieties of recutting.

Type V. Similar to type III of 1851-56 but with side ornaments partly cut away.

A5	1c blue, type I	Imperf. 5
A5	1c blue, type Ib	Imperf. 5A
A5	1c blue, type I	Perf. 15 18
A5	1c bright blue	Perf. 12 40
A6	1c blue, type Ia	Imperf. 6
A6	1c blue, type Ia	Perf. 15 19
A7	1c blue, type II	Imperf. 7
A7	1c blue, type II	Perf. 15 20
A8	1c blue, type III	Imperf. 8
A8	1c blue, type IIIa	Imperf. 8A
A8	1c blue, type III	Perf. 15 21
A8	1c blue, type IIIa	Perf. 15 22
A9	1c blue, type IV	Imperf. 9
A9	1c blue, type IV	Perf. 15 23
A20	1c blue, type V	Perf. 15 24
A20	1c blue, type V	Perf. 15, laid paper .24b

A10 Washington, Type I.

A10 Type I. There is an outer frame line at top and bottom.

A21 Type II. The outer line has been removed at top and bottom.

Type IIa. The side frame lines extend only to the top and bottom of the stamp design. All type IIa stamps are from plates X and XI (each exists in 3 states), and these plates produced only type IIa. The side frame lines were recut individually for each stamp, thus being broken between the stamps vertically.

A11 Jefferson, Type I. There are projections on all four sides.

A22 Type II The projections at top and bottom are partly cut away. Several minor types could be made according to the extent of cutting of the projections.

Nos. 40-47 are reprints produced by the Continental Bank Note Co. for the Centennial Exposition of 1876. The stamps are on white paper without gum, perf 12. They were not good for postal use. They also exist imperforate.

A10	3c orange brown, type I	Imperf.	10
A10	3c dull red, type I	Imperf.	11
A10	3c claret, type I	Imperf.	11a
A10	3c rose, type I	Perf. 15	25
A10	3c scarlet	Perf. 12	41
A21	3c dull red, type II	Perf. 15	26
A21	3c dull red, type IIa	Perf. 15	26a

IDENTIFIER

A11	5c red brown, type I	Imperf.	12
A11	5c brick red, type I	Perf. 15	27
A11	5c red brown, type I	Perf. 15	28
A11	5c Indian red, type I	Perf. 15	28A
A11	5c brown, type I	Perf. 15	29
A22	5c orange brown, type II	Perf. 15	30
A22	5c brown, type II	Perf. 15	30A
A22	5c orange brown, type II	Perf. 12	42

A12 Washington, Type I. De-

A16 Washington

A12 Type I. The 'shells' at the lower corners are practically complete. The outer line below the label is very nearly complete. The outer lines are broken above the middle of the top label and the "X" in each upper corner

A13 Type II. The design is complete at the top. The outer line at the bottom is broken in the middle. The shells are partly cut away

A14 Type III. The outer lines are broken above the top label and the "X" numerals. The outer line at the bottom and the shells are partly cut away as in Type II.

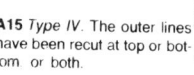
A15 Type IV. The outer lines have been recut at top or bottom, or both.

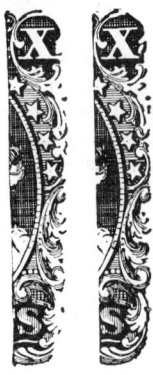
A23 Type V.. The side ornaments are slightly cut away. Usually only one pearl remains at each end of the lower label but some copies show two or three pearls at the right side. At the bottom the outer line is complete and the shells nearly so. The outer lines at top are complete except over the right "X".

A12	10c green, type I	Imperf.	13
A12	10c green, type I	Perf. 15	31
A12	10c blue green	Perf. 12	43
A13	10c green, type II	Imperf.	14
A13	10c green, type II	Perf. 15	32
A14	10c green, type III	Imperf.	15
A14	10c green, type III	Perf. 15	33
A15	10c green, type IV	Imperf.	16
A15	10c green, type IV	Perf. 15	34
A23	10c green, type V	Perf. 15	35
A16	12c black	Imperf.	17
A16	12c black, plate II	Perf. 15	36
A16	12c black, plate III		36b
A16	12c greenish black	Perf. 12	44

A17 Washington

A18 Franklin

A19 Washington

A17	24c gray lilac	Perf. 15	37
A17	24c gray	Perf. 15	37a
A17	24c red lilac	Perf. 15	37b
A17	24c gray lilac	Imperf.	37c
A17	24c blackish violet	Perf. 12	45
A18	30c orange	Perf. 15	38
A18	30c orange	Imperf.	38a
A18	30c yellow orange	Perf. 12	46
A19	90c blue	Perf. 15	39
A19	90c blue	Imperf.	39a
A19	90c deep blue	Perf. 12	47

ISSUES of 1861-75

This series is divided into three groups known as "First Designs," "Second Designs" and "Grills." The first issue is printed on thin, semi-transparent paper; the paper used for the second and grilled issues is usually thicker and opaque.

A24 Franklin

A24a

A24 A dash has been added under the tip of the ornament at right of the numeral in upper left corner.

A24a	1c indigo, thin paper	Perf. 12	.55
A24	1c blue	Perf. 12	.63
A24	1c ultramarine	Perf. 12	.63a
A24	1c dark blue	Perf. 12	.63b
A24	1c blue	Same, laid paper	.63c
A24	1c blue	Grill 11x14 mm.	.85A
A24	1c blue	Grill 11x13 mm.	.86
A24	1c dull blue	same	.86a
A24	1c blue	Grill 9x13 mm.	.92
A24	1c pale blue	same	.92a
A24	1c blue	No grill, hard white paper	.102

A25a

A25 Washington

A25 Ornaments at corners have been enlarged and end in a small ball.

A25a	3c brown rose, thin paper	See illustration A25a	.56
A25	3c pink	See illustration A25	.64
A25	3c pigeon blood pink	No grill, perf. 12	.64a
A25	3c rose pink	Same	.64b
A25	3c lake	Same	.66
A25	3c scarlet	Same	.74
A25	3c rose	Same	.65
A25	3c rose	Grilled all over	.79
A25	3c rose	Grill 18x15 mm.	.82
A25	3c rose	Grill 13x16 mm.	.83
A25	3c rose	Grill 12x14 mm.	.85
A25	3c rose	Grill 11x14 mm.	.85C
A25	3c rose	Grill 11x13 mm.	.88
A25	3c lake red	same	.88a
A25	3c red	Grill 9x13 mm.	.94
A25	3c rose	same	.94a
A25	3c brown red	No grill, hard white paper	.104

A26 Jefferson

A26a

A26 A leaflet has been added to the foliated ornaments at each corner.

A26a	5c brown, thin paper	See illustration A26a	.57
A26	5c buff	See illustration A26	.67
A26	5c brown yellow	No grill	.67a
A26	5c olive yellow	No grill	.67b
A26	5c red brown	No grill	.75
A26	5c brown	No grill	.76
A26	5c dark brown	No grill	.76a
A26	5c brown	Laid paper	.76b
A26	5c brown	Grilled all over	.80
A26	5c dark brown	Same	.80a
A26	5c brown	Grill 9x13 mm.	.95
A26	5c black brown	same	.95a
A26	5c brown	No grill, hard white paper	.105

IDENTIFIER

A27 *Washington*

A27a

A27 A heavy curved line has been cut below the stars and an outer line added to the ornaments above them.

A27a	10c dark green, thin paper	See illustration A27a .**58**
A27a		Same used **62B**
A27	10c yellow green	See illustration A27 .. **68**
A27	10c dark green	same **68a**
A27	10c green	Grill 11x14 mm. ...**85D**
A27	10c green	Grill 11x13 mm. **89**
A27	10c yellow green	Grill 9x13 mm. **96**
A27	10c dark green	same **96a**
A27	10c green	No grill, hard white paper **106**

A28a *Washington*

A28 *Washington*

A28a	12c black, thin paper	See illustration A28a .**59**
A28	12c black	See illustration A28 .. **69**
A28	12c black	Grill 11x14 mm. ...**85E**
A28	12c black	Grill 11x13 mm. **90**
A28	12c black	Grill 9x13 mm. **97**
A28	12c black	Hard white paper, no grill **107**

A29 *Washington*

A30 *Franklin*

A29	24c dark violet	Thin paper, no grill ..**60**
A29	24c violet	Same **70c**
A29	24c grayish lilac	Same **70d**
A29	24c red lilac	No grill **70**
A29	24c brown lilac	No grill **70a**
A29	24c steel blue	No grill **70b**
A29	24c lilac	No grill **78**
A29	24c grayish lilac	No grill **78a**
A29	24c gray	No grill **78b**
A29	24c blackish violet	No grill **78c**
A29	24c gray lilac	Grill 9x13 mm. **99**
A29	24c deep violet	Hard white paper, no grill **109**
A30	30c red orange	Thin paper, no grill ..**61**
A30	30c orange	No grill **71**
A30	30c orange	Grilled all over **81**
A30	30c orange	Grill 9x13 mm. **100**
A30	30c brownish orange	Hard white paper, no grill **110**

A31 *Washington*

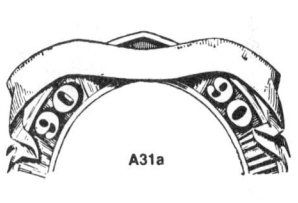

A31a

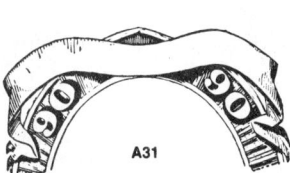

A31

Parallel lines form an angle above the ribbon with "U.S. Postage"; between these lines a row of dashes has been added and a point of color to the apex of the lower line.

A31a	90c dull blue, thin paper	See illustration A31a .**62**
A31a	90c dull blue	Imperf., pair **62a**
A31	90c blue	See illustration A31 ..**72**
A31	90c pale blue	Same **72a**
A31	90c dark blue	Same **72b**
A31	90c blue	Grill 9x13 mm. **101**
A31	90c blue	Hard white paper, no grill **111**

ISSUES of 1861-75

A32 Jackson   **A33** Lincoln

Perf. 12, Unwmkd.

A32	2c black	No grill	73
A32	2c black	Laid paper	73d
A32	2c black	Grill 12x14 mm	84
A32	2c black	Grill 11x14 mm	85B
A32	2c black	Grill 11x13 mm	87
A32	2c black	Grill 9x13 mm	93
A32	2c black	Hard white paper, no grill	103
A33	15c black	No grill	77
A33	15c black	Grill 11x14 mm	85F
A33	15c black	Grill 11x13 mm	91
A33	15c black	Grill 9x13 mm	98
A33	15c black	Hard white paper, no grill	108

ISSUES of 1869-80

A34 Franklin

A34	1c buff	Grill 9½x9 mm	112
A34	1c buff	No grill	112b
A34	1c buff	No grill, hard white paper	123
A34	1c buff	No grill, soft porous paper	133
A34	1c brown orange	Same without gum	133a

A35 Pony Express   **A36** Baldwin 4-4-0 Locomotive, c. 1857

A35	2c brown	Grill 9½x9 mm	113
A35	2c brown	No grill	113b
A35	2c brown	No grill, hard white paper	124

A36	3c ultramarine	Grill 9½x9 mm	114
A36	3c ultramarine	No grill	114a
A36	3c blue	No grill, hard white paper	125

A37 Washington   **A38** Shield and Eagle

A39 S. S. Adriatic

A37	6c ultramarine	Grill 9½x9 mm	115
A37	6c blue	No grill, hard white paper	126
A38	10c yellow	Grill 9½x9 mm	116
A38	10c yellow	No grill, hard white paper	127
A39	12c green	Grill 9½x9 mm	117
A39	12c green	No grill, hard white paper	128

A40 Landing of Columbus.

A40 Type I. Picture unframed

A40a Type II. Picture framed

Type III, same as Type I but without the fringe of brown shading lines around central vignette.

A40	15c brown & blue, type I	Grill 9½x9 mm	118
A40	15c brown & blue, type I	No grill	118a
A40	15c brown & blue, type III	No grill, hard white paper	129
A40a	15c brown & blue, type II	Grill 9½x9 mm	119

IDENTIFIER

A41 The Declaration of Independence

A44 Franklin

A42 Shield, Eagle and Flags.

A43 Lincoln

A44

A44a *With secret mark.* In the pearl at the left of the numeral "1" there is a small dash.

A44b—*Re-engraved.* The vertical lines in the upper part of the stamp have been so deepened that the background often appears to be solid. Lines of shading have been added to the upper arabesques.

A41	24c green & violet	Grill 9½x9 mm.....120	
A41	24c green & violet	No grill 120a	
A41	24c green & violet	No grill, hard white paper 130	
A42	30c blue & carmine	Grill 9½x9 mm.....121	
A42	30c blue & carmine	No grill 121a	
A42	30c blue & carmine	No grill, hard white paper 131	
A43	90c carmine & black	Grill 9½x9 mm.....122	
A43	90c carmine & black	No grill 122a	
A43	90c carmine & black	No grill, hard white paper 132	
A44	1c ultramarine	With grill 134	
A44	1c ultramarine	No grill 145	
A44a	1c ultramarine	White wove paper ..156	
A44a	1c ultramarine	With grill........156e	
A44a	1c ultramarine	Hard white paper, without gum 167	
A44a	1c dark ultra.	Soft porous paper...182	
A44a	1c dark ultra.	Soft porous paper, without gum (See Note I)..........192	
A44b	1c gray blue	206	

A45

45a—*With secret mark.* Under the scroll at the left of "U.S." there is a small diagonal line.

A45 *Jackson*

ISSUES of 1870-88

The secret mark shown in the detail of A45a is seldom found on the actual stamps. Stamps Nos. 146 and 157 are best identified by color which is red brown for No. 146 and brown for No. 157.

Note I: Special printings of 1880-83—All denominations of this series were printed on special order from the Post Office Department during the period the stamps were current. The paper being the same as used on the then current issue, the special printings are extremely difficult to identify. The 2c brown, 7c scarlet vermilion, 12c blackish purple and 24c dark violet are easily distinguished by the soft porous paper as these denominations were never previously printed on soft paper. The other denominations can be distinguished by shades only, those of the special printings being slightly deeper and richer than the regular issue. The special printings except No. 211B were issued without gum. The only certain way to identify them is by comparison with stamps previously established as special printings.

IDENTIFIER

A45	2c red brown	With grill 135
A45	2c red brown	No grill 146
A45a	2c brown	White wove paper ..157
A45a	2c brown	With grill.........157c
A45a	2c dark brown	Hard white paper, without gum 168
A45a	2c black brown	Soft porous paper, without gum 193
A45a	2c vermilion	Yellowish paper 178
A45a	2c vermilion	Imperf............178a
A45a	2c vermilion	With grill.........178c
A45a	2c vermilion	Soft porous paper...183
A45a	2c carmine vermilion	Hard white paper, without gum 180
A45a	2c scarlet vermilion	Soft porous paper (See note I)......203

A46

 A46 Washington

A46a—With secret mark. The under part of the tail of the left ribbon is heavily shaded.

A46b—Re-engraved. The shading at the sides of the central oval appears only about one half the previous width. A short horizontal dash has been cut about 1 mm. below the "TS" of "CENTS".

A46	3c green	With grill 136
A46	3c green	No grill 147
A46	3c green	Imperf., pair 147c
A46a	3c green	White wove paper ..158
A46a	3c blue green	Hard white paper, without gum 169
A46a	3c green	Soft porous paper...184
A46a	3c green	Same, imperf......184a
A46a	3c blue green	Soft porous paper, without gum (See Note I)..........194
A46b	3c blue green	Re-engraved 207
A46b	3c vermilion	214

A47

A47a—With secret mark. The first four vertical lines of the shading in the lower part of the left ribbon have been strengthened.

A47b—Re-engraved. 6c. On the original stamps four vertical lines can be counted from the edge of the panel to the outside of the stamp. On the re-engraved stamps there are but three lines in the same place.

A47 Lincoln

A47	6c carmine	With grill 137
A47	6c carmine	No grill 148
A47a	6c dull pink	No grill, white wove paper 159
A47a	6c dull pink	With grill 159b
A47a	6c dull rose	Hard white paper, without gum 170
A47a	6c pink	Soft porous paper...186
A47a	6c dull rose	Soft porous paper, without gum (See Note I)..........195
A47b	6c rose	Re-engraved 208
A47b	6c brown red	................208a

A48 Edwin McMasters Stanton

A49 Thomas Jefferson

A48

A48a—With secret mark. Two small semi-circles are drawn around the ends of the lines which outline the ball in the lower right hand corner.

A49

A49a—With secret mark: A small semi-circle in the scroll at the right end of the upper label.

IDENTIFIER

A49b *Re-engraved.* On the original stamps there are five vertical lines between the left side of the oval and the edge of the shield. There are only four lines on the re-engraved stamps. In the lower part of the re-engraved stamps the horizontal lines of the background have been strengthened.

A50

A50a—*With secret mark.* The balls of the figure "2" are crescent shaped.

A50 *Henry Clay*

A51

A51a—*With secret mark.* In the lower part of the triangle in the upper left corner two lines have been made heavier forming a "V". This mark can be found on some of the Continental and American (1879) printings, but not all stamps show it.

A51 *Webster.*

A51	15c orange	With grill 141
A51	15c bright orange	No grill 152
A51a	15c yellow orange	White wove paper ..163
A51a	15c yellow orange	With grill 163a
A51a	15c bright orange	Hard white paper, without gum 174
A51a	15c red orange	Soft porous paper...189
A51a	15c orange	(See Note I) 199

A48	7c vermilion	With grill 138
A48	7c vermilion	No grill 149
A48a	7c orange verm.	White wove paper ..160
A48a	7c reddish verm.	Hard white paper, without gum 171
A48a	7c scarlet verm.	Soft porous paper, without gum 196
A49	10c brown	With grill 139
A49	10c brown	No grill 150
A49	10c brown	Soft porous paper...187
A49a	10c brown	White wove paper ..161
A49a	10c brown	With grill 161c
A49a	10c pale brown	Hard white paper, without gum 172
A49a	10c brown	Soft porous paper...188
A49a	10c deep brown	(See Note I on page 7) 197
A49b	10c brown	Re-engraved 209
A49b	10c black brown	Re-engraved 209b
A50	12c dull violet	With grill 140
A50	12c dull violet	No grill 151
A50a	12c blackish violet	White wove paper ..162
A50a	12c blackish violet	With grill 162a
A50a	12c dark violet	Hard white paper, without gum 173
A50a	12c blackish purple	Soft porous paper, without gum 198

A52 *General Winfield Scott.*

A53 *Hamilton,* by Giuseppe

A54 *Perry,* by William Wal-

Secret marks were added to the dies of the 24c, 30c and 90c but new plates were not made from them. The various printings of these stamps can be distinguished only by the shades and paper.

A52	24c purple	With grill 142
A52	24c purple	No grill 153
A52	24c dull purple	Hard white paper, without gum 175
A52	24c dark violet	Soft porous paper, without gum 200
A53	30c black	With grill 143
A53	30c black	No grill 154
A53	30c full black	Soft porous paper...190

A53	30c gray black	White wove paper, no grill	165
A53	30c greenish black	White wove paper	165a
A53	30c greenish black	With grill	165c
A53	30c greenish black	Hard white paper, without gum	176
A53	30c greenish black	Soft porous paper, without gum (See Note I)	201
A53	30c orange brown		217
A54	90c carmine	With grill	144
A54	90c carmine	No grill	155
A54	90c carmine	Soft porous paper	191
A54	90c rose carmine	White wove paper	166
A54	90c violet carmine	Hard white paper, without gum	177
A54	90c dull carmine	Soft porous paper, without gum (See Note I)	202
A54	90c purple		218

ISSUES of 1875-88

A55 Taylor

A56 Garfield.

Perf. 12, Unwmkd.

A55	5c blue	Yellowish wove paper, no grill	179
A55	5c blue	With grill	179c
A55	5c bright blue	Hard, white wove paper, without gum	181
A55	5c blue	Soft porous paper	185
A55	5c deep blue	Soft porous paper, without gum (See Note I)	204
A56	5c yellow brown		205
A56	5c gray brown	Soft porous paper, without gum (See Note I)	205C
A56	5c indigo		216

A57 Washington.

A58 Jackson

A57	2c red brown		210
A57	2c pale red brown	Soft porous paper, with gum (See Note I)	211B
A57	2c green		213
A58	4c blue green		211
A58	4c deep blue green	Soft porous paper, without gum (See Note I)	211D
A58	4c carmine		215

A59 Franklin

A59	1c ultramarine		212

ISSUES of 1890-93

A60 Franklin

A61 Washington

A62 Jackson

A63 Lincoln

A64 Grant

A65 Garfield

A66 William T. Sherman.

A67 Daniel Webster

IDENTIFIER

A68 Henry Clay, after   A69 Jefferson, after bust by

A87 Franklin.   A88 Washington.

A70 Perry, after statue by

A60	1c dull blue	219
A61	2c lake	219D
A61	2c carmine	220
A62	3c purple	221
A63	4c dark brown	222
A64	5c chocolate	223
A65	6c brown red	224
A66	8c lilac	225
A67	10c green	226
A68	15c indigo	227
A69	30c black	228
A70	90c orange	229

A89 Jackson.   A90 Lincoln.

A91 Grant.   A92 Garfield.

ISSUES of 1894 to 1899

This series, the first to be printed by the Bureau of Engraving and Printing, closely resembles the 1890 series but is identified by the triangles which have been added to the upper corners of the designs.

The Catalogue divides this group into three separate series, the first of which was issued in 1894 and is unwatermarked. In 1895 the paper used was watermarked with the double line letters USPS (United States Postal Service). The stamps show one complete letter of the watermark or parts of two or more letters.

This watermark appears on all United States stamps issued from 1895 until 1910.

In 1898 the colors of some of the denominations were changed, which created the third series noted in the Catalogue.

Other than the watermark, or lack of it, there are three types of the corner triangles used on the 2 cent stamps and two variations of designs are noted on the 10 cent and $1 denominations. In the following list all of these variations are illustrated and described immediately preceding the denominations on which they appear.

A93 Sherman.   A94 Webster.

A95 Clay.   A96 Jefferson.

A97 Perry.

Wmkd. USPS (191) Horizontally

or USPS Vertically

(Actual size of letter)

A98 James Madison   A99 John Marshall

A87	1c ultramarine	Unwmkd	246
A87	1c blue	Unwmkd	247
A87	1c blue	Wmkd	264
A87	1c deep green	Wmkd	279
A87	1c on 1c yellow green	"CUBA"	Cuba 221
A87	1c deep green	"GUAM"	Guam 1
A87	1c yellow green	"PHILIPPINES"	Phil. 213
A87	1c yellow green	"PORTO RICO"	P.R. 210
A87	1c yellow green	"PUERTO RICO"	P.R. 215

Type I (Triangle I). The horizontal lines of the ground work run across the triangle and are of the same thickness within it as without.

Type II (Triangle II). The horizontal lines cross the triangle but are thinner within it than without.

Type III (Triangle III). The horizontal lines do not cross the double lines of the triangle. The lines within the triangle are thin, as in Type II. Two varieties of Type III are known, but the variations are minor.

A88	2c pink, type I	Unwmkd	248
A88	2c carmine lake, type I	Unwmkd	249
A88	2c carmine, type I	Unwmkd	250
A88	2c carmine, type I	Wmkd. USPS	265
A88	2c carmine, type II	Unwmkd	251
A88	2c carmine, type II	Wmkd	266
A88	2c carmine, type III	Unwmkd	252
A88	2c carmine, type III	Wmkd	267
A88	2c red, type III	Wmkd	279B
A88	2c rose carmine, type III	Wmkd	279c
A88	2c orange red, type III	Wmkd	279d
A88	2c	Booklet pane of 6, wmkd., single stamps with 1 or 2 straight edges	279e
A88	2c on 2c carmine, type III	"CUBA"	Cuba 222
A88	2½c on 2c red, type III	"CUBA"	Cuba 223
A88	2c carmine, type III	"GUAM"	Guam 2
A88	2c orange red, type III	"PHILIPPINES"	Phil. 214
A88	2c carmine, type III	"PHILIPPINES"	Phil. 214a
A88		Same, booklet pane of 6	Phil. 214b
A88	2c carmine, type III	"PORTO RICO"	P.R. 211
A88	same	"PUERTO RICO"	P.R. 216
A89	3c purple	Unwmkd	253
A89	3c purple	Wmkd	268
A89	3c on 3c purple	"CUBA"	Cuba 224
A89	3c purple	"GUAM"	Guam 3
A89	3c purple	" PHILIPPINES "	Phil. 215
A90	4c dark brown	Unwmkd	254
A90	4c dark brown	Wmkd	269
A90	4c rose brown	Wmkd	280
A90	4c lilac brown	Wmkd	280a
A90	4c orange brown	Wmkd	280b
A90	4c lilac brown	"GUAM"	Guam 4
A90	4c orange brown	" PHILIPPINES"	Phil. 220
A91	5c chocolate	Unwmkd	255
A91	5c chocolate	Wmkd	270
A91	5c dark blue	Wmkd	281
A91	5c on 5c blue	"CUBA"	Cuba 225
A91	5c blue	"GUAM"	Guam 5
A91	5c blue	"PHILIPPINES"	Phil. 216
A91	5c blue	"PORTO RICO"	P.R. 212
A92	6c dull brown	Unwmkd	256
A92	6c dull brown	Wmkd. USPS	271
A92	6c dull brown	Wmkd. USIR	271a
A92	6c lake	Wmkd. USPS	282
A92	6c purplish lake	Wmkd	282a
A92	6c lake	"GUAM"	Guam 6
A92	6c lake	"PHILIPPINES"	Phil. 221
A93	8c violet brown	Unwmkd	257
A93	8c violet brown	Wmkd. USPS	272
A93	8c violet brown	Wmkd. USIR	272a
A93	8c violet brown	"GUAM"	Guam 7
A93	8c violet brown	"PHILIPPINES"	Phil. 222
A93	8c violet brown	"PORTO RICO"	P.R. 213

IDENTIFIER

Type I. The tips of the foliate ornaments do not impinge on the white curved line below "ten cents."

Type II. The tips of the ornaments break the curved line below the "e" of "ten" and the "t" of "cents".

A94	10c dark green	Unwmkd............258	
A94	10c dark green	Wmkd..............273	
A94	10c brown, type I	Wmkd............282C	
A94	10c orange brown, type II	Wmkd..............283	
A94	10c on 10c brown, type I	"CUBA"....Cuba 226	
A94	Same, type II	"CUBA"...Cuba226A	
A94	10c brown, type I	"GUAM".....Guam 8	
A94	10c brown, type II	"GUAM".....Guam 9	
A94	10c brown, type I	"PHILIPPINES" ....Phil. 217	
A94	10c orange brown, type II	"PHILIPPINES" ....Phil. 217A	
A94	10c brown, type I	"PORTO RICO" ............P.R. 214	
A95	15c dark blue	Unwmkd............259	
A95	15c dark blue	Wmkd..............274	
A95	15c olive green	Wmkd..............284	
A95	15c olive green	"GUAM"....Guam 10	
A95	15c olive green	"PHILIPPINES" ....Phil. 218	
A95	15c light olive green	"PHILIPPINES" ....Phil. 218a	
A96	50c orange	Unwmkd............260	
A96	50c orange	Wmkd..............275	
A96	50c orange	"GUAM"....Guam 11	
A96	50c orange	"PHILIPPINES" ....Phil. 219	

A97 *Type I* The circles enclosing "$1" are broken where they meet the curved line below One Dollar
A97 *Type II* The circles are complete.

A97	$1 black, type I	Unwmkd...........261	
A97	$1 black, type I	Wmkd..............276	
A97	$1 black, type II	Unwmkd..........261A	
A97	$1 black, type II	Wmkd.............276A	
A97	$1 black, type I	"GUAM"....Guam 12	
A97	$1 black, type II	"GUAM"....Guam 13	
A97	$1 black, type I	"PHILIPPINES" ....Phil. 223	
A98	$2 bright blue	Unwmkd............262	
A98	$2 bright blue	Wmkd..............277	
A98	$2 dark blue	Wmkd.............277a	
A98	$2 dark blue	"PHILIPPINES" ....Phil. 224	
A99	$5 dark green	Unwmkd............263	
A99	$5 dark green	Wmkd..............278	
A99	$5 dark green	"PHILIPPINES" ....Phil. 225	

ISSUES of 1902-17

A115 Franklin

A116 Washington

A117 Jackson

A118 Grant

A119 Lincoln

A120 Garfield

A121 Martha Washington

A122 Daniel Webster

A123 Benjamin Harrison

A124 Henry Clay

A125 Jefferson

A126 David G. Farragut

54 IDENTIFIER

A127 *Madison*, after portrait A128 *Marshall*, after engrav-

Unless otherwise noted all stamps are Perf. 12 and Wmkd. (191)

Single stamps from booklet panes show 1 or 2 straight edges.

A115	1c blue green		...300
A115	1c	Booklet pane of 6	.300b
A115	1c blue green	Imperf.	...314
A115	1c blue green	Perf. 12 Horiz., pair	316
A115	1c blue green	Perf. 12 vert., pair.	.318
A115	1c blue green	"CANAL ZONE PANAMA"...C.Z. 4	
A115	1c blue green	"PHILIPPINES" ...Phil. 226	
A116	2c carmine		...301
A116	2c	Booklet pane of 6	.301c
A116	2c carmine	"PHILIPPINES" ...Phil. 227	
A116	2c carmine	same, booklet pane of 6	Phil. 227a
A117	3c bright violet		...302
A117	3c bright violet	"PHILIPPINES" ...Phil. 228	
A118	4c brown		...303
A118	4c brown	Imperf.	...314A
A118	4c brown	"PHILIPPINES" ...Phil. 229	
A118	4c orange brown	"PHILIPPINES" ...Phil. 229a	
A119	5c blue		...304
A119	5c blue	Imperf.	...315
A119	5c blue	Perf. 12 horiz, pair	.317
A119	5c blue	"CANAL ZONE PANAMA"...C.Z. 6	
A119	5c blue	"PHILIPPINES" ...Phil. 230	
A120	6c claret		...305
A120	6c brownish lake	"PHILIPPINES" ...Phil. 321	
A121	8c violet black		...306
A121	8c violet black	"CANAL ZONE PANAMA"...C.Z. 7	
A121	8c violet black	"PHILIPPINES" ...Phil. 232	
A122	10c pale red brown		...307
A122	10c pale red brown	"CANAL ZONE PANAMA"...C.Z. 8	
A122	10c pale red brown	"PHILIPPINES" ...Phil. 233	
A122	10c red brown	"PHILIPPINES" ...Phil. 233a	
A123	13c purple black		...308
A123	13c purple black	"PHILIPPINES" ...Phil. 234	
A124	15c olive green		...309
A124	15c olive green	"PHILIPPINES" ...Phil. 235	
A125	50c orange		...310
A125	50c orange	"PHILIPPINES" ...Phil. 236	
A126	$1 black		...311
A126	$1 black	"PHILIPPINES" ...Phil. 237	
A127	$2 dark blue		...312
A127	$2 dark blue	Unwmkd., Perf. 10	.479
A127	$2 dark blue	"PHILIPPINES" ...Phil. 238	
A128	$5 dark green		...313
A128	$5 light green	Unwmkd., Perf. 10	.480
A128	$5 dark green	"PHILIPPINES" ...Phil. 239	

ISSUE of 1903

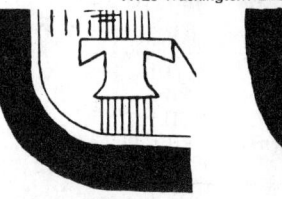

A129 *Washington*. Designed

Die I   Die II

Specialists recognize over a hundred shades of this stamp in various hues of vermilion, red, carmine and lake. The Scott Catalogue lists only the most striking differences.

The Government coil stamp, No. 322 should not be confused with the scarlet vermilion coil of the International Vending Machine Co., which is perforated 12½ to 13.

A129	2c carmine	Wmkd.	...319
A129	2c lake	Die I	...319a
A129	2c carmine rose	Die I	...319b
A129	2c scarlet	Die II	...319c
A129	2c lake	Die II	...319f
A129	2c various shades	Booklet pane of 6, die I	...319g
A129	same	Same, die II	...319h
A129	2c carmine	Die II	...319i
A129	2c carmine	Imperf.	...320
A129	2c lake	Imperf.	...320a
A129	2c scarlet	Imperf.	...320b
A129	2c carmine	Perf. 12 horiz.	...321
A129	2c carmine	Perf. 12 vert.	...322
A129	2c carmine	"CANAL ZONE PANAMA"...C.Z. 5	
A129	2c scarlet	Same	...C.Z. 5a
A129	2c carmine	"PHILIPPINES" ...Phil. 240	
A129	2c carmine	Same, booklet pane of 6	Phil. 240a

ISSUES OF 1908-09

This series introduces for the first time the single line watermark USPS. Only a small portion of several letters is often all that can be seen on a single stamp.

A138 *Franklin*

A139 *Washington*

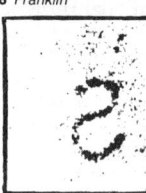
Wmk. 190

A138	1c green	Perf. 12, double line wmk.	331
A138	1c green	Perf. 12, single line wmk.	374
A138	1c green	Perf. 12, bluish paper	357
A138	1c green	Imperf., double line wmk.	343
A138	1c green	Imperf., single line wmk.	383
A138	1c green	Perf. 12 horiz., double line wmk.	348
A138	1c green	Perf. 12 horiz., single line wmk.	385
A138	1c green	Perf. 12 vert., double line wmk.	352
A138	1c green	Perf. 12 vert., single line wmk.	387
A138	1c green	Perf. 8½ horiz., single line wmk.	390
A138	1c green	Perf. 8½ vert., single line wmk.	392
A139	2c carmine	Perf. 12, double line wmk.	332
A139	2c carmine	Perf. 12, single line wmk.	375
A139	2c carmine	Perf. 12, bluish paper	358
A139	2c carmine	Perf. 11, double line wmk.	519
A139	2c carmine	Imperf., double line wmk	344
A139	2c carmine	Imperf., single line wmk.	384
A139	2c carmine	Perf. 12 horiz., double line wmk.	349
A139	2c carmine	Perf. 12 horiz., single line wmk.	386
A139	2c carmine	Perf. 12 vert., double line wmk.	353
A139	2c carmine	Perf. 12 vert., single line wmk.	388
A139	2c carmine	Perf. 8½ horiz. single line wmk.	391
A139	2c carmine	Perf. 8½ vert., single line wmk.	393

Single stamps from booklet panes show 1 or 2 straight edges.

A138	1c green	Booklet pane of 6	**331a**
A138	1c green	Booklet pane of 6	**374a**
A139	2c carmine	Booklet pane of 6	**332a**
A139	2c carmine	Booklet pane of 6	**375a**

ISSUES of 1908-21
FLAT BED AND ROTARY PRESS STAMPS

The Rotary Press Stamps are printed from plates that are curved to fit around a cylinder. This curvature produces stamps that are slightly larger, either horizontally or vertically, than those printed from flat plates. Designs of stamps from flat plates measure about 18½-19 mm. wide by 22 mm. high. When the impressions are placed sidewise on the curved plates the designs are 19½-20 mm. wide; when they are place vertically the designs are 22½ to 23 mm. high. A line of color (not a guide line) shows where the curved plates meet or join on the press.

Rotary Press Coil Stamps were printed from plates of 170 subjects for stamps coiled sidewise, and from plates of 150 subjects for stamps coiled endwise.

A140 *Washington*, after bust

1c	A138	Portrait of Franklin, value in words	
1c	A140	Portrait of Washington, value in numerals	
2c	A139	Portrait of Washington, value in words.	
2c	A140	Portrait of Washington, value in numerals	
A140	1c green	Perf. 12, single line wmk.	405
A140	1c green	Same, booklet pane of 6	405b
A140	1c green	Perf. 11, flat plate, Unwmkd.	498
A140	1c green	Same, booklet pane of 6	498e
A140	1c green	Same, booklet pane of 30	498f
A140	1c green	Perf. 11, rotary press measuring 19mm. x22½mm., Unwmkd.	544
A140	1c green	Same, measuring 19½ to 20mm x 22mm.	545
A140	1c gray green	Perf. 11, offset, Unwmkd.	525
A140	1c dark green	Same	525a
A140	1c gray green	Perf. 12½	536

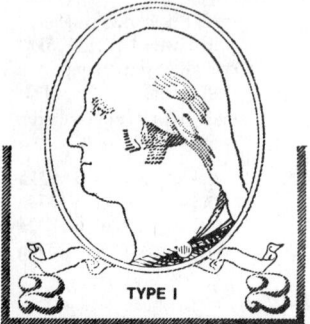  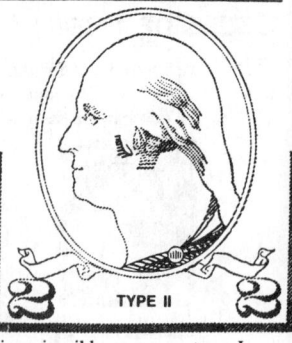

Type Ia. The design characteristics are similar to type I except that all of the lines of the design are stronger.

The toga button, toga rope and rope shading lines are heavy.

The latter characteristics are those of type II, which, however, occur only on impressions from rotary plates.

Used only on flat plates 10208 and 10209.

Type II. Shading lines in ribbons as on type I.

The toga button, rope and rope shading lines are heavy.

The shading lines of the face at the lock of hair end in a strong vertical curved line.

Used on rotary press printings only.

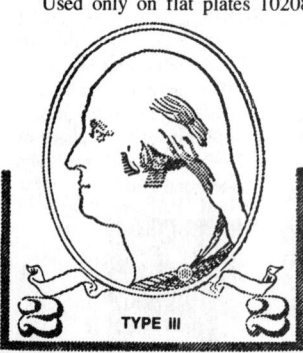 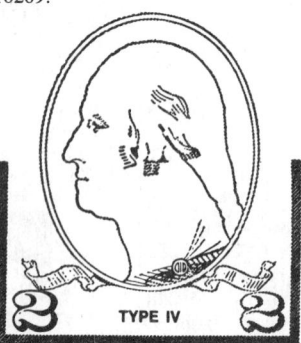 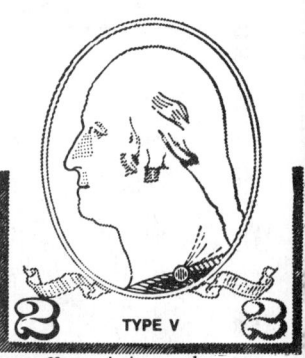

Type III. Two lines of shading in the curves of the ribbons.

Other characteristics similar to type II.

Used on rotary press printings only.

Type IV. Top line of the toga rope is broken.

The shading lines in the toga button are so arranged that the curving of the first and last form "CIID".

The line of color in the left "2" is very thin and usually broken. Used on offset printings only.

Type V. Top line of the toga is complete.

There are five vertical shading lines in the toga button. The line of color is the left "2" is very thin and usually broken.

The shading dots on the nose are as shown on the diagram.

Used on offset printings only.

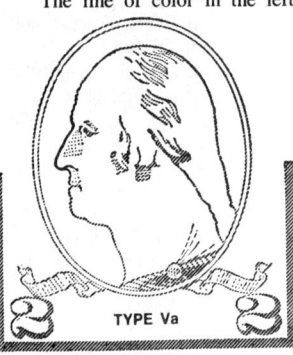 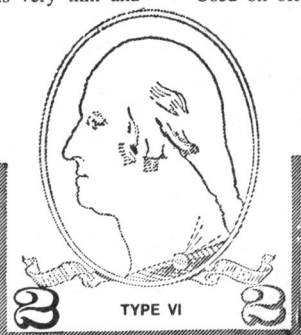 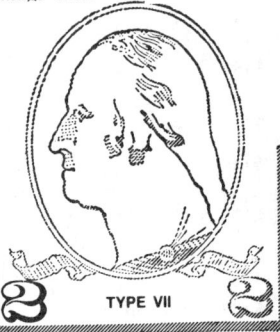

Type Va. Characteristics are the same as type V except in the shading dots of the nose. The third row of dots from the bottom has four dots instead of six. The overall height is ⅓ mm. shorter than type V.

Used on offset printings only.

Type VI. General characteristics the same as type V except that the line of color in the left "2" is very heavy. Used on offset printings only.

Type VII. The line of color in the left "2" is invariably continuous, clearly defined and heavier than in type V or Va but not as heavy as type VI.

An additional vertical row of dots has been added to the upper lip.

Numerous additional dots have been added to the hair on top of the head.

Used on offset printings only.

IDENTIFIER

A140	1c green	Perf. 11x10 538	A140	2c rose red	Perf. 12x10, single line wmk., type I **425d**
A140	1c green	Perf. 10x11 542			
A140	1c green	Perf. 10, single line wmk. 424	A140	2c rose red	Same, perf. 10, booklet pane of 6.**425e**
A140	1c green	Same, perf. 12x10 .**424a**	A140	2c carmine	Perf. 10, unwmkd., type I 463
A140	1c green	Same, perf. 10x12 .**424b**			
A140	1c green	Same, booklet pane of 6 .... **424d**	A140	2c carmine	Same, booklet pane of 6 .... **463a**
A140	1c green	Perf. 10, flat plate, unwmkd. 462	A140	2c carmine	Imperf., flat plate, single line wmk., type I 409
A140	1c green	Same, booklet pane of 6 .... **462a**	A140	2c carmine	Imperf., rotary press, single line wmk., type I 459
A140	1c green	Perf. 10, rotary press, unwmkd. 543			
A140	1c green	Imperf., single line wmk. 408	A140	2c carmine	Imperf., unwmkd., type I 482
A140	1c green	Imperf., unwmkd. ...481	A140	2c deep rose	Same, type Ia **482A**
A140	1c green	Imperf., offset 531	A140	2c carmine rose	Imperf., offset, unwmkd., type IV **532**
A140	1c green	Perf. 10 horiz., flat plate, single line wmk. 441	A140	2c carmine rose	Same, type V 533
			A140	2c carmine	Same, type Va 534
A140	1c green	Same, rotary press ..448	A140	2c carmine	Same, type VI **534A**
A140	1c green	Perf. 10 horiz., rotary press, unwmkd. ...486	A140	2c carmine	Same, type VII ...**534B**
			A140	2c carmine rose	Perf. 10 horiz., flat plate, single line wmk., type I 442
A140	1c green	Perf. 10 vert., flat plate, single line wmk. 443			
			A140	2c red	Same, rotary press ..449
A140	1c green	Same, rotary press ..452	A140	2c carmine	Same, type III 450
A140	1c green	Perf. 10 vert., rotary press, unwmkd. ...490	A140	2c carmine	Perf. 10 horiz., rotary press, unwmkd., type II 487
A140	1c green	Perf. 8½ horiz, single line wmk. .410			
			A140	2c carmine	Same, type III 488
A140	1c green	Perf. 8½ vert., same 412	A140	2c carmine	Perf. 10 vert., flat plate, single line wmk., type I 444
A140	2c carmine	Perf. 12, type I, single line wmk. .406			
A140	2c carmine	Same, booklet pane of 6 .... **406a**	A140	2c red	Same, rotary press ..453
			A140	2c carmine	Same, type II 454
A140	2c pale car. red	Perf. 11, single line wmk., type I 461	A140	2c carmine	Same, type III 455
			A140	2c carmine	Perf. 10 vert., rotary press, unwmkd., type II 491
A140	2c rose	Perf. 11, flat plate, unwmkd., type I .499			
A140	2c rose	Same, booklet pane of 6 .... **499e**	A140	2c carmine	Same, type III 492
			A140	2c carmine	Perf. 8½ horiz., type I 411
A140	2c rose	Same, booklet pane of 30 .... **499f**	A140	2c carmine	Perf. 8½ vert., type I 413
A140	2c deep rose	Perf. 11, unwmkd., type Ia 500			
			A140	3c deep violet	Perf. 12, double line wmk., type I 333
A140	2c carmine rose	Perf. 11, rotary press, unwmkd., type III **546**	A140	3c deep violet	Perf. 12, single line wmk., type I 376
A140	2c carmine	Perf. 11, offset, unwmkd., type IV **526**	A140	3c deep violet	Perf. 12, bluish paper, type I 359
A140	2c carmine	Same, type V 527			
A140	2c carmine	Same, type Va 528	A140	3c light violet	Perf. 11, unwmkd., type I 501
A140	2c carmine	Same, type VI **528A**			
A140	2c carmine	Same, type VII ...**528B**	A140	3c light violet	Same, booklet pane of 6 .... **501b**
A140	2c carmine rose	Perf. 11x10, type II 539	A140	3c dark violet	Perf. 11, unwmkd., type II 502
A140	2c carmine rose	Same, type III 540			
A140	2c rose red	Perf. 10, single line wmk., type I 425	A140	3c dark violet	Same, booklet pane of 6 .... **502b**
A140	2c carmine rose	Same **425a**			
A140	2c carmine	Same **425b**	A140	3c violet	Perf. 11, offset, type III 529
A140	2c red	Same **425c**			

IDENTIFIER

Types of THREE CENTS

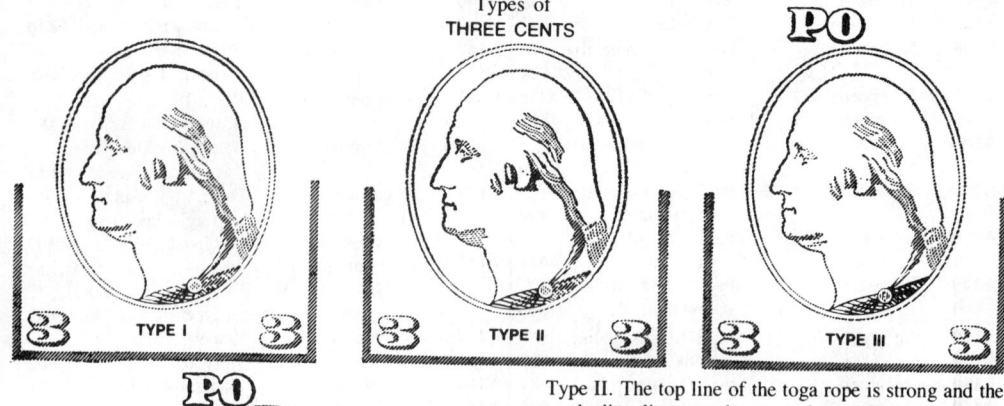

Type I. The top line of the toga rope is weak and the rope shading lines are thin. The 5th line from the left is missing. The line between the lips is thin.

Type II. The top line of the toga rope is strong and the rope shading lines are heavy and complete.
The line between the lips is heavy.
Used on both flat plate and rotary press printings.

Type III. The top line of the toga rope is strong but the 5th shading line is missing as in type I.
Center shading line of the toga button consists of two dashes with a central dot.
The "P" and "O" of "POSTAGE" are separated by a line of color.
The frame line at the bottom of the vignette is complete.
Used on offset printings only.

Type IV. The shading lines of the toga rope are complete.
The second and fourth shading lines in the toga button are broken in the middle and the third line is continuous with a dot in the center.
The "P" and "O" of "POSTAGE" are joined.
The frame line at the bottom of the vignette is broken.
Used on offset printings only.

A140	3c purple	Same, type IV 530
A140	3c violet	Perf. 11x10, type II.541
A140	3c deep violet	Perf. 10, single line wmk., type I 426
A140	3c violet	Perf. 10, unwmkd., type I..........464
A140	3c deep violet	Imperf., double line wmk., type I 345
A140	3c violet	Imperf., unwmkd., type I..........483
A140	3c violet	Same, type II 484
A140	3c violet	Imperf., offset, type IV 535
A140	3c deep violet	Perf. 12 vert., single line wmk., type I.389
A140	3c violet	Perf. 10 vert., flat plate, single line wmk., type I 445
A140	3c violet	Perf. 10 vert., rotary press, single line wmk., type I 456
A140	3c violet	Perf. 10 vert., rotary press, unwmkd., type I..........493
A140	3c violet	Same, type II 494
A140	3c violet	Perf. 10 horiz., type I..........489
A140	3c deep violet	Perf. 8½ vert., type I..........394
A140	4c orange brown	Perf. 12, double line wmk............334
A140	4c orange brown	Perf. 12, bluish paper 360
A140	4c brown	Perf. 12, single line wmk............377
A140	4c brown	Perf. 11, unwmkd...503
A140	4c brown	Perf. 10, single line wmk............427
A140	4c orange brown	Perf. 10, unwmkd...465
A140	4c orange brown	Imperf............346
A140	4c orange brown	Perf. 12 horiz......350
A140	4c orange brown	Perf. 12 vert......354
A140	4c brown	Perf. 10 vert., flat plate, single line wmk............446
A140	4c brown	Same, rotary press ..457
A140	4c orange brown	Perf. 10 vert., rotary press, unwmkd. ..495
A140	4c brown	Perf. 8½ vert., single line wmk. .395

IDENTIFIER

A140	5c blue	Perf. 12, double line wmk. 335	
A140	5c blue	Perf. 12 bluish paper 361	
A140	5c blue	Perf. 12, single line wmk. 378	
A140	5c blue	Perf. 11, unwmkd...504	
A140	5c rose (error)	Same 505	
A140	5c carmine (error)	Perf. 10, unwmkd ..467	
A140	5c blue	Perf. 10, single line wmk. 428	
A140	5c blue	Perf. 12x10 ....428a	
A140	5c blue	Perf. 10, unwmkd...466	
A140	5c blue	Imperf.............347	
A140	5c carmine (error)	Imperf.............485	
A140	5c blue	Perf. 12 horiz. 351	
A140	5c blue	Perf. 12 vert. 355	
A140	5c blue	Perf. 10 vert., flat plate, single line wmk............447	
A140	5c blue	Same, rotary press ..458	
A140	5c blue	Perf. 10 vert., rotary press, unwmkd...496	
A140	5c blue	Perf. 8½ vert. 396	
A140	6c red orange	Perf. 12, double line wmk. 336	
A140	6c red orange	Perf. 12, bluish paper 362	
A140	6c red orange	Perf. 12, single line wmk. 379	
A140	6c red orange	Perf. 11, unwmkd...506	
A140	6c red orange	Perf. 10, single line wmk. 429	
A140	6c red orange	Perf. 10, unwmkd...468	
A140	7c black	Perf. 12, single line wmk. 407	
A140	7c black	Perf. 11, unwmkd...507	
A140	7c black	Perf. 10, single line wmk. 430	
A140	7c black	Perf. 10, unwmkd...469	
A140	8c olive green	Perf. 12, double line wmk. 337	
A140	8c olive green	Perf. 12, bluish paper 363	
A140	8c olive green	Perf. 12, single line wmk. 380	
A140	10c yellow	Perf. 12, double line wmk. 338	
A140	10c yellow	Perf. 12, bluish paper 364	
A140	10c yellow	Perf. 12, single line wmk. 381	
A140	10c yellow	Perf. 12 vert. 356	
A140	13c blue green	Perf. 12, double line wmk. 339	
A140	13c blue green	Perf. 12, bluish paper 365	
A140	15c pale ultra.	Perf. 12, double line wmk. 340	
A140	15c pale ultra.	Perf. 12, bluish paper 366	
A140	15c pale ultra.	Perf. 12, single line wmk. 382	

A140	50c violet	341	
A140	$1 violet brown	342	

ISSUES of 1912-19

A148   A149

Franklin

Designs of 8c to $1.00 denominations differ only in figures of value.

A148	8c pale olive green	Perf. 12, single line wmk. 414	
A148	8c olive bister	Perf. 11, unwmkd...508	
A148	8c pale olive grn.	Perf. 10, single line wmk. 431	
A148	8c olive green	Perf. 10, unwmkd...470	
A148	9c salmon red	Perf. 12, single line wmk. 415	
A148	9c salmon red	Perf. 11, unwmkd...509	
A148	9c salmon red	Perf. 10, single line wmk. 432	
A148	9c salmon red	Perf. 10, unwmkd...471	
A148	10c orange yellow	Perf.12, single line wmk. 416	
A148	10c orange yellow	Perf. 11, unwmkd...510	
A148	10c orange yellow	Perf. 10, single line wmk. 433	
A148	10c orange yellow	Perf. 10, unwmkd...472	
A148	10c orange yellow	Perf. 10 vert., same...........497	
A148	11c light green	Perf. 11, unwmkd...511	
A148	11c dark green	Perf. 11, unwmkd..511a	
A148	11c dark green	Perf. 10, single line wmk. 434	
A148	11c dark green	Perf. 10, unwmkd...473	
A148	12c claret brown	Perf. 12, single line wmk. 417	
A148	12c claret brown	Perf. 11, unwmkd...512	
A148	12c brown carmine	Same 512a	
A148	12c claret brown	Perf. 10, single line wmk. 435	
A148	12c copper red	Same 435a	
A148	12c claret brown	Perf. 10, unwmkd...474	
A148	13c apple green	Perf. 11, unwmkd...513	
A148	15c gray	Perf. 12, single line wmk. 418	
A148	15c gray	Perf. 11, unwmkd...514	
A148	15c gray	Perf. 10, single line wmk. 437	
A148	15c gray	Perf. 10, unwmkd...475	
A148	20c ultramarine	Perf. 12, single line wmk. 419	
A148	20c light ultra.	Perf. 11, unwmkd...515	
A148	20c ultramarine	Perf. 10, single line wmk. 438	
A148	20c light ultra.	Perf. 10, unwmkd...476	

IDENTIFIER

A148	30c orange red	Perf. 12, single line wmk. 420
A148	30c orange red	Perf. 11, unwmkd. . .516
A148	30c orange red	Perf. 10, single line wmk. 439
A148	30c orange red	Perf. 10, unwmkd. 476A
A148	50c violet	Perf. 12, single line wmk. 421
A148	50c violet	Perf. 12, double line wmk. 422
A148	50c red violet	Perf. 11, unwmkd. . .517
A148	50c violet	Perf. 10, single line wmk. 440
A148	50c light violet	Perf. 10, unwmkd. . .477
A148	$1 violet brown	Perf. 12, double line wmk. 423
A148	$1 violet brown	Perf. 11, unwmkd. . .518
A148	$1 deep brown	Same 518b
A148	$1 violet black	Perf. 10, double line wmk. 460
A148	$1 violet black	Perf. 10, unwmkd. . .478

ISSUES of 1918-20

Perf. 11. Unwmkd.

A149	$2 org. red & blk.	523
A149	$2 car. & blk.	547
A149	$5 dp. grn. & blk.	524

ISSUES of 1922-32

A154 Nathan Hale

A155 Franklin

A156 Warren G. Harding

A157 Washington

A158 Lincoln

A159 Martha Washington

A160 Theodore Roosevelt

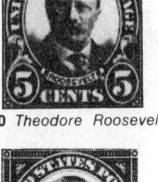

A161 Garfield

A162 McKinley

A163 Grant

A164 Jefferson

A165 Monroe

A166 Hayes

A167 Cleveland

A168 American Indian

A169 Statue of Liberty

A170 Golden Gate

A171 Niagara Falls

A172 Buffalo

A173 Arlington Amphitheater and Tomb of the Unknown Soldier

IDENTIFIER

A174 *Lincoln Memorial, after*

A175 *United States Capitol,*

A176 *"America"*

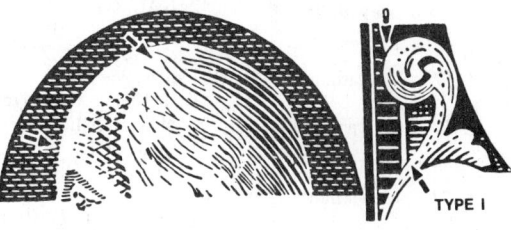
TYPE I

No heavy hair lines at top center of head. Outline of left acanthus scroll generally faint at top and toward base at left side.

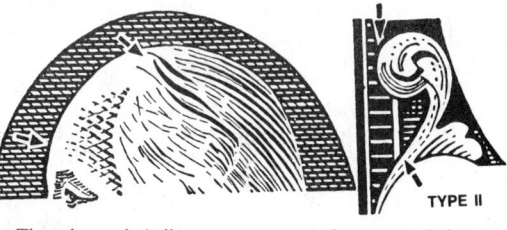
TYPE II

Three heavy hair lines at top center of head; two being outstanding in the white area. Outline of left acanthus scroll very strong and clearly defined at top (under left edge of lettered panel) and at lower curve (above and to left of numeral oval).

Unwmkd.

A154	½c olive brown	Perf. 11	551
A154	½c olive brown	Perf. 11x10½	653
A154	½c olive brown	"CANAL ZONE"	C.Z. 70
A155	1c deep green	Perf. 11, flat plate	552
A155	1c deep green	Booklet pane of 6	552a
A155	1c green	Perf. 11, rotary press 19¾x22¼mm.	594
A155	1c green	Same, 19¼x22¾mm. (used).	596
A155	1c green	Perf. 11x10, rotary press	578
A155	1c green	Perf. 10	581
A155	1c green	Perf. 11x10½	632
A155	1c green	Booklet pane of 6	632a
A155	1c green	Overprt. Kans.	658
A155	1c green	Overprt. Nebr.	669
A155	1c green	Imperf.	575
A155	1c green	Perf. 10 vert.	597
A155	1c yellow green	Perf. 10 horiz.	604
A155	1c deep green	"CANAL ZONE" type A	C.Z. 71
A155	1c deep green	Same, booklet pane of 6	C.Z. 71e
A155	1c green	"CANAL ZONE" type B	C.Z. 100
A156	1½c yellow brown	Perf. 11	553
A156	1½c yellow brown	Perf. 11x10½	633
A156	1½c brown	Overprt. Kans.	659
A156	1½c brown	Overprt. Nebr.	670
A156	1½c brown	Perf. 10	582
A156	1½c brown	Perf. 10 vert.	598
A156	1½c yellow brown	Perf. 10 horiz.	605
A156	1½c yellow brown	Imperf., flat plate	576
A156	1½c yellow brown	Imperf., rotary press	631
A156	1½c yellow brown	"CANAL ZONE"	C.Z. 72
A157	2c carmine	Perf. 11, flat plate	554
A157	2c carmine	Same, booklet pane of 6	554c
A157	2c carmine	Perf. 11, rotary press	595
A157	2c carmine	Perf. 11x10	579
A157	2c carmine	Perf. 11x10½, type I	634
A157	2c carmine	Perf. 11x10½, type II	634A
A157	2c carmine lake	Same, type I	634b
A157	2c carmine lake	Same, booklet pane of 6	634d
A157	2c carmine	Overprt. Molly Pitcher	646
A157	2c carmine	Overprt. Hawaii 1778-1928	647
A157	2c carmine	Overprt. Kans.	660
A157	2c carmine	Overprt. Nebr.	671
A157	2c carmine	Perf. 10	583
A157	2c carmine	Same, booklet pane of 6	583a
A157	2c carmine	Imperf.	577
A157	2c carmine	Perf. 10 vert., type I	599
A157	2c carmine	Same, type II	599A
A157	2c carmine	Perf. 10 horiz.	606
A157	2c carmine	"CANAL ZONE" type A	C.Z. 73
A157	2c carmine	Same, booklet pane of 6	C.Z. 73a
A157	2c carmine	"CANAL ZONE" type B, perf. 11	C.Z. 84
A157	2c carmine	Same, booklet pane of 6	C.Z. 84d

IDENTIFIER

A157	2c carmine	"CANAL ZONE" type B, perf. 10 . . . . .C.Z. 97	A165	10c orange	Perf. 11 562
A157	2c carmine	Same, booklet pane of 6 . . . . . . .C.Z. 97b	A165	10c orange	Perf. 11x10½ 642
A157	2c carmine	"CANAL ZONE" type B, perf. 11x10½ . . . .C.Z. 101	A165	10c orange yellow	Overprt. Kans. 668
			A165	10c orange yellow	Overprt. Nebr. 679
			A165	10c orange	Perf. 10 591
			A165	10c orange	Perf. 10 vert. 603
A157	2c carmine	Same, booklet pane of 6 . . . . . .C.Z. 101a	A165	10c orange	"CANAL ZONE" type A, perf. 11 . . . . .C.Z. 75
A158	3c violet	Perf. 11 555	A165	10c orange	Same, type B . .C.Z. 87
A158	3c violet	Perf. 11x10½ 635	A165	10c orange	Same, perf. 10 .C.Z. 99
A158	3c bright violet	Same 635a	A165	10c orange	Same, perf. 11x10½ . . . . .C.Z. 104
A158	3c violet	Overprt. Kans. 661	A166	11c light blue	Perf. 11 563
A158	3c violet	Overprt. Nebr. 672	A166	11c light blue	Perf. 11x10½ 692
A158	3c violet	Perf. 10 584	A167	12c brown violet	Perf. 11 564
A158	3c violet	Perf. 10 vert. 600	A167	12c brown violet	Perf. 11x10½ 693
A158	3c violet	"CANAL ZONE" perf. 11 . . . . .C.Z. 85	A167	12c brown violet	"CANAL ZONE" type A . . . . . .C.Z. 76
A158	3c violet	"CANAL ZONE" perf. 10 . . . . .C.Z. 98	A167	12c brown violet	Same, type B . .C.Z. 88
			A168	14c blue	Perf. 11 565
A158	3c violet	"CANAL ZONE" perf. 11x10½C.Z. 102	A168	14c dark blue	Perf. 11x10½ 695
			A168	14c dark blue	"CANAL ZONE" type A, perf. 11 . . . . .C.Z. 77
A159	4c yellow brown	Perf. 11 556
A159	4c yellow brown	Perf. 11x10½ 636
A159	4c yellow brown	Overprt. Kans. 662	A168	14c dark blue	Same, type B . .C.Z. 89
A159	4c yellow brown	Overprt. Nebr. 673	A168	14c dark blue	Same, perf. 11x10½ . . . . .C.Z. 116
A159	4c yellow brown	Perf. 10 585
A159	4c yellow brown	Perf. 10 vert. 601	A169	15c gray	Perf. 11 566
A160	5c dark blue	Perf. 11 557	A169	15c gray	Perf. 11x10½ 696
A160	5c dark blue	Perf. 11x10½ 637	A169	15c gray	"CANAL ZONE" . . . . .C.Z. 90
A160	5c dark blue	Overprt. Hawaii 1778-1928 648
A160	5c deep blue	Overprt. Kans. 663	A170	20c carmine rose	Perf. 11 567
A160	5c deep blue	Overprt. Nebr. 674	A170	20c carmine rose	Perf. 10½x11 698
A160	5c blue	Perf. 10 586	A170	20c carmine rose	"CANAL ZONE" . . . . .C.Z. 92
A160	5c dark blue	Perf. 10 vert. 602
A160	5c dark blue	"CANAL ZONE" type A, perf. 11 . . . . .C.Z. 74	A171	25c yellow green	Perf. 11 568
			A171	25c blue green	Perf. 10½x11 699
			A172	30c olive brown	Perf. 11 569
A160	5c dark blue	Same, type B . .C.Z. 86	A172	30c brown	Perf. 10½x11 700
A160	5c dark blue	Same, perf. 11x10½ . . . .C.Z. 103	A172	30c olive brown	"CANAL ZONE" type A . . . . . .C.Z. 79
A161	6c red orange	Perf. 11 558	A172	30c olive brown	"CANAL ZONE" type B . . . . . .C.Z. 93
A161	6c red orange	Perf. 11x10½ 638
A161	6c red orange	Overprt. Kans. 664	A173	50c lilac	Perf. 11 570
A161	6c red orange	Overprt. Nebr. 675	A173	50c lilac	Perf. 10½x11 701
A161	6c red orange	Perf. 10 587	A173	50c lilac	"CANAL ZONE" type A . . . . . .C.Z. 80
A161	6c deep orange	Perf. 10 vert. 723
A162	7c black	Perf. 11 559	A173	50c lilac	"CANAL ZONE" type B . . . . . .C.Z. 94
A162	7c black	Perf. 11x10½ 639
A162	7c black	Overprt. Kans. 665	A174	$1 violet black	Perf. 11 571
A162	7c black	Overprt. Nebr. 676	A174	$1 violet brown	"CANAL ZONE" type A . . . . . .C.Z. 81
A162	7c black	Perf. 10 588
A163	8c olive green	Perf. 11 560	A174	$1 violet brown	"CANAL ZONE" type B . . . . . .C.Z. 95
A163	8c olive green	Perf. 11x10½ 640
A163	8c olive green	Overprt. Kans. 666	A175	$2 deep blue	Perf. 11 572
A163	8c olive green	Overprt. Nebr. 677	A176	$5 car. & blue	Perf. 11 573
A163	8c olive green	Perf. 10 589
A164	9c rose	Perf. 11 561
A164	9c orange red	Perf. 11x10½ 641
A164	9c light rose	Overprt. Kans. 667
A164	9c light rose	Overprt. Nebr. 678
A164	9c rose	Perf. 10 590

REGULAR ISSUES of 1925-26, 1930 and 1932

A186 Harrison

A187 Wilson

A186	13c green	Perf. 11 622
A186	13c yellow green	Perf. 11x10½ 694
A187	17c black	Perf. 11 623
A187	17c black	Perf. 10½x11 697
A187	17c black	"CANAL ZONE" .... C.Z. 91

A203 Harding

A204 Taft

A203	1½c brown	Perf. 11x10½ 684
A203	1½c brown	Perf. 10 vert. 686
A204	4c brown	Perf. 11x10½ 685
A204	4c brown	Perf. 10 vert. 687

A226 Washington, after 1796

A226	3c deep violet	Perf. 11x10½ 720
A226	3c deep violet	Booklet pane of 6 .720b
A226	3c deep violet	Perf. 10 vert. 721
A226	3c deep violet	Perf. 10 horiz. 722
A226	3c deep violet	"CANAL ZONE" .... C.Z. 115

PRESIDENTIAL ISSUE of 1938

A275 Benjamin Franklin,

A276 George Washington,

A277 Martha Washington,

A278 John Adams

A279 Thomas Jefferson,

A280 James Madison

A281 The White House,

A282 James Monroe

A283 John Quincy Adams,

A284 Andrew Jackson,

A285 Martin Van Buren,

A286 William H. Harrison,

A287 John Tyler

A288 James K. Polk,

A289 Zachary Taylor

A290 Millard Fillmore

IDENTIFIER

291 Franklin Pierce

A292 James Buchanan,

A305 Warren G. Harding,  A306 Calvin Coolidge.

Rotary Press Printing
Unwmkd.

A275	½c deep orange	Perf. 11x10½ 803
A275	½c red orange	"CANAL ZONE" ..........C.Z. 118
A276	1c green	Perf. 11x10½ 804
A276	1c green	Booklet pane of 6 804b
A276	1c green	Perf. 10 vert. 839
A276	1c green	Perf. 10 horiz. 848
A277	1½c bister brown	Perf. 11x10½ 805
A277	1½c bister brown	Perf. 10 vert. 840
A277	1½c bister brown	Perf. 10 horiz. 849
A277	1½c bister brown	"CANAL ZONE" ..........C.Z. 119
A278	2c rose carmine	Perf. 11x10½ 806
A278	2c	Booklet pane of 6 806b
A278	2c rose carmine	Perf. 10 vert. 841
A278	2c rose carmine	Perf. 10 horiz. 850
A279	3c deep violet	Perf. 11x10½ 807
A279	3c deep violet	Booklet pane of 6 807a
A279	3c deep violet	Perf. 10 vert. 842
A279	3c deep violet	Perf. 10 horiz. 851
A280	4c red violet	Perf. 11x10½ 808
A280	4c red violet	Perf. 10 vert. 843
A281	4½c dark gray	Perf. 11x10½ 809
A281	4½c dark gray	Perf. 10 vert. 844
A282	5c bright blue	Perf. 11x10½ 810
A282	5c bright blue	Perf. 10 vert. 845
A283	6c red orange	Perf. 11x10½ 811
A283	6c red orange	Perf. 10 vert. 846
A284	7c sepia	Perf. 11x10½ 812
A285	8c olive green	Perf. 11x10½ 813
A286	9c rose pink	Perf. 11x10½ 814
A287	10c brown red	Perf. 11x10½ 815
A287	10c brown red	Perf. 10 vert. 847
A288	11c ultramarine	Pref. 11x10½ 816
A289	12c bright violet	Perf. 11x10½ 817
A290	13c blue green	Perf. 11x10½ 818
A291	14c blue	Perf. 11x10½ 819
A292	15c blue gray	Perf. 11x10½ 820
A293	16c black	Perf. 11x10½ 821
A294	17c rose red	Perf. 11x10½ 822
A295	18c brn. carmine	Perf. 11x10½ 823
A296	19c bright violet	Perf. 11x10½ 824
A297	20c bright blue green	Perf. 11x10½ 825
A298	21c dull blue	Perf. 11x10½ 826
A299	22c vermilion	Perf. 11x10½ 827
A300	24c gray black	Perf. 11x10½ 828
A301	25c dp. red lilac	Perf. 11x10½ 829
A302	30c deep ultra.	Perf. 11x10½ 830
A303	50c lt. red violet	Perf. 11x10½ 831

A293 Abraham Lincoln,

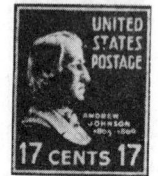
A294 Andrew Johnson,

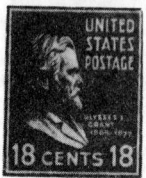
A295 Ulysses S. Grant,

A296 Rutherford B. Hayes,

A297 James A. Garfield,

A298 Chester A. Arthur,

A299 Grover Cleveland,

A300 Benjamin Harrison,

A301 William McKinley,

A302 Theodore Roosevelt,

A303 William Howard Taft,

A304 Woodrow Wilson,

IDENTIFIER

Flat Plate Printing
Perf. 11

A304	$1 pur. & blk.	Unwmkd. 832
A304	$1 pur. & blk.	Wmkd. USIR 832b
A304	$1 red vio. & blk.	Thick white paper, smooth colorless gum 832c
A305	$2 yel. grn. & blk.	833
A306	$5 car. & blk.	834

LIBERTY ISSUE 1954-73

A477 Benjamin Franklin

A478 George Washington,

A478a Palace of the Governors, Santa Fe

A479 Mount Vernon

A480 Thomas Jefferson

A481 Bunker Hill Monument and Massachusetts Flag, 1776

A482 Statue of Liberty

A483 Abraham Lincoln

A484 The Hermitage

A485 James Monroe

A486 Theodore Roosevelt,

A487 Woodrow Wilson

A488 Statue of Liberty (Rotary and flat plate printing).

A489 Design slightly altered; see position of torch (Giorgi press printing).

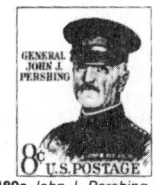
A489a John J. Pershing

A490 The Alamo

A491 Independence Hall,

A491a Statue of Liberty,

A492 Benjamin Harrison,

A493 John Jay

A494 Monticello

A496 Robert E. Lee

A497 John Marshall

A498 Susan B. Anthony

A495 Paul Revere

66 IDENTIFIER

A499 Patrick Henry

A500 Alexander Hamilton,

A496	30c black	Perf. 11x10½	**1049**
A497	40c brown red	Same	**1050**
A498	50c bright purple	Same	**1051**
A499	$1 purple	Same	**1052**
A500	$5 black	Perf. 11	**1053**

ISSUE of 1962-66

Unwmkd.

A477	½c red orange	Perf. 11x10½	**1030**
A478	1c dark green	Perf. 11x10½	**1031**
A478	1c dark green	Perf. 10 vert.	**1054**
A478	1c dark green	Imperf., pair	**1054b**
A478a	1¼c turquoise	Perf. 10½x11	**1031A**
A478a	1¼c turquoise	Perf. 10 horiz.	**1054A**
A479	1½c brown carmine	Perf. 10½x11	**1032**
A480	2c carmine rose	Perf. 11x10½	**1033**
A480	2c carmine rose	Perf. 10 vert.	**1055**
A480	2c carmine rose	Same, tagged	**1055a**
A481	2½c gray blue	Perf. 11x10½	**1034**
A481	2½c gray blue	Perf. 10 vert.	**1056**
A482	3c deep violet	Perf. 11x10½	**1035**
A482	3c deep violet	Same, tagged	**1035b**
A482	3c deep violet	Booklet pane of 6	**1035a**
A482	3c deep violet	Perf. 10 vert.	**1057**
A482	3c deep violet	Same, tagged	**1057b**
A482	3c deep violet	Imperf., pair	**1057a**
A482	3c deep violet	Imperf., size: 24x28mm	**1075a**
A483	4c red violet	Perf. 11x10½	**1036**
A483	4c red violet	Same, tagged	**1036b**
A483	4c red violet	Booklet pane of 6	**1036a**
A483	4c red violet	Perf. 10 vert.	**1058**
A483	4c red violet	Imperf. pair	**1058a**
A484	4½c blue green	Perf. 10½x11	**1037**
A484	4½c blue green	Perf. 10 horiz.	**1059**
A485	5c deep blue	Perf. 11x10½	**1038**
A486	6c carmine	Same	**1039**
A487	7c rose carmine	Same	**1040**
A488	8c dk. violet blue & carmine	Perf. 11	**1041**
A488	8c dk. violet blue & carmine	Imperf., size: 24x28mm	**1075b**
A489	8c dk. violet blue & car. rose	Perf. 11	**1042**
A489a	8c brown	Perf. 11x10½	**1042A**
A490	9c rose lilac	Perf. 10½x11	**1043**
A491	10c rose lake	Same	**1044**
A491	10c rose lake	Same, tagged	**1044b**
A491a	11c carmine & dk. vio. blue	Perf. 11	**1044A**
A491a		Same, tagged	**1044c**
A492	12c red	Perf. 11x10½	**1045**
A492	12c red	Same, tagged	**1045a**
A493	15c rose lake	Same	**1046**
A493	15c rose lake	Same, tagged	**1046a**
A494	20c ultramarine	Perf. 10½x11	**1047**
A495	25c green	Perf. 11x10½	**1048**
A495	25c green	Perf. 10 vert.	**1059A**
A495	25c green	Same, tagged	**1059b**

A646 Andrew Jackson, de-

A650 George Washington,

A646	1c green	Perf. 11x10½, untagged	**1209**
A646	1c green	Same, tagged	**1209a**
A646	1c green	Perf. 10 vert., untagged	**1225**
A646	1c green	Same, tagged	**1225a**
A650	5c dk. bl. gray	Perf. 11x10½, untagged	**1213**
A650	5c dk. bl. gray	Same, tagged	**1213b**
A650	5c dk. bl. gray	Booklet pane of 5+ label, untagged	**1213a**
A650	5c dk. bl. gray	Same, tagged	**1213c**
A650	5c dk. bl. gray	Perf. 10 vert. untagged	**1229**
A650	5c dk. bl. gray	Same, tagged	**1229a**

PROMINENT AMERICANS ISSUE 1965-75

A710 Thomas Jefferson

A711 Albert Gallatin

A712 Frank Lloyd Wright and Guggenheim Museum, New York

A713 Francis Parkman

A714 Abraham Lincoln

IDENTIFIER

A715 *George Washington,*

A715a *George Washington,*

A818b *Amadeo P. Giannini.*

A722 *Frederick Douglass,*

A716 *Franklin D. Roosevelt,*

A727a *Franklin D. Roosevelt* (vertical coil)

A723 *John Dewey*

A724 *Thomas Paine*

A725 *Lucy Stone*

A726 *Eugene O'Neill*

A816 *Benjamin Franklin and his signature*

A717 *Albert Einstein*

A718 *Andrew Jackson*

A718a *Henry Ford and 1909 Model T*

A727 *John Bassett Moore*

A719 *John F. Kennedy*

A817a *Fiorello H. LaGuardia and New York skyline*

**Unwmkd.
Rotary Press Printing**

A720 *Oliver Wendell Holmes*

A818 *Ernest (Ernie) Taylor Pyle*

A818a *Dr. Elizabeth Blackwell*

A721 *George C. Marshall,*

A710	1c green	Perf. 11x10½, tagged **1278**
A710	1c green	Booklet pane of 8 **1278a**
A710	1c green	Booklet pane of 4+2 labels **1278b**
A710	1c green	Perf. 11x10½, untagged **1278c**
A710	1c green	Perf. 10, vert., tagged **1299**
A710	1c green	Untagged (Bureau precanceled) ...**1299a**
A711	1¼c light green	Perf. 11x10½, untagged **1279**
A712	2c dk. bl. gray	Perf. 11x10½, tagged **1280**
A712	2c dk. bl. gray	Booklet pane of 5+ label **1280a**
A712	2c dk. bl. gray	Perf. 11x10½, untagged (Bureau precanceled) ...**1280b**
A712	2c dk. bl. gray	Booklet pane of 6 **1280c**

A713	3c violet	Perf. 10½x11, tagged 1281	A817a	14c gray brown	Perf. 11x10½ 1397
A713	3c violet	Same, untagged (Bureau precanceled) 1281a	A817a	14c gray brown	Untagged (Bureau Precanceled) ...1397a
A713	3c violet	Perf. 10 horiz., tagged 1297	A720	15c maroon	Perf. 11x10½, tagged 1288
A713	3c violet	Same, untagged (Bureau Precanceled) ...1297b	A720	15c maroon	Untagged (Bureau precanceled) ...1288a
A714	4c black	Perf. 11x10½, untagged 1282	A720	15c dark rose claret	Perf. 10 (Bklt. panes only) 1288B
A714	4c black	Same, tagged 1282a	A720	15c dark rose claret	Booklet pane of 8 .1288c
A714	4c black	Perf. 10, vert., tagged 1303	A818	16c brown	Tagged 1398
A714	4c black	Same, untagged (Bureau precanceled) 1303a	A818	16c brown	Untagged (Bureau precanceled) ...1398a
A715	5c blue	Perf. 11x10½, untagged 1283	A818a	18c violet	Perf. 11x10½ 1399
			A721	20c deep olive	Perf. 11x10½, untagged 1289
A715	5c blue	Same, tagged 1283a	A721	20c deep olive	Tagged 1289a
A715	5c blue	Perf. 10 vert., tagged 1304	A818b	21c green	Perf. 11x10½ 1400
			A722	25c rose lake	Perf. 11x10½, untagged 1290
A715	5c blue	Same, untagged (Bureau precanceled) 1304a	A722	25c rose lake	Tagged 1290a
			A723	30c red lilac	Perf. 10½x11, untagged 1291
A715a	5c blue	Perf. 11x10½, tagged 1283B	A723	30c red lilac	Tagged 1291a
			A724	40c blue black	Perf. 11x10½, untagged 1292
A715a	5c blue	Untagged (Bureau precanceled) ...1283d	A724	40c blue black	Tagged 1292a
			A725	50c rose magenta	Perf. 11x10½, untagged 1293
A716	6c gray brown	Perf. 10½x11, tagged 1284	A725	50c rose magenta	Tagged 1293a
A716	6c gray brown	Tagged 1284a	A726	$1 dull purple	Perf. 11x10½, untagged 1294
A716	6c gray brown	Booklet pane of 8 1284b	A726	$1 dull purple	Tagged 1294a
A716	6c gray brown	Booklet pane of 5+ label 1284c	A726	$1 dull purple	Perf. 10 vert., tagged 1305C
A716	6c gray brown	Perf. 10 horiz., tagged 1298	A727	$5 gray black	Perf. 11x10½, untagged 1295
A727a	6c gray brown	Perf. 10 vert., tagged 1305	A727	$5 gray black	Tagged 1295a
A727a	6c gray brown	Untagged (Bureau precanceled) ...1305b			
A816	7c bright blue	Perf. 10½x11, tagged 1393D			
A816	7c bright blue	Same, untagged (Bureau precanceled)....1393e			
A717	8c violet	Perf. 11x10½, untagged 1285	A815 Dwight D. Eisenhower.		A815a
A717	8c violet	Tagged 1285a	A815	6c dark blue gray	Perf. 11x10½, tagged 1393
A718	10c lilac	Perf. 11x10½, tagged 1286	A815	6c dk. bl. gray	Booklet pane of 8 1393a
A718	10c lilac	Untagged (Bureau precanceled) ...1286b	A815	6c dk. bl. gray	Booklet pane of 5+label 1393b
A718a	12c black	Perf. 10½x11, tagged 1286A	A815	6c dk. bl. gray	Untagged (Bureau precanceled)....1393c
A718a	12c black	Untagged (Bureau precanceled)....1286c	A815	6c dk. bl. gray	Perf. 10, vert., tagged 1401
A719	13c brown	Perf. 11x10½, tagged 1287	A815	6c dk. bl. gray	Same, untagged (Bureau precanceled) ...1401a
A719	13c brown	Untagged (Bureau precanceled) ...1287a			

IDENTIFIER

A815	8c deep claret	Perf. 11x10½ (Bklt. panes only)	1395
A815	8c deep claret	Booklet pane of 8	1395a
A815	8c deep claret	Booklet pane of 6	1395b
A815	8c deep claret	Booklet pane of 4+ 2 labels	1395c
A815	8c deep claret	Booklet pane of 7+label	1395d
A815	8c deep claret	Perf. 10 vert., tagged	1402
A815	8c deep claret	Same, untagged (Bureau precanceled)	1402b
A815a	8c blk., red & bl. gray	Perf. 11	1394

FLAG ISSUE, 1968-71

A760 Flag and White House.

A760	6c dark blue, red & green	Perf. 11, size: 19x22mm.	1338
A760	6c dark blue, red & green	Perf. 11x10½, size: 18¼x21mm.	1338D
A760	6c dark blue, red & green	Perf. 10 vert., size: 18¼x21mm.	1338A
A760	8c multicolored	Perf. 11x10½	1338F
A760	8c multicolored	Perf. 10 vert.	1338G

REGULAR ISSUE 1970-76

A817 U.S. Postal Service Emblem.

A923 50-Star and 13-Star Flags.

A924 Jefferson Memorial and quotation from Declaration of Independence.

A925 Mail Transport and "Zip Code"

A926 Liberty Bell.

A817	8c multicolored	Perf. 11x10½	1396
A923	10c red & blue	Perf. 11x10½	1509
A923	10c red & blue	Perf. 10 vert.	1519
A924	10c blue	Perf. 11x10½	1510
A924	10c blue	Same, untagged (Bureau precanceled)	1510a
A924	10c blue	Booklet pane of 5+label	1510b
A924	10c blue	Booklet pane of 8	1510c
A924	10c blue	Booklet pane of 6	1510d
A924	10c blue	Perf. 10 vert.	1520
A924	10c blue	Same, untagged (Bureau precanceled)	1520a
A925	10c multicolored	Perf. 11x10½	1511
A926	6.3c brick red	Perf. 10 vert.	1518
A926	6.3c brick red	Same, untagged (Bureau precanceled)	1518a

AMERICANA ISSUE 1975-81

A984 Inkwell and Quill.

A985 Speaker's Stand.

A987 Early Ballot Box.

A988 Books, Bookmark, Eyeglasses.

A994 Dome of Capitol.

A995 Contemplation of Justice.

69

IDENTIFIER

A996 Early American Printing Press.

A997 Torch, Statue of Liberty

A1013a Kerosene Table Lamp

A1014 Railroad Conductors Lantern, c. 1850

Coil Stamps

A998 Liberty Bell.

A999 Eagle and Shield.

A1014a Six-string guitar

A1199 Weaver violins

A1001 Ft. McHenry Flag.

A1002 Head, Statue of Liberty.

A1015 Saxhorns.

A1016 Drum.

A1006 Old North Church.

A1007 Ft. Nisqually.

A1008 Sandy Hook Lighthouse.

A1009 Morris Township School No. 2, Devil's Lake

A1017 Steinway Grand Piano, 1857.

A1011 Iron "Betty" Lamp Plymouth Colony, 17th-18th Centuries

A1013 Rush Lamp and Candle Holder

A984	1c dark blue, greenish	Perf. 11x10½	.....**1581**
A984	1c dark blue, greenish	Same, untagged (Bureau Precanceled)	...**1581a**
A984	1c dark blue, greenish	Perf. 10 vert	......**1811**
A985	2c red brown, greenish	Perf. 11x10½	.....**1582**
A985	2c red brown, greenish	Same, untagged (Bureau Precanceled)	...**1582a**
A987	3c olive, greenish	Perf. 11x10½	.....**1584**
A987	3c olive, greenish	Same, untagged (Bureau Precanceled)	....**1584a**
A988	4c rose magenta, cream	Perf. 11x10½	.....**1585**
A988	4c rose magenta, cream	Same, untagged (Bureau Precanceled)	...**1585a**

IDENTIFIER

A994	9c slate green	Perf. 11x10½ (Bklt. panes only)	1590
A994	9c slate green	Perf. 10 (Bklt. panes only)	1590a
A994	9c slate green, gray	Perf. 11x10½	1591
A994	9c slate green, gray	Same, untagged (Bureau Precanceled)	1591a
A994	9c slate green, gray	Perf. 10 vert.	1616
A994	9c slate green, gray	Same, untagged (Bureau Precanceled)	1616a
A995	10c violet, gray	Perf. 10 vert.	1617
A995	10c violet, gray	Perf. 11x10½	1592
A995	10c violet, gray	Same, untagged (Bureau Precanceled)	1592a
A996	11c orange, gray	Perf. 11x10½	1593
A997	12c red brown, beige	Perf. 10 vert	1816
A997	12c red brown, beige	Same, untagged (Bureau precanceled)	1816a
A998	13c brown	Perf. 11x10½	1595
A998	13c brown	Booklet pane of 6	1595a
A998	13c brown	Booklet pane of 7 + label	1595b
A998	13c brown	Booklet pane of 8	1595c
A998	13c brown	Booklet pane of 5 + label	1595d
A998	13c brown	Perf. 10 vert.	1618
A998	13c brown	Same, untagged (Bureau Precanceled)	1618a
A999	13c multicolored	Perf. 11x10½	1596
A1001	15c gray, dark blue & red	Perf. 11	1597
A1001	15c gray, dark blue & red	Perf. 11x10½ (Bklt. panes only)	1598
A1001	15c gray, dark blue & red	Booklet pane of 8	1598a
A1001	15c gray, dark blue & red	Perf. 10 vert.	1618C
A1002	16c blue	Perf. 11x10½	1599
A1002	16c blue	Perf. 10 vert.	1619
A1006	24c red, blue	Perf. 11x10½	1603
A1007	28c brown, blue	Perf. 11x10½	1604
A1008	29c blue, blue	Perf. 11x10½	1605
A1009	30c green	Perf. 11x10½	1606
A1011	50c black & orange	Perf. 11	1608
A1013	$1 brown, orange & yellow, tan	Perf. 11	1610
A1013a	$2 dark green & red, tan	Perf. 11	1611
A1014	$5 red brown, yellow & orange, tan	Perf. 11	1612

A1014a	3.1c brown, yellow	Perf. 10 vert	1613
A1014a	3.1c brown, yellow	Same, untagged (Bureau precanceled)	1613a
A1199	3.5c purple, yellow	Perf. 10 vert	1813
A1199	3.5c purple, yellow	Same, untagged (Bureau precanceled)	1813a
A1015	7.7c brown, bright yellow	Perf. 10 vert.	1614
A1015	7.7c brown, bright yellow	Same, untagged (Bureau Precanceled)	1614a
A1016	7.9c carmine, yellow	Perf. 10 vert.	1615
A1016	7.9c carmine, yellow	Same, untagged (Bureau Precanceled)	1615a
A1017	8.4c dark blue, yellow	Perf. 10 vert.	1615C
A1017	8.4c dark blue, yellow	Same, untagged (Bureau Precanceled)	1615d

FLAG ISSUE
1975-77

A1018 13-star Flag over Independence Hall.

A1018a Flag over Capitol.

A1018	13c dark blue & red	Perf. 11x10½	1622
A1018	13c dark blue & red	Perf. 10 vert.	1625
A1018a	13c blue & red	Perf. 11x10½ (Bklt. panes only)	1623
A1018a	13c blue & red	Booklet pane of 7 #1623 + 1 #1590	1623a
A1018a	13c blue & red	Perf. 10 (Bklt. panes only)	1623b
A1018a	13c blue & red	Booklet pane of 7 #1623b + 1 #1590a	1623c

REGULAR ISSUE
1978

A1123 Indian Head Penny, 1877

A1209 Dolley Madison

IDENTIFIER

A1126 *Red Masterpiece and Medallion Roses*

A1123	13c	brown & blue green, bister	Perf. 11 .... **1734**
A1126	15c	multicolored	Perf. 10 (Bklt. panes only) **1737**
A1126	15c	multicolored	Booklet pane of 8. **1737a**
A1209	15c	red brown & sepia	Perf. 11 .... **1822**

REGULAR ISSUE
1978-85

A1124 *"A" Eagle*

A1207 *"B" Eagle*

A1332 *"C" Eagle*

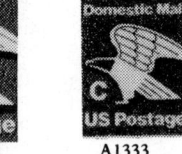

A1333

A1496 *"D" Eagle*

A1497 *"D" Eagle (Booklet)*

A1124	(15c)	orange	Perf. 11 .... **1735**
A1124	(15c)	orange	Perf. 11x10½ (Bklt. panes only) **1736**
A1124	(15c)	orange	Booklet pane of 8. **1736a**
A1124	(15c)	orange	Perf. 10 vert **1743**
A1207	(18c)	violet	Perf. 11x10½ **1818**
A1207	(18c)	violet	Perf. 10 (Bklt. panes only) **1819**
A1207	(18c)	violet	Booklet pane of 8. **1819a**
A1207	(18c)	violet	Perf. 10 vert **1820**

A1332	(20c)	brown	Perf. 11x10½ **1946**
A1332	(20c)	brown	Perf. 10 vert **1947**
A1333	(20c)	brown	Perf. 11x10½ (Bklt. panes only) **1948**
A1333	(20c)	brown	Booklet pane of 10 **1948a**
A1496	(22c)	green	Perf. 11 .... **2111**
A1496	(22c)	green	Perf. 10 vert **2112**
A1497	(22c)	green	Perf. 11 (Bklt. panes only) **2113**
A1497	(22c)	green	Booklet pane of 10 **2113a**

REGULAR ISSUE
1980

A1127 *Virginia*

A1128 *Rhode Island*

A1129 *Massachusetts*

A1130 *Illinois*

A1131 *Texas*

A1127	15c	sepia, yellow	Perf. 11 (Bklt. panes only) **1738**
A1128	15c	sepia, yellow	Perf. 11 (Bklt. panes only) **1739**
A1129	15c	sepia, yellow	Perf. 11 (Bklt. panes only) **1740**
A1130	15c	sepia, yellow	Perf. 11 (Bklt. panes only) **1741**
A1131	15c	sepia, yellow	Perf. 11 (Bklt. panes only) **1142**

IDENTIFIER

GREAT AMERICANS ISSUE
1980-86

 A1231 Dorothea Dix
 A1551 Margaret Mitchell
 A1232 Igor Stravinsky
 A1233 Henry Clay
 A1553 Dr. Paul Dudley White
 A1234 Carl Schurz
 A1554
 A1235 Pearl Buck
 A1555 Hugo Black
 A1236 Walter Lippmann
A1237 Abraham Baldwin
A1238 Henry Knox
 A1239 Sylvanus Thayer
 A1240 Richard Russell
 A1241 Alden Partridge
 A1242 Crazy Horse
 A1243 Sinclair Lewis
 A1244 Rachel Carson

 A1562 Belva Ann Lockwood
 A1245 George Mason
 A1246 Sequoyah
 A1247 Ralph Bunche
 A1248 Thomas H. Gallaudet
 A1249 Harry S. Truman
 A1250 John J. Audubon
A1566 Jack London
A1251 Frank C. Laubach
 A1252 Charles R. Drew

 A1253 Robert Millikan
 A1254 Grenville Clark
 A1255 Lillian M. Gilbreth
 A1256 Chester W. Nimitz
 A1574 John Harvard
 A1577 Dr. Bernard Revel

 A1578 William Jennings Bryan

IDENTIFIER

A1231	1c black	Perf. 11	1844
A1551	1c		2168
A1232	2c brown black	Perf. 10½x11	1845
A1233	3c olive green	Perf. 10½x11	1846
A1553	3c		2170
A1234	4c violet	Perf. 10½x11	1847
A1554	4c		2171
A1235	5c henna brown	Perf. 10½x11	1848
A1555	5c green		2172
A1236	6c	Perf. 11	1849
A1237	7c bright carmine	Perf. 10½x11	1850
A1238	8c olive black	Perf. 10½x11	1851
A1239	9c dark green	Perf. 10½x11	1852
A1240	10c Prussian blue	Perf. 10½x11	1853
A1241	11c dark blue	Perf. 11	1854
A1242	13c light maroon	Perf. 10½x11	1855
A1243	14c slate green	Perf. 11	1856
A1244	17c green	Perf. 10½x11	1857
A1562	17c		2179
A1245	18c dark blue	Perf. 10½x11	1858
A1246	19c brown	Perf. 10½x11	1859
A1247	20c claret	Perf. 10½x11	1860
A1248	20c green	Perf. 10½x11	1861
A1249	20c black	Perf. 11	1862
A1250	22c dark chalky blue	Perf. 11	1863
A1566	25c blue	Perf. 11	2183
A1251	30c olive gray	Perf. 11	1864
A1252	35c gray	Perf. 10½x11	1865
A1253	37c blue	Perf. 10½x11	1866
A1254	39c rose lilac	Perf. 11	1867
A1255	40c dark green	Perf. 11	1868
A1256	50c brown	Perf. 11	1869
A1574	56c		2191
A1577	$1		2194
A1578	$2		2195

REGULAR ISSUE
1981

A1267 Bighorn A1268 Puma
A1269 Harbor Seal A1270 Bison
A1271 Brown bear A1272 Polar bear
A1273 Elk (wapiti) A1274 Moose
A1275 White-tailed deer A1276 Pronghorn

A1267	18c dark brown	Perf. 11 (Bklt. panes only) **1880**
A1268	18c dark brown	Perf. 11 (Bklt. panes only) **1881**
A1269	18c dark brown	Perf. 11 (Bklt. panes only) **1882**
A1270	18c dark brown	Perf. 11 (Bklt. panes only) **1883**
A1271	18c dark brown	Perf. 11 (Bklt. panes only) **1884**
A1272	18c dark brown	Perf. 11 (Bklt. panes only) **1885**
A1273	18c dark brown	Perf. 11 (Bklt. panes only) **1886**
A1274	18c dark brown	Perf. 11 (Bklt. panes only) **1887**
A1275	18c dark brown	Perf. 11 (Bklt. panes only) **1888**
A1276	18c dark brown	Perf. 11 (Bklt. panes only) **1889**

IDENTIFIER

FLAG AND ANTHEM ISSUE
1981

A1277

A1278

A1279 *Field of 1777 flag*

A1280

A1281

A1498

A1499 *Of the People, By the People, For the People*

A1277	18c multicolored	Perf. 11	**1890**
A1278	18c multicolored	Perf. 10 vert	**1891**
A1279	6c multicolored	Perf. 11 (Bklt. panes only)	**1892**
A1280	18c multicolored	Perf. 11 (Bklt. panes only)	**1893**
A1280	18c multicolored	Booklet pane of 8.	**1893a**
A1281	20c black, dark blue & red	Perf. 11	**1894**
A1281	20c black, dark blue & red	Perf. 11x10½ (Bklt. panes only)	**1896**
A1281	20c black, dark blue & red	Booklet pane of 6.	**1896a**
A1281	20c black, dark blue & red	Booklet pane of 8.	**1896b**
A1498	22c blue, red & black	Perf. 11	**2114**
A1498	22c blue, red & black	Perf. 10 vert	**2115**
A1499	22c blue, red & black	Perf. 10 horiz. (Bklt. panes only)	**2116**
A1499	22c blue, red & black	Booklet pane of 5.	**2116a**

TRANSPORTATION ISSUE
1981-86

A1283 *Omnibus*

A1284 *Locomotive*

A1284a *Handcar*

A1506 *School Bus*

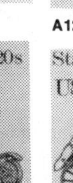

A1285 *Stagecoach*

A1508 *Buckboard*

A1286 *Motorcycle*

A1287 *Sleigh*

A1288 *Bicycle*

A1288a *Baby Buggy*

A1511 *Ambulance*

A1510 *Tricycle*

A1289 *Mail Wagon*

A1512 *Oil Wagon*

A1290 *Hansom Cab*

A1291 *RR Caboose*

A1513 *Stutz Bearcat*

A1514 *Stanley Steamer*

A1515 *Pushcart*

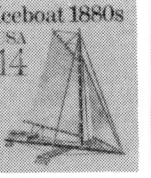
A1517 *Iceboat*

A1292 *Electric Auto*

A1518 Dog Sled

A1293 Surrey

A1294 Fire Pumper

A1283	1c violet	Perf. 10 vert **1897**
A1284	2c black	Perf. 10 vert **1897A**
A1284a	3c dark green	Perf. 10 vert **1898**
A1506	3.4c dark bluish green	Perf. 10 vert **2123**
A1506	3.4c dark bluish green	Same, untagged (Bureau precanceled)... **2123a**
A1285	4c reddish brown	Perf. 10 vert **1898A**
A1285	4c reddish brown	Same, untagged (Bureau precanceled)..**1898Ab**
A1508	4.9c brown black	Perf. 10 vert **2125**
A1508	4.9c brown black	Same, untagged Bureau precanceled)... **2125a**
A1286	5c gray green	Perf. 10 vert **1899**
A1287	5.2c carmine	Perf. 10 vert **1900**
A1287	5.2c carmine	Same, untagged Bureau precanceled)... **1900a**
A1288	5.9c blue	Perf. 10 vert....... **1901**
A1288	5.9c blue	Same, untagged Bureau precanceled)... **1901a**
A1510	6c red brown	Perf. 10 vert **2127**
A1510	6c red brown	Same, untagged (Bureau precanceled)... **2127a**
A1288a	7.4c brown	Perf. 10 vert **1902**
A1288a	7.4c brown	Same, untagged (Bureau precanceled)... **1902a**
A1511	8.3c green	Perf. 10 vert **2128**
A1511	8.3c green	Same, untagged (Bureau precanceled)... **2128a**
A1289	9.3c carmine rose	Perf. 10 vert **1903**
A1289	9.3c carmine rose	Same, untagged Bureau precanceled)... **1903a**
A1512	10.1c slate blue	Perf. 10 vert **2129**
A1512	10.1c slate blue	Same, untagged Bureau precanceled)... **2129a**
A1290	10.9c purple	Perf. 10 vert **1904**
A1290	10.9c purple	Same, untagged (Bureau precanceled)... **1904a**
A1291	11c red	Perf. 10 vert **1905**
A1291	11c red	Same, untagged (Bureau precanceled)... **1905a**
A1513	11c dark green	Perf. 10 vert **2130**
A1514	12c dark blue	Perf. 10 vert **2131**
A1514	12c dark blue	Same, untagged (Bureau precanceled)... **2131a**
A1515	12.5c olive green	Perf. 10 vert **2132**
A1515	12.5c olive green	Same, untagged (Bureau precanceled)... **2132a**
A1517	14c sky blue	Perf. 10 vert **2134**
A1292	17c ultramarine	Perf. 10 vert **1906**
A1292	17c ultramarine	Same, untagged (Bureau precanceled)... **1906a**
A1518	17c	**2135**
A1293	18c dark brown	Perf. 10 vert **1907**
A1294	20c vermilion	Perf. 10 vert **1908**

REGULAR ISSUE
1983-85

A1296 *Eagle and Moon*

A1505 *Eagle and Half Moon*

A1296	$9.35	multicolored	Perf. 10 vert. (Bklt. panes only) **1909**
A1296	$9.35	multicolored	Booklet pane of 3 .... **1909a**
A1505	$10.75	multicolored	Perf. 10 vert. (Bklt. panes only) **2122**
A1505	$10.75	multicolored	Bklt. pane of 3 .... **2122a**

REGULAR ISSUE
1982-85

A1334 *Rocky Mountain Bighorn*

A1390 *Consumer Education*

A1334	20c	dark blue	Perf. 11 (Bklt. panes only) **1949**
A1390	20c	sky blue	Perf. 10 vert **2005**

A1500 *Frilled Dogwinkle*

A1501 *Reticulated Helmet*

A1502 *New England Neptune* **A1503** *Calico Scallop* **A1504** *Lightning Whelk*

A1500	22c black & brown	Perf. 10 (Bklt. panes only) **2117**
A1501	22c black & brown	Perf. 10 (Bklt. panes only) **2118**
A1502	22c black & brown	Perf. 10 (Bklt. panes only) **2119**
A1503	22c black & brown	Perf. 10 (Bklt. panes only) **2120**
A1504	22c black & brown	Perf. 10 (Bklt. panes only) **2121**
A1504	22c black & brown	Booklet pane of 10 .... **2121a**

REGULAR ISSUE
1985-86

A1532 *George Washington, Washington Monument*

A1533 *Sealed Envelopes*

A1532	18c multicolored	Perf. 10 vert **2149**
A1532	18c multicolored	Same, untagged (Bureau precanceled) ... **2149a**
A1533	21.1c multicolored	Perf. 10 vert **2150**
A1533	21.1c multicolored	Same, untagged (Bureau precanceled) ... **2150a**

A1588 Muskellunge

A1589 Atlantic Cod

A1590 Largemouth Bass

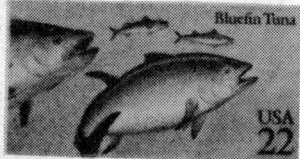
A1591 Bluefin Tuna

A1592 Catfish

A1588	22c multicolored	Perf. 10 horiz. (Bklt. panes only)	**2205**
A1589	22c multicolored	Perf. 10 horiz. (Bklt. panes only)	**2206**
A1590	22c multicolored	Perf. 10 horiz. (Bklt. panes only)	**2207**
A1591	22c multicolored	Perf. 10 horiz. (Bklt. panes only)	**2208**
A1592	22c multicolored	Perf. 10 horiz. (Bklt. panes only)	**2209**
A1592	22c multicolored	Booklet pane of 5 #2205-2209..........	**2209a**

INDEX OF COMMEMORATIVE ISSUES

Entry	Number
Adams, Abigail	2146
Addams, Jane	878
Aeronautics Conference	649-650
Aging Together	2011
Air Mail, 50th Anniversary	C74
Alabama Statehood	1375
Alaska Purchase	C70
Alaska Statehood	C53, 2066
Alaska Territory	800
Alaska-Yukon Pacific	370-371
Alcoholism	1927
Alcott, Louisa May	862
Alexander, Matthew	2222
Alexandria, Va.	C40
Alger, Horatio	2010
Alliance for Progress	1234
Allied Nations	907
Alta California	1725
Amateur Radio	1260
American Arts	1484-1487, 1553
American Bald Eagle	1387
American Bankers Assn.	987
American Bicentennial	1456-1459, 1476-1483, 1543-1546, 1559-1568, 1629-1631, 1633-1682, 1686-1694, 1704, 1716-1720, 1722, 1726, 1728, 1753, 1937-1938, 2052
American Chemical Society	1002, 1685
American Dance	1749-1752
American Folk Art	1706-1709, 1745-1748, 1834-1837, 2138-2141
American Indian	1364
American Legion	1369
American Militia	1568
American Philatelic Society	730, 731, 750
American Quilts	1745-1748
American Revolution	1432
AMERIPEX 86	2145
Angus Cattle	1504
Annapolis, Maryland	984
Antarctic Treaty	1431
Anthony, Susan B.	784
Anti-pollution	1410-1413
Appleseed, Johnny	1317
Apollo 8 (moon orbit)	1371
Apollo Soyuz Space Project	1569-1570
Appomattox Surrender	1182
Apprenticeship	1201
Arbor Day	717
Architects' Institute, American	1089
Architecture, American	1779-1782, 1838-1841, 1928-1931, 2019-2022
Arctic Explorations	1128
Arizona Statehood	1192
Arkansas River Navigation	1358
Arkansas Statehood	782, 2167
Armed Forces	1067
Armstrong, Edwin	2056
Army	785-789
Army, Continental	1565
Army, World War II	934
Articles of Confederation	1726
Artists	884-888
Atlantic Cable	1112
Atoms for Peace	1070, 1200
Audubon, John James	874, 1241
Authors	859-863
Automobile Association (AAA)	1007
Automated Post Office	1164
Bailey, Liberty Hyde	1100
Balloons	2032-2035
Baltimore & Ohio Railroad	1006
Bankers Assn., American	987
Banking and Commerce	1577-1578
Banneker, Benjamin	1804
Bar Assn., American	1022
Barton, Clara	967
Barrymore, John, Ethel & Lionel	2012
Bartholdi, Frederic Auguste	2147
Baseball	855, 1381
Basketball-Naismith	1189
Beautification of America	1318, 1365-1368
Bell, Alexander Graham	893
Bethune, Mary McLeod	2137
Biglin Brothers	1335
Bill of Rights	1312
Birds & Flowers, State	1953-2002
Bissell, Emily	1823
Black Heritage	1804, 1875, 2016, 2044, 2073, 2137
Blair, Montgomery	C66
Blood Donor	1425
Bolivar, Simon	1110-1111
Boone, Daniel	1357
Boston Tea Party	1480-1483
Botanical Congress	1376-1379
Boulder Dam	774
Boys' Clubs of America	1163
Boy Scouts	995, 1145
Braddock's Field	688
Brooklyn, Battle of	1003
Brooklyn Bridge	2041
Brussels International Exhibition	1104
Bunker Hill, Battle of	1564
Burbank, Luther	876
Burgoyne	644, 1728
Butterflies	1712-1715
Byrd Antarctic	733
Cadillac landing at Detroit	1000
California Gold	954
California-Pacific Exposition	773
California Settlement (Bicentenary)	1373
California Statehood	997
Camp Fire Girls	1167
Canada Centenary	1324
Canada-U.S. Friendship	961
Cancer	1263, 1754
CAPEX '78	1757
CARE	1439
Carnegie, Andrew	1171
Carolina-Charleston	683
Carolina Charter	1230
Carver, George Washington	953
Cassatt, Mary	1322
Cather, Willa	1487
Catt, Carrie Chapman	959
Century of Progress	728-729
Champions of Liberty	1096, 1110-1111, 1117-1118, 1125-1126, 1136-1137, 1146-1147, 1159-1160, 1165-1166, 1168-1169, 1174-1175
Chanute, Octave	C93-C94
Chaplains, Four	956
Chautauqua	1505
Chemical Society, American	1002
Chemistry	1685
Cherokee Strip	1360
Chief Joseph	1364
Child, International Year of	1772
Children's Friendship	1085
Chinese Resistance	906
Christmas	1205, 1240, 1254-1257, 1276, 1321, 1336, 1363, 1384, 1414-1418, 1444-1445, 1471-1472, 1507-1508, 1550-1552, 1579-1580, 1701-1703, 1729-1730, 1768-1769, 1799-1800, 1842-1843, 1939- 40, 2025-2030, 2063-2064, 2107-2108, 2165-2166, 2244-2245
Churchill, Winston S.	1264
Circus, American	1309
City Mail Delivery	1238
Civil Service	2053
Civil War Centennial	1178-1182
Civilian Conservation Corps	2037
Clark, George Rogers	651
Clemens, Samuel L.	863
Clemente, Roberto	2097
Coast and Geodetic Survey	1088
Coast Guard	936
Cohan, George M.	1756
Collective Bargaining	1558
Colonial Craftsmen	1456-1459
Colorado Statehood	1001, 1711
Columbia University	1029
Columbian Exposition	230-245
Commercial Aviation	1684
Communications for Peace	1173
Composers	879-883
Comstock, Henry	1130
Confederate Veterans, United	998
Confederation, Articles of	1726
Connecticut Tercentenary	772
Constitution Ratifaction	835
Constitution, Sesquicentennial	798
"Constitution," U.S. Frigate	951
Consumer Education	2005
Continental Army	1565
Continental Congress	1543-1546
Continental Marines	1567
Continental Navy	1566
Contributors to the Cause	1559-1562
Cook, Capt. James	1732-1733
Cooper, James Fenimore	860
Copernicus, Nicolaus	1488
Copley, John Singleton	1273
Coral Reefs	1827-1830
Coronado Expedition	898
Corregidor	925
Credit Union Act	2075
Credo	1139-1144
Crime Prevention	2102
Crippled, Hope for	1385
Crockett, Davy	1330
Curtiss, Glenn	C100
Daniel Boone	1357
Dante	1268
Dare, Virginia	796
Dartmouth College Case	1380
Davy Crockett	1330
Declaration of Independence	627, 1691-1694
Defense, National	899-902
De Galvez, Gen. Bernardo	1825
De Leon, Ponce	2024
Dental Health	1135
Desert Plants	1942-1945
Devils Tower	1084
Dickinson, Emily	1436
Dirksen, Everett	1874
Disabled Veterans & Servicemen	1421-1422
Disney, Walt	1355
Doctors	949
Dogs	2098-2101
Drug Abuse, Prevent.	1438
Duck Decoys	2138-2141
Dulles, John Foster	1172
Dunbar, Paul L.	1554
Eakins, Thomas	1335
Earhart, Amelia	C68
Eastman, George	1062
Echo I	1173
Edison, Thomas A.	654-656, 945
Education	1833
Educators	869-873
Einstein, Albert	1774
Eisenhower, Dwight D.	1383
Electric Light	654-656
Electronics Progress	1500-1502, C86
Elephant Herd, African	1388
Eliot, Charles W.	871
Elks (B.P.O.E.)	1342
Ellington, Duke	2211
Eliot, T.S.	2239
Emancipation Proclamation	1233
Emerson, Ralph Waldo	861
Endangered Flora	1783-1786
Energy	1547, 1723-1724, 2006-2009
Engineers, American Society of Civil	1012
Ericsson, John	628
Erie Canal	1325
Erikson, Leif	1359
Everglades	952
Explorers	2024, 2093
EXPO '74	1527
Fairbanks, Douglas	2088
Fallen Timbers, Battle of	680
Family Planning	1455
Family Unity	2104
Farnsworth, Philo T.	2058
Federal Deposit Insurance Corporation	2071
Fields, W.C.	1803
Fine Arts	1259
Finnish Independence	1334
Flags, Foreign	909-921
Flags, U.S.	1094, 1132, 1153, 1208, 1338-1338A, 1338D, 1338F, 1338G, 1345-1354
Flags, 50 States	1633-1682
Florida Settlement	1271
Florida Statehood	927
Flowers	1876-1879, 2076-2079
Flowers & Birds, State	1953-2002
Flushing Remonstrance	1099
Folk Art, American	1706-1709, 1745-1748, 1775-1778, 1834-1837, 2138-2141
Folklore, American	1317, 1330, 1357, 1370, 1470, 1548
Food for Peace	1231
Football, Intercollegiate	1382
Forest Conservation	1122

80 INDEX OF COMMEMORATIVE ISSUES

Forestry Congress, 5th World 1156
Fort Bliss 976
Fort Duquesne 1123
Fort Harrod 1542
Fort Kearny 970
Fort Snelling 1409
Fort Sumter 1178
Fort Ticonderoga 1071
Foster, Stephen Collins 879
Four Freedoms 908
Four-H Clubs 1005
Francis of Assisi 2023
Francisco, Peter 1562
Franklin, Benjamin 1073, 1690
Freedom from Hunger 1231
Freedom of the Press 1119
French Alliance 1753
Frost, Robert 1526
Fulton, Robert 1270
Future Farmers 1024
Gadsden Purchase 1028
Galvez, Gen. Bernardo de 1825
Gandhi, Mahatma 1174-1175
Gardening-Horticulture 1100
Garibaldi, Giuseppe 1168-1169
Geophysical Year 1107
George, Walter F. 1170
Georgia Bicentennial 726
German Immigration 2040
Gershwin, George 1484
Gettysburg Address 978
Gettysburg, Battle of 1180
Girl Scouts 974, 1199
Goddard, Robert H. C69
Gold Star Mothers 969
Golden Gate Exposition 852
Gompers, Samuel 988
Grand Army of the Republic 985
Grand Coulee Dam 1009
Grandma Moses 1370
Grange 1323
Great River Road 1319
Greely, Adolphus W. 2221
Greeley, Horace 1177
Griffith, D. W. 1555
Gunston Hall 1108
Gutenberg Bible 1014
Haida Canoe 1389
Hamilton, Alexander 1086
Hammarskjold, Dag 1203-1204
Handicapped 1155
Handy, W.C. 1372
Hanson, John 1941
Harding, Warren G. 610-613
Harnett, William M. 1386
Harris, Joel Chandler 980
Harrison, William Henry 996
Hawaii Sesquicentennial 647-648
Hawaii Statehood C55, 2080
Hawaii Territory 799
Hawthorne, Nathaniel 2047
Health Research 2087
HemisFair '68 1340
Herbert, Victor 881
Herkimer at Oriskany 1722
Higher Education 1206
Hispanic Americans 2103
Historic Preservation 1440-1443
Hoban, James 1935-1936
Homemakers 1253
Homer, Winslow 1207
Homestead Act 1198
Hoover, Herbert C. 1269
Hopkins, Mark 870
Horse Racing 1528
Horses 2155-2158
Horticulture 1100
Houston, Sam 1242
Howe, Elias 892
Hudson-Fulton 372-373
Hughes, Charles Evans 1195
Huguenot-Walloon 614-616
Hull, Cordell 1235
Humane Treatment of Animals 1307
Hunger, Help End 2164
Idaho Statehood 896
Illinois Statehood 1339
Independence, Skilled Hands for. 1717-1720
Independence Spirit, Rise of 1476-1479
Indian Centenary 972
Indian Masks, Pacific Northwest. 1834-1837
Indiana Statehood 1308
Indiana Territory 996
International Cooperation Year 1266
International Peace Garden 2014
International Philatelic Exhibitions . . . 630, 778, 1075-1076, 1310-1311, 1632, 2145
Intl. Telecommunication Union 1274
International Women's Year 1571
International Year of the Disabled 1925
International Youth Year 2160-2163
Interphil 76 1632
Inventors 889-893, 2055-2058
Inventors 889-893
Iowa Statehood 942
Iowa Territory 838
Irving, Washington 859
Iwo Jima 929
Jackson, Andrew 941
Jamestown Exposition 328-330
Jamestown Festival 1091
Japan 1021, 1158
Jeffers, Robinson 1485
Johnny Appleseed 1317
Johnson, Lyndon B. 1503
Jones, Bobby 1933
Jones, Casey 993
Jones, John Paul 1789
Joplin, Scott 2044
Joseph, Chief 1364
Jupiter Balloon C54
Kane, Elisha Kent 2220
Kansas City, Mo. 994
Kansas Statehood 1183
Kansas Territory 1061
Kearny Expedition 944
Keller, Helen & Sullivan, Anne 1824
Kennedy, John F. 1246
Kennedy, Robert F. 1770
Kentucky 904, 1542
Kern, Jerome 2110
Key, Francis Scott 962
King, Martin Luther, Jr. 1771
Knoxville World's Fair 2006-2009
Kosciuszko, Gen. Tadeusz 734
Kossuth, Lajos 1117-1118
Labor Day 1082
Lafayette, Marquis de 1010, 1097, 1716
Land-Grant Colleges 1065, 1206
Lanier, Sidney 1446
Law and Order 1343
Lee, Jason 964
Legend of Sleepy Hollow 1548
Leon, Ponce de 2024
Lewis & Clark Expedition 1063
Lexington-Concord 617-619, 1563
Liberty Bell C57
Libraries, America's 2015
Library of Congress 2004
Lincoln, Abraham 367-369, 906, 978, 1113-1116, C59
Lincoln-Douglas Debates 1115
Lindbergh Flight 1710
Lions International 1326
Long, Crawford W. 875
Longfellow, Henry Wadswoth 864
Louisiana Purchase Exposition 323-327
Louisiana Purchase Sesquicentennial . . 1020
Louisiana Statehood 1197
Louisiana World Exposition 2086
Love 1475, 1951, 2072, 2143, 2202
Low, Juliette Gordon 974
Lowell, James Russell 866
Ludington, Sybil 1559
Luther, Martin 2065
Maass, Clara 1699
MacArthur, Gen. Douglas 1424
MacDowell, Edward 882
Mackinac Bridge 1109
Magna Carta 1265
Magsaysay, Ramon 1096
Mail Order Business 1468
Maine Statehood 1391
Malaria 1194
Mann, Horace 869
Mannerheim, Baron Gustf. 1165-1166
Marine Corps Reserve 1315
Mariner 10 1557
Marines, Continental 1567
Marines, World War II 929
Marquette, Jacques 1356
Maryland Tercentenary 736
Masaryk, Thomas G. 1147-1148
Massachusetts Bay Colony 682
Masters, Edgar Lee 1405
Mayo, Drs. William & Charles 1251
Mazzei, Philip C98
McCormack, John 2090
McCormick, Cyrus Hall 891
McDowell, Dr. Ephraim 1138
McLoughlin, John 964
McMahon, Brien 1200
Medal of Honor 2045
Mellon, Andrew W. 1072
Melville, Herman 2094
Merchant Marine 939
Metropolitan Opera 2054
Mexican Independence 1157
Michael, Moina 977
Michigan Centenary 775
Migratory Bird Treaty 1306
Military Services Bicentenary . . . 1565-1568
Military Uniforms 1565-1568
Militia, American 1568
Millay, Edna St. Vincent 1926
Mineral Heritage 1538-1541
Minnesota Statehood 1106
Minnesota Territory 981
Mississippi Statehood 1337
Mississippi Territory 955
Missouri Statehood 1426
Mobile, Battle of 1826
Monmouth, Battle of 646
Monroe, James 1105
Montana Statehood 858
Moon Landing, First C76
Mother's Day 737-738
Morse, Samuel F. B. 890
Moses, Horace 2095
Motion Pictures 926
Mott, Lucretia 959
Mt. Rushmore 1011
Muir, John 1245
Music, American 1252
Naismith-Basketball 1189
Nassau Hall 1083
Nation of Readers 2106
National Academy of Science 1237
National Archives 2081
National Capital Sesquicentennial . 989-992
National Grange 1323
National Guard 1017
National Letter Writing Week . . . 1805-1810
National Park Service 1314
National Parks 740-749
National Parks Centennial . . 1448-1454, C84
National Recovery Administration 732
National Stamp Exhibition 735, 1934
NATO 1008, 1127
Natural History Museum 1387-1390
Navaho Art 2235-2238
Naval Aviation 1185
Naval Review 1091
Navy 790-794
Navy, Continental 1566
Navy, World War II 935
Nebraska Statehood 1328
Nebraska Territory 1060
Netherlands 2003
Nevada Settlement 999
Nevada Statehood 1248
Nevin, Ethelbert 883
Newburgh 727
Newspaper Boys 1015
New Hampshire Stone Face 1068
New Jersey 1247
New Mexico Statehood 1191
New Orleans, Battle of 1261
New York City 1027, C38
New York Coliseum 1076
New York World's Fair 853, 1244
Norris, George W. 1184
Norse-American 620-621
North Dakota Statehood 858
Northwest Ordinance 795
Northwest Territory 837
Nursing 1190
Ochs, Adolph S. 1700
Oglethorpe, James Edward 726
Ohio River Canalization 681
Ohio Statehood 1018
Oklahoma Statehood 1092
Olympics . . 716, 718-719, 1146, 1460-1462, 1695-1698, C85, 1790-1794, 2048-2051, C97, 2067-2070, 2082-2085, C101-C112
Olympics, Special 1788, 2142
Orchids 2076-2079
Oregon Statehood 1124
Oregon Territory 783, 964
Organized Labor 1831
Oriskany Battle 1722
Osteopathic Medicine 1469
Overland Mail 1120
Overrun Countries 909-921
Owls, American 1760-1763

INDEX OF COMMEMORATIVE ISSUES

Paderewski, Ignacy Jan......... 1159-1160
Palomar Observatory............... 966
Panama Canal..................... 856
Panama-Pacific Exposition...... 397-404
Pan-American Exposition........ 294-299
Pan American Games............... C56
Pan American Union............... 895
Papanicolaou, Dr. George......... 1754
Parent Teacher Assn.............. 1463
Patton, Gen. George S............ 1026
Peace Bridge..................... 1721
Peace Corps...................... 1447
Peace, Search for................ 1326
Peace Sesquicentennial............ 727
Peary, Robert E.................. 2222
Penn, William.................... 724
Pennsylvania Academy............. 1064
Performing Arts.... 1755-1756, 1801, 1803,
       2012, 2088, 2090, 2110
Perkins, Frances................. 1821
Perry, Commodore Matthew C....... 1021
Petroleum........................ 1134
Pharmacy......................... 1473
Photography...................... 1758
Physical Fitness................. 2043
Physical Fitness-Sokol........... 1262
Pilgrims' Landing................ 1420
Pilgrim Tercentenary.......... 548-550
Pioneer 10....................... 1556
Pitcher, Molly.................... 646
Poe, Edgar Allen................. 986
Poets......................... 864-868
Polio............................ 1087
Polish Millennium................ 1313
Pony Express................ 894, 1154
Poor, Salem...................... 1560
Poppy, Memorial................... 977
Post, Wiley.................... C95-C96
Postal Service Bicentenary.... 1572-1575
Postal Service Employees...... 1489-1498
Poultry Industry.................. 968
Powell, John Wesley.............. 1374
Presidents................... 2216-2219
Priestley, Joseph................ 2038
Printing.......................... 857
Professional Management.......... 1920
Project Mercury.................. 1193
PTA.............................. 1463
Public Education................. 2159
Public Hospitals................. 2210
Pueblo Pottery............... 1706-1709
Puerto Rican Elections............ 983
Puerto Rico Territory............. 801
Pulaski, Gen. Casimir............. 690
Pulitzer, Joseph................. 946
Quilts....................... 1745-1748
Railroad Engineers................ 993
Railroad, Transcontinental........ 922
Range Conservation............... 1176
Rayburn, Sam..................... 1202
Readers, Nation of............... 2106
Red Cross..... 702, 967, 1016, 1238, 1910
Reed, Walter..................... 877
Register and Vote........... 1249, 1344
Religious Freedom................ 1099
Remington, Frederic..... 888, 1187, 1934
Reptiles, Age of................. 1390
Retarded Children................ 1549
Reuter, Ernst............... 1136-1137
Rhode Island Tercentenary......... 777
Riley, James Whitcomb............. 868
Rise of Spirit of Independence... 1476-1479
Roanoke Voyages.................. 2093
Robinson, Jackie................. 2016
Rodgers, Jimmie.................. 1755
Rogers, Will................ 975, 1801
Roosevelt, Eleanor.......... 1236, 2105
Roosevelt, Franklin D...... 930-933, 1950
Roosevelt, Theodore............... 856
Ross, Betsy...................... 1004
Rotary International............. 1066
Rough Riders...................... 973
Rural America............... 1504-1506
Rural Electrification Administration.. 2144
Russell, Charles M........... 1176, 1243
Ruth, Babe....................... 2046
Sagamore Hill.................... 1023
Saint-Gaudens, Augustus........... 1131, 2091
Salomon, Haym.................... 1561
Salvation Army................... 1267
Sandburg, Carl................... 1731
San Juan......................... 1437
San Martin, Jose de.......... 1125-1126
Saratoga, Surrender at............ 1728
Save Our Air, Cities, Soil, Water . 1410-1413

Savings and Loans................ 1911
Savings Bonds.................... 1320
Sawyer, Tom...................... 1470
Science & Industry............... 2031
Science, National Academy of..... 1237
Scientists................... 874-878
Scott, Blanche Stuart............. C99
Search for Peace................. 1326
SEATO............................ 1151
Seattle World's Fair............. 1196
Seeing Eye Dogs.................. 1787
Serra, Junipero................... C116
Servicemen.................. 1320, 1422
Sevier, John...................... 941
Shakespeare, William.............. 1250
Shiloh, Battle of................. 1179
Shipbuilding..................... 1095
Silver Centenary................. 1130
SIPEX........................ 1310-1311
Skilled Hands for Independence . 1717-1720
Skylab........................... 1529
Sleepy Hollow.................... 1548
Sloan, John...................... 1433
Smith, Alfred E................... 937
Smithsonian Institution........... 943
Smokey the Bear.................. 2096
Social Security Act.............. 2153
Society of Philatelic Americans... 797
Soil and Water Conservation...... 2074
Soil Conservation................ 1133
Sokol-Physical Fitness........... 1262
Soo Locks........................ 1069
Sound Recording.................. 1705
Sousa, John Philip................ 880
South Carolina Tercentenary...... 1407
South Dakota Statehood............ 858
Space Accomplishments.. 1331-1332, 1556,
                   1759, 1912-1919
Space Achievement Decade..... 1434-1435
Sperry, Lawrence & Elmer.......... C114
Spirit of '76................. 1629-1631
Stamp Centenary................... 948
Stamp Collecting....... 1474, 2198-2201
Stanton, Elizabeth................ 959
State Birds & Flowers........ 1953-2002
State Flags.................. 1633-1682
Statehood, North Dakota, South Dakota,
     Montana, Washington.......... 858
Statue of Liberty Centenary...... 2224
Statue of Liberty....... 1075, C58, C63
Steamship Savannah................ 923
Steel Industry................... 1090
Stefansson, Vilhjalmer........... 2223
Steinbeck, John.................. 1773
Steinmetz, Charles............... 2055
Steuben, Baron Friedrich von...... 689
Stevenson, Adlai................. 1275
Stone, Harlan Fiske............... 965
Stone Mountain Memorial.......... 1408
Streetcars................... 2059-2062
Stuart, Gilbert................... 884
Stuyvesant, Peter................. 971
Sullivan, Anne & Keller, Helen.... 1824
Sullivan, Maj. Gen. John.......... 657
Sun Yat-sen................. 906, 1188
Sweden-U.S. Treaty............... 2036
Swedish-Finnish Settlement........ 836
Swedish Pioneers.................. 958
Taft, Robert A................... 1161
Talking Pictures................. 1727
Tanner, Henry Ossawa............. 1486
Teachers......................... 1093
Telegraph Centenary............... 924
Telephone Centenary.............. 1683
Tennessee Statehood............... 941
Tennessee Valley Authority....... 2042
Tesla, Nikola.................... 2057
Texas Independence................ 776
Texas Republic................... 2204
Texas Statehood................... 938
Thirteenth Amendment.............. 902
Thoreau, Henry David............. 1327
Thorpe, Jim...................... 2089
Ticonderoga...................... 1071
Toleware, Pennsylvania...... 1775-1778
Tom Sawyer....................... 1470
Touro Synagogue.................. 2017
Traffic Safety................... 1272
Trans-Mississippi Exposition.... 285-293
Trans-Mississippi Philatelic
  Exposition..................... 751
Transpacific Airmail 50th Anniv.... C115
Treaty of Paris.................. 2052
Trees, American.............. 1764-1767
Trucking Industry................ 1025
Truman, Harry S.................. 1499

Trumbull, John................... 1361
Truth, Sojourner................. 2203
Tubman, Harriet.................. 1744
Turners, American Society of...... 979
Twain, Mark....................... 863
United Confederate Veterans....... 998
United Nations, 25th anniv....... 1419
United Nations Conference......... 928
U.S.-Canada Friendship............ 961
U.S.-Canada Peace Bridge......... 1721
U.S.-Japan Treaty................ 1158
U.S.-Netherlands
  Diplomatic Relations........... 2003
U.S.-Sweden Treaty............... 2036
Universal Postal Union........ C42-C44
UPU Centenary................ 1530-1537
Urban Planning................... 1333
Utah Settlement................... 950
Valley Forge................ 645, 1729
Vermont Sesquicentennial.......... 643
Vermont Statehood................. 903
Verrazano-Narrows Bridge......... 1258
Verville, Alfred V................ C113
Veterans, Korean War............. 2152
Veterans, Vietnam War............ 1802
Veterans, World War I............ 2154
Veterans, World War II............ 940
Veterans Adminstration........... 1825
Veterans of Foreign Wars......... 1525
Victory, World War I.............. 537
Vietnam Veterans' Memorial....... 2109
Viking Missions to Mars.......... 1759
Virgin Islands.................... 802
Virginia Capes, Battle of........ 1938
Voice of America................. 1329
Voluntarism...................... 2039
Volunteer Firemen................. 971
Walker, Dr. Mary................. 2013
Washington, Booker T......... 873, 1074
Washington, D.C........... 989-992, C64
Washington, George 704-715, 854, 947, 948,
                  1003, 1704, 1729, 1952
Washington & Lee Univ............. 982
Washington Statehood.............. 858
Washington Territory............. 1019
Water Conservation............... 1150
Waterfowl Conservation........... 1362
Waterfowl Conservation Act....... 2092
Wayne, Gen. Anthony............... 680
Webster, Daniel.............. 725, 1380
Webster, Noah.................... 1121
West, Benjamin................... 1553
West Virginia Statehood.......... 1232
Wharton, Edith................... 1832
Wharton, Joseph.................. 1920
Wheat............................ 1506
Wheatland........................ 1081
Wheels of Freedom................ 1162
Whistler, James McNeill........... 885
White Plains, Battle of........... 629
White, William Allen.............. 960
Whitman, Walt..................... 867
Whitney, Eli...................... 889
Whittier, John Greenleaf.......... 865
Wilderness, Battle of the........ 1181
Wildlife 1077-1079, 1098, 1392, 1427-1430,
                  1464-1467, 1921-1924
Wiley, Harvey W.................. 1080
Willard, Frances E................ 872
Win the War....................... 905
Winter Special Olympics.......... 2142
Wisconsin Statehood............... 957
Wisconsin Tercentenary............ 739
Wolf Trap Farm Park.......... 1452, 2018
Woman Suffrage................... 1406
Women............................ 1152
Women, Armed Services............ 1013
Women, Progress................... 959
Women's Clubs.................... 1316
Woodcarving................. 2270-2273
Woodson, Carter G................ 2073
Wool Industry.................... 1423
Workmen's Compensation........... 1186
World Peace...................... 1129
World Peace through Law.......... 1576
World Refugee Year............... 1149
World's Fair... 853, 1196, 1244, 2006-2009,
                                    2086
Wright Brothers........... C45, C91-C92
Wyoming Statehood................. 897
Yorktown, Battle of.............. 1937
Yorktown, Surrender of............ 703
Young, Whitney, Moore, Jr........ 1875
Youth Month....................... 963
Youth, Support Our............... 1342
Zaharias, Babe................... 1932

UNITED STATES
NATIONAL ALBUM

The SCOTT UNITED STATES NATIONAL POSTAGE STAMP ALBUM is "The" Album demanded by serious collectors of United States material.

The NATIONAL POSTAGE STAMP ALBUM comes complete with famous Scott hand-crafted sturdy binder and Scott Album pages. Each page includes spaces with the Scott Catalogue number and a description or photo of every stamp.

The SCOTT NATIONAL POSTAGE STAMP ALBUM provides spaces for commemoratives, definitives, air post, special delivery, registration, certified mail, postage due, parcel post, special handling, officials, newspapers, offices abroad, hunting permits, confederates and much more!

Available in U.S.A. and Canada from your favorite dealer, bookstore or stamp collecting accessory retailer or write:

SCOTT. Publishing Company

P.O. Box 828, Sidney, OH 45365

POSTMASTERS' PROVISIONALS

The Act of Congress of March 3, 1845 reads: "For every single letter in manuscript or communicated in writing or by marks asked or communicated in writing or by marks, not exceeding 300 miles, five cents; and for any distance over 300 miles be charged double these rates; and for a treble letter, triple; quadruple these rates; and every letter or parcel not exceeding a single letter, and every additional weight of half an ounce, shall be charged with postage as follows: ... postage. All drop letters, or letters placed in any post office, not for transmission in the mail but for delivery only, shall be charged with postage at the rate of two cents each.

Circulars were charged 2 cents; magazines and pamphlets, 2½ cents; newspapers with the mail but not exceeding...

Between the time of the Act of 1845, effecting uniform postage rates, and the Act of March 3, 1847, authorizing the postmaster-general to issue stamps, postmasters in various cities issued provisional stamps.

Before adhesive stamps were introduced, mail was marked "Paid" or "Due" either with pen and ink or handstamps of various designs. Sometimes the word suffixed, but usually the amount of the postage and date were added. They may be found separately applied and also in one handstamp. These "Stampless Covers" are found in numerous types and usually carry the town postmark.

New York Postmaster Robert H. Morris issued the first postmaster provisional in July, 1845. Other postmasters soon followed. The provisionals served until superseded by the federal government's 5c and 10c stamps issued July 1, 1847.

Postmasters recognized the provisionals as indicating postage prepaid. On several provisionals the signature or initials of the postmaster vouched for their legitimate use.

On July 12, 1845, Postmaster Morris sent examples of his new stamp to the postmasters of Boston, Philadelphia, Albany and Washington, asking that they be treated as unpaid until they reached the New York office. Starting in that year the New York stamps were distributed to other offices. Postmaster General Cave Johnson reportedly authorized this practice with the understanding that these stamps were to be sold for letters directed to or passing through New York. This was an experiment to test the practicality of the use of adhesive postage stamps.

PRICES FOR ENVELOPES ARE FOR ENTIRES.

ALEXANDRIA, VA.
Daniel Bryan, Postmaster.

A1

All known copies cut to shape.
Type I—40 asterisks in circle.
Type II—39 asterisks in circle.

			Typeset	Imperforate
1846				
1X1	A1	5c buff, type I		17,500.
	a.	5c buff, type II		35,000.
		On cover (I or II)		85,000.
1X2	"	5c blue, type I, on cover		

CANCELLATIONS.
Red circular town
Black "PAID"
Black ms. accounting number
("No. 45," "No. 70")

The few copies of Nos. 1X1 and 1X1a known on cover are generally not tied by postmark and some are uncanceled. The price for "on cover" is for a stamp obviously belonging on a cover which bears the proper circular dated town, boxed "5" and straight line "PAID" markings.

No. 1X2 is unique. It is canceled with a black straight line "PAID" marking which is repeated on the cover. The cover also bears a black circular "Alexandria Nov. 25" postmark.

ANNAPOLIS, MD.
Martin F. Revell, Postmaster.
ENVELOPE.

E1

Printed in upper right corner of envelope.

1846			
2XU1	E1	5c carmine red, white	45,000.

No. 2XU1 exists in two sizes of envelope. Envelopes and letter sheets are known showing the circular design stamped in blue and figure "2" handstamped in blue or red. They were used locally. Price $1500.
A letter sheet is known showing the circular design and figure "5" handstamped in red. Used from Annapolis to Washington. Price $2000.
Similar circular design in blue without numeral or "PAID" is known to have been used as a postmark.

BALTIMORE, MD.
James Madison Buchanan, Postmaster.

Signature of Postmaster
A1

83

Printed from plate of 10 (5x2) separately engraved sub-
stamps (Pos. 1-6, 8, ...) ...imprint "Eng'd by Thos. Chubbuck, Bratto," be-
...middle stamp of the lower row (Pos. 8).

1846   *Imperforate*

5X1	A1	5c buff	13,500.	5,000.
		On cover		8,000.

CANCELLATIONS
Red straight line "PAID"
Red pen

The red pen-marks are small and lightly applied. They may have been used to invalidate a sample sheet since each plate position is known so canceled.

LOCKPORT, N. Y.
Hezekiah W. Scovell, Postmaster.

A1

"Lockport, N.Y." oval and "PAID" separately hand-stamped in red, "5" in black ms.

1846   *Imperforate*

6X1	A1	5c red, buff, on cover	60,000.

CANCELLATION
Black ms. "X"

One copy of No. 6X1 is known. Small fragments of two other copies adhering to one cover have been found.

MILLBURY, MASS.
Asa H. Waters, Postmaster.

George Washington
A1

Printed from a woodcut, singly, on a hand press.

1846   *Imperforate.*

7X1	A1	5c bluish	50,000.	17,500.
		On cover		30,000.

CANCELLATIONS
Red straight line "PAID"
Red circular "MILBURY, MS.",
  date in center

NEW HAVEN, CONN.
Edward A. Mitchell, Postmaster.
ENVELOPES.

E1

Printed from... stamps (Pos. 1-6, 8, ...)

3X1	A1	5c black		
3X2	"	On cover		3,500.
3X3	"	10c ...		5,500.
3X4	"	...		40,000.

Nos. 3X3-3X4 ...

CANCELLATIONS
Blue "5" in oval
Blue "10" in oval
Black pen

Prices are a general guide by either pen or ms. ...less. Items of blue ... considerably more, ... or quality of attractive-ness...

ENVELOPES

James M. Buchanan

PAID
5
E1

The "PAID" and "5" in oval were handstamped in blue or red, always both in the same color on the entire. "James M. Buchanan" was handstamped in black or red. The paper is manila, buff, white, salmon or ...ish. Manila is by far the most frequently found 5c ...ope. All 10c envelopes are rare, with manila or buff the more frequent. Of the 10c on salmon, only one example is known.

Prices are intended as guides. The general attractiveness of the envelope and the clarity of the handstamps primarily determine the value.

The color listed is that of the "PAID" and "5" in ...

1845   Various Papers   Handstamped

3XU1	E1	5c blue	
3XU2	"	5c red	12...
3XU3	"	10c blue	12...
3XU4	"	10c red	

CANCELLATIONS
Blue circular town | Blue "5" in oval
                         | Red "5" in oval

The second "5" in oval on the unlisted "5 + 5" envelopes is believed not to be part of the basic prepaid marking, but envelopes bearing this marking merit a premium over the prices for Nos. 3XU1-3XU2.

BOSCAWEN, N. H.
Worcester Webster, Postmaster.

PAID
5
CENTS
A1

Typeset.   *Imperforate.*

1846 (?)
4X1	A1	5c dull blue, *yellowish*, on cover with ms. postal markings.	60,000.

One copy known, uncancelled on cover with ms. postal markings.

BRATTLEBORO, VT.
Frederick N. Palmer, Postmaster.

Initials of Postmaster
A1

POSTMASTERS' PROVISIONALS

Impressed from a brass handstamp at upper right of envelope.

Signed in blue, black, magenta or red ms., as indicated in parenthesis.

1845

8XU1	E1	5c red, *white* (Bl or M)	—
		Cut square	4,000.
		Cut to shape	2,000.
8XU2	"	5c red, *light bluish* (Bk)	32,000.
8XU3	"	5c dull blue, *buff* (Bl)	22,500.
8XU4	"	5c dull blue, *white* (Bk)	22,500.
8XU5	"	5c dull blue, *buff* (R)	—

Prices of Nos. 8XU1-8XU5 are a guide to value. They are based on auction realizations and take condition into consideration. All New Haven envelopes are of almost equal rarity. An entire of No. 8XU2 is the finest example known. The other envelopes and cut squares are priced according to condition as much as rarity.

Reprints

Twenty reprints in dull blue on white paper, signed by E. A. Mitchell in lilac rose ink, were made in 1871 for W. P. Brown and others. Thirty reprints in carmine on hard white paper, signed in dark blue or red, were made in 1874 for Cyrus B. Peets, Chief Clerk for Mitchell. Unsigned reprints were made for N. F. Seebeck and others about 1872.

Edward A. Mitchell, grandson of the Postmaster, in 1923 delivered reprints in lilac on soft white wove paper, dated "1923" in place of the signature.

In 1932, the New Haven Philatelic Society bought the original handstamp and gave it to the New Haven Colony Historical Society. To make the purchase possible (at the $1000 price) it was decided to print 260 stamps from the original handstamp. Of these, 130 were in red and 130 in dull blue, all on hard, white wove paper.

According to Carroll Alton Means' booklet on the New Haven Provisional Envelope, after this last reprinting the brass handstamp was so treated that further reprints cannot be made. The reprints were sold originally at $5 each. A facsimile signature of the postmaster, "E. A. Mitchell," (blue on the red reprints, black on the blue) was applied with a rubber handstamp. These 260 reprints are all numbered to correspond with the number of the booklet issued then.

NEW YORK, N. Y.
Robert H. Morris, Postmaster.

George Washington
A1

Printed by Rawdon, Wright & Hatch from a plate of 40 (5x8). The die for Washington's head on the contemporary bank notes was used for the vignette. It had a small flaw—a line extending from the corner of the mouth down the chin—which is quite visible on the paper money. This was corrected for the stamp.

The stamps were usually initialed "ACM" (Alonzo Castle Monson) in magenta ink as a control before being sold or passed through the mails. There are four or five styles of these initials. The most common is "ACM" without periods. The scarcest is "A.C.M.", believed written by Marcena Monson. The rare initials "RHM" (Robert H. Morris, the postmaster) and "MMJr" (Marcena Monson) are listed separately.

The stamps were printed on a variety of wove papers varying in thickness from pelure to thick, and in color from gray to bluish and blue. Some stamps appear to have a slight ribbing or mesh effect. A few also show letters of a double-line papermaker's watermark, a scarce variety. The blue paper is listed separately since it is the rarest and most distinctve. All used true blue copies carry "ACM" without periods; of the three unused copies, two lack initials.

Earliest known use: July 15, 1845.

1845		Engraved	*Imperforate*	
9X1	A1	5c bluish	700.00	325.00
		On cover		450.00
		On cover to foreign country		1,500.
		Pair	2,000.	800.00
		Pair on cover		1,250.
		Pair on cover to foreign country		3,500.
		Strip of three		3,000.
		Strip of four	6,000.	
		Block of four		6,000.
		Double transfer at bottom (Pos. 2)	1,000.	425.00
		Double transfer at top (Pos. 7)	1,000.	425.00
		Bottom frame line double (Pos. 31)	1,000.	425.00
		Top frame line double (Pos. 36)	1,000.	425.00
	a.	Blue paper	5,500.	1,850.
		On cover, blue paper		3,500.
		Pair, blue paper		5,000.
	b.	Signed "RHM"	10,000.	2,250.
	c.	Signed "MMJr", on cover		—
	d.	Without signature	1,350.	600.00

Known used from Albany, Boston, Jersey City, N.J., New Hamburgh, N.Y., Philadelphia, Sing Sing, N.Y., Washington, D.C., and Hamilton, Canada, as well as by route agents on the Baltimore R.R. Covers originating in New Hamburgh are known only with No. 9X1b; some also bear the U.S. City Despatch Post carrier.

CANCELLATIONS

Black pen	350.00	Red "U.S." in	
Blue pen	350.00	octagon frame	
Magenta pen	+50.00	(Carrier)	+650.00
Red grid	+50.00	Red Baltimore	
Red town	+100.00	R.R.	—

Another plate of nine subjects (3x3) was made from the original die. Each subject differs slightly from the others, with Position 8 showing the white stock shaded by crossed diagonal lines. Prints were struck from this plate in black on deep blue and white papers, as well as in blue, green, scarlet and brown on white bond paper.

ENVELOPES.

Postmaster Morris, according to a newspaper report of July 7, 1845, issued envelopes. The design was not stated and no example has been seen.

PROVIDENCE, R. I.
Welcome B. Sayles, Postmaster.

A1   A2

Engraved on copper plate containing 12 stamps (3x4). Upper right corner stamp (Pos. 3) "TEN"; all others "FIVE". The stamps were engraved directly on the plate, each differing from the other. The "TEN" and Pos. 4, 5, 6, 9, 11 and 12 have no period after "CENTS".

Yellowish White Handmade Paper

1846, Aug. 24				*Imperforate*
10X1	A1	5c gray black	200.00	1,000.
		On cover, tied by postmark		12,000.
		On cover, pen canceled		3,500.
		Two on cover		—
		Pair		425.00
		Block of four		875.00
10X2	A2	10c gray black	950.00	
		On cover, pen canceled		—
	a.	Se-tenant with 5c		1,200.
		Complete sheet		3,850.

POSTMASTERS' PROVISIONALS

CANCELLATIONS

Black pen check mark
Red circular town
Red straight line "PAID" (2 types)
Red "5"

All canceled copies of Nos. 10X1-10X2, whether or not bearing an additional handstamped cancellation, are obliterated with a black pen check mark. All genuine covers must bear the red straight line "PAID," the red circular town postmark, and the red numeral "5" or "10" rating mark.

Reprints were made in 1898. In general, each stamp bears one of the following letters on the back: B. O. G. E. R. T. D. U. R. B. I. N. However, some reprint sheets received no such printing on the reverse. All reprints are without gum. Price for 5c, $50; for 10c, $125; for sheet, $725.

ST. LOUIS, MO.

John M. Wimer, Postmaster.

Missouri Coat of Arms
A1   A2   A3

Printed from a copper plate of 6 (2x3) subjects separately engraved by J. M. Kershaw.

The plate in its first state, referred to as Plate I, comprised: three 5c stamps in the left vertical row and three 10c in the right vertical row. The stamps vary slightly in size, measuring from 17¾ to 18¼ by 22 to 22½ mm.

Later a 20c denomination was believed necessary. So two of the 5c stamps, types I (pos. 1) and II (pos. 3) were changed to 20c by placing the plate face down on a hard surface and hammering on the back of the parts to be altered until the face was driven flush at those points. The new numerals were then engraved. Both 20c stamps show broken frame lines and the paw of the right bear on type II is missing. The 20c type II (pos. 3) also shows retouching in the dashes under "SAINT" and "LOUIS." The characteristics of types I and II of the 5c also serve to distinguish the two types of the 20c. This altered, second state of the plate is referred to as Plate II. It is the only state to contain the 20c.

The demand for the 20c apparently proved inadequate, and the plate was altered again. The "20" was erased and "5" engraved in its place, resulting in noticeable differences from the 5c stamps from Plate I. In type I (pos. 1) reengraved, the "5" is twice as far from the top frame line as in the original state, and the four dashes under "SAINT" and "LOUIS" have disappeared except for about half of the upper dash under each word. In type II (pos. 3) reengraved, the ornament in the flag of the "5" is a diamond instead of a triangle; the diamond in the bow is much longer than in the first state, and the ball of the "5," originally blank, contains a large dot. At right of the shading of the "5" is a short curved line which is evidently a remnant of the "0" of "20." Type III (pos. 5) of the 5c was slightly retouched. This second alteration of the plate is referred to as Plate III.

Type characteristics common to Plates I, II and III:

5 Cent. Type I (pos. 1). Haunches of both bears almost touch frame lines.
    Type II (pos. 3). Bear at right almost touches frame line, but left bear is about ¼ mm. from it.
    Type III (pos. 5). Haunches of both bears about ½ mm. from frame lines. Small spur on "S" of "POST."
10 Cent. Type I (pos. 2). Three dashes below "POST OFFICE."
    Type II (pos. 4). Three pairs of dashes.
    Type III (pos. 6). Pairs of dashes (with rows of dots between) at left and right. Dash in center with row of dots above it.
20 Cent. Type I. See 5c Type I.
    Type II. See 5c Type II.

Wove Paper Colored Through

1845, Nov.–1846 *Imperforate*

11X1	A1	5c *greenish*	5,000.	2,350.
		On cover		4,000.
		Pair		5,250.
		Two on cover		7,000.
		Strip of three on cover		9,500.
11X2	A2	10c *greenish*	4,500.	2,000.
		On cover		3,000.
		Pair on cover		6,500.
		Strip of three on cover		9,000.
11X3	A3	20c *greenish*		25,000.
		On cover		

Three varieties of the 5c and three of the 10c were printed from Plate I. One variety of the 5c, three of the 10c, and two of the 20c were printed from Plate II.

1846

11X4	A1	5c *gray lilac*	—	3,500.
		On cover		5,000.
11X5	A2	10c *gray lilac*	4,500.	1,750.
		On cover		2,750.
		Pair		5,000.
		Strip of 3		8,250.
		Strip of three on cover		13,500.
		Pair (II & III) se-tenant with 5c (III)		17,000.
11X6	A3	20c *gray lilac*		10,000.
		On cover		13,500.
		Pair on cover		30,000.
		Se-tenant with 10c, on cover		27,500.
		Strip of 3, 20c + 20c + 5c se-tenant		40,000.

One variety of the 5c, three of the 10c and two of the 20c. Printed from Plate II.

1846 *Pelure Paper*

11X7	A1	5c *bluish*	—	5,000.
		On cover		6,500.
		Pair		
		Two on cover		12,500.
11X8	A2	10c *bluish*		5,000.
		On cover		6,500.
	a.	Impression of 5c on back		

Three varieties of the 5c and three of the 10c. Printed from Plate III.

CANCELLATIONS on Nos. 11X1 to 11X8.

Black pen
Ms. initials of postmaster (✱ 11X2, type I)
Red circular town
Red straight line "PAID"
Red grid (✱ 11X7)

Prices for used off-cover stamps are for fine to very fine pen-canceled copies. Handstamp canceled copies sell for much more. Prices for stamps on cover are approximate quotations for fine to very fine stamps pen canceled. Covers with the stamps tied by handstamp sell at considerable premiums depending upon the condition of the stamps and the general attractiveness of the cover. In general, covers with multiple frankings (unless separately priced) are valued at the "on cover" price of the highest item, plus the "off cover" price of the other stamps.

TUSCUMBIA, ALA.

ENVELOPE.

E1

1858   Handstamped at upper right of envelope
12XU1 E1 3c dull red, *buff*   6,500.

No. 12XU1 also exists with a 3c 1857 stamp affixed at upper right over the provisional handstamp, tied by black circular "TUSCUMBIA, ALA." town postmark. Price $2,000.

See also Confederate States Nos. 84XU1-84XU3.

Start your
U.S. COLLECTION
with.... SCOTT

Scott's U.S. Minuteman Stamp Album!

FEATURES...

★ The famous Scott Catalogue identification number for every stamp.

★ Exciting stories of almost every stamp.

★ Attractive vinyl binder.   ★ Supplemented annually.

"A must for every collector of United States postage stamps."

Available at your local dealer or direct from Scott Publishing Co.

Scott Publishing Company
P.O. Box 828, Sidney, OH 45365

Know Your Options

Buying or Selling, Explore Your Options With Andrew Levitt, Philatelic Consultant

Levitt Offers You:

An unbiased client/consultant relationship.

$200,000,000 and 25 years experience buying, placing and appraising important properties.

Full market coverage from auctions to tax-free donations.

Professionalism, integrity and confidentiality.

ANDREW LEVITT
Philatelic Consultant

Box 342-SS
Danbury, CT 06813
(203) 743-5291

Life member: APS, ASDA, Collectors Club of N.Y., U.S. Classics Society, Philatelic Foundation

Fully insured, Letter of Credit Available.

POSTAGE

General Issues.

All issues from 1847 to 1894 are Unwatermarked.

Benjamin Franklin
A1

This issue was authorized by an Act of Congress, approved March 3, 1847, to take effect July 1, 1847, from which date the use of Postmasters' Stamps or any which were not authorized by the Postmaster General became illegal.
Earliest known use: 5c, July 7; 10c, July 2, 1847.
This issue was declared invalid as of July 1, 1851.

Produced by Rawdon, Wright, Hatch & Edson.
Plates of 200 subjects in two panes of 100 each.

Thin Bluish Wove Paper.

1847, July 1 Cat. No.			Engraved	Imperforate. Unused	Used
1	A1	5c	red brown	4,000.	650.00
			pale brown	4,000.	650.00
			brown	4,000.	650.00
	a.	5c	dark brown	4,000.	650.00
			grayish brown	4,000.	650.00
			blackish brown	4,000.	650.00
	b.	5c	orange brown	4,500.	750.00
			brown orange		1,200.
	c.	5c	red orange	10,000.	1,850.
			On cover		850.00
			Pair	9,500.	1,500.
			Pair on cover		1,750.
			Strip of three	15,000.	3,000.
			Block of four	35,000.	30,000.
			Block of four on cover		42,500.
			Dot in 'S' in upper right corner (Plate I)	5,500.	850.00
	(A)		Double transfer of top frame line (80RI)		800.00
	(B)		Double transfer of top and bottom frame lines (90RI)		800.00
	(C)		Double transfer of bottom frame line and lower part of left frame line		800.00
	(D)		Double transfer of top, bottom and left frame lines, also numerals		1,100.

80RI(A)
Double transfer of top frame line.

90RI(B)
Double transfer of top and bottom frame lines

(C)
Double transfer of bottom frame line and lower part of left frame line

(D)
Double transfer of top, bottom and left frame lines, also numerals.

CANCELLATIONS

Red	650.00	U. S. Express Mail	+100.00
Blue	+25.00	"Way"	+250.00
Black	+35.00	"Steamboat"	+350.00
Magenta	+150.00	"Steam"	+200.00
Orange	+150.00	"Steamship"	+300.00
Ultramarine	+100.00	Hotel	+2000.00
Ultra., town	+250.00	Numeral	+50.00
Violet	+250.00	Canada	+1200.00
Green	+750.00	Wheeling, Va., grid	+600.00
"Paid"	+50.00		
"Free"	+150.00	Pen	375.00
Railroad	+200.00		

POSTAGE, 1847, 1875

George Washington
A2

2	A2	10c	**black**	18,500.	2,000.
			gray black	18,500.	2,000.
			greenish black		2,000.
			On cover		2,350.
			On cover with 5c No. 1		18,500.
			Pair	40,000.	4,500.
			Pair on cover		6,000.
			Strip of three		10,500.
			Block of four	120,000.	50,000.
		a.	Diagonal half used as 5 cents on cover		15,000.
		b.	Vertical half used as 5 cents on cover		21,000.
		c.	Horizontal half used as 5 cents on cover		25,000.
			Short transfer at top	18,500.	2,000.
			Vertical line through second "F" of "OFFICE" (68RI)		2,500.
			With "Stick Pin" in tie (52LI)		2,500.
			With "harelip" (57LI)		2,500.
		(A)	Double transfer in "X" at lower right (1RI)		2,500.
		(B)	Double transfer in "Post Office" (31RI)		2,500.
		(C)	Double transfer in "X" at lower right (2RI)		2,500.
		(D)	Double transfer of left and bottom frame line (41RI)		2,500.

1RI
(A)
Double transfer in "X" at lower right

31RI
(B)
Double transfer in "Post Office"

2RI
(C)
Double transfer in "X" at lower right

41RI
(D)
Double transfer of left and bottom frame line.

CANCELLATIONS.

Red	2,000.	U.S. Express Mail	+350.00
Blue	+50.00	"Way"	+400.00
Orange	+150.00	Numeral	+100.00
Black	+100.00	"Steam"	+350.00
Magenta	+200.00	"Steamship"	+450.00
Violet	+250.00	"Steamboat"	+650.00
Green	+1000.00	"Steamer 10"	+1000.00
Ultramarine	+200.00	Canada	+1250.00
"Paid"	+100.00	Panama	—
"Free"	+300.00	Wheeling, Va., grid	+1500.00
Railroad	+350.00	Pen	1250.00

1875   REPRODUCTIONS

Actually, official imitations made from new plates of 50 subjects made by the Bureau of Engraving and Printing by order of the Post Office Department for display at the Centennial Exposition of 1876. These were not good for postal use.

Reproductions. The letters R. W. H. & E. at the bottom of each stamp are less distinct on the reproductions than on the originals.

Original   Reproduction

5c. On the originals the left side of the white shirt frill touches the oval on a level with the top of the "F" of "Five". On the reproductions it touches the oval about on a level with the top of the figure "5".

DANIEL F. KELLEHER CO., INC.

Stanley J. Richmond, prop.
Established 1885

Since 1885 America's oldest philatelic auction house has successfully brought together both buyer and seller for better quality rare United States and Foreign stamps, covers, autographs and collections. Daniel F. Kelleher Co., Inc. offers you important reasons for choosing us as your auction house, whether you wish to purchase, consign or sell your better philatelic items or collections.

- Liberal Advances to $1,000,000.00 always available for better items or collections
- Prompt payment made to seller and consignor
- Professional staff to advise you.
- Personal attention to lotting and descriptions by Stanley J. Richmond, lending his worldwide reputation and contacts to the sale of your better philatelic items or collections.

Contact us today to assist with your needs to buy or sell better quality rare philatelic material.

Daniel F. Kelleher Co., Inc.

Member:
Collectors Club, New York
U.S. Classics Society
Philatelic Foundation

40 Broad St.
Suite 830
Boston, Massachusetts 02109
Bank references on request

617-523-3676
617-742-0883
617-542-4450

FOR AUCTION INFORMATION - BUYING OR SELLING -
CIRCLE #35 ON THE READER SERVICE CARD.

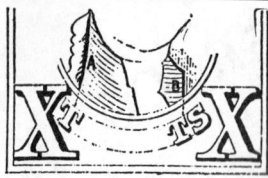

Original

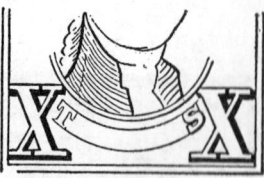

Reproduction

10c. On the originals line of coat (A) points to "T" of TEN and (B) it points between "T" and "S" of CENTS. On the reproductions line of coat (A) points to right tip of "X" and line of coat (B) points to center of "S".
On the reproductions the eyes have a sleepy look, the line of the mouth is straighter, and in the curl of the hair near the left cheek is a strong black dot, while the originals have only a faint one.
(See Nos. 948a and 948b for 1947 reproductions—5c blue and 10c brown orange in larger size.)

A3

A4

Imperforate.
Bluish paper, without gum.

3	A3	5c red brown (4779)		1,300.
		brown		1,300.
		dark brown		1,300.
		Pair		3,000.
		Block of four		8,000.
4	A4	10c black (3883)		1,700.
		gray black		1,700.
		Pair		3,750.
		Block of four		11,000.

1851-56   *Imperforate.*
Produced by Toppan, Carpenter, Casilear & Co.

Stamps of the 1847, 1851-56 series were printed from plates consisting of 200 subjects and the sheets were divided into panes of 100 each. In order that each stamp in the sheet could be identified easily in regard to its relative position it was devised that the stamps in each pane be numbered from one to one hundred, starting with the top horizontal row and numbering consecutively from left to right. Thus the first stamp at the upper left corner would be No. 1 and the last stamp at the bottom right corner, would be No. 100. The left and right panes are indicated by the letters "L" or "R". The number of the plate is designated by Roman numerals. As an example, the scarce type III, 1c 1851 being the 99th stamp in the right pane of Plate No. 2 is listed as (99 R II), *i.e.* 99th stamp, right pane, Plate No. 2.

One plate of the one cent and several plates of the three cents were extensively recut after they had been in use. The original state of the plate is called "Early" and the recut state is termed "Late". Identification of "Early" state or "Late" state is explained by the addition of the letters "E" or "L" after the plate numbers. The sixth stamp of the right pane of Plate No. I from the "Early" state would be **6 R I E**. The same plate position from the "Late" state would be **6 R I L**.

The position of the stamp in the sheet is placed within parentheses, for example: (99 R II).

The different values of this issue were intended primarily for the payment of specific rates, though any value might be used in making up a rate. The 1c was to pay the postage on newspapers, drop letters and circulars, and the one cent carrier fee in some cities from 1856. The 3c stamp represented the rate on ordinary letters and two of them made up the rate for distances over 3000 miles. The 5c was originally intended for registration fee but the fee was usually paid in cash. Occasionally two of them were used to pay the rate over 3000 miles, after it was changed in April, 1855. Singles paid the "Shore to ship" rate to certain foreign countries and, from 1857, triples paid the 15c rate to France. Ten cents was the rate to California and points distant more than 3000 miles. The 12c was for quadruple the ordinary rate. The 24c represented the single letter rate to Great Britain. Thirty cents was the rate to Germany. The 90c was apparently intended to facilitate the payment of large amounts of postage.

Act of Congress, March 3, 1851. "From and after June 30, 1851, there shall be charged the following rates: Every single letter not exceeding 3000 miles, prepaid postage, 3 cents; not prepaid, 5 cents; for any greater distance, double these rates. Every single letter or paper conveyed wholly or in part by sea, and to or from a foreign country over 2500 miles, 20 cents; under 2500 miles, 10 cents. Drop or local letters, 1 cent each. Letters uncalled for and advertised, to be charged 1 cent in addition to the regular postage."

Act of Congress, March 3, 1855. "For every single letter, in manuscript or paper of any kind, in writing, marks or signs, conveyed in the mail between places in the United States not exceeding 3000 miles, 3 cents; and for any greater distance, 10 cents. Drop or local letters, 1 cent."

Act of March 3, 1855, effective April 1, 1855, also said: "the foregoing rates to be prepaid on domestic letters." The Act also made the prepayment of postage on domestic letters compulsory.

The Act of March 3, 1855, effective July 1, 1855, authorized the Postmaster to establish a system for the registration of valuable letters, and to require prepayment of postage on such letters as well as registration fee of 5 cents. Stamps to prepay the registry fee were not required until June 1, 1867.

Franklin
A5

A5

POSTAGE, 1851-56   93

ONE CENT. Issued July 1, 1851.
   Type I. Has complete curved lines outside the labels with "U. S. Postage" and "One Cent". The scrolls below the lower label are turned under, forming little balls. The ornaments at top are substantially complete.
   Type Ib. As I, but balls below bottom label are not so clear. Plume-like scrolls at bottom are incomplete.

5	A5	1c **blue**, type I (7 R I E)	100,000.	22,500.
		On cover, single (7 R I E)		32,500.
		On cover, pair, one stamp (7 R I E)		
		On cover strip of three, one stamp (7 R I E)		60,000.

CANCELLATIONS.

		Red town	—
Blue	+500.00	Red "Paid"	—
Red grid	+1000.00		

5A	"	1c **blue**, type Ib, *July 1, 1851* (Best examples, 6R, 8R, IE)	12,000.	4,500.
		On cover		5,500.
		blue, type Ib (Less distinct 3R, 4R, 5R, 9R, Plate IE)	9,000.	3,500.
		Pair	20,000.	7,500.
		On cover		4,250.
		Block of four, combination pair type Ib and pair type IIIa (8, 9-18, 19 R I E)		—

CANCELLATIONS (on best examples).

Blue town	+100.00	Pen 6 or 8 RIE	2,000.00
Red Carrier	—	Pen (3, 4, 5 or 9 RIE)	1,400.00

A6

   Type Ia. Same as I at bottom but top ornaments and outer line at top are partly cut away.

6	A6	1c **blue**, type Ia, *April 19, 1857*	15,000.	5,500.
		On cover		6,500.
		Pair		11,500.
		Vertical pair, combination types Ia and III	—	—
		Vertical pair, combination types Ia and IIIa	18,000.	—
		Block of 4, combination types Ia and IIIa	43,500.	
		"Curl on shoulder" (97L IV)	15,500.	5,750.
		"Curl in C" (97 R IV)	15,500.	5,750.

   Type Ia comes only from the bottom row of both panes of Plate IV. All type Ia stamps have the flaw below "U" of "U.S." But this flaw also appears on some stamps of types III and IIIa, Plate IV.

CANCELLATIONS.

		Black Carrier	+350.00
Blue	+100.00	Red Carrier	+350.00
		Pen	2,350.00

A7

   Type II. The little balls of the bottom scrolls and the bottoms of the lower plume ornaments are missing. The side ornaments are complete.

7	A7	1c **blue**, type II, (Plates IE, II); *July 1, 1851*	450.00	85.00
		On cover		100.00
		Pair	950.00	185.00
		Strip of three	1,500.	285.00

Pair, combination types II and IIIa (Plate IE)	2,300.	700.00
Plate III, *May, 1856*	—	300.00
On cover (Plate III)	—	500.00
Pair (Plate III)	—	700.00
Plate IV, *April, 1857*	500.00	100.00
On cover (Plate IV)	—	125.00
Pair (Plate IV)	1,050.	225.00
"Curl in hair" (3 R, 4 R IV)	650.00	150.00
Block of four (Plate I E)	—	—
Block of four (Plate II)	2,100.	600.00
Block of four (Plate III)	—	—
Block of four, combination, type II and type IIIa	—	—
Margin block of 8, Impt. & P# (Plate II)	—	—
Double transfer (Plate IE or II)	500.00	100.00
Double transfer (4 R IL)	1,000.	250.00
Double transfer (89 R II)	550.00	110.00
Double transfer (Plate III)	—	325.00
Double transfer (10 R IV)	—	150.00
Double transfer, one inverted (71 LIE)	750.00	225.00
Triple transfer, one inverted (91 LIE)	750.00	225.00
Cracked Plate (2L, 12L, 13L, 23L and 33L, Plate II)	650.00	200.00
Perf. 12½, unofficial	—	3,500.

   In addition to the cracked plates listed above (Plate II) there exist a number of surface cracks coming from the rare Plate III.

CANCELLATIONS.

		"Way"	+35.00
Blue	+2.50	Numeral	+15.00
Red	+5.00	Railroad	+50.00
Magenta	+15.00	"Steam"	+50.00
Ultramarine	+20.00	"Steamboat"	+70.00
Green	+225.00	Red Carrier	+15.00
1855 year date	+10.00	Black Carrier	+25.00
1856 year date	+5.00	U. S. Express Mail	+25.00
1857 year date	+2.50	Printed Precancel-	
1858 year date	—	lation "PAID"	+325.00
"Paid"	+5.00	Pen	45.00

A8

   Type III. The top and bottom curved lines outside the labels are broken in the middle. The side ornaments are substantially complete.
   Type IIIa. Similar to III with the outer line broken at top or bottom but not both. The outside ornaments are substantially complete.

8	A8	1c **blue**, type III (99 R II)	7,000.	2,500.
		Pair, combination types III (99RII) and II	—	—
		Pair, combination types III (99RII) and IIIa	10,000.	—
		Block of 4, combination type III (99RII) and 3 of type II	17,500.	
		On cover (99 R II)		5,000.

CANCELLATIONS.

		"Paid"	—
Blue	+100.00	Red Carrier	+250.00

   The finest example of type III is 99 R II. All other stamps of this type come from Plate IV and show the breaks in the lines less clearly defined.

8	A8	1c **blue**, type III (Plate IV) *April, 1857*	5,250.	1,450.
		On cover		1,750.
		Pair		2,900.
		Pair, combination types III and IIIa		—
		Strip of three		5,000.
		Block of four, combination types III and IIIa		—

POSTAGE, 1851-56

CANCELLATIONS.

Blue	+50.00	Red Carrier	+150.00
		Black Carrier	+200.00
		Pen	650.00

Examples of type III with wide breaks in outer lines command higher prices than those with small breaks.

8A	A8	1c **blue**, type IIIa (Plate IE)		1,700.	575.00
		On cover			750.00
		Pair		——	1,200.
		Double transfer, one inverted (81 L I E)		2,100.	725.00
		Plate I E (100 R)		——	——
		Plate II (100 R)		——	——
		Plate IV, *April, 1857*		1,900.	625.00
		On cover (Plate IV)		——	850.00
		Pair (Plate IV)		——	1,250.
		Vertical pair, combination types IIIa and II (Plate IV)		——	——
		Block of four (Plate IV)		——	6,000.

CANCELLATIONS.

		"Paid"	+75.00
Blue	+25.00	Black Carrier	+150.00
Red	+50.00	Red Carrier	+125.00
		Pen	300.00

Stamps of type IIIa with bottom line broken command higher prices than those with top line broken. See note after type III on width of break of outer lines.

A9

Type IV. Similar to II, but with the curved lines outside the labels recut at top or bottom or both.

9	A9	1c **blue**, type IV, *June 8, 1852*		300.00	75.00
		On cover			95.00
		Pair		625.00	160.00
		Strip of three		975.00	265.00
		Block of four		1,500.	850.00
		Margin block of 8, Impt. & P# (Plate I)		——	
		Double transfer		325.00	77.50
		Triple transfer, one inverted (71LIL, 81LIL and 91LIL)		450.00	125.00
		Cracked plate		450.00	125.00
		Perf. 12½, unofficial			2,500.

VARIETIES OF RECUTTING.

Stamps of this type were printed from Plate I after it had been recut in 1852. All but one stamp (4 R) were recut and all varieties of recutting are listed below:

Recut once at top and once at bottom, (113 on plate)	300.00	75.00
Recut once at top, (40 on plate)	310.00	77.50
Recut once at top and twice at bottom, (29 on plate)	320.00	80.00
Recut twice at bottom, (11 on plate)	325.00	85.00
Recut once at bottom, (8 on plate)	335.00	90.00
Recut once at bottom and twice at top, (4 on plate)	350.00	95.00
Recut twice at bottom and twice at top, (2 on plate)	400.00	125.00
Pair, combination, type II (4RIL) and type IV	1750.00	700.00

CANCELLATIONS.

Blue	+2.50	Railroad	+75.00
Red	+7.50	"Steam"	+60.00
Ultramarine	+12.50	Numeral	+10.00
Brown	+12.50	"Steamboat"	+75.00
Green	+200.00	"Steamship"	+60.00
Violet	+50.00	Red Carrier	+10.00
1853 year date	+150.00	Black Carrier	+25.00
1855 year date	+10.00	U. S. Express Mail	+60.00
1856 year date	+7.50	Express Company	——
1857 year date	+10.00	Packet boat	——
"Paid"	+10.00	Printed precancellation "PAID"	+450.00
"U. S. PAID"	+50.00	Printed precancellation "paid"	+450.00
"Way"	+35.00	Pen	40.00
"Free"	+50.00		

These 1c stamps were often cut apart carelessly, destroying part or all of the top and bottom lines. This makes it difficult to determine whether a stamp is type II or IV without plating the position. Such mutilated examples sell for much less.

Washington
A10

THREE CENTS. Issued July 1, 1851.

Type I. There is an outer frame line at top and bottom.

10	A10	3c **orange brown**, type I		1,200.	50.00
		deep orange brown		1,200.	50.00
		copper brown		1,350.	60.00
		On cover			75.00
		Pair		2,500.	105.00
		Strip of three		4,000.	200.00
		Block of four		8,500.	
		Double transfer			65.00
		Triple transfer			175.00
		Gash on shoulder			60.00
		Dot in lower right diamond block (69 L V E)			65.00
		On part-India paper			200.00

VARIETIES OF RECUTTING.

All of these stamps were recut at least to the extent of four frame lines and usually much more. Some of the most prominent varieties are listed below (others are described in "The 3c Stamp of U.S. 1851-57 Issue," by Carroll Chase):

Recut inner frame lines	1250.00	65.00
No inner frame lines	1300.00	67.50
Left inner line only recut		72.50
Right inner line only recut		67.50
1 line recut in upper left triangle	1300.00	67.50
2 lines recut in upper left triangle		72.50
3 lines recut in upper left triangle		87.50
5 lines recut in upper left triangle (47 L O)		200.00
1 line recut in lower left triangle		80.00
1 line recut in lower right triangle		75.00
2 lines recut in lower right triangle (57 L O)		175.00
2 lines recut in upper left triangle, 1 line recut in lower right triangle		——
1 line recut in upper right triangle		75.00

POSTAGE, 1851-56

Upper part of top label and diamond block recut	1,300.	55.00
Top label and right diamond block joined		57.50
Top label, left diam. block joined		60.00
Lower label and right diamond block joined		57.50
2 lines recut at top of upper right diamond block		62.50
1 line recut at bottom of lower left diamond block (34 R II E)		70.00

CANCELLATIONS.

		"Free"	+50.00	
Blue	+2.00	Numeral	+15.00	
Red	+5.00	Railroad	+50.00	
Orange	+10.00	U. S. Express Mail	+20.00	
Brown	+10.00	"Steam"	+35.00	
Ultramarine	+20.00	"Steamship"	+60.00	
Green	+175.00	"Steamboat"	+60.00	
Violet	+40.00	Packet Boat	+300.00	
1851 year dat	+60.00	Blue Carrier		
1852 year dat	+60.00	(New Orleans)	+300.00	
"Paid"	+5.00	Green Carrier		
"Way"	+40.00	(New Orleans)	+600.00	
"Way" with		Canadian		
numeral	+150.00	Territorial	+175.00	
		Pen	35.00	

11	A10	3c	dull red (1853-54-55), type I	130.00	7.00
			orange red (1855)	130.00	7.00
			rose red (1854-55)	130.00	7.00
			brownish carmine (1852 and 1856)	145.00	8.50
		a.	3c claret (1857)	160.00	10.00
			deep claret (1857)	185.00	13.50
			On cover, dull red		9.00
			On patriotic cover		200.00
			On propaganda cover		350.00
			Pair	270.00	15.00
			Strip of three	425.00	30.00
			Block of four	675.00	300.00
			Margin block of 8, Impt. & P#		
		c.	Vertical half used as 1c on cover		2,750.
		d.	Diagonal half used as 1c on cover		2,250.
		e.	Double impression		
			Double transfer in "Three Cents"	150.00	8.00
			Double transfer line through "Three Cents" and rosettes double (92 L I L)	225.00	35.00
			Triple transfer (92 L II L)	200.00	25.00
			Double transfer, "Gents" instead of "Cents" (66 R II L)	200.00	25.00
			Gash on shoulder	140.00	7.50
			Dot on lower right diamond block 69 L V L)	175.00	20.00
			Cracked plate (51L, 74L, 84L, 94L, 96L, and 9R, Plate V L)	375.00	60.00
			Worn plate	130.00	7.00
			Perf. 12½, unofficial		1,250.

VARIETIES OF RECUTTING.

All of these stamps were recut at least to the extent of three frame lines and usually much more. Some of the most prominent varieties are listed below (others are described in "The 3c Stamp of U.S. 1851-57 Issue," by Carroll Chase):

Recut inner frame lines	130.00	7.00
No inner frame lines	130.00	7.00
Right inner lines only recut	140.00	7.25
1 line recut in upper left triangle	140.00	7.25
2 lines recut in upper left triangle	140.00	7.25
3 lines recut in upper left triangle	150.00	8.00
5 lines recut in upper left triangle	—	65.00
1 line recut in lower left triangle	160.00	8.00
1 line recut in lower right triangle	140.00	7.50
1 line recut in upper right triangle	—	10.00
Recut button on shoulder (10 R II L)	—	40.00
Lines on bust and bottom of medallion circle recut (47 R VI)	300.00	100.00
Upper part of top label and diamond block recut	140.00	7.25
Top label and right diamond block joined	140.00	7.25
Top label and left diamond block joined	150.00	9.50
Lower label and right diamond block joined	150.00	9.50
1 extra vertical line outside of left frame line (29L, 39L, 49L, 59L, 69L, 79L, Plate III)	145.00	8.50
2 extra vertical lines outside of left frame line 89L, 99L, Plate III	180.00	20.00

1 extra vertical line outside of right frame line (58L, 68L, 78L, 88L, 98L, Plate III)	155.00	9.00
No inner line and frame line close to design at right (9L, 19L, Plate III)	165.00	12.50
No inner line and frame line close to design at left (70L, 80L, 90L, 100L, Plate III)	150.00	10.00

CANCELLATIONS.

		"Free"	+25.00
Blue	+.25	Numeral	+7.50
Red	+1.00	Railroad	+20.00
Orange	+5.00	U. S. Express Mail	+5.00
Brown	+2.00	"Steam"	+15.00
Magenta	+15.00	"Ship"	+20.00
Ultramarine	+15.00	"New York Ship"	+35.00
Green	+80.00	"Steamboat"	+45.00
Violet	+25.00	"Steamship"	+45.00
Purple	+25.00	Packet boat	+120.00
Olive	+30.00	Express Company	+120.00
Yellow	+100.00	Black Carrier	+60.00
1852 year date	+250.00	Red Carrier	
1853 year date	+90.00	(New York)	+50.00
1855 year date	+10.00	Green Carrier	
1858 year date	+.50	(New Orleans)	+350.00
1859 year date	—	Blue Carrier	
"Paid"	+1.00	(New Orleans)	+200.00
"Way"	+10.00	Canada	
"Way" with		Territorial	+70.00
numeral	+60.00	Pen	4.00

Thomas Jefferson
A11

FIVE CENTS. Earliest known use Mar. 24, 1856.
Type I. Projections on all four sides.

12	A11	5c	red brown, type I	9,500.	1,300.
			dark red brown	9,500.	1,300.
			single on cover		3,000.
			Pair	20,000.	2,750.
			Strip of three	34,000.	4,500.
			Block of four	110,000.	35,000.

CANCELLATIONS.

		"Paid"	+50.00
Red	+50.00	"Steamship"	+200.00
Magenta	+125.00	U. S. Express Mail	+150.00
Blue	+25.00	Express Company	+300.00
Green	+600.00	"Steamboat"	+250.00
1856 year date	+25.00	Railroad	+250.00
1857 year date	+25.00	Pen	600.00
1858 year date	—		

Washington
A12

POSTAGE, 1851-56

A12

TEN CENTS. Earliest known use May 12, 1855

Type I. The "shells" at the lower corners are practically complete. The outer line below the label is very nearly complete. The outer lines are broken above the middle of the top label and the "X" in each upper corner.

Types I, II, III and IV have complete ornaments at the sides of the stamps, and three pearls at each outer edge of the bottom panel.

Type I comes only from the bottom row of both panes of Plate I.

13	A12	10c	**green,** type I	8,500.	700.00
			dark green	8,500.	700.00
			yellowish green	8,500.	700.00
			On cover		1,000.
			On patriotic cover		5,000.
			Pair	18,000.	1,550.
			Strip of three		—
			Pair, combination types I & III	11,000.	—
			Pair, combination type I and type IV		—
			Vertical strip of three, combination type I, type II, type III		—
			Block of four, combination type I and type III	25,000.	—
			Block of four, combination types I, III and IV		—
			Double transfer (100 R I)	9,000.	775.00
			"Curl" in left "X" (99 R I)	9,000.	775.00

CANCELLATIONS.

Blue	+25.00	"Paid"	+50.00
Red	+50.00	"Steamship"	+150.00
Magenta	+150.00	Railroad	+175.00
Orange	—	Territorial	+400.00
1855 year date	+25.00	Numeral	+50.00
1856 year date	+25.00	U. S. Express Mail	
1857 year date	+25.00	Pen	325.00

A13

Type II. The design is complete at the top. The outer line at the bottom is broken in the middle. The shells are partly cut away.

14	A13	10c	**green,** type II	1,700.	275.00
			dark green	1,700.	275.00
			yellowish green	1,700.	275.00
			On cover		350.00
			Pair	3,500.	600.00
			Strip of 3		—
			Block of four	9,000.	4,000.
			Pair, combination type II and type III	3,600.	600.00
			Pair, combination type II and type IV	12,500.	2,000.
			Vertical strip of three, combination types II, III and IV		—
			Block of four, combination type II and type III		2,750.
			Block of four, combination types II and IV		—
			Block of four, combination types II, III, and IV		9,000.
			Double transfer (31L, 51L and 20 R, Plate I)	1,750.	325.00
			"Curl" opposite "X" (10 R I)	1,800.	350.00

CANCELLATIONS.

Blue	+10.00	"Paid"	+25.00
Red	+25.00	"Way"	+50.00
Brown	+25.00	"Free"	+75.00
Ultramarine	+75.00	Railroad	+75.00
Magenta	+75.00	Steamship	+75.00
Green	+200.00	Steamboat	+100.00
1855 year date	—	Numeral	+50.00
1856 year date	+50.00	Territorial	+150.00
1857 year date	+10.00	Express Company	+200.00
1858 year date	+10.00	U. S. Express Mail	+75.00
		Pen	150.00

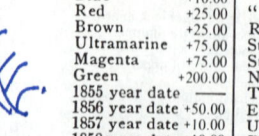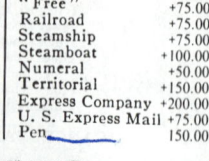

A14

Type III. The outer lines are broken above the top label and the "X" numerals. The outer line at the bottom and the shells are partly cut away as in Type II.

15	A14	10c	**green,** type III	1,750.	285.00
			dark green	1,750.	285.00
			yellowish green	1,750.	285.00
			On cover		400.00
			Pair	3,600.	600.00
			Strip of 3		—
			Pair, combination type III and type IV	12,500.	2,000.
			Double transfer at top and at bottom		
			"Curl" on forehead (85 L I)	1,850.	350.00
			"Curl" to right of left "X" (87 R I)	1,850.	350.00

CANCELLATIONS.

Blue	+10.00	"Paid"	+25.00
Red	+25.00	Steamship	+75.00
Magenta	+75.00	U. S. Express Mail	+75.00
Brown	+25.00	Express Company	+200.00
Orange	+35.00	Packet boat	
Green	+200.00	Canada (on cover)	+1000.00
1855 year date	—	Territorial	+150.00
1856 year date	+50.00	Railroad	+75.00
1857 year date	+10.00	Numeral	+50.00
1858 year date	+10.00	Pen	150.00

A15

Type IV. The outer lines have been recut at top or bottom or both.

16	A15	10c	**green,** type IV	10,000.	1,450.
			dark green	10,000.	1,450.
			yellowish green	10,000.	1,450.
			On cover		2,250.
			On patriotic cover		—
			Pair		3,350.
			Block of four (54-55, 64-65L)		

VARIETIES OF RECUTTING.

Eight stamps on Plate I were recut. All are listed below.
Outer line recut at top (65L, 74L, 86L, and 3R, Plate I) 9500.00 1350.00
Outer line recut at bottom (54L, 55L, 76L, Plate I) 9750.00 1400.00
Outer line recut at top and bottom (64 L I) 10,500.00 1500.00
Positions 65LI and 86LI have both "X" ovals recut at top, as well as the outer line.

CANCELLATIONS.

Blue	+50.00	"Paid"	
Red	+100.00	Steamship	
Brown	—	Territorial	
1857 year date	—	Express Company	+750.00
1859 year date	—	Numeral	+100.00
		Pen	700.00

Types I, II, III and IV occur on the same sheet, so it is possible to obtain pairs and blocks showing combinations of types. For listings of type combinations in pairs and blocks, see Nos. 13-15.

Washington
A16

17	A16	12c **black,** *July 1, 1851*		1,850.	250.00
		gray black		1,850.	250.00
		intense black		1,850.	250.00
		Single, on cover		1,300.	
		Single on cover with No. 11		1,000.	
		Pair		3,900.	525.00
		Pair, on cover			625.00
		Block of four		11,000.	2,750.
		a. Diagonal half used as 6c on cover			5,500.
		b. Vertical half used as 6c on cover			8,500.
		c. Printed on both sides			3,500.
		Double transfer		1,950.	275.00
		Triple transfer (5 R I & 49 R I)		2,300.	325.00
		Not recut in lower right corner		1,900.	275.00
		Recut in lower left corner (43L, 53L, 63L, 73L and 100L, Plate I)		2,100.	300.00
		On part-India paper		—	475.00

CANCELLATIONS.

Red	+20.00	Steamship	+100.00
Blue	+5.00	Steamboat	+125.00
Brown	+20.00	Supplementary Mail	
Magenta	+65.00	Type A	+75.00
Orange	+40.00	Railroad	+75.00
Green	+300.00	"Honolulu" in red	+400.00
"Paid"	+25.00	U. S. Express Mail	+125.00
"Way"	+75.00	Pen	125.00

SAME DESIGNS AS 1851-56 ISSUES.
Printed by Toppan, Carpenter & Co.

1857-61   Perf. 15

18	A5	1c **blue,** type I (Plate XII), *Jan. 25, 1861*		675.00	350.00
		On cover			450.00
		On patriotic cover			900.00
		Pair		1,400.	750.00
		Strip of three		2,250.	1,250.
		Block of four		4,750.	
		Pair, combination types I & II		1,200.	550.00
		Pair, combination types I and IIIa		1,400.	600.00
		Block of four, combination types I and II		2,650.	1,500.
		Block of four, combination types I, II and IIIa		3,250.	2,000.
		Double transfer		725.00	400.00
		Cracked plate (91 R XII)		—	475.00

Plate XII consists of types I and II. A few positions are type IIIa.

CANCELLATIONS.

		"Paid"	+25.00
Blue	+10.00	Black Carrier	+85.00
Red	+35.00	Red Carrier	+75.00
Violet	+100.00	Pen	175.00

19	A6	1c **blue,** type Ia (Plate IV), *July 26, 1857*		9,500.	2,250.
		On cover			3,250.
		Pair		20,000.	4,750.
		Strip of three		33,000.	7,250.

---

vertical pair, types Ia & II ... 600.00
tical pair, types Ia & IIIa ... 10,000.
of four, combination, pair
a and types III or IIIa
shoulder" (97 L IV)

is stamp exist with perforations not the design at any point. Such mand very high prices.

ly from the bottom row of both IV. Examples called "Ashbrook etimes offered as varieties of hey are varieties of type IIIa

CANCELLATIONS.
Red Carrier ... IV and 96 R IV which are

20	A7	1c **blue,** type II (Plate ...)			1000.00
		On cover			135.00
		Pair	1857	425.00	175.00
		Strip of three			280.00
		Block of four		900.00	435.00
		Double transfer (Plate II)		1,400.	1,250.
		Cracked plate (2L, 12L, 13L, 23L & 33L, Plate II)		200.	150.00
		Double transfer (4 R I L)			250.00
		Plate IV, *July 26, 1857*		475.00	300.00
		On cover (Plate IV)			200.00
		Pair (Plate IV)		1,000.	335.00
		Strip of three (Plate IV)			300.00
		Double transfer (10 R IV)			225.00
		"Curl in hair" (3 R, 4 R IV)			175.00
		Plate XI, *Jan. 12, 1861*		525.00	225.00
		On cover (Plate XI)			650.00
		On patriotic cover (Plate XI)		1,100.	375.00
		Pair (Plate XI)			
		Strip of three (Plate XI)			
		Double transfer (Plate XI)		425.00	135.00
		Plate XII, *Jan. 25, 1861*			175.00
		On cover (Plate XII)			450.00
		On patriotic cover (Plate XII)		900.00	280.00
		Pair (Plate XII)		1,400.	435.00
		Strip of three (Plate XII)		2,200.	1,250.
		Block of four (Plate XII)			

CANCELLATIONS.

		1863 year date	+200.00
Blue	+5.00	"Paid"	+15.00
Red	+20.00	Railroad	+60.00
Green	+200.00	"Way"	+75.00
1857 year date	+10.00	Steamboat	+75.00
1858 year date	+5.00	Red Carrier	+35.00
1861 year date	+5.00	Black Carrier	+50.00
		Pen	65.00

21	A8	1c **blue,** type III, (99 R II), *July 26, 1857*		—	5,500.
		On cover			7,500.
		Pair, combination type III (99 R II) and type II			—
		Pair, combination types III (99 R II) and IIIa			—
		Strip of three, combination type III (99 R II) and types II and IIIa			—
		Block of 12, combination one type III (99 R II), others type II			—
21	A8	1c **blue,** type III (Plate IV), *July 26, 1857*		4,000.	1,150.
		On cover			1,600.
		Pair		8,250.	2,400.
		Strip of three			3,500.
		Block of four			
		Pair, types III & IIIa		4,750.	1,500.
		Vertical pair, types III & II			—
		Block of 4, types III & IIIa			—
		Top & bottom lines broken (46 L XII)		—	

CANCELLATIONS.

Blue	+25.00	"Paid"	+50.00
Red	+50.00	Black Carrier	+175.00
Green	+350.00	Red Carrier	+150.00
1858 year date	+25.00	Pen	450.00

22	A8	1c **blue,** type IIIa (Plate IV), *July 26, 1857*		625.00	225.00
		On cover			275.00
		On patriotic cover			600.00
		Pair		1,300.	475.00
		Vertical pair, combination types IIIa and II (Plate IV)		1,250.	400.00
		Strip of three		2,100.	700.00
		Block of four		3,750.	3,750.
		Block of four, combination types IIIa and II (Plate IV)		3,250.	—

1857-61

Pair	225.00	47.50
Strip of three	340.00	75.00
Block of four	475.00	275.00
Margin block of 8, Impt. & P#	3,250.	
Double transfer at top (8R and 10R, Plate VII)	150.00	45.00
Double transfer at bottom (52R I X)	185.00	55.00
Curl on shoulder, (57R, 58R, 59R, 98R, 99R, Plate VII)	150.00	37.50
With "Earring" below ear (10 L IX)	200.00	55.00
"Curl" over "C" of "Cent"	160.00	37.50
"Curl" over "E" of "Cent" (41R and 81R VIII)	170.00	45.00
"Curl in hair," 23L VII; 39, 69L VIII; 34, 74R IX	150.00	32.50
Horizontal dash in hair (24L VII)	200.00	50.00
Horizontal dash in hair (36L VIII)	200.00	50.00
Long double "curl" in hair (52, 92R VIII)	185.00	45.00
b. Laid paper	450.00	150.00
c. Imperf. horizontally (pair)		
Plate V, Jan. 2, 1858		
On cover (Plate V)	300.00	70.00
Pair (Plate V)		110.00
Strip of three (Plate V)	—	—
Block of four (Plate V)	—	—
"Curl" in "O" of "ONE" (62 L V)	—	—
"Curl" on shoulder (48 L V)	—	—

Type Va: Stamps from Plate V with almost complete ornaments at right side and no side scratches.

CANCELLATIONS.

Blue	+1.00	"Free"		+25.00
Red	+5.00	Railroad		+50.00
Green	+100.00	Numeral		+7.50
Brown	+5.00	Express Company		+90.00
Magenta	+15.00	Steamboat		+55.00
Ultramarine	+10.00	"Steam"		+30.00
1857 year date	+70.00	Steamship		+40.00
1858 year date	+1.00	Packet boat		
1859 year date	+1.00	Supplementary Mail Types A, B, or C		+55.00
1860 year date	+1.00	"Way"		+30.00
1861 year date	+1.00	Red Carrier		+7.50
1863 year date	+80.00	Black Carrier		+12.50
Printed Precancellation		Blue Carrier		+50.00
"CUMBERLAND, ME." (on cover)		Brown Carrier		—
		"Old Stamps—Not Recognized"		+1000.00
		Territorial		+80.00
"Paid"	+3.50	Pen		10.00

25 A10 3c **rose**, type I, Feb. 28, 1857 650.00 27.50
rose red 650.00 27.50
claret 700.00 32.50
dull red 650.00 27.50
On cover   37.50
On patriotic cover   275.00
Pair 1,350. 57.50
Strip of three 2,150. 95.00
Block of four 3,250. 3,500.

All type I stamps were printed from [...] of the plates used for the imperfs., so [m]any varieties exist both imperf. and perf.

a. Imperf. vertically (pair)   3,500.
b. Imperf. horizontally (pair)   6,000.
Gash on shoulder 675.00 30.00
Double transfer 700.00 32.00
Double transfer "Gents" instead of "Cents" (66R II L) — 50.00
Triple transfer (92L II L) — 60.00
Worn plate 650.00 27.50
Cracked plate 900.00 100.00

VARIETIES OF RECUTTING.

Recut inner frame lines 650.00 27.50
Recut inner frame line only at right   28.50
1 extra vertical line outside of left frame line (29L, 39L, 49L, 59L, 69L, 79L, Plate III) — 32.50
2 extra vertical lines outside of left frame line (89L, 99L, Plate III) — 40.00
1 extra vertical line outside of right frame line (58L, 68L, 78L, 88L, 98L, Plate III) — 32.50
No inner line and frame line close to design at right (9L, 19L, Plate III) — 40.00

250.00
300.00
Double transfer 750.00
Plate II (100 R) 1,500. 525.00
Plate XI, Jan. 25
XII, Jan. 1
On cover 1,600. 550.00
On patriotic 2,400. 825.00
Pair 4,000.
Vertical pair, types IIIa and [...]
Strip of [...] 4,250. 2,500.
Block (Plate XI) 750.00 300.00
Block (46 L XII) — —

[...]ATIONS.
1861 year date —
+5.00 1863 year date —
+20.00 " Paid " +25.00
[...]een +225.00 Red Carrier +35.00
1857 year date — Black Carrier +50.00
1858 year date — Blue Carrier +100.00
Pen 90.00

23 A9 1c **blue**, type IV, July 25, 1857 1,750. 285.00
On cover   450.00
Pair 3,650. 600.00
Strip of three 5,650. 950.00
Block of four — 4,000.
Double transfer 1,800. 300.00
Triple transfer, one inverted (71LIL, 81LIL and 91LIL) 2,350. 425.00
Cracked plate 2,250. 400.00

VARIETIES OF RECUTTING.

Recut once at top and once at bottom, (113 on plate) 1500.00 250.00
Recut once at top, (40 on plate) 1525.00 255.00
Recut once at top and twice at bottom, (21 on plate) 1550.00 260.00
Recut twice at bottom, (11 on plate) 1600.00 275.00
Recut once at bottom, (8 on plate) 1650.00 285.00
Recut once at bottom and twice at top, (4 on plate) 1700.00 300.00
Recut twice at top and twice at bottom, (2 on plate) 1800.00 325.00
Pair, combination, type II (4 R I L) and type IV   1200.00

CANCELLATIONS.

		Black Carrier	+60.00
Blue	+5.00	Railroad	+85.00
Red	+25.00	"Way"	+90.00
"Paid"	+25.00	Steamboat	+135.00
Red Carrier	+40.00	"Steam"	+100.00
		Pen	125.00

A20

Type V. Similar to type III of 1851-56 but with side ornaments partly cut away.

24 A20 1c **blue**, type V (Plates VII, VIII, IX, X) Nov. 17, 1857 110.00 22.50
On cover   35.00
On patriotic cover   250.00

No inner line and...
to design at left...
100L, Plate III...
Lines on bust and...
medallion circle...
Recut button (10R2...
Other varieties of...
"The 3c Stamp...
by Carroll Chase...

CANCELLATIONS.

Blue	+1.00
Red	+5.00
Orange	+5.00
Brown	+5.00
Ultramarine	+7.50
Green	+150.00
1857 year date	+1.00
1858 year date	+1.00
1859 year date	+1.00
"Paid"	+2.50
"Way"	+20.00
Railroad	+25.00
Numeral	+7.50
"Steam"	+20.00

Steam...
Steamboat...
Packet Boat ...A21
Supplementary Ma...
  Type A +40...
U. S. Express Mail +5.00
Express Company +65.00
Black Carrier +30.00
"Old Stamps—Not
  Recognized" +1000.00
Territorial +35.00
Printed
  precancellation
  "Cumberland,
  Me." (on cover)
Pen 15.00

1857-61

3c dull red, type IIa, July 11, 185...   110.00   30.0...
  brownish carmine   120.00   175.00
  rose   225.00   42.50
  claret   350.00   70.00
  On cover   550.00   120.00
  On patriotic cover   25.00
  Pair ... of three   60.00
  ... k of four   55.00
  ... e transfer
  ... transfer of rosettes and lower
  ... stamp (91R XI L)   120.00   21.00
  ... er above lower   125.00   22.00
                     25.00
                     30.00
  CANCEL ...ght   110.00   25.00
                     20.00

Blue	+1.00		+40.00
Red	+5.00		+2.50
Orange	+5.00	Stea...	+5.00
Brown	+5.00	Steamboa...	+25.00
Ultramarine	+7.50	Steamship	+15.00
Violet	+12.50	"Way"	+17.50
Green	+135.00	Railroad	+17.50
1857 year date	+2.50	U. S. Express Mail	+65.00
1858 or 1859		Express Company	+65.00
year date	+1.50	Packet boat	+65.00
"Paid"	+2.50	Black Carrier	+30.00
"Paid All"	+15.00	Red Carrier	+20.00
"Free"	+20.00	Territorial	+25.00
		Pen	10.00

Type II. The outer frame line has been removed at top and bottom. The side frame lines were recut so as to be continuous from the top to the bottom of the plate.

Type IIa. The side frame lines extend only to the top and bottom of the stamp design. All Type IIa stamps are from plates X and XI (each of which exists in three states), and these plates produced only Type IIa. The side frame lines were recut individually for each stamp, thus being broken between the stamp vertically.

26	A21	3c dull red, type II, 1857	45.00	2.75
		red	45.00	2.75
		rose	45.00	2.75
		brownish carmine	50.00	3.00
		claret	60.00	3.50
		orange brown	—	—
		On cover		3.50
		On patriotic cover		75.00
		On Confederate patriotic cover		1,200.
		On pony express cover		
		Pair	92.50	5.75
		Strip of three	140.00	9.00
		Block of four	200.00	50.00
		Margin block of 8, Impt. & P#		
	b.	Imperf. vertically (pair)	4,000.	3,500.
	c.	Imperf. horizontally (pair)		3,500.
	d.	Horizontal pair, imperf. between		3,500.
	e.	Double impression		4.00
		Double transfer		
		Double transfer, rosettes double and line through "Postage"	—	40.00
		Left frame line double	50.00	3.75
		Right frame line double	50.00	3.75
		Cracked plate	375.00	60.00
		Damaged transfer above lower left rosette	50.00	3.25
		Same, retouched	55.00	3.50
		1 line recut in upper left triangle	—	16.50
		5 lines recut in upper left triangle		
		Inner line recut at right		32.50
		Worn plate	50.00	3.00

27	A11	5c brick red, type I, Oct. 6, 1858	7,500.	1,000.
				1,600.
		On cover		4,000.
		On patriotic cover		2,100.
		Pair	15,500.	3,500.
		Strip of three		14,500.
		Block of four	45,000.	

CANCELLATIONS.

		"Paid"	+25.00
Blue	+25.00	Supplementary Mail	
Red	+50.00	Type A	+100.00
Ultramarine	+150.00	"Steamship"	+100.00
1859 year date	+25.00	Pen	450.00
1860 year date	+25.00		

28	A11	5c red brown, type I, Aug. 23, 1857	1,350.	275.00
		pale red brown	1,350.	275.00
	b.	Bright red brown	1,850.	400.00
		On cover		450.00
		Pair	2,750.	575.00
		Strip of three		900.00
		Block of four	10,000.	2,500.

CANCELLATIONS.

		"Paid"	+35.00
Blue	+10.00	Railroad	+75.00
Red	+25.00	"Short Paid"	
1857 year date	+20.00	Pen	120.00
1858 year date	+10.00		

28A	A11	5c Indian red, type I, Mar. 31, 1858	9,000.	1,400.
		On cover		2,600.
		Pair		2,900.
		Strip of three		4,500.
		Block of four		

CANCELLATIONS.

		1858 year date	+50.00
Red	+50.00	1859 year date	+25.00
		Pen	600.00

29	A11	5c brown, type I, July 4, 1859	725.00	225.00
		pale brown	725.00	225.00
		deep brown	725.00	225.00
		yellowish brown	725.00	225.00
		On cover		325.00
		Pair	1,500.	475.00
		Strip of three	2,350.	725.00
		Block of four	4,500.	2,750.

CANCELLATIONS.

		1859 year date	+5.00
Blue	+5.00	1860 year date	+5.00
Red	+15.00	"Paid"	+15.00
Brown	+15.00	"Steam"	+75.00
Magenta	+50.00	Steamship	+85.00
Green	+250.00	Numeral	+50.00
		Pen	95.00

eku: Sept.15

"Steam"	+12.50
Steamer	
Steamboat	+22.50
Steamship	+22.50
"Way"	+12.50
Railroad	+15.00
U. S. Express Mail	+20.00
Express Company	+65.00
Packet boat	+65.00
Supplementary Mail	
Types A, B or C	+75.00
Black Carrier	+30.00
Red Carrier	+25.00
"Southn. Letter Unpaid"	
Territorial	+20.00
"Old Stamps—Not Recognized"	+500.00

Blue	+.10
Red	+1.50
Orange	+1.50
Brown	+1.50
Ultramarine	+2.00
Violet	+6.00
Green	+50.00
1857–1861 year date	+.25
Printed Circular Precancellation	
"Cumberland, Me." (on cover)	
"Paid"	+.25
"Paid All"	+15.00
"Free"	+20.00
"Collect"	+40.00
Numeral	+2.50

UNITED STATES
NATIONAL ALBUM

The SCOTT UNITED STATES NATIONAL POSTAGE STAMP ALBUM is "The" Album demanded by serious collectors of United States material.

The NATIONAL POSTAGE STAMP ALBUM comes complete with famous Scott hand-crafted sturdy binder and Scott Album pages. Each page includes spaces with the Scott Catalogue number and a description or photo of every stamp.

The SCOTT NATIONAL POSTAGE STAMP ALBUM provides spaces for commemoratives, definitives, air post, special delivery, registration, certified mail, postage due, parcel post, special handling, officials, newspapers, offices abroad, hunting permits, confederates and much more!

Available in U.S.A. and Canada from your favorite dealer, bookstore or stamp collecting accessory retailer or write:

SCOTT Publishing Company

P.O. Box 828, Sidney, OH 45365

POSTAGE, 1857–61

Jefferson
A22

FIVE CENTS.

Type II. The projections at top and bottom are partly cut away. Several minor types could be made according to the extent of cutting of the projections.

30	A22	5c **orange brown**, Type II, *May 8, 1861*		750.00	900.00
		deep orange brown		750.00	900.00
		On cover			2,250.
		On patriotic cover			4,000.
		Pair		1,550.	2,250.
		Strip of three		2,500.	—
		Block of four		4,000.	—

CANCELLATIONS.

Blue	+25.00	Steamship	+110.00
Red	+50.00	Supp. Mail A	+150.00
"Paid"	+75.00	Railroad	—
		Pen	300.00

30A	A22	5c **brown**, type II, *Mar. 4, 1860*		450.00	175.00
		dark brown		450.00	175.00
		yellowish brown		450.00	175.00
		On cover			250.00
		On patriotic cover			
		Pair		925.00	360.00
		Strip of three		1,450.	575.00
		Block of four		2,400.	2,500.
		b. Printed on both sides		3,750.	3,000.
		Cracked plate			—

CANCELLATIONS.

		"Steamship"	+50.00
Blue	+5.00	"Steam"	+40.00
Red	+20.00	Express Company	+250.00
Magenta	+40.00	Railroad	—
Green	+250.00	Packet boat	—
"Paid"	+20.00	Pen	75.00
Supp. Mail, A	+50.00		

31	A12	10c **green**, type I, *July 27, 1857*		5,000.	525.00
		dark green		5,000.	525.00
		bluish green		5,000.	525.00
		yellowish green		5,000.	525.00
		On cover			800.00
		On patriotic cover			2,500.
		Pair		10,500.	1,100.
		Pair combination, type I and type III		6,800.	700.00
		Pair, combination, type I and type IV			—
		Strip of three			—
		Vertical strip of 3, combination, type I, type III, type II			—
		Block of four, combination, type I and type III		15,000.	—
		Block of four, combination, types I, III and IV			—
		Double transfer (100R I)		5,500.	600.00
		"Curl" in left "X" (99R I)		5,500.	600.00

Type I comes only from the bottom row of both panes of Plate I.

CANCELLATIONS.

		Supplementary Mail	
Blue	+10.00	Type A	—
Red	+25.00	"Steamship"	+100.00
Green	+225.00	Pen	250.00

Act of February 27, 1861. Ten cent rate of postage to be prepaid on letters conveyed in the mail from any point in the United States east of the Rocky Mountains to any State or Territory on the Pacific Coast and vice versa, for each half-ounce.

32	A13	10c **green**, type II, *July 27, 1857*		1,650.	170.00
		dark green		1,650.	170.00
		bluish green		1,650.	170.00
		yellowish green		1,650.	170.00

On cover		
On pony express cover		
Pair		3,4—
Strip of 3		
Block of four	9,000.	3,500.
Pair, combination, types II & III	3,500.	370.00
Pair, combination, types II & IV	17,500.	1,850.
Vertical strip of three, combination types II, III and IV		—
Block of four, combination, type II and type III	8,000.	1,650.
Block of four, combination types II and IV		—
Block of 4, types II, III, IV	35,000.	—
Double transfer (31L, 51L and 20R, Plate I)	1,750.	195.00
"Curl opposite left X" (10R I)		235.00

CANCELLATIONS.

		1857 year date	+5.00
Blue	+5.00	Steamship	+50.00
Red	+20.00	Packet boat	—
Brown	+20.00	Railroad	—
Green	+225.00	Express Company	—
"Paid"	+20.00	Pen	70.00

33	A14	10c **green**, type III, *July 27, 1857*		1,750.	180.00
		dark green		1,750.	180.00
		bluish green		1,750.	180.00
		yellowish green		1,750.	180.00
		On cover			250.00
		Pair		3,600.	375.00
		Strip of 3			
		Pair, combination types III & IV			1,950.
		"Curl" on forehead (85L I)			235.00
		"Curl in left X" (87R I)			235.00

CANCELLATIONS.

		"Paid"	+20.00
Blue	+5.00	"Steam"	+45.00
Red	+20.00	Steamboat	—
Brown		Steamship	+50.00
Ultramarine	+35.00	Numeral	+15.00
1857 year date	+5.00	Packet boat	—
		Pen	75.00

34	A15	10c **green**, type IV, *July 27, 1857*		15,000.	1,550.
		dark green		15,000.	1,550.
		bluish green		15,000.	1,550.
		yellowish green		15,000.	1,550.
		On cover			2,250.
		Pair			3,450.
		Block of four (54-55, 64-65L)			

VARIETIES OF RECUTTING.

Eight stamps on Plate I were recut. All are listed below.

Outer line recut at top (65L, 74L, 86L and 3R, Plate I)	12,500.00	1350.00
Outer line recut at bottom (54L, 55L, 76L, Plate I)	13,000.00	1400.00
Outer line recut at top and bottom (64L I)	13,500.00	1450.00

CANCELLATIONS.

		Steamship	+150.00
Blue	+25.00	Packet boat	—
Red	+50.00	Pen	700.00

Types I, II, III and IV occur on the same sheet, so it is possible to obtain pairs and blocks showing combinations of types. For listings of type combinations in pairs and blocks, see Nos. 31-33.

A23
(Two typical examples)

POSTAGE, 1857-61

Type V. The side ornaments are slightly cut away. Usually only one pearl remains at each end of the lower label, but some copies show two or three pearls at the right side. At the bottom the outer line is complete and the shells nearly so. The outer lines at top are complete except over the right "X".

35	A23	10c **green**, type V, (Plate II),		
		May 9, 1859	175.00	57.50
		dark green	175.00	57.50
		yellowish green	175.00	57.50
		On cover		85.00
		On patriotic cover		600.00
		On pony express cover		
		Pair	360.00	120.00
		Block of four	750.00	500.00
		Margin block of 8, Impt. & P#	9,000.	
		Double transfer at bottom (47R II)	225.00	75.00
		Small "Curl" on forehead (37, 78L II)	210.00	65.00
		Curl in "e" of "cents" (93L II)	225.00	75.00
		Curl in "t" of "cents" (73R II)	225.00	75.00

CANCELLATIONS.

Red	+2.50	Steamship	+35.00
Brown	+2.50	"Steam"	+30.00
Blue	+1.50	Numerals	+15.00
Orange	+5.00	Supplementary Mail	
Magenta	+20.00	Type A or C	+60.00
Green	+125.00	Express Company	+135.00
1859 year date	+5.00	"Southn Letter Unpaid"	—
"Paid"	+5.00	Territorial	—
Red carrier	—	Pen	30.00
Railroad	+40.00		

TWELVE CENTS. Printed from two plates.

Plate I. Outer frame lines complete.
Plate III. Outer frame lines noticeably uneven or broken, sometimes partly missing. Imperforate stamps, Plate III, are from a trial printing.

36	A16	12c **black** (Plate I), *July 30, 1857*	300.00	80.00
		gray black	300.00	80.00
		Single on cover		450.00
		Single on cover with No. 26		150.00
		Pair on cover		200.00
		Pair on patriotic cover		
		Pair	675.00	170.00
		Block of four	1,650.	750.00
		a. Diagonal half used as 6c on cover		
		c. Horizontal pair, imperf. between (I)		
		Not recut in lower right corner	335.00	85.00
		Recut in lower left corner (43L, 53L, 63L, 73L and 100L)	350.00	90.00
		Double transfer	375.00	95.00
		Triple transfer	450.00	

CANCELLATIONS.

Blue	+2.50	Supplementary Mail	
Red	+7.50	Type A	+60.00
Brown	+7.50	Express Company	
Magenta	+20.00	Railroad	+60.00
Green	+250.00	Numeral	+20.00
1857 year date	+20.00	"Southn Letter Unpaid"	—
"Paid"	+10.00	Pen	40.00

36b	A16	12c **black** (Plate III), *Dec. 3, 1859*	225.00	95.00
		intense black	225.00	95.00
		Single on cover		550.00
		Single on cover with No. 26		175.00
		Pair on cover		250.00
		Pair	475.00	200.00
		Block of four	1,100.	1,100.
		Double frame line at right	250.00	100.00
		Double frame line at left	250.00	100.00
		Vertical line through rosette (95R II)	375.00	125.00

Washington
A17

37	A17	24c **gray lilac**, *1860*	600.00	200.00
		a. 24c gray	600.00	200.00
		On cover		1,100.
		On patriotic cover		3,500.
		Pair	1,250.	450.00
		Block of four, gray lilac	3,000.	5,000.
		Margin block of 12, Impt. & P#	30,000.	
		b. 24c red lilac	1,000.	
		b. Block of four, red lilac	6,000.	
		c. Imperforate	1,150.	
		c. Pair, imperforate	4,750.	

CANCELLATIONS. eku: July 8

		"Free"	+100.00
Blue	+10.00	Supplementary Mail	
Red	+20.00	Type A	+100.00
Magenta	+45.00	Railroad	+150.00
Violet	+75.00	Packet Boat	+200.00
Green	+450.00	Red Carrier	—
1860 year date	+15.00	Numeral	+40.00
"Paid"	+25.00	"Southn Letter Unpaid"	—
"Paid All"	+50.00	Pen	120.00

Franklin
A18

38	A18	30c **orange**, *Aug. 8, 1860*	750.00	285.00
		yellow orange	750.00	285.00
		reddish orange	750.00	285.00
		On cover		2,250.
		On patriotic cover		8,500.
		Pair	1,550.	650.00
		Block of four	4,250.	6,500.
		a. Imperforate	2,500.	
		a. Pair, imperforate	6,000.	
		Double transfer (89 L I and 99 L I)	850.00	325.00
		Recut at bottom (52L I)	900.00	375.00
		Cracked plate		

CANCELLATIONS.

		"Free"	—
Blue	+10.00	Black town	+25.00
Red	+25.00	Supplementary Mail	
Magenta	+60.00	Type A	+75.00
Violet	+75.00	Steamship	—
Green	+450.00	Express Company	—
1860 year date	+25.00	"Southn Letter Unpaid"	—
"Paid"	+35.00	Pen	175.00

The 30c was first printed in black. It was not perforated or gummed. Evidence that any were issued is unsatisfactory. It is listed in the Trial Color Proofs section.

Washington
A19

39	A19	90c **blue,** *1860*	1,450.	2,750.
		deep blue	1,450.	2,750.
		On cover		70,000.
		Pair	3,000.	
		Block of four	10,000.	
a.		Imperforate	3,500.	
a.		Pair, imperforate	10,000.	
		Double transfer at bottom	1,600.	
		Double transfer at top	1,600.	
		Short transfer at bottom right and left (13L I and 68R I)	1,450.	

CANCELLATIONS.   eku: Sept.11

Blue	+100.00	"Paid"	
Red	+250.00	Red Carrier	
1861 year date	—	Pen	1000.00

Genuine cancellations on the 90c are rare.
Nos. 37b, 37c, 38a and 39a were probably not regularly issued but came from trial printings.

1875   REPRINTS OF 1857-60 ISSUE.

Issued for the Centennial Exposition of 1876. These were not good for postal use.

Perf. 12.

Produced by the Continental Bank Note Co.

White paper, without gum.

The 1, 3, 10 and 12c were printed from new plates of 100 subjects each differing from those used for the regular issue.

40	A5	1c bright blue (*3846*)	550.00
		Pair	1,200.
		Block of four	3,000.
		Cracked plate (*91*)	700.00
		Double transfer (*94*)	700.00
41	A10	3c scarlet (*479*)	2,850.
42	A22	5c orange brown (*878*)	950.00
		Pair	2,750.
		Vertical margin strip of 4, Impt. & P#	9,500.
43	A12	10c blue green (*516*)	2,250.
		Pair	6,500.
44	A16	12c greenish black (*489*)	2,600.
		Pair	6,000.
45	A17	24c blackish violet (*479*)	2,850.
46	A18	30c yellow orange (*480*)	2,850.
47	A19	90c deep blue (*454*)	4,250.

Nos. 40 to 47 exist imperforate.
Numbers in parentheses are quantities issued.

1861   Produced by the National Bank Note Co.

Franklin
A24a

Jefferson
A26a

Washington
A27a

Washington
A28a

Washington
A31a

Plates of 200 subjects in two panes of 100 each.

Perf. 12.

The paper of Nos. 55-62 is thin and semitransparent. That of the following issues is thicker and more opaque, except Nos. 62B, 70c, and 70d.
It is doubtful that Nos. 55-62 were regularly issued.

55	A24a	1c **indigo**	17,000.
56	A25a	3c **brown rose**	700.00
		Pair	1,450.
		Block of four	3,000.
		Margin of 8, Impt. & P#	15,000.
a.		Imperf., pair	1,750.
57	A26a	5c **brown**	12,500.
58	A27a	10c **dark green**	5,500.
59	A28a	12c **black**	35,000.

104

60	A29	24c dark violet			.00.
61	A30	30c Block of			
62	A31a	90c red oran		5,500.	450.00
		dull blu		5,500.	450.00
1861		a. Imper			750.00
62B	A27a	10c d			2,000.
				10,500.	1,000.
				23,000.	5,000.
		4 R IV		6,000.	525.00

TIONS			
+50.00		Steamship	+100.00
+25.00		Express Company	+200.00
+50.00		Supplementary Mail Type A	+125.00

62B unused cannot be distinguished from No. 58 which does not exist used.

Designs modified (except 24c and 30c).

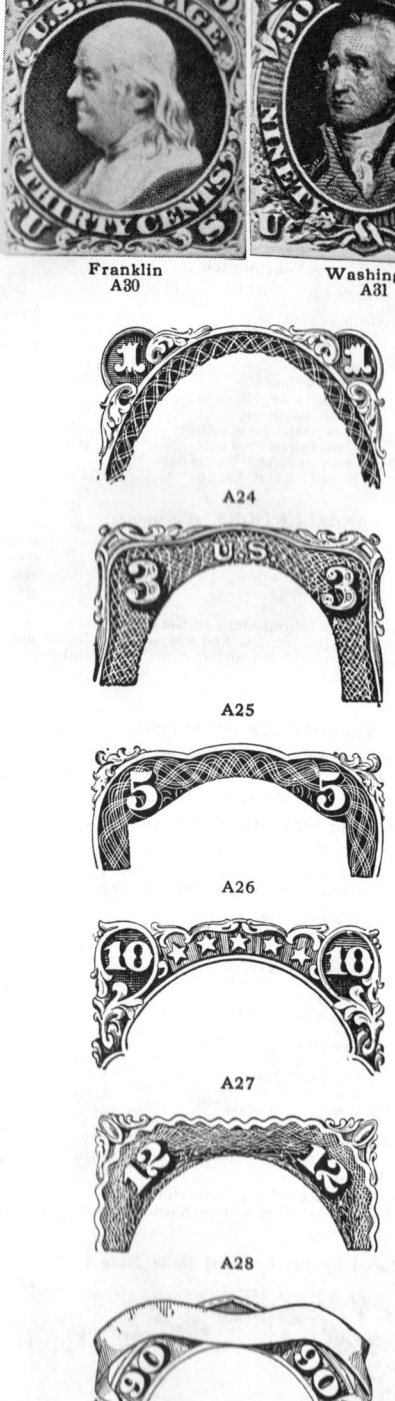

Franklin A24

Washington A25

Jefferson A26

Washington A27

Washington A28

Washington A29

Franklin A30

Washington A31

A24

A25

A26

A27

A28

A31

in·teg·ri·ty (in·teg´·rə·tē) n.

1. Uprightness of character; probity; honesty.
2. Unimpaired state; soundness. 3. Undivided or unbroken state; completeness.
4. Products and services as provided by Champagne Incorporated.

Use our reply card to send for your **FREE** fully illustrated **NET PRICE SALE** catalogue today.

- *Aggressive buyers of quality U.S. stamps.*
- *Expert appraisals and collection consultation.*
- *Personalized want list service.*

CHAMPAGNE, INCORPORATED
DAVID AND LAUREN CHAMPAGNE
POST OFFICE BOX 67
NEWTON, MASSACHUSETTS 02160
617 965 7250

POSTAGE, 1861-62

1861-62

1c. A dash has been added under the tip of the ornament at right of the numeral in upper left corner.

3c. Ornaments at corners have been enlarged and end in a small ball.

5c. A leaflet has been added to the foliated ornaments at each corner.

10c. A heavy curved line has been cut below the stars and an outer line added to the ornaments above them.

12c. Ovals and scrolls have been added to the corners.

90c. Parallel lines form an angle above the ribbon with "U. S. Postage"; between these lines a row of dashes has been added and a point of color to the apex of the lower line.

Patriotic Covers covering a wide range of historical interest were used during the Civil War period, in the North as well as the South, and are collected in State groups as well as generally. There are known to be over 11,000 varieties.

During the war, these stamps were used as small change until Postage Currency was issued.

The Act of Congress of March 3, 1863, effective July 1, 1863, created a rate of three cents for each half ounce, first class domestic mail. This Act was the first law which established uniform rate of postage regardless of the distance. This rate remained in effect for twenty years.

Perf. 12.

63	A24	**1c blue**, *Aug. 17, 1861*		100.00	17.50
		pale blue		100.00	17.50
		bright blue		100.00	17.50
		a. 1c ultramarine		185.00	40.00
		b. 1c dark blue		150.00	25.00
		indigo		300.00	65.00
		On cover (single)			27.50
		On prisoner's letter			175.00
		On patriotic cover			
		Pair		205.00	37.50
		Block of four		450.00	125.00
		Margin block of 8, Impr. & P#		2,400.	
		Double transfer			25.00
		Dot in "U"		110.00	20.00
		c. Laid paper, horiz. or vert.		—	150.00
		d. Vertical pair, imperf. horiz.			
		e. Printed on both sides		—	2,500.

CANCELLATIONS.

Blue	+1.00	Supp. Mail, A, B	+30.00
Red	+5.00	Steamship	+35.00
Magenta	+10.00	Steam	+30.00
Green	+90.00	Express Company	+85.00
Violet	+25.00	Red Carrier	+5.00
1861 year date	+7.50	Black Carrier	+10.00
1865 year date	+1.00	Railroad	+30.00
1866 year date	+1.00	Numeral	+10.00
"Free"	+20.00	"Steamboat"	+50.00
"Paid"	+2.50	Printed Precancel	
"Paid All"	+15.00	"CUMBERLAND, ME." (on cover)	1,500.

64	A25	**3c pink**		3,250.	250.00
		On cover (pink)			350.00
		On patriotic cover (pink)			650.00
		Block of four (pink)		16,000.	
		a. 3c pigeon blood pink		—	1,200.
		a. On cover (pigeon blood pink)			2,250.
		a. On patriotic cover (pig. bld. pink)			3,500.
		b. 3c rose pink		250.00	45.00
		b. On cover (rose pink)			65.00
		b. On patriotic cover (rose pink)			150.00
		b. Block of four (rose pink)		1,300.	275.00

CANCELLATIONS.

	No. 64	No. 64b		No. 64	No. 64b
Blue	+10.00	+5.00	"Paid"	+25.00	+10.00
Red	+25.00	+10.00	"Ship"	+85.00	+30.00
Green	+500.00	+150.00	"Free"	+125.00	+50.00
1861 date	—		Railroad	+125.00	+50.00
			Steamboat	+175.00	+75.00
			Supp. Mail, B	+150.00	

65	A25	**3c rose** *1861*			
		bright rose		45.00	1.10
		dull red		45.00	1.10
		rose red		45.00	1.10
		brown red		45.00	1.10
		pale brown red		45.00	1.10
		On cover			1.50
		On patriotic cover			40.00
		On prisoner's letter			200.00
		On pony express cover			

Pair		92.50	2.25
Block of four		200.00	15.00
Margin block of 8, Impt. & P#		1,750.	
b. Laid paper, horiz. or vert.		200.00	25.00
c. Imperf., pair		450.00	—
c. Margin block of 8, Impt. & P#			
d. Vertical pair, imperf. horiz.		1,200.	750.00
e. Printed on both sides		1,650.	1,000.
f. Double impression			1,200.
Double transfer		55.00	2.50
Cracked plate			

CANCELLATIONS. eku: Aug.17

Blue	+10	"Collect"	+35.00
Ultramarine	+2.75	"Ship"	+15.00
Brown	+2.50	"U. S. Ship"	+35.00
Red	+2.50	"Steam"	+12.00
Violet	+4.50	Steamship	+15.00
Magenta	+4.50	Steamboat	+20.00
Green	+45.00	"Ship Letter"	+35.00
Olive	+12.00	Red Carrier	+15.00
Orange	+10.00	Blue Carrier	+25.00
1861 year date	+.50	Black Carrier	+20.00
1867 or 1868 year date	+.50	Numeral	+3.00
		Supplementary Mail	
"Paid"	+.35	Types A, B or C	+15.00
"Paid All"	+7.50	Express Company	+40.00
"Mails Suspended"	—	Army Field Post	+60.00
Railroad	+12.50	Packet Boat	+40.00
"Way"	+20.00	"Registered"	+30.00
"Free"	+20.00	"Postage Due"	+25.00
		"Advertised"	+15.00
		Territorial	+25.00
		St. Thomas	
		China	—

66	A25	**3c lake**		1,650.	
		Pair		3,400.	
		Block of four		7,000.	
		a. Imperf., (pair)		1,850.	
		a. Margin block of 8, Impt. & P#		—	
		Double transfer		1,900.	

Nos. 66 and 66a were not regularly issued. John N. Luff recorded the plate number as 34.

67	A26	**5c buff**, *Aug. 19, 1861*		4,000.	375.00
		a. 5c brown yellow		4,000.	375.00
		b. 5c olive yellow		4,000.	375.00
		On cover			700.00
		On patriotic cover			3,500.
		Pair		8,250.	800.00
		Block of four		50,000.	9,000.

CANCELLATIONS.

Red	+25.00	"Paid"	+25.00
Blue	+10.00	Supplementary Mail	
Magenta	+50.00	Type A	+100.00
1861 year date	+10.00	Express Company	+250.00
		Numeral	+50.00
		"Steamship"	+100.00

68	A27	**10c yellow green**, *Aug. 20, 1861*		235.00	27.50
		deep yellow green on thin paper green		325.00	40.00
				235.00	27.50
		a. 10c dark green		250.00	28.50
		blue green		250.00	30.00
		On cover			45.00
		On patriotic cover			350.00
		Pair		475.00	57.50
		Block of four		1,100.	250.00
		Margin block of 8, Impt. & P#		5,000.	
		b. Vertical pair, imperf. horiz.			3,500.
		Double transfer		275.00	35.00

CANCELLATIONS.

Blue	+1.00	"Free"	+25.00
Red	+2.50	Numeral	+7.50
Purple	+5.00	Red Carrier	+45.00
Magenta	+5.00	Railroad	+20.00
Brown	+2.50	Steamship	+15.00
Green	+110.00	"Steamboat"	+35.00
1865 year date	+3.50	Supplementary Mail	
"Paid"	+2.50	Types A or D	+30.00
"Collect"	+32.50	Express Company	+70.00
"Short Paid"	+50.00	China	—
"P.D." in circle	+30.00	Japan	+200.00
		St. Thomas	—

69	A28	**12c black**, *Aug. 1861*		425.00	50.00
		gray black		425.00	50.00
		intense black		450.00	55.00
		On cover			85.00
		On patriotic cover			800.00
		Pair		875.00	105.00

POSTAGE, 1861-62, 1861-66

Block of four		2,000.	500.00
Double transfer of top frame line		500.00	60.00
Double transfer of bottom frame line		500.00	60.00
Double transfer of top and bottom frame lines		525.00	65.00

Earliest known use: Aug. 20

CANCELLATIONS.
Blue	+2.00	"Paid"	+5.00
Red	+5.00	"Registered"	+35.00
Purple	+10.00	Supplementary Mail	
Magenta	+10.00	Types A, B or C	+45.00
Green	+175.00	Express Company	+175.00
1861 year date	+5.00	Railroad	+50.00
		Numeral	+15.00

70 A29 24c red lilac, *Jan. 7, 1862*   500.00   72.50
    On cover   200.00
    On patriotic cover   3,000.
    Pair   1,050.   150.00
    Block of four   3,500.   750.00
  a. 24c brown lilac   425.00   60.00
    Block of four   3,000.
  b. 24c steel blue ('61)   3,500.   275.00
    Block of four   15,500.
  c. 24c violet, *Aug. 20, 1861*   3,500.   550.00
  d. 24c grayish lilac   1,000.   275.00
  b. On cover (steel blue)   800.00
    Scratch under "A" of "Postage"   85.00

There are numerous shades of the 24c stamp in this and the following issue.

Color changelings, especially of No. 78, are frequently offered as No. 70b.

Nos. 70c and 70d are on a thinner, harder and more transparent paper than Nos. 70, 70a, 70b or the latter Nos. 78, 78a, 78b and 78c. No. 60 is distinguished by its distinctive dark color.

CANCELLATIONS. (No. 70)
Blue	+2.50	1865 year date	+5.00
Red	+5.00	"Paid"	+15.00
Magenta	+15.00	Supplementary Mail	
Brown	+5.00	Types A or B	+75.00
Green	+300.00	Express Company	+350.00

71 A30 30c orange, *Aug. 20, 1861*   450.00   65.00
    deep orange   450.00   65.00
    On cover   500.00
    On patriotic cover   3,500.
    Pair   925.00   150.00
    Block of four   2,250.   900.00
  a. Printed on both sides

CANCELLATIONS.
Blue	+2.50	Railroad	—
Magenta	+15.00	Packet Boat	—
Brown	+10.00	"Steamship"	+75.00
Red	+15.00	Supplementary Mail	
"Paid"	+25.00	Type A	+75.00
"Paid All"	+35.00	Express Company	+350.00
		Japan	

72 A31 90c blue, *Aug., 1861*   1,200.   250.00
  a. 90c pale blue   1,200.   250.00
  b. 90c dark blue   1,300.   275.00
    dull blue   1,200.   250.00
    On cover   13,500.
    Pair   2,500.   550.00
    Block of four   6,250.   2,500.

Earliest known use: Nov. 27

CANCELLATIONS.
Blue	+10.00	"Paid"	+25.00
Red	+25.00	"Registered"	+75.00
Green	+450.00	Express Company	+500.00
1865 year date	+15.00	Supplementary Mail	
		Type A	+100.00

Nos. 65c, 68a, 69, 71 and 72 exist as imperforate sheet-margin singles with pen cancel. They were not regularly issued.

The 90c was distributed to several post offices in the last two weeks of August, 1861. However, the earliest known use is Nov. 27, 1861.

Owing to the Civil War, stamps and stamped envelopes in current use or available for postage in 1860, were demonetized by various post office orders, beginning in August, 1861, and extending to early January, 1862.

"A reasonable time after hostilities began in 1861 was given for the return to the Department of all these (1851-56) stamps in the hands of postmasters, and as early as 1863 the Department issued an order declining to longer redeem them."

P. O. Department Bulletin.

The Act of Congress, approved March 3, 1863, abolished carriers' fees and established a prepaid rate of two cents for drop letters, making necessary the 2-cent Jackson (No. 73).

Free City Delivery was authorized by the Act of Congress of March 3, 1863, effective in 49 cities with 449 carriers, beginning July 1, 1863.

Produced by the National Bank Note Co.

1861–66   **Perf. 12**

DESIGNS AS 1861 ISSUE.

Andrew Jackson
A32

Earliest known use: 2c, July 6, 1863.

73 A32 2c black, *July 1863*   100.00   20.00
    gray black   100.00   20.00
    intense black   110.00   25.00
    On cover   40.00
    On prisoner's letter   —
    On patriotic cover   1,000.
    Pair   210.00   42.50
    Block of four   475.00   350.00
    Margin block of 8, Impt. & P#   8,000.
  a. Half used as 1c on cover, diagonal, vert. or horiz.   1,650.
  d. Laid paper   —
  e. Printed on both sides   4,000.
    Double transfer   120.00   22.50
    Major double transfer of top left corner   250.00
    Major overall double transfer ("Atherton shift")   6,000.
    Triple transfer   —
    Short transfer   105.00   21.00
    Cracked plate   —

CANCELLATIONS.
Blue	+1.00	"Paid"	+10.00
Brown	+5.00	Numeral	+15.00
Red	+7.50	Railroad	+85.00
Magenta	+12.50	"Steam"	+40.00
Ultramarine	+12.50	Steamship	+65.00
Orange	+10.00	"Steamboat"	+65.00
Green	+265.00	"Ship Letter"	—
1863 year date	+5.00	Black Carrier	+20.00
Printed		Blue Carrier	+35.00
Precancellation	—	Supplementary Mail	
"Jefferson, Ohio"	—	Types A or B	+60.00
		Express Company	+200.00
"PAID ALL"	+40.00	"Short Paid"	+130.00
		China	—

74 A25 3c scarlet*   4,000.
    Block of four   18,500.
    With 4 horiz. black pen strokes   1,750.
  a. Imperf., pair   3,750.

Nos. 74 and 74a were not regularly issued. John N. Luff recorded the plate number as 19.

POSTAGE, 1861-66, 1867

75	A26	5c **red brown**, *Jan. 2, 1862*	1,200.	200.00
		dark red brown	1,200.	200.00
		On cover		475.00
		On patriotic cover		2,500.
		Pair	2,500.	425.00
		Block of four	8,500.	2,750.
		Double transfer	1,400.	235.00

CANCELLATIONS.

Blue	+10.00	"Paid"	+25.00
Red	+25.00	Supplementary Mail	
Magenta	+50.00	Type A	+50.00
		Express Company	+300.00

76	A26	5c **brown**, *Feb. 3, 1863*	285.00	50.00
		pale brown	285.00	50.00
		a. 5c dark brown	350.00	65.00
		On cover		120.00
		On patriotic cover		800.00
		Pair	575.00	110.00
		Block of four	1,400.	400.00
		a. Block of four	1,650.	
		Double transfer of top frame line	350.00	65.00
		Double transfer of bottom frame line	350.00	65.00
		Double transfer of top and bottom frame lines	375.00	70.00
		b. Laid paper		—

CANCELLATIONS.

Blue	+2.50	"Paid"	+15.00
Magenta	+5.00	"Short Paid"	+75.00
Red	+5.00	Supplementary Mail	
Brown	+5.00	Type A or F	+55.00
Green	+225.00	Express Company	+175.00
1865 year date	+10.00	"Steamship"	+65.00
		Packet boat	—

Abraham Lincoln
A33

77	A33	15c **black**, *1866*	450.00	60.00
		full black	450.00	60.00
		On cover		175.00
		Pair	925.00	125.00
		Block of four	14,000.	—
		Margin block of 8, Impt. & P#		
		Double transfer	500.00	70.00
		Cracked plate		—

CANCELLATIONS. eku: Apr.14

Blue	+2.50	"Paid"	+15.00
Magenta	+10.00	"Short Paid"	+85.00
Red	+10.00	"Insufficiently Paid"	+150.00
Brown	+10.00	"Ship"	+50.00
Green	+250.00	Steamship	+50.00
Ultramarine	+25.00	Supplementary Mail	
		Type A	+70.00

78	A29	24c **lilac**, *Feb. 20, 1863*	250.00	47.50
		dark lilac	250.00	47.50
		a. 24c grayish lilac	250.00	47.50
		b. 24c gray	250.00	47.50
		c. 24c blackish violet	3,500.	550.00
		On cover		200.00
		Pair	525.00	100.00
		Block of four	1,200.	450.00
		d. Printed on both sides		3,000.
		Scratch under "A" of "Postage"	325.00	65.00

CANCELLATIONS.

Blue	+2.50	"Paid"	+12.50
Red	+7.50	Numeral	+17.50
Magenta	+10.00	Supplementary Mail	
Green	+275.00	Type A	+50.00
		"Free"	+75.00

Nos. 73, 76–78 exist as imperforate sheet-margin singles, all with pen cancel except No. 76 which is uncanceled. They were not regularly issued.

SAME DESIGNS AS 1861-66 ISSUES.

1867 Printed by the National Bank Note Co.

Perf. 12.

Grill

Embossed with grills of various sizes.

A peculiarity of the United States issues from 1867 to 1870 is the grill or embossing. The object was to break the fibre of the paper so that the ink of the cancelling stamp would soak in and make washing for a second using impossible. The exact date at which grilled stamps came into use is unsettled. Luff's "Postage Stamps of the United States" places the date as probably August 8, 1867. Some authorities believe that more than one size of grill probably existed on one of the grill rolls.

GRILL WITH POINTS UP.

Grills A and C were made by a roller covered with ridges shaped like an inverted V. Pressing the ridges into the stamp paper forced the paper into the pyramidal pits between the ridges, causing irregular breaks in the paper. Grill B was made by a roller with raised bosses.

A. Grill Covering the Entire Stamp.

79	A25	3c **rose**	1,650.	425.00
		On cover		750.00
		Pair	3,500.	1,000.
		Block of four	10,000.	—
		a. Imperf., pair	1,650.	
		a. Block of four	3,750.	
		a. Margin block of 8, Impt. & P#	10,000.	
		b. Printed on both sides		

CANCELLATIONS.

Earliest known use, Aug. 13, 1867.

Blue	+25.00	Railroad	—

An essay which is often mistaken for No. 79 shows the points of the grill as small squares faintly impressed in the paper but not cutting through it. On the issued stamp the grill generally breaks through the paper. Copies without defects are rare.

No. 79a was not regularly issued.

80	A26	5c **brown**	40,000.	—
		a. 5c dark brown		37,500.
81	A30	30c **orange**		32,500.

B. Grill about 18x15 mm.

(22x18 points.)

| 82 | A25 | 3c **rose** | | 45,000. |

Start your
U.S. COLLECTION
with .... SCOTT

Scott's U.S. Minuteman Stamp Album!

FEATURES . . .

★ The famous Scott Catalogue identification number for every stamp.

★ Exciting stories of almost every stamp.

★ Attractive vinyl binder.   ★ Supplemented annually.

"A must for every collector of United States postage stamps."

Available at your local dealer or direct from Scott Publishing Co.

Scott Publishing Company
P.O. Box 828, Sidney, OH 45365

POSTAGE, 1867

C. Grill about 13x16 mm.
(16 to 17 by 18 to 21 points.)

The grilled area on each of four C grills in the sheet may total about 18x15mm. when a normal C grill adjoins a fainter grill extending to the right or left edge of the stamp. This is caused by a partial erasure on the grill roller when it was changed to produce C grills instead of the all-over A grill.

83	A25	3c **rose**	1,600.	350.00
		On cover		450.00
		Pair	3,300.	750.00
		Block of four	8,500.	
		a. Imperf., pair	*1,650.*	
		Double grill	3,500.	1,500.
		Grill with points down	3,000.	650.00

CANCELLATIONS.

Blue +10.00

No. 83a was not regularly issued.
A 1c blue (A24) with "c" grill points down exists unused. It was not issued. Experts consider it an essay.

GRILL WITH POINTS DOWN.

The grills were produced by rollers with the surface covered, or partly covered, by pyramidal bosses. On the D, E and F grills the tips of the pyramids are vertical ridges. On the Z grill the ridges are horizontal.

D. Grill about 12x14mm.
(15 by 17 to 18 points.)

84	A32	2c **black**	2,750.	850.00
		On cover		1,300.
		Pair	5,600.	1,750.
		Block of four	*13,000.*	
		Double transfer		
		Split grill		900.00

CANCELLATIONS.

Red +75.00 | "Paid All" +100.00

85	A25	3c **rose**	1,250.	400.00
		On cover		500.00
		Pair	2,600.	825.00
		Block of four	*7,500.*	
		Double grill		
		Split grill		400.00

CANCELLATIONS.

Blue +10.00 | "Paid" +50.00
Green +200.00

Z. Grill about 11x14 mm.
(13 to 14 by 17 to 18 points.)

85A	A24	1c **blue**	—	—
85B	A32	2c **black**	1,100.	325.00
		On cover		500.00
		Pair	2,300.	700.00
		Block of four	*7,500.*	
		Double transfer	1,050.	350.00
		Double grill		

CANCELLATIONS.

Blue +10.00 | Black Carrier +75.00
Red +50.00 | "Paid All" +75.00

85C	A25	3c **rose**	3,000.	900.00
		On cover		1,200.
		Block of four	*13,000.*	
		Double grill	*4,000.*	

CANCELLATIONS.

Green +250.00 | Red +75.00
Blue +25.00 | "Paid" +50.00

85D	A27	10c **green**	—	25,000.
85E	A28	12c **black**	1,450.	500.00
		On cover		900.00
		Block of four	—	
		Double transfer of top frame line		550.00
85F	A33	15c **black**	—	—

E. Grill about 11x13 mm.
(14 by 15 to 17 points.)

86	A24	1c **blue**	700.00	225.00
		a. 1c dull blue	700.00	225.00
		On cover		300.00
		Pair	1,450.	475.00
		Block of four	3,200.	1,100.
		Double grill		350.00
		Split grill	750.00	250.00

CANCELLATIONS.

Blue	+5.00	"Paid"	+20.00
Red	+25.00	Steamboat	+85.00
Green	+140.00	Red Carrier	+60.00

87	A32	2c **black**	325.00	65.00
		intense black	350.00	70.00
		gray black	325.00	65.00
		On cover		95.00
		Pair	675.00	135.00
		Block of four	1,600.	
		a. Half used as 1c on cover, diagonal or vertical		2,000.
		Double grill	450.00	100.00
		Triple grill		
		Split grill	375.00	80.00
		Grill with points down		
		Double transfer	350.00	70.00

CANCELLATIONS.

Blue	+2.50	"Paid"	+10.00
Purple	+15.00	Steamship	+60.00
Brown	+10.00	Black Carrier	+35.00
Red	+15.00	"Paid All"	+20.00
Green	+175.00	"Short Paid"	+65.00
		Japan	

88	A25	3c **rose**	225.00	9.50
		pale rose	225.00	9.50
		rose red	225.00	9.50
		a. 3c lake red	250.00	11.00
		On cover		13.50
		Pair	460.00	20.00
		Block of four	975.00	100.00
		Double grill	325.00	35.00
		Triple grill		
		Split grill	250.00	11.00
		Very thin paper	235.00	11.00

CANCELLATIONS.

Blue	+.25	"Paid"	+3.00
Red	+3.00	"Way"	+20.00
Ultramarine	+3.00	Numeral	+2.00
Green	+80.00	Steamboat	+35.00
		Railroad	+25.00
		Express Company	+80.00

89	A27	10c **green**	1,100.	170.00
		dark green	1,100.	170.00
		blue green	1,100.	170.00
		On cover		250.00
		Pair	2,300.	350.00
		Block of four	5,500.	*1,100.*
		Double grill	1,700.	300.00
		Split grill	1,200.	180.00
		Double transfer		190.00
		Very thin paper	1,150.	180.00

CANCELLATIONS.

Blue	+5.00	"Paid"	+15.00
Red	+20.00	Steamship	+50.00
		Japan	+225.00

90	A28	12c **black**	1,300.	175.00
		gray black	1,300.	175.00
		intense black	1,300.	175.00
		On cover		300.00
		Pair	2,700.	360.00
		Block of four	6,750.	*1,200.*
		Double transfer of top frame line	1,400.	190.00
		Double transfer of bottom frame line	1,400.	190.00
		Double transfer of top and bottom frame lines	1,450.	210.00
		Double grill	1,850.	350.00
		Split grill	1,400.	185.00

CANCELLATIONS.

Blue	+5.00	Railroad	+60.00
Red	+20.00	"Paid"	+20.00
Green	+225.00		

POSTAGE, 1867

91	A33	15c **black**		2,750.	425.00
		gray black		2,750.	425.00
		On cover			650.00
		Pair		5,600.	900.00
		Block of four		12,500.	3,500.
		Double grill		———	600.00
		Split grill		———	450.00

CANCELLATIONS.

Blue	+10.00	"Paid"	+30.00
Red	+50.00	Supplementary Mail Type A	+100.00

F. Grill about 9x13 mm.
(11 to 12 by 15 to 17 points.)

92	A24	1c **blue**		285.00	90.00
		a. 1c pale blue		285.00	90.00
		dark blue		285.00	90.00
		On cover			130.00
		Pair		585.00	185.00
		Block of four		1,350.	500.00
		Double transfer		310.00	110.00
		Double grill			175.00
		Split grill		300.00	95.00
		Very thin paper		295.00	95.00

CANCELLATIONS.

Blue	+2.50	"Paid"	+10.00
Red	+10.00	Red Carrier	+25.00
Green	+175.00	"Paid All"	+15.00

93	A32	2c **black**		110.00	22.50
		gray black		110.00	22.50
		On cover			35.00
		Pair		225.00	47.50
		Block of four		525.00	200.00
		Margin block of 8, Impr. & P#		———	
		a. Half used as 1c on cover, diagonal, vertical or horizontal			1,600.
		Double transfer		120.00	25.00
		Double grill		———	100.00
		Split grill		120.00	25.00
		Very thin paper		120.00	25.00

CANCELLATIONS.

Blue	+2.50	"Paid"	+5.00
Red	+7.50	"Paid All"	+15.00
Green	+200.00	Black Carrier	+20.00
Japan	———	Red Carrier	+30.00

94	A25	3c **red**		75.00	2.50
		rose red		75.00	2.50
		a. 3c rose		75.00	2.50
		On cover			3.25
		Pair		160.00	5.25
		Block of four		350.00	45.00
		Margin block of 8, Impt. & P#		2,400.	
		b. Imperf., pair		650.00	
		c. Vertical pair, imperf. horiz.		900.00	
		d. Printed on both sides		950.00	
		Double transfer		100.00	4.00
		Double grill		150.00	20.00
		Triple grill		———	100.00
		End roller grill		———	120.00
		Split grill		80.00	2.75
		Quadruple split grill		225.00	50.00
		Grill with points up			
		Very thin paper		80.00	2.75

CANCELLATIONS.

Blue	+.10	"Paid"	+2.25
Ultramarine	+3.00	"Paid All"	+12.50
Red	+3.50	"Free"	+20.00
Violet	+5.50	Railroad	+30.00
Green	+70.00	Steamboat	+40.00
Numeral	+3.00	Packet boat	+60.00
		Express Company	+50.00

95	A26	5c **brown**		800.00	200.00
		a. 5c dark brown		850.00	225.00
		On cover			350.00
		Pair		1,650.	425.00
		Block of four		3,600.	1,150.
		Double transfer of top frame line		———	———
		Double grill			
		Split grill		900.00	225.00
		Very thin paper		850.00	210.00

CANCELLATIONS.

Blue	+5.00	Green	+200.00
Magenta	+30.00	"Paid"	+25.00
Violet	+35.00	"Free"	+50.00
Red	+30.00	"Steamship"	+100.00

96	A27	10c **yellow green**		600.00	100.00
		green		600.00	100.00
		a. 10c dark green		600.00	100.00
		blue green		600.00	100.00
		On cover			165.00
		Pair		1,250.	210.00
		Block of four		3,250.	800.00
		Double transfer		———	———
		Double grill		———	200.00
		Split grill		650.00	110.00
		Quadruple split grill			325.00
		Very thin paper		625.00	110.00

CANCELLATIONS.

Blue	+2.50	"Paid"	+10.00
Red	+15.00	"Free"	+50.00
Magenta	+20.00	Steamship	+75.00
Green	+175.00	Japan	+250.00
		China	———

97	A28	12c **black**		625.00	105.00
		gray black		625.00	105.00
		On cover			185.00
		Pair		1,300.	220.00
		Block of four		3,350.	1,100.
		Double transfer of top frame line		650.00	120.00
		Double transfer of bottom frame line		650.00	120.00
		Double transfer of top and bottom frame lines		———	140.00
		Double grill		———	225.00
		Triple grill			350.00
		Split grill		675.00	120.00
		End roller grill		———	———
		Very thin paper		650.00	110.00

CANCELLATIONS.

Blue	+2.50	"Paid"	+15.00
Red	+15.00	"Insufficiently	
Magenta	+20.00	Prepaid"	+100.00
Brown	+15.00	"Paid All"	+25.00
Green	+200.00	Supplementary Mail Type A	+50.00

98	A33	15c **black**		625.00	110.00
		gray black		625.00	110.00
		On cover			185.00
		Pair		1,300.	230.00
		Block of four		3,500.	1,000.
		Margin block of 8, Impt. & P#		25,000.	
		Double transfer of upper right corner		———	
		Double grill		———	225.00
		Split grill		650.00	120.00
		Quadruple split grill		1,200.	325.00
		Very thin paper		650.00	115.00

CANCELLATIONS.

Blue	+2.50	"Paid"	+20.00
Magenta	+20.00	"Insufficiently	
Red	+15.00	Prepaid"	+135.00
Green	+225.00	"Insufficiently	
Orange	+20.00	Paid"	+135.00
		Japan	+300.00
		Supplementary Mail Type A	+60.00

99	A29	24c **gray lilac**		1,150.	450.00
		gray		1,150.	450.00
		On cover			800.00
		Pair		2,350.	950.00
		Block of four		5,750.	4,000.
		Margin block of 8, Impt. & P#		30,000.	
		Double grill		1,650.	700.00
		Split grill		1,250.	475.00

CANCELLATIONS.

Blue	+10.00	Red	+50.00
		"Paid"	+50.00

100	A30	30c **orange**		1,300.	350.00
		deep orange		1,300.	350.00
		On cover			1,000.
		Pair		2,700.	725.00
		Block of four		7,000.	3,000.
		Double grill		1,850.	600.00
		Split grill		1,400.	400.00

CANCELLATIONS.

Blue	+10.00	"Paid"	+50.00
Red	+50.00	Supplementary Mail Type A	+100.00
Magenta	+75.00		
		Japan	+400.00

POSTAGE, 1867, 1875, 1869

101	A31	90c **blue**	4,000.	900.00
		dark blue	4,000.	900.00
		On cover		
		Pair	8,250.	1,900.
		Block of four	18,000.	5,000.
		Double grill	5,500.	
		Split grill	4,150.	950.00

CANCELLATIONS.

Blue	+25.00	Japan	+600.00
Red	+50.00	"Paid"	+50.00

RE-ISSUE OF 1861-66 ISSUES

Issued for the Centennial Exposition of 1876.
Produced by the National Bank Note Co.

1875 *Perf. 12*

Without grill, hard white paper, with white crackly gum.

The 1, 2, 5, 10 and 12c were printed from new plates of 100 subjects each.

102	A24	1c 1c blue (*3195*)	500.00	800.00
		Block of four	3,500.	
103	A32	2c black (*979*)	2,500.	4,000.
		Block of four	13,500.	
104	A25	3c brown red (*465*)	3,250.	4,250.
		Block of four	16,000.	
105	A26	5c brown (*672*)	1,800.	2,250.
		Block of four	10,000.	
106	A27	10c green (*451*)	2,100.	3,750.
		Block of four	12,500.	
107	A28	12c black (*389*)	3,000.	4,500.
		Block of four	15,000.	
108	A33	15c black (*397*)	3,000.	4,750.
		Block of four	15,000.	
109	A29	24c deep violet (*346*)	4,000.	6,000.
		Block of four	19,000.	
110	A30	30c brownish orange (*346*)	4,500.	7,000.
		Block of four	22,500.	
111	A31	90c blue (*317*)	5,750.	18,500.

These stamps can be distinguished from the 1861-66 issue by the brighter colors, the sharper proof-like impressions and the paper which is very white instead of yellowish.

Numbers in parentheses are quantities issued.

1869 Produced by the National Bank Note Co.

Plates for the 1c, 2c, 3c, 6c, 10c and 12c consisted of 300 subjects in two panes of 150 each. For the 15c, 24c, 30c and 90c plates of 100 subjects each.

> NOTE. Stamps of the 1869 issue without grill cannot be guaranteed except when unused and with the original gum.

Franklin
A34

Perf. 12.
G. Grill measuring 9½x9mm.
(12 by 11 to 11½ points)
Hard Wove Paper.

112	A34	1c **buff**, *Mar. 27, 1869*	225.00	60.00
		brown orange	225.00	60.00
		dark brown orange	225.00	60.00
		On cover, single		150.00
		Pair	465.00	125.00
		Block of four	1,000.	450.00
		Margin block of 4, arrow	1,100.	
		Margin block of 10, Impt. & P#		
		Double transfer		
	b.	Without grill, original gum	750.00	
		Double grill	450.00	150.00
		Split grill	250.00	70.00

CANCELLATIONS.

Blue	+2.50	"Paid"	+35.00
Ultramarine	+15.00	Steamship	+50.00
Magenta	+15.00	Black town	+10.00
Purple	+15.00	Blue town	+20.00
Red	+17.50	Red town	+50.00
Green	+150.00	Black Carrier	+60.00
		Japan	+225.00

Post Horse and Rider
A35

113	A35	2c **brown**, *Mar. 27, 1869*	160.00	25.00
		pale brown	160.00	25.00
		dark brown	160.00	25.00
		yellow brown	160.00	25.00
		On cover, single		60.00
		Pair	325.00	52.50
		Block of four	725.00	275.00
		Margin block of 4, arrow	775.00	
		Margin block of 10, Impt. & P#		
	b.	Without grill, original gum	600.00	
	c.	Half used as 1c on cover, diagonal, vertical or horizontal		
	d.	Printed on both sides		
		Double grill		125.00
		Split grill	185.00	35.00
		Quadruple split grill		200.00
		Double transfer		30.00

CANCELLATIONS.

Blue	+1.00	Steamship	+50.00
Red	+15.00	Black town	+10.00
Orange	+15.00	Blue town	+20.00
Magenta	+12.50	Japan	+200.00
Purple	+12.50	Blue Carrier	+75.00
Ultramarine	+15.00	Black Carrier	+60.00
Green	+175.00	China	
"Paid"	+15.00	Printed	
"Paid All"	+25.00	Precancellation "Jefferson, Ohio"	

CANCELLATIONS.

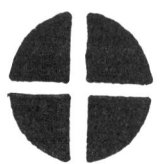    

The common type of cancellation on the 1869 issue is the block or cork similar to illustrations above. Japanese cancellations seen on this issue (not illustrated) resulted from the sale of U. S. stamps in Japanese cities where post offices were maintained for mail going from Japan to the United States.

THE FINEST IN UNITED STATES STAMPS & COVERS

Known as expert buyers and sellers of premium quality United States stamps, covers, proofs and specialized nineteenth- and twentieth-century varieties.

You may telephone and let us know your special requirements or send your want lists. We can help you build your collection.

Expertising and appraisals for estates and insurance.

Visit us at all major stamp shows.

And we are always seeking finer collections and individual stamps. Call if you wish to sell.

RICHARD A. CHAMPAGNE LTD.

POST OFFICE BOX 372 • NEWTON, MASSACHUSETTS 02160
617-969-5719
Members: ASDA, APS, USPCS, PRA and CCNY.

POSTAGE, 1869

Locomotive
A36

114	A36	3c **ultramarine,** *March 27, 1869*		135.00	5.50
		pale ultramarine		135.00	5.50
		dark ultramarine		135.00	5.50
		blue		135.00	5.50
		dark blue		135.00	5.50
		On cover			12.00
		Pair		275.00	11.50
		Block of four		625.00	125.00
		Margin block of 4, arrow		675.00	
		Margin block of 10, Impt. & P#		7,000.	
		a. Without grill, original gum		600.00	—
		b. Vertical one-third used as 1c on cover			—
		c. Vertical two-thirds used as 2c on cover			—
		d. Double impression			—
		Double transfer		150.00	6.50
		Double grill		275.00	45.00
		Triple grill		—	100.00
		Split grill		145.00	6.50
		Quadruple split grill		325.00	60.00
		End roller grill		—	—
		Gray paper		—	—
		Cracked plate		—	—

CANCELLATIONS.

Blue	+.25	"Paid"	+10.00
Ultramarine	+3.00	"Paid All"	+15.00
Magenta	+5.00	"Steamboat"	—
Purple	+5.00	"Steamship"	+40.00
Violet	+5.00	Ship	+35.00
Red	+7.00	Railroad	+30.00
Brown	+3.00	Packet Boat	+100.00
Green	+125.00	Black Carrier	+30.00
Orange	+7.00	Blue Carrier	+40.00
Black town	+2.50	Express Company	—
Blue town	+4.00	"Way"	—
Red town	+25.00	"Free"	+30.00
Numeral	+10.00	Alaska	—
		Japan	+150.00

Washington
A37

115	A37	6c **ultramarine,** *1869*		775.00	90.00
		pale ultramarine		775.00	90.00
		On cover			300.00
		Pair		1,600.	190.00
		Block of four		4,000.	1,000.
		Margin block of 4, arrow		4,500.	
		Double grill		—	300.00
		Split grill		825.00	100.00
		Quadruple split grill		—	400.00
		Double transfer			100.00
		b. Vertical half used as 3c on cover		—	

CANCELLATIONS. eku: Apr. 26

		"Paid"	+15.00
Blue	+5.00	"Paid All"	+25.00
Brown	+10.00	Black town	+20.00
Magenta	+20.00	"Short Paid"	+75.00
Purple	+20.00	Steamship	+35.00
Red	+30.00	Railroad	+35.00
Green	+225.00	Japan	+175.00

Shield and Eagle
A38

116	A38	10c **yellow,** *April 1, 1869*		850.00	95.00
		yellowish orange		850.00	95.00
		On cover			325.00
		Pair		1,750.	200.00
		Block of four		4,500.	1,150.
		Margin block of 4, arrow		5,000.	
		Double grill		—	275.00
		Split grill		900.00	105.00
		End roller grill		—	—

CANCELLATIONS.

		"Paid"	+15.00
Blue	+5.00	"Paid All"	+30.00
Magenta	+20.00	"Insufficiently Paid"	+125.00
Purple	+20.00	Supplementary Mail	
Red	+30.00	Type A	+55.00
Ultramarine	+30.00	Express Company	—
Green	+225.00	St. Thomas	—
Black town	+20.00	Hawaii	—
Steamship	+45.00	Japan	+200.00
Railroad	+45.00	China	—

S.S. "Adriatic"
A39

117	A39	12c **green,** *April 5, 1869*		750.00	90.00
		bluish green		750.00	90.00
		yellowish green		750.00	90.00
		On cover			325.00
		Pair		1,550.	190.00
		Block of four		4,000.	850.00
		Margin block of 4, arrow		4,500.	
		Double grill		—	275.00
		Split grill		800.00	100.00
		End roller grill		—	—

CANCELLATIONS.

		"Paid"	+25.00
Blue	+5.00	"Paid All"	+40.00
Magenta	+20.00	"Too Late"	+100.00
Purple	+20.00	"Insufficiently	
Brown	+15.00	Paid"	+125.00
Red	+30.00	Black town	+20.00
Green	+225.00	Japan	+175.00
Numeral	—		

FANCY CANCELS

BUYING — **SELLING**

N.Y.C. SEEING EYE

Ask for a selection on approval. Send two philatelic references or a deposit, a description of what you would like to see, and a price range. Available on and off cover. When selling, come to someone who knows and can give you the best price.

WRITE OR CALL . . .

Edward Hines

P.O. Box 2177, Danbury, CT 06813
Phone 203-743-6707

POSTAL HISTORY
- BUYING AND SELLING -

Post Cards • Railroad Postmarks
Postmarks by States - Ala. thru Wisc.
Registered Covers
Ships & Naval Cancels
Flag Cancels • Advertising Covers
Philatelic Supplies • Auxiliary Markings
Discontinued Post Offices

Write or call for a FREE copy of our next...
NET PRICE POSTAL HISTORY CATALOGUE. 6-8 ANNUALLY.
To receive the next 6 cats. include $2 to offset mailing.

- U.S. POSTAL HISTORY APPROVAL SERVICE
  All Areas. Please include references.
- WANT LISTS SOLICITED
- BUYING, TOP PRICES PAID! WRITE OR CALL US!

 Satisfaction Guaranteed.
Refunds Cheerfully Made.

 RUSTCO, INC.
P.O. Box 742
Lima, Ohio 45802
Phone (419) 229-2662

"Established full-time, full-service business in 1976"
Member: IFPD, OPHS, MPOS, APS, USCS, etc.

Why Are
ScottMounts Superior?
Because . . .

- They're completely interchangeable with Showgard® mounts, and come with more mounts to the package.
- They're made of two welded sheets of 100 percent inert polystyrol foil.
- They're center-split across the back for easy insertion of your stamps.
- The Black-backed mounts are totally opaque for perfect stamp framing.
- Crystal clear mount faces eliminate distracting distortions.
- Double layers of gum assure stay-put bonding, yet they're easily peeled off.
- They come packed in their own reuseable storage trays.

See for yourself. Try a package of ScottMounts today.

Available from your local dealer or direct from Scott.

P.O. Box 828
Sidney, OH 45365

POSTAGE, 1869

Landing of Columbus
A40

A40

118	A40	15c **brown & blue**, type I, Picture		
		unframed, *April 2, 1869*	1,750.	250.00
		dark brown & blue	1,750.	250.00
		On cover		1,300.
		Pair	3,650.	525.00
		Block of four	12,000.	20,000.
		a. Without grill, original gum	3,500.	
		Double grill	—	450.00
		Split grill	1,900.	300.00

CANCELLATIONS.

Blue	+10.00	"Paid"	+50.00
Red	+40.00	"Insufficiently Paid"	+150.00
Brown	+25.00	Black town	+50.00
		Steamship	+100.00

A40a

119	A40a	15c **brown & blue**, type II, Picture		
		framed,	850.00	120.00
		dark brown & blue	850.00	120.00
		On cover		800.00
		Pair	1,750.	260.00
		Block of four	4,000.	3,500.
		Margin block of 8, Impt. & P#	20,000.	
		b. Center inverted	130,000.	17,500.
		c. Center double, one inverted	—	—
		Double transfer		
		Double grill	1,750.	275.00
		Split grill	1,000.	150.00

CANCELLATIONS.
Earliest known use, May 23, 1869.

Blue	+10.00	"Paid"	+20.00
Purple	+35.00	"Paid All"	+35.00
Magenta	+35.00	Black town	+30.00
Red	+35.00	"Steamship"	+60.00
Brown	+20.00	Supp. Mail, A, F	+40.00
Green	+250.00	Japan	+275.00

The Declaration of Independence
A41

120	A41	24c **green & violet**, *April 7, 1869*	2,500.	450.00
		bluish green & violet	2,500.	450.00
		On cover		9,500.
		Pair	5,250.	950.00
		Block of four	14,000.	18,000.
		a. Without grill, original gum	5,000.	
		b. Center inverted	110,000.	16,500.
		b. On cover		—
		b. Block of four		—
		b. Imperf.	—	—
		Double grill	—	1,000.
		Split grill	2,750.	500.00

No. 120b, imperf., is without grill.

CANCELLATIONS.

		Red town	+150.00
Red	+75.00	"Paid All"	+100.00
Blue	+25.00	"Steamship"	+175.00
Black town	+50.00	Supp. Mail, A	+125.00

Shield, Eagle and Flags
A42

121	A42	30c **blue & carmine**, *May 15, 1869*	2,250.	225.00
		blue & dark carmine	2,250.	225.00
		On cover		11,000.
		Pair	4,600.	475.00
		Block of four	12,000.	1,150.
		a. Without grill, original gum	3,750.	
		a. Block of four	18,500.	
		b. Flags inverted	105,000.	45,000.
		Double grill	—	500.00
		Split grill	2,400.	250.00
		Double paper (without grill), original gum	2,750.	

CANCELLATIONS.

		Black town	+35.00
Red	+50.00	Steamship	+75.00
Blue	+10.00	"Steam"	+60.00
Brown	+25.00	Supplementary Mail	
Green	+400.00	Type A	+75.00
"Paid"	+50.00	Japan	+400.00
"Paid All"	+75.00	China	—

Lincoln
A43

122	A43	90c **carmine & black**	7,000.	1,200.
		carmine rose & black	7,000.	1,200.
		On cover		—
		Pair	16,000.	3,000.
		Block of four	65,000.	25,000.
		a. Without grill, original gum	13,500.	
		Split grill	—	—

Earliest known use: May 10, 1869.

CANCELLATIONS.

| | | Red | +200.00 |
| Blue | +100.00 | Black town | +200.00 |

THERE MUST BE A REASON

PROBITY

SAGACITY

ERUDITION

INTRINSICALITY

EFFICACIOUSNESS

The above are some rarely seen words for some of the many simple reasons so many collectors have bought and sold with confidence in William A. Fox Auctions for the past quarter of a century. Auction excellence clearly defined.

Whether buying or selling contact us.
We know you will be pleased with the results.

William A. Fox Auctions, Inc.
676 MORRIS AVENUE
SPRINGFIELD, NEW JERSEY 07081

TELEPHONE (201) 467-2366

POSTAGE, 1875, 1880, 1870-71

1875   RE-ISSUE OF 1869 ISSUE.
Issued for the Centennial Exposition of 1876.
Produced by the National Bank Note Co.
Perf. 12.
Without grill, hard white paper, with white crackly gum.
A new plate of 150 subjects was made for the 1c and for the frame of the 15c. The frame on the 15c is the same as type I but without the fringe of brown shading lines around central vignette.

123	A34	1c buff (*8252)	325.00	225.00
		Block of four	1,850.	
		On cover		1,250.
124	A35	2c brown (4755)	375.00	325.00
		Block of four	2,250.	
125	A36	3c blue (1406)	3,000.	1,400.

CANCELLATION.

			Supplementary Mail Type F	—
126	A37	6c blue (2226)	850.00	550.00
		Block of four	12,500.	
127	A38	10c yellow (1947)	1,400.	1,200.
		Block of four	9,000.	
128	A39	12c green (1584)	1,500.	1,200.
		Block of four	12,500.	
129	A40	15c brown & blue, Type III, (1981)	1,300.	550.00
		Block of four	20,000.	
		a. Imperf. horizontally	1,600.	
130	A41	24c green & violet (2091)	1,250.	550.00
131	A42	30c blue & carmine (1535)	1,750.	1,000.
132	A43	90c carmine & black (1356)	5,500.	6,000.
		Block of four	32,500.	

Numbers in parentheses are quantities issued.
*This quantity probably includes the 1880 Re-issue No. 133.

1880   RE-ISSUE OF 1869 ISSUE.
Produced by the American Bank Note Co.
Without grill, soft porous paper.

133	A34	1c **buff**, issued with gum	200.00	135.00
		Block of four, with gum	950.00	
		a. 1c brown orange, issued without gum	175.00	120.00
		a. Block of four, without gum	800.00	
		Margin block of 10, Impt. & P#	17,500.	
		On cover		1,850.

1870-71
Produced by the National Bank Note Company.
Plates of 200 subjects in two panes of 100 each.
Perf. 12

Franklin
A44

A44

Jackson
A45

A45

Washington
A46

A46

Lincoln
A47

A47

Edwin M. Stanton
A48

A48

Jefferson
A49

A49

Henry Clay
A50

A50

Daniel Webster
A51

A51

Two varieties of grill are known on this issue.

H. Grill about 10x12 mm. (11 to 13 by 14 to 16 points.) On all values 1c to 90c.

I. Grill about 8½x10 mm. (10 to 11 by 10 to 13 points.) On 1, 2, 3, 6 and 7c.

On the 1870–71 stamps the grill impressions are usually faint or incomplete. This is especially true of the H grill, which often shows only a few points.

Prices are for stamps showing well defined grills.

Killer cancellation of the oval grid type with letters or numeral centers was first used in 1876 Bank Note issues. By order of the Postmaster-General (July 23, 1860) it was prohibited to use the town mark as a cancelling instrument, and a joined town and killer cancellation was developed.

Numeral cancellations—see "Postal Markings—Examples."

White Wove Paper, Thin to Medium Thick.

134	A44	1c **ultramarine,** *April 1870*	450.00	50.00
		pale ultramarine	450.00	50.00
		dark ultramarine	450.00	50.00
		On cover		75.00
		Pair	925.00	105.00
		Block of four	2,000.	300.00
		Double transfer	475.00	60.00
		Double grill		110.00
		Split grill	500.00	60.00
		Quadruple split grill		175.00
		End roller grill		300.00

CANCELLATIONS.

		"Paid"	+10.00
Blue	+2.50	"Paid All"	+20.00
Red	+10.00	"Steamship"	+45.00
Green	+100.00		

135	A45	2c **red brown,** *April 1870*	300.00	35.00
		pale red brown	300.00	35.00
		dark red brown	300.00	35.00
		On cover		55.00
		Pair	610.00	72.50
		Block of four	1,300.	200.00
	a.	Diagonal half used as 1c on cover		
		Double grill	450.00	70.00
		Split grill	325.00	40.00
		Quadruple split grill	*1,000.*	120.00
		End roller grill	*650.00*	225.00

CANCELLATIONS.

		"Paid"	+5.00
Blue	+1.00	"Paid All"	+10.00
Red	+5.00	Numeral	+5.00
Brown	+3.00	China	
Green	+100.00		

POSTAGE, 1870-71

136	A46	3c **green,** *April 12, 1870*	250.00	9.50
		pale green	250.00	9.50
		yellow green	250.00	9.50
		deep green	250.00	9.50
		On cover		15.00
		Pair	510.00	19.00
		Block of four	1,100.	75.00
		Margin block of 10, Impt. & P#	5,000.	
		Margin block of 12, Impt. & P#	6,000.	
		Printed on both sides	—	
		Double transfer	—	11.00
		Double grill	400.00	40.00
		Split grill	275.00	9.50
		Quadruple split grill	—	60.00
		End roller grill	—	150.00
		Cracked plate	—	45.00
		b. Imperf., pair	1,200.	—
		b. Margin block of 12, Impt. & P#	—	

CANCELLATIONS.
Blue	+.25	"Paid"	+2.50
Purple	+2.50	Railroad	+10.00
Magenta	+2.50	"Steamship"	+20.00
Red	+3.50	"Paid All"	+15.00
Orange	+3.50	Numeral	+4.00
Brown	+1.50	"Free"	+25.00
Green	+45.00		

137	A47	6c **carmine,** *April 1870*	1,500.	250.00
		pale carmine	1,500.	250.00
		carmine rose	1,500.	250.00
		On cover		500.00
		Pair	3,100.	525.00
		Block of four	7,250.	
		Double grill	—	450.00
		Split grill	1,550.	275.00
		Quadruple split grill	—	500.00
		End roller grill	2,750.	550.00

CANCELLATIONS.
Blue	+5.00	" Paid "	+35.00
Red	+35.00		

138	A48	7c **vermilion,** *Mar. 1871*	1,000.	225.00
		deep vermilion	1,000.	225.00
		On cover		450.00
		Pair	2,100.	475.00
		Block of four	4,750.	
		Double grill	—	400.00
		Split grill	1,050.	250.00
		Quadruple split grill	—	450.00
		End roller grill	—	500.00

CANCELLATIONS.
Blue	+5.00	Red	+35.00
Purple	+20.00	Green	+200.00
		"Paid"	+25.00

The 7c stamps, Nos. 138 and 149, were issued for a 7c rate of July 1, 1870, to Prussia, German States and Austria, including Hungary, via Hamburg (on the Hamburg-American Line steamers), or Bremen (on North German Lloyd ships), but issue was delayed by the Franco-Prussian War. The rate for this service was reduced to 6c in 1871. For several months there was no 7c rate, but late in 1871 the Prussian closed mail rate via England was reduced to 7c which revived an important use for the 7c stamps. The rate to Denmark direct via Baltic Lloyd ships, or via Bremen and Hamburg as above, was 7c from Jan. 1, 1872.

139	A49	10c **brown,** *April 1870*	1,350.	375.00
		yellow brown	1,350.	375.00
		dark brown	1,350.	375.00
		On cover		700.00
		Pair	2,800.	800.00
		Block of four	10,000.	
		Double grill	—	750.00
		Split grill	1,400.	400.00
		End roller grill		800.00

CANCELLATIONS.
Blue	+5.00	"Steamship"	+50.00
Red	+30.00	"Honolulu Paid All"	—

140	A50	12c **dull violet,** *April 18, 1870*	12,000.	1,500.
		On cover		4,500.
		Pair	25,000.	3,200.
		Block of four	55,000.	
		Split grill	—	1,600.
		End roller grill	—	4,500.

CANCELLATIONS.
Blue	+50.00	"Paid all"	—
Red	+100.00		

141	A51	15c **orange,** *April 1870*	1,700.	675.00
		bright orange	1,700.	675.00
		deep orange	1,700.	675.00
		On cover		1,350.
		Pair	3,500.	1,450.
		Block of four	10,000.	
		Double grill	—	—
		Split grill	1,850.	725.00

CANCELLATIONS.
Blue	+10.00	Red	+75.00
Purple	+50.00	Green	+300.00

General Winfield Scott
A52

142	A52	24c **purple**	—	10,500.
		On cover		
		Block of four		
		Split grill		

CANCELLATIONS
Red	+500.00	

Alexander Hamilton
A53

143	A53	30c **black,** *April 1870*	3,750.	800.00
		full black	3,750.	800.00
		On cover		2,000.
		Pair	7,750.	1,750.
		Block of four	18,000.	
		Double grill	—	—
		End roller grill		1,750.

CANCELLATIONS.
Blue	+25.00	
Red	+100.00	

POSTAGE, 1870-71   121

Commodore Oliver Hazard Perry
A54

144	A54	90c **carmine,** *April 12, 1870*		5,000.	700.00
		dark carmine		5,000.	700.00
		On cover			
		Pair		10,500.	1,500.
		Block of four		25,000.	4,000.
		Double grill			
		Split grill			750.00

CANCELLATIONS.

Blue	+25.00
Red	+75.00

1870–71 Produced by the National Bank Note Co.

White Wove Paper, Thin to Medium Thick.

Perf. 12.

Issued (except 3c and 7c) in April, 1870.

Without Grill.

145	A44	1c **ultramarine**		145.00	6.50
		pale ultramarine		145.00	6.50
		dark ultramarine		145.00	6.50
		gray blue		145.00	6.50
		On cover			10.00
		Pair		300.00	14.00
		Block of four		625.00	50.00
		Double transfer			9.00
		Worn plate		145.00	6.50

CANCELLATIONS.

Blue	+.25	"Paid"	+3.00
Ultramarine	+1.50	"Paid All"	+15.00
Magenta	+1.00	"Steamship"	+25.00
Purple	+1.00	Railroad	+20.00
Brown	+1.00	Numeral	+2.00
Red	+3.00		
Green	+55.00		

146	A45	2c **red brown**		50.00	4.50
		pale red brown		50.00	4.50
		dark red brown		50.00	4.50
		orange brown		52.50	4.75
		On cover			6.50
		Pair		105.00	9.25
		Block of four		225.00	30.00
	a.	Half used as 1c on cover, diagonal or vertical			
	c.	Double impression			
		Double transfer			6.00

CANCELLATIONS.

Blue	+.10	"Paid"	+2.00
Purple	+.75	"Paid All"	+10.00
Red	+2.50	Numeral	+2.00
Green	+55.00	"Steamship"	+22.50
Brown	+1.00	Black Carrier	+12.50
		Japan	
		China	
		Curacao	

147	A46	3c **green,** *Mar. 13, 1870*		100.00	50
		pale green		100.00	50
		dark green		100.00	50
		yellow green		105.00	55
		On cover			1.00
		Pair		205.00	1.05
		Block of four		425.00	9.00
		Margin block of 10, Impt. & P#		1,750.	
	a.	Printed on both sides			1,500.
	b.	Double impression			1,000.
		Double transfer			4.50
		Short transfer at bottom		92.50	75
		Cracked plate			25.00
		Worn plate		90.00	50
	c.	Imperf., pair		700.00	
	c.	Margin block of 10, Impt. & P#			

CANCELLATIONS.

Blue	+.5	"Paid"	+2.00
Purple	+.35	"Paid All"	+10.00
Magenta	+.35	"Free"	+15.00
Brown	+1.50	Numeral	+2.00
Red	+2.50	Railroad	+10.00
Ultramarine	+2.00	Express Company	
Green	+35.00	"Steamboat"	+20.00
		"Steamship"	+17.50
		Ship	+15.00
		Japan	+75.00

148	A47	6c **carmine**		185.00	12.00
		dark carmine		185.00	12.00
		rose		185.00	12.00
		brown carmine		185.00	12.00
		violet carmine		210.00	15.00
		On cover			30.00
		Pair		375.00	24.50
		Block of four		850.00	125.00
	a.	Vertical half used as 3c on cover			
	b.	Double impression			1,250.
		Double transfer			
		Double paper			

CANCELLATIONS.

Blue	+.25	"Paid"	+3.00
Purple	+1.00	"Steamship"	+25.00
Violet	+1.00	"Paid All"	+15.00
Ultramarine	+2.00	Numeral	
Brown	+1.00	Supplementary Mail	
Red	+3.00	Type A or D	+25.00
Green	+90.00	China	
		Japan	+150.00

149	A48	7c **vermilion,** *Mar. 1871*		300.00	50.00
		deep vermilion		300.00	50.00
		On cover			110.00
		Pair		625.00	105.00
		Block of four		1,400.	450.00
		Cracked plate			

CANCELLATIONS.

Blue	+2.50	Ultramarine	+12.50
Purple	+7.50	Red	+10.00
		Japan	+150.00

150	A49	10c **brown**		185.00	12.00
		dark brown		185.00	12.00
		yellow brown		185.00	12.00
		On cover			27.50
		Pair		375.00	25.00
		Block of four		900.00	125.00
		Margin block of 10, Impt. & P#			
		Double transfer			47.50

CANCELLATIONS.

Blue	+.25	Brown	+3.00
Purple	+2.00	"Paid All"	+20.00
Magenta	+2.00	"Steamship"	+20.00
Ultramarine	+4.00	Supplementary Mail	
Red	+4.00	Type A or D	+25.00
Green	+120.00	Japan	+120.00
Orange	+4.00	China	
		St. Thomas	

POSTAGE, 1870-71, 1873

151	A50	12c	**dull violet**	475.00	55.00
			violet	475.00	55.00
			dark violet	475.00	55.00
			On cover		350.00
			Pair	975.00	115.00
			Block of four	2,750.	600.00

CANCELLATIONS.

Blue	+2.50	"Paid All"	+25.00
Magenta	+7.50	"Steamship"	+50.00
Red	+10.00	Supplementary Mail	
Green	+150.00	Type A or D	+40.00

152	A51	15c	**bright orange**	450.00	55.00
			deep orange	450.00	55.00
			On cover		225.00
			Pair	925.00	115.00
			Block of four	2,000.	550.00

CANCELLATIONS.

Blue	+2.50	"Paid"	+12.50
Magenta	+7.50	"Steamship"	+40.00
Ultramarine	+10.00	Supplementary Mail	
Red	+12.50	Type A or F	+30.00
		China	

153	A52	24c	**purple**	525.00	75.00
			bright purple	525.00	75.00
			On cover		1,600.
			Pair	1,100.	175.00
			Block of four	4,500.	2,500.
			Double paper		

CANCELLATIONS.

Red	+10.00	"Paid"	+25.00
Blue	+2.50	Town	+15.00
Purple	+7.50	"Steamship"	
China		Supplementary Mail	
		Types A, D or F	+30.00

154	A53	30c	**black**	900.00	85.00
			full black	900.00	85.00
			On cover		700.00
			Pair	1,850.	185.00
			Block of four	7,000.	

CANCELLATIONS.

Magenta	+15.00	"Steamship"	+55.00
Red	+25.00	Supplementary Mail	
Brown	+15.00	Type A	+40.00
Blue	+2.50		

155	A54	90c	**carmine**	1,100.	165.00
			dark carmine	1,100.	165.00
			On cover		
			Pair	2,250.	340.00
			Block of four	7,000.	1,100.

CANCELLATIONS.

Blue	+5.00	Town	+20.00
Purple	+15.00	Supplementary Mail	
Magenta	+15.00	Type A or F	+40.00
Green	+275.00	Japan	
Red	+30.00		

1873 Printed by the Continental Bank Note Co.

Plates of 200 subjects in two panes of 100 each.

Issued in July (?), 1873.

Perf. 12.

Designs of the 1870-71 Issue with secret marks on the values from 1c to 15c, as described and illustrated:

The object of secret marks was to provide a simple and positive proof that these stamps were produced by the Continental Bank Note Company and not by their predecessors.

Franklin
A44a

1c. In the pearl at the left of the numeral "1" there is a small crescent.

Jackson
A45a

2c. Under the scroll at the left of "U. S." there is a small diagonal line. This mark seldom shows clearly. The stamp, No. 157, can be distinguished by its color.

Washington
A46a

3c. The under part of the upper tail of the left ribbon is heavily shaded.

Lincoln
A47a

6c. The first four vertical lines of the shading in the lower part of the left ribbon have been strengthened.

Stanton
A48a

7c. Two small semi-circles are drawn around the ends of the lines which outline the ball in the lower right hand corner.

Jefferson
A49a

10c. There is a small semi-circle in the scroll at the right end of the upper label.

Clay
A50a

12c. The balls of the figure "2" are crescent shaped.

POSTAGE, 1873

Webster
A51a

15c. In the lower part of the triangle in the upper left corner two lines have been made heavier forming a "V". This mark can be found on some of the Continental and American (1879) printings, but not all stamps show it.

Secret marks were added to the dies of the 24c, 30c and 90c but new plates were not made from them. The various printings of the 30c and 90c can be distinguished only by the shades and paper.

J. Grill about 7x9½mm. exists on all values except 90c. Grill was composed of truncated pyramids and was so strongly impressed that some points often broke through the paper.

White Wove Paper, Thin to Thick.
Without Grill

156	A44a	1c **ultramarine**	45.00	1.75
		pale ultramarine	45.00	1.75
		dark ultramarine	50.00	1.75
		gray blue	45.00	1.75
		blue	45.00	1.75
		On cover		3.00
		Pair	92.50	3.75
		Block of four	200.00	20.00
		Margin block of 12, Impt. & P#	2,500.	
		Double transfer	55.00	4.00
		Double paper	200.00	
		Ribbed paper	50.00	2.50
		Paper with silk fibers		15.00
	e.	With grill	1,100.	
		Cracked plate		
	f.	Imperf., pair		500.00
		Paper cut with "cogwheel" punch	275.00	

CANCELLATIONS.

Blue	+10	Railroad	+12.00
Purple	+35	"Free"	+12.00
Magenta	+35	Black carrier	+15.00
Ultramarine	+1.00	Numeral	+2.50
Red	+3.50	Alaska	
Orange	+3.50	Japan	
Brown	+1.50	Printed "G."	
Green	+60.00	Precancellation	
"Paid All"	+7.00	(Glastonbury, Conn.)	+200.00
"Paid"	+1.00	Printed Star Precancellation (Glen Allen, Va.)	+100.00

157	A45a	2c **brown**	130.00	7.00
		dark brown	130.00	7.00
		dark reddish brown	130.00	7.00
		yellowish brown	130.00	7.00
		With secret mark	140.00	7.50
		On cover		12.50
		Pair	265.00	14.50
		Block of four	600.00	70.00
		Margin block of 12, Impt. & P#		
		Margin block of 14, Impt. & P( )		
		Double paper	200.00	20.00
		Ribbed paper	140.00	8.50
	c.	With grill	850.00	600.00
	d.	Double impression		
	e.	Vertical half used as 1c on cover		
		Double transfer		9.50

CANCELLATIONS.

Blue	+.25	"P. D." in circle	+15.00
Magenta	+1.00	Town	+2.00
Purple	+1.00	Numeral	+1.50
Red	+1.00	Black Carrier	+8.50
Orange	+3.50	"Steamship"	+15.00
Green	+60.00	Supplementary Mail	
"Paid"	+2.50	Type F	+5.00
"Insufficiently Paid"		China	
		Japan	+100.00
"Paid All"	+13.50	Printed Star Precancellation (Glen Allen, Va.)	

158	A46a	3c **green**	35.00	15
		bluish green	35.00	15
		yellow green	35.00	15
		dark yellow green	35.00	10
		dark green	35.00	15
		olive green	45.00	2.50
		On cover		30
		Pair	72.50	35
		Block of four	160.00	7.50
		Margin strip of 5, Impt. & P#	225.00	
		Margin strip of 6, Impt. & P#	300.00	
		Margin block of 10, Impt. & P#	1,300.	
		Margin block of 12, Impt. & P#	2,000.	
		Margin block of 14, Impt. & P#	2,650.	
		Double paper	65.00	5.00
		Paper cut with "cogwheel" punch	150.00	150.00
		Ribbed paper	40.00	1.00
		Paper with silk fibers		4.00
	e.	With grill	150.00	
		End roller grill	300.00	200.00
	f.	Imperf. with grill (pair)	600.00	
	g.	Imperf. without grill (pair)	700.00	
	h.	Horizontal pair, imperf. vert.		
	i.	Horizontal pair, imperf. between		1,300.
	j.	Double impression		600.00
	k.	Printed on both sides		
		Cracked plate		27.50
		Double transfer		4.00
		Short transfer		2.25

CANCELLATIONS.

Blue	+2	Railroad	+7.00
Magenta	+20	"R. P. O."	+1.50
Purple	+20	"P. D." in circle	
Ultramarine	+1.25	"Steamboat"	
Red	+2.50	"Steamship"	
Orange	+2.50	Supplementary Mail	
Green	+25.00	Type D	+11.00
Town	+5	Supplementary Mail	
"Paid"	+2.50	Type F	+8.50
"Paid All"	+20.00	Express Company	
"Free"	+15.00	Black Carrier	+8.00
Numeral	+1.00	Red Carrier	+25.00
China		Japan	+65.00
		Alaska	

159	A47a	6c **dull pink**	175.00	8.00
		brown rose	175.00	8.00
		On cover		35.00
		Pair	360.00	16.50
		Block of four	775.00	85.00
		Margin block of 12, Impt. & P#	12,000.	
		Double paper		9.00
		Ribbed paper		9.00
		Paper with silk fibers		25.00
	b.	With grill	600.00	
		End roller grill	1,000.	

CANCELLATIONS.

Blue	+25	"Paid"	+7.00
Magenta	+1.50	"Paid All"	
Purple	+1.50	Supplementary Mail	
Ultramarine	+2.50	Types D, E or F	+15.00
Red	+6.50	Japan	+100.00
Green	+80.00	China	
Numeral	+1.50	Railroad	
		"R. P. O."	+2.00

160	A48a	7c **orange vermilion**	375.00	55.00
		vermilion	375.00	55.00
		On cover		300.00
		Pair	775.00	115.00
		Block of four	1,700.	
		Margin block of 12, Impt. & P#		
	a.	With grill	1,350.	
		Double transfer of "7 cents" (1R XXII)		150.00
		Double transfer in lower left corner		70.00
		Double paper		
		Ribbed paper		70.00
		Paper with silk fibers		90.00

CANCELLATIONS.

Blue	+2.50	Purple	+10.00
Red	+7.50	Brown	+5.00
		"Paid"	+15.00

161	A49a	10c **brown**	175.00	9.00
		dark brown	175.00	9.00
		yellow brown	175.00	9.00
		On cover		25.00
		Pair	360.00	18.50
		Block of four	800.00	85.00
		Margin block of 10, Impt. & P#	6,500.	
		Block of 12, Impt. & P#	7,500.	

POSTAGE, 1873, 1875

Double paper		300.00	
Ribbed paper		——	15.00
Paper with silk fibers		——	20.00
c. With grill		1,750.	
d. Horizontal pair, imperf. between		——	2,500.
Double transfer		——	25.00

CANCELLATIONS.

Blue	+.50	"Paid"	+4.00
Purple	+1.50	"P. D." in circle	+20.00
Red	+4.00	"Steamship"	+15.00
Magenta	+1.50	Supplementary Mail	
Orange	+4.00	Type E	+7.00
Brown	+1.50	Supplementary Mail	
Green	+100.00	Type F	+2.50
		Japan	+100.00
		China	——
		Alaska	——

162	A50a	12c **blackish violet**		550.00	60.00
		On cover			300.00
		Pair		1,150.	125.00
		Block of four		3,000.	600.00
		a. With grill		3,000.	
		Ribbed paper		——	60.00

CANCELLATIONS.

Blue	+2.50	Supplementary Mail	
Ultramarine	+15.00	Type D	+15.00
Brown	+5.00	Japan	+200.00
Red	+15.00		

163	A51a	15c **yellow orange**		525.00	50.00
		pale orange		525.00	50.00
		reddish orange		525.00	50.00
		On cover			250.00
		Pair		1,100.	105.00
		Block of four		2,700.	500.00
		Double paper		——	
		Paper with silk fibers		650.00	70.00
		Vertical ribbed paper		575.00	60.00
		a. With grill		3,000.	

CANCELLATIONS.

Blue	+2.50	Supplementary Mail	
Purple	+10.00	Type F	+10.00
Red	+15.00	"Steamship"	——
		Numeral	+7.50
		Puerto Rico	——
		China	——

It is generally accepted as fact that the Continental Bank Note Co. printed and delivered a quantity of 24c stamps. They are impossible to distinguish from those printed by the National Bank Note Co.

165	A53	30c **gray black**		550.00	50.00
		greenish black		550.00	50.00
		On cover			650.00
		Pair		1,150.	105.00
		Block of four		2,750.	550.00
		Double transfer		——	65.00
		Double paper		——	
		Ribbed paper		600.00	60.00
		Paper with silk fibers		——	——
		c. With grill		3,000.	

CANCELLATIONS.

Purple	+7.50	"Steamship"	——
Blue	+2.50	Supplementary Mail	
Red	+15.00	Type E	+10.00
Brown	+7.50	Supplementary Mail	
Magenta	+7.50	Type F	+5.00

166	A54	90c **rose carmine**		1,150.	170.00
		pale rose carmine		1,150.	170.00
		On cover			7,500.
		Pair		2,400.	360.00
		Block of four		5,500.	1,750.

CANCELLATIONS.

Blue	+10.00	Supplementary Mail	
Purple	+15.00	Type F	+30.00
Red	+30.00		

SPECIAL PRINTING OF 1873 ISSUE.
Produced by the Continental Bank Note Co.
Issued for the Centennial Exposition of 1876.

1875 *Perf. 12.*
Hard, white wove paper, without gum.

167	A44a	1c ultramarine	7,000.	
168	A45a	2c dark brown	3,250.	
169	A46a	3c blue green	9,000.	——
		On cover		——
170	A47a	6c dull rose	8,000.	
171	A48a	7c reddish vermilion	2,000.	
172	A49a	10c pale brown	7,500.	
173	A50a	12c dark violet	2,750.	
		Horizontal pair	——	
174	A51a	15c bright orange	7,500.	
175	A52	24c dull purple	1,750.	
		Horizontal pair	——	
176	A53	30c greenish black	6,750.	
177	A54	90c violet carmine	6,750.	

Although perforated, these stamps were usually cut apart with scissors. As a result, the perforations are often much mutilated and the design is frequently damaged.

These can be distinguished from the 1873 issue by the shades; also by the paper, which is very white instead of yellowish.

These and the subsequent issues listed under the heading of "Special Printings" are special printings of stamps then in current use which, together with the reprints and re-issues, were made for sale to collectors. They were available for postage.

REGULAR ISSUE.
Printed by the Continental Bank Note Co.

1875 Yellowish Wove Paper. *Perf. 12*

178	A45a	2c **vermilion**, *June 1875*		135.00	4.50
		On cover			8.50
		Pair		275.00	9.50
		Block of four		575.00	60.00
		Margin block of 12, Impt. & P#		——	
		Margin block of 14, Impt. & P#		——	
		a. Imperf., (pair)		600.00	
		b. Margin block of 12, Impt. & P#		——	
		b. Half used as 1c on cover		——	
		Double transfer		——	——
		Double paper		——	——
		Ribbed paper		——	——
		c. With grill		250.00	
		Paper with silk fibers		175.00	7.50

CANCELLATIONS.

Blue	+10	"Paid"	+8.00
Purple	+25	"Steamship"	——
Magenta	+25	Supplementary Mail	
Red	+6.00	Type F	+5.50
		Black Carrier	+15.00
		Railroad	+12.50

Zachary Taylor
A55

179	A55	5c **blue**, *June 1875*		150.00	8.00
		dark blue		150.00	8.00
		bright blue		150.00	8.00
		light blue		150.00	8.00
		greenish blue		165.00	9.50
		On cover			20.00
		Pair		310.00	17.50
		Block of four		650.00	100.00
		Cracked plate		——	100.00
		Double transfer		——	13.50
		Double paper		200.00	
		Ribbed paper		——	——
		c. With grill		300.00	
		End roller grill		——	
		Paper with silk fibers		——	15.00

POSTAGE, 1875, 1879 125

CANCELLATIONS.			
Blue	+25	Railroad	+17.50
Ultramarine	+3.00	"Steamship"	+12.50
Purple	+1.50	Ship	+12.50
Magenta	+1.50	Supplementary Mail	
Red	+5.00	Type E	+5.00
Green	+70.00	Supplementary Mail	
Numeral	+5.00	Type F	+2.00
		China	—
		Japan	+100.00
		Peru	—

The five cent rate to foreign countries in the Universal Postal Union began on July 1, 1875. No. 179 was issued for that purpose.

1875 SPECIAL PRINTING OF 1875 ISSUE

Produced by the **Continental Bank Note Co.**
Issued for the Centennial Exposition of 1876.
Hard, White Wove Paper, without gum.

| 180 | A45a | 2c carmine vermilion | 17,000. | |
| 181 | A55 | 5c bright blue | 32,500. | |

1879 Printed by the **American Bank Note Company.**

The Continental Bank Note Co. was consolidated with the American Bank Note Co. on February 4, 1879. The American Bank Note Company used many plates of the Continental Bank Note Company to print the ordinary postage, Departmental and Newspaper stamps. Therefore, stamps bearing the Continental Company's imprint were not always its product.

The A. B. N. Co. also used the 30c and 90c plates of the N. B. N. Co. Some of No. 190 and all of No. 217 were from. A. B. N. Co. plate 405.

Early printings of No. 188 were from Continental plates 302 and 303 which contained the normal secret mark of 1873. After those plates were re-entered by the A. B. N. Co. in 1880, pairs or multiple pieces contained combinations of normal, hairline or missing marks. The pairs or other multiples usually found contain at least one hairline mark which tended to disappear as the plate wore.

A. B. N. Co. plates 377 and 378 were made in 1881 from the National transfer roll of 1870. No. 187 from these plates has no secret mark.

SAME AS 1870-75 ISSUES.
Perf. 12.
Soft Porous Paper.

182	A44a	1c **dark ultramarine**	100.00	1.20
		blue	100.00	1.20
		gray blue	100.00	1.20
		On cover		1.75
		Pair	205.00	2.50
		Block of four	425.00	25.00
		Margin block of 10, Impt. & P#	3,250.	
		Double transfer	—	5.00

CANCELLATIONS.			
Blue	+5	Railroad	+12.50
Magenta	+10	Printed "G,"	
Purple	+10	Precancellation	
Red	+7.00	(Glastonbury,	
Green	+35.00	Conn.)	+100.00
"Paid"	+4.00	Printed Star	
Supplementary		Precancellation	
Mail Type F	+10.00	(Glen Allen, Va.)	+75.00

183	A45a	2c **vermilion**	45.00	1.20
		orange vermilion	45.00	1.20
		On cover		1.75
		Pair	90.00	2.50
		Block of four	200.00	20.00
		Margin block of 10, Impt. & P#	1,250.	
		Margin block of 12, Impt. & P#	1,700.	
	a.	Double impression	—	500.00
		Double transfer		

CANCELLATIONS.			
Blue	+10	Numeral	+4.00
Purple	+20	Railroad	+15.00
Magenta	+20	Supplementary Mail	
Red	+6.00	Type F	+8.00
"Paid"	+5.00	China	—
"Paid All"	—	Printed Star	
"Ship"	—	Precancellation	
		(Glen Allen, Va.)	—

184	A46a	3c **green**	37.50	10
		light green	37.50	10
		dark green	37.50	10
		On cover		20
		Pair	75.00	20
		Block of four	155.00	6.00
		Margin block of 10, Impt. & P#	900.00	
		Margin block of 12, Impt. & P#	1,100.	
		Margin block of 14, Impt. & P#	1,400.	
	a.	Imperf., pair	500.00	
	b.	Double impression		
		Double transfer	—	4.00
		Short transfer	—	5.00

CANCELLATIONS.			
Blue	+2	Numeral	+2.00
Magenta	+15	Railroad	+12.50
Purple	+15	"Steamboat"	—
Violet	+15	Supplementary Mail	
Brown	+1.00	Type F	+8.00
Red	+7.50	Printed Star	
Green	+25.00	Precancellation	
"Paid"	+3.00	(Glen Allen,	
"Free"	+15.00	Va.)	—
		China	+60.00

185	A55	5c **blue**	190.00	7.50
		light blue	190.00	7.50
		bright blue	190.00	7.50
		dark blue	190.00	7.50
		On cover		17.50
		Pair	390.00	15.50
		Block of four	825.00	100.00
		Margin block of 12, Impt. & P#	5,000.	

CANCELLATIONS.			
Blue	+25	Numeral	+2.00
Purple	+1.00	Supplementary Mail	
Magenta	+1.00	Type F	+1.50
Ultramarine	+3.50	"Steamship"	+35.00
Red	+7.50	China	+60.00
Railroad	+20.00	Peru	—
		Panama	—

186	A47a	6c **pink**	400.00	11.00
		dull pink	400.00	11.00
		brown rose	400.00	11.00
		On cover		30.00
		Pair	825.00	22.50
		Block of four	1,800.	300.00

CANCELLATIONS.			
Blue	+50	Supplementary Mail	
Purple	+1.00	Type F	+4.00
Magenta	+1.00	Railroad	+22.50
Red	+12.00	Numeral	+4.00
		China	+70.00

187	A49	10c **brown**, *without secret mark*	650.00	13.00
		yellow brown	650.00	13.00
		On cover		30.00
		Pair	1,350.	27.00
		Block of four	3,250.	
		Double transfer	—	25.00

CANCELLATIONS.			
Blue	+50	"Paid"	+3.50
Magenta	+1.50	Supplementary Mail	
Red	+10.00	Type F	+3.00
		China	+70.00

188	A49a	10c **brown**, *with secret mark*	375.00	14.00
		yellow brown	375.00	14.00
		black brown	450.00	22.50
		On cover		25.00
		Pair	775.00	29.00
		Block of four	1,750.	120.00
		Pair, one stamp No. 187		150.00
	c.	Vertical pair, imperf. between		
		Double transfer	—	25.00
		Cracked plate		

CANCELLATIONS			
Blue	+50	Red	+10.00
Ultramarine	+3.00	Green	+70.00
Purple	+2.00	"Paid"	+7.50
Magenta	+2.00	Supp. Mail Type F	+5.00
		Numeral	+3.00

POSTAGE, 1879, 1880, 1882, 1881-82

189	A51a	15c **red orange**	150.00	14.00
		orange	150.00	14.00
		yellow orange	150.00	14.00
		On cover		75.00
		Pair	310.00	29.00
		Block of four	650.00	100.00
		Margin block of 12, Impt. & P#	6,000.	

CANCELLATIONS.

		"Steamship"	+22.50
Blue	+1.00	Supplementary Mail	
Purple	+3.00	Type F	+5.00
Magenta	+3.00	Japan	+120.00
Ultramarine	+5.00	China	—
Red	+12.00		

190	A53	30c **full black**	450.00	25.00
		greenish black	450.00	25.00
		On cover		400.00
		Pair	875.00	52.50
		Block of four	1,850.	200.00
		Margin block of 10, Impt. & P#	8,250.	

CANCELLATIONS.

		Supplementary Mail	
Blue	+1.50	Type F	+6.00
Purple	+3.00	"Steamship"	+35.00
Magenta	+3.00	Tahiti	—
Red	+20.00	Samoa	—

191	A54	90c **carmine**	1,000.	140.00
		rose	1,000.	140.00
		carmine rose	1,000.	140.00
		On cover		5,000.
		Pair	2,050.	290.00
		Block of four	4,750.	675.00
	b.	Imperf., pair	3,250.	

CANCELLATIONS.

		Red	+35.00
Blue	+10.00	Supplementary Mail	
Purple	+20.00	Type F	+20.00

No. 191b, imperforate, was not regularly issued.

SPECIAL PRINTING OF 1879 ISSUE.
Produced by the American Bank Note Co.

1880   Perf. 12

Soft porous paper, without gum.

192	A44a	1c dark ultramarine	8,500.
193	A45a	2c black brown	5,500.
194	A46a	3c blue green	13,000.
195	A47a	6c dull rose	9,000.
196	A48a	7c scarlet vermilion	2,000.
197	A49a	10c deep brown	8,500.
198	A50a	12c blackish purple	4,000.
199	A51a	15c orange	8,000.
200	A52	24c dark violet	2,750.
201	A53	30c greenish black	6,750.
202	A54	90c dull carmine	6,750.
203	A45a	2c scarlet vermilion	16,000.
204	A55	5c deep blue	28,500.

No. 197 was printed from Continental plate 302 (or 303) after plate was re-entered, therefore stamp may show normal, hairline or missing secret mark.

The Post Office Department did not keep separate records of the 1875 and 1880 Special Printings of the 1873 and 1879 issues, but the total quantity sold of both is recorded. The 1880 Special Printing is much the rarer.

Number Issued of 1875 and 1880 Special Printings.

1c ultramarine & dark ultramarine	(388)
2c dark brown & black brown	(416)
2c carmine vermilion & scarlet vermilion	(917)
3c blue green	(267)
5c bright blue & deep blue	(317)
6c dull rose	(185)
7c reddish vermilion & scarlet vermilion	(473)
10c pale brown & deep brown	(180)
12c dark violet & blackish purple	(282)
15c bright orange & orange	(169)
24c dull purple & dark violet	(286)
30c greenish black	(179)
90c violet carmine & dull carmine	(170)

REGULAR ISSUE.
Printed by the American Bank Note Co.

1882   Perf. 12

James A. Garfield
A56

205	A56	5c **yellow brown**, *April 10, 1882*	90.00	4.00
		brown	90.00	4.00
		gray brown	90.00	4.00
		On cover		12.50
		Pair	185.00	8.25
		Block of four	375.00	65.00
		Margin strip of 5, Impt. & P#	600.00	
		Margin strip of 6, Impt. & P#	750.00	
		Margin block of 12, Impt. & P#	3,500.	

CANCELLATIONS.

		Supplementary Mail	
Purple	+50	Type F	+2.50
Magenta	+50	Red Express Co.	—
Blue	+25	China	+125.00
Red	+7.00		
"Ship"	—	Samoa	+150.00
Numeral	+2.00	Puerto Rico	—

SPECIAL PRINTING.
Printed by the American Bank Note Co.

1882   Perf. 12

Soft porous paper, without gum.

205C	A56	5c gray brown	16,500.	
		Block of four	—	

DESIGNS OF 1873 RE-ENGRAVED.

A44b

1881-82

1c. The vertical lines in the upper part of the stamp have been so deepened that the background often appears to be solid. Lines of shading have been added to the upper arabesques.

206	A44b	1c **gray blue**, *August, 1881*	30.00	40
		ultramarine	30.00	40
		dull blue	30.00	40
		slate blue	30.00	40
		On cover		75
		Pair	62.50	85
		Block of four	130.00	10.00
		Margin strip of 5, Impt. & P#	225.00	
		Margin strip of 6, Impt. & P#	275.00	
		Margin block of 10, Impt. & P#	1,000.	
		Margin block of 12, Impt. & P#	1,250.	
		Double transfer	45.00	4.00
		Punched with eight small holes in a circle		175.00
		Margin block of 10, Impt. & P# (8-hole punch)	3,750.	

CANCELLATIONS.

		"Paid"	+4.75
Purple	+10	"Paid All"	+12.00
Magenta	+10	Numeral	+3.50
Blue	+20	Supp. Mail Type F	+5.00
Red	+3.00	Railroad	+10.0
Green	+35.00	Printed Star Precancel	
Orange	+3.00	(Glen Allen, Va.)	+55.0
		China	—

POSTAGE, 1881-82, 1883   127

A46b

3c. The shading at the sides of the central oval appears only about one-half the previous width. A short horizontal dash has been cut about 1 mm. below the "TS" of "CENTS".

207	A46b	3c **blue green,** *July 16, 1881*	35.00	12
		green	35.00	12
		yellow green	35.00	12
		On cover		35
		Pair	72.50	25
		Block of four	150.00	25.00
		Margin strip of 5, Impt. & P#	275.00	
		Margin block of 10, Impt. & P#	1,250.	
		Double transfer		7.50
		Cracked plate	—	
		Punched with eight small holes in a circle	200.00	

CANCELLATIONS.

Purple	+10	Numeral	+2.50
Magenta	+10	"Ship"	—
Blue	+25	Railroad	+5.00
Brown	+1.50	Supplementary Mail	
Red	+2.50	Type F	+8.00
"Paid"	+3.00	Printed Star	
"Paid All"	—	Precancellation (Glen Allen, Va.)	—

Lincoln
A47b

6c. On the original stamps four vertical lines can be counted from the edge of the panel to the outside of the stamp. On the re-engraved stamps there are but three lines in the same place.

208	A47b	6c **rose,** *June, 1882*	210.00	45.00
		dull rose	210.00	45.00
		On cover (rose)		125.00
		Pair (rose)	425.00	95.00
		Block of four (rose)	900.00	300.00
a.		6c brown red	185.00	55.00
		On cover (brown red)		175.00
		Pair (brown red)	375.00	120.00
		Block of four (brown red)	800.00	350.00
a.		Margin strip of 6, Impt. & P#	1,800.	
a.		Margin block of 10, Impt. & P#		
a.		Margin block of 12, Impt. & P#		
		Double transfer	275.00	60.00

CANCELLATIONS.

		Blue	+4.00
Magenta	+2.50	Red	+15.00
Purple	+2.50	Supp. Mail Type F	+10.00

Jefferson
A49b

10c. On the original stamps there are five vertical lines between the left side of the oval and the edge of the shield. There are only four lines on the re-engraved stamps. In the lower part of the latter, also, the horizontal lines of the background have been strengthened.

209	A49b	10c **brown,** *April, 1882*	67.50	2.25
		yellow brown	67.50	2.25
		orange brown	67.50	2.25
		purple brown	75.00	2.50
		olive brown	75.00	2.50
		On cover		7.50
		Pair	137.50	4.75
		Block of four	300.00	22.50
		Margin strip of 5, Impt. & P#	450.00	
		Margin strip of 6, Impt. & P#	575.00	
		Margin block of 10, Impt. & P#	1,850.	
		Margin block of 12, Impt. & P#	2,250.	
b.		10c black brown	90.00	6.75
		On cover		30.00
		Pair		17.50
		Block of four		
c.		Double impression		

CANCELLATIONS.

		"Paid"	+2.50
Purple	+25	Supplementary Mail	
Magenta	+25	Type F	+3.00
Blue	+75	Express Company	—
Red	+3.50	Japan	+75.00
Green	+35.00	China	—
Numeral	+2.00	Samoa	—

1883 Printed by the American Bank Note Company.

Perf. 12.

Washington
A57

Nos. 210-211 were issued to meet the reduced first class rate of 2 cents for each half ounce, and the double rate, which Congress approved Mar. 3, 1883, effective Oct. 1, 1883.

210	A57	2c **red brown,** *Oct. 1, 1883*	28.50	8
		dark red brown	28.50	8
		orange brown	28.50	8
		On cover		25
		Pair	58.50	20
		Block of four	120.00	9.00
		Margin strip of 5, Impt. & P#	190.00	
		Margin strip of 6, Impt. & P#	250.00	
		Margin block of 10, Impt. & P#	950.00	
		Margin block of 12, Impt. & P#	1,200.	
b.		Imperf., pair		
		Double transfer	35.00	1.25

CANCELLATIONS.

		Numeral	+2.50
Purple	+10	"Paid"	+3.00
Magenta	+10	Railroad	+5.00
Blue	+20	Express Company	—
Violet	+30	Supplementary Mail	
Brown	+30	Type F	+5.00
Red	+3.50	"Ship"	—
Green	+25.00	"Steamboat"	—
		China	—

Jackson
A58

211	A58	4c **blue green,** *Oct. 1, 1883*	130.00	7.50
		deep blue green	130.00	7.50
		On cover		40.00
		Pair	265.00	16.00
		Block of four	550.00	65.00
		Margin strip of 6, Impt. & P#	1,100.	
		Margin block of 12, Impt. & P#	4,000.	

POSTAGE, 1883, 1887, 1888

    a. Imperf. (pair) —
    Double transfer — —
    Cracked plate —

CANCELLATIONS.

		Blue	+1.00
Purple	+1.00	Numeral	+2.00
Magenta	+1.00	Supp. Mail Type F	+5.00
Green	+35.00		

SPECIAL PRINTING
Printed by the American Bank Note Company.

1883   *Perf. 12*

Soft porous paper.

211B	A57	2c **pale red brown**, with gum	700.00	—
		Block of four	3,000.	
		c. Horizontal pair, imperf. between	2,250.	
211D	A58	4c **deep blue green**, without gum	12,500.	

The quantity issued of Nos. *211B* and *211D* is not definitely known, but 2,000 of each were delivered.

REGULAR ISSUE.
Printed by the American Bank Note Company.

1887   *Perf. 12*

Franklin
A59

212	A59	1c **ultramarine**, *June 1887*	50.00	65
		bright ultramarine	50.00	65
		On cover		1.50
		Pair	100.00	1.35
		Block of four	210.00	20.00
		Margin strip of 5, Impt. & P#	325.00	
		Margin strip of 6, Impt. & P#	400.00	
		Margin block of 10, Impt. & P#	*1,200.*	
		Margin block of 12, Impt. & P#	*1,500.*	
		a. Imperf., pair	750.00	325.00
		Double transfer	—	

CANCELLATIONS.

		Numeral	+2.00
Purple	+10	Railroad	+10.00
Magenta	+10	Supplementary Mail	
Blue	+10	Type F	+5.00
Red	+5.50	China	—

213	A57	2c **green**, *Sept. 10, 1887*	20.00	8
		bright green	20.00	8
		dark green	20.00	8
		On cover		20
		Pair	41.00	18
		Block of four	90.00	7.50
		Margin strip of 5, Impt. & P#	130.00	
		Margin strip of 6, Impt. & P#	165.00	
		Margin block of 10, Impt. & P#	700.00	
		Margin block of 12, Impt. & P#	850.00	
		a. Imperf., pair	750.00	325.00
		b. Printed on both sides	—	
		Double transfer	—	3.00

CANCELLATIONS.

		Railroad	+12.00
Purple	+10	Numeral	+2.00
Magenta	+10	"Steam"	—
Blue	+90	"Steamboat"	—
Red	+5.00	Supp. Mail Type F	+7.50
Green	+25.00	China	—
"Paid"	+5.00	Japan	—

214	A46b	3c **vermilion**, *Oct. 3, 1887*	42.50	37.50
		On cover (single)		85.00
		Pair	87.50	80.00
		Block of four	180.00	200.00
		Margin strip of 5, Impt. & P#	275.00	
		Margin strip of 6, Impt. & P#	325.00	
		Margin block of 10, Impt. & P#	*1,100.*	
		Margin block of 12, Impt. & P#	*1,300.*	

CANCELLATIONS.

		Blue	+10.00
Purple	+5.00	Supplementary Mail	
Magenta	+5.00	Type F	+15.00
Green	+150.00	Railroad	+30.00

1888 Printed by the American Bank Note Company.

Perf. 12.

SAME AS 1870-83 ISSUES.

215	A58	4c **carmine**, *Nov. 1888*	130.00	11.00
		rose carmine	130.00	11.00
		pale rose	130.00	11.00
		On cover		35.00
		Pair	265.00	23.00
		Block of four	550.00	75.00
		Margin strip of 5, Impt. & P#	800.00	
		Margin strip of 6, Impt. & P#	*1,000.*	
		Margin block of 10, Impt. & P#	*3,500.*	
		Margin block of 12, Impt. & P#	*4,250.*	

CANCELLATIONS.

		Magenta	+2.00
Blue	+1.00	Supplementary Mail	
Red	+5.00	Type F	+5.00
Purple	+2.00		

216	A56	5c **indigo**, *Feb. 1888*	120.00	6.50
		deep blue	120.00	6.50
		On cover		25.00
		Pair	240.00	13.50
		Block of four	480.00	60.00
		Margin strip of 5, Impt. & P#	700.00	
		Margin strip of 6, Impt. & P#	850.00	
		Margin block of 10, Impt. & P#	*3,500.*	
		Margin block of 12, Impt. & P#	*4,000.*	
		b. Imperf., pair	*1,000.*	

CANCELLATIONS.

		Supplementary Mail	
Purple	+1.00	Type F	+3.00
Magenta	+1.00	China	+85.00
Blue	+1.00	Japan	+85.00
Samoa	—	Puerto Rico	+75.00

217	A53	30c **orange brown**, *Jan. 1888*	300.00	70.00
		deep orange brown	300.00	70.00
		On cover		*1,400.*
		Pair	625.00	150.00
		Block of four	*1,400.*	325.00
		Margin strip of 5, Impt. & P#	*2,100.*	
		Margin block of 10, Impt. & P#	*6,750.*	
		Margin block of 12, Impt. & P#	—	
		a. Imperf., pair	*1,350.*	

CANCELLATIONS.

		Supplementary Mail	
Blue	+5.00	Type F	+10.00
Magenta	+10.00	"Paid All"	+25.00
		"Paid"	+15.00

218	A54	90c **purple**, *Feb. 1888*	675.00	130.00
		bright purple	675.00	130.00
		On cover		*7,500.*
		Pair	*1,375.*	270.00
		Block of four	*3,000.*	600.00
		Margin strip of 5, Impt. & P#	*4,250.*	
		Margin block of 10, Impt. & P#	*22,500.*	
		Margin block of 12, Impt. & P#	—	
		a. Imperf., pair	—	

CANCELLATIONS.

		Supplementary Mail	
Blue	+10.00	Type F	+25.00
Purple	+15.00		

Nos. *216b*, *217a* and *218a* were not regularly issued.

POSTAGE, 1890-93

1890-93

Printed by the American Bank Note Company.

Plates for the 1c and 2c were of 400 subjects in four panes of 100 each. All other values were from plates of 200 subjects in two panes of 100 each.

Franklin
A60

Washington
A61

Jackson
A62

Lincoln
A63

Grant
A64

Garfield
A65

William T. Sherman
A66

Daniel Webster
A67

Henry Clay
A68

Jefferson
A69

Perry
A70

Perf. 12.

219	A60	1c **dull blue,** *Feb. 22, 1890*	18.50	10
		deep blue	18.50	10
		ultramarine	18.50	12
		On cover		35
		Block of four	75.00	3.50
		Margin strip of 5, Impt. & P#	120.00	
		Margin strip of 6, Impt. & P#	145.00	
		Margin strip of 7, Impt. & P#	175.00	
		Margin block of 10, Impt. & P#	475.00	
		Margin block of 12, Impt. & P#	600.00	
		Margin block of 14, Impt. & P#	750.00	
		c. Imperf. (pair)	225.00	
		Double transfer		

CANCELLATIONS.
Samoa ——— | China ———

219D	A61	2c **lake,** *Feb. 22, 1890*	135.00	45
		On cover		1.25
		Block of four	550.00	7.00
		Margin strip of 5, Impt. & P#	750.00	
		Margin block of 10, Impt. & P#	2,750.	
		e. Imperf. (pair)	100.00	
		Double transfer		

CANCELLATION.
Supplementary Mail Type F   3.00

220	A61	2c **carmine,** *1890*	15.00	5
		dark carmine, rose or car rose	15.00	5
		On cover		15
		Block of four	60.00	1.50
		Margin strip of 5, Impt. & P#	100.00	
		Margin strip of 6, Impt. & P#	125.00	
		Margin strip of 7, Impt. & P#	160.00	
		Margin block of 10, Impt. & P#	450.00	
		Margin block of 12, Impt. & P#	550.00	
		Margin block of 14, Impt. & P#	700.00	
		a. Cap on left "2"		
		(Plates 235-36, 246-47-48)	35.00	1.00
		Pair, cap on left, one normal		
		a. Margin block of 12, Impt. & P#	*1,200.*	
		c. Cap on both "2's" (Plates 245, 246)	110.00	8.00
		Pair, cap on left, cap on both		
		d. Imperf. (pair)	100.00	
		d. Imperf. (pair), without gum	40.00	
		d. Margin block of 12, Impt. & P#		
		Double transfer		3.00

CANCELLATIONS.
Blue   +5 | Supplementary Mail
Purple   +5 | Types F or G   +3.00
                    | China   +20.00

POSTAGE, 1890-93, 1893

221	A62	3c **purple,** *Feb. 22, 1890*	47.50	4.50
		bright purple	47.50	4.50
		dark purple	47.50	4.50
		On cover		12.50
		Block of four	200.00	30.00
		Margin strip of 5, Impt. & P#	325.00	
		Margin block of 10, Impt. & P#	1,750.	
		a. Imperf. (pair)	275.00	

CANCELLATION

| Samoa | — |

222	A63	4c **dark brown,** *June 2, 1890*	47.50	1.50
		blackish brown	47.50	1.50
		On cover		12.50
		Block of four	200.00	13.50
		Margin strip of 5, Impt. & P#	325.00	
		Margin block of 10, Impt. & P#	1,850.	
		a. Imperf. (pair)	250.00	
		Double transfer	65.00	

CANCELLATION

| China | +40.00 |

223	A64	5c **chocolate,** *June 2, 1890*	47.50	1.50
		yellow brown	47.50	1.50
		On cover		10.00
		Block of four	200.00	12.50
		Margin strip of 5, Impt. & P#	325.00	
		Margin block of 10, Impt. & P#	1,850.	
		b. Imperf., pair, yellow brown	275.00	
		Double transfer	65.00	1.75

CANCELLATIONS.

| China | +35.00 | Supplementary Mail |
| Samoa | — | Types F or G | +3.00 |

224	A65	6c **brown red,** *Feb. 22, 1890*	50.00	15.00
		dark brown red	50.00	15.00
		On cover		30.00
		Block of four	205.00	70.00
		Margin strip of 5, Impt. & P#	340.00	
		Margin block of 10, Impt. & P#	1,850.	
		a. Imperf. (pair)	275.00	

CANCELLATION

| Supplementary Mail Type F | +3.00 |

225	A66	8c **lilac,** *Mar. 21, 1893*	35.00	8.50
		grayish lilac	35.00	8.50
		magenta	35.00	8.50
		On cover		25.00
		Block of four	145.00	50.00
		Margin strip of 5, Impt. & P#	250.00	
		Margin block of 10, Impt. & P#	1,300.	
		a. Imperf. (pair)	1,250.	

The 8c was issued because the registry fee was reduced from 10 to 8 cents effective Jan. 1, 1893.

226	A67	10c **green,** *Feb. 22, 1890*	90.00	1.75
		bluish green	90.00	1.75
		dark green	90.00	1.75
		On cover		7.50
		Block of four	375.00	20.00
		Margin strip of 5, Impt. & P#	625.00	
		Margin block of 10, Impt. & P#	3,000.	
		a. Imperf. (pair)	400.00	
		Double transfer	—	—

CANCELLATIONS.

| Samoa | — | Supplementary Mail Types F or G | +2.50 |

227	A68	15c **indigo,** *Feb. 22, 1890*	135.00	15.00
		deep indigo	135.00	15.00
		On cover		60.00
		Block of four	550.00	75.00
		Margin strip of 5, Impt. & P#	900.00	
		Margin block of 10, Impt. & P#	5,750.	
		a. Imperf. (pair)	750.00	
		Double transfer	—	—
		Triple transfer	—	—

CANCELLATION

| Supplementary Mail Type F | +3.00 |

228	A69	30c **black,** *Feb. 22, 1890*	190.00	18.50
		gray black	190.00	18.50
		full black	190.00	18.50
		On cover		275.00
		Block of four	800.00	90.00
		Margin strip of 5, Impt. & P#	1,300.	
		Margin block of 10, Impt. & P#	9,000.	
		a. Imperf. (pair)	1,350.	
		Double transfer	—	—

CANCELLATION

| Supplementary Mail Type F | +5.00 |

229	A70	90c **orange,** *Feb. 22, 1890*	325.00	90.00
		yellow orange	325.00	90.00
		red orange	325.00	90.00
		On cover		2,500.
		Block of four	1,400.	375.00
		Margin strip of 5, Impt. & P#	2,350.	
		Margin block of 10, Impt. & P#	18,500.	
		a. Imperf. (pair)	2,750.	
		Short transfer at bottom	—	—

CANCELLATION

| Supplementary Mail Type F or G | +10.00 |

Imperforate stamps of this issue were not regularly issued. The imperforate 1c, 2c, 4c, 5c and 6c values exist in many trial colors. Price slightly less than for those in normal colors.

COLUMBIAN EXPOSITION ISSUE.

Issued to commemorate the World's Columbian Exposition held at Chicago, Ill., from May 1, 1893 to October 30, 1893, which was to celebrate the 400th anniversary of the discovery of America by Christopher Columbus.

Columbus in Sight of Land
A71

Landing of Columbus
A72

POSTAGE, 1893   131

"Santa Maria," Flagship of Columbus
A73

Fleet of Columbus
A74

Columbus Soliciting Aid from Queen Isabella
A75

Columbus Welcomed at Barcelona
A76

Columbus Restored to Favor
A77

Columbus Presenting Natives
A78

Columbus Announcing His Discovery
A79

Columbus at La Rábida
A80

POSTAGE, 1893

Recall of Columbus
A81

Columbus Describing His Third Voyage
A84

Queen Isabella Pledging Her Jewels
A82

Queen Isabella and Columbus
A85

Columbus in Chains—A83

Columbus—A86

No. 57   **AMERICAN BANK NOTE COMPANY**

Type of imprint and plate number.

Exposition Station Cancellation.
Condition is extremely important in evaluating Nos. 230–245. Prices are for stamps free from faults and with the design well clear of the perforations. Stamps of superior quality command substantial premiums.

1893 Printed by the American Bank Note Company.
Plates of 200 subjects in two panes of 100 each (1c, 2c).
Plates of 100 subjects in two panes of 50 each (2c–$5).

Issued (except 8c) Jan. 2, 1893.
Perf. 12.

230	A71	1c **deep blue**	21.00	30
		blue	21.00	30
		pale blue	21.00	30
		On cover		75
		On cover or card, Expo. sta. canc.		175.00
		Block of four	85.00	6.00
		Margin strip of 3, Impt. & P#	82.50	
		Margin strip of 4, Impt. & P#	125.00	
		Margin block of 6, Impt. & P#	350.00	
		Margin block of 8, Impt., letter & P#	550.00	
		Double transfer	30.00	50
		Cracked plate	100.00	

CANCELLATION
| China

231	A72	2c **brown violet**	20.00	6
		deep brown violet	20.00	6
		gray violet	20.00	6
		On cover		25
		On cover or card, Expo. sta. cancel		150.00
		Block of four	82.50	3.00
		Margin strip of 3, Impt. & P#	80.00	
		Margin strip of 4, Impt. & P#	115.00	
		Margin block of 6, Impt. & P#	300.00	
		Margin block of 8, Impt., letter & P#	500.00	
		b. Imperf., pair	1,200.	
		Double transfer	30.00	25
		Triple transfer	75.00	
		Quadruple transfer	110.00	
		Third figure to left of Columbus shows broken hat	65.00	20
		Broken frame line	25.00	8
		Recut frame lines	25.00	
		Cracked plate	100.00	

CANCELLATIONS.
China   ——| Supp. Mail, G

Samuel Shaskan

Philatelist

Superb Used United States

Want Lists Promptly Filled

. . . They

Speak For

Themselves!

P.O. Box 8145, Stamford, Connecticut 06905 USA.   (203) 359-8144

Member APS, USPCS

POSTAGE, 1893

232	A73	3c **green**	45.00	15.00	
		dull green	45.00	15.00	
		dark green	45.00	15.00	
		On cover		30.00	
		On cover, Expo. station canc.		300.00	
		Block of four	185.00	75.00	
		Margin strip of 3, Impt. & P#	180.00		
		Margin strip of 4, Impt. & P#	265.00		
		Margin block of 6, Impt. & P#	650.00		
		Margin block of 8, Impt., letter & P#	1,050.		
		Double transfer		75.00	
		CANCELLATIONS.			
		China ——— | Supp. Mail, F, G		+7.50	
233	A74	4c **ultramarine**	65.00	6.00	
		dull ultramarine	65.00	6.00	
		deep ultramarine	65.00	6.00	
		On cover		20.00	
		On cover, Expo. station canc.		400.00	
		Block of four	265.00	35.00	
		Margin strip of 3, Impt. & P#	260.00		
		Margin strip of 4, Impt. & P#	375.00		
		Margin block of 6, Impt. & P#	950.00		
		Margin block of 8, Impt., letter & P#	1,800.		
		a. **4c blue** (error)	6,500.	2,500.	
		a. Block of four (error)	28,500.		
		a. Margin strip of 4, Impt., letter & P#	37,500.		
		Double transfer	110.00		
		CANCELLATIONS.			
		——— | Supp. Mail, G		+3.00	
		No. 233a exists in two shades.			
234	A75	5c **chocolate**	75.00	7.00	
		dark chocolate	75.00	7.00	
		pale brown	75.00	7.00	
		yellow brown	75.00	7.00	
		On cover		20.00	
		On cover, Expo. station canc.		400.00	
		Block of four	310.00	45.00	
		Margin strip of 3, Impt. & P#	300.00		
		Margin strip of 4, Impt. & P#	425.00		
		Margin block of 6, Impt. & P#	1,350.		
		Margin block of 8, Impt., letter & P#	2,500.		
		Double transfer	110.00		
		CANCELLATIONS.			
		China ——— | Supp. Mail, F		+3.00	
235	A76	6c **purple**	65.00	20.00	
		dull purple	65.00	20.00	
		a. 6c red violet	65.00	20.00	
		On cover		45.00	
		On cover, Expo. station canc.		450.00	
		Block of four	265.00	85.00	
		Margin strip of 3, Impt. & P#	260.00		
		Margin strip of 4, Impt. & P#	375.00		
		Margin block of 6, Impt. & P#	1,050.		
		Margin block of 8, Impt., letter & P#	1,900.		
		Double transfer	100.00	25.00	
		CANCELLATIONS.			
		China ——— | Supp. Mail, F		+5.00	
236	A77	8c **magenta**, *Mar. 1893*	50.00	8.00	
		light magenta	50.00	8.00	
		dark magenta	50.00	8.00	
		On cover		20.00	
		On cover, Expo. station canc.		450.00	
		Block of four	205.00	40.00	
		Margin strip of 3, Impt. & P#	200.00		
		Margin strip of 4, Impt. & P#	285.00		
		Margin block of 6, Impt. & P#	650.00		
		Margin block of 8, Impt., letter & P#	1,050.		
		Double transfer		65.00	
		CANCELLATIONS. eku: Mar. 3			
		China ——— | Supp. Mail, F		+4.50	
237	A78	10c **black brown**	110.00	6.50	
		dark brown	110.00	6.50	
		gray black	110.00	6.50	
		On cover		30.00	
		On cover, Expo. station canc.		500.00	
		Block of four	450.00	40.00	
		Margin strip of 3, Impt. & P#	440.00		
		Margin strip of 4, Impt. & P#	625.00		
		Margin block of 6, Impt. & P#	3,000.		
		Margin block of 8, Impt., letter & P#	4,500.		
		Double transfer	175.00	10.00	
		Triple transfer			
		Supplementary Mail Types F or G		+4.00	
238	A79	15c **dark green**	200.00	65.00	
		green	200.00	65.00	
		dull green	200.00	65.00	
		On cover		200.00	
		On cover, Expo. station canc.		900.00	
		Block of four	850.00	300.00	
		Margin strip of 3, Impt. & P#	850.00		
		Margin strip of 4, Impt. & P#	1,150.		
		Margin block of 6, Impt. & P#	4,750.		
		Margin block of 8, Impt., letter & P#	7,500.		
		Double transfer			
		CANCELLATIONS.			
		China +75.00 | Supp. Mail, F, G		+10.00	
239	A80	30c **orange brown**	275.00	90.00	
		bright orange brown	275.00	90.00	
		On cover		375.00	
		On cover, Expo. station canc.		1,500	
		Block of four	1,150.	425.00	
		Margin strip of 3, Impt. & P#	1,100.		
		Margin strip of 4, Impt. & P#	1,600.		
		Margin block of 6, Impt. & P#	7,000.		
		Margin block of 8, Impt., letter & P#	10,500.		
		CANCELLATIONS.			
		Supplementary Mail Types F or G		+25.00	
240	A81	50c **slate blue**	325.00	140.00
		dull slate blue	325.00	140.00
		On cover		600.00
		On cover, Expo. station canc.		2,250
		Block of four	1,350.	650.00
		Margin strip of 3, Impt. & P#	1,300.	
		Margin strip of 4, Impt. & P#	1,900.	
		Margin block of 6, Impt. & P#	9,500.	
		Margin block of 8, Impt., letter & P#	14,000.	
		Double transfer		
		Triple transfer		
		CANCELLATIONS.		
		Supplementary Mail Types F or G		+30.00
241	A82	$1 **salmon**	1,000.	550.00
		dark salmon	1,000.	550.00
		On cover		1,900
		On cover, Expo. station canc.		4,500
		Block of four	4,250.	2,500
		Margin strip of 3, Impt. & P#	4,000.	
		Margin strip of 4, Impt. & P#	6,000.	
		Margin block of 6, Impt. & P#	19,500.	
		Margin block of 8, Impt., letter & P#	27,500.	
		Double transfer		
		CANCELLATIONS.		
		Supplementary Mail Types F or G		+50.00
242	A83	$2 **brown red**	1,100.	500.00
		deep brown red	1,100.	500.00
		On cover		1,850
		On cover, Expo. station canc.		4,500
		Block of four	4,750.	2,250
		Margin strip of 3, Impt. & P#	4,400.	
		Margin strip of 4, Impt. & P#	6,600.	
		Margin block of 6, Impt. & P#	21,000.	
		Margin block of 8, Impt., letter & P#	30,000.	
		CANCELLATIONS.		
		Supplementary Mail Type G		+50.00
243	A84	$3 **yellow green**	2,300.	1,100
		pale yellow green	2,300.	1,100
		a. $3 olive green	2,300.	1,100
		On cover		2,500
		On cover, Expo. station canc.		6,250
		Block of four	10,500.	5,500
		Margin strip of 3, Impt. & P#	9,500.	
		Margin strip of 4, Impt. & P#	13,500.	
		Margin block of 6, Impt. & P#	45,000.	
		Margin block of 8, Impt., letter & P#	70,000.	
244	A85	$4 **crimson lake**	3,100.	1,450
		a. $4 rose carmine	3,100.	1,450
		pale aniline rose	3,100.	1,450
		On cover		3,750
		On cover, Expo. station canc.		8,500
		Block of four	14,500.	7,000
		Margin strip of 3, Impt. & P#	13,500.	
		Margin strip of 4, Impt. & P#	19,000.	
		Margin block of 6, Impt. & P#	90,000.	
		Margin block of 8, Impt., letter & P#	130,000.	
245	A86	$5 **black**	3,250.	1,700
		grayish black	3,250.	1,700
		On cover		4,500
		On cover, Expo. station canc.		12,000
		Block of four	14,500.	9,000
		Margin strip of 3, Impt. & P#	14,000.	
		Margin strip of 4, Impt. & P#	20,000.	
		Margin block of 6, Impt. & P#	100,000.	
		Margin block of 8, Impt., letter & P#	150,000.	

Nos. 230–245 exist imperforate; not issued.

BUREAU ISSUES

In the following listings of postal issues mostly printed by the Bureau of Engraving and Printing at Washington, D.C., the editors acknowledge with thanks the use of material prepared by the Catalogue Listing Committee of the Bureau Issues Association.

The Bureau-printed stamps until 1965 were engraved except the Offset Issues of 1918–19 (Nos. 525–536). Engraving and lithography were combined for the first time for the Homemakers 5c (No. 1253). The Bureau used photogravure first in 1971 on the Missouri 8c (No. 1426).

Stamps in this section which were not printed by the Bureau begin with Nos. 909–921 and are so noted.

"*On cover*" listings carry through No. 550. Beyond this point a few covers of special significance are listed. Many Bureau Issue stamps are undoubtedly scarce properly used on cover. Most higher denominations exist almost exclusively on pieces of package wrapping and usually in combination with other values. Collector interest in covers is generally limited to fancy cancellations, attractive corner cards, use abroad and other special usages.

Plate number blocks are priced unused. Although many exist used, and are scarcer in that condition, they command only a fraction of the price of the unused examples because they are less sought after.

IMPRINTS AND PLATE NUMBERS.

In listing the Bureau of Engraving & Printing Imprints, the editors have followed the classification of types adopted by the Bureau Issues Association. Types I, II, IV, V and VIII occur on postage issues and are illustrated below. Types III, VI and VII occur only on Special Delivery plates, so are illustrated with the listings of those stamps; other types are illustrated with the listings of the issues on which they occur.

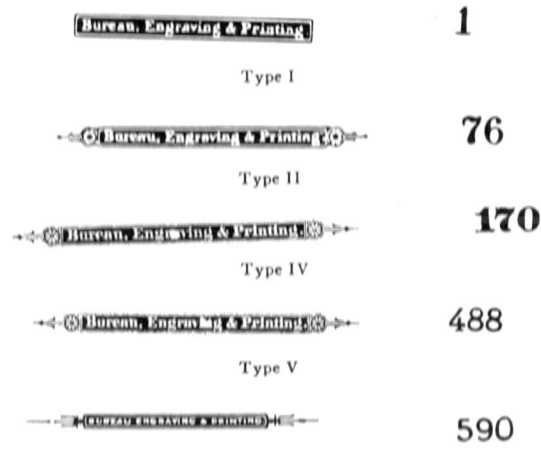

In listing Imprint blocks and strips, the editors have designated for each stamp the various types known to exist. If, however, the Catalogue listing sufficiently describes the Imprint, no type number is given. Thus a listing reading: "Imprint, P# & A" in the 1912-14 series would not be followed by a type number as the description is self-explanatory. Prices are for the commonest types.

PLATE POSITIONS.

At the suggestion of the Catalogue Listing Committee of the Bureau Issues Association, all plate positions of these issues are indicated by giving the plate number first, next the pane position, and finally the stamp position. For example: 20234 L. L. 58.

POSTAGE, 1894

Franklin
A87

Washington
A88

Clay
A95

Jefferson
A96

Jackson
A89

Lincoln
A90

Perry
A97

James Madison
A98

Grant
A91

Garfield
A92

John Marshall
A99

Sherman
A93

Webster
A94

1894   **REGULAR ISSUE.**

Plates for the issues of 1894, 1895 and 1898 were of two sizes:

400 subjects for all 1c, 2c and 10c denominations; 200 subjects for all 6c, 8c, 15c, 50c, $1.00, $2.00 and $5.00, and both 400 and 200 subjects for the 3c, 4c and 5c denominations; all issued in panes of 100 each.

Dates of issue of the 1894, 1895 and 1898 denominations are taken from the Report of the Third Assistant Postmaster General, dated June 30, 1899.

Perf. 12.
Unwatermarked.

246	A87	1c	**ultramarine,** *Oct. 1894*	21.00	3.00
			bright ultramarine	21.00	3.00
			dark ultramarine	21.00	3.00
			On cover		15.00
			Block of four	85.00	17.50
			Margin strip of 3, Impt. & P#, T I	90.00	
			Margin block of 6, Impt. & P#, T I	300.00	
			Double transfer	30.00	4.00

CANCELLATIONS.
China ———

POSTAGE, 1894

247	A87	1c **blue**		52.50	1.25
		bright blue		52.50	1.25
		dark blue		52.50	1.25
		On cover			15.00
		Block of four		225.00	12.50
		Margin strip of 3, Impt. & P#, T I or II		225.00	
		Margin block of 6, Impt. & P#, T I or II		600.00	
		Double transfer		—	3.50

TWO CENTS.

Type I (Triangle I). The horizontal lines of the ground work run across the triangle and are of the same thickness within it as without.

Type II (Triangle II). The horizontal lines cross the triangle but are thinner within it than without.

Type III (Triangle III). The horizontal lines do not cross the double lines of the triangle. The lines within the triangle are thin, as in Type II. Two varieties of Type III are known but the variations are minor. For further information see the March, 1937 issue of the "Bureau Specialist."

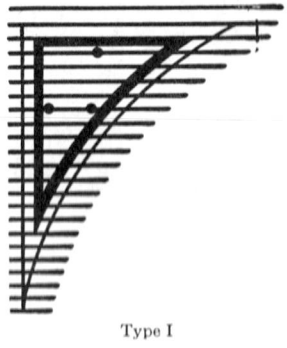

Type I

248	A88	2c **pink,** type I, *Oct. 1894*		17.50	2.00
		pale pink		17.50	2.00
		On cover			12.50
		Block of four		72.50	15.00
		Margin strip of 3, Impt. & P#, T I or II		75.00	
		Margin block of 6, Impt. & P#, T I or II		200.00	
		a. Vert. pair, imperf. horiz.		2,000.	
		Double transfer		—	
249	A88	2c **carmine lake,** type I		125.00	1.35
		dark carmine lake		125.00	1.35
		On cover			10.00
		Block of four		525.00	15.00
		Margin strip of 3, Impt. & P#, T I or II		525.00	
		Margin block of 6, Impt. & P#, T I or II		1,250.	
		Double transfer		—	2.00
250	A88	2c **carmine,** type I		21.00	25
		dark carmine		21.00	25
		scarlet		21.00	25
		On cover			2.00
		Block of four		85.00	3.00
		Margin strip of 3, Impt. & P#, T I or II		85.00	
		Margin block of 6, Impt. & P#, T I or II		300.00	
		a. Vert. pair, imperf. horiz.		1,500.	
		b. Horizontal pair, imperf. between		1,500.	
		Double transfer		—	1.50
251	A88	2c **carmine,** type II		165.00	2.50
		dark carmine		165.00	2.50
		On cover			15.00
		Block of four		675.00	22.50
		Margin strip of 3, Impt. & P#, T II		675.00	
		Margin block of 6, Impt. & P#, T II		2,100.	
252	A88	2c **carmine,** type III		85.00	3.25
		pale carmine		85.00	3.25
		On cover			15.00
		Block of four		350.00	40.00
		Margin strip of 3, Impt. & P#, T II or IV		350.00	
		Margin block of 6, Impt. & P#, T II or IV		1,200.	
		a. Horiz. pair, imperf. vert.		1,350.	
		b. Horiz. pair, imperf. between		1,500.	
253	A89	3c **purple,** *Sept. 1894*		80.00	6.25
		dark purple		80.00	6.25
		On cover			20.00
		Block of four		325.00	40.00
		Margin block of 4, arrow, R or L		350.00	
		Margin strip of 3, Impt. & P#, T I or II		325.00	
		Margin block of 6, Impt. & P#, T I or II		1,000.	
		a. Imperf., pair		350.00	
		a. Block of four		750.00	
		a. Margin block of 6, Impt. & P#		—	
254	A90	4c **dark brown,** *Sept. 1894*		90.00	2.50
		brown		90.00	2.50
		On cover			20.00
		Block of four		375.00	20.00
		Margin block of 4, arrow, R or L		385.00	

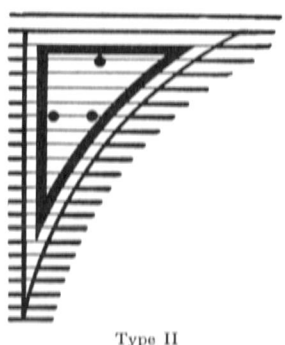

Type II

Type III

137

POSTAGE, 1894

		Margin strip of 3, Impt. & P#, T I or II	375.00	
		Margin block of 6, Impt. & P#, T I or II	1,250.	
	a.	Imperf., pair	350.00	
	a.	Block of four	750.00	
	a.	Margin block of 6, Impt. & P#	—	

CANCELLATIONS.

Supplementary Mail Type F   +2.00

255	A91	5c **chocolate,** *Sept. 1894*	75.00	3.50
		deep chocolate	75.00	3.50
		yellow brown	75.00	3.50
		On cover		15.00
		Block of four	310.00	20.00
		Margin block of 4, arrow, R or L	325.00	
		Margin strip of 3, Impt. & P#, T I, II or IV	300.00	
		Margin block of 6, Impt. & P#, T I, II or IV	875.00	
	b.	Imperf., pair	350.00	
	b.	Block of four	750.00	
	b.	Margin block of 6, Impt. & P#	—	
	c.	Vert. pair, imperf. horiz.	900.00	
		Worn plate, diagonal lines missing in oval background	75.00	3.50
		Double transfer	90.00	4.00

CANCELLATIONS.

Supplementary Mail Type G   +2.00
China   —

256	A92	6c **dull brown,** *July 1894*	140.00	15.00
		On cover		45.00
		Block of four	575.00	80.00
		Margin block of 4, arrow, R or L	600.00	
		Margin strip of 3, Impt. & P#, T I	575.00	
		Margin block of 6, Impt. & P#, T I	1,500.	550.00
	a.	Vert. pair, imperf. horiz.	850.00	
	a.	Margin block of 6, Impt. & P#, T I	10,000.	
257	A93	8c **violet brown,** *Mar. 1895*	100.00	10.00
		bright violet brown	100.00	10.00
		On cover		35.00
		Block of four	410.00	60.00
		Margin block of 4, arrow, R or L	425.00	
		Margin strip of 3, Impt. & P#, T I	410.00	
		Margin block of 6, Impt. & P#, T I	1,000.	
258	A94	10c **dark green,** *Sept. 1894*	175.00	7.50
		green	175.00	7.50
		dull green	175.00	7.50
		On cover		35.00
		Block of four	750.00	40.00
		Margin strip of 3, Impt. & P#, T I	750.00	
		Margin block of 6, Impt. & P#, T I	2,400.	
	a.	Imperf., pair	650.00	
	a.	Block of four	1,400.	
	a.	Margin block of 6, Impt. & P#	—	
		Double transfer	225.00	8.50

CANCELLATIONS.

China   —
Supplementary Mail Types F or G   +2.00

259	A95	15c **dark blue,** *Oct. 1894*	250.00	45.00
		indigo	250.00	45.00
		On cover		120.00
		Block of four	1,050.	250.00
		Margin block of 4, arrow, R or L	1,100.	
		Margin strip of 3, Impt. & P#, T I	1,100.	
		Margin block of 6, Impt. & P#, T I	3,750.	

CANCELLATIONS.

China   —

260	A96	50c **orange,** *Nov. 1894*	325.00	75.00
		deep orange	325.00	75.00
		On cover		350.00
		Block of four	1,400.	450.00
		Margin block of 4, arrow, R or L	1,500.	
		Margin strip of 3, Impt. & P#, T I	1,400.	
		Margin block of 6, Impt. & P#, T I	6,000.	

CANCELLATIONS.

Supplementary Mail Types F or G   —
China   —

Type I

Type II

ONE DOLLAR.

Type I. The circles enclosing "$1" are broken where they meet the curved line below "One Dollar".

Type II. The circles are complete.

The fifteen left vertical rows of impressions from plate 76 are Type I, the balance being Type II.

261	A97	$1 **black,** type I, *Nov. 1894*	850.00	250.00
		grayish black	850.00	250.00
		On cover		1,000.
		Block of four	3,500.	1,100.
		Margin block of 4, arrow, L	3,750.	
		Margin strip of 3, Impt. & P#, T II	3,500.	
		Margin block of 6, Impt. & P#, T II	15,000.	
261A	A97	$1 **black,** type II, *Nov. 1894*	1,850.	475.00
		On cover		3,000.
		Block of four	7,500.	2,750.
		Margin block of 4, arrow, R	7,750.	
		Horizontal pair, types I and II	3,250.	1,000.
		Block of four, two each of types I and II	6,750.	—
		Margin strip of 3, Impt. & P#, T II, one stamp No. 261	6,000.	
		Margin block of 6, Impt. & P#, T II, two stamps No. 261	25,000.	
262	A98	$2 **bright blue,** *Dec. 1894*	2,100.	600.00
		dark blue	2,200.	625.00
		On cover		3,000.
		Block of four	8,500.	2,600.
		Margin block of 4, arrow, R or L	9,000.	
		Margin strip of 3, Impt. & P#, T II	8,750.	
		Margin block of 6, Impt. & P#, T II	35,000.	
263	A99	$5 **dark green,** *Dec. 1894*	3,250.	1,050.
		On cover		6,000.
		Block of four	14,000.	5,000.
		Margin block of 4, arrow, R or L	15,000.	
		Margin strip of 3, Impt. & P#, TII	15,000.	

The "Imperf. horizontally" variety No. 248a, and the imperforate varieties Nos. 253a, 254a, 255b and 258a were not regularly issued.

POSTAGE, 1895   139

REGULAR ISSUE.

1895   Perf. 12

Wmkd. USPS (191) Horizontally

or USPS Vertically,

(Actual size of letter)

repeated in rows, thus

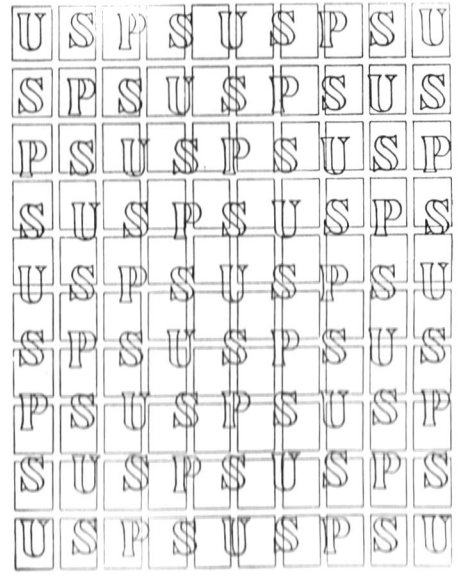

The letters stand for "U.S. Postage Stamp."
Plates for the 1895 issue were of two sizes:—
400 subjects for all 1c, 2c and 10c denominations; 200 subjects for all 4c, 5c, 6c, 8c, 15c, 50c, $1.00, $2.00 and $5.00; and both 400 and 200 subjects for the 3c denomination; all issued in panes of 100 each.
Printings from the 400 subject plates show the watermark reading horizontally, on the 200 subject printings the watermark reads vertically (with the tops and bottoms of the letters toward the vertical sides of the stamps.)

264	A87	1c **blue**, *Apr. 1895*	5.00	10
		dark blue	5.00	10
		pale blue	5.00	10
		On cover		1.00
		Block of four	20.00	2.00
		Margin strip of 3, Impt. & P#, T I, II, IV or V	20.00	
		Margin block of 6, Impt. & P#, T I, II, IV or V	175.00	
		b. Horiz. pair, imperf. vert.	—	
		c. Imperf. (pair)	325.00	
		c. Block of four	700.00	
		Double transfer		1.00

CANCELLATIONS.
China   — | Philippines —
                   | Samoa   —

265	A88	2c **carmine**, type I, *May 1895*	22.50	65
		deep carmine	22.50	65
		On cover		3.00
		Block of four	95.00	6.00
		Margin strip of 3, Impt. & P#, T II	95.00	
		Margin block of 6, Impt. & P#, T II	350.00	
		Double transfer	40.00	5.00
266	A88	2c **carmine**, type II	20.00	2.50
		On cover		6.50
		Block of four	82.50	18.50
		Horizontal pair, types II and III	55.00	10.00
		Margin strip of 3, Impt. & P#, T II or IV	82.50	
		Margin block of 6, Impt. & P#, T II or IV	325.00	
267	A88	2c **carmine**, type III	4.50	5
		deep carmine	4.50	5
		On cover		20
		Block of four	18.50	1.00
		Margin strip of 3, Impt. & P#, T II, IV or V	17.50	
		Margin block of 6, Impt. & P#, T II, IV or V	125.00	
		a. Imperf. (pair)	300.00	
		a. Block of four	650.00	
		Double transfer	15.00	1.50
		Triple transfer	—	
		Triangle at upper right without shading	25.00	7.50

CANCELLATIONS.
China   — | Philippines —
Hawaii — | Samoa   —

The three left vertical rows of impressions from plate 170 are Type II, the balance being Type III.

268	A89	3c **purple**, *Oct. 1895*	32.50	1.00
		dark purple	32.50	1.00
		On cover		10.00
		Block of four	132.50	7.50
		Margin block of 4, arrow, R or L	140.00	
		Margin strip of 3, Impt. & P#, T II or V	135.00	
		Margin block of 6, Impt. & P#, T II or IV	575.00	
		a. Imperf. (pair)	350.00	
		a. Block of four	800.00	
		Double transfer	45.00	3.50

CANCELLATIONS.
Guam   — | Philippines —
China   — |

269	A90	4c **dark brown**, *June 1895*	35.00	1.10
		dark yellow brown	35.00	1.10
		On cover		12.50
		Block of four	140.00	10.00
		Margin block of 4, arrow, R or L	145.00	
		Margin strip of 3, Impt. & P#, T I, II, IV or V	140.00	
		Margin block of 6, Impt. & P#, T I, II, IV or V	600.00	
		a. Imperf. (pair)	350.00	
		a. Block of four	800.00	
		Double transfer	40.00	3.50

CANCELLATIONS.
Philippines — | Samoa —
China   — |

270	A91	5c **chocolate**, *June 11, 1895*	32.50	1.75
		deep brown	32.50	1.75
		chestnut	32.50	1.75
		On cover		7.50
		Block of four	135.00	10.00
		Margin block of 4, arrow, R or L	145.00	
		Margin strip of 3, Impt. & P#, T I, II, IV or V	135.00	
		Margin block of 6, Impt. & P#, T I, II, IV or V	600.00	
		b. Imperf. (pair)	350.00	
		b. Block of four	800.00	
		Double transfer	50.00	4.00
		Worn plate, diagonal lines missing in oval background	40.00	2.50

CANCELLATIONS.
China   — | Supp. Mail, G   +2.50

POSTAGE, 1895, 1898

271	A92	6c **dull brown,** *Aug. 1895*		65.00	3.50
		claret brown		65.00	3.50
		On cover			30.00
		Block of four		265.00	25.00
		Margin block of 4, arrow, R or L		275.00	
		Margin strip of 3, Impt. & P#, T I, IV or V		265.00	
		Margin block of 6, Impt. & P#, T I, IV or V		1,100.	
		Very thin paper		70.00	3.50
		a. Wmkd. USIR		*1,850.*	350.00
		b. Imperf. (pair)		400.00	
		b. Block of four		850.00	
		CANCELLATION			
			Philippines	—	
272	A93	8c **violet brown,** *July 1895*		40.00	1.00
		dark violet brown		40.00	1.00
		On cover			17.50
		Block of four		165.00	7.50
		Margin block of 4, arrow, R or L		170.00	
		Margin strip of 3, Impt. & P#, T I, IV or V		165.00	
		Margin block of 6, Impt. & P#, T I, IV or V		700.00	
		a. Wmkd. USIR		700.00	110.00
		a. Wmkd. USIR, P# strip of 3		*3,000.*	
		b. Imperf. (pair)		550.00	
		b. Block of four		1,150.	
		Double transfer		60.00	3.00
		CANCELLATIONS.			
		China	Puerto Rico, 1898	—	
		Guam	Samoa	—	
		Philippines	Supplementary Mail Type G	—	+2.50
273	A94	10c **dark green,** *June 1895*		55.00	1.20
		green		55.00	1.20
		On cover			20.00
		Block of four		230.00	10.00
		Margin strip of 3, Impt. & P#, T I or IV		230.00	
		Margin block of 6, Impt. & P#, T I or IV		1,150.	
		a. Imperf. (pair)		450.00	
		a. Block of four		950.00	
		Double transfer		75.00	4.00
		CANCELLATIONS.			
		China	Philippines	—	
		Cuba	Supplementary Mail Types F or G	—	+2.00
274	A95	15c **dark blue,** *Sept. 1895*		160.00	8.25
		indigo		160.00	8.25
		On cover			65.00
		Block of four		650.00	50.00
		Margin block of 4, arrow, R or L		700.00	
		Margin strip of 3, Impt. & P#, T I or IV		650.00	
		Margin block of 6, Impt. & P#, T I or IV		3,000.	
		a. Imperf. (pair)		1,450.	
		a. Block of four		3,000.	
		CANCELLATIONS.			
		China	Supplementary Mail Type G	—	+3.00
		Philippines		—	
275	A96	50c **orange,** *Nov. 1895*		235.00	20.00
		a. 50c red orange		250.00	22.50
		On cover			250.00
		Block of four		950.00	100.00
		a. Block of four		1,050.	120.00
		Margin block of 4, arrow, R or L		1,050.	
		Margin strip of 3, Impt. & P#, T I		950.00	
		Margin block of 6, Impt. & P#, T I		6,000.	
		b. Imperf. (pair)		1,600.	
		b. Block of four		*3,350.*	
		CANCELLATIONS.			
		China	Supplementary Mail Types F or G	—	+5.00
276	A97	$1 **black,** type I, *Aug. 1895*		550.00	65.00
		greenish black		550.00	65.00
		On cover			950.00
		Block of four		2,300.	300.00
		Margin block of 4, arrow, L		2,500.	
		Margin strip of 3, Impt. & P#, T II		2,400.	
		Margin block of 6, Impt. & P#, T II		10,000.	
		b. Imperf. (pair)		*2,750.*	
		b. Block of four		*6,000.*	
		CANCELLATION			
			Philippines	—	

276A	A97	$1 **black,** type II, *Aug. 1895*		1,200.	125.00
		greenish black		1,200.	125.00
		On cover			1,250.
		Block of four		5,000.	600.00
		Margin block of 4, arrow, R		5,250.	
		Horizontal pair, types I and II		2,150.	300.00
		Block of four, two each of types I and II		4,500.	750.00
		Margin strip of 3, Impt. & P#, T II, one stamp No. 276		4,500.	
		Margin block of 6, Impt. & P#, T II, two stamps No. 276		20,000.	
		CANCELLATIONS.			
			China	—	

The fifteen left vertical rows of impressions from plate 76 are Type I, the balance being Type II.

277	A98	$2 **bright blue,** *Aug. 1895*		900.00	275.00
		On cover			2,250
		Block of four		3,750.	1,250
		Margin block of 4, arrow, R or L		4,000.	
		Margin strip of 3, Impt. & P#, T II		4,000.	
		Margin block of 6, Impt. & P#, T II		18,500.	
		a. $2 dark blue		950.00	285.00
		a. Block of four		4,000.	1,350.
		b. Imperf. (pair)		*3,500.*	
		b. Block of four		*7,500.*	
		CANCELLATIONS.			
			Supplementary Mail Type G	—	
278	A99	$5 **dark green,** *Aug. 1895*		2,000.	400.0
		On cover			5,000
		Block of four		8,250.	2,250
		Margin block of 4, arrow, R or L		8,500.	
		Margin strip of 3, Impt. & P#, T II		8,500.	
		Margin block of 6, Impt. & P#, T II		60,000.	
		a. Imperf. (pair)		*6,000.*	
		a. Block of four		*13,000.*	

The "Imperf. vertically" variety No. 264b and the imperforate varieties of all the denominations in the 1895 issue were not regularly issued.

REGULAR ISSUE.

1898 Perf. 12

Wmkd. USPS (191) Horizontally

or USPS Vertically.

Plates for the 1898 issue were of two sizes:—

400 subjects for the 1c and 2c denominations; 200 subjects for all 5c, 6c and 15c denominations; and both 400 and 200 for the 4c and 0c denominations; all issued in panes of 100 each.

Printings from the 400 subject plates show the watermark reading horizontally, on the 200 subject plate printings the watermark reads vertically.

In January, 1898, the color of the 1-cent stamp was changed to green and in March, 1898, that of the 5-cents to dark blue in order to conform to the colors assigned these values by the Universal Postal Union. These changes necessitated changing the colors of the 10c and 15c denominations in order to avoid confusion.

279	A87	1c **deep green,** *Jan. 1898*		10.00	
		green		10.00	
		yellow green		10.00	
		dark yellow green		10.00	
		On cover			50
		Block of four		41.00	1.75
		Strip of 3, Impt. & P#, T V		42.50	—
		Block of 6, Impt. & P#, T V		175.00	
		Double transfer		15.00	1.25
		CANCELLATIONS.			
		China	Puerto Rico, 1898	—	
		Guam	Philippines	—	

POSTAGE, 1898

279B	A88	2c **red,** type III	9.00	5
		On cover		15
		Block of four (red)	36.50	75
		Margin strip of 3, Impt. & P#, T V (red)	35.00	
		Margin block of 6, Impt. & P#, T V (red)	160.00	
		c. 2c rose carmine, type III	150.00	30.00
		c. Block of four (rose carmine)	625.00	—
		c. Margin strip of 3, Impt. & P#, T V (rose carmine)	625.00	
		c. Margin block of 6, Impt. & P#, T V (rose carmine)	2,250.	
		d. 2c orange red, type III	9.50	12
		d. Block of four (orange red)	38.50	1.25
		d. Margin strip of 3, Impt. & P#, T V (orange red)	37.50	
		d. Margin block of 6, Impt. & P#, T V (orange red)	175.00	
		e. Booklet pane of six	350.00	200.00
		Double transfer	20.00	1.25
		f. 2c deep red, type III	20.00	75

CANCELLATIONS.

Puerto Rico, 1898	—	Supplementary Mail Type G	+4.00
Philippines, 1898	—	Cuba, 1898	—
Guam, 1899 or 1900	—	China	—
		Samoa	—

280	A90	4c **rose brown,** *Oct. 1898*	30.00	70
		a. 4c lilac brown	30.00	70
		brownish claret	30.00	70
		b. 4c orange brown	30.00	70
		On cover		12.50
		Block of four	122.50	7.50
		Margin block of 4, arrow, R or L	127.50	
		Margin strip of 3, Impt. & P#, T V	125.00	
		Margin block of 6, Impt. & P#, T V	600.00	
		Double transfer	40.00	1.50
		Extra frame line at top (Plate 793 R 62)	50.00	5.00

CANCELLATIONS.

Supplementary Mail Type G	+3.00
China	—
Philippines	—

281	A91	5c **dark blue,** *Mar. 1898*	35.00	65
		blue	35.00	65
		bright blue	35.00	65
		On cover		10.00
		Block of four	142.50	5.00
		Margin block of 4, arrow, R or L	150.00	
		Margin strip of 3, Impt. & P#, T V	145.00	
		Margin block of 6, Impt. & P#, T V	650.00	
		Double transfer	50.00	2.50
		Worn plate diagonal lines missing in oval background	40.00	85

CANCELLATIONS.

Puerto Rico, 1898	—	Supplementary Mail Type G	+4.00
		China	—
		Cuba	—
		Guam	—
		Philippines	—

282	A92	6c **lake,** *Dec. 1898*	45.00	2.00
		claret	45.00	2.00
		On cover		15.00
		Block of four	185.00	20.00
		Margin block of 4, arrow, R or L	200.00	
		Margin strip of 3, Impt. & P#, T V	200.00	
		Margin block of 6, Impt. & P#, T V	900.00	
		a. 6c purplish lake	50.00	2.50
		a. Block of four	205.00	30.00
		a. Margin block of 4, arrow	220.00	
		a. Margin strip of 3, Impt. & P#, T V	210.00	
		a. Margin block of 6, Impt. & P#, T V	1,100.	
		Double transfer	60.00	3.50

CANCELLATIONS.

Supplementary Mail Type G	+4.00
China	—
Philippines	—

TEN CENTS.

Type I. The tips of the foliate ornaments do not impinge on the white curved line below "ten cents".

282C	A94	10c **brown,** type I, *Nov. 1898*	160.00	2.00
		dark brown	160.00	2.00
		On cover		15.00
		Block of four	650.00	20.00
		Margin strip of 3, Impt. & P#, T IV or V	650.00	
		Margin block of 6, Impt. & P#, T IV or V	2,500.	
		Double transfer	200.00	4.50

CANCELLATIONS.

Supplementary Mail Type G	+2.50

Type II. The tips of the ornaments break the curved line below the "e" of "ten" and the "t" of "cents".

283	A94	10c **orange brown,** type II	90.00	1.75
		brown	90.00	1.75
		yellow brown	90.00	1.75
		On cover		15.00
		Block of four	365.00	15.00
		Margin block of 4, arrow, R or L	375.00	—
		Margin strip of 3, Impt. & P#, T V	375.00	
		Margin block of 6, Impt. & P#, T V	1,500.	
		Pair, type I and type II	15,000.	850.00

CANCELLATIONS.

Supplementary Mail Type G	+2.50	China	—
		Puerto Rico	—

On the 400 subject plate 932, all the subjects are Type I except the following: U. L. 20; U. R. 11, 12, 13; L. L. 61, 71, 86, these seven being Type II.

284	A95	15c **olive green,** *Nov. 1898*	120.00	6.75
		dark olive green	120.00	6.75
		On cover		35.00
		Block of four	490.00	35.00
		Margin block of 4, arrow, R or L	500.00	
		Margin strip of 3, Impt. & P#, T IV	500.00	
		Margin block of 6, Impt. & P#, T IV	2,250.	

CANCELLATIONS.

Supplementary Mail Types F or G	+2.50	China	—
		Samoa	—

TRANS-MISSISSIPPI EXPOSITION ISSUE.

Issued to commemorate the Trans-Mississippi Exposition held in Omaha, Nebraska, June 1 to November 1, 1898.

Jacques Marquette on the Mississippi
A100

POSTAGE, 1898

Farming in the West
A101

Indian Hunting Buffalo
A102

John Charles Frémont on the Rocky Mountains
A103

Troops Guarding Wagon Train
A104

Hardships of Emigration
A105

Western Mining Prospector
A106

Western Cattle in Storm
A107

Mississippi River Bridge, St. Louis
A108

POSTAGE, 1898, 1901 143

Exposition Station Cancellation

Condition is extremely important in evaluating Nos. 285–293. Prices are for stamps free from faults and with the design well clear of the perforations. Stamps of superior quality command substantial premiums.

Plates of 100 (10x10) subjects, divided vertically into 2 panes of 50.

285	A100	1c	**dark yellow green**	27.50	5.50
			yellow green	27.50	5.50
			green	27.50	5.50
			On cover		10.00
			On card, Expo. station canc.		225.00
			Block of four	112.50	25.00
			Margin block of 4, arrow, R or L	115.00	
			Margin pair, Impt. & P#, T VIII	70.00	
			Margin strip of 3, Impt. & P#, T VIII	110.00	
			Margin block of 4, Impt. & P#, T VIII	225.00	
			Margin block of 6, Impt. & P#, T VIII	325.00	
			Double transfer	40.00	7.00

CANCELLATIONS.
Supplementary | China
Mail, Types | Philippines
F or G +1.50 | Puerto Rico, 1898

286	A101	2c	**copper red**	25.00	1.50
			brown red	25.00	1.50
			light brown red	25.00	1.50
			On cover		2.00
			On cover, Expo. station canc.		200.00
			Block of four	102.50	9.00
			Margin block of 4, arrow, R or L	105.00	
			Margin pair, Impt. & P#, T VIII	65.00	
			Margin strip of 3, Impt. & P#, T VIII	105.00	
			Margin block of 4, Impt. & P#, T VIII	210.00	
			Margin block of 6, Impt. & P#, T VIII	300.00	
			Double transfer	40.00	2.50
			Worn plate	30.00	1.75

CANCELLATIONS.
China | Puerto Rico, 1898
Hawaii | Philippines

287	A102	4c	**orange**	140.00	22.50
			deep orange	140.00	22.50
			On cover		70.00
			On cover, Expo. station canc.		400.00
			Block of four	575.00	100.00
			Margin block of 4, arrow, R or L	600.00	
			Margin pair, Impt. & P#, T VIII	350.00	
			Margin strip of 3, Impt. & P#, T VIII	550.00	
			Margin block of four, Impt. & P#, T VIII	1,100.	
			Margin block of 6, Impt. & P#, T VIII	1,700.	

CANCELLATIONS.
Supplementary Mail | China
Types F or G +5.00 | Philippines

288	A103	5c	**dull blue**	125.00	20.00
			bright blue	125.00	20.00
			On cover		60.00
			On cover, Expo. station canc.		400.00
			Block of four	525.00	90.00
			Margin block of 4, arrow, R or L	550.00	
			Margin pair, Impt. & P#, T VIII	300.00	
			Margin strip of 3, Impt. & P#, T VIII	475.00	
			Margin block of four, Impt. & P#, T VIII	1,000.	
			Margin block of 6, Impt. & P#, T VIII	1,500.	

CANCELLATIONS.
Supplementary | China
Mail Types | Philippines
F or G +5.00 | Puerto Rico, 1898

289	A104	8c	**violet brown**	165.00	40.00
			dark violet brown	165.00	40.00
			On cover		125.00
			On cover, Expo. station canc.		750.00
			Block of four	660.00	185.00
			Margin block of 4, arrow, R or L	675.00	
			Margin pair, Impt. & P#, T VIII	400.00	
			Margin strip of 3, Impt. & P#, T VIII	650.00	
			Margin block of 4, Impt. & P#, T VIII	1,750.	
			Margin block of 6, Impt. & P#, T VIII	2,650.	
		a.	Vert. pair, imperf. horiz.	12,000.	

CANCELLATIONS.
Philippines ——— | Samoa ———

290	A105	10c	**gray violet**	185.00	20.00
			blackish violet	185.00	20.00
			On cover		90.00
			On cover, Expo. station canc.		750.00
			Block of four	750.00	95.00
			Margin block of 4, arrow, R or L	775.00	
			Margin pair, Impt. & P#, T VIII	450.00	
			Margin strip of 3, Impt. & P#, T VIII	700.00	
			Margin block of 4, Impt. & P#, T VIII	2,250.	
			Margin block of 6, Impt. & P#, T VIII	3,500.	

CANCELLATIONS.
China ——— | Supplementary Mail
Philippines ——— | Type G +5.00

291	A106	50c	**sage green**	725.00	165.00
			dark sage green	725.00	165.00
			On cover		1,200.
			Block of four	3,000.	950.00
			Margin block of 4, arrow, R or L	3,250.	
			Margin pair, Impt. & P#, T VIII	1,750.	
			Margin strip of 3, Impt. & P#, T VIII	2,850.	
			Margin block of 4, Impt. & P#, T VIII	13,500.	
			Margin block of 6, Impt. & P#, T VIII	20,000.	

CANCELLATIONS.
Cuba ——— | Supplementary Mail
Philippines ——— | Types F or G +25.00

292	A107	$1	**black**	1,750.	625.00
			On cover		3,750.
			Block of four	7,500.	3,500.
			Margin block of 4, arrow, R or L	8,000.	
			Margin pair, Impt. & P#, T VIII	4,250.	
			Margin strip of 3, Impt. & P#, T VIII	7,250.	
			Margin block of 4, Impt. & P#, T VIII	40,000.	
			Margin block of 6, Impt. & P#, T VIII	52,500.	

CANCELLATION.
Philippines ——— |

293	A108	$2	**orange brown**	2,650.	875.00
			dark orange brown	2,650.	875.00
			On cover		8,500.
			Block of four	12,500.	4,250.
			Margin block of 4, arrow, R or L	13,500.	
			Margin pair, Impt. & P#, T VII	6,500.	
			Margin strip of 3, Impt. & P#, T VIII	10,500.	
			Margin block of 4, Impt. & P#, T VII	80,000.	
			Margin block of 6, Impt. & P#, T VIII	115,000.	

PAN-AMERICAN EXPOSITION ISSUE.

Issued to commemorate the Pan-American Exposition held at Buffalo, N. Y., May 1 to Nov. 1, 1901. On sale May 1–Oct. 31, 1901.

Fast Lake Navigation (Steamship "City of Alpena") A109

144　POSTAGE, 1901

Empire State Express
A110

Electric Automobile in Washington
A111

Bridge at Niagara Falls
A112

Canal Locks at Sault Ste. Marie
A113

Fast Ocean Navigation (Steamship "St. Paul")
A114

Exposition Station Cancellation.

Note on condition and pricing above No. 285 also applies to Nos. 294–299.

Plates of 200 subjects in two panes of 100 each.

1901, May 1 Wmkd. USPS (191)　　*Perf. 12*

294	A109	1c **green & black**	20.00	4.00
		dark blue green & black	20.00	4.00
		On cover		5.50
		On cover or card, Expo. sta. canc.		110.00
		Block of four	80.00	20.00
		Margin block of 4, top arrow & markers	82.50	
		Margin block of 4, bottom arrow & markers & black P#	85.00	
		Margin strip of 3, Impt. & P#, T V	85.00	
		Margin block of 6, Impt. & P#, T V	275.00	
		Margin strip of 5, bottom two P#, T V Impt., arrow & markers	140.00	
		Margin block of 10, bottom, Impt., T V, two P#, arrow & markers	525.00	
	a.	Center inverted	10,000.	4,500.
	a.	Center inverted, on cover		15,000.
	a.	Center inverted, block of 4	42,500.	
	a.	Same, Margin strip of 3, Impt. & P#	44,000.	
		Double transfer	27.50	6.00

295	A110	2c **carmine & black**	20.00	1.10
		carmine & gray black	20.00	1.10
		rose carmine & black	20.00	1.10
		scarlet & black	20.00	1.10
		On cover		1.75
		On cover or card, Expo. sta. canc.		95.00
		Block of four	80.00	6.00
		Margin block of 4, top arrow & markers	82.50	
		Margin block of 4, bottom arrow & markers and black P#	85.00	
		Margin strip of 3, Impt. & P#, T V	85.00	
		Margin block of 6, Impt. & P#, T V	275.00	
		Margin strip of 5, bottom, Impt., T V, two P#, arrow & markers	140.00	
		Margin block of 10, bottom, Impt., T V, two P#, arrow & markers	525.00	
	a.	Center inverted	45,000.	13,500.
	a.	Center inverted, block of four	200,000.	
		Double transfer	27.50	2.50

296	A111	4c **deep red brown & black**	110.00	20.00
		chocolate & black	110.00	20.00
		On cover		45.00
		On cover, Expo. station canc.		325.00
		Block of four	450.00	85.00
		Margin block of 4, top arrow & markers	460.00	
		Margin block of 4, bottom arrow & markers & black P#	475.00	
		Margin strip of 3, Impt. & P#, T V	450.00	
		Margin block of 6, Impt. & P#, T V	2,500.	
		Margin strip of 5, bottom Impt., T V two P#, arrow & markers	725.00	
		Margin block of 10, bottom, Impt., TV, two P#, arrow & markers	4,750.	
	a.	Center inverted	13,000.	
	a.	Center inverted, block of 4	57,500.	
	a.	Same, Margin strip of 4, Impt. & P#	67,500.	

No. 296a was not regularly issued. See No. 296a-S. "Specimen" Stamps.

297	A112	5c **ultramarine & black**	125.00	20.00
		dark ultramarine & black	125.00	20.00
		On cover		45.00
		On cover, Expo. station canc.		325.00
		Block of four	500.00	85.00
		Margin block of 4, top arrow & markers	510.00	
		Margin block of 4, bottom arrow & markers & black P#	525.00	
		Margin strip of 3, Impt. & P#, T V	500.00	
		Margin block of 6, Impt. & P#, T V	2,750.	
		Margin strip of 5, bottom Impt., T V two P#, arrow & markers	800.00	
		Margin block of 10, bottom Impt., T V, two P#, arrow & markers	5,000.	

298	A113	8c **brown violet & black**	150.00	75.00
		purplish brown & black	150.00	75.00
		On cover		120.00
		On cover, Expo. station canc.		625.00
		Block of four	625.00	375.00
		Margin block of 4, top arrow & markers	635.00	

POSTAGE, 1901, 1902–03

Margin block of 4, bottom arrow & markers & black P#	650.00	
Margin strip of 3, Impt. & P#, T V	625.00	
Margin block of 6, Impt. & P#, T V	4,750.	
Margin strip of 5, bottom Impt., T V, two P#, arrow & markers	1,000.	
Margin block of 10, bottom, Impt., T V, two P#, arrow & markers	8,000.	

299	A114	10c	**yellow brown & black**	225.00	35.00
			dark yellow brown & black	225.00	35.00
			On cover		135.00
			On cover, Expo. station canc.;850.00		
			Block of four	925.00	175.00
			Margin block of 4, top arrow & markers	950.00	
			Margin block of 4, bottom arrow & markers & black P#	975.00	
			Margin strip of 3, Impt. & P#, T V	950.00	
			Margin block of 6, Impt. & P#, T V	7,500.	
			Margin strip of 5, bottom Impt., T V, two P#, arrow & markers	1,500.	
			Margin block of 10, bottom Impt., T V, two P#, arrow & markers	11,500.	

Martha Washington
A121

Daniel Webster
A122

Franklin
A115

Washington
A116

Benjamin Harrison
A123

Henry Clay
A124

Jackson
A117

Grant
A118

Jefferson
A125

David G. Farragut
A126

Lincoln
A119

Garfield
A120

Madison
A127

Marshall
A128

REGULAR ISSUE.

Plates of 400 subjects in four panes of 100 each for all values from 1c to 15c inclusive. Certain plates of 1c, 2c type A129, 3c and 5c show a round marker in margin opposite the horizontal guide line at right or left.

Plates of 200 subjects in two panes of 100 each for 15c, 50c, $1, $2 and $5.

POSTAGE, 1902–03, 1906–08, 1908

1902–03   **Wmkd. USPS (191)**

Perf. 12.

Many stamps of this issue are known with blurred printing due to having been printed on dry paper.

300	A115	1c	**blue green,** *Feb. 1903*	10.00	5
			green	10.00	5
			deep green	10.00	5
			gray green	10.00	5
			yellow green	10.00	6
			On cover		15
			Block of four	40.00	2.00
			Margin strip of 3, Impt. & P#, T V	40.00	
			Margin block of 6, Impt. & P#, T V	185.00	
		b.	Booklet pane of six, *Mar. 6, 1907*	500.00	250.00
			Double transfer	15.00	1.75
			Worn plate	10.50	25
			Cracked plate		
301	A116	2c	**carmine,** *Jan. 17, 1903*	12.50	5
			bright carmine	12.50	5
			deep carmine	12.50	5
			carmine rose	12.50	8
			On cover		15
			Block of four	50.00	2.00
			Margin strip of 3, Impt. & P#, T V	50.00	
			Margin block of 6, Impt. & P#, T V	200.00	
		c.	Booklet pane of six, *Jan. 24, 1903*	425.00	250.00
			Double transfer	20.00	1.50
			Cracked plate		
302	A117	3c	**bright violet,** *Feb. 1903*	45.00	3.00
			violet	45.00	3.00
			deep violet	45.00	3.00
			On cover		12.50
			Block of four	185.00	17.50
			Margin strip of 3, Impt. & P#, T V	185.00	
			Margin block of 6, Impt. & P#, T V	850.00	
			Double transfer	85.00	5.00
			Cracked plate		
303	A118	4c	**brown,** *Feb. 1903*	45.00	1.00
			dark brown	45.00	1.00
			yellow brown	45.00	1.00
			orange brown	45.00	1.00
			red brown	45.00	1.00
			On cover		12.50
			Block of four	185.00	8.50
			Margin strip of 3, Impt. & P#, T V	185.00	
			Margin block of 6, Impt. & P#, T V	850.00	
			Double transfer	80.00	3.50
304	A119	5c	**blue,** *Jan. 1903*	55.00	1.00
			pale blue	55.00	1.00
			bright blue	55.00	1.00
			dark blue	55.00	1.00
			On cover		8.50
			Block of four	225.00	6.00
			Margin strip of 3, Impt. & P#, T V	225.00	
			Margin block of 6, Impt. & P#, T V	950.00	
			Double transfer	90.00	4.00
			Cracked plate		
305	A120	6c	**claret,** *Feb. 1903*	60.00	2.25
			deep claret	60.00	2.25
			brownish lake	75.00	2.25
			dull brownish lake	60.00	2.25
			On cover		15.00
			Block of four	245.00	20.00
			Margin strip of 3, Impt. & P#, T V	245.00	
			Margin block of 6, Impt. & P#, T V	1,000.	
			Double transfer	90.00	3.50
306	A121	8c	**violet black,** *Dec. 1902*	35.00	2.00
			black	35.00	2.00
			slate black	35.00	2.00
			gray lilac	35.00	2.00
			lavender	45.00	2.50
			On cover		10.00
			Block of four	145.00	15.00
			Margin strip of 3, Impt. & P#, T V	145.00	
			Margin block of 6, Impt. & P#, T V	700.00	
			Double transfer	47.50	3.00
307	A122	10c	**pale red brown,** *Feb. 1903*	60.00	1.50
			red brown	60.00	1.50
			dark red brown	60.00	1.50
			On cover		10.00
			Block of four	245.00	8.00
			Margin strip of 3, Impt. & P#, T V	245.00	
			Margin block of 6, Impt. & P#, T V	1,150.	
			Double transfer	110.00	15.00
308	A123	13c	**purple black,** *Nov. 18, 1902*	35.00	8.50
			brown violet	35.00	8.50
			On cover		25.00
			Block of four	145.00	40.00
			Margin strip of 3, Impt. & P#, T V	145.00	
			Margin block of 6, Impt. & P#, T V	650.00	
309	A124	15c	**olive green,** *May 27, 1903*	135.00	6.00
			dark olive green	135.00	6.00
			On cover		50.00
			Block of four	550.00	60.00
			Margin block of 4, arrow	575.00	
			Margin strip of 3, Impt. & P#, T V	550.00	
			Margin block of 6, Impt. & P#, T V	3,000.	
			Double transfer	210.00	12.00
310	A125	50c	**orange,** *Mar. 23, 1903*	450.00	25.00
			deep orange	450.00	25.00
			On cover		350.00
			Block of four	1,900.	125.00
			Margin block of 4, arrow	2,000.	
			Margin strip of 3, Impt. & P#, T V	1,900.	
			Margin block of 6, Impt. & P#, T V	7,500.	
311	A126	$1	**black,** *June 5, 1903*	800.00	60.00
			grayish black	800.00	60.00
			On cover		1,000.
			Block of four	3,300.	275.00
			Margin block of 4, arrow	3,400.	
			Margin strip of 3, Impt. & P#, T V	3,300.	
			Margin block of 6, Impt. & P#, T V	16,500.	
312	A127	$2	**dark blue,** *June 5, 1903*	1,050.	200.00
			blue	1,050.	200.00
			On cover		2,000.
			Block of four	4,400.	850.00
			Margin block of 4, arrow	4,600.	
			Margin strip of 3, Impt. & P#, T V	4,500.	
			Margin block of 6, Impt. & P#, T V	25,000.	
313	A128	$5	**dark green,** *June 5, 1903*	2,750.	650.00
			On cover		4,250.
			Block of four	11,500.	3,000.
			Margin block of 4, arrow	12,000.	
			Margin strip of 3, Impt. & P#, T V	12,000.	
			Margin block of 6, Impt. & P#, T V	62,500.	

For listings of designs A127 and A128 with Perf. 10 see Nos. 479 and 480.

1906–08   *Imperf.*

314	A115	1c	**blue green,** *Oct. 2, 1906*	30.00	21.00
			green	30.00	21.00
			deep green	30.00	21.00
			On cover		30.00
			Block of four	120.00	90.00
			Corner margin block of four	125.00	92.50
			Margin block of 4, arrow	130.00	95.00
			Margin block of 4, arrow & round marker	175.00	
			Center line block	250.00	125.00
			Margin block of 6, Impt. & P#	275.00	
			Double transfer	55.00	30.00
314A	A118	4c	**brown,** *April 1908*	17,500.	9,000.
			On cover		22,500.
			Pair	45,000.	
			Guide line pair	95,000.	

This stamp was issued imperforate but all copies were privately perforated with large oblong perforations at the sides. (Schermack type III).

315	A119	5c	**blue,** *May 12, 1908*	550.00	250.00
			On cover		2,000.
			Block of four	2,250.	1,200.
			Corner margin block of four	2,350.	
			Margin block of 4, arrow	2,400.	
			Margin block of 4, arrow & round marker	2,850.	
			Center line block	3,000.	
			Margin block of 6, Impt. & P#	4,750.	

COIL STAMPS.

Warning! Imperforate stamps have been fraudulently perforated to resemble coil stamps and part-perforate varieties.

1908   *Perf. 12 Horizontally*

316	A115	1c	**blue green,** pair, *Feb. 18, 1908*	22,500.	—
			Guide line pair	55,000.	—
317	A119	5c	**blue,** pair, *Feb. 24, 1908*	5,000.	—
			Guide line pair	7,000.	

POSTAGE, 1908, 1903, 1906, 1908, 1904   147

318	A115	1c	**blue green**, pair, *July 31, 1908*	4,000.	—
			Guide line pair	6,000.	—
			Double transfer		

Coil stamps for use in vending and affixing machines are perforated on two sides only, either horizontally or vertically. They were first issued in 1908, using perf. 12. This was changed to 8½ in 1910, and to 10 in 1914.

Imperforate sheets of certain denominations were sold to the vending machine companies which applied a variety of private perforations and separations. (See Vending and Affixing Machine Perforations section of this catalogue.)

Several values of the 1902 and later issues are found on an apparently coarse-ribbed paper. This is caused by worn blankets on the printing presses and is not a true paper variety.

Washington
A129

Plate of 400 subjects in four panes of 100 each.

1903   Wmkd.      (191)   *Perf. 12*

Die I   Die II

319	A129	2c	**carmine**, Die I, *Nov. 12, 1903*	6.00	5
			bright carmine	6.00	5
			carmine lake	6.00	5
			On cover		10
			Block of four	24.50	2.00
			Margin strip of 3, Impt. & P#, T V (carmine)	23.00	
			Margin block of 6, Impt. & P#, T V (carmine)	100.00	
	a.		2c lake, Die I	—	—
			On cover	—	—
			Block of four (lake)	—	—
			Margin strip of 3, Impt. & P#, T V (lake)	—	
			Margin block of 6, Impt. & P#, T V (lake)	—	
	b.		2c carmine rose, Die I	10.00	20
			On cover		50
			Block of four (carmine rose)	41.00	4.00
			Margin strip of 3, Impt. & P#, T V (carmine rose)	42.50	
			Margin block of 6, Impt. & P#, T V (carmine rose)	200.00	
	c.		2c scarlet, Die I	6.00	6
			On cover		10
			Block of four (scarlet)	24.50	2.00
			Margin strip of 3, Impt. & P#, T V (scarlet)	23.00	
			Margin block of 6, Impt. & P#, T V (scarlet)	100.00	
	d.		Vert. pair, imperf. horiz.	1,200.	
	e.		Vertical pair, imperf. between	550.00	
			Vertical pair, rouletted between	600.00	
	f.		2c lake, Die II	6.50	10
			On cover		20
			Block of four	26.50	3.50
			Double transfer	15.00	2.00

	g.	Booklet pane of six, car., Die I	110.00	20.00
	g.	Booklet pane of six, lake (I)	—	—
	g.	Booklet pane of six, car. rose (I)	—	
	g.	Booklet pane of six, scarlet (I)	110.00	
	h.	Booklet pane of six, car., Die II	200.00	
	h.	Booklet pane of six, lake, (II)	140.00	
	i.	2c carmine, Die II	35.00	—
	j.	2c carmine rose, Die II	—	—
	k.	2c scarlet, Die II	—	

During the use of this stamp, the Postmaster at San Francisco discovered in his stock sheets of No. 319, each of which had the horizontal perforations missing between the two top rows of stamps. To facilitate their separation, the imperf. rows were rouletted, and the stamps sold over the counter. So vertical pairs are found with regular perforations all around and rouletted between.

1906   *Imperf.*

320	A129	2c	**carmine**, *Oct. 2, 1906*	30.00	21.00
			On cover		30.00
			Block of four, carmine	120.00	85.00
			Corner margin block of four, carmine	122.50	
			Margin block of 4, arrow, carmine	125.00	—
			Center line block, carmine	225.00	—
			Margin block of 6, Impt. & P#, T V, carmine	300.00	
	a.		2c lake, Die II	90.00	35.00
			On cover		75.00
			Block of four, lake	360.00	160.00
			Corner margin block of four, lake	365.00	
			Margin block of 4, arrow, lake	375.00	
			Center line block, lake	750.00	
			Margin block of 6, Impt. & P#, T V, lake	1,100.	
	b.		2c scarlet	30.00	21.00
			On cover		30.00
			Block of four, scarlet	120.00	
			Corner margin block of four, scarlet	122.50	
			Margin block of 4, arrow, scarlet	125.00	—
			Center line block, scarlet	225.00	—
			Margin block of 6, Impt. & P#, T V, scarlet	300.00	
			Die II, scarlet		
			Double transfer	40.00	25.00

COIL STAMPS.
1908   *Perf. 12 Horizontally*

| 321 | A129 | 2c | **carmine**, pair, *Feb. 18, 1908* | 35,000. | — |
| | | | Guide line pair | | |

Perf. 12 Vertically

322	A129	2c	**carmine**, pair, *July 31, 1908*	5,250.	—
			Guide line pair	7,500.	
			Double transfer		

This Government Coil Stamp should not be confused with those of the International Vending Machine Co., which are perforated 12½ to 13.

LOUISIANA PURCHASE EXPOSITION ISSUE.

Issued to commemorate the Louisiana Purchase Exposition held at St. Louis, Mo., Apr. 30–Dec. 1, 1904.

Robert R. Livingston
A130

148 POSTAGE, 1904, 1907

Thomas Jefferson
A131

James Monroe
A132

William McKinley
A133

Map of Louisiana Purchase
A134

Plates of 100 (10x10) subjects, divided vertically into 2 panes of 50.

Exposition Station Cancellation

Note on condition and pricing preceding No. 285 also applies to Nos. 323–327.

Wmkd. USPS (191)

1904, Apr. 30   Perf. 12

323	A130	1c green	27.50	5.00
		dark green	27.50	5.00
		On cover		8.50
		On card, Expo. station canc.		55.00
		Block of four	110.00	25.00
		Margin block of 4, arrow, R or L	115.00	
		Margin pair, Impt. & P#, T V	70.00	
		Margin strip of 3, Impt. & P#, T V	110.00	
		Margin block of 4, Impt. & P#, T V	180.00	
		Margin block of 6, Impt. & P#, T V	275.00	
		Diagonal line through left "1" (2138 L 2)	50.00	15.00
		Double transfer	—	—
324	A131	2c carmine	25.00	1.50
		bright carmine	25.00	1.50
		On cover		3.00
		On cover, Expo. station canc.		85.00
		Block of four	100.00	12.50
		Margin block of 4, arrow, R or L	105.00	
		Margin pair, Impt. & P#, T V	65.00	
		Margin strip of 3, Impt. & P#, T V	105.00	
		Margin block of 4, Impt. & P#, T V	180.00	
		Margin block of 6, Impt. & P#, T V	275.00	
		a. Vertical pair, imperf. horiz.	6,000.	
325	A132	3c violet	95.00	35.00
		On cover		45.00
		On cover, Expo. station canc.		300.00
		Block of four	380.00	165.00
		Margin block of 4, arrow, R or L	400.00	
		Margin pair, Impt. & P#, T V	235.00	
		Margin strip of 3, Impt. & P#, T V	350.00	
		Margin block of 4, Impt. & P#, T V	625.00	
		Margin block of 6, Impt. & P#, T V	950.00	
		Double transfer	—	—
326	A133	5c dark blue	110.00	25.00
		On cover		50.00
		On cover, Expo. station canc.		350.00
		Block of four	440.00	120.00
		Margin block of 4, arrow, R or L	450.00	
		Margin pair, Impt. & P#, T V	275.00	
		Margin strip of 3, Impt. & P#, T V	425.00	
		Margin block of 4, Impt. & P#, T V	750.00	
		Margin block of 6, Impt. & P#, T V	1,100.	
327	A134	10c red brown	190.00	35.00
		dark red brown	190.00	35.00
		On cover		100.00
		On cover, Expo. station canc.		525.00
		Block of four	775.00	165.00
		Margin block of 4, arrow, R or L	800.00	
		Margin pair, Impt. & P#, T V	475.00	
		Margin strip of 3, Impt. & P#, T V	725.00	
		Margin block of 4, Impt. & P#, T V	1,600.	
		Margin block of 6, Impt. & P#, T V	2,500.	

JAMESTOWN EXPOSITION ISSUE.

Issued to commemorate the Jamestown Exposition held at Hampton Roads, Va., April 26 to December 1, 1907.

Captain John Smith
A135

Founding of Jamestown
A136

POSTAGE, 1907, 1908-09 149

Pocahontas
A137

Plates of 200 subjects in two panes of 100 each.

Exposition Station Cancellation

1907		Wmkd. USPS (191)			
		Perf. 12.			
328	A135	1c **green,** *Apr. 26, 1907*		20.00	4.00
		dark green		20.00	4.00
		On cover			7.50
		On card, Expo. station canc.			75.00
		Block of four		80.00	35.00
		Margin block of 4, arrow		82.50	
		Margin strip of 3, Impt. & P#, T V		75.00	
		Margin block of 6, Impt. & P#, T V		300.00	
		Double transfer		27.50	6.50
329	A136	2c **carmine,** *Apr. 26, 1907*		27.50	3.00
		bright carmine		27.50	3.00
		On cover			6.00
		On cover, Expo. station canc.			100.00
		Block of four		110.00	17.50
		Margin block of 4, arrow		112.50	
		Margin strip of 3, Impt. & P#, T V		100.00	
		Margin block of 6, Impt. & P#, T V		425.00	
		Double transfer		40.00	5.00
330	A137	5c **blue,** *Apr. 26, 1907*		125.00	30.00
		deep blue		125.00	30.00
		On cover			65.00
		On cover, Expo. station canc.			500.00
		Block of four		500.00	130.00
		Margin block of 4, arrow		510.00	
		Margin strip of 3, Impt. & P#, T V		450.00	
		Margin block of 6, Impt. & P#, T V		2,900.	
		Double transfer		145.00	45.00

Earliest known use: May 10, 1907.

1908-09 REGULAR ISSUE

Plates of 400 subjects in four panes of 100 each for all values 1c to 15c inclusive.

Plates of 200 subjects in two panes of 100 each for 50c and $1 denominations.

In 1909 the Bureau prepared certain plates with horizontal spacings of 3mm. between the outer six vertical rows and 2mm. between the others. This was done to try to counteract the effect of unequal shrinkage of the paper. *However, shrinkage did occur and intermediate spacings are frequently found.* The listings of 2mm. and 3mm. spacings are for exact measurements. Intermediate spacings sell for approximately the same as the cheaper of the two listed spacings. All such plates were marked with an open star added to the imprint and exist on the 1c, 2c, 3c, 4c, and 5c denominations only. A small solid star was added to the imprint and plate number for 1c plate No. 4980, 2c plate No. 4988 and for the 2c Lincoln. All other plates for this issue are spaced 2mm. throughout.

There are several types of some of the 2c and 3c stamps of this and succeeding issues. These types are described under the dates at which they first appeared. The differences between the types are usually minute and difficult to distinguish. Illustrations of Types I-VII of the 2c (A140) and Types I-IV of the 3c (A140) are reproduced by permission of H. L. Lindquist.

China Clay Paper. A small quantity of Nos. 331-340 was printed on paper containing a high mineral content (5-20%), instead of the specified 2%. The minerals, principally aluminum silicate, produced China clay paper. It is thick, hard and grayish, often darker than "bluish" paper.

☆ 4968

Imprint, plate number and open star.

★ 4976

Imprint, plate number and small solid star.

A 5557

Imprint, plate number and "A".

A 5805

"A" and number only.

988

Number only.

The above illustrations are the several styles used on plates of issues from 1908 to date.

Franklin
A138

Washington
A139

Wmkd. USPS (191)

1908-09		Perf. 12			
331	A138	1c **green,** *Dec. 1908*		8.00	5
		bright green		8.00	5
		dark green		8.00	5
		yellow green		8.00	5
		On cover			40
		Block of four (2mm. spacing)		32.50	1.50
		Block of four (3mm. spacing)		33.50	1.75
		Margin block of 6, Impt. & P#, T V		90.00	
		Margin block of 6, Impt. & P# & star		80.00	
		Margin block of 6, Impt. & P# & small solid star (plate 4980)		1,000.	
	a.	Booklet pane of six, *Dec. 2, 1908*		150.00	35.00
		Double transfer		12.00	1.00
		Cracked plate			

POSTAGE, 1908-09

	a. Booklet pane of six, *Dec. 2, 1908*	150.00	35.00
	Double transfer	12.00	1.00
	Cracked plate		
	No. 331 exists in horizontal pair, imperforate between, a variety resulting from booklet experiments. Not regularly issued.		
332	A139 2c **carmine**, *Nov. 1908*	7.50	5
	light carmine	7.50	5
	dark carmine	7.50	5
	On cover		10
	Block of four (2mm. spacing)	31.00	75
	Block of four (3mm. spacing)	32.50	85
	Margin block of 6, Impt. & P#, T V	80.00	
	Margin block of 6, Impt. & P# & star	75.00	
	Margin block of 6, Impt. & P# & small solid star (plate 4988)	950.00	
	a. Booklet pane of six	120.00	35.00
	Double transfer	15.00	1.50
	Double transfer, design of 1c (plate 5299)	1,250.	
	Rosette crack		
	Cracked plate		

Washington—A140

TYPE I

THREE CENTS.

Type I. The top line of the toga rope is weak and the rope shading lines are thin. The 5th line from the left is missing. The line between the lips is thin. (For descriptions of 3c types II, III and IV, see notes and illustrations preceding Nos. 484, 529–530.)

Used on both flat plate and rotary press printings.

333	A140 3c **deep violet**, type I, *Dec. 1908*	30.00	3.00
	violet	30.00	3.00
	light violet	30.00	3.00
	On cover		7.50
	Block of four (2mm. spacing)	122.50	16.00
	Block of four (3mm. spacing)	125.00	17.50
	Margin block of 6, Impt. & P#, T V	350.00	
	Margin block of 6, Impt. & P# & star	375.00	
	Double transfer	45.00	7.50
334	A140 4c **orange brown**, *Dec. 1908*	32.50	1.00
	brown	32.50	1.00
	light brown	32.50	1.00
	dark brown	32.50	1.00
	On cover		6.00
	Block of four (2mm. spacing)	132.50	7.50
	Block of four (3mm. spacing)	135.00	8.50
	Margin block of 6, Impt. & P#, T V	375.00	
	Margin block of 6, Impt. & P# & star	375.00	
	Double transfer	65.00	4.00

335	A140 5c **blue**, *Dec. 1908*	45.00	2.00
	bright blue	45.00	2.00
	dark blue	45.00	2.00
	On cover		7.50
	Block of four (2mm. spacing)	182.50	12.00
	Block of four (3mm. spacing)	185.00	10.00
	Margin block of 6, Impt. & P#, T V	600.00	
	Margin block of 6, Impt. & P# & star	625.00	
	Double transfer	50.00	4.50
336	A140 6c **red orange**, *Jan. 1909*	50.00	4.50
	pale red orange	50.00	4.50
	orange	70.00	4.50
	On cover		20.00
	Block of four	210.00	30.00
	Margin block of 6, Impt. & P#, T V	900.00	
337	A140 8c **olive green**, *Dec. 1908*	37.50	2.50
	deep olive green	37.50	2.50
	On cover		15.00
	Block of four	152.50	15.00
	Margin block of 6, Impt. & P#, T V	475.00	
	Double transfer	60.00	6.00
338	A140 10c **yellow**, *Jan. 1909*	65.00	1.50
	On cover		10.00
	Block of four	265.00	7.50
	Margin block of 6, Impt. & P#, T V	1,000.	
	Double transfer		
	Very thin paper		
339	A140 13c **blue green**, *Jan. 1909*	35.00	22.50
	deep blue green	35.00	22.50
	On cover		100.00
	Block of four	145.00	110.00
	Margin block of 6, Impt. & P#, T V	475.00	
	Line through "TAG" of "POSTAGE" (4948 L. R. 96)	70.00	40.00
340	A140 15c **pale ultramarine**, *Jan. 1909*	60.00	5.75
	ultramarine	60.00	5.75
	On cover		90.00
	Block of four	250.00	40.00
	Margin block of 6, Impt. & P#, T V	650.00	
341	A140 50c **violet**, *Jan. 13, 1909*	300.00	15.00
	dull violet	300.00	15.00
	On cover		1,500.
	Block of four	1,250.	85.00
	Margin block of 4, arrow, right or left	1,350.	
	Margin block of 6, Impt. & P#, T V	7,500.	
342	A140 $1 **violet brown**, *Jan. 29, 1909*	450.00	85.00
	light violet brown	450.00	85.00
	On cover		2,000.
	Block of four	1,900.	400.00
	Margin block of 4, arrow, right or left	2,000.	400.00
	Margin block of 6, Impt. & P#, T V	12,500.	
	Double transfer		

For listings of other perforated stamps of **A138**, **A139** and **A140** see

Nos. 357 to 366   Bluish paper
"   374 to 382, 405 to 407   Single line wmk. Perf. 12
"   424 to 430   Single line wmk. Perf. 10
"   461   Single line wmk. Perf. 11
"   462 to 469   Unwmkd. Perf. 10
"   498 to 507   Unwmkd. Perf. 11
"   519   Double line wmk. Perf. 11
"   525 to 530 and 536   Offset printing
"   538 to 546   Rotary press printing

Imperf.

343	A138 1c **green**, *Dec. 1908*	8.00	3.50
	dark green	8.00	3.50
	yellowish green	8.00	3.50
	On cover		7.50
	Block of four (2mm. or 3mm. spacing)	32.00	15.00
	Margin block of 4, arrow, 2mm. or 3mm.	35.00	15.50
	Corner margin block of four, 2mm. or 3mm.	32.50	15.50
	Center line block	50.00	20.00
	Margin block of 6, Impt. & P#, T V	80.00	35.00
	Margin block of 6, Impt. & P# & star	90.00	37.50

Critters like these...
have a home in Texas!!

URGENTLY NEEDED!
Pay 100% Scott for
XF NH perforated stamps
#331-547 ... others
wanted too!

Sam Houston Philatelics

14654 Memorial, Houston, TX 77079
MAILING ADDRESS
P.O. Box 820087, Houston, TX 77282

ALWAYS BUYING...

Call Toll-free 1-800-231-5926
Texas 1-713-493-6386
Bob Dumaine-Owner

See our Business Reply Card in the back of this catalogue or
circle Reader Service Card **#83** for Free Price Lists and Auction Catalogues.

Stamp Monthly QUIZ

1 How can I keep this catalogue up-to-date?

2 Where can I find out what's happening at Scott under its new ownership?

3 What is the only monthly publication that gives a comprehensive listing of *all* new issues with the Scott number for each stamp?

4 Where can I find the most interesting and exciting writing in philately today?

ANSWERS: 1, 2, 3 and 4 — SCOTT STAMP MONTHLY

To order you subscription today, return the subscription card inside the back cover of this catalogue or send your name and address along with $18 for 12 issues or $32 for 24 issues *(50% off the cover price)* to:

SCOTT P.O. Box 828, Sidney, Ohio 45365

In Canada add $8 per year for postage. Outside U.S./Canada add $23 per year for postage.
Please allow 6 to 8 weeks for delivery of first issue.

POSTAGE, 1908-09, 1908-10, 1909

344	A139		Margin block of 6, Impt. & P# & small solid star (plate 4980)	750.00	
			Double transfer	20.00	7.00
		2c	carmine, *Dec. 10, 1908*	11.00	3.00
			light carmine	11.00	3.00
			dark carmine	11.00	3.00
			On cover		5.00
			Block of four (2mm. or 3mm. spacing)	44.00	13.00
			Margin block of 4, arrow, 2mm. or 3mm.	47.50	14.00
			Corner margin block of four, 2mm. or 3mm.	45.00	14.00
			Center line block	65.00	25.00
			Margin block of 6, Impt. & P#, T V	145.00	
			Margin block of 6, Impt. & P# & star	130.00	
			Double transfer	20.00	5.00
			Double transfer, design of 1c (plate 5299)	1,250.	
345	A140	3c	deep violet, type I, *Mar. 3, 1909*	22.50	13.50
			violet	22.50	13.50
			On cover		30.00
			Block of four	90.00	57.50
			Corner margin block of four	95.00	60.00
			Margin block of 4, arrow	100.00	60.00
			Center line block	135.00	80.00
			Margin block of 6, Impt. & P#, T V	300.00	110.00
			Double transfer	35.00	20.00
346	A140	4c	orange brown, *Feb. 25, 1909*	40.00	20.00
			brown	40.00	20.00
			On cover		50.00
			Block of four (2mm. or 3mm. spacing)	160.00	85.00
			Margin block of 4, arrow, 2mm. or 3mm.	175.00	90.00
			Corner margin block of four 2mm. or 3 mm.	165.00	90.00
			Center line block	240.00	100.00
			Margin block of 6, Impt. & P#, T V	400.00	150.00
			Margin block of 6, Impt. & P# & star	450.00	
			Double transfer	75.00	30.00
347	A140	5c	blue, *Feb. 25, 1909*	60.00	35.00
			dark blue	60.00	35.00
			On cover		100.00
			Block of four	240.00	125.00
			Corner margin block of four	245.00	135.00
			Margin block of 4, arrow	260.00	150.00
			Center line block	400.00	175.00
			Margin block of 6, Impt. & P#, T V	650.00	250.00
			Cracked plate		

For listings of other imperforate stamps of designs A138, A139 and A140 see

Nos. 383, 384, 408, 409 and 459 Single line wmk.
" 481 to 485 Unwmkd.
" 531 to 535 Offset printing

1908-10
COIL STAMPS
Perf. 12 Horizontally

348	A138	1c	green, *Dec. 29, 1908*	22.50	13.00
			dark green	22.50	13.00
			On cover		22.50
			Pair	55.00	35.00
			Guide line pair	175.00	85.00
349	A139	2c	carmine, *Jan. 1909*	45.00	6.00
			dark carmine	45.00	6.00
			On cover		12.50
			Pair	105.00	16.00
			Guide line pair	225.00	40.00
			Double transfer, design of 1c (plate 5299)		
350	A140	4c	orange brown, *Aug. 15, 1910*	110.00	65.00
			On cover		100.00
			Pair	250.00	150.00
			Guide line pair	750.00	250.00
351	A140	5c	blue, *Jan. 1909*	130.00	80.00
			dark blue	130.00	80.00
			On cover		135.00
			Pair	290.00	185.00
			Guide line pair	800.00	350.00

1909
Perf. 12 Vertically

352	A138	1c	green, *Jan. 1909*	55.00	18.50
			dark green	55.00	18.50
			On cover		35.00
			Pair (2mm. spacing)	135.00	45.00
			Pair (3mm. spacing)	130.00	42.50
			Guide line pair	275.00	85.00
			Double transfer		
353	A139	2c	carmine, *Jan. 12, 1909*	45.00	6.00
			dark carmine	45.00	6.00
			On cover		15.00
			Pair (2mm. spacing)	110.00	17.50
			Pair (3mm. spacing)	105.00	15.00
			Guide line pair	275.00	50.00
354	A140	4c	orange brown, *Feb. 23, 1909*	120.00	50.00
			On cover		75.00
			Pair (2mm. spacing)	285.00	100.00
			Pair (3mm. spacing)	275.00	95.00
			Guide line pair	750.00	200.00
355	A140	5c	blue, *Feb. 23, 1909*	130.00	70.00
			On cover		110.00
			Pair	300.00	150.00
			Guide line pair	800.00	250.00
356	A140	10c	yellow, *Jan. 7, 1909*	1,300.	375.00
			On cover		3,000.
			Pair	3,250.	950.00
			Guide line pair	7,500.	2,250.

These Government Coil Stamps, Nos. 352-355, should not be confused with those of the International Vending Machine Co., which are perf. 12½-13.

For listings of other coil stamps of designs A138, A139 and A140 see

Nos. 385 to 396, 410 to 413, 441 to 459 Single line wmk.
Nos. 486 to 496 Unwmkd.

BLUISH PAPER.

This was made with 35 per cent rag stock instead of all wood pulp. The bluish color goes through the paper showing clearly on the back as well as on the face.

1909
Perf. 12.

357	A138	1c	green, *Feb. 16, 1909*	110.00	100.00
			On cover		200.00
			Block of four (2mm. spacing)	450.00	425.00
			Block of four (3mm. spacing)	850.00	
			Margin block of 6, Impt. & P#, T V	1,150.	
			Margin block of 6, Impt. & P# & star	3,250.	
358	A139	2c	carmine, *Feb. 16, 1909*	100.00	75.00
			On cover		200.00
			Block of four (2mm. spacing)	410.00	325.00
			Block of four (3mm. spacing)	450.00	
			Margin block of 6, Impt. & P#, T V	1,100.	
			Margin block of 6, Impt. & P# & star	1,750.	
			Double transfer		
359	A140	3c	deep violet, type I	1,650.	1,250.
			On cover		2,000.
			Block of four	6,750.	
			Margin block of 6, Impt. & P# T V	16,500.	
360	A140	4c	orange brown	14,000.	
			Block of four	57,500.	
			Margin strip of 3, Impt. & P#, T V	60,000.	
361	A140	5c	blue	3,500.	4,000.
			Block of four	15,000.	
			Margin block of 6, Impt. & P#, T V	35,000.	
362	A140	6c	red orange	1,000.	650.00
			On cover		
			Block of four	4,250.	
			Margin block of 6, Impt. & P#, T V	11,000.	
363	A140	8c	olive green	14,000.	
			Block of four	57,500.	
			Margin strip of 3, Impt. & P#, T V	55,000.	
364	A140	10c	yellow	1,050.	700.00
			On cover		
			Block of four	4,500.	
			Margin block of 6, Impt. & P#, T V	12,000.	
365	A140	13c	blue green	2,100.	1,100.
			On cover		1,750.
			Block of four	8,750.	5,500.
			Margin block of 6, Impt. & P# T V	17,500.	
366	A140	15c	pale ultramarine	950.00	700.00
			On cover		
			Block of four	4,000.	
			Margin block of 6, Impt. & P#, T V	9,500.	

POSTAGE, 1909, 1910-11

LINCOLN MEMORIAL ISSUE.

Issued to commemorate the 100th anniversary of the birth of Abraham Lincoln.

Lincoln
A141

1909

Wmkd. USPS (191)

Plates of 400 subjects in four panes of 100 each.

Perf. 12

367	A141	2c **carmine**, *Feb. 12, 1909*	7.00	2.75
		bright carmine	7.00	2.75
		On cover		4.50
		Block of four (2mm. spacing)	28.00	12.00
		Block of four (3mm. spacing)	28.00	11.50
		Margin block of 6, Impt. & P# & small solid star	160.00	
		Double transfer	11.00	4.00

Imperf.

368	A141	2c **carmine**, *Feb. 12, 1909*	35.00	30.00
		On cover		42.50
		Block of four (2mm. or 3mm. spacing)	140.00	125.00
		Corner margin block of four	150.00	
		Margin block of 4, arrow	160.00	135.00
		Center line block	210.00	150.00
		Margin block of 6, Impt. & P# & small solid star	300.00	
		Double transfer	55.00	35.00

BLUISH PAPER.
Perf. 12.

369	A141	2c **carmine**, *Feb. 1909*	275.00	200.00
		On cover		300.00
		Block of four (2mm. or 3mm. spacing)	1,150.	850.00
		Margin block of 6, Impt. & P# & small solid star	4,250.	

ALASKA-YUKON-PACIFIC EXPOSITION ISSUE.

Issued to commemorate the Alaska-Yukon Pacific Exposition, held at Seattle, Wash., June 1–Oct. 16, 1909.

William H. Seward
A142

1909   *Perf. 12*

Wmkd. USPS (191)

Plates of 280 subjects in four panes of 70 each.

370	A142	2c **carmine**, *June 1, 1909*	12.00	2.25
		bright carmine	12.00	2.25
		On cover		5.00
		On cover, Expo. station canc.		75.00
		Block of four	52.00	11.00
		Margin block of 6, Impt. & P# T V	300.00	
		Double transfer (5249 U.L.8)	17.50	5.00

Imperf.

371	A142	2c **carmine**, *June 1909*	50.00	35.00
		On cover		45.00
		On cover, Expo. station canc.		175.00
		Block of four	220.00	145.00
		Corner margin block of four	225.00	
		Margin block of 4, arrow	230.00	150.00
		Center line block	300.00	160.00
		Margin block of 6, Impt. & P#, T V	400.00	
		Double transfer	65.00	40.00

Earliest known use: June 13.

HUDSON-FULTON CELEBRATION ISSUE.

Issued to commemorate the tercentenary of the discovery of the Hudson River and the centenary of Robert Fulton's steamship, the "Clermont."

Henry Hudson's "Half Moon" and Fulton's Steamship "Clermont"—A143

1909   Wmkd. USPS (191)   *Perf. 12*

Plates of 240 subjects in four panes of 60 each.

372	A143	2c **carmine**, *Sept. 25, 1909*	16.00	4.75
		On cover		9.00
		Block of four	64.00	20.00
		Margin block of 6, Impt. & P#, T V	350.00	
		Double transfer (5393 and 5394)	21.00	6.00

Imperf.

373	A143	2c **carmine**, *Sept. 25, 1909*	55.00	35.00
		On cover		45.00
		Block of four	220.00	145.00
		Corner margin block of four	225.00	
		Margin block of 4, arrow	250.00	155.00
		Center line block	375.00	175.00
		Margin block of 6, Impt. & P#, T V	450.00	
		Double transfer (5393 and 5394)	70.00	40.00

REGULAR ISSUE.

1910-11   DESIGNS OF 1908-09 ISSUES.

In this issue the Bureau used three groups of plates:

(1) The old standard plates with uniform 2mm. spacing throughout (6c, 8c, 10c and 15c values);

(2) Those having an open star in the margin and showing spacings of 2mm. and 3mm. between stamps (for all values 1c to 10c); and

(3) A third set of plates with uniform spacing of approximately 2¾mm. between all stamps. These plates have imprints showing

a. "Bureau of Engraving & Printing", "A" and number.
b. "A" and number only.
c. Number only.
        (See above No. 331)

These were used for the 1c, 2c, 3c, 4c and 5c values.

On or about Nov. 1, 1910 the Bureau began using paper watermarked with single-lined letters,

(Actual size of letter)

POSTAGE, 1910–11, 1911, 1910

repeated in rows, this way:

[watermark pattern diagram showing U S P S letters repeated in rows]

1910-11   Wmkd. **USPS** (190)   *Perf. 12*
Plates of 400 subjects in four panes of 100 each.

374	A138	1c green, *Nov. 23, 1910*	7.50	6
		light green	7.50	6
		dark green	7.50	6
		On cover		8
		Block of four (2mm. spacing)	31.50	3.00
		Block of four (3mm. spacing)	31.00	2.75
		Margin block of 6, Impt. & P#, & star	85.00	
		Margin block of 6, Impt. & P# & "A"	100.00	
	a.	Booklet pane of six, *Oct. 7, 1910*	135.00	30.00
		Double transfer	12.50	2.50
		Cracked plate		
		Pane of sixty	1,200.	

Panes of 60 of No. 374 were regularly issued in Washington, D. C. during Sept. and Oct., 1912. They were made from the six outer vertical rows of imperforate "Star Plate" sheets that had been rejected for use in vending machines on account of the 3 mm. spacing. These panes have sheet margins on two adjoining sides and are imperforate along the other two sides. Both sheet margins show the plate number, imprint and star.

375	A139	2c carmine, *Nov. 23, 1910*	7.00	5
		bright carmine	7.00	5
		dark carmine	7.00	5
		lake	125.00	
		On cover		6
		Block of four (2mm. spacing)	29.00	1.25
		Block of four (3mm. spacing)	28.00	1.00
		Margin block of 6, Impt. & P# & star	85.00	
		Margin block of 6, Impt. & P# & "A"	95.00	
	a.	Booklet pane of six, *Nov. 30, 1910*	110.00	25.00
		Cracked plate		
		Double transfer	12.50	2.50
		Double transfer, design of 1c (plate 5299)		1,000.
376	A140	3c deep violet, type I, *Jan. 16, 1911*	17.50	1.50
		violet	17.50	1.50
		lilac	20.00	1.65
		On cover		7.50
		Block of four (2mm. spacing)	72.50	8.50
		Block of four (3mm. spacing)	70.00	8.00
		Margin block of 6, Impt. & P# & star	165.00	
		Margin block of 6, P# only	200.00	
377	A140	4c brown, *Jan. 20, 1911*	25.00	50
		dark brown	25.00	50
		orange brown	25.00	50
		On cover		7.50
		Block of four (2mm. spacing)	102.50	3.25
		Block of four (3mm. spacing)	100.00	3.00

		Margin block of 6, Impt. & P# & star	225.00	
		Margin block of 6, P# only	250.00	
		Double transfer		
378	A140	5c blue, *Jan. 25, 1911*	25.00	50
		light blue	25.00	50
		dark blue	25.00	50
		bright blue	25.00	50
		On cover		5.00
		Block of four (2mm. spacing)	102.50	5.00
		Block of four (3mm. spacing)	100.00	4.00
		Margin block of 6, Impt. & P#, T V	275.00	
		Margin block of 6, Impt. & P# & star	265.00	
		Margin block of 6, "A" & P#	325.00	
		Margin block of 6, P# only	325.00	
		Double transfer		
379	A140	6c red orange, *Jan. 25, 1911*	35.00	75
		light red orange	35.00	75
		On cover		12.50
		Block of four (2mm. spacing)	145.00	8.50
		Block of four (3mm. spacing)	142.50	8.00
		Margin block of 6, Impt. & P# T V	500.00	
		Margin block of 6, Impt. & P# & star	450.00	
380	A140	8c olive green, *Feb. 8, 1911*	115.00	13.50
		dark olive green	115.00	12.50
		On cover		40.00
		Book of four (2mm. spacing)	475.00	60.00
		Block of four (3mm. spacing)	475.00	57.50
		Margin block of 6, Impt. & P# T V	1,250.	
		Margin block of 6, Impt. & P# & star	1,750.	
381	A140	10c yellow, *Jan. 24, 1911*	110.00	4.00
		On cover		17.50
		Block of four (2mm. spacing)	450.00	25.00
		Block of four (3mm. spacing)	450.00	22.50
		Margin block of 6, Impt. & P#, T V	1,300.	
		Margin block of 6, Impt. & P# & star	1,250.	
382	A140	15c pale ultramarine, *Mar. 1, 1911*	260.00	15.00
		On cover		100.00
		Block of four	1,050.	90.00
		Margin block of 6, Impt. & P#, T V	2,500.	

1911   *Imperf.*

383	A138	1c green, *Jan. 3, 1911*	4.00	3.00
		dark green	4.00	3.00
		yellowish green	4.00	3.00
		bright green	4.00	3.00
		On cover		5.00
		Block of four (2mm. or 3mm. spacing)	16.00	13.00
		Corner margin block of four	17.00	
		Margin block of 4, arrow	17.50	13.50
		Center line block	35.00	16.00
		Margin block of 6, Impt. & P# & star	65.00	27.50
		Margin block of 6, Impt. & P# & "A"	125.00	
		Double transfer	10.00	6.00
384	A139	2c carmine, *Jan. 3, 1911*	6.00	2.00
		light carmine	6.00	2.00
		dark carmine	6.00	2.00
		On cover		2.50
		Horizontal pair	17.50	6.00
		Block of four (2mm. or 3mm. spacing)	36.00	12.00
		Corner margin block of four	37.00	
		Margin block of 4, arrow	37.00	18.00
		Center line block	75.00	30.00
		Margin block of 6, Impt. & P# & star	200.00	
		Margin block of 6, Impt. & P# & "A"	250.00	
		Double transfer, design of 1c (plate 5299)	1,250.	
		Double transfer	12.00	2.75
		Cracked plate	30.00	

COIL STAMPS.

1910   *Perf. 12 Horizontally*

385	A138	1c green, *Nov. 1, 1910*	21.00	12.00
		dark green	21.00	12.00
		On cover		25.00
		Pair	52.00	27.50
		Guide line pair	200.00	85.00

POSTAGE, 1910, 1910-11, 1910, 1910-13, 1913   155

386	A139	2c **carmine**, *Nov. 1, 1910*	40.00	11.00
		light carmine	40.00	11.00
		On cover		20.00
		Pair	100.00	27.50
		Guide line pair	375.00	65.00

1910-11   *Perf. 12 Vertically.*

387	A138	1c **green**, *Nov. 1, 1910*	70.00	22.50
		On cover		35.00
		Pair (2mm. spacing)	175.00	50.00
		Pair (3mm. spacing)	185.00	52.50
		Guide line pair	350.00	120.00
388	A139	2c **carmine**, *Nov. 1, 1910*	550.00	75.00
		On cover		200.00
		Pair (2mm. spacing)	1,600.	200.00
		Pair (3mm. spacing)	1,650.	225.00
		Guide line pair	3,750.	550.00

Stamps sold as No. 388 frequently are privately perforated copies of 384, or copies of 375, with horizontal perforations removed.

389	A140	3c **deep vio.**, type I, *Jan. 24, 1911*	13,000.	5,250.
		On cover		8,000.
		Pair	40,000.	

This is the rarest coil, only a small supply being used at Orangeburg, N. Y.
(See note above No. 316.)

Perf. 8½ Horizontally.

390	A138	1c **green**, *Dec. 12, 1910*	4.50	3.25
		dark green	4.50	3.25
		On cover		6.00
		Pair	10.00	7.00
		Guide line pair	27.50	11.00
		Double transfer		
391	A139	2c **carmine**, *Dec. 23, 1910*	32.50	8.50
		light carmine	32.50	8.50
		On cover		20.00
		Pair	75.00	20.00
		Guide line pair	175.00	50.00

1910-13   *Perf. 8½ Vertically.*

392	A138	1c **green**, *Dec. 12, 1910*	20.00	15.00
		dark green	20.00	15.00
		On cover		40.00
		Pair	45.00	35.00
		Guide line pair	110.00	60.00
		Double transfer		
393	A139	2c **carmine**, *Dec. 16, 1910*	40.00	6.00
		dark carmine	40.00	6.00
		On cover		15.00
		Pair	90.00	15.00
		Guide line pair	200.00	25.00
394	A140	3c **deep violet**, type I, *Sept. 18, 1911*	50.00	27.50
		violet	50.00	27.50
		red violet	50.00	27.50
		On cover		75.00
		Pair (2mm. spacing)	115.00	65.00
		Pair (3mm. spacing)	110.00	62.50
		Guide line pair	300.00	110.00
395	A140	4c **brown**, *Apr. 15, 1912*	50.00	27.50
		dark brown	50.00	27.50
		On cover		75.00
		Pair (2mm. spacing)	115.00	65.00
		Pair (3mm. spacing)	110.00	62.50
		Guide line pair	300.00	110.00
396	A140	5c **blue**, *Mar. 1913*	50.00	27.50
		dark blue	50.00	27.50
		On cover		75.00
		Pair	110.00	65.00
		Guide line pair	300.00	120.00

PANAMA-PACIFIC EXPOSITION ISSUE.

Issued to commemorate the Panama-Pacific Exposition held at San Francisco, Cal., Feb. 20-Dec. 4, 1915.

Vasco Nunes de Balboa
A144

Pedro Miguel Locks, Panama Canal
A145

Golden Gate
A146

Discovery of San Francisco Bay
A147

Exposition Station Cancellation.

1913   Wmkd. USPS (190)

Plates of 280 subjects in four panes of 70 each.
Perf. 12.

397	A144	1c **green**, *Jan. 1, 1913*	17.50	1.75
		deep green	17.50	1.75
		yellowish green	17.50	1.75
		On cover		2.50
		On card, Expo. station 1915 canc.		50.00
		Block of four	70.00	7.50
		Margin block of 6, P# only	175.00	
		Double transfer	27.50	3.00
398	A145	2c **carmine**, *Jan. 1913*	20.00	50
		deep carmine	20.00	50
		lake	225.00	
		On cover		1.00
		On cover, Expo. station 1915 canc.		65.00
		Block of four	80.00	5.00
		Margin block of 6, P# only	300.00	
		Double transfer	35.00	2.00
399	A146	5c **blue**, *Jan. 1, 1913*	80.00	11.00
		dark blue	80.00	11.00
		On cover		25.00
		On cover, Expo. station 1915 canc.		300.00
		Block of four	325.00	55.00
		Margin block of 6, P# only	2,250.	

POSTAGE, 1913, 1914–15, 1912–14, 1912

400	A147	10c	**orange yellow,** *Jan. 1, 1913*	150.00	25.00
			On cover		50.00
			On cover, Expo. station 1915 canc.		400.00
			Block of four	625.00	110.00
			Margin block of 6, P# only	3,000.	
400A	A147	10c	**orange,** *Aug.1913*	250.00	20.00
			On cover		60.00
			On cover, Expo. station 1915 canc.		425.00
			Block of four	1,050.	85.00
			Margin block of 6, P# only	9,500.	

1914–15   Perf. 10

401	A144	1c	**green,** *Dec.1914*	27.50	6.50
			dark green	27.50	6.50
			On cover		15.00
			On card, Expo. station 1915 canc.		120.00
			Block of four	110.00	30.00
			Margin block of 6, P# only	375.00	
402	A145	2c	**carmine,** *Feb.1915*	90.00	1.50
			deep carmine	90.00	1.50
			red	90.00	1.50
			On cover		5.00
			On cover, Expo. station 1915 canc.		185.00
			Block of four	365.00	13.50
			Margin block of 6, P# only	1,850.	
403	A146	5c	**blue,** *Feb. 1915*	190.00	17.50
			dark blue	190.00	17.50
			On cover		35.00
			On cover, Expo. station 1915 canc.		450.00
			Block of four	775.00	75.00
			Margin block of 6, P# only	4,500.	
404	A147	10c	**orange,** *July 1915*	1,400.	70.00
			On cover		120.00
			On cover, Expo. station 1915 canc.		850.00
			Block of four	5,650.	310.00
			Margin block of 6, P# only	15,000.	

REGULAR ISSUE.

Washington
A140

Wmkd. USPS (190)

1912–14   Perf. 12

The plates for this and later issues were the so-called "A" plates with uniform spacing of 2¾mm. between stamps.

Plates of 400 subjects in four panes of 100 each for all values 1c to 50c inclusive.

Plates of 200 subjects in two panes of 100 each for $1 and some of the 50c (No. 422) denomination.

405	A140	1c	**green,** *Feb.1912*	7.00	6
			light green	7.00	6
			dark green	7.00	6
			yellowish green	7.00	6
			On cover		10
			Block of four	28.50	1.00
			Margin block of 6, Impt. & P# & "A"	140.00	
			Margin block of 6, "A" & P#	125.00	
			Margin block of 6, P# only	115.00	
		a.	Vert. pair, imperf. horiz.	650.00	
		b.	Booklet pane of six, *Feb. 8, 1912*	65.00	7.50
			Cracked plate	25.00	
			Double transfer	12.00	

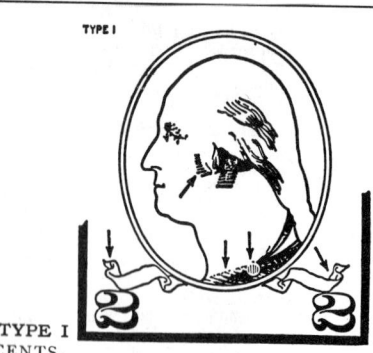

TYPE I

TYPE I
TWO CENTS.

Type I. There is one shading line in the first curve of the ribbon above the left "2" and one in the second curve of the ribbon above the right "2".

The button of the toga has only a faint outline.

The top line of the toga rope, from the button to the front of the throat, is also very faint.

The shading lines of the face terminate in front of the ear with little or no joining, to form a lock of hair.

Used on both flat plate and rotary press printings.

406	A140	2c	**carmine,** type I, *Feb. 1912*	6.00	5
			bright carmine	6.00	5
			dark carmine	6.00	5
			lake	150.00	25.00
			On cover		5
			Block of four	24.50	75
			Margin block of 6, Impt. & P# & "A"	165.00	
			Margin block of 6, "A" & P#	150.00	
			Margin block of 6, P# only	140.00	
			Margin block of 6, Electrolytic, (Pl. 6023)	350.00	
		a.	Booklet pane of six, *Feb. 8, 1912*	70.00	17.50
		b.	Double impression		
			Double transfer	12.50	1.00
407	A140	7c	**black,** *Apr.1914*	100.00	8.00
			grayish black	100.00	8.00
			intense black	100.00	8.00
			On cover		30.00
			Block of four	410.00	45.00
			Margin block of 6, P# only	1,250.	

1912   Imperf.

408	A140	1c	**green,** *Mar.1912*	1.50	60
			yellowish green	1.50	60
			dark green	1.50	60
			On cover		1.10
			Block of four	6.00	2.50
			Corner margin block of four	6.25	2.65
			Margin block of 4, arrow	6.25	2.65
			Center line block	11.00	6.50
			Margin block of 6, Impt. & P# & "A", T, B or L	70.00	13.00
			Margin block of 6, Impt. & P# & "A", at right	750.00	
			Margin block of 6, "A" & P#	35.00	
			Margin block of 6, P# only	25.00	5.50
			Double transfer	4.00	1.20
			Cracked plate		
409	A140	2c	**carmine,** type I, *Feb.1912*	1.65	60
			deep carmine	1.65	60
			scarlet	1.65	60
			On cover		1.00
			Block of four	6.60	2.75
			Corner margin block of four	6.75	
			Margin block of 4, arrow	6.75	3.25
			Center line block	12.50	7.00
			Margin block of 6, Impt. & P# & "A"	75.00	10.00
			Margin block of 6, "A" & P#	65.00	
			Margin block of 6, P# only	50.00	
			Cracked plate (Plates 7580, 7582)	25.00	

In December, 1914, the Post Office at Kansas City, Missouri, had on hand a stock of imperforate sheets of 400 of stamps Nos. 408 and 409, formerly sold for use in vending machines, but not then in demand. In order to make them salable, they were rouletted with ordinary tracing wheels and were sold over the counter with official approval of the Post Office Department given January 5, 1915. These stamps were sold until the supply was exhausted. Except for one full sheet of 400 of each value, all were cut into panes of 100 before being rouletted and sold. They are known as "Kansas City Roulettes".

POSTAGE, 1912, 1912–14, 1912, 1914–15   157

1912 COIL STAMPS.
Perf. 8½ Horizontally

410	A140	1c green, *Mar.1912*		6.25	3.50
		dark green		6.25	3.50
		On cover			6.50
		Pair		13.50	8.00
		Guide line pair		35.00	14.00
		Double transfer			
411	A140	2c carmine, type I, *Mar.1912*		7.75	3.75
		deep carmine		7.75	3.75
		On cover			7.50
		Pair		16.50	8.50
		Guide line pair		42.50	14.00
		Double transfer		12.00	6.00

Perf. 8½ Vertically.

412	A140	1c green, *Mar. 18, 1912*		21.00	5.00
		deep green		21.00	5.00
		On cover			10.00
		Pair		44.00	12.00
		Guide line pair		90.00	20.00
413	A140	2c carmine, type I, *Mar.1912*		30.00	60
		dark carmine		30.00	60
		On cover			5.00
		Pair		65.00	4.00
		Guide line pair		165.00	12.50
		Double transfer		60.00	2.50

Franklin
A148

Wmkd. USPS (190)

1912–14 Perf. 12

414	A148	8c pale olive green, *Feb. 1912*		35.00	1.50
		olive green		35.00	1.50
		On cover			15.00
		Block of four		145.00	12.00
		Margin block of 6, Impt. & P#		475.00	
415	A148	9c salmon red, *Apr.1914*		47.50	15.00
		rose red		47.50	15.00
		On cover			45.00
		Block of four		195.00	75.00
		Margin block of 6, P# only		750.00	
416	A148	10c orange yellow, *Jan.1912*		35.00	30
		yellow		35.00	30
		brown yellow		150.00	
		On cover			2.50
		Block of four		145.00	1.75
		Margin block of 6, Impt. & P# & "A"		525.00	
		Margin block of 6, "A" & P#		550.00	
		Double transfer			
417	A148	12c claret brown, *Apr.1914*		40.00	4.50
		deep claret brown		40.00	4.50
		On cover			20.00
		Block of four		165.00	22.50
		Margin block of 6, P# only		550.00	
		Double transfer		55.00	7.50
		Triple transfer		75.00	10.00
418	A148	15c gray, *Feb.1912*		75.00	3.50
		dark gray		75.00	3.50
		On cover			10.00
		Block of four		310.00	20.00
		Margin block of 6, Impt. & P#		750.00	
		Margin block of 6, "A" & P#		800.00	
		Margin block of 6, P# only		850.00	
		Double transfer			
419	A148	20c ultramarine, *Apr.1914*		175.00	16.00
		dark ultramarine		175.00	16.00
		On cover			110.00
		Block of four		725.00	75.00
		Margin block of 6, P# only		2,000.	

420	A148	30c orange red, *Apr.1914*		110.00	16.00
		dark orange red		110.00	16.00
		On cover			125.00
		Block of four		450.00	75.00
		Margin block of 6, P# only		1,750.	
421	A148	50c violet, *Apr. 29, 1914*		500.00	17.50
		bright violet		500.00	17.50
		On cover			1,000.
		Block of four		2,100.	85.00
		Margin block of 6, P# only		9,000.	

1912 Wmkd. USPS (191)

422	A148	50c violet, *Feb. 12, 1912*		250.00	17.50
		On cover			1,000.
		Block of four		1,050.	80.00
		Margin block of 4, arrow, R or L		1,250.	
		Margin block of 6, Impt. & P# & "A"		5,500.	
423	A148	$1 violet brown, *Feb. 12, 1912*		575.00	70.00
		On cover			2,000.
		Block of four		2,400.	300.00
		Margin block of 4, arrow, R or L		2,500.	
		Margin block of 6, Impt. & P# & "A"		12,500.	
		Double transfer (5782 L. 66)		650.00	80.00

During the United States occupation of Vera Cruz, Mexico, from April to November, 1914, letters sent from there show Provisional Postmarks.

For other listings of perforated stamps of design A148, see:

Nos. 431 to 440	Single line wmk.	Perf. 10
" 460	Double line wmk.	Perf. 10
" 470 to 478	Unwmkd.	Perf. 10
" 508 to 518	Unwmkd.	Perf. 11

1914–15 Wmkd. USPS (190) Perf. 10

Plates of 400 subjects in four panes of 100 each.

424	A140	1c green, *Sept. 5, 1914*		2.75	6
		bright green		2.75	6
		deep green		2.75	6
		yellowish green		2.75	6
		On cover			10
		Block of four		11.00	75
		Margin block of 6, P# only		45.00	
		Block of ten with imprint "COIL STAMPS" and number (6581-82, 85, 89)		175.00	
		Cracked plate			
		Double transfer		7.50	1.00
		a. Perf. 12x10		300.00	250.00
		b. Perf. 10x12			125.00
		c. Vert. pair, imperf. horiz.		425.00	250.00
		d. Booklet pane of six, *Jan. 6, 1914*		4.00	75
		e. Vert. pair, imperf. btwn.			

Most copies of No. 424b are precancelled Dayton, Ohio, to which the price applies.

425	A140	2c rose red, type I, *Sept. 5, 1914*		2.50	5
		dark rose red		2.50	5
		carmine rose		2.50	5
		carmine		2.50	5
		dark carmine		2.50	5
		scarlet		2.50	5
		red			6
		On cover			6
		Block of four		10.00	35
		Margin block of 6, P# only		30.00	
		Block of ten with imprint "COIL STAMPS" and number (6566-73)		175.00	
		Cracked plate		15.00	
		Double transfer			
		c. Perf. 10x12			250.00
		d. Perf. 12x10			3.00
		e. Booklet pane of six, *Jan. 6, 1914*		15.00	

The aniline inks used on some printings of Nos. 425, 426 and 435 caused a pink tinge to permeate the paper and appear on the back. These are called "pink backs."

426	A140	3c deep violet, type I, *Sept. 18, 1914*		12.50	1.25
		violet		12.50	1.25
		bright violet		12.50	1.25
		3c reddish violet		12.50	1.25
		On cover			3.00
		Block of four		52.50	6.50
		Margin block of 6, P# only		135.00	
427	A140	4c brown, *Sept. 7, 1914*		32.50	40
		dark brown		32.50	40
		orange brown		32.50	40

POSTAGE, 1914-15, 1914, 1915-16

		yellowish brown	32.50	40	
		On cover		2.50	
		Block of four	132.50	3.75	
		Margin block of 6, P# only	400.00		
		Double transfer	60.00	2.50	
428	A140	5c **blue**, *Sept. 14, 1914*	27.50	40	
		bright blue	27.50	40	
		dark blue	27.50	40	
		indigo blue	27.50	50	
		On cover		1.25	
		Block of four	112.50	2.50	
		Margin block of 6, P# only	285.00		
		a. Perf. 12x10		400.00	
429	A140	6c **red orange**, *Sept. 28, 1914*	37.50	1.20	
		deep red orange	37.50	1.20	
		pale red orange	37.50	1.20	
		On cover		8.50	
		Block of four (2mm. spacing)	160.00	11.00	
		Block of four (3mm. spacing)	155.00	10.00	
		Margin block of 6, Impt. & P# & star	300.00		
		Margin block of 6, P# only	350.00		
430	A140	7c **black**, *Sept. 10, 1914*	90.00	4.25	
		gray black	90.00	4.25	
		intense black	90.00	4.25	
		On cover		35.00	
		Block of four	375.00	25.00	
		Margin block of 6, P# only	850.00		
431	A148	8c **pale olive green**, *Sept. 26, 1914*	35.00	1.50	
		olive green	35.00	1.50	
		On cover		5.00	
		Block of four	145.00	10.00	
		Margin block of 6, Impt. & "A"	400.00		
		Margin block of 6, "A" & P#	450.00		
		Double impression			
		Double transfer			
432	A148	9c **salmon red**, *Oct. 6, 1914*	50.00	8.50	
		dark salmon red	50.00	8.50	
		On cover		20.00	
		Block of four	210.00	40.00	
		Margin block of 6, P# only	550.00		
433	A148	10c **orange yellow**, *Sept. 9, 1914*	45.00	25	
		golden yellow	45.00	25	
		On cover		7.50	
		Block of four	200.00	1.50	
		Margin block of 6, Impt. & "A"	550.00		
		Margin block of 6, "A" & P#	550.00		
		Margin block of 6, P# only	550.00		
434	A148	11c **dark green**, *Aug. 11, 1915*	22.50	7.00	
		bluish green	22.50	7.00	
		On cover		20.00	
		Block of four	90.00	32.50	
		Margin block of 6, P# only	200.00		
435	A148	12c **claret brown**, *Sept. 10, 1914*	25.00	4.50	
		deep claret brown	25.00	4.50	
		On cover		17.50	
		Block of four	100.00	25.00	
		Margin block of 6, P# only	250.00		
		a. 12c copper red	27.50	4.50	
		a. On cover		17.50	
		a. Block of four	110.00	25.00	
		a. Margin block of 6, P# only	275.00		
		b. Vertical pair, imperf. between	650.00		
		Double transfer	40.00	7.50	
		Triple transfer	50.00	9.00	
437	A148	15c **gray**, *Sept. 16, 1914*	115.00	7.25	
		dark gray	115.00	7.25	
		On cover		50.00	
		Block of four	475.00	40.00	
		Margin block of 6, Impt. & "A"	850.00		
		Margin block of 6, "A" & P#	875.00		
		Margin block of 6, P# only	850.00		
438	A148	20c **ultramarine**, *Sept. 19, 1914*	225.00	4.00	
		dark ultramarine	225.00	4.00	
		On cover		100.00	
		Block of four	950.00	25.00	
		Margin block of 6, P# only	2,500.		
439	A148	30c **orange red**, *Sept. 19, 1914*	275.00	20.00	
		dark orange red	275.00	20.00	
		On cover		150.00	
		Block of four	1,150.	95.00	
		Margin block of 6, P# only	3,500.		
440	A148	50c **violet**, *Dec. 10, 1915*	800.00	20.00	
		On cover		1,000.	
		Block of four	3,300.	85.00	
		Margin block of 6, P# only	11,000.		

COIL STAMPS

1914 — *Perf. 10 Horizontally*

441	A140	1c **green**, *Nov. 14, 1914*	1.00	90
		deep green	1.00	90
		On cover		2.00
		Pair	2.25	2.00
		Guide line pair	7.50	3.50
442	A140	2c **carmine**, type I, *July 22, 1914*	10.00	7.50
		deep carmine	10.00	7.50
		On cover		12.50
		Pair	21.00	17.50
		Guide line pair	55.00	35.00

1914 — *Perf. 10 Vertically*

443	A14	1c **green**, *May 29, 1914*	20.00	6.00
		deep green	20.00	6.00
		On cover		12.00
		Pair	47.50	13.50
		Guide line pair	110.00	30.00
444	A140	2c **carmine**, type I, *Apr. 25, 1914*	30.00	1.50
		deep carmine	30.00	1.50
		red	30.00	1.50
		On cover		2.50
		Pair	70.00	4.00
		Guide line pair	175.00	9.50
445	A140	3c **violet**, type I, *Dec. 18, 1914*	225.00	110.00
		deep violet	225.00	110.00
		On cover		200.00
		Pair	500.00	250.00
		Guide line pair	1,100.	400.00
446	A140	4c **brown**, *Oct. 2, 1914*	130.00	35.00
		On cover		75.00
		Pair	300.00	80.00
		Guide line pair	650.00	140.00
447	A140	5c **blue**, *July 30, 1914*	45.00	22.50
		On cover		35.00
		Pair	105.00	55.00
		Guide line pair	225.00	100.00

No. 443 represents stamps from coils. Part of a sheet of No. 424 is also known which is perforated vertically and imperforate horizontally.

ROTARY PRESS STAMPS.

The Rotary Press Stamps are printed from plates that are curved to fit around a cylinder. This curvature produces stamps that are slightly larger, either horizontally or vertically, than those printed from flat plates. Designs of stamps from flat plates measure about 18½-19 mm. wide by 22 mm. high. When the impressions are placed sidewise on the curved plates the designs are 19½-20 mm. wide; when they are placed vertically the designs are 22½ to 23 mm. high. A line of color (not a guide line) shows where the curved plates meet or join on the press.

Rotary Press Coil Stamps were printed from plates of 170 subjects for stamps coiled sidewise, and from plates of 150 subjects for stamps coiled endwise.

Double paper listings of Rotary Press stamps have been discontinued and deleted from this catalogue. Collectors are referred to the note on "Rotary Press Double Paper" in the "Information for Collectors" in the front of the catalogue.

ROTARY PRESS COIL STAMPS.

Stamp designs 18½ to 19 mm. wide by 22½ mm. high.

1915-16 — *Perf. 10 Horizontally*

448	A140	1c **green**, *Dec. 12, 1915*	7.50	3.00
		light green	7.50	3.00
		On cover		6.50
		Pair	16.50	7.00
		Joint line pair	45.00	17.50

6568 COIL STAMPS

Type of plate number and imprint used for the 12 special 1c and 2c plates designed for the production of coil stamps.

POSTAGE, 1915–16, 1914–16, 1914, 1915, 1916–17   159

TYPE II

TWO CENTS.
Type II. Shading lines in ribbons as on type I.
The toga button, rope and rope shading lines are heavy.
The shading lines of the face at the lock of hair end in a strong vertical curved line.
Used on rotary press printings only.

TYPE III

Type III. Two lines of shading in the curves of the ribbons.
Other characteristics similar to type II.
Used on rotary press printings only.

449	A140	2c **red**, type I, *Dec. 5, 1915*	1,600.	160.00
		carmine rose, type I	—	275.00
		On cover, type I		3.00
		Pair, type I	3,500.	375.00
		Joint line pair, type I	7,500.	750.00
450	A140	2c **carmine**, type III, *Feb. 1916*	11.00	3.00
		carmine rose, type III	11.00	3.00
		red, type III	11.00	3.00
		On cover, type III		7.00
		Pair, type III	23.00	8.00
		Joint line pair, type III	60.00	15.00

1914–16   *Perf. 10 Vertically*

Stamp designs 19½ to 20 mm. wide by 22 mm. high.

452	A140	1c **green**, *Nov. 11, 1914*	10.00	1.75
		On cover		3.00
		Pair	22.50	4.00
		Joint line pair	72.50	8.00
453	A140	2c **carmine rose**, type I, *July 3, 1914*	120.00	4.50
		On cover, type I		10.00
		Pair, type I	250.00	11.00
		Joint line pair, type I	575.00	35.00
		Cracked plate, type I		
454	A140	2c **red**, type II, *June, 1915*	115.00	13.50
		carmine, type II	115.00	13.50
		On cover, type II		35.00
		Pair, type II	240.00	35.00
		Joint line pair, type II	575.00	90.00
455	A140	2c **carmine**, type III, *Dec. 1915*	10.00	1.00
		carmine rose, type III	10.00	1.00
		On cover, type III		2.00
		Pair, type III	21.00	2.50
		Joint line pair, type III	60.00	5.00

Fraudulently altered copies of Type III (Nos. 455, 488, 492 and 540) have had one line of shading scraped off to make them resemble Type II (Nos. 454, 487, 491 and 539).

456	A140	3c **violet**, type I, *Feb. 2, 1916*	300.00	95.00
		deep violet	300.00	95.00
		red violet	300.00	95.00
		On cover		175.00
		Pair	650.00	225.00
		Joint line pair	1,300.	400.00
457	A140	4c **brown**, *Feb. 18, 1916*	30.00	18.00
		light brown	30.00	18.00
		On cover		40.00
		Pair	65.00	45.00
		Joint line pair	165.00	75.00
		Cracked plate	60.00	—
458	A140	5c **blue**, *Mar. 9, 1916*	30.00	18.00
		On cover		40.00
		Pair	65.00	45.00
		Joint line pair	165.00	75.00
		Double transfer	—	—

1914   *Imperf.*
Horizontal Coil

459	A140	2c **carmine**, type I, *June 30, 1914*	450.00	600.00
		On cover		—
		Pair	950.00	1,350.
		Joint line pair	2,100.	3,250.

Most line pairs of No. 459 are creased. Uncreased pairs command a premium.

FLAT PLATE PRINTINGS
Wmkd. **USPS** (191)

1915   *Perf. 10*

460	A148	$1 **violet black**, *Feb. 8, 1915*	975.00	95.00
		On cover		1,500.
		Block of four	4,100.	425.00
		Margin block of 4, arrow, R or L	4,250.	
		Margin block of 6, Impt. & P# & "A"	12,500.	
		Double transfer (5782 L. 66)	1,050.	105.00

Wmkd. **USPS** (190)

1915   *Perf. 11*

461	A140	2c **pale car. red**, type I, *June 17, 1915*	100.00	85.00
		On cover		500.00
		Block of four	410.00	375.00
		Margin block of 6, P# only	950.00	

Fraudulently perforated copies of No. 409 are offered as No. 461.

FLAT PLATE PRINTINGS

Plates of 400 subjects in four panes of 100 each for all values 1c to 50c inclusive.
Plates of 200 subjects in two panes of 100 each for $1, $2 and $5 denominations.
The Act of Oct. 3, 1917, effective Nov. 2, 1917, created a 3 cent rate. Local rate, 2 cents.

1916–17   *Perf. 10*   Unwmkd.

462	A140	1c **green**, *Sept. 27, 1916*	8.50	20
		light green	8.50	20
		dark green	8.50	20
		bluish green	8.50	20
		On cover		40
		Block of four	34.00	2.00
		Margin block of 6, P# only	150.00	
	a.	Booklet pane of six, *Oct. 15, 1916*	12.00	1.00
463	A140	2c **carmine**, type I, *Sept. 25, 1916*	4.25	10
		dark carmine	4.25	10
		rose red	4.25	10
		On cover		15
		Block of four	17.50	1.25
		Margin block of 6, P# only	120.00	
	a.	Booklet pane of six, *Oct. 8, 1916*	75.00	15.00
		Double transfer	9.00	1.00
464	A140	3c **violet**, type I, *Nov. 11, 1916*	80.00	11.00
		deep violet	80.00	11.00
		On cover		25.00
		Block of four	325.00	60.00
		Margin block of 6, P# only	1,350.	
		Double transfer in "CENTS"	110.00	
465	A140	4c **orange brown**, *Oct. 7, 1916*	40.00	1.75
		deep brown	40.00	1.75
		brown	40.00	1.75
		On cover		5.00
		Block of four	165.00	15.00
		Margin block of 6, P# only	650.00	
		Double transfer		
466	A140	5c **blue**, *Oct. 17, 1916*	75.00	1.75
		dark blue	75.00	1.40
		On cover		12.50
		Block of four	310.00	12.00
		Margin block of 6, P# only	900.00	

POSTAGE, 1916–17, 1917, 1916–17

467	A140	5c **carmine** (error in plate of 2c) *Mar. 7, 1917*	750.00	525.00
		On cover		1,500.
		Block of 9, middle stamp the error	1,000.	850.00
		Block of 12, two middle stamps errors	1,750.	1,500.
		Margin block of six 2c stamps (#463), P#7942	135.00	

No. 467 is an error caused by using a 5c transfer roll in re-entering three subjects: 7942 U. L. 74, 7942 U. L. 84, 7942 L. R. 18; the balance of the subjects on the plate being normal 2c entries. No. 467 imperf. is listed as No. 485.

468	A140	6c **red orange**, *Oct. 10, 1916*	95.00	7.50
		On cover		35.00
		Block of four	385.00	40.00
		Margin block of 6, P# only	1,150.	
		Double transfer		
469	A140	7c **black**, *Oct. 10, 1916*	125.00	13.00
		gray black	125.00	13.00
		On cover		40.00
		Block of four	510.00	70.00
		Margin block of 6, P# only	1,350.	
470	A148	8c **olive green**, *Nov. 13, 1916*	50.00	6.50
		dark olive green	50.00	6.50
		On cover		25.00
		Block of four	210.00	35.00
		Margin block of 6, Impt. & P# & "A"	525.00	
		Margin block of 6, "A" & P#	575.00	
471	A148	9c **salmon red**, *Nov. 16, 1916*	57.50	16.00
		On cover		35.00
		Block of four	235.00	65.00
		Margin block of 6, P# only	650.00	
472	A148	10c **orange yellow**, *Oct. 17, 1916*	110.00	1.00
		On cover		7.50
		Block of four	450.00	7.50
		Margin block of 6, P# only	1,350.	
473	A148	11c **dark green**, *Nov. 16, 1916*	30.00	17.50
		On cover		40.00
		Block of four	125.00	85.00
		Margin block of 6, P# only	325.00	
474	A148	12c **claret brown**, *Oct. 10, 1916*	50.00	5.00
		On cover		20.00
		Block of four	200.00	25.00
		Margin block of 6, P# only	550.00	
		Double transfer	60.00	7.50
		Triple transfer	80.00	12.00
475	A148	15c **gray**, *Nov. 16, 1916*	175.00	12.00
		dark gray	175.00	12.00
		On cover		60.00
		Block of four	725.00	75.00
		Margin block of 6, P# only	2,500.	
		Margin block of 6, Impt. & & "A"	—	
476	A148	20c **light ultramarine**, *Dec. 5, 1916*	250.00	12.50
		ultramarine	250.00	12.50
		On cover		150.00
		Block of four	1,050.	75.00
		Margin block of 6, P# only	3,500.	
476A	A148	30c **orange red**		
		Block of four	—	—
		Margin block of 6, P# only	—	
477	A148	50c **light violet**, *Mar. 2, 1917*	1,400.	75.00
		On cover		1,200.
		Block of four	5,750.	375.00
		Margin block of 6, P# only	25,000.	
478	A148	$1 **violet black**, *Dec. 22, 1916*	950.00	20.00
		On cover		1,500.
		Block of four	4,000.	100.00
		Margin block of 4, arrow, R or L	4,250.	
		Margin block of 6, Impt. & P# & "A"	13,000.	
		Double transfer (5782 L. 66)	1,050.	27.50

TYPES OF 1902–03 ISSUE.

1917   Perf. 10   Unwmkd.

479	A127	$2 **dark blue**, *Mar. 22, 1917*	500.00	45.00
		On cover		1,000.
		Block of four	2,000.	200.00
		Margin block of 4, arrow, R or L	2,100.	
		Margin block of 6, P# only	6,000.	
		Double transfer		
480	A128	$5 **light green**, *Mar. 22, 1917*	400.00	47.50
		On cover		1,000.
		Block of four	1,600.	210.00
		Margin block of 4, arrow, R or L	1,700.	
		Margin block of 6, P# only	4,500.	

1916–17   *Imperf.*

481	A140	1c **green**, *Nov. 1916*	1.00	75
		bluish green	1.00	75
		deep green	1.00	75
		On cover		1.25
		Block of four	4.00	3.25
		Corner margin block of four	4.25	
		Margin block of 4, arrow	4.50	2.50
		Center line block	10.00	
		Margin block of 6, P# only	15.00	5.00
		Margin block of 6, Electrolytic (Pl. 13376-13377)	350.00	
		Double transfer	4.00	2.00

During September, 1921, the Bureau of Engraving and Printing issued a 1c stamp printed from experimental electrolytic plates made in accordance with patent granted to George U. Rose. Tests at that time did not prove satisfactory and the method was discontinued. Four plates were made, viz., 13376, 13377, 13389 and 13390 from which stamps were issued. They are difficult to distinguish from the normal varieties. (See No. 498).

TYPE Ia

TWO CENTS.

Type Ia. The design characteristics are similar to type I except that all of the lines of the design are stronger.

The toga button, toga rope and rope shading lines are heavy. The latter characteristics are those of type II, which, however, occur only on impressions from rotary plates.

Used only on flat plates 10208 and 10209.

482	A140	2c **carmine**, type I, *Dec. 8, 1916*	1.25	1.25
		deep carmine	1.25	1.25
		carmine rose	1.25	1.25
		deep rose	1.25	1.25
		On cover		2.25
		Block of four	5.00	5.00
		Corner margin block of four	5.25	5.25
		Margin block of 4, arrow	5.50	5.50
		Center line block	8.00	
		Margin block of 6, P# only	25.00	12.00
		Cracked plate	—	
482A	A140	2c **deep rose**, type Ia		6,000.
		On cover		9,000.

The imperforate, type Ia, was issued but all known copies were privately perforated with large oblong perforations at the sides. (Schermack type III)

Earliest known use: Feb. 27, 1920.

TYPE II

Canceled equals Precanceled?

 Catalogue Value ~~6¢~~ $50

Catalogue Value ~~8¢~~ $300

 Catalogue Value ~~$17.50~~ $500

Catalogue Value ~~10¢~~ $1,000

Obviously Not!

Are you missing out on gems like these? Bureau precancels were introduced late in 1916 in an effort to reduce the costs of local precanceling. These "experimentals" were used in three cities.

In May 1923 Bureau Precanceling became part of the printing process, preceding gumming and perforating. This was the real start of the collecting field that now numbers over 9,400 stamps. To find out if you have some of the rarities in your collection or to learn about this exciting philatelic area, send $2 for the Precancel Stamp Society Bureau Precancel Catalog.

A few Local Types are illustrated in this Catalogue on page 38. Hundreds of types are listed at more than $100 each. Thousands more sell at 100 to 2000 times the Scott Catalogue value as used stamps. To identify these send $15 for the Fourth edition of the P.S.S. Town and Type Catalog of Local Precancels.

Precancel Stamp Society
12045 Hickory Hills Court, Oakton, VA 22124

POSTAGE, 1916-17, 1916-19, 1916-22, 1917-19

THREE CENTS.

Type II. The top line of the toga rope is strong and the rope shading lines are heavy and complete. The line between the lips is heavy. Used on both flat plate and rotary press printings.

483	A140	3c **violet**, type I, *Oct. 13, 1917*		15.00	8.50
		light violet, type I		15.00	8.50
		On cover, type I			15.00
		Block of four, type I		60.00	36.00
		Corner margin block of four, type I		62.50	
		Margin block of 4, arrow, type I		62.50	
		Center line block, type I		90.00	
		Margin block of 6, P# only, type I		175.00	
		Double transfer, type I		25.00	——
		Triple transfer, type I			
484	A140	3c **violet**, type II		11.00	4.00
		deep violet, type II		11.00	4.00
		On cover, type II			7.50
		Block of four, type II		44.00	17.50
		Corner margin block of four, type II		45.00	
		Margin block of 4, arrow, type II		45.00	
		Center line block, type II		65.00	
		Margin block of 6, P# only, type II		135.00	
		Double transfer, type II		20.00	7.50
485	A140	5c **carmine** (error), *Mar. 1917*		13,000.	
		Block of 9, middle stamp the error		15,000.	
		Block of 12, two middle stamps errors		28,500.	
		Margin block of six 2c stamps (#482), P#7942		300.00	

(*See note under No. 467.*)

ROTARY PRESS COIL STAMPS.
(*See note over No. 448.*)

1916-19   *Perf. 10 Horizontally.*

Stamp designs 18½ to 19 mm. wide by 22½ mm. high.

486	A140	1c **green**, *Jan. 1918*		1.00	15
		yellowish green		1.00	15
		On cover			35
		Pair		2.25	35
		Joint line pair		4.50	75
		Cracked plate			
		Double transfer		4.00	1.50
487	A140	2c **carmine**, type II, *Nov. 15, 1916*		18.00	2.50
		On cover, type II			5.00
		Pair, type II		37.50	6.00
		Joint line pair, type II		135.00	20.00
		Cracked plate			

(*See note after No. 455*)

488	A140	2c **carmine**, type III, *1919*		3.00	1.50
		carmine rose, type III		3.00	1.50
		On cover, type II			3.00
		Pair, type III		6.50	3.50
		Joint line pair, type III		20.00	8.00
		Cracked plate, type III		20.00	7.50
489	A140	3c **violet**, type I, *Oct. 10, 1917*		5.50	1.00
		dull violet		5.50	1.00
		bluish violet		5.50	1.00
		On cover			2.00
		Pair		11.50	2.50
		Joint line pair		35.00	7.00

1916-22   *Perf. 10 Vertically.*

Stamp designs 19½ to 20 mm. wide by 22 mm. high.

490	A140	1c **green**, *Nov. 17, 1916*		75	15
		yellowish green		75	15
		On cover			25
		Pair		1.75	35
		Joint line pair		4.75	75
		Double transfer			
		Cracked plate (horizontal)		12.00	——
		Cracked plate (vertical) retouched		14.00	——
		Rosette crack		16.50	——
491	A140	2c **carmine**, type II, *Nov. 17, 1916*		1,450.	200.00
		On cover, type II			300.00
		Pair, type II		3,100.	450.00
		Joint line pair, type II		7,000.	

(*See note after No. 455*)

492	A140	2c **carmine**, type III		9.00	15
		carmine rose, type III		9.00	15
		On cover, type III			25
		Pair, type III		19.00	40
		Joint line pair, type III		55.00	2.00
		Double transfer, type III			
		Cracked plate			
493	A140	3c **violet**, type I, *July 23, 1917*		21.00	3.00
		reddish violet, type I		21.00	3.00
		On cover, type I			6.00
		Pair, type I		43.50	7.50
		Joint line pair, type I		140.00	25.00
494	A140	3c **violet**, type II, *Feb. 4, 1918*		11.50	60
		dull violet, type II		11.50	60
		gray violet, type II		11.50	60
		On cover, type II			1.00
		Pair, type II		24.00	1.50
		Joint line pair, type II		75.00	3.50
495	A140	4c **orange brown**, *Apr. 15, 1917*		12.50	3.50
		On cover			5.00
		Pair		26.00	8.00
		Joint line pair		85.00	13.50
		Cracked plate		35.00	5.00
496	A140	5c **blue**, *Jan. 15, 1919*		4.50	60
		On cover			1.00
		Pair		9.50	1.50
		Joint line pair		30.00	4.50
497	A148	10c **orange yellow**, *Jan. 31, 1922*		26.50	8.50
		On cover			15.00
		Pair		55.00	18.50
		Joint line pair		150.00	37.50

FLAT PLATE PRINTINGS.

Plates of 400 subjects in four panes of 100 each.

TYPES OF 1914-15 ISSUE.

1917-19   **Unwmkd.**   *Perf. 11*

498	A140	1c **green**, *Mar. 1917*		25	5
		light green		25	5
		dark green		25	5
		yellowish green		25	5
		On cover			5
		Block of four		1.00	25
		Margin block of 6, P# only		15.00	
		Margin block of 6, Electrolytic (Pl. 13376-7, 13389-90) *see note after No. 481*		250.00	
	a.	Vertical pair, imperf. horiz.		175.00	
	b.	Horizontal pair, imperf. between		75.00	
	c.	Vertical pair, imperf. between		450.00	
	d.	Double impression		150.00	
	g.	Perf. 10 at top or bottom		500.00	——
		Cracked plate (10656 U. L. and 10645 L. R.)		10.00	——
		Double transfer		7.50	2.00
	e.	Booklet pane of six, *Apr. 6, 1917*		1.75	35
	f.	Booklet pane of thirty		550.00	
499	A140	2c **rose**, type I, *Mar. 1917*		25	5
		dark rose, type I		25	5
		carmine rose, type I		25	5
		On cover, type I			6
		Block of four, type I		1.00	20
		Margin block of 6, P# only, type I		14.00	
	a.	Vertical pair, imperf. horiz., type I		150.00	
	b.	Horiz. pair, imperf. vert., type I		150.00	100.00
	c.	Vert. pair, imperf. btwn., type I		500.00	225.00
	e.	Booklet pane of six, type I, *Mar. 31, 1917*		2.00	50
	f.	Booklet pane of thirty, type I		9,000.	
	g.	Double impression, type I		125.00	——
		Double impression, type I, 15 mm. wide			
		Cracked plate, type I		——	——
		Recut in hair, type I		——	——
		Double transfer, type I		6.00	——
500	A140	2c **deep rose**, type Ia		275.00	130.00
		On cover, type Ia			225.00
		Block of four, type Ia		1,150.	550.00
		Margin block of 6, P# only, type Ia		2,250.	
		Margin block of 6, P#, two stamp type I (P# 10208 L.L)		6,750.	
		Pair, types I and Ia (10208 L. L. 95 or 96)		1,350.	
501	A140	3c **light violet**, type I, *Mar. 1917*		17.50	10
		violet, type I		17.50	10
		dark violet, type I		17.50	10
		reddish violet, type I		17.50	10
		On cover, type I			12
		Block of four, type I		70.00	1.60
		Margin block of 6, P# only, type I		175.00	
	b.	Blkt. pane of 6, type I, *Oct. 17, 1917*		75.00	15.00
	c.	Vert. pair, imper. horiz., type I		300.00	
	d.	Double impression		150.00	
		Double transfer, type I		25.00	
502	A140	3c **dark violet**, type II		20.00	25
		violet, type II		20.00	25
		On cover, type II			40
		Block of four, type II		80.00	1.75
		Margin block of 6, P# only, type II		210.00	
	b.	Blkt. pane of 6, type II, *Feb. 25, 1918*		50.00	10.00
	c.	Vert. pair, imperf. horiz., type II		250.00	125.00
	d.	Double impression		125.00	
	e.	Perf. 10 at top or bottom		425.00	——

POSTAGE, 1917–19, 1917, 1918

503	A140	4c **brown**, *Mar. 1917*	13.00	20
		dark brown	13.00	20
		orange brown	13.00	20
		yellow brown	13.00	20
		On cover		50
		Block of four	52.50	85
		Margin block of 6, P# only	175.00	
		b. Double impression		
		Double transfer	30.00	2.00
504	A140	5c **blue**, *Mar. 1917*	10.00	8
		light blue	10.00	8
		dark blue	10.00	8
		On cover		20
		Block of four	40.00	75
		Margin block of 6, P# only	140.00	
		a. Horizontal pair, imperf. between	1,250.	
		Double transfer	20.00	
505	A140	5c **rose** (error), *Mar. 23, 1917*	550.00	400.00
		On cover		1,000.
		Block of 9, middle stamp the error	750.00	600.00
		Block of 12, two middle stamps errors	1,300.	
		Margin block of six 2c stamps (#499), P# 7942	35.00	
		(*See note under No. 467.*)		
506	A140	6c **red orange**, *Mar. 1917*	15.00	30
		orange	15.00	30
		On cover		2.50
		Block of four	60.00	1.35
		Margin block of 6, P# only	210.00	
		a. Perf. 10 at top or bottom	500.00	250.00
		Double transfer		
507	A140	7c **black**, *Mar. 1917*	32.50	1.50
		gray black	32.50	1.50
		intense black	32.50	1.50
		On cover		7.50
		Block of four	132.50	8.50
		Margin block of 6, P# only	325.00	
		Double transfer		
508	A148	8c **olive bister**, *Mar. 1917*	13.50	70
		dark olive green	13.50	70
		olive green	13.50	70
		On cover		2.50
		Block of four	55.00	4.00
		Margin block of 6, Impt. & P# & "A"	225.00	
		Margin block of 6, "A" & P#	275.00	
		Margin block of 6, P# only	200.00	
		b. Vertical pair, imperf. between		
		c. Perf. 10 at top or bottom		500.00
509	A148	9c **salmon red**, *Mar. 1917*	17.50	2.75
		salmon	17.50	2.75
		On cover		12.50
		Block of four	72.50	14.00
		Margin block of 6, P# only	190.00	
		Double transfer	35.00	4.50
		a. Perf. 10 at top or bottom		300.00
510	A148	10c **orange yellow**, *Mar. 1917*	20.00	10
		golden yellow	20.00	10
		On cover		2.00
		Block of four	82.50	75
		Margin block of 6, "A" & P#	350.00	
		Margin block of 6, P# only	250.00	
511	A148	11c **light green**, *May 1917*	10.00	3.75
		green	10.00	3.75
		dark green	11.00	3.75
		On cover		8.00
		Block of four	41.00	17.50
		Margin block of 6, P# only	120.00	
		Double transfer	15.00	5.00
		a. Perf. 10 at top or bottom	650.00	275.00
512	A148	12c **claret brown**, *May 1917*	10.50	45
		a. 12c brown carmine	11.00	45
		On cover		4.00
		Block of four	42.50	3.00
		Margin block of 6, P# only	140.00	
		Double transfer	20.00	3.00
		Triple transfer	30.00	5.00
		b. Perf. 10 at top or bottom		300.00
513	A148	13c **apple green**, *Jan. 10, 1919*	12.00	7.00
		pale apple green	12.00	7.00
		deep apple green	14.00	7.50
		On cover		17.50
		Block of four	48.00	35.00
		Margin block of 6, P# only	135.00	
514	A148	15c **gray**, *May 1917*	47.50	1.00
		dark gray	47.50	1.00
		On cover		25.00
		Block of four	195.00	10.00
		Margin block of 6, P# only	650.00	
		Double transfer		
515	A148	20c **light ultramarine**, *May 1917*	60.00	30
		deep ultramarine	62.50	30
		gray blue	60.00	30
		On cover		40.00
		Block of four	245.00	2.00
		Margin block of 6, P# only	750.00	
		b. Vertical pair, imperf. between	325.00	
		c. Double impression	400.00	
		Double transfer		
		d. Perf. 10 at top or bottom	1,200.	
516	A148	30c **orange red**, *May 1917*	47.50	95
		dark orange red	47.50	95
		On cover		100.00
		Block of four	195.00	6.00
		Margin block of 6, P# only	575.00	
		Double transfer		
		a. Perf. 10 at top or bottom	850.00	
517	A148	50c **red violet**, *May 1917*	90.00	65
		violet	110.00	65
		light violet	115.00	75
		On cover		200.00
		Block of four	365.00	3.00
		Margin block of 6, P# only	1,350.	
		b. Vertical pair, imperf. between	1,750.	750.00
		Double transfer	165.00	2.50
		c. Perf. 10 at top or bottom		700.00
518	A148	$1 **violet brown**, *May 1917*	75.00	1.75
		violet black	75.00	1.75
		b. $1 deep brown	650.00	200.00
		On cover		200.00
		Block of four	310.00	8.00
		Margin block of 4, arrow right or left	320.00	
		Margin block of 6, Impt. & P# & "A"	1,200.	
		Double transfer (5782 L. 66)	100.00	2.50

TYPE OF 1908-09 ISSUE.

1917 Wmkd. USPS (191)

This is the result of an old stock of No. 344 which was returned to the Bureau in 1917 and perforated with the then current gauge 11.

Perf. 11.

519	A139	2c **carmine**, *Oct. 10, 1917*	250.00	275.00
		On cover		1,750.
		Block of four	1,050.	
		Margin block of 6, T V, Impt. & P#	2,500.	

Franklin
A149

Plates of 100 subjects.
Unwmkd. *Perf. 11*

1918, Aug.

523	A149	$2 **orange red & black**	1,100.	200.00
		red orange & black	1,100.	200.00
		On cover		2,000.
		Block of four	4,500.	850.00
		Margin block of 4, arrow	4,600.	
		Center line block	4,750.	950.00
		Margin block of 8, two P# & arrow	18,500.	
524	A149	$5 **deep green & black**	450.00	30.00
		On cover		1,500.
		Block of four	1,850.	125.00
		Margin block of 4, arrow	1,900.	130.00
		Center line block	2,000.	140.00
		Margin block of 8, two P# & arrow	6,000.	

For other listing of design A149 see No. 547.

1918-20   OFFSET PRINTING

Plates of 400, 800 or 1600 subjects in panes of 100 each, as follows:

No. 525 — 400 and 1600 subjects.
No. 526 — 400, 800 and 1600 subjects.
No. 529 — 400 subjects only.
No. 531 — 400 subjects only.
No. 532 — 400, 800 and 1600 subjects.
No. 535 — 400 subjects only.
No. 536 — 400 and 1600 subjects.

TYPES OF 1917-19 ISSUE.
Unwmkd.   *Perf. 11.*

525	A140	1c gray green, *Dec. 1918*	2.25	60
		emerald	4.00	1.50
		On cover		1.25
		Block of four	9.25	2.75
		Margin block of 6, P# only	30.00	
		a. 1c dark green	2.75	1.25
		c. Horizontal pair, imperf. betwee	60.00	
		d. Double impression	15.00	15.00
		"Flat nose"		

TYPE IV

TWO CENTS.

Type IV. Top line of the toga rope is broken.

The shading lines in the toga button are so arranged that the curving of the first and last form "(IID)".

The line of color in the left "2" is very thin and usually broken.

Used on offset printings only.

TYPE V

Type V. Top line of the toga is complete.

There are five vertical shading lines in the toga button.

The line of color in the left "2" is very thin and usually broken.

The shading dots on the nose are as shown on the diagram.

Used on offset printings only.

TYPE Va

Type Va. Characteristics are the same as type V except in the shading dots of the nose. The third row of dots from the bottom has four dots instead of six. The overall height is ⅓ mm. shorter than type V.

Used on offset printings only.

TYPE VI

Type VI. General characteristics the same as type V except that the line of color in the left "2" is very heavy.
Used on offset printings only.

TYPE VII

Type VII. The line of color in the left "2" is invariably continuous, clearly defined and heavier than in type V or Va but not as heavy as type VI.

An additional vertical row of dots has been added to the upper lip.

Numerous additional dots have been added to the hair on top of the head.

Used on offset printings only.

Dates of issue of types after type IV are not known but official records show the first plate of each type to have been certified as follows:

  Type IV............Mar. 6, 1920
  "   V............Mar. 20, 1920
  "   Va...........May 4, 1920
  "   VI...........June 24, 1920
  "   VII..........Nov. 3, 1920

POSTAGE, 1918-20

526	A140	2c **carmine**, type IV, *Mar. 15, 1920*	30.00	4.00
		rose carmine, type IV	30.00	4.00
		On cover, type IV		10.00
		Block of four, type IV	122.50	18.00
		Margin block of 6, P# only, type IV	250.00	
		Gash on forehead, type IV	40.00	6.50
		Malformed "2" at left, type IV (10823 L. R. 93)	40.00	7.50
527	A140	2c **carmine**, type V	17.50	1.00
		bright carmine, type V	17.50	1.00
		rose carmine, type V	17.50	1.00
		On cover		2.00
		Block of four, type V	71.00	6.50
		Block of 6, P# only, type V	150.00	
		a. Double impression, type V	45.00	8.50
		b. Vert. pair, imperf. horiz., type V	600.00	
		c. Horiz. pair, imperf. vert., type V		
		Line through "2" & "EN", type V	32.50	7.50
528	A140	2c **carmine**, type Va	8.00	15
		On cover, type Va		35
		Block of four, type Va	32.00	2.00
		Block of 6, P# only, type Va	65.00	
		Block of 6, monogram over P#	90.00	
		c. Double impression, type Va	25.00	
		g. Vert. pair, imperf. between		
		Retouches in "P" of Postage type Va	12.00	
		Retouched on toga, type Va	25.00	
		Variety "CRNTS", type Va	22.50	
528A	A140	2c **carmine**, type VI	50.00	1.00
		bright carmine, type VI	50.00	1.00
		On cover, type VI		3.00
		Block of four, type VI	200.00	5.00
		Margin block of 6, P# only, type VI	375.00	
		Block of 6, monogram over P#	500.00	
		d. Double impression, type VI	100.00	
		f. Vert. pair, imperf. horiz., type VI		
		h. Vert. pair, imperf. between		
528B	A140	2c **carmine**, type VII	20.00	12
		On cover, type VII		15
		Block of four, type VII	82.50	1.10
		Margin block of 6, P# only, type VII	160.00	
		e. Double impression, type VII	45.00	
		Retouched on cheek, type VII	35.00	

TYPE IV

Type IV. The shading lines of the toga rope are complete. The second and fourth shading lines in the toga button are broken in the middle and the third line is continuous with a dot in the center.
The "P" and "O" of "POSTAGE" are joined.
The frame line at the bottom of the vignette is broken.
Used on offset printings only.

529	A140	3c **violet**, type III, *March 1918*	3.00	10
		light violet, type III	3.00	10
		dark violet, type III	3.00	10
		On cover, type III		12
		Block of four, type III	12.00	55
		Margin block of 6, P# only, type III	70.00	
		a. Double impression, type III	20.00	
		b. Printed on both sides, type III	350.00	
530	A140	3c **purple**, type IV	70	6
		light purple, type IV	70	6
		deep purple, type IV	70	6
		violet, type IV	70	10
		On cover, type IV		10
		Block of four, type IV	3.00	30
		Margin block of 6, P# only, type IV	12.00	
		a. Double impression, type IV	12.50	4.00
		b. Printed on both sides, type IV	150.00	
		"Blister" under "U.S.," type IV	3.50	
		Recut under "U.S.," type IV	3.50	

Earliest known use, June 30, 1918.

1918-20   *Imperf.*

Dates of issue of 2c types are not known, but official records show that the first plate of each type known to have been issued imperforate was certified as follows:

Type IV............Mar. 1920   Type Va..........May 25, 1920
  "   V............May 4, 1920   "   VI..........July 26, 1920
                                     "   VII.........Dec. 2, 1920

531	A140	1c **green**, *Jan. 1919*	10.00	8.00
		gray green	10.00	8.00
		On cover		12.50
		Block of four	40.00	33.50
		Corner margin block of four	42.00	
		Margin block of 4, arrow	42.00	35.00
		Center line block	75.00	
		Margin block of 6, P# only	100.00	
532	A140	2c **carmine rose**, type IV	47.50	27.50
		On cover, type IV		35.00
		Block of four, type IV	190.00	110.00
		Corner margin block of four, type IV	200.00	
		Margin block of 4, arrow, type IV	200.00	
		Center line block, type IV	230.00	
		Margin block of 6, P# only, type IV	350.00	
533	A140	2c **carmine**, type V	235.00	70.00
		On cover, type V		95.00
		Block of four, type V	950.00	300.00
		Corner margin block of 4, type V	1,000.	
		Margin block of 4, arrow, type V	1,000.	
		Center line block, type V	1,150.	375.00
		Margin block of 6, P# only, type V	2,000.	
534	A140	2c **carmine**, type Va	12.50	9.00
		carmine rose, type Va	12.50	9.00
		On cover, type Va		13.50
		Block of four, type Va	50.00	40.00
		Corner margin block of four, type Va	51.00	
		Margin block of 4, arrow, type Va	51.00	
		Center line block, type Va	65.00	
		Margin block of 6, P# only, type Va	110.00	
		Block of 6, monogram over P#	225.00	
534A	A140	2c **carmine**, type VI	40.00	25.00
		On cover, type VI		35.00

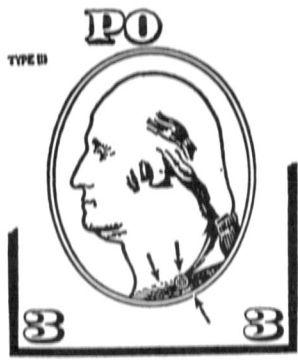

TYPE III

THREE CENTS.

Type III. The top line of the toga rope is strong but the 5th shading line is missing as in type I.
Center shading line of the toga button consists of two dashes with a central dot.
The "P" and "O" of "POSTAGE" are separated by a line of color.
The frame line at the bottom of the vignette is complete.
Used on offset printings only.

166　POSTAGE, 1918–20, 1919, 1920, 1921, 1923, 1920

		Block of four, type VI	160.00	110.00
		Corner block of four, type VI	165.00	
		Block of 4, arrow, type VI	165.00	
		Center line block, type VI	200.00	
		Block of 6, P# only, type VI	350.00	
534B	A140	2c **carmine**, type VII	1,550.	425.00
		On cover, type VII		625.00
		Block of four, type VII	6,250.	1,800.
		Corner margin block of four, type VII	6,300.	
		Margin block of 4, arrow, type VII	6,400.	
		Center line block, type VII	7,250.	
		Margin block of 6, P# only, type VII	12,500.	2,750.

Copies of the 2c type VII with Schermack III vending machine perforations, have been cut down at sides to simulate the rarer No. 534B imperforate.

535	A140	3c **violet**, type IV, *1918*	8.50	6.50
		On cover		10.00
		Block of four	34.00	27.50
		Corner margin block of four	35.00	
		Margin block of 4, arrow	35.00	
		Center line block	50.00	
		Margin block of 6, P# only	70.00	
a.		Double impression	80.00	—

CANCELLATIONS.
　　　　　　　　　　| Haiti　　　　　—

1919　　　　　*Perf. 12½*

536	A140	1c **gray green**, *Aug. 1919*	15.00	13.50
		On cover		40.00
		Block of four	62.50	65.00
		Margin block of 6, P# only	200.00	
a.		Horiz. pair, imperf. vert.	*400.00*	

VICTORY ISSUE.
Victory of the Allies in World War I.

"Victory" and Flags of Allies
A150

Designed by Charles A. Huston.

FLAT PLATE PRINTING.
Plates of 400 subjects in four panes of 100 each.

1919, Mar. 3　　　*Perf. 11*　　　Unwmkd.

537	A150	3c **violet**	11.00	4.25
		On cover		6.00
		Block of four	45.00	17.50
		Margin block of 6, P# only	150.00	
a.		3c deep red violet	325.00	40.00
		On cover		100.00
		Block of four	1,350.	175.00
		Margin block of 6, P# only	3,000.	
b.		3c light reddish violet	11.00	4.25
c.		3c red violet	40.00	11.00
		Double transfer	—	—

REGULAR ISSUE.
ROTARY PRESS PRINTINGS.
(*See note over No. 448.*)

1919　　　*Perf. 11x10*　　　Unwmkd.

Issued in sheets of 170 stamps (coil waste).
Stamp designs 19½ to 20mm. wide by 22 to 22¼mm. high.

538	A140	1c **green**, *June 1919*	10.00	9.00
		yellowish green	10.00	9.00
		bluish green	10.00	9.00
		On cover		20.00
		Block of four	41.00	37.50
		Margin block of 4, P# & "S 30"	100.00	
		Margin block of 4, P# only	110.00	
		Margin block of 4, star & P#	135.00	
a.		Vert. pair, imperf. horiz.	50.00	50.00
a.		Margin block of 4, P# only	700.00	
		Double transfer	25.00	20.00

539	A140	2c **carmine rose**, type II	2,350.	750.00
		On cover, type II	9,500.	—
		Block of four, type II		
		Margin block of 4, type II, P# & "S 20"	*15,000.*	

(*See note after No. 455*)

540	A140	2c **carmine rose**, type III, *June 14, 1919*	11.00	9.00
		carmine	11.00	9.00
		On cover, type III		22.50
		Block of four, type III	45.00	37.50
		Margin block of 4, type III, P# & "S 30"	110.00	
		Margin block of 4, type III, P# & "S 30" inverted	650.00	
		Margin block of 4, type III, P# only	115.00	
		Margin block of 4, type III, star & P#	150.00	
a.		Vert. pair, imperf. horiz., type III	50.00	50.00
a.		Margin block of 4, type III P# only	500.00	
a.		Margin block of 4, type III, Star & P#	550.00	
b.		Horiz. pair, imperf. vert., type III	550.00	
		Double transfer, type III	30.00	30.00
541	A140	3c **violet**, type II, *June 1919*	37.50	35.00
		gray violet, type II	37.50	35.00
		On cover		90.00
		Block of four	155.00	145.00
		Margin block of 4, P# only	400.00	

1920, May 26　　　*Perf. 10x11*

Plates of 400 subjects in four panes of 100 each.
Stamp design 19 mm. wide by 22½ to 22¾ mm. high.

542	A140	1c **green**	10.00	1.00
		bluish green	10.00	1.00
		On cover		2.00
		Block of four	40.00	6.00
		Vertical margin block of 6, P# opposite center horizontal row	165.00	

1921, May　　　*Perf. 10*

Plates of 400 subjects in four panes of 100 each.
Stamp design 19 mm. wide by 22½ mm. high.

543	A140	1c **green**	60	6
		deep green	60	6
		On cover		10
		Block of four	2.40	25
		Vertical margin block of 6, P# opposite center horizontal row	45.00	
		Corner margin block of 4, P# only	20.00	
a.		Horizontal pair, imperf. between	550.00	
		Double transfer	—	—
		Triple transfer	—	—

1923　　　*Perf. 11*

Stamp design 19 mm. wide by 22½ mm. high.

544	A140	1c **green**	6,500.	1,500.
		On cover		2,500.

1921, May

Issued in sheets of 170 stamps (coil waste).
Stamp designs 19½ to 20 mm. wide by 22 mm. high.

545	A140	1c **green**	135.00	110.00
		yellowish green	135.00	110.00
		On cover		600.00
		Block of four	550.00	500.00
		Margin block of 4, P# & "S 30"	1,100.	
		Margin block of 4, P# only	1,150.	
		Margin block of 4, star & P#	1,200.	
546	A140	2c **carmine rose**, type III	100.00	90.00
		deep carmine rose	100.00	90.00
		On cover		500.00
		Block of four	410.00	400.00
		Margin block of 4, P# & "S 30"	850.00	
		Margin block of 4, P# only	875.00	
		Margin block of 4, star & P#	900.00	
a.		Perf. 10 on left side	350.00	
		Recut in hair	140.00	120.00

FLAT PLATE PRINTING

1920, Nov. 1　　Plates of 100 subjects　　*Perf. 11*

547	A149	$2 **carmine & black**	400.00	40.00
		lake & black	400.00	40.00
		On cover (commercial)		750.00
		on flown cover (philatelic)		250.00
		Block of four	1,650.	165.00
		Margin block of 4, arrow	1,700.	
		Center line block	2,000.	—
		Margin block of 8, two P#, & arrow	7,000.	

PILGRIM TERCENTENARY ISSUE.

Issued to commemorate the tercentenary of the Landing of the Pilgrims at Plymouth, Mass.

The "Mayflower"
A151

Landing of the Pilgrims
A152

Signing of the Compact
A153

Designed by Charles A. Huston.

Plates of 280 subjects in four panes of 70 each.

1920, Dec. 21   Perf. 11   Unwmkd.

548	A151	1c **green**	5.50	3.00
		dark green	5.50	3.00
		On cover		4.00
		Block of four	22.00	13.00
		Margin block of 6, P# only	55.00	
		Double transfer		
549	A152	2c **carmine rose**	8.50	2.25
		carmine	8.50	2.25
		rose	8.50	2.25
		On cover		2.75
		Block of four	34.00	9.25
		Margin block of 6, P# only	80.00	

CANCELLATIONS.
| China

550	A153	5c **deep blue**	52.50	18.50
		dark blue	52.50	18.50
		On cover		25.00
		Block of four	210.00	75.00
		Margin block of 6, P# only	650.00	

REGULAR ISSUE.

Nathan Hale
A154

Franklin
A155

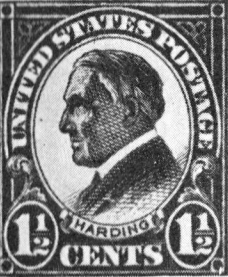

Warren G. Harding
A156

Washington
A157

Lincoln
A158

Martha Washington
A159

Theodore Roosevelt
A160

Garfield
A161

POSTAGE, 1922-25

McKinley
A162

Grant
A163

Jefferson
A164

Monroe
A165

Hayes
A166

Cleveland
A167

American Indian
A168

Statue of Liberty
A169

Golden Gate
A170

Niagara Falls
A171

Buffalo
A172

Arlington Amphitheater
A173

Lincoln Memorial
A174

United States Capitol
A175

Head of Freedom Statue, Capitol Dome
A176

POSTAGE, 1922-25

Plates of 400 subjects in four panes of 100 each for all values 1c to 50c inclusive.
Plates of 200 subjects for $1 and $2. The sheets were cut along the horizontal guide line into two panes, upper and lower, of 100 subjects each.
Plates of 100 subjects for the $5.00 denomination, and sheets of 100 subjects were issued intact.
The Bureau of Engraving and Printing in 1925 in experimenting to overcome the loss due to uneven perforations, produced what is known as the "Star Plate". The vertical rows of designs on these plates are spaced 3 mm. apart in place of 2¾ mm. as on the regular plates. These plates were identified with a star added to the plate number

Designed by Charles Aubrey Huston.

FLAT PLATE PRINTINGS.

1922-25			Perf. 11.	Unwmkd.	
551	A154	½c	**olive brown,** *Apr. 4, 1925*	15	6
			pale olive brown	15	6
			deep olive brown	15	6
			Block of four	60	35
			Margin block of 6, P# only	7.00	
			"Cap" on fraction bar (Pl. 17041)	75	25
552	A155	1c	**deep green,** *Jan. 17, 1923*	2.25	5
			green	2.25	5
			pale green	2.25	5
			Block of four	9.00	35
			Margin block of 6, P# only	25.00	
		a.	Booklet pane of six, *Aug. 11, 1923*	5.50	50
			Double transfer	6.00	
553	A156	1½c	**yellow brown,** *Mar. 19, 1925*	3.50	20
			pale yellow brown	3.50	20
			brown	3.50	20
			Block of four	14.00	1.00
			Margin block of 6, P# only	40.00	2.25
			Double transfer		
554	A157	2c	**carmine,** *Jan. 15, 1923*	1.75	5
			light carmine	1.75	5
			Block of four	7.00	20
			Margin block of 6, P# only	25.00	
			Margin block of 6, P# & small 5 point star, top only	600.00	
			Margin block of 6, P# & large 5 point star, side only	100.00	
			Same, large 5-pt. star, top	750.00	
			Same, large 6-pt. star, top	1,000.	
			Same, large 6-pt. star, side only (Pl. 17196)	1,250.	
		a.	Horiz. pair, imperf. vert	175.00	
		b.	Vert. pair, imperf. horiz.	500.00	
		c.	Booklet pane of six, *Feb. 10, 1923*	7.00	1.00
			Double transfer	4.00	1.00
		d.	Perf. 10 at top or bottom		
555	A158	3c	**violet,** *Feb. 12, 1923*	21.00	1.25
			deep violet	21.00	1.25
			dark violet	21.00	1.25
			red violet	21.00	1.25
			bright violet	21.00	1.25
			Block of four	85.00	5.25
			Margin block of 6, P# only	210.00	
556	A159	4c	**yellow brown,** *Jan. 15, 1923*	21.00	20
			brown	21.00	20
			Block of four	85.00	1.35
			Margin block of 6, P# only	225.00	
		a.	Vert. pair, imperf. horiz.		
			Double transfer		
		b.	Perf. 10 at top or bottom	425.00	
557	A160	5c	**dark blue,** *Oct. 27, 1922*	21.00	8
			deep blue	21.00	8
			Block of four	85.00	75
			Margin block of 6, P# only	250.00	
		a.	Imperf., pair	700.00	
		b.	Horiz. pair, imperf. vert.		
			Double transfer (15571 U.L. 86)		375.00
		c.	Perf. 10 at top or bottom		
558	A161	6c	**red orange,** *Nov. 20, 1922*	40.00	85
			pale red orange	40.00	85
			Block of four	160.00	4.25
			Margin block of 6, P# only	425.00	
			Double transfer (Plate 14169 L. R. 60 and 70)	65.00	3.50
			Same, recut	65.00	3.50
559	A162	7c	**black,** *May 1, 1923*	10.00	75
			gray black	10.00	75
			Block of four	40.00	3.00
			Margin block of 6, P# only	90.00	
			Double transfer		
560	A163	8c	**olive green,** *May 1, 1923*	55.00	85
			pale olive green	55.00	85
			Block of four	220.00	4.25
			Margin block of 6, P# only	725.00	
			Margin block of 6, P# & large 5 point star, side only		
			Double transfer		
561	A164	9c	**rose,** *Jan. 15, 1923*	17.00	1.25
			pale rose	17.00	1.25
			Block of four	68.00	6.00
			Margin block of 6, P# only	210.00	
			Double transfer		
562	A165	10c	**orange,** *Jan. 15, 1923*	22.50	10
			pale orange	22.50	10
			Block of four	90.00	50
			Margin block of 6, P# only	300.00	
		a.	Vert. pair, imperf. horiz.	500.00	
		b.	Imperf., pair	650.00	
		c.	Perf. 10 at top or bottom		600.00
563	A166	11c	**light blue,** *Oct. 4, 1922*	2.00	25
			greenish blue	2.00	25
			light bluish green	2.00	25
			light yellow green	2.00	40
			Block of four	8.00	1.25
			Margin block of 6, P# only	35.00	
		d.	Imperf., pair		
564	A167	12c	**brown violet,** *Mar. 20, 1923*	8.50	8
			deep brown violet	8.50	8
			Block of four	34.00	80
			Margin block of 6, P# only	90.00	
			Margin block of 6, P# & large 5 point star, side only	150.00	
			Margin block of 6, P# & large 6 point star, side only	300.00	
		a.	Horiz. pair, imperf. vert.	650.00	
		b.	Imperf., pair		
			Double transfer, (14404 U.L. 73 & 74)	20.00	1.00
565	A168	14c	**blue,** *May 1, 1923*	5.00	85
			deep blue	5.00	85
			Block of four	20.00	3.75
			Margin block of 6, P# only	60.00	
			Double transfer		

Horizontal pairs of No. 565 are known with spacings up to 3¾mm. instead of 2mm. between. These are from the 5th and 6th vertical rows of the upper right pane of Plate 14515 and also between stamps Nos. 3 and 4 of the same pane. A plate block of Pl. 14512 is known with 3 mm. spacing.

566	A169	15c	**gray,** *Nov. 11, 1922*	22.50	6
			light gray	22.50	6
			Block of four	90.00	40
			Margin block of 6, P# only	275.00	
			Margin block of 6, P# & large 5 point star, side only	475.00	
567	A170	20c	**carmine rose,** *May 1, 1923*	25.00	6
			deep carmine rose	25.00	6
			Block of four	100.00	50
			Margin block of 6, P# only	300.00	
			Margin block of 6, P# & large 5 point star, side only	700.00	
		a.	Horiz. pair, imperf. vert.	750.00	
			Double transfer (Pl. 18925)	60.00	2.50
568	A171	25c	**yellow green,** *Nov. 11, 1922*	22.50	50
			green	22.50	50
			deep green	22.50	50
			Block of four	90.00	2.25
			Margin block of 6, P# only	250.00	
		b.	Vert. pair, imperf. horiz.	850.00	
			Perf. 10 at one side		
			Double transfer		
569	A172	30c	**olive brown,** *Mar. 20, 1923*	45.00	35
			Block of four	180.00	2.75
			Margin block of 6, P# only	450.00	
			Double transfer (16065 U.R. 52)	65.00	2.50
570	A173	50c	**lilac,** *Nov. 11, 1922*	75.00	12
			dull lilac	75.00	12
			Block of four	300.00	75
			Margin block of 6, P# only	900.00	
571	A174	$1	**violet black,** *Feb. 12, 1923*	50.00	45
			violet brown	50.00	45
			Block of four	200.00	2.00
			Margin block of 4, arrow, top or bottom	210.00	
			Margin block of 6, P# only	500.00	
			Double transfers, Pl. 18642 L. 30 and Pl. 18682	110.00	2.50
572	A175	$2	**deep blue,** *Mar. 20, 1923*	145.00	11.00
			Block of four	590.00	45.00
			Margin block of 4, arrow, top or bottom	600.00	
			Margin block of 6, P# only	1,650.	
573	A176	$5	**carmine & blue,** *Mar. 20, 1923*	375.00	15.00
			carmine lake & dark blue	375.00	15.00
			Block of four	1,500.	65.00

170 POSTAGE, 1922-25, 1923-25, 1923-26, 1923-29

			Margin block of 4, arrow	1,550.	
			Center line block	1,600.	85.00
			Margin block of 8, two P# & arrow	5,500.	

For other listings of perforated stamps of designs A154 to A176 see

Nos. 578 & 579	Perf. 11x10
" 581 to 591	Perf. 10
" 594 to 596	Perf. 11
" 632 to 642, 653, 692 to 696	Perf. 11x10½
" 697 to 701	Perf. 10½x11

This series also includes Nos. 622-623 (perf. 11).

1923-25   Imperf.

575	A155	1c	green, *March 20, 1923*	10.00	3.50
			deep green	10.00	3.50
			Block of four	40.00	15.00
			Corner margin block of four	41.00	
			Margin block of 4, arrow	42.50	
			Center line block	50.00	
			Margin block of 6, P# only	100.00	
576	A156	1½c	yellow brown, *Apr. 4, 1925*	2.25	1.75
			pale yellow brown	2.25	1.75
			brown	2.25	1.75
			Block of four	9.00	7.50
			Corner margin block of four	9.50	
			Margin block of 4, arrow	10.00	
			Center line block	17.50	12.50
			Margin block of 6, P# only	30.00	
			Double transfer		

The 1½c A156 Rotary press imperforate is listed as No. 631.

577	A157	2c	carmine	2.50	2.00
			light carmine	2.50	2.00
			Block of four	10.00	8.50
			Corner margin block of four	10.50	
			Margin block of 4, arrow	11.00	
			Center line block	20.00	
			Margin block of 6, P# only	30.00	
			Margin block of 6, P# & large 5 point star	110.00	

ROTARY PRESS PRINTINGS.
(See note over No. 448).

1923-26   Perf. 11x10

Issued in sheets of 70 or 100 stamps, coil waste. Stamp designs 19¾x22¼ mm.

578	A155	1c	green	80.00	65.00
			On cover		150.00
			Margin block of 4, star & P#	750.00	
579	A157	2c	carmine	57.50	50.00
			deep carmine	57.50	50.00
			On cover		175.00
			Margin block of 4, star & P#	450.00	
			Recut in eye, plate 14731	75.00	75.00

Perf. 10.

Plates of 400 subjects in four panes of 100 each.
Stamp designs 19x22½ mm.

581	A155	1c	green, *Apr. 21, 1923*	9.50	65
			yellow green	9.50	65
			pale green	9.50	65
			Block of four	38.00	3.00
			Margin block of 4, P# only	125.00	
582	A156	1½c	brown, *Mar. 19, 1925*	5.00	60
			dark brown	5.00	60
			Block of four	20.00	2.75
			Margin block of 4, P# only	45.00	
			Pair with full horiz. gutter btwn.	135.00	
			Pair with full vert. gutter btwn.	135.00	

No. 582 was available in full sheets of 400 subjects but was not regularly issued in that form.

583	A157	2c	carmine, *Apr. 14, 1924*	2.50	5
			deep carmine	2.50	5
			Block of four	10.00	50
			Margin block of 4, P# only	30.00	
		a.	Booklet pane of six, *Aug. 27, 1926*	75.00	25.00
584	A158	3c	violet, *Aug. 1, 1925*	27.50	1.75
			Block of four	110.00	8.00
			Margin block of 4, P# only	250.00	
585	A159	4c	yellow brown, *Mar. 1925*	17.00	40
			deep yellow brown	17.00	40
			Block of four	68.00	2.00
			Margin block of 4, P# only	175.00	
586	A160	5c	blue, *Dec. 1924*	16.00	18
			deep blue	16.00	18
			Block of four	64.00	90
			Margin block of 4, P# only	165.00	
		a.	Horizontal pair, imperf. between		
			Double transfer		

587	A161	6c	red orange, *Mar. 1925*	7.50	40
			pale red orange	7.50	40
			Block of four	30.00	2.25
			Margin block of 4, P# only	70.00	
588	A162	7c	black, *May 29, 1926*	11.50	5.00
			Block of four	46.00	25.00
			Margin block of 4, P# only	110.00	
589	A163	8c	olive green, *May 29, 1926*	26.00	3.00
			pale olive green	26.00	3.00
			Block of four	105.00	14.00
			Margin block of 4, P# only	250.00	
590	A164	9c	rose, *May 29, 1926*	4.50	2.25
			Block of four	18.00	11.00
			Margin block of 4, P# only	45.00	
591	A165	10c	orange, *June 8, 1925*	70.00	10
			Block of four	280.00	70
			Margin block of 4, P# only	650.00	

Perf. 11

Issued in sheets of 70 or 100 stamps, coil waste of Nos. 597, 599. Stamp designs approximately 19¾x22¼ mm.

594	A155	1c	green	7,000.	1,850.
			On cover		2,750.
595	A157	2c	carmine	200.00	175.00
			deep carmine	200.00	175.00
			On cover		400.00
			Margin block of 4, star & P#	1,500.	
			Recut in eye, plate 14731		

Perf. 11

Stamp design approximately 19¼x22¾ mm.

| 596 | A155 | 1c | green | | 13,500. |

Most copies of No. 596 carry the Bureau precancel "Kansas City, Mo."

COIL STAMPS, ROTARY PRESS
1923-29   Perf. 10 Vertically.

Stamp designs approximately 19¾x22¼ mm.

597	A155	1c	green, *July 18, 1923*	35	6
			yellow green	35	6
			Pair	75	12
			Joint line pair	2.25	25
			Gripper cracks	3.00	1.00
			Double transfer	3.00	1.00
598	A156	1½c	brown, *Mar. 19, 1925*	75	10
			deep brown	75	10
			Pair	1.60	25
			Joint line pair	5.25	50

TYPE I

TYPE II

TYPE I   TYPE II

Type I—No heavy hair lines at top center of head. Outline of left acanthus scroll generally faint at top and toward base at left side.

Type II—Three heavy hair lines at top center of head; two being outstanding in the white area. Outline of left acanthus scroll very strong and clearly defined at top (under left edge of lettered panel) and at lower curve (above and to left of numeral oval). This type appears only on Nos. 599A and 634A.

599	A157	2c **carmine**, type I, *Jan. 1923*	30	5
		deep carmine, type I	30	5
		Pair, type I	65	12
		Joint line pair, type I	2.00	20
		Double transfer, type I	2.00	1.00
		Gripper cracks, type I	2.50	2.50
599A	A157	2c **carmine**, type II, *Mar. 1929*	140.00	12.00
		Pair, type II	290.00	25.00
		Joint line pair, type II	800.00	60.00
		Joint line pair, types I & II	900.00	120.00
600	A158	3c **violet**, *May 10, 1924*	8.00	8
		deep violet	8.00	8
		Pair	17.00	20
		Joint line pair	35.00	85
		Cracked plate	—	
601	A159	4c **yellow brown**, *Aug. 5, 1923*	4.00	40
		brown	4.00	40
		Pair	8.50	1.00
		Joint line pair	27.50	2.00
602	A160	5c **dark blue**, *Mar. 5, 1924*	1.50	18
		Pair	3.10	40
		Joint line pair	9.00	60
603	A165	10c **orange**, *Dec. 1, 1924*	4.00	8
		Pair	8.50	25
		Joint line pair	27.50	1.00

The 6c design A161 coil stamp is listed as No. 723.

1923-25   *Perf. 10 Horizontally*
Stamp designs 19¼-19½mm. wide by 22-22½mm. high.

604	A155	1c **yellow green**	25	8
		green, *July 19, 1924*	25	10
		Pair	55	20
		Joint line pair	3.00	35
605	A156	1½c **yellow brown**, *May 9, 1925*	30	15
		brown	30	15
		Pair	65	35
		Joint line pair	2.75	50
606	A157	2c **carmine**, *Dec. 31, 1925*	30	12
		Pair	65	25
		Joint line pair	2.00	35
		Cracked plate	7.50	3.50

HARDING MEMORIAL ISSUE.

Issued as a tribute to the memory of President Warren G. Harding, who died in San Francisco, Aug. 2, 1923.
Plates of 400 subjects in four panes of 100 each.

Warren Gamaliel Harding
A177

FLAT PLATE PRINTINGS.

Stamp designs 19¼mm. wide by 22¼mm. high.
1923   *Perf. 11*

610	A177	2c **black**, *Sept. 1, 1923*	75	10
		intense black	75	10
		grayish black	75	10
		Margin block of 6, P#	30.00	
	a.	Horiz. pair, imperf. vert.	800.00	
		Double transfer	3.00	50

Imperf.

611	A177	2c **black**, *Nov. 15, 1923*	12.00	6.00
		Corner margin block of four	50.00	25.00
		Margin block of 4, arrow	50.00	26.00
		Center line block	85.00	55.00
		Margin block of 6, P#	140.00	—

ROTARY PRESS PRINTINGS.

Stamp designs 19¼mm. wide by 22¾mm. high.

Perf. 10.

612	A177	2c **black**, *Sept. 12, 1923*	25.00	2.50
		gray black	25.00	2.50
		Margin block of 4, P#	350.00	
		Pair with full vertical gutter between	350.00	

Perf. 11.

613	A177	2c **black**		13,500.

HUGUENOT-WALLOON TERCENTENARY ISSUE.

Issued to commemorate the 300th anniversary of the settling of the Walloons, and in honor of the Huguenots.

Ship "Nieu Nederland"
A178

Walloons Landing at Fort Orange (Albany)
A179

Jan Ribault Monument at Mayport, Fla.
A180

POSTAGE, 1924, 1925

Designed by Charles Aubrey Huston.
FLAT PLATE PRINTINGS.
Plates of 200 subjects in four panes of 50 each.

1924, May 1   *Perf. 11*

614	A178	1c **dark green**		5.00	4.50
		green		5.00	4.50
		Margin block of 6, P#		50.00	
		Double transfer		12.00	9.00
615	A179	2c **carmine rose**		8.00	3.50
		dark carmine rose		8.00	3.50
		Margin block of 6, P#		85.00	
		Double transfer		17.50	6.00
616	A180	5c **dark blue**		50.00	22.50
		deep blue		50.00	22.50
		Margin block of 6, P#		450.00	
		Added line at bottom of white circle around right numeral, so-called "broken circle" (15754 UR 2, 3, 4, 5)		75.00	27.50

LEXINGTON-CONCORD ISSUE.

Issued to commemorate the 150th anniversary of the Battle of Lexington-Concord.

Washington at Cambridge
A181

"Birth of Liberty," by Henry Sandham
A182

The Minute Man, by Daniel Chester French
A183

Plates of 200 subjects in four panes of 50 each.

1925, Apr. 4   *Perf. 11*

617	A181	1c **deep green**		5.00	5.00
		green		5.00	5.00
		Margin block of 6, P#		50.00	
618	A182	2c **carmine rose**		9.00	7.50
		pale carmine rose		9.00	7.50
		Margin block of 6, P#		95.00	
619	A183	5c **dark blue**		45.00	20.00
		blue		45.00	20.00
		Margin block of 6, P#		400.00	
		Line over head (16807 L. L. 48)		75.00	30.00

NORSE-AMERICAN ISSUE.

Issued to commemorate the centenary of the arrival in New York, on Oct. 9, 1825, of the sloop "Restaurationen" with the first group of immigrants from Norway.

Sloop "Restaurationen"
A184

Viking Ship
A185

Designed by Charles Aubrey Huston.
Plates of 100 subjects.

1925, May 18   *Perf. 11*

620	A184	2c **carmine & black**		7.50	5.00
		deep carmine & black		7.50	5.00
		Margin block of 4, arrow		31.00	
		Center line block		35.00	
		Margin block of 8, two P# & arrow		225.00	
		Margin block of 8, carmine P# & arrow; black P# omitted		2,750.	
621	A185	5c **dark blue & black**		25.00	22.50
		Margin block of 4, arrow		102.50	
		Center line block		120.00	
		Margin block of 8, two P# & arrow		750.00	

POSTAGE, 1925–26, 1926 173

REGULAR ISSUE.

Benjamin Harrison
A186

Woodrow Wilson
A187

Plates of 400 subjects in four panes of 100 each.

1925–26   Perf. 11

622	A186	13c	**green,** *Jan. 11, 1926*	17.50	65
			light green	17.50	65
			Margin block of 6, P# only	200.00	
			Margin block of 6, P# & large 5 point star	1,250.	
623	A187	17c	**black,** *Dec. 28, 1925*	25.00	35
			gray black	25.00	35
			Margin block of 6, P# only	250.00	

SESQUICENTENNIAL EXPOSITION ISSUE.

Issued in connection with the Sesquicentennial Exposition held at Philadelphia, Pa., from June 1 to Dec. 1, 1926, to commemorate the 150th anniversary of the Declaration of Independence.

Liberty Bell
A188

Designed by Charles Aubrey Huston.
Plates of 200 subjects in four panes of 50 each.

1926   Perf. 11

627	A188	2c	**carmine rose,** *May 10, 1926*	4.00	60
			On cover, Expo. station canc.		3.50
			Margin block of 6, P#	50.00	
			Double transfer		

ERICSSON MEMORIAL ISSUE.

Issued as a memorial to John Ericsson, builder of the "Monitor" and in connection with the unveiling of his statue by the Crown Prince of Sweden at Washington, D. C., May 29, 1926.

Statue of John Ericsson
A189

Designed by Charles Aubrey Huston.
Plates of 200 subjects in four panes of 50 each.

1926   Perf. 11

628	A189	5c	**gray lilac,** *May 29, 1926*	10.00	5.00
			Margin block of 6, P#	110.00	

BATTLE OF WHITE PLAINS ISSUE.

Issued to commemorate the 150th anniversary of the Battle of White Plains, N. Y.

Alexander Hamilton's Battery
A190

Designed by Charles Aubrey Huston.
Plates of 400 subjects in four panes of 100 each.

1926   Perf. 11

629	A190	2c	**carmine rose,** *Oct. 18, 1926*	2.50	2.25
			Margin block of 6, P#	50.00	
			a. Vertical pair, imperf. between	1,250.	

INTERNATIONAL PHILATELIC EXHIBITION ISSUE.
SOUVENIR SHEET.

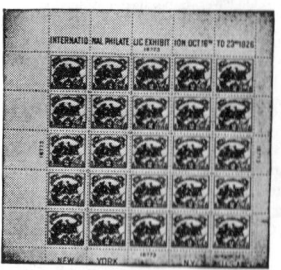

A190a

Plates of 100 subjects in four panes of 25 each, separated by one inch wide gutters with central guide lines.

1926, Oct. 18   **Perf. 11**

630	A190a	2c carmine rose, sheet of 25	500.00	425.00
		Dot over first "S" of "States"		
		18774 LL9 or 18773 LL11, sheet	525.00	450.00

Issued in sheets measuring 158–160¼ x 136–146½ mm. containing 25 stamps with inscription "International Philatelic Exhibition, Oct. 16 to 23, 1926" in top margin. Issued to commemorate the International Philatelic Exhibition in New York, Oct. 16 to 23, 1926.

REGULAR ISSUE.
ROTARY PRESS PRINTINGS.
(See note over No. 448.)

Plates of 400 subjects in four panes of 100 each.
Stamp designs 18½ to 19 mm. wide by 22¼ mm. high.

1926   *Imperf.*

631	A156	1½c yellow brown, *Aug. 27, 1926*	2.25	2.10
		light brown	2.25	2.10
		Gutter block of four	10.00	9.00
		Margin block with dash (left, right, top or bottom)	11.00	9.25
		Center block with crossed gutters and dashes	25.00	
		Margin block of 4, P#	70.00	
		Without gum breaker ridges	3.25	

1926–34   **Perf. 11x10½.**

632	A155	1c green, *June 10, 1927*	15	5
		yellow green	15	5
		Margin block of 4, P#	2.00	
		a. Booklet pane of six, *Nov. 2, 1927*	2.50	25
		Booklet of 4 with full gutter btwn.	150.00	
		b. Vertical pair, imperf. between	150.00	75.00
		Cracked plate	—	—
633	A156	1½c yellow brown, *May 17, 1927*	2.50	8
		deep brown	2.50	8
		Block of four	10.00	75
		Margin block of 4, P#	90.00	
634	A157	2c carmine, type I, *Dec. 10, 1926*	15	5
		Margin block of 4, type I, P# opposite corner stamp	1.20	
		Vertical margin block of 10, P# opposite third horizontal row from top or bottom (Experimental Electric Eye plates)	5.00	
		Margin block of 4, Electric Eye marking	65	25
		Pair with full vertical gutter between	200.00	
		b. 2c carmine lake, type I	3.00	1.00
		b. Margin block of 4, P#	30.00	
		c. Horizontal pair, type I, imperf. between	2,000.	
		d. Booklet pane of six, type I, *Feb. 25, 1927*	1.00	15
		Recut face, type I, 20234 LL58	—	

No. 634, Type I, exists on a thin, tough experimental paper.

634A	A157	2c carmine, type II, *Dec. 1928*	350.00	25.00
		On cover		50.00
		Margin block of 4, type II, P#	2,100.	—
		Pair with full horiz. gutter btwn.	1,000.	—
		Pair with full vert. gutter btwn.	1,000.	—

No. 634A, Type II, was available in full sheet of 400 subjects but was not regularly issued in that form.

635	A158	3c violet, *Feb. 3, 1927*	50	5
		Margin block of 4, P#	7.00	
		a. 3c bright violet, *Feb. 7, 1934*. re-issue, Plates 21185 & 21186	30	5
		a. Margin block of 4, P#	4.00	
		a. Gripper cracks	4.00	2.00
636	A159	4c yellow brown, *May 17, 1927*	3.50	8
		Block of four	14.00	75
		Margin block of 4, P#	100.00	
		Pair with full vert. gutter btwn.	200.00	
637	A160	5c dark blue, *Mar. 24, 1927*	3.00	5
		Margin block of 4, P#	21.00	
		Pair with full vert. gutter btwn.	275.00	
		Double transfer	—	—
638	A161	6c red orange, *July 27, 1927*	3.00	5
		Margin block of 4, P#	21.00	
		Pair with full horiz. gutter btwn.	—	—
		Pair with full vert. gutter btwn.	200.00	
639	A162	7c black, *Mar. 24, 1927*	3.00	8
		Margin block of 4, P#	21.00	
		a. Vertical pair, imperf. between	125.00	80.00
640	A163	8c olive green, *June 10, 1927*	3.00	5
		olive bister	3.00	5
		Margin block of 4, P#	21.00	
641	A164	9c orange red, *1931*	3.00	5
		salmon rose	3.00	5
		rose, *May 17, 1927*	3.00	5
		Margin block of 4, P#	21.00	
		Pair with full vert. gutter btwn.	—	—
642	A165	10c orange, *Feb. 3, 1927*	5.50	5
		Margin block of 4, P#	35.00	
		Double transfer	—	—

The 2c, 5c and 8c imperf. (dry print) are printer's waste. See No. 653.

VERMONT SESQUICENTENNIAL ISSUE.

Battle of Bennington, 150th anniv. and State independence.

Green Mountain Boy
A191

FLAT PLATE PRINTING.

Plates of 400 subjects in four panes of 100 each.

1927   **Perf. 11**

643	A191	2c carmine rose, *Aug. 3, 1927*	1.50	1.65
		Margin block of 6, P#	40.00	

BURGOYNE CAMPAIGN ISSUE.

Issued to commemorate the Battles of Bennington, Oriskany, Fort Stanwix and Saratoga.

Surrender of Gen. John Burgoyne
A192

Plates of 200 subjects in four panes of 50 each.

1927			Perf. 11.		
644	A192	2c **carmine rose**, *Aug. 3, 1927*		5.00	3.75
		Margin block of 6, P#		65.00	

VALLEY FORGE ISSUE.

Issued to commemorate the 150th anniversary of Washington's encampment at Valley Forge, Pa.

Washington at Prayer
A193

Plates of 400 subjects in four panes of 100 each.

1928			Perf. 11		
645	A193	2c **carmine rose**, *May 26, 1928*		1.10	65
		Margin block of 6, P#		40.00	

BATTLE OF MONMOUTH ISSUE.

Issued to commemorate the 150th anniversary of the Battle of Monmouth, N. J., and a memorial to Molly Pitcher, the heroine of the battle.

No. 634 Overprinted **MOLLY PITCHER**

ROTARY PRESS PRINTING.

1928			Perf. 11x10½		
646	A157	2c **carmine**, *Oct. 20, 1928*		1.50	1.50
		Margin block of 4, P#		40.00	
		Wide spacing, vert. pair		35.00	

The normal space between a vertical pair of the overprints is 18mm., but pairs are known with the space measuring 28mm.

HAWAII SESQUICENTENNIAL ISSUE.

Issued to commemorate the Sesquicentennial Celebration of the discovery of the Hawaiian Islands.

Nos. 634 and 637 Overprinted **HAWAII 1778 - 1928**

ROTARY PRESS PRINTING.

1928, Aug. 13			Perf. 11x10½		
647	A157	2c **carmine**		7.00	6.00
		Margin block of 4, P#		150.00	
		Wide spacing, vert. pair		125.00	
648	A160	5c **dark blue**		20.00	17.50
		Margin block of 4, P#		300.00	

Nos. 647-648 were sold at post offices in Hawaii and at the Postal Agency in Washington, D.C. They were valid throughout the nation.

Normally the overprints were placed 18mm. apart vertically, but pairs exist with a space of 28mm. between the overprints.

AERONAUTICS CONFERENCE ISSUE.

Issued in commemoration of the International Civil Aeronautics Conference at Washington, D. C., Dec. 12 to 14, 1928, and of the twenty-fifth anniversary of the first airplane flight by the Wright brothers, Dec. 17, 1903.

Wright Airplane
A194

Globe and Airplane
A195

FLAT PLATE PRINTING.

Plates of 200 subjects in four panes of 50 each.

1928, Dec. 12			Perf. 11		
649	A194	2c **carmine rose**		1.50	1.40
		Margin block of 6, P#		17.50	
650	A195	5c **blue**		8.50	5.00
		Margin block of 6, P#		90.00	
		Plate flaw "prairie dog" (19658 L. L. 50)		50.00	20.00

GEORGE ROGERS CLARK ISSUE.

Issued to commemorate the 150th anniversary of the surrender of Fort Sackville, the present site of Vincennes, Ind., to George Rogers Clark

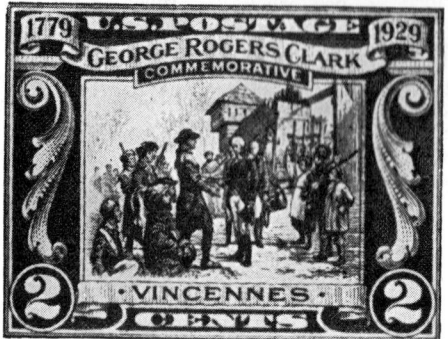

Surrender of Fort Sackville
A196

Plates of 100 subjects in two panes of 50 each.

1929			*Perf. 11*		
651	A196	2c	**carmine & black,** *Feb. 25, 1929*	85	80
			Margin block of 4, arrow (line only) right or left	3.50	
			Margin block of 6, two P# & "Top"	16.00	—
			Margin block of 10, red P# only	—	—
			Double transfer (19721 R. 14,29 & 44)	7.50	5.00

REGULAR ISSUE.
Type of 1922-26 Issue.
ROTARY PRESS PRINTING.
Plates of 400 subjects in four panes of 100 each.

1929			*Perf. 11x10½*		
653	A154	½c	**olive brown,** *May 25, 1929*	5	5
			Damaged plate, (19652 L. L. 72)	1.50	75
			Retouched plate, (19652 L. L. 72)	1.50	75
			Margin block of 4, P#	1.00	—
			Pair with full horizontal gutter between	125.00	

ELECTRIC LIGHT'S GOLDEN JUBILEE ISSUE.

Issued to commemorate the 50th anniversary of the invention of the first incandescent electric lamp by Thomas Alva Edison on October 21, 1879.

Edison's First Lamp
A197

Designed by Alvin R. Meissner.
FLAT PLATE PRINTING.
Plates of 400 subjects in four panes of 100 each.

1929			*Perf. 11*		
654	A197	2c	**carmine rose,** *June 5, 1929*	90	1.00
			Margin block of 6, P#	35.00	—

ROTARY PRESS PRINTING.
Perf. 11x10½.

655	A197	2c	**carmine rose,** *June 11, 1929*	85	25
			Margin block of 4, P#	55.00	—

ROTARY PRESS COIL STAMP.
Perf. 10 Vertically.

656	A197	2c	**carmine rose,** *June 11, 1929*	20.00	2.00
			Pair	42.50	4.50
			Joint line pair	90.00	20.00

SULLIVAN EXPEDITION ISSUE.

Issued to commemorate the 150th anniversary of the Sullivan Expedition in New York State during the Revolutionary War.

Major General John Sullivan
A198

FLAT PLATE PRINTING.
Plates of 400 subjects in four panes of 100 each.

1929			*Perf. 11.*		
657	A196	2c	**carmine rose,** *June 17, 1929*	1.00	90
			lake	40.00	—
			Margin block of 6, P#	35.00	—

REGULAR ISSUE.

Nos. 632 to 642 Overprinted **Kans.**

Officially issued May 1, 1929.

Some values are known cancelled as early as April 15.

Special issue prepared by overprinting the abbreviations "Kans." and "Nebr." on stamps of the 1926-27 series. This special issue was authorized as a measure of preventing losses from post office burglaries. Approximately a year's supply was printed and issued to postmasters. The P. O. Dept. found it desirable to discontinue the State overprinted stamps after the initial supply was used.

ROTARY PRESS PRINTING.

1929			*Perf. 11x10½*		
658	A155	1c	**green**	2.00	1.65
			Margin block of 4, P#	25.00	—
		a.	Vertical pair, one without ovpt.	300.00	—
			Wide spacing, pair	40.00	
659	A156	1½c	**brown**	3.00	3.00
			Margin block of 4, P#	40.00	—
		a.	Vertical pair, one without ovpt.	325.00	—
			Wide spacing, pair	90.00	

POSTAGE, 1929

660	A157	2c **carmine**	3.00	65
		Margin block of 4, P#	40.00	
		Wide spacing, pair	60.00	
661	A158	3c **violet**	17.50	12.00
		Margin block of 4, P#	175.00	—
		a. Vertical pair, one without ovpt.	*400.00*	
662	A159	4c **yellow brown**	17.50	7.50
		Margin block of 4, P#	175.00	
		a. Vertical pair, one without ovpt.	*400.00*	
663	A160	5c **deep blue**	13.00	9.00
		Margin block of 4, P#	150.00	
664	A161	6c **red orange**	27.50	17.50
		Margin block of 4, P#	400.00	
665	A162	7c **black**	27.50	22.50
		Margin block of 4, P#	400.00	
		a. Vertical pair, one without ovpt.	*400.00*	
666	A163	8c **olive green**	85.00	72.50
		Margin block of 4, P#	800.00	
667	A164	9c **light rose**	13.00	11.00
		Margin block of 4, P#	175.00	
668	A165	10c **orange yellow**	21.00	11.00
		Margin block of 4, P#	325.00	
		Pair with full horizontal gutter between		

676	A162	7c **black**	21.00	15.00
		Margin block of 4, P#	275.00	—
677	A163	8c **olive green**	30.00	22.50
		Margin block of 4, P#	375.00	
		Wide spacing, pair	225.00	
678	A164	9c **light rose**	35.00	25.00
		Margin block of 4, P#	400.00	
		a. Vertical pair, one without ovpt.	*600.00*	
		Wide spacing, pair	200.00	
679	A165	10c **orange yellow**	100.00	17.50
		Margin block of 4, P#	900.00	—

Nos. 658, 659, 660, 669, 670, 671, 672, 673, 677 and 678 are known with the overprints on vertical pairs spaced 32mm. apart instead of the normal 22mm.

BATTLE OF FALLEN TIMBERS ISSUE.

Issued as a memorial to Gen. Anthony Wayne and to commemorate the 135th anniversary of the Battle of Fallen Timbers, Ohio.

General Wayne Memorial
A199

FLAT PLATE PRINTING.

Plates of 400 subjects in four panes of 100 each.

1929   Perf. 11.

680	A199	2c **carmine rose**, *Sept. 14, 1929*	1.00	1.00
		deep carmine rose	1.00	1.00
		Margin block of 6, P#	40.00	—

Overprinted **Nebr.**

Issued May 1, 1929.

669	A155	1c **green**	2.00	2.00
		Margin block of 4, P#	25.00	
		a. Vertical pair, one without ovpt.	*275.00*	
		Wide spacing, pair	45.00	45.00
		No period after "Nebr." (19338, 19339 L.R. 26, 36)		
670	A156	1½c **brown**	3.00	2.25
		Margin block of 4, P#	40.00	
		Wide spacing, pair	45.00	
671	A157	2c **carmine**	2.00	85
		Margin block of 4, P#	25.00	
		Wide spacing, pair	65.00	
672	A158	3c **violet**	12.00	8.75
		Margin block of 4, P#	150.00	
		a. Vertical pair, one without ovpt.	*400.00*	
		Wide spacing, pair	100.00	
673	A159	4c **yellow brown**	17.50	11.00
		Margin block of 4, P#	200.00	
		Wide spacing, pair	150.00	
674	A160	5c **deep blue**	16.00	13.50
		Margin block of 4, P#	210.00	
675	A161	6c **red orange**	40.00	19.00
		Margin block of 4, P#	500.00	

OHIO RIVER CANALIZATION ISSUE.

Issued to commemorate the completion of the Ohio River Canalization Project, between Cairo, Ill. and Pittsburgh, Pa.

Lock No. 5, Monongahela River
A200

Plates of 400 subjects in four panes of 100 each.

1929   Perf. 11

681	A200	2c **carmine rose**, *Oct. 19, 1929*	80	80
		Margin block of 6, P#	32.50	—

FOR YOU IT'S FREE

- **FREE** weekly list of U.S. stamps for sale
- **FREE** weekly collecting information
- **FREE** weekly stamp stories
- **NEW** and advanced collectors served
- **FREE** insured shipping of your purchases
- **FREE** no interest layaway on big purchases
- **VISA** and MasterCard can be used
- **NEXT** four weeks lists free by simply asking

Charlie and Rosalie Wonderlin
P.O. Box 1243
Bloomington, Illinois 61702
309-454-1501

MASSACHUSETTS BAY COLONY ISSUE.

Issued in commemoration of the 300th anniversary of the founding of the Massachusetts Bay Colony.

Massachusetts Bay Colony Seal
A201

Plates of 400 subjects in four panes of 100 each.

1930   *Perf. 11*

682	A201	2c **carmine rose,** *April 8, 1930*		80	60
		Margin block of 6, P#		40.00	

CAROLINA-CHARLESTON ISSUE.

Issued in commemoration of the 260th anniversary of the founding of the Province of Carolina and the 250th anniversary of the city of Charleston, S.C.

Gov. Joseph West and Chief Shadoo, a Kiawah
A202

Plates of 400 subjects in four panes of 100 each.

1930   *Perf. 11.*

683	A202	2c **carmine rose,** *April 10, 1930*		1.65	1.60
		Margin block of 6, P#		65.00	

REGULAR ISSUE.

Harding   Taft
A203   A204

Type of 1922–26 Issue.

ROTARY PRESS PRINTING.

1930   *Perf. 11x10½*

684	A203	1½c **brown,** *Dec. 1, 1930*		25	5
		yellow brown		25	5
		Margin block of 4, P#		1.50	
		Pair with full horiz. gutter btwn.		175.00	
		Pair with full vert. gutter btwn.			
685	A204	4c **brown,** *June 4, 1930*		60	6
		deep brown		60	6
		Margin block of 4, P#		10.00	
		Gouge on right "4" (20141 U.L.24)		3.00	90
		Recut right "4" (20141 U.L.24)		3.00	1.00
		Pair with full horiz. gutter btwn.			

ROTARY PRESS COIL STAMPS.
Perf. 10 Vertically.

686	A203	1½c **brown,** *Dec. 1, 1930*		1.90	7
		Pair		4.00	16
		Joint line pair		7.00	50
687	A204	4c **brown,** *Sept. 18, 1930*		3.00	50
		Pair		6.25	1.10
		Joint line pair		12.50	1.75

BRADDOCK'S FIELD ISSUE.

Issued in commemoration of the 175th anniversary of the Battle of Braddock's Field, otherwise the Battle of Monongahela.

Statue of Colonel George Washington
A205

Designed by Alvin R. Meissner.

FLAT PLATE PRINTING.

Plates of 400 subjects in four panes of 100 each.

1930   *Perf. 11.*

688	A205	2c **carmine rose,** *July 9, 1930*		1.40	1.40
		Margin block of 6, P#		55.00	

VON STEUBEN ISSUE.

Issued in commemoration of the 200th anniversary of the birth of Baron Friedrich Wilhelm von Steuben (1730–1794) and his participation in the American Revolution.

General von Steuben
A206

FLAT PLATE PRINTING.

Plates of 400 subjects in four panes of 100 each.

1930 *Perf. 11*

689	A206	2c	carmine rose, *Sept. 17, 1930*	80	75
			Margin block of 6, P#	35.00	
		a.	Imperf. (pair)	2,250.	
		a.	Margin block of 6, P#, imperf.	10,000.	

PULASKI ISSUE.

Issued to commemorate the 150th anniversary (in 1929) of the death of Gen. Casimir Pulaski, Polish patriot and hero of the American Revolutionary War.

General Casimir Pulaski
A207

Plates of 400 subjects in four panes of 100 each.

1931 *Perf. 11*

690	A207	2c	carmine rose, *Jan. 16, 1931*	25	18
			deep carmine rose	25	18
			Margin block of 6, P#	17.50	

REGULAR ISSUE.

TYPE OF 1922-26 ISSUES.

ROTARY PRESS PRINTING.

1931 *Perf. 11x10½.*

692	A166	11c	light blue, *Sept. 4, 1931*	3.00	10
			Margin block of 4, P#	19.00	
			Retouched forehead		
			(20617 L. L. 2,3)	12.00	1.50
693	A167	12c	brown violet, *Aug. 25, 1931*	6.50	6
			violet brown	6.50	6
			Margin block of 4, P#	35.00	
694	A186	13c	yellow green, *Sept. 4, 1931*	2.50	10
			light yellow green	2.50	10
			blue green	2.50	10
			Block of four	10.00	75
			Margin block of 4, P#	18.00	
			Pair with full vert. gutter btwn.	150.00	
695	A168	14c	dark blue, *Sept. 8, 1931*	4.00	30
			Margin block of 4, P#	25.00	
696	A169	15c	gray, *Aug. 27, 1931*	10.00	6
			dark gray	10.00	6
			Margin block of 4, P#	60.00	

Perf. 10½x11.

697	A187	17c	black, *July 25, 1931*	5.00	25
			Margin block of 4, P#	30.00	
698	A170	20c	carmine rose, *Sept. 8, 1931*	12.00	5
			Margin block of 4, P#	65.00	
			Double transfer (20538 L. R. 26)	35.00	
699	A171	25c	blue green, *July 25, 1931*	11.00	8
			Margin block of 4, P#	62.50	
700	A172	30c	brown, *Sept. 8, 1931*	18.50	7
			Block of four	74.00	60
			Margin block of 4, P#	100.00	
			Retouched in head (20552 U.L. 83)	40.00	1.50
			Cracked plate (20552 U.R. 30)	40.00	1.50
701	A173	50c	lilac, *Sept. 4, 1931*	55.00	7
			red lilac	55.00	7
			Block of four	220.00	50
			Margin block of 4, P#	300.00	

RED CROSS ISSUE.

Issued in commemoration of the fiftieth anniversary of the founding of the American Red Cross Society.

"The Greatest Mother"
A208

FLAT PLATE PRINTING.

Plates of 200 subjects in two panes of 100 each.

1931 *Perf. 11*

702	A208	2c	black & red, *May 21, 1931*	15	12
			Margin block of 4, arrow		
			right or left	75	
			Margin block of 4, two P#	2.25	
			Red cross omitted		
			Double transfer	2.50	1.00

The cross tends to shift, appearing in many slightly varied positions.

YORKTOWN ISSUE.

Issued in commemoration of the Sesquicentennial of the surrender of Cornwallis at Yorktown.

Rochambeau, Washington, de Grasse
A209

POSTAGE, 1931, 1932

First Plate Layout.
    Border and vignette plates of 100 subjects in two panes of 50 subjects each.
Second Plate Layout.
    Border plates of 100 subjects in two panes of 50 each, separated by a 1 inch wide vertical gutter with central guide line and vignette plates of 50 subjects.
Issued in panes of 50 subjects.

1931   *Perf. 11*

703	A209	2c **carmine rose & black,** *Oct. 19, 1931*	40	35
		Margin block of 4, arrow marker, right or left	1.70	
		Center line block	1.85	
		Margin block of 4, two P#	3.50	
		Margin block of 4, two P# & arrow & marker block	3.50	
		Margin block of 6, two P# & "TOP", arrow & marker	4.75	
		Margin block of 8, two P# & "TOP"	6.00	
	a.	2c lake & black	3.50	50
	b.	2c dark lake & black	275.00	
	b.	Margin block of 4, two P#	1,650.	
	c.	Imperf. vertically, pair	2,500.	
		Double transfer	2.50	1.25

WASHINGTON BICENTENNIAL ISSUE.
200th anniversary of the birth of George Washington.
Various Portraits of George Washington.

By Charles Willson
Peale, 1777
A210

From Houdon Bust,
1785
A211

By Charles Willson
Peale, 1772
A212

By Gilbert Stuart,
1796
A213

By Charles Willson
Peale, 1777
A214

By Charles Peale Polk
A215

By Charles Willson
Peale, 1795
A216

By John Trumbull, 1792
A217

By John Trumbull, 1780
A218

By Charles B. J. F.
Saint Memin, 1798
A219

By W. Williams, 1794
A220

By Gilbert Stuart, 1795
A221

ROTARY PRESS PRINTINGS.
Plates of 400 subjects in four panes of 100 each.

1932, Jan. 1   *Perf. 11x10½*

Broken Circle

704	A210	½c **olive brown**	8	5
		Margin block of 4, P#	4.00	
		Broken circle (20500 U. R. 8)	60	15
705	A211	1c **green**	13	5
		Margin block of 4, P#	5.00	
		Gripper cracks (20742 U. L. and U. R.)	3.00	2.00

POSTAGE, 1932

706	A212	1½c **brown**	55	8
		Margin block of 4, P#	22.50	
707	A213	2c **carmine rose**	10	5
		Margin block of 4, P#	1.50	
		Pair with full vert. gutter between		
		Gripper cracks (20752 L. R.), (20755 L. L. and L. R.), (20756 L. L.), (20774 L. R.), (20792 L. L. and L. R.), (20796 L. L. and L. R.)	2.00	75

Double Transfer

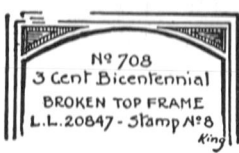

708	A214	3c **deep violet**	60	6
		Margin block of 4, P#	16.00	
		Double transfer	2.00	75
		Broken top frame line (20847 L. L. 8)	4.50	1.00

Retouch in Eyes

709	A215	4c **light brown**	25	6
		Margin block of 4, P#	5.00	
		Double transfer (20568 L. R. 60)	1.50	25
		Retouch in eyes (20568 L. R. 89)	2.00	35
		Broken bottom frame line (20568 L. R. 100)	1.50	50

Cracked Plate

710	A216	5c **blue**	2.25	10
		Margin block of 4, P#	24.00	
		Cracked plate (20637 U. R. 80)	6.00	1.25
711	A217	6c **red orange**	5.00	6
		Margin block of 4, P#	75.00	

Double Transfer

712	A218	7c **black**	30	20
		Margin block of 4, P#	6.00	
		Double transfer (20563 U. L. 1 or 20564 L. L. 91)	1.50 4.50	30 90
713	A219	8c **olive bistre**		
		Margin block of 4, P#	70.00	
		Pair, gutter between		
714	A220	9c **pale red**	4.00	25
		orange red	4.00	25
		Margin block of 4, P#	45.00	7.00
715	A221	10c **orange yellow**	15.00	10
		Margin block of 4, P#	150.00	

OLYMPIC WINTER GAMES ISSUE.

Issued in honor of the 3rd Olympic Winter Games, held at Lake Placid, N. Y., February 4–13, 1932.

Ski Jumper
A222

FLAT PLATE PRINTING.

Plates of 400 subjects in four panes of 100 each.

1932		*Perf. 11*		
716	A222	2c **carmine rose**, *Jan. 25, 1932*	50	25
		carmine	50	25
		Margin block of 6, P#	17.50	
		Cracked plate (20823 UR 41, 42; UL 48, 49, 50)	6.00	2.50
		Recut (20823 U.R. 61)	5.00	2.50
		Colored "snowball" (20815 U.R. 64)	30.00	5.00

ARBOR DAY ISSUE.

Issued in commemoration of the sixtieth anniversary of the first observance of Arbor Day in the state of Nebraska in April, 1872, and of the centenary of the birth of Julius Sterling Morton, who conceived the plan and the name "Arbor Day", while he was a member of the Nebraska State Board of Agriculture.

Boy and Girl Planting Tree
A223

ROTARY PRESS PRINTING.

Plates of 400 subjects in four panes of 100 each.

1932		*Perf. 11x10½*		
717	A223	2c **carmine rose**, *April 22, 1932*	18	8
		Margin block of 4, P#	12.50	

OLYMPIC GAMES ISSUE.

Issued in honor of the 10th Olympic Games, held at Los Angeles, Calif., July 30 to Aug. 14, 1932.

Runner at Starting Mark
A224

Myron's Discobolus
A225

Designed by Victor S. McCloskey, Jr.

ROTARY PRESS PRINTING.
Plates of 400 subjects in four panes of 100 each.

1932, June 15			Perf. 11x10½	
718	A224	3c **violet**	2.00	6
		deep violet	2.00	6
		Margin block of 4, P#	25.00	
		Gripper cracks (20906 U.L. 1)	5.00	1.00
719	A225	5c **blue**	3.25	30
		deep blue	3.25	30
		Margin block of 4, P#	40.00	
		Gripper cracks (20868 U.L. and U.R.)	5.00	1.25

Washington, by Gilbert Stuart
A226

REGULAR ISSUE.
ROTARY PRESS PRINTING.
Plates of 400 subjects in four panes of 100 each.

1932			Perf. 11x10½	
720	A226	3c **deep violet**, June 16, 1932	15	5
		light violet	15	5
		Margin block of 4, P#	1.50	
		Pair with full vert. gutter btwn.	200.00	
		Pair with full horiz. gutter btwn.	200.00	
		b. Booklet pane of six, July 25, 1932	22.50	5.00
		c. Vertical pair, imperf. between	225.00	
		Double transfer	1.50	50
		Recut lines on nose	3.00	1.00
		Gripper cracks	1.75	50

ROTARY PRESS COIL STAMPS.
1932			Perf. 10 Vertically	
721	A226	3c **deep violet**, June 24, 1932	3.00	8
		light violet	3.00	8
		Pair	6.25	20
		Joint line pair	14.00	75
		Gripper cracks		
		Recut lines on nose		
		Recut lines around eyes		

1932			Perf. 10 Horizontally	
722	A226	3c **deep violet**, Oct. 12, 1932	1.85	45
		light violet	1.85	45
		Pair	3.85	1.00
		Joint line pair	10.00	1.75

TYPE OF 1922-26 ISSUES.
1932			Perf. 10 Vertically.	
723	A161	6c **deep orange**, Aug. 18, 1932	12.50	25
		Pair	26.00	60
		Joint line pair	75.00	2.50

WILLIAM PENN ISSUE.
Issued in commemoration of the 250th anniversary of the arrival in America of William Penn (1644–1718), English Quaker and founder of Pennsylvania.

William Penn
A227

FLAT PLATE PRINTING.
Plates of 400 subjects in four panes of 100 each
1932			Perf. 11	
724	A227	3c **violet**, Oct. 24, 1932	35	25
		Margin block of 6, P#	18.50	
		a. Vert. pair, imperf. horiz.		

DANIEL WEBSTER ISSUE.
Issued in commemoration of the 150th anniversary of the birth of Daniel Webster (1782–1852), statesman.

Daniel Webster
A228

FLAT PLATE PRINTING.
Plates of 400 subjects in four panes of 100 each.
1932			Perf. 11	
725	A228	3c **violet**, Oct. 24, 1932	50	40
		light violet	50	40
		Margin block of 6, P#	30.00	

GEORGIA BICENTENNIAL ISSUE.
Issued in commemoration of the 200th anniversary of the founding of the Colony of Georgia and in honor of James Edward Oglethorpe, who landed from England, Feb. 12, 1733, and personally supervised the establishing of the colony.

Gen. James Edward Oglethorpe
A229

FLAT PLATE PRINTING.

Plates of 400 subjects in four panes of 100 each.

1933   *Perf. 11.*

726	A229	3c **violet,** *Feb. 12, 1933*		35	25
		Margin block of 6, P#		20.00	—
		Margin block of 10, "CS" & P#		25.00	
		Bottom margin block of 20, no P#			

PEACE OF 1783 ISSUE.

Issued to commemorate the 150th anniversary of the issuance by George Washington of the official order containing the Proclamation of Peace marking officially the ending of hostilities in the War for Independence.

Washington's Headquarters
at Newburgh, N. Y.
A230

ROTARY PRESS PRINTING

Plates of 400 subjects in four panes of 100 each.

1933   *Perf. 10½x11*

727	A230	3c **violet,** *April 19, 1933*		15	10
		Margin block of 4, P#		6.50	—
		Margin block of 4, horizontal gutter between		75.00	—
		Block of 4, vertical gutter between		85.00	—

No. 727 was available in full sheets of 400 subjects with gum, but was not regularly issued in that form.

CENTURY OF PROGRESS ISSUES.

Issued to commemorate the "Century of Progress" International Exhibition at Chicago, which opened June 1, 1933, and the centenary of the incorporation of Chicago as a city.

Restoration of Fort Dearborn
A231

Federal Building
A232

ROTARY PRESS PRINTING.

Plates of 400 subjects in four panes of 100 each.

1933, May 25   *Perf. 10½x11*

728	A231	1c **yellow green**		12	6
		On cover, Expo. station canc.			50
		Margin block of 4, P#		2.50	—
		Block of 4, horizontal gutter between		75.00	—
		Block of 4, vertical gutter between		75.00	—
		Gripper cracks (21133 U.R. and L.R.)		2.00	—
729	A232	3c **violet**		18	5
		On cover, Expo. station canc.			50
		Margin block of 4, P#		3.50	—
		Block of 4, horizontal gutter between		100.00	—
		Block of 4, vertical gutter between		100.00	—

Nos. 728 and 729 were available in full sheets of 400 subjects with gum, but were not regularly issued in that form.

AMERICAN PHILATELIC SOCIETY ISSUE.

SOUVENIR SHEETS.

A231a

A232a

FLAT PLATE PRINTING.

Plates of 225 subjects in nine panes of 25 each.

1933   *Imperf.*
Without Gum.

730	A231a	1c **deep yellow green,** sheet of twenty-five, *Aug. 25*		35.00	35.00
	a.	Single stamp		1.00	50
731	A232a	3c **deep violet,** sheet of twenty-five		30.00	30.00
	a.	Single stamp		85	50

Issued in sheets measuring 134 x 120 mm. containing twenty-five stamps, inscribed in the margins: PRINTED BY THE TREASURY DEPARTMENT, BUREAU OF ENGRAVING AND PRINTING,—UNDER AUTHORITY OF JAMES A. FARLEY, POSTMASTER-GENERAL, AT CENTURY OF PROGRESS,—IN COMPLIMENT TO THE AMERICAN PHILATELIC SOCIETY FOR ITS CONVENTION AND EXHIBITION—CHICAGO, ILLINOIS, AUGUST, 1933. PLATE NO. 21145 [or 21159 (1c) 21146 or 21160 (3c)].

See also Nos. 766-767.

NATIONAL RECOVERY ACT ISSUE.

Issued to direct attention to and arouse the support of the Nation for the National Recovery Act.

Group of Workers
A233

ROTARY PRESS PRINTING.

Plates of 400 subjects in four panes of 100 each.

1933   Perf. 10½x11.

732	A233	3c violet, *Aug. 15, 1933*	14	5
		Margin block of 4, P#	1.75	—
		Gripper cracks (21151 U.L. and U.R.)		
		(21153 U.R. and L.R.)	2.00	—
		Recut at right (21151 U.R. 47)	2.50	

BYRD ANTARCTIC ISSUE.

Issued in connection with the Byrd Antarctic Expedition of 1933 and for use on letters mailed through the Little America Post Office established at the Base Camp of the Expedition in the territory of the South Pole.

A Map of the World
(on van der Grinten's Projection)
A234
Designed by Victor S. McCloskey, Jr.

FLAT PLATE PRINTING.

Plates of 200 subjects in four panes of 50 each

1933   Perf. 11.

733	A234	3c dark blue, *Oct. 9, 1933*	85	85
		Margin block of 6, P#	25.00	—
		Double transfer (21167 L.R. 2)	3.50	1.50

In addition to the postage charge of 3 cents, letters sent by the ships of the expedition to be cancelled in Little America were subject to a service charge of 50 cents each. See also No. 753.

KOSCIUSZKO ISSUE.

Issued to commemorate Gen. Tadeusz Kosciuszko (1746–1807), Polish soldier and statesman who served in the American Revolution, and to mark the 150th anniversary of the granting to him of American citizenship.

Statue of General Tadeusz Kosciuszko
A235
Designed by Victor S. McCloskey, Jr.

FLAT PLATE PRINTING.

Plates of 400 subjects in four panes of 100 each

1934   Perf. 11.

734	A235	5c blue, *Oct. 13, 1933*	85	40
		Margin block of 6, P#	45.00	—
	a.	Horiz. pair, imperf. vert.	1,750.	—
		Cracked plate		

NATIONAL STAMP EXHIBITION ISSUE.
SOUVENIR SHEET.

A235a

TYPE OF BYRD ISSUE.

Plates of 150 subjects in 25 panes of six each.

1934   Imperf.

Without Gum.

735	A235a	3c dark blue, sheet of six, *Feb. 10*	22.50	20.00
	a.	Single stamp	2.50	2.50

Issued in sheets measuring 87x93 mm. containing six stamps, inscribed in the margins: "Printed by the Treasury Department, Bureau of Engraving and Printing, under authority of James A. Farley, Postmaster General, in compliment to the National Stamp Exhibition of 1934. New York, N. Y., February 10-18, 1934. Plate No. 21184." Plate No. 21187 was used for sheets printed at the Exhibition, but all these were destroyed.

See also No. 768.

MARYLAND TERCENTENARY ISSUE.

Issued to commemorate the 300th anniversary of the founding of Maryland.

"The Ark" and "The Dove"
A236

Designed by Alvin R. Meissner.

FLAT PLATE PRINTING.

Plates of 400 subjects in four panes of 100 each.

1934			Perf. 11.		
736	A236	3c	**carmine rose,** *Mar. 23, 1934*	20	20
			Margin block of 6, P#	13.50	
			Double transfer (21190 U.L. 1)		
		a.	Horiz. pair, imperf. between	1,000.	

MOTHERS OF AMERICA ISSUE.

Issued to commemorate Mother's Day.

Adaptation of Whistler's Portrait of his Mother
A237

Designed by Victor S. McCloskey, Jr.

Plates of 200 subjects in four panes of 50 each.

ROTARY PRESS PRINTING.

1934			Perf. 11x10½.		
737	A237	3c	**deep violet,** *May 2, 1934*	15	6
			Margin block of 4, P#	1.75	

FLAT PLATE PRINTING.

Perf. 11.

738	A237	3c	**deep violet,** *May 2, 1934*	20	20
			Margin block of 6, P#	7.25	

See also No. 754.

WISCONSIN TERCENTENARY ISSUE.

Issued to commemorate the 300th anniversary of the arrival of Jean Nicolet, French explorer, on the shores of Green Bay. According to historical records, Nicolet was the first white man to reach the territory now comprising the State of Wisconsin.

Nicolet's Landing
A238

Designed by Victor S. McCloskey, Jr.

FLAT PLATE PRINTING.

Plates of 200 subjects in four panes of 50 each.

1934			Perf. 11.		
739	A238	3c	**deep violet,** *July 7, 1934*	20	12
			violet	20	12
			Margin block of 6, P#	7.00	
		a.	Vert. pair, imperf. horiz.	250.00	
		b.	Horiz. pair, imperf. vert.	325.00	

See also No. 755.

NATIONAL PARKS ISSUE.

Issued to commemorate "National Parks Year".

El Capitan, Yosemite (California)
A239

View of Grand Canyon (Arizona)
A240

Mt. Rainier and Mirror Lake (Washington)
A241

Cliff Palace, Mesa Verde Park (Colorado)
A242

Old Faithful, Yellowstone (Wyoming)
A243

Crater Lake (Oregon)
A244

Great Head, Acadia Park (Maine)
A245

Great White Throne, Zion Park (Utah)
A246

Mt. Rockwell (Mt. Sinopah) and Two Medicine Lake, Glacier National Park (Montana)
A247

POSTAGE, 1934

Great Smoky Mountains
(North Carolina)
A248

FLAT PLATE PRINTING.

Plates of 200 subjects in four panes of 50 each.

1934			Perf. 11	Unwmkd.	
740	A239	1c	green, *July 16, 1934*	10	6
			light green	10	6
			Margin block of 6, P#	1.50	
			Recut	2.00	.75
		a.	Vert. pair, imperf. horiz., with gum	450.00	
741	A240	2c	red, *July 24, 1934*	15	6
			orange red	15	6
			Margin block of 6, P#	2.00	
		a.	Vert. pair, imperf. horiz., with gum	375.00	
		b.	Horiz. pair, imperf. vert., with gum	400.00	
			Double transfer	1.75	
742	A241	3c	deep violet, *Aug. 3, 1934*	20	6
			Margin block of 6, P#	3.00	
			Recut	2.00	
		a.	Vert. pair, imperf. horiz., with gum	500.00	
743	A242	4c	brown, *Sept. 25, 1934*	55	50
			light brown	55	50
			Margin block of 6, P#	11.00	
		a.	Vert. pair, imperf. horiz., with gum	650.00	
744	A243	5c	blue, *July 30, 1934*	1.10	90
			light blue	1.10	90
			Margin block of 6, P#	16.00	
		a.	Horiz. pair, imperf. vert., with gum	400.00	
745	A244	6c	dark blue, *Sept. 5, 1934*	2.00	1.25
			Margin block of 6, P#	30.00	
746	A245	7c	black, *Oct. 2, 1934*	1.00	1.00
			Margin block of 6, P#	20.00	
		a.	Horiz. pair, imperf. vert., with gum	600.00	
			Double transfer	5.00	2.00
747	A246	8c	sage green, *Sept. 18, 1934*	2.85	2.50
			Margin block of 6, P#	30.00	
748	A247	9c	red orange, *Aug. 27, 1934*	3.00	90
			orange	3.00	90
			Margin block of 6, P#	30.00	
749	A248	10c	gray black, *Oct. 8, 1934*	5.00	1.35
			gray	5.00	1.35
			Margin block of 6, P#	50.00	

Imperforate varieties of the 2c and 5c exist as errors of the perforated Parks set, but are virtually impossible to distinguish from gummed copies from the imperforate sheets of 200. (See note above No. 752).

AMERICAN PHILATELIC SOCIETY ISSUE.

SOUVENIR SHEET.

A248a

Plates of 120 subjects in 20 panes of 6 stamps each

1934					Imperf.	
750	A24	3c	deep violet, sheet of six, *Aug. 28*		40.00	35.00
		a.	Single stamp		4.50	4.50

Issued in sheets measuring 97x99 mm. containing six stamps, inscribed in the margins: PRINTED BY THE TREASURY DEPARTMENT, BUREAU OF ENGRAVING AND PRINTING,—UNDER AUTHORITY OF JAMES A. FARLEY, POSTMASTER GENERAL,—IN COMPLIMENT TO THE AMERICAN PHILATELIC SOCIETY FOR ITS CONVENTION AND EXHIBITION,—ATLANTIC CITY, NEW JERSEY, AUGUST, 1934. PLATE NO. 21303.

TRANS-MISSISSIPPI PHILATELIC EXPOSITION ISSUE.

SOUVENIR SHEET.

A248b

Plates of 120 subjects in 20 panes of 6 stamps each.

1934					Imperf.	
751	A248b	1c	green, sheet of six, *Oct. 10*		15.00	15.00
		a.	Single stamp		1.75	1.75

Issued in sheets measuring 94x99 mm. containing six stamps, inscribed in the margins: PRINTED BY THE TREASURY DEPARTMENT, BUREAU OF ENGRAVING AND PRINTING,—UNDER AUTHORITY OF JAMES A. FARLEY, POSTMASTER GENERAL,—IN COMPLIMENT TO THE TRANS-MISSISSIPPI PHILATELIC EXPOSITION AND CONVENTION, OMAHA, NEBRASKA,—OCTOBER, 1934. PLATE NO. 21341.

POSTAGE, 1935

SPECIAL PRINTING.
(Nos. 752 to 771 inclusive)
Issued March 15, 1935.

"Issued for a limited time in full sheets as printed, and in blocks thereof, to meet the requirements of collectors and others who may be interested."—*From Postal Bulletin No. 16614.*

Issuance of the following 20 stamps in complete sheets resulted from the protest of collectors and others at the practice of presenting, to certain government officials, complete sheets of unsevered panes, imperforate (except Nos. 752 and 753) and generally ungummed.

Gutter or line pairs sell for half the price of gutter or line blocks of four.

Designs of Commemorative Issues.
Without Gum.

NOTE. In 1940 the P. O. Department offered to and did gum full sheets of Nos. 754 to 771 sent in by owners.

TYPE OF PEACE ISSUE.

Issued in sheets of 400, consisting of four panes of 100 each, with vertical and horizontal gutters between and plate numbers at outside corners at sides.

ROTARY PRESS PRINTING.

1935   *Perf. 10½x11*   **Unwmkd.**

752	A230	3c **violet**		20	15
		Horiz. gutter block of four		9.00	
		Vert. gutter block of four		15.00	
		Gutter block of four with dash (left or right)		10.00	
		Gutter block of four with dash (top or bottom)		15.00	
		Center block with crossed gutters and dashes		35.00	
		Margin block of 4, P#		16.00	

No. 752 is similar to No. 727. Positive identification is by blocks or pairs showing wide gutters between stamps. These wide gutters occur only on No. 752.

TYPE OF BYRD ISSUE

Issued in sheets of 200, consisting of four panes of 50 each, with vertical and horizontal guide lines in gutters between panes, and plate numbers centered at top and bottom of each pane. This applies to Nos. 753-765 and 771.

FLAT PLATE PRINTING.
Perf. 11.

753	A234	3c **dark blue**		60	60
		Horiz. line block of four		7.00	
		Vert. line block of four		80.00	
		Margin block of 4, arrow & guide line (left or right)		7.50	
		Margin block of 4, arrow & guideline (top or bottom)		82.50	
		Center line block		87.50	30.00
		Margin block of 6, P# (Number at top or bottom)		25.00	

No. 753 is similar to No. 733. Positive identification is by blocks or pairs showing guide line between stamps. These lines between stamps are found only on No. 753.

TYPE OF MOTHERS OF AMERICA ISSUE.
Issued in sheets of 200.

FLAT PLATE PRINTING.
Imperf.

754	A237	3c **deep violet**		1.00	60
		Horiz. or vert. line block of four		4.25	
		Margin block of 4, arrow & guideline (left, right, top or bottom)		4.50	
		Center line block		10.00	
		Margin block of 6, P# (Number at top or bottom)		35.00	

TYPE OF WISCONSIN ISSUE.
Issued in sheets of 200.

FLAT PLATE PRINTING.
Imperf.

755	A238	3c **deep violet**		1.00	60
		Horiz. or vert. line block of four		4.25	
		Margin block of 4, arrow & guideline (left, right, top or bottom)		4.50	
		Center line block		10.00	
		Margin block of 6, P# (Number at top or bottom)		35.00	

TYPES OF NATIONAL PARKS ISSUE
Issued in sheets of 200.

FLAT PLATE PRINTING.
Imperf.

756	A239	1c **green**		30	20
		Horiz. or vert. line block of four		1.30	
		Margin block of 4, arrow & guideline (left, right, top or bottom)		1.40	
		Center line block		3.50	
		Margin block of 6, P# (Number at top or bottom)		5.50	

See note above No. 766.

757	A240	2c **red**		40	35
		Horiz. or vert. line block of four		1.70	
		Margin block of 4, arrow & guideline (left, right, top or bottom)		1.75	
		Center line block		5.00	
		Margin block of 6, P# (Number at top or bottom)		6.50	
		Double transfer			
758	A241	3c **deep violet**		75	70
		Horiz. or vert. line block of four		3.20	
		Margin block of 4, arrow & guideline (left, right, top or bottom)		3.25	
		Center line block		6.50	
		Margin block of 6, P# (Number at top or bottom)		20.00	
759	A242	4c **brown**		2.00	2.00
		Horiz. or vert. line block of four		8.25	
		Margin block of 4, arrow & guideline (left, right, top or bottom)		8.50	
		Center line block		11.00	
		Margin block of 6, P# (Number at top or bottom)		27.50	
760	A243	5c **blue**		2.75	2.25
		Horiz. or vert. line block of four		12.50	
		Margin block of 4, arrow & guideline (left, right, top or bottom)		13.00	
		Center line block		17.50	
		Margin block of 6, P# (Number at top or bottom)		35.00	
		Double transfer			
761	A244	6c **dark blue**		4.00	2.75
		Horiz. or vert. line block of four		16.50	
		Margin block of 4, arrow & guideline left, right, top or bottom)		17.00	
		Center line block		22.50	
		Margin block of 6, P# (Number at top or bottom)		47.50	
762	A245	7c **black**		3.00	2.50
		Horiz. or vert. line block of four		12.50	
		Margin block of 4, arrow & guideline (left, right, top or bottom)		13.00	
		Center line block		18.50	
		Margin block of 6, P# (Number at top or bottom)		42.50	
		Double transfer			

POSTAGE, 1935

763	A246	8c **sage green**	3.50	2.75
		Block of four	14.00	11.00
		Horiz. or vert. line block of four	14.50	—
		Margin block of 4, arrow & guideline (left, right, top or bottom)	15.00	—
		Center line block	20.00	—
		Margin block of 6, P# (Number at top or bottom)	55.00	—
764	A247	9c **red orange**	3.75	2.75
		Block of four	15.00	11.00
		Horiz. or vert. line block of four	15.50	—
		Margin block of 4, arrow & guideline (left, right, top or bottom)	16.00	—
		Center line block	21.00	—
		Margin block of 6, P# (Number at top or bottom)	60.00	—
765	A248	10c **gray black**	6.25	5.50
		Block of four	25.00	22.00
		Horiz. or vert. line block of four	25.50	—
		Margin block of 4, arrow & guideline (left, right, top or bottom)	26.00	—
		Center line block	32.50	—
		Margin block of 6, P# (Number at top or bottom)	72.50	—

SOUVENIR SHEETS.
TYPE OF CENTURY OF PROGRESS ISSUE.

Issued in sheets of 9 panes of 25 stamps each, with vertical and horizontal gutters between panes. This applies to Nos. 766–770.

Note. Single items from these sheets are identical with other varieties, 766 and 730, 766a and 730a, 767 and 731, 767a and 731a, 768 and 735, 768a and 735a, 769 and 756, 770 and 758. Positive identification is by blocks or pairs showing wide gutters between stamps. These wide gutters occur only on Nos. 766 to 770 and measure, horizontally, 13 mm. on Nos. 766-767; 16 mm. on No. 768, and 23 mm. on Nos. 769-770.

FLAT PLATE PRINTING.
Imperf.

766	A231a	1c **yellow green**, pane of twenty-five	45.00	45.00
	a.	Single stamp	1.00	50
		Block of four	4.00	2.25
		Horiz. gutter block	13.00	—
		Vert. gutter block	15.00	—
		Block with crossed gutters	20.00	—
		Block of 50 stamps (two panes)	105.00	—
767	A232a	3c **violet**, pane of twenty-five	40.00	35.00
	a.	Single stamp	85	50
		Horiz. gutter block	12.00	—
		Vert. gutter block	14.00	—
		Block with crossed gutters	19.00	—
		Block of 50 stamps (two panes)	95.00	—

NATIONAL EXHIBITION ISSUE.
TYPE OF BYRD ISSUE.
Issued in sheets of 25 panes of 6 stamps each.
FLAT PLATE PRINTING.
Imperf.

768	A235a	3c **dark blue**, pane of six	30.00	25.00
	a.	Single stamp	3.25	2.75
		Horiz. gutter block	16.00	—
		Vert. gutter block	17.00	—
		Block of four with crossed gutters	18.50	—
		Block of 12 stamps (two panes)	65.00	—

TYPES OF NATIONAL PARKS ISSUE.
Issued in sheets of 20 panes of 6 stamps each.
FLAT PLATE PRINTING.
Imperf.

769	A248b	1c **green**, pane of six	15.00	12.00
	a.	Single stamp	1.75	1.75
		Horiz. or vert. gutter block	14.00	—
		Block of four with crossed gutters	15.00	—
		Block of 12 stamps (two panes)	31.00	—
770	A248a	3c **deep violet**, pane of six	35.00	25.00
	a.	Single stamp	3.75	3.75
		Horiz. or vert. gutter block	25.00	—
		Block of four with crossed gutters	26.50	—
		Block of 12 stamps (two panes)	75.00	—

TYPE OF AIR POST SPECIAL DELIVERY
Issued in sheets of 200.
FLAT PLATE PRINTING.
Imperf.

771	APSD116c	**dark blue**	3.00	3.00
		Horiz. or vert. line block of four	13.00	13.00
		Margin block of 4, arrow & guide line (left, right, top or bottom)	15.00	15.00
		Center line block	35.00	—
		Margin block of 6, P# (Number at top or bottom)	65.00	—

CONNECTICUT TERCENTENARY ISSUE.

Issued in commemoration of the 300th anniversary of the settlement of Connecticut.

The Charter Oak—A249
ROTARY PRESS PRINTING.
Plates of 200 subjects in four panes of 50 each.

1935		Perf. 11x10½		Unwmkd.
772	A249	3c **violet**, April 26, 1935	15	6
		rose violet	15	8
		Margin block of 4, P#	2.00	—
		Defect in "¢" (21395 U.R. 4)	1.00	25

CALIFORNIA PACIFIC EXPOSITION ISSUE.

Issued in commemoration of the California Pacific Exposition at San Diego.

View of San Diego Exposition—A250
ROTARY PRESS PRINTING.
Plates of 200 subjects in four panes of 50 each.

1935		Perf. 11x10½		Unwmkd.
773	A250	3c **purple**, May 29, 1935	12	6
		On cover, Expo. station canc.		50
		Margin block of 4, P#	2.00	—
		Pair with full vertical gutter between		—

BOULDER DAM ISSUE.

Issued to commemorate the dedication of Boulder Dam.

Boulder Dam
(Hoover Dam)
A251

FLAT PLATE PRINTING.

Plates of 200 subjects in four panes of 50 each.

1935		Perf. 11	Unwmkd.	
774	A251	3c **purple,** *Sept. 30, 1935*	12	6
		deep purple	12	6
		Margin block of 6, P#	2.75	

MICHIGAN CENTENARY ISSUE.

Advance celebration of Michigan Statehood centenary. Michigan was admitted to the Union Jan. 26, 1837.

Michigan State Seal
A252

Designed by Alvin R. Meissner.

ROTARY PRESS PRINTING.

Plates of 200 subjects in four panes of 50 each.

1935		Perf. 11x10½	Unwmkd.	
775	A252	3c **purple,** *Nov. 1, 1935*	12	6
		Margin block of 4, P#	2.00	

TEXAS CENTENNIAL ISSUE.

Issued in commemoration of the centennial of Texas independence.

Sam Houston, Stephen F. Austin and the Alamo
A253

Designed by Alvin R. Meissner.

ROTARY PRESS PRINTING.

Plates of 200 subjects in four panes of 50 each.

1936		Perf. 11x10½.	Unwmkd.	
776	A253	3c **purple,** *March 2, 1936*	12	6
		On cover, Expo. station canc.		50
		Margin block of 4, P#	2.00	

RHODE ISLAND TERCENTENARY ISSUE

Issued in commemoration of the 300th anniversary of the settlement of Rhode Island.

Statue of Roger Williams
A254

ROTARY PRESS PRINTING.

Plates of 200 subjects in four panes of 50 each.

1936		Perf. 10½x11	Unwmkd.	
777	A254	3c **purple,** *May 4, 1936*	15	6
		rose violet	15	6
		Margin block of 4, P#	2.00	
		Pair with full gutter between	200.00	

THIRD INTERNATIONAL PHILATELIC EXHIBITION ISSUE.
SOUVENIR SHEET.

A254a

TYPES OF CONNECTICUT, CALIFORNIA, MICHIGAN AND TEXAS ISSUES.
Plates of 120 subjects in thirty panes of 4 each.
FLAT PLATE PRINTING.

1936, May 9		Imperf.	Unwmkd.	
778	A254a	**violet**, sheet of four	3.50	3.50
	a.	3c type A249	70	60
	b.	3c type A250	70	60
	c.	3c type A252	70	60
	d.	3c type A253	70	60

Issued in sheets measuring 98x66 mm. containing four stamps, inscribed in the margins: "Printed by the Treasury Department, Bureau of Engraving and Printing, under authority of James A. Farley, Postmaster General, in compliment to the third International Philatelic Exhibition of 1936. New York, N. Y., May 9-17, 1936. Plate No. 21557 (or 21558)."

ARKANSAS CENTENNIAL ISSUE.

Issued in commemoration of the 100th anniversary of the State of Arkansas.

Arkansas Post, Old and New State Houses
A255

ROTARY PRESS PRINTING.
Plates of 200 subjects in four panes of 50 each.

1936		Perf. 11x10½	Unwmkd.	
782	A255	3c **purple**, *June 15, 1936*	12	6
		Margin block of 4, P#	2.00	

OREGON TERRITORY ISSUE

Issued in commemoration of the 100th anniversary of the opening of the Oregon Territory, 1836.

Map of Oregon Territory—A256

ROTARY PRESS PRINTING.
Plates of 200 subjects in four panes of 50 each.

1936		Perf. 11x10½	Unwmkd.	
783	A256	3c **purple**, *July 14, 1936*	12	6
		Margin block of 4, P#	2.00	
		Double transfer (21579 U.L. 3)	1.50	50

SUSAN B. ANTHONY ISSUE.

Issued in honor of Susan Brownell Anthony (1820–1906), woman-suffrage advocate, on the 16th anniversary of the ratification of the 19th Amendment which grants American women the right to vote.

Susan B. Anthony
A257

ROTARY PRESS PRINTING
Plates of 400 subjects in four panes of 100 each.

1936		Perf. 11x10½	Unwmkd.	
784	A257	3c **dark violet**, *Aug. 20, 1936*	10	5
		Margin block of 4, P#	75	
		Period missing after "B"		
		(21590 L.R. 100)	1.00	25

ARMY ISSUE.

Issued in honor of the United States Army.

Generals George Washington, Nathanael Greene and Mt. Vernon
A258

Maj. Gen. Andrew Jackson, Gen. Winfield Scott and the Hermitage
A259

192　POSTAGE, 1936-37

Generals William T. Sherman, Ulysses S. Grant and Philip H. Sheridan
A260

Generals Robert E. Lee, "Stonewall" Jackson and Stratford Hall
A261

U. S. Military Academy, West Point
A262

ROTARY PRESS PRINTING.

Plates of 200 subjects in four panes of 50 each.

1936–37		Perf. 11x10½.	Unwmkd.	
785	A258	1c **green,** *Dec. 15, 1936*	10	6
		yellow green	10	6
		Margin block of 4, P#	1.00	
		Pair with full vertical gutter between		
786	A259	2c **carmine,** *Jan. 15, 1937*	15	6
		Margin block of 4, P#	1.10	
787	A260	3c **purple,** *Feb. 18, 1937*	20	8
		Margin block of 4, P#	1.50	
788	A261	4c **gray,** *March 23, 1937*	65	15
		Margin block of 4, P#	13.00	
789	A262	5c **ultramarine,** *May 26, 1937*	1.00	15
		Margin block of 4, P#	15.00	

NAVY ISSUE.

Issued in honor of the United States Navy.

John Paul Jones and John Barry
A263

Stephen Decatur and Thomas MacDonough
A264

Admirals David G. Farragut and David D. Porter
A265

Admirals William T. Sampson, George Dewey and Winfield S. Schley
A266

POSTAGE, 1936-37, 1937   193

Seal of U. S. Naval Academy
and Naval Cadets
A267

ROTARY PRESS PRINTING.

Plates of 200 subjects in four panes of 50 each.

1936-37		Perf. 11x10½	Unwmkd.	
790	A263	1c **green**, *Dec. 15, 1936*	10	6
		yellow green	10	6
		Margin block of 4, P#	1.00	
791	A264	2c **carmine**, *Jan. 15, 1937*	15	6
		Margin block of 4, P#	1.10	
792	A265	3c **purple**, *Feb. 18, 1937*	20	8
		Margin block of 4, P#	1.50	
793	A266	4c **gray**, *March 23, 1937*	65	15
		Margin block of 4, P#	13.00	
794	A267	5c **ultramarine**, *May 26, 1937*	1.00	15
		Margin block of 4, P#	15.00	
		Pair with full vert. gutter btwn.		

VIRGINIA DARE ISSUE.

Issued to commemorate the 350th anniversary of the birth of Virginia Dare and the settlement at Roanoke Island. Virginia was the first child born in America of English parents (Aug. 18, 1587).

Virginia Dare and Parents
A269

FLAT PLATE PRINTING.

Plates of 192 subjects in four panes of 48 each, separated by 1¼ inch wide gutters with central guide lines.

1937		Perf. 11.	Unwmkd.	
796	A269	5c **gray blue**, *Aug. 18, 1937*	35	25
		Margin block of 6, P#	10.00	

SOCIETY OF PHILATELIC AMERICANS ISSUE.

SOUVENIR SHEET.

A269a

TYPE OF NATIONAL PARKS ISSUE.

Plates of 36 subjects.

FLAT PLATE PRINTING.

1937		*Imperf.*	Unwmkd.	
797	A269a	10c **blue green**, *Aug. 26*	1.25	85

Issued in sheets measuring 67x78 mm., one stamp in center of each sheet inscribed in margins: "Printed by the Treasury Department, Bureau of Engraving and Printing—Under the Authority of James A. Farley, Postmaster General —In Compliment to the 43rd Annual Convention of the Society of Philatelic Americans—Asheville, N. C., August 26-28, 1937. Plate Number 21695 (6)."

ORDINANCE OF 1787 SESQUICENTENNIAL ISSUE.

Issued in commemoration of the 150th anniversary of the adoption of the Ordinance of 1787 and the creation of the Northwest Territory.

Manasseh Cutler, Rufus Putnam
and Map of Northwest Territory
A268

ROTARY PRESS PRINTING.

Plates of 200 subjects in four panes of 50 each.

1937		Perf. 11x10½	Unwmkd.	
795	A268	3c **red violet**, *July 13, 1937*	12	6
		Margin block of 4, P#	2.00	

CONSTITUTION SESQUICENTENNIAL ISSUE.

Issued in commemoration of the 150th anniversary of the signing of the Constitution on September 17, 1787.

"Adoption of the Constitution"
A270

ROTARY PRESS PRINTING
Plates of 200 subjects in four panes of 50 each.

1937		Perf. 11x10½		Unwmkd.	
798	A270	3c **bright red violet,** *Sept. 17, 1937*		15	7
		Margin block of 4, P#		1.65	—

TERRITORIAL ISSUES
Hawaii

Statue of Kamehameha I, Honolulu
A271

Alaska

Mt. McKinley
272

Puerto Rico

La Fortaleza, San Juan
A273

Virgin Islands

Charlotte Amalie Harbor, St. Thomas
A274

ROTARY PRESS PRINTING.
Plates of 200 subjects in panes of 50 each.

1937		Perf. 10½x11.		Unwmkd.	
799	A271	3c **violet,** *Oct. 18, 1937*		15	7
		Margin block of 4, P#		2.00	—

Perf. 11x10½.

800	A272	3c **violet,** *Nov. 12, 1937*		15	7
		Margin block of 4, P#		2.00	—
		Pair with full gutter between		—	
801	A273	3c **bright violet,** *Nov. 25, 1937*		15	7
		Margin block of 4, P#		2.00	—
802	A274	3c **light violet,** *Dec. 15, 1937*		15	7
		Margin block of 4, P#		2.00	—
		Pair with full vertical gutter between		275.00	

POSTAGE, 1938-43   195

PRESIDENTIAL ISSUE

Benjamin Franklin
A275

George Washington
A276

Martha Washington
A277

John Adams
A278

Thomas Jefferson
A279

James Madison
A280

The White House
A281

James Monroe
A282

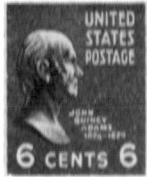
John Quincy Adams
A283

Andrew Jackson
A284

Martin Van Buren
A285

William H. Harrison
A286

John Tyler
A287

James K. Polk
A288

Zachary Taylor
A289

Millard Fillmore
A290

Franklin Pierce
A291

James Buchanan
A292

Abraham Lincoln
A293

Andrew Johnson
A294

Ulysses S. Grant
A295

Rutherford B. Hayes
A296

James A. Garfield
A297

Chester A. Arthur
A298

POSTAGE, 1938–43

Grover Cleveland
A299

Benjamin Harrison
A300

William McKinley
A301

Theodore Roosevelt
A302

William Howard Taft
A303

Woodrow Wilson
A304

Warren G. Harding
A305

Calvin Coolidge
A306

ROTARY PRESS PRINTING.

Ordinary and Electric Eye Plates of 400 subjects in four panes of 100 each.

(For details of Electric Eye Markings, see Information for Collectors in first part of this Catalogue).

1938-43 Perf. 11x10½. **Unwmkd.**

803	A275	½c **deep orange,** *May 19, 1938*		5	5
		Margin block of 4, P#		40	
804	A276	1c **green,** *April 25, 1938*		6	5
		1c light green		6	5
		Margin block of 4, P#		25	
		b. Booklet pane of six		1.75	20
		Pair with full vertical gutter between		125.00	
805	A277	1½c **bistre brown,** *May 5, 1938*		6	5
		buff ('43)		6	5
		Margin block of 4, P#		30	
		a. Horiz. pair, imperf. between		200.00	10.00
		Pair with full horizontal gutter between		150.00	
		Pair with full vertical gutter between			
806	A278	2c **rose carmine,** *June 3, 1938*		6	5
		rose pink ('43)		6	5
		Margin block of 4, P# opposite corner stamp		35	
		Vertical margin block of 10, P# opposite third horizontal row (Experimental Electric Eye plates)		4.50	
		b. Booklet pane of six		4.25	50
		Recut at top of head, Pl. 22156 U.L. 3		3.00	1.50
		Pair with full horiz. gutter btwn.			
		Pair with full vert. gutter btwn.			
807	A279	3c **deep violet,** *June 16, 1938*		10	5
		Margin block of 4, P# opposite corner stamp		50	25
		Vertical margin block of 10, P# opposite third horizontal row (Experimental Electric Eye plates)		25.00	
		a. Booklet pane of six		8.50	50
		b. Horiz. pair, imperf. between		350.00	
		c. Imperf., pair		2,100.	
		Pair with full vertical gutter between		150.00	
		Pair with full horizontal gutter between		225.00	
808	A280	4c **red violet,** *July 1, 1938*		45	5
		rose violet ('43)		45	5
		Margin block of 4, P#		2.00	
809	A281	4½c **dark gray,** *July 11, 1938*		20	6
		gray ('43)		20	6
		Block of four		80	50
		Margin block of 4, P#		1.60	
810	A282	5c **bright blue,** *July 21, 1938*		40	5
		light blue		40	5
		Margin block of 4, P#		1.80	
		Pair full vert. gutter btwn.			
811	A283	6c **red orange,** *July 28, 1938*		45	5
		Margin block of 4, P#		2.00	
812	A284	7c **sepia,** *August 4, 1938*		50	5
		violet brown		50	5
		Margin block of 4, P#		2.20	
813	A285	8c **olive green,** *August 11, 1938*		65	5
		light olive green ('43)		65	5
		olive ('42)		65	5
		Margin block of 4, P#		2.75	
814	A286	9c **rose pink,** *August 18, 1938*		70	5
		pink ('43)		70	5
		Margin block of 4, P#		3.00	
		Pair with full vertical gutter between			
815	A287	10c **brown red,** *September 2, 1938*		50	5
		pale brown red ('43)		50	5
		Margin block of 4, P#		2.20	
816	A288	11c **ultramarine,** *September 8, 1938*		1.00	8
		bright ultramarine		1.00	8
		Margin block of 4, P#		4.50	
817	A289	12c **bright violet,** *September 14, 1938*		1.90	6
		Margin block of 4, P#		8.00	
818	A290	13c **blue green,** *September 22, 1938*		2.00	8
		deep blue green		2.00	8
		Margin block of 4, P#		8.50	
819	A291	14c **blue,** *October 6, 1938*		1.75	10
		Margin block of 4, P#		7.50	
820	A292	15c **blue gray,** *October 13, 1938*		75	5
		Margin block of 4, P#		3.25	
821	A293	16c **black,** *October 20, 1938*		1.75	35
		Margin block of 4, P#		7.50	
822	A294	17c **rose red,** *October 27, 1938*		1.50	12
		deep rose red		1.50	12
		Block of four		6.00	75
		Margin block of 4, P#		7.00	
823	A295	18c **brown carmine,** *Nov. 3, 1938*		3.25	8
		rose brown ('43)		3.25	8
		Block of four		13.00	75
		Margin block of 4, P#		14.00	
824	A296	19c **bright violet,** *November 10, 1938*		2.00	50
		Margin block of 4, P#		9.00	

Used pairs of No. 805b are Bureau precanceled St. Louis, Mo., and generally with gum.

POSTAGE, 1938-43, 1938-54   197

825	A297	20c	**bright blue green,** November 10, 1938	1.20	5
			deep blue green ('43)	1.20	5
			Margin block of 4, P#	5.75	—
826	A298	21c	**dull blue,** *November 22, 1938*	2.25	10
			Block of four	9.00	1.25
			Margin block of 4, P#	10.50	—
827	A299	22c	**vermillion,** *November 22, 1938*	2.25	50
			Margin block of 4, P#	11.50	—
828	A300	24c	**gray black,** *December 2, 1938*	7.00	25
			Block of four	28.00	1.50
			Margin block of 4, P#	30.00	—
829	A301	25c	**deep red lilac,** *December 2, 1938*	1.40	5
			rose lilac ('43)	1.40	5
			Margin block of 4, P#	6.00	—
			Pair with full vert. gutter btwn.	—	—
830	A302	30c	**deep ultramarine,** *Dec. 8, 1938*	9.00	5
			blue	25.00	—
			deep blue	125.00	—
			Block of four	36.00	50
			Margin block of 4, P#	37.50	—
831	A303	50c	**light red violet,** *Dec. 8, 1938*	13.50	6
			Margin block of 4, P#	57.50	—

FLAT PLATE PRINTING.

1938-54   Plates of 100 subjects.   *Perf. 11*

832	A304	$1	**purple & black,** *August 29, 1938*	12.50	10
			Margin block of 4, bottom or side arrow	51.00	—
			Top margin block of 4, 2P#	55.00	—
			Center line block	55.00	4.00
			Top margin block of 20, 2P#, arrow, 2 TOP, 2 registration markers and denomination	265.00	—
		a.	Vert. pair, imperf. horiz.	1,000.	
		b.	Wmkd. USIR ('51)	350.00	90.00
			Margin block of 4, 2P#	1,850.	
		c.	$1 red vio. & black, *Aug. 31, 1954*	9.00	15
		c.	Top or bottom margin block of 4, 2P#	40.00	
		d.	As "c", vert. pair, imperf. horiz.	1,000.	
		e.	Vertical pair, imperf. between	2,500.	
		f.	As "c", vert. pair, imperf. btwn.	7,000.	

No. 832c is dry printed from 400-subject flat plates on thick white paper with smooth, colorless gum.

FOR YOU IT'S FREE

• **FREE** weekly list of U.S. stamps for sale
• **FREE** weekly collecting information
• **FREE** weekly stamp stories
• **NEW** and advanced collectors served
• **FREE** insured shipping of your purchases
• **FREE** no interest layaway on big purchases
• **VISA** and MasterCard can be used
• **NEXT** four weeks lists free by simply asking

Charlie and Rosalie Wonderlin
P.O. Box 1243
Bloomington, Illinois 61702
309-454-1501

833	A305	$2	**yellow green & black,** *Sept. 29, 1938*	32.50	6.00
			green & black ('43)	32.50	6.00
			Margin block of 4, bottom or side arrow	135.00	—
			Top margin block of 4, 2 P#	165.00	—
			Center line block	140.00	35.00
			Top margin block of 20, 2 P#, arrow, 2 TOP, 2 registration markers and denominations	700.00	—
834	A306	$5	**car. & black,** *Nov. 17, 1938*	125.00	5.50
		a.	$5 red brown & black	800.00	175.00
			Margin block of four, bottom or side arrow	510.00	—
			Top margin block of 4, 2 P#	575.00	—
			Center line block	525.00	35.00
			Top margin block of 20, 2 P#, arrow, 2 TOP, 2 registration markers and denominations	2,750.	

Top plate number blocks of Nos. 832, 833 and 834 are found both with and without top arrow or registration markers.

CONSTITUTION RATIFICATION ISSUE.

Issued in commemoration of the 150th anniversary of the ratification of the United States Constitution.

Old Courthouse, Williamsburg, Va.
A307

ROTARY PRESS PRINTING.

Plates of 200 subjects in four panes of 50 each.
1938   *Perf. 11x10½.*   Unwmkd.

835	A307	3c	**deep violet,** *June 21, 1938*	25	8
			Margin block of 4, P#	5.50	—

SWEDISH-FINNISH TERCENTENARY ISSUE.

Issued in commemoration of the tercentenary of the founding of the Swedish and Finnish Settlement at Wilmington, Delaware.

"Landing of the First Swedish and Finnish Settlers in America," by Stanley M. Arthurs
A308

FLAT PLATE PRINTING.

Plates of 192 subjects in four panes of 48 each, separated by 1¼ inch wide gutters with central guide lines.
1938   *Perf. 11*   Unwmkd.

836	A308	3c	**red violet,** *June 27, 1938*	25	10
			Margin block of 6, P#	6.00	—

NORTHWEST TERRITORY SESQUICENTENNIAL ISSUE.

Issued in commemoration of the sesquicentennial of the settlement of the Northwest Territory.

"Colonization of the West," by Gutzon Borglum
A309
ROTARY PRESS PRINTING.
Plates of 400 subjects in four panes of 100 each.

1938			Perf. 11x10½.	Unwmkd.	
837	A309	3c	**bright violet,** *July 15, 1938*	25	8
			rose violet	25	8
			Margin block of 4, P#	15.00	—

IOWA TERRITORY CENTENNIAL ISSUE.

Issued in commemoration of the 100th anniversary of the establishment of Iowa Territory.

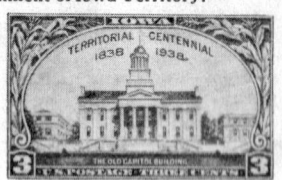

Old Capitol, Iowa City
A310
ROTARY PRESS PRINTING.
Plates of 200 subjects in four panes of 50 each.

1938			Perf. 11x10½.	Unwmkd.	
838	A310	3c	**violet,** *August 24, 1938*	25	8
			Margin block of 4, P#	9.00	—
			Pair with full vertical gutter between		

REGULAR ISSUE.
ROTARY PRESS COIL STAMPS.
Types of 1938.

1939			Perf. 10 Vertically.	Unwmkd.	
839	A276	1c	**green,** *Jan. 20, 1939*	25	6
			light green	25	6
			Pair	50	14
			Joint line pair	1.50	25
840	A277	1½c	**bister brown,** *Jan. 20, 1939*	30	6
			buff	30	6
			Pair	60	12
			Joint line pair	1.50	25
841	A278	2c	**rose carmine,** *Jan. 20, 1939*	30	5
			Pair	60	10
			Joint line pair	1.75	15
842	A279	3c	**deep violet,** *Jan. 20, 1939*	75	5
			violet	75	5
			Pair	1.50	11
			Joint line pair	3.00	15
			Gripper cracks		
			Thin translucent paper	2.00	—
843	A280	4c	**red violet,** *Jan. 20, 1939*	9.00	35
			Pair	18.00	70
			Joint line pair	35.00	2.00
844	A281	4½c	**dark gray,** *Jan. 20, 1939*	60	45
			Pair	1.20	90
			Joint line pair	4.00	1.50
845	A282	5c	**bright blue,** *Jan. 20, 1939*	6.50	35
			Pair	13.00	70
			Joint line pair	30.00	1.50
846	A283	6c	**red orange,** *Jan. 20, 1939*	1.40	20
			Pair	2.80	40
			Joint line pair	8.75	80
847	A287	10c	**brown red,** *Jan. 20, 1939*	15.00	40
			Pair	30.00	80
			Joint line pair	60.00	2.75

Perf. 10 Horizontally.

848	A276	1c	**green,** *Jan. 27, 1939*	1.00	12
			Pair	2.00	25
			Joint line pair	3.75	50
849	A277	1½c	**bister brown,** *Jan. 27, 1939*	1.50	40
			Pair	3.00	80
			Joint line pair	4.75	1.10
850	A278	2c	**rose carmine,** *Jan. 27, 1939*	3.50	50
			Pair	7.00	1.00
			Joint line pair	9.00	1.40
851	A279	3c	**deep violet,** *Jan. 27, 1939*	2.75	45
			Pair	5.50	90
			Joint line pair	7.50	1.40

GOLDEN GATE INTERNATIONAL EXPOSITION ISSUE.

Issued in commemoration of the Golden Gate International Exposition at San Francisco.

"Tower of the Sun"
A311
ROTARY PRESS PRINTING.
Plates of 200 subjects in four panes of 50 each.

1939			Perf. 10½x11.	Unwmkd.	
852	A311	3c	**bright purple,** *Feb. 18, 1939*	12	6
			On cover, Expo. station canc.		6.75
			Margin block of 4, P#	1.75	—

NEW YORK WORLD'S FAIR ISSUE.

Issued to commemorate the New York World's Fair.

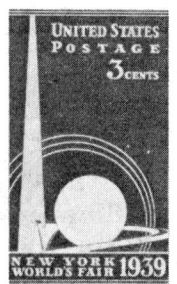

Trylon and Perisphere
A312

POSTAGE, 1939   199

ROTARY PRESS PRINTING.
Plates of 200 subjects in four panes of 50 each.

1939			Perf. 10½x11		Unwmkd.	
853	A312	3c	deep purple, *April 1, 1939*		15	6
			On cover, Expo. station canc.			30
			Margin block of 4, P#		2.00	—

WASHINGTON INAUGURATION ISSUE.

Issued in commemoration of the sesquicentennial of the inauguration of George Washington as First President.

Washington Taking Oath of Office, Federal Building, New York City
A313

FLAT PLATE PRINTING.
Plates of 200 subjects in four panes of 50 each.

1939			Perf. 11.		Unwmkd.	
854	A313	3c	bright red violet, *April 30, 1939*		35	10
			Margin block of 6, P#		4.25	—

BASEBALL CENTENNIAL ISSUE.

Issued in commemoration of the centennial of Baseball.

Sandlot Baseball Game
A314

Designed by William A. Roach.
ROTARY PRESS PRINTING.
Plates of 200 subjects in four panes of 50 each.

1939			Perf. 11x10½		Unwmkd.	
855	A314	3c	violet, *June 12, 1939*		35	8
			Margin block of 4, P#		4.00	—

PANAMA CANAL ISSUE.

25th anniversary of the opening of the Panama Canal.

Theodore Roosevelt, Gen. George W. Goethals and Ship in Gaillard Cut
A315

Designed by William A. Roach.
FLAT PLATE PRINTING.
Plates of 200 subjects in four panes of 50 each.

1939			Perf. 11.		Unwmkd.	
856	A315	3c	deep red violet, *August 15, 1939*		30	8
			Margin block of 6, P#		6.00	—

PRINTING TERCENTENARY ISSUE.

Issued in commemoration of the 300th anniversary of printing in Colonial America. The Stephen Daye press is in the Harvard University Museum.

Stephen Daye Press
A316

Designed by William K. Schrage.
ROTARY PRESS PRINTING.
E. E. Plates of 200 subjects in four panes of 50 each.

1939			Perf. 10½x11.		Unwmkd.	
857	A316	3c	violet, *Sept. 25, 1939*		15	8
			Margin block of 4, P#		1.65	—

50th ANNIVERSARY OF STATEHOOD ISSUE.

Issued in commemoration of the 50th anniversary of the admission to statehood of North Dakota, South Dakota, Montana and Washington.

Map of North and South Dakota, Montana and Washington
A317

ROTARY PRESS PRINTING.
E. E. Plates of 200 subjects in four panes of 50 each.

1939			Perf. 11x10½.		Unwmkd.	
858	A317	3c	rose violet, *November 2, 1939*		15	8
			Margin block of 4, P#		1.65	—

FAMOUS AMERICANS ISSUES.
ROTARY PRESS PRINTING.
E. E. Plates of 280 subjects in four panes of 70 each.
1940   Perf. 10½x11.   Unwmkd.
AUTHORS.
Issued in honor of famous American authors.

Washington Irving
A318

James Fenimore Cooper
A319

Ralph Waldo Emerson
A320

Louisa May Alcott
A321

Samuel L. Clemens
(Mark Twain)
A322

POETS.
Issued in honor of famous American poets

Henry Wadsworth
Longfellow
A323

John Greenleaf Whittier
A324

James Russell Lowell
A325

Walt Whitman
A326

James Witcomb Riley
A327

859	A318	1c **bright blue green,** *Jan. 29, 1940*	8	6
		Margin block of 4, P#	1.10	
860	A319	2c **rose carmine,** *Jan. 29, 1940*	10	8
		Margin block of 4, P#	1.25	
861	A320	3c **bright red violet,** *Feb. 5, 1940*	12	6
		Block of four	48	40
		Margin block of 4, P#	2.00	
862	A321	5c **ultramarine,** *Feb. 5, 1940*	35	30
		Margin block of 4, P#	11.00	
863	A322	10c **dark brown,** *Feb. 13, 1940*	2.50	2.35
		Margin block of 4, P#	50.00	
864	A323	1c **bright blue green,** *Feb. 16, 1940*	12	8
		Margin block of 4, P#	1.75	
865	A324	2c **rose carmine,** *Feb. 16, 1940*	10	8
		Margin block of 4, P#	1.75	
866	A325	3c **bright red violet,** *Feb. 20, 1940*	18	6
		Block of four	72	50
		Margin block of 4, P#	3.50	
867	A326	5c **ultramarine,** *Feb. 20, 1940*	35	25
		Margin block of 4, P#	11.00	
868	A327	10c **dark brown,** *Feb. 24, 1940*	3.25	3.00
		Margin block of 4, P#	45.00	

EDUCATORS.
Issued in honor of famous American educators.

Horace Mann
A328

Mark Hopkins
A329

Charles W. Eliot
A330

Frances E. Willard
A331

Booker T. Washington
A332

869	A328	1c **bright blue green,** *March 14, 1940*	9	8
		Margin block of 4, P#	1.75	—
870	A329	2c **rose carmine,** *March 14, 1940*	10	6
		Margin block of 4, P#	1.40	—
871	A330	3c **bright red violet,** *March 28, 1940*	30	6
		Block of four	1.20	60
		Margin block of 4, P#	3.25	—
872	A331	5c **ultramarine,** *March 28, 1940*	50	35
		Margin block of 4, P#	12.00	—
873	A332	10c **dark brown,** *April 7, 1940*	2.25	2.25
		Margin block of 4, P#	32.50	—

SCIENTISTS.
Issued in honor of famous American scientists.

John James Audubon
A333

Dr. Crawford W. Long
A334

Luther Burbank
A335

Dr. Walter Reed
A336

Jane Addams
A337

874	A333	1c **bright blue green,** *April 8, 1940*	8	6
		Margin block of 4, P#	1.00	—
875	A334	2c **rose carmine,** *April 8, 1940*	10	6
		Margin block of 4, P#	1.20	—
876	A335	3c **bright red violet,** *April 17, 1940*	10	6
		Margin block of 4, P#	1.75	—
877	A336	5c **ultramarine,** *April 17, 1940*	30	25
		Block of four	1.20	2.00
		Margin block of 4, P#	9.00	—
878	A337	10c **dark brown,** *April 26, 1940*	2.00	2.00
		Margin block of 4, P#	32.50	—

COMPOSERS.
Issued in honor of famous American composers.

Stephen Collins Foster
A338

John Philip Sousa
A339

Victor Herbert
A340

Edward A. MacDowell
A341

Ethelbert Nevin
A342

ARTISTS.
Issued in honor of famous American artists.

Gilbert Charles Stuart
A343

James A. McNeill Whistler
A344

Augustus Saint-Gaudens
A345

Daniel Chester French
A346

Frederic Remington
A347

879	A338	1c **bright blue green,** *May 3, 1940*		8	6
		Margin block of 4, P#		1.25	—
880	A339	2c **rose carmine,** *May 3, 1940*		10	6
		Margin block of 4, P#		1.25	—
881	A340	3c **bright red violet,** *May 13, 1940*		15	6
		Block of four		60	35
		Margin block of 4, P#		1.75	—
882	A341	5c **ultramarine,** *May 13, 1940*		60	30
		Margin block of 4, P#		12.50	—
883	A342	10c **dark brown,** *June 10, 1940*		5.00	2.25
		Margin block of 4, P#		50.00	—
884	A343	1c **bright blue green,** *Sept. 5, 1940*		8	6
		Margin block of 4, P#		1.10	—
885	A344	2c **rose carmine,** *Sept. 5, 1940*		10	6
		Margin block of 4, P#		1.10	—
886	A345	3c **bright red violet,** *Sept. 16, 1940*		10	6
		Margin block of 4, P#		1.25	—
887	A346	5c **ultramarine,** *Sept. 16, 1940*		40	22
		Margin block of 4, P#		11.50	—
888	A347	10c **dark brown,** *Sept. 30, 1940*		2.50	2.25
		Margin block of 4, P#		35.00	—

POSTAGE, 1940   203

INVENTORS.

Issued in honor of famous American inventors.

Eli Whitney
A348

Samuel F. B. Morse
A349

Cyrus Hall McCormick
A350

Elias Howe
A351

Alexander Graham Bell
A352

889	A348	1c	bright blue green, *October 7, 1940*	12	8
			Margin block of 4, P#	2.50	
890	A349	2c	rose carmine, *October 7, 1940*	10	6
			Margin block of 4, P#	1.30	
891	A350	3c	bright red violet, *October 14, 1940*	20	6
			Margin block of 4, P#	2.50	
892	A351	5c	ultramarine, *October 14, 1940*	1.25	40
			Margin block of 4, P#	20.00	
893	A352	10c	dark brown, *October 28, 1940*	14.50	3.25
			Margin block of 4, P#	100.00	

PONY EXPRESS ISSUE.

Issued in commemoration of the 80th anniversary of the Pony Express.

Pony Express Rider
A353

ROTARY PRESS PRINTING.

E. E. Plates of 200 subjects in four panes of 50 each.

1940			Perf. 11x10½.		Unwmkd.
894	A353	3c	henna brown, *April 3, 1940*	50	15
			Margin block of 4, P#	6.50	

PAN AMERICAN UNION ISSUE.

Issued in commemoration of the 50th anniversary of the founding of the Pan American Union.

The Three Graces (Botticelli)
A354

ROTARY PRESS PRINTING.

E. E. Plates of 200 subjects in four panes of 50 each.

1940			Perf. 10½x11.		Unwmkd.
895	A354	3c	light violet, *April 14, 1940*	40	12
			Margin block of 4, P#	5.50	

IDAHO STATEHOOD ISSUE.

Issued in commemoration of the 50th anniversary of admission of Idaho to statehood.

Idaho State Capitol
A355

ROTARY PRESS PRINTING.

E. E. Plates of 200 subjects in four panes of 50 each.

1940			Perf. 11x10½		Unwmkd.
896	A355	3c	bright violet, *July 3, 1940*	20	8
			Margin block of 4, P#	3.50	

WYOMING STATEHOOD ISSUE.

Issued in commemoration of the 50th anniversary of admission of Wyoming to statehood.

Wyoming State Seal
A356

ROTARY PRESS PRINTING.
E. E. Plates of 200 subjects in four panes of 50 each.
1940   *Perf. 10½x11*   Unwmkd.

897	A356	3c **brown violet**, *July 10, 1940*	20	8
		Margin block of 4, P#	2.75	

CORONADO EXPEDITION ISSUE.

Issued in commemoration of the 400th anniversary of the Coronado Expedition.

"Coronado and His Captains"
Painted by Gerald Cassidy
A357

ROTARY PRESS PRINTING.
E. E. Plates of 200 subjects in four panes of 50 each.
1940   *Perf. 11x10½.*   Unwmkd.

898	A357	3c **violet**, *Sept. 7, 1940*	20	8
		Margin block of 4, P#	2.75	

NATIONAL DEFENSE ISSUE.

Issued in connection with the National Defense Program.

Statue of Liberty   90-millimeter Anti-aircraft Gun
A358   A359

Torch of Enlightenment
A360

ROTARY PRESS PRINTING.
E. E. Plates of 400 subjects in four panes of 100 each.
1940, Oct. 16   *Perf. 11x10½*   Unwmkd.

899	A358	1c **bright blue green**	5	5
		Margin block of 4, P#	70	
		a. Vertical pair, imperf. between	500.00	
		b. Horizontal pair, imperf. between	45.00	
		Pair with full vertical gutter between	200.00	
		Cracked plate (22684 U.R. 10)	3.00	
		Gripper cracks	3.00	
900	A359	2c **rose carmine**	6	5
		Margin block of 4, P#	70	
		a. Horizontal pair, imperf. between	50.00	
		Pair with full vertical gutter between	275.00	
901	A360	3c **bright violet**	12	5
		Margin block of 4, P#	1.40	
		a. Horizontal pair, imperf. between	25.00	
		Pair with full vertical gutter between		

THIRTEENTH AMENDMENT ISSUE.

Issued to commemorate the 75th anniversary of the 13th Amendment to the Constitution abolishing slavery.

Emancipation Monument;
Lincoln and Kneeling Slave,
by Thomas Bell
A361

Designed by William A. Roach.

ROTARY PRESS PRINTING.
E. E. Plates of 200 subjects in four panes of 50 each.
1940   *Perf. 10½x11*   Unwmkd.

902	A361	3c **deep violet**, *October 20, 1940*	25	15
		dark violet	25	15
		Margin block of 4, P#	6.00	

VERMONT STATEHOOD ISSUE.

Issued in commemoration of the 150th anniversary of the admission of Vermont to statehood.

State Capitol, Montpelier
A362

Designed by Alvin R. Meissner.

ROTARY PRESS PRINTING.
E. E. Plates of 200 subjects in four panes of 50 each.
1941   *Perf. 11x10½*   Unwmkd.

903	A362	3c **light violet**, *March 4, 1941*	22	10
		Margin block of 4, P#	2.50	

POSTAGE, 1942, 1943, 1943-44   205

KENTUCKY STATEHOOD ISSUE.

Issued in commemoration of the 150th anniversary of the admission of Kentucky to statehood.

Daniel Boone and Three Frontiersmen,
from Mural by Gilbert White
A363

Designed by William A. Roach.
ROTARY PRESS PRINTING.
E. E. Plates of 200 subjects in four panes of 50 each.
1942   Perf. 11x10½.   Unwmkd.
904   A363   3c violet, June 1, 1942   15   12
              Margin block of 4, P#   2.25

ALLIED NATIONS ISSUE

Allegory of Victory
A366
Designed by Leon Helguera.
ROTARY PRESS PRINTING.
E. E. Plates of 400 subjects in four panes of 100 each.
1943   Perf. 11x10½.   Unwmkd.
907   A366   2c rose carmine, January 14, 1943   8   5
              Margin block of 4, P#   50
              Pair with full vert. or horiz. gutter
               between   225.00

FOUR FREEDOMS ISSUE

Liberty Holding the Torch of Freedom
and Enlightenment
A367
Designed by Paul Manship.
ROTARY PRESS PRINTING.
E. E. Plates of 400 subjects in four panes of 100 each.
1943   Perf. 11x10½.   Unwmkd.
908   A367   1c bright blue green, Feb. 12, 1943   6   5
              Margin block of 4, P#   1.00

WIN THE WAR ISSUE.

American Eagle
A364
ROTARY PRESS PRINTING.
E. E. Plates of 400 subjects in four panes of 100 each.
1942   Perf. 11x10½.   Unwmkd.
905   A364   3c violet, July 4, 1942   10   5
              light violet   10   5
         a. 3c purple   20.00 8.00
              Margin block of 4, P#   60
              Pair with full vert. or horiz.
               gutter between   175.00

CHINESE RESISTANCE ISSUE

Issued to commemorate the Chinese people's five years of resistance to Japanese aggression.

Map of China, Abraham Lincoln and
Sun Yat-sen, Founder of the Chinese Republic
A365
ROTARY PRESS PRINTING.
E. E. Plates of 200 subjects in four panes of 50 each.
1942   Perf. 11x10½.   Unwmkd.
906   A365   5c bright blue, July 7, 1942   35   30
              Margin block of 4, P#   18.50

OVERRUN COUNTRIES ISSUE

Printed by the American Bank Note Co.
**FRAMES ENGRAVED,
CENTERS OFFSET PRINTING.
FLAT PLATE PRINTING.**
Plates of 200 subjects in four panes of 50 each.

Due to the failure of the printers to divulge detailed information as to printing processes used, the editors omit listings of irregularities, flaws, blemishes and "errors" which are numerous in this issue. These include shifted prints (not true double prints), etc. An exception is made for the widely recognized "KORPA" variety.

1943-44   Perf. 12   Unwmkd.

Flag of Poland
A368
909   A368   5c blue violet, bright red & black,
              June 22, 1943   35   20
              Margin block of 4,
               Inscribed "Poland"   8.00
              Top margin block of 6, with red
               & blue violet guide markings
               and "Poland"   9.00
              Bottom margin block of 6, with
               red & black guide markings   2.15

POSTAGE, 1943-44

Flag of Czechoslovakia
A368a

910	A368a	5c	**blue violet, blue, bright red & black,** *July 12, 1943*	30	15
			Margin block of 4, inscribed "Czechoslovakia"	4.00	—
			Top margin block of 6, with red & blue violet guide markings and "Czechoslovakia"	5.00	—

Flag of Norway
A368b

911	A368b	5c	**blue violet, dark rose, deep blue & black,** *July 27, 1943*	25	12
			Margin block of 4, inscribed "Norway"	2.50	—
			Bottom margin block of 6 with dark rose & blue violet guide markings	1.75	—

Flag of Luxembourg
A368c

912	A368c	5c	**blue violet, dark rose, light blue & black,** *August 10, 1943*	25	12
			Margin block of 4, inscribed "Luxembourg"	2.50	—
			Top margin block of 6 with light blue & blue violet guide markings & "Luxembourg"	3.25	—

Flag of Netherlands
A368d

913	A368d	5c	**blue violet, dark rose, blue & black,** *August, 24, 1943*	25	12
			Margin block of 4, inscribed "Netherlands"	2.50	—
			Bottom margin block of 6 with blue & blue violet guide markings	1.75	—

Flag of Belgium
A368e

914	A368e	5c	**blue violet, dark rose, yellow & black,** *Sept. 14, 1943*	25	12
			Margin block of 4, inscribed "Belgium"	2.50	—
			Top margin block of 6, with yellow & blue violet guide markings and "Belgium"	3.25	—

Flag of France
A368f

915	A368f	5c	**blue violet, deep blue, dark rose & black,** *Sept. 28, 1943*	25	10
			Margin block of 4, inscribed "France"	2.50	—
			Bottom margin block of 6 with dark rose & blue violet guide markings	1.75	—

Flag of Greece
A368g

916	A368g	5c	**blue violet, pale blue & black,** *Oct. 12, 1943*	85	60
			Margin block of 4, inscribed "Greece"	20.00	—
			Top margin block of 6 with pale blue & blue violet guide markings & "Greece"	22.50	—

Flag of Yugoslavia
A368h

917	A368h	5c	**blue violet, blue, dark rose & black,** *Oct. 26, 1943*	50	40
			Margin block of 4, inscribed "Yugoslavia"	7.50	—
			Bottom margin block of 6 with dark rose & blue violet guide markings	3.25	—

Flag of Albania
A368i

918	A368i	5c	**blue violet, dark red & black,** *Nov. 9, 1943*	50	40
			Margin block of 4, inscribed "Albania"	7.50	—
			Top margin block of 6, with dark red & blue violet guide markings & "Albania"	9.00	—

POSTAGE, 1943-44, 1944

Flag of Austria
A368j

919	A368j	5c **blue violet, red & black,** Nov. 23, 1943	30	25
		Margin block of 4, inscribed "Austria"	5.50	—
		Bottom margin block of 6, with red & blue violet guide markings	2.00	—

Flag of Denmark
A368k

920	A368k	5c **blue violet, red & black,** Dec. 7, 1943	50	50
		Margin block of 4, inscribed "Denmark"	7.50	—
		Top margin block of 6, with red & blue violet guide markings & "Denmark"	9.00	—

Flag of Korea
A368m

921	A368m	5c **blue violet, red, black & light blue,** Nov. 2, 1944	28	25
		Margin block of 4, inscribed "Korea"	7.00	—
		Top margin block of 6 with blue & black guide markings and "Korea"	7.75	—
		Stamp inscribed "KORPA"	25.00	20.00

TRANSCONTINENTAL RAILROAD ISSUE.

Issued to commemorate the 75th anniversary of the completion of the first transcontinental railroad.

"Golden Spike Ceremony" Painted by John McQuarrie
A369
Engraved.
ROTARY PRESS PRINTING.
E. E. Plates of 200 subjects in four panes of 50 each.
1944 *Perf. 11x10½* Unwmkd.

922	A369	3c **violet,** May 10, 1944	20	15
		Margin block of 4, P#	2.50	—

STEAMSHIP ISSUE.

Issued to commemorate the 125th anniversary of the first steamship to cross the Atlantic Ocean.

"Savannah"
A370
ROTARY PRESS PRINTING.
E. E. Plates of 200 subjects in four panes of 50 each.
1944 *Perf. 11x10½.* Unwmkd.

923	A370	3c **violet,** May 22, 1944	15	15
		Margin block of 4, P#	2.50	—

TELEGRAPH ISSUE.

Issued to commemorate the 100th anniversary of the first message transmitted by telegraph

Telegraph Wires and Morse's First Transmitted Words "What Hath God Wrought"
A371
ROTARY PRESS PRINTING.
E. E. Plates of 200 subjects in four panes of 50 each.
1944 *Perf. 11x10½* Unwmkd.

924	A371	3c **bright red violet,** May 24, 1944	12	10
		Margin block of 4, P#	1.60	—

PHILIPPINE ISSUE.

Issued to commemorate the final resistance of the United States and Philippine defenders on Corregidor to the Japanese invaders in 1942.

Aerial View of Corregidor, Manila Bay
A372
ROTARY PRESS PRINTING
E. E. Plates of 200 subjects in four panes of 50 each.
1944 *Perf. 11x10½.* Unwmkd.

925	A372	3c **deep violet,** Sept. 27, 1944	12	12
		Block of 4, P#	3.00	—

MOTION PICTURE ISSUE.

Issued to commemorate the 50th anniversary of motion pictures.

Motion Picture Showing for
Armed Forces in South Pacific
A373
ROTARY PRESS PRINTING.
E. E. Plates of 200 subjects in four panes of 50 each.

1944		Perf. 11x10½		Unwmkd.	
926	A373	3c **deep violet**, *Oct. 31, 1944*		12	10
		Margin block of 4, P#		2.00	

FLORIDA STATEHOOD ISSUE.

Centenary of the admission of Florida to statehood.

State Seal, Gates of St. Augustine
and Capitol at Tallahassee
A374
ROTARY PRESS PRINTING.
E. E. Plates of 200 subjects in four panes of 50 each.

1945		Perf. 11x10½		Unwmkd.	
927	A374	3c **bright red violet**, *March 3, 1945*		10	8
		Margin block of 4, P#		1.00	

UNITED NATIONS CONFERENCE ISSUE.

United Nations Conference, San Francisco, Calif.

"Toward United Nations, April 25, 1945"
A375
ROTARY PRESS PRINTING.
E. E. Plates of 200 subjects in four panes of 50 each.

1945		Perf. 11x10½.		Unwmkd.	
928	A375	5c **ultramarine**, *April 25, 1945*		12	8
		Margin block of 4, P#		70	

IWO JIMA (MARINES) ISSUE.

Issued to commemorate the battle of Iwo Jima and to honor the achievements of the United States Marines.

Marines Raising
American Flag on Mount
Suribachi, Iwo Jima
A376
ROTARY PRESS PRINTING.
E. E. Plates of 200 subjects in four panes of 50 each.

1945		Perf. 10½x11		Unwmkd.	
929	A376	3c **yellow green**, *July 11, 1945*		10	5
		Margin block of 4, P#		50	

FRANKLIN D. ROOSEVELT ISSUE.

Issued in tribute to Franklin Delano Roosevelt (1882–1945).

Roosevelt and Hyde Park Residence
A377

Roosevelt and the "Little White House"
at Warm Springs, Ga.
A378

Roosevelt and White House
A379

Roosevelt, Map of Western Hemisphere
and Four Freedoms
A380

ROTARY PRESS PRINTING.

E. E. Plates of 200 subjects in four panes of 50 each.

1945-46		Perf. 11x10½.		Unwmkd.	
930	A377	1c blue green, *July 26, 1945*		5	5
		Margin block of 4, P#		30	
931	A378	2c carmine rose, *August 24, 1945*		8	8
		Margin block of 4, P#		40	
932	A379	3c purple, *June 27, 1945*		10	8
		Margin block of 4, P#		65	
933	A380	5c bright blue, *Jan. 30, 1948*		12	8
		Margin block of 4, P#		75	

2¢ 23314 5x10

ARMY ISSUE.

Issued to commemorate the achievements of the United States Army in World War II.

United States Troops Passing Arch of Triumph, Paris
A381

ROTARY PRESS PRINTING.

E. E. Plates of 200 subjects in four panes of 50 each.

1945		Perf. 11x10½.		Unwmkd.	
934	A381	3c olive, *Sept. 28, 1945*		10	5
		Margin block of 4, P#		60	

NAVY ISSUE.

Issued to commemorate the achievements of the United States Navy in World War II.

United States Sailors—A382

ROTARY PRESS PRINTING.

E. E. Plates of 200 subjects in four panes of 50 each.

1945		Perf. 11x10½.		Unwmkd.	
935	A382	3c blue, *Oct. 27, 1945*		10	5
		Margin block of 4, P#		60	

COAST GUARD ISSUE.

Issued to commemorate the achievements of the United States Coast Guard in World War II.

Coast Guard Landing Craft and Supply Ship
A383

ROTARY PRESS PRINTING.

E. E. Plates of 200 subjects in four panes of 50 each.

1945		Perf. 11x10½		Unwmkd.	
936	A383	3c bright blue green, *Nov. 10, 1945*		10	5
		Margin block of 4, P#		60	

ALFRED E. SMITH ISSUE.

Issued in honor of Alfred E. Smith, governor of New York.

Alfred E. Smith
A384

ROTARY PRESS PRINTING.

E. E. Plates of 400 subjects in four panes of 100 each.

1945		Perf. 11x10½.		Unwmkd.	
937	A384	3c purple, *Nov. 26, 1945*		10	5
		Margin block of 4, P#		50	
		Pair with full vert. gutter btwn.			

TEXAS STATEHOOD ISSUE.

Issued to commemorate the 100th anniversary of the admission of Texas to statehood.

Flags of the United States and the State of Texas
A385

ROTARY PRESS PRINTING.

E. E. Plates of 200 subjects in four panes of 50 each.

1945		Perf. 11x10½		Unwmkd.	
938	A385	3c dark blue, *Dec. 29, 1945*		10	5
		Margin block of 4, P#		50	

MERCHANT MARINE ISSUE.

Issued to commemorate the achievements of the United States Merchant Marine in World War II.

Liberty Ship Unloading Cargo—A386

ROTARY PRESS PRINTING.

E. E. Plates of 200 subjects in four panes of 50 each.

1946		Perf. 11x10½		Unwmkd.	
939	A386	3c blue green, *Feb. 26, 1946*		10	5
		Margin block of 4, P#		50	

POSTAGE, 1946, 1947

VETERANS OF WORLD WAR II ISSUE.
Issued to honor all veterans of World War II.

Honorable Discharge Emblem
A387
ROTARY PRESS PRINTING.
E. E. Plates of 400 subjects in four panes of 100 each.
1946   *Perf. 11x10½.*   Unwmkd.
940   A387   3c **dark violet**, *May 9, 1946*   10   5
            Margin block of 4, P#   55

TENNESSEE STATEHOOD ISSUE.
Issued to commemorate the 150th anniversary of the admission of Tennessee to statehood.

Andrew Jackson, John Sevier and State Capitol, Nashville—A388
ROTARY PRESS PRINTING.
E. E. Plates of 200 subjects in four panes of 50 each.
1946   *Perf. 11x10½.*   Unwmkd.
941   A388   3c **dark violet**, *June 1, 1946*   10   5
            Margin block of 4, P#   50

IOWA STATEHOOD ISSUE.
Centenary of the admission of Iowa to statehood.

Iowa State Flag and Map—A389
ROTARY PRESS PRINTING.
E. E. Plates of 200 subjects in four panes of 50 each.
1946   *Perf. 11x10½.*   Unwmkd.
942   A389   3c **deep blue**, *August 3, 1946*   10   5
            Margin block of 4, P#   50

SMITHSONIAN INSTITUTION ISSUE.
Issued to commemorate the 100th anniversary of the establishment of the Smithsonian Institution, Washington, D. C.

Smithsonian Institution—A390

ROTARY PRESS PRINTING.
E. E. Plates of 200 subjects in four panes of 50 each.
1946   *Perf. 11x10½.*   Unwmkd.
943   A390   3c **violet brown**, *August 10, 1946* 10   5
            Margin block of 4, P#   50

KEARNY EXPEDITION ISSUE.
Issued to commemorate the 100th anniversary of the entry of General Stephen Watts Kearny into Santa Fe.

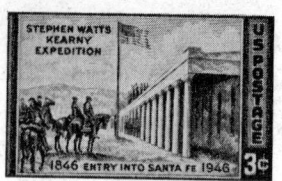

"Capture of Santa Fe" by Kenneth M. Chapman
A391
ROTARY PRESS PRINTING.
E. E. Plates of 200 subjects in four panes of 50 each.
1946   *Perf. 11x10½.*   Unwmkd.
944   A391   3c **brown violet**, *October 16, 1946* 10   5
            Margin block of 4, P#   50

THOMAS A. EDISON ISSUE.
Centenary of the birth of Thomas Alva Edison (1847–1931), inventor.

Thomas A. Edison—A392
ROTARY PRESS PRINTING.
E. E. Plates of 280 subjects in four panes of 70 each.
1947   *Perf. 10½x11*   Unwmkd.
945   A392   3c **bright red violet**, *Feb. 11, 1947* 10   5
            Margin block of 4, P#   50

JOSEPH PULITZER ISSUE.
Centenary of the birth of Joseph Pulitzer (1847– 1911), journalist.

Joseph Pulitzer and Statue of Liberty—A393

POSTAGE, 1947   211

Designed by Victor S. McCloskey, Jr.
ROTARY PRESS PRINTING.
E. E. Plates of 200 subjects in four panes of 50 each.
1947   Perf. 11x10½.   Unwmkd.
946 A393 3c purple, April 10, 1947   10   5
           Margin block of 4, P#   50

POSTAGE STAMP CENTENARY ISSUE.

Issued to commemorate the centenary of the first postage stamps issued by the United States Government

Washington and Franklin,
Early and Modern Mail-carrying Vehicles
A394
Designed by Leon Helguera.
ROTARY PRESS PRINTING.
E. E. Plates of 200 subjects in four panes of 50 each.
1947   Perf. 11x10½.   Unwmkd.
947 A394 3c deep blue, May 17, 1947   10   5
           Margin block of 4, P#   50

CENTENARY INTERNATIONAL PHILATELIC EXHIBITION ISSUE.

SOUVENIR SHEET.

A395
FLAT PLATE PRINTING.
Plates of 30 subjects.
1947   Imperf.   Unwmkd.
948 A395 Sheet of two, May 19, 1947   1.50   1.00
     a. 5c blue, type A1   35   30
     b. 10c brown orange, type A2   50   30

Sheet inscribed below stamps: "100th Anniversary United States Postage Stamps" and in the margins:

"PRINTED BY THE TREASURY DEPARTMENT, BUREAU OF ENGRAVING AND PRINTING.— UNDER AUTHORITY OF ROBERT E. HANNEGAN, POSTMASTER GENERAL.— IN COMPLIMENT TO THE CENTENARY INTERNATIONAL PHILATELIC EXHIBITION.— NEW YORK, N. Y., MAY 17-25, 1947."

Sheet size varies: 96-98 × 66-68mm.

DOCTORS ISSUE.

Issued to honor the physicians of America.

"The Doctor" by Sir Luke Fildes
A396
Designed by Charles R. Chickering.
ROTARY PRESS PRINTING.
E. E. Plates of 200 subjects in four panes of 50 each.
1947   Perf. 11x10½   Unwmkd.
949 A396 3c brown violet, June 9, 1947   10   5
           Margin block of 4, P#   50

UTAH ISSUE.

Issued to commemorate the centenary of the settlement of Utah.

Pioneers Entering the Valley of Great Salt Lake
A397
Designed by Charles R. Chickering.
ROTARY PRESS PRINTING.
E. E. Plates of 200 subjects in four panes of 50 each.
1947   Perf. 11x10½.   Unwmkd.
950 A397 3c dark violet, July 24, 1947   10   5
           Margin block of 4, P#   50

U. S. FRIGATE CONSTITUTION ISSUE.

Issued to commemorate the 150th anniversary of the launching of the U. S. frigate Constitution ("Old Ironsides").

Naval Architect's Drawing
of Frigate Constitution
A398
Designed by Andrew H. Hepburn.
ROTARY PRESS PRINTING.
E. E. Plates of 200 subjects in four panes of 50 each.
1947   Perf. 11x10½.   Unwmkd.
951 A398 3c blue green, Oct. 21, 1947   10   5
           Margin block of 4, P#   50

EVERGLADES NATIONAL PARK ISSUE.

Issued to commemorate the dedication of the Everglades National Park, Florida, December 6, 1947.

Great White Heron and Map of Florida
A399
Designed by Robert I. Miller, Jr.
ROTARY PRESS PRINTING.
E. E. Plates of 200 subjects in four panes of 50 each.
1947   Perf. 10½x11.   Unwmkd.

| 952 | A399 | 3c bright green, *Dec. 5, 1947* Margin block of 4, P# | 10 50 | 5 |

GEORGE WASHINGTON CARVER ISSUE

Issued to commemorate the fifth anniversary of the death of Dr. George Washington Carver, (1864–1943), botanist.

Dr. George Washington Carver—A400
ROTARY PRESS PRINTING.
E. E. Plates of 280 subjects in four panes of 70 each.
1948   Perf. 10½x11.   Unwmkd.

| 953 | A400 | 3c bright red violet, *Jan. 5, 1948* Margin block of 4, P# | 10 50 | 5 |

CALIFORNIA GOLD CENTENNIAL ISSUE.

Centenary of the discovery of gold in California

Sutter's Mill, Coloma, California—A401
Designed by Charles R. Chickering.
ROTARY PRESS PRINTING.
E. E. Plates of 200 subjects in four panes of 50 each.
1948   Perf. 11x10½.   Unwmkd.

| 954 | A401 | 3c dark violet, *Jan. 24, 1948* Margin block of 4, P# | 10 50 | 5 |

MISSISSIPPI TERRITORY ISSUE.

Issued to commemorate the 150th anniversary of the establishment of the Mississippi Territory.

Map, Seal of Mississippi Territory and Gov. Winthrop Sargent
A402
Designed by William K. Schrage.
ROTARY PRESS PRINTING.
E. E. Plates of 200 subjects in four panes of 50 each.
1948   Perf. 11x10½.   Unwmkd.

| 955 | A402 | 3c brown violet, *Apr. 7, 1948* Margin block of 4, P# | 10 50 | 5 |

FOUR CHAPLAINS ISSUE.

Issued in honor of George L. Fox, Clark V. Poling, John P. Washington and Alexander D. Goode, the four chaplains who sacrificed their lives in the sinking of the S. S. Dorchester, February 3, 1943.

Four Chaplains and Sinking S. S. Dorchester
A403
Designed by Charles R. Chickering.
ROTARY PRESS PRINTING.
E. E. Plates of 200 subjects in four panes of 50 each.
1948   Perf. 11 x 10½.   Unwmkd.

| 956 | A403 | 3c gray black, *May 28, 1948* Margin block of 4, P# | 10 50 | 5 |

WISCONSIN CENTENNIAL ISSUE.

Issued to commemorate the centenary of the admission of Wisconsin to statehood.

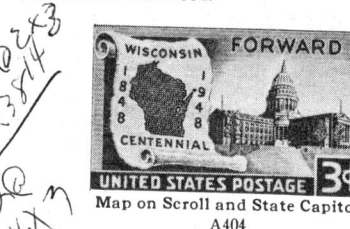

Map on Scroll and State Capitol
A404
Designed by Victor S. McCloskey, Jr.
ROTARY PRESS PRINTING.
E. E. Plates of 200 subjects in four panes of 50 each.
1948   Perf. 11 x 10½.   Unwmkd.

| 957 | A404 | 3c dark violet, *May 29, 1948* Margin block of 4, P# | 10 50 | 5 |

POSTAGE, 1948 213

SWEDISH PIONEER ISSUE.

Issued to commemorate the centenary of the coming of the Swedish pioneers to the Middle West.

Swedish Pioneer with Covered Wagon
Moving Westward
A405

Designed by Charles R. Chickering.
ROTARY PRESS PRINTING
E. E. Plates of 200 subjects in four panes of 50 each.
1948   Perf. 11x10½   Unwmkd.
958   A405   5c deep blue, *June 4, 1948*   15   10
           Margin block of 4, P#   1.00

PROGRESS OF WOMEN ISSUE.

Issued to commemorate a century of progress of American Women.

Elizabeth Stanton, Carrie Chapman Catt
and Lucretia Mott—A406
Designed by Victor S. McCloskey, Jr.
ROTARY PRESS PRINTING
E. E. Plates of 200 subjects in four panes of 50 each.
1948   Perf. 11x10½   Unwmkd.
959   A406   3c dark violet, *July 19, 1948*   10   5
           Margin block of 4, P#   50

WILLIAM ALLEN WHITE ISSUE

Issued to honor William Allen White, (1868–1944), writer and journalist.

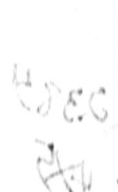 

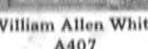
William Allen White
A407
ROTARY PRESS PRINTING
E. E. Plates of 280 subjects in four panes of 70 each.
1948   Perf. 10½x11   Unwmkd.
960   A407   3c bright red violet, *July 31, 1948*   10   6
           Margin block of 4, P#   60

UNITED STATES - CANADA FRIENDSHIP ISSUE.

Issued to commemorate a century of friendship between the United States and Canada.

Niagara Railway Suspension Bridge—A408
Designed by Leon Helguera, modeled by V. S. McCloskey, Jr.
ROTARY PRESS PRINTING
E. E. Plates of 200 subjects in four panes of 50 each.
1948   Perf. 11x10½   Unwmkd.
961   A408   3c blue, *Aug. 2, 1948*   10   5
           Margin block of 4, P#   50

FRANCIS SCOTT KEY ISSUE.

Issued to honor Francis Scott Key (1779–1843), Maryland lawyer and author of "The Star-Spangled Banner" (1813).

Francis Scott Key
and American Flags of 1814 and 1948
A409
Designed by Victor S. McCloskey, Jr.
ROTARY PRESS PRINTING
E. E. Plates of 200 subjects in four panes of 50 each.
1948   Perf. 11x10½   Unwmkd.
962   A409   3c rose pink, *Aug. 9, 1948*   10   5
           Margin block of 4, P#   50

SALUTE TO YOUTH ISSUE.

Issued to honor the Youth of America and to publicize "Youth Month," September, 1948.

Girl and Boy Carrying Books
A410
ROTARY PRESS PRINTING
E. E. Plates of 200 subjects in four panes of 50 each.
1948   Perf. 11x10½   Unwmkd.
963   A410   3c deep blue, *Aug. 11, 1948*   10   6
           Margin block of 4, P#   50

OREGON TERRITORY ISSUE.

Issued to commemorate the centenary of the establishment of Oregon Territory.

John McLoughlin, Jason Lee
and Wagon on Oregon Trail
A411
ROTARY PRESS PRINTING
E. E. Plates of 200 subjects in four panes of 50 each.
1948   Perf. 11x10½   Unwmkd.
964 A411 3c brown red, Aug. 14, 1948   10   10
            Margin block of 4, P#   90

HARLAN F. STONE ISSUE

Issued to honor Harlan Fiske Stone (1872–1946) of New York, associate justice of the Supreme Court, 1925–1941, and chief justice, 1941–1946.

Chief Justice Harlan F. Stone
A412
E. E. Plates of 280 subjects in four panes of 70 each.
1948   Perf. 10½x11   Unwmkd.
965 A412 3c bright violet, Aug. 25, 1948   10   8
            Margin block of 4, P#   1.70

PALOMAR MOUNTAIN OBSERVATORY ISSUE.

Issued to commemorate the dedication of the Palomar Mountain Observatory, August 30, 1948.

Observatory,
Palomar Mountain,
California
A413
Designed by Victor S. McCloskey, Jr.
ROTARY PRESS PRINTING
E. E. Plates of 280 subjects in four panes of 70 each.
1948   Perf. 10½x11   Unwmkd.
966 A413 3c blue, Aug. 30, 1948   12   10
            Margin block of 4, P#   2.50
        a. Vert. pair, imperf. btwn.   800.00

CLARA BARTON ISSUE.

Issued to honor Clara Barton (1821–1912), who founded the American Red Cross in 1882.

Clara Barton and Cross
A414
Designed by Charles R. Chickering.
ROTARY PRESS PRINTING
E. E. Plates of 200 subjects in four panes of 50 each.
1948   Perf. 11x10½   Unwmkd.
967 A414 3c rose pink, Sept. 7, 1948   10   8
            Margin block of 4, P#   60

POULTRY INDUSTRY CENTENNIAL ISSUE.

Issued to commemorate the centenary of the establishment of the American Poultry Industry.

Light Brahma Rooster
A415
Designed by Charles R. Chickering.
ROTARY PRESS PRINTING.
E. E. Plates of 200 subjects in four panes of 50 each.
1948   Perf. 11x10½.   Unwmkd.
968 A415 3c sepia, Sept. 9, 1948   12   8
            Margin block of 4, P#   80

GOLD STAR MOTHERS ISSUE.

Issued to honor the mothers of deceased members of the United States armed forces.

Star and Palm Frond
A416

POSTAGE, 1948 215

Designed by Charles R. Chickering.
ROTARY PRESS PRINTING.
E. E. Plates of 200 subjects in four panes of 50 each.
1948 Perf. 10½x11. Unwmkd.
969 A416 3c orange yellow, Sept. 21, 1948 12 8
  Margin block of 4, P# 65 ——

FORT KEARNY ISSUE.

Centenary of the establishment of Fort Kearny, Neb.

Fort Kearny and Pioneer Group—A417
ROTARY PRESS PRINTING.
E. E. Plates of 200 subjects in four panes of 50 each.
1948 Perf. 11x10½. Unwmkd.
970 A417 3c violet, Sept. 22, 1948 12 8
  Margin block of 4, P# 65 ——

VOLUNTEER FIREMEN ISSUE.

Issued to commemorate the 300th anniversary of the organization of the first volunteer firemen in America by Peter Stuyvesant.

Peter Stuyvesant,
Early and Modern Fire Engines
A418
ROTARY PRESS PRINTING.
E. E. Plates of 200 subjects in four panes of 50 each.
1948 Perf. 11x10½ Unwmkd.
971 A418 3c bright rose carmine, Oct. 4, 1948 12 8
  Margin block of 4, P# 75 ——

INDIAN CENTENNIAL ISSUE.

Issued to commemorate the centenary of the arrival in Indian Territory, later Oklahoma, of the Five Civilized Indian Tribes: Cherokee, Chickasaw, Choctaw, Muscogee and Seminole.

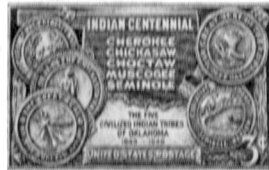

Map of Indian Territory and Seals of Five Tribes
A419

ROTARY PRESS PRINTING.
E. E. Plates of 200 subjects in four panes of 50 each.
  Perf. 11x10½. Unwmkd.
1948
972 A419 3c dark brown, Oct. 15, 1948 12 8
  Margin block of 4, P# 75 ——

ROUGH RIDERS ISSUE.

Issued to commemorate the 50th anniversary of the organization of the Rough Riders of the Spanish-American War.

Statue of Capt. William O. (Bucky) O'Neill
by Solon H. Borglum
A420
Designed by Victor S. McCloskey, Jr.
ROTARY PRESS PRINTING.
E. E. Plates of 200 subjects in four panes of 50 each.
1948 Perf. 11x10½. Unwmkd.
973 A420 3c violet brown, Oct. 27, 1948 12 10
  Margin block of 4, P# 1.20 ——

JULIETTE LOW ISSUE.

Issued to honor Juliette Gordon Low (1860–1927), founder of the Girl Scouts of America. Mrs. Low organized the first troop of Girl Guides in 1912 at Savannah. The name was changed to Girl Scouts in 1913 and headquarters moved to New York.

Juliette Gordon Low and Girl Scout Emblem
A421
Designed by William K. Schrage.
ROTARY PRESS PRINTING.
E. E. Plates of 200 subjects in four panes of 50 each.
1948 Perf. 11x10½. Unwmkd.
974 A421 3c blue green, Oct. 29, 1948 12 8
  Margin block of 4, P# 65 ——

WILL ROGERS ISSUE.

Issued to honor Will Rogers, (1879–1935), humorist and political commentator.

Will Rogers—A422

POSTAGE, 1948, 1949

ROTARY PRESS PRINTING.
E. E. Plates of 280 subjects in four panes of 70 each.
1948		Perf. 10½x11.		Unwmkd.	
975	A422	3c bright red violet, Nov. 4, 1948		12	8
		Margin block of 4, P#		1.00	

FORT BLISS CENTENNIAL ISSUE.
Issued to commemorate the centenary of the establishment of Fort Bliss at El Paso, Texas.

Fort Bliss and Rocket Firing
A423
Designed by Charles R. Chickering.
ROTARY PRESS PRINTING.
E. E. Plates of 280 subjects in four panes of 70 each.
1948		Perf. 10½x11.		Unwmkd.	
976	A423	3c henna brown, Nov. 5, 1948		15	8
		Margin block of 4, P#		1.50	

MOINA MICHAEL ISSUE.
Issued to honor Moina Michael (1870–1944), educator who originated (1918) the Flanders Field Poppy Day idea as a memorial to the war dead.

Moina Michael and Poppy Plant
A424
ROTARY PRESS PRINTING.
E. E. Plates of 200 subjects in four panes of 50 each.
1948		Perf. 11x10½		Unwmkd.	
977	A424	3c rose pink, Nov. 9, 1948		12	8
		Margin block of 4, P#		65	

GETTYSBURG ADDRESS ISSUE.
Issued to commemorate the 85th anniversary of Abraham Lincoln's address at Gettysburg, Pennsylvania.

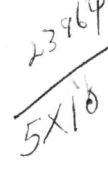

Abraham Lincoln and Quotation
from Gettysburg Address
A425

Designed by Charles R. Chickering.
ROTARY PRESS PRINTING.
E. E. Plates of 200 subjects in four panes of 50 each.
1948		Perf. 11x10½.		Unwmkd.	
978	A425	3c bright blue, Nov. 19, 1948		12	8
		Margin block of 4, P#		70	

AMERICAN TURNERS ISSUE.
Issued to commemorate the centenary of the formation of the American Turners Society.

Torch and Emblem of American Turners
A426
Designed by Alvin R. Meissner.
ROTARY PRESS PRINTING.
E. E. Plates of 200 subjects in four panes of 50 each.
1948		Perf. 10½x11.		Unwmkd.	
979	A426	3c carmine, Nov. 20, 1948		12	8
		Margin block of 4, P#		55	

JOEL CHANDLER HARRIS ISSUE.
Issued to commemorate the centenary of the birth of Joel Chandler Harris (1848–1908), Georgia writer, creator of "Uncle Remus" and newspaperman.

Joel Chandler Harris—A427
ROTARY PRESS PRINTING.
E. E. Plates of 280 subjects in four panes of 70 each.
1948		Perf. 10½x11.		Unwmkd.	
980	A427	3c bright red violet, Dec. 9, 1948		12	8
		Margin block of 4, P#		85	

MINNESOTA TERRITORY ISSUE.
Issued to commemorate the centenary of the establishment of Minnesota Territory.

Pioneer and Red River Oxcart—A428

POSTAGE, 1949, 1950 217

ROTARY PRESS PRINTING.
E. E. Plates of 200 subjects in four panes of 50 each.
1949   Perf. 11x10½.   Unwmkd.
981   A428   3c blue green, Mar. 3, 1949   10   5
              Margin block of 4, P#   50

WASHINGTON AND LEE UNIVERSITY ISSUE.

Bicentenary of Washington and Lee University.

George Washington, Robert E. Lee and University Building, Lexington, Va.—A429
ROTARY PRESS PRINTING.
E. E. Plates of 200 subjects in four panes of 50 each.
1949   Perf. 11x10½.   Unwmkd.
982   A429   3c ultramarine, April 12, 1949   10   5
              Margin block of 4, P#   50

PUERTO RICO ELECTION ISSUE.

Issued to commemorate the first gubernatorial election in the Territory of Puerto Rico, Nov. 2, 1948.

Puerto Rican Farmer
Holding Cogwheel and Ballot Box—A430
ROTARY PRESS PRINTING.
E. E. Plates of 200 subjects in four panes of 50 each.
1949   Perf. 11x10½.   Unwmkd.
983   A430   3c green, April 27, 1949   10   5
              Margin block of 4, P#   50

ANNAPOLIS TERCENTENARY ISSUE.

Issued to commemorate the 300th anniversary of the founding of Annapolis, Maryland

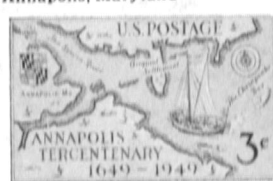

James Stoddert's 1718 Map of Regions
about Annapolis, Redrawn
A431
ROTARY PRESS PRINTING.
E. E. Plates of 200 subjects in four panes of 50 each.
1949   Perf. 11x10½.   Unwmkd.
984   A431   3c aquamarine, May 23, 1949   10   5
              Margin block of 4, P#   50

G.A.R. ISSUE.

Issued to commemorate the final encampment of the Grand Army of the Republic, Indianapolis, August 28 to September 1, 1949.

Union Soldier
and G. A. R. Veteran of 1949
A432
Designed by Charles R. Chickering.
ROTARY PRESS PRINTING.
E.E. Plates of 200 subjects in four panes of 50 each.
1949   Perf. 11x10½   Unwmkd.
985   A432   3c bright rose carmine, Aug. 29, 1949 10   5
              Margin block of 4, P#   50

EDGAR ALLAN POE ISSUE.

Issued to commemorate the centenary of the death of Edgar Allan Poe (1809–1849), Boston-born poet, story writer and editor.

Edgar Allan Poe—A433
ROTARY PRESS PRINTING.
E. E. Plates of 280 subjects in four panes of 70 each.
1949   Perf. 10½x11   Unwmkd.
986   A433   3c bright red violet, Oct. 7, 1949   10   5
              Margin block of 4, P#   60
              Thin outer frame line at top, inner
              line missing (24143 L.L. 42)   10.00

AMERICAN BANKERS ASSOCIATION ISSUE.

Issued to commemorate the 75th anniversary of the formation of the American Bankers Association.

Coin, Symbolizing Fields of Banking Service
A434
Designed by Charles R. Chickering.
ROTARY PRESS PRINTING.
E. E. Plates of 200 subjects in four panes of 50 each.
1950   Perf. 11x10½.   Unwmkd.
987   A434   3c yellow green, Jan. 3, 1950   10   5
              Margin block of 4, P#   50

SAMUEL GOMPERS ISSUE.

Issued to commemorate the centenary of the birth of Samuel Gompers (1850–1924), British-born American labor leader.

Samuel Gompers—A435
ROTARY PRESS PRINTING.
E. E. Plates of 280 subjects in four panes of 70 each.
1950   Perf. 10½x11.   Unwmkd.

988	A435	3c bright red violet, Jan. 27, 1950	10	5
		Margin block of 4, P#	65	

NATIONAL CAPITAL SESQUICENTENNIAL ISSUE.

Issued to commemorate the 150th anniversary of the establishment of the National Capital, Washington D. C.

Statue of Freedom on Capitol Dome—A436

Executive Mansion—A437

Supreme Court Building—A438

United States Capitol—A439

ROTARY PRESS PRINTING.
E. E. Plates of 200 subjects in four panes of 50 each.
1950   Perf. 10½x11, 11x10½.   Unwmkd.

989	A436	3c bright blue, Apr. 20, 1950	10	5
		Margin block of 4, P#	50	
990	A437	3c deep green, June 12, 1950	10	5
		Margin block of 4, P#	50	
991	A438	3c light violet, Aug. 2, 1950	10	5
		Margin block of 4, P#	50	
992	A439	3c bright red violet, Nov. 22, 1950	10	5
		Margin block of 4, P#	50	
		Gripper cracks (24285 U.L. 11)	1.50	50

RAILROAD ENGINEERS ISSUE.

Issued to honor the Railroad Engineers of America. Stamp portrays John Luther (Casey) Jones (1864–1900), locomotive engineer killed in train wreck near Vaughn, Miss.

"Casey" Jones and
Locomotives of 1900 and 1950
A440
ROTARY PRESS PRINTING.
E. E. Plates of 200 subjects in four panes of 50 each.
1950   Perf. 11x10½.   Unwmkd.

993	A440	3c violet brown, April 29, 1950	10	5
		Margin block of 4, P#	50	

KANSAS CITY, MISSOURI, CENTENARY ISSUE.

Issued to commemorate the centenary of the incorporation of Kansas City, Missouri.

Kansas City Skyline, 1950
and Westport Landing, 1850
A441
ROTARY PRESS PRINTING.
E. E. Plates of 200 subjects in four panes of 50 each.
1950   Perf. 11x10½.   Unwmkd.

994	A441	3c violet, June 3, 1950	10	5
		Margin block of 4, P#	50	

BOY SCOUTS ISSUE.

Issued to honor the Boy Scouts of America on the occasion of the second National Jamboree, Valley Forge, Pa.

Three Boys, Statue of Liberty and Scout Badge
A442
ROTARY PRESS PRINTING.
E. E. Plates of 200 subjects in four panes of 50 each.
1950   Perf. 11x10½   Unwmkd.
995   A442   3c sepia, *June 30, 1950*   10   6
             Margin block of 4, P#   55

INDIANA TERRITORY ISSUE.

Issued to commemorate the 150th anniversary of the establishment of Indiana Territory.

Gov. William Henry Harrison and First Indiana Capitol, Vincennes
A443
ROTARY PRESS PRINTING.
E. E. Plates of 200 subjects in four panes of 50 each.
1950   Perf. 11x10½.   Unwmkd.
996   A443   3c bright blue, *July 4, 1950*   10   5
             Margin block of 4, P#   50

CALIFORNIA STATEHOOD ISSUE.

Issued to commemorate the centenary of the admission of California to statehood.

Gold Miner, Pioneers and S. S. Oregon
A444
ROTARY PRESS PRINTING.
E. E. Plates of 200 subjects in four panes of 50 each.
1950   Perf. 11x10½.   Unwmkd.
997   A444   3c yellow orange, *Sept. 9, 1950*   10   5
             Margin block of 4, P#   50

UNITED CONFEDERATE VETERANS FINAL REUNION ISSUE.

Issued to commemorate the final reunion of the United Confederate Veterans, Norfolk, Virginia, May 30, 1951.

Confederate Soldier
and United Confederate Veteran
A445
ROTARY PRESS PRINTING.
E. E. Plates of 200 subjects in four panes of 50 each.
1951   Perf. 11x10½.   Unwmkd.
998   A445   3c gray, *May 30, 1951*   10   5
             Margin block of 4, P#   50

NEVADA CENTENNIAL ISSUE.

Issued to commemorate the centenary of the settlement of Nevada.

Carson Valley, c. 1851
A446
Designed by Charles R. Chickering.
ROTARY PRESS PRINTING.
E. E. Plates of 200 subjects in four panes of 50 each.
1951   Perf. 11x10½.   Unwmkd.
999   A446   3c light olive green, *July 14, 1951*   10   5
             Margin block of 4, P#   50

LANDING OF CADILLAC ISSUE.

Issued to commemorate the 250th anniversary of the landing of Antoine de la Mothe Cadillac at Detroit.

Detroit Skyline and Cadillac Landing
A447
ROTARY PRESS PRINTING.
E. E. Plates of 200 subjects in four panes of 50 each.
1951   Perf. 11x10½   Unwmkd.
1000   A447   3c blue, *July 24, 1951*   10   5
              Margin block of 4, P#   50

COLORADO STATEHOOD ISSUE.

Issued to commemorate the 75th anniversary of the admission of Colorado to statehood.

Colorado Capitol, Mount of the Holy Cross, Columbine and Bronco Buster by Proctor
A448
ROTARY PRESS PRINTING.
E. E. Plates of 200 subjects in four panes of 50 each.

1951			Perf. 11x10½.		Unwmkd.
1001	A448	3c	blue violet, Aug. 1, 1951	10	5
			Margin block of 4, P#	50	—

AMERICAN CHEMICAL SOCIETY ISSUE.

Issued to commemorate the 75th anniversary of the formation of the American Chemical Society.

A. C. S. Emblem and Symbols of Chemistry
A449
ROTARY PRESS PRINTING.
E. E. Plates of 200 subjects in four panes of 50 each.

1951			Perf. 11x10½.		Unwmkd.
1002	A449	3c	violet brown, Sept. 4, 1951	10	5
			Margin block of 4, P#	50	—

BATTLE OF BROOKLYN ISSUE.

Issued to commemorate the 175th anniversary of the Battle of Brooklyn.

Gen. George Washington Evacuating Army; Fulton Ferry House at Right
A450
ROTARY PRESS PRINTING.
E. E. Plates of 200 subjects in four panes of 50 each.

1951			Perf. 11x10½.		Unwmkd.
1003	A450	3c	violet, Dec. 10, 1951	10	5
			Margin block of 4, P#	50	—

BETSY ROSS ISSUE.

Issued to commemorate the 200th anniversary of the birth of Betsy Ross, maker of the first American flag.

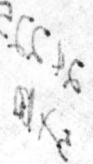 

Betsy Ross Showing Flag to Gen. George Washington, Robert Morris and George Ross
A451
ROTARY PRESS PRINTING.
E. E. Plates of 200 subjects in four panes of 50 each.

1952			Perf. 11x10½.		Unwmkd.
1004	A451	3c	carmine rose, Jan. 2, 1953	10	5
			Margin block of 4, P#	50	—

4-H CLUB ISSUE.

Issued to honor the 4-H Club movement.

Farm, Club Emblem, Boy and Girl
A452
ROTARY PRESS PRINTING.
E. E. Plates of 200 subjects in four panes of 50 each.

1952			Perf. 11x10½.		Unwmkd.
1005	A452	3c	blue green, Jan. 15, 1952	10	5
			Margin block of 4, P#	60	—

B. & O. RAILROAD ISSUE.

Issued to commemorate the 125th anniversary of the granting of a charter to the Baltimore and Ohio Railroad Company by the Maryland Legislature.

Charter and Three Stages of Rail Transportation
A453
ROTARY PRESS PRINTING.
E. E. Plates of 200 subjects in four panes of 50 each.

1952			Perf. 11x10½		Unwmkd.
1006	A453	3c	bright blue, Feb. 28, 1952	10	5
			Margin block of 4, P#	50	—

POSTAGE, 1952

A. A. A. ISSUE.

Issued to commemorate the 50th anniversary of the formation of the American Automobile Association.

School Girls and Safety Patrolman
Automobiles of 1902 and 1952
A454
ROTARY PRESS PRINTING.
E. E. Plates of 200 subjects in four panes of 50 each.
1952   Perf. 11x10½.   Unwmkd.
1007 A454 3c deep blue, *March 4, 1952*   10   5
        Margin block of 4, P#   60

NATO ISSUE

Issued to commemorate the third anniversary of the signing of the North Atlantic Treaty.

Torch of Liberty and Globe
A455
ROTARY PRESS PRINTING.
E. E. Plates of 400 subjects in four panes of 100 each.
1952   Perf. 11x10½.   Unwmkd.
1008 A455 3c deep violet, *April 4, 1952*   10   5
        Margin block of 4, P#   55

GRAND COULEE DAM ISSUE.

Issued to commemorate 50 years of Federal cooperation in developing the resources of rivers and streams in the West.

Spillway, Grand Coulee Dam
A456
ROTARY PRESS PRINTING.
E. E. Plates of 200 subjects in four panes of 50 each.
1952   Perf. 11x10½.   Unwmkd.
1009 A456 3c blue green, *May 15, 1952*   10   5
        Margin block of 4, P#   50

LAFAYETTE ISSUE.

Issued to commemorate the 175th anniversary of the arrival of Marquis de Lafayette in America.

Marquis de Lafayette,
Flags, Cannon and Landing Party
A457
Designed by Victor S. McCloskey, Jr.
ROTARY PRESS PRINTING.
E. E. Plates of 200 subjects in four panes of 50 each.
1952   Perf. 11x10½.   Unwmkd.
1010 A457 3c bright blue, *June 13, 1952*   10   5
        Margin block of 4, P#   50

MT. RUSHMORE MEMORIAL ISSUE.

Issued to commemorate the 25th anniversary of the dedication of the Mt. Rushmore National Memorial in the Black Hills of South Dakota.

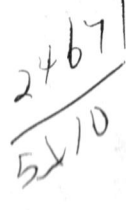

Sculptured Heads on Mt. Rushmore
A458
Designed by William K. Schrage.
ROTARY PRESS PRINTING.
E. E. Plates of 200 subjects in four panes of 50 each.
1952   Perf. 10½x11.   Unwmkd.
1011 A458 3c blue green, *Aug. 11, 1952*   10   5
        Margin block of 4, P#   60

ENGINEERING CENTENNIAL ISSUE.

Issued to commemorate the centenary of the founding of the American Society of Civil Engineers.

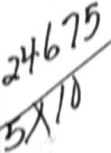

George Washington Bridge and Covered Bridge of 1850's
A459

POSTAGE, 1952, 1953

ROTARY PRESS PRINTING.
E. E. Plates of 200 subjects in four panes of 50 each.
1952   Perf. 11x10½.   Unwmkd.
1012 A459 3c violet blue, Sept. 6, 1952   10   5
      Margin block of 4, P#   50

SERVICE WOMEN ISSUE.

Issued to honor the women in the United States Armed Services.

Women of the Marine Corps, Army, Navy and Air Force
A460
ROTARY PRESS PRINTING.
E. E. Plates of 200 subjects in four panes of 50 each.
1952   Perf. 11x10½.   Unwmkd.
1013 A460 3c deep blue, Sept. 11, 1952   10   5
      Margin block of 4, P#   50

GUTENBERG BIBLE ISSUE.

Issued to commemorate the 500th anniversary of the printing of the first book, the Holy Bible, from movable type, by Johann Gutenberg.

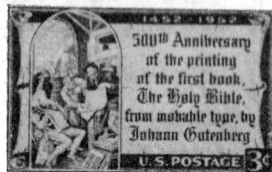

Gutenberg Showing Proof to the Elector of Mainz
A461
ROTARY PRESS PRINTING.
E. E. Plates of 200 subjects in four panes of 50 each.
1952   Perf. 11x10½.   Unwmkd.
1014 A461 3c violet, Sept. 30, 1952   10   5
      Margin block of 4, P#   50

NEWSPAPER BOYS ISSUE.

Issued to honor the newspaper boys of America.

Newspaper Boy, Torch
and Group of Homes
A462
ROTARY PRESS PRINTING.
E. E. Plates of 200 subjects in four panes of 50 each.
1952   Perf. 11x10½.   Unwmkd.
1015 A462 3c violet, Oct. 4, 1952   10   5
      Margin block of 4, P#   50

RED CROSS ISSUE.

Issued to honor the International Red Cross.

Globe, Sun and Cross
A463
ROTARY PRESS PRINTING.
Cross Typographed
E. E. Plates of 200 subjects in four panes of 50 each.
1952   Perf. 11x10½.   Unwmkd.
1016 A463 3c deep blue & carmine,
      Nov. 21, 1952   10   5
      Margin block of 4, P#   50

NATIONAL GUARD ISSUE.

Issued to honor the National Guard of the United States.

National Guardsman,
Amphibious Landing and Disaster Service
A464
ROTARY PRESS PRINTING.
E. E. Plates of 200 subjects in four panes of 50 each.
1953   Perf. 11x10½   Unwmkd.
1017 A464 3c bright blue, Feb. 23, 1953   10   5
      Margin block of 4, P#   50

OHIO STATEHOOD ISSUE.

Sesquicentennial of Ohio statehood.

Ohio Map, State Seal, Buckeye Leaf
A465
ROTARY PRESS PRINTING.
E. E. Plates of 280 subjects in four panes of 70 each.
1953   Perf. 11x10½   Unwmkd.
1018 A465 3c chocolate, Mar. 2, 1953   10   5
      Margin block of 4, P#   80

POSTAGE, 1953   223

WASHINGTON TERRITORY ISSUE.

Issued to commemorate the centenary of the organization of Washington Territory.

Medallion, Pioneers and Washington Scene
A466
ROTARY PRESS PRINTING.

1953		Perf. 11x10½.		Unwmkd.	
1019	A466	3c green, Mar. 2, 1953		10	5
		Margin block of 4, P#		50	—

LOUISIANA PURCHASE ISSUE

Issued to commemorate the 150th anniversary of the Louisiana Purchase, 1803.

James Monroe, Robert R. Livingston and
Marquis Francois de Barbé-Marbois
A467
ROTARY PRESS PRINTING.

1953		Perf. 11x10½.		Unwmkd.	
1020	A467	3c violet brown, April 30, 1953		10	5
		Margin block of 4, P#		50	—

OPENING OF JAPAN CENTENNIAL ISSUE.

Issued to commemorate the centenary of Commodore Matthew Calbraith Perry's negotiations with Japan, which opened her doors to foreign trade.

Commodore Matthew C. Perry
and First Anchorage off Tokyo Bay
A468
ROTARY PRESS PRINTING.
E. E. Plates of 200 subjects in four panes of 50 each.

1953		Perf. 11x10½.		Unwmkd.	
1021	A468	5c green, July 14, 1953		15	10
		Margin block of 4, P#		1.40	

AMERICAN BAR ASSOCIATION ISSUE.

Issued to commemorate the 75th anniversary of the formation of the American Bar Association.

Section of Frieze, Supreme Court Room
A469
ROTARY PRESS PRINTING.
E. E. Plates of 200 subjects in four panes of 50 each.

1953		Perf. 11x10½.		Unwmkd.	
1022	A469	3c rose violet, Aug. 24, 1953		10	5
		Margin block of 4, P#		50	—

SAGAMORE HILL ISSUE.

Issued to commemorate the opening of Sagamore Hill, Theodore Roosevelt's home, as a national shrine.

Home of Theodore Roosevelt
A470
ROTARY PRESS PRINTING.
E. E. Plates of 200 subjects in four panes of 50 each.

1953		Perf. 11x10½.		Unwmkd.	
1023	A470	3c yellow green, Sept. 14, 1953		10	5
		Margin block of 4, P#		50	—

FUTURE FARMERS ISSUE.

Issued to commemorate the 25th anniversary of the organization of Future Farmers of America.

Agricultural Scene and Future Farmer
A471
ROTARY PRESS PRINTING.
E. E. Plates of 200 subjects in four panes of 50 each.

1953		Perf. 11x10½.		Unwmkd.	
1024	A471	3c deep blue, Oct. 13, 1953		10	5
		Margin block of 4, P#		50	—

TRUCKING INDUSTRY ISSUE.

Issued to commemorate the 50th anniversary of the Trucking Industry in the United States.

Truck, Farm and Distant City
A472
ROTARY PRESS PRINTING.
E. E. Plates of 200 subjects in four panes of 50 each.
1953   Perf. 11x10½.   Unwmkd.
1025   A472   3c violet, Oct. 27, 1953   10   5
           Margin block of 4, P#   50

GENERAL PATTON ISSUE

Issued to honor Gen. George S. Patton, Jr. (1885–1945), and the armored forces of the United States Army.

Gen. George S. Patton, Jr., and Tanks in Action
A473
ROTARY PRESS PRINTING.
E. E. Plates of 200 subjects in four panes of 50 each.
1953   Perf. 11x10½.   Unwmkd.
1026   A473   3c blue violet, Nov. 11, 1953   10   5
           Margin block of 4, P#   60

NEW YORK CITY ISSUE.

Issued to commemorate the 300th anniversary of the founding of New York City.

Dutch Ship in New Amsterdam Harbor
A474
ROTARY PRESS PRINTING.
E. E. Plates of 200 subjects in four panes of 50 each.
1953   Perf. 11x10½.   Unwmkd.
1027   A474   3c bright red violet, Nov. 20, 1953   10   5
           Margin block of 4, P#   60

GADSDEN PURCHASE ISSUE.

Issued to commemorate the centenary of James Gadsden's purchase of territory from Mexico to adjust the U. S.-Mexico boundary.

Map and Pioneer Group—A475
ROTARY PRESS PRINTING.
E. E. Plates of 200 subjects in four panes of 50 each.
1953   Perf. 11x10½.   Unwmkd.
1028   A475   3c copper brown, Dec. 30, 1953   10   5
           Margin block of 4, P#   50

COLUMBIA UNIVERSITY ISSUE.

Issued to commemorate the 200th anniversary of the founding of Columbia University.

Low Memorial Library—A476
ROTARY PRESS PRINTING.
E. E. Plates of 200 subjects in four panes of 50 each.
1954   Perf. 11x10½.   Unwmkd.
1029   A476   3c blue, Jan. 4, 1954   10   5
           Margin block of 4, P#   50

Wet and Dry Printings

In 1953 the Bureau of Engraving and Printing began experiments in printing on "dry" paper (moisture content 5–10 per cent). In previous "wet" printings the paper had a moisture content of 15–35 per cent.

The new process required a thicker, stiffer paper, special types of inks and greater pressure to force the paper into the recessed plates. The "dry" printings show whiter paper, a higher sheen on the surface, feel thicker and stiffer, and the designs stand out more clearly than on the "wet" printings.

Nos. 832c and 1041 (flat plate) were the first "dry" printings to be issued of flat-plate, regular-issue stamps. No. 1063 was the first rotary press stamp to be produced entirely by "dry" printing.

Stamps printed by both the "wet" and "dry" process are Nos. 1030, 1031, 1035, 1035a, 1036, 1039, 1049, 1050–1052, 1054, 1055, 1057, 1058, C34–C36, C39, C39a, J78, J80–J84, QE1–QE3, RF26. The "wet" printed 4c coil, No. 1058, exists only precancelled.

All postage stamps have been printed by the "dry" process since the late 1950's.

LIBERTY ISSUE.

Benjamin Franklin   George Washington
A477   A478

POSTAGE, 1954-68

Palace of the Governors, Santa Fe
A478a

Mount Vernon
A479

John J. Pershing
A489a

The Alamo, San Antonio
A490

Thomas Jefferson
A480

Bunker Hill Monument and Massachusetts Flag, 1776
A481

Independence Hall
A491

Statue of Liberty
A491a

Statue of Liberty
A482

Abraham Lincoln
A483

Benjamin Harrison
A492

John Jay
A493

The Hermitage, Home of Andrew Jackson, near Nashville
A484

James Monroe
A485

Monticello, Home of Thomas Jefferson, near Charlottesville, Va.
A494

Theodore Roosevelt
A486

Woodrow Wilson
A487

Paul Fevere
A495

Robert E. Lee
A496

Statue of Liberty
A488   A489

John Marshall
A497

Susan B. Anthony
A498

POSTAGE, 1954–68

Patrick Henry
A499

Alexander Hamilton
A500

ROTARY PRESS PRINTING.
E. E. Plates of 400 subjects in four panes of 100 each.

1954–68 Perf. 11x10½ Unwmkd.

1030	A477	½c red orange, Oct. 20, 1954	5	5
		Margin block of 4, P#	30	
1031	A478	1c dark green, Aug. 26, 1954	5	5
		Margin block of 4, P#	25	
		Pair with full vert. or horiz. gutter between	150.00	

Perf. 10½x11

1031A	A478a	1¼c turquoise, June 17, 1960	5	5
		Margin block of 4, P#	1.75	
1032	A479	1½c brown carmine, Feb. 22, 1956	8	5
		Margin block of 4, P#	7.50	

Perf. 11x10½.

1033	A480	2c carmine rose, Sept. 15, 1954	5	5
		Margin block of 4, P#	25	
		Pair with full vert. or horiz. gutter between		
1034	A481	2½c gray blue, June 17, 1959	8	5
		Margin block of 4, P#	2.00	
1035	A482	3c deep violet, June 24, 1954	8	5
		Margin block of 4, P#	40	
		Pair with full vert. or horiz. gutter between	150.00	
	a.	Booklet pane of 6, June 30, 1954	3.00	50
	b.	Tagged, July 6, 1966	25	20
	c.	Imperf., pair	750.00	
	d.	Horiz. pair, imperf. between	1,000.	
1036	A483	4c red violet, Nov. 19, 1954	10	5
		Margin block of 4, P#	50	
		Pair with full vert. gutter between		
	a.	Booklet pane of 6, July 31, 1958	2.00	50
	b.	Tagged, Nov. 2, 1963	75	16

Perf. 10½x11.

1037	A484	4½c blue green, March 16, 1959	15	8
		Margin block of 4, P#	1.75	

Perf. 11x10½.

1038	A485	5c deep blue, Dec. 2, 1954	17	5
		Margin block of 4, P#	75	
		Pair with full vert. gutter btwn.	200.00	
1039	A486	6c carmine, Nov. 18, 1955	40	5
		Margin block of 4, P#	2.00	
1040	A487	7c rose carmine, Jan. 10, 1956	25	5
		Margin block of 4, P#	1.50	

Luminescence (Tagged) see Information for Collectors.

FLAT PLATE OR ROTARY PRESS PRINTING.
Plates of 400 subjects in four panes of 100 each.
Perf. 11.

1041	A488	8c dark violet blue & carmine, Apr. 9, 1954	30	6
		Margin block of 4, 2 P# (flat plate)	5.00	
		Margin block of 4, 2 P# (rotary)	5.00	
		Corner margin block of 4, blue P# only	—	
		Corner margin block of 4, red P# only	—	
	a.	Carmine dbl. impression	1,200.	

FLAT PRINTING PLATES
Frame: 24912-13-14-15, 24926, 24929-30, 24932-33.
Vignette: 24916-17-18-19-20, 24935-36-37, 24939.

ROTARY PRINTING PLATES
Frame: 24923-24, 24928, 24940, 24942.
Vignette: 24921-22, 24927, 24938.

GIORI PRESS PRINTING.
Plates of 400 subjects in four panes of 100 each.
Redrawn design.
Perf. 11

1042	A489	8c dark violet blue & carmine rose, March 22, 1958	30	5
		Margin block of 4, P#	1.75	

ROTARY PRESS PRINTING.
E. E. Plates of 400 subjects in four panes of 100 each.
Perf. 11x10½

1042A	A489a	8c brown, Nov. 17, 1961	25	5
		Margin block of 4, P#	1.50	

Perf. 10½x11

1043	A490	9c rose lilac, June 14, 1956	30	5
		Margin block of 4, P#	1.50	
1044	A491	10c rose lake, July 4, 1956	35	5
		Margin block of 4, P#	1.65	
	b.	Tagged, July 6, 1966	1.50	1.25

GIORI PRESS PRINTING
Plates of 400 subjects in four panes of 100 each.
Perf. 11

1044A	A491a	11c carmine & dark violet blue, June 15, 1961	30	6
		Margin block of 4, P#	1.50	
	c.	Tagged, Jan. 11, 1967	2.00	1.60

ROTARY PRESS PRINTING.
E. E. Plates of 400 subjects in four panes of 100 each.
Perf. 11x10½

1045	A492	12c red, June 6, 1959	55	5
		Marginal block of 4, P#	2.75	
	a.	Tagged, 1968	55	15
1046	A493	15c rose lake, Dec. 12, 1958	85	5
		Margin block of 4, P#	3.75	
	a.	Tagged, July 6, 1966	90	22

Perf. 10½x11

1047	A494	20c ultramarine, April 13, 1956	90	5
		Margin block of 4, P#	4.50	

Perf. 11x10½

1048	A495	25c green, April 18, 1958	2.75	5
		Margin block of 4, P#	12.00	

POSTAGE, 1954-68, 1954-73, 1954

1049	A496	30c black, *Sept. 21, 1955*	2.00	8
		Margin block of 4, P#	8.50	
1050	A497	40c brown red, *Sept. 24, 1955*	3.00	10
		Margin block of 4, P#	13.00	
1051	A498	50c bright purple, *Aug. 25, 1955*	3.25	5
		Margin block of 4, P#	14.00	
		Cracked plate (25231 U.L.)		
1052	A499	$1 purple, *Oct. 7, 1955*	10.00	6
		Margin block of 4, P#	42.50	

FLAT PLATE PRINTING.

Plates of 400 subjects in four panes of 100 each.

Perf. 11

1053	A500	$5 black, *March 19, 1956*	100.00	8.00
		Margin block of 4, P#	425.00	

ROTARY PRESS COIL STAMPS.

1954-73 Perf. 10 Vertically Unwmkd.

1054	A478	1c dark green, *Oct. 8, 1954*	35	12
		Pair	70	24
		Joint line pair	2.00	35
		b. Imperf. (pair)	2,250.	

Perf. 10 Horizontally

1054A	A478a	1¼c turquoise, *June 17, 1960*	25	20
		Pair	50	40
		Joint line pair	3.00	1.00

Perf. 10 Vertically.

1055	A480	2c carmine rose, *Oct. 22, 1954*	10	5
		Pair	20	10
		Joint line pair	75	20
		a. Tagged, *May 6, 1968*	10	5
		b. Imperf., pair (Bureau precanceled)		450.00
		c. As "a," imperf. pair	500.00	
1056	A481	2½c gray blue, *Sept. 9, 1959*	55	35
		Pair	1.10	70
		Joint line pair	7.50	1.20
1057	A482	3c deep violet, *July 20, 1954*	15	5
		Pair	30	10
		Joint line pair	1.00	15
		Gripper cracks		
		a. Imperf. (pair)	600.00	
		a. Imperf., joint line pair	850.00	
		b. Tagged, *Oct. 1966*	75	25

No. 1057a measures about 19½x22mm.; No. 1035c, about 18¾x22½mm.

1058	A483	4c red violet, *July 31, 1958*	15	5
		Pair	30	10
		Joint line pair	1.20	20
		a. Imperf. (pair)	100.00	100.00
		a. Imperf., joint line pair	200.00	

Perf. 10 Horizontally.

1059	A484	4½c blue green, *May 1, 1959*	3.25	1.20
		Pair	6.50	2.40
		Joint line pair	20.00	3.00

Perf. 10 Vertically

1059A	A495	25c green, *Feb. 25, 1965*	70	30
		Pair	1.40	60
		Joint line pair	3.25	1.20
		b. Tagged, *April 3, 1973*	50	20
		c. Imperf., pair	40.00	

NEBRASKA TERRITORY ISSUE.

Issued to commemorate the centenary of the establishment of the Nebraska Territory.

"The Sower," Mitchell Pass and Scotts Bluff
A507

ROTARY PRESS PRINTING.

E. E. Plates of 200 subjects in four panes of 50 each.

1954 Perf. 11x10½. Unwmkd.

1060	A507	3c violet, *May 7, 1954*	10	5
		Margin block of 4, P#	50	

KANSAS TERRITORY ISSUE.

Issued to commemorate the centenary of the establishment of the Kansas Territory

Wheat Field and Pioneer Wagon Train
A508

ROTARY PRESS PRINTING.

E. E. Plates of 200 subjects in four panes of 50 each.

1954 Perf. 11x10½ Unwmkd.

1061	A508	3c brown orange, *May 31, 1954*	10	5
		Margin block of 4, P#	50	

GEORGE EASTMAN ISSUE.

Issued to commemorate the birth centenary of George Eastman (1854-1932), inventor of photographic dry plates, flexible film and the Kodak camera; Rochester, N. Y., industrialist.

George Eastman
A509

ROTARY PRESS PRINTING

E. E. Plates of 280 subjects in four panes of 70 each.

1954 Perf. 10½x11 Unwmkd.

1062	A509	3c violet brown, *July 12, 1954*	10	5
		Margin block of 4, P#	60	

LEWIS AND CLARK EXPEDITION.

Issued to commemorate the 150th anniversary of the Lewis and Clark expedition.

Meriwether Lewis, William Clark and Sacagawea Landing on Missouri Riverbank
A510
ROTARY PRESS PRINTING.
E. E. Plates of 200 subjects in four panes of 50 each.
1954   *Perf. 11x10½.*   Unwmkd.

1063 A510 3c **violet brown**, *July 28, 1954*   10   5
            Margin block of 4, P#   50

PENNSYLVANIA ACADEMY OF THE FINE ARTS ISSUE

Issued to commemorate the 150th anniversary of the founding of the Pennsylvania Academy of the Fine Arts, Philadelphia.

Charles Willson Peale in his Museum, Self-portrait
A511
ROTARY PRESS PRINTING.
E. E. Plates of 200 subjects in four panes of 50 each.
1955   *Perf. 10½x11*   Unwmkd.

1064 A511 3c **rose brown**, *Jan. 15, 1955*   10   5
            Margin block of 4, P#   50

LAND GRANT COLLEGES ISSUE

Issued to commemorate the centenary of the founding of Michigan State College and Pennsylvania State University, first of the land grant institutions.

Open Book and Symbols of Subjects Taught
A512
ROTARY PRESS PRINTING.
E. E. Plates of 200 subjects in four panes of 50 each.
1955   *Perf. 11x10½*   Unwmkd.

1065 A512 3c **green**, *Feb. 12, 1955*   10   5
            Margin block, P#   50

ROTARY INTERNATIONAL ISSUE

Issued to commemorate the 50th anniversary of the founding of Rotary International.

Torch, Globe and Rotary Emblem—A513
ROTARY PRESS PRINTING.
E. E. Plates of 200 subjects in four panes of 50 each.
1955   *Perf. 11x10½*   Unwmkd.

1066 A513 8c **deep blue**, *Feb. 23, 1955*   20   12
            Margin block of 4, P#   1.50

ARMED FORCES RESERVE ISSUE

Issued to honor the Armed Forces Reserve.

Marine, Coast Guard, Army, Navy and Air Force Personnel
A514
ROTARY PRESS PRINTING.
E. E. Plates of 200 subjects in four panes of 50 each.
1955   *Perf. 11x10½*   Unwmkd.

1067 A514 3c **purple**, *May 21, 1955*   10   5
            Margin block of 4, P#   50

NEW HAMPSHIRE ISSUE

Issued to honor New Hampshire on the occasion of the sesquicentennial of the discovery of the "Old Man of the Mountains."

Great Stone Face
A515
ROTARY PRESS PRINTING.
E. E. Plates of 200 subjects in four panes of 50 each.
1955   *Perf. 10½x11*   Unwmkd.

1068 A515 3c **green**, *June 21, 1955*   10   5
            Margin block of 4, P#   50

SOO LOCKS ISSUE

Centenary of the opening of the Soo Locks.

Map of Great Lakes and Two Steamers
A516
ROTARY PRESS PRINTING.

E. E. Plates of 200 subjects in four panes of 50 each.

1955		Perf. *11x10½*		Unwmkd.	
1069	A516	3c **blue**, *June 28, 1955*		10	5
		Margin block of 4, P#		50	

ATOMS FOR PEACE ISSUE

Issued to promote an Atoms for Peace policy.

Atomic Energy Encircling the Hemispheres
A517
Designed by George R. Cox.
ROTARY PRESS PRINTING.

E. E. Plates of 200 subjects in four panes of 50 each.

1955		Perf. *11x10½*		Unwmkd.	
1070	A517	3c **deep blue**, *July 28, 1955*		12	5
		Margin block of 4, P#		70	

FORT TICONDEROGA ISSUE

Issued to commemorate the bicentenary of Fort Ticonderoga, New York.

Map of the Fort, Ethan Allen and Artillery
A518
Designed by Enrico Arno.
ROTARY PRESS PRINTING.

E. E. Plates of 200 subjects in four panes of 50 each.

1955		Perf. *11x10½*		Unwmkd.	
1071	A518	3c **light brown**, *Sept. 18, 1955*		10	5
		Margin block of 4, P#		50	

ANDREW W. MELLON ISSUE.

Issued to commemorate the centenary of the birth of Andrew W. Mellon (1855–1937), U.S. Secretary of the Treasury (1921–32), financier and art collector.

Andrew W. Mellon
A519
Designed by Victor S. McCloskey, Jr.
ROTARY PRESS PRINTING.

E. E. Plates of 280 subjects in four panes of 70 each.

1955		Perf. *10½x11.*		Unwmkd.	
1072	A519	3c **rose carmine**, *Dec. 20, 1955*		10	5
		Margin block of 4, P#		60	

BENJAMIN FRANKLIN ISSUE.

Issued to commemorate the 250th anniversary of the birth of Benjamin Franklin.

"Franklin Taking Electricity from the Sky,"
by Benjamin West
A520
Designed by Charles R. Chickering.
ROTARY PRESS PRINTING.

E. E. Plates of 200 subjects in four panes of 50 each.

1956		Perf. *10½x11*		Unwmkd.	
1073	A520	3c **bright carmine**, *Jan. 17, 1956*		10	5
		Margin block of 4, P#		50	

BOOKER T. WASHINGTON ISSUE

Issued to commemorate the centenary of the birth of Booker T. Washington (1856–1915), black educator, founder and head of Tuskegee Institute in Alabama.

Log Cabin
A521
Designed by Charles R. Chickering.
ROTARY PRESS PRINTING.

E. E. Plates of 200 subjects in four panes of 50 each.

1956		Perf. *11x10½.*		Unwmkd.	
1074	A521	3c **deep blue**, *April 5, 1956*		10	5
		Margin block of 4, P#		50	

FIFTH INTERNATIONAL PHILATELIC EXHIBITION ISSUES.

Issued to commemorate the Fifth International Philatelic Exhibition (FIPEX), New York City, April 28-May 6, 1956.

SOUVENIR SHEET.

A522
FLAT PLATE PRINTING.
Plates of 24 subjects.

1956		*Imperf.*	Unwmkd.	
1075	A522	Sheet of two, *April 28, 1956*	4.00	3.50
		a. A482 3c deep violet	1.35	1.10
		b. A488 8c dark violet blue & carmine	1.75	1.50

No. 1075 measures 108x73 mm. Nos. 1075a and 1075b measure 24x28 mm. Below the stamps appears the signature of Arthur E. Summerfield, Postmaster General of the United States. Marginal inscription reads: "In compliment to 5th International Philatelic Exhibition, 1956. New York, N. Y. Apr. 28 - May 6."

Inscriptions printed in dark violet blue; scrolls and stars in carmine.

New York Coliseum and Columbus Monument—A523
Designed by William K. Schrage.
ROTARY PRESS PRINTING.
E. E. Plates of 200 subjects in four panes of 50 each.

1956		*Perf. 11x10½*	Unwmkd.	
1076	A523	3c deep violet, *April 30, 1956*	10	5
		Margin block of 4, P#	50	—

WILDLIFE CONSERVATION ISSUE.

Issued to emphasize the importance of Wildlife Conservation in America.

Wild Turkey—A524

Pronghorn Antelope
A525

King Salmon
A526
Designed by Robert W. (Bob) Hines.
ROTARY PRESS PRINTING.
E. E. Plates of 200 subjects in four panes of 50 each.

1956		*Perf. 11x10½*	Unwmkd.	
1077	A524	3c **rose lake**, *May 5, 1956*	12	5
		Margin block of 4, P#	65	—
1078	A525	3c **brown**, *June 22, 1956*	12	5
		Margin block of 4, P#	65	—
1079	A526	3c **blue green**, *Nov. 9, 1956*	12	5
		Margin block of 4, P#	65	—

PURE FOOD AND DRUG LAWS ISSUE.

Issued to commemorate the 50th anniversary of the passage of the Pure Food and Drug Laws.

Harvey Washington Wiley
A527
Designed by Robert L. Miller.
ROTARY PRESS PRINTING.
E. E. Plates of 200 subjects in four panes of 50 each.

1956		*Perf. 10½x11*	Unwmkd.	
1080	A527	3c **dark blue green**, *June 27, 1956*	10	5
		Margin block of 4, P#	50	—

WHEATLAND ISSUE.

Pres. Buchanan's Home, Lancaster, Pa.
A528
ROTARY PRESS PRINTING.
E. E. Plates of 200 subjects in four panes of 50 each.

1956			Perf. 11x10½		Unwmkd.	
1081	A528	3c	black brown, Aug. 5, 1956		10	5
			Margin block of 4, P#		50	

LABOR DAY ISSUE.

Issued to commemorate Labor Day.

Mosaic, AFL-CIO Headquarters
A529

Designed by Victor S. McCloskey, Jr.
ROTARY PRESS PRINTING.
E. E. Plates of 200 subjects in four panes of 50 each.

1956			Perf. 10½x11		Unwmkd.	
1082	A529	3c	deep blue, Sept. 3, 1956		10	5
			Margin block of 4, P#		50	

NASSAU HALL ISSUE.

Issued to commemorate the 200th anniversary of Nassau Hall, Princeton University.

Nassau Hall, Princeton, N. J.
A530
ROTARY PRESS PRINTING.
E. E. Plates of 200 subjects in four panes of 50 each.

1956, Sept. 22			Perf. 11x10½		Unwmkd.	
1083	A530	3c	black, orange		10	5
			Margin block of 4, P#		50	

DEVILS TOWER ISSUE.

Issued to commemorate the 50th anniversary of the Federal law providing for protection of American natural antiquities. Devils Tower National Monument, Wyoming, is an outstanding example.

Devils Tower—A531
Designed by Charles R. Chickering.
ROTARY PRESS PRINTING.
E. E. Plates of 200 subjects in four panes of 50 each.

1956			Perf. 10½x11		Unwmkd.	
1084	A531	3c	violet, Sept. 24, 1956		10	5
			Margin block of 4, P#		50	
			Pair with full horiz. gutter btwn.			

CHILDREN'S ISSUE

Issued to promote friendship among the children of the world.

Children of the World—A532
Designed by Ronald Dias.
ROTARY PRESS PRINTING.
E. E. Plates of 200 subjects in four panes of 50 each.

1956			Perf. 11x10½		Unwmkd.	
1085	A532	3c	dark blue, Dec. 15, 1956		10	5
			Margin block of 4, P#		50	

ALEXANDER HAMILTON ISSUE.

Issued to commemorate the 200th anniversary of the birth of Alexander Hamilton (1755–1804).

Alexander Hamilton and Federal Hall—A533
Designed by William K. Schrage.
ROTARY PRESS PRINTING.
E. E. Plates of 200 subjects in four panes of 50 each.

1957			Perf. 11x10½		Unwmkd.	
1086	A533	3c	rose red, Jan. 11, 1957		10	5
			Margin block of 4, P#		50	

POLIO ISSUE.

Issued to honor "those who helped fight polio," and on the occasion of the 20th anniversary of the National Foundation for Infantile Paralysis and the March of Dimes.

Allegory—A534
Designed by Charles R. Chickering.
ROTARY PRESS PRINTING.
E. E. Plates of 200 subjects in four panes of 50 each.
1957 Perf. 10½x11 Unwmkd.

1087	A534	3c red lilac, *Jan. 15, 1957*	10	5
		Margin block of 4, P#	50	—

COAST AND GEODETIC SURVEY ISSUE.

Issued to commemorate the 150th anniversary of the establishment of the Coast and Geodetic Survey.

Flag of Coast and Geodetic Survey
and Ships at Sea—A535
Designed by Harold E. MacEwen.
ROTARY PRESS PRINTING.
E. E. Plates of 200 subjects in four panes of 50 each.
1957 Perf. 11x10½ Unwmkd.

1088	A535	3c dark blue, *Feb. 11, 1957*	10	5
		Margin block of 4, P#	50	—

ARCHITECTS ISSUE.

Issued to commemorate the centenary of the American Institute of Architects.

Corinthian Capital and
Mushroom Type Head and Shaft—A536
Designed by Robert J. Schultz.
ROTARY PRESS PRINTING.
E. E. Plates of 200 subjects in four panes of 50 each.
1957 Perf. 11x10½ Unwmkd.

1089	A536	3c red lilac, *Feb. 23, 1957*	10	5
		Margin block of 4, P#	50	—

STEEL INDUSTRY ISSUE.

Issued to commemorate the centenary of the steel industry in America.

American Eagle and Pouring Ladle
A537
Designed by Anthony Petruccelli.
ROTARY PRESS PRINTING.
E. E. Plates of 200 subjects in four panes of 50 each.
1957 Perf. 10½x11 Unwmkd.

1090	A537	3c bright ultramarine, *May 22, 1957*	10	5
		Margin block of 4, P#	50	—

INTERNATIONAL NAVAL REVIEW ISSUE.

Issued to commemorate the International Naval Review and the Jamestown Festival.

Aircraft Carrier and Jamestown Festival Emblem
A538
Designed by Richard A. Genders.
ROTARY PRESS PRINTING.
E. E. Plates of 200 subjects in four panes of 50 each.
1957 Perf. 11x10½. Unwmkd.

1091	A538	3c blue green, *June 10, 1957*	10	5
		Margin block of 4, P#	50	—

OKLAHOMA STATEHOOD ISSUE.

Issued to commemorate the 50th anniversary of the admission of Oklahoma to Statehood.

Map of Oklahoma,
Arrow and Atom Diagram
A539

POSTAGE, 1957

Designed by William K. Schrage.
ROTARY PRESS PRINTING.
E. E. Plates of 200 subjects in four panes of 50 each.
1957   Perf. 11x10½   Unwmkd.
1092 A539 3c dark blue, June 14, 1957   10   5
            Margin block of 4, P#   60

SCHOOL TEACHERS ISSUE.

Issued to honor the school teachers of America.

Teacher and Pupils
A540

ROTARY PRESS PRINTING.
E. E. Plates of 200 subjects in four panes of 50 each.
1957   Perf. 11x10½   Unwmkd.
1093 A540 3c rose lake, July 1, 1957   10   5
            Margin block of 4, P#   50

FLAG ISSUE.

"Old Glory" (48 Stars)
A541

Designed by Victor S. McCloskey, Jr.
GIORI PRESS PRINTING
Plates of 200 subjects in four panes of 50 each.
1957   Perf. 11   Unwmkd.
1094 A541 4c dark blue & deep carmine,
            July 4, 1957   10   5
            Margin block of 4, P#   60

SHIPBUILDING ISSUE.

Issued to commemorate the 350th anniversary of shipbuilding in America.

"Virginia of Sagadahock" and Seal of Maine
A542

Designed by Ervine Metzel, Mrs. William Zorach, A. M. Main, Jr., and George F. Cary II.
ROTARY PRESS PRINTING
E. E. Plates of 280 subjects in four panes of 70 each.
1957   Perf. 10½x11   Unwmkd.
1095 A542 3c deep violet, Aug. 15, 1957   10   5
            Margin block of 4, P#   70

CHAMPION OF LIBERTY ISSUE.

Issued to honor Ramon Magsaysay (1907–1957), President of the Philippines.

Ramon Magsaysay
A543

Designed by Arnold Copeland, Ervine Metzl and William H. Buckley.
GIORI PRESS PRINTING
Plates of 192 subjects in four panes of 48 each.
1957   Perf. 11   Unwmkd.
1096 A543 8c carmine, ultramarine & ochre,
            Aug. 31, 1957   22   15
            Margin block of 4, two P#   1.75
            Margin block of 4, ultra. P#
            omitted

LAFAYETTE BICENTENARY ISSUE.

Issued to commemorate the bicentenary of the birth of the Marquis de Lafayette (1757–1834).

Marquis de Lafayette
A544

Designed by Ervine Metzl.
ROTARY PRESS PRINTING
E. E. Plates of 200 subjects in four panes of 50 each.
1957   Perf. 10½x11   Unwmkd.
1097 A544 3c rose lake, Sept. 6, 1957   10   5
            Margin block of 4, P#   50

WILDLIFE CONSERVATION ISSUE.

Issued to emphasize the importance of Wildlife Conservation in America.

Whooping Cranes
A545

Designed by Bob Hines and C. R. Chickering.
GIORI PRESS PRINTING
Plates of 200 subjects in four panes of 50 each.
1957   Perf. 11   Unwmkd.
1098   A545   3c blue, ocher & green, *Nov. 22, 1957*   10   5
                Margin block of 4, P#   65   ——

RELIGIOUS FREEDOM ISSUE.

Issued to commemorate the 300th anniversary of the Flushing Remonstrance.

Bible, Hat and
Quill Pen
A546

Designed by Robert Geissmann.
ROTARY PRESS PRINTING.
E. E. Plates of 200 subjects in four panes of 50 each.
1957   Perf. 10½x11   Unwmkd.
1099   A546   3c black, *Dec. 27, 1957*   10   5
                Margin block of 4, P#   50   ——

GARDENING-HORTICULTURE ISSUE.

Issued to honor the garden clubs of America and in connection with the centenary of the birth of Liberty Hyde Bailey horticulturist.

"Bountiful Earth"
A547

Designed by Denver Gillen.
ROTARY PRESS PRINTING.
E. E. Plates of 200 Subjects in four panes of 50 each.
1958   Perf. 10½x11   Unwmkd.
1100   A547   3c green, *March 15, 1958*   10   5
                Margin block of 4, P#   50   ——

BRUSSELS EXHIBITION ISSUE.

Issued in honor of the opening of the Universal and International Exhibition at Brussels, April 17.

U. S. Pavilion at Brussels
A551

Designed by Bradbury Thompson.
ROTARY PRESS PRINTING.
E. E. Plates of 200 subjects in four panes of 50 each.
1958   Perf. 11x10½   Unwmkd.
1104   A551   3c deep claret, *April 17, 1958*   10   5
                Margin block of 4, P#   50   ——

JAMES MONROE ISSUE.

Issued to commemorate the bicentenary of the birth of James Monroe (1758–1831), fifth President of the United States.

James Monroe
A552

Designed by Frank P. Conley.
ROTARY PRESS PRINTING.
E. E. Plates of 280 subjects in four panes of 70 each.
1958   Perf. 11x10½   Unwmkd.
1105   A552   3c purple, *April 28, 1958*   10   5
                Margin block of 4, P#   60   ——

MINNESOTA STATEHOOD ISSUE.

Issued to commemorate the centenary of Minnesota's admission to statehood.

Minnesota Lakes and Pines
A553

POSTAGE, 1958   235

Designed by Homer Hill.
ROTARY PRESS PRINTING.
E. E. Plates of 200 subjects in four panes of 50 each.
1958   Perf. 11x10½   Unwmkd.
1106   A553   3c green, *May 11, 1958*   10   5
              Margin block of four, P#   50

GEOPHYSICAL YEAR ISSUE.

Issued to commemorate the International Geophysical Year, 1957-58.

Solar Disc and Hands from Michelangelo's
"Creation of Adam"
A554
Designed by Ervine Metzl.
GIORI PRESS PRINTING
Plates of 200 subjects in four panes of 50 each.
1958   Perf. 11   Unwmkd.
1107   A554   3c black & red orange, *May 31, 1958*   10   5
              Margin block of 4, P#   75

GUNSTON HALL ISSUE.

Issued for the bicentenary of Gunston Hall and to honor George Mason, author of the Constitution of Virginia and the Virginia Bill of Rights.

Gunston Hall Virginia—A555
Designed by Rene Clarke.
ROTARY PRESS PRINTING.
E. E. Plates of 200 subjects in four panes of 50 each.
1958   Perf. 11x10½   Unwmkd.
1108   A555   3c light green, *June 12, 1958*   10   5
              Margin block of 4, P#   50

MACKINAC BRIDGE ISSUE

Issued to commemorate the dedication of Mackinac Bridge, Michigan.

Mackinac Bridge
A556

Designed by Arnold J. Copeland.
ROTARY PRESS PRINTING.
E. E. Plates of 200 subjects in four panes of 50 each.
1958   Perf. 10½x11   Unwmkd.
1109   A556   3c bright greenish blue,
              June 25, 1958   10   5
              Margin block of 4, P#   50

CHAMPION OF LIBERTY ISSUE

Issued in honor of Simon Bolivar, South American freedom fighter.

Simon Bolívar
A557
ROTARY PRESS PRINTING.
E. E. Plates of 280 subjects in four panes of 70 each.
1958   Perf. 10½x11   Unwmkd.
1110   A557   4c olive bister, *July 24, 1958*   10   5
              Margin block of 4, P#   60

GIORI PRESS PRINTING
Plates of 288 subjects in four panes of 72 each.
Perf. 11
1111   A557   8c carmine, ultramarine & ochre,
              July 24, 1958   25   15
              Margin block of 4, two P#   5.00
              Corner block of 4, ocher P# only

ATLANTIC CABLE CENTENNIAL ISSUE

Issued to commemorate the centenary of the Atlantic Cable, linking the Eastern and Western hemispheres.

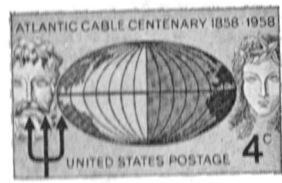

Neptune, Globe and Mermaid
A558
Designed by George Giusti.
ROTARY PRESS PRINTING.
E. E. Plates of 200 subjects in four panes of 50 each.
1958   Perf. 11x10½   Unwmkd.
1112   A558   4c reddish purple, *Aug. 15, 1958*   10   5
              Margin block of 4, P#   50

LINCOLN SESQUICENTENNIAL ISSUE

Issued to commemorate the sesquicentennial of the birth of Abraham Lincoln. No. 1114 also commemorates the centenary of the founding of Cooper Union, New York City. No. 1115 marks the centenary of the Lincoln-Douglas Debates.

Lincoln
by George Healy
A559

Lincoln
by Gutzon Borglum
A560

Lincoln and Stephen A. Douglas Debating,
from Painting by Joseph Boggs Beale
A561

Daniel Chester French Statue of Lincoln
as Drawn by Fritz Busse
A562

Designed by Ervine Metzl.
ROTARY PRESS PRINTING.
E. E. Plates of 200 subjects in four panes of 50 each.

1958-59		Perf. 10½x11		Unwmkd.
1113	A559	1c green, *Feb. 12, 1959*	5	5
		Margin block of 4, P#	40	
1114	A560	3c purple, *Feb. 27, 1959*	10	6
		Margin block of 4, P#	60	

		Perf. 11x10½		
1115	A561	4c sepia, *Aug. 27, 1958*	10	5
		Margin block, P#	55	
1116	A562	4c dark blue, *May 30, 1959*	10	5
		Margin block of 4, P#	65	

CHAMPION OF LIBERTY ISSUE

Issued in honor of Lajos Kossuth, Hungarian freedom fighter.

Lajos Kossuth—A563
ROTARY PRESS PRINTING.
E. E. Plates of 280 subjects in four panes of 70 each.

1958		Perf. 10½x11		Unwmkd.
1117	A563	4c green, *Sept. 19, 1958*	10	5
		Margin block of 4, P#	60	

GIORI PRESS PRINTING
Plates of 288 subjects in four panes of 72 each.
Perf. 11

1118	A563	8c carmine, ultramarine & ocher,		
		Sept. 19, 1958	22	12
		Margin block of 4, two P#	3.50	

FREEDOM OF PRESS ISSUE

Issued in honor of Journalism and freedom of the press in connection with the 50th anniversary of the first School of Journalism at the University of Missouri.

Early Press and Hand Holding Quill—A564
Designed by Lester Beall and Charles Goslin.
ROTARY PRESS PRINTING.
E. E. Plates of 200 subjects in four panes of 50 each.

1958		Perf. 10½x11		Unwmkd.
1119	A564	4c black, *Sept. 22, 1958*	10	5
		Margin block of 4, P#	50	

OVERLAND MAIL ISSUE

Issued to commemorate the centenary of Overland Mail Service.

Mail Coach and Map of Southwest U. S.
A565

Designed by William H. Buckley.
ROTARY PRESS PRINTING.
E. E. Plates of 200 subjects in four panes of 50 each.
1958   Perf. 11 x 10½   Unwmkd.
1120   A565   4c crimson rose, Oct. 10, 1958   10   5
              Margin block of 4, P#   50

NOAH WEBSTER ISSUE

Issued to commemorate the bicentenary of the birth of Noah Webster (1758–1843), lexicographer and author.

Noah Webster
A566

Designed by Charles R. Chickering.
ROTARY PRESS PRINTING.
E. E. Plates of 280 subjects in four panes of 70 each.
1958   Perf. 10½x11   Unwmkd.
1121   A566   4c dark carmine rose, Oct. 16, 1958   10   5
              Margin block of 4, P#   50

FOREST CONSERVATION ISSUE

Issued to publicize forest conservation and the protection of natural resources and to honor Theodore Roosevelt, a leading forest conservationist, on the centenary of his birth.

Forest Scene
A567

Designed by Rudolph Wendelin.
GIORI PRESS PRINTING
Plates of 200 subjects in four panes of 50 each.
1958   Perf. 11   Unwmkd.
1122   A567   4c green, yellow & brown,
              Oct. 27, 1958   10   5
              Margin block of 4, P#   60

FORT DUQUESNE ISSUE.

Issued to commemorate the bicentennial of Fort Duquesne (Fort Pitt) at future site of Pittsburgh.

British Capture of Fort Duquesne, 1758; Brig. Gen. John Forbes on Litter, Colonel Washington Mounted
A568

Designed by William H. Buckley and Douglas Gorsline.
ROTARY PRESS PRINTING.
E. E. Plates of 200 subjects in four panes of 50 each.
1958   Perf. 11x10½   Unwmkd.
1123   A568   4c blue, Nov. 25, 1958   10   5
              Margin block of 4, P#   50

OREGON STATEHOOD ISSUE.

Issued to commemorate the centenary of Oregon's admission to Statehood.

Covered Wagon and Mt. Hood
A569

Designed by Robert Hallock.
ROTARY PRESS PRINTING.
E E. Plates of 200 subjects in four panes of 50 each.
1959   Perf. 11x10½   Unwmkd.
1124   A569   4c blue green, Feb. 14, 1959   10   5
              Margin block of 4, P#   50

CHAMPION OF LIBERTY ISSUE.

Issued to honor José de San Martin, South American soldier and statesman.

José de San Martin
A570

ROTARY PRESS PRINTING.
E. E. Plates of 280 subjects in four panes of 70 each.
1959, Feb. 25   Perf. 10½x11   Unwmkd.
1125   A570   4c blue   10   5
              Margin block of 4, P#   55
       a. Horiz. pair, imperf. between   1,850.

POSTAGE, 1959

GIORI PRESS PRINTING.
Plates of 288 subjects in four panes of 72 each.
Perf. 11

1126	A570	8c carmine, ultramarine & ocher	20	12
		Margin block of 4, P#	1.75	

NATO ISSUE

Issued to commemorate the 10th anniversary of the North Atlantic Treaty Organization.

NATO Emblem—A571
Designed by Stevan Dohanos.
ROTARY PRESS PRINTING.
E. E. Plates of 280 subjects in four panes of 70 each.
1959   *Perf. 10½x11*   Unwmkd.

1127	A571	4c blue, *April 1, 1959*	10	5
		Margin block of 4, P#	50	

ARCTIC EXPLORATIONS ISSUE

Issued to commemorate the conquest of the Arctic by land by Rear Admiral Robert Edwin Peary in 1909 and by sea by the submarine "Nautilus" in 1958.

North Pole, Dog Sled and "Nautilus"—A572
Designed by George Samerjan.
ROTARY PRESS PRINTING.
E. E. Plates of 200 subjects in four panes of 50 each.
1959, Apr. 6   *Perf. 11x10½*   Unwmkd.

1128	A572	4c bright greenish blue	13	5
		Margin block of 4, P#	85	

WORLD PEACE THROUGH WORLD TRADE ISSUE

Issued in conjunction with the 17th Congress of the International Chamber of Commerce, Washington, D. C., April 19-25.

Globe and Laurel—A573

Designed by Robert Baker.
ROTARY PRESS PRINTING.
E. E. Plates of 200 subjects in four panes of 50 each.
1959   *Perf. 11x10½*   Unwmkd.

1129	A573	8c rose lake, *Apr. 20, 1959*	20	1
		Margin block of 4, P#	1.50	

SILVER CENTENNIAL ISSUE

Issued to commemorate the centenary of the discovery of silver at the Comstock Lode, Nevada.

Henry Comstock at Mount Davidson Site—A574
Designed by Robert L. Miller and W. K. Schrage.
ROTARY PRESS PRINTING.
E. E. Plates of 200 subjects in four panes of 50 each.
1959   *Perf. 11x10½*   Unwmkd.

1130	A574	4c black, *June 8, 1959*	10	5
		Margin block of 4, P#	50	

ST. LAWRENCE SEAWAY ISSUE

Issued to commemorate the opening of the St. Lawrence Seaway.

Great Lakes, Maple Leaf and Eagle Emblems—A575
GIORI PRESS PRINTING
Plates of 200 subjects in four panes of 50 each.
1959   *Perf. 11*   Unwmkd.

1131	A575	4c red & dark blue, *June 26, 1959*	10	5
		Margin block of 4, P#	50	
		Pair with full horiz. gtter btwn.		

49-STAR FLAG ISSUE

U. S. Flag, 1959—A576
Designed by Stevan Dohanos.
GIORI PRESS PRINTING
Plates of 200 subjects in four panes of 50 each.
1959   *Perf. 11*   Unwmkd.

1132	A576	4c ocher, dark blue & deep carmine, *July 4, 1959*	10	5
		Margin block of 4, P#	50	

SOIL CONSERVATION ISSUE

Issued as a tribute to farmers and ranchers who use soil and water conservation measures.

Modern Farm—A577
Designed by Walter Hortens.
GIORI PRESS PRINTING
Plates of 200 subjects in four panes of 50 each.
1959   Perf. 11   Unwmkd.
1133 A577 4c blue, green & ocher,
           Aug. 26, 1959   10   5
           Margin block of 4, P#   65

PETROLEUM INDUSTRY ISSUE

Issued to commemorate the centenary of the completion of the nation's first oil well at Titusville, Pa.

Oil Derrick—A578
Designed by Robert Foster.
ROTARY PRESS PRINTING.
E. E. Plates of 200 subjects in four panes of 50 each.
1959   Perf. 10½x11   Unwmkd.
1134 A578 4c brown, Aug. 27, 1959   10   5
           Margin block of 4, P#   50

DENTAL HEALTH ISSUE

Issued to publicize Dental Health and for the centenary of the American Dental Association.

Children
A579
Designed by Charles Henry Carter.
ROTARY PRESS PRINTING.
E. E. Plates of 200 subjects in four panes of 50 each.
1959   Perf. 11x10½   Unwmkd.
1135 A579 4c green, Sept. 14, 1959   10   5
           Margin block of 4, P#   50

CHAMPION OF LIBERTY ISSUE

Issued to honor Ernst Reuter, Mayor of Berlin, 1948-53.

Ernst Reuter
A580
ROTARY PRESS PRINTING.
E. E. Plates of 280 Subjects in four panes of 70 each.
1959, Sept. 29   Perf. 10½x11   Unwmkd.
1136 A580 4c gray   10   5
           Margin block of 4, P#   60

GIORI PRESS PRINTING.
Plates of 288 subjects in four panes of 72 each.
Perf. 11.
1137 A580 8c carmine, ultramarine & ochre 20   12
           Margin block of 4, P#   1.75

DR. EPHRAIM McDOWELL ISSUE.

Issued to honor Dr. Ephraim McDowell (1771–1830) on the 150th anniversary of the first successful ovarian operation in the United States, performed at Danville, Ky., 1809.

Dr. Ephraim McDowell
A581
Designed by Charles R. Chickering.
ROTARY PRESS PRINTING.
E. E. Plates of 280 subjects in four panes of 70 each.
1959   Perf. 10½x11   Unwmkd.
1138 A581 4c rose lake, Dec. 3, 1959   10   5
           Margin block of 4, P#   50
      a. Vert. pair, imperf. btwn.   700.00
      b. Vert. pair, imperf. horiz.   600.00

AMERICAN CREDO ISSUE

Issued to re-emphasize the ideals upon which America was founded and to honor those great Americans who wrote or uttered the credos.

Quotation from Washington's Farewell Address, 1796
A582

POSTAGE, 1960-61, 1960

Benjamin Franklin Quotation
A583

Thomas Jefferson Quotation
A584

Francis Scott Key Quotation
A585

Abraham Lincoln Quotation
A586

Patrick Henry Quotation
A587

Designed by Frank Conley.
GIORI PRESS PRINTING.
Plates of 200 subjects in four panes of 50 each.

1960-61		Perf. 11		Unwmkd.	
1139	A582	4c dark violet blue, & carmine, Jan. 20, 1960		18	5
		Margin block of 4, P#		1.00	
1140	A583	4c olive bister & green, March 31, 1960		18	5
		Margin block of 4, P#		1.00	
1141	A584	4c gray & vermilion, May 18, 1960		18	5
		Margin block of 4, P#		1.00	
1142	A585	4c carmine & dark blue, Sept. 14, 1960		18	5
		Margin block of 4, P#		1.00	
1143	A586	4c magenta & green, Nov. 19, 1960		18	5
		Margin block of 4, P#		1.00	
1144	A587	4c green & brown, Jan. 11, 1961		18	5
		Margin block of 4, P#		1.00	

1144	A587	4c green & brown, Jan. 11, 1961		18	5
		Block of four		72	20
		Margin block of 4, P#		1.00	

BOY SCOUT JUBILEE ISSUE

Issued to commemorate the 50th anniversary of the Boy Scouts of America.

Boy Scout Giving Scout Sign—A588
Designed by Norman Rockwell.
GIORI PRESS PRINTING
Plates of 200 subjects in four panes of 50 each.

1960		Perf. 11		Unwmkd.	
1145	A588	4c red, dark blue & dark bister, Feb. 8, 1960		10	5
		Margin block of 4, P#		50	

OLYMPIC WINTER GAMES ISSUE

Issued to commemorate the opening of the 8th Olympic Winter Games, Squaw Valley, Feb. 18-29, 1960.

Olympic Rings and Snowflake—A589
Designed by Ervine Metzl.
ROTARY PRESS PRINTING.
E. E. Plates of 200 subjects in four panes of 50 each.

1960		Perf. 10½x11		Unwmkd.	
1146	A589	4c dull blue, Feb. 18, 1960		10	5
		Margin block of 4, P#		50	

CHAMPION OF LIBERTY ISSUE

Issued to honor Thomas G. Masaryk, founder and president of Czechoslovakia (1918-35), on the 110th anniversary of his birth.

Thomas G. Masaryk
A590

POSTAGE, 1960   241

ROTARY PRESS PRINTING
E. E. Plates of 280 subjects in four panes of 70 each.

1960		Perf. 10½x11	Unwmkd.	
1147	A590	4c blue, March 7, 1960	10	5
		Margin block of 4, P#	60	
	a.	Vert. pair, imperf. between	2,100.	

GIORI PRESS PRINTING
Plates of 288 subjects in four panes of 72 each.
Perf. 11

1148	A590	8c carmine, ultramarine & ocher, March 7, 1960	20	12
		Margin block of 4, P#	1.75	
	a.	Horiz. pair, imperf. between		

WORLD REFUGEE YEAR ISSUE

Issued to publicize World Refugee Year, July 1, 1959–June 30, 1960.

Family Walking Toward New Life
A591

Designed by Ervine Metzl.

ROTARY PRESS PRINTING.
E. E. Plates of 200 subjects in four panes of 50 each.

1960		Perf. 11x10½	Unwmkd.	
1149	A591	4c gray black, Apr. 7, 1960	10	5
		Margin block of 4, P#	50	

WATER CONSERVATION ISSUE

Issued to stress the importance of water conservation and to commemorate the 7th Watershed Congress, Washington, D. C.

Water: From Watershed to Consumer
A592

Designed by Elmo White.

GIORI PRESS PRINTING.
Plates of 200 subjects in four panes of 50 each.

1960		Perf. 11	Unwmkd.	
1150	A592	4c dark blue, brown orange & green, Apr. 18, 1960	10	5
		Margin block of 4, P#	65	

SEATO ISSUE

Issued to honor the South-East Asia Treaty Organization and to publicize the SEATO Conference, Washington, D.C., May 31–June 3.

SEATO Emblem
A593

Designed by John Maass.

ROTARY PRESS PRINTING
E.E. plates of 280 subjects in four panes of 70 each.

1960		Perf. 10½x11	Unwmkd.	
1151	A593	4c blue, May 31, 1960	10	5
		Margin block of 4, P#	50	
	a.	Vertical pair, imperf. between	225.00	

AMERICAN WOMAN ISSUE

Issued to pay tribute to American women and their accomplishments in civic affairs, education, arts and industry.

Mother and Daughter
A594

Designed by Robert Sivard.

ROTARY PRESS PRINTING
E.E. Plates of 200 subjects in four panes of 50 each.

1960		Perf. 11x10½	Unwmkd.	
1152	A594	4c deep violet, June 2, 1960	10	5
		Margin block of 4, P#	50	

50-STAR FLAG ISSUE

U.S. Flag, 1960
A595

Designed by Stevan Dohanos.
GIORI PRESS PRINTING
Plates of 200 subjects in four panes of 50 each.
1960		Perf. 11		Unwmkd.	
1153	A595	4c dark blue & red, July 4		10	5
		Margin block of 4, P#		50	

PONY EXPRESS CENTENNIAL ISSUE

Issued to commemorate the centenary of the Pony Express.

Pony Express Rider
A596

Designed by Harold von Schmidt.
ROTARY PRESS PRINTING
E. E. Plates of 200 subjects in four panes of 50 each.
1960		Perf. 11x10½		Unwmkd.	
1154	A596	4c sepia, July 19, 1960		10	5
		Margin block of 4, P#		50	

EMPLOY THE HANDICAPPED ISSUE

Issued to promote the employment of the physically handicapped and to publicize the Eighth World Congress of the International Society for the Welfare of Cripples, New York City.

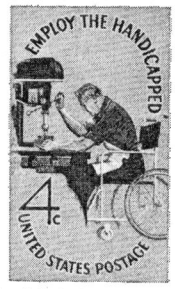

Man in Wheelchair Operating Drill Press
A597

Designed by Carl Bobertz.
ROTARY PRESS PRINTING
E. E. Plates of 200 subjects in four panes of 50 each.
1960		Perf. 10½x11		Unwmkd.	
1155	A597	4c dark blue, Aug. 28, 1960		10	5
		Margin block of 4, P#		50	

WORLD FORESTRY CONGRESS ISSUE

Issued to commemorate the Fifth World Forestry Congress, Seattle, Washington, Aug. 29–Sept. 10.

World Forestry
Congress Seal
A598

ROTARY PRESS PRINTING
E. E. Plates of 200 subjects in four panes of 50 each.
1960, Aug. 29		Perf. 10½x11		Unwmkd.	
1156	A598	4c green		10	5
		Margin block of 4, P#		50	

MEXICAN INDEPENDENCE ISSUE

Issued to commemorate the 150th anniversary of Mexican Independence.

Independence Bell
A599

Designed by Leon Helguera and Charles R. Chickering.
GIORI PRESS PRINTING
Plates of 200 subjects in four panes of 50 each.
1960		Perf. 11		Unwmkd.	
1157	A599	4c green & rose red, Sept. 16, 1960		10	5
		Margin block of 4, P#		50	

U.S.-JAPAN TREATY ISSUE

Issued to commemorate the centenary of the United States-Japan Treaty of Amity and Commerce.

Washington Monument and Cherry Blossoms
A600

POSTAGE, 1960   243

Designed by Gyo Fujikawa.
GIORI PRESS PRINTING
Plates of 200 subjects in four panes of 50 each.
1960, Sept. 28   Perf. 11   Unwmkd.
1158   A600   4c blue & pink   10   5
              Margin block of 4, P#   50

CHAMPION OF LIBERTY ISSUE

Issued to honor Ignacy Jan Paderewski, Polish statesman and musician.

Ignacy Jan Paderewski
A601
ROTARY PRESS PRINTING
E. E. Plates of 280 subjects in four panes of 70 each.
1960, Oct. 8   Perf. 10½x11   Unwmkd.
1159   A601   4c blue   10   5
              Margin block of 4, P#   55

GIORI PRESS PRINTING
Plates of 288 subjects in four panes of 72 each.
Perf. 11
1160   A601   8c carmine, ultramarine & ocher   20   12
              Margin block of 4, P#   1.75

SENATOR TAFT MEMORIAL ISSUE

Issued in memory of Senator Robert A. Taft (1889–1953) of Ohio.

Robert A. Taft
A602
Designed by William K. Schrage.
ROTARY PRESS PRINTING
E. E. Plates of 280 subjects in four panes of 70 each.
1960   Perf. 10½x11   Unwmkd.
1161   A602   4c dull violet, Oct. 16, 1960   10   5
              Margin block of 4, P#   50

WHEELS OF FREEDOM ISSUE

Issued to honor the automotive industry and in connection with the National Automobile Show, Detroit, Oct. 15–23.

Globe and Steering Wheel with Tractor, Car and Truck
A603
Designed by Arnold J. Copeland.
ROTARY PRESS PRINTING
E. E. Plates of 200 subjects in four panes of 50 each.
1960   Perf. 11x10½   Unwmkd.
1162   A603   4c dark blue, Oct. 15, 1960   10   5
              Margin block of 4, P#   50

BOYS' CLUBS OF AMERICA ISSUE

Issued to commemorate the centenary of the Boys' Clubs of America movement.

Profile of Boy
A604
Designed by Charles T. Coiner.
GIORI PRESS PRINTING
Plates of 200 subjects in four panes of 50 each.
1960   Perf. 11   Unwmkd.
1163   A604   4c indigo, slate & rose red,
              Oct. 18, 1960
              Margin block of 4, P#   10   5
                                             50

FIRST AUTOMATED POST OFFICE IN THE U.S.A. ISSUE

Issued to publicize the opening of the first automated post office in the United States at Providence, R.I.

Architect's Sketch of New Post Office, Providence, R.I.
A605

POSTAGE, 1960

Designed by Arnold J. Copeland and
Victor S. McCloskey, Jr.
GIORI PRESS PRINTING
Plates of 200 subjects in four panes of 50 each.
1960		Perf. 11		Unwmkd.	
1164	A605	4c dark blue & carmine, *Oct. 20, 1960*		10	5
		Margin block of 4, P#		50	

CHAMPION OF LIBERTY ISSUE

Issued to honor Baron Karl Gustaf Emil Mannerheim (1867-1951), Marshal and President of Finland.

Baron Gustaf Mannerheim
A606
ROTARY PRESS PRINTING
E. E. Plates of 280 subjects in four panes of 70 each.
1960, Oct. 26		Perf. 10½x11		Unwmkd.	
1165	A606	4c blue		10	5
		Margin block of 4, P#		55	

GIORI PRESS PRINTING
Plates of 288 subjects in four panes of 72 each.
Perf. 11
1166	A606	8c carmine, ultramarine & ocher	20	12
		Margin block of 4, P#	1.75	

CAMP FIRE GIRLS ISSUE

Issued to commemorate the 50th anniversary of the Camp Fire Girls' movement and in connection with the Golden Jubilee Convention celebration of the Camp Fire Girls.

Camp Fire Girls Emblem
A607
Designed by H. Edward Oliver.
GIORI PRESS PRINTING
Plates of 200 subjects in four panes of 50 each.
1960, Nov. 1		Perf. 11		Unwmkd.	
1167	A607	4c dark blue & bright red		10	5
		Margin block of 4, P#		50	

CHAMPION OF LIBERTY ISSUE

Issued to honor Giuseppe Garibaldi (1807-1882), Italian patriot and freedom fighter.

Giuseppe Garibaldi
A608
ROTARY PRESS PRINTING
E. E. Plates of 280 subjects in four panes of 70 each.
1960, Nov. 2		Perf. 10½x11		Unwmkd.	
1168	A608	4c green		10	5
		Margin block of 4, P#		55	

GIORI PRESS PRINTING
Plates of 288 subjects in four panes of 72 each.
Perf. 11
1169	A608	8c carmine, ultramarine & ocher	20	12
		Margin block of 4, P#	1.75	

SENATOR GEORGE MEMORIAL ISSUE

Issued in memory of Senator Walter F. George (1878-1957) of Georgia.

Walter F. George
A609
Designed by William K. Schrage.
ROTARY PRESS PRINTING
E.E. Plates of 280 subjects in four panes of 70 each.
1960		Perf. 10½x11		Unwmkd.	
1170	A609	4c dull violet, *Nov. 5, 1960*		10	5
		Margin block of 4, P#		50	

ANDREW CARNEGIE ISSUE

Issued to honor Andrew Carnegie (1835-1919), industrialist and philanthropist.

Andrew Carnegie
A610

POSTAGE, 1960, 1961

Designed by Charles R. Chickering.
ROTARY PRESS PRINTING
E.E. Plates of 280 subjects in four panes of 70 each.
1960   Perf. 10½x11   Unwmkd.
1171 A610 4c deep claret, Nov. 25, 1960   10   5
            Margin block of 4, P#   50

JOHN FOSTER DULLES MEMORIAL ISSUE

Issued in memory of John Foster Dulles (1888–1959), Secretary of State (1953–1959).

John Foster Dulles
A611
Designed by William K. Schrage.
ROTARY PRESS PRINTING
E. E. Plates of 280 subjects in four panes of 70 each.
1960   Perf. 10½x11   Unwmkd.
1172 A611 4c dull violet, Dec. 6, 1960   10   5
            Margin block of 4, P#   55

ECHO I— COMMUNICATIONS FOR PEACE ISSUE

Issued to commemorate the world's first communications satellite, Echo I, placed in orbit by the National Aeronautics and Space Administration, Aug. 12, 1960.

Radio Waves Connecting Echo I and Earth
A612
Designed by Ervine Metzl.
ROTARY PRESS PRINTING
E. E. Plates of 200 subjects in four panes of 50 each.
1960, Dec. 15   Perf. 11x10½   Unwmkd.
1173 A612 4c deep violet, Dec. 15, 1960   35   12
            Margin block of 4, P#   2.25

CHAMPION OF LIBERTY ISSUE

Issued to honor Mohandas K. Gandhi, leader in India's struggle for independence.

Mahatma Gandhi—A613

ROTARY PRESS PRINTING
E.E. Plates of 280 subjects in four panes of 70 each.
1961, Jan. 26   Perf. 10½x11   Unwmkd.
1174 A613 4c red orange   10   5
            Margin block of 4, P#   55

GIORI PRESS PRINTING
Plates of 288 subjects in four panes of 72 each.
                   Perf. 11
1175 A613 8c carmine, ultramarine & ocher   20   12
            Margin block of 4, P#   2.00

RANGE CONSERVATION ISSUE

Issued to stress the importance of range conservation and to commemorate the meeting of the American Society of Range Management, Washington, D. C. "The Trail Boss" from a drawing by Charles M. Russell is the Society's emblem.

The Trail Boss and Modern Range
614
Designed by Rudolph Wendelin.
GIORI PRESS PRINTING
Plates of 200 subjects in four panes of 50 each.
1961, Feb. 2   Perf. 11   Unwmkd.
1176 A614 4c blue, slate & brown orange   10   5
            Margin block of 4, P#   65

HORACE GREELEY ISSUE

Issued to honor Horace Greeley (1811–1872), publisher and editor.

Horace Greeley
A615
Designed by Charles R. Chickering.
ROTARY PRESS PRINTING
E. E. Plates of 280 subjects in four panes of 70 each.
1961   Perf. 10½x11   Unwmkd.
1177 A615 4c dull violet, Feb. 3, 1961   10   5
            Margin block of 4, P#   55

CIVIL WAR CENTENNIAL ISSUE

Issued to commemorate the centenaries of the firing on Fort Sumter (No. 1178), the Battle of Shiloh (No. 1179), the Battle of Gettysburg (No. 1180), the Battle of the Wilderness (No. 1181) and the surrender at Appomattox (No. 1182).

Sea Coast Gun of 1861—A616

Rifleman at Battle of Shiloh, 1862—A617

Blue and Gray at Gettysburg, 1863—A618

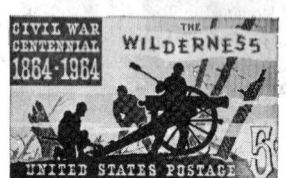

Battle of the Wilderness, 1864—A619

Appomattox, 1865—A620

Designed by Charles R. Chickering (Sumpter),
Noel Sickles (Shiloh),
Roy Gjertson (Gettysburg),
B. Harold Christenson (Wilderness),
Leonard Fellman (Appomattox).

ROTARY PRESS PRINTING

E.E. Plates of 200 subjects in four panes of 50 each.

1961-65		Perf. 11x10½		Unwmkd.	
1178	A616	4c light green, *Apr. 12, 1961*		18	5
		Margin block of 4, P#		1.10	
1179	A617	4c *peach blossom, Apr. 7, 1962*		15	5
		Margin block of 4, P#		1.00	

GIORI PRESS PRINTING

Plates of 200 subjects in four panes of 50 each.

Perf. 11

1180	A618	5c **gray & blue,** *July 1, 1963*	15	5
		Margin block of 4, P#	1.00	
1181	A619	5c **dark red & black,** *May 5, 1964*	15	5
		Margin block of 4, P#	1.00	
		Margin block of 4, Mr. Zip and "Use Zip Code$$	85	
1182	A620	5c **Prus. blue & black,** *Apr. 9, 1965*	15	5
		Margin block of 4, P#	1.10	
		Margin block of 4, Mr. Zip and "Use Zip Code"	90	
	a.	Horiz. pair, imperf. vert.		

KANSAS STATEHOOD ISSUE

Issued to commemorate the centenary of the admission of Kansas to statehood.

Sunflower, Pioneer Couple and Stockade
A621

GIORI PRESS PRINTING

Plates of 200 subjects in four panes of 50 each.

1961		Perf. 11		Unwmkd.	
1183	A621	4c **brown, dark red & green,** *yellow, May 10, 1961*		10	5
		Margin block of 4, P#		55	

SENATOR NORRIS ISSUE

Issued to commemorate the centenary of the birth of Senator George W. Norris (1861-1944), of Nebraska.

Senator George W. Norris and Norris Dam
A622

Designed by C. R. Chickering.

ROTARY PRESS PRINTING

E. E. Plates of 200 subjects in four panes of 50 each.

1961		Perf. 11x10½		Unwmkd.	
1184	A622	4c **blue green,** *July 11, 1961*		10	5
		Margin block of 4, P#		55	

NAVAL AVIATION ISSUE

Issued to commemorate the 50th anniversary of Naval Aviation.

Navy's First Plane (Curtiss A-1 of 1911) and Naval Air Wings
A623
Designed by John Maass.
ROTARY PRESS PRINTING

E.E. Plates of 200 subjects in four panes of 50 each.
1961   Perf. 11x10½   Unwmkd.
1185   A623   4c **blue**, *Aug. 20, 1961*   10   5
              Margin block of 4, P#   55   —
              Pair with full vertical gutter
              between   150.00

WORKMEN'S COMPENSATION ISSUE

Issued to commemorate the 50th anniversary of the first successful Workmen's Compensation Law, enacted by the Wisconsin legislature.

Scales of Justice, Factory, Worker and Family
A624
Designed by Norman Todhunter.
ROTARY PRESS PRINTING

E. E. Plates of 200 subjects in four panes of 50 each.
1961   Perf. 10½x11   Unwmkd.
1186   A624   4c **ultramarine**, *grayish, Sept. 4, 1961*   10   5
              Margin block of 4, P#   55   —
              Margin block of 4, P# inverted   75   —

FREDERIC REMINGTON ISSUE

Issued to commemorate the centenary of the birth of Frederic Remington (1861-1909), artist of the West. The design is from an oil painting, Amon Carter Museum of Western Art, Fort Worth, Texas.

"The Smoke Signal"
A625

Designed by Charles R. Chickering.
GIORI PRESS PRINTING
Panes of 200 subjects in four panes of 50 each.
1961   Perf. 11   Unwmkd.
1187   A625   4c **multicolored**, *Oct. 4, 1961*   12   5
              Margin block of 4, P#   1.00   —

REPUBLIC OF CHINA ISSUE

Issued to commemorate the 50th anniversary of the Republic of China.

Sun Yat-sen
A626
ROTARY PRESS PRINTING

E.E. Plates of 200 subjects in four panes of 50 each.
1961   Perf. 10½x11   Unwmkd.
1188   A626   4c **blue**, *Oct. 10, 1961*   10   5
              Margin block of 4, P#   55   —

NAISMITH-BASKETBALL ISSUE

Issued in honor of basketball and to commemorate the centenary of the birth of James A. Naismith (1861–1939), Canada-born director of physical education, who invented the game in 1891 at Y.M.C.A. College, Springfield, Mass.

Basketball
A627
Designed by Charles R. Chickering.
ROTARY PRESS PRINTING

E.E. Plates of 200 subjects in four panes of 50 each.
1961   Perf. 10½x11   Unwmkd.
1189   A627   4c **brown**, *Nov. 6, 1961*   10   5
              Margin block of 4, P#   55   —

NURSING ISSUE

Issued to honor the nursing profession.

Student Nurse Lighting Candle
A628

Designed by Alfred Charles Parker.
GIORI PRESS PRINTING
Plates of 200 subjects in four panes of 50 each.

1961, Dec. 28		Perf. 11		Unwmkd.	
1190	A628	4c **blue, green, orange & black**		10	5
		Margin block of 4, two P#		70	

NEW MEXICO STATEHOOD ISSUE

Issued to commemorate the 50th anniversary of New Mexico's admission to statehood.

Shiprock
A629

Designed by Robert J. Jones.
GIORI PRESS PRINTING
Plates of 200 subjects in four panes of 50 each.

1962, Jan. 6		Perf. 11		Unwmkd.	
1191	A629	4c **lt. blue, maroon & bister**		10	5
		Margin block of 4, P#		55	

ARIZONA STATEHOOD ISSUE

Issued to commemorate the 50th anniversary of the admission of Arizona to statehood.

Giant Saguaro Cactus
A630

Designed by Jimmie E. Ihms and James M. Chemi.
GIORI PRESS PRINTING
Plates of 200 subjects in four panes of 50 each.

1962, Feb. 14		Perf. 11		Unwmkd.	
1192	A630	4c **carmine, violet blue & green**		10	
		Margin block of 4, P#		65	

PROJECT MERCURY ISSUE

Issued to commemorate the first orbital flight of a U.S. astronaut, Feb. 20, 1962. The flight was made by Lt. Col. John H. Glenn, Jr.

"Friendship 7" Capsule and Globe—A631

GIORI PRESS PRINTING
Plates of 200 subjects in four panes of 50 each.

1962		Perf. 11		Unwmkd.	
1193	A631	4c **dark blue & yellow**, Feb. 20, 1962		10	10
		Margin block of 4, P#		65	

Imperfs. are printers waste.

MALARIA ERADICATION ISSUE

Issued for the World Health Organization's drive to eradicate malaria.

Great Seal of U.S. and W.H.O. Symbol—A632
Designed by Charles R. Chickering.
GIORI PRESS PRINTING
Plates of 200 subjects in four panes of 50 each.

1962		Perf. 11		Unwmkd.	
1194	A632	4c **blue & bister**, March 30, 1962		10	5
		Margin block of 4, P#		55	

CHARLES EVANS HUGHES ISSUE

Issued to commemorate the centenary of the birth of Charles Evans Hughes (1862–1948), Governor of New York, Chief Justice of the U.S.

Charles Evans Hughes—A633

POSTAGE, 1962

Designed by Charles R. Chickering.
ROTARY PRESS PRINTING
E.E. Plates of 200 subjects in four panes of 50 each.
1962   *Perf. 10½x11*   Unwmkd.
1195   A633   4c **buff**, *Apr. 11, 1962*   10   5
     Margin block of 4, P#   55

SEATTLE WORLD'S FAIR ISSUE

Issued to publicize the "Century 21" International Exposition, Seattle, Wash., Apr. 21–Oct. 21.

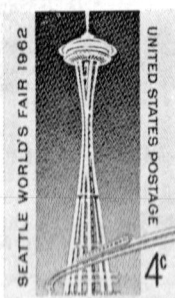

"Space Needle" and Monorail—A634
Designed by John Maass.
GIORI PRESS PRINTING
Plates of 200 subjects in four panes of 50 each.
1962   *Perf. 11*   Unwmkd.
1196   A634   4c **red & dark blue**, *Apr. 25, 1962*   10   5
     Margin block of 4, P#   65

LOUISIANA STATEHOOD ISSUE

Issued to commemorate the sesquicentennial of Louisiana statehood.

Riverboat on the Mississippi—A635
Designed by Norman Todhunter.
GIORI PRESS PRINTING
Plates of 200 subjects in four panes of 50 each.
1962   *Perf. 11*   Unwmkd.
1197   A635   4c **blue, dark slate green & red**,
     Apr. 30, 1962   10   5
     Margin block of 4, P#   55

HOMESTEAD ACT ISSUE

Issued to commemorate the centenary of the Homestead Act.

Sod Hut and Settlers—A636

Designed by Charles R. Chickering.
ROTARY PRESS PRINTING
E.E. Plates of 200 subjects in four panes of 50 each.
1962   *Perf. 11x10½*   Unwmkd.
1198   A636   4c **slate**, *May 20, 1962*   10   5
     Margin block of 4, P#   55

GIRL SCOUTS ISSUE

Issued to commemorate the 50th anniversary of the Girl Scouts of America.

Senior Girl Scout and Flag—A637
Designed by Ward Brackett.
ROTARY PRESS PRINTING
E.E. Plates of 200 subjects in four panes of 50 each.
1962   *Perf. 11x10½*   Unwmkd.
1199   A637   4c **rose red**, *July 24, 1962*   10   5
     Margin block of 4, P#   55
     Pair with full vertical gutter
     between   250.00

SENATOR BRIEN McMAHON ISSUE

Issued to honor Sen. Brien McMahon (1903–1952) of Connecticut for his role in opening the way to peaceful uses of atomic energy through the Atomic Energy Act establishing the Atomic Energy Commission.

Brien McMahon and Atomic Symbol—A638
Designed by V. S. McCloskey, Jr.
ROTARY PRESS PRINTING
E.E. Plates of 200 subjects in four panes of 50 each.
1962   *Perf 11x10½*   Unwmkd.
1200   A638   4c **purple**, *July 28, 1962*   10   5
     Margin block of 4, P#   65

APPRENTICESHIP ISSUE

Issued to publicize the National Apprenticeship Program and to commemorate the 25th anniversary of the National Apprenticeship Act.

Machinist Handing Micrometer to Apprentice
A639

Designed by Robert Geissmann.
ROTARY PRESS PRINTING
E.E. Plates of 200 subjects in four panes of 50 each.
1962   Perf. 11x10½   Unwmkd.
1201 A639 4c yellow bister, Aug. 31, 1962   10   5
             Margin block of 4, P#   55

SAM RAYBURN ISSUE

Issued to honor Sam Rayburn (1882–1961), Speaker of the House of Representatives.

Sam Rayburn and Capitol
A640
Designed by Robert L. Miller.
GIORI PRESS PRINTING
Plates of 200 subjects in four panes of 50 each.
1962, Sept. 16   Perf. 11   Unwmkd.
1202 A640 4c dark blue & red brown   10   5
             Margin block of 4, P#   55

DAG HAMMARSKJOLD ISSUE

Issued to honor Dag Hammarskjold, Secretary General of the United Nations, 1953–61.

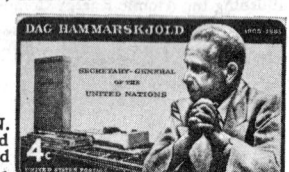

U.N. Headquarters and Dag Hammarskjold
A641
Designed by Herbert M. Sanborn.
GIORI PRESS PRINTING
Plates of 200 subjects in four panes of 50 each.
1962   Perf. 11   Unwmkd.
1203 A641 4c black, brown & yellow, Oct. 23, 1962   10   5
             Margin block of 4, two P#   70

Hammarskjold Special Printing

No. 1204 was issued following discovery of No. 1203 with yellow background inverted.
GIORI PRESS PRINTING
Plates of 200 subjects in four panes of 50 each.
1962   Perf. 11   Unwmkd.
1204 A641 4c black, brown & yellow (yellow
             inverted), Nov. 16, 1962   12   8
             Margin block of 4, two P#, yellow #
             inverted   4.00

The inverted yellow impression is shifted to the right in relation to the black and brown impression. Stamps of first vertical row of UL and LL panes show no yellow at left side for a space of 11–11½mm. in from the perforations. Stamps of first vertical row of UR and LR panes show vertical no-yellow strip 9¾mm. wide, covering UN Building. On all others, the vertical no-yellow strip is 3½mm. wide, and touches UN Building.

CHRISTMAS ISSUE

Wreath and Candles
A642
Designed by Jim Crawford.
GIORI PRESS PRINTING
Plates of 400 subjects in four panes of 100 each. Panes of 90 and 100 exist without plate numbers due to provisional use of smaller paper.
1962   Perf. 11   Unwmkd.
1205 A642 4c green & red, Nov. 1, 1962   10   5
             Margin block of 4, P#   50

HIGHER EDUCATION ISSUE

Issued to publicize higher education's role in American cultural and industrial development in connection with the centenary celebrations of the signing of the law creating land-grant colleges and universities.

Map of U.S. and Lamp
A643
Designed by Henry K. Bencsath.
GIORI PRESS PRINTING
Plates of 200 subjects in panes of 50 each.
1962   Perf. 11   Unwmkd.
1206 A643 4c blue green & black, Nov. 14, 1962   10   5
             Margin block of 4, two P#   55

WINSLOW HOMER ISSUE

Issued to honor Winslow Homer (1836–1910), painter, showing his oil, "Breezing Up," which hangs in the National Gallery, Washington, D. C.

"Breezing Up"
A644
Designed by Victor S. McCloskey, Jr.
GIORI PRESS PRINTING
Plates of 200 subjects in four panes of 50 each.
1962   Perf. 11   Unwmkd.
1207 A644 4c multicolored, Dec. 15, 1962   15   5
             Margin block of 4, P#   1.00
       a. Horiz. pair, imperf. between

FLAG ISSUE

Flag over White House
A645
Designed by Robert J. Jones.
GIORI PRESS PRINTING
Plates of 400 subjects in four panes of 100 each.

1963–66		Perf. 11		Unwmkd.	
1208	A645	5c blue & red, *Jan. 9, 1963*		12	5
		Margin block of 4, P#		55	
		a. Tagged, *Aug. 25, 1966*		25	5
		b. Horiz. pair, imperf. between, tagged		900.00	
		Pair with full horiz. gutter between		———	

REGULAR ISSUE

Andrew Jackson
A646

George Washington
A650
Designed by William K. Schrage.
ROTARY PRESS PRINTING
E. E. Plates of 400 subjects in four panes of 100 each.

1962–66		Perf. 11x10½		Unwmkd.	
1209	A646	1c green, *March 22, 1963*		5	5
		Margin block of 4, P#		25	
		a. Tagged, *July 6, 1966*		6	5
		Pair with full vert. gutter btwn.		———	
1213	A650	5c dark blue gray, *Nov. 23, 1962*		12	5
		Margin block of 4, P#		75	
		a. Booklet pane of 5 + label		2.00	75
		b. Tagged, *Oct. 28, 1963*		65	30
		c. As "a," tagged, *Oct. 28, 1963*		1.25	50
		Pair with full vert. gutter btwn.		———	

COIL STAMPS (Rotary Press)

1962–66		Perf. 10 Vertically			
1225	A646	1c green, *May 31, 1963*		20	5
		Pair		40	10
		Joint line pair		85	12
		a. Tagged, *July 6, 1966*		12	5
1229	A650	5c dark blue gray, *Nov. 23, 1962*		1.75	5
		Pair		3.50	10
		Joint line pair		4.75	15
		a. Tagged, *Oct. 28, 1963*		1.25	6
		b. Imperf., pair		350.00	

See Luminescence note in "Information for Collectors" at front of book.

CAROLINA CHARTER ISSUE

Issued to commemorate the tercentenary of the Carolina Charter granting to eight Englishmen lands extending coast-to-coast roughly along the present border of Virginia to the north and Florida to the south. Original charter on display at Raleigh.

First Page of Carolina Charter
A662
Designed by Robert L. Miller.
GIORI PRESS PRINTING
Plates of 200 subjects in four panes of 50 each.

1963		Perf. 11		Unwmkd.	
1230	A662	5c dk. car. & brown, *Apr. 6, 1963*		12	5
		Margin block of 4, P#		60	

FOOD FOR PEACE–FREEDOM FROM HUNGER ISSUE

Issued for the American "Food for Peace" program and the "Freedom from Hunger" campaign of the U.N. Food and Agriculture Organization.

Wheat
A663
Designed by Stevan Dohanos.
GIORI PRESS PRINTING
Plates of 200 subjects in four panes of 50 each.

1963		Perf. 11		Unwmkd.	
1231	A663	5c green, buff & red, *June 4, 1963*		12	5
		Margin block of 4, P#		60	

WEST VIRGINIA STATEHOOD ISSUE

Issued to commemorate the centenary of the admission of West Virginia to statehood.

Map of West Virginia and State Capitol
A664

252   POSTAGE, 1963

Designed by Dr. Dwight Mutchler.
GIORI PRESS PRINTING
Plates of 200 subjects in four panes of 50 each.
1963   Perf. 11   Unwmkd.
1232   A664   5c green, red & black, *June 20, 1963*   12   5
              Margin block of 4, P#   60

EMANCIPATION PROCLAMATION ISSUE

Issued to commemorate the centenary of President Lincoln's Emancipation Proclamation freeing about 3,000,000 slaves in 10 southern states.

Severed Chain
A665
Designed by Georg Olden.
GIORI PRESS PRINTING
Plates of 200 subjects in four panes of 50 each.
1963, Aug. 16   Perf. 11   Unwmkd.
1233   A665   5c dark blue, black & red   12   5
              Margin block of 4, P#   60

ALLIANCE FOR PROGRESS ISSUE

Issued to commemorate the second anniversary of the Alliance for Progress, which aims to stimulate economic growth and raise living standards in Latin America.

Alliance Emblem
A666
Designed by William K. Schrage.
GIORI PRESS PRINTING
Plates of 200 subjects in four panes of 50 each.
1963   Perf. 11   Unwmkd.
1234   A666   5c ultramarine & green, *Aug. 17, 1963*   12   5
              Margin block of 4, P#   60

CORDELL HULL ISSUE

Issued to honor Cordell Hull (1871–1955), Secretary of State (1933–44).

Cordell Hull
A667

Designed by Robert J. Jones.
ROTARY PRESS PRINTING
E.E. Plates of 200 subjects in four panes of 50 each.
1963   Perf. 10½x11   Unwmkd.
1235   A667   5c blue green, *Oct. 5, 1963*   12   5
              Margin block of 4, P#   60

ELEANOR ROOSEVELT ISSUE

Issued to honor Mrs. Franklin D. Roosevelt (1884–1962).

Eleanor Roosevelt
A668
Designed by Robert L. Miller.
ROTARY PRESS PRINTING
E. E. Plates of 200 subjects in four panes of 50 each.
1963, Oct. 11   Perf. 11x10½   Unwmkd.
1236   A668   5c bright purple   12   5
              Margin block of 4, P#   60

SCIENCE ISSUE

Issued to honor the sciences and in connection with the centenary of the National Academy of Science.

"The Universe"
A669
Designed by Antonio Frasconi.
GIORI PRESS PRINTING
Plates of 200 subjects in four panes of 50 each.
1963   Perf. 11   Unwmkd.
1237   A669   5c Prussian blue & black, *Oct. 14, 1963*   12   5
              Margin block of 4, P#   60

CITY MAIL DELIVERY ISSUE

Issued to commemorate the centenary of free city mail delivery.

Letter Carrier, 1863
A670

Designed by Norman Rockwell.
GIORI PRESS PRINTING
Plates of 200 subjects in four panes of 50 each.
Tagged

1963			Perf. 11		Unwmkd.	
1238	A670	5c	gray, dk. blue & red, Oct. 26, 1963		12	5
			Margin block of 4, P#		60	—

RED CROSS CENTENARY ISSUE

Issued to commemorate the centenary of the International Red Cross.

Cuban Refugees on S.S. Morning Light and
Red Cross Flag—A671
Designed by Victor S. McCloskey, Jr.
GIORI PRESS PRINTING
Plates of 200 subjects in four panes of 50 each.

1963			Perf. 11		Unwmkd.	
1239	A671	5c	bluish black & red, Oct. 29, 1963		12	5
			Margin block of 4, P#		60	—

CHRISTMAS ISSUE

National Christmas Tree
and White House
A672

Designed by Lily Spandorf; modified by
Norman Todhunter.
GIORI PRESS PRINTING
Plates of 400 subjects in four panes of 100 each.

1963			Perf. 11		Unwmkd.	
1240	A672	5c	dk. blue, bluish black & red, Nov. 1, 1963		12	5
			Margin block of 4, P#		60	—
		a.	Tagged, Nov. 2, 1963		1.00	40
			Pair with full horiz. gutter between		—	

JOHN JAMES AUDUBON ISSUE

Issued to honor John James Audubon (1785–1851) ornithologist and artist. The birds pictured are actually Collie's magpie jays.

"Columbia Jays"
by Audubon
A673

Designed by Robert L. Miller.
GIORI PRESS PRINTING
Plates of 200 subjects in four panes of 50 each.

1963			Perf. 11		Unwmkd.	
1241	A673	5c	dark blue & multicolored, Dec. 7, 1963		12	5
			Margin block of 4, P#		60	—

SAM HOUSTON ISSUE

Issued to commemorate the centenary of the death of Sam Houston (1793–1863), soldier, president of Texas, U.S. senator.

Sam Houston
A674

Designed by Tom Lea.
ROTARY PRESS PRINTING
E.E. Plates of 200 subjects in four panes of 50 each.

1964			Perf. 10½x11		Unwmkd.	
1242	A674	5c	black, Jan. 10, 1964		12	5
			Margin block of 4, P#		60	—
			Margin block of 4, Mr. Zip and "Use Zip Code"		50	—

CHARLES M. RUSSELL ISSUE

Issued to commemorate the centenary of the birth of Charles M. Russell (1864–1926), painter. The design is from a painting, Thomas Gilcrease Institute of American History and Art, Tulsa, Okla.

"Jerked Down"
A675

Designed by William K. Schrage.
GIORI PRESS PRINTING
Plates of 200 subjects in four panes of 50 each.

1964			Perf. 11		Unwmkd.	
1243	A675	5c	multicolored, March 19, 1964		15	5
			Margin block of 4, P#		75	—
			Margin block of 4, Mr. Zip and "Use Zip Code"		75	—

NEW YORK WORLD'S FAIR ISSUE

Issued to publicize the New York World's Fair, 1964–65.

Mall with Unisphere and "Rocket Thrower" by
Donald De Lue
A676
Designed by Robert J. Jones.
ROTARY PRESS PRINTING
E.E. Plates of 200 subjects in four panes of 50 each.
1964   Perf. 11x10½   Unwmkd.
1244 A676 5c blue green, *Apr. 22, 1964*   12   5
             On cover, Expo. station canc.   15
             Margin block of 4, P#   60   —
             Margin block of 4, Mr. Zip
                and "Use Zip Code"   55   —

JOHN MUIR ISSUE

Issued to honor John Muir (1838–1914), naturalist and conservationist.

John Muir and Redwood Forest
A677
Designed by Rudolph Wendelin.
GIORI PRESS PRINTING
Plates of 200 subjects in four panes of 50 each.
1964   Perf. 11   Unwmkd.
1245 A677 5c brown, green, yel. grn. & olive,
                 Apr. 29, 1964   12   5
             Margin block of 4, P#   60   —

KENNEDY MEMORIAL ISSUE

Issued in memory of President John Fitzgerald Kennedy, 1917–63.

John F. Kennedy and Eternal Flame
A678

Designed by Raymond Loewy/William Snaith, Inc.
Photograph by William S. Murphy.
ROTARY PRESS PRINTING
E.E. Plates of 200 subjects in four panes of 50 each.
1964   Perf. 11x10½
1246 A678 5c blue gray, *May 29, 1964*   12   5
             Margin block of 4, P#   60   —

NEW JERSEY TERCENTENARY ISSUE

Issued to commemorate the 300th anniversary of English colonization of New Jersey. The design is from a mural by Howard Pyle in the Essex County Courthouse, Newark, N. J.

Philip Carteret Landing at Elizabethtown,
and Map of New Jersey
A679
Designed by Douglas Allen.
ROTARY PRESS PRINTING
E. E. Plates of 200 subjects in four panes of 50 each.
1964   Perf. 10½x11   Unwmkd.
1247 A679 5c brt. ultramarine, *June 15, 1964* 12   5
             Margin block of 4, P#   60   —
             Margin block of 4, Mr. Zip and
                "Use Zip Code"   50   —

NEVADA STATEHOOD ISSUE

Issued to commemorate the centenary of the admission of Nevada to statehood.

Virginia City and Map of Nevada
A680
Designed by William K. Schrage.
GIORI PRESS PRINTING
Plates of 200 subjects in four panes of 50 each.
1964   Perf. 11
1248 A680 5c red, yellow & blue, *July 22, 1964* 12   5
             Margin block of 4, P#   60   —
             Margin block of 4, Mr. Zip and
                "Use Zip Code"   50   —

POSTAGE, 1964

REGISTER AND VOTE ISSUE

Issued to publicize the campaign to draw more voters to the polls.

Flag
A681
Designed by Victor S. McCloskey, Jr.
GIORI PRESS PRINTING
Plates of 200 subjects in four panes of 50 each.

1964		Perf. 11		Unwmkd.	
1249	A681	5c dk. blue & red, *Aug. 1, 1964*		12	5
		Margin block of 4, P#		60	
		Margin block of 4, Mr. Zip and "Use Zip Code"		50	

SHAKESPEARE ISSUE

Issued to commemorate the 400th anniversary of the birth of William Shakespeare (1564-1616).

William Shakespeare
A682
Designed by Douglas Gorsline.
ROTARY PRESS PRINTING
E. E. Plates of 200 subjects in four panes of 50 each.

1964		Perf. 10½x11		Unwmkd.	
1250	A682	5c black brown, tan, *Aug. 14, 1964*		12	5
		Margin block of 4, P#		60	
		Margin block of 4, Mr. Zip and "Use Zip Code"		50	

DOCTORS MAYO ISSUE

Issued to honor Dr. William James Mayo (1861-1939) and his brother, Dr. Charles Horace Mayo (1865-1939), surgeons who founded the Mayo Foundation for Medical Education and Research in affiliation with the University of Minnesota at Rochester, Minn. Heads on stamp are from a sculpture by James Earle Fraser.

Drs. William and
Charles Mayo
A683

ROTARY PRESS PRINTING

E.E. Plates of 200 subjects in four panes of 50 each.

1964		Perf. 10½x11		Unwmkd.	
1251	A683	5c green, *Sept. 11, 1964*		12	5
		Margin block of 4, P#		60	
		Margin block of 4, Mr. Zip and "Use Zip Code"		50	

AMERICAN MUSIC ISSUE

Issued in tribute to American Music on the 50th anniversary of the founding of the American Society of Composers, Authors and Publishers (ASCAP).

Lute, Horn, Laurel, Oak and Music Score
A684
Designed by Bradbury Thompson.
GIORI PRESS PRINTING
Plates of 200 subjects in four panes of 50 each.

1964		Perf. 11		Unwmkd.	
		Gray Paper with Blue Threads			
1252	A684	5c red, black & blue, *Oct. 15, 1964*		12	5
		Margin block of 4, P#		60	
		Margin block of 4, Mr. Zip and "Use Zip Code"		50	
	a.	Blue omitted		1,500.	

HOMEMAKERS ISSUE

Issued to honor American women as homemakers and to commemorate the 50th anniversary of the passage of the Smith-Lever Act. By providing economic experts under an extension service of the U.S. Department of Agriculture, this legislation helped to improve homelife.

Farm Scene Sampler
A685
Designed by Norman Todhunter.
Plates of 200 subjects in four panes of 50 each.
Engraved (Giori Press); Background Lithographed

1964		Perf. 11		Unwmkd.	
1253	A685	5c multicolored, *Oct. 26, 1964*		12	5
		Margin block of 4, P#		60	
		Margin block of 4, Mr. Zip and "Use Zip Code"		50	

CHRISTMAS ISSUE

Holly
A686

Mistletoe
A687

Poinsettia
A688

Sprig of Conifer
A689

Designed by Thomas F. Naegele.
GIORI PRESS PRINTING
Plates of 400 subjects in four panes of 100 each. Panes contain 25 subjects each of Nos. 1254–1257

1964			Perf. 11	Unwmkd.	
1254	A686	5c	**green, carmine & black,** *Nov. 9*	50	5
			Margin block of 4, P# adjoining #1254	3.25	—
			Margin block of 4, Mr. Zip and "Use Zip Code" adjoining # 1254	3.00	—
		a.	Tagged, *Nov. 10*	1.50	50
1255	A687	5c	**carmine, green & black,** *Nov. 9*	50	5
			Margin block of 4, P# adjoining #1255	3.25	—
			Margin block of 4, Mr. Zip and "Use Zip Code" adjoining # 1255	3.00	—
		a.	Tagged, *Nov. 10*	1.50	50
1256	A688	5c	**carmine, green & black,** *Nov. 9*	50	5
			Margin block of 4, P# adjoining #1256	3.25	—
			Margin block of 4, Mr. Zip and "Use Zip Code" adjoining #1256	3.00	—
		a.	Tagged, *Nov. 10*	1.50	50
1257	A689	5c	**black, green & carmine,** *Nov. 9*	50	5
			Margin block of 4, P# adjoining #1257	3.25	—
			Margin block of 4, Mr. Zip and "Use Zip Code" adjoining #1257	3.00	—
		a.	Tagged, *Nov. 10*	1.50	50
		b.	Block of four, #1254-1257	2.75	1.25
		c.	Block of four, tagged	6.50	3.00

VERRAZANO-NARROWS BRIDGE ISSUE

Issued to commemorate the opening of the Verrazano-Narrows Bridge connecting Staten Island and Brooklyn.

Verrazano-Narrows Bridge and Map of New York Bay
A690

ROTARY PRESS PRINTING
E.E. Plates of 200 subjects in four panes of 50 each.

1964			Perf. 10½x11	Unwmkd	
1258	A690	5c	**blue green,** *Nov. 21*	12	5
			Margin block of 4, P#	60	—
			Margin block of 4, Mr. Zip and "Use Zip Code"	50	—

FINE ARTS ISSUE

Abstract Design by Stuart Davis
A691

GIORI PRESS PRINTING
Plates of 200 subjects in four panes of 50 each.

1964			Perf. 11	Unwmkd	
1259	A691	5c	**ultra., black & dull red,** *Dec. 2*	12	5
			Margin block of 4, two P#	75	—
			Margin block of 4, Mr. Zip and "Use Zip Code"	50	—

AMATEUR RADIO ISSUE

Issued to honor the radio amateurs on the 50th anniversary of the American Radio Relay League.

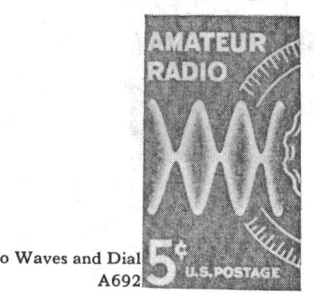

Radio Waves and Dial
A692

Designed by Emil J. Willett.
ROTARY PRESS PRINTING
E.E. Plates of 200 subjects in four panes of 50 each.

1964			Perf. 10½x11	Unwmkd	
1260	A692	5c	**red lilac,** *Dec. 15*	12	5
			Margin block of 4, P#	75	—
			Margin block of 4, Mr. Zip and "Use Zip Code"	50	—

BATTLE OF NEW ORLEANS ISSUE

Issued to commemorate the sesquicentennial of the Battle of New Orleans, Chalmette Plantation, Jan. 8–18 1815, which established 150 years of peace and friendship between the United States and Great Britain.

General Andrew Jackson and Sesquicentennial Medal
A693

POSTAGE, 1965

Designed by Robert J. Jones.
GIORI PRESS PRINTING
Plates of 200 subjects in four panes of 50 each.
1965   Perf. 11   Unwmkd.
1261 A693 5c dp. carmine, violet blue & gray,
              Jan. 8   12   5
              Margin block of 4, P#   75   —
              Margin block of 4, Mr. Zip and
                 "Use Zip Code"   50   —

PHYSICAL FITNESS—SOKOL ISSUE

Issued to publicize the importance of physical fitness and to commemorate the centenary of the founding of the Sokol (athletic) organization in America.

Discus Thrower
A694

Designed by Norman Todhunter.
GIORI PRESS PRINTING
Plates of 200 subjects in four panes of 50 each.
1965   Perf. 11   Unwmkd.
1262 A694 5c maroon & black, Feb. 15   12   5
              Margin block of 4, P#   75   —
              Margin block of 4, Mr. Zip and
                 "Use Zip Code"   50   —

CRUSADE AGAINST CANCER ISSUE

Issued to publicize the "Crusade Against Cancer" and to stress the importance of early diagnosis.

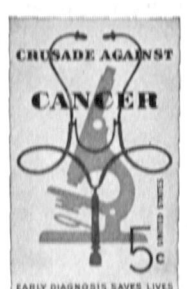

Microscope and Stethoscope
A695

Designed by Stevan Dohanos.
GIORI PRESS PRINTING
Plates of 200 subjects in four panes of 50 each.
1965   Perf. 11   Unwmkd.
1263 A695 5c black, purple & red orange, Apr. 1   12   5
              Margin block of 4, two P#   75   —
              Margin block of 4, Mr. Zip and "Use
                 Zip Code"   50   —

CHURCHILL MEMORIAL ISSUE

Issued in memory of Sir Winston Spencer Churchill (1874–1965), British statesman and World War II leader.

Winston Churchill
A696

Designed by Richard Hurd.
ROTARY PRESS PRINTING
E.E. Plates of 200 subjects in four panes of 50 each.
1965   Perf. 10½x11   Unwmkd.
1264 A696 5c black, May 13   12   5
              Margin block of 4, P#   75   —
              Margin block of 4, Mr. Zip and "Use
                 Zip Code"   50   —

MAGNA CARTA ISSUE

Issued to commemorate the 750th anniversary of the Magna Carta, the basis of English and American common law.

Procession of Barons and King John's Crown
A697

Designed by Brook Temple.
GIORI PRESS PRINTING
Plates of 200 subjects in four panes of 50 each.
1965   Perf. 11   Unwmkd.
1265 A697 5c black, yellow ocher & red lilac,
              June 15   12   5
              Margin block of 4, two P#   75   —
              Margin block of 4, Mr. Zip and "Use
                 Zip Code"   50   —
              Corner block of 4, black P# omitted   —

INTERNATIONAL COOPERATION YEAR ISSUE

Issued for the International Cooperation Year, 1965, and to commemorate the 20th anniversary of the United Nations.

International Cooperation Year Emblem
A698

Designed by Herbert M. Sanborn and Olav S. Mathiesen.
GIORI PRESS PRINTING
Plates of 200 subjects in four panes of 50 each.

1965			Perf. 11	Unwmkd.	
1266	A698	5c	dull blue & black, *June 26*	12	5
			Margin block of 4, P#	75	
			Margin block of 4, Mr. Zip and "Use Zip Code"	50	

SALVATION ARMY ISSUE

Issued to commemorate the centenary of the founding of the Salvation Army by William Booth in London.

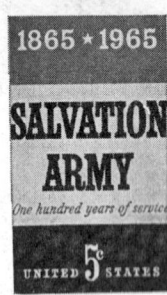

A699
Designed by Sam Marsh.
GIORI PRESS PRINTING
Plates of 200 subjects in four panes of 50 each.

1965			Perf. 11	Unwmkd.	
1267	A699	5c	red, black & dark blue, *July 2*	12	5
			Margin block of 4, P#	75	
			Margin block of 4, Mr. Zip and "Use Zip Code"	50	

DANTE ISSUE

Issued to commemorate the 700th anniversary of the birth of Dante Alighieri (1265–1321), Italian poet.

Dante after a 16th Century Painting
A700
Designed by Douglas Gorsline.
ROTARY PRESS PRINTING
E. E. Plates of 200 subjects in four panes of 50 each.

1965			Perf. 10½x11	Unwmkd.	
1268	A700	5c	maroon, *July 17*	12	5
			Margin block of 4, P#	75	
			Margin block of 4, Mr. Zip and "Use Zip Code"	50	

HERBERT HOOVER ISSUE

Issued in memory of President Herbert Clark Hoover (1874–1964).

Herbert Hoover
A701

Designed by Norman Todhunter; photograph by Fabian Bachrach, Sr.
ROTARY PRESS PRINTING
E.E. Plates of 200 subjects in four panes of 50 each.

1965			Perf. 10½x11	Unwmkd.	
1269	A701	5c	rose red, *Aug. 10*	12	5
			Margin block of 4, P#	75	
			Margin block of 4, Mr. Zip and "Use Zip Code"	50	

ROBERT FULTON ISSUE

Issued to commemorate the 200th anniversary of the birth of Robert Fulton (1765–1815), inventor of the first commercial steamship.

Robert Fulton and the Clermont
A702

Designed by John Maass; bust by Jean Antoine Houdon.
GIORI PRESS PRINTING
Plates of 200 subjects in four panes of 50 each.

1965			Perf. 11	Unwmkd.	
1270	A702	5c	black & blue, *Aug. 19*	12	5
			Margin block of 4, P#	75	
			Margin block of 4, Mr. Zip and "Use Zip Code"	50	

FLORIDA SETTLEMENT ISSUE

Issued to commemorate the 400th anniversary of the settlement of Florida, and the first permanent European settlement in the continental United States, St. Augustine, Fla. Similar stamp issued by Spain, No. 1312.

Spanish Explorer, Royal Flag of Spain and Ships
A703

Designed by Brook Temple.
GIORI PRESS PRINTING
Plates of 200 subjects with four panes of 50 each.

1965		Perf. 11	Unwmkd.		
1271	A703	5c red, yellow & black, *Aug. 28*		12	5
		Margin block of 4, three P#	1.00		
		Margin block of 4, Mr. Zip and "Use Zip Code"	55		
	a.	Yellow omitted	600.00		

TRAFFIC SAFETY ISSUE

Issued to publicize traffic safety and the prevention of traffic accidents.

Traffic Signal
A704

Designed by Richard F. Hurd.
GIORI PRESS PRINTING
Plates of 200 subjects in four panes of 50 each.

1965		Perf. 11	Unwmkd.		
1272	A704	5c emerald, black & red, *Sept. 3*		12	5
		Margin block of 4, two P#	1.00		
		Margin block of 4, Mr. Zip and "Use Zip Code"	55		

JOHN SINGLETON COPLEY ISSUE

Issued to honor John Singleton Copley (1738–1815), painter. The portrait of the artist's daughter is from the oil painting "The Copley Family," which hangs in the National Gallery of Art, Washington, D.C.

Elizabeth Clarke Copley
A705

Designed by John Carter Brown.
GIORI PRESS PRINTING
Plates of 200 subjects in four panes of 50 each.

1965		Perf. 11	Unwmkd.		
1273	A705	5c black, brown & olive, *Sept. 17*		15	5
		Margin block of 4, P#	1.25		
		Margin block of 4, Mr. Zip and "Use Zip Code"	80		

INTERNATIONAL TELECOM-MUNICATION UNION ISSUE

Issued to commemorate the centenary of the International Telecommunication Union.

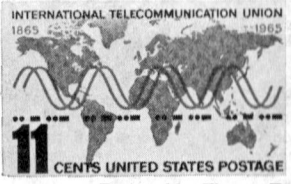

Galt Projection
World Map and
Radio Sine Wave
A706

Designed by Thomas F. Naegele.
GIORI PRESS PRINTING
Plates of 200 subjects with four panes of 50 each.

1965		Perf. 11	Unwmkd.		
1274	A706	11c black, carmine & bister, *Oct. 6*		50	25
		Margin block of 4, 2 P#	9.00		
		Margin block of 4, Mr. Zip and "Use Zip Code"	4.00		

ADLAI STEVENSON ISSUE

Issued in memory of Adlai Ewing Stevenson (1900–65), governor of Illinois, U.S. ambassador to the U.N.

Adlai E. Stevenson
A707

Designed by George Samerjan; photograph by Philippe Halsman.
LITHOGRAPHED, ENGRAVED (Giori)
Plates of 200 subjects in four panes of 50 each.

1965		Perf. 11	Unwmkd.		
1275	A707	5c pale blue, black, carmine & violet blue, *Oct. 23*		12	5
		Margin block of 4, P#	75		

CHRISTMAS ISSUE

Angel with Trumpet, 1840
Weather Vane
A708

Designed by Robert Jones after a watercolor by Lucille Gloria Chabot of the 1840 weather vane from the People's Methodist Church, Newburyport, Mass.
GIORI PRESS PRINTING
Plates of 400 subjects in four panes of 100 each.

1965		Perf. 11	Unwmkd.		
1276	A708	5c carmine, dark olive green & bister, *Nov. 2*		12	5
		Margin block of 4, P#	60		
		Margin block of 4, Mr. Zip and "Use Zip Code"	50		
		Pair with full vert. gutter btwn.			
	a.	Tagged, *Nov. 15*		50	15

PROMINENT AMERICANS ISSUE

Thomas Jefferson
A710

Albert Gallatin
A711

Oliver Wendell Holmes
A720

George Catlett Marshall
A721

Frank Lloyd Wright and Guggenheim Museum, New York
A712

Francis Parkman
A713

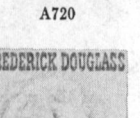
Frederick Douglass
A722

John Dewey
A723

Abraham Lincoln
A714

George Washington
A715

Thomas Paine
A724

Lucy Stone
A725

George Washington (redrawn)
A715a

Franklin D. Roosevelt
A716

Eugene O'Neill
A726

John Bassett Moore
A727

Designers: 1c, Robert Geissmann, after portrait by Rembrandt Peale. 1¼c, Robert Gallatin. 2c, Patricia Amarantides; photograph by Blackstone-Shelburne. 3c, Bill Hyde. 4c, Bill Hyde; photograph by Mathew Brady. 5c, Bill Hyde, after portrait by Rembrandt Peale. 5c, No 1283B, Redrawn by Stevan Dohanos. 6c, 30c, Richard L Clark. 8c, Frank Sebastiano; photograph by Philipp Halsman. 10c, Lester Beall. 12c, Norman Todhunter 13c, Stevan Dohanos; photograph by Jacques Lowe. 15c Richard F. Hurd. 20c, Robert Geissmann. 25c, Walte DuBois Richards. 40c, Robert Geissmann, after portrait by John Wesley Jarvis. 50c, Mark English. $1, Norman Todhunter. $5, Tom Laufer.

ROTARY PRESS PRINTING

E.E. Plates of 400 subjects in four panes of 100 each.

Albert Einstein
A717

Andrew Jackson
A718

1965–78   Perf. 11x10½, 10½x11   Unwmkd

Types of 15c:
I. Necktie barely touches coat at bottom; crosshatching of tie strong a complete. Flag of "5" is true horizontal. Crosshatching of "15" is colorle when visible.
II. Necktie does not touch coat at bottom; LL to UR crosshatching lir strong, UL to LR lines very faint. Flag of "5" slants down slightly at rig Crosshatching of "15" is colored and visible when magnified.
A third type, used only for No. 1288B, is smaller in overall size and "15c" ¾mm. closer to head.

Henry Ford and 1909 Model T
A718a

John F. Kennedy
A719

POSTAGE, 1965–78

1278	A710	1c **green,** tagged, *Jan. 12, 1968*	5	5
		Margin block of 4, P#	25	
		Margin block of 4, "Use Zip Codes"	20	—
		Margin block of 6, "Mail Early in the Day"	32	
	a.	Booklet pane of 8, *Jan. 12, 1968*	1.00	25
	b.	Bklt. pane of 4 + 2 labels, *May 10, 1971*	75	20
	c.	Untagged (Bureau precanceled)		7
1279	A711	1¼c **light green,** *Jan. 30, 1967*	10	5
		Margin block of 4, P#	25.00	
1280	A712	2c **dark blue gray,** tagged, *June 8, 1966*	5	5
		Margin block of 4, P#	30	
		Margin block of 4, "Use Zip Codes"	20	—
		Margin block of 6, "Mail Early in the Day"	32	
	a.	Bklt. pane of 5 + label, *Jan. 8, 1968*	1.20	40
	b.	Untagged (Bureau precanceled)		10
	c.	Bklt. pane of 6, *May 7, 1971*	1.00	35
		Pair with full vert. gutter btwn.	—	
1281	A713	3c **violet,** tagged, *Sept. 16, 1967*	6	5
		Margin block of 4, P#	40	
		Margin block of 4, "Use Zip Codes"	1.20	—
		Margin block of 6, "Mail Early in the Day"	1.40	
	a.	Untagged (Bureau precanceled)		12
1282	A714	4c **black,** *Nov. 19, 1965*	8	5
		Margin block of 4, P#	40	
	a.	Tagged, *Dec. 1, 1965*	8	5
		Pair with full horiz. gutter between	—	
1283	A715	5c **blue,** *Feb. 22, 1966*	10	5
		Margin block of 4, P#	50	
		Pair with full vert. gutter btwn.	—	
	a.	Tagged, *Feb. 23, 1966*	10	5
1283B	A715a	5c **blue,** tagged, *Nov. 17, 1967*	12	5
		Margin block of 4, P#	1.00	
	d.	Untagged (Bureau precanceled)		15
1284	A716	6c **gray brown,** *Jan. 29, 1966*	18	5
		Margin block of 4, P#	80	
		Margin block of 4, "Use Zip Codes"	3.50	—
		Margin block of 6, "Mail Early in the Day"	4.25	
		Pair with full horiz. gutter btwn.	150.00	
		Pair with full vert. gutter btwn.	150.00	
	a.	Tagged, *Dec. 29, 1966*	12	5
	b.	Booklet pane of 8, *Dec. 28, 1967*	1.50	50
	c.	Bklt. pane of 5 + label, *Jan. 9, 1968*	1.25	50
1285	A717	8c **violet,** *March 14, 1966*	25	5
		Margin block of 4, P#	1.25	
		Margin block of 4, "Use Zip Codes"	1.50	—
		Margin block of 6, "Mail Early in the Day"	1.75	
	a.	Tagged, *July 6, 1966*	16	5
1286	A718	10c **lilac,** tagged, *March 15, 1967*	25	5
		Margin block of 4, P#	2.00	
		Margin block of 4, "Use Zip Codes"	1.75	—
		Margin block of 6, "Mail Early in the Day"	2.25	
	b.	Untagged (Bureau precanceled)		20
1286A	718a	12c **black,** tagged, *July 30, 1968*	30	5
		Margin block of 4, P#	1.50	
		Margin block of 4, "Use Zip Codes"	1.30	—
		Margin block of 6, "Mail Early in the Day"	1.90	
	c.	Untagged (Bureau precanceled)		25
1287	A719	13c **brown,** tagged, *May 29, 1967*	30	5
		Margin block of 4, P#	1.65	
	a.	Untagged (Bureau precanceled)		25
1288	A720	15c **maroon,** type I, tagged, *Mar. 8, 1968*	30	6
		Margin block of 4, P#	1.50	
		Margin block of 4, "Use Zip Codes"	1.45	—
		Margin block of 6, "Mail Early in the Day"	2.00	
	a.	Untagged (Bureau precanceled)		30
	d.	Type II	30	6
1288B	A720	15c **dark rose claret,** tagged, perf. 10 (from blkt. pane)	30	5
	c.	Booklet pane of 8, *June 14, 1978*	2.40	1.25

No. 1288B issued in booklets only. All stamps have one or two straight edges. Plates made from redrawn die.

1289	A721	20c **deep olive,** *Oct. 24, 1967*	55	6
		Margin block of 4, P#	2.50	
		Margin block of 4, "Use Zip Codes"	2.25	—
		Margin block of 6, "Mail Early in the Day"	3.50	
	a.	Tagged, *Apr. 3, 1973*	40	6
1290	A722	25c **rose lake,** *Feb. 14, 1967*	60	5
		Margin block of 4, P#	2.75	
		Margin block of 4, "Use Zip Codes"	2.50	—
		Margin block of 6, "Mail Early in the Day"	3.75	
	a.	Tagged, *Apr. 3, 1973*	50	5
1291	A723	30c **red lilac,** *Oct. 21, 1968*	75	8
		Margin block of 4, P#	3.50	
		Margin block of 4, "Use Zip Codes"	3.25	—
		Margin block of 6, "Mail Early in the Day"	5.00	
	a.	Tagged, *Apr. 3, 1973*	60	6
1292	A724	40c **blue black,** *Jan. 29, 1969*	95	10
		Margin block of 4, P#	4.25	
		Margin block of 4, "Use Zip Codes"	4.00	—
		Margin block of 6, "Mail Early in the Day"	6.00	
	a.	Tagged, *Apr. 3, 1973*	80	8
1293	A725	50c **rose magenta,** *Aug. 13, 1968*	1.00	5
		Margin block of 4, P#	4.50	
		Margin block of 4, "Use Zip Codes"	4.25	—
		Margin block of 6, "Mail Early in the Day"	6.50	
		Pair with full vert. gutter btwn.	—	
	a.	Tagged, *Apr. 3, 1973*	1.00	5
1294	A726	$1 **dull purple,** *Oct. 16, 1967*	2.40	8
		Margin block of 4, P#	10.50	
		Margin block of 4, "Use Zip Codes"	10.00	—
		Margin block of 6, "Mail Early in the Day"	13.50	
	a.	Tagged, *Apr. 3, 1973*	2.00	8
1295	A727	$5 **gray black,** *Dec. 3, 1966*	12.50	2.00
		Margin block of 4, P#	50.00	
	a.	Tagged, *Apr. 3, 1973*	10.00	2.00

No. 1283B is redrawn; highlights, shadows softened.
See Luminescence note.

COIL STAMPS

1967–75		Tagged	Perf. 10 Horizontally	
1297	A713	3c **violet,** *Nov. 4, 1975*	12	5
		Pair	24	10
		Joint line pair	60	8
	a.	Imperf., pair	35.00	
	b.	Imperf., joint line pair	50.00	
	c.	As "b," imperf. pair		10.00
1298	A716	6c **gray brown,** *Dec. 28, 1967*	30	5
		Pair	60	12
		Joint line pair	3.00	25
	a.	Imperf., pair	2,250.	

Franklin D. Roosevelt
A727a

Revised design by Robert J. Jones and Howard C. Mildner.

COIL STAMPS

1966–78		Tagged	Perf. 10 Vertically	
1299	A710	1c **green,** *Jan. 12, 1968*	6	5
		Pair	12	10
		Joint line pair	35	8
	a.	Untagged (Bureau precanceled)		7
	b.	Imperf., pair	50.00	
	b.	Imperf., joint line pair	75.00	
1303	A714	4c **black,** *May 28, 1966*	15	5
		Pair	30	10
		Joint line pair	2.25	20
	a.	Untagged (Bureau precanceled)		15
	b.	Imperf., pair	500.00	
	b.	Imperf., joint line pair	750.00	
1304	A715	5c **blue,** *Sept. 8, 1966*	15	5
		Pair	30	10
		Joint line pair	90	20
	a.	Untagged (Bureau precanceled)		15
	b.	Imperf., pair	250.00	
	b.	Imperf., joint line pair	375.00	
1304C	A715a	5c **blue,** *1981*	15	5
		Pair	35	10
		Line pair	75	
	d.	Imperf., pair		

262   POSTAGE, 1966-78

1305	A727a	6c	**gray brown,** *Feb. 28, 1968*	20	5
			Pair	40	10
			Joint line pair	1.25	8
		a.	Imperf., pair	85.00	
		a.	Imperf., joint line pair	125.00	
		b.	Untagged (Bureau precanceled)		20
1305E	A720	15c	**rose claret,** type I, *June 14, 1978*	30	5
			Pair	60	10
			Joint line pair	1.65	30
		f.	Untagged (Bureau precanceled)		30
		g.	Imperf., pair	30.00	
		h.	Pair, imperf. between	200.00	
		i.	Type II	30	5
1305C	A726	$1	**dull purple,** *Jan. 12, 1973*	2.25	20
			Pair	4.50	40
			Joint line pair	6.50	70
		d.	Imperf., pair	2,000.	

Sesquicentennial Seal; Map of
Indiana with 19 Stars and
old Capitol at Corydon
A730

Clown
A731

INDIANA STATEHOOD ISSUE

Issued to commemorate the sesquicentennial of Indiana statehood.

Designed by Paul A. Wehr.
GIORI PRESS PRINTING
Plates of 200 subjects in four panes of 50 each.

1966			Perf. 11		Unwmkd.	
1308	A730	5c	**ocher, brown & violet blue,** *Apr. 16*		12	5
			Margin block of 4, two P#		75	
			Margin block of 4, Mr. Zip and "Use Zip Code"		60	

MIGRATORY BIRD TREATY ISSUE

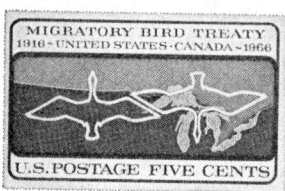

Migratory Birds over
Canada-U.S. Border
A728

Designed by Burt E. Pringle.
GIORI PRESS PRINTING
Plates of 200 subjects in four panes of 50 each.

1966			Perf. 11		Unwmkd.	
1306	A728	5c	**black, crimson & dark blue,** *March 16*		12	5
			Margin block of 4, two P#		75	
			Margin block of 4, Mr. Zip and "Use Zip Code"		60	

AMERICAN CIRCUS ISSUE

Issued to honor the American Circus on the centenary of the birth of John Ringling.

Designed by Edward Klauck.
GIORI PRESS PRINTING
Plates of 200 subjects in four panes of 50 each.

1966			Perf. 11		Unwmkd.	
1309	A731	5c	**multicolored,** *May 2*		12	5
			Margin block of 4, two P#		90	
			Margin block of 4, Mr. Zip and "Use Zip Code"		60	

HUMANE TREATMENT OF ANIMALS ISSUE

Issued to promote humane treatment of all animals and to commemorate the centenary of the American Society for the Prevention of Cruelty to Animals.

Mongrel
A729

Designed by Norman Todhunter.
LITHOGRAPHED, ENGRAVED (Giori)
Plates of 200 subjects in four panes of 50 each.

1966			Perf. 11		Unwmkd.	
1307	A729	5c	**orange brown & black,** *Apr. 9*		12	5
			Margin block of 4, P#		90	
			Margin block of 4, Mr. Zip and "Use Zip Code"		60	

SIXTH INTERNATIONAL PHILATELIC EXHIBITION ISSUES

Issued to commemorate the Sixth International Philatelic Exhibition (SIPEX), Washington, D.C., May 21-30.

Stamped Cover
A732

Designed by Thomas F. Naegele.
LITHOGRAPHED, ENGRAVED (Giori)
Plates of 200 subjects in four panes of 50 each.

1966						Perf. 11
1310	A732	5c	**multicolored,** *May 21*		12	5
			Margin block of 4, P#		90	
			Margin block of 4, Mr. Zip and "Use Zip Code"		60	

POSTAGE, 1966

SOUVENIR SHEET

A733
Designed by Brook Temple.
LITHOGRAPHED, ENGRAVED (Giori)
Plates of 24 subjects.

1966 *Imperf.*
1311   A733   5c **multicolored**, *May 23*   30   15

No. 1311 measures 108x74mm. Below the stamp appears a line drawing of the Capitol and Washington Monument. Marginal inscriptions and drawing are green.

BILL OF RIGHTS ISSUE

Issued to commemorate the 175th anniversary of the Bill of Rights.

"Freedom" Checking "Tyranny"
A734
Designed by Herbert L. Block (Herblock).
GIORI PRESS PRINTING
Plates of 200 subjects in four panes of 50 each.

1966 *Perf. 11* Unwmkd.
1312 A734 5c **carmine, dark & light blue**, *July 1* 12 5
         Margin block of 4, two P#   75
         Margin block of 4, Mr. Zip and "Use
           Zip Code" 60

POLISH MILLENNIUM ISSUE

Issued to commemorate the thousandth anniversary of the adoption of Christianity in Poland.

Polish Eagle and Cross
A735
Designed by Edmund D. Lewandowski.
ROTARY PRESS PRINTING
E.E. Plates of 200 subjects in four panes of 50 each.

1966 *Perf. 10½x11* Unwmkd.
1313 A735 5c **red**, *July 30* 12 5
         Margin block of 4, P#   90
         Margin block of 4, Mr. Zip and "Use
           Zip Code" 60

NATIONAL PARK SERVICE ISSUE

Issued to commemorate the 50th anniversary of the National Park Service of the Interior Department. The design "Parkscape U.S.A." identifies National Park Service facilities.

National Park Service Emblem
A736

Designed by Thomas H. Geismar.
LITHOGRAPHED, ENGRAVED (Giori)
Plates of 200 subjects in four panes of 50 each.

1966				Perf. 11	
1314	A736	5c yellow, black & green, *Aug. 25*		12	5
		Margin block of 4, P#		75	—
		Margin block of 4, Mr. Zip and "Use Zip Code"		60	—
		a. Tagged, *Aug. 26.*		30	15

MARINE CORPS RESERVE ISSUE

Issued to commemorate the 50th anniversary of the founding of the U.S. Marine Corps Reserve.

Combat Marine, 1966; Frogman; World War II Flier;
World War I "Devil Dog" and Marine, 1775
A737

Designed by Stella Grafakos.
LITHOGRAPHED, ENGRAVED (Giori)
Plates of 200 subjects in four panes of 50 each.

1966				Perf. 11	
1315	A737	5c black, bister, red & ultra., *Aug. 29*		12	5
		Margin block of 4, P#		1.00	—
		Margin block of 4, Mr. Zip and "Use Zip Code"		60	—
		a. Tagged, *Aug. 29*		30	15
		b. Black & bister (engraved) missing		—	

GENERAL FEDERATION OF WOMEN'S CLUBS ISSUE

Issued to honor 75 years of service by the General Federation of Women's Clubs.

Women of 1890 and 1966
A738

Designed by Charles Henry Carter.
GIORI PRESS PRINTING
Plates of 200 subjects in four panes of 50 each.

1966				Perf. 11	
1316	A738	5c black, pink & blue, *Sept. 12*		12	5
		Margin block of 4, two P#		1.00	—
		Margin block of 4, Mr. Zip and "Use Zip Code"		60	—
		a. Tagged, *Sept. 13*		30	15

AMERICAN FOLKLORE ISSUE

Johnny Appleseed

Issued to honor Johnny Appleseed (John Chapman 1774–1845), who wandered over 100,000 square miles planting apple trees, and who gave away and sold seedlings to Midwest pioneers.

Johnny Appleseed
A739

Designed by Robert Bode.
GIORI PRESS PRINTING
Plates of 200 subjects in four panes of 50 each.

1966				Perf. 11	
1317	A739	5c green, red & black, *Sept. 24*		12	5
		Margin block of 4, two P#		1.00	—
		Margin block of 4, Mr. Zip and "Use Zip Code"		60	—
		a. Tagged, *Sept. 26*		30	15

BEAUTIFICATION OF AMERICA ISSUE

Issued to publicize President Johnson's "Plant for a more beautiful America" campaign.

Jefferson Memorial, Tidal Basin and Cherry Blossoms
A740

Designed by Miss Gyo Fujikawa
GIORI PRESS PRINTING
Plates of 200 subjects in four panes of 50 each.

1966			Perf. 11	Unwmkd.	
1318	A740	5c emerald, pink & black, *Oct. 5*		12	5
		Margin block of 4, two P#		1.00	—
		Margin block of 4, Mr. Zip and "Use Zip Code"		75	—
		a. Tagged, *Oct. 5*		30	15

GREAT RIVER ROAD ISSUE

Issued to publicize the 5,600-mile Great River Road connecting New Orleans with Kenora, Ontario, and following the Mississippi most of the way.

Map of Central United States with Great River Road
A741

Designed by Herbert Bayer.
LITHOGRAPHED, ENGRAVED (Giori)
Plates of 200 subjects in four panes of 50 each.

1966
1319   A741   5c **vermilion, yellow, blue & green,** *Oct. 21*   12   5
    Margin block of 4, P#   1.00
    Margin block of 4, Mr. Zip and "Use Zip Code"   60
    a. Tagged, *Oct. 22*   30   15

SAVINGS BOND—SERVICEMEN ISSUE

Issued to commemorate the 25th anniversary of U.S. Savings Bonds, and to honor American servicemen.

Statue of Liberty and "Old Glory"
A742

Designed by Steven Dohanos, photo by Bob Noble.
LITHOGRAPHED, ENGRAVED (Giori)
Plates of 200 subjects in four panes of 50 each.

1966   Perf. 11   Unwmkd.
1320   A742   5c **red, dark blue, light blue & black,** *Oct. 26*   12   5
    Margin block of 4, P#   1.00
    Margin block of 4, Mr. Zip and "Use Zip Code"   60
    a. Tagged, *Oct. 27*   30   15
    b. Red, dark blue & black omitted   3,500.

CHRISTMAS ISSUE

Madonna and Child, by Hans Memling
A743

Modeled by Howard C. Mildner after "Madonna and Child with Angels," by the Flemish artist Hans Memling (c.1430-1494), Mellon Collection, National Gallery of Art, Washington, D.C.

LITHOGRAPHED, ENGRAVED (Giori)
Plates of 400 subjects in four panes of 100 each.

1966   Perf. 11   Unwmkd.
1321   A743   5c **multicolored,** *Nov. 1*   12   5
    Margin block of 4, P#   75
    Margin block of 4, Mr. Zip and "Use Zip Code"   60
    a. Tagged, *Nov. 2*   25   10

MARY CASSATT ISSUE

Issued to honor Mary Cassatt (1845-1926), painter. The original painting "The Boating Party" is in the National Gallery of Art, Washington, D.C.

"The Boating Party"
A744

Designed by Robert J. Jones.
GIORI PRESS PRINTING
Plates of 200 subjects in four panes of 50 each.

1966   Perf. 11   Unwmkd.
1322   A744   5c **multicolored,** *Nov. 17*   20   5
    Margin block of 4, two P#   2.75
    Margin block of 4, Mr. Zip and "Use Zip Code"   1.20
    a. Tagged, *Nov. 17*   45   15

NATIONAL GRANGE ISSUE

Issued to commemorate the centenary of the founding of the National Grange, American farmers' organization.

Grange Poster, 1870
A745

Designed by Lee Pavão.
GIORI PRESS PRINTING
Plates of 200 subjects in four panes of 50 each.
Tagged

1967   Perf. 11   Unwmkd.
1323   A745   5c **orange, yellow, brown, green & black,** *April 17*   12   5
    Margin block of 4, two P#   90
    Margin block of 4, Mr. Zip and "Use Zip Code"   60

CANADA CENTENARY ISSUE

Issued to commemorate the centenary of Canada's emergence as a nation.

Canadian Landscape
A746

Designed by Ivan Chermayeff.
GIORI PRESS PRINTING
Plates of 200 subjects in four panes of 50 each.
Tagged

1967			Perf. 11		Unwmkd.
1324	A746	5c lt. blue, dp. green, ultra., olive & black, May 25	12	5
		Margin block of 4, two P#	90	—
		Margin block of 4, Mr. Zip and "Use Zip Code"	60	—

ERIE CANAL ISSUE

Issued to commemorate the 150th anniversary of the Erie Canal ground-breaking ceremony at Rome, N.Y. The canal links Lake Erie and New York City.

Stern of Early Canal Boat
A747

Designed by George Samerjan.
LITHOGRAPHED, ENGRAVED (Giori)
Plates of 200 subjects in four panes of 50 each.

1967			Tagged	Perf. 11	
1325	A747	5c ultra., greenish blue, black & crimson, July 4	12	5
		Margin block of 4, P#	90	—
		Margin block of 4, Mr. Zip and "Use Zip Code"	60	—

"SEARCH FOR PEACE"—LIONS ISSUE

Issued to publicize the search for peace. "Search for Peace" was the theme of an essay contest for young men and women sponsored by Lions International on its 50th anniversary.

Peace Dove
A748

Designed by Bradbury Thompson.
GIORI PRESS PRINTING
Plates of 200 subjects in four panes of 50 each.

1967			Tagged		Perf. 1
		Gray Paper with Blue Threads			
1326	A748	5c blue, red & black, July 5	12	
		Margin block of 4, P#	90	—
		Margin block of 4, Mr. Zip and "Use Zip Code"	60	—

HENRY DAVID THOREAU ISSUE

Issued to commemorate the 150th anniversary of the birth of Henry David Thoreau (1817–1862), writer.

Henry David Thoreau
A749

Designed by Leonard Baskin.
GIORI PRESS PRINTING
Plates of 200 subjects in four panes of 50 each.

1967			Tagged		Perf. 11
1327	A749	5c carmine, black & blue green, July 12	12	5
		Margin block of 4, P#	90	—
		Margin block of 4, Mr. Zip and "Use Zip Code"	60	—

NEBRASKA STATEHOOD ISSUE

Issued to commemorate the centenary of the admission of Nebraska to Statehood.

Hereford Steer and Ear of Corn
A750

Designed by Julian K. Billings.
LITHOGRAPHED, ENGRAVED (Giori)
Plates of 200 subjects in four panes of 50 each.

1967			Tagged		Perf. 11
1328	A750	5c dark red brown, lemon & yellow, July 29	12	5
		Margin block of 4, P#	90	—
		Margin block of 4, Mr. Zip and "Use Zip Code"	60	—

VOICE OF AMERICA ISSUE

Issued to commemorate the 25th anniversary of the radio branch of the United States Information Agency (USIA).

Radio Transmission Tower and Waves
A751
Designed by Georg Olden.
LITHOGRAPHED, ENGRAVED (Giori)
Plates of 200 subjects in four panes of 50 each.

1967			Tagged		Perf. 11	
1329	A751	5c	red, blue, black & carmine, *Aug. 1*		12	5
			Margin block of 4, P#		1.00	
			Margin block of 4, Mr. Zip and "Use Zip Code"		60	

AMERICAN FOLKLORE ISSUE
Davy Crockett

Issued to honor Davy Crockett (1786–1836), frontiersman, hunter, and congressman from Tennessee who died at the Alamo.

Davy Crockett and Scrub Pine
A752
Designed by Robert Bode.
LITHOGRAPHED, ENGRAVED (Giori)
Plates of 200 subjects in four panes of 50 each.

1967			Tagged		Perf. 11	
1330	A752	5c	green, black, & yellow, *Aug. 17*		12	5
			Margin block of 4, P#		1.00	
			Margin block of 4, Mr. Zip and "Use Zip Code"		60	
		a.	Vertical pair, imperf. between			

ACCOMPLISHMENTS IN SPACE ISSUE

Issued to commemorate United States' accomplishments in space. Nos. 1331–1332 are printed se-tenant in horizontal rows of 5 in panes of 50. In the upper and lower left panes the astronaut stamp is first, third and fifth, the spaceship second and fourth. This arrangement is reversed in the upper and lower right panes.

Space-Walking Astronaut
A753

Designed by Paul Calle.
LITHOGRAPHED, ENGRAVED (Giori)
Plates of 200 subjects in four panes of 50 each.

1967			Tagged		Perf. 11	
1331	A753	5c	multicolored, *Sept. 29*		90	25
		a.	Pair, #1331-1332		2.00	1.50
			Block of four, 2 #1331 + 2 #1332		4.00	4.00
			Marg. block of 4, P# adjoining #1331		8.00	
			Margin block of 4, Mr. Zip and "Use Zip Code" adjoining #1331		5.25	

Gemini 4 Capsule
A754

1332	A754	5c	multicolored, *Sept. 29*		90	25
			Margin block of 4, P# adjoining #1332		8.00	
			Margin block of 4, Mr. Zip and "Use Zip Code" adjoining #1332		5.25	
			Red stripes of flag on capsule omitted (29322, 29325 U.L. 19)		250.00	

URBAN PLANNING ISSUE

Issued to publicize the importance of Urban Planning in connection with the International Conference of the American Institute of Planners, Washington, D.C., Oct. 1–6.

View of Model City
A755
Designed by Francis Ferguson.
LITHOGRAPHED, ENGRAVED (Giori)
Plates of 200 subjects in four panes of 50 each.

1967			Tagged		Perf. 11	
1333	A755	5c	dark blue, light blue & black, *Oct. 2*		15	5
			Margin block of 4, P#		1.25	
			Margin block of 4, Mr. Zip and "Use Zip Code"		1.00	

		Block of four		60	20
		Margin block of 4, P#		3.00	
		Margin block of 4, Mr. Zip and "Use Zip Code"		1.25	

FINNISH INDEPENDENCE ISSUE

Issued to commemorate the 50th anniversary of Finland's independence.

Finnish Coat of Arms
A756

Designed by Bradbury Thompson.
ENGRAVED (Giori)
Plates of 200 subjects in four panes of 50 each.

1967		Tagged	Perf. 11	
1334	A756	5c blue, Oct. 6	15	5
		Margin block of 4, P#	1.25	—
		Margin block of 4, Mr. Zip and "Use Zip Code"	1.00	—

THOMAS EAKINS ISSUE

Issued to honor Thomas Eakins (1844–1916), painter and sculptor. The original painting is in the National Gallery of Art, Washington, D.C.

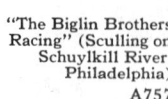

"The Biglin Brothers Racing" (Sculling on Schuylkill River, Philadelphia)
A757

Printed by Photogravure & Color Co., Moonachie, N.J.
PHOTOGRAVURE
Plates of 200 subjects in four panes of 50 each.

1967		Tagged	Perf. 12	
1335	A757	5c gold & multicolored, Nov. 2	18	5
		Margin block of 4, 6 P#	1.50	—

Plate number blocks from upper left or lower left panes show clipped corner of margin.

CHRISTMAS ISSUE

Madonna and Child, by Hans Memling
A758

LITHOGRAPHED, ENGRAVED (Giori)
Plates of 200 subjects in four panes of 50 each.

1967		Tagged	Perf. 11	
1336	A758	5c multicolored, Nov. 6	12	5
		Margin block of 4, P#	60	—
		Margin block of 4, Mr. Zip and "Use Zip Code"	50	—

See note on painting above No. 1321.

MISSISSIPPI STATEHOOD ISSUE

Issued to commemorate the 150th anniversary of Mississippi statehood.

Magnolia
A759

Designed by Andrew Bucci.
GIORI PRESS PRINTING
Plates of 200 subjects in four panes of 50 each.

1967		Perf. 11	Unwmkd	
		Tagged		
1337	A759	5c brt. greenish blue, green & red brown, Dec. 11	15	5
		Margin block of 4, 2 P#	1.00	—
		Margin block of 4, Mr. Zip and "Use Zip Code"	90	—

FLAG ISSUE

Flag and White House
A760
Designed by Stevan Dohanos.
GIORI PRESS PRINTING
Plates of 400 subjects in four panes of 100 each.

1968		Tagged	Perf. 11	
		Size: 19x22mm.		
1338	A760	6c dark blue, red & green, Jan. 24	12	5
		Margin block of 4, P#	60	—
		Margin block of 4, "Use Zip Code"	50	—
		Margin block of 6, "Mail Early in the Day"	70	—
	c.	Vert. pair, imperf. horiz.	225.00	
	k.	Vert. pair, imperf. btwn.	300.00	

MULTICOLOR HUCK PRESS
Panes of 100 (10x10) each.

1970–71		Tagged	Perf. 11x10½	
		Size: 18¼x21mm.		
1338D	A760	6c dark blue, red & green, Aug. 7, 1970	20	5
		Margin block of 20*	4.25	—
	e.	Horiz. pair, imperf. between	175.00	

* Margin blocks of 20 come in four versions: (1) 2 P#, 3 ME, 3 zip; (2) 3 P#, 2 ME, 2 zip; (3) 2 P#, 3 ME, 2 zip; (4) 3 P#, 2 ME, 3 zip.

1338F	A760	8c dk. blue, red & slate green, May 10, 1971	20	5
		Margin block of 20*	4.25	—
	i.	Imperf., vert. pair	70.00	
	j.	Horiz. pair, imperf. between	70.00	

* Margin block of 20: See note after No. 1338D.

COIL STAMPS
MULTICOLOR HUCK PRESS

1969–71		Tagged	Perf. 10 Vertically	
		Size: 18¼x21mm.		
1338A	A760	6c dk. blue, red & green, May 30, 1969	20	5
		Pair	40	10
	b.	Imperf., pair	650.00	
1338G	A760	8c dk. blue, red & slate green, May 10, 1971	20	5
		Pair	40	10
	h.	Imperf., pair	50.00	

ILLINOIS STATEHOOD ISSUE

Issued to commemorate the 150th anniversary of Illinois statehood.

Farm Buildings and Fields of Ripening Grain
A761

Designed by George Barford.
LITHOGRAPHED, ENGRAVED (Giori)
Plates of 200 subjects in four panes of 50 each.

1968		Tagged		Perf. 11	
1339	A761	6c dk. blue, blue, red & ocher, *Feb. 12*		18	5
		Margin block of 4, P#		1.00	
		Margin block of 4, Mr. Zip and "Use Zip Code"		80	

HEMISFAIR '68 ISSUE

Issued to publicize the HemisFair '68 exhibition at San Antonio, Texas, Apr. 6–Oct. 6, commemorating the 250th anniversary of San Antonio.

Map of North and South America and Lines Converging on San Antonio
A762

Designed by Louis Macouillard.
LITHOGRAPHED, ENGRAVED (Giori)
Plates of 200 subjects in four panes of 50 each.

1968		Tagged		Perf. 11	
1340	A762	6c blue, rose red & white, *Mar. 30*		18	5
		Margin block of 4, P#		1.00	
		Margin block of 4, Mr. Zip and "Use Zip Code"		80	
		Margin block of 6, "Mail Early in the Day"		1.20	
	a.	White omitted		1,500.	

AIRLIFT ISSUE

Issued to pay for airlift of parcels from and to U.S. ports to servicemen overseas and in Alaska, Hawaii and Puerto Rico. Valid for all regular postage. On Apr. 26, 1969, the Post Office Department ruled that henceforth No. 1341 "may be used toward paying the postage or fees for special services on *airmail* articles."

Eagle Holding Pennant
A763

Designed by Steven Dohanos after a late 19th century wood carving, part of the Index of American Design, National Gallery of Art.
LITHOGRAPHED, ENGRAVED (Giori)
Plates of 200 subjects in four panes of 50 each.

1968		Perf. 11		Unwmkd.	
1341	A763	$1 sepia, dk. blue, ocher & brown red, *Apr. 4*		5.00	3.00
		Margin block of 4, P#		25.00	
		Margin block of 4, Mr. Zip and "Use Zip Code"		21.00	
		Margin block of 6, "Mail Early in the Day"		32.50	
		Pair with full horiz. gutter btwn.			

"SUPPORT OUR YOUTH"—ELKS ISSUE

Issued to publicize the Support Our Youth program, and to honor the Benevolent and Protective Order of Elks, which extended its youth service program in observance of its centennial year.

Girls and Boys
A764

Designed by Edward Vebell.
LITHOGRAPHED, ENGRAVED (Giori)
Plates of 200 subjects in four panes of 50 each.

1968		Tagged		Perf. 11	
1342	A764	6c ultramarine & orange red, *May 1*		18	5
		Margin block of 4, P#		1.00	
		Margin block of 4, Mr. Zip and "Use Zip Code"		80	
		Margin block of 6, "Mail Early in the Day"		1.20	

LAW AND ORDER ISSUE

Issued to publicize the policeman as protector and friend and to encourage respect for law and order.

Policeman and Boy
A765

Designed by Ward Brackett.
GIORI PRESS PRINTING
Plates of 200 subjects in four panes of 50 each

1968		Tagged		Perf. 11	
1343	A765	6c blue & black, *May 17*		18	5
		Margin block of 4, P#		1.00	
		Margin block of 4, Mr. Zip and "Use Zip Code"		80	
		Margin block of 6, "Mail Early in the Day"		1.20	

REGISTER AND VOTE ISSUE

Issued to publicize the campaign to draw more voters to the polls. The weather vane is from an old house in the Russian Hill section of San Francisco, Cal.

Eagle Weather Vane
A766

Designed by Norman Todhunter and Bill Hyde; photograph by M. Halberstadt.

LITHOGRAPHED, ENGRAVED (Giori)
Plates of 200 subjects in four panes of 50 each.

1968			Perf. 11		Unwmkd.
			Tagged		
1344	A766	6c	**black, yellow & orange,** *June 27*	18	5
			Margin block of 4, P#	1.00	
			Margin block of 4, Mr. Zip and "Use Zip Code"	80	
			Margin block of 6, "Mail Early in the Day"	1.20	

HISTORIC FLAG SERIES

Issued to show flags carried by American colonists and by citizens of the new United States. Nos. 1345–1354 are printed se-tenant in vertical rows of 10 in panes of 50. The flag sequence on the 2 upper panes is as listed. On the 2 lower panes the sequence is reversed with the Navy Jack in the first row and the Fort Moultrie flag in the 10th.

Ft. Moultrie, 1776
A767

Ft. McHenry, 1795–1818
A768

Washington's Cruisers, 1775
A769

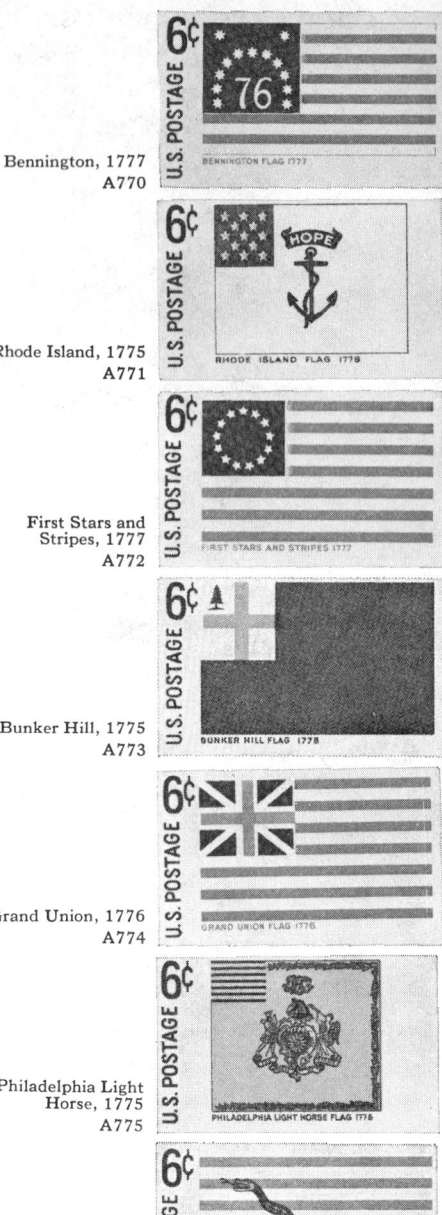

Bennington, 1777
A770

Rhode Island, 1775
A771

First Stars and Stripes, 1777
A772

Bunker Hill, 1775
A773

Grand Union, 1776
A774

Philadelphia Light Horse, 1775
A775

First Navy Jack, 1775
A776

ENGR. (Giori) (#1345–1348, 1350);
ENGR. & LITHO. (#1349, 1351–1354)
Plates of 200 subjects in four panes of 50 each.

1968, July 4			Perf. 11	Unwmkd.	
			Tagged		
1345	A767	6c	**dark blue**	1.00	50
1346	A768	6c	**dark blue & red**	1.00	50
1347	A769	6c	**dark blue & olive green**	60	50

POSTAGE, 1968

348	A770	6c dark blue & red		60	40
349	A771	6c dark blue, yellow & red		60	45
350	A772	6c dark blue & red		60	35
351	A773	6c dark blue, olive green & red		60	35
352	A774	6c dark blue & red		60	35
353	A775	6c dark blue, yellow & red		80	35
354	A776	6c dark blue, red & yellow		80	40
		a. Strip of ten (#1345-#1354)		8.25	7.50
		Margin block of 20, P#, inscriptions (#1345-1354)		18.00	

WALT DISNEY ISSUE

Issued in memory of Walt Disney (1901–1966), cartoonist, film producer and creator of Mickey Mouse.

Walt Disney and Children of the World
A777

Designed by C. Robert Moore; portrait by Paul E. Wenzel.
Printed by Achrovure Division of Union-Camp Corp., Englewood, N.J.
Plates of 400 subjects in eight panes of 50 each.
PHOTOGRAVURE
Perf. 12

1968		Tagged		Unwmkd.	
355	A777	6c **multicolored**, *Sept. 11*		20	5
		Margin block of 4, 5P#	1.25		
		Margin block of 4, 5P# and 5 dashes	1.25		
		Margin block of 4, Mr. Zip and "Use Zip Code"	1.00		
		Margin block of 6, "Mail Early in the Day"	1.35		
		a. Ocher omitted ("Walt Disney," "6c," etc.)	800.00		
		b. Vert. pair, imperf. horiz.	900.00		
		c. Imperf, pair	1,100.		
		d. Black omitted	1,750.		
		e. Horiz. pair, imperf. between	3,250.		
		f. Blue omitted	1,850.		

FATHER MARQUETTE ISSUE

Issued to honor Father Jacques Marquette (1637–1675), French Jesuit missionary, who together with Louis Jolliet explored the Mississippi River and its tributaries.

Father Marquette and Louis Jolliet Exploring the Mississippi
A778

Designed by Stanley W. Galli.
Plates of 200 subjects in four panes of 50 each.
GIORI PRESS PRINTING

1968		Tagged		*Perf. 11*	
1356	A778	6c **black, apple green & orange brown**, *Sept. 20*		20	5
		Margin block of 4, P#		1.00	
		Margin block of 4, Mr. Zip and "Use Zip Code"		85	
		Margin block of 6, "Mail Early in the Day"		1.35	

AMERICAN FOLKLORE ISSUE
Daniel Boone

Issued to honor Daniel Boone (1734–1820), frontiersman and trapper.

Pennsylvania Rifle, Powder Horn, Tomahawk Pipe and Knife
A779

Designed by Louis Macouillard.
LITHOGRAPHED, ENGRAVED (Giori)
Plates of 200 subjects in four panes of 50 each.

1968		Tagged		*Perf. 11*	
1357	A779	6c **yellow, deep yellow, maroon & black**, *Sept. 26*		20	5
		Margin block of 4, P#		1.00	
		Margin block of 4, Mr. Zip and "Use Zip Code"		85	
		Margin block of 6, "Mail Early in the Day"		1.35	

ARKANSAS RIVER NAVIGATION ISSUE

Issued to commemorate the opening of the Arkansas River to commercial navigation.

Ship's Wheel, Power Transmission Tower and Barge
A780

Designed by Dean Ellis.
LITHOGRAPHED, ENGRAVED (Giori)
Plates of 200 subjects in four panes of 50 each.

1968, Oct. 1		Tagged		*Perf. 11*	
1358	A780	6c **bright blue, dark blue & black**		20	5
		Margin block of 4, P#		1.00	
		Margin block of 4, Mr. Zip and "Use Zip Code"		85	
		Margin block of 6, "Mail Early in the Day"		1.35	

LEIF ERIKSON ISSUE

Issued in memory of Leif Erikson, 11th century Norse explorer, called the first European to set foot on the American continent, at a place he called Vinland. The Leif Erikson statue by the American sculptor A. Stirling Calder is in Reykjavik, Iceland.

Leif Erikson by A. Stirling Calder
A781
Designed by Kurt Weiner.
LITHOGRAPHED & ENGRAVED
Plates of 200 subjects in four panes of 50 each.

1968, Oct. 9		Tagged		Perf. 11	
1359	A781	6c light gray brown & black brown		20	5
		Margin block of 4, P#		1.00	
		Margin block of 4, Mr. Zip and "Use Zip Code"		85	
		Margin block of 6, "Mail Early in the Day"		1.35	

The luminescent element is in the light gray brown ink of the background. The engraved parts were printed on a rotary currency press.

CHEROKEE STRIP ISSUE

Issued to commemorate the 75th anniversary of the opening of the Cherokee Strip to settlers, Sept. 16, 1893.

Racing for Homesteads in Cherokee Strip, 1893
A782
Designed by Norman Todhunter.
ROTARY PRESS PRINTING
E.E. Plates of 200 subjects in four panes of 50 each.

1968		Tagged		Perf. 11x10½	
1360	A782	6c brown, Oct. 15		20	5
		Margin block of 4, P#		1.00	
		Margin block of 4, Mr. Zip and "Use Zip Code"		85	
		Margin block of 6, "Mail Early in the Day"		1.35	

JOHN TRUMBULL ISSUE

Issued to honor John Trumbull (1756–1843), painter. The stamp design shows Lt. Thomas Grosvenor and his attendant Peter Salem. The original painting hangs at Yale University, New Haven, Connecticut.

Detail from "The Battle of Bunker's Hill"
A783
Modeled by Robert J. Jones.
LITHOGRAPHED, ENGRAVED (Giori)
Plates of 200 subjects in four panes of 50 each.

1968		Tagged Perf. 11		Unwmkd.	
1361	A783	6c multicolored, Oct. 18		25	5
		Margin block of 4, P#		1.25	
		Margin block of 4, Mr. Zip and "Use Zip Code"		1.10	
		Margin block of 6, "Mail Early in the Day"		1.60	

WATERFOWL CONSERVATION ISSUE

Issued to publicize waterfowl conservation.

Wood Ducks
A784
Designed by Stanley W. Galli.
LITHOGRAPHED, ENGRAVED (Giori)
Plates of 200 subjects in four panes of 50 each.

1968		Tagged		Perf. 11	
1362	A784	6c black & multicolored, Oct. 24		25	5
		Margin block of 4, P#		1.75	
		Margin block of 4, Mr. Zip and "Use Zip Code"		1.25	
		Margin block of 6, "Mail Early in the Day"		1.75	
		a. Vertical pair, imperf. between		750.00	
		b. Red & dark blue omitted		1,750.	

CHRISTMAS ISSUE

"The Annunciation" by the 15th century Flemish painter Jan van Eyck is in the National Gallery of Art, Washington, D. C.

Angel Gabriel, from "The Annunciation" by Jan van Eyck
A785

Designed by Robert J. Jones.
ENGRAVED (Multicolor Huck)
Panes of 50 (10x5).

1968			Tagged		Perf. 11	
1363	A785	6c	**multicolored**, *Nov. 1*	20	5	
			Margin block of 10, 7P# and 3 "Mail Early"	2.75		
			Margin block of 10, 8P# and 2 "Mail Early"	2.75		
		a.	Untagged, *Nov. 2*	20	5	
		b.	Imperf., pair (tagged)	450.00		
		c.	Light yellow omitted	150.00		
		d.	Imperf. pair, untagged	600.00		

AMERICAN INDIAN ISSUE

Issued to honor the American Indian and to commemorate the opening of the National Portrait Gallery, Washington, D. C. Chief Joseph (Indian name, Thunder Traveling over the Mountains), a leader of the Nez Percé, was born in eastern Oregon about 1840 and died at the Colesville Reservation in Washington State in 1904.

Chief Joseph, by Cyrenius Hall
A786

Designed by Robert J. Jones; lettering by Crimilda Pontes.
LITHOGRAPHED, ENGRAVED (Giori)
Plates of 200 subjects in four panes of 50 each.

1968			Tagged		Perf. 11	
1364	A786	6c	**black & multicolored**, *Nov. 4*	30	5	
			Margin block of 4, P#	1.35		
			Margin block of 4, Mr. Zip and "Use Zip Code"	1.25		
			Margin block of 6, "Mail Early in the Day"	2.00		

BEAUTIFICATION OF AMERICA ISSUE

Issued to publicize the Natural Beauty Campaign for more beautiful cities, parks, highways and streets. Nos. 1365–1368 are printed in blocks of four in panes of 50. In the upper and lower left panes Nos. 1365 and 1367 appear in first, third and fifth place, Nos. 1366 and 1368 in second and fourth place. This arrangement is reversed in the upper and lower right panes.

Capitol, Azaleas and Tulips
A787 PLANT for more BEAUTIFUL CITIES

Washington Monument, Potomac River and Daffodils
PLANT for more BEAUTIFUL PARKS A788

Poppies and Lupines along Highway
A789 PLANT for more BEAUTIFUL HIGHWAYS

Blooming Crabapples Lining Avenue
PLANT for more BEAUTIFUL STREETS A790

Designed by Walter DuBois Richards.
LITHOGRAPHED, ENGRAVED (Giori)
Plates of 200 subjects in four panes of 50 each.

1969, Jan. 16			Tagged		Perf. 11	
1365	A787	6c	**multicolored**	90	15	
			Marg. block of 4, P# adjoining #1365	7.50		
			Margin block of 4, Mr. Zip and "Use Zip Code" adjoining #1365	6.00		
			Margin block of 6, "Mail Early in the Day" adjoining #1365	7.50		
1366	A788	6c	**multicolored**	90	15	
			Marg. block of 4, P# adjoining #1366	7.50		
			Margin block of 4, Mr. Zip and "Use Zip Code" adjoining #1366	6.00		
			Margin block of 6, "Mail Early in the Day" adjoining #1366	7.50		
1367	A789	6c	**multicolored**	90	15	
			Marg. block of 4, P# adjoining #1367	7.50		
			Margin block of 4, Mr. Zip and "Use Zip Code" adjoining #1367	6.00		
			Margin block of 6, "Mail Early in the Day" adjoining #1367	7.50		
1368	A790	6c	**multicolored**	90	15	
			Marg. block of 4, P# adjoining #1368	7.50		
			Margin block of 4, Mr. Zip and "Use Zip Code" adjoining #1368	6.00		
			Margin block of 6, "Mail Early in the Day" adjoining #1368	7.50		
		a.	Block of 4, #1365-1368	4.50	3.50	

AMERICAN LEGION ISSUE

Issued to commemorate the 50th anniversary of the American Legion.

Eagle from Great Seal
A791

Designed by Robert Hallock.
LITHOGRAPHED, ENGRAVED (Giori)
Plates of 200 subjects in four panes of 50 each.

1969			Tagged	Perf. 11	
1369	A791	6c	red, blue & black, *Mar. 15*	20	5
			Margin block of 4, P#	1.10	—
			Margin block of 4, Mr. Zip and "Use Zip Code"	85	—
			Margin block of 6, "Mail Early in the Day"	1.35	—

AMERICAN FOLKLORE ISSUE

Grandma Moses

Issued to honor Grandma Moses (Anna Mary Robertson Moses, 1860–1961), primitive painter of American life.

July Fourth, by Grandma Moses
A792

Designed by Robert J. Jones.
LITHOGRAPHED, ENGRAVED (Giori)
Plates of 200 subjects in four panes of 50 each.

1969			Tagged	Perf. 11	
1370	A792	6c	multicolored, *May 1*	25	5
			Margin block of 4, P#	1.35	—
			Margin block of 4, Mr. Zip and "Use Zip Code"	1.10	—
			Margin block of 6, "Mail Early in the Day"	1.65	—
		a.	Horizontal pair, imperf. between	450.00	
		b.	Black ("6c U.S. Postage") & Prus. blue ("Grandma Moses") omitted (engraved)	1,000.	

APOLLO 8 ISSUE

Issued to commemorate the Apollo 8 mission, which first put men into orbit around the moon, Dec. 21–27 1968. The astronauts were: Col. Frank Borman, Capt James Lovell and Maj. William Anders.

Moon Surface and Earth
A793

Designed by Leonard E. Buckley after a photograph by the Apollo 8 astronauts.
GIORI PRESS PRINTING
Plates of 200 subjects in four panes of 50 each.

1969			Tagged	Perf. 11	
1371	A793	6c	black, blue & ocher, *May 5*	30	6
			Margin block of 4, P#	1.50	—
			Margin block of 4, Mr. Zip and "Use Zip Code"	1.30	—
			Margin block of 6, "Mail Early in the Day"	2.10	—

W. C. HANDY ISSUE

Issued to honor W. C. Handy (1873–1958), jazz musician and composer.

William Christopher Handy
A794

Designed by Bernice Kochan.
LITHOGRAPHED, ENGRAVED (Giori)
Plates of 200 subjects in four panes of 50 each.

1969			Tagged	Perf. 11	
1372	A794	6c	violet, dp. lilac & blue, *May 17*	20	5
			Margin block of 4, P#	1.00	—
			Margin block of 4, Mr. Zip and "Use Zip Code"	85	—
			Margin block of 6, "Mail Early in the Day"	1.35	—

CALIFORNIA SETTLEMENT ISSUE

Issued to commemorate the 200th anniversary of the settlement of California.

Carmel Mission Belfry
A795

POSTAGE, 1969   275

Designed by Leonard Buckley and Howard C. Mildner.
LITHOGRAPHED, ENGRAVED (Giori)
Plates of 200 subjects in four panes of 50 each.
1969   Tagged   Perf. 11
1373 A795 6c orange, red, black & light blue, July 16   20   5
            Margin block of 4, P#   1.00   —
            Margin block of 4, Mr. Zip and "Use
              Zip Code"   85   —
            Margin block of 6, "Mail Early in the
              Day"   1.35   —

JOHN WESLEY POWELL ISSUE

Issued to honor John Wesley Powell (1834–1902), geologist who explored the Green and Colorado Rivers 1869–1875, and ethnologist.

Major Powell Exploring Colorado River, 1869
A796
Designed by Rudolph Wendelin.
LITHOGRAPHED, ENGRAVED (Giori)
Plates of 200 subjects in four panes of 50 each.
1969   Tagged   Perf. 11
1374 A796 6c black, ocher & light blue, Aug. 1   20   5

            Margin block of 4, P#   1.00   —
            Margin block of 4, Mr. Zip and "Use
              Zip Code"   85   —
            Margin block of 6, "Mail Early in the
              Day"   1.35   —

ALABAMA STATEHOOD ISSUE

Issued to commemorate the 150th anniversary of Alabama statehood.

Camellia and Yellow-shafted Flicker
A797
Designed by Bernice Kochan
LITHOGRAPHED, ENGRAVED (Giori)
Plates of 200 subjects in four panes of 50 each.
1969   Tagged   Perf. 11
1375 A797 6c magenta, rose red, yellow, dark
                green & brown, Aug. 2   20   5
            Margin block of 4, P#   1.00   —
            Margin block of 4, Mr. Zip and "Use
              Zip Code"   85   —
            Margin block of 6, "Mail Early in the
              Day"   1.35   —

BOTANICAL CONGRESS ISSUE

Issued to publicize the 11th International Botanical Congress, Seattle, Wash., Aug. 24–Sept. 2. Nos. 1376–1379 are printed in blocks of four in panes of 50. In upper and lower left panes Nos. 1376 and 1378 appear in first, third and fifth place; Nos. 1377 and 1379 in second and fourth place. This arrangement is reversed in upper and lower right panes.

Douglas Fir
(Northwest)
A798

Ocotillo
(Southwest)
A800

Lady's-slipper
(Northeast)
A799

Franklinia
(Southeast)
A801

Designed by Stanley Galli.
LITHOGRAPHED, ENGRAVED (Giori)
Plates of 200 subjects in four panes of 50 each.
1969, Aug. 23   Tagged   Perf. 11
1376 A798 6c multicolored   1.10   15
            Margin block of 4, P# adjoining
              #1376   8.50   —
            Margin block of 4, Mr. Zip and "Use
              Zip Code" adjoining #1376   6.50   —
            Margin block of 6, "Mail Early in the
              Day" adjoining #1376   8.50   —
1377 A799 6c multicolored   1.10   15
            Margin block of 4, P# adjoining
              #1377   8.50   —
            Margin block of 4, Mr. Zip and "Use
              Zip Code" adjoining #1377   6.50   —
            Margin block of 6, "Mail Early in the
              Day" adjoining #1377   8.50   —
1378 A800 6c multicolored   1.10   15
            Margin block of 4, P# adjoining
              #1378   8.50   —
            Margin block of 4, Mr. Zip and "Use
              Zip Code" adjoining #1378   6.50   —
            Margin block of 6, "Mail Early in the
              Day" adjoining #1378   8.50   —
1379 A801 6c multicolored   1.10   15
            Margin block of 4, P# adjoining
              #1379   8.50   —
            Margin block of 4, Mr. Zip and "Use
              Zip Code" adjoining #1379   6.50   —
            Margin block of 6, "Mail Early in the
              Day" adjoining #1379   8.50   —
         a. Block of four, #1376–1379   5.50   5.00

DARTMOUTH COLLEGE CASE ISSUE

Issued to commemorate the 150th anniversary of the Dartmouth College Case, which Daniel Webster argued before the Supreme Court, reasserting the sanctity of contracts.

Daniel Webster and Dartmouth Hall
A802

Designed by John R. Scotford, Jr.
ROTARY PRESS PRINTING
E.E. Plates of 200 subjects in four panes of 50 each.

1969			Tagged	Perf. 10½x11	
1380	A802	6c	green, *Sept. 22*	20	5
			Margin block of 4, P#	1.35	
			Margin block of 4, Mr. Zip and "Use Zip Code"	85	
			Margin block of 6, "Mail Early in the Day"	1.35	

PROFESSIONAL BASEBALL ISSUE

Issued to commemorate the centenary of professional baseball.

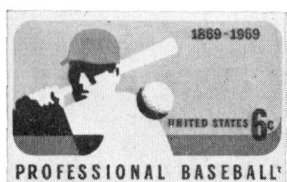

Batter
A803
Designed by Alex Ross.
LITHOGRAPHED, ENGRAVED (Giori)
Plates of 200 subjects in four panes of 50 each.

1969			Tagged	Perf. 11	
1381	A803	6c	yel., red, blk. & grn., *Sept. 24*	25	5
			Margin block of 4, P#	1.75	
			Margin block of 4, Mr. Zip and "Use Zip Code"	1.10	
			Margin block of 6, "Mail Early in the Day"	1.65	
		a.	Black omitted ("1869-1969, United States, 6c, Professional Baseball")	*1,000.*	

INTERCOLLEGIATE FOOTBALL ISSUE

Issued to commemorate the centenary of intercollegiate football.

Football Player and Coach
A804

Designed by Robert Peak.
LITHOGRAPHED, ENGRAVED (Giori)
Plates of 200 subjects in four panes of 50 each.

1969			Tagged	Perf. 11	
1382	A804	6c	red & green, *Sept. 26*	25	5
			Margin block of 4, P#	1.75	
			Margin block of 4, Mr. Zip and "Use Zip Code"	1.10	
			Margin block of 6, "Mail Early in the Day"	1.65	

The engraved parts were printed on a rotary currency press.

DWIGHT D. EISENHOWER ISSUE

Issued in memory of Gen. Dwight David Eisenhower, 34th President (1890–1969).

Dwight D. Eisenhower
A805

Designed by Robert J. Jones; photograph by Bernie Noble.
GIORI PRESS PRINTING
Plates of 128 subjects in 4 panes of 32 each.

1969			Tagged	Perf. 11	
1383	A805	6c	blue, black & red, *Oct. 14*	20	5
			Margin block of 4, P#	1.00	
			Margin block of 4, Mr. Zip and "Use Zip Code"	85	
			Margin block of 6, "Mail Early in the Day"	1.35	

CHRISTMAS ISSUE

The painting, painted about 1870 by an unknown primitive artist, is the property of the N.Y. State Historical Association, Cooperstown, N.Y.

Winter Sunday in Norway, Maine
A806

Designed by Stevan Dohanos.
ENGRAVED (Multicolor Huck)
Panes of 50 (5x10)

1969			Tagged	Perf. 11x10½	
1384	A806	6c	dark green & multi., *Nov. 3*	18	5
			Margin block of 10, 5P#, 2 to 3 zip, 2-3 Mail Early	2.25	
		a.	Precanceled	60	6
		b.	Imperf. pair	*1,500.*	
		c.	Light green omitted	35.00	
		d.	Lt. grn., red & yel omitted	*1,200.*	
		e.	Yellow omitted		

No. 1384a is an experimental precancel printed in four cities with the names between bars: in black or green, "ATLANTA, GA" and in green only "BALTIMORE, MD", "MEMPHIS, TN" and "NEW HAVEN, CT". They were sold freely to the public and could be used on any class of mail at all post offices during the experimental program and thereafter.

HOPE FOR CRIPPLED ISSUE

Issued to encourage the rehabilitation of crippled children and adults and to honor the National Society for Crippled Children and Adults (Easter Seal Society) on its 50th anniversary.

Cured Child
A807

Designed by Mark English.
LITHOGRAPHED, ENGRAVED (Giori)
Plates of 200 subjects in four panes of 50 each. Perf. 11

1969			Tagged		
1385	A807	6c	multicolored, *Nov. 20*	18	5
			Margin block of 4, P#	1.00	
			Margin block of 4, Mr. Zip and "Use Zip Code"	.80	
			Margin block of 6, "Mail Early in the Day"	1.20	

WILLIAM M. HARNETT ISSUE

Issued to honor William M. Harnett (1848–1892), painter. The painting hangs in the Museum of Fine Arts, Boston.

"Old Models"
A808

Designed by Robert J. Jones.
LITHOGRAPHED, ENGRAVED (Giori)
Plates of 128 subjects in 4 panes of 32 each. Perf. 11

1969			Tagged		
1386	A808	6c	multicolored, *Dec. 3*	18	5
			Margin block of 4, P#	1.20	
			Margin block of 4, Mr. Zip and "Use Zip Code"	.80	
			Margin block of 6, "Mail Early in the Day"	1.20	

NATURAL HISTORY ISSUE

Issued in connection with the 1969–1970 celebration of the centenary of the American Museum of Natural History in New York City. Nos. 1387–1390 are printed in blocks of four in panes of 32. Nos. 1387–1388 alternate in first row, Nos. 1389–1390 in second row. This arrangement is repeated throughout the pane.

American Bald Eagle
A809
AMERICAN BALD EAGLE

AFRICAN ELEPHANT HERD
African Elephant Herd
A810

Tlingit Chief in Haida Ceremonial Canoe
A811
HAIDA CEREMONIAL CANOE

THE AGE OF REPTILES
Brontosaurus, Stegosaurus and Allosaurus from Jurassic Period
A812

Designers: No. 1387 (eagle), Walter Richards; No. 1388 (elephants), Dean Ellis; No. 1389 (Haida canoe), Paul Rabut; No. 1390 (Age of Reptiles) detail from mural by Rudolph Zallinger in Yale's Peabody Museum, adapted by Robert J. Jones.

LITHOGRAPHED, ENGRAVED (Giori)
Plates of 128 subjects in 4 panes of 32 each (4x8).

1970, May 6			Tagged	Perf. 11	
1387	A809	6c	multicolored	22	12
			Margin block of 4, P# adjoining #1387	1.75	
			Margin block of 4, Mr. Zip and "Use Zip Code" adjoining #1387	1.10	
			Margin block of 6, "Mail Early in the Day" adjoining #1387	1.50	
1388	A810	6c	multicolored	22	12
			Margin block of 4, P# adjoining #1388	1.75	
1389	A811	6c	multicolored	22	12
			Margin block of 4, P# adjoining #1389	1.75	
			Margin block of 4, Mr. Zip and "Use Zip Code" adjoining #1389	1.10	
			Margin block of 6, "Mail Early in the Day" adjoining #1389	1.50	
1390	A812	6c	multicolored	22	12
			Margin block of 4, P# adjoining #1390	1.75	
			Margin block of 4, Mr. Zip and "Use Zip Code" adjoining #1390	1.10	
			Margin block of 6, "Mail Early in the Day" adjoining #1390	1.50	
		a.	Block of four (#1387-1390)	1.00	1.00

MAINE STATEHOOD ISSUE

Issued to commemorate the sesquicentennial of Maine Statehood. The painting by Edward Hopper (1882–1967) hangs in the Metropolitan Museum of Art, New York City.

The Lighthouse at Two Lights, Maine,
by Edward Hopper
A813

Designed by Stevan Dohanos.
LITHOGRAPHED, ENGRAVED (Giori)
Plates of 200 subjects in four panes of 50 each.

1970		Tagged	Perf. 11	
1391	A813	6c **black & multicolored**, *July 9*	18	5
		Margin block of 4, P#	1.10	
		Margin block of 4, Mr. Zip and "Use Zip Code"	80	
		Margin block of 6, "Mail Early in the Day"	1.20	

WILDLIFE CONSERVATION ISSUE

Issued to emphasize the importance of wildlife conservation in America.

American Buffalo
A814

Designed by Robert Lougheed.
ROTARY PRESS PRINTING
E.E. Plates of 200 subjects in four panes of 50 each.

1970		Tagged	Perf. 11x10½	
1392	A814	6c **light brown**, *July 20*	18	5
		Margin block of 4, P#	1.10	
		Margin block of 4, Mr. Zip and "Use Zip Code"	80	
		Margin block of 6, "Mail Early in the Day"	1.20	

REGULAR ISSUE

Dwight David Eisenhower

Dot between "R" and "U"	No Dot between "R" and "U"
A815	A815a

Benjamin Franklin
A816

U.S. Postal Service
Emblem—A817

Fiorello H. LaGuardia
A817a

Ernest Taylor Pyle
A818

Dr. Elizabeth Blackwell
A818a

Amadeo P. Giannini
A818b

Designers: Nos. 1393-1395, 1401-1402, Robert Geissman; photograph by George Tames. 7c, Bill Hyde. No. 1396, Raymond Loewy/William Smith, Inc. 14c, Robert Geissman; photograph by George Fayer. 16c, Robert Geissman; photograph by Alfred Eisenstadt. 18c, Robert Geissman; painting by Joseph Kozlowski. 21c, Robert Geissman.

ROTARY PRESS PRINTING
E.E. Plates of 400 subjects in four panes of 100 each.

1970-74		Tagged	Perf. 11x10½	
1393	A815	6c **dark blue gray**, *Aug. 6, 1970*	12	5
		Margin block of 4, P#	60	
		Margin block of 4, "Use Zip Codes"	50	
		Margin block of 6, "Mail Early in the Day"	80	
	a.	Booklet pane of 8	1.25	50
	b.	Booklet pane of 5 + label	1.20	35
	c.	Untagged (Bureau precanceled)		10

Perf. 10½x11

1393D	A816	7c **bright blue**, *Oct. 20, 1972*	14	5
		Margin block of 4, P#	1.35	
		Margin block of 4, "Use Zip Codes"	60	
		Margin block of 6, "Mail Early in the Day"	95	
	e.	Untagged (Bureau precanceled)		10

GIORI PRESS PRINTING
Plates of 400 subjects in four panes of 100 each.
Perf. 11

1394	A815a	8c **black, red & blue gray**, *May 10, 1971*	16	5
		Margin block of 4, P#	1.00	
		Margin block of 4, "Use Zip Codes"	70	
		Margin block of 6, "Mail Early in the Day"	1.00	
		Pair with full vert. gutter btwn.		

ROTARY PRESS PRINTING
Perf. 11x10½

1395	A815	8c **deep claret**, (from blkt. pane)		16	5
		a. Booklet pane of 8, *May 10, 1971*		2.00	1.25
		b. Booklet pane of 6, *May 10, 1971*		1.00	75
		c. Booklet pane of 4 + 2 labels ('72), *Jan. 28, 1972*		1.00	50
		d. Booklet pane of 7 + label ('72), *Jan. 28, 1972*		1.75	1.00

No. 1395 was issued only in booklets. All stamps have one or two straight edges.

PHOTOGRAVURE (Andreotti)
Plates of 400 subjects in four panes of 100 each.
Perf. 11x10½

1396	A817	8c **multicolored**, *July 1, 1971*		25	5
		Margin block of 12, 6P#		5.00	
		Margin block of 20, 6P#, "Mail Early in the Day," "Use Zip Codes" and rectangular color contents (UL pane)		7.50	
		Margin block of 4, "Use Zip Codes"		1.20	
		Margin block of 4, "Mail Early in the Day"		1.20	

ROTARY PRESS PRINTING
E. E. Plates of 400 subjects in four panes of 100 each.

1397	A817a	14c **gray brown**, *Apr. 24, 1972*		32	5
		Margin block of 4, P#		2.35	
		Margin block of 4, "Use Zip Codes"		1.40	
		Margin block of 6, "Mail Early in the Day"		2.00	
		a. Untagged (Bureau precanceled)			25
1398	A818	16c **brown**, *May 7, 1971*		35	5
		Margin block of 4, P#		2.35	
		Margin block of 4, "Use Zip Codes"		1.60	
		Margin block of 6, "Mail Early in the Day"		2.30	
		a. Untagged (Bureau precanceled)			25
1399	A818a	18c **violet**, *Jan. 23, 1974*		40	6
		Margin block of 4, P#		2.25	
		Margin block of 4, "Use Zip Codes"		1.80	
		Margin block of 6, "Mail Early in the Day"		2.60	
1400	A818b	21c **green**, *June 27, 1973*		45	6
		Margin block of 4, P#		2.25	
		Margin block of 4, "Use Zip Codes"		2.00	
		Margin block of 6, "Mail Early in the Day"		2.85	

COIL STAMPS
ROTARY PRESS PRINTING

1970-71   Tagged   *Perf. 10 Vert.*

1401	A815	6c **dark blue gray**, *Aug. 6, 1970*		20	5
		Pair		40	10
		Joint line pair		1.00	15
		a. Untagged (Bureau precanceled)			10
		b. Imperf. pair		1,000.	
1402	A815	8c **deep claret**, *May 10, 1971*		22	5
		Pair		44	10
		Joint line pair		1.00	20
		a. Imperf., pair		50.00	
		a. Joint line pair		75.00	
		b. Untagged (Bureau precanceled)			20
		c. Pair, imperf. between			

EDGAR LEE MASTERS ISSUE

Issued to honor Edgar Lee Masters (1869–1950), poet.

Edgar Lee Masters
A819

Designed by Fred Otnes.

LITHOGRAPHED, ENGRAVED (Giori)

E.E. Plates of 200 subjects in four panes of 50 each.

1970   Tagged   *Perf. 11*

1405	A819	6c **black & olive bister**, *Aug. 22*		18	5
		Margin block of 4, P#		1.00	
		Margin block of 4, Mr. Zip and "Use Zip Code"		80	
		Margin block of 6, "Mail Early in the Day"		1.20	

WOMAN SUFFRAGE ISSUE

Issued to commemorate the 50th anniversary of the 19th Amendment, which gave the vote to women.

Suffragettes, 1920, and Woman Voter, 1970—A820

Designed by Ward Brackett.

GIORI PRESS PRINTING

Plates of 200 subjects in four panes of 50 each.

1970   Tagged   *Perf. 11*

1406	A820	6c **blue**, *Aug. 26*		18	5
		Margin block of 4, P#		1.00	
		Margin block of 4, Mr. Zip and "Use Zip Code"		80	
		Margin block of 6, "Mail Early in the Day"		1.20	

SOUTH CAROLINA ISSUE

Issued to commemorate the 300th anniversary of the founding of Charles Town (Charleston), the first permanent settlement of South Carolina. Against a background of pine wood the line drawings of the design represent the economic and historic development of South Carolina: the spire of St. Phillip's Church, Capitol, state flag, a ship, 17th century man and woman, a Fort Sumter cannon, barrels, cotton, tobacco and yellow jasmine.

Symbols of South Carolina
A821

Designed by George Samerjan.
LITHOGRAPHED, ENGRAVED (Giori)
Plates of 200 subjects in four panes of 50 each.

1970			Tagged	Perf. 11	
1407	A821	6c bister, black & red, *Sept. 12*		18	5
		Margin block of 4, P#		1.00	
		Margin block of 4, Mr. Zip and "Use Zip Code"		80	
		Margin block of 6, "Mail Early in the Day"		1.20	

STONE MOUNTAIN MEMORIAL ISSUE

Issued to commemorate the dedication of the Stone Mountain Confederate Memorial, Georgia, May 9, 1970.

Robert E. Lee, Jefferson Davis and "Stonewall" Jackson
A822

Designed by Robert Hallock.
GIORI PRESS PRINTING
Plates of 200 subjects in four panes of 50 each.

1970			Tagged	Perf. 11	
1408	A822	6c gray, *Sept. 19*		18	5

		Margin block of 4, P#		1.00	
		Margin block of 4, Mr. Zip and "Use Zip Code"		80	
		Margin block of 6, "Mail Early in the Day"		1.20	

FORT SNELLING ISSUE

Issued to commemorate the 150th anniversary of Fort Snelling, Minnesota, which was an important outpost for the opening of the Northwest.

Fort Snelling, Keelboat and Tepees
A823

Designed by David K. Stone.
LITHOGRAPHED, ENGRAVED (Giori)
Plates of 200 in four panes of 50 each.

1970			Tagged	Perf. 11	
1409	A823	6c yellow & multicolored, *Oct. 17*		18	5
		Margin block of 4, P#		1.00	
		Margin block of 4, Mr. Zip and "Use Zip Code"		80	
		Margin block of 6, "Mail Early in the Day"		1.20	

ANTI-POLLUTION ISSUE

Issued to focus attention on the problems of pollution. Nos. 1410–1413 are printed in blocks of four in panes of 50. In upper and lower left panes Nos. 1410 and 1412 appear in first, third and fifth place; Nos. 1411 and 1413 in second and fourth place. This arrangement is reversed in upper and lower right panes.

Globe and Wheat
A824

Globe and City
A825

Globe and Bluegill
A826

Globe and Seagull
A827

Designed by Arnold Copeland and Walter DuBois Richards. Printed by Bureau of Engraving and Printing at Guilford Gravure, Inc., Guilford, Conn.

PHOTOGRAVURE
Plates of 200 Subjects in four panes of 50 each.

1970, Oct. 28			Tagged	Perf. 11x10½	
1410	A824	6c multicolored		45	13
		Margin block of 10, 5 P# adjoining #1410, 1412		6.00	
		Margin block of 4, Mr. Zip and "Use Zip Code" adjoining #1410		2.75	
		Margin block of 6, "Mail Early in the Day" adjoining #1410		3.50	
1411	A825	6c multicolored		45	13
		Margin block of 10, 5 P# adjoining #1411, 1413		6.00	
		Margin block of 4, Mr. Zip and "Use Zip Code" adjoining #1411		2.75	
		Margin block of 6, "Mail Early in the Day" adjoining #1411		3.50	
1412	A826	6c multicolored		45	13
		Margin block of 4, Mr. Zip and "Use Zip Code" adjoining #1412		2.75	
		Margin block of 6, "Mail Early in the Day" adjoining #1412		3.50	
1413	A827	6c multicolored		45	13
		Margin block of 4, Mr. Zip and "Use Zip Code" adjoining #1413		2.75	
		Margin block of 6, "Mail Early in the Day" adjoining #1413		3.50	
		a. Block of four, #1410-1413		2.50	2.00

POSTAGE, 1970 281

CHRISTMAS ISSUE

Nos. 1415–1418 are printed in blocks of four in panes of 50. In upper and lower left panes Nos. 1415 and 1417 appear in first, third and fifth place; Nos. 1416 and 1418 in second and fourth place. This arrangement is reversed in upper and lower right panes.

Nativity, by Lorenzo Lotto
A828

Tin and Cast-iron Locomotive
A829

Toy Horse on Wheels
A830

Mechanical Tricycle
A831

Doll Carriage
A832

Designers: No. 1414, Howard C. Mildner, from a painting by Lorenzo Lotto (1480-1556) in the National Gallery of Art, Washington, D.C. Nos. 1415-1418, Stevan Dohanos, from a drawing (locomotive) by Charles Hemming and from "Golden Age of Toys" by Fondin and Remise.
Printed by Guilford Gravure, Inc., Guilford, Conn.

PHOTOGRAVURE

Plates of 200 subjects in four panes of 50 each.

1970, Nov. 5   Tagged   Perf. 10½x11

1414	A828	6c **multicolored**	20	5
		Margin block of 8, 4 P#	2.25	
		Margin block of 4, Mr. Zip and "Use Zip Code"	1.20	
		Margin block of 6, "Mail Early in the Day"	1.50	
	a.	Precanceled	35	8
	b.	Black omitted	900.00	
	c.	As "a," blue omitted	1,400.	

Perf. 11x10½

1415	A829	6c **multicolored**	85	10
		Margin block of 8, 4 P# adjoining #1415, 1417	8.50	
		Margin block of 4, Mr. Zip and "Use Zip Code" adjoining #1415	4.50	
		Margin block of 6, "Mail Early in the Day" adjoining #1415	6.50	
	a.	Precanceled	2.00	15
	b.	Black omitted	1,500.	

1416	A830	6c **multicolored**	85	10
		Margin block of 8, 4 P# adjoining #1416, 1418	8.50	
		Margin block of 4, Mr. Zip and "Use Zip Code" adjoining #1416	4.50	
		Margin block of 6, "Mail Early in the Day" adjoining #1416	6.50	
	a.	Precanceled	2.00	15
	b.	Black omitted	1,500.	
	c.	Imperf., pair (#1416, 1418)		

1417	A831	6c **multicolored**	85	10
		Margin block of 4, Mr. Zip and "Use Zip Code" adjoining #1417	4.50	
		Margin block of 6, "Mail Early in the Day" adjoining #1417	6.50	
	a.	Precanceled	2.00	15
	b.	Black omitted	1,500.	

1418	A832	6c **multicolored**	85	10
		Margin block of 4, Mr. Zip and "Use Zip Code" adjoining #1418	4.50	
		Margin block of 6, "Mail Early in the Day" adjoining #1418	6.50	
	a.	Precanceled	2.00	15
	b.	Block of four, #1415-1418	4.50	3.50
	c.	As "b," precanceled	9.00	6.00
	d.	Black omitted	1,500.	

The precanceled stamps, Nos. 1414a-1418a, were furnished to 68 cities. The plates include two straight (No. 1414a) or two wavy (Nos. 1415a-1418a) black lines that make up the precancellation. Unused prices are for copies with gum and used prices are for copies with an additional cancellation or without gum.

UNITED NATIONS ISSUE

Issued to commemorate the 25th anniversary of the United Nations.

"U.N." and U.N. Emblem
A833

Designed by Arnold Copeland.

LITHOGRAPHED, ENGRAVED (Giori)

Plates of 200 subjects in four panes of 50 each.

1970			Tagged	Perf. 11	
1419	A833	6c	**black, verm. & ultra.**, *Nov. 20*	18	5
			Margin block of 4, P#	1.25	
			Margin block of 4, Mr. Zip and "Use Zip Code"	80	
			Margin block of 6, "Mail Early in the Day"	1.20	
			Pair with full horiz. gutter btwn.		

LANDING OF THE PILGRIMS ISSUE

Issued to commemorate the 350th anniversary of the landing of the Mayflower.

Mayflower and Pilgrims
A834

Designed by Mark English.

LITHOGRAPHED, ENGRAVED (Giori)

Plates of 200 subjects in four panes of 50 each.

1970			Tagged	Perf. 11	
1420	A834	6c	**blk., org., yel., magenta, bl. & brn.**, *Nov. 21*	18	5
			Margin block of 4, P#	1.25	
			Margin block of 4, Mr. Zip and "Use Zip Code"	80	
			Margin block of 6, "Mail Early in the Day"	1.20	
		a.	Orange & yellow omitted	1,250.	

DISABLED AMERICAN VETERANS AND SERVICEMEN ISSUE

No. 1421 commemorates the 50th anniversary of the Disabled Veterans of America Organization; No. 1422 honors the contribution of servicemen, particularly those who were prisoners of war, missing or killed in action. Nos. 1421–1422 are printed se-tenant in horizontal rows of 10 in panes of 50, four panes to a sheet.

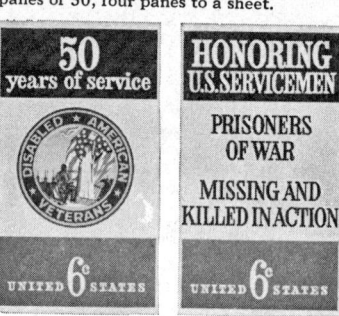

Disabled American
Veterans Emblem
A835   A836

Designed by Stevan Dohanos.

LITHOGRAPHED, ENGRAVED (Giori)

Plates of 200 subjects in four panes of 50 each.

1970, Nov. 24			Tagged	Perf. 11	
1421	A835	6c	**dk. blue, red & multicolored**	20	10
		a.	Pair, #1421-1422	50	65
			Block of four, 2 #1421 + 2 #1422	1.00	1.40
			Margin block of 4, P# No. adjoining #1421	3.00	
			Margin block of 4, Mr. Zip and "Use Zip Code" adjoining #1421	1.25	
			Margin block of 6, "Mail Early in the Day" adjoining #1421	1.60	

ENGRAVED

1422	A836	6c	**dark blue, black & red**	20	10
			Margin block of 4, P# adjoining #1422	3.00	
			Margin block of 4, Mr. Zip and "Use Zip Code" adjoining #1422	1.25	
			Margin block of 6, "Mail Early in the Day" adjoining #1422	1.60	

AMERICAN WOOL INDUSTRY ISSUE

Issued to commemorate the 450th anniversary of the introduction of sheep to the North American continent and the beginning of the American wool industry.

Ewe and Lamb
A837

Designed by Dean Ellis.

LITHOGRAPHED, ENGRAVED (Giori)

Plates of 200 subjects in four panes of 50 each.

1971			Tagged	Perf. 11	
1423	A837	6c	**multicolored**, *Jan. 19*	18	5
			Block of four	72	20
			Margin block of 4, P#	1.00	

GEN. DOUGLAS MacARTHUR ISSUE

Issued in honor of Gen. Douglas MacArthur (1880–1964), Chief of Staff, Supreme Commander for the Allied Powers in the Pacific Area during World War II and Supreme Commander in Japan after the war.

Gen. Douglas MacArthur
A838

Designed by Paul Calle; Wide World photograph.

GIORI PRESS PRINTING

Plates of 200 subjects in four panes of 50 each.

		Tagged		Perf. 11	
1971					
1424	A838	6c black, red & dark blue, Jan. 26	18	5
		Margin block of 4, P#	1.00	—
		Margin block of 4, Mr. Zip and "Use Zip Code"	80	—
		Margin block of 6, "Mail Early in the Day"	1.20	—

BLOOD DONOR ISSUE

Salute to blood donors and spur to increased participation in the blood donor program.

"Giving Blood Saves Lives"
A839

Designed by Howard Munce.

LITHOGRAPHED, ENGRAVED (Giori)

Plates of 200 subjects in four panes of 50 each.

		Tagged		Perf. 11	
1971					
1425	A839	6c blue, scarlet & indigo, Mar. 12	18	5
		Margin block of 4, P#	1.00	—
		Margin block of 4, Mr. Zip and "Use Zip Code"	80	—
		Margin block of 6, "Mail Early in the Day"	1.20	—

MISSOURI SESQUICENTENNIAL ISSUE

Sesquicentennial of Missouri's admission to the Union. The stamp design shows a Pawnee facing a hunter-trapper and a group of settlers. It is from a mural by Thomas Hart Benton in the Harry S. Truman Library, Independence, Mo.

"Independence and the Opening of the West," Detail, by Thomas Hart Benton—A840

Designed by Bradbury Thompson.

PHOTOGRAVURE (Andreotti)

Plates of 200 subjects in four panes of 50 each.

		Tagged		Perf. 11x10½	
1971					
1426	A840	8c multicolored, May 8	20	5
		Margin block of 12, 6P#	3.50	—
		Margin block of 4, Mr. Zip and "Use Zip Code"	1.10	—
		Margin block of 4, "Mail Early in the Day"	1.00	—

See note on Andreotti printings and their color control markings in Information for Collectors under Printing, Photogravure.

WILDLIFE CONSERVATION ISSUE

Nos. 1427–1430 are printed in blocks of 4 in panes of 32. Nos. 1427–1428 alternate in first row, Nos. 1429–1430 in second row. This arrangement repeated throughout pane.

Trout
A841

Alligator
A842

Polar Bear and Cubs
A843

California Condor
A844

284 POSTAGE, 1971

Designed by Stanley W. Galli.
LITHOGRAPHED, ENGRAVED (Giori)
Plates of 128 subjects in 4 panes of 32 each (4x8).

1971, June 12			Tagged		Perf. 11	
1427	A841	8c	**multicolored**		30	10
			Margin block of 4, P# adjoining 1427	1.75		
			Margin block of 4, Mr. Zip and "Use Zip Code" adjoining #1427		1.40	—
			Margin block of 6, "Mail Early in the Day" adjoining #1427		2.00	—
1428	A842	8c	**multicolored**		30	10
			Margin block of 4, P# adjoining 1428	1.75		
			Margin block of 4, Mr. Zip and "Use Zip Code" adjoining #1428		1.40	—
			Margin block of 6, "Mail Early in the Day" adjoining #1428		2.00	—
1429	A843	8c	**multicolored**		30	10
			Margin block of 4, P# adjoining 1429	1.75		
			Margin block of 4, Mr. Zip and "Use Zip Code" adjoining #1429		1.40	—
			Margin block of 6, "Mail Early in the Day" adjoining #1429		2.00	—
1430	A844	8c	**multicolored**		30	10
			Margin block of 4, P# adjoining 1430	1.75		
			Margin block of 4, Mr. Zip and "Use Zip Code" adjoining #1430		1.40	—
			Margin block of 6, "Mail Early in the Day" adjoining #1430		2.00	—
		a.	Block of four, #1427-1430		1.30	1.00
		b.	As "a", light green & dark green omitted from #1427-1428		3,000.	
		c.	As "a", red omitted from #1427 1429-1430			

ANTARCTIC TREATY ISSUE

Map of Antarctica—A845

Designed by Howard Koslow; adapted from emblem on official documents of Consultative Meetings.
GIORI PRESS PRINTING
Plates of 200 subjects in four panes of 50 each.

1971			Tagged		Perf. 11	
1431	A845	8c	**red & dark blue,** *June 23*		25	5
			Margin block of 4, P#		1.50	—
			Margin block of 4, Mr. Zip and "Use Zip Code"		1.10	—
			Margin block of 6, "Mail Early in the Day"		1.65	—

AMERICAN REVOLUTION BICENTENNIAL

Bicentennial of the American Revolution.

Bicentennial Commission Emblem—A846
Designed by Chermayeff & Geismar.
LITHOGRAPHED, ENGRAVED (Giori)
Plates of 200 subjects in four panes of 50 each.

1971			Tagged		Perf. 11	
1432	A846	8c	**gray, red, blue & black,** *July 4*		50	5
			Margin block of 4, P#		3.25	—
			Margin block of 4, Mr. Zip and "Use Zip Code"		2.25	—
			Margin block of 6, "Mail Early in the Day"		3.50	—
		a.	Gray & black omitted		1,000.	
		b.	Gray ("U.S. Postage 8c") omitted			—

JOHN SLOAN ISSUE

Issued to honor John Sloan (1871–1951), painter. The painting hangs in the Phillips Gallery, Washington, D.C.

The Wake of the Ferry—A847
Designed by Bradbury Thompson.
LITHOGRAPHED, ENGRAVED (Giori)
Plates of 200 subjects in four panes of 50 each.

1971			Tagged		Perf. 11	
1433	A847	8c	**multicolored,** *Aug. 2*		20	5
			Margin block of 4, P#		1.50	—
			Margin block of 4, Mr. Zip and "Use Zip Code"		1.00	—
			Margin block of 6, "Mail Early in the Day"		1.20	—

SPACE ACHIEVEMENT DECADE ISSUE

Issued to commemorate a decade of space achievements and the Apollo 15 moon exploration mission, July 26–Aug. 7. Nos. 1434-1435 are printed se-tenant in horizontal rows of 5 in panes of 50. In the upper and lower left panes the earth and sun stamp is first, third and fifth, the rover second and fourth. This arrangement is reversed in the upper and lower right panes.

Earth, Sun and Landing Craft on Moon
A848

Lunar Rover and Astronauts
A849

POSTAGE, 1971

Designed by Robert McCall.
LITHOGRAPHED, ENGRAVED (Giori)
Plates of 200 subjects in four panes of 50 each.

1971, Aug. 2			Tagged		Perf. 11	
1434	A848	8c	**black, blue, gray, yellow & red**	20	10	
		a.	Pair, #1434-1435	50	35	
			Block of four, 2 #1434 + 2 #1435	1.00	70	
			Block of 4, P# adjoining #1434	1.75		
			Margin block of 4, Mr. Zip and "Use Zip Code" adjoining #1434	1.10		
			Margin block of 6, "Mail Early in the Day" adjoining #1434	1.50		
		b.	As "a," blue & red (litho.) omitted	2,000.		
1435	A849	8c	**black, blue, gray, yellow & red**	20	10	
			Margin block of 4, P# adjoining #1435	1.75		
			Margin block of 4, Mr. Zip and "Use Zip Code" adjoining #1435	1.10		
			Margin block of 6, "Mail Early in the Day" adjoining #1435	1.50		

EMILY DICKINSON ISSUE

Issued to honor Emily Elizabeth Dickinson (1830–1886), poet.

Emily Dickinson—A850
Designed by Bernard Fuchs after a photograph.
LITHOGRAPHED, ENGRAVED (Giori)
Plates of 200 subjects in four panes of 50 each.

1971			Tagged		Perf. 11	
1436	A850	8c	**multicolored,** *greenish, Aug. 28*	18	5	
			Margin block of 4, P#	1.25		
			Margin block of 4, Mr. Zip and "Use Zip Code"	85		
			Margin block of 6, "Mail Early in the Day"	1.20		
		a.	Black & olive (engr.) omitted	850.00		
		b.	Pale rose omitted			

SAN JUAN ISSUE

Issued for the 450th anniversary of San Juan, Puerto Rico.

Sentry Box, Morro Castle, San Juan—A851
Designed as a woodcut by Walter Brooks.

LITHOGRAPHED, ENGRAVED (Giori)
Plates of 200 subjects in four panes of 50 each.

1971			Tagged		Perf. 11	
1437	A851	8c	**pale brown, black, yellow & dark brown,** *Sept. 12*	18	5	
			Margin block of 4, P#	1.25		
			Margin block of 4, Mr. Zip and "Use Zip Code"	85		
			Margin block of 6, "Mail Early in the Day"	1.20		

PREVENT DRUG ABUSE ISSUE

Drug Abuse Prevention Week, Oct. 3–9.

Young Woman Drug Addict—A852
Designed by Miggs Burroughs.
PHOTOGRAVURE (Andreotti)
Plates of 200 subjects in four panes of 50 each.

1971			Tagged		Perf. 10½x11	
1438	A852	A8c	**blue, deep blue & black,** *Oct. 4*	18	5	
			Margin block of 6, 3P#	1.85		
			Margin block of 4, "Use Zip Code"	85		
			Margin block of 6, "Mail Early in the Day"	1.20		

CARE ISSUE

25th anniversary of CARE, a U.S.-Canadian Cooperative for American Relief everywhere.

Hands Reaching for CARE—A853
Designed by Soren Noring.
PHOTOGRAVURE (Andreotti)
Plates of 200 subjects in four panes of 50 each.

1971			Tagged		Perf. 10½x11	
1439	A853	8c	**blue, blk., vio. & red lilac,** *Oct. 27*	18	5	
			Margin block of 8, 4P#	2.10		
			Margin block of 4, Mr. Zip and "Use Zip Code"	85		
			Margin block of 6, "Mail Early in the Day"	1.20		

HISTORIC PRESERVATION ISSUE

Nos. 1440–1443 are printed in blocks of 4 in panes of 32. Nos. 1440–1441 alternate in first row, Nos. 1442–1443 in second row. This arrangement is repeated throughout the pane.

Decatur House, Washington, D. C.
A854

Whaling Ship Charles W. Morgan, Mystic, Conn.
A855

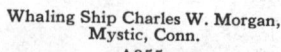

Cable Car, San Francisco
A856

San Xavier del Bac Mission, Tucson, Ariz.
A857

Designed by Melbourne Brindle.
LITHOGRAPHED, ENGRAVED (Giori)

1971, Oct. 29			Tagged		*Perf. 11*	
1440	A854	8c	black brown & ocher, *buff*		25	12
			Margin block of 4, P# adjoining #1440		1.85	——
			Margin block of 4, Mr. Zip and "Use Zip Code" adjoining #1440		1.20	——
			Margin block of 6, "Mail Early in the Day" adjoining #1440		1.60	——
1441	A855	8c	black brown & ocher, *buff*		25	12
			Margin block of 4, P# adjoining #1441		1.85	——
			Margin block of 4, Mr. Zip and "Use Zip Code" adjoining #1441		1.20	——
			Margin block of 6, "Mail Early in the Day" adjoining #1441		1.60	——
1442	A856	8c	black brown & ocher, *buff*		25	12
			Margin block of 4, P# adjoining #1442		1.85	——
			Margin block of 4, Mr. Zip and "Use Zip Code" adjoining #1442		1.20	——
			Margin block of 6, "Mail Early in the Day" adjoining #1442		1.60	——
1443	A857	8c	black brown & ocher, *buff*		25	12
			Margin block of 4, P# adjoining #1443		1.85	——
			Margin block of 4, Mr. Zip and "Use Zip Code" adjoining #1443		1.20	——
			Margin block of 6, "Mail Early in the Day" adjoining #1443		1.60	——
		a.	Block of four (#1440-1443)		1.20	1.20
		b.	As "a," black brown omitted		2,250.	
		c.	As "a," ocher omitted		——	

CHRISTMAS ISSUE

Adoration of the Shepherds, by Giorgione
A858

"Partridge in a Pear Tree"
A859

PHOTOGRAVURE (Andreotti)

Plates of 200 subjects in four panes of 50 each.

1971, Nov. 10			Tagged	*Perf. 10½x11*	
1444	A858	8c	**gold & multicolored**	18	5
			Margin block of 12, 6P#	2.50	——
			Margin block of 4, Mr. Zip and "Use Zip Code"	85	——
			Margin block of 4, "Mail Early in the Day"	85	——
		a.	Gold omitted	600.00	
1445	A859	8c	**dark green, red & multicolored**	18	5
			Margin block of 12, 6P#	2.50	——
			Margin block of 4, Mr. Zip and "Use Zip Code"	85	——
			Margin block of 4, "Mail Early in the Day"	85	——

Designers: No. 1444, Bradbury Thompson, using a painting by Giorgione in the National Gallery of Art, Washington, D. C. No. 1445, Jamie Wyeth.

SIDNEY LANIER ISSUE

Issued to honor Sidney Lanier (1842–1881), poet, musician, lawyer and educator.

Sidney Lanier
A860

Designed by William A. Smith.

GIORI PRESS PRINTING

Plates of 200 subjects in four panes of 50 each.

1972		Tagged		Perf. 11	
1446	A860	8c **black, brown & light blue**, *Feb. 3*		18	5
		Margin block of 4, P#		1.00	
		Margin block of 4, Mr. Zip and "Use Zip Code"		85	
		Margin block of 6, "Mail Early in the Day"		1.20	

PEACE CORPS ISSUE

Issued to honor the Peace Corps.

Peace Corps Poster,
by David Battle
A861

Designed by Bradbury Thompson.

PHOTOGRAVURE (Andreotti)

Plates of 200 subjects in four panes of 50 each.

1972		Tagged		Perf. 10½x11	
1447	A861	8c **dk. blue, lt. blue & red**, *Feb. 11*		18	5
		Margin block of 6, 3 P#		1.50	
		Margin block of 4, Mr. Zip and "Use Zip Code"		85	
		Margin block of 6, "Mail Early in the Day"		1.20	

NATIONAL PARKS CENTENNIAL ISSUE

Centenary of Yellowstone National Park, the first National Park, and of the entire National Park System. The four 2c stamps were issued for Cape Hatteras, N.C., National Seashore; 6c for Wolf Trap Farm, Vienna, Va.; 8c for Yellowstone National Park, Wyo., and 15c for Mt. McKinley National Park, Alaska. See No. C84.

A862   A863

Cape Hatteras National Seashore
A864   A865

Wolf Trap Farm, Va.
A866

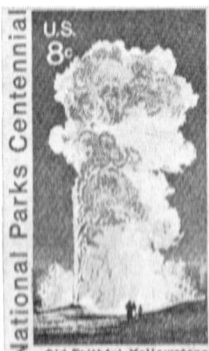

Old Faithful, Yellowstone
A867

Mt. McKinley,
Alaska
A868

Designers: 2c, Walter D. Richards; 6c, Howard Koslow; 8c, Robert Handville; 15c, James Barkley.

LITHOGRAPHED, ENGRAVED (Giori)

Plates of 400 subjects in 4 panes of 100 each. Panes contain 25 subjects each of Nos. 1448–1451.

1972		Tagged		Perf. 11	
1448	A862	2c **black & multi.**, *Apr. 5*		6	6
		Margin block of 4, P# adjoining #1448		1.60	
		Margin block of 4, "Use Zip Codes" adjoining #1448		50	
		Margin block of 8, "Mail Early in the Day" adjoining #1448		80	

POSTAGE, 1972

1449	A863	2c **black & multi.**, *Apr. 3*		6	6
		Margin block of 4, P# adjoining #1449		1.60	
		Margin block of 4, "Use Zip Codes" adjoining #1449		50	
		Margin block of 8, "Mail Early in the Day" adjoining #1449		80	
1450	A864	2c **black & multi.**, *Apr. 5*		6	6
		Margin block of 4, P# adjoining #1450		1.60	
		Margin block of 4, "Use Zip Codes" adjoining #1450		50	
		Margin block of 8, "Mail Early in the Day" adjoining #1450		80	
1451	A865	2c **black & multi.**, *Apr. 5*		6	6
		Margin block of 4, P# adjoining #1451		1.60	
		Margin block of 4, "Use Zip Codes" adjoining #1451		50	
		Margin block of 8, "Mail Early in the Day" adjoining #1451		80	
		a. Block of four (#1448-1451)		25	30
		b. As "a," black (litho.) omitted		2,000.	

Plates of 200 subjects in four panes of 50 each

1452	A866	6c **black & multicolored**, *June 26*	16	8
		Margin block of 4, P#	1.25	
		Margin block of 4, Mr. Zip and "Use Zip Code"	70	
		Margin block of 6, "Mail Early in the Day"	1.00	

Plates of 128 subjects in four panes of 32 (8x4)

1453	A867	8c **blk., blue, brn. & multi.**, *March 1*	18	5
		Block of four	72	20
		Margin block of 4, P#	1.00	
		Margin block of 4, Mr. Zip and "Use Zip Code"	85	
		Margin block of 6, "Mail Early in the Day"	1.20	

Plates of 200 subjects in four panes of 50 each

1454	A868	15c **black & multi.**, *July 28*	35	22
		Margin block of 4, P#	2.75	
		Margin block of 4, Mr. Zip	1.65	
		Margin block of 6, Mail Early	2.25	

FAMILY PLANNING ISSUE

Family
A869

LITHOGRAPHED, ENGRAVED (Giori)
Plates of 200 subjects in four panes of 50 each.

1972			Tagged		Perf. 11
1455	A869	8c **black & multi.**, *Mar. 18*		16	5
		Margin block of 4, P#		1.00	
		Margin block of 4, Mr. Zip and "Use Zip Code"		70	
		Margin block of 6, "Mail Early in the Day"		1.00	
		a. Yellow omitted			

AMERICAN BICENTENNIAL ISSUE
Colonial American Craftsmen

Nos. 1456–1459 are printed in blocks of four in panes of 50. In upper and lower left panes Nos. 1456 and 1458 appear in first, third and fifth place; Nos. 1457 and 1459 in second and third place. This arrangement is reversed in upper and lower right panes.

Glass Blower
A870

Silversmith
A871

Wigmaker
A872

Hatter
A873

Designed by Leonard Everett Fisher.
ENGRAVED
E. E. Plates of 200 subjects in four panes of 50 each.

1972, July 4			Tagged	Perf. 11x10½	
1456	A870	8c **deep brown**, *dull yellow*		30	8
		Margin block of 4, P# adjoining #1456		1.75	
		Margin block of 4, Mr. Zip and "Use Zip Code" adjoining #1456		1.40	
		Margin block of 6, Bicentennial emblem* adjoining #1456		2.00	
1457	A871	8c **deep brown**, *dull yellow*		30	8
		Margin block of 4, P# adjoining #1457		1.75	
		Margin block of 4, Mr. Zip and "Use Zip Code" adjoining #1457		1.40	
		Margin block of 6, Bicentennial emblem* adjoining #1457		2.00	
1458	A872	8c **deep brown**, *dull yellow*		30	8
		Margin block of 4, P# adjoining #1458		1.75	
		Margin block of 4, Mr. Zip and "Use Zip Code" adjoining #1458		1.40	
		Margin block of 6, Bicentennial emblem* adjoining #1458		2.00	
1459	A873	8c **deep brown**, *dull yellow*		30	8
		Margin block of 4, P# adjoining #1459		1.75	
		Margin block of 4, Mr. Zip and "Use Zip Code" adjoining #1459		1.40	
		Margin block of 6, Bicentennial emblem* adjoining #1459		2.00	
		a. Block of 4, #1456-1459		1.25	1.25
		First day cover, #1459a			2.50

* Bicentennial Commission emblem and inscription: USA BICENTENNIAL/HONORS COLONIAL/AMERICAN CRAFTSMEN.

POSTAGE, 1972

OLYMPIC GAMES ISSUE

11th Winter Olympic Games, Sapporo, Japan, Feb. 3–13 and 20th Summer Olympic Games, Munich, Germany, Aug. 26–Sept. 11. See No. C85.

Bicycling and Olympic Rings—A874

Bobsledding and Olympic Rings—A875

Running and Olympic Rings—A876

Designed by Lance Wyman.
PHOTOGRAVURE (Andreotti)
Plates of 200 subjects in four panes of 50 each.

1972, Aug. 17   Tagged   Perf. 11x10½

1460	A874	6c black, blue, red, emerald & yellow	16	12
		Margin block of 10, 5P#	2.25	
		Margin block of 4, Mr. Zip and "Use Zip Code"	75	
		Margin block of 6, "Mail Early in the Day"	1.10	
		Plate flaw (broken red ring) (33312 U.L. 43)	7.50	
1461	A875	8c black, blue, red, emerald & yellow	16	5
		Margin block of 10, 5#	2.25	
		Margin block of 4, Mr. Zip and "Use Zip Code"	70	
		Margin block of 6, "Mail Early in the Day"	1.00	
1462	A876	15c black, blue, red, emerald & yel.	35	18
		Margin block of 10, 5P#	4.50	
		Margin block of 4, Mr. Zip and "Use Zip Code"	1.60	
		Margin block of 6, "Mail Early in the Day"	2.25	

PARENT TEACHER ASSN. ISSUE

75th anniversary of the Parent Teacher Association.

Blackboard—A877

Designed by Arthur S. Congdon, III.
PHOTOGRAVURE (Andreotti)
Plates of 200 subjects in four panes of 50 each.

1972   Tagged   Perf. 11x10½

1463	A877	8c yellow & black, Sept. 15	16	5
		Margin block of 4, two P#	1.00	
		Margin block of 4, yel. P# reversed	1.75	
		Margin block of 4, Mr. Zip and "Use Zip Code"	70	
		Margin block of 6, "Mail Early in the Day"	1.00	

WILDLIFE CONSERVATION ISSUE

Nos. 1464–1467 are printed in blocks of 4 in panes of 32. Nos. 1464–1465 alternate in first row, Nos. 1468–1469 in second row. This arrangement repeated throughout pane.

Fur Seals—A878   Cardinal—A879

Brown Pelican—A880   Bighorn Sheep—A881

POSTAGE, 1972

Designed by Stanley W. Galli.
LITHOGRAPHED, ENGRAVED (Giori)
Plates of 128 subjects in 4 panes of 32 (4x8).

1972, Sept. 20		Tagged	Perf. 11	
1464	A878	8c **multicolored**	25	8
		Margin block of 4, P# adjoining #1464	1.40	
		Margin block of 4, Mr. Zip and "Use Zip Code" adjoining #1464	1.10	
		Margin block of 6, "Mail Early in the Day" adjoining #1464	1.60	
1465	A879	8c **multicolored**	25	8
		Margin block of 4, P# adjoining #1465	1.40	
		Margin block of 4, Mr. Zip and "Use Zip Code" adjoining #1465	1.10	
		Margin block of 6, "Mail Early in the Day" adjoining #1465	1.60	
1466	A880	8c **multicolored**	25	8
		Margin block of 4, P# adjoining #1466	1.40	
		Margin block of 4, Mr. Zip and "Use Zip Code" adjoining #1466	1.10	
		Margin block of 6, "Mail Early in the Day" adjoining #1466	1.60	
1467	A881	8c **multicolored**	25	8
		Margin block of 4, P# adjoining #1467	1.40	
		Margin block of 4, Mr. Zip and "Use Zip Code" adjoining #1467	1.10	
		Margin block of 6, "Mail Early in the Day" adjoining #1467	1.60	
		a. Block of four (#1464-1467)	1.10	85
		b. As "a," brown omitted	3,500.	
		c. As "a," green & blue omitted		

MAIL ORDER BUSINESS ISSUE

Centenary of mail order business, originated by Aaron Montgomery Ward, Chicago. Design based on Headsville, West Va., post office in Smithsonian Institution, Washington, D.C.

Rural Post Office Store
A882

Designed by Robert Lambdin.
PHOTOGRAVURE (Andreotti)
Plates of 200 subjects in four panes of 50 each.

1972		Tagged	Perf. 11x10½	
1468	A882	8c **multicolored**, Sept. 27	16	5
		Margin block of 12, 6 P#	2.75	
		Margin block of 4, Mr. Zip and "Use Zip Code"	70	
		Margin block of 4, "Mail Early in the Day"	1.00	

The tagging on No. 1468 consists of a vertical bar of phosphor 10 mm. wide.

OSTEOPATHIC MEDICINE ISSUE

75th anniversary of the American Osteopathic Association, founded by Dr. Andrew T. Still (1828–1917), who developed the principles of osteopathy in 1874.

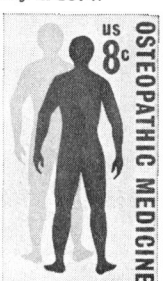

Man's Quest for Health
A883

Designed by V. Jack Ruther.
PHOTOGRAVURE (Andreotti)
Plates of 200 subjects in four panes of 50 each.

1972		Tagged	Perf. 10½x11	
1469	A883	8c **multicolored**, Oct. 9	16	5
		Margin block of 6, 3 P#	1.35	
		Margin block of 4, Mr. Zip and "Use Zip Code"	70	
		Margin block of 6, "Mail Early in the Day"	1.00	

AMERICAN FOLKLORE ISSUE
Tom Sawyer

Tom Sawyer, by Norman Rockwell
A884

Designed by Bradbury Thompson.
LITHOGRAPHED, ENGRAVED (Giori)
Plates of 200 subjects in four panes of 50 each.

1972		Tagged	Perf. 11	
1470	A884	8c **black, red, yellow, tan, blue & rose red**, Oct. 13	16	5
		Margin block of 4, P#	1.00	
		Margin block of 4, Mr. Zip and "Use Zip Code"	70	
		Margin block of 6, "Mail Early in the Day"	1.00	
		a. Horiz. pair, imperf. between	2,000.	
		b. Red & black (engr.) omitted	1,000.	
		c. Yellow, tan, blue & rose red (litho.) omitted	1,500.	

CHRISTMAS ISSUE

Angels from "Mary, Queen of Heaven"
A885

Santa Claus
A886

Designers: No. 1471, Bradbury Thompson, using detail from a painting by the Master of the St. Lucy legend, in the National Gallery of Art, Washington, D.C. No. 1472, Stevan Dohanos.

PHOTOGRAVURE (Andreotti)
Plates of 200 subjects in four panes of 50 each.

1972, Nov. 9		Tagged	Perf. 10½x11	
1471	A885	8c multicolored	16	5
		Margin block of 12, 6 P#	2.75	
		Margin block of 4, Mr. Zip and "Use Zip Code"	70	
		Margin block of 4, "Mail Early in the Day"	70	
		a. Pink omitted	450.00	
		b. Black omitted		
1472	A886	8c multicolored	16	5
		Margin block of 12, 6 P#	2.75	
		Margin block of 4, Mr. Zip and "Use Zip Code"	70	
		Margin block of 4, "Mail Early in the Day"	70	

PHARMACY ISSUE

Honoring American druggists in connection with the 120th anniversary of the American Pharmaceutical Association.

Mortar and Pestle, Bowl of Hygeia, 19th Century Medicine Bottles—A887

Designed by Ken Davies.

LITHOGRAPHED, ENGRAVED (Giori)
Plates of 200 subjects in four panes of 50 each.

1972		Tagged	Perf. 11	
1473	A887	8c black & multicolored, Nov. 10	16	5
		Margin block of 4, P#	1.00	
		Margin block of 4, Mr. Zip and "Use Zip Code"	70	
		Margin block of 6, "Mail Early in the Day"	1.00	
		a. Blue & orange omitted	1,100.	
		b. Blue omitted		

STAMP COLLECTING ISSUE

Issued to publicize stamp collecting.

U.S. No. 1 under Magnifying Glass—A888

Designed by Frank E. Livia.

LITHOGRAPHED, ENGRAVED (Giori)
Plates of 160 subjects in four panes of 40 each.

1972		Tagged	Perf. 11	
1474	A888	8c multicolored, Nov. 17	16	5
		Margin block of 4, P#	1.00	
		Margin block of 4, Mr. Zip and "Use Zip Code"	70	
		Margin block of 6, "Mail Early in the Day"	1.00	
		a. Black (litho.) omitted	900.00	

LOVE ISSUE

"Love," by Robert Indiana—A889

Designed by Robert Indiana.

PHOTOGRAVURE (Andreotti)
Plates of 200 Subjects in four panes of 50 each.

1973, Jan. 26		Tagged	Perf. 11x10½	
1475	A889	8c red, emerald & violet blue	16	5
		Margin block of 6, 3 P#	1.35	
		Margin block of 4, Mr. Zip and "Use Zip Code"	70	
		Margin block of 6, "Mail Early in the Day"	1.00	

AMERICAN BICENTENNIAL ISSUE

Communications in Colonial Times

Printer and Patriots Examining Pamphlet—A890

Posting a Broadside—A891

Postrider—A892

Drummer—A893

Designed by William A. Smith.

POSTAGE, 1973

GIORI PRESS PRINTING
Plates of 200 subjects in four panes of 50 each.

1973			Tagged		Perf. 11	
1476	A890	8c	ultra., greenish blk. & red, *Feb. 16*	20	5	
			Margin block of 4, P#	1.35	—	
			Margin block of 4, Mr. Zip and "Use Zip Code"	90	—	
			Margin block of 6, "Mail Early in the Day"	1.30	—	
1477	A891	8c	black, vermilion & ultra., *Apr. 13*	20	5	
			Margin block of 4, P#	1.35	—	
			Margin block of 4, Mr. Zip and "Use Zip Code"	90	—	
			Margin block of 6, "Mail Early in the Day"	1.30	—	
			Margin block of 6, Bicentennial emblem and "USA Bicentennial Era"	1.30	—	
			Pair with full horiz. gutter btwn.			

LITHOGRAPHED, ENGRAVED (Giori)

1478	A892	8c	blue, black, red & green, *June 22*	20	5
			Margin block of 4, P#	1.35	—
			Margin block of 4, Mr. Zip and "Use Zip Code"	90	—
			Margin block of 6, "Mail Early in the Day"	1.30	—
			Margin block of 6, Bicentennial emblem and "USA Bicentennial Era"	1.30	—
1479	A893	8c	blue, black, yellow & red, *Sept. 28*	20	5
			Margin block of 4, P#	1.35	—
			Margin block of 4, Mr. Zip and "Use Zip Code"	90	—
			Margin block of 6, "Mail Early in the Day"	1.30	—
			Margin block of 6, Bicentennial emblem and "USA Bicentennial Era"	1.30	—

AMERICAN BICENTENNIAL ISSUE

Boston Tea Party

Nos. 1480–1483 are printed in blocks of four in panes of 50. In upper and lower left panes Nos. 1480 and 1482 appear in first, third and fifth place, Nos. 1481 and 1483 appear in second and fourth place. This arrangement is reversed in upper and lower right panes.

British Merchantman—A894   British Three-master—A895

Boats and Ship's Hull—A896   Boat and Dock—A897

Designed by William A. Smith.

LITHOGRAPHED, ENGRAVED (Giori)
Plates of 200 subjects in four panes of 50 each.

1973, July 4			Tagged		Perf. 11	
1480	A894	8c	black & multicolored	20	10	
			Margin block of 4, P# adjoining #1480	1.35	—	
			Margin block of 4, Mr. Zip and "Use Zip Code" adjoining #1480	1.00	—	
			Margin block of 6, "Mail Early in the Day" adjoining #1480	1.50	—	
			Margin block of 6, Bicentennial emblem and "USA Bicentennial Era"	1.50	—	
1481	A895	8c	black & multicolored	20	10	
			Margin block of 4, P# adjoining #1481	1.35	—	
			Margin block of 4, Mr. Zip and "Use Zip Code" adjoining #1481	1.00	—	
			Margin block of 6, "Mail Early in the Day" adjoining #1481	1.50	—	
			Margin block of 6, Bicentennial emblem and "USA Bicentennial Era" adjoining #1481	1.50	—	
1482	A896	8c	black & multicolored	20	10
			Margin block of 4, P# adjoining #1482	1.35	—
			Margin block of 4, Mr. Zip and "Use Zip Code" adjoining #1482	1.00	—
			Margin block of 6, "Mail Early in the Day" adjoining #1482	1.50	—
			Margin block of 6, Bicentennial emblem and "USA Bicentennial Era" adjoining #1482	1.50	—
1483	A897	8c	black & multicolored	20	10
			Margin block of 4, P# adjoining #1483	1.35	—
			Margin block of 4, Mr. Zip and "Use Zip Code" adjoining #1483	1.00	—
			Margin block of 6, "Mail Early in the Day" adjoining #1483	1.50	—
			Margin block of 6, Bicentennial emblem and "USA Bicentennial Era" adjoining #1483	1.50	—
		a.	Block of 4, #1480-1483	85	80
		b.	As "a," black (engraved) omitted	2,500.	
		c.	As "a," black (litho.) omitted	1,800.	

AMERICAN ARTS ISSUE

George Gershwin (1899–1937), composer (No. 1484); Robinson Jeffers (1887–1962), poet (No. 1485); Henry Ossawa Tanner (1859–1937), black painter (No. 1486); Willa Cather (1873–1947), novelist (No. 1487).

Gershwin, Sportin' Life,
Porgy and Bess
A898

Robinson Jeffers,
Man and Children
of Carmel with Burro
A899

Henry Ossawa Tanner,
Palette and Rainbow
A900

Willa Cather, Pioneer Family
and Covered Wagon
A901
Designed by Mark English.

PHOTOGRAVURE (Andreotti)
Plates of 160 subjects in four panes of 40 each.

1973		Tagged	Perf. 11	
1484	A898	8c dp. green & multi., *Feb. 28*	16	5
		Margin block of 12, 6 P#	2.75	—
		Margin block of 4, Mr. Zip, "Use Zip Code" and "Mail Early in the Day"	70	—
		Margin block of 16, 6 P#, Mr. Zip and slogans	3.50	—
		a. Vertical pair, imperf. horiz.	400.00	
1485	A899	8c **Prussian blue & multi.,** *Aug. 13*	16	5
		Margin block of 12, 6 P#	2.75	—
		Margin block of 4, Mr. Zip, "Use Zip Code" "Mail Early in the Day"	70	—
		Margin block of 16, 6 P#, Mr. Zip and slogans	3.50	—
		a. Vertical pair, imperf. horiz.	450.00	
1486	A900	8c **yellow brown & multi.,** *Sept. 10*	16	5
		Margin block of 12, 6 P#	2.75	—
		Margin block of 4, Mr. Zip, "Use Zip Code" "Mail Early in the Day"	70	—
		Margin block of 16, 6 P#, Mr. Zip and slogans	3.50	—
1487	A901	8c **deep brown & multi.,** *Sept. 20*	16	5
		Margin block of 12, 6 P#	2.75	—
		Margin block of 4, Mr. Zip, "Use Zip Code" "Mail Early in the Day"	70	—
		Margin block of 16, 6 P#, Mr. Zip and slogans	3.50	—
		a. Vertical pair, imperf. horiz.	400.00	

COPERNICUS ISSUE

500th anniversary of the birth of Nicolaus Copernicus (1473–1543), Polish astronomer.

Nicolaus Copernicus
A902

Designed by Alvin Eisenman after 18th century engraving.

LITHOGRAPHED, ENGRAVED (Giori)
Plates of 200 subjects in four panes of 50 each.

1973		Tagged	Perf. 11	
1488	A902	8c **black & orange,** *Apr. 23*	16	5
		Margin block of 4, P#	1.00	—
		Margin block of 4, Mr. Zip and "Use Zip Code"	70	—
		Margin block of 6, "Mail Early in the Day"	1.00	—
		a. Orange omitted	1,200.	
		b. Black (engraved) omitted	1,500.	

The orange can be chemically removed.

POSTAL SERVICE EMPLOYEES ISSUE

A tribute to U.S. Postal Service employees. Nos. 1489-1498 are printed se-tenant in horizontal rows of 10. Emerald inscription on back, printed beneath gum in water-soluble ink, includes Postal Service emblem,
"People Serving You" and a statement, differing for each of the 10 stamps, about some aspect of postal service.
Each stamp in top or bottom row has a tab with blue inscription enumerating various jobs in postal service.

Stamp Counter A903 — Mail Collection A904 — Letter Facing on Conveyor Belt A905 — Parcel Post Sorting A906 — Mail Canceling A907

Manual Letter Routing A908 — Electronic Letter Routing A909 — Loading Mail on Truck A910 — Mailman A911 — Rural Mail Delivery A912

Designed by Edward Vebell.
PHOTOGRAVURE (Andreotti)
Plates of 200 subjects in four panes of 50 each.

1973, Apr. 30			Tagged	Perf. 10½x11	
1489	A903	8c	multicolored	20	12
1490	A904	8c	"	20	12
1491	A905	8c	"	20	12
1492	A906	8c	"	20	12
1493	A907	8c	multicolored	20	12
			Margin block of 10, 5 P# adjoining #1489-1493	2.25	

1494	A908	8c	multicolored	20	12
1495	A909	8c	"	20	12
1496	A910	8c	"	20	12
1497	A911	8c	"	20	12
1498	A912	8c	multicolored	20	12
			Margin block of 10, 5 P# adjoining #1494-1498	2.25	—
			Margin block of 20, 5 P# and 10 tabs	4.50	—
		a.	Strip of 10 (#1489-1498)	2.25	2.00

The tagging on Nos. 1489-1498 consists of a ½-inch horizontal band of phosphor.

HARRY S. TRUMAN ISSUE

Harry S. Truman, 33rd President (1884-1972).

Designed by Bradbury Thompson; photograph by Leo Stern.
GIORI PRESS PRINTING
Plates of 128 subjects in four panes of 32 each.

1973			Tagged		Perf. 11
1499	A913	8c	carmine rose, black & blue, May 8	16	5
			Margin block of 4, P#	1.00	—

ELECTRONICS PROGRESS ISSUE

See No. C86.

Harry S. Truman A913

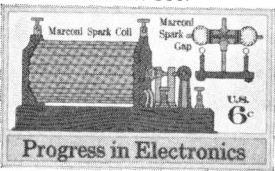

Marconi's Spark Coil and Spark Gap—A914

POSTAGE, 1973, 1973-74 295

Transistors and Printed Circuit Board—A915

Microphone, Speaker, Vacuum Tube and TV Camera Tube—A916

Designed by Walter and Naiad Einsel.

LITHOGRAPHED, ENGRAVED (Giori)
Plates of 200 subjects in four panes of 50 each.

1973, July 10			Tagged	Perf. 11	
1500	A914	6c	lilac & multicolored	12	10
			Margin block of 4, P#	1.25	
			Margin block of 4, Mr. Zip and "Use Zip Code"	.55	
			Margin block of 6, "Mail Early in the Day"	.80	
1501	A915	8c	tan & multicolored	16	5
			Margin block of 4, P#	1.00	
			Margin block of 4, Mr. Zip and "Use Zip Code"	.70	
			Margin block of 6, "Mail Early in the Day"	1.00	
		a.	Black (inscriptions & "U.S. 8c") omitted	750.00	
		b.	Tan (background) & lilac omitted	1,250.	
1502	A916	15c	gray green & multicolored	30	20
			Margin block of 4, P#	3.00	
			Margin block of 4, Mr. Zip and "Use Zip Code"	1.50	
			Margin block of 6, "Mail Early in the Day"	1.90	
		a.	Black (inscriptions & "U.S. 15c") omitted	1,500.	

LYNDON B. JOHNSON ISSUE

Lyndon B. Johnson (1908-1973), 36th President.

Lyndon B. Johnson
A917

Designed by Bradbury Thompson, portrait by Elizabeth Shoumatoff.

PHOTOGRAVURE (Andreotti)
Plates of 128 subjects in four panes of 32 each.

1973, Aug. 27				Perf. 11	
1503	A917	8c	black & multicolored, Aug. 27	16	5
			Margin block of 12, 6 P#	2.50	
		a.	Horiz. pair, imperf. vert.	400.00	

RURAL AMERICA ISSUE

Centenary of the introduction of Aberdeen Angus cattle into the United States (No. 1504); of the Chautauqua Institution (No. 1505); and of the introduction of hard winter wheat into Kansas by Mennonite immigrants (No. 1506).

Angus and Longhorn Cattle—A918

Chautauqua Tent and Buggies—A919

Wheat Fields and Train—A920

No. 1504 modeled by Frank Waslick after painting by F. C. "Frank" Murphy. Nos. 1505-1506 designed by John Falter.

LITHOGRAPHED, ENGRAVED (Giori)
Plates of 200 subjects in four panes of 50 each.

1973-74			Tagged	Perf. 11	
1504	A918	8c	multicolored, Oct. 5, 1973	16	5
			Margin block of 4, P#	1.00	
			Margin block of 4, Mr. Zip and "Use Zip Code"	.70	
			Margin block of 6, "Mail Early in the Day"	1.00	
		a.	Green & red brown omitted	700.00	
1505	A919	10c	multicolored, Aug. 6, 1974	20	5
			Margin block of 4, P#	1.00	
			Margin block of 4, Mr. Zip and "Use Zip Code"	.90	
			Margin block of 6, "Mail Early in the Day"	1.30	
1506	A920	10c	multicolored, Aug. 16, 1974	20	5
			Margin block of 4, P#	1.00	
			Margin block of 4, Mr. Zip and "Use Zip Code"	.90	
			Margin block of 6, "Mail Early in the Day"	1.30	
		a.	Black and blue (engr.) omitted	600.00	

CHRISTMAS ISSUE

Small Cowper Madonna, by Raphael
A921

Christmas Tree in Needlepoint
A922

Designers: No. 1507, Bradbury Thompson, using a painting in the National Gallery of Art, Washington, D.C. No. 1508, Dolli Tingle.

PHOTOGRAVURE (Andreotti)
Plates of 200 subjects in four panes of 50 each.

1973, Nov. 7		Tagged	Perf. 10½x11	
1507	A921	8c **multicolored**	16	5
		Margin block of 12, 6 P#	2.10	
		Margin block of 4, Mr. Zip and "Use Zip Code"	70	
		Margin block of 4, "Mail Early in the Day"	70	
1508	A922	8c **multicolored**	16	5
		Margin block of 12, 6 P#	2.10	
		Margin block of 4, Mr. Zip and "Use Zip Code"	70	
		Margin block of 4, "Mail Early in the Day"	70	
		a. Vertical pair, imperf. between	600.00	
		Pair with full horiz. gutter btwn.	—	

The tagging on Nos. 1507-1508 consists of a 20x12mm. horizontal bar of phosphor.

50-Star and 13-Star Flags
A923

Jefferson Memorial and Signature
A924

Mail Transport
A925

Liberty Bell
A926

Designers: No. 1509, Ren Wicks. No. 1510, Dean Ellis. No. 1511, Randall McDougall. 6.3c, Frank Lionetti.

MULTICOLOR HUCK PRESS
Panes of 100 (10x10).

1973-74		Tagged	Perf. 11x10½	
1509	A923	10c **red & blue,** *Dec. 8, 1973*	20	5
		Margin block of 20, 4-6 P#, 2-3 "Mail Early" and 2-3 "Use Zip Code"	5.50	—
		a. Horizontal pair, imperf. between	65.00	—
		b. Blue omitted	250.00	
		c. Imperf., vert. pair	750.00	

ROTARY PRESS PRINTING
E.E. Plates of 400 subjects in four panes of 100 each.

1510	A924	10c **blue,** *Dec. 14, 1973*	20	5
		Margin block of 4, P#	1.00	—
		Margin block of 4, "Use Zip Codes"	90	—
		Margin block of 6, "Mail Early in the Day"	1.30	—
		a. Untagged (Bureau precanceled)		20
		b. Booklet pane of 5 + label	1.50	30
		c. Booklet pane of 8	1.60	30
		d. Booklet pane of 6, *Aug. 5, 1974*	2.50	30
		e. Vert. pair, imperf. horiz.	250.00	
		f. Vert. pair, imperf. between	—	

PHOTOGRAVURE (Andreotti)
Plates of 400 subjects in four panes of 100 each.

1511	A925	10c **multicolored,** *Jan. 4, 1974*	20	5
		Margin block of 8, 4 P#	2.25	
		Margin block of 4, "Use Zip Codes"	90	—
		Margin block of 6, "Mail Early in the Day"	1.30	—
		a. Yellow omitted	60.00	
		Pair with full horiz. gutter btwn.	—	

COIL STAMPS
ROTARY PRESS PRINTING

1973-74		Tagged	Perf. 10 Vert.	
1518	A926	6.3c **brick red,** *Oct. 1, 1974*	13	7
		Pair	26	14
		Joint line pair	35	—
		a. Untagged (Bureau precanceled)		13
		b. Imperf., pair	120.00	
		c. As "a," imperf., pair		65.00

A total of 129 different Bureau precancels were used by 117 cities.

MULTICOLOR HUCK PRESS

1519	A923	10c **red & blue,** *Dec. 8, 1973*	25	5
		Pair	50	10
		a. Imperf., pair	20.00	

ROTARY PRESS PRINTING

1520	A924	10c **blue,** *Dec. 14, 1973*	20	5
		Pair	40	10
		Joint line pair	50	—
		a. Untagged (Bureau precanceled)		25
		b. Imperf., pair	40.00	

POSTAGE, 1974

VETERANS OF FOREIGN WARS ISSUE

75th anniversary of Veterans of Spanish-American and Other Foreign Wars.

Emblem and Initials of Veterans of Foreign Wars—A928
Designed by Robert Hallock.
GIORI PRESS PRINTING
Plates of 200 subjects in 4 plates of 50 each.

1974		Tagged	Perf. 11	
1525	A928	10c **red & dark blue,** *Mar. 11*	20	5
		Margin block of 4, P#	1.25	
		Margin block of 4, Mr. Zip and "Use Zip Code"	85	
		Margin block of 6, "Mail Early in the Day"	1.25	

ROBERT FROST ISSUE

Centenary of the birth of Robert Frost (1873-1963), poet.

Robert Frost—A929

Designed by Paul Calle; photograph by David Rhinelander.
ROTARY PRESS PRINTING
E. E. Plates of 200 subjects in four panes of 50 each.

1974		Tagged	Perf. 10½x11	
1526	A929	10c **black,** *Mar. 26*	20	5
		Margin block of 4, P#	1.00	
		Margin block of 4, Mr. Zip and "Use Zip Code"	90	
		Margin block of 6, "Mail Early in the Day"	1.30	

EXPO '74 WORLD'S FAIR ISSUE

EXPO '74 World's Fair "Preserve the Environment," Spokane, Wash., May 4–Nov. 4.

"Cosmic Jumper" and "Smiling Sage"
A930

Designed by Peter Max.
PHOTOGRAVURE (Andreotti)
Plates of 160 subjects in four panes of 40 each.

1974		Tagged	Perf. 11	
1527	A930	10c **multicolored,** *Apr. 18*	20	5
		Margin block of 12, 6 P#	2.60	
		Margin block of 4, Mr. Zip, "Use Zip Code" and "Mail Early in the Day"	90	
		Margin block of 16, 6 P#, Mr. Zip and slogans	3.50	

HORSE RACING ISSUE

Centenary of the Kentucky Derby, Churchill Downs.

Horses Rounding Turn
A931

Designed by Henry Koehler.
PHOTOGRAVURE (Andreotti)
Plates of 200 subjects in four panes of 50 each.

1974		Tagged	Perf. 11x10½	
1528	A931	10c **yellow & multicolored,** *May 4*	20	5
		Margin block of 12, 6 P#	2.60	
		Margin block of 4, Mr. Zip and "Use Zip Code"	90	
		Margin block of 4, "Mail Early in the Day"	90	
	a.	Blue ("Horse Racing") omitted	1,000.	
	b.	Red ("U.S. postage 10 cents") omitted		

SKYLAB ISSUE

First anniversary of the launching of Skylab I, honoring all who participated in the Skylab project.

Skylab
A932

Designed by Robert T. McCall.
LITHOGRAPHED, ENGRAVED (Giori)
Plates of 200 subjects in four panes of 50 each.

1974		Tagged	Perf. 11	
1529	A932	10c **multicolored,** *May 14*	20	5
		Margin block of 4, P#	1.00	
		Margin block of 4, Mr. Zip and "Use Zip Code"	90	
		Margin block of 6, "Mail Early in the Day"	1.30	
	a.	Vert. pair, imperf. between		

UNIVERSAL POSTAL UNION ISSUE

Centenary of Universal Postal Union. Nos. 1530–1537 are arranged in blocks of 8 (4x2), four blocks to a pane (8x4). In the first row Nos. 1530–1537 are in sequence as listed. In the second row Nos. 1534–1537 are followed by Nos. 1530–1533. Every row of 8 and every horizontal block of 8 contains all 8 designs. All four panes have this arrangement. The letter writing designs are from famous works of art; some are details. The quotation on every second stamp, "Letters mingle souls," is from a letter by poet John Donne.

Michelangelo, from "School of Athens," by Raphael, 1509
A933

"Five Feminine Virtues," by Hokusai, c. 1811
A934

"Old Scraps," by John Fredrick Peto, 1894
A935

"The Lovely Reader," by Jean Etienne Liotard, 1746
A936

"Lady Writing Letter," by Gerard Terborch, 1654
A937

Inkwell and Quill, from "Boy with a Top," by Jean-Baptiste Simeon Chardin, 1738
A938

Mrs. John Douglas, by Thomas Gainsborough, 1784
A939

Don Antonio Noriega, by Francisco de Goya, 1801
A940

Designed by Bradbury Thompson.
PHOTOGRAVURE (Andreotti)
Plates of 128 subjects in four panes of 32 each.

1974, June 6   Tagged   Perf. 11

1530	A933	10c	multicolored	20	18
1531	A934	10c	"	20	18
1532	A935	10c	"	20	18
1533	A936	10c	"	20	18
1534	A937	10c	"	20	18
1535	A938	10c	"	20	18
1536	A939	10c	"	20	18
1537	A940	10c	multicolored	20	18

a. Block or strip of 8 (#1530–1537)   1.60   2.00
b. As "a," (block), imperf. vert.   4,500.
Margin block of 16, 5 P# adjoining #1530–1534, "Mail Early in the Day" adjoining #1535 and Mr. Zip and "Use Zip Code" adjoining #1537   3.40   —
Margin block of 16, 5 P# adjoining #1533–1537, "Mail Early in the Day" adjoining #1532 and Mr. Zip and "Use Zip Code" adjoining #1530   3.40   —
Margin block of 16, 5 P# adjoining #1534–1537, 1530, "Mail Early in the Day" adjoining #1531 and Mr. Zip and "Use Zip Code" adjoining #1533   3.40   —
Margin block of 16, 5 P# adjoining #1537, 1530–1533, "Mail Early in the Day" adjoining #1536 and Mr. Zip and "Use Zip Code" adjoining #1534   3.40   —
Margin block of 10, 5 P# as above; no slogans   2.60   —

MINERAL HERITAGE ISSUE

Panes contain 12 blocks of 4 (3x4). The sequence of stamps in first horizontal row is Nos. 1538–1541, 1538– 1539. In second row Nos. 1540–1541 are followed by Nos. 1538–1541. All four panes have this arrangement.

Petrified Wood
A941

Amethyst
A943

Tourmaline
A942

Rhodochrosite
A944

Designed by Leonard F. Buckley.
LITHOGRAPHED, ENGRAVED (Giori)
Plates of 192 subjects in four panes of 48 (6x8).

1974, June 13		Tagged	Perf. 11	
1538	A941 10c	**blue & multicolored**	20	10
		Margin block of 4, P# adjoining #1538	1.50	—
		Margin block of 4, Mr. Zip and "Use Zip Code" adjoining #1538	90	—
		Margin block of 6, "Mail Early in the Day" adjoining #1538	1.30	—
	a.	Light blue & yellow omitted		
1539	A942 10c	**blue & multicolored**	20	10
		Margin block of 4, P# adjoining #1539	1.50	—
		Margin block of 4, Mr. Zip and "Use Zip Code" adjoining #1539	90	—
		Margin block of 6, "Mail Early in the Day" adjoining #1539	1.30	—
	a.	Light blue omitted		
	b.	Black & purple omitted		
1540	A943 10c	**blue & multicolored**	20	10
		Margin block of 4, P# adjoining #1540	1.50	—
		Margin block of 4, Mr. Zip and "Use Zip Code" adjoining #1540	90	—
		Margin block of 6, "Mail Early in the Day" adjoining #1540	1.30	—
	a.	Light blue & yellow omitted		
1541	A944 10c	**blue & multicolored**	20	10
		Margin block of 4, P# adjoining #1541	1.50	—
		Margin block of 4, Mr. Zip and "Use Zip Code" adjoining #1541	90	—
		Margin block of 6, "Mail Early in the Day" adjoining #1541	1.30	—
	a.	Block of 4, #1538-1541	80	80
	b.	As "a," lt. blue & yellow omitted	2,000.	—
	c.	Light blue omitted		
	d.	Black & red omitted		

KENTUCKY SETTLEMENT ISSUE

Bicentenary of Fort Harrod, first settlement in Kentucky.

Covered Wagons
at Fort Harrod
A945

Designed by David K. Stone.
LITHOGRAPHED, ENGRAVED (Giori)
Plates of 200 subjects in four panes of 50 each.

1974		Tagged	Perf. 11	
1542	A945 10c	**green & multicolored,** *June 15*	20	5
		Margin block of 4, P#	1.20	—
		Margin block of 4, Mr. Zip and "Use Zip Code"	90	—
		Margin block of 6, "Mail Early in the Day"	1.30	—
	a.	Dull black (litho.) omitted	800.00	
	b.	Green (engr. & litho.), black (engr. & litho.) & blue omitted	3,000.	

POSTAGE, 1974

AMERICAN REVOLUTION BICENTENNIAL ISSUE
First Continental Congress

Nos. 1543–1546 are printed in blocks of four in panes of 50. Nos. 1543–1544 alternate in first row, Nos. 1545–1546 in second row. This arrangement is repeated throughout the pane.

Carpenters' Hall, Philadelphia
A946

"We ask but for peace..."
A947

"Deriving their just powers..."
A948

Independence Hall
A949

Designed by Frank P. Conley
GIORI PRESS PRINTING
Plates of 200 subjects in four panes of 50 each.

1974, July 4			Tagged		Perf. 11	
1543	A946	10c	dark blue & red		20	10
			Margin block of 4, P# adjoining #1543		1.20	—
			Margin block of 4, Mr. Zip and "Use Zip Code" adjoining #1543		90	—
			Margin block of 6, "Mail Early in the Day" adjoining #1543		1.30	—
			Margin block of 6, Bicentennial Emblem and "USA Bicentennial Era" adjoining #1543		1.30	—
1544	A947	10c	gray, dark blue & red		20	10
			Margin block of 4, P# adjoining #1544		1.20	—
			Margin block of 4, Mr. Zip and "Use Zip Code" adjoining #1544		90	—
			Margin block of 6, "Mail Early in the Day" adjoining #1544		1.30	—
			Margin block of 6, Bicentennial Emblem and "USA Bicentennial Era" adjoining #1544		1.30	—
1545	A948	10c	gray, dark blue & red		20	10
			Margin block of 4, Mr. Zip and "Use Zip Code" adjoining #1545		90	—
			Margin block of 6, "Mail Early in the Day" adjoining #1545		1.30	—
			Margin block of 6, Bicentennial Emblem and "USA Bicentennial Era" adjoining #1545		1.30	—
1546	A949	10c	red & dark blue		20	10
			Margin block of 4, P# adjoining #1546		1.20	—
			Margin block of 4, Mr. Zip and "Use Zip Code" adjoining #1546		90	—
			Margin block of 6, "Mail Early in the Day" adjoining #1546		1.30	—
			Margin block of 6, Bicentennial Emblem and "USA Bicentennial Era" adjoining #1546		1.30	—
	a.		Block of four, #1543-1546		80	80

ENERGY CONSERVATION ISSUE

Publicizing the importance of conserving all forms of energy.

Molecules and Drops of Gasoline and Oil
A950

Designed by Robert W. Bode.
LITHOGRAPHED, ENGRAVED (Giori)
Plates of 200 subjects in four panes of 50 each.

1974			Tagged		Perf. 11	
1547	A950	10c	multicolored, Sept. 23		20	5
			Margin block of 4, P#		1.00	—
			Margin block of 4, Mr. Zip and "Use Zip Code"		90	—
			Margin block of 6, "Mail Early in the Day"		1.30	—
	a.		Blue & orange omitted		700.00	
	b.		Orange & green omitted		600.00	
	c.		Green omitted		700.00	

AMERICAN FOLKLORE ISSUE
Legend of Sleepy Hollow

The Headless Horseman in pursuit of Ichabod Crane from *Legend of Sleepy Hollow*, by Washington Irving.

Headless Horseman and Ichabod—A951
Designed by Leonard Everett Fisher.
LITHOGRAPHED, ENGRAVED (Giori)
Plates of 200 subjects in four panes of 50 each.

1974			Tagged		Perf. 11	
1548	A951	10c	dk. bl., blk., org. & yel., Oct. 10		20	5
			Margin block of 4, P#		1.00	—
			Margin block of 4, Mr. Zip and "Use Zip Code"		90	—
			Margin block of 6, "Mail Early in the Day"		1.30	—

RETARDED CHILDREN ISSUE

Retarded Children Can Be Helped, theme of annual convention of the National Association of Retarded Citizens.

Retarded Child—A952
Designed by Paul Calle.
GIORI PRESS PRINTING
Plates of 200 subjects in four panes of 50 each.

1974			Tagged		Perf. 11
1549	A952	10c	**brown red & dark brown**, Oct. 12	20	5
			Margin block of 4, P#	1.00	
			Margin block of 4, Mr. Zip and "Use Zip Code"	90	
			Margin block of 6, "Mail Early in the Day"	1.30	

CHRISTMAS ISSUE

Angel—A953

"The Road—Winter," by Currier and Ives—A954

Dove Weather Vane atop Mount Vernon—A955

Designers: No. 1550, Bradbury Thompson, using detail from the Pérussia altarpiece painted by anonymous French artist, 1480, in Metropolitan Museum of Art, New York City. No. 1551, Stevan Dohanos, using Currier and Ives print from drawing by Otto Knirsch. No. 1552, Don Hedin and Robert Geissman.

PHOTOGRAVURE (Andreotti)
Plates of 200 subjects in four panes of 50 each.

1974, Oct. 23			Tagged	Perf. 10½x11	
1550	A953	10c	**multicolored**	20	5
			Margin block of 10, 5 P#	2.25	
			Margin block of 4, Mr. Zip and "Use Zip Code"	90	
			Margin block of 6, "Mail Early in the Day"	1.30	

Perf. 11x10½

1551	A954	10c	**multicolored**	20	5
			Margin block of 12, P#	2.60	
			Margin block of 4, Mr. Zip and "Use Zip Code"	90	
			Margin block of 4, "Mail Early in the Day"	90	

Imperf., Paper Backing Rouletted

1974, Nov. 15   Untagged
Self-adhesive; Inscribed "Precanceled"

1552	A955	10c	**multicolored**	20	8
			Margin block of 20, 6 P# and 5 slogans	5.50	
			Margin block of 12, 6 P# and 5 different slogans	3.25	

Unused price of No. 1552 is for copy on rouletted paper backing as issued. Used price is for copy on piece, with or without postmark.
Die cutting includes crossed slashes through dove, applied to prevent removal and re-use of the stamp. The stamp will separate into layers if soaked.
Two different machines were used to roulette the sheet.

AMERICAN ARTS ISSUE

Benjamin West (1738–1820), painter (No. 1553); Paul Laurence Dunbar (1872–1906), poet (No. 1554); David Lewelyn Wark Griffith (1875–1948), motion picture producer (No. 1555).

Benjamin West,
Self-portrait
A956

Paul Laurence Dunbar
A957

David Lewelyn Griffith
A958

Designed by Bradbury Thompson (No. 1553); Walter D. Richards (No. 1554); Fred Otnes (No. 1555).

PHOTOGRAVURE (Andreotti)
Plates of 200 subjects in four panes of 50 each.

1975			Tagged	Perf. 10½x11	
1553	A956	10c	**multicolored**, Feb. 10	20	5
			Margin block of 10, 5 P#	2.20	
			Margin block of 4, Mr. Zip and "Use Zip Code"	90	
			Margin block of 6, "Mail Early in the Day"	1.30	

POSTAGE, 1975

Perf. 11

1554	A957	10c	multicolored, *May 1*	20	5
			Margin block of 10, 5 P#	2.20	
			Margin block of 4, Mr. Zip and "Use Zip Code"	90	
			Margin block of 6, "Mail Early in the Day"	1.30	
		a.	Imperf., pair	1,400.	

LITHOGRAPHED, ENGRAVED (Giori)
Perf. 11

1555	A958	A10c	brown & multicolored, *May 27*	20	5
			Margin block of 4, P#	1.00	
			Margin block of 4, Mr. Zip and "Use Zip Code"	90	
			Margin block of 6, "Mail Early in the Day"	1.30	
		a.	Brown (engraved) omitted	750.00	

SPACE ISSUES

U.S. space accomplishments with unmanned craft. Pioneer 10 passed within 81,000 miles of Jupiter, Dec. 10, 1973. Mariner 10 explored Venus and Mercury in 1974 and Mercury again in 1975.

Pioneer 10 Passing Jupiter
A959

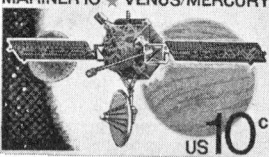

Mariner 10, Venus and Mercury
A960

Designed by Robert McCall (No. 1556); Roy Gjertson (No. 1557).

LITHOGRAPHED, ENGRAVED (Giori)
Plates of 200 subjects in four panes of 50 each.

1975			Tagged	Perf. 11	
1556	A959	10c	violet blue, yellow & red, *Feb. 28*	20	5
			Margin block of 4, P#	1.00	
			Margin block of 4, Mr. Zip and "Use Zip Code"	90	
			Margin block of 6, "Mail Early in the Day"	1.30	
		a.	Red & yellow (litho.) omitted	1,250.	
		b.	Blue omitted	1,400.	
1557	A960	10c	black, red, ultra. & bister, *Apr. 4*	20	5
			Margin block of 4, P#	1.00	
			Margin block of 4, Mr. Zip and "Use Zip Code"	90	
			Margin block of 6, "Mail Early in the Day"	1.30	
		a.	Red omitted	400.00	
		b.	Ultra. & bister omitted	2,250.	

COLLECTIVE BARGAINING ISSUE

Collective Bargaining law, enacted 1935, in Wagner Act.

"Labor and Management"
A961

Designed by Robert Hallock.

PHOTOGRAVURE (Andreotti)
Plates of 200 subjects in four panes of 50 each.

1975			Tagged	Perf. 11	
1558	A961	10c	multicolored, *March 13*	20	5
			Margin block of 8, 4 P#	1.80	
			Margin block of 4, Mr. Zip and "Use Zip Code"	90	
			Margin block of 6, "Mail Early in the Day"	1.30	

Imperfs exist from printer's waste.

AMERICAN BICENTENNIAL ISSUE

Contributors to the Cause

Sybil Ludington, age 16, rallied militia, Apr. 26, 1777; Salem Poor, black freeman, fought in Battle of Bunker Hill; Haym Salomon, Jewish immigrant, raised money to finance Revolutionary War; Peter Francisco, Portuguese-French immigrant, joined Continental Army at 15. Emerald inscription on back, printed beneath gum in water-soluble ink, gives thumbnail sketch of portrayed contributor.

Sybil Ludington—A962

Salem Poor—A963

Haym Salomon—A964

Peter Francisco—A965

Designed by Neil Boyle.

PHOTOGRAVURE (Andreotti)
Plates of 200 subjects in four panes of 50 each.

1975, Mar. 25			Tagged	Perf. 11x10½	
1559	A962	8c	multicolored	16	13
			Margin block of 10, 5 P#	2.00	
			Margin block of 4, Mr. Zip and "Use Zip Code"	70	
			Margin block of 6, "Mail Early in the Day"	1.10	
		a.	Back inscriptions omitted	300.00	

POSTAGE, 1975

1560	A963	10c	**multicolored**	20	5
			Margin block of 10, 5 P#	2.50	
			Margin block of 4, Mr. Zip and "Use Zip Code"	90	
			Margin block of 6, "Mail Early in the Day"	1.30	
		a.	Back inscription omitted	300.00	
1561	A964	10c	**multicolored**	20	5
			Margin block of 10, 5 P#	2.50	
			Margin block of 4, Mr. Zip and "Use Zip Code"	90	
			Margin block of 6, "Mail Early in the Day"	1.30	
		a.	Back inscription omitted	400.00	
		b.	Red omitted	325.00	
1562	A965	18c	**multicolored**	36	20
			Margin block of 10, 5 P#	5.00	
			Margin block of 4, Mr. Zip and "Use Zip Code"	1.65	
			Margin block of 6, "Mail Early in the Day"	2.40	

Lexington-Concord Battle

Bicentenary of the Battle of Lexington and Concord.

"Birth of Liberty,"
by Henry Sandham
A966

Designed by Bradbury Thompson.
PHOTOGRAVURE (Andreotti)
Plates of 160 subjects in four panes of 40 each.

1975			Tagged	*Perf. 11*	
1563	A966	10c	**multicolored**, *Apr. 19*	20	5
			Margin block of 12, 6 P#	2.60	
			Margin block of 4, Mr. Zip, "Use Zip Code" and "Mail Early in the Day"	90	
			Margin block of 16, 6 P#, Mr. Zip and slogans	3.50	
		a.	Vert. pair, imperf. horiz.	600.00	

Bunker Hill Battle

Bicentenary of the Battle of Bunker Hill.

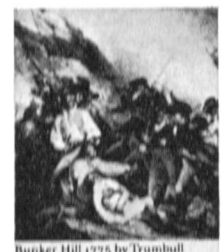

Battle of Bunker Hill,
by John Trumbull
A967

Designed by Bradbury Thompson.

PHOTOGRAVURE (Andreotti)
Plates of 160 subjects in four panes of 40 each.

1975			Tagged	*Perf. 11*	
1564	A967	10c	**multicolored**, *June 17*	20	5
			Margin block of 12, 6 P#	2.60	
			Margin block of 4, Mr. Zip, "Use Zip Code" and "Mail Early in the Day"	90	
			Margin block of 16, 6 P#, Mr. Zip and slogans	3.50	

Military Uniforms

Bicentenary of U.S. Military Services. Nos. 1565–1568 are printed in blocks of four in panes of 50. Nos. 1565–1566 alternate in one row, Nos. 1567–1568 in next row.

Soldier with Flintlock Musket, Uniform Button	Sailor with Grappling Hook, First Navy Jack, 1775
A968	A969

Marine with Musket, Full-rigged Ship	Militaman with Musket and Powder Horn
A970	A971

Designed by Edward Vebell.
PHOTOGRAVURE (Andreotti)
Plates of 200 subjects in four panes of 50 each.

1975, July 4			Tagged	*Perf. 11*	
1565	A968	10c	**multicolored**	20	8
			Margin block of 12, 6 P# adjoining Nos. 1565-1566	2.60	
			Margin blocks of 20, 6 P# adjoining Nos. 1565-1566, Mr. Zip and slogans	4.40	
			Margin block of 4, Mr. Zip and "Use Zip Code" adjoining No. 1565	90	
			Margin block of 4, "Mail Early in the Day" adjoining No. 1565	90	
1566	A969	10c	**multicolored**	20	8
			Margin block of 4, Mr. Zip and "Use Zip Code" adjoining No. 1566	90	
			Margin block of 4, "Mail Early in the Day" adjoining No. 1566	90	
1567	A970	10c	**multicolored**	20	8
			Margin block of 12, 6 P# adjoining Nos. 1567-1568	2.60	
			Margin block of 20, 6 P# adjoining Nos. 1567-1568, Mr. Zip and slogans	4.40	
			Margin block of 4, Mr. Zip and "Use Zip Code" adjoining No. 1567	90	

			Margin block of 4, "Mail Early in the Day" adjoining No. 1567	90	
1568	A971	10c	multicolored	20	8
			Margin block of 4, Mr. Zip and "Use Zip Code" adjoining No. 1568	90	
			Margin block of 4, "Mail Early in the Day" adjoining No. 1568	90	
		a.	Block of 4, #1565-1568	80	80
			#1565-1568@		90

APOLLO SOYUZ SPACE ISSUE

Apollo Soyuz space test project, Russo-American cooperation, launched July 15; link-up, July 17. Nos. 1569–1570 are printed se-tenant in horizontal rows of 3 in panes of 24. In the first row of the pane No. 1569 is in first and third space, No. 1570 is second space; in the second row No. 1570 is in first and third space, No. 1569 in second space, etc.

Participating U.S. and U.S.S.R. crews: Thomas P. Stafford, Donald K. Slayton, Vance D. Brand, Aleksei A. Leonov, Valery N. Kubasov.

See Russia Nos. 4339–4340.

Apollo and Soyuz after Link-up, and Earth—A972

Spacecraft before Link-up, Earth and Project Emblem
A973

Designed by Robert McCall (No. 1569) and Anatoly M. Aksamit of USSR (No. 1570).

PHOTOGRAVURE (Andreotti)
Plates of 96 subjects in four panes of 24 each.

1975, July 15			Tagged		Perf. 11
1569	A972	10c	multicolored	20	10
		a.	Pair, #1569-1570	40	25
			Block of four, 2 #1569 + 2 #1570	80	80
			Margin block of 12, 6 P#	2.60	
			Margin block of 4, Mr. Zip, "Use Zip Code" adjoining No. 1569; "Mail Early in the Day" adjoining No. 1570	90	
			Margin block of 16, 6 P#, Mr. Zip "Use Zip Code" adjoining No. 1569, "Mail Early in the Day" adjoining No. 1570	3.40	
		b.	As "a," vert. pair imperf. horiz.	1,250.	
			Pair with full horiz. gutter btwn.		
1570	A973	10c	multicolored	20	10
			Margin block of 4, Mr. Zip, "Use Zip Code" adjoining No. 1570; "Mail Early in the Day" adjoining No. 1569	90	
			Margin block of 16, 6 P#, Mr. Zip, "Use Zip Code" adjoining No. 1570, "Mail Early in the Day" adjoining No. 1569	3.40	

INTERNATIONAL WOMEN'S YEAR ISSUE

International Women's Year 1975.

Worldwide Equality for Women
A974

Designed by Miriam Schottland.

PHOTOGRAVURE (Andreotti)
Plates of 200 subjects in four panes of 50 each.

1975			Tagged		Perf. 11x10½
1571	A974	10c	blue, orange & dark blue, Aug. 26	20	5
			Margin block of 6, 3 P#	1.40	
			Margin block of 4, Mr. Zip and "Use Zip Code"	90	
			Margin block of 4, "Mail Early in the Day"	1.30	

U.S. POSTAL SERVICE BICENTENNIAL ISSUE

Nos. 1572–1575 are printed in blocks of four in panes of 50. Nos. 1572–1573 alternate in first row, Nos. 1574–1575 in second row. This arrangement is repeated throughout the pane.

Stagecoach and Trailer Truck
A975

Old and New Locomotives
A976

Early Mail Plane and Jet
A977

Satellite for Transmission of Mailgrams
A978

POSTAGE, 1975

Designed by James L. Womer.
PHOTOGRAVURE (Andreotti)
Plates of 200 subjects in four panes of 50 each.

1975, Sept. 3			Tagged	Perf. 11x10½	
1572	A975	10c	multicolored	20	8
			Margin block of 12, 6 P# adjoining Nos. 1572, 1574	2.60	
			Margin block of 20, 6 P# adjoining Nos. 1572, 1574, Mr. Zip and slogans	4.40	
			Margin block of 4, Mr. Zip and "Use Zip Code" adjoining No. 1572	90	
			Margin block of 4, "Mail Early in the Day" adjoining No. 1572	90	
1573	A976	10c	multicolored	20	8
			Margin block of 12, 6 P# adjoining Nos. 1573, 1575	2.60	
			Margin block of 20, 6 P# adjoining Nos. 1573, 1575, Mr. Zip and slogans	4.40	
			Margin block of 4, Mr. Zip and "Use Zip Code" adjoining No. 1573	90	
			Margin block of 4, "Mail Early in the Day" adjoining No. 1573	90	
1574	A977	10c	multicolored	20	8
			Margin block of 4, Mr. Zip and "Use Zip Code" adjoining No. 1574	90	
			Margin block of 4, "Mail Early in the Day" adjoining No. 1574	90	
1575	A978	10c	multicolored	20	8
			Margin block of 4, Mr. Zip and "Use Zip Code" adjoining No. 1575	90	
			Margin block of 4, "Mail Early in the Day" adjoining No. 1575	90	
		a.	Block of 4, #1572-1575	80	80
		b.	As "a", red ("10c") omitted		

WORLD PEACE THROUGH LAW ISSUE

A prelude to 7th World Law Conference of the World Peace Through Law Center at Washington, D.C., Oct. 12–17.

Law Book, Gavel, Olive Branch and Globe
A979

Designed by Melbourne Brindle.
GIORI PRESS PRINTING
Plates of 200 subjects in four panes of 50 each.

1975			Tagged	Perf. 11	
1576	A979	10c	green, Prussian blue & rose brown, Sept. 29	20	5
			Margin block of 4, P#	1.00	
			Margin block of 4, Mr. Zip and "Use Zip Code"	90	
			Margin block of 6, "Mail Early in the Day"	1.30	

BANKING AND COMMERCE ISSUE

Banking and commerce in the U.S., and for the Centennial Convention of the American Bankers Association.

Engine Turning, Indian Head Penny, Seated Liberty Quarter, Morgan-type Silver Dollar and $20 Gold Double Eagle

A980   A981

LITHOGRAPHED, ENGRAVED (Giori)
Plates of 160 subjects in four panes of 40 each.

1975, Oct. 6				Perf. 11	
1577	A980	10c	multicolored	20	8
		a.	Pair, #1577-1578	40	20
		b.	Brown & blue (litho) omitted	1,000.	
			Block of four, 2 #1577 + 2 #1578	80	75
			Margin block of 4, P# adjoining #1577	1.00	
			Margin block of 4, Mr. Zip and "Use Zip Code" adjoining #1577	90	
			Margin block of 6, "Mail Early in the Day" adjoining #1577	1.30	
1578	A981	10c	multicolored	20	8
			Margin block of 4, P# adjoining #1578	1.00	
			Margin block of 4, Mr. Zip and "Use Zip Code" adjoining #1578	90	
			Margin block of 6, "Mail Early in the Day" adjoining #1578	1.30	

CHRISTMAS ISSUE

Madonna and Child,
by Domenico Ghirlandaio
A982

Christmas Card, by
Louis Prang, 1878
A983

Designed by Steven Dohanos.
PHOTOGRAVURE (Andreotti)
Plates of 200 subjects in four panes of 50 each.

1975, Oct. 14		Tagged	Perf. 11	
1579	A982(10c)	**multicolored**	20	5
		Margin block of 12, 6 P#	2.60	—
		Margin block of 4, Mr. Zip and "Use Zip Code"	90	—
		Margin block of 4, "Mail Early in the Day"	90	—
	a.	Imperf., pair	125.00	
		Plate flaw ("d" damaged) (36741-36746 L.L. 47)	5.00	—
1580	A983(10c)	**multicolored**	20	5
		Margin block of 12, 6 P#	2.60	—
		Margin block of 4, Mr. Zip and "Use Zip Code"	90	—
		Margin block of 4, "Mail Early in the Day"	90	—
	a.	Imperf., pair	125.00	
	b.	Perf. 10½x11	50	5

AMERICANA ISSUE

Inkwell and Quill
A984

Speaker's Stand
A985

Early Ballot Box
A987

Books, Bookmark,
Eyeglasses
A988

Dome of Capitol
A994

Contemplation of
Justice, by
J. E. Fraser
A995

Early American
Printing Press
A996

Liberty Bell
A998

Eagle and Shield
A999

Fort McHenry
Flag (15 Stars)
A1001

Head, Statue of Liberty
A1002

Old North Church,
Boston
A1006

Fort Nisqually,
Wash.
A1007

Sandy Hook Lighthouse,
N.J.
A1008

POSTAGE, 1975-79   307

Morris Township School No. 2, Devils Lake
A1009

Iron "Betty" Lamp, Plymouth Colony, 17th–18th Centuries
A1011

Rush Lamp and Candle Holder
A1013

Kerosene Table Lamp
A1013a

Railroad Conductor's Lantern, c. 1850
A1014

Torch, Statue of Liberty—A997

ROTARY PRESS PRINTING
E.E. Plates of 400 subjects in four panes of 100 each.

1975-81		Tagged	Perf. 11x10½

Size: 18½x22½mm.

1581	A984	1c dark blue, greenish, Dec. 8, 1977	5	5
		Margin block of 4, P#	25	
		Margin block of 4, "Use Zip Code"	22	
		Margin block of 6, "Mail Early ..."	32	
		Pair with full vert. gutter btwn.		
	a.	Untagged (Bureau precanceled)		5
1582	A985	2c red brown, greenish, Dec. 8, 1977	5	5
		Margin block of 4, P#	25	
		Margin block of 4, "Use Zip Code"	22	
		Margin block of 6, "Mail Early ..."	32	
	a.	Untagged (Bureau precanceled)		6
	b.	Cream paper, 1981	5	5
1584	A987	3c olive, greenish, Dec. 8, 1977	6	5
		Margin block of 4, P#	30	
		Margin block of 4, "Use Zip Code"	28	
		Margin block of 6, Mail Early	38	
	a.	Untagged (Bureau precanceled)		6
1585	A988	4c rose magenta, cream, Dec. 8, 1977	8	5
		Margin block of 4, P#	40	
		Margin block of 4, "Use Zip Code"	35	
		Margin block of 6, "Mail Early ..."	50	
	a.	Untagged (Bureau precanceled)		8

Size: 17½x20½mm.

| 1590 | A994 | 9c slate green (from bklt. pane), Mar. 11, 1977 | 75 | 20 |
| | a. | Perf. 10 (from bklt. pane) | 25.00 | 6.00 |

Size: 18½x22½mm.

1591	A994	9c slate green, gray, Nov. 24, 1975	18	5
		Margin block of 4, P#	90	
		Margin block of 4, "Use Zip Code"	80	
		Margin block of 6, "Mail Early in the Day"	1.20	
	a.	Untagged (Bureau precanceled)		18
1592	A995	10c violet, gray, Nov. 17, 1977	20	5
		Margin block of 4, P#	1.00	
		Margin block of 4, "Use Zip Code"	90	
		Margin block of 6, "Mail Early in the Day"	1.50	
	a.	Untagged (Bureau precanceled)		25
1593	A996	11c orange, gray, Nov. 13, 1975	22	5
		Margin block of 4, P#	1.10	
		Margin block of 4, "Use Zip Code"	1.00	
		Margin block of 6, "Mail Early in the Day"	1.50	
1594	A997	12c red brown, beige, Apr. 8, 1981	24	5
		P# block of 4	1.15	
		Zip block of 4	1.10	
		Mail Early block of 6	1.60	
1595	A998	13c brown (from bklt. pane), Oct. 31, 1975	26	5
	a.	Booklet pane of 6	1.60	50
	b.	Booklet pane of 7 + label	1.80	50
	c.	Booklet pane of 8	2.10	50
	d.	Booklet pane of 5 + label, Apr. 2, 1976	1.30	50
	e.	Vert. pair, imperf. btwn.		

PHOTOGRAVURE (Andreotti)
Plates of 400 subjects in four panes of 100 each.
Perf. 11

1596	A999	13c multicolored, Dec. 1, 1975	26	5
		Margin block of 12, 6 P#	3.38	
		Margin block of 20, 6 P# and slogans	5.45	
		Margin block of 4, "Use Zip Code"	1.25	
		Margin block of 4, "Mail Early in the Day"	1.25	
	a.	Imperf., pair	40.00	
	b.	Yellow omitted	175.00	
		Pair with full horiz. gutter btwn.		

ENGRAVED (Combination Press)
Plates of 460 subjects (20x23) in panes of 100 (10x10)

1597	A1001	15c gray, dark blue & red, June 30, 1978	30	5
		Margin block of 6, P#	2.10	
		Margin block of 20, 1 or 2 P#	8.50	
	a.	Imperf., vert. pair	20.00	
	b.	Gray omitted		

Plate number appears 3 times on each plate of 23 rows. With no separating gutters, each pane has only left or right sheet margin. Plate numbers appear on both margins; there are no slogans. Margin blocks of 20 have one or two plate numbers.

ENGRAVED
Perf. 11x10½

1598	A1001	15c gray, dark blue & red (from bklt. pane), June 30, 1978	30	5
	a.	Booklet pane of 8	3.75	60
1599	A1002	16c blue, Mar. 31, 1978	32	5
		Margin block of 4, P#	2.25	
		Margin block of 4, "Use Correct Zip Code"*	1.45	
		Margin block of 4, copyright	1.45	
1603	A1006	24c red, blue, Nov. 14, 1975	48	9
		Margin block of 4, P#	2.75	
		Margin block of 4, "Use Zip Code"	2.15	
		Margin block of 6, "Mail Early in the Day"	3.00	
1604	A1007	28c brown, blue, Aug. 11, 1978	56	8
		Margin block of 4, P#	3.25	
		Margin block of 4, "Use Correct Zip Code"*	2.50	
		Margin block of 4, copyright	2.50	
1605	A1008	29c blue, light blue, Apr. 14, 1978	58	8
		Margin block of 4, P#	3.25	
		Margin block of 4, "Use Correct Zip Code"*	2.65	
		Margin block of 4, copyright	2.65	

POSTAGE, 1975-79

1606	A1009	30c	green, blue, Aug. 27, 1979	60	8
			Margin block of 4, P#	3.00	—
			Margin block of 4, "Use Correct Zip Code"®	2.70	—
			Margin block of 4, © "United States Postal Service 1979"	2.70	—

Perf. 11
ENGRAVED

1608	A1011	50c	black & orange, tan, Sept. 11, 1979	1.00	25
			Margin block of 4, P#	5.00	—
			Margin block of 4, "Use Correct Zip Code"®	4.50	—
			Margin block of 4, © "United States Postal Service 1979"	4.50	—
		a.	Black omitted		—
1610	A1013	$1	brown, orange & yellow, tan, July 2, 1979	2.00	25
			Margin block of 4, P#	9.00	—
			Margin block of 4, "Use Correct Zip Code"®	9.00	—
			Margin block of 4, © "United States Postal Service 1979"	9.00	—
		a.	Brown (engraved) omitted	500.00	
		b.	Tan, orange & yellow omitted	400.00	
		c.	Brown inverted		
1611	A1013a	$2	dark green & red, tan, Nov. 16, 1978	4.00	50
			Margin block of 4, P#	18.00	—
			Margin block of 4, "Use Correct Zip Code"®	17.00	—
			Margin block of 4, © "United States Postal Service 1978"	17.00	—
1612	A1014	$5	red brown, yellow & orange, tan, Aug. 23, 1979	10.00	2.00
			Margin block of 4, P#	45.00	—
			Margin block of 4, "Use Correct Zip Code"®	45.00	—
			Margin block of 4, © "United States Postal Service 1979"	45.00	—

Nos. 1590, 1590a, 1595, 1598, 1623 and 1623b were issued only in booklets. All stamps have one or two straight edges.

Six-string Guitar
A1014a

Saxhorns
A1015

Drum
A1016

Steinway Grand Piano, 1857
A1017

Designers: 3.1c, George Mercer. 7.7c, Susan Robb. 7.9c, Bernard Glassman. 10c, Walter Brooks. 15c, V. Jack Ruther.

COIL STAMPS

1975-79 Perf. 10 Vertically

1613	A1014a	3.1c	brown, yellow, Oct. 25, 1979	20	10
			Pair	40	16
			Joint line pair	1.75	
		a.	Untagged (Bureau precanceled)		10
		b.	Imperf., pair	950.00	
1614	A10157	.7c	brown, bright yellow, Nov. 20, 1976	20	8
			Pair	40	16
			Joint line pair	1.00	
		a.	Untagged (Bureau precanceled)		16
		b.	As "a," imperf., pair		450.00

A total of 159 different Bureau precancels were used by 153 cities.

1615	A10167	.9c	carmine, yellow, Apr. 23, 1976	20	8
			Pair	40	16
			Joint line pair	1.10	
		a.	Untagged (Bureau precanceled)		16
		b.	Imperf., pair	450.00	

A total of 108 different Bureau precancels were used by 107 cities.

1615C	A10178	.4c	dark blue, yellow, July 13, 1978	25	8
			Pair	50	16
			Joint line pair	2.00	30
		d.	Untagged (Bureau precanceled)		16
		e.	As "d," pair, imperf. between	30.00	
		f.	As "d," imperf., pair	17.50	

A total of 145 different Bureau precancels were used by 144 cities.

1616	A994	9c	slate green, gray, Mar. 5, 1976	22	5
			Pair	44	10
			Joint line pair	90	20
		a.	Imperf., pair	100.00	
		b.	Untagged (Bureau precanceled)		18
		c.	As "b," imperf., pair		150.00
1617	A995	10c	violet, gray, Nov. 4, 1977	20	5
			Pair	40	10
			Joint line pair	1.25	
		a.	Untagged (Bureau precanceled)		25
		b.	Imperf., pair	65.00	
1618	A998	13c	brown, Nov. 25, 1975	26	5
			Pair	52	10
			Joint line pair	1.00	25
		a.	Untagged (Bureau precanceled)		25
		b.	Imperf., pair	25.00	
1618C	A1001	15c	gray, dark blue & red, June 30, 1978	40	5
			Pair	80	10
		d.	Imperf., pair	20.00	
		e.	Pair, imperf. between	150.00	
		f.	gray omitted	65.00	
1619	A1002	16c	ultramarine, Mar. 31, 1978	32	5
			Pair	65	10
			Joint line pair	1.50	—

No. 1619 was printed on two different presses. Huck press printings have white background without bluish tinge, are a fraction of a millimeter smaller and have block instead of overall tagging. Cottrell press printings show a joint line. See Nos. 1811, 1813, 1816.

13-Star Flag over Independence Hall
A1018

Flag over Capitol
A1018a

Designers: No. 1622, Melbourne Brindle. No. 1623, Esther Porter.

MULTICOLOR HUCK PRESS
Panes of 100 (10x10) each.

1975-77 Perf. 11x10½

1622	A1018	13c	dark blue & red, Nov. 15, 1975	26	5
			Margin block of 20	5.50	
		a.	Horiz. pair, imperf. between	75.00	
		b.	Vert. pair, imperf.		
		c.	Perf. 11, 1981	30	5

See note after No. 1338D.

No. 1622c has floating plate markings at sides of sheet. No. 1622 at top and bottom.

ENGRAVED

1623	A1018a	13c	blue & red (from bklt. pane), Mar. 11, 1977	26	5
		a.	Booklet pane of 8 (1 #1590 + 7 #1623)	2.50	60
		b.	Perf. 10 (from bklt. pane)	1.50	1.00
		c.	Booklet pane of 8, perf. 10 (1 #1590a + 7 #1623b)	37.50	
		d.	Se-tenant pair, #1590 & #1623	1.50	—

COIL STAMP

1975, Nov. 15   *Perf. 10 Vertically*

1625	A1018 13c	dark blue & red	30	5
		Pair	60	10
	a.	Imperf., pair	20.00	

AMERICAN BICENTENNIAL ISSUE
The Spirit of '76

Designed after painting by Archibald M. Willard in Abbot Hall, Marblehead, Massachusetts. Nos. 1629-1631 printed se-tenant in panes of 50 (10x5). Left panes contain 3 No. 1631a and one No. 1629; right panes contain one No. 1631 and 3 No. 1631a.

Drummer Boy   Old Drummer   Fifer
A1019   A1020   A1021

Designed by Vincent E. Hoffman.

PHOTOGRAVURE (Andreotti)
Plates of 200 subjects in four panes of 50 each.

1976, Jan. 1   Tagged   *Perf. 11*

1629	A1019 13c	blue violet & multi.	26	8
1630	A1020 13c	blue violet & multi.	26	8
1631	A1021 13c	" " "	26	8
	a.	Strip of 3, #1629-1631	78	60
	b.	As "a," imperf.	2,000.	
	c.	Imperf., vert. pair	1,100.	
		Margin block of 12, 5 P#	3.40	—
		Margin block of 20, 5 P# and slogans	5.50	—

INTERPHIL ISSUE

Interphil 76 International Philatelic Exhibition, Philadelphia, Pa., May 29–June 6.

"Interphil 76"
A1022
Designed by Terrence W. McCaffrey.

LITHOGRAPHED, ENGRAVED (Giori)
Plates of 200 subjects of four panes of 50 each.

1976   Tagged   *Perf. 11*

1632	A1022 13c	dark blue, red & ultra., *Jan. 17*	26	5
		Margin block of 4, P#	1.30	—
		Margin block of 4, Mr. Zip and "Use Zip Code"	1.20	—
		Margin block of 6, "Mail Early in the Day"	1.70	—

Scott Album Supplement Schedule

January
U.S. Commemorative Plate Blocks
Regular & Air Plate Blocks
U.N. Singles & Postal Stationery
U.N. Imprint Blocks
National Hingeless

March
Austria
France
Germany

April
Great Britain
British Europe
Channel Islands
Ireland
Monaco & Fr. Andorra
Korea
Israel Singles
Israel Tabs

May
Switzerland
Liechtenstein
Greece
Scandinavia & Finland

June
Japan
Portugal
Spain & Sp. Andorra
Italy
San Marino
Vatican City

July
Belgium
Netherlands
Luxembourg
U.S.S.R.
Czechoslovakia
Poland
Hungary

August
Australia & Dep.
New Zealand
New Zealand Dep.
Mexico
Br. America Vol. 1
Br. America Vol. 2

November
National
Minuteman
American
Canada
Master Canada
International

December
U.S. Booklet Panes
U.S. Commemorative Singles
U.S. Blocks of 4
U.S. Postal Stationery
U.S. Postal Cards

Scott Publishing Company
P.O. Box 828
Sidney, OH 45365

All supplements are available from your local dealer or direct from Scott.

POSTAGE, 1976

AMERICAN BICENTENNIAL ISSUE

State Flags—A1023–A1072

Designed by Walt Reed.
PHOTOGRAVURE (Andreotti)
Plates of 200 subjects in four panes of 50 each.

1976, Feb. 23   Tagged   Perf. 11
Multicolored

1633	A1023 13c	Delaware	45	30
1634	A1024 13c	Pennsylvania	45	30
1635	A1025 13c	New Jersey	45	30
1636	A1026 13c	Georgia	45	30
1637	A1027 13c	Connecticut	45	30
1638	A1028 13c	Massachusetts	45	30
1639	A1029 13c	Maryland	45	30
1640	A1030 13c	South Carolina	45	30
1641	A1031 13c	New Hampshire	45	30
1642	A1032 13c	Virginia	45	30
1643	A1033 13c	New York	45	30
1644	A1034 13c	North Carolina	45	30
1645	A1035 13c	Rhode Island	45	30
1646	A1036 13c	Vermont	45	30
1647	A1037 13c	Kentucky	45	30
1648	A1038 13c	Tennessee	45	30
1649	A1039 13c	Ohio	45	30
1650	A1040 13c	Louisiana	45	30
1651	A1041 13c	Indiana	45	30
1652	A1042 13c	Mississippi	45	30
1653	A1043 13c	Illinois	45	30
1654	A1044 13c	Alabama	45	30
1655	A1045 13c	Maine	45	30

POSTAGE, 1976

1656	A1046 13c	*Missouri*	45	30
1657	A1047 13c	*Arkansas*	45	30
1658	A1048 13c	*Michigan*	45	30
1659	A1049 13c	*Florida*	45	30
1660	A1050 13c	*Texas*	45	30
1661	A1051 13c	*Iowa*	45	30
1662	A1052 13c	*Wisconsin*	45	30
1663	A1053 13c	*California*	45	30
1664	A1054 13c	*Minnesota*	45	30
1665	A1055 13c	*Oregon*	45	30
1666	A1056 13c	*Kansas*	45	30
1667	A1057 13c	*West Virginia*	45	30
1668	A1058 13c	*Nevada*	45	30
1669	A1059 13c	*Nebraska*	45	30
1670	A1060 13c	*Colorado*	45	30
1671	A1061 13c	*North Dakota*	45	30
1672	A1062 13c	*South Dakota*	45	30
1673	A1063 13c	*Montana*	45	30
1674	A1064 13c	*Washington*	45	30
1675	A1065 13c	*Idaho*	45	30
1676	A1066 13c	*Wyoming*	45	30
1677	A1067 13c	*Utah*	45	30
1678	A1068 13c	*Oklahoma*	45	30
1679	A1069 13c	*New Mexico*	45	30
1680	A1070 13c	*Arizona*	45	30
1681	A1071 13c	*Alaska*	45	30
1682	A1072 13c	*Hawaii*	45	30
	a.	Pane of 50	25.00	
		Pane of 50, 6 P# adjoining Nos. 1633, 1638, 1643, 1648, 1653, 1658; "Mail Early in the Day" adjoining No. 1663, Mr. Zip and "Use Zip Code" adjoining No. 1678	25.00	
		Pane of 50, 6 P# adjoining Nos. 1637, 1642, 1647, 1652, 1657, 1662; "Mail Early in the Day" adjoining No. 1667, Mr. Zip and "Use Zip Code" adjoining No. 1682	25.00	
		Pane of 50, 6 P# adjoining Nos. 1653, 1658, 1663, 1668, 1673, 1678 "Mail Early in the Day" adjoining No. 1648, Mr. Zip and "Use Zip Code" adjoining No. 1633	25.00	
		Pane of 50, 6 P# adjoining Nos. 1657, 1662, 1667, 1672, 1677, 1682; "Mail Early in the Day" adjoining No. 1652, Mr. Zip and "Use Zip Code" adjoining No. 1637	25.00	

COMMERCIAL AVIATION ISSUE

50th anniversary of first contract airmail flights: Dearborn, Mich. to Cleveland, Ohio, Feb. 15, 1926; and Pasco, Wash. to Elko, Nev., Apr. 6, 1926.

Ford-Pullman Monoplane and Laird Swallow Biplane—A1074

Designed by Robert E. Cunningham.

PHOTOGRAVURE (Andreotti)

Plates of 200 subjects in four panes of 50 each.

1976, Mar. 19		Tagged	*Perf. 11*	
1684	A1074 13c	blue & multicolored	26	5
		Margin block of 10, 5 P#	2.90	
		Margin block of 4, Mr. Zip and "Use Zip Code"	1.20	
		Margin block of 6, "Mail Early in the Day"	1.70	

TELEPHONE CENTENNIAL ISSUE

Centenary of first telephone call by Alexander Graham Bell, March 10, 1876.

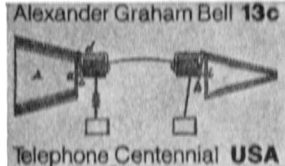

Bell's Telephone Patent Application, 1876—A1073

Designed by George Tscherny.

ENGRAVED (Giori)

Plates of 200 subjects in four panes of 50 each.

1976, Mar. 10		Tagged	*Perf. 11*	
1683	A1073 13c	black, purple & red, *tan*	26	5
		Margin block of 4, P#	1.30	
		Margin block of 4, "Mr. Zip and "Use Zip Code"	1.20	
		Margin block of 6, "Mail Early in the Day"	1.70	

CHEMISTRY ISSUE

Honoring American chemists, in conjunction with the centenary of the American Chemical Society.

Various Flasks, Separatory Funnel, Computer Tape—A1075

Designed by Ken Davies.

PHOTOGRAVURE (Andreotti)

Plates of 200 subjects in four panes of 50 each.

1976, Apr. 6		Tagged	*Perf. 11*	
1685	A1075 13c	multicolored	26	5
		Margin block of 12, 6 P#	3.40	
		Margin block of 4, Mr. Zip and "Use Zip Code"	1.20	
		Margin block of 4, "Mail Early in the Day"	1.20	

AMERICAN BICENTENNIAL ISSUES

SOUVENIR SHEETS

Designs, from Left to Right, No. 1686: a. Two American officers. b. Gen. Benjamin Lincoln. c. George Washington. d. John Trumbull, Col. Cobb, von Steuben, Lafayette, Thomas Nelson. e. Alexander Hamilton, John Laurens, Walter Stewart (all vert.).

No. 1687: a. John Adams, Roger Sherman, Robert R. Livingston. b. Jefferson, Franklin. c. Thomas Nelson, Jr., Francis Lewis, John Witherspoon, Samuel Huntington. d. John Hancock, Charles Thomson. e. George Read, John Dickinson, Edward Rutledge (a, d, vert., b, c, e, horiz.).

No. 1688: a. Boatsman. b. Washington. c. Flag bearer. d. Men in boat. e. Men on shore (a, d, horiz., b, c, e, vert.).

No. 1689: a. Two officers. b. Washington. c. Officer, black horse. d. Officer, white horse. e. Three soldiers (a, c, e, horiz., b, d, vert.).

Surrender of Cornwallis at Yorktown, by John Trumbull—A1076

Declaration of Independence, by John Trumbull—A1077

Washington Crossing the Delaware, by Emmanuel Leutze/Eastman Johnson—A1078

Washington Reviewing Army at Valley Forge, by William T. Trego—A1079

Designed by Vincent E. Hoffman.
LITHOGRAPHED
Plates of 30 subjects in six panes of 5 each.

1976, May 29   Tagged   Perf. 11

1686	A1076	13c sheet of 5	4.50	
	a.	13c multicolored	65	40
	b.	13c "	65	40
	c.	13c "	65	40
	d.	13c "	65	40
	e.	13c "	65	40
	f.	"USA/13c" omitted on "b," "c" & "d," imperf.		
	g.	"USA/13c" omitted on "a" & "e"		
	h.	Imperf., untagged		
	i.	"USA/13c" omitted on "b," "c" & "d"		
	j.	"USA/13c" double on "b"		
	k.	"USA/13c" omitted on "c" & "d"		
	l.	"USA/13c" omitted on "e" untagged		
	m.	"USA/13c" omitted, imperf.		

1687	A1077	18c sheet of 5	6.00	
	a.	18c multicolored	80	55
	b.	18c "	80	55
	c.	18c "	80	55
	d.	18c "	80	55
	e.	18c "	80	55
	f.	Design & marginal inscriptions omitted		
	g.	"USA/18c" omitted on "a" & "c"		
	h.	"USA/18c" omitted on "b," "d" & "c"		
	i.	"USA/18c" omitted on "d"		
	j.	Black omitted in design		
	k.	"USA/18c" omitted, imperf., untagged		
	m.	"USA/18c" omitted on "b" & "e"		

POSTAGE, 1976   313

1688	A1078	24c sheet of 5	7.50		
		a. 24c multicolored	1.00	75	
		b. 24c "	1.00	75	
		c. 24c "	1.00	75	
		d. 24c "	1.00	75	
		e. 24c "	1.00	75	
		f. "USA/24c" omitted, imperf.			
		g. "USA/24c" omitted on "d" & "e"			
		h. Design & marginal inscriptions omitted			
		i. "USA/24c" omitted on "a," "b" & "c"			
		j. Imperf., untagged			
		k. "USA/24c" of "d" & "e" inverted			
1689	A1079	31c sheet of 5	9.00		
		a. 31c multicolored	1.25	90	
		b. 31c "	1.25	90	
		c. 31c "	1.25	90	
		d. 31c "	1.25	90	
		e. 31c "	1.25	90	
		f. "USA/31c" omitted, imperf.			
		g. "USA/31c" omitted on "a" & "c"			
		h. "USA/31c" omitted on "b," "d" & "e"			
		i. "USA/31c" omitted on "e"			
		j. Black omitted in design			
		k. Imperf., untagged			
		l. "USA/31c" omitted on "b" & "d"			
		m. "USA/31c" omitted on "a," "b" & "e"			
		n. As "m," imperf., untagged			
		p. As "h," imperf., untagged			

Issued in connection with Interphil 76 International Philatelic Exhibition, Philadelphia, Pa., May 29–June 6. Size of sheets: 153x204mm.; size of stamps: 25x39½mm., 39½x25mm.
Nos. 1688-1689 exist with inverted perforations.

Benjamin Franklin

American Bicentennial; Benjamin Franklin (1706–1790), deputy postmaster general for the colonies (1753–1774) and statesman. Design based on marble bust by anonymous Italian sculptor after terra cotta bust by Jean Jacques Caffieri, 1777. Map published by R. Sayer and J. Bennett in London. See Canada No. 691.

Franklin and Map of North America, 1776—A1080

Designed by Bernard Reilander (Canada).
LITHOGRAPHED, ENGRAVED (Giori)
Plates of 200 subjects in four panes of 50 each.

1976, June 1	Tagged		Perf. 11	
1690	A1080 13c **ultramarine & multicolored**	26	5
	Margin block of 4, P#	1.30	
	Margin block of 4, Mr. Zip and "Use Zip Code"	1.20	
	Margin block of 6, "Mail Early in the Day"	1.70	
	a. Light blue omitted	450.00	

Declaration of Independence

Designed after painting in the Rotunda of the Capitol, Washington, D.C. Nos. 1691–1694 printed se-tenant in sheets of 50 (10x5). Left panes contain 10 No. 1694a and 5 each of Nos. 1691–1692; right panes contain 5 each of Nos. 1693–1694 and 10 No. 1694a.

Declaration of Independence, by John Trumbull
A1081   A1082   A1083   A1084

Designed by Vincent E. Hoffman.
PHOTOGRAVURE (Andreotti)
Plates of 200 subjects in four panes of 50 each.

1976, July 4	Tagged		Perf. 11	
1691	A1081 13c **blue & multicolored**	26	8
	Margin block of 20, 5 P# adjoining Nos. 1691-1694 & 1691, "Mail Early in the Day" adjoining No. 1693, Mr. Zip and "Use Zip Code" adjoining No. 1692	5.50	
	Margin block of 16, 5 P# as above, "Mail Early in the Day"	4.50	
1692	A1082 13c **blue & multicolored**	26	8
	Margin block of 8, "Mail Early in the Day" adjoining No. 1692	2.30	
	Margin block of 4, Mr. Zip and "Use Zip Code" adjoining No. 1692	1.15	
1693	A1083 13c **blue & multicolored**	26	8
	Margin block of 8, "Mail Early in the Day" adjoining No. 1693	2.30	
	Margin block of 4, Mr. Zip and "Use Zip Code" adjoining No. 1693	1.15	
1694	A1084 13c **blue & multicolored**	26	8
	Margin block of 20, 5 P# adjoining Nos. 1691-1694 & 1694, "Mail Early in the Day" adjoining No. 1692, Mr. Zip and "Use Zip Code" adjoining No. 1693	5.50	
	Margin block of 16, 5 P# as above, "Mail Early in the Day$$	4.50	
	a. Strip of 4, #1691-1694	1.10	75

OLYMPIC GAMES ISSUE

12th Winter Olympic Games, Innsbruck, Austria, Feb. 4–15, and 21st Summer Olympic Games, Montreal, Canada, July 17–Aug. 1. Nos. 1695–1698 are printed in blocks of four in panes of 50. Nos. 1695–1696 alternate in one row, Nos. 1697–1698 in other row.

Diving
A1085

Skiing
A1086

Running
A1087

Skating
A1088

Designed by Donald Moss.
PHOTOGRAVURE (Andreotti)
Plates of 200 subjects in four panes of 50 each.

1976, July 16		Tagged	Perf. 11	
1695	A1085 13c	**multicolored**	26	8
		Margin block of 12, 6 P# adjoining Nos. 1695-1696	3.40	—
		Margin block of 20, 6 P# adjoining Nos. 1695-1696, Mr. Zip and slogans	5.50	—
		Margin block of 4, Mr. Zip and "Use Zip Code" adjoining No. 1695	1.20	—
		Margin block of 4, "Mail Early in the Day" adjoining No. 1695	1.20	—
1696	A1086 13c	**multicolored**	26	8
		Margin block of 4, Mr. Zip and "Use Zip Code" adjoining No. 1696	1.20	—
		Margin block of 4, "Mail Early in the Day" adjoining No. 1696	1.20	—
1697	A1087 13c	**multicolored**	26	8
		Margin block of 12, 6 P# adjoining Nos. 1697-1698	3.40	—
		Margin block of 20, 6 P# adjoining Nos. 1697-1698, Mr. Zip and slogans	5.50	—
		Margin block of 4, Mr. Zip and "Use Zip Code" adjoining No. 1697	1.20	—
		Margin block of 4, "Mail Early in the Day" adjoining No. 1697	1.20	—
1698	A1088 13c	**multicolored**	26	8
		Margin block of 4, Mr. Zip and "Use Zip Code" adjoining No. 1698	1.20	—
		Margin block of 4, "Mail Early in the Day" adjoining No. 1698	1.20	—
	a.	Block of 4, #1695-1698	1.10	1.00
	b.	As "a," imperf.	1,250.	

CLARA MAASS ISSUE

Clara Louise Maass (1876–1901), volunteer in fight against yellow fever, birth centenary.

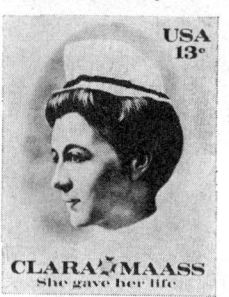

Clara Maass and
Newark German Hospital Pin
A1089

Designed by Paul Calle.
PHOTOGRAVURE (Andreotti)
Plates of 160 subjects in four panes of 40 each.

1976, Aug. 18		Tagged	Perf. 11	
1699	A1089 13c	**multicolored**	26	6
		Margin block of 12, 6 P#	3.40	—
		Margin block of 4, Mr. Zip, "Use Zip Code" and "Mail Early in the Day"	1.20	—
		Margin block of 16, 6 P#, Mr. Zip and slogans	4.20	—
	a.	Horiz. pair, imperf. vert.	600.00	

ADOLPH S. OCHS ISSUE

Adolph S. Ochs (1858–1935), publisher of the New York Times, 1896–1935.

Adolph S. Ochs
A1090

Designed by Bradbury Thompson; photograph by S. J. Woolf.
GIORI PRESS PRINTING
Plates of 128 subjects in four panes of 32 (8x4).

1976, Sept. 18		Tagged	Perf. 11	
1700	A1090 13c	**black & gray**	26	5
		Margin block of 4, P#	1.30	—
		Margin block of 4, Mr. Zip and "Use Zip Code"	1.20	—
		Margin block of 6, "Mail Early in the Day"	1.70	—

CHRISTMAS ISSUE

Nativity,
by John Singleton Copley
A1091

"Winter Pastime,"
by Nathaniel Currier
A1092

Designers: No. 1701, Bradbury Thompson after 1776 painting in Museum of Fine Arts, Boston. No. 1702, Stevan Dohanos after 1855 lithograph in Museum of the City of New York.

PHOTOGRAVURE (Andreotti)
Plates of 200 subjects in four panes of 50 each.

1976, Oct. 27		Tagged, Overall	Perf. 11	
1701	A1091 13c	**multicolored**	26	5
		Margin block of 12, 6 P#	3.40	
		Margin block of 4, Mr. Zip and "Use Zip Code"	1.20	
		Margin block of 4, "Mail Early in the Day"	1.20	
	a.	Imperf., pair	100.00	
1702	A1092 13c	**multicolored**	26	5
		Margin block of 10, 5 P#	3.00	
		Margin block of 4, Mr. Zip and "Use Zip Code"	1.20	
		Margin block of 6, "Mail Early in the Day"	1.70	
	a.	Imperf., pair	125.00	

Plates of 230 (10x23) subjects in panes of 50 (5x10)

Tagged, Block

1703	A1092 13c	**multicolored**	26	5
		Margin block of 20 5-8 P#	5.70	
	a.	Imperf., pair	150.00	
	b.	Vert. pair, imperf. btwn.		

No. 1702 has overall tagging. Lettering at base is black and usually ½ mm. below design. As a rule, no "snowflaking" in sky or pond. Pane of 50 has margins on 4 sides with slogans.
No. 1703 has block tagging the size of printed area. Lettering at base is gray black and usually ¾ mm. below design. "Snowflaking" generally in sky and pond.

COMBINATION PRESS

Cylindrical plates consist of 23 rows of subjects, 10 across for commemoratives (230 subjects), 20 across for definitives (460 subjects), with margins on the two outer edges only. Guillotining through the perforations creates individual panes of 50 or 100 with one margin. Failure of the guillotine to separate through the perforations resulted in straight edges on some stamps. Perforating teeth along the center column and the tenth rows were removed for issues released on or after May 31, 1984 (the 10c Richard Russell, for definitives; the 20c Horace Moses, for commemoratives), creating panes with straight edged stamps on three sides.
Three sets of plate numbers, copyright notices (starting with No. 1787), and zip insignia (starting with No. 1927) are arranged identically on the left and right sides of the plate so that each pane has at least one of each marking. The markings adjacent to any particular row are repeated either seven or eight rows away on the cylinder. Fifteen combinations of the three marginal markings and blank rows are possible on panes.

AMERICAN BICENTENNIAL ISSUE

Washington at Princeton

Washington's Victory over Lord Cornwallis at Princeton, N.J., bicentenary.

Washington, Nassau Hall,
Hessian Prisoners and
13-star Flag, by
Charles Willson Peale
A1093

Designed by Bradbury Thompson.

PHOTOGRAVURE (Andreotti)
Plates of 160 subjects in four panes of 40 each.

1977, Jan. 3		Tagged	Perf. 11	
1704	A1093 13c	**multicolored**	26	5
		Margin block of 10, 5 P#	2.90	
		Margin block of 4, Mr. Zip and "Use Zip Code", "Mail Early in the Day"	1.20	
	a.	Horiz. pair, imperf. vert.	450.00	

SOUND RECORDING ISSUE

Centenary of the invention of the phonograph by Thomas Alva Edison and development of sophisticated recording industry.

Tin Foil Phonograph
A1094

Designed by Walter and Naiad Einsel.

LITHOGRAPHED, ENGRAVED (Giori)
Plates of 200 subjects in four panes of 50 each.

1977, March 23		Tagged	Perf. 11	
1705	A1094 13c	**black & multicolored**	26	5
		Margin block of 4, P#	1.30	
		Margin block of 4, Mr. Zip and "Use Zip Code"	1.20	
		Margin block of 6, "Mail Early in the Day"	1.70	

AMERICAN FOLK ART ISSUE
Pueblo Pottery

Pueblo art, 1880–1920, from Museums in New Mexico, Arizona and Colorado.

Nos. 1706–1709 are printed in blocks and strips of four in panes of 40. In the first row Nos. 1706–1709 are in sequence as listed. In the second row Nos. 1708–1709 are followed by Nos. 1706–1709, 1708–1709.

Zia Pot
A1095

San Ildefonso Pot
A1096

Hopi Pot
A1097

Acoma Pot
A1098

Designed by Ford Ruthling.

PHOTOGRAVURE (Andreotti)
Plates of 160 subjects in four panes of 40 each.

1977, Apr. 13   Tagged   Perf. 11

1706	A1095 13c	**multicolored**	26	8
		Margin block of 10, 5 P#	3.00	—
		Margin block of 16, 5 P#; Mr. Zip and slogans adjoining Nos. 1706-1707	5.00	—
		Margin block of 6, Mr. Zip and "Use Zip Code" "Mail Early in the Day" adjoining Nos. 1706-1707	1.70	—
1707	A1096 13c	**multicolored**	26	8
1708	A1097 13c	**multicolored**	26	8
		Margin block of 16, 5 P#; Mr. Zip and slogans adjoining Nos. 1708-1709	5.00	—
		Margin block of 6, Mr. Zip and "Use Zip Code" "Mail Early in the Day" adjoining Nos. 1708-1709	1.70	—
1709	A1098 13c	**multicolored**	26	8
		a. Block of strip of 4, #1706-1709	1.05	1.00
		b. As "a", imperf. vert.	2,000.	

LINDBERGH FLIGHT ISSUE

Charles A. Lindbergh's solo transatlantic flight from New York to Paris, 50th anniversary.

Spirit of St. Louis
A1099

Designed by Robert E. Cunningham.

PHOTOGRAVURE (Andreotti)
Plates of 200 subjects in four panes of 50 each.

1977, May 20   Tagged   Perf. 11

1710	A1099 13c	**multicolored**	26	5
		Margin block of 12, 6 P#	3.65	—
		Margin block of 4, Mr. Zip and "Use Zip Code"	1.20	—
		Margin block of 4, "Mail Early in the Day"	1.20	—
		a. Imperf., pair	2,000.	

COLORADO STATEHOOD ISSUE

Issued to honor Colorado as the "Centennial State." It achieved statehood in 1876.

Columbine and
Rocky Mountains
A1100

Designed by V. Jack Ruther.

PHOTOGRAVURE (Andreotti)
Plates of 200 subjects in four panes of 50 each.

1977, May 21   Tagged   Perf. 11

1711	A1100 13c	**multicolored**	26	5
		Margin block of 12, 6 P#	3.65	—
		Margin block of 4, Mr. Zip and "Use Zip Code"	1.20	—
		Margin block of 4, "Mail Early in the Day"	1.20	—
		a. Horiz. pair, imperf. btwn.		

Perforations do not run through the sheet margin on about 10 percent of the sheets of No. **1711**.

BUTTERFLY ISSUE

Nos. 1712–1715 are printed in blocks of 4, in panes of 50. Nos. 1712–1713 alternate in first row, Nos. 1714–1715 in second row. This arrangement is repeated throughout the pane. Butterflies represent different geographic U.S. areas.

Swallowtail—A1101   Checkerspot—A1102

Dogface—A1103   Orange-Tip—A1104

Designed by Stanley Galli.
PHOTOGRAVURE (Andreotti)
Plates of 200 subjects in four panes of 50 each.

1977, June 6		Tagged	Perf. 11	
1712	A1101	13c tan & multicolored	26	8
		Margin block of 12, 6 P# adjoining Nos. 1712, 1714	3.65	
		Margin block of 20, 6 P# adjoining Nos. 1712, 1714, Mr. Zip and slogans	6.00	
		Margin block of 4, Mr. Zip and "Use Zip Code" adjoining No. 1712	1.20	
		Margin block of 4, "Mail Early in the Day" adjoining No. 1712	1.20	
1713	A1102	13c tan & multicolored	26	8
		Margin block of 12, 6 P# adjoining Nos. 1713, 1715	3.65	
		Margin block of 20, 6 P# adjoining Nos. 1713, 1715	6.00	
		Margin block of 4, Mr. Zip and "Use Zip Code" adjoining No. 1713	1.20	
		Margin block of 4, "Mail Early in the Day" adjoining No. 1713	1.20	
1714	A1103	13c tan & multicolored	26	8
		Margin block of 4, Mr. Zip and "Use Zip Code" adjoining No. 1714	1.20	
		Margin block of 4, "Mail Early in the Day" adjoining No. 1714	1.20	
1715	A1104	13c tan & multicolored	26	8
		Margin block of 4, Mr. Zip and "Use Zip Code" adjoining No. 1715	1.20	
		Margin block of 4, "Mail Early in the Day" adjoining No. 1715	1.20	
	a.	Block of 4, #1712-1715	1.05	90
	b.	As 'a', imperf. horiz.		

AMERICAN BICENTENNIAL ISSUES
Marquis de Lafayette

200th anniversary of Lafayette's Landing on the coast of South Carolina, north of Charleston.

Designed by Bradbury Thompson.
GIORI PRESS PRINTING
Plates of 160 subjects in four panes of 40 each.

1977, June 13		Tagged	Perf. 11	
1716	A1105	13c blue, black & red	26	5
		Margin block of 4, P#	1.30	
		Margin block of 4, Mr. Zip and "Use Zip Code"	1.20	
		Margin block of 6, "Mail Early in the Day"	1.70	

Marquis de Lafayette
A1105   US Bicentennial 13c

POSTAGE, 1977

Skilled Hands for Independence

Nos. 1717–1720 are printed se-tenant in blocks of four, in panes of 50. Nos. 1717–1718 alternate in first row, Nos. 1719–1720 in second row. This arrangement is repeated throughout the pane.

Seamstress—A1106   Blacksmith—A1107

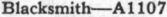

Wheelwright—A1108   Leatherworker—A1109

Designed by Leonard Everett Fisher.
PHOTOGRAVURE (Andreotti)
Plates of 200 subjects in four panes of 50 each.

1977, July 4		Tagged	Perf. 11	
1717	A1106	13c **multicolored**	26	8
		Margin block of 12, 6 P# adjoining Nos. 1717, 1719	3.65	—
		Margin block of 20, 6 P# adjoining Nos. 1717, 1719, Mr. Zip and slogans	5.75	—
		Margin block of 4, Mr. Zip and "Use Zip Code" adjoining No. 1717	1.20	—
		Margin block of 4, "Mail Early in the Day" adjoining No. 1717	1.20	—
1718	A1107	13c **multicolored**	26	8
		Margin block of 12, 6 P# adjoining Nos. 1718, 1720	3.65	—
		Margin block of 20, 6 P# adjoining Nos. 1718, 1720	5.75	—
		Margin block of 4, Mr. Zip and "Use Zip Code" adjoining No. 1718	1.20	—
		Margin block of 4, "Mail Early in the Day" adjoining No. 1718	1.20	—
1719	A1108	13c **multicolored**	26	8
		Margin block of 4, Mr. Zip and "Use Zip Code" adjoining No. 1719	1.20	—
		Margin block of 4, "Mail Early in the Day" adjoining No. 1719	1.20	—
1720	A1109	13c **multicolored**	26	8
		Margin block of 4, Mr. Zip and "Use Zip Code" adjoining No. 1720	1.20	—
		Margin block of 4, "Mail Early in the Day" adjoining No. 1720	1.20	—
		a. Block of 4, #1717-1720	1.05	90

PEACE BRIDGE ISSUE

50th anniversary of the Peace Bridge, connecting Buffalo (Fort Porter), N.Y. and Fort Erie, Ontario.

Peace Bridge and Dove
A1110

Designed by Bernard Brussel-Smith (wood-cut).
ENGRAVED
Plates of 200 subjects in four panes of 50 each.

1977, Aug. 4		Tagged	Perf. 11x10½	
1721	A1110	13c **blue**	26	5
		Margin block of 4, P#	1.30	—
		Margin block of 4, Mr. Zip and "Use Zip Code"	1.20	—
		Margin block of 6, "Mail Early in the Day"	1.80	—

AMERICAN BICENTENNIAL ISSUE

Battle of Oriskany

200th anniversary of the Battle of Oriskany, American Militia led by Brig. Gen. Nicholas Herkimer (1728–1777).

Herkimer at Oriskany, by Frederick Yohn
A1111

Designed by Bradbury Thompson after painting in Utica, N.Y. Public Library.
PHOTOGRAVURE (Andreotti)
Plates of 160 subjects in four panes of 40 each.

1977, Aug. 6		Tagged	Perf. 11	
1722	A1111	13c **multicolored**	26	5
		Margin block of 10, 5 P#	3.10	—
		Margin block of 6, Mr. Zip and "Use Zip Code" and "Mail Early in the Day"	1.80	—

ENERGY ISSUE

Conservation and development of nation's energy resources. Nos. 1723-1724 printed se-tenant vertically.

"Conservation"	"Development"
A1112	A1113

Designed by Terrance W. McCaffrey.
PHOTOGRAVURE (Andreotti)
Plates of 160 subjects in four panes of 40 each.

1977, Oct. 20   Tagged   Perf. 11
1723   A111213c   multicolored   26   8
       a. Pair, #1723-1724   52   35
       Margin block of 12, 6 P#   3.65
       Margin block of 4, Mr. Zip, "Use
         Zip Code" and "Mail Early in
         the Day"   1.20
1724   A111313c   multicolored   26   8

ALTA CALIFORNIA ISSUE

Founding of El Pueblo de San José de Guadalupe, first civil settlement in Alta California, 200th anniversary.

Farm Houses—A1114
Designed by Earl Thollander.
LITHOGRAPHED, ENGRAVED (Giori)
Plates of 200 subjects in four panes of 50 each.

1977, Sept. 9   Tagged   Perf. 11
1725   A111413c   black & multicolored   26   5
       Margin block of 4, P#   1.30
       Margin block of 4, Mr. Zip and
         "Use Zip Code"   1.20
       Margin block of 6, "Mail Early in
         the Day"   1.80

AMERICAN BICENTENNIAL ISSUE
Articles of Confederation

200th anniversary of drafting the Articles of Confederation, York Town, Pa.

Members of Continental Congress in Conference—A1115

Designed by David Blossom.
ENGRAVED (Giori)
Plates of 200 subjects in four panes of 50 each.

1977, Sept. 30   Tagged   Perf. 11
1726   A111513c   red & brown, cream   26   5
       Margin block of 4, P#   1.30
       Margin block of 4, Mr. Zip and "Use
         Zip Code"   1.20
       Margin block of 6, "Mail Early in
         the Day"   1.80

TALKING PICTURES ISSUE

50th anniversary of talking pictures.

Movie Projector and Phonograph
A1116
Designed by Walter Einsel.
LITHOGRAPHED, ENGRAVED (Giori)
Plates of 200 subjects in four panes of 50 each.

1977, Oct. 6   Tagged   Perf. 11
1727   A111613c   multicolored   26   5
       Margin block of 4, P#   1.30
       Margin block of 4, Mr. Zip and
         "Use Zip Code"   1.20
       Margin block of 6, "Mail Early in
         the Day"   1.80

AMERICAN BICENTENNIAL ISSUE
Surrender at Saratoga

200th anniversary of Gen. John Burgoyne's surrender at Saratoga.

Surrender of Burgoyne, by John Trumbull
A1117
Designed by Bradbury Thompson.
PHOTOGRAVURE (Andreotti)
Plates of 160 subjects in four panes of 40 each.

1977, Oct. 7   Tagged   Perf. 11
1728   A111713c   multicolored   26   5
       Margin block of 10, 5 P#   3.10
       Margin block of 6, Mr. Zip, "Use
         Zip Code" and "Mail Early in
         the Day"   1.80

CHRISTMAS ISSUE

Washington at
Valley Forge
A1118

Rural Mailbox
A1119

Designers: No. 1729, Stevan Dohanos, after painting by J. C. Leyendecker. No. 1730, Dolli Tingle.

1977, Oct. 21 Tagged *Perf. 11*
PHOTOGRAVURE (Combination Press)

1729	A1118 13c **multicolored**	26	5
	Margin block of 20, 5-8 P#	5.70	
	a. Imperf., pair	80.00	

See third paragraph after No. 1703.

PHOTOGRAVURE (Andreotti)
Plates of 400 subjects in 4 panes of 100 each.

1730	A1119 13c **multicolored**	26	5
	Margin block of 10, 5 P#	3.10	
	Margin block of 4, Mr. Zip and "Use Zip Code"	1.20	
	Margin block of 6, "Mail Early in the Day"	1.80	
	a. Imperf., pair	300.00	

CARL SANDBURG ISSUE

Carl Sandburg (1878-1967), poet, biographer and collector of American folk songs, birth centenary.

Carl Sandburg,
by William A. Smith, 1952
A1120

Designed by William A. Smith.
GIORI PRESS PRINTING
Plates of 200 subjects in four panes of 50 each.

1978, Jan. 6 Tagged *Perf. 11*

1731	A1120 13c **black & brown**	26	5
	Margin block of 4, P#	1.30	
	Margin block of 4, Mr. Zip	1.20	
	Margin block of 4, copyright	1.20	

CAPTAIN COOK ISSUE

Capt. James Cook, 200th anniversary of his arrival in Hawaii, at Waimea, Kauai, Jan. 20, 1778, and of his anchorage in Cook Inlet, near Anchorage, Alaska, June 1, 1778. Nos. 1732-1733 printed in panes of 50, containing 25 each of Nos. 1732-1733 including 5 No. 1732a.

Capt. Cook, by Nathaniel Dance
A1121

"Resolution" and "Discovery,"
by John Webber—A1122

GIORI PRESS PRINTING
Plates of 200 subjects in four panes of 50 each.

1978, Jan. 20 Tagged *Perf. 11*

1732	A1121 13c **dark blue**	26	8
	a. Pair, #1732-1733	55	30
	b. As "a," imperf. between		
	Margin block of 4, P#	1.30	
	Margin block of 4, Mr. Zip	1.20	
	Margin block of 4, copyright	1.20	
	Margin block of 20, 10 each, #1732-1733, P# adjoining #1732, and slogans	5.75	
1733	A1122 13c **green**	26	8
	a. Vert. pair, imperf. horiz.		
	Margin block of 4, P#	1.30	
	Margin block of 4, Mr. Zip	1.20	
	Margin block of 4, copyright	1.20	
	Margin block of 20, 10 each #1732-1733, P# adjoining #1733, and slogans	5.75	

Indian Head
Penny, 1877
A1123

Eagle
A1124

Red Masterpiece
and Medallion
Roses
A1126

ENGRAVED (Giori)
Plates of 600 subjects in four panes of 150 each.

1978 Tagged *Perf. 11*

1734	A1123 13c **brown & blue green**, *bister, Jan. 11, 1978*	26	10
	Margin block of 4, P#	3.25	
	Margin block of 4, "Use Correct Zip Code"®	2.00	
	Margin block of 4, copyright	2.00	
	a. Horiz. pair, imperf. vert.	400.00	

PHOTOGRAVURE (Andreotti)
Plates of 400 subjects in four panes of 100 each.

1735	A1124(15c) **orange**, *May 22, 1978*	30	5
	Margin block of 4, P#	1.50	
	Margin block of 4, "Use Zip Code"	1.30	
	Margin block of 6, "Mail Early in the Day"	1.90	
	a. Imperf., vert. pair	90.00	
	b. Vert. pair, imperf. horiz.	500.00	

ENGRAVED
Perf. 11x10½

1736	A1124(15c) **orange** (from booklet pane)	30	5
	a. Booklet pane of 8, *May 22, 1978*	2.40	60

POSTAGE, 1978 321

Perf. 10

1737	A1126	15c	multicolored (from booklet pane)	30	6
	a.		Booklet pane of 8, July 11, 1978	2.40	60
	b.		As "a", imperf.		

Nos. 1736, 1737 issued in booklets only. All stamps have one or two straight edges.

A1127

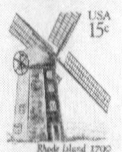
A1128

A1129

A1130

A1131

Designed by Ronald Sharpe.

ENGRAVED

1980, Feb. 7		Tagged		Perf. 11	
1738	A1127	15c	sepia, yellow	30	5
1739	A1128	15c	sepia, yellow	30	5
1740	A1129	15c	sepia, yellow	30	5
1741	A1130	15c	sepia, yellow	30	5
1742	A1131	15c	sepia, yellow	30	5
	a.		Booklet pane of 10	3.50	60

Nos. 1738-1742 issued in booklets only. All stamps have one or two straight edges.

COIL STAMP

1978			Perf. 10 Vert.	
1743	A1124	(15c)orange, May 22, 1978	30	5
		Pair	60	
		Joint line pair	1.00	
	a.	Imperf. pair	90.00	

BLACK HERITAGE ISSUE
Harriet Tubman

Harriet Tubman (1820-1913), born a slave, helped more than 300 slaves escape to freedom.

Harriet Tubman and
Cart Carrying Slaves
A1133

Designed by Jerry Pinkney after photograph.
PHOTOGRAVURE (Andreotti)
Plates of 200 subjects in four panes of 50 each.

1978, Feb. 1		Tagged		Perf. 10½x11	
1744	A1133	13c	multicolored	26	5
		Margin block of 12, 6 P#	3.65	
		Margin block of 4, Mr. Zip	1.20	
		Margin block of 4, copyright	1.20	

AMERICAN FOLK ART ISSUE
Quilts

Nos. 1745-1748 are printed in blocks of four. Nos. 1745-1746 alternate in first row, Nos. 1747-1748 in second.

Basket Design

A1134 A1135

A1136 A1137

Designed by Christopher Pullman after 1875 quilt made in New York City.
PHOTOGRAVURE (Andreotti)
Plates of 192 subjects in four panes of 48 (6x8).

1978, March 8				Perf. 11	
1745	A1134	13c	multicolored	26	8
		Margin block of 12, 6 P#, adjoining Nos. 1745, 1747	3.65	
		Margin block of 16, 6 P# adjoining Nos. 1745, 1747, Mr. Zip and copyright	5.00	
		Margin block of 4, Mr. Zip adjoining No. 1745, copyright No. 1747	1.20	
		Margin block of 4, Mr. Zip adjoining No. 1747, copyright No. 1745	1.20	
1746	A1135	13c	multicolored	26	8
		Margin block of 12, 6 P#, adjoining Nos. 1746, 1748	3.65	
		Margin block of 16, 6 P# adjoining Nos. 1746, 1748, Mr. Zip and copyright	5.00	
		Margin block of 4, Mr. Zip adjoining No. 1746, copyright No. 1748	1.20	
		Margin block of 4, Mr. Zip adjoining No. 1748, copyright No. 1746	1.20	
1747	A1136	13c	multicolored	26	8
1748	A1137	13c	multicolored	26	8
	a.	Block of 4, #1745-1748	1.05	75

AMERICAN DANCE ISSUE

Nos. 1749-1752 printed se-tenant in blocks of four. Nos. 1749-1750 alternate in first row, Nos. 1751-1752 in second.

Theater A1139

Ballet A1138

Modern Dance A1141

Folk Dance A1140

Designed by John Hill.
PHOTOGRAVURE (Andreotti)
Plates of 192 subjects in four panes of 48 (6x8).
1978, Apr. 26   Perf. 11

1749	A1138 13c	multicolored	26	8
		Margin block of 12, 6 P#, adjoining Nos. 1749, 1751	3.65	—
		Margin block of 16, 6 P#, adjoining Nos. 1749, 1751, Mr. Zip and copyright	5.00	—
		Margin block of 4, Mr. Zip adjoining No. 1749, copyright No. 1751	1.20	—
		Margin block of 4, Mr. Zip adjoining No. 1751, copyright No. 1749	1.20	—
1750	A1139 13c	multicolored	26	8
		Margin block of 12, 6 P#, adjoining Nos. 1750, 1752	3.65	—
		Margin block of 16, 6 P# adjoining Nos. 1750, 1752, Mr. Zip and copyright	5.00	—
		Margin block of 4, Mr. Zip adjoining No. 1750, copyright No. 1752	1.20	—
		Margin block of 4, Mr. Zip adjoining No. 1752, copyright No. 1750	1.20	—
1751	A1140 13c	multicolored	26	8
1752	A1141 13c	multicolored	26	8
	a.	Block of 4, #1749-1752	1.05	75

AMERICAN BICENTENNIAL ISSUE
French Alliance

Bicentenary of French Alliance, signed in Paris, Feb. 6, 1778 and ratified by Continental Congress, May 4, 1778.

King Louis XVI and Benjamin Franklin, by Charles Gabriel Sauvage—A1142

Designed by Bradbury Thompson after 1785 porcelain sculpture in Du Pont Winterthur Museum, Delaware.
GIORI PRESS PRINTING
Plates of 160 subjects in four panes of 40 each.
1978, May 4   Tagged   Perf. 11

1753	A1142 13c	blue, black & red	26	5
		Margin block of 4, P#	1.30	—
		Margin block of 4, Mr. Zip	1.20	—
		Margin block of 4, copyright	1.20	—

EARLY CANCER DETECTION ISSUE

George Papanicolaou, M.D. (1883–1962), cytologist and developer of Pap Test, early cancer detection in women.

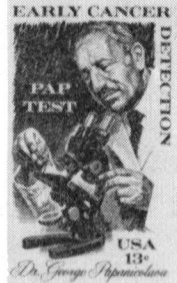

Dr. Papanicolaou, His Signature and Microscope
A1143
Designed by Paul Calle.
Engraved
Plates of 200 subjects in four panes of 50 each.

1978, May 13		Tagged	Perf. 10½x11	
1754	A1143 13c	brown	26	5
		Margin block of 4, P#	1.30	
		Margin block of 4, Mr. Zip	1.20	
		Margin block of 4, copyright	1.20	

PERFORMING ARTS ISSUE

Jimmie Rodgers (1897–1933), the "Singing Brakeman, Father of Country Music" (No. 1755); George M. Cohan (1878–1942), actor and playwright (No. 1756).

Jimmie Rodgers with Guitar and Brakeman's Cap, Locomotive	George M. Cohan, "Yankee Doodle Dandy" and Stars
A1144	A1145

Designed by Jim Sharpe.
PHOTOGRAVURE (Andreotti)
Plates of 200 subjects in four panes of 50 each.

1978		Tagged	Perf. 11	
1755	A1144 13c	multicolored, May 24	26	5
		Margin block of 12, 6 P#	3.65	
		Margin block of 4, Mr. Zip	1.20	
		Margin block of 4, copyright	1.20	
1756	A1145 15c	multicolored, July 3	30	5
		Margin block of 12, 6 P#	4.20	
		Margin block of 4, Mr. Zip	1.40	
		Margin block of 4, copyright	1.40	

CAPEX ISSUE

CAPEX '78, Canadian International Philatelic Exhibition, Toronto, Ont., June 9–18. No. 1757 has black inscriptions on green panel: "Canadian International Exhibition, Toronto" and in French and English "This tribute features wildlife that share the Canadian-United States Border." Signature of Postmaster General William F. Bolger. Size: 108x74mm.

Wildlife from Canadian-United States Border—A1146
Designed by Stanley Galli.
LITHOGRAPHED, ENGRAVED (Giori)
Plates of 24 subjects in four panes of 6 each.

1978, June 10		Tagged	Perf. 11	
1757	A1146	Block of 8, **multicolored**	2.10	2.50
	a.	13c *Cardinal*	26	10
	b.	13c *Mallard*	26	10
	c.	13c *Canada goose*	26	10
	d.	13c *Blue jay*	26	10
	e.	13c *Moose*	26	10
	f.	13c *Chipmunk*	26	10
	g.	13c *Red fox*	26	10
	h.	13c *Raccoon*	26	10
	i.	Yel, grn, red, brn, bl, blk (litho) omitted		
		Margin block of 8, P#	2.75	
		Margin block of 8, Mr. Zip and copyright	2.75	
		Pane of 6 (No. 1757), P#, Mr. Zip and copyright	15.00	

PHOTOGRAPHY ISSUE

Photography's contribution to communications and understanding.

Camera, Lens, Color Filters, Adapter Ring, Studio Light Bulb and Album—A1147
Designed by Ben Somoroff.
PHOTOGRAVURE (Andreotti)
Plates of 160 subjects in four panes of 40 each.

1978, June 26		Tagged	Perf. 11	
1758	A1147 15c	multicolored	30	5
		Margin block of 12, 6 P#	4.20	
		Margin block of 4, Mr. Zip and copyright	1.40	
		Margin block of 16, 6 P#, Mr. Zip and copyright	5.60	

VIKING MISSIONS TO MARS ISSUE

Second anniversary of landing of Viking 1 on Mars.

Viking 1 Lander Scooping up Soil on Mars—A1148
Designed by Robert McCall.
LITHOGRAPHED, ENGRAVED (Giori)
Plates of 200 subjects in four panes of 50 each.

1978, July 20		Tagged		*Perf. 11*	
1759	A1148 15c	multicolored		30	5
		Margin block of 4, P#		1.50	—
		Margin block of 4, Mr. Zip		1.40	—
		Margin block of 4, copyright		1.40	—

AMERICAN OWLS ISSUE

Nos. 1760–1763 are printed in blocks of four. Nos. 1760–1761 alternate in one horizontal row. Nos. 1762–1763 in the next.

Great Gray Owl	Saw-whet Owl
A1149	A1150

Barred Owl	Great Horned Owl
A1151	A1152

Designed by Frank J. Waslick.
LITHOGRAPHED, ENGRAVED (Giori)
Plates of 200 subjects in four panes of 50 each.

1978, Aug. 26		Tagged		*Perf. 11*	
1760	A1149 15c	multicolored		30	8
		Margin block of 4, P# adjoining #1760		1.50	—
		Margin block of 4, Mr. Zip adjoining #1760		1.40	—
		Margin block of 4, copyright adjoining #1760		1.40	—
1761	A1150 15c	multicolored		30	
		Margin block of 4, P# adjoining #1761		1.50	—
		Margin block of 4, Mr. Zip adjoining #1761		1.40	—
		Margin block of 4, copyright adjoining #1761		1.40	—
1762	A1151 15c	multicolored		30	
		Margin block of 4, P# adjoining #1762		1.50	—
		Margin block of 4, Mr. Zip adjoining #1762		1.40	—
		Margin block of 4, copyright adjoining #1762		1.40	—
1763	A1152 15c	multicolored		30	
		Margin block of 4, P# adjoining #1763		1.50	—
		Margin block of 4, Mr. Zip adjoining #1763		1.40	—
		Margin block of 4, copyright adjoining #1763		1.40	—
	a.	Block of four, #1760-1763		1.25	85

AMERICAN TREES ISSUE

Nos. 1764–1767 are printed se-tenant in blocks of four. Nos. 1764–1765 alternate in first row, Nos. 1766–1767 in second.

Giant Sequoia	White Pine
A1153	A1154

White Oak	Gray Birch
A1155	A1156

Designed by Walter D. Richards.
PHOTOGRAVURE (Andreotti)
Plates of 160 subjects in four panes of 40 each.

1978, Oct. 9		Tagged		*Perf. 11*	
1764	A1153 15c	multicolored		30	8
		Margin block of 12, 6 P# adjoining #1764, 1766		4.20	—
		Margin block of 16, 6 P# adjoining #1764, 1766, Mr. Zip and copyright		5.40	—
		Margin block of 4, Mr. Zip adjoining #1764, copyright #1766		1.40	—
		Margin block of 4, Mr. Zip adjoining #1766, copyright #1764		1.40	—

POSTAGE, 1978-79

1765	A11541	5c multicolored		30	8
		Margin block of 12, 6 P# adjoining #1765, 1767		4.20	
		Margin block of 16, 6 P# adjoining #1765, 1767, Mr. Zip and copyright		5.40	
		Margin block of 4, Mr. Zip adjoining #1765, copyright #1767		1.40	
		Margin block of 4, Mr. Zip adjoining #1767, copyright #1765		1.40	
1766	A11551	5c multicolored		30	8
1767	A11561	5c multicolored		30	8
	a.	Block of 4, #1764-1767		1.25	85
	b.	As "a," imperf. horiz.			

CHRISTMAS ISSUE

Christmas USA 15c

Madonna and Child with Cherubim, by Andrea della Robbia
A1157

Child on Hobby Horse and Christmas Trees
A1158

Designed by Bradbury Thompson (#1768) after terra cotta sculpture in National Gallery, Washington, D.C., and by Dolli Tingle (#1769).

PHOTOGRAVURE (Andreotti)
Plates of 400 subjects in four panes of 100 each.

1978, Oct. 18   Perf. 11

1768	A115715c	blue & multicolored		30	5
		Margin block of 12, 6 P#		4.20	
		Margin block of 4, "Use Correct Zip Code"		1.40	
		Margin block of 4, copyright		1.40	
	a.	Imperf. pair		175.00	
1769	A115815c	red & multicolored		30	5
		Margin block of 12, 6 P#		4.20	
		Margin block of 4, "Use Correct Zip Code"		1.40	
		Margin block of 4, copyright		1.40	
	a.	Imperf. pair		100.00	
	b.	Vert. pair, imperf. horiz.			

ROBERT F. KENNEDY ISSUE

Plates of 192 subjects in four panes of 48 (8x6).

Robert F. Kennedy
A1159

Designed by Bradbury Thompson after photograph by Stanley Tretick.

ENGRAVED
Plates of 192 subjects in four panes of 48 (8x6).

1979, Jan. 12   Tagged   Perf. 11

1770	A115915c	blue		30	5
		Margin block of 4, P#		1.50	
		Margin block of 4, Mr. Zip		1.40	
		Margin block of 4, copyright		1.40	

BLACK HERITAGE ISSUE

Martin Luther King, Jr.

Dr. Martin Luther King, Jr. (1929–1968), Civil Rights leader.

Martin Luther King, Jr. and Civil Rights Marchers
A1160

Designed by Jerry Pinkney.
PHOTOGRAVURE (Andreotti)
Plates of 200 subjects in four panes of 50 each.

1979, Jan. 13   Tagged   Perf. 11

1771	A116015c	multicolored		30	5
		Margin block of 12, 6 P#		4.20	
		Margin block of 4, Mr. Zip		1.40	
		Margin block of 4, copyright		1.40	
	a.	Imperf. pair			

YEAR OF THE CHILD ISSUE

International Year of the Child.

Children of Different Races—A1161
Designed by Paul Calle.
ENGRAVED
Plates of 200 subjects in four panes of 50 each.

1979, Feb. 15   Tagged   Perf. 11

1772	A116115c	orange red		30	5
		Margin block of 4, P#		1.50	
		Margin block of 4, Mr. Zip		1.40	
		Margin block of 4, copyright		1.40	

JOHN STEINBECK ISSUE

John Ernst Steinbeck (1902–1968), novelist.

John Steinbeck
A1162

Designed by Bradbury Thompson after photograph by Philippe Halsman.

ENGRAVED
Plates of 200 subjects in four panes of 50 each.

1979, Feb. 27		Tagged	Perf. 10½x11	
1773	A116215c	dark blue	30	5
		Margin block of 4, P#	1.50	—
		Margin block of 4, Mr. Zip	1.40	—
		Margin block of 4, copyright	1.40	—

ALBERT EINSTEIN ISSUE

Albert Einstein (1879–1955), theoretical physicist.

Albert Einstein Einstein
A1163 USA 15c

Designed by Bradbury Thompson after photograph by Hermann Landshoff.

ENGRAVED
Plates of 200 subjects in four panes of 50 each.

1979, Mar. 4		Tagged	Perf. 10½x11	
1774	A116315c	chocolate	30	5
		Margin block of 4, P#	1.50	—
		Margin block of 4, Mr. Zip	1.40	—
		Margin block of 4, copyright	1.40	—
		Pair, horiz. gutter btwn.		—

AMERICAN FOLK ART ISSUE
Pennsylvania Toleware, c. 1800

Coffeepot
A1164

Tea Caddy
A1165

Sugar Bowl
A1166

Coffeepot
A1167

Designed by Bradbury Thompson.

PHOTOGRAVURE (Andreotti)
Plates of 160 subjects in four panes of 40 each.

1979, Apr. 19		Tagged	Perf. 11	
1775	A116415c	multicolored	30	8
		Margin block of 10, 5 P#	3.50	—
		Margin block of 16, 5 P#; Mr. Zip and copyright adjoining Nos. 1775-1776	5.40	—
		Margin block of 6, Mr. Zip and copyright adjoining Nos. 1775-1776	2.25	—
1776	A116515c	multicolored	30	8
1777	A116615c	multicolored	30	8
		Margin block of 16, 5 P#; Mr. Zip and copyright adjoining Nos. 1777-1778	5.40	—
		Margin block of 6, Mr. Zip and copyright adjoining Nos. 1777-1778	2.25	—
1778	A116715c	multicolored	30	8
	a.	Block of 4, #1775-1778	1.25	85
	b.	As "a," imperf. horiz.		—

AMERICAN ARCHITECTURE ISSUE

Nos. 1779–1782 printed se-tenant in blocks of four. Nos. 1779–1780 alternate in first row, Nos. 1781–1782 in second.

Virginia Rotunda,
by Thomas Jefferson
A1168

Baltimore Cathedral,
by Benjamin Latrobe
A1169

Boston State House,
by Charles Bulfinch
A1170

Philadelphia Exchange,
by William Strickland
A1171

Designed by Walter D. Richards.
ENGRAVED (Giori)
Plates of 192 subjects in four panes of 48 (6x8).

1979, June 4		Tagged	Perf. 11	
1779	A116815c	black & brick red	30	8
		Margin block of 4, P# adjoining #1779	1.50	—
		Margin block of 4, Mr. Zip adjoining #1779	1.40	—
		Margin block of 4, copyright adjoining #1779	1.40	—
1780	A116915c	black & brick red	30	8
		Margin block of 4, P# adjoining #1780	1.50	—
		Margin block of 4, Mr. Zip adjoining #1780	1.40	—
		Margin block of 4, copyright adjoining #1780	1.40	—

1781	A1170 15c	black & brick red	30	8	
		Margin block of 4, P# adjoining #1781	1.50	—	
		Margin block of 4, Mr. Zip adjoining #1781	1.40	—	
		Margin block of 4, copyright adjoining #1781	1.40	—	
1782	A1171 15c	black & brick red	30	8	
		Margin block of 4, P# adjoining #1782	1.50	—	
		Margin block of 4, Mr. Zip adjoining #1782	1.40	—	
		Margin block of 4, copyright adjoining #1782	1.40	—	
	a.	Block of 4, #1779-1782	1.25	.85	

ENDANGERED FLORA ISSUE

Nos. 1783–1786 are printed in blocks of four. Nos. 1783–1784 alternate in one horizontal row. Nos. 1785–1786 in the next.

Persistent Trillium
A1172

Hawaiian Wild Broadbean
A1173

Contra Costa Wallflower
A1174

Antioch Dunes Evening Primrose
A1175

Designed by Frank J. Waslick.

PHOTOGRAVURE (Andreotti)

Plates of 200 subjects in four panes of 50 each.

1979, June 7   Tagged   Perf. 11

1783	A1172 15c	multicolored	30	8	
		Margin block of 12, 6 P# adjoining Nos. 1783-1784	4.20	—	
		Margin block of 20, 6 P#, Mr. Zip and copyright adjoining Nos. 1783-1784	6.75	—	
		Marginal block of 4, Mr. Zip adjoining No. 1783	1.40	—	
		Margin block of 4, copyright adjoining No. 1783	1.40	—	
1784	A1173 15c	multicolored	30	8	
		Margin block of 4, Mr. Zip adjoining No. 1784	1.40	—	
		Margin block of 4, copyright adjoining No. 1784	1.40	—	
1785	A1174 15c	multicolored	30	8	
		Margin block of 12, 6 P# adjoining Nos. 1785-1786	4.20	—	
		Margin block of 20, 6 P#, Mr. Zip and copyright adjoining Nos. 1785-1786	6.75	—	
		Margin block of 4, Mr. Zip adjoining No. 1785	1.40	—	
		Margin block of 4, copyright adjoining No. 1785	1.40	—	
1786	A1175 15c	multicolored	30	8	
		Margin block of 4, Mr. Zip adjoining No. 1786	1.40	—	
		Margin block of 4, copyright adjoining No. 1786	1.40	—	
	a.	Block of 4, #1783-1786	1.25	.85	
	b.	As "a," imperf.	1,000.		

SEEING EYE DOGS ISSUE

First guide dog program in the United States, 50th anniversary.

German Shepherd Leading Man
A1176

Designed by Joseph Csatari.

PHOTOGRAVURE (Combination Press)

Plates of 230 (10x23) subjects in panes of 50 (10x5).

1979, June 15   Tagged   Perf. 11

1787	A1176 15c	multicolored	30	5	
		Margin block of 20, 5-8 P#, 1-2 copyright	6.50	—	
		Margin block of 4, copyright	1.40	—	
	a.	Imperf. pair	850.00		
		See 3rd note after No. 1703.			

Child Holding Winner's Medal
A1177

John Paul Jones, by Charles Willson Peale
A1178

SPECIAL OLYMPICS ISSUE

Special Olympics for special children, Brockport, N.Y., Aug. 8–13.

Designed by Jeff Cornell.

PHOTOGRAVURE (Andreotti)

Plates of 200 subjects in four panes of 50 each.

1979, Aug. 9   Tagged   *Perf. 11*

1788	A1177 15c	multicolored	30	5
		Margin block of 10, 5 P#	3.50	—
		Margin block of 4, Mr. Zip	1.40	—
		Margin block of 4, copyright	1.40	—

JOHN PAUL JONES ISSUE

John Paul Jones (1747–1792), Naval Commander, American Revolution.

Designed by Bradbury Thompson after painting in Independence National Historical Park, Philadelphia.
Printed by J. W. Fergusson and Sons, Richmond, Va.

PHOTOGRAVURE (Champlain)

Plates of 200 subjects in four panes of 50 each.

1979, Sept. 23   Tagged   *Perf. 11×12*

1789	A1178 15c	multicolored	30	5
		P# block of 10, 5 P#	3.50	—
		Zip block of 4	1.40	—
		Copyright block of 4	1.40	—
	a.	Perf. 11	30	6
	b.	Perf. 12		
	c.	Vert. pair, imperf. horiz.	200.00	
	d.	As "a," vert. pair, imperf. horiz.	150.00	

Imperfs exist from printer's waste.

OLYMPIC GAMES ISSUE

22nd Summer Olympic Games, Moscow, July 19–Aug. 3, 1980. Nos. 1791–1794 printed se-tenant. Nos. 1791–1792 alternate in one horizontal row, Nos. 1793–1794 in next.

Decathlon, Javelin
A1179

Running
A1180

Swimming, Women's
A1181

Rowing
A1182

Equestrian
A1183

Designed by Robert M. Cunningham.

PHOTOGRAVURE

Plates of 200 subjects in four panes of 50 each.

1979, Sept. 5   Tagged   *Perf. 11*

1790	A1179 10c	multicolored	25	22
		P# block of 12, 6 P#	3.75	—
		Zip block of 4	1.10	—
		Copyright block of 4	1.10	—

1979, Sept. 28

1791	A1180 15c	multicolored	35	8
		P# block of 12, 6 P# adjoining Nos. 1791, 1793	4.75	—
		Zip block of 4	1.60	—
		Copyright block of 4	1.60	—
		P# block of 20, 6 P#, zip, copyright adjoining Nos. 1791, 1793	8.00	—
1792	A1181 15c	multicolored	35	8
		P# block of 12, 6 P# adjoining Nos. 1792, 1794	4.75	—
		Zip block of 4	1.60	—
		Copyright block of 4	1.60	—
		P# block of 20, 6 P#, zip, copyright adjoining Nos. 1792, 1794	8.00	—
1793	A1182 15c	multicolored	35	8
		Zip block of 4	1.60	—
		Copyright block of 4	1.60	—
1794	A1183 15c	multicolored	35	8
		Zip block of 4	1.60	—
		Copyright block of 4	1.60	—
	a.	Block of 4, #1791-1794	1.50	85
	b.	As "a," imperf.	2,000.	

OLYMPIC GAMES ISSUE

13th Winter Olympic Games, Lake Placid, N.Y., Feb. 12-24. Nos. 1795-1798 printed se-tenant. Nos. 1795-1796 alternate in one horizontal row, Nos. 1797-1798 in next.

Speed Skating
A1184

Downhill Skiing
A1185

Ski Jump
A1186

Hockey Goaltender
A1187

Designed by Robert M. Cunningham

Plates of 200 subject in four panes of 50 each.

PHOTOGRAVURE

1980, Feb. 1		Tagged	Perf. 11×10½	
1795	A1184 15c	multicolored	45	8
		P# block of 12, 6 P# adjoining #1795, 1797	6.50	
		Zip block of 4, adjoining #1795	2.00	
		Copyright block of 4, adjoining #1795	2.00	
		P# block of 20, 6 P# adjoining #1795, 1797, zip and copyright	10.50	
	a.	Perf. 11	1.50	
1796	A1185 15c	multicolored	45	8
		P# block of 12, 6 P#, #1796, 1798	6.50	
		Zip block of 4, adjoining #1796	2.00	
		Copyright block of 4, adjoining #1796	2.00	
		P# block of 20, 6 P# adjoining 1796, 1798, zip and copyright	10.50	
	a.	Perf. 11	1.50	
1797	A1186 15c	multicolored	45	8
		Zip block of 4, adjoining #1797	2.00	
		Copyright block of 4, adjoining #1797	2.00	
	a.	Perf. 11	1.50	
1798	A1187 15c	multicolored	45	8
		Zip block of 4, adjoining #1798	2.00	
		Copyright block of 4, adjoining #1798	2.00	
	a.	Perf. 11	1.50	
	b.	Block of 4, #1795-1798	1.90	.85
	c.	Block of 4, #1795a-1798a	6.25	

CHRISTMAS ISSUE

Virgin and Child by Gerard David
A1188

Santa Claus, Christmas Tree Ornament
A1189

Designed by Bradbury Thompson (#1799) after painting in National Gallery of Art, Washington, D.C. and by Eskil Ohlsson (#1800).

PHOTOGRAVURE (Andreotti)

Plates of 400 subjects in four panes of 100 each.

1979, Oct. 18		Tagged		Perf. 11	
1799	A1188 15c	multicolored		30	5
		P# block of 12, 6 P#		4.25	
		Zip block of 4		1.40	
		Copyright block of 4		1.40	
		P# block of 20, 6 P#, zip, copyright		6.75	
	a.	Imperf. pair		100.00	
	b.	Vert. pair, imperf. horiz.		1,000.	
1800	A1189 15c	multicolored		30	5
		P# block of 12, 6 P#		4.25	
		Zip block of 4		1.40	
		Copyright block of 4		1.40	
		P# block of 20, 6 P#, zip, copyright		6.75	
	a.	Green & yellow omitted			
	b.	Green, yellow & tan omitted			

PERFORMING ARTS ISSUE

Will Rogers (1879 - 1935), actor and humorist.

Will Rogers
A1190
Designed by Jim Sharpe.
Plates of 200 subjects in four panes of 50 each.
PHOTOGRAVURE (Andreotti)

1979, Nov. 4		Tagged		Perf. 11
1801	A1190 15c	multicolored	30	5
		P# block of 12, 6 P#	4.25	
		Zip block of 4	1.40	
		Copyright block of 4	1.40	
		P# block of 12, 6 P#, zip, copyright	6.75	
	a.	Imperf. pair	325.00	

VIETNAM VETERANS ISSUE

A tribute to veterans of the Vietnam War.

Ribbon for Vietnam Service Medal
A1191
Designed by Stevan Dohanos.
PHOTOGRAVURE (Andreotti)
Plates of 200 subjects in four panes of 50 each.

1979, Nov. 11		Tagged		Perf. 11
1802	A1191 15c	multicolored	30	5
		P# block of 10, 5 P#	3.50	
		Zip block of 4	1.40	
		Copyright block of 4	1.40	

PERFORMING ARTS ISSUE

W.C. Fields (1800-1946), actor and comedian.

W.C. Fields—A1192
Designed by Jim Sharpe.
Plates of 200 subjects in four panes of 50 each.
PHOTOGRAVURE

1980, Jan. 29		Tagged		Perf. 11
1803	A1192 15c	multicolored	30	5
		P# block of 12, 6 P#	4.25	
		Zip block of 4	1.40	
		Copyright block of 4	1.40	
		P# block of 20, 6 P#, zip, copyright	6.75	

BLACK HERITAGE ISSUE

Benjamin Banneker

Benjamin Banneker (1731-1806), astronomer and mathematician.

Benjamin Banneker—A1193
Designed by Jerry Pinkney.
Plates of 200 subjects in four panes of 50 each.
PHOTOGRAVURE

1980, Feb. 15		Tagged		Perf. 11
1804	A1193 15c	multicolored	30	5
		P# block of 12, 6 P#	4.25	
		Zip block of 4	1.40	
		Copyright block of 4	1.40	
		Plate block of 20, 6 P#, zip, copyright	6.75	
	a.	Horiz. pair, imperf. vert.		

Imperfs exist from printer's waste.

NATIONAL LETTER WRITING WEEK ISSUE

National Letter Writing Week, Feb. 24-Mar. 1. Nos. 1805-1810 are printed vertically se-tenant.

Letters
Preserve Memories
A1194

Letters
Lift Spirits
A1196

P.S.
Write Soon
A1195

Letters
Shape Opinions
A1197

Designed by Randall McDougall.

Plates of 240 subjects in four panes of 60 (10× 6) each.

PHOTOGRAVURE

1980, Feb. 25		Tagged		Perf. 11	
1805	A1194	15c	multicolored	30	8
			P# block of 36, 6 P# adjoining #1805	11.00	
			Zip block of 12, adjoining #1805	4.00	
			Copyright block of 12, adjoining #1805	4.00	
1806	A1195	15c	purple & multi	30	8
1807	A1196	15c	multicolored	30	8
1808	A1195	15c	green & multi	30	8
1809	A1197	15c	multicolored	30	8
1810	A1198	15c	red & multi	30	8
			P# block of 36, 6 P# adjoining #1810	11.00	
			Zip block of 12, adjoining #1810	4.00	
			Copyright block of 12, adjoining #1810	4.00	
		a.	Vertical strip of 6, #1805-1810	1.80	1.25

AMERICANA TYPE

Weaver Violins—A1199
Designer: 3.5c, George Mercer.

COIL STAMPS

1980-81			Engraved		Perf. 10 Vertically	
1811	A984	1c	dark blue, greenish, Mar. 6, 1980		5	5
			Pair		10	10
			Joint line pair		15	15
		a.	Imperf. pair		135.00	
1813	A1199	3.5	purple, yellow, June 23, 1980		8	5
			Pair		16	10
			Joint line pair		30	
		a.	Untagged (Bureau precanceled, lines only			10
		b.	Imperf. pair		250.00	
1816	A997	12c	red brown, beige, Apr. 8, 1981		24	5
			Pair		50	10
			Joint line pair		75	
		a.	Untagged (Bureau precanceled, lines only)			25
		b.	Imperf. pair		150.00	

Eagle-A1207

PHOTOGRAVURE

Plates of 400 subjects in four panes of 100 each.

1981, Mar. 15			Tagged	Perf. 11x10½	
1818	A1207(18c)		violet	36	5
			P# block of 4	1.80	
			Zip block of 4	1.60	
			Mail Early block of 6	2.50	

ENGRAVED
Perf. 10

1819	A1207(18c)		violet (from booklet pane)	36	5
		a.	Booklet pane of 8	4.50	1.50

COIL STAMP
Perf. 10 Vert.

1820	A1207(18c)		violet	36	5
			Pair	72	10
			Joint line pair	1.00	
		a.	Imperf. pair	75.00	

Frances Perkins
A1208

Dolley Madison
A1209

FRANCES PERKINS ISSUE

Frances Perkins (1882-1965), Secretary of Labor, 1933-1945 (first woman cabinet member).

Designed by F.R. Petrie.

ENGRAVED

Plates of 200 subjects in four panes of 50 each.

1980, Apr. 10		Tagged	*Perf. 10½×11*	
1821	A1208 15c	**Prussian blue**	30	5
		P# block of 4	1.50	—
		Zip block of 4	1.40	—
		Copyright block of 4	1.40	—

DOLLEY MADISON ISSUE

Dolley Madison (1768-1849), First Lady, 1809-1817.

Designed by Esther Porter.

ENGRAVED

Plates of 600 subjects in four panes of 150 each.

1980, May 20		Tagged	*Perf. 11*	
1822	A1209 15c	**red brown & sepia**	30	5
		P# block of 4	1.50	—
		Zip block of 4	1.40	—
		Copyright block of 4	1.40	—

Emily Bissell
A1210

Helen Keller and
Anne Sullivan—A1211

EMILY BISSELL ISSUE

Emily Bissell (1861-1948), social worker; introduced Christmas seals in United States.

Designed by Stevan Dohanos.

ENGRAVED

Plates of 200 subjects in four panes of 50 each.

1980, May 31		Tagged	*Perf. 11*	
1823	A1210 15c	**black & red**	30	5
		P# block of 4	1.50	—
		Zip block of 4	1.40	—
		Copyright block of 4	1.40	—
	a.	Vert. pair, imperf. horiz.	600.00	

HELEN KELLER ISSUE

Helen Keller (1880-1968), blind and deaf writer and lecturer taught by Ann Sullivan (1867-1936).

Designed by Paul Calle.

LITHOGRAPHED AND ENGRAVED

Plates of 200 subjects in four panes of 50 each.

1980, June 27		Tagged	*Perf. 11*	
1824	A1211 15c	**multicolored**	30	5
		P# block of 4	1.50	—
		Zip block of 4	1.40	—
		Copyright block of 4	1.40	—

Veterans Administration
Emblem—A1212

Gen. Bernardo de Galvez
A1213

VETERANS ADMINISTRATION ISSUE

Veterans Administration, 50th anniversary.

Designed by Malcolm Grear.

PHOTOGRAVURE

Plates of 200 subjects in four panes of 50 each.

1980, July 21		Tagged	*Perf. 11*	
1825	A1212 15c	**carmine & violet blue**	30	5
		P# block of 4, 2 P#	1.50	—
		Zip block of 4	1.40	—
		Copyright block of 4	1.40	—
	a.	Horiz. pair, imperf. vert.	800.00	

BERNARDO DE GALVEZ ISSUE

Gen. Bernardo de Galvez (1746-1786), helped defeat British in Battle of Mobile, 1780.

Designed by Roy H. Andersen.
ENGRAVED
Plates of 200 subjects in four panes of 50 each.

1980, July 23		Tagged	Perf. 11	
1826	A1213 15c	**multicolored**	30	5
		P# block of 4	1.50	——
		Zip block of 4	1.40	——
		Copyright block of 4	1.40	——
	a.	Red, brown & blue (engr.) omitted	——	

CORAL REEFS ISSUE

Nos. 1827-1830 are printed in blocks of four. Nos. 1827-1828 alternate in one horizontal row. Nos. 1829-1830 in the next.

Brain Coral, Beaugregory Fish
A1214

Elkhorn Coral, Porkfish
A1215

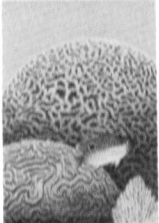

Chalice Coral, Moorish Idol
A1216

Finger Coral, Sabertooth Blenny
A1217

Designed by Chuck Ripper.
PHOTOGRAVURE
Plates of 200 subjects in four panes of 50 each.

1980, Aug. 26		Tagged	Perf. 11	
1827	A1214 15c	**multi**	30	8
		P# block of 12, 6 P# adjoining #1827, 1828	4.50	——
		Zip block of 4, adjoining #1827	1.40	——
		Copyright block of 4, adjoining #1827	1.40	——
1828	A1215 15c	**multi**	30	8
		Zip block of 4, adjoining #1828	1.40	——
		Copyright block of 4, adjoining #1828	1.40	——
1829	A1216 15c	**multi**	30	8
		P# block of 12, 6 P# adjoining #1829, 1830	4.50	——
		Zip block of 4, adjoining #1829	1.40	——
		Copyright block of 4, adjoining #1829	1.40	——
1830	A1217 15c	**multi**	30	8
		Zip block of 4, adjoining #1830	1.40	——
		Copyright block of 4, adjoining #1830	1.40	——
	a.	Block of 4, #1827-1830	1.20	85
	b.	As "a," imperf.	2,000.	
	c.	As "a," imperf. btwn., vert		
	d.	As 'a' imperf. vert.		

American Bald Eagle
A1218

Edith Wharton
A1219

ORGANIZED LABOR ISSUE

Designed by Peter Cocci.
PHOTOGRAVURE
Plates of 200 subjects in four panes of 50 each.

1980, Sept. 1		Tagged	Perf. 11	
1831	A1218 15c	**multi**	30	5
		P# block of 12, 6 P#	4.50	——
		Zip block of 4	1.40	——
		Copyright block of 4	1.40	——
	a.	Imperf. pair	750.00	

EDITH WHARTON ISSUE

Edith Wharton (1862-1937), novelist.

Designed by Bradbury Thompson after 1905 photograph.

ENGRAVED

Plates of 200 subjects in four panes of 50 each.

1980, Sept. 5		Tagged	Perf. 10½×11	
1832	A1219 15c	**purple**	30	5
		P# block of 4	1.50	—
		Zip block of 4	1.40	—
		Copyright block of 4	1.40	—

EDUCATION ISSUE

"Homage to the Square: Glow"
by Josef Albers—A1220

Designed by Bradbury Thompson

PHOTOGRAVURE

Plates of 200 subjects in four panes of 50 each.

1980, Sept. 12		Tagged	Perf. 11	
1833	A1220 15c	**multi**	30	5
		P# block of 6, 3 P#	2.25	—
		Zip block of 4	1.40	—
		Copyright block of 4	1.40	—
	a.	Horiz. pair, imperf. vert.	400.00	

AMERICAN FOLK ART ISSUE

Pacific Northwest Indian Masks

Heiltsuk,
Bella Bella Tribe
A1221

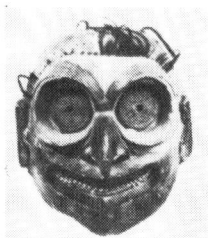

Chilkat Tlingit Tribe
A1222

Tlingit Tribe
A1223

Bella Coola Tribe
A1224

Designed by Bradbury Thompson after photographs.

PHOTOGRAVURE

Plates of 160 subjects in four panes of 40 each.

1980, Sept. 25		Tagged	Perf. 11	
1834	A1221 15c	**multi**	30	8
1835	A1222 15c	**multi**	30	8
1836	A1223 15c	**multi**	30	8
1837	A1224 15c	**multi**	30	8
		P# block of 10, 5 P#	3.50	—
		Zip, copyright block of 6	2.25	—
	a.	Block of 4, #1834-1837	1.20	85

AMERICAN ARCHITECTURE ISSUE

Smithsonian
A1225

Trinity Church
A1226

POSTAGE, 1980 335

Penn Academy
A1227

Lyndhurst
A1228

Designed by Walter D. Richards.
ENGRAVED (Giori)
Plates of 160 subjects in four panes of 40 each.

1980, Oct. 9		Tagged	Perf. 11	
1838	A1225 15c	black & red	30	8
1839	A1226 15c	black & red	30	8
1840	A1227 15c	black & red	30	8
1841	A1228 15c	black & red	30	8
	P# block of 4		1.50	
	Zip block of 4		1.40	
	Copyright block of 4		1.40	
a.	Block of 4, #1838-1841		1.20	.85

CHRISTMAS ISSUE

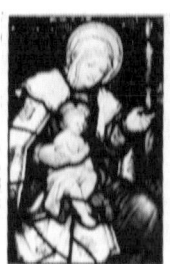

Madonna and Child   Wreath and Toys
A1229   A1230

Designed by Esther Porter (#1842) after Epiphany Window, Washington Cathedral, and by Bob Timberlake (#1843).

1980, Oct. 31 Tagged *Perf. 11*
PHOTOGRAVURE
Plates of 200 subjects in four panes of 50 each.

1842	A1229 15c	multi	30	5
	P# block of 12, 6 P#		4.25	
	Zip block of 4		1.40	
	Copyright block of 4		1.40	
a.	Imperf. pair		100.00	
	Pair with full vert. gutter btwn.			

PHOTOGRAVURE (Combination Press)
Plates of 230 subjects (10x23) in panes of 50 (10x5).

1843	A1230 15c	multi	30	5
	P# block of 20, 5-8 P#, 1-2 copyright		6.50	
	Copyright block of 4		1.40	
a.	Imperf. pair		100.00	

See 3rd note after No. 1703.

GREAT AMERICANS ISSUE

A1231   A1232   A1233

A1234   A1235   A1236

A1237   A1238   A1239

A1240   A1241   A1242

A1243   A1244   A1245

POSTAGE

A1246 A1247 A1248
A1249 A1250 A1251
A1252 A1253 A1254
A1255 A1256

Designers: 1c, Bernie Fuchs. 2c, Burt Silverman. 3c, 17c, 40c, Ward Brackett. 4c, 7c, 10c, 18c, 30c, Richard Sparks. 6c, No. 1862, Dennis Lyall. 8c, Arthur Lidov. 9c, 11c. Robert Alexander Anderson. 13c, Brad Holland. 14c, Bradbury Thompson. 19c, 39c, Roy H. Andersen. No. 1860, Jim Sharpe. No. 1861, 22c, 50c, 37c, Christopher Calle. 35c, Nathan Jones.

ENGRAVED
Perf. 10½ x 11
Perf. 11 (1c, 6c-11c, 14c, No. 1862, 22c, 30c, 39c, 40c, 50c)
1980-1985   Tagged

1844	A1231	1c	**black,** *Sept. 23, 1983*	5	5
			P# block of 20, 1-2 P		
			1-2 copyright	1.00	—
		a.	Imperf. pair		
1845	A1232	2c	**brn blk** *Nov. 18, 1982*	5	5
			P# block of 4	20	—
			Zip block of 4	18	—
			Copyright block of 4	18	—
1846	A1233	3c	**olive green,** *July 13, 1983*	6	5
			P# block of 4	30	—
			Zip block of 4	28	—
			Copyright block of 4	28	—
1847	A1234	4c	**violet,** *June 3, 1983*	8	5
			P# block of 4	40	—
			Zip block of 4	35	—
			Copyright block of 4	35	—
1848	A1235	5c	**henna brown,** *June 25, 1983*	10	5
			P# block of 4	50	—
			Zip block of 4	45	—
			Copyright block of 4	45	—
1849	A1236	6c	**orange vermilion,** *Sept. 19, 1985*	12	5
			P# block of 20, 1-2		
			1-2 zip, 1-2 copyright	2.75	—
1850	A1237	7c	**bright carmine,** *Jan. 25, 1985*	14	5
			P# block of 20, 1-2		
			1-2 zip, 1-2 copyright	3.00	—
1851	A1238	8c	**olive black,** *July 25, 1985*	16	5
			P# block of 4	80	—
			Zip block of 4	70	—
			Copyright block of 4	70	—
1852	A1239	9c	**dark green,** *June 7, 1985*	18	5
			P# block of 20, 1-2		
			1-2 zip, 1-2 copyright	4.00	—
1853	A1240	10c	**Prus. blue,** *May 31, 1984*	20	5
			P# block of 20, 1-2 P		
			1-2 copyright, 1-2 zip	4.50	—
1854	A1241	11c	**dark blue,** *Feb. 12, 1985*	22	5
			P# block of 4	1.10	—
			Zip block of 4	1.00	—
			Copyright block of 4	1.00	—
1855	A1242	13c	**lt. maroon,** *Jan. 15, 1982*	26	5
			P# block of 4	1.30	—
			Zip block of 4	1.20	—
			Copyright block of 4	1.20	—
1856	A1243	14c	**slate green,** *Mar. 21, 1985*	28	5
			P# block of 20, 1-2		
			1-2 zip, 1-2 copyright	6.00	—
		a.	Vert. pair, imperf. horiz.		
		b.	Horiz. pair, imperf. btwn.	15.00	
1857	A1244	17c	**green,** *May 28, 1981*	34	5
			P# block of 4	1.75	—
			Zip block of 4	1.60	—
			Copyright block of 4	1.60	—
1858	A1245	18c	**dark blue,** *May 7, 1981*	36	5
			P# block of 4	1.75	—
			Zip block of 4	1.60	—
			Copyright block of 4	1.60	—
1859	A1246	19c	**brown,** *Dec. 27, 1980*	38	7
			P# block of 4	2.00	—
			Zip block of 4	1.80	—
			Copyright block of 4	1.80	—
1860	A1247	20c	**claret,** *Jan. 12, 1982*	40	5
			P# block of 4	2.00	—
			Zip block of 4	1.80	—
			Copyright block of 4	1.80	—
1861	A1248	20c	**green,** *June 10, 1983*	40	5
			P# block of 4	2.00	—
			Zip block of 4	1.75	—
			Copyright block of 4	1.75	—
1862	A1249	20c	**black,** *Jan. 26, 1984*	40	5
			P# block of 20, 1-2 P		
			1-2 copyright, 1-2 zip	8.50	—
1863	A1250	22c	**dark chalky blue,** *Apr. 23, 1985*	44	5
			P# block of 20, 1-2		
			1-2 zip, 1-2 copyright	9.25	—
1864	A1251	30c	**olive gray** *Sept. 2, 1984*	60	8
			P# block of 20, 1-2 P		
			1-2 copyright, 1-2 zip	12.50	—
1865	A1252	35c	**gray,** *June 3, 1981*	70	8
			P# block of 4	3.50	—
			Zip block of 4	3.25	—
			Copyright block of 4	3.25	—
1866	A1253	37c	**blue,** *Jan. 26, 1982*	75	5
			P# block of 4	3.75	—
			Zip block of 4	3.35	—
			Copyright block of 4	3.35	—
1867	A1254	39c	**rose lilac,** *May 20, 1985*	80	8
			P# block of 20, 1-2		
			1-2 zip, 1-2 copyright	17.00	—
1868	A1255	40c	**dark green,** *Feb 24, 1984*	80	10
			P# block of 20, 1-2 P ,		
			1-2 copyright, 1-2 zip	17.50	—
1869	A1256	50c	**brown,** *Feb. 22, 1985*	1.00	10
			P# block of 4	5.00	—
			Zip block of 4	4.50	—
			Copyright block of 4	4.50	—

POSTAGE 337

A1261   A1262

EVERETT DIRKSEN (1896-1969)
Senate minority leader, 1960-1969.
Designed by Ron Adair

ENGRAVED
Plates of 200 subjects in four panes of 50 each.

1981, Jan. 4		Tagged		Perf. 11	
1874	A1261 15c	gray		30	5
		P# block of 4		1.50	
		Zip block of 4		1.40	
		Copyright block of 4		1.40	

WHITNEY MOORE YOUNG, Jr. (1921-1971)
Black Heritage
Civil Rights leader.
Designed by Jerry Pinkney.

PHOTOGRAVURE

1981, Jan. 30		Tagged		Perf. 11	
1875	A1262 15c	multi		30	5
		P# block of 4		1.50	
		Zip block of 4		1.40	
		Copyright block of 4		1.40	

Flower Issue
Rose   Camellia
A1263   A1264

Dahlia   Lily
A1265   A1266

Designed by Lowell Nesbitt.

PHOTOGRAVURE
Plates of 192 subjects in four panes of 48 (8×6).

1981, Apr. 23		Tagged		Perf. 11	
1876	A1263 18c	multicolored		36	8
1877	A1264 18c	multicolored		36	8
1878	A1265 18c	multicolored		36	8
1879	A1266 18c	multicolored		36	8
		P# block of 4		1.75	—
		Zip block of 4		1.50	—
		Copyright block of 4		1.50	—
	a.	Block of 4, #1876-1879		1.50	85

A1267-A1276
Designs from photographs by Jim Brandenburg.

ENGRAVED

1981, May 14   Tagged   Perf. 11
Dark brown

1880	A1267 18c	Bighorn	36	5
1881	A1268 18c	Puma	36	5
1882	A1269 18c	Harbor seal	36	5
1883	A1270 18c	Bison	36	5
1884	A1271 18c	Brown bear	36	5
1885	A1272 18c	Polar bear	36	5
1886	A1273 18c	Elk (wapiti)	36	5
1887	A1274 18c	Moose	36	5
1888	A1275 18c	White-tailed deer	36	5
1889	A1276 18c	Pronghorn	36	5
	a.	Booklet pane of 10	3.60	

Nos. 1880-1889 issued in booklet only. All stamps have one or two straight edges.

UNITED STATES
1985

AMERIPEX '86   **Public Education**

Scott 2145

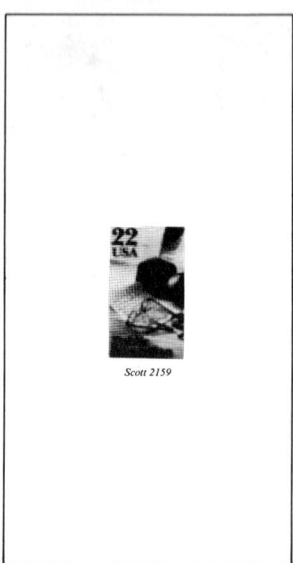
Scott 2159

COLLECT THE SCOTT WAY... WITH SCOTT'S

U.S. COMM. & COMM. AIR PLATE BLOCK
ALBUM

FEATURING:

- Spaces for all 20th Century commemoratives beginning with the 1901 Pan American Exposition to date, in separate parts. Collect any size block you like because there are no borders around floating plate blocks.

- Each stamp pictured or described and arranged in order by Scott number.

- Chemically neutralized paper protects your stamps for generations.

- Paper just the right thickness to make collecting a pleasure.

- Yearly supplement available.

Pages only Part 1 (1901-40) $24.95
Part 2 (1940-59) $24.95
Part 3 (1959-68) $24.95
Part 4 (1969-73) $22.95
Part 5 (1973-80) $24.95
Part 6 (1980-85) $24.95

AVAILABLE NOW AT
YOUR LOCAL DEALER
OR DIRECT FROM:

P.O. BOX 828, SIDNEY, OH 45365

Flag and Anthem Issue

A1277

A1278

A1279

A1280

Designed by Peter Cocci.
ENGRAVED
Plates of 460 subjects (20x23) in panes of 100 (10x10).

1981, Apr. 24		Tagged		Perf. 11	
1890	A1277	18c **multi**		36	5
		P# block of 20, 1-2 P#		7.50	
	a.	Imperf. pair		100.00	

See third paragraph after No. 1703.

Coil Stamp
Perf. 10 Vert.

1891	A1278	18c **multi**		36	5
		Pair		72	10
		P# strip of 3, P# 4, 5		5.50	
		P# strip of 3, P# 2		7.50	
		P# strip of 3, P# 1		50.00	
		P# strip of 3, P# 3, 7		175.00	
		P# strip of 3, P# 6			
	a.	Imperf. pair		20.00	

Booklet Stamps
Perf. 11

1892	A1279	6c **multi**		12	10
1893	A1280	18c **multi**		36	5
	a.	Booklet pane of 8			
		(2 #1892, 6 #1893)		2.40	
	b.	As "a," vert. imperf. btwn.		65.00	

Flag Over Supreme Court

A1281

Designed by Dean Ellis
ENGRAVED
Plates of 460 subjects (20x23) in panes of 100 (10x10).

1981, Dec. 17		Tagged		Perf. 11	
1894	A1281	20c **blk., dk. blue & red**		40	5
		P# block of 20, 1-2 P#		8.50	
	a.	Vert. pair, imperf.		15.00	
	b.	Vert. pair, imperf. horiz.			
	c.	Dark blue omitted			
	d.	Black omitted			

Coil Stamp
Perf. 10 Vert.

1895	A1281	20c **blk., dk. blue & red**		40	5
		Pair		80	10
		P# strip of 3, P# 1-3, 5, 6, 8-10, 12-14		5.50	
		P# strip of 3, P# 4		12.50	
		P# strip of 3, P# 11		25.00	
	a.	Imperf. pair		6.00	
	b.	Black omitted		50.00	
	c.	Blue omitted			
	d.	Pair, imperf. btwn.			
	e.	Untagged (Bureau precanceled)			45
		P# strip of 3, line, P# 14		6.50	

BOOKLET STAMP
Perf. 11x10½

1896	A1281	20c **blk., dk. blue & red**		40	5
	a.	Booklet pane of 6		2.50	
	b.	Booklet pane of 10		4.25	

TRANSPORTATION ISSUE

A1283

A1284

A1284a

A1285

A1286

A1287

A1288

A1288a

A1289

340   POSTAGE

A1290   A1291   A1292

A1293   Amoskeg Engine A1294

Designers: 1c, 2c, 5.9c, 10.9c, 18c, David Stone. 3c, 5c, 5.2c, Walter Brooks. 4c, 7.4c, 9.3c, 11c, 20c, Jim Schleyer. 17c Chuck Jaquays.

COIL STAMPS
ENGRAVED

1981-84   Tagged   *Perf. 10 vert.*

1897	A1283	1c	**violet,** *Aug. 19, 1983*		5	5
			Pair		10	10
			P# strip of 3, line, P# 1-6		85	
1897A	A1284	2c	**black,** *May 20, 1982*		10	5
			Pair		20	10
			P# strip of 3, line, P# 2-4, 6, 8, 10		75	
		e.	Imperf. pair			
1898	A1284a	3c	**dark green,** *Mar. 25, 1983*		15	5
			Pair		30	5
			P# strip of 3, line, P# 1-4		1.00	
1898A	A1285	4c	**reddish brown,** *Aug. 19, 1982*		12	5
			Pair		24	10
			P# strip of 3, line, P# 1-6		2.00	
		b.	Untagged (Bureau precanceled)			12
			P# strip of 3, line, P# 3-6			4.00
		c.	As 'b' imperf. pair			
1899	A1286	5c	**gray green,** *Oct. 10, 1983*		15	5
			Pair		30	10
			P# strip of 3, line, P# 1-4		2.00	
		a.	Imperf. pair			
1900	A1287	5.2	**carmine,** *Mar. 21, 1983*		20	5
			Pair		40	10
			P# strip of 3, line, P# 1,2		4.00	
			P# strip of 3, line, P# 3, 5		15.00	
		a.	Untagged (Bureau precanceled)			20
			P# strip of 3, line, P# 1-6			3.50
1901	A1288	5.9	**blue,** *Feb. 17, 1982*		20	5
			Pair		40	10
			P# strip of 3, line, P# 3, 4		3.00	
		a.	Untagged (Bureau Precanceled, lines only)			20
			P# strip of 3, line, P# 3-6			10.00
		b.	As 'a', imperf. pair			250.00
1902	A1288a	7.4	**brown,** *Apr. 7, 1984*		20	8
			Pair		40	16
			P# strip of 3, P# 2		3.50	
		a.	Untagged (Bureau precanceled)			20
			P# strip of 3, P# 2			4.00
1903	A1289	9.3	**carmine rose,** *Dec. 15*		20	8
			Pair		40	16
			P# strip of 3, line, P# 1-4		4.00	
			P# strip of 3, line, P# 5, 6		20.00	
		a.	Untagged (Bureau precanceled, lines only)			20
			P# strip of 3, line, P# 4-6			3.00
			P# strip of 3, line, P# 2-3			5.00
			P# strip of 3, line, P# 1,8			8.50
		b.	As "a," imperf. pair			50.00
1904	A1290	10.9	**purple,** *Mar. 26, 1982*		25	5
			Pair		50	10
			P# strip of 3, line, P# 1, 2		4.00	
		a.	Untagged (Bureau precanceled, lines only)			25
			P# strip of 3, line, P# 1, 2			9.00
			P# strip of 3, line, P# 3, 4			
		b.	As "a," imperf. pair			65.00
1905	A1291	11c	**red,** *Feb. 3, 1984*		25	8
			Pair		50	16
			P# strip of 3, P# 1		4.00	
		a.	Untagged (Bureau precanceled)			25
			P# strip of 3, P# 1			5.00
1906	A1292	17c	**ultramarine,** *June 25*		35	5
			Pair		70	10
			P# strip of 3, line, P# 3-6		4.00	
		a.	Untagged (Bureau precanceled, Presorted First Class)			35
			P# strip of 3, line, P# 1-2, 7			10.00
			Three diff. precancel styles exist.			
		b.	Imperf. pair			
		c.	As "a," imperf. pair			
1907	A1293	18c	**dark brown,** *May 18*		36	5
			Pair		72	10
			P# strip of 3, line, P# 2, 5, 6, 8-10, 13, 14		4.00	
			P# strip of 3, line, P# 3, 4, 7, 11, 12, 15-18		7.00	
			P# strip of 3, line, P# 1		10.00	
		a.	Imperf. pair		60.00	
1908	A1294	20c	**vermilion,** *Dec. 10*		40	5
			Pair		80	10
			P# strip of 3, line, P# 3-11, 13, 15, 16		6.00	
			P# strip of 3, line, P# 1		10.00	
			P# strip of 3, line, P# 12, 14		35.00	
			P# strip of 3, line, P# 2		100.00	
		a.	Imperf. pair		40.00	

See No *2228*

Eagle and Moon A1296

Booklet Stamp
PHOTOGRAVURE

1983, Aug. 12   *Perf. 10 Vert.*

1909	A1296	9.35	**multi**		20.00	6.00
		a.	Booklet pane of 3		62.50	

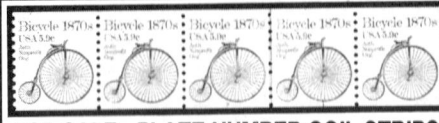

FOR SALE - PLATE NUMBER COIL STRIPS

AL HAAKE

R.R. 1, Box 65, Germantown, IL 62245

BUYING - PLATE NUMBER COIL STRIPS

"Come to one of the biggest for your plate coil needs"

FREE — BUY/SELL PRICE LIST — FREE

COIL NUMBER STRIP HEADQUARTERS

- Strips of 3 and 5
- All Flags; Everything
- Every Plate Number Priced
- All Transportations
- Mint and Precancelled
- Discounts

PRICE LIST FREE - SEND STAMPED ENVELOPE

CATALOG SPECIALS - Number Strips (3) F-VF NH
- All 24 Transportations, Mint..................... $43.00
- All 15 Transportations, Precancels............ $48.00
- All 18 Diff. 18¢ Surreys (Sc. #1907)......... $95.00

Strips (5) add 20%; VF-S add 40%.

Dr. Robert Rabinowitz, APS, BIA
37-P Stanwick Pl., Stamford, CT 06905

BUYING   SELLING
PLATE
COILS

FREE CATALOG

Sam Houston Philatelics

14654 Memorial Dr.   P.O. Box 820407
Houston, TX 77079   Houston, TX 77282

Toll Free 1-800-231-5926 • Texas 1-713-493-6386

CIRCLE READER SERVICE CARD #83

GO FOR TRANSPORTATION COILS...

All Mint, F-VF, NH; For XF-Sup Plate Strips add 30%.

Scott# Description	Sgl	Pair	No.+ L/Pr	PS3	PS5
1897 1¢ Omnibus	.10	.20	.50	.60	.65
1897A 2¢ Locomotive	.15	.30	.50	.60	.65
1898 3¢ Handcar	.25	.50	.75	1.00	1.05
1898A 4¢ Stagecoach	.15	.30	1.60	1.75	1.85
1899 5¢ Motorcycle	.20	.40	1.55	1.75	1.85
1900 5.2¢ Sleigh	.25	.50	3.25	3.50	3.75
1901 5.9¢ Bicycle	.25	.50	3.25	3.50	3.75
			No/L		
1902 7.4¢ B/Buggy	.25	.50	2.75	3.50	3.75
1903 9.3¢ Mail Wagon	.25	.50	3.25	3.50	3.75
1904 10.9¢ Hansom Cab	.25	.50	3.70	3.95	4.25
			No/L		
1905 11¢ Caboose	.25	.50	2.75	3.50	3.75
1906 17¢ Elec. Car	.35	.70	3.15	3.50	3.75
1907 18¢ Surry	.35	.70	3.60	3.95	4.25
1908 20¢ Fire Pumper	.35	.70	3.15	3.50	3.75
2123 3.4¢ School Bus	.25	.50	2.25	2.50	2.65
2125 4.9¢ Buckboard	.25	.50	2.25	2.50	2.65
			No/L		
2127 6¢ Tricycle	.25	.50	2.25	2.50	2.65
2128 8.3¢ Ambulance	.25	.50	2.25	2.50	2.65
			No/L		
2129 10.9¢ Oil Wagon	.25	.50	2.75	3.50	3.75
2130 11¢ Stutz Bearcat	.30	.60	2.20	2.50	2.65
2131 12¢ S/Steamer	.30	.60	2.20	2.50	2.65
			No/L		
2132 12.5¢ Push Cart	.35	.70	2.40	2.75	3.00
2134 14¢ Ice Boat	.30	.60	2.20	2.50	2.80

FILL IN YOUR SETS or BUY COMPLETE SETS.

PRE-CANCELLED TRANSPORTATION COILS

Scott # Description	Sgl	Pair	No.+ L/Pr	PS3	PS5
1898Ab 4¢ Stagecoach	.25	.50	2.75	3.00	3.25
1900a 5.2¢ Sleigh	.25	.50	3.70	3.95	4.25
1901a 5.9¢ Bicycle	.25	.50	4.70	6.95	8.00
			No/L		
1902a 7.4¢ B/Buggy	.25	.50	3.25	3.95	4.25
1903a 9.3¢ Mail Wagon	.25	.50	3.70	3.95	4.25
1904a 10.9¢ Hansom Cab	.30	.60	5.65	8.95	9.95
			No/L		
1905a 11¢ Caboose	.25	.50	3.25	3.95	4.25
1906a 17¢ Elec. Car	.35	.70	3.60	3.95	4.25
2123a 3.4¢ School Bus	.30	.60	2.95	3.25	3.50
2125a 4.9¢ Buckboard	.30	.60	2.95	3.25	3.50
			No/L		
2127a 6¢ Tricycle	.30	.60	2.50	3.25	3.50
2128a 8.3¢ Ambulance	.30	.60	2.95	3.25	3.50
			No/L		
2129a 10.1¢ Oil Wagon	.30	.60	2.95	3.50	3.75
2131a 12¢ S/Steamer	.35	.70	2.65	3.00	3.25
			No/L		
2132a 12.5¢ Push Cart	.40	.80	2.75	3.50	3.85

Send SASE today for your free check-off chart . . . the most comprehensive modern coil price list offered to date!

		Plt. strips
COMPLETE SETS	Singles Pairs	of (3) as listed
(23) Diff. Transp. coils	4.95 10.95	55.95 All 3 sets 66.95
(15) Diff precancelled	3.95 7.95	48.95 All 3 sets 54.95

COMPLETE ALL ABOVE (6) SETS - $115.00

TERMS: Minimum order $10.00, send 30¢ for current price lists. Postage payment accepted; MasterCard, VISA accepted; send account number and expiration date. PA residents add 6% sales tax. Add $1.00 insurance. Prices subject to change. - WE BUY! - We are active and constant buyers of better U.S. & Foreign singles, sets & collections, especially earlier U.S. material. Write with description for our high offer.

You are fully protected by our "Money Back" guarantee in effect for 20 years. 24 Hour Service. Phone Orders Welcome From 9:00 to 5:00 Daily.

 CHARGE IT!

For FREE Comprehensive U.S. Price List, Circle # 10 on Reader Service Card.

DALE ENTERPRISES, INC.
P.O. Box 539-C
Emmaus, PA 18049

Phone: (215) 433-3303   BIA

AMERICAN RED CROSS CENTENNIAL

A1297

Designed by Joseph Csatari.
PHOTOGRAVURE
Plates of 200 subjects in four panes of 50.

1981, May 1	Tagged	Perf. 10½x11	
1910	A1297 18c **multi**	36	5
	P# block of 4	1.75	—
	Zip block of 4	1.60	—
	Copyright block of 4	1.60	—

SAVINGS & LOAN SESQUICENTENNIAL

A1298

Designed by Don Hedin.
PHOTOGRAVURE
Plates of 200 subjects in four panes of 50.

1981, May 8	Tagged	Perf. 11	
1911	A1298 18c **multi**	36	5
	P# block of 4	1.75	—
	Zip block of 4	1.60	—
	Copyright block of 4	1.60	—

SPACE ACHIEVEMENT ISSUE

A1299   A1300   A1301   A1302

A1303   A1304   A1305   A1306

Designs: A1299, Moon walk. A1300—A1301, A1304-A1305, Columbia space shuttle. A1302, Skylab. A1303, Pioneer II. A1306, Telescope. Se-tenant in blocks of 8.

Designed by Robert McCall
PHOTOGRAVURE
Plates of 192 subjects in four panes of 48 each.

1981, May 21	Tagged	Perf. 11	
1912	A1299 18c **multi**	36	10
1913	A1300 18c **multi**	36	10
1914	A1301 18c **multi**	36	10
1915	A1302 18c **multi**	36	10
1916	A1303 18c **multi**	36	10
1917	A1304 18c **multi**	36	10
1918	A1305 18c **multi**	36	10
1919	A1306 18c **multi**	36	10
	P# block of 8, 6 P#	3.50	
	Zip, copyright block of 8	3.25	—
a.	Block of 8, #1912-1919	3.00	2.25
b.	As "a," imperf.		

POSTAGE, 1981 343

PROFESSIONAL MANAGEMENT ISSUE

Joseph Wharton
(Founder of Wharton
School of Business)
A1307

Professional management education centenary.

Designed by Rudolph de Harak.
PHOTOGRAVURE
Plates of 200 subject in four panes of 50 each.
1981, June 18   Tagged   Perf. 11

1920	A1307 18c **blue & black**		36	5
	P# block of 4, 2 P#		1.75	
	Zip block of 4		1.60	
	Copyright block of 4		1.60	

PRESERVATION OF WILDLIFE HABITATS ISSUE

Great Blue Heron
A1308

Badger
A1309

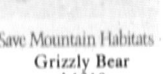

Grizzly Bear
A1310

Ruffed Grouse
A1311

Designed by Chuck Ripper
PHOTOGRAVURE
Plates of 200 subjects in four panes of 50 each.
1981, June 26   Tagged   Perf. 11

1921	A1308 18c **multi**	36	8
1922	A1309 18c **multi**	36	8
1923	A1310 18c **multi**	36	8
1924	A1311 18c **multi**	36	8
	P# block of 4, 5 P#	1.75	
	Zip block of 4	1.60	
	Copyright block of 4	1.60	
	a. Block of 4, #1921-1924	1.50	85

INTERNATIONAL YEAR OF THE DISABLED ISSUE

Man Using
Microscope
A1312

Designed by Martha Perske
PHOTOGRAVURE
Plates of 200 subjects in four panes of 50 each.
1981, June 29   Tagged   Perf. 11

1925	A1312 18c **multi**	36	5
	P# block of 4, 6 P#	1.75	
	Zip block of 4	1.60	
	Copyright block of 4	1.60	
	a. Vert. pair, imperf. horiz.	2,500.	

EDNA ST. VINCENT MILLAY ISSUE

A1313

Designed by Glenora Case Richards
LITHOGRAPHED AND ENGRAVED
Plates of 200 subjects in four panes of 50 each.
1981, July 10   Tagged   Perf. 11

1926	A1313 18c **multi**	36	5
	P# block of 4, 7 P#	1.75	
	Zip block of 4	1.60	
	Copyright block of 4	1.60	
	a. Black (engr., inscriptions) omitted	500.00	

ALCOHOLISM

A1314

Designed by John Boyd

ENGRAVED

Plates of 230 (10x23) subjects in panes of 50 (5x10)
1981, Aug. 19   Tagged   Perf. 11

1927	A1314 18c **blue & black**	36	5
	P# block of 20, 1-2 P#, 1-2 copyright, 1-2 Zip	25.00	
	a. Imperf., pair	400.00	

AMERICAN ARCHITECTURE

New York University Library
by Stanford White
A1315

Biltmore House
By Richard Morris Hunt
A1316

Palace of the Arts
by Bernard Maybeck
A1317

National Farmer's Bank
by Louis Sullivan
A1318
Designed by
Walter D. Richards

ENGRAVED

1981, Aug. 28		Tagged	Perf. 11	
1928	A1315 18c **black & red**		36	8
1929	A1316 18c **black & red**		36	8
1930	A1317 18c **black & red**		36	8
1931	A1318 18c **black & red**		36	8
	P# block of 4		1.75	—
	Zip block of 4		1.60	—
	Copyright block of 4		1.60	—
	a. Block of 4, #1928-1931		1.50	.85

Coming Through
the Rye—A1321

Designed by Paul Calle

LITHOGRAPHED AND ENGRAVED
Plates of 200 in four panes of 50

1981, Oct. 9		Tagged	Perf. 11	
1934	A1321 18c **gray, olive green & brown**		36	5
	P# block of 4, 3 P#		1.75	—
	Zip block of 4		1.60	—
	Copyright block of 4		1.60	—
	a. Vert. pair, imperf. btwn.		350.00	
	b. Brown omitted		700.00	

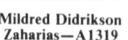

Mildred Didrikson
Zaharias—A1319

Robert Tyre
Jones—A1320

Designed by Richard Gangel

Plates of 200 subjects in four panes of 50 each.

1981, Sept. 22		Tagged	Perf. 10½x11	
1932	A1319 18c **purple**		36	5
	P# block of 4		1.75	—
	Zip block of 4		1.60	—
	Copyright block of 4		1.60	—
1933	A1320 18c **green**		36	5
	P# block of 4		1.75	—
	Zip block of 4		1.60	—
	Copyright block of 4		1.60	—

JAMES HOBAN

Irish-American Architect
of the White House—A1322

Designed by Ron Mercer and Walter D. Richards

PHOTOGRAVURE
Plates of 200 in four panes of 50

1981, Oct. 13		Tagged	Perf. 11	
1935	A1322 18c **multi**		50	25
	P# block of 4, 6 P#		3.00	—
	Zip block of 4		2.25	—
	Copyright block of 4		2.25	—
1936	A1322 20c **multi**		40	5
	P# block of 4, 6 P#		2.00	—
	Zip block of 4		1.75	—
	Copyright block of 4		1.75	—

AMERICAN BICENTENNIAL

Battle of Yorktown
A1323

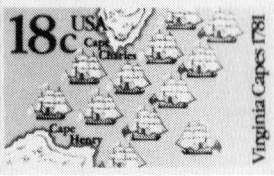
Battle of the
Virginia Capes
A1324

Designed by Cal Sacks
LITHOGRAPHED AND ENGRAVED
Plates of 200 in four panes of 50

					P# block of 4, 7 P#	1.75	—
1981, Oct. 16		Tagged	Perf. 11		Zip block of 4	1.60	—
					Copyright block of 4	1.60	—
1937	A1323 18c multicolored		36	6	a. Pair, #1937-1938	72	15
1938	A1324 18c multicolored		36	6	b. As "a," black (engr., inscriptions) omitted	800.00	

CHRISTMAS

Madonna and Child, Botticelli   Felt Bear on Sleigh
A1325   A1326

Designed by Bradbury Thompson (#1939)
and by Naiad Einsel (#1940)

PHOTOGRAVURE
Plates of 400 in four panes of 100 (#1939)
Plates of 200 in four panes of 50 (#1940)

1981, Oct. 28		Tagged	Perf. 11		
1939	A1325(20c)multi		40	5	
	P# block of 4, 6 P#		2.00		
	Zip block of 4		1.75		
	Copyright block of 4		1.75		
	a. Imperf. pair		200.00		
1940	A1326(20c)multi		40	5	
	P# block of 4, 5 P#		2.00		
	Zip block of 4		1.75		
	Copyright block of 4		1.75		
	a. Imperf. pair		200.00		
	b. Vert. pair, horiz. imperf.				

JOHN HANSON

First President of the
Continental Congress
A1327
Designed by Ron Adair
PHOTOGRAVURE
Plates of 200 in panes of 50

1981, Nov. 5		Tagged		Perf. 11	
1941	A1327 20c multicolored		40	5	
	P# block of 4, 5 P#		2.00		
	Zip block of 4		1.75		
	Copyright block of 4		1.75		

Agave
A1329

Barrel Cactus   Beavertail Cactus   Saguaro
A1328   A1330   A1331

DESERT PLANTS

Designed by Frank J. Waslick

LITHOGRAPHED AND ENGRAVED

Plates of 160 in four panes of 40

1981 Dec. 11	Tagged		Perf. 11	
1942	A1328 20c multi		40	6
1943	A1329 20c multi		40	6
1944	A1330 20c multi		40	6
1945	A1331 20c multi		40	6
	P# block of 4, 7 P#		2.00	—
	Zip block of 4		1.75	—
	Copyright block of 4		1.75	—
	a. Block of 4, #1942-1945		1.60	85

A1332

A1333

Designed by Bradbury Thompson

PHOTOGRAVURE

Plates of 400 in panes of 100

1981, Oct. 11	Tagged	Perf. 11x10½	
1946	A1332(20c) brown	40	5
	P# block of 4	2.00	—
	Zip block of 4	1.75	—
	Copyright block of 4	1.75	—

COIL STAMP
Perf. 10 Vert.

1947	A1332(20c) brown	40	5
	Pair	80	10
	Joint line pair	1.00	
	a. Imperf. pair	—	

BOOKLET STAMPS
Perf. 11x10½

1948	A1333(20c) brown	40	5
	a. Booklet pane of 10	4.25	

Rocky Mountain Bighorn
A1334

ENGRAVED

1982, Jan. 8	Tagged	Perf. 11	
1949	A1334 20c dark blue (from bklt. pane)	40	5
	a. Booklet pane of 10	4.00	—

Franklin D. Roosevelt
A1335

Designed by Clarence Holbert

ENGRAVED

Plates of 192 in four panes of 48

1982, Jan. 3	Tagged	Perf. 11	
1950	A1335 20c blue	40	5
	P# block of 4	2.00	—
	Zip block of 4	1.75	—
	Copyright block of 4	1.75	—

LOVE ISSUE

A1336

Designed by Mary Faulconer

PHOTOGRAVURE

Plates of 200 in four panes of 50

1982, Feb. 1	Tagged	Perf. 11x10½	
1951	A1336 20c Multicolored	40	5
	P# block of 4, 5 P#	2.00	—
	Zip block of 4	1.75	—
	Copyright block of 4	1.75	—
	a. Perf. 11	50	5
	b. Imperf. pair	300.00	
	c. Blue omitted	—	

GEORGE WASHINGTON

A1337

Designed by Mark English

PHOTOGRAVURE

Plates of 200 in four panes of 50

1982, Feb. 22	Tagged	Perf. 11	
1952	A1337 20c multicolored	40	5
	P# block of 4, 6 P#	2.00	—
	Zip block of 4	1.75	—
	Copyright block of 4	1.75	—

STATE BIRDS AND FLOWERS ISSUE

State Birds and Flowers—A1338-A1387
Designed by Arthur and Alan Singer.

PHOTOGRAVURE (Andreotti)
Plates of 200 subjects in four panes of 50 each.

			Tagged		Perf. 10½x11	
1982, Apr. 14						
1953	A1338	20c	Alabama		40	25
1954	A1339	20c	Alaska		40	25
1955	A1340	20c	Arizona		40	25
1956	A1341	20c	Arkansas		40	25
1957	A1342	20c	California		40	25
1958	A1343	20c	Colorado		40	25
1959	A1344	20c	Connecticut		40	25
1960	A1345	20c	Delaware		40	25
1961	A1346	20c	Florida		40	25
1962	A1347	20c	Georgia		40	25
1963	A1348	20c	Hawaii		40	25
1964	A1349	20c	Idaho		40	25
1965	A1350	20c	Illinois		40	25
1966	A1351	20c	Indiana		40	25
1967	A1352	20c	Iowa		40	25
1968	A1353	20c	Kansas		40	25
1969	A1354	20c	Kentucky		40	25
1970	A1355	20c	Louisiana		40	25
1971	A1356	20c	Maine		40	25
1972	A1357	20c	Maryland		40	25
1973	A1358	20c	Massachusetts		40	25
1974	A1359	20c	Michigan		40	25
1975	A1360	20c	Minnesota		40	25
1976	A1360	20c	Mississippi		40	25
1977	A1361	20c	Missouri		40	25
1978	A1362	20c	Montana		40	25
1979	A1363	20c	Nebraska		40	25
1980	A1364	20c	Nevada		40	25
1981	A1364	20c	New Hampshire		40	25
1982	A1365	20c	New Jersey		40	25
1983	A1366	20c	New Mexico		40	25
1984	A1369	20c	New York		40	25
1985	A1370	20c	North Carolina		40	25
1986	A1371	20c	North Dakota		40	25
1987	A1372	20c	Ohio		40	25
1988	A1373	20c	Oklahoma		40	25
1989	A1374	20c	Oregon		40	25
1990	A1375	20c	Pennsylvania		40	25
1991	A1376	20c	Rhode Island		40	25
1992	A1377	20c	South Carolina		40	25
1993	A1378	20c	South Dakota		40	25
1994	A1379	20c	Tennessee		40	25
1995	A1380	20c	Texas		40	25
1996	A1381	20c	Utah		40	25
1997	A1382	20c	Vermont		40	25
1998	A1383	20c	Virginia		40	25
1999	A1384	20c	Washington		40	25
2000	A1385	20c	West Virginia		40	25
2001	A1386	20c	Wisconsin		40	25
2002	A1387	20c	Wyoming		40	25

    a. 1953a-2002a, any single, perf. 11   50   30
    b. Pane of 50, perf. 10½x11   20.00
    c. Pane of 50, perf. 11   25.00
    d. Pane of 50, imperf.

US-NETHERLANDS

200th Anniv. of Diplomatic
Recognition by The Netherlands—A1388
Designed by Heleen Tigler Wybrandi-Raue

PHOTOGRAVURE
Plates of 230 (10x23) subjects in panes of 50 (5x10)

			Tagged		Perf. 11	
1982, Apr. 20						
2003	A1388	20c	verm., brt. blue & gray blk.		40	5

    P# block of 20, 1-2 P#,
    1-2 copyright, 1-2 zip   8.50
    a. Imperf. pair   500.00

LIBRARY OF CONGRESS

A1389
Designed by Bradbury Thompson
ENGRAVED
Plates of 200 subjects in four panes of 50

1982, Apr. 21	Tagged		Perf. 11
2004 A1389 20c red & black	40	5
P# block of 4	2.00	
Zip block of 4	1.75	—
Copyright block of 4	1.75	—

A1390
Designed by John Boyd
ENGRAVED
Coil Stamp

1982, Apr. 27	Tagged		Perf. 10 vert.
2005 A1390 20c sky blue	40	5
Pair	80	6
P# strip of 3, line, P# 1-4	10.00	
a. Imperf. pair	65.00	

KNOXVILLE WORLD'S FAIR

A1391　　　　A1392

A1393　　　　A1394

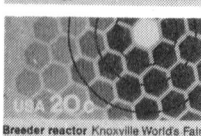 

Designed by Charles Harper
PHOTOGRAVURE
Plates of 200 in four panes of 50

1982, Apr. 29	Tagged		Perf. 11
2006 A1391 20c multi	40	8
2007 A1392 20c multi	40	8
2008 A1393 20c multi	40	8
2009 A1394 20c multi	40	8
P# block of 4, 5 P#	2.00	
Zip block of 4	1.75	—
Copyright block of 4	1.75	—
a. Block of 4, #2006-2009	1.60	85

AMERICAN AUTHOR, 1832-1899

A1395
Designed by Robert Hallock
ENGRAVED
Plates of 200 in four panes of 50

1982, Apr. 30	Tagged		Perf. 11
2010 A1395 20c red & black, tan	40	5
P# block of 4	2.00	
Zip block of 4	1.75	—
Copyright block of 4	1.75	—

AGING TOGETHER

A1396
Designed by Paul Calle
ENGRAVED
Plates of 200 in four panes of 50

1982, May 21	Tagged		Perf. 11
2011 A1396 20c brown	40	5
P# block of 4	2.00	
Zip block of 4	1.75	—
Copyright block of 4	1.75	—

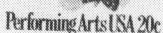

John, Lionel and Ethel Barrymore　　A1398
A1397

PERFORMING ARTS

Designed by Jim Sharpe
PHOTOGRAVURE
Plates of 200 in four panes of 50

1982, June 8	Tagged		Perf. 11
2012 A1397 20c multicolored	40	5
P# block of 4, 6 P#	2.00	—
Zip block of 4	1.75	—
Copyright block of 4	1.75	—

WOMENS RIGHTS

Designed by Glenora Richards
PHOTOGRAVURE
Plate of 200 in four panes of 50

1982, June 10	Tagged		Perf. 11
2013 A1398 20c multicolored	40	5
P# block of 4, 6 P#	2.00	—
Zip block of 4	1.75	—
Copyright block of 4	1.75	—

Dunseith, ND-Boissevain, Manitoba
A1399
Designed by Gyo Fujikawa
LITHOGRAPHED AND ENGRAVED
Plate of 200 in four panes of 50

1982, June 30	Tagged		Perf. 11
2014 A1399 20c multicolored	40	5
P# block of 4, 5 P#	2.00	—
Zip block of 4	1.75	—
Copyright block of 4	1.75	—
a. Black, green & brown (engr.) omitted	—	

A1400   A1401
Designed by Bradbury Thompson
ENGRAVED
Plate of 200 subjects in four panes of 50

1982, July 13	Tagged		Perf. 11
2015 A1400 20c red & black	40	5
P# block of 4	2.00	—
Zip block of 4	1.75	—
Copyright block of 4	1.75	—
a. Vert. pair, imperf. horiz.		

JACKIE ROBINSON

Designed by Jerry Pinkney
PHOTOGRAVURE
Plate of 200 subjects in four panes of 50

1982, Aug. 2	Tagged		Perf. 10½x11
2016 A1401 20c multicolored	40	5
P# block of 4, 5 P#	2.00	—
Zip block of 4	1.75	—
Copyright block of 4	1.75	—

TOURO SYNAGOGUE

Oldest Existing Synagogue Building in the U.S.
A1402
Designed by Donald Moss and Bradbury Thompson
PHOTO. AND ENGRAVED
Plates of 230 (10x23) subjects in panes of 50 (5x10)

1982, Aug. 22	Tagged		Perf. 11
2017 A1402 20c multi	40	5
P# block of 20, 6-12 #, 1-2 copyright, 1-2 zip	8.50	—
a. Imperf. pair		

WOLF TRAP FARM PARK

A1403
Designed by Richard Schlecht
PHOTOGRAVURE
Plates of 200 in four panes of 50

1982, Sept. 1	Tagged		Perf. 11
2018 A1403 20c multi	40	5
P# block of 4, 5 P#	2.00	—
Zip block of 4	1.75	—
Copyright block of 4	1.75	—

POSTAGE

A1404

A1405

A1408

A1406

A1407

A1409

Designed by Walter D. Richards

Designed by Ned Seidler.
Printed by American Bank Note Co. and J.W. Ferguson and Sons.

ENGRAVED
Plates of 160 subjects in four panes of 40

Plates of 200 subjects in four panes of 50 each

PHOTOGRAVURE

1982, Sept. 30		Tagged		Perf. 11
2019	A1404 20c	black & brown	40	8
2020	A1405 20c	black & brown	40	8
2021	A1406 20c	black & brown	40	8
2022	A1407 20c	black & brown	40	8
		P# block of 4	2.00	
		Zip block of 4	1.75	
		Copyright block of 4	1.75	
	a.	Block of 4, #2019-2022	1.60	85

1982, Oct. 7		Tagged		Perf. 11
2023	A1408 20c	multi	40	5
		P# block of 4, 6 P#	2.00	
		Zip block of 4	1.75	
		Copyright block of 4	1.75	

Designed by Richard Schlecht

PHOTOGRAVURE (Combination press)
Plates of 230 subjects (10x23) in panes of 50 (5x10)

1982, Oct. 12		Tagged		Perf. 11
2024	A1409 20c	multi	40	5
		P# block of 20, 5 or 10 P#, 1-2 zip, 1-2 copyright	8.50	
	a.	Imperf. pair		

See 3rd note after No. 1703.

A1410

A1411

A1412

A1413

A1414

A1415

1982, Nov. 3   **Tagged**

2025	A1410 13c	multi	26	5
		P# block of 4	1.30	
		Zip block of 4	1.20	
		Copyright block of 4	1.20	
	a.	Imperf. pair		

1982, Oct. 28   **Tagged**

2026	A1411 20c	multi	40	5
		P# block of 20, 5 or 10 P#, 1-2 copyright, 1-2 zip	8.50	
	a.	Imperf. pair		

2027	A1412 20c	multi	40	5
2028	A1413 20c	multi	40	5
2029	A1414 20c	multi	40	5
2030	A1415 20c	multi	40	5
		P# block of 4, 4 P#	2.00	
		Zip block of 4	1.75	
		Copyright block of 4	1.75	
	a.	Block of 4, #2027-2030	1.60	85
	b.	As "a," imperf.		
	c.	As "a," imperf. horiz.		

POSTAGE

SCIENCE & INDUSTRY

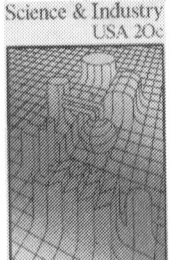

A1416
Designed by Saul Bass

LITHOGRAPHED AND ENGRAVED
Plates of 200 in four panes of 50

1983, Jan. 19		Tagged	Perf. 11	
2031	A1416	20c multi	40	5
		P# block of 4, 4P#	2.00	
		Zip block of 4	1.75	
		Copyright block of 4	1.75	
	a.	Black (engr.) omitted	—	

BALLOONS

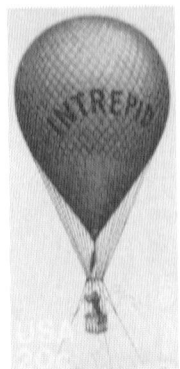

Intrepid
A1417

Explorer II
A1420

A1418

A1419
Designed by David Meltzer

PHOTOGRAVURE
Plates of 160 in four panes of 40

1983, Mar. 31		Tagged	Perf. 11	
2032	A1417	20c multi	40	8
2033	A1418	20c multi	40	8
2034	A1419	20c multi	40	8
2035	A1420	20c multi	40	8
		P# block of 4, 5P#	2.00	
		Zip block of 4	1.75	
		Copyright block of 4	1.75	
	a.	Block of 4, #2032-2035	1.60	85
	b.	As "a," imperf.	—	

US—SWEDEN

Benjamin Franklin—A1421

Designed by Czeslaw Slania, court engraver of Sweden

ENGRAVED
Plates of 200 in four panes of 50

1983, Mar. 24		Tagged	Perf. 11	
2036	A1421	20c blue, blk & red brn	40	5
		P# block of 4	2.00	
		Zip block of 4	1.75	
		Copyright block of 4	1.75	

CCC, 50th Anniv.

A1422

Designed by David K. Stone

PHOTOGRAVURE
Plates of 200 in four panes of 50

1983, Apr. 5		Tagged	Perf. 11	
2037	A1422	20c multi	40	5
		P# block of 4, 6P#	2.00	
		Zip block of 4	1.75	
		Copyright block of 4	1.75	
	a.	Imperf. pair	—	

JOSEPH PRIESTLEY

Discoverer of Oxygen—A1423

Designed by Dennis Lyall

Printed by American Bank Note Company and J.W. Fergusson And Sons

PHOTOGRAVURE
Plates of 200 in four panes of 50

1983, Apr. 13		Tagged	Perf. 11	
2038	A1423	20c multi	40	5
		P# block of 4, 6P#	2.00	
		Zip block of 4	1.75	
		Copyright block of 4	1.75	

VOLUNTARISM

A1424

Designed by Paul Calle
ENGRAVED
Plates of 230 (10x23) subjects in panes of 50 (5x10)

		Tagged	Perf. 11	
1983, Apr. 20			40	5
2039	A1424	20c red & black		
		P# block of 20, 1-2 P#,		
		1-2 copyright, 1-2 zip	8.50	—

US—GERMANY

A1425

Designed by Richard Schlecht
ENGRAVED
Plates of 200 in four panes of 50

		Tagged	Perf. 11	
1983, Apr. 29			40	5
2040	A1425	20c brown		
		P# block of 4	2.00	—
		Zip block of 4	1.75	—
		Copyright block of 4	1.75	—

BROOKLYN BRIDGE

A1426
Designed by Howard Koslow
ENGRAVED
Plates of 200 in four panes of 50

		Tagged	Perf. 11	
1983, May. 5			40	5
2041	A1426	20c blue		
		P# block of 4	2.00	—
		Zip block of 4	1.75	—
		Copyright block of 4	1.75	—

TVA

Norris Hydroelectric Dam—A1427

Designed by Howard Koslow
PHOTOGRAVURE AND ENGRAVED
Plates of 230 in panes of 50

		Tagged	Perf. 11	
1983, May 18			40	5
2042	A1427	20c multi		
		P# block of 20, 5-10 P#,		
		1-2 copyright, 1-2 zip	8.50	—

Runners, Electrocardiograph tracing—A1428

Designed by Donald Moss
PHOTOGRAVURE
Plates of 230 in panes of 50

		Tagged	Perf. 11	
1983, May 14			40	5
2043	A1428	20c multi		
		P# block of 20, 4-8 P#,		
		1-2 copyright, 1-2 zip	8.50	—

SCOTT JOPLIN (1868-1917)
Black Heritage

A1429

Designed by Jerry Pinkney
PHOTOGRAVURE
Plates of 200 in four panes of 50

		Tagged	Perf. 11	
1983, June 9			40	5
2044	A1429	20c multi		
		P# block of 4, 6P#	2.00	—
		Zip block of 4	1.75	—
		Copyright block of 4	1.75	—
	a.	Imperf. pair		

MEDAL OF HONOR

A1430

Designed by Dennis J. Hom
TYPOGRAPHED AND ENGRAVED
Plates of 160 in four panes of 40

		Tagged	Perf. 11	
1983, June 7			40	5
2045	A1430	20c multi		
		P# block of 4, 5P#	2.00	—
		Zip block of 4	1.75	—
		Copyright block of 4	1.75	—
	a.	Red omitted		

POSTAGE, 1983   353

A1431   A1432

GEORGE HERMAN RUTH (1895-1948)

Designed by Richard Gangel
ENGRAVED
Plates of 200 in four panes of 50

1983, July 6		Tagged	Perf. 10½x11	
2046	A1431	20c blue	40	5
		P# block of 4	2.00	—
		Zip block of 4	1.75	—
		Copyright block of 4	1.75	—

NATHANIEL HAWTHORNE (1804-1864)

Designed by Bradbury Thompson after 1851 painting by
Cephus Giovanni Thompson
PHOTOGRAVURE
Plates of 200 in four panes of 50

1983, July 8		Tagged	Perf. 11	
2047	A1432	20c multi	40	5
		P# block of 4, 4P#	2.00	—
		Zip block of 4	1.75	—
		Copyright block of 4	1.75	—

LOS ANGELES OLYMPICS
July 28-August 12, 1984

A1433

A1434

A1435

A1436

Designed by Bob Peake
PHOTOGRAVURE
Plates of 200 in four panes of 50

1983, July 28		Tagged	Perf. 11	
2048	A1433	13c multi	26	5
2049	A1434	13c multi	26	5
2050	A1435	13c multi	26	5
2051	A1436	13c multi	26	5
		P# block of 4, 4P#	1.30	—
		Zip block of 4	1.15	—
		Copyright block of 4	1.15	—
	a.	Block of 4, #2048-2051	1.05	65

SIGNING OF TREATY OF PARIS

John Adams, B. Franklin, John Jay, David Hartley
A1437

Designed by David Blossom based on unfinished painting
by Benjamin West in Winterthur Museum.
PHOTOGRAVURE
Plates of 160 in four panes of 40

1983, Sept. 2		Tagged	Perf. 11	
2052	A1437	20c multi	40	5
		P# block of 4, 4P#	2.00	—
		Zip block of 4	1.75	—
		Copyright block of 4	1.75	—

CIVIL SERVICE

A1438

Designed by MDB Communications, Inc.
PHOTOGRAVURE AND ENGRAVED
Plates of 230 in four panes of 50

1983, Sept. 9		Tagged	Perf. 11	
2053	A1438	20c buff, blue & red	40	5
		P# block of 20, 2P#	8.50	—

METROPOLITAN OPERA

Original State Arch and Current 5-arch Entrance
A1439

Designed by Ken Davies
LITHOGRAPHED AND ENGRAVED
Plates of 200 in four panes of 50

1983, Sept. 14		**Tagged**	*Perf. 11*	
2054	A1439	20c yel & maroon	40	5
		P# block of 4	2.00	—
		Zip block of 4	1.75	—
		Copyright block of 4	1.75	—

AMERICAN INVENTORS

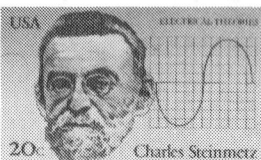

Charles Steinmetz
and Curve on Graph
A1440

Edwin Armstrong
and Frequency Modulator
A1441

Nikola Tesla
and Induction Motor
A1442

Philo T. Farnsworth
and First
Television Camera
A1443

Designed by Dennis Lyall
LITHOGRAPHED AND ENGRAVED
Plates of 200 in four panes of 50

1983, Sept. 21		**Tagged**	*Perf. 11*	
2055	A1440	20c multi	40	8
2056	A1441	20c multi	40	8
2057	A1442	20c multi	40	8
2058	A1443	20c multi	40	8
		P# block of 4, 2 P#	2.00	—
		Zip block of 4	1.75	—
		Copyright block of 4	1.75	—
	a.	Block of 4, #2055-2058	1.60	85
	b.	As "a," black omitted	—	

STREET CARS

A1444

A1445

A1446

A1447

Designed by Richard Leech
PHOTOGRAVURE AND ENGRAVED
Plates of 200 in four panes of 50

1983, Oct. 8		**Tagged**	*Perf. 11*	
2059	A1444	20c multi	40	8
2060	A1445	20c multi	40	8
2061	A1446	20c multi	40	8
2062	A1447	20c multi	40	8
		P# block of 4, 5#	2.00	—
		Zip block of 4	1.75	—
		Copyright block of 4	1.75	—
	a.	Block of 4, #2059-2062	1.60	85
	b.	As "a," black omitted	—	

CHRISTMAS

Niccolini-Cowper
Madonna, by Raphael
A1448

Santa Claus
A1449

Designed by Bradbury Thompson (#2063), and
John Berkey (#2064)
PHOTOGRAVURE
Plates of 200 in four panes of 50 (#2063),
Plates of 230 in panes of 50 (#2064)

1983, Oct. 28		**Tagged**	*Perf. 11*	
2063	A1448	20c multi	40	5
		P# block of 4, 5#	2.00	—
		Zip block of 4	1.75	—
		Copyright block of 4	1.75	—
2064	A1449	20c multi	40	5
		P# block of 20, 5-10 P#, 1-2 copyright, 1-2 zip	8.50	—
	a.	Imperf. pair	—	

POSTAGE, 1983-84   355

German Religious Leader, Founder of Lutheran Church (1483-1546)
A1450

Caribou and Alaska Pipeline
A1451

MARTIN LUTHER
Designed by Bradbury Thompson
Printed by American Bank Note Company
and J.W. Fergusson And Sons
PHOTOGRAVURE
Plates of 200 in four panes of 50

1983, Nov.11		Tagged	Perf. 11	
2065	A1450	20c multi	40	5
		P# block of 4, 5#	2.00	
		Zip block of 4	1.75	—
		Copyright block of 4	1.75	—

25th ANNIVERSARY OF ALASKA STATEHOOD
Designed by Bill Bond
Printed by American Bank Note Company
and J.W. Fergusson
And Sons
PHOTOGRAVURE
Plates of 200 in four panes of 50

1984, Jan. 3		Tagged	Perf. 11	
2066	A1451	20c multi	40	5
		P# block of 4, 5#	2.00	
		Zip block of 4	1.75	—
		Copyright block of 4	1.75	—

14th WINTER OLYMPIC GAMES, SARAJEVO, JUGOSLAVIA, FEB. 8-19

Ice Dancing — A1452   Alpine Skiing — A1453

Nordic Skiing
A1454

Hockey
A1455

Designed by Bob Peak
PHOTOGRAVURE
Plates of 200 in four panes of 50

1984, Jan. 6		Tagged	Perf. 10½ x 11	
2067	A1452	20c multi	40	8
2068	A1453	20c multi	40	8
2069	A1454	20c multi	40	8
2070	A1455	20c multi	40	8
		P# block of 4, 4#	2.00	
		Zip block of 4	1.75	—
		Copyright block of 4	1.75	—
		a. Block of 4, #2067-2070	1.60	85

Pillar, Dollar Sign
A1456

FEDERAL DEPOSIT INSURANCE CORPORATION, 50TH ANNIVERSARY
Designed by Michael David Brown
PHOTOGRAVURE
Plates of 200 in four panes of 50
(1 pane each #2071, 2074, 2075 and 2081)

1984, Jan. 12		Tagged	Perf. 11	
2071	A1456	20c multi	40	5
		P# block of 4, 6#, UL only	2.00	
		Zip block of 4	1.75	—
		Copyright block of 4	1.75	—

LOVE
Designed by Bradbury Thompson
PHOTOGRAVURE AND ENGRAVED
Plates of 230 in four panes of 50

1984, Jan. 31		Tagged	Perf. 11 x 10½	
2072	A1457	20c multi	40	5
		P# block of 20, 6-12#, 1-2 copyright, 1-2 zip	8.50	—
		a. Horiz. pair, imperf. vert.		—

Carter G. Woodson
(1875-1950),
Black Historian
A1458

A1459

BLACK HERITAGE
Designed by Jerry Pinkney
Printed by American Bank Note Company
PHOTOGRAVURE
Plates of 200 in four panes of 50

1984, Feb. 1		Tagged	Perf. 11	
2073	A1458	20c multi	40	5
		P# block of 4, 6#	2.00	—
		Zip block of 4	1.75	—
		Copyright block of 4	1.75	—
		a. Horiz. pair, imperf. vert.	—	

SOIL & WATER CONSERVATION
Designed by Michael David Brown
See #2071 for printing information.

1984, Feb. 6		Tagged	Perf. 11	
2074	A1459	20c multi	40	5
		P# block of 4, 6#, UR only	2.00	—
		Zip block of 4	1.75	—
		Copyright block of 4	1.75	—

50TH ANNIVERSARY OF CREDIT UNION ACT

Dollar Sign, Coin—A1460

Designed by Michael David Brown
See #2071 for printing information.

1984, Feb. 10		Tagged	Perf. 11	
2075	A1460	20c multi	40	5
		P# block of 4, 6#, LR only	2.00	—
		Zip block of 4	1.75	—
		Copyright block of 4	1.75	—

ORCHIDS

Wild Pink
A1461

Yellow Lady's-slipper
A1462

Spreading Pogonia
A1463

Pacific Calypso
A1464

Designed by Manabu Saito
PHOTOGRAVURE
Plates of 192 in four panes of 48

1984, Mar. 5		Tagged	Perf. 11	
2076	A1461	20c multi	40	8
2077	A1462	20c multi	40	8
2078	A1463	20c multi	40	8
2079	A1464	20c multi	40	8
		P# block of 4, 5#	2.00	—
		Zip block of 4	1.75	—
		Copyright block of 4	1.75	—
		a. Block of 4, #2076-2079	1.60	85

25th ANNIVERSARY OF HAWAII STATEHOOD

Eastern Polynesian Canoe, Golden
Plover, Mauna Loa Volcano—A1465

Designed by Herb Kane
Printed by American Bank Note Company
PHOTOGRAVURE
Plates of 200 in four panes of 50

1984, Mar. 12		Tagged	Perf. 11	
2080	A1465	20c multi	40	5
		P# block of 4, 5#	2.00	—
		Zip block of 4	1.75	—
		Copyright block of 4	1.75	—

50TH ANNIVERSARY, NATIONAL ARCHIVES

Abraham Lincoln, George Washington—A1466

Designed by Michael David Brown
See #2071 for printing information

1984, Apr. 16		Tagged	Perf. 11	
2081	A1466	20c multi	40	5
		P# block of 4, 6#, LL only	2.00	—
		Zip block of 4	1.75	—
		Copyright block of 4	1.75	—

LOS ANGELES SUMMER OLYMPICS
July 28-August 12

Diving
A1467

Long Jump
A1468

Wrestling
A1469

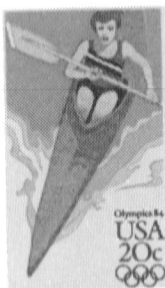
Kayak
A1470

Designed by Bob Peak
PHOTOGRAVURE
Plates of 200 in four panes of 50

1984, May 4			Tagged	Perf. 11	
2082	A1467	20c multi		40	8
2083	A1468	20c multi		40	8
2084	A1469	20c multi		40	8
2085	A1470	20c multi		40	8
		P# block of 4, 4#		2.00	
		Zip block of 4		1.75	
		Copyright block of 4		1.75	
		a. Block of 4, #2082-2085		1.60	.85

LOUISIANA WORLD EXPOSITION
New Orleans, May 12-Nov. 11

Bayou Wildlife—A1471

Designed by Chuck Ripper
PHOTOGRAVURE
Plates of 160 in four panes of 40

1984, May 11		Tagged	Perf. 11	
2086	A1471	20c multi	40	5
		P# block of 4, 5#	2.00	
		Zip block of 4	1.75	
		Copyright block of 4	1.75	

HEALTH RESEARCH

Lab Equipment—A1472

Designed by Tyler Smith
Printed by American Bank Note Company
PHOTOGRAVURE
Plates of 200 in four panes of 50

1984, May 17		Tagged	Perf. 11	
2087	A1472	20c multi	40	5
		P# block of 4, 5#	2.00	
		Zip block of 4	1.75	
		Copyright block of 4	1.75	

Actor Douglas
Fairbanks
(1883-1939)
A1473

A1474

PERFORMING ARTS
Designed by Jim Sharpe
PHOTOGRAVURE AND ENGRAVED
Plates of 230 in panes of 50

1984, May 23		Tagged	Perf. 11	
2088	A1473	20c multi	40	5
		P# block of 20, 5-10#, 1-2 copyright, 1-2 zip	8.50	

JIM THORPE, 1888-1953
Designed by Richard Gangel
ENGRAVED
Plates of 200 in four panes of 50

1984, May 24		Tagged	Perf. 11	
2089	A1474	20c brown	40	5
		P# block of 4	2.00	
		Zip block of 4	1.75	
		Copyright block of 4	1.75	

PERFORMING ARTS

John McCormack
(1884-1945),
Operatic Tenor
A1475

Designed by Jim Sharpe (U.S.) and Ron Mercer (Ireland)
PHOTOGRAVURE
Plates of 200 in four panes of 50

1984, June 6		Tagged	Perf. 11	
2090	A1475	20c multi	40	5
		P# block of 4, 5#	2.00	—
		Zip block of 4	1.75	—
		Copyright block of 4	1.75	—

See Ireland, No. 594

25TH ANNIVERSARY OF ST. LAWRENCE SEAWAY

Aerial View of Seaway, Freighters
A1476
Designed by Ernst Barenscher (Canada)
Printed by American Bank Note Company
PHOTOGRAVURE
Plates of 200 in four panes of 50

1984, June 26		Tagged	Perf. 11	
2091	A1476	20c multi	40	5
		P# block of 4, 4#	2.00	—
		Zip block of 4	1.75	—
		Copyright block of 4	1.75	—

50TH ANNIVERSARY OF WATERFOWL PRESERVATION ACT

"Mallards Dropping In"
by Jay N. Darling
A1477
Design adapted from Darling's work (#RW1)
by Donald M. McDowell
ENGRAVED
Plates of 200 in four panes of 50

1984, July 2		Tagged	Perf. 11	
2092	A1477	20c multi	40	5
		P# block of 4	2.00	—
		Zip block of 4	1.75	—
		Copyright block of 4	1.75	—
		a. Horiz. pair, imperf. vert.		—

The Elizabeth
A1478

A1479

ROANOKE VOYAGES
Designed by Charles Lundgren
Printed by American Bank Note Company
PHOTOGRAVURE
Plates of 200 in four panes of 50

1984, July 13		Tagged	Perf. 11	
2093	A1478	20c multi	40	5
		P# block of 4, 5#	2.00	—
		Zip block of 4	1.75	—
		Copyright block of 4	1.75	—

HERMAN MELVILLE (1819-1891), AUTHOR
Designed by Bradbury Thompson
ENGRAVED
Plates of 200 in four panes of 50

1984, Aug. 1		Tagged	Perf. 11	
2094	A1479	20c sage green	40	5
		P# block of 4	2.00	—
		Zip block of 4	1.75	—
		Copyright block of 4	1.75	—

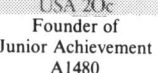

Founder of
Junior Achievement
A1480

Smokey the Bear
A1481

HORACE MOSES (1862-1947)
Designed by Dennis Lyall
PHOTOGRAVURE AND ENGRAVED
Plates of 200 in panes of 50

1984, Aug. 6		Tagged	Perf. 11	
2095	A1480	20c orange & dark brown	40	5
		P# block of 20, 1-2#, 1-2 copyright, 1-2 zip	8.50	—

SMOKEY THE BEAR
Designed by Rudolph Wendelin
LITHOGRAPHED AND ENGRAVED
Plates of 200 in panes of 50

1984, Aug. 13		Tagged	Perf. 11	
2096	A1481	20c multi	40	5
		P# block of 4, 5#	2.00	—
		Zip block of 4	1.75	—
		Copyright block of 4	1.75	—
		a. Horiz. pair, imperf. btwn.		—
		b. Vert. pair, imperf. btwn.		—
		c. Block of 4, imperf. btwn. vert. and horiz.		—

ROBERTO CLEMENTE (1934-1972)

Clemente Wearing
Pittsburgh Pirates Cap,
Puerto Rican Flag
A1482

Designed by Juan Lopez-Bonilla
PHOTOGRAVURE
Plates of 200 in panes of 50

1984, Aug. 17	Tagged	Perf. 11	
2097 A1482	20c multi	40	5
	P# block of 4, 6#	2.00	—
	Zip block of 4	1.75	—
	Copyright block of 4	1.75	—
	a. Horiz. pair, imperf. vert.	—	

DOGS

Beagle and Boston Terrier
A1483

Chesapeake Bay Retriever
and Cocker Spaniel
A1484

Alaskan Malamute
and Collie
A1485

Black and Tan Coonhound
and American Foxhound
A1486

Designed by Roy Andersen
PHOTOGRAVURE
Plates of 160 in panes of 40

1984, Sept. 7		Tagged	Perf. 11	
2098	A1483	20c multi	40	8
2099	A1484	20c multi	40	8
2100	A1485	20c multi	40	8
2101	A1486	20c multi	40	8
		P# block of 4, 4#	2.00	—
		Zip block of 4	1.75	—
		Copyright block of 4	1.75	—
		a. Block of 4, #2098-2101	1.60	85

CRIME PREVENTION

McGruff, the Crime Dog
A1487
Designed by Randall McDougall
Printed by American Bank Note Company
PHOTOGRAVURE
Plates of 200 in panes of 50

1984, Sept. 26	Tagged	Perf. 11	
2102 A1487	20c multi	40	5
	P# block of 4, 4#	2.00	—
	Zip block of 4	1.75	—
	Copyright block of 4	1.75	—

HISPANIC AMERICANS

A1488
Designed by Robert McCall
PHOTOGRAVURE
Plates of 160 in four panes of 40

1984, Oct. 31	Tagged	Perf. 11	
2103 A1488	20c multi	40	5
	P# block of 4, 5 #	2.00	—
	Zip block of 4	1.75	—
	Copyright block of 4	1.75	—

FAMILY UNITY

Stick Figures
A1489

Designed by Molly LaRue
PHOTOGRAVURE AND ENGRAVED
Plates of 230 in panes of 50

1984, Oct. 1	Tagged	Perf. 11	
2104 A1489	20c multi	40	5
	P# block of 20, 3-6#,		
	1-2 copyright, 1-2 zip	8.50	—

ELEANOR ROOSEVELT (1884-1962)

A1490

Designed by Bradbury Thompson
ENGRAVED
Plates of 192 in panes of 48

1984, Oct. 11			Tagged	Perf. 11	
2105	A1490	20c	dp bl	40	5
			P# block of 4	2.00	—
			Zip block of 4	1.75	—
			Copyright block of 4	1.75	—

NATION OF READERS

Abraham Lincoln Reading to Son, Tad
A1491

Designed adapted from Matthew Brady
daguerrotype by Bradbury Thompson
ENGRAVED
Plates of 200 in panes of 50

1984, Oct. 16			Tagged	Perf. 11	
2106	A1491	20c	brown & maroon	40	5
			P# block of 4	2.00	—
			Zip block of 4	1.75	—
			Copyright block of 4	1.75	—

CHRISTMAS

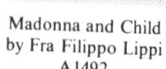

Madonna and Child
by Fra Filippo Lippi
A1492

Santa Claus
A1493

Designed by Bradbury Thompson (#2107) and
Danny La Boccetta (#2108)
PHOTOGRAVURE
Plates of 200 in panes of 50

1984, Oct. 30			Tagged	Perf. 11	
2107	A1492	20c	multi	40	5
			P# block of 4, 5 #	2.00	—
			Zip block of 4	1.75	—
			Copyright block of 4	1.75	—
2108	A1493	20c	multi	40	5
			P# block of 4, 5 #	2.00	—
			Zip block of 4	1.75	—
			Copyright block of 4	1.75	—

VIETNAM VETERANS' MEMORIAL

Memorial and Visitors
A1494

Designed by Paul Calle
ENGRAVED
Plates of 160 in panes of 40

1984, Nov. 10			Tagged	Perf. 10½	
2109	A1494	20c	multi	40	5
			P# block of 4	2.00	—
			Zip block of 4	1.75	—
			Copyright block of 4	1.75	—

PERFORMING ARTS

Jerome Kern (1885-1945), Composer
A1495

Designed by Jim Sharpe
Printed by the American Bank Note Company
PHOTOGRAVURE
Plates of 200 in four panes of 50

1985, Jan. 23			Tagged	Perf. 11	
2110	A1495	22c	multi	44	5
			P# block of 4, 5 #	2.20	—
			Zip block of 4	2.00	—
			Copyright block of 4	2.00	—

POSTAGE

A1496 A1497
Designed by Bradbury Thompson
PHOTOGRAVURE
Plates of 460 (20 x 23) in panes of 100

1985, Feb. 1   Tagged   *Perf. 11*

2111	A1496 (22c)	green	44	5
		P# block of 20, 1-2 #, 1-2 Zip, 1-2 Copyright	9.25	—
		a. Vert. pair, imperf.	—	

COIL STAMP
Perf. 10 Vert.

2112	A1496 (22c)	green	44	5
		Pair	88	10
		P# strip of 3, line. P# 1, 2	3.50	
		a. Imperf. pair	30.00	

BOOKLET STAMP
Perf. 11

2113	A1497 (22c)	green	44	5
		a. Booklet pane of 10	4.40	—

A1498 Flag Over Capital Dome A1499
Designed by Frank Waslick
ENGRAVED
Plates of 400 subjects in panes of 100

1985, Mar. 29   Tagged   *Perf. 11*

2114	A1498	22c blue, red & black	44	5
		P# block of 4	2.20	
		Zip block of 4	2.00	—
		Copyright block of 4	2.00	—

COIL STAMP
Perf. 10 Vert.

2115	A1498	22c blue, red & black	44	5
		Pair	88	10
		P# strip of 3, P# 1-8, 10, 11	3.00	
		a. Imperf. pair	20.00	

BOOKLET STAMP
Perf. 10 Horiz.

2116	A1499	22c blue, red & black	44	5
		a. Booklet pane of 5	2.20	

BOOKLET STAMPS

Frilled Dogwinkle   Reticulated Helmet
A1500   A1501

 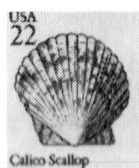

New England Neptune   Calico Scallop
A1502   A1503

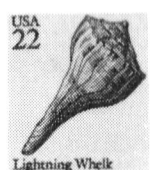

Lightning Whelk
A1504
Designed by Pete Cocci
ENGRAVED

1985, Apr. 4   Tagged   *Perf. 10*

2117	A1500	22c black & brown	44	5
2118	A1501	22c black & multi	44	5
2119	A1502	22c black & brown	44	5
2120	A1503	22c black & violet	44	5
2121	A1504	22c black & multi	44	5
		a. Booklet pane of 10	4.40	—

Eagle and Half Moon
A1505
Designed by Young & Rubicam
PHOTOGRAVURE

1985, Apr. 29   Tagged   *Perf. 10 Vert.*

2122	A1505	$10.75 multi	22.00	—
		a. Booklet pane of 3	67.50	—

TRANSPORTATION ISSUE

2129	A1512	10.1c **slate blue,** *Apr. 18*		22	5
		Pair		44	10
		P# strip of 3, P# 1		3.50	
		a. Untagged (Bureau precancel)			22
		P# strip of 3, P# 1			4.50
2130	A1513	11c **dark green,** *June 11*		22	5
		Pair		44	10
		P# strip of 3, line, P# 1-4		2.50	
2131	A1514	12c **dark blue,** *Apr. 2*		24	5
		Pair		48	10
		P# strip of 3, line, P# 1, 2		2.50	
		a. Untagged (Bureau precancel)			24
		P# strip of 3, line, P# 1, 2			3.50
2132	A1515	12.5c **olive green,** *Apr. 18*		25	5
		Pair		50	10
		P# strip of 3, P# 1		3.00	
		a. Untagged (Bureau precancel)			25
		P# strip of 3, P# 1			4.50
		b. As "a" imperf. pair			100.00
2134	A1517	14c **sky blue,** *Mar. 23*		28	5
		Pair		58	10
		P# strip of 3, line, P# 1-4		1.50	
		a. Imperf. pair		50.00	
2135	A1518	17c Dog sled, *Aug. 20, 1986*		34	5
		Pair		68	10

This is an expanding set. Numbers will change if necessary.

Designers: 3.4c, Lou Nolan. 4.9c, 14c, William H. Bond. 6c, 8.3c, 10.1c, 12.5c, James Schleyer. 11c, 12c, Ken Dallison.

COIL STAMPS
ENGRAVED

1985			Tagged	*Perf. 10 Vert.*	
2123	A1506	3.4c **dark bluish green,** *June 8*		8	5
		Pair		16	10
		P# strip of 3, line, P# 1, 2		1.25	
		a. Untagged (Bureau precancel)		20	20
		P# strip of 3, line, P# 1, 2			1.50
2125	A1508	4.9c **brown black,** *June 21*		10	5
		Pair		20	10
		P# strip of 3, line, P# 3, 4		1.25	
		a. Untagged (Bureau precancel)			10
		P# strip of 3, line, P# 1-6			2.00
2127	A1510	6c **red brown,** *May 6*		12	5
		Pair		24	10
		P# strip of 3, P# 1		1.50	
		a. Untagged (Bureau precancel)			12
		P# strip of 3, P# 1, 2			3.50
2128	A1511	8.3c **green,** *June 21*		16	5
		Pair		32	10
		P# strip of 3, line, P# 1, 2		3.00	
		a. Untagged (Bureau precancel)			16
		P# strip of 3, line, P# 1-4			3.50

BLACK HERITAGE

Mary McLeod Bethune (1875-1955), Educator — A1520
Designed by Jerry Pinkney from a photograph
Printed by American Bank Note Compnay
PHOTOGRAVURE
Plates of 200 in four panes of 50

1985, Mar. 5			Tagged	*Perf. 11*	
2137	A1520	22c **multi**		44	5
		P# block of 4, 6 #		2.20	—
		Zip block of 4		2.00	—
		Copyright block of 4		2.00	—

AMERICAN FOLK ART ISSUE
Duck Decoys

Broadbill A1521

Mallard A1522

Canvasback A1523

Redhead A1524

Designed by Stevan Dohanos
Printed by American Bank Note Company and
J.W. Fergusson & Sons
PHOTOGRAVURE
Plates of 200 in four panes of 50

1985, Mar. 22   Tagged   *Perf. 11*

2138	A1521	22c multi	44	8
2139	A1522	22c multi	44	8
2140	A1523	22c multi	44	8
2141	A1524	22c multi	44	8
		P# block of 4, 5 #	2.20	—
		Zip block of 4	2.00	—
		Copyright block of 4	2.00	—
		a. Block of 4, #2138-2141	1.80	1.00

WINTER SPECIAL OLYMPICS

Ice Skater, Emblem, Skier — A1525
Designed by Jeff Carnell
PHOTOGRAVURE
Plates of 160 in four panes of 40

1985, Mar. 25   Tagged   *Perf. 11*

2142	A1525	22c multi	44	5
		P# block of 4, 6 #	2.20	—
		Zip block of 4	2.00	—
		Copyright block of 4	2.00	—

LOVE

A1526
Designed by Corita Kent
PHOTOGRAVURE
Plates of 200 in four panes of 50

1985, Apr. 17   Tagged   *Perf. 11*

2143	A1526	22c multi	44	5
		P# block of 4, 6 #	2.20	—
		Zip block of 4	2.00	—
		Copyright block of 4	2.00	—

RURAL ELECTRIFICATION ADMINISTRATION

REA Power Lines, Farmland — A1527
Designed by Gary Slaght
PHOTOGRAVURE & ENGRAVED
Plates of 200 in four panes of 50

1985, May 11   Tagged   *Perf. 11*

2144	A1527	22c multi	44	5
		P# block of 20, 5-10 #, 1-2 Zip, 1-2 Copyright	9.25	—

AMERIPEX '86

U.S. No. 134 — A1528
Designed by Richard D. Sheaff
LITHOGRAPHED & ENGRAVED
Plates of 192 in four panes of 48

1985, May 25   Tagged   *Perf. 11*

2145	A1528	22c multi	44	5
		P# block of 4, 3 #	2.20	—
		Zip block of 4	2.00	—
		Copyright block of 4	2.00	—
		a. Red, black & blue omitted		

364 POSTAGE

Abigail Adams (1744-1818)
A1529
Designed by Bart Forbes
PHOTOGRAVURE
Plates of 200 in four panes of 50

1985, June 14			Tagged		Perf. 11
2146	A1529	22c	multi	44	5
			P# block of 4, 4 #	2.20	—
			Zip block of 4	2.00	—
			Copyright block of 4	2.00	—
		a.	Imperf. pair	—	

ARCHITECT, SCULPTOR

Frederic Auguste Bartholdi (1834-1904), Statue of Liberty
A1530
Designed by Howard Paine from paintings by
Jose Frappa and James Dean.
LITHOGRAPHED & ENGRAVED
Plates of 200 in four panes of 50

1985, July 18			Tagged		Perf. 11
2147	A1530	22c	multi	44	5
			P# block of 4, 5 #	2.20	—
			Zip block of 4	2.00	—
			Copyright block of 4	2.00	—

COIL STAMPS

George Washington, Washington Monument
A1532

Sealed Envelopes
A1533

Designed by Thomas Szumowski (#2149) based on a portrait by Gilbert Stuart, and Richard Sheaff (#2150).
PHOTOGRAVURE

1985					Perf. 10 Vertically
2149	A1532	18c	multi	36	8
			Pair	72	16
			P# strip of 3, P# 1112, 3333	2.50	
		a.	Untagged (Bureau Precancel)		36
			P# strip of 3, P# 11121, 33333		4.00
		b.	Imperf. pair	—	
		c.	As "a," imperf. pair		—
2150	A1533	21.1c	multi	45	8
			Pair	90	16
			P# strip of 3, P# 111111	3.50	
		a.	Untagged (Bureau Precancel)		45
			P# strip of 3, P# 111111, 111121		4.50

Issue dates: 18c, Nov. 6. 21.1c, Oct. 22.

KOREAN WAR VETERANS

American Troops Marching
A1535
Designed by Dick Sheaff from a photograph by
David D. Duncan
ENGRAVED
Plates of 200 in four panes of 50

1985, July 26			Tagged		Perf. 11
2152	A1535	22c	gray green & rose red	44	5
			P# block of 4	2.20	—
			Zip block of 4	2.00	—
			Copyright block of 4	2.00	—

SOCIAL SECURITY ACT, 50th ANNIV.

Men, Women, Children, Corinthian Columns
A1536
Designed by Robert Brangwynne
Printed by American Bank Note Company and
J.W. Fergusson & Sons
PHOTOGRAVURE
Plates of 200 in four panes of 50

1985, Aug. 14			Tagged		Perf. 11
2153	A1536	22c	deep & light blue	44	5
			P# block of 4, 2 #	2.20	—
			Zip block of 4	2.00	—
			Copyright block of 4	2.00	—

POSTAGE 365

WORLD WAR I VETERANS

The Battle of Marne, France
A1537
Designed by Dick Sheaff from Harvey Dunn's
charcoal drawing
ENGRAVED
Plates of 200 in four panes of 50

1985, Aug. 26			Tagged		Perf. 11	
2154	A1537	22c	gray green & rose red		44	5
			P# block of 4		2.20	—
			Zip block of 4		2.00	—
			Copyright block of 4		2.00	—

HORSES

Quarter Horse
A1538

Morgan
A1539

Saddlebred
A1540

Appaloosa
A1541

Designed by Roy Andersen
PHOTOGRAVURE
Plates of 160 in four panes of 40

1985, Sept. 25			Tagged		Perf. 11	
2155	A1538	22c	multi		44	8
2156	A1539	22c	multi		44	8
2157	A1540	22c	multi		44	8
2158	A1541	22c	multi		44	8
			P# block of 4, 5#		2.20	—
			Zip block of 4		2.00	—
			Copyright block of 4		2.00	—
		a.	Block of 4, #2155-2158		1.80	1.00

PUBLIC EDUCATION IN AMERICA

Quill Pen, Apple, Spectacles, Penmanship Quiz
A1542
Designed by Uldis Purins
Printed by American Bank Note Company and
J.W. Fergusson & Sons
PHOTOGRAVURE
Plates of 200 in four panes of 50

1985, Oct. 1			Tagged		Perf. 11	
2159	A1542	22c	multi		44	5
			P# block of 4, 5 #		2.20	—
			Zip block of 4		2.00	—
			Copyright block of 4		2.00	—

INTERNATIONAL YOUTH YEAR

YMCA Youth
Camping, Cent.
A1543   YMCA Youth Camping

Boy Scouts,
75th Anniv.
A1544

Big Brothers/Big Sisters
Federation, 40th Anniv.
A1545

Camp Fire Inc.,
75th Anniv.
A1546

POSTAGE
366

Designed by Dennis Luzak
Printed by American Bank Note Company and
J.W. Fergusson & Sons
PHOTOGRAVURE
Plates of 200 in four panes of 50

1985, Oct. 7   Tagged   Perf. 11

2160	A1543	22c multi		44	8
2161	A1544	22c multi		44	8
2162	A1545	22c multi		44	8
2163	A1546	22c multi		44	8
		P# block of 4, 5 #	2.20	—
		Zip block of 4	2.00	—
		Copyright block of 4	2.00	—
		a. Block of 4, #2160-2163	1.80	1.00

HELP END HUNGER

Youths and Elderly Suffering from
Malnutrition — A1547
Designed by Jerry Pinkney
Printed by the American Bank Note Company
PHOTOGRAVURE
Plates of 200 in four panes of 50

1985, Oct. 16   Tagged   Perf. 11

2164	A1547	22c multi	44	5
		P# block of 4, 5 #	2.20	—
		Zip block of 4	2.00	—
		Copyright block of 4	2.00	—

CHRISTMAS 1985

Genoa Madonna, Enameled   Poinsettia Plants
Terra-Cotta   A1549
by Luca Della Robbia
(1400-1482) — A1548

Designed by Bradbury Thompson (#2165) and
James Dean (#2166)
PHOTOGRAVURE
Plates of 200 in panes of 50

1985, Oct. 31   Tagged   Perf. 11

2165	A1548	22c multi	44	5
		P# block of 4, 4 #	2.20	—
		Zip block of 4	2.00	—
		Copyright block of 4	2.00	—
		a. Imperf. pair	—	

2166	A1549	22c multi	44	5
		P# block of 4, 5 #	2.20	—
		Zip block of 4	2.00	—
		Copyright block of 4	2.00	—
		a. Imperf. pair	—	

ARKANSAS
STATEHOOD SESQUICENTENNARY

Old State House, Little Rock
A1550
Designed by Gideon Shyrock
Printed by the American Bank Note Company and J.W.
Fergusson & Sons
PHOTOGRAVURE
Plates of 200 in four panes of 50

1986, Jan. 3   Tagged   Perf. 11

2167	A1550	22c multi		44	5
		P# block of 4, 6#	2.25	—
		Zip block of 4	2.00	—
		Copyright block of 4	2.00	—

GREAT AMERICANS ISSUE

 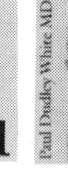  
A1551   A1553   A1554

A1555   A1562   A1566

A1574   A1577   A1578

Designers: 1c, Ron Adair. 3c, 4c, 5c, 17c, Christopher Calle. 25c,
Richard Sparks. 56c, Robert Anderson. $1, $2, Tom Broad.
ENGRAVED
Perf. 11

1986   Tagged

2168	A1551	1c	brnh verm, *June 30*	5	5
			P# block of 4	20	—
			Zip block of 4	18	—
			Copyright block of 4	18	—
2170	A1553	3c	*Sept. 15*	6	5
			P# block of 4	30	—
			Zip block of 4	28	—
			Copyright block of 4	28	—
2171	A1554	4c	bl vio, *July 14*	8	5
			P# block of 4	40	—
			Zip block of 4	35	—
			Copyright block of 4	35	—
2172	A1555	5c	dk ol grn, *Feb. 27*	10	5
			P# block of 4	50	—
			Zip block of 4	45	—
			Copyright block of 4	45	—

POSTAGE

2179	A1562	17c	dl bl grn, *June 18*	34	5	
			P# block of 4	1.75	—	
			Zip block of 4	1.60	—	
			Copyright block of 4	1.60	—	
2183	A1566	25c	bl, *Jan. 11*	50	6	
			P# block of 4	2.50	—	
			Zip block of 4	2.25	—	
			Copyright block of 4	2.25	—	
2191	A1574	56c	*Sept. 3*	1.10	8	
			P# block of 4	5.50	—	
			Zip block of 4	5.00	—	
			Copyright block of 4	5.00	—	
2194	A1577	$1	*Sept. 23*	2.00	25	
			P# block of 4	10.00	—	
			Zip block of 4	9.00	—	
			Copyright block of 4	9.00	—	
2195	A1578	$2	brt vio, *Mar. 19*	4.00	50	
			P# block of 4	20.00	—	
			Zip block of 4	18.00	—	
			Copyright block of 4	18.00	—	

Boy Examining Stamp Collection
A1582

No. 836 Under Magnifying Glass, Sweden Nos. 268, 271
A1583

1986 Presidents Miniature Sheet
A1584
Designed by Richard Sheaff and Eva Jern (#2200)

BOOKLET STAMPS
LITHOGRAPHED & ENGRAVED

1986, Jan. 23   Tagged   Perf. 10 Vert. on 1 or 2 Sides

2198	A1581	22c	multi	44	5
2199	A1582	22c	multi	44	5
2200	A1583	22c	multi	44	5
2201	A1584	22c	multi	44	5
		a. Bklt. pane of 4, #2198-2201		1.80	—
		b. As "a," black omitted on Nos. 2198, 2201		50.00	

UNITED STATES—SWEDEN
STAMP COLLECTING

Handstamped Cover, Philatelic Memorabilia
A1581

LOVE ISSUE

A1585

Designed by
Saul Mandel
Plates of 200
in four panes of 50

PHOTOGRAVURE

1986, Jan. 30   Tagged   *Perf. 11*
2202 A1585 22c **multi**   44   5
              P# block of 4, 5#   2.25   —
              Zip block of 4   2.00   —
              Copyright block of 4 2.00   —

BLACK HERITAGE ISSUE

Sojourner Truth
(c. 1797-1883),
Human Rights Activist
A1586

Designed by
Jerry Pinkney
Plates of 200
in four panes of 50

PHOTOGRAVURE

1986, Feb. 4   Tagged   *Perf. 11*
2203 A1586 22c **multi**   44   5
              P# block of 4, 6#   2.25   —
              Zip block of 4   2.00   —
              Copyright block of 4 2.00   —

REPUBLIC OF TEXAS, 150th Anniv.

Texas State Flag and Silver Spur
A1587
Designed by Don Adair
Printed by the American Bank Note Co.
and J.W. Fergusson & Sons

PHOTOGRAVURE
Plates of 200 in four panes of 50

1986, Mar. 2   Tagged   *Perf. 11*
2204 A1587 22c **dark blue, dark red & grayh black**   44   5
              P# block of 4, 3 #   2.20   —
              Zip block of 4   2.00   —
              Copyright block of 4 2.00   —

FISH

Muskellunge—A1588

Atlantic Cod—A1589

Largemouth Bass—A1590

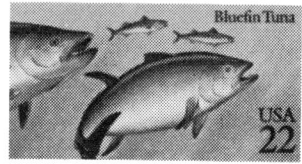

Bluefin Tuna—A1591

Catfish—A1592
Designed by Chuck Ripper

BOOKLET STAMPS
PHOTOGRAVURE

1986, Mar. 21   Tagged   *Perf. 10 Horiz.*
2205 A1588 22c **multi**   44   5
2206 A1589 22c **multi**   44   5
2207 *A1590* 22c **multi**   44   5
2208 A1591 22c **multi**   44   5
2209 A1592 22c **multi**   44   5
         a. Bklt. pane of 5, #2205-2209   2.25   —

POSTAGE

PUBLIC HOSPITALS

A1593
Designed by Uldris Purins
Printed by the American Bank Note Co. and J.W. Fergusson & Sons
PHOTOGRAVURE
Plates of 200 in four panes of 50

1986, Apr. 11		Tagged	Perf. 11	
2210	A1593	22c multi	44	5
		P# block of 4, 5#	2.20	—
		Zip block of 4	2.00	—
		Copyright block of 4	2.00	—

PERFORMING ARTS

Edward Kennedy "Duke" Ellington (1899-1974), Jazz Composer
A1594
Designed by Jim Sharpe
Printed by the American Bank Note Co. and J.W. Fergusson & Sons
PHOTOGRAVURE
Plates of 200 in four panes of 50

1986, Apr. 29		Tagged	Perf. 11	
2211	A1594	22c multi	44	5
		P# block of 4, 6#	2.20	—
		Zip block of 4	2.00	—
		Copyright block of 4	2.00	—
	a.	Vert. pair, imperf. horiz.		

AMERIPEX '86 ISSUE
Miniature Sheets

AMERIPEX 86
International
Stamp Show
Chicago, Illinois
May 22-June 1, 1986

35 Presidents—A1599a

AMERIPEX 86
International
Stamp Show
Chicago, Illinois
May 22-June 1, 1986

A1599b

A1599c

A1599 d

Designs: No. 2216a, George Washington. No. 2216b, John Adams. No. 2216c, Thomas Jefferson. No. 2216d, James Madison. No. 2216e, James Monroe. No. 2216f, John Quincy Adams. No. 2216g, Andrew Jackson. No. 2216h, Martin Van Buren. No. 2216i, William H. Harrison. No. 2217a, John Tyler. No. 2217b, James Knox Polk. No. 2217c, Zachary Taylor. No. 2217d, Millard Fillmore. No. 2217e, Franklin Pierce. No. 2217f, James Buchanon. No. 2217g, Abraham Lincoln. No. 2217h, Andrew Johnson. No. 2217i, Ulysses S. Grant. No. 2218a, Rutherford B. Hayes. No. 2218b, James A. Garfield. No. 2218c, Chester A. Arthur. No. 2218d, Grover Cleveland. No. 2218e, Benjamin Harrison. No. 2218f, William McKinley. No. 2218g, Theodore Roosevelt. No. 2218h, William H. Taft. No. 2218i, Woodrow Wilson. No. 2219a, Warren G. Harding. No. 2219b, Calvin Coolidge. No. 2219c, Herbert Hoover. No. 2219d, Franklin Delano Roosevelt. No. 2219e, White House. No. 2219f, Harry S. Truman. No. 2219g, Dwight D. Eisenhower. No. 2219h, John F. Kennedy. No. 2219i, Lyndon B. Johnson.

Designed by Jerry Dadds
LITHOGRAPHED & ENGRAVED
1986, May 22   Tagged   Perf. 11

2216	A1599a	Sheet of 9	4.00	—
		a.-i. 22c, any single	44	20
2217	A1599b	Sheet of 9	4.00	—
		a.-i. 22c, any single	44	20
2218	A1599c	Sheet of 9	4.00	—
		a.-i. 22c, any single	44	20
2219	A1599d	Sheet of 9	4.00	—
		a.-i. 22c, any single	44	20

Issued in conjunction with AMERIPEX '86 Intl. Philatelic Exhibition, Chicago, IL May 22-June 1. Sheet size: 120x207mm.

Elisha Kent Kane
A1600

Adolphus W. Greely
A1601

Vilhjalmur Stefansson
A1602

POSTAGE

Robert E. Peary, Matthew Henson
A1603

Designed by Dennis Lyall
Printed by the American Bank Note Company and J.W. Ferguson & Sons
PHOTOGRAVURE
Plates of 200 in four panes of 50

1986, May 28		Tagged		Perf. 11	
2220	A1600	22c multi		44	8
2221	A1601	22c multi		44	8
2222	A1602	22c multi		44	8
2223	A1603	22c multi		44	8
		P# block of 4, 5#		2.20	—
		Zip block of 4		2.00	—
		Copyright block of 4		2.00	—
	a.	Block of 4, #2220-2223		1.80	1.00

NAVAJO ART

A1605 A1606

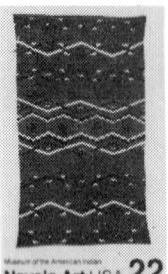 

A1607 A1608

Designed by Derry Noyes
LITHOGRAPHED & ENGRAVED
Plates of 200 in four panes of 50

1986, Sept. 4		Tagged		Perf. 11	
2235	A1605	22c multi		44	8
2236	A1606	22c multi		44	8
2237	A1607	22c multi		44	8
2238	A1608	22c multi		44	8
		P# block of 4, 5#		2.20	—
		Zip block of 4		2.00	—
		Copyright block of 4		2.00	—
	a.	Block of 4, #2235-2238		1.80	1.00

STATUE OF LIBERTY, CENT.

A1604

Designed by Howard Paine
ENGRAVED
Plates of 200 in four panes of 50

1986, July 4		Tagged		Perf. 11	
2224	A1604	22c scar & dk bl		44	5
		P# block of 4, 2#		2.20	—
		Zip block of 4		2.00	—
		Copyright block of 4		2.00	—

TRANSPORTATION ISSUE

Reduced Size

COIL STAMPS
ENGRAVED

1986		Tagged		Perf. 10 Vert.	
2228	A1285	4c reddish brown, 1986		8	5
		Pair		16	10

On No. 2228 "Stagecoach 1890s" is 17mm long, on No. 1898A, 19½mm long.

This is an expanding set. Numbers will change if necessary.

LITERARY ARTS

T.S. Eliot (1888-1965), Poet
A1609

Designed by Bradbury Thompson
ENGRAVED
Plates of 200 in four panes of 50

1986, Sept. 26		Tagged			
2239	A1609	22c		44	5
		P# block of 4		2.20	—
		Zip block of 4		2.00	—
		Copyright block of 4		2.00	—

AMERICAN FOLK ART ISSUE
Woodcarved Figurines

A1610   A1611

A1612   A1613

Designed by Bradbury Thompson
Printed by the American Bank Note Company and J.W. Ferguson & Sons

PHOTOGRAVURE
Plates of 200 in four panes of 50

1986, Oct. 1   Tagged

2240	A1610	22c	multi	44	8
2241	A1611	22c	multi	44	8
2242	A1612	22c	multi	44	8
2243	A1613	22c	multi	44	8
			P# block of 4, 5#	2.20	—
			Zip block of 4	2.00	—
			Copyright block of 4	2.00	—
		a.	Block of 4, #2240-2243	1.80	1.00

CHRISTMAS 1986

Madonna, National Gallery,   Village Scene
by Perugino (c. 1450-1513)

A1614   A1615

Designed by Dolli Tingle (#2244)
and Bradbury Thompson (#2245)

PHOTOGRAVURE
Plates of 200 in four panes of 50

1986, Oct. 24   Tagged   *Perf.*

2244	A1614	22c	multi	44	5
			P# block of 4, 6#	2.20	—
			Zip block of 4	2.00	—
			Copyright block of 4	2.00	—
2245	A1615	22c	multi	44	5
			P# block of 4, 5#	2.20	—
			Zip block of 4	2.00	—
			Copyright block of 4	2.00	—

EVEN IF YOUR COLLECTION DOESN'T HAVE AN INVERTED JENNY

★AMERICANA★ WILL BUY IT!

★ **TOP CASH PRICES PAID!** ★

- ★ We Buy All U.S. STAMPS 1847-1938, etc.
- ★ We Buy All U.S. ERRORS - Old or New...All Kinds
- ★ We Buy All BRITISH, WESTERN EUROPE, JAPAN, ISRAEL, All WORLDWIDE.
- ★ We Buy All Singles, Plate Blocks, Sheets, Covers, Proofs, Essays, BOB, Ducks, Possessions, etc.
- ★ We Buy All Lots, Collections, Accumulations, Estates, etc.
- ★ All 19th & 20th Century, Mint or Used; all Grades!
- ★ No Lot Too Small or Too Large!
- ★ $200. to $200,000. - SHIP TODAY for FASTEST OFFER!
- ★ Nice Graf Zepps C13-15, NH, Paying $1700-$2500/up!
- ★ SHIP INSURED OR REGISTERED FOR PROMPT CASH OFFER
- ★ OR SHIP FOR FAST AUCTION DISPOSAL (Consignments Welcome).

Public Stamp AUCTIONS & Mail Bid SALES
Ask For FREE ILLUSTRATED CATALOG
U.S., BRITISH, W. EUROPE, WORLDWIDE

Visit Our Tarzana Store! | **AMERICANA** | Your Want List is Welcome!

STAMP & COIN CO., INC.
JAY TELL, President
18385-SP Ventura Blvd. (in Tarzana Square)
TARZANA, CALIF. 91356
"Buying and Selling Since 1958"

Telephone 818-705-1100

AIR POST STAMPS

Air mail in the U. S. Post Office system developed in three stages: pioneer period (with many unofficial or semi-official flights before 1918), government flights and contract air mail (C.A.M.). Contract air mail began on Feb. 15, 1926. All C.A.M. contracts were canceled on Feb. 19, 1934, and air mail was carried by Army planes for six months. After that the contract plan was resumed.

No. C3 first used on airplane mail service between Washington, Philadelphia and New York, on May 15, 1918, but was valid for ordinary postage. The rate of postage was 24 cents per ounce, which included immediate individual delivery.

Rate of postage was reduced to 16 cents for the first ounce and 6 cents for each additional ounce, which included 10 cents for immediate individual delivery, on July 15, 1918, by Postmaster General's order of June 26, 1918. No. C2 was first used for air mail in the tri-city service on July 15.

Rate of postage was reduced on December 15, 1918, by Postmaster General's order of November 30, 1918, to 6 cents per ounce. No. C1 was first used for air mail (same three-way service) on Dec. 16.

Nos. C4 to C6 were issued primarily for use in the new night-flying air mail service between New York and San Francisco, but valid for all purposes. Three zones were established; the first from New York to Chicago, the second from Chicago to Cheyenne, and the third from Cheyenne to San Francisco, and the rate of postage was 8 cents an ounce for each zone. Service was inaugurated on July 1, 1924.

These stamps were placed on sale at the Philatelic Agency at Washington on the dates indicated in the listings but were not issued to postmasters at that time.

Curtiss Jenny
AP1
FLAT PLATE PRINTINGS
Engraved

Plates of 100 subjects.

Airplane Radiator and
Wooden Propeller
AP2

Air Service Emblem
AP3

DeHavilland Biplane
AP4

Plates of 400 subjects in four panes of 100 each.

1918			Perf. 11	Unwmkd.	
C1	AP1	6c	orange, Dec. 10	120.00	45.00
			pale orange	120.00	45.00
			On cover		65.00
			First flight cover, Dec. 16		2,750.
			Margin block of 4, arrow top or left	500.00	195.00
			Center line block	550.00	210.00
			Margin block of 6, arrow & P#	1,200.	500.00
			Double transfer (#9155-14)	175.00	65.00
C2	AP1	16c	green, July 11	160.00	52.50
			dark green	160.00	52.50
			On cover		70.00
			First flight cover, July 15		800.00
			Margin block of 4, arrow top or left	675.00	230.00
			Center line block	725.00	250.00
			Margin block of 6, arrow & P#	2,250.	700.00
C3	AP1	24c	carmine rose & blue, May 13	160.00	65.00
			dark carmine rose & blue	160.00	65.00
			On cover		80.00
			First flight cover, May 15		750.00
			Margin block of 4, arrow top or left	675.00	285.00
			Margin block of 4, arrow bottom	700.00	300.00
			Margin block of 4, arrow right	775.00	350.00
			Center line block	750.00	325.00
			Margin block of 4, red P# only	775.00	375.00
			Margin block of 12, two P#, arrow & two "TOP"	2,600.	1,200.
			Margin block of 12, two P#, arrow & blue "TOP" only	10,000.	
		a.	Center inverted	115,000.	
		a.	Same, in block of four	475,000.	
		a.	Same, center line block	525,000.	
		a.	Same, margin block of 4, blue P#	525,000.	

1923			Perf. 11	Unwmkd.	
C4	AP2	8c	dark green, Aug. 15	45.00	20.00
			deep green	45.00	20.00
			On cover		35.00
			Margin block of 6, P#	600.00	300.00
			Double transfer	75.00	35.00
C5	AP3	16c	dark blue, Aug. 17	160.00	50.00
			On cover		65.00
			Margin block of 6, P#	3,250.	650.00
			Double transfer	200.00	70.00
C6	AP4	24c	carmine, Aug. 21	200.00	40.00
			On cover		55.00
			Margin block of 6, P#	4,250.	850.00
			Double transfer (Pl. 14841)	250.00	55.00

Map of United States and Two Mail Planes—AP5

The Act of Congress of February 2, 1925, created a rate of 10 cents per ounce for distances to 1000 miles, 15 cents per ounce for 1500 miles and 20 cents for more than 1500 miles on contract air mail routes.

AIR POST STAMPS

Plates of 200 subjects in four panes of 50 each.

1926–27			Perf. 11		Unwmkd.
C7	AP5	10c	**dark blue,** *Feb. 13, 1926*	4.50	50
			light blue	4.50	50
			Margin block of 6, P#	55.00	20.00
			Double transfer (11 UL 18246)	10.00	2.00
C8	AP5	15c	**olive brown,** *Sept. 18, 1926*	5.50	2.75
			light brown	5.50	2.75
			Margin block of 6, P#	65.00	25.00
C9	AP5	20c	**yellow green,** *Jan. 25, 1927*	16.00	2.25
			green	16.00	2.25
			Margin block of 6, P#	165.00	40.00

Lindbergh's Plane "Spirit of St. Louis" and Flight Route
AP6

A tribute to Col. Charles A. Lindbergh, who made the first non-stop (and solo) flight from New York to Paris, May 20-21, 1927.

Plates of 200 subjects in four panes of 50 each.

1927			Perf. 11		Unwmkd.
C10	AP6	10c	**dark blue,** *June 18*	13.00	3.00
			Margin block of 6, P#	200.00	35.00
		a.	Bklt. pane of 3, *May 26, 1928*	100.00	60.00
			Double transfer	20.00	5.00

First day covers of No. C10a and other airmail booklet panes are listed in the Booklet Panes section of this catalogue.

Beacon on Rocky Mountains
AP7

Issued to meet the new rate, effective August 1, of 5 cents per ounce.

Plates of 100 subjects in two panes of 50 each.

1928			Perf. 11.		Unwmkd.
C11	AP7	5c	**carmine and blue,** *July 25*	6.00	65
			On cover, first day of 5c airmail rate, *Aug. 1*		3.00
			Margin block of 4, arrow, (line) right or left	30.00	3.00
			Margin block of 8, two P# only	250.00	25.00
			Margin block of 6, two P# & red "TOP"	65.00	10.00
			Margin block of 6, two P# & blue "TOP"	65.00	10.00
			Margin block of 6, two P# & double "TOP"	150.00	15.00
		a.	Vert. pair, imperf. btwn.	*5,500.*	
			Recut frame line at left	12.00	1.50
			Double transfer	—	—

Winged Globe—AP8

Plates of 200 subjects in tour panes of 50 each.

1930			Perf. 11		Unwmkd.

Stamp design 46½x19mm.

C12	AP8	5c	**violet,** *Feb. 10*	17.50	45
			Margin block of 6, P#	250.00	40.00
		a.	Horiz. pair, imperf. btwn.	*4,500.*	
			Double transfer (Pl. 20189)	27.50	1.75

See Nos. C16-C17, C19.

GRAF ZEPPELIN ISSUE

Zeppelin Over Atlantic Ocean
AP9

Zeppelin Between Continents
AP10

Zeppelin Passing Globe
AP11

Issued for use on mail carried on the first Europe-Pan-America round trip flight of the Graf Zeppelin in May, 1930. They were withdrawn from sale June 30, 1930.

Plates of 200 subjects in four panes of 50 each.

1930, Apr. 19			Perf. 11		Unwmkd.
C13	AP9	65c	**green**	350.00	275.00
			On cover or card		325.00
			Block of four	1,500.	1,300.
			Margin block of 6, P#	3,250.	2,500.
C14	AP10	$1.30	**brown**	800.00	550.00
			On cover		600.00
			Block of four	3,300.	2,300.
			Margin block of 6, P#	6,750.	4,750.
C15	AP11	$2.60	**blue**	1,300.	800.00
			On cover		850.00
			Block of four	5,300.	3,350.
			Margin block of 6, P#	11,000.	7,000.

WE BUY

UNITED STATES
BRITISH COMMONWEALTH
AND
GENERAL FOREIGN

STAMPS

We specialize in buying and effectively marketing entire philatelic properties, not just a select few items. If you have ANY worthwhile collection, accumulation, dealer's stock or estate holding you wish to sell, please call toll free:

1-800-221-7966
(CALIFORNIA RESIDENTS CALL 1-800-831-7698)

If you are actively collecting or accumulating stamps, we offer approximately sixty nationally advertised sales each year. Additionally, our direct mail offerings provide a comprehensive source of virtually every phase of philately. Write today for a free copy of our price list.

 Dealers in Rare Stamps and Coins Since 1938

Pacific Stamp & Coin Sales, Inc.

8353 La Mesa Blvd.   La Mesa, California 92041-9990
Telephone: (619) 463-5707

ROTARY PRESS PRINTING

Plates of 200 subjects in four panes of 50 each.

1931-32 Perf. 10½x11 Unwmkd.

Stamp design 47½x19mm.

C16	AP8	5c **violet,** *Aug. 19, 1931*	10.00	50
		Block of four	40.00	2.75
		Margin block of 4, P#	135.00	25.00

Issued to conform with new air mail rate of 8 cents per ounce which became effective July 6, 1932.

C17	AP8	8c **olive bister,** *Sept. 26, 1932*	4.00	30
		Block of four	16.00	1.65
		Margin block of 4, P#	45.00	5.00

CENTURY OF PROGRESS ISSUE

"Graf Zeppelin," Federal Building at Chicago Exposition and Hangar at Friedrichshafen
AP12

Issued in connection with the flight of the airship "Graf Zeppelin" in October, 1933, to Miami, Akron and Chicago and from the last city to Europe.

FLAT PLATE PRINTING

Plates of 200 subjects in four panes of 50 each.

1933 Perf. 11 Unwmkd.

C18	AP12	50c **green,** *Oct. 2*	110.00	95.00
		On cover		110.00
		Block of four	450.00	400.00
		Margin block of 6, P#	1,100.	700.00

Type of 1930 Issue.
ROTARY PRESS PRINTING.

Issued to conform with new air mail rate of 6 cents per ounce which became effective July 1, 1934.

Plates of 200 subjects in four panes of 50 each.

1934 Perf. 10½x11 Unwmkd.

C19	AP8	6c **dull orange,** *June 30*	4.25	12
		On cover, first day of 6c airmail rate, *July 1*		10.00
		Block of four	18.00	70
		Margin block of 4, P#	27.50	
		Pair with full vert. gutter btwn.	425.00	

TRANSPACIFIC ISSUES

"China Clipper" over Pacific
AP13

Issued to pay postage on mail transported by the Transpacific air mail service, inaugurated Nov. 22, 1935.

FLAT PLATE PRINTING

Plates of 200 subjects in four panes of 50 each.

1935 Perf. 11 Unwmkd.

C20	AP13	25c **blue,** *Nov. 22*	1.50	1.25
		Margin block of 6, P#	25.00	

"China Clipper" over Pacific
AP14

Issued primarily for use on the Transpacific service to China, but valid for all air mail purposes.

FLAT PLATE PRINTING

Plates of 200 subjects in four panes of 50 each.

1937 Perf. 11. Unwmkd

C21	AP14	20c **green,** *Feb. 15*	15.00	2.25
		dark green	15.00	2.25
		Block of four	60.00	12.50
		Margin block of 6, P#	150.00	
C22	AP14	50c **carmine,** *Feb. 15*	14.00	6.50
		Block of four	56.00	27.50
		Margin block of 6, P#	140.00	

Eagle Holding Shield, Olive Branch and Arrows
AP15

FLAT PLATE PRINTING

Frame plates of 100 subjects in two panes of 50 each separated by a 1½-inch wide vertical gutter with central guide line, and vignette plates of 50 subjects. Some plates were made of iron, then chromed; several of these carry an additional imprint, "E.I." (Electrolytic Iron).

Issued in panes of 50 each.

1938 Perf. 11. Unwmkd.

C23	AP15	6c **dark blue & carmine,** *May 14*	50	6
		Margin block of 4, bottom or side arrow	2.25	55
		Margin block of 4, 2 P#	11.00	
		Center line block	2.75	95
		Top margin block of 10, with two P#, arrow, two "TOP" and two registration markers	17.50	
	a.	Vert. pair, imperf. horiz.	350.00	
	b.	Horiz. pair, imperf. vert.	8,500.	
	c.	ultramarine & carmine	200.00	

Top plate number blocks of No. C23 are found both with and without top arrow.

TRANSATLANTIC ISSUE

Winged Globe
AP16

Inauguration of Transatlantic air mail service.

FLAT PLATE PRINTING

Plates of 200 subjects in four panes of 50 each.

1939 Perf. 11 Unwmkd.

C24	AP16	30c **dull blue,** *May 16*	16.00	1.50
		Margin block of 6, P#	210.00	

AIR POST STAMPS 377

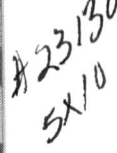

Twin-Motored Transport Plane
AP17

ROTARY PRESS PRINTING

E. E. Plates of 200 subjects in four panes of 50 each.

			1941–44	Perf. 11x10½		Unwmkd.	
C25	AP17	6c	**carmine**, *June 25, 1941*			15	5
			Margin block of 4, P#			1.00	
			Pair with full vertical gutter between			225.00	
			a. Booklet pane of three, *March, 18, 1943*			6.50	1.00
			b. Horiz. pair, imperf. between			2,000.	
C26	AP17	8c	**olive green**, *March 21, 1944*			20	5
			Margin block of 4, P#			1.25	
			Pair with full horiz. gutter btwn.			325.00	
C27	AP17	10c	**violet**, *August 15, 1941*			1.65	20
			Margin block of 4, P#			12.50	
C28	AP17	15c	**brown carmine**, *Aug. 19, 1941*			3.75	35
			Margin block of 4, P#			18.50	
C29	AP17	20c	**bright green**, *August 27, 1941*			2.75	30
			Margin block of 4, P#			16.50	
C30	AP17	30c	**blue**, *Sept. 25, 1941*			3.50	30
			Margin block of 4, P#			17.50	
C31	AP17	50c	**orange**, *Oct. 29, 1941*			20.00	4.00
			Margin block of 4, P#			100.00	

DC-4 Skymaster
AP18

ROTARY PRESS PRINTING

E. E. Plates of 200 subjects in four panes of 50 each.

			1946	Perf. 11x10½		Unwmkd.	
C32	AP18	5c	**carmine**, *September 25*			15	5
			Margin block of 4, P#			75	

DC-4 Skymaster
AP19

ROTARY PRESS PRINTING

E. E. Plates of 400 subjects in four panes of 100 each.

			1947	Perf. 10½x11		Unwmkd.	
C33	AP19	5c	**carmine**, *March 26*			12	5
			Margin block of 4, P#			75	

Pan American Union Building, Washington, D.C.,
and Martin 2-0-2
AP20

Statue of Liberty, New York Skyline
and Lockheed Constellation
AP21

San Francisco-Oakland Bay Bridge
and Boeing B377 Stratocruiser
AP22

Designed by Victor S. McCloskey, Jr., Leon Helguera and William K. Schrage.

ROTARY PRESS PRINTING

E. E. Plates of 200 subjects in four panes of 50 each.

			1947	Perf. 11x10½		Unwmkd.	
C34	AP20	10c	**black**, *August 30*			30	6
			Margin block of 4, P#			2.25	
C35	AP21	15c	**bright blue green**, *Aug. 20*			35	5
			blue green			35	5
			Margin block of 4, P#			2.50	
			Pair with full horiz. gutter btwn.			400.00	
			a. Horiz. pair, imperf. between			2,000.	
C36	AP22	25c	**blue**, *July 30*			1.60	12
			Margin block of 4, P#			7.50	

ROTARY PRESS COIL STAMP

Type of 1947.

			1948	*Perf. 10 Horizontally.*		Unwmkd.	
C37	AP19	5c	**carmine**, *Jan. 15*			2.00	1.10
			Pair			4.00	2.25
			Joint line pair			13.50	3.00

NEW YORK CITY ISSUE

Map of Five Boroughs,
Circular Band and Planes
AP23

Issued to commemorate the 50th anniversary of the consolidation of the five boroughs of New York City.

ROTARY PRESS PRINTING

E. E. Plates of 400 subjects in four panes of 100 each.

			1948	Perf. 11x10½		Unwmkd.	
C38	AP23	5c	**bright carmine**, *July 31*			18	18
			Margin block of 4, P#			20.00	

Type of 1947.

ROTARY PRESS PRINTING

E. E. Plates of 400 subjects in four panes of 100 each.

			1949	Perf. 10½x11		Unwmkd.	
C39	AP19	6c	**carmine**, *Jan. 18*			18	5
			Margin block of 4, P#			85	
			a. Booklet pane of 6, *Nov. 18*			12.00	5.00

ALEXANDRIA BICENTENNIAL ISSUE

Home of John Carlyle,
Alexandria Seal and Gadsby's Tavern
AP24

Issued to commemorate the 200th anniversary of the founding of Alexandria, Virginia.

ROTARY PRESS PRINTING

E. E. Plates of 200 subjects in four panes of 50 each.

1949			Perf. 11x10½.		Unwmkd.	
C40	AP24	6c	carmine, *May 11*		18	10
			Margin block of 4, P#		95	—

ROTARY PRESS COIL STAMP

Type of 1947.

1949			Perf. 10 Horizontally.		Unwmkd.	
C41	AP19	6c	carmine, *Aug. 25*		4.50	5
			Pair		9.00	15
			Joint line pair		20.00	1.35

UNIVERSAL POSTAL UNION ISSUE

Post Office Department Building
AP25

Globe and Doves Carrying Messages
AP26

Boeing Stratocruiser and Globe
AP27

Issued to commemorate the 75th anniversary of the formation of the Universal Postal Union.

ROTARY PRESS PRINTING

E. E. Plates of 200 subjects in four panes of 50 each.

1949			Perf. 11x10½.		Unwmkd.	
C42	AP25	10c	violet, *Nov. 18*		35	35
			Margin block of 4, P#		3.25	—
C43	AP26	15c	ultramarine, *Oct. 7*		50	50
			Margin block of 4, P#		2.75	—
C44	AP27	25c	rose carmine, *Nov. 30*		85	85
			Margin block of 4, P#		11.00	—

WRIGHT BROTHERS ISSUE

Wilbur and Orville Wright and their Plane, 1903
AP28

Issued to commemorate the 46th anniversary of the first successful flight in a motor-powered airplane, made Dec. 17, 1903, at Kill Devil Hill near Kitty Hawk, N.C., by Wilbur Wright (1867–1912) and his brother Orville (1871–1948) of Dayton, O. The plane flew 852 feet in 59 seconds.

ROTARY PRESS PRINTING

E. E. Plates of 200 subjects in four panes of 50 each.

1949			Perf. 11x10½		Unwmkd.	
C45	AP28	6c	magenta, *Dec. 17*		20	10
			Margin block of 4, P#		1.00	—

Diamond Head, Honolulu, Hawaii
AP29

ROTARY PRESS PRINTING

E. E. Plates of 200 subjects in four panes of 50 each.

1952, Mar. 26			Perf. 11x10½		Unwmkd.	
C46	AP29	80c	bright red violet		11.00	1.50
			Margin block of 4, P#		55.00	—

POWERED FLIGHT ISSUE

First Plane and Modern Plane
AP30

Issued to commemorate the 50th anniversary of powered flight.

ROTARY PRESS PRINTING

E. E. Plates of 200 subjects in four panes of 50 each.

1953			Perf. 11x10½		Unwmkd.	
C47	AP30	6c	carmine, *May 29*		16	10
			Margin block of 4, P#		85	—

Eagle in Flight
AP31

Issued primarily for use on domestic post cards.

ROTARY PRESS PRINTING

E. E. Plates of 400 subjects in four panes of 100 each.

1954			Perf. 11x10½.		Unwmkd.	
C48	AP31	4c	bright blue, *Sept. 3*		12	8
			Margin block of 4, P#		5.00	—

AIR POST STAMPS

AIR FORCE ISSUE

B-52 Stratofortress and F-104 Starfighters
AP32

Designed by Alexander Nagy, Jr.

Issued to commemorate the 50th anniversary of the U. S. Air Force.

ROTARY PRESS PRINTING

E. E. Plates of 200 subjects in four panes of 50 each.

1957		Perf. 11 x 10½	Unwmkd.	
C49	AP32	6c **blue**, *Aug. 1*	20	10
		Margin block of 4, P#	1.50	

Type of 1954

Issued primarily for use on domestic post cards.

1958		Perf. 11x10½	Unwmkd.	
C50	AP31	5c **red**, *July 31*	22	15
		Margin block of 4, P#	5.00	

Silhouette of Jet Airliner
AP33

Designed by William H. Buckley and Sam Marsh.

ROTARY PRESS PRINTING

E. E. Plates of 400 subjects in four panes of 100 each.

1958		Perf. 10½x11	Unwmkd.	
C51	AP33	7c **blue**, *July 31*	22	5
		Margin block of 4, P#	1.30	
		a. Booklet pane of 6	15.00	6.50

ROTARY PRESS COIL STAMP
Perf. 10 Horizontally

C52	AP33	7c **blue**, *July 31*	4.50	20
		Pair	9.00	50
		Joint line pair	22.50	1.25

ALASKA STATEHOOD ISSUE

Big Dipper, North Star and Map of Alaska
AP34

Designed by Richard C. Lockwood.

Issued to commemorate Alaska's admission to statehood.

ROTARY PRESS PRINTING

E. E. Plates of 200 subjects in four panes of 50 each.

1959		Perf. 11x10½	Unwmkd.	
C53	AP34	7c **dark blue**, *Jan. 3*	25	12
		Margin block of 4, P#	1.50	

BALLOON JUPITER ISSUE

Balloon and Crowd
AP35

Designed by Austin Briggs.

Issued to commemorate the centenary of the carrying of mail by the balloon Jupiter from Lafayette to Crawfordsville, Ind.

GIORI PRESS PRINTING

Plates of 200 subjects in four panes of 50 each.

1959		Perf. 11	Unwmkd.	
C54	AP35	7c **dark blue & red**, *Aug. 17*	25	12
		Margin block of 4, P#	1.50	

HAWAII STATEHOOD ISSUE

Alii Warrior, Map of Hawaii and Star of Statehood
AP36

Designed by Joseph Feher.

Issued to commemorate Hawaii's admission to statehood.

ROTARY PRESS PRINTING

E. E. Plates of 200 subjects in four panes of 50 each.

1959		Perf. 11 x 10½.	Unwmkd.	
C55	AP36	7c **rose red**, *Aug. 21*	25	12
		Margin block of 4, P#	1.50	

PAN AMERICAN GAMES ISSUE

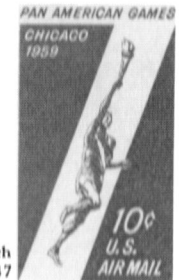

Runner Holding Torch
AP37

Designed by Suren Ermoyan.

Issued to commemorate the 3rd Pan American Games at Chicago, Aug. 27–Sept. 7, 1959.

GIORI PRESS PRINTING

Plates of 200 subjects in four panes of 50 each.

1959		Perf. 11	Unwmkd.	
C56	AP37	10c **violet blue & bright red**, *Aug. 27*	40	40
		Margin block of 4, P#	5.00	

AIR POST STAMPS

Liberty Bell
AP38

Statue of Liberty
AP39

Abraham Lincoln
AP40

GIORI PRESS PRINTING

Plates of 200 subjects in four panes of 50 each.

1959–66			Perf. 11	Unwmkd.	
C57	AP38	10c	**black & green,** *June 10, 1960*	3.00	1.00
			Margin block of 4, P#	15.00	
C58	AP39	15c	**black & orange,** *Nov. 20, 1959*	75	6
			Margin block of 4, P#	4.00	
C59	AP40	25c	**black & maroon,**		
			Apr. 22, 1960	75	6
			Margin block of 4, P#	4.00	
		a.	Tagged, *Dec. 29, 1966*	75	15

See Luminescence data in Information for Collectors section.

Type of 1958
ROTARY PRESS PRINTING

E. E. Plates of 400 subjects in four panes of 100 each.

1960			Perf. 10½x11	Unwmkd.	
C60	AP33	7c	**carmine,** *Aug. 12*	30	5
			Margin block of 4, P#	1.50	
			Pair with full horiz. gutter btwn.		
		a.	Booklet pane of 6, *Aug. 19*	20.00	7.00

Type of 1958
ROTARY PRESS COIL STAMP

1960			Perf. 10 Horizontally	Unwmkd.	
C61	AP33	7c	**carmine,** *Oct. 22*	8.00	25
			Pair	16.00	55
			Joint line pair	50.00	3.25

Type of 1959–60 and

Statue of Liberty
AP41

GIORI PRESS PRINTING

Plates of 200 subjects in four panes of 50 each.

1961–67			Perf. 11	Unwmkd.	
C62	AP38	13c	**black & red,** *June 28, 1961*	65	10
			Margin block of 4, P#	7.00	
		a.	Tagged, *Feb. 15, 1967*	80	25

C63	AP41	15c	**black & orange,** *Jan. 13, 1961*	40	8
			Margin block of 4, P#	2.25	
		a.	Tagged, *Jan. 11, 1967*	50	12
		b.	As "a," horiz. pair, imperf. vert.	15,000.	

Jet Airliner over Capitol
AP42

Designed by Henry K. Bencsath.

ROTARY PRESS PRINTING

E.E. Plates of 400 subjects in four panes of 100 each.

1962–65			Perf. 10½x11	Unwmkd.	
C64	AP42	8c	**carmine,** *Dec. 5, 1962*	22	5
			Margin block of 4, P#	1.10	
		a.	Tagged, *Aug. 1, 1963*	22	5
		a.	Pair with full horiz. gutter between		
		b.	Booklet pane of 5 + label	7.50	1.25
		c.	As "b," tagged, *1964*	2.25	50

Nos. C64a and C64c were made by overprinting Nos. C64 and C64b with phosphorescent ink. No. C64a was first issued at Dayton, O., for experiments in high speed mail sorting. The tagging is visible in ultraviolet light.

COIL STAMP; ROTARY PRESS
Perf. 10 Horizontally

C65	AP42	8c	**carmine,** *Dec. 5, 1962*	50	8
			Pair	1.00	20
			Joint line pair	4.00	35
		a.	Tagged, *Jan. 14, 1965*	60	10

MONTGOMERY BLAIR ISSUE

Montgomery Blair
AP43

Designed by Robert J. Jones

Issued to honor Montgomery Blair (1813–1883), Postmaster General (1861–64), who called the first International Postal Conference, Paris, 1863, forerunner of the U.P.U.

GIORI PRESS PRINTING

Plates of 200 subjects in four panes of 50 each.

1963			Perf. 11	Unwmkd.	
C66	AP43	15c	**dull red, dk. brn. & bl.,** *May 3*	1.30	75
			Margin block of 4, P#	7.00	

Bald Eagle
AP44

Designed by V. S. McCloskey, Jr.

Issued primarily for use on domestic post cards.

ROTARY PRESS PRINTING

E.E. Plates of 400 subjects in four panes of 100 each.

1963–67			Perf. 11x10½	Unwmkd.	
C67	AP44	6c	**red,** *July 12, 1963*	20	15
			Margin block of 4, P#	3.50	
		a.	Tagged, *Feb. 15, 1967*	3.00	50

AIR POST STAMPS

AMELIA EARHART ISSUE

Amelia Earhart and
Lockheed Electra
AP45

Designed by Robert J. Jones.

Issued to honor Amelia Earhart (1898–1937), first woman to fly across the Atlantic.

GIORI PRESS PRINTING

Plates of 200 subjects in four panes of 50 each.

1963		Perf. 11	Unwmkd.	
C68	AP45	8c carmine & maroon, *July 24*	30	15
		Block of four	1.60	60
		Margin block of 4, P#	3.00	

ROBERT H. GODDARD ISSUE

Robert H. Goddard, Atlas Rocket and Launching tower, Cape Kennedy
AP46

Designed by Robert J. Jones.

Issued to honor Dr. Robert H. Goddard (1882–1945), physicist and pioneer rocket researcher.

GIORI PRESS PRINTING

Plates of 200 subjects in four panes of 50 each.

1964		Tagged	Perf. 11	
C69	AP46	8c blue, red & bister, *Oct. 5*	90	15
		Margin block of 4, P#	5.00	
		Margin block of 4, Mr. Zip and "Use Zip Code"	4.25	

Luminescence

Air Post stamps issued after mid-1964 are tagged.

ALASKA PURCHASE ISSUE

Tlingit Totem,
Southern Alaska
AP47

Designed by Willard R. Cox

Issued to commemorate the centenary of the Alaska Purchase. The totem pole shown is in the Alaska State Museum, Juneau.

GIORI PRESS PRINTING

Plates of 200 subjects in four panes of 50 each.

1967		Perf. 11	Unwmkd.	
C70	AP47	8c brown, *March 30*	45	20
		Margin block of 4, P#	4.00	
		Margin block of 4, Mr. Zip and "Use Zip Code"	2.20	

"Columbia Jays" by John
James Audubon
AP48

Fifty-Star Runway
AP49

GIORI PRESS PRINTING

Designed by Robert J. Jones.

Plates of 200 subjects in four panes of 50 each.

1967			Perf. 11	
C71	AP48	20c multicolored, *Apr. 26*	1.50	15
		Margin block of 4, P#	8.50	
		Margin block of 4, Mr. Zip and "Use Zip Code"	6.75	

See note over No. 1241.

ROTARY PRESS PRINTING

Designed by Jaan Born.

E. E. Plates of 400 subjects in four panes of 100 each.

1968		Perf. 11x10½	Unwmkd.	
C72	AP49	10c carmine, *Jan. 5*	30	5
		Margin block of 4, P#	2.25	
		Margin block of 4, "Use Zip Codes"	1.40	
		Margin block of 6, "Mail Early in the Day"	2.00	
	b.	Booklet pane of 8	4.00	75
	c.	Booklet pane of 5 + label, *Jan. 6*	2.50	75

ROTARY PRESS COIL STAMP
Perf. 10 Vertically

C73	AP49	10c carmine, *Jan. 5*	65	5
		Pair	1.30	10
		Joint line pair	4.50	20
	a.	Imperf., pair	550.00	

$1 Air Lift

This stamp, listed as No. 1341, was issued Apr. 4, 1968, to pay for airlift of parcels to and from U.S. ports to servicemen overseas and in Alaska, Hawaii and Puerto Rico. It was "also valid for paying regular rates for other types of mail," the Post Office Department announced to the public in a philatelic release dated Mar. 10, 1968. The stamp is inscribed "U.S. Postage" and is untagged.

On Apr. 26, 1969, the P.O.D. stated in its Postal Manual (for postal employees) that this stamp "may be used toward paying the postage or fees for special services on *airmail* articles." On Jan. 1, 1970, the Department told postal employees through its Postal Bulletin that this $1 stamp "can only be used to pay the airlift fee or toward payment of postage or fees on *airmail* articles."

Some collectors prefer to consider No. 1341 an airmail stamp.

50th ANNIVERSARY OF AIR MAIL ISSUE

Curtiss Jenny
AP50

Designed by Hordur Karlsson.

Issued to commemorate the 50th anniversary of regularly scheduled air mail service.

LITHOGRAPHED, ENGRAVED (GIORI)
Plates of 200 subjects in four panes of 50 each.

1968				Perf. 11	
C74	AP50	10c **blue, black & red,** *May 15*		60	15
		Margin block of 4, P#		5.00	—
		Margin block of 4, Mr. Zip and "Use Zip Code"		2.60	—
		Margin block of 6, "Mail Early in the Day"		3.75	—
		a. Red (tail stripe) omitted			

"USA" and Jet—AP51

Designed by John Larrecq.

LITHOGRAPHED, ENGRAVED (GIORI)
Plates of 200 subjects in four panes of 50 each.

1968				Perf. 11	
C75	AP51	20c **red, blue & black,** *Nov. 22*		85	6
		Margin block of 4, P#		5.00	—
		Margin block of 4, Mr. Zip and "Use Zip Code"		4.00	—
		Margin block of 6, "Mail Early in the Day"		5.00	—

MOON LANDING ISSUE

First Man on the Moon—AP52

Designed by Paul Calle.

Issued to commemorate man's first landing on the moon July 20, 1969, by U.S. astronauts Neil A. Armstrong and Col. Edwin E. Aldrin, Jr., with Lieut. Col. Michael Collins piloting Apollo 11.

LITHOGRAPHED, ENGRAVED (GIORI)
Plates of 128 subjects in four panes of 32 each.

1969				Perf. 11	
C76	AP52	10c **yellow, black, lt. blue, ultra., rose red & carmine,** *Sept. 9*		30	15
		Margin block of 4, P#		2.50	—
		Margin block of 4, Mr. Zip and "Use Zip Code"		1.40	—
		Margin block of 6, "Mail Early in the Day"		2.10	—
		a. Rose red (litho.) omitted		400.00	—

On No. C76a, the lithographed rose red is missing from the entire vignette—the dots on top of the yellow areas as well as the flag shoulder patch.

Silhouette of Delta Wing Plane—AP53

Silhouette of Jet Airliner
AP54

Winged Airmail Envelope
AP55

Statue of Liberty—AP56

Designed by George Vander Sluis (9c, 11c), Nelson Gruppo (13c) and Robert J. Jones (17c).

ROTARY PRESS PRINTING
E. E. Plates of 400 subjects in four panes of 100 each.

1971-73				Perf. 10½ x 11	
C77	AP53	9c **red,** *May 15, 1971*		22	15
		Margin block of 4, P#		2.00	—
		Margin block of 4, "Use Zip Codes"		1.00	—
		Margin block of 6, "Mail Early in the Day"		1.50	—

No. C77 issued primarily for use on domestic post cards.

Perf. 11x10½

C78	AP54	11c **carmine,** *May 7, 1971*		30	5
		Margin block of 4, P#		1.75	—
		Margin block of 4, "Use Zip Codes"		1.30	—
		Margin block of 6, "Mail Early in the Day"		2.00	—
		Pair with full vert. gutter btwn.			
		a. Booklet pane of 4 + 2 labels		1.50	40
		b. Untagged (Bureau precanceled)			25
C79	AP55	13c **carmine,** *Nov. 16, 1973*		32	10
		Margin block of 4, P#		1.65	—
		Margin block of 4, "Use Zip Codes"		1.35	—
		Margin block of 6, "Mail Early in the Day"		2.00	—
		a. Booklet pane of 5 + label, *Dec. 27, 1973*		1.35	70
		b. Untagged (Bureau precanceled)			30

No. C78b precanceled "WASHINGTON D.C." (or "DC"), No. C79b "WASHINGTON DC" only; both for use of Congressmen.

GIORI PRESS PRINTING
Panes of 200 subjects in four panes of 50 each.

Perf. 11

C80	AP56	17c **bluish black, red, & dark green,** *July 13, 1971*		55	15
		Margin block of 4, P#		2.75	—
		Margin block of 4, Mr. Zip and "Use Zip Code"		2.35	—
		Margin block of 6, "Mail Early in the day"		3.40	—

AIR POST STAMPS

"USA" & Jet Type of 1968
LITHOGRAPHED, ENGRAVED (GIORI)
Plates of 200 subjects in four panes of 50 each.
Perf. 11

C81	AP51 21c **red, blue & black,** *May 21, 1971*	55	10
	Margin block of 4, P#	2.75	—
	Margin block of 4, Mr. Zip and "Use Zip Code"	2.35	—
	Margin block of 6, "Mail Early in the Day"	3.40	—

COIL STAMPS
ROTARY PRESS PRINTING

1971-73   *Perf. 10 Vertically*

C82	AP54 11c **carmine,** *May 7, 1971*	40	6
	Pair	80	24
	Joint line pair	2.25	32
	a. Imperf., pair	200.00	
	a. Joint line pair	300.00	
C83	AP55 13c **carmine,** *Dec. 27, 1973*	40	10
	Pair	80	25
	Joint line pair	2.10	
	a. Imperf., pair	100.00	
	a. Joint line pair	150.00	

NATIONAL PARKS CENTENNIAL ISSUE
City of Refuge, Hawaii

Kii Statue and Temple
AP57
Designed by Paul Rabut.

Issued to commemorate the centenary of national parks. This 11c honors the City of Refuge National Historical Park, established in 1961 at Honaunau, island of Hawaii.

LITHOGRAPHED, ENGRAVED (GIORI)
Plates of 200 subjects in four panes of 50 each.

1972   *Perf. 11*

C84	AP57 11c **orange & multicolored,** *May 3*	30	15
	Margin block of 4, P#	2.00	—
	Margin block of 4, Mr. Zip and "Use Zip Code"	1.50	—
	Margin block of 6, "Mail Early in the Day"	2.00	—
	a. Blue & green (litho.) omitted	1,500.	

OLYMPIC GAMES ISSUE

Skiing and Olympic Rings
AP58
Designed by Lance Wyman.

Issued to commemorate the 11th Winter Olympic Games, Sapporo, Japan, Feb. 3-13, and the 20th Summer Olympic Games, Munich, Germany, Aug. 26–Sept. 11.

PHOTOGRAVURE (Andreotti)
Plates of 200 subjects in four panes of 50 each.

1972   *Perf. 11x10½*

C85	AP58 11c **black, blue, red, emerald & yellow,** *Aug. 17*	30	15
	Margin block of 10, 5 P#	3.50	—
	Margin block of 4, "Use Zip Code"	1.25	—
	Margin block of 6, "Mail Early in the Day"	1.90	—

ELECTRONICS PROGRESS ISSUE

De Forest Audions
AP59
Designed by Walter and Naiad Einsel.
LITHOGRAPHED, ENGRAVED (GIORI)
Plates of 200 subjects in four panes of 50 each.

1973   *Perf. 11*

C86	AP59 11c **vermilion, lilac, pale lilac, olive, brown, dp. carmine & black,** *July 10*	30	15
	Margin block of 4, P#	1.75	—
	Margin block of 4, Mr. Zip and "Use Zip Code"	1.35	—
	Margin block of 6, "Mail Early in the Day"	2.00	—
	a. Verm. & olive (litho.) omitted	1,750.	

Statue of Liberty—AP60

Mt. Rushmore National Memorial—AP61
Designed by Robert (Gene) Shehorn.
GIORI PRESS PRINTING
Panes of 200 subjects in four panes of 50 each.

1974   *Perf. 11*

C87	AP60 18c **carmine, black & ultramarine** *Jan. 11*	45	45
	Margin block of 4, 2 P#	2.50	—
	Margin block of 4, Mr. Zip and "Use Zip Code"	1.90	—
	Margin block of 6, "Mail Early in the Day"	2.85	—
C88	AP61 26c **ultramarine, black & carmine,** *Jan. 2*	60	15
	Margin block of 4, P#	2.85	—
	Margin block of 4, Mr. Zip and "Use Zip Code"	2.50	—
	Margin block of 6, "Mail Early in the Day"	3.75	—

AIR POST STAMPS

Plane and Globes—AP62

Plane, Globes and Flags
AP63
Designed by David G. Foote.
GIORI PRESS PRINTING
Panes of 200 subjects in four panes of 50 each.
1976, Jan. 2   *Perf. 11*

C89	AP62 25c	red, blue & black	60	18
		Margin block of 4, P#	3.25	
		Margin block of 4, Mr. Zip and "Use Zip Code"	2.60	
		Margin block of 6, "Mail Early in the Day"	3.75	
C90	AP63 31c	red, blue & black	62	10
		Margin block of 4, P#	3.25	
		Margin block of 4, Mr. Zip and "Use Zip Code"	2.75	
		Margin block of 6, "Mail Early in the Day"	4.00	

WRIGHT BROTHERS ISSUE

Orville and
Wilbur Wright,
and Flyer A
AP64

Wright Brothers,
Flyer A
and Shed
AP65

Designed by Ken Dallison.
75th anniversary of first powered flight, Kill Devil Hill, N.C., Dec. 17, 1903. Nos. C91–C92 printed se-tenant vertically.
LITHOGRAPHED, ENGRAVED (GIORI)
Plates of 400 subjects in four panes of 100 each.
1978, Sept. 23   *Perf. 11*

C91	AP64 31c	ultra. & multicolored	90	15
C92	AP65 31c	ultra. & multicolored	90	15
	a.	Pair, #C91-C92	1.85	65
		Margin block of 4, P#	4.50	
		Margin block of 4, "Use Correct Zip Code"	3.75	
		Margin block of 4, copyright	3.75	
	b.	As "a," ultra. & black (engr.) omitted		
	c.	As "a," black (engr.) omitted		

OCTAVE CHANUTE ISSUE

Chanute and
Biplane
Hang-glider
AP66

Biplane
Hang-glider
and Chanute
AP67

Designed by Ken Dallison.
Octave Chanute (1832–1910), civil engineer and aviation pioneer. Nos. C93–C94 printed se-tenant vertically.
LITHOGRAPHED, ENGRAVED (GIORI)
Plates of 400 subjects in four panes of 100 each.
1979, Mar. 29   Tagged   *Perf. 1*

C93	AP66 21c	blue & multicolored	90	3:
C94	AP67 21c	blue & multicolored	90	3:
	a.	Pair, #C93-C94	1.85	7:
		Margin block of 4, P#	6.50	
		Margin block of 4, Mr. Zip	3.75	
		Margin block of 4, copyright	3.75	
	b.	As "a," ultra & black (engr.) omitted 3,000.		

WILEY POST ISSUE

Wiley Post and "Winnie Mae"—AP68

NR-105-W, Post in Pressurized Suit, Portrait—AP69

Designed by Ken Dallison.
Wiley Post (1899–1935), first man to fly around th world alone and high-altitude flying pioneer. Nos. C95– C96 printed se-tenant vertically.
LITHOGRAPHED, ENGRAVED (GIORI)
Plates of 400 subjects in four panes of 100 each.
1979, Nov. 20   Tagged   *Perf. 1*

C95	AP68 25c	blue & multicolored	90	35
C96	AP69 25c	blue & multicolored	90	35
	a.	Pair, #C95-C96	1.85	85
		Margin block of 4, P#	7.50	
		Margin block of 4, Mr. Zip	3.75	
		Margin block of 4, copyright	3.75	

OLYMPIC GAMES ISSUE

High Jump—AP70
Designed by Robert M. Cunningham.
PHOTOGRAVURE
22nd Olympic Games, Moscow, July 19–Aug. 3, 1980.
Plates of 200 subjects in four panes of 50 each.

1979, Nov. 1		Tagged		*Perf. 11*
C97	AP70 31c **multi**		90	30
	P# block of 12, 6 P#		12.00	
	Zip block of 4		3.75	
	Copyright block of 4		3.75	

PHILIP MAZZEI (1730—1816)

Italian-born political writer
AP71
Designed by Sante Graziani
PHOTOGRAVURE
Plates of 200 subjects in four panes of 50 each.

1980, Oct. 13		Tagged		*Perf. 11*
C98	AP71 40c **multi**		90	30
	P# block of 12, 6 P#		12.00	
	Zip block of 4		3.75	
	Copyright block of 4		3.75	
	a. Perf. 10½x11 ('82)		2.00	
	b. Imperf. pair		2,250.	

BLANCHE STUART SCOTT (1886-1970)

First woman pilot —AP72
Designed by Paul Calle.
PHOTOGRAVURE
Plates of 200 subjects in four panes of 50.

1980, Dec. 30		Tagged		*Perf. 11*
C99	AP72 28c **multi**		70	15
	P# block of 12, 6 P#		9.00	
	Zip block of 4		3.00	
	Copyright block of 4		3.00	

GLENN CURTISS (1878-1930)

Aviation pioneer and aircraft designer —AP73
Designed by Ken Dallison.
PHOTOGRAVURE
Plates of 200 subjects in four panes of 50.

1980, Dec. 30		Tagged		*Perf. 11*
C100	AP73 35c **multi**		75	15
	P# block of 12, 6 P#		10.00	
	Zip block of 4		3.25	
	Copyright block of 4		3.25	

SUMMER OLYMPICS 1984

Women's Gymnastics
AP74

Hurdles
AP75

Women's Basketball
AP76

Soccer
AP77

AIR POST STAMPS

Shot Put
AP78

Men's Gymnastics
AP79

Women's Swimming
AP80

Weight Lifting
AP81

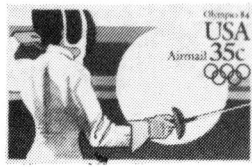

Women's Fencing
AP82

Cycling
AP83

Women's Volleyball
AP84

Pole Vaulting
AP85

Designed by Robert Peak
23rd Olympic Games, Los Angeles, July 28-Aug. 12, 1984.

PHOTOGRAVURE
Plates of 200 subjects in four panes of 50.

1983, June 17		Tagged	Perf. 11	
C101	AP74	28c multi	56	28
C102	AP75	28c multi	56	28
C103	AP76	28c multi	56	28
C104	AP77	28c multi	56	28
		P# block of 4, 5 P#	2.75	—
		Zip block of 4	2.50	—
		Copyright block of 4	2.50	—
		a. Block of 4, #C101-C104	2.25	1.75

1983, Apr. 8		Tagged	Perf. 11	
C105	AP78	40c multi	80	40
C106	AP79	40c multi	80	40
C107	AP80	40c multi	80	40
C108	AP81	40c multi	80	40
		P# block of 4, 5 P#	4.00	—
		Zip block of 4	3.75	—
		Copyright block of 4	3.75	—
		a. Block of 4, #C105-C108	3.50	2.00
		b. As "a," imperf.	—	

1983, Nov. 4		Tagged	Perf. 11	
C109	AP82	35c multi	70	35
C110	AP83	35c multi	70	35
C111	AP84	35c multi	70	35
C112	AP85	35c multi	70	35
		P# block of 4, 4#	3.50	—
		Zip block of 4	3.25	—
		Copyright block of 4	3.25	—
		a. Block of 4, #C109-C112	3.00	1.85

AVIATION PIONEERS

Alfred V. Verville (1890-1970),
Inventor, Verville-Sperry
R-3 Army Racer
AP86

Lawrence (1892-1931), Aircraft Designer,
and Elmer (1860-1930), Designer and Pilot,
Sperry, First Seaplane
AP87

Designed by Ken Dallison (#C113) and
Howard Koslow (#C114)
PHOTOGRAVURE
Plates of 200 in four panes of 50
(2 panes each, #C113 and #C114)

1985, Feb. 13		Tagged	Perf. 11	
C113	AP86	33c **multi**	66	20
		P# block of 4, 5 #	3.50	—
		Zip block of 4	3.00	—
		Copyright block of 4	3.00	—
		a. Imperf. pair	—	
C114	AP87	39c **multi**	78	20
		P# block of 4, 5 #	4.00	—
		Zip block of 4	3.50	—
		Copyright block of 4	3.50	—
		a. Imperf. pair	—	

TRANSPACIFIC AIRMAIL
50th Anniversary

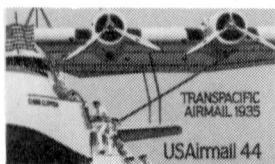

Martin M-130 China Clipper
AP88
Designed by Chuck Hodgson
PHOTOGRAVURE
Plates of 200 in four panes of 50

1985, Feb. 15		Tagged	Perf. 11	
C115	AP88	44c multi	88	20
		P# block of 4, 5 #	4.50	—
		Zip block of 4	4.00	—
		Copyright block of 4	4.00	—
	a.	Imperf. pair	—	

FR. JUNIPERO SERRA (1713-1784)
Foremost California Missionary

Outline Map of Southern California, Portrait,
San Gabriel Mission
AP89
Designed by Robert Schlect from a Spanish stamp
PHOTOGRAVURE
Plates of 200 in eight panes of 50

1985, Aug. 22		Tagged	Perf. 11	
C116	AP89	44c multi	88	20
		P# block of 4	4.50	—
		Zip block of 4	4.00	—
		Copyright block of 4 .	4.00	—
	a.	Imperf. pair	—	

UNITED STATES
WORLDWIDE COLLECTIONS
If you spend over $25.00 per month
you should subscribe to the
"Money's Worth" list.
FOR 3 FREE ISSUES
write or call:
Warren A. Wasson
11329 N. Central, Dallas, TX 75243
Phone 214/369-1427

UNITED STATES
1982-85
Great Americans

 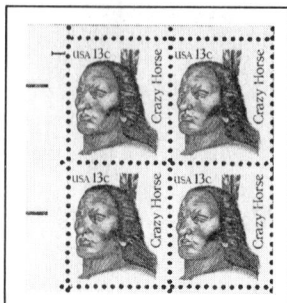

COLLECT THE SCOTT WAY... WITH SCOTT'S

U.S. REG. & REG. AIR PLATE BLOCK
ALBUM

FEATURING:

- Spaces for the first airmail issue of 1918 (Scott C1-C3), the 1922-25 regulars (beginning with Scott 551) and all subsequent Regular and Regular Air Plate Blocks listed in the Scott "Specialized Catalogue of United States Stamps".
- Each stamp pictured or described and arranged in order by Scott number.
- A handsome, sturdy binder is standard with this album - not tacked on at an extra cost.
- Chemically neutralized paper protects your stamps for generations.
- Paper just the right thickness to make collecting a pleasure.
- Yearly supplement available.

$34.95 Album through 1985

AVAILABLE NOW AT
YOUR LOCAL DEALER
OR DIRECT FROM:

P.O. BOX 828, SIDNEY, OH 45365

AIR POST SPECIAL DELIVERY STAMPS

Great Seal of United States
APSD1

No. CE1 was issued for the prepayment of the air ostage and the special delivery fee in one stamp. First ay sale was at the American Air Mail Society Convenon.

FLAT PLATE PRINTING.
Plates of 200 subjects in four panes of 50 each.
934, Aug. 30   *Perf.* 11   Unwmkd.

E1	APSD116c **dark blue**		75	85
	blue		75	85
	First day cover, Chicago *(40,171)*		25.00	
	First day cover, Washington, D.C., *Aug. 31*			3.50
	Margin block of 6, P#	20.00		

For imperforate variety see No. 771.

1936, Feb. 10   Type of 1934.

Frame plates of 100 subjects in two panes of 50 each separated by a 1½ inch wide vertical gutter with central guide line, and vignette plates of 50 subjects.

The "seal" design for No. CE2 was from a new engraving, slightly smaller than that used for No. CE1.

Top plate number blocks of No. CE2 are found both with and without top arrow.

Issued in panes of 50 each.

CE2	APSD116c **red & blue**		40	25
	First day cover, Washington, D.C. *(72,981)*			17.50
	Margin block of 4, two P#	8.50		
	Margin block of 4, two P#, blue dotted registration marker	65.00		
	Same, arrow, red registration marker	50.00		
	Margin block of 4, bottom or side arrow	2.00	1.75	
	Center line block	2.25	2.75	
	Margin block of 10, two P#, two "TOP" and two registration markers	15.00	6.00	
a.	Horiz. pair, imperf. vert.	3,250.		

Quantities issued: No. CE1, 9,215,750. No. CE2, 72,517,850.

AIR POST SEMI-OFFICIAL STAMPS

Buffalo Balloon

This stamp was privately issued by John F. B. Lillard, a Nashville reporter. It was used on covers carried on a balloon ascension of June 18, 1877, which began at Nashville and landed at Gallatin, Tenn., and possibly on other flights. The balloon was owned and piloted by Samuel Archer King. The stamp was reported to have been engraved by (Mrs. ?) J. H. Snively and printed in strips from a single die. Lillard wrote that 300 were printed and 23 used.

Buffalo Balloon
CS1

1877, June 18   Typographed   *Imperf.*

CL1	CS1	5c **deep blue**		4,500
		On cover with 3c #158		20,000
		On cover with 1c #156 & 2c #178		20,000
a.	Tête bêche pair, vertical			9,500

A black proof exists of No. CL1.

"R.F." OVERPRINTS

Authorized as a control mark by the United States Fleet Post Office during 1944-45 for the accommodation of and exclusive use by French naval personnel on airmail correspondence to the United States and Canada. All "R.F." (Republique Francaise) mail had to be posted at the North African naval bases and had to bear the return address, rank and/or serial number of a French officer or seaman. It also had to be censored.

All "R.F." overprints were handstamped by the French naval authorities after the stamps were affixed for mailing. The stamps had to be cancelled by a special French naval cancellation. The status of unused copies seems questionable; they are alleged to have been handstamped at a later date.

Several types of "R.F." overprints other than those illustrated are known, but their validity is doubtful.

United States No. C25 Handstamped in Black

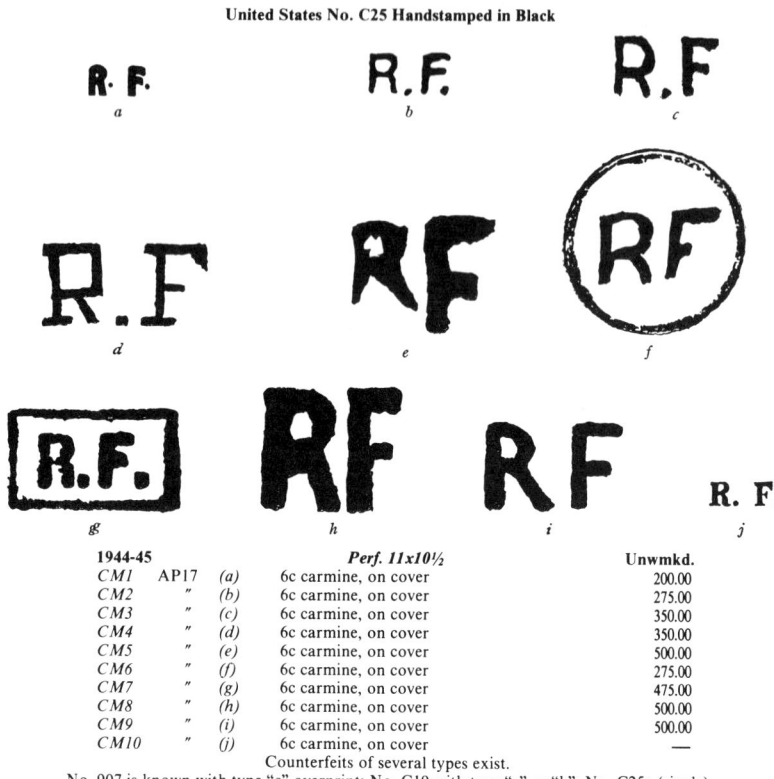

1944-45			*Perf. 11x10½*	Unwmkd.
CM1	AP17	(a)	6c carmine, on cover	200.00
CM2	"	(b)	6c carmine, on cover	275.00
CM3	"	(c)	6c carmine, on cover	350.00
CM4	"	(d)	6c carmine, on cover	350.00
CM5	"	(e)	6c carmine, on cover	500.00
CM6	"	(f)	6c carmine, on cover	275.00
CM7	"	(g)	6c carmine, on cover	475.00
CM8	"	(h)	6c carmine, on cover	500.00
CM9	"	(i)	6c carmine, on cover	500.00
CM10	"	(j)	6c carmine, on cover	—

Counterfeits of several types exist.

No. 907 is known with type "c" overprint; No. C19 with type "e" or "h"; No. C25a (single) with type "c", and No. C26 with type "b" or "f." Type "i" exists in several variations.

STAMPED ENVELOPES
No. UC5 Handstamped in Black

1944-45				
UCM1	UC2	(a)	6c orange, *white*, entire	300.00
UCM2	"	(b)	6c orange, *white*, entire	400.00
UCM3	"	(d)	6c orange, *white*, entire	450.00
UCM4	"	(f)	6c orange, *white*, entire	450.00
UCM5	"	(h)	6c orange, *white*, entire	500.00

SPECIAL DELIVERY STAMPS

Special Delivery service was instituted by the Act of Congress of March 3, 1885, and put into operation on October 1, 1885. The Act limited the service to free delivery offices and such others as served places with a population of 4000 or more, and its privileges were thus operative in but 555 post offices. The Act of August 4, 1886 made the stamps and service available at all post offices and upon any article of mailable matter. To consume the supply of stamps of the first issue, No. E2 was withheld until Sept. 6, 1888.

A Special Delivery stamp, when affixed to any stamped letter or article of mailable matter, secures faster delivery during daytime and evening at most post offices.

Messenger Running
SD1

Messenger Running
SD2

ENGRAVED.

Unwatermarked

Perf. 12.

Printed by the American Bank Note Co.

Plates of 100 subjects in two panes of 50 each.

1885

E1	SD1	10c **blue**, *Oct. 1, 1885*	250.00	30.00
		deep blue	250.00	30.00
		On cover		50.00
		First day cover		8,000.
		Margin block of 8, Impt. & P# 495 or 496	12,000.	
		Margin strip of 4, same	1,600.	
		Double transfer at top	350.00	50.00

1888

E2	SD2	10c **blue**, *Sept. 6, 1888*	250.00	7.50
		deep blue	250.00	7.50
		On cover		25.00
		Margin block of 8, Impt. & P# 73 or 552	12,000.	
		Margin strip of 4, same	1,600.	

Earliest known use: Dec. 18, 1888.

COLUMBIAN EXPOSITION ISSUE.

From January 24, 1893, until January 5, 1894, the special delivery stamp was printed in orange; the issue in that color continued until May 19, 1894, when the stock on hand was exhausted. The stamp in blue was not issued from January 24, 1893 to May 19, 1894. However, on January 5, 1894, printing of the stamp in blue was resumed. Presumably it was reissued from May 19, 1894 until the appearance of E4 on October 10, 1894. The emissions of the blue stamp of this design before January 24, 1893 and after January 5, 1894 are indistinguishable.

1893

E3	SD2	10c **orange**, *Jan. 24, 1893*	165.00	14.00
		deep orange	165.00	14.00
		On cover		60.00
		Margin block of 8, Impt. & P# 73 or 552	7,250.	
		Margin strip of 4, same	1,200.	

Earliest known use: Feb. 11, 1893.

TYPES OF IMPRINT AND PLATE NUMBER.

–◆《BUREAU ENGRAVING & PRINTING》◆– **77**

Type III

–◆《BUREAU ENGRAVING & PRINTING》◆– **257**

Type VI

–◆《BUREAU ENGRAVING & PRINTING》◆– **381**

Type VII

SPECIAL DELIVERY

Helmet of Mercury
SD5

1908

Plates of 280 subjects in four panes of 70 each.

E7	SD5	10c **green,** *Dec. 12, 1908*	60.00	27.50
		dark green	60.00	27.50
		yellowish green	60.00	27.50
		On cover		85.00
		Margin block of 6, T V		
		Impt. & P#	925.00	—
		Margin strip of 3, same	250.00	
		Double transfer	85.00	35.00

Earliest known use: Dec. 14, 1908.

1911   Wmkd. USPS (190)   Perf. 1.

Plates of 200 subjects in four panes of 50 each.

E8	SD4	10c **ultramarine,** *Jan., 1911*	90.00	4.00
		pale ultramarine	90.00	4.00
		dark ultramarine	90.00	4.00
	b.	10c violet blue	90.00	4.00
		On cover		17.50
		Margin block of 6, T VII		
		Impt. & P#	2,750.	—
		Margin block of 6, P# only	2,500.	—
		Top frame line missing (Pl. 5514)	120.00	5.00

Earliest known use: Feb. 13, 1911.

1914   **Perf. 10.**

E9	SD4	10c **ultramarine,** *Sept., 1914*	175.00	5.25
		pale ultramarine	175.00	5.25
		blue	175.00	5.25
		On cover		30.00
		Margin block of 6, T VII		
		Impt. & P#	5,000.	—
		Margin block of 6, P# only	4,250.	—
		Margin block of 8, T VII		
		Impt. & P# (side)	—	

Earliest known use: Oct. 26, 1914.

1916   **Perf. 10.**   Unwmkd

E10	SD4	10c **pale ultramarine,** *Oct. 19, 1916*	325.00	21.00
		ultramarine	300.00	21.00
		blue	300.00	21.00
		On cover		65.00
		Margin block of 6, T VII		
		Impt. & P# 5520	6,250.	—
		Margin block of 6, P# only	5,750.	—

Earliest known use: Nov. 4, 1916.

1917   **Perf. 11**   Unwmkd

E11	SD4	10c **ultramarine,** *May 2, 1917*	15.00	30
		pale ultramarine	15.00	30
		dark ultramarine	15.00	30
	b.	10c gray violet	15.00	30
	c.	10c blue	30.00	50
		On cover		3.00
		Margin block of 6, T VII		
		Impt. & P#	850.00	—
		Margin block of 6, P# only	200.00	—
		Margin block of 8, T VII		
		Impt. & P# (side)	—	
	d.	Perf. 10 at left	—	

Earliest known use: June 12, 1917.

The aniline ink used on some printings of No. E11 permeated the paper causing a pink tinge to appear on the back. Such stamps are called "pink backs."

Messenger Running—SD3
Printed by the Bureau of Engraving and Printing.

1894   Line under "TEN CENTS".

E4	SD3	10c **blue,** *Oct. 10, 1894*	725.00	17.50
		dark blue	725.00	17.50
		bright blue	725.00	17.50
		On cover		100.00
		Block of four	3,400.	
		Margin block of 4, arrow	3,500.	
		Margin block of 6, T III Impt. & P# 77	14,500.	
		Margin strip of 3, same	3,500.	
	a.	Imperf., pair	5,500.	
		Double transfer	—	

Earliest known use: Nov. 21, 1894.

1895   Wmkd. USPS (191)

E5	SD3	10c **blue,** *Aug. 16, 1895*	135.00	2.50
		dark blue	135.00	2.50
		deep blue	135.00	2.50
		On cover		17.50
		Margin block of 4, arrow	600.00	
		Margin block of 6, T III, VI or VII Impt. & P#	4,500.	
		Margin strip of 3, same	625.00	
	a.	Imperf., pair	4,500.	
	b.	Printed on both sides	1,250.	
		Double transfer	—	25.00
		Line of color through "POSTAL DELIVERY", from bottom row of Plates 1257-1260	200.00	15.00
		Dots in curved frame above messenger (Pl. 882)	175.00	10.00

Earliest known use: Oct. 3, 1895.

1902   Messenger on Bicycle—SD4

E6	SD4	10c **ultramarine,** *Dec. 9, 1902*	90.00	2.50
		dark ultramarine	90.00	2.50
		pale ultramarine	90.00	2.50
		blue	90.00	2.50
		On cover		10.00
		P# block of 6, "09"	2,750.	
		Margin block of 4, arrow	450.00	
		Margin block of 6, T VII Impt. & P#	3,000.	
		Margin strip of 3, same	400.00	
		Double transfer	—	
		Damaged transfer under "N" of "CENTS"	150.00	5.00

Earliest known use: Jan. 22, 1903.
No. E6 was re-issued in 1909 from new plates 5240, 5243-5245. After a few months use the Bureau added "09" to these plate numbers. The stamp can be identified only by plate number.

Motorcycle Delivery
SD6

FLAT PLATE PRINTING.

1922			Perf. 11	Unwmkd.	
E12	SD6	10c	**gray violet,** *July 12, 1922*	22.50	15
		a.	10c deep ultramarine	30.00	20
			On cover		1.00
			First day cover		500.00
			Margin block of 6, P# only	375.00	—
			Double transfer	45.00	1.00

Post Office Truck
SD7

1925			Perf. 11	Unwmkd.	

Issued to facilitate special delivery service for parcel post.

E13	SD6	15c	**deep orange,** *April 11, 1925*	22.50	65
			On cover		10.00
			First day cover		250.00
			Margin block of 6, P# only	250.00	—
			Double transfer	35.00	1.50
E14	SD7	20c	**black,** *April 25, 1925*	3.00	1.75
			On cover		2.25
			First day cover		125.00
			Margin block of 6, P# only	37.50	

Motorcycle Type of 1922

ROTARY PRESS PRINTING.

1927			Perf. 11x10½	Unwmkd.	
E15	SD6	10c	**gray violet,** *Nov. 29, 1927*	70	5
		a.	10c red lilac	70	5
		b.	10c gray lilac	70	5
			violet	70	5
			On cover		25
			First day cover		90.00
			Margin block of 4, P# only	5.25	—
		c.	Horizontal pair, imperf. between	275.00	
			Gouged plate	—	
			Cracked plate 19280 LR	50.00	

The design of No. E15 (rotary printing) measures 36½x21¾ mm. Design of stamps from the flat plates measures 36x21⅛ mm.

Motorcycle Type of 1922

ROTARY PRESS PRINTING.

1931			Perf. 11x10½.	Unwmkd.	
E16	SD6	15c	**orange,** *Aug. 13, 1931*	80	8
			On cover		25
			First day cover, Washington, D.C.		125.00
			First day cover, Easton, Pa., *Aug. 6, 1931*		1,000.
			Margin block of 4, P# only	6.50	—

Design of No. E16 measures 36¾x22¼ mm.
Design of No. E13 measures 36½x22½mm.

Motorcycle Type of 1922

ROTARY PRESS PRINTING.

E. E. Plates of 200 subjects in four panes of 50 each.

1944, Oct. 30			Perf. 11x10½	Unwmkd.	
E17	SD6	13c	**blue**	65	6
			First day cover		12.00
			Margin block of 4, P#	4.00	—
E18	SD6	17c	**orange yellow**	5.00	2.25
			First day cover		12.00
			First day cover, Nos. E17 & E18		30.00
			Margin block of 4, P#	28.50	—

Truck Type of 1925

ROTARY PRESS PRINTING.

E. E. Plates of 200 subjects in four panes of 50 each.

1951			Perf. 11x10½.	Unwmkd.	
E19	SD7	20c	**black,** *Nov. 30, 1951*	2.00	12
			First day cover		5.00
			Margin block of 4, P#	12.00	—

Design of No. E19 measures 36¼x22mm.
Design of No. E14 measures 35½x21½mm.

Special Delivery Letter, Hand to Hand
SD8

ROTARY PRESS PRINTING.

E. E. Plates of 200 subjects in four panes of 50 each.

1954			Perf. 11x10½	Unwmkd.	
E20	SD8	20c	**deep blue,** *Oct. 13, 1954*	60	8
			light blue	—	—
			First day cover, Boston *(194,043)*		3.00
			Margin block of 4, P#	4.00	—

SPECIAL DELIVERY—REGISTRATION—CERTIFIED MAIL

1957
E21	SD8	30c **lake,** *Sept. 3, 1957*	90	5
		First Day cover, Indianapolis *(111,451)*		2.25
		Margin block of 4, P#	5.00	—

Arrows
SD9
Designed by Norman Yves.
GIORI PRESS PRINTING
Plates of 200 subjects in four panes of 50 each.

1969   *Perf. 11*   Unwmkd.

E22	SD9	45c **carmine & violet blue,** *Nov. 21*	2.25	20
		First day cover, New York, N.Y.		3.50
		Margin block of 4, P#	11.00	—
		Margin block of 4, Mr. Zip and "Use Zip Code"	9.50	—
		Margin block of 6, "Mail Early in the Day"	14.00	—

1971   *Perf. 11*

E23	SD9	60c **vio. blue & carmine,** *May 10*	1.20	12
		First day cover, Phoenix, Ariz. *(129,562)*		3.50
		Margin block of 4, P#	5.50	—
		Margin block of 4, Mr. Zip and "Use Zip Code"	5.00	—
		Margin block of 6, "Mail Early in the Day"	7.50	—

REGISTRATION STAMP

The Registry System for U.S. mail went into effect July 1, 1855, the fee being 5 cents. On June 30, 1863, the fee was increased to 20 cents.

On Jan. 1, 1869, the fee was reduced to 15 cents and on Jan. 1, 1874, to 8 cents. On July 1, 1875, the fee was increased to 10 cents. On Jan. 1, 1893 the fee was again reduced to 8 cents and again it was increased to 10 cents on Nov. 1, 1909.

Early registered covers with various stamps, rates and postal markings are receiving the attention of collectors.

Registry stamps (10c ultramarine) were issued on Dec. 1, 1911, to prepay registry fees (not postage), but ordinary stamps were valid for registry fees then as now. These special stamps were abolished May 28, 1913, by order of the Postmaster General, who permitted their use until supplies on hand were exhausted.

Eagle
RS1

ENGRAVED
Wmkd. USPS (190)

1911   *Perf. 12*

F1	RS1	10c **ultramarine,** *Dec. 1, 1911*	75.00	4.50
		pale ultramarine	75.00	4.50
		On cover		40.00
		First day cover		8,000.
		Block of four	310.00	75.00
		Margin block of 6, Impt., P# & "A"	1,850.	350.00

CERTIFIED MAIL STAMP

Certified Mail service was started on June 6, 1955, for use on first-class mail for which no indemnity value is claimed but for which proof of mailing and proof of delivery are available at less cost than registered mail. The mailer receives one receipt and the addressee signs another when the postman delivers the letter. The second receipt is kept on file at the Post Office for six months. The 15c Certified Mail charge is in addition to regular postage, whether surface mail, air mail or special delivery.

Letter Carrier
CM1
ROTARY PRESS PRINTING

E. E. Plates of 200 subjects in four panes of 50 each.

1955   *Perf. 10½x11*   Unwmkd.

FA1	CM1	15c **red,** *June 6, 1955*	50	30
		First day cover		3.25
		Margin block of 4, P#	6.25	—

POSTAGE DUE STAMPS

For affixing, by a postal clerk, to any piece of mailable matter, to denote the amount to be collected from the addressee because of insufficient prepayment of postage.

Prior to July, 1879, whenever a letter was unpaid, or insufficiently prepaid, the amount of postage due was written by hand or handstamped on the envelope, and the deficiency collected by the carrier. No vouchers were given for money thus collected.

Postage Due Stamps were authorized by the Act of Congress, approved March 3, 1879, effective July 1, 1879.

Printed by the American Bank Note Co.

Engraved

Plates of 200 subjects in two panes of 100 each.

Figure of Value in Oval
D1

1879			Perf. 12		Unwmkd.	
J1	D1	1c	brown		25.00	5.00
			pale brown		25.00	5.00
			deep brown		25.00	5.00
			Block of four		100.00	25.00
J2	"	2c	brown		165.00	4.00
			pale brown		165.00	4.00
			Block of four		700.00	
J3	"	3c	brown		20.00	2.50
			pale brown		20.00	2.50
			deep brown		20.00	2.50
			yellowish brown		22.50	3.50
			Block of four		85.00	11.00
J4	"	5c	brown		250.00	20.00
			pale brown		250.00	20.00
			deep brown		250.00	20.00
			Block of four		1,050.	
J5	"	10c	brown, Sept. 19		325.00	10.00
			pale brown		325.00	10.00
			deep brown		325.00	10.00
			Block of four		1,400.	
		a.	Imperf., pair		1,600.	
J6	"	30c	brown, Sept. 19		140.00	20.00
			pale brown		140.00	20.00
			Block of four		575.00	
J7	"	50c	brown, Sept. 19		200.00	30.00
			pale brown		200.00	30.00
			Block of four		825.00	

Special Printing.

1879			Perf. 12	Unwmkd.
		Soft porous paper.		
		Printed by the American Bank Note Co.		
J8	D1	1c	deep brown (4,420)	5,500.
J9	"	2c	deep brown (1,361)	3,500.
J10	"	3c	deep brown (436)	3,250.
J11	"	5c	deep brown (249)	2,750.
J12	"	10c	deep brown (174)	1,600.
J13	"	30c	deep brown (179)	1,600.
J14	"	50c	deep brown (179)	1,600.

1884-87			Perf. 12.	Unwmkd.	
J15	D1	1c	red brown	25.00	2.50
			pale red brown	25.00	2.50
			deep red brown	25.00	2.50
			Block of four	105.00	12.00
J16	"	2c	red brown	32.50	2.50
			pale red brown	32.50	2.50
			deep red brown	32.50	2.50
			Block of four	135.00	12.00
J17	"	3c	red brown	425.00	90.00
			deep red brown	425.00	90.00
			Block of four	1,800.	
J18	"	5c	red brown	200.00	10.00
			pale red brown	200.00	10.00
			deep red brown	200.00	10.00
			Block of four	825.00	
J19	"	10c	red brown, March 15, 1887	165.00	5.00
			deep red brown	165.00	5.00
			Block of four	675.00	
J20	"	30c	red brown	90.00	22.50
			deep red brown	90.00	22.50
			Block of four	375.00	110.00
J21	"	50c	red brown	900.00	125.00
			Block of four	3,750.	

1891			Perf. 12.	Unwmkd.	
J22	D1	1c	bright claret	10.00	50
			light claret	10.00	50
			dark claret	10.00	50
			Block of four	42.50	2.25
		a.	Imperforate, pair	450.00	
J23	"	2c	bright claret	12.50	45
			light claret	12.50	45
			dark claret	12.50	45
			Block of four	52.50	2.25
		a.	Imperforate, pair	450.00	
J24	"	3c	bright claret	25.00	2.75
			dark claret	25.00	2.75
			Block of four	105.00	15.00
		a.	Imperforate, pair	450.00	
J25	"	5c	bright claret	27.50	2.75
			light claret	27.50	2.75
			dark claret	27.50	2.75
			Block of four	115.00	15.00
		a.	Imperforate, pair	450.00	
J26	"	10c	bright claret	60.00	7.50
			light claret	60.00	7.50
			Block of four	250.00	35.00
		a.	Imperforate, pair	450.00	
J27	"	30c	bright claret	225.00	85.00
			Block of four	925.00	
		a.	Imperforate, pair	525.00	
J28	"	50c	bright claret	250.00	85.00
			dark claret	250.00	85.00
			Block of four	1,050.	
		a.	Imperforate, pair	525.00	

The imperforate varieties, Nos. J22a-J28a, were not regularly issued.

POSTAGE DUE

Printed by the Bureau of Engraving and Printing.

D2

1894			**Perf. 12**	**Unwmkd.**	
J29	D2	1c **vermilion**		475.00	85.00
		pale vermilion		475.00	85.00
		Block of four		1,900.	350.00
		Margin block of 6, Impt. & P#		5,000.	
J30	"	2c **vermilion**		200.00	35.00
		deep vermilion		200.00	35.00
		Block of four		810.00	
		Margin block of 6, Impt. & P#		2,250.	

1894					
J31	D2	1c **deep claret,** *Aug. 14, 1894*		15.00	3.00
		claret		15.00	3.00
		lake		15.00	3.00
		Block of four		62.50	13.00
		Margin block of 6, Impt. & P#		375.00	
		a. Imperf., pair		225.00	
		a. Block of four		500.00	
		b. Vertical pair, imperf. horiz.			
J32	"	2c **deep claret,** *July 20, 1894*		12.50	1.75
		claret		12.50	1.75
		lake		12.50	1.75
		Block of four		52.50	8.00
		Margin block of 6, Impt. & P#		325.00	
J33	"	3c **deep claret,** *Apr. 27, 1895*		65.00	17.50
		lake		65.00	17.50
		Block of four		275.00	
		Margin block of 6, Impt. & P#		850.00	
J34	"	5c **deep claret,** *Apr. 27, 1895*		70.00	22.50
		claret		70.00	22.50
		Block of four		300.00	
		Margin block of 6, Impt. & P#		950.00	
J35	"	10c **deep claret,** *Sept. 24, 1894*		70.00	12.50
		Block of four		300.00	
		Margin block of 6, Impt. & P#		900.00	
J36	"	30c **deep claret,** *Apr. 27, 1895*		175.00	45.00
		claret		175.00	45.00
		Block of four		725.00	
		a. 30c carmine		165.00	42.50
		a. Block of four (carmine)		675.00	
		b. 30c pale rose		150.00	42.50
		b. Block of four (pale rose)		625.00	
		Margin block of 6, Impt. & P#		2,100.	
J37	"	50c **deep claret,** *Apr. 27, 1895*		425.00	100.00
		Block of four		1,750.	
		a. 50c pale rose		375.00	80.00
		a. Block of four (pale rose)		1,550.	
		Margin block of 6, Impt. & P#		5,000.	

Shades are numerous in the 1894 and later issues.

Wmkd. USPS **(191) Horizontally or Vertically.**

1895				**Perf. 12**	
J38	D2	1c **deep claret,** *Aug. 29, 1895*		4.50	30
		claret		4.50	30
		carmine		4.50	30
		lake		4.50	30
		Block of four		18.50	1.40
		Margin block of 6, Impt. & P#		190.00	
J39	"	2c **deep claret,** *Sept. 14, 1895*		4.50	20
		claret		4.50	20
		carmine		4.50	20
		lake		4.50	20
		Block of four		18.50	1.00
		Margin block of 6, Impt. & P#		190.00	
		Double transfer			

In October, 1895, the Postmaster at Jefferson, Iowa, surcharged a few 2 cent stamps with the words "Due 1 cent" in black on each side, subsequently dividing the stamps vertically and using each half as a 1 cent stamp. Twenty of these were used.

J40	D2	3c **deep claret,** *Oct. 30, 1895*		27.50	1.00
		claret		27.50	1.00
		rose red		27.50	1.00
		carmine		27.50	1.00
		Block of four		112.50	4.50
		Margin block of 6, Impt. & P#		425.00	
J41	"	5c **deep claret,** *Oct. 15, 1895*		27.50	1.00
		claret		27.50	1.00
		carmine rose		27.50	1.00
		Block of four		112.50	4.50
		Margin block of 6, Impt. & P#		450.00	
J42	"	10c **deep claret,** *Sept. 14, 1895*		30.00	2.00
		claret		30.00	2.00
		carmine		30.00	2.00
		lake		30.00	2.00
		Block of four		122.50	8.50
		Margin block of 6, Impt. & P#		550.00	
J43	"	30c **deep claret,** *Aug. 21, 1897*		225.00	17.50
		claret		225.00	17.50
		Block of four		925.00	
		Margin block of 6, Impt. & P#		3,750.	
J44	"	50c **deep claret,** *Mar. 17, 1896*		150.00	18.50
		claret		150.00	18.50
		Block of four		625.00	80.00
		Margin block of 6, Impt. & P#		2,250.	

Wmkd. USPS **(190)**

1910-12				**Perf. 12**	
J45	D2	1c **deep claret,** *Aug. 30, 1910*		17.50	2.00
		a. 1c rose carmine		16.00	1.75
		Block of four (2 or 3mm spacing)		72.50	9.00
		Margin block of 6, Impt. & P# & star		400.00	
J46	"	2c **deep claret,** *Nov. 25, 1910*		17.50	15
		lake		17.50	15
		a. 2c rose carmine		16.00	15
		Block of four (2 or 3mm spacing)		72.50	75
		Margin block of 6, Impt. & P# & star		350.00	
		Margin block of 6, P# only		375.00	
		Double transfer			
J47	"	3c **deep claret,** *Aug. 31, 1910*		325.00	15.00
		lake		325.00	15.00
		Block of four (2 or 3mm spacing)		1,350.	65.00
		Margin block of 6, Impt. & P# & star		3,850.	
J48	"	5c **deep claret,** *Aug. 31, 1910*		50.00	2.50
		a. 5c rose carmine			
		Block of four (2 or 3mm spacing)		190.00	11.00
		Margin block of 6, Impt. & P# & star		600.00	
J49	"	10c **deep claret,** *Aug. 31, 1910*		65.00	7.50
		a. 10c rose carmine			
		Block of four (2 or 3mm spacing)		275.00	32.50
		Margin block of 6, Impt. & P# & star		1,150.	
J50	"	50c **deep claret,** *Sept. 23, 1912*		550.00	65.00
		Block of four (2 or 3mm spacing)		2,350.	
		Margin block of 6, Impt. & P# & star		6,500.	

1914-15				**Perf. 10**	
J52	D2	1c **carmine lake**		35.00	7.50
		deep carmine lake		35.00	7.50
		a. 1c dull rose		35.00	7.50
		Block of four (2 or 3mm spacing)		145.00	32.00
		Margin block of 6, Impt. & P# & star		550.00	75.00
J53	"	2c **carmine lake**		25.00	20
		a. 2c dull rose		25.00	20
		b. 2c vermilion		25.00	20
		Block of four		105.00	1.00
		Margin block of 6, P# only		350.00	7.50

POSTAGE DUE

J54	D2	3c **carmine lake**	350.00	15.00
		a. 3c dull rose	350.00	15.00
		Block of four (2 or 3mm spacing)	1,450.	—
		Margin block of 6, Impt. & P# & star	4,500.	—
J55	"	5c **carmine lake**	20.00	1.50
		a. 5c dull rose	20.00	1.50
		carmine rose	20.00	1.50
		deep claret		
		Block of four (2 or 3mm spacing)	82.50	7.00
		Margin block of 6, Impt. & P# & star	285.00	30.00
J56	"	10c **carmine lake**	32.50	1.00
		a. 10c dull rose	32.50	1.00
		carmine rose	32.50	1.00
		Block of four (2 or 3mm spacing)	132.50	4.75
		Margin block of 6, Impt. & P# & star	675.00	30.00
J57	"	30c **carmine lake**	125.00	12.00
		Block of four (2 or 3mm spacing)	525.00	50.00
		Margin block of 6, Impt. & P# & star	2,350.	125.00
J58	"	50c **carmine lake**	5,000.	350.00
		Block of four (2 or 3mm spacing)	21,000.	1,500.
		Margin block of 6, Impt. & P# & star	36,000.	

J66	"	30c **carmine rose**	50.00	40
		a. 30c deep claret	50.00	40
		claret brown	50.00	40
		Block of four (2 or 3mm spacing)	210.00	1.75
		Margin block of 6, Impt. & P# & star	525.00	—
		Margin block of 6, P# only	550.00	—
J67	"	50c **carmine rose**	65.00	12
		a. 50c rose red	65.00	12
		b. 50c deep claret	65.00	15
		claret brown	65.00	15
		Block of four (2 or 3mm spacing)	275.00	50
		Margin block of 6, Impt. & P# & star	750.00	7.50
		Margin block of 6, P# only	800.00	8.50

1925

J68	D2	½c **dull red,** *Apr. 13, 1925*	50	6
		Block of four	2.00	24
		Margin block of 6, P# only	11.00	50

1916   Perf. 10   Unwmkd.

J59	D2	1c **rose**	850.00	150.00
		Block of four (2 or 3mm spacing)	3,500.	650.00
		Margin block of 6, Impt. & P# & star	7,250.	
J60	"	2c **rose**	70.00	6.00
		Block of four	290.00	—
		Margin block of 6, P# only	800.00	25.00

1917-23   Perf. 11.   Unwmkd.

J61	D2	1c **carmine rose**	1.50	8
		dull rose	1.50	8
		a. 1c rose red	1.50	15
		b. 1c deep claret	1.50	8
		claret brown	1.50	8
		Block of four (2 or 3mm spacing)	6.25	35
		Margin block of 6, Impt. & P# & star	85.00	75
		Margin block of 6, P# only	40.00	65
J62	"	2c **carmine rose**	1.25	5
		a. 2c rose red	1.25	5
		b. 2c deep claret	1.25	5
		claret brown	1.25	5
		Block of four	5.25	20
		Margin block of 6, P# only	35.00	60
		Double transfer		
J63	"	3c **carmine rose**	7.50	8
		a. 3c rose red	7.50	7
		b. 3c deep claret	7.50	25
		claret brown	7.50	25
		Block of four (2 or 3mm spacing)	32.50	30
		Margin block of 6, Impt. & P# & star	100.00	2.25
		Margin block of 6, P# only	85.00	1.50
J64	"	5c **carmine**	7.50	8
		carmine rose	7.50	8
		a. 5c rose red	7.50	8
		b. 5c deep claret	7.50	5
		claret brown	7.50	10
		Block of four (2 or 3mm spacing)	32.50	32
		Margin block of 6, Impt. & P# & star	100.00	2.85
		Margin block of 6, P# only	85.00	1.50
J65	D2	10c **carmine rose**	10.00	20
		a. 10c rose red	10.00	6
		b. 10c deep claret	10.00	6
		claret brown	10.00	6
		Block of four (2 or 3mm spacing)	42.50	85
		Margin block of 6, Impt. & P# & star	125.00	4.50
		Margin block of 6, P# only	135.00	2.00
		Double transfer		

D3

D4

1930-31   Perf. 11.   Unwmkd.

Design measures 19 × 22 mm.

J69	D3	½c **carmine**	3.50	70
		Block of four	14.00	3.00
		Margin block of 6, P#	35.00	7.50
J70	"	1c **carmine**	2.50	15
		Block of four	10.00	75
		Margin block of 6, P#	27.50	2.00
J71	"	2c **carmine**	3.50	15
		Block of four	14.00	75
		Margin block of 6, P#	40.00	2.00
J72	"	3c **carmine**	25.00	1.00
		Block of four	100.00	4.25
		Margin block of 6, P#	240.00	10.00

POSTAGE DUE

J73	D3	5c	carmine	20.00	1.50
			Block of four	80.00	6.50
			Margin block of 6, P#	225.00	15.00
J74	"	10c	carmine	42.50	50
			Block of four	170.00	2.25
			Margin block of 6, P#	400.00	7.50
J75	"	30c	carmine	120.00	1.00
			Block of four	480.00	5.00
			Margin block of 6, P#	1,000.	15.00
J76	"	50c	carmine	140.00	30
			Block of four	560.00	1.30
			Margin block of 6, P#	1,150.	10.00

Design measures 22 x 19 mm.

J77	D4	$1	carmine	30.00	6
			Block of four	120.00	24
		a.	$1 scarlet	25.00	6
		a.	Block of four, scarlet	100.00	25
			Margin block of 6, P#	275.00	
J78	"	$5	carmine	40.00	12
			Block of four	160.00	48
		a.	$5 scarlet	35.00	12
		a.	Block of four, scarlet	140.00	48
			Margin block of 6, P#	375.00	

Postage due stamps printed by both the "wet" and "dry" process are Nos. J78, J80–J84. See note on Wet and Dry Printings following No. 1029.

Type of 1930-31 Issue.
Rotary Press Printing
Ordinary and Electric Eye Plates.
Design measures 19 x 22½ mm.

1931-32   *Perf. 11x10½.*   Unwmkd.

J79	D3	½c	dull carmine	1.25	8
		a.	½c scarlet	1.25	8
			Margin block of 4, P#	22.50	1.00
J80	"	1c	dull carmine	15	5
		a.	1c scarlet	15	5
			Margin block of 4, P#	2.00	25
			Pair with full vertical gutter between		
J81	"	2c	dull carmine	15	5
		a.	2c scarlet	15	5
			Margin block of 4, P#	2.00	25
J82	"	3c	dull carmine	25	5
		a.	3c scarlet	25	5
			Margin block of 4, P#	3.00	30
J83	"	5c	dull carmine	35	5
		a.	5c scarlet	35	5
			Margin block of 4, P#	4.00	35
J84	"	10c	dull carmine	1.10	5
		a.	10c scarlet	1.10	5
			Margin block of 4, P#	8.50	45
J85	"	30c	dull carmine	8.50	8
		a.	30c scarlet	8.50	8
			Margin block of 4, P#	45.00	90
J86	"	50c	dull carmine	9.50	6
		a.	50c scarlet	9.50	6
			Margin block of 4, P#	57.50	90

Design measures 22½ x 19 mm.

1956   *Perf. 10½x11*

J87	D4	$1	scarlet	40.00	20
			Margin block of 4, P#	300.00	2.50

D5
Rotary Press Printing

Denominations added in black by rubber plates in an operation similar to precanceling.

1959, June 19   *Perf. 11x10½*   Unwmkd.

J88	D5	½c	carmine rose	1.25	85
			Margin block of 4, P#	125.00	
J89	"	1c	carmine rose	5	5
			Margin block of 4, P#	50	
		a.	"1 CENT" omitted	350.00	
		b.	Pair, one without "1 CENT"		
J90	"	2c	carmine rose	6	5
			Margin block of 4, P#	60	
J91	"	3c	carmine rose	7	5
			Margin block of 4, P#	70	
		a.	Pair, one without "3 CENTS"		
J92	"	4c	carmine rose	8	5
			Margin block of 4, P#	1.25	
J93	"	5c	carmine rose	10	5
			Margin block of 4, P#	75	
		a.	Pair, one without "5 CENTS"		
J94	"	6c	carmine rose	12	5
			Margin block of 4, P#	1.40	
		a.	Pair, one without "6 CENTS"		
			Pair with full vert. gutter btwn.		
J95	"	7c	carmine rose	14	6
			Margin block of 4, P#	1.60	
J96	"	8c	carmine rose	16	5
			Margin block of 4, P#	1.75	
		a.	Pair, one without "8 CENTS"		
J97	"	10c	carmine rose	20	5
			Margin block of 4, P#	1.25	
J98	"	30c	carmine rose	70	5
			Margin block of 4, P#	5.50	
J99	"	50c	carmine rose	1.10	5
			Margin block of 4, P#	6.50	

Straight Numeral Outlined in Black.

J100	D5	$1	carmine rose	2.00	5
			Margin block of 4, P#	10.00	
J101	"	$5	carmine rose	8.00	15
			Margin block of 4, P#	40.00	

The 2c, 4c, 7c and 8c exist in vertical pairs with numerals widely spaced. This spacing was intended to accommodate the gutter, but sometimes fell within the pane.

Rotary Press Printing
1978, Jan. 2   *Perf. 11x10½*
Denomination in Black

J102	D5	11c	carmine rose	22	5
			Margin block of 4, P#	1.10	
J103	"	13c	carmine rose	26	5
			Margin block of 4, P#	1.30	
J104	D5	17c	carmine rose, *June 10, 1985*	34	5
			Margin block of 4, P#	1.70	

BUYING AND SELLING CLASSIC & 20TH CENTURY U.S.

POSTAGE DUES - NEWSPAPERS - OFFICIALS - SAVINGS - REVENUES - POSSESSIONS
MINT - USED - MULTIPLES - COVERS - ESSAYS - PROOFS - SPECIMENS
WRITE, CALL, OR SHIP. LOTS HELD INTACT PENDING ACCEPTANCE OF MY PROMPT OFFER.

Price Lists Available
Want Lists Accepted.

LEWIS KAUFMAN
Box 255, Kiamesha Lake, NY 12751 • (914) 794-8013

OFFICES IN CHINA

U. S. POSTAL AGENCY IN CHINA.

Postage stamps of the 1917-19 U.S. series (then current) were issued to the U. S. Postal Agency, Shanghai, China, surcharged (as illustrated) at double the original value of the stamps. The surcharges on the 1919 issue are in black, except on the 7-cent and $1 which are surcharged in red ink.

These stamps were intended for sale at Shanghai at their surcharged value in local currency, valid for prepayment on mail despatched from the United States Postal Agency at Shanghai to addresses in the United States.

Stamps were first issued May 24, 1919, and were placed on sale at Shanghai on July 1, 1919. These stamps were not issued to postmasters in the United States. The Shanghai post office, according to the U.S.P.O. Bulletin was closed in December, 1922. After the closing of the Shanghai office, the stamps were on sale at the Philatelic Agency in Washington, D. C. for a short time.

The postmarks of the China office were "U.S. Postal Agency Shanghai China" and "U.S.Pos. Service Shanghai China".

United States Stamps Nos. 498 to 518 Surcharged

SHANGHAI 2¢ CHINA

1919   *Perf. 11*   Unwmkd.

K1	A140	2c on 1c **green**	20.00	22.50
		Block of four	82.50	100.00
		Margin block of six, P#	275.00	
K2	"	4c on 2c **rose**, type I	20.00	22.50
		Block of four	82.50	100.00
		Margin block of six, P#	275.00	
K3	"	6c on 3c **violet**, type II	37.50	50.00
		Block of four	155.00	235.00
		Margin block of six, P#	450.00	
K4	"	8c on 4c **brown**	45.00	50.00
		Block of four	185.00	235.00
		Margin block of six, P#	550.00	
K5	"	10c on 5c **blue**	50.00	57.50
		Block of four	210.00	250.00
		Margin block of six, P#	525.00	
K6	"	12c on 6c **red orange**	60.00	72.50
		Block of four	250.00	325.00
		Margin block of six, P#	700.00	
K7	"	14c on 7c **black**	65.00	80.00
		Block of four	270.00	375.00
		Margin block of six, P#	800.00	
K8	A148	16c on 8c **olive bister**	50.00	55.00
	a.	16c on 8c olive green	45.00	47.50
		Block of four	210.00	275.00
		Margin block of six, P#	600.00	
K9	"	18c on 9c **salmon red**	50.00	60.00
		Block of four	210.00	300.00
		Margin block of six, P#	650.00	
K10	"	20c on 10c **orange yellow**	45.00	52.50
		Block of four	190.00	250.00
		Margin block of six, P#	600.00	
K11	"	24c on 12c **brown carmine**	52.50	62.50
	a.	24c on 12c claret brown	67.50	77.50
		Block of four (brown carmine)	220.00	300.00
		Margin block of six, P#	800.00	
K12	"	30c on 15c **gray**	65.00	80.00
		Block of four	270.00	375.00
		Margin block of six, P#	1,000.	
K13	"	40c on 20c **deep ultramarine**	100.00	125.00
		Block of four	425.00	600.00
		Margin block of six, P#	1,300.	
K14	"	60c on 30c **orange red**	90.00	110.00
		Block of four	375.00	525.00
		Margin block of six, P#	1,000.	
K15	"	$1 on 50c **light violet**	600.00	500.00
		Block of four	2,500.	2,250.
		Margin block of six, P#	10,000.	
K16	"	$2 on $1 **violet brown**	425.00	425.00
		Block of four	1,750.	2,000.
		Margin block of four, arrow, right or left	1,850.	
		Margin block of six, P#	7,500.	
	a.	Double surcharge	2,500.	2,250.

United States Stamps Nos. 498 and 528B Locally Surcharged

SHANGHAI 2 Cts. CHINA

1922, July 3

K17	A140	2c on 1c **green**	90.00	75.00
		Block of four	365.00	350.00
		Margin block of six, P#	725.00	
K18	"	4c on 2c **carmine**, type VII	80.00	70.00
		Block of four	325.00	350.00
		Margin block of six, P#	675.00	
		"SHANGHAI" omitted		
		"CHINA" only		

OFFICIAL STAMPS

Official stamps were authorized by Act of Congress, approved March 3, 1873, abolishing the franking privilege. Stamps of special design for each government department to prepay postage on official matter were issued July 1, 1873. These stamps were supplanted on May 1, 1879, by penalty envelopes and on July 5, 1884, were declared obsolete.

DESIGNS. All Official stamps have name of department at top. Large numerals form the central design of the Post Office Department stamps. Those for the other departments picture the same busts used in the regular postage issue: 1c Franklin, 2c Jackson, 3c Washington, 6c Lincoln, 7c Stanton, 10c Jefferson, 12c Clay, 15c Webster, 24c Scott, 30c Hamilton, 90c Perry, $2, $10 and $20 Seward.

Designs of the various denominations are not identical, but resemble those illustrated.

PLATES. Plates of 200 subjects in two panes of 100 were used for Post Office Department 1c, 3c, 6c Treasury Department 1c, 2c, 3c, and War Department 2c, 3c. Plates of 10 subjects were used for State Department $2, $5, $10 and $20. Plates of 100 subjects were used for all other Official stamps.

CANCELLATIONS. Odd or Town cancellations on Departmental stamps are relatively much scarcer than those appearing on the general issues of the same period. Town cancellations, especially on the 1873 issue, are scarce. The "Kicking Mule" cancellation is found used on stamps of the War Department and has also been seen on some stamps of the other Departments. Black is usual.

CONDITION. Examples that are fresh, well centered and (if unused) have original gum, sell at much higher prices.

Practically all official stamps exist imperforate but little is known of their history.

SPECIAL PRINTING. In 1875 a Special printing of the Official stamps was made along with those of the regular issues. These stamps were overprinted "SPECIMEN". They are listed in the "Specimen" Stamps section.

Printed by the Continental Bank Note Co.
Thin Hard Paper.
Engraved
1873　　　　　Perf. 12　　　　Unwmkd.

AGRICULTURE.

Franklin
O1

O1	O1	1c **yellow**		55.00	30.00
		golden yellow		57.50	32.50
		olive yellow		60.00	35.00
		On cover			—
		Block of four		275.00	
		Ribbed paper		60.00	35.00

CANCELLATIONS.

	Town	+7.50
Magenta +7.50		
Purple +7.50		
Blue +5.00		

O2	O1	2c **yellow**		37.50	13.50
		golden yellow		40.00	14.50
		olive yellow		45.00	15.50
		On cover			1,100.
		Block of four		175.00	
		Ribbed paper		40.00	16.50

CANCELLATIONS.

	Town	+5.00
Blue + 3.00		
Red +15.00		
Magenta + 5.00		

O3	"	3c **yellow**		30.00	3.50
		golden yellow		32.50	4.00
		olive yellow		37.50	4.50
		On cover			600.00
		Block of four		145.00	
		Ribbed paper		35.00	6.00
		Double transfer		—	—

CANCELLATIONS.

	Town	+ 4.00
Blue + .50	"Paid"	+27.50
Purple + 1.00	Railroad	+75.00
Magenta + 1.00	Numeral	+35.00
Violet + 1.00		
Red + 12.00		
Green +125.00		

OFFICIAL STAMPS 401

04	O1	6c **yellow**		40.00	12.50	O11	O2	2c **carmine**	150.00	70.00
		golden yellow		42.50	13.50			deep carmine	150.00	70.00
		olive yellow		45.00	15.00			On cover		1,500.
		On cover			700.00			Block of four	1,500.	
		Pair on cover			—			Double transfer		—
		Block of four		185.00						

CANCELLATIONS.

		Town	+7.00
Blue	+3.00	Express Company	—
Magenta	+4.00		
Violet	+4.00		

CANCELLATIONS.

		Red	+50.00
Blue	+10.00		

05	"	10c **yellow**		95.00	47.50	O12	"	3c **carmine**	175.00	65.00
		golden yellow		100.00	50.00			a. 3c violet rose	150.00	65.00
		olive yellow		110.00	52.00			On cover		700.00
		On cover			—			Block of four	950.00	
		Block of four		425.00						

CANCELLATIONS.

		Town	+15.00
Purple	+5.00		
Blue	+5.00		

CANCELLATIONS.

		Town	+25.00
Blue	+10.00		
Purple	+10.00		

06	"	12c **yellow**		130.00	70.00	O13	"	6c **carmine**	275.00	140.00
		golden yellow		160.00	75.00			pale carmine	275.00	140.00
		olive yellow		170.00	85.00			deep carmine	275.00	140.00
		On cover			—			On cover		2,000.
		Block of four		650.00				Block of four	2,250.	

CANCELLATIONS.

		Town	+20.00
Purple	+10.00		
Blue	+10.00		

CANCELLATIONS.

		Town	+50.00
Purple	+15.00		

O7	"	15c **yellow**		90.00	47.50	O14	"	10c **carmine**	250.00	150.00
		golden yellow		95.00	50.00			pale carmine	250.00	150.00
		olive yellow		100.00	55.00			deep carmine	250.00	150.00
		Block of four		410.00	—			Block of four	2,250.	

CANCELLATIONS.

Purple	+10.00

CANCELLATIONS.

		Purple	+15.00
Blue	+15.00		

O8	"	24c **yellow**		110.00	55.00	
		golden yellow		125.00	60.00	
		Block of four		500.00		

1873   INTERIOR.

Franklin
O3

CANCELLATIONS.

	Purple	+10.00

O9	"	30c **yellow**		150.00	85.00	O15	O3	1c **vermilion**	15.00	2.25
		golden yellow		160.00	90.00			dull vermilion	15.00	2.25
		olive yellow		170.00	100.00			bright vermilion	15.00	2.25
		Block of four		650.00				On cover		125.00
								Block of four	65.00	—
								Ribbed paper	18.50	4.50

CANCELLATIONS.

	Red	+35.00

1873   EXECUTIVE.

Franklin
O2

CANCELLATIONS.

		Town	+3.00
Purple	+ 1.00		
Blue	+ 1.00		
Red	+12.50		
Ultramarine	+ 8.00		

O10	O2	1c **carmine**		225.00	85.00	O16	"	2c **vermilion**	12.00	1.50
		deep carmine		225.00	85.00			dull vermilion	12.00	1.50
		On cover			1,300.			bright vermilion	12.00	1.50
		Block of four		5,000.				On cover		60.00
								Block of four	55.00	12.50

CANCELLATIONS.

		Town	+30.00
Purple	+10.00		
Blue	+10.00		
Red	+50.00		

CANCELLATIONS.

		Town	+2.00
Purple	+ .75		
Blue	+ .75		
Red	+ 6.00		

OFFICIAL STAMPS

O17	O3	3c **vermilion**		20.00	1.50
		dull vermilion		20.00	1.50
		bright vermilion		20.00	1.50
		On cover			40.00
		Block of four		85.00	
		Ribbed paper		25.00	4.00

CANCELLATIONS.

Purple	+ 1.00	Town	+ 2.00
Blue	+ 1.00	Express Company	+75.00
Red	+15.00	"Paid"	+20.00
Green	+65.00	Fort	

O18	"	6c **vermilion**		15.00	1.50
		dull vermilion		15.00	1.50
		bright vermilion		15.00	1.50
		scarlet vermilion		15.00	2.00
		On cover			85.00
		Block of four		65.00	

CANCELLATIONS.

Purple	+ 1.00	Town	+2.00
Blue	+ 1.00	Express Company	
Red	+15.00	Railroad	
		Fort	

O19	"	10c **vermilion**		12.50	3.50
		dull vermilion		12.50	3.50
		bright vermilion		12.50	3.50
		On cover			225.00
		Block of four		55.00	

CANCELLATIONS.

Purple	+ 1.00	Town	+4.00
Blue	+ 1.00	Fort	

O20	"	12c **vermilion**		20.00	2.50
		bright vermilion		20.00	2.50
		On cover			275.00
		Block of four		87.50	

CANCELLATIONS.

Purple	+ 1.00	Town	+4.00
Magenta	+ 1.00	Fort	
Blue	+ 1.00		
Red	+15.00		

O21	"	15c **vermilion**		37.50	7.25
		bright vermilion		37.50	7.25
		On cover			450.00
		Block of four		160.00	
		Double transfer		55.00	17.50

CANCELLATIONS.

Blue	+1.50	Town	+5.00
Purple	+1.50		

O22	"	24c **vermilion**		27.50	5.50
		dull vermilion		27.50	5.50
		bright vermilion		27.50	5.50
		On cover			500.00
		Block of four		125.00	

CANCELLATIONS.

Purple	+ 1.50	Town	+5.00
Blue	+ 1.50		
Red	+15.00		

O23	"	30c **vermilion**		37.50	5.75
		bright vermilion		37.50	5.75
		On cover			
		Block of four		160.00	

CANCELLATIONS.

Purple	+ 2.00	Town	+5.00
Blue	+ 2.00		
Red	+15.00		

O24	"	90c **vermilion**		85.00	12.50
		bright vermilion		85.00	12.50
		On cover			
		Block of four		400.00	120.00
		Double transfer			

CANCELLATIONS.

Purple	+4.00	Town	+7.50
Blue	+4.00		

1873

JUSTICE.

Franklin
O4

O25	O4	1c **purple**		35.00	17.50
		dark purple		35.00	17.50
		On cover			600.00
		Block of four		160.00	

CANCELLATIONS.

Violet	+ 3.00	Town	+ 7.50
Blue	+ 3.00		
Red	+20.00		

O26	"	2c **purple**		57.50	20.00
		light purple		57.50	20.00
		On cover			
		Block of four		250.00	

CANCELLATIONS.

Violet	+ 4.00	Town	+10.00
Blue	+ 4.00		
Red	+20.00		

O27	"	3c **purple**		60.00	7.00
		dark purple		60.00	7.00
		bluish purple		60.00	7.00
		On cover			400.00
		Block of four		260.00	
		Double transfer			

CANCELLATIONS.

Purple	+ 2.00	Town	+5.00
Magenta	+ 2.00		
Blue	+ 2.00		
Red	+ 12.00		
Green	+100.00		

O28	"	6c **purple**		52.50	10.00
		light purple		52.50	10.00
		bluish purple		52.50	10.00
		On cover			500.00
		Block of four		240.00	

CANCELLATIONS.

Violet	+ 2.00	Town	+7.50
Purple	+ 2.00		
Blue	+ 2.00		
Red	+15.00		

O29	"	10c **purple**		60.00	25.00
		bluish purple		60.00	25.00
		On cover			1,200.00
		Block of four		275.00	
		Double transfer			

CANCELLATIONS.

Violet	+4.00	Town	+10.00
Blue	+4.00		

O30	"	12c **purple**		40.00	12.00
		dark purple		40.00	12.00
		On cover			800.00
		Block of four		175.00	

CANCELLATIONS.

Purple	+2.00	Town	+7.50
Blue	+2.00		

OFFICIAL STAMPS

O31	O4	15c **purple**		95.00	47.50
		On cover			900.00
		Block of four		550.00	
		Double transfer			

CANCELLATIONS.

		Town	+10.00
Blue	+5.00		
Purple	+5.00		

O32	"	24c **purple**		275.00	120.00
		On cover			1,100.
		Block of four			

CANCELLATIONS.

		Town	+30.00
Violet	+ 10.00		
Purple	+ 10.00		
Blue	+ 10.00		
Red	+ 35.00		

O33	"	30c **purple**		250.00	85.00
		On cover			
		Block of four		1,300.	
		Double transfer at top			

CANCELLATIONS.

		Town	+30.00
Blue	+ 10.00		
Purple	+ 10.00		
Red	+ 35.00		

O34	"	90c **purple**		375.00	175.00
		dark purple		375.00	175.00
		Block of four			

CANCELLATIONS

		Violet	+25.00
Blue	+25.00		

1873   NAVY.

Franklin
O5

O35	O5	1c **ultramarine**		30.00	10.00
		dark ultramarine		30.00	10.00
		a. 1c dull blue		37.50	12.00
		On cover			250.00
		Block of four		135.00	

CANCELLATIONS.

		Town	+ 7.50
Violet	+ 2.00	Steamship	+100.00
Blue	+ 2.00		
Red	+20.00		

O36	"	2c **ultramarine**		20.00	8.00
		dark ultramarine		20.00	8.00
		a. 2c dull blue		27.50	10.00
		gray blue		22.50	10.00
		On cover			200.00
		Block of four		90.00	
		Double transfer			

The 2c deep green, both perforated and imperforate, is a trial color proof.

CANCELLATIONS.

		Town	+10.00
Purple	+ 1.50	Steamship	+85.00
Violet	+ 1.50		
Blue	+ 1.50		
Red	+15.00		
Green	+75.00		

O37	O5	3c **ultramarine**		24.00	3.00
		pale ultramarine		24.00	3.00
		dark ultramarine		24.00	3.00
		a. 3c dull blue		30.00	4.50
		On cover			150.00
		Block of four		105.00	
		Double transfer			

CANCELLATIONS.

		Town	+ 5.00
Violet	+ 1.50	Blue town	+15.00
Blue	+ 1.50	Steamship	+50.00
Red	+15.00		

O38	"	6c **ultramarine**		20.00	4.50
		bright ultramarine		20.00	4.50
		a. 6c dull blue		27.50	6.50
		On cover			225.00
		Block of four		90.00	
		Vertical line through "N" of "Navy" (Pos. 2 & 6, plate 53)		50.00	12.50
		Double transfer			

CANCELLATIONS.

		Town	+ 5.00
Violet	+ 1.50	Steamship	+65.00
Purple	+ 1.50		
Blue	+ 1.50		
Red	+17.50		
Green	+75.00		

O39	"	7c **ultramarine**		150.00	60.00
		dark ultramarine		150.00	60.00
		a. 7c dull blue		175.00	75.00
		On cover			
		Block of four		700.00	
		Double transfer			

CANCELLATIONS.

		Town	+15.00
Blue	+10.00		
Violet	+10.00		
Magenta	+10.00		
Red	+40.00		

O40	"	10c **ultramarine**		26.00	10.00
		dark ultramarine		26.00	10.00
		a. 10c dull blue		30.00	12.00
		On cover			1,350.
		Block of four		125.00	
		Cracked plate		65.00	
		Ribbed paper		30.00	15.00

CANCELLATIONS.

		Town	+10.00
Violet	+ 2.00	Steamship	+85.00
Blue	+ 2.00		
Brown	+20.00		
Purple	+ 2.00		
Red	+25.00		

O41	"	12c **ultramarine**		37.50	8.25
		pale ultramarine		37.50	8.25
		dark ultramarine		37.50	8.25
		On cover			1,500.
		Block of four		170.00	
		Double transfer of left side		85.00	

CANCELLATIONS.

		Town	+10.00
Purple	+ 2.50	Supplementary Mail	+80.00
Magenta	+ 2.50	Steamship	+100.00
Blue	+ 2.50		
Red	+25.00		

O42	"	15c **ultramarine**		65.00	22.50
		dark ultramarine		65.00	22.50
		Block of four		350.00	

CANCELLATIONS.

		Town	+20.00
Blue	+ 2.50		
Red	+35.00		

OFFICIAL STAMPS

O43	O5	24c **ultramarine**		65.00	30.00
		dark ultramarine		65.00	30.00
		a. 24c dull blue		75.00	—
		Block of four		350.00	

CANCELLATIONS.

		Town	+ 20.00
Magenta	+ 5.00	Steamship	+100.00
Blue	+ 5.00		
Green	+150.00		

O44	"	30c **ultramarine**		55.00	12.50
		dark ultramarine		55.00	12.50
		Block of four		275.00	
		Double transfer		90.00	25.00

CANCELLATIONS.

		Town	+ 10.00
Blue	+ 4.00	Supplementary	
Red	+30.00	Mail	+125.00
Purple	+ 4.00		
Violet	+ 4.00		

O45	"	90c **ultramarine**		275.00	80.00
		Block of four		1,300.	
		a. Double impression			2,000.

CANCELLATIONS.

		Town	+25.00
Purple	+15.00		

1873   **POST OFFICE.**

Numeral of Value
O6

Stamps of the Post Office Department are often on paper with a gray surface. This is due to insufficient wiping of the plates during printing.

O47	O6	1c **black**		7.25	3.00
		gray black		7.25	3.00
		On cover			50.00
		Block of four		32.50	—

CANCELLATIONS.

		Town	+3.50
Purple	+ 1.00		
Magenta	+ 1.00		
Blue	+ 1.00		
Red	+12.50		

O48	"	2c **black**		7.00	2.50
		gray black		7.00	2.50
		On cover			50.00
		Block of four		32.50	
		a. Double impression		300.00	

CANCELLATIONS.

		Town	+3.50
Magenta	+ 1.00	Blue town	+7.50
Purple	+ 1.00		
Blue	+ 1.00		
Red	+12.50		

O49	"	3c **black**		2.50	.75
		gray black		2.50	.75
		On cover			25.00
		Block of four		11.50	5.00
		Cracked plate		—	—
		Double transfer at bottom		—	—
		Double paper		—	—
		Vertical ribbed paper		—	—

				Town	+1.50
Purple	+ .75	Railroad	+25.00
Magenta	+ .75	"Paid"	+12.00
Violet	+ .75		
Blue	+ .75		
Ultramarine	+ 1.50		
Red	+10.00		
Green	+60.00		

O50	O6	6c **black**		7.00	1.65
		gray black		7.00	1.65
		On cover			75.00
		Block of four		32.50	—
		a. Diagonal half used as 3c on cover			2,750.
		Vertical ribbed paper		—	7.50

CANCELLATIONS.

		Town	+ 2.50
Purple	+ .75	"Paid"	+15.00
Magenta	+ .75		
Blue	+ .75		
Red	+12.00		

O51	"	10c **black**		32.50	16.50
		gray black		32.50	16.50
		On cover			400.00
		Block of four		150.00	—

CANCELLATIONS.

		Red	+15.00
Purple	+3.50	Town	+10.00
Magenta	+3.50		
Blue	+3.50		

O52	"	12c **black**		17.50	3.75
		gray black		17.50	3.75
		On cover			425.00
		Block of four		75.00	—

CANCELLATIONS.

		Town	+4.00
Purple	+ 1.00		
Magenta	+ 1.00		
Blue	+ 1.00		
Red	+ 12.50		

O53	"	15c **black**		20.00	6.50
		gray black		20.00	6.50
		On cover			1,000.
		Block of four		90.00	—
		a. Imperf., pair		600.00	
		Double transfer		30.00	12.00

CANCELLATIONS.

		Town	+7.50
Purple	+1.50		
Magenta	+1.50		
Blue	+1.50		

O54	"	24c **black**		25.00	8.25
		gray black		25.00	8.25
		On cover			600.00
		Block of four		110.00	—
		Double paper		—	—

CANCELLATIONS.

		Town	+7.50
Purple	+ 1.50		
Blue	+ 1.50		
Red	+20.00		

O55	"	30c **black**		25.00	7.00
		gray black		25.00	7.00
		On cover			800.00
		Block of four		110.00	—

CANCELLATIONS.

		Town	+12.50
Purple	+ 1.50		
Blue	+ 1.50		
Red	+20.00		
Magenta	+ 1.50		

O56	"	90c **black**		40.00	11.00
		gray black		40.00	11.00
		Block of four		185.00	—
		Double transfer		—	—
		Double paper		—	—

CANCELLATIONS.

		Town	+6.50
Purple	+1.50		
Magenta	+1.50		
Blue	+1.50		

OFFICIAL STAMPS

1873

STATE.

Franklin
O7

O57	O7	1c **dark green**	35.00	10.00
		dark yellow green	35.00	10.00
		light green	35.00	10.00
		On cover		
		Block of four	200.00	

CANCELLATIONS.

		Town	+7.50
Violet	+2.00		
Purple	+2.00		
Blue	+2.00		
Red	+17.50		

O58	"	2c **dark green**	80.00	25.00
		dark yellow green	80.00	25.00
		yellow green		
		On cover		650.00
		Block of four		
		Double transfer		

CANCELLATIONS.

		Town	+10.00
Purple	+ 5.00	Blue town	+20.00
Blue	+ 5.00		
Red	+30.00		
Green	+75.00		

O59	"	3c **bright green**	30.00	7.50
		yellow green	30.00	7.50
		dark green	30.00	7.50
		On cover		450.00
		First day cover, *July 1, 1875*		
		Block of four	150.00	
		Double paper		

CANCELLATIONS.

		Town	+ 6.50
Purple	+ 1.50	Blue town	+10.00
Blue	+ 1.50		
Red	+10.00		

O60	"	6c **bright green**	27.50	7.50
		dark green	27.50	7.50
		yellow green	27.50	7.50
		On cover		550.00
		Block of four	125.00	
		Double transfer		

CANCELLATIONS.

		Town	+7.50
Purple	+ 2.00		
Red	+10.00		

O61	"	7c **dark green**	55.00	15.00
		dark yellow green	55.00	15.00
		On cover		1,000.
		Block of four	425.00	
		Ribbed paper	70.00	20.00

CANCELLATIONS.

		Town	+10.00
Purple	+ 2.00		
Blue	+ 2.00		
Red	+25.00		

O62	"	10c **dark green**	35.00	12.50
		bright green	35.00	13.50
		yellow green		
		On cover		1,200.
		Block of four	300.00	

CANCELLATIONS.

		Town	+ 5.00
Purple	+ 2.50	Blue town	+10.00
Magenta	+ 2.50	Numeral	+15.00
Blue	+ 2.50		
Red	+25.00		

O63	O7	12c **dark green**	70.00	27.50
		dark yellow green		1,400.
		On cover		
		Block of four	350.00	

CANCELLATIONS.

		Town	+15.00
Purple	+ 5.00		
Blue	+5.00		
Red	+30.00		

O64	"	15c **dark green**	55.00	15.00
		dark yellow green	55.00	15.00
		On cover		
		Block of four	325.00	

CANCELLATIONS.

		Town	+15.00
Purple	+ 2.50		
Blue	+ 2.50		
Red	+20.00		

O65	"	24c **dark green**	150.00	75.00
		On cover		1,750.
		dark yellow green	150.00	70.00
		Block of four	850.00	

CANCELLATIONS.

		Town	+25.00
Purple	+15.00		
Blue	+15.00		
Red	+65.00		

O66	"	30c **dark green**	135.00	60.00
		dark yellow green	135.00	60.00
		On cover		
		Block of four		

CANCELLATIONS.

		Town	+20.00
Purple	+ 5.00	Blue town	+30.00
Blue	+ 5.00		
Red	+35.00		

O67	"	90c **dark green**	300.00	120.00
		dark yellow green		
		Block of four		

CANCELLATIONS.

		Town	+40.00
Purple	+15.00		
Blue	+15.00		
Red	+75.00		

William H. Seward—O8

OFFICIAL STAMPS

O68	O8	$2 **green & black**		500.00	250.00
		yellow green & black		500.00	250.00
		On cover			
		Block of four		17,000.	

CANCELLATIONS.

			Town	+ 75.00
Blue	+ 25.00		Blue town	+150.00
Red	+125.00		Manuscript	*125.00*
Purple	+ 25.00			

O69	"	$5 **green & black**		4,250.	2,000.
		dark green & black		4,250.	2,000.
		yellow green & black		4,250.	2,000.
		Block of four		20,000.	

CANCELLATIONS.

Blue	+250.00		Manuscript	*1000.00*

O70	"	$10 **green & black**		2,750.	1,300.
		dark green & black		2,750.	1,300.
		yellow green & black		2,750.	1,300.
		Block of four		14,000.	

CANCELLATIONS.

Blue	+200.00		Manuscript	*700.00*

O71	"	$20 **green & black**		2,250.	1,100.
		dark green & black		2,250.	1,100.
		yellow green & black		2,250.	1,100.
		Block of four		12,500.	
		Block of four, ms. cancel			4,000.

CANCELLATIONS.

Blue	+200.00		Manuscript	*550.00*

The design of Nos. O68 to O71 measures 25½ x 39½ mm.

1873   **TREASURY.**

Franklin
O9

O72	O9	1c **brown**		12.00	1.75
		dark brown		12.00	1.75
		yellow brown		12.00	1.75
		On cover			85.00
		Block of four		50.00	
		Double transfer		20.00	3.50

CANCELLATIONS.

			Town	+2.00
Purple	+ 1.00		Blue town	+4.00
Magenta	+ 1.00			
Blue	+ 1.00			
Red	+10.00			

O73	"	2c **brown**		18.00	1.75
		dark brown		18.00	1.75
		yellow brown		18.00	1.75
		On cover			75.00
		Block of four		80.00	
		Double transfer			5.00
		Cracked plate		35.00	

CANCELLATIONS.

			Town	+2.00
Purple	+ 1.00		Blue town	+4.00
Magenta	+ 1.00			
Blue	+ 1.00			
Red	+10.00			

O74	O9	3c **brown**		10.00	1.00
		dark brown		10.00	1.00
		yellow brown		10.00	1.00
		On cover			40.00
		First day cover, *July 1, 1873*			
		Block of four		45.00	
		Double paper			
		Shaded circle outside of right frame line			

CANCELLATIONS.

			Town	+ 1.00
Purple	+ .50		Railroad	+20.00
Magenta	+ .50		"Paid"	+10.00
Blue	+ .50			
Ultramarine	+2.00			
Red	+3.50			

O75	"	6c **brown**		17.50	1.00
		dark brown		17.50	1.00
		yellow brown		17.50	1.00
		On cover			125.00
		Block of four		80.00	
		Worn plate		18.50	2.00
		Double transfer			

CANCELLATIONS.

			Town	+1.50
Purple	+ .50			
Magenta	+ .50			
Blue	+ .50			
Ultramarine	+ 1.50			
Red	+ 5.00			
Green	+20.00			

O76	"	7c **brown**		35.00	11.00
		dark brown		35.00	11.00
		yellow brown		35.00	11.00
		On cover			750.00
		Block of four		150.00	

CANCELLATIONS.

			Town	+ 7.50
Purple	+ 2.00		Blue town	+12.50
Blue	+ 2.00			
Green	+60.00			

O77	"	10c **brown**		35.00	3.50
		dark brown		35.00	3.50
		yellow brown		35.00	3.50
		On cover			375.00
		Block of four		150.00	
		Double paper			
		Double transfer			

CANCELLATIONS.

			Town	+4.00
Purple	+ 1.00		Blue town	+8.50
Magenta	+ 1.00			
Blue	+ 1.00			
Ultramarine	+ 4.00			
Red	+12.00			

O78	"	12c **brown**		35.00	1.50
		dark brown		35.00	1.50
		yellow brown		35.00	1.50
		On cover			500.00
		Block of four		150.00	

CANCELLATIONS.

			Town	+2.50
Purple	+ .50			
Blue	+ .50			
Red	+10.00			
Green	+35.00			

O79	"	15c **brown**		35.00	3.25
		yellow brown		35.00	3.25
		On cover			850.00
		Block of four		150.00	

CANCELLATIONS.

			Town	+ 2.50
Blue	+ 1.00		Blue town	+ 7.50
Purple	+ 1.00		Numeral	+15.00
Red	+10.00			

OFFICIAL STAMPS

O80	O9	24c **brown**	165.00	55.00
		dark brown	165.00	55.00
		yellow brown	165.00	55.00
		Block of four	700.00	
		Double transfer at top		

CANCELLATIONS.

		Town	+15.00
Blue	+5.00	Blue town	+25.00
Magenta	+5.00		

O81	"	30c **brown**	50.00	3.25
		dark brown	50.00	3.25
		yellow brown	50.00	3.25
		On cover		1,000.
		Block of four	225.00	
		Short transfer at top right		

CANCELLATIONS.

		Black town	+3.50
Blue	+ 1.00	Blue town	+7.50
Red	+12.00		
Purple	+ 1.00		

O82	"	90c **brown**	55.00	3.00
		dark brown	55.00	3.00
		yellow brown	55.00	3.00
		Block of four	250.00	35.00
		Double paper		

CANCELLATIONS.

		Town	+3.50
Purple	+1.00	Blue town	+7.50
Magenta	+1.00		
Blue	+1.00		
Brown	+7.50		

1873   WAR.

Franklin
O10

O83	O10	1c **rose**	50.00	3.25
		rose red	50.00	3.25
		On cover		125.00
		Pair on cover		125.00
		Block of four	225.00	

CANCELLATIONS.

		Town	+ 3.50
Purple	+ 1.00	Fort	+50.00
Blue	+ 1.00	Numeral	+12.50
Red	+15.00	"Paid"	

O84	"	2c **rose**	47.50	5.00
		rose red	47.50	5.00
		On cover		60.00
		Block of four	210.00	
		Ribbed paper	60.00	6.50

CANCELLATIONS.

		Town	+ 4.00
Purple	+ 1.50	Fort	+50.00
Magenta	+ 1.50		
Blue	+ 1.50		
Red	+15.00		

O85	O10	3c **rose**	45.00	1.00
		rose red	45.00	1.00
		On cover		30.00
		Block of four	210.00	

CANCELLATIONS.

		Town	+ 1.50
Blue	+ 1.00	Fort	+40.00
Purple	+ 1.00	"Paid"	+12.00
Magenta	+ 1.00		
Green	+35.00		

O86	"	6c **rose**	225.00	4.00
		pale rose	225.00	4.00
		On cover		50.00
		Block of four	950.00	

CANCELLATIONS.

		Town	+ 3.50
Purple	+ 1.50	Blue town	+ 6.50
Blue	+ 1.50	Fort	+40.00
Red	+15.00		

O87	"	7c **rose**	45.00	30.00
		pale rose	45.00	30.00
		rose red	45.00	30.00
		On cover		
		Block of four	200.00	

CANCELLATIONS.

		Town	+7.50
Purple	+2.50		
Blue	+3.50		

O88	"	10c **rose**	15.00	3.00
		rose red	15.00	3.00
		On cover		
		Block of four	67.50	
		Cracked plate		

CANCELLATIONS.

		Town	+ 3.50
Purple	+1.00	Fort	+40.00
Blue	+1.00		

O89	"	12c **rose**	45.00	2.00
		On cover		300.00
		Block of four	190.00	
		Ribbed paper	55.00	5.00

CANCELLATIONS.

		Town	+ 3.00
Purple	+ 1.00	Fort	+35.00
Magenta	+ 1.00		
Blue	+ 1.00		
Red	+10.00		

O90	"	15c **rose**	12.00	1.20
		pale rose	12.00	1.20
		rose red	12.00	1.20
		On cover		325.00
		Block of four	52.50	15.00
		Ribbed paper	17.50	3.00

CANCELLATIONS.

		Town	+ 2.50
Purple	+ 1.00	Fort	+30.00
Blue	+ 1.00	Express Company	
Red	+10.00		

O91	"	24c **rose**	12.50	1.75
		pale rose	12.50	1.75
		rose red	12.50	1.75
		On cover		
		Block of four	55.00	

CANCELLATIONS.

		Town	+2.50
Purple	+1.00	Fort	+3.50
Blue	+1.00		

O92	"	30c **rose**	14.00	1.50
		rose red	14.00	1.50
		On cover		
		Block of four	58.50	20.00
		Ribbed paper	17.50	4.00

CANCELLATIONS.

		Town	+ 2.50
Purple	+1.00	Fort	+35.00
Magenta	+1.00		
Blue	+1.00		

OFFICIAL STAMPS

O93	O10	90c rose		35.00	10.00
		rose red		35.00	10.00
		On cover			1,000.
		Block of four		150.00	

CANCELLATIONS.

Purple	+2.00	Town	+ 7.50
Magenta	+2.00	Fort	+90.00
Blue	+2.00		

Printed by the American Bank Note Co.

1879   Soft Porous Paper.

AGRICULTURE.

O94	O1	1c yellow (issued without gum)	1,350.	
		Block of four	6,000.	
O95	"	3c yellow	170.00	30.00
		On cover		
		Block of four	725.00	

CANCELLATIONS.

Purple	+5.00	Town	+17.50
Blue	+5.00		

INTERIOR.

O96	O3	1c vermilion	120.00	65.00
		pale vermilion	120.00	65.00
		Block of four	525.00	

CANCELLATIONS.

Blue	+5.00	Town	+15.00

O97	"	2c vermilion	2.50	75
		pale vermilion	2.50	75
		scarlet vermilion	2.50	75
		On cover		35.00
		Block of four	12.00	

CANCELLATIONS.

		Town	+ 1.50
Purple	+ .50	Blue town	+ 3.00
Blue	+ .50	Fort	+25.00
Red	+5.00		

O98	"	3c vermilion	2.00	60
		pale vermilion	2.00	60
		On cover		30.00
		Block of four	9.00	

CANCELLATIONS.

		Town	+1.50
Purple	+ .50	Blue town	+3.00
Blue	+ .50	Numeral	+5.00
Red	+5.00		

O99	"	6c vermilion	3.00	1.00
		pale vermilion	3.00	1.00
		scarlet vermilion	3.00	1.00
		On cover		200.00
		Block of four	14.00	

CANCELLATIONS.

		Town	+1.50
Purple	+ .50		
Blue	+ .50		
Red	+5.00		

O100	"	10c vermilion	27.50	17.50
		pale vermilion	27.50	17.50
		On cover		350.00
		Block of four	120.00	

CANCELLATIONS.

		Town	+10.00
Purple	+5.00		
Blue	+5.00		

O101	"	12c vermilion	50.00	30.00
		pale vermilion	50.00	30.00
		On cover		550.00
		Block of four	210.00	
O102	"	15c vermilion	135.00	70.00
		Block of four	575.00	
		On cover		
		Double transfer	175.00	

CANCELLATIONS.

Purple	+5.00	

O103	O3	24c vermilion	1,100.
		Block of four	4,750.

1879   ### JUSTICE.

O106	O4	3c bluish purple	40.00	17.50
		deep bluish purple	40.00	17.50
		On cover		550.00
		Block of four	185.00	

CANCELLATIONS.

Blue	+5.00	

O107	"	6c bluish purple	100.00	60.00
		Block of four	450.00	

CANCELLATIONS.

Blue	+10.00	Town	+20.00

POST OFFICE.

O108	O6	3c black	7.50	1.40
		gray black	7.50	1.40
		On cover		35.00
		Block of four	32.50	10.00

CANCELLATIONS.

		Town	+ 2.00
Blue	+ 1.00	"Paid"	+12.00
Purple	+ 1.00		
Violet	+ 1.00		
Magenta	+ 1.00		
Green	+40.00		

TREASURY.

O109	O9	3c brown	23.50	2.50
		yellow brown	23.50	2.50
		On cover		110.00
		Block of four	100.00	

CANCELLATIONS.

		Town	+2.00
Purple	+1.50	Numeral	+7.50
Blue	+1.50		

O110	"	6c brown	42.50	17.50
		yellow brown	42.50	17.50
		dark brown	42.50	17.50
		On cover		300.00
		Block of four	180.00	

CANCELLATIONS

Purple	+6.00
Magenta	+6.00
Blue	+6.00

O111	"	10c brown	60.00	15.00
		yellow brown	60.00	15.00
		dark brown	60.00	15.00
		On cover		900.00
		Block of four	250.00	

CANCELLATIONS.

		Town	+7.50
Purple	+2.50		
Blue	+2.50		

O112	"	30c brown	700.00	135.00
		Block of four	3,250.	

CANCELLATIONS.

		Town	+50.00
Blue	+25.00		

O113	"	90c brown	725.00	135.00
		dark brown	725.00	135.00
		Block of four	3,500.	

CANCELLATIONS.

		Town	+75.00
Purple	+25.00		
Blue	+25.00		

OFFICIAL STAMPS

WAR

1879					
O114	O10	1c rose red		1.75	75
		rose		1.75	75
		dull rose red		1.75	75
		brown rose		1.75	75
		On cover			50.00
		Block of four		8.00	4.00

CANCELLATIONS.

		Town		+ 1.00
Purple	+.50	Fort		+25.00
Blue	+.50			

O115	"	2c rose red		2.75	1.00
		dark rose red		2.75	1.00
		dull vermilion		2.75	1.25
		On cover			40.00
		Pair on cover			
		Block of four		12.00	6.00

CANCELLATIONS.

		Town		+ 2.00
Blue	+.50	Fort		+25.00
Purple	+.50			
Magenta	+.50			
Green	+35.00			

O116	"	3c rose red		2.75	65
		dull rose red		2.75	65
		On cover			35.00
		Pair on cover			40.00
		Block of four		12.00	4.00
		a. Imperf., (pair)		800.00	
		b. Double impression		500.00	
		Double transfer		6.00	4.00

CANCELLATIONS.

		Town		+ 1.00
Purple	+.50	Fort		+25.00
Violet	+.50			
Blue	+.50			
Red	+5.00			

O117	"	6c rose red		2.50	70
		dull rose red		2.50	70
		dull vermilion			
		On cover			50.00
		Block of four		10.50	6.00

CANCELLATIONS.

		Town		+ 1.00
Purple	+.50	Fort		+25.00
Blue	+.50	Numeral		+ 7.50

O118	"	10c rose red		17.50	6.00
		dull rose red		17.50	6.00
		On cover			
		Block of four		72.50	

CANCELLATIONS.

	Town		+ 5.00
	Fort		+45.00

O119	"	12c rose red		14.00	1.75
		dull rose red		14.00	1.75
		brown rose		14.00	1.75
		On cover			
		Block of four		57.50	15.00

CANCELLATIONS.

		Town		+ 2.50
Purple	+ 1.00	Fort		+40.00
Violet	+ 1.00			
Red	+10.00			

O120	"	30c rose red		40.00	25.00
		dull rose red		40.00	25.00
		On cover			
		Block of four		170.00	

CANCELLATIONS.

	Town	+10.00
	Fort	+80.00

POSTAL SAVINGS MAIL

The Act of Congress, approved June 25, 1910, establishing postal savings depositories, provided:

" Sec. 2. That the Postmaster General is hereby directed to prepare and issue special stamps of the necessary denominations for use, in lieu of penalty or franked envelopes, in the transmittal of free mail resulting from the administration of this act."

The use of postal savings official stamps was discontinued by the Act of Congress, approved September 23, 1914. The unused stamps in the hands of postmasters were returned and destroyed.

O11

Engraved.

1910-11   Wmkd. USPS (191)

Perf. 12.

O121	O11	2c black, *Dec. 22, 1910*		9.00	1.10
		On cover			10.00
		Block of four (2mm. spacing)		40.00	6.00
		Block of four (3mm. spacing)		38.50	5.00
		Margin block of 6, Impt. & P# & Star		225.00	
		Double transfer		12.50	2.00
O122	"	50c dark green, *Feb. 1, 1911*		100.00	32.50
		On cover			150.00
		Block of four (2mm. spacing)		425.00	175.00
		Block of four (3mm. spacing)		410.00	175.00
		Margin block of 4, arrow		440.00	
		Margin block of 6, Impt. & P# & Star		2,100.	
O123	"	$1 ultramarine, *Feb. 1, 1911*		95.00	9.50
		On cover			85.00
		Block of four (2mm. spacing)		410.00	50.00
		Block of four (3mm. spacing)		400.00	50.00
		Margin block of 4, arrow		425.00	
		Margin block of 6, Impt. & P# & Star		1,850.	350.00

Wmkd. USPS (190)

O124	O11	1c dark violet, *March 27, 1911*		4.00	1.00
		On cover			10.00
		Block of four (2mm. spacing)		17.50	4.50
		Block of four (3mm. spacing)		17.00	4.25
		Margin block of 6, Impt. & P# & Star		120.00	
O125	"	2c black		30.00	3.50
		On cover			17.50
		Block of four (2mm. spacing)		125.00	17.50
		Block of four (3mm. spacing)		122.50	17.50
		Margin block of 6, Impt. & P# & Star		550.00	
		Double transfer		25.00	4.50
O126	"	10c carmine, *Feb. 1, 1911*		8.50	1.00
		On cover			10.00
		Block of four (2mm. spacing)		37.50	5.50
		Block of four (3mm. spacing)		36.00	5.00
		Margin block of 6, Impt. & P# & Star		250.00	
		Double transfer		15.00	2.50

OFFICIAL MAIL

O12

Designed by Bradbury Thompson

ENGRAVED

1983, Jan. 12   *Perf. 11x10½*

O127	O12	1c red, bl & blk		5	75
		FDC, Washington, DC		25	
		P# block of 4, UL or UR			
O128	O12	4c red, bl & blk		8	75
		FDC, Washington, DC		40	
		P# block of 4, LR only			
O129	O12	13c red, bl & blk		26	60
		FDC, Washington, DC		1.30	
		P# block of 4, UR only			
O129A	O12	14c red, bl & blk, *May 15, 1985*		28	65
		FDC, Washington, DC			
O130	O12	17c red, bl & blk		34	75
		FDC, Washington, DC		1.70	
		P# block of 4, LL only		2.00	
O132	O12	$1 red, bl & blk			2.25
		FDC, Washington, DC		10.00	
		P# block of 4, UL only		10.00	
O133	O12	$5 red, bl & blk			12.50
		FDC, Washington, DC		50.00	
		P# block of 4, LL only			

Coil Stamp
Perf. 10 Vert.

O135	O12	20c red, bl & blk		40	40
		FDC, Washington, DC			75
		Pair		80	
		P# strip of 3, P# 1		10.00	
		a. Imperf. pair		—	
O136	O12	22c red, bl & blk, *May 15, 1985*		44	80
		FDC, Washington, DC			
		Pair		90	

O13

1985, Feb. 4   *Perf. 11*

O138	O13	(14c) red, bl & blk		28	65
		FDC, Washington, DC			
		P# block of 4, LR only		1.40	—

Coil Stamp
Perf. 10 Vert.

O139	O13	(22c) red, bl & blk		44	80
		FDC, Washington, DC			
		Pair		90	
		P# strip of 3, P# 1		10.00	

OFFICIALS - NEWSPAPER
POSTAGE DUE - SAVINGS
POSTAL STATIONERY -
U.S. AND DEPENDENCIES!

FOR COMPLETE LIST OF FAIR PRICES
FOR F-VF STAMPS SEND 56¢ SASE.

COMPLETE 36 PAGE BUYING LIST $2.00
(Refunded when we pay for the first shipment)

AJAX STAMP CO.
Box 69S, Caseville, MI 48725

FSDA   BIA, ARA

OFFICIALS and NEWSPAPER
... stamps are our specialties. Buying or selling — we know the market. Send us your wantlist, or contact us if you wish to sell your collection.

Robert L. Markovits'
Quality Investors, Ltd.
RARE STAMPS OF THE WORLD
BOX 891, MIDDLETOWN, N.Y. 10940
TELEPHONE: (914) 343-2174

NEWSPAPER AND PERIODICAL STAMPS

First issued in September, 1865, for prepayment of postage on bulk shipments of newspapers and periodicals. From 1875 on, the stamps were affixed to memorandums of mailing, cancelled and retained by the post office. Discontinued on July 1, 1898.

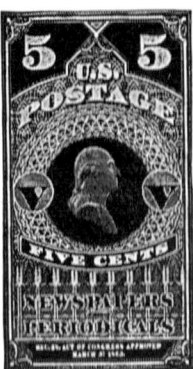

Washington
N1

Franklin
N2

Lincoln
N3

(Illustrations N1, N2 and N3 are half the size of the stamps.)

Printed by the National Bank Note Co.
Typographed, Embossed
Plates of 20 subjects in two panes of 10 each.
1865   *Perf. 12*   Unwmkd.
Thin hard paper, without gum.
Size of design: 51x95 mm.
Colored Border.

PR1	N1	5c **dark blue**	160.00	
		a. 5c light blue	175.00	
		blue	160.00	
		Block of four	725.00	
PR2	N2	10c **blue green**	85.00	
		a. 10c green	85.00	
		Block of four	400.00	
		b. Pelure Paper	90.00	
PR3	N3	25c **orange red**	85.00	
		a. 25c carmine red	85.00	
		Block of four	400.00	
		b. Pelure paper	90.00	

White Border.
Yellowish paper.

PR4	N1	5c **light blue**	35.00	30.00
		blue	35.00	30.00
		a. 5c dark blue	35.00	30.00
		Block of four	175.00	
		b. Pelure paper	40.00	

REPRINTS OF 1865 ISSUE.
Printed by the Continental Bank Note Co.
1875   *Perf. 12*
Hard white paper, without gum.
5c White Border, 10c and 25c Colored Border.

PR5	N1	5c **dull blue** (6395)	65.00	
		dark blue	65.00	
		Block of four	325.00	
		a. Printed on both sides		
PR6	N2	10c **dark bluish green** (8515)	40.00	
		deep green	40.00	
		Block of four	185.00	
		a. Printed on both sides	1,500.	
PR7	N3	25c **dark carmine** (7434)	65.00	
		dark carmine red	65.00	
		Block of four	325.00	

1880   **Printed by the American Bank Note Co.**
Soft porous paper.
White Border.

PR8	N1	5c **dark blue**	125.00	
		Block of four	525.00	

The Continental Bank Note Co. made another special printing from new plates, which did not have the colored border. These exist imperforate and perforated, but they were not regularly issued.

Statue of Freedom on Capitol Dome,
by Thomas Crawford
N4

"Justice"
N5

Clio
N8

Ceres
N6

Minerva
N9

"Victory"
N7

Vesta
N10

NEWSPAPERS

"Peace"
N11

"Commerce"
N12

Hebe
N13

Indian Maiden
N14

Printed by the Continental Bank Note Co.
Plates of 100 subjects in two panes of 50 each.
Size of design: 24x35 mm.

1875, Jan. 1   Engraved   *Perf. 12*
Thin hard paper

PR9	N4	2c	black	8.00	8.00
			gray black	8.00	8.00
			greenish black	8.00	8.00
			Block of four	40.00	55.00
PR10	"	3c	black	11.00	11.00
			gray black	11.00	11.00
			Block of four	55.00	65.00
PR11	"	4c	black	9.00	9.00
			gray black	9.00	9.00
			greenish black	9.00	9.00
			Block of four	45.00	
PR12	"	6c	black	12.50	12.50
			gray black	12.50	12.50
			greenish black	12.50	12.50
			Block of four	60.00	
PR13	"	8c	black	17.50	17.50
			gray black	17.50	17.50
			greenish black	17.50	17.50
PR14	"	9c	black	40.00	40.00
			gray black	40.00	40.00
			Double transfer at top	50.00	50.00
PR15	"	10c	black	17.50	15.00
			gray black	17.50	15.00
			greenish black	17.50	15.00
			Block of four	85.00	
PR16	N5	12c	rose	40.00	30.00
			pale rose	40.00	30.00
PR17	"	24c	rose	50.00	35.00
			pale rose	50.00	35.00
PR18	"	36c	rose	55.00	40.00
			pale rose	55.00	40.00
PR19	"	48c	rose	100.00	65.00
			pale rose	100.00	65.00
PR20	"	60c	rose	50.00	40.00
			pale rose	50.00	40.00
PR21	"	72c	rose	125.00	90.00
			pale rose	125.00	90.00
PR22	"	84c	rose	200.00	100.00
			pale rose	200.00	100.00
PR23	"	96c	rose	110.00	85.00
			pale rose	110.00	85.00
PR24	N6	$1.92	dark brown	130.00	90.00
PR25	N7	$3	vermilion	175.00	110.00
PR26	N8	$6	ultramarine	325.00	150.00
			dull ultramarine	325.00	150.00
PR27	N9	$9	yellow	425.00	185.00
PR28	N10	$12	blue green	500.00	250.00
PR29	N11	$24	dark gray violet	500.00	275.00
PR30	N12	$36	brown rose	550.00	325.00
PR31	N13	$48	red brown	700.00	425.00
PR32	N14	$60	violet	700.00	375.00

NEWSPAPER

1875 Special Printing of 1875 Issue.
Perf. 12.
Hard white paper, without gum.

PR33	N4	2c gray black (19,514*)	60.00
		Horizontally ribbed paper	60.00
PR34	"	3c gray black (6952)	65.00
		Block of four	—
		Horizontally ribbed paper	75.00
PR35	"	4c gray black (4451)	80.00
		Block of four	400.00
PR36	"	6c gray black (2348)	110.00
PR37	"	8c gray black (1930)	130.00
PR38	"	9c gray black (1795)	150.00
PR39	"	10c gray black (1499)	185.00
		Horizontally ribbed paper	200.00
PR40	N5	12c pale rose (1313)	210.00
PR41	"	24c pale rose (411)	275.00
PR42	"	36c pale rose (330)	375.00
PR43	"	48c pale rose (268)	425.00
PR44	**	60c pale rose (222)	500.00
PR45	"	72c pale rose (174)	650.00
PR46	"	84c pale rose (164)	675.00
PR47	"	96c pale rose (141)	800.00
PR48	N6	$1.92 dark brown (41)	2,400.
PR49	N7	$3 vermilion (20)	5,000.
PR50	N8	$6 ultramarine (14)	6,000.
PR51	N9	$9 yellow (4)	11,000.
PR52	N10	$12 blue green (5)	10,000.
PR53	N11	$24 dark gray violet (2)	—
PR54	N12	$36 brown rose (2)	—
PR55	N13	$48 red brown (1)	—
PR56	N14	$60 violet (1)	—

All values of this issue, Nos. PR33 to PR56, exist imperforate but were not regularly issued.
Numbers in parenthesis are quantities issued.
*This quantity may include the 1883 Re-issue.

1879 Printed by the American Bank Note Co.
Soft porous paper.
Unwatermarked.
Perf. 12.

PR57	N4	2c black	4.00	3.50
		gray black	4.00	3.50
		greenish black	4.00	3.50
		Block of four	18.50	
		Imperf., (pair)	—	—
		Double transfer at top	6.00	6.00
		Cracked plate	—	—
PR58	"	3c black	5.00	4.50
		gray black	5.00	4.50
		intense black	5.00	4.50
		Block of four	25.00	
		Imperf., (pair)	—	—
		Double transfer at top	6.00	6.00
PR59	"	4c black	5.00	4.50
		gray black	5.00	4.50
		intense black	5.00	4.50
		greenish black	5.00	4.50
		Block of four	25.00	
		Imperf., (pair)	—	—
		Double transfer at top	6.00	6.00

PR60	N4	6c black	10.50	9.00
		gray black	10.50	9.00
		intense black	10.50	9.00
		greenish black	10.50	9.00
		Block of four	47.50	
		Imperf., (pair)	—	—
		Double transfer at top	12.50	12.50
PR61	"	8c black	10.50	9.00
		gray black	10.50	9.00
		greenish black	10.50	9.00
		Block of four	47.50	
		Imperf., (pair)	—	—
		Double transfer at top	12.50	12.50
PR62	"	10c black	10.50	9.00
		gray black	10.50	9.00
		greenish black	10.50	9.00
		Block of four	47.50	
		Imperf., (pair)	—	—
		Double transfer at top	12.50	
PR63	N5	12c red	30.00	20.00
		Block of four	135.00	
PR64	"	24c red	30.00	18.50
		Block of four	135.00	
PR65	"	36c red	110.00	85.00
		Block of four	475.00	
PR66	"	48c red	80.00	50.00
PR67	"	60c red	60.00	50.00
		Block of four	275.00	
	a.	Imperf., (pair)	500.00	
PR68	"	72c red	145.00	90.00
PR69	"	84c red	110.00	75.00
		Block of four	—	
PR70	"	96c red	80.00	55.00
		Block of four	375.00	
PR71	N6	$1.92 pale brown	65.00	50.00
		brown	65.00	50.00
		Block of four	300.00	
		Cracked plate	120.00	
		Imperf., (pair)	—	
PR72	N7	$3 red vermilion	65.00	50.00
		Block of four	300.00	
		Imperf., (pair)	—	
PR73	N8	$6 blue	110.00	75.00
		ultramarine	110.00	75.00
		Imperf., (pair)	—	
PR74	N9	$9 orange	70.00	50.00
		Imperf., (pair)	—	
PR75	N10	$12 yellow green	110.00	75.00
		Imperf., (pair)	—	
PR76	N11	$24 dark violet	145.00	100.00
		Imperf., (pair)	—	
PR77	N12	$36 Indian red	185.00	120.00
		Imperf., (pair)	—	
PR78	N13	$48 yellow brown	250.00	150.00
		Imperf., (pair)	—	
PR79	N14	$60 purple	275.00	150.00
		bright purple	275.00	150.00
		Imperf., (pair)	—	

Imperforate stamps of this issue, except No. PR67a, were not regularly issued.

1883 Special Printing of 1879 Issue.

PR80	N4	2c intense black	130.00	
		Block of four	600.00	

NEWSPAPER

Printed by the American Bank Note Co.
Perf. 12

1885, July 1   Unwmkd.

PR81	N4	1c **black**	5.50	3.50
		gray black	5.50	3.50
		intense black	5.50	3.50
		Block of four	25.00	
		Imperf., (pair)		
		Double transfer at top	7.00	4.00
PR82	N5	12c **carmine**	17.50	8.50
		deep carmine	17.50	8.50
		rose carmine	17.50	8.50
		Block of four	75.00	
		Imperf., (pair)		
PR83	"	24c **carmine**	20.00	12.50
		deep carmine	20.00	12.50
		rose carmine	20.00	12.50
		Block of four	85.00	
		Imperf., (pair)		
PR84	"	36c **carmine**	30.00	15.00
		deep carmine	30.00	15.00
		rose carmine	30.00	15.00
		Block of four	130.00	
		Imperf., (pair)		
PR85	"	48c **carmine**	40.00	25.00
		deep carmine	40.00	25.00
		Block of four	170.00	
		Imperf., (pair)		
PR86	"	60c **carmine**	60.00	35.00
		deep carmine	60.00	35.00
		Block of four	275.00	
		Imperf., (pair)		
PR87	"	72c **carmine**	70.00	40.00
		deep carmine	70.00	40.00
		rose carmine	70.00	40.00
		Block of four	300.00	
		Imperf., (pair)		
PR88	"	84c **carmine**	140.00	85.00
		rose carmine	140.00	85.00
		Block of four	575.00	
		Imperf., (pair)		
PR89	"	96c **carmine**	100.00	70.00
		rose carmine	100.00	70.00
		Block of four	450.00	
		Imperf., (pair)		

Imperforate stamps of the 1885 issue were not regularly issued.

Printed by the Bureau of Engraving and Printing
Perf. 12
Soft wove paper.

1894   Unwmkd.

PR90	N4	1c **intense black**	30.00
		Block of four	135.00
		Double transfer at top	40.00
PR91	"	2c **intense black**	30.00
		Block of four	140.00
		Double transfer at top	40.00
PR92	"	4c **intense black**	40.00
		Block of four	175.00
PR93	"	6c **intense black**	750.00
		Block of four	
PR94	"	10c **intense black**	75.00
		Block of four	350.00
PR95	N5	12c **pink**	375.00
		Block of four	1,750.
PR96	"	24c **pink**	350.00
		Block of four	1,600.
PR97	"	36c **pink**	2,200.
		Block of four	
PR98	"	60c **pink**	2,200.
		Block of four	
PR99	"	96c **pink**	3,500.
PR100	N7	$3 **scarlet**	4,500.
		Block of four	
PR101	N8	$6 **pale blue**	5,250. 3,000.

Statue of Freedom on Capitol Dome,
by Thomas Crawford
N15

"Justice"
N16

"Victory"
N17

NEWSPAPER

Clio
N18

"Commerce"
N21

Vesta
N19

Indian Maiden
N22

"Peace"
N20

				Unwmkd.	
1895, Feb. 1		*Perf. 12*			
		Size of designs:			
		1c to 50c, 21x34 mm.			
		$2 to $100, 24x35 mm.			
PR102	N15	1c	black	17.50	5.00
			Block of four	75.00	25.00
PR103	"	2c	black	18.50	5.00
			gray black	18.50	5.00
			Block of four	85.00	
			Double transfer at top	25.00	
PR104	"	5c	black	25.00	8.50
			gray black	25.00	8.50
			Block of four	110.00	
PR105	"	10c	black	55.00	25.00
			Block of four	240.00	
PR106	N16	25c	carmine	75.00	25.00
			Block of four	325.00	
PR107	"	50c	carmine	175.00	75.00
			Block of four	725.00	
PR108	N17	$2	scarlet	200.00	45.00
PR109	N18	$5	ultramarine	325.00	135.00
PR110	N19	$10	green	300.00	150.00
PR111	N20	$20	slate	600.00	275.00
PR112	N21	$50	dull rose	625.00	275.00
PR113	N22	$100	purple	700.00	325.00

NEWSPAPER - POSTAL NOTE

1895-97   Wmkd. USPS (191)
Perf. 12.

PR114	N15	1c **black**, *Jan. 11, 1896*	2.50	2.00
		gray black	2.50	2.00
		Block of four	12.00	
PR115	"	2c **black**, *Nov. 21, 1895*	2.50	1.50
		gray black	2.50	1.50
		Block of four	12.00	
PR116	"	5c **black**, *Feb. 12, 1896*	4.00	3.00
		gray black	4.00	3.00
		Block of four	17.50	
PR117	"	10c **black**, *Sept. 13, 1895*	2.50	2.00
		gray black	2.50	2.00
		Block of four	12.00	
PR118	N16	25c **carmine**, *Oct. 11, 1895*	4.00	3.75
		lilac rose	4.00	3.75
		Block of four	17.50	
PR119	"	50c **carmine**, *Sept. 19, 1895*	5.00	3.50
		rose carmine	5.00	3.50
		lilac rose	5.00	4.00
		Block of four	20.00	
PR120	N17	$2 **scarlet**, *Jan. 23, 1897*	7.50	9.50
		scarlet vermilion	7.50	9.50
		Block of four	35.00	
PR121	N18	$5 **dark blue**, *Jan. 16, 1896*	17.50	22.50
		a. $5 light blue	85.00	45.00
		Block of four	75.00	
PR122	N19	$10 **green**, *Mar. 5, 1896*	15.00	25.00
		Block of four	65.00	
PR123	N20	$20 **slate**, *Jan. 27, 1896*	16.00	27.50
		Block of four	70.00	
PR124	N21	$50 **dull rose**, *July 31, 1897*	17.50	27.50
		Block of four	80.00	
PR125	N22	$100 **purple**, *Jan. 23, 1896*	20.00	35.00
		Block of four	90.00	

Nos. PR102-PR125 were printed from plates with guide lines and arrows both vertical and horizontal.

In 1899 the Government sold 26,989 sets of these stamps, but, as the stock of high values was not sufficient to make up the required number, an additional printing was made of the $5, $10, $20, $50 and $100. These are virtually indistinguishable from earlier printings.

The use of newspaper and periodical stamps was discontinued on July 1, 1898.

POSTAL NOTE STAMPS

Postal notes were issued in amounts up to $10 to supplement the regular money order service. Postal note stamps were affixed and cancelled by the clerk to make up fractions of a dollar. They were discontinued March 31, 1951.

MO1
ROTARY PRESS PRINTING.
1945, Feb. 1   Perf. 11x10½   Unwmkd.

PN1	MO1	1c **black**	10	5
PN2	"	2c "	15	5
PN3	"	3c "	20	5
PN4	"	4c "	25	5
PN5	"	5c "	35	5
PN6	"	6c "	40	5
PN7	"	7c "	50	5
PN8	"	8c "	65	5
PN9	MO1	9c **black**	70	5
PN10	"	10c "	85	5
PN11	"	20c "	1.65	5
PN12	"	30c "	2.25	5
PN13	"	40c "	2.75	6
PN14	"	50c "	3.25	5
PN15	"	60c "	4.50	5
PN16	"	70c "	5.00	5
PN17	"	80c "	6.00	8
PN18	"	90c "	6.50	8

Blocks of four and plate number blocks of four are priced at 4 and 15 times the unused single price.
Postal note stamps exist on postal note cards with first day cancellation.

Plate Nos.

1c	155950-51	7c	156075-76	40c	156283-84
2c	156003-04	8c	156077-78	50c	156322-23
3c	156062-63	9c	156251-52	60c	156324-25
4c	155942-43	10c	156274-75	70c	156344-45
5c	156261-62	20c	156276-77	80c	156326-27
6c	156064-65	30c	156303-04	90c	156352-53

PARCEL POST STAMPS

The Act of Congress approved Aug. 24, 1912, created postage rates on fourth-class mail weighing 4 ounces or less at 1 cent per ounce or fraction. On mail over 4 ounces, the rate was by the pound. These rates were to be prepaid by distinctive postage stamps. Under this provision, the Post Office Dept. prepared 12 parcel post and 5 parcel post due stamps, usable only on parcel post packages starting Jan. 1, 1913.

With the approval of the Interstate Commerce Commission, the Postmaster General directed, in Order No. 7241 dated June 26, 1913, and effective July 1, 1913, that regular postage stamps should be valid on parcels. Parcel post stamps then became usable as regular stamps.

Parcel post and parcel post due stamps remained on sale, but no further printings were made. Remainders, consisting of 3,510,345 of the 75c, were destroyed in September, 1921.

The 20c was the first postage stamp of any country to show an airplane.

Post Office Clerk
PP1

City Carrier
PP2

Railway Postal Clerk
PP3

Rural Carrier
PP4

Mail Train and Mail Bag on Rack
PP5

Steamship "Kronprinz Wilhelm"
and Mail Tender,
New York
PP6

Automobile Service
PP7

Airplane Carrying Mail
PP8

Manufacturing
(Steel Plant, South Chicago)
PP9

Dairying
PP10

Harvesting
PP11

Fruit Growing
(Florida Orange Grove)
PP12

PARCEL POST STAMPS

TEN

6161 Plate number and imprint consisting of value in words.

Engraved.

Marginal imprints, consisting of value in words, were added to the plates on January 27, 1913.

Plates of 180 subjects in four panes of 45 each.

1912-13   Wmkd. USPS (190)   Perf. 12.

Q1	PP1	1c **carmine rose,** *Nov. 27, 1912*			
		(209,691,094)	4.00	.90	
		carmine	4.00	.90	
		First day cover, *July 1, 1913*		800.00	
		On cover, 1913-25		5.00	
		Block of four	16.50	5.00	
		Margin block of 4, Impt. & P#	30.00		
		Margin block of 6, Impt. & P#	85.00		
		Margin block of 6, P# only	95.00		
		Double transfer	9.00	3.00	
Q2	PP2	2c **carmine rose,** *Nov. 27, 1912*			
		(206,417,253)	4.50	.70	
		carmine	4.50	.70	
		lake			
		First day cover, *July 1, 1913*		800.00	
		On cover, 1913-25		5.00	
		Block of four	18.50	3.50	
		Margin block of 4, Impt. & P#	35.00		
		Margin block of 6, Impt. & P#	95.00		
		Margin block of 6, P# only	115.00		
		Double transfer			
Q3	PP3	3c **carmine,** *Apr. 5, 1913* (29,027,433)	10.00	5.00	
		deep carmine	10.00	5.00	
		First day cover, *July 1, 1913*		2,500.	
		On cover, 1913-25		17.50	
		Block of four	40.00	25.00	
		Margin block of 4, Impt. & P#	65.00		
		Margin block of 6, Impt. & P#	185.00		
		Margin block of 6, P# only	175.00		
		Margin block of 8, Impt. & P# (side)	225.00		
		Retouched at lower right corner			
		(No. 6257LL7)	25.00	12.50	
		Double transfer (No. 6257LL6)	25.00	12.50	
Q4	PP4	4c **carmine rose,** *Dec. 12, 1912*			
		(76,743,813)	25.00	2.00	
		carmine	25.00	2.00	
		First day cover, *July 1, 1913*		2,500.	
		On cover, 1913-25		60.00	
		Block of four	105.00		
		Margin block of 4, Impt. & P#	250.00		
		Margin block of 6, Impt. & P#	775.00		
		Margin block of 6, P# only	750.00		
		Double transfer			
Q5	PP5	5c **carmine rose,** *Nov. 27, 1912*			
		(108,153,993)	25.00	1.25	
		carmine	25.00	1.25	
		First day cover, *July 1, 1913*		2,500.	
		On cover, 1913-25		40.00	
		Block of four	105.00	10.00	
		Margin block of 4, Impt. & P#	250.00		
		Margin block of 6, Impt. & P#	775.00		
		Margin block of 6, P# only	750.00		
		Double transfer	50.00	5.00	
Q6	PP6	10c **carmine rose,** *Dec. 9, 1912*			
		(56,896,653)	40.00	1.75	
		carmine	40.00	1.75	
		On cover, 1913-25		50.00	
		Block of four	165.00	20.00	
		Margin block of 4, Impt. & P#	300.00		
		Margin block of 6, Impt. & P#	1,000.		
		Margin block of 6, P# only	950.00		
		Double transfer			
Q7	PP7	15c **carmine rose,** *Dec. 16, 1912*			
		(21,147,033)	65.00	9.00	
		carmine	65.00	9.00	
		First day cover, *July 1, 1913*		350.00	
		On cover, 1913-25		60.00	
		Block of four	265.00		
		Margin block of 4, Impt. & P#	500.00		
		Margin block of 6, Impt. & P#	1,900.		
		Margin block of 8, Impt. & P#	2,400.		
		Margin block of 6, P# only	1,850.		
Q8	PP8	20c **carmine rose,** *Dec. 16, 1912*			
		(17,142,393)	140.00	17.50	
		carmine	140.00	17.50	
		On cover, 1913-25		750.00	
		Block of four	575.00	100.00	
		Margin block of 4, Impt. & P#	1,050.		
		Margin block of 6, Impt. & P#	5,250.		
		Margin block of 8, Impt. & P# (side)	5,750.		
		Margin block of 6, P# only	5,250.		
Q9	PP9	25c **carmine rose,** *Nov. 27, 1912*			
		(21,940,653)	75.00	4.50	
		carmine	75.00	4.50	
		On cover, 1913-25		300.00	
		Block of four	310.00	35.00	
		Margin block of 6, Impt. & P#	2,500.		
		Margin block of 8, Impt. & P# (side)	3,000.		
		Margin block of 6, P# only	2,350.		
Q10	PP10	50c **carmine rose,** *Mar. 15, 1913*			
		(2,117,793)	210.00	35.00	
		carmine	210.00	35.00	
		On cover, 1913-25		200.00	
		Block of four	850.00		
		Margin block of 4, Impt. & P#	1,500.		
		Margin block of 6, Impt. & P#	12,000.		
Q11	PP11	75c **carmine rose,** *Dec. 18, 1912*			
		(2,772,615)	70.00	25.00	
		carmine	70.00	25.00	
		On cover, 1913-25		125.00	
		Block of four	285.00		
		Margin block of 6, Impt. & P#	2,750.		
		Margin block of 8, Impt. & P# (side)	3,000.		
		Margin block of 6, P# only	2,650.		
Q12	PP12	$1 **carmine rose,** *Jan. 3, 1913*			
		(1,053,273)	400.00	20.00	
		carmine	400.00	20.00	
		On cover, 1913-25		1,100.	
		Block of four	1,650.	100.00	
		Margin block of 6, Impt. & P#	15,000.		
		Margin block of 8, Impt. & P# (side)	16,500.		
		Margin block of 6, P# only	15,000.		

The 1c, 2c and 4c are known in parcel post usage postmarked Jan. 1, 1913.

SPECIAL HANDLING STAMPS

The Postal Service Act, approved February 28, 1925, provided for a special handling stamp of the 25 cent denomination for use on fourth-class mail matter, which would secure for such mail matter the expeditious handling accorded to mail matter of the first class.

PP13
FLAT PLATE PRINTING.
Plates of 200 subjects in four panes of 50.

1925–29   Perf. 11.   Unwmkd.

QE1	PP13 10c yellow green, *June 25, 1928*	1.50	90
	First day cover		55.00
	Block of four	6.00	5.00
	Margin block of 6, P# only	25.00	
QE2	PP13 15c yellow green, *June 25, 1928*	1.65	90
	First day cover		55.00
	Block of four	6.60	5.00
	Margin block of 6, P# only	35.00	
QE3	" 20c yellow green, *June 25, 1928*	2.00	1.75
	First day cover		55.00
	Block of four	8.00	9.00
	Margin block of 6, P# only	40.00	
QE4	" 25c yellow green ('29)	20.00	7.50
	Block of four	80.00	35.00
	Margin block of 6, P# only	240.00	
	a. 25c deep green, *Apr. 11, 1925*	25.00	4.50
	a. First day cover		225.00
	a. Block of four	100.00	25.00
	a. Margin block of 6, P# only	310.00	
	"A" and "T" of "States" joined at top (Pl. 17103)	45.00	20.00
	"A" and "T" of "States" and "T" and "A" of "Postage" joined at top (Pl. 17103)	45.00	45.00

Special Handling stamps printed by both the "wet" and "dry" process are Nos. QE1-QE3. See note on Wet and Dry Printings following No. 1029.

POSTAL INSURANCE LABELS

Postal insurance labels were issued to pay insurance on parcels for loss or damage. The label comes in a booklet of one which also carries instructions for use and a receipt form for possible claim. The booklets were sold by vending machine.

PPI1

1965, Aug.   Typographed   *Rouletted 9 at Top*

QI1   PPI1(10c) dark red   120.00   —

No. QI1 paid insurance up to $10. It was sold at the Canoga Park, Calif., automatic post office which opened Aug. 19, 1965. The "V" stands for "Vended."

PPI2

1966, March 26   Lithographed   *Perf. 11 at Top*

QI2   PPI2(20c) **red**   75   —

No. QI2 paid insurance up to $15. The rate increased from 20c to 25c on Apr. 18, 1976, and to 40c on July 18, 1976.

POSTMARK OF

MAILING OFFICE

FEE PAID THROUGH
VENDING MACHINE
PPI3

1978   Lithographed   *Perf. 11 at Top*

QI3   PPI3(40c) **black**   80   —
QI4   " (50c) **green**   1.00   —

The rate increased to 50c on May 29, 1978.

QI5   PPI3(45c) **red**, *1981*   90   —

PARCEL POST POSTAGE DUE STAMPS

Parcel Post Due stamps were prepared in conformity with the Act of Congress, approved August 24, 1912, at the same time the Parcel Post stamps were issued. (See note over Q1.)

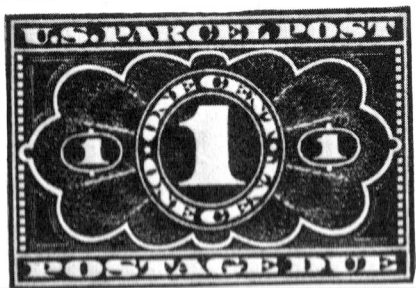

PPD1

Engraved.

Plates of 180 subjects in four panes of 45.

Wmkd. USPS (190)

1912   **Perf. 12**

JQ1	PPD1	1c **dark green,** *Nov. 27, 1912*		9.00	3.00
		(7,322,400)		9.00	3.00
		yellowish green		9.00	3.00
		On cover, 1913-25			150.00
		Block of four		36.50	20.00
		Margin block of 6, P#		550.00	
JQ2	"	2c **dark green,** *Dec. 9, 1912*			
		(3,132,000)		80.00	15.00
		yellowish green		80.00	15.00
		On cover, 1913-25			200.00
		Block of four		325.00	85.00
		Margin block of 6, P#		2,750.	
JQ3	PPD1	5c **dark green,** *Nov. 27, 1912*			
		(5,840,100)		11.50	3.50
		yellowish green		11.50	3.50
		On cover, 1913-25			185.00
		Block of four		47.50	20.00
		Margin block of 6, P#		675.00	
JQ4	"	10c **dark green,** *Dec. 12, 1912*			
		(2,124,540)		150.00	35.00
		yellowish green		150.00	35.00
		On cover, 1913-25			650.00
		Block of four		625.00	200.00
		Margin block of 6, P#		6,750.	
JQ5	"	25c **dark green,** *Dec. 16, 1912*			
		(2,117,700)		75.00	3.50
		yellowish green		75.00	3.50
		On cover, 1913-25			
		Block of four		310.00	20.00
		Margin block of 6, P#		2,750.	

FIRST DAY COVERS

All envelopes or cards are postmarked Washington, D.C., unless otherwise stated.

Prices are for covers bearing single stamps. Blocks of 4 on first day covers usually sell for about 1½ the price for singles; Plate Number blocks of 4 at about 3 times; Plate Number blocks of 6 at about 4 times; coil line pairs at about 3 times.

Dates given are those on which the stamps were first *officially* placed on sale. Instances are known of stamps being sold in advance, contrary to regulations.

Numbers in parentheses are quantities canceled on first day.

Listings since 1922 are all exclusively for covers canceled at cities officially designated by the Post Office Department or Postal Service. Some tagged varieties are exceptions.

Airmail first day covers are listed in the Air Post section of this catalogue. Booklet pane first day covers are listed in the Booklet Panes section.

Printed cachets on covers before No. 772 sell at a substantial premium. Prices for covers from No. 772 onward are for those with the most common cachets and addressed. Unaddressed covers command a premium. Those without cachets sell at a substantial discount.

1851-57
5A	1c blue, type Ib, *July 1, 1851*, Boston, Mass.	18,500.00
7	1c blue, type II, *July 1, 1851, any city*	13,000.00
	same on printed circular	2,500.00
10	3c orange brown, *July 1, 1851, any city*	7,000.00
24	1c blue, type V, *Nov. 17, 1857, any city*	—

1883
210	2c red brown, *Oct. 1, 1883, any city*	1700.00
211	4c blue green, *Oct. 1, 1883, any city*	8500.00

1890
219D	2c lake, *Feb. 22, 1890, any city*	14,500.00

1893 COLUMBIAN EXPOSITION ISSUE
230	1c deep blue, *Jan. 2, 1893, any city*	3000.00
231	2c brown violet, *Jan. 2, 1893, any city*	2400.00
232	3c green, *Jan. 2, 1893, any city*	6000.00
233	4c ultramarine, *Jan. 2, 1893, any city*	6000.00
234	5c chocolate, *Jan. 2, 1893, any city*	6250.00
235	6c purple, *Jan. 2, 1893, any city*	6750.00
237	10c black brown, *Jan. 2, 1893, any city*	7500.00
242	$2 brown red, *Jan. 2, 1893, any city*	15,000.00

Jan. 1, 1893, postmarks are known on the Columbian issue. As that day was a Sunday, specialists recognize both Jan. 1 and 2 as "first day."

1898 TRANS-MISSISSIPPI EXPOSITION ISSUE
285	1c green, *June 17, 1898, any city*	4500.00
286	2c copper red, *June 17, 1898, any city*	4000.00
288	5c dull blue, *June 17, 1898, any city*	5000.00
289	8c violet brown, *June 17, 1898, any city*	7500.00
	285-290, all six on one cover, *June 17, 1898, any city*	13,000.00
291	50c sage green, *June 17, 1898, any city*	9000.00

1901 PAN AMERICAN EXPOSITION ISSUE
294	1c green & black, *May 1, 1901, any city*	3500.00
295	2c carmine & black, *May 1, 1901, any city*	3000.00
296	4c deep red brown & black, *May 1, 1901*	4250.00
297	5c ultra. & blk., *May 1, 1901, any city*	4500.00
	294 to 299, Complete set of six on one cover *May 1, 1901, any city*	10,000.00

1903
301	2c carmine, *Jan. 17, 1903, any city*	2750.00

1904 LOUISIANA PURCHASE EXPOSITION ISSUE
323	1c green, *Apr. 30, 1904, any city*	3000.00
324	2c carmine, *Apr. 30, 1904, any city*	2750.00
325	3c violet, *Apr. 30, 1904, any city*	3250.00
326	5c dark blue, *Apr. 30, 1904, any city*	4250.00
327	10c red brown, *Apr. 30, 1904, any city*	6500.00
	323-327, all five on one cover, *Apr. 30, 1904, any city*	12,500.00

1907 JAMESTOWN EXPOSITION ISSUE
328	1c green, *Apr. 26, 1907, any city*	3250.00
329	2c carmine, *Apr. 26, 1907, any city*	4000.00

1909 LINCOLN ISSUE
367	2c carmine, *Feb. 12, 1909, any city*	350.00
	Imperf.	
368	2c carmine, *Feb. 12, 1909, any city*	1900.00

1909 ALASKA—YUKON ISSUE
370	2c carmine, *June 1, 1909, any city*	1800.00

1909 HUDSON-FULTON ISSUE
372	2c carmine, *Sept. 25, 1909, any city*	850.00
	Imperf.	
373	2c carmine, *Sept. 25, 1909, any city*	2000.00

1913 PANAMA-PACIFIC ISSUE
397	1c green, *Jan. 1, 1913, any city*	3250.00
399	5c blue, *Jan. 1, 1913*	4000.00
	397, 399 & 400, all 3 on one cover, San Francisco	5000.00

1916-22 COIL STAMP
497	10c orange yellow, *Jan. 31, 1922, any city*	1750.00

1918-20 OFFSET PRINTING
526	2c carmine, type IV, *Mar. 15, 1920*	800.00

1919 VICTORY ISSUE
537	3c violet, *Mar. 3, 1919, any city*	700.00

1920 REGULAR ISSUE
Perf. 10x11
542	1c green, *May 26, 1920*	700.00

1920 PILGRIM TERCENTENARY ISSUE
548	1c green, *Dec. 21, 1920, any city*	700.00
549	2c carmine rose, *Dec. 21, 1920, any city*	625.00
	Plymouth, Mass.	900.00
	548 to 550, Complete set of three on one cover, *Dec. 21, 1920, any city*	2000.00
	Washington, D.C.	2500.00

1922-26 Perf. 11
551	½c Hale, *April 4, 1925*, (Block of 4)	22.50
	New Haven, Conn.	35.00
552	1c Franklin, *Jan. 17, 1923*	32.50
	Philadelphia, Pa.	65.00
553	1½c Harding, *Mar. 19, 1925*	35.00
554	2c Washington, *Jan. 15, 1923*	45.00
555	3c Lincoln, *Feb. 12, 1923*	37.50
	Hodgenville, Ky.	225.00
556	4c Martha Washington, *Jan. 15, 1923*	50.00
557	5c Roosevelt, *Oct. 27, 1922*	125.00
	New York, N.Y.	250.00
	Oyster Bay, N.Y.	675.00
558	6c Garfield, *Nov. 20, 1922*	200.00
559	7c McKinley, *May 1, 1923*	100.00
	Niles, O.	200.00
560	8c Grant, *May 1, 1923*	100.00
561	9c Jefferson, *Jan. 15, 1923*	100.00
562	10c Monroe, *Jan. 15, 1923*	100.00
563	11c Hayes, *Oct. 4, 1922*	550.00
	Fremont, O.	1000.00
564	12c Cleveland, *Mar. 20, 1923*	135.00
	Boston, Mass. (Philatelic Exhibition)	165.00
	Caldwell, N.J.	200.00
565	14c Indian, *May 1, 1923*	300.00
	Muskogee, Okla.	850.00
566	15c Statue of Liberty, *Nov. 11, 1922*	350.00
567	20c Golden Gate, *May 1, 1923*	400.00
	San Francisco, Cal.	900.00
568	25c Niagara Falls, *Nov. 11, 1922*	600.00
569	30c Bison, *Mar. 20, 1923*	725.00
570	50c Arlington, *Nov. 11, 1922*	1000.00

571	**$1 Lincoln Memorial,** *Feb. 12, 1923*	4000.00
	Springfield, Ill.	5000.00
572	**$2 U.S. Capitol,** *Mar. 20, 1923*	10,000.00
573	**$5 America,** *Mar. 20, 1923*	11,000.00

Imperf.
576	**1½c Harding,** *April 4, 1925*	45.00

Perf. 10
581	**1c Franklin,** *Oct. 17, 1923, not precanceled*	2,000.00
582	**1½c Harding,** *Mar. 19, 1925*	47.50
584	**3c Lincoln,** *Aug. 1, 1925*	55.00
585	**4c Martha Washington,** *Apr. 4, 1925*	55.00
586	**5c Roosevelt,** *April 4, 1925*	55.00
587	**6c Garfield,** *April 4, 1925*	70.00
588	**7c McKinley,** *May 29, 1926*	70.00
589	**8c Grant,** *May 29, 1926*	72.50
590	**9c Jefferson,** *May 29, 1926*	75.00
591	**10c Monroe,** *June 8, 1925*	100.00

ROTARY PRESS COIL STAMPS
Perf. 10 Vertically
597	**1c Franklin,** *July 18, 1923*	450.00
598	**1½c Harding,** *Mar. 19, 1925*	55.00
599	**2c Washington,** *Jan. 15, 1923*	850.00
600	**3c Lincoln,** *May 10, 1924*	72.50
602	**5c Roosevelt,** *Mar. 5, 1924*	75.00
603	**10c Monroe,** *Dec. 1, 1924*	95.00

Perf. 10 Horizontally
604	**1c Franklin,** *July 19, 1924*	85.00
605	**1½c Harding,** *May 9, 1925*	55.00
606	**2c Washington,** *Dec. 31, 1923*	80.00

1923
610	**2c Harding,** *Sept. 1, 1923* (Perf. 11)	40.00
	Marion, O.	22.50
611	**2c Harding,** *Nov. 15, 1923* (Imperf.)	100.00
612	**2c Harding,** *Sept. 12, 1923* (Perf. 10)	110.00

1924
Perf. 11
614	**1c Huguenot-Walloon,** *May 1, 1924*	
	Albany, N.Y.	
	Allentown, Pa.	
	Charleston, S.C.	
	Jacksonville, Fla.	
	Lancaster, Pa.	
	Mayport, Fla.	
	New Rochelle, N.Y.	
	New York, N.Y.	
	Philadelphia, Pa.	
	Reading, Pa.	@27.50
615	**2c Huguenot-Walloon,** *May 1, 1924*	
	Albany, N.Y.	
	Allentown, Pa.	
	Charleston, S.C.	
	Jacksonville, Fla.	
	Lancaster, Pa.	
	Mayport, Fla.	
	New Rochelle, N.Y.	
	New York, N.Y.	
	Philadelphia, Pa.	
	Reading, Pa.	@35.00
616	**5c Huguenot-Walloon,** *May 1, 1924*	
	Albany, N.Y.	
	Allentown, Pa.	
	Charleston, S.C.	
	Jacksonville, Fla.	
	Lancaster, Pa.	
	Mayport, Fla.	
	New Rochelle, N.Y.	
	New York, N.Y.	
	Philadelphia, Pa.	
	Reading, Pa.	@70.00
	614 to 616, set of three on one cover, *any city*	140.00

1925
617	**1c Lexington-Concord,** *April 4, 1925*	27.50
	Boston, Mass.	27.50
	Cambridge, Mass.	27.50
	Concord, Mass.	27.50
	Concord Junction, Mass.	35.00
	Lexington, Mass.	35.00
618	**2c Lexington-Concord,** *April 4, 1925*	35.00
	Boston, Mass.	35.00
	Cambridge, Mass.	35.00
	Concord, Mass.	35.00
	Concord Junction, Mass.	35.00
	Lexington, Mass.	50.00

Honestly, If you have a Postal History Collection or Covers for Sale...

Why not sell to a man with an established reputation of Honesty, Integrity, a fair and equitable buyer!

AL ZIMMERMAN IS YOUR MAN!

He knows and understands the care and love you have put into your collection. He is ready to offer the best price, fastest payment and the most courteous service.

I WANT TO BUY U.S. COVERS

...ACCEPTING COVER CONSIGNMENTS FOR PUBLIC AUCTION

(Minimum value $1000)

AL ZIMMERMAN

843 Van Nest Avenue
The Bronx, New York 10462

Phone (212) 822-7333

619	5c **Lexington-Concord,** *April 4, 1925*		50.00
	Boston, Mass.		70.00
	Cambridge, Mass.		70.00
	Concord, Mass.		70.00
	Concord Junction, Mass.		70.00
	Lexington, Mass.		80.00
	617 to 619, set of three on one cover, Concord Junction, Mass., or Lexington, Mass.		175.00
	Set of three on one cover, any other city		130.00
1925			
620	2c **Norse-American,** *May 18, 1925*		
	Algona, Iowa		
	Benson, Minn.		
	Decorah, Iowa		
	Minneapolis, Minn.		
	Northfield, Minn.		
	St. Paul, Minn.		@25.00
621	5c **Norse-American,** *May 18, 1925*		
	Algona, Iowa		
	Benson, Minn.		
	Decorah, Iowa		
	Minneapolis, Minn.		
	Northfield, Minn.		
	St. Paul, Minn.		@45.00
	620 and 621, set of two on one cover, *any city*		70.00
1925-26			
622	13c **Harrison,** *Jan. 11, 1926*		35.00
	Indianapolis, Ind.		47.50
	North Bend, Ohio *(500)*		250.00
623	17c **Wilson,** *Dec. 28, 1925*		
	New York, N.Y.		
	Princeton, N.J.		
	Staunton, Va.		@30.00
1926			
627	2c **Sesquicentennial,** *May 10, 1926*		
	Boston, Mass.		
	Philadelphia, Pa.		@14.00
628	5c **Ericsson,** *May 29, 1926*		
	Chicago, Ill.		
	Minneapolis, Minn.		
	New York, N.Y.		@22.50
629	2c **White Plains,** New York, N.Y., *Oct. 18, 1926*		6.25
	New York, N.Y., Inter-Philatelic Exhibition Agency cancellation		6.25
	White Plains, N.Y.		6.25
	Washington, D.C., *Oct. 28, 1926*		3.50
630	Sheet of 25, *Oct. 18, 1926*		1,500.00
	Sheet of 25, *Oct. 28, 1926*		500.00
1926-34		*Imperf.*	
631	1½c **Harding,** *Aug. 27, 1926*		35.00
		Perf. 11x10½	
632	1c **Franklin,** *June 10, 1927*		55.00
633	1½c **Harding,** *May 17, 1927*		55.00
634	2c **Washington,** *Dec. 10, 1926*		57.50
635	3c **Lincoln,** *Feb. 3, 1927*		47.50
635a	3c bright violet, *Feb. 7, 1934*		22.50
636	4c **Martha Washington,** *May 17, 1927*		55.00
637	5c **Roosevelt,** *Mar. 24, 1927*		55.00
638	6c **Garfield,** *July 27, 1927*		65.00
639	7c **McKinley,** *Mar. 24, 1927*		67.50
640	8c **Grant,** *June 10, 1927*		70.00
641	9c **Jefferson,** *May 17, 1927*		85.00
642	10c **Monroe,** *Feb. 3, 1927*		90.00
1927		*Perf. 11*	
643	2c **Vermont,** *Aug. 3, 1927*		
	Bennington, Vt.		@6.00
644	2c **Burgoyne,** *Aug. 3, 1927*		
	Albany, N.Y.		
	Rome, N.Y.		
	Syracuse, N.Y.		
	Utica, N.Y.		@16.50
1928			
645	2c **Valley Forge,** *May 26, 1928*		5.00
	Cleveland, O.		100.00
	Lancaster, Pa.		5.00
	Norristown, Pa.		5.00
	Philadelphia, Pa.		5.00
	Valley Forge, Pa.		5.00
	West Chester, Pa.		5.00
	Cleveland, Midwestern Philatelic Sta. cancellation		5.00

		Perf. 11x10½	
646	2c **Molly Pitcher,** *Oct. 20, 1928*		
	Freehold, N.J.		
	Red Bank, N.J.		@17.50
1928		*Perf. 11x10½*	
647	2c **Hawaii,** *Aug. 13, 1928*		17.50
	Honolulu, Hawaii		20.00
648	5c **Hawaii,** *Aug. 13, 1928*		32.50
	Honolulu, Hawaii		40.00
	647 and 648, set of two on one cover		60.00
		Perf. 11	
649	2c **Aero Conf.,** *Dec. 12, 1928*		10.00
650	5c **Aero Conf.,** *Dec. 12, 1928*		15.00
	649 and 650, set of two on one cover		27.50
1929			
651	2c **Clark,** Vincennes, Indiana, *Feb. 25, 1929*		7.50
	Washington, *Feb. 26, 1929,* First day of sale by Philatelic Agency		3.00
	Charlottesville, Va., *Feb. 26, 1929*		6.00
		Perf. 11x10½	
653	½c olive brown, *May 25, 1929* (Block of Four)		30.00
		Perf. 11	
654	2c **Electric Light,** Menlo Park, N.J., *June 5, 1929*		13.00
	Washington, *June 6, 1929,* first day of sale by Philatelic Agency		5.50
		Perf. 11x10½	
655	2c **Electric Light,** *June 11, 1929*		90.00
		Perf. 10 Vertically	
656	2c **Electric Light,** *June 11, 1929*		100.00
		Perf. 11 Vertically	
657	2c **Sullivan,** Auburn, N.Y., *June 17, 1929*		
	Binghamton, N.Y.		
	Canajoharie, N.Y.		
	Canandaigua, N.Y.		
	Elmira, N.Y.		
	Geneva, N.Y.		
	Geneseo, N.Y.		
	Horseheads, N.Y.		
	Owego, N.Y.		
	Penn Yan, N.Y.		
	Perry, N.Y.		
	Seneca Falls, N.Y.		
	Waterloo, N.Y.		
	Watkins Glen, N.Y.		
	Waverly, N.Y.		@4.50
	Washington, D.C., *June 18, 1929*		2.50
1929		**KANSAS AND NEBRASKA**	
658	1c **Kansas,** *May 1, 1929*		27.50
	Newton, Kan., *April 15, 1929*		200.00
659	1½c **Kansas,** *May 1, 1929*		27.50
	Colby, Kan., *April 16, 1929*		—
660	2c **Kansas,** *May 1, 1929*		27.50
	Colby, Kan., *April 16, 1929*		—
661	3c **Kansas,** *May 1, 1929*		30.00
	Colby, Kan., *April 16, 1929*		—
662	4c **Kansas,** *May 1, 1929*		32.50
	Colby, Kan., *April 16, 1929*		—
663	5c **Kansas,** *May 1, 1929*		35.00
	Colby, Kan., *April 16, 1929*		—
664	6c **Kansas,** *May 1, 1929*		42.50
	Newton, Kan., *April 15, 1929*		350.00
665	7c **Kansas,** *May 1, 1929*		42.50
	Colby, Kan., *April 16, 1929*		—
666	8c **Kansas,** *May 1, 1929*		80.00
	Newton, Kan., *April 15, 1929*		350.00
667	9c **Kansas,** *May 1, 1929*		72.50
	Colby, Kan., *April 16, 1929*		—
668	10c **Kansas,** *May 1, 1929*		85.00
	Colby, Kan., *April 16, 1929*		—
	658 to 668, set of eleven on one cover, Washington, D.C., *May 1, 1929*		800.00
669	1c **Nebraska,** *May 1, 1929*		27.50
	Beatrice, Neb., *April 15, 1929*		—
670	1½c **Nebraska,** *May 1, 1929*		25.00
	Hartington, Neb., *April 15, 1929*		160.00
671	2c **Nebraska,** *May 1, 1929*		25.00
	Auburn, Neb., *April 15, 1929*		—
	Beatrice, Neb., *April 15, 1929*		—
	Hartington, Neb., *April 15, 1929*		160.00

FIRST DAY COVERS 425

672	3c **Nebraska,** *May 1, 1929*		32.50
	Beatrice, Neb., *April 15, 1929*		175.00
	Hartington, Neb., *April 15, 1929*		175.00
673	4c **Nebraska,** *May 1, 1929*		37.50
	Beatrice, Neb., *April 15, 1929*		175.00
	Hartington, Neb., *April 15, 1929*		175.00
674	5c **Nebraska,** *May 1, 1929*		37.50
	Beatrice, Neb., *April 15, 1929*		175.00
	Hartington, Neb., *April 15, 1929*		175.00
675	6c **Nebraska,** *May 1, 1929*		55.00
	Ravenna, Neb., *April 17, 1929*		—
	Wahoo, Neb., *April 17, 1929*		—
676	7c **Nebraska,** *May 1, 1929*		57.50
	Auburn, Neb., *April 17, 1929*		—
677	8c **Nebraska,** *May 1, 1929*		60.00
	Humbolt, Neb., *April 17, 1929*		—
	Pawnee City, Neb., *April 17, 1929*		—
678	9c **Nebraska,** *May 1, 1929*		62.50
	Cambridge, Neb., *April 17, 1929*		—
679	10c **Nebraska,** *May 1, 1929*		70.00
	Tecumseh, Neb., *April 18, 1929*		—
	669 to 679, set of eleven on one cover,		
	Washington, D.C., *May 1, 1929*		850.00
	Perf. 11		
680	2c **Fallen Timbers,** Erie, Pa., *Sept. 14, 1929*		
	Maumee, O.		
	Perrysburg, O.		
	Toledo, O.		
	Waterville, O.		
	Washington, D.C., *Sept. 16, 1929*		@5.00
681	2c **Ohio River,** Cairo, Ill., *Oct. 19, 1929*		
	Cincinnati, O.		
	Evansville, Ind.		
	Homestead, Pa.		
	Louisville, Ky.		
	Pittsburgh, Pa.		
	Wheeling, W. Va.		
	Washington, D.C., *Oct. 21, 1929*		@4.50
1930			
682	2c **Massachusetts Bay Colony,** Boston, Mass.		
	April 8, 1930 (60,000)		5.25
	Salem, Mass.		5.25
	Washington, D.C., *April 11, 1930*		2.00
683	2c **Carolina-Charleston,** Charleston, S.C.		
	April 10, 1930		5.50
	Washington, D.C., *April 11, 1930*		2.00
	Perf. 11x10½		
684	1½c **Harding,** Marion, O., *Dec. 1, 1930*		6.25
	Washington, D.C., *Dec. 2, 1930*		2.50
685	4c **Taft,** Cincinnati, O., *June 4, 1930*		10.00
	Washington, D.C., *June 5, 1930*		4.00
	Perf. 10 Vertically		
686	1½c **Harding,** Marion, Ohio, *Dec. 1, 1930*		7.50
	Washington, D.C., *Dec. 2, 1930*		3.00
687	4c **Taft,** *Sept. 18, 1930*		30.00
	Perf. 11		
688	2c **Braddock,** Braddock, Pa., *July 9, 1930*		6.00
	Washington, D.C., *July 10, 1930*		2.75
689	2c **Von Steuben,** New York, N.Y., *Sept. 17, 1930*		6.00
	Washington, D.C., *Sept. 18, 1930*		2.75
1931			
690	2c **Pulaski,** Brooklyn, N.Y., *Jan. 16, 1931*		
	Buffalo, N.Y.		
	Chicago, Ill.		
	Cleveland, O.		
	Detroit, Mich.		
	Gary, Ind.		
	Milwaukee, Wis.		
	New York, N.Y.		
	Pittsburgh, Pa.		
	Savannah, Ga.		
	South Bend, Ind.		
	Toledo, O.		@5.00
	Washington, D.C., *Jan. 17, 1931*		2.75
1931		***Perf. 11x10½***	
692	11c **Hayes,** *Sept. 4, 1931*		80.00
693	12c **Cleveland,** *Aug. 25, 1931*		80.00
694	13c **Harrison,** *Sept. 4, 1931*		85.00
695	14c **Indian,** *Sept. 8, 1931*		85.00
696	15c **Liberty,** *Aug. 27, 1931*		100.00

	Perf. 10½x11		
697	17c **Wilson,** *July 25, 1931,* Brooklyn, N.Y.		1300.00
	Washington, D.C., *July 27*		325.00
698	20c **Golden Gate,** *Sept. 8, 1931*		185.00
699	25c **Niagara Falls,** *July 25, 1931,* Brooklyn, N.Y.		1300.00
	Washington, D.C., *July 27*		350.00
700	30c **Bison,** *Sept. 8, 1931*		275.00
701	50c **Arlington,** *Sept. 4, 1931*		425.00
1931			
702	2c **Red Cross,** *May 21, 1931*		4.00
	Dansville, N.Y.		4.00
703	2c **Yorktown,** *Oct. 19, 1931,* Wethersfield, Conn.		5.00
	Yorktown, Va.		5.00
	Washington, D.C., *Oct. 20*		3.00
1932	**WASHINGTON BICENTENNIAL ISSUE**		
704	½c *Jan. 1, 1932*		5.00
705	1c *Jan. 1, 1932*		5.50
706	1½c *Jan. 1, 1932*		5.50
707	2c *Jan. 1, 1932*		5.50
708	3c *Jan. 1, 1932*		5.75
709	4c *Jan. 1, 1932*		5.75
710	5c *Jan. 1, 1932*		6.00
711	6c *Jan. 1, 1932*		6.75
712	7c *Jan. 1, 1932*		6.75
713	8c *Jan. 1, 1932*		6.75
714	9c *Jan. 1, 1932*		7.75
715	10c *Jan. 1, 1932*		10.00
	704 to 715, Complete set of twelve on one cover,		
	Washington, D.C., *Jan. 1, 1932*		100.00
1932			
716	2c **Olympic Winter Games,**		
	Jan. 25, 1932, Lake Placid, N.Y.		7.50
	Washington, D.C., *Jan. 26*		1.50
717	2c **Arbor Day,** *April 22, 1933,* Nebraska City, Neb.		5.00
	Washington, D.C., *April 23*		1.50
	Adams, N.Y., *April 23*		6.50
718	3c **Olympic Summer Games,**		
	June 15, 1932, Los Angeles, Cal.		7.50
	Washington, D.C., *June 16*		2.75
719	5c **Olympic Summer Games,**		
	June 15, 1932, Los Angeles, Cal.		9.50
	Washington, D.C., *June 16*		2.75
	718, 719 on one cover, Los Angeles, Cal.		16.00
	718, 719 on one cover, Washington, D.C.		4.50
720	3c **Washington,** *June 16, 1932*		10.00
721	3c **Washington Coil,** Sideways, *June 24, 1932*		20.00
722	3c **Washington Coil,** Endways, *Oct. 12, 1932*		20.00
723	6c **Garfield Coil,** Sideways, *Aug. 18, 1932*		
	Los Angeles, Cal.		20.00
	Washington, D.C., *Aug. 19*		6.00
724	3c **William Penn,** *Oct. 24, 1932,* New Castle, Del.		
	Chester, Pa.		
	Philadelphia, Pa.		@3.00
	Washington, D.C., *Oct. 25*		1.25
725	3c **Daniel Webster,** *Oct. 24, 1932,* Franklin, N.H.		
	Exeter, N.H.		
	Hanover, N.H.		@3.00
	Washington, D.C., *Oct. 25*		1.25
1933			
726	3c **Gen. Oglethorpe,** *Feb. 12, 1933,* Savannah,		
	Ga., *(200,000)*		@3.00
	Washington, D.C., *Feb. 13*		1.25
727	3c **Peace Proclamation,**		
	April 19, 1933, Newburgh, N.Y. *(349,571)*		3.50
	Washington, D.C., *April 20*		1.20
728	1c **Century of Progress,** *May 25, 1933,* Chicago, Ill.		3.00
	Washington, D.C., *May 26*		1.00
729	3c **Century of Progress,** *May 25, 1933,* Chicago, Ill.		3.00
	Washington, D.C., *May 26*		1.00
	728, 729 on one cover		6.50
	Covers mailed May 25 bearing		
	Nos. 728 and 729 total 232,251.		
730	1c **American Philatelic Society,** sheet of 25,		
	Aug. 25, 1933, Chicago, Ill.		120.00
730a	1c **A.P.S.,** single, imperf., Chicago, Ill.		3.25
	Washington, D.C., *Aug. 28*		1.25
731	3c **American Philatelic Society,** sheet of 25,		
	Aug. 25, 1933, Chicago, Ill.		120.00
731a	3c **A.P.S.,** single, imperf., Chicago, Ill.		3.25
	Washington, D.C., *Aug. 28*		1.25
	730a, 731a on one cover		5.50
	Covers mailed Aug. 25 bearing		
	Nos. 730a and 731a total 65,218.		

FIRST DAY COVERS

732	3c **National Recovery Administration,** *Aug. 15, 1934*		
	Washington, D.C. *(65,000)*		3.25
	Nira, Iowa, *Aug. 17*		2.50
733	3c **Byrd Antarctic,** *Oct. 9, 1933*		6.00
734	5c **Kosciuszko,** *Oct. 13, 1933,* Boston, Mass. *(23,025)*		5.50
	Buffalo, N.Y. *(14,981)*		7.00
	Chicago, Ill, *(26,306)*		5.50
	Detroit, Mich. *(17,792)*		6.50
	Pittsburgh, Pa. *(6,282)*		37.50
	Kosciuszko, Miss. *(27,093)*		6.50
	St. Louis, Mo. *(17,872)*		6.50
	Washington, D.C., *Oct. 14*		3.00
1934			
735	3c **National Exhibition,** sheet of 6, Byrd imperf.,		
	Feb. 10, 1934, New York, N.Y.		55.00
	Washington, D.C., *Feb. 19*		27.50
735a	3c **National Exhibition,** single, imperf.,		
	New York, N.Y., *Feb. 10, 1934*		
	(450,715)		6.00
	Washington, D.C., *Feb. 19*		2.75
736	3c **Maryland Tercentenary,**		
	Mar. 23, 1934 St. Mary's City, Md. *(148,785)*		1.60
	Washington, D.C., *Mar. 24*		.60
	Perf. 11x10½		
737	3c **Mothers of America,** *May 2, 1934,* any city		1.60
	Perf. 11		
738	3c **Mothers of America,** *May 2, 1934,* any city		1.60
	737, 738 on one cover		4.00
	Covers mailed at Washington, May 2 bearing Nos. 737 and 738 total 183,359.		
739	3c **Wisconsin,** *July 7, 1934,* Green Bay, Wisconsin *(130,000)*		1.60
	Washington, D.C., *July 9*		.75
740	1c **Parks, Yosemite,** *July 16, 1934*		2.25
	Yosemite, California *(60,000)*		2.75
741	2c **Parks, Grand Canyon,** *July 24, 1934*		2.25
	Grand Canyon, Arizona *(75,000)*		2.75
742	3c **Parks, Mt. Rainier,** *August 3, 1934*		2.50
	Longmire, Washington, *(64,500)*		3.00
743	4c **Parks, Mesa Verde,** *Sept. 25, 1934*		3.25
	Mesa Verde, Colorado *(51,882)*		3.50
744	5c **Parks, Yellowstone,** *July 30, 1934*		3.25
	Yellowstone, Wyoming *(87,000)*		3.50
745	6c **Parks, Crater Lake,** *Sept. 5, 1934*		4.00
	Crater Lake, Oregon *(45,282)*		4.25
746	7c **Parks, Arcadia** *October 2, 1934*		4.00
	Bar Harbor, Maine *(51,312)*		4.25
747	8c **Parks, Zion,** *Sept. 18, 1934*		4.25
	Zion, Utah, *(43,650)*		4.75
748	9c **Parks, Glacier Park,** *August 17, 1934*		4.50
	Glacier Park, Montana *(52,626)*		4.75
749	10c **Parks, Smoky Mountains,** *Oct. 8, 1934*		10.00
	Sevierville, Tennessee *(39,000)*		11.00
	Imperf.		
750	3c **American Philatelic Society,** sheet of 6, *Aug. 28, 1934,* Atlantic City, N.J.		55.00
750a	3c **A.P.S.,** single, *Aug. 28, 1934,* Atlantic City, N.J. *(40,000)*		6.25
	Washington, D.C., *Sept. 4*		4.00
751	1c **Trans-Mississippi Philatelic Expo.,** sheet of 6, *Oct. 10, 1934,* Omaha, Neb.		40.00
751a	1c **Trans-Miss. Phil. Expo.,** single, Omaha. Neb., *Oct. 10, 1934 (125,000)*		4.50
	Washington, D.C., *Oct. 15*		2.00
1935	**SPECIAL PRINTING**		
	Nos. 752 to 771 inclusive issued March 15, 1935.		
752	3c **Peace Commemoration**		10.00
753	3c **Byrd**		12.00
754	3c **Mothers of America**		12.00
755	3c **Wisconsin Tercentenary**		12.00
756	1c **Parks, Yosemite**		12.00
757	2c **Parks, Grand Canyon**		12.00
758	3c **Parks, Mount Rainier**		13.00
759	4c **Parks, Mesa Verde**		13.00
760	5c **Parks, Yellowstone**		13.00
761	6c **Parks, Crater Lake**		13.00
762	7c **Parks, Acadia**		13.00
763	8c **Parks, Zion**		15.00
764	9c **Parks, Glacier Park**		15.00
765	10c **Parks, Smoky Mountains**		15.00
766a	1c **Century of Progress**		11.00
	Pane of 25		250.00
767a	3c **Century of Progress**		11.00
	Pane of 25		250.00
768a	3c **Byrd**		13.00
	Pane of 6		250.00
769a	1c **Parks, Yosemite**		8.00
	Pane of 6		250.00
770a	3c **Parks, Mount Rainier**		10.00
	Pane of 6		250.00
771	15c **Airmail Special Delivery**		25.00
772	3c **Connecticut Tercentenary,**		
	April 26, 1935, Hartford, Conn. *(217,800)*		8.00
	Washington, D.C., *April 27*		1.25
773	3c **California Exposition,**		
	May 29, 1935, San Diego, Cal. *(214,042)*		8.00
	Washington, D.C., *May 31*		1.25
774	3c **Boulder Dam,** *Sept. 30, 1935,* Boulder City, Nev. *(166,180)*		10.00
	Washington, D.C., *Oct. 1*		2.00
775	3c **Michigan Centenary,** *Nov. 1, 1935,* Lansing, Mich. *(176,962)*		8.00
	Washington, D.C., *Nov. 2*		1.25
1936			
776	3c **Texas Centennial,**		
	March 2, 1936, Gonzales, Texas *(319,150)*		12.50
	Washington, D.C., *March 3*		1.25
777	3c **Rhode Island Tercentenary,**		
	May 4, 1936, Providence, R.I. *(245,400)*		8.00
	Washington, D.C., *May 5*		1.25
778	**TIPEX** souvenir sheet, *May 9, 1936 (297,194)*		
	New York, N.Y. (TIPEX cancellation)		13.00
	Washington, D.C., *May 11*		3.50
782	3c **Arkansas Centennial,**		
	June 15, 1936, Little Rock, Ark. *(376,693)*		8.00
	Washington, D.C, *June 16*		1.00
783	3c **Oregon Territory Centennial,**		
	July 14, 1936, Astoria, Ore. *(91,110)*		
	Daniel, Wyo, *(67,013)*		8.50
	Lewiston, Idaho. *(86,100)*		8.00
	Missoula, Mont. *(59,883)*		8.50
	Walla Walla, Wash. *(106,150)*		8.00
	Washington, D.C., *July 15*		1.25
784	3c **Susan Anthony,** *August 26, 1936 (178,500)*		15.00
1936-37			
785	1c **Army,** *December 15, 1936*		5.00
786	2c **Army,** *January 15, 1937*		5.00
787	3c **Army,** *February 18, 1937*		5.00
788	4c **Army,** *March 23, 1937*		5.00
789	5c **Army,** *May 26, 1937,*		
	West Point, N.Y., *(160,000)*		5.50
	Washington, D.C., *May 27*		1.25
790	1c **Navy,** *December 15, 1936*		5.00
791	2c **Navy,** *January 15, 1937*		5.00
792	3c **Navy,** *February 18, 1937*		5.00
793	4c **Navy,** *March 23, 1937*		5.50
794	5c **Navy,** *May 26, 1937,*		
	Annapolis, Md., *(202,806)*		5.50
	Washington, D.C., *May 27*		1.25
	Covers for both Nos. 785 and 790 total 390,740; Nos. 786 and 791 total 292,570; Nos. 787 and 792 total 320,888; Nos. 788 and 793 total 331,000.		
1937			
795	3c **Ordinance of 1787,** *July 13, 1937*		
	Marietta, Ohio *(130,531)*		6.00
	New York, N.Y. *(125,134)*		6.00
	Washington, D.C., *July 14*		1.20
796	5c **Virginia Dare,** *Aug. 18, 1937,* Manteo, N.C. *(226,730)*		7.00
797	10c **Souvenir Sheet,** *Aug. 26, 1937,* Asheville, N.C. *(164,215)*		6.00
798	3c **Constitution,** *Sept. 17, 1937,* Philadelphia, Pa. *(281,478)*		6.50
799	3c **Hawaii,** *Oct. 18, 1937,* Honolulu, Hawaii *(320,334)*		7.00
800	3c **Alaska,** *Nov. 12, 1937,* Juneau, Alaska *(230,370)*		7.00
801	3c **Puerto Rico,** *Nov. 25, 1937,* San Juan, P.R. *(244,054)*		7.00
802	3c **Virgin Islands,** *Dec. 15, 1937,* Charlotte Amalie, V.I. *(225,469)*		7.00
1938	**PRESIDENTIAL ISSUE**		
803	½c *May 19, 1938,* Philadelphia, Pa. *(224,901)*		1.25
804	1c *April 25, 1938 (124,037)*		2.00
805	1½c *May 5, 1938 (128,339)*		2.00
806	2c *June 13, 1938 (127,806)*		2.00
807	3c *June 16, 1938 (118,097)*		2.00
808	4c *July 1, 1938 (118,765)*		2.00
809	4½c *July 11, 1938 (115,820)*		2.50
810	5c *July 21, 1938 (98,282)*		2.25

FIRST DAY COVERS 427

811	6c *July 28, 1938 (97,428)*	2.25	
812	7c *Aug. 4, 1938 (98,414)*	2.50	
813	8c *Aug. 11, 1938 (94,857)*	2.50	
814	9c *Aug. 18, 1938 (91,229)*	2.65	
815	10c *Sept. 2, 1938 (83,707)*	2.75	
816	11c *Sept. 8, 1938 (63,966)*	2.75	
817	12c *Sept. 14, 1938 (62,935)*	3.00	
818	13c *Sept. 22, 1938 (58,965)*	3.00	
819	14c *Oct. 6, 1938 (49,819)*	3.25	
820	15c *Oct. 13, 1938 (52,209)*	3.25	
821	16c *Oct. 20, 1938 (59,566)*	3.50	
822	17c *Oct. 27, 1938 (55,024)*	3.75	
823	18c *Nov. 3, 1938 (53,124)*	4.25	
824	19c *Nov. 10, 1938 (54,124)*	4.25	
825	20c *Nov. 10, 1938 (51,971)*	4.50	
826	21c *Nov. 22, 1938 (44,367)*	5.00	
827	22c *Nov. 22, 1938 (44,358)*	5.25	
828	24c *Dec. 2, 1938 (46,592)*	5.25	
829	25c *Dec. 2, 1938 (45,691)*	6.50	
830	30c *Dec. 8, 1938 (43,528)*	10.00	
831	50c *Dec. 8, 1938 (41,984)*	20.00	
832	$1 *Aug. 29, 1938 (24,618)*	55.00	
832c	$1 *Aug. 31, 1954 (20,202)*	30.00	
833	$2 *Sept. 29, 1938 (19,895)*	110.00	
834	$5 *Nov. 17, 1938 (15,615)*	175.00	
1938			
835	3c **Constitution,** *June 21, 1938,* Philadelphia, Pa. *(232,873)*	6.50	
836	3c **Swedes and Finns,** *June 27, 1938,* Wilmington, Del. *(225,617)*	6.00	
837	3c **Northwest Sesqui.,** *July 15, 1938,* Marietta, Ohio *(180,170)*	6.00	
838	3c **Iowa,** *Aug. 24, 1938,* Des Moines, Iowa *(209,860)*	6.00	
1939	**COIL STAMPS**		
	Perf 10 Vertically		
839	1c Pair, *Jan. 20, 1939*	7.00	
840	1½c Pair, *Jan. 20, 1939*	7.00	
841	2c Pair, *Jan. 20, 1939*	7.00	
842	3c Pair, *Jan. 20, 1939*	8.00	
843	4c Pair, *Jan. 20, 1939*	10.00	
844	4½c Pair, *Jan. 20, 1939*	10.00	
845	5c Pair, *Jan. 20, 1939*	11.00	
846	6c Pair, *Jan. 20, 1939*	16.00	
847	10c Pair, *Jan. 20, 1939*	22.00	
	839 to 847, set of 9 pairs on one cover, *Jan. 20, 1939*	125.00	
	Perf. 10 Horizontally		
848	1c Pair, *Jan. 27, 1939*	7.00	
849	1½c Pair, *Jan. 27, 1939*	9.00	
850	2c Pair, *Jan. 27, 1939*	11.00	
851	3c Pair, *Jan. 27, 1939*	13.50	
	848 to 851, set of 4 pairs on one cover, *Jan. 27, 1939*	55.00	
1939			
852	3c **Golden Gate Expo,** *Feb. 18, 1939,* San Francisco, Cal. *(352,165)*	5.00	
853	3c **N.Y. World's Fair,** *Apr. 1, 1939,* New York, N.Y. *(585,565)*	8.00	
854	3c **Washington Inauguration,** *Apr. 30, 1939,* New York, N.Y. *(395,644)*	5.00	
855	3c **Baseball Centennial,** *June 12, 1939,* Cooperstown, N.Y. *(398,199)*	18.00	
856	3c **Panama Canal,** *Aug. 15, 1939,* U.S.S. Charleston, Canal Zone *(230,974)*	5.00	
857	3c **Printing Tercentenary,** *Sept. 25, 1939,* New York, N.Y. *(295,270)*	5.00	
858	3c **50th Statehood Anniversary,** Bismarck, N.D. *Nov. 2, 1939 (142,106)* Pierre, S.D., *Nov. 2, 1939 (150,429)* Helena, Mont., *Nov. 8, 1939 (130,273)* Olympia, Wash., *Nov. 11, 1939 (150,429)*	@5.00	
1940	**FAMOUS AMERICANS**		
859	1c **Washington Irving,** *Jan. 29, 1940,* Tarrytown, N.Y. *(170,969)*	1.75	
860	2c **James Fenimore Cooper,** *Jan. 29, 1940,* Cooperstown, N.Y. *(154,836)*	1.75	
861	3c **Ralph Waldo Emerson,** *Feb. 5, 1940,* Boston, Mass. *(185,148)*	1.75	
862	5c **Louisa May Alcott,** *Feb. 5, 1940,* Concord, Mass. *(134,325)*	4.50	
863	10c **Samuel L. Clemens,** *Feb. 13, 1940,* Hannibal, Mo. *(150,492)*	7.50	
864	1c **Henry W. Longfellow,** *Feb. 16, 1940,* Portland, Me. *(160,508)*	1.75	
865	2c **John Greenleaf Whittier,** *Feb. 16, 1940,* Haverhill, Mass. *(148,423)*	1.75	

866	3c **James Russell Lowell,** *Feb. 20, 1940,* Cambridge, Mass. *(148,735)*	1.75	
867	5c **Walt Whitman,** *Feb. 20, 1940,* Camden, N.J. *(134,185)*	4.00	
868	10c **James Whitcomb Riley,** *Feb. 24, 1940,* Greenfield, Ind. *(131,760)*	7.50	
869	1c **Horace Mann,** *March 14, 1940,* Boston, Mass. *(186,854)*	1.75	
870	2c **Mark Hopkins,** *March 14, 1940,* Williamstown, Mass. *(140,286)*	1.75	
871	3c **Charles W. Eliot,** *March 28, 1940,* Cambridge, Mass. *(155,708)*	1.75	
872	5c **Frances E. Willard,** *March 28, 1940,* Evanston, Ill. *(140,483)*	4.00	
873	10c **Booker T. Washington,** *April 7, 1940,* Tuskegee Institute, Ala. *(163,507)*	7.50	
874	1c **John James Audubon,** *April 8, 1940,* St. Francisville, La. *(144,123)*	1.75	
875	2c **Dr. Crawford W. Long,** *April 8, 1940,* Jefferson, Ga. *(158,128)*	1.75	
876	3c **Luther Burbank,** *April 17, 1940,* Santa Rosa, Cal. *(147,033)*	2.75	
877	5c **Dr. Walter Reed,** *April 17, 1940,* Washington, D.C. *(154,464)*	4.00	
878	10c **Jane Addams,** *April 26, 1940,* Chicago, Ill. *(132,375)*	7.50	
879	1c **Stephen Collins Foster,** *May 3, 1940,* Bardstown, Ky. *(183,461)*	1.75	
880	2c **John Philip Sousa,** *May 3, 1940,* Washington, D.C. *(131,422)*	1.75	
881	3c **Victor Herbert,** *May 13, 1940,* New York, N.Y. *(198,200)*	1.75	
882	5c **Edward A. MacDowell,** *May 13, 1940,* Peterborough, N.H. *(135,155)*	4.00	
883	10c **Ethelbert Nevin,** *June 10, 1940,* Pittsburgh, Pa. *(121,951)*	7.00	
884	1c **Gilbert Charles Stuart,** *Sept. 5, 1940,* Narragansett, R.I. *(131,965)*	1.75	
885	2c **James A. McNeill Whistler,** *Sept. 5, 1940,* Lowell, Mass. *(130,962)*	1.75	
886	3c **Augustus Saint-Gaudens,** *Sept. 16, 1940,* New York, N.Y. *(138,200)*	1.75	
887	5c **Daniel Chester French,** *Sept. 16, 1940,* Stockbridge, Mass. *(124,608)*	3.50	
888	10c **Frederic Remington,** *Sept. 16, 1940,* Canton, N.Y. *(116,219)*	7.00	
889	1c **Eli Whitney,** *Oct. 7, 1940,* Savannah, Ga. *(140,868)*	1.75	
890	2c **Samuel F.B. Morse,** *Oct. 7, 1940,* New York, N.Y. *(135,388)*	1.75	
891	3c **Cyrus Hall McCormick,** *Oct. 14, 1940,* Lexington, Va. *(137,415)*	1.75	
892	5c **Elias Howe,** *Oct. 14, 1940,* Spencer, Mass. *(126,334)*	4.50	
893	10c **Alexander Graham Bell,** *Oct. 28, 1940,* Boston, Mass. *(125,372)*	12.50	
1940			
894	3c **Pony Express,** *April 3, 1940,* St. Joseph, Mo. *(194,589)* Sacramento, Cal. *(160,849)*	6.00 6.00	
895	3c **Pan American Union,** *April 14, 1940 (182,401)*	4.50	
896	3c **Idaho Statehood,** *July 3, 1940,* Boise, Idaho *(156,429)*	4.50	
897	3c **Wyoming Statehood,** *July 10, 1940* Cheyenne, Wyo. *(156,709)*	4.50	
898	3c **Coronado Expedition,** *Sept. 7, 1940,* Albuquerque, N.M. *(161,012)*	4.50	
899	1c **Defense,** *Oct. 16, 1940*	4.25	
900	2c **Defense,** *Oct. 16, 1940*	4.25	
901	3c **Defense,** *Oct. 16, 1940*	4.25	
	899 to 901 on one cover *(450,083)*	12.50	
902	3c **Thirteenth Amendment,** *Oct. 20, 1940,* World's Fair, N.Y. *(156,146)*	5.00	
1941			
903	3c **Vermont Statehood,** *March 4, 1941,* Montpelier, Vt. *(182,423)*	4.50	
1942			
904	3c **Kentucky Statehood,** *June 1, 1942,* Frankfort, Ky. *(155,730)*	4.00	
905	3c **"Win the War",** *July 4, 1942 (191,168)*	3.75	
906	5c **Chinese Resistance,** *July 7, 1942,* Denver, Colo. *(168,746)*	5.75	

FIRST DAY COVERS

1943
907	2c United Nations, *Jan. 14, 1943 (178,865)*	3.50
908	1c Four Freedoms, *Feb. 12, 1943 (193,800)*	3.50
909	5c Poland, *June 22, 1943,*	
	Chicago, Ill. *(88,170)*	6.00
	Washington, D.C. *(136,002)*	5.00
910	5c Czechoslovakia, *July 12, 1943 (145,112)*	5.00
911	5c Norway, *July 27, 1943 (130,054)*	4.00
912	5c Luxemburg, *Aug. 10, 1943 (166,367)*	4.00
913	5c Netherlands, *Aug. 24, 1943 (148,763)*	4.00
914	5c Belgium, *Sept. 14, 1943 (154,220)*	4.00
915	5c France, *Sept. 28, 1943 (163,478)*	4.00
916	5c Greece, *Oct. 12, 1943 (166,553)*	4.00
917	5c Yugoslavia, *Oct. 26, 1943 (161,835)*	4.00
918	5c Albania, *Nov. 9, 1943 (162,275)*	4.00
919	5c Austria, *Nov. 23, 1943 (172,285)*	4.00
920	5c Denmark, *Dec. 7, 1943 (173,784)*	4.00

1944
921	5c Korea, *Nov. 2, 1944 (192,860)*	5.00
922	3c Railroad, *May 10, 1944,*	
	Ogden, Utah *(151,324)*	
	Omaha, Neb. *(171,000)*	
	San Francisco, Cal. *(125,000)*	@6.00
923	3c Steamship, *May 22, 1944,*	
	Kings Point, N.Y. *(152,324)*	
	Savannah, Ga. *(181,472)*	@4.00
924	3c Telegraph, *May 24, 1944,*	
	Washington, D.C. *(141,907)*	
	Baltimore, Md. *(136,480)*	@3.50
925	3c Philippines, *Sept. 27, 1944 (214,865)*	3.50
926	3c Motion Picture, *Oct. 31, 1944,*	
	Hollywood, Cal. *(190,660)*	
	New York, N.Y. *(176,473)*	@3.50

1945
927	3c Florida, *March 3, 1945,*	
	Tallahassee, Fla. *(228,435)*	3.50
928	5c United Nations Conference, *April 25, 1945,*	
	San Francisco, Cal. *(417,450)*	3.50
929	3c Iwo Jima, *July 11, 1945 (391,650)*	5.25

1945-46
930	1c Roosevelt, *July 26, 1945,*	
	Hyde Park, N.Y. *(390,219)*	2.50
931	2c Roosevelt, *Aug. 24, 1945,*	
	Warm Springs, Ga. *(426, 142)*	2.50
932	3c Roosevelt, *June 27, 1945 (391,650)*	2.50
933	5c Roosevelt, *Jan. 30, 1945 (466,766)*	3.00
	930 to 933 on one cover	10.00
934	3c Army, *Sept. 28, 1945 (392,300)*	3.50
935	3c Navy, *Oct. 27, 1945,*	
	Annapolis, Md. *(460,352)*	3.50
936	3c Coast Guard, *Nov. 10, 1945*	
	New York, N.Y. *(405,280)*	3.50
937	3c Alfred E. Smith, *Nov. 26, 1945*	
	New York, N.Y. *(424,950)*	2.50
938	3c Texas, *Dec. 29, 1945,*	
	Austin, Tex. *(397,860)*	3.50

1946
939	3c Merchant Marine, *Feb. 26, 1946 (432,141)*	2.50
940	3c Veterans of WWII, *May 9 1946 (492,786)*	2.50
941	3c Tennessee, *June 1, 1946,*	
	Nashville, Tenn. *(463,512)*	2.50
942	3c Iowa, *Aug. 3, 1946,*	
	Iowa City, Iowa *(517,505)*	2.50
943	3c Smithsonian, *Aug. 10, 1946 (402,448)*	2.50
944	3c Kearny Expedition, *Oct. 16, 1946,*	
	Santa Fe, N.M. *(384,300)*	2.50

1947
945	3c Thomas A. Edison, *Feb. 11, 1947,*	
	Milan, Ohio *(632,473)*	2.50
946	3c Joseph Pulitzer, *Apr. 10, 1947,*	
	New York, N.Y. *(580,870)*	2.50
947	3c Stamp Centenary, *May 17, 1947,*	
	New York, N.Y. *(712,873)*	2.50
948	5c and 10c Centenary Exhibition Sheet, *May 19, 1947,*	
	New York, N.Y. *(502,175)*	3.00
949	3c Doctors, *June 9, 1947,*	
	Atlantic City, N.J. *(508,016)*	1.50
950	3c Utah, *July 24, 1947,*	
	Salt Lake City, Utah *(456,416)*	1.50
951	3c "Constitution", *Oct. 21, 1947,*	
	Boston, Mass. *(683,416)*	1.50
952	3c Everglades Park, *Dec. 5, 1947,*	
	Florida City, Fla. *(466,647)*	1.50

1948
953	3c Carver, *Jan. 5, 1948,*	
	Tuskegee Institute, Ala. *(402,179)*	1.50
954	3c California Gold, *Jan. 24, 1948,*	
	Coloma, Calif. *(526,154)*	1.50
955	3c Mississippi Territory, *April 7, 1948,*	
	Natchez, Miss. *(434, 804)*	1.50
956	3c Four Chaplains, *May 28, 1948,*	
	Washington, D.C. *(459,070)*	1.50
957	3c Wisconsin Centennial, *May 29, 1948,*	
	Madison, Wis. *(470,280)*	1.50
958	5c Swedish Pioneers, *June 4, 1948,*	
	Chicago, Ill. *(364,318)*	1.50
959	3c Women's Progress, *July 19, 1948,*	
	Seneca Falls, N.Y. *(401,923)*	1.50
960	3c William Allen White, *July 31, 1948,*	
	Emporia, Kans. *(385,648)*	1.50
961	3c U.S.-Canada Friendship, *Aug. 2, 1948,*	
	Niagara Falls, N.Y. *(406,467)*	1.50
962	3c Francis Scott Key, *Aug. 9, 1948,*	
	Frederick, Md. *(505,930)*	1.50
963	3c Salute to Youth, *Aug. 11, 1948,*	
	Washington, D.C. *(347,070)*	1.50
964	3c Oregon Territory Establishment, *Aug. 14, 1948,*	
	Oregon City, Ore. *(365,898)*	1.50
965	3c Harlan Fiske Stone, *Aug. 25, 1948,*	
	Chesterfield, N.H. *(362,170)*	1.50
966	3c Palomar Observatory, *Aug. 30, 1948,*	
	Palomar Mountain, Calif. *(401,365)*	1.50
967	3c Clara Barton, *Sept. 7, 1948,*	
	Oxford, Mass. *(362,000)*	1.25
968	3c Poultry Industry, *Sept. 9, 1948,*	
	New Haven, Conn. *(475,000)*	1.25
969	3c Gold Star Mothers, *Sept. 21, 1948,*	
	Washington, D.C. *(386,064)*	1.50
970	3c Fort Kearny, *Sept. 22, 1948,*	
	Minden, Neb. *(429,633)*	1.50
971	3c Volunteer Firemen, *Oct. 4, 1948,*	
	Dover, Del. *(399,630)*	1.50
972	3c Indian Centennial, *Oct. 15, 1948,*	
	Muskogee, Okla. *(459,528)*	1.25
973	3c Rough Riders, *Oct. 27, 1948,*	
	Prescott, Ariz. *(399, 198)*	1.25
974	3c Juliette Low, *Oct. 29, 1948,*	
	Savannah, Ga. *(476, 573)*	1.25
975	3c Will Rogers, *Nov. 4, 1948,*	
	Claremore, Okla. *(450,350)*	1.25
976	3c Fort Bliss, *Nov. 5, 1948,*	
	El Paso, Tex. *(421,000)*	1.25
977	3c Moina Michael, *Nov. 9, 1948,*	
	Athens, Ga. *(374,090)*	1.25
978	3c Gettysburg Address, *Nov. 19, 1948,*	
	Gettysburg, Pa. *(511,990)*	1.25
979	3c American Turners Society, *Nov. 20, 1948,*	
	Cincinnati, Ohio *(434,090)*	1.25
980	3c Joel Chandler Harris, *Dec. 9, 1948,*	
	Eatonton, Ga. *(426,199)*	1.25
981	3c Minnesota Territory, *May 3, 1949,*	
	St. Paul, Minn. *(458,750)*	1.25
982	3c Washington and Lee University, *April 12, 1949,* Lexington, Va. *(447,910)*	1.25
983	3c Puerto Rico Election, *April 27, 1949,*	
	San Juan, P.R. *(390,416)*	1.25
984	3c Annapolis, Md., *May 23, 1949,*	
	Annapolis, Md. *(441,802)*	1.25
985	3c G.A.R., *Aug. 29, 1949,*	
	Indianapolis, Ind. *(471,696)*	1.25
986	3c Edgar Allan Poe, *Oct. 7, 1949,*	
	Richmond, Va. *(371,020)*	1.25

1950
987	3c American Bankers Association, *Jan. 3, 1950,*	
	Saratoga Springs, N.Y. *(388,622)*	1.25
988	3c Samuel Gompers, *Jan. 27, 1950,*	
	Washington, D.C. *(332,023)*	1.25
989	3c National Capital Sesquicentennial (Freedom), *April 20, 1950,*	
	Washington, D.C. *(371,743)*	1.25
990	3c National Capital Sesquicentennial (Executive), *June 12, 1950,*	
	Washington, D.C. *(376,789)*	1.25
991	3c National Capital Sesquicentennial (Judicial), *Aug. 2, 1950,*	
	Washington, D.C. *(324,007)*	1.25
992	3c National Capital Sesquicentennial, (Legislative), *Nov. 22, 1950,*	
	Washington, D.C. *(352,215)*	1.25

FIRST DAY COVERS

993	3c **Railroad Engineers,** *April 29, 1950,* Jackson, Tenn. *(420,830)*	1.25
994	3c **Kansas City Centenary,** *June 3, 1950,* Kansas City, Mo. *(405,390)*	1.25
995	3c **Boy Scouts,** *June 30, 1950,* Valley Forge, Pa. *(622,972)*	2.00
996	3c **Indiana Territory Sesquicentennial,** *July 4, 1950,* Vincennes, Ind. *(359,643)*	1.25
997	3c **California Statehood,** *Sept. 9, 1950,* Sacramento, Cal. *(391,919)*	1.25
1951		
998	3c **United Confederate Veterans,** *May 30, 1951,* Norfolk, Va. *(374,235)*	1.25
999	3c **Nevada Centennial,** *July 14, 1951,* Genoa, Nev. *(336,890)*	1.25
1000	3c **Landing of Cadillac,** *July 24, 1951,* Detroit, Mich. *(323,094)*	1.25
1001	3c **Colorado Statehood,** *Aug. 1, 1951,* Minturn, Colo. *(311,568)*	1.25
1002	3c **American Chemical Society,** *Sept. 4, 1951,* New York, N.Y. *(436,419)*	1.25
1003	3c **Battle of Brooklyn,** *Dec. 10, 1951,* Brooklyn, N.Y. *(420,000)*	1.25
1952		
1004	3c **Betsy Ross,** *Jan. 2, 1952,* Philadelphia, Pa. *(314,312)*	1.25
1005	3c **4-H Club,** *Jan. 15, 1952,* Springfield, Ohio *(383,290)*	1.25
1006	3c **B. & O. Railroad,** *Feb. 28, 1952,* Baltimore, Md. *(441,600)*	1.50
1007	3c **American Automobile Association,** *March 4, 1952,* Chicago, Ill. *(520,123)*	85
1008	3c **NATO,** *April 4, 1952,* Washington, D.C. *(313,518)*	85
1009	3c **Grand Coulee Dam,** *May 15, 1952,* Grand Coulee, Wash. *(341,680)*	85
1010	3c **Lafayette,** *June 13, 1952,* Georgetown, S.C. *(349,102)*	85
1011	3c **Mt. Rushmore Memorial,** *Aug. 11, 1952,* Keystone, S.D. *(337,027)*	85
1012	3c **Civil Engineers,** *Sept. 6, 1952,* Chicago, Ill. *(318,483)*	85
1013	3c **Service Women,** *Sept. 11, 1952,* Washington, D.C. *(308,062)*	85
1014	3c **Gutenberg Bible,** *Sept. 30, 1952,* Washington, D.C. *(387,078)*	85
1015	3c **Newspaper Boys,** *Oct. 4, 1952,* Philadelphia, Pa. *(626,000)*	85
1016	3c **Red Cross,** *Nov. 21, 1952,* New York, N.Y. *(439,252)*	85
1953		
1017	3c **National Guard,** *Feb. 23, 1953,* Washington, D.C. *(387,618)*	85
1018	3c **Ohio Sesquicentennial,** *March 2, 1953,* Chillicothe, Ohio *(407,983)*	85
1019	3c **Washington Territory,** *March 2, 1953,* Olympia, Wash. *(344,047)*	85
1020	3c **Louisiana Purchase,** *April 30, 1953,* St. Louis, Mo *(425,600)*	82
1021	5c **Opening of Japan,** *July 14, 1953,* Washington, D.C. *(320,541)*	85
1022	3c **American Bar Association,** *Aug. 24, 1953,* Boston, Mass. *(410,036)*	85
1023	3c **Sagamore Hill,** *Sept. 14, 1953,* Oyster Bay, N.Y. *(379,750)*	1.00
1024	3c **Future Farmers,** *Oct. 13, 1953,* Kansas City, Mo. *(424,193)*	85
1025	3c **Trucking Industry,** *Oct. 27, 1953,* Los Angeles, Calif. *(875,021)*	85
1026	3c **Gen. G.S. Patton, Jr.,** *Nov. 11, 1953,* Fort Knox, Ky. *(342,600)*	85
1027	3c **New York City,** *Nov. 20, 1953,* New York, N.Y. *(387,914)*	85
1028	3c **Gadsden Purchase,** *Dec. 30, 1953,* Tucson, Ariz. *(363,250)*	85
1954		
1029	3c **Columbia University,** *Jan. 4, 1954,* New York, N.Y. *(550,745)*	85
1954-67	**LIBERTY ISSUE**	
1030	½c *Oct. 20, 1955,* Washington, D.C. *(223,122)* Block of four	85
1031	1c *Aug. 26, 1954,* Chicago, Ill. *(272,581)*	85

1031A	1¼c *June 17, 1960,* Santa Fe, N.M. (total for #1031A, 1054A and combination covers, *501,848*)	85
	1031A and 1054A on one cover	1.50
1031	1½c *Feb. 22, 1956,* Mount Vernon, Va. *(270,109)*	60
1033	2c *Sept. 15, 1954,* San Francisco, Cal. *(307,300)*	60
1034	2½c *June 17, 1959,* Boston, Mass. *(315,060)*	60
1035	3c *June 24, 1954,* Albany, N.Y. *(340,001)*	60
1035b	3c Tagged, *July 6, 1966*	15.00
1036	4c *Nov. 19, 1954,* New York, N.Y. *(374,064)*	60
1036b	4c Tagged, *Nov. 2, 1963,* Washington, D.C. No. 1036b was supposed to have been issued at Dayton Nov. 2, but a mix-up delayed its issuance there until Nov. 4. About 510 Covers received the Nov. 2 cancellation.	50.00
1037	4½c *Mar. 16, 1959,* Hermitage, Tenn. *(320,000)*	60
1038	5c *Dec. 2, 1954,* Fredericksburg, Va. *(255,650)*	60
1039	6c *Nov. 18, 1955,* New York, N.Y. *(257,551)*	65
1040	7c *Jan. 10, 1956,* Staunton, Va. *(200,111)*	70
1041	8c *April 9, 1954,* Washington, D.C. *(340,077)*	80
1042	8c (Giori press), *Mar. 22, 1958,* Cleveland, O. *(223,899)*	60
1042A	8c **Pershing,** *Nov. 17, 1961,* New York, N.Y. *(321,031)*	60
1043	9c *June 14, 1956,* San Antonio, Texas *(207,086)*	1.50
1044	10c *July 4, 1956,* Philadelphia, Pa., *(220,930)*	90
1044b	10c Tagged, *July 6, 1966*	15.00
1044A	11c *June 15, 1961,* Washington, D.C. *(238,905)*	90
1044c	11c Tagged, *Jan. 11, 1967*	22.50
1045	12c *June 6, 1959,* Oxford, O. *(225,869)*	90
1045a	12c Tagged, *May 6, 1968*	25.00
1046	15c *Dec. 12, 1958,* Washington, D.C. *(205,860)*	1.00
1046a	15c Tagged, *July 6, 1966*	20.00
1047	20c *Apr. 13, 1956,* Charlottesville, Va. *(147,860)*	1.20
1048	25c *April 18, 1958,* Boston, Mass. *(196,530)*	1.30
1049	30c *Sept. 21, 1955,* Norfolk, Va. *(120,166)*	1.50
1050	40c *Sept. 24, 1955,* Richmond, Va. *(113,972)*	1.75
1051	50c *Aug. 25, 1955,* Louisville, Ky. *(110,220)*	6.00
1052	$1 *Oct. 7, 1955,* Joplin, Mo. *(80,191)*	13.00
1053	$5 *Mar. 19, 1956,* Paterson, N.J. *(34,272)*	75.00
1954-65	**COIL STAMPS**	
1054	1c *Oct. 8, 1954,* Baltimore, Md. *(196,318)* Strip of three	75
1054A	1¼c *June 17, 1960,* Santa Fe, N.M. (total for #1054A, 1031A and combination covers *(501,848)*	1.00
1055	2c *Oct. 22, 1954,* St. Louis, Mo. *(162,050)* Pair	75
1055a	2c Tagged, *May 6, 1968* pair	11.00
1056	2½c *Sept. 9, 1959,* Los Angeles, Calif. *(198,680)*	1.20
1057	3c *July 20, 1954,* Washington, D.C. *(137,139)*	75
1058	4c *July 31, 1958,* Mandan, N.D. *(184,079)*	75
1059	4½c *May 1, 1959,* Denver, Colo. *(202,454)*	1.75
1059A	25c *Feb. 25, 1965,* Wheaton, Md. *(184,954)*	1.20
1059b	25c Tagged, *Apr. 3, 1973,* New York, N.Y.	14.00
1954		
1060	3c **Nebraska Territory,** *May 7, 1954,* Nebraska City, Neb. *(401,015)*	75
1061	3c **Kansas Territory,** *May 31, 1954,* Fort Leavenworth, Kans. *(349,145)*	45
1062	3c **George Eastman,** *July 12, 1954,* Rochester, N.Y. *(630,448)*	75
1063	3c **Lewis & Clark Expedition,** *July 28, 1954,* Sioux City, Iowa *(371,557)*	75
1955		
1064	3c **Pennsylvania Academy of the Fine Arts,** *Jan. 15, 1955,* Philadelphia, Pa. *(307,040)*	75
1065	3c **Land Grant Colleges,** *Feb. 12, 1955,* East Lansing, Mich. *(419,241)*	75
1066	8c **Rotary International,** *Feb. 23, 1955,* Chicago, Ill. *(350,625)*	90
1067	3c **Armed Forces Reserve,** *May, 21, 1955,* Washington, D.C. *(300,436)*	75
1068	3c **New Hampshire,** *June 21, 1955,* Franconia, N.H. *(330,630)*	75
1069	3c **Soo Locks,** *June 28, 1955,* Sault Sainte Marie, Mich. *(316,616)*	75
1070	3c **Atoms for Peace,** *July 28, 1955,* Washington, D.C. *(351,940)*	75
1071	3c **Fort Ticonderoga,** *Sept. 18, 1955,* Fort Ticonderoga, N.Y. *(342,946)*	75
1072	3c **Andrew W. Mellon,** *Dec. 20, 1955,* Washington, D.C. *(278,897)*	75

1956

1073	3c **Benjamin Franklin,** *Jan. 17, 1956,* Philadelphia, Pa. *(351,260)*		75
1074	3c **Booker T. Washington,** *Apr. 5, 1956,* Booker T. Washington Birthplace, Va. *(272,659)*		75
1075	11c **FIPEX Souvenir Sheet,** *Apr. 28, 1956,* New York, N.Y. *(429,327)*		7.50
1076	3c **FIPEX,** *Apr. 30, 1956,* New York, N.Y. *(526,090)*		75
1077	3c **Wildlife (Turkey),** *May 5, 1956,* Fond du Lac, Wis. *(292,121)*		1.10
1078	3c **Wildlife (Antelope),** *June 22, 1956,* Gunnison, Colo. *(294,731)*		1.10
1079	3c **Wildlife (Salmon),** *Nov. 9, 1956,* Seattle, Wash. *(346,800)*		1.10
1080	3c **Pure Food and Drug Laws,** *June 27, 1956,* Washington, D.C. *(411,761)*		80
1081	3c **Wheatland,** *Aug. 5, 1956,* Lancaster, Pa. *(340,142)*		80
1082	3c **Labor Day,** *Sept. 3, 1956,* Camden, N.J. *(338,450)*		80
1083	3c **Nassau Hall,** *Sept. 22, 1956,* Princeton, N.J. *(350,756)*		80
1084	3c **Devils Tower,** *Sept. 24, 1956,* Devils Tower, Wyo. *(285,090)*		80
1085	3c **Children,** *Dec. 15, 1956,* Washington, D.C. *(305,125)*		80

1957

1086	3c **Alexander Hamilton,** *Jan. 11, 1957,* New York, N.Y. *(305,117)*		80
1087	3c **Polio,** *Jan. 15, 1957,* Washington, D.C. *(307,630)*		80
1088	3c **Coast & Geodetic Survey,** *Feb. 11, 1957,* Seattle, Wash. *(309,931)*		80
1089	3c **Architects,** *Feb. 23, 1957,* New York, N.Y. *(368,840)*		80
1090	3c **Steel Industry,** *May 22, 1957,* New York, N.Y. *(473,284)*		80
1091	3c **Naval Review,** *June 10, 1957,* U.S.S. Saratoga, Norfolk, Va. *(365,933)*		80
1092	3c **Oklahoma Statehood,** *June 14, 1957,* Oklahoma City, Okla. *(327,172)*		80
1093	3c **School Teachers,** *July 1, 1957,* Philadelphia, Pa. *(357,986)* (Spelling error) Philadelphia		80 4.50
1094	4c **Flag,** *July 4, 1957,* Washington, D.C. *(523,879)*		80
1095	3c **Shipbuilding,** *Aug. 15, 1957,* Bath, Maine *(347,432)*		80
1096	8c **Ramon Magsaysay,** *Aug. 31, 1957,* Washington, D.C. *(334,558)*		80
1097	3c **Lafayette Bicentenary,** *Sept. 6, 1957,* Easton, Pa. *(260,421)* Fayetteville, N.C. *(230,000)* Louisville, Ky. *(207,856)*		@80
1098	3c **Wildlife (Whooping Cranes),** *Nov. 22, 1957,* New York, N.Y. *(342,970)* New Orleans, La. *(154,327)* Corpus Christi, Tex. *(280,990)*		@1.00
1099	3c **Religious Freedom,** *Dec. 27, 1957,* Flushing, N.Y. *(357,770)*		80

1958

1100	3c **Gardening-Horticulture,** *Mar. 15, 1958,* Ithaca, N.Y. *(451,292)*		80
1104	3c **Brussels Exhibition,** *April 17, 1958,* Detroit, Mich. *(428,073)*		80
1105	3c **James Monroe,** *April 28, 1958,* Montross, Va. *(326,988)*		80
1106	3c **Minnesota Statehood,** *May 11, 1958,* Saint Paul, Minn. *(475,552)*		80
1107	3c **International Geophysical Year,** *May 31, 1958,* Chicago, Ill. *(397,000)*		80
1108	3c **Gunston Hall,** *June 12, 1958,* Lorton, Va. *(349,801)*		80
1109	3c **Mackinac Bridge,** *June 25, 1958,* "Mackinac Bridge, Mich." *(445,605)*		80
1110	4c **Simon Bolivar,** *July 24, 1958,* Washington, D.C.		80
1111	8c **Simon Bolivar,** *July 24, 1958* Washington, D.C. 1110 and 1111, set of two on one cover First day cancellation was applied to 708, 777 covers bearing No. 1110, No. 1111. or both.		80 2.25
1112	4c **Atlantic Cable,** *Aug. 15, 1958,* New York, N.Y. *(365,072)*		80

1958-59

1113	1c **Lincoln Sesquicentennial,** *Feb. 12, 1959,* Hodgenville, Ky. *(379,862)*		80
1114	3c **Lincoln Sesquicentennial,** *Feb. 12, 1959,* New York, N.Y. *(437,737)*		80
1115	4c **Lincoln-Douglas Debates,** *Aug. 27, 1958,* Freeport, Ill. *(373,063)*		80
1116	4c **Lincoln Sesquicentennial,** *May, 30, 1959,* Washington, D.C. *(894,887)*		80

1958

1117	4c **Lajos Kossuth,** *Sept. 19, 1958,* Washington, D.C.		80
1118	8c **Lajos Kossuth,** *Sept. 19, 1958,* Washington, D.C. 1117 and 1118, set of two on one cover First day cancellation was applied to 722, 188 covers bearing No. 1117, No. 1118, or both.		80 2.25
1119	4c **Freedom of Press,** *Sept. 22, 1958,* Columbia, Mo. *(411,752)*		80
1120	4c **Overland Mail,** *Oct. 10, 1958,* San Francisco, Cal. *(352,760)*		80
1121	4c **Noah Webster,** *Oct. 16, 1958,* West Hartford, Conn. *(364,608)*		80
1122	4c **Forest Conservation,** *Oct. 27, 1958,* Tucson, Ariz. *(405,959)*		80
1123	4c **Fort Duquesne,** *Nov. 25, 1958,* Pittsburgh, Pa. *(421,764)*		80

1959

1124	4c **Oregon Statehood,** *Feb. 14, 1959,* Astoria, Ore. *(452,764)*		80
1125	4c **San Martin,** *Feb. 25, 1959,* Washington, D.C.		80
1126	8c **San Martin,** *Feb. 25, 1959,* Washington, D.C. 1125 and 1126, set of two on one cover First day cancellation was applied to 910, 208 covers bearing No. 1125, No. 1126, or both.		80 2.25
1127	4c **NATO** *April, 1, 1959,* Washington, D.C. *(361,040)*		80
1128	4c **Arctic Exploration,** *April 6, 1959,* Cresson, Pa. *(397,770)*		80
1129	8c **World Trade,** *April 20, 1959,* Washington, D.C. *(503,618)*		80
1130	4c **Silver Centennial,** *June 8, 1959,* Virginia City, Nev. *(337,233)*		80
1131	4c **St. Lawrence Seaway,** *June 26, 1959,* Massena, N.Y. *(543,211)*		80
1132	4c **Flag (49 stars),** *July 4, 1959,* Auburn, N.Y. *(523,773)*		80
1133	4c **Soil Conservation,** *Aug. 26, 1959,* Rapid City, S.D. *(400,613)*		80
1134	4c **Petroleum Industry,** *Aug. 27, 1959,* Titusville, Pa. *(801,859)*		80
1135	4c **Dental Health,** *Sept. 14, 1959,* New York, N.Y. *(649,813)*		80
1136	4c **Reuter,** *Sept. 29, 1959,* Washington, D.C.		80
1137	8c **Reuter,** *Sept. 29, 1959,* Washington, D.C. 1136 and 1137, set of two on one cover First day cancellation was applied to 1,207,933 covers bearing No. 1136, No. 1137, or both.		80 2.25
1138	4c **Dr. Ephraim McDowell,** *Dec. 3, 1959,* Danville, Ky. *(344,603)*		80

1960-61

1139	4c **Washington "Credo,"** *Jan. 20, 1960,* Mount Vernon, Va. *(438,335)*		1.25
1140	4c **Franklin "Credo,"** *March 31, 1960,* Philadelphia, Pa. *(497,913)*		1.00
1141	4c **Jefferson "Credo,"** *May 18, 1960,* Charlottesville, Va. *(454,903)*		1.00
1142	4c **Francis Scott Key "Credo,"** *Sept. 14, 1960,* Baltimore, Md. *(501,129)*		1.25
1143	4c **Lincoln "Credo,"** *Nov. 19, 1960,* New York, N.Y. *(467,780)*		1.25
1144	4c **Patrick Henry "Credo,"** *Jan. 11, 1961,* Richmond, Va. *(415,252)*		1.25
1145	4c **Boy Scouts,** *Feb. 8, 1960,* Washington, D.C. *(1,419,955)*		1.25
1146	4c **Olympic Winter Games,** *Feb. 18, 1960,* Olympic Valley, Calif. *(516,456)*		80

FIRST DAY COVERS

1147	4c **Masaryk**, *Mar. 7, 1960*, Washington, D.C.	80
1148	4c **Masaryk**, *Mar. 7, 1960*, Washington, D.C.	80
	1147 and 1148, set of two on one cover	2.25
	First day cancellation was applied to 1,710,726 covers bearing No. 1147, No. 1148, or both.	
1149	4c **World Refugee Year**, *Apr. 7, 1960*, Washington, D.C. *(413,298)*	80
1150	4c **Water Conservation**, *Apr. 18, 1960*, Washington, D.C. *(648,988)*	80
1151	4c **SEATO**, *May 31, 1960*, Washington, D.C. *(514,926)*	80
1152	4c **American Woman**, *June 2, 1960*, Washington, D.C. *(830,385)*	80
1153	4c **50-Star Flag**, *July 4, 1960*, Honolulu, Hawaii *(820,900)*	80
1154	4c **Pony Express Centennial**, *July 19, 1960*, Sacramento, Calif. *(520,223)*	80
1155	4c **Employ the Handicapped**, *Aug. 28, 1960*, New York, N.Y. *(439,638)*	80
1156	4c **World Forestry Congress**, *Aug. 29, 1960*, Seattle, Wash. *(350,848)*	80
1157	4c **Mexican Independence**, *Sept. 16, 1960*, Los Angeles, Calif. *(360,297)*	80
1158	4c **U.S.-Japan Treaty**, *Sept. 28, 1960*, Washington, D.C. *(545,150)*	80
1159	4c **Paderewski**, *Oct. 8, 1960*, Washington, D.C.	80
1160	8c **Paderewski**, *Oct. 8, 1960*, Washington, D.C.	80
	1159 and 1160 on one cover	2.25
	First day cancellation was applied to 1,057,438 covers bearing No. 1159, No. 1160, or both.	
1161	4c **Robert A. Taft**, *Oct. 10, 1960*, Cincinnati, Ohio *(312,116)*	80
1162	4c **Wheels of Freedom**, *Oct. 15, 1960*, Detroit, Mich. *(380,551)*	80
1163	4c **Boys' Clubs**, *Oct. 18, 1960*, New York, N.Y. *(435,009)*	80
1164	4c **Automated P.O.**, *Oct. 20, 1960*, Providence, R.I. *(458,237)*	80
1165	4c **Mannerheim**, *Oct. 26, 1960*, Washington, D.C.	80
1166	8c **Mannerheim**, *Oct. 26, 1960*, Washington, D.C.	80
	1165 and 1166 on one cover	2.25
	First day cancellation was applied to 1,168,770 covers bearing No. 1165, No. 1166, or both.	
1167	4c **Camp Fire Girls**, *Nov. 1, 1960*, New York, N.Y. *(324,944)*	80
1168	4c **Garibaldi**, *Nov. 2, 1960*, Washington, D.C.	80
1169	4c **Garibaldi**, *Nov. 2, 1960*, Washington, D.C.	80
	1168 and 1169 on one cover	2.25
	First day cancellation was applied to 1,001,490 covers bearing No. 1168, No. 1169, or both.	
1170	4c **Senator George**, *Nov. 25, 1960*, New York, N.Y. *(318,180)*	80
1171	4c **Andrew Carnegie**, *Nov. 25, 1960*, New York, N.Y. *(318,180)*	80
1172	4c **John Foster Dulles**, *Dec. 6, 1960*, Washington, D.C. *(400,055)*	80
1173	4c **Echo I**, *Dec. 15, 1960*, Washington, D.C. *(583,747)*	1.75

1961-65

1174	4c **Gandhi**, *Jan. 26, 1961*, Washington, D.C.	80
1175	8c **Gandhi**, *Jan. 26, 1961*, Washington, D.C.	80
	1174 and 1175 on one cover	2.25
	First day cancellation was applied to 1,013,515 covers bearing No. 1174, No. 1175, or both.	
1176	4c **Range Conservation**, *Feb. 2, 1961*, Salt Lake City, Utah *(357,101)*	75
1177	4c **Horace Greeley**, *Feb. 3, 1961*, Chappaqua, N.Y. *(359,205)*	75
1178	4c **Fort Sumter**, *Apr. 12, 1961*, Charleston, S.C. *(602,599)*	1.75
1179	4c **Battle of Shiloh**, *Apr. 7, 1962*, Shiloh, Tenn. *(526,062)*	1.75
1180	5c **Battle of Gettysburg**, *July 1, 1963*, Gettysburg, Pa. *(600,205)*	1.75

1181	5c **Battle of Wilderness**, *May 5, 1964*, Fredericksburg, Va. *(450,904)*	1.75
1182	5c **Appomattox**, *Apr. 9, 1965*, Appomattox, Va. *(653,121)*	1.75
1183	4c **Kansas Statehood**, *May 10, 1961*, Council Grove, Kansas *(480,561)*	75
1184	4c **Senator Norris**, *July 11, 1961*, Washington, D.C. *(482,875)*	75
1185	4c **Naval Aviation**, *Aug. 20, 1961*, San Diego, Calif. *(416,391)*	90
1186	4c **Workmen's Compensation**, *Sept. 4, 1961*, Milwaukee, Wis, *(410,236)*	75
1187	4c **Frederic Remington**, *Oct. 4, 1961*, Washington, D.C. *(723,443)*	75
1188	4c **China Republic**, *Oct. 10, 1961*, Washington, D.C. *(463,900)*	75
1189	4c **Naismith-Basketball**, *Nov. 6, 1961*, Springfield, Mass. *(479,917)*	1.50
1190	4c **Nursing**, *Dec. 28, 1961*, Washington, D.C. *(964,005)*	75

1962

1191	4c **New Mexico Statehood**, *Jan. 6, 1962*, Sante Fe, N.M. *(365,330)*	75
1192	4c **Arizona Statehood**, *Feb. 14, 1962*, Phoenix, Ariz. *(508,216)*	75
1193	4c **Project Mercury**, *Feb. 20, 1962*, Cape Canaveral, Fla. *(3,000,000)*	1.50
	Any city	5.00
1194	4c **Malaria Eradication**, *Mar. 30, 1962*, Washington, D.C. *(554,175)*	75
1195	4c **Charles Evans Hughes**, *Apr. 11, 1962*, Washington, D.C. *(544,424)*	75
1196	4c **Seattle World's Fair**, *Apr. 25, 1962*, Seattle, Wash. *(771,856)*	75
1197	4c **Louisiana Statehood**, *Apr. 30, 1962*, New Orleans, La. *(436,681)*	75
1198	4c **Homestead Act**, *May 20, 1962*, Beatrice, Nebr. *(487,450)*	75
1199	4c **Gil Scouts**, *July 24, 1962*, Burlington, VT. *(634,347)*	1.00
1200	4c **Brien McMahon**, *July 28, 1962*, Norwalk, Conn. *(384,419)*	75
1201	4c **Apprenticeship**, *Aug. 31, 1962*, Washington, D.C. *(1,003,548)*	75
1202	4c **Sam Rayburn**, *Sept. 16, 1962*, Bonham, Texas *(401,042)*	75
1203	4c **Dag Hammarskjold**, *Oct. 23, 1962*, New York, N.Y. *(500,683)*	75
1204	4c **Hammarskjold**, yellow inverted, *Nov. 16, 1962*, Washington, D.C. (about 75,000)	6.00
1205	4c **Christmas**, *Nov. 1, 1962*, Pittsburgh, Pa. *(491,312)*	75
1206	4c **Higher Education**, *Nov. 14, 1962*, Washington, D.C. *(627,347)*	75
1207	4c **Winslow Homer**, *Dec. 15, 1962*, Gloucester, Mass. *(498,866)*	75

1963-66

1208	5c **Flag**, *Jan. 9, 1963*, Washington, D.C. *(696,185)*	75
1208a	5c **Tagged**, *Aug. 25, 1966*	11.50

1962-66   **REGULAR ISSUE**

1209	1c **Jackson**, *Mar. 22, 1963*, New York, N.Y. *(392,363)*	75
1209a	1c **Tagged**, *July 6, 1966*, Washington, D.C.	5.75
1213	5c **Washington**, *Nov. 23, 1962*, New York, N.Y. *(360,531)*	75
1213b	5c **Tagged**, *Oct. 28, 1963*, Dayton, Ohio, (about 15,000)	5.75
1225	1c **Coil**, *May 31, 1963*, Chicago, Ill. *(238,952)*	75
1225a	1c **Coil, tagged**, *July 6, 1966*, Washington, D.C., Pair	5.75
1229	5c **Coil**, *Nov. 23, 1962*, New York, N.Y. *(184,627)*	75
1229a	5c **Coil, tagged**, *Oct. 28, 1963*, Dayton, Ohio, (about 2,000)	20.00

1963

1230	5c **Carolina Charter**, *Apr. 6, 1963*, Edenton, N.C. *(426,200)*	75
1231	5c **Food for Peace**, *June 4, 1963*, Washington, D.C. *(624,342)*	75
1232	5c **West Virginia Statehood**, *June 20, 1963*, Wheeling, W. Va. *(413,389)*	75
1233	5c **Emancipation Proclamation**, *Aug. 16, 1963*, Chicago, Ill. *(494,886)*	75

FIRST DAY COVERS

1234	5c **Alliance for Progress,** *Aug. 17, 1963,* Washington, D.C. *(528,095)*	75
1235	5c **Cordell Hull,** *Oct. 5, 1963* Carthage, Tenn. *(391,631)*	75
1236	5c **Eleanor Roosevelt,** *Oct. 11, 1963,* Washington, D.C. *(860,155)*	75
1237	5c **Science,** *Oct. 14, 1963,* Washington, D.C. *(504,503)*	75
1238	5c **City Mail Delivery,** *Oct. 26, 1963,* Washington, D.C. *(544,806)*	75
1239	5c **Red Cross,** *Oct. 29, 1963,* Washington, D.C. *(557,678)*	75
1240	5c **Christmas,** *Nov. 1, 1963,* Santa Claus, Ind. *(458,619)*	75
1240a	5c **Christmas,** tagged, *Nov. 2, 1963,* Washington, D.C. (about *500*)	75.00
	Note below No. 1936b also applies to No. 1240a.	
1241	5c **Audubon,** *Dec. 7, 1963,* Henderson, Ky. *(518,855)*	75
1964		
1242	5c **Sam Houston,** *Jan. 10, 1964,* Houston, Tex. *(487,986)*	75
1243	5c **Charles Russel,** *Mar. 19, 1964,* Great Falls, Mont. *(658,745)*	75
1244	5c **N.Y. World's Fair,** *Apr. 22, 1964,* World's Fair, N.Y. *(1,656,346)*	75
1245	5c **John Muir,** *Apr. 29, 1964,* Martinez, Calif. *(446,925)*	75
1246	5c **John F. Kennedy,** *May 29, 1964,* Boston, Mass. *(2,003,096)*	75
	Any city	75
1247	5c **New Jersey Tercentenary,** *June 15, 1964,* Elizabeth, N.J. *(526,879)*	75
1248	5c **Nevada Statehood,** *July 22, 1964,* Carson City, Nev. *(584,973)*	75
1249	5c **Register & Vote,** *Aug. 1, 1964,* Washington, D.C. *(533,439)*	75
1250	5c **Shakespeare,** *Aug. 14, 1964,* Stratford, Conn. *(524,053)*	75
1251	5c **Drs. Mayo,** *Sept. 11, 1964,* Rochester, Minn. *(674,846)*	75
1252	5c **American Music,** *Oct. 15, 1964,* New York, N.Y. *(466,107)*	75
1253	5c **Homemakers,** *Oct. 26, 1964,* Honolulu, Hawaii *(435,392)*	75
1254	5c **Christmas (holly),** *Nov. 9, 1964,* Bethlehem, Pa.	75
1254a	5c Tagged, *Nov. 10, 1964,* Dayton, O.	12.50
1255	5c **Christmas (mistletoe),** *Nov. 9, 1964,* Bethlehem, Pa.	75
1255a	5c Tagged, *Nov. 10, 1964,* Dayton, O.	12.50
1256	5c **Christmas (poinsettia),** *Nov. 9, 1964,* Bethlehem, Pa.	75
1256a	5c Tagged, *Nov. 10, 1964,* Dayton, O.	12.50
1257	5c **Christmas (conifer),** *Nov. 9, 1964,* Bethlehem, Pa.	75
1257a	5c Tagged, *Nov. 10, 1964,* Dayton, O.	12.50
	Nos. 1254-1257, block of four on one cover	3.00
	Nos. 1254a-1257a, block of four on one cover	57.50
	First day cancellation was applied to 794,900 covers bearing Nos. 1254-1257 in singles or block and (at Dayton) to about 2,700 covers bearing Nos. 1254a-1257a in singles or multiples.	
1258	5c **Verrazano-Narrows Bridge,** *Nov. 21, 1964,* Staten Island, N.Y. *(619,082)*	
1259	5c **Fine Arts,** *Dec. 2, 1964,* Washington, D.C. *(558,046)*	75
1260	5c **Amateur Radio,** *Dec. 15, 1964,* Anchorage, Alaska *(452,255)*	75
1965		
1261	5c **Battle of New Orleans,** *Jan. 8,* New Orleans, La. *(466,029)*	75
1262	5c **Physical Fitness-Sokol,** *Feb. 15,* Washington, D.C. *(864,848)*	75
1263	5c **Cancer Crusade,** *Apr. 1,* Washington, D.C. *(744,485)*	75
1264	5c **Churchill,** *May 13,* Fulton, Mo. *(773,580)*	75
1265	5c **Magna Carta,** *June 15,* Jamestown, Va. *(479,065)*	75
1266	5c **Intl. Cooperation Year,** *June 26,* San Francisco, Cal. *(402,925)*	75

1267	5c **Salvation Army,** *July 2,* New York, N.Y. *(634,228)*	75
1268	5c **Dante,** *July 17,* San Francisco, Cal. *(424,893)*	75
1269	5c **Herbet Hoover,** *Aug. 10,* West Branch, Iowa *(698,182)*	75
1270	5c **Robert Fulton,** *Aug. 19,* Clermont, N.Y. *(550,330)*	75
1271	5c **Florida Settlement,** *Aug. 28,* St. Augustine, Fla. *(465,000)*	75
1272	5c **Traffic Safety,** *Sept. 3,* Baltimore, Md. *(527,075)*	75
1273	5c **Copley,** *Sept. 17,* Washington, D.C. *(613,484)*	75
1274	5c **Intl. Telecommunication Union,** *Oct. 6,* Washington, D.C. *(332,818)*	75
1275	5c **Adlai Stevenson,** *Oct. 23,* Bloomington, Ill. *(755,656)*	75
1276	5c **Christmas,** *Nov. 2,* Silver Bell, Ariz. *(705,039)*	75
1276a	5c Tagged, *Nov. 15,* Washington, D.C. (about *300*)	42.50
1965-78	**PROMINENT AMERICANS ISSUE**	
1278	1c *Jan. 12, 1968,* Jeffersonville, Ind.	60
	First day cancellation was applied to 655,680 covers bearing Nos. 1278, 1278a or 1299.	
1279	1¼c *Jan. 30, 1967,* Gallatin, Mo. *(439,010)*	60
1280	2c *June 8, 1966,* Spring Green, Wis. *(460,427)*	60
1281	3c *Sept. 16, 1967,* Boston, Mass. *(518,355)*	60
1282	4c *Nov. 19, 1965,* New York, N.Y. *(445,629)*	60
1282a	4c Tagged, *Dec. 1, 1965,* Dayton, O. (about *2,000*) Washington, D.C. *(1,200)*	32.50
1283	5c *Feb. 22, 1966,* Washington, D.C. *(525,372)*	60
1283a	5c Tagged, *Feb. 23, 1966,* Washington, D.C. (about *900*)	22.50
	Dayton, Ohio (about *200*)	57.50
1283B	5c Redrawn, *Nov. 17, 1967,* New York, N.Y. *(328,983)*	45
1284	6c *Jan. 29, 1966,* Hyde Park, N.Y. *(448,631)*	45
1284a	6c Tagged, *Dec. 29, 1966,* Washington, D.C.	20.00
1285	8c *Mar. 14, 1966,* Princeton, N.J. *(366,803)*	50
1285a	8c Tagged, *July 6, 1966*	14.00
1286	10c *Mar. 15, 1967,* Hermitage, Tenn. *(255,945)*	60
1286A	12c *July 30, 1968,* Greenfield Village, Mich. *(342,850)*	50
1287	13c *May 29, 1967,* Brookline, Mass. *(391,195)*	65
1288	15c *Mar. 8, 1968,* Washington, D.C. *(322,970)*	60
1288B	15c *June 14, 1978,* Boston, Mass.	65
	First day cancellation was applied to 387,119 covers bearing No. 1288B or 1305E.	
1289	20c *Oct. 24, 1967,* Lexington, Va. *(221,206)*	80
1289a	20c Tagged, *Apr. 3, 1973,* New York, N.Y.	12.50
1290	25c *Feb. 14, 1967,* Washington, D.C. *(213,730)*	1.00
1290a	25c Tagged, *Apr. 3, 1973,* New York, N.Y.	14.00
1291	30c *Oct. 21, 1968,* Burlington, Vt. *(162,790)*	1.20
1291a	30c Tagged, *Apr. 3, 1973,* New York, N.Y.	14.00
1292	40c *Jan. 29, 1968,* Philadelphia, Pa. *(157,947)*	1.60
1292a	40c Tagged, *Apr. 3, 1973,* New York, N.Y.	15.00
1293	50c *Aug. 13, 1968,* Dorchester, Mass. *(140,410)*	3.25
1293a	50c Tagged, *Apr. 3, 1973,* New York, N.Y.	20.00
1294	$1 *Oct. 16, 1967,* New London, Conn. *(103, 102)*	7.50
1294a	$1 Tagged, *Apr. 3,* New York, N.Y.	22.50
1295	$5 *Dec. 3, 1966,* Smyrna, Del. *(41,130)*	60.00
1295a	$5 Tagged, *Apr. 3, 1973,* New York, N.Y.	70.00
	First day cancellation was applied to 17,533 covers bearing one or more of Nos. 1059b, 1289a, 1290a, 1291a, 1292a, 1293a, 1294a and 1295a.	
1297	3c *Nov. 4, 1975,* Pendleton, Ore. *(166,798)*	75
1298	6c Perf. 10 Horiz., *Dec. 28, 1967,* Washington, D.C.	75
	First day cancellation was applied to 312,330 covers bearing Nos. 1298 to 1284b.	
1299	1c *Jan. 12, 1968,* Jeffersonville, Ind.	75
1303	4c *May 28, 1966,* Springfield, Ill. *(322,563)*	75
1304	5c *Sept. 8, 1966,* Cincinnati, N.Y.	75
1305	6c Perf. 10 vert., *Feb. 28, 1968,* Washington, D.C. *(317,199)*	75
1305E	15c *June 14, 1978,* Boston, Mass.	75
1305C	$1 *Jan. 12, 1973,* Hempstead, N.Y. *(121,217)*	3.00
1966		
1306	5c **Migratory Bird Treaty,** *Mar. 16, 1966,* Pittsburg, Pa. *(555,685)*	75
1307	5c **Humane Treatment of Animals,** *Apr. 9, 1966,* New York, N.Y. *(524,420)*	75
1308	5c **Indiana Statehood,** *Apr. 16, 1966,* Corydon, Ind. *(575,557)*	75
1309	5c **Circus,** *May 2, 1966,* Delavan, Wis. *(754,076)*	75
1310	5c **SIPEX,** *May 21, 1966,* Washington, D.C. *(637,802)*	75
1311	5c **SIPEX, Souvenir Sheet,** *May 23, 1966,* Washington, D.C. *(700,882)*	75
1312	5c **Bill of Rights,** *July 1, 1966,* Miami Beach, Fla. *(562,920)*	75

FIRST DAY COVERS 433

1313	5c **Polish Millennium**, *July 30, 1966,* Washington, D.C. *(715,603)*	75
1314	5c **National Park Service**, *Aug. 25, 1966,* Yellowstone National Park, Wyo. *(528,170)*	75
1314a	5c **Tagged**, *Aug. 26, 1966*	20.00
1315	5c **Marine Corps Reserve**, *Aug. 29, 1966,* Washington, D.C. *(585,923)*	75
1315a	5c **Tagged**, *Aug. 29, 1966,* Washington, D.C.	20.00
1316	5c **Gen. Fed. of Women's Clubs**, *Sept. 12, 1966,* New York, N.Y. *(383,334)*	75
1316a	5c **Tagged**, *Sept. 13, 1966*	22.50
1317	5c **Johnny Appleseed**, *Sept. 24, 1966,* Leominster, Mass. *(794,610)*	75
1317a	5c **Tagged**, *Sept. 26, 1966*	22.50
1318	5c **Beautification of America**, *Oct. 5, 1966,* Washington, D.C. *(564,440)*	75
1318a	5c **Tagged**, *Oct. 5, 1966,* Washington, D.C.	20.00
1319	5c **Great River Road**, *Oct. 21, 1966,* Baton Rouge, La. *(330,933)*	75
1319a	5c **Tagged**, *Oct. 22, 1966*	22.50
1320	5c **Savings Bond-Servicemen**, *Oct. 26, 1966,* Sioux City, Iowa *(444,421)*	75
1320a	5c **Tagged**, *Oct. 27, 1966*	22.50
1321	5c **Christmas**, *Nov. 1, 1966,* Christmas, Mich. *(537,650)*	75
1321a	5c **Tagged**, *Nov. 2, 1966*	9.50
1322	5c **Mary Cassatt**, *Nov. 17, 1966,* Washington, D.C. *(593,389)*	75
1322a	5c **Tagged**, *Nov. 17, 1966,* Washington, D.C.	20.00
1967		
1323	5c **National Grange**, *Apr. 17, 1967,* Washington, D.C. *(603,460)*	75
1324	5c **Canada Centenary**, *May 25, 1967,* Montreal, Canada *(711,795)*	75
1325	5c **Erie Canal**, *July 4, 1967,* Rome, N.Y. *(784,611)*	75
1326	5c **Search for Peace-Lions**, *July 5, 1967,* Chicago, Ill. *(393,197)*	75
1327	5c **Thoreau**, *July 12, 1967,* Concord, Mass. *(696,789)*	75
1328	5c **Nebraska Statehood**, *July 29, 1967,* Lincoln, Nebr. *(1,146,957)*	75
1329	5c **Voice of America**, *Aug. 1, 1967,* Washington, D.C. *(455,190)*	75
1330	5c **Davy Crockett**, *Aug. 17, 1967,* San Antonio, Tex. *(462,291)*	75
1331-1332	5c **Space Accomplishments**, *Sept. 29, 1967,* Kennedy Space Center, Fla. *(667,267)*	@2.50
	1331a	8.00
1333	5c **Urban Planning**, *Oct. 2, 1967,* Washington, D.C. *(389,009)*	75
1334	5c **Finland Independence**, *Oct. 6, 1967,* Finland, Minn. *(408,532)*	75
1335	5c **Thomas Eakins**, *Nov. 2, 1967,* Washington, D.C. *(648,054)*	75
1336	5c **Christmas**, *Nov. 6, 1967,* Bethlehem, Ga. *(462,118)*	75
1337	5c **Mississippi Statehood**, *Dec. 11, 1967,* Natchez, Miss. *(379,612)*	75
1968-71		
1338	6c **Flag (Giori)**, *Jan. 24, 1968,* Washington, D.C. *(412,120)*	75
1338A	6c **Flag coil**, *May 30, 1969,* Chicago, Ill. *(248,434)*	75
1338D	6c **Flag (Huck)** *Aug. 7, 1970,* Washington, D.C. *(365,280)*	75
1338F	9c **Flag**, *May 10, 1971,* Washington, D.C.	75
1338G	8c **Flag coil**, *May 10, 1971,* Washington, D.C. First day cancellation (May 10) was applied to 235,543 covers bearing either No. 1338F or 1338G.	
1339	6c **Illinois Statehood**, *Feb. 12, 1968,* Shawneetown, Ill. *(761,640)*	75
1340	6c **HemisFair '68**, *Mar. 30, 1968,* San Antonio, Tex. *(469,909)*	75
1341	$1 **Airlift**, *Apr. 4, 1968,* Seattle, Wash. *(105,088)*	6.50
1342	6c **Youth-Elks**, *May 1, 1968,* Chicago, Ill. *(354,711)*	75
1343	6c **Law and Order**, *May 17, 1968,* Washington, D.C. *(407,081)*	75
1344	6c **Register and Vote**, *June 27, 1968,* Washington, D.C. *(355,685)*	75
1345-1354	6c **Historic Flag series of 10**, *July 4, 1968,* Pittsburgh, Pa.	@4.00
	1354a	12.00
	First day cancellation was applied to 2,924,962 covers bearing one or more of Nos. 1345-1354.	

1355	6c **Disney**, *Sept. 11, 1968,* Marceline, Mo. *(499,505)*	1.00
1356	6c **Marquette**, *Sept. 20, 1968,* Sault Ste. Marie, Mich. *(379,710)*	75
1357	6c **Daniel Boone**, *Sept. 26, 1968,* Frankfort, Ky. *(333,440)*	75
1358	6c **Arkansas River**, *Oct. 1, 1968,* Little Rock, Ark. *(358,025)*	75
1359	6c **Leif Erikson**, *Oct. 9, 1968,* Seattle, Wash. *(376,565)*	75
1360	6c **Cherokee Strip**, *Oct. 15, 1968,* Ponca, Okla. *(339,330)*	75
1361	6c **John Trumbull**, *Oct. 18, 1968,* New Haven, Conn. *(378,285)*	75
1362	6c **Waterfowl Conservation**, *Oct. 24, 1968,* Cleveland, Ohio *(349,719)*	75
1363	6c **Christmas**, tagged, *Nov. 1, 1968,* Washington, D.C. *(739,055)*	75
1363a	**Untagged**, *Nov. 2, 1968,* Washington, D.C.	6.50
1364	6c **American Indian**, *Nov. 4, 1968,* Washington, D.C. *(415,964)*	75
1969		
1365-1368	6c **Beautification of America**, *Jan. 16, 1969,* Washington, D.C.	@2.00
	1368a	5.00
	First day cancellation was applied to 1,094,184 covers bearing one or more of Nos. 1365-1368.	
1369	6c **American Legion**, *Mar. 15, 1959,* Washington, D.C. *(632,035)*	75
1370	6c **Grandma Moses**, *May 1, 1969,* Washington, D.C. *(367,880)*	75
1371	6c **Apollo 8**, *May 5, 1969,* Houston, Texas *(908,634)*	2.00
1372	6c **W.C. Handy**, *May 17, 1969,* Memphis, Tenn. *(398,216)*	75
1373	6c **California Bicentenary**, *July 16, 1969,* San Diego, Calif. *(530,210)*	75
1374	6c **J.W. Powell**, *Aug. 1, 1969,* Page, Ariz. *(434,433)*	75
1375	6c **Alabama Statehood**, *Aug. 2, 1969,* Huntsville, Ala. *(485,801)*	75
1376-1379	6c **Botanical Congress**, *Aug. 23, 1969,* Seattle, Wash.	@2.00
	1379a	7.00
	First day cancellation was applied to 737,935 covers bearing one or more of Nos. 1376-1379.	
1380	6c **Dartmouth Case**, *Sept. 22, 1969,* Hanover N.H. *(416,327)*	75
1381	6c **Professional Baseball**, *Sept. 24, 1969,* Cincinnati, Ohio *(414,942)*	1.50
1382	6c **Intercollegiate Football**, *Sept. 26, 1969,* New Brunswick, N.J. *(414,860)*	1.50
1383	6c **Dwight D. Eisenhower**, *Oct. 14, 1969,* Abilene, Kans. *(1,009,560)*	75
1384	6c **Christmas**, *Nov. 3, 1969,* Christmas, Fla. *(555,500)*	75
1385	6c **Hope for Crippled**, *Nov. 20, 1969,* Columbus, Ohio *(342,676)*	75
1386	6c **William M. Harnett**, *Dec. 3, 1969,* Boston, Mass. *(408,860)*	75
1970-74		
1387-1390	6c **National History**, *May 6, 1970,* New York, N.Y.	@2.00
	1390a	3.00
	First day cancellation was applied to 834,260 covers bearing one or more of Nos. 1387-1390.	
1391	6c **Maine Statehood**, *July 9, 1970,* Portland, Maine, *(472,165)*	75
1392	6c **Wildlife Conservation**, *July 20, 1970,* Custer, S.D. *(309,418)*	1.00
1393	6c **Eisenhower**, *Aug. 6, 1970,* Washington, D.C.	75
1393D	7c **Franklin**, *Oct. 20, 1972,* Philadelphia, Pa. *(309,276)*	75
1394	8c **Eisenhower** (multi.) *May 10, 1971,* Washington, D.C.	75
1395	8c **Eisenhower** (claret), *May 10, 1971,* Washington, D.C.	75
1396	8c **Postal Service Emblem**, *July 1, 1971,* any city (est. 16,300,000)	75
1397	14c **Fiorello H. LaGuardia**, *Apr. 24, 1972,* New York, N.Y. *(180,114)*	85
1398	16c **Ernie Pyle**, *May 7, 1971,* Washington, D.C. *(444,410)*	75
1399	18c **Elizabeth Blackwell**, *Jan. 23, 1974,* Geneva, N.Y. *(217,938)*	1.25

FIRST DAY COVERS

1400	21c **Amadeo Giannini**, *June 27, 1973*, San Mateo, Calif. *(282,520)*		1.00
1401	6c **Eisenhower coil**, *Aug. 6, 1970*, Washington, D.C.		75
1402	8c **Eisenhower coil**, *May 10, 1971*, Washington, D.C.		75
1405	6c **Edgar Lee Masters**, *Aug. 22, 1970*, Petersburg Ill. *(372,804)*		75
1406	6c **Woman Suffrage**, *Aug. 26, 1970*, Adams, Mass. *(508,142)*		75
1407	6c **South Carolina Anniv.** *Sept. 12, 1970*, Charleston, S.C. *(533,000)*		75
1408	6c **Stone Mt. Memorial**, *Sept. 19, 1970*, Stone Mountain, Ga. *(558,546)*		75
1409	6c **Fort Snelling**, *Oct. 17, 1970*, Fort Snelling, Minn. *(497,611)*		75
1410-1413	6c **Anti-Pollution**, *Oct. 28, 1970*, San Clemente, Calif.		@1.40
	1413a		4.25
	First day cancellation was applied to 1,033, 147 covers bearing one or more of Nos. 1410-1413.		
1414-1418	6c **Christmas**, *Nov. 5, 1970*, Washington, D.C.		@1.40
	1414-1418 on one cover		
	First day cancellation was applied to 2,014,450 covers bearing one or more of Nos. 1414-1418 or 1414a-1418a.		
1419	6c **United Nations**, *Nov. 20, 1970*, New York, N.Y. *(474,070)*		75
1420	6c **Pilgrims' Landing**, *Nov. 21, 1970*, Plymouth, Mass. *(629,850)*		75
1421	6c **Disabled Veterans**, *Nov. 24, 1970*, Cincinnati, Ohio, or Montgomery, Ala.		75
1422	6c **U.S. Servicemen**, *Nov. 24, 1970*, Cincinnati, Ohio, or Montgomery, Ala.		75
	1421-1422 se-tenant on one cover		1.20
	First day cancellation was applied to 476,610 covers at Cincinnati and 336,417 at Montgomery, each cover bearing one or both of Nos. 1421-1422.		

1971

1423	6c **Wool Industry**, *Jan. 19, 1971*, Las Vegas, Nev. *(379,911)*		75
1424	6c **MacArthur**, *Jan. 26, 1971*, Norfolk, Va. *(720,015)*		75
1425	6c **Blood Donor**, *Mar. 12, 1971*, New York, N.Y. *(644,497)*		75
1426	8c **Missouri Sesquicentennial**, *May 8, 1971*, Independence, Mo. *(551,000)*		75
1427-1430	8c **Wildlife Conservation**, *June 12, 1971*, Avery Island, La.		@1.75
	1430a		3.00
	First day cancellation was applied to 679,483 covers bearing one or more of Nos. 1427-1430.		
1431	8c **Antarctic Treaty**, *June 23, 1971*, Washington D.C. *(419,200)*		75
1432	8c **American Revolution Bicentennial**, *July 4, 1971*, Washington, D.C. *(434,930)*		75
1433	8c **John Sloan**, *Aug. 2, 1971*, Lock Haven, Pa. *(482,265)*		75
1434-1435	8c **Space Achievement Decade**, *Aug. 2, 1971*, se-tenant, Kennedy Space Center, Fla. *(1,403,644)*		1.75
	Houston, Texas *(811,560)*		2.00
	Huntsville, Ala. *(524,000)*		2.25
1436	8c **Emily Dickinson**, *Aug. 28, 1971*, Amherst, Mass. *(498,180)*		75
1437	8c **San Juan**, *Sept. 12, 1971*, San Juan, P.R. *(501,668)*		75
1438	8c **Drug Abuse**, *Oct. 4, 1971*, Dallas, Texas *(425,330)*		75
1439	8c **CARE**, *Oct. 27, 1971*, New York, N.Y. *(402,121)*		75
1440-1443	8c **Historic Preservation**, *Oct. 29, 1971*, San Diego, Calif.		@1.50
	1443a		3.00
	First day cancellation was applied to 783,242 covers bearing one or more of Nos. 1440-1443.		
1444-1445	8c **Christmas**, *Nov. 10, 1971*, Washington, D.C.		@75
	1444-1445 on one cover		1.20
	First day cancellation was applied to 348,038 covers with No. 1444 (Nativity) and 580,062 with No. 1445 (partridge).		

1972

1446	8c **Sidney Lanier**, *Feb. 3, 1972*, Macon Ga. *394,800)*		75
1447	8c **Peace Corps**, *Feb. 11, 1972*, Washington, D.C. *(453,660)*		75
1448-1451	2c **National Parks Centennial**, *Apr. 5, 1972*, Hatteras, N.C., block of 4 *(505,697)*		1.25
1452	6c **National Parks**, *June 26, 1972*, Vienna, Va. *(403,396)*		75
1453	8c **National Parks**, *Mar. 1, 1972* Yellowstone National Park, Wyo.		75
	Washington, D.C. *(847,500)*		75
1454	15c **National Parks**, *July 28, 1972*, Mt. McKinley National Park, Alaska *(491,456)*		75
1455	8c **Family Planning**, *Mar. 18, 1972*, New York, N.Y. *(691,385)*		75
1456-1459	8c **Colonial Craftsmen** (Rev. Bicentennial), *July 4, 1972*, Williamsburg, Va.		@1.00
	1459a		2.50
1460	6c **Olympics**, *Aug. 17, 1972*, Washington, D.C.		75
1461	8c **Winter Olympics**, *Aug. 17, 1972*, Washington, D.C.		85
1462	15c **Olympics**, *Aug. 17, 1972*, Washington, D.C.		1.00
	1460-1462 and C85 on one cover		2.75
	First day cancellation was applied to 971,536 covers bearing one or more of Nos. 1460-1462 and C85.		
1463	8c **P.T.A.**, *Sept. 15, 1972*, San Francisco, Cal. *(523,454)*		75
1464-1467	8c **Wildlife**, *Sept. 20, 1972*, Warm Springs Ore.		@2.00
	1467a		3.00
	First day cancellation was applied to 733,778 covers bearing one or more of Nos. 1464-1467.		
1468	8c **Mail Order**, *Sept. 27, 1972*, Chicago, Ill. *(759,666)*		75
1469	8c **Osteopathy**, *Oct. 9, 1972*, Miami, Fla. *(607,160)*		75
1470	8c **Tom Sawyer**, *Oct. 13, 1972*, Hannibal, Mo. *(459,013)*		75
1471-1472	8c **Christmas**, *Nov. 9, 1972*, Washington, D.C.		@75
	1471-1472 on one cover		1.00
	First day cancellation was applied to 713,821 covers bearing one or more of Nos. 1471-1472.		
1473	8c **Pharmacy**, *Nov. 10, 1972*, Cincinnati, Ohio *(804,320)*		75
1474	8c **Stamp Collecting**, *Nov. 17, 1972*, New York, N.Y. *(434,680)*		75

1973

1475	8c **Love**, *Jan. 26, 1973*, Philadelphia, Pa. *(422,492)*		75
1476	8c **Pamphleteer** (Rev. Bicentennial), *Feb. 16, 1973*, Portland, Ore. *(431,784)*		75
1477	8c **Broadside** (Rev. Bicentennial), *April 27, 1973*, Atlantic City, N.J. *(423,437)*		75
1478	8c **Post Rider** (Rev. Bicentennial), *June 22, 1973*, Rochester, N.Y. *(586,850)*		75
1479	8c **Drummer** (Rev. Bicentennial), *Sept. 28, 1973*, New Orleans, La. *(522,427)*		75
1480-1483	8c **Boston Tea Party** (Rev. Bicentennial), *July 4, 1973*, Boston, Mass.		@1.75
	1483a		3.75
	First day cancellation was applied to 897,870 covers bearing one or more of Nos. 1480-1483.		
1484	8c **George Gershwin**, *Feb. 28, 1973*, Beverly Hills, Calif. *(448,814)*		75
1485	8c **Robinson Jeffers**, *Aug. 13, 1973*, Carmel, Calif. *(394,261)*		75
1486	8c **Henry O. Tanner**, *Sept. 10, 1973*, Pittsburgh, Pa. *(424,065)*		75
1487	8c **Willa Cather**, *Sept. 20, 1973*, Red Cloud, Nebr. *(435,784)*		75
1488	8c **Nicolaus Copernicus**, *April 23, 1973*, Washington, D.C. *(734,190)*		75
1489-1498	8c **Postal People**, *April 30, 1973*, any city		@1.10
	1498a		6.00
	First day cancellation was applied at Boston to 1,205,212 covers bearing one or more of Nos. 1489-1498. Cancellations at other cities unrecorded.		
1499	8c **Harry S. Truman**, *May 8, 1973*, Independence, Mo. *(938,636)*		75
1500	6c **Electronics**, *July 10, 1973*, New York, N.Y.		75
1501	8c **Electronics**, *July 10, 1973*, New York, N.Y.		75
1502	15c **Electronics**, *July 10, 1973*, New York, N.Y.		80
	1500-1502 and C86 on one cover		3.50
	First day cancellation was applied to 1,197,700 covers bearing one or more of Nos. 1500-1502 and C86.		
1503	8c **Lyndon B. Johnson**, *Aug. 27, 1973*, Austin Texas *(701,490)*		75

FIRST DAY COVERS 435

1973-74
1504   8c **Angus Cattle**, *Oct. 5, 1973*, St. Joseph, Mo. *(521,427)* ... 75
1505 10c **Chautauqua**, *Aug. 6, 1974*, Chautauqua, N.Y. *(411,105)* ... 75
1506 10c **Wheat**, *Aug. 16, 1974*, Hillsboro, Kans. *(468,280)* ... 75
1507-1508 8c **Christmas**, *Nov. 7, 1973*, Washington, D.C. ... @75
    1507-1508 on one cover ... 1.00
    First day cancellation was applied to 807,468 covers bearing one or both of Nos. 1507-1508.
1509 10c **Crossed Flags**, *Dec. 8, 1973*, San Francisco, Calif. ... 75
    First day cancellation was applied to 341,528 covers bearing one or more of Nos. 1509 and 1519.
1510 10c **Jefferson Memorial**, *Dec. 14, 1973*, Washington, D.C. ... 75
    First day cancellation was applied to 686,300 covers bearing one or more of Nos. 1510, 1510b, 1510c, 1520.
1511 10c **Zip Code**, *Jan. 4, 1974*, Washington, D.C. *(335,220)* ... 75
1518 6.3c **Bell Coil**, *Oct. 1, 1974*, Washington, D.C. *(221,141)* ... 75
1519 10c **Crossed Flags coil**, *Dec. 8, 1973*, San Francisco, Calif. ... 75
1520 10c **Jefferson Memorial coil**, *Dec. 14, 1973*, Washington, D.C. ... 75

1974
1525 10c **Veterans of Foreign Wars**, *Mar. 11, 1974*, Washington, D.C. *(543,598)* ... 75
1526 10c **Robert Frost**, *Mar. 26, 1974*, Derry, N.H. *(500,425)* ... 75
1527 10c **EXPO '74**, *April 18, 1974*, Spokane, Wash. *(565,548)* ... 75
1528 10c **Horse Racing**, *May 4, 1974*, Louisville, Ky. *(623,983)* ... 75
1529 10c **Skylab**, *May 14, 1974*, Houston, Tex. *(972,326)* ... 1.25
1530-1537 10c **UPU Centenary**, *June 6, 1974*, Washington, D.C. ... @1.10
    1537a ... 4.25
    First day cancellation was applied to 1,374,765 covers bearing one or more of Nos. 1530-1537.
1538-1541 10c **Mineral Heritage**, *June 13, 1974*, Lincoln, Neb. ... @1.50
    1541a ... 3.00
    First day cancellation was applied to 865,368 covers bearing one or more of Nos. 1538-1541.
1542 10c **Kentucky Settlement**, *June 15, 1974*, Harrodsburg, Ky. *(478,239)* ... 75
1543-1546 10c **Continental Congress** (Rev. Bicentennial), *July 4, 1974*, Philadelphia ... @90
    1546a ... 2.75
    First day cancellation was applied to 2,124,957 covers bearing one or more of Nos. 1543-1546.
1547 10c **Energy Conservation**, *Sept. 23, 1974*, Detroit, Mich. *(587,210)* ... 75
1548 10c **Sleepy Hollow**, *Oct. 10, 1974*, North Tarrytown, N.Y. *(514,836)* ... 75
1549 10c **Retarded Children**, *Oct. 12, 1974*, Arlington Tex. *(412,882)* ... 75
1550-1551 10c **Christmas**, *Oct. 23, 1974*, New York, N.Y. *(634,990)* ... @75
    1550-1551 on one cover ... 1.10
1552 10c **Christmas**, *Nov. 15, 1974*, New York, N.Y. *(477,410)* ... 75

1975
1553 10c **Benjamin West**, *Feb. 10, 1975*, Swarthmore, Pa. *(465,017)* ... 75
1554 10c **Paul L. Dunbar**, *May 1, 1975*, Dayton, Ohio *(397,347)* ... 75
1555 10c **D.W. Griffith**, *May 27, 1975*, Beverly Hills, Calif. *(424,167)* ... 75
1556 10c **Pioneer-Jupiter**, *Feb. 28, 1975*, Mountain View, Calif. *(594,896)* ... 1.25
1557 10c **Mariner 10**, *Apr. 4, 1975*, Pasadena, Calif. *(563,636)* ... 1.25
1558 10c **Collective Bargaining**, *Mar. 13, 1975*, Washington, D.C. *(412,329)* ... 75
1559   8c **Sybil Ludington** (Rev. Bicentennial), *Mar. 25, 1975*, Carmel, N.Y. *(394,550)* ... 75

1560 10c **Salem Poor** (Rev. Bicentennial, *Mar. 25, 1975*, Cambridge, Mass. *(415,565)* ... 75
1561 10c **Haym Salomon** (Rev. Bicentennial), *Mar. 25, 1975*, Chicago, Ill. ... 75
1562 18c **Peter Francisco** (Rev. Bicentennial), *Mar. 25, 1975*, Greensboro, N.C. *(415,000)* ... 75
1563 10c **Lexington-Concord** (Rev. Bicentennial), *Apr. 19, 1975*, Lexington, Mass., or Concord, Mass, *(975,020)* ... 75
1564 10c **Bunker Hill** (Rev. Bicentennial), *June 17, 1975*, Charlestown, Mass. *(557,130)* ... 75
1565-1568 10c **Military Services** (Rev. Bicentennial), *July 4, 1975*, Washington, D.C. ... @90
    1568a ... 2.40
    First day cancellation was applied to 1,134,831 covers bearing one or more of Nos. 1565-1568.
1569-1470 10c **Apollo-Soyuz**, *July 15, 1975*, Kennedy Space Center, Fla. *(1,427,046)* ... @1.00
    1569a ... 3.00
1571 10c **International Women's Year**, *Aug. 26, 1975*, Seneca Falls, N.Y. *(476,769)* ... 75
1572-1575 10c **Postal Service Bicentenary**, *Sept. 3, 1975*, Philadelphia, Pa. ... @75
    1575a ... 2.40
    First day cancellation was applied to 969,000 covers bearing one or more of Nos. 1572-1575.
1576 10c **World Peace through Law**, *Sept. 29, 1975*, Washington, D.C. ... 75
1577-1578 10c **Banking-Commerce**, *Oct. 6, 1975*, New York, N.Y. *(555,580)* ... @75
    1577a ... 1.00
1579-1580 10c **Christmas**, *Oct. 14, 1975*, Washington ... @75
    1579-1580 on one cover ... 1.10
    First day cancellation was applied to 730,079 covers bearing one or more of Nos. 1579-1580.

1975-79   **AMERICANA ISSUE**
1581   1c *Dec. 8, 1977*, St. Louis, Mo. ... 40
1582   2c *Dec. 8, 1977*, St. Louis, Mo. ... 40
1584   3c *Dec. 8, 1977*, St. Louis, Mo. ... 40
1585   4c *1572-1575*, block of 4 on one cover ... 2.40
    Dec. 8, 1977, St. Louis, Mo. ... 40
    First day cancellation was applied to 530,033 covers bearing one or more of Nos. 1581-1582, 1584-1585.
1590   9c *Mar. 11, 1977*, New York, N.Y. ... 1.00
1591   9c *Nov. 24, 1975*, Washington, D.C. *(190,117)* ... 60
1592 10c *Nov. 17, 1977*, New York, N.Y. *(359,050)* ... 60
1594 11c *Nov. 13, 1975*, Philadelphia, Pa. *(217,755)* ... 60
1594 12c *Apr. 8, 1981*, Dallas, TX ... 60
    First day cancellation was applied to 280,930 covers bearing Nos. 1594 or 1816.
1595 13c *Oct. 31, 1975*, Cleveland, Ohio ... 60
1596 13c *Dec. 1, 1975*, Juneau, Alaska *(418,272)* ... 60
1597 15c *June 30, 1978*, Baltimore, Md. ... 65
1598 15c *June 30, 1978*, Baltimore, Md. ... 65
    First day cancellation was applied to 315,359 covers bearing Nos. 1597, 1598, or 1618C.
1599 16c *Mar. 31, 1978*, New York, N.Y. ... 65
1603 24c *Nov. 14, 1975*, Boston, Mass. *(208,973)* ... 75
1604 28c *Aug. 11, 1978*, Tacoma, Wash. *(159,639)* ... 1.20
1605 29c *Apr. 14, 1978*, Atlantic City, N.J. *(193,476)* ... 1.10
1606 30c *Aug. 27, 1979*, Devils Lake, N.D. *(186,882)* ... 1.10
1608 50c *Sept. 11, 1979*, San Juan, P.R. *(159,540)* ... 1.50
1610 $1 *July 2, 1979*, San Francisco, Calif. ... 3.00
1611 $2 *Nov. 16, 1978*, New York, N.Y. *(173,596)* ... 5.00
1612 $5 *Aug. 23, 1989*, Boston, Mass. *(129,192)* ... 10.00

COIL STAMPS
1613   3.1c *Oct. 25, 1979*, Shreveport, La. *(230,403)* ... 40
1614   7.7c *Nov. 20, 1976*, New York, N.Y. *(285,290)* ... 60
1615   7.9c *Apr. 23, 1976*, Miami, Fla. *(193,270)* ... 60
1615C 8.4c *July 13, 1978*, Interlochen, Mich. *(200,392)* ... 60
1616   9c *May 5, 1976*, Milwaukee, Wis. *(128,171)* ... 60
1617 10c *Nov. 4, 1977*, Tampa, Fla. *(184,954)* ... 60
1618 13c **Liberty Bell**, *Nov. 25, 1975*, Allentown, Pa. *(320,387)* ... 65
1618C 15c *June 30, 1978*, Boston, Mass. ... 65
1619 13c *Mar. 31, 1978*, New York, N.Y. ... 60

FIRST DAY COVERS

1975
1622	13c	**13-Star Flag,** *Nov. 15, 1975*, Philadelphia, Pa.	65
1623	13c	*Mar. 11, 1977*, New York, N.Y. *(242,208)*	1.00
1625	13c	**13-Star Flag coil,** *Nov. 15, 1975*, Philadelphia	65
		First day cancellation was applied to 362,959 covers bearing Nos. 1622 or 1625.	

1976
1629-1631	13c	**Spirit of '76,** *Jan. 1, 1976*, Pasadena, CA	@65
		1631a	1.75
		First day cancellation was applied to 1,013,067 covers bearing one or more of Nos. 1629-1631.	
1632	13c	**Interphil '76,** *Jan. 17, 1976*, Philadelphia, Pa. *(519,902)*	65
1633-1682	13c	**State Flags,** *Feb. 23, 1976*, Washington, D.C.	@1.75
		1682a	32.50
1683	13c	**Telephone,** *Mar. 10, 1976*, Boston, Mass. *(662,515)*	65
1684	13c	**Commercial Aviation,** *Mar. 19, 1976*, Chicago Ill. *(631,555)*	65
1685	13c	**Chemistry,** *April 6, 1976*, New York, N.Y.	65
1686	13c	**Bicentennial Souvenir Sheet of 5, Surrender of Cornwallis,** *May 29, 1976*, Philadelphia, Pa.	6.00
1687	18c	**Bicentennial Souvenir Sheet of 5, Declaration of Independence,** *May 29, 1976*, Philadelphia, Pa.	7.50
1688	24c	**Bicentennial Souvenir Sheet of 5, Declaration of Independence,** *May 29, 1976*, Philadelphia, Pa.	8.50
1689	31c	**Bicentennial Souvenir Sheet of 5, Washington at Valley Forge,** *May 29, 1976*, Philadelphia, Pa.	9.50
		First day cancellation was applied to 879,890 covers bearing one of Nos. 1686-1689.	
1690	13c	**Franklin,** *June 1, 1976*, Philadelphia, Pa. *(588,740)*	65
1691-1694	13c	**Declaration of Independence,** *July 4, 1976*, Philadelphia, Pa.	@65
		1694a	2.00
		First day cancellation was applied to 2,093,880 covers bearing one or more of Nos. 1691-1694.	
1695-1698	13c	**Olympic Games,** *July 16, 1976*, Lake Placid, N.Y.	@75
		1698a	2.00
1699	13c	**Clara Maass,** *Aug. 18, 1976*, Belleville, N.J. *(646,506)*	75
1700	13c	**Adolph S. Ochs,** *Sept. 18, 1976*, New York, N.Y. *(582,580)*	75
1701-1703	13c	**Christmas,** *Oct 27, 1976*, Boston, Mass. (No. 1701, 540,050; No. 1702, 181,410; No. 1703, 330,450)	@65
		1701 and 1702 or 1703 on one cover	1.20

1977
1704	13c	**Washington at Princeton,** *Jan. 3, 1977*, Princeton, N.J.	65
1705	13c	**Sound Recording,** *Mar. 23, 1977*, Washington, D.C. *(632,216)*	65
1706-1709	13c	**Pueblo Art,** *Apr. 13, 1977*, Santa Fe, N.M. *(1,194,554)*	@75
		1709a	2.00
1710	13c	**Lindbergh Flight,** *May 20, 1977*, Roosevelt Sta., N.Y. *(3,985,989)*	75
1711	13c	**Colorado Statehood,** *May 21, 1977*, Denver, Colo. *(510,880)*	65
1712-1715	13c	**Butterflies,** *June 6, 1977*, Indianapolis Ind. *(1,218,278)*	@75
		1715a	2.00
1716	13c	**Lafayette's Landing,** *June 13, 1977*, Charleston, S.C. *(514,506)*	65
1717-1720	13c	**Skilled Hands,** *July 4, 1977*, Cincinnati, Ohio *(1,263,568)*	@65
		1720a	1.75
1721	13c	**Peace Bridge,** *Aug. 4, 1977*, Buffalo, N.Y. *(512,995)*	65
1722	13c	**Battle of Oriskany,** *Aug. 6, 1977*, Utica, N.Y. *(605,906)*	65
1723-1724	13c	**Energy Conservation,** *Oct. 20, 1977*, Washington, D.C. *(410,299)*	@65
		1723a	1.00
1725	13c	**Alta California,** *Sept. 9, 1977*, San Jose, Calif. *(709,457)*	65
1726	13c	**Articles of Confederation,** *Sept. 30, 1977*, York, Pa. *(605,455)*	65
1727	13c	**Talking Pictures,** *Oct. 6, 1977*, Hollywood, Calif. *(570,195)*	75
1728	13c	**Surrender at Saratoga,** *Oct. 7, 1977*, Schuylerville, N.Y. *(557,529)*	65
1729	13c	**Christmas (Valley Forge),** *Oct. 21, 1977*, Valley Forge, Pa. *(583,139)*	65
1730	13c	**Christmas (mailbox),** *Oct. 21, 1977*, Ohama, Nebr. *(675,786)*	65

1978
1731	13c	**Carl Sandburg,** *Jan. 6*, Galesburg, Ill. *(493,826)*	65
1732-1733	13c	**Captain Cook,** *Jan. 20*, Honolulu, Hawaii, or Anchorage, Alaska	@75
		1732a	1.50
		First day cancellation was applied to 823,855 covers at Honolulu, and 672,804 at Anchorage, each cover bearing one or both of Nos. 1732-1733.	
1734	13c	**Indian Head Penny,** *Jan. 11*, Kansas City, Mo. *(512,426)*	1.00

1978-80   **REGULAR ISSUE**
1735	(15c)	**"A" Eagle,** *May 22*, Memphis, Tenn.	65
1736	(15c)	**"A" Eagle,** *May 22*, Memphis, Tenn.	65
1737	15c	**Roses,** *July 11*, Shreveport, La. *(445,003)*	65
1738-1742	15c	**Windmills,** *Feb. 7, 1980*, Lubbock, TX *(708,411)*	65
1743	15c	**"A" Eagle coil,** *May 22*, Memphis, Tenn.	65
		First day cancellation was applied to 689,049 covers bearing Nos. 1734, 1736 or 1743.	

1978
1744	13c	**Harriet Tubman,** *Feb. 1*, Washington, D.C. *(493,495)*	1.00
1745-1748	13c	**American Quilts,** *Mar. 8*, Charleston, W. Va.	@75
		1748a	2.00
		First day cancellation was applied to 1,081,827 covers bearing one or more of Nos. 1745-1748.	
1749-1752	13c	**American Dance,** *April 26*, New York, N.Y.	@75
		1752a	1.75
1753	13c	**French Alliance,** *May 4*, York, Pa. *(705,240)*	65
1754	13c	**Papanicolaou,** *May 13*, Washington, D.C. *(535,584)*	65
1755	13c	**Jimmie Rodgers,** *May 24*, Meridian, Miss. *(599,287)*	65
1756	15c	**George M. Cohan,** *July 3*, Providence, R.I. *(740,750)*	65
1757		**CAPEX souv. sheet,** *June 10*, Toronto, Canada *(1,994,067)*	3.00
1758	15c	**Photography,** *June 26*, Las Vegas, Nev. *(684,987)*	65
1759	15c	**Viking Missions,** *July 20*, Hampton, Va. *(805,051)*	1.10
1760-1763	15c	**American Owls,** *Aug. 26*, Fairbanks, Alas. *(1,690,474)*	@75
		1763a	2.00
1764-1767	15c	**American Trees,** *Oct. 9*, Hot Springs National Park, Ark. *(1,139,100)*	@75
		1767a	2.00
1768	15c	**Christmas (Madonna),** *Oct. 18*, Washington, D.C. *(553,064)*	65
1769	15c	**Christmas (Hobby Horse),** *Oct. 18*, Holly, Mich. *(603,008)*	65

1979-80
1770	15c	**Robert Kennedy,** *Jan. 12*, Washington, D.C. *(624,582)*	65
1771	15c	**Martin L. King,** *Jan. 13*, Atlanta, Ga. *(726,149)*	65
1772	15c	**Year of Child,** *Feb. 15*, Philadelphia, Pa. *(716,782)*	65
1773	15c	**John Steinbeck,** *Feb. 27*, Salinas, Calif. *(709,073)*	65
1774	15c	**Albert Einstein,** *Mar. 4*, Princeton, N.J. *(641,423)*	65
1775-1778	15c	**Toleware,** *Apr. 19*, Lancaster, Pa. *(1,581,962)*	@75
		1778a	2.00
1779-1782	15c	**American Architecture,** *June 4*, Kansas City, Mo. *(1,219,258)*	@75
		1782a	2.00
1783-1786	15c	**Endangered Flora,** *June 7*, Milwaukee, Wis.	@75
		1786a	2.00

FIRST DAY COVERS 437

1787	15c **Guide Dogs,** *June 15,* Morristown, N.J. *(588,826)*	65
1788	15c **Special Olympics,** *Aug. 9,* Brockport, N.Y. *(651,344)*	65
1789	15c **John Paul Jones,** *Sept. 23,* Annapolis, Md. *(587,018)*	65
1790	10c **Olympic Javelin,** *Sept. 5,* Olympia, Wash. *(305,122)*	1.00
1791-1794	15c **Olympics 1980,** *Sept. 28,* Los Angeles, Calif. *(1,561,366)*	@75
	1794a	2.00
1795-1798	15c **Winter Olympics,** *Feb. 1, 1980,* Lake Placid, N.Y.	@75
	1798b	2.00
1799	15c **Christmas (Madonna),** *Oct. 18,* Washington, D.C. *(686,990)*	65
1800	15c **Christmas (Santa Claus),** *Oct. 18,* North Pole, Alaska *(511,829)*	65
1801	15c **Will Rogers,** *Nov. 4,* Claremore, Okla. *(1,643,151)*	65
1802	15c **Viet Nam Veterans,** *Nov. 11,* Washington, D.C. *(445,934)*	1.25
1980		
1803	15c **W.C. Fields,** *Jan. 29,* Beverly Hills, CA *(633,303)*	65
1804	15c **Benjamin Banneker,** *Feb. 15,* Annapolis, MD *(647, 126)*	65
1805-1810	15c **Letter Writing,** *Feb. 24,* Washington, DC *(1,083,360)*	@65
	1810a	3.00
1980-81	**DEFINITIVES**	
1811	1c **Quill Pen,** coil, *Mar. 6, 1980,* New York, NY	40
1813	3.5c **Violins,** coil, *June 23, 1980,* Williamsburg, PA FD cancel was applied to 716,988 covers bearing Nos. 183 or U590.	50
1816	12c **Torch,** coil, *Apr. 8, 1981,* Dallas TX	60
1818	(18c) **"B" Eagle,** *Mar. 15, 1981,* San Francisco, CA FD cancel was applied to 511,688 covers bearing Nos. 1818-1820, U592 or UX88.	75
1819	(18c) **"B" Eagle,** bklt. single, *Mar. 15, 1981,* San Francisco, CA	75
1820	(18c) **"B" Eagle,** coil, *Mar. 15, 1981,* San Francisco, CA	75
1980		
1821	15c **Frances Perkins,** *Apr. 10,* Washington, DC *(678,966)*	65
1822	15c **Dolley Madison,** *May 20,* Washington, DC *(331,048)*	65
1823	15c **Emily Bissel,** *May 31,* Wilmington, DE *(649,509)*	65
1824	15c **Helen Keller, Anne Sullivan,** *June 27,* Tuscumbia, AL *(713,061)*	80
1825	15c **Veterans Administration,** *July 21,* Washington, DC *(634,101)*	65
1826	15c **Bernardo de Galvez,** *July 23,* New Orleans, LA *(658,061)*	65
1827-1830	15c **Coral Reefs,** *Aug. 26,* Charlotte Amalie, VI *(1,195,126)*	@85
	1830a	2.00
1831	15c **Organized Labor,** *Sept. 1,* Washington, DC *(759,973)*	65
1832	15c **Edith Wharton,** *Sept. 5,* New Haven, CT *(633,917)*	65
1833	15c **Education,** *Sept. 12,* Washington, DC *(672,592)*	65
1834-1837	15c **Indian Masks,** *Sept. 25,* Spokane, WA *(2,195,136)*	@75
	1837a	2.00
1838-1841	15c **Architecture,** *Oct. 9,* New York, NY *(2,164,721)*	75
	1841a	2.00
1842	15c **Christmas (Madonna),** *Oct. 31,* Washington, DC *(718,614)*	65
1843	15c **Christmas (Toys),** *Oct. 31,* Christmas, MI *(755,108)*	65
1980-85	**GREAT AMERICANS ISSUE**	
1844	1c **Dorothea Dix,** *Sept. 23, 1983 (164,140)*	60
1845	2c **Igor Stravinsky,** *Nov. 18, 1982,* New York, NY *(504,719)*	60
1846	3c **Henry Clay,** *July 13, 1983,* Washington, DC *(204,320)*	60
1847	4c **Carl Schurz,** *June 3, 1983,* Watertown, WI *(165,010)*	60
1848	5c **Pearl Buck,** *June 23, 1983,* Hillsboro, WV *(231,852)*	60

1849	6c **Walter Lippman,** *Sept. 19, 1985,* Minneapolis, MN *(371,990)*	60
1850	7c **Abraham Baldwin,** *Jan. 25, 1985,* Athens, GA *(402,285)*	60
1851	8c **Henry Knox,** *July 25, 1985,* Thomaston, ME *(315,937)*	60
1852	9c **Sylvanus Thayer,** *June 7, 1985,* Braintree, MA *(345,649)*	60
1853	10c **Richard Russell,** *May 31, 1984,* Winder, GA *(183,581)*	65
1854	11c **Alden Partridge,** *Feb. 12, 1985,* Northfield, VT *(442,311)*	65
1855	13c **Crazy Horse,** *Jan. 15, 1982,* Crazy Horse, SD	65
1856	14c **Sinclair Lewis,** *Mar. 21, 1985,* Sauk Centre, MN *(308,612)*	65
1857	17c **Rachel Carson,** *May 28, 1981,* Springdale, PA *(273,686)*	75
1858	18c **George Mason,** *May 7, 1981,* Gunston Hall, VA *(461,937)*	75
1859	19c **Sequoyah,** *Dec. 27, 1980,* Tahlequah, OK *(241,325)*	80
1860	20c **Ralph Bunche,** *Jan. 12, 1982,* New York, NY	75
1861	20c **Thomas Gallaudet,** *June 10, 1983,* West Hartford, CT *(261,336)*	75
1862	20c **Harry S. Truman,** *Jan. 26, 1984,* Washington, DC *(267,631)*	75
1863	22c **John J. Audubon,** *Apr. 23, 1985,* New York, NY *(516,249)*	80
1864	30c **Frank Laubach,** *Sept. 2, 1984,* Benton, PA *(118,974)*	85
1865	35c **Charles Drew,** *June 3, 1981,* Washington, DC *(383,882)*	1.00
1866	37c **Robert Millikan,** *Jan. 26, 1982,* Pasadena, CA	1.00
1867	39c **Grenville Clark,** *Mar. 20, 1985,* Hanover, NH *(297,797)*	1.00
1868	40c **Lillian Gilbreth,** *Feb. 24, 1984,* Montclair, NJ *(110,588)*	1.00
1869	50c **Chester W. Nimitz,** *Feb. 22, 1985,* Fredericksburg, TX *(376,166)*	1.25
	DEFINITIVES	
1880-1889	18c **Animals,** *May 14,* Boise, ID	75
1890	18c **Flag-Anthem (grain),** *Apr. 24,* Portland, ME	75
1891	18c **Flag-Anthem (sea),** *Apr. 24,* Portland, ME	75
1892	6c **Star Circle,** *Apr. 24,* Portland, ME	75
1893	18c **Flag-Anthem (mountain),** *Apr. 24,* Portland, ME FDC cancel was applied to 691,526 covers bearing Nos. 1890-1893 & 1893a.	75
1894	20c **Flag-Court,** *Dec. 17,* Washington, DC	75
1895	20c **Flag-Court,** coil, *Dec. 17,* Washington, DC	75
1896	20c **Flag-Court,** p. 11x10½, *Dec. 17,* Washington, DC *(185,543)*	75
1981-84	**TRANSPORTATION ISSUE**	
1897	1c **Omnibus,** *Aug. 19, 1983,* Arlington, VA *(109,463)*	60
1897A	2c **Locomotive,** *May 20, 1982,* Chicago, IL *(290,020)*	60
1898	3c **Handcar,** *Mar. 25, 1983,* Rochester, NY *(77,900)*	60
1898A	4c **Stagecoach,** *Aug. 19, 1982,* Milwaukee, WI *(152,940)*	60
1899	5c **Motorcycle,** *Oct. 10, 1983,* San Francisco, CA *(188,240)*	60
1900	5.2c **Sleigh,** *Mar. 21, 1983,* Memphis, TN *(141,979)*	60
1901	5.9c **Bicycle,** *Feb. 17, 1982,* Wheeling, WV *(814,419)*	60
1902	7.4c **Baby Buggy,** *Apr. 7, 1984,* San Diego, CA	65
1903	9.3c **Mail Wagon,** *Dec. 15, 1981,* Shreveport, LA	65
1904	10.9c **Hansom,** *May 26, 1982,* Chattanooga, TN	65
1905	11c **Railroad Caboose,** *Feb. 3, 1984,* Chicago, IL *(172,753)*	65
1906	17c **Electric Auto,** *June 25, 1982,* Greenfield Village, MI *(239,458)*	75
1907	18c **Surrey,** *May 18, 1981,* Notch, MO *(207,801)*	75
1908	20c **Fire Pumper,** *Dec. 10, 1981,* Alexandria, VA *(304,668)*	65
1909	$9.53 **Eagle,** *Aug. 12, 1983,* Kennedy Space Center, FL *(77,858)*	25.00
1981		
1910	18c **Red Cross,** *May 1,* Washington, DC *(874,972)*	75
1911	18c **Savings & Loan,** *May 8,* Chicago, IL *(740,910)*	75
1912-1919	18c **Space Achievement,** *May 21,* Kennedy Space Center, FL *(7,027,549)*	@75
	1919a	5.00
1920	18c **Professional Management,** *June 18,* Philadelphia, PA *(713,096)*	75
1921-1924	18c **Wildlife Habitats,** *June 26,* Reno, NV *(2,327,609)*	@75
	1924a	2.50

FIRST DAY COVERS

1925	18c **Year of Disabled,** *June 29,* Milford, MI *(714,244)*		75
1926	18c **Edna St. V. Millay,** *July 10,* Austerlitz, NY *(725,978)*		75
1927	18c **Alcoholism,** *Aug. 19,* Washington, DC *(874,972)*		75
1928-1931	18c **Architecture,** *Aug. 28,* New York, NY *(1,998,208)*		@75
	1931a		2.00
1932	18c **Babe Zaharias,** *Sept. 22,* Pinehurst, NC		75
1933	18c **Bobby Jones,** *Sept. 22,* Pinehurst, NC		75
	FD cancel was applied to 1,231,543 covers bearing No. 1932 or 1933.		
1934	18c **Frederic Remington,** *Oct. 9,* Oklahoma City, OK *(1,367,099)*		75
1935	18c **James Hoban,** *Oct. 13,* Washington, DC		75
1936	20c **James Hoban,** *Oct. 13,* Washington, DC		75
	FD cancel was applied to 635,012 covers bearing No. 1935 or 1936.		
1937-1938	18c **Yorktown—Va. Capes Battle,** *Oct. 16,* Yorktown, VA *(1,098,278)*		@75
	1938a		1.00
1939	(20c) **Christmas (Madonna),** *Oct. 28,* Chicago, IL *(481,395)*		75
1940	(20c) **Christmas (Teddy Bear),** *Oct. 28,* Christmas Valley, OR *(517,898)*		75
1941	20c **John Hanson,** *Nov. 5,* Frederick, MD *(605,616)*		75
1942-1945	20c **Desert Plants,** *Dec. 11,* Tucson, AZ		@75
	1945a *(1,770,187)*		2.50
	REGULAR ISSUE		
1946	(20c) "C" **Eagle,** *Oct. 11,* Memphis, TN		75
1947	(20c) "C" **Eagle,** coil, *Oct. 11,* Memphis, TN		75
1948	(20c) "C" **Eagle,** bklt. single, *Oct. 11,* Memphis, TN		75
1982			
1949	20c **Bighorn,** *Jan. 8,* Bighorn, MT		75
1950	20c **F.D. Roosevelt,** *Jan. 30,* Hyde Park, NY		75
1951	20c **Love,** *Feb. 1,* Boston, MA *(325,727)*		75
1952	20c **Washington,** *Feb. 22,* Mt. Vernon, VA		75
1953-2002	20c **Birds-Flowers,** *Apr. 14,* Washington, DC, or State Capital		@1.00
	2002b		75
2003	20c **U.S.-Netherlands,** *Apr. 20,* Washington, DC		75
2004	20c **Library of Congress,** *Apr. 21,* Washington, DC		75
2005	20c **Consumer Education,** *Apr. 27,* Washington, DC		75
2006-2009	20c **Knoxville Fair,** *Apr. 29,* Knoxville, TN		@75
	2009a		2.50
2010	20c **Horatio Alger,** *Apr. 30,* Willow Grove, PA		75
2011	20c **Aging,** *May 21,* Sun City, AZ *(510,677)*		75
2012	20c **Barrymotes,** *June 8,* New York, NY		75
2013	20c **Dr. Mary Walker,** *June 10,* Oswego, NY		75
2014	20c **Peace Garden,** *June 30,* Dunseith, ND		75
2015	20c **America's Libraries,** *July 13,* Philadelphia, PA		75
2016	20c **Jackie Robinson,** *Aug. 2,* Cooperstown, NY		75
2017	20c **Touro Synagogue,** *Aug. 22,* Newport, RI *(517,264)*		85
2018	20c **Wolf Trap Farm Parks,** *Sept. 1,* Vienna, VA *(704,361)*		75
2019-2022	20c **Architecture,** *Sept. 30,* Washington, DC *(1,552,567)*		75
	2022b		2.50
2023	20c **St. Francis,** *Oct. 7,* San Francisco, CA *(530,275)*		75
2024	20c **Ponce de Leon,** *Oct. 2,* San Juan, PR *(530,275)*		75
2025	13c **Puppy, Kitten,** *Nov. 3,* Danvers, MA *(239,219)*		75
2026	20c **Christmas (Madonna),** *Oct. 28,* Washington, DC *(462,982)*		75
2027-2030	20c **Christmas (Children),** *Oct. 28,* Snow, OK *(676,950)*		@75
	2030a		2.50
1983			
2031	20c **Science & Industry,** *Jan. 19,* Chicago, IL *(526,693)*		75
2032-2035	20c **Balloon,** *Mar. 31,* Albuquerque, NM or Wash., DC *(989,305)*		75
	2035a		2.50
2036	20c **U.S.-Sweden,** *Mar. 25,* Philadelphia, PA *(526,373)*		75
2037	20c **Civilian Conservation Corps.,** *Apr. 5,* Luray, VA *(483,824)*		75
2038	20c **Joseph Priestley,** *Jan. 13,* Northumberland, PA *(673,266)*		75
2039	20c **Voluntarism,** *Apr. 20,* Washington, DC *(574,708)*		75
2040	20c **U.S.-Germany,** *Apr. 29,* Germantown, PA *(611,109)*		75
2041	20c **Brooklyn Bridge,** *Mar. 5,* Brooklyn, NY *(815,450)*		75
2042	20c **TVA,** *Mar. 18,* Knoxville, TN *(837,588)*		75
2043	20c **Physical Fitness,** *May 14,* Houston, TX *(501,336)*		75
2044	20c **Scott Joplin,** *June 9,* Sedalia, MO *(472,667)*		75
2045	20c **Medal of Honor,** *June 7,* Washington, DC *(1,623,995)*		75
2046	20c **Babe Ruth,** *July 6,* Chicago, IL *(1,277,907)*		75
2047	20c **Nathaniel Hawthorne,** *July 8,* Salem, MA *(442,793)*		75
2048-2051	13c **Summer Olympics,** *July 28,* South Bend, IN *(909,332)*		@75
	2051a		2.50
2052	20c **Treaty of Paris,** *Sept. 2,* Washington, DC *(651,208)*		75
2053	20c **Civil Service,** *Sept. 9,* Washington, DC *(422,206)*		75
2054	20c **Metropolitan Opera,** *Sept. 14,* New York, NY *(807,609)*		75
2055-2058	20c **American Inventors,** *Sept. 21,* Arlington, VA *(1,006,516)*		@75
	2058a		2.50
2059-2062	20c **Streetcars,** *Oct. 8,* Kennebunkport, ME *(1,116,909)*		75
	2062a		2.50
2063	20c **Christmas (Madonna),** *Oct. 28,* Washington, DC *(361,874)*		75
2064	20c **Christmas (Santa),** *Oct. 28,* Santa Claus, IN *(388,749)*		75
2065	20c **Martin Luther,** *Nov. 11,* Washington, DC *(463,777)*		75
1984			
2066	20c **Alaska Statehood,** *Jan. 3,* Fairbanks, AK *(816,591)*		75
2067-2070	20c **Winter Olympics,** *Jan. 6,* Lake Placid, NY *(1,245,807)*		@75
	2070a		2.50
2071	20c **Federal Deposit Ins. Corp.,** *Jan. 12,* Washington, DC *(536,329)*		75
2072	20c **Love,** *Jan. 31,* Washington, DC *(327,727)*		75
2073	20c **Carter Woodson,** *Feb. 1,* Washington, DC *(387,583)*		75
2074	20c **Soil & Water Conservation,** *Feb. 6,* Denver, CO *(426,101)*		75
2075	20c **Credit Union Act,** *Feb. 10,* Salem, MA *(523,583)*		75
2076-2079	20c **Orchids,** *Mar. 5,* Miami FL		@75
	2079a *(1,063,237)*		2.50
2080	20c **Hawaii Statehood,** *Mar. 12,* Honolulu, HI *(546,930)*		75
2081	20c **National Archives,** *Apr. 16,* Washington, DC *(414,415)*		75
2082-2085	20c **Olympics 1984,** *May 4,* Los Angeles, CA		@75
	2085a *(1,172,313)*		2.50
2086	20c **Louisiana Exposition,** *May 11,* New Orleans, LA *(467,408)*		75
2087	20c **Health Research,** *May 17,* New York, NY *(845,007)*		75
2088	20c **Douglas Fairbanks,** *May 23,* Denver CO *(547,134)*		75
2089	20c **Jim Thorpe,** *May 24,* Shawnee, OK *(568,544)*		75
2090	20c **John McCormack,** *June 6,* Boston, MA *(464,117)*		75
2091	20c **St. Lawrence Seaway,** *June 26,* Massena, NY *(550,173)*		75
2092	20c **Waterfowl Preservation Act,** *July 2,* Des Moines, IA *(549,388)*		75
2093	20c **Roanoke Voyages,** *July 13,* Manteo, NC *(443,725)*		75
2094	20c **Herman Melville,** *Aug. 1,* New Bedford, MA *(378,293)*		75
2095	20c **Horace A. Moses,** *Aug. 6,* Bloomington, IN *(439,386)*		75
2096	20c **Smokey the Bear,** *Aug. 13,* Capitan, NM *(506,833)*		75
2097	20c **Roberto Clemente,** *Aug. 17,* Carolina, PR *(547,387)*		75
2098-2101	20c **Dogs,** *Sept. 7,* New York, NY *(1,157,373)*		@75
	2101a		2.50
2102	20c **Crime Prevention,** *Sept. 26,* Washington, DC *(427,564)*		75
2103	20c **Hispanic Americans,** *Oct. 31,* Washington, DC *(416,796)*		75
2104	20c **Family Unity,** *Oct. 1,* Shaker Heights, OH *(400,659)*		75
2105	20c **Eleanor Roosevelt,** *Oct. 11,* Hyde Park, NY *(479,919)*		75
2106	20c **Nation of Readers,** *Oct. 16,* Washington, DC *(437,559)*		75
2107	20c **Christmas (Madonna),** *Oct. 30,* Washington, DC *(386,385)*		75
2108	20c **Christmas (Santa),** *Oct. 30,* Jamaica, NY *(430,843)*		75
2109	20c **Vietnam Veterans' Memorial,** *Nov. 10,* Washington, DC *(434,489)*		75
1985			
2110	22c **Jerome Kern,** *Jan. 23,* New York, NY *(503,855)*		80
	REGULAR ISSUE		
2111	(22c) "D" **Eagle,** *Feb. 1,* Los Angeles, CA		80
2112	(22c) "D" **Eagle,** coil, *Feb. 1,* Los Angeles, CA		80
2113	(22c) "D" **Eagle,** bklt. single, *Feb. 1,* Los Angeles, CA		80

First Day cancel was applied to 513,027 covers bearing Nos. 2111-2113.

FIRST DAY COVERS 439

DEFINITIVES
2114	22c **Flag Over Capitol Dome**, *Mar. 29*, Washington, DC	80
2115	22c **Flag Over Capitol Dome, coil**, *Mar. 29*, Washington, DC	80

First Day Cancel was applied to 268,161 covers bearing Nos. 2114-2115.

2116	22c **Flag Over Capitol Dome, bklt. single**, *Mar. 29*, Waubeka, WI *(234,318)*	80
2117-2121	22c **Seashells**, *Apr. 4*, Boston, MA *(426,290)*	@80
2122	$10.75 **Eagle and Half Moon**, *Apr. 29*, San Francisco, CA *(93,154)*	30.00

1985   TRANSPORTATION ISSUE
2123	3.4c **School Bus**, *June 8*, Arlington, VA *(131,480)*	60
2125	4.9c **Buckboard**, *June 21*, Reno, NV	60
2127	6c **Tricycle**, *May 6*, Childs, MD *(151,494)*	60
2128	8.3c **Ambulance**, *June 21*, Reno, NV	60
2129	10.1c **Oil Wagon**, *Apr. 18*, Oil Center, NM	65
2130	11c **Stutz Super Bearcat**, *June 11*, Baton Rouge, LA *(135,037)*	65
2131	12c **Stanley Steamer**, *Apr. 2*, Kingfield, ME *(173,998)*	65
2132	12.5c **Pushcart**, *Apr. 18*, Oil Center, NM	65
2134	14c **Ice Boat**, *Mar. 23*, Rochester, NY *(324,710)*	65
2135	17c **Dog Sled**, *Aug. 20*, Anchorage, AK	75

1985
2137	22c **Mary McLeod Bethune**, *Mar. 5*, Washington, DC *(413,244)*	80
2138-2141	22c **Duck Decoys**, *Mar. 22*, Shelburne, VT *(932,249)*	@80
	2141a	2.75
2142	22c **Winter Special Olympics**, *Mar. 25*, Park City, UT *(253,074)*	80
2143	22c **Love**, *Apr. 17*, Hollywood, CA *(283,072)*	80
2144	22c **Rural Electrification Administration**, *May 11*, Madison, SD *(472,895)*	80
2145	22c **Ameripex '85**, *May 25*, Rosemont, IL *(457,038)*	80
2146	22c **Abigail Adams**, *June 14*, Quincy, MA *(491,026)*	80
2147	22c **Frederic Auguste Bartholdi**, *July 18*, New York, NY *(594,896)*	80
2149	18c **George Washington, Washington Monument**, *Nov. 6*, Washington, DC *(376,238)*	80
2150	21.1c **Sealed Envelopes**, *Oct. 22*, Washington, DC *(119,941)*	80
2152	22c **Korean War Veterans**, *July 26*, Washington, DC *(391,754)*	80
2153	22c **Social Security Act**, *Aug. 14*, Baltimore, MD *(265,143)*	80
2154	22c **World War I Veterans**, *Aug. 26*, Milwaukee, WI *(234,435)*	80
2155-2158	22c **Horses**, *Sept. 25*, Lexington, KY *(1,135,368)*	@80
	2158a	2.75
2159	22c **Public Education in America**, *Oct. 1*, Boston, MA *(356,030)*	80
2160-2163	22c **International Youth Year**, *Oct. 7*, Chicago, IL *(1,202,541)*	@80
	2163a	2.75
2164	22c **Help End Hunger**, *Oct. 15*, Washington, DC *(299,485)*	80
2165	22c **Christmas (Madonna & Child)**, *Oct. 30*, Detroit, MI	80
2166	22c **Christmas (Poinsettia)**, *Oct. 30*, Nazareth, MI *(524,929)*	80

1986
2167	22c **Arkansas Statehood**, *Jan. 3*, Little Rock, AR *(364,729)*	80

GREAT AMERICANS ISSUE
2168	1c **Margaret Mitchell**, *Sept. 17*, New York, NY	80
2170	3c **Dr. Paul Dudley White**, *Sept. 15*, Washington, DC	80
2171	4c **Father Flanagan**, *July 14*, Boys Town, NE	80
2172	5c **Hugo Black**, *Feb. 27*, Washington, DC *(303,012)*	80
2179	17c **Belva Ann Lockwood**, *June 18*, Middleport, NY	80
2183	25c **Jack London**, *Jan. 11*, Glen Ellen, CA *(358,686)*	85
2191	56c **John Harvard**, *Sept. 3*, Boston, MA	1.25
2194	$1 **Dr. Barnard Revel**, *Sept. 23*, New York, NY	2.00
2195	$2 **William Jennings Bryan**, *Mar. 19*, Salem, IL *(123,430)*	3.00
2198-2201	22c **Stamp Collecting**, *Jan. 23*, State College, PA	@80
2202	22c **Love**, *Jan. 30*, New York, NY	80
2203	22c **Sojourner Truth**, *Feb. 4*, New Paltz, NY *(342,985)*	80
2204	22c **Republic of Texas**, *Mar. 2*, San Antonio, TX	80
2205-2209	22c **Fish**, *Mar. 21*, Seattle, WA	@80
2210	22c **Public Hospitals**, *Apr. 11*, New York, NY	80
2211	22c **Duke Ellington**, *Apr. 29*, New York, NY	80

2216-2219	22c **Presidential Souvenir Sheets of 9**, *May 22*, Chicago, IL	@3.00
	2216a-2219i	@80
2220-2223	22c **Polar Explorers**, *May 28*, North Pole, AK	@80
	2223a	2.75
2224	22c **Statue of Liberty**, *July 4*, New York, NY	80
2235-2238	22c **Navajo Art**, Window Rock, AZ	@80
	2238a	2.75
2239	22c **T.S. Eliot**, *Sept. 26*, St. Louis, MO	80
2240-2243	22c **Woodcarved Figurines**, *Oct. 1*, Washington, DC	@80
	2243a	2.75
2244	22c **Christmas (Madonna)**, *Oct. 24*, Washington, DC	80
2245	22c **Christmas (Winter Village)**, *Oct. 24*, Snow Hill, MD	80

FIRST DAY COVERS

See first day cover pages for postage issues for introductory notes.

1918
C1 6c orange, *Dec. 10*	16,000.00
C2 16c green, *July 11*	16,000.00
C3 24c carmine rose & blue, *May 13*	19,000.00

1923
C4 8c dark green, *Aug. 15*	350.00
C5 16c dark blue, *Aug. 17*	750.00
C6 24c carmine, *Aug. 21*	900.00

1926-27
C7 10c dark blue, *Feb. 13, 1926,*	
Chicago, Ill.	65.00
Detroit, Mich.	75.00
Cleveland, Ohio	75.00
Dearborn, Mich.	135.00
C8 15c olive brown, *Sept. 18, 1926,*	135.00
	75.00
C9 20c yellow green, *Jan. 25, 1927,*	115.00
New York, N.Y.	125.00
C10 10c dark blue, *June 18, 1927,*	25.00
St. Louis, Mo.	25.00
Little Falls, Minn.	35.00
Detroit, Mich.	35.00

1928-30
C11 5c carmine & blue, *July 25, 1928,* pair	50.00
single stamp	150.00
C12 5c violet, *Feb. 10, 1930*	20.00
C13 65c green, *April 19, 1930*	1,850.00
C14 $1.30 brown, *April 19, 1930*	1,400.00
C15 $2.60 blue, *April 19, 1930*	2,000.00
C13-C15 on one cover	13,500.00

1931-33
C16 5c violet, *Aug. 19, 1931*	200.00
C17 8c olive bister, *Sept. 26, 1932*	20.00
C18 50c green, *Oct. 2, 1933,* New York, N.Y. (3,500)	275.00
Akron, Ohio, *Oct. 4*	425.00
Washington, D.C., *Oct. 5*	375.00
Miami, Fla., *Oct. 6*	250.00
Chicago, Ill., *Oct. 7*	375.00

1934-37
C19 6c dull orange, *June 30, 1934*	
Baltimore, Md.	200.00
New York, N.Y.	650.00
C20 25c blue, *Nov. 22, 1935 (10,910)*	40.00
San Francisco, Cal. (15,000)	35.00
C21 20c green, *Feb. 15, 1937*	40.00
C22 50c carmine, *Feb. 15, 1937*	40.00
C21-C22 on one cover	75.00
First day covers of Nos. C21 and C22 total 40,000.	

1938-39
C23 6c dark blue & carmine, *May 14, 1938,*	
Dayton, Ohio (116,443)	15.00
St. Petersburg, Fla. (95,121)	15.00
Washington, D.C., *May 15*	3.50
C24 30c dull blue, *May 16, 1939*	
New York, N.Y. (68,634)	45.00

1941-44
C25 6c carmine, *June 25, 1941 (99,986)*	2.25
C26 8c olive green, *March 21, 1944 (147,484)*	3.75
C27 10c violet, *Aug. 15, 1941,*	
Atlantic City, N.J. (87,712)	7.00
C28 15c brown carmine, *Aug. 19, 1941,*	
Baltimore, Md. (74,000)	10.00
C29 20c bright green, *Aug. 27, 1941,*	
Philadelphia, Pa. (66,225)	10.00
C30 30c blue, *Sept. 25, 1941,*	
Kansas City, Mo. (57,175)	16.00
C31 50c orange, *Oct. 29, 1941,*	
St. Louis, Mo. (54,580)	40.00

1946-48
C32 5c carmine, *Sept. 25, 1946*	2.00
First day covers of both Nos. C32 and UC14 (5c stamped envelope) total 396,669.	
C33 5c carmine, *March 26, 1947 (342,634)*	2.00
C34 10c black, *Aug. 30, 1947 (265,773)*	2.00
C35 15c bright blue green, *Aug. 20, 1947,*	
New York, N.Y. (230,338)	2.75
C36 25c blue, *July 30, 1947,*	
San Francisco, Cal. (201,762)	3.50
C37 5c carmine, coil, *Jan. 15, 1948 (192,084)*	2.00
C38 5c New York City, *July 31, 1948*	
New York, N.Y. (371,265)	1.75

1949
C39 6c carmine, *Jan. 18 (266,790)*	1.50
C40 6c Alexandria Bicentennial, *May 11,*	
Alexandria, Va. (386,717)	1.25
C41 6c carmine coil, *Aug. 25 (240,386)*	1.25
C42 10c U.P.U., *Nov. 18,*	
New Orleans, La. (270,000)	1.75
C43 15c U.P.U., *Oct. 7,*	
Chicago, Ill. (246,833)	2.25
C44 25c U.P.U., *Nov. 30,*	
Seattle, Wash. (220,215)	2.75
C45 6c Wright Brothers, *Dec. 17,*	
Kitty Hawk, N.C. (378,585)	3.75

1952-59
C46 80c Hawaii, *March 26, 1952,*	
Honolulu, Hawaii, (89,864)	17.50
C47 6c Powered Flight, *May 29, 1953,*	
Dayton, Ohio (359,050)	1.50
C48 4c bright blue, *Sept. 3, 1954,*	
Philadelphia, Pa. (295,720)	75
C49 6c Air Force, *Aug. 1, 1957 (356,683)*	1.75
C50 5c red, *July 31, 1958,*	
Colorado Springs, Colo. (207,954)	80
C51 7c blue, *July 31, 1958,*	
Philadelphia, Pa. (204,401)	75
C52 7c blue coil, *July 31, 1958,*	
Miami, Fla. (181,603)	90
C53 7c Alaska Statehood, *Jan. 3, 1959,*	
Juneau, Alaska (489,752)	65
C54 7c Balloon Jupiter, *Aug. 17, 1959,*	
Lafayette, Ind. (383,556)	1.10
C55 7c Hawaii Statehood, *Aug. 21, 1959,*	
Honolulu, Hawaii (533,464)	1.00
C56 10c Pan American Games, *Aug. 27, 1959,*	
Chicago, Ill. (302,306)	90

1959-66
C57 10c Liberty Bell, *June 10, 1960,*	
Miami, Fla. (246,509)	1.50
C58 15c Statue of Liberty, *Nov. 20, 1959,*	
New York, N.Y. (259,412)	1.10
C59 25c Abraham Lincoln, *April 22, 1960,*	
San Francisco, Cal. (211,235)	1.50
C59a 25c Tagged, *Dec. 29, 1966 (about 3,000)*	12.50
C60 7c carmine, *Aug. 12, 1960,*	
Arlington, Va. (247,190)	70
C61 7c carmine coil, *Oct. 22, 1960,*	
Atlantic City, N.J. (197,995)	1.00

1961-67
C62 13c Liberty Bell, *June 28, 1961,*	
New York, N.Y. (316,166)	80
C62a 13c Tagged, *Feb. 15, 1967*	10.00
C63 15c Redrawn Statue of Liberty, *Jan. 13, 1961*	
Buffalo, N.Y. (192,976)	1.00
C63a 15c Tagged, *Jan. 11, 1967*	12.00
C64 8c carmine, *Dec. 5, 1962 (288,355)*	60
C64a 8c Tagged, *Aug. 1, 1963,*	
Dayton, Ohio (262,720)	50
C65 8c carmine coil, *Dec. 5, 1962 (220,173)*	80
C65a 8c Tagged, *Jan. 14, 1965,*	
New Orleans, La.	—

1963-69

C66 **15c Montgomery Blair,** *May 3, 1963,*
  Silver Spring, Md. *(260,031)* — 1.35
C67 **6c Bald Eagle,** *July 12, 1963,*
  Boston, Mass. *(268,265)* — 50
C67a **6c Tagged,** *Feb. 15, 1967* — 12.50
C68 **8c Amelia Earhart,** *July 24, 1963,*
  Atchison, Kan. *(437,996)* — 2.50
C69 **8c Robert H. Goddard,** *Oct. 5, 1964,*
  Roswell, N.M. *(421,020)* — 2.75
C70 **8c Alaska Purchase,** *March 30, 1967,*
  Sitka, Alaska *(554,784)* — 70
C71 **20c Audubon,** *April 26, 1967,*
  Audubon (Station of N.Y.C.), N.Y. *(227,930)* — 2.00
C72 **10c carmine,** *Jan. 5, 1968,*
  San Francisco, Cal. — 60
C73 **10c carmine coil,** *Jan. 5, 1968,*
  San Francisco, Cal. — 60
C74 **10c Air Mail Service,** *May 15, 1968 (521,084)* — 1.50
C75 **20c USA and Jet,** *Nov. 22, 1968,*
  New York, N.Y. *(276,244)* — 1.10
C76 **10c Moon Landing,** *Sept. 9, 1969 (8,743,070)* — 3.50

1971-73

C77 **9c red,** *May 15, 1971,*
  Kitty Hawk, N.C. — 50
First day cancellation was applied to 379,442 covers of Nos. C77 and UXC10.
C78 **11c carmine,** *May 7, 1971,*
  Spokane, Wash. — 50
C79 **13c carmine,** *Nov. 16, 1973,*
  New York, N.Y. *(282,550)* — 55
First day cancellation was applied to 464,750 covers of Nos. C78, C78a and C82, and to 204,756 covers of Nos. C79a and C83.
C80 **17c Statue of Liberty,** *July 13, 1971,*
  Lakehurst, N.J. *(172,269)* — 60
C81 **21c USA and Jet,** *May 21, 1971 (293,140)* — 75
C82 **11c carmine coil,** *May 7, 1971,*
  Spokane, Wash. — 50
C83 **13c carmine coil,** *Dec. 27, 1973,*
  Chicago, Ill. — 50
C84 **11c National Parks Centennial,** *May 3, 1972,*
  Honaunau, Hawaii *(364,816)* — 65
C85 **11c Olympics,** *Aug. 17, 1972* — 50
First day cancellation was applied to 971,536 covers of Nos. 1460-1462 and C85.
C86 **11c Electronics,** *July 10, 1973,*
  New York, N.Y. — 50
First day cancellation was applied to 1,197,700 covers of Nos. 1500-1502 and C86.

1974-79

C87 **18c Statue of Liberty,** *Jan. 11, 1974,*
  Hempstead, N.Y. *(216,902)* — 65
C88 **26c Mt. Rushmore,** *Jan. 2, 1974,*
  Rapid City, S.D. *(210,470)* — 85
C89 **25c Plane and Globes,** *Jan. 2, 1976,*
  Honolulu, Hawaii — 85
C90 **31c Plane, Globes and Flag,** *Jan. 2, 1976,*
  Honolulu, Hawaii — 85
C91-C92 **31c Wright Brothers,** *Sept. 23, 1978,*
  Dayton, Ohio — @1.15
  C92a — 2.30
C93-C94 **21c Octave Chanute,** *Mar. 29, 1979,*
  Chanute, Kan. — @1.00
  C94a — 2.00
First day cancellation was applied to 459,235 covers bearing Nos. C93, C94 or pair.
C95-C96 **25c Wiley Post,** *Nov. 20, 1979,*
  Oklahoma City, Okla. — @1.00
  C96a — 2.00
C97 **31c Olympics,** *Nov. 1, 1979,*
  Colorado Springs, CO — 1.15

1980-83

C98 **40c Philip Mazzei,** *Oct. 13, 1980* — 1.35
C99 **28c Blanche Stuart Scott,** *Dec. 30, 1980,*
  Hammondsport, NY — 1.10
C100 **35c Glenn Curtiss,** *Dec. 30, 1980,*
  Hammondsport, NY — 1.25
C101-C104 **28c Olympics,** *June 17, 1983,*
  San Antonio, TX — @1.10
  C104a — 3.75
C105-C108 **40c Olympics,** *April 8, 1983,*
  Los Angeles, CA *(1,001,657)* — @1.35
  C108a — 5.00
C109-C112 **35c Olympics,** *Nov. 4, 1983,*
  Colorado Springs, CO — @1.25
  C112a — 4.50

1985

C113 **33c Alfred V. Verville,** *Feb. 13,* Garden City, NY — 1.25
C114 **39c Lawrence & Elmer Sperry,** *Feb. 13,*
  Garden City, NY — 1.35
C115 **44c Transpacific Air Mail,** *Feb. 15,*
  San Francisco, CA *(269,229)* — 1.35
C116 **44c Junipero Serra,** *Aug. 22,* San Diego, CA — 1.35

BOOKLETS AND BOOKLET PANES

Most booklet panes issued before 1962 consist of a vertical block of six stamps which is perforated vertically through the center. The panes are perforated horizontally on all but the bottom edge. The two sides and bottom are straight edge. Exceptions to the 6-stamp pane of 1900-1962 are the 1918 American Expeditionary Force panes (30 stamps); the Lindbergh and 6c 1943 air mails (3 stamps) and the Savings Stamps (10). The 5-stamp pane was introduced in 1962; the 8-stamp pane in 1967, and the 4-stamp and 7-stamp panes in 1971.

Flat plate booklet panes, with the exceptions noted above, are made of stamps printed from specially designed plates of 180 or 360 subjects and are collected in plate positions. There are nine collectible plate positions on the 180-subject sheet and 12 collectible positions on the 360-subject sheet.

Rotary booklet panes are made of stamps printed from specially designed plates of 180 or 360 subjects and are collected in plate positions. There are five collectible plate positions on the 360-subject sheet which was printed before the electric eye plates came into use, and 20 collectible positions on the Type II "new design" 360-subject rotary sheet. There are 23 collectible positions in the rotary air mail 180-subject sheet as well as the Type IV "modified design" 360-subject sheet, and five collectible positions on Defense and War Savings 300-subject sheets.

The generally accepted method of designating the various positions of the panes on the sheet as illustrated and explained hereafter, is that suggested by George H. Beans in the May, 1913, issue of *Everybody's Philatelist*.

Some collectors take all varieties possible, the majority collecting unused ordinary panes (A) and Plate Number panes (D), hence listings are limited to these.

Dr. William R. Bush, Dr. Robert Marks and the Bureau Issues Association helped the editors extensively in compiling the listings and preparing the illustrations of booklets, covers and plate layouts.

Prices are for complete panes with selvage, and for panes of six unless otherwise stated.

BOOKLET PANES

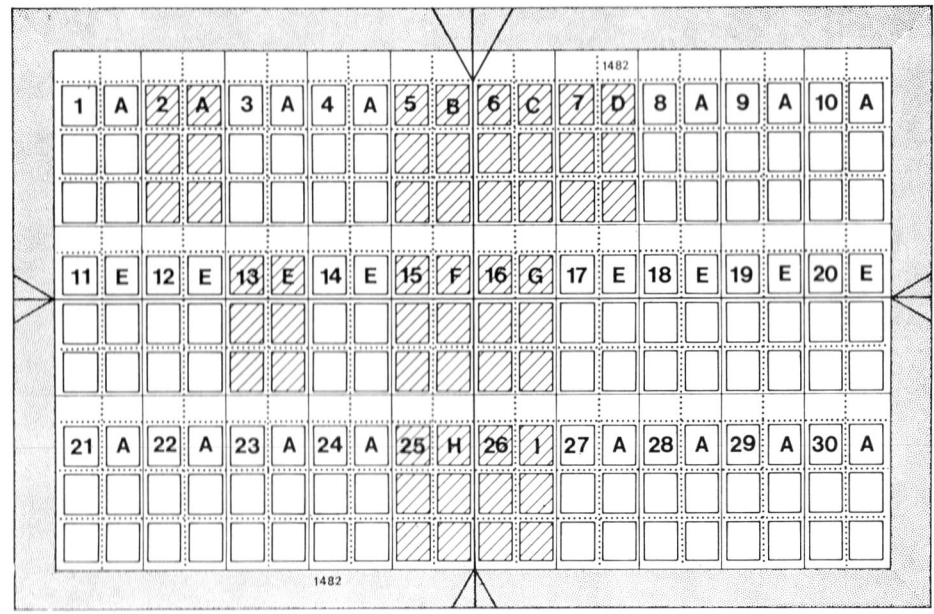

The 180-Subject Plate — 9 Collectible Positions

Beginning at upper left and reading from left to right, the panes are designated from 1 to 30. All positions not otherwise identifiable are designated by the letter A: Pane 1A, 2A, 3A, 4A, etc.

The identifiable positions are as follows:

A The ordinary booklet pane without distinguishing features. Occurs in Position 1, 2, 3, 4, 8, 9, 10, 21, 22, 23, 24, 27, 28, 29, 30.
B Split arrow and guide line at right. Occurs in Position 5 only.
C Split arrow and guide line at left. Occurs in Position 6 only.
D Plate number pane. Occurs in Position 7 only.
E Guide line pane showing horizontal guide line between stamps 1-2 and 3-4 of the pane. Occurs in Positions 11, 12, 13, 14, 17, 18, 19, and 20.
F Guide line through pane and at right. Occurs in Position 15 only.
G Guide line through pane and at left. Occurs in Position 16 only.
H Guide line at right. Occurs in Position 25 only.
I Guide line at left. Occurs in Position 26 only.

Only positions B, F and H or C, G and I may be obtained from the same sheet, depending on whether the knife which separated the panes fell to right or left of the line.

Side arrows, bottom arrows, or bottom plate numbers are seldom found because the margin of the sheets is usually cut off, as are the sides and bottom of each pane.

In the illustrations, the dotted lines represent the rows of perforations, the unbroken lines represents the knife cut.

BOOKLET PANES

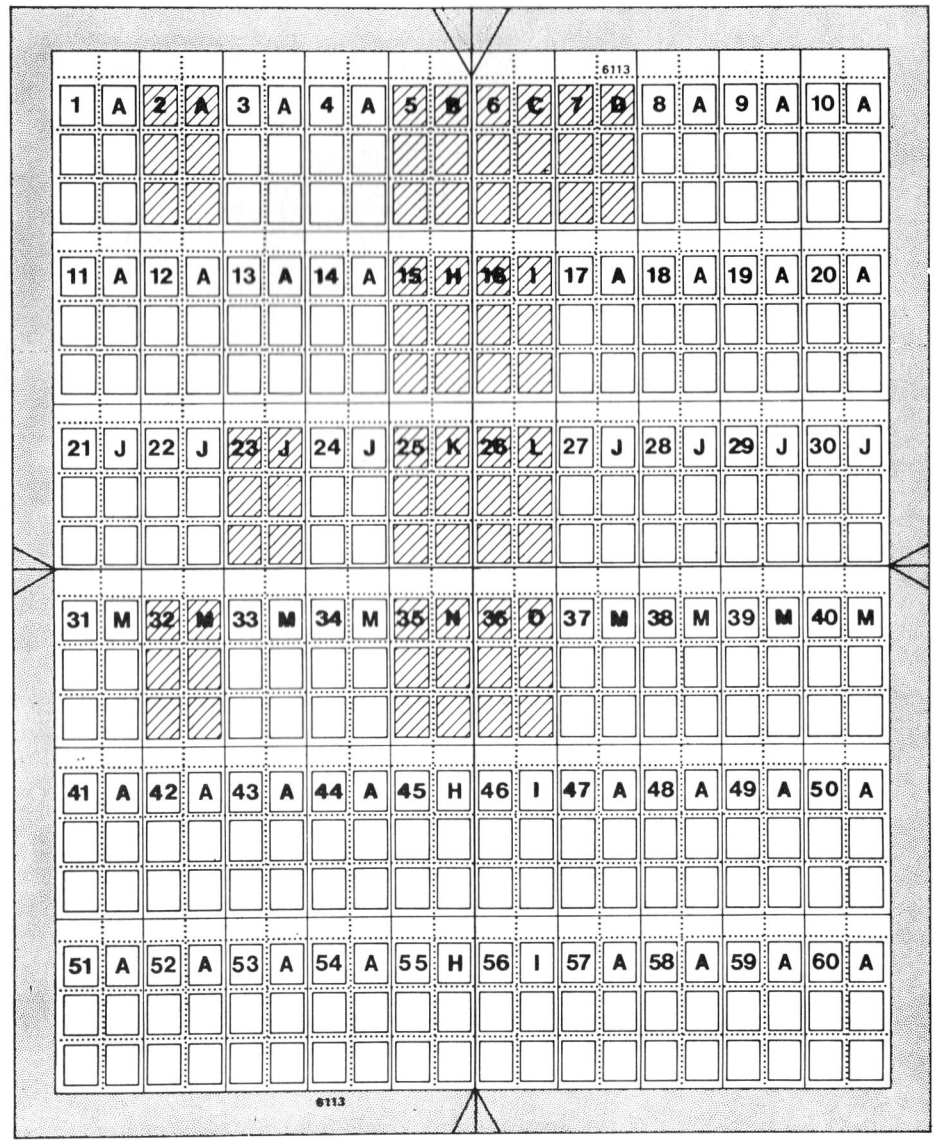

The 360-Subject Plate —— 12 Collectible Positions

BOOKLET PANES

As with the 180 - Subject Sheets, the position of the various panes is indicated by numbers beginning in the upper left corner with the No. 1 and reading from left to right to No. 60.

The identifiable positions are as follows:

- **A** The ordinary booklet pane without distinguishing features. Occurs in Positions 1, 2, 3, 4, 8, 9, 10, 11, 12, 13, 14, 17, 18, 19, 20, 41, 42, 43, 44, 47, 48, 49, 50, 51, 52, 53, 54, 57, 58, 59, and 60.
- **B** Split arrow and guide line at right. Occurs in Position 5 only.
- **C** Split arrow and guide line at left. Occurs in Position 6 only.
- **D** Plate number pane. Occurs in Position 7 only.
- **E**
- **F** } Do not occur in the 360-Subject Plate.
- **G**
- **H** Guide line at right. Occurs in Positions 15, 45, and 55.
- **I** Guide line at left. Occurs in Positions 16, 46, and 56.
- **J** Guide line at bottom. Occurs in Positions 21, 22, 23, 24, 27, 28, 29 and 30.
- **K** Guide line at right and bottom. Occurs in Position 25 only.
- **L** Guide line at left and bottom. Occurs in Position 26 only.
- **M** Guide line at top. Occurs in Positions 31, 32, 33, 34, 37, 38, 39 and 40.
- **N** Guide line at top and right. Occurs in Position 35 only.
- **O** Guide line at top and left. Occurs in Position 36 only.

Only one each of Positions B or C, K, L, N or O; four positions of H or I, and eight or nine positions of J or M may be obtained from each 360 subject sheet, depending on whether the knife fell to the right or left, top or bottom of the guide lines.

Because the horizontal guide line appears so close to the bottom row of stamps on panes Nos. 21 to 30, Positions M, N, and O occur with great deal less frequency than Positions J, K and L.

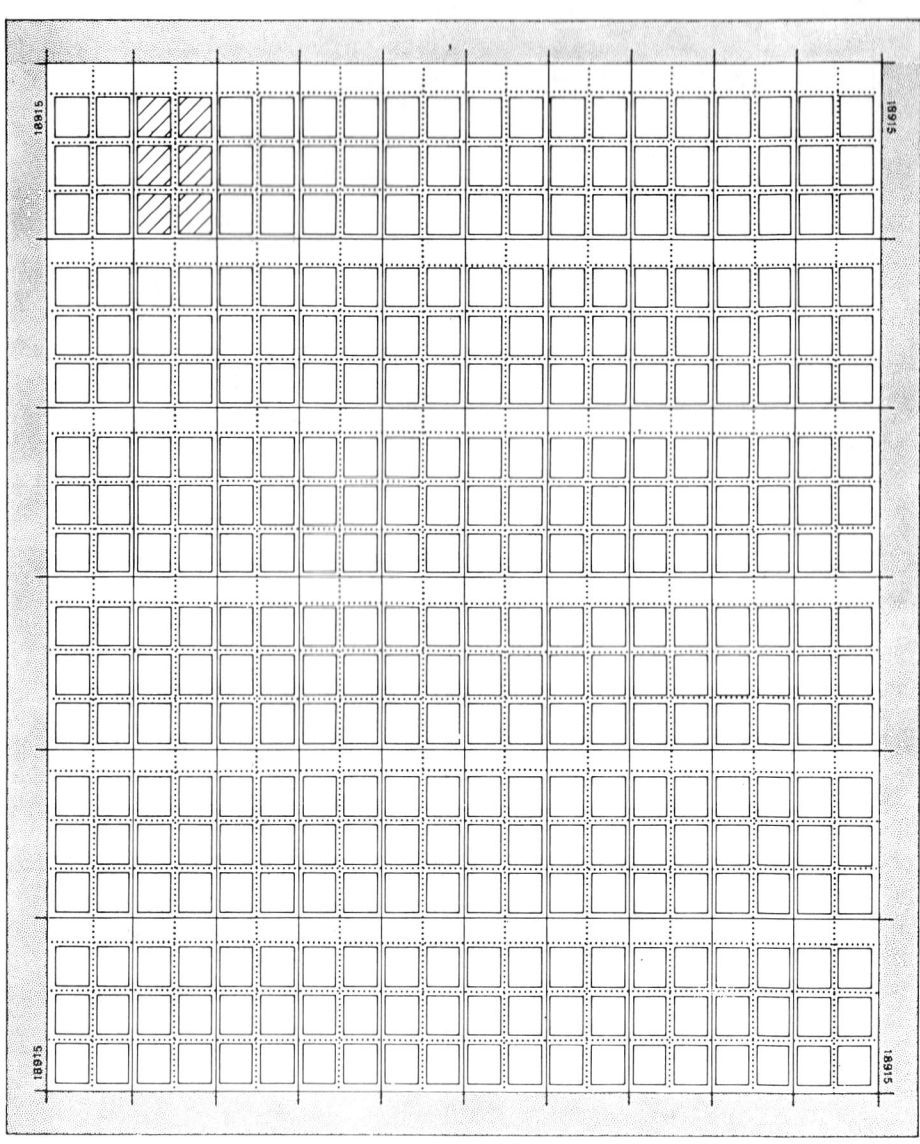

**The 360-subject Rotary Press Plate
(before Electric Eye)
Position A only.**

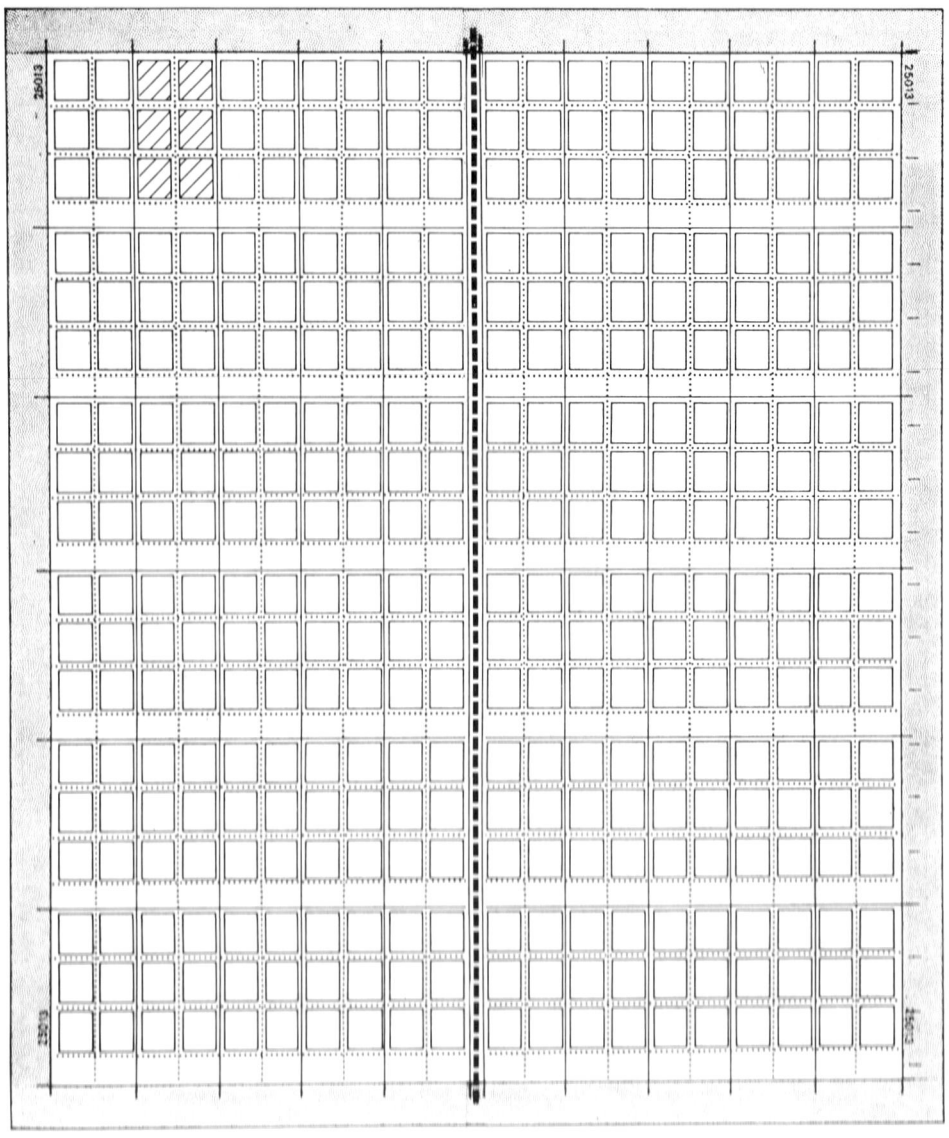

The 360-Subject Rotary Press Plate
Electric Eye

A modified design was put into use in 1956. The new plates have 20 frame bars instead of 17.

448 BOOKLET PANES

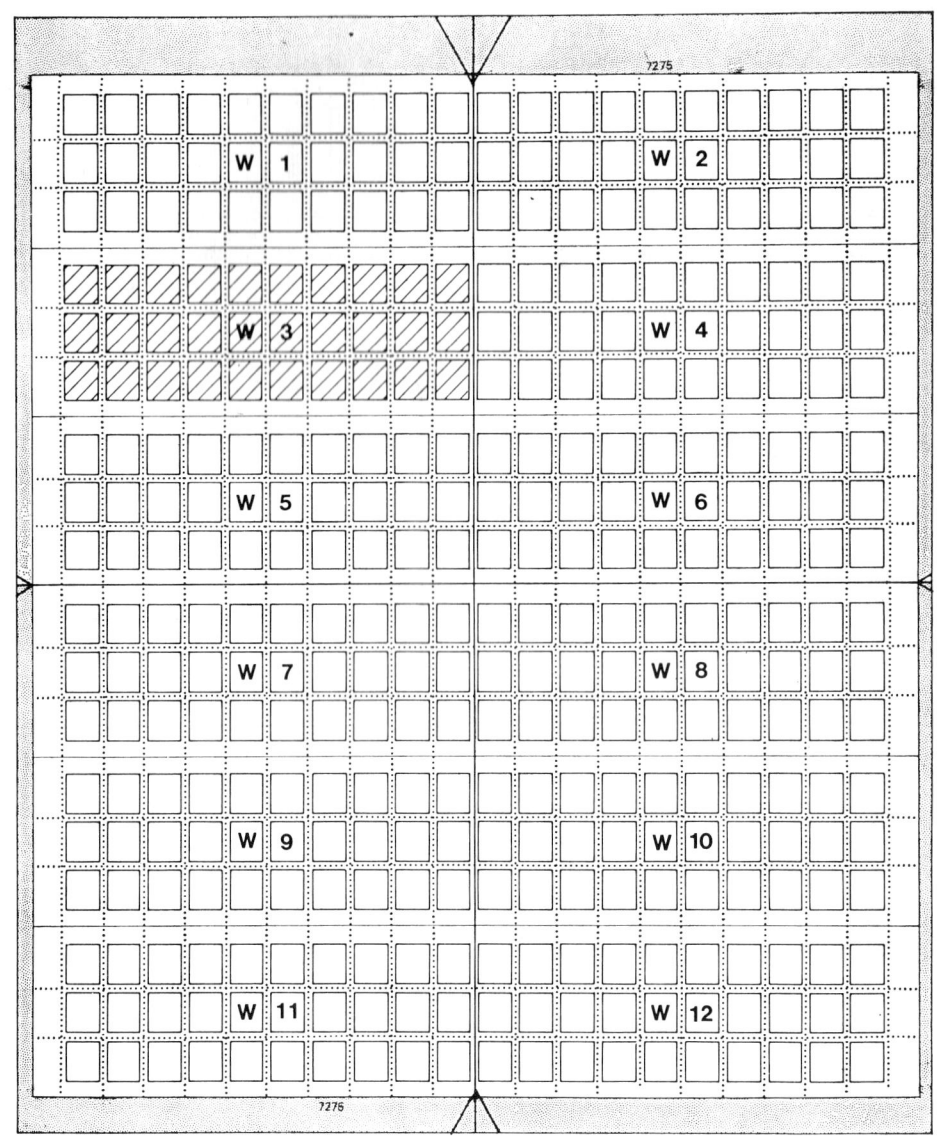

The A.E.F. Plate —— 360-subject Flat Plate
10 Collectible Positions

BOOKLET PANES

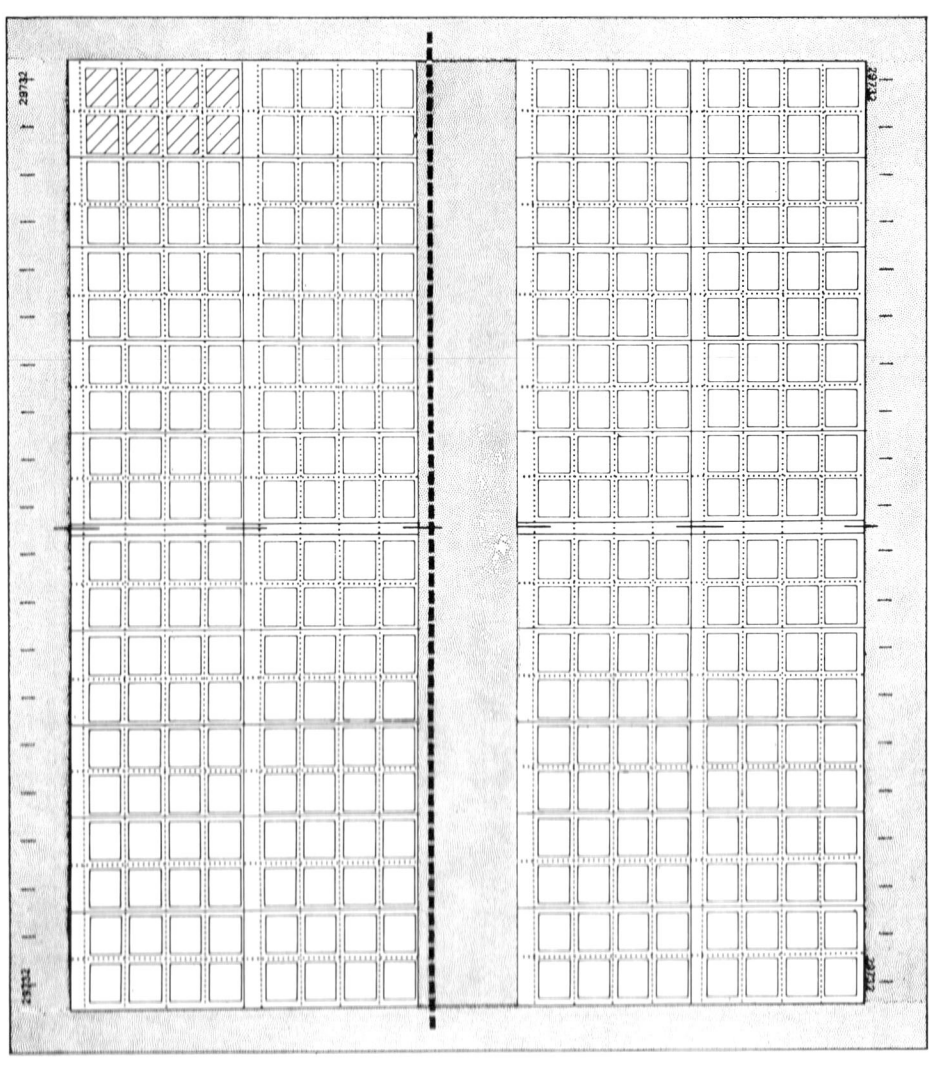

The 320-subject plate

BOOKLET PANES

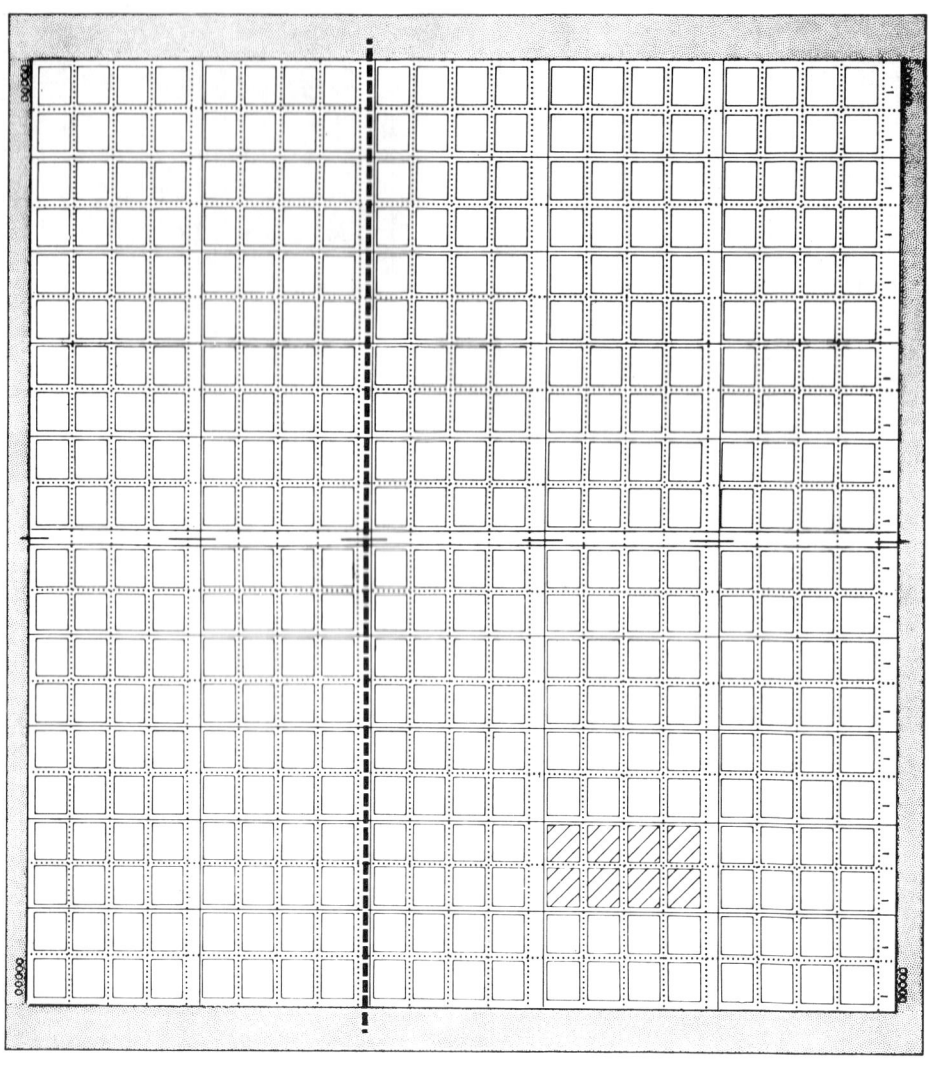

The 400-subject plate
The 300-subject plate with double labels has the same layout.

BOOKLET PANES

Lindbergh Booklet Plate - 180 Subjects
11 Collectible Positions.

BOOKLET PANES

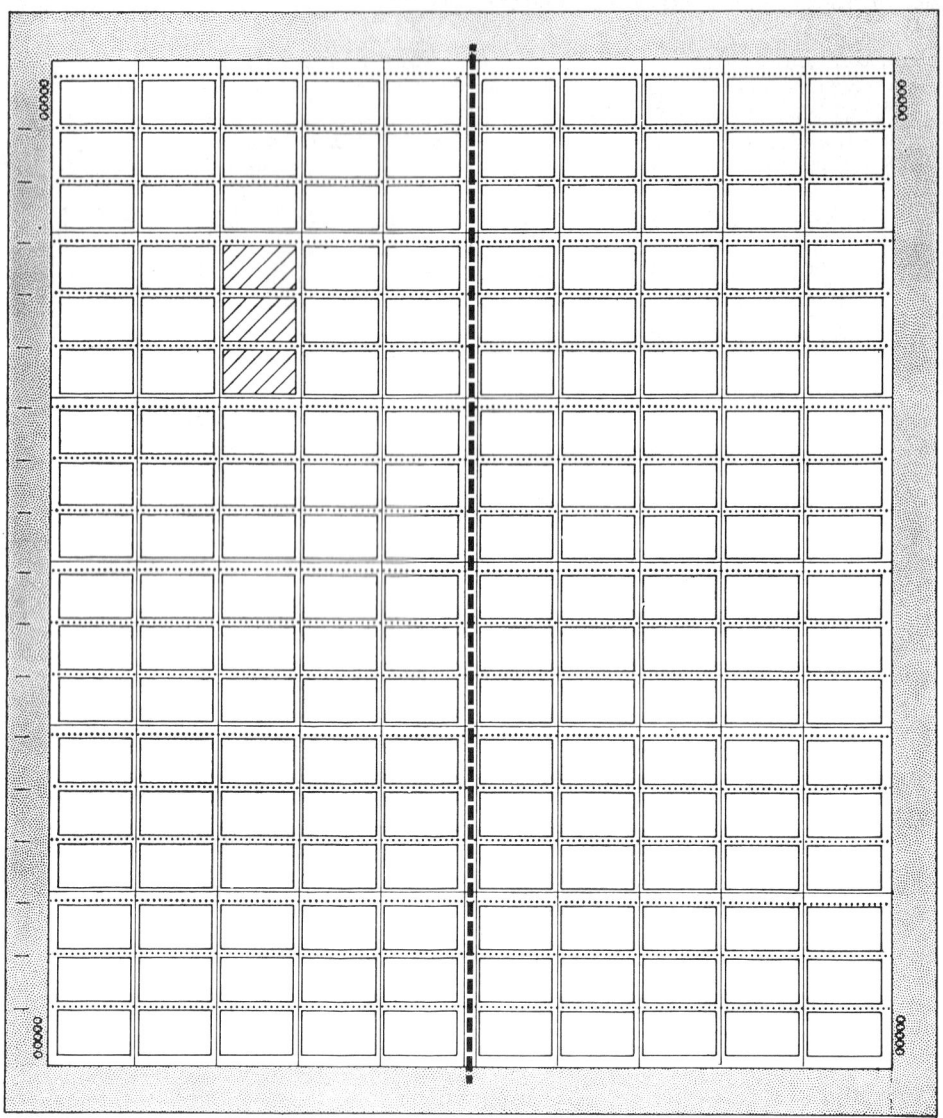

**Airmail 180-subject Rotary Press Plate
Electric Eye**

SAVINGS STAMPS

Booklet panes of Postal Savings Stamps and Savings Stamps are listed in detail in the Savings Stamps section of this Catalogue.

453

Booklet Covers

Front covers of booklets of postage and airmail issues are illustrated and numbered. At left is the Booklet Cover number (BC2A); at right, the catalogue numbers of the Booklet Panes (300b, 331a). The text of the inside and back covers changes. When more than one combination of covers exists, the number of possible booklets is noted in parenthesis after the booklet listing.

900

Text only cover.
25c booklet contains 2 panes of six 2c stamps.
49c booklet contains 4 panes of six 2c stamps.
97c booklet contains 8 panes of six 2c stamps.
Booklets sold for 1c more than the face value of the stamps.

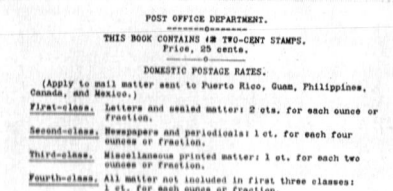

BC1A   279Be

BC1B   279Be

BC1C   279Be

900-1908

Text cover with price added in upper corners.
25c booklets contain 4 panes of six 1c stamps or 2 panes of six 2c stamps.
49c booklet contains 4 panes of six 2c stamps.
97c booklet contains 8 panes of six 2c stamps.

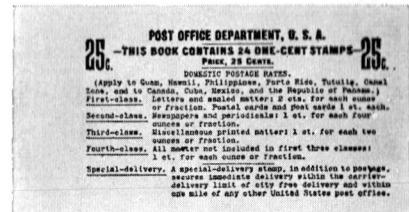

BC2A   300b, 331a

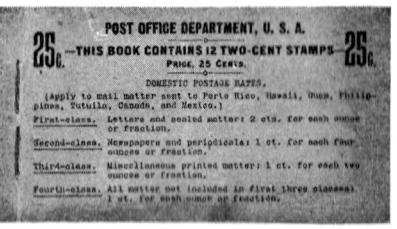

BC2B   279Be, 301c, 319, 332a

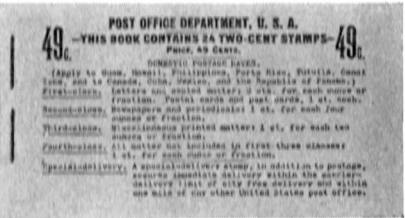

BC2C   279Be, 301c, 319, 332a

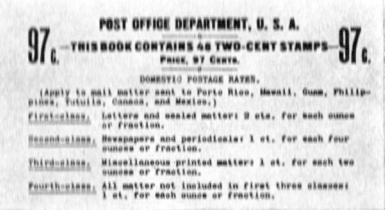

BC2D   279Be, 301c, 319, 332a

BOOKLET COVERS

1908–1912   Postrider

25c booklet contains 2 panes of six 2c stamps.
49c booklet contains 4 panes of six 2c stamps.
97c booklet contains 8 panes of six 2c stamps.

BC3A   331a, 374a, 405b

BC3B   332a, 375a, 406a

BC3C   332a, 375a, 406a

BC3D   332a, 375a, 406a

1912–1939   Washington P.O.

Price of booklet in large numerals behind contents information.

25c booklet contains 4 panes of six 1c stamps.
73c booklet contains 4 panes of six 1c stamps and panes of six 2c stamps.
97c booklet contains 16 panes of six 1c stamps.

BC4A   405b, 424d, 462a, 498e

BC4B   405b, 424d, 462a, 498e, 552a, 632a

BC4C   405b, 424d, 462a 498e, 552a 632a, 804b

1912–1939   Small Postrider

Large background numerals.

25c booklets contain 4 panes of six 1c stamps or 2 panes of six 2c stamps.
49c booklet contains 4 panes of six 2c stamps.
73c booklet contains 4 panes of six 1c stamps and panes of six 2c stamps.
97c booklets contain 16 panes of six 1c stamps or panes of six 2c stamps.

BOOKLET COVERS 455

BC5A   632a, 804b

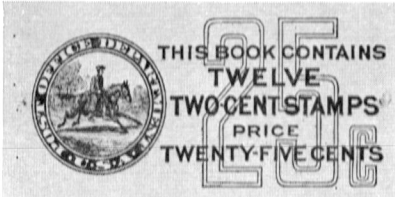

BC5B   406a, 425e, 463a, 499e, 554c,
                     583a, 634d, 806b

BC5C   406a, 425e, 463a, 499e, 554c,
                     583a, 634d, 806b

BC5D   632a, 804b

BC5E   632a, 804b

BC5F   406a, 425e, 463a 499e, 634d
                                  806b

1917-1927   **Oval designs**

25c booklet contains 4 panes of six 1c stamps.
37c booklet contains 2 panes of six 3c stamps.
97c booklet contains 8 panes of six 2c stamps.

BC6A   498e, 552a

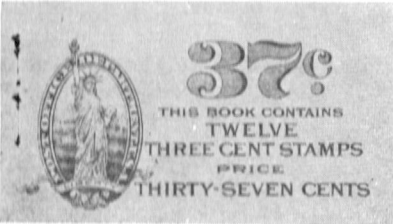

BC6B   501b, 502b

BC6C   499d, 554c, 583a, 634d

BOOKLET COVERS

1918   **A.E.F.**

$3 booklet contains 10 panes of thirty 1c stamps.
$6 booklet contains 10 panes of thirty 2c stamps.
Booklets sold for face value.

300
1 CENT POSTAGE STAMPS
$3.

BC7A   498

300
2 CENT POSTAGE STAMPS
$6.

BC7B   499

1928   **Postrider and Wings**

61c booklet contains 2 panes of three 10c stamps.

BC8   C10a

BOOKLET COVERS

1932–1954 **Post Office Seal**
Large background numerals.
25c booklet contains 2 panes of six 2c stamps.
37c booklet contains 2 panes of six 3c stamps.
49c booklet contains 4 panes of six 2c stamps.
73c booklets contain 4 panes of six 3c stamps or 4 panes of six 1c stamps and 4 panes of six 2c stamps.

BC9A   806b

BC9B   720b, 807a, 1035a

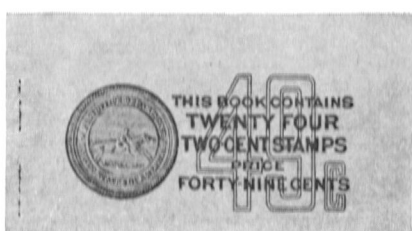

BC9C   806b

BC9D   720b, 807a, 1035a

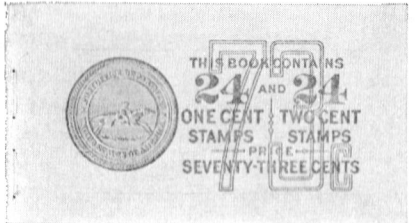

BC9E   804b

1958
97c booklet contains 4 panes of six 4c stamps.

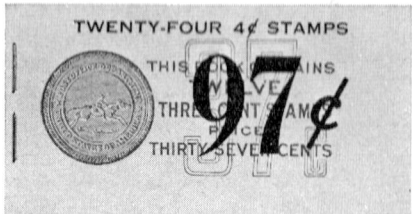

BC9F   1036a

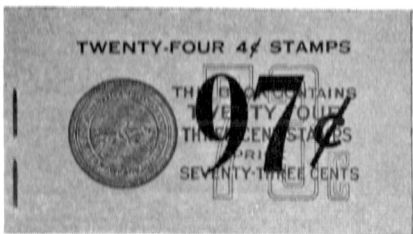

BC9G   1036a

BC9H   1036a

BOOKLET COVERS

1943 **Postrider and Wings**
Large background numerals.
37c booklet contains 2 panes of three 6c stamps.
73c booklet contains 4 panes of three 6c stamps.

BC10A   C25a

BC10B   C25a

1949–1963 **U.S. Airmail Wings**
The 73c and 85c booklets were the last sold for 1c over face value.
    73c booklet contains 2 panes of six 6c stamps.
    85c booklet contains 2 panes of six 7c stamps.
    80c booklet contains 2 panes of five 8c stamps.
    $2 booklet contains 5 panes of five 8c stamps.

BC11A   C39a

BC11B   C51a

BC11C   C51a, C60a

BC11D   C64b, C64c

BC11E   C64b

1962–1963 **Small Postrider**
$1 booklet contains 4 panes of five 5c stamps.

BC12A   1213a

BOOKLET COVERS

1963–1964 Mr. Zip

$1 booklet contains 4 panes of five 5c stamps.
$2 booklet contains 5 panes of five 8c stamps.

BC13A   1213a, 1213c

BC13B   C64b, C64c

1967–1968

$2 booklet contains 4 panes of eight 6c stamps and 1 pane of eight 1c stamps.
$4 booklet contains 5 panes of eight 10c stamps.

BC14A   1284b

BC14B   C72b

1968–1971

$1 booklets contain 2 panes of five 10c stamps or 2 panes of six 8c stamps and 1 pane of four 1c stamps; 3 panes of five 6c stamps and 1 pane of five 2c stamps or 2 panes of four 11c stamps and 1 pane of six 2c stamps.

BC15A   C72c

BC15B   1395b

BC15C   1284c, 1393b

BC15D   C78a

BOOKLET COVERS

1970-1971 Eisenhower

$2 booklet contains 4 panes of eight 6c stamps and 1 pane of eight 1c stamps.

$1.92 booklet contains 3 panes of eight 8c stamps.

BC16A 1393a

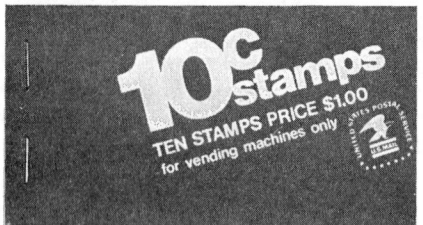

BC17B 1510b

BC16B 1395a

BC17C 1510c

BC17D 1510d

1972-1974 Postal Service Emblem

$2 booklet contains 3 panes of seven 8c stamps and 1 pane of four 8c stamps.

$1 booklet contains 2 panes of five 10c stamps.

$4 booklet contains 5 panes of eight 10c stamps.

$1.25 booklet contains 1 pane of five 13c stamps and 1 pane of six 10c stamps.

1973

$1.30 booklet contains 2 panes of five 13c stamps.

BC17A 1395d

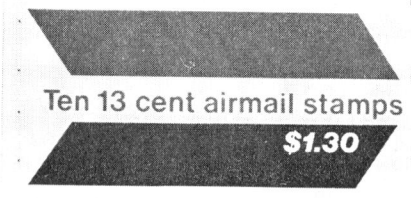

BC18 C79a

BOOKLET COVERS

1975–1976
- 90c booklet contains 1 pane of six 13c stamps and 1 pane of six 2c stamps.
- $1.30 booklet contains 2 panes of five 13c stamps.
- $2.99 booklet contains 2 panes of eight 13c stamps and 1 pane of seven 13c stamps.

BC19A   1595a, 1595d BC19B   1595c

1977–1978
- $1 booklet contains 1 pane of one 9c stamp and seven 13c stamps.
- $1.20 booklet contains 1 pane of eight 15c stamps.
- $2.40 booklet contains 2 panes of eight 15c stamps.
- $3.60 booklet contains 3 panes of eight 15c stamps.

BC20   1623a BC21   1598a

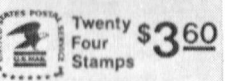

BC22   1738a BC23   1288c

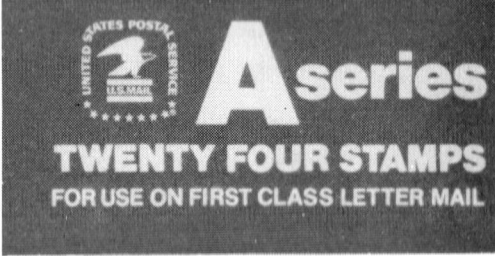

BC24   1736a

1980

$3 booklet contains 2 panes of ten 15c stamps.

BC25   1742a

BOOKLET COVERS

1981-82
$4.32 booklet contains 3 panes of eight B stamps.
$4 booklet contains 2 panes of ten C stamps.
$4.40 booklet contains 2 panes of ten D stamps.

BC26　　　　　　　　　　　　1819a, 1948a, 2113a

1981
$1.20 booklet contains 1 pane of two 6c and six 18c stamps.
$3.60 booklet contains 2 panes of ten 18c stamps.

BC28　　　　　　　　　　　　1889a

1982
$1.20 booklet contains 2 panes of six 20c stamps.
$2 booklet contains 1 pane of ten 20c stamps.
$4 booklet contains 2 panes of ten 20c stamps.

BC27　　　1893a　　　BC29　　1896a　　BC30　　1949a

BC29B　　　　　　　　　　　　1896b

1983

$28.05 booklet contains 1 pane of three $9.35 stamps.
$32.25 booklet contains 1 pane of three $10.75 stamps.

BC31   1909a

1985

$1.10 booklet contains one pane of five 22c stamps.
$2.20 booklet contains two panes of five 22c stamps.
$4.40 booklet contains two panes of ten 22c stamps.

BC32   2116a

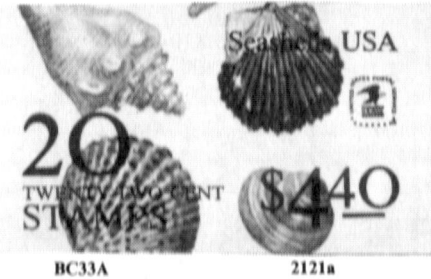

BC33A   2121a

BC33B   2121a

Seven different seashell configurations are possible on BC33A.

1986

$1.76 booklet contains 2 panes of four 22c stamps.
$2.20 booklet contains 2 panes of five 22c stamps.

BC34   2201a

BC35   2209a

BOOKLET PANES

Washington
A88

1900	Wmkd.	USPS or USPS (vertical)	(191)	Horizontally or Vertically.

Perf. 12.

279Be	A88	2c orange red, *April 16*	350.00	200.00
		2c red	350.00	200.00
		With plate number (D)	700.00	

180- and 360-Subject Plates. All plate positions exist, except J, K, and L, due to the horizontal guide line being placed too far below stamps to appear on the upper panes.

Booklets

BK1	BC1A	25c black, *cream*	—
BK2	"	25c black, *buff*	—
BK3	BC1B	49c green, *cream*	—
BK4	"	49c black, *buff*	—
BK5	BC1C	97c red, *cream*	—
BK6	"	97c black, *gray*	—
BK7	BC2B	25c black, *cream* (3)	—
BK8	BC2C	49c black, *buff* (3)	—
BK9	BC2D	97c black, *gray* (3)	—

BK1-BK6 and one type each of BK7-BK9 exist with specimen overprints handstamped on cover and individual stamps.
All covers of BK7-BK9 exist with "Philippines" overprint in 50mm or 48mm.

Franklin   Washington
A115   A116

1903-1907		**Wmkd. (191) Vertically.**		
300b	A115	1c blue green, *March 6, 1907*	500.00	250.00
		With plate number (D)	1000.00	

180-Subject Plates only. All plate positions exist.

Booklet

	BK10	BC2A	25c black, *green* (6)	—
301c	A116	2c carmine, *Jan. 24, 1903*	425.00	250.00
		With plate number (D)	1100.00	

180-Subject Plates only. All plate positions exist.

Booklets

BK11	BC2B	25c black, *cream*	—
BK12	BC2C	49c black, *buff*	—
BK13	BC2D	97c black, *gray*	—

Washington
A129

1903		**Wmkd. (191) Vertically.**		
319g	A129	2c carmine, Die I, *Dec. 3, 1903*	110.00	20.00
319ga	"	2c lake (I)	—	—
319gb	"	2c carmine rose (I)	—	
319gc	"	2c scarlet (I)	110.00	
319h	"	2c carmine, Die II	200.00	
319ha	"	2c lake (II)	140.00	
		With plate number, Die I (D)	200.00	
		With plate number, Die II (D)	300.00	
		Wmk. horizontal	135.00	30.00

180-Subject Plates only. All plate positions exist.

BK14	BC2B	25c black, *cream* (11)	—
BK15	BC2C	49c black, *buff*, (11)	—
BK16	"	49c black, *pink*	—
BK17	BC2D	97c black, *gray* (11)	—

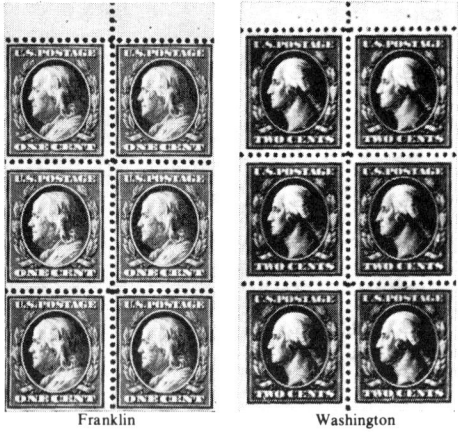

Franklin   Washington
A138   A139

1908		**Wmkd. (191) Vertically.**		
331a	A138	1c green, *Nov. 18, 1908*	150.00	35.00
		With plate number (D)	200.00	

180- and 360-Subject Plates. All plate positions exist.

BOOKLET PANES 465

		Booklets		
	BK18 BC2A	25c black, *green* (3)	—	
	BK19 BC3A	25c black, *green*	—	
332a	A139	2c carmine, *Nov. 16, 1908*	120.00	35.00
		With plate number (D)	165.00	

180- and 360-Subject Plates. All plate positions exist.

Booklets

BK20	BC2B	25c black, *cream* (2)	—
BK21	BC2C	49c black, *buff* (2)	—
BK22	"	49c black, *pink*	—
BK23	BC2D	97c black, *gray* (3)	—
BK24	BC3B	25c black, *cream*	—
BK25	BC3C	49c black, *pink*	—
BK26	BC3D	97c black, *gray*	—

1910		Wmkd. (190) Vertically		*Perf. 12*
374a	A138	1c green, *Oct. 7, 1910*	135.00	30.00
		With plate number (D)	175.00	

360-Subject Plates only. All plate positions exist.

Booklet

	BK27	BC3A	25c black, *green* (2)	—	
375a	A139	2c carmine, *Nov. 30, 1910*		110.00	25.00
		With plate number (D)		150.00	

360-Subject Plates only. All plate positions exist.

Booklets

BK28	BC3B	25c black, *cream* (2)	—
BK29	BC3C	49c black, *pink* (2)	—
BK30	BC3D	97c black, *gray* (2)	—

Washington
A140

1912		**Wmkd. (190) Vertically.**		
405b	A140	1c green, *Feb. 8, 1912*	65.00	7.50
		With plate number (D)	90.00	

360-Subject Plates only. All plate positions exist.

Ordinary Booklets

BK31	BC3A	25c black, *green* (2)	—
BK32	BC4A	25c black, *green* (3)	—
BK33	BC4C	97c green, *lavender*	—

Combination Booklet

BK34	BC4B	73c red, 4 #405b (1c) + 4 #406a (2c)	—
406a	A140	2c carmine, *Feb. 8, 1912*	70.00	17.50
		With plate number (D)	90.00	

360-Subject Plates only. All plate positions exist.

Ordinary Booklets

BK35	BC3B	25c black, *cream* (2)	—
BK36	BC3C	49c black, *pink* (2)	—
BK37	BC3D	97c black, *gray* (2)	—
BK38	BC5B	25c red, *buff* (3)	—
BK39	BC3C	49c red, *pink* (3)	—
BK40	BC5F	97c red, *blue*, (3)	—

Combination Booklet
See No. BK34.

1914		**Wmkd. (190) Vertically.**		*Perf. 10*
424d	A140	1c green, *Jan. 6, 1914*	4.00	75
		Double transfer, Plate 6363	—	—
		With plate number (D)	7.00	
		Cracked plate		
		Imperf.		

360-Subject Plates only. All plate positions exist.

Ordinary Booklets

| BK41 | BC4A | 25c green, *green* (3) | — |
| BK42 | BC4C | 97c green, *lavender* (2) | — |

Combination Booklet

BK43	BC4B	73c red, 4 #424d (1c) + 4 #425e (2c) (3)	—
425e	A140	2c carmine, *Jan. 6, 1914*	15.00	3.00
		With plate number (D)	22.50	

360-Subject Plates only. All plate positions exist.

Ordinary Booklets

BK44	BC5B	25c red, *buff* (3)	—
BK45	BC5C	49c red, *pink* (3)	—
BK46	BC5F	97c red, *blue* (3)	—

Combination Booklet
See No. BK43.

1916		**Unwatermarked**		*Perf. 10*
462a	A140	1c green *Oct. 15, 1916*	12.00	1.00
		Cracked plate at right	50.00	—
		Cracked plate at left	50.00	
		With plate number (D)	17.50	

360-Subject Plates only. All plate positions exist.

Ordinary Booklets

| BK47 | BC4A | 25c green, *green* | — |
| BK48 | BC4C | 97c green, *lavender* | — |

Combination Booklets

BK49	BC4B	73c red, 4 #462a (1c) + 4 #463a (2c) (2)	—
463a	A140	2c carmine, *Oct. 8, 1916*	75.00	15.00
		With plate number (D)	110.00	

360-Subject Plates only. All plate positions exist.

Ordinary Booklets

BK50	BC5B	25c red, *buff*	—
BK51	BC5C	49c red, *pink*	—
BK52	BC5F	97c red, *blue*	—

Combination Booklets
See No. BK49.

1917-18		**Unwatermarked**		*Perf. 11*
498e	A140	1c green, *Apr. 6, 1917*	1.75	35
		Double transfer	—	—
		With plate number (D)	2.75	60

360-Subject Plates only. All plate positions exist.

BOOKLET PANES

		Ordinary Booklets		
BK53	BC4A	25c green, *green* (2)	—	
BK54	BC4C	97c green, *lavender* (4)	—	
BK55	BC6A	25c green, *green* (5)	—	
		Combination Booklets		
BK56	BC4B	73c red, 4 #498e (1c) + 4 #499e (2c) (4)	—	
BK57	BC4B	73c red, 4 #498e (1c) + 4 #554c (2c) (3)	—	

499e   A140   2c rose, type I, *Mar. 31, 1917*   2.00   50
       With plate number (D)   3.00   90
       360-Subject Plates only. All plate positions exist.

Ordinary Booklets

| BK58 | BC5B | 25c red, *buff* (5) | — |
| BK59 | BC5C | 49c red, *pink* (4) | — |

| BK60 | BC5F | 97c red, *blue* (3) | — |
| BK61 | BC6C | 97c red, *blue* (2) | — |

Combination Booklets
See No. BK56.

501b   A140   3c violet, type I, *Oct. 17, 1917*   75.00   15.00
       With plate number (D)   100.00
       360-Subject Plates only. All plate positions exist.

Booklet

| BK62 | BC6B | 37c violet, *sage* | — |

502b   A140   3c violet, type II, *Feb. 25, 1918*   50.00   10.00
       With plate number (D)   70.00
       360-Subject Plates only. All plate positions exist.

Booklet

| BK63 | BC6B | 37c violet, *sage* | — |

Washington—A140

A.E.F. Panes of 30

498f   A140   1c green (pane of 30), *Jan. 1, 1918*   550.00

Booklet

| BK64 | BC7A | $3 black, *green* | — |

499f   A140   2c rose, (pane of 30) type I, *Jan. 1, 1918*   9,000.00

Booklet

| BK65 | BC7B | $6 black, *pink* | |

Nos. 498f and 499f were for use of the American Expeditionary Force in France.

They were printed from the ordinary 360-Subject Plates, the sheet being cut into 12 leaves of 30 stamps each in place of 60 leaves of 6 stamps each, and, of course, the lines of perforations changed accordingly.

The same system as used for designating plate positions on the ordinary booklet panes is used for designating the war booklet, only each war booklet pane is composed of 5 ordinary panes. Thus, No. 1 war booklet pane would be composed of positions 1, 2, 3, 4, and 5 of an ordinary pane.

The following varieties are noted, the figures in parentheses indicating the number of ordinary booklet panes:

W 1	(1 to 5)	Split arrow and guide line at right.
W 2	(6 to 10)	Split arrow and guide line at left. Plate number over fourth stamp.
W 3	(11 to 15)	Guide line at right.
W 4	(16 to 20)	Guide line at left.
W 5	(21 to 25)	Guide line at right and at bottom. Arrow at lower left.
W 6	(26 to 30)	Guide line at left and at bottom. Arrow at lower right.
W 7	(31 to 35)	Guide line at right and top. Arrow at upper left.
W 8	(36 to 40)	Guide line at left and top. Arrow at upper right.
W 9	(41 to 45)	Guide line at right.
W10	(46 to 50)	Guide line at left.
W11	(51 to 55)	Guide line at right. Arrow at lower right.
W12	(56 to 60)	Guide line at left. Arrow at lower left.

The A. E. F. booklet panes were bound at side margins which accounts for side arrows being found. More often than not, the positions are not found on the sheets as when knifing them apart, very little attention was paid to the location of the margins. Positions W3 and W4 cannot be distinguished from W9 and W10.

Franklin   Washington
A155   A157

1923   **Unwatermarked**   *Perf. 11*

552a   A155   1c deep green, *Aug. 11, 1923*   5.50   50
       With plate number (D)   8.50
       360-Subject Plates only. All plate positions exist.

Ordinary Booklets

| BK66 | BC6A | 25c green, *green* (2) | — |
| BK67 | BC4C | 97c green, *lavender* (3) | — |

Combination Booklet

| BK68 | BC4B | 73c white, *red*, 4 #552a (1c) + 4 #554c (2c) (3) | — |

554c   A157   2c carmine, *Feb. 10, 1923*   7.00   1.00
       With plate number (D)   11.00
       360-Subject Plates only. All plate positions exist.

BOOKLET PANES

Ordinary Booklets

BK69	BC5B	25c red, *buff* (3)	—
BK70	BC5C	49c red, *pink* (3)	—
BK71	BC6C	97c red, *blue* (3)	—

Combination Booklets
See Nos. BK57 and BK68.

ROTARY PRESS PRINTINGS.

The rotary press booklet panes were printed from specially prepared plates of 360-subjects in arrangement as before, but without the guide lines and the plate numbers are at the sides instead of at the top as on the flat plates. The only varieties possible are the ordinary pane (A) and Partial plate numbers appearing at the right or left of the upper or lower stamps of a booklet pane when the trimming of the sheets is off center. The note applies to Nos. 583a, 632a, 634d, 720b, 804b, 806b and 807a, before Electric Eyes.

1926 *Perf. 10.*

583a A157 2c carmine, *Aug. 27, 1926* 75.00 25.00
First day cover 1,200.00

Ordinary Booklets

BK72	BC5B	25c red, *buff* (2)	—
BK73	BC5C	49c red, *pink*	—
BK74	BC6C	97c red, *blue*	—

1927 *Perf. 11×10½*

632a A155 1c green, *Nov. 2, 1927* 2.50 25

Ordinary Booklets

BK75	BC5A	25c green, *green* (3)	—
BK76	BC4C	97c green, *lavender*	—
BK77	BC5E	97c green, *lavender*	—

Combination Booklets

| BK78 | BC4B | 73c red, 4 #632a (1c) + 4 #634d (2c) | — |
| BK79 | BC5D | 73c red, 4 #632a (1c) + 4 #634d (2c) (2) | — |

634d A157 2c carmine, type I, *Feb. 25, 1927* 1.00 15

Ordinary Booklets

BK80	BC5B	25c red, *buff* (2)	—
BK81	BC5C	49c red, *pink* (2)	—
BK82	BC5F	97c red, *blue* (2)	—
BK83	BC6C	97c red, *blue*	—

Combination Booklets
See Nos. BK78 and BK79.

Washington—A226

1932
720b A226 3c deep violet, *July 25, 1932* 22.50 5.00
First day cover 100.00

Ordinary Booklets

| BK84 | BC9B | 37c violet, *buff* (2) | — |
| BK85 | BC9D | 73c violet, *pink* (2) | — |

Washington Adams
A276 A278

Jefferson
A279

In 1942 plates were changed to the Type II "new design" and the E. E. marks may appear at the right or left margins of panes of Nos. 804b, 806b and 807a. Panes printed from E. .E. plates have 2½mm. vertical gutter; those from pre-E. E. plates have 3mm. vertical gutter.

1939-42 *Perf. 11×10½*

804b A276 1c green (3mm. vert. gutter), *Jan. 27, 1939* 1.75 30
First day cover 20.00

Ordinary Booklets

BK86	BC5A	25c green, *green*	—
BK87	BC5E	97c green, *lavender*	—
BK88	BC4C	97c green, *lavender*	—

Combination Booklet

| BK89 | BC5D | 73c red, 4 #804b (1c) + 4 #806b (2c) | — |

BOOKLET PANES

804b	A276	1c green (2½mm. vert. gutter), April 14, 1942	1.75	20
		Horiz. pair, if perf. only at bottom	—	
		Ordinary Booklets		
	BK90	BC5A 25c green, *green*	—	
	BK91	BC5E 97c green, *lavender*	—	
		Combination Booklets		
	BK92	BC5D 73c red, 4 #804b (1c) + 4 #806b (2c)	—	
	BK93	BC9E 73c red, 4 #804b (1c) + 4 #806b (2c)	—	
806b	A278	2c rose carmine (3mm. vert. gutter), Jan. 27, 1939	4.50	85
		First day cover		20.00
		Ordinary Booklets		
	BK94	BC5B 25c red, *buff*	—	
	BK95	BC5C 49c red, *pink*	—	
	BK96	BC5F 97c red, *blue*	—	
		Combination Booklets		
		See No. BK89.		
806b	A278	2c rose carmine, (2½mm. vert. gutter), April 25, 1942	4.25	50
		Ordinary Booklets		
	BK97	BC5F 97c red, *blue*	—	
	BK98	BC9A 25c red, *buff*	—	
	BK99	BC9C 49c red, *pink*	—	
		Combination Booklets		
		See Nos. BK92 and BK93.		
807a	A279	3c deep violet (3mm. vert. gutter), Jan. 27, 1939	9.50	1.50
		First day cover		24.00
		Booklets		
	BK100	BC9B 37c violet, *buff*	—	
	BK101	BC9D 73c violet, *pink*	—	
807a	A279	3c deep violet, (2½mm. vert. gutter), Mar. 6, 1942	8.50	50
		With full vert. gutter (6mm.) btwn.	—	
		Booklets		
	BK102	BC9B 37c violet, *buff* (3)	—	
	BK103	BC9D 73c violet, *pink* (3)	—	

		Booklets		
	BK104	BC9B 37c violet, *buff*	9.00	
	BK105	BC9D 73c violet, *pink*	15.00	
1036a	A483	4c red violet, *July 31, 1958*	2.00	50
		First day cover, Wheeling, W. Va. (135,825)		5.00
		Imperf. horizontally	—	
		Booklets		
	BK106	BC9F 97c on 37c violet, *buff*	—	
	BK107	BC9G 97c on 73c violet, *pink*	—	
	BK108	BC9H 97c blue, *yellow*	10.00	
	BK109	" 97c blue, *pink* (3)	10.00	

Slogan 2

Slogan 1   Slogan 3

Washington
A650

1962-64   ***Perf. 11×10½***

Plate of 300 stamps, 60 labels.

1213a	A650	5c dark blue gray, pane of 5+label, slogan 1, *Nov. 23, 1962*	5.50	2.00
		First day cover, New York, N. Y. (111,452)		5.00
		With slogan 2, *1963*	10.00	3.50
		With slogan 3, *1964*	2.00	75
		Imperf. vertically	—	
		Booklets		
	BK110	BC12A $1 blue, slogan 1	—	
	BK111	" $1 blue, slogan 2	—	
	BK112	BC13A $1 blue, slogan 2	—	
	BK113	" $1 blue, slogan 3 (4)	10.00	
1213c	A650	As No. 1213a, tagged, slogan 2, *Oct. 28, 1963*	50.00	7.50
		First day cover, Dayton, O.		100.00
		Washington, D.C. (750)		115.00
		With slogan 3, *1964*	1.25	50
		Booklets		
	BK114	BC13A $1 blue, slogan 2	—	
	BK115	" $1 blue, slogan 3 (4)	6.00	

Statue of Liberty   Lincoln
A482   A483

1954-58   ***Perf. 11×10½***

1035a	A482	3c deep violet, *June 30, 1954*	3.00	50
		First day cover		6.00

BOOKLET PANES

Jefferson
A710

An experimental moisture-resistant gum was used on 1,000,000 panes of No. 1278a and 4,000,000 of No. 1393a released in March, 1971. This dull finish gum shows no breaker ridges. The booklets lack interleaving. This gum was also used for Nos. 1395c, 1395d, 1288Bc and all panes from No. 1510b on unless noted.

Oliver Wendell Holmes
A720

Wright
A712

Slogan 4

Slogan 5

Roosevelt—A716

			1967-78	Tagged		Perf. 11×10½	
1278a	A710		1c green, pane of 8, *Jan. 12, 1968*		1.00	25	
			First day cover, Jeffersonville, Ind.			2.50	
			Dull finish gum		2.00		
			Combination Booklets				
			See Nos. BK116, BK117B, BK118 and BK119.				
1278b	A710		1c green, pane of 4+2 labels, slogans 5 & 4, *May 10, 1971*		.75	20	
			First day cover, Washington, D.C.			15.00	
			Combination Booklet				
			See No. BK122.				
1280a	A712		2c dark blue gray, pane of 5+label, slogan 4, *Jan. 8, 1968*		1.20	40	
			First day cover, Buffalo, N.Y.			2.50	
			(147,244)				
			With slogan 5		1.20	40	
			Combination Booklets				
			See Nos. BK117 and BK120.				
1280c	A712		2c dark blue gray, pane of 6, *May 7, 1971*		1.00	35	
			First day cover, Spokane, Wash.			15.00	
			Dull finish gum		1.00		
			Combination Booklets				
			See Nos. BK127 and BKC22.				

The 1c and 6c panes of 8, Nos. 1278a and 1284b, were printed from 320-subject plates and from 400-subject plates, both with electric eye markings. The 2c and 6c panes of 5 stamps plus label, Nos. 1280a and 1284c, were printed from 360-subject plates.

				Perf. 10½×11			
1284b	A716		6c gray brown, pane of 8, *Dec. 28, 1967*		1.50	50	
			First day cover, Washington, D.C.			3.50	
			Combination Booklet				
	BK116	BC14C	$2 brown, 4 #1284b (6c)+ 1 #1278a (1c)		8.50		
1284c	A716		6c gray brown, pane of 5+label, slogan 4, *Jan. 9, 1968*		1.25	50	
			First day cover, Washington, D.C.			110.00	
			With slogan 5		1.25	50	
			Combination Booklet				
	BK117	BC15C	$1 brown, 3 #1284c (6c) + 1 #1280a (2c) (2)		6.00		

No. BK117 contains panes with slogan 4, slogan 5 or combinations of 4 and 5.

				Perf. 10			
1288c	A720		15c dark rose claret, pane of 8, *June 24, 1978*		2.40	1.25	
			First day cover, Boston, Mass.			4.00	
1288e			As "c," vert. imperf. btwn.		125.00		
			Booklet				
	BK117A	BC23	$3.60 red & light blue		8.00		

BOOKLET PANES

Eisenhower—A815

Plate of 400 subjects for No. 1393a. Plate of 300 stamps and 60 labels for No. 1393b.

1970		Tagged	Perf. 11×10½	
1393a	A815	6c dark gray, pane of 8, *Aug. 6*	1.25	50
		First day cover, Washington, D.C.		3.75
		Dull finish gum	1.75	

Combination Booklets

BK117B	BC14A	$2 blue, 4 #1393a (6c) + 1 #1278a (1c)	—	
BK118	BC16A	$2 blue, 4 #1393a (6c) + 1 #1278a (1c)	7.00	
BK119	"	$2 blue, dull finish gum, 4 #1393a (6c) + 1 #1278a (1c)	10.00	

1393b	A815	6c dark blue gray, pane of 5+label, slogan 4, *Aug. 6*	1.20	35
		With slogan 5	1.20	35
		First day cover, Washington, D.C. (either slogan)		2.00

Combination Booklet

BK120	BC15C	$1 blue, 3 #1393b (6c) + 1 #1280a (2c)	5.50	

No. BK120 contains panes with slogan 4, slogan 5 or combinations of 4 and 5.

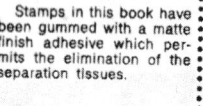

Slogans 6 and 7

Eisenhower
A815a

1971-72		Tagged	Perf. 11×10½	
1395a	A815a	8c deep claret, pane of 8, *May 10, 1971*	2.00	1.25
		First day cover, Washington, D.C.		3.50

Booklet

BK121	BC16B	$1.92 claret	7.00	

1395b	A815a	8c deep claret, pane of 6, *May 10, 1971*	1.00	75
		First day cover, Washington, D.C.		3.00

Combination Booklet

BK122	BC15B	$1 claret, 2 #1395b (8c) + 1 #1278b (1c)	4.75	

Dull Finish Gum

1395c	A815a	8c deep claret, pane of 4+2 labels, slogans 6 and 7, *Jan. 28, 1972*	1.00	50
		First day cover, Casa Grande, Ariz.		2.25

BOOKLET PANES

1395d A815 8c deep claret, pane of 7+label,
             slogan 4, *Jan. 28, 1972*   1.75   1.00
             With slogan 5   1.75   1.00
             First day cover, Casa Grande, Ariz.   2.50

The first day cancellation was applied to 181,601 covers bearing Nos. 1395c or 1395d.

Combination Booklet

BK123 BC17A $2 claret, *yellow*, 3
              #1395d + 1 #1395c   7.50

Plate of 400 subjects for No. 1395a. Plate of 360 subjects for No. 1395b. Plate of 300 subjects (200 stamps and 100 double-size labels) for No. 1395c. Plate of 400 subjects (350 stamps and 50 labels) for No. 1395d.

Slogan 9

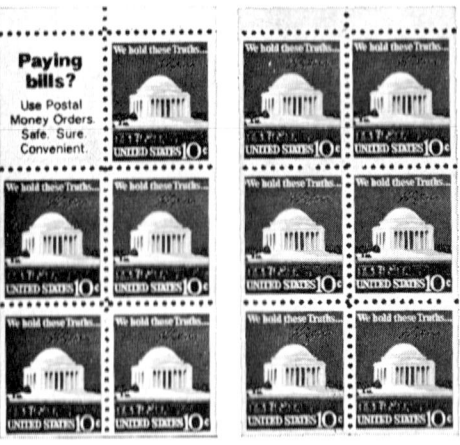

Slogan 8

Jefferson Memorial—A924

			Perf. 11×10½	
1973-74		**Tagged**		
1510b	A924	10c blue, pane of 5+label, slogan 8, *Dec. 14, 1973*	1.50	30
		First day cover, Washington, D.C.		2.75
		Booklet		
BK124	BC17B	$1 red & blue	3.50	
1510c	A924	10c blue, pane of 8, *Dec. 14, 1973*	1.60	30
		First day cover, Washington, D.C.		3.00
		Booklet		
BK125	BC17C	$4 red & blue	9.00	
1510d	A924	10c blue, pane of 6, *Aug. 5, 1974*	2.50	30
		First day cover, Oakland, Calif.		3.00
		Combination Booklet		
BK126	BC17D	$1.25 red & blue, 1 #1510d (10c) + 1 #C79a (13c)	6.00	

Liberty Bell
A998

			Perf. 11×10½	
1975-78		**Tagged**		
1595a	A998	13c brown, pane of 6, *Oct. 31, 1975*	1.60	50
		First day cover, Cleveland, Ohio		2.00
		Combination Booklet		
BK127	BC19A	90c red & blue, 1 #1595a (13c) + 1 #1280c (2c)	3.00	
1595b	A998	13c brown, pane of 7+label, slogan 8, *Oct. 31, 1975*	1.80	50
		First day cover, Cleveland, Ohio		2.75
1595c	A998	13c brown, pane of 8, *Oct. 31, 1975*	2.10	50
		First day cover, Cleveland, Ohio		2.50
		Combination Booklet		
BK128	BC19B	$2.99 red & blue, 2 #1595c (13c) + 1 #1595b (13c)	6.50	
1595d	A998	13c brown, pane of 5+label, slogan 9, *Apr. 2, 1976*	1.30	50
		First day cover, Liberty, Mo.		2.25
		Booklet		
BK129	BC19A	$1.30 red & blue	3.00	

472 BOOKLET PANES

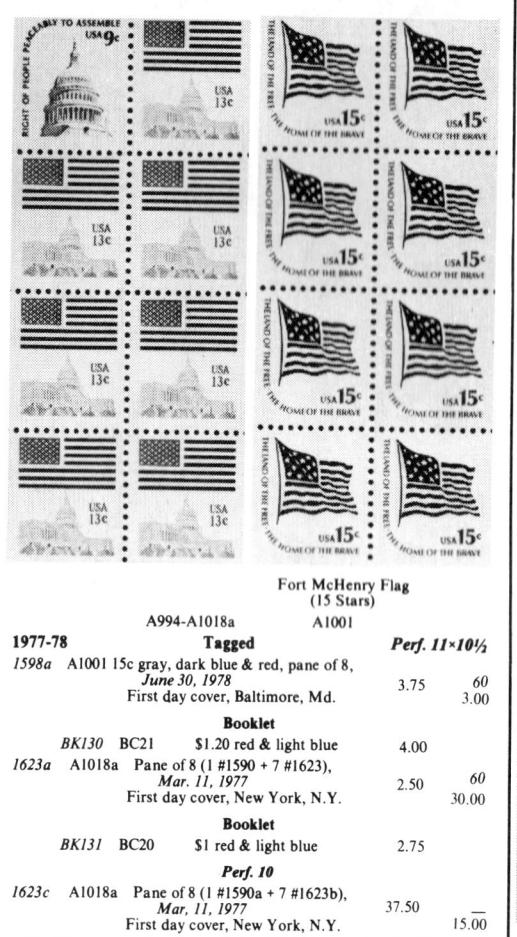

Fort McHenry Flag
(15 Stars)
A994-A1018a   A1001

1977-78		**Tagged**		***Perf. 11×10½***
1598a	A1001	15c gray, dark blue & red, pane of 8, June 30, 1978	3.75	60
		First day cover, Baltimore, Md.		3.00
		Booklet		
	BK130	BC21	$1.20 red & light blue	4.00
1623a	A1018a	Pane of 8 (1 #1590 + 7 #1623), Mar. 11, 1977	2.50	60
		First day cover, New York, N.Y.		30.00
		Booklet		
	BK131	BC20	$1 red & light blue	2.75
		Perf. 10		
1623c	A1018a	Pane of 8 (1 #1590a + 7 #1623b), Mar. 11, 1977	37.50	—
		First day cover, New York, N.Y.		15.00

First day cancellation was applied to 242,208 covers bearing Nos. 1623a or 1623c.

		Booklet		
	BK132	BC20	$1 red & light blue	45.00

Red Masterpiece and Medallion Roses
A1126
Perf. 10

1737a	A1126	15c multicolored, pane of 8, July 11, 1978	2.40	60
		First day cover, Shreveport, La.		3.00
1737b		As "a," imperf.	—	
		Booklet		
	BK134	BC22	$2.40 rose red & yellow green	5.00

Windmills A1127-A1131

1980		**Tagged**		***Perf. 11***
1742a	A1131	15c sepia, *yellow,* pane of 10, Feb. 7	3.50	60
		Booklet		
	BK135	BC25	$3 lt. blue & dark blue, blue	7.25

Eagle
A1124

1978		**Tagged**		***Perf. 11×10½***
1736a	A1124	(15c) orange, pane of 8, *May 22, 1978*	2.40	60
		First day cover, Memphis, Tenn.		3.00
		Booklet		
	BK133	BC24	$3.60 deep orange	8.00

BOOKLET PANES 473

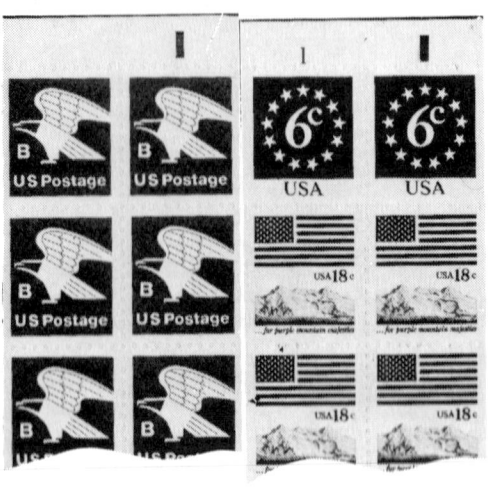

A1207   A1279-A1280

1889a	A1267- A1276	18c dark brown, pane of 10, May 14 First day cover, Boise, ID		3.60	— 7.00
		Booklet			
	BK137	BC28	$3.60 gray & olive	7.50	
1893a	A1279- A1280	Pane of 8 (2 #1892, 6 #1893), Apr. 24 First day cover, Portland, ME		2.40	— 3.00
1893b		As "a," vert. imperf. btwn.		65.00	
		Booklet			
	BK138	BC27	$1.20 blue & red	2.50	

A1281

1896a	A1281	20c black, dark blue & red, pane of 6, Dec. 17, 1981		2.50	—
		First day cover, Washington, D.C.			8.00
		Booklet			
	BK139	BC29	$1.20 blue & red	2.75	
1896b	A1281	20c black, dark blue & red, pane of 10, June 1, 1982		4.25	—
		First day cover, Washington, D.C.			—
		Scored perforation		4.25	—
		Booklets			
	BK140	BC29	$2 blue & red	4.50	—
	BK140A	BC29B	$4 blue & red	8.50	—

A1267-A1276

A1296

1983

1909a	A1296	$9.35 multi, pane of 3, Aug. 12, 1983		62.50	—
		First day cover, Kennedy Space Center, FL			—
		Booklet			
	BK140B	BC31	$28.05 blue & red	65.00	

1981

1819a	A1207	(18c) violet, pane of 8, Mar. 15	4.50	3.00	*1.50*	
		First day cover, San Francisco, CA			4.00	
		Booklet				
	BK136	BC26	$4.32 dull violet		14.50	

BOOKLET PANES

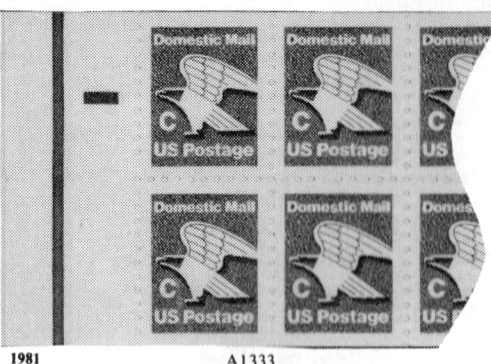

1981 A1333

1948a	A1333	(20c) brown, pane of 10, *Oct. 11, 1981*	4.25	—
		First day cover, Memphis, TN		

Booklet

BK141	BC26	$4	9.00

1982 A1334

1949a	A1334	20c dark blue, pane of 10, *Jan. 8, 1982*	4.00	—
		First day cover, Bighorn, MI		8.00
1949b		As "a," vert. imperf. btwn.	85.00	

Booklet

BK142	BC30	$4	8.50

A1497

1985 **Perf. 11**

2113a	A1497	(22c) green, pane of 10	4.40	—
		Feb. 1, 1985		9.00
		First day cover, Los Angeles, CA		

Booklet

BK143	BC26	$4.40 green	9.50

A1499

Perf. 10 Horiz.

2116a	A1499	22c blue, red & black,	2.20	—
		pane of 5, *Mar. 29, 1985*		4.50
		First day cover, Waubeka, WI		

Booklets

BK144	BC32	$1.10	2.50
BK145	BC32	$2.20	5.00

A1505

BOOKLET PANES

1986

2201a	A1581-A1584	22c	multicolored, pane of 4, *Jan. 23, 1986*	1.80	—
			First day cover, State College, PA		3.75

Booklet

| BK149 | BC34 | $1.76 | 4.25 |

A1500-A1504

Perf. 10

2121a	A1500-A1504	22c	multicolored, pane of 10, *Apr. 4, 1985*	4.40	—
			First day cover, Boston, MA		9.00

Booklets

| BK146 | BC33A | $4.40 multi | 9.50 |
| BK147 | BC33B | $4.40 multi | 9.50 |

Perf. 10 Vert.

2122a	A1505	$10.75	multicolored, pane of 3, *Apr. 29, 1985*	67.50	—
			First day cover, San Francisco, CA		—

Booklet

| BK148 | BC31 | $32.25 | 70.00 |

A1581-A1584

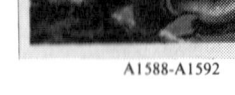

A1588-A1592

2209a	A1588-A1592	22c	multicolored, pane of 5, *Mar. 21, 1986*	2.25	—
			First day cover, Seattle, WA		4.00

Booklet

| BK150 | BC35 | $2.20 | 5.00 |

BOOKLET PANES

AIR POST STAMPS.

Spirit of St. Louis
AP6
FLAT PLATE PRINTING.

1928   *Perf. 11.*

C10a	AP6	10c dark blue, *May 26*	100.00	60.00
		First day cover, Washington, D.C.		925.00
		First day cover, Cleveland, Midwestern Philatelic Sta. cancel		900.00
		Tab at bottom		—

No. C10a was printed from specially designed 180-subject plates arranged exactly as a 360-subject plate—each pane of three occupying the relative position of a pane of six in a 360-subject plate. Plate numbers appear at the sides, therefore Position D does not exist except partially on panes which have been trimmed off center All other plate positions common to a 360-subject plate are known.

Booklet

BKC1	BC8	61c blue	—

AP17

1943   **ROTARY PRESS PRINTINGS.**

C25a	AP17	6c carmine, *Mar. 18, 1943*	6.50	1.00
		First day cover, Washington, D.C.		25.00

180-Subject Plates Electric Eye Convertible.

Booklets

BKC2	BC10A	37c red	—
BKC3	BC10B	73c red	—

AP19

1949   *Perf. 10½×11.*

C39a	AP19	6c carmine, *Nov. 18, 1949*	12.00	5.00
		First day cover, New York, N.Y.		10.00

Booklet

BKC4	BC11A	73c red (2)	—

AP33

1958

C51a	AP33	7c blue, *July 31, 1958*	15.00	6.50
		First day cover, San Antonio, Tex. (119,769)		9.50

Booklets

BKC5	BC11B	85c on 73c red	—
BKC6	BC11C	85c blue	—

BOOKLET PANES

477

1960

C60a	AP33	7c carmine, *Aug. 19, 1960*	20.00	7.00
		First day cover, St. Louis, Mo.		9.50
		(143,363)		

Booklets

| BKC7 | BC11C | 85c blue | — |
| BKC8 | " | 85c red | — |

1962-64 AP42

C64b	AP42	8c carmine, pane of 5+label, slogan 1, *Dec. 5, 1962*	7.50	1.25
		First day cover, Washington, D.C. (146,835)		2.00
		With slogan 2, *1963*	25.00	5.00
		With slogan 3, *1964*	12.50	1.25

Booklets

BKC9	BC11D	80c black, *pink*, slogan 1	—
BKC10	BC11E	$2 red, *pink*, slogan 1	—
BKC11	BC11D	80c black, *pink*, slogan 3 (2)	—
BKC12	BC11E	$2 red, *pink*, slogan 2	—
BKC13	BC13B	$2 red, *pink*, slogan 2	—
BKC14	"	$2 red, slogan 3	—
BKC15	"	$2 red, *pink*, slogan 3	—

| C64c | AP42 | As No. C64b, tagged, slogan 3, *1964* | 2.25 | .50 |

Plate of 360 subjects (300 stamps, 60 labels).

Booklets

BKC16	BC11D	80c black (2)	6.00
BKC17	"	80c black, *pink*	6.00
BKC18	BC13B	$2 red, *pink*	13.00
BKC19	"	$2 red (3)	13.00

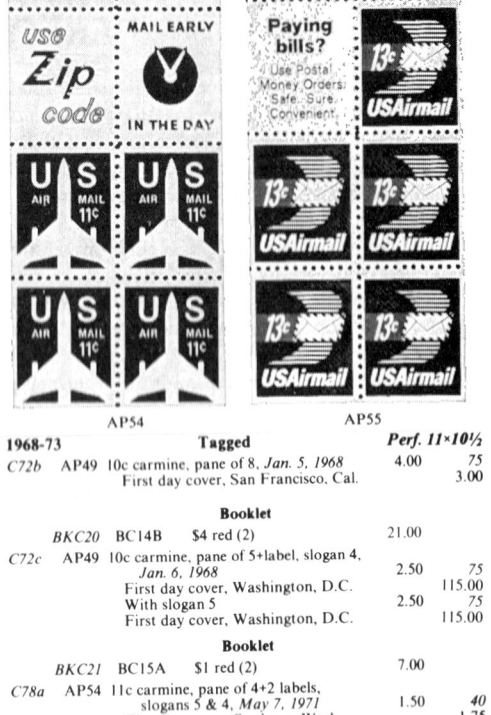

AP54   AP55

1968-73   Tagged   Perf. 11×10½

C72b	AP49	10c carmine, pane of 8, *Jan. 5, 1968*	4.00	75
		First day cover, San Francisco, Cal.		3.00

Booklet

| BKC20 | BC14B | $4 red (2) | 21.00 |

C72c	AP49	10c carmine, pane of 5+label, slogan 4, *Jan. 6, 1968*	2.50	75
		First day cover, Washington, D.C.		115.00
		With slogan 5	2.50	75
		First day cover, Washington, D.C.		115.00

Booklet

| BKC21 | BC15A | $1 red (2) | 7.00 |

C78a	AP54	11c carmine, pane of 4+2 labels, slogans 5 & 4, *May 7, 1971*	1.50	40
		First day cover, Spokane, Wash.		1.75

Combination Booklet

| BKC22 | BC15D | $1 red, 2 #C78a (11c) + 1 #1280c (2c) | 5.00 |

C79a	AP55	13c carmine, pane of 5+label, slogan 8, *Dec. 27, 1973*	1.35	70
		First day cover, Chicago, Ill.		1.75

Booklet

| BKC23 | BC18 | $1.30 blue & red | 3.00 |

Combination Booklet

See No. BK126.

No. C72b, the 8-stamp pane, was printed from 320-subject plate and from 400-subject plate; No. C72c, C78a and C79a from 360-subject plates.

AP49

VENDING AND AFFIXING MACHINE PERFORATIONS

Imperforate sheets of 400 were first issued in 1906 on the request of several makers of vending and affixing machines. The machine manufacturers made coils from the imperforate sheets and applied various perforations to suit the particular needs of their machines. These privately applied perforations were used for many years and form a chapter of postal history.

Unused prices are for pairs, used prices for singles. "On cover" prices are for single stamps commercially used in the proper period.

The 2mm. and 3mm. spacings refer only to the 1908-11 issues. Prices for intermediate spacings would roughly correspond to the lower-priced of the two listed spacings.

Many varieties are suspected or known to have been perforated for philatelic purposes and not actually used in machines. These are indicated by an asterisk before the number. Several of these privately applied perforation varieties exist in blocks, which were not produced in the regular course of business. They are generally valued as a multiple of the coil pairs contained with a slight premium for plate numbers attached.

Counterfeits are prevalent, especially of items having a basic imperf. priced far lower than the vending machine coil.

The Vending and Affixing Machine Perforations Committee of the Bureau Issues Association compiled these listings.

THE BRINKERHOFF COMPANY.
Sedalia, Mo.
Manufacturers of Vending Machines.

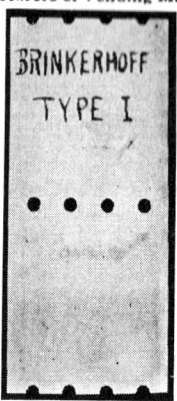

Perforations Type I.
Stamps were cut into strips and joined before being perforated.

		Unused Pair	Used Single
	On Issue of 1906-08.		
314	1c blue green	70.00	12.00
	Guide line pair	85.00	
320	2c carmine	60.00	12.00
	Guide line pair	85.00	
*320a	2c lake	50.00	10.00
	Guide line pair	75.00	
	On Issue of 1908-09		
*343	1c green	45.00	9.00
	Guide line pair	65.00	
*344	2c carmine	45.00	9.00
	Guide line pair	65.00	
	On cover		125.00
*345	3c deep violet	60.00	
	Guide line pair	80.00	
*346	4c orange brown	80.00	35.00
	Guide line pair	120.00	
*347	5c blue	90.00	35.00
	Guide line pair	125.00	
	On Lincoln Issue of 1909.		
*368	2c carmine, coiled endwise	60.00	15.00
	Guide line pair	80.00	

		Unused Pair	Used Single
	On Alaska-Yukon Issue of 1909.		
*371	2c carmine, coiled sideways	200.00	
	On Issue of 1912.		
*408	1c green	20.00	7.00
	Guide line or paste-up pair	35.00	
*409	2c carmine	20.00	7.00
	Guide line or paste-up pair	35.00	

 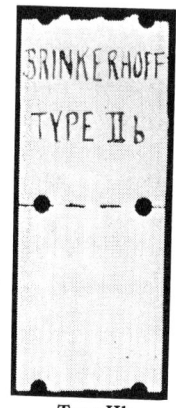

Type IIa. One knife cut.   **Type IIb.** Two knife cuts.

Perforations Type II.
The Type II perforations consist of two holes. The knife cuts separating the stamps were applied by the vending machine and were of two types as illustrated above. All items listed below are known without knife cuts, but did not pass through the vending machine.

Type			Unused Pair	Used Single
		On Issue of 1906-08.		
314	II	1c blue green	45.00	
	IIa	1c blue green	40.00	4.00
		Guide line pair	50.00	
	*IIb	1c blue green	85.00	
320	II	2c carmine	60.00	
	IIa	2c carmine	25.00	5.00
		Guide line pair	40.00	
320a	II	2c lake	65.00	
	IIa	2c lake	25.00	5.00
		On cover		350.00
		Guide line or paste-up pair	40.00	
	*IIb	2c lake	100.00	

VENDING AND AFFIXING MACHINE PERFORATIONS 479

Type			Unused Pair	Used Single
		On Issue of 1908-09.		
343	II	1c green	32.50	
		Guide line pair	45.00	
	IIa	1c green	10.00	1.25
		Paste-up pair	15.00	
	IIb	1c green	11.50	
		Paste-up pair	16.50	
344	II	2c carmine	40.00	
		Paste-up pair	60.00	
		On cover, pair		550.00
	IIa	2c carmine	7.50	1.00
		Guide line pair	12.50	
		On cover		175.00
	IIb	2c carmine	12.50	2.00
		Guide line or paste-up pair	17.50	
*345	II	3c deep violet	45.00	
	*IIa	3c deep violet	40.00	4.00
		Guide line pair	55.00	
	*IIb	3c deep violet	85.00	
*346	II	4c orange brown	80.00	
		Guide line pair	100.00	
	*IIa	4c orange brown	75.00	
		Guide line or paste-up pair	100.00	
	*IIb	4c orange brown	100.00	15.00
*347	II	5c blue	120.00	
		Guide line pair	150.00	
	*IIa	5c blue	100.00	40.00
		On cover		650.00
	*IIb	5c blue	110.00	
		On Lincoln Issue of 1909.		
368	II	2c carmine	70.00	
		Guide line pair	90.00	
	IIa	2c carmine	60.00	6.00
		Guide line pair	75.00	
	IIb	2c carmine	65.00	7.50
		Guide line pair	85.00	
		On Alaska-Yukon Issue of 1909.		
371	II	2c carmine, coiled sideways	75.00	
		Guide line or paste-up pair	100.00	
	II	2c carmine, coiled endwise	175.00	
		Guide line pair	200.00	
	IIa	2c carmine, coiled sideways	85.00	10.00
		On cover		400.00
		Guide line or paste-up pair	100.00	
		On Hudson-Fulton Issue of 1909.		
*373	II	2c carmine, coiled sidewise	165.00	
		Guide line pair	225.00	
		On Issue of 1911.		
383	II	1c green	10.00	
		Guide line pair	13.50	
	IIa	1c green	15.00	4.00
	IIb	1c green	10.00	
		Guide line pair	15.00	
384	II	2c carmine	7.50	
		Guide line pair	10.00	
	IIa	2c carmine	25.00	
	IIb	2c carmine	20.00	3.50
		On Issue of 1912.		
408	II	1c green	60.00	
		Guide line pair	80.00	
		On cover		175.00
	*IIa	1c green	70.00	
		Guide line pair	85.00	
	IIb	1c green	5.00	2.25
		Guide line pair	7.00	
409	II	2c carmine	70.00	
		Guide line pair	100.00	
	*IIa	2c carmine	75.00	
		Guide line pair	110.00	
	IIb	2c carmine	5.00	
		Guide line pair	7.00	

THE FARWELL COMPANY.
Chicago, Ill.

A wholesale dry goods firm using Schermack (Mailometer) affixing machines. In 1911 the Farwell Company began to make and perforate their own coils. These were sometimes wrongly called "Chambers" perforations.

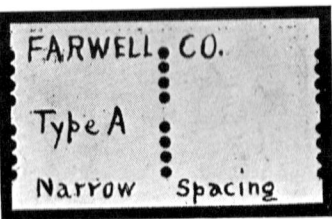

Type A.

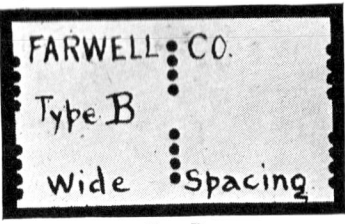

Type B.

Stamps were perforated in sheets, then cut into strips and coiled. Blocks exist.

The following listings are grouped according to the number of holes, further divided into two types of spacing, narrow and wide. The type symbols (3A2) indicate 3 holes over 2 holes with narrow, type A, spacing between groups. Types A and B occurred in different rows on the same sheet.

Left margin or paste-up stamps sometimes show different perforation type on the two sides.

			Unused Pair Spacing 2mm. / 3mm.	Used Single
		Group 1, no spacing.		
		On Issue of 1911.		
384		2c carmine, 7 holes	450.00	200.00
		On cover		1100.00
384		2c carmine, 6 holes	550.00	
		Group 2, two and three holes.		
		On Issue of 1911.		
	Type			
383	2B3	1c green	200.00	75.00
	3A2	1c green	200.00	
		Guide line pair	325.00	
384	2A3	2c carmine	200.00 / 200.00	
		On cover		850.00
	2B3	2c carmine	200.00	75.00
		On cover		
	3A2	2c carmine	200.00 / 200.00	60.00
		On cover		850.00
		Guide line pair	325.00	
	3B2	2c carmine	200.00	
		Guide line pair	325.00	
		Group 3, three and four holes.		
		On Issue of 1911.		
383	3B4	1c green		100.00
	4B3	1c green	150.00 / 150.00	30.00
384	3B4	2c carmine	75.00	
		On cover		500.00
		Guide line pair	150.00	
	4B3	2c carmine	225.00	50.00
		On cover		550.00

VENDING AND AFFIXING MACHINE PERFORMATIONS

			Unused Pair Spacing		Used
			2 mm.	3 mm.	Single

Group 4, four and four holes.
On Issue of 1908-09.

343	*A	1c green	80.00		
	*B	1c green	70.00		
344	*A	2c carmine	80.00		
	*B	2c carmine	65.00		

On Lincoln Issue of 1909.

| 368 | *A | 2c carmine | 200.00 | | |
| | *B | 2c carmine | — | | |

On Issue of 1911.

383	A	1c green	15.00	14.00	
		Guide line pair	25.00		
	B	1c green	15.00	14.00	—
		Guide line pair	25.00		
384	A	2c carmine	20.00	15.00	2.50
		Guide line pair	30.00		
	B	2c carmine	22.50	17.50	2.50
		Guide line pair	35.00		
		On cover			175.00

On Issue of 1912.

408	A	1c green		10.00	1.00
		On cover			65.00
		Guide line pair		15.00	
	B	1c green		10.00	1.25
		Guide line pair		15.00	
409	A	2c carmine		5.00	.75
		On cover			65.00
		Guide line pair		7.50	
	B	2c carmine		7.50	1.00
		On cover			65.00
		Guide line pair		10.00	

On Issue of 1916-17.

| 482 | A | 2c carmine | 100.00 | | 10.00 |
| | B | 2c carmine | 120.00 | | 10.00 |

Group 5, four and five holes.
On Issue of 1911.

383	4A5	1c green	90.00		
		Guide line pair	125.00		
384	4A5	2c carmine	65.00	70.00	—
		Guide line pair	100.00		

On Issue of 1912.

408	4A5	1c green		75.00	
		Guide line pair		100.00	
	*5A4	1c green		125.00	
		Guide line pair		175.00	
409	*4A5	2c carmine		125.00	—
	*5A4	2c carmine		125.00	
		Guide line pair		175.00	

INTERNATIONAL VENDING MACHINE CO.
Baltimore, Md.

Similar to the Government Coil stamp No. 322, but perforated 12½ to 13.

On Issue of 1906.

| 320b | | 2c scarlet | 500.00 |

On Issue of 1908–09.

343	1c green	—
344	2c carmine	—
345	3c deep violet	—
346	4c orange brown	—
347	5c blue	—

THE MAILOMETER COMPANY.
Detroit, Mich.

Formerly the Schermack Mailing Machine Co., then Mail-om-eter Co., and later the Mail-O-Meter Co. Their round-hole perforations were developed in an attempt to get the Bureau of Engraving and Printing to adopt a larger perforation for coil stamps.

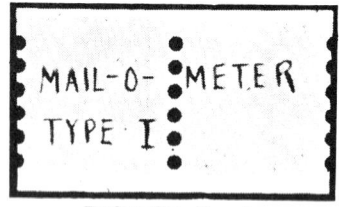

Perforations Type I.

Used experimentally in Detroit and Chicago in August, 1909. Later used regularly in the St. Louis branch.

			Unused Pair Spacing		Used
			2 mm.	3 mm.	Single

On Issue of 1906-08.

*320		2c carmine	100.00		
*320a		2c lake	75.00		
		Guide line pair	90.00		
*320b		2c scarlet	75.00		

On Issue of 1908-09.

343		1c green	10.00	11.00	10.00
		On cover			150.00
		Guide line pair	13.50		
344		2c carmine	10.00	11.00	1.50
		On cover, St. Louis			65.00
		On cover, Detroit or Chicago			125.00
		Guide line pair	13.50		
345		3c deep violet	30.00		5.00
		Guide line pair	40.00		
346		4c orange brown	60.00	50.00	9.00
		Guide line pair	85.00		
347		5c blue	85.00		10.00
		Guide line pair	110.00		

On Lincoln Issue of 1909.

| *368 | | 2c carmine | 75.00 | 60.00 | 35.00 |
| | | Guide line or paste-up pair | 95.00 | | |

On Alaska-Yukon Issue of 1909.

| *371 | | 2c carmine | 80.00 | | 25.00 |
| | | Guide line pair | 100.00 | | |

On Hudson-Fulton Issue of 1909.

| *373 | | 2c carmine | 80.00 | | 25.00 |
| | | Guide line or paste-up pair | 100.00 | | |

On Issue of 1911.

383		1c green	5.00	3.75	1.00
		Guide line pair	6.50		
384		2c carmine	9.00	8.00	1.50
		On cover			50.00
		Guide line pair	12.50		

On Issue of 1912.

*408		1c green		4.50	1.25
		Guide line pair		6.00	
*409		2c carmine		4.50	1.25
		Guide line pair		6.00	

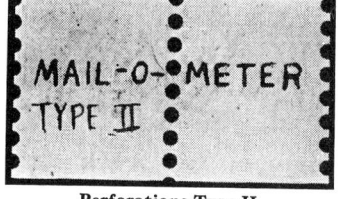

Perforations Type II.

Used experimentally in Detroit from 1909 to 1911.

On Issue of 1906-08.

| *320 | | 2c carmine | 90.00 | | |
| *320b | | 2c scarlet | 175.00 | | |

On Issue of 1908-09.

343		1c green	13.00	12.00	4.00
		Guide line pair	17.50		
344		2c carmine	21.00	20.00	4.00
		On cover			185.00
		Guide line pair	27.50		
*345		3c deep violet	100.00		15.00
*346		4c orange brown	120.00	110.00	
*347		5c blue	150.00		

VENDING AND AFFIXING MACHINE PERFORATIONS

		Unused Pair Spacing 2 mm.	3 mm.	Used Single
	On Lincoln Issue of 1909.			
*368	2c carmine	85.00	80.00	
	On Alaska-Yukon Issue of 1909.			
*371	2c carmine		90.00	
	On Hudson-Fulton Issue of 1909.			
*373	2c carmine		100.00	
	Guide line or paste-up pair		120.00	
	On Issue of 1911.			
383	1c green	50.00	45.00	10.00
	Guide line or paste-up pair		60.00	
384	2c carmine		60.00	12.50
	On cover			175.00

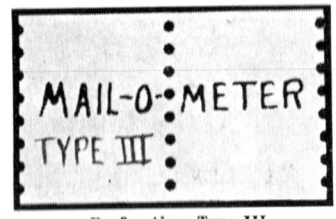

Perforations Type III.

Used experimentally in Detroit in 1910.

	On Issue of 1906-08.			
*320	2c carmine		110.00	
*320b	2c scarlet		125.00	
	On Issue of 1908-09.			
343	1c green	30.00	25.00	
	Guide line pair	40.00		
344	2c carmine	40.00	35.00	
	Guide line pair	55.00		
*345	3c deep violet		90.00	
*346	4c orange brown	130.00	120.00	
*347	5c blue		325.00	
	On Lincoln Issue of 1909.			
*368	2c carmine	90.00	80.00	25.00
	On Alaska-Yukon Issue of 1909.			
*371	2c carmine		110.00	
	On Hudson-Fulton Issue of 1909.			
*373	2c carmine		100.00	

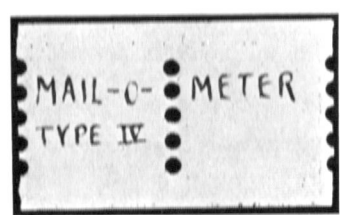

Perforations Type IV.

Used in St. Louis branch office.
Blocks exist but were not regularly produced or issued.

	On Issue of 1906-08.			
*320	2c carmine		120.00	35.00
*320b	2c scarlet		100.00	25.00

		Unused Pair Spacing 2 mm.	3 mm.	Used Single
	On Issue of 1908-09			
343	1c green	15.00	13.00	4.00
	Guide line pair	22.50		
344	2c carmine	22.50	20.00	3.50
	Guide line or paste-up pair	32.50		
345	3c deep violet	60.00		
	Guide line or paste-up pair	75.00		
346	4c orange brown	80.00	75.00	
	Guide line pair	110.00		
347	5c blue	135.00		
	Guide line pair	175.00		
	On Lincoln Issue of 1909.			
*368	2c carmine	75.00	65.00	12.50
	Guide line or paste-up pair	100.00		
	On Alaska-Yukon Issue of 1909.			
*371	2c carmine		200.00	
	Guide line pair		225.00	
	On Hudson-Fulton Issue of 1909.			
*373	2c carmine		200.00	
	Guide line pair		225.00	
	On Issue of 1911.			
383	1c green	2.75	2.50	60
	On cover			65.00
	Guide line pair	4.00		
384	2c carmine	7.50	6.50	40
	On cover			60.00
	Guide line pair	10.00		
	On Issue of 1912.			
408	1c green		2.00	40
	On cover			10.00
	Guide line or paste-up pair		3.00	
409	2c carmine		2.25	25
	On cover			10.00
	Guide line or paste-up pair		3.75	
	On Issue of 1916-17			
482	2c carmine	70.00		25.00
	On cover			225.00
	Guide line pair	100.00		
483	3c violet, type I	75.00		—
	On cover			200.00
	Paste-up pair	100.00		

THE SCHERMACK COMPANY.

Detroit, Mich.

These perforations were developed by the Schermack Mailing Machine Co. before it became the Mailometer Co. The Type III perforation was used in Mailometer affixing machines from 1909 through 1927.

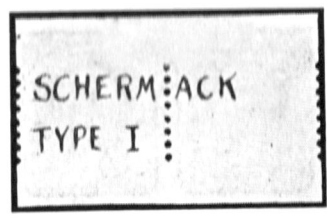

Perforations Type I. Eight Holes.

Perforated in sheets, then cut into strips and coiled.

VENDING AND AFFIXING MACHINE PERFORATIONS

		Unused Pair Spacing 2mm. 3mm.	Used Single
	On Issue of 1906-08.		
314	1c blue green	100.00	15.00
	Guide line pair	125.00	
	*Seven holes	325.00	
	*Six holes	225.00	
	*Guide line pair	300.00	
320	2c carmine	65.00	15.00
	On cover		—
	Guide line pair	90.00	
	Seven holes	225.00	
	On cover		—
	Guide line or paste-up pair	300.00	
	*Six holes	175.00	
*320a	2c lake	150.00	45.00
	*Seven holes	225.00	
	*Six holes	200.00	
*315	5c blue	1350.00	
	On Issue of 1908-09.		
*343	1c green		20.00
	Guide line pair	75.00	
*344	2c carmine		
	Guide line pair	75.00	
*345	3c deep violet		
	Guide line pair	85.00	
*346	4c orange brown	85.00	
	Guide line pair	125.00	
*347	5c blue	85.00	
	Guide line pair	110.00	
	On Lincoln Issue of 1909.		
*368	2c carmine	85.00 80.00	30.00
	Guide line pair	95.00	
	*Seven holes	275.00	
	*Six holes	275.00	

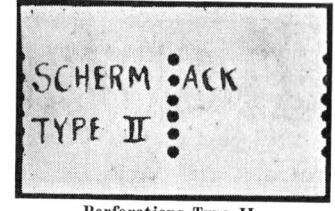

Perforations Type II.

Cut into strips and joined before being perforated.

	On Issue of 1906–08.		
314	1c blue green	80.00	30.00
	Guide line pair	100.00	
320	2c carmine	60.00	25.00
	Guide line pair	75.00	
*320a	2c lake	100.00	40.00
	Guide line pair	120.00	
*315	5c blue	1350.00	550.00
	Guide line pair	—	
	On Issue of 1908–09.		
*343	1c green	65.00 60.00	
	Guide line pair	90.00	
*344	2c carmine	65.00	
	Guide line pair	90.00	
*345	3c deep violet	75.00	
	Guide line pair	100.00	
*346	4c orange brown	85.00	
	Guide line pair	110.00	
*347	5c blue	135.00	
	Guide line pair	175.00	
	On Issue of 1912		
*368	2c carmine	75.00 70.00	20.00
	Guide line pair	95.00	
	On Issue of 1912.		
*383	1c green	—	

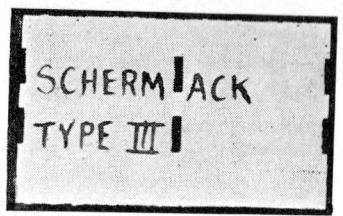

Perforations Type III.

Blocks exist but were not regularly produced or issued.

		Unused Pair Spacing 2mm. 3mm.	Used Single
	On Issue of 1906-08.		
314	1c blue green	15.00	1.00
	On cover		75.00
	Guide line or paste-up pair	20.00	
320	2c carmine	20.00	2.50
	On cover		75.00
	Guide line pair	30.00	
*320a	2c lake	25.00	1.00
	On cover		75.00
	Guide line or paste-up pair	30.00	
*320b	2c scarlet	25.00	2.75
	Guide line pair	30.00	
*314A	4c brown	45,000.00	9000.00
	On cover		22,500.00
	Guide line pair	95,000.00	
*315	5c blue	1100.00	
	On Issue of 1908-09.		
*343	1c green	5.00 6.00	40
	On cover		20.00
	Guide line or paste-up pair	7.00	
*344	2c carmine	5.00 6.00	40
	On cover		20.00
	Guide line or paste-up pair	7.00	
*345	3c deep violet	20.00 150.00	2.50
	Guide line pair	25.00	
*346	4c orange brown	30.00 20.00	2.50
	Guide line or paste-up pair	40.00	
*347	5c blue	40.00	7.50
	Guide line pair	50.00	
	On Lincoln Issue of 1909.		
*368	2c carmine	50.00 45.00	4.00
	On cover		200.00
	Guide line or paste-up pair	65.00	
	On Alaska-Yukon Issue of 1909.		
*371	2c carmine	70.00	
	Guide line or paste-up pair	85.00	
	On Hudson-Fulton Issue of 1909.		
*373	2c carmine	70.00	
	Guide line or paste-up pair	85.00	
	On Issue of 1911.		
*383	1c green	2.25 2.00	40
	On cover		17.50
	Guide line or paste-up pair	5.00	
*384	2c carmine	6.00 5.00	30
	On cover		17.50
	Guide line pair	7.50	

VENDING AND AFFIXING MACHINE PERFORATIONS

		Unused Pair Spacing 2 mm. / 3 mm.	Used Single
	On Issue of 1912.		
408	1c green	75	20
	On cover		15.00
	Guide line or paste-up pair	1.00	
409	2c carmine	75	15
	On cover		15.00
	Guide line or paste-up pair	1.00	
	On Issue of 1916-17.		
481	1c green	2.25	15
	On cover		15.00
	Guide line or paste-up pair	3.00	
482	2c carmine, type I	2.75	30
	On cover		15.00
	Guide line or paste-up pair	3.75	
482A	2c carmine, type I a	—	6000.00
	On cover		9000.00
483	3c violet, type I	10.00	1.50
	On cover		55.00
	Guide line or paste-up pair	15.00	
484	3c violet, type II	15.00	2.00
	On cover		75.00
	Guide line or paste-up pair	20.00	
	On Issue of 1918-20.		
531	1c green	10.00	2.00
	On cover		65.00
	Guide line or paste-up pair	15.00	
532	2c carmine, type IV	35.00	2.00
	On cover		85.00
	Guide line or paste-up pair	45.00	
533	2c carmine, type V	350.00	40.00
	On cover		300.00
	Guide line or paste-up pair	500.00	
534	2c carmine, type Va	15.00	1.00
	On cover		85.00
	Guide line or paste-up pair	20.00	
534A	2c carmine, type VI	35.00	2.00
	On cover		85.00
	Guide line or paste-up pair	45.00	
534B	2c carmine, type VII	800.00	140.00
	On cover		450.00
	Guide line pair	1500.00	
535	3c violet, type IV	12.50	2.00
	On cover		60.00
	Guide line or paste-up pair	15.00	
	On Issue of 1923-26.		
575	1c green	125.00	4.00
	Unused single	6.50	
	On cover		65.00
	Precanceled	3.00	50
576	1½c yellow brown	4.50	60
	Guide line or paste-up pair	6.25	
	Precanceled	3.00	20
577	2c carmine	6.00	4.25	20
	On cover		20.00
	Guide line or paste-up pair	6.00	
	On Harding Issue of 1923.		
611	2c black	50.00	12.50
	On cover		75.00
	Guide line or paste-up pair	60.00	

U. S. AUTOMATIC VENDING COMPANY.

New York City.

This firm also used coil strips of manila paper, folded so as to form small "pockets," each "pocket" containing one 1c stamp and two 2c stamps, usually imperforate. The manila "pockets" were perforated type II, coiled sideways.

Separations Type I.

Cut into strips and joined before being perforated.

		Unused Pair	Used Single
	On Issue of 1906-08.		
	Coiled Endwise.		
314	1c blue green	30.00	5.00
	On cover		225.00
	Guide line or paste-up pair	40.00	
320	2c carmine	35.00	4.00
	Guide line pair	45.00	
*320a	2c lake	50.00	4.50
	Guide line or paste-up pair	60.00	
320b	2c scarlet	35.00	3.50
	On cover		225.00
	Guide line pair	45.00	
315	5c blue	1150.00	
	On cover		
	Guide line pair	1350.00	
	On Issue of 1908-09.		
	Coiled Endwise.		
343	1c green	6.00	75
	On cover		45.00
	Guide line or paste-up pair	8.00	
344	2c carmine	7.00	75
	On cover		45.00
	Guide line or paste-up pair	9.00	
*345	3c deep violet	30.00	4.00
	On cover		175.00
	Guide line or paste-up pair	40.00	
*346	4c orange brown	45.00	4.50
	Guide line or paste-up pair	55.00	
347	5c blue	85.00	15.00
	On cover		275.00
	Guide line or paste-up pair	110.00	

484 VENDING AND AFFIXING MACHINE PERFORATIONS

		Unused Pair	Used Single
	On Lincoln Issue of 1909.		
368	2c carmine, coiled endwise	50.00	4.00
	On cover		200.00
	Guide line or paste-up pair	60.00	
	On Alaska-Yukon Issue of 1909.		
*371	2c carmine, coiled sideways	60.00	5.00
	Guide line pair	75.00	
	On Issue of 1911		
383	1c green	4.00	1.25
	On cover		30.00
	Guide line or paste-up pair	6.00	
*384	2c carmine	10.00	2.25
	Guide line pair	15.00	
	On Issue of 1912.		
*408	1c green	5.00	—
	Guide line pair	7.00	
*409	2c carmine	6.00	1.25
	Guide line pair	8.00	

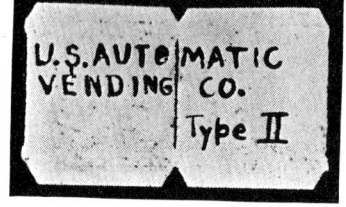

Separations Type II.

Similar to Type I but with notches further apart and a longer slit.

Cut into strips and joined before being perforated.

Coiled Sideways.

		Unused Pair Spacing 2 mm. 3 mm.	Used Single
	On Issue of 1906-08.		
*314	1c blue green	27.50	4.00
	Guide line or paste-up pair	37.50	
*320	2c carmine	45.00	
*320b	2c scarlet	32.50	2.75
	Guide line pair	40.00	
*315	5c blue	1050.00	
	Guide line pair	1250.00	
	On Issue of 1908-09.		
343	1c green	7.50	2.00
	Guide line pair	9.00	
344	2c carmine	10.00	
	Guide line pair	13.50	
*345	3c deep violet	35.00	
	Guide line pair	50.00	
*346	4c orange brown	50.00	40.00
	Guide line pair	65.00	
*347	5c blue	90.00	
	Guide line pair	110.00	
	On Lincoln Issue of 1909.		
368	2c carmine	60.00	55.00	10.00
	Guide line or paste-up pair	75.00	
	On Alaska-Yukon Issue of 1909.		
*371	2c carmine	85.00	
	Guide line or paste-up pair	100.00	
	On Hudson-Fulton Issue of 1909.		
*373	2c carmine	70.00	6.00
	On cover		250.00
	Guide line or paste-up pair	85.00	

		Unused Pair Spacing 2 mm. 3 mm.	Used Single
	On Issue of 1911.		
383	1c green	6.50	5.50
	Guide line pair	9.00	
384	2c carmine	12.00	10.00
	Guide line pair	15.00	
	On Issue of 1912.		
408	1c green	4.50	1.00
	Guide line or paste-up pair	7.00	
409	2c carmine	6.00	2.00
	Guide line pair	8.50	

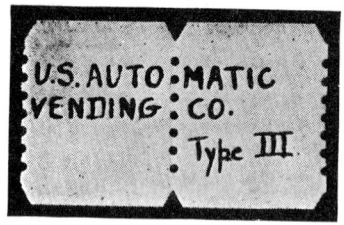

Perforations Type III.

Cut into strips and joined before being perforated.

		2 mm. 3 mm.	Used Single
	On Issue of 1906-08.		
*314	1c blue green	40.00	5.00
	Guide line pair	50.00	
*320	2c carmine	60.00	
*320b	2c scarlet	50.00	5.00
	Guide line pair	65.00	
*315	5c blue	1150.00	
	Guide line pair	1350.00	
	On Issue of 1908-09.		
343	1c green	10.00	9.00	2.50
	Guide line or paste-up pair	14.00	
344	2c carmine	10.00	2.00
	Guide line pair	14.00	
*345	3c deep violet	40.00	
	Guide line pair	50.00	
*346	4c orange brown	55.00	50.00	6.00
	Guide line pair	70.00	
*347	5c blue	75.00	
	Guide line pair	90.00	
	On Lincoln Issue of 1909.		
*368	2c carmine	60.00	50.00	10.00
	Guide line pair	75.00	
	On Alaska-Yukon Issue of 1909.		
*371	2c carmine	70.00	10.00
	Guide line or paste-up pair	85.00	
	On Hudson-Fulton Issue of 1909.		
*373	2c carmine	70.00	10.00
	Guide line or paste-up pair	85.00	
	On Issue of 1911.		
383	1c green	5.00	5.00	1.25
	Guide line pair	7.50	
384	2c carmine	6.00	6.00	1.25
	Guide line pair	8.00	
	On Issue of 1912.		
408	1c green	2.75	
	Guide line pair	3.75	
409	2c carmine	3.50	
	Guide line pair	4.75	
	On 1914 Rotary Press Coil.		
459	2c carmine	8000.00	4500.00

IMPERFORATE COIL STAMPS

The imperforate coil stamps were made from imperforate sheets of the regular issues, and were issued in coils of 500 or 1,000. The numbers assigned below are those of the regular imperforate stamps to which "S" or "E" has been added to indicate that the stamps are coiled horizontally (side by side), or vertically (end to end). These coil stamps are virtually indistinguishable from the corresponding imperforate stamps, although they can be authenticated by experts, particularly when in strips of four or longer. Many genuine imperforate coil stamps bear authenticating signatures of contemporary experts and professionals.

FLAT PLATE PRINTING.

1908 Wmkd. USPS (191)
Imperf.

314E	A115	1c blue green, pair	250.00	—
		Strip of 4	650.00	—
		Guide line pair	—	—
		Guide line strip of 4	—	—
314S	"	1c blue green, pair	—	—
		Strip of 4	—	—
		Guide line pair	—	—
		Guide line strip of 4	—	—
320E	A129	2c carmine, pair	—	—
		Strip of 4	—	—
		Guide line pair	—	—
		Guide line strip of 4	—	—
320S	"	2c carmine, pair	—	—
		Strip of 4	—	—
		Guide line pair	—	—
		Guide line strip of 4	—	—

1908-10 *Imperf.*

343E	A138	1c green, pair	22.00	8.50
		Strip of 4	50.00	—
		Guide line pair	30.00	—
		Guide line strip of 4	65.00	—
343S	"	1c green, pair	42.50	—
		Strip of 4	105.00	—
		Guide line pair	70.00	—
		Guide line strip of 4	—	—
344E	A139	2c carmine, pair	27.50	20.00
		Strip of 4	65.00	—
		Guide line pair	40.00	—
		Guide line strip of 4	75.00	—
		Double transfer, design of 1c	1250.00	—
344S	"	2c carmine, pair (2mm. spacing)	27.50	20.00
		Strip of 4	—	—
		Guide line pair	—	—
		Guide line strip of 4	30.00	—
		Pair (3mm. spacing)	—	—
		Strip of 4	45.00	—
		Guide line pair	—	—
		Guide line strip of 4	—	—
346E	A140	4c orange brown, pair	110.00	—
		Strip of 4	250.00	—
		Guide line pair	135.00	75.00
		Guide line strip of 4	—	—
347E	"	5c blue, pair	150.00	—
		Strip of 4	325.00	—
		Guide line pair	185.00	—
		Guide line strip of 4	375.00	—

1909 *Imperf.*

368E	A141	2c carmine, *Lincoln*, pair	85.00	—
		Strip of 4	200.00	—
		Guide line pair	150.00	—
		Guide line strip of 4	325.00	—
368S	A141	2c carmine, *Lincoln*, pair	150.00	—
		Strip of 4	—	—
		Guide line pair	—	—
		Guide line strip of 4	—	—

1910 Wmkd. USPS (190)
Imperf.

383E	A138	1c green, pair	11.00	—
		Strip of 4	25.00	—
		Guide line pair	15.00	—
		Guide line strip of 4	50.00	—
		Double transfer	—	—
383S	"	1c green, pair (2mm. spacing)	12.00	—
		Strip of 4	26.00	—
		Guide line pair	—	—
		Guide line strip of 4	—	—
		Pair (3mm. spacing)	12.00	—
		Strip of 4	26.00	—
		Guide line pair	—	—
		Guide line strip of 4	15.00	—
384E	A139	2c carmine, pair	12.50	—
		Strip of 4	27.50	—
		Guide line pair	17.50	—
		Guide line strip of 4	32.50	—
		Double transfer, design of 1c	1000.00	—
384S	"	2c carmine, pair (2mm. spacing)	25.00	—
		Strip of 4	60.00	—
		Guide line pair	—	—
		Guide line strip of 4	—	—
		Pair (3mm. spacing)	22.50	—
		Strip of 4	55.00	—
		Guide line pair	30.00	—
		Guide line strip of 4	—	—

1912 Wmkd. USPS (190)
Imperf.

408E	A140	1c green, pair	3.50	—
		Strip of 4	—	—
		Guide line pair	—	—
		Guide line strip of 4	—	—
408S	"	1c green, pair	3.75	—
		Strip of 4	—	—
		Guide line pair	—	—
		Guide line strip of 4	—	—
409E	"	2c carmine, pair	3.75	—
		Strip of 4	—	—
		Guide line pair	—	—
		Guide line strip of 4	—	—
409S	"	2c carmine, pair	5.00	—
		Strip of 4	—	—
		Guide line pair	—	—
		Guide line strip of 4	—	—
		Double transfer	—	—

COMMEMORATIVE STAMPS
QUANTITIES ISSUED

Cat. No.	Quantity	Cat. No.	Quantity	Cat. No.	Quantity
230	449,195,550	630 (sheet of 25)	107,398	733	5,735,944
231	1,464,588,750	643	39,974,900	734	45,137,700
232	11,501,250	644	25,628,450	735 (sheet of six)	811,404
233	19,181,550	645	101,330,328	735a	4,868,424
234	35,248,250	646	9,779,896	736	46,258,300
235	4,707,550	647	5,519,897	737	193,239,100
236	10,656,550	648	1,459,897	738	15,432,200
237	16,516,950	649	51,342,273	739	64,525,400
238	1,576,950	650	10,319,700	740	84,896,350
239	617,250	651	16,684,674	741	74,400,200
240	243,750	654	31,679,200	742	95,089,000
241	55,050	655	210,119,474	743	19,178,650
242	45,550	656	133,530,000	744	30,980,100
243	27,650	657	51,451,880	745	16,923,350
244	26,350	658	13,390,000	746	15,988,250
245	27,350	659	8,240,000	747	15,288,700
285	70,993,400	660	87,410,000	748	17,472,600
286	159,720,800	661	2,540,000	749	18,874,300
287	4,924,500	662	2,290,000	750 (sheet of six)	511,391
288	7,694,180	663	2,700,000	750a	3,068,346
289	2,927,200	664	1,450,000	751 (sheet of six)	793,551
290	4,629,760	665	1,320,000	751a	4,761,306
291	530,000	666	1,530,000	752	3,274,556
292	56,900	667	1,130,000	753	2,040,760
293	56,200	668	2,860,000	754	2,389,288
294	91,401,500	669	8,220,000	755	2,294,948
295	209,759,700	670	8,990,000	756	3,217,636
296	5,737,100	671	73,220,000	757	2,746,640
297	7,201,300	672	2,110,000	758	2,168,088
298	4,921,700	673	1,600,000	759	1,822,684
299	5,043,700	674	1,860,000	760	1,724,576
323	79,779,200	675	980,000	761	1,647,696
324	192,732,400	676	850,000	762	1,682,948
325	4,542,600	677	1,480,000	763	1,638,644
326	6,926,700	678	530,000	764	1,625,224
327	4,011,200	679	1,890,000	765	1,644,900
328	77,728,794	680	29,338,274	766 (pane of 25)	98,712
329	149,497,994	681	32,680,900	766a	2,467,800
330	7,980,594	682	74,000,800	767 (pane of 25)	85,914
367	148,387,191	683	25,215,574	767a	2,147,850
368	1,273,900	688	25,609,470	768 (pane of six)	267,200
369	637,000	689	66,487,000	768a	1,603,200
370	152,887,311	690	96,559,400	769 (pane of six)	279,960
371	525,400	702	99,074,600	769a	1,679,760
372	72,634,631	703	25,006,400	770 (pane of six)	215,920
373	216,480	704	87,969,700	770a	1,295,520
397	} 334,796,926	705	1,265,555,100	771	1,370,560
401		706	304,926,800	772	70,726,800
398	} 503,713,086	707	4,222,198,300	773	100,839,600
402		708	456,198,500	774	73,610,650
399	} 29,088,726	709	151,201,300	775	75,823,900
403		710	170,565,100	776	124,324,500
400	} 16,968,365	711	111,739,400	777	67,127,650
404		712	83,257,400	778 (sheet of four)	2,809,039
537	99,585,200	713	96,506,100	778a	2,809,039
548	137,978,207	714	75,709,200	778b	2,809,039
549	196,037,327	715	147,216,000	778c	2,809,039
550	11,321,607	716	51,102,800	778d	2,809,039
610	1,459,487,085	717	100,869,300	782	72,992,650
611	770,000	718	168,885,300	783	74,407,450
612	99,950,300	719	52,376,100	784	269,522,200
614	51,378,023	724	49,949,000	785	105,196,150
615	77,753,423	725	49,538,500	786	93,848,500
616	5,659,023	726	61,719,200	787	87,741,150
617	15,615,000	727	73,382,400	788	35,794,150
618	26,596,600	728	348,266,800	789	36,839,250
619	5,348,800	729	480,239,300	790	104,773,450
620	9,104,983	730 (sheet of 25)	456,704	791	92,054,550
621	1,900,983	730a	11,417,600	792	93,291,650
627	307,731,900	731 (sheet of 25)	441,172	793	34,552,950
628	20,280,500	731a	11,029,300	794	36,819,050
629	40,639,485	732	1,978,707,300	795	84,825,250

COMMEMORATIVE STAMPS, QUANTITIES ISSUED

Cat. No.	Quantity	Cat. No.	Quantity	Cat. No.	Quantity
796	25, 040, 400	925	50, 129, 350	1005	115, 945, 000
797	5, 277, 445	926	53, 479, 400	1006	112, 540, 000
798	99, 882, 300	927	61, 617, 350	1007	117, 415, 000
799	78, 454, 450	928	75, 500, 000	1008	2, 899, 580, 000
800	77, 004, 200	929	137, 321, 000	1009	114, 540, 000
801	81, 292, 450	930	128, 140, 000	1010	113, 135, 000
802	76, 474, 550	931	67, 255, 000	1011	116, 255, 000
835	73, 043, 650	932	133, 870, 000	1012	113, 860, 000
836	58, 564, 368	933	76, 455, 400	1013	124, 260, 000
837	65, 939, 500	934	128, 357, 750	1014	115, 735, 000
838	47, 064, 300	935	138, 863, 000	1015	115, 430, 000
852	114, 439, 600	936	111, 616, 700	1016	136, 220, 000
853	101, 699, 550	937	308, 587, 700	1017	114, 894, 600
854	72, 764, 550	938	170, 640, 000	1018	118, 706, 000
855	81, 269, 600	939	135, 927, 000	1019	114, 190, 000
856	67, 813, 350	940	260, 339, 100	1020	113, 990, 000
857	71, 394, 750	941	132, 274, 500	1021	89, 289, 600
858	66, 835, 000	942	132, 430, 000	1022	114, 865, 000
859	56, 348, 320	943	139, 209, 500	1023	115, 780, 000
860	53, 177, 110	944	114, 684, 450	1024	115, 244, 600
861	53, 260, 270	945	156, 540, 510	1025	123, 709, 600
862	22, 104, 950	946	120, 452, 600	1026	114, 789, 600
863	13, 201, 270	947	127, 104, 300	1027	115, 759, 600
864	51, 603, 580	948	10, 299, 600	1028	116, 134, 600
865	52, 100, 510	949	132, 902, 000	1029	118, 540, 000
866	51, 666, 580	950	131, 968, 000	1060	115, 810, 000
867	22, 207, 780	951	131, 488, 000	1061	113, 603, 700
868	11, 835, 530	952	122, 362, 000	1062	128, 002, 000
869	52, 471, 160	953	121, 548, 000	1063	116, 078, 150
870	52, 366, 440	954	131, 109, 500	1064	116, 139, 800
871	51, 636, 270	955	122, 650, 500	1065	120, 484, 800
872	20, 729, 030	956	121, 953, 500	1066	53, 854, 750
873	14, 125, 580	957	115, 250, 000	1067	176, 075, 000
874	59, 409, 000	958	64, 198, 500	1068	125, 944, 400
875	57, 888, 600	959	117, 642, 500	1069	122, 284, 600
876	58, 273, 180	960	77, 649, 600	1070	133, 638, 850
877	23, 779, 000	961	113, 474, 500	1071	118, 664, 600
878	15, 112, 580	962	120, 868, 500	1072	112, 434, 000
879	57, 322, 790	963	77, 800, 500	1073	129, 384, 550
880	58, 281, 580	964	52, 214, 000	1074	121, 184, 600
881	56, 398, 790	965	53, 958, 100	1075	2, 900, 731
882	21, 147, 000	966	61, 120, 010	1076	119, 784, 200
883	13, 328, 000	967	57, 823, 000	1077	123, 159, 400
884	54, 389, 510	968	52, 975, 000	1078	123, 138, 800
885	53, 636, 580	969	77, 149, 000	1079	109, 275, 000
886	55, 313, 230	970	58, 332, 000	1080	112, 932, 200
887	21, 720, 580	971	56, 228, 000	1081	125, 475, 000
888	13, 600, 580	972	57, 932, 000	1082	117, 855, 000
889	47, 599, 580	973	53, 875, 000	1083	122, 100, 000
890	53, 766, 510	974	63, 834, 000	1084	118, 180, 000
891	54, 193, 580	975	67, 162, 200	1085	100, 975, 000
892	20, 264, 580	976	64, 561, 500	1086	115, 299, 450
893	13, 726, 580	977	64, 079, 500	1087	186, 949, 627
894	46, 497, 400	978	63, 388, 000	1088	115, 235, 000
895	47, 700, 000	979	62, 285, 000	1089	106, 647, 500
896	50, 618, 150	980	57, 492, 610	1090	112, 010, 000
897	50, 034, 400	981	99, 190, 000	1091	118, 470, 000
898	60, 943, 700	982	104, 790, 000	1092	102, 230, 000
902	44, 389, 550	983	108, 805, 000	1093	102, 410, 000
903	54, 574, 550	984	107, 340, 000	1094	84, 054, 400
904	63, 558, 400	985	117, 020, 000	1095	126, 266, 000
906	21, 272, 800	986	122, 633, 000	1096	39, 489, 600
907	1, 671, 564, 200	987	130, 960, 000	1097	122, 990, 000
908	1, 227, 334, 200	988	128, 478, 000	1098	174, 372, 800
909	19, 999, 646	989	132, 090, 000	1099	114, 365, 000
910	19, 999, 646	990	130, 050, 000	1100	122, 765, 200
911	19, 999, 646	991	131, 350, 000	1104	113, 660, 200
912	19, 999, 646	992	129, 980, 000	1105	120, 196, 580
913	19, 999, 646	993	122, 315, 000	1106	120, 805, 200
914	19, 999, 646	994	122, 170, 000	1107	125, 815, 200
915	19, 999, 646	995	131, 635, 000	1108	108, 415, 200
916	14, 999, 646	996	121, 860, 000	1109	107, 195, 200
917	14, 999, 646	997	121, 120, 000	1110	115, 745, 280
918	14, 999, 646	998	119, 120, 000	1111	39, 743, 640
919	14, 999, 646	999	112, 125, 000	1112	114, 570, 200
920	14, 999, 646	1000	114, 140, 000	1113	120, 400, 200
921	14, 999, 646	1001	114, 490, 000	1114	91, 160, 200
922	61, 303, 000	1002	117, 200, 000	1115	114, 860, 200
923	61, 001, 450	1003	116, 130, 000	1116	126, 500, 000
924	60, 605, 000	1004	116, 175, 000	1117	120, 561, 280

COMMEMORATIVE STAMPS, QUANTITIES ISSUED

Cat. No.	Quantity	Cat. No.	Quantity	Cat. No.	Quantity
1118	44, 064, 576	1207	117, 870, 000	1362	142, 245, 000
1119	118, 390, 200	1230	129, 945, 000	1363	1, 410, 580, 000
1120	125, 770, 200	1231	135, 620, 000	1364	125, 100, 000
1121	114, 114, 280	1232	137, 540, 000	1365–1368	192, 570, 000
1122	156, 600, 200	1233	132, 435, 000	1369	148, 770, 000
1123	124, 200, 200	1234	135, 520, 000	1370	139, 475, 000
1124	120, 740, 200	1235	131, 420, 000	1371	187, 165, 000
1125	133, 623, 280	1236	133, 170, 000	1372	125, 555 ,000
1126	45, 569, 088	1237	130, 195, 000	1373	144, 425, 000
1127	122, 493, 280	1238	128, 450, 000	1374	135, 875, 000
1128	131, 260, 200	1239	118, 665, 000	1375	151, 110, 000
1129	47, 125, 200	1240	1, 291, 250, 000	1376–1379	159, 195, 000
1130	123, 105, 000	1241	175, 175, 000	1380	129, 540, 000
1131	126, 105, 050	1242	125, 995, 000	1381	130, 925, 000
1132	209, 170, 000	1243	128, 025, 000	1382	139, 055, 000
1133	120, 835, 000	1244	145, 700, 000	1383	150, 611, 200
1134	115, 715, 000	1245	120, 310, 000	1384	1, 709, 795, 000
1135	118, 445, 000	1246	511, 750, 000	1385	127, 545, 000
1136	111, 685, 000	1247	123, 845, 000	1386	145, 788, 800
1137	43, 099, 200	1248	122, 825, 000	1387–1390	201, 794, 200
1138	115, 444, 000	1249	453, 090, 000	1391	171, 850, 000
1139	126, 470, 000	1250	123, 245, 000	1392	142, 205, 000
1140	124, 560, 000	1251	123, 355, 000	1405	137, 660, 000
1141	115, 455, 000	1252	126, 970, 000	1406	135, 125, 000
1142	122, 060, 000	1253	121, 250, 000	1407	135, 895, 000
1143	120, 540, 000	1254–1257	1, 407, 760, 000	1408	132, 675, 000
1144	113, 075, 000	1258	120, 005, 000	1409	134, 795, 000
1145	139, 325, 000	1259	125, 800, 000	1410–1413	161, 600, 000
1146	124, 445, 000	1260	122, 230, 000	1414–1414a	683, 730, 000
1147	113, 792, 000	1261	115, 695, 000	1415–1418, 1415a–1418a	489, 255, 000
1148	44, 215, 200	1262	115, 095, 000	1419	127, 610, 000
1149	113, 195, 000	1263	119, 560, 000	1420	129, 785, 000
1150	121, 805, 000	1264	125, 180, 000	1421–1422	134, 380, 000
1151	115, 353, 000	1265	120, 135, 000	1423	136, 305, 000
1152	111, 080, 000	1266	115, 405, 000	1424	134, 840, 000
1153	153, 025, 000	1267	115, 855, 000	1425	130, 975, 000
1154	119, 665, 000	1268	115, 340, 000	1426	161, 235, 000
1155	117, 855, 000	1269	114, 840, 000	1427–1430	175, 679, 600
1156	118, 185, 000	1270	116, 140, 000	1431	138, 700, 000
1157	112, 260, 000	1271	116, 900, 000	1432	138, 165, 000
1158	125, 010, 000	1272	114, 085, 000	1433	152, 125, 000
1159	119, 798, 000	1273	114, 880, 000	1434–1435	176, 295, 000
1160	42, 696, 000	1274	26, 995, 000	1436	142, 845, 000
1161	106, 610, 000	1275	128, 495, 000	1437	148, 755, 000
1162	109, 695, 000	1276	1, 139, 930, 000	1438	139, 080, 000
1163	123, 690, 000	1306	116, 835, 000	1439	130, 755, 000
1164	123, 970, 000	1307	117, 470, 000	1440–1443	170, 208, 000
1165	124, 796, 800	1308	123, 770, 000	1444	1, 074, 350, 000
1166	42, 076, 800	1309	131, 270, 000	1445	979, 540, 000
1167	116, 210, 000	1310	122, 285, 000	1446	137, 355, 000
1168	126, 252, 000	1311	14, 680, 000	1447	150, 400, 000
1169	42, 746, 400	1312	114, 160, 000	1448–1451	172, 730, 000
1170	124, 117, 000	1313	128, 475, 000	1452	104, 090, 000
1171	119, 840, 000	1314	119, 535, 000	1453	164, 096, 000
1172	117, 187, 000	1315	125, 110, 000	1454	53, 920, 000
1173	124, 390, 000	1316	114, 853, 200	1455	153, 025, 000
1174	112, 966, 000	1317	124, 290, 000	1456–1459	201, 890, 000
1175	41, 644, 200	1318	128, 460, 000	1460	67, 335, 000
1176	110, 850, 000	1319	127, 585, 000	1461	179, 675, 000
1177	98, 616, 000	1320	115, 875, 000	1462	46, 340, 000
1178	101, 125, 000	1321	1, 173, 547, 420	1463	180, 155, 000
1179	124, 865, 000	1322	114, 015, 000	1464–1467	198, 364, 800
1180	79, 905, 000	1323	121, 105, 000	1468	185, 490, 000
1181	125, 410, 000	1324	132, 045, 000	1469	162, 335, 000
1182	112, 845, 000	1325	118, 780, 000	1470	162, 789, 950
1183	106, 210, 000	1326	121, 985, 000	1471	1, 003, 475, 000
1184	110, 810, 000	1327	111, 850, 000	1472	1, 017, 025, 000
1185	116, 995, 000	1328	117, 225, 000	1473	165, 895, 000
1186	121, 015, 000	1329	111, 515, 000	1474	166, 508, 000
1187	111, 600, 000	1330	114, 270, 000	1475	320, 055, 000
1188	110, 620, 000	1331–1332	120, 865, 000	1476	166, 005, 000
1189	109, 110, 000	1333	110, 675, 000	1477	163, 050, 000
1190	145, 350, 000	1334	110, 670, 000	1478	159, 005, 000
1191	112, 870, 000	1335	113, 825, 000	1479	147, 295, 000
1192	121, 820, 000	1336	1, 208, 700, 000	1480–1483	196, 275, 000
1193	289, 240, 000	1337	113, 330, 000	1484	139, 152, 000
1194	120, 155, 000	1339	141, 350, 000	1485	128, 048, 000
1195	124, 595, 000	1340	144, 345, 000	1486	146, 008, 000
1196	147, 310, 000	1342	147, 120, 000	1487	139, 608, 000
1197	118, 690, 000	1343	130, 125, 000	1488	159, 475, 000
1198	122, 730, 000	1344	158, 700, 000	1489–1498	486, 020, 000
1199	126, 515, 000	1345–1354	228, 040, 000	1499	157, 052, 800
1200	130, 960, 000	1355	153, 015, 000	1500	53, 005, 000
1201	120, 055, 000	1356	132, 560, 000	1501	159, 775, 000
1202	120, 715, 000	1357	130, 385, 000	1502	39, 005, 000
1203	121, 440, 000	1358	132, 265, 000	1503	152, 624, 000
1204	40, 270, 000	1359	128, 710, 000	1504	145, 840, 000
1205	861, 970, 000	1360	124, 775, 000	1505	151, 335, 000
1206	120, 035, 000	1361	128, 295, 000	1506	141, 085, 000

COMMEMORATIVE STAMPS, QUANTITIES ISSUED

Cat. No.	Quantity	Cat. No.	Quantity	Cat. No.	Quantity
1507	885,160,000	1695–1698	185,715,000	1790	67,195,000
1508	939,835,000	1699	130,592,000	1791-1794	186,905,000
1525	143,930,000	1700	158,332,800	1795-1798	208,295,000
1526	145,235,000	1701	809,955,000	1799	873,710,000
1527	135,052,000	1702–1703	963,370,000	1800	931,880,000
1528	156,750,000	1704	150,328,000	1801	161,290,000
1529	164,670,000	1705	176,830,000	1802	172,740,000
1530–1537	190,156,800	1706–1709	195,976,000	1803	168,995,000
1538–1541	167,212,800	1710	208,820,000	1804	160,000,000
1542	156,265,000	1711	192,250,000	1805-1810	232,134,000
1543–1546	195,585,000	1712–1715	219,830,000	1821	163,510,000
1547	148,850,000	1716	159,852,000	1822	256,620,000
1548	157,270,000	1717–1720	188,310,000	1823	95,695,000
1549	150,245,000	1721	163,625,000	1824	153,975,000
1550	835,180,000	1722	156,296,000	1825	160,000,000
1551	882,520,000	1723–1724	158,676,000	1826	103,850,000
1552	213,155,000	1725	154,495,000	1827-1830	204,715,000
1553	156,995,000	1726	168,050,000	1831	166,545,000
1554	146,365,000	1727	156,810,000	1832	163,310,000
1555	148,805,000	1728	153,736,000	1833	160,000,000
1556	173,685,000	1729	882,260,000	1834-1837	152,404,000
1557	158,600,000	1730	921,530,000	1838-1841	152,720,000
1558	153,355,000	1731	156,560,000	1842	692,500,000
1559	63,205,000	1732–1733	202,155,000	1843	718,715,000
1560	157,865,000	1744	156,525,000	1874	160,155,000
1561	166,810,000	1745–1748	165,182,400	1875	159,505,000
1562	44,825,000	1749–1752	157,598,400	1876-1879	210,633,000
1563	144,028,000	1753	102,856,000	1910	165,175,000
1564	139,928,000	1754	152,270,000	1911	107,240,000
1565–1568	179,855,000	1755	94,600,000	1912-1919	337,819,000
1569–1570	161,863,200	1756	151,570,000	1920	99,420,000
1571	145,640,000	1757	15,170,400	1921-1924	178,930,000
1572–1575	168,655,000	1758	161,228,000	1925	100,265,000
1576	146,615,000	1759	158,880,000	1926	99,615,000
1577–1578	146,196,000	1760–1763	186,550,000	1927	97,535,000
1579	739,430,000	1764–1767	168,136,000	1928-1931	167,308,000
1580	878,690,000	1768	963,120,000	1932	101,625,000
1629–1631	219,455,000	1769	916,800,000	1922	99,170,000
1632	157,825,000	1770	159,297,600	1934	101,155,000
1633–1682	436,005,000	1771	166,435,000	1935	101,200,000
1683	159,915,000	1772	162,535,000	1936	167,360,000
1684	156,960,000	1773	155,000,000	1937-1938	162,420,000
1685	158,470,000	1774	157,310,000	1939	597,720,000
1686	1,990,000	1775–1778	174,096,000	1940	792,600,000
1687	1,983,000	1779–1782	164,793,600	1941	167,130,000
1688	1,953,000	1783–1786	163,055,000	1942-1945	191,560,000
1689	1,903,000	1787	161,860,000		
1690	164,890,000	1788	165,775,000		
1691–1694	208,035,000	1789	160,000,000		

AIR POST STAMPS
QUANTITIES ISSUED

Cat. No.	Quantity	Cat. No.	Quantity	Cat. No.	Quantity
C1	3,395,854	C32	864,753,100	C64	
C2	3,793,887	C33	971,903,700	C65	
C3	2,134,888	C34	207,976,550	C66	42,245,000
C4	6,414,576	C35	756,186,350	C67	
C5	5,309,275	C36	132,956,100	C68	63,890,000
C6	5,285,775	C37	33,244,500	C69	62,255,000
C7	42,092,800	C38	38,449,100	C70	55,710,000
C8	15,597,307	C39	5,070,095,200	C71	*50,000,000
C9	17,616,350	C40	75,085,000	C72	
C10	20,379,179	C41	260,307,500	C73	
C11	106,887,675	C42	21,061,300	C74	*60,000,000
C12	97,641,200	C43	36,613,100	C75	
C13	93,536	C44	16,217,100	C76	152,364,800
C14	72,428	C45	80,405,000	C77	
C15	61,296	C46	18,876,800	C78	
C16	57,340,050	C47	78,415,000	C79	
C17	76,648,803	C48	50,483,977	C80	
C18	324,070	C49	63,185,000	C81	
C19	302,205,100	C50	72,480,000	C82	
C20	10,205,400	C51	1,326,960,000	C83	
C21	12,794,600	C52	157,035,000	C84	78,210,000
C22	9,285,300	C53	90,055,200	C85	96,240,000
C23	349,946,500	C54	79,290,000	C86	58,705,000
C24	19,768,150	C55	84,815,000	C87	
C25	4,746,527,700	C56	38,770,000	C88	
C26	1,744,878,650	C57	39,960,000	C89	
C27	67,117,400	C58	98,160,000	C90	
C28	78,434,800	C59		C91–C92	
C29	42,359,850	C60	1,289,460,000	C93–C94	
C30	59,880,850	C61	87,140,000	C95–C96	
C31	11,160,600	C62		C97	
		C63			

* Quantity ordered printed.

CARRIERS' STAMPS

The term "Carriers' Stamps" is applied to certain stamps of the United States used to defray delivery to a post office on letters going to another post office, and for collection and delivery in the same city (local letters handled only by the carrier department). A less common usage was for collection fee to the addressee at the post office ("drop letters"). During the period when these were in use, the ordinary postage fee defrayed the carriage of mail matter from post office to post office only.

In many of the larger cities the private ("Local") posts delivered mail to the post office or to an addressee in the city direct for a fee of 1 or 2 cents (seldom more), and adhesive stamps were often employed to indicate payment. In some cases mail was delivered by private posts from the post office to the addressee as well. (See introduction to "Local Stamps" section.)

In 1851 the Federal Government, under the acts of 1825 and 1836, undertook to deliver letters in many cities and so issued Carriers' stamps for local delivery service. This Act of Congress of Mar. 3, 1851, effective July 1, 1851 (succeeding Act of 1836) provided for the collecting and delivering of letters to the post office by carriers, "for which not exceeding 1 or 2 cents shall be charged."

Carriers' stamps were issued under the authority of, or derived from, the postmaster general. The "Official Issues" (Nos. L01–L02) were general issues of which No. L02 was valid for postage at face value, and No. L01 at the value set upon sale, in any post office. They were issued under the direct authority of the postmaster general. The "Semi-official Issues" were valid in the city in which they were issued either directly by or sanctioned by the local postmaster under authority derived from the postmaster general.

These "Official" and "Semi-official" Carriers' stamps prepaid the fees of official letter carriers who were appointed by the postmaster general and were under heavy bond to the United States for the faithful performance of their duties. Some of the letter carriers received fixed salaries from the government. Others were paid from the fees received for the delivery and collection of letters carried by them. After discontinuance of carrier fees on June 30, 1863, all carriers of the United States Post Office were government employees, paid by salary at a yearly rate.

Some Carriers' stamps are often found on cover with the regular government stamps and have the official post office cancellation applied to them as well. Only Williams' City Post in Cincinnati used its own cancellation, which is sometimes found on No. L02. Honour's City Express and the other Charleston, S. C., Carrier stamps almost always have the stamp uncanceled or canceled with pen, or less frequently pencil.

Prices for Carriers' stamps on cover are for covers having the stamp tied by a handstamped cancellation.

Carriers' stamps, either uncanceled or pen-canceled, **on covers to which they apparently belong** deserve **a premium of approximately 25 percent** over the prices for the respective uncanceled or canceled off-cover stamps.

Stamps are listed "On cover" **only** when they are known to exist tied by a handstamped cancellation.

All Carriers' stamps are imperforate and on wove paper, either white or colored through, unless otherwise stated.

Counterfeits exist of many Carriers' stamps.

OFFICIAL ISSUES.
Franklin Carrier.

Franklin
OC1

Engraved and printed by Toppan, Carpenter, Casilear & Co.

Plate of 200 subjects divided into two panes of 100 each, one left, one right.

1851		Imperf.		Unwmkd.	
LO1	OC1	(1c) dull blue (shades), rose, September, 1851		1,850.	2,500.
		On cover			4,500.
		Cracked plate		2,250.	
		Double transfer			
		Pair		4,000.	5,500.
		Strip of three		6,250.	9,500.

CANCELLATIONS.

Philadelphia		New Orleans	
Red star	2,500.	Blue grid	——
Blue town	——	Black grid	——
New York		Green grid	——
Red town	——		

Of the entire issue of 310,000 stamps, 250,000 were sent to New York, 50,000 to New Orleans, 10,000 to Philadelphia. However, the quantity sent to each city is not indicative of proportionate use. More appear to have been used in Philadelphia than in the other two cities. The use in all three cities was notably limited.

Eagle Carrier.

Eagle
OC2

Engraved and printed by Toppan, Carpenter, Casilear & Co.

Plate of 200 subjects divided into two panes of 100 each, one upper, one lower.

1851		Imperf.	Unwmkd.	
LO2	OC2	1c blue (shades), Nov. 17, 1851	20.00	20.00
		On cover, used alone		100.00
		On cover with block of 3, 1c #9		1,000.
		On cover with 3c #11		150.00
		On cover with 3c #26		150.00
		On cover with strip of 3, 3c #26		400.00
		On 3c envelope #U2, #U9 or U10		175.00
		Pair	42.50	
		Block of four	90.00	
		Double transfer		

CANCELLATIONS.

Red star	20.00	Red town	——
Black grid	+5.00	Blue squared target	——
Red grid	——	Red squared target	——
Black town	+5.00	Railroad	——
Blue town	+5.00	Black carrier (Type C32)	——
		Red carrier (Type C32)	——

Used principally in Philadelphia. Also known used from Cincinnati, Baltimore, Boston, Washington, D. C., and Kensington, Pa. One cover bearing a strip of 3 is known used from Andalusia, Pa.

GOVERNMENT REPRINTS

Made for the Centennial Exposition of 1876.
Printed by the Continental Bank Note Co.
First reprinting—10,000 copies, on April 2, 1875.
Second reprinting—10,000 copies, on Dec. 22, 1875.

The first reprinting of the Franklin stamp was on the rose paper of the original, obtained from Toppan, Carpenter, Casilear & Co. The second was on slightly thicker, softer paper of paler tint. The Franklin reprints are in dark blue instead of the dull or deep blue of the originals. First and second reprints and originals all differ under ultraviolet light.

Reprints of the Eagle stamp are on the same hard white paper used for reprints and special printings of the postage issue, and on a coarse wove paper. Originals are on yellowish paper with brown gum.

Franklin Reprints.
Imperf. Without gum.

1875			
LO3	OC1	(1c) blue, rose	40.00
		Block of four	175.00
		Cracked plate	60.00

SPECIAL PRINTING
Perf. 12. Without gum.

LO4	OC1	(1c) blue	2,250.
		Pair	8,500.

Eagle Reprints.
Imperf. Without gum.

LO5	OC2	1c blue	20.00
		Block of four	90.00

SPECIAL PRINTING
Perf. 12. Without gum.

LO6	OC2	1c blue	120.00
		Block of four	550.00

SEMI-OFFICIAL ISSUES.
All are imperforate.
Baltimore, Md.

C1

1850-55				Typographed	
	Settings of 10 (2x5) varieties.				
1LB1	C1	1c red (shades), bluish		100.00	60.00
		On cover			250.00
1LB2	"	1c blue (shades), bluish		125.00	90.00
		On cover			300.00
		a. Bluish laid paper		——	——
1LB3	"	1c blue (shades)		75.00	50.00
		On cover			250.00
		Block of four		500.00	
		a. Laid paper		150.00	100.00
		On cover			300.00
1LB4	"	1c green		——	600.00
		On cover			1,000.
		Pair		——	——
1LB5	"	1c red		350.00	275.00
		On cover			550.00
		On cover with 3c #11			650.00

CANCELLATIONS on Nos. 1LB1 to 1LB5.

Black grid	——	Blue town	——
Blue grid	——	Black numeral	——
Black cross	——	Blue numeral	——
Black town	——	Black pen	——

CARRIERS

C2

1856   Typographed

1LB6	C2	1c **blue** (shades)		90.00	60.00
		On cover with 3c #26			250.00
1LB7	"	1c **red** (shades)		65.00	40.00
		On cover			350.00
		On cover with 3c #26			250.00
		Block of four		600.00	

C3

Plate of 10 (2x5); 10 Varieties

The sheet consisted of at least four panes of 10 placed horizontally, the two center panes tête bêche. This makes possible five horizontal tête bêche gutter pairs.

1857   Typographed

1LB8	C3	1c **black** (shades)		25.00	20.00
		On cover			150.00
		On cover with 3c #26			125.00
		On 3c envelope #U10			150.00
		Block of four		125.00	
		a. "SENT", Pos. 7		35.00	25.00
		b. Short rays, Pos. 2		35.00	25.00
		Tête bêche gutter pair		400.00	

CANCELLATIONS.

Black pen (or pencil)	20.00	Black town	22.50
Blue town	22.50	Black Steamship	—

1LB9	"	1c **red** (shades)		40.00	30.00
		On cover with 3c #26			150.00
		On 3c envelope #U9			200.00
		On 3c envelope #U10			
		a. "SENT", Pos. 7		50.00	40.00
		b. Short rays, Pos. 2		50.00	40.00

CANCELLATIONS on Nos 1LB6–7, 1LB9:

Black town	—	Blue numeral	—
Blue town	—	Black pen	—

Boston, Mass.

C6

Several Varieties

Pelure Paper

1849–50   Typeset

3LB1	C6	1c **blue**		120.00	75.00
		On cover			200.00
		On cover with 5c #1			1,200.

C7

Typeset
Several Varieties
Wove Paper Colored Through

3LB2	C7	1c **blue** (shades), *grayish*		135.00	65.00
		On cover			175.00
		On cover with 3c #10			300.00
		On cover with 3c #11			225.00
3LB3	"	1c **blue** (shades), *bluish*		125.00	65.00
		On cover			250.00
		On cover with 3c #11			275.00
		On 3c envelope #U9			275.00

CANCELLATIONS on Nos. 3LB1–3LB3:

Black small fancy circle	—	Black diamond grid	—
		Red diamond grid	—
Red small fancy circle		Red town	—

Charleston, S. C.

John H. Honour was appointed a letter carrier at Charleston, in 1849, and engaged his brother-in-law, E. J. Kingman, to assist him. They separated in 1851, dividing the carrier business of the city between them. At the same time Kingman was appointed a letter carrier. In March, 1858, Kingman retired, being replaced by Joseph G. Martin. In the summer of 1858, John F. Steinmeyer, Jr., was added to the carrier force. When Honour retired in 1860, John C. Beckman was appointed in his place.

Each of these carriers had stamps prepared. These stamps were sold by the carriers. The Federal Government apparently encouraged their use.

Honour's City Express.

C8

Wove Paper Colored Through

1849   Typographed

4LB1	C8	2c **brown rose**		1,300.	1,300.
		Cut to shape			600.00
4LB2	"	2c **yellow**			1,300.
		On cover with 10c #2			5,500.

CANCELLATIONS on Nos. 4LB1–4LB2:

Red grid   — | Red town   —

C10

1854   Wove Paper   Typeset

4LB3	C10	2c **black**			650.00
		On cover with 3c #11			1,400.

CANCELLATIONS.

Black "PAID"   — | Black pen   650.00

C11

Several Varieties

1849–50   Wove Paper Colored Through   Typeset

4LB5	C11	2c **bluish**, pelure		400.00	300.00
		On cover with pair 5c #1b			3,500.
		On cover with 3c #11			600.00
4LB7	"	2c **yellow**		400.00	400.00
		On cover			1,500.

CANCELLATIONS on Nos. 4LB5, 4LB7.

Red town	—
Black pen	—
Red crayon	—

The varieties of type C11 on bluish wove (thicker) paper and pink, pelure paper are not believed genuine.

C13   C14   C15

Several varieties of each type

1851–58   Wove Paper Colored Through   Typeset

4LB8	C13	2c **bluish**		175.00	100.00
		On cover			250.00
		On cover with 3c #11			350.00
		On cover with 3c #26			350.00
		Horiz. pair			1,000.
		a. Period after "PAID"		300.00	150.00
		b. "Cens"			700.00
		c. "Conours" and "Bents"			

CARRIERS

4LB9	C13	2c *bluish*, pelure	375.00	425.00
4LB11	C14	(2c) *bluish*	—	250.00
		On cover with 3c #11		2,500.
4LB12	"	(2c) *bluish*, pelure	—	250.00
4LB13	C15	(2c) *bluish* ('58)	250.00	125.00
		On cover with 3c #26		1,200.
	a.	Comma after "PAID"		300.00
	b.	No period after "Post"		300.00

A 2c of type C13 exists on pink pelure paper. It is believed not to have been issued by the post, but to have been created later and perhaps accidentally.

CANCELLATIONS on Nos. 4LB8 to 4LB13.

Black town	—	Black pen	—
Blue town	—	Black pencil	—
Red town	—	Red crayon	—

Kingman's City Post.

C16   C17

Several varieties of each

1851(?)-58(?)   Wove Paper Colored Through   Typeset

4LB14	C16	2c *bluish*	450.00	450.00
		On cover with 3c #26		1,250.
4LB15	C17	2c *bluish*	450.00	450.00
		On cover		1,400.
		Vertical pair		
		Vertical strip of three	2,200.	

CANCELLATIONS on Nos. 4LB14-4LB15

Black town	—
Black pen	—

Martin's City Post.

C18

Several varieties

1858   Wove Paper Colored Through   Typeset

4LB16	C18	2c *bluish*	2,750.

Beckman's City Post.

Same as C19, but inscribed "Beckmann's City Post."

1860

4LB17	C19	2c **black**, on cover	—

No. 4LB17 is unique. It is on cover with 3c No. 26, both tied by black circle townmark: "CHARLESTON, S.C. JUN 18, 1860".

Steinmeyer's City Post.

C19   C20

Several varieties of C19; C20 printed from plate of 10 (2x5) varieties.

1859   Wove Paper Colored Through   Typeset

4LB18	C19	2c *bluish*	2,500.	
4LB19	C20	2c *bluish*	1,500.	—
4LB20	"	2c *pink*	75.00	
		Block of four	350.00	
		Sheet of ten	1,000.	
4LB21	"	2c *yellow*	85.00	
		Block of four	400.00	
		Sheet of ten	1,500.	

Cancellation on Nos. 4LB19-4LB21: Black pen.

Cincinnati, Ohio
Williams' City Post.

Organized by C. C. Williams, who was appointed and commissioned by the Postmaster General.

C20a

1854   Wove Paper   Lithographed

9LB1	C20a	2c **brown**	500.00	500.00
		On cover		1,000.
		On cover with 1c #9		2,250.
		Pair	1.500.	

CANCELLATIONS.

Red squared target	—	Blue company circle	—
Black pen	—		

Cleveland, Ohio
Bishop's City Post.

Organized by Henry S. Bishop, "Penny Postman" who was appointed and commissioned by the Postmaster General.

C20b   C20c

1854   Wove Paper   Lithographed

10LB1	C20b	**blue**	400.00	400.00
		On cover		1,500.

Vertically Laid Paper.

10LB2	C20c	2c *bluish*	400.00	400.00
		On cover		1,250.
		Pair		1,750.

CANCELLATIONS on Nos. 10LB1-10LB2.

Red town	—	Black pencil	—
Red boxed numeral	—	Black pen	—

Louisville, Ky.

Carrier Service was first established by the Louisville Post Office about 1854, with one carrier. David B. Wharton, appointed a carrier in 1856, issued an adhesive stamp in 1857, but as he was soon thereafter replaced in the service, it is not believed that any of these stamps were used. Brown & McGill, carriers who succeeded Wharton, issued stamps in April, 1858.

Wharton's U.S.P.O. Despatch.

C21

Lithographed by Robyn & Co.
Sheet of 50 subjects in two panes of 25 (5x5) each, one upper, one lower

1857

5LB1	C21	(2c) *bluish green*		35.00
		Block of four		150.00
		Pane of 25		950.00
		Sheet of 50		2,000.

CARRIERS

Brown & McGill's U. S. P. O. Despatch.

C22

Lithographed by Hart & Maypother.

1858

5LB2	C22	(2c) *blue* (shades)	100.00	150.00
		On cover with 3c #26		1,100.
		Block of four	650.00	
5LB3	"	(2c) *black*	600.00	1,750.

CANCELLATIONS on Nos. 5LB2 and 5LB3

Blue town   —
Black pencil   —

New York, N. Y.

UNITED STATES CITY DESPATCH POST.

By an order made on August 1, 1842, the Postmaster General established a carrier service in New York known as the "United States City Despatch Post". Local delivery service had been authorized by the Act of Congress of July 2, 1836.

Greig's City Despatch Post was sold to the U. S. P. O. Department and on August 16, 1842, began operation as the "United States City Despatch Post" under the superintendence of Alexander M. Greig who was appointed a U. S. letter carrier for that purpose.

The Greig circular introducing this service stated that letter boxes had been placed throughout the city, that letters might be sent prepaid or collect, and that registry service was available for an extra 3 cents.

The City Despatch Post stamps were accepted for the service of the United States City Despatch Post. The stamps thus used bear the cancellations of the New York Post Office, usually "U.S." in an octagon:

Occasionally they bear a circle with the date and the words "U.S. CITY DESPATCH POST" or infrequently a New York town postmark.

No. 6LB3 was the first stamp issued by authority of the U.S.P.O. Department. The 3c denomination included 1 cent in lieu of drop letter postage until June 30, 1845, and the maximum legal carrier fee of 2 cents. Service was discontinued late in November, 1846.

C23

Engraved and printed by Rawdon, Wright & Hatch.
Plate of 42 (6x7) subjects.

1842   Wove Paper Colored Through

6LB1	C23	3c *grayish*		750.00
		On cover		2,500.

CANCELLATIONS.

Red circle "U.S." in City Despatch	—	Red "U.S." in octagon	—

Used copies which do not bear the official cancellation of the New York Post Office and unused copies are classed as Local stamps. See No. 40L1.

C24

Engraved by Rawdon, Wright & Hatch.
Plate of 100 subjects.

1842-45   Wove Paper (unsurfaced) Colored Through

6LB2	C24	3c *rosy buff*	550.00	
6LB3	"	3c *light blue*	300.00	200.00
		On cover		500.00
		Pair	700.00	
6LB4	"	3c *green*	2,000.	

Some authorities consider No. 6LB2 to be an essay, and No. 6LB4 a color changeling.

Glazed Paper, Surface Colored.

6LB5	C24	3c *dark blue* (shades)	100.00	75.00
		On cover		300.00
		Pair		300.00
		Strip of three		500.00
		Block of four	2,000.	
a.		Double impression		500.00
		Ribbed paper	—	
		Double transfer	—	—
6LB6	"	3c *bluish green*	125.00	75.00
		On cover		300.00
		Five on cover		2,500.
		Pair		250.00
		Strip of three	—	
		Strip of four	—	
		Strip of five	—	
a.		Double impression		550.00
		Ribbed paper	—	
		Double transfer	—	

No. 6LB6 has been noted on cover with the 5c New York signed "R.H.M.", No. 9X1b.

C25

1846   No. 6LB6 Surcharged in Red

6LB7	C25	2c on 3c *bluish green*, on cover		5,000.

The City Dispatch 2c red formerly listed as No. 6LB8 is now listed under Local Stamps as No. 160L1.

U. S. MAIL

C27

Issued by the Postmaster at New York, N.Y.

1849   Wove Paper, Colored Through   Typographed

6LB9	C27	1c *rose*	50.00	25.00
		On cover		150.00
		On cover with 5c #1		1,250.
		Pair	—	
		Block of four	—	

1849-50   Glazed Surface Paper.

6LB10	C27	1c *yellow*	45.00	25.00
		On cover		125.00
		On cover with 5c #1		
		Pair	—	
		Block of four	—	
6LB11	"	1c *buff*	40.00	25.00
		On cover		100.00
		On cover with 5c #1		
a.		Pair, one stamp sideways	1,000.	

CARRIERS

CANCELLATIONS on Nos. 6LB9 to 6LB11.	
Red town —	Red "N.Y. U.S.
Red grid —	CITY MAIL"
Red "PAID" —	in circle —
Black numeral	Black pen —
in circle —	Black pencil —

Philadelphia, Pa.

C28
Several Varieties.
Thick Wove Paper Colored Through

1849-50			Typeset
7LB1	C28	1c rose (with "L P")	175.00
		On cover	500.00
7LB2	"	1c rose (with "S")	500.00
7LB3	"	1c rose (with "H")	175.00
		On cover	400.00
7LB4	"	1c rose (with "L S")	175.00
7LB5	"	1c rose (with "J J")	2,000.

C29
Several Varieties.

7LB6	C29	1c rose	150.00	125.00
		On cover		400.00
7LB7	"	1c blue, glazed	600.00	
7LB8	"	1c vermilion, glazed	600.00	
7LB9	"	1c yellow, glazed	1,350.	

Cancellations on Nos. 7LB1-7LB9: Normally these stamps were left uncanceled on the letter, but occasionally were accidentally tied by the Philadelphia town postmark which was normally struck in blue ink.

A 1c black on buff (unglazed) of type C29 is believed to be a color changeling.

C30
Settings of 25 (5x5) varieties.

1850-52		(Five basic types)	Lithographed	
7LB11	C30	1c gold, black, glazed	60.00	55.00
		On cover		200.00
		On cover with 5c #1		
		On cover with 3c #10		
		Block of four	500.00	
7LB12	"	1c blue	200.00	100.00
		On cover		250.00
		Pair		
7LB13	"	1c black	—	500.00
		On cover		1,000.
		On cover with 3c #11		1,200.

CANCELLATION on Nos. 7LB11-7LB13.
Red star — |

C31
Handstamped

7LB14	C31	1c blue, buff	1,000.

No. 7LB14 was handstamped on coarse dark buff paper on which rectangles in the approximate size of the type C31 handstamp had been ruled in pencil. The stamps so produced were later cut out and show traces of the adjoining handstamp markings as well as parts of the penciled rectangle.

1855(?)
7LB16	C31	1c black	1,650.
		On cover with strip of 3, 1c #9	—

C32

1856(?)			Handstamped	
7LB18	C32	1c black	1,200.	1,300.
		On cover (cut diamond-shaped) with pair 1c #7 and single 1c #9		2,750.
		On cover with strip of 3, 1c #9		
		On cover with 3c #11		2,750.

CANCELLATIONS on Nos. 7LB16, 7LB18
Black circled grid — | Black town —

Nos. 7LB16 and 7LB18 were handstamped on the sheet margins of U.S. 1851 1c stamps, cut out and used as adhesives. The paper therefore has some surface bluing, and some stamps show parts of the plate imprint. Prices are for stamps cut square unless otherwise mentioned.

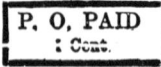

The authenticity of stamps of these designs, typeset and on thin wove paper, is in doubt. Those seen are uncanceled, either off cover or affixed to stampless covers of the early 1850's.

ENVELOPES

Handstamps of types C31 and C32 were also used to make stamped envelopes and letter sheets or circulars. These same types were also used as postmarks or cancellations in the same period. A handstamp similar to C32, but with "U.S.P. DESPATCH" in serif capitals, is believed to have been used only as a postmark.

Type C31 exists struck in blue or red, type C32 in blue, black or red. When found on cover, on various papers, struck alone, they are probably postmarks and not prepaid stamped envelopes. As such, these entire covers, depending upon the clarity of the handstamp and the general attractiveness of the letter are priced between $100 and $200.

When found on envelopes with the Carrier stamp canceled by a handstamp (such as type C31 struck in blue on a buff envelope canceled by the red solid star cancellation) they can be regarded as probably having been sold as prepaid envelopes. Price approximately $600.

St. Louis, Mo.

C36   C37

1849		White Wove Paper	Lithographed	
		Two Types		
8LB1	C36	2c black	2,000.	2,750.

CANCELLATION
Black town — |

1857			Lithographed.	
8LB2	C37	2c blue		2,500.
		On cover		

CANCELLATIONS.
Black boxed "1ct"— |
Black pen — |

LOCAL STAMPS

This listing of Local stamps includes stamps issued by Local Posts (city delivery), Independent Mail Routes and Services, Express Companies and other private posts which competed with, or supplemented, official services.

The Independent Mail Routes began using stamps early in 1844 and were put out of business by an Act of March, 1845, which became effective July 1, 1845. By this Act, the Government reduced the zones to two, reduced the rates to 5c and 10c and applied them to weight instead of the number of sheets of paper which composed a letter.

Most of the Local Posts still in business were forced to discontinue service by an Act of 1861, except Boyd's and Hussey's which were able to continue about 20 years longer because of the particular nature of their business. Other posts appeared illegally and sporadically after 1861 and were quickly suppressed.

City posts generally charged 1c to deliver a letter to the Post Office (usually the letter bore a government stamp as well) and 2c for intracity delivery (such letters naturally bore only local stamps). These usages are not catalogued separately because the value of a cover is determined as much by its attractiveness as its franking, rarity being the basic criterion.

Only a few Local Posts used special handstamps for canceling. The stamps frequently were left uncanceled, were canceled by pen, or less often by pencil. **Prices for stamps on cover are for covers having the stamp tied by a handstamped cancellation, either private or governmental.** Local stamps, either uncanceled or pen canceled, **on covers to which they apparently belong** deserve **a premium of about 25 percent** over the prices for the respective uncanceled or canceled off-cover stamp.

The absence of any specific cancellation listed indicates that no company handstamp is known so used, and that the canceling, if any, was done by pen, pencil or government handstamp.

Stamps are listed "on cover" **only** when they are known to exist tied by private or governmental handstamp. Local stamps used on letters directed out of town (and consequently bearing government stamps) sometimes, because of their position, are tied together with the government stamp by the cancellation used to cancel the latter.

Prices for envelopes are for entires unless specifically mentioned where entires are unknown.

All Local stamps are imperforate and on wove paper, either white or colored through, unless otherwise stated.

Counterfeits exist of many Local stamps, but most of these are crude reproductions and would deceive only the novice.

Adams & Co.'s Express, California

This post started in September, 1849, operating only on the Pacific Coast.

Cancellation (1L1-1L2): Black Express Co.
Nos. 1L1—1L2 were the earliest adhesive franks issued west of the Mississippi River.

Glazed Surface Cardboard.

1L3	L2	25c *pink*	20.00
		Block of four	90.00
		Retouched flaw above LR "25"	100.00

No. 1L.3 was probably never placed in use as a postage stamp.

L1

L2

D. H. Haskell, Manager

Nos. 1L2-1L5 Printed in Sheets of 40 (8x5).

			Lithographed	
1854				
1L1	L1	25c *blue*	150.00	—
		On cover		—
1L2	L2	25c black (initials in black)	45.00	—
		Block of four	200.00	
		a. Initials in red		—
		b. Without initials		—

L3

LOCALS

Overprinted in red "Over our California lines only"
1L4	L3	25c black	175.00

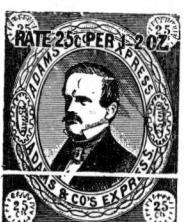 

L4   L.5

1L5	L4	25c black (black surcharge)	300.00	
1L6	L5	25c black	300.00	
		Pair	750.00	

NEWSPAPER STAMP.

L6

1LP1	L6	claret	300.00	400.00

Cancellation: Blue company oval.

ENVELOPES.

L6a   L6b

Typographed

1LU1	L6a	25c blue (cut square)		
1LU2	L6b	50c black (on U.S. No. U9)	250.00	400.00
1LU3	"	50c black (on U.S. No. U9)	250.00	400.00
1LU4	"	50c black, *buff*		

No.1LU2 exists cut out and apparently used as an adhesive.
Cancellation: Blue company oval.

Adams' City Express Post, New York, N.Y.

L7   L8

1850-51   **Typographed**

2L2	L7	2c buff	250.00	250.00
2L3	L8	1c gray	300.00	300.00
2L4	"	2c gray	275.00	275.00

Nos. 2L3-2L4 were reprinted in black and in blue on white wove paper. Some students claim that the 1c and 2c in blue exist as originals.

Allen's City Dispatch, Chicago, Ill.

Established by Edwin Allen for intracity delivery of letters and circulars. The price of the stamps is believed to have been determined on a quantity basis. Uncanceled and canceled remainders were sold to collectors after suppression of the post.

L9

1882		**Typographed**		**Perf.10.**
		Sheet of 100		
3L1	L9	pink	3.00	8.00
		On cover		125.00
3L2	"	black	7.00	
		On cover		150.00
		a. Horizontal pair, imperf. between		—
3L3	"	red, *yellow*	50	2.00
		On cover		100.00
		a. Imperf., pair		
		b. Horizontal pair, imperf. between		—
3L4	"	purple	50.00	

Cancellations: Violet company oval. Violet "eagle."

American Express Co., New York, N.Y.

Believed by some researchers to have been established by Smith & Dobson in 1856, and short-lived.

L10

		Glazed Surface Paper		**Typeset**
4L1	L10	2c green		—

American Letter Mail Co.

Lysander Spooner established this independent mail line operating to and from New York, Philadelphia and Boston.

L12
Sheet of 20 (5x4)

1844				**Engraved**
5L1	L12	5c black, thin paper (2nd printing)	4.00	15.00
		Thick paper (1st printing)	15.00	25.00
		On cover		85.00
		Pair on cover		—
		Block of four, thin paper	20.00	
		Sheet of 20, thin paper	100.00	

No. 5L1 has been extensively reprinted in several colors.
Cancellations: Red dotted star (2 types). Red "PAID".

LOCALS

L13
Engraved

5L2	L13	black, *gray*	45.00	45.00
		On cover		150.00
		Pair on cover		—
		Block of four	250.00	
5L3	"	blue, *gray*	225.00	225.00
		On cover		300.00

Cancellations: Red "PAID". Red company oval.

A. W. Auner's Despatch Post, Philadelphia, Pa.

L13a

1851   **Typeset**
Cut to shape
154L1   L13a   black, *grayish*   1,000.00 1,000.00

Baker's City Express Post, Cincinnati, Ohio.

L14

1849
6L1   L14   2c *pink*   750.00

Barnard's Cariboo Express, British Columbia

The adhesives were used on British Columbia mail and the post did not operate in the United States, so the formerly listed PAID and COLLECT types are omitted. This company had an arrangement with Wells, Fargo & Co. to exchange mail at San Francisco.

Barnard's City Letter Express, Boston, Mass.
Established by Moses Barnard.

L19

1845
7L1   L19   *yellow*, glazed paper   300.00 300.00
7L2   "   red   750.00

Barr's Penny Dispatch, Lancaster, Pa.
Established by Elias Barr.

L20

1855   **Typeset**
Five varieties of each.
8L1   L20   red   250.00 250.00
                On cover   2500.00
8L2   "   black, *green*   45.00
                Pair   100.00

Bayonne City Dispatch, Bayonne City, N.J.

Organized April 1, 1883, to carry mail, with three daily deliveries. Stamps sold at 80 cents per 100.

L21

1883   **Electrotyped**
Sheet of 10
9L1   L21   1c black   100.00 100.00
                On cover   300.00
Cancellation: Purple concentric circles.
ENVELOPE.
1883, May 15   **Handstamped**
9LU1   L21   1c purple, *amber*   100.00 500.00

Bentley's Dispatch, New York, N.Y.

Established by H. W. Bentley, who acquired Cornwell's Madison Square Post Office, operating until 1856, when the business was sold to Lockwood. Bentley's postmark was double circle handstamp.

L22   L22a

1856 (?)   **Glazed Surface Paper**
10L1   L22   gold   1,500.00 1,500.00
10L2   L22a   gold   1,500.00
Cancellation: Black "PAID."

Berford & Co.'s Express, New York, N.Y.

Organized by Richard G. Berford and Loring L. Lombard.
Carried letters, newspapers and packages by steamer to Panama and points on the West Coast, North and South America. Agencies in West Indies, West Coast of South America, Panama, Hawaii, etc.

L23

LOCALS

1851
11L1	L23	3c black	500.00	500.00
		On cover		—
11L2	"	6c green	500.00	500.00
		On cover		750.00
11L3	"	10c violet	500.00	500.00
		On cover		—
		Pair	1,250.00	
		Horiz. tete beche pair	1,500.00	
11L4	"	25c red	500.00	500.00
		On cover		—

Prices of cut to shape copies are about half of those quoted. Cancellation: Red "B & Co. Paid" (sometimes impressed without ink). Dangerous counterfeits exist of Nos. 11L1-11L4.

Bicycle Mail Route, California.

During the American Railway Union strike, Arthur C. Banta, Fresno agent for Victor bicycles, established this post to carrry mail from Fresno to San Francisco and return, employing messengers on bicycles. The first trip was made from Fresno on July 6, 1894. Service was discontinued on July 18 when the strike ended. In all, 380 letters were carried. Stamps were used on covers with U.S. Government adhesive stamps and on stamped envelopes.

(Illustration reduced size.)
L24
Printed from single die. Sheet of six.
Error of spelling "SAN FRANSISCO".

1894   Typographed   *Rouletted 10*
12L1	L24	25c green	50.00	75.00
		On cover		1100.00

(Illustration reduced size.)
L25
Retouched die. Spelling error corrected.

12L2	L25	25c green	20.00	40.00
		On cover		850.00
		Block of 4	85.00	
		Pane of 6	165.00	
		a. "Horiz." pair, imperf. "vert "	65.00	

ENVELOPES.
12LU1	L25	25c brown, on 2c No. U311	85.00	*1350.00*
12LU2	"	25c brown, on 2c No. U312	85.00	*1350.00*

Cancellation: Two black parallel bars 2mm. apart. Stamps and envelopes were reprinted from the defaced die.

Bigelow's Express, Boston, Mass.

Authorities consider items of this design to be express company labels rather than stamps.

Bishop's City Post, Cleveland, Ohio
See Carriers' Stamps, Nos. 10LB1-12LB2.

Blizzard Mail

Organized March, 1888, to carry mail to New York City during the interruption of U.S. mail by the Blizzard of 1888. Used March 12-16.

L27
1888, Mar. 12   Quadrille Paper   Typographed
163L1	L27	5c black	250.00

D.O. Blood & Co., Philadelphia, Pa.
I. Philadelphia Despatch Post

Operated by Robertson & Co., predecessor of D.O. Blood & Co.

L28   L29
Initialed "R & Co."

1843   Handstamped
Cut to Shape
15L1	L28	3c red, *bluish*		750.00
		On cover		2500.00
15L2	"	3c black		750.00
		On cover		—

Cancellations on Nos. 15L1-15L2: Red "3". Red pattern of segments.

Without shading in background.
Initialed "R & Co"

1843   Lithographed
15L3	L29	(3c) *grayish*		200.00
		On cover		500.00
		a. Double impression		—

Cancellation on No. 15L3: Red "3".

The design shows a messenger stepping over the Merchants' Exchange Building, which then housed the Government Post Office, implying that the private post gave faster service.

LOCALS

II. D.O. Blood & Co.

Formed by Daniel Otis Blood and Walter H. Blood in 1845. Successor to Philadelphia Despatch Post which issued Nos. 15L1-15L3.

L30
Initialed "Dob & Cos" or "D.O.B. & Co."

1845   **Shading in background.**

15L4	L30	(3c) *grayish*	100.00	
		On cover		500.00

L31   L32

1845

15L5	L31	(2c) black	75.00	75.00
		On cover		350.00
		Block of four	350.00	

1846

15L6	L32	(2c) black	—	90.00
		On cover		500.00

Cancellations on Nos. 15L4-15L6: Black dot pattern. Black cross. Red "PAID".
Dangerous counterfeits exist of Nos. 15L3-15L6.

L33

L34   L35

1846-47

15L7	L33	(1c) black	75.00	55.00
		On cover		300.00
15L8	L34	(1c) black	60.00	40.00
		On cover		275.00
15L9	L35	(1c) black	40.00	30.00
		On cover		275.00
		Block of four		

Prices for Nos. 15L7-15L9 cut to shape are half of those quoted.
"On cover" listings of Nos. 15L7-15L9 are for stamps tied by government town postmarks, either Philadelphia, or rarely Baltimore.

L36   L37

1848

15L10	L36	black and blue	75.00	75.00
		On cover		250.00
15L11	L37	*pale green*	—	40.00
		On cover		150.00

Cancellation: Black grid.

L38   L39

L40   L41

1848-54

15L12	L38	(1c) gold, *black*, glazed	40.00	25.00
		On cover		100.00
15L13	L39	1c bronze, *black*, glazed ('50)	7.50	6.00
		On cover		75.00
		On cover, acid tied		25.00
		Block of four	50.00	
15L14	L40	(1c) bronze, *lilac* ('54)	3.50	2.50
		On cover		75.00
		On cover, acid tied		25.00
		Block of four	35.00	
		a. Laid paper	—	—
15L15	"	(1c) blue & pink, *bluish* ('53)	9.00	6.00
		On cover		85.00
		On cover, acid tied		40.00
		Block of four	60.00	
		a. Laid paper	—	—
15L16	"	(1c) bronze, *black*, glazed ('54)	12.00	9.00
		On cover		90.00
		On cover, acid tied		40.00
15L17	L41	(1c) bronze, *black*, glazed	15.00	8.00
		On cover		90.00
		On cover, acid tied		40.00

Cancellations: Black grid (No. 15L12, 15L17). Nos. 15L13-15L16 were almost always canceled with an acid which discolored both stamp and cover.

"On cover" prices for Nos. 15L13-15L17 are minimum quotations for stamps tied by government postmarks to stampless covers or covers bearing contemporary government stamps, usually the 3c denomination. Covers with less usual frankings such as 5c or 10c 1847, or 1c or 10c 1851-57, merit substantial premiums.

III. Blood's Penny Post

Blood's Penny Post was acquired by the general manager, Charles Kochersperger, in 1855, when Daniel O. Blood died.

Henry Clay
L42

1855   **Engraved by Draper, Welsh & Co.**

15L18	L42	(1c) black	5.00	5.00
		On cover		75.00
		Block of four	50.00	

Cancellations: Black circular "Blood's Penny Post". Black "1" in frame. Red "1" in frame.

ENVELOPES.

L43   L44

1850-60		**Embossed**		
15LU1	L43	red, *white*	30.00	50.00
		a. pink, *white*		50.00
		b. Impressed on U.S. Env. No. U9		200.00
15LU2	″	red, *buff*	—	65.00
15LU3	L44	red, *white*	30.00	45.00
15LU4	″	red, *buff*	30,00	45.00

L45

15LU5	L45	red, *white*	20.00	50.00
		Used with 3c No. 11		125.00
		a. Impressed on U.S. Env. No. U7		175.00
		b. Impressed on U.S. Env. No. U9		175.00
		c. Impressed on U.S. Env. No. U1		250.00
		d. Impressed on U.S. Env. No. U3		—
		e. Impressed on U.S. Env. No. U2		200.00
15LU6	″	red, *amber*	20.00	30.00
15LU6A	″	red, *buff*		65.00
		Used with 10c No.2		—
		b. red, *brown*		—
		Laid Paper.		
15LU7	L45	red, *white*	20.00	60.00
15LU8	″	red, *amber*	20.00	60.00
		Used with 3c No. 25		125.00
15LU9	″	red, *buff*	20.00	60.00
15LU10	″	red, *blue*	200.00	200.00

Nos. 15LU1—15LU9 exist in several envelope sizes.
Cancellations: Black grid (Nos. 15LU1-15LU4). Black company circle (2 sizes and types). When on government envelope, the Blood stamp was often left uncanceled.

Bouton's Post, New York, N.Y.
I. Franklin City Despatch Post.
Organized by John R. Bouton.

L46

1847		**Glazed Surface Paper**	**Typographed**
16L1	L46	(2c) *green*	500.00
		a. "Bouton" in blk. ms. vert. at side	500.00

II. Bouton's Manhattan Express.
Acquired from William V. Barr.

L47

1847			**Typographed**
17L1	L47	2c *pink*	350.00
		Cut to shape	80.00

III. Bouton's City Dispatch Post.
(Sold to Swart's in 1849.)

Zachary Taylor

Corner leaves   Corner dots
L48   L49

1848				**Lithographed**
18L1	L48	2c black	—	150.00
		On cover		600.00
18L2	L49	2c *gray blue*	100.00	75.00
		On cover		600.00

Cancellations on Nos. 18L1-18L2: Red "PAID BOUTON".

Boyce's City Express Post, New York, N.Y.

L50
Center background has 17 parallel lines

1852		**Glazed Surface Paper**		**Typographed**
19L1	L50	2c *green*	350.00	300.00
		On cover		1250.00

Boyd's City Express, New York, N.Y.

Boyd's City Express, as a post, was established by John T. Boyd, on June 17, 1844. In 1860 the post was briefly operated by John T. Boyd, Jr., under whose management No. 20L15 was issued. For about six months in 1860 the post was suspended. It was then sold to William and Mary Blackham who resumed operation on Dec. 24, 1860. The Blackham issues began with No. 20L16.

Boyd's had arrangements to handle local delivery mail for Pomeroy, Letter Express, Brooklyn City Express Post, Staten Island Express Post and possibly others.

L51 (Type I)
Types I to VI, IX and X have a rectangular frame of fine lines surrounding the design.

1844		**Glazed Surface Paper**	**Lithographed**
20L1	L51	2c *green,* type I	175.00
		On cover	400.00
		Cancellation: Red "FREE".	

LOCALS

503

L52 (Type II)
Plain background. Map on globe.

1844
20L2 L52 2c *yellow green*, type II   75.00
           On cover   150.00
           Cancellation: Red "FREE".

L53 (Type III)
Plain background. Only globe shaded.

1845
20L3 L53 2c *bluish green*, type III   ——   85.00
           On cover   150.00
           Cancellation: Red "FREE".

L54 (Type IV)
Inner oval frame of two thin lines. Netted background, showing but faintly on late impressions.

1845
20L4 L54 2c *green*, type IV   10.00   10.00
           On cover   75.00
           On cover with 5¢ #1   1000.00
           Double transfer   20.00
           Diagonal half used as 1c on cover   ——

1847
20L5 L54 2c *gold, cream*, type IV   50.00
   Types IV to IX (except No. 20L23) were also obtainable die cut. An extra charge was made for such stamps. In general, genuine Boyd die-cuts sell for 75% of rectangular cut copies. Stamps hand cut to shape are worth much less.

L55 (Type V)
No period after "CENTS". Inner oval frame has heavy inner line.

1848
20L7 L55 2c *green*, type V (glazed)   5.00   8.00
           On cover   75.00
           Block of four   25.00
           a. 2c *yellow green*, type V   8.00
              On cover   85.00
           Cancellation: Black grid.
   No. 20L7a is on unglazed surface-colored paper.

L56 (Type VI)
Period after "CENTS." Inner frame as in type V.

1852   Lithographed
20L8 L56 2c *green*, type VI   15.00   20.00
           On cover   50.00
           Vert. strip of 3 on cover   300.00
20L9 "   2c *gold*, type VI   8.00   20.00
           On cover   60.00
           Block of four   35.00
   Cancellations on Nos. 20L8-20L9: Black cork. Black "PAID J.T.B."
   No. 20L8 was reprinted in 1862 on unglazed paper, and about 1880 on glazed paper without rectangular frame.

L57 (Type VII)
Period after "CENTS." Inner oval frame has heavy outer line. Eagle's tail pointed. Upper part of "2" open, with heavy downstroke at left shorter than one at right . "2C" closer than "T2".

1854
20L10 L57 2c *green*, type VII   20.00   15.00
            On cover   75.00
            Cancellation: Black "PAID J.T.B."

L58 (Type VIII)
Outer oval frame of three lines, outermost heavy. Solid background

1856   Unglazed Paper   Colored Through   Typographed
20L11 L58 2c *olive green*, type VIII   20.00   15.00
            On cover   80.00

1857
20L12 L58 2c *brick red, white*, type VIII 15.00   15.00
            On cover   100.00
20L13 "   2c *dull orange, white*, type VIII 20.00   20.00
            On cover   110.00
   Cancellation on Nos. 20L11-20L13: Black "PAID J.T.B."
   Nos. 20L11-20L13 were reprinted in the 1880's for sale to collectors. They were printed from a new small plate of 25 on lighter weight paper and in colors of ink and paper lighter than the originals.

L59 (Type IX)

Similar to type VII, but eagle's tail square. Upper part of "2" closed (in well printed specimens) forming a symmetrical "o" with downstrokes equal. "T2" closer than "2C".

1857   Glazed Surface Paper   **Lithographed**
20L14   L59   2c *green,* type IX   6.00   5.00
                  On cover   75.00
                  Pair on cover
                  Block of four   30.00
                  a. Serrate perf.

The serrate perf. is probably of private origin.
No. 20L15 was made by altering the stone of type IX, and many traces of the "S" of "CENTS" remain.

1860
20L15   L59   1c *green,* type IX   1.00   15.00
                  On cover   90.00
                  Block of four   5.00
                  a. "CENTS" instead of "CENT"

Cancellation on Nos. 20L14-20L15: Black "PAID J.T.B."

L60 (Type X)
Center dots before "POST" and after "CENTS".

1860
20L16   L60   2c *red,* type X   5.00   7.00
                  On cover   65.00
                  Block of four   25.00
                  a. Tete beche pair   20.00
20L17   "   1c *lilac,* type X   5.00   7.00
                  On cover   125.00
                  Block of four   20.00
                  a. "CENTS" instead of "CENT"   15.00   20.00
                      Two on cover (No. 20L17a)
                  b. Tete beche pair   35.00
                  c. "1" inverted
20L18   "   1c *blue gray,* type X   5.00   10.00
                  On cover   100.00
                  Block of four   25.00
                  a. "CENTS" instead of "CENT"   15.00   20.00
                    On cover   200.00
                  b. Tete beche pair   35.00

Cancellations on Nos. 20L16-20L18: Black company oval. Black company circle. Black "PAID" in circle.

1861
20L19   L60   2c *gold,* type X   40.00
                  Block of four
                  a. Tete beche pair
20L20   "   2c *gold, green,* type X   12.00
                  Block of four   50.00
                  a. Tete beche pair   35.00
20L21   "   2c *gold, dark blue,* type X   5.00
                  On cover   100.00
                  Block of four   22.50
                  a. Tete beche pair   25.00
20L22   "   2c *gold, crimson,* type X   10.00
                  Block of four   45.00
                  a. Tete beche pair   30.00

1863   **Typographed**
20L23   L58   2c *red,* type VIII   5.00   10.00
                  On cover   100.00
                  Block of four   25.00
                  a. Tete beche pair   35.00

Cancellations: Black company. Black "PAID"in circle.
No. 20L23 *was reprinted from a new stone on paper of normal color. See note after No. 20L13.*

L61 (Type XI)
No period or center dots.

1867   **Typographed.**
20L24   L61   1c *lilac,* type XI   5.00   10.00
                  On cover   100.00
                  Block of four   25.00
20L25   "   1c *blue,* type XI   4.00   10.00
                  On cover   100.00
                  Block of four   20.00

Cancellation on Nos. 20L24-20L25: Black company.

Boyd's City Dispatch.
(Change in Name.)

L62

1874   Glazed Surface Paper   **Lithographed**
20L26   L62   2c light blue   12.00   12.00
                  On cover   100.00
                  Block of four   60.00

The 2c black on wove paper, type L62, is a cut-out from the Bank Notices envelope, No. 20LU45.

                  Surface Colored Paper.
20L28   L62   2c *red*   40.00
20L29   "   2c *blue, red*   40.00

The adhesives of type L62 were made from the third state of the envelope die.
Nos. 20L28 and 20L29 are color trials, possibly used postally.

                 L63   **L64**

1876   **Lithographed**
20L30   L63   2c lilac, *roseate*
                  Laid Paper
20L31   L63   2c lilac, *roseate*
                  Perf. 12½.
20L32   L63   2c lilac, *roseate*   8.00   12.00
                  On cover   100.00
                  a. 2c lilac, *grayish*   8.00   12.00
                  Laid Paper.
20L33   L63   2c lilac, *roseate*   8.00
                  a. 2c lilac, *grayish*   10.00
                  Glazed Surface Paper.
20L34   L63   2c brown, *yellow*   12.00   12.00
                  a. Imperf. horizontally

1877   **Laid Paper**   **Perf. 11, 12, 12½**
20L35   L64   (1c) violet, *lilac*   8.00   8.00
                  On cover   100.00
                  a. (1c) red lilac, *lilac*   8.00   8.00
                  b. (1c) gray lilac, *lilac*   6.00   6.00
                  c. Vert. pair, imperf. horiz.   *100.00*
20L36   "   (1c) gray, *roseate*   8.00   8.00
                  On cover   125.00
                  a. (1c) gray, *grayish*   8.00

LOCALS

Boyd's Dispatch.
(Change in Name.)

L65
Mercury Series—Type I
Lithographed.
Printed in sheets of 100.
Inner frame line at bottom broken below foot of Mercury.
Printed by C.O. Jones.

				Imperf.
1878		**Wove Paper**		*Imperf.*
20L37	L65	pink	50.00	50.00
		Surface Colored Wove Paper.		
20L38	L65	orange red	110.00	110.00
20L39	"	crimson	110.00	110.00
		Laid Paper.		
20L40	L65	salmon	150.00	
20L41	"	lemon	150.00	150.00
20L42	"	lilac pink		150.00

Nos. 20L37-20L42 are color trials, some of which may have been used postally.

Surface Colored Paper.
Perf. 12

20L43	L65	crimson	17.50	17.50
		On cover		100.00
20L43A	"	orange red	50.00	—

Wove Paper.
Perf. 11, 11½, 12, 12½ and Compound

20L44	L65	pink	1.00	1.00
		On cover		75.00
		a. Horizontal pair, imperf. between	—	—

1879 **Perf. 11, 11½, 12**

20L45	L65	blue	4.00	4.00
		On cover		85.00
20L46	"	blue, blue	12.00	15.00
		On cover		100.00

1880 **Perf. 11, 12, 13½**

20L47	L65	lavender	2.50	2.50
		On cover		85.00
20l48	"	blue, lavender		

1881 **Laid Paper** **Perf. 12, 12½, 14**

20L49	L65	pink		
20L50	"	lilac pink	3.00	3.00
		On cover		85.00

L65a
Mercury Series—Type II.
No break in frame, the great toe raised, other toes touching line.
Printed by J. Gibson.

1881		**Wove Paper**	**Perf. 12, 16 & Compound.**	
20L51	L65a	blue	5.00	5.00
20L52	"	pink		
		On cover		100.00
		Laid Paper		
20L53	L65a	pink	3.00	3.00
		On cover		100.00
20L54	"	lilac pink	3.00	3.00
		On cover		100.00

L65b
Mercury Series—Type III.
No break in frame, the great toe touching.
Printed by the "Evening Post".

1882		**Wove Paper**	**Perf. 10, 11½, 12, 16 & Compound.**	
20L55		L65b blue	3.00	3.00
		On cover		100.00
20L56	"	pink	35	2.00
		On cover		100.00

Cancellation on Nos. 20L37-20L56: Purple company.

Boyd's City Post
ENVELOPES.

L66
Imprinted in upper right corner.
Used envelopes show Boyd's handstamps.

1864		**Laid Paper**	**Embossed**
20LU1	L66	red, *white*	40.00
20LU2	"	red, *amber*	35.00
20LU3	"	red, *yellow*	—
20LU4	"	blue, *white*	60.00
20LU5	"	blue, *amber*	50.00
20LU6	"	blue, *yellow*	—
		Several shades of red and blue.	
20LU7	L66	deep blue, *orange*	— 350.00

Reprinted on pieces of white, fawn and oriental buff papers, vertically, horizontally or diagonally laid.

Wove Paper

20LU8	L66	red, *cream*	65.00	
20LU9	"	red, *orange*	—	150.00
20LU10	"	blue, *cream*	65.00	150.00
20LU11	"	blue, *orange*	—	
20LU11A	"	blue, *amber*		1250.00

Boyd's City Dispatch.

L67 (A) L67 (B)

A. First state of die. Lines and letters sharp and clear. Trefoils at sides pointed and blotchy, middle leaf at right long and thick at end.

B. Second state. Lines and letters thick and rough. Lobes of trefoils rounded and definitely outlined. Stamp impressed normally in upper right corner of envelope; in second state rarely in upper left.

1867		**Laid Paper**	**Typographed**	
20LU12	L67	2c red, *white* (A) (B)	25.00	40.00
20LU13	"	2c red, *amber* (B)	25.00	40.00
20LU14	"	2c red, *cream* (B)	25.00	40.00
20LU15	"	2c red, *yellow* (A) (B)	25.00	50.00
20LU16	"	2c red, *orange* (B)	30.00	50.00

LOCALS

Wove Paper
20LU17	L67	2c red, *white* (A) (B)	25.00	—
20LU18	"	2c red, *cream* (A) (B)	25.00	40.00
20LU19	"	2c red, *yellow* (A)	25.00	40.00
20LU20	"	2c red, *orange* (A)	30.00	50.00
20LU21	"	2c red, *blue* (A) (B)	50.00	75.00

Design as Type L62
First state of die, showing traces of old address.
1874   **Laid Paper.**
| 20LU22 | L62 | red, *amber* | | |
| 20LU23 | " | 2c red, *cream* | 30.00 | 30.00 |

Wove Paper
| 20LU24 | L62 | 2c red, *amber* | | |
| 20LU25 | " | 2c red, *yellow* | | 30.00 |

Second state of die, no traces of address.
1875   **Laid Paper**
| 20LU26 | L62 | 2c red, *amber* | | |
| 20LU27 | " | 2c red, *cream* | 30.00 | — |

Wove Paper
| 20LU28 | L62 | 2c red, *amber* | | |

L68   L69

1877   **Laid Paper**
| 20LU29 | L68 | 2c red, *amber* | | 90.00 |

Stamp usually impressed in upper left corner of envelope.
1878   **Laid Paper**
| 20LU30 | L69 | (1c) red, *amber* | 25.00 | 45.00 |

Wove Paper
| 20LU31 | L69 | (1c) red, *cream* | | |
| 20LU32 | " | (1c) red, *yellow* | | |

Boyd's Dispatch

L70   L71

Mercury Series—Type IV.
Shading omitted in banner. No period after "Dispatch." Short line extends to left from great toe.
1878   **Laid Paper**
20LU33	L70	black, *white*	25.00	60.00
20LU34	"	black, *amber*		45.00
20LU35	"	black, *cream*	30.00	60.00
20LU36	"	red, *white*		30.00
20LU37	"	red, *amber*	20.00	25.00
20LU38	"	red, *cream*	20.00	45.00
20LU39	"	red, *yellow green*		
20LU40	"	red, *orange*		80.00
20LU41	"	red, *fawn*		

Wove Paper.
| 20LU42 | L70 | red, *white* | 10.00 | — |

Mercury Series—Type V.
Colorless crosshatching lines in frame work
1878   **Laid Paper**
| 20LU43 | L71 | red, *white* | — | — |
| 20LU44 | " | red, *cream* | 6.00 | 20.00 |

BANK NOTICES
IMPORTERS' AND TRADERS' NATIONAL BANK
1874   Thin to Thick White Wove Paper
           Incomplete Year Date on Card
| 20LU45 | L62 | 2c black | | 40.00 |

1875-83   Complete Year Date on Card
20LU46	L62	2c black		40.00
20LU47	L63	2c black ('76-'77)		40.00
20LU48	L69	2c black ('78)		40.00
20LU49	L70	2c black ('79)		40.00
20LU50	L70	2c black ('80)		40.00
20LU51	L71	2c black ('81)		—
20LU52	L71	2c black ('82)		—
20LU53	L71	2c black ('83)		—

1880   **NATIONAL PARK BANK**
| 20LU54 | L71 | black, 120x65mm. | | — |

The Bank Notices are in the class of postal cards.
No postmarks or cancellations were used on Bank Notices.

Bradway's Despatch, Millville, N.J.
Operated by Isaac Bradway

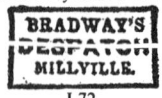

L72

1857   **Typographed**
| 21L1 | L72 | gold, *lilac* | 750.00 | 750.00 |

Brady & Co., New York, N.Y.
Operated by Abner S. Brady at 97 Duane St. Successor to Clark & Co.

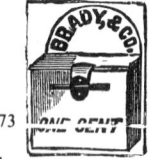

L73

1857   **Typographed**
| 22L1 | L73 | 1c red, *yellow* | 175.00 | 150.00 |
| | | On cover | | 1000.00 |

Cancellations: Blue boxed "PAID." Blue company oval.
Reprints exist.

Brady & Co.'s Penny Post, Chicago, Ill.

L74

1860 (?)   **Lithographed**
| 23L1 | L74 | 1c violet | | 100.00 |

The authenticity of this stamp has not been fully established.

Brainard & Co.
Established by Charles H. Brainard in 1844, operating between New York, Albany and Troy. Exchanged mail with Hale & Co. by whom Brainard had been employed.

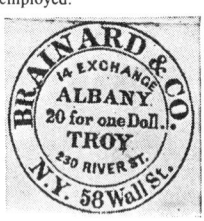

L75

LOCALS

1844   Typographed
24L1   L75   black   100.00   125.00
24L2   "   blue   150.00   175.00
           On Cover   350.00

Prices for Nos. 21L1-24L2 cut to shape are one half of prices quoted.

Brigg's Despatch, Philadelphia, Pa.
Established by George W. Briggs

         L76   L77

1847
25L1   L76   (2c) *yellow buff*   500.00
25L2   "   (2c) *blue*, cut to shape   1000.00

1848
25L4   L77   (2c) gold, *yellow*, glazed   400.00
25L5   "   (2c) gold, *black*, glazed   400.00
25L6   "   (2c) gold, *pink*

Handstamps formerly illustrated as types L78 and L79 are included in the section "Local Handstamped Covers" at the end of the Local Stamp listings. They were used as postmarks and there is no evidence that any prepaid handstamped envelopes or letter sheets were ever sold.

Broadway Post Office, New York, N.Y.
Started by James C. Harriott in 1848. Sold to Dunham & Lockwood in 1855.

               L80

1849(?)   Typographed
26L1   L80   (1c) gold, *black*, glazed   300.00   250.00
           On cover
           Pair on cover   2500.00

1851(?)
26L2   L80   (1c) black   35.00   60.00
           On cover   750.00
           Pair on cover   2000.00
           Block of four   300.00

Cancellation: Black oval "Broadway City Express Post-Office 2 Cts".

Bronson & Forbes' City Express Post, Chicago, Ill.
Operated by W.H. Bronson and G.F. Forbes.

               L81

1855   Typographed
27L1   L81   green   85.00   110.00
           On cover   300.00
27L2   "   lilac   750.00

Cancellation: Black circle "Bronson & Forbes' City Express Post" (2 types).

Brooklyn City Express Post, Brooklyn, N.Y.
According to the foremost students of local stamps, when this concern was organized its main asset was the business of Kidder's City Express Post, of which Isaac C. Snedeker was the proprietor.

               L82

1855-64   Glazed Surface Paper   Typographed
28L1   L82   1c *blue* (shades)   12.00   30.00
           On cover   150.00
           a. Tete beche pair   40.00
28L2   "   1c *green*   12.00   30.00
           On cover   150.00
           a. Tete beche pair   40.00

               L83

No. 28L5 has frame (dividing) lines around design.
28L3   L83   2c *crimson*   —   40.00
           On cover   150.00
28L4   "   2c *pink*   12.00   30.00
           On cover   200.00
           Block of four   55.00
           a. Tete beche pair   40.00
28L5   "   2c *dark blue*   40.00   30.00
           On cover   175.00
           Block of four   225.00
28L6   "   2c *orange*   —   —
           On cover
           a. Tete beche pair   100.00

Unsurfaced Paper Colored Through
28L7   L83   2c *pink*   100.00
           Cancellation: Black ring.

Reprints exist of Nos. 28L1-28L4, 28L6.

Browne & Co.'s City Post Office, Cincinnati, Ohio
Operated by John W.S. Browne.

         L84   L85

1852-55   Lithographed
29L1   L84   1c black (Brown & Co.)   85.00   50.00
           On cover   600.00
           Pair   350.00
29L2   L85   2c black (Browne & Co.)   120.00   100.00
           On cover   750.00
           Pair   500.00

Cancellations: Black, blue or red circle "City Post*". Red, bright blue or dull blue circle "Browne & Co. City Post Paid".

Browne's Easton Despatch, Easton, Pa.
Established by William J. Browne.

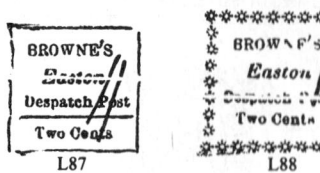

L87   L88

1857			Glazed Surface Paper	Typeset
30L1	L87	2c red	—	500.00
30L2	L88	2c red	—	600.00

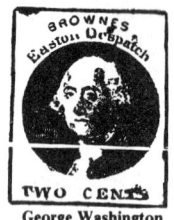

George Washington
L89

			Wove Paper	Engraved.
30L3	L89	2c black	100.00	350.00
		Pair		275.00
		Block of four		1000.00

Cancellation on No. 30L3: Black oval "Browne's Despatch Easton Pa."

Brown's City Post, New York, N.Y.
Established by stamp dealer William P. Brown for philatelic purposes.

L86

1876		Glazed Surface Paper		Typographed
31L1	L86	1c *bright red*	40.00	50.00
		On cover		250.00
31L2	"	1c *yellow*	40.00	50.00
		On cover		250.00
31L3	"	1c *green*	40.00	50.00
		On cover		250.00
31L4	"	1c *violet*	40.00	50.00
		On cover		250.00
31L5	"	1c *vermilion*	40.00	50.00
		On cover		250.00

Cancellation: Black circle "Brown's Despatch Paid".

Bury's City Post, New York, N.Y.

L90   L91

1857		Embossed without color	
32L1	L90	1c *blue*	1250.00
		Handstamped	
32L2	L91	*blue*	200.00

Bush's Brooklyn City Express, Brooklyn, N.Y.

L91a

1848(?)		Cut to shape		Handstamped
157L1	L91a	2c red, *green*, glazed		1500.00

See Bush handstamp in Local Handstamped Covers section.

California City Letter Express Co., San Francisco, Calif.

Organized by J.W. Hoag, proprietor of the Contra-Costa Express, for local delivery. Known also as the California Letter Express Co.

L92

L93

1862-66		Typeset		
33L1	L92	10c red	—	750.00
33L2	"	10c blue	—	1000.00
33L3	"	10c green	—	—
33L4	L93	10c red	—	—
33L5	"	10c blue	—	—
33L6	"	10c green	1000.00	750.00
33L7	"	10c red (no side ornaments, "Hoogs & Madison's" in one line)		1000.00
33L8	"	10c blue (Same as 33L7)		1000.00

California Penny Post Co.

Established in 1855 by J. P. Goodwin and partners. At first confined its operations to San Francisco, Sacramento, Stockton and Marysville, but branches were soon established at Benicia, Coloma, Nevada, Grass Valley and Mokelumne Hill. Operation was principally that of a city delivery post, as it transported mail to the General Post Office and received mail for local delivery. Most of the business of this post was done by means of prepaid envelopes

L94   L95

LOCALS

1855 **Lithographed**
34L1	L94	2c blue	175.00	200.00
		On cover		1500.00
		Block of four	750.00	
34L1A	L95	3c blue	600.00	
34L2	"	5c blue	50.00	100.00
		On cover		1000.00
		Block of four	250.00	
34L3	"	10c blue	200.00	—
		On cover		3000.00

Cancellation: Blue circle "Penny Post Co."

L96
34L4	L96	5c blue	300.00	325.00
		On cover		1000.00
		Strip of three	1000.00	

ENVELOPES.

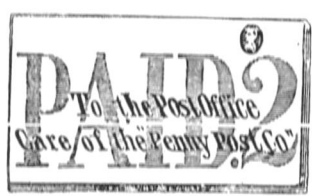

L97

1855-59 (Illustration reduced size.)
34LU1	L97	2c black, *white*	150.00	750.00
		a. Impressed on 3c U.S. env. No. U10	200.00	750.00
34LU2	"	5c blue, *blue*	120.00	
34LU3	"	5c black, *buff*	120.00	
		a. Impressed on 3c U.S. env. No. U10		750.00
34LU4	"	7c black, *buff*	120.00	

L98
34LU6	L98	7c verm. on 3c U.S. env. U9	90.00	500.00
34LU7	"	7c verm. on 3c U.S. env. U10	90.00	600.00

PENNY-POSTAGE PAID, 5.

L98A
34LU8	L98A	5c black, *white*	100.00	400.00
34LU9	"	5c black, *buff*	100.00	400.00
		a. Impressed on 3c U.S. env. No. U10		600.00
34LU10	"	7c black, *white*	100.00	400.00
		a. Impressed on 3c U.S. env. No. U10		750.00
34LU11	"	7c black, *buff*		400.00
		a. Impressed on 3c U.S. env. No. U10		1000.00
34LU11C	"	black, *buff*, "Collect Penny Postage" (no denomination)		750.00

L98B
34LU11B	L98B	7c black on 3c U.S. env. No. U10	850.00
34LU12	"	7c black on 3c U.S. env. No. U9	600.00

OCEAN PENNY POSTAGE.
PAID 5.

L98C
| 34LU13 | L98C | 5c black, *buff* | | 750.00 |

L98D
34LU13A	L98D	5c black, *buff*		—
34LU14	"	7c black, *buff*	100.00	750.00
34LU15	"	7c black on 3c U.S. env. No. U9	125.00	1000.00

The non-government envelopes of types L97, L98A, L98C and L98D bear either 1c No. 9 or 3c No. 11 adhesives. These adhesives are normally canceled with the government postmark of the town of original mailing. Prices are for covers of this kind. The U.S. adhesives are seldom canceled with the Penny Post cancellation. When they are, the cover brings a higher price.

Carnes' City Letter Express, San Francisco, Calif.

Established by George A. Carnes, former post office clerk.

L99   L100

1864 **Typographed**
35L1	L99	(5c) rose	30.00	50.00
		On cover		1500.00

Cancellations: Black dots. Blue dots. Blue "Paid". Blue oval "Wm. A. Frey".

Overprinted "X" in Blue
35L2	L99	10c rose	40.00

Lithographed
35L3	L100	5c bronze	15.00
		a. Tete beche pair	40.00
35L4	"	5c gold	15.00
		a. Tete beche pair	40.00
35L5	"	5c silver	15.00
		a. Tete beche pair	40.00
35L6	"	5c black	15.00
		a. Tete beche pair	40.00
35L7	"	5c blue	15.00
		a. Tete beche pair	40.00
35L8	"	5c red	15.00
		a. Tete beche pair	40.00

Printed in panes of 15 (3x5), the last two horizontal rows being tete beche.

LOCALS

G. Carter's Despatch, Philadelphia, Pa.
Operated by George Carter.

L101

1849-51
36L1
	L101	2c black	—	45.00
		On cover		*150.00*
	a.	Ribbed paper	—	75.00

No. 36L1 exists on paper with a blue, green, red or maroon wash. The origin and status are unclear.
Cancellation: Black circle "Carter's Despatch".

ENVELOPE

L102

36LU1   L102   blue, *buff*   500.00
          Known only used with 3c No.11.

Cheever & Towle, Boston, Mass.
Sold to George H. Barker in 1851.

L104

1849(?)
37L1
	L104	2c blue	200.00	200.00
		On cover		750.00

Cancellation: Red oval "Towle's City Despatch Post 7 State Street".

Chicago Penny Post, Chicago, Ill.

L105

1862   **Typographed**
38L1   L105   (1c) orange brown   185.00   250.00
                On cover   *1,000.00*

Cancellation: Black circle "Chicago Penny Post A. E. Cooke Sup't".

Cincinnati City Delivery, Cincinnati, Ohio
Operated by J. Staley, who also conducted the St. Louis City Delivery Co. He established the Cincinnati post in January, 1883. The government suppressed both posts after a few weeks. Of the 25,000 Cincinnati City Delivery stamps printed, about 5,000 were sold for postal use. The remainders, both canceled and uncanceled, were sold to collectors.

L106

1883   **Typographed**   *Perf. 11*
39L1   L106   (1c) carmine   2.00   20.00
           a. Imperf., pair
        Cancellation: Purple target.

City Despatch Post, New York, N.Y.
The City Despatch Post was started Feb. 1, 1842, by Alexander M. Greig. Greig's Post extended to 23rd St. Its operations were explained in a circular which throws light on the operations of all Local Posts:

**New York City Despatch Post,
Principal Office, 46 William Street.**

"The necessity of a medium of communication by letter from one part of the city to another being universally admitted, and the Penny Post, lately existing having been relinquished, the opportunity has been embraced to reorganize it under an entirely new proprietary and management, and upon a much more comprehensive basis, by which Despatch, Punctuality and Security—those essential elements of success—may at once be attained, and the inconvenience now experienced be entirely removed.

"***Branch Offices—Letter boxes are placed throughout every part of the city in conspicuous places; and all letters deposited therein not exceeding two ounces in weight, will be punctually delivered three times a day *** at three cents each.

"***Post-Paid Letters.—Letters which the writers desire to send free, must have a free stamp affixed to them. An ornamental stamp has been prepared for this purpose *** 36 cnts per dozen or 2 dolls. 50c per hundred.***

"No money must be put in boxes. All letters intended to be sent forward to the General Post Office for the inland mails must have a free stamp affixed to them.

"Unpaid Letters.—Letters not having a free stamp will be charged three cents, payable by the party to whom they are addressed, on delivery.

"Registry and Despatch.—A Registry will be kept for letters which it may be wished to place under special charge. Free stamps must be affixed for such letters for the ordinary postage, and three cents additional be paid (or an additional fee stamp be affixed), for the Registration."

The City Despatch Post ceased to operate as a private carrier on August 15, 1842. It was replaced by the "United States City Despatch Post" which began operation on August 16, 1842, as a Government carrier.

No. 40L1 was issued by Alexander M. Greig; No. 40L2 and possibly No. 40L3 by Abraham Mead; Nos. 40L4-40L8 probably by Charles Cole.

        L106a   Cancellation

Engraved by Rawdon, Wright & Hatch.
Plate of 42 (6x7) subjects.
This was the first adhesive stamp used in the United States. Issued on Feb. 1, 1842. This stamp was also used as a carrier stamp—see No. 6LB1.

1842
40L1	L106a 3c *grayish*	300.00	150.00
	On cover		600.00
	On first day cover		4500.00
	Block of four	1400.00	

Cancellations: Red framed "FREE" (see illustration above). Red circle "City Despatch Post" (2 types).

1847   **Glazed Surface Paper**
40L2	L106a 2c *green*	100.00	60.00
	On cover		150.00
40L3	" 2c *pink*		600.00
	On cover		1750.00

Cancellations: Red framed "FREE". Black framed "FREE". Red circle "City Despatch Post".
Die reprints of No. 40L1 were made in 1892 on various colored papers.

L107
Similar to L106a with "CC" at sides.

1847-50
40L4	L107 2c *green*	350.00	90.00
	On cover		225.00
	a. "C" at right inverted		200.00
	b. "C" at left sideways		200.00
	c. "C" at right only		
40L5	" 2c *grayish*		165.00
	On cover		650.00
	a. "C" at right inverted		250.00
	b. "C" at left sideways		250.00
	c. "C" in ms. between "Two" and "Cents"		200.00
40L6	" 2c *vermilion*	450.00	175.00
	On cover		500.00
	a. "C" at right inverted		250.00
	b. "C" at left sideways		250.00
40L7	" 2c *yellow*		1000.00
40L8	" 2c *buff*		650.00
	a. "C" at right inverted		750.00
	b. "C" at left sideways		750.00

Cancellations: Red framed "FREE". Black framed "FREE". Black "PAID". Red "PAID". Red circle company. Black grid of 4 short parallel bars.

City Dispatch, New York, N.Y.

L107a

1846   **Typographed**
160L1	L107a 2c *red*	800.00	750.00
	On cover		1750.00
	Pair	2000.00	
	Cancellation: Red "PAID".		

City Dispatch, Philadelphia, Pa.

Justice
L108

1860   **Thick to Thin Wove Paper**   **Lithographed**
41L1	L108 1c *black*	5.00	20.00
	On cover		350.00
	Block of four	25.00	

Cancellations: Black circle "Penny Post Philada." Black circled grid of X's.

City Dispatch, St. Louis, Mo.

L109
Initials in black ms.

1851   **Lithographed**
42L1	L109 2c *blue*		1750.00

City Dispatch Post Office, New Orleans, La.
Stamps sold at 5c each, or 30 for $1.

L110

1847   **Glazed Surface Paper**   **Typeset**
43L1	L110 (5c) *green*	1000.00	
	On cover		
43L2	" (5c) *pink*	1000.00	
	On cover		

City Express Post, Philadelphia, Pa.

L111   L112

184-(?)   **Typeset**
44L1	L111 2c *black*	1000.00	
44L2	L112 (2c) *pink*	500.00	
44L3	" (2c) *red, yellow*	3000.00	

City Letter Express Mail, Newark, N.J.
Began business under the management of Augustus Peck at a time when there was no free city delivery in Newark.

L113

LOCALS

1856   **Lithographed**
45L1   L113   1c red   125.00   200.00
                 On cover   500.00
45L2   "   2c red (on cover)   —

On No. 45L2, the inscription reads "City Letter/Express/City Delivery" in three lines across the top.

City Mail Co., New York, N.Y.

There is evidence that Overton & Co. owned this post.

L114

1845
46L1   L114   (2c) *grayish*   1500.00   1000.00
                On cover   1500.00
                Cancellation: Red "PAID".

City One Cent Dispatch, Baltimore, Md.

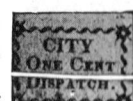
L115

1851
47L1   L115   1c *pink* (on cover)   —

Clark & Co., New York, N.Y.
(See Brady & Co.)

L116

1857   **Typographed**
48L1   L116   1c red, *yellow*   150.00   125.00
                On cover   750.00
                Cancellation: Blue boxed "PAID".

Clark & Hall, St. Louis, Mo.

Established by William J. Clark and Charles F. Hall.

L117
Several varieties

1851   **Typeset**
49L1   L117   1c *pink*   750.00

Clarke's Circular Express, New York, N.Y.

Established by Marion M. Clarke.

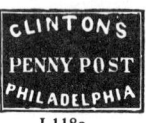
George Washington
L118

Impression handstamped through inked ribbon.
Cut squares from envelopes or wrappers.

1865-68(?)
50LU1   L118   blue, wove paper   350.00
               a. diagonally laid paper   —
50LU2   "   black, diag. laid paper   350.00
               Cancellation: Blue dated company circle.

Clinton's Penny Post, Philadelphia, Pa.

L118a
Typographed
161L1   L188a(1c) black   —

Cook's Dispatch, Baltimore, Md.

Established by Isaac Cook.

L119

1853
51L1   L119   (1c) green, *white*   500.00
                On cover   3000.00
                Cancellation: Red straight-line "I cook"

Cornwell's Madison Square Post Office, New York, N.Y.

Established by Daniel H. Cornwell. Sold to H.W. Bentley.

L120

1856   **Typographed**
52L1   L120   (1c) red, *blue*   75.00   —
52L2   "   (1c) red   100.00   100.00
                On cover   1000.00
                Pair   250.00

Cancellation: Black oval "Cornwall's Madison Square Post Office". Covers also bear black boxed "Paid Swarts".

Cressman & Co.'s Penny Post, Philadelphia, Pa.

L121

1856   **Glazed Surface Paper**
53L1   L121   (1c) gold, *black*   —   125.00
                Pair   400.00
53L2   "   (1c) gold, *lilac*   1750.00
                On cover   3750.00

Cancellation: Acid. (See D.O. Blood & Co. Nos. 15L13-15L16.)

LOCALS 513

Crosby's City Post, New York, N.Y.
Established by Oliver H. Crosby. Stamps printed by J.W. Scott & Co.

L123

			Typographed	
1870				
54L1	L123	2c carmine (shades)	1.00	25.00
		On cover		250.00
		Sheet of 25		25.00

Cancellation: Black oval "Crosby's City Post".

Cummings' City Post, New York, N.Y.
Established by A. H. Cummings.

L124

			Typographed	
1844		Glazed Surface Paper		
55L1	L124	2c rose		500.00
		On cover		
55L2	"	2c green		250.00
		On cover		600.00
55L3	"	2c yellow		275.00
		On cover		500.00

Cancellations: Red boxed "FREE". Red boxed "PAID AHC". Black cork (3 types).

L125

| 55L4 | L125 | 2c green | 750.00 | 750.00 |
| 55L5 | " | 2c olive | 750.00 | 750.00 |

L126

55L7	L126	2c vermilion	2000.00	
		On cover		3500.00
		Same as L124, but "Cummings" erased on cliche.		
55L8	L124	2c vermilion		5000.00

Cutting's Despatch Post, Buffalo, N.Y.
Established by Thomas S. Cutting.

L127

1847		Cut to shape.	
		Glazed Surface Paper	
56L1	L127	2c vermilion	2500.00

Davis's Penny Post, Baltimore, Md.
Established by William D. Davis and brother.

L128

1856		Several varieties	Typeset	
57L1	L128	(1c) lilac		400.00
		On cover		1500.00

Cancellation: Red company circle.

Deming's Penny Post, Frankford, Pa.
Established by Sidney Deming.

L129

1854			Lithographed	
58L1	L129	(1c) grayish	750.00	750.00

Douglas' City Despatch, New York, N.Y.
Established by George H. Douglas.

L130   L131

Printed in sheets of 25.

			Typographed	Perf. 11½	
1879					
59L1	L130	(1c) pink		4.00	5.00
		On cover			150.00
59L2	"	(2c) blue		4.00	5.00
		a. Imperf.		8.00	
		b. Printed on both sides			
			Perf. 12½		
59L3	L131	1c vermilion		3.50	8.00
		On cover			100.00
		a. Imperf.		30	
59L4	"	1c orange		3.50	8.00
59L5	"	1c blue		4.00	8.00
		On cover			100.00
		a. Imperf.		30	
59L6	"	1c slate blue		4.00	8.00
		a. Imperf.		30	

Imperforates are believed to be remainders sold by the printer.

Dupuy & Schenck, New York, N.Y.
Established by Henry J. Dupuy and Jacob H. Schenck, formerly carriers for City Despatch Post and U. S. City Despatch Post.

Beehive
L132

514   LOCALS

1846-48			Engraved	
60L1	L132	(1c) black, glazed paper	125.00	125.00
60L2	"	(1c) *gray*	85.00	75.00
		On cover		500.00
		Cancellation: Red "PAID".		

Eagle City Post, Philadelphia. Pa.
Established by W. Stait, an employee of Adams' Express Co.

L133
Black "WS" manuscript control.

1847		**Pelure Paper**		Typeset
61L1	L133	(2c) *grayish*	1500.00	
		Cut to shape		500.00

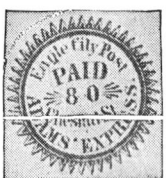 

L134   L135
Two types: 39 and 46 points around circle.

1848			Lithographed	
61L2	L134	(2c) black	40.00	60.00
		On cover		350.00
		Block of four	175.00	
		a. Tete beche pair		150.00
		`Paper varies in thickness.		
1850				
61L3	L135	(1c) red, *bluish*	75.00	75.00
		On cover		200.00
61L4	"	(1c) blue, *bluish*	65.00	65.00
		On cover		200.00
		Block of four	450.00	

Cancellations on Nos. 61L2-61L4: Red "PAID" in large box. Red circular "Stait's at Adams Express."

East River Post Office, New York, N. Y.
Established by Jacob D. Clark and Henry Wilson in 1850, and sold to Sigmund Adler in 1852.

L136   L137

1852			Typographed
62L1	L136	(1c) *rose* (on cover)	200.00
1852-54			Lithographed
62L3	L137	(1c) *green*, glazed	200.00

L138

1855				
62L4	L138	(1c) *green*, glazed	100.00	125.00
		On cover		750.00
		Pair	300.00	

Eighth Avenue Post Office. New York, N. Y.

L139

1852			Typographed
63L1	L139 red		2500.00

Empire City Dispatch, New York, N. Y.
Established by J. Bevan & Son and almost immediately suppressed by the Government.

L140

1881		**Perf. 12**	Typographed	Laid Paper
64L1	L140	*green*		1.00
		Block of four		5.00
		a. Imperf.		
		b. Horiz. or vert. pair, imperf. between		35.00

Essex Letter Express, New York, N. Y.

L141

1856		**Glazed Surface Paper**	Typographed
65L1	L141	2c *red*	250.00

Some authories doubt that No. 65L1 was placed in use.

Faunce's Penny Post, Atlantic City, N. J.
Established in 1884 by Ancil Faunce to provide local delivery of letters to and from the post office. Discontinued in 1887.

L141a

1885		Die cut.		
152L1	L141a	(1c) black, *red*		110.00	175.00
		On cover			900.00

Jabez Fearey & Co's Mustang Express, Newark, N. J.
Established by Jabez Fearey, Local Agent of the Pacific & Atlantic Telegraph Co.

L142

LOCALS

1870		Glazed Surface Paper	Typeset
66L1	L142	red	100.00

Some authorities consider this item to be an express company label rather than a stamp.

Fiske & Rice

Authorities consider items of this design to be express company labels rather than stamps.

Floyd's Penny Post, Chicago, Ill.

Established by John R. Floyd early in 1860, operated by him until June 20, 1861, then continued by Charles W. Mappa.

John R. Floyd
L144

1860			Typographed	
68L1	L144	(1c) blue (shades)	—	50.00
		On cover		*1200.00*
		Pair		*150.00*
68L2	"	(1c) brown	—	80.00
		On cover		*1400.00*
68L3	"	(1c) green	—	100.00
		On cover		*1400.00*

Cancellations: Black circle "Floyd's Penny Post Chicago". Black circle "Floyd's Penny Post" and sunburst. Black or blue oval "Floyd's Penny Post Chicago".

Franklin City Despatch Post, N. Y.

(See Bouton's Manhattan Express.)

Frazer & Co., Cincinnati, Ohio.

Established by Hiram Frazer. Stamps used while he was a Cincinnati letter carrier.

L145
Cut to shape

1845		Glazed Surface Paper	
69L1	L145	2c green	750.00
		On cover	*1250.00*

L146

1845-51		Wove Paper	Lithographed	
69L2	L146	2c *pink*	—	200.00
69L3	"	2c *green*	200.00	200.00
69L4	"	2c *yellow*	200.00	200.00
69L5	"	2c *grayish*	200.00	200.00

Some stamps of type L146 show manual erasure of "& Co."

L147

1848-51				
69L6	L147	2c *rose*	600.00	
69L7	"	2c *blue* (shades)	600.00	600.00
69L8	"	2c *yellow*	1000.00	

Freeman & Co.'s Express, New York, N. Y.

L147a

1855 (?)			Lithographed
164L1	L145a	(25c) blue	500.00

Friend's Boarding School.
Barnesville, Ohio.

(Barclay W. Stratton, Supt.)

On Nov. 6, 1877 the school committee decided to charge the students one cent for each letter carried to or from the post office, one and a half miles away. Adhesive labels were prepared and sold for one cent each. Their sale and use continued until 1884.

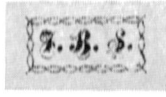

L147b

Several varieties and sizes of frame.

1877		Typographed		
151L1	L147b	(1c) black	65.00	—
		On cover		*150.00*

No. 151L1 was usually affixed to the back of the envelope and left uncanceled.

Gahagan & Howe City Express, San Francisco, Calif.

Established by Dennis Gahagan and C. E. B. Howe, as successors to John C. Robinson, proprietor of the San Francisco Letter Express. Sold in 1865 to William E. Loomis, who later purchased the G. A. Carnes business. Loomis used the adhesive stamps and handstamps of these posts, changing the Carnes stamp by erasing his name.

L148   L149

1849-70				Typeset
70L1	L148	5c light blue	50.00	60.00
70L2	L149	(5c) blue	50.00	55.00
		a. Tete beche pair	125.00	

Sheets of No. 70L2 contain five vertical rows of four, the first two rows being reversed against the others, making horizontal tete beche pairs with wide margins between. The pairs were not evenly locked up in the form.

LOCALS

L150

70L3	L150	(5c) black	25.00	20.00
		Pair		45.00
		Strip of three		75.00
		Overprinted "X" in Blue		
70L4	L150	10c black	85.00	

Cancellations: Blue or black oval "Gahagan & Howe". Blue or black oval "San Francisco Letter Express" and horseman (Robinson). Blue or black oval "PAID" (Loomis).

Glen Haven Daily Mail, Glen Haven, N.Y.

Glen Haven was located at the head of Skaneateles Lake, Cayuga County, N.Y., until 1910 when the City of Syracuse, having purchased the land for reservoir purposes, razed all the buildings.

Glen Haven, by 1848, had becom a famous Water Cure resort, with many sanitariums conducted there. The hamlet had a large summer colony interested in dress reform under the leadership of Amelia Jenks Bloomer; also antislavery, and other reform movements.

A local post was established by the hotel and sanitarium managements for their guests' convenience to deliver mail to the U.S. post offices at Homer or Scott, N.Y. The local stamps were occasionally pen canceled. They are known tied to cover with the Homer or Scott town postmark when the local stamp was placed adjacent to the government stamp and received the cancellation accidentally. The local stamps are only known used in conjunction with government stamps.

L151   L152

1854-58   Typeset.
Several varieties of each.
71L1	L151	1c dark green	300.00	
		a. Gien instead of Glen	500.00	
		Glazed Surface Paper		
71L2	L152	1c green	400.00	400.00
		On cover		750.00

Links at corners   Varying ornaments at corners
L153   L153a
Several varieties of each.
Glazed Surface Paper
71L3	L153	1c green	125.00	125.00
		On cover		600.00
		Pair		500.00
71L4	L153a	1c green	200.00	200.00
		On cover		600.00

Gordon's City Express, New York, N. Y.
Established by Samuel B. Gordon.

L154

1848-52		**Surface Colored Paper**	**Typographed**	
72L1	L154	2c vermilion	750.00	750.00
		On cover		1000.00
72L2	"	2c green	75.00	75.00
		On cover		350.00
		Glazed Surface Paper		
72L3	L154	2c green	85.00	85.00
		On cover		350.00

Cancellation: Small black or red "PAID".

Grafflin's Baltimore Despatch, Baltimore, Md.
Established by Joseph Grafflin.

L155

1856			**Lithographed**	
73L1	L155	1c black	85.00	125.00
		On cover		400.00
		Block of four	600.00	

Originals show traces of a fine horizontal line through tops of most of the letters in "BALTIMORE".

Guy's City Despatch, Philadelphia, Pa.
Established by F. A. Guy, who employed eight carriers.

L156
Sheets of 25 (5x5)
1879		**Typographed**	**Perf. 11, 12, 12½**	
74L1	L156	(1c) pink	12.00	12.00
		On cover		300.00
		a. Imperf., pair		
74L2	"	(1c) blue	15.00	20.00
		On cover		250.00
		a. Imperf., pair		

When Guy's City Despatch was suppressed, the remainders were sold to a New York stamp dealer.

Hackney & Bolte Penny Post, Atlantic City, N. J.
Established in 1886 by Evan Hackney and Charles Bolte to provide delivery of mail to and from the post office. Discontinued in 1887.

L156a

		Die cut		
153L1	L156a	(1c) black on red	125.00	175.00
		On cover		900.00
		On cover with 2c No. 210		1000.00

Hale & Co.

Established by James W. Hale at New York, N.Y., to carry mail to points in New England, New York State, Philadelphia and Baltimore. Stamps sold at 6 cents each or "20 for $1.00."

L157

1838		**Wove Paper (several thicknesses)**		**Typographed**
75L1	L157	(6c) light blue (shades)	30.00	17.50
		Cut to shape		9.00
		On cover		150.00
		Cut to shape on cover		50.00
		Strip of 3 on cover		250.00
75L2	"	(6c) red, *bluish*	100.00	85.00
		Cut to shape		40.00
		On cover		200.00
		Cut to shape on cover		100.00
		Pair on cover		

Same Handstamped in Black or Red, "City Despatch Office, 23 State St."

75L3	L157	(6c) red, *bluish* (Bk), cut to shape	400.00
		Pair, partly cut to shape	1,000.00
75L4	"	(6c) blue (R), cut to shape	400.00

L158

Same as Type L157 but street address omitted.

75L5	L158	(6c) blue (shades)	15.00	10.00
		Cut to shape		5.00
		On cover		100.00
		Cut to shape on cover		40.00
		Pair on cover		175.00
		Block of four		75.00
		Sheet of 20 (5x4)		450.00

Cancellations on Nos. 75L1-75L5: Large red "PAID". Red, black or blue oval "Hale & Co." (several types and cities). Small red ornamental framed box (several types). Red negative monogram "WE' '.

Hall & Mills' Despatch Post, New York, N.Y.

Established by Gustavus A. Mills and A. C. Hall.

L159

Several Varieties.

1847		**Glazed Surface Paper.**		**Typeset**
76L1	L159	(2c) *green*	250.00	250.00
		On cover		500.00
		On cover with 5¢ #1		2000.00

T.A. Hampton City Despatch, Philadelphia, Pa.

L159a   L159b

Several Varieties of L159a.

1847		**Cut to shape**		**Typeset**
77L1	L159a	(2c) black	350.00	350.00
		On cover		900.00
77L2	L159b	black		800.00

A handstamp similar to type L159b with denomination "2cts" or "3c" instead of "PAID." in center has been used as a postmark.

Hanford's Pony Express, New York, N.Y.

Established by John W. Hanford.

L160

1845		**Glazed Surface Paper**		**Typographed**
78L1	L160	2c *orange yellow* (shades)	65.00	85.00
		Cut to shape		35.00
		On cover		500.00

Cancellation: Small red "PAID".

The handstamp in black or red formerly listed as Nos. 78LU1-78LU6 is illustrated in the Local Handstamped Covers section. It was used as a postmark and there is no evidence that any prepaid handstamped envelopes or letterheets were ever sold.

George S. Harris City Despatch Post, Philadelphia, Pa.

L160a   L160b

1847 (?)				**Typeset**
79L1	L160a	(2c) black		500.00
79L2	L160b	black		750.00

Hartford, Conn. Mail Route

L161

Plate of 12 (6x2) varieties.

1844		**Glazed Surface Paper**	**Engraved**	
80L1	L161	(5c) *yellow*	250.00	150.00
		Pair		400.00
		On cover		1000.00
80L3	"	*pink*	300.00	300.00

Chemically affected copies of No. 80L1 appear as buff, and of No. 80L3 as salmon.

Cancellations are usually initials or words ("S", "W", "South", etc.) in black ms. This may indicate destination or routing.

Hill's Post, Boston, Mass.
Established by Oliver B. Hill

L162

1849			**Typographed**
81L1	L162	1c *rose*	750.00

A. M. Hinkley's Express Co., New York, N.Y.

Organized by Abraham M. Hinkley, Hiram Dixon and Hiram M. Dixon, in 1855, and business transferred to the Metropolitan Errand & Carrier Express Co. in same year.

L163

Sheets of 64 (8x8).

1855			**Lithographed**
82L1	L163	1c red, *bluish*	200.00

It is doubtful that No. 82L1 was ever placed in use.
Reprints exist on white paper somewhat thicker than the originals.

Homan's Empire Express, New York, N.Y.
Established by Richard S. Homan.

 L164

Several varieties

1852				**Typeset**
83L1	L164	*yellow*	400.00	400.00
		a. "1" for "I" in "PAID"		500.00

Hopedale Penny Post, Milford, Mass.

Hopedale was a large farm community southwest of Milford, Mass. The community meeting of Feb. 2, 1849, voted to arrange for regular transportation of mail to the nearest post office, which was at Milford, a mile and a half distant, at a charge of 1c a letter. A complete history of this community may be found in "The Hopedale Community," published in 1897.

Rayed asterisks in corners	Plain asterisks in corners
L165	L166

Several varieties of Types L165-L166.

1849		**Glazed Surface Paper**		**Typeset**
84L1	L165	(1c) *pink*	300.00	300.00
84L2	L166	(1c) *pink*	300.00	300.00

Types L165 and L166 probably were printed together in a single small plate.

L167

		Wove Paper		**Typographed**
84L3	L167	(1c) *yellow*	400.00	400.00
		On cover		1,250.00
84L4	"	(1c) *pink*	450.00	450.00
		Pair	1100.00	

J. A. Howell's City Despatch, Philadelphia, Pa.

L167a

184 ?			**Typographed**
165L1	L167a	black	—

Hoyt's Letter Express, Rochester, N.Y.

David Hoyt, agent at Rochester for the express company of Livingston, Wells & Pomeroy, operated a letter and package express by boats on the Genesee Canal between Dansville, N.Y., and Rochester, where connection was also made with Pomeroy's Letter Express.

L168

Several varieties

1844		**Glazed Surface Paper**		**Typeset**
85L1	L168	(5c) *vermilion*	300.00	300.00
		a. "LETTCR" instead of "LETTER"		450.00

Humboldt Express, Nevada

A branch of Langton's Pioneer Express, connecting with the main line of Pioneer Express at Carson City, Nevada, and making tri-weekly trips to adjacent points.

L169

1863			**Lithographed**	
86L1	L169	25c brown	250.00	300.00
		Pair		700.00
		On cover (U.S. Envelopes Nos. U34 or U35)		7500.00

Cancellations: Blue oval "Langton's Pioneer Express Unionville". Red "Langton & Co."

Hussey's Post, New York City, N.Y.
Established by George Hussey.
Reprints available for postage are so described.

L170   L171

LOCALS

1854
				Lithographed	
87L1	L170	(1c) blue			50.00
		On cover			250.00

1856
87L2	L171	(1c) black		150.00	50.00
		On cover			300.00
87L3	"	(1c) red			35.00
		On cover			275.00

Cancellation on Nos. 87L1-87L3: Black "FREE".

L172

L173

1858
87L4	L172	1c brown red	17.50	25.00
		On cover		150.00
		Pair		400.00
87L5	"	1c black	50.00	—
		On cover		—

Cancellation on Nos. 87L4-87L5: Black circle "1ct PAID HUSSEY 50 Wm. ST", date in center.

1858
87L6	L173	(1c) black	2.00	
		On cover		
87L7	"	(1c) rose red	2.00	
		On cover		
87L8	"	(1c) red	8.00	
		On cover		

Type L173 was printed in sheets of 46: 5 horizontal rows of 8, one row of 6 sideways at bottom. Type L173 saw little, if any, commercial use and was probably issued mainly for collectors. Covers exist, many with apparently contemporary corner cards. On cover stamps bear a black HUSSEY'S POST handstamp, but most if not all of Nos. 87L6-87L8 were cancelled after the post ceased to operate.

L174

L175

1858
			Typographed	
87L9	L174	(1c) blue	2.00	

1859
			Lithographed	
87L10	L175	1c rose red	10.00	20.00
		On cover		200.00

No. 87L10 in orange red is not known to have been placed in use.

Cancellations: Black "FREE". Black company circle "1 CT PAID HUSSEY 50 WM ST.", no date in center (smaller than cancel on Nos. 87L4-87L5).

87L11	L175	1c lake		
87L12	"	1c black		

1862
87L13	L176	1c black	15.00	
87L14	"	1c blue	7.00	10.00
		On cover		125.00
87L15	"	1c green	8.00	
		On cover		125.00
87L16	"	1c red	15.00	
87L17	"	1c red brown	15.00	
87L18	"	1c brown	15.00	
87L19	"	1c lake	17.50	
87L20	"	1c purple	12.00	
87L21	"	1c yellow	12.00	

1862
Similar to L174 but has condensed "50" and shows a short flourish line over the "I" of "DELIVERY".

87L22	L177	(1c) blue	70	—
		On cover		—

L178

Similar to L171, but no dots in corners
L179

1863
87L23	L178	(1c) blue	5.00	
87L24	L179	(1c) black	2.00	
87L25	"	(1c) red	5.00	

See also No. 87L52.

L180

L182

87L26	L180	1c brown red	4.00	—
		Block of four	20.00	
		On cover		125.00

A so-called "reprint" of No. 87L26, made for J. W. Scott, has a colored flaw extending diagonally upward from the "I" in "CITY".

Reprints of types L173, L174, L178, L179 and L180 were made in 1875-76 on thicker paper in approximately normal colors and were available for postage.

1863   Dated 1863
87L27	L182	1c blue	8.00	10.00
		On cover		100.00
87L28	"	1c green	12.00	—
		On cover		—
87L29	"	1c yellow	15.00	—
87L30	"	1c brown	10.00	
87L31	"	1c red brown	10.00	
87L32	"	1c red	10.00	
87L33	"	1c black	20.00	
87L34	"	1c violet	20.00	
87L35	"	2c brown	10.00	12.00
		On cover		100.00

The 2c blue dated 1863 exists only as a counterfeit.

1865   Dated 1865.
87L38	L182	2c blue	12.00	12.00
		On cover		225.00

1867   Dated 1867.
87L39	L182	2c blue	20.00	20.00
		On cover		225.00

1868   Dated 1868.
87L40	L182	2c blue	17.50	17.50
		On cover		225.00

1869   Dated 1870.
87L41	L182	2c blue	20.00	20.00
		On cover		225.00

1871   Dated 1871.
87L42	L182	2c blue	22.50	22.50
		On cover		225.00

520   LOCALS

1872		L183	Wove Paper	L184	
87L43	L183	black		2.00	5.00
		On cover			100.00
87L44	"	red lilac		6.00	
		On cover			100.00
87L45	"	blue		5.00	—
87L46	"	green		6.00	—
		On cover			100.00

Sheets contain four panes of 28 each. Double periods after "A.M." on two stamps in two panes, and on four stamps in the other two panes.
Covers show postmark reading: "HUSSEY'S SPECIAL—MESSENGER EXPRESS—PAID—54 PINE ST."

1872			Thick Laid paper		
87L47	L184	black		5.00	8.00
		Block of four		22.50	
		On cover			
87L48	"	yellow		9.00	10.00
87L49	"	red brown		7.00	
		On cover			100.00
87L50	"	red		6.00	8.00
		On cover			

L185

1873			Thin Wove Paper	
87L51	L185	2c black	7.00	8.00
		On cover		85.00

A reprint of No. 87L51, believed to have been made for J. W. Scott, shows a 4mm. break in the bottom frameline under "54."

Type of 1863
1875   Thick Wove Paper
87L52   L179 (1c) blue   —

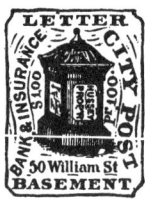
L186

L186 in imitation of L180, but no corner dots, "S" for "$", etc. etc.

1875
87L53   L186 1c black   1.00
Some authorities believe Nos. 87L52-87L53 are imitations made from new stones. Attributed to J. W. Scott.

 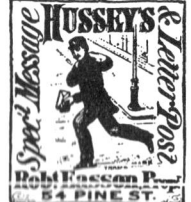

"Copyright 1877"
L188   L188a

1877			Thick Wove Paper.		
87L55	L188	black		75.00	—
		On cover			500.00

Error of design, used provisionally. Stamp was never copyrighted. Printed singly.

87L56	L188a	black		50.00	
		Thin Wove Paper			
87L57	L188a	blue		10.00	
87L58	"	rose		6.00	
		On cover			—
			Perf. 12½.		
87L59	L188a	blue		2.00	5.00
	a. Imperf. horizontally, pair				125.00
		On cover			
87L60	"	rose		2.00	5.00
		On cover			125.00

L189   L190   L191

L189—"TRADE MARK" small.
L190—"TRADE MARK" medium.
L191—"TRADE MARK" larger, touching "s" of "Easson".

1878		Wove Paper	Perf. 11, 11½, 11x12, 12		
87L61	L189	blue		5.00	—
		On cover			125.00
87L62	"	carmine		8.50	—
		On cover			75.00
87L63	"	black		50.00	

Nos. 87L61-87L63 exist imperforate.
Perf. 11, 12, 12½, 14, 16 and Compound

87L64	L190	blue		2.00	5.00
		On cover			75.00
87L65	"	red		2.00	5.00
		On cover			50.00
87L66	"	black		—	

Nos. 87L64-87L66 imperf. are reprints.

1879   Perf. 11, 12, and Compound
87L67	L191	blue		2.00	5.00
		On cover			75.00
87L69	"	black		—	
1880			Imperf.		
87L70	L191	blue		—	
		On cover			225.00
87L71	"	red		—	
87L72	"	black		—	

The authenticity of Nos. 87L69-87L72 has not been fully established.

L192

Two types of L192: I. Imprint "N. F. Seebeck, 97 Wall St. N.Y." is in lower tablet below "R Easson, etc." II. Imprint in margin below stamp.

1880		Glazed Surface Wove Paper		Perf. 12
87L73	L192	brown, type I	5.00	8.00
	a. brown, type II		5.00	8.00
	b. Horiz. pair, imperf. between		20.00	
	c. Imperf., pair		20.00	
	On cover			150.00
	Block of four, type I		—	
87L74	"	ultramarine, type I	7.00	8.00
	a. Imperf., pair		—	
	b. deep blue, type II		20.00	

LOCALS

87L75	L192	red, type II	1.00	
		On cover		85.00
		Block of four	5.00	
1882		***Perf. 16, 12x16***		
87L76	L192	brown, type I	6.00	10.00
		On cover		
87L77	"	ultramarine, type I	6.00	10.00
		On cover		85.00

Cancellations: Violet 3-ring target. Violet ornamental "T".
Imperforate impressions of Type I in various colors, on horizontally laid paper, ungummed, are color trials.

SPECIAL DELIVERY STAMPS.

L181

1863   **Typographed; Numerals Inserted Separately.**
Glazed Surface Paper

87LE1	L181	5c red	1.25	7.50
		On cover		150.00
87LE2	"	10c gold, *green*	1.25	8.50
		On cover		150.00
87LE3	"	15c gold, *black*	1.25	10.00
		On cover		200.00
87LE4	"	20c black	1.25	10.00
		On cover		200.00
87LE5	"	25c gold, *blue*	1.25	8.50
		On cover		200.00
87LE6	"	30c gold, *red*		
87LE7	"	50c *green*		

Nos. 87LE1-87LE7 on cover show Hussey handstamp cancellations in various types.
Nos. 87LE4 and 87LE5 are on unglazed paper, the latter surface colored. Ten minor varieties of each value, except the 30c and 50c, which have the figures in manuscript. Printed in two panes of 10, certain values exist in horizontal cross-gutter tete beche pairs.
Originals of the 5c to 20c have large figures of value. The 25c has condensed figures with decimal point. Reprints exist with both large and condensed figures. Reprints of the 25c also exist with serifs on large figures.
Most of the Hussey adhesives are known on cover, tied with Hussey Express postmarks. Many of these were cancelled after the post ceased to operate as a mail carrier. "On cover" prices are for original stamps used while the post was operating.

WRAPPERS

L192a

1856   **Handstamped.**
Inscribed: "82 Broadway"

87LUP1	L192	black, *white*		175.00
1858		Inscribed: "50 William St. Basement"		
87LUP2	L192a	black, *manila*		175.00
87LUP3	"	black, *white*		175.00

Jefferson Market P. O., New York, N. Y.
Established by Godfrey Schmidt.

L193

1850		**Glazed Surface Paper**		**Lithographed**
88L1	L193	(2c) pink	600.00	450.00
88L2	"	(2c) blue		500.00
		On cover		1250.00

Jenkins' Camden Dispatch, Camden, N. J.
Established by Samuel H. Jenkins and continued by William H. Jenkins.

George Washington
L194   L195

1853		**Lithographed**		
89L1	L194	black (fine impression)	60.00	60.00
		On cover		500.00
		Block of four	300.00	
89L2	"	yellow (coarse impression)		300.00
		Typeset		
89L3	L195	1c *bluish*		

Type L194 printed on envelopes at upper left is considered a corner card.
Some authorities believe No. 89L3 is bogus.

Johnson & Co.'s City Despatch Post,
Baltimore, Md.
Operated by Ezekiel C. Johnson, letter carrier.

L196

1848				**Typeset**
90L1	L196	2c *lavender*		2000.00

Jones' City Express, Brooklyn, N. Y.

George Washington
L197

1845		**Glazed Surface Paper**		**Engraved**
91L1	L197	2c *pink*	350.00	350.00
		On cover		850.00

Cancellation: Red oval "Boyd's City Express Post".

Kellogg's Penny Post & City Despatch,
Cleveland, Ohio.

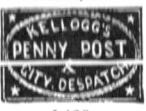

L198

1853				**Typographed**
92L1	L198	(1c) vermilion		400.00
		On cover		600.00

Cancellation: Black grid.

Kidder's City Express Post, Brooklyn, N.Y.

In 1847, Henry A. Kidder took over the post of Walton & Co., and with the brothers Isaac C. Snedeker and George H. Snedeker increased its scope. In 1851, the business was sold to the Snedekers. It was operated under the old name until 1853 when the Brooklyn City Express Post was founded.

L199

Stamps bear black manuscript "I S" control in two styles.

1847		Glazed Surface Paper	Typographed	
93L1	L199	2c *pale blue*	275.00	225.00
		On cover		450.00
		Block of four	1400.00	
		Cancellation: Red "PAID".		
		Reprinted on green paper.		

Kurtz Union Despatch Post, New York, N. Y.

L200

Typeset; "T" in Black Ms.

1853		Glazed Surface Paper		
94L1	L200	2c *green*	3500.00	

Langton & Co.
(See Humboldt Express.)

Ledger Dispatch, Brooklyn, N.Y.

Established by Edwin Pidgeon. Stamps reported to have been sold at 80 cents per 100. Suppressed after a few months.

L201

1882		Rouletted 12 in color	Typographed	
95L1	L201	rose (shades)	50.00	—
		Block of four	300.00	

Letter Express.

Established by Henry Wells. Carried mail for points in Western New York, Chicago, Detroit and Duluth.

L202   L203

1844		Glazed Surface Paper	Typographed	
96L1	L202	5c *pink*	100.00	75.00
		Pair	250.00	200.00
		Block of four	750.00	
96L2	"	5c *green*	—	75.00
		Pair		200.00
96L3	L203	10c Pink	150.00	100.00
		Pair		300.00
	a.	Bisect on cover		750.00

No. 96L3a was sold as a horizontal or vertical bisect. It is known used singly for 5c (rare), or as two bisects for 10c (extremely rare). Stamps are known almost exclusively tied with black ms. "X" covering the cut, and can be authenticate by experts.

L204

| 96L4 | L204 | 10c *scarlet* | — | 300.00 |

Cancellations: Red large partly boxed "PAID". Red boxed "Boyd's City Express Post".

Locomotive Express Post.

L205

1847 (?)			Handstamped	
97L1	L205	black	—	

Wm. E. Loomis Letter Express, San Francisco, Calif.

William E. Loomis established this post as the successor to the Gahagan & Howe City Express, which he bought in 1865. He continued to use the Gahagan & Howe stamps unchanged. Later Loomis bought Carnes' City Letter Express. He altered the Carnes stamp by erasing "CARNES'" from the plate and adding the address below the oval: "S.E. cor. Sans'e & Wash'n."

L206

1868			Typographed	
98L1	L206	(5c) rose	35.00	125.00

McGreely's Express, Alaska.

Established in 1898 by S.C. Marcuse to carry letters and packages by motorboat between Dyea and Skagway, Alaska.

L208

LOCALS

1898   Typographed   *Perf. 14*
155L1   L208   25c blue   10.00
               Block of four   50.00
The status of No. 155L1 is questioned.

McIntires's City Express Post, New York, N. Y.
Established by William H. McIntire.

Mercury
L207

1859   Lithographed
99L1   L207   2c pink   10.00   30.00
               Block of four   60.00
               On cover   300.00
             a. Period after CENTS omitted
Cancellation: Black oval "McIntires's City Express Post Paid".

McMillan's City Dispatch Post, Chicago, Ill.

L208a

1855   Typeset
100L1   L208a   *rose*

Magic Letter Express, Richmond, Va.
Established by Evans, Porter & Co.

L209

1865   Typographed
101L1   L209   2c *brown*   750.00
101L2   "   5c *brown*

Mason's New Orleans City Express, New Orleans, La.
J. Mason, proprietor.

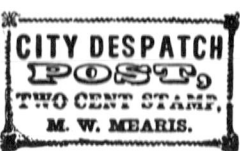

L210

1850-57   Typeset
102L1   L210   ½c *blue* (value changed to "1"
               in black ms.)   750.00
               On cover   2000.00
102L2   "   2c *yellow*   250.00
               On cover   1250.00
Cancellations: Red grid. Small red circle "Mason's City Express".

Mearis' City Despatch Post, Baltimore, Md.
Established by Malcom W. Mearis.

L211   L212

Black ms. initials " M W M" control on all stamps

1846   Typeset
103L1   L211   1c *gray*   300.00   300.00
               On cover   750.00
103L2   L212   1c *gray*   400.00
103L3   "   c *gray*   400.00
             a. Horiz. pair, Nos. 103L2-
               103L3 se-tenant   1500.00

L213

103L4   L213   1c *gray*   400.00
103L5   "   2c *gray*   400.00
             a. Horiz. pair, Nos. 103L4-
               103L5 se-tenant   1500.00

L214

103L6   L214   1c *gray*   500.00
Corner ornaments of Nos. 103L1-103L differ on each stamp. All varieties probably contained in one plate.

Menant & Co.'s Express, New Orleans, La.

L215

1853 (?)   Typographed
104L1   L215   2c dark red   750.00

Mercantile Library Association, New York, N. Y.
Stamps paid for special delivery service of books ordered from the library, and of forms especially provided to subscribers. The forms bore a government stamp on the outside, a library stamp inside.

L216

LOCALS

1870-75				Lithographed
105L1	L216	5c maroon	45.00	50.00
105L2	"	5c yellow	50.00	50.00
105L3	"	5c blue	50.00	50.00
		Pair		125.00
105L5	"	6c maroon	125.00	
105L6	"	10c yellow	85.00	100.00

No. 105L5 is slightly larger than the 5c and 10c stamps.

The stamps "on cover" are affixed to cutouts from order blanks showing order number, title of book desired, and subscriber's name and address. When canceled, the stamps and order blanks show a dull blue double-lined oval inscribed "MERCANTILE LIBRARY ASSOCIATION" and date in center. The stamps are really more a form of receipt for a prepaid parcel delivery service than postage stamps.

POSTAL CARD
Printed on U. S. Postal Card, First Issue.

| 105LU1 | L216 | 10c yellow | 500.00 |

Messenkope's Union Square Post Office, New York, N. Y.

Established by Charles F. Messenkope in 1849 and sold to Joseph E. Dunham in 1850.

L217

1849		Glazed Surface Paper		Lithographed
106L1	L217	(1c) green	60.00	60.00
		On cover		175.00
		Two on cover (2c rate)		350.00
		On cover with 5¢ #1		1200.00
106L2	"	(2c) pink	400.00	350.00
		On cover		500.00

Some examples of No. 106L1 are found with "MESSENKOPES" crossed through in black ms. in an apparent attempt (by Dunham ?) to obliterate it.

Cancellations: Red "PAID". Red oval "DUNHAMS UNION SQUARE POST OFFICE". Red grid of dots.

Metropolitan Errand and Carrier Express Co., New York, N. Y.

Organized Aug. 1, 1855, by Abraham M. Hinkley, Hiram Dixon, and others.

L218

Printed in sheets of 100 (10x10), each stamp separated by thin ruled lines.

1855		Thin to Medium Wove Paper		Engraved
107L1	L218	1c red orange (shades)	10.00	15.00
		Cut to shape	2.50	3.50
		Pair	30.00	
		Block of four	75.00	
		On cover		225.00
107L2	"	5c red orange	85.00	
		Cut to shape	30.00	
107L3	"	10c red orange	85.00	
		Cut to shape	30.00	
107L4	"	20c red orange	125.00	
		Cut to shape	40.00	

Cancellations: Black, blue or green boxed "PAID".
Nos. 107L1-107L4 have been extensively reprinted in brown and in blue on paper much thicker than the originals.

ENVELOPE

L219

		Wide Diagonally Laid Paper	Embossed.
107LU1	L219	2c red, amber	65.00

No. 107LU1 has been reprinted on amber wove, diagonally laid or horizontally laid paper with narrow lines. The embossing is sharper than on the original.

Metropolitan Post Office, New York, N. Y.

Established by Lemuel Williams who later took William H. Laws as a partner.

L220

L221   L222

Nos. 108L1-108L5 were issued die cut, and only exist thus.

1852-53		Glazed Surface Paper		Embossed
108L1	L220	(2c) red (L. Williams)	350.00	350.00
108L2	L221	(2c) red (address and name erased)	400.00	400.00
108L3	L222	(2c) red	100.00	75.00
		On cover		900.00
108L3A	"	(2c) blue	350.00	350.00
		On cover		800.00

L223
Wove Paper

108L4	L223	1c red	60.00	70.00
		On cover		225.00
108L5	"	1c blue	60.00	70.00
		On cover		200.00

Cancellations: Black circle "METROPOLITAN P. O."
Black boxed "PAID W. H. LAWS."

G. A. Mills' Despatch Post, New York, N. Y.

Established by Gustavus A. Mills at 6 Wall St., succeeding Hall & Mills.

L224
Several varieties.

LOCALS

525

1847		**Glazed Surface Paper**		**Typeset**
109L1	L224	(2c) *green*	200.00	200.00
		On cover		500.00

Moody's Penny Dispatch, Chicago, Ill.
Robert J. Moody, proprietor.

L225

Several varieties.

1856		**Glazed Surface Paper**		**Typeset**
110L1	L225	(1c) *red*, "CHICAGO" 8mm.	200.00	175.00
		Vert. strip of 3 showing 3 varieties: period, colon, comma after "Dispatch"		1500.00
		On cover		1000.00
	a.	"CHICAGO" 12½mm.		200.00

Cancellations: Black or blue circle "Moody's Despatch".

New York City Express Post, New York, N.Y.

L226

Several varieties

1847		**Glazed Surface Paper**		**Engraved**
111L1	L226	2c *green*	250.00	150.00
		Cut to shape	60.00	60.00
		On cover		600.00
		Cut to shape on cover		125.00
		Wove Paper		
111L2	L226	2c *orange*	500.00	500.00
		On cover		1000.00

One Cent Despatch, Baltimore, Md., Washington, D.C.

Established by J.H. Wiley to deliver mail in Washington, Georgetown and Baltimore. Made as many as five deliveries daily at 1 cent if prepaid, or 2 cents payable on delivery.

L227

Two types: I. Courier's letter points to "O" of "ONE."
II. Letter points to "N" of "ONE."

1856		**Washington, D.C.**		**Lithographed**
		Inscribed at bottom "Washington City"		
112L1	L227	1c *violet*	100.00	60.00
		On cover		650.00
		Horiz. pair, Types I & II se-tenant		600.00
		Baltimore, Maryland.		
		No name at bottom		
112L2	L227	1c *red*	100.00	85.00
		On cover		800.00

Cancellation on Nos. 112L1-112L2: Black circle "City Despatch".

Overton & Co.

Carried mail principally between New York and Boston; also to Albany. Stamps sold for 6c each, 20 for $1.

L229

1844				
113L1	L229	(6c) *greenish*	200.00	150.00
		On cover		350.00
		Pair		400.00

Cancellation: Black "PAID".
A variety of this stamp has "FREE" below the design.

Penny Express Co.

Little information is available on this post, but a sheet is known carrying the ms. initials of Henry Reed of the Holladay staff. The post was part of the Holladay Overland Mail and Express Co. system.

In 1866 in the West the "short-bit" or 10 cents was the smallest currency generally used. The word "penny" is believed to refer to the "half-bit" or 5 cents (nickel)

L230

Printed in sheets of 32 (8x4).

1866				**Lithographed**
114L1	L230	5c *black*		100.00
	a.	Initialed "HR", black ms. As "a", block of four		
114L2	"	5c *blue*		5.00
		Block of four		21.00
114L3	"	5c *red*		5.00
		Block of four		21.00

Nos. 114L1-114L3 lack gum and probably were never placed in use.

Philadelphia Despatch Post, Philadelphia, Pa.
See D.O. Blood & Co.

Pinkney's Express Post, New York, N.Y.

L231

1851		**Glazed Surface Paper**		**Typographed**
115L1	L231	2c *green*		1000.00
		Cut to shape		600.00

Pips Daily Mail, Brooklyn, N.Y.

L232

LOCALS

1862 (?)			Lithographed	
116L1	L232	1c black	75.00	
116L2	"	1c *buff*	60.00	—
116L3	"	1c *yellow*	60.00	
116L4	"	1c *dark blue*	60.00	
116L5	"	1c *rose*	65.00	
		Block of four	—	

Pomeroy's Letter Express.

Established in 1844 by George E. Pomeroy. Carried mail principally to points in New York State. Connected with Letter Express for Western points.

L233

Engraved by John E. Gavit, Albany, N. Y. (Seen as "GAVIT" in bottom part of stamp). Sheets of 40 (8x5).

1844		Surface Colored Wove Paper		
117L1	L233	5c *yellow*	3.00	15.00
		On cover		125.00
		Pair		100.00
		Pair on cover		300.00
117L2	"	*yellow* (value incomplete)		100.00
		On cover		200.00
		Thin Bond Paper		
117L3	L233	5c blue	1.50	25.00
		On cover		100.00
117L4	"	5c black	1.50	25.00
		On cover		125.00
		Strip of four on cover		500.00
117L5	"	5c red	1.50	35.00
		On cover		—
117L6	"	5c lake	100.00	100.00
		On cover		—
		Pair on cover		—
117L7	"	5c orange	5.00	—

Cancellations: Large red partly boxed "PAID" (Nos. 117L1, 117L6). Red "Cd" (Nos. 117L1-117L2, 117L4); stamps are considered "tied to cover" by this "Cd" when the impression shows through the letter paper.

All stamps except No. 117L2 have "20 for $1" in tablet at the bottom. On No. 117L2 the value is incomplete.

Remainders (reprints?) of Nos. 117L1, 117L3, 117L4 and 117L5 are plentiful in unused condition, including multiples and sheets. A 5c black on yellow paper colored through and a 5c brown were prepared for use but never issued. No. 117L2 was never reprinted.

P. O. Paid, Philadelphia, Pa.
See note in Carriers' Stamps Section.

Price's City Express,
New York, N. Y.

L235   L236

1857-58		Glazed Surface Paper	Lithographed
119L1	L235	2c *vermilion*	100.00
		On cover	750.00
119L2	"	2c green	85.00

1858				
		Sheets of 108 (12x9).		
119L3	L236	2c *green*	5.00	55.00
		On cover		—
		Block of four	25.00	

Cancellation on No. 119L3: Black oval "Price's City Express".

Price's Eighth Avenue Post Office,
New York, N. Y.

Established by James Price at 350 Eighth Avenue, in 1854, and sold to Russell in the same year.

L237

1854			Lithographed
120L1	L237	(2c) red, *bluish*	200.00

Priest's Despatch
Philadelphia, Pa.

Established by Solomon Priest.

L238   L239

1851		Glazed Surface Paper	Typographed	
121L1	L238	(2c) silver, *vermilion*	300.00	300.00
121L2	"	(2c) gold, *dark blue*	500.00	
		Wove Paper		
121L2A	L238	(2c) bronze, *bluish*	250.00	250.00
121L3	"	(2c) *yellow*	150.00	
121L4	"	(2c) *rose*	150.00	
121L5	"	(2c) *blue*	150.00	
121L6	L239	(2c) *yellow*	150.00	
121L7	"	(2c) *blue*	150.00	
121L8	"	(2c) *rose*	150.00	
121L9	"	(2c) *emerald*	250.00	

Prince's Letter Dispatch, Portland, Maine.

Established by J. H. Prince of Portland. Mail carried nightly by messenger travelling by steamer to Boston. Stamp engraved by Lowell of Lowell & Brett, Boston, his name appearing in the design below the steamship.

L240

Printed in sheets of 40 (5x8).

1861			Lithographed	
122L1	L240	black	5.00	50.00
		On cover		750.00
		Block of four	25.00	
		Sheet of forty	275.00	

LOCALS

527

Private Post Office, San Francisco, Calif.
ENVELOPES.

L241
(Illustration reduced size.)
Impressed on U. S. Envelopes, 1863-64 Issue.

1864				Typographed
123LU1	L241	15c blue, *orange*		
		(on U. S. No. U56)		350.00
123LU2	"	15c blue, *buff*		
		(on U. S. No. U54)		350.00
	a.	15c blue, *buff*		
		(on U. S. No. U58)		150.00
	b.	15c blue, *buff*		
		(on U. S. No. U59)		150.00
123LU3	"	25c blue, *buff*		
		(on U. S. No. U54)		350.00

Providence Despatch, Providence, R.I.

L242

1849			Typeset
124L1	L242	black	2000.00

Public Letter Office, San Francisco, Calif.
ENVELOPES.

L243
(Illustration reduced size.)
Impressed on U. S. Envelopes, 1863-64 Issue.

1864			Typeset
125LU1	L243	black	200.00
125LU2	"	blue	200.00
125LU3	"	15c blue	250.00
125LU4	"	25c blue	250.00

**Reed's City Despatch Post,
San Francisco, Calif.**

Pioneer San Francisco private post. Also serving Adams & Co. for city delivery.

L244

1853-54		Glazed Surface Paper	Lithographed
126L1	L244	*green*, on cover	
126L2	"	*blue*	3000.00

Cancellation: Blue double-circle "Adams & Co. San Francisco".

Ricketts & Hall, Baltimore, Md.
Successors to Cook's Dispatch

L244a

1857		Cut to shape		Typographed
127L1	L244a 1c red, *bluish*		750.00	900.00

Robinson & Co., Brooklyn, N. Y.

L245

1855-56			Typographed
128L1	L245 1c *blue*		300.00 300.00
	On cover		4000.00

Cancellation: Blue "PAID".

**Roche's City Dispatch,
Wilmington, Del.**

L246

1850		Glazed Surface Paper	Typographed
129L1	L246 (2c) *green*		750.00
	Cut to shape		400.00
	On cover		1250.00

A black negative handstamp similar to type L246 served solely as a postmark and no evidence exists that any prepaid handstamped envelopes or lettersheets were ever sold.

Rogers' Penny Post, Newark, N.J.

Established by Alfred H. Rogers, bookseller, at 194 Broad St., Newark, N.J.

L246a
Cut to shape

1856		Glazed Surface Paper	Handstamped
162L1	L246a *(1c) green*		

See Rogers' handstamp in Local Handstamp Covers section.

Russell Eighth Avenue Post Office, New York, N. Y.
(See Price's Eighth Avenue Post Office.)

L247

LOCALS

1854-58			Wood Engraving	
130L1	L247	(2c) blue, *rose*	150.00	125.00
		On cover		400.00
130L2	"	(2c) *yellow*	175.00	150.00
		On cover		400.00
130L3	"	(2c) red, *bluish*	250.00	200.00
		On cover		500.00
130L4	"	(2c) blue green, *green*		——

St. Louis City Delivery Company, St. Louis, Mo.
(See Cincinnati City Delivery)

L249

1883			Typographed.	Perf. 12.
131L1	L249	(1c) red	1.00	1.50
		Block of four	5.00	
		On cover		150.00
		a. Imperf., pair		
		Cancellation: Purple target.		

Smith & Stephens' City Delivery, St. Louis, Mo.

L284
Typeset

| 158L1 | L284 | 1c *pale rose* | | —— |

Spaulding's Penny Post, Buffalo, N. Y.

L283   L283a

1848-49				
156L1	L283	2c vermilion		1250.00
156L2	L283a	2c carmine		2000.00

Spence & Brown Express Post, Philadelphia, Pa.

L285   L286
(Illustrations reduced size)

1847 (?)				Typeset
159L1	L285	2c *bluish*	750.00	750.00
1848			Lithographed	
159L2	L286	(2c) black	600.00	600.00

Squier & Co. City Letter Dispatch, St. Louis, Mo.
(Jordon & Co.)

This post began to operate as a local carrier on July 6, 1859 and was discontinued in the early part of 1860. Squier & Co. used imperforate stamps; their successors (Jordan & Co.) about Jan. 1 1860, used the roulettes.

L248

1859			Lithographed	*Imperforate*
132L1	L248	1c green	——	75.00
		On cover		500.00
1860			Rouletted 19	
132L2	L248	1c rose brown	75.00	75.00
		On cover		400.00
132L3	"	1c brownish purple	75.00	75.00
		On cover		400.00
132L4	"	1c green	75.00	75.00
		On cover		400.00

Cancellation: Black circle "Jordan's Penny Post Saint Louis".

Staten Island Express Post, Staten Island, N. Y.
Established by Hagadorn & Co., with office at Stapleton, Staten Island. Connected with Boyd for delivery in New York City.

L250

1849				Typographed
133L1	L250	3c vermilion	350.00	300.00
133L2	"	6c vermilion	——	1250.00

Stringer & Morton's City Despatch, Baltimore, Md.
According to an advertisement in the Baltimore newspapers, dated October 19, 1850, this post aimed to emulate the successful posts of other cities, and divided the city into six districts, with a carrier in each district. Stamps were made available throughout the city.

L251

1850			Glazed Surface Paper	
134L1	L251	(1c) gold, *black*	100.00	——
		On cover		750.00

Cancellation: Black circle "Baltimore City Despatch & Express Paid".

Sullivan's Dispatch Post, Cincinnati, Ohio

L252

1853			Glazed Surface Paper	Lithographed
135L1	L252	(2c) *green*		1500.00
			Wove Paper	
135L2	L252	(2c) bluish black		1500.00
135L3	"	(2c) green	——	1200.00

Nos. 135L1-135L2 are either die cut octagonally or cut round. They do not exist cut square.

LOCALS

Swarts' City Dispatch Post, New York, N.Y.

Established by Aaron Swarts, at Chatham Square, in 1847, becoming one of the largest local posts in the city.

The postmarks of Swarts' Post Office are often found on stampless covers, as this post carried large quantities of mail without using adhesive stamps.

Zachary Taylor L253		George Washington L254	
1849-53		Glazed Surface Paper	Lithographed
136L1	L253 (2c) *light green*	—	100.00
	On cover		250.00
136L2	" (2c) *dark green*	—	75.00
	On cover		200.00
		Wove Paper	
136L3	L253 (2c) pink	—	20.00
	On cover		125.00
136L4	" (2c) red (shades)	20.00	15.00
	On cover		125.00
136L5	" (2c) pink, *blue*	—	35.00
	On cover		175.00
136L6	" (2c) red, *blue*	—	35.00
	On cover		175.00
136L7	" (2c) black, *blue gray*	100.00	85.00
	On cover		175.00
136L8	" (2c) blue	—	90.00
	On cover		300.00
136L9	L254 (1c) red	—	20.00
	On cover		175.00
136L10	" (1c) pink	—	15.00
	On cover		175.00
136L11	" (1c) red, *bluish*	—	25.00
	On cover		175.00
136L12	" (1c) pink, *bluish*	—	35.00
	On cover		175.00
	Bouton's Stamp with Red ms. "Swarts" at Top		
136L13	L49 2c *gray blue*	250.00	250.00
	On cover		500.00

L255

Printed in sheets of 25 (5x5). Five minor varieties, the stamps in each vertical row being identical.

136L14	L255 1c blue	—	40.00
	On cover		200.00
	a. Thin paper	5.00	
	As "a," block of four	25.00	
136L15	" 1c red	—	50.00
	On cover		250.00
136L16	" 1c red, *bluish*	—	75.00
	On cover		350.00
136L17	" 1c black, on cover		1250.00

Nos. 136L3-136L4, 136L9-136L10, 136L14-136L15 have been reprinted.

Cancellations: Red boxed "PAID" (mostly on Nos. 136L1-136L8, 136L13). Black boxed "PAID SWARTS" (mostly on Nos. 136L9-136L12). Black oval "Swarts Post Office Chatham Square" (Nos. 136L9-136L12). Black oval "Swarts B Post Chatham Square". Black grids (5-bar rectangle, 6-bar circle, solid star, hollow star, star in circle, etc). Other handstamp postmarks of the post have been found as cancellations. Government town postmarks exist on almost all Swarts stamps.

Teese & Co. Penny Post, Philadelphia, Pa.

L256

Printed in sheet of 200 divided into two panes of 100. Each pane includes setting of 20, repeated 5 times. Vertical or horizontal tete beche pairs appear twice in each setting. Twenty varieties.

1852		Wove Paper	Lithographed
137L1	L256 (1c) blue, *bluish*	6.50	35.00
	On cover		400.00
	Block of four	35.00	
	a. Tete beche pair	45.00	

Telegraph Despatch P. O., Philadelphia, Pa.

L257

1848			
138L1	L257 1c black, *yellowish*		600.00
138L2	" 2c black, *yellowish*		2000.00

The 2c differs in design, including the address, "Office No. 6 Sth 8 St" at bottom.

Third Avenue Post Office, New York, N. Y.

Established by S. Rotheneim, a former carrier for Boyd's City Express. All stamps were cut to shape by hand before being sold and exist only in that form.

L258

1855		Glazed Surface Paper	Handstamped
139L1	L258 2c green	250.00	250.00
	On cover		700.00
139L1A	" 2c blue, *green*	400.00	
139L2	" 2c maroon	400.00	
	Unsurfaced Paper colored through.		
139L3	L258 2c *yellow*	200.00	
139L4	" 2c *blue*	450.00	
139L5	" 2c *brown*	450.00	
139L6	" 2c *buff*	250.00	
139L7	" 2c *pink*	450.00	
139L8	" 2c *green*	400.00	400.00

Cancellation on No. 139L1: Black "PAID".

Union Post, New York, N. Y.

L259

1846		Thick Glazed Surface Paper	Handstamped
140L3	L259 blue, *green* ("UNOIN")	3000.00	
140L4	" red, *blue* ("UNION")	2000.00	
	On cover		

Type L259 was used also as a postmark, usually struck in blue.

Union Square Post Office, New York, N. Y.

Established by Joseph E. Dunham about 1850. In 1851 Dunham acquired Messenkope's Union Square Post Office, operating the combined posts until 1854 or 1855. The business was sold in 1855 to Phineas C. Godfrey.

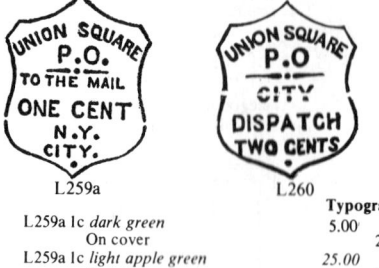

		L259a	L260		
1852				**Typographed**	
141L1	L259a 1c *dark green*			5.00	20.00
	On cover				250.00
141L2	L259a 1c *light apple green*			25.00	20.00
	On cover				200.00
141L3	L260 2c *rose*			1.50	
	Block of four			8.50	

Walton & Co.'s City Express, Brooklyn, N. Y.
Operated by Wellington Walton

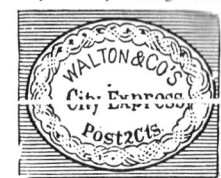

L261

1846		**Glazed Surface Paper**		**Lithographed**
142L1	L261 2c *pink*		400.00	300.00
	On cover			700.00

Cancellations: Black "PAID / W. W." Black oblong quad (ties stamp "through" to cover).

Wells, Fargo and Co.

Wells, Fargo & Company entered the Western field about July 1, 1852, to engage in business on the Pacific Coast, and soon began to acquire other express businesses, eventually becoming the most important express company in its territory.

The Central Overland, California and Pikes Peak Express Company, inaugurated in 1860, was the pioneer Pony Express system and was developed to bring about quicker communication between the extreme portions of the United States. Via water the time was 28 to 30 days, with two monthly sailings, and by the overland route the time was 28 days. In 1860 the pioneer Pony Express carried letters only, reducing the time for the 2,100 miles (St. Joseph to San Francisco) to about 12 days. The postage rate was originally $5 the half-ounce.

About April 1, 1861, Wells, Fargo & Company became agents for the Central Overland, California and Pikes Peak Express Company and issued $2 red and $4 green stamps.

The rates were cut in half about July 1, 1861, and new stamps were issued: the $1 red, $2 green and $4 black, and the $1 garter design.

The revival of the Pony Express in 1862, known as the "Virginia City Pony" resulted in the appearance of the "cents" values, first rate.

Advertisement in the Placerville newspaper, Aug. 7, 1862: "Wells, Fargo & Co.'s Pony Express. On and after Monday, the 11th inst., we will run a Pony Express Daily between Sacramento and Virginia City, carrying letters and exchange papers, through from San Francisco in 24 hours, Sacramento in 15 hours and Placerville in 10 hours. Rates: All letters to be enclosed in our franks, and TEN CENTS PREPAID, in addition, for each letter weighing half an ounce or less, and ten cents for each additional half-ounce."

Wells, Fargo & Company used various handstamps to indicate mail transit. These are illustrated and described in the handbook, "Wells, Fargo & Co.'s Handstamps and Franks" by V. M. Berthold, published by Scott Stamp & Coin Co., Ltd. (out of print). The history of the Pony Express, a study of the stamps and reprints, and a survey of existing covers are covered in "The Pony Express," by M. C. Nathan and Winthrop S. Boggs, published by the Collectors Club, 22 E. 35th., New York, N.Y. 10016.

Wells Fargo stamps of types L262-L264 were lithographed by Britton & Rey, San Francisco.

L262

Printed in sheets of 40 (8x5), two panes of 20 (4x5) each.

1861		**(April to July 1)**		**Lithographed**
143L1	L262 $2 red		125.00	250.00
	On U. S. envelope No. U10			—
	On U. S. envelope No. U16			—
	On U. S. envelope No. U17			*6000.00*
	On U. S. envelope No. U18			*6000.00*
	On U. S. envelope No. U32 (patriotic cover)			*13,000.00*
	On U. S. envelope No. U33			*6000.00*
	On U. S. envelope No. U65			—
143L2	" $4 green		225.00	400.00
	Block of four			—
	On U. S. envelope No. U33			—
1861		**(July 1 to Nov.)**		
143L3	L262 $1 red		60.00	135.00
	Block of four		325.00	
	On U. S. envelope No. U11			—
	On U. S. envelope No. U15			*4500.00*
	On U. S. envelope No. U17			*4500.00*
	On U. S. envelope No. U32			*6000.00*
	On U. S. envelope No. U33			*6000.00*
	On U. S. envelope No. U35			*4500.00*
	On U. S. envelope No. U40			*6000.00*
	On U. S. envelope No. U41			*5000.00*
143L4	" $2 green		175.00	250.00
	Block of four		900.00	
	On U. S. envelope No. U41			*11,000.00*
143L5	" $4 black		150.00	500.00
	Block of four			—

Cancellations: Blue, black or magenta express company.

Nos. 143L1-143L5 and 143L7-143L9 were reprinted in 1897. The reprints are retouched. Shades vary from originals. Originals and reprints are fully described in "The Pony Express," by M. C. Nathan and W. S. Boggs (Collectors Club).

L263

Printed in sheets of 16 (4x4)

		Thin Wove Paper		
1861				
143L6	L263 $1 blue		300.00	600.00
	On 10c U.S. envelope No. U40			*17,500.00*

No. 143L6 apparently used only from east to west.
One counterfeit has a horizontal line bisecting the shield. Another, without the line, is sometimes called a reprint.

L264

PARK CITIES STAMPS

STAMP DEALER

SPECIALIZING IN . . .

UNITED STATES LOCALS
REVENUES - TAX PAID
MATCH & MEDICINE
CINDERELLAS
STATE REVENUES

Excellent, Comprehensive Stock.
We Welcome Your Want List.

BUYING & SELLING

Paying Highest Prices For The Above.
Ship with price or for our prompt offer.

PARK CITIES STAMPS

Byron J. Sandfield • Phone 214-361-4322
6440 N. Central, Suite 609
Dallas, TX 75206

Member: ARA, TPA, U.S. Classic Society.

LOCALS

Printed in sheets of 40 (8x5), four panes of 10, each pane 2x5.

1862-64

143L7	L264	10c brown (shades)	30.00	75.00
		Pair	75.00	350.00
		Block of four	250.00	
		On U. S. envelope No. U26		5000.00
		On U. S. envelope No. U34		4500.00
		On U.S. envelope No. U35		3500.00
		On cover with 3c #65		
143L8	"	25c blue	50.00	75.00
		Pair	125.00	
		Block of four	350.00	
		On plain cover		2250.00
		On U.S. envelope No. U10		
		On U.S. envelope No. U34		3500.00
		On U.S. envelope No. U35		4000.00
143L9	"	25c red	20.00	40.00
		Pair	60.00	
		Block of four	150.00	
		On U.S. envelope No. U9		
		On U.S. envelope No. U10		4000.00
		On U.S. envelope No. U34		4000.00
		On U.S. envelope No U35		4000.00
		Pair on U.S.envelope No. U35		9000.00

Cancellations on Nos. 143L7-143L9: Blue or black express company. Black town.

NEWSPAPER STAMPS

L265

L266

L267

L268

L269

L270

1861-70

143LP1	L265	black	250.00	300.00
143LP2	L266	blue	350.00	
143LP3	L267	blue	10.00	
		a. Thin paper	20.00	
143LP4	L268	blue	25.00	

Rouletted 10.

143LP5	L267	blue	15.00	25.00
		On wrapper		
		Block of four	75.00	
		a. Thin paper		
143LP6	L268	blue	15.00	
		a. Tete beche	100.00	

Type L267 was printed in sheets of 50 (5x10).

1883-88 *Perf. 11, 12, 12½*

143LP7	L268	blue	7.50	
143LP8	L269	blue	12.50	17.50
143LP9	L270	blue	1.50	2.00
		On wrapper		
		a. Vertical pair, imperf. between	60.00	
		b. Horiz. pair, imperf. vert.		
		Double transfer		

FOR PUBLISHERS' USE

L271

1876

143LP10	L271	blue		Typographed
			5.00	15.00
		Block of four	25.00	
		On wrapper		500.00

Cancellation: Blue company

ENVELOPES

1862

143LU1	L264	10c red	—	750.00
143LU2	"	10c blue	—	750.00
143LU3	"	25c red	350.00	
		On "Gould & Curry" overall advertising envelope	350.00	

Westervelt's Post, Chester, N. Y.

Operated by Charles H. Westervelt. Rate was 1 cent for letters and 2 cents for packages carried to the post office. Local and government postage required prepayment.

L273
Several varieties

1863 (?)

144L1	L273	(1c) *flesh*	20.00	Typeset
		On cover		500.00
144L2	"	lavender	25.00	
		On cover		

Indian Chief
L274

General U. S. Grant
L275

Six varieties

1864 (?)

144L9	L274	(1c) red, *pink*	20.00	Typeset
		On cover		500.00

Six varieties

1865 Typographed

144L29	L275	2c *yellow*	20.00	
144L30	"	2c gray green	25.00	
144L40	"	2c red, *pink*	25.00	

All of the Westervelt stamps are believed to have a philatelic flavor, although it is possible that Nos. 144L1-144L2 were originally issued primarily for postal purposes. It is possible that Nos. 144L29-144L30 and 144L40 were used in the regular course of business, particularly No. 144L9. However, the large number of varieties on various colors of paper, which exist both as originals as well as contemporary and near-contemporary reprints, are believed to have been produced solely for sale to collectors. Type L275 was certainly issued primarily for sale to collectors. Many of the unlisted colors in all three types exist only as reprints. Forgeries of all three types also exist.

LOCALS

533

L276
ENVELOPES
Impressed at top left.

1865			Typographed
144LU1	L276	red, *white*	——
144LU2	"	red brown, *orange*	200.00
144LU3	"	black *bluish*	——
144LU4	"	black, *buff*	——
144LU5	"	black, *white*	——

It is possible that Nos. 114LU1-144LU5 were corner cards and had no franking value.

Westtown, Westtown, Pa.

The Westtown School at Westtown, Pa., is the oldest of the secondary schools in America, managed by the Society of Friends. It was established in 1799. In 1853 the school authorities decided that all outgoing letters carried by stage should pay a fee of 2 cents. Prepaid stamps were placed on sale at the school. Stamps were usually affixed to the reverse of the letter sheets or envelopes.

At first, letters were usually mailed at West Chester, Pa. After March 4, 1859, letters were sent from Street Road Post Office, located at the railroad station. Later this became the Westtown Post Office. The larger stamp was the first used. The smaller stamp came into use about 1867.

L277 L.277a

Several types of each, with and without hyphen.

1853-67(?)			Lithographed	
145L1	L277 (2c) gold		30.00	——
145L2	L277a (2c) gold		10.00	*10.00*
	On cover			*110.00*
	Block of four		500.00	
	a. Tete beche pair		*100.00*	

No. 145L1 in red brown is a color changeling.

Whittelsey's Express, Chicago, Ill.
Operated by Edmund A. and Samuel M. Whittelsey.

George Washington
L.278

1857		Typographed	
146L1	L.278 2c red	375.00	*600.00*
	Block of four	——	

Cancellation: Blue oval "Whittelsey's Express".

Williams' City Post, Cincinnati, Ohio
See Carriers' Stamps, No. 9LB1.

Wood & Co. City Despatch, Baltimore, Md.
Operated by W. Wood.

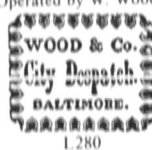

L.280

1856			Typeset
148L1	L280 (1c) *yellow*	——	750.00

W. Wyman, Boston, Mass.
Established to carry mail between Boston and New York.

L281

1844			Lithographed	
149L1	L281 5c black		——	125.00
	On cover			500.00

No. 149L1 may have been sold singly at 6 cents each.

Zieber's One Cent Dispatch, Pittsburgh, Pa.

L282

1851			Typeset
150L1	L282 1c *gray blue*	——	2000.00

Cancellation: Acid

For Local 151L1 see under
Friend's Boarding School.

For Local 152L1 see under
Faunce's Penny Post.

For Local 153L1 see under
Hackney & Bolte Penny Post.

For Local 154L1 see under
A. W. Auner's Despatch Post.

For Local 155L1 see under
McGreely's Express.

For Local 156L1-2 see under
Spaulding's Penny Post.

For Local 157L1 see under
Bush's Brooklyn City Express.

For Local 158L1 see under
Smith & Stephens City Delivery.

For Local 159L1-2 see under
Spence & Brown Express Post.

For Local 160L1 see under
City Dispatch, New York City.

For Local 161L1 see under
Clinton's Penny Post.

For Local 162L1 see under
Rogers' Penny Post.

For Local 163L1 see under
Blizzard Mail.

For Local 164L1 see under
Freeman & Co.'s Express, New York City.

For Local 165L1 see under
J. A. Howell's City Despatch

LOCAL HANDSTAMPED COVERS

In 1836–1860 when private companies carried mail, many of them used handstamps on the covers they carried. Examples of these handstamps are shown on this and following pages.

Accessory Transit Co. of Nicaragua.

Black

Red, Black or Blue
A sub-variety shows "Leland" below "MAILS"
in lower right corner.

1853   Blue

Barker's City Post, Boston, Mass.

1856–57   Black
Also known with "10" instead of "34" Court Square.

E. N. Barry's Despatch Post, New York City, N.Y.

1852 (?)   Black

Bates & Co., New Bedford, Mass.
(Agent for Hale & Co. at New Bedford)

1845   Red

Branch Post Office, New York City, N. Y.
(Swarts' Chatham Square Post Office)

1847   Red

Brigg's Despatch, Philadelphia, Pa.

1848   Black, Red or Blue

HANDSTAMPED COVERS

Bush's Brooklyn City Express, Brooklyn, N. Y.

1848   Red

Cover shows red PAID.

City Despatch & Express, Baltimore, Md.

1856   Black

Cover shows black PAID.

City Despatch Post, New York City, N. Y.
(Used by Mead, successor to
United States City Despatch Post.)

1848   Black

City Dispatch Post, Baltimore, Md.

Red brown

City Despatch & Express, Baltimore, Md.

1850   Black

Cole's City Despatch P.O., New York City, N. Y.
(Used by Cole with some of the
City Despatch Post stamps.)

1848   Black or Red

Dunhams Post Office, New York City, N. Y.
(See Union Square Post Office).

Red

Gay, Kinsley & Co., Boston, Mass.
(A package express)

Red

Hanford's Pony Express Post,
New York, N.Y.

1845   Black or Red

Hartford Penny Post, Hartford, Conn.

1853   Black

536 HANDSTAMPED COVERS

Hudson Street Post Office,
New York City, N. Y.

1850   Red

Cover shows red PAID.

Jones & Russell's Pikes Peak Express Co.,
Denver, Colo.

1859–60   Black

Kenyon's Letter Office, 91 Wall St., New York City

1859   Red

Letter Express, San Francisco, Cal.
(See Gahagan & Howe, San Francisco, Cal.)

Blue

Libbey & Co.'s City Post, Boston, Mass.

    LIBBEY & CO'S
    CITY POST.
    10 COURT SQUARE

1852   Black or Red

Cover has 3c 1851 postmarked Boston, Mass.

Manhattan Express, New York City, N. Y.
(W. V. Barr. See also Bouton's Manhattan Express.)

1847   Red

New York Penny Post,
New York City, N. Y.

1840–41   Black or red

Also known with hour indicated

Noisy Carriers, San Francisco, Cal.

Blue or Green

Blue

Black or Red

HANDSTAMPED COVERS

Pony Express.

1860   Blue or Red

Blue
(Enlarged)

Black or Carmine

Blue or Red

Black, Blue or Green

Black

1853-56   Black or Blue

Northern Liberties News Rooms, Philadelphia, Pa.

1836   Black   Black

Press printed
Two types

Overton & Co.'s City Mail, New York City, N. Y.

1845   Red

from
St. Joseph, Mo.	Black or Green
Denver City, K. T.	Black
Leavenworth City, K. T.	Black
San Francisco, Cal.	Blue

Black or Green

Red

1860   Blue

Rogers' Penny Post, Newark, N. J.

1856   Black or Red

Spark's Post Office, New York City, N. Y.

Spaulding's Penny Post, Buffalo, N. Y.

1848   Black

Spence & Brown Express Post, Philadelphia, Pa.

1848   Black

Stait's Despatch Post, Philadelphia, Pa.
(Eagle City Post)

1850   Black

Red

HANDSTAMPED COVERS

Stone's City Post, New York City, N. Y.

1859   Red

J. W. Sullivan's Newspaper Office
San Francisco, Cal.

1854   Black or Red

Towle & Co. Letter Delivery, Boston, Mass.

1847   Red

Towle's City Dispatch Post, Boston, Mass.

1849   Red

Towle's City Post, Boston, Mass.

1849   (Also 10 Court Sq.)
Red
Cover shows PAID.

TELEGRAPH STAMPS

THESE stamps were issued by the individual companies for use on their own telegrams, and can usually be divided into three classes: Free franking privileges issued to various railroad, newspaper and express company officials, etc., whose companies were large users of the lines; those issued at part cost to the lesser officials of the same type companies; and those bearing values which were usually sold to the general public. Some of the companies on occasion granted the franking privilege to stockholders and minor State (not Federal) officials. Most Telegraph Stamps were issued in booklet form and will be found with one or more straight edges.

American Rapid Telegraph Company.

Organized February 21st, 1879, in New York State. Its wires extended as far north as Boston, Mass., and west to Cleveland, Ohio. It was amalgamated with the Bankers and Merchants Telegraph Co., but when that company was unable to pay the fixed charges, the properties of the American Rapid Telegraph Company were sold on March 11th, 1891, to a purchasing committee comprised of James W. Converse and others. This purchasing committee deeded the property and franchise of the American Rapid Telegraph Company to the Western Union Telegraph Company on June 25th, 1894. Issued three types of stamps-Telegram, Collect and Duplicate. Telegram stamps were issued in sheets of 100 and were used to prepay messages which could be dropped in convenient boxes for collection. Collect and duplicate stamps were issued in alternate rows on the same sheet of 100 subjects. Collect stamps were attached to telegrams sent collect, the receiver of which paid the amount shown by the stamps, while the Duplicate stamps were retained by the Company as vouchers. Remainders with punched cancellations were bought up by a New York dealer.

T1

Engraved and Printed by the American Bank Note Co.

1881 Perf. 12

"Prepaid Telegram" Stamps

			Unused	Used	Punched
1T1	T1	1c black	4.50	3.00	8
		Block of four	20.00		40
1T2	"	3c orange	12.00	8.00	50
		Block of four			4.00
1T3	"	5c bistre brown	85	30	8
		Block of four	4.00		40
		a. 5c brown	85	40	10
		Block of four	4.00		50
1T4	"	10c purple	5.00	3.00	7
		Block of four	22.50		15
1T5	"	15c green	2.00	60	8
		Block of four	9.00		40
1T6	"	20c red	2.00	50	5
		Block of four			25
1T7	"	25c rose	3.00	75	10
		Block of four	13.00		50
1T8	"	50c blue	5.00	3.00	60
		Block of four			3.50

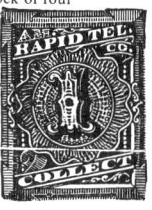

T2

"Collect" Stamps

			Unused	Used	Punched
1T9	T2	1c brown	2.50	2.00	10
1T10	"	5c blue	1.50	50	10
1T11	"	15c red brown	1.00	40	25
1T12	"	20c olive green	75	50	10

T3

"Office Coupon" Stamps

			Unused	Used	Punched
1T13	T3	1c brown	4.00	1.50	10
		a. Pair, se-tenant with "Collect"			1.50
		Block of four, same as "a"			3.25
1T14	"	5c blue	3.00	1.50	10
		a. Pair, se-tenant with "Collect"	7.00		2.25
		Block of four, same as "a"	15.00		5.00
1T15	"	15c red brown	5.00	2.00	20
		a. Pair, se-tenant with "Collect"	9.00		2.50
		Block of four, same as "a"	20.00		5.50
1T16	"	20c olive green	5.00	2.00	10
		a. Pair, se-tenant with "Collect"			2.50
		Block of four, same as "a"			5.50

Atlantic Telegraph Company

Organized 1884 at Portland, Maine. Its lines extended from Portland, Me., to Boston, Mass., and terminated in the office of the Baltimore and Ohio Telegraph Company at Boston. Later bought out by the Baltimore and Ohio Telegraph Co. Stamps issued by the Atlantic Telegraph Company could also be used for messages destined to any point on the Baltimore and Ohio system. Stamps were printed in panes of six and a full book sold for $10. Remainders of these stamps, without control numbers, were purchased by a Boston dealer and put on the market about 1932.

T4

TELEGRAPHS 541

1888		Perf. 13	Unused	Used	Remainders (no control numbers)
2T1	T4	1c green	2.50	—	2.00
		Pane of six	—	—	14.00
2T2	"	5c blue	2.50	—	2.00
		Pane of six	—	—	14.00
		a. Imperf. vert., pair	—	—	
		b. Imperf. horiz., pair	20.00	—	
2T3	"	10c purple brown	2.50	—	2.00
		Pane of six	—	—	14.00
		a. Horiz. Pair, imperf. between	30.00	—	
2T4	"	25c carmine	2.50	—	2.25
		Pane of six	—	—	16.00

Baltimore & Ohio Telegraph Companies.

"The Baltimore & Ohio Telegraph Co. of the State of New York" was incorporated May 17, 1882. Organization took place under similar charter in 26 other states. It absorbed the National Telegraph Co. and several others. Extended generally along the lines of the Baltimore & Ohio Railroad, but acquired interests in other states. Company absorbed in 1887 by the Western Union Telegraph Co. Stamps were issued in booklet form and sold for $5.00 and $10.00, containing all denominations.

T5

T6

Engraved by the American Bank Note Co.
Perf. 12

1885				
3T1	T5	1c vermilion	20.00	10.00
		Pane of six	140.00	
3T2	"	5c blue	25.00	17.50
3T3	"	10c red brown	12.00	8.00
		Pane of six	75.00	
3T4	"	25c orange	22.50	12.00
3T5	T6	brown	1.00	
		Pane of four	6.00	
1886				
3T6	T6	black	1.00	
		Pane of four	6.00	

Imprint of Kendall Bank Note Co.
1886		Thin Paper. Perf. 14.		
3T7	T5	1c green	4.00	.50
		a. Thick paper	6.00	.85
		b. Imperf., pair	60.00	
3T8	"	5c blue	3.00	.75
		a. Thick paper	5.00	.75
		b. Imperf., pair		50.00
3T9	"	10c brown	4.00	.60
		a. Thick paper	5.00	.85
3T10	"	25c deep orange	12.50	.75
		a. Thick paper	12.50	1.00

Used copies of Nos. 3T7-3T20 normally have heavy grid cancellations. Lightly canceled copies command a premium.

Lithographed by A. Hoen & Co.
Imprint of firm
Perf. 12.

1886				
3T11	T5	1c green	2.50	.25
		Pane of six	17.50	—
3T12	"	5c blue	5.00	.25
		Pane of six	35.00	
		a. Imperf., pair	—	
3T13	"	10c dark brown	4.00	.40
		Pane of six	25.00	—
		a. Vertical pair, imperf. between		50.00

Wmkd. "A. HOEN AND CO. BALTIMORE" in double lined capitals in sheet.
Perf 12.

3T14	T5	1c green	7.00	1.00
		Pane of six	45.00	—
3T15	"	5c blue	12.50	1.00
		Pane of six	80.00	—
		a. Imperf., pair	40.00	—
3T16	"	10c dark brown	9.00	.85
		Pane of six	60.00	—

Lithographed by Forbes Co., Boston.
Imprint of firm.
Perf. 12½.

1887				
3T17	T5	1c green	15.00	1.00
3T18	"	5c blue	17.50	1.50
3T19	"	10c brown	12.50	1.50
3T20	"	25c yellow	15.00	1.00
		a. 25c orange	15.00	1.00

Baltimore & Ohio — Connecticut River Telegraph Companies.

The Connecticut River Telegraph Co. ran from New Haven to Hartford. An agreement was entered wherein the Baltimore & Ohio System had mutual use of their lines. This agreement terminated when the Baltimore & Ohio System was absorbed by the Western Union. The Connecticut River Telegraph Company then joined the United Lines. In 1885 stamps (black on yellow) were issued and sold in booklets for $10. In 1887 the Connecticut River Telegraph Co. had extended its lines to New Boston, Mass., and new books of stamps (black on blue) were issued for use on this extension. Remainders were cancelled with bars and sold to a New York dealer.

T7

1885		Perf. 11	Unused	Used	Remainders (Bar canc.)
4T1	T7	1c yellow	3.00	7.50	.30
		Pane of ten	35.00		4.00
		a. Imperf., pair	40.00		
		b. Imperf. horizontally, pair			
4T2	"	5c yellow	3.00	7.50	.25
		Pane of ten	35.00		3.00
		a. Horizontal pair, imperf. between			
		b. Vertical pair, imperf. between			35.00
		c. Imperf., pair			35.00
4T3	"	1c blue	6.00	—	2.00
		Pane of ten	65.00		22.50
4T4	"	5c blue	6.00	—	2.00
		Pane of ten	65.00		22.50

California State Telegraph Company.

Incorporated June 17, 1854 as the California Telegraph Company and constructed a line from Nevada through Grass Valley to Auburn. Extended to run from San Francisco to Marysville via San Jose and Stockton. Later absorbed Northern Telegraph Co. and thus extended to Eureka. It was incorporated as the California State Telegraph Company on April 6, 1861. At the time of its lease to the Western Union on May 16, 1867 the California State consisted of the following companies which had been previously absorbed: Alta California Telegraph Co., Atlantic and Pacific States Telegraph Co., National Telegraph Co., Northern California Telegraph Co., Overland Telegraph Co., Placervelle and Humboldt Telegraph Co. Tuolumne Telegraph Co. Stamps were issued in booklets, six to a pane. Remainers of Nos. 5T1 and 5T4, without frank numbers are known.

TELEGRAPHS

T8

1870

			Perf. 13½		
5T1	T8	black & blue		45.00	
		Pane of six		285.00	
		a. Without number		40.00	

T9 T10

			Perf. 12, 13		
1870					
5T2	T9	black & red, without number		110.00	110.00
1871			Dated "1871"		
5T3	T9	black & red, without number		200.00	
		a. Imperf., pair		—	
5T4	T10	black & salmon, blue number		100.00	—
		Pane of six		—	
1872					
5T5	T10	green & red, red number			
		(No year date)		100.00	—
		Pane of six		—	
1873			Dated "1873".		
5T6	T10	red & salmon, blue number		140.00	140.00
1874			Dated "1874".		
5T7	T10	blue & salmon, black number		55.00	—
		Pane of six		—	
1875			Dated "1875".		
5T8	T10	brown & green, black number		100.00	—
		Pane of six		—	

City & Suburban Telegraph Company.
(New York City and Suburban Printing Telegraph Company.)

Organized 1855. Extended only through New York City and Brooklyn. Sold out to the American Telegraph Co. Stamps were sold to the public for prepayment of messages, which could be dropped in convenient boxes for collection. Stamps were issued in sheets of 60 having a face value of $1.00. These were arranged in six vertical rows of ten, the horizontal rows having the following denominations: 2c, 1c, 1c, 1c, 2c, 3c.

Counterfeits are known both in black and blue, mostly on pelure or hard white paper. Originals are on soft wove paper, somewhat yellowish scalloped edge is more sharply etched on the counterfeits.

T11

			Typographed		
			Imperf.		
6T1	T11	1c black		110.00	100.00
		Pair		—	
		Block of four		—	
6T2	"	2c black		175.00	140.00
		Pair		—	
		Pair, 2c + 1c		350.00	
6T3	"	3c black		275.00	225.00
		Pair		—	
		Strip of three, 1c, 2c and 3c		1000.00	

Colusa, Lake & Mendocino Telegraph Company.

Was organized in California early in 1873. First known as the Princeton, Colusa and Grand Island Telegraph Co. In May, 1873 they completed their line from Princeton through Colusa, at which point it was connected with the Western Union office, to Grand Island. On Feb. 10, 1875 it was incorporated as the Colusa, Lake & Mendocino Telegraph Co. Its lines were extended into the counties of Colusa, Lake, Mendocino and Napa. Eventually reached a length of 260 miles. Went out of business in 1892. Stamps were issued for prepayment of mesages and were sold in books. When sold they were stamped "P.L.W." (the superintendent's initials) in blue. The 5c value was printed 10 to a pane, being two horizontal rows of five. Of the 10c and 25c nothing definite is known about the settings.

T11a

			Perf. 12.		
1876					
7T1	T11a	5c black		175.00	—
		Block of four		750.00	
		Pane of ten		2000.00	
		Without "P.L.W."		225.00	
7T2	"	10c black		9000.00	—
7T3	"	25c red		9000.00	—

Commercial Union Telegraph Company.

Incorporated in New York State on March 31, 1886. Its lines ran from Albany through Troy to Berlin, N.Y., thence to North Adams, Mass. The lines of this Company, which was controlled by the Postal Telegraph Company, were later extended throughout Northern New York and the States of Massachusetts, Vermont, New Hampshire and Maine. Stamps issued in panes of four.

T12

T13

TELEGRAPHS

T14
Lithographed by A. C. Goodwin.
1891 *Perf. 12.*

8T1	T12	25c yellow	12.50	
		Pane of four	55.00	
8T2	T13	25c green	10.00	
		Pane of four	45.00	
		a. Imperf. vertically (pair)	40.00	
8T3	T14	lilac rose	25.00	

Mutual Union Telegraph Company

Incorporated October 4, 1880. Extended over 22 states. Absorbed about 1883 by the Western Union Telegraph Co. Franks issued for use of stockholders, in books, four to a pane.

T15
Engraved by Van Campen Engraving Co., New York.
1882-83 *Perf. 14.*

9T1	T15	blue	18.00	18.00
		Pane of four	75.00	
		a. Imperf. horizontally (pair)	60.00	
		b. Imperf., pair	60.00	
9T2	"	carmine	20.00	
		Pane of four	85.00	

North American Telegraph Company

Incorporated October 15, 1885 to run from Chicago to Minneapolis, later being extended into North and South Dakota. Absorbed In 1929 by the Postal System.
Apparently these stamps were not cancelled when used. Issued in panes of four.

T15a
1899-1907 *Perf. 12.*

10T1	T15a	violet	(1899)	50.00
		Pane of four		210.00
10T2	"	green	(1901)	60.00
10T3	"	dark brown	(1902)	80.00
10T4	"	blue	(1903)	60.00
10T5	"	violet	(1904)	50.00
		Pane of four		210.00
		a. Imperf. vertically (pair)		200.00
10T6	"	red brown	(1905)	40.00
10T7	"	rose	(1906)	50.00
10T8	"	green	(1907)	225.00

Nos. 10T1 to 10T8 are known imperforate.

Northern Mutual Telegraph Company.

Incorporated in New York State as the Northern Mutual Telegraph and Telephone Company on June 20, 1882. Its line, which consisted of a single wire, extended from Syracuse to Ogdensburg via Oswego, Watertown and Clayton, a distance of 170 miles. It was sold to the Bankers and Merchants Telegraph Company in 1883. Stamps were in use for a few days only in April, 1883. Issued in panes of 35 having a face value of $5.00. Seven horizontal rows of five covering all denominations as follows: 2 rows of 25c, 1 of 20c, 2 of 10c, 2 of 5c. The remainders and plates were purchased by a New York dealer in 1887.

T16
1883 *Perf. 14*

11T1	T16	5c yellow brown	4.00	
		Block of four	17.50	
11T2	"	10c yellow brown	4.00	
		Block of four	17.50	
11T3	"	20c yellow brown	10.00	
		Horizontal pair	22.50	
11T4	"	25c yellow brown	4.00	
		Block of four	17.50	
		Pane of 35	225.00	

The first reprints are lighter in color than the originals, perf. 14 and the gum is yellowish instead of white. The pane makeup differs in the reprints. The second reprints are darker than the originals, perf. 12. Price 75c each.

Northern New York Telegraph Company.

Organized about 1892. Extended from Malone, N.Y. to Massena, N.Y. Re-incorporated as the New York Union Telegraph Co. on April 2, 1896.

T16a
Typographed by Charles H. Smith, Brushton, N.Y.
1894-95 *Rouletted.*

12T1	T16a	green (overprinted in red "Frank 1894")	60.00	
		Pane of six	375.00	
12T2	"	red (overprinted in black "Frank 1895")	125.00	
		Pane of six	775.00	
12T3	"	1c yellow (overprinted in black "One")	80.00	
		Pane of six	500.00	
12T4	"	10c blue (overprinted in red "10")	100.00	
		Pane of six	650.00	

Some specialists believe that Nos. 12T1-12T4 were not issued and probably are essays.

Pacific Mutual Telegraph Company.

Incorporated in Missouri on June 21, 1883. Operated between St. Louis and Kansas City, Mo., during the years 1884 and 1885. It had 15 offices, 425 miles of poles and 850 miles of wire. The controlling interests were held by the Bankers and Merchants Telegraph Company. The name was changed on Sept. 10, 1910 to Postal Telegraph-Cable Company of Missouri. Stamps were issued in booklets having a face value of $10 and containing 131 stamps as follows: 50-1c, 20-5c, 45-10c, 16-25c. They are not known used.

T17
1883
Perf. 12.

13T1	T17	1c black		22.50
13T2	"	1c slate		35
		Block of four		1.50
		a. 1c gray		35
		Block of four		1.50
13T3	"	5c *buff*		40
		Block of four		1.75
13T4	"	10c *green*		25
		Block of four		1.25
		a. Horizontal pair, imperf. between		
13T5	"	25c *salmon buff*		.30
		Block of four		1.50

Pacific Postal Telegraph-Cable Company.

The Pacifc Postal Telegraph-Cable Company was the Pacific Coast Department of the Postal Telegraph-Cable Company, and was organized in 1886. Its first wire ran from San Francisco to New Westminster, B.C., where it touched the lines of the Canadian Pacific Railway Company, then the only connection between the Eastern and Western Postal systems. Later the Postal's own wires spanned the continent and the two companies were united.

Stamps issued in booklet form in vertical panes of five.

T16b
Perf. 12 x Imperf.

14T1	T16b	10c brown	30.00	25.00
		Pane of five	150.00	
14T2	"	15c black	20.00	15.00
		Pane of five	105.00	
14T3	"	25c rose red	30.00	25.00
		Pane of five	160.00	
14T4	"	40c green	25.00	20.00
		Pane of five	135.00	
14T5	"	50c blue	30.00	25.00
		Pane of five	160.00	

These stamps were issued with three sizes of frank numbers; large closely spaced, small closely spaced and small widely spaced figures.

They also exist without frank numbers.

Postal Telegraph Company.

Organized in New York in 1881. Reorganized in 1891 as the Postal Telegraph-Cable Co. The Postal Telegraph Co stamps of 1885 were issued in sheets of 100. Some years after the reorganization a New York dealer purchased the remainders which were cancelled with a purple star. The Postal Telegraph-Cable Co. issued frank stamps in booklets, usually four stamps to a pane. This company was merged with the Western Union Telegraph Company in 1943.

T18 T19

T20 T21

Engraved by Hamilton Bank Note Co.

1885
Perf. 14.

				Unused	Used	Remainders (Purple Star)
15T1	T18	10c green		1.75	—	25
		Block of four		8.00		1.25
		a. Horizontal pair, imperf. between				20.00
		b. 10c deep green		1.75	—	25
		Block of four		8.00		1.25
15T2	T19	15c orange red		2.50	—	60
		Block of four		12.00		3.00
		a. Horizontal pair, imperf. between		25.00		
15T3	T20	25c blue		1.00	4.00	15
		Block of four		5.00		75
		a. Horizontal pair, imperf. between		30.00		
15T4	T21	50c brown		1.50	—	60
		Block of four		7.00		3.00

The 25c in ultramarine and the 50c in black were printed and perforated 16 but are not known to have been issued. Price about $5 each.

T22 T22a

Typographed by Moss Engraving Co.
1892-1920
Perf. 14
Signature of A.B. Chandler.

15T5	T22	blue gray	(1892)	15.00	
		a. Imperf., pair		50.00	
		Perf. 13 to 14½ and Compound.			
15T6	T22	gray lilac	(1892)	15.00	
15T7	"	red	(1893)	12.00	10.00
		Pane of four		50.00	
15T8	"	red brown	(1893)	4.00	3.00
		Perf. 12.			
15T9	T22	violet brown	(1894)	6.00	
15T10	"	gray green	(1894)	4.00	
		a. Imperf., pair		20.00	
15T11	"	blue	(1895)	15.00	
15T12	"	rose	(1895)	70.00	
15T13	T22a	slate green	(1896)	5.00	
		Pane of four		17.50	
15T14	"	brown	(1896)	60.00	

Nos. 15T11 and 15T12 are from a new die resembling T22 but without shading under "Postal Telegraph Co."

TELEGRAPHS

Signature of Albert B. Chandler.

15T15	T22a	lilac brown	(1897)	1.25
		Pane of four		5.50
15T16	"	orange	(1897)	50.00

Typographed by Knapp & Co.

15T17	T22a	pale blue	(1898)	1.25
		Pane of four		5.50
15T18	"	rose	(1898)	70.00

Typographed by Moss Engraving Co.
Perf. 12.

15T19	T22a	orange brown	(1899)	1.25
		Pane of four		5.50

Perf. 11

15T20	T22a	blue	(1900)	2.50	2.50
		a. "I" "Complimentary" omitted		40	

The variety 15T20a represents a different die with many variations in the design

Perf.14.

15T21	T22a	sea green	(1901)	40	40
		Pane of four		1.75	
		a. Horiz. pair, imperf. between			

Signature of John W. Mackay.

15T22	T22a	chocolate	(1902)	.50
		Pane of four		2.50

Signature of Clarence H. Mackay.

15T23	T22a	blue	(1903)	2.50	2.50

Perf. 12.

15T24	T22a	blue, *blue*	(1904)	2.00	2.00
		Pane of four		9.00	
15T25	"	blue, *yellow*	(1905)	3.50	
		Pane of four		15.00	
15T26	"	blue, *light blue*	(1906)	2.50	
		Pane of four		11.00	
		a. Imperf. vertically, pair			

T22b

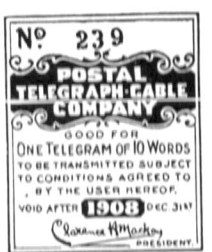

T22c

Perf. 12.

15T27	T22b	*yellow* (laid paper)	(1907)	25.00
		Pane of four		105.00
15T28	"	blue, *pink*(laid paper)	(1907)	17.50
		Pane of four		75.00

"One Telegram of 10 Words."

15T29	T22c	blue	(1908)	25.00
		Pane of four		105.00
15T30	"	yellow	(1908)	70.00
		Pane of four		300.00
15T31	"	black	(1908)	22.50
		Pane of four		95.00
15T32	"	brown	(1909)	17.50
		Pane of four		75.00
		a. Date reads "1908"		100.00
15T33	"	olive green	(1909)	12.50
		Pane of four		55.00
15T34	"	dark blue	(1910)	17.50
15T35	"	dark brown	(1910)	15.00
15T36	"	violet	(1911)	90.00
15T37	"	blue	(1912)	100.00
15T38	"	violet	(1913)	100.00

Perf. 14

15T39	T22c	violet (not dated)	(1914)	40.00
		a. Red violet		40.00
		Pane of four		170.00

"One Telegram."
Perf. 12

15T40	T22c	blue,	(1908)	30.00
		Pane of four		125.00
15T41	"	lilac	(1909)	15.00
		Pane of four		60.00
15T42	"	*yellow* (laid paper)	(1910)	60.00
15T43	"	violet	(1910)	10.00
		a. Red violet		10.00
		Pane of four		
		Pane of eight		90.00
15T44	"	dark blue,	(1911)	25.00
		Pane of four		100.00
15T45	"	light violet,	(1912)	20.00
		Pane of four		85.00

Perf. 14.

15T46	T22c	dark blue	(1913)	20.00
		Pane of eight		165.00
		a. Imperf. vertically, pair		60.00
		b. Perf. 12		40.00
15T47	"	dark blue, (not dated)	(1914)	20
		Pane of four		1.50
		Pane of eight		1.75

In panes of four the stamps are 4½ mm. apart horizontally, panes of eight 5½ mm. There are two types of design T22c, one with and one without spurs on colored curved lines above "O" of "Postal" and below "M" of "Company". Both types are known of 15T47.

Nos. 15T39 and 15T47 Overprinted with date in double line numerals, all four numerals complete on each stamp.

15T47A	T22c	violet	(1916)	250.00
15T48	"	dark blue	(1917)	500.00
15T49	"	dark blue	(1918)	550.00
15T49A	"	dark blue	(1919)	70.00
15T49B	"	dark blue	(1920)	60.00

No. 15T49B is overprinted "1920" in small single line numerals.

T22d

1907
Perf. 12

15T50	T22d	1c dark brown		20.00	20.00
		Pane of four		85.00	
15T51	"	2c dull violet		20.00	20.00
		Pane of four		85.00	
15T52	"	5c green		20.00	20.00
		Pane of four		85.00	
15T53	"	25c light red		20.00	20.00
		Pane of four		85.00	

T22e

1931
Perf. 14

15T54	T22e	25c gray blue	(1931)	25
		Pane of six		1.50

1932

Stamp of 1931 overprinted "1932" and control number in red.

15T55	T22e	25c gray blue		25.00
		Pane of six		160.00

Many varieties between Nos. 15T5 and 15T55 are known without frank numbers.

TELEGRAPHS

1900
OFFICIAL.
Inscribed "Supts."
Perf. 11, 12.

15TO1	T22c	magenta		75	75

For Use of Railroad Superintendents.
Perf. 12.
"C. G. W." (Chicago, Great Western Railroad) at top

15TO2	T22c	carmine	(1908)	30.00	
		Pane of four		120.00	
15TO3	"	carmine	(1909)	40.00	
15TO4	"	carmine	(1910)	60.00	
15TO5	"	carmine	(1911)	35.00	
15TO6	"	carmine	(1912)	40.00	

Perf. 14.

15TO7	"	carmine	(1913)	60.00	
	a. Perf. 12				
15TO8	T22c	dull red (not dated)	(1914)	20	
		Pane of eight		1.60	

Perf. 12.
"E. P." (El Paso and Northeastern Railroad) at top

15TO9	T22C	orange	(1908)	60.00	

"I. C." (Illinois Central Railroad) at top

15TO10	T22c	green	(1908)	25.00	
		Pane of four		110.00	
15TO11	"	yellow green	(1909)	8.00	
		Pane of four			
		Pane of eight		65.00	
15TO12	"	dark green	(1910)	40.00	
15TO13	"	dark green	(1911)	35.00	
		Pane of four		140.00	
		Pane of eight		285.00	
15TO14	"	dark green	(1912)	60.00	
15TO15	"	dark green	(1913)	110.00	

Perf. 14.

15TO16	T22c	dark green (1914) (not dated)		2.00	
		Pane of four		9.00	
		Pane of eight		17.50	
	a. Green (spurs)			1.25	
		Pane of four		6.00	
	b. Line under "PRESIDENT"				
	(no spurs)			20	
		Pane of eight		2.00	
	(See note after No. 15T47.)				

Both types of design T22c are known of 15TO16.

Perf. 12
"O. D." (Old Dominion Steamship Co.) at top

15TO17	T22c	violet	(1908)	150.00	

"P. R." (Pennsylvania Railroad) at top

15TO18	T22c	orange brown	(1908)	9.00	
		Pane of four		37.50	
		Pane of eight		75.00	
15TO19	"	orange brown	(1909)	25.00	
		Pane of four		110.00	
		Pane of eight		225.00	
15TO20	"	orange brown	(1910)	15.00	
		Pane of four		65.00	
		Pane of eight		125.00	
15TO21	"	orange brown	(1911)	45.00	
15TO22	"	orange brown	(1912)	35.00	

Perf. 14.

15TO23	T22c	orange brown	(1913)	17.50	
		Pane of eight		145.00	
	a. Perf. 12			60.00	

"P. R. R." (Pennsylvania Rail Road) at top

15TO24	T22c	orange (not dated) (1914)		15.00	
		Pane of eight		125.00	

Perf. 12.
"S. W." (El Paso Southwestern Railroad) at top

15TO25	T22c	yellow	(1909)	60.00	
15TO26	"	yellow	(1910)	175.00	
15TO27	"	yellow	(1911)	60.00	
15TO28	"	yellow	(1912)	60.00	
		Pane of four		265.00	

Nos. 15TO1 to 15TO17 and 15TO25 to 15TO28 are without frank numbers.

T O1
Lithographed.
1942 Unwmkd.

15TO29	TO1	5c pink		6.00	3.00
		Pane of eight		50.00	
15TO30	"	25c pale blue		7.00	4.00
		Pane of eight		57.50	

The stamps were issued in booklets to all Postal Telegraph employees in the Armed Forces for use in the United States. They were discontinued Oct. 8, 1943. Used copies normally bear manuscript cancellations.

Western Union Telegraph Company.

Organized by consolidation in 1856. Now extends throughout the United States. Frank stamps have been issued regularly since 1871 in booklet form. The large size, early issues, were in panes of four, 1871-1913; the medium size, later issues, were in panes of six, 1914-32; and the recent small size issues are in panes of nine, 1933 to 1946.

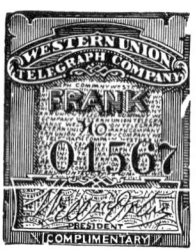 

T23   T24

Engraved by the National Bank Note Co.
1871-94 *Perf. 12.*
Signature of William Orton.

16T1	T23	green	(1871) (not dated)	20.00	
16T2	"	red	(1872) (not dated)	20.00	
		Pane of four		85.00	
16T3	"	blue	(1873) (not dated)	20.00	
		Pane of four		85.00	
16T4	"	brown	(1874) (not dated)	20.00	
		Pane of four		85.00	
16T5	T24	deep green	(1875)	20.00	
16T6	"	red	(1876)	17.50	
		Pane of four		75.00	
16T7	"	violet	(1877)	20.00	
16T8	"	gray brown	(1878)	22.50	

Signature of Norvin Green.

16T9	T24	blue	(1879)	22.50	
		Pane of four		100.00	

Engraved by the American Bank Note Co.

16T10	T24	lilac rose	(1880)	15.00	
		Pane of four		65.00	
16T11	"	green	(1881)	12.00	
		Pane of four		50.00	
16T12	"	blue	(1882)	7.50	
		Pane of four		35.00	
16T13	"	yellow brown	(1883)	15.00	
		Pane of four		65.00	
16T14	"	gray violet	(1884)	40	30
		Pane of four		2.00	

546

TELEGRAPHS

16T15	T24	green	(1885)	2.00	1.25
		Pane of four		10.00	
16T16	"	brown violet	(1886)	2.25	
		Pane of four		11.00	
16T17	"	red brown	(1887)	4.00	
		Pane of four		20.00	
16T18	"	blue	(1888)	2.00	
		Pane of four		10.00	
16T19	"	olive green	(1889)	1.25	80
		Pane of four		5.00	
16T20	"	purple	(1890)	60	40
		Pane of four		3.00	
16T21	"	brown	(1891)	80	
		Pane of four		4.00	
16T22	"	vermilion	(1892)	1.25	
		Pane of four		6.00	
16T23	"	blue	(1893)	60	25
		Pane of four		3.00	

Signature of Thos. T. Eckert.

16T24	T24	green	(1894)	50	40
		Pane of four		2.50	

T25

Engraved by the International Bank Note Co.

1895-1913   Perf. 14.

16T25	T25	dark brown	(1895)	50	35
		Pane of four		2.50	
16T26	"	violet	(1896)	50	35
		Pane of four		2.50	
16T27	"	rose red	(1897)	50	40
		Pane of four		2.50	
16T28	"	yellow green	(1898)	50	40
		Pane of four		2.50	
16T29	"	olive green	(1899)	40	40
		Pane of four		1.75	

Perf. 13.

16T30	T25	red violet	(1900)	50	45
		Pane of four		2.25	
16T31	"	brown	(1901)	40	
		Pane of four		2.00	

Perf. 14.

16T32	T25	blue	(1902)	5.00	
		Pane of four		25.00	

Signature of R.C. Clowry.

16T33	T25	blue	(1902)	5.00	
		Pane of four		25.00	
16T34	"	green	(1903)	50	40
		Pane of four		2.25	
16T35	"	red violet	(1904)	50	
		Pane of four		2.25	
16T36	"	carmine rose	(1905)	40	30
		Pane of four		1.75	
16T37	"	blue	(1906)	40	30
		Pane of four		2.00	
		a. Vertical pair, imperf.. between		30.00	
16T38	"	orange brown	(1907)	40	30
		Pane of four		1.75	
16T39	"	violet	(1908)	75	40
		Pane of four		4.00	
16T40	"	olive green	(1909)	1.00	
		Pane of four		5.00	

Perf. 12.

16T41	T25	buff	(1910)	50	40
		Pane of four		2.25	

Engraved by the American Bank Note Co.
Signature of Theo. N. Vail.

16T42	T24	green	(1911)	10.00	
		Pane of four		50.00	
16T43	"	violet	(1912)	6.00	
		Pane of four		30.00	

Imprint of Kihn Brothers Bank Note Company
Perf. 14.

16T44	T24	brown	(1913)	10.00	
		Pane of four		50.00	
		a. Vert. pair, imperf. between		35.00	
		b. Horiz. pair, imperf. between		40.00	

T26   T27

Engraved by the E.A. Wright Bank Note Co.
Signature of Theo. N. Vail.

1914-15   Perf. 12.

16T45	T26	5c brown	(1914)	1.00	
		Pane of six		7.00	
		a. Vert. pair, imperf. between		—	
		b. Horiz. pair, imperf. between		—	
16T46	"	25c slate	(1914)	4.00	4.00
		Pane of six		25.00	

Signature of Newcomb Carlton.

16T47	T26	5c orange	(1915)	1.25	
		Pane of six		8.00	
		orange yellow		5.00	
16T48	"	25c olive green	(1915)	4.00	
		Pane of six		25.00	
		a. Imperf. horizontally (pair)		45.00	

Engraved by the American Bank Note Co.

1916-32

16T49	T27	5c light blue	(1916)	1.50	
		Pane of six		10.00	
16T50	"	25c carmine lake	(1916)	1.50	
		Pane of six		10.00	

Engraved by the Security Bank Note Co.
Perf. 11.

16T51	T27	5c yellow brown	(1917)	1.00	
		Pane of six		6.50	
16T52	"	25c deep green	(1917)	2.50	
		Pane of six		16.00	
16T53	"	5c olive green	(1918)	60	
		Pane of six		4.00	
16T54	"	25c dark violet	(1918)	1.50	
		Pane of six		9.50	
16T55	"	5c brown	(1919)	1.25	
		Pane of six		8.00	
16T56	"	25c blue	(1919)	2.50	
		Pane of six		16.00	

Engraved by the E.A. Wright Bank Note Co.
Perf. 12.

16T57	T27	5c dark green	(1920)	50	
		Pane of six		3.25	
16T58	"	25c olive green	(1920)	60	
		Pane of six		4.00	

547

TELEGRAPHS

Engraved by the Security Bank Note Co.

16T59	T27	5c carmine rose	(1921)	40	
		Pane of six		2.75	
16T60	"	25c deep blue	(1921)	75	
		Pane of six		5.00	
16T61	"	5c yellow brown	(1922)	40	
		Pane of six		2.75	
		a. Horizontal pair, imperf. between		12.00	
16T62	"	25c claret	(1922)	1.00	
		Pane of six		7.00	
16T63	"	5c olive green	(1923)	50	
		Pane of six		3.25	
16T64	"	25c dull violet	(1923)	1.00	
		Pane of six		7.00	
16T65	"	5c brown	(1924)	1.25	
		Pane of six		8.00	
16T66	"	25c ultramarine	(1924)	3.00	
		Pane of six		20.00	
16T67	"	5c olive green	(1925)	40	
		Pane of six		2.75	
16T68	"	25c carmine rose	(1925)	75	
		Pane of six		5.00	
16T69	"	5c blue	(1926)	45	
		Pane of six		3.25	
16T70	"	25c light brown	(1926)	1.25	
		Pane of six		8.00	
16T71	"	5c carmine	(1927)	60	
		Pane of six		4.00	
16T72	"	25c green	(1927)	4.00	
		Pane of six		27.50	

Engraved by the E. A. Wright Bank Note Co.
Without Imprint.

16T73	T27	5c yellow brown	(1928)	35	
		Pane of six		2.25	
16T74	"	25c dark blue	(1928)	75	
		Pane of six		5.00	

Engraved by the Security Bank Note Co.
Without Imprint.

16T75	T27	5c dark green	(1929)	25	25
		Pane of six		1.50	
16T76	"	25c red violet	(1929)	75	50
		Pane of six		5.00	
16T77	"	5c olive green	(1930)	20	15
		Pane of six		1.25	
16T78	"	25c carmine	(1930)	20	12
		Pane of six		1.40	
		a. Imperf. vertically (pair)		17.50	
16T79	"	5c brown	(1931)	10	8
		Pane of six		90	
16T80	"	25c blue	(1931)	15	10
		Pane of six		1.00	
16T81	"	5c green	(1932)	12	8
		Pane of six		85	
16T82	"	25c rose carmine	(1932)	12	8
		Pane of six		85	

1933-40
Lithographed by Oberly & Newell Co.
Without Imprint.
Perf. 14x12½.

16T83	T28	5c pale brown	(1933)	25	
		Pane of nine		2.50	
16T84	"	25c green	(1933)	25	
		Pane of nine		2.50	

Lithographed by Security Bank Note Co.
Without Imprint.
Perf. 12
Signature of R. B. White.

16T85	T28	5c lake	(1934)	15	
		Pane of nine		1.50	
16T86	"	25c dark blue	(1934)	15	
		Pane of nine		1.50	
16T87	"	5c yellow brown	(1935)	12	
		Pane of nine		1.25	
16T88	"	25c lake	(1935)	15	
		Pane of nine		1.50	
16T89	"	5c blue	(1936)	20	15
		Pane of nine		2.00	
16T90	"	25c apple green	(1936)	15	10
		Pane of nine		1.50	
16T91	"	5c bistre brown	(1937)	20	
		Pane of nine		2.00	
16T92	"	25c carmine rose	(1937)	20	
		Pane of nine		2.00	
16T93	"	5c green	(1938)	20	15
		Pane of nine		2.00	
16T94	"	25c blue	(1938)	25	15
		Pane of nine		2.50	
16T95	"	5c dull vermilion	(1939)	60	
		Pane of nine		6.00	
		a. Horiz. pair, imperf. between			
16T96	"	25c bright violet	(1939)	50	
		Pane of nine		5.00	
16T97	"	5c light blue	(1940)	40	
		Pane of nine		4.00	
16T98	"	25c bright green	(1940)	40	
		Pane of nine		4.00	

TELEGRAPH STAMPS
● Singles ● Booklet Panes
● Proofs ● Unlisted
● Used on Telegram
BOUGHT & SOLD
How may we help you?
WHITTIER PHILATELIC SERVICES
Eric Jackson
(213) 698-3193 or 698-2888
P.O. Box 651, Whittier, CA 90608

Samuel F. B. Morse
T29

Plates of 90 stamps.
Stamp designed by Nathaniel Yontiff.
Unlike the frank stamps, Nos. 16T99 to 16T103 were sold to the public in booklet form for use in prepayment of telegraph services.

T28

TELEGRAPHS

Engraved by Security Bank Note Co. of Philadelphia

1940
Unwmkd.
Perf. 12.

16T99	T29	1c yellow green	1.00	
		Pane of five	6.00	
		a. Imperf. pair		
16T100	"	2c chestnut	1.75	1.00
		Pane of five	10.00	
		a. Imperf. pair		
16T101	"	5c deep blue	3.00	
		Pane of five	18.00	
		a. Vert. pair, imperf. btwn.	45.00	
		b. Imperf. pair		
16T102	"	10c orange	3.50	
		Pane of five	20.00	
		a. Imperf. pair		
16T103	"	25c bright carmine	4.00	
		Pane of five	25.00	
		a. Imperf. pair		

Type of 193_-40

1941
Perf. 12½
Lithographed
Without Imprint
Signature of R.B. White

16T104	T28	5c dull rose lilac	.25
		Pane of nine	2.50
16T105	"	25c vermilion	.25
		Pane of nine	2.50

1942
Signature of A.N. Williams

16T106	T28	5c brown	.30
		Pane of nine	3.00
16T107	"	25c ultramarine	.30
		Pane of nine	3.00

1943

16T108	T28	5c salmon	.30
		Pane of nine	3.00
16T109	"	25c red violet	.25
		Pane of nine	2.50

1944

16T110	T28	5c light green	.30
		Pane of nine	3.00
16T111	"	25c buff	.25
		Pane of nine	2.50

1945

16T112	T28	5c light blue	.35
		Pane of nine	3.50
16T113	"	25c light green	.35
		Pane of nine	3.50

1946

16T114	T28	5c light bistre brown	1.00
		Pane of nine	10.00
16T115	"	25c rose pink	1.00
		Pane of nine	10.00

Many of the stamps between 16T1 and 16T98 and 16T104 to 16T115 are known without frank numbers. Several of them are also known with more than one color used in the frank number and with handstamped and manuscript numbers. The numbers are also found in combination with various letters: O, A, B, C, D, etc.

Western Union discontinued the use of Telegraph stamps with the 1946 issue.

United States
Telegraph-Cable-Radio Carriers

Booklets issued to accredited representatives to the World Telecommunications Conferences, Atlantic City, New Jersey, 1947. Valid for messages to points outside the United States. Issued by All America Cables & Radio, Inc., The Commercial Cable Company, Globe Wireless, Limited, Mackay Radio and Telegraph Company, Inc., R C A Communications, Inc., Tropical Radio Telegraph Company and The Western Union Telegraph Company.

TX1
Lithographed
Perf. 12½.

1947
Unwmkd.

17T1	TX1	5c olive bistre	5.00	
		Pane of nine	50.00	
		Pane of 8+1 No. 17T2	325.00	
17T2	"	10c olive bistre	250.00	
17T3	"	50c olive bistre	7.00	
		Pane of nine	85.00	

UNLISTED ISSUES

Several telegraph or wireless companies other than those listed above have issued stamps or franks, but as evidence of actual use is lacking, they are not listed. Among these are:

American District Telegraph Co.
American Telegraph Typewriter Co.
Continental Telegraph Co.
Marconi Wireless Telegraph Co.
Telepost Co.
Tropical Radio Telegraph Co.
United Fruit Co. Wireless Service.
United Wireless Telegraph Co.

Scott Stamp Monthly

The only magazine that updates Scott Catalogues every month with new Scott Numbers for the latest issues. Get the stories behind the stamps in lively, colorful features. Get Scott Stamp Monthly today.

Send name, address and $18 for twelve issues to:

Scott Publishing Company
P.O. Box 828, Sidney, Ohio 45365

SANITARY FAIR STAMPS

The United States Sanitary Commission was authorized by the Secretary of War on June 9, 1861, and approved by President Lincoln on June 13, 1861. It was a committee of inquiry, advice and aid dealing with the health and general comfort of Union troops, supported by public contributions.

Many Sanitary Fairs were held to raise funds for the Commission, and eight issued stamps. The first took place in 1863 at Chicago when no stamp was issued. Some Sanitary Fairs advertised on envelopes.

Sanitary Fair stamps occupy a position midway between United States semi-official carrier stamps and the private local posts. Although Sanitary Fair stamps were not valid for U.S. postal service, they were prepared for, sold and used at the fair post offices, usually with the approval and participation of the local postmaster.

The Commission undertook to forward soldiers' unpaid and postage due letters. These letters were handstamped "Forwarded by the U.S. Sanitary Commission."

Details about the Sanitary Fair stamps may be found in the following publications:

American Journal of Philately, Jan. 1889, by J. W. Scott
The Collector's Journal, Aug.–Sept. 1909, by C. E. Severn
Scott's Monthly Journal, Jan. 1927 (reprint, Apr. 1973), by Elliott Perry
Stamps, April 24th, 1937, by Harry M. Konwiser
Pat Paragraphs, July, 1939, by Elliott Perry
Covers, Aug. 1952, by George B. Wray

The listings were compiled originally by H. M. Konwiser and Dorsey F. Wheless.

Albany, New York.
Army Relief Bazaar.

SF1

Panes of 12 (Narrow Spacing), or 25 (Wide Spacing)
1864, Feb. 22–Mar. 30   Litho.   Imperf.
Thin White Paper

WV1	SF1	10c rose	40.00
		Block of four	175.00
		Pane of 12	675.00
		Pane of 25	1100.00
		Used on cover (tied "Albany")	850.00
WV2	"	10c black	175.00
		Block of five	1100.00

Imitations are typographed in red, blue, black or green on a thin white or ordinary white paper, also on colored papers and are:
(*a*) Eagle with topknot, printed in sheets of 30 (6x5).
(*b*) Eagle without shading around it.
(*c*) Eagle with shading around it, but with a period instead of a circle in "C" of "Cents", and "Ten Cents" is smaller.

Boston, Mass.
National Sailors' Fair.

SF2

1864, Nov. 9–22   Die Cut   Lithographed
WV3 SF2 10c green   150.00

Brooklyn, N. Y.
Brooklyn Sanitary Fair.

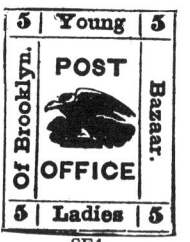
SF3

1864, Feb. 22–Mar. 8   Litho.   Imperf.
WV4	SF3	green	300.00	
		Block of four	1350.00	
		Block of six	2000.00	
		On cover, Fair postmark on envelope		1100.00
WV5	"	black		
		On cover, Fair postmark on envelope		1500.00

Imitations: (*a*) Typographed and shows "Sanitary" with a heavy cross bar to "T" and second "A" with a long left leg. (*b*) Is a rough typograph print without shading in letters of "Fair".

SF4   SF5

SANITARY FAIR

1863, Dec.		Typeset	Imperf.
WV6	SF4	5c black, *rosy buff*	325.00
WV7	SF5	10c green	450.00
		a. Tête bêche pair	1250.00

New York, N. Y.
Metropolitan Fair.

SF6

1864, Apr. 4–27		Engraved	Imperf.
		Thin White Paper	
WV8	SF6	10c blue	35.00
		Sheet of four	185.00
WV9	"	10c red	375.00
		Pair	900.00
WV10	"	10c black	750.00

Engraved and printed by John E. Gavit of Albany, N. Y. from a steel plate composed of four stamps, 2x2. Can be plated by the positions of scrolls and dots around "Ten Cents".

Philadelphia, Pa.
Great Central Fair.

SF7

1864, June 7–28   Engraved   Perf. 12
Printed by Butler & Carpenter, Philadelphia
Sheets of 126 (14x9)

WV11	SF7	10c blue	15.00	110.00
		Block of four	67.50	
		On cover tied with Fair postmark		900.00
		On cover with 3c #65, Fair and Philadelphia postmarks		1500.00
WV12	"	20c green	7.50	90.00
		Block of four	32.50	
		Block of 12	135.00	
		On cover tied with Fair postmark		800.00
WV13	"	30c black	16.50	75.00
		Block of four	75.00	
		On cover tied with Fair postmark		750.00

Imprint "Engraved by Butler & Carpenter, Philadelphia" on right margin adjoining three stamps.
Used examples of Nos. WV11–WV13 have Fair cancellation.
Imitation of No. WV13 comes typographed in blue or green on thick paper.
White and amber envelopes were sold by the fair inscribed "Great Central Fair for the Sanitary Commission," showing picture of wounded soldier, doctors and ambulance marked "U. S. Sanitary Commission." Same design and inscription are known on U. S. envelope No. U46.

Springfield, Mass.
Soldiers' Fair.

SF8

1864, Dec. 19–24		Typographed	Imperf.
WV14	SF8	10c lilac	75.00
		Horizontal strip of four	350.00
		On unaddressed cover, Fair postmark on envelope	250.00

Design by Thomas Chubbuck, engraver of the postmaster provisional stamp of Brattleboro, Vt.
Imitations: (a) Without designer's name in lower right corner, in lilac on laid paper. (b) With designer's name, but roughly typographed, in lilac on white wove paper. Originals show 5 buttons on uniform.

Stamford, Conn.
Soldiers' Fair.

SF9
Sheets of 8

1864
WV15	SF9	15c pale brown	450.00	475.00

Originals have tassels at ends of ribbon inscribed "SOLDIERS FAIR."
Imitations have leaning "s" in "CENTS" and come in lilac, brown, green, also black on white paper, green on pinkish paper and other colors.

PROOFS
New York Metropolitan Fair

1864   Plate on India
                        Mounted
                        on Card
WV10P 10c black   225.00

Philadelphia Great Central Fair

1864
		LARGE DIE (1)	PLATE		
			(4) Card	(5) Wove, Imperf.	(6) Wove, Perf.
WV11P	10c blue	40.00			
	Block of four	200.00			
WV11TC–WV13TC	10c, 30c greenish black, se-tenant vert., glazed paper	450.00			
WV12P	20c green	45.00			
	Block of four	200.00			
WV12TC	20c carmine				35.00
	Block of four				175.00
WV12TC	20c vermilion, India on card	275.00			
WV12TC	20c vermilion			22.50	35.00
	Block of four			115.00	175.00

		LARGE DIE (1)	PLATE				LARGE DIE (1)	PLATE	
		(4) Card	(5) Wove, Imperf.	(6) Wove, Perf.			(4) Card	(5) Wove, Imperf.	(6) Wove, Perf.
WV12TC	20c orange		22.50		WV12TC	20c lt. ultramarine		22.50	
	Block of four		115.00			Block of four		125.00	
WV12TC	20c brown orange,				WV12TC	20c purple		22.50	
	opaque paper		22.50			Block of four		125.00	
	Block of four		115.00		WV12TC	20c claret			35.00
WV12TC	20c red brown			35.00		Block of four			200.00
	Block of four			175.00	WV12TC	20c brown black			35.00
WV12TC	20c black brown		25.00			Block of four			175.00
	Block of four		125.00		WV12TC	20c greenish black, glazed paper	225.00		
WV12TC	20c olive		22.50		WV12TC	20c gray black, opaque paper		22.50	
	Block of four		100.00			Block of four		125.00	
WV12TC	20c yellow green		22.50		WV12TC	20c gray black			35.00
	Block of four		125.00			Block of four			175.00
WV12TC	20c light green			35.00	WV12TC	20c black, experimental double paper		25.00	
	Block of four			175.00		Block of four		140.00	
WV12TC	20c blue, India on card	275.00			WV13P	30c black		22.50	
WV12TC	20c bright blue		22.50	35.00		Block of four		125.00	
	Block of four		125.00	175.00					

STAMPED ENVELOPES AND WRAPPERS

STAMPED ENVELOPES were first issued on July 1, 1853. They have always been made by private contractors, after public bidding, usually at four year intervals. They have always been sold to the public at postage value plus cost of manufacture. They have appeared in many sizes and shapes, made of a variety of papers, with a number of modifications.

George F. Nesbitt & Co. made the government envelopes during the 1853-70 period. The Nesbitt seal or crest on the tip of the top flap was officially ordered discontinued July 7, 1853.

Watermarks in envelope paper, illustrated on opposite page, have been mandatory since their first appearance in 1853. One important exception, started in 1919 and lasted until the manila newspaper wrappers were discontinued in October 1934. The envelope contractor, due to inability to obtain watermarked Manila paper, was permitted to buy unwatermarked stock in the open market, a procedure that accounts for the wide range of shades and weights in this paper, including glazed and unglazed brown (kraft) paper. A diagonally laid paper has been used for some envelopes beginning with number U571.

A few stamped envelopes, in addition to the Manila items noted above, have been found without watermarks or with unauthorized watermarks. Such unusual watermarks or lack of watermarks are errors, bidders' samples or "specimen" envelopes, and most of them are quite rare.

Watermarks have usually been changed with every four year contract, and thus serve to identify the envelope contractor, and since 1911, the manufacturer of the paper.

Envelope paper watermarks can be seen by spreading the envelope open and holding it against the light.

COLORS IN ENVELOPE PAPER.

Stamped envelopes have usually been supplied in several colors and qualities of paper, some of which blend into each other and require study for identification. The following are the principal colors and their approximate years of use for stamped envelopes and wrappers:

Amber:	1870-1920 and 1929-1943; in two qualities; a pale yellow color; its intentional use in the Nesbitt series is doubtful.
Amber-Manila:	1886-98; same as Manila-amber.
Blue:	1874-1943; usually in two qualities; light and dark shades.
Buff:	1853-70; called cream, 1870-78; and oriental buff, 1886-1920; varies widely in shades.
Canary:	1873-78; another designation given to lemon.
Cream:	1870-78; see buff; second quality in 1c and 2c envelopes.
Fawn:	1874-86; very dark buff, almost light chocolate.
Lemon:	1873-78; Post Office official envelopes only, same as canary.
Manila:	1861-1934; second quality envelopes 1886-1928, and most wrappers; light and dark shades 1920-34; also kraft colored paper in later years.
Manila-Amber:	1886-98; amber shade of Manila quality.
Orange:	1861-80; second and third qualities only.
Oriental Buff:	1886-1920; see buff.
White:	1853-date; two qualities 1915-date; three qualities 1915-25; many shades including ivory, light gray, and bluish; far more common than any other color of paper.

Laid paper was used almost exclusively from 1853 to 1915, but there were a few exceptions, mostly in the Manila papers. Wove paper has been the rule since 1915.

EMBOSSING AND PRINTING DIES.

Stamped envelopes have always been embossed, with the colorless areas slightly raised above the colored (or printed) flat background. While this process was not made mandatory in the original act, custom and tradition have firmly established this policy. It is an unusual procedure, seldom seen in other printed matter. Embossed impressions without color and those where the colored lines are raised are not unusual. The method of making envelope embossings has few counterparts in the typographic industries, and hence is not well understood, even by stamp collectors.

Three types of dies are used, closely inter-related in their derivation, MASTER dies, HUB dies and WORKING (or PRINTING) dies. These types and the ways in which they are made, have undergone many changes with the years, and some of the earlier techniques are unrecorded and rather vague. No attempt will be made to describe other than the present day methods. As an aid to clarity, the design illustrated herewith is the interlocked monogram US, within a single circular border. Dies with curved faces for rotary printing are extensively used, as well as with straight faces for flat printing; only the latter will be described, since the basic principles are the same for both.

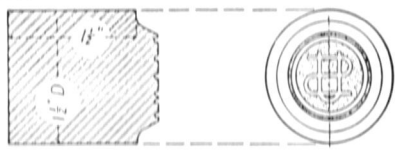

Fig. 1
Master Die for Envelope Stamps
Colorless Lines are Recessed Below the Printing Surface.
It Reads Backward.

The MASTER die (Fig. 1) is engraved on the squared end of a small soft steel cylinder, before hardening. The lines that are to remain colorless are cut or engraved into the face of this die, leaving the flat area of the face to carry the printing ink. The monogram is reversed, reading backward, as with any printing type or plate. Instead of engraving, a master die may be made by transfer under heavy pressure, usually for some modification in design, in which case it is called a sub-master or supplementary-master die. Sub-master dies are sometimes made without figures of value, when the balance of the design is as desired, and only the figures of value engraved by hand. Various other combinations of transfer and engraving are known, always resulting in a reversed design, with recessed lines and figures, from which proofs can be pulled, and which accurately represents the printing surface that is desired in the eventual working die. The soft steel of a master die, after engraving and transferring is completed, is hardened by heat treatments before it can be used for making hubs.

554 ENVELOPE WATERMARKS (More before No. U534)

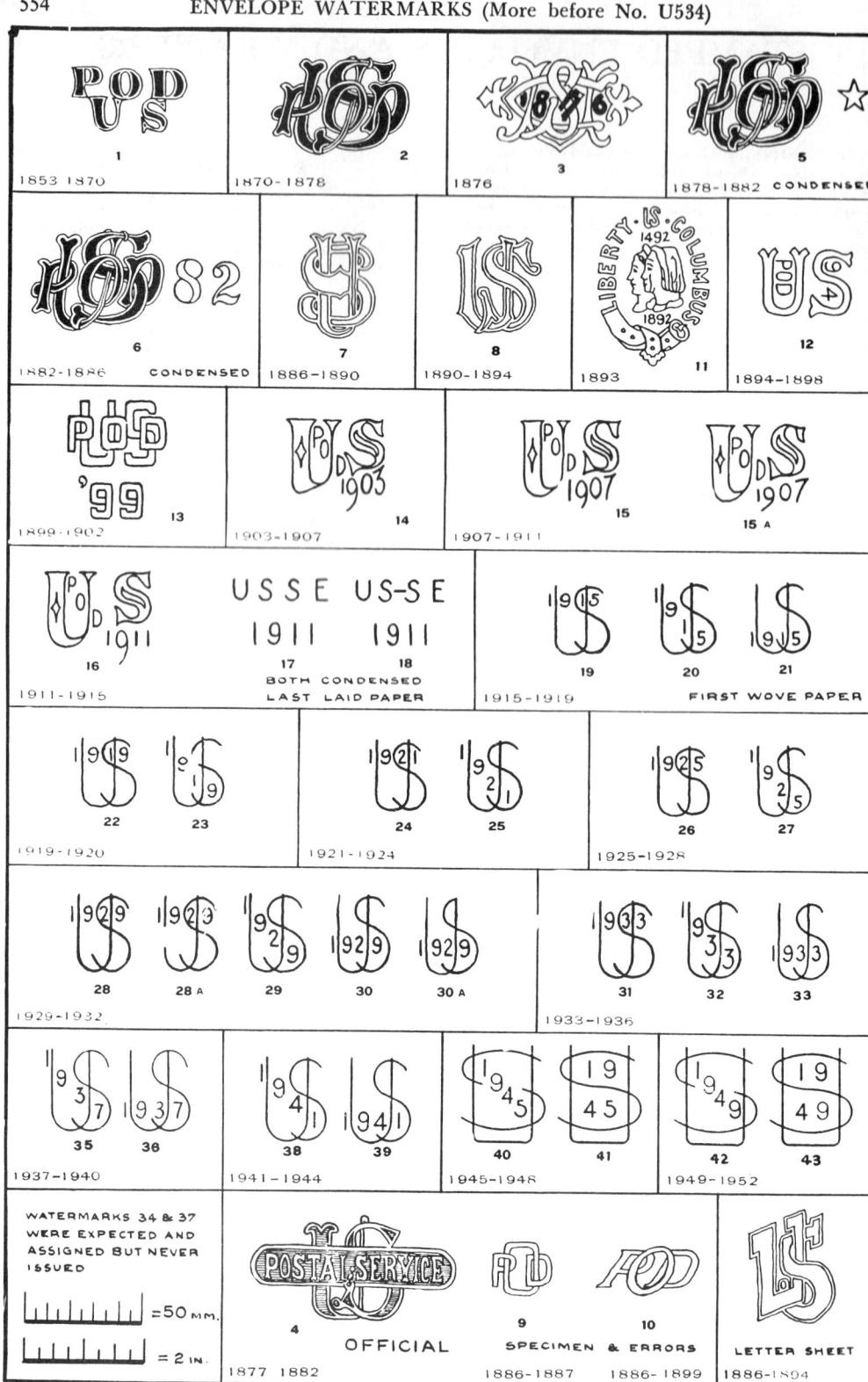

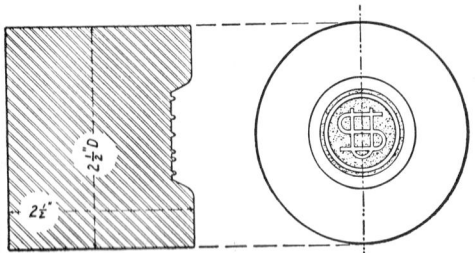

Fig. 2
Hub Die for Envelope Stamps
Colorless Lines Protrude above the Surface.
The Monogram Reads Forward.

The HUB die (Fig. 2), also called HOB die, is made from soft steel by transfer under pressure from the hardened master or sub-master die, which serves as a matrix or pattern. Since it is a transfer from the master die, the colorless lines protrude from the surface and it reads forward. This transfer impression of the hub die is made in a depression at the end of a sturdy cylinder, as it is subject to extremely hard service in making many working dies.

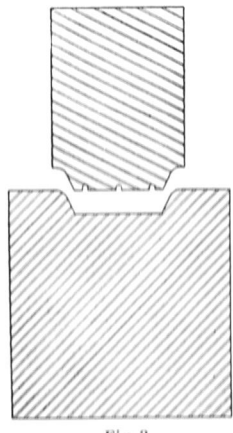

Fig. 3
Pressure Transfer from Master Die to Hub Die

Above, Hardened Steel Master Die with Recessed Monogram.
Below, Soft Steel Hub Die Blank.

Fig. 3 shows the relative position of the hardened steel master die as it enters the depression in the soft steel hub die blank. Some surplus metal may be squeezed out as the master die is forced into the hub blank, and require removal, leading to possible minor differences between the hub and master dies. At the completion of the pressure transfer the engraver may need to touch up the protruding surfaces to eliminate imperfections, to make letters and figures more symmetrical, and to improve the facial lines of the bust.

A hub die may be made by normal transfer, as above the figures of value then ground off, and thus be ready for use in making a sub-master die without figures of value, and in which the figures of value may be engraved or punched. Since a hub die may be used to make a hundred or more working dies, it must be exceedingly sturdy and withstand terrific punishment without damage. Duplicate hub dies are frequently made from master dies, as stand-bys or reserves. After completion, hub dies are hardened. Hub dies cannot be engraved, nor can proof impressions be taken from them.

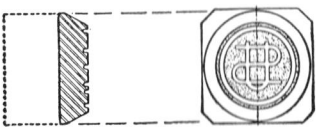

Fig. 4
Working or Printing Die for Envelope Stamps
An exact Replica of the Master Die, except for size and shape of shank, which is designed for Printers' lock-up.
It Reads Backward.

The WORKING, or PRINTING, die (Fig. 4) is like the type or plate that printers use, and may be thin to clamp to a base block, or type-high with square sides to lock in a printer's form. Its face reads backward, i.e., in reverse, and it is an exact replica of the master die as well as an exact matrix of the hub die.

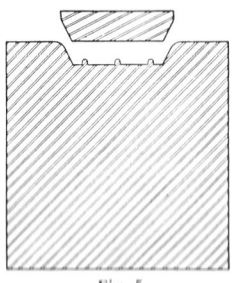

Fig. 5
Pressure Transfer from Hub to Working Die

Above, Soft Steel Blank for Working Die.
Below, Hardened Steel Hub Die with Protruding Lines.

The process of pressure transfer is shown in Fig. 5, where the soft steel blank of the working die is entering the depression on the top end of the hardened hub die. In fact the pressure transfer of working dies from hub dies closely resembles that of minting coins, and many of these envelope stamp dies are made at the United States Mint in Philadelphia.

In some cases even working dies may be made without figures of value, and the figures of value individually engraved thereon. This is known to be the case in Die B of the 6c orange airmail stamped envelope die, where the size and position of the "6" has eleven variations.

There are some known instances, as in the case of the 4c and 5c envelopes dies of 1903 and 1907, where the engraved master dies were used as printing dies, since the anticipated demand did not justify the expense of making hub dies.

While working envelope dies are heat treated to the hardest temper known, they do wear down eventually to a point where impressions deteriorate and are unsatisfactory, due to shallow recesses or to broken areas, and such dies are destroyed. In many cases these printing dies can be reworked, or deepened, by annealing the steel, touching up the lines or busts by hand engraving to restore the letters or renew the facial contour lines, and then rehardened for subsequent use. This recutting is the principal cause for minor die varieties in envelope stamps. When working dies are no longer useful, they are mutilated and eventually melted down into scrap metal.

The average "life" (in number of good impressions obtained) of a hardened steel working die, as used in envelope printing and embossing machines is around 30,000,000 on flat bed presses, and 43,000,000 on rotary presses. The present production of stamped envelopes is approximately 2,000,000,000 annually, indicating that 60 to 75 working dies are worn out each year, and require replacement with new dies or a reworking of old dies. Some 200 to 250 working dies are in constant use, since most envelope printing presses are set up for a special size, type or value, and few can be operated continuously at maximum capacity.

Master and hub dies of obsolete envelope issues are kept in the vaults of the Bureau of Engraving and printing in Washington, as are the original dies of adhesive stamps, revenue paper, government securities and paper currency.

PRINTING ENVELOPE STAMPS.

Embossed envelope stamps are not printed against a rigid flat platen, as is the normal printed page, but against a somewhat flexible or resilient platen or make-ready (Fig. 6). This resilient platen is hard enough to produce a clear full impression from the ink on the face of the working die, and soft enough to push the paper into the uninked recesses that correspond to the engraved lines cut into the master die. The normal result is raised lines or embossments without ink or color, standing out in relief against an inked or colored background. The method differs from the usual embosssing technique, where rigid dies are used on both sides of the paper, as in notarial seals. The use of the resilient platen in envelope embossing permits far higher operating speeds than can be obtained with rigid embossing dies, without the need of such accurate register between the printing surface and the platen.

When these recessed lines in a working die become filled with ink or other foreign material, the paper is not pushed in, the plugged area receives ink, and the corresponding colorless line does not appear on the stamp. This accounts for missing letters, lines or figures, and is a printing error, not a die variety.

An ALBINO impression is where two or more envelope blanks are fed into the printing press. The one adjacent to the printing die receives the color and the embossing, while the others are embossed only. Albinos are printing errors and are worth more than normal, inked impressions. Albinos of earlier issues, canceled while current, are scarce.

Before Jan. 1, 1965, stamped envelopes were printed by two processes: (1.) The rotary, with curved dies, on Huckins and Harris presses. (2.) The flat process, with straight dies, as illustrated, on the O'Connell-type press, which is a redesigned Hartford press. The flat bed presses include a gumming and folding attachment, while the rotary presses, running at higher speeds, require separate folding machines.

Different master dies in every denomination are required for Huckins, Harris and flat bed presses. This difference gives rise to most of the major die varieties in envelope stamps.

Web-fed equipment which converts paper from a roll into finished envelopes in a continuous operation has produced envelopes starting with Nos. U547 and UC37. Albino impressions do not occur on envelopes produced by web-fed equipment.

Some authorities claim that Nos. U37, U48, U49, U110, U124, U125, U130, U133A, U137A, U137B, U137C, W138, U145, U162, U178A, U185, U220, U285, U286, U298, U299, UO3, UO32, UO38, UO45 and UO45A (with asterisk* before number), were not regularly issued and are not known to have been used.

Wrappers are listed with envelopes of corresponding design, and are numbered with the prefix "W" instead of "U."

Prices for cut squares are for copies with fine margins on all sides. Prices for unused entires are for those without printed or manuscript address. A "full corner" includes back and side flaps and commands a premium.

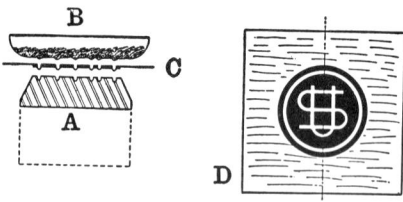

Fig. 6

Printing Process for Embossed Envelope Stamps

A. Working Die, Carrying ink on its surface.
B. Resilient Platen, or Make-ready, Pushing Paper into uninked recesses, so that lines of Embossed Monogram receive no color.
C. Paper of Envelope Blank, after Printing and Embossing. Heavy line shows deposit of ink on surface of paper, but Embossed Lines are not inked.
D. Front view of Embossed impression.

Washington
U1

Die 1

"THREE" in short label with curved ends; 13mm. wide at top. (Twelve varieties.)

U2
Die 2

"THREE" in short label with straight ends; 15½mm. wide at top. (Three varieties.)

U3
Die 3

"THREE" in short label with octagon ends. (Two varieties.)

U4
Die 4

"THREE" in wide label with straight ends; 20 mm. wide at top.

U5
Die 5

"THREE" in medium wide label with curved ends; 14½ mm. wide at top (10 varieties). A sub-variety shows curved lines at either end of label omitted; both T's have longer cross stroke; R is smaller (20 varieties).

U6

Four varieties.

U7
Die 1

"TEN" in short label; 15½ mm. wide at top.

ENVELOPES

U8
Die 2

"TEN" in wide label; 20 mm. wide at top.
Printed by George F. Nesbitt & Co., New York, N.Y.
1853-55   On Diagonally Laid Paper.
(Early printings of Nos. U1, U3 on Horizontally Laid Paper.)

U1	U1	3c **red,** die 1, *white*	150.00	10.00
		Entire	750.00	17.50
U2	"	3c **red,** die 1, *buff*	50.00	4.50
		Entire	500.00	8.50
U3	U2	3c **red,** die 2, *white*	475.00	25.00
		Entire	1,800.	40.00
U4	"	3c **red,** die 2, *buff*	150.00	10.00
		Entire	900.00	15.00
U5	U3	3c **red,** die 3, *white* ('54)	2,500.	300.00
		Entire	7,500.	400.00
U6	"	3c **red,** die 3, *buff* ('54)	100.00	17.50
		Entire	600.00	40.00
U7	U4	3c **red,** die 4, *white*	450.00	45.00
		Entire	*3,000.*	75.00
U8	"	3c **red,** die 4, *buff*	850.00	70.00
		Entire	3,000.	85.00
U9	U5	3c **red,** die 5, *white* ('54)	10.00	70
		Entire	40.00	2.50
U10	"	3c **red,** die 5, *buff* ('54)	5.50	65
		Entire	30.00	2.00
U11	U6	6c **red,** *white*	80.00	40.00
		Entire	150.00	80.00
U12	"	6c **red,** *buff*	60.00	35.00
		Entire	140.00	125.00
U13	"	6c **green,** *white*	140.00	70.00
		Entire	230.00	110.00
U14	"	6c **green,** *buff*	140.00	50.00
		Entire	250.00	110.00
U15	U7	10c **green,** die 1, *white* ('55)	90.00	35.00
		Entire	200.00	80.00
U16	"	10c **green,** die 1, *buff* ('55)	45.00	25.00
		Entire	125.00	60.00
	a.	10c pale green, die 1, *buff*	45.00	20.00
		Entire	125.00	60.00
U17	U8	10c **green,** die 2, *white* ('55)	125.00	60.00
		Entire	200.00	90.00
	a.	10c pale green, die 2, *white*	120.00	60.00
		Entire	150.00	80.00
U18	"	10c **green,** die 2, *buff* ('55)	55.00	25.00
		Entire	110.00	50.00
	a.	10c pale green, die 2, *buff*	55.00	25.00
		Entire	100.00	50.00

Nos. U9, U10, U11, U12, U13, U14, U17, and U18 have been reprinted on white and buff paper, vertically laid, and are not known entire. The originals are on diagonally laid paper. Price, set of 8 reprints, $125.

Franklin
U9
Die 1
Period after "POSTAGE." (Eleven varieties.)

Franklin
U10
Die 2
Bust touches inner frame-line at front and back.

Franklin
U11
Die 3
No period after "POSTAGE." (Two varieties.)

ENVELOPES

Washington
U12

Nine varieties of type U12.
Envelopes are on diagonally laid paper.
Wrappers on vertically or horizontally laid paper.
Wrappers of the 1 cent denomination were authorized by an Act of Congress, February 27, 1861, and were issued in October, 1861. These were suspended in 1863, and their use resumed in June, 1864.

1860-61

U19	U9	1c **blue,** die 1, *buff*	18.00	7.50
		Entire	40.00	14.00
W20	"	1c **blue,** die 1, *buff*	40.00	27.50
		Entire	75.00	50.00
W21	"	1c **blue,** die 1, *manila* ('61)	25.00	25.00
		Entire	50.00	50.00
W22	"	1c **blue,** die 1, *orange* ('61)	1,000.	
		Entire	1,600.	
U23	U10	1c **blue,** die 2, *orange*	300.00	325.00
		Entire	375.00	375.00
U24	U11	1c **blue,** die 3, *buff*	150.00	75.00
		Entire	250.00	150.00
W25	"	1c **blue,** die 3, *manila* ('61)	950.00	750.00
		Entire	5,000.	2,250.
U26	U12	3c **red,** *white*	14.00	8.00
		Entire	20.00	14.00
U27	"	3c **red,** *buff*	12.00	6.00
		Entire	18.00	12.00
U28	U12+U9	3c+1c **red & blue** *white*	275.00	175.00
		Entire	400.00	300.00
U29	"	3c+1c **red & blue,** *buff*	175.00	150.00
		Entire	325.00	350.00
U30	U12	6c **red,** *white*	1,750.	1,000.
		Entire	2,500.	
U31	"	6c **red,** *buff*	1,250.	750.00
		Entire	2,000.	3,000.
U32	"	10c **green,** *white*	600.00	225.00
		Entire	6,500.	325.00
U33	"	10c **green,** *buff*	550.00	150.00
		Entire	1,800.	350.00

Nos. U26, U27, U30 to U33 have been reprinted on the same papers as the reprints of the 1853-55 issue, and are not known entire. Price, set of 6 reprints, $160.

Washington
U13

17 varieties for Nos. U34-U35; 2 varieties for No. U36.

Washington
U14

Washington
U15

Washington
U16

Envelopes are on diagonally laid paper.
U36 comes on vertically or horizontally laid paper. It appeared in August, 1861, and was withdrawn in 1864. Total issue 211,800.

1861

U34	U13	3c **pink,** *white*	10.00	2.50
		Entire	25.00	7.00
U35	"	3c **pink,** *buff*	9.00	2.50
		Entire	25.00	7.00
U36	"	3c **pink,** *blue* (Letter Sheet)	50.00	27.50
		Entire	125.00	50.00
U37	"	3c **pink,** *orange*	1,900.	
		Entire	3,000.	

ENVELOPES

U38	U14	6c	**pink,** *white*	75.00	70.00
			Entire	125.00	140.00
U39	"	6c	**pink,** *buff*	45.00	45.00
			Entire	90.00	125.00
U40	U15	10c	**yellow green,** *white*	20.00	18.00
			Entire	40.00	37.50
		a.	10c blue green, *white*	20.00	20.00
			Entire	40.00	35.00
U41	"	10c	**yellow green,** *buff*	17.50	16.00
			Entire	40.00	35.00
		a.	10c blue green, *buff*	16.00	16.00
			Entire	32.50	35.00
U42	U16	12c	**red & brown,** *buff*	140.00	110.00
			Entire	275.00	400.00
		a.	12c lake & brown, *buff*	600.00	
U43	"	20c	**red & blue,** *buff*	125.00	125.00
			Entire	350.00	500.00
U44	"	24c	**red & green,** *buff*	130.00	125.00
			Entire	450.00	500.00
		a.	24c lake & green, *salmon*	150.00	130.00
			Entire	450.00	750.00
U45	"	40c	**black & red,** *buff*	175.00	200.00
			Entire	500.00	900.00

Nos. U38 and U39 have been reprinted on the same papers as the reprints of the 1853-55 issue, and are not known entire. Price, set of 2 reprints, $30.

Jackson
U17
Die 1

"U. S. POSTAGE" above. Downstroke and tail of "2" unite near the point (seven varieties.)

Jackson
U18
Die 2

"U. S. POSTAGE" above. The downstroke and tail of the "2" touch but do not merge.

Jackson
U19
Die 3

"U. S. POST" above. Stamp 24-25mm. wide. (Sixteen varieties.)

Jackson
U20
Die 4

"U. S. POST" above. Stamp 25½-26¼mm. wide. (Twenty-five varieties.)

Envelopes are on diagonally laid paper.
Wrappers on vertically or horizontally laid paper.

1863-64

U46	U17	2c	**black,** die 1, *buff*	22.50	11.00
			Entire	47.50	25.00
W47	"	2c	**black,** die 1, *dark manila*	27.50	20.00
			Entire	45.00	42.50
U48	U18	2c	**black,** die 2, *buff*	1,000.	
			Entire	2,500.	
U49	"	2c	**black,** die 2, *orange*	800.00	
			Entire	1,600.	
U50	U19	2c	**black,** die 3, *buff* ('64)	6.00	5.00
			Entire	18.00	10.00
W51	"	2c	**black,** die 3, *buff* ('64)	110.00	100.00
			Entire	170.00	150.00
U52	"	2c	**black,** die 3, *orange* ('64)	7.50	4.50
			Entire	15.00	8.50
W53	"	2c	**black,** die 3, *dark manila* ('64)	16.50	14.00
			Entire	50.00	50.00
U54	U20	2c	**black,** die 4, *buff* ('64)	7.50	6.50
			Entire	13.50	9.00
W55	"	2c	**black,** die 4, *buff* ('64)	50.00	35.00
			Entire	90.00	75.00
U56	"	2c	**black,** die 4, *orange* ('64)	5.50	4.50
			Entire	7.50	7.00
W57	"	2c	**black,** die 4, *light manila* ('64)	6.50	6.50
			Entire	14.00	15.00

ENVELOPES

Washington
U21
79 varieties for Nos. U58-U61; 2 varieties for Nos. U63-U65

Washington
U22

1870-71

Printed by George H. Reay, Brooklyn, N. Y.
The engravings in this issue are finely executed.

Franklin
U23
Bust points to the end of the "N" of "ONE"

Jackson
U24
Bust narrow at back. Small, thick figures of value.

Washington
U25
Queue projects below bust.

1864-65

U58	U21	3c **pink,** *white*		3.00	90
		Entire		5.00	2.00
U59	"	3c **pink,** *buff*		2.50	65
		Entire		5.00	2.00
U60	"	3c **brown,** *white* ('65)		25.00	17.50
		Entire		55.00	60.00
U61	"	3c **brown,** *buff* ('65)		25.00	15.00
		Entire		60.00	50.00
U62	"	6c **pink,** *white*		30.00	18.00
		Entire		60.00	40.00
U63	"	6c **pink,** *buff*		22.50	15.00
		Entire		50.00	40.00
U64	"	6c **purple,** *white* ('65)		25.00	17.50
		Entire		42.50	40.00
U65	"	6c **purple,** *buff* ('65)		25.00	15.00
		Entire		45.00	40.00
U66	U22	9c **lemon,** *buff* ('65)		225.00	150.00
		Entire		450.00	325.00
U67	"	9c **orange,** *buff* ('65)		60.00	60.00
		Entire		140.00	175.00
		a. 9c orange yellow, *buff*		75.00	70.00
		Entire		110.00	200.00
U68	"	12c **brown,** *buff* ('65)		200.00	175.00
		Entire		400.00	725.00
U69	"	12c **red brown,** *buff* ('65)		65.00	45.00
		Entire		90.00	160.00
U70	"	18c **red,** *buff* ('65)		65.00	45.00
		Entire		170.00	500.00
U71	"	24c **blue,** *buff* ('65)		60.00	50.00
		Entire		160.00	500.00
U72	"	30c **green,** *buff* ('65)		40.00	40.00
		Entire		150.00	500.00
		a. 30c yellow green, *buff*		40.00	50.00
		Entire		150.00	550.00
U73	"	40c **rose,** *buff* ('65)		50.00	125.00
		Entire		200.00	700.00

Lincoln
U26
Neck very long at the back.

Clay
U29
Ear partly concealed by hair, mouth large, chin prominent.

Stanton
U27
Bust pointed at the back; figures "7" are normal.

Webster
U30
Has side whiskers.

Jefferson
U28
Queue forms straight line with the bust.

Scott
U31
Straggling locks of hair at top of head; ornaments around the inner oval end in squares.

ENVELOPES

Hamilton
U32

Back of bust very narrow, chin almost straight; labels containing figures of value are exactly parallel.

Perry
U33

Front of bust very narrow and pointed; inner lines of shields project very slighly beyond the oval.

1870-71

U74	U23	1c **blue**, *white*	20.00	15.00
		Entire	40.00	25.00
		a. 1c ultramarine, *white*	40.00	20.00
		Entire	70.00	42.50
U75	"	1c **blue**, *amber*	20.00	15.00
		Entire	40.00	10.00
		a. 1c ultramarine, *amber*	30.00	18.00
		Entire	52.50	42.50
U76	"	1c **blue**, *orange*	10.00	8.00
		Entire	20.00	12.00
W77	"	1c **blue**, *manila*	25.00	20.00
		Entire	50.00	40.00
U78	U24	2c **brown**, *white*	20.00	9.00
		Entire	45.00	11.00
U79	"	2c **brown**, *amber*	9.00	5.00
		Entire	25.00	11.00
U80	"	2c **brown**, *orange*	5.00	4.00
		Entire	9.00	5.00
W81	"	2c **brown**, *manila*	12.00	12.00
		Entire	25.00	20.00
U82	U25	3c **green**, *white*	3.00	.50
		Entire	5.00	2.00
U83	"	3c **green**, *amber*	3.00	1.25
		Entire	7.00	2.50
U84	"	3c **green**, *cream*	6.00	2.00
		Entire	12.00	4.00
U85	U26	6c **dark red**, *white*	10.00	8.00
		Entire	15.00	10.00
		a. 6c vermilion, *white*	9.00	9.00
		Entire	14.00	10.00
U86	U26	6c **dark red**, *amber*	14.00	8.00
		Entire	20.00	11.00
		a. 6c vermilion, *amber*	14.00	8.00
		Entire	22.50	11.00
U87	"	6c **dark red**, *cream*	17.00	9.00
		Entire	30.00	20.00
		a. 6c vermilion, *cream*	19.00	9.00
		Entire	30.00	16.00
U88	U27	7c **vermilion**, *amber* ('71)	20.00	100.00
		Entire	40.00	500.00
U89	U28	10c **olive black**, *white*	250.00	175.00
		Entire	350.00	600.00
U90	"	10c **olive black**, *amber*	250.00	175.00
		Entire	350.00	600.00
U91	"	10c **brown**, *white*	35.00	40.00
		Entire	60.00	60.00
U92	"	10c **brown**, *amber*	50.00	40.00
		Entire	75.00	60.00
		a. 10c dark brown, *amber*	50.00	40.00
		Entire	75.00	70.00
U93	U29	12c **plum**, *white*	65.00	45.00
		Entire	180.00	325.00
U94	"	12c **plum**, *amber*	75.00	45.00
		Entire	150.00	400.00
U95	"	12c **plum**, *cream*	150.00	110.00
		Entire	275.00	
U96	U30	15c **red orange**, *white*	40.00	55.00
		Entire	100.00	
		a. 15c orange, *white*	40.00	
		Entire	110.00	
U97	"	15c **red orange**, *amber*	110.00	125.00
		Entire	325.00	
		a. 15c orange, *amber*	110.00	
		Entire	325.00	
U98	"	15c **red orange**, *cream*	135.00	160.00
		Entire	250.00	
		a. 15c orange, *cream*	150.00	
		Entire	250.00	
U99	U31	24c **purple**, *white*	75.00	60.00
		Entire	150.00	
U100	"	24c **purple**, *amber*	125.00	200.00
		Entire	300.00	
U101	"	24c **purple**, *cream*	125.00	200.00
		Entire	250.00	
U102	U32	30c **black**, *white*	45.00	65.00
		Entire	175.00	
U103	"	30c **black**, *amber*	125.00	175.00
		Entire	400.00	
U104	"	30c **black**, *cream*	135.00	225.00
		Entire	275.00	
U105	U33	90c **carmine**, *white*	110.00	150.00
		Entire	160.00	
U106	"	90c **carmine**, *amber*	200.00	250.00
		Entire	700.00	
U107	"	90c **carmine**, *cream*	200.00	300.00
		Entire	700.00	

Printed by Plimpton Manufacturing Co.

U34
Die 1

Bust forms an angle at the back near the frame. Lettering poorly executed. Distinct circle in "O" of "Postage".

U35
Die 2
Lower part of bust points to the end of the "E" in "ONE".
Head inclined downward.

U36
Die 1
Bust narrow at back. Thin numerals. Head of "P" narrow. Bust broad at front, ending in sharp corners.

U37
Die 2
Bust broad. Figures of value in long ovals.

U38
Die 3
Similar to die 2 but the figure "2" at the left touches the oval.

U39
Die 4
Similar to die 2 but the "O" of "TWO" has the center netted instead of plain and the "G" of "POSTAGE" and the "C" of "CENTS" have diagonal crossline.

U40
Die 5
Bust broad: numerals in ovals short and thick.

ENVELOPES

U41
Die 6
Similar to die 5 but the ovals containing the numerals are much heavier. A diagonal line runs from the upper part of the "U" to the white frame-line.

U42
Die 7
Similar to die 5 but the middle stroke of "N" in "CENTS" is as thin as the vertical strokes.

U43
Die 8
Bottom of bust cut almost semi-circularly.

U44
Die 1
Thin lettering, long thin figures of value.

U45
Die 2
Thick lettering, well-formed figures of value, queue does not project below bust.

U46
Die 3
Top of head egg-shaped; knot of queue well marked and projects triangularly.

ENVELOPES

Die 1
Figures of value with thick, curved tops.

Taylor U47

Die 2
Figures of value with long, thin tops.

U48
Neck short at back.

U50
Die 1
Very large head.

U49
Figures of value turned up at the ends

U51
Die 2
Knot of queue stands out prominently.

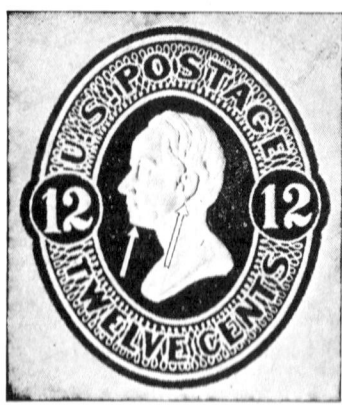

U52
Ear prominent, chin receding.

U53
No side whiskers, forelock projects above head.

U54
Hair does not project; ornaments around the inner oval end in points.

U55
Back of bust rather broad, chin slopes considerably; labels containing figures of value are not exactly parallel.

U56
Front of bust sloping; inner lines of shields project considerably into the inner oval.

1874-86

U108	U34	1c **dark blue,** die 1, *white*	60.00	25.00
		Entire	80.00	60.00
		a. light blue, die 1, *white*		
U109	"	1c **dark blue,** die 1, *amber*	70.00	45.00
		Entire	100.00	60.00
U110	"	1c **dark blue,** die 1, *cream*	475.00	
U111	"	1c **dark blue,** die 1, *orange*	11.00	8.00
		Entire	20.00	15.00
		a. 1c light blue, die 1, *orange*	15.00	7.00
		Entire	14.00	10.00
W112	"	1c **dark blue,** die 1, *manila*	30.00	19.00
		Entire	50.00	50.00
U113	U35	1c **light blue,** die 2, *white*	50	25
		Entire	1.10	75
		a. 1c dark blue, die 2, *white*	5.00	3.00
		Entire	10.00	7.00
U114	"	1c **light blue,** die 2, *amber*	1.75	1.00
		Entire	3.00	2.00
		a. 1c dark blue, die 2, *amber*	10.00	5.00
		Entire	14.00	7.00
U115	"	1c **blue,** die 2, *cream*	2.00	1.25
		Entire	3.00	2.00
		a. 1c dark blue, die 2, *cream*	10.00	3.00
		Entire	12.00	9.00
U116	"	1c **light blue,** die 2, *orange*	25	10
		Entire	35	30
		a. 1c dark blue, die 2, *orange*	85	50
		Entire	4.00	3.50
U117	"	1c **light blue,** die 2, *blue* ('80)	2.25	1.75
		Entire	2.75	2.50
U118	"	1c **light blue,** die 2, *fawn* ('79)	2.25	1.75
		Entire	3.00	2.65
U119	"	1c **light blue,** die 2, *manila* ('86)	2.25	1.50
		Entire	2.75	1.95

ENVELOPES

W120	U35	1c **light blue,** die 2, *manila*	50	35
		Entire	75	65
		a. 1c dark blue, die 2, *manila*	2.00	1.25
		Entire	3.00	2.50
U121	"	1c **light blue,** die 2, *amber manila* ('86)	3.50	3.50
		Entire	4.50	4.00
U122	U36	2c **brown,** die 1, *white*	65.00	22.50
		Entire	80.00	65.00
U123	"	2c **brown,** die 1, *amber*	30.00	17.50
		Entire	55.00	55.00
U124	"	2c **brown,** die 1, *cream*	350.00	
U125	"	2c **brown,** die 1, *orange*	5,500.	
		Entire	9,000.	
W126	"	2c **brown,** die 1, *manila*	50.00	25.00
		Entire	60.00	50.00
W127	"	2c **vermilion,** die 1, *manila*	800.00	225.00
		Entire	1,000.	
U128	U37	2c **brown,** die 2, *white*	25.00	14.00
		Entire	50.00	50.00
U129	"	2c **brown,** die 1, *amber*	40.00	15.00
		Entire	50.00	32.50
U130	"	2c **brown,** die 2, *cream*	15,000.	
W131	"	2c **brown,** die 2, *manila*	7.50	6.00
		Entire	9.00	9.00
U132	U38	2c **brown,** die 3, *white*	45.00	15.00
		Entire	60.00	45.00
U133	"	2c **brown,** die 3, *amber*	150.00	47.50
		Entire	175.00	75.00
U133A	"	2c **brown,** die 3, *cream*	30,000.	
U134	U39	2c **brown,** die 4, *white*	500.00	85.00
		Entire	525.00	115.00
U135	"	2c **brown,** die 4, *amber*	250.00	75.00
		Entire	300.00	110.00
U136	"	2c **brown,** die 4, *orange*	25.00	20.00
		Entire	45.00	30.00
W137	"	2c **brown,** die 4, *manila*	45.00	22.50
		Entire	50.00	30.00
U137A	"	2c **vermilion,** die 4, *white*	15,000.	
U137B	"	2c **vermilion,** die 4, *amber*	15,000.	
U137C	"	2c **vermilion,** die 4, *orange*	15,000.	
W138	"	2c **vermilion,** die 4, *manila*	5,000.	
U139	U40	2c **brown,** die 5, *white* ('75)	35.00	25.00
		Entire	35.00	25.00
U140	"	2c **brown,** die 5, *amber* ('75)	50.00	40.00
		Entire	65.00	42.50
W141	"	2c **brown,** die 5, *manila* ('75)	22.50	17.00
		Entire	25.00	25.00
U142	"	2c **vermilion,** die 5, *white* ('75)	3.00	1.50
		Entire	3.75	2.00
		a. 2c pink, die 5, *white*	6.50	4.50
		Entire	9.00	6.50
U143	"	2c **vermilion,** die 5, *amber* ('75)	2.50	1.25
		Entire	3.25	3.00
U144	"	2c **vermilion,** die 5, *cream* ('75)	4.25	3.50
		Entire	6.00	4.50
U145	"	2c **vermilion,** die 5, *orange* ('75)	5,000.	
		Entire	7,500.	
U146	"	2c **vermilion,** die 5, *blue* ('80)	85.00	22.50
		Entire	125.00	110.00
U147	"	2c **vermilion,** die 5, *fawn* ('75)	3.50	3.00
		Entire	5.75	4.00
W148	"	2c **vermilion,** die 5, *manila* ('75)	2.00	1.50
		Entire	3.00	2.50
U149	U41	2c **vermilion,** die 6, *white* ("78)	25.00	14.00
		Entire	32.50	20.00
		a. 2c pink, die 6, *white*	25.00	14.00
		Entire	35.00	17.00
U150	"	2c **vermilion,** die 6, *amber* ('78)	15.00	9.00
		Entire	22.50	12.00
U151	"	2c **vermilion,** die 6, *blue* ('80)	5.00	4.00
		Entire	6.00	6.00
		a. 2c pink, die 6, *blue*	6.00	4.00
		Entire	7.50	6.00
U152	"	2c **vermilion,** die 6, *fawn* ('78)	5.00	3.00
		Entire	6.50	5.00
U153	U42	2c **vermilion,** die 7, *white* ('76)	35.00	20.00
		Entire	55.00	27.50
U154	"	2c **vermilion,** die 7, *amber* ('76)	175.00	50.00
		Entire	190.00	70.00
W155	"	2c **vermilion,** die 7, *manila* ('76)	7.50	6.00
		Entire	10.00	8.00
U156	U43	2c **vermilion,** die 8, *white* ('81)	325.00	90.00
		Entire	475.00	225.00
U157	"	2c **vermilion,** die 8, *amber* ('81)	10,000.	10,000.
		Entire	30,000.	
W158	"	2c **vermilion,** die 8, *manila* ('81)	50.00	40.00
		Entire	90.00	75.00
U159	U44	3c **green,** die 1, *white*	14.00	3.00
		Entire	17.00	9.00
U160	"	3c **green,** die 1, *amber*	17.00	5.00
		Entire	20.00	8.00

U161	U44	3c **green,** die 1, *cream*	25.00	6.00
		Entire	30.00	12.00
U162	"	3c **green,** die 1, *blue*	30,000.	
U163	U45	3c **green,** die 2, *white*	45	10
		Entire	1.00	35
U164	"	3c **green,** die 2, *amber*	45	20
		Entire	1.45	55
U165	"	3c **green,** die 2, *cream*	3.75	2.00
		Entire	6.50	4.25
U166	"	3c **green,** die 2, *blue*	4.00	2.50
		Entire	7.50	5.50
U167	"	3c **green,** die 2, *fawn* ('75)	2.00	1.00
		Entire	4.50	2.50
U168	U46	3c **green,** die 3, *white* ('81)	325.00	27.50
		Entire	1,500.	50.00
U169	"	3c **green,** die 3, *amber*	150.00	80.00
		Entire	240.00	110.00
U170	"	3c **green,** die 3, *blue* ('81)	6,000.	1,000.
		Entire	10,000.	3,000.
U171	"	3c **green,** die 3, *fawn* ('81)	20,000.	650.00
		Entire		10,000.
U172	U47	5c **blue,** die 1, *white* ('75)	4.50	4.00
		Entire	8.00	7.50
U173	"	5c **blue,** die 1, *amber* ('75)	6.00	4.50
		Entire	8.00	5.00
U174	"	5c **blue,** die 1, *cream* ('75)	70.00	32.50
		Entire	85.00	75.00
U175	"	5c **blue,** die 1, *blue* ('75)	5.00	5.00
		Entire	10.00	9.50
U176	"	5c **blue,** die 1, *fawn* ('75)	75.00	40.00
		Entire	160.00	
U177	"	5c **blue,** die 2, *white* ('75)	3.50	2.50
		Entire	7.50	6.00
U178	"	5c **blue,** die 2, *amber* ('75)	3.50	2.50
		Entire	9.00	8.00
U178A	"	5c **blue,** die 2, *cream* ('76)	1,200.	
		Entire	2,000.	
U179	"	5c **blue,** die 2, *blue* ('75)	7.50	4.50
		Entire	9.50	9.00
U180	"	5c **blue,** die 2, *fawn* ('75)	60.00	30.00
		Entire	85.00	80.00
U181	U48	6c **red,** *white*	2.50	1.75
		Entire	7.00	6.00
		a. 6c vermilion, *white*	2.50	1.75
		Entire	6.00	6.00
U182	"	6c **red,** *amber*	3.50	2.75
		Entire	11.00	8.50
		a. 6c vermilion, *amber*	5.50	3.00
		Entire	11.00	7.50
U183	"	6c **red,** *cream*	12.00	8.00
		Entire	16.00	16.00
		a. 6c vermilion, *cream*	12.00	8.00
		Entire	16.00	16.00
U184	"	6c **red,** *fawn* ('75)	11.00	7.00
		Entire	17.00	14.00
U185	U49	7c **vermilion,** *white*	750.00	
U186	"	7c **vermilion,** *amber*	60.00	45.00
		Entire	95.00	
U187	U50	10c **brown,** die 1, *white*	15.00	10.00
		Entire	35.00	
U188	"	10c **brown,** die 1, *amber*	40.00	22.50
		Entire	60.00	
U189	U51	10c **chocolate,** die 2, *white* ('75)	2.50	1.75
		Entire	5.00	5.00
		a. bister brown, die 2, *white*	2.75	2.00
		Entire	5.00	5.00
		b. yellow ocher	600.00	
		Entire	750.00	
U190	"	10c **chocolate,** die 2, *amber* ('75)	3.75	3.50
		Entire	6.50	5.00
		a. bister brown, die 2, *amber*	3.50	3.00
		Entire	6.50	5.00
		b. yellow ocher	600.00	
		Entire	750.00	
U191	"	10c **brown,** die 2, *oriental buff* ('86)	5.00	4.50
		Entire	6.00	5.00
U192	"	10c **brown,** die 2, *blue* ('86)	5.50	4.00
		Entire	6.50	5.00
		a. 10c gray black, die 2, *blue*	5.00	4.50
		Entire	6.00	4.50
		b. 10c red brown, die 2, *blue*	5.50	4.00
		Entire	7.00	6.00
U193	"	10c **brown,** die 2, *manila* ('86)	4.50	4.00
		Entire	9.00	8.00
		a. 10c red brown, die 2, *manila*	4.50	4.00
		Entire	7.50	5.50
U194	"	10c **brown,** die 2, *amber manila* ('86)	4.50	4.00
		Entire	9.00	8.00
		a. 10c red brown, die 2, *amber manila*	4.50	4.00
		Entire	9.00	9.00

ENVELOPES

U195	U52	12c **plum**, *white*	95.00	50.00
		Entire	140.00	
U196	"	12c **plum**, *amber*	125.00	100.00
		Entire	175.00	
U197	"	12c **plum**, *cream*	140.00	100.00
		Entire	600.00	
U198	U53	15c **orange**, *white*	25.00	20.00
		Entire	60.00	45.00
U199	"	15c **orange**, *amber*	85.00	65.00
		Entire	140.00	
U200	"	15c **orange**, *cream*	275.00	200.00
		Entire	750.00	
U201	U54	24c **purple**, *white*	120.00	70.00
		Entire	175.00	
U202	"	24c **purple**, *amber*	130.00	70.00
		Entire	175.00	
U203	"	24c **purple**, *cream*	110.00	85.00
		Entire	600.00	
U204	U55	30c **black**, *white*	42.50	20.00
		Entire	55.00	40.00
U205	"	30c **black**, *amber*	40.00	35.00
		Entire	75.00	*150.00*
U206	"	30c **black**, *cream* ('75)	275.00	200.00
		Entire	650.00	
U207	"	30c **black**, *oriental buff* ('81)	65.00	50.00
		Entire	95.00	
U208	"	30c **black**, *blue* ('81)	75.00	50.00
		Entire	85.00	
U209	"	30c **black**, *manila* ('81)	50.00	50.00
		Entire	80.00	
U210	"	30c **black**, *amber manila* ('86)	50.00	50.00
		Entire	85.00	
U211	U56	90c **carmine**, *white* ('75)	75.00	50.00
		Entire	90.00	70.00
U212	"	90c **carmine**, *amber* ('75)	90.00	150.00
		Entire	150.00	
U213	"	90c **carmine**, *cream* ('75)	900.00	
		Entire	1,500.	
U214	"	90c **carmine**, *oriental buff* ('86)	140.00	170.00
		Entire	200.00	
U215	"	90c **carmine**, *blue* ('86)	120.00	150.00
		Entire	175.00	
U216	"	90c **carmine**, *manila* ('86)	85.00	150.00
		Entire	150.00	
U217	U56	90c **carmine**, *amber manila* ('86)	80.00	125.00
		Entire	160.00	

U58
Double line under "POSTAGE".

1876

Printed by Plimpton Manufacturing Co.

U218	U57	3c **red**, *white*	45.00	17.50
		Entire	55.00	35.00
U219	"	3c **green**, *white*	35.00	10.00
		Entire	45.00	25.00
U220	U58	3c **red**, *white*	15,000.	
		Entire	20,000.	
U221	"	3c **green**, *white*	40.00	12.00
		Entire	70.00	32.50

Note: No. U206 has watermark #2; No. U207 watermark #6 or #7. No. U213 has watermark #2; No. U214 watermark #7. These envelopes cannot be positively identified except by the watermark.

Garfield
U59

1882-86
Printed by Plimpton Manufacturing Co. and Morgan Envelope Co.

U222	U59	5c **brown**, *white*	1.75	75
		Entire	2.50	2.50
U223	"	5c **brown**, *amber*	2.25	1.25
		Entire	5.00	3.00
U224	"	5c **brown**, *oriental buff* ('86)	75.00	35.00
		Entire	80.00	
U225	"	5c **brown**, *blue*	30.00	20.00
		Entire	50.00	35.00
U226	"	5c **brown**, *fawn*	150.00	
		Entire	200.00	

U57
Single line under "POSTAGE".

Washington
U60

1883, October

U227	U60	2c **red**, *white*	2.25	75
		Entire	3.00	1.00
		a. 2c brown (error), *white*, entire	*1,000.*	
U228	"	2c **red**, *amber*	2.75	90
		Entire	4.00	3.00
U229	"	2c **red**, *blue*	4.00	2.50
		Entire	5.50	3.25
U230	"	2c **red**, *fawn*	3.50	1.25
		Entire	5.00	2.75

U62
Retouched die.
Wavy lines thick and blurred.

1884, June

U236	U62	2c **red**, *white*	3.00	1.25
		Entire	5.50	3.25
U237	"	2c **red**, *amber*	6.00	3.00
		Entire	9.50	4.00
U238	"	2c **red**, *blue*	8.50	4.75
		Entire	12.50	5.00
U239	"	2c **red**, *fawn*	6.00	3.00
		Entire	9.00	4.50

Washington
U61
Wavy lines fine and clear.

1883, November

Four Wavy Lines in Oval

U231	U61	2c **red**, *white*	1.25	40
		Entire	3.50	75
U232	"	2c **red**, *amber*	1.75	75
		Entire	3.25	2.25
U233	"	2c **red**, *blue*	3.00	2.00
		Entire	6.50	3.25
U234	"	2c **red**, *fawn*	2.50	1.10
		Entire	4.50	2.00
W235	"	2c **red**, *manila*	4.25	2.50
		Entire	8.00	4.50

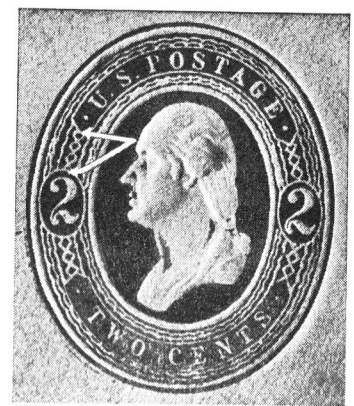

U63
3½ links over left "2".

U240	U63	2c **red**, *white*	27.50	15.00
		Entire	35.00	30.00
U241	"	2c **red**, *amber*	475.00	225.00
		Entire	550.00	350.00
U242	"	2c **red**, *fawn*	*5,000.*	
		Entire	*7,500.*	

ENVELOPES 571

U64
2 links below right "2".

U243	U64	2c **red,** *white*	40.00	25.00
		Entire	50.00	45.00
U244	"	2c **red,** *amber*	80.00	45.00
		Entire	120.00	80.00
U245	"	2c **red,** *blue*	200.00	75.00
		Entire	250.00	110.00
U246	"	2c **red,** *fawn*	175.00	75.00
		Entire	225.00	150.00

Jackson
U66
Die 1

Die 1
Numeral at left is
2¾ mm. wide.

Die 2
Numeral at left is
3¼ mm. wide

1883-86

U250	U66	4c **green,** die 1, *white*	1.50	1.40
		Entire	3.00	3.00
U251	"	4c **green,** die 1, *amber*	1.75	1.25
		Entire	3.50	3.00
U252	"	4c **green,** die 1, *oriental buff* ('86)	3.50	3.00
		Entire	7.50	5.50
U253	"	4c **green,** die 1, *blue* ('86)	3.50	2.50
		Entire	7.50	5.00
U254	"	4c **green,** die 1, *manila* ('86)	5.50	3.00
		Entire	8.50	6.00
U255	"	4c **green,** die 1, *amber manila* ('86)	12.50	6.00
		Entire	17.50	11.00
U256	"	4c **green,** die 2, *white*	2.75	1.25
		Entire	7.00	4.00
U257	"	4c **green,** die 2, *amber*	6.00	3.00
		Entire	9.00	7.50
U258	"	4c **green,** die 2, *manila* ('86)	3.00	2.25
		Entire	7.00	7.00
U259	"	4c **green,** die 2, *amber manila* ('86)	3.75	2.25
		Entire	7.00	6.50

1884, May

U260	U61	2c **brown,** *white*	6.00	1.75
		Entire	7.50	4.25
U261	"	2c **brown,** *amber*	6.50	2.00
		Entire	9.00	2.50
U262	"	2c **brown,** *blue*	8.00	3.25
		Entire	10.00	5.00
U263	"	2c **brown,** *fawn*	6.50	3.00
		Entire	7.50	5.00
W264	"	2c **brown,** *manila*	7.50	5.75
		Entire	12.00	9.00

1884, June   Retouched Die.

U265	U62	2c **brown,** *white*	7.75	2.50
		Entire	11.00	5.00
U266	"	2c **brown,** *amber*	35.00	12.50
		Entire	40.00	15.00
U267	"	2c **brown,** *blue*	6.00	3.25
		Entire	8.00	5.00
U268	"	2c **brown,** *fawn*	7.00	4.00
		Entire	8.50	5.00
W269	"	2c **brown,** *manila*	12.00	8.50
		Entire	15.00	9.00

2 Links Below Right "2"

U270	U64	2c **brown,** *white*	50.00	27.50
		Entire	70.00	70.00
U271	"	2c **brown,** *amber*	145.00	75.00
		Entire	190.00	120.00
U272	"	2c **brown,** *fawn*	*1,750.*	*900.00*
		Entire	*2,500.*	*1,400.*

U65
Round "O" in "TWO".

U247	U65	2c **red,** *white*	600.00	175.00
		Entire	825.00	400.00
U248	"	2c **red,** *amber*	1,200.	475.00
		Entire	1,700.	600.00
U249	"	2c **red,** *fawn*	375.00	175.00
		Entire	500.00	275.00

ENVELOPES

U273	U65	2c **brown**, *white*		90.00	45.00
		Entire		110.00	85.00
U274	"	2c **brown**, *amber*		95.00	45.00
		Entire		110.00	75.00
U275	"	2c **brown**, *blue*			2,350.
U276	"	2c **brown**, *fawn*		525.00	350.00
		Entire		750.00	500.00

Washington
U67
Die 1
Extremity of bust below the queue forms a point.

U68
Die 2

1884-86 Extremity of bust is rounded.
Similar to U61. Two wavy lines in oval

U277	U67	2c **brown**, die 1, *white*		15	10
		Entire		35	12
	a.	2c brown lake, die 1, *white*		15.00	7.50
		Entire		17.50	12.00
U278	"	2c **brown**, die 1, *amber*		20	10
		Entire		65	40
	a.	2c brown lake, die 1, *amber*		25.00	8.00
		Entire		27.50	9.00
U279	"	2c **brown**, die 1, *oriental buff* ('86)		1.75	1.00
		Entire		2.50	1.50
U280	"	2c **brown**, die 1, *blue*		85	70
		Entire		1.40	1.30
U281	"	2c **brown**, die 1, *fawn*		1.25	1.00
		Entire		2.25	1.00
U282	"	2c **brown**, die 1, *manila* ('86)		6.00	2.00
		Entire		7.00	4.00
W283	"	2c **brown**, die 1, *manila*		3.50	1.75
		Entire		6.00	5.00
U284	"	2c **brown**, die 1, *amber manila* ('86)		3.75	2.25
		Entire		5.00	4.50
U285	"	2c **red**, die 1, *white*		450.00	
		Entire		550.00	
U286	U67	2c **red**, die 1, *blue*		150.00	
		Entire		175.00	
W287	"	2c **red**, die 1, *manila*		75.00	
		Entire		90.00	
U288	U68	2c **brown**, die 2, *white*		110.00	15.00
		Entire		250.00	65.00
U289	"	2c **brown**, die 2, *amber*		7.00	5.00
		Entire		12.00	9.00
U290	"	2c **brown**, die 2, *blue*		400.00	100.00
		Entire		450.00	110.00
U291	"	2c **brown**, die 2, *fawn*		15.00	12.00
		Entire		20.00	14.00
W292	"	2c **brown**, die 2, *manila*		15.00	12.00
		Entire		18.00	15.00

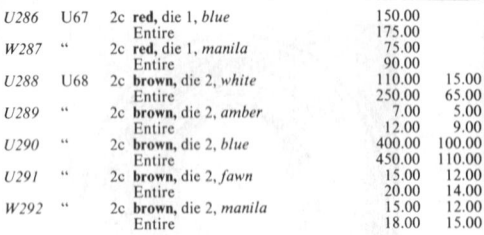

Gen. U. S. Grant
US1

1886 **Printed by American Bank Note Co.**
Issued August 18, 1886. Withdrawn June 30, 1894.
Letter Sheet, 160x271mm. Stamp in upper right corner.
Creamy White Paper.

U293	US1	2c **green**, *white*, entire	17.00	4.50
		Perforation varieties:		
		83 perforations at top	17.00	4.50
		41 perforations at top	17.00	4.50
		33 perforations at top	25.00	7.50

All with 41 perforations at top.

Inscribed: Series 1	17.00	4.50
Inscribed: Series 2	17.00	4.50
Inscribed: Series 3	17.00	4.50
Inscribed: Series 4	17.00	4.50
Inscribed: Series 5	17.00	4.50
Inscribed: Series 6	17.00	4.50
Inscribed: Series 7	17.00	4.50

Franklin
U69

ENVELOPES

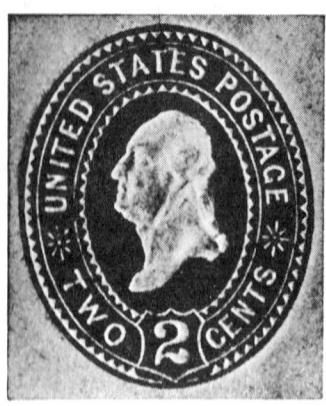

Washington
U70
Die 1

Bust points between third and fourth notches of inner oval "G" of "POSTAGE" has no bar.

U71
Die 2

Bust points between second and third notches of inner oval; "G" of "POSTAGE" has a bar; ear is indicated by one heavy line; one vertical line at corner of mouth.

U72
Die 3

Frame same as die 2; upper part of head more rounded; ear indicated by two curved lines with two locks of hair in front; two vertical lines at corner of mouth.

Jackson
U73

Grant
U74
Die 1

There is a space between the beard and the collar of the coat. A button is on the collar.

U75
Die 2

The collar touches the beard and there is no button.

ENVELOPES

1887-94
Printed by Plimpton Manufacturing Co. and Morgan Envelope Co., Hartford, Conn.; James Purcell, Holyoke, Mass.

U294	U69	1c **blue**, *white*	30	5
		Entire	50	20
U295	"	1c **dark blue**, *white* ('94)	5.00	1.25
		Entire	7.50	5.00
U296	"	1c **blue**, *amber*	1.75	60
		Entire	3.00	1.50
U297	"	1c **dark blue**, *amber* ('94)	30.00	12.00
		Entire	35.00	17.00
U298	"	1c **blue**, *oriental buff*	1,500.	
		Entire	2,800.	
U299	"	1c **blue**, *blue*	1,850.	
		Entire	3,500.	
U300	"	1c **blue**, *manila*	30	5
		Entire	60	25
W301	"	1c **blue**, *manila*	15	5
		Entire	45	20
U302	"	1c **dark blue**, *manila* ('94)	16.00	5.00
		Entire	20.00	7.00
W303	"	1c **dark blue**, *manila* ('94)	9.00	6.00
		Entire	12.00	7.50
U304	"	1c **blue**, *amber manila*	2.25	1.40
		Entire	4.00	2.25
U305	U70	2c **green**, die 1, *white*	5.00	4.00
		Entire	10.00	8.00
U306	"	2c **green**, die 1, *amber*	12.00	6.00
		Entire	18.00	10.00
U307	"	2c **green**, die 1, *oriental buff*	45.00	20.00
		Entire	60.00	30.00
U308	"	2c **green**, die 1, *blue*	1,800.	400.00
		Entire		3,000.
U309	"	2c **green**, die 1, *manila*	1,250.	250.00
		Entire	4,000.	400.00
U310	"	2c **green**, die 1, *amber manila*	1,100.	350.00
		Entire	4,000.	1,750.
U311	U71	2c **green**, die 2, *white*	20	5
		Entire	25	10
U312	"	2c **green**, die 2, *amber*	25	5
		Entire	35	10
U313	"	2c **green**, die 2, *oriental buff*	35	8
		Entire	50	20
U314	"	2c **green**, die 2, *blue*	35	8
		Entire	55	20
U315	"	2c **green**, die 2, *manila*	50	20
		Entire	1.25	50
W316	"	2c **green**, die 2, *manila*	75	50
		Entire	2.50	80
U317	"	2c **green**, die 2, *amber manila*	55	18
		Entire	1.85	40
U318	U72	2c **green**, die 3, *white*	75.00	8.50
		Entire	85.00	25.00
U319	"	2c **green**, die 3, *amber*	100.00	11.00
		Entire	110.00	25.00
U320	"	2c **green**, die 3, *oriental buff*	110.00	18.00
		Entire	120.00	30.00
U321	"	2c **green**, die 3, *blue*	125.00	25.00
		Entire	135.00	30.00
U322	"	2c **green**, die 3, *manila*	100.00	40.00
		Entire	120.00	65.00
U323	"	2c **green**, die 3, *amber manila*	225.00	60.00
		Entire	250.00	75.00
U324	U73	4c **carmine**, *white*	80	50
		Entire	1.75	1.40
	a.	4c **lake**, *white*	1.25	50
		Entire	1.75	1.50
	b.	4c **scarlet**, *white* ('94)	1.25	50
		Entire	2.00	1.50
U325	"	4c **carmine**, *amber*	1.25	60
		Entire	2.50	1.50
	a.	4c **lake**, *amber*	1.25	60
		Entire	2.00	1.00
	b.	4c **scarlet**, *amber* ('94)	1.25	75
		Entire	3.00	1.50
U326	"	4c **carmine**, *oriental buff*	3.00	1.50
		Entire	5.00	2.50
	a.	4c **lake**, *oriental buff*	3.00	1.50
		Entire	5.00	3.00
U327	"	4c **carmine**, *blue*	3.00	1.50
		Entire	4.00	2.50
	a.	4c **lake**, *blue*	3.25	1.50
		Entire	4.00	2.50
U328	"	4c **carmine**, *manila*	3.75	2.50
		Entire	6.00	4.00
	a.	4c **lake**, *manila*	4.00	2.50
		Entire	6.00	4.00
	b.	4c **pink**, *manila*	5.50	2.50
		Entire	7.00	4.00
U329	"	4c **carmine**, *amber manila*	2.00	1.50
		Entire	5.00	2.50
	a.	4c **lake**, *amber manila*	2.00	1.25
		Entire	4.25	2.25
	b.	4c **pink**, *amber manila*	3.50	1.25
		Entire	6.00	6.00
U330	U74	5c **blue**, die 1, *white*	1.25	1.25
		Entire	4.00	4.50
U331	"	5c **blue**, die 1, *amber*	1.75	1.25
		Entire	5.00	4.00
U332	"	5c **blue**, die 1, *oriental buff*	2.50	2.00
		Entire	7.00	3.75
U333	"	5c **blue**, die 1, *blue*	3.00	2.50
		Entire	5.25	4.50
U334	U75	5c **blue**, die 2, *white* ('94)	4.50	2.50
		Entire	6.50	6.00
U335	"	5c **blue**, die 2, *amber* ('94)	3.00	3.00
		Entire	10.00	10.00
U336	U55	30c **red brown**, *(Hamilton) white*	27.50	30.00
		Entire	35.00	175.00
	a.	30c **yellow brown**, *white*	35.00	25.00
		Entire	45.00	200.00
	b.	30c **chocolate**, *white*	25.00	30.00
		Entire	40.00	200.00
U337	"	30c **red brown**, *amber*	25.00	25.00
		Entire	35.00	200.00
	a.	30c **yellow brown**, *amber*	35.00	30.00
		Entire	45.00	200.00
	b.	30c **chocolate**, *amber*	35.00	30.00
		Entire	45.00	200.00
U338	"	30c **red brown**, *oriental buff*	24.00	25.00
		Entire	30.00	200.00
	a.	30c **yellow brown**, *oriental buff*	20.00	20.00
		Entire	25.00	200.00
U339	"	30c **red brown**, *blue*	20.00	20.00
		Entire	25.00	200.00
	a.	30c **yellow brown**, *blue*	25.00	15.00
		Entire	30.00	200.00
U340	"	30c **red brown**, *manila*	25.00	15.00
		Entire	30.00	175.00
	a.	30c **brown**, *manila*	25.00	15.00
		Entire	35.00	175.00
U341	"	30c **red brown**, *amber manila*	22.50	18.00
		Entire	30.00	175.00
	a.	30c **yellow brown**, *amber manila*	18.00	15.00
		Entire	30.00	175.00
U342	U56	90c **purple**, *(Perry) white*	37.50	35.00
		Entire	50.00	250.00
U343	"	90c **purple**, *amber*	37.50	35.00
		Entire	65.00	250.00
U344	"	90c **purple**, *oriental buff*	45.00	35.00
		Entire	65.00	250.00
U345	"	90c **purple**, *blue*	45.00	35.00
		Entire	75.00	250.00
U346	"	90c **purple**, *manila*	40.00	35.00
		Entire	75.00	250.00
U347	"	90c **purple**, *amber manila*	40.00	35.00
		Entire	80.00	250.00

Columbus and Liberty
U76

Four dies were used for the 1c, 2c and 5c:
1. Meridian behind Columbus' head. Period after "CENTS".
2. No meridian. With period.
3. With meridian. No period.
4. No meridian. No period.

1893

U348	U76	1c **deep blue**, *white*	1.10	45
		Entire	2.00	60
U349	"	2c **violet**, *white*	70	20
		Entire	1.60	35
	a.	2c **dark slate** (error), *white*	650.00	
		Entire		

ENVELOPES

U350	U76	5c **chocolate,** *white*		5.00	4.00
		Entire		10.00	8.00
		a. 5c slate brown (error), *white*		500.00	250.00
		Entire		550.00	500.00
U351	"	10c **slate brown,** *white*		32.50	15.00
		Entire		50.00	40.00

Franklin
U77

Washington
U78
Die 1

Bust points to first notch of inner oval and is only slightly concave below.

U79
Die 2

Bust points to middle of second notch of inner oval and is quite hollow below. Queue has ribbon around it.

U80
Die 3

Same as die 2, but hair flowing. No ribbon on queue.

Lincoln
U81
Die 1

Bust pointed but not draped.

U82
Die 2

Bust broad and draped.

576   ENVELOPES

U83
Die 3
Head larger, inner oval has no notches.

Grant
U84
Similar to design of 1887-95 but smaller.

1899				
U352	U77	1c **green,** *white*	30	10
		Entire	50	25
U353	"	1c **green,** *amber*	3.00	85
		Entire	5.00	1.75
U354	"	1c **green,** *oriental buff*	7.00	1.75
		Entire	8.00	3.00
U355	"	1c **green,** *blue*	7.00	1.50
		Entire	8.00	4.00
U356	"	1c **green,** *manila*	65	30
		Entire	2.00	75
W357	"	1c **green,** *manila*	65	30
		Entire	2.75	1.75
U358	U78	2c **carmine,** die 1, *white*	1.50	60
		Entire	5.00	2.00
U359	"	2c **carmine,** die 1, *amber*	12.50	7.00
		Entire	17.00	9.00
U360	"	2c **carmine,** die 1, *oriental buff*	12.50	6.00
		Entire	15.00	7.00
U361	"	2c **carmine,** die 1, *blue*	40.00	15.00
		Entire	45.00	20.00
U362	U79	2c **carmine,** die 2, *white*	15	5
		Entire	30	20
		a. 2c dark lake, die 2, *white*	20.00	20.00
		Entire	25.00	25.00
U363	"	2c **carmine,** die 2, *amber*	45	5
		Entire	1.25	40
U364	"	2c **carmine,** die 2, *oriental buff*	35	10
		Entire	1.25	40
U365	U79	2c **carmine,** die 2, *blue*	75	35
		Entire	2.00	1.25
W366	"	2c **carmine,** die 2, *manila*	2.50	90
		Entire	3.00	2.00
U367	U80	2c **carmine,** die 3, *white*	2.00	75
		Entire	4.50	3.00
U368	"	2c **carmine,** die 3, *amber*	5.00	2.00
		Entire	8.50	6.00
U369	"	2c **carmine,** die 3, *oriental buff*	17.00	5.00
		Entire	22.50	11.00
U370	"	2c **carmine,** die 3, *blue*	6.50	5.00
		Entire	15.00	7.00
U371	U81	4c **brown,** die 1, *white*	12.50	7.00
		Entire	15.00	11.00
U372	"	4c **brown,** die 1, *amber*	12.50	7.00
		Entire	20.00	17.50
U373	U82	4c **brown,** die 2, *white*	3,000.	300.00
		Entire	3,500.	
U374	U83	4c **brown,** die 3, *white*	6.00	4.00
		Entire	12.00	8.00
U375	"	4c **brown,** die 3, *amber*	30.00	8.00
		Entire	35.00	12.00
W376	"	4c **brown,** die 3, *manila*	9.00	5.00
		Entire	11.00	8.00
U377	U84	5c **blue,** *white*	7.50	3.00
		Entire	8.50	4.00
U378	"	5c **blue,** *amber*	9.00	5.00
		Entire	12.00	7.50

Franklin
U85

Washington
U86
One short and two long vertical lines
at the right of "CENTS."

ENVELOPES

Grant
U87

U89
Re-cut Die.

The three lines at the right of "CENTS" and at the left of "TWO" are usually all short; the lettering is heavier and the ends of the ribbons slightly changed.

1904   **Re-cut Die.**

U395	U89	2c **carmine**, *white*	25	8
		Entire	50	25
		2c pink, *white*	4.00	2.00
U396	"	2c **carmine**, *amber*	5.50	20
		Entire	6.00	60
		2c pink, *amber*	7.00	2.00
U397	"	2c **carmine**, *oriental buff*	3.75	50
		Entire	4.50	75
		2c pink, *oriental buff*	5.00	2.00
U398	"	2c **carmine**, *blue*	2.00	50
		Entire	2.50	80
		2c pink, *amber*	4.00	2.00
W399	"	2c **carmine**, *manila*	9.00	4.50
		Entire	13.00	5.00
		2c pink, *manila*	13.00	5.00

Lincoln
U88

1903
Printed by Hartford Manufacturing Co., Hartford, Conn.

U379	U85	1c **green**, *white*	40	6
		Entire	60	20
U380	"	1c **green**, *amber*	8.00	1.50
		Entire	11.00	2.00
U381	"	1c **green**, *oriental buff*	7.00	1.50
		Entire	10.00	2.00
U382	"	1c **green**, *blue*	8.25	1.40
		Entire	9.00	2.00
U383	"	1c **green**, *manila*	2.00	75
		Entire	3.00	1.00
W384	"	1c **green**, *manila*	80	20
		Entire	1.00	50
U385	U86	2c **carmine**, *white*	25	5
		Entire	40	25
		2c pink, *white*	1.25	75
U386	"	2c **carmine**, *amber*	1.00	10
		Entire	2.00	40
		2c pink, *amber*	2.50	1.10
U387	"	2c **carmine**, *oriental buff*	1.00	25
		Entire	1.50	30
		2c pink, *oriental buff*	1.90	85
U388	"	2c **carmine**, *blue*	80	40
		Entire	2.00	50
		2c pink, *blue*	2.50	1.50
W389	"	2c **carmine**, *manila*	10.00	5.00
		Entire	12.00	6.00
U390	U87	4c **chocolate**, *white*	12.00	4.50
		Entire	14.00	7.00
U391	"	4c **chocolate**, *amber*	12.00	5.00
		Entire	14.00	7.00
W392	U87	4c **chocolate**, *manila*	11.00	5.00
		Entire	14.00	11.00
U393	U88	5c **blue**, *white*	11.00	4.00
		Entire	13.00	10.00
U394	"	5c **blue**, *amber*	12.00	5.50
		Entire	15.00	12.50

Franklin
U90

U90
Die 1

U90
Die 2

U90
Die 3

U90
Die 4

Die 1. Wide "D" in "UNITED".
Die 2. Narrow "D" in "UNITED".
Die 3. Wide "S-S" in "STATES" (1910).
Die 4. Sharp angle at back of bust,
   "N" and "E" of "ONE" are parallel (1912).

1907-16
   Printed by Mercantile Corp. and Middle West Supply Co., Dayton, Ohio.

U400	U90	1c green, *white*, die 1		20	5
		Entire		25	15
		a. Die 2		40	15
		Entire		50	25
		b. Die 3		50	25
		Entire		75	45
		c. Die 4		50	20
		Entire		60	25
U401	"	1c green, *amber*, die 1		40	20
		Entire		60	30
		a. Die 2		65	25
		Entire		1.00	55
		b. Die 3		70	35
		Entire		1.25	65
		c. Die 4		60	30
		Entire		75	40
U402	"	1c green, *oriental buff*, die 1		65	20
		Entire		85	35
		a. Die 2		1.00	40
		Entire		1.25	45
		b. Die 3		2.00	65
		Entire		2.25	80
		c. Die 4		1.50	40
		Entire		1.75	60
U403	"	1c green, *blue*, die 1		1.85	50
		Entire		2.25	90
		a. Die 2		1.85	70
		Entire		2.50	1.00
		b. Die 3		2.25	85
		Entire		2.75	1.00
		c. Die 4		1.85	75
		Entire		3.00	1.25
U404	"	1c green, *manila*, die 1		1.75	70
		Entire		2.50	1.10
		a. Die 2		1.85	70
		Entire		4.00	1.25
W405	"	1c green, *manila*, die 1		40	10
		Entire		50	15
		a. Die 2		20.00	15.00
		Entire		21.00	17.50
		b. Die 3		1.50	1.00
		Entire		4.00	3.00
		c. Die 4		20.00	17.50
		Entire		20.00	20.00

Washington
U91

U91
Die 1

U91
Die 2

U91
Die 3

U91
Die 4

U91
Die 5

U91
Die 6

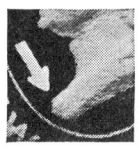
U91
Die 7

U91
Die 8

Die 1. Oval "O" in "TWO" and "C" in "CENTS".
   front of bust broad.
Die 2. Similar to 1 but hair re-cut in two distinct locks
   at top of head.
Die 3. Round "O" in "TWO" and "C" in "CENTS",
   coarse lettering.
Die 4. Similar to 3 but lettering fine and clear, hair lines
   clealy embossed. Inner oval thin and
   clear.
Die 5. All "S"s wide (1910).
Die 6. Similar to 1 but front of bust narrow (1913).
Die 7. Similar to 6 but upper corner of front of bust cut
   away (1916).
Die 8. Similar to 7 but lower stroke of "S" in "CENTS" is a
   straight line. Hair as in Die 2 (1916).

U406	U91	2c **brown red**, *white*, die 1		25	6
		Entire		50	15
		a. Die 2		20.00	7.50
		Entire		50	25
		b. Die 3		30	20
		Entire		40	25
U407	"	2c **brown red**, *amber*, die 1		3.50	1.00
		Entire		5.00	2.50
		a. Die 2		75.00	30.00
		Entire		90.00	50.00
		b. Die 3		1.75	60
		Entire		2.50	90

ENVELOPES 579

U408	U91	2c **brown red,** *oriental buff,* die 1	4.50	1.25
		Entire	5.00	3.00
		a. Die 2	85.00	40.00
		Entire	100.00	75.00
		b. Die 3	4.00	1.00
		Entire	4.50	2.00
U409	"	2c **brown red,** *blue,* die 1	2.75	50
		Entire	4.00	1.00
		a. Die 2	100.00	75.00
		Entire	120.00	85.00
		b. Die 3	2.25	50
		Entire	3.00	1.00
W410	"	2c **brown red,** *manila,* die 1	25.00	15.00
		Entire	30.00	20.00
U411	"	2c **carmine,** *white,* die 1	10	5
		Entire	25	12
		a. Die 2	20	8
		Entire	50	35
		b. Die 3	40	25
		Entire	75	40
		c. Die 4	20	15
		Entire	40	25
		d. Die 5	30	20
		Entire	60	45
		e. Die 6	20	8
		Entire	40	25
		f. Die 7	9.00	7.50
		Entire	11.00	8.00
		g. Die 8	9.50	7.00
		Entire	11.00	7.50
		h. 2c carmine, die 1, with added impression of 1c green (#U400), die 1, entire	175.00	
		i. 2c carmine, die 1, with added impression of 4c black (#U416a), entire	140.00	
U412	"	2c **carmine,** *amber,* die 1	8	6
		Entire	30	10
		a. Die 2	12	10
		Entire	40	15
		b. Die 3	70	30
		Entire	1.25	60
		c. Die 4	20	15
		Entire	40	35
		d. Die 5	35	20
		Entire	70	40
		e. Die 6	15	10
		Entire	50	20
		f. Die 7	7.00	5.00
		Entire	8.50	6.50
U413	"	2c **carmine,** *oriental buff,* die 1	40	20
		Entire	50	25
		a. Die 2	45	45
		Entire	60	35
		b. Die 3	2.75	1.75
		Entire	5.00	4.00
		c. Die 4	10	10
		d. Die 5	35	15
		Entire	80	45
		e. Die 6	30	25
		Entire	75	45
		f. Die 7	30.00	15.00
		Entire	37.50	22.50
		g. Die 8	6.50	5.00
		Entire	9.00	6.50
U414	"	2c **carmine,** *blue,* die 1	10	6
		Entire	30	10
		a. Die 2	25	20
		Entire	55	30
		b. Die 3	40	35
		Entire	1.00	55
		c. Die 4	10	8
		Entire	30	15
		d. Die 5	35	30
		Entire	80	40
		e. Die 6	25	15
		Entire	70	30
		f. Die 7	8.50	4.25
		Entire	13.00	12.00
		g. Die 8	7.50	4.00
		Entire	9.50	7.50
W415	U91	2c **carmine,** *manila,* die 1	2.00	80
		Entire	4.00	2.00
		a. Die 2	1.75	90
		Entire	2.50	1.15
		b. Die 5	1.75	90
		Entire	3.00	2.25
		c. Die 7	30.00	24.00
		Entire	37.50	30.00

U90—4c U90—4c
Die 1 Die 2

4c—Die 1. "F" close to (1 mm.) left "4".
4c—Die 2. "F" far from (1¼ mm.) left "4".

U416	U90	4c **black,** *white,* die 2	1.50	50
		Entire	4.00	1.00
		a. Die 1	2.75	1.50
		Entire	5.00	2.75
U417	"	4c **black,** *amber,* die 2	2.50	1.60
		Entire	5.00	3.00
		a. Die 1	2.85	1.60
		Entire	5.50	3.25

U91—5c U91—5c
Die 1 Die 2

5c—Die 1. Tall "F" in "FIVE".
4c—Die 2. Short "F" in "FIVE".

U418	U91	5c **blue,** *white,* die 2	2.75	1.35
		Entire	5.00	3.25
		a. Die 1	2.75	1.35
		Entire	5.50	3.50
		b. 5c blue, *buff,* die 2 (error)	500.00	
		c. 5c blue, *blue,* die 2 (error)	500.00	
		d. 5c blue, *blue,* die 1 (error)	600.00	
		Entire	1,000.	
U419	"	5c **blue,** *amber,* die 2	9.00	6.50
		Entire	12.00	7.50
		a. Die 1	8.50	6.00
		Entire	11.00	9.00

On July 1, 1915 the use of laid paper was discontinued and wove paper was substituted. Nos. U400 to W405 and U411 to U419 exist on both papers; U406 to W410 come on laid only. Nos. U429 and U430 exist on laid paper.

Franklin
U92

Die 1　　　　Die 2　　　　　　Die 3

Die 4　　　　Die 5

(The 1c and 4c dies are the same except for figures of value.)
Die 1. UNITED nearer inner circle than outer circle.
Die 2. Large U; large NT closely spaced.
Die 3. Knob of hair at back of neck. Large NT widely spaced.
Die 4. UNITED nearer outer circle than inner circle.
Die 5. Narrow oval C, (also O and G).

Some of the engraved dies of this series represent printing methods now obsolete, others are still in service. Some are best distinguished in the entire envelope. Many electrotypes were used.

Printed by Middle West Supply Co. and International Envelope Corp., Dayton, Ohio.

1916-32

U420	U92	1c **green,** *white,* die 1		6	5
		Entire		20	10
		a. Die 2		50.00	40.00
		Entire, size 8		75.00	50.00
		b. Die 3		8	5
		Entire		25	10
		c. Die 4		12	10
		Entire		30	15
		d. Die 5		12	10
		Entire		50	25
U421	"	1c **green,** *amber,* die 1		30	30
		Entire		40	35
		a. Die 2		200.00	125.00
		Entire, size 8		375.00	150.00
		b. Die 3		80	50
		Entire		1.25	85
		c. Die 4		70	40
		Entire		1.20	1.05
		d. Die 5		55	30
		Entire		85	70
U422	"	1c **green,** *oriental buff,* die 1		1.10	75
		Entire		1.40	1.20
		a. Die 4		2.50	1.00
		Entire		3.50	2.50
U423	"	1c **green,** *blue,* die 1		35	8
		Entire		45	15
		a. Die 3		50	40
		Entire		80	65
		b. Die 4		80	30
		Entire		1.25	55
		c. Die 5		50	20
		Entire		80	40
U424	"	1c **green,** *manila,* (unglazed) die 1		4.00	2.00
		Entire		5.00	3.00
W425	"	1c **green,** *manila,* (unglazed) die 1		8	6
		Entire		10	8
		a. Die 3		100.00	100.00
		Entire		125.00	125.00
U426	"	1c **green,** (glazed) *brown* ('20), die 1		16.00	8.50
		Entire		30.00	15.00
W427	"	1c **green,** (glazed) *brown* ('20), die 1		50.00	
		Entire		60.00	
U428	"	1c **green,** (unglazed) *brown* ('20), die 1		5.00	4.50
		Entire		7.50	6.00

All manila envelopes of circular dies are unwatermarked. Manila paper, including that of Nos. U424 and W425, exists in many shades.

Washington
U93

Die 1　　　　　Die 2　　　　　Die 3

Die 4　　　　　Die 5　　　　　Die 6

Die 7　　　　　Die 8　　　　　Die 9

(The 1½c, 2c, 3c, 5c, and 6c dies are the same except for figures of value.)

Die 1. Letters broad. Numerals vertical. Large head (9¼ mm.) from tip of nose to back of neck. E closer to inner circle than N of cents.
Die 2. Similar to 1; but U far from left circle.
Die 3. Similar to 2; but all inner circles very thin (Rejected die).
Die 4. Similar to 1; but C very close to left circle.
Die 5. Small head (8¾ mm.) from tip of nose to back of neck. T and S of CENTS close at bottom.
Die 6. Similar to 5; but T and S of CENTS far apart at bottom. Left numeral slopes to right.
Die 7. Large head. Both numerals slope to right. Clean cut lettering. All letters T have short top strokes.
Die 8. Similar to 7; but all letters T have long top strokes.
Die 9. Narrow oval C (also O and G).

ENVELOPES

581

U429	U93	2c **carmine**, *white*, die 1		5	5	U436	U93	3c **dark violet**, *white*, die 1	10	5
		Entire		20	5			Entire	25	10
		a. Die 2		5.00	4.00			*a.* 3c purple ('32), die 1	35	25
		Entire		11.00	6.00			Entire	65	30
		b. Die 3		20.00	15.00			*b.* 3c dark violet, die 5	50	10
		Entire		30.00	20.00			Entire	1.50	30
		c. Die 4		5.00	5.00			*c.* 3c dark violet, die 6	60	25
		Entire		7.00	6.00			Entire	1.75	35
		d. Die 5		25	15			*d.* 3c dark violet, die 7	45	10
		Entire		40	35			Entire	1.50	30
		e. Die 6		25	15			*e.* 3c purple ('32), die 7	30	10
		Entire		60	35			Entire	1.25	20
		f. Die 7		30	15			*f.* 3c purple ('32), die 9	10	5
		Entire		60	40			Entire	35	10
		g. Die 8		25	10			*g.* 3c carmine (error), die 1	17.00	17.00
		Entire		50	35			Entire	20.00	20.00
		h. Die 9		15	6			*h.* 3c carmine (error), die 5	17.00	17.00
		Entire		40	30			Entire	20.00	20.00
		i. 2c green, die 1 (error), *white*, entire		3,500.				*i.* 3c dark violet, die 1, with added impression of 1c green (#U420), die 1, entire	350.00	
		j. 2c carmine, die 1, with added impression of 1c green (#U420), die 1, entire		275.00				*j.* 3c dark violet, die 1, with added impression of 2c carmine (#U429), die 1, entire	300.00	
		k. 2c carmine, die 1, with added impression of 4c black (#U416a), entire		350.00		U437	"	3c **dark violet**, *amber*, die 1	1.60	40
								Entire	2.50	1.00
		l. 2c carmine, die 1, with added impression of 1c green (#U400), die 1, entire		350.00				*a.* 3c purple ('32), die 1	15	5
								Entire	45	25
								b. 3c dark violet, die 5	3.00	1.00
U430	"	2c **carmine**, *amber*, die 1		12	6			Entire	5.00	2.50
		Entire		30	10			*c.* 3c dark violet, die 6	3.50	1.00
		a. Die 2		5.00	5.00			Entire	5.00	2.50
		Entire		12.00	8.00			*d.* 3c dark violet, die 7	2.50	80
		b. Die 4		15.00	8.00			Entire	3.50	1.75
		Entire		20.00	10.00			*e.* 3c purple ('32), die 7	50	10
		c. Die 5		25	25			Entire	80	50
		Entire		80	60			*f.* 3c purple ('32), die 9	35	10
		d. Die 6		45	15			Entire	60	25
		Entire		85	40			*g.* 3c carmine (error), die 5	225.00	150.00
		e. Die 7		35	20			Entire	275.00	160.00
		Entire		70	35			*h.* 3c black (error), die 1	100.00	
		f. Die 8		35	20			Entire	125.00	
		Entire		65	35	U438	"	3c **dark violet**, *oriental buff*, die 1	16.00	75
		g. Die 9		25	8			Entire	20.00	1.00
		Entire		60	35			*a.* Die 5	16.00	75
U431	"	2c **carmine**, *oriental buff*, die 1		50	20			Entire	19.00	85
		Entire		2.50	50			*b.* Die 6	17.00	1.25
		a. Die 2		70.00	20.00			Entire	25.00	2.00
		Entire		80.00	50.00			*c.* Die 7	20.00	3.00
		b. Die 4		20.00	15.00			Entire	25.00	7.00
		Entire		30.00	18.00	U439	"	3c **dark violet**, *blue*, die 1	3.50	55
		c. Die 5		90	75			Entire	7.50	2.75
		Entire		2.75	95			*a.* 3c purple ('32), die 1	18	5
		d. Die 6		95	80			Entire	40	10
		Entire		2.75	1.10			*b.* 3c dark violet, die 5	3.75	2.00
		e. Die 7		1.00	80			Entire	7.00	3.00
		Entire		3.00	1.10			*c.* 3c dark violet, die 6	3.50	2.50
U432	"	2c **carmine**, *blue*, die 1		10	5			Entire	6.50	2.75
		Entire		40	20			*d.* 3c dark violet, die 7	5.00	2.75
		b. Die 2		15.00	10.00			Entire	9.50	6.00
		Entire		22.00	18.00			*e.* 3c purple ('32), die 7	30	20
		c. Die 3		65.00	60.00			Entire	60	30
		Entire		110.00	75.00			*f.* 3c purple ('32), die 9	30	10
		d. Die 4		15.00	15.00			Entire	80	40
		Entire		20.00	17.00			*g.* 3c carmine (error), die 5	200.00	200.00
		e. Die 5		30	10			Entire	250.00	225.00
		Entire		75	30	U440	U92	4c **black**, *white*, die 1	60	35
		f. Die 6		20	16			Entire	1.75	1.50
		Entire		95	45			*a.* 4c black with added impression of 2c carmine (#U429), die 1, entire	150.00	
		g. Die 7		30	15					
		Entire		95	45	U441	"	4c **black**, *amber*, die 1	1.50	55
		h. Die 8		35	20			Entire	2.75	1.25
		Entire		60	45	U442	"	4c **black**, *blue*, ('21), die 1	1.50	40
		i. Die 9		30	20			Entire	3.00	1.35
		Entire		1.65	45	U443	U93	5c **blue**, *white*, die 1	1.50	50
U432A	"	2c **car**, *manila*, die 1, entire		20,000.				Entire	3.25	2.25
W433	"	2c **carmine**, *manila*, die 1		15	7	U444	"	5c **blue**, *amber*, die 1	1.75	75
		Entire		20	10			Entire	3.50	2.50
W434	"	2c **carmine**, (glazed) *brown* ('20), die 1		65.00	40.00	U445	"	5c **blue**, *blue*, ('21), die 1	1.75	75
		Entire		77.50	45.00			Entire	3.75	2.75
W435	"	2c **carmine**, (unglazed) *brown* ('20), die 1		65.00	40.00					
		Entire		75.00	45.00					

The provisional 2c surcharges of 1920-21 were made at central post offices with canceling machines using slugs provided by the Post Office Department.

Double or triple surcharge listings of 1920-25 are for specimens with surcharge directly or partly upon the stamp.

1920-21

Surcharged on 1874-1920 Envelopes indicated by Numbers in Parentheses.

Type 1.
Surcharged in Black.

U446	U93	2c on 3c **dark violet**, *white*		
		(U436, die 1)	7.50	7.50
		Entire	9.00	8.00
		a. Die 5	7.50	7.50
		Entire	9.00	8.00

Surcharged

Type 2.
Rose Surcharge.

U447	U93	2c on 3c **dark violet**, *white*		
		(U436, die 1)	4.00	4.00
		Entire	5.00	4.50
		b. Die 6	4.00	4.00
		Entire	7.00	4.25

Black Surcharge.

U447A	U93	2c on 2c **carmine**, *white* (U429)	1,200.	
U447C	"	2c on 2c **carmine**, *amber* (U430)		
U448	"	2c on 3c **dark violet**, *white* (U436)	1.50	1.50
		Entire	1.75	1.75
U449	"	2c on 3c **dark violet**, *amber* (U437)	3.50	3.50
		Entire	4.00	4.00
U450	"	2c on 3c **dark violet**, *oriental buff* (U438)	10.00	10.00
		Entire	12.00	7.00
U451	"	2c on 3c **dark violet**, *blue* (U439)	8.50	6.00
		Entire	9.00	6.50

Type 2 exists in three city sub-types.

Type 3.
Bars 2 mm. apart.

U451A	U90	2c on 1c **green**, *white* (U400, die 1)	900.00	
U452	U92	2c on 1c **green**, *white* (U420)	600.00	
		Entire	700.00	
		a. Double surcharge, type 3	700.00	
U453	U91	2c on 2c **carmine**, *white* (U411, die 1)	600.00	
		Entire	700.00	
		a. Die 4	600.00	
		Entire	700.00	
U453B	U91	2c on 2c **carmine**, *blue* (U414e, die 6)	500.00	
		Entire	375.00	
U453C	"	2c on 2c **carmine**, *oriental buff* (U413e, die 6)	450.00	400.00
		Entire	500.00	
		d. Die 1	450.00	
		Entire	475.00	
U454	U93	2c on 2c **carmine**, *white* (U429)	50.00	
		Entire	60.00	
U455	"	2c on 2c **carmine**, *amber* (U430, die 1)	600.00	
		Entire	650.00	
U456	U93	2c on 2c **carmine**, *oriental buff* (U431)	125.00	
		Entire	150.00	
		a. Double surcharge, type 3	140.00	
U457	"	2c on 2c **carmine**, *blue* (U432)	140.00	
		Entire	150.00	
U458	"	2c on 3c **dark violet**, *white* (U436)	15	8
		Entire	35	15
		a. Double surcharge	7.00	4.00
		b. Triple surcharge	20.00	
		c. Double surcharge, one in magenta	40.00	
		d. Double surcharge, types 2 & 3	60.00	
U459	"	2c on 3c **dark violet**, *amber* (U437)	1.50	50
		Entire	2.50	1.00
		a. Double surcharge, type 3	12.00	
		b. Double surcharge, types 2 & 3	55.00	
U460	"	2c on 3c **dark violet**, *oriental buff* (U438)	1.75	50
		Entire	2.50	75
		a. Double surcharge	7.50	
		b. Triple surcharge	17.50	
U461	"	2c on 3c **dark violet**, *blue* (U439)	2.00	60
		Entire	3.00	1.00
		a. Double surcharge	12.00	
U462	U87	2c on 4c **chocolate**, *white* (U390)	225.00	75.00
		Entire	250.00	125.00
U463	"	2c on 4c **chocolate**, *amber* (U391)	225.00	50.00
		Entire	250.00	125.00
U463A	U90	2c on 4c **black**, *white* (U416)	550.00	250.00
		Entire	650.00	
U464	U93	2c on 5c **blue**, *white* (U443)	450.00	
		Entire	550.00	

Type 3 exists in 11 city sub-types.

Type 4.
Same as Type 3, but bars 1½ mm. apart.

U465	U92	2c on 1c **green**, *white* (U420)	600.00	
		Entire	750.00	
U466	U91	2c on 2c **carmine**, *white* (U411e, die 6)	2,000.	
		Entire	2,500.	
U466A	U93	2c on 2c **carmine**, *white* (U429)	150.00	
		Entire	200.00	
		c. Die 5	300.00	
U466B	"	2c on 2c **carmine**, *amber* (U430, die 1)	1,000.	
		Entire	1,250.	
U467	U45	2c on 2c **green**, die 2, *white* (U163)	175.00	
		Entire	200.00	
U468	U93	2c on 3c **dark violet**, *white* (U436)	25	15
		Entire	60	30
		a. Double surcharge	10.00	
		b. Triple surcharge	15.00	
		c. Inverted surcharge	50.00	
		d. Double surcharge, types 2 & 4	45.00	
		e. 2c on 3c carmine (error), *white* (U436h)	250.00	
		Entire	275.00	
U469	U93	2c on 3c **dark violet**, *amber* (U437)	1.50	90
		Entire	2.00	1.25
		a. Double surcharge, types 2 & 4	35.00	
U470	"	2c on 3c **dark violet**, *oriental buff* (U438)	3.00	1.50
		Entire	4.00	2.50
		a. Double surcharge, type 4	11.00	
		b. Double surcharge, types 2 & 4	35.00	

ENVELOPES 583

U471	U93	2c on 3c **dark violet,** *blue* (U439)	2.50	80
		Entire	3.50	2.00
		a. Double surcharge, type 4	12.00	
		b. Double surcharge, types 2 & 4	95.00	
U472	U87	2c on 4c **chocolate,** *white* (U390)	7.50	5.00
		Entire	15.00	7.50
		a. Double surcharge	25.00	
U473	"	2c on 4c **chocolate,** *amber* (U391)	10.00	5.00
		Entire	14.00	7.50

Type 4 exists in 30 city sub-types.

1 CENT

Double Surcharge, Type 4 and 1c as above.

U474	U93	2c on 1c **dark violet,** *white* (U436)	150.00	
		Entire	175.00	
U475	"	2c on 1c on 3c **dark violet,** *amber* (U437, die 1)	140.00	
		Entire	155.00	

2

Type 5.

U476	U93	2c on 3c **dark violet,** *amber* (U437, die 1)	70.00	
		Entire	80.00	
		a. Double surcharge		

Surcharged **2**

Type 6.

U477	U93	2c on 3c **dark violet,** *white* (U436)	70.00	
		Entire	80.00	
U478	"	2c on 3c **dark violet,** *amber* (U437, die 1)	125.00	
		Entire	150.00	

Handstamped Surcharged in Black or Violet

Type 7.

U479	U93	2c on 3c **dark violet,** *white* (Bk) (U436)	250.00	
		Entire	300.00	
U480	"	2c on 3c **dark violet,** *white* (V) (U436, die 7)	500.00	
		Entire	550.00	

1925   **Type of 1916-32 Issue.**

U481	U93	1½c **brown,** die 1, *white* (Washington)	10	6
		Entire	50	10
		a. Die 8	15	10
		Entire	55	15
		b. 1½c purple, die 1, *white* (error) ('34)	50.00	
		Entire	60.00	
U482	"	1½c **brown,** die 1, *amber*	75	20
		Entire	1.25	45
		a. Die 8	85	35
		Entire	1.40	65

U483	U93	1½c **brown,** die 1, *blue*	1.25	60
		Entire	1.50	90
		a. Die 8	1.40	65
		Entire	1.65	1.00
U484	"	1½c **brown,** die 1, *manila*	4.00	2.00
		Entire	8.00	5.00
W485	"	1½c **brown,** die 1, *manila*	60	10
		Entire	90	40
		a. With added impression of W433	100.00	—

The manufacture of newspaper wrappers was discontinued in 1934.

New rates on printed matter effective Apr. 15, 1925, resulted in revaluing some of the current envelopes.

Under the caption "Revaluation of Surplus Stocks of the 1 cent envelopes", W. Irving Glover, Third Assistant Postmaster-General, distributed through the Postal Bulletin a notice to postmasters authorizing the surcharging of envelopes under stipulated conditions.

Surcharging was permitted "at certain offices where the excessive quantities of 1 cent stamped envelopes remained in stock on April 15, 1925."

Envelopes were revalued by means of post office cancelling machines equipped with special dies designed to imprint "1½" in the center of the embossed stamp and four vertical bars over the original numerals "1" in the lower corners.

Postmasters were notified that the revaluing dies would be available for use only in the International and "Universal" Model G machines and that the overprinting of surplus envelopes would be restricted to post offices having such cancelling equipment available.

1925   **Envelopes of Preceding Issues Surcharged**

1½ |||| ||||

Type 8.
On Envelopes of 1887.

U486	U71	1½c on 2c **green,** *white* (U311)	400.00	
		Entire	450.00	
U487	U71	1½c on 2c **green,** *amber* (U312)	550.00	
		Entire	600.00	

On Envelopes of 1899.

U488	U77	1½c on 1c **green,** *white* (U352)	400.00	
		Entire	500.00	
U489	"	1½c on 1c **green,** *amber* (U353)	45.00	30.00
		Entire	50.00	35.00

On Envelopes of 1907-16

U490	U90	1½c on 1c **green,** *white* (U400, die 1)	2.50	2.00
		Entire	3.50	3.00
		a. Die 2	7.00	5.00
		Entire	9.00	7.00
		b. Die 4	3.00	1.75
		Entire	4.00	3.00
U491	"	1½c on 1c **green,** *amber* (U401, die 1)	3.50	1.50
		Entire	6.00	4.00
		a. Die 2	50.00	45.00
		Entire	55.00	50.00
		b. Die 4	3.50	1.75
		Entire	6.00	4.00
U492	"	1½c on 1c **green,** *oriental buff* (U402a, die 2)	125.00	40.00
		Entire	150.00	45.00
		a. Die 4	125.00	35.00
		Entire	150.00	40.00
U493	"	1½c on 1c **green,** *blue* (U403c, die 4)	55.00	25.00
		Entire	65.00	27.50
		a. Die 2	75.00	40.00
		Entire	90.00	50.00
U494	"	1½c on 1c **green,** *manila* (U404, die 1)	175.00	60.00
		Entire	200.00	75.00

On Envelopes of 1916-20

U495	U92	1½c on 1c **green,** *white* (U420, die 1)	25	15
		Entire	50	25
		a. Die 3	1.10	50
		b. Die 4	1.50	50
		c. Double surcharge	3.00	1.50

ENVELOPES

U496	U92	1½c on 1c **green,** *amber* (U421)		10.00	10.00
		Entire		14.00	12.00
U497	"	1½c on 1c **green,** *oriental buff*			
		(U422, die 1)		2.50	1.50
		Entire		4.00	1.75
U498	"	1½c on 1c **green,** *blue* (U423)		75	50
		Entire		1.50	80
U499	"	1½c on 1c **green,** *manila* (U424, die 1)		7.00	4.50
		Entire		12.00	5.00
U500	"	1½c on 1c **green,** *brown*			
		(unglazed) (U428, die 1)		40.00	20.00
		Entire		45.00	22.50
U501	"	1½c on 1c **green,** *brown* (glazed)			
		(U426, die 1)		40.00	15.00
		Entire		42.50	17.00
U502	U93	1½c on 2c **carmine,** *white*			
		(U429, die 1)		160.00	—
		Entire		185.00	—
U503	"	1½c on 2c **carmine,** *oriental buff*			
		(U431c, die 5)		175.00	—
		Entire		200.00	—
		a. Double surcharge		—	
U504	"	1½c on 2c **carmine,** *blue*			
		(U432f, die 6)		165.00	—
		Entire		200.00	—

On Envelopes of 1925.

U505	U93	1½c on 1½c **brown,** *white*			
		(U481, die 1)		325.00	
		Entire		400.00	
		a. Die 8		375.00	
		Entire		400.00	
U506	"	1½c on 1½c **brown,** *blue*			
		(U483a, die 8)		250.00	
		Entire		275.00	

The paper of No. U500 is not glazed and appears to be the same as that used for the wrappers of 1920.

Type 8 exists in 20 city sub-types.

Surcharged

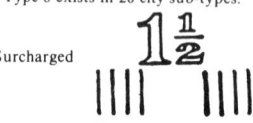

Type 9.
Black Surcharge.

On Envelope of 1887.

U507	U69	1½c on 1c **blue,** *white* (U294)		800.00	
		Entire		850.00	

On Envelope of 1899.

U508	U77	1½c on 1c **green,** *amber* (U353)		35.00	
		Entire		45.00	

On Envelope of 1903.

U508A	U85	1½c on 1c **green,** *white* (U379)		1,000.	
		Entire		1,200.	
U509	"	1½c on 1c **green,** *amber* (U380)		4.00	2.50
		Entire		9.00	3.00
		a. Double surcharge		16.00	
		Entire		18.00	
U509B	"	1½c on 1c **green,** *oriental buff*			
		(U381)		35.00	15.00
		Entire		40.00	16.00

On Envelopes of 1907-16.

U510	U90	1½c on 1c **green,** *white*			
		(U400, die 1)		1.25	75
		Entire		2.00	95
		a. Double surcharge		5.00	
		b. Die 2		5.00	3.00
		Entire		7.00	5.00
		c. Die 3		14.00	7.00
		Entire		20.00	10.00
		d. Die 4		2.50	1.00
		Entire		5.00	2.00
U511	"	1½c on 1c **green,** *amber*			
		(U401, die 1)		90.00	50.00
		Entire		100.00	37.50
U512	"	1½c on 1c **green,** *oriental buff*			
		(U402, die 1)		3.00	1.50
		Entire		5.00	3.00
		a. Die 4		15.00	12.00
		Entire		20.00	14.00
U513	"	1½c on 1c **green,** *blue*			
		(U403, die 1)		3.00	1.75
		Entire		5.00	3.00
		a. Die 4		3.00	2.00
		Entire		3.00	2.00
U514	"	1½c on 1c **green,** *manila*			
		(U404, die 1)		12.50	4.00
		Entire		22.50	12.00
		a. Die 3		35.00	30.00
		Entire		40.00	35.00

On Envelopes of 1916-20.

U515	U92	1½c on 1c **green,** *white* (U420)		25	15
		Entire		50	25
		a. Double surcharge		5.00	
		b. Inverted surcharge		7.50	
		c. Triple surcharge		8.50	
U516	"	1½c on 1c **green,** *amber* (U421)		27.50	15.00
		Entire		35.00	20.00
U517	"	1½c on 1c **green,** *oriental buff*			
		(U422)		2.50	60
		Entire		3.00	75
U518	"	1½c on 1c **green,** *blue* (U423)		2.50	75
		Entire		3.00	95
		a. Double surcharge		7.00	
U519	"	1½c on 1c **green,** *manila*			
		(U424, die 1)		10.00	6.00
		Entire		12.00	7.50
		a. Double surcharge		20.00	
U520	U93	1½c on 2c **carmine,** *white* (U429)		90.00	—
		Entire		110.00	—

Magenta Surcharge

U521	U92	1½c on 1c **green,** *white* (U420)		2.25	1.50
		Entire		2.50	2.00
		a. Double surcharge		15.00	

Sesquicentennial Exposition Issue.

Issued to commemorate the 150th anniversary of the Declaration of Independence.

Liberty Bell
U94

Die 1. The center bar of "E" of "postage" is shorter than top bar.
Die 2. The center bar of "E" of "postage" is of same length as top bar.

1926, July 27

U522	U94	2c **carmine,** *white,* die 1		1.25	50
		Entire		2.00	95
		Entire, 1st day cancel, Washington, D.C.			32.50
		Entire, 1st day cancel, Philadelphia			30.00
		a. Die 2		8.00	4.00
		Entire		11.00	6.50

Washington Bicentennial Issue.

200th anniversary of the birth of George Washington.

Mount Vernon
U95

ENVELOPES 585

1932
    2c Die 1. "S" of "Postage" normal.
    2c Die 2. "S" of "Postage" raised.

U523	U95	1c **olive green**, *white, Jan. 1*	1.25	40
		Entire	1.75	2.00
		Entire, 1st day cancel		18.00
U524	"	1½c **chocolate**, *white, Jan. 1*	3.00	1.50
		Entire	3.75	2.00
		Entire, 1st day cancel		18.00
U525	"	2c **carmine**, die 1, *white, Jan. 1*	40	5
		Entire	60	10
		Entire, 1st day cancel		15.00
		a. 2c carmine, die 2, *white*	75.00	10.00
		Entire	100.00	35.00
		b. 2c carmine, die 1, *blue* (error) entire	7,500.	
U526	"	3c **violet**, *white, June 16*	3.00	35
		Entire	3.50	40
		Entire, 1st day cancel		18.00
U527	"	4c **black**, *white, Jan. 1*	22.50	14.00
		Entire	30.00	20.00
		Entire, 1st day cancel		30.00
U528	"	5c **dark blue**, *white, Jan. 1*	4.50	2.50
		Entire	6.00	4.00
		Entire, 1st day cancel		20.00

1932, Aug. 18
    Type of 1916-32 Issue.

U529	U93	6c **orange**, die 7, *white*	3.75	2.00
		Entire	6.00	3.50
		Entire, 1st day cancel		17.50
U530	"	6c **orange**, die 7, *amber*	7.50	6.00
		Entire	11.00	7.50
		Entire, 1st day cancel		17.50
U531	"	6c **orange**, die 7, *blue*	7.50	6.00
		Entire	10.00	7.00
		Entire, 1st day cancel		17.50

Franklin
U96

Washington
U97

Die 1   Die 2

Die 3

Die 1. Short (3½ mm.) and thick "1" in thick circle.
Die 2. Tall (4½ mm.) and thin "1" in thin circle; upper and lower bars of E in ONE long and 1 mm. from circle
Die 3. As in Die 2, but E normal and 1½ mm. from circle.
    Printed by International Envelope Corp.

1950

U532	U96	1c **green**, *white*, die 1, *Nov. 16, 1950*	4.00	1.50
		Entire	5.00	2.00
		Entire, 1st day cancel		2.50
		a. Die 2	4.00	2.00
		Entire	6.00	2.50
		b. Die 3	4.00	2.00
		Entire	6.00	2.50
		b. Precanceled		60
		Entire, precanceled		90

Die 1   Die 2

Die 3   Die 4

Die 1. Thick "2" in thick circle; toe of "2" is acute right angle.
Die 2. Thin "2" in thin circle; toe of "2" is almost right angle; line through left stand of "N" in UNITED and stand of "E" in POSTAGE goes considerably below tip of chin; "N" of UNITED is tall; "O" of TWO is high.
Die 3. Figure "2" as in Die 2. Short UN in UNITED thin crossbar in A of STATES.
Die 4. Tall UN in UNITED; thick crossbar in A of STATES; otherwise like Die 3.

U533	U97	2c **carmine**, *white*, die 3	65	8
		Entire	95	10
		a. Die 1, *Nov. 17, 1950*	75	25
		Entire	1.25	40
		Entire, 1st day cancel		85
		b. Die 2	1.30	80
		Entire	1.70	85
		c. Die 4	1.20	50
		Entire	1.40	60

Die 1   Die 2

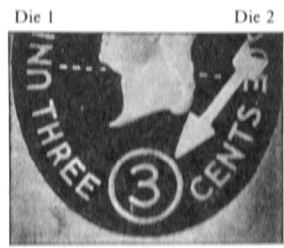
Die 3

ENVELOPES

ENVELOPE WATERMARKS

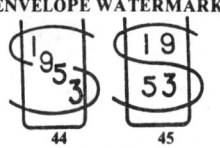  

44	45	46	48	49	50
1953-1956		1957-1960	1961-1964		1965-1968

A watermark introduced in 1970 resembles Wmk. 48, differing in size and shape of letters, spacing of lines and size of star, which matches the letters in height.
Earlier watermarks are illustrated at the beginning of the Stamped Envelopes and Wrappers section.

Die 4   Die 5

Die 1. Thick and tall (4½ mm.) "3" in thick circle; long top bars and short stems in T's of STATES.
Die 2. Thin and tall (4½ mm.) "3" in medium circle; short top bars and long stems in T's of STATES
Die 3. Thin and short (4 mm.) "3" in thin circle; lettering wider than Dies 1 and 2; line from left stand of N to stand of E is distinctly below tip of chin.
Die 4. Figure and letters as in Die 3. Line hits tip of chin; short N in UNITED and thin crossbar in A of STATES.
Die 5. Figure, letter and chin line as in Die 4; but tall N in UNITED and thick crossbar in A of STATES.

U534	U97	3c **dark violet,** *white*, die 4	35	10
		Entire	40	15
		a. Die 1, *Nov. 18, 1950*	1.00	30
		Entire	1.60	80
		Entire, 1st day cancel		2.00
		b. Die 2, *Nov. 19, 1950*	65	25
		Entire	1.25	30
		c. Die 3	50	25
		Entire	95	35
		d. Die 5	50	30
		Entire	75	35

Washington
U98

1951

U535	U98	1½c **brown,** *white*	4.00	2.50
		Entire	4.75	3.00
		Precanceled		35
		Entire, precanceled		75

Die 1   Die 2   Die 3

Die 1. Head high in oval (2mm. below T of STATES). Circle near (1 mm.) bottom of colored oval.
Die 2. Head low in oval (3 mm.). Circle 1½ mm. from edge of oval. Right leg of A in POSTAGE shorter than left. Short leg on P.
Die 3. Head centered in oval (2½ mm.). Circle as in Die 2. Legs of A of POSTAGE about equal. Long leg on P.

1958

U536	U96	4c **red violet,** *white*, die 1,		
		July 31	60	6
		Entire	75	8
		Entire, 1st day cancel,		
		Montpelier, Vt. *(163,746)*		1.50
		a. Die 2	75	6
		Entire	90	8
		b. Die 3	75	6
		Entire	90	8

Nos. U429, U429f, U429h,
U533, U533a-U533c
Surcharged in Red
at Left of Stamp

b

1958

U537	U93	2c + 2c **carmine,** *white*, die 1	2.75	1.00
		Entire	3.25	—
		a. Die 7	8.00	—
		Entire	10.00	—
		b. Die 9	3.00	1.00
		Entire	4.00	—
U538	U97	2c + 2c **carmine,** *white*, die 1	75	18
		Entire	80	25
		a. Die 2	1.00	—
		Entire	1.20	—
		b. Die 3	80	15
		Entire	1.00	20
		c. Die 4	80	—
		Entire	1.00	—

Nos. U436a, U436e-U436f,
U534, U534b-U534d
Surcharged in Green
at Left of Stamp

U539	U93	3c + 1c **purple,** *white*, die 1	14.00	—
		Entire	15.00	—
		a. Die 7	12.00	—
		Entire	14.00	—
		b. Die 9	20.00	—
		Entire	22.50	—
U540	U97	3c + 1c **dark violet,** *white*, die 3	50	10
		Entire	60	12
		a. Die 2		
		Entire	750.00	—
		b. Die 4	75	10
		Entire	85	15
		c. Die 5	75	10
		Entire	85	15

Benjamin Franklin   George Washington
U99   U100

ENVELOPES

Die 1   Die 2

Dies of 1¼c

Die 1. The "4" is 3 mm. high. Upper leaf in left cluster is 2 mm. from "U."
Die 2. The "4" is 3½ mm. high. Leaf clusters are larger. Upper leaf at left is 1 mm. from "U."

1960

U541	U99	1¼c turquoise, white, die 1, June 25, 1960	70	50
		Entire	80	55
		Entire, 1st day cancel, Birmingham, Ala. (211,500)		1.50
		Precanceled		5
		Entire, precanceled		10
		a. Die 2, precanceled		1.50
		Entire, precanceled		1.60
U542	U100	2½c dull blue, white, May 28, 1960	80	50
		Entire	90	60
		Entire, 1st day cancel, Chicago, Ill. (196,977)		1.50
		Precanceled		10
		Entire, precanceled		12

Pony Express Centennial Issue

Pony Express Rider
U101
White Outside, Blue Inside

1960

U543	U101	4c brown, July 19, 1960	50	15
		Entire	60	20
		Entire, 1st day cancel, St. Joseph, Mo. (407,160)		2.25

Abraham Lincoln
U102

Die 1   Die 2   Die 3

Die 1. Center bar of E of POSTAGE is above the middle. Center bar of E of STATES slants slightly upward. Nose sharper, more pointed. No offset ink specks inside envelope on back of die impression.
Die 2. Center bar of E of POSTAGE in middle. P of POSTAGE has short stem. Ink specks on back of die impression.
Die 3. Fl of FIVE closer than Die 1 or 2. Second T of STATES seems taller than ES. Ink specks on back of die impression.

1962

U544	U102	5c dark blue, white, die 2, Nov. 19, 1962	80	20
		Entire	90	25
		Entire, 1st day cancel, Springfield, Ill. (163,258)		1.50
		a. Die 1	85	25
		Entire	95	30
		b. Die 3	90	30
		Entire	1.00	35
		c. Die 2 with albino 4c impression, entire	40.00	
		d. Die 3 with albino 4c impression, entire	55.00	

No. U536 Surcharged in Green
at left of Stamp

a

1962

Two types of surcharge:
Type I. "U.S. POSTAGE" 18½ mm. high. Serifs on cross of T both diagonal. Two lines of shading in C of CENT.
Type II. "U.S. POSTAGE" 17½ mm. high. Right serif on cross of T is vertical. Three shading lines in C.

U545	U96	4c + 1c red vio., white, die 1, type I, Nov. 1962	1.30	50
		Entire	1.50	60
		a. Type II	1.30	40
		Entire	1.50	50

New York World's Fair Issue
Issued to publicize the New York World's Fair, 1964-65

Globe with Satellite Orbit
U103

1964

U546	U103	5c maroon, Apr. 22, 1964	50	20
		Entire	60	25
		Entire, 1st day cancel World's Fair N.Y. (466,422)		1.50

Liberty Bell
U104

Old Ironsides
U105

Eagle
U106

Head of Statue of Liberty
U107

Printed by the United States Envelope Company, Williamsburg, Pa. Designed (6c) by Howard C. Mildner and (others) by Robert J. Jones.

1965-69

U547	U104	1¼c **brown,** *Jan. 6, 1965*	70	6
		Entire	80	15
		Entire, 1st day cancel, Washington, D.C.		1.50
U548	"	1⁴⁄₁₀c **brown,** *March 26, 1968*	65	6
		Entire	85	15
		Entire, 1st day cancel, Springfield, Mass. *(134,832)*		1.50
U548A	"	1⁴⁄₁₀c **orange,** *June 16, 1969*	75	8
		Entire	85	15
		Entire, 1st day cancel, Washington, D.C.		1.50
U549	U105	4c **bright blue,** *Jan. 6, 1965*	75	10
		Entire	95	15
		Entire, 1st day cancel, Washington, D.C.		1.50
U550	U106	5c **bright purple,** *Jan. 5, 1965*	75	5
		Entire	85	8
		Entire, 1st day cancel, Williamsburg, Pa. *(246,496)*		1.50
	a.	Tagged, *Aug. 15, 1967*	60	5
		Entire	1.25	20
		Entire, tagged, 1st day cancel		5.00

Tagged

U551	U107	6c **light green,** *Jan. 4, 1968*	70	5
		Entire	80	8
		Entire, 1st day cancel, New York, N.Y. *(184,784)*		1.75

No. U550a has a 9x29 mm. panel at left of stamp that glows yellow green under ultraviolet light.
First day covers of the 1¼c and 4c total 451,960.

Nos. U549-U550 Surcharged Types "b" and "a" in Red or Green at Left of Stamp

1968, Feb. 5

U552		4c + 2c **bright blue** (R)	2.75	50
		Entire	3.25	1.10
		Entire, 1st day cancel		7.00
U553	U106	5c + 1c **bright purple** (G)	2.00	1.50
		Entire	2.50	2.00
	a.	Tagged	2.00	1.50
		Entire	3.00	2.00
		Entire, 1st day cancel		7.00

Tagged

Envelopes from No. U554 onward are tagged, with the tagging element in the ink unless otherwise noted.

Herman Melville Issue

Issued to honor Herman Melville (1819-1891), writer, and the whaling industry.

Moby Dick
U108

1970, Mar. 7

U554	U108	6c **blue**	45	6
		Entire	55	10
		Entire, 1st day cancel, New Bedford, Mass. *(433,777)*		1.75

Youth Conference Issue

Issued to publicize the White House Conference on Youth, Estes Park, Colo., Apr. 18-22.

Conference Emblem Symbolic of Man's Expectant Soul and of Universal Brotherhood—U109

Printed by United States Envelope Company, Williamsburg, Pa. Designed by Chermayeff and Geismar Associates.

1971, Feb. 24

U555	U109	6c **light blue**	60	6
		Entire	70	60
		Entire, 1st day cancel, Washington, D.C. *(264,559)*		1.50

Liberty Bell Type of 1965 and U110

Eagle
U110

ENVELOPES

Printed by the United States Envelope Co., Williamsburg, Pa. Designed (8c) by Bradbury Thompson.

1971

U556	U104 1⁷/₁₀c	deep lilac, untagged, May 10	25	8
		Entire	30	10
		Entire, 1st day cancel, Baltimore, Md. (150,767)		1.50
U557	U110	8c ultramarine, May 6	40	5
		Entire	50	8
		Entire, 1st day cancel, Williamsburg, Pa. (193,000)		1.75

Nos. U551 and U555 Surcharged in Green at Left of Stamp

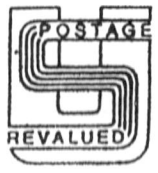

c

1971

U561	U107	6c + (2c) light green, May 16	90	20
		Entire	1.00	30
		Entire, 1st day cancel, Washington, D.C.		3.00
U562	U109	6c + (2c) light blue, May 16	2.25	20
		Entire	2.50	50
		Entire, 1st day cancel, Washington, D.C.		4.00

Bowling Issue

Issued as a salute to bowling and in connection with the 7th World Tournament of the International Bowling Federation, Milwaukee, Wis.

Bowling Ball and Pin—U111
Designed by George Giusti.

1971, Aug. 21

U563	U111	8c rose red	40	8
		Entire	50	10
		Entire, 1st day cancel, Milwaukee, Wis. (281,242)		2.00

Aging Conference Issue

White House Conference on Aging, Washington, D.C., Nov. 28-Dec. 2, 1971.

Conference Symbol—U112
Designed by Thomas H. Geismar.

1971, Nov. 15

U564	U112	8c light blue	40	8
		Entire	50	10
		Entire, 1st day cancel, Washington, D.C. (125,000)		1.75

International Transportation Exhibition Issue

U.S. International Transportation Exhibition, Dulles International Airport, Washington, D.C., May 27-June 4.

Transportation Exhibition Emblem—U113
(Size of actual stamp: 64x70 mm.)
Emblem designed by Toshihiki Sakow.

1972, May 2

U565	U113	8c ultramarine & rose red	40	5
		Entire	60	15
		Entire, 1st day cancel, Washington, D.C.		1.75

No. U557 Surcharged Type "b" in Ultramarine at Left of Stamp

1973, Dec. 1

U566	U110	8c + 2c brt. ultramarine	35	5
		Entire	45	10
		Entire, 1st day cancel, Washington, D.C.		2.00

Liberty Bell—U114

1973, Dec. 5

U567	U114	10c emerald	35	5
		Entire	40	8
		Entire, 1st day cancel, Philadelphia, Pa. (142,141)		1.25

"Volunteer Yourself"
U115
Designed by Norman Ives.

1974, Aug. 23   Untagged

U568	U115	1⁸/₁₀c blue green	15	8
		Entire	30	12
		Entire, 1st day cancel, Cincinnati, Ohio		1.25

Tennis Centenary Issue

Centenary of tennis in the United States.

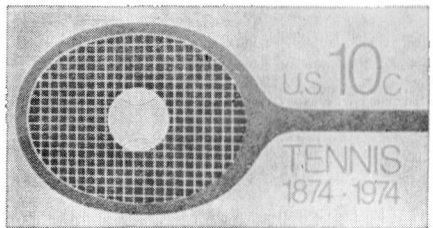

Tennis Racquet
U116
Designed by Donald Moss.

1974, Aug. 31
U569	U116 10c	**yellow, brt. blue & light green**	24	10
		Entire	35	12
		Entire, 1st day cancel, Forest Hills, N.Y. *(245,000)*		2.00

Bicentennial Era Issue

The Seafaring Tradition—Compass Rose—U118

The American Homemaker—Quilt Pattern—U119

The American Farmer—Sheaf of Wheat—U120

The American Doctor, Mortar—U121

The American Craftsman, Tools, c.1750—U122

Designs (in brown on left side of envelope): 10c, Norwegian sloop Restaurationen. No. U572, Spinning wheel. No. U573, Plow. No. U574, Colonial era medical instruments and bottle. No. U575, Shaker rocking chair.
Designed by Arthur Congdon.

1975-76   Embossed

U571	U118 10c	**brown & blue,** *light brown, Oct. 13, 1975*	24	10
		Entire	40	15
		Entire, 1st day cancel, Minneapolis, Minn. *(255,304)*		1.50
		a. Brown ("10c/USA") omitted, entire		—
U572	U119 13c	**brown & blue green,** *light brown, Feb. 2, 1976*	30	13
		Entire	50	15
		Entire, 1st day cancel, Biloxi, Miss. *(196,647)*		80
		a. Brown ("13c/USA") omitted, entire		—
U573	U120 13c	**brown & bright green,** *light brown, Mar. 15, 1976*	30	13
		Entire	50	15
		Entire, 1st day cancel, New Orleans, La. *(214,563)*		1.50
		a. Brown ("13c/USA") omitted, entire		—
U574	U121 13c	**brn. & org.,** *light brown, June 30, 1976*	30	13
		Entire	50	15
		Entire, 1st day cancel, Dallas, Texas		1.50
U575	U122 13c	**brn. & car.,** *lt. brown, Aug. 6, 1976*	30	13
		Entire	50	15
		Entire, 1st day cancel, Hancock, Mass.		1.50
		a. Brown ("13c/USA") omitted, entire		—

Liberty Tree, Boston, 1646
U123
Designed by Leonard Everett Fisher.

1975, Nov. 8   Embossed

U576	U123 13c	**orange brown**	30	13
		Entire	40	15
		Entire, 1st day cancel, Memphis, Tenn. *(226,824)*		80

ENVELOPES 591

Star and Pinwheel—U124

U125

U126

Eagle—U127

Uncle Sam—U128

Designers: 2c, Rudolph de Harak. 2.1c, Norman Ives. 2.7c, Ann Sforza Clementino. 15c, George Mercer.

1976-78				Embossed	
U577	U124	2c **red,** untagged, *Sept. 10, 1976*		20	5
		Entire		30	10
		Entire, 1st day cancel, Hempstead, N.Y. *(81,388)*			70
U578	U125	2.1c **green,** untagged, *June 3, 1977*		20	5
		Entire		30	10
		Entire, 1st day cancel, Houston, Tex. *(120,280)*			70

U579	U126	2.7c **green,** untagged, *July 5, 1978*	25	5
		Entire	35	15
		Entire, 1st day cancel, Raleigh, N.C. *(92,687)*		75
U580	U127(15c)	**orange,** *May 22, 1978*	35	15
		Entire	48	18
		Entire, 1st day cancel, Memphis, Tenn.		85
U581	U128	15c **red,** *June 3, 1978*	35	15
		Entire	48	18
		Entire, 1st day cancel, Williamsburg, Pa. *(176,000)*		85

Bicentennial Issue

Centennial Envelope, 1876
U129

1976, Oct. 15				Embossed	
U582	U129	13c **emerald**		30	13
		Entire		40	15
		Entire, 1st day cancel, Los Angeles, Cal. *(277,222)*			80

Golf Issue

Golf Club in Motion and Golf Ball—U130
Designed by Guy Salvato.

1977, Apr. 7			Photogravure and Embossed	
U583	U130	13c **black, blue & yellow green**	30	13
		Entire	40	10
		Entire, 1st day cancel, Augusta, Ga. *(252,000)*		1.10
	a. Black omitted, entire			
	b. Black & blue omitted, entire			

Energy Issue
Conservation and development of national resources.

"Conservation"—U131

"Development"— U132
Designed by Terrance W. McCaffrey.

1977, Oct. 20				Embossed	
U584	U131	13c	black, red & yellow	30	13
			Entire	40	15
			Entire, 1st day cancel, Ridley Park, Pa.		80
		a.	Red & yellow omitted, entire	—	
		b.	Yellow omitted, entire	—	
U585	U132	13c	black, red & yellow	30	13
			Entire	40	15
			Entire, 1st day cancel, Ridley Park, Pa.		80

First day cancellation applied to 353,515 of Nos. U584 and U585. Envelopes exist with black omitted, and with red and black omitted.

Nos. U584—U585 have a luminescent panel at left of stamp which glows green under ultraviolet light.

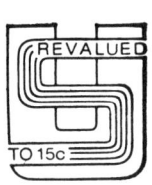 

Olive Branch and Star—U133
Designed by George Mercer.

1978, July 28				Embossed	
			Black Surcharge		
U586	U133	15c on 16c blue		35	15
			Entire	48	18
			Entire, 1st day cancel, Williamsburg, Pa. (193,153)		75
		a.	Surcharge omitted, entire	—	—
		b.	Surch. on No. U581, entire	—	—

Auto Racing Issue

Indianapolis 500 Racing Car—U134
Designed by Robert Peak.

1978, Sept. 2				Embossed	
U587	U134	15c	red, blue & black	35	15
			Entire	48	18
			Entire, 1st day cancel, Ontario, Cal. (209,147)		1.00
		a.	Black omitted, entire	200.00	
		b.	Black & blue omitted, entire	—	
		c.	Red omitted, entire	—	

No. U576 Surcharged Like No. U586

1978, Nov. 28				Embossed	
U588	U123	15c on 13c orange brown		35	15
			Entire	48	18
			Entire, 1st day cancel, Williamsburg, Pa. (137,500)		75

U135   Weaver Violins U136

U137   Eagle-U138

U139   Eagle—U140

1979, May 18		Untagged		Embossed	
U589	U135	3.1c ultramarine, untagged		12	5
			Entire	20	10
			Entire, 1st day cancel, Denver, Colo. (117,575)		60

1980, June 23		Untagged		Embossed	
U590	U136	3.5c purple, untagged		15	8
			Entire	25	15
			Entire, 1st day cancel, Williamsburg, Pa.		65

1982, Feb. 17		Untagged		Embossed	
U591	U137	5.9c brown, untagged		16	8
			Entire	20	10
			Entire, 1st day cancel, Wheeling, WV		70

1981, Mar. 15				Embossed	
U592	U138(18c) violet			45	18
			Entire	55	22
			Entire, 1st day cancel, Memphis, TN (179,171)		80

1981, Apr. 2				Embossed	
U593	U139	18c dark blue		45	18
			Entire	55	22
			Entire, 1st day cancel, Star City, IN (160,439)		80

1981, Oct. 11				Embossed	
U594	U140(20c) brown			40	10
			Entire	48	15
			Entire, 1st day cancel, Memphis, TN (304,404)		80

ENVELOPES

Veterinary Medicine Issue
Honoring Veterinary Medicine.

Seal of Veterinarians—U141
Design at left side of envelope shows 5 animals and bird in brown, "Veterinary Medicine" in gray.
Designed by Guy Salvato.

1979, July 24			Embossed	
U595	U141	15c brown & gray	35	15
		Entire	48	18
		Entire, 1st day cancel, Seattle, WA (209,658)		75

Olympic Games Issue
22nd Olympic Games, Moscow, July 19—Aug. 3, 1980.

U142
Design (multicolored on left side of envelope) shows two soccer players with ball.
Designed by Robert M. Cunningham.

1979, Dec. 10			Embossed	
U596	U142	15c red, green & black	35	15
		Entire	48	18
		Entire, 1st day cancel, East Rutherford, NJ (179,336)		75
	a.	Red & grn omitted, untagged	200.00	
	b.	Black omitted, untagged	200.00	
	c.	Black & green omitted	200.00	

Highwheeler Bicycle
U143
Design (blue on left side of envelope) shows racing bicycle.
Designed by Robert Hallock.

1980, May 16			Embossed	
U597	U143	15c blue & rose claret	35	15
		Entire	48	18
		Entire, 1st day cancel, Baltimore, MD (173,978)		75
	a.	Blue ("15c USA") omitted		

AMERICA'S CUP
Yacht
U144
Designed by Cal Sachs.

1980, Sept. 15			Embossed	
U598	U144	15c blue & red	35	15
		Entire	48	18
		Entire, 1st day cancel, Newport, RI (192,220)		75

Italian Honeybee and Orange Blossoms—U145
Designed by Jerry Pinkney.

Bee and petals colorless embossed.

1980, Oct. 10			Photogravure and Embossed	
U599	U145	15c brown, green & yel.	35	15
		Entire	48	18
		Entire, 1st day cancel, Paris, IL (202,050)		75
	a.	Brown ("USA 15c") omitted		

U146
Design: Hand and braille colorless embossed.
Designed by John Boyd

1981, Aug. 13			Embossed	
U600	U146	18c blue & red	45	18
		Entire	55	22
		Entire, 1st day cancel, Arlington, VA (175,966)		80

Capital Dome   U147

1981, Nov. 13			Embossed	
U601	U147	20c deep magenta	45	10
		Entire	48	15
		Entire, first day cancel, Los Angeles, CA		80

U148
Designed by Bradbury Thompson

1982, June 15   Embossed
U602   U148   20c   **dark blue, black & magenta**   45   10
     Entire   48   15
     Entire, first day cancel,
       Washington, DC *(163,905)*   80

U149
Designed by John Boyd

1982, Aug. 6   Embossed
U603   U149   20c   **purple & black**   45   10
     Entire   48   15
     Entire, first day cancel,
       Washington, DC *(110,679)*   80

U150

1983, Mar. 21   Embossed
U604   U150   5.2c orange   15   10
     Entire   20   15
     Entire, first day cancel,
       Memphis, TN   80

U151

1983, Aug. 3   Embossed
U605   U151   20c red, blue & black   40   10
     Entire   48   15
     Entire, first day cancel,
       Portland, OR   80

Small Business USA 20c

U152

Designed by Peter Spier and Pat Taylor

Design shows storefronts at lower left. Stamp and design continue on back of envelope.

1984, May 7
U606   U152   20c multi   40   10
     Entire   48   15
     Entire, first day cancel,
       Washington, DC   80

                                                   Bison
U153   U154
Designed by Bradbury Thompson

1985, Feb. 1   Embossed
U607   U153   (22c)   dp grn   44   12
     Entire   55   18
     Entire, first day cancel,
       Washington, DC   1.10

                Designed by George Mercer
1985, Feb. 25   Embossed
U608   U154   22c   vio brn   44   12
     Entire   55   18
     Entire, first day cancel,
       Washington, DC   1.10

Frigate U.S.S. Constitution
                         U155
Designed by Cal Sacks

1985, May 3   Embossed
U609   U155   6c   grn blue   12   5
     Entire   15   6
     Entire, first day cancel,
       Washington, DC   30

ENVELOPES
1983-85

Scott U604

Scott U605

Scott U607

COLLECT THE SCOTT WAY... WITH SCOTT'S

U. S. POSTAL STATIONERY
ALBUM

FEATURING:

- Spaces for cut squares of every major postal stationery item in the Scott "Specialized Catalogue of United States Stamps" including regular and commemoratives as well as airpost, and officials. Spaces for folded entires of aerogrammes.

- Each stamp pictured or described and arranged in order by Scott number.

- A handsome, sturdy binder is standard with this album - not tacked on at an extra cost.

- Chemically neutralized paper protects your stamps for generations.

- Paper just the right thickness to make collecting a pleasure.

- Yearly supplement available.

$39.95 Album through 1985

AVAILABLE NOW AT YOUR LOCAL DEALER OR DIRECT FROM:

P.O. BOX 828, SIDNEY, OH 45365

AIR POST STAMPED ENVELOPES AND AIR LETTER SHEETS

All envelopes have carmine and blue borders, unless noted. There are seven types of borders:

Carmine Diamond in Upper Right Corner.

a. Diamonds measure 9 to 10 mm. parallel to edge of envelope and 11 to 12 mm. along oblique side (with top flap open). Sizes 5 and 13 only.
b. Like "a" except diamonds measure 7 to 8 mm. along oblique side (with top flap open). Sizes 5 and 13 only.
c. Diamonds measure 11 to 12 mm. parallel to edge of envelope. Size 8 only.

Blue Diamond in Upper Right Corner.

d. Lower points of top row of diamonds point to left. Size 8 only.
e. Lower points of top row of diamonds point to right. Size 8 only.

Diamonds Omitted in Upper Right Corner (1965 Onward)

f. Blue diamond above at left of stamp.
g. Red diamond above at left of stamp.

UC1
Die 1 (5¢)
Vertical rudder is not semi-circular but slopes down to the left. The tail of the plane projects into the G of POSTAGE. Border types a, b, c, d and e.

UC2
Die 2 (5¢ and 8¢)
Vertical rudder is semi-circular. The tail of the plane touches but does not project into the G of POSTAGE. Border types b, d, and e for the 5¢; b and d for the 8¢.

Die 2 (6¢): Same as UC2 except three types of numeral.
2a. The numeral "6" is 6½ mm. wide.
2b. The numeral "6" is 6 mm. wide.
2c. The numeral "6" is 5½ mm. wide.

Eleven working dies were used in printing the 6¢. On each, the numeral "6" was engraved by hand, producing several variations in position, size and thickness.

Nos. UC1 and UC2 occur with varying size blue blobs, caused by a shallow printing die. They are not constant.

Border types b and d for dies 2a and 2b; also without border (June 1944 to Sept. 1945) for dies 2a, 2b and 2c.

Die 3 (6¢): Vertical rudder leans forward. S closer to O than to T of POSTAGE. E of POSTAGE has short center bar. Border types b and d, also without border.

No. UC1 with 1933 and 1937 watermarks and No. UC2 with 1929 and 1933 watermarks were issued in Puerto Rico.

No. UC1 in blue black, with 1925 watermark #26 and border type a, is a proof.

1929-44

UC1	UC1	5¢ **blue**, *white*, die 1, *Jan. 12, 1929*		2.75	1.50
		Entire, border a or b		4.00	2.00
		Entire, border c, d or e		7.50	5.00
		First day cancel, border a, entire			40.00
		1933 wmk. #33, border d, entire		600.00	600.00
		1933 wmk. #33, border b, entire		—	—
		1937 wmk. #36, border d, entire		—	850.00
		1937 wmk. #36, border b, entire		—	—
		Bicolored border omitted, entire		500.00	
UC2	UC2	5¢ **blue**, *white*, die 2		10.00	3.00
		Entire, border b		12.00	4.00
		Entire, border e		12.50	7.50
		1929 wmk. #28, border d, entire		—	1,400.
		1933 wmk. #33, border d, entire		500.00	—
		1933 wmk. #33, border d, entire		250.00	—
UC3	"	6¢ **orange**, *white*, die 2a, *July 1, 1934*		1.00	15
		Entire, bicolored border		1.25	30
		Entire, without border		1.50	40
		Entire, 1st day cancel			14.00
	a.	6¢ orange, *white*, die 2a, with added impression of 3¢ purple (#U436a), entire without border		2,000.	
UC4	"	6¢ **orange**, *white*, die 2b ('42)		1.40	75
		Entire, bicolored border, 1941 wmk. #39		50.00	12.50
		Entire, without border		2.75	1.25
UC5	"	6¢ **orange**, *white*, die 2c ('44)		60	25
		Entire, without border		85	35
UC6	"	6¢ **orange**, *white*, die 3 ('42)		65	25
		Entire, bicolored border		1.00	55
		Entire, without border		2.00	45
		Entire, carmine of border omitted		900.00	
		Double impression, entire		250.00	
	a.	6¢ orange, *blue*, die 3 (error) Entire, without border		—	2,000.
UC7	"	8¢ **olive green**, *white*, die 2, *Sept. 26, 1932*		11.00	2.50
		Entire, bicolored border		14.00	5.00
		Entire, 1st day cancel			11.00

AIR 6¢ MAIL

Surcharged in black on envelopes indicated by number in parenthesis.

1945

UC8	U93	6¢ on 2¢ **carmine**, *white* (U429)	80	40
		Entire	1.25	75
	a.	6¢ on 1¢ green (error), *white* (U420)	1,350.	
		Entire	2,000.	
	b.	6¢ on 3¢ purple (error), *white* (U436a)	1,350.	
		Entire	2,000.	
	c.	6¢ on 3¢ purple (error), *amber* (U437a)	2,250.	
		Entire	3,000.	
	d.	6¢ on 3¢ violet (error), *white* (U526)	2,250.	
		Entire	3,000.	
UC9	U95	6¢ on 2¢ **carmine**, *white* (U525)	50.00	25.00
		Entire	75.00	35.00

Ten surcharge varieties are found on Nos. UC8-UC9.

ENVELOPES

Surcharged in Black
on 6c Air Post Envelopes
without borders

REVALUED
5¢
P.O. DEPT.

1946

UC10	UC2	5c on 6c **orange**, *white*, die 2a	2.25	1.00
		Entire	3.50	2.00
		a. Double surcharge	40.00	
UC11	"	5c on 6c **orange**, *white*, die 2b	7.50	4.00
		Entire	9.00	5.00
UC12	"	5c on 6c **orange**, *white*, die 2c	50	40
		Entire	90	50
		a. Double surcharge	35.00	20.00
UC13	"	5c on 6c **orange**, *white*, die 3	75	40
		Entire	90	50
		a. Double surcharge	35.00	

The 6c borderless envelopes and the revalued envelopes were issued primarily for use to and from members of the armed forces. The 5c rate came into effect Oct. 1, 1946.
Ten surcharge varieties are found on Nos. UC10-UC13.

DC-4 Skymaster—UC3

1946
Envelopes with borders types b and d.
Die 1. The end of the wing at the right is a smooth curve. The juncture of the front end of the plane and the engine forms an acute angle. The first T of STATES and the E's of UNITED STATES lean to the left.
Die 2. The end of the wing at the right is a straight line. The juncture of the front end of the plane and the engine is wide open. The first T of STATES and the E's of UNITED STATES lean to the right.

UC14	UC3	5c **carmine**, *white*, die 1, Sept. 25, 1946	55	8
		Entire, bicolored border	80	15
		Entire, 1st day cancel		2.50
		Entire, bicolored border omitted		
UC15	"	5c **carmine**, *white*, die 2	65	15
		Entire, bicolored border	90	25

No. UC14, printed on flat bed press, measures 21½ mm. high.
No. UC15, printed on rotary press, measures 22 mm. high.

DC-4 Skymaster UC4

Typographed, Without Embossing.
Letter Sheets for Foreign Postage.

1947-55

UC16	UC4	10c **bright red**, *pale blue*, "Air Letter" on face, 2-line inscription on back, entire	6.00	5.00
		Entire, 1st day cancel, Apr. 29, 1947		7.50
		Die cutting reversed, entire	110.00	
UC16a	UC4	10c **bright red**, *pale blue*, Sept. 1951, "Air Letter" on face, 4-line inscription on back, entire	9.00	8.50
		Die cutting reversed, entire	275.00	
		b. 10c chocolate, *pale blue*, entire	350.00	
UC16c	"	10c **bright red**, *pale blue*, Nov. 1953, "Air Letter" and "Aerogramme" inscription on back, 4-line inscription on back, entire	50.00	7.50
		Die cutting reversed, entire		
UC16d	"	10c **bright red**, *pale blue*, 1955, "Air Letter" and "Aerogramme" inscription on back, 3-line inscription on back, entire	7.50	7.50
		Die cutting reversed, entire	60.00	
		Dark blue (inscriptions & border diamonds) omitted		

Printed on protective tinted paper containing colorless inscription, UNITED STATES FOREIGN AIR MAIL multiple, repeated in parallel vertical or horizontal lines.

Postage Stamp Centenary Issue.

Issued to commemorate the centenary of the first postage stamps issued by the United States Government.

Washington and Franklin,
Early and Modern Mail-carrying Methods
UC5

Two dies: Rotary, design measures 22¼ mm. high; and flat bed press, design 21¼ mm. high.

1947, May 21   **For Domestic Postage**   **Embossed**

UC17	UC5	5c **carmine**, *white* (rotary)	40	25
		Entire, bicolored border b	50	30
		Entire, 1st day cancel		2.00
		a. Flat plate printing	50	30

1950   **Type of 1946.**
Type I: 6's lean to right.
Type II: 6's upright.

UC18	UC3	6c **carmine**, *white*, type I, Sept. 22, 1950	25	8
		Entire, bicolored border	50	15
		Entire, 1st day cancel		1.25
		a. Type II	75	25
		Entire	1.00	30

Several other types differ slightly from the two listed.

Nos. UC14, UC15, UC18
Surcharged in Red
at Left of Stamp

REVALUED
6¢
P. O. DEPT.

1951

UC19	UC3	6c on 5c **carmine**, *white*, die 1	85	50
		Entire	1.25	75
UC20	"	6c on 5c **carmine**, *white*, die 2	80	50
		Entire	1.15	70
		a. 6c on 6c car. *white* (error) entire	1,000.	
		b. Double surcharge	225.00	

ENVELOPES

Nos. UC14 and UC15
Surcharged in Red
at Left of Stamp

1952

UC21	UC3	6c on 5c **carmine**, *white*, die 1		22.50	12.00
		Entire		25.00	14.00
UC22	"	6c on 5c **carmine**, *white*, die 2, Aug. 29, 1952		3.00	1.75
		Entire		4.00	3.00
		a. Double surcharge		55.00	

Same Surcharge in Red on No. UC17

UC23	UC5	6c on 5c **carmine**, *white*		
		Entire	750.00	

The 6c on 4c black (No. U440) is believed to be a favor printing.

Fifth International Philatelic Exhibition Issue.

FIPEX, the Fifth International Philatelic Exhibition, New York, N.Y., Apr. 28—May 6, 1956.

Eagle in Flight
UC6

1956, May 2

UC25	UC6	6c **red**		55	25
		Entire		80	40
		Entire, 1st day cancel, New York, N.Y. *(363,239)*			1.10

Two types exist, differing slightly in the clouds at top.

1958, July 31   Skymaster Type of 1946

UC26	UC3	7c **blue**, *white*		40	20
		Entire		70	40
		Entire, 1st day cancel, Dayton, O. *(143,428)*			2.00

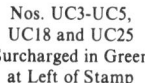

Nos. UC3-UC5,
UC18 and UC25
Surcharged in Green
at Left of Stamp

1958

UC27	UC2	6c + 1c **orange**, *white*, die 2a		130.00	100.00
		Entire, without border		150.00	120.00
UC28	"	6c + 1c **orange**, *white*, die 2b		45.00	55.00
		Entire, without border		55.00	60.00
UC29	"	6c + 1c **orange**, *white*, die 2c		25.00	30.00
		Entire		30.00	40.00
UC30	UC3	6c + 1c **carmine**, *white*, type I		65	30
		Entire		90	40
		a. Type II		75	30
		Entire		85	40
UC31	UC6	6c + 1c **red**, *white*		85	40
		Entire		1.20	70

Jet Airliner
UC7
Letter Sheet for Foreign Postage

1958-59   Typographed, Without Embossing

Type I: Back inscription in 3 lines.
Type II: Back inscription in 2 lines

UC32	UC7	10c **blue & red**, *blue*, II, *May, 1959*, entire		6.00	3.00
		b. Red omitted, II, entire			
		c. Blue omitted, II, entire		750.00	
UC32a	"	10c **blue & red**, *blue*, I, *Sept. 12, 1958*, entire		9.00	3.00
		Entire, 1st day cancel, St. Louis, Mo. *(92,400)*			3.25
		Die cutting reversed, entire		75.00	

Silhouette of Jet Airliner
UC8

1958, Nov. 21   Embossed

UC33	UC8	7c **blue**, *white*		60	12
		Entire		70	15
		Entire, 1st day cancel, New York, N.Y. *(208,980)*			1.50

1960, Aug. 18

UC34	UC8	7c **carmine**, *white*		60	12
		Entire		70	15
		Entire, 1st day cancel, Portland, Ore. *(196,851)*			1.50

Jet Airliner and Globe
UC9

ENVELOPES 599

Letter Sheet for Foreign Postage
Typographed, Without Embossing

1961, June 16
UC35 UC9 11c **red & blue,** *blue, entire*   2.25   1.50
                Entire, 1st day cancel,
                  Johnstown, Pa. *(163,460)*   2.50
             a. Red omitted, entire   500.00
             b. Blue omitted, entire   500.00
                Die cutting reversed, entire   35.00

Jet airliner
UC10

1962, Nov. 17   Embossed
UC36 UC10 8c **red,** *white*   50   8
                Entire   80   15
                Entire, 1st day cancel,
                  Chantilly, Va. *(194,810)*   80

Jet Airliner
UC11

1965-67
UC37 UC11 8c **red,** *Jan. 7*   35   6
                Entire, border "f"   50   10
                Entire, border "g"   5.00
                Entire, 1st day cancel,
                  Chicago, Ill. *(226,178)*   60
             a. Tagged, *Aug. 15, 1967*   85   30
                Entire   1.75   75
                Tagged, 1st day cancel   6.00

No. UC37a has a ⅜ x 1-inch panel at left of stamp that glows orange red under ultraviolet light.

Pres. John F. Kennedy and Jet Plane
UC12
Letter Sheets for Foreign Postage
Typographed, Without Embossing

1965, May 29
UC38 UC12 11c **red & dark blue,** *blue, entire*   3.25   1.00
                Entire, 1st day cancel, Boston,
                  Mass. *(337,422)*   1.50
                Die cutting reversed, entire   50.00

1967, May 29
UC39 UC12 13c **red & dark blue,** *blue, entire*   3.00   .75
                Entire, 1st day cancel,
                  Chicago, Ill. *(211,387)*   1.50
             a. Red omitted   400.00
             b. Dark blue omitted   400.00
                Die cutting reversed, entire

Jet Liner
UC13

                Designed by Robert J. Jones.
1968, Jan. 8   **Tagged**   Embossed
UC40 UC13 10c **red**   50   6
                Entire   80   15
                Entire, 1st day cancel,
                  Chicago, Ill. *(157,553)*   75

No. UC37 Surcharged in Red
at Left of Stamp

1968, Feb. 5
UC41 UC11 8c + 2c **red**   55   15
                Entire   90   40
                Entire, 1st day cancel, Washington, D.C.   8.50

Human Rights Year Issue

Issued for International Human Rights Year, and to commemorate the 20th anniversary of the United Nations' Declaration of Human Rights.

Globes and Flock of Birds—UC14
Printed by Acrovure Division of Union-Camp Corporation, Englewood, N.J. Designed by Antonio Frasconi.
Letter Sheet for Foreign Postage
1968, Dec. 3   **Tagged**   Photogravure
UC42 UC14 13c **gray, brown, orange & black,**
                  blue, entire   7.50   2.00
                Entire, 1st day cancel,
                  Washington, D.C. *(145,898)*   2.75
             a. Orange omitted
             b. Brown omitted
             c. Black omitted

No. UC42 has a luminescent panel ⅜ x 1 inch on the right globe. The panel glows orange red under ultraviolet light.

Jet Plane—UC15
Printed by United States Envelope Co., Williamsburg, Pa. Designed by Robert Geissmann.
Center Circle Luminescent
1971, May 6   Embossed (Plane)
UC43 UC15 11c **red & blue**   50   10
                Entire   60   13
                Entire, 1st day cancel,
                  Williamsburg, Pa. *(187,000)*   90

Birds in Flight—UC16
Printed by Bureau of Engraving and Printing. Designed by Soren Noring.

Letter Sheet for Foreign Postage

1971		Tagged		Photogravure
UC44	UC1615c	gray, red, white & blue, *blue*, entire, *May 28*	1.50	.90
		Entire, 1st day cancel, Chicago, Ill. *(130,669)*		1.35
		Die cutting reversed, entire	25.00	
	a.	"AEROGRAMME" added to inscription, entire, *Dec. 13*	1.50	.90
		Entire, 1st day cancel, Philadelphia, Pa.		1.35
		Die cutting reversed, entire	25.00	

Folding instructions (2 steps) in capitals on No. C44; (4 steps) in upper and lower case on No. UC44a.

On Nos. UC44—UC44a the white rhomboid background of "USA postage 15c" is luminescent. No. UC44 is inscribed: "VIA AIR MAIL-PAR AVION". "postage 15c" is in gray. See No. UC46.

No. UC40 Surcharged in Green at Left of Stamp

1971, June 28 — Embossed

UC45	UC13 10c + (1c) red		
	Entire	1.50	.20
		1.90	.25
	Entire, 1st day cancel, Washington, D.C.		8.50

Hot Air Ballooning Championships Issue
Hot Air Ballooning World Championships, Albuquerque, N.M., Feb. 10-17, 1973.

"usa" Type of 1971
Design: Three balloons and cloud at left in address section; no birds beside stamp. Inscribed "INTERNATIONAL HOT AIR BALLOONING." "postage 15c" in blue.

Printed by Bureau of Engraving and Printing. Designed by Soren Noring (vignette) and Esther Porter (balloons).

Letter Sheet for Foreign Postage

1973, Feb. 10		Tagged	Photogravure (Andreotti)
UC46	UC1615c	red, white & blue, *blue*, entire	75 .40
		Entire, 1st day cancel, Albuquerque, N.M. *(210,000)*	.70

Folding instructions as on No. UC44a. See notes after No. UC44.

Bird in Flight
UC17

1973, Dec. 1			Luminescent Ink	
UC47	UC1713c	rose red		
		Entire	28	10
		Entire, 1st day cancel, Memphis, Tenn. *(132,658)*	40	13
				55

Printed by the Bureau of Engraving and Printing. Designed by Bill Hyde.

Letter Sheet for Foreign Postage.

1974, Jan. 4		Tagged		Photogravure
UC48	UC1818c	red & blue, *blue*, entire		70 .30
		Entire, 1st day cancel, Atlanta, Ga. *(119,615)*		.80
	a.	Red omitted, entire		—
		Die cutting reversed, entire		—

25th Anniversary of NATO Issue.
25th anniversary of the North Atlantic Treaty Organization.

"USA" **postage 18c**
UC19

Design: "NATO" and NATO emblem at left in address section.
Printed by Bureau of Engraving and Printing. Designed by Soren Noring.

Letter Sheet for Foreign Postage

1974, Apr. 4		Tagged	Photogravure (Andreotti)
UC49	UC1918c	red & blue, *blue*, entire	70 .25
		Entire, 1st day cancel, Washington, D.C.	.80

"USA"—UC20

Printed by Bureau of Engraving and Printing. Designed by Robert Geissmann.

Letter Sheet for Foreign Postage

1976, Jan. 16		Tagged		Photogravure
UC50	UC2022c	red & blue, *blue*, entire		70 .25
		Entire, 1st day cancel, Tempe, Ariz. *(118,303)*		.90
		Die cutting reversed, entire	25.00	

"USA"—UC21

Printed by Bureau of Engraving and Printing. Designed by Soren Noring.

Letter Sheet for Foreign Postage

1978, Nov. 3		Tagged		Photogravure
UC51	UC2122c	blue, *blue*, entire		70 .25
		Entire, 1st day cancel, St. Petersburg, Fla. *(86,099)*		.90
		Die cutting reversed, entire	25.00	

22nd Olympic Games, Moscow, July 19 — Aug. 3, 1980.

UC22

Design (multicolored in bottom left corner) shows discus thrower.
Printed by Bureau of Engraving and Printing. Designed by Robert M. Cunningham.
Letter Sheet for Foreign Postage.

1979, Dec. 5		Tagged		Photogravure
UC52	UC22	22c **red, black & green**, *bluish*, entire		1.50 22
		Entire, 1st day cancel, Bay Shore, N.Y.		90

"USA"—UC23

Design (brown): lower left, Statue of Liberty. Inscribed "Tour the United States." Folding area shows tourist attractions.
Printed by Bureau of Engraving and Printing.
Designed by Frank J. Waslick.
Letter Sheet for Foreign Postage

1980, Dec. 29		Tagged		Photogravure
UC53	UC23	30c **blue, red & brn.**, *blue*, entire	60	30
		Entire, 1st day cancel, San Francisco, CA		1.10
	a.	Red ("30") omitted Die cutting reversed, entire	—	

1981, Sept. 21		Tagged		Photogravure
UC54	UC23	30c **yel., mag., blue & black**, *blue*, entire	60	30
		First day cancel, Honolulu, HI		1.10

UC24

"Made in USA...world's best buys!"
Printed by Bureau of Engraving and Printing.
Designed by Frank J. Waslick.
Letter Sheet for Foreign Postage

1982, Sept. 16		Tagged		Photogravure
UC55	UC24	30c **multi.**, *blue*, entire	60	30
		First day cancel, Seattle, WA		1.10

World Communications Year

World Map Showing Locations of Satellite Tracking Stations—UC25

Printed by Bureau of Engraving and Printing.
Designed by Esther Porter.
Letter Sheet for Foreign Postage

1983, Jan. 7		Tagged		Photogravure
UC56	UC25	30c multi, *blue*, entire	60	30
		First day cancel, Anaheim, CA		1.10

1984 Olympics

UC26
Printed by the Bureau of Engraving & Printing
Designed by Bob Peak
Letter Sheet for Foreign Postage

Design: Woman equestrian at lower left with montage of competitive events on reverse folding area.

1983, Oct. 14		Tagged		Photogravure
UC57	UC26	30c multi, *blue*, entire	60	30
		First day cancel, Los Angeles, CA		1.10

WEATHER SATELLITES, 25th Anniv.

Landsat Infrared and Thermal Mapping Bands
UC27
Printed by the Bureau of Engraving & Printing
Designed by Esther Porter
Letter Sheet for Foreign Postage

Design: Landsat orbiting the earth at lower left with three Landsat photographs on reverse folding area. Inscribed: "Landsat views the Earth."

1985, Feb. 14		Tagged	Photogravure	
UC58	UC27	36c	multi, *blue*, entire	72	36
			First day cancel,		
			Goddard Flight Center, MD		1.35

NATIONAL TOURISM WEEK

Urban Skyline
UC28
Printed by the Bureau of Engraving & Printing
Designed by Dennis Luzak
Letter Sheet for Foreign Postage

Design: Inscribed "Celebrate America" at lower left and "Travel ... the perfect freedom" on folding area. Skier, Indian chief, cowboy, jazz trumpeter and pilgrims on reverse folding area.

1985, May 21		Tagged	Photogravure	
UC59	UC28	36c	multi, *blue*, entire	72	36
			First day cancel,		
			Washington, DC		1.35

Mark Twain (1835-1910), Author, and Halley's Comet

Comet Tail Viewed from Space — UC29

Printed by the Bureau of Engraving & Printing.
Designed by Dennis Luzak.
Letter sheet for foreign postage.

Design: Portrait of Twain at lower left and inscribed "I came in with Halley's Comet in 1835. It is coming again next year, and I expect to go out with it. It will be the greatest disappointment of my life if I don't go out with Halley's Comet." "1835 . Mark Twain . 1910 . Halley's Comet . 1985" and Twain, Huckleberry Finn, steamboat and comet on reverse folding areas.

1985, Dec. 4		Tagged	Photogravure	
UC60	UC29	36c	multi, entire	72	36
			First day cancel,		
			Washington, DC		1.35

ENVELOPES

OFFICIAL ENVELOPES.

By the Act of Congress, January 31, 1873, the franking privilege of officials was abolished as of July 1, 1873 and the Postmaster General was authorized to prepare official envelopes. At the same time official stamps were prepared for all Departments. Department envelopes became obsolete July 5, 1884. After that, government offices began to use franked envelopes of varied design. These indicate no denomination and lie beyond the scope of this Catalogue.

Printed by George H. Reay, Brooklyn, N.Y.

1873

UO1	UO1	2c **black**, *lemon*	7.50	4.00
		Entire	11.00	7.00
UO2	UO2	3c **black**, *lemon*	2.25	2.00
		Entire	6.00	4.00
UO3	"	3c **black**, *white*	*5,000.*	
		Entire	*15,000.*	
UO4	UO3	6c **black**, *lemon*	7.00	5.00
		Entire	12.00	9.00

Post Office Department.

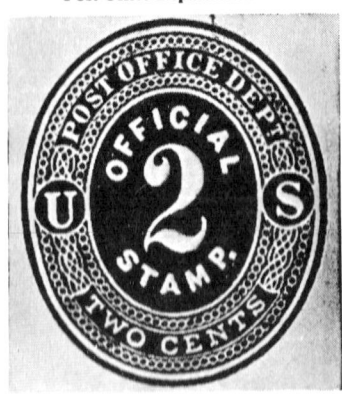

UO1
Numeral 9 mm. high.

UO2
Numeral 9 mm. high.

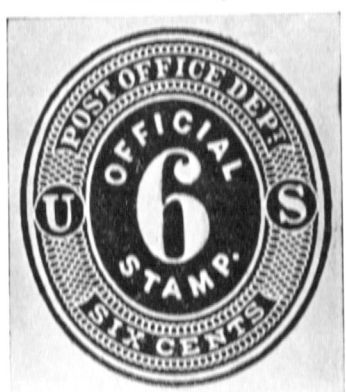

UO3   Numeral 9½ mm. high.

UO4
Numeral 9¼ mm. high.

UO5
Numeral 9¼ mm. high.

UO6   Numeral 10½ mm. high.

ENVELOPES

Printed by Plimpton Manufacturing Co., Hartford, Conn.
1874-79

UO5	UO4	2c **black,** *lemon*	2.50	2.00
		Entire	5.00	3.00
UO6	"	2c **black,** *white*	35.00	20.00
		Entire	45.00	22.50
UO7	UO5	3c **black,** *lemon*	1.50	30
		Entire	2.00	60
UO8	"	3c **black,** *white*	400.00	425.00
		Entire	500.00	
UO9	"	3c **black,** *amber*	25.00	20.00
		Entire	25.00	20.00
UO10	"	3c **black,** *blue*	12,500.	
		Entire	15,000.	
UO11	"	3c **blue,** *blue* ('75)	10,000.	
		Entire	9,000.	
UO12	UO6	6c **black,** *lemon*	2.00	1.00
		Entire	4.00	3.00
UO13	"	6c **black,** *white*	425.00	
		Entire	550.00	

Fakes exist of Nos. UO3, UO8 and UO13.

Jackson
UO9
Bust narrow at the back.

Postal Service

UO7

1877

UO14	UO7	**black,** *white*	1.50	90
		Entire	2.00	1.50
UO15	"	**black,** *amber*	15.00	10.00
		Entire	80.00	15.00
UO16	"	**blue,** *amber*	19.00	12.00
		Entire	75.00	20.00
UO17	"	**blue,** *blue*	2.50	3.00
		Entire	4.00	3.50

Washington
UO10
Queue projects below the bust.

War Department.

Franklin
UO8
Bust points to the end of "N" of "ONE".

Lincoln
UO11
Neck very long at the back.

ENVELOPES 605

Jefferson
UO12
Queue forms straight line with bust

Scott
UO15

Clay
UO13
Ear partly concealed by hair, mouth large, chin prominent.

Hamilton
UO16
Back of bust very narrow; chin almost straight; the labels containing the letters "U S" are exactly parallel.

Printed by George H. Reay.

1873

UO18	UO8	1c **dark red,** *white*	400.00	150.00
		Entire	500.00	200.00
UO19	UO9	2c **dark red,** *white*	450.00	150.00
		Entire	525.00	
UO20	UO10	3c **dark red,** *white*	27.50	15.00
		Entire	40.00	30.00
UO21	"	3c **dark red,** *amber*	7,500.	
		Entire	12,000.	
UO22	"	3c **dark red,** *cream*	275.00	75.00
		Entire	350.00	90.00
UO23	UO11	6c **dark red,** *white*	110.00	35.00
		Entire	140.00	
UO24	"	6c **dark red,** *cream*	950.00	150.00
		Entire	1,500.	500.00
UO25	UO12	10c **dark red,** *white*	1,200.	160.00
		Entire	2,500.	300.00
UO26	UO13	12c **dark red,** *white*	75.00	20.00
		Entire	90.00	
UO27	UO14	15c **dark red,** *white*	75.00	20.00
		Entire	90.00	
UO28	UO15	24c **dark red,** *white*	80.00	15.00
		Entire	90.00	
UO29	UO16	30c **dark red,** *white*	250.00	50.00
		Entire	275.00	75.00

1873

UO30	UO8	1c **vermilion,** *white*	100.00	
		Entire	175.00	
WO31	"	1c **vermilion,** *manila*	4.00	1.75
		Entire	7.50	5.00

Webster
UO14
Has side whiskers.

UO32	UO9	2c	**vermilion,** *white*	125.00	
			Entire	3,000.	
WO33	"	2c	**vermilion,** *manila*	100.00	
			Entire	150.00	
UO34	UO10	3c	**vermilion,** *white*	40.00	15.00
			Entire	90.00	—
UO35	"	3c	**vermilion,** *amber*	50.00	
			Entire	150.00	
UO36	"	3c	**vermilion,** *cream*	4.00	2.00
			Entire	12.00	8.00
UO37	UO11	6c	**vermilion,** *manila*	45.00	
			Entire	60.00	
UO38	"	6c	**vermilion,** *cream*	200.00	
			Entire	4,000.	
UO39	UO12	10c	**vermilion,** *white*	115.00	
			Entire	250.00	
UO40	UO13	12c	**vermilion,** *white*	75.00	
			Entire	135.00	
UO41	UO14	15c	**vermilion,** *white*	110.00	
			Entire	1,500.	
UO42	UO15	24c	**vermilion,** *white*	200.00	
			Entire	275.00	
UO43	UO16	30c	**vermilion,** *white*	300.00	
			Entire	425.00	

UO19
Bottom serif on "S" is short;
queue does not project below bust.

UO17
Bottom serif on "S" is thick and short; bust at bottom below hair forms a sharp point.

UO20
Neck very short at the back

UO18
Bottom serif on "S" is thick and short;
front part of bust is rounded.

UO21
Knot of queue stands out prominently

ENVELOPES 607

UO22
Ear prominent, chin receding.

UO23
Has no side whiskers; forelock projects above head.

UO24
Back of bust rather broad; chin slopes considerably; the label containing letters "U S" are not exactly parallel.
Printed by Plimpton Manufacturing Co.

1875

UO44	UO17	1c red, white	70.00	55.00
		Entire	80.00	
UO45	"	1c red, amber	400.00	
UO45A	"	1c red, orange	12,000.	
WO46	"	1c red, manila	1.00	50
		Entire	2.50	2.50

UO47	UO18	2c red, white	50.00	
		Entire	60.00	
UO48	"	2c red, amber	15.00	3.00
		Entire	20.00	10.00
UO49	"	2c red, orange	22.50	6.00
		Entire	25.00	12.00
WO50	"	2c red, manila	50.00	30.00
		Entire	75.00	
UO51	UO19	3c red, white	6.50	3.00
		Entire	7.00	5.00
UO52	"	3c red, amber	5.00	3.00
		Entire	6.00	5.00
UO53	"	3c red, cream	2.00	1.00
		Entire	2.50	1.50
UO54	"	3c red, blue	1.25	50
		Entire	1.50	75
UO55	"	3c red, fawn	65	50
		Entire	1.50	90
UO56	UO20	6c red, white	20.00	10.00
		Entire	50.00	
UO57	"	6c red, amber	50.00	15.00
		Entire	60.00	
UO58	"	6c red, cream	75.00	40.00
		Entire	100.00	
UO59	UO21	10c red, white	75.00	40.00
		Entire	100.00	
UO60	"	10c red, amber	650.00	
		Entire	750.00	
UO61	UO22	12c red, white	15.00	15.00
		Entire	50.00	
UO62	"	12c red, amber	400.00	
		Entire	450.00	
UO63	"	12c red, cream	325.00	
		Entire	450.00	
UO64	UO23	15c red, white	80.00	30.00
		Entire	110.00	
UO65	"	15c red, amber	450.00	
		Entire	500.00	
UO66	"	15c red, cream	450.00	
		Entire	500.00	
UO67	UO24	30c red, white	90.00	50.00
		Entire	110.00	
UO68	"	30c red, amber	650.00	
		Entire	750.00	
UO69	"	30c red, cream	675.00	
		Entire	800.00	

POSTAL SAVINGS ENVELOPES.

Issued under the Act of Congress, approved June 25, 1910, in lieu of penalty or franked envelopes. Unused remainders, after October 5, 1914, were overprinted with the Penalty Clause.

Regular stamped envelopes, redeemed by the Government, were also overprinted for official use.

UO25

1911

UO70	UO25	1c green, white	40.00	5.00
		Entire	50.00	25.00
UO71	"	1c green, oriental buff	110.00	30.00
		Entire	125.00	40.00
UO72	"	2c carmine, white	4.00	75
		Entire	6.50	3.00
	a.	2c carmine, manila (error)	1,200.	
		Entire	1,650.	

OFFICIAL WRAPPERS.
Included in listings of Official Envelopes with prefix letters WO instead of UO.

OFFICIAL MAIL

UO26

1983, Jan. 12   **Embossed**
UO73 UO26   20c blue, entire   50   ―――
               FDC, Washington, DC   75

UO27

1985, Feb. 26   **Embossed**
UO74 UO27   22c blue, entire   55   ―――
               FDC, Washington, DC   80

POSTAL CARDS

Prices are for (1), unused cards as sold by the Post Office, without printed or written address or message.
(2), unused cards with printed or written address or message. Used price applies after 1952.
*(3), used cards with Post Office cancellation, when current.
Starting with No. UX21, all postal cards have been printed by the Government Printing Office.
Nos. UX1-UX48 are typographed; others are lithographed (offset) unless otherwise stated.
Numerous printing varieties exist. Varieties of surcharged cards include (a) inverted surcharge at lower left, (b) double surcharge, one inverted at lower left, (c) surcharge in other abnormal positions, including back of card. Such varieties command a premium.
Colored cancellations sell for more than black in some instances.
All prices are for entire cards.

*Used prices for international rate cards are for proper usage. Those domestically used sell for less.

Liberty—PC1
Size: 130x76 mm.

1873 Wmkd. Large "U S P O D" in Monogram, (90 x 60 mm.)

		(1)	(2)	(3)
UX1	PC1	1c brown on buff, May 13, 1873	250.00	40.00	15.00
		First day cancel, Boston, New York or Washington			2250.00

Wmkd. Small "U S P O D" in Monogram, (53 x 36 mm.)

UX3 PC1 1c brown on buff, July 6, 1875   50.00   10.00   1.25
     a. Without watermark

The watermarks on Nos. UX1, UX3 and UX4 are found in normal position, inverted, reversed, and inverted and reversed. They are often dim, especially on No. UX4.
No. UX3a is not known unused. Cards offered as such are either unwatermarked proofs, or have partial or vague watermarks. See also No. UX65.

Liberty
PC2

1875
Since 1875 it has been possible to purchase postal cards in sheets for multiple printing, hence pairs, strips and blocks are available.

Inscribed: "WRITE THE ADDRESS . . ."
Wmkd. Small "U S P O D" in Monogram.
UX4 PC2 1c black on buff, Sept. 28   1250.00   500.00   185.00

Unwmkd.

			(1)	(2)	(3)
UX5	PC2	1c black on buff, Sept. 30	40.00	3.00	30

For other postal card of type PC2 see No. UX7.

1879   Liberty
     PC3

UX6	PC3	2c blue on buff, Dec. 1, 1879	15.00	5.00	15.00
		a. 2c dark blue on buff	17.50	7.50	16.00

See also Nos. UX13 and UX16.

1881   Design of PC2.
Inscribed: "NOTHING BUT THE ADDRESS."

UX7	PC2	1c black on buff, Oct. 17 (?)	40.00	3.00	25
		a. 23 teeth below "ONE CENT"	500.00	175.00	25.00
		b. Printed on both sides	525.00		350.00

Jefferson
PC4

610 POSTAL CARDS

1885

			(1)	(2)	(3)
UX8	PC4	1c brown on buff, *Aug. 24*	25.00	4.00	75
	a.	1c orange brown on buff	25.00	5.00	75
	b.	1c red brown on buff	25.00	5.00	75
	c.	1c chocolate on buff	50.00	12.50	5.00
	d.	Double impression			
	e.	Double impression, one inverted	525.00		
	f.	Printed both sides	500.00		

PC5
Head of Jefferson facing right, centered on card.

1886

UX9	PC5	1c black on buff, *Dec. 1, 1886*	8.00	1.00	40
	a.	1c black on dark buff	15.00	4.00	75
	b.	Double impression	400.00		
	c.	Double impression, one inverted	850.00		

Grant
PC6

1891

Size: 155 x 95 mm.

UX10	PC6	1c black on buff, *Dec. 16, 1891*	22.50	3.00	50
	a.	Double impression, one inverted	550.00		
	b.	Double impression	550.00		

Two types exist of No. UX10.

Size: 117 x 75 mm.

UX11	PC6	1c blue on grayish white, *Dec. 16, 1891*	8.50	2.50	1.25
	b.	Double impression, one inverted	170.00		

(Cards printed in black instead of blue are invariably proofs.)

1894

PC7
Head of Jefferson facing left.
Small wreath and name below.
Size: 140 x 89 mm.

			(1)	(2)	(3)
UX12	PC7	1c black on buff, *Jan. 2, 1894*	22.00	1.00	25
	a.	Double impression	200.00		

1897

Design of PC 3.
Size: 140 x 89 mm.

| UX13 | PC3 | 2c bl. on cream, *Jan. 25, 1897* | 90.00 | 40.00 | 60.00 |

PC8
Head same as PC 7. Large wreath and name below.
1897 Size: 139 x 82 mm.

UX14	PC8	1c black on buff, *Dec. 1, 1897*	17.50	1.25	25
	a.	Double impression, one inverted	—	600.00	650.00
	b.	Printed both sides		—	—
	c.	Double impression	300.00	—	—

John Adams
PC9
1898 Size: 126 x 74 mm.

| UX15 | PC9 | 1c black on buff, *Mar. 31* | 25.00 | 5.00 | 10.00 |

Design same as PC 3, without frame around card.
Size: 140 x 82 mm.

| UX16 | PC3 | 2c black on buff, 1898 | 7.50 | 4.00 | 8.50 |

POSTAL CARDS 611

McKinley
PC10
1902
UX17   PC10   1c black on buff   (1) 4500.00   (2) 2500.00   (3) 2000.00
Earliest known use: May 27, 1902.

McKinley
PC11
1902
UX18   PC11   1c black on buff   7.50   .75   .30
Earliest known use: July 15, 1902.
Two types exist of Nos. UX18–UX20.

McKinley
PC12
1907
UX19   PC12   1c black on buff   22.50   1.00   .30
Earliest known use: June 28, 1907.

1908   Same design,
correspondence space at left.
UX20   PC12   1c black on buff,
Jan. 2, 1908   35.00   4.00   3.25

1910   **PC13**
McKinley, background shaded.
                     (1)   (2)   (3)
UX21   PC13   1c blue on bluish   80.00   10.00   3.00
     a. 1c bronze blue on bluish
                     150.00   25.00   10.00

     b. Double impression   250.00
     c. Triple impression   300.00
     d. Double impression,
          one inverted   375.00
     e. Four arcs above and
          below "IS" of inscrip-
          tion to left of stamp im-
          pression are pointed   600.00   350.00   350.00
A No. UX21 card exists with Philippines No. UX11 printed on the back.

                 PC14
1910
UX22   PC14   Same design, white background.
         1c blue on bluish,
         Apr. 13, 1910   10.00   .75   .25
     a. Double impression   150.00
     b. Triple impression   175.00
     c. Triple impression,
          one inverted
     See also No. UX24.

             PC15
1911   Head of Lincoln solid background.
             Size: 127x76mm.
UX23   PC15   1c red on cream, *Jan. 21*   6.00   1.50   4.00
     a. Triple impression   450.00
For other postal card of type PC15 see No. UX26.

612 POSTAL CARDS

Design same as PC 14.
Size: 140x82mm.

			(1)	(2)	(3)
UX24	PC14	1c red on cream, *Aug. 10*	6.00	75	25
		a. Double impression	200.00		
		b. Triple impression	250.00		

Grant—PC16

UX25	PC16	2c red on cream, *Oct. 27, 1911*	1.25	20	6.50
		a. Double impression			

For other postal card of type PC16 see No. UX36.

1913
Design same as PC 15.
Size: 127 x 76 mm.

UX26	PC15	1c green on cream, *July 29*	5.50	1.00	4.00

Jefferson—PC17
Die I — End of queue small, sloping sharply downward to right.

Die II (re-cut)—End of queue large and rounded.

1914-16
Size: 140x82mm.

UX27	PC17	1c green on buff, Die I, *June 4, 1914*	25	15	10
		a. 1c green on cream	3.00	40	30
		b. Double impression	125.00		

On gray, rough surfaced card.

UX27C	PC17	1c green, Die I, *1916*	1250.00		
UX27D	"	1c dark green, Die II, *Dec. 22, 1916*	1450.00	175.00	90.00

Lincoln—PC19

1917-18
Size: 127 x 76 mm.

			(1)	(2)	(3)
UX28	PC19	1c green on cream, *Mar. 14, 1917*	60	30	30
		a. 1c green on dk. buff	1.00	30	50
		b. Double impression			

No. UX28 was printed also on light buff and canary.

Jefferson
PC20

Die I. Rough, coarse impression. End of queue slopes sharply downward to right. Left basal ends of "2" form sharp points.

Die II. Clear fine lines in hair. Left basal ends of "2" form balls.

Size: 140 x 82 mm.

UX29	PC20	2c red on buff, Die I, *Oct. 22, 1917*	27.50	3.00	1.00
		a. 2c lake on cream, Die I	30.00	5.00	2.00
		c. 2c vermilion on buff, Die I	150.00	45.00	30.00
UX30	"	2c red on cream, Die II, *Jan. 23, 1918*	15.00	2.50	1.00

POSTAL CARDS

2c Postal Cards of 1917–18 Revalued.

Surcharged in one line by canceling machine at Washington, D. C.

1920
UX31 PC20 1c on 2c red on cream,   (1)   (2)   (3)
    Die II, *April, 1920* 2750.00 1750.00 2500.00

Surcharged in two lines by canceling machine (46 Types)

UX32 PC20 1c on 2c red on buff, Die I,
   April, 1920 35.00 7.50 7.50
   a. 1c on 2c vermilion on buff 75.00   50.00
   b. Double surcharge —   50.00
UX33 " 1c on 2c red on cream, Die II,
   April, 1920 5.00 1.00 1.00
   a. Inverted surcharge 50.00
   b. Double surcharge 35.00 25.00 30.00
   c. Double surcharge, one inverted 275.00
   d. Triple surcharge 275.00

Prices for surcharge varieties of Nos. UX32 and UX33 are for cards having the surcharges *on the stamp.* Copies having the surcharge inverted in the lower left corner, either alone or in combination with a normal surcharge, exist in many of the 46 types.

Surcharged in Two Lines by Press Printing.

UX34 PC20 1c on 2c red on buff, Die I 300.00 60.00 25.00
   g. Double surcharge 375.00
UX35 " 1c on 2c red on cream, Die II 150.00 25.00 20.00

Surcharges were prepared from (a) special dies fitting International and Universal post office canceling machines (Nos. UX31-UX33), and (b) printing press dies (Nos. UX34-UX35). There are 38 canceling machine types on Die I, and 44 on Die II. There are two printing press types of each die.

UX36 PC16 1c on 2c red on cream (UX25) 3500.00

Unused copies of No. UX36 (New York surcharge) were probably made by favor. Used copies of No. UX36 (Los Angeles surcharge) are unquestionably authentic. Surcharges on other numbers exist, but their validity is doubtful.

McKinley
PC21

Franklin
PC22

1926
UX37 PC21 3c red on buff, *Feb. 1, 1926* 2.00 25 25
   First day cancel, Washington, D.C.   200.00
   a. 3c red on yellow 2.00 25 4.00

1951
UX38 PC22 2c carmine rose on buff, *Nov. 16, 1951* 30 25 25
   First day cancel   4.00
   a. Double impression 200.00

Nos. UX27 and UX28 Surcharged by Canceling Machine at Left of Stamp in Light Green

REVALUED 2¢ P. O. DEPT.

1952, Jan. 1   (1)   (2)   (3)
UX39 PC17 2c on 1c green on buff 50 25 25
   First day cancel, any city   20.00
   a. Surcharged vertically, reading down 6.00 2.00 7.50
   b. Double surcharge 12.00   15.00
UX40 PC19 2c on 1c green on cream 60 30 30
   a. Surcharged vertically, reading down 6.00 3.00 5.00

Nos. UX27 and UX28 with Similar Surcharge Typographed at Left of Stamp in Dark Green.

1952
UX41 PC17 2c on 1c green on buff 3.50 75 1.50
   a. Inverted surcharge at lower left 75.00 35.00 100.00
UX42 PC19 2c on 1c green on cream 4.50 2.00 2.00
   a. Surcharged on back 65.00

Type of 1917
Size: 127 x 76 mm.

UX43 PC19 2c carmine on buff, *July 31, 1952* 25 15 20
   First day cancel   2.50

Torch and Arm of Statue of Liberty
PC23

1956
Issued to commemorate the Fifth International Philatelic Exhibition (FIPEX), New York City, Apr. 28–May 6, 1956.

UX44 PC23 2c deep carmine & dark violet blue on buff, *May 4, 1956* 25 20
   First day cancel, New York, N. Y. (557,474)   1.25
   a. 2c lilac rose & dark violet blue on buff 1.00   40
   b. Dark violet blue omitted 300.00   200.00
   c. Double impression of dark violet blue 15.00   10.00

Statue of Liberty
PC24   PC25

POSTAL CARDS

1956   For international use.

		(1)		(3)
UX45	PC24	4c deep red & ultramarine on buff, *Nov. 16, 1956*	75	10
		First day cancel, New York, N. Y. *(129,841)*		1.25

Issued at the American Stamp Dealers' Association National Postage Stamp Show, New York City, Nov. 16–18.

1958–61

UX46	PC25	3c purple on buff, *Aug. 1, 1958*	40	20
		First day cancel, Philadelphia, Pa. *(180,610)*		1.25
	a.	"N GOD WE TRUST"	10.00	12.50
	b.	Double impression	300.00	
	c.	Precanceled with 3 printed purple lines, *1961*	3.00	2.00

Issued at the convention and exhibition of the American First Day Cover Society, Philadelphia, Pa.

On No. UX46c, the precanceling lines are incorporated with the design. The earliest known postmark on this experimental card is Sept. 15, 1961.

No. UX38 Surcharged by Canceling Machine at Left of Stamp in Black

ONE CENT ADDITIONAL PAID

1958

UX47	PC22	2c+1c carmine rose on buff	140.00	165.00

The surcharge was applied to 750,000 cards for the use of the General Electric Co., Owensboro, Ky. A variety of the surcharge shows the D of PAID beneath the N of ADDITIONAL. All known examples of No. UX47 have a printed advertisement on the back and a small punch hole near lower left corner.

Lincoln—PC26

1962–66

UX48	PC26	4c red violet on white, *Nov. 19, 1962*	25	20
		First day cancel, Springfield, Ill. *(162,939)*		1.50
	a.	Tagged, *June 25, 1966*	50	20
		Tagged, first day cancel, Bellevue, Ohio		—

No. UX48a was printed with luminescent ink.
See note on Luminescence in "Information for Collectors."

Map of Continental United States
PC27

1963   Designed by Suren H. Ermoyan.

Issued to attract tourists to the U.S.

		(1)		(3)
UX49	PC27	7c bl. & red on white, *Aug. 30*	1.25	50
		First day cancel, New York, N. Y.		1.00
	a.	Blue omitted		

First day cancellation was applied to 270,464 of Nos. UX49 and UY19. See Nos. UX54, UX59.

Flags and Map of U.S.—PC28

Designed by Gerald N. Kurtz.

1964   Precanceled with 3 printed blue lines.

Issued to commemorate the 175th anniversary of the U.S. Customs Service.

UX50	PC28	4c red & blue on white, *Feb. 22*	40	50
		First day cancel, Washington, D.C. *(313,275)*		1.00
	a.	Blue omitted	350.00	
	b.	Red omitted		

Americans "Moving Forward" (Street Scene)
PC29

Designed by Gerald N. Kurtz.

1964   Precanceled with a blue and 2 red printed lines

Issued to publicize the need to strengthen the U.S. Social Security system. Released in connection with the 15th conference of the International Social Security Association at Washington, D.C.

UX51	PC29	4c dull blue & red on white, *Sept. 26*	40	20
		First day cancel, Washington, D.C. *(293,650)*		1.00
	a.	Red omitted		
	b.	Blue omitted	550.00	

Coast Guard Flag—PC30

Designed by Muriel R. Chamberlain.

1965   Precanceled with 3 printed red lines

Issued to commemorate the 175th anniversary of the U.S. Coast Guard.

UX52	PC30	4c blue & red on white, *Aug. 4*	30	20
		First day cancel, Newburyport, Mass. *(338,225)*		1.00
	a.	Blue omitted		—

POSTAL CARDS 615

Crowd and Census Bureau Punch Card
PC31
Designed by Emilio Grossi.
1965 Precanceled with 3 bright blue printed lines
UX53 PC31 4c bright blue & black on white,
Oct. 21   30   20
First day cancel, Philadelphia,
Pa. (275,100)   1.00

Map Type of 1963
1967, Dec. 4
UX54 PC27 8c blue & red on white   1.00   50
First day cancel, Washington,
D.C.   50

First day cancellation was applied to 268,077 of Nos. UX54 and UY20.

Lincoln
PC33
Designed by Robert J. Jones.
Luminescent Ink
1968 Precanceled with 3 printed green lines
UX55 PC33 5c emerald on white, Jan. 4   25   15
First day cancel, Hodgenville,
Ky.   1.00
a. Double impression

First day cancellation was applied to 274,000 of Nos. UX55 and UY21.

Woman Marine, 1968, and Marines of
Earlier Wars
PC34
Designed by Muriel R. Chamberlain.
1968, July 26
Issued to commemorate the 25th anniversary of the Women Marines.
UX56 PC34 5c rose red & grn. on white   15   20
First day cancel, San Francisco,
Cal. (205,714)   1.00

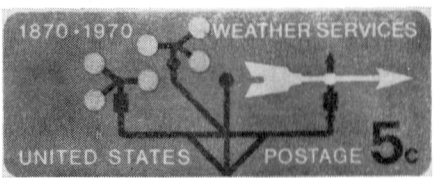

Weather Vane
PC35
Designed by Robert Geissmann.
1970 Tagged
Issued to commemorate the centenary of the Army's Signal Service, the Weather Services (Weather Bureau).
UX57 PC35 5c blue, yellow, red & black on
white, Sept. 1   30   15
First day cancel, Fort Myer,
Va. (285,800)   1.00
a. Yellow & black omitted   700.00
b. Blue omitted   500.00
c. Black omitted   600.00

Paul Revere—PC36
Designed by Howard C. Mildner after statue near Old North Church, Boston.
Luminescent Ink
1971 Precanceled with 3 printed brown lines.
Issued to honor Paul Revere, Revolutionary War patriot.
UX58 PC36 6c brown on white, May 15   25   20
First day cancel, Boston, Mass.   1.00
a. Double impression   300.00

First day cancellation was applied to 340,000 of Nos. UX58 and UY22.

Map Type of 1963
1971 Tagged
UX59 PC27 10c bl. & red on white, June 10 1.50 50
First day cancel, New York,
N.Y.   1.00

First day cancellation was applied to 297,000 of Nos. UX59 and UXC11.

New York Hospital, New York City—PC37
Designed by Dean Ellis.

Issued as a tribute to America's hospitals in connection with the 200th anniversary of New York Hospital.
1971 Tagged
UX60 PC37 6c bl. & multi. on white, Sept. 16 25 20
First day cancel, New York,
N.Y. (218,200)   1.00
a. Blue & yellow omitted   700.00

U.S.F. Constellation—PC38

Monument Valley—PC39

Gloucester, Mass.—PC40

Tourism Year of the Americas 1972.
Designed by Melbourne Brindle.

1972, June 29		Tagged		
		Size: 152½x108½mm.		
UX61	PC38	6c black on buff (*Yosemite, Mt. Rushmore, Niagara Falls, Williamsburg on back*)	30	50
		First day cancel, any city		40
		a. Address side blank	300.00	
UX62	PC39	6c black on buff (*Monterey, Redwoods, Gloucester, U.S.F. Constellation on back*)	30	50
		First day cancel, any city		40
UX63	PC40	6c black on buff (*Rodeo, Mississippi Riverboat, Grand Canyon, Monument Valley on back*)	30	50
		First day cancel, any city		40

Nos. UX61-UX63, UXC12-UXC13 went on sale throughout the United States. They were sold as souvenirs without postal validity at Belgica Philatelic Exhibition in Brussels and were displayed at the American Embassies in Paris and Rome. This is reflected in the first day cancel.

Nos. UX61-UX63 have a luminescent panel at left of stamp which glows green under ultraviolet light.

Varieties of the pictorial back printing include: black omitted (UX62), black and pale salmon omitted (UX63), and back inverted in relation to address side (UX63).

John Hanson—PC41
Designed by Thomas Kronen after statue by Richard Edwin Brooks in Maryland Capitol.
Luminescent Ink

1972		Precanceled with 3 printed blue lines		
UX64	PC41	6c blue on white, *Sept. 1*	25	15
		First day cancel, Baltimore, Md.		1.00

Liberty Type of 1873
Centenary of first U.S. postal card.

1973		Tagged		
UX65	PC1	6c magenta on white, *Sept. 14*	25	15
		First day cancel, Washington, D.C. (*289,950*)		1.00

Samuel Adams—PC42
Designed by Howard C. Mildner.
Luminescent Ink

1973		Precanceled with 3 printed orange lines		
UX66	PC42	8c orange, *Dec. 16*	25	15
		First day cancel, Boston, Mass. (*147,522*)		1.00

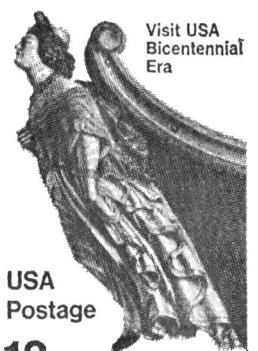

Ship's Figurehead, 1883
PC43

Design is after a watercolor by Elizabeth Moutal of the oak figurehead by John Rogerson from the barque Edinburgh.

1974		Tagged		
UX67	PC43	12c multicolored, *Jan. 4*	35	25
		First day cancel, Miami, Fla. (*138,500*)		1.00

No. UX67 has a luminescent panel at left of stamp which glows green under ultraviolet light.

POSTAL CARDS 617

Charles Thomson
PC44

John Witherspoon
PC45

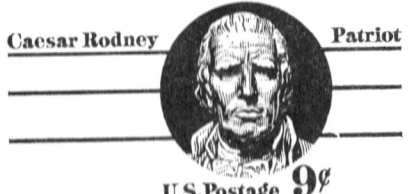

Caesar Rodney
PC46

Designed by Howard C. Mildner.
Luminescent Ink

1975-76   Precanceled with 3 printed emerald lines
UX68 PC44 7c emerald, *Sept. 14, 1975*   25   10
        First day cancel,
            Bryn Mawr, Pa.   75

Precanceled with 3 printed brown lines
UX69 PC45 9c yellow brown, *Nov. 10, 1975* 25   10
        First day cancel, Princeton,
            N.J.   75

Precanceled with 3 printed blue lines
UX70 PC46 9c blue on white, *July 1, 1976* 25   10
        First day cancel, Dover, Del.   75
    a. Double impression

First day cancellation applied to 231,919 of Nos. UX68 and UY25; 254,239 of Nos. UX69 and UY26; 304,061 of Nos. UX70 and UY27.

Federal Court House,
Galveston, Texas—PC47

Designed by Donald Moss.
The Court House, completed in 1861, is on the National Register of Historic Places.
1977, July 20   Tagged
UX71 PC47 9c multicolored on white   25   10
        First day cancel, Galveston,
            Tex. (245,535)   75

Nathan Hale—PC48
Designed by Howard C. Mildner.
Luminescent Ink
1977, Oct. 14   Precanceled with 3 printed green lines
UX72 PC48 9c green   25   10
        First day cancel, Coventry,
            Conn.   75

First day cancellation applied to 304,592 of Nos. UX72 and UY28.

Cincinnati Music Hall—PC49
Designed by Clinton Orlemann.
Centenary of Cincinnati Music Hall, Cincinnati, Ohio.
1978, May 12   Tagged
UX73 PC49 10c multicolored   25   10
        First day cancel, Cincin-
            nati, O. (300,000)   75

John Hancock—PC50
Designed by Howard Behrens.
Luminescent Ink
Precanceled with 3 printed brown orange lines.
1978
UX74 PC50 (10c) brown orange, *May 19* 25   10
        First day cancel,
            Quincy, Mass. (299,623)   75

Inscribed "U.S. Postage 10¢"
UX75 PC50 10c brown orange on white,
            June 20   25   10
        First day cancel, Quincy,
            Mass. (187,120)   75

POSTAL CARDS

US Coast Guard Eagle USA 14c

Coast Guard Cutter Eagle
PC51
Designed by Carl G. Evers.

1978, Aug. 4   Tagged
UX76   PC51   14c multicolored   30   15
     First day cancel, Seattle,
     Wash. *(196,400)*   75

Molly Pitcher, Monmouth, 1778

Molly Pitcher Firing Cannon at Monmouth
PC52
Designed by David Blossom.

Bicentennial of Battle of Monmouth, June 28, 1778, and to honor Molly Pitcher (Mary Ludwig Hays).

1978, Sept. 8   Tagged   Lithographed
UX77   PC52   10c multicolored   25   10
     First day cancel, Freehold,
     N.J. *(180,280)*   75

George Rogers Clark, Vincennes, 1779

Clark and his Frontiersmen Approaching Fort Sackville—PC53
Designed by David Blossom.

Bicentenary of capture of Fort Sackville from the British by George Rogers Clark.

1979, Feb. 23   Tagged   Lithographed
UX78   PC53   10c multicolored   25   10
     First day cancel, Vincennes,
     Ind.   75

Casimir Pulaski, Savannah, 1779

Gen. Casimir Pulaski—PC54
Bicentenary of the death of Gen. Casimir Pulaski (1748–1779), Polish nobleman who served in American Revolutionary Army.

1979, Oct. 11   Tagged   Lithographed
UX79   PC54   10c multicolored   25   15
     First day cancel,
     Savannah, GA *(210,000)*   75

Olympic Games Issue

Sprinter—PC55
Designed by Robert M. Cunningham.

22nd Olympic Games, Moscow, July 19–Aug. 3, 1980.

1979, Sept. 17   Tagged   Lithographed
UX80   PC55   10c multicolored   50   25
     First day cancel, Eugene, Ore.   75

Historic Preservation

Iolani Palace, Honolulu—PC56

1979, Oct. 1   Tagged   Lithographed
UX81   PC56   10c multicolored   25   10
     First day cancel,
     Honolulu, HI *(242,804)*   75

POSTAL CARDS 619

Women's
Figure Skating
PC57

13th Winter Olympic Games, Lake Placid, N.Y., Feb. 12-24.
Designed by Robert M. Cunningham.

1980, Jan. 15	Tagged	Lithographed		
UX82 PC57	14c multicolored		50	25
	First day cancel,			
	Atlanta, GA (160,977)			75

Salt Lake Temple, Salt Lake City—PC58

1980, Apr. 5	Tagged	Lithographed		
UX83 PC58	10c multicolored		22	10
	First day cancel,			
	Salt Lake City, UT (325,260)			75

Landing of Rochambeau, 1780
Rochambeau's Fleet—PC59

Count Jean-Baptiste de Rochambeau's landing at Newport,
R.I. (American Revolution) bicentenary.
Designed by David Blossom.

1980, July 11	Tagged	Lithographed		
UX84 PC59	10c multicolored		22	10
	First day cancel, Newport, R.I (180,567)			75

Battle of Kings Mountain, 1780
Whig Infantrymen—PC60
Bicentenary of the Battle
of Kings Mountain (American Revolution).
Designed by David Blossom.

1980, Oct. 7	Tagged	Lithographed		
UX85 PC60	10c multicolored		22	10
	First day cancel, Kings			
	Mountain, NC (136,130)			75

Golden Hinde—PC61

Drake's Golden Hinde 1580

300th anniversary of Sir Francis Drake's
circumnavigation (1578-1580).
Designed by Charles J. Lundgren.

1980, Nov. 21				
UX86 PC61	19c multicolored		42	15
	First day cancel, San			
	Rafael, CA (290,547)			75

Battle of Cowpens, 1781

Cols. Washington and Tarleton—PC62
Bicentenary of the Battle
of Cowpens (American Revolution).
Designed by David Blossom.

1981, Jan. 17				
UX87 PC62	10c multicolored		22	10
	First day cancel,			
	Cowpens, SC (160,000)			75

Eagle—PC63
Luminescent Ink

1981, Mar. 15   **Precanceled with 3 printed violet lines**
UX88 PC63   (12c) violet   28   12
              First day cancel,
              Memphis, TN   75
              See No. 1818, FDC section.

Isaiah Thomas—PC64
Designed by Chet Jezierski.

1981, May 5   **Precanceled with 3 printed lines**
UX89 PC64   12c lt blue   28   12
              First day cancel,
              Worchester, MA *(185,610)*   75

PC65
Bicentenary of the Battle at Eutaw Springs (American Revolution)
Designed by David Blossom

1981, Sept. 8   **Lithographed**
UX90 PC65   12c multicolored   28   12
              First day cancel,
              Eutaw Springs, SC *(115,755)*   75

Lewis and Clark Expedition, 1806
PC66
Designed by David Blossom

1981, Sept. 23
UX91 PC66   12c multicolored   28   12
              First day cancel,
              Saint Louis, MO   75

Robert Morris—PC67

1981   **Precanceled with 3 printed lines**
UX92 PC67   (13c) buff, *Oct. 11*   30   12
              First day cancel, Memphis, TN   55
              See No. 1946, FDC section.
              Inscribed: U.S. Postage 13¢

UX93 PC67   13c buff, *Nov.10*   30   12
              First day cancel, Philadelphia, PA   55

"Swamp Fox" Francis Marion, 1782

General Francis Marion (1732?-1795)
PC68
Designed by David Blossom

1982, Apr. 3   **Lithographed**
UX94 PC68   13c multicolored   30   12
              First day cancel, Marion, SC *(141,162)*   55

Rene Robert Cavelier, Sieur de la Salle
(1643-1687)—PC69
Designed by David Blossom

1982, Apr. 7		**Lithographed**		
UX95	PC69	13c multicolored	30	12
		First day cancel,		
		New Orleans, LA		55

PC70
Designed by Melbourne Brindle

1982, June 18		**Lithographed**		
UX96	PC70	13c brown, red & cream, *buff*	30	12
		First day cancel, Philadelphia, PA		55

Historic Preservation
PC71
Designed by Clint Orlemann

1982, Oct. 14		**Lithographed**		
UX97	PC71	13c multicolored	30	12
		First day cancel, St. Louis, MO		55

Gen. Oglethorpe Meeting
Chief Tomo-Chi-Chi of the Yamacraw
PC72
Designed by David Blossom

1983, Feb. 12		**Lithographed**		
UX98	PC72	13c multicolored	30	12
		First day cancel, Savannah, GA		55

PC73
Designed by Walter Brooks

1983, Apr. 19		**Lithographed**		
UX99	PC73	13c multicolored	30	12
		First day cancel,		
		Washington, DC (125,056)		55

Olympics 84, Yachting
PC74
Designed by Bob Peak

1983, Aug. 5		**Lithographed**		
UX100	PC74	13c multicolored	30	12
		First day cancel,		
		Long Beach, CA		55

POSTAL CARDS

The Ark and the Dove
PC75

Designed by David Blossom

1984, Mar. 25   **Lithographed**
UX101 PC75   13c multicolored   30   12
                   First day cancel,
                   St. Clement's Island, MD   55

Runner Carrying Olympic Torch
PC76
Designed by Robert Peak

1984, Apr. 30   **Lithographed**
UX102 PC76   13c multicolored   30   12
                  First day cancel,
                  Los Angeles, CA   55

Father Baraga and Indian Guide in Canoe
PC77
Designed by David Blossom

1984, June 29   **Lithographed**
UX103 PC77   13c multicolored   30   12
                 First day cancel,
                 Marquette, MI   55

Dominguez Adobe at Rancho San Pedro
PC78
Designed by Earl Thollander

1984, Sept. 16   **Lithographed**
UX104 PC78   13c multicolored   30   12
                 First day cancel,
                Compton, CA   55

Charles Carroll (1737-1832)
PC79
Designed by Richard Sparks

1985, Feb. 1   **Precanceled with 3 printed lines**
UX105 PC79   (14c)   pale grn   28   14
                         First day cancel,
                         New Carrollton, MD   58
                    Inscribed: USA 14
1985, Mar. 6   **Precanceled with 3 printed lines**
UX106 PC79   14c   pale grn   28   14
                      First day cancel,
                      Annapolis, MD   58

Clipper Flying Cloud
PC80
Designed by Richard Schlecht

1985, Feb. 27   **Lithography**
UX107 PC80   25c   multi   50   25
                    First day cancel,
                    Salem, MA   95

POSTAL CARDS

Issued Sept. 16, 1984

Scott UX104

COLLECT THE SCOTT WAY... WITH SCOTT'S

UNITED STATES POSTAL CARD
ALBUM

Newly Available - Postal card blank pages, 40 pages for $6.00

FEATURING:

- Spaces for every known variety of postal card, reply postal card, airpost postal card, and official postal card issued by the United States and listed in the Scott "Specialized Catalogue of United States Stamps". Pages made of extra heavy paper to support the weight of your cards.

- Each stamp pictured or described and arranged in order by Scott number.

- A handsome, sturdy binder is standard with this album - not tacked on at an extra cost.

- Chemically neutralized paper protects your stamps for generations.

- Paper just the right thickness to make collecting a pleasure.

- Yearly supplement available.

$49.95 Album through 1985

AVAILABLE NOW AT YOUR LOCAL DEALER OR DIRECT FROM:

SCOTT

P.O. BOX 828, SIDNEY, OH 45365

POSTAL CARDS

George Wythe (1726-1806)
PC81
Designed by Chet Jezierski from a portrait by John Fergusson

1985, June 20   **Precanceled with 3 printed lines**
UX108 PC81   14c   brt apple grn   28   14
     First day cancel,
     Williamsburg, VA   58

Francis Vigo (1747-1836)
PC84
Designed by David Blossom

1986, May 24   **Lithographed**
UX111 PC84   14c   multi   28   14
     First day cancel, Vincennes, IN   58

Arrival of Thomas Hooker and Hartford Congregation
PC82
Settlement of Connecticut, 350th Anniv.
Designed by David Blossom

1986, Apr. 18   **Lithographed**
UX109 PC82   14c   **multi**   28   14
     First day cancel, Hartford, CT   58

Roger Williams (1603-1683), Clergyman,
Landing at Providence
PC85
Settling of Rhode Island, 350th Anniv.
Designed by David Blossom

1986, June 26   **Lithographed**
UX112 PC85   14c   multi   28   14
     First day cancel, Providence, RI   58

Stamp Collecting
PC83
Designed by Ray Ameijide

1986, May 23   **Lithographed**
UX110 PC83   14c   **multi**   28   14
     First day cancel, Chicago, IL   58

Miners, Shake Rag Street Housing
PC86
Wisconsin Territory Sesquicentennial
Designed by David Blossom

1986, July 3   **Lithographed**
UX113 PC86   14c   multi   28   14
     First day cancel, Mineral Point, WI   58

POSTAL CARDS

PAID REPLY POSTAL CARDS.

These are sold to the public as two unsevered cards, one for message and one for reply. These are listed first as unsevered cards and then as severed cards. Prices are for

(1) unused cards (both unsevered and severed) without printed or written address or message.
(2) unused cards (both unsevered and severed) with printed or written address or message. Used price applies after 1952.
(3) used unsevered cards, Message Card with Post Office cancellation and Reply Card uncancelled; and used severed cards with cancellation when current.

Unsevered cards sell for a premium if never folded.

International Paid Reply Cards sell for more if used to or from foreign countries. If used internationally and unsevered, they sell for considerably more than catalogue prices. International cards are Nos. UY2, UY11, UY12, UY16, UY19–UY20, UY24.

PM2

PM1

PR1

Head of Grant, card framed.

1892, Oct. 25   Size: 140x89mm.   (1)   (2)   (3)
UY1   PM1+PR1 1c+1c black on buff,
                unsevered   25.00 7.00 3.00
      a. Message card printed on both
         sides, reply card blank 200.00
      b. Message card blank, reply
         card printed on both sides 200.00
      c. Cards joined at bottom   100.00 40.00 50.00
      m. PM1 Message card
         detached   4.00 1.50   .75
      r. PR1 Reply card detached   4.00 1.50   .75

For other postal cards of types PM1 and PR1 see No. UY3.

Liberty
PR2

1893, Mar. 1   (1)   (2)   (3)
UY2   PM2+PR2 2c+2c blue on grayish
                white, unsevered   12.00 6.00 10.00
      a. 2c+2c dark blue on grayish
         white, unsevered   12.00 6.00 10.00
      b. Message card printed on both
         sides, reply card blank   250.00
      c. Message card blank,
         reply card printed on
         both sides   —
      d. Message card normal,
         reply card blank   250.00
      m. PM2 Message card
         detached   2.50 1.00 1.00
      r. PR2 Reply card detached   2.50 1.00 1.00

For other postal cards of types PM2 and PR2 see No. UY11.

Design same as PM1 and PR1,
without frame around card.

1898, Sept.   Size: 140x82mm.
UY3   PM1+PR1 1c+1c black on buff,
                unsevered   40.00 10.00 6.00
      a. Message card normal,
         reply card blank   200.00
      b. Message card printed
         on both sides, reply
         card blank   200.00
      c. Message card blank, reply
         card printed on both sides 200.00
      d. Message card without
         "Detach annexed card/
         for answer"   100.00   —   100.00
      e. Message card blank,
         reply card normal   200.00
      m. PM1 Message card
         detached   5.00 2.25 1.25
      r. PR1 Reply card detached   5.00 2.25 1.25

PM3

PR3

1904, March 31

		(1)	(2)	(3)
UY4	PM3+PR3	1c+1c black on buff, unsevered	25.00	3.50	1.75
	a.	Message card normal, reply card blank	225.00		
	b.	Message card printed on both sides, reply card blank	—		
	c.	Message card blank, reply card normal	225.00		
	d.	Message card blank, reply card printed on both sides	—	150.00	125.00
	m.	PM3 Message card detached	5.00	1.00	40
	r.	PR3 Reply card detached	4.00	1.00	35

PM4

PR4

1910, Sept. 14
Double frame line around instructions.

		(1)	(2)	(3)
UY5	PM4+PR4	1c+1c blue on bluish, unsevered	75.00	15.00	4.50
	a.	Message card normal, reply card blank	150.00		
	m.	PM4 Message card detached	4.00	2.00	1.00
	r.	PR4 Reply card detached	4.00	2.00	1.50

1911, Oct. 27   Same designs.

UY6	PM4+PR4	1c+1c green on cream, unsevered	75.00	25.00	15.00
	a.	Message card normal, reply card blank	—		
	m.	PM4 Message card detached	15.00	8.00	2.00
	r.	PR4 Reply card detached	15.00	6.00	3.00

1915, Sept. 18   Same designs.
Single frame line around instructions.

UY7	PM4+PR4	1c+1c green on cream, unsevered	75	25	20
	a.	1c+1c dark green on buff, unsevered	75	25	20
	m.	PM4 Message card detached	25	15	20
	r.	PR4 Reply card detached	25	15	20

PM5

PR5

POSTAL CARDS

		(1)	(2)	(3)
1918, Aug. 2				
UY8 PM5+PR5	2c+2c red on buff, unsevered	50.00	17.50	25.00
m.	PM5 Message card detached	10.00	5.00	3.50
r.	PR5 Reply card detached	10.00	5.00	3.50

1 CENT

Same Surcharged

1920, April
Fifteen canceling machine types.

UY9 PM5+PR5	1c on 2c+1c on 2c red on buff, unsevered	12.50	3.00	5.00
a.	Message card normal, reply card no surcharge	65.00	—	—
b.	Message card normal, reply card double surcharge	55.00	—	—
c.	Message card double surcharge, reply card normal	55.00	—	—
d.	Message card no surcharge, reply card normal	55.00	—	—
e.	Message card no surcharge, reply card double surcharge	55.00	—	—
m.	PM5 Message card detached	2.50	1.00	1.50
r.	PR5 Reply card detached	2.50	1.00	2.00

One press printed type.

UY10 PM5+PR5	1c on 2c+1c on 2c red on buff, unsevered	225.00	100.00	125.00
a.	Message card no surcharge, reply card normal	—	—	—
m.	PM5 Message card detached	60.00	25.00	30.00
r.	PR5 Reply card detached	60.00	25.00	30.00

Designs same as PM2 and PR2.
1924, March 18   Size: 139x89mm.

UY11 PM2+PR2	2c+2c red on cream, unsevered	1.50	1.00	1.00
m.	PM2 Message card detached	50	25	25
r.	PR2 Reply card detached	50	25	25

PM6   PR6

1926, Feb. 1

UY12 PM6+PR6	3c+3c red on buff, unsevered	5.00	2.00	2.00
a.	3c+3c red on yellow, unsevered	5.00	2.00	2.00
m.	PM6 Message card detached	1.50	1.00	1.00
r.	PR6 Reply card detached	1.50	1.00	1.00

1951, Dec. 29   Type of 1910
Single frame line around instructions.

UY13 PM4+PR4	2c+2c carmine rose on buff, unsevered	1.00	40	50
	First day cancel, Washington, D.C.			3.00
m.	PM4 Message card detached	30	25	20
r.	PR4 Reply card detached	30	25	20

No. UY7a
Surcharged by
Canceling Machine
Below Stamp
in Green

REVALUED
2¢
P. O. DEPT.

		(1)	(2)	(3)
1952, Jan. 1				
UY14 PM4+PR4	2c on 1c+2c on 1c green on buff, unsevered	1.00	50	40
a.	Surcharge vertical at left of stamps	5.00	4.00	5.00
b.	Surcharge horizontal at left of stamps	12.50	6.00	10.00
c.	Inverted surcharge horizontal at left of stamps	125.00	65.00	85.00
d.	Message card normal, reply card no surcharge	25.00	—	35.00
e.	Message card normal, reply card double surcharge	30.00	—	—
f.	Message card no surcharge, reply card normal	25.00	—	25.00
g.	Message card double surcharge, reply card normal	20.00	—	20.00
h.	Both cards, dbl. surch.	25.00	—	25.00
m.	PM4 Message card detached	40	25	20
r.	PR4 Reply card detached	40	25	20

No. UY7a with Similar Surcharge (horizontal)
Typographed at Left of Stamp in Dark Green.

1952

UY15 PM4+PR4	2c on 1c+2c on 1c green on buff, unsevered	60.00	25.00	30.00
a.	Surcharge on message card only	100.00		
m.	PM4 Message card detached	10.00	4.00	5.00
r.	PR4 Reply card detached	10.00	4.00	5.00

On No. UY15a, the surcharge also appears on blank side of card.

1956   Liberty Type of Postal Card, 1956
For international use.

UY16 PC24	4c+4c carmine & dark violet blue on buff, unsevered, *Nov. 16, 1956*		75	50
	First day cancel, New York, N. Y. (127,874)			1.50
a.	Message card printed on both halves	100.00		
b.	Reply card printed on both halves	85.00		—
m.	Message card detached	40		25
r.	Reply card detached	40		25

See note after UX45.

1958   Liberty Type of Postal Card, 1956

UY17 PC25	3c+3c purple on buff, unsevered, *July 31, 1958*		2.50	25
	First day cancel, Boise, Idaho (136,768)			1.00
a.	One card blank	125.00		—

Both halves of No. UY17 are identical, inscribed as No. UX46, "This side of card is for address."

Lincoln Type of Postal Card, 1962
Precanceled with 3 printed red violet lines.

1962

UY18 PC26	4c+4c red violet on white, unsevered, *Nov. 19, 1962* (107,746)	2.00		75
	First day cancel, Springfield, Ill.			2.25
a.	Tagged, *Mar. 7, 1967*	4.50		2.50
a.	First day cancel, Dayton, OH			30.00

Both halves of No. UY18 are identical, inscribed as No. UX48, "This side of card is for address."
No. UY18a was printed with luminescent ink.

Map Type of Postal Card, 1963

1963   **For International Use.**   (1)   (3)

UY19   PC27   7c+7c blue & red on white,
unsevered, *Aug. 30, 1963*   1.75   1.00
First day cancel, New York   1.50
a. Message card normal, reply
card blank   125.00   100.00
b. Message card blank, reply
card normal   125.00
m. Message card detached   75   50
r. Reply card detached   75   50

Message card inscribed "Postal Card With Paid Reply" in English and French. Reply card inscribed "Reply Postal Card Carte Postale Reponse".

Map Type of Postal Card, 1963

1967, Dec. 4   **For International Use**

UY20   PC27   8c+8c blue & red on white,
unsevered   1.75   35
First day cancel, Washington, D.C.   1.50
m. Message card detached   75   75
r. Reply card detached   75   75

Message card inscribed "Postal Card With Paid Reply" in English and French. Reply card inscribed "Reply Postal Card Carte Postale Résponse."

Lincoln Type of Postal Card, 1968

1968   **Tagged**

UY21   PC33   5c+5c emerald on white, unsevered,
Jan. 4, 1968   1.00   40
First day cancel,
Hodgenville, Ky.   1.50

Paul Revere Type of Postal Card, 1971
Luminescent Ink

1971   **Precanceled with 3 printed brown lines.**

UY22   PC36   6c+6c brown on white, unsevered,
May 15   75   25
First day cancel, Boston, Mass.   1.25

John Hanson Type of Postal Card, 1972
Luminescent Ink

1972   **Precanceled with 3 printed blue lines.**

UY23   PC41   6c+6c blue on white, unsevered,
Sept. 1   60   25
First day cancel,
Baltimore, Md.   75

Samuel Adams Type of Postal Card, 1973
Luminescent Ink

1973   **Precanceled with 3 printed orange lines**

UY24   PC42   8c+8c orange on white,
unsevered, *Dec. 16*   50   25
First day cancel,
Boston, Mass. *(105,369)*   1.00

Thomson, Witherspoon, Rodney, Hale & Hancock Types of Postal Cards, 1975–78
Luminescent Ink

1975–78   **Precanceled with 3 printed emerald lines**

UY25   PC44   7c+7c emerald, unsevered,
Sept. 14, 1975   60   40
First day cancel,
Bryn Mawr, Pa.   80

Precanceled with 3 printed yellow brown lines

UY26   PC45   9c+9c yellow brown, unsevered,
Nov. 10, 1975   60   25
First day cancel,
Princeton, N.J.   1.25

Precanceled with 3 printed blue lines

UY27   PC46   9c+9c blue on white, unsevered,
July 1, 1976   60   30
First day cancel, Dover, Del.   1.00

Precanceled with 3 printed green lines

UY28   PC48   9c+9c green on white, unsevered,
Oct. 14, 1977   60   25
First day cancel,
Coventry, Conn.   1.25

Inscribed "U.S. Domestic Rate"

Precanceled with 3 printed brown orange lines

UY29   PC50   (10c+10c) brn. orange on white,
unsevered,
May 19, 1978   8.50   4.50
First day cancel,
Quincy, Mass.   2.00

Inscribed "U.S. Postage 10¢"

Precanceled with 3 printed brown orange lines

UY30   PC50   10c+10c brn. orange on white,
unsevered,
June 20, 1978   50   25
First day cancel,
Quincy, Mass.   1.50

a. One card "Domestic Rate,"
other "Postage 10¢"

Eagle Type of 1981
Inscribed "U.S. Domestic Rate"
Luminescent Ink

1981, Mar. 15   **Precanceled with 3 printed violet lines**

UY31   PC63   (12c+12c) violet, unsevered   55   15
First day cancel, Memphis, TN   1.10

Isaiah Thomas Type
Luminescent Ink

1981, May 5   **Precanceled with 3 printed lines**

UY32   PC64   12c+12c lt blue   55   15
First day cancel,
Worcester, MA   1.10
a. Small die on one side   3.00

Morris Type of 1981
Inscribed "U.S. Domestic Rate"

1981   **Precanceled with 3 printed lines**

UY33   PC67   (13c+13c) buff, *Oct. 11*   55   15
First day cancel, Memphis, TN   85

Inscribed "U.S. Postage 13¢"

UY34   PC67   13c+13c buff, *Nov. 10*   55   15
First day cancel, Philadelphia, PA   85

Charles Carroll Type of 1985
Inscribed: U.S. Domestic Rate

1985   **Precanceled with 3 printed lines**

UY35   PC79   (14c + 14c) pale grn, *Feb. 1*   56   18
First day cancel,
New Carrollton, MD   90

Inscribed: USA

UY36   PC79   14c + 14c pale green, *Mar. 6*   56   18
First day cancel,
Annapolis, MD   90

George Wythe Type of 1985

1985, June 20   **Precanceled with 3 printed lines**

UY37   PC81   14c + 14c brt apple grn   56   18
First day cancel,
Williamsburg, VA   90

AIR POST POSTAL CARDS

AIR POST POSTAL CARDS.

Eagle in Flight
APC1

1949		Typographed	(1)	(2)	(3)
UXC1	APC1	4c orange red on buff, *Jan. 10, 1949*		35	20	30
		First day cancel, Washington, D.C. *(236,620)*				4.00

1958		Type of Air Post Stamp, 1954.			
UXC2	AP31	5c red on buff, *July 31, 1958*	1.50		40
		First day cancel, Wichita, Kans. *(156,474)*				3.00

1960		Type of 1958 Redrawn Lithographed (Offset).		
UXC3	AP31	5c red on buff, bicolored border, *June 18, 1960*	5.50	1.25
		First day cancel, Minneapolis, Minn. *(228,500)*		2.75

Size of stamp of No. UXC3: 18½x21mm.; on No. UXC2: 19x22mm. White cloud around eagle enlarged and finer detail of design on No. UXC3. Inscription "AIR MAIL—POSTAL CARD" has been omitted and blue and red border added on No. UXC3.

Bald Eagle—APC2
Precanceled with 3 printed red lines.

1963				
UXC4	APC2	6c red on white, bicolored border, *Feb. 15, 1963*	40	20
		First day cancel, Maitland, Fla. *(816,803)*		2.25

Emblem of Commerce Department's Travel Service
APC3

1966

Issued at the Sixth International Philatelic Exhibition (SIPEX), Washington, D.C., May 21–30.

			(1)	(3)
UXC5	APC3	11c blue & red on white, *May 27*	50	25
		First day cancel, Washington, D.C. *(272,813)*		2.00

Four photographs at left on address side show: Mt. Rainier, New York skyline, Indian on horseback and Miami Beach. The card has blue and red border. See also No. UXC8, UXC11.

Virgin Islands and Territorial Flag—APC4
Designed by Burt Pringle.

1967
Lithographed

Issued to commemorate the 50th anniversary of the purchase of the Virgin Islands.

UXC6	APC4	6c multi. on white, *Mar. 31*	35	25
		First day cancel, Charlotte Amalie, V. I. *(346,906)*		1.75
a.	Red & yellow omitted		—	

Borah Peak, Lost River Range, Idaho, and Scout Emblem
APC5

Designed by Stevan Dohanos.

1967, Aug. 4
Lithographed

Issued to commemorate the 12th Boy Scout World Jamboree, Farragut State Park, Idaho, Aug. 1–9.

UXC7	APC5	6c bl., yel., blk. & red on white	35	20
		First day cancel, Farragut State Park, ID *(471,585)*		1.50
a.	Blue omitted		—	
b.	Blue & black omitted		—	
c.	Red & yellow omitted		—	

Travel Service Type of 1966

1967

Issued in connection with the American Air Mail Society Convention, Detroit, Mich.

UXC8	APC3	13c blue & red on white, *Sept. 8*	1.10	50
		First day cancel, Detroit, Mich. *(178,189)*		1.75

Stylized Eagle
APC6

Designed by Muriel R. Chamberlain.

1968–69   Precanceled with 3 printed red lines.

			(1)	(3)
UXC9	APC6	8c blue & red, *March 1*	55	30
		First day cancel, New York, N.Y. *(179,923)*		1.50
		a. Tagged, *Mar. 19, 1969*	1.50	2.00
		Tagged, first day cancel		15.00

Tagged

1971   Precanceled with 3 printed blue lines.

UXC10	APC6	9c red & blue, *May 15*	40	30
		First day cancel, Kitty Hawk, N.C.		2.00

Travel Service Type of 1966

1971   Tagged

UXC11	APC3	15c blue & red, *June 10*	1.00	50
		First day cancel, New York, N.Y.		1.75

U.S. AIR MAIL 9 CENTS
Grand Canyon—APC7

U.S. AIR MAIL 15 CENTS
Niagara Falls—APC8
Tourism Year of the Americas 1972.
Designed by Melbourne Brindle.

1972, June 29   Tagged   Lithographed
Size: 152½x108½mm.

UXC12	APC7	9c black on buff (*Statue of Liberty, Hawaii, Alaska, San Francisco on back*)	45	30
		First day cancel, any city		1.50
UXC13	APC8	15c black on buff (*Mt. Vernon, Washington, D.C., Lincoln, Liberty Bell on back*)	55	35
		First day cancel, any city		1.50
		a. Address side blank	400.00	

See note after No. UX63. Nos. UXC12–UXC13 have a luminescent panel at left of stamp which glows orange under ultraviolet light.

Stylized Eagle—APC9

Eagle Weather Vane
APC10

Designed by David G. Foote (11c) and Stevan Dohanos (18c).

1974, Jan. 4   Tagged   Lithographed

			(1)	(3)
UXC14	APC9	11c ultramarine & red	50	25
		First day cancel, State College, Pa. *(160,500)*		1.25
UXC15	APC10	18c multicolored	70	35
		First day cancel, Miami, Fla. *(132,114)*		1.50

Angel Gabriel Weather Vane
APC11

Designed by Stevan Dohanos.

1975, Dec. 17   Tagged   Lithographed

UXC16	APC11	21c multicolored	70	40
		First day cancel, Kitty Hawk, N.C.		1.50

Nos. UXC14–UXC16 have a luminescent panel at left of stamp which glows orange under ultraviolet light.

Curtiss (JN4H) Jenny—APC12
Designed by Keith Ferris.

1978, Sept. 16   Tagged   Lithographed

UXC17	APC12	21c multicolored	70	35
		First day cancel, San Diego, Cal. *(174,886)*		1.75

No. UXC17 has luminescent panel at left of stamp which glows green under ultraviolet light.

Gymnast
APC13
22nd Olympic Games, Moscow,
July 19–Aug. 3, 1980.
Designed by Robert M. Cunningham.

1979, Dec. 1	Tagged	Lithographed		
UXC18	APC13 21c multicolored		75	35
	First day cancel, Fort Worth, Tex.			1.25

Pangborn, Herndon and Miss Veedol—APC14
First non-stop transpacific flight by Clyde Pangborn and
Hugh Herndon, Jr., 50th anniversary
Designed by Ken Dallison.

1981, Jan. 2	Tagged	Lithographed		
UXC19	APC14 28c multicolored		60	30
	First day cancel, Wenatchee, WA			1.00

Gliders—APC15
Designed by Robert E. Cunningham

1982, Mar. 5	Tagged	Lithographed		
UXC20	APC15 28c magenta, yel, blue & black		60	30
	FDC, Houston, TX (106,932)			1.00

Speedskater—APC16
Designed by Robert Peak

1983, Dec. 29		Lithographed		
UXC21	APC16 28c multicolored		60	30
	First day cancel, Milwaukee, WI			1.00

Martin M-130 China Clipper Seaplane
APC17
Designed by Chuck Hodgson

1985, Feb. 15		Lithographed		
UXC22	APC17 33c multi		66	45
	First day cancel, San Francisco, CA			1.10

Chicago Skyline—APC18
AMERIPEX '86, Chicago, May 22–June 1
Designed by Ray Ameijide

1986, Feb. 1	Tagged	Lithographed		
UXC23	APC18 33c multi		66	45
	First day cancel, Chicago, IL			1.10

OFFICIAL POSTAL CARDS

PO1

1913 Size: 126x76mm.
UZ1 PO1 1c black on white, *July, 1913* 225.00 125.00

All No. UZ1 cards have printed address and printed form on message side.

PO2

1983-1985
UZ2 PO2 13c blue, *Jan. 12* 26 —
          FDC, Washington, DC   75
UZ3 PO2 14c blue, *Feb. 26, 1985* 28 —
          FDC, Washington, DC   80

U.S. REVENUES
BACK-OF-THE-BOOK
OUTSTANDING STOCK

- Revenues
- Tax Paids
- Cinderellas
- Officials
- Match/Medicine
- Documentaries
- Proofs & Essays
- State Revenues
- Early U.S. Stamps

If you have any of the above items, please contact us. We are always ready to buy!

GOLDEN PHILATELICS

Myrna Golden • Jack Golden

(516) 791-1804

Post Office Box 484
Cedarhurst, New York 11516

ARA   BIA

U.S. REVENUES, B-O-B

Excellent stock of 1st, 2nd, 3rd issue Revenues, Reds & Greens; Postage Dues; Officials, Postal Stationery, etc.

- Send SASE for our FREE PRICE LIST.
  - Auctions • Auction Consignments accepted.
  - Want Lists Solicited • Satisfaction Guaranteed

Call or write...

HOUSTONIAN STAMP COMPANY

3000 Wilcrest, Suite 145
Houston, Texas 77042
Ph. 713-556-9412 or 713-784-9847

SCOTT REVENUE PAGES R, RB, RC, RD, RE, RF, RFV, RG, RH, RI, RJA, RK, RL, RV, RVB, RY, PN, PS, S, WS, TS, 132 pages with binder $46; without binder.. 40.00
SPRINGER MATCH & MEDICINE PAGES face varieties, Scott compatible.... 8.00
SPRINGER TELEGRAPH PAGES, Scott compatible............................... 6.00
UNITED STATES REVENUE STAMPS by Rickerson, 64pp, 20pp ill., perfect bound... 6.00
THE BOSTON REVENUE BOOK by Toppan et al, 423 pp, hardbound.......... 35.00
PRIVATE DIE PROPRIETARY MEDICINE STAMPS by Griffenhagen, 78 pp Illustrated.. 6.00
A HANDBOOK FOR UNITED STATES REVENUE STAMPED PAPER by Einstein et al, 99 pp, perfect bound.. 14.00
Above prices include postage. Other books in stock.

- CUSTOM STAMP APPROVALS AGAINST WANT LISTS •

REVENUE SPECIALIST
P.O. Box 15565,
Chattanooga, TN 37415
ARA • ASDA • APS • SPMC

REVENUE STAMPS

The Commissioner of Internal Revenue advertised for bids for revenue stamps in August, 1862, and the contract was awarded to Butler & Carpenter of Philadelphia.

Nos. R1–R102 were used to pay taxes on documents and proprietary articles including playing cards. Until Dec. 25, 1862, the law stated that a stamp could be used only for payment of the tax upon the particular instrument or article specified on its face. After that date, stamps, except the Proprietary, could be used indiscriminately.

Most stamps of the first issue appeared in the latter part of 1862 or early in 1863. The 5c and 10c Proprietary were issued in the fall of 1864, and the 6c Proprietary on April 13, 1871.

Plate numbers and imprints are usually found at the bottom of the plate on all denominations except 25c and $1 to $3.50. On these it is nearly always at the left of the plate. The imprint reads "Engraved by Butler & Carpenter, Philadelphia" or "Jos. R. Carpenter".

Plates were of various sizes: 1c and 2c, 210 subjects (14x15); 3c to 20c, 170 subjects (17x10); 25c to 30c, 102 subjects (17x6); 50c to 70c, 85 subjects (17x5); $1 to $1.90, 90 subjects (15x6); $2 to $10, 73 subjects (12x6); $15 to $50, 54 subjects (9x6); $200, 8 subjects (2x4).

The paper varies, the first employed being thin, hard and brittle until September, 1869, from which time it acquired a softer texture and varied from medium to very thick. Early printings of some revenue stamps occur on paper which appears to have laid lines. Some are found on experimental silk paper, first employed about August, 1870.

Canceling was usually done with pen and ink and all values quoted are for stamps canceled in that way. Handstamped cancellations as a rule sell for more than pen. Printed cancellations are scarce and command much higher prices. Herringbone, punched or other types of cancellation which break the surface of the paper adversely affect prices.

Some of the stamps were in use eight years and were printed several times. Many color variations occurred, particularly if unstable pigments were used and the color was intended to be purple or violet, such as the 4c Proprietary, 30c and $2.50 stamps. Before 1868 dull colors predominate on these and the early red stamps. In later printings of the 4c Proprietary, 30c and $2.50 stamps, red predominates in the mixture and on the dollar values the red is brighter. The early $1.90 stamp is dull purple, imperforate or perforated. In a later printing, perforated only, the purple is darker.

Where a stamp is known in a given form or variety but insufficient information is available on which to base a price, its existence is indicated by a dash.

Part perforate stamps are understood to be imperforate horizontally unless otherwise stated.

Part perforate stamps with an asterisk (*) exist imperforate horizontally or vertically.

Part perforate PAIRS should be imperforate between the stamps as well as imperforate at opposite ends. See illustration **Type A** under "Information For Collectors—Perforations."

All imperforate or part perforate stamps listed are known in pairs or larger multiples. Certain unlisted varieties of this nature exist as singles and specialists believe them genuine.

Prices are for fine specimens. Imperforate and part-perforate singles in very fine or better condition and with large margins usually command substantial premiums.

Documentary revenue stamps were no longer required after Dec. 31, 1967.

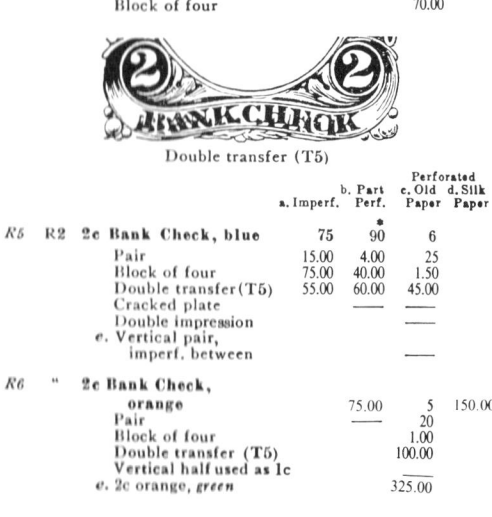

First Issue.

George Washington
R1 — Engraved
1862-71

R2 — Imperf. or Perf. 12

				a. Imperf.	b. Part Perf.	c. Old Paper	d. Silk Paper
R1	R1	1c Express, red		50.00	35.00	1.00	45.00
		Pair		130.00	100.00	2.50	
		Block of four		400.00	375.00	10.00	
		Double transfer					
		Short transfer				100.00	
R2	"	1c Playing Cards, red		750.00	375.00	100.00	
		Pair		1600.00	800.00	225.00	
		Block of four				550.00	
		Cracked plate					
R3	"	1c Proprietary, red		500.00	100.00	.35	4.50
		Pair		1750.00	250.00	.75	
		Block of four			700.00	2.00	

				a. Imperf.	b. Part Perf.	c. Old Paper	d. Silk Paper
R4	R1	1c Telegraph, red		275.00		8.00	
		Pair		700.00		20.00	
		Block of four				70.00	

Double transfer (T5)

				a. Imperf.	b. Part Perf.	c. Old Paper	d. Silk Paper
R5	R2	2c Bank Check, blue		75	90	6	
		Pair		15.00	4.00	.25	
		Block of four		75.00	40.00	1.50	
		Double transfer (T5)		55.00	60.00	45.00	
		Cracked plate					
		Double impression					
		e. Vertical pair, imperf. between					
R6	"	2c Bank Check, orange			75.00	5	150.00
		Pair				.20	
		Block of four				1.00	
		Double transfer (T5)				100.00	
		Vertical half used as 1c					
		e. 2c orange, *green*				325.00	

Michael E. Aldrich
The Revenue Specialist

offers you...

U.S. REVENUE:

Buying-Selling
Consignments
Free Price List
Public & Mail Auctions

MICHAEL E. ALDRICH
P.O. BOX 13323
ST. PAUL, MN 55113
(612) 644-5523

"Deal with the Dealer who deals exclusively in Revenues"

U.S. REVENUES

★ We offer one of America's best stocks of U.S. Back-Of-The-Book with special emphasis on all Scott-listed revenue stamps.

★ We publish price lists for everyone - from beginning to advanced collectors. A current copy is yours FREE on request. Please indicate whether you are a beginning or advanced collector.

★ We gladly accept want lists.

★ We are always buying revenue and telegraph stamps, including taxpaid revenues. What do you have for sale?

Write for a FREE copy of our new illustrated price list.

RICHARD FRIEDBERG

Masonic Building, Suite A-106
Meadville, PA. 16335 ★ 814-724-5824

Member: ASDA, APS, SPA, ARA, USPCS, 1869 PRA

REVENUES

Double transfer (T7)

			a. Imperf.	b. Part Perf.	Perforated c. Old Paper	d. Silk Paper
R7	R2	2c Certificate, blue	10.00		20.00	
		Pair	30.00		50.00	
		Block of four	125.00		150.00	
		Double transfer (T7)	150.00		160.00	
		Cracked plate			30.00	
R8	"	2c Certificate, orange			20.00	
		Pair			125.00	
		Block of four			—	
		Double transfer (T7)			250.00	
R9	"	2c Express, blue	10.00	*12.00	25	
		Pair	30.00	30.00	75	
		Block of four	90.00	125.00	2.50	
		Double transfer	50.00		15.00	
		Cracked plate			—	
R10	"	2c Express, orange			6.00	27.50
		Pair			14.00	
		Block of four			35.00	
		Double transfer			21.00	
R11	"	2c Playing Cards, blue		130.00	2.50	
		Pair		400.00	10.00	
		Block of four			40.00	
		Cracked plate			—	
R12	"	2c Playing Cards, orange			25.00	
		Pair			—	

Double transfer (T13)

Double transfer (T13a)

R13	R2	2c Proprietary, blue	120.00	35	10.00	
		Pair	260.00	80		
		Block of four	750.00	5.00		
		Double transfer(T13)		70.00		
		Complete double transfer (T13a)		100.00		
		Cracked plate		25.00		
		Horizontal half used as 1c		—		
		e. 2c ultramarine		120.00		
		Pair		260.00		
		Block of four		700.00		
		Double transfer		—		
R14	"	2c Proprietary, orange		30.00		
		Pair		—		
		Block of four		—		
		Double transfer (T13)		110.00		
		Complete double transfer (T13a)		350.00		

Double transfer (T15)

Double transfer (T15a)

			a. Imperf.	b. Part Perf.	Perforated c. Old Paper	d. Silk Paper
R15	R2	2c U. S. Internal Revenue, orange ('64)			5	6
		Pair			10	
		Block of four			40	
		Double transfer (T15)			60.00	
		Double transfer (T15a)			45.00	
		Double transfer			12.00	
		Triple transfer			40.00	
		Cracked plate			—	
		Half used as 1c				
		e. 2c orange, green			350.00	

R3

R16	R3	3c Foreign Exchange, green		130.00	2.50	13.00
		Pair			5.75	
		Block of four			45.00	
		Double transfer			—	
R17	"	3c Playing Cards, green ('63)	5000.00		100.00	
		Pair	15,000.00		275.00	
		Block of four			700.00	
R18	"	3c Proprietary, green		175.00	1.75	11.00
		Pair		450.00	4.50	—
		Block of four			15.00	
		Double transfer			8.00	
		Double impression			—	
		e. Printed on both sides				
R19	"	3c Telegraph, green	45.00	16.00	2.25	—
		Pair	160.00	35.00	6.00	
		Block of four	600.00	150.00	50.00	
R20	"	4c Inland Exchange, brown ('63)			1.50	13.00
		Pair			4.50	
		Block of four			20.00	
		Double transfer at top			4.00	
R21	"	4c Playing Cards, slate ('63)			300.00	
		Pair			750.00	
		Block of four			1750.00	
R22	"	4c Proprietary, purple		170.00	2.50	17.50
		Pair		425.00	6.00	
		Block of four			25.00	
		Double transfer at top			7.50	
		Double transfer at bottom			11.00	

There are shade and color variations of Nos. R21–R22. See foreword of Revenue Stamps section.

REVENUES

			a. Imperf.	b. Part Perf.	Perforated c. Old Paper	d. Silk Paper
R23	R3	5c Agreement, red			20	90
		Pair			40	2.50
		Block of four			1.25	12.50
		Double transfer in numerals			25.00	
R24	"	5c Certificate, red	2.50	8.00	10	25
		Pair	25.00	60.00	20	90
		Block of four	125.00	200.00	60	6.00
		Double transfer in upper label			10.00	
		Double transfer throughout			70.00	
		Triple transfer (No. 121)			35.00	
		Impression of No. R3 on back			—	
R25	"	5c Express, red	3.50	4.00*	25	
		Pair	12.00	40.00	60	
		Block of four	60.00	100.00	2.00	
		Double transfer			5.00	
R26	"	5c Foreign Exchange, red	—		25	100.00
		Pair	—		75	
		Block of four			10.00	
		Double transfer at top			—	
		Double transfer at bottom			—	
R27	"	5c Inland Exchange, red	3.50	3.00	10	5.50
		Pair	20.00	15.00	20	
		Block of four	50.00	50.00	1.25	
		Dbl. transfer at top	60.00	40.00	25.00	
		Cracked plate	60.00	60.00	30.00	
R28	"	5c Playing Cards, red ('63)			12.00	
		Pair			26.00	
		Block of four			60.00	
		Double impression			250.00	
R29	"	5c Proprietary, red ('64)			16.00	35.00
		Pair			40.00	
		Block of four			120.00	
R30	"	6c Inland Exchange, orange ('63)			90	20.00
		Pair			10.00	
		Block of four			60.00	
R31	"	6c Proprietary, orange ('71)			2500.00	
R32	"	10c Bill of Lading, blue	45.00	125.00	85	
		Pair	125.00	450.00	2.00	
		Block of four	325.00		7.00	
		Double transfer (Nos. 33 & 143)			—	
		Half used as 5c			200.00	
R33	"	10c Certificate, blue	90.00	95.00*	20	2.25
		Pair	225.00	225.00	45	
		Block of four	1000.00	—	1.50	
		Double transfer			7.00	
		Cracked plate			15.00	
R34	"	10c Contract, blue		90.00	20	1.50
		Pair		225.00	50	4.00
		Block of four		—	2.00	50.00
		Complete double transfer			70.00	
		Vertical half used as 5c			200.00	
		e. 10c ultramarine		225.00	50	
		Pair			1.25	
		Block of four			15.00	
R35	"	10c Foreign Exchange, blue			3.00	—
		Pair			7.00	
		Block of four			35.00	
		e. 10c ultramarine			6.50	
		Pair			15.00	
		Block of four			35.00	

			a. Imperf.	b. Part Perf.	Perforated c. Old Paper	d. Silk Paper
R36	R3	10c Inland Exchange, blue	120.00	3.00*	15	13.00
		Pair	275.00	10.00	35	—
		Block of four	750.00	50.00	1.50	—
		Half used as 5c			200.00	
R37	"	10c Power of Attorney, blue	300.00	17.00	25	
		Pair	650.00	65.00	60	
		Block of four	1800.00	200.00	3.50	
		Half used as 5c			200.00	
R38	"	10c Proprietary, blue ('64)			13.00	
		Pair			30.00	
		Block of four			75.00	
R39	"	15c Foreign Exchange, brown ('63)			12.00	
		Pair			45.00	
		Block of four			225.00	
		Double impression			500.00	
R40	"	15c Inland Exchange, brown	25.00	10.00	1.00	
		Pair	95.00	30.00	2.25	
		Block of four	325.00	150.00	8.00	
		Double transfer			5.00	
		Cracked plate	40.00		—	
		Double impression		—	550.00	
R41	"	20c Foreign Exchange, red	40.00		30.00	
		Pair	125.00		70.00	
		Block of four	500.00		200.00	
R42	"	20c Inland Exchange, red	12.00	16.00	30	—
		Pair	50.00	45.00	70	—
		Block of four	160.00	150.00	12.50	
		Half used as 10c			200.00	

R4

R5

R43	R4	25c Bond, red	80.00	5.00	1.50	
		Pair	350.00	35.00	4.00	
		Block of four		200.00	40.00	
R44	"	25c Certificate, red	5.00	5.00*	10	1.50
		Pair	35.00	30.00	20	—
		Block of four	300.00	150.00	2.50	—
		Double transfer, top or bottom			2.00	
		Triple transfer			—	
		e. Printed on both sides			—	
		f. Impression of No. R48 on back			6500.00	
R45	"	25c Entry of Goods, red	15.00	30.00*	40	6.75
		Pair	55.00	—	35.00	
		Block of four	300.00			
		Top frame line double	60.00	75.00	10.00	
R46	"	25c Insurance, red	8.00	9.00	20	2.25
		Pair	35.00	20.00	50	—
		Block of four	500.00	175.00	5.00	
		Double impression			—	
		Cracked plate			15.00	

REVENUES

			a. Imperf.	b. Part Perf.	Perforated c. Old Paper	d. Silk Paper
R47	R4	25c Life Insurance, red	30.00	100.00	4.00	
		Pair	90.00	500.00	75.00	
		Block of four	—	—		
R48	"	25c Power of Attorney, red	5.00	15.00	20	
		Pair	40.00	55.00	50	
		Block of four	300.00	200.00	6.00	
		Double transfer			1.00	
		Bottom frame line double			3.00	
R49	"	25c Protest, red	20.00	125.00	5.00	
		Pair	80.00	300.00	25.00	
		Block of four	350.00		100.00	
R50	"	25c Warehouse Receipt, red	35.00	125.00	20.00	
		Pair	100.00	300.00	65.00	
		Block of four	750.00		200.00	
R51	"	30c Foreign Exchange, lilac	60.00	300.00	35.00	
		Pair	250.00	750.00	150.00	
		Block of four	—	—		
		Double transfer			70.00	
		Top frame line double			—	
R52	"	30c Inland Exchange, lilac	35.00	40.00	2.00	
		Pair	100.00	150.00	25.00	
		Block of four	—	—	100.00	
		Double transfer			—	

There are shade and color variations of Nos. R51-R52. See foreword of "Revenues" section.

			a. Imperf.	b. Part Perf.	c. Old Paper	d. Silk Paper
R53	R4	40c Inland Exchange, brown	425.00	3.50	2.00	—
		Pair		15.00	5.00	
		Block of four		150.00	100.00	
		Double transfer			35.00	25.00
R54	R5	50c Conveyance, blue	10.00	1.00	10	2.25
		Pair	50.00	30.00	25	6.00
		Block of four	250.00	100.00	2.50	
		Double transfer			6.00	
		Cracked plate			15.00	
		e. 50c ultramarine			20	—
		Pair			1.00	
		Block of four			10.00	
R55	"	50c Entry of Goods, blue		10.00	20	10.00
		Pair		60.00	50	
		Block of four		—	20.00	
		Double transfer			4.00	
		Cracked plate			20.00	
R56	"	50c Foreign Exchange, blue	35.00	30.00	4.00	
		Pair	85.00	80.00	30.00	
		Block of four			100.00	
		Double impression			—	
		Double transfer at left			10.00	
		Half used as 25c			200.00	
R57	"	50c Lease, blue	20.00	50.00	5.00	
		Pair	80.00	130.00	100.00	
		Block of four	650.00	400.00	225.00	
R58	"	50c Life Insurance, blue	25.00	50.00	60	
		Pair	80.00		5.00	
		Block of four	400.00		30.00	
		Double transfer	25.00		10.00	
		Double impression			—	

Cracked Plate (C59)

			a. Imperf.	b. Part Perf.	Perforated c. Old Paper	d. Silk Paper
R59	R5	50c Mortgage, blue	10.00	1.50	30	18.00
		Pair	40.00	40.00	70	
		Block of four	160.00	150.00	5.00	
		Cracked plate (C59)		40.00	15.00	
		Scratched plate, diagonal	40.00	30.00	15.00	
		Double transfer			3.00	
		Double impression			—	
R60	"	50c Original Process, blue	2.50		25	1.25
		Pair	45.00		60	—
		Block of four	300.00		2.50	
		Double transfer at top			5.00	
		Double transfer at bottom			8.00	
		Cracked plate			10.00	
R61	"	50c Passage Ticket, blue	60.00	100.00	50	
		Pair	175.00	225.00	5.00	
		Block of four			90.00	
R62	"	50c Probate of Will, blue	30.00	40.00	15.00	
		Pair	80.00	90.00	40.00	
		Block of four	375.00	350.00		
R63	"	50c Surety Bond, blue	120.00	2.00	15	
		Pair	800.00	12.00	1.00	
		Block of four		75.00	8.00	
		e. 50c ultramarine			80	
		Pair			5.00	
		Block of four			50.00	
R64	"	60c Inland Exchange, orange	75.00	40.00	5.00	17.50
		Pair	175.00	90.00	12.00	
		Block of four	600.00	300.00	75.00	
R65	"	70c Foreign Exchange, green	300.00	80.00	5.00	17.50
		Pair		225.00	20.00	50.00
		Block of four		1000.00	150.00	
		Cracked plate			25.00	
		e. Vert. pair, imperf. between				

R6   R7

			a. Imperf.	b. Part Perf.	c. Old Paper	d. Silk Paper
R66	R6	$1 Conveyance, red	10.00	250.00	1.75	22.50
		Pair	40.00	1250.00	5.00	
		Block of four	250.00		20.00	
		Double transfer	25.00		5.50	
		Right frame line double	70.00		15.00	
		Top frame line double			12.00	
R67	"	$1 Entry of Goods, red	25.00		1.25	17.50
		Pair	80.00		4.00	
		Block of four	275.00		40.00	
R68	"	$1 Foreign Exchange, red	45.00		50	10.00
		Pair	120.00		1.25	
		Block of four			9.00	
		Double transfer			4.00	
		Left frame line double	125.00		12.50	
		Diagonal half used as 50c				200.00
R69	"	$1 Inland Exchange, red	10.00	225.00	35	1.25
		Pair	45.00	1500.00	1.50	5.00
		Block of four	425.00		8.00	20.00
		Double transfer at bottom			3.50	
		Double transfer of top shields	75.00		30.00	

			a.Imperf.	b. Part Perf.	Perforated c.Old Paper	d.Silk Paper
R70	R6	$1 Lease, red	30.00		1.00	
		Pair	80.00		5.00	
		Block of four	350.00		40.00	
		Double transfer at bottom	40.00		7.50	
		Cracked plate			25.00	
R71	"	$1 Life Insurance, red	130.00		4.00	
		Pair	275.00		10.00	
		Block of four	600.00		45.00	
		Right frame line double	250.00		17.50	
R72	"	$1 Manifest, red	50.00		20.00	
		Pair	120.00		45.00	
		Block of four	275.00		120.00	
R73	"	$1 Mortgage, red	18.00		125.00	
		Pair	50.00		275.00	
		Block of four	250.00		600.00	
		Double transfer at left	—		150.00	
		Bottom frame line double	75.00		200.00	
R74	"	$1 Passage Ticket, red	150.00		125.00	
		Pair	325.00		275.00	
		Block of four	700.00		700.00	
R75	"	$1 Power of Attorney, red	60.00		1.25	
		Pair	140.00		4.00	
		Block of four	325.00		18.00	
		Double transfer			7.50	
		Recut			10.00	
R76	"	$1 Probate of Will, red	55.00		30.00	
		Pair	140.00		75.00	
		Block of four	550.00		200.00	
		Right frame line double	125.00		60.00	
R77	R7	$1.30 Foreign Exchange, orange ('63)	1850.00		50.00	
		Pair			125.00	
		Block of four			—	

Double transfer (T78)

			a.Imperf.	b. Part Perf.	Perforated c.Old Paper	d.Silk Paper
R78	R7	$1.50 Inland Exchange, blue	20.00		2.25	
		Pair	80.00		40.00	
		Block of four	250.00		225.00	
		Double transfer (T78)			8.50	
R79	R7	$1.60 Foreign Exchange, green ('63)	600.00		80.00	
		Pair	3000.00		—	
R80	"	$1.90 Foreign Exchange, purple ('63)	1700.00		60.00	90.00
		Pair			130.00	
		Block of four			350.00	

There are many shade and color variations of No. R80. See foreword of "Revenues" section.

R8

R81	R8	$2 Conveyance, red	85.00	700.00	1.25	10.00
		Pair	200.00	—	5.00	
		Block of four	600.00		35.00	
		Cracked plate			—	
		Half used as $1			—	
R82	"	$2 Mortgage, red	75.00		2.00	22.50
		Pair	180.00		6.00	
		Block of four	450.00		35.00	
		Double transfer			10.00	
		Half used as $1			—	
R83	"	$2 Probate of Will, red ('63)	2100.00		40.00	
		Pair	4400.00		90.00	
		Block of four			225.00	
		Double transfer			60.00	
R84	"	$2.50 Inland Exchange, purple ('63)	850.00		2.50	10.00
		Pair	—		8.00	25.00
		Block of four			75.00	350.00
		Double impression				

There are many shade and color variations of Nos. R84c and R84d. See foreword of "Revenues" section.

R85	R8	$3 Charter Party, green	90.00		3.00	25.00
		Pair	260.00		40.00	65.00
		Block of four	—		150.00	
		Double transfer at top				
		Double transfer at bottom			9.00	
		Half used as $1.50			—	
		e. Printed on both sides			2000.00	
		g. Impression of No. RS208 on back			4000.00	
R86	"	$3 Manifest, green	85.00		20.00	
		Pair	210.00		50.00	
		Block of four	1000.00		150.00	
		Double transfer			30.00	
R87	"	$3.50 Inland Exchange, blue ('63)	850.00		45.00	
		Pair	2300.00		120.00	
		Block of four			350.00	

Start your
U.S. COLLECTION
with.... SCOTT

Scott's U.S. Minuteman Stamp Album!

FEATURES...

★ The famous Scott Catalogue identification number for every stamp.

★ Exciting stories of almost every stamp.

★ Attractive vinyl binder. ★ Supplemented annually.

"A must for every collector of United States postage stamps."

Available at your local dealer or direct from Scott Publishing Co.

Scott Publishing Company
P.O. Box 828, Sidney, OH 45365

REVENUES

QUALITY MATERIAL AT FAIR MARKET PRICES

YOU AND YOUR COLLECTION . . .

. . . can benefit from our experience in both buying and selling, appraisals, expertizing, mail sales, attendance at major stamp shows, auction representation, and periodic price lists.

YOUR WANT LISTS . . .

. . . can be filled from our extensive and specialized inventory of all types of U.S. Revenues. All Scott-listed revenues are represented in stock, including embossed and revenue stamped paper and match & medicine. All types of Taxpaid revenues, including beer stamps, tobacco, cigar, butter and oleo stamps, etc., are available. State revenues and possessions revenues are also well represented. We deal in U.S. local posts and telegraph stamps as well.

BUYING OR SELLING
contact

ERIC JACKSON
WHITTIER PHILATELIC SERVICES
6727 S. Washington Ave., P.O. Box 651, Whittier, CA 90608
(213) 698-3193 or 2888

MEMBER

BUREAU ISSUES ASSOCIATION
AMERICAN PHILATELIC CONGRESS
CONFEDERATE STAMP ALLIANCE
ESSAY-PROOF SOCIETY
U.S. POSSESSIONS PHIL. SOC.

AMERICAN REVENUE ASSOCIATION
STATE REVENUE SOCIETY
CHECK COLLECTORS ROUNDTABLE
CINDERELLA STAMP CLUB
COLLECTORS CLUB OF NEW YORK

REVENUES 641

R9

R10

			a.Imperf.	b.Part Perf.	Perforated c.Old Paper	d.Silk Paper
R99	R10	$20 Probate of Will, orange	900.00		850.00	
		Pair	1900.00		1750.00	
		Block of four	4250.00		3750.00	
R100	"	$25 Mortgage, red ('63)	700.00		80.00	125.00
		Pair	1500.00		190.00	
		Block of four	—		900.00	
		e. Horiz. pair, imperf. between			1000.00	
R101	"	$50 U.S. Internal Revenue, green ('63)	150.00		85.00	
		Pair	325.00		190.00	
		Block of four	800.00		450.00	
		Cracked plate			—	

R11

			a.Imperf.	b.Part Perf.	c.Old Paper	d.Silk Paper
R102	R11	$200 U.S. Internal Revenue, green & red ('64)	1000.00		550.00	
		Pair	2250.00		1200.00	
		Block of four	5500.00		2750.00	

DOCUMENTARY STAMPS
Second Issue.

After release of the First Issue revenue stamps, the Bureau of Internal Revenue received many reports of fraudulent cleaning and re-use. The Bureau ordered a Second Issue with new designs and colors, using a patented "chameleon" paper which is usually violet or pinkish, with silk fibers.

While designs are different from those of the first issue, stamp sizes and make up of the plates are the same for corresponding denominations.

R12

R12a

George Washington

Engraved and printed by Jos. R. Carpenter, Philadelphia.

Various Frames and Numeral Arrangements

1871 *Perf. 12*

			Single	Pair	Block of Four
R103	R12	1c blue & black	25.00	60.00	150.00
		a. Inverted center	1300.00		
R104	"	2c blue & black	1.00	3.00	15.00
		a. Inverted center	4500.00		
R105	R12a	3c blue & black	12.00	27.50	60.00
R106	"	4c blue & black	45.00	110.00	
		Horiz. or vert. half used as 2c	—		
R107	"	5c blue & black	1.00	2.50	10.00
		a. Inverted center	1850.00		

			a.Imperf.	b.Part Perf.	Perforated c.Old Paper	d.Silk Paper
R88	R9	$5 Charter Party, red	225.00		4.00	22.50
		Pair	500.00		50.00	
		Block of four	—		150.00	
		Right frame line double	350.00		50.00	
		Top frame line double	300.00		50.00	
R89	"	$5 Conveyance, red	30.00		3.00	20.00
		Pair	95.00		10.00	
		Block of four	500.00		25.00	
R90	"	$5 Manifest, red	80.00		80.00	
		Pair	225.00		200.00	
		Block of four	1000.00		500.00	
		Left frame line double	125.00		125.00	
R91	"	$5 Mortgage, red	80.00		15.00	
		Pair	400.00		60.00	
		Block of four	—		—	
R92	"	$5 Probate of Will, red	375.00		15.00	
		Pair	800.00		70.00	
		Block of four	1750.00		300.00	
R93	"	$10 Charter Party, green	350.00		20.00	
		Pair	900.00		60.00	
		Block of four	—		300.00	
		Double transfer			60.00	
R94	"	$10 Conveyance, green	70.00		50.00	
		Pair	160.00		120.00	
		Block of four	400.00		600.00	
		Double transfer at top	100.00		80.00	
		Right frame line double	125.00			
R95	"	$10 Mortgage, green	325.00		20.00	
		Pair	700.00		80.00	
		Block of four	—		—	
		Top frame line double	350.00		50.00	
R96	"	$10 Probate of Will, green	800.00		20.00	
		Pair	—		60.00	
		Block of four	—		250.00	
		Double transfer at top			45.00	
R97	R10	$15 Mortgage, blue	900.00		100.00	
		Pair	2100.00		275.00	
		Block of four	4500.00		2500.00	
		e. $15 ultramarine			150.00	
		Pair			300.00	
		Block of four Milky blue			150.00	
R98	"	$20 Conveyance, orange	45.00		25.00	40.00
		Pair	130.00		70.00	100.00
		Block of four	300.00		225.00	

REVENUES

			Single	Pair	Block of Four
R108	R12a	6c blue & black	65.00	150.00	450.00
R109	"	10c blue & black	75	2.00	6.00
		Double impression of medallion	—		
		Half used as 5c	—		
		a. Inverted center	1650.00		
R110	"	15c blue & black	20.00	42.50	95.00
R111	"	20c blue & black	4.00	9.00	35.00
		a. Inverted center	7500.00		

			Single	Pair	Block of Four
R119	R13b	$1.30 blue & black	200.00	500.00	
R120	"	$1.50 blue & black	10.00	30.00	—
		a. Sewing machine perf.	350.00	—	
R121	"	$1.60 blue & black	300.00	750.00	
R122	"	$1.90 blue & black	120.00	275.00	
R123	R13c	$2 blue & black	10.00	25.00	100.00
		Double transfer	15.00		
R124	"	$2.50 blue & black	18.00	45.00	525.00
R125	"	$3 blue & black	30.00	80.00	
		Double transfer	—		
R126	"	$3.50 blue & black	100.00	250.00	

R13

R13a

R112	R13	25c blue & black	50	1.50	7.50
		Double transfer, position 57	15.00		
		a. Inverted center	9500.00		
		b. Sewing machine perf.	90.00	250.00	750.00
		c. Perf. 8	250.00		
R113	"	30c blue & black	45.00	100.00	275.00
R114	"	40c " "	27.50	90.00	
R115	R13a	50c blue & black	50	1.25	6.50
		Double transfer	15.00		
		a. Sewing machine perf.	90.00	200.00	1200.00
		b. Inverted center	650.00	1800.00	
		Inverted center, punch cancellation	200.00	500.00	
R116	"	60c blue & black	55.00	150.00	
		Double transfer, design of 70c	125.00		
R117	"	70c blue & black	22.50	80.00	
		a. Inverted center	3000.00		

R13d

R13e

R127	R13d	$5 blue & black	15.00	40.00	150.00
		a. Inverted center	2150.00		
		Inverted center, punch cancel	600.00		
R128	"	$10 blue & black	100.00	225.00	
R129	R13e	$20 " "	300.00	650.00	
R130	"	$25 " "	300.00	650.00	
R131	"	$50 " "	325.00	700.00	

R13b

R13c

R13f

R118	R13b	$1 blue & black	2.50	6.00	20.00
		a. Inverted center	5250.00		
		Inverted center, punch cancellation	1000.00		

R132	R13f	$200 blue, black & red	5250.00

REVENUES

R13g

R133 R13g $500 blk., green & red   15,000.00

Inverted Centers: Fraudulently produced inverted centers exist, some excellently made.

Third Issue.

Confusion resulting from the fact that all denominations of the Second Issue were uniform in color, caused the ordering of a new printing with values in distinctive colors.
Plates used were those of the preceding issue.

Engraved and printed by Jos. R. Carpenter, Philadelphia.

Various Frames and Numeral Arrangements.

Violet 'Chameleon' Paper with Silk Fibers.

1871-72   Perf. 12.

			Single	Pair	Block of Four
R134	R12	1c claret & black ('72)	20.00	50.00	175.00
R135	"	2c orange & black	5	12	1.00
		Double transfer			
		Double impression of frame			
		Frame printed on both sides	1000.00		
		Double impression of head	150.00		
		a. 2c vermilion & black (error)	400.00		
		b. Inverted center	250.00	600.00	
R136	R12a	4c brown & black ('72)	27.50	70.00	
R137	"	5c orange & black	20	40	1.00
		a. Inverted center	1500.00		
R138	"	6c orange & black ('72)	27.50	60.00	150.00
R139	"	15c brown & black ('72)	7.50	20.00	110.00
		a. Inverted center	8000.00		
R140	R13	30c orange & black ('72)	10.00	25.00	
		Double transfer			
		a. Inverted center	1350.00		
R141	"	40c brown & black ('72)	17.50	50.00	125.00
R142	"	60c orange & black ('72)	45.00	100.00	225.00
		Double transfer, design of 70c	150.00		

			Single	Pair	Block of Four
R143	R13	70c green & black ('72)	27.50	75.00	
R144	R13b	$1 green & black ('72)	1.00	3.00	25.00
		a. Inverted center	7000.00		
R145	R13c	$2 vermilion & black ('72)	18.00	40.00	140.00
		Double transfer	25.00		
R146	"	$2.50 claret & black ('72)	30.00	70.00	175.00
		a. Inverted center	15,000.00		
R147	"	$3 green & black ('72)	30.00	80.00	250.00
		Double transfer			
R148	R13d	$5 vermilion & black ('72)	16.00	40.00	100.00
R149	"	$10 green & black ('72)	85.00	200.00	700.00
R150	R13e	$20 orange & black ('72)	375.00	800.00	
		a. $20 vermilion & black (error)	500.00		

(See note on Inverted Centers after No. R133.)

1874   Perf. 12

R151	R12	2c orange & black, green	6	12	60
		a. Inverted center	325.00		

Liberty
R14

1875-78   Silk Paper   Wmkd. U S I R (191R)
            a. Perf.   b. Perf. c. Rouletted 6

R152	R14	2c blue, *blue*	6	6	32.50
		Pair	15	15	125.00
		Block of four	50	60	
		Double transfer	5.00	5.00	
		d. Vert. pair, imperf. horiz.	100.00		
		e. Imperf., pair	250.00		

The watermarked paper came into use in 1878.

1898   Postage Stamps of 1895-98 Overprinted:

I. R.   I. R.
  a   b

Overprint "a" exists in two or possibly more settings, with upright rectangular periods, as illustrated, or with square periods. Overprint "b" has 4 stamps with small period in each sheet of 100.

Wmkd. USPS (191)

Perf. 12.   Unused Used

R153	A87	1c green, red overprint (a)	1.00	90
		Block of four	6.00	5.00
		Margin strip of 3, Impt. & P #	17.50	
		Margin block of 6, Impt. & P #	50.00	
R154	"	1c green, red overprint (b)	12	10
		Block of four	50	45
		Margin strip of 3, Impt. & P #	9.00	
		Margin block of 6, Impt. & P #	40.00	
		a. Overprint inverted	7.50	6.00
		a. Block of four	32.50	
		a. Margin strip of 3, Impt. & P #	40.00	
		a. Margin block of 6, Impt. & P #	90.00	
		b. Overprint on back instead of face, inverted		
		c. Pair, one without overprint		
R155	A88	2c carmine, blue overprint (b)	15	6
		Block of four	65	30
		Margin strip of 3, Impt. & P #	8.50	
		Margin block of 6, Impt. & P #	30.00	
		a. Overprint inverted	90	65
		a. Block of four	4.00	3.00
		b. Pair, one without overprint	400.00	
		c. Overprint on back instead of face, inverted	400.00	

Handstamped Type "b" in Magenta

R156	A93	8c *violet brown*		2000.00
R157	A94	10c *dark green*		2250.00
R158	A95	15c *dark blue*		2750.00

Nos. R156-R158 were emergency provisionals, privately prepared, not officially issued.

REVENUES

Privately Prepared Provisionals

I. R.
L. H. C.

No. 285 Overprinted in Red

1898   *Perf. 12*   Wmk. 191

R158A A100 1c dark yellow green — 3500.00
    Same Overprinted "I.R./P.I.D. & Son" in Red.
R158B A100 1c dark yellow green — 6000.00

Nos. R158A-R158B were overprinted with federal government permission by the Purvis Printing Co. upon order of Capt. L. H. Chapman of the Chapman Steamboat Line. Both the Chapman Line and P. I. Daprix & Son operated freight-carrying steamboats on the Erie Canal. The Chapman Line touched at Syracuse, Utica, Little Falls and Fort Plain; the Daprix boat ran between Utica and Rome. Overprintings of 250 of each stamp were made.

Dr. Kilmer & Co. provisional overprints are listed under "Private Die Medicine Stamps," Nos. RS307–RS315.

Newspaper Stamp No. PR121 Surcharged in Red:

1898   *Perf. 12.*

		Unused	Used
R159 N18	$5 dark blue, surcharge reading down	150.00	125.00
	Block of four	650.00	550.00
	a. Margin strip of 3, Impt. & P #	—	
	a. "OCUMENTARY"	300.00	200.00
R160 "	$5 dark blue, surcharge reading up	75.00	50.00
	Block of four	350.00	—
	Margin strip of 3, Impt. & P #	—	
	a. "OCUMENTARY"	300.00	200.00

Battleship
R15

There are two styles of rouletting for the proprietary and documentary stamps of the 1898 issue, an ordinary rouletting 5½ and one by which small rectangles of the paper are cut out, usually called hyphen-hole perforation 7. Several stamps are known with an apparent roulette 14 caused by slippage of a hyphen-hole 7 rouletting wheel.

1898   Wmkd. USIR (191R)
      Rouletted 5½, 7.

			r. Rouletted 5½		p. Hyphen Hole Perf. 7	
			Unused	Used	Unused	Used
R161 R15	½c orange		1.50	5.00		
	Block of four		7.00	35.00		
R162 "	½c dark gray		15	10		
	Block of four		75	50		
	a. Vert. pair, imperf. horiz.		40.00			
R163 "	1c pale blue		8	5	25	15
	Block of four		40	25	2.50	1.25
	Double transfer		—			
	a. Vert. pair, imperf. horiz.		7.50			
R164 "	2c carmine rose		10	5	30	10
	Block of four		45	25	2.50	50
	Double transfer		1.00	25		
	a. Vert. pair, imperf. horiz.		30.00			
	b. Imperf., pair		125.00			
	c. Horiz. pair, imperf. vert.		—			
R165 R15	3c dark blue		70	12	2.00	25
	Block of four		3.50	75	9.00	1.50
	Double transfer		—			
R166 "	4c pale rose		25	10	60	25
	Block of four		1.25	50	3.00	1.50
	a. Vert. pair, imperf. horiz.		75.00			
R167 "	5c lilac		15	6	40	15
	Block of four		75	30	2.00	1.00
	a. Pair, imperf. horiz. or vert.		125.00	75.00		
R168 "	10c dark brown		20	6	40	15
	Block of four		1.00	30	2.00	75
	a. Vert. pair, imperf. horiz.		20.00	20.00		
	b. Horiz. pair, imperf. vert.		—			
R169 "	25c purple brown		20	10	50	20
	Block of four		1.00	50	2.50	1.00
	Double transfer		—			
R170 "	40c blue lilac		30.00	1.00	40.00	10.00
	Block of four		150.00	50.00	175.00	100.00
	Cut cancellation			15		
R171 "	50c slate violet		2.50	12	4.00	20
	Block of four		12.50	2.00	25.00	2.00
	a. Imperf., pair		300.00			
	b. Horiz. pair, imperf. between		—			
R172 "	80c bistre		15.00	25	40.00	15.00
	Block of four		75.00	30.00	175.00	100.00
	Cut cancellation			8		

Numerous double transfers exist on this issue.

Commerce
R16

R173 R16	$1 dark green	2.50	10	—	30
	Block of four	—	50		1.50
	a. Vert. pair, imperf. horiz.				
	b. Horiz. pair, imperf. vert.	—	250.00		
R174 "	$3 dark brown	5.50	20	—	1.00
	Block of four	—	1.25		4.50
	Cut cancellation		12		25
	a. Horiz. pair, imperf. vert.	300.00			

Rouletted 5½.

R175 R16	$5 orange red	—	1.00
	Block of four	—	6.00
	Cut cancellation		18
R176 "	$10 black	22.50	2.25
	Block of four		12.00
	Cut cancellation		50
	a. Horiz. pair, imperf. vert.	—	
R177 "	$30 red	110.00	70.00
	Block of four		325.00
	Cut cancellation		25.00
R178 "	$50 gray brown	45.00	2.50
	Block of four		12.00
	Cut cancellation		1.25

REVENUES

John Marshall
R17

Alexander Hamilton
R18

James Madison
R19

Various Portraits in Various Frames, Each Inscribed "Series of 1898."

1899	Without Gum			Imperf.
R179 R17	$100 yellow brown & black		50.00	25.00
	Vertical strip of four		—	110.00
	Cut cancellation			12.00
	Vertical strip of four, cut canc.	—	45.00
R180 R18	$500 carmine lake & black			400.00
	Vertical strip of four		—	1700.00
	Cut cancellation			175.00
	Vertical strip of four, cut canc.	400.00	750.00
R181 R19	$1000 green & black			300.00
	Vertical strip of four		—	1300.00
	Cut cancellation			90.00
	Vertical strip of four, cut canc.		400.00

1900	Hyphen-hole Perf. 7		
	Allegorical Figure of Commerce.		
R182 R16	$1 carmine	4.50	40
	Block of four	—	2.25
	Cut cancellation		10
	Block of four, cut canc.		50
R183 "	$3 lake (fugitive ink)	50.00	35.00
	Block of four	—	175.00
	Cut cancellation		7.00
	Block of four, cut canc.		30.00

Surcharged in Black with Open Numerals of Value.

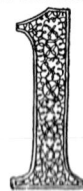

R184 R16	$1 gray	2.50	12
	Block of four	—	55
	Cut cancellation		6
	Block of four, cut canc.		30
	a. Horiz. pair, imperf. vert		
	b. Surcharge omitted	100.00	
	Surcharge omitted, cut canc.		80.00
R185 "	$2 gray	2.25	12
	Block of four	11.00	50
	Cut cancellation		6
	Block of four, cut canc.		30

R186 R16	$3 gray	20.00	10.00
	Block of four	—	45.00
	Cut cancellation		1.50
	Block of four, cut canc.		7.00
R187 "	$5 gray	12.00	4.00
	Block of four	—	17.50
	Cut cancellation		25
	Block of four, cut canc.		1.25
R188 "	$10 gray	35.00	9.00
	Block of four	—	40.00
	Cut cancellation		3.00
	Block of four, cut canc.		14.00
R189 "	$50 gray	500.00	300.00
	Block of four		1400.00
	Cut cancellation		65.00
	Block of four, cut canc.		275.00

1902 Surcharged in Black with Ornamental Numerals of Value.

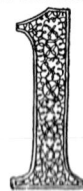

Warning: If Nos. R190–R194 are soaked, the center part of the surcharged numeral may wash off. Before the surcharging, a square of soluble varnish was applied to the middle of some stamps.

R190 R16	$1 green	5.00	2.00
	Block of four	—	10.00
	Cut cancellation		20
	Block of four, cut canc.		85
	a. Inverted surcharge		135.00
R191 "	$2 green	4.75	1.00
	Block of four	—	5.00
	Cut cancellation		20
	Block of four, cut canc.		1.00
	a. Surcharged as No. R185	40.00	40.00
	b. Surcharged as No. R185, in violet	—	—
	c. Double surcharge	100.00	
R192 "	$5 green	27.50	11.00
	Block of four	—	50.00
	Cut cancellation		1.75
	Block of four, cut canc.		8.00
	a. Surcharge omitted	50.00	
	b. Pair, one without surcharge	300.00	
R193 "	$10 green	200.00	125.00
	Block of four		550.00
	Cut cancellation		25.00
	Block of four, cut canc.		110.00
R194 "	$50 green	900.00	625.00
	Block of four		
	Cut cancellation		200.00
	Block of four, cut canc.		850.00

R20

Wmk. 190

Offset Printing.
Inscribed "Series of 1914."

1914 Wmkd. USPS (190) Perf. 10.

R195 R20	½c rose	4.00	2.00
	Block of four	17.50	9.00
R196 "	1c rose	1.00	12
	Block of four	4.50	50
	Creased transfer, left side	—	
R197 "	2c rose	1.00	10
	Block of four	4.50	45
	Double impression	—	
R198 "	3c rose	22.50	17.50
	Block of four	100.00	80.00
R199 "	4c rose	5.50	90
	Block of four	25.00	4.00
	Recut U. L. corner	—	

REVENUES

R200	R20	5c rose	2.00	12
		Block of four	9.00	75
R201	"	10c rose	1.75	8
		Block of four	8.00	35
R202	"	25c rose	10.00	40
		Block of four	45.00	1.75
R203	"	40c rose	6.00	50
		Block of four	30.00	2.25
R204	"	50c rose	2.50	10
		Block of four	11.00	45
R205	"	80c rose	35.00	6.00
		Block of four	160.00	26.00

Wmkd. USIR (191R)

R206	R20	½c rose	1.10	45
		Block of four	5.00	2.00
R207	"	1c rose	12	5
		Block of four	55	18
		Double impression	—	—
R208	"	2c rose	15	5
		Block of four	65	20
R209	"	3c rose	1.00	20
		Block of four	4.50	85
R210	"	4c rose	2.00	30
		Block of four	9.00	1.35
R211	"	5c rose	1.00	.10
		Block of four	4.50	45
R212	"	10c rose	35	6
		Block of four	1.65	30
R213	"	25c rose	3.25	60
		Block of four	15.00	2.75
R214	"	40c rose	27.50	6.00
		Block of four	125.00	26.00
		Cut cancellation		45
R215	"	50c rose	6.50	12
		Block of four	30.00	45
R216	"	80c rose	35.00	7.50
		Block of four	150.00	35.00
		Cut cancellation		1.00

Liberty
R21
Inscribed "Series 1914."
Engraved.

R217	R21	$1 green	8.00	12
		Block of four	—	50
		Cut cancellation		5
		Block of four, cut canc.		25
		a. $1 yellow green		12
R218	"	$2 carmine	16.00	15
		Block of four	—	1.00
		Cut cancellation		6
		Block of four, cut canc.		25
R219	"	$3 purple	25.00	1.00
		Block of four	—	4.50
		Cut cancellation		20
		Block of four, cut canc.		1.00
R220	"	$5 blue	20.00	1.50
		Block of four	85.00	7.00
		Cut cancellation		50
		Block of four, cut canc.		2.50
R221	"	$10 orange	40.00	4.00
		Block of four	—	18.00
		Cut cancellation		75
		Block of four, cut canc.		3.50
R222	"	$30 vermilion	80.00	9.00
		Block of four	—	40.00
		Cut cancellation		1.85
		Block of four, cut canc.		8.00
R223	"	$50 violet	800.00	550.00
		Block of four		
		Cut cancellation		225.00

Portrait Types of 1899 Inscribed "Series of 1915" (#R224), or "Series of 1914."

1914-15 Without Gum Perf. 12

R224	R19	$60 brown (*Lincoln*)	—	100.00
		Cut cancellation		45.00
		Vertical strip of four, cut canc.		200.00

R225	R17	$100 green (*Washington*)	—	40.00
		Cut cancellation		15.00
		Vertical strip of four, cut canc.		65.00
R226	R18	$500 blue (*Hamilton*)	—	450.00
		Cut cancellation		200.00
		Vertical strip of four, cut canc.		850.00
R227	R19	$1000 orange (*Madison*)	—	450.00
		Cut cancellation		200.00
		Vertical strip of four, cut canc.		850.00

The stamps of types R17, R18 and R19 in this and subsequent issues are issued in vertical strips of four which are imperforate at the top, bottom and right side; therefore, single copies are always imperforate on one or two sides.

R22

1917 Offset Printing. Perf. 11

Wmkd. USIR (191R)

Size: 21x18mm.

Two types of design R22 are known.
Type I—With dot in centers of periods before and after "CENTS".
Type II—Without such dots.
First printings were done by commercial companies, later printings by the Bureau of Engraving and Printing.

R228	R22	1c carmine rose	12	
		Block of four	55	4
		Double impression	7.00	4.00
R229	"	2c carmine rose	8	
		Block of four	40	2
		Double impression	7.50	5.00
R230	"	3c carmine rose	25	1
		Block of four	1.10	
		Double impression	—	7
R231	"	4c carmine rose	12	
		Block of four	60	2
		Double impression	—	—
R232	"	5c carmine rose	15	
		Block of four	70	2
R233	"	8c carmine rose	1.50	1
		Block of four	7.00	5
R234	"	10c carmine rose	15	
		Block of four	75	2
		Double impression		5.00
R235	"	20c carmine rose	30	
		Block of four	1.40	2
		Double impression	—	—
R236	"	25c carmine rose	60	
		Block of four	2.60	2
		Double impression	—	—
R237	"	40c carmine rose	1.00	
		Block of four	—	3
		Double impression	8.00	5.00
R238	"	50c carmine rose	1.25	
		Block of four	5.25	2
		Double impression	—	—
R239	"	80c carmine rose	3.00	
		Block of four	13.00	3
		Double impression	40.00	—

Liberty Type of 1914 without "Series 1914."
1917-33 Engraved
Size: 18½x27½mm.

R240	R21	$1 yellow green	3.75	
		Block of four	—	2
		a. $1 green	4.50	
R241	"	$2 rose	8.00	
		Block of four	—	3
R242	"	$3 violet	17.50	40
		Block of four	—	1.75
R243	"	$4 yellow brown ('33)	10.00	80
		Block of four	—	3.25
		Cut cancellation		12
		Block of four, cut canc.		50
R244	"	$5 dark blue	8.00	15
		Block of four	—	75
		Cut cancellation		
R245	"	$10 orange	15.00	50
		Block of four	—	3.00
		Cut cancellation		12
		Block of four, cut canc.		60

REVENUES

Portrait Types of 1899 without "Series of" and Date.

1917   **Without Gum**   *Perf. 12*

			Unused	Used
R246	R17	$30 deep orange, green numerals (*Grant*)	25.00	2.00
		Vertical strip of four		—
		Cut cancellation		55
		Vertical strip of four, cut canc.		3.00
		a. Imperf., pair	—	—
		b. Numerals in blue	—	1.75
		Numerals in blue, cut canc.		90
R247	R19	$60 brown (*Lincoln*)	30.00	6.00
		Vertical strip of four		—
		Cut cancellation		80
		Vertical strip of four cut canc.		5.00
R248	R17	$100 green (*Washington*)	20.00	70
		Vertical strip of four		—
		Cut cancellation		35
		Vertical strip of four, cut canc.		1.90
R249	R18	$500 blue, red numerals (*Hamilton*)	—	30.00
		Vertical strip of four		—
		Cut cancellation		7.00
		Vertical strip of four, cut canc.		45.00
		Double transfer	—	50.00
		a. Numerals in orange	—	70.00
R250	R19	$1000 orange (*Madison*)	80.00	10.00
		Vertical strip of four		—
		Cut cancellation		3.50
		Vertical strip of four, cut canc.		16.00
		a. Imperf., pair	—	—

See note after No. R227.

1928-29   **Offset Printing**   *Perf. 10*

			Unused	Used
R251	R22	1c carmine rose	1.75	1.00
		Block of four	8.00	4.50
R252	"	2c carmine rose	50	15
		Block of four	2.50	65
R253	"	4c carmine rose	5.00	3.50
		Block of four	22.50	15.00
R254	"	5c carmine rose	1.00	30
		Block of four	4.50	1.50
R255	"	10c carmine rose	1.50	90
		Block of four	7.00	4.00
R256	"	20c carmine rose	5.00	4.00
		Block of four	22.50	18.00
		Double impression	—	—

Engraved.

			Unused	Used
R257	R21	$1 green	40.00	25.00
		Block of four	—	—
		Cut cancellation		5.00
R258	"	$2 rose	12.50	1.50
		Block of four	—	7.00
R259	"	$10 orange	65.00	30.00
		Block of four	—	—
		Cut cancellation		17.50

1929   **Offset Printing**   *Perf. 11x10*

			Unused	Used
R260	R22	2c carmine rose ('30)	2.50	2.00
		Block of four	11.00	9.00
		Double impression	—	—
R261	"	5c carmine rose ('30)	1.75	1.50
		Block of four	8.00	7.00
R262	"	10c carmine rose	7.00	6.00
		Block of four	30.00	25.00
R263	"	20c carmine rose	12.50	8.00
		Block of four	55.00	35.00

Types of 1917-33 Overprinted in Black   SERIES 1940

1940   Wmkd. USIR (191R)   *Perf. 11.*

Offset Printing.

			Unused	Used (uncut)	Used (cut canc.)	Used (perforated Initials)
R264	R22	1c rose pink	1.40	90	35	20
R265	"	2c rose pink	1.40	90	40	30
R266	"	3c rose pink	4.00	2.25	70	50
R267	"	4c rose pink	1.75	25	12	8
R268	"	5c rose pink	2.00	40	25	15
R269	"	8c rose pink	12.00	10.00	3.00	2.00
R270	"	10c rose pink	65	15	8	5
R271	"	20c rose pink	1.10	20	10	5
R272	"	25c rose pink	2.25	30	10	6
R273	"	40c rose pink	2.25	25	8	5
R274	"	50c rose pink	2.75	25	8	5
R275	"	80c rose pink	4.00	40	20	10

Engraved.

			Unused	Used (uncut)	Used (cut canc.)	Used (perforated Initials)
R276	R21	$1 green	12.50	30	10	8
R277	"	$2 rose	12.50	45	10	8
R278	"	$3 violet	12.50	11.00	2.00	1.25
R279	"	$4 yellow brown	30.00	16.00	2.50	1.25
R280	"	$5 dark blue	17.50	4.25	50	15
R281	"	$10 orange	45.00	13.00	1.25	35

Types of 1917 Handstamped in Green "Series 1940".

1940   *Perf. 12.*   Wmk. 191R

Without Gum

			Unused	Used
R282	R17	$30 vermilion	400.00	275.00
R283	R19	$60 brown	550.00	375.00
		a. As #R285a	—	—
R284	R17	$100 green	800.00	700.00
R285	R18	$500 blue	1150.00	950.00 800.00
		Double transfer	1250.00	
		a. With black 2-line handstamp in larger type	1500.00	1100.00
		Double transfer	—	
		b. Blue handstamp; double transfer	—	
R286	R19	$1000 orange	550.00	300.00 200.00

Alexander Hamilton   Levi Woodbury
R23   R24

Various Portraits.
Engraved.

1940   Wmkd. USIR (191R)

Perf. 11.

Plates of 400 subjects, issued in panes of 100.

Size: 19x22mm.

Overprinted in Black   SERIES 1940

The "sensitive ink" varieties are in a bluish-purple overprint showing minute flecks of gold.

			Unused	Used (uncut)	Used (cut canc.)	Used (perforated Initials)
R288	R23	1c carmine	2.50	1.75	1.00	60
		Sensitive ink	20.00	—		
R289	"	2c carmine (*Oliver Wolcott, Jr.*)	3.00	2.00	1.00	75
		Sensitive ink	20.00	—		
R290	"	3c carmine (*Samuel Dexter*)	10.00	4.50	3.00	2.00
		Sensitive ink	30.00	—		
R291	"	4c carmine (*Albert Gallatin*)	25.00	17.50	4.00	3.50
R292	"	5c carmine (*G. W Campbell*)	2.25	60	25	18
R293	"	8c carmine (*Alexander Dallas*)	35.00	30.00	16.00	11.00
R294	"	10c carmine (*William H. Crawford*)	1.50	30	12	10
R295	"	20c carmine (*Richard Rush*)	2.00	1.75	1.00	75
R296	"	25c carmine (*S. D. Ingham*)	1.75	20	12	10
R297	"	40c carmine (*Louis McLane*)	17.50	9.00	3.50	2.00
R298	"	50c carmine (*Wm. J. Duane*)	2.25	10	6	5
R299	"	80c carmine (*Roger B. Taney*)	45.00	40.00	20.00	15.00

648 REVENUES

Plates of 200 subjects, issued in panes of 50.
Size: 21½ x 36¼ mm.

			Unused	Used (uncut)	Used (cut canc.)	Used (perforated initials)
R300	R24	$1 carmine	—	10	6	5
		Sensitive ink	50.00			
R301	"	$2 carmine (*Thomas Ewing*)	—	20	8	6
		Sensitive ink	70.00			
R302	"	$3 carmine (*Walter Forward*)	—	50.00	10.00	7.00
		Sensitive ink	120.00			
R303	"	$4 carmine (*J. C. Spencer*)	—	17.50	3.50	1.50
R304	"	$5 carmine (*G. M. Bibb*)	—	70	30	20
R305	"	$10 carmine (*R. J. Walker*)	—	2.50	70	25
R305A	"	$20 carmine (*Wm. M. Meredith*)	600.00	500.00	300.00	175.00
		b. Imperf., pair	750.00			

Thomas Corwin
R25
(Overprint: "SERIES 1940")

Perf. 12
Various Frames and Portraits.
Plates of 16 subjects, issued in strips of 4.
Without Gum
Size: 28½ x 42 mm.

R306	R25	$30 carmine	600.00	500.00	300.00	175.00
R306A	"	$50 carmine (*James Guthrie*)	750.00	35.00	15.00	9.00
R307	"	$60 carmine (*Howell Cobb*)	—	800.00	650.00	—
		a. Vert. pair, imperf. between	—	40.00	22.50	15.00
R308	"	$100 carmine (*P. F. Thomas*)	—	37.50	17.50	8.50
R309	"	$500 carmine (*J. A. Dix*)	—	500.00	300.00	175.00
R310	"	$1000 carmine (*S. P. Chase*)	—	250.00	115.00	90.00

The $30 to $1,000 denominations in this and following similar issues, and the $2,500, $5,000 and $10,000 stamps of 1952–58 have straight edges on one or two sides. They were issued without gum through No. R723.

Documentary Stamps of 1940
Overprinted in Black
SERIES 1941

1941   **Perf. 11**   **Wmk. 191R**
Size: 19 x 22 mm.

R311	R23	1c carmine	1.65	1.50	70	60
R312	"	2c carmine	1.65	60	40	35
R313	"	3c carmine	4.25	2.50	1.25	85
R314	"	4c carmine	2.50	60	30	12
R315	"	5c carmine	60	10	8	6
R316	"	8c carmine	9.50	4.25	2.75	2.25
R317	"	10c carmine	90	20	10	8
R318	"	20c carmine	1.75	40	20	15
R319	"	25c carmine	1.00	10	5	5
R320	"	40c carmine	5.75	1.65	1.00	60
R321	"	50c carmine	1.50	10	5	5
R322	"	80c carmine	30.00	5.00	2.00	1.50

Size: 21½ x 36¼ mm.

R323	R24	$1 carmine	5.00	10	6	5
R324	"	$2 carmine	6.00	12	5	5
R325	"	$3 carmine	10.00	1.75	35	30
R326	"	$4 carmine	12.50	7.50	85	70
R327	"	$5 carmine	20.00	30	10	8
R328	"	$10 carmine	30.00	1.50	25	20
R329	"	$20 carmine	90.00	75.00	20.00	15.00

Perf. 12
Without Gum
Size: 28½ x 42 mm.

			Unused	Used (uncut)	Used (cut canc.)	Used (perforated initials)
R330	R25	$30 carmine	—	16.00	9.00	6.00
R331	"	$50 carmine	100.00	70.00	40.00	20.00
R332	"	$60 carmine	—	30.00	7.50	5.00
R333	"	$100 carmine	—	13.00	4.00	2.75
R334	"	$500 carmine	—	135.00	75.00	40.00
R335	"	$1000 carmine	—	100.00	30.00	20.00

Documentary Stamps of 1940
Overprinted in Black
SERIES 1942

1942   **Perf. 11**   **Wmk. 191R**
Size: 19 x 22 mm.

R336	R23	1c carmine	25	20	10	8
R337	"	2c carmine	25	20	10	8
R338	"	3c carmine	45	30	22	15
R339	"	4c carmine	70	35	25	20
R340	"	5c carmine	35	10	6	5
R341	"	8c carmine	3.25	2.00	1.00	1.00
R342	"	10c carmine	60	10	6	5
R343	"	20c carmine	85	25	15	15
R344	"	25c carmine	1.00	10	5	5
R345	"	40c carmine	3.00	75	50	30
R346	"	50c carmine	2.00	8	5	5
R347	"	80c carmine	8.00	5.50	2.50	1.75

Size: 21½ x 36¼ mm.

R348	R24	$1 carmine	4.50	10	5	5
R349	"	$2 carmine	5.50	10	5	5
R350	"	$3 carmine	9.00	1.25	25	20
R351	"	$4 carmine	11.00	3.00	30	25
R352	"	$5 carmine	18.00	35	7	5
R353	"	$10 carmine	30.00	1.50	10	5
R354	"	$20 carmine	50.00	22.50	12.00	10.00

Perf. 12
Without Gum
Size: 28½ x 42 mm.

R355	R25	$30 carmine	—	18.00	6.00	5.00
R356	"	$50 carmine	150.00	110.00	70.00	50.00
R357	"	$60 carmine	150.00	125.00	60.00	45.00
R358	"	$100 carmine	—	50.00	21.00	14.00
R359	"	$500 carmine	—	150.00	100.00	45.00
R360	"	$1000 carmine	—	100.00	50.00	40.00

Documentary Revenue Stamps of 1940
Overprinted in Black
SERIES 1943

1943   **Perf. 11**   **Wmk. 191R**
Size: 19 x 22 mm.

R361	R23	1c carmine	40	20	12	10
R362	"	2c carmine	35	12	8	6
R363	"	3c carmine	1.50	1.25	50	30
R364	"	4c carmine	70	40	25	20
R365	"	5c carmine	30	15	8	5
R366	"	8c carmine	2.75	2.50	1.50	1.00
R367	"	10c carmine	35	10	7	6
R368	"	20c carmine	1.25	35	25	20
R369	"	25c carmine	85	15	8	6
R370	"	40c carmine	3.50	1.25	90	60
R371	"	50c carmine	1.10	10	5	5
R372	"	80c carmine	6.75	4.25	1.10	90

Size: 21½ x 36¼ mm.

R373	R24	$1 carmine	3.75	8	5	5
R374	"	$2 carmine	5.50	10	6	5
R375	"	$3 carmine	9.00	1.50	30	10
R376	"	$4 carmine	11.00	2.00	40	30
R377	"	$5 carmine	16.00	30	8	6
R378	"	$10 carmine	25.00	1.65	50	35
R379	"	$20 carmine	45.00	9.00	3.50	2.25

Perf. 12
Without Gum
Size: 28½ x 42 mm.

R380	R25	$30 carmine	—	15.00	4.00	3.00
R381	"	$50 carmine	—	22.00	8.00	5.00
R382	"	$60 carmine	—	35.00	11.00	6.00
R383	"	$100 carmine	—	10.00	5.50	3.50
R384	"	$500 carmine	—	110.00	75.00	60.00
R385	"	$1000 carmine	—	140.00	45.00	37.50

Documentary Revenue Stamps of 1940
Overprinted in Black
Series 1944

1944   **Perf. 11**   **Wmk. 191R**
Size: 19 x 22 mm.

R386	R23	1c carmine	25	15	12	10
R387	"	2c carmine	20	12	8	8
R388	"	3c carmine	25	15	10	8

REVENUES

			Unused	Used (uncut)	Used (cut canc.)	Used (perforated initials)
R389	R23	4c carmine	35	30	12	10
R390	"	5c carmine	30	10	6	5
R391	"	8c carmine	1.25	75	45	40
R392	"	10c carmine	40	6	5	5
R393	"	20c carmine	55	20	15	12
R394	"	25c carmine	1.00	10	6	5
R395	"	40c carmine	1.75	30	25	20
R396	"	50c carmine	1.75	10	5	5
R397	"	80c carmine	6.00	3.25	1.00	80

Size: 21½ x 36¼ mm.

R398	R24	$1 carmine	3.75	8	5	5
R399	"	$2 carmine	5.00	10	7	5
R400	"	$3 carmine	7.50	1.25	45	10
R401	"	$4 carmine	12.00	7.00	1.00	90
R402	"	$5 carmine	12.00	25	10	7
R403	"	$10 carmine	25.00	70	25	10
R404	"	$20 carmine	45.00	10.00	3.00	2.00

Perf. 12.
Without Gum
Size: 28½ x 42 mm.

R405	R25	$30 carmine	50.00	20.00	4.50	3.00
R406	"	$50 carmine	20.00	7.50	3.00	2.50
R407	"	$60 carmine	90.00	35.00	7.00	5.00
R408	"	$100 carmine	—	8.00	4.00	3.00
R409	"	$500 carmine	—	450.00	325.00	250.00
R410	"	$1000 carmine	—	125.00	50.00	40.00

Documentary Revenue Stamps of 1940
Overprinted in Black — Series **1945**
1945 Perf. 11 Wmk. 191R
Size: 19x22mm.

R411	R23	1c carmine	15	10	8	5
R412	"	2c carmine	15	10	8	6
R413	"	3c carmine	30	25	15	10
R414	"	4c carmine	25	15	10	8
R415	"	5c carmine	25	6	5	5
R416	"	8c carmine	2.75	1.00	60	30
R417	"	10c carmine	50	10	5	5
R418	"	20c carmine	3.00	55	40	15
R419	"	25c carmine	90	10	6	5
R420	"	40c carmine	2.75	60	40	35
R421	"	50c carmine	1.90	10	6	5
R422	"	80c carmine	10.00	5.50	2.85	1.75

Size: 21½ x 36¼ mm.

R423	R24	$1 carmine	3.75	8	6	6
R424	"	$2 carmine	5.00	12	8	6
R425	"	$3 carmine	7.50	2.25	80	60
R426	"	$4 carmine	11.00	2.50	50	30
R427	"	$5 carmine	12.00	30	15	10
R428	"	$10 carmine	25.00	1.00	25	18
R429	"	$20 carmine	40.00	7.50	3.00	2.50

Perf. 12.
Without Gum
Size: 28½ x 42mm.

R430	R25	$30 carmine	—	17.50	4.50	2.00
R431	"	$50 carmine	—	20.00	10.00	5.50
R432	"	$60 carmine	75.00	30.00	10.00	8.00
R433	"	$100 carmine	—	10.00	6.00	4.00
R434	"	$500 carmine	150.00	110.00	60.00	50.00
R435	"	$1000 carmine	100.00	70.00	25.00	17.50

Documentary Stamps of 1940
Overprinted in Black — Series **1946**
1946 Perf. 11 Wmk. 191R
Size: 19 x 22 mm.

R436	R23	1c carmine	15	10	5	5
R437	"	2c carmine	20	18	6	5
R438	"	3c carmine	25	15	10	8
R439	"	4c carmine	30	25	8	6
R440	"	5c carmine	25	8	6	5
R441	"	8c carmine	90	75	25	10
R442	"	10c carmine	60	8	6	5
R443	"	20c carmine	1.00	40	12	6
R444	"	25c carmine	1.00	15	8	6
R445	"	40c carmine	1.10	70	30	15
R446	"	50c carmine	2.00	8	6	5
R447	"	80c carmine	5.00	3.25	60	45

Size: 21½ x 36¼ mm.

R448	R24	$1 carmine	3.75	12	8	5
R449	"	$2 carmine	5.50	15	10	8
R450	"	$3 carmine	8.00	4.50	85	35
R451	"	$4 carmine	10.00	7.00	2.00	1.00
R452	"	$5 carmine	11.00	40	15	10
R453	"	$10 carmine	22.00	1.25	30	18
R454	"	$20 carmine	40.00	7.50	2.00	1.50

Perf. 12.
Without Gum
Size: 28½ x 42 mm.

R455	R25	$30 carmine	40.00	10.00	4.00	2.50
R456	"	$50 carmine	20.00	8.00	4.00	2.50
R457	"	$60 carmine	40.00	12.00	8.00	6.00
R458	"	$100 carmine	—	8.00	3.00	3.00
R459	"	$500 carmine	—	75.00	30.00	22.50
R460	"	$1000 carmine	—	70.00	25.00	15.00

Documentary Stamps of 1940
Overprinted in Black — Series **1947**
1947 Perf. 11 Wmk. 191R
Size: 19 x 22 mm.

R461	R23	1c carmine	40	18	8	5
R462	"	2c carmine	30	15	8	5
R463	"	3c carmine	35	20	15	5
R464	"	4c carmine	35	30	12	5
R465	"	5c carmine	25	15	5	5
R466	"	8c carmine	75	30	20	10
R467	"	10c carmine	60	12	8	5
R468	"	20c carmine	1.00	30	15	5
R469	"	25c carmine	1.10	25	12	8
R470	"	40c carmine	1.75	60	20	10
R471	"	50c carmine	1.75	12	8	5
R472	"	80c carmine	3.50	2.75	60	20

Size: 21½ x 36¼ mm.

R473	R24	$1 carmine	3.75	20	6	6
R474	"	$2 carmine	5.00	20	10	8
R475	"	$3 carmine	6.75	4.00	1.00	60
R476	"	$4 carmine	8.00	3.50	40	30
R477	"	$5 carmine	11.00	40	12	10
R478	"	$10 carmine	25.00	2.00	60	20
R479	"	$20 carmine	40.00	7.50	1.00	70

Perf. 12.
Without Gum
Size: 28½ x 42 mm.

R480	R25	$30 carmine	60.00	17.50	4.00	2.00
R481	"	$50 carmine	30.00	9.00	4.00	2.50
R482	"	$60 carmine	—	22.50	14.00	6.00
R483	"	$100 carmine	30.00	8.00	4.00	2.00
R484	"	$500 carmine	—	100.00	50.00	35.00
R485	"	$1000 carmine	—	70.00	35.00	22.50

Documentary Stamps of 1940
Overprinted in Black — Series **1948**
1948 Perf. 11 Wmk. 191R
Size: 19x22mm.

R486	R23	1c carmine	15	12	8	6
R487	"	2c carmine	18	15	8	6
R488	"	3c carmine	30	25	12	10
R489	"	4c carmine	25	15	10	8
R490	"	5c carmine	25	10	6	5
R491	"	8c carmine	50	30	18	12
R492	"	10c carmine	50	10	6	5
R493	"	20c carmine	90	30	12	8
R494	"	25c carmine	90	15	8	6
R495	"	40c carmine	1.75	75	30	20
R496	"	50c carmine	1.75	12	6	5
R497	"	80c carmine	4.00	3.00	1.35	50

Size: 21½x36¼mm.

R498	R24	$1 carmine	3.75	18	8	6
R499	"	$2 carmine	5.00	15	8	6
R500	"	$3 carmine	7.00	2.00	40	25
R501	"	$4 carmine	10.00	2.25	75	40
R502	"	$5 carmine	11.00	50	20	10
R503	"	$10 carmine	20.00	1.00	25	15

  a. Pair one dated "1946"

| R504 | " | $20 carmine | 40.00 | 7.50 | 3.00 | 1.25 |

Perf. 12.
Without Gum
Size: 28½x42mm.

| R505 | R25 | $30 carmine | 40.00 | 15.00 | 5.00 | 2.50 |
| R506 | " | $50 carmine | 40.00 | 12.50 | 6.00 | 2.50 |

  a. Vertical pair, imperf. between

| R507 | " | $60 carmine | 50.00 | 17.50 | 9.00 | 5.00 |

  a. Vertical pair, imperf. between

| R508 | " | $100 carmine | — | 10.00 | 4.00 | 2.50 |

  a. Vertical pair, imperf. between 350.00

| R509 | " | $500 carmine | 125.00 | 75.00 | 40.00 | 20.00 |
| R510 | " | $1000 carmine | 80.00 | 50.00 | 27.50 | 18.00 |

REVENUES

1949
Documentary Stamps of 1940 Overprinted in Black
Series 1949
Perf. 11 — Wmk. 191R
Size: 19 x 22 mm.

			Unused	Used (uncut)	Used (cut canc.)	Used (perforated initials)
R511	R23	1c carmine	10	8	6	6
R512	"	2c carmine	15	12	8	6
R513	"	3c carmine	18	12	10	8
R514	"	4c carmine	20	15	10	8
R515	"	5c carmine	25	15	10	8
R516	"	8c carmine	45	30	20	18
R517	"	10c carmine	35	20	12	10
R518	"	20c carmine	50	40	30	25
R519	"	25c carmine	75	45	25	20
R520	"	40c carmine	1.90	1.00	40	30
R521	"	50c carmine	1.90	18	6	5
R522	"	80c carmine	3.75	3.00	1.50	75

Size: 21½ x 36¼ mm.

R523	R24	$1 carmine	3.75	25	12	10
R524	"	$2 carmine	4.50	1.00	40	25
R525	"	$3 carmine	7.50	5.00	2.00	1.00
R526	"	$4 carmine	7.50	4.75	2.75	1.50
R527	"	$5 carmine	10.00	1.50	60	40
R528	"	$10 carmine	20.00	2.50	1.00	85
R529	"	$20 carmine	40.00	6.00	2.00	1.00

Perf. 12.
Without Gum
Size: 28½ x 42 mm.

R530	R25	$30 carmine	50.00	18.00	5.00	3.00
R531	"	$50 carmine	—	30.00	10.00	6.00
R532	"	$60 carmine	—	35.00	18.00	7.00
R533	"	$100 carmine	—	15.00	3.00	2.50
R534	"	$500 carmine	—	140.00	75.00	40.00
R535	"	$1000 carmine	—	80.00	35.00	20.00

1950
Documentary Stamps of 1940 Overprinted in Black
Series 1950
Perf. 11 — Wmk. 191R
Size: 19 x 22 mm.

R536	R23	1c carmine	10	6	5	5
R537	"	2c carmine	15	8	5	5
R538	"	3c carmine	15	12	6	5
R539	"	4c carmine	20	15	10	8
R540	"	5c carmine	25	12	8	6
R541	"	8c carmine	40	30	20	12
R542	"	10c carmine	50	15	10	8
R543	"	20c carmine	75	35	25	12
R544	"	25c carmine	1.00	35	25	20
R545	"	40c carmine	2.00	1.00	40	25
R546	"	50c carmine	2.25	20	8	5
R547	"	80c carmine	3.50	3.00	85	50

Size: 21½ x 36¼ mm.

R548	R24	$1 carmine	3.50	20	12	8
R549	"	$2 carmine	4.00	1.50	35	15
R550	"	$3 carmine	5.50	3.00	1.25	75
R551	"	$4 carmine	8.00	4.00	2.50	1.25
R552	"	$5 carmine	10.00	60	30	18
R553	"	$10 carmine	20.00	6.50	80	50
R554	"	$20 carmine	40.00	7.00	2.50	1.50

Perf. 12.
Without Gum
Size: 28½ x 42 mm.

R555	R25	$30 carmine	—	30.00	10.00	8.00
R556	"	$50 carmine	—	11.00	6.00	3.50

a. Vert. pair, imperf. horiz.

R557	"	$60 carmine	—	40.00	12.00	6.00
R558	"	$100 carmine	—	17.50	5.00	3.00
R559	"	$500 carmine	—	100.00	40.00	30.00
R560	"	$1000 carmine	—	60.00	25.00	18.00

1951
Documentary Stamps of 1940 Overprinted in Black
Series 1951
Perf. 11 — Wmk. 191R
Size: 19 x 22 mm.

R561	R23	1c carmine	10	8	6	5
R562	"	2c carmine	15	8	5	5
R563	"	3c carmine	15	12	8	6
R564	"	4c carmine	20	12	8	6
R565	"	5c carmine	25	12	8	6
R566	"	8c carmine	40	30	20	15
R567	"	10c carmine	50	15	10	8
R568	"	20c carmine	90	35	25	15
R569	"	25c carmine	1.00	35	25	15
R570	"	40c carmine	1.75	70	40	25
R571	"	50c carmine	1.75	18	10	6
R572	"	80c carmine	2.50	2.00	1.25	70

Size: 21½ x 36¼ mm.

R573	R24	$1 carmine	3.50	20	15	10
R574	"	$2 carmine	4.00	25	18	12
R575	"	$3 carmine	7.00	3.50	1..5	1.00
R576	"	$4 carmine	9.00	4.00	2.50	1.25
R577	"	$5 carmine	9.00	35	30	20
R578	"	$10 carmine	20.00	2.25	1.00	75
R579	"	$20 carmine	40.00	6.00	3.00	3.50

Perf. 12.
Without Gum
Size: 28½ x 42 mm.

R580	R25	$30 carmine	—	10.00	5.00	3.50

a. Imperf., pair 750.00

R581	"	$50 carmine	—	12.50	6.00	4.00
R582	"	$60 carmine	—	30.00		12.50
R583	"	$100 carmine	—	12.50	6.00	5.00
R584	"	$500 carmine	125.00	70.00	37.50	22.50
R585	"	$1000 carmine	—	75.00	30.00	25.00

1952
Documentary Stamps and Types of 1940 Overprinted in Black
Series 1952

Designs: 55c, $1.10, $1.65, $2.20, $2.75, $3.30, L. J. Gage; $2500, William Windom; $5000, C. J. Folger; $10,000, W. Q. Gresham.

Size: 19 x 22 mm.
Perf. 11 — Wmk. 191R

R586	R23	1c carmine	10	6	5	5
R587	"	2c carmine	12	10	5	5
R588	"	3c carmine	12	10	6	5
R589	"	4c carmine	15	12	8	6
R590	"	5c carmine	15	10	6	5
R591	"	8c carmine	30	25	12	8
R592	"	10c carmine	35	15	8	6
R593	"	20c carmine	50	35	20	18
R594	"	25c carmine	90	35	25	20
R595	"	40c carmine	1.50	70	50	40
R596	"	50c carmine	1.75	20	8	6
R597	"	55c carmine	9.00	4.00	1.25	1.00
R598	"	80c carmine	4.00	2.00	75	65

Size: 21½ x 36¼ mm.

R599	R24	$1 carmine	3.00	1.50		35
R600	"	$1.10 carmine	18.00	10.00		
R601	"	$1.65 carmine	75.00	40.00		
R602	"	$2 carmine	4.50	30		10
R603	"	$2.20 carmine	55.00	45.00		
R604	"	$2.75 carmine	75.00	40.00		
R605	"	$3 carmine	8.00	3.00	1.50	1.25

a. Horiz. pair, imperf. btwn. —

R606	"	$3.30 carmine	55.00	40.00		
R607	"	$4 carmine	10.00	3.50	2.00	1.50
R608	"	$5 carmine	10.00	1.00	40	35
R609	"	$10 carmine	22.00	1.00	40	35
R610	"	$20 carmine	35.00	8.00	2.75	2.25

Perf. 12.
Without Gum
Size: 28½ x 42 mm.

R611	R25	$30 carmine	—	12.00	5.00	4.00
R612	"	$50 carmine	—	12.00	5.00	4.00
R613	"	$60 carmine	—	30.00	10.00	8.00
R614	"	$100 carmine	—	8.00	3.00	2.00
R615	"	$500 carmine	—	75.00	50.00	30.00
R616	"	$1000 carmine	—	30.00	15.00	10.00
R617	"	$2500 carmine	—	125.00	100.00	75.00
R618	"	$5000 carmine	—	800.00	600.00	500.00
R619	"	$10,000 carmine	—	400.00	300.00	225.00

1953
Documentary Stamps and Types of 1940 Overprinted in Black
Series 1953
Perf. 11 — Wmk. 191R
Size: 19 x 22 mm.

R620	R23	1c carmine	10	8	5	5
R621	"	2c carmine	10	8	5	5
R622	"	3c carmine	12	10	6	5
R623	"	4c carmine	15	10	8	5
R624	"	5c carmine	15	10	6	5
R625	"	8c carmine	30	20	15	12
R626	"	10c carmine	35	18	6	5
R627	"	20c carmine	50	40	20	15
R628	"	25c carmine	75	50	25	20
R629	"	40c carmine	1.25	75	40	30
R630	"	50c carmine	1.50	15	6	5
R631	"	55c carmine	2.00	1.25		

a. Horiz. pair, imperf. vert. 275.00

R632	"	80c carmine	2.50	1.50	1.20	1.00

Size: 21½ x 36¼ mm.

R633	R24	$1 carmine	2.75	25	12	10

REVENUES 651

			Unused	Used (uncut)	Used (cut canc.)	Used (perforated initials)
R634	R24	$1.10 carmine	4.00	2.50	2.00	1.50
		a. Horiz. pair, imperf. vert.	300.00			
		b. Imperf., pair	450.00			
R635	"	$1.65 carmine	5.00	3.50		
R636	"	$2 carmine	4.50	45	25	20
R637	"	$2.20 carmine	6.00	5.00	2.50	2.00
R638	"	$2.75 carmine	8.00	6.00	3.50	
R639	"	$3 carmine	6.00	3.00	1.50	1.25
R640	"	$3.30 carmine	12.00	7.00		
R641	"	$4 carmine	8.00	5.50	1.75	1.50
R642	"	$5 carmine	10.00	60	40	30
R643	"	$10 carmine	20.00	1.50	1.00	85
R644	"	$20 carmine	40.00	15.00	3.00	2.00

Perf. 12.
Without Gum
Size: 28½ x 42 mm.

R645	R25	$30 carmine	—	12.00	5.00	4.00
R646	"	$50 carmine	—	20.00	5.00	4.00
R647	"	$60 carmine	—	45.00		
R648	"	$100 carmine	35.00	12.00	5.00	3.50
R649	"	$500 carmine	—	90.00	30.00	20.00
R650	"	$1000 carmine	100.00	50.00	20.00	15.00
R651	"	$2500 carmine	400.00	300.00	225.00	200.00
R652	"	$5000 carmine	—	800.00	700.00	550.00
R653	"	$10,000 carmine	—	600.00	400.00	150.00

Types of 1940
Without Overprint
1954 Perf. 11 Wmk. 191R
Size: 19 x 22mm.

R654	R23	1c carmine	6	5	5	5
		a. Horiz. pair, imperf. vert.	—			
R655	R23	2c carmine	8	6	5	5
R656	"	3c carmine	12	10	5	5
R657	"	4c carmine	12	10	5	5
R658	"	5c carmine	13	8	5	5
R659	"	8c carmine	25	20	12	10
R660	"	10c carmine	25	15	6	5
R661	"	20c carmine	50	35	15	12
R662	"	25c carmine	60	40	18	15
R663	"	40c carmine	90	60	40	35
R664	"	50c carmine	1.00	15	10	8
		a. Horiz. pair, imperf. vert.	200.00			
R665	"	55c carmine	1.15	1.10		
R666	"	80c carmine	1.75	1.65	1.00	80

Size: 21½ x 36¼ mm.

R667	R24	$1 carmine	1.00	20	10	8
R668	"	$1.10 carmine	2.75	2.35		
R669	"	$1.65 carmine	100.00	75.00		
R670	"	$2 carmine	1.75	45	25	20
R671	"	$2.20 carmine	4.50	3.75		
R672	"	$2.75 carmine	100.00	75.00		
R673	"	$3 carmine	3.00	2.00	1.00	75
R674	"	$3.30 carmine	6.50	5.00		
R675	"	$4 carmine	4.00	3.50	2.00	1.50
R676	"	$5 carmine	10.00	50	30	20
R677	"	$10 carmine	20.00	1.50	80	70
R678	"	$20 carmine	40.00	6.00	3.00	1.50

Documentary Stamps and Type of 1940
Overprinted in Black
1954 Perf. 12 **Series 1954** Wmk. 191R
Without Gum
Size: 28½ x 42 mm.

R679	R25	$30 carmine	—	12.00	4.00	3.00
R680	"	$50 carmine	—	15.00	9.00	4.50
R681	"	$60 carmine	—	17.50	10.00	6.00
R682	"	$100 carmine	—	7.00	4.00	3.00
R683	"	$500 carmine	—	60.00	22.50	15.00
R684	"	$1000 carmine	—	40.00	15.00	12.00
R685	"	$2500 carmine	—	125.00	70.00	35.00
R686	"	$5000 carmine	—	400.00	325.00	225.00
R687	"	$10,000 carmine	—	350.00	100.00	90.00

Documentary Stamps and Type of 1940
Overprinted in Black
1955 Perf. 12 **Series 1955** Wmk. 191R
Without Gum
Sizes: 28½x42mm.

R688	R25	$30 carmine	—	9.00	4.00	
R689	"	$50 carmine	—	13.50	9.00	4.00
R690	"	$60 carmine	—	16.50	5.00	4.00
R691	"	$100 carmine	—	7.00	5.00	3.50
R692	"	$500 carmine	—	90.00	30.00	20.00
R693	"	$1000 carmine	—	35.00	17.50	12.50
R694	"	$2500 carmine	—	100.00	60.00	40.00
R695	"	$5000 carmine	—	400.00	325.00	200.00
R696	"	$10,000 carmine	—	400.00	150.00	80.00

Documentary Stamps and Type of 1940
Overprinted in Black "Series 1956"
1956 Perf. 12 Wmk. 191R
Without Gum
Size: 28½ x 42 mm.

			Unused	Used (uncut)	Used (cut canc.)	Used (perforated initials)
R697	R25	$30 carmine	—	13.50	9.00	3.50
R698	"	$50 carmine	—	15.00	10.00	3.50
R699	"	$60 carmine	—	30.00	5.00	3.50
R700	"	$100 carmine	—	10.00	5.00	4.00
R701	"	$500 carmine	—	62.50	25.00	15.00
R702	"	$1000 carmine	—	50.00	15.00	9.00
R703	"	$2500 carmine	—	200.00	90.00	60.00
R704	"	$5000 carmine	—	800.00	700.00	600.00
R705	"	$10,000 carmine	—	300.00	150.00	100.00

Documentary Stamps and Type of 1940
Overprinted in Black "Series 1957"
1957 Perf. 12 Wmk. 191R
Without Gum
Size: 28½ x 42 mm.

R706	R25	$30 carmine	—	27.50	10.00	5.00
R707	"	$50 carmine	—	15.00	6.00	4.00
R708	"	$60 carmine	—	85.00		40.00
R709	"	$100 carmine	—	12.50	8.00	4.00
R710	"	$500 carmine	175.00	75.00	50.00	30.00
R711	"	$1000 carmine	—	65.00	30.00	
R712	"	$2500 carmine	—	450.00	300.00	225.00
R713	"	$5000 carmine	—	450.00	300.00	150.00
R714	"	$10,000 carmine	—	300.00	150.00	100.00

Documentary Stamps and Type of 1940
Overprinted in Black "Series 1958"
1958 Perf. 12 Wmk. 191R
Without Gum
Size: 28½x42mm.

R715	R25	$30 carmine	—	15.00	10.00	
R716	"	$50 carmine	—	16.00	14.00	6.00
R717	"	$60 carmine	—	25.00		10.00
R718	"	$100 carmine	—	10.00	5.00	
R719	"	$500 carmine	100.00	45.00		18.00
R720	"	$1000 carmine	—	55.00	30.00	
R721	"	$2500 carmine	—	600.00	375.00	275.00
R722	"	$5000 carmine	—	1250.00	1100.00	1000.00
R723	"	$10,000 carmine	—	650.00	550.00	300.00

Documentary Stamps and Type of 1940 Without Overprint.
1958 Perf. 12 Wmk. 191R
With Gum
Size: 28½ x 42mm.

R724	R25	$30 carmine	35.00	6.00	4.50	3.00
		a. Vert. pair, imperf. horiz.	—			
R725	"	$50 carmine	35.00	5.00	2.50	2.00
		a. Vert. pair, imperf. horiz.	—			
R726	"	$60 carmine	—	20.00	10.00	
R727	"	$100 carmine	17.50	4.75	3.00	2.25
R728	"	$500 carmine	80.00	25.00	10.00	7.50
R729	"	$1000 carmine	50.00	20.00	10.00	7.50
		a. Vert. pair, imperf. horiz.	—			
R730	"	$2500 carmine	—	125.00	75.00	
R731	"	$5000 carmine	—	125.00	85.00	60.00
R732	"	$10,000 carmine	—	100.00	50.00	25.00

Internal Revenue Building, Washington, D.C.
R26

Centenary of the Internal Revenue Service.
Giori Press Printing
1962, July 2 Perf. 11 Unwmkd.

R733	R26	10c vio.bl. & brt.grn.	1.00	20	10	8
		Margin block of 4, P #	15.00			

1963 "Established 1862" Removed

R734	R26	10c vio.bl. & brt.grn.	3.00	10	5	5
		Margin block of 4, P #	35.00			

Documentary revenue stamps were no longer required after Dec. 31, 1967.

PROPRIETARY STAMPS.

Stamps for use on proprietary articles were included in the first general issue of 1862–71. They are R3, R13, R14, R18, R22, R29, R31 and R38.

Several varieties of "violet" paper were used in printing Nos. RB1–RB10. One is grayish with a slight greenish tinge, called "intermediate" paper by specialists. It should not be confused with the "green" paper, which is truly green.

All prices prior to 1898 are for used copies. Printed cancellations on proprietary stamps command sizable premiums.

George Washington
RB1   RB1a

Engraved and printed by Jos. R. Carpenter Philadelphia.

1871-74   Perf. 12

RB1b
a. Violet Paper   b. Green Paper
                     (1874)

			a. Violet Paper (1871)	b. Green Paper (1874)
RB1	RB1	1c green & black	3.50	5.75
		Pair	8.00	14.00
		Block of four	20.00	35.00
		c. Imperf.	100.00	
		Imperf. pair	250.00	
		Imperf. block of four	600.00	
		d. Inverted center	2500.00	
RB2	"	2c green & black	4.00	12.00
		Pair	10.00	27.50
		Block of four	22.50	65.00
		Double transfer	—	
		c. Inverted center	40,000.00	9500.00
		Vert. half used as 1c	—	
RB3	RB1a	3c green & black	10.00	35.00
		Pair	25.00	80.00
		Block of four	60.00	175.00
		Double transfer	—	
		c. Sewing machine perf.	125.00	
		d. Inverted center	15,000.00	
RB4	"	4c green & black	7.00	12.50
		Pair	18.00	30.00
		Block of four	40.00	70.00
		Double transfer	—	
		c. Inverted center	16,500.00	
		Vert. half used as 2c	—	
RB5	"	5c green & black	90.00	95.00
		Pair	225.00	225.00
		Block of four	500.00	500.00
		c. Inverted center	40,000.00	
RB6	"	6c green & black	27.50	70.00
		Pair	65.00	150.00
		Block of four	150.00	400.00
		Double transfer	—	
RB7	"	10c green & black ('73)	125.00	35.00
		Pair	300.00	75.00
		Block of four	—	175.00
		Double transfer	—	
RB8	RB1b	50c green & black ('73)	550.00	800.00
		Pair	1300.00	
RB9	"	$1 green & black ('73)	1200.00	3000.00
		Pair	—	

(See note on Inverted Centers after No. R133.)

RB1c

REVENUES

		a. Violet Paper	b. Green Paper
RB10	RB1c $5 green & black ('73)	2500.00	—
	Pair	5500.00	—

When the Carpenter contract expired Aug. 31, 1875, the proprietary stamps remaining unissued were delivered to the Bureau of Internal Revenue. Until the taxes expired, June 30, 1883, the B.I.R. issued 34,315 of the 50c, 6,585 of the $1 and 2,109 of the $5, Nos. RB8–RB10. No. RB19, the 10c blue, replaced No. RB7b, the 10c on green paper, after 336,000 copies were issued, exhausting the supply in 1881.

George Washington
RB2   RB2a

1875-81
Engraved and printed by the National Bank Note Co.

			Silk Paper	Wmkd. USIR (191R)	
			a. Perf.	b. Perf.	c. Rouletted 6
RB11	RB2	1c green	1.25	25	30.00
		Pair	3.00	75	65.00
		Block of four	8.00	2.00	150.00
		d. Vertical pair, imperf. between		200.00	
RB12	"	2c brown	1.50	1.00	45.00
		Pair	3.50	3.00	100.00
		Block of four	8.00	7.00	250.00
RB13	RB2a	3c orange	8.50	2.00	45.00
		Pair	20.00	5.00	100.00
		Block of four	45.00	12.00	225.00
		d. Horizontal pair, imperf. between			
RB14	"	4c red brown	4.00	3.75	
		Pair	9.00	9.00	
		Block of four	22.00	20.00	
RB15	"	4c red		3.25	45.00
		Pair		7.00	100.00
		Block of four		20.00	
RB16	"	5c black	80.00	70.00	725.00
		Pair	170.00	150.00	—
		Block of four	375.00	325.00	—
RB17	"	6c violet blue	18.00	12.00	125.00
		Pair	40.00	30.00	275.00
		Block of four	90.00	65.00	—
RB18	"	6c violet		18.00	150.00
		Pair		40.00	325.00
		Block of four		90.00	—
RB19	"	10c blue ('81)		175.00	
		Pair		375.00	
		Block of four		800.00	

No. RB19 was produced by the Bureau of Engraving and Printing after taking over the stamp printing contract in 1880.

Battleship
RB3
Inscribed "Series of 1898," and "Proprietary."

Wmkd. USIR (191R)

1898
Engraved   Rouletted 5½, 7
See note on rouletting preceding No. R161.

			r. Rouletted 5½		p. Hyphen Hole Perf. 7	
			Unused	Used	Unused	Used
RB20	RB3	⅛c yellow green	6	6	12	10
		Block of four	25	25	55	50
		Double transfer	—	—		
		a. Vert. pair, imperf. horiz.	—	—		

			r. Rouletted 5½		p. Hyphen Hole Perf. 7	
			Unused	Used	Unused	Used
RB21	RB3	⅛c brown	6	6	12	10
	a.	⅛c red brown	6	6		
	b.	⅛c yellow brown	6	6	12	10
	c.	⅛c orange brown	6	6	12	10
	d.	⅛c bistre	6	6		
		Block of four	25	25	55	50
		Double transfer	—	—		
	e.	Vert. pair, imperf. horiz.		—		
	f.	Printed on both sides		—		
RB22	"	⅜c deep orange	12	8	25	15
		Block of four	60	32	1.25	—
	a.	Horiz. pair, imperf. vert.	9.00			
	b.	Vert. pair, imperf. horiz.				
RB23	"	⅝c deep ultramarine	12	10	25	15
		Block of four	60	40	1.25	75
		Double transfer	1.50			
	a.	Vert. pair, imperf. horiz.	50.00			
	b.	Horiz. pair, imperf. vert.	200.00			
RB24	"	1c dark green	30	15	12.00	5.00
		Block of four	1.50	75	—	—
	a.	Vert. pair, imperf. horiz.				
RB25	"	1¼c violet	10	8	20	12
		Block of four	45	35	90	90
	a.	1¼c brown violet	12	10	20	12
	b.	Vertical pair, imperf. between				
RB26	"	1⅞c dull blue	2.00	65	7.50	—
		Block of four	10.00	—	50.00	—
		Double transfer	—			
RB27	"	2c violet brown	35	18	75	25
		Block of four	1.75	—	4.00	—
		Double transfer	—			
	a.	Horiz. pair, imperf. vert.	25.00			
RB28	"	2½c lake	40	12	50	20
		Block of four	2.00	60	—	—
	a.	Vert. pair, imperf. horiz.	30.00			
RB29	"	3¾c olive gray	5.00	2.50	10.00	5.00
		Block of four	25.00	—	55.00	25.00
RB30	"	4c purple	2.00	75	—	—
		Block of four	10.00	3.75	—	—
		Double transfer	—			
RB31	"	5c brown orange	2.00	75	10.00	6.00
		Block of four	10.00	4.00	—	—
	a.	Vert. pair, imperf. horiz.	—	225.00		
	b.	Horiz. pair, imperf. vert.	—			

See note after No. RS315 regarding St. Louis Provisional Labels of 1898.

RB4
Inscribed "Series of 1914"
Wmkd. USPS (190)

1914
Offset Printing   Perf. 10

RB32	RB4	¼c black			15	10
		Block of four			70	50
RB33	"	⅜c black			1.00	70
		Block of four			4.50	
RB34	"	⅝c black			15	10
		Block of four			65	50
RB35	"	⅝c black			2.00	1.25
		Block of four			9.00	
RB36	"	1¼c black			1.50	75
		Block of four			7.00	
RB37	"	1⅞c black			20.00	12.00
		Block of four			90.00	
RB38	"	2½c black			2.75	2.00
		Block of four			12.50	9.00
RB39	"	3⅛c black			60.00	45.00
		Block of four			250.00	
RB40	"	3¾c black			20.00	12.00
		Block of four			90.00	

RB41	RB4	4c black		35.00	22.50
		Block of four		150.00	
RB42	"	4⅜c black		700.00	—
		Block of four		—	
RB43	"	5c black		75.00	50.00
		Block of four		325.00	

Wmkd. USIR (191R)

RB44	RB4	⅛c black		12	10
		Block of four		55	45
RB45	"	¼c black		12	10
		Block of four		55	45
		Double impression		12.50	
RB46	"	⅜c black		50	30
		Block of four		2.25	1.50
RB47	"	½c black		2.25	1.65
		Block of four		10.00	
RB48	"	⅝c black		10	8
		Block of four		50	35
RB49	"	1c black		3.00	2.25
		Block of four		13.00	10.00
RB50	"	1¼c black		30	20
		Block of four		1.50	1.00
RB51	"	1½c black		2.50	1.75
		Block of four		11.00	8.00
RB52	"	1⅞c black		75	55
		Block of four		3.25	2.50
RB53	"	2c black		4.00	3.25
		Block of four		18.00	
RB54	"	2½c black		1.00	85
		Block of four		4.50	4.00
RB55	"	3c black		3.00	2.50
		Block of four		14.00	
RB56	"	3⅛c black		3.50	2.50
		Block of four		15.00	
RB57	"	3¾c black		7.50	6.00
		Block of four		32.50	
RB58	"	4c black		25	18
		Block of four		1.15	90
		Double impression		—	
RB59	"	4⅜c black		9.00	6.00
		Block of four		40.00	
RB60	"	5c black		2.25	2.00
		Block of four		10.00	
RB61	"	6c black		40.00	30.00
		Block of four		175.00	
RB62	"	8c black		11.00	9.00
		Block of four		47.50	
RB63	"	10c black		7.50	6.00
		Block of four		32.50	
RB64	"	20c black		15.00	11.00
		Block of four		65.00	

RB5

1919   Offset Printing   Perf. 11

RB65	RB5	1c dark blue		10	8
		Block of four		50	40
		Double impression		17.50	—
RB66	"	2c dark blue		12	8
		Block of four		55	40
		Double impression		—	
RB67	"	3c dark blue		60	40
		Block of four		2.75	1.50
		Double impression		—	
RB68	"	4c dark blue		90	40
		Block of four		4.00	
RB69	"	5c dark blue		90	45
		Block of four		4.00	2.50
RB70	"	8c dark blue		9.00	7.00
		Block of four		40.00	
RB71	"	10c dark blue		1.75	1.25
		Block of four		7.50	5.50
RB72	"	20c dark blue		3.25	2.25
		Block of four		15.00	
RB73	"	40c dark blue		18.00	6.00
		Block of four		75.00	

FUTURE DELIVERY STAMPS.

Issued to facilitate the collection of a tax upon each sale, agreement of sale or agreement to sell any products or merchandise at any exchange or board of trade, or other similar place for future delivery.

Documentary Stamps of 1917 Overprinted in Black or Red

FUTURE DELIVERY Type I

Wmkd. USIR (191R)

1918-34   Offset Printing   Perf. 11.

Overprint Horizontal
(Lines 8mm. apart)

RC1	R22	2c carmine rose		75	10
		Block of four		3.50	50
RC2	"	3c carmine rose ('34)		25.00	20.00
		Cut cancellation			10.00
RC3	"	4c carmine rose		90	10
		Block of four		4.00	50
		Double impression of stamp			10.00
RC3A	"	5c carmine rose ('33)		—	2.50
		Block of four			12.00
RC4	"	10c carmine rose		1.75	10
		Block of four		8.00	50
		a. Double overprint		—	4.00
		b. "FUTURE" omitted		—	
		c. "DELIVERY FUTURE"			25.00
RC5	"	20c carmine rose		2.00	10
		Block of four		9.00	50
		a. Double overprint			20.00
RC6	"	25c carmine rose		8.00	40
		Block of four		32.50	1.75
		Cut cancellation			6
		Block of four, cut canc.			25
RC7	"	40c carmine rose		6.00	40
		Block of four		25.00	1.75
		Cut cancellation			6
		Block of four, cut canc.			25
RC8	"	50c carmine rose		2.00	12
		Block of four		9.00	55
		a. "DELIVERY" omitted			
RC9	"	80c carmine rose		13.00	5.00
		Block of four		55.00	22.50
		Cut cancellation			70
		Block of four, cut canc.			3.00
		a. Double overprint			25.00
		a. Cut cancellation			6.00

Engraved.

Overprint Vertical, Reading Up.
(Lines 2mm. apart)

RC10	R21	$1 green (R)		—	15
		Block of four			75
		Cut cancellation			5
		a. Overprint reading down		275.00	
		b. Black overprint		—	
		Black ovpt., cut canc.		125.00	
RC11	"	$2 rose		—	15
		Block of four			75
		Cut cancellation			5
RC12	"	$3 violet (R)		—	1.00
		Block of four			4.50
		Cut cancellation			12
		Block of four, cut canc.			50
		a. Overprint reading down		—	50.00
RC13	"	$5 dark blue (R)		—	25
		Block of four			1.25
		Cut cancellation			8
		Block of four, cut canc.			35
RC14	"	$10 orange		—	50
		Block of four			2.25
		Cut cancellation			15
		Block of four, cut canc.			75
		a. "DELIVERY FUTURE"		—	
RC15	"	$20 olive bistre		—	3.00
		Block of four			14.00
		Cut cancellation			45
		Block of four, cut canc.			2.00

REVENUES

Overprint Horizontal.
(Lines 11½mm. apart)
Perf. 12.
Without Gum

RC16	R17	$30 vermilion, green numerals		—	2.75
		Vertical strip of four			—
		Cut cancellation			1.00
		Vertical strip of four, cut canc.			4.50
		a. Numerals in blue	50.00		2.50
		Cut cancellation			1.00
		b. Imperf., blue numerals			—
RC17	R19	$50 olive green *(Cleveland)*		—	90
		Vertical strip of four			—
		Cut cancellation			40
		Vertical strip of four, cut canc.			1.75
		a. $50 olive bister		—	90
		Cut cancellation			40
RC18	"	$60 brown		—	1.50
		Vertical strip of four			—
		Cut cancellation			75
		Vertical strip of four, cut canc.			3.50
		a. Vert. pair, imperf. horiz.			400.00
RC19	R17	$100 yellow green ('34)		—	20.00
		Vertical strip of four			—
		Cut cancellation			5.00
		Vertical strip of four, cut canc.			21.00
RC20	R18	$500 blue, red numerals (R)	50.00		8.00
		Vertical strip of four			—
		Cut cancellation			3.50
		Vertical strip of four, cut canc.			16.00
		Double transfer			15.00
		a. Numerals in orange		—	60.00
		a. Cut cancellation			10.00
		a. Double transfer			15.00
RC21	R19	$1000 orange		—	3.50
		Vertical strip of four			20.00
		Cut cancellation			1.50
		Vertical strip of four, cut canc.			7.50
		a. Vert. pair, imperf. horiz.			500.00
		See note after No. R227.			

1923-1924   Offset Printing.   *Perf. 11.*
Overprint Horizontal.
(Lines 2mm. apart)

RC22	R22	1c carmine rose		35	10
		Block of four		1.50	50
RC23	"	80c carmine rose		—	1.25
		Block of four		—	6.00
		Cut cancellation			20
		Block of four, cut canc.			85

FUTURE DELIVERY

Documentary Stamps of 1917 Overprinted

1925-1934   Engraved.   Type II

RC25	R21	$1 green (R)	5.00		50
		Block of four		—	2.25
		Cut cancellation			6
		Block of four, cut canc.			30
RC26	"	$10 orange (Bk) ('34)		—	10.00
		Cut cancellation			5.00

Overprint Type I
1928-29   Offset Printing.   *Perf. 10*

RC27	R22	10c carmine rose		850.00
RC28	"	20c carmine rose		850.00

STOCK TRANSFER STAMPS.

Issued to facilitate the collection of a tax on all sales or agreements to sell, or memoranda of sales or delivery of, or transfers of legal title to shares or certificates of stock.

STOCK TRANSFER

Documentary Stamps of 1917 Overprinted in Black or Red

Wmkd. USIR (191R)

1918-22   Offset Printing.   *Perf. 11*
Overprint Horizontal.
(Lines 8mm. apart)

RD1	R22	1c carmine rose		25	10
		Block of four		1.20	45
		a. Double overprint		—	—
RD2	R22	2c carmine rose		10	5
		Block of four		—	20
		a. Double overprint		—	5.00
		a. Cut cancellation			2.50
		Double impression of stamp		—	
RD3	"	4c carmine rose		12	5
		Block of four		50	20
		a. Double overprint		—	4.00
		a. Cut cancellation		—	2.00
		b. "STOCK" omitted		—	10.00
		d. Ovpt. lines 10mm. apart			
		Double impression of stamp			6.00
RD4	"	5c carmine rose		15	5
		Block of four		60	25
RD5	"	10c carmine rose		12	5
		Block of four			25
		a. Double overprint		—	5.00
		a. Cut cancellation			2.50
		b. "STOCK" omitted			—
		Double impression of stamp			—
RD6	"	20c carmine rose		20	5
		Block of four		95	25
		a. Double overprint		—	6.00
		b. "STOCK" double			—
		Double impression of stamp			6.00
RD7	"	25c carmine rose		60	10
		Block of four		—	50
		Cut cancellation			5
RD8	"	40c carmine rose ('22)		50	6
		Block of four			30
RD9	"	50c carmine rose		25	5
		Block of four		70	25
		a. Double overprint			—
		Double impression of stamp			—
RD10	"	80c carmine rose		65	20
		Block of four		—	1.00
		Cut cancellation			5

Engraved.
Overprint Vertical, Reading Up.
(Lines 2mm. apart)

RD11	R21	$1 green (R)		25.00	6.00
		Block of four		—	—
		Cut cancellation			45
		Block of four, cut canc.			2.25
		a. Overprint reading down		—	10.00
		a. Cut cancellation			4.00
RD12	"	$1 green (Bk)		1.25	5
		Block of four		—	25
		a. Pair, one without overprint		—	
		b. Overprinted on back instead of face, inverted			—
		c. Overprint reading down		—	5.00
		d. $1 yellow green		—	6
RD13	"	$2 rose		1.25	5
		Block of four		—	25
		a. Overprint reading down		—	10.00
		a. Cut cancellation			1.50
		b. Vert. pair, imperf. horiz.		500.00	
		c. "TRANSFER STOCK"			—
RD14	"	$3 violet (R)		4.50	75
		Block of four		—	20
		Block of four, cut canc.			1.00
RD15	"	$4 yellow brown		3.25	5
		Block of four		—	25
		Cut cancellation			5
RD16	"	$5 dark blue (R)		2.00	5
		Block of four		—	25
		Cut cancellation			5
		Block of four, cut canc.			15
		a. Overprint reading down		—	75
		a. Cut cancellation			15
RD17	"	$10 orange		3.25	12
		Block of four		15.00	60
		Cut cancellation			5
		Block of four, cut canc.			20
		a. "TRANSFER STOCK"			—
		b. "TRANSFER" omitted			—
RD18	"	$20 olive bistre ('21)		27.50	15.00
		Block of four		125.00	75.00
		Cut cancellation			3.00
		Block of four, cut canc.			15.00

Overprint Horizontal.
(Lines 11½mm. apart)
Perf. 12.
Without Gum

1918

RD19	R17	$30 vermilion, green numerals		11.00	3.50
		Vertical strip of four			15.00
		Cut cancellation			1.00
		Vertical strip of four, cut canc.			6.00
		a. Numerals in blue			50.00

REVENUES

RD20	R19	$50 olive green (*Cleveland*)	60.00	45.00
		Vertical strip of four		200.00
		Cut cancellation		10.00
		Vertical strip of four, cut canc.		45.00
RD21	"	$60 brown	45.00	14.00
		Vertical strip of four		65.00
		Cut cancellation		5.00
		Vertical strip of four, cut canc.		21.00
RD22	R17	$100 green	12.00	4.00
		Vertical strip of four		15.00
		Cut cancellation		1.50
		Vertical strip of four, cut canc.		7.00
RD23	R18	$500 blue (R)	—	95.00
		Vertical strip of four		—
		Cut cancellation		40.00
		Vertical strip of four, cut canc.		175.00
		Double transfer		110.00
		a. Numerals in orange		100.00
RD24	R19	$1000 orange	—	65.00
		Vertical strip of four		275.00
		Cut cancellation		22.50
		Vertical strip of four, cut canc.		100.00
		See note after No. R227.		

1928   Offset Printing.   *Perf. 10.*
Overprint Horizontal.
(Lines 8mm. apart)

RD25	R22	2c carmine rose	25	5
		Block of four	1.10	25
RD26	"	4c carmine rose	25	5
		Block of four	1.10	25
RD27	"	10c carmine rose	30	6
		Block of four	1.25	25
		a. Inverted overprint		1000.00
RD28	"	20c carmine rose	45	6
		Block of four	2.00	25
		Double impression of stamp		—
RD29	"	50c carmine rose	80	10
		Block of four	3.25	45

Engraved.
Overprint Vertical, Reading Up
(Lines 2mm. apart)

RD30	R21	$1 green	1.40	5
		Block of four	—	25
		a. $1 yellow green	—	—
RD31	"	$2 carmine rose	1.40	5
		Block of four	—	25
		a. Pair, one without overprint	150.00	
RD32	"	$10 orange	6.25	15
		Block of four	—	75
		Cut cancellation		5
		Perf. 11 at top or bottom		—

STOCK TRANSFER

Overprinted Horizontally in Black

1920   Offset Printing   *Perf. 11*

RD33	R22	2c carmine rose	2.25	40
		Block of four	10.00	2.00
RD34	"	10c carmine rose	35	5
		Block of four	1.50	20
		a. "TRANSFER STOCK"		40.00
RD35	"	20c carmine rose	35	5
		Block of four	1.50	25
		a. Pair, one without overprint	175.00	—
		b. "TRANSFER STOCK"		75.00
		c. "TRANSFER" omitted		65.00
RD36	"	50c carmine rose	85	8
		Block of four	3.75	35

Engraved.

RD37	R21	$1 green	10.00	4.50
		Block of four	—	20.00
		Cut cancellation		25
		Block of four, cut canc.		65
RD38	"	$2 rose	7.50	4.50
		Block of four	35.00	20.00
		Cut cancellation		25
		Block of four, cut canc.		1.10

Offset Printing.
Perf. 10.

RD39	R22	2c carmine rose	2.25	25
		Block of four	10.00	40
		Double impression of stamp	—	
RD40	"	10c carmine rose	65	6
		Block of four	3.00	25
RD41	"	20c carmine rose	85	6
		Block of four	3.50	25

SERIES 1940

Documentary Stamps
of 1917–33
Overprinted in Black

1940   *Perf. 11*   Wmk. 191R

			Unused	Used (uncut)	Used (cut canc.)	Used (perforated initials)
RD42	R22	1c rose pink	1.25	40	20	15
		a. "Series 1940" inverted	—	225.00	100.00	
RD43	"	2c rose pink	75	25	8	6
RD45	"	4c rose pink	75	6	5	5
RD46	"	5c rose pink	1.00	6	5	5
RD48	"	10c rose pink	1.25	8	5	5
RD49	"	20c rose pink	4.00	8	5	5
RD50	"	25c rose pink	4.00	25	12	10
RD51	"	40c rose pink	2.00	50	15	10
RD52	"	50c rose pink	2.75	8	6	5
RD53	"	80c rose pink	40.00	20.00	6.00	5.00

Engraved.

RD54	R21	$1 green	7.50	15	8	5
RD55	"	$2 rose	7.50	15	8	6
RD56	"	$3 violet	—	1.40	8	6
RD57	"	$4 yellow brown	9.00	25	5	5
RD58	"	$5 dark blue	11.00	25	12	5
RD59	"	$10 orange	30.00	3.00	50	40
RD60	"	$20 olive bistre	55.00	16.00	5.00	3.50

Nos. RD19-RD24 Handstamped in Blue "Series 1940"

1940   *Perf. 12*   Wmk. 191R

Without Gum

RD61	R17	$30 vermilion	300.00	150.00	110.00
RD62	R19	$50 olive green	400.00	100.00	80.00
		a. Double overprint			325.00
RD63	"	$60 brown	400.00	100.00	85.00
RD64	R17	$100 green	350.00	100.00	60.00
RD65	R18	$500 blue	1250.00	800.00	350.00
RD66	R19	$1000 orange	1750.00		1250.00

Alexander Hamilton   Levi Woodbury
ST1   ST2

Various Portraits

Engraved.

Overprinted in Black   SERIES 1940

1940   *Perf. 11*   Wmk. 191R

Size: 19 x 22 mm.

RD67	ST1	1c bright green	3.75	1.10	40	25
RD68	"	2c bright green (*Oliver Wolcott, Jr.*)	1.40	40	12	10
RD70	"	4c bright green (*Albert Gallatin*)	3.50	1.65	45	20
RD71	"	5c bright green (*G. W. Campbell*)	2.50	75	15	8
		a. Without overprint		—		
RD73	"	10c bright green (*William H. Crawford*)	3.50	55	18	8

REVENUES

			Unused	Used (uncut)	Used (cut canc.)	Used (perforated initials)
RD74	ST1	20c bright green (*Richard Rush*)	3.25	50	15	10
RD75	"	25c bright green (*S. D. Ingham*)	12.00	3.75	60	35
RD76	"	40c bright green (*Louis McLane*)	25.00	18.00	1.50	85
RD77	"	50c bright green (*Wm. J. Duane*)	3.25	65	30	25
RD78	"	80c bright green (*R. B. Taney*)	35.00	21.00	10.00	1.75

Size: 21½ x 36¼ mm.

RD79	ST2	$1 bright green	6.50	1.10	35	25
		a. Without overprint				150.00
RD80	"	$2 bright green (*Thomas Ewing*)	7.50	3.25	35	25
RD81	"	$3 bright green (*Walter Forward*)	16.00	4.25	50	8
RD82	"	$4 bright green (*J. C. Spencer*)	——	100.00	50.00	40.00
RD83	"	$5 bright green (*G. M. Bibb*)	16.00	6.50	30	20
RD84	"	$10 bright green (*R. J. Walker*)	——	16.00	50	40
RD85	"	$20 bright green (*Wm. M. Meredith*)	——	22.50	4.50	2.50

Nos. RD67–RD85 exist imperforate, without overprint.

Thomas Corwin
ST3
Perf. 12.
Overprinted "SERIES 1940"
Various Frames and Portraits
Without Gum
Size: 28½ x 42 mm.

RD86	ST3	$30 bright green	——	80.00	40.00	22.50
RD87	"	$50 bright green (*James Guthrie*)	——	100.00	35.00	30.00
RD88	"	$60 bright green (*Howell Cobb*)	——	140.00	55.00	40.00
RD89	"	$100 bright green (*P. F. Thomas*)	——	110.00	50.00	30.00
RD90	"	$500 bright green (*J. A. Dix*)	——	375.00	300.00	
RD91	"	$1000 bright green (*S. P. Chase*)	——	275.00	250.00	225.00

Stock Transfer Stamps of 1940 Overprinted in Black   SERIES 1941
1941   Perf. 11   Wmk. 191R
Size: 19 x 22 mm.

RD92	ST1	1c bright green	35	25	15	40
RD93	"	2c bright green	15	8	6	20
RD95	"	4c bright green	15	6	5	20
RD96	"	5c bright green	15	6	5	20
RD98	"	10c bright green	25	6	6	30
RD99	"	20c bright green	60	6	5	70
RD100	"	25c bright green	70	10	8	80
RD101	"	40c bright green	80	15	8	90

			Unused	Used (uncut)	Used (cut canc.)	Used (perforated initials)
RD102	ST1	50c bright green	1.65	8	5	5
RD103	"	80c bright green	7.25	2.75	25	12

Size: 21½ x 36¼ mm.

RD104	ST2	$1 bright green	4.50	8	5	5
RD105	"	$2 bright green	5.50	12	8	5
RD106	"	$3 bright green	7.50	70	30	5
RD107	"	$4 bright green	13.00	4.00	25	15
RD108	"	$5 bright green	16.50	30	10	6
RD109	"	$10 bright green	27.50	2.00	70	15
RD110	"	$20 bright green	——	25.00	6.00	90

Perf. 12.
Without Gum
Size: 28½ x 42 mm.

RD111	ST3	$30 bright green	85.00	70.00	16.00	9.00
RD112	"	$50 bright green	——	75.00	18.00	9.00
RD113	"	$60 bright green	160.00	100.00		
RD114	"	$100 bright green	——	45.00	18.00	8.00
RD115	"	$500 bright green	——	325.00		150.00
RD116	"	$1000 bright green	——	275.00		165.00

Stock Transfer Stamps of 1940   SERIES 1942
Overprinted in Black
1942   Perf. 11   Wmk. 191R
Size: 19 x 22 mm.

RD117	ST1	1c bright green	25	12	10	7
RD118	"	2c bright green	12	8	6	5
RD119	"	4c bright green	2.00	70	50	40
RD120	"	5c bright green	25	6	5	5
		a. Overprint inverted (Cut cancel.)			225.00	
RD121	"	10c bright green	60	6	5	5
RD122	"	20c bright green	85	8	6	5
RD123	"	25c bright green	1.00	8	6	5
RD124	"	40c bright green	1.90	18	10	8
RD125	"	50c bright green	2.50	6	5	5
RD126	"	80c bright green	5.50	3.00	1.00	20

Size: 21½ x 36¼ mm.

RD127	ST2	$1 bright green	5.50	6	5	5
RD128	"	$2 bright green	8.50	12	8	6
RD129	"	$3 bright green	10.00	50	10	6
RD130	"	$4 bright green	16.00	10.00	35	18
RD131	"	$5 bright green	12.00	30	10	5
		a. Double ovpt.				——
RD132	"	$10 bright green	27.50	4.00	65	20
RD133	"	$20 bright green	55.00	20.00	3.25	1.00

Perf. 12.
Without Gum
Size: 28½ x 42 mm.

RD134	ST3	$30 bright green	——	35.00	12.00	6.00
RD135	"	$50 bright green	——	55.00	16.00	6.00
RD136	"	$60 bright green	——	75.00		30.00
RD137	"	$100 bright green	——	60.00	20.00	10.00
RD138	"	$500 bright green	——			
RD139	"	$1000 bright green	——	200.00	150.00	

Stock Transfer Stamps of 1940   SERIES 1943
Overprinted in Black
1943   Perf. 11   Wmk. 191R
Size: 19 x 22 mm.

RD140	ST1	1c bright green	25	18	15	10
RD141	"	2c bright green	30	15	6	5
RD142	"	4c bright green	90	10	8	5
RD143	"	5c bright green	30	8	6	5
RD144	"	10c bright green	35	6	5	5
RD145	"	20c bright green	80	8	6	5
RD146	"	25c bright green	1.65	18	12	8
RD147	"	40c bright green	1.65	25	10	8
RD148	"	50c bright green	1.65	6	5	5
RD149	"	80c bright green	5.00	2.25	1.25	75

Size: 21½ x 36¼ mm.

RD150	ST2	$1 bright green	4.50	8	6	5
RD151	"	$2 bright green	6.00	20	10	5
RD152	"	$3 bright green	7.00	65	10	5
RD153	"	$4 bright green	16.00	9.00	35	15
RD154	"	$5 bright green	18.00	35	20	6
RD155	"	$10 bright green	27.50	2.75	75	5
RD156	"	$20 bright green	45.00	20.00	10.00	2.75

REVENUES

		Unused	Used (uncut)	Used (cut canc.)	Used (perforated initials)
		Perf. 12.			
		Without Gum			
		Size: 28½ x 42 mm.			
RD157	ST3	$30 bright green 175.00	75.00	20.00	17.50
RD158	"	$50 bright green —	75.00	20.00	12.00
RD159	"	$60 bright green —	90.00	40.00	35.00
RD160	"	$100 bright green —	45.00	15.00	10.00
RD161	"	$500 bright green —	175.00	90.00	
RD162	"	$1000 bright green —	165.00	125.00	90.00

Stock Transfer Stamps of 1940
Overprinted in Black   **Series 1944**

1944		**Perf. 11**		**Wmk. 191R**	
		Size: 19x22 mm.			
RD163	ST1	1c bright green 40	30	15	12
RD164	"	2c bright green 30	12	10	8
RD165	"	4c bright green 35	20	15	12
RD166	"	5c bright green 30	6	5	5
RD167	"	10c bright green 25	8	6	5
RD168	"	20c bright green 45	15	10	8
RD169	"	25c bright green 90	30	16	10
RD170	"	40c bright green 3.75	3.00	1.25	1.00
RD171	"	50c bright green 2.00	15	10	6
RD172	"	80c bright green 3.25	2.50	1.25	1.00
		Size: 21½ x 36¼ mm.			
RD173	ST2	$1 bright green 3.25	20	10	8
RD174	"	$2 bright green —	30	15	8
RD175	"	$3 bright green 9.00	60	25	8
RD176	"	$4 bright green 13.00	2.75	18	10
RD177	"	$5 bright green 11.00	50	30	15
RD178	"	$10 bright green 25.00	2.50	45	20
RD179	"	$20 bright green 50.00	4.75	3.00	1.50
		Perf. 12.			
		Without Gum			
		Size: 28½ x 42 mm.			
RD180	ST3	$30 bright green 50.00	35.00	11.00	9.00
RD181	"	$50 bright green 50.00	30.00	11.00	8.00
RD182	"	$60 bright green 125.00	75.00		30.00
RD183	"	$100 bright green —	35.00	15.00	8.00
RD184	"	$500 bright green —	300.00	225.00	175.00
RD185	"	$1000 bright green —		175.00	150.00
RD185A	"	$2500 bright green (William Windom) —			
RD185B	"	$5000 bright green (C. J. Folger) —			
RD185C	"	$10,000 bright green (W. Q. Gresham) —		800.00	

Stock Transfer Stamps of 1940
Overprinted in Black   **Series 1945**

1945		**Perf. 11**		**Wmk. 191R**	
		Size: 19 x 22 mm.			
RD186	ST1	1c bright green 12	10	6	5
RD187	"	2c bright green 20	15	8	6
RD188	"	4c bright green 15	8	6	5
RD189	"	5c bright green 18	8	5	5
RD190	"	10c bright green 35	30	10	8
RD191	"	20c bright green 40	25	20	12
RD192	"	25c bright green 90	35	25	20
RD193	"	40c bright green 1.50	18	12	8
RD194	"	50c bright green 1.50	18	8	6
RD195	"	80c bright green 2.50	1.50	70	65
		Size: 21½ x 36¼ mm.			
RD196	ST2	$1 bright green 6.00	12	8	6
RD197	"	$2 bright green 8.50	15	10	8
RD198	"	$3 bright green 11.00	35	12	10
RD199	"	$4 bright green 11.00	1.00	45	40
RD200	"	$5 bright green 9.00	20	15	8
RD201	"	$10 bright green 18.00	3.25	75	60
RD202	"	$20 bright green 30.00	3.75	1.00	85
		Perf. 12.			
		Without Gum			
		Size: 28½ x 42 mm.			
RD203	ST3	$30 bright green 60.00	30.00	16.00	13.00
RD204	"	$50 bright green 40.00	10.00	4.00	3.00
RD205	"	$60 bright green 100.00	65.00	20.00	15.00
RD206	"	$100 bright green —	20.00	12.00	7.00
RD207	"	$500 bright green ——	200.00	135.00	100.00
RD208	"	$1000 bright green —	225.00		125.00

RD208A	ST3	$2500 bright green —	—		
RD208B	"	$5000 bright green —	—		
RD208C	"	$10,000 bright green —		800.00	

Stock Transfer Stamps and Type of 1940
Overprinted in Black   **Series 1946**

1946		**Perf. 11**		**Wmk. 191R**	
		Size: 19 x 22 mm.			
RD209	ST1	1c bright green 10	8	6	5
		a. Pair, one dated "1945" 375.00			
RD210	"	2c bright green 12	6	5	5
RD211	"	4c bright green 15	8	6	5
RD212	"	5c bright green 18	6	5	5
RD213	"	10c bright green 30	6	5	5
RD214	"	20c bright green 65	12	10	8
RD215	"	25c bright green 75	12	10	8
RD216	"	40c bright green 1.00	25	15	12
RD217	"	50c bright green 1.25	20	12	10
RD218	"	80c bright green 2.75	2.50	90	80
		Size: 21½ x 36¼ mm.			
RD219	ST2	$1 bright green 3.00	20	8	6
RD220	"	$2 bright green 4.00	20	15	12
RD221	"	$3 bright green 6.00	50	30	18
RD222	"	$4 bright green 7.50	2.50	1.00	85
RD223	"	$5 bright green 11.00	40	20	18
RD224	"	$10 bright green 20.00	85	25	15
RD225	"	$20 bright green 35.00	20.00	7.00	5.00
		Perf. 12.			
		Without Gum			
		Size: 28½ x 42 mm.			
RD226	ST3	$30 bright green 45.00	25.00	12.00	9.00
RD227	"	$50 bright green 45.00	25.00	10.00	7.00
RD228	"	$60 bright green 100.00	60.00	22.50	10.00
RD229	"	$100 bright green 60.00	30.00	10.00	8.00
RD230	"	$500 bright green —	125.00		65.00
RD231	"	$1000 bright green —	110.00		75.00
RD232	"	$2500 bright green —	—		
RD233	"	$5000 bright green —	—		
RD234	"	$10,000 bright green —		800.00	

Stock Transfer Stamps and Type of 1940
Overprinted in Black   **Series 1947**

1947		**Perf. 11**		**Wmk. 191R**	
		Size: 19 x 22 mm.			
RD235	ST1	1c bright green 35	30	8	6
RD236	"	2c bright green 25	15	8	8
RD237	"	4c bright green 15	15	6	5
RD238	"	5c bright green 20	10	5	5
RD239	"	10c bright green 30	15	6	5
RD240	"	20c bright green 55	20	15	12
RD241	"	25c bright green 80	25	18	15
RD242	"	40c bright green 1.10	35	25	18
RD243	"	50c bright green 1.40	10	5	5
RD244	"	80c bright green 6.00	4.50	2.00	1.75
		Size: 21½ x 36¼ mm.			
RD245	ST2	$1 bright green 3.00	25	15	12
RD246	"	$2 bright green 4.50	35	15	12
RD247	"	$3 bright green 7.00	75	35	30
RD248	"	$4 bright green 15.00	3.25	85	70
RD249	"	$5 bright green 10.00	70	30	20
RD250	"	$10 bright green 17.50	2.75	1.10	90
RD251	"	$20 bright green 35.00	15.00		4.50
		Perf. 12.			
		Without Gum			
		Size: 28½ x 42 mm.			
RD252	ST3	$30 bright green 50.00	22.50	7.00	4.00
RD253	"	$50 bright green 100.00	70.00	20.00	12.50
RD254	"	$60 bright green 100.00	75.00	30.00	25.00
RD255	"	$100 bright green —	21.00	10.00	8.00
RD256	"	$500 bright green —	175.00	75.00	60.00
RD257	"	$1000 bright green —	75.00	35.00	25.00
RD258	"	$2500 bright green —		300.00	
RD259	"	$5000 bright green —		350.00	
RD260	"	$10,000 bright green —		65.00	
		a. Horiz. pair, imperf. vert.			

Stock Transfer Stamps of 1940
Overprinted in Black   **Series 1948**

1948		**Perf. 11**		**Wmk. 191R**	
		Size: 19x22mm.			
RD261	ST1	1c bright green 12	10	6	5
RD262	"	2c bright green 15	8	6	5

REVENUES

			Unused	Used (uncut)	Used (cut canc.)	Used (perforated initials)
RD263	ST1	4c bright green	20	15	12	8
RD264	"	5c bright green	20	8	6	5
RD265	"	10c bright green	25	8	6	5
RD266	"	20c bright green	60	15	10	8
RD267	"	25c bright green	70	20	15	12
RD268	"	40c bright green	1.00	30	25	20
RD269	"	50c bright green	1.75	12	8	8
RD270	"	80c bright green	5.00	4.00	1.00	90

Size: 21½ x 36¼ mm.

RD271	ST2	$1 bright green	3.00	20	12	10
RD272	"	$2 bright green	6.00	30	15	15
RD273	"	$3 bright green	6.00	2.00	50	40
RD274	"	$4 bright green	7.50	5.00	1.50	1.50
RD275	"	$5 bright green	11.00	90	25	20
RD276	"	$10 bright green	18.00	2.50	75	60
RD277	"	$20 bright green	35.00	10.00	4.50	

Perf. 12.
Without Gum
Size: 28½ x 42 mm.

RD278	ST3	$30 brt. green	50.00	25.00	18.00	10.00
RD279	"	$50 brt. green	40.00	25.00	9.00	6.00
RD280	"	$60 brt. green	75.00	55.00	20.00	15.00
RD281	"	$100 brt. green	—	12.00	6.00	4.00
RD282	"	$500 brt. green	—	125.00	75.00	35.00
RD283	"	$1000 brt. green	—	75.00	30.00	25.00
RD284	"	$2500 brt. green	250.00	200.00	150.00	
RD285	"	$5000 brt. green	—	200.00	150.00	
RD286	"	$10,000 brt. green	—		60.00	

Stock Transfer Stamps of 1940
Overprinted in Black — Series 1949

1949 Perf. 11 Wmk. 191R
Size: 19 x 22 mm.

RD287	ST1	1c bright green	15	15	6	5
RD288	"	2c bright green	15	10	5	5
RD289	"	4c bright green	20	15	6	5
RD290	"	5c bright green	20	10	6	5
RD291	"	10c bright green	35	10	5	5
RD292	"	20c bright green	70	15	10	8
RD293	"	25c bright green	85	25	12	10
RD294	"	40c bright green	1.65	55	20	15
RD295	"	50c bright green	2.00	15	6	5
RD296	"	80c bright green	4.00	3.00	1.75	1.20

Size: 21½ x 36¼ mm.

RD297	ST2	$1 bright green	3.00	20	10	8
RD298	"	$2 bright green	5.50	40	18	15
RD299	"	$3 bright green	9.00	2.75	45	40
RD300	"	$4 bright green	11.00	5.25	2.00	1.50
RD301	"	$5 bright green	16.00	1.00	25	20
RD302	"	$10 bright green	25.00	2.25	1.25	1.00
RD303	"	$20 bright green	50.00	10.00	5.00	4.00

Perf. 12.
Without Gum
Size: 28½ x 42 mm.

RD304	ST3	$30 bright green	—	35.00	12.00	
RD305	"	$50 bright green	—	35.00	12.00	9.00
RD306	"	$60 bright green	125.00	70.00	25.00	
RD307	"	$100 bright green	—	35.00	20.00	12.00
RD308	"	$500 bright green	—	110.00	45.00	35.00
RD309	"	$1000 bright green	—	60.00	40.00	25.00
RD310	"	$2500 bright green	—		125.00	
RD311	"	$5000 bright green	—		100.00	
RD312	"	$10,000 bright green	—		30.00	225.00

  a. Pair, one without overprint

Stock Transfer Stamps of 1940
Overprinted in Black — Series 1950

1950 Perf. 11 Wmk. 191R
Size: 19 x 22 mm.

RD313	ST1	1c bright green	15	10	5	5
RD314	"	2c bright green	15	10	5	5
RD315	"	4c bright green	20	10	6	5
RD316	"	5c bright green	20	10	5	5
RD317	"	10c bright green	70	10	5	5
RD318	"	20c bright green	85	15	6	5
RD319	"	25c bright green	1.65	25	12	10
RD320	"	40c bright green	2.00	35	20	18
RD321	"	50c bright green	3.25	15	6	5
RD322	"	80c bright green	2.75	2.50	1.50	1.00

			Unused	Used (uncut)	Used (cut canc.)	Used (perforated initials)

Size: 21½ x 36¼ mm.

RD323	ST2	$1 bright green	3.50	20	8	6
RD324	"	$2 bright green	6.75	30	12	10
RD325	"	$3 bright green	9.00	2.00	60	50
RD326	"	$4 bright green	11.00	6.00	2.25	1.75
RD327	"	$5 bright green	15.00	85	20	18
RD328	"	$10 bright green	25.00	3.25	85	75
RD329	"	$20 bright green	40.00	12.00		4.00

Perf. 12.
Without Gum
Size: 28½ x 42 mm.

RD330	ST3	$30 bright green	60.00	35.00	20.00	12.00
RD331	"	$50 bright green	70.00	50.00		18.00
RD332	"	$60 bright green	—	75.00	30.00	
RD333	"	$100 bright green	—	30.00	20.00	10.00
RD334	"	$500 bright green	—	100.00		75.00
RD335	"	$1000 bright green	—	65.00	30.00	20.00
RD336	"	$2500 bright green	—		425.00	
RD337	"	$5000 bright green	—	350.00	225.00	
RD338	"	$10,000 bright green	—		60.00	

Stock Transfer Stamps of 1940
Overprinted in Black — Series 1951

1951 Perf. 11 Wmk. 191R
Size: 19 x 22 mm.

RD339	ST1	1c bright green	15	10	5	5
RD340	"	2c bright green	15	10	5	5
RD341	"	4c bright green	20	15	5	5
RD342	"	5c bright green	20	10	5	5
RD343	"	10c bright green	35	10	5	5
RD344	"	20c bright green	80	25	12	10
RD345	"	25c bright green	1.10	30	15	12
RD346	"	40c bright green	2.00	2.00	50	40
RD347	"	50c bright green	2.00	30	8	6
RD348	"	80c bright green	3.50	2.50	1.25	1.00

Size: 21½ x 36¼ mm.

RD349	ST2	$1 bright green	4.50	25	6	5
RD350	"	$2 bright green	5.50	40	18	12
RD351	"	$3 bright green	9.00	4.00		
RD352	"	$4 bright green	11.00	6.00		1.50
RD353	"	$5 bright green	15.00	1.10	25	20
RD354	"	$10 bright green	25.00	6.00	2.00	1.50
RD355	"	$20 bright green	45.00	10.00	6.00	4.50

Perf. 12.
Without Gum
Size: 28½ x 42 mm.

RD356	ST3	$30 bright green	—	27.50		10.00
RD357	"	$50 bright green	—	25.00		10.00
RD358	"	$60 bright green	—	150.00		70.00
RD359	"	$100 bright green	—	20.00	15.00	
RD360	"	$500 bright green	—	90.00		50.00
RD361	"	$1000 bright green	—	50.00		30.00
RD362	"	$2500 bright green	—	450.00	200.00	150.00
RD363	"	$5000 bright green	—	450.00	175.00	
RD364	"	$10,000 bright green	—	100.00	50.00	

Stock Transfer Stamps of 1940
Overprinted in Black — Series 1952

1952 Perf. 11 Wmk. 191R
Size: 19 x 22 mm.

RD365	ST1	1c bright green	20.00	10.00	1.50	1.25
RD366	"	10c bright green	15.00	7.50	1.00	90
RD367	"	20c bright green	350.00			
RD368	"	25c bright green	400.00			
RD369	"	40c bright green	40.00	15.00	6.00	3.00

Size: 21½ x 36¼ mm.

RD370	ST2	$4 bright green	750.00	350.00		
RD371	"	$10 bright green	1500.00			
RD372	"	$20 bright green	2000.00			

Stock Transfer Stamps were discontinued in 1952.

CORDIALS, WINES, Etc.

RE1
Inscribed "Series of 1914"

Wmkd. USPS (190)

1914		Offset Printing	Perf. 10	
		Size: 19½ x 22¼ mm.		
RE1	RE1	¼c green	35	25
RE2	"	½c green	25	15
RE3	"	1c green	30	20
RE4	"	1½c green	1.25	60
RE5	"	2c green	2.50	1.75
RE6	"	3c green	1.10	50
RE7	"	4c green	1.25	1.10
RE8	"	5c green	50	25
RE9	"	6c green	3.00	1.25
RE10	"	8c green	1.65	60
RE11	"	10c green	1.65	1.40
RE12	"	20c green	1.50	60
RE13	"	24c green	6.00	3.50
RE14	"	40c green	1.25	35

RE1a
Imperf.
Without Gum
Size: 47x40mm.

RE15	RE1a	$2 green	2.25	15
		a. Double impression		90.00

1914		Wmkd. USIR (191R)	Perf. 10	
RE16	RE1	¼c green	2.00	1.75
RE17	"	½c green	1.00	90
RE18	"	1c green	12	8
RE19	"	1½c green	25.00	20.00
RE20	"	2c green	10	8
RE21	"	3c green	1.15	90
RE22	"	4c green	65	55
RE23	"	5c green	5.50	5.00
RE24	"	6c green	30	20
RE25	"	8c green	60	25
RE26	"	10c green	25	12
RE27	"	20c green	50	25
RE28	"	24c green	5.50	50
RE29	"	40c green	12.00	7.50

Imperf.
Without Gum

RE30	RE1a	$2 green	15.00	2.00

Perf. 11.

RE31	RE1	2c green	40.00	30.00

WINE STAMPS.

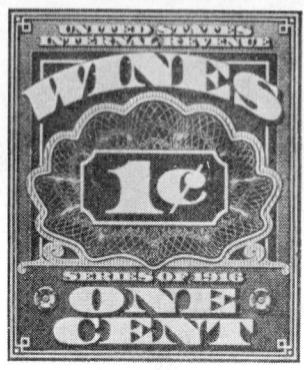

RE2
Inscribed: "Series of 1916".

Wmkd. USIR (191R)

1916		Offset Printing	Rouletted 3½	
		Without Gum		
		Plates of 100 subjects.		
		Size: Approximately 40 x 47 mm.		
RE32	RE2	1c green	35	30
RE33	"	3c green	3.50	3.00
RE34	"	4c green	30	25
RE35	"	6c green	1.00	75
RE36	"	7½c green	5.00	3.00
RE37	"	10c green	70	40
RE38	"	12c green	1.75	1.65
RE39	"	15c green	1.75	1.50
RE40	"	18c green	22.50	20.00
RE41	"	20c green	30	25
RE42	"	24c green	2.00	1.50
RE43	"	30c green	2.25	2.00
RE44	"	36c green	13.00	10.00
RE45	"	50c green	60	40
RE46	"	60c green	2.25	2.00
RE47	"	72c green	30.00	27.50
RE48	"	80c green	75	55
RE49	"	$1.20 green	6.00	4.50
RE50	"	$1.44 green	4.50	2.00
RE51	"	$1.60 green	17.50	14.00
RE52	"	$2 green	1.25	1.25

RE3
Engraved

Plates of 50 subjects.

RE53	RE3	$4 green	60	18
RE54	"	$4.80 green	2.75	2.25
RE55	"	$9.60 green	60	25

Nos. RE32 to RE55 exist in many shades. Size variations of 1c to $2 are believed due to offset printing. These designs in light green, rouletted 7, were re-issued in 1933-34. See Nos. RE60 to RE83.

REVENUES 661

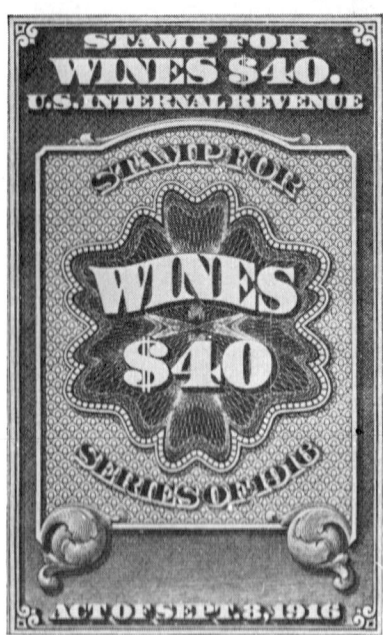

RE4
Perf. 11½ at left.

Size: Approximately 51 x 81 mm
Plates of 6 subjects.

RE56	RE4	$20 green	70.00	30.00
RE57	"	$40 green	150.00	40.00
RE58	"	$50 green	30.00	25.00
RE59	"	$100 green	200.00	125.00

Stamps of design RE4 have an adjoining tablet at right for affixing additional stamps. See also Nos. RE107A-RE107D.

Same designs as Issue of 1916-18.

1933   *Rouletted 7*   Wmk. 191R

Offset Printing

RE60	RE2	1c light green	1.75	25
RE61	"	3c light green	5.50	1.75
RE62	"	4c light green	65	15
RE63	"	6c light green	7.00	3.00
RE64	"	7½c light green	1.00	15
RE65	"	10c light green	90	8
RE66	"	12c light green	3.50	75
RE67	"	15c light green	1.50	10
RE69	"	20c light green	1.75	5
RE70	"	24c light green	1.75	5
		a. Double impression	—	
RE71	"	30c light green	1.75	6
RE72	"	36c light green	5.50	35
RE73	"	50c light green	2.75	25
RE74	"	60c light green	3.25	8
RE75	"	72c light green	6.00	30
RE76	"	80c light green	5.50	10
RE77	"	$1.20 light green	7.75	1.25
RE78	"	$1.44 light green	4.50	2.50
RE79	"	$1.60 light green	125.00	55.00
RE80	"	$2 light green	22.50	3.00

Engraved

RE81	RE3	$4 light green	18.00	5.25
RE82	"	$4.80 light green	21.00	11.50
RE83	"	$9.60 light green	125.00	60.00

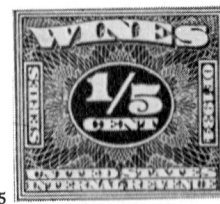

RE5

1934–40   *Rouletted 7*   Wmk. 191R

Inscribed: "Series of 1934".
Size: Approximately 28x25 mm.
Offset Printing
Plates of 200 and 224 subjects.
Issued With and Without Gum.

RE83A	RE5	1/5c green ('40)	50	12
RE84	"	½c green	50	20
RE85	"	1c green	50	15
RE86	"	1¼c green	1.25	65
RE87	"	1½c green	5.50	3.00
RE88	"	2c green	1.25	30
RE89	"	2½c green	1.50	50
RE90	"	3c green	4.50	3.50
RE91	"	4c green	1.25	15
RE92	"	5c green	50	10
RE93	"	6c green	1.65	25
RE94	"	7½c green	1.00	15
RE95	"	10c green	35	6
RE96	"	12c green	1.00	10
RE96A	"	14 2/5c green ('40)	70.00	3.00
RE97	"	15c green	60	10
RE98	"	18c green	1.10	12
RE99	"	20c green	1.00	6
RE100	"	24c green	1.10	10
RE101	"	30c green	90	8

Size: Approximately 39x45 mm.
Plates of 100 subjects.
Issued Without Gum

RE102	RE2	40c green	1.00	25
RE102A	"	43 1/5c green ('40)	7.50	1.75
RE103	"	48c green	7.00	1.25
RE104	"	$1 green	12.00	9.00
RE105	"	$1.50 green	20.00	12.00
		Perforated initials		5.00

Engraved

Size: Approximately 39 x 46mm.
Plates of 50 subjects

RE106	RE3	$2.50 green	25.00	13.00
		Perforated initials		5.00
RE107	"	$5 green	18.00	7.50
		Perforated initials		2.00

Stamps of types RE5 and RE2 overprinted "Rectified Spirits / Puerto Rico" are listed under Puerto Rico.

Inscribed: "Series of 1916"
Size: Approximately 51 x 81mm.
Plates of 6 subjects.

1934   *Perf. 11½ at left.*

RE107A	RE4	$20 yellow green	1300.00
RE107B	"	$40 yellow green	1500.00

Perf. 12½ at left.

RE107C	RE4	$50 yellow green	400.00
RE107D	"	$100 yellow green	300.00

The serial numbers of Nos. RE107A-RE107D are much thinner than on Nos. RE56-RE59.

RE6

REVENUES

Offset Printing
Size: 28 x 25mm.
Inscribed "Series of 1941",

1942-44   *Rouletted 7*   Wmk. 191R

RE108	RE6	1/5c green & black	65	30
RE109	"	¼c green & black	1.00	50
RE110	"	½c green & black	1.10	75

a. Imperf. vertically (pair) 50.00

RE111	"	1c green & black	60	30
RE112	"	2c green & black	2.25	1.75
RE113	"	3c green & black	2.25	1.75
RE114	"	3½c green & black		2250.00
RE115	"	3¾c green & black	3.75	1.75
RE116	"	4c green & black	1.25	1.00
RE117	"	5c green & black	1.25	1.00
RE118	"	6c green & black	1.25	1.00
RE119	"	7c green & black	2.00	1.25
RE120	"	7½c green & black	2.25	1.75
RE121	"	8c green & black	2.25	1.25
RE122	"	9c green & black	3.25	2.50
RE123	"	10c green & black	2.75	70
RE124	"	11¼c green & black	3.00	2.25
RE125	"	12c green & black	3.50	2.75
RE126	"	14c green & black	13.00	6.00
RE127	"	15c green & black	3.25	1.50

a. Imperf. vert., pair

RE128	"	16c green & black	3.75	2.75
RE129	"	19-1/5c green & black	90.00	3.50
RE130	"	20c green & black	3.00	90
RE131	"	24c green & black	3.00	10
RE132	"	28c green & black	1200.00	500.00
RE133	"	30c green & black	90	8
RE134	"	32c green & black	45.00	3.50
RE135	"	36c green & black	1.65	8
RE136	"	40c green & black	1.25	12
RE137	"	45c green & black	2.00	18
RE138	"	48c green & black	6.00	2.00
RE139	"	50c green & black	7.50	3.50
RE140	"	60c green & black	2.00	12
RE141	"	72c green & black	5.75	60
RE142	"	80c green & black	17.50	3.00
RE143	"	84c green & black		30.00
RE144	"	90c green & black	8.00	10
RE145	"	96c green & black	8.00	12

See also Nos. RE182D-RE194.

RE7
Denomination Spelled Out in Two Lines

1942-47   Size: 39 x 45½mm.   Engraved

RE146	RE7	$1.20 yellow green & black	2.75	10
RE147	"	$1.44 yellow green & black	1.25	6
RE148	"	$1.50 yellow green & black	80.00	45.00
RE149	"	$1.60 yellow green & black	5.75	90
RE150	"	$1.68 yellow green & black	55.00	40.00
RE151	"	$1.80 yellow green & black	2.25	8

a. Vertical pair, one without denomination —

RE152	"	$1.92 yellow green & black	35.00	30.00
RE153	"	$2.40 yellow green & black	6.00	50
RE154	"	$3 yellow green & black	45.00	22.50
RE155	"	$3.36 yellow green & black	—	27.50
RE156	"	$3.60 yellow green & black	—	5.50
RE157	"	$4 yellow green & black	15.00	4.50
RE158	"	$4.80 yellow green & black	—	2.50
RE159	"	$5 yellow green & black	10.00	7.00
RE160	"	$7.20 yellow green & black	16.00	40
RE161	"	$10 yellow green & black	100.00	55.00

RE162	RE7	$20 yellow green & black	100.00	70.00
RE163	"	$50 yellow green & black	100.00	50.00
		Perforated initials		18.00
RE164	"	$100 yellow green & black	250.00	30.00
RE165	"	$200 yellow green & black	90.00	18.00
		Perforated initials		7.50
RE165B	"	$400 yellow green & black	—	1200.00
RE166	"	$500 yellow green & black	—	125.00
		Perforated initials		25.00
RE167	"	$600 yellow green & black	—	125.00
RE168	"	$900 yellow green & black		1250.00
		Perforated initials		550.00
RE169	"	$1000 yellow green & black		150.00
RE170	"	$2000 yellow green & black		500.00
RE171	"	$3000 yellow green & black		160.00
RE172	"	$4000 yellow green & black		550.00

Denomination Repeated, Spelled Out in One Line.

1949-54

RE173	RE7	$1 yellow green & black	2.75	1.50
RE174	"	$2 yellow green & black	4.00	1.50
RE175	"	$4 yellow green & black	425.00	250.00
RE176	"	$5 yellow green & black		60.00
RE177	"	$6 yellow green & black		375.00
RE178	"	$7 yellow green & black		45.00
RE179	"	$8 yellow green & black	400.00	250.00
RE180	"	$10 yellow green & black	15.00	5.00
		Perforated initials		1.00
RE181	"	$20 yellow green & black	15.00	3.00
		Perforated initials		1.00
RE182	"	$30 yellow green & black	550.00	475.00

Other denominations of engraved stamps, type RE7, that were printed and delivered to the Internal Revenue Service were: $7.14, $9, $12, $40, $60, $70, $80, $300, $700 and $800. None are reported in collectors' hands.

Types of 1941-54.
1951-54   Size: 28 x 25mm.   Offset Printing

RE182D	RE6	1 7/10 c green & black		3250.00
RE183	"	3⅖c green & black	40.00	27.50
RE184	"	8¼c green & black	20.00	17.50
RE185	"	13 2/5 c green & black	60.00	50.00
RE186	"	17c green & black	12.00	12.00
RE187	"	20⅖c green & black	60.00	35.00
RE188	"	33⅗c green & black	60.00	45.00
RE189	"	38¼c green & black	65.00	45.00
RE190	"	40⅘c green & black	3.00	40.00
RE191	"	51c green & black	3.00	50
RE192	"	67c green & black	10.00	4.00
RE193	"	68c green & black	2.50	50
RE194	"	80⅖c green & black	75.00	70.00

Engraved
Size: 39 x 45½mm.

Denomination Spelled Out in Two Lines in Small Letters
Two types of $1.60 ⅘:

   I. The "4" slants sharply. Loop of "5" almost closes to form oval. Each numeral 2mm. high.
   II. The "4" is less slanted. Loop of "5" more open and nearly circular. Each numeral 2½ mm high.

RE195	RE7	$1.50¾ yellow green & black	40.00	30.00
RE196	"	$1.60⅘ yellow green & black (I)	3.00	25

a. "DOLLLAR"   35.00   12.50
b. As "a," horiz. pair, one without denomination   400.00
c. Type II   350.00   100.00

RE197	"	$1.88 3/10 yellow green & black	90.00	50.00

Denomination Spelled Out in Two Lines in Slightly Larger Letters Same as Nos. RE146-RE172

RE198	RE7	$1.60⅘ yellow green & black (II)	25.00	5.00

a. First line larger letters, second line small letters   450.00
b. Type I ('53)   50.00   20.00

RE199	"	$2.01 yellow green & black	3.00	35
RE200	"	$2.68 yellow green & black	3.00	35
RE201	"	$4.08 yellow green & black	40.00	25.00
RE202	"	$5.76 yellow green & black	200.00	75.00
RE203	"	$8.16 yellow green & black	12.00	4.00
RE204	"	$9.60 yellow green & black		1850.00

Other denominations that were printed but not delivered to the Internal Revenue Service were: 6 7/10c, 10 1/5c and $90. None are reported in collectors' hands.

Wine stamps were discontinued on Dec. 31, 1954.

REVENUES

PLAYING CARD STAMPS.

Stamps for use on packs of playing cards were included in the first general issue of 1862–71. They are Nos. R2, R11, R12, R17, R21 and R28.

The tax on playing cards was repealed effective June 22, 1965.

"ON HAND...."
RF1

"ACT OF...."
RF2

Engraved.
1894   Rouletted 5½   Unwmkd.

RF1	RF1	2c lake	35	25
		a. Horizontal pair, imperf. between	150.00	—
		b. Horiz. pair, imperf. vert.	—	—
RF2	RF2	2c ultramarine	4.00	2.00
		a. 2c blue		3.00
		b. Imperf., pair	125.00	
		c. Imperf. horizontally	100.00	100.00
		d. Rouletted 12½	50.00	50.00
		e. Imperf. horizontally, rouletted 12½ vertically, pair	80.00	80.00

1896–99   Wmkd. USIR (191R)
Rouletted 5½, 7.

RF3	RF2	2c blue	3.00	30
		a. 2c ultramarine ('99)	4.50	75
		b. Imperf., pair	50.00	

1902   Perf. 12

RF4	RF2	2c deep blue		25.00

No. RF4 is known with cancellation date "1899" but that is due to the use of an old cancelling plate. The stamp was first used in 1902.

ACT OF 1917

Stamp of 1896-99
Surcharged in Rose
7 CENTS

1917   Rouletted 7   Wmk. 191R
RF5	RF2	7c on 2c ultramarine	750.00	600.00
		a. Inverted surcharge		

The surcharge on No. RF5 was handstamped at the Internal Revenue Office in New York City.

The surcharges on Nos. RF6 to RF13 inclusive, and No. RF15 were applied by the manufacturers, together with their initials, dates, etc., thus forming a combination of surcharge and precancellation. The surcharge on No. RF16 was made by the Bureau of Engraving and Printing. After it appeared the use of the combinations was continued but only as cancellations.

Surcharged in Black   **17**
1917
RF6	RF2	(7c) on 2c blue		30.00
		a. Inverted surcharge		30.00

The "17" indicated that the 7 cent tax had been paid according to the Act of 1917.

Surcharged in Black   **7**
RF7	RF2	7c on 2c blue		275.00
		a. Inverted surcharge		275.00

Surcharged Vertically in Red or Violet   **7 CTS.**
RF8	RF2	7c on 2c blue		450.00
		a. Double surcharge		500.00

Surcharged Vertically, Reading up in Black, Violet or Red   **7 CENTS**
RF9	RF2	7c on 2c blue		7.00
		a. Double surcharge		35.00
		b. Numeral omitted		25.00
		c. Surcharge reading down		8.00
		d. As "c", numeral omitted		25.00
		e. As "c", double surcharge		100.00
		f. Double surcharge, one inverted		100.00
		g. Surcharge and "A.D." in violet		100.00
		h. Surcharge and "A.D." in red, "U.S.P.C." in black		250.00
		i. Surcharge and "A.D." in red reading up, "U.S.P.C." in black reading down		300.00

"A.D." stands for Andrew Dougherty, the name of a playing card company. "U.S.P.C." stands for United States Playing Card Co.

On Nos. RF9g-RF9i, surcharge and company initials were applied simultaneously.

Surcharged in Carmine   **7c**
RF10	RF2	7c on 2c blue		35.00
		a. Inverted surcharge		25.00
		b. Double surcharge		175.00
		c. Double surcharge, inverted		135.00
		d. Triple surcharge		—

RF3

REVENUES

1918 Size: 21x40 mm.
Imperf.
RF11 RF3 blue 35.00 25.00
    Block of four 150.00 110.00

Private Roulette 14.
RF12 RF3 blue 125.00
    a. Rouletted 13 in red 500.00
    b. Rouletted 6½ 150.00
    c. Perf. 12 horiz., imperf. vert. 90.00
    d. Perf. 12 on 4 sides

Nos. RF11 and RF12 served as 7c stamps when used before April 1, 1919, and as 8c stamps when used after that date.

Surcharged like No. RF9 in Violet, Red or Black
Private Roulette 9½.
RF13 RF3 7c blue 25.00
    a. Inverted surcharge 25.00
    b. Double surcharge 160.00
    c. Double surcharge, inverted 160.00

REVENUE ACT OF 1918
Stamp of 1896-99 Surcharged in Magenta or Rose **8 CENTS**

1919 *Rouletted 7.*
RF14 RF2 8c on 2c ultramarine 65.00
    a. Double surcharge 125.00
    b. Inverted surcharge 125.00

The surcharge on No. RF14 was handstamped at the Internal Revenue Office in New York City.

Surcharged in Carmine **8**
RF15 RF2 8c on 2c blue (inverted surcharge) 325.00
    a. Double surcharge, inverted 425.00

No. RF15 is surcharged only with large "8c" inverted, and overprinted with date and initials. No. RF16 is often found with additional impression of large "8c," as on No. RF15, but in this usage the large "8c" is a cancellation.

Surcharged in Carmine **8 Cts.**
RF16 RF2 8c on 2c blue 25.00 50
    a. Inverted surcharge
    See note after No. RF5.

RF4
Size: 19x22mm.
1922 *Rouletted 7.*
RF17 RF4 (8c) blue 9.00 1.00

Surcharged in Carmine, Blue or Black **8c**
RF18 RF4 8c blue 27.50
    a. Inverted surcharge 27.50

RF5

1924 *Rouletted 7.*
RF19 RF5 10c blue 6.00 25
    Block of four 27.50

ROTARY PRESS COIL STAMP
1926 *Perf. 10 Vertically.*
RF20 RF5 10c blue 15
RF20 exists only precanceled.

FLAT PLATE PRINTING.
1927 *Perf. 11*
RF21 RF5 10c blue 8.00 4.00
    Block of four 35.00

1929 *Perf. 10*
RF22 RF5 10c blue 7.00 3.00

RF6

ROTARY PRESS COIL STAMP.
1929 *Perf. 10 Horizontally*
RF23 RF6 10c light blue 10
No. RF23 exists only precanceled.

FLAT PLATE PRINTING.
1930 *Perf. 10*
RF24 RF6 10c blue 7.00 1.00
    Block of four 30.00 10.00
    a. Horiz. pair, imperf. vert. 150.00

1931 *Perf. 11.*
RF25 RF6 10c blue 7.50 1.00

RF7

ROTARY PRESS COIL STAMP.
1940 *Perf. 10 vertically*
RF26 RF7 blue .... — 25
No. RF26 exists in both wet and dry printings. See note after No. 1029.

RF8

ROTARY PRESS COIL STAMPS
Wmkd. USIR (191R)
1940 *Perf. 10 Horizontally.*
RF27 RF8 blue 10

REVENUES 665

FLAT PLATE PRINTING.
Perf. 11.

RF28	RF8	blue	5.00	1.00

ROTARY PRESS PRINTING.
Perf. 10x11.

RF29	RF8	blue	125.00	75.00
		a. Imperforate (P. C. Co.)		125.00

PLAYING CARD STAMPS
FOR THE VIRGIN ISLANDS.

These stamps were overprinted by the Bureau of Engraving and Printing. Shipments of 10,000 each of Nos. RFV1-RFV3 were sent to the Virgin Islands on June 17, 1920, Jan. 16, 1926, and Mar. 5, 1934, respectively.

U. S. Playing Card Stamp No. RF3
Overprinted in Carmine

VIRGIN ISLANDS 4 CTS.

Wmkd. USIR (191R)

1920 — Engraved. — *Rouletted 7.*
RFV1 RF2 4c on 2c blue — 120.00

U. S. Playing Card Stamp No. RF17
Overprinted in Carmine

VIRGIN ISLANDS 4 cts.

1926 — *Rouletted 7.*
RFV2 RF4 4c blue — 35.00

Same Overprint on U.S. Type RF4.

1934 — *Perf. 11.*
RFV3 RF4 4c light blue — 85.00

The above stamp with perforation 11 was not issued in the United States without the overprint.

SILVER TAX STAMPS.

The Silver Purchase Act of 1934 imposed a 50 per cent tax on the net profit realized on a transfer of silver bullion. The tax was paid by affixing stamps to the transfer memorandum. Congress authorized the Silver Tax stamps on Feb. 20, 1934. They were discontinued on June 4, 1963.

Documentary Stamps of 1917 Overprinted **SILVER TAX**

1934 — *Perf. 11* — Wmk. 191R
Offset Printing.

RG1	R22	1c carmine rose	60	30
RG2	"	2c carmine rose	85	35
		a. Double impression of stamp		
RG3	"	3c carmine rose	1.00	45
RG4	"	4c carmine rose	1.00	50
RG5	"	5c carmine rose	1.25	75
RG6	"	8c carmine rose	1.75	1.00
RG7	"	10c carmine rose	1.75	1.00
RG8	"	20c carmine rose	3.50	2.50
RG9	"	25c carmine rose	3.50	3.00
RG10	"	40c carmine rose	5.00	4.25
RG11	"	50c carmine rose	6.00	5.00
		a. Double impression of stamp	30.00	
RG12	"	80c carmine rose	9.00	6.00

Engraved.

RG13	R21	$1 green	9.00	7.00
RG14	"	$2 rose	12.00	10.00
RG15	"	$3 violet	25.00	20.00
RG16	"	$4 yellow brown	17.50	13.00
RG17	"	$5 dark blue	22.50	12.00
RG18	"	$10 orange	37.50	12.00

Perf. 12.
Without Gum

RG19	R17	$30 vermilion	—	30.00
		Cut cancellation		17.50
RG20	R19	$60 brown	—	50.00
		Vertical strip of four		210.00
		Cut cancellation		25.00
RG21	R17	$100 green	90.00	30.00
		Vertical strip of four		125.00
RG22	R18	$500 blue	250.00	200.00
		Vertical strip of four		
		Cut cancellation		95.00
RG23	R19	$1000 orange	—	100.00
		Cut cancellation		60.00

See note after R227.

Same Overprint, spacing 11 mm. between words "SILVER TAX."

1936 — Without Gum — *Perf. 12*

RG26	R17	$100 green	110.00	50.00
		Vertical strip of four		
RG27	R19	$1000 orange		475.00

Documentary Stamps of 1917 Handstamped "SILVER TAX" in Violet, Large Block Letters, in Two Lines
Offset Printing.

1939 — *Perf. 11* — Wmk. 191R

RG28	R22	3c rose pink	—	
RG30	"	10c rose pink	—	
RG32	"	80c rose pink	—	

Other handstamps exist on various values. One has letters 4mm. high, 2mm. wide with "SILVER" and "TAX" applied in separate operations. Another has "Silver Tax" in two lines in a box.

Engraved.
Overprint Typewritten In Black
Perf. 11.

RG35	R21	$3 violet	—	
RG36	"	$5 dark blue	—	

Typewritten overprints also exist on 2c, 3c, 20c, 50c and in red on $5.

SERIES 1940

Type of Documentary Stamps 1917, Overprinted in Black **SILVER TAX**

Offset Printing.

1940 — *Perf. 11*

RG37	R22	1c rose pink	8.50	—
RG38	"	2c rose pink	8.50	—
RG39	"	3c rose pink	8.50	—
RG40	"	4c rose pink	10.00	—
RG41	"	5c rose pink	6.00	—
RG42	"	8c rose pink	10.00	—
RG43	"	10c rose pink	8.50	—
RG44	"	20c rose pink	10.00	—
RG45	"	25c rose pink	8.50	—
RG46	"	40c rose pink	15.00	—
RG47	"	50c rose pink	15.00	—
RG48	"	80c rose pink	15.00	—

Engraved.

RG49	R21	$1 green	40.00	—
RG50	"	$2 rose	60.00	—
RG51	"	$3 violet	90.00	—
RG52	"	$4 yellow brown	200.00	—
RG53	"	$5 dark blue	225.00	—
RG54	"	$10 orange	300.00	—

Nos. RG19-RG20, RG26 Handstamped in Blue "Series 1940"

1940 — Without Gum — *Perf. 12*

RG55	R17	$30 vermilion	—	1100.00
RG56	R19	$60 brown	—	1750.00
RG57	R17	$100 green	—	1350.00

REVENUES

Alexander Hamilton
RG1

Levi Woodbury
RG2

Thomas Corwin
RG3

Overprinted in Black SERIES 1941
Engraved.

1941 Perf. 11 Wmk. 191R
Size: 19 x 22 mm.

RG58	RG1	1c gray	.90	—
RG59	"	2c gray (Oliver Wolcott, Jr.)	.90	—
RG60	"	3c gray (Samuel Dexter)	1.00	—
RG61	"	4c gray (Albert Gallatin)	1.25	—
RG62	"	5c gray (G. W. Campbell)	1.50	—
RG63	"	8c gray (A. J. Dallas)	2.00	—
RG64	"	10c gray (Wm. H. Crawford)	2.50	—
RG65	"	20c gray (Richard Rush)	3.75	—
RG66	"	25c gray (S. D. Ingham)	5.50	—
RG67	"	40c gray (Louis McLane)	9.00	—
RG68	"	50c gray (Wm. J. Duane)	11.00	—
RG69	"	80c gray (Roger B. Taney)	20.00	15.00

Size: 21½ x 36¼ mm.

RG70	RG2	$1 gray	20.00	—
RG71	"	$2 gray (Thomas Ewing)	60.00	27.50
RG72	"	$3 gray (Walter Forward)	45.00	32.50
RG73	"	$4 gray (J. C. Spencer)	55.00	—
RG74	"	$5 gray (G. M. Bibb)	60.00	40.00
RG75	"	$10 gray (R. J. Walker)	80.00	50.00
RG76	"	$20 gray (Wm. M. Meredith)	150.00	—

Perf. 12
Without Gum
Size: 28½ x 42 mm.

RG77	RG3	$30 gray	110.00	60.00
RG78	"	$50 gray (James Guthrie)	—	45.00
RG79	"	$60 gray (Howell Cobb)	550.00	100.00
		Cut cancellation		75.00
RG80	"	$100 gray (P. F. Thomas)	—	175.00
		Vertical strip of four		—
		Cut cancellation		75.00
RG81	"	$500 gray (J. A. Dix)	—	600.00
RG82	"	$1000 gray (S. P. Chase)	—	300.00
		Cut cancellation		

Silver Purchase Stamps of 1941
Overprinted in Black   SERIES 1942

1942 Perf. 11 Wmk. 191R
Size: 19 x 22 mm.

RG83	RG1	1c gray	.40	—
RG84	"	2c gray	.50	—
RG85	"	3c gray	.50	—
RG86	"	4c gray	.55	—
RG87	"	5c gray	.65	—
RG88	"	8c gray	1.00	—
RG89	"	10c gray	2.25	—
RG90	"	20c gray	3.25	—
RG91	"	25c gray	6.50	—
RG92	"	40c gray	7.50	—
RG93	"	50c gray	7.50	—
RG94	"	80c gray	20.00	—

Size: 21½ x 36¼ mm.

RG95	RG2	$1 gray	20.00	—
		a. Overprint "SERIES 5942"	250.00	—
RG96	"	$2 gray	22.50	—
		a. Overprint "SERIES 5942"	250.00	—
RG97	"	$3 gray	40.00	—
		a. Overprint "SERIES 5942"		—
RG98	"	$4 gray	42.50	—
		a. Overprint "SERIES 5942"		—
RG99	"	$5 gray	45.00	—
		a. Overprint "SERIES 5942	250.00	—
RG100	"	$10 gray	100.00	—
RG101	"	$20 gray	200.00	—
		a. Overprint "SERIES 5942"		—

Perf. 12
Without Gum
Size: 28½ x 42 mm.

RG102	RG3	$30 gray	300.00	275.00
RG103	"	$50 gray	300.00	275.00
RG104	"	$60 gray	—	275.00
		Cut cancellation		225.00
RG105	"	$100 gray	—	200.00
		Cut cancellation		150.00
RG106	"	$500 gray	—	—
RG107	"	$1000 gray	—	—
		Cut cancellation		—

Silver Purchase Stamps of 1941 without Overprint.

1944 Perf. 11 Wmk. 191R
Size: 19 x 22 mm.

RG108	RG1	1c gray	.20	.15
RG109	"	2c gray	.25	—
RG110	"	3c gray	.35	—
RG111	"	4c gray	.45	—
RG112	"	5c gray	.90	—
RG113	"	8c gray	1.25	—
RG114	"	10c gray	1.25	—
RG115	"	20c gray	3.00	—
RG116	"	25c gray	3.00	—
RG117	"	40c gray	5.50	—
RG118	"	50c gray	5.50	—
RG119	"	80c gray	7.00	—

Size: 21½ x 36¼ mm.

RG120	RG2	$1 gray	13.50	6.00
RG121	"	$2 gray	22.50	15.00
RG122	"	$3 gray	27.50	9.00
RG123	"	$4 gray	32.50	27.50
RG124	"	$5 gray	32.50	12.50
RG125	"	$10 gray	45.00	22.50
		Cut cancellation		9.00
RG126	"	$20 gray	175.00	—

Perf. 12.
Without Gum
Size: 28½ x 42 mm.

RG127	RG3	$30 gray	110.00	85.00
		Vertical strip of four		—
		Cut cancellation		50.00
RG128	"	$50 gray	375.00	325.00
		Vertical strip of four		—
RG129	"	$60 gray	—	125.00
		Cut cancellation		75.00
RG130	"	$100 gray	—	30.00
		Vertical strip of four		—
		Cut cancellation		15.00
RG131	"	$500 gray	—	250.00
		Cut cancellation		175.00
RG132	"	$1000 gray	—	150.00
		Vertical strip of four		—
		Cut cancellation		75.00

CIGARETTE TUBES STAMPS

These stamps were for a tax on the hollow tubes of cigarette paper, each with a thin cardboard mouthpiece attached. They were sold in packages so buyers could add loose tobacco to make cigarettes.

CIGTTE.

Documentary Stamp of 1917 Overprinted

TUBES

Wmkd. USIR (191R)

1919   Offset Printing   Perf. 11

RH1	R22	1c carmine rose	.35	.25
		Block of four	1.50	—
		a. Without period	7.00	4.50

1929   Perf. 10

RH2	R22	1c carmine rose	15.00	5.00

RH1

1933		*Perf. 11*	Wmk. 191R	
RH3	RH1	1c rose	1.00	30
		Block of four	4.50	
RH4	"	2c rose	2.00	90

POTATO TAX STAMPS.

These stamps were required under the Agricultural Adjustment Act of Dec. 1, 1935. Their use ended Jan. 6, 1936, when this act was declared unconstitutional. Potato growers were given allotments and for excess had to pay ¾ cent a pound.

Young Woman
RI1

Engraved.

1935		*Perf. 11.*	Unwmkd.
RI1	RI1	¾c carmine rose	15
RI2	"	1½c black brown	30
RI3	"	2¼c yellow green	30
RI4	"	3c light violet	40
RI5	"	3¾c olive bistre	40
RI6	"	7½c orange brown	1.00
RI7	"	11¼c deep orange	1.25
RI8	"	18¾c violet brown	3.00
RI9	"	37½c red orange	3.25
RI10	"	75c blue	3.75
RI11	"	93¾c rose lake	5.00
RI12	"	$1.12½ green	7.00
RI13	"	$1.50 yellow brown	8.00

TOBACCO SALE TAX STAMPS.

These stamps were required to pay the tax on the sale of tobacco in excess of quotas set by the Secretary of Agriculture. The tax was 25 per cent of the price for which the excess tobacco was sold. It was intended to affect tobacco harvested after June 28, 1934 and sold before May 1, 1936. The tax was stopped when the Agricultural Adjustment Act was declared unconstitutional by the Supreme Court on Dec. 1, 1935.

Prices for unused stamps are for copies with original gum.

Stamps and Types of 1917 Documentary Issue Overprinted **TOBACCO SALE TAX**

Wmkd. USIR **(191R)**

1934		Offset Printing	*Perf. 11*	
RJ1	R22	1c carmine rose	30	15
RJ2	"	2c carmine rose	35	20
RJ3	"	5c carmine rose	1.20	40
RJ4	"	10c carmine rose	1.50	40
		a. Inverted overprint	8.00	6.00
RJ5	R22	25c carmine rose	4.00	1.50
RJ6	"	50c carmine rose	4.00	1.50

Engraved.

RJ7	R21	$1 green	7.00	1.60
RJ8	"	$2 rose	12.50	1.75
RJ9	"	$5 dark blue	15.00	4.00
RJ10	"	$10 orange	25.00	10.00
RJ11	"	$20 olive bistre	60.00	12.00

On No. RJ11 the overprint is vertical, reading up.

NARCOTIC TAX STAMPS

The Revenue Act of 1918 imposed a tax of 1 cent per ounce or fraction thereof on opium, coca leaves and their derivatives. The tax was paid by affixing Narcotic stamps to the drug containers. The tax lasted from Feb. 25, 1919, through Apr. 30, 1971.

Members of the American Revenue Association compiled the listings in this section.

Documentary Stamps of 1914 Handstamped "NARCOTIC" in Magenta, Blue or Black

Offset Printing

1919		*Perf. 10*	Wmk. 191R	
RJA1	R20	1c rose	50.00	35.00

The overprint was applied by District Collectors of Internal Revenue. It is always in capital letters and exists in various type faces and sizes, including: 21½x2½mm., serif; 21x2¼mm., sans-serif boldface; 15½x2½mm., sans-serif; 13x2mm., sans-serif.

The ½c, 2c, 3c, 4c, 5c, 10c, 25c and 50c with similar handstamp in serif capitals measuring about 20x2¼mm. are bogus.

Documentary Stamps of 1917 Handstamped "NARCOTIC", "Narcotic", "NARCOTICS" or "ACT / NARCOTIC / 1918" in Magenta, Black, Blue, Violet or Red

Offset Printing

1919		*Perf. 11*	Wmk. 191R	
RJA9	R22	1c carmine rose	1.50	1.00
RJA10	"	2c " "	4.00	3.00
RJA11	"	3c " "	15.00	12.00
RJA12	"	4c " "	7.00	5.00
RJA13	"	5c " "	10.00	10.00
RJA14	"	8c " "	7.50	12.00
RJA15	"	10c " "	35.00	6.00
RJA16	"	20c " "	35.00	30.00
RJA17	"	25c " "	30.00	25.00
RJA18	"	40c " "	65.00	55.00
RJA19	"	50c " "	15.00	15.00
RJA20	"	80c " "	75.00	55.00

Engraved

RJA21	R21	$1 green	35.00	25.00
RJA22	"	$2 rose		—
RJA23	"	$3 violet		—
RJA24	"	$5 dark blue		—
RJA25	"	$10 orange		—

The overprints were applied by District Collectors of Internal Revenue. They are known in at least 20 type faces and sizes of which the majority read "NARCOTIC" in capital letters. Two are in upper and lower case letters. Experts have identified 14 by city. The 3-line handstamp was used in Seattle; "NARCOTICS" in Philadelphia. Most handstamps are not found on all denominations.

No. R228 Overprinted in Black:
"NARCOTIC / E. L. CO. / 3-19-19"

1919		*Perf. 11*	Wmk. 191R
		"NARCOTIC" 14½mm. wide.	
RJA26	R22	1c carmine rose	300.00

Overprinted by Eli Lilly Co., Indianapolis, for that firm's use.

No. R228 Overprinted in Black:
"J W & B / NARCOTIC"

1919		*Perf. 11*	Wmk. 191R
		"NARCOTIC" 14½mm. wide.	
RJA27	R22	1c carmine rose	225.00

Overprinted by John Wyeth & Brother, Philadelphia, for that firm's use.

REVENUES

Nos. R228, R231-R232 Handstamped in Blue:
"P-W-R-Co. / NARCOTIC"

1919   *Perf. 11*   Wmk. 191R

RJA28	R22	1c carmine rose	225.00
RJA28A	"	4c " "	—
RJA29	"	5c " "	—

The handstamp was applied by the Powers-Weightmann-Rosengarten Co., Philadelphia, for that firm's use.

Proprietary Stamps of 1919 Handstamped
"NARCOTIC" in Blue

Offset Printing

1919   *Perf. 11*   Wmk. 191R

RJA30	RB5	1c dark blue	—
RJA31	"	2c " "	—
RJA32	"	4c " "	—

No. RB65 is known with "Narcotic" applied in red ms.

Documentary Stamps of 1917
Overprinted in Black

NARCOTIC
17½ mm. wide

Offset Printing

1919   *Perf. 11*   Wmk. 191R

RJA33	R22	1c carmine rose (6,900,000)	75	50
RJA34	"	2c " " (3,650,000)	1.50	1.00
RJA35	"	3c " " (388,400)	25.00	15.00
RJA36	"	4c " " (2,400,000)	5.00	3.50
RJA37	R22	5c carmine rose (2,400,000)	12.00	10.00
RJA38	"	8c " " (1,200,000)	17.50	13.00
RJA39	"	10c " " (3,400,000)	3.00	2.50
RJA40	"	25c " " (700,000)	17.50	13.00

Overprint Reading Up
Engraved

RJA41	R21	$1 green (270,000)	20.00	12.00

The overprint of Nos. RJA33-RJA41 has been counterfeited. In the genuine the C's are not slanted.

NT1
Offset Printing

1919–1970   *Imperf., Rouletted*   Wmk. 191R

			a. Imperf.	b. Rouletted 7
RJA42	NT1	1c violet	3.00	10
		d. 1c purple		5.00

NT2

			a. Imperf.	b. Rouletted 7
RJA43	NT2	1c violet	50	15
		d. 1c purple	3.00	2.00
RJA44	"	2c violet	1.00	40
		d. 2c purple		4.00
RJA45	"	3c violet ('64)	—	65.00

NT3

			a. Imperf.	b. Rouletted 7
RJA46	NT3	1c violet	2.00	65
		d. 1c purple		4.50
RJA47	"	2c violet	1.50	50
		d. 2c purple		6.00
RJA48	"	3c violet	250.00	
RJA49	"	4c " ('42)	—	7.50
		d. 4c purple		25.00
RJA50	"	5c violet	40.00	3.25
		d. 5c purple		10.00
RJA51	"	6c violet		65
		d. 6c purple		7.00

			a. Imperf.	b. Rouletted 7
RJA52	NT3	8c violet	50.00	3.00
		d. 8c purple		20.00
RJA53	"	9c violet ('53)	60.00	6.50
RJA54	"	10c violet	25.00	50
		d. 10c purple		6.00
RJA55	"	16c violet	45.00	2.50
		d. 16c purple		11.50
RJA56	"	18c violet ('61)	70.00	5.00
RJA57	"	19c " ('61)	100.00	15.00
RJA58	"	20c "	250.00	100.00

Nos. RJA47–RJA58 have "CENTS" below the value.

NT4

			a. Imperf.	b. Rouletted 7	c. Rouletted 3½
RJA59	NT4	1c violet	45.00	10.00	4.00
RJA60	"	2c "		20.00	
RJA61	"	3c "	40.00	18.50	
RJA62	"	5c "		25.00	
RJA63	"	6c "	60.00	20.00	
RJA64	"	8c "		45.00	
RJA65	"	9c " ('61)	12.50	10.00	
RJA66	"	10c "	11.00	15.00	
RJA67	"	16c "	15.00	10.00	
RJA68	"	18c " ('61)	325.00	375.00	
RJA69	"	19c "	10.00	110.00	
RJA70	"	20c "	300.00	110.00	
RJA71	"	25c "	—	20.00	4.00
RJA72	"	40c "	325.00		65.00
RJA73	"	$1 green		1.25	
RJA74	"	$1.28 green	20.00	10.00	
RJA75	"	$4 grn, unwmkd. ('70)	750.00		

On Nos. RJA60–RJA75 the value tablet is solid.

NT5

Denomination added in black by rubber plate in an operation similar to precanceling.

1963   **Engraved**   Unwmkd.   *Imperf.*

RJA76	NT5	1c violet	50.00

Denomination on Stamp Plate

1964   **Offset Printing**   *Imperf.*

RJA77	NT5	1c violet	5.00

CONSULAR SERVICE FEE STAMPS

Act of Congress, April 5, 1906, effective June 1, 1906, provided that every consular officer should be provided with special adhesive stamps printed in denominations determined by the Department of State.

Every document for which a fee was prescribed had to have attached a stamp or stamps representing the amount collected, and such stamps were used to show payment of these prescribed fees.

These stamps were usually affixed close to the signature, or at the lower left corner of the document. If no document was issued, the stamp or stamps were attached to a receipt for the amount of the fee and canceled either with pen and ink or rubber stamp showing the date of cancellation and bearing the initials of the canceling officer or name of the Consular Office. These stamps were not sold to the public uncanceled. Their use was discontinued Sept. 30, 1955.

CS1

CS2

CS3

1906		*Perf. 12*	*Unwmkd.*	
RK1	CS1	25c dark green		20.00
RK2	"	50c carmine		27.50
RK3	"	$1 dark violet		5.00
RK4	"	$2 brown		4.00
RK5	"	$2.50 dark blue		.85
RK6	"	$5 brown red		15.00
		a. Horizontal half used as $2.50		—
RK7	"	$10 orange		30.00
		Perf. 10.		
RK8	CS1	25c dark green		20.00
RK9	"	50c carmine		25.00
RK10	"	$1 dark violet		125.00
RK11	"	$2 brown		40.00
RK12	"	$2.50 dark blue		12.50
RK13	"	$5 brown red		37.50
		Perf. 11.		
RK14	CS1	25c dark green		27.50
RK15	"	50c carmine		50.00
RK16	"	$1 dark violet		1.50
		a. Diagonal half used as 50c.		—
RK17	"	$2 brown		1.75
RK18	"	$2.50 dark blue		.40
RK19	"	$5 brown red		3.00
		a. Diagonal half used as $2.50		30.00
RK20	"	$9 gray		9.00
RK21	"	$10 orange		17.50
		a. Diagonal half used as $5		50.00

For $2 black of type CS1, see No. RN-Y1 in Revenue Stamped Paper section.

1924			*Perf. 11*
RK22	CS2	$1 violet	32.50
RK23	"	$2 brown	35.00
RK24	"	$2.50 blue	7.00
RK25	"	$5 brown red	27.50
RK26	"	$9 gray	125.00
1925-52			*Perf. 10*
RK27	CS3	$1 violet	10.00
RK28	"	$2 brown	25.00
RK29	"	$2.50 ultramarine	1.10
RK30	"	$5 carmine	8.00
RK31	"	$9 gray	21.00
		Perf. 11.	
RK32	CS3	25c green('37)	27.50
RK33	"	50c orange ('34)	25.00
RK34	"	$1 violet	2.25
		a. Diagonal half used as 50c	2.00
RK35	"	$2 brown	30
RK36	"	$2.50 blue	25
		a. $2.50 ultramarine	3.00
RK37	"	$5 carmine	10.00
RK38	"	$9 gray	40.00
RK39	"	$10 blue gray ('37)	50.00
RK40	"	$20 violet ('52)	

CUSTOMS FEE STAMPS
New York Custom House

Issued to indicate the collection of miscellaneous customs fees. Use was discontinued on February 28, 1918. The stamps were not utilized in the collection of customs duties.

Silas Wright
CF1
Size: 48mm. x 34 mm.
Engraved

Each of these eight stamps has its own distinctive background.

1887								*Rouletted 5½*
RL1	CF1	20c dull rose		35				
		a. 20c red, perf. 10.		—	RL4	CF1	50c dark blue	3.50
		b. Vertical half used as 10c		—	RL5	"	60c red violet	1.00
		c. 20c red, rouletted 7		100.00	RL6	"	70c brown violet	22.50
RL2	"	30c orange		90	RL7	"	80c brown	50.00
RL3	"	40c green		1.75	RL8	"	90c black	70.00

EMBOSSED REVENUE STAMPED PAPER
INCLUDING COLONIAL EMBOSSED REVENUES

Some of the American Colonies of Great Britain used embossed stamps in raising revenue, as Britain had done from 1694. The British government also imposed stamp taxes on the Colonies, and in the early 19th century the U.S. government and some of the states enacted similar taxes.

Under one statute or another, these stamps were required on such documents as promissory notes, bills of exchange, insurance policies, bills of lading, bonds, protests, powers of attorney, stock certificates, letters patent, writs, conveyances, leases, mortgages, charter parties, commissions and liquor licenses.

A few of these stamps were printed, but most were colorless impressions resembling a notary public's seal.

The scant literature of these stamps includes E. B. Sterling's revenue catalogue of 1888, and "New Discovery from British Archives on the 1765 Tax Stamps for America," edited by Adolph Koeppel and published (1962) by the American Revenue Association.

Prices are for stamps of clear impression on entire documents in good condition. Parts of documents, cut squares or poor impressions sell for much less. Prices represent actual sales wherever possible. Prices in italics are tentative. A dash in the price column indicates that few copies are known or information for pricing is inadequate.

Colin MacR. Makepeace originally compiled the listings in this section.

EMBOSSED REVENUE STAMPED PAPER

I. COLONIAL ISSUES.
A. MASSACHUSETTS.
Act of January 8, 1755
In effect May 1, 1755—April 30, 1757

EP1

EP2   EP2 as photographed

EP3   EP4

		Typographed	
RM1	EP1	½p red	2000.00
		Embossed	
RM2	EP2	2p	450.00
RM3	EP3	3p	110.00
RM4	EP4	4p	500.00

A second die of EP2 with no fin on the under side of the codfish has been seen. There were at least two dies of the ½p.

B. NEW YORK
Act of December 1, 1756
In effect January 1, 1757—December 31, 1760

EP9

		Typographed	
RM9	EP9	½p red	2500.00
		Embossed	
RM10	EP9	1p	450.00
RM11	"	2p	200.00
RM12	"	3p	400.00
RM13	"	4p	300.00

II. BRITISH REVENUES FOR USE IN AMERICA.
Act of March 22, 1765
In effect November 1, 1765—May 1, 1766.

A. ALMANAC STAMPS

EP15
Engraved

RM15	EP15	2p red	
RM16	"	4p red	
RM17	"	8p red	

Proofs of all of these stamps printed in the issued color are known. Full size facsimile reproductions in the color of the originals were made about 1876 of the proof sheets of the 8p stamp, Plates 1 and 2, Dies 1 to 50 inclusive.

B. PAMPLETS AND NEWSPAPER STAMPS.

EP18
Engraved

RM18	EP18	½p red	1750.00
RM19	"	1p red	
RM20	"	2p red	

Proofs of all of these stamps printed in the issued color are known. Full size facsimile reproductions in the color of the originals were made about 1876 of the proof sheets of the 1p stamp, Plates 3 and 4, Dies 51 to 100 inclusive.

C. GENERAL ISSUE.

EP24   EP25

EP26   EP27

EMBOSSED REVENUE STAMPED PAPER

EP28
EP29
EP30
EP31
EP33
EP34
EP35
Embossed

RM24	EP24		3p	1250.00
RM25	EP25		4p	3000.00
RM26	EP26		6p	2000.00
RM27	EP27		1sh	1000.00
RM28	EP28		1sh 6p	1250.00
RM29	EP29		2sh	3000.00
RM30	EP30		2sh 3p	2150.00
RM31	EP31		2sh 6p	800.00
	a. Not on document			500.00
RM33	EP33		4sh	2500.00
RM34	EP34		5sh	2500.00
RM35	EP35		10sh	3250.00

Proofs exist of similar 1sh, 1sh6p and 2sh6p stamps inscribed "AMERICA CONT.& c."

	Various Similar Designs	
RM36	£1	
RM37	£2	
RM38	£3	—
RM39	£4	—
RM40	£6	—
RM41	£10	—

The £1 to £10 denominations probably exist only as proofs.

D. PLAYING CARDS STAMP.

Type similar to EP29, with Arms of George III Encircled by Garter.

RM42 1sh —

All of these were embossed without color and most of them were embossed directly on the document except the 2sh 6p which was generaly embossed on a rectangular piece of bluish or brownish stiff paper or cardboard only slightly larger than the stamp which was attached to the document by a small piece of metal. Three dies exist of the 3p; two of the 4p, 6p, 1sh, 1sh6p, 2sh and 2sh3p.

All of these stamps have the word "America" somewhere in the design and this is the feature which distinguishes them from the other British revenues. The stamps of the general issue are occasionally found with a design of a British revenue stamp struck over the American design, as a number of them were afterwards re-struck and used elsewhere as British revenues.

These stamps are sometimes called the "Teaparty" or "Tax on Tea" stamps. This, however, is a misnomer, as the act under which these stamps were issued laid no tax on tea. The tax on tea was levied by an act passed two years later, and the duties imposed by that act were not collected by stamps.

It must be remembered that these stamps were issued under an act applicable to all of the British colonies in America which included many which are not now part of the United States. Copies have been seen which were used in Quebec, Nova Scotia and in the West Indies. So great was the popular clamor against taxiation by a body in which the colonists had no representation that ships bringing the stamps from England were not allowed to land them in some of the colonies, the stamps were destroyed in others, and in practically all of those which are now a part of the United States the "Stamp Masters" who were to administer the act were forced to resign and to take oath that they would never carry out the duties of the offices. Notwithstanding the very general feeling about these stamps there is evidence that a very small number of them were actually used on ships' documents for one vessel clearing from New York and for a very small number of vessels clearing from the Savannah River. Florida was at this time under military government and the only known copy of these stamps used in what is now the United States, a 4p (#RM25), was used there.

III. ISSUES OF THE UNITED STATES.
A. FIRST FEDERAL ISSUE.
Act of July 6, 1797
In effect July 1, 1798—Feburary 28, 1801.

The distinguishing feature of the stamps of this issue is the name of a state in the design. These stamps were issued by the Federal Government, however, and not by the states. The design, with the exception of the name of the state, was the same for each denomination; but different denominations had the shield and the eagle in different positions. The design of only one denomination of these stamps is illustrated.

In addition to the eagle and shield design on the values from four cents to ten dollars there are two other stamps for each state, similar in design to one another, one of which is illustrated. All of these stamps are embossed without color.

In the following table of these stamps, the catalogue number is given first and then the price immediately below it. Prices are for clearly impressed examples.

EMBOSSED REVENUE STAMPED PAPER

673

State	4c	10c	20c	25c	30c	50c	75c	$1.00
Connecticut	RM45 20.00	RM46 20.00	RM47 160.00	RM48 24.00	RM49 —	RM50 120.00	RM51 —	RM52 750.00
Delaware	RM58 90.00	RM59 135.00	RM60 225.00	RM61 135.00	RM62 —	RM63 250.00	RM64 —	RM65 —
Georgia	RM71 135.00	RM72 55.00	RM73 —	RM74 65.00	RM75 —	RM76 120.00	RM77 —	RM78 —
Kentucky	RM84 15.00	RM85 15.00	RM86 145.00	RM87 15.00	RM88 475.00	RM89 90.00	RM90 70.00	RM91 —
Maryland	RM97 32.50	RM98 11.00	RM99 175.00	RM100 11.00	RM101 325.00	RM102 25.00	RM103 25.00	RM104 375.00
Massachusetts	RM110 8.00	RM111 8.00	RM112 75.00	RM113 8.00	RM114 —	RM115 50.00	RM116 160.00	RM117 90.00
New Hampshire	RM123 25.00	RM124 25.00	RM125 75.00	RM126 32.50	RM127 190.00	RM128 110.00	RM129 100.00	RM130 425.00
New Jersey	RM136 250.00	RM137 135.00	RM138 —	RM139 100.00	RM140 425.00	RM141 250.00	RM142 —	RM143 —
New York	RM149 25.00	RM150 15.00	RM151 25.00	RM152 10.00	RM153 18.00	RM154 22.50	RM155 55.00	RM156 110.00
North Carolina	RM162 27.50	RM163 22.50	RM164 300.00	RM165 40.00	RM166 —	RM167 110.00	RM168 150.00	RM169 275.00
Pennsylvania	RM175 30.00	RM176 17.50	RM177 22.50	RM178 17.50	RM179 20.00	RM180 17.50	RM181 17.50	RM182 70.00
Rhode Island	RM188 27.50	RM189 22.50	RM190 85.00	RM191 40.00	RM192 225.00	RM193 100.00	RM194 325.00	RM195 165.00
South Carolina	RM201 40.00	RM202 32.50	RM203 —	RM204 70.00	RM205 —	RM206 80.00	RM207 425.00	RM208 —
Tennessee	RM214 165.00	RM215 65.00	RM216 —	RM217 185.00	RM218 —	RM219 475.00	RM220 —	RM221 —
Vermont	RM227 50.00	RM228 25.00	RM229 165.00	RM230 40.00	RM231 135.00	RM232 110.00	RM233 375.00	RM234 750.00
Virginia	RM240 17.50	RM241 15.00	RM242 65.00	RM243 17.50	RM244 250.00	RM245 25.00	RM246 25.00	RM247 —

The Act calls for a $2, $4, $5 and $10 stamp for each state, none of which has been seen except the $4 Connecticut RM54, the $4 Maryland RM106, the $10 New Jersey RM147, the $2, $5, and $10 New York RM157, RM159, and RM160, the $5 South Carolina RM211 and the $10 Vermont RM238.

The Act also calls for a "Ten cents per centum" and a "Six mills per dollar" stamp for each state, none of which has been seen except the former Pennsylvania RM187.

A press and a set of dies, one die for each denomination, were prepared and sent to each state where it was the duty of the Supervisors of the Revenue to stamp all documents presented to them upon payment of the proper tax. The Supervisors were also to have on hand for sale blank paper stamped with the different rates of duty to be sold to the public upon which the purchaser could later write or print the proper type of instrument corresponding with the value of the stamp impressed thereon. So far as is now known there was no distinctive watermark for the paper sold by the government. The Vermont set of dies is in the Vermont Historical Society at Montpelier.

B. SECOND FEDERAL ISSUE.
Act of April 23, 1800
In effect March 1, 1801—June 30, 1802.

		(a) Government watermark in italics; laid paper	(b) Government watermark in Roman; wove paper	(c) No Government watermark
RM260	4c	15.00	15.00	50.00
RM261	10c	15.00	15.00	50.00
RM262	20c	55.00	50.00	85.00
RM263	25c	15.00	15.00	17.50
RM264	30c	37.50	55.00	500.00
RM265	50c	55.00	45.00	85.00

EMBOSSED REVENUE STAMPED PAPER

		(a) Government watermark in italics; laid paper	(b) Government watermark in Roman; wove paper	(c) No Government watermark
RM266	75c	30.00	40.00	100.00
RM267	$1	100.00	120.00	90.00
RM269	$4			500.00
RM271	$10		500.00	

The distinguishing feature of the stamps of this issue is the counter stamp, the left stamp shown in the illustration which usually appears on a document below the other stamp. In the right stamp the design of the eagle and the shield are similar to their design in the same denomination of the First Federal Issue but the name of the state is omitted and the denomination appears below instead of above the eagle and the shield. All of these stamps were embossed without color.

All the paper which was furnished by the government contained the watermark vertically along the edge of the sheet, "GEN STAMP OFFICE", either in Roman capitals on wove paper or in italic capitals on laid paper. The wove paper also had in the center of each half sheet either the watermark "W. Y. & Co." or "Delaware". William Young & Co. who owned the Delaware Mills made the government paper. The laid paper omitted the watermark "Delaware". The two stamps were separately impressed. The design of the eagle and shield differed in each value.

All the stamping was done in Washington, the right stamp being put on in the General Stamp Office and the left one or counter stamp in the office of the Commissioner of the Revenue as a check on the stamping done in the General Stamp Office. The "Com. Rev. C. S." in the design of the counter stamp stands for "Commissioner of the Revenue, Counter Stamp."

The Second Federal issue was intended to include $2 and $5 stamps, but these denominations have not been seen.

C. THIRD FEDERAL ISSUE.
Act of August 2, 1813
In effect January 1, 1814—December 31, 1817

		a. Watermark	b. Unwmkd.
RM275	5c	10.00	15.00
RM276	10c	10.00	10.00
RM277	25c	10.00	10.00
RM278	50c	10.00	10.00
RM279	75c	13.00	17.50
RM280	$1	13.00	27.50
RM281	$1.50	13.00	32.50
RM282	$2	27.50	27.50
RM283	$2.50	27.50	55.00
RM284	$3.50	65.00	45.00
RM285	$4		110.00
RM286	$5	37.50	50.00

The distinguishing features of the stamps of this issue is the absence of the name of a state in the design and the absence of the counter stamp. Different values show different positions of the eagle. All stamps of this issue were embossed without color at Washington. The paper with the watermark "Stamp U. S." was sold by the government. Unwatermarked paper may be either wove or laid.

IV. ISSUES BY VARIOUS STATES.

A. DELAWARE.
Act of June 19, 1793
In effect October 1, 1793—Feburary 7, 1794

EP50   EP51

EP53

RM291	EP50	5c	800.00
RM292	EP51	20c	1000.00
RM294	EP53	50c	

In some cases a reddish ink was used in impressing the stamp and in other cases the impressions are colorless.

Besides the denominations listed, 3c, 33c, and $1 stamps were called for by the taxing act. Stamps of these denominations have not been seen.

B. VIRGINIA.
Act of February 20, 1813
In effect May 1, 1813—April 30, 1815
Act of December 21, 1814
In effect May 1, 1815—February 27, 1816

EP60   EP61

EMBOSSED REVENUE STAMPED PAPER

			a. Die cut	b. On Document
RM305	EP61	4c	17.50	
RM306	EP60	6c	17.50	
RM307	EP61	10c		
RM308	EP60	12c	17.50	
RM309	EP61	20c		
RM310	"	25c	17.50	100.00
RM311	"	37c	17.50	
RM312	"	45c		
RM313	"	50c	17.50	
RM314	"	70c		
RM315	"	75c	17.50	
RM316	"	95c		
RM317	"	100c		
RM318	"	120c		
RM319	"	125c	17.50	
RM323	EP60	175c	17.50	
RM325	EP61	200c	17.50	

All of these stamps are colorless impressions and with some exceptions as noted below those issued the 1813 Act cannot be distinguished from those issued under the 1814 Act. The 10c, 20c, 45c, 70c, 95c, 120c, 145c, 150c, 170c and 190c denominations were issued only under the 1813 Act and the 6c, 12c, and 37c denominations were issued only under the 1814 Act. The other denominations were common to both Acts.

RM311, the 37c denomination, has the large lettering of EP60 but the 37 is to the left and the XXXVII to the right as in EP61. The design of the dogwood branch and berries is similar but not identical in all values.

When the tax on the document exceeded "two hundred cents", two or more stamps were impressed or attached to the document. For instance a document has been seen with RM312 and RM325 both impressed on it to make up the $2.45 rate, and another with RM315 and RM325.

Since both the Virginia and the Third Federal Acts to some extend taxed the same kind of document, and since during the period from Jan. 1, 1814, to Feb. 27, 1816, both Acts were in effect in Virginia, some instruments have both Virginia and Third Federal stamps on them.

The circular die cut Virginia stamps about 29 mm. in diameter were cut out of previously stamped paper which after the Act was repealed, was presented for redemption at the office of the Auditor of Public Accounts. They were threaded on fine twine and until recently preserved in his office as required by law. Watermarked die cut Virginia stamps are all cut out of Third Federal watermarked paper.

Besides the denominations listed, 145c, 150c, and 170c stamps were called for by the 1813 Act, and a 195c by both the 1813 and 1814 Acts. Stamps of these four denominations have not been seen.

C. MARYLAND.
1. Act of February 11, 1818
In effect May 1, 1818—March 7, 1819

EP70

RM362	EP70	30c red (printed), unused	100.00
		Sheet of 4, unused	550.00

The Act called for six other denominations, none of which has been seen. The Act imposing this tax was held unconstitutional by the United States Supreme Court in the case of McCulloch vs. Maryland.

2. Act of March 10, 1845
In effect May 10, 1845—March 10, 1856.

EP71

RM370	EP71	10c	8.00
RM371	"	15c	6.00
RM372	"	25c	6.00
RM373	"	50c	6.00
RM374	"	75c	6.00
RM375	"	$1	6.00
RM376	"	$1.50	12.00
RM377	"	$2	15.00
RM378	"	$2.50	15.00
RM379	"	$3.50	35.00
RM380	"	$4	60.00
RM381	"	$5.50	35.00
RM382	"	$6	35.00

Nos. RM370-RM382 are embossed without color with a similar design for each value. They vary in size from 20 mm. in diameter for the 10c to 33 mm. for the $6.

V. FEDERAL LICENSES TO SELL LIQUOR, ETC.

1. Act of June 5, 1794
In effect September 1, 1794—June 30, 1802

EP80

| RM400 | EP80 | $5 | 350.00 |

Provisionals are in existence using the second issue Connecticut Supervisors' stamp with the words "Five Dollars" written or printed over it or the second issue of the New Hampshire Supervisors' stamp without the words "Five Dollars".

2. Act of August 2, 1813
In effect January 1, 1814 — December 31, 1817.

EP81

RM451	EP81	$10	375.00
RM452	"	12	300.00
RM453	"	15	250.00
RM454	"	18	275.00
RM455	"	20	275.00
RM456	"	22.50	300.00
RM457	"	25	250.00
RM458	"	30	—
RM459	"	37.50	325.00

The Act of December 23, 1814, increased the basic rates of $10, $12, $15, $20 and $25 by 50 per cent, effective February 1, 1815. This increase applied to the unexpired portions of the year so far as licenses then in effect were concerned and these licenses were required to be brought in and to have the payment of the additional tax endorsed on them.

VI. FEDERAL LICENSES TO WORK A STILL.
Act of July 24, 1813.
In effect January 1, 1814-December 31, 1817.

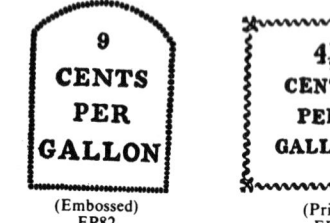

	(Embossed) EP82		a. Embossed	(Printed EP83	b. Printed
RM466		4½c			800.00
RM468		9c	550.00		375.00
RM471		18c			—
RM480		52c	350.00		
RM488		$1.08	350.00		

The statute under which these were issued provided for additional rates of 2½c, 5c, 10c, 16c, 21c, 25c, 26c, 32c, 35c, 36c, 42c, 50c, 54c, 60c, 64c, 70c, 84c, $1.04, $1.05, $1.20, $1.35, $1.40, $2.10, $2.16 and $2.70 per gallon of the capacity of the still. Stamps of these denominations have not been seen.

VII. SUPERVISORS' AND CUSTOM HOUSE SEALS.
1. Supervisors' Seals Act of March 3, 1791.
In effect July 1, 1792 — March 2, 1799.

EP90

		Check Letter	State	
RM501	EP90	"B"	South Carolina	30.00
RM503	"	"D"	Virginia	—
RM506	"	"G"	Pennsylvania	70.00
RM508	"	"I"	New York	22.50
RM509	"	"K"	Connecticut	25.00
RM510	"	"L"	Rhode Island	75.00
RM511	"	"M"	Massachusetts	22.50
RM512	"	"N"	New Hampshire	—
RM514	"	"P"	Kentucky	—

2. Supervisors' Seals Act of March 2, 1799.
In effect from March 2, 1799.

EP91

RM552	EP91	North Carolina	—
RM553	"	Virginia	—
RM554	"	Maryland	50.00
RM556	"	Pennsylvania	—
RM558	"	New York	22.50
RM559	"	Connecticut	22.50
RM560	"	Rhode Island	27.50
RM561	"	Massachusetts	22.50
RM562	"	New Hampshire	70.00

3. Custom House Seals.

EP92

RM575	EP92	Custom House, Philadelphia	60.00

Although no value is expressed in the Supervisors' and Custom House seals, and they do not evidence the payment of a tax in the same way that the other stamps do, some collectors of stamped paper include them in their collections if they are on instruments evidencing the payment of a tax. They were all embossed without color and, as to Supervisors' seals issued under the Act of 1791, the only difference in design is that at the left of the eagle there was a different check letter for each state. Custom House seals used in the other cities are in existence, but, in view of the doubtful status of Custom House seals as revenue stamps, it is not proposed to list them.

REVENUE STAMPED PAPER

These stamps were printed in various denominations and designs on checks, drafts, receipts, insurance policies, bonds, stock certificates, etc. They were authorized by Act of Congress of July 1, 1862, effective Oct. 1, 1862, and were used until July 1, 1882, except for the Spanish-American War series of 1898.

Most of these stamps were lithographed; some were engraved. They were printed by private firms under supervision of government representatives from stones or dies loaned by the Bureau of Internal Revenue. Types A-F were printed by, or the stones originated with, the American Phototype Co., New York (1865-75); type G, American Graphic Co., New York (1875); types H-L, Joseph R. Carpenter, Philadelphia (1869-75); types M-N, Bureau of Engraving and Printing (1874); type O, St. Louis Lithograph Co., St. Louis.

Samples of these stamps were produced with special dies for types B-G and P. For each sample die a section of the design was removed and replaced by the word "Sample." Types G and P-W exist with a redemption clause added by typography or rubber stamp.

Multiples or single impressions on various plain papers are usually considered proofs or printers' waste. For further information see "Handbook for United States Revenue Stamped Paper," published (1979) by the American Revenue Association.

Illustration size varies, with actual size quoted for each type.

Prices for types A-O are for clear impressions on plain entire checks and receipts. Attractive documents with vignettes sell for more. Prices for types P-W are for stamps on documents with attractive engravings, usually stock certificates, bonds and insurance policies. Examples on plain documents and cut squares sell for less.

Type A
Size: 22 x 25 mm.

1862-82			Unused	Used
RN-A1	A	2c black	65.00	50.00
		a. Printed on both sides		30.00
RN-A2	"	2c orange		100.00
RN-A8	"	2c purple (shades)		600.00
RN-A9	"	2c green		600.00

Same Type with 1 Entire and 53 to 57 Partial Impressions in Vertical Format ("Tapeworm")

			Full Document	Strip with Bank Names
RN-A10	A	2c orange, 56 partial impressions	800.00	200.00
	a.	53 partial impressions	1,000.	275.00
	b.	54 partial impressions	1,100.	300.00
	d.	57 partial impressions	1,100.	300.00
		Cut square, stamp only		60.00

No. RN-A10 was used by the Mechanics' National Bank of New York on a bank specie clerk's statement. It was designed so that the full stamp or one of the repeated bottom segments fell on each line opposite the name of a bank.

Size: 31 x 48 mm.

Eagle
Type B

RN-B1	B	2c orange	3.00	1.00
		yellow orange	3.00	1.00
		deep orange	3.00	1.00
		a. Printed on both sides	—	20.00
		b. Double impression	350.00	
		c. Printed on back		
		d. With 10 centimes blue French handstamp, right	300.00	
RN-B2	"	2c black	65.00	25.00
		slate	75.00	35.00
RN-B3	"	2c blue	75.00	30.00
		light blue	75.00	25.00
RN-B4	"	2c brown	—	45.00
RN-B5	"	2c bronze	65.00	25.00
RN-B6	"	2c green (shades)	75.00	25.00
RN-B7	"	2c yellow	6.00	2.50
RN-B10	"	2c red	75.00	25.00
		pale red	75.00	25.00
RN-B11	"	2c purple	75.00	35.00
RN-B13	"	2c violet (shades)	85.00	45.00
		a. 2c violet brown	100.00	75.00

"Good only for checks and drafts payable at sight."
in Rectangular Tablet at Base

RN-B16	B	2c orange	40.00	12.50
		a. With 2c org. red Nevada	325.00	325.00

"Good only for checks and drafts payable at sight."
in Octagonal Tablet at Base

RN-B17	B	2c orange	40.00	12.50
		a. Tablet inverted	—	650.00
		b. With 2c org. red Nevada	85.00	35.00
		c. With 2c green Nevada	100.00	35.00
		d. With 2c dull vio. Nevada		—

"Good when issued for the payment of money."
in Octagonal Tablet at Base

RN-B20	B	2c orange	60.00	5.00
		a. Printed on both sides	30.00	7.50

"Good when issued for the payment of money" in two lines at base in orange

RN-B23	B	2c orange		600.00

"Good when the amount does not exceed $100."
in Octagonal Tablet at Base

RN-B24	B	2c orange	175.00	60.00

Washington — Type C

REVENUE STAMPED PAPER

		Size: 22 x 25 mm.			
RN-C1	C	2c orange		5.00	2.00
		red orange		5.00	2.00
		yellow orange		5.00	2.00
		salmon		6.00	2.50
		brown orange		6.00	2.50
		a. "Good when used..." vert. at left black			
RN-C2	"	2c brown		30.00	10.00
		a. 2c buff		30.00	10.00
RN-C5	"	2c pale red		50.00	17.50
		red		50.00	22.50
		a. 2c pink			17.50
RN-C6	"	2c yellow		7.50	3.00
RN-C8	"	2c green			

"Good only for Sight Draft"
in two lines in color of stamp

RN-C9	C	2c orange, legend at lower right	75.00	35.00
RN-C11	C	2c brown, legend at lower left	75.00	35.00
RN-C13	C	2c orange, legend at lower left	40.00	12.50

"Good only for Receipt for Money Paid"
in two lines in color of stamp

RN-C15	C	2c orange, legend at lower right	—	
RN-C16	C	2c orange, legend at lower left		135.00

"Good when issued for the payment of money"
in one line at base in color of stamp.

RN-C17	C	2c orange (shades)		250.00

"Good when issued for the/Payment of Money" in two tablets at lower left and right.

RN-C19	C	2c orange		250.00
		a. Printed on both sides		30.00

"Good/only for Bank/Check"
in 3-part Band

RN-C21	C	2c orange	50.00	10.00
		yellow		20.00
		a. Inverted		650.00
		b. With 2c red org. Nevada	70.00	30.00
		c. Printed on back		
RN-C22	"	2c brown	—	22.50
		a. Printed on back		125.00
RN-C23	"	2c red		650.00

"Good when the amount does not exceed $100"
in tablet at lower right.

RN-C26	C	2c orange		175.00

Franklin
Type D

Size: 80 x 43 mm.

RN-D1	D	2c orange (shades)	2.00	60
		a. Double impression		
		b. Printed on back	—	300.00
		c. Inverted		350.00
RN-D2	"	2c yellow	10.00	4.00
RN-D3	"	2c brown	7.50	3.00
		light brown	7.50	3.00
		a. 2c buff	7.50	3.00
RN-D5	"	2c red		

"Good only for/Bank Check"
in panels within circles at left and right

RN-D7	D	2c orange	20.00	7.50
		a. Printed on back		—

"Good only for / Bank Check"
in two lines at lower right in color of stamp

RN-D8	D	2c orange		325.00

"Good only for Sight Draft"
in two lines at lower left in color of stamp

RN-D9	D	2c orange	150.00	50.00

Franklin
Type E

Size: 28 x 50 mm.

RN-E4	E	2c orange	5.00	3.00
		a. Double impression		350.00
		Broken die, lower R or L	40.00	20.00
		"Good only for sight draft"		
		in two lines at base in orange		
RN-E5	E	2c orange	65.00	17.50
		"Good only for/Bank Check"		
		in colorless letters in two lines above and below portrait		
RN-E7	E	2c orange	50.00	15.00

Franklin
Type F

Size: 56 x 34 mm.

RN-F1	F	2c orange	8.00	3.00
RN-F2	"	2c yellow	10.00	5.00
		a. Inverted		—

Liberty
Type G

Size: 80 x 48 mm.

REVENUE STAMPED PAPER

679

RN-G1	G	2c orange	1.25	25
		a. Printed on back	50.00	35.00
RN-G2	"	2c yellow	10.00	10.00
		Imprint: "Graphic Co., New York" at left and right in minute type.		
RN-G3	G	2c orange	100.00	85.00

Eagle
Type H
Size: 32 x 50mm.

RN-H3	H	2c orange	7.50	2.00
		a. Inverted		
		b. Double impression		400.00
		c. "Good when used..." added in 2 lines at base, black		400.00
		d. As "*c.*" legend added in 1 line upward at left, black		—
		e. As "*c.*" legend added in 1 line horiz., black		500.00
		f. "Good for bank check..." added in black		125.00

"Good for check or sight draft only" at left and right in color of stamp.

RN-H5	H	2c orange		750.00

Type I
Design R2 of 1862-72 adhesive revenues.
Size: 20 x 23mm.
"BANK CHECK"

RN-I1	R2	2c orange		175.00

"U.S. INTER. REV."

RN-I2	R2	2c orange	600.00	300.00

Washington
Type J

Size: 105 x 40mm.
Background of medallion crosshatched, filling oval except for bust.

RN-J4	J	2c orange	10.00	4.00
		pale orange	10.00	4.00
		deep orange	20.00	7.50
		a. Double impression		
		b. "Good only for..." added vert. at left in red org.		450.00
RN-J5	"	2c red	35.00	12.00

"Good for check or sight draft only" curved, below.

RN-J9	J	2c red		650.00
		Background shaded below bust and at left.		
RN-J11	J	2c orange	50.00	15.00

Washington
Type K
Size: 84 x 33mm.

RN-K4	"	2c gray	35.00	7.50
		pale gray	35.00	7.50
RN-K5	"	2c brown	150.00	100.00
RN-K6	"	2c orange	15.00	7.50
RN-K8	"	2c red		250.00
RN-K11	"	2c olive	175.00	150.00
		pale olive		125.00

Washington
Type L
Size: 50 x 33mm.

RN-L1	L	2c blue (shades)	200.00	140.00
RN-L3	"	2c gray	25.00	10.00
		pale gray	25.00	10.00
RN-L4	"	2c green	225.00	175.00
		light green	225.00	175.00
RN-L5	"	2c orange	12.50	5.00
RN-L6	"	2c olive		65.00
		gray olive		30.00
RN-L10	"	2c red	12.50	5.00
		a. 2c violet red	15.00	5.00
RN-L13	"	2c brown		95.00

Washington Size: 68 x 37mm.
Type M

RN-M1		2c yellow	37.50	10.00
RN-M2	M	2c orange	35.00	7.50
		a. Printed on back, inverted.		
RN-M3	"	2c green		225.00
RN-M4	"	2c gray		500.00

REVENUE STAMPED PAPER

Eagle, Numeral and Monitor
Type N   Size: 107 x 48mm.

RN-N3	N	2c orange	50.00	12.00
		a. Printed on back	150.00	100.00
		b. Inverted		150.00
RN-N4	"	2c light brown		150.00

Liberty
Type O

RN-O2	O	2c orange	1000.00	1250.00

Type P
Frame as Type B, Lincoln in center
Size: 32 x 49 mm.

			Unused (full document)	Used (full document)	Cut Square
RN-P2	P	5c brown		300.00	50.00
RN-P4	"	5c yellow		40.00	6.00
RN-P5	"	5c orange	50.00	35.00	4.00
RN-P6	"	5c red (shades)	150.00	150.00	20.00

The 5c green, type P, only exists in combination with a 25c green or 50c green. See Nos. RN-T2, RN-V1

Size: 28 x 56mm.

Madison
Type Q

RN-Q1	Q	5c orange	100.00	75.00	15.00
		brownish orange	100.00	75.00	
RN-Q2	Q	5c brown			150.00

Type R
Frame as Type B, Lincoln in center
Size: 32 x 49mm.

RN-R2	R	10c red	—	550.00	100.00
RN-R3	"	10c orange		350.00	40.00

"Good when the premium does not exceed $10" in tablet at base

RN-R6	R	10c orange	—	300.00	30.00
RN-R7	"	10c orange, motto without tablet			450.00

Washington
Type S   Size: 33 x 54mm.

"Good when the premium does not exceed $10" in tablet at base.

			Unused (full doc.)	Used (full doc.)	Cut Square
RN-S1	S	10c orange no motto or tablet		4000.00	
RN-S2	S	10c orange		3000.00	250.00

Eagle
Type T   Size: 33 x 40mm.

RN-T1	T	25c black	—		—
RN-T2	"	25c green		700.00	
RN-T3	"	25c red	150.00	75.00	7.50
RN-T4	"	25c orange	125.00	60.00	6.00
		light orange	125.00	60.00	6.00
		brown orange		70.00	7.50

RN-T2 includes a 5c green, type P, and a 25c green, type T, obliterating an RN-V4.

"Good when the premium does not exceed $50" in tablet at base.

RN-T6	T	25c orange	450.00	325.00	35.00
RN-T7	"	25c org., motto without tablet			300.00

"Good when the amount insured shall not exceed $1000" in tablet at base.

RN-T8	T	25c deep orange	550.00	475.00	75.00

Franklin
Type U
Size: 126 x 65mm.

RN-U1	U	25c orange	35.00	25.00	4.00
RN-U2	"	25c brown	45.00	30.00	5.00

REVENUE STAMPED PAPER

"Good when the premium does not exceed $50" in tablet at lower right.

			Unused (full document)	Used (full document)	Cut Square
RN-U3	U	25c orange			250.00

Tablet at lower left.

RN-U4	U	25c yellow	550.00	450.00	75.00
RN-U5	"	25c red	600.00		250.00
RN-U6	"	25c orange	500.00	400.00	50.00

Tablet at base.

| RN-U7 | U | 25c brown | 500.00 | | 175.00 |
| RN-U9 | " | 25c orange | 550.00 | | 200.00 |

Type V
As Type T, Lincoln in center
Size: 32 x 41 mm.

RN-V1	V	50c green		135.00	40.00
RN-V2	"	50c brown		300.00	50.00
RN-V4	"	50c orange	125.00	75.00	10.00
		deep orange	125.00	75.00	10.00
RN-V5	"	50c red	600.00		200.00

RN-V1 includes a 50c green, type V, and a 5c green, type P, obliterating an RN-W2.

"Good when the amount insured shall not exceed $5000" in tablet at base.

RN-V6	V	50c orange	400.00	325.00	50.00
RN-V9	"	50c red		--	--
RN-V10	"	50c orange, motto without tablet			150.00

Washington
Type W

Size: 34 x 73mm.

			Unused (full document)	Used (full document)	Cut Square
RN-W2	W	$1 orange (shades)	125.00	65.00	10.00
RN-W4	"	$1 light brown	175.00	150.00	30.00

SPANISH-AMERICAN WAR SERIES.

Many of these stamps were used for parlor car tax and often were torn in two or more parts.

Liberty
Type X

1898 Size: 68 x 38mm.

			New	Used	Partial
RN-X1	X	1c rose	500.00		50.00
		dark red			50.00
RN-X4	"	1c orange	120.00		
		a. On pullman ticket	350.00		20.00
		b. As "a," printed on back			50.00
RN-X5	"	1c green	50.00	30.00	
		a. On parlor car ticket	50.00	20.00	
		b. On pullman ticket	500.00		15.00
RN-X6	"	2c yellow	5.00	2.00	
		pale olive		1,000.	
RN-X7	"	2c orange	75	25	
		pale orange	75	25	
		a. Printed on back only	125.00	100.00	
		c. Printed on front and back			
		d. Vertical		85.00	
		e. Double impression			
		f. On pullman ticket	500.00	200.00	
		g. Inverted			

No. RN-X1 exists only as a four-part unused pullman ticket or as a used half of a two-part ticket. Nos. RN-X4a and RN-X5b exist as unused two-part tickets and as used half portions. No. RN-X7f exists as an unused four-part ticket and as a used two-piece portion with nearly complete stamp design.

CONSULAR FEE
Type of Consular Fee Stamps

1906 (?)
| RN-Y1 | CS1 | $2 black |

PRIVATE DIE PROPRIETARY STAMPS

The extraordinary demands of the Civil War upon the Federal Treasury resulted in Congress devising an passing the Revenue Act of 1862. The Government provided revenue stamps to be affixed to boxes or packages matches, and to proprietary medicines, perfumery, playing cards-as well as to documents, et cetera.

But manufacturers were permitted, at their expense, to have dies engraved and plates made for their exclusive us Many were only too willing to do this because a discount or premium of from 5% to 10% was allowed on orders fro the dies which often made it possible for them to undersell their competitors and too, the considerable advertisir value of the stamps could not be overlooked. These are now known as private die proprietary stamps.

The face value of the stamp used on matches was determined by the number, i.e., 1c for each 100 matches o fraction thereof. Medicines and perfumery were taxed at the rate of 1c for each 25 cents of the retail price or fractio thereof up o $1 and 2c for each 50 cents or fraction above that amount. Playing cards were first taxed at the same ra but subsequently the tax was 5c for a deck of 52 cards and 10c for a greater number of cards or double decks.

The stamp tax was repealed on Mar. 3, 1883, effective July 1, 1883.

The various papers were:
- *a.* Old paper, 1862-71. First Issue. Hard and brittle varying from thick to thin.
- *b.* Silk paper, 1871-77. Second Issue. Soft and porous with threads of silk, mostly red, blue and black, up to ¼ inch in length.
- *c.* Pink paper, 1877-78. Third Issue. Soft paper colored pink ranging from pale to deep shades.
- *d.* Watermarked paper, 1878-83. Fourth Issue. Soft porous paper showing part of "USIR".
- *e.* Experimental silk paper. Medium smooth paper, containing minute fragments of silk threads either blue alone or blue and red (infrequent), widely scattered, sometimes but a single fiber on a stamp.

Early printings of some private die revenue stamps are on paper which appears to have laid lines.

These stamps were usually torn in opening the box or container. Prices quoted are for specimens which are damaged, but are reasonably attractive. Specimens in fine to very fine condition sell for 30% to 100% more.

PRIVATE DIE MATCH STAMPS.

Arnold & Co. — RO14 — 1864-83
Thos. Allen — RO5 — Perf. 12
Wm. Bond & Co. — RO32/RO33

			a. Old Paper.	b. Silk Paper.	c. Pink Paper.	d. Wmkd. USIR (191R)
A						
RO1	1c	blue, Akron Match Co.	100.00			
RO2	1c	orange, Alexander's Matches	6.00	45.00		
RO3	1c	blue, Alexander's Matches	1200.00			
RO4	1c	blue, Allen's, J. J., Sons			2.00	
RO5	1c	green, Allen, Thos.	75.00			
RO6	1c	blue, Allen & Powers	3.50	15.00	3.00	
RO7	1c	blue, Alligator Match Co.			15.00	
RO8	1c	blue, Alligator Match Co. (Rouletted)			60.00	
RO9	1c	black, American Fusee Co.	2.50	4.00	2.50	
RO10	1c	black, American Match Co.	65.00	15.00		
RO11	3c	black, American Match Co.	275.00	90.00		
		e. Experimental silk paper	400.00			
		f. Double transfer	—			
RO12	1c	black, American Match Co. (Eagle)	40.00			
RO13	3c	green, American Match Co. (Rock Island)	1500.00			
RO14	1c	black, Arnold & Co.		22.50		
B						
RO15	1c	green, Bagley & Dunham				12.50
RO16	1c	blue, Barber, Geo. & O. C.	50.00			
RO17	1c	blue, Barber Match Co.	15.00	50	9.00	50
		u. 1c ultramarine	125.00			
		e. Experimental silk paper	40.00			
		t. Double transfer	—			
RO18	1c	blue, Barber Match Co. (Rouletted)				900.00
RO19	3c	black, Barber Match Co.	110.00	75.00		
		e. Experimental silk paper	150.00			
RO20	1c	blue, Barber & Peckham	30.00			
RO21	3c	black, Barber & Peckham	150.00			
RO22	1c	blue, Bauer & Beudel	50.00	80.00		
		u. 1c ultramarine	70.00			
RO23	1c	orange, A. B. & S. (A. Beecher & Son)	4.00	35.00		
		e. Experimental silk paper	30.00			
RO24	1c	brown, Bendel, B. & Co.	2.25			275.00
RO25	12c	brown, Bendel, B. & Co.	100.00			
RO26	1c	brown, Bendel, H.	4.00	1.50	50	
RO27	12c	brown, Bendel, H.	325.00			

Nos. RO26-RO27 are RO24-RO25 altered to read "H. Bendel doing business as B. Bendel & Co."

RO28	1c	blue, Bentz, H. & M.	20.00			
RO29	1c	black, Bent & Lea	20.00			
		e. Experimental silk paper	15.00			
		t. Double transfer at left	—			
RO30	1c	green, B. J. & Co. (Barber, Jones & Co.)		35.00		
RO31	1c	black, Bock, Schneider & Co.	5.00			
RO32	4c	black, Bond, Wm. & Co.	180.00			
RO33	4c	green, Bond, Wm. & Co.	90.00	100.00	10.00	

PRIVATE DIE PROPRIETARY

Charles Busch RO47	W.D. Curtis RO68	Eichele & Co. RO78	Excelsior Match RO83	Gardner, Beer & Co. RO86	Charles S. Hale RO106

			a. Old Paper.	b. Silk Paper.	c. Pink Paper.	d. Wmkd. USIR (191R)
RO34	1c	lilac, Bousfield & Poole	80.00			
RO35	1c	black, Bousfield & Poole	10.00	3.00		
		e. Experimental silk paper	30.00			
		t. Double transfer				
RO36	3c	lilac, Bousfield & Poole	1300.00			
RO37	3c	black, Bousfield & Poole	120.00	75.00		
		Experimental silk paper	—			
RO38	1c	black, Boutell & Maynard	90.00			
RO39	1c	green, Bowers & Dunham				130.00
RO40	1c	blue, Bowers & Dunham				50.00
RO41	1c	lake, B. & N. (Brocket & Newton) die I	25.00			
RO42	1c	lake, B.& N. (Brocket & Newton) die II	4.00			
		The initials "B. & N." measure 5¼ mm. across the top in Die I, and 4¼ mm. in Die II.				
RO43	1c	black, Brown & Durling	700.00			
RO44	1c	green, Brown & Durling	40.00			
RO45	1c	black, Buck, L.W. & Co.	500.00			
		e. Experimental silk paper	400.00			
RO46	1c	black, Burhans, D.& Co.	100.00	1000.00		
		e. Experimental silk paper	300.00			
RO47	1c	black, Busch, Charles				15.00
RO48	1c	black, Byam, Carlton & Co., (41x75mm.) (Two heads to left) (Imperf.)	1300.00			
RO49	1c	black, Byam, Carlton & Co., (19x23mm.)	15.00	3.00		40
		e. Experimental silk paper	35.00			
		i. Imperf. horizontally (pair)				130.00
		t. Double transfer				
RO50	1c	black, Byam, Carlton & Co., 2 heads to left, buff wrapper, 131x99 mm.	1000.00			
RO51	1c	black, Byam, Carlton & Co., 2 heads to left, buff wrapper 131x89 mm.	140.00			
RO52	1c	black, Byam, Carlton & Co., 1 head to right, white wrapper (94x54mm.)	50.00			
RO53	1c	black, Byam, Carlton & Co., 1 head to right, buff wrapper (94x54mm.)	125.00			
RO54	1c	black, Byam, Carlton & Co., 2 heads to right, buff wrapper (81x50mm.)	5.00			
		h. Right block reading up	20.00			
RO55	1c	black, Byam, Carlton & Co., 1 head to left, white wrapper (94x56mm.)	17.50			
RO56	1c	black, Byam, Carlton & Co., 2 heads to left, buff wrapper (95x57mm.)	2.25			

			a. Old Paper.	b. Silk Paper.	c. Pink Paper.	d. Wmkd. USIR (191R)
		— C —				
RO57	1c	green, Cannon Match Co.	15.00			
RO58	1c	lake, Cardinal Match Co.				4.00
RO59	1c	lake, C., F.E. (Frank E. Clark)	45.00	45.00		
		e. Experimental silk paper	50.00			
RO60	3c	black, Chicago Match Co.	150.00			
RO61	1c	green, Clark, Henry A.	50.00			
RO62	1c	green, Clark, James L.	60	15.00		60
		t. Double transfer				
RO63	1c	green, Clark, James L. (Rouletted)				250.00
RO64	1c	lake, Clark Match Co.	4.00			
RO65	1c	black, Cramer & Kemp	20.00			
RO66	1c	blue, Cramer & Kemp	50.00	3.00		
		e. Experimental silk paper	125.00			
		u. 1c ultramarine	150.00			
RO67	1c	black, Crown Match Co.	10.00			
RO68	1c	green, Curtis, W.D.	100.00	75.00		
		e. Experimental silk paper	110.00			
		— D —				
RO69	1c	black, Davis, G.W.H.	35.00			
RO70	1c	carmine, Davis, G.W.H.				40.00
RO71	1c	blue, Doolittle, W.E.	200.00			
RO72	1c	green, Dunham, E.P.				40.00
		— E —				
RO73	1c	black, Eaton, James	25.00	85	7.00	85
		e. Experimental silk paper	50.00			
RO74	1c	black, Eaton, James (Rouletted)				35.00
RO75	1c	carmine, Eddy, E.B., die I				8.00
		r. Die II				25.00
		Die II shows eagle strongly recut; ribbon across bottom is narrower; color is deeper.				
RO76	1c	black, Eichele, Aug.	45.00			
RO77	1c	blue, Eichele, P., & Co.	40.00	4.50		
		u. 1c ultramarine	150.00			
		e. Experimental silk paper	65.00			
RO78	1c	blue, Eichele & Co.	2.00	10.00		1.50
RO79	1c	blue, Eichele & Co. (Rouletted)				100.00
RO80	1c	blue, Eisenhart, J.W.	25.00	50.00		17.50
RO81	1c	black, Excelsior M. Co., Watertown	65.00			
RO82	1c	black, Excelsior M. Co., Syracuse	3.00	8.50		4.00
RO83	1c	blue, Excelsior Match, Baltimore	25.00	60.00		
		u. 1c ultramarine	150.00			
		— F —				
RO84	1c	black, Farr, G., & Co.	50.00			
RO85	1c	brown, Frank, L.				40.00
		— G —				
RO86	1c	black, Gardner, Beer & Co.				90.00
RO87	1c	black, Gates, Wm. die I	4.00	2.50		

PRIVATE DIE PROPIETARY

684

			a. Old Paper.	b. Silk Paper.	c. Pink Paper.	d. Wmkd. USIR (191R)
RO88	1c	black, Gates, Wm. die 2	22.50	2.50		
		t. Double transfer				
		e. Experimental silk paper	50.00			
		The shirt collar is colorless in Die 1, and shaded in Die 2. Other differences exist.				
RO89	3c	black, Gates, Wm.	40.00	30.00		
		e. Experimental silk paper	—			
		t. Double transfer		45.00		
RO90	6c	black, Gates, Wm.	75.00			
RO91	3c	black, Gates, Wm. (three 1c stamps)		75.00		
RO92	1c	black, Gates, Wm., Sons		15.00	4.00	40
RO93	1c	black, Gates, Wm., Sons (Rouletted)				750.00
RO94	3c	black, Gates, Wm., Sons (three 1c stamps)	75.00	110.00		60.00
RO95	1c	green, Goldback, A. & Co.	22.50			
RO96	1c	green, Goldback, A.		45.00	1750.00	
RO97	1c	black, Gorman, T. & Bro.	200.00			
		t. Double transfer	—			
RO98	1c	green, Gorman, T. & Bro.	17.50	13.00		
		t. Double transfer	—			
RO99	1c	green, Gorman, Thomas		2.75	15.00	27.50
RO100	1c	green, Greenleaf & Co.	50.00	50.00		
RO101	3c	carmine, Greenleaf & Co.	75.00	110.00		
RO102	5c	orange, Greenleaf & Co.	100.00	900.00		
RO103	1c	black, Griggs & Goodwill		20.00		
RO104	1c	green, Griggs & Goodwill		7.50		
		t. Double transfer	—			
RO105	1c	black, Griggs & Scott	5.00	25.00		
		e. Experimental silk paper	30.00			

H

RO106	1c	green, Hale, Charles S.			100.00	
RO107	1c	blue, Henning & Bonhack	85.00			
RO108	1c	red, Henry, W.E. & Co.			20.00	
RO109	1c	black, Henry, W.E. & Co.				4.00
RO110	1c	green, Hotchkiss, J.G.		4.00	30.00	6.00
RO111	1c	lake, Howard, B. & H.D.	60.00			
RO112	1c	blue, Howard, B. & H.D.	5.00			
		u. 1c ultramarine	75.00			
RO113	1c	black, Hunt, L.G.	100.00	550.00		
		e. Experimental silk paper	100.00			
RO114	1c	lake, Hutchinson, D.F., Jr.				8.00

I

RO115	1c	blue, Ives Matches	3.50	3.50		
		u. 1c ultramarine	67.50			
		t. Double transfer	—			
RO116	1c	blue, Ives, P.T.		2.50	15.00	2.50
RO117	1c	blue, Ives, P.T. (Rouletted)				200.00
RO118	8c	blue, Ives, P.T.	75.00			
		u. 8c ultramarine	400.00			
RO119	1c	green, Ives & Judd		8.00	30.00	50.00
RO120	1c	green, Ives & Judd Match Co.				60.00
		t. Double transfer				200.00

K

RO121	1c	green, Kirby & Sons		30.00		
RO122	1c	black, Kyle, W.S.	10.00	6.00		
		t. Double transfer	—			

L

			a. Old Paper.	b. Silk Paper.	c. Pink Paper.	d. Wmkd. USIR (191R)
RO123	1c	black, Lacour's Matches	10.00	30.00		
		e. Experimental silk paper	50.00			
RO124	1c	green, Leeds, Robinson & Co.				40.00
RO125	1c	blue, Leigh, H.				4.50
RO126	1c	black, Leigh & Palmer		17.50	45.00	30.00
RO127	1c	blue, Loehr, John		15.00		
RO128	1c	blue, Loehr, Joseph		1.50	8.00	1.75

M

RO129	1c	black, Macklin, J.J. & Co. (Rouletted)	3500.00			
RO130	1c	blue, Mansfield, F. & Co.		2.50	5.00	6.50
RO131	1c	blue, Maryland M. Co.		65.00		2250.00
RO132	1c	blue, Matches, (head Franklin)	2.25	1.75		
		u. 1c ultramarine	150.00			
		t. Double transfer	80.00			
		e. Experimental silk paper	40.00			
RO133	1c	black, Messinger, A.		1.00	8.00	1.00

N

RO134	1c	blue, National M. Co.				50.00
RO135	1c	lake, Newton, F.P.		1.00	4.50	1.00
RO136	1c	blue, N.Y. Match Co. (Shield)	150.00	4.00		
RO137	1c	vermilion, N.Y. Match Co. (Eagle)	35.00	2250.00		
		e. Experimental silk paper	55.00			
RO138	1c	green, N.Y. Match Co. (Size 22x60mm.)	20.00	4.00		
		e. Experimental silk paper	30.00			
RO139	5c	blue, N.Y. Match Co. (Size 22x60mm.)		900.00		
RO140	4c	green, N. & C. (Newbauer & Co.)		2.50	85.00	2.50

O

RO141	1c	blue, Orono Match Co.	15.00	20.00		
		u. 1c ultramarine	150.00			

P

RO142	1c	green, Park City Match Co.	30.00	30.00		
		e. Experimental silk paper	75.00			
RO143	3c	orange, Park City Match Co.	30.00			
RO144	1c	blue, Penn Match Co.				25.00
RO145	1c	green, Pierce Match Co.	1000.00			
RO146	1c	black, P.M. Co. (Portland M. Co.)	17.50			
RO147	1c	black, Portland M. Co. (wrapper)	40.00			

Price of No. RO147 applies to commonest date (Dec. 1866); all others are much rarer.

RO148	1c	blue, Powell, V.R.		2.50		5.00
		u. 1c ultramarine	135.00			
		e. Experimental silk paper	30.00			
		t. Double transfer	—			

Ives & Judd Match Co.
RO120

Leeds, Robinson & Co.
RO124

"Matches"
RO132

V.R. Powell
RO148

Standard Match Co.
RO170

Washington Match Co.
RO181

PRIVATE DIE PROPIETARY

			a. Old Paper.	b. Silk Paper.	c. Pink Paper.	d. Wmkd. USIR (191R)
RO149	1c	black, Powell, V.R. (buff wrapper) uncut	1500.00			
RO150	1c	black, Powell, V. R. (buff wrapper) cut to shape	650.00			
RO151	1c	black, Powell, V. R. (white wrapper) cut to shape	1000.00			

R

RO152	1c	black, Reading M. Co.				5.00
RO153	1c	black, Reed & Thompson				4.50
RO154	1c	red, Richardson, D. M.	70.00			
RO155	1c	black, Richardson, D. M.	2.50	1.50		
	e.	Experimental silk paper	20.00			
	t.	Double transfer		25.00		
RO156	3c	vermilion, Richardson, D.M.	80.00			
RO157	3c	blue, Richardson, D. M.	3.50	2.00		
	e.	Experimental silk paper	25.00			
RO158	1c	black, Richardson Match Co.		75	3.50	75
RO159	3c	blue, Richardson Match Co.		55.00		
RO160	1c	blue, Roeber, H. & W.	6.00	1.50		
	u.	1c ultramarine	65.00			
	t.	Double transfer	175.00			
RO161	1c	blue, Roeber, Wm.		1.25	4.00	1.25
RO162	1c	blue, Roeber, Wm. (Rouletted)				70.00
RO163	1c	black, Russell, E. T.	2.50	8.50		
	e.	Experimental silk paper	30.00			
RO164	1c	lake, R. C. & W. (Ryder, Crouse & Welch)				40.00

S

San Francisco Match Co.
RO165

RO165	12c	blue, San Francisco Match Co.	325.00			
RO166	1c	vermilion, Schmitt & Schmittdiel	2.00	40.00		2.00
RO167	3c	blue, Schmitt & Schmittdiel	25.00 8.00	30.00		12.00
RO168	1c	blue, Smith, E. K.				
RO169	1c	blue, Smith, E. K. (Rouletted)				900.00
RO170	1c	black, Standard Match Co.				22.50
RO171	1c	black, Stanton, H.	8.00	3.50	8.50	5.00
	e.	Experimental silk paper	25.00			
RO172	1c	black, Star Match	3.00	10	20	10
	e.	Experimental silk paper	15.00			
	t.	Double transfer				15.00
RO173	1c	blue, Swift & Courtney	1.25	1.25		
	u.	1c ultramarine	25.00			
	e.	Experimental silk paper	7.50			
	t.	Double transfer				
RO174	1c	blue, Swift & Courtney & Beecher Co.		40	1.50	40
	t.	Double transfer				
RO175	1c	black, S. C. B. C. (Flag)				60.00

T

			a. Old Paper.	b. Silk Paper.	c. Pink Paper.	d. Wmkd. USIR (191R)
RO176	1c	blue, Trenton M. Co.				4.00
RO177	1c	green, T., E. R. (E. R. Tyler)	8.00	2.75		
	e.	Experimental silk paper	25.00			
	t.	Double transfer				

U

RO178	1c	green, Underwood, Alex. & Co.	45.00	110.00		
	e.	Experimental silk paper	100.00			
RO179	1c	black, Union Match Co.				40.00
RO180	1c	black , U. S. M. Co. (Universal Safety M. Co.)	1.50	15.00		
	e.	Experimental silk paper	20.00			

W

RO181	1c	black, Washington Match Co.		22.50		
RO182	1c	black, Wilmington Parlor Match Co.	40.00	2000.00		
	e.	Experimental silk paper	40.00			
RO183	1c	black, Wise & Co.	800.00			

Z

RO184	1c	black, Zaiss, F. & Co.	65	2.00	1.00	
RO185	1c	green, Zisemann, Griesheim & Co.	500.00			
RO186	1c	blue, Zisemann, Griesheim & Co.	80.00	15.00		
	u.	1c ultramarine	175.00			

PRIVATE DIE CANNED FRUIT STAMP.

T. Kensett & Co.
RP1
Perf. 12

1867				
RP1	1c	green, Kensett, T. & Co.	600.00	

PRIVATE DIE MEDICINE STAMPS.

Anglo-American Drug Co.
RS1
Perf. 12

1862-83						
RS1	1c	black, Anglo-American Drug Co.				45.00
RS2	1c	brown, carmine, Ayer J. C. & Co. (imperf.)	1750.00			
RS3	1c	green, Ayer, J. C. & Co. (imperf.)	2000.00			
RS4	1c	black, Ayer, J. C. & Co (imperf.)	45.00	45.00	725.00	35.00
	t.	Double transfer				
RS5	1c	blue, Ayer, J. C. & Co. (imperf.)	1750.00			
RS6	1c	orange Ayer, J. C. & Co. (imperf.)	2000.00			

PRIVATE DIE PROPRIETARY

			a. Old Paper.	b. Silk Paper.	c. Pink Paper.	d. Wmkd. USIR (191R)
RS7	1c	gray lilac, Ayer, J.C. & Co. (imperf.)	2000.00			
RS8	4c	red, Ayer, J.C. & Co. (die cut)	1750.00			
RS9	4c	blue, Ayer, J.C. & Co. (die cut)	2.50	2.50		2.50
		u. 4c ultramarine (die cut)	150.00			
RS10	4c	blue, Ayer, J.C. & Co. (imperf.)	350.00	325.00		350.00
RS11	4c	purple, Ayer, J.C. & Co. (die cut)	2250.00			
RS12	4c	green, Ayer, J.C. & Co. (die cut)	1500.00			
RS13	4c	vermilion, Ayer, J.C. & Co. (die cut)	1750.00			

The 4c in black was printed and sent to Ayer & Co. It may exist but has not been seen by collectors.

B

RS14	4c	green, Barham, P.C. Co., wmkd. lozenges		60.00		
RS15	1c	vermilion, Barnes, D.S.	90.00			
RS16	2c	vermilion, Barnes, D.S.	55.00			
RS17	4c	vermilion, Barnes, D.S.	250.00			
RS18	1c	black, Barnes, D.S.	15.00			
RS19	2c	black, Barnes, D.S.	50.00			
RS20	4c	black, Barnes, D.S.	65.00			
RS21	1c	black, Barnes, Demas	12.00			
RS22	2c	black, Barnes, Demas	40.00			
RS23	4c	black, Barnes, Demas	15.00			
RS24	1c	black, Barnes & Co., Demas	6.00	.275.00		
RS25	2c	black, Barnes, Demas & Co.	5.00	225.00		
		e. Experimental silk paper	35.00			
RS26	4c	black, Barnes, Demas & Co.	5.00			
RS27	4c	black, Barr, T.H. & Co.	7.50			
		t. Double transfer	75.00			
RS28	2c	green, Barry's Tricopherous	8.00	9.00		
RS29	2c	green, Barry's Proprietary	2.25	95.00		2.75
		t. Double transfer				
RS30	1c	lake, Bennett, D.M.	5.00			
		e. Experimental silk paper	35.00			
RS31	1c	green, Blow, W.T.	200.00	55.00	275.00	45.00
		e. Experimental silk paper	250.00			
RS32	1c	black, Brandreth, (perf.)	250.00	300.00		
RS33	1c	black, Brandreth, (imperf.)	2.00	1.00		
		e. Experimental silk paper	10.00			
RS34	1c	black, Brandreth, Allcock's (41x50 mm. imperf.)		100.00		
RS35	1c	black, Brandreth, Allcock's (24x30 mm. imperf.)	85	3.00		.85
		p. Perf.				
RS36	1c	blue, Brown, C.F.	125.00	45.00		55.00
RS37	2c	black, Brown, Fred Co. (imperf.) die I, "E" of "Fred" incomplete	85.00	45.00	750.00	40.00
		e. Experimental silk paper	150.00			
RS38	2c	black, Brown, Fred Co. (imperf.) die II, "E" of "Fred" normal		55.00		
		Die II shows recutting in the "E" of "Fred" and "Genuine".				
RS39	1c	black, Brown, John I. & Son	6.00	17.50		4.00

RS40	2c	green, Brown, John I. & Son	6.00	6.00	150.00	150.00
		e. Experimental silk paper	40.00			
		t. Double transfer	—			
RS41	4c	brown, Brown, John I. & Son				
RS42	1c	black, Bull, John	150.00	60.00		800.00
		e. Experimental silk paper	125.00	9.00	200.00	7.00
RS43	4c	blue, Bull, John	125.00			
		u. 4c ultramarine	150.00	7.00	175.00	4.50
		e. Experimental silk paper	250.00			
RS44	1c	black, Burdsal, J.S. & Co., wrapper white paper	175.00	40.00		22.50
RS45	1c	black, Burdsal, J.S. & Co., wrapper orange paper	450.00			275.00
RS46	4c	black, Burnett, Joseph & Co.	65.00	5.00	165.00	5.00

C

RS47	4c	black, Campion, J.W. & Co. (imperf.)		300.00		250.00
		p. Pair, perf. horiz.				600.00
RS48	4c	black, Campion, J.W. & Co. (die cut)		120.00	175.00	70.00
RS49	4c	green, Cannon & Co. (imperf.)		65.00	200.00	55.00
RS50	1c	vermilion, Centaur Co.			40.00	5.00
RS51	2c	black, Centaur Co.			8.00	1.00
RS52	4c	black, Centaur Co.				35.00
RS53	1c	black, Chase, A.W., Son & Co.		55.00		1250.00
RS54	2c	black, Chase, A.W., Son & Co.		65.00		
RS55	4c	black, Chase, A.W., Son & Co.		95.00		
RS56	3c	blue, Clarke, Wm. E				70.00
RS57	6c	black, Clarke, Wm. E.				55.00
RS58	4c	black, Clark, R.C. & C.S. (A.B.C.)		7.00		12.00
RS59	1c	black, Collins Bros.	8.00	135.00		
RS60	1c	black, Comstock, W.H.				2.00
RS61	4c	blue, Cook & Bernheimer		4.00		70.00
RS62	1c	black, Crittenton, Chas. N.				
RS63	1c	blue, Crittenton, Chas. N.			10.00	3.50
RS64	2c	black, Crittenton, Chas. N.		50.00	25.00	3.00
RS65	4c	black, Crook, Oliver & Co.	60.00	10.00		
		e. Experimental silk paper	10.00			
RS66	1c	black, Curtis, Jeremiah, & Son, die I, small numerals		55.00		
RS67	1c	black, Curtis, Jeremiah, & Son, die II, large numerals				80.00
RS68	2c	black, Curtis, Jeremiah, & Son	7.00	7.00	80.00	125.00
		t. Double transfer				
RS69	1c	black, Curtis & Brown	3.50	2.50		
RS70	2c	black, Curtis & Brown		75.00		
RS71	1c	black, Curtis & Brown Mfg. Co.			90.00	2.50
RS72	2c	black, Curtis & Brown Mfg. Co.		950.00		450.00

D

RS73	2c	green, Dalley's Horse Salve	60.00	60.00		60.00
RS74	1c	black, Dalley's Pain Ext.	5.00	5.00		6.00
		h. Error, $100 instead of $1.00	200.00			7.50
RS75	1c	blue, Davis, Perry & Son	5.00	2.00	150.00	2.00
		u. 1c ultramarine	65.00			
		e. Experimental silk paper	40.00			
RS76	2c	brown red, Davis, Perry & Son	80.00			

Dr. C.F. Brown
RS36

Wm. E. Clarke
RS56

Barry's Tricopherous
RS28

Herrick's Pills & Plasters
RS118

Holman Liver Pad Co.
RS126

PRIVATE DIE PROPRIETARY

			a. Old Paper	b. Silk Paper	c. Pink Paper	d. Wmkd. USIR (191R)
RS77	2c	black, Davis, Perry & Son	50.00			
RS78	2c	dull purple, Davis, Perry & Son	4.50			
RS78A	2c	slate, Davis, Perry & Son	8.00			2.50
RS79	2c	dull red, Davis, Perry & Son	50.00			
RS80	2c	brown, Davis, Perry & Son	—			
RS81	4c	brown, Davis, Perry & Son	7.00	2.00		1.50
RS82	2c	black, Drake, P. H. & Co.	800.00			
RS83	4c	black, Drake, P. H. & Co.	25.00	40.00		
		e. Experimental silk paper	85.00			

F

RS84	1c	lake, Fahnestock, B. A. (imperf.)	90.00	85.00		
RS85	4c	black, Father Mathew T. M. Co.				3.50
RS86	1c	green, Flanders, A. H. (perf.)	10.00			9.00
RS87	1c	green, Flanders, A. H. (part perf.)	20.00	1.25	25.00	1.25
RS88	1c	black, Fleming Bros. (Vermifuge) (imperf.)	8.50	15.00		20.00
		e. Experimental silk paper	50.00			
RS89	1c	black, Fleming Bros. (L. Pills) (imperf.)	1500.00			
RS90	1c	blue, Fleming Bros. (L. Pills) (imperf.)	2.50	2.50		2.00
		u. 1c ultramarine	125.00			
		t. Double transfer		40.00		40.00
RS91	4c	black, Fowle, Seth W. & Son.	10.00	2.00		3.00
		i. Vertical pair, imperf. between				

G

RS92	3c	black, Green, G. G.				2.25
		h. Tete beche pair				200.00
RS93	3c	black, Green, G. G. (rouletted)				100.00

H

RS94	4c	black, Hall & Co. Reuben P.	15.00	14.00		16.00
RS95	1c	green, Hall & Ruckel	60	60	17.50	75
		e. Experimental silk paper	10.00			
RS96	3c	black, Hall & Ruckel	1.25	1.25	45.00	1.50
RS97	1c	black, Harter, Dr. & Co.	15.00	10.00		
		e. Experimental silk paper	50.00			
RS98	1c	black, Harter, Dr.		85	8.00	85
		t. Double impression				
RS99	4c	black, Hartman, S. B. & Co.	150.00	40.00	175.00	650.00
RS100	6c	black, Hartman, S. B. & Co.	200.00	140.00		
RS101	1c	black, Hazeltine, E. T.				10.00
RS102	2c	blue, "		22.50		
RS103	4c	black, Hazeltine, E. T.	200.00	15.00		12.00
		e. Experimental silk paper	250.00			
		i. Imperf. (pair)	600.00			
RS104	3c	black, H., E. (Edward Heaton)				30.00
RS105	3c	brown, H., E. (Edward Heaton)				9.00
RS106	2c	blue, Helmbold	65	175.00		
		t. Double transfer				
RS107	3c	green, Helmbold	25.00	20.00		
RS108	4c	black, Helmbold	3.00	100.00		
		t. Double transfer				
RS109	6c	black, Helmbold	2.00	2.50		
		e. Experimental silk	15.00			
RS110	2c	blue, Helmbold A. L.	85.00	95.00		85.00
RS111	4c	black, Helmbold, A.L.	20.00	100.00		6.00
RS112	2c	violet, Henry, John F.	150.00			
RS113	4c	bistre, Henry, John F.	400.00			
RS114	1c	black, Henry, John F.	35.00	35	3.50	35
		e. Experimental silk paper	65.00			
RS115	2c	blue, Henry, John F.	27.50	4.00	80.00	4.00
		u. 2c ultramarine	35.00			
RS116	4c	red, Henry, John F.	90.00	50	10.00	40
		e. Experimental silk paper	35.00			
RS117	1c	black, Herrick's Pills	60.00	25.00	60.00	25.00
		e. Experimental silk paper	110.00			
RS118	1c	red, Herrick's Pills & Plasters,	90	2.00	40.00	90
RS119	1c	black, Hetherington, J. E.				10.00
RS120	2c	black, Hetherington, J. E.				225.00

			a. Old Paper	b. Silk Paper	c. Pink Paper	d. Wmkd. USIR (191R)
RS121	3c	black, Hetherington, J. E.				15.00
		i. Imperf.				175.00
RS122	2c	black, Hiscox & Co.				10.00
RS123	4c	black, Hiscox & Co.		75.00	150.00	950.00
RS124	1c	blue, Holloway's Pills, (perf.)	6.50			
RS125	1c	blue, Holloway's Pills, (imperf.)	165.00			
RS126	1c	green, Holman Liver Pad Co.				15.00
RS127	4c	green, Holman Liver Pad Co.				5.00
RS128	2c	blue, Home Bitters Co.				125.00
		t. Double transfer				
RS129	3c	green, Home Bitters Co.		80.00	100.00	65.00
RS130	4c	green, Home Bitters Co.		150.00		175.00
RS131	4c	black, Hop Bitters Co.				5.00
RS132	4c	black, Hostetter & Smith (imperf.)	50.00	30.00	65.00	17.50
		t. Double transfer				
RS133	6c	black, Hostetter & Smith (imperf.)	70.00			
		e. Experimental silk paper	125.00			
RS134	4c	black, Howe, S. D. (Duponco's Pills)	75.00	135.00		
RS135	4c	red, Howe, S. D. (Duponco's Pills)		225.00		
RS136	4c	green, Howe, S. D. (Duponco's Pills)		200.00		
		RS135 and RS136 were never used.				
RS137	4c	blue, Howe, S. D. (Arabian Milk)		4.00		110.00
RS138	1c	black, Hull, C. E. & Co.	85.00	2.50	25.00	4.00
RS139	2c	violet, Husband, T. J. (imperf.)	375.00			
RS140	2c	vermilion, Husband, T. J. (imperf.)	7.00	4.00		5.00
RS141	4c	green, Hutchings & Hillyer (imperf.)	15.00	17.50		
		e. Experimental silk paper	70.00			

I

RS142	1c	black, Ingham, H. A. & Co.				45.00

J

RS143	4c	green, Jackson, J. A. & Co.	450.00	150.00		
RS144	1c	blue, Jayne, D. & Son (imperf.)		800.00		300.00
		p. Perf.	800.00			
RS145	2c	black, Jayne, D. & Son (imperf.)	1250.00	1000.00		650.00
		p. Perf.	1750.00			
RS146	4c	green, Jayne, D. & Son (imperf.)	1250.00	900.00	850.00	250.00
		p. Perf.	1750.00			
RS147	1c	blue, Jayne, D. & Son (die cut)	1.25	4.00	125.00	3.00
		p. Perf. and die cut	40.00			
		On horizontally laid paper				
RS148	2c	black, Jayne, D. & Son (die cut)	3.50	4.00	65.00	4.50
		e. Experimental silk paper	25.00			
		p. Perf. and die cut	20.00			
		t. Double transfer	40.00	40.00	80.00	40.00
RS149	4c	green, Jayne, D. & Son (die cut)	3.00	3.00	65.00	3.00
		e. Experimental silk paper	50.00			
		p. Perf. and die cut	35.00			
		On vertically laid paper				
		t. Double transfer				
RS150	1c	vermilion, Johnson, I. S. & Co.		35	7.50	30
		t. Double transfer		15.00		15.00
RS151	1c	black, Johnston, Holloway & Co.		1.75		1.75
RS152	2c	green, Johnston, Holloway & Co.		1.25		1.25

K

RS153	4c	black, Kelly, J.B. & Co. (imperf.)	1250.00			
		e. Experimental silk paper	1250.00			
RS154	4c	blue, Kendall, B. J. & Co.				20.00
RS155	2c	green, Kennedy, Dr	35.00	2.50	22.50	2.50
		t. Double transfer				

PRIVATE DIE PROPRIETARY

			a. Old Paper.	b. Silk Paper.	c. Pink Paper.	d. Wmkd. USIR (191R)
RS156	6c	black, Kennedy, Dr.		4.00	50.00	4.00
RS157	2c	black, Kennedy & Co.		2.50	55.00	2.50
RS158	1c	green, Kennedy, (K & Co.)				3.50
RS159	4c	blue, Kerr, Jas. C	2500.00	120.00		120.00
RS160	6c	black, Kerr, Jas. C.	300.00			

L

RS161	4c	black, Lawrence & Martin				17.50
RS162	1c	blue, Lee & Osgood	6.00	7.50		8.00
RS163	4c	blue, Lippman, J. & Bro.	1000.00	1250.00		
		e. Experimental silk paper	1000.00			
RS164	1c	black, Littlefield, Alvah	75	75		15.00
		e. Experimental silk paper	12.00			
		t. Double transfer	30.00			
RS165	4c	green, Littlefield, Alvah	500.00	120.00		
RS166	1c	black, Low, Prof.		1.50	10.00	1.50
		t. Double transfer		—	50.00	40.00
RS167	1c	black, Lyon Mfg. Co.		10.00	150.00	12.00
RS168	2c	black, Lyon Mfg. Co.		4.50	100.00	4.50
		i. Vertical pair, imperf. between				500.00

M

RS169	4c	black, McCullough, J.		60.00		75.00
RS170	1c	black, McLean, J.H.	2.00	75	10.00	75
		e. Experimental silk paper	40.00			
		i. Imperf. horizontally				
		t. Double transfer				25.00
RS171	1c	violet, Manhattan Med. Co.				20.00
		u. 1c purple				20.00
RS172	2c	black, Manhattan Med. Co.		17.50	27.50	10.00
RS173	1c	blue, Mansfield & Higbee		12.00		
		i. Pair, imperf. between		90.00		
		j. Block of four, imperf. between		120.00		
RS174	1c	blue, Mansfield, S. & Co.		22.50	110.00	10.00
		i. Pair, imperf. between		90.00	200.00	125.00
		j. Block of four, imperf. between		100.00	250.00	150.00

Nos. RS173-RS174 are perf. on 4 sides. The i. and j. varieties served as 2c or 4c stamps. Straightedged copies from severed pairs or blocks are worth much less.

Johnston, Holloway & Co.
RS152

S. Mansfield &Co.
RS174

J.B. Rose & Co.
RS205

RS175	2c	blue, Marsden, T.W.	2000.00			
RS176	4c	black, Marsden, T.W.	225.00			
RS177	2c	black, Mercado & Seully (imperf.)	2000.00			
RS178	1c	black, Merchant's Gargling Oil	150.00	13.00	225.00	17.50
		e. Experimental silk paper	225.00			

			a. Old Paper.	b. Silk Paper.	c. Pink Paper.	d. Wmkd. USIR (191R)
RS179	2c	green, Merchant's Gargling Oil	135.00	17.50	225.00	20.00
		e. Experimental silk paper	175.00			
		t. Double transfer, over design of RO11				2000.00
RS180	3c	black, Mette & Kanne				250.00
RS181	4c	black, Mishler Herb Bitters Co.				75.00
		p. Imperf. at ends				80.00
RS182	4c	black, Moody Michel & Co. (imperf.)		125.00		
RS183	1c	vermilion, Moore, C. C.				3.50
RS184	2c	black, Moore C.C.			60.00 2000.00	22.50
RS185	1c	black, Morehead's Mag. Plaster	17.50			
RS186	4c	black, Morehead's Neurodyne	750.00			

N

RS187	4c	black, New York Pharmacal Assn.		7.00	25.00	4.00

P

RS188	6c	black, Perl, Dr. M. & Co. (cut to shape)	950.00			
RS189	1c	green, Pierce, R.V.		10.00	110.00	20.00
RS190	2c	black, Pierce, R.V.	20.00	3.00	22.50	3.50
		e. Experimental silk paper	60.00			
		t. Double transfer				—
RS191	4c	black, Pieters, Bennett & Co.	275.00	1000.00		
		e. Experimental silk paper	275.00			
RS192	6c	black, Pieters, Bennett & Co.	850.00			
		i. Imperf.				—

R

RS193	2c	black, Radway & Co.	2.50	2.50	6.00	3.00
		e. Experimental silk paper	30.00			
		t. Double transfer		50.00	125.00	—
RS194	1c	blue, Ransom, D. & Co.	2.00	1.75		
		e. Experimental silk paper	40.00			
		t. Double transfer				
RS195	2c	black, Ransom, D. & Co.	12.50	14.00		
		e. Experimental silk paper	55.00			
RS196	1c	blue, Ransom, D., Son & Co.		2.00	10.00	1.50
		t. Double transfer				
RS197	2c	black, Ransom, D., Son & Co.		8.00	50.00	7.00
RS198	1c	black, Redding's Russia Salve		4.00		4.00
		t. Double transfer		75.00		
RS199	2c	blue, Ring's Veg. Ambrosia (imperf.)	1250.00			
		p. Perf.	900.00			
RS200	4c	black, Ring's Veg. Ambrosia (imperf.)	1000.00	900.00		
RS201	2c	blue, Ring's Veg. Ambrosia (die cut)		15.00		
RS202	4c	black, Ring's Veg. Ambrosia (die cut)	10.00	10.00		15.00
		e. Experimental silk paper	45.00			
RS203	4c	black, Ring's Veg. Ambrosia (perf.)		900.00		950.00
		k. Perf. and die cut				
		p. Part perf.	1000.00			—
RS204	2c	black, Rose, J.B. & Co.		2.50	20.00	1750.00
		t. Double transfer		30.00		
RS205	4c	black, Rose, J.B. & Co.		85.00		
		t. Double transfer		—		
RS206	2c	green, Rumford Chemical Works				2.00
RS207	2c	green, Rumford Chemical Works (imperf.)				17.50

Merchant's Gargling Oil
RS178

New York Pharmacal Association
RS187

Redding's Russia Salve
RS198

PRIVATE DIE PROPRIETARY

		a. Old Paper.	b. Silk Paper.	c. Pink Paper.	d. Wmkd. USIR (191R)

S

RS208	1c	green, Sands, A.B. & D.	8.00	8.00		
		e. Experimental silk paper	50.00			
RS209	2c	green, Sands, M.P. J. & H.M.		12.00	85.00	10.00
RS210	4c	black, Scheetz's Bitter Cordial (perf.)		250.00		
RS211	4c	black, Scheetz's Bitter Cordial (imperf.)		950.00		
RS212	1c	green, Schenck's Mandrake Pills (imperf.)	3.50	6.00	75.00	3.00
		e. Experimental silk paper				
		t. Double transfer	30.00			
RS213	6c	black, Schenck's Pulmonic Syrup (imperf.)	3.00	3.00	85.00	85.00
		e. Experimental silk paper	40.00			
		p. Perforated				
		t. Double transfer		50.00		
RS214	4c	black, Schenck, J.H. & Son				5.00
RS215	1c	lake, Schwartz, J.E. & Co. (imperf.)		70.00	200.00	45.00

Seabury & Johnson RS216

RS216	1c	black, Seabury & Johnson				45.00
RS217	1c	black, Seabury & Johnson ("porous" obliterated by pen)				2.00
		h. Printed obliteration				1.50
RS218	1c	lake, Seabury & Johnson				1100.00
RS219	4c	blue, Sigesmond, S. Brown				65.00
RS220	1c	black, Scovill, A.L. & Co.	75	1.25		
		e. Experimental silk paper	10.00			
		r. Printed on both sides		750.00		
		t. Double transfer				
RS221	4c	green, Scovill, A.L. & Co.	1.50	1.75		
		e. Experimental silk paper	10.00			
RS222	8c	black, Seelye, D.H. & Co. (imperf.)	6.00			
RS223	1c	black, Simmons, M.A., Iuka, Miss.		60.00		1500.00
RS224	1c	black, Simmons, M.A., St. Louis, Mo.				85.00
RS225	4c	black, Smith, S.N. & Co.	25.00			22.50
RS226	1c	blue, Soule, E.L. & Co., New York (wrapper)		45.00		
RS227	1c	blue, Soule, E.L. & Co. Syracuse (wrapper)	50.00	20.00		
		u. 1c ultramarine	150.00			
RS228	1c	brown, Stevens, H.R.		12.00		
RS229	2c	chocolate, Stevens, H.R.		3.50		
RS230	6c	black, Stevens, H.R.		80.00	2.50	
RS231	6c	orange, Swaim, Jas. (die cut), manuscript signature		1000.00		
RS232	8c	orange, Swaim, Jas. (imperf.)		750.00		
		h. Manuscript signature		700.00		
RS233	8c	orange, Swaim, Jas. (die cut)	225.00			
		h. Manuscript signature	700.00			
RS234	8c	orange, Swaim, Wm. (imperf.)	1750.00	1500.00		800.00
		k. Without signature	375.00	375.00		
RS235	8c	orange, Swaim, Wm. (die cut)	500.00	130.00		120.00
		h. Signature inverted		750.00		
		l. Manuscript signature				
RS236	4c	black, Swett, G.W. (die cut)	8.00			
RS237	4c	green, Swett, G.W. (perf.)	150.00			700.00
RS238	4c	green, Swett, G.W. (perf. and die cut)	225.00			950.00

John L. Thompson
RS242

H.H. Warner & Co.
RS254

J.H. Zeilin & Co.
RS277

		a. Old Paper.	b. Silk Paper.	c. Pink Paper.	d. Wmkd. USIR (191R)

T

RS239	2c	vermilion, Tallcot, Geo				8.00
RS240	4c	black, Tallcot, Geo		50.00	1250.00	15.00
RS241	4c	red, Tarrant & Co.		1.50	60.00	1.50
RS242	1c	black, Thompson, John L.	2.00	2.00		2.00
		e. Experimental silk paper	45.00			
		t. Double transfer				

U

RS243	4c	black, U.S. Prop. Med. Co.	45.00	75.00		
		e. Experimental silk paper	75.00			
RS244	6c	black, U.S. Prop. Med. Co.	600.00			
RS245	1c	black, U.S. Prop. Med. Co. white wrapper	13.00	13.00		
		e. Experimental silk paper	500.00			
RS246	1c	black, U.S. Prop. Med. Co. yellow wrapper	55.00	125.00		
RS247	1c	black, U.S. Prop. Med. Co. orange wrapper	125.00	650.00		
RS248	1c	black, U.S. Prop. Med. Co. orange red wrapper	400.00	900.00		

V

RS249	4c	blk., Van Duzer, S.R.	22.50	20.00		95.00
RS250	6c	black, Van Duzer, S.R.				45.00
RS251	1c	black, Vogeler, A. & Co.		50		50
RS252	1c	vermilion, Vogeler, Meyer & Co.			2.50	20

W

RS253	4c	black, Walker, J.	25.00	12.50		12.50
		e. Experimental silk paper	60.00			
		t. Double transfer				
RS254	1c	brown, W.,H.H. & Co. (H.H. Warner & Co.)				4.00
RS255	6c	brown, W.,H.H. & Co. (H.H. Warner & Co.) (19x26mm.)				55.00
RS256	2c	brown, W., H.H. & Co (H.H. Warner & Co.) (88x11 mm.)				22.50
RS257	4c	brown, W., H.H. & Co. (H.H. Warner & Co.) (95x18 mm.)				30.00
RS258	6c	brown, same				3.50
		t. Double transfer				40.00
RS259	1c	black, Weeks & Potter	4.50			1.50
RS260	2c	black, Weeks & Potter	80.00			
RS261	4c	black, Weeks & Potter	15.00	20.00		5.00
RS262	2c	red, Weeks & Potter			20.00	5.00
RS263	4c	black, Wells, Richardson & Co.				12.00
RS264	4c	black, West India Mfg. Co., die I	225.00	180.00		250.00
		r. Die II				180.00

Die II shows evidence of retouching, particularly in the central disk.

RS265	1c	green, Wilder, Edward (imperf.)	500.00	150.00		200.00
RS266	1c	green, Wilder, Edward (die cut)	40.00	30.00		17.50
		e. Experimental silk paper	135.00			

			a. Old Paper.	b. Silk Paper.	c. Pink Paper.	d. Wmkd. USIR (191R)
RS266A	4c	vermilion, Wilder, Edward (imperf.)				
		e. Experimental silk paper	——			
RS267	4c	vermilion, Wilder, Edward (die cut)	100.00	300.00		
		e. Experimental silk paper	100.00			
RS268	4c	lake, Wilder, Edward (imperf.)		150.00		450.00
RS269	4c	lake, Wilder, Edward (die cut)	350.00	5.00		6.00
RS270	12c	blue, Wilson, E.A.		50.00		250.00
RS271	4c	black, Wilson, Thos. E.	*2500.00*			
RS272	1c	green, World Dispen. Med. Assn.				17.50
RS273	2c	black, World Dispen. Med. Assn.				2.50
RS274	1c	green, Wright's Indian Veg. Pills	1.00	1.00	17.50	1.00
		e. Experimental silk paper	20.00			
		t. Double transfer				——

Z

			a.	b.	c.	d.
RS275	2c	red, Zeilin, J.H. & Co. (perf.)		400.00		
RS276	2c	green, Zeilin, J.H. & Co. (perf.)		30.00		
RS277	2c	green, Zeilin, J.H. & Co. (imperf.)	190.00	3.50	100.00	2.00

1898-1900

See rouletting note preceding No. R161.

			r. Rouletted 5½ Unused	Used	h. Hyphen Hole Perf. 7 Unused	Used
RS278	2½c	carmine, Antikamnia Co.			1.50	1.50
RS279	4c	black, Branca Bros	6.00	6.00	5.00	5.00
RS280	¼c	carmine, Emerson Drug Co.			3.00	75
RS281	⅝c	green, Emerson Drug Co.			3.00	1.00
RS282	1¼c	violet brown, Emerson Drug Co.			3.50	2.00
RS283	2½c	brown orange, Emerson Drug Co.			3.50	2.00
RS284	1¼c	black, Fletcher, C.H.	25	25	20	20
RS285	2½c	black, Hostetter Co. (imperf.)	40	40		
RS286	⅝c	carmine, Johnson & Johnson	10	10	10	10
RS287	⅝c	green, Lanman & Kemp	6.00	2.00	6.00	2.00
RS288	1¼c	brown, Lanman & Kemp	10.00	6.00	10.00	6.00
RS289	1⅞c	blue, Lanman & Kemp	10.00	3.00	10.00	3.00
RS290	⅛c	dark blue, Lee, J. Ellwood, Co.			1.75	1.75
RS291	⅝c	carmine, Lee, J. Ellwood, Co.			75	75
RS292	1¼c	dark green, Lee, J. Ellwood, Co.			1.50	1.50
RS293	2½c	orange, Lee, J. Ellwood, Co.			1.75	1.75
RS294	5c	chocolate, Lee. J. Ellwood, Co.			1.75	1.75
RS295	⅝c	black, Marchand, Chas.	4.00	4.00	5.00	5.00
RS296	1¼c	black, Marchand, Chas.	1.00	1.00	1.00	1.00
RS297	1⅞c	black, Marchand, Chas.	1.50	1.50	2.00	2.00
RS298	2½c	black, Marchand, Chas.	75	75	1.00	1.00
RS299	3⅛c	black, Marchand, Chas	5.00	5.00	5.00	5.00
RS300	4⅜c	black, Marchand, Chas.	10.00	10.00	10.00	10.00
RS301	7½c	black, Marchand, Chas.	8.00	8.00	8.00	8.00
RS302	2½c	carmine, Od Chemical Co.				60
RS303	⅝c	blue, Piso Co.	15	15	15	15
RS304	⅝c	blue, Radway & Co.	50	50	45	45
RS305	3⅛c	brown, Warner's Safe Cure Co.	60	60	50	50
RS306	1¼c	pink, Williams Medicine Co., Dr.			80	80

Dr. Kilmer & Co., Provisionals.

Postage Stamps of 1895-98, Nos. 279, 279B and 268, Precancel Overprinted in Black:

a	b	c
Dr. K. & Co. I. R. 7-5-'98.	Dr. K. & Co. I. R. Binghamton, N. Y. 7-11-'98	Dr. K. & Co. I. R. Binghamton, N. Y. 7-7-'98

1898 *Perf. 12* **Wmk. 191**

Overprint "a," Large "I.R." Dated July 5, 1898.

RS307	A87	1c deep green	60.00
RS308	A88	2c red	35.00
RS309	A89	3c purple	40.00

Overprint "b," Small "I.R.," "Dr. K. & Co." with Serifs. Dated July 6, 7, 9, 11 to 14, 1898.

RS310	A87	1c deep green	40.00
RS311	A88	2c red	20.00
RS312	A89	3c purple	35.00

Overprint "c," Small "I.R.," "Dr. K. & Co." without Serifs. Dated July 7, 9, 11 to 14, 1898.

RS313	A87	1c deep green	50.00
RS314	A88	2c red	20.00
RS315	A89	3c purple	25.00

Many varieties of the Kilmer overprints exist. For the complete listing see "The Case of Dr. Kilmer," by Morton Dean Joyce.

St. Louis Provisional Labels, 1898

Ten proprietary drug companies of St. Louis prepared and used labels to denote payment of July 1, 1898, Proprietary Revenue tax because the government issue of "Battleship" stamps (Nos. RB20-RB31) was not available on the effective date. An illustrated descriptive list of these labels, compiled by Morton Dean Joyce, appeared in the December, 1970, issue of Scott's Monthly Journal.

PRIVATE DIE PERFUMERY STAMPS.

Corning & Tappan RT4

C.B. Woodworth & Son RT20

R. & G.A. Wright RT23

1864-81 *Perf. 12*

			a. Old Paper.	b. Silk Paper.	c. Pink Paper.	d. Wmkd. USIR (191R)
RT1	2c	blue, Bazin X, (die cut)	450.00			
		This stamp was never placed in use.				
RT2	1c	black, Corning & Tappan (imperf.)				500.00
		h. Die cut, 19mm. diameter				80.00
		k. Die cut, 21mm. diameter				90.00
RT3	1c	black, Corning & Tappan, (perf.)				250.00
RT4	1c	blue, Corning & Tappan, (perf.)				1.50
RT5	2c	vermilion, Fetridge & Co. (cut to shape)	90.00			
RT6	1c	black, Hoyt, E.W. & Co. (imperf.)		1000.00	800.00	100.00
RT7	1c	black, Hoyt, E.W. & Co. (die cut)		17.50	17.50	7.00
RT8	2c	black, Hoyt, E.W. & Co. (imperf.)				250.00
RT9	2c	black, Hoyt, E.W. & Co. (die cut)				45.00
RT10	4c	black, Hoyt, E.W. & Co. (imperf.)		900.00	200.00	500.00
RT11	4c	black, Hoyt, E.W. & Co. (die cut)		65.00	50.00	40.00
RT12	1c	vermilion, Kidder & Laird				5.50
RT13	2c	vermilion, Kidder & Laird				7.00

PRIVATE DIE PROPRIETARY

			a. Old Paper.	b. Silk Paper.	c. Pink Paper.	d. Wmkd. USIR (191R)
RT14	3c	black, Laird, Geo. W (imperf.)		325.00	500.00	425.00
		t. Double transfer		450.00	600.00	
		p. Perf.	900.00		—	
		As "p," double transfer	—			
RT15	3c	black, Laird, Geo. W (die cut)	700.00	70.00	400.00	75.00
		p. Perf. and die cut	750.00			
		t. Double transfer		—	550.00	
RT16	1c	black, Lanman & Kemp		3.50	100.00	3.50
		t. Double transfer		—		
RT17	2c	brown, Lanman & Kemp		22.50		5.00
RT18	3c	green, Lanman & Kemp		3.50		7.00
RT19	1c	vermilion, Tetlow's Perfumery				1.50
RT20	1c	green, Woodworth, C. B. & Son		4.00	12.00	4.00
		t. Double transfer		—	—	—
RT21	2c	blue, Woodworth, C. B. & Son		85.00	750.00	6.00
RT22	1c	blue, Wright, R. & G. A.	4.00	4.00		40.00
		e. Experimental silk paper	20.00			
RT23	2c	black, Wright, R. & G. A.	8.50	15.00		85.00
RT24	3c	lake, Wright, R. & G. A.	22.50	50.00		100.00
RT25	4c	grn. Wright, R. & G. A.	60.00	65.00		125.00
RT26	1c	green, Young, Ladd & Coffin (imperf.)		65.00	65.00	60.00
RT27	1c	green, Young, Ladd & Coffin (perf.)		15.00	12.50	10.00
RT28	2c	blue, Young, Ladd & Coffin (imperf.)		85.00	65.00	45.00
RT29	2c	blue, Young, Ladd & Coffin (perf.)		50.00	60.00	10.00
RT30	3c	vermilion Young, Ladd & Coffin (imperf.)		80.00	90.00	50.00
RT31	3c	vermilion Young, Ladd & Coffin (perf.)		25.00	3.50	1.50
RT32	4c	brown, Young, Ladd & Coffin (imperf.)			80.00	30.00
RT33	4c	brown, Young, Ladd & Coffin (perf.)		30.00	9.00	3.00

PRIVATE DIE PLAYING CARD STAMPS.

Eagle Card Co. RU7	Victor E. Mauger & Petrie RU13	Russell, Morgan & Co. RU16

1864-83

			a. Old Paper.	b. Silk Paper.	c. Pink Paper.	d. Wmkd. USIR (191R)
RU1	5c	brown, Caterson Brotz & Co.				2000.00
		This stamp was never placed in use.				
RU2	2c	orange, Dougherty, A	40.00			
RU3	4c	black, Dougherty, A	30.00			
RU4	5c	blue, Dougherty, A (20x26mm.)	35	35		7.50
		u. 5c ultramarine	75.00			
		t. Double transfer	—			
RU5	5c	blue, Dougherty, A (18x23mm.)				40
RU6	10c	blue, Dougherty, A	30.00			
RU7	5c	black, Eagle Card Co.				75.00
RU8	5c	black, Goodall, Chas.	125.00	1.50		
		e. Experimental silk paper	200.00			
RU9	5c	black, Hart, Samuel & Co.	3.50	3.50		
RU10	2c	blue, Lawrence & Cohen	55.00			
RU11	5c	green, Lawrence & Cohen	2.50	2.00		
		e. Experimental silk paper	35.00			
RU12	5c	black, Levy, John J.	15.00	20.00		
		e. Experimental silk paper	60.00			
RU13	5c	blue, Mauger, Victor E., & Petrie	1.00	1.00		30
RU14	5c	black, N. Y. Consolidated Card Co.	2.00	8.00		2.00
RU15	5c	black, Paper Fabrique Co.	3.50	12.00		3.50
RU16	5c	black, Russell, Morgan & Co.				5.00

BOATING STAMPS

Required on applications for the certificate of number for motorboats of more than 10hp, starting April 1, 1960. The pictorial upper part of the $3 stamp is attached to the temporary certificate and kept by the boat owner. The lower part (stub), showing number only, is affixed to the application and sent by the Post Office to the Coast Guard which issues permanent certificate. The $3 fee is for three years. The $1 stamp covers charges for reissuance of a lost or destroyed certificate of number.

Outboard and Inboard Motorboats
B1
Offset Printing, Number Typographed

1960		Rouletted		Unwmkd.
RVB1	B1	$1 rose red, black number	30.00	
		Margin block of 4, P#	130.00	
RVB2	"	$3 blue, red number	45.00	25.00
		Margin block of 4, P#	200.00	

MOTOR VEHICLE USE REVENUE STAMPS

When affixed to a motor vehicle, permitted use of that vehicle for a stated period.

RV1

Wmkd. USIR (191R)

OFFSET PRINTING

Perf. 11.

1942   **With Gum on Back**
RV1	RV1	$2.09 light green *(February)*	1.25	.40

With Gum on Face.
Inscriptions on Back.

RV2	RV1	$1.67 light green *(March)*	12.50	7.00
RV3	″	$1.25 light green *(April)*	11.00	6.00
RV4	″	84c light green *(May)*	12.50	6.00
RV5	″	42c light green *(June)*	11.00	6.00

1942   With Gum and Control Number on Face.
Inscriptions on Back.

RV6	RV1	$5 rose red *(July)*	2.50	75
RV7	″	$4.59 rose red *(August)*	20.00	10.00
RV8	″	$4.17 rose red *(September)*	25.00	10.00
RV9	″	$3.75 rose red *(October)*	22.50	10.00
RV10	″	$3.34 rose red *(November)*	21.00	10.00
RV11	″	$2.92 rose red *(December)*	20.00	—

1943
RV12	RV1	$2.50 rose red *(January)*	25.00	8.00
RV13	″	$2.09 rose red *(February)*	18.00	6.00
RV14	″	$1.67 rose red *(March)*	15.00	—
RV15	″	$1.25 rose red *(April)*	15.00	6.00
RV16	″	84c rose red *(May)*	15.00	6.00
RV17	″	42c rose red *(June)*	12.50	—
RV18	″	$5 yellow *(July)*	3.00	75
RV19	″	$4.59 yellow *(August)*	25.00	10.00
RV20	″	$4.17 yellow *(September)*	37.50	10.00
RV21	″	$3.75 yellow *(October)*	35.00	10.00
RV22	″	$3.34 yellow *(November)*	40.00	10.00
RV23	″	$2.92 yellow *(December)*	50.00	10.00

1944
RV24	RV1	$2.50 yellow *(January)*	50.00	12.50
RV25	″	$2.09 yellow *(February)*	32.50	8.00
RV26	″	$1.67 yellow *(March)*	25.00	8.00
RV27	″	$1.25 yellow *(April)*	25.00	6.00
RV28	″	84c yellow *(May)*	20.00	—
RV29	″	42c yellow *(June)*	20.00	—

Gum on Face
Control Number and Inscriptions on Back

RV30	RV1	$5 violet *(July)*	2.50	50
RV31	″	$4.59 violet *(August)*	40.00	12.50
RV32	″	$4.17 violet *(September)*	30.00	12.50
RV33	″	$3.75 violet *(October)*	30.00	10.00
RV34	″	$3.34 violet *(November)*	20.00	8.00
RV35	″	$2.92 violet *(December)*	22.50	8.00

1945
RV36	RV1	$2.50 violet *(January)*	22.50	7.00
RV37	″	$2.09 violet *(February)*	20.00	6.00
RV38	″	$1.67 violet *(March)*	17.50	6.00
RV39	″	$1.25 violet *(April)*	17.50	5.00
RV40	″	84c violet *(May)*	15.00	4.00
RV41	″	42c violet *(June)*	12.50	4.00

Daniel Manning
RV2

OFFSET PRINTING
Gum on Face
Control Number and Inscriptions on Back

1945   *Perf. 11*   **Wmk. 191R**
RV42	RV2	$5 bright blue green & yellow green *(July)*	2.50	50
RV43	″	$4.59 bright blue green & yellow green *(August)*	30.00	—
RV44	″	$4.17 bright blue green & yellow green *(Sept.)*	30.00	—
RV45	″	$3.75 bright blue green & yellow green *(October)*	25.00	—
RV46	″	$3.34 bright blue green & yellow green *(November)*	20.00	—
RV47	″	$2.92 bright blue green & yellow green *(December)*	17.50	—

1946
RV48	″	$2.50 bright blue green & yellow green *(January)*	20.00	—
RV49	″	$2.09 bright blue green & yellow green *(February)*	20.00	—
RV50	″	$1.67 bright blue green & yellow green *(March)*	15.00	—
RV51	″	$1.25 bright blue green & yellow green *(April)*	12.00	—
RV52	″	84c bright blue green & yellow green *(May)*	12.00	—
RV53	″	42c bright blue green & yellow green *(June)*	8.00	—

UNITED STATES
NATIONAL ALBUM

The SCOTT UNITED STATES NATIONAL POSTAGE STAMP ALBUM is "The" Album demanded by serious collectors of United States material.

The NATIONAL POSTAGE STAMP ALBUM comes complete with famous Scott hand-crafted sturdy binder and Scott Album pages. Each page includes spaces with the Scott Catalogue number and a description or photo of every stamp.

The SCOTT NATIONAL POSTAGE STAMP ALBUM provides spaces for commemoratives, definitives, air post, special delivery, registration, certified mail, postage due, parcel post, special handling, officials, newspapers, offices abroad, hunting permits, confederates and much more!

Available in U.S.A. and Canada from your favorite dealer, bookstore or stamp collecting accessory retailer or write:

SCOTT. Publishing Company

P.O. Box 828, Sidney, OH 45365

U.S. DUCKS SALE

SOMETHING FOR EVERY DUCK COLLECTOR

Important note: We make every effort to keep well-stocked in Ducks. However, at times we may be out of a particular item so alternatives appreciated. Ducks on license prices are for full license. NG means No gum, unsigned stamps.

★★ Please add 25% for Plate # Singles RW1-25 mint or used.
Add 15% for RW26-52 ★★

We are buying all Federal Ducks, all conditions. Ship insured for offer

Please add $1.50 for P&H. As always, satisfaction guaranteed or return for replacement or refund. Photocopies can be provided on more expensive items. Layaway plan available (⅓ down, balance within 90 days). Prices subject to change. Tel. #(617) 484-5073. (12-8 P.M. EST).

H. F. JOHNSON
23 Harriet Avenue
Belmont, MA 02178

Scott #	Wounded Used	F-VF Used	Premium Used	License Used	F-VF NG	Wounded Mint	F-VF Mint	VF-XF NH	Superb NH	F-VF NH PB	XF NH PB
RW1	29.95	49.50	69.50	115.	115.	185.	250.	350.	450.	POR	POR
RW2	59.00	89.00	130.	200.	169.	210.	289.	389.	495.	POR	POR
RW3	25.95	45.00	62.50	95.00	75.00	89.00	139.	199.	250.	POR	POR
RW4	13.95	19.00	37.50	60.00	49.00	60.00	95.00	150.	210.	1600.	2000.
RW5	13.95	19.00	37.50	60.00	49.00	70.00	110.	180.	250.	1800.	POR
RW6	7.95	13.00	22.50	35.00	32.50	55.00	85.00	125.	165.	995.	POR
RW7	7.95	13.00	22.50	35.00	32.50	55.00	85.00	125.	165.	950.	POR
RW8	7.95	13.00	22.50	35.00	32.50	55.00	85.00	125.	165.	900.	POR
RW9	7.95	13.00	22.50	35.00	32.50	55.00	85.00	125.	165.	800.	POR
RW10	7.95	13.00	22.50	30.00	27.00	22.50	35.00	55.00	75.00	450.	600.
RW11	7.95	13.00	22.50	30.00	27.00	22.50	35.00	55.00	75.00	400.	550.
RW12	4.50	9.95	15.00	25.00	21.00	16.00	24.00	35.00	45.00	275.	375.
RW13	3.95	6.95	10.00	17.00	17.00	16.00	24.00	35.00	45.00	250.	325.
RW14	3.95	6.95	10.00	17.00	17.00	16.00	24.00	35.00	45.00	275.	350.
RW15	3.95	6.95	10.00	17.00	17.00	16.00	24.00	35.00	45.00	300.	400.
RW16	3.95	6.95	10.00	17.00	14.00	18.00	30.00	40.00	55.00	275.	350.
RW17	3.00	5.50	8.95	15.00	14.00	20.00	35.00	40.00	55.00	350.	450.
RW18	3.00	4.95	7.50	13.00	14.00	20.00	30.00	40.00	55.00	350.	450.
RW19	3.00	4.95	7.50	13.00	14.00	20.00	35.00	45.00	55.00	395.	475.
RW20	3.00	4.95	7.50	13.00	14.00	20.00	35.00	45.00	55.00	350.	435.
RW21-2 ea.	2.00	4.00	7.00	12.00	15.00	25.00	40.00	50.00	60.00	395.	465.
RW23	2.00	4.00	7.00	12.00	15.00	25.00	35.00	45.00	55.00	395.	465.
RW24	2.00	4.00	7.00	12.00	15.00	25.00	35.00	45.00	55.00	395.	465.
RW25	2.00	4.00	7.00	12.00	17.50	25.00	35.00	45.00	55.00	395.	475.
RW26	2.00	4.00	7.00	12.00	20.00	32.50	45.00	60.00	75.00	350.	425.
RW27	2.00	4.00	7.00	12.00	25.00	32.50	50.00	60.00	75.00	350.	450.
RW28	2.00	4.00	7.00	12.00	25.00	45.00	65.00	80.00	90.00	400.	475.
RW29	2.00	4.50	7.00	13.00	30.00	45.00	65.00	80.00	90.00	400.	475.
RW30	2.00	4.50	7.00	13.00	30.00	45.00	65.00	80.00	90.00	400.	475.
RW31	2.00	4.50	7.00	13.00	30.00	45.00	65.00	75.00	85.00	POR	POR
RW32	2.00	4.50	7.00	13.00	35.00	45.00	65.00	75.00	85.00	325.	395.
RW33	2.00	4.00	7.00	13.00	35.00	45.00	65.00	75.00	85.00	350.	425.
RW34	2.00	4.00	7.00	11.00	30.00	45.00	65.00	75.00	85.00	350.	425.
RW35	2.00	4.00	7.00	11.00	22.50	30.00	37.50	45.00	55.00	200.	250.
RW36	2.00	4.00	7.00	11.00	17.50	25.00	32.00	40.00	50.00	195.	250.
RW37											
RW38	2.00	4.00	7.00	11.00	15.00	17.50	22.50	27.50	35.00	110.	175.
RW39	1.75	3.00	6.00	11.00	9.00	17.50	22.50	27.50	35.00	80.00	100.
RW40	1.75	3.00	6.00	10.00	9.00	14.00	20.00	25.00	30.00	80.00	100.
RW41-2 ea.	1.75	3.00	6.00	10.00	5.00	7.00	10.00	12.50	15.00	45.00	65.00
RW43-5 ea.	1.75	3.00	6.00	10.00	5.00	6.00	9.00	10.00	11.00	40.00	50.00
RW46-52 ea.	1.75	3.00	6.00	10.00	7.00	8.00	11.00	12.00	13.00	45.00	55.00

We also have small supplies of most State Ducks. Write for quotes and availability. We also specialize in U.S. Washington-Franklins (331-547) in Mint and Used condition. Write for lists.

DUCK STAMPS
FEDERAL ★ STATE ★ PRINTS
Mint ★ Used ★ Singles ★ Plate Blocks

WE BUY...
Duck Stamps in any quantity and condition!

YES!...
We have the NEW Scott Federal & State Duck Stamp Albums in stock for $39.95 delivered.

EXTENSIVE CATALOG FREE!

14654 Memorial Dr., Houston, TX 77079
● (713) 493-6386 ● (800) 231-5926
Bob Dumaine - "Duck Specialist"
CIRCLE READER SERVICE CARD #83

Special Selection of . . .
HIGH-QUALITY, U.S. FEDERAL
DUCK STAMPS

● U.S. Stamps, Covers and FDC's.
● State & Federal Duck Stamp Prints.

BUYING - TOP QUALITY PHILATELIC MATERIAL!
Call or write for our prompt offer. Top Prices Paid!

New Jersey Stamp Trading Co.
Philip Gigante, owner
STORE: 254 Comly Road, Lincoln Park, NJ 07035
MAILING: P.O. Box 285, Towaco, NJ 07082

PHONE (201) 263-2648
Member ASDA, APS, NJSDA, ANA, AFDCS

HUNTING PERMIT STAMPS

Authorized by Act of Congress, approved March 16, 1934, to license hunters, the receipts going to maintain waterfowl life in the United States. Sales to collectors were made legal June 15, 1935. The 1934 issue was designed by J. N. Darling, 1935 by Frank W. Benson, 1936 by Richard E. Bishop, 1937 by J. D. Knap, 1938 by Roland Clark, 1939 by Lynn Bogue Hunt, 1940 by Francis L. Jaques, 1941 by E. R. Kalmbach, 1942 by A. Lassell Ripley, 1943 by Walter E. Bohl, 1944 by Walter A. Weber, 1945 by Owen J. Gromme, 1946 by Robert W. Hines, 1947 by Jack Murray, 1948 by Maynard Reece, 1949 by "Roge" E. Preuss, 1950 by Walter A. Weber, 1951 by Maynard Reece, 1952 by John H. Dick, 1953 by Clayton B. Seagears, 1954 by Harvey D. Sandstrom, 1955 by Stanley Stearns, 1956 by Edward J. Bierly, 1957 by Jackson Miles Abbott, 1958 by Leslie C. Kouba, 1959 by Maynard Reece, 1960 by John A. Ruthven, 1961–62 by Edward A. Morris, 1963 by Edward J. Bierly, 1964 by Stanley Stearns, 1965 by Ron Jenkins, 1966 by Stanley Stearns, 1967 by Leslie C. Kouba, 1968 by C. G. Pritchard, 1969 by Maynard Reece, 1970 by Edward J. Bierly, 1971 by Maynard Reece, 1972 by Arthur M. Cook, 1973 by Lee LeBlanc, 1975 by James L. Fisher, 1976 by Alderson Magee, 1977 by Martin R. Murk, 1978 by Albert Earl Gilbert, 1979 by Kenneth L. Michaelsen, 1980 by Richard W. Plasschaert, 1981 by John S. Wilson, 1982 by David A. Maass, 1983 by Phil Scholer, 1984 by William C. Morris.

Used price is for stamp signed by hunter. Plate number blocks of six have margins on two sides.

Department of Agriculture.

Mallards Alighting—HP1
Engraved: Flat Plate Printing.
Issued in panes of 28 subjects.
Various Designs.

	Perf. 11.	Unwmkd.		
1934	Inscribed "Void after June 30, 1935".			
RW1	HP1	$1 blue	350.00	75.00
		P# block of 6	6000.00	
		a. Imperf. (pair)	4000.00	
		b. Vert. pair, imperf. horiz.		—
1935	Inscribed "Void after June 30, 1936".			
RW2		$1 rose lake (Canvasbacks Taking to Flight)	450.00	125.00
		P# block of 6	700.00	
1936	Inscribed "Void after June 30, 1937".			
RW3		$1 brown black (Canada Geese in Flight)	250.00	50.00
		P# block of 6	3000.00	
1937	Inscribed "Void after June 30, 1938".			
RW4		$1 light green (Scaup Ducks Taking to Flight)	150.00	25.00
		P# block of 6	1750.00	
1938	Inscribed "Void after June 30, 1939".			
RW5		$1 light violet (Pintail Drake and Hen Alighting)	175.00	25.00
		P# block of 6	1850.00	

Department of the Interior.

Green-winged Teal—HP2

1939	Inscribed "Void after June 30, 1940".			
RW6	HP2	$1 chocolate	110.00	20.00
		P# block of 6	1100.00	
1940	Inscribed "Void after June 30, 1941".			
RW7		$1 sepia (Black Mallards)	100.00	20.00
		P# block of 6	1000.00	
1941	Inscribed "Void after June 30, 1942".			
RW8		$1 brown carmine (Family of Ruddy Ducks)	100.00	20.00
		P# block of 6	900.00	
1942	Inscribed "Void after June 30, 1943".			
RW9		$1 violet brown (Baldpates)	100.00	20.00
		P# block of 6	800.00	
1943	Inscribed "Void After June 30, 1944".			
RW10		$1 deep rose (Wood Ducks)	50.00	15.00
		P# block of 6	375.00	
1944	Inscribed "Void after June 30, 1945".			
RW11		$1 red orange (White-fronted Geese)	55.00	15.00
		P# block of 6	325.00	
1945	Inscribed "Void after June 30, 1946"			
RW12		$1 black (Shoveller Ducks in Flight)	30.00	7.50
		P# block of 6	225.00	
1946	Inscribed "Void after June 30, 1947"			
RW13		$1 red brown (Redhead Ducks)	30.00	7.50
		P# block of 6	225.00	
1947	Inscribed "Void after June 30, 1948".			
RW14		$1 black (Snow Geese)	30.00	7.50
		P# block of 6	225.00	
1948	Inscribed "Void after June 30, 1949".			
RW15		$1 bright blue (Buffleheads in Flight)	30.00	7.50
		P# block of 6	225.00	

Goldeneye Ducks
HP3

1949	Inscribed "Void after June 30, 1950".			
RW16	HP3	$2 bright green	30.00	7.50
		P# block of 6	225.00	

Start your
U.S. COLLECTION
with .... SCOTT

Scott's U.S. Minuteman Stamp Album!

FEATURES...

★ The famous Scott Catalogue identification number for every stamp.

★ Exciting stories of almost every stamp.

★ Attractive vinyl binder. ★ Supplemented annually.

"A must for every collector of United States postage stamps."

Available at your local dealer or direct from **Scott Publishing Co.**

Scott Publishing Company
P.O. Box 828, Sidney, OH 45365

HUNTING PERMIT STAMPS

1950	Inscribed "Void after June 30, 1951".			
RW17	$2 **violet** (Trumpeter Swans in Flight)	45.00	6.00	
	P# block of 6	325.00		
1951	Inscribed "Void after June 30, 1952."			
RW18	$2 **gray black** (Gadwall Ducks)	45.00	5.00	
	P# block of 6	325.00		
1952	Inscribed "Void after June 30, 1953."			
RW19	$2 **deep ultramarine** (Harlequin Ducks)	45.00	5.00	
	P# block of 6	325.00		
1953	Inscribed "Void after June 30, 1954."			
RW20	$2 **dark rose brown** (Blue-winged Teal)	45.00	5.00	
	P# block of 6	325.00		
1954	Inscribed "Void after June 30, 1955."			
RW21	$2 **black** (Ring-necked Ducks)	50.00	5.00	
	P# block of 6	350.00		
1955	Inscribed "Void after June 30, 1956."			
RW22	$2 **dark blue** (Blue Geese)	50.00	5.00	
	P# block of 6	350.00		
1956	Inscribed: "Void after June 30, 1957."			
RW23	$2 **black** (American Merganser)	50.00	5.00	
	P# block of 6	350.00		
1957	Inscribed: "Void after June 30, 1958."			
RW24	$2 **emerald** (American Eider)	50.00	5.00	
	P# block of 6	350.00		
1958	Inscribed: "Void after June 30, 1959."			
RW25	$2 **black** (Canada Geese)	50.00	5.00	
	P# block of 6	350.00		

Labrador Retriever Carrying Mallard Drake
HP4

Giori Press Printing.
Issued in panes of 30 subjects.

1959	Inscribed: "Void after June 30, 1960."			
RW26 HP4	$3 **blue, ocher & black**	60.00	3.50	
	P# block of 4	300.00		

Redhead Ducks
HP5

1960	Inscribed: "Void after June 30, 1961."			
RW27 HP5	$3 **red brown, dark blue & bister**	60.00	3.50	
	P# block of 4	300.00		
1961	Inscribed: "Void after June 30, 1962."			
RW28	$3 **Mallard Hen and Ducklings**	70.00	3.50	
	P# block of 4	350.00		

Pintail Drakes Coming in for Landing
HP6

1962	Inscribed: "Void after June 30, 1963."			
RW29 HP6	$3 **dark blue, dark red brown & black**	85.00	4.50	
	P# block of 4	400.00		
1963	Inscribed: "Void after June 30, 1964."			
RW30	$3 **Pair of Brant Landing**	85.00	4.50	
	P# block of 4	400.00		
1964	Inscribed: "Void after June 30, 1965."			
RW31	$3 **Hawaiian Nene Geese**	80.00	4.50	
	P# block of 6	2500.00		
1965	Inscribed: "Void after June 30, 1966."			
RW32	$3 **Three Canvasback Drakes**	80.00	4.50	
	P# block of 4	375.00		

Whistling Swans
HP7

1966	Inscribed: "Void after June 30, 1967."			
RW33 HP7	$3 **multicolored**	80.00	3.50	
	P# block of 4	375.00		
1967	Inscribed "Void after June 30, 1968."			
RW34	$3 **Old Squaw Ducks**	80.00	3.50	
	P# block of 4	375.00		
1968	Inscribed: "Void after June 30, 1969."			
RW35	$3 **Hooded Mergansers**	50.00	3.50	
	P# block of 4	250.00		

White-winged Scoters
HP8

1969	Inscribed: "Void after June 30, 1970."			
RW36 HP8	$3 **multicolored**	45.00	3.50	
	P# block of 4	225.00		
1970	**Engraved & Lithographed**			
	Inscribed: "Void after June 30, 1971."			
RW37	$3 **Ross's Geese**	40.00	3.50	
	P# block of 4	200.00		
1971	Inscribed: "Void after June 30, 1972"			
RW38	$3 **Three Cinnamon Teal**	30.00	3.25	
	P# block of 4	140.00		

HUNTING PERMIT STAMPS

1972		Inscribed: "Void after June 30, 1973"			
RW39		$5 Emperor Geese		20.00	3.25
		P# block of 4		90.00	
1973		Inscribed: "Void after June 30, 1974"			
RW40		$5 Steller's Eiders		20.00	3.25
		P# block of 4		90.00	
1974		Inscribed: "Void after June 30, 1975"			
RW41		$5 Wood Ducks		15.00	3.25
		P# block of 4		70.00	
1975		Inscribed: "Void after June 30, 1976"			
RW42		$5 Canvasback Decoy, 3 Flying Canvasbacks		12.50	3.25
		P# block of 4		55.00	
		Engraved			
1976		Inscribed "Void after June 30, 1977"			
RW43		$5 Family of Canada Geese		10.00	3.25
		P# block of 4		50.00	
1977		Inscribed: "Void after June 30, 1978"			
RW44		$5 Pair of Ross's Geese		10.00	3.25
		P# block of 4		50.00	

Gray inscription on back of Nos. RW13–RW34: "It is unlawful to hunt waterfowl unless you sign your name in ink on the face of this stamp". Additional wording on Nos. RW26–RW27: "Duck stamp dollars buy wetlands to perpetuate waterfowl," and on Nos. RW28–RW34: "Duck stamp dollars buy wetlands for waterfowl." Back inscription on Nos. RW35–RW36 reads: "Buy duck stamps / Save wetlands / Send in *all* bird bands / Sign your duck stamp."

Back inscription of Nos. RW37–RW51 repeats 4-line message of Nos. RW35–RW36 and also includes in two added lines the "It is unlawful . . ." warning.

No. RW21 and following issues are printed on dry, pregummed paper and the back inscription is printed on top of the gum.

QUANTITIES ISSUED

RW1	635,001	RW17	1,903,644	RW33	1,805,341
RW2	448,204	RW18	2,167,767	RW34	1,934,697
RW3	603,623	RW19	2,296,628	RW35	1,837,139
RW4	783,039	RW20	2,268,446	RW36	2,072,108
RW5	1,002,715	RW21	2,184,550	RW37	2,420,244
RW6	1,111,561	RW22	2,369,940	RW38	2,441,664
RW7	1,260,810	RW23	2,332,014	RW39	2,179,628
RW8	1,439,967	RW24	2,355,190	RW40	2,113,594
RW9	1,383,629	RW25	2,176,425	RW41	2,190,268
RW10	1,169,352	RW26	1,626,115	RW42	2,218,589
RW11	1,487,029	RW27	1,725,634	RW43	2,248,394
RW12	1,725,505	RW28	1,344,236	RW44	2,180,625
RW13	2,016,841	RW29	1,147,212	RW45	2,196,758
RW14	1,722,677	RW30	1,448,191	RW46	2,209,572
RW15	2,127,603	RW31	1,573,155	RW47	2,103,021
RW16	1,954,734	RW32	1,558,197	RW48	1,940,578

Hooded Merganser Drake HP9

1978		Inscribed: "Void after June 30, 1979"			
RW45	HP9	$5 multicolored		10.00	3.25
		P# block of 4		50.00	
1979		Inscribed: "Void after June 30, 1980"			
RW46		$7.50 Green-winged Teal		15.00	3.25
		P# block of 4		75.00	
1980		Inscribed: "Void after June 30, 1981"			
RW47		$7.50 Mallards		15.00	3.25
		P# block of 4		75.00	
1981		Inscribed: Void after June 30, 1982			
RW48		$7.50 Ruddy Ducks		15.00	3.25
		P# block of 4		75.00	
1982		Inscribed: Void after June 30, 1983			
RW49		$7.50 Canvasbacks		15.00	3.25
		P# block of 4		75.00	
1983		Inscribed: Void after June 30, 1984			
RW50		$7.50 Pintails		15.00	2.50
		P# block of 4		75.00	
1984		Inscribed: "Void after June 30, 1985"			
RW51		$7.50 Wigeons		15.00	2.50
		P# block of 4		75.00	
1985		Inscribed: "Void after June 30, 1986"			
RW52	$7.50	Cinnamon teal		15.00	2.50
		P# block of 4		75.00	
1986		Inscribed: "Void after June 30, 1987"			
RW53	$7.50	Fulvous whistling duck		15.00	2.50
		P# block of 4		75.00	

The Duck Stops Here

NATIONAL WILDLIFE GALLERIES

is recognized as one of the major publishers and distributors of Federal & State Duck Stamps and Duck Stamp Prints. We buy, sell and trade mint, uncancelled & used Federal & State Duck Stamps in singles, plate blocks and/or framed sets. Call or write for FREE price list.

11000-33 METRO PARKWAY, DEPT. 9, FT. MYERS, FL 33912
PHONE (813) 275-0500

Sam Houston Philatelics price list.

STATE DUCK STAMPS
★ PRICE LIST ★

Catalog numbers used are those of Sam Houston Philatelics and not Scott Publishing Co. Prices subject to change due to volatile market conditions. Complete Catalog of State and Federal Duck Stamps, Albums, Prints and Literature FREE for asking! We are also major purchasers of all Duck Stamps!

ALL STAMPS MINT NEVER HINGED

ALABAMA
AL1	1979	10.00
AL2	1980	8.00
AL3	1981	8.00
AL4	1982	8.00
AL5	1983	8.00
AL6	1984	12.50
AL7	1985	7.00
AL8	1986	7.00

ALASKA
AK1	1985	12.00
AK2	1986	7.00

ARKANSAS
AR1	1981	20.00
AR1a	1981	20.00
AR2	1982	15.00
AR2a	1982	20.00
AR3	1983	12.50
AR4	1984	7.50
AR4a	1984	50.00
AR5	1985	7.50
AR5a	1985	50.00
AR6	1986	7.50

CALIFORNIA
CA1	1971	350.00
CA2	1972	WTD
CA3	1973	5.00
CA4	1974	5.00
CA5	1975	20.00
CA6	1976	5.00
CA7	1977	20.00
CA7A	1977	5.00
CA8	1978	35.00
CA9	1979	6.00
CA9a	1979	30.00
CA10	1980	5.50
CA10a	1980	30.00
CA11	1981	6.75
CA12	1982	6.75
CA13	1983	6.75
CA14	1984	9.00
CA15	1985	9.00
CA16	1986	9.00

DELAWARE
DE1	1980	25.00
DE2	1981	18.50
DE3	1982	15.00
DE4	1983	7.00
DE5	1984	7.00
DE6	1985	7.00
DE7	1986	7.00

FLORIDA
FL1	1979	25.00
FL2	1980	5.00
FL3	1981	5.00
FL4	1982	5.00
FL5	1983	5.00
FL6	1984	5.00
FL7	1985	5.00
FL8	1986	5.00

GEORGIA
GA1	1985	7.50
GA2	1986	7.50

ILLINOIS
IL1	1975	150.00
IL2	1976	25.00
IL3	1977	25.00
IL4	1978	25.00
IL5	1979	25.00
IL6	1980	25.00
IL7	1981	25.00
IL7a	1981	295.00
IL8	1982	15.00
IL9	1983	12.00
IL10	1984	11.00
IL11	1985	8.00
IL12	1986	7.00

INDIANA
IN1	1976	7.00
IN2	1977	7.00
IN3	1978	7.00
IN4	1979	7.00
IN5	1980	7.00
IN6	1981	7.00
IN7	1982	7.00
IN8	1983	7.00
IN9	1984	7.00
IN10	1985	7.00
IN11	1986	7.00

IOWA
IA1	1972	150.00
IA2	1973	50.00
IA2a	1973	150.00
IA3	1974	50.00
IA4	1975	50.00
IA5	1976	14.50
IA6	1977	14.50
IA7	1978	75.00
IA8	1979	425.00
IA9	1980	50.00
IA10	1981	17.50
IA11	1982	10.00
IA12	1983	9.50
IA13	1984	9.00
IA13a	1984	100.00
IA14	1985	7.50
IA15	1986	7.50

KENTUCKY
KY1	1985	7.00
KY2	1986	7.00

MAINE
ME1	1984	12.00
ME2	1985	8.50
ME3	1986	4.00

MARYLAND
MD1	1974	20.00
MD2	1975	4.00
MD3	1976	4.00
MD4	1977	4.00
MD5	1978	4.00
MD6	1979	4.00
MD7	1980	4.00
MD8	1981	4.00
MD9	1982	4.00
MD10	1983	4.00
MD11	1984	8.00
MD12	1985	8.00
MD13	1986	8.00

MASSACHUSETTS
MA1	1974	10.00
MA2	1975	10.00
MA3	1976	10.00
MA4	1977	10.00
MA5	1978	7.50
MA6	1979	7.50
MA7	1980	7.50
MA8	1981	4.50
MA9	1982	4.50
MA10	1983	3.00
MA11	1984	3.00
MA12	1985	3.00
MA13	1986	3.00

MICHIGAN
MI1	1976	40.00
MI2	1977	225.00
MI3	1978	55.00
MI4	1979	20.00
MI5	1980	15.00
MI6	1981	15.00
MI7	1982	15.00
MI8	1983	15.00
MI9	1984	9.50
MI10	1985	6.00
MI11	1986	5.00

MINNESOTA
MN1	1977	5.00
MN2	1978	5.00
MN3	1979	5.00
MN4	1980	5.00
MN5	1981	5.00
MN6	1982	5.00
MN7	1983	5.00
MN8	1984	5.00
MN9	1985	5.00
MN10	1986	6.50

MISSISSIPPI
MS1	1976	15.00
MS2	1977	4.00
MS3	1978	4.00
MS4	1979	4.00
MS5	1980	4.00
MS6	1981	4.00
MS7	1982	4.00
MS8	1983	4.00
MS9	1984	4.00
MS10	1985	4.00
MS11	1986	4.00

MISSOURI
MO1	1979	250.00
MO2	1980	60.00
MO3	1981	20.00
MO4	1982	15.00
MO5	1983	10.00
MO6	1984	5.00
MO7	1985	5.00
MO8	1986	5.00

MONTANA
MT1	1986	6.50

NEVADA
NV1	1979	22.50
NV2	1980	3.50
NV3	1981	3.50
NV4	1982	3.50
NV5	1983	3.50
NV6	1984	3.50
NV7	1985	3.50
NV8	1986	3.50

NEW HAMPSHIRE
NH1	1983	27.50
NH2	1984	10.00
NH3	1985	6.00
NH4	1986	6.00

NEW JERSEY
NJ1	1984	10.50
NJ1A	1984	20.00
NJ2	1985	6.00
NJ2A	1985	10.00
NJ3	1986	3.75
NJ3A	1986	7.00

NEW YORK
NY1	1985	10.00
NY2	1986	7.50

NORTH CAROLINA
NC1	1983	15.00
NC2	1984	10.00
NC3	1985	10.00
NC4	1986	7.00

NORTH DAKOTA
ND1	1982	25.00
ND2	1983	15.00
ND3	1984	12.50
ND4	1985	12.50
ND5	1986	11.00

OHIO
OH1	1982	50.00
OH2	1983	20.00
OH3	1984	10.00
OH4	1985	7.25
OH5	1986	7.25

OKLAHOMA
OK1	1980	22.50
OK2	1981	12.00
OK3	1982	6.00
OK4	1983	6.00
OK5	1984	6.00
OK6	1985	6.00
OK7	1986	6.00

OREGON
OR1	1984	15.00
OR2	1985	10.00
OR3	1986	7.00

PENNSYLVANIA
PA1	1983	15.00
PA2	1984	10.00
PA3	1985	7.00
PA4	1986	7.00

SOUTH CAROLINA
SC1	1981	40.00
SC2	1982	40.00
SC3	1983	55.00
SC4	1984	25.00
SC5	1985	15.00
SC6	1986	7.50

SOUTH DAKOTA
SD1	1976	10.00
SD2	1977	6.00
SD3	1978	3.00

TENNESSEE
TN1	1979	50.00
TN1A	1979	295.00
TN2	1980	15.00
TN2A	1980	40.00
TN3	1981	8.00
TN4	1982	14.00
TN5	1983	14.00
TN6	1984	14.00
TN7	1985	8.00
TN8	1986	8.00

TEXAS
TX1	1981	45.00
TX2	1982	30.00
TX3	1983	50.00
TX4	1984	10.00
TX5	1985	7.00
TX6	1986	7.00

UTAH
UT1	1986	5.00

VERMONT
VT1	1986	7.00

WASHINGTON
WA1	1986	7.00

WISCONSIN
WI1	1978	55.00
WI2	1979	95.00
WI3	1980	5.00
WI4	1981	5.00
WI5	1982	5.00
WI6	1983	5.00
WI7	1984	5.00
WI8	1985	5.00
WI9	1986	5.00

WYOMING
WY1	1985	7.00

CANADA
1985	$4	7.50
1986	$4	5.75

Sam Houston Philatelics

14654 Memorial Dr., Houston, TX 77079 • (713) 493-6396 • (800) 231-5926
VISA, MASTERCARD, AMEX Accepted.
CIRCLE READER SERVICE CARD #83

Advertisement. The above numbers are not Scott numbers, but are Sam Houston Philatelics numbers.

DISTILLED SPIRITS EXCISE TAX STAMPS

Charles S. Fairchild, Secretary of Treasury 1887-89
Actual size: 89½ x 63½mm.

DS1
Offset Printing

1950   **Wmk. 191R**   *Rouletted 7*
Inscribed "STAMP FOR SERIES 1950"

			Used	Punched Cancel
RX1	DS1	1c yellow green & black	25.00	20.00
RX2	"	3c yellow green & black	100.00	90.00
RX3	"	5c yellow green & black	25.00	20.00
RX4	"	10c yellow green & black	20.00	15.00
RX5	"	25c yellow green & black	8.00	6.00
RX6	"	50c yellow green & black	8.00	6.00
RX7	"	$1 yellow green & black	1.50	1.00
RX8	"	$3 yellow green & black	20.00	15.00
RX9	"	$5 yellow green & black	7.00	5.00
RX10	"	$10 yellow green & black	2.00	1.25
RX11	"	$25 yellow green & black	12.50	9.00
RX12	"	$50 yellow green & black	8.00	5.00
RX13	"	$100 yellow green & black	3.00	2.00
RX14	DS1	$300 yellow green & black	30.00	25.00
RX15	"	$500 yellow green & black	20.00	15.00
RX16	"	$1,000 yellow green & black	10.00	8.00
RX17	"	$1,500 yellow green & black	70.00	50.00
RX18	"	$2,000 yellow green & black	3.50	3.00
RX19	"	$3,000 yellow green & black	25.00	20.00
RX20	"	$5,000 yellow green & black	25.00	20.00
RX21	"	$10,000 yellow green & black	40.00	27.50
RX22	"	$20,000 yellow green & black	40.00	35.00
RX23	"	$30,000 yellow green & black	85.00	60.00
RX24	"	$40,000 yellow green & black	700.00	500.00
RX25	"	$50,000 yellow green & black	100.00	75.00

1952   **Type of 1950.**
Inscription 'STAMP FOR SERIES 1950" omitted

RX28	DS1	5c yellow green & black	—	40.00
RX29	"	10c yellow green & black	—	4.00
RX30	"	25c yellow green & black	—	17.50
RX31	"	50c yellow green & black	—	15.00
RX32	"	$1 yellow green & black	20.00	1.00
RX33	"	$3 yellow green & black	35.00	22.50
RX34	"	$5 yellow green & black	40.00	27.50
RX35	"	$10 yellow green & black	—	1.50
RX36	"	$25 yellow green & black	25.00	10.00
RX37	"	$50 yellow green & black	—	30.00
RX38	"	$100 yellow green & black	20.00	2.50
RX39	"	$300 yellow green & black	—	7.00
RX40	"	$500 yellow green & black	—	35.00
RX41	"	$1,000 yellow green & black	—	6.00
RX43	"	$2,000 yellow green & black	—	65.00
RX44	"	$3,000 yellow green & black	—	600.00
RX45	"	$5,000 yellow green & black	—	45.00
RX46	"	$10,000 yellow green & black	—	90.00

Seven other denominations with "Stamp for Series 1950" omitted were prepared but are not known to have been put into use: 1c, 3c, $1,500, $20,000, $30,000, $40,000 and $50,000

Copies listed as used have staple holes.

Distilled Spirits Excise Tax stamps were discontinued in 1959.

701

FIREARMS TRANSFER TAX STAMPS

Documentary Stamp of 1917
Overprinted Vertically in Black.
Reading Up

NATIONAL FIREARMS ACT

Two types of $200:
  I. Serial number with serifs, not preceded by zeros. Tips of 6 lines project into left margin.
  II. Gothic serial number preceded by zeros. Five line tips in left margin.

1934-74   **Wmk. 191R**
Size: 28x42mm.
Without Gum

Engraved

		Wmkd.	USIR	(191R)
1934			Without Gum	
			Perf. 11	
RY1	R21	$1 green		300.00 300.00

RY2   RY1 $200 dull blue & red, type II,
     #3001-up, unwmkd. ('74)   250.00   120.00
   a. $200 dark blue & red, type I,
     #1-1500   2000.00   —
   b. $200 dull blue & red, type II,
     #1501-3000 ('50)   750.00   —

issued in vertical strips of 4 which are imperforate at top, bottom and right side.

Eagle, Shield and Stars from U.S. Seal
RY1   RY2
(Type I)

1938   **Perf. 11**
Size : 28x33½mm.
RY3   RY2 $1 green   75.00   —

1960, July 1   Size: 29x34mm.   **Perf. 11**
RY4   RY2 $5 red   10.00   —

No. RY4 was issued in sheets of 50 (10x5) with straight edge on four sides of sheet.
The watermark is hard to see on many copies of Nos. RY2-RY4.

RECTIFICATION TAX STAMPS

Actual size: 89½x64mm.
RT1
Offset Printing

1946   *Rouletted 7*   **Wmk. 191R**
                                                 Punched
                                    Unused   Used   Cancel

RZ1	RT1	1c blue & black	7.00	3.00	1.50
RZ2	"	3c blue & black	25.00	8.00	7.50
RZ3	"	5c blue & black	15.00	2.50	1.25
RZ4	"	10c blue & black	15.00	2.50	1.25
RZ5	"	25c blue & black	15.00	3.00	2.00
RZ6	"	50c blue & black	20.00	5.00	3.00
RZ7	"	$1 blue & black	20.00	4.00	2.00
RZ8	"	$3 blue & black	—	20.00	10.00
RZ9	"	$5 blue & black	30.00	12.00	6.00
RZ10	"	$10 blue & black	25.00	4.00	1.00
RZ11	"	$25 blue & black	—	10.00	3.00
RZ12	"	$50 blue & black	—	7.50	3.50
RZ13	"	$100 blue & black	—	10.00	3.00
RZ14	"	$300 blue & black	—	10.00	7.50
RZ15	"	$500 blue & black	—	10.00	7.00
RZ16	"	$1000 blue & black	—	16.50	15.00
RZ17	"	$1500 blue & black	—	45.00	35.00
RZ18	"	$2000 blue & black	—	75.00	55.00

Copies listed as used have staple holes.

DIE AND PLATE PROOFS

NORMAL COLORS

PROOFS are known in many styles other than those noted in this section. For the present, however listings are restricted to die proofs, large and small, and plate proofs on India paper and cardboard. The listing of normal color proofs includes several that differ somewhat from the colors of the issued stamps.

Large Die Proofs are so termed because of the relatively large piece of paper on which they are printed which is about the size of the die block, 40 mm. by 50 mm. or larger. The margins of this group of proofs usually are from 15 to 20 mm. in width though abnormal examples prevent the acceptance of these measurements as a complete means of identification. These proofs were prepared in most cases by the original contracting companies and often show the imprint thereof and letter and numbers of identification. They are listed under "DIE-Large (1)." The India paper on which these proofs are printed is of an uneven texture and in some respects resembles hand-made paper. These large die proofs were mounted on cards though many are found removed from the card. Large Die Proofs autographed by the engraver or officially approved are worth much more.

Prices for die proofs of the bicolored 1869 issue are for examples which are completely printed. Occasionally the vignette has been cut out and affixed to an impression of the border.

Die Proofs of all United States stamps of later issues exist. Only those known outside of government ownership are listed.

Small Die Proofs are so called because of the small piece of paper on which they are printed. Proofs of stamps issued prior to 1904, are reprints, and not in all cases from the same dies as the large die proofs. The margins are extremely narrow, seldom being more than from 3 to 5mm. in width. These 302 small die proofs are from sets prepared for 85 ("Roosevelt presentation") albums in 1904 by the Bureau of Engraving and Printing but bear no imprint to this effect. The white wove paper on which they are printed is of a fibrous nature. These are listed under "DIE-Small (2)."

A special printing of 413 different small die proofs was made in 1915 for the Panama-Pacific Exposition. These have small margins (2½ to 3 mm.) and are on soft yellowish wove paper. They are extremely scarce as only 3 to 5 of each are known and a few, such as the 1861 5c buff, exist only in this special printing. They are listed under "DIE-Small (2a)."

Plate Proofs are, quite obviously, impressions taken from finished plates and differ from the stamps themselves chiefly in their excellence of impression and the paper on which they are printed. Some of the colors vary.

Hybrids are plate proofs of all issues before 1894 which have been cut to shape, mounted and pressed on large cards to resemble large die proofs. These sell for somewhat less than the corresponding large die proofs.

India Paper is a thin, soft, opaque paper which wrinkles when wet. It varies in thickness and shows particles of bamboo.

Cardboard is a plain, clear white card of good quality, which is found in varying thicknesses for different printings. Plate proofs on cardboard were made in five printings in 1879-93. Quantities range from 500 to 2,500 of the cardboard proofs listed between Nos. 3P and 245P.

Margin blocks with full imprint and plate number are indicated by the abbreviation "P # blk. of —."

Numbers have been assigned to all proofs consisting of the number of the regular stamp with the suffix letter "P" to denote Proof.

Proofs in other than accepted or approved colors exist in a large variety of shades, colors and papers produced at various times by various people for many different reasons. The field is large. The task of listing has been begun under "Trial Colors" following the regular proofs.

The editors are indebted to the Essay-Proof Society, through co-operation of its catalogue advisory committee, for help in preparing this section.

PROOFS

1845 New York.

		DIE			PLATE	
		(1) Large	(2) Small	(2a)	(3) India	(4) Card
9X1P	5c black on India paper	500.00	300.00		250.00	
	a. With scar on neck		275.00			
	b. Dot in "P" of "POST" and scar on neck	375.00	"			
	c. As "b" on Bond	"	"		250.00	
	d. As "b" on glazed paper		"			

The above listed Large Die varieties have an additional impression of the portrait medallion. Plate proofs from the sheet of 9 also exist on white and bluish bond paper. Price $125.

Providence, R. I.

10X1P	5c black			325.00
10X2P	10c black			425.00
	Sheet of 12			4000.00

General Issues.

1847
1P	5c red brown on India paper	950.00	750.00	500.00
	a. White bond paper	"	"	
	b. Colored bond paper	"	"	
	c. White laid paper	"	"	
	d. Bluish laid paper	"	"	
	e. Yellowish wove paper	"	"	
	f. Bluish wove paper	"	"	
	g. White wove paper	"	"	
	h. Card		"	
	i. Glazed paper			
2P	10c black on India paper			600.00
	a. White bond paper	"	"	
	b. Colored bond paper	"	"	
	c. White laid paper	"	"	
	d. Bluish laid paper	"	"	
	e. Yellowish wove paper	"	"	
	g. White wove paper	"	"	
	h. Card		"	
	i. Glazed paper			

Original die proofs are generally found cut to stamp size. Plate proofs overprinted "Specimen" sell for about half the above figures.

Reproductions of 1847 Issue

Actually, official imitations made about 1875 from new dies and plates by order of the Post Office Department.

3P	5c red brown	900.00	400.00	1300.00	285.00	200.00
	Block of four				1350.00	900.00
	a. On bond paper		650.00			
4P	10c black	900.00	400.00	1300.00	285.00	200.00
	Block of four				1350.00	900.00
	a. On bond paper		650.00			

1851-60
5P	1c blue, type I	5000.00				
11P	3c red, type I, brush obliteration		"		600.00	
	Block of four				3000.00	
12P	5c brown, type I		525.00	1500.00		
13P	10c green, type I		"	"		
17P	12c black					
24P	1c blue, type V (pl. 9)				750.00	
	Pair				2100.00	
26P	3c red, type II (pl. 20)				600.00	
30P	5c brown, type II				525.00	
35P	10c green, type V				575.00	

		DIE			PLATE	
		(1) Large	(2) Small	(2a)	(3) India	(4) Card
36P	12c black, plate III (broken frame lines)				475.00	
	Block of four				2400.00	
37P	24c lilac	2200.00		1500.00	475.00	
	Pair				1200.00	
38P	30c orange	"	550.00	"	475.00	
	Pair				1200.00	
39P	90c blue	"	"	"	700.00	
	Pair				1500.00	

Plate proofs of 24P to 39P are from the original plates. They may be distinguished from the 40P to 47P by the type in the case of the 1c, 3c, 10c and 12c, and by the color in the case of the 5c, 24c, 30c and 90c.

The 3c plate proofs (No. 11) are on proof paper and nearly all known copies have a vertical brush stroke obliteration.

Reprints of 1857-60 Issue

40P	1c bright blue, type I (new plate)	400.00	425.00	1400.00	125.00	90.00
	Block of four				600.00	450.00
41P	3c scarlet, type I (new plate)	"	"	"	125.00	90.00
	Block of four				600.00	450.00
42P	5c orange brown type II (plate II)	"	"		125.00	90.00
	Block of four				600.00	450.00
	P # blk. of 8				1500.00	---
43P	10c blue green, type I (new plate)	"	"	"	125.00	90.00
	Block of four				600.00	450.00
44P	12c greenish black (new plate, frame line complete)	"	"	"	175.00	90.00
	Block of four				700.00	450.00
45P	24c blksh vio (pl.I)	"	"	"	125.00	90.00
	Block of four				600.00	450.00
	P# blk. of 8				1500.00	
46P	30c yel org (pl. I)	"	"	"	125.00	90.00
	Block of four				600.00	450.00
	P# blk. of 8				1750.00	
47P	90c deep blue (pl. I)	"	"	"	175.00	125.00
	Block of four				700.00	600.00
	P# blk. of 8				1750.00	1700.00

Nos. 40P-47P, large die, exist only as hybrids.

1861 FIRST DESIGNS.

55P	1c indigo	1350.00	350.00		325.00	
	Block of four				1600.00	
56P	3c red	"	"	1750.00	200.00	
	Block of four				1200.00	
57P	5c brown	"	"		200.00	
	Block of four				1200.00	
	P # blk. of 12				4500.00	
58P	10c dark green	"	"		200.00	
	Block of four				1200.00	
59P	12c black	"	500.00	"	400.00	
	Block of four				2000.00	
60P	24c violet	900.00	400.00	"	200.00	
	Block of four				1200.00	
61P	30c red orange	1750.00	"	"	400.00	
	Block of four				2250.00	
62P	90c blue	1350.00	"	"	400.00	
	Block of four				2250.00	

1861 SECOND DESIGNS (Regular Issue)

63P	1c blue	700.00	275.00	1600.00	95.00	60.00
	Block of four			"	425.00	425.00
	P # blk. of 8			"	2000.00	---
	Indigo					
64P	3c pink	3500.00				
65P	3c rose	1000.00	---	"	175.00	165.00
	Block of four				1000.00	
	P # blk. of 8				2500.00	
	a. 3c dull red				175.00	
66P	3c lake		325.00	"	200.00	
	Block of four				1100.00	
	P # blk. of 8				2500.00	
67P	5c buff			"		
76P	5c brown	700.00	250.00	"	85.00	50.00
	Block of four				400.00	250.00
	P # blk. of 8				1400.00	
68P	10c green		650.00	"	120.00	50.00
	Block of four				550.00	250.00
	P # blk. of 8				1600.00	
69P	12c black		700.00	"	120.00	50.00
	Block of four				550.00	250.00
	P # blk. of 8				1600.00	
70P	24c red lilac			2100.00		400.00
78P	24c lilac			"	150.00	125.00
	Block of four				750.00	600.00
	P # blk. of 8				2000.00	---

PROOFS

		DIE			PLATE	
		(1) Large	(2) Small	(2a)	(3) India	(4) Card
71P	30c orange	500.00	300.00	1600.00	95.00	50.00
	Block of four				450.00	250.00
	P ♯ blk. of 8				1800.00	—
72P	90c blue	500.00	"	"	95.00	50.00
	Block of four				450.00	250.00
	P ♯ blk. of 8				1800.00	—

1861–66

73P	2c black, die I	3000.00			185.00	
	Block of four				900.00	
	P ♯ blk. of 8				2500.00	—
	a. Die II	2500.00	1500.00	5000.00	165.00	135.00
	a. Block of four				800.00	700.00
	a. P ♯ blk. of 8				2250.00	—
74P	3c scarlet	2250.00	450.00	1600.00	165.00	200.00
	Block of four				800.00	900.00
	P ♯ blk. of 8					—
77P	15c black	1250.00	550.00	2500.00	95.00	65.00
	Block of four				450.00	300.00
	P ♯ blk. of 8				1600.00	—

The listed plate proofs of the 1c (63P), 5c (76P), 10c (68P) and 12c (69P) are from the 100 subject re-issue plates of 1875. The 2c Die II has a small dot on the left cheek.

1869

112P	1c buff	1400.00	650.00	1800.00	100.00	110.00
	Block of four				450.00	500.00
	P ♯ blk. of 10				1350.00	—
113P	2c brown	"		"	70.00	75.00
	Block of four				300.00	325.00
	P ♯ blk. of 10				1100.00	—
114P	3c ultramarine	1750.00	"	"	80.00	85.00
	Block of four				350.00	400.00
	P ♯ blk. of 10				1450.00	—
115P	6c ultramarine	1500.00	"	"	80.00	90.00
	Block of four				350.00	475.00
	P ♯ blk. of 10				1450.00	—
116P	10c yellow	"	"	"	80.00	90.00
	Block of four				350.00	475.00
	P ♯ blk. of 10				1450.00	—
117P	12c green	"	"	"	85.00	100.00
	Block of four				400.00	525.00
	P ♯ blk. of 10				1600.00	—
119P	15c brown & blue (type II)	850.00	700.00	2100.00	225.00	
	Block of four				1100.00	
	P ♯ blk. of 8				2650.00	
129P	15c Re-issue (type III)	"	"	"	450.00	130.00
	Block of four				2100.00	700.00
	P ♯ blk. of 8				5500.00	—
	a. Center inverted (100)					6000.00
	a. Block of four					25,000.00
	a. P ♯ blk. of 8					65,000.00
120P	24c green & violet	"	"	"	250.00	225.00
	Block of four				1100.00	1100.00
	P ♯ blk. of 8				2650.00	—
	a. Center inverted (100)					6000.00
	a. Block of four					25,000.00
	a. P ♯ blk. of 8					65,000.00
121P	30c bl. & carmine	1400.00	"	"	250.00	275.00
	Block of four				1100.00	1500.00
	P ♯ blk. of 8				2650.00	—
	a. Flags inverted (100)					6000.00
	a. Block of four					25,000.00
	a. P ♯ blk. of 8					75,000.00
122P	90c carmine & black	850.00	"	"	325.00	275.00
	Block of four				1500.00	1500.00
	P ♯ blk. of 8				3200.00	—
	a. Center inverted (100)					6000.00
	a. Block of four					25,000.00
	a. P ♯ blk. of 8					65,000.00

Large die proofs of Nos. 119, 129, 120 and 122 exist only as hybrids.

1880

133P	1c dark buff	1400.00			150.00	
	Block of four				700.00	
	P ♯ blk. of 10				2000.00	

1870–71 National Bank Note Co.

145P	1c ultramarine	450.00	250.00	800.00	40.00	
	Block of four				175.00	
	P ♯ blk. of 12				800.00	
146P	2c red brown	450.00			40.00	
	Block of four				175.00	
	P ♯ blk. of 12				800.00	
147P	3c green	500.00			45.00	
	Block of four				200.00	
	P ♯ blk. of 12				800.00	
148P	6c carmine	600.00			80.00	
	Block of four				350.00	
	P ♯ blk. of 12				1350.00	
149P	7c vermilion	375.00			35.00	
	Block of four				150.00	
	P ♯ blk. of 12				700.00	
150P	10c brown	500.00			90.00	
	Block of four				400.00	
	P ♯ blk. of 12				1500.00	
151P	12c violet	400.00			40.00	
	Block of four				175.00	
	P ♯ blk. of 12				850.00	
152P	15c orange	450.00			65.00	
	Block of four				300.00	
	P ♯ blk. of 12				1150.00	
153P	24c purple	"			65.00	
	Block of four				300.00	
	P ♯ blk. of 12				1150.00	
154P	30c black	"			90.00	
	Block of four				400.00	
	P ♯ blk. of 12				1450.00	
155P	90c carmine	"			100.00	
	Block of four				450.00	
	P ♯ blk. of 12				1600.00	

Secret Marks on 24, 30 and 90c Dies of the Bank Note Issues

National — 24c. Rays of lower star normal
Continental — 24c. Rays of lower star strengthened

National
30c. Lower line does not join point of shield

Continental and American
30c. Lower line joins point of shield and bottom line of shield thicker

National — 90c. Rays of star in upper right normal
Continental and American — 90c. Rays of star in upper right strengthened

PROOFS

1873 — Continental Bank Note Co.

		DIE			PLATE	
		(1) Large	(2) Small	(2a)	(3) India	(4) Card
156P	1c ultramarine	750.00			110.00	200.00
	Block of four				500.00	
	P ♯ blk. of 14				2100.00	
157P	2c brown	600.00	265.00	800.00	70.00	35.00
	Block of four				325.00	175.00
	P ♯ blk. of 12				1200.00	—
158P	3c green	"	"	"	110.00	225.00
	Block of four				500.00	
	P ♯ blk. of 14				2100.00	
159P	6c pink	1000.00	300.00	"	225.00	300.00
	Block of four				1000.00	
	P ♯ blk. of 12				3750.00	
160P	7c orange vermilion	450.00	265.00	"	70.00	25.00
	Block of four				325.00	120.00
	P ♯ blk. of 14				1500.00	—
161P	10c brown	750.00	285.00	"	125.00	300.00
	Block of four				600.00	
	P♯ blk. of 14				2400.00	
162P	12c blackish violet	400.00	265.00	"	80.00	35.00
	Block of four				400.00	160.00
	P ♯ blk. of 14				1750.00	—
163P	15c yellow orange	650.00	"	"	110.00	40.00
	Block of four				500.00	200.00
	P♯ blk. of 12				1800.00	—
164P	24c violet	"	"	"	100.00	55.00
	Block of four				450.00	250.00
	P ♯ blk. of 12				1750.00	—
165P	30c gray black	"	"	"	80.00	35.00
	Block of four				400.00	160.00
	P ♯ blk. of 12				1500.00	—
166P	90c rose carmine	"	"	"	110.00	75.00
	Block of four				500.00	350.00
	P ♯ blk. of 12				1850.00	—

Die Proofs of the 24c, 30c and 90c show secret marks, as illustrated, but as plates of these denominations were not made from these dies, plate proofs can be identified only by color.

182P	1c gray blue	850.00			120.00	
	Block of four				525.00	
	P ♯ blk. of 12				1850.00	
183P	2c vermilion	500.00	275.00	750.00	50.00	25.00
	Block of four				225.00	125.00
	P ♯ blk. of 12				825.00	—
185P	5c blue	600.00	"	750.00	110.00	40.00
	Block of four				500.00	185.00
	P ♯ blk. of 12				1800.00	—

1881-82 — American Bank Note Co

205P	5c yellow brown	350.00	275.00	750.00	70.00	30.00
	Block of four				310.00	140.00
	P ♯ blk. of 12				1100.00	—
206P	1c blue	550.00	"	"	70.00	35.00
	Block of four				310.00	160.00
	P ♯ blk. of 12				1100.00	—
207P	3c blue green	"	"	"	70.00	35.00
	Block of four				310.00	160.00
	P ♯ blk. of 12				1100.00	—
208P	6c rose	1100.00	"	"	175.00	90.00
	Block of four				850.00	400.00
	a. 6c brown red				—	100.00
209P	10c brown	"	"	"	75.00	50.00
	Block of four				325.00	225.00
	P ♯ blk. of 12				1200.00	—

1883

210P	2c red brown	550.00	"	"	65.00	45.00
	Block of four				285.00	200.00
	P ♯ blk. of 12				1100.00	—
211P	4c green	"	"	"	80.00	55.00
	Block of four				350.00	250.00
	P ♯ blk. of 12				1350.00	—

1887-88

212P	1c ultramarine	950.00	"	"	200.00	1850.00
	Block of four				900.00	—
	P ♯ blk. of 12				3250.00	
213P	2c green	600.00	"	"	70.00	50.00
	Block of four				310.00	225.00
	P ♯ blk. of 12				1150.00	—
214P	3c vermilion	650.00	"	"	80.00	55.00
	Block of four				350.00	250.00
	P ♯ blk. of 12				1350.00	—

Nos. 207P-1 & 214P-1 inscribed: "Worked over by new company, June 29th, 1881."

215P	4c carmine	900.00	275.00	750.00	200.00	80.00
	Block of four				950.00	350.00
	P ♯ blk. of 12				—	—

		DIE			PLATE	
		(1) Large	(2) Small	(2a)	(3) India	(4) Card
216P	5c indigo	900.00	275.00	750.00	125.00	50.00
	Block of four				600.00	225.00
	P ♯ blk. of 12				—	—
217P	30c org. brown	1000.00	"	"	125.00	50.00
	Block of four				600.00	225.00
	P ♯ blk. of 10				—	—
218P	90c purple	"	"	"	175.00	80.00
	Block of four				800.00	350.00
	P ♯ blk. of 10					

1890-93

219P	1c ultramarine	300.00	275.00	550.00	50.00	70.00
	Block of four				225.00	310.00
	P ♯ blk. of 12				900.00	1200.00
219D-P	2c lake	800.00	"	"	175.00	350.00
	Block of four				800.00	1500.00
	P ♯ blk. of 12				3000.00	6000.00
220P	2c carmine	700.00	"	"	450.00	300.00
	Block of four				2000.00	1300.00
	P ♯ blk. of 12				7000.00	4500.00
221P	3c purple	300.00	"	"	70.00	45.00
	Block of four				310.00	200.00
	P ♯ blk. of 12				1200.00	1100.00
222P	4c dark brown	"	"	"	70.00	45.00
	Block of four				310.00	200.00
	P ♯ blk. of 12				1200.00	1100.00
223P	5c chocolate	"	"	"	65.00	40.00
	Block of four				285.00	175.00
	P ♯ blk. of 12				1100.00	1150.00
224P	6c brown red	"	"	"	65.00	40.00
	Block of four				285.00	175.00
	P ♯ blk. of 12				1100.00	1400.00
225P	8c lilac	850.00	"	"	110.00	225.00
	Block of four				500.00	1000.00
	P ♯ blk. of 12				2000.00	3750.00
226P	10c green	300.00	"	"	80.00	80.00
	Block of four				350.00	350.00
	P ♯ blk. of 12				1300.00	1350.00
227P	15c indigo	400.00	"	"	90.00	80.00
	Block of four				400.00	350.00
	P ♯ blk. of 12				1500.00	1600.00
228P	30c black	"	"	"	90.00	90.00
	Block of four				400.00	400.00
	P ♯ blk. of 12				1500.00	1600.00
229P	90c orange	"	"	"	125.00	100.00
	Block of four				550.00	450.00
	P ♯ blk. of 12				2000.00	2100.00

1893 — COLUMBIAN ISSUE.

230P	1c blue	800.00	450.00	1100.00	85.00	45.00
	Block of four				375.00	225.00
	P ♯ blk. of 8				950.00	700.00
231P	2c violet	"	"	"	500.00	175.00
	Block of four				2200.00	750.00
	P ♯ blk. of 8				5000.00	2100.00
232P	3c green	"	"	"	115.00	100.00
	Block of four				500.00	450.00
	P ♯ blk. of 8				1350.00	1200.00
233P	4c ultramarine	"	"	"	115.00	100.00
	Block of four				500.00	450.00
	P ♯ blk. of 8				1350.00	1200.00
233a-P	4c blue (error) on thin card	2750.00				
234P	5c chocolate	800.00	"	"	115.00	100.00
	Block of four				500.00	450.00
	P ♯ blk. of 8				1350.00	1250.00
235P	6c purple	"	"	"	125.00	100.00
	Block of four				550.00	450.00
	P ♯ blk. of 8				1750.00	1200.00
236P	8c magenta	"	"	"	125.00	225.00
	Block of four				550.00	1050.00
	P ♯ blk. of 8				1750.00	2750.00
237P	10c black brown	"	"	"	125.00	100.00
	Block of four				550.00	450.00
	P ♯ blk. of 8				1750.00	1200.00
238P	15c dark green	"	"	"	125.00	125.00
	Block of four				550.00	550.00
	P ♯ blk. of 8				1750.00	1750.00
239P	30c orange brown	"	"	"	175.00	145.00
	Block of four				800.00	675.00
	P ♯ blk. of 8				2500.00	2500.00
240P	50c slate blue	"	"	"	250.00	175.00
	Block of four				1100.00	800.00
	P ♯ blk. of 8				3000.00	2400.00
241P	$1 salmon	1000.00	550.00	1200.00	300.00	250.00
	Block of four				1450.00	1100.00
	P ♯ blk. of 8				4000.00	

PROOFS

		DIE			PLATE	
		(1) Large	(2) Small	(2a)	(3) India	(4) Card
242P	$2 brown red	1000.00	550.00	1200.00	325.00	275.00
	Block of four				1400.00	1200.00
	P ♯ blk. of 8				4250.00	3500.00
243P	$3 yellow green	"	"	"	425.00	325.00
	Block of four				2000.00	1500.00
	P ♯ blk. of 8				5750.00	4250.00
244P	$4 crimson lake	"	"	"	500.00	400.00
	Block of four				2200.00	1800.00
	P ♯ blk. of 8				6000.00	5250.00
245P	$5 black	"	"	"	600.00	500.00
	Block of four				2600.00	2200.00
	P ♯ blk. of 8				7000.00	6500.00

This set also exists as Large Die proofs, not die sunk, but printed directly on thin card. Set price $8650. 1c through 50c, $400 each; $1 through $5, $850 each.

1894 Bureau of Engraving and Printing.

246P	1c ultramarine	375.00				
247P	1c blue	250.00	250.00	650.00		150.00
	Block of four					650.00
	P ♯ blk. of 6					1200.00
250P	2c carmine (triangle I)					150.00
	Block of four					700.00
	P ♯ blk. of 6					1350.00
251P	2c carmine (triangle II)	"				
252P	2c carmine (triangle III)	400.00		"	275.00	
	Block of four				1200.00	
253P	3c purple (triangle I)	400.00				
253P	3c purple (triangle II)	325.00				
254P	4c dark brown	250.00	"	"		
255P	5c chocolate		"	"		
256P	6c brown				300.00	
	Block of four				1300.00	
	P ♯ blk. of 6				2250.00	
257P	8c violet brown	275.00	250.00	650.00		
258P	10c green		"	"		
259P	15c dark blue	300.00	"	"		
260P	50c orange	450.00	210.00	"		
261A-P	$1 black	475.00	350.00	725.00		
262P	$2 dark blue	"	"	"		550.00
	Block of four					2250.00
	P ♯ blk. of 6					3500.00
263P	$5 dark green	650.00	375.00	725.00	600.00	
	Block of four				2400.00	
	P ♯ blk. of 6				3750.00	

258P to 263P (small die) are from the type II die.

1898-99

279P	1c green	700.00	375.00	700.00		
279B-P	2c orange red		"			
280P	4c rose brown	"	"	"		
281P	5c blue	"	"	"		
282P	6c lake	"	"			
283P	10c orange brown (type II)	800.00	"	"		
283a-P	10c brown (type II)	"				
284P	15c olive green (type II)	"	"	"		

1898 TRANS-MISSISSIPPI ISSUE.

285P	1c green	1100.00	650.00	900.00		
286P	2c copper red	"	"	"		1000.00
287P	4c orange	"	"	"		
288P	5c dull blue	"	"	"		
289P	8c violet brown	"	"	"		
290P	10c gray violet	"	"	"		
291P	50c sage green	"	"	"		
292P	$1 black	1200.00	"	"		
293P	$2 orange brown	"	"	"		2000.00
	Block of four					9000.00

1901 PAN-AMERICAN ISSUE.

294P	1c green & black	575.00	575.00	800.00
295P	2c carmine & black	"	"	"
296P	4c chocolate & black	"	"	"

		DIE		
		(1) Large	(2) Small	(2a)
297P	5c ultramarine & black	575.00	575.00	800.00
298P	8c brown violet & black	"	"	"
299P	10c yellow brown & black	"	"	"

1902-03

300P	1c green	750.00	300.00	650.00
301P	2c carmine	"	"	"
302P	3c purple	"	"	"
303P	4c orange brown	"	"	"
304P	5c blue	"	"	"
305P	6c lake	"	"	"
306P	8c violet black	"	"	"
307P	10c orange brown	"	"	"
308P	13c deep violet brown	"	"	"
309P	15c olive green	"	"	"
310P	50c orange	"	"	"
311P	$1 black	"	"	"
312P	$2 blue	"	"	"
313P	$5 green	850.00	375.00	800.00

1903

319P	2c carmine, Die I	950.00		900.00
319i-P	2c carmine, Die II	"	700.00	

1904 LOUISIANA PURCHASE ISSUE

323P	1c green	1400.00	750.00	900.00
324P	2c carmine	"	"	"
325P	3c violet	"	"	"
326P	5c dark blue	"	"	"
327P	10c brown	"	"	"

1907 JAMESTOWN EXPOSITION ISSUE

328P	1c green	1300.00	900.00	1100.00
329P	2c carmine	"	"	"
330P	5c blue	"	"	"

1908-09

331P	1c green	850.00	600.00	650.00
332P	2c carmine	"	"	"
333P	3c deep violet	"	"	"
334P	4c brown	"	"	"
335P	5c blue	"	"	"
336P	6c red orange	"	"	"
337P	8c olive green	"	"	"
338P	10c yellow	"	"	"
339P	13c blue green	"	"	"
340P	15c pale ultramarine	"	"	"
341P	50c violet	"	"	"
342P	$1 violet black	"	"	"

1909 LINCOLN MEMORIAL ISSUE.

367P	2c carmine	1100.00	900.00	1000.00

1909 ALASKA-YUKON ISSUE.

370P	2c carmine	1100.00	900.00	1000.00

1909 HUDSON-FULTON ISSUE.

372P	2c carmine	1100.00	900.00	1000.00

1912-13 PANAMA-PACIFIC ISSUE

397P	1c green	1250.00	1100.00	1100.00
398P	2c carmine	"	"	"
399P	5c blue	"	"	"
400P	10c org. yellow	"	"	"
400A-P	10c orange	1350.00	1100.00	1200.00
398A-P	2c carmine (*Inscribed* "*Gatun Locks*")			4750.00

Plates were made of this design and a large supply of stamps printed. It was discovered that the view shown did not in fact represent the Gatun Locks, but those of San Pedro Miguel. The stamps and plates were destroyed and the die altered to read Panama Canal. Only three impressions of the original die exist.

PROOFS 707

1912-19

		DIE		
		(1) Large	(2) Small	(2a)
405P	1c green	750.00	600.00	800.00
406P	2c carmine	"	"	"
407P	7c black	"	"	"
414P	8c olive green	"	"	"
415P	9c salmon red	"	"	"
416P	10c orange yellow	"	"	"
434P	11c dark green	"	"	"
417P	12c claret brown	"	"	"
513P	13c apple green	"		
418P	15c gray	"	"	"
419P	20c ultramarine	"	"	"
420P	30c orange red	"	"	"
421P	50c violet	"	"	"
423P	$1 violet black	"	"	"

1918-20

524P	$5 deep green & black	1500.00
547P	$2 carmine & black	"

1919   VICTORY ISSUE.

537P	3c violet	1100.00	850.00

1920   PILGRIM ISSUE

548P	1c green	1250.00	1000.00
549P	2c carmine rose	"	"
550P	5c deep blue	"	"

1922-26

		LARGE DIE		PLATE	
		(1) India	(1a) White Wove	(3) White Wove	(4) Card
551P	½c olive brown	800.00	"	—	
552P	1c deep green	"	500.00	—	
553P	1½c yellow brown	"	"	—	
554P	2c carmine	"	"	—	
555P	3c violet	"	"	—	
556P	4c yellow brown	"	"	—	
557P	5c dark blue	"	"	—	
558P	6c red orange	"	"	—	
559P	7c black	"	"	—	
560P	8c olive green	"	"	—	
561P	9c rose	"	"	—	
562P	10c orange	"	"	—	
563P	11c light blue	1200.00	"	—	
564P	12c brown violet	750.00	"	—	
622P	13c green	1000.00	"	—	
565P	14c dark blue	750.00	"	—	
566P	15c gray	1000.00	"	—	
623P	17c black	800.00	"	—	
567P	20c carmine rose	"	"	—	
568P	25c deep green	"	"	—	
569P	30c olive brown	"	"	—	
570P	50c lilac	"	"	—	
571P	$1 violet brown	"	"	—	
572P	$2 deep blue	1100.00	"	—	
573P	$5 carmine & dark blue	"	"		

		SMALL DIE
		(2) India
572P	$2 deep blue	—

No. 573P1 exists only as a hybrid.

		LARGE DIE		SMALL DIE
		(1) India	(1a) White Wove	(2) White or Yellowish Wove
611P 1923,	Harding 2c black	1000.00	700.00	700.00
614P 1924,	Huguenot-Walloon, 1c dark green	650.00	600.00	600.00
615P "	Huguenot-Walloon, 2c carmine rose	"	"	"
616P "	Huguenot-Walloon, 5c dark blue	"	"	"
617P 1925,	Lexington-Concord, 1c deep green	"	"	"
618P "	Lexington-Concord, 2c carmine rose	"	"	"

		LARGE DIE		SMALL DIE
		(1) India	(1a) White Wove	(2) White or Yellowish Wove
619P 1925,	Lexington-Concord, 5c dark blue	650.00	600.00	600.00
620P "	Norse-American, 2c car. & blk.	750.00	750.00	750.00
621P "	Norse-American, 5c dk. bl. & blk.	"	"	"
627P 1926,	Sesquicentennial, 2c carmine rose	700.00	650.00	"
628P "	Ericsson, 5c gray lilac	"	"	"
629P "	White Plains, 2c carmine rose	"	"	"
643P 1927,	Vermont, 2c carmine rose	"	"	"
644P "	Burgoyne, 2c carmine rose	"	"	"
645P 1928,	Valley Forge, 2c carmine rose	"	.	"
649P "	Aeronautics, 2c carmine rose	1250.00	900.00	900.00
650P "	Aeronautics, 5c blue	"	"	"
651P 1929,	Clark, 2c carmine & black	800.00	700.00	650.00
654P "	Edison, 2c carmine rose	"	"	"
657P "	Sullivan, 2c carmine rose	750.00	"	"
680P "	Fallen Timbers, 2c carmine rose	"	"	"
681P "	Ohio River Canalization, 2c carmine rose	750.00	"	"
682P 1930,	Massachusetts Bay, 2c carmine rose	"	"	"
683P "	Carolina-Charleston, 2c carmine rose	"	"	"
684P "	1½c brown	650.00	"	"
685P "	4c brown	650.00	"	"
688P "	Braddock's Field, 2c carmine rose	750.00	"	"
689P "	von Steuben, 2c carmine rose	"	"	"
690P 1931,	Pulaski, 2c carmine rose	"	"	"
702P "	Red Cross, 2c black & red	"	"	"
703P "	Yorktown, 2c carmine rose & black	1000.00	"	"
704P 1932,	Bicentennial, ½c olive brown	850.00	800.00	750.00
705P "	Bicentennial, 1c green	"	"	"
706P "	Bicentennial, 1½c brown	"	"	"
707P "	Bicentennial, 2c carmine rose	"	"	"
708P "	Bicentennial, 3c deep violet	"	"	"
709P "	Bicentennial, 4c light brown	"	"	"
710P "	Bicentennial, 5c blue	"	"	"
711P "	Bicentennial, 6c red orange	"	"	"
712P "	Bicentennial, 7c black	"	"	"
713P "	Bicentennial, 8c olive bistre	"	"	"
714P "	Bicentennial, 9c pale red	"	"	"
715P "	Bicentennial, 10c org. yellow	"	"	"
716P "	Winter Games, 2c carmine rose	1000.00	850.00	800.00
717P "	Arbor Day, 2c carmine rose	800.00	800.00	700.00
718P "	Olympic Games, 3c violet	1000.00	850.00	800.00
719P "	Olympic Games, 5c blue	"	"	"
720P "	3c deep violet	700.00	"	"
724P "	Penn, 3c violet	"	650.00	650.00
725P "	Webster, 3c violet	"	"	"
726P 1933,	Georgia, 3c violet	"	"	"
727P "	Peace, 3c violet	"	"	"

708 — PROOFS

			LARGE DIE		SMALL DIE
			(1) India	(1a) White Wove	(2) White or Yellowish Wove
728P	1933,	Century of Progress, 1c yellow green	700.00	650.00	650.00
729P	"	Century of Progress, 3c violet	"	"	"
732P	"	N. R. A., 3c violet		"	"
733P	"	Byrd Antarctic, 3c dark blue		650.00	"
734P	"	Kosciuszko, 5c blue		"	"
736P	1934,	Maryland, 3c carmine rose		"	"
737P	"	Mothers Day, 3c deep violet	800.00	"	"
739P	"	Wisconsin, 3c deep violet		"	"
740P	"	Parks, 1c green		"	"
741P	"	" 2c red		"	"
742P	"	" 3c violet		"	"
743P	"	" 4c brown		"	"
744P	"	" 5c blue		"	"
745P	"	" 6c dark blue		"	"
746P	"	" 7c black		"	"
747P	"	" 8c sage green		"	"
748P	"	Parks, 9c red orange		"	"
749P	"	Parks, 10c gray black		"	"
772P	1935,	Conn. 3c violet		"	"
773P	"	San Diego, 3c purple		"	"
774P	"	Boulder Dam, 3c purple		"	"
775P	"	Michigan, 3c purple		"	"
776P	1936,	Texas, 3c purple		"	"
777P	"	Rhode Is., 3c purple		"	"
782P	"	Arkansas, 3c pur.	"	"	"
783P	"	Oregon, 3c purple		600.00	"
784P	"	Anthony, 3c violet		"	"
785P	"	Army, 1c green		"	"
786P	1937,	" 2c carmine		"	"
787P	"	" 3c purple	800.00	"	"
788P	"	" 4c gray		"	"
789P	"	" 5c ultramarine	800.00	"	"
790P	1936,	Navy, 1c green		"	"
791P	1937,	" 2c car.	"	"	"
792P	"	" 3c purple		"	"
793P	"	" 4c gray		"	"
794P	"	" 5c ultramarine		"	"
795P	"	Ordinance, 3c red violet		"	"
796P	"	Virginia Dare, 5c gray blue	800.00	"	"
797P	"	S.P.A. Sheet, 10c blue green		"	"
798P	"	Constitution, 3c red violet		"	"
799P	"	Hawaii, 3c violet		"	"
800P	"	Alaska, 3c violet		"	"
801P	"	Puerto Rico, 3c bright violet	"	"	"
802P	"	Virgin Is., 3c light violet		"	"
803P	1938,	½c deep orange	1000.00	"	"
804P	"	1c green		"	"
805P	"	1½c bistre brown		"	"
806P	"	2c rose carmine		"	"
807P	"	3c deep violet		"	"
808P	"	4c red violet		"	"
809P	"	4½c dark gray		"	"
810P	"	5c bright blue	"	"	"
811P	"	6c red orange		"	"
812P	"	7c sepia		"	"
813P	"	8c olive green		"	"
814P	"	9c rose pink		"	"
815P	"	10c brown red		"	"
816P	"	11c ultramarine		"	"
817P	"	12c bright violet	"	"	"
818P	"	13c blue green		"	"
819P	"	14c blue		"	"
820P	"	15c blue gray		"	"
821P	"	16c black	"	"	"
822P	"	17c rose red		"	"
823P	"	18c brown carmine		"	"
824P	"	19c bright violet		"	"
825P	"	20c bright blue green		"	"
826P	"	21c dull blue		"	"
827P	"	22c vermilion		"	"
828P	"	24c gray black		"	"
829P	"	25c deep red lilac		"	"
830P	"	30c deep ultramarine		"	"
831P	"	50c light red violet		"	"
832P	"	$1 purple & black		"	"
833P	1938,	$2 yellow green & black			800.00
834P	"	$5 carmine & black			"
835P	"	3c deep violet Constitution			600.00
836P	"	3c red violet, Delaware			"
837P	"	N.W. Territory, 3c bright violet			
838P	"	Iowa, 3c violet	850.00		"
852P	1939,	Golden Gate, 3c bright purple			"
853P	"	World's Fair, 3c deep purple			"
854P	"	Inauguration, 3c bright red violet			"
855P	"	Baseball, 3c violet			"
856P	"	Panama Canal, 3c deep red violet			"
857P	"	Printing, 3c violet			"
858P	"	Statehood, 3c rose violet			"
859P	1940,	Authors, 1c bright blue green			800.00
860P	"	Authors, 2c rose carmine			"
861P	"	Authors, 3c bright red violet			"
862P	"	Authors, 5c ultramarine		"	"
863P	"	Authors, 10c dark brown			"
864P	"	Poets, 1c bright blue green			"
865P	"	Poets, 2c rose carmine			"
866P	"	Poets, 3c bright red violet			"
867P	"	Poets, 5c ultramarine			"
868P	"	Poets, 10c dark brown			"
869P	"	Educators, 1c bright blue green			"
870P	"	Educators, 2c rose carmine			"
871P	"	Educators, 3c bright red violet			"
872P	"	Educators, 5c ultramarine			"
873P	"	Educators, 10c dark brown			"
874P	"	Scientists, 1c bright blue green			"
875P	"	Scientists, 2c rose carmine	900.00		"
876P	"	Scientists, 3c bright red violet			"
877P	"	Scientists, 5c ultramarine			"
878P	"	Scientists, 10c dark brown			"
879P	"	Composers, 1c bright blue green			"
880P	"	Composers, 2c rose carmine			"
881P	"	Composers, 3c bright red violet			"
882P	"	Composers, 5c ultramarine	900.00		"
883P	"	Composers, 10c dark brown			"
884P	"	Artists, 1c bright blue green			"
885P	"	Artists, 2c rose carmine			"
886P	"	Artists, 3c bright red violet			"
887P	"	Artists, 5c ultramarine			"
888P	"	Artists, 10c dark brown			"
889P	"	Inventors, 1c bright blue green			"
890P	"	Inventors, 2c rose carmine			"
891P	"	Inventors, 3c bright red violet		"	"
892P	"	Inventors, 5c ultramarine			"
893P	"	Inventors, 10c dark brown			"

PROOFS

	LARGE DIE (1) India	SMALL DIE (1a) White Wove	(2) White or Yellowish Wove
894P 1940, Pony Express, 3c henna brown			500.00
895P " Pan American, 3c light violet			"
896P " Idaho, 3c bright violet			"
897P " Wyoming, 3c brown violet			"
898P " Coronado, 3c violet			"
899P " Defense, 1c bright blue green	600.00		"
900P " Defense, 2c rose carmine			"
901P " Defense, 3c bright violet			"
902P " Emancipation, 3c deep violet		"	
903P 1941, Vermont, 3c light violet			"
904P 1942, Kentucky, 3c violet			"
905P " Win the War, 3c violet			"
906P " China, 5c bright blue			"
907P 1943, Allied Nations, 2c rose carmine			"
908P " Four Freedoms, 1c bright blue green		"	"
922P 1944, Railroad, 3c violet			"
923P " Steamship, 3c violet			"
924P " Telegraph, 3c bright red violet		"	"
925P " Corregidor, 3c deep violet			"
926P " Motion Picture, 3c deep violet			"
927P 1945, Florida, 3c bright red violet			"
928P " United Nations, 5c ultramarine			"
929P " Iwo Jima, 3c yellow green			"
930P " Roosevelt, 1c blue green			"
931P " Roosevelt, 2c carmine rose			"
932P " Roosevelt, 3c purple			"
934P " Army, 3c olive		"	"
935P " Navy, 3c blue		"	"
941P 1946, Tennessee		"	
942P " Iowa		"	
944P " Kearny		"	
945P 1947, Edison		"	
946P " Pulitzer		"	
949P " Doctors		"	
951P " Constitution		"	
958P 1948, Wisconsin		"	
959P " Women		"	
962P " Key		"	
965P " Stone		"	
973P " Rough Riders		"	
981P 1949 Minnesota Terr., 3c blue green		"	—
983P " Puerto Rico		"	
991P 1950, Supreme Court		"	
992P " Capitol		"	
1000P 1951, Cadillac		"	
1001P " Colorado		"	
1002P " Chemical, 3c violet brown		"	
1003P " Brooklyn		"	
1004P 1952, Betsy Ross		"	
1005P " 4-H Clubs		"	
1007P " A.A.A.		"	
" " 3c deep blue		"	—
1009P " Grand Coulee Dam, 3c blue green		"	
1011P " Mt. Rushmore, 3c blue green		"	
1017P 1953, National Guard, 3c bright blue		"	
1018P " Ohio Statehood, 3c chocolate		"	—
1019P " Washington		"	
1020P " Louisiana		"	
1021P " Japan		"	
1022P " American Bar		"	
1026P " Gen. Patton, 3c blue violet		"	—
1029P 1954, Columbia		"	

	LARGE DIE (1) India	SMALL DIE (1a) White Wove	(2) White or Yellowish Wove
	LIBERTY ISSUE		
1031P 1954, Washington	600.00		
1032P " Mount Vernon		"	
1033P " Jefferson			—
1036P " Lincoln		"	
1038P " Monroe		"	
1039P " Roosevelt			—
1047P " Monticello		"	
1050P " Marshall		"	
1051P " Anthony		"	
1052P " Henry		"	
1053P " Hamilton		"	
1060P 1954, Nebraska		"	
1062P " Eastman		"	
1063P " Lewis & Clark		"	
1068P 1955, New Hampshire		"	
1073P 1956, Franklin		"	
1074P " Washington		"	
1076P " FIPEX, 3c deep violet			—
1077P " Turkey		"	
1078P " Antelope		"	
1079P " Salmon		"	
1081P " Wheatland		"	
1082P " Labor Day		"	
1083P " Nassau Hall		"	
1085P " Children		"	
1086P 1957, Hamilton, 3c rose red		"	—
1087P " Polio		"	
1090P " Steel		"	

AIR POST.

		DIE (1) Large	(2) Small
1918			
C1P	6c orange	8750.00	
C2P	16c green	7250.00	
C3P	24c carmine rose & blue	8750.00	
1923			
C4P	8c dark green	5000.00	
C5P	16c dark blue	"	
C6P	24c carmine		
1926-27			
C7P	10c dark blue	3500.00	
C8P	15c olive brown	"	
C9P	20c yellow green		
1927	**LINDBERGH ISSUE**		
C10P	10c dark blue	3500.00	3500.00
1930			
C11P	5c car. & blue	3500.00	
C12P	5c violet	3000.00	
1930	**ZEPPELIN ISSUE**		
C13P	65c green	8500.00	7500.00
	a. on wove	"	

PROOFS

		DIE	
		(1) Large	(2) Small
C14P	1.30 brown	8750.00	7750.00
	a. on wove	"	"
C15P	2.60 blue	"	"
	a. on wove	"	

1932
| C17P | 8c olive bistre | 2500.00 |

1933 — CENTURY OF PROGRESS ISSUE
| C18P | 50c green | 5250.00 | 5250.00 |

1935–39
C20P	25c blue on wove		2500.00
C21P	20c green on wove		"
C22P	50c carmine on wove		"
C23P	6c dark blue & carm. on wove		"
C24P	30c dull blue	3250.00	"

1941–53
C25P	6c carmine on wove	"
C26P	8c olive green on wove	"
C27P	10c violet on wove	"
C28P	15c brown carmine on wove	"
C29P	20c brt. grn. on wove	"
C30P	30c blue on wove	"
C31P	50c orange on wove	"
C46P	80c brt. red violet	1500.00
C47P	6c carmine	"
C48P	4c brt. blue	

AIR POST SPECIAL DELIVERY

1934
| CE1P | 16c dk. blue on wove | 2300.00 |
| CE2P | 16c red & blue on wove | " |

SPECIAL DELIVERY

		DIE			PLATE	
1885		(1) Large	(2) Small	(2a)	(3) India	(4) Card
E1P	10c blue	500.00	250.00	1000.00	60.00	50.00
	Block of four				275.00	225.00
	P ♯ blk. of 8					

1888
E2P	10c blue	"	"	"	60.00	50.00
	Block of four				275.00	225.00
	P ♯ blk. of 8				700.00	

1893
E3P	10c orange	1100.00	300.00	1100.00	110.00	120.00
	Block of four				475.00	525.00
	P ♯ blk. of 8					1500.00

1894
| E4P | 10c blue | 400.00 | 250.00 | 1100.00 | |

1902
| E6P | 10c ultramarine | 900.00 | " | 1000.00 |

1908
| E7P | 10c green | 1750.00 | 900.00 | 1100.00 |

		LARGE DIE	
		(1) India	(1a) White Wove
1922			
E12P	10c deep ultra.	1250.00	1100.00

1925
| E13P | 15c deep orange | " |
| E14P | 20c black | " |

1911 — REGISTRATION
		DIE			PLATE
		(1) Large	(2) Small	(2a)	(3) India	(4) Card
F1P	10c ultramarine	2500.00	1000.00	1100.00

1879 — POSTAGE DUE
J1P	1c brown	115.00	100.00	400.00	35.00	15.00
	Block of four				175.00	100.00
	P ♯ blk. of 12				750.00	

		DIE			PLATE	
		(1) Large	(2) Small	(2a)	(3) India	(4) Card
J2P	2c brown	115.00	100.00	400.00	32.50	15.00
	block of four				150.00	100.00
	P ♯ blk. of 12				750.00	
	2c dark brown	—				
J3P	3c brown	115.00	100.00	400.00	32.50	15.00
	block of four				150.00	100.00
	P ♯ blk. of 12				750.00	
	3c dark brown	—	—			
J4P	5c brown	115.00	100.00	400.00	32.50	15.00
	block of four				150.00	100.00
	P ♯ blk. of 12				750.00	
	5c dark brown	—				
J5P	10c brown	115.00	100.00	400.00		15.00
	10c dark brown	—			50.00	
	block of four				250.00	100.00
	P ♯ blk. of 12				1200.00	
J6P	30c brown	115.00	100.00	400.00		15.00
	30c dark brown	—			50.00	
	block of four				250.00	100.00
	P ♯ blk. of 12				1200.00	
J7P	50c brown	115.00	100.00	400.00		15.00
	50c dark brown	—			50.00	
	block of four				250.00	100.00
	P ♯ blk. of 12				1200.00	

1887
J15P	1c red brown			400.00		20.00
	Block of four					
	P ♯ blk. of 12					
J16P	2c red brown			"		20.00
	Block of four					
	P ♯ blk. of 12					
J17P	3c red brown			"		30.00
	Block of four					
	P ♯ blk. of 12					
J18P	5c red brown			"		20.00
	Block of four					
	P ♯ blk. of 12					
J19P	10c red brown			"	30.00	40.00
	Block of four				150.00	
	P ♯ blk. of 12				600.00	
J20P	30c red brown			"	30.00	25.00
	Block of four				150.00	
	P ♯ blk. of 12				600.00	
J21P	50c red brown			"	75.00	40.00
	Block of four				350.00	
	P ♯ blk. of 12					

1891–93
J22P	1c bright claret	140.00	125.00	400.00	20.00	25.00
	Block of four				110.00	125.00
	P ♯ blk. of 12					
J23P	2c bright claret	"	"	"	20.00	25.00
	Block of four				110.00	125.00
	P ♯ blk. of 12					
J24P	3c bright claret	"	"	"	20.00	25.00
	Block of four				110.00	125.00
	P ♯ blk. of 12					
J25P	5c bright claret	"	"	"	20.00	25.00
	Block of four				110.00	125.00
	P ♯ blk. of 12					
J26P	10c bright claret	"	"	"	20.00	25.00
	Block of four				110.00	125.00
	P ♯ blk. of 12					
J27P	30c bright claret	"	"	"	45.00	25.00
	Block of four				225.00	125.00
	P ♯ blk. of 12					
J28P	50c bright claret	"	"	"	30.00	20.00
	Block of four				140.00	100.00
	P ♯ blk. of 12					

1894
J31P	1c claret	165.00	120.00	350.00		
J32P	2c claret	"	"	"		125.00
	Block of four					650.00
	P ♯ blk. of 6					1000.00
J33P	3c claret	"	"	"		
J34P	5c "	"	"	"		
J35P	10c "	"	"	"		
J36P	30c "	"	"	"		
J37P	50c "	"	"	"		

1930–31
J69P	½c deep carmine	400.00		
J70P	1c	"	"	
J71P	2c	"	"	
J72P	3c	"	"	
J73P	5c	"	"	
J74P	10c	"	"	
J75P	30c	"	"	
J76P	50c	"	"	
J77P	$1	"	"	
J78P	$5	"	"	

PROOFS

1912 PARCEL POST POSTAGE DUE.

		DIE			PLATE	
		(1) Large	(2) Small	(2a)	(3) India	(4) Card
JQ1P	1c dark green	500.00	400.00	600.00		
JQ2P	2c "	"	"	"		
JQ3P	5c dark green	"	"	"		
JQ4P	10c "	"	"	"		
JQ5P	25c "	"	"	"		

1851 CARRIERS.

		DIE			PLATE	
LO1P	1c bl. (*Franklin*)	700.00	200.00	700.00	60.00	30.00
	Block of four				300.00	150.00
	Cracked plate					
LO2P	1c blue (*Eagle*)	"	"	"	60.00	30.00
	Block of four				300.00	150.00
	P ♯ blk. of 8				1200.00	

Nos. LO1P (1)–LO2P (1) exist only as hybrids.

1873 OFFICIAL.

AGRICULTURE.

		(1) Large	(2) Small	(2a)	(3) India	(4) Card
O1P	1c yellow	90.00	62.50	275.00	10.00	8.00
	Block of four				50.00	60.00
	P ♯ blk. of 12					--
O2P	2c yellow	"	"	"	10.00	8.00
	Block of four				50.00	60.00
	P ♯ blk. of 10					--
O3P	3c yellow	"	"	"	10.00	8.00
	Block of four				50.00	60.00
	P ♯ blk. of 12					--
O4P	6c yellow	"	"	"	10.00	8.00
	Block of four				50.00	60.00
	P ♯ blk. of 12					--
O5P	10c yellow	"	"	"	10.00	8.00
	Block of four				50.00	60.00
	P ♯ blk. of 12					--
O6P	12c yellow	"	"	"	10.00	8.00
	Block of four				50.00	60.00
	P ♯ blk. of 12					--
O7P	15c yellow	"	"	"	10.00	8.00
	Block of four				50.00	60.00
	P ♯ blk. of 12					--
O8P	24c yellow	"	"	"	10.00	8.00
	Block of four				50.00	60.00
	P ♯ blk. of 12					--
O9P	30c yellow	"	"	"	10.00	13.00
	Block of four				50.00	90.00
	P ♯ blk. of 12					--

EXECUTIVE.

O10P	1c carmine	110.00	80.00	275.00	16.00	11.50
	Block of four				75.00	65.00
	P ♯ blk. of 14					--
O11P	2c carmine	"	"	"	16.00	11.50
	Block of four				75.00	65.00
	P ♯ blk. of 12					--
O12P	3c carmine	"	"	"	16.00	11.50
	Block of four				75.00	65.00
	P ♯ blk. of 12					--
O13P	6c carmine	"	"	"	30.00	17.50
	Block of four				150.00	90.00
	P ♯ blk. of 10					--
O14P	10c carmine	"	"	"	25.00	11.50
	Block of four				120.00	65.00
	P ♯ blk. of 12					--

INTERIOR

O15P	1c vermilion	90.00	60.00	275.00	10.00	8.00
	Block of four				70.00	60.00
	P ♯ blk. of 12					--
O16P	2c vermilion	"	"	"	10.00	8.00
	Block of four				70.00	60.00
	P ♯ blk. of 10					--
O17P	3c vermilion	"	"	"	10.00	8.00
	Block of four				70.00	60.00
	P ♯ blk. of 10					--
O18P	6c vermilion	"	"	"	20.00	17.50
	Block of four				95.00	85.00
	P ♯ blk. of 12					--
O19P	10c vermilion	"	"	"	10.00	8.00
	Block of four				70.00	60.00
	P ♯ blk. of 12					--
O20P	12c vermilion	"	"	"	10.00	8.00
	Block of four				70.00	60.00
	P ♯ blk. of 10					--
O21P	15c vermilion	"	"	"	10.00	8.00
	Block of four				70.00	60.00
	P ♯ blk. of 12					--
O22P	24c vermilion	"	"	"	10.00	8.00
	Block of four				70.00	60.00
	P ♯ blk. of 12					--
O23P	30c vermilion	"	"	"	10.00	8.00
	Block of four				70.00	60.00
	P ♯ blk. of 12					--

		DIE			PLATE	
		(1) Large	(2) Small	(2a)	(3) India	(4) Card
O24P	90c vermilion	90.00	60.00	275.00	12.00	10.00
	Block of four				100.00	90.00
	P ♯ blk. of 12					--

JUSTICE.

O25P	1c purple	90.00	60.00	275.00	10.00	8.00
	Block of four				60.00	60.00
	P ♯ blk. of 12					--
O26P	2c purple	"	"	"	10.00	8.00
	Block of four				60.00	60.00
	P ♯ blk. of 12					--
O27P	3c purple	"	"	"	10.00	8.00
	Block of four				60.00	60.00
	P ♯ blk. of 12					--
O28P	6c purple	"	"	"	10.00	8.00
	Block of four				60.00	60.00
	P ♯ blk. of 12					--
O29P	10c purple	"	"	"	10.00	8.00
	Block of four				60.00	60.00
	P ♯ blk. of 10					--
O30P	12c purple	"	"	"	10.00	8.00
	Block of four				60.00	60.00
	P ♯ blk. of 12					--
O31P	15c purple	"	"	"	10.00	8.00
	Block of four				60.00	60.00
	P ♯ blk. of 10					--
O32P	24c purple	"	"	"	13.00	10.00
	Block of four				90.00	70.00
	P ♯ blk. of 12					--
O33P	30c purple	"	"	"	13.00	10.00
	Block of four				90.00	70.00
	P ♯ blk. of 12					--
O34P	90c purple	"	"	"	17.50	10.00
	Block of four				100.00	70.00
	P ♯ blk. of 10					--

NAVY.

O35P	1c ultramarine	90.00	60.00	275.00	11.00	8.00
	Block of four				60.00	60.00
	P ♯ blk. of 12					--
O36P	2c ultramarine	"	"	"	11.00	8.00
	Block of four				60.00	60.00
	P ♯ blk. of 12					--
O37P	3c ultramarine	"	"	"	11.00	8.00
	Block of four				60.00	60.00
	P ♯ blk. of 10					--
O38P	6c ultramarine	"	"	"	27.50	20.00
	Block of four				135.00	100.00
	P ♯ blk. of 10					--
O39P	7c ultramarine	"	"	"	13.00	13.00
	Block of four				80.00	80.00
	P ♯ blk. of 10					--
O40P	10c ultramarine	"	"	"	11.00	8.00
	Block of four				60.00	60.00
	P ♯ blk. of 12					--
O41P	12c ultramarine	"	"	"	11.00	8.00
	Block of four				60.00	60.00
	P ♯ blk. of 12					--
O42P	15c ultramarine	"	"	"	11.00	8.00
	Block of four				60.00	60.00
	P ♯ blk. of 12					--
O43P	24c ultramarine	"	"	"	13.00	8.00
	Block of four				80.00	60.00
	P ♯ blk. of 12					--
O44P	30c ultramarine	"	"	"	22.50	11.00
	Block of four				115.00	80.00
	P ♯ blk. of 12					--
O45P	90c ultramarine	"	"	"	14.00	11.00
	Block of four				85.00	80.00
	P ♯ blk. of 12					--

POST OFFICE

O47P	1c black	90.00	60.00	275.00	9.00	8.00
	Block of four				60.00	60.00
	P ♯ blk. of 10					--
O48P	2c black	"	"	"	9.00	8.00
	Block of four				60.00	60.00
	P ♯ blk. of 14					--
O49P	3c black	"	"	"	9.00	8.00
	Block of four				60.00	60.00
	P ♯ blk. of 12					--
O50P	6c black	"	"	"	9.00	8.00
	Block of four				60.00	60.00
	P ♯ blk. of 12					--
O51P	10c black	"	"	"	11.00	11.00
	Block of four				70.00	70.00
	P ♯ blk. of 12					--
O52P	12c black	"	"	"	9.00	9.00
	Block of four				60.00	60.00
	P ♯ blk. of 12					--
O53P	15c black	"	"	"	9.00	11.00
	Block of four				60.00	70.00
	P ♯ blk. of 12					--

PROOFS

		DIE			PLATE	
		(1) Large	(2) Small	(2a)	(3) India	(4) Card
O54P	24c black	90.00	60.00	275.00	9.00	8.00
	Block of four				60.00	60.00
	P # blk. of 12				—	—
O55P	30c black	"	"	"	9.00	8.00
	Block of four				60.00	60.00
	P # blk. of 12				—	—
O56P	90c black	"	"	"	9.00	8.00
	Block of four				60.00	60.00
	P # blk. of 12				—	—

STATE.

O57P	1c green	90.00	60.00	275.00	11.00	10.00
	Block of four				75.00	65.00
	P # blk. of 12				—	—
O58P	2c green	"	"	"	11.00	10.00
	Block of four				75.00	65.00
	P# blk. of 10				—	—
O59P	3c green	"	"	"	11.00	10.00
	Block of four				75.00	65.00
	P # blk. of 10				—	—
O60P	6c green	"	"	"	35.00	22.50
	Block of four				175.00	125.00
	P # blk. of 12				—	—
O61P	7c green	"	"	"	11.00	10.00
	Block of four				75.00	65.00
	P # blk. of 12				—	—
O62P	10c green	"	"	"	11.00	10.00
	Block of four				75.00	65.00
	P # blk. of 12				—	—
O63P	12c green	"	"	"	11.00	10.00
	Block of four				75.00	65.00
	P # blk. of 10				—	—
O64P	15c green	"	"	"	11.00	10.00
	Block of four				75.00	65.00
	P # blk. of 12				—	—
O65P	24c green	"	"	"	22.50	10.00
	Block of four				110.00	60.00
	P # blk. of 12				—	—
O66P	30c green	"	"	"	22.50	14.00
	Block of four				110.00	85.00
	P # blk. of 12				—	—
O67P	90c green	"	"	"	22.50	14.00
	Block of four				110.00	85.00
	P # blk. of 12				—	—
O68P	$2 green & black	175.00	150.00	300.00	100.00	60.00
	Block of four				450.00	300.00
	Sheet of ten				1350.00	—
	a. Invtd. center					1250.00
O69P	$5 green & black	"	"	300.00	100.00	60.00
	Block of four				450.00	300.00
	Sheet of ten				1350.00	—
	a. Invtd. center					1250.00
O70P	$10 green & black	"	"	350.00	100.00	60.00
	Block of four				450.00	—
	Sheet of ten				1350.00	—
O71P	$20 green & black	"	"	350.00	100.00	60.00
	Block of four				450.00	300.00
	Sheet of ten				1350.00	—
	a. Invtd. center					1250.00

O68P–O71P Large Dies exist as hybrids only.

TREASURY.

O72P	1c brown	90.00	60.00	275.00	9.00	8.00
	Block of four				60.00	60.00
	P # blk. of 12				—	—
O73P	2c brown	"	"	"	9.00	8.00
	Block of four				60.00	60.00
	P # blk. of 12				—	—
O74P	3c brown	"	"	"	9.00	8.00
	Block of four				60.00	60.00
	P # blk. of 14				—	—
O75P	6c brown	"	"	"	25.00	25.00
	Block of four				125.00	125.00
	P # blk. of 12				—	—
O76P	7c brown	"	"	"	9.00	8.00
	Block of four				60.00	60.00
	P # blk. of 12				—	—
O77P	10c brown	"	"	"	9.00	8.00
	Block of four				60.00	60.00
	P # blk. of 12				—	—
O78P	12c brown	"	"	"	9.00	8.00
	Block of four				60.00	60.00
	P # blk. of 12				—	—
O79P	15c brown	"	"	"	9.00	8.00
	Block of four				60.00	60.00
	P # blk. of 12				—	—
O80P	24c brown	"	"	"	22.50	17.50
	Block of four				110.00	90.00
	P # blk. of 12				—	—
O81P	30c brown	"	"	"	22.50	17.50
	Block of four				110.00	90.00
	P # blk. of 12				—	—
O82P	90c brown	90.00	60.00	275.00	13.00	8.00
	Block of four				90.00	60.00
	P # blk. of 12				—	—

WAR.

O83P	1c rose	90.00	60.00	275.00	17.00	8.00
	Block of four				85.00	60.00
	P # blk. of 12				—	—
O84P	2c rose	"	"	"	17.00	8.00
	Block ot four				85.00	60.00
O85P	3c rose	"	"	"	17.00	8.00
	Block of four				85.00	60.00
O86P	6c rose	"	"	"	17.50	8.00
	Block of four				85.00	60.00
	P # blk. of 12				—	—
O87P	7c rose	"	"	"	17.00	8.00
	Block of four				85.00	60.00
	P # blk. of 10				—	—
O88P	10c rose	"	"	"	17.00	8.00
	Block of four				85.00	60.00
	P # blk. of 10				—	—
O89P	12c rose	"	"	"	17.00	8.00
	Block of four				85.00	60.00
	P # blk. of 12				—	—
O90P	15c rose	"	"	"	17.00	8.00
	Block of four				85.00	60.00
	P # blk. of 12				—	—
O91P	24c rose	"	"	"	17.00	8.00
	Block of four				85.00	60.00
	P # blk. of 10				—	—
O92P	30c rose	"	"	"	17.00	20.00
	Block of four				85.00	110.00
	P # blk. of 10				—	—
O93P	90c rose	"	"	"	17.00	8.00
	Block of four				85.00	60.00
	P # blk. of 12				—	—

O83-O93 Exist in a plum snade.

1911   POSTAL SAVINGS MAIL.

O124P	1c dark violet	350.00	250.00	400.00
O121P	2c black	"	"	"
O126P	10c carmine	"	"	"
O122P	50c dark green	"	"	"
O123P	$1 ultramarine	"	"	"

1911   POSTAL SAVINGS.

PS1P	10c orange	900.00		400.00
PS4P	10c deep blue	"		"

1872   POST OFFICE SEALS.

OX1P	green	250.00	150.00	75.00	50.00
	Block of four			325.00	
	a. Wove paper	70.00			
	b. Glazed paper		150.00		

1877

OX3P	brown			22.50	
	Block of four			100.00	

1879

OX4P	brown	2250.00	85.00	17.50	
	Block of four			80.00	

1888-94

OX6b-P	chocolate	110.00	

1901-03

OX10P	yellow brown	75.00	
OX10a-P	gray brown	"	
OX10b-P	red brown	"	
OX10c-P	dark brown	"	
OX10d-P	orange brown	"	

1865   NEWSPAPERS.

				PLATE	
				(3) Wove	(4) Card
				Paper	
PR2P	10c green	275.00	125.00	60.00	72.50
	Block of four			300.00	375.00
	P # blk. of 6			—	—
PR3P	25c orange red	"	"	65.00	72.50
	Block of four			325.00	375.00
	P # blk. of 6			—	—
PR4P	5c blue	"	"	60.00	72.50
	Block of four			300.00	375.00
	P # blk. of 6			—	—

1875

PR5P	5c dark blue		475.00	40.00
PR6P	10c deep green		"	45.00
PR7P	25c dark carmine red		"	

PROOFS

		DIE			PLATE	
		(1) Large	(2) Small	(2a)	(3) India	(4) Card
PR9P	2c black	90.00	50.00	275.00	11.00	7.00
	Block of four				50.00	40.00
	P # blk. of 8				—	—
PR10P	3c black	"	"	"	11.00	7.00
	Block of four				50.00	40.00
	P # blk. of 8				—	—
PR11P	4c black	"	"	"	11.00	7.00
	Block of four				50.00	40.00
	P # blk. of 8				—	—
PR12P	6c black	"	"	"	11.00	7.00
	Block of four				50.00	40.00
	P # blk. of 8				—	—
PR13P	8c black	"	"	"	11.00	7.00
	Block of four				50.00	40.00
	P # blk. of 8				—	—
PR14P	9c black	"	"	"	11.00	7.00
	Block of four				50.00	40.00
	P # blk. of 8				—	—
PR15P	10c black	"	"	"	11.00	7.00
	Block of four				50.00	40.00
	P # blk. of 8				—	—
PR16P	12c rose	"	"	"	11.00	9.00
	Block of four				50.00	50.00
	P # blk. of 8				—	—
PR17P	24c rose	"	"	"	11.00	9.00
	Block of four				50.00	50.00
	P # blk. of 8				—	—
PR18P	36c rose	"	"	"	11.00	9.00
	Block of four				50.00	50.00
	P # blk. of 8				—	—
PR19P	48c rose	"	"	"	11.00	9.00
	Block of four				50.00	50.00
	P # blk. of 8				—	—
PR20P	60c rose	"	"	"	11.00	9.00
	Block of four				50.00	50.00
	P # blk. of 8				—	—
PR21P	72c rose	"	"	"	11.00	9.00
	Block of four				50.00	50.00
	P # blk. of 8				—	—
PR22P	84c rose	"	"	"	11.00	9.00
	Block of four				50.00	50.00
	P # blk. of 8				—	—
PR23P	96c rose	"	"	"	11.00	9.00
	Block of four				50.00	50.00
	P # blk. of 8				—	—
PR24P	$1.92 dark brown	"	"	"	16.00	11.00
	Block of four				80.00	65.00
	P # blk. of 8				—	—
PR25P	$3 vermilion	"	"	"	16.00	11.00
	Block of four				80.00	65.00
	P # blk. of 8				—	—
PR26P	$6 ultramarine	"	"	"	16.00	11.00
	Block of four				80.00	65.00
	P # blk. of 8				—	—
PR27P	$9 yellow	"	"	"	16.00	11.00
	Block of four				80.00	65.00
	P # blk. of 8				—	—
PR28P	$12 blue green	"	"	"	18.00	11.00
	Block of four				90.00	65.00
	P # blk. of 8				—	—
PR29P	$24 dark gray					
	violet	"	"	"	20.00	13.00
	Block of four				100.00	90.00
	P # blk. of 8				—	—
PR30P	$36 brown rose	"	"	"	22.00	13.00
	Block of four				110.00	90.00
	P # blk. of 8				—	—
PR31P	$48 red brown	"	"	"	30.00	13.00
	Block of four				150.00	90.00
	P # blk. of 8				—	—
PR32P	$60 violet	"	"	"	35.00	18.00
	Block of four				175.00	100.00
	P # blk. of 8				—	—

1879

PR57P	2c deep black	90.00			15.00	7.00
	Block of four				80.00	40.00
PR58P	3c deep black	90.00			16.00	7.00
	Block of four				80.00	40.00
PR59P	4c deep black	90.00			13.00	7.00
	Block of four				65.00	40.00
PR60P	6c deep black	"			13.00	7.00
	Block of four				65.00	40.00
PR61P	8c deep black	"			13.00	7.00
	Block of four				65.00	40.00
PR62P	10c deep black	"			13.00	7.00
	Block of four				65.00	40.00
PR63P	12c red	"			13.00	9.00
	Block of four				65.00	60.00
PR64P	24c red	"			13.00	9.00
	Block of four				65.00	60.00
PR65P	36c red	"			13.00	9.00
	Block of four				65.00	60.00
PR66P	48c red	"			13.00	9.00
	Block of four				65.00	60.00
PR67P	60c red	"			13.00	9.00
	Block of four				65.00	60.00
PR68P	72c red	"			13.00	9.00
	Block of four				65.00	60.00
PR69P	84c red	"			13.00	9.00
	Block of four				65.00	60.00
PR70P	96c red	"			13.00	9.00
	Block of four				65.00	60.00
PR71P	$1.92 pale brown	"			16.00	12.50
	Block of four				80.00	80.00
PR72P	$3 red verm.	"			16.00	12.50
	Block of four				80.00	80.00
PR73P	$6 blue	"			16.00	12.50
	Block of four				80.00	80.00
PR74P	$9 orange	"			16.00	12.50
	Block of four				80.00	80.00
PR75P	$12 yel. green	"			16.00	12.50
	Block of four				80.00	80.00
PR76P	$24 dark violet	"			20.00	12.50
	Block of four				100.00	80.00
PR77P	$36 Indian red	"			21.00	12.50
	Block of four				110.00	80.00
PR78P	$48 yel. brown	"			30.00	12.50
	Block of four				150.00	80.00
PR79P	$60 purple	"			30.00	12.50
	Block of four				150.00	80.00

1885

PR81P	1c black	110.00	70.00	275.00	18.00	13.00
	Block of four				90.00	65.00
	P # blk. of 8				—	300.00
PR82P	12c carmine		90.00	"	30.00	13.00
	Block of four		"	"	140.00	
PR83P	24c carmine		"	"	30.00	13.00
	Block of four				140.00	
PR84P	36c carmine		"	"	30.00	13.00
	Block of four				140.00	
PR85P	48c carmine		"	"	30.00	13.00
	Block of four				140.00	
PR86P	60c carmine		"	"	30.00	13.00
	Block of four				140.00	
PR87P	72c carmine		"	"	30.00	13.00
	Block of four				140.00	
PR88P	84c carmine		"	"	30.00	13.00
	Block of four				140.00	
PR89P	96c carmine		"	"	30.00	13.00
	Block of four				140.00	

1895

PR102P	1c black	135.00	110.00	300.00		
PR103P	2c "	"	"	"		
PR104P	5c "	"	"	"		
PR105P	10c "	"	"	"		
PR106P	25c carmine	"	"	"		
PR107P	50c "	"	"	"		
PR108P	$2 scarlet	"	"	"		
PR109P	$5 blue	"	"	"		
PR110P	$10 green	"	"	"		
PR111P	$20 slate	"	"	"		
PR112P	$50 carmine	"	"	"		
PR113P	$100 purple	"	"	"		

POSTAL SAVINGS

1940

PS7P	10c deep ultra. on wove	1150.00
PS8P	25c dk. car. rose on wove	"
PS9P	50c dk. bl. green on wove	"
PS10P	$1 gray black on wove	"

1941

PS11P	10c rose red on wove	850.00
PS12P	25c blue green on wove	"
PS13P	50c ultramarine on wove	"
PS14P	$1 gray black on wove	"
PS15P	$5 sepia on wove	"

PROOFS

		DIE ON INDIA			PLATE	
		(1) Large	(2) Small	(2a)	(3) India	(4) Card
1912-13		**PARCEL POST.**				
Q1P	1c carmine rose	900.00	700.00		900.00	
Q2P	2c	"	"		"	
Q3P	3c	"	"		"	
Q4P	4c	"	"		"	
Q5P	5c	"	"		"	
Q6P	10c	"	"		"	
Q7P	15c	"	"		"	
Q8P	20c	"	"		"	
Q9P	25c	"	"		"	
Q10P	50c	"	"		"	
Q11P	75c	"	"		"	
Q12P	$1	"	"		"	
1925-28		**SPECIAL HANDLING.**				
QE1P	10c yellow grn.	850.00				
QE2P	15c	"	"			
QE3P	20c	"	"			
QE4a-P	25c deep green	"				

REVENUE PROOFS.
NORMAL COLORS.
1862-68 by Butler & Carpenter, Philadelphia.
1868-75 by Joseph R. Carpenter, Philadelphia.

In the following listings the so-called small die proofs on India paper may be, in fact probably are, plate proofs. The editors shall consider them die proofs, however, until they see them in pairs or blocks. Many revenue proofs on India are mounted on card.

1862-71   FIRST ISSUE

		DIE ON INDIA		PLATE	
		(1) Large	(2) Small	(3) India	(4) Card
R1P	1c Express, red			170.00	160.00
	Block of four				675.00
R2P	1c Playing Cards, red	600.00		140.00	160.00
	Block of four			600.00	675.00
R3P	1c Proprietary, red			130.00	100.00
	Block of four				450.00
R4P	1c Telegraph, red				60.00
	Block of four				250.00
R5P	2c Bank Check, blue	525.00			65.00
	Block of four				275.00
R6P	2c Bank Check, orange			140.00	
	Block of four			600.00	
R7P	2c Certificate, blue				60.00
	Block of four				250.00
R8P	2c Certificate, orange			160.00	
	Block of four			650.00	
R9P	2c Express, blue				60.00
	Block of four				250.00
R10P	2c Express, orange	600.00		140.00	
	Pair			600.00	
R11P	2c Playing Cards, blue				80.00
	Block of four				350.00
R13P	2c Proprietary, blue	400.00			60.00
	Block of four				250.00
R15P	2c U. S. I. R., orange			700.00	
R16P	3c Foreign Exchange, green	600.00		400.00	80.00
	Block of four				350.00
R17P	3c Playing Cards green	400.00			200.00
	Block of four				875.00
R18P	3c Proprietary, green			140.00	60.00
	Block of four			600.00	250.00
R19P	3c Telegraph, green	600.00		500.00	60.00
	Block of four				250.00
R20P	4c Inland Exchange, brown			450.00	60.00
	Block of four				250.00
R21P	4c Playing Cards, violet	400.00			200.00
	Block of four				875.00
R22P	4c Proprietary, violet	600.00		250.00	135.00
	Block of four			1100.00	600.00
R23P	5c Agreement, red				75.00
	Block of four				350.00
R24P	5c Certificate, red			200.00	250.00
	Block of four			825.00	
R25P	5c Express, red	250.00			70.00
	Block of four				325.00
R26P	5c Foreign Exchange, red				450.00
R27P	5c Inland Exchange, red	250.00			60.00
	Block of four				275.00
R28P	5c Playing Cards, red	—		235.00	450.00
	Block of four			900.00	
R30P	6c Inland Exchange, orange			130.00	75.00
	Block of four			550.00	325.00
R32P	10c Bill of Lading, blue				75.00
	Block of four				325.00
R33P	10c Certificate, blue			300.00	75.00
	Block of four				325.00
R34P	10c Contract, blue				75.00
	Block of four				325.00
R35P	10c Foreign Exchange, blue				75.00
	Block of four				325.00
R36P	10c Inland Exchange, blue				75.00
	Block of four				325.00
R37P	10c Power of Attorney, blue				75.00
	Block of four				325.00
R38P	10c Proprietary, blue			160.00	
	Block of four			650.00	
R39P	15c Foreign Exchange, brown			210.00	475.00
	Block of four			875.00	
R40P	15c Inland Exchange, brown			275.00	75.00
	Block of four				325.00
R41P	20c Foreign Exchange, red	600.00		185.00	200.00
	Block of four			775.00	850.00
R42P	20c Inland Exchange, red	600.00	250.00	350.00	75.00
	Block of four				325.00
R43P	25c Bond, red				350.00
	Block of four				
R44P	25c Certificate, red				75.00
	Block of four				325.00
R45P	25c Entry of Goods, red				400.00
R46P	25c Insurance, red				75.00
	Block of four			150.00	325.00
R47P	25c Life Insurance, red				75.00
	Block of four				325.00
R48P	25c Power of Attorney, red				75.00
	Block of four				325.00
R49P	25c Protest, red				75.00
	Block of four				325.00
R50P	25c Warehouse Receipt, red				75.00
	Block of four				325.00
R51P	30c Foreign Exchange, lilac			250.00	225.00
	Block of four			1050.00	1200.00
R52P	30c Inland Exchange, lilac			140.00	120.00
	Block of four			600.00	500.00
R53P	40c Inland Exchange, brown			200.00	140.00
	Block of four				600.00
R54P	50c Conveyance, blue	250.00			140.00
	Block of four				600.00
R55P	50c Entry of Goods, blue			140.00	90.00
	Block of four			600.00	400.00
R56P	50c Foreign Exchange, blue			140.00	90.00
	Block of four			600.00	400.00

PROOFS

		DIE ON INDIA	PLATE
		(1) Large (2) Small	(3) India (4) Card
R57P	50c Lease, blue	140.00	80.00
	Block of four	600.00	350.00
R58P	50c Life Insurance, blue	140.00	80.00
	Block of four	600.00	350.00
R59P	50c Mortgage, blue		200.00
	Block of four		850.00
R60P	50c Original Process, blue	140.00	80.00
	Block of four	600.00	350.00
R61P	50c Passage Ticket, blue		120.00
	Block of four		500.00
R62P	50c Probate of Will, blue	140.00	120.00
	Block of four	600.00	500.00
R63P	50c Surety Bond, blue		120.00
	Block of four		500.00
R64P	60c Inland Exchange, orange	120.00	90.00
	Block of four		400.00
R65P	70c Foreign Exchange, green	275.00	125.00
	Block of four		525.00
R66P	$1 Conveyance, red		100.00
	Block of four		425.00
R67P	$1 Entry of Goods, red 500.00		100.00
	Block of four		425.00
R68P	$1 Foreign Exchange red		80.00
	Block of four		350.00
R69P	$1 Inland Exchange, red		120.00
	Block of four		500.00
R70P	$1 Lease, red		700.00
R71P	$1 Life Insurance, red		80.00
	Block of four		350.00
R72P	$1 Manifest, red	130.00	80.00
	Block of four	——	350.00
R73P	$1 Mortgage, red		120.00
	Block of four		500.00
R74P	$1 Passage Ticket, red		700.00
	Block of four		2900.00
R75P	$1 Power of Attorney, red		210.00
	Block of four		900.00
R76P	$1 Probate of Will, red		80.00
	Block of four		350.00
R77P	$1.30 Foreign Exchange, orange	300.00	225.00
	Block of four	1250.00	950.00
R78P	$1.50 Inland Exchange, blue	250.00	100.00
	Block of four	1050.00	425.00
R79P	$1.60 Foreign Exchange green	300.00	225.00
	Block of four		950.00
R80P	$1.90 Foreign Exchange, violet	300.00	225.00
	Block of four	1300.00	950.00
R81P	$2 Conveyance, red	275.00	80.00
	Block of four		350.00
R82P	$2 Mortgage, red	275.00	80.00
	Block of four	——	350.00
R83P	$2 Probate of Will, red		250.00
	Block of four		
R84P	$2.50 Inland Exchange, violet	400.00	350.00
	Block of four		——
R85P	$3 Charter Party, green		275.00 140.00
	Block of four		1150.00 600.00
R86P	$3 Manifest, green 350.00		400.00 140.00
	Block of four		600.00
R87P	$3.50 Inland Exchange, blue		400.00 225.00
	Block of four		950.00

		DIE ON INDIA	PLATE
		(1) Large (2) Small	(3) India (4) Card
R88P	$5 Charter Party, red		160.00 120.00
	Block of four		150.00 500.00
R89P	$5 Conveyance, red		600.00 120.00
	Block of four		500.00
R90P	$5 Manifest, red 300.00		120.00
	Block of four		500.00
R91P	$5 Mortgage, red		" 120.00
	Block of four		500.00
R92P	$5 Probate of Will, red	"	120.00
	Block of four		500.00
R93P	$10 Charter Party, green		275.00 120.00
	Block of four		500.00
R94P	$10 Conveyance, green		120.00
	Block of four		500.00
R95P	$10 Mortgage, green		120.00
	Block of four		500.00
R96P	$10 Probate of Will, green		160.00
	Block of four		600.00
R97P	$15 Mortgage, dark blue ——		225.00
	Block of four		950.00
R97e-P	$15 Mortgage, ultramarine	475.00	
	Block of four		——
	$15 Mortgage, milky blue	400.00	
R98P	$20 Conveyance, orange		425.00 200.00
	Block of four		1800.00 850.00
R99P	$20 Probate of Will, orange		450.00
	Block of four		
R100P	$25 Mortgage, red		375.00 275.00
	Block of four		1150.00
R101P	$50 U. S. I. R., green		450.00 475.00
	Block of four		2000.00
R102P	$200 U. S. I. R., green & red	1700.00	

1871-72   SECOND ISSUE.

		DIE ON INDIA	PLATE
		(1) Large (2) Small	(3) India (4) Card
R105P	3c blue & black		27.50 20.00
	Block of four		120.00 90.00
R109P	10c blue & black		27.50 20.00
	Block of four		120.00 90.00
R111P	20c blue & black		27.50 20.00
	Block of four		120.00 90.00
R112P	25c blue & black		27.50 20.00
	Block of four		120.00 90.00
R115P	50c blue & black		65.00 20.00
	Block of four		300.00 90.00
R119P	$1.30 blue & black		65.00 50.00
	Block of four		300.00 225.00
R120P	$1.50 blue & black		35.00 30.00
	Block of four		160.00 130.00
R121P	$1.60 blue & black		80.00 80.00
	Block of four		350.00 350.00
R122P	$1.90 blue & black		65.00 50.00
	Block of four		300.00 225.00
R126P	$3.50 blue & black		120.00 135.00
	Block of four		525.00 575.00
R130P	$25 blue & black		210.00 160.00
	Block of four		900.00 700.00

PROOFS

	DIE ON INDIA		PLATE	
	(1) Large	(2) Small	(3) India	(4) Card
R131P	$50 blue & black		225.00	200.00
	Block of four		1000.00	900.00
R132P	$200 blue, red			
	& black	3500.00 2750.00	2500.00	
R133P	$500 green, red			
	& black	" "		
	$5000 green, orange			
	& black	6500.00		
	$5000 light green, yellow			
	& black	"		
	$5000 blue, red			
	& black	8500.00		
	$5000 light green, scarlet &			
	black	"		

The $5000 revenue stamp was approved but never issued.
The "small die proofs" formerly listed under Nos. R103P-R131P are plate proofs from the sheets listed under "Trial Color Proofs."

1871-72 THIRD ISSUE.

R134P	1c claret & black		22.50
	Block of four		100.00
R135P	2c orange & black	24.00	22.50
	Block of four	105.00	100.00
R136P	4c brown & black	27.50	22.50
	Block of four	120.00	100.00
R137P	5c orange & black	27.50	22.50
	Block of four	120.00	100.00
R138P	6c orange & black	27.50	22.50
	Block of four	120.00	100.00
R139P	15c brown & black	27.50	22.50
	Block of four	120.00	100.00
R140P	30c orange & black	35.00	27.50
	Block of four	150.00	120.00
R141P	40c brown & black	35.00	27.50
	Block of four	150.00	120.00
R142P	60c orange & black	95.00	80.00
	Block of four	400.00	350.00
	a. Center inverted		450.00
	Same, block of four		2000.00
	Double transfer, design of 70c		2000.00
R143P	70c green & black	65.00	55.00
	Block of four	285.00	250.00
R144P	$1 green & black	55.00	55.00
	Block of four	250.00	250.00
R145P	$2 vermilion & black	120.00	160.00
	Block of four	500.00	675.00
R146P	$2.50 claret & black	70.00	55.00
	Block of four	300.00	250.00
R147P	$3 green & black	95.00	100.00
	Block of four	400.00	425.00
R148P	$5 vermilion & black	95.00	80.00
	Block of four	400.00	350.00
R149P	$10 green & black	120.00	80.00
	Block of four	500.00	350.00
R150P	$20 orange & black	175.00	225.00
	Block of four	750.00	950.00

The "small die proofs" formerly listed under Nos. R134P-R150P are plate proofs from the sheets listed under "Trial Color Proofs."

1875 National Bank Note Co., New York City.

R152P	2c blue		
	(Liberty)	450.00	110.00
	Block of four		475.00

1898 DOCUMENTARY.

| R173P | $1 dark green | 475.00 |
| R176P | $10 black | 575.00 |

1899

| R180P | $500 carmine lake & black | 1200.00 |

1914

| R197P | 2c rose | — |

1914-15

| R226P | $500 blue | 675.00 |

1952

| R597P | 55c carmine | " |

PROPRIETARY.

1871-75 Joseph R. Carpenter, Philadelphia.

	DIE ON INDIA		PLATE		
	(2) Small	(3) India	(4) Card	(5) Bond
RB1P	1c green & black	— —		18.00	18.00
	Block of four			80.00	80.00
RB2P	2c green & black	175.00		18.00	
	Block of four			80.00	
RB3P	3c green & black	22.50		18.00	
	Block of four	100.00		80.00	
RB4P	4c green & black	22.50		18.00	
	Block of four	100.00		80.00	
RB5P	5c green & black	22.50		18.00	
	Block of four	100.00		80.00	
RB6P	6c green & black	22.50		18.00	
	Block of four	100.00		80.00	
RB7P	10c green & black	22.50		18.00	
	Block of four	100.00		80.00	
RB8P	50c green & black	600.00		725.00	
RB9P	$1 green & black	700.00			
RB10P	$5 green & black	850.00		1000.00	

The "small die proofs" formerly listed under Nos. RB1P-RB7P are from the composite plate proofs listed under "Trial Color Proofs."

1875-83 National Bank Note Co., New York City.

	DIE ON INDIA		PLATE	
	(1) Large	(2) Small	(3) India	(4) Card
RB11P	1c green	600.00	"	70.00	—
	Block of four			300.00	
RB12P	2c brown	"	"	70.00	—
	Pair			150.00	
RB13P	3c orange	"	"	75.00	—
	Pair			165.00	
	Block of four			—	
RB14P	4c red brown	"	"	70.00	—
	Pair			150.00	
	Block of four			—	
RB15P	4c red	"			
RB16P	5c black	"	"	75.00	—
	Pair			165.00	
	Block of four			—	
RB17P	6c violet blue	"	"	70.00	—
	Pair			150.00	
RB18P	6c blue	"	"	200.00	—
	Pair			425.00	
RB19P	10c blue	"			

No. RB19P was produced by the Bureau of Engraving and Printing.

PLAYING CARDS.
1896 Bureau of Engraving & Printing.

RF2P	2c ultramarine	145.00
	a. 2c blue	"

HUNTING PERMIT.

	DIE (Wove)	
	(1) Large	(2) Small
RW1P	1934, $1 blue	—	2250.00
RW2P	1935, $1 rose lake		"
RW3P	1936, $1 brown black		"
RW4P	1937, $1 light green	—	"
RW5P	1938, $1 light violet		"
RW6P	1939, $1 chocolate		"
RW7P	1940, $1 sepia		"
RW8P	1941, $1 brown carmine		"
RW9P	1942, $1 violet brown		"
RW10P	1943, $1 deep rose		"
RW11P	1944, $1 red orange		"
RW12P	1945, $1 black		3100.00
RW13P	1946, $1 red brown		"
RW14P	1947, $1 black		"
RW15P	1948, $1 bright blue		"
RW19P	1952, $2 deep ultra.		"
RW23P	1956, $2 black	—	

TELEGRAPH.
1881 AMERICAN RAPID TELEGRAPH CO.

	DIE	PLATE
	(2) Small	(3) India
1T1P	1c black	60.00	25.00
	Pair		52.50
1T2P	3c orange		25.00
	Pair	60.00	52.50
1T3P	5c bistre brown		25.00
	Pair		52.50
1T4P	10c purple	60.00	25.00
	Pair		52.50
1T5P	15c green		25.00
	Pair		52.50

PROOFS

		DIE	PLATE
		(2) Small	(3) India
1T6P	20c red	60.00	25.00
	Pair		52.50
1T7P	25c rose	60.00	25.00
	Pair		52.50
1T8P	50c blue		35.00
	Pair		72.50

"Collect"

		DIE		PLATE
		(1) Large	(2) Small	(3) India
1T9P	1c brown			25.00
	Pair, se-tenant with 1T13P			52.50
	Same, block of four			110.00
1T10P	5c blue			25.00
	Pair, se-tenant with 1T14P			52.50
	Same, block of four			110.00
1T11P	15c red brown			25.00
	Pair, se-tenant with 1T15P			52.50
	Same, block of four			110.00
1T12P	20c olive green			25.00
	Pair, se-tenant with 1T16P			52.50
	Same, block of four			110.00

Office Coupon.

1T13P	1c brown	25.00
1T14P	5c blue	25.00
1T15P	15c red brown	25.00
1T16P	20c olive green	25.00

1885 BALTIMORE & OHIO TELEGRAPH CO.

3T1P	1c vermilion	25.00
	Pair	55.00
3T2P	5c blue	25.00
	Pair	55.00
3T3P	10c red brown	25.00
	Pair	55.00
3T4P	25c orange	25.00
	Pair	55.00

1886

3T6P	black			30.00
	Pair			62.50
3T7P	1c green			30.00
3T8P	5c blue			30.00
3T9P	10c brown			30.00
3T10P	25c orange			30.00

1885 POSTAL TELEGRAPH CO.

15T1P	10c green		50.00	30.00
15T2P	15c orange red			30.00
15T3P	25c blue	60.00		30.00
15T4P	50c brown		60.00	30.00

WESTERN UNION TELEGRAPH CO.

16T1P	(1871)	green		15.00
		Pair		32.50
16T2P	(1872)	red		15.00
		Pair		32.50
16T3P	(1873)	blue		15.00
		Pair		32.50
16T4P	(1874)	brown		15.00
		Pair		32.50
16T5P	(1875)	deep green		15.00
16T6P	(1876)	red		15.00
16T7P	(1877)	violet		--
16T8P	(1878)	gray brown		18.00
16T9P	(1879)	blue		13.00
16T10P	(1880)	lilac rose		15.00
16T11P	(1881)	green		15.00
16T12P	(1882)	blue		18.00
16T13P	(1883)	yellow brown		15.00
16T14P	(1884)	gray violet		18.00
16T15P	(1885)	green		18.00
16T16P	(1886)	brown violet		12.00
		Pair		25.00
16T17P	(1887)	red brown		12.00
		Pair		25.00
16T18P	(1888)	blue		12.00
		Pair		25.00
16T19P	(1889)	olive green		15.00
16T22P	(1892)	vermilion		15.00
16T30P	(1900)	red violet		25.00
16T44P	(1913)	brown	--	--

TRIAL COLOR PROOFS

The listings of trial color proofs include several that are similar to the colors of the issued stamps.

New York.
All on India paper unless otherwise stated.
Original Die.

1845

		DIE		PLATE
		(1) Large	(2) Small	(5) Bond
9X1TC	5c dull dark violet	275.00		
"	5c brown violet	"		
"	5c deep rose violet	"		
"	5c deep blue	"		200.00
"	5c dark green	"		"
"	5c orange yellow	"		"
"	5c brown	"		"
"	5c scarlet	"		"

With "Scar" on Neck.

| 9X1TC | 5c dull blue | 200.00 | |
| " | 5c vermilion | " | |

With "Scar" and dot in "P" of "POST"

9X1TC	5c sapphire	450.00	
"	5c dull gray blue	300.00	
"	5c deep blue on Bond	250.00	
"	5c deep ultramarine on thin glazed card	"	
"	5c deep green	"	300.00
"	5c deep green on Bond		250.00
"	5c dull dark green	"	300.00
"	5c org. verm.	"	
"	5c orange vermilion on thin glazed card	"	
"	5c dark red org.	"	
"	5c dull brown red on Bond		250.00
"	5c dark brown red	"	300.00
"	5c dull dark brown	"	
"	5c dull dark brown on Bond		250.00
"	5c sepia	"	
"	5c brown black on thin glazed card	"	

The above listed Large Die varieties, except those on thin glazed card, have an additional impression of the portrait medallion. Plate proofs are from the small sheet of 9.

Providence, R. I.

1846

		Plate on Card
10X1TC	5c gray blue	275.00
"	5c green	"
"	5c brown carmine	"
"	5c brown	"
10X2TC	10c gray blue	400.00
"	10c green	"
"	10c brown carmine	"
"	10c brown	"
	Sheet of 12, any color	3750.00

General Issues.

1847

		DIE				SMALL	
		LARGE					
		India	Bond	Wove	Thin Glazed Card	India	Bond
1TC	5c violet	900.00					
"	5c dull bl.	"					
"	5c deep blue		800.00	800.00		625.00	
"	5c deep ultra.				800.00		
"	5c bl. green	"					
"	5c dull blue green	"					
"	5c dull grn.	"				600.00	
"	5c dk. grn.	"					
"	5c yellow green	"					
"	5c org. yel.	"					
"	5c deep yellow	"					
"	5c orange vermilion	"					
"	5c scarlet vermilion	"					
"	5c rose lake	"				625.00	
"	5c black brown	"					

		DIE				SMALL	
		LARGE					
		India	Bond	Wove	Thin Glazed Card	India	Bond
1TC	5c dull rose lake						625.00
"	5c brn. red	900.00					
"	5c black	"	800.00		800.00	675.00	
2TC	10c violet	"					
"	10c dull blue	"					
"	10c dp. blue	"		800.00	"	"	
"	10c dull gray blue	"					
"	10c blue green	"					
"	10c dull blue green	"					
"	10c dull green	"					
"	10c dk. grn.	"					
"	10c yel. grn.	"					
"	10c dull yel.	"					
"	10c org. yel.	"				"	
"	10c orange vermilion	"					
"	10c scar. verm.	"					
"	10c golden brown	"					
"	10c lt. brn.	"					
"	10c dk. brn.	"					
"	10c red brown	"					
"	10c dull red	"				"	
"	10c rose lake	"					
"	10c dull rose lake	"					
"	10c blk. brn.	"					
"	10c yel. grn. on blue pelure paper						

		DIE		PLATE	
		(1) Large	(2) Small	(3) India	(4) Card
1TC	5c orange			600.00	
"	5c black			"	
2TC	10c orange			"	
"	10c deep brown			"	

1875

3TC	5c dull rose lake			550.00
"	5c black	900.00		
"	5c green	"		
4TC	10c green	"		750.00

		DIE		PLATE	
		(1) Large	(2) Small	(3) India	(5) Wove Paper

1856-60

11TC	3c black			1250.00	
12TC	5c pale brown			275.00	
"	5c rose brown			"	
"	5c dp. red brown			1400.00	
"	5c dark olive bistre			275.00	
"	5c olive brown			"	
"	5c olive green			"	
"	5c deep orange			"	
"	5c black			1400.00	
13TC	10c black	2650.00			
37TC	24c claret brown			600.00	
"	24c red brown			"	
"	24c orange			"	
"	24c deep yellow			"	
"	24c yellow			"	
"	24c deep blue			"	
"	24c black			"	
"	24c violet black			"	
38TC	30c black	2350.00		1400.00	
	Block of four			9000.00	
39TC	90c rose lake			625.00	
"	90c henna brown			"	
"	90c orange red			"	
"	90c brown orange		"		
"	90c sepia			"	
"	90c dark green			"	
"	90c dark violet brown			"	
"	90c black		"	1250.00	675.00

1875

40TC	1c orange vermilion			400.00	
"	1c orange			"	
"	1c yellow orange			"	
"	1c orange brown			"	

TRIAL COLOR PROOFS

		DIE		PLATE	
		(1) Large	(2) Small	(3) India	(5) Wove Paper
40TC	1c dark brown				400.00
"	1c dull violet				"
"	1c violet				"
"	1c red violet				"
"	1c gray				"
41TC	3c red			—	

		PLATE	
1861		(5) Wove Paper, Imperf.	(6) Wove Paper, Perf.
63TC	1c rose	30.00	32.50
"	1c deep orange red	30.00	32.50
"	1c deep red orange	30.00	
"	1c dark orange		32.50
"	1c yellow orange	30.00	
"	1c orange brown	30.00	32.50
"	1c dark brown	30.00	
"	1c yellow green		32.50
"	1c green	30.00	
"	1c blue green	30.00	32.50
"	1c gray lilac	30.00	32.50
"	1c gray black	30.00	32.50
"	1c slate black	30.00	
"	1c blue	30.00	
"	1c light blue	30.00	

There are many trial color impressions of the issues of 1861 to 1883 made for experimentation with various patent papers, grills, etc. Some are fully perforated, gummed and with grill.

		DIE		PLATE	
1861		(1) Large	(2) Small	(3) India	(4) Card
55TC	1c ultramarine	2250.00		400.00	
56TC	3c black	2000.00			
"	3c black on regular paper				400.00
"	3c scarlet		"	300.00	
"	3c pink	2850.00			
"	3c orange red	2000.00			
"	3c dk. org. red		"		
57TC	5c black	1750.00			
"	5c light brown			300.00	
"	5c dark brown			"	
58TC	10c black		"		
"	10c green			300.00	
"	10c light green			300.00	
59TC	12c scarlet		"		
60TC	24c scarlet		"		
"	24c green		"		
"	24c orange		"		
"	24c red brown		"		
"	24c orange brown		"		
"	24c orange yellow		"		
"	24c rose red		"		
"	24c gray		"		
"	24c steel blue	2250.00			
"	24c blue	1750.00			
61TC	30c black		"		
"	30c green		"		
"	30c dull gray blue		"		
"	30c violet brown		"		
"	30c scarlet		"		
"	30c dull rose		"		
62TC	90c black		"		
"	90c blue green on regular paper				275.00

1861-62					
63TC	1c black		600.00		
"	1c red		"		
"	1c brown		"		
65TC	3c black	1400.00			
"	3c blk. on glazed		"		
"	3c blue green		"		
"	3c orange		"		
"	3c brown		"		
"	3c dark blue		"		
"	3c ochre		"		
"	3c green		"		
"	3c dull red		"		
"	3c slate		"		
"	3c red brown		"		
"	3c deep pink		"		
"	3c rose pink		"		
"	3c dark rose		"		
68TC	10c orange		"		
"	10c red brown		"		
"	10c dull pink		"		
"	10c scarlet		"		
"	10c black		"	550.00	
69TC	12c scarlet verm.		"		
"	12c brown		"		
"	12c red brown		"		
"	12c green		"		
"	12c orange yellow		"		
"	12c black		"		

		DIE		PLATE	
		(1) Large	(2) Small	(3) India	(4) Card
71TC	30c rose	1400.00			
"	30c black		600.00		
72TC	90c black		"		
"	90c ultramarine		"		
"	90c bluish gray		"		
"	90c violet gray		"		
"	90c red brown		"		
"	90c orange		"		
"	90c yellow orange		"		
"	90c scarlet		"		
"	90c green		"		
1863					
73TC	2c light blue			300.00	
"	2c dull chalky bl.	4000.00			
"	2c green		"		
"	2c olive green			"	
"	2c dull yellow		"		
"	2c dark orange		"		
"	2c vermilion			"	
"	2c scarlet		"		"
"	2c dull red			"	
"	2c dull rose			"	
"	2c brown		"		
"	2c gray black			"	
"	2c ultramarine		"		
76TC	5c black	1350.00	500.00		
"	5c orange yellow		"		
"	5c dark orange		"		
"	5c green		"		
"	5c ultramarine		"		
"	5c gray		"		
78TC	24c black		"		
1866					
77TC	15c deep blue	1750.00		300.00	
"	Block of four			1500.00	
"	15c dark red		"		
"	15c orange red		"		
"	15c dark orange		"		
"	15c yellow orange		"		
"	15c yellow		"		
"	15c sepia		"		
"	15c orange brown		"		
"	15c red brown		"		
"	15c blue green		"		
"	15c dusky blue		"		
"	15c gray black		"		
1869					
112TC	1c black	2250.00			
113TC	2c black		"		
114TC	3c black		"		
115TC	6c deep dull blue		"		
"	6c black		"		
116TC	10c black		"		
"	10c dull dk. violet		"		
"	10c deep green		"		
"	10c dull dk. orange		"		
"	10c dull rose		"		
"	10c copper red		"		
"	10c chocolate		"		
"	10c dk. Pruss. bl.		"		
117TC	12c black		"		
118TC	15c dull dk. violet		"		
"	15c deep blue		"		
"	15c dull red brown		"		
"	15c black		"		
"	15c dark blue gray		"		
120TC	24c black		"		
121TC	30c deep blue & deep green		"		
"	30c dp. brn. & blue		"		
"	30c golden brown & carmine lake		"		
"	30c carmine lake & dull violet		"		
"	30c carmine lake & green		"		
"	30c carmine lake & brown		"		
"	30c carmine lake & black		"		
"	30c dull orange red & dp. green		"		
"	30c deep ochre & golden brown		"		
"	30c dull violet & golden brown		"		
"	30c blk. & dp. green		"		
122TC	90c brn. & dp. grn.		"		
"	90c green & black				1500.00

TRIAL COLOR PROOFS

		DIE		PLATE	
		(1) Large	(2) Small	(3) India	(4) Card
1870-71					
145TC	1c yellow orange	800.00	"		
"	1c red brown		"		
"	1c red violet		"		
"	1c green		"		
146TC	2c black		"		
147TC	3c brown			200.00	
"	3c dark brown			"	
"	3c dark red			"	
"	3c light ultramarine			"	
"	3c violet brown			"	
"	3c bistre			"	
"	3c dull red violet			"	
"	3c orange			"	
148TC	6c deep magenta		"		
"	6c ultramarine		"		
"	6c carmine		"		
"	6c maroon		"		
149TC	7c black		"		
150TC	10c blue		"		
"	10c dull pale blue		"		
"	10c ultramarine		"		
"	10c blue green		"		
"	10c carmine		"		
"	10c bistre		"		
"	10c dull red		"		
"	10c red orange		"		
"	10c yellow brown		"		
"	10c brown orange		"		
151TC	12c orange		"		
"	12c orange brown		"		
"	12c brown red		"		
"	12c dull red		"		
"	12c carmine		"		
"	12c blue		"		
"	12c light blue		"		
"	12c ultramarine		"		
"	12c green		"		
153TC	24c dark brown		"		
155TC	90c carmine		"		
"	90c ultramarine		"		
"	90c black		"		
1873					
156TC	1c black			15.00	
"	Block of four			65.00	
"	1c scarlet		—		
157TC	2c black			15.00	
"	Block of four			65.00	
"	2c dull blue	800.00			
158TC	3c black			12.00	
"	Block of four			55.00	
159TC	6c black		250.00	30.00	
"	Block of four			150.00	
"	6c deep green		225.00		
"	6c deep brown		"		
"	6c dull red		"		
"	6c dull gray blue		"		
160TC	7c black		250.00	75.00	
"	Block of four			325.00	
"	7c deep green		225.00		
"	7c deep brown		"		
"	7c dull gray blue		"		
"	7c dull red		"		
161TC	10c black		250.00		
"	10c deep green		225.00		
"	10c deep brown		"		
"	10c dull gray blue		"		
"	10c dull red		"		
162TC	12c black		250.00		
"	12c deep green		225.00		
"	12c dull gray blue		"		
"	12c deep brown		"		
"	12c dull red		"		
163TC	15c black		250.00		
"	15c deep green		225.00		
"	15c dull gray blue		"		
"	15c deep brown		"		
"	15c dull red		"		
164TC	24c black		250.00		
"	24c deep green		225.00		
"	24c dull gray blue		"		
"	24c deep brown		"		
"	24c dull red		"		
165TC	30c black		250.00		
"	30c deep green		225.00		
"	30c dull gray blue		"		
"	30c deep brown		"		
"	30c dull red		"		
166TC	90c black		250.00		
"	90c deep green		225.00		
"	90c dull gray blue		"		
"	90c deep brown		"		
"	90c dull red		"		

		DIE		PLATE	
		(1) Large	(2) Small	(3) India	(4) Card
1875					
179TC	5c black	850.00	250.00	25.00	
"	Block of four			125.00	
"	5c deep green		225.00		
"	5c dull gray blue		"		
"	5c deep brown		"		
"	5c dull red		"		
"	5c scarlet	1000.00			

Small die proofs of 1873-75 issues are "Goodall" prints.

1881-82

206TC	1c deep green	900.00	200.00		
"	1c black		"	125.00	
"	1c ultramarine		"		
"	1c dk. yel. green		"		

		LARGE DIE		PLATE	
1882-87		(1) India	(2) Card	(3) India	(4) Card
212TC	1c indigo	800.00			
"	1c carmine	"	700.00		
"	1c green	"			
"	1c deep green	"	"		
"	1c copper brown	"	"		
"	1c chestnut brown	"	"		
210TC	2c brown red	"	"		
"	2c dp. dull orange	"	"		
"	2c chestnut brown	"	"		
"	2c violet rose	"	"		
"	2c indigo	"	"		
"	2c black	"	"		
"	2c pale ultramarin	"	"		
"	2c olive green	"	"		
"	2c olive brown	"	"		
"	2c lake				140.00
"	2c rose lake				"
"	2c dark carmine				"
"	2c deep red				"
214TC	3c green	750.00			
"	3c dark brown	"	"		
"	3c chestnut brown	"	"		
"	3c dull red brown	"	"		

All of 214TC above bear inscription "Worked over by new company, June 29th, 1881."

211TC	4c green	900.00	"		
"	4c chestnut brown	"	"		
"	4c orange brown	"	"		
"	4c pale ultra.	"	"		
"	4c dark brown	"	"		
"	4c black	"	"		
205TC	5c chestnut brown	"	"		
"	5c dp. dull orange	"	"		
"	5c pale ultra.	"	"		
"	5c deep green	"	"		
"	5c green	"	"	200.00	
"	5c carmine	"	"		225.00
"	5c carmine lake	"	"		
"	5c blue black	"	"		
"	5c black on glazed	"	"		
208TC	6c dp. dull orange	"	"		
"	6c indigo	"	"		
"	6c org. vermilion	"	"		
"	6c dark violet	"	"		
"	6c chestnut brown	"	"		
"	6c carmine	"	"		
209TC	10c carmine	"	"		
"	10c orange brown	"	"		
"	10c dp. dull orange	"	"		
"	10c chestnut brown	"	"		
"	10c indigo	"	"		
"	10c pale ultra.	"	"		
"	10c black (glazed)	"	"		
189TC	15c org. vermilion	"	"		
"	15c orange brown	"	"		
"	15c chestnut brown	"	"		
"	15c dark brown	"	"		
"	15c deep green	"	"		
"	15c black	"	"		
190TC	30c black	"	"		
"	30c org. vermilion	"	"		
"	30c dark brown	"	"		
"	30c deep green	"	"		
"	30c dull red brown	"	"		
"	30c green	"	"		
191TC	90c carmine	"	"		
"	90c dark brown	"	"		
"	90c dp. dull orange	"	"		
"	90c indigo	"	"		
"	90c dull red brown	"	"		
"	90c black	"	"		

TRIAL COLOR PROOFS

		DIE		PLATE	
		(1) India	(2) Card	(3) India	(4) Card
1890-93					
219TC	1c green	550.00			
"	1c dull violet	"			
220TC	2c dull violet	"			
"	2c blue green	"			
"	2c slate black	"			
222TC	4c org. brn. on wove			—	—
"	4c yel. brn. on wove			—	—
"	4c green				
223TC	5c bl. on glossy wove	"			
"	5c dark brown on glossy wove	"			
"	5c bister on wove	"			—
"	5c sepia on wove	"			—
"	5c blk. brn. on wove	"			—
224TC	6c deep orange red	"			
"	6c org. red on wove				120.00
"	6c vio. blk. on wove				"
"	6c yellow on wove				"
"	6c olive grn. on wove				"
"	6c purple on wove				"
"	6c red org. on wove				"
"	6c brown on wove				"
"	6c red brn. on wove				"
"	6c org. brn. on wove				"
"	6c blk. brn. on wove				"
"	6c slate grn. on wove				"
"	6c brn. olive on wove				"
225TC	8c dark violet red	550.00			
"	8c metallic green	"			
"	8c salmon	"			
"	8c orange brown	"			
"	8c light green	"			
"	8c blue	"			
"	8c steel blue	"			
1893					
231TC	2c sepia	850.00	850.00		
"	2c orange brown		"		
"	2c deep orange		"		
"	2c light brown		"		
"	2c blue green		"		
"	2c bright rose red		"		
"	2c rose violet		"		
232TC	3c sepia		"		
"	3c blackish green		"	800.00	
"	3c black		"		
233TC	4c sepia		"		
"	4c deep orange		"		
"	4c light brown		"		
"	4c blue green		"		
"	4c rose red		"		
"	4c rose violet		"		
234TC	5c black	"			
"	5c dark violet	"	"		
"	5c rose violet	"	"		
"	5c red violet	"			
"	5c brown violet	"			
"	5c deep blue	"			
"	5c deep ultra.	"			
"	5c green	"			
"	5c deep green	"			
"	5c blue green	"			
"	5c dk. olive green	"			
"	5c deep orange	"			
"	5c orange red	"			
"	5c orange brown	"	"		
"	5c bright rose red	"			
"	5c claret	"			
"	5c brown rose	"			
"	5c dull rose brown	"			
"	5c sepia	"			
237TC	10c bright rose red	1000.00			
"	10c claret	"			
239TC	30c sepia		1000.00		
"	30c black				350.00
240TC	50c sepia		"		
242TC	$2 blackish brown				1000.00

		DIE	
		(1) Large	(2) Small
1894			
255TC	5c black	900.00	
257TC	8c black	"	
258TC	10c olive	"	
259TC	15c red violet	"	
"	15c dark red orange	1000.00	
261A-TC	$1 lake	"	
262TC	$2 black	"	
"	$2 dull violet	"	

		DIE		PLATE	
		(1) Large	(2) Small	(3) India	(4) Card
262TC	$2 violet	1000.00			
"	$2 turquoise blue	"			
"	$2 orange brown	"			
"	$2 olive green	"			
"	$2 sepia	"			
"	$2 greenish black	"			
263TC	$5 black	"			
"	$5 dark yellow	"			
"	$5 orange brown	"			
"	$5 olive green	"			
"	$5 dull violet	"			
"	$5 sepia	"			
"	$5 brown red	"			
1898					
283TC	10c orange	"			
"	10c sepia	"			
1898					
286TC	2c purple				1100.00
"	2c black				"
"	2c blue				"
"	2c brown				"
"	2c deep carmine rose				"
290TC	10c black	1200.00	1000.00		
291TC	50c black	"	"		
293TC	$2 black	5000.00			
1903					
319TC	2c black, Die I	900.00			
1907					
330TC	5c ultramarine	1600.00			
"	5c black	1700.00			
1908					
332TC	2c dull violet	450.00			
"	2c light ultra.	"			
"	2c bright ultra.	"			
"	2c light green	"			
"	2c dark olive green	"			
"	2c golden yellow	"			
"	2c dull orange	"			
"	2c rose carmine	"			
"	2c ultramarine	"			
"	2c ultra. on buff	"			
"	2c ultra. on green	"			
"	2c green on pink	"			
"	2c green on rose	"			
"	2c dk. green on grn	"			
1909					
342TC	$1 carmine lake	1200.00	1100.00		
"	$1 pink	"	"		
1912-13					
400TC	10c brown red	1350.00		"	
1918					
524TC	$5 carmine & blk.	1350.00			
1919					
513TC	13c violet	550.00			
"	13c lilac	"			
"	13c violet brown	"			
"	13c light ultra.	"			
"	13c ultramarine	"			
"	13c deep ultra.	"			
"	13c green	"			
"	13c dark green	"			
"	13c olive green	"			
"	13c orange yellow	"			
"	13c orange	"			
"	13c red orange	"			
"	13c ochre	"			
"	13c salmon red	"			
"	13c brown carmine	"			
"	13c claret brown	"			
"	13c brown	"			
"	13c black brown	"			
"	13c gray	"			
"	13c black	"			
1920					
547TC	$2 green & black	1300.00			
1922-25					
554TC	2c black (bond paper)				500.00
561TC	9c red orange	900.00			
563TC	11c deep green	"			

TRIAL COLOR PROOFS

		DIE (1) Large	2) Small	PLATE (3) India	(4) Card
565TC	14c dark brown	900.00			
566TC	15c black		"		
1923					
611TC	2c Harding, green	1000.00			
1926					
622TC	13c black		"		
628TC	5c Ericsson, dull dusky blue		"		
"	gray blue			1000.00	
1932					
718TC	3c Olympic, car.		"		
720TC	3c black (bond paper)			750.00	
1935					
773TC	3c San Diego, org. red (yel. glazed card)		"		
1936-43					
785TC	1c Army, black (bond paper)			750.00	
788TC	4c Army, dk.brn.	900.00			
789TC	5c Army, blue	"			
793TC	4c Navy, dk. brn.	"			
798TC	3c Constitution, blk. (bond paper)			"	
799TC	3c Hawaii, black (bond paper)			"	
800TC	3c Alaska, black (bond paper)			"	
"	(India paper)				
801TC	3c Puerto Rico, blk	800.00			
"	(bond paper)			"	
"	(India paper)				
802TC	3c Virgin Islands, black (bond paper)			"	
815TC	10c sepia		"		
836TC	3c Swedes & Finns, purple		"		
837TC	3c Northwest Terr., dark purple		"		
854TC	3c Inauguration, purple		"		
862TC	5c Authors, dull bl.		"		
866TC	3c Poets, dark blue violet		"		
963TC	3c Youth, violet	650.00			
964TC	3c Oregon, dull violet		"		
968TC	3c Poultry, red brown		"		

Air Post.

1923-47

C5TC	16c dark green	4500.00
C8TC	15c orange	4000.00
C32TC	5c blue	4000.00
C35TC	15c brown violet	4000.00

Air Post Special Delivery.

1934

| CE1TC | 16c black | 3600.00 |

Special Delivery.

1885-1902

E1TC	10c black	1000.00	
"	10c dark brown	"	
"	10c org. yellow (wove paper)		1100.00
E2TC	10c black	900.00	
"	10c green	"	
"	10c olive yellow		600.00
E6TC	10c orange	1000.00	
"	10c black	"	
"	10c rose red	1500.00	

1922-25

| E12TC | 10c black | 1100.00 |
| E14TC | 20c black | " |

Registration

1911

| FITC | 10c black (glazed card) | 900.00 |

		DIE (1) Large (2) Small	PLATE (3) India (4) Card
	Carriers.		
LO1TC	deep green	200.00	
	Block of four	950.00	
	a. orange (wove paper)		350.00
LO2TC	deep green	200.00	
	Block of four	950.00	
	a. orange (wove paper)	"	

1879 ## Postage Due.

J1TC	1c black	225.00		25.00
"	1c gray black	"		
"	1c ultramarine	"		
"	1c blue	"		
"	1c blue green	"		
"	1c orange	"	75.00	
"	1c red orange	"		
"	1c olive bistre	"		
J2TC	2c black	"		
"	2c gray black	"		
"	2c ultramarine	"		
"	2c blue	"		
"	2c blue green	"		
"	2c orange	"	"	
"	2c red orange	"		
"	2c sepia	"		
J3TC	3c black	"		
"	3c gray black	"	"	
"	3c ultramarine	"		
"	3c blue	"		
"	3c blue green	"		
"	3c orange	"		
"	3c red orange	"		
"	3c light brown	"		
J4TC	5c black	"		
"	5c gray black	"		
"	5c ultramarine	"		
"	5c blue	"		
"	5c blue green	"		
"	5c orange	"	"	
"	5c red orange	"		
J5TC	10c black	"		
"	10c gray black	"		
"	10c blue	"		
"	10c olive yellow	"		
"	10c blue green	"		
"	10c orange	"	"	
"	10c red orange	"		
"	10c olive bistre	"		
"	10c sepia	"		
"	10c gray	"		
J6TC	30c black	"		
"	30c gray black	"	"	
"	30c blue	"		
"	30c olive yellow	"	"	
"	30c blue green	"		
"	30c orange	"		
"	30c red orange	"		
"	30c olive bistre	"		
"	30c sepia	"	"	
J7TC	50c black	"		
"	50c gray black	"		
"	50c blue	"	"	
"	50c olive yellow	"	"	
"	50c blue green	"		
"	50c orange	"	"	
"	50c red orange	"		
"	50c olive bistre	"		
"	50c sepia	"		
"	50c gray	"		

Agriculture ## Official.

O1TC	1c black	190.00	65.00
O2TC	2c black	"	"
O3TC	3c black	"	
	3c deep green	"	
O4TC	6c black	"	125.00
O5TC	10c black	"	
O6TC	12c black	"	65.00
O9TC	30c black	"	

Executive

O11TC	2c black	"	"
"	2c deep brown	"	
"	2c brown carmine	"	75.00
O12TC	3c black	"	"
"	3c deep green	"	

TRIAL COLOR PROOFS

	DIE		PLATE	
	(1) Large	(2) Small	(3) India	(4) Card

O13TC	6c black		80.00	
O14TC	10c black		80.00	

Interior

O16TC	2c black	190.00		
"	2c deep brown	"		
O17TC	3c black	"	80.00	
"	3c deep green	"		

Justice

O27TC	3c black	"	"	
"	3c deep green	"		
"	3c bistre yellow		"	
"	3c dull orange		"	
"	3c black violet		"	

Navy

O35TC	1c black		"	
O36TC	2c black	"		
"	2c deep brown	"		
"	2c dp. green on wove paper, perf.			250.00
"	2c dp. green on wove paper, imperf.			250.00
O37TC	3c black	"	"	
"	3c deep green	"		

Post Office

O48TC	2c deep brown	"
O49TC	3c deep green	"
O50TC	6c deep brown	"
"	6c brown carmine	"

State

O57TC	1c black	"
"	1c lt. ultramarine	"
O58TC	2c black	"
"	2c deep brown	"
O59TC	3c black	"
O67TC	90c black	"
O68TC	$2 violet & black	1000.00
"	$2 brown red & black	"
"	$2 orange red & slate blue	"

Treasury

O72TC	1c black	190.00	
"	1c lt. ultramarine	"	
O73TC	2c black	"	
O74TC	3c black	"	
"	3c deep green	"	
O75TC	6c black	"	
O77TC	10c black	"	
O78TC	12c black	"	
O79TC	15c black	"	
O82TC	90c black	"	

War

O83TC	1c black	"	80.00	
"	1c lt. ultramarine	"		
O84TC	2c black	"	"	75.00
"	2c deep brown	"		
O85TC	3c black	"		
"	3c deep green	"		
O86TC	6c black	"	"	
O89TC	12c black	"	"	

Postal Savings Mail.

1910

O121TC	2c lake	250.00

The so-called "Goodall" set of Small Die proofs on India Paper in five colors.

		(a) Black	(b) Deep green	(c) Dull gray blue	(d) Deep brown	(e) Dull red
Agriculture						
O1TC	1c	175.00	160.00	160.00	160.00	160.00
O2TC	2c	"	"	"	"	"
O3TC	3c	"	"	"	"	"
O4TC	6c	"	"	"	"	"
O5TC	10c	"	"	"	"	"
O6TC	12c	"	"	"	"	"
O7TC	15c	"	"	"	"	"
O8TC	24c	"	"	"	"	"
O9TC	30c	"	"	"	"	"
Executive						
O10TC	1c	"	"	"	"	"
O11TC	2c	"	"	"	"	"
O12TC	3c	"	"	"	"	"
O13TC	6c	"	"	"	"	"
O14TC	10c	"	"	"	"	"

		(a) Black	(b) Deep green	(c) Dull gray blue	(d) Deep brown	(e) Dull red
Interior						
O15TC	1c	175.00	160.00	160.00	160.00	160.00
O16TC	2c	"	"	"	"	"
O17TC	3c	"	"	"	"	"
O18TC	6c	"	"	"	"	"
O19TC	10c	"	"	"	"	"
O20TC	12c	"	"	"	"	"
O21TC	15c	"	"	"	"	"
O22TC	24c	"	"	"	"	"
O23TC	30c	"	"	"	"	"
O24TC	90c	"	"	"	"	"
Justice						
O25TC	1c	"	"	"	"	"
O26TC	2c	"	"	"	"	"
O27TC	3c	"	"	"	"	"
O28TC	6c	"	"	"	"	"
O29TC	10c	"	"	"	"	"
O30TC	12c	"	"	"	"	"
O31TC	15c	"	"	"	"	"
O32TC	24c	"	"	"	"	"
O33TC	30c	"	"	"	"	"
O34TC	90c	"	"	"	"	"
Navy						
O35TC	1c	"	"	"	"	"
O36TC	2c	"	"	"	"	"
O37TC	3c	"	"	"	"	"
O38TC	6c	"	"	"	"	"
O39TC	7c	"	"	"	"	"
O40TC	10c	"	"	"	"	"
O41TC	12c	"	"	"	"	"
O42TC	15c	"	"	"	"	"
O43TC	24c	"	"	"	"	"
O44TC	30c	"	"	"	"	"
O45TC	90c	"	"	"	"	"
Post Office						
O47TC	1c	"	"	"	"	"
O48TC	2c	"	"	"	"	"
O49TC	3c	"	"	"	"	"
O50TC	6c	"	"	"	"	"
O51TC	10c	"	"	"	"	"
O52TC	12c	"	"	"	"	"
O53TC	15c	"	"	"	"	"
O54TC	24c	"	"	"	"	"
O55TC	30c	"	"	"	"	"
O56TC	90c	"	"	"	"	"
State						
O57TC	1c	"	"	"	"	"
O58TC	2c	"	"	"	"	"
O59TC	3c	"	"	"	"	"
O60TC	6c	"	"	"	"	"
O61TC	7c	"	"	"	"	"
O62TC	10c	"	"	"	"	"
O63TC	12c	"	"	"	"	"
O64TC	15c	"	"	"	"	"
O65TC	24c	"	"	"	"	"
O66TC	30c	"	"	"	"	"
O67TC	90c	"	"	"	"	"
O68TC	$2 scarlet frame, green center				800.00	"
"	$2 " black center					"
"	$2 " blue center					"
"	$2 green frame, brown center					"
"	$2 brown frame, green center					"
"	$2 " black center					"
Treasury						
O72TC	1c	175.00	160.00	160.00	160.00	160.00
O73TC	2c	"	"	"	"	"
O74TC	3c	"	"	"	"	"
O75TC	6c	"	"	"	"	"
O76TC	7c	"	"	"	"	"
O77TC	10c	"	"	"	"	"
O78TC	12c	"	"	"	"	"
O79TC	15c	"	"	"	"	"
O80TC	24c	"	"	"	"	"
O81TC	30c	"	"	"	"	"
O82TC	90c	"	"	"	"	"
War						
O83TC	1c	"	"	"	"	"
O84TC	2c	"	"	"	"	"
O85TC	3c	"	"	"	"	"
O86TC	6c	"	"	"	"	"
O87TC	7c	"	"	"	"	"
O88TC	10c	"	"	"	"	"
O89TC	12c	"	"	"	"	"
O90TC	15c	"	"	"	"	"
O91TC	24c	"	"	"	"	"
O92TC	30c	"	"	"	"	"
O93TC	90c	"	"	"	"	"

TRIAL COLOR PROOFS

1872 — **Official Seals.**

OX1TC	ultramarine	Die on India	200.00
"	blue	Die on card, colored border	300.00
"	deep blue	Die on card, colored border	
"	deep green	Die on card, colored border	
"	chocolate	Die on glossy bond	200.00
"	chocolate	Die on card, colored border	300.00
"	carmine	Die on India	200.00
"	brown	Die on India	
"	red violet	Die on India	—

1877

OX3TC	blue	Die on India	120.00
"	green	Die on India	"
"	green	Plate on bond	"
"	orange	Die on India	"
"	red orange	Die on India	"
"	black	Die on India	"

Newspapers.

1865 (2) Small Die   (5) Thick, cream, wove paper

PR2TC	10c black	67.50
"	10c lake	
"	10c blue green	"
"	10c blue	"
PR3TC	25c black	"
"	25c lake	"
"	25c blue green	"
"	25c blue	"
"	25c ochre	200.00
"	25c brick red	"
PR4TC	5c black	"
"	5c lake	"
"	5c blue green	"
"	5c blue	"

1875   (1) Die on India   (3) Plate on India

PR9TC	2c dark carmine	35.00	
"	2c brown rose		"
"	2c scarlet		"
"	2c orange brown	110.00	"
"	2c black brown		"
"	2c sepia		"
"	2c orange yellow		"
"	2c dull orange		"
"	2c green		"
"	2c blue green	"	
"	2c light ultramarine		"
"	2c light blue		"
"	2c dark violet		"
"	2c violet black		"
PR10TC	3c rose lake	"	
PR16TC	12c dark carmine		"
"	12c brown rose	"	"
"	12c scarlet	"	"
"	12c orange brown		"
"	12c sepia	"	"
"	12c orange yellow		"
"	12c dull orange		
"	12c green	"	"
"	12c light ultramarine	"	"
"	12c light blue		"
"	12c dark violet	"	"
"	12c violet black	"	"
"	12c black		
PR17TC	24c sepia		
"	24c green	"	"
"	24c black	"	"
PR18TC	36c black	"	"
"	36c sepia	"	"
"	36c green	"	
PR19TC	48c black	"	"
"	48c sepia	"	
"	48c green	"	"
PR20TC	60c black	"	"
PR21TC	72c black	"	"
PR22TC	84c black	"	"
PR23TC	96c black	"	
PR24TC	$1.92 dark carmine	"	
"	$1.92 brown rose	"	
"	$1.92 scarlet	"	
"	$1.92 orange brown	"	
"	$1.92 sepia	"	
"	$1.92 orange yellow	"	
"	$1.92 dull orange	"	
"	$1.92 green	"	
"	$1.92 light ultramarine	"	
"	$1.92 dark violet	"	
"	$1.92 violet black	"	
"	$1.92 black	"	
PR25TC	$3 dark carmine	"	
"	$3 brown rose	"	

		(1) Die on India	(3) Plate on India
PR25TC	$3 scarlet		35.00
"	$3 orange brown		"
"	$3 sepia		"
"	$3 orange yellow	110.00	"
"	$3 dull orange		"
"	$3 green	"	"
"	$3 light ultramarine	"	"
"	$3 light blue	"	
"	$3 dark violet	"	"
"	$3 violet black	"	"
"	$3 black	"	"
PR26TC	$6 dark carmine	"	"
"	$6 brown rose	"	"
"	$6 scarlet	"	"
"	$6 orange brown	"	"
"	$6 dark brown	"	
"	$6 sepia	"	"
"	$6 orange yellow	"	"
"	$6 dull orange	"	"
"	$6 green	"	"
"	$6 light ultramarine	"	"
"	$6 light blue	"	"
"	$6 dark violet	"	"
"	$6 violet black	"	"
"	$6 black	"	"
PR27TC	$9 dark carmine	"	"
"	$9 brown rose	"	"
"	$9 scarlet	"	"
"	$9 orange brown	"	"
"	$9 sepia	"	"
"	$9 orange yellow	"	"
"	$9 dull orange	"	"
"	$9 green	"	"
"	$9 light ultramarine	"	"
"	$9 light blue	"	"
"	$9 dark violet	"	"
"	$9 violet black	"	"
"	$9 black	"	"
PR28TC	$12 black	"	"
"	$12 sepia	"	"
"	$12 orange brown	"	"
PR29TC	$24 black	"	"
"	$24 black brown	"	
"	$24 orange brown	"	"
"	$24 green	"	"
PR30TC	$36 dark carmine	"	"
"	$36 black	"	"
"	$36 black brown	"	"
"	$36 orange brown	"	"
"	$36 sepia	"	"
"	$36 violet	"	"
"	$36 green	"	"
PR31TC	$48 violet brown	"	"
"	$48 black	"	"
"	$48 sepia	"	"
"	$48 green	"	"
PR32TC	$60 dark carmine	"	40.00
"	$60 scarlet	"	"
"	$60 sepia	"	"
"	$60 green	"	"
"	$60 light ultramarine	"	"
"	$60 black	"	"
"	$60 violet black	"	
"	$60 orange brown	"	
"	$60 orange yellow	"	"
"	$60 dull orange	"	
"	$60 brown rose	"	

1885

PR81TC	1c salmon	"	
"	1c scarlet		120.00
"	1c dark brown		"
"	1c violet brown		"
"	1c dull orange		"
"	1c green		"
"	1c light blue		"

1894

PR106TC	25c deep carmine		150.00
"	25c dark carmine		"
PR107TC	50c black		"
PR108TC	$2 deep scarlet		"
"	$2 dark scarlet		"
PR109TC	$5 light ultramarine		"
"	$5 dark ultramarine		"
PR110TC	$10 black		"
PR112TC	$50 black		"
"	$50 deep rose		"
"	$50 dark rose		"
PR113TC	$100 black		"

TRIAL COLOR PROOFS

The so-called "Goodall" set of Small Die proofs on India Paper in five colors.

		(a) Black	(b) Deep green	(c) Dull gray blue	(d) Deep brown	(e) Dull red
PR 9TC	2c	150.00	125.00	125.00	125.00	125.00
PR10TC	3c	"	"	"	"	"
PR11TC	4c	"	"	"	"	"
PR12TC	6c	"	"	"	"	"
PR13TC	8c	"	"	"	"	"
PR14TC	9c	"	"	"	"	"
PR15TC	10c	"	"	"	"	"
PR16TC	12c	"	"	"	"	"
PR17TC	24c	"	"	"	"	"
PR18TC	36c	"	"	"	"	"
PR19TC	48c	"	"	"	"	"
PR20TC	60c	"	"	"	"	"
PR21TC	72c	"	"	"	"	"
PR22TC	84c	"	"	"	"	"
PR23TC	96c	"	"	"	"	"
PR24TC	$1.92	"	"	"	"	"
PR25TC	$3	"	"	"	"	"
PR26TC	$6	"	"	"	"	"
PR27TC	$9	"	"	"	"	"
PR28TC	$12	"	"	"	"	"
PR29TC	$24	"	"	"	"	"
PR30TC	$36	"	"	"	"	"
PR31TC	$48	"	"	"	"	"
PR32TC	$60	"	"	"	"	"

1925 Special Handling.

QE4TC	25c apple green	600.00
"	25c olive green	"
"	25c light blue green	"
"	25c dark blue	"
"	25c orange yellow	"
"	25c orange	"
"	25c dull rose	"
"	25c carmine lake	"
"	25c brown	"
"	25c gray brown	"
"	25c dark violet brown	"
"	25c gray black	"
"	25c black	"

THE "ATLANTA" SET OF PLATE PROOFS.

A set in five colors on thin card reprinted in 1881 for display at the International Cotton Exhibition in Atlanta, Ga.

1847 Designs (Reproductions)

		Black	Scarlet	Brown	Green	Blue
3TC	5c	300.00	300.00	300.00	300.00	300.00
4TC	10c	"	"	"	"	"

1851-60 Designs

40TC	1c	150.00	135.00	135.00	135.00	135.00
41TC	3c	"	"	"	"	"
42TC	5c	"	"	"	"	"
43TC	10c	"	"	"	"	"
44TC	12c	"	"	"	"	"
45TC	24c	"	"	"	"	"
46TC	30c	"	"	"	"	"
47TC	90c	"	"	"	"	"

1861-66 Designs

102TC	1c	125.00	115.00	115.00	115.00	115.00
103TC	2c	200.00	200.00	200.00	200.00	200.00
104TC	3c	125.00	115.00	115.00	115.00	115.00
105TC	5c	"	"	"	"	"
106TC	10c	"	"	"	"	"
107TC	12c	"	"	"	"	"
108TC	15c	"	"	"	"	"
109TC	24c	"	"	"	"	"
110TC	30c	"	"	"	"	"
111TC	90c	"	"	"	"	"

1869 Designs

123TC	1c	200.00	175.00	175.00	175.00	175.00
124TC	2c	"	"	"	"	"
125TC	3c	"	"	"	"	"
126TC	6c	"	"	"	"	"
127TC	10c	"	"	"	"	"
128TC	12c	"	"	"	"	"
129TC	15c black frame, scarlet center	450.00				
"	15c " green center	"				
"	15c scarlet frame, black center	"				
"	15c " blue center	"				
"	15c brown frame, black center	"				
"	15c " green center	"				
"	15c " blue center	"				
"	15c green frame, black center	"				

		Black	Scarlet	Brown	Green	Blue
129TC	15c green frame, blue center	450.00				
"	15c blue frame, black center	"				
"	15c blue frame, brown center	"				
"	15c " green center	"				
130TC	24c black frame, scarlet center	"				
"	24c " green center	"				
"	24c " blue center	"				
"	24c scarlet frame, black center	"				
"	24c " blue center	"				
"	24c brown frame, black center	"				
"	24c " blue center	"				
"	24c green frame, black center	"				
"	24c " brown center	"				
"	24c " blue center	"				
"	24c blue frame, brown center	"				
"	24c " green center	"				
131TC	30c black frame, scarlet center	"				
"	30c " green center	"				
"	30c " blue center	"				
"	30c scarlet frame, black center	"				
"	30c " green center	"				
"	30c " blue center	"				
"	30c brown frame, black center	"				
"	30c " scarlet center	"				
"	30c " blue center	"				
"	30c green frame, black center	"				
"	30c " brown center	"				
"	30c blue frame, scarlet center	"				
"	30c " brown center	"				
"	30c " green center	"				
132TC	90c black frame, scarlet center	500.00				
"	90c " brown center	"				
"	90c " green center	"				
"	90c scarlet frame, blue center	"				
"	90c brown frame, black center	"				
"	90c " blue center	"				
"	90c green frame, brown center	"				
"	90c " blue center	"				
"	90c blue frame, brown center	"				
"	90c " green center	"				

1873-75 Designs

156TC	1c	60.00	55.00	55.00	55.00	55.00
157TC	2c	"	"	"	"	"
158TC	3c	65.00	60.00	60.00	60.00	60.00
159TC	6c	"	"	"	"	"
160TC	7c	60.00	55.00	55.00	55.00	55.00
161TC	10c	"	"	"	"	"
162TC	12c	"	"	"	"	"
163TC	15c	"	"	"	"	"
164TC	24c	"	"	"	"	"
165TC	30c	65.00	60.00	60.00	60.00	60.00
166TC	90c	60.00	55.00	55.00	55.00	55.00
179TC	5c	75.00	70.00	70.00	70.00	70.00

Postage Due

J1TC	1c	60.00	55.00	55.00	55.00	55.00
J2TC	2c	"	"	"	"	"
J3TC	3c	"	"	"	"	"
J4TC	5c	"	"	"	"	"
J5TC	10c	"	"	"	"	"
J6TC	30c	"	"	"	"	"
J7TC	50c	"	"	"	"	"

Carriers

LO1TC	1c Franklin	100.00	90.00	90.00	90.00	90.00
LO2TC	1c Eagle	"	"	"	"	"

Agriculture

O1TC	1c	45.00	40.00	40.00	40.00	40.00
O2TC	2c	"	"	"	"	"
O3TC	3c	"	"	"	"	"
O4TC	6c	55.00	50.00	50.00	50.00	50.00
O5TC	10c	45.00	40.00	40.00	40.00	40.00
O6TC	12c	"	"	"	"	"
O7TC	15c	"	"	"	"	"
O8TC	24c	"	"	"	"	"
O9TC	30c	"	"	"	"	"

Executive

O10TC	1c	"	"	"	"	"
O11TC	2c	"	"	"	"	"
O12TC	3c	"	"	"	"	"
O13TC	6c	55.00	50.00	50.00	50.00	50.00
O14TC	10c	45.00	40.00	40.00	40.00	40.00

Interior

O15TC	1c	"	"	"	"	"
O16TC	2c	"	"	"	"	"
O17TC	3c	"	"	"	"	"
O18TC	6c	55.00	50.00	50.00	50.00	50.00
O19TC	10c	45.00	40.00	40.00	40.00	40.00
O20TC	12c	"	"	"	"	"

TRIAL COLOR PROOFS

		Black	Scarlet	Brown	Green	Blue
O21TC	15c	45.00	40.00	40.00	40.00	40.00
O22TC	24c	"	"	"	"	"
O23TC	30c	60.00	55.00	55.00	55.00	55.00
O24TC	90c	45.00	40.00	40.00	40.00	40.00

Justice
O25TC	1c	"	"	"	"	"
O26TC	2c	"	"	"	"	"
O27TC	3c	"	"	"	"	"
O28TC	6c	55.00	50.00	50.00	50.00	50.00
O29TC	10c	45.00	40.00	40.00	40.00	40.00
O30TC	12c	"	"	"	"	"
O31TC	15c	"	"	"	"	"
O32TC	24c	"	"	"	"	"
O33TC	30c	60.00	55.00	55.00	55.00	55.00
O34TC	90c	45.00	40.00	40.00	40.00	40.00

Navy
O35TC	1c	"	"	"	"	"
O36TC	2c	"	"	"	"	"
O37TC	3c	"	"	"	"	"
O38TC	6c	55.00	50.00	50.00	50.00	50.00
O39TC	7c	45.00	40.00	40.00	40.00	40.00
O40TC	10c	"	"	"	"	"
O41TC	12c	"	"	"	"	"
O42TC	15c	"	"	"	"	"
O43TC	24c	"	"	"	"	"
O44TC	30c	60.00	55.00	55.00	55.00	55.00
O45TC	90c	45.00	40.00	40.00	40.00	40.00

Post Office
O48TC	2c	"	"	"	"	"
O49TC	3c	"	"	"	"	"
O50TC	6c	"	"	"	"	"
O51TC	10c	"	"	"	"	"
O52TC	12c	"	"	"	"	"
O53TC	15c	"	"	"	"	"
O54TC	24c	"	"	"	"	"
O55TC	30c	"	"	"	"	"
O56TC	90c	"	"	"	"	"

State
O57TC	1c	"	"	"	"	"
O58TC	2c	"	"	"	"	"
O59TC	3c	"	"	"	"	"
O60TC	6c	55.00	50.00	50.00	50.00	50.00
O61TC	7c	45.00	40.00	40.00	40.00	40.00
O62TC	10c	"	"	"	"	"
O63TC	12c	"	"	"	"	"
O64TC	15c	"	"	"	"	"
O65TC	24c	"	"	"	"	"
O66TC	30c	60.00	55.00	55.00	55.00	55.00
O67TC	90c	45.00	40.00	40.00	40.00	40.00
O68TC	$ 2.00 scarlet frame, black center	850.00				
"	$ 2.00 " blue center	"				
"	$ 2.00 brown frame, black center	"				
"	$ 2.00 " blue center	"				
"	$ 2.00 green frame, brown center	"				
"	$ 2.00 blue frame, brown center	"				
"	$ 2.00 " green center	"				
O69TC	$ 5.00 scarlet frame, black center	"				
"	$ 5.00 " blue center	"				
"	$ 5.00 brown frame, black center	"				
"	$ 5.00 " blue center	"				
"	$ 5.00 green frame, brown center	"				
"	$ 5.00 blue frame, brown center	"				
"	$ 5.00 " green center	"				
O70TC	$10.00 scarlet frame, black center	"				
"	$10.00 " blue center	"				
"	$10.00 brown frame, black center	"				
"	$10.00 " blue center	"				
"	$10.00 green frame, brown center	"				
"	$10.00 blue frame, brown center	"				
"	$10.00 " green center	"				
O71TC	$20.00 scarlet frame, black center	"				
"	$20.00 " blue center	"				
"	$20.00 brown frame, black center	"				
"	$20.00 " blue center	"				
"	$20.00 green frame, brown center	"				
"	$20.00 blue frame, brown center	"				
"	$20.00 " green center	"				

Treasury
		Black	Scarlet	Brown	Green	Blue
O72TC	1c	45.00	40.00	40.00	40.00	40.00
O73TC	2c	"	"	"	"	"
O74TC	3c	"	"	"	"	"
O75TC	6c	55.00	50.00	50.00	50.00	50.00
O76TC	7c	45.00	40.00	40.00	40.00	40.00
O77TC	10c	"	"	"	"	"
O78TC	12c	"	"	"	"	"
O79TC	15c	"	"	"	"	"
O80TC	24c	45.00	40.00	40.00	40.00	40.00
O81TC	30c	60.00	55.00	55.00	55.00	55.00
O82TC	90c	45.00	40.00	40.00	40.00	40.00

War
O83TC	1c	"	"	"	"	"
O84TC	2c	"	"	"	"	"
O85TC	3c	"	"	"	"	"
O86TC	6c	55.00	50.00	50.00	50.00	50.00
O87TC	7c	45.00	40.00	40.00	40.00	40.00
O88TC	10c	"	"	"	"	"
O89TC	12c	"	"	"	"	"
O90TC	15c	"	"	"	"	"
O91TC	24c	"	"	"	"	"
O92TC	30c	60.00	55.00	55.00	55.00	55.00
O93TC	90c	45.00	40.00	40.00	40.00	40.00

Newspapers
PR9TC	2c	45.00	30.00	30.00	30.00	30.00
PR10TC	3c	"	"	"	"	"
PR11TC	4c	"	"	"	"	"
PR12TC	6c	"	"	"	"	"
PR13TC	8c	"	"	"	"	"
PR14TC	9c	"	"	"	"	"
PR15TC	10c	"	"	"	"	"
PR16TC	12c	"	"	"	"	"
PR17TC	24c	"	"	"	"	"
PR18TC	36c	"	"	"	"	"
PR19TC	48c	"	"	"	"	"
PR20TC	60c	"	"	"	"	"
PR21TC	72c	"	"	"	"	"
PR22TC	84c	"	"	"	"	"
PR23TC	96c	"	"	"	"	"
PR24TC	$ 1.92	"	"	"	"	"
PR25TC	$ 3.00	"	"	"	"	"
PR26TC	$ 6.00	"	"	"	"	"
PR27TC	$ 9.00	"	"	"	"	"
PR28TC	$12.00	"	"	"	"	"
PR29TC	$24.00	"	"	"	"	"
PR30TC	$36.00	"	"	"	"	"
PR31TC	$48.00	"	"	"	"	"
PR32TC	$60.00	"	"	"	"	"

REVENUES.

Several lists of revenue proofs in trial colors have been published, but the accuracy of some of them is questionable. The following listings are limited to items seen by the editors. The list is not complete.

1862–71   FIRST ISSUE.

R3TC	1c Proprietary, black	Plate on India	80.00
"	1c " carmine	Plate on Card	110.00
"	1c " dull red	Plate on Bond	"
"	1c " dull yel.	Plate on Bond	"
"	1c " vio. rose	Plate on Bond	"
"	1c " deep blue	Plate on Bond	"
"	1c " red on blue, perf. & gum	Plate on Bond	"
R7TC	2c Certificate, ultra.	Plate on Card	
R11TC	2c Playing Cards, black	Die on India	65.00
R13TC	2c Proprietary, black	Plate on India	400.00
R15TC	2c U.S.I.R., violet rose	Plate on Bond	75.00
"	2c " light green	Plate on Bond	110.00
"	2c " pale blue	Plate on Card	"
"	2c " black	Plate on India	"
R16TC	3c Foreign Exchange, green on blue	Plate on Bond	"
"	3c Foreign Exchange, blue	Plate on Gold-beater's Skin	"
R18TC	3c Proprietary, black	Die on India	300.00
R21TC	4c Playing Cards, black	Die(?) on India	"
R22TC	4c Proprietary, black	Plate on India	110.00
"	4c " black	Die on India	350.00
"	4c " red lilac	Plate on Card	110.00
R24TC	5c Certificate, carmine	Plate on India	110.00
R26TC	5c Foreign Exchange, orange	Plate on India	110.00
R28TC	5c Playing Cards, black	Die(?) on India	300.00
R30TC	6c Inland Exchange, black	Die on India	350.00
R31TC	6c Proprietary, black	Die on India	—

726

TRIAL COLOR PROOFS

R32TC	10c Bill of Lading, greenish blue	Die on India	350.00
R35TC	10c Foreign Exchange, black	Die(?) on India	"
R37TC	10c Power of Attorney, greenish blue	Die on India	"
R38TC	10c Proprietary, black	Die on India	"
R43TC	25c Bond, carmine	Plate on Card	90.00
R46TC	25c Insurance, dull red	Plate on Bond	150.00
"	25c " dull red	Plate on Goldbeater's Skin	210.00
"	25c " vermilion	Plate on Goldbeater's Skin	"
"	25c " vermilion	Plate on Bond	170.00
"	25c " blue	Plate on Bond	"
"	25c " blue	Plate on Goldbeater's Skin	215.00
"	25c " dark blue	Plate on Bond	155.00
"	25c " dark blue	Plate on Goldbeater's Skin	215.00
"	25c " green	Plate on Goldbeater's Skin	215.00
R51TC	30c Foreign Exchange, violet	Plate on India	130.00
"	30c violet gray	Plate on India	"
"	30c black	Plate on India	155.00
"	30c red	Plate on India	"
R52TC	30c Inland Exchange, deep red lilac	Plate on India	"
R55TC	50c Entry of Goods, orange	Plate on Bond	275.00
"	50c green	Plate on Bond	"
"	50c red	Plate on Bond	340.00
R58TC	50c Life Insurance, ultramarine	Plate on India	85.00
R60TC	50c Original Process, black	Die(?) on India	280.00
R64TC	60c Inland Exchange, green	Die(?) on India	—
R65TC	70c Foreign Exchange, orange	Die(?) on India	—
R65TC	70c Foreign Exchange, black	Die(?) on India	285.00
R66TC	$1 Conveyance, carmine	Plate on India	85.00
R67TC	$1 Entry of Goods, carmine	Plate on India	60.00
R68TC	$1 Foreign Exchange, carmine	Plate on India	"
R69TC	$1 Inland Exchange, carmine	Plate on India	"
R70TC	$1 Lease, carmine	Plate on India	130.00
R71TC	$1 Life Insurance, carmine	Plate on India	75.00
R72TC	$1 Manifest, carmine	Plate on India	80.00
R73TC	$1 Mortgage, carmine	Plate on India	85.00
R74TC	$1 Passage Ticket, carmine	Plate on India	120.00
R75TC	$1 Power of Attorney, carmine	Plate on India	"
R76TC	$1 Probate of Will, carmine	Plate on India	60.00
R78TC	$1.50 Inland Exchange, black	Die on India	475.00
R80TC	$1.90 Foreign Exchange, black	Plate on India	155.00
R81TC	$2 Conveyance, carmine	Plate on Card	85.00
R82TC	$2 Mortgage, carmine	Plate on Card	"
R84TC	$2.50 Inland Exchange, black	Die(?) on India	120.00
R87TC	$3.50 Inland Exchange, black	Die on India	400.00
R88TC	$5 Charter Party, carmine	Plate on India	85.00
R89TC	$5 Conveyance, carmine	Plate on India	90.00
R91TC	$5 Mortgage, carmine	Plate on India	"
R95TC	$10 Mortgage, yel. green	Plate on India	—
R98TC	$20 Conveyance, red orange	Plate on Card	120.00
"	$20 red orange	Plate on Card	220.00
R99TC	$20 Probate of Will, red orange	Plate on Card	275.00
"	$20 black	Plate on Card	"
R101TC	$50 U.S.I.R., orange	Plate on Bond	"
"	$50 U.S.I.R., deep blue	Plate on Bond	"
R102TC	$200 U.S.I.R., black & red	Plate on India	1400.00
"	$200 gray brown & red	Plate on India	"
"	$200 green & brown red	Plate on India	"

SECOND ISSUE.

R104TC	2c pale blue & black	Plate on Bond	60.00
R132TC	$200 green, red & black	Die on India	2500.00
"	$200 orange	Die on India	"
"	$200 blue	Die on India	"
"	$200 green	Die on India	"
R133TC	$500 green, yel. & black	Die on India	"
"	$500 black	Plate on Card	3250.00
"	$500 yellow & black	Plate on Card	2500.00
"	$500 red, green & black	Plate on Bond	3000.00
"	$500 blue, scarlet & black	Plate on Bond	2500.00

THIRD ISSUE.

R134TC	1c brown & black	Plate on Card	60.00

1875   National Bank Note Co., New York Cit

R152TC	2c(Liberty), green	Die on India	600.00
"	2c " brown	Die on India	"
"	2c " black	Die on India	"

1898

R161TC	½c green	Large die on India	750.00
R163TC	1c green	Large die on India	"
"	1c black	Large die on India	"
R165TC	3c green	Small die on India	650.00
R169TC	25c green	Large die on India	"
R170TC	40c black	Large die on India	"
R172TC	80c green	Large die on India	"

1898

R174TC	$3 black	Die on India	"
R176TC	$10 green	Die on India	"

1899

R179TC	$100 dark green & black	Die on India	850.00
R181TC	$1000 dark blue & black	Die on India	"

1914

R195TC	½c black	Small die on Wove	—
R196TC	1c blue green	Small die on Wove	—
R198TC	3c ultramarine	Small die on Wove	—
R199TC	4c brown	Small die on Wove	—
R200TC	5c blue	Small die on Wove	—
R201TC	10c yellow	Small die on Wove	—
R202TC	25c dull violet	Small die on Wove	—
R203TC	40c blue green	Small die on Wove	—
R204TC	50c red brown	Small die on Wove	—
R205TC	80c orange	Small die on Wove	—

Proprietary.

1871–75

RB1TC	1c blue & black	Plate on Bond	70.00
"	1c scarlet & black	Plate on Bond	"
"	1c orange & black	Plate on Bond	"
"	1c orange & ultramarine	Plate on Granite Bond	60.00
RB3TC	3c blue & black, with gum	Plate on Bond	"
"	3c blue & black	Plate on Gray Bond	"
RB8TC	50c green & brown	Die on India	675.00
"	50c green & purple	Die on India	"
"	50c green & brown red	Die on India	"
"	50c green & violet	Die on India	"
"	50c green & dk. carmine	Die on India	"
"	50c ultramarine & red	Die on India	"
RB9TC	$1 green & brown	Die on India	"
"	$1 green & purple	Die on India	"
"	$1 green & violet brown	Die on India	"
"	$1 green & brown red	Die on India	"
"	$1 green & violet	Die on India	"
"	$1 green & dk. carmine	Die on India	"

1875–83

RB11TC	1c brown	Die on India	500.00
"	1c black	Die on India	"
RB12TC	2c green	Die on India	"
"	2c black	Die on India	"
"	2c brown	Die on India	"
RB13TC	3c brown	Die on India	"
"	3c green	Die on India	"
"	3c black	Plate on India	150.00
RB14TC	4c dark brown	Die on India	450.00
"	4c green	Die on India	"
"	4c black	Die on India	"
"	4c black	Plate on India	150.00
RB16TC	5c green	Die on India	450.00
RB17TC	6c green	Plate on India	150.00
"	6c black	Die on India	450.00
"	6c black	Plate on India	150.00
"	6c violet brown	Die on India	550.00
RB19TC	10c black	Die on India	550.00

TRIAL COLOR PROOFS

SECOND, THIRD AND PROPRIETARY ISSUES.
Stamps Nos. R103 to R131, R134 to R150 and RB1 to RB7.

A special composite plate was made and impressions taken in various colors and shades. Although all varieties in all colors must have been made, only those seen by the editors are listed.

PLATE PROOFS ON INDIA PAPER. CENTERS IN BLACK.

1871-75		a. Dark Purple	b. Dull Purple	c. Red Purple	d. Brown	e. Black Brown	f. Orange Brown	g. Light Blue	h. Dark Blue	i. Ultramarine	j. Bright Yellow Green, on Card	k. Yellow Green	l. Dark Yellow Green	m. Emerald Green
R103TC	1c	60.00	60.00		60.00	60.00		60.00	70.00	70.00		70.00		
R104TC	2c	"	"		"	"		"	"	"		"	70.00	
R105TC	3c	"	"		"	"		"	"	"		"		
R106TC	4c	"	"		"	"	65.00	"	"	"		"		
R107TC	5c	"	"		"	"	"	"	"	"		"		
R108TC	6c	"	"		"	"	"	"	"	"		"		
R109TC	10c	"	"		"	"		"	"	"		"		
R110TC	15c	"	"		"	"	"	"	"	"		"		
R111TC	20c	"	"		"	"		"	"	"		"		
R112TC	25c	"	"		"	"		"	"	"		"	70.00	
R113TC	30c	"	"		"	"		"	"	"		"		
R114TC	40c	"	"		"	"	"	"	"	"		"		
R115TC	50c	"	"		"	"		"	"	"		"		
R116TC	60c	"	"		"	"		"	"	"		"		
R117TC	70c	"	"		"	"		"	"	"		"		
R118TC	$1	70.00	70.00		70.00	70.00		80.00	82.50	82.50		77.50		
R119TC	$1.30	"	"		"	"		"	"	"	72.50	"		
R120TC	$1.50	"	"		"	"		"	"	"	"	"		
R121TC	$1.60	"	"		"	"		"	"	"		"		
R122TC	$1.90	"	"		"	"		"	"	"	"	"		
R123TC	$2	"	"		"	"		"	"	"	"	"		
R124TC	$2.50	"	"		"	"		"	"	"	"	"		
R125TC	$3	"	"		"	"		"	"	"	"	"		
R126TC	$3.50	"	"	75.00	"	"		"	"	"		"		
R127TC	$5	"	"		"	"		"	"	"		"		
R128TC	$10	"	"		"	"		"	"	"	"	75.00		
R129TC	$20	95.00	95.00		95.00	95.00		87.50	87.50	87.50		85.00		85.00
R130TC	$25	100.00	100.00		100.00	100.00		90.00	87.50	87.50		"		"
R131TC	$50	95.00	95.00		95.00	95.00		87.50	87.50	87.50	85.00	"		"
RB1TC	1c	67.50	67.50		65.00	65.00		75.00	75.00	75.00		70.00	70.00	
RB2TC	2c	"	"		"	"		70.00	70.00	70.00	70.00	"		
RB3TC	3c	"	"		"	"		"	"	"		"	"	
RB4TC	4c	"	"		"	"		"	"	"		"	"	
RB5TC	5c	"	"		"	"		"	"	"	"	"	"	
RB6TC	6c	"	"		"	"		"	"	"		"	"	
RB7TC	10c	"	"		"	"		"	"	"	"	"	"	

SECOND, THIRD AND PROPRIETARY ISSUES.

Stamps Nos. R103 to R131, R134 to R150 and RB1 to RB7.

PLATE PROOFS ON INDIA PAPER. CENTERS IN BLACK.

1871-75		n. Green	o. Dark Green	p. Blue Green	q. Light Orange	r. Dark Orange	s. Deep Orange	t. Scarlet	u. Carmine	v. Dark Carmine	w. Purplish Carmine	x. Dark Brown Red	y. Dark Brown Orange, Goldbeater's Skin
R103TC	1c	65.00	65.00	65.00	65.00	65.00	65.00	65.00	65.00			65.00	90.00
R104TC	2c	"	"	"	"	"	"	"	"			"	"
R105TC	3c	"	"	"	"	"	"	"	"			"	"
R106TC	4c	"	"	"	"	"	"	"	"			"	"
R107TC	5c	"	"	"	"	"	"	"	"	65.00	65.00	"	"
R108TC	6c	"	"	"	"	"	"	"	"	"	"	"	"
R109TC	10c	"	"	"	"	"	"	"	"			"	
R110TC	15c	"	"	"	"	"	"	"	"	"		"	
R111TC	20c	"	"	"	"	"	"	"	"		"	"	"
R112TC	25c	"	"	"	"	"	"	"	"			"	"
R113TC	30c	"	"	"	"	"	"	"	"	"	"	"	"
R114TC	40c	"	"	"	"	"	"	"	"			"	
R115TC	50c	"	"	"	"	"	"	"	"			"	
R116TC	60c	"	"	"	"	"	"	"	"	"		"	"
R117TC	70c	"	"	"	"	"	"	"	"			"	
R118TC	$1	72.50	72.50	72.50	72.50	72.50	72.50	77.50	77.50		77.50	77.50	"
R119TC	$1.30	"	"	"	"	"	"	"	"			"	
R120TC	$1.50	"	"	"	"	"	"	"	"			"	
R121TC	$1.60	"	"	"	"	"	"	"	"			"	
R122TC	$1.90	"	"	"	"	"	"	"	"			"	
R123TC	$2	"	"	"	"	"	"	"	"		"	"	100.00
R124TC	$2.50	"	"	"	"	"	"	"	"	77.50		"	
R125TC	$3	"	"	"	"	"	"	"	"			"	
R126TC	$3.50	"	"	"	"	"	"	87.50	"			"	
R127TC	$5	"	"	"	"	"	"	72.50	72.50		72.50	"	"
R128TC	$10	"	"	"	"	"	"	"	77.50			"	
R129TC	$20	"	"	"	"	85.00	85.00	87.50	"	87.50		"	
R130TC	$25	"	"	"	"	"	"	"	"			87.50	300.00	"
R131TC	$50	"	"	"	"	"	"	"	"			77.50	
RB1TC	1c	65.00	65.00	65.00	65.00	65.00	65.00	65.00	65.00			65.00	
RB2TC	2c	"	"	"	"	"	"	"	"			"	
RB3TC	3c	"	"	"	"	"	"	"	"			"	
RB4TC	4c	"	"	"	"	"	"	"	"			"	
RB5TC	5c	"	"	"	"	"	"	"	"			"	
RB6TC	6c	"	"	"	"	"	"	"	"			"	
RB7TC	10c	"	"	"	"	"	"	"	"			"	

TRIAL COLOR PROOFS

1898
RB21TC	¼c green	Large die on India	500.00
RB22TC	⅜c green	Large die on India	"
RB26TC	1⅞c green	Large die on India	"
"	1⅞c black	Large die on India	"
RB27TC	2c green	Small die on India	350.00
RB31TC	5c green	Small die on India	"

1918-29 Stock Transfer.
RD20TC	$50 black	Die on India	350.00
"	$50 blue	Die on India	"

1894 Playing Cards.
RF1TC	2c black (On hand)	Die on India	"
RF2TC	2c lake (Act of)	Die on India	"

Telegraph.

American Rapid Telegraph Co.

		DIE		PLATE	
		(2) Small	(3) India	(4) Card	
1T1TC	1c green	50.00			
"	1c brown	"			
"	1c red	"			
"	1c blue	"			
"	1c bluish green	"			
1T3TC	5c green	"			
"	5c black	"			
"	5c red	"			
"	5c blue	"			
"	5c bluish green	"			
1T5TC	15c red	"			
"	15c black	"			
"	15c brown	"			
"	15c bluish green	"			
1T6TC	20c green	"			
"	20c black	"			
"	20c brown	"			
"	20c blue	"			
"	20c bluish green	"			

Collect.

		DIE		PLATE	
		(1) Large	(2) Small	(3) India	(4) Card
1T10TC	5c red		50.00		
"	5c black		"		
"	5c brown		"		
"	5c green		"		
"	5c bluish green		"		
1T11TC	15c red		"		
"	15c black		"		
"	15c brown		"		
"	15c green		"		
"	15c blue		"		
"	15c bluish green		"		

Office Coupon.

1T14TC	5c red	50.00	
"	5c black	"	
"	5c brown	"	
"	5c green	"	
"	5c bluish green	"	

		DIE		PLATE	
		(1) Large	(2) Small	(3) India	(4) Card
1T15TC	15c red		50.00		
"	15c black		"		
"	15c brown		"		
"	15c green		"		
"	15c blue		"		
"	15c bluish green		"		

Baltimore & Ohio Telegraph Co.
3T2TC	5c dark olive	60.00	
3T4TC	25c dark olive	60.00	

Postal Telegraph Co.
5T1TC	10c brown red	60.00	
"	10c red	60.00	
"	10c blue	"	
"	10c black	"	
"	10c orange		60.00
15T2TC	15c black	"	50.00
"	15c red	50.00	
"	15c blue	"	"
"	25c brown red	60.00	
15T3TC	25c black	"	
"	25c red	"	
"	25c ultramarine		35.00
"	25c brown	"	"
15T4TC	50c dull blue	"	
"	50c black	"	"
"	50c red	"	
"	50c blue	"	
15T6TC	red brown		"

Western Union Telegraph Co.
16T1TC	lilac (1871)	18.00	18.00
"	Pair	40.00	40.00
"	orange	18.00	18.00
"	Pair	40.00	40.00
"	black	18.00	18.00
"	Pair	40.00	40.00
"	violet brown		18.00
"	Pair		40.00
"	light olive		18.00
"	Pair		40.00
"	brown		18.00
"	Pair		40.00
"	orange brown		18.00
"	Pair		40.00
"	blue green		18.00
"	Pair		40.00
16T6TC	violet blue (1876)	18.00	18.00
16T7TC	orange yellow (1877)		18.00
"	Pair		40.00
"	dark brown		18.00
"	Pair		40.00
"	black		18.00
"	Pane of four		—
16T8TC	dark brown (1878)		—
16T9TC	blue (1879)		—
16T10TC	violet brown (1880)		—
"	rose		—
16T22TC	black (1892)		25.00

SOUVENIR CARDS

These cards were issued as souvenirs of the philatelic gatherings at which they were distributed by the United States Postal Service, its predecessor the United States Post Office Department, or the Bureau of Engraving and Printing. They were not valid for postage.

Most of the cards bear reproductions of United States stamps with the design enlarged or altered by removal of denomination, country name and "Postage" or "Air Mail." The cards are not perforated.

A forerunner of the souvenir cards is the **1938** Philatelic Truck souvenir sheet which the Post Office Department issued and distributed in various cities visited by the Philatelic Truck. It shows the White House, printed in blue on white paper. Issued with and without gum. Price, with gum, $85; without gum, $15.

1954

1 Postage Stamp Design Exhibition, National Philatelic Museum, Mar. 13, 1954, Philadelphia. Card of 4. Monochrome views of Washington, D.C. Inscribed: "Souvenir sheet designed, engraved and printed by members, Bureau, Engraving and Printing. / Reissued by popular request" 1,750.

SOUVENIR CARDS

1960

2. Barcelona, 1st International Philatelic Congress, Mar. 26–Apr. 5, 1960. Enlarged vignette, Landing of Columbus from No. 231. Printed in black (P.O.D.) — 375.00

1966

3. SIPEX, 6th International Philatelic Exhibition, May 21–30, 1966, Washington, D.C. Card of 3. Multicolored views of Washington, D.C. Inscribed: "Sixth International Philatelic Exhibition / Washington, D.C. / Designed, Engraved, and Printed by Union Members of Bureau of Engraving and Printing" — 200.00

1968

4. EFIMEX, International Philatelic Exhibition, Nov. 1–9, 1968, Mexico City. No. 292 enlarged to 58x 37½mm. Card inscribed in Spanish (P.O.D.) — 4.00

1969

5. SANDIPEX, San Diego Philatelic Exhibition, July 16–20, 1969, San Diego, Cal. Card of 3. Multicolored views of Washington, D.C. Inscribed: "Sandipex—San Diego 200th Anniversary—1769–1969" (B.E.P.) — 85.00
6. A.S.D.A. National Postage Stamp Show, Nov. 21–23, 1969, New York. Card of 4. No. E4 reengraved. Denomination and "United States" removed (B.E.P.) — 30.00

1970

7. INTERPEX, Mar. 13–15, 1970, New York. Card of 4. Nos. 1027, 1035, C35 and C38 reengraved. Denomination, etc. removed (B.E.P.) — 70.00
8. COMPEX, Combined Philatelic Exhibition of Chicagoland, May 29–31, 1970, Chicago. Card of 4 No. C18 reengraved. Denomination, etc. removed (B.E.P.) — 20.00
9. PHILYMPIA, London International Stamp Exhibition, Sept. 18–26 1970. Card of 3, Nos. 548–550 enlarged 1½ times (P.O.D.) — 3.00
10. HAPEX, American Philatelic Society Convention, Nov. 5–8, 1970, Honolulu, Hawaii. Card of 3, Nos. 799, C46 and C55 reengraved. Denomination, etc. removed (B.E.P.) — 20.00

1971

11. INTERPEX, Mar. 12–14, 1971, New York. Card of 4 No. 1193 reengraved. Denomination removed. Background tint includes enlargements of Nos. 1331–1332, 1371 and C76 (B.E.P.) — 3.50
12. WESTPEX, Western Philatelic Exhibition, Apr. 23–25, 1971, San Francisco. Card of 4, Nos. 740, 852, 966 and 997. Denomination, etc. removed (B.E.P.) — 3.50
13. NAPEX 71, National Philatelic Exhibition, May 21–23, 1971, Washington, D.C. Card of 3, Nos. 990, 991, 992. Denomination, etc. removed (B.E.P.) — 3.50
14. TEXANEX 71, Texas Philatelic Association and American Philatelic Society conventions, Aug. 26–29, 1971, San Antonio, Tex. Card of 3, Nos. 938, 1043 and 1242. Denomination, etc. removed (B.E.P.) — 4.00
15. EXFILIMA 71, 3rd Inter-American Philatelic Exhibition, Nov. 6–14, 1971, Lima, Peru. Card of 3. Nos. 1111 and 1126 with denomination, etc. removed. Reproduction of Peru No. 300. Card inscribed in Spanish (U.S.P.S.) — 2.25
16. A.S.D.A. National Postage Stamp Show, Nov. 19–21, 1971, New York. Card of 3, Nos. C13–C15. Denomination, etc. removed (B.E.P.) — 3.50
17. ANPHILEX '71, Anniversary Philatelic Exhibition, Nov. 26–Dec. 1, 1971, New York. Card of 2, Nos. 1–2. Denomination, etc. removed (B.E.P.) — 2.00

1972

18. INTERPEX, Mar. 17–19, 1972, New York. Card of 4 No. 1173. Denomination, etc. removed. Background tint includes enlargements of Nos. 976, 1434–1435 and C69 (B.E.P.) — 2.00
19. NOPEX, Apr. 6–9, 1972, New Orleans. Card of 4 No. 1020. Denomination, etc. removed. Background tint includes enlargements of Nos. 323–327 (B.E.P.) — 2.00
20. BELGICA 72, Brussels International Philatelic Exhibition, June 24–July 9, 1972, Brussels, Belgium. Card of 3. No. 914 enlarged to 55x34mm. Nos. 1026 and 1104 with denomination, etc. removed. Card inscribed in Flemish and French (U.S.P.S.) — 2.25
21. Olympia Philatelie München 72, Aug. 18–Sept. 10, 1972, Munich, Germany. Card of 4, Nos. 1460–1462 and C85 enlarged to 54x32mm. Card inscribed in German (U.S.P.S.) — 2.25
22. EXFILBRA 72, 4th Inter-American Philatelic Exhibition, Aug. 26–Sept. 2, 1972, Rio de Janeiro, Brazil. Card of 3. No. C14 enlarged to 69½x 28½mm. and reproductions of Brazil Nos. C18–C19. Card inscribed in Portuguese (U.S.P.S.) — 2.25
23. National Philatelic Forum VI, Aug. 28–30, 1972, Washington, D.C. Card of 4 No. 1396 enlarged to 26x31mm. (U.S.P.S.) — 2.50
24. SEPAD '72, Oct. 20–22, 1972, Philadelphia. Card of 4 No. 1044 reengraved, denomination, etc. removed (B.E.P.) — 3.00
25. A.S.D.A. National Postage Stamp Show, Nov. 17–19, 1972, New York. Card of 4, Nos. 883, 863, 868 and 888. Denomination, etc. removed (B.E.P.) — 2.00
26. STAMP EXPO, Nov. 24–26, 1972, San Francisco. Card of 4 No. C36 re-engraved with denomination, etc. removed (B.E.P.) — 2.50

1973

27. INTERPEX, Mar. 9–11, 1973, New York. Card of 4 No. 976. Denomination, etc. removed (B.E.P.) — 3.00
28. IBRA 73 International Philatelic Exhibition, Munich, May 11–20, 1973. No. C13 enlarged to 70x 29mm. (U.S.P.S.) — 3.00
29. COMPEX 73, May 25–27, 1973, Chicago. Card of 4 No. 245. Denomination, etc. removed (B.E.P.) — 2.00
30. APEX 73, International Airmail Exhibition, Manchester, England, July 4–7, 1973. Card of 3. No. C3a enlarged to 34x29mm., enlarged reproductions of Newfoundland No. C4 and Honduras No. C12 (U.S.P.S.) — 2.00
31. POLSKA 73, World Philatelic Exhibition, Poznan, Poland, Aug. 19–Sept. 2, 1973. Card of 3. No. 1488 enlarged to 32x55mm., enlarged reproductions of Poland Nos. 1944–1945. Card inscribed in Polish (U.S.P.S.) — 3.50
32. NAPEX 73, Sept. 14–16, 1973, Washington, D.C. Card of 4 No. C3. Denomination. etc. removed. Background tint includes montage of enlarged reproductions of C4–C6 (B.E.P.) — 2.50
33. A.S.D.A. National Postage Stamp Show, Nov. 16–18, 1973, New York. Card of 4 No. 908 reengraved. Denomination, etc. removed. Foreground includes enlarged reproductions of Nos. 1139–1144 (B.E.P.) — 2.50
34. STAMP EXPO NORTH, Dec. 7–9, 1973, San Francisco. Card of 4 No. C20. Denomination, etc. removed. (B.E.P.) — 2.50

A card of 10, Nos. 1489–1498, was distributed to postal employees. Not available to public. Size: about 14x11 inches.

1974

35. National Hobby Industry Trade Show, Feb. 3–6, 1974, Chicago. Card of 4; block of Nos. 1456–1459 reduced to 61x39mm. Enlarged reproductions of silversmith (from No. 1457) and glassmaker (from No. 1456) (U.S.P.S.) — 3.50
36. MILCOPEX 1974, Mar. 8–10, 1974, Milwaukee. Card of 4 No. C43. Denomination, etc. removed (B.E.P.) — 3.50
37. INTERNABA 1974, June 6, 1974, Basel, Switzerland. Card of 8, strip of Nos. 1530–1537 reduced to 175x35mm. Card inscribed in German, French, and Italian (U.S.P.S.) — 4.00
38. STOCKHOLMIA 74, International Philatelic Exhibition, September 21–29, 1974, Stockholm, Sweden. Card of 3 No. 836 enlarged to 34x35mm., enlarged reproductions of Sweden Nos. 300 and 767. Card inscribed in Swedish. (U.S.P.S.) — 4.00
39. EXFILMEX 74, Interamerican Philatelic Exposition, Oct. 26–Nov. 3, 1974, Mexico City. Card of 2. No. 1157 enlarged to 39x61 mm. Enlarged reproduction of Mexico No. 910. Card inscribed in Spanish. (U.S.P.S.) — 4.00

1975

40. ESPANA 75, World Stamp Exhibition, Apr. 4–13, Madrid. Card of 3 No. 233 enlarged to 52x34 mm., No. 1271 and Spain No. 1312 reduced to 16x27 mm. Card inscribed in Spanish. (U.S.P.S.) — 3.00
41. NAPEX 75, May 9–11, 1975, Washington, D.C. Card of 4 No. 708. Denomination, etc. removed. (B.E.P.) — 10.00
42. ARPHILA 75, June 6–16, 1975, Paris. Card of 3. Designs of No. 1187 enlarged to 32x55 mm., No. 1207 enlarged to 55x32 mm. Reproduction of France No. 1117. Card inscribed in French. (U.S.P.S.) — 3.00
43. International Women's Year, 1975. Card of 3 Nos. 872, 878, and 959. Denomination, etc. removed. Reproduction of 1886 dollar bill. (B.E.P.) — 35.00

SOUVENIR CARDS

44 A.S.D.A. National Postage Stamp Show, Nov. 21-23, 1975. Bicentennial series. Card of 4 No. 1003 reengraved. Denomination, etc. removed. Bicentennial insignia, Trumbull's Washington with his words, "...and maintain the liberty which we have derived from our ancestors" (B.E.P.) ... 50.00

1976

45 WERABA 76, Third International Space Stamp Exhibition, April 1-4, 1976, Zurich, Switzerland. Card of 2, Nos. 1434 and 1435 se-tenant enlarged to 114x32 mm. Quotation "Man is his own star..." (U.S.P.S.) ... 5.00

46 INTERPHIL 76, Seventh International Philatelic Exhibition, May 29-June 6, 1976. Philadelphia, Pa. Bicentennial series. Card of 4 No. 120. Denominations, etc. removed. Bicentennial insignia. Bust of Jefferson with words "...that all men are created equal." Reading of the Declaration of Independence. (B.E.P.) ... 10.00

An Interphil '76 card issued by the American Revolution Bicentennial Administration was bound into the Interphil program. It shows an altered No. 1044 in black brown, the Bicentennial emblem and a view of Independence Hall. Printed by B.E.P.

48 Bicentennial Exposition on Science and Technology, May 30-Sept. 6, 1976, Kennedy Space Center, Fla. No. C76 enlarged to 75x41 mm. (U.S.P.S.) ... 5.00

49 STAMP EXPO 76, June 11-13, 1976, Los Angeles, Calif. Bicentennial series. Card of 4, Nos. 1351, 1352, 1345 and 1348 se-tenant vertically. Denominations, etc. removed (B.E.P.) ... 9.00

50 Colorado Statehood Centennial, August 1, 1976. Card of 3, Nos. 743 and 288 denominations, etc. removed and No. 1670 (Colorado state flag) enlarged. (U.S.P.S.) ... 5.00

51 HAFNIA 76, International Stamp Exhibition, Copenhagen, Denmark, August 20-29, 1976. Card of 2. No. 5 and Denmark No. 2 enlarged. Card inscribed in Danish and English. (U.S.P.S.) ... 4.50

52 ITALIA 76, International Philatelic Exhibition, Oct. 14-24, 1976, Milan, Italy. Card of 3. No. 1168 and Italy Nos. 578 and 601. Card inscribed in Italian. (U.S.P.S.) ... 4.50

53 NORDPOSTA 76, North German Stamp Exhibition, Oct. 30-31, Hamburg, Germany. Card of 3. No. 689 and Germany Nos. B366 and B417. Card inscribed in German. (U.S.P.S.) ... 4.50

1977

54 MILCOPEX, Milwaukee Philatelic Society, Mar. 4-6, Milwaukee. Card of 2, Nos. 733 and 1128. (B.E.P.) ... 3.75

55 ROMPEX 77, Rocky Mountain Philatelic Exhibition, May 20-22, Denver. Card of 4. No. 1001. (B.E.P.) ... 4.00

56 AMPHILEX 77, International Philatelic Exhibition, May 26-June 5, Amsterdam, Netherlands. Card of 3. No. 1027 and Netherlands Nos. 41 and 294. Card inscribed in Dutch. (U.S.P.S.) ... 4.50

57 SAN MARINO 77, International Philatelic Exhibition, San Marino, Aug. 28-Sept. 4. Card of 3. Nos. 1-2 and San Marino No. 1. Card inscribed in Italian. (U.S.P.S.) ... 4.50

58 PURIPEX 77, Silver Anniversary Philatelic Exhibit, Sept. 2-5, San Juan, Puerto Rico. Card of 4 No. 801. (B.E.P.) ... 3.50

59 A.S.D.A. National Postage Stamp Show, Nov. 15-20, New York. Card of 4 No. C45. (B.E.P.) ... 4.50

1978

60 ROCPEX 78, International Philatelic Exhibition, Mar. 20-29, Taipei, Taiwan. Card of 6. Nos. 1706-1709 and China Nos. 1812 and 1816. Card inscribed in Chinese. (U.S.P.S.) ... 5.50

61 NAPOSTA '78 Philatelic Exhibition, May 20-25, Frankfurt, Germany. Card of 3. Nos. 555, 563 and Germany No. 1216. Card inscribed in German. (U.S.P.S.) ... 5.50

62 CENJEX 78, Federated Stamp Clubs of New Jersey, 30th annual exhibition, June 23-25, Freehold, N. J. Card of 9. Nos. 646, 680, 689, 1086, 1716 and 4 No. 785. (B.E.P.) ... 5.50

1979

63 BRASILIANA 79, International Philatelic Exhibition, Sept. 15-23, Rio de Janeiro. Card of 3. Nos. C91-C92 and Brazil No. 1295. Card inscribed in Portuguese. (U.S.P.S.) ... 7.50

64 JAPEX 79, International Philatelic Exhibition, Nov. 2-4, Tokyo. Card of 2. No. 1158 and Japan No. 1024. Card inscribed in Japanese. (U.S.P.S.) ... 7.50

1980

65 LONDON 1980, International Philatelic Exhibition, May 6-14, London. No. 329 enlarged. (U.S.P.S.) ... 6.50

66 NORWEX 80, International Stamp Exhibition, June 13-22, Oslo. Card of 3. Nos. 620-621 and Norway No. 658. Card inscribed in Norwegian. (U.S.P.S.) ... 5.50

67 NAPEX 80, July 4-6, Washington, D.C. Card of 4. No. 573. (B.E.P.) ... 15.00

68 A.S.D.A. Stamp Festival, Sept. 25-28, 1980, New York, N.Y. Card of 4 No. 962. (B.E.P.) ... 17.50

69 ESSEN 80, Third International Stamp Fair, Nov. 15-19, Essen, West Germany. Card of 2. No. 1014 and Germany No. 723. Card inscribed in German. (U.S.P.S.) ... 5.50

1981

70 STAMP EXPO '81 SOUTH, Mar. 20-22, Anaheim, Calif. Card of 6. Nos. 1331-1332, 4 of No. 1287. (B.E.P.) ... 15.00

71 WIPA 1981, International Stamp Exhibition, May 22-31, Vienna, Austria. Card of 2. No. 1252 and Austria No. 789. Card inscribed in German. (U.S.P.S.) ... 5.00

72 National Stamp Collecting Month, October, 1981. Card of 2. Nos. 245 and 1918, enlarged. (U.S.P.S.) ... 5.00

73 PHILATOKYO '81, International Stamp Exhibition, Oct. 9-18. Tokyo. Card of 2. No. 1531 and Japan No. 800. Card inscribed in Japanese. (U.S.P.S.) ... 6.00

74 NORDPOSTA 81, North German Stamp Exhibition, Nov. 7-8. Hamburg, Germany. Card of 2. No. 923 and Germany No. B538. Card inscribed in German. (U.S.P.S.) ... 5.00

1982

75 MILCOPEX '82, Milwaukee Philatelic Association Exhibition, Mar. 5-7, Milwaukee, Wis. Card of 4. No. 1137. (B.E.P.) ... 15.00

76 CANADA 82, international philatelic youth exhibition, May 20-24, Toronto. Card of 2. No. 116 and Canada No. 15. Card inscribed in French and English. (U.S.P.S.) ... 5.00

77 PHILEXFRANCE '82, International Philatelic Exhibition, June 11-21, Paris, Card of 2. No. 1753 and France No. 1480. Card inscribed in French. (U.S.P.S.) ... 4.00

78 National Stamp Collecting Month, October. Card of 1. No. C3a. (U.S.P.S.) ... 6.00

79 ESPAMER '82, International Philatelic Exhibition, Oct. 12-17, San Juan, P.R. Card of 4. No. 244. Card inscribed in English and Spanish (B.E.P.) ... 30.00

80 ESPAMER '82, International Philatelic Exhibition, Oct. 12-17, San Juan, P.R. Card of 3. Nos. 801, 1437 and 2024. Card inscribed in Spanish and English. (U.S.P.S.) ... 6.00

1983

81 Joint stamp issues, Sweden and U.S.A. Mar. 24. Card of 3. Nos. 958, 2036 and Sweden No. 1453, all enlarged. Card inscribed in Swedish and English. (U.S.P.S.) ... 5.00

82 Joint stamp issues, Germany and U.S.A. Apr. 29. Card of 2. No. 2040 and Germany No. 1397, both enlarged. Card inscribed in German and English. (U.S.P.S.) ... 5.00

83 TEMBAL 83, International Philatelic Exhibition, Mar. 21-29, Basel. Card of 2. No. C71 and Switzerland, Basel No. 3L1, both enlarged. Card inscribed in German. (U.S.P.S.) ... 5.00

84 TEXANEX-TOPEX '83 Exhibition, June 17-19, San Antonio, Texas. Card of 5. No. 1660, enlarged, and No. 776, block of 4, both with denomination removed. (B.E.P.) ... 15.00

85 BRASILIANA 83, International Philatelic Exhibition, July 29-Aug. 7, Rio de Janeiro. Card of 2. No. 2 and Brazil No. 1, both enlarged. Card inscribed in Portuguese (U.S.P.S.) ... 5.00

86 BANGKOK 83, International Philatelic Exhibition, Aug. 4-13, Bangkok, Thailand. Card of 2. No. 210 and Thailand No. 1, both enlarged. Card inscribed in Thai. (U.S.P.S.) ... 5.00

87 International Philatelic Memento, 1983-84. Card of one. No. 1387, enlarged. (U.S.P.S.) ... 2.50

88 National Stamp Collecting Month, October. Card of 1. No. 293, enlarged and bicolored. (U.S.P.S.) ... 5.00

89 Philatelic Show '83, Boston, Oct. 21-23. Card of 2, Nos. 718-719. (B.E.P.) ... 15.00

90 ASDA 1983, National Postage Stamp Show, New York, Nov. 17-20. Card of 4, No. 881. Denominations, etc. removed. (B.E.P.) ... 15.00

1984

91 ESPANA 84, World Exhibition of Philately. Madrid, Apr. 27-May 6. Card of 4, No. 241. Denominations removed. Enlarged vignette, Landing of Columbus, from No. 231 at right. Card inscribed in English and Spanish (B.E.P.) ... 12.00

1984

92 ESPANA 84, International Philatelic Exhibition, Madrid, Apr. 27-May 6. Card of 2, No. 233 and Spain No. 428, both enlarged. Card inscribed in Spanish. (U.S.P.S.) ... 5.00
93 Stamp Expo '84 South, Anaheim, Calif., Apr. 27-29. Card of 4, Nos. 1791-1794, with Olympic torch. (B.E.P.) ... 12.00
94 COMPEX '84, Rosemont, Ill., May 25-27. Card of 4, No. 728. (B.E.P.) ... 12.00
95 HAMBURG '84, International Exhibition for 19th UPU Congress, Hamburg, Germany, June 19-26. Card of 2, No. C66 and Germany No. 669, both enlarged. Card inscribed in English, French and German. (U.S.P.S.) ... 5.00
96 St. Lawrence Seaway, 25th anniversary, June 26. Card of 2, No. 1131 and Canada No. 387, both enlarged. Card inscribed in English and French. (U.S.P.S.) ... 5.00
97 AUSIPEX '84, Australia's first international exhibition, Melbourne, Sept. 21-30. Card of 2, No. 290 and Western Australia No. 1, both enlarged. Card inscribed in English. (U.S.P.S.) ... 5.00
98 National Stamp Collecting Month, October. Card of 1, No. 2104, enlarged and tricolored. Card inscribed in English. (U.S.P.S.) ... 5.00
99 PHILAKOREA '84, Seoul, Oct. 22-31. Card of 2, No. 741 and Korea No. 994, both enlarged. Card inscribed in Korean and English. (U.S.P.S.) ... 5.00

1985

100 ASDA 1984, National Postage Stamp Show, New York, NY, Nov. 15-18. Card of 4, No. 1470. Denominations removed. (B.E.P.) ... 10.00
101 International Philatelic Memento, 1985. Card of 1, No. 2, enlarged. (U.S.P.S.) ... 3.00
102 OLYMPHILEX '85. International Philatelic Exhibition, Lausanne, Switzerland, Mar. 18-24. Card of 2, No. C106 and Switzerland No. 746, both enlarged. Card inscribed in French and English. (U.S.P.S.) ... 5.00
103 ISRAPHIL '85. International Philatelic Exhibition, Tel Aviv, Israel, May 14-22. Card of 2, No. 566 and Israel No. 33, both enlarged. Card inscribed in Hebrew and English. (U.S.P.S.) ... 5.00
104 LONG BEACH '85, Numismatic and Philatelic Exposition, Long Beach, CA, Jan. 31-Feb. 3. Card of 4, No. 954, plus a Series 1865 $20 Gold Certificate. Stamp denominations removed. (B.E.P.) ... 10.00
105 MILCOPEX '85, Milwaukee Philatelic Society annual stamp show, Milwaukee, WI, Mar. 1-3. Card of 4, No. 880. Denominations, etc., removed. (B.E.P.) ... 10.00
106 NAPEX '85, National Philatelic Exhibition, Arlington, VA, June 7-9. Card of 4, No. 2014. Denominations defaced with diagonal lines. (B.E.P.) ... 10.00
107 ARGENTINA '85, International Philatelic Exhibition, Buenos Aires, July 5-14. Card of 2, No. 1737 and Argentina No. B27, both enlarged. Card inscribed in Spanish. (U.S.P.S.) ... 4.00
108 MOPHILA '85, International Philatelic Exhibition, Hamburg, Sept. 11-15. Card of 2, No. 296 and Germany No. B595, both enlarged. Card inscribed in German. (U.S.P.S.) ... 4.00
109 ITALIA '85, International Phialtelic Exhibition, Rome, Oct. 25-Nov. 3. Card of 2, No. 1107 and Italy No. 830, both enlarged. Card inscribed in Italian. (U.S.P.S.) ... 4.00

1986

110 Statue of Liberty Centennial, National Philatelic Memento, 1986. Card of 1, No. C87, enlarged, (U.S.P.S.) ... 2.00
111 Garfield Perry Stamp Club, National Stamp Show, Cleveland, OH, Mar. 21-23. Card of 4, No. 306. Denominations, etc., removed (B.E.P.) ... 8.00
112 AMERIPEX '86, International Philatelic Exhibition, Chicago, IL, May 22-June 1. Card of 3, Nos. 134, 2052 and 1474. Denominations, etc., removed, or stamp enlarged. (B.E.P.) ... 8.00

COMMEMORATIVE PANELS

The Postal Service began issuing commemorative panels Sept. 20, 1972, with the Wildlife Conservation issue, Nos. 1464–1467. Each panel is devoted to a separate issue. It includes unused examples of the stamp or stamps, usually a block of four; reproductions of steel engravings, and background information on the subject of the issue.

1972
1CP	Wildlife Conservation, #1464–1467	11.00
2CP	Mail Order, #1468	11.00
3CP	Osteopathic Medicine, #1469	11.00
4CP	Tom Sawyer, #1470	11.00
5CP	Pharmacy, #1473	11.00
6CP	Christmas, 1972 (angel), #1471	12.50
7CP	Santa Claus, #1472	12.50
8CP	Stamp Collecting, #1474	11.00

1973
9CP	Love, #1475	11.00
10CP	Pamphleteers, #1476	12.50
11CP	George Gershwin, #1484	12.50
12CP	Posting a Broadside, #1477	12.50
13CP	Copernicus, #1488	11.00
14CP	Postal Service Employees, #1489–1498	12.50
15CP	Harry S. Truman, #1499	20.00
16CP	Postrider, #1478	22.00
17CP	Boston Tea Party, #1480–1483	33.00
18CP	Electronics Progress, #1500–1502, C86	12.50
19CP	Robinson Jeffers, #1485	12.50
20CP	Lyndon B. Johnson, #1503	20.00
21CP	Henry O. Tanner, #1486	12.50
22CP	Willa Cather, #1487	12.50
23CP	Drummer, #1479	22.00
24CP	Angus and Longhorn Cattle, #1504	11.00
25CP	Christmas, 1973 (Madonna), #1507	12.50
26CP	Christmas Tree, needlepoint, #1508	12.50

1974
27CP	Veterans of Foreign Wars, #1525	11.00
28CP	Robert Frost, #1526	11.00
29CP	EXPO '74, #1527	11.00
30CP	Horse Racing, #1528	11.00
31CP	Skylab, #1529	12.50
32CP	Universal Postal Union, #1530–1537	16.50
33CP	Mineral Heritage, #1538–1541	12.50
34CP	Kentucky Settlement (Ft. Harrod), #1542	11.00
35CP	First Continental Congress, #1543–1546	11.00
36CP	Chautauqua, #1505	11.00
37CP	Kansas Wheat, #1506	11.00
38CP	Energy Conservation, #1547	11.00
39CP	Sleepy Hollow Legend, #1548	11.00
40CP	Retarded Children, #1549	11.00
41CP	Christmas, 1974 (Currier-Ives), #1551	18.75
42CP	Christmas, 1974 (angel), #1550	13.75

1975
43CP	Benjamin West, #1553	11.00
44CP	Pioneer 10, #1556	13.50
45CP	Collective Bargaining, #1558	11.00
46CP	Contributors to the Cause, #1559–1562	11.00
47CP	Mariner 10, #1557	13.50
48CP	Lexington-Concord Battle, #1563	13.50
49CP	Paul Laurence Dunbar, #1554	11.00
50CP	D. W. Griffith, #1555	11.00
51CP	Battle of Bunker Hill, #1564	13.50
52CP	Military Services (uniforms), #1565–1568	16.50
53CP	Apollo Soyuz, #1569–1570	13.50
54CP	World Peace through Law, #1576	11.00
55CP	International Women's Year, #1571	11.00
56CP	Postal Service 200 Years, #1572–1575	13.50
57CP	Banking and Commerce, #1577–1578	11.00
58CP	Early Christmas Card, #1580	13.75
59CP	Christmas, 1975 (Madonna), #1579	13.75

1976
60CP	Spirit of '76, #1629–1631	16.50
61CP	Interphil '76, #1632	13.50
62CP	State Flags, block of 4 from #1633–1682	17.50
63CP	Telephone Centenary, #1683	11.00
64CP	Commercial Aviation, #1684	11.00
65CP	Chemistry, #1685	11.00
66CP	Benjamin Franklin, #1690	13.50
67CP	Declaration of Independence, #1691–1694	13.50
68CP	12th Winter Olympics, #1695–1698	12.50
69CP	Clara Maass, #1699	12.50
70CP	Adolph S. Ochs, #1700	11.00
71CP	Christmas, 1976 (Currier print), #1702	13.50
72CP	Christmas, 1976 (Copley Nativity), #1701	13.50

1977
73CP	Washington at Princeton, #1704	19.00
74CP	Sound Recording, #1705	22.50
75CP	Pueblo Art, #1706–1709	—
76CP	Lindbergh Flight, #1710	
77CP	Colorado Statehood, #1711	22.50
78CP	Butterflies, #1712–1715	22.50
79CP	Lafayette, #1716	22.50
80CP	Skilled Hands for Independence, #1717–1720	22.50
81CP	Peace Bridge, #1721	22.50
82CP	Battle of Oriskany, #1722	22.50
83CP	Energy Conservation-Development, #1723–1724	22.50
84CP	Alta California, #1725	22.50
85CP	Articles of Confederation, #1726	22.50
86CP	Talking Pictures, #1727	22.50
87CP	Surrender at Saratoga, #1728	22.50
88CP	Christmas, 1977 (Washington at Valley Forge), #1729	22.50
89CP	Christmas, 1977 (rural mailbox), #1730	22.50

1978
90CP	Carl Sandburg, #1731	11.00
91CP	Captain Cook, #1732–1733	27.50
92CP	Harriet Tubman, #1744	11.00
93CP	American Quilts, #1745–1748	22.50
94CP	American Dance, #1749–1752	11.00
95CP	French Alliance, #1753	11.00
96CP	Pap Test, #1754	11.00
97CP	Jimmie Rodgers, #1755	11.00
98CP	Photography, #1758	11.00
99CP	George M. Cohan, #1756	11.00
100CP	Viking Missions, #1759	27.50
101CP	American Owls, #1760–1763	22.50
102CP	American Trees, #1764–1767	22.50
103CP	Christmas, 1978 (Madonna), #1768	11.00
104CP	Christmas, 1978 (hobby-horse), #1769	11.00

1979
105CP	Robert F. Kennedy, #1770	9.00
106CP	Martin Luther King, Jr., #1771	9.00
107CP	Year of the Child, #1772	10.00
108CP	John Steinbeck, #1773	9.00
109CP	Albert Einstein, #1774	9.00
110CP	Pennsylvania Toleware, #1775–1778	12.50
111CP	American Architecture, #1779–1782	12.50
112CP	Endangered Flora, #1783–1786	9.00
113CP	Seeing Eye Dogs, #1787	9.00
114CP	Special Olympics, #1788	9.00
115CP	John Paul Jones, #1789	9.00
116CP	Olympic Games, #1790–1794	25.00
117CP	Christmas, 1979 (Madonna), #1799	11.00
118CP	Christmas, 1979 (Santa Claus), #1800	11.00
119CP	Will Rogers, #1801	9.00
120CP	Viet Nam Veterans, #1802	8.00

"SPECIMEN" STAMPS

These are regular stamps overprinted "Specimen." Each number has a suffix letter "S" to denote Specimen. The number is that of the regular stamp, and the second letter "A", etc., indicates the type of overprint.

Type A *Specimen* 12 mm. long.

Type B *Specimen.* 15 mm. long.

Type C *Specimen.* 30 mm. long.

Type D SPECIMEN Capital Letters.

Type E Specimen. Initial Capital.

Type F *Specimen.* 22 mm. long

Type G SPECIMEN 14 mm. long

Type H SPECIMEN 16 mm. long

Type I *Specimen* 20 mm. long.

REGULAR ISSUES.

Overprinted *Specimen* in Black.

Type A. Overprint 12mm. long.

1851–56
7S A	1c blue, Type II	200.00
11S A	3c dull red, Type I	950.00

1857–60
21S A	1c blue, Type III	1500.00
24S A	1c blue, Type V	1000.00
26S A	3c dull red, Type II	"
30S A	5c orange brown, Type II	"
35S A	10c green, Type V	1100.00
36bS A	12c black	1000.00
37S A	24c lilac	"
38S A	30c orange	"
26S F	3c dull red, Type II	1500.00
26S I	3c dull red, Type II	"

1861
63S A	1c blue	425.00
65S A	3c rose	"
68S A	10c dark green	"
70S A	24c red lilac	"
72S A	90c blue	"
73S A	2c black	525.00
76S A	5c brown	425.00

Specimen.

1861–66 Type B. Overprint 15mm. long.
Black, except as noted.
63S B	1c blue (1300)	120.00
	Without period	120.00
65S B	3c rose (1500)	"
68S B	10c dark green (1600)	"
69S B	12c black (Orange) (1300)	"
71S B	30c orange (1400)	"
72S B	90c blue (1394)	"
73S B	2c black (Vermilion) (1306)	275.00
	Without period	
76S B	5c brown (1306)	120.00
77S B	15c black (Vermilion) (1808)	200.00
78S B	24c lilac (1300)	120.00

1867–68
86S A	1c blue	400.00
85E-S A	12c black	"

93S A	2c black	500.00
94S A	3c rose	400.00
95S A	5c brown	"
98S A	15c black	450.00
100S A	30c orange	400.00

1869
112S A	1c buff	525.00
113S A	2c brown	"
115S A	6c ultramarine	"
116S A	10c yellow	"
117S A	12c green	"
119S A	15c brown & blue	675.00
120S A	24c green & violet	"
	a. Without grill	
121S A	30c blue & carmine	675.00
	a. Without grill	
122S A	90c carmine & black	950.00
	a. Without grill	

1870–71
145S A	1c ultramarine	350.00
146S A	2c red brown	"
147S A	3c green	"
147S B	3c green	450.00
148S A	6c carmine	350.00
149S A	7c vermilion	"
150S A	10c brown	"
151S A	12c dull violet	"
152S A	15c bright orange	"
154S A	90c carmine	"
155S B	90c carmine (Blue)	450.00

1873
159S B	6c dull pink	375.00
160S B	7c orange vermilion (Blue)	350.00
162S B	12c blackish violet (Blue)	"

Overprinted SPECIMEN in Red.
Type D.

1879
189S D	15c red orange	80.00
190S D	30c full black	"
191S D	90c carmine	"
	a. Overprint in black brown	

1881–82
205S D	5c yellow brown	"
206S D	1c gray blue	"
207S D	3c blue green	"
208S D	6c brown red	"
209S D	10c brown	"

SPECIMEN

1883
210S D	2c red brown	100.00	
211S D	4c blue green	"	

Handstamped **Specimen.** in Dull Purple.
Type E.

1890-93
219S E	1c dull blue	100.00
220S E	2c carmine	"
221S E	3c purple	"
222S E	4c dark brown	"
223S E	5c chocolate	"
224S E	6c dull red	"
225S E	8c lilac	"
226S E	10c green	"
227S E	15c blue	"
228S E	30c black	"
229S E	90c orange	135.00

1893 COLUMBIAN ISSUE.
230S E	1c deep blue	400.00
	Double overprint	
231S E	2c violet	400.00
232S E	3c green	"
233S E	4c ultramarine	"
234S E	5c chocolate	"
235S E	6c purple	"
236S E	8c magenta	"
237S E	10c black brown	"
238S E	15c dark green	"
239S E	30c orange brown	"
240S E	50c slate blue	"
241S E	$1 salmon	500.00
242S E	$2 brown red	"
243S E	$3 yellow green	550.00
244S E	$4 crimson lake	575.00
245S E	$5 black	675.00

Overprinted **Specimen.** in Magenta.
Type F.

230S F	1c deep blue	550.00
232S F	3c green	"
233S F	4c ultramarine	"
234S F	5c chocolate	"
235S F	6c purple	"
237S F	10c black brown	"
243S F	$3 yellow green	700.00

Overprinted Type H in Black or Red.

231S H	2c violet (Bk)	625.00
233S H	4c ultramarine (R)	"
234S H	5c chocolate (R)	"

Overprinted Type I in Black or Red.

231S I	2c violet (R)	"
232S I	3c green (R)	"
233S I	4c ultramarine (R)	"
234S I	5c chocolate (Bk)	"
235S I	6c purple (R)	"
236S I	8c magenta (Bk)	"
237S I	10c black brown (R)	"
238S I	15c dark green (R)	"
239S I	30c orange brown (Bk)	"
240S I	50c slate blue (R)	"

1895   Type E
264S E	1c blue	90.00
267S E	2c carmine	"
268S E	3c purple	"
269S E	4c dark brown	100.00
270S E	5c chocolate	90.00
271S E	6c dull brown	"
272S E	8c violet brown	"
273S E	10c dark green	"
274S E	15c dark blue	"
275S E	50c orange	"
276S E	$1 black, Type I	325.00
277S E	$2 dark blue	300.00
278S E	$5 dark green	400.00

1898-99
279S E	1c deep green	90.00
279B-S E	2c orange red	
	a. Booklet pane of 6	525.00
280S E	4c rose brown	160.00

281S E	5c dark blue	80.00
282S E	6c lake	"
282C-S E	10c brown, Type I	"
283S E	10c brown, Type II	
284S E	15c olive green	80.00

1898 TRANS-MISSISSIPPI ISSUE.
285S E	1c dark yellow green	250.00
286S E	2c copper red	"
287S E	4c orange	"
288S E	5c dull blue	"
289S E	8c violet brown	"
290S E	10c gray violet	"
291S E	50c sage green	300.00
292S E	$1 black	450.00
293S E	$2 orange brown	625.00

1901 PAN-AMERICAN ISSUE.
294S E	1c green & black	235.00
295S E	2c carmine	"
296S E	4c chocolate & black	"
	a. Center inverted	4500.00
297S E	5c ultramarine & black	235.00
298S E	8c brown violet & black	"
299S E	10c yellow brown & black	"

1902
300S E	1c blue green	90.00
301S E	2c carmine	"
302S E	3c bright violet	"
303S E	4c brown	"
304S E	5c blue	"
305S E	6c claret	"
306S E	8c violet black	"
307S E	10c pale red brown	"
308S E	13c purple black	"
309S E	15c olive green	"
310S E	50c orange	"
311S E	$1 black	200.00
312S E	$2 dark blue	300.00
313S E	$5 dark green	400.00

1903
319S E	2c carmine	110.00

1904 LOUISIANA PURCHASE ISSUE.
323S E	1c green	350.00
324S E	2c carmine	"
325S E	3c violet	"
326S E	5c dark blue	"
327S E	10c red brown	"

SPECIAL DELIVERY STAMPS

Overprinted **SPECIMEN.** in Red.

1885   Type D.
E1S D	10c blue	110.00

Handstamped **Specimen.** in Dull Purple.

1888   Type E.
E2S E	10c blue	110.00

1893
E3S E	10c orange	150.00

1894
E4S E	10c blue	225.00

1895
E5S E	10c blue	150.00

1902
E6S E	10c ultramarine	150.00

POSTAGE DUE STAMPS.

Overprinted SPECIMEN· in Red.
Type D.

1879
J1S D	1c brown	250.00
J2S D	2c brown	"
J3S D	3c brown	"
J4S D	5c brown	"

1884
J15S D	1c red brown	45.00
J16S D	2c red brown	"
J17S D	3c red brown	"
J18S D	5c red brown	"
J19S D	10c red brown	"
J20S D	30c red brown	"
J21S D	50c red brown	"

1895

Overprinted Specimen. in Dull Purple.
Type E.

J38S E	1c deep claret	65.00
J39S E	2c deep claret	"
J40S E	3c deep claret	"
J41S E	5c deep claret	"
J42S E	10c deep claret	"
J43S E	30c deep claret	"
J44S E	50c deep claret	"

Official Stamps.

Special printings of Official stamps were made in 1875 at the time the other Reprints, Re-issues and Special Printings were printed. They are ungummed.

Although perforated, these stamps were sometimes (but not always) cut apart with scissors. As a result the perforations may be mutilated and the design damaged.

Number issued indicated in brackets.

All values exist imperforate.

Overprinted SPECIMEN in Block Letters.
Type D.
Perf. 12.
Thin, hard white paper.

1875

AGRICULTURE.
Carmine Overprint.

O1S D	1c yellow (15,234)	5.00
	a. "Sepcimen" error	475.00
	b. Small dotted "i" in "Specimen"	165.00
	c. Ribbed paper	15.00
O2S D	2c yellow (4,192)	11.00
	a. "Sepcimen" error	525.00
O3S D	3c yellow (389)	45.00
	a. "Sepcimen" error	1900.00
O4S D	6c yellow (373)	80.00
	a. "Sepcimen" error	
O5S D	10c yellow (390)	80.00
	a. "Sepcimen" error	1900.00
O6S D	12c yellow (379)	75.00
	a. "Sepcimen" error	1900.00
O7S D	15c yellow (370)	75.00
	a. "Sepcimen" error	1900.00
O8S D	24c yellow (352)	75.00
	a. "Sepcimen" error	1900.00
O9S D	30c yellow (354)	75.00
	a. "Sepcimen" error	1900.00

EXECUTIVE.
Blue Overprint.

O10S D	1c carmine (14,652)	7.00
	a. Small dotted "i" in "Specimen"	175.00
	b. Ribbed paper	13.50
O11S D	2c carmine (7,430)	10.00
O12S D	3c carmine (3,735)	15.00
O13S D	6c carmine (3,485)	"
O14S D	10c carmine (3,461)	"

INTERIOR.
Blue Overprint.

O15S D	1c vermilion (7,194)	9.50
O16S D	2c vermilion (1,263)	15.00
	a. "Sepcimen" error	1150.00
O17S D	3c vermilion (88)	325.00
O18S D	6c vermilion (83)	300.00
O19S D	10c vermilion (82)	"
O20S D	12c vermilion (75)	325.00
O21S D	15c vermilion (78)	"
O22S D	24c vermilion (77)	"
O23S D	30c vermilion (75)	"
O24S D	90c vermilion (77)	"

JUSTICE.
Blue Overprint.

O25S D	1c purple (19,729)	8.00
	a. "Sepcimen" error	450.00
	b. Small dotted "i" in "Specimen"	150.00
	c. Ribbed paper	10.00
O26S D	2c purple (3,395)	10.00
	a. "Sepcimen" error	750.00
O27S D	3c purple (178)	140.00
	a. "Sepcimen" error	2450.00
O28S D	6c purple (163)	140.00
O29S D	10c purple (163)	135.00
O30S D	12c purple (154)	135.00
	a. "Sepcimen" error	2450.00
O31S D	15c purple (157)	160.00
	a. "Sepcimen" error	2450.00
O32S D	24c purple (150)	175.00
	a. "Sepcimen" error	2450.00
O33S D	30c purple (150)	175.00
	a. "Sepcimen" error	2450.00
O34S D	90c purple (152)	175.00

NAVY.
Carmine Overprint.

O35S D	1c ultramarine (9,182)	8.25
	a. "Sepcimen" error	375.00
	b. Broken "i" in "Specimen"	165.00
O36S D	2c ultramarine (1,748)	13.00
	a. "Sepcimen" error	475.00
	b. Broken "i" in "Specimen"	575.00
O37S D	3c ultramarine (126)	175.00
O38S D	6c ultramarine (116)	200.00
O39S D	7c ultramarine (501)	80.00
	a. "Sepcimen" error	1200.00
O40S D	10c ultramarine (112)	200.00
	a. "Sepcimen" error	2400.00
O41S D	12c ultramarine (107)	185.00
	a. "Sepcimen" error	2400.00
O42S D	15c ultramarine (107)	185.00
	a. "Sepcimen" error	2400.00
O43S D	24c ultramarine (106)	180.00
	a. "Sepcimen" error	2400.00
O44S D	30c ultramarine (104)	180.00
	a. "Sepcimen" error	2400.00
O45S D	90c ultramarine (102)	180.00

POST OFFICE.
Carmine Overprint

O47S D	1c black (6,015)	9.00
	a. "Sepcimen" error	450.00
	b. Inverted overprint	375.00
O48S D	2c black (590)	32.00
	a. "Sepcimen" error	1200.00
O49S D	3c black (91)	240.00
	a. "Sepcimen" error	2400.00
O50S D	6c black (87)	240.00
O51S D	10c black (177)	165.00
	a. "Sepcimen" error	1950.00
O52S D	12c black (93)	240.00
O53S D	15c black (82)	260.00
	a. "Sepcimen" error	2400.00
O54S D	24c black (84)	240.00
	a. "Sepcimen" error	2400.00
O55S D	30c black (81)	250.00
O56S D	90c black (82)	250.00
	a. "Sepcimen" error	2400.00

STATE.
Carmine Overprint.

O57S D	1c bluish green (21,672)	8.00
	a. "Sepcimen" error	275.00
	b. Small dotted "i" in "Specimen"	225.00
	c. Ribbed paper	10.00
O58S D	2c bluish green (5,145)	11.00
	a. "Sepcimen" error	375.00
O59S D	3c bluish green (793)	23.00
	a. "Sepcimen" error	1200.00
O60S D	6c bluish green (467)	55.00
	a. "Sepcimen" error	1300.00
O61S D	7c bluish green (791)	23.00
	a. "Sepcimen" error	1200.00
O62S D	10c bluish green (346)	100.00
O63S D	12c bluish green (280)	110.00
	a. "Sepcimen" error	1950.00
O64S D	15c bluish green (257)	110.00
O65S D	24c bluish green (253)	110.00
	a. "Sepcimen" error	1950.00

738 SPECIMEN

O66S D	30c bluish green (249)		110.00
	a. "Sepcimen" error		2000.00
O67S D	90c bluish green (245)		110.00
	a. "Sepcimen" error		2000.00
O68S D	$2 green & black (32)		2000.00
O69S D	$5 green & black (12)		3750.00
O70S D	$10 green & black (8)		4450.00
O71S D	$20 green & black (7)		4750.00

TREASURY
Blue Overprint

O72S D	1c dark brown (2,185)		12.00
O73S D	2c dark brown (309)		75.00
O74S D	3c dark brown (84)		240.00
O75S D	6c dark brown (85)		275.00
O76S D	7c dark brown (198)		155.00
O77S D	10c dark brown (82)		240.00
O78S D	12c dark brown (75)		250.00
O79S D	15c dark brown (75)		250.00
O80S D	24c dark brown (99)		240.00
O81S D	30c dark brown (74)		360.00
O82S D	a. Short transfer at top right		—
	90c dark brown (72)		360.00

WAR.
Blue Overprint

O83S D	1c deep rose (4,610)		10.00
	a. "Sepcimen" error		375.00
O84S D	2c deep rose (1,618)		15.00
	a. "Sepcimen" error		675.00
O85S D	3c deep rose (118)		200.00
	a. "Sepcimen" error		2000.00
O86S D	6c deep rose (111)		240.00
	a. "Sepcimen" error		2000.00
O87S D	7c deep rose (539)		40.00
	a. "Sepcimen" error		975.00
O88S D	10c deep rose (119)		190.00
	a. "Sepcimen" error		2000.00
O89S D	12c deep rose (105)		240.00
	a. "Sepcimen" error		2000.00
O90S D	15c deep rose (105)		240.00
	a. "Sepcimen" error		2000.00
O91S D	24c deep rose (106)		240.00
	a. "Sepcimen" error		2000.00
O92S D	30c deep rose (104)		240.00
	a. "Sepcimen" error		2000.00
O93S D	90c deep rose (106)		240.00
	a. "Sepcimen" error		2000.00

SOFT POROUS PAPER.
EXECUTIVE.
Blue Overprint.

O10xS D	1c violet rose		25.00
	Broken "i" in "Specimen"		200.00

NAVY.
Carmine Overprint

O35xS D	1c gray blue		30.00
	deep blue		35.00
	Broken "i" in "Specimen"		200.00
	a. Double overprint		550.00

STATE.

O57xS D	1c yellow green		110.00

The total number issued of the 1c Executive, 1c Navy, 1c State Departments possibly includes the soft paper "Specimen" printings.

SAVINGS STAMPS.

Overprinted Vertically
Reading Down in Red   **Specimen**

1911
PS4S	10c deep blue		—

1917-18 Handstamped "SPECIMEN" in Violet

WS1S	25c deep green		—
WS2S	$5 deep green		—

NEWSPAPER STAMPS.

Overprinted **Specimen.** in Red.

1865 Type C. Overprint 30mm. long.

PR5S C	5c dark blue		140.00
	a. Triple overprint		260.00
PR2S C	10c blue green		150.00
RP3S C	25c carmine red		165.00

Handstamped **Specimen** in Black.

1875 Type A.

PR9S A	2c black		185.00
PR11S A	4c black		"
PR12S A	6c black		"
PR16S A	12c rose		"

Overprinted **Specimen.** in Black,
except as noted.

1875 Type B. Overprint 15mm. long.

PR9S B	2c black		45.00
PR10S B	3c black		"
PR11S B	4c black		"
PR12S B	6c black		"
PR13S B	8c black		"
PR14S B	9c black		"
	a. Overprint in blue		—
PR15S B	10c black		45.00
PR16S B	12c rose		"
PR17S B	24c rose		"
PR18S B	36c rose		"
PR19S B	48c rose		"
	a. Overprint in blue		62.50
PR20S B	60c rose		45.00
PR21S B	72c rose		"
	a. Overprint in blue		62.50
PR22S B	84c rose		45.00
	a. Overprint in blue		—
PR23S B	96c rose		45.00
	a. Overprint in blue		—
PR24S B	$1.92 dark brown		45.00
PR25S B	$3 vermilion		45.00
	a. Overprint in blue		62.50
PR26S B	$6 ultramarine		45.00
	a. Overprint in blue		—
PR27S B	$9 yellow		45.00
	a. Overprint in blue		—
PR28S B	$12 dark green		45.00
	a. Overprint in blue		—
PR29S B	$24 dark gray violet		45.00
	a. Overprint in blue		60.00
PR30S B	$36 brown rose		62.00
PR31S B	$48 red brown		"
PR32S B	$60 violet		"

Overprinted **SPECIMEN.** in Red

1875 Type D.

PR14S D	9c black		30.00

1879
PR57S D	2c black		25.00
PR58S D	3c black		"
PR59S D	4c black		"
PR60S D	6c black		"
PR61S D	8c black		"
PR62S D	10c black		"
	a. Double overprint		250.00
PR63S D	12c red		25.00
PR64S D	24c red		"
PR65S D	36c red		"
PR66S D	48c red		"
PR67S D	60c red		"
PR68S D	72c red		"
PR69S D	84c red		"
PR70S D	96c red		"
PR71S D	$1.92 pale brown		"
PR72S D	$3 red vermilion		"
PR73S D	$6 blue		"
PR74S D	$9 orange		"
PR75S D	$12 yellow green		"
PR76S D	$24 dark violet		"
PR77S D	$36 Indian red		"
PR78S D	$48 yellow brown		"
PR79S D	$60 purple		"

1885
PR81S D	1c black		"

SPECIMEN

Handstamped **Specimen.** in Dull Purple.
Type E.

1879

PR57S E	2c black	22.50	
PR58S E	3c black		"
PR59S E	4c black		"
PR60S E	6c black		"
PR61S E	8c black		"
PR62S E	10c black		"
PR63S E	12c red		"
PR64S E	24c red		"
PR65S E	36c red		"
PR66S E	48c red		"
PR67S E	60c red		"
PR68S E	72c red		"
PR69S E	84c red		"
PR70S E	96c red		"
PR71S E	$1.92 pale brown		"
PR72S E	$3 red vermilion		"
PR73S E	$6 blue		"
PR74S E	$9 orange		"
PR75S E	$12 yellow green		"
PR76S E	$24 dark violet		"
PR77S E	$36 Indian red		"
PR78S E	$48 yellow brown		"
PR79S E	$60 purple		"

1885

PR81S E	1c black	"

Wmkd. USPS (191)

1895

PR114S E	1c black	35.00	
PR115S E	2c black		"
PR116S E	5c black		"
PR117S E	10c black		"
PR118S E	25c carmine		"
PR119S E	50c carmine		"
PR120S E	$2 scarlet		"
PR121S E	$5 dark blue		"
PR122S E	$10 green	42.50	
PR123S E	$20 slate		"
PR124S E	$50 dull rose		"
PR125S E	$100 purple		"

REVENUE STAMPS.

SPECIMEN
Type G.

1862   Overprint. 14 mm. long.

R5S G	2c Bank Check, blue (Red)	300.00
R15S A	2c U.S.I.R., orange	

SPECIMEN
Type H.

Overprint. 16 mm. long.

R23S H	5c Agreement, red (Black)	300.00
R34S H	10c Contract, blue (Red)	"
R35eS H	10c Foreign Exchange, ultramarine (Red)	"
R36S H	10c Inland Exchange, blue (Red)	"
R46S H	25c Insurance, red (Black)	"
R52S H	30c Inland Exchange, lilac (Red)	"
R53S H	40c Inland Exchange, brown (Red)	"
R68S H	$1 Foreign Exchange, red (Black)	"

Specimen (script)

Type I.

1898   Overprint. 20 mm. long.

R153S I	1c green (Red)	175.00

1875

RB11S H	1c green (Red)	250.00

PRIVATE MATCH STAMP

Overprinted with Type G in Red **SPECIMEN**

RO133bS G	A. Messinger, 1c black	120.00

VARIOUS OVERPRINTS.

Overprinted with control numbers in carmine.

7890
Type J.

1861

63S J	A24	1c pale blue (overprint 9012)	200.00
65S J	A25	3c brown red (overprint 7890)	"
68S J	A27	10c green (overprint 5678)	"
69S J	A28	12c gray black (overprint 4567)	"
71S J	A30	30c orange (overprint 2345)	"
72S J	A31	90c pale blue (overprint 1234)	"

     a. Pair, one without overprint   —

1861–66

73S J	A32	2c black (overprint 8901)	275.00
76S J	A26	5c brown (overprint 6789)	200.00
77S J	A33	15c black (overprint 235)	250.00
78S J	A29	24c gray lilac (overprint 3456)	200.00

Special Printings Overprinted in Red or Blue   **SAMPLE.**

Type K.

1889

212S K	A59	1c ultramarine (red)	75.00
210S K	A57	2c red brown (blue)	"
210S K	A57	2c lake (blue)	"
210S K	A57	2c rose lake (blue)	"
210S K	A57	2c scarlet (blue)	"
214S K	A46b	3c vermilion (blue)	"
211S K	A58	4c blue green (red)	"
205S K	A56	5c yellow brown (red)	"
208S K	A47b	6c brown red (blue)	"
209S K	A49b	10c brown (red)	"
		Without overprint	80.00
189S K	A51a	15c orange (blue)	75.00
190S K	A53	30c full black (red)	"
191S K	A54	90c carmine (blue)	"

Special Printings Overprinted in Red or Blue   **SAMPLE A.**

Type L.

212S L	A59	1c ultramarine (red)	75.00
210S L	A57	2c rose lake (blue)	"
214S L	A46b	3c purple (red)	"
211S L	A58	4c dark brown (red)	"
205S L	A56	5c gray brown (blue)	"
208S L	A47b	6c vermilion (blue)	"
209S L	A49b	10c green (red)	"
		Without overprint	100.00
189S L	A51a	15c blue (red)	75.00
		Without overprint	100.00
190S L	A53	30c full black (red)	75.00
191S L	A54	90c orange (blue)	"

Overprinted with Type K together with "A" in Black manuscript.

191S M	A54	90c carmine (blue)	140.00
209S M	A49b	10c brown (red)	"
211S M	A58	4c blue green (red)	"

"SAMPLE A" in manuscript (red or black)

216S N	A56	5c indigo	160.00

Regular Issues
Overprinted
in Blue or Red

UNIVERSAL POSTAL CONGRESS
Type O.

1897

125 sets were distributed to delegates to the Universal Postal Congress held in Washington, D. C., May 5 to June 15, 1897.

264S O	A87	1c blue	135.00
267S O	A88	2c carmine	"
268S O	A89	3c purple	"
269S O	A90	4c dark brown	"
270S O	A91	5c chestnut	"
271S O	A92	6c claret brown	"
272S O	A93	8c violet brown	"
273S O	A94	10c dark green	"
274S O	A95	15c dark blue	"
275S O	A96	50c red orange	"
276S O	A97	$1 black, Type I	500.00
276A-S O	"	$1 black, Type II	450.00
277S O	A98	$2 dark blue	325.00
278S O	A99	$5 dark green	500.00

SPECIAL DELIVERY

E5S O	SD3	10c blue (R)	250.00

POSTAGE DUE

J38S O	D2	1c deep claret	125.00
J39S O	"	2c "	"
J40S O	"	3c "	"
J41S O	"	5c "	"
J42S O	"	10c "	"
J43S O	"	30c "	"
J44S O	"	50c "	"

NEWSPAPERS.

PR114S O	N15	1c black	85.00
PR115S O	"	2c black	"
PR116S O	"	5c black	"
PR117S O	"	10c black	"
PR118S O	N16	25c carmine	"
PR119S O	"	50c carmine	"
PR120S O	N17	$2 scarlet	"
PR121S O	N18	$5 dark blue	85.00
PR122S O	N19	$10 green	"
PR123S O	N20	$20 slate	"
PR124S O	N21	$50 dull rose	"
PR125S O	N22	$100 purple	"

ENVELOPES.
UNIVERSAL POSTAL CONGRESS
Overprinted Type P.

U294S P		1c blue on white	100.00
U296S P		1c blue on amber	"
U300S P		1c blue on manila	"
W301S P		1c blue on manila	"
U304S P		1c blue on amber manila	"
U311S P		2c green, Die 2, on white	"
U312S P		2c green, Die 2, on amber	"
U313S P		2c green, Die 2, on oriental buff	"
U314S P		2c green, Die 2, on blue	"
U315S P		2c green, Die 2, on manila	"
W316S P		2c green, Die 2, on manila	"
U317S P		2c green, Die 2, on amber manila	"
U324S P		4c carmine on white	"
U325S P		4c carmine on amber	120.00
U330S P		5c blue, Die 1, on white	110.00
U331S P		5c blue, Die 1, on amber	"

Two settings of type P overprint are found.

POSTAL CARDS.
Overprinted UNIVERSAL POSTAL CONGRESS.
Type Q.

UX12S Q		1c black on buff	400.00
UX13S Q		2c blue on cream	..

PAID REPLY POSTAL CARDS
Overprinted with Type Q.

UY1S Q		1c black on buff	"
UY2S Q		2c blue on grayish white	"

As Nos. UY1S-UY2S were made by overprinting unsevered reply cards, prices are for unsevered cards.

SAVINGS STAMPS

POSTAL SAVINGS STAMPS.
Issued by the Post Office Department.
Redeemable in the form of credits to Postal Savings accounts. The Postal Savings system was discontinued Mar. 28, 1966.

PS1
Size of design: 18 x 21½ mm

| | | 1911 | Wmkd. | USPS | (191) | Perf. 12. |

Engraved.
Plates of 400 subjects in four panes of 100 each.
FLAT PLATE PRINTING.

PS1	PS1	10c orange, *Jan. 3, 1911*	10.00	75
		Block of four, 2 mm. spacing	40.50	
		Block of four, 3 mm. spacing	41.50	
		Margin strip of 3, Impt. open star & P #	50.00	
		Margin block of 6, Impt. open star & P #	500.00	

Plate Nos.
5504 5506 5698 5703
5505 5507 5700 5704

1911   Unwmkd.
Imprinted on Deposit Card, Size of design: 137 x 79 mm.

| PS2 | PS1 | 10c orange, *Jan. 3, 1911* | 90.00 | 35.00 |

A 10c deep blue with head of Washington in circle imprinted on deposit card (design 136x79mm.) exists, but there is no evidence that it was ever placed in use.

| | | 1911 | Wmkd. | USPS | (190) | Perf. 12. |

PS4	PS1	10c deep blue, *Aug. 14, 1911*	5.50	75
		Block of four, 2 mm. spacing	22.50	
		Block of four, 3 mm. spacing	24.00	
		Margin strip of 3, Impt. open star & P #	30.00	
		Margin block of 6, Impt. open star & P #	185.00	

Plate Nos.
5504 5506 5698 5703
5505 5507 5700 5704

1911   Unwmkd.
Imprinted on Deposit Card, Size of design: 133 x 78 mm.

| PS5 | PS1 | 10c deep blue | 90.00 | 25.00 |

1936		Perf. 11		Unwmkd.
PS6	PS1	10c deep blue	4.50	1.00
		a. 10c violet blue	"	1.00
		Block of four	18.50	
		Margin block of 6, Impt. solid star & P #	125.00	

Plate Nos. 21485 21486

PS2
Size of design: 19 x 22 mm.

| 1940 | | Perf. 11 | | Unwmkd. |

Engraved.
Plates of 400 subjects in four panes of 100 each.
FLAT PLATE PRINTING.

PS7	PS2	10c deep ultramarine, *April 3, 1940*	12.00
		Block of four	48.00
		Margin block of 6, P #	225.00
		Plate Nos. 22540 22541	
PS8	PS2	25c dark carmine rose, *April 1, 1940*	16.00
		Block of four	64.00
		Margin block of 6, P #	300.00
		Plate Nos. 22542 22543	
PS9	PS2	50c dark blue green, *April 1, 1940*	45.00
		Block of four	180.00
		Margin block of 6, P #	775.00
		Plate No. 22544	
PS10	PS2	$1 gray black, *April 1, 1940*	85.00
		Block of four	340.00
		Margin block of 6, P #	1750.00
		Plate No. 22545	

Nos. PS11–PS15 redeemable in the form of United States Treasury Defense, War or Savings Bonds.

Minute Man
PS3
Size of design: 19 x 22½ mm.

| 1941 | | Perf. 11x10½ | | Unwmkd. |

E.E. Plates of 400 subjects in four panes of 100 each.
ROTARY PRESS PRINTING.

PS11	PS3	10c rose red, *May 1, 1941*	65	65
		a. 10c carmine rose		65
		Block of four	2.60	
		Margin block of 4, P #	9.00	
		b. Bklt. pane of 10, *July 30, 1941,* trimmed horizontal edges		60.00
		As "*b*," with Electric Eye marks at left		65.00
		c. Booklet pane of 10, perf. horizontal edges		125.00
		As "*c*," with Electric Eye marks at left		140.00

741

742 — SAVINGS STAMPS

Plate Nos. of sheet stamps

22714	22722	148245
22715	22723	148246

Plate Nos. of booklet panes

147084	147085	148241	148242

PS12 PS3 **25c blue green,** *May 1, 1941* ... 3.00
 Block of four ... 12.00
 Margin block of 4, P # ... 22.00
 b. Bklt. pane of 10, *July 30, 1941* ... 60.00
  Booklet pane with Electric
   Eye marks at left ... 65.00

Plate Nos. of sheet stamps

22716	22724	148247
22717	22725	148248

Plate Nos. of booklet panes

147087	147088	148243	148244

PS13 PS3 **50c ultramarine,** *May 1, 1941* ... 9.00
 Block of four ... 36.00
 Margin block of 4, P # ... 50.00

Plate Nos.

22718	22719	22726	22727

PS14 PS3 **$1 gray black,** *May 1, 1941* ... 16.00
 Block of four ... 64.00
 Margin block of 4, P # ... 110.00

Plate Nos.

22720	22728

Perf. 11.
FLAT PLATE PRINTING.
Size: 36x46 mm.
Plates of 100 subjects in four panes of 25 each.

PS15 PS3 **$5 sepia,** *May 1, 1941* ... 45.00
 Block of four ... 180.00
 Margin block of 6, P # at top
  or bottom ... 550.00

Plate Nos.

22730	22733	22736
22731	22734	22737
22732	22735	22740

SAVINGS STAMPS.
Issued by the Post Office Department.

Redeemable in the form of United States Savings Bonds. Sale of Savings Stamps was discontinued June 30, 1970.

Minute Man
S1
Size of design: 19x22½ mm.

1954–57 *Perf. 11x10½* Unwmkd.
E.E. Plates of 400 subjects in four panes of 100 each.
ROTARY PRESS PRINTING.

S1 S1 **10c rose red,** *Nov. 30, 1954* ... 60
 Block of four ... 2.40
 Margin block of 4, P # ... 3.50
 a. Booklet pane of 10, *Apr. 22, 1955* ... 150.00
  Booklet pane with Electric Eye
   marks at left ... 175.00

Plate Nos. of sheet stamps

164991	165917	166643	167089	168765
164992	165918	166644	167090	168766

Plate Nos. of booklet panes

165218	165954	167001
165219	165955	167002

S2 S1 **25c blue green,** *Dec. 30, 1954* ... 2.50
 Block of four ... 10.00
 Margin block of 4, P # ... 25.00
 a. Booklet pane of 10, *Apr. 15, 1955* ... 375.00
  Booklet pane with Electric Eye
   marks at left ... 425.00

Plate Nos. of sheet stamps

165007	165008	165919	165920

Plate Nos. of booklet panes

165220	165221	165956	165957

S3 S1 **50c ultramarine,** *Dec. 31, 1956* ... 6.00
 Block of four ... 24.00
 Margin block of 4, P# ... 35.00

Plate Nos.

165050	166741	166941
165051	166742	166942

S4 S1 **$1 gray black,** *March 13, 1957* ... 18.00
 Block of four ... 72.00
 Margin block of 4, P# ... 90.00

Plate Nos.

166097	166683
166098	166684

Perf. 11
FLAT PLATE PRINTING
Size: 36x46 mm.
Plates of 100 subjects in four panes of 25 each.

S5 S1 **$5 sepia,** *Nov. 30, 1956* ... 65.00
 Block of four ... 260.00
 Margin block of 6, P# at top
  or bottom ... 800.00

Plate No. 166068

Minute Man and
48-Star Flag
S2

1958 *Perf. 11* Unwmkd.
GIORI PRESS PRINTING
Plates of 400 subjects in four panes of 100 each.

S6 S2 **25c dark blue & carmine,** *Nov. 18, 1958* ... 75
 Block of four ... 3.00
 Margin block of 4, P# ... 7.50
 a. Booklet pane of 10, *Nov. 18, 1958* ... 70.00

Plate Nos. of sheet stamps

166921	166925	166946	166949	167014

Minute Man and
50-Star Flag
S3

SAVINGS STAMPS

1961   *Perf. 11*   Unwmkd.
Plates of 400 subjects in four panes of 100 each.

S7	S3	25c dark blue & carmine	75
		Block of four	3.00
		Margin block of 4, P #	7.50
		a. Booklet pane of 10	300.00

Plate Nos. of sheet stamps
167473   167476   167486   167489   169089

Plate Nos. of booklet panes
167495   167502

WAR SAVINGS STAMPS.

Issued by the Treasury Department.

Redeemable in the form of United States Treasury War Certificates, Defense Bonds or War Bonds.

WS1

Size of design: 28 x 18½ mm.

1917   *Perf. 11*   Unwmkd.

Engraved.

Plates of 300 subjects in six panes of 50 each.

FLAT PLATE PRINTING.

WS1	WS1	25c deep green, *Dec. 1, 1917*	10.00
		Block of four	42.50
		Margin strip of 3, P # only	50.00
		Margin block of 6, P # only	500.00

Plate Nos.

56800	57076	57336	58801	59156
56810	57077	57382	58802	61207
56811	57149	57395	58803	61208
56817	57150	57396	58804	61209
57074	57151	57399	59044	61210
57075	57152	57443	59045	

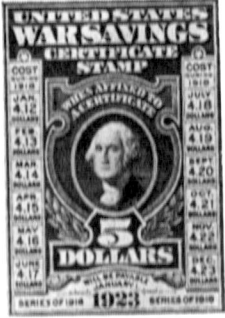

George Washington
WS2

Size of design: 39 x 55 mm.

1918   *Perf. 11*   Unwmkd.

Engraved.

Plates of 80 subjects in four panes of 20 each.

FLAT PLATE PRINTING.

WS2	WS2	$5 deep green, *Nov. 17, 1917*	90.00
		Block of four	375.00
		Margin copy with P # only	100.00
		b. Vertical pair, imperf. horizontally	

Plate Nos.

56914	57170	58434	60662	61265
56915	57171	58435	60665	61266
56916	57172	58436	60666	61267
56917	57173	58437	60667	61268
57066	57174	58438	60668	61360
57067	57175	58726	60846	61361
57068	57176	58727	60847	61362
57069	57333	58728	60848	61363
57070	57334	58729	60849	61364
57071	57343	59071	60850	61365
57072	57344	60257	60851	61366
57073	57345	60258	60852	61367
57145	57346	60259	60899	61388
57146	57347	60260	61203	61435
57147	57348	60659	61204	61502
57148	58431	60660	61205	
57169	58433	60661	61206	

Rouletted 7.

WS3	WS2	$5 deep green	1000.00
		Block of four	4200.00
		Margin copy with P # only	1050.00

Benjamin Franklin
WS3

Size of design: 27 x 36 mm.

1919   *Perf. 11*   Unwmkd.

Engraved.

Plates of 150 subjects in six panes of 25 each.

FLAT PLATE PRINTING.

WS4	WS3	$5 deep blue, *July 3, 1919*	275.00
		Block of four	1150.00
		Margin copy with P # only	300.00
		Margin copy with inverted P #	325.00

Plate Nos.

61882	61910	61970	61998	62010
61883	61911	61971	62007	62011
61884	61912	61972	62008	62012
61885	61913	61997	62009	62013

George Washington
WS4

Size of design: 36 x 41½ mm.

1920   *Perf. 11*   Unwmkd.

Engraved.

Plates of 100 subjects in four panes of 25 each.

FLAT PLATE PRINTING.

WS5	WS4	$5 carmine, *Dec. 11, 1919*	475.00
		Block of four	2000.00
		Margin copy with P # only	500.00

Plate Nos.

67545	67549	69349	69673	69678
67546	67550	69350	69674	69679
67547	67551	69351	69675	69680
67548	67552	69352	69677	69829

SAVINGS STAMPS

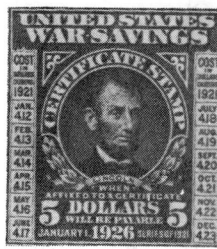

Abraham Lincoln
WS5

Size of design: 39½ x 42 mm.

1921 Perf. 11 Unwmkd.

Engraved.

Plates of 100 subjects in four panes of 25 each.

FLAT PLATE PRINTING.

WS6	WS5	**$5 orange, green,** *Dec. 21, 1920*	2500.00
		Block of four	11,000.00
		Margin copy with P # only	2650.00

Plate Nos.

| 73129 | 73131 | 73133 | 73135 |
| 73130 | 73132 | 73134 | 73136 |

Minute Man
WS6

Size of design: 19 x 22½ mm.

1942 Perf. 11x10½ Unwmkd.

Plates of 400 subjects in four panes of 100 each.

ROTARY PRESS PRINTING.

WS7	WS6	**10c rose red,** *Oct. 29, 1942*	50
		a. 10c carmine rose	50
		Block of four	2.00
		Margin block of 4, P #	5.00
		b. Booklet pane of 10, *Oct. 27, 1942*	40.00
		Booklet pane with Electric Eye marks at left	45.00

Plate Nos. of sheet stamps

149492	149495	150706	155311
149493	150206	150707	155312
149494	150207		

Plate Nos. of booklet panes

| 149655 | 149656 | 149657 | 150664 |

WS8	WS6	**25c dark blue green,** *Oct. 15, 1942*	1.25
		Block of four	5.00
		Margin block of 4, P #	12.50
		b. Booklet pane of 10, *Nov. 6, 1942*	55.00
		Booklet pane with Electric Eye marks at left	60.00

Plate Nos. of sheet stamps

149587	150320	155313	155813
149588	150321	155314	156517
149589	150708	155812	156518
149590	150709		

Plate Nos. of booklet panes

| 149658 | 149659 | 149660 | 150666 |

WS9	WS6	**50c deep ultramarine,** *Nov. 12, 1942*	4.50
		Block of four	18.00
		Margin block of 4, P #	32.50

Plate Nos.

| 149591 | 149592 | 149593 | 149594 |

WS10	WS6	**$1 gray black,** *Nov. 17, 1942*	12.50
		Block of four	50.00
		Margin block of 4, P #	65.00

Plate Nos.

| 149595 | 149596 | 149597 | 149598 |

Type of 1942.

Size : 36 x 46 mm.

1945 Perf. 11 Unwmkd.

FLAT PLATE PRINTING.

Plates of 100 subjects in four panes of 25 each

WS11	WS6	**$5 violet brown**	55.00
		Block of four	220.00
		Margin block of 6, P # at top or bottom	600.00

Plate Nos.

| 150131 | 150132 | 150133 | 150134 |
| 150291 | | | |

Type of 1942.

Coil Stamps.

1943 Perf. 10 Vertically. Unwmkd.

WS12	WS6	**10c rose red,** *Aug. 5, 1943*	2.00
		Pair	4.25
		Line pair	12.00

Plate Nos.

| 153286 | 153287 |

WS13	WS6	**25c dark blue green,** *Aug. 5, 1943*	4.00
		Pair	8.50
		Line pair	20.00

Plate Nos.

| 153289 | 153290 |

TREASURY SAVINGS STAMP.

Issued by the Treasury Department.

Redeemable in the form of War Savings Stamps or Treasury Savings Certificates.

Alexander Hamilton
TS1

Size of design: 33½ x 33½ mm.

1921 Perf. 11 Unwmkd.

Engraved.

FLAT PLATE PRINTING.

TS1	TS1	**$1 red, green,** *Dec. 21, 1920*	2750.00
		Block of four	11,500.00
		Margin copy with P #	2850.00

Plate Nos.

| 73196 | 73198 | 73200 | 73202 |
| 73197 | 73199 | 73201 | 73203 |

ENCASED POSTAGE STAMPS

In 1862 John Gault of Boston patented the idea of encasing postage stamps in metal frames behind a shield of transparent mica, and using them for advertising. The scarcity of small change during the Civil War made these encased stamps popular. Many firms impressed their names and products on the back of these stamp frames in embossed letters. Prices are for fine specimens with mica intact, although signs of circulation and handling are to be expected.

Types of Encased Stamps.

Aerated Bread Co., New York (1)

1	1c	1650.00

Ayer's Cathartic Pills, Lowell, Mass. (3)

Varieties with long and short arrows below legend occur on all denominations.

2	1c	150.00
3	3c	135.00
4	5c	275.00
5	10c	400.00
6	12c	650.00
7	24c	1900.00

Take Ayer's Pills (2)

8	1c	145.00
9	3c	135.00
10	5c	185.00
	a. Ribbed frame	800.00
11	10c	375.00
12	12c	900.00

Ayer's Sarsaparilla (4)

Three varieties: "AYER'S"; small, medium and large.

13	1c, medium "Ayer's"	145.00
	a. Small	350.00
14	2c	—
15	3c, small "Ayer's"	150.00
	a. Medium	135.00
	b. Large	275.00
	c. Ribbed frame, medium	500.00
16	5c, medium "Ayer's"	200.00
	a. Large	450.00
17	10c, medium "Ayer's"	300.00
	a. Ribbed frame, medium	800.00
	b. Small	450.00
	c. Large	600.00
18	12c, medium "Ayer's"	750.00
	a. Small	1200.00
19	24c, medium "Ayer's"	2000.00
20	30c, medium "Ayer's"	2750.00

The authenticity of No. 14 is questioned.

Bailey & Co., Philadelphia

21	1c	600.00
22	3c	625.00
23	5c	850.00
24	10c	800.00
25	12c	1500.00

Joseph L. Bates, Boston (5)

Two varieties: FANCY GOODS as one word or two.

26	1c, one word	225.00
	a. Two words	275.00
27	3c, one word	450.00
	a. Two words	500.00
28	5c, one word	750.00
	a. Two words	600.00
	b. Ribbed frame, one word	850.00
29	10c, one word	400.00
	a. Two words	425.00
	b. Ribbed frame, one word	800.00
30	12c, two words	900.00

Brown's Bronchial Troches (6)

31	1c	675.00
32	3c	300.00
33	5c	275.00
34	10c	425.00
35	12c	800.00
36	24c	1900.00
37	30c	3500.00

F. Buhl & Co., Detroit

38	1c	500.00
39	3c	800.00
40	5c	750.00
41	10c	1000.00
42	12c	1300.00
43	24c	2500.00

Burnett's Cocoaine Kalliston (7)

44	1c	250.00
45	3c	250.00
46	5c	375.00
47	10c	400.00
48	12c	800.00
49	24c	2250.00
50	30c	3000.00
51	90c	7500.00

Burnett's Cooking Extracts (8)

52	1c	—
53	3c	190.00
54	5c	250.00
55	10c	300.00
	a. Ribbed frame	650.00
56	12c	700.00
57	24c	1800.00
58	30c	3000.00

A. M. Claflin, Hopkinton, R. I.

59	1c	1500.00
60	3c	3750.00
61	5c	3250.00
62	10c	4500.00
63	12c	5500.00

H. A. Cook, Evansville, Ind.

64	5c	900.00
65	10c	900.00

Dougan, Hatter, New York (9)

66	1c	1650.00
67	3c	1250.00
68	5c	1500.00
69	10c	2000.00

Drake's Plantation Bitters (10)

70	1c	200.00
71	3c	165.00
72	5c	250.00
	a. Ribbed frame	600.00
73	10c	300.00
	a. Ribbed frame	750.00
74	12c	750.00
75	24c	2000.00
76	30c	3000.00
77	90c	8500.00

ENCASED POSTAGE STAMPS

Ellis, McAlpin & Co., Cincinnati (15)

78	1c	1250.00
79	3c	1000.00
80	5c	1250.00
81	10c	1400.00
82	12c	1300.00
83	24c	2400.00

C. G. Evans, Philadelphia

84	1c	625.00
85	3c	625.00
86	5c	900.00
87	10c	1000.00

Gage Bros. & Drake, Tremont House, Chicago (20)

88	1c	350.00
89	3c	375.00
90	5c	325.00
91	10c	375.00
	a. Ribbed frame	900.00
92	12c	750.00

J. Gault (11)

93	1c	150.00
	a. Ribbed frame	500.00
94	2c	3000.00
95	3c	125.00
	a. Ribbed frame	550.00
96	5c	185.00
	a. Ribbed frame	500.00
97	10c	300.00
	a. Ribbed frame	600.00
98	12c	650.00
	a. Ribbed frame	1100.00
99	24c	1650.00
	a. Ribbed frame	2500.00
100	30c	2650.00
	a. Ribbed frame	3200.00
101	90c	7000.00

L. C. Hopkins & Co., Cincinnati

102	1c	1000.00
103	3c	1250.00
104	5c	1100.00
105	10c	1500.00

Hunt & Nash, Irving House, New York (12)

106	1c	375.00
107	3c	375.00
	a. Ribbed frame	800.00
108	5c	400.00
	a. Ribbed frame	600.00
109	10c	425.00
	a. Ribbed frame	600.00
110	12c	750.00
	a. Ribbed frame	1250.00
111	24c	2000.00
	a. Ribbed frame	2800.00
112	30c	3250.00

Kirkpatrick & Gault, New York (13)

113	1c	325.00
114	3c	425.00
115	5c	250.00
116	10c	300.00
117	12c	800.00
118	24c	2250.00
119	30c	3000.00
120	90c	8000.00

Lord & Taylor, New York (14)

121	1c	575.00
122	3c	700.00
123	5c	700.00
124	10c	1000.00
125	12c	1800.00
126	24c	2750.00
127	30c	3750.00
128	90c	8500.00

Mendum's Family Wine Emporium, New York (16)

129	1c	375.00
130	3c	700.00
131	5c	500.00
132	10c	600.00
	a. Ribbed frame	1100.00
133	12c	1350.00

B. F. Miles, Peoria

| 134 | 1c | 3000.00 |
| 135 | 5c | 3000.00 |

John W. Norris, Chicago

136	1c	1350.00
137	3c	1200.00
138	5c	1150.00
139	10c	1600.00

No. American Life Insurance Co., N. Y.

Two varieties: inscription in curved line or straight line.

140	1c, curved	325.00
	a. Straight	350.00
141	3c, curved	475.00
	a. Straight	400.00
142	5c, straight	500.00
	a. Ribbed frame	950.00
143	10c, straight	500.00
	a. Curved	700.00
	b. Curved, ribbed frame	1200.00
144	12c, straight	1000.00

Pearce, Tolle & Holton, Cincinnati

145	1c	2400.00
146	3c	1500.00
147	5c	1800.00
148	10c	2000.00
149	12c	2150.00
150	24c	2750.00

Sands Ale

151	5c	1700.00
152	10c	2000.00
153	12c	2300.00
154	30c	4250.00

Schapker & Bussing, Evansville, Ind. (17)

155	1c	550.00
156	3c	700.00
157	5c	650.00
158	10c	700.00
159	12c	1250.00

John Shillito & Co., Cincinnati (18)

160	1c	600.00
161	3c	500.00
162	5c	500.00
163	10c	700.00
164	12c	1750.00

S. Steinfeld, New York (19)

165	1c	900.00
166	5c	950.00
167	10c	1400.00
168	12c	2000.00

N. G. Taylor & Co., Philadelphia

169	1c	900.00
170	3c	850.00
171	5c	1100.00
172	10c	1500.00
173	12c	2000.00

Weir and Larminie, Montreal

174	1c	1500.00
175	3c	1900.00
176	5c	1500.00
177	10c	1400.00

White, the Hatter, New York

178	1c	1200.00
179	3c	1000.00
180	5c	1100.00
181	10c	1200.00

POSTAGE CURRENCY

Small coins disappeared from circulation in 1861-62 as cash was hoarded. To ease business transactions, merchants issued notes of credit, promises to pay, tokens, store cards, etc. U.S. Treasurer Francis E. Spinner made a substitute for small currency by affixing postage stamps, singly and in multiples, to Treasury paper. He arranged with the Post Office to replace worn stamps with new when necessary.

The next step was to print the stamps on Treasury paper. On July 17, 1862, Congress authorized the issue of such "Postage Currency." It was not money, but a means of making stamps negotiable.

Postage Currency remained in use until 1876 when Congress authorized the minting of silver coins to redeem the outstanding fractional currency

Prices quoted are for notes in crisp, new condition, not creased or worn.
Creased or worn copies sell for 25 to 75 per cent less.

FIRST GENERAL ISSUE

August 21, 1862 to May 27, 1863

Front Engraved and Printed by the National Bank Note Co.

This series has on each note a facsimile of the postage stamp then current. In the 25c and 50c denominations the 5c and 10c stamps are engraved overlapping each other, five in a row, respectively.

Back Engraved and Printed by The American Bank Note Co.
"A B Co." on Back

Perforated Edges—Perf. 12.

1	5c	Bust of Jefferson on 5c stamp, brown	50.00
		a. Inverted back	200.00
2	10c	Bust of Washington on 10c stamp, green	35.00
3	25c	Five 5c stamps, brown	45.00
4	50c	Five 10c stamps, green	50.00
		a. Perforated 14	100.00
		b. Inverted back	200.00

Imperforate Edges.

5	5c	Bust of Jefferson on 5c stamp	17.50
		a. Inverted back	200.00
6	10c	Bust of Washington on 10c stamp	15.00
		a. Inverted back	200.00
7	25c	Five 5c stamps	30.00
		a. Inverted back	200.00
8	50c	Five 10c stamps	50.00
		a. Inverted back	200.00

Back Printed by the Government
Without "A B Co." on Back

Perforated Edges—Perf. 12.

9	5c	Bust of Jefferson on 5c stamp	50.00
		a. Inverted back	250.00
10	10c	Bust of Washington on 10c stamp	50.00
		a. Inverted back	250.00
11	25c	Five 5c stamps	100.00
		a. Inverted back	250.00
12	50c	Five 10c stamps	120.00

Imperforate Edges.

13	5c	Bust of Jefferson on 5c stamp	50.00
		a. Inverted back	300.00
14	10c	Bust of Washington on 10c stamp	85.00
		a. Inverted back	250.00
15	25c	Five 5c stamps	120.00
16	50c	Five 10c stamps	135.00
		a. Inverted back	250.00

INTERNATIONAL REPLY COUPONS

Coupons produced by the Universal Postal Union for member countries to provide for payment of postage on a return letter from a foreign country. Exchangeable for a stamp representing single-rate ordinary postage to a foreign country under the terms of contract as printed on the face of the coupon in French and the language of the issuing country and on the reverse in four, five or six other languages.

Postmasters are instructed to apply a postmark indicating date of sale to the left circle on the coupon. When offered for exchange for stamps, the receiving postmaster is instructed to cancel the right circle.

The following is a list of all varieties issued by the Universal Postal Union for any or all member countries.

Type A — Face.

1907-20   Watermarked
"25c Union Postale Universelle 25c".
A1 Face   — Name of country in letters 1½ mm. high.
    Reverse — Printed rules between paragraphs German text contains four lines.
1907-20
A2 Face   — Same as A1.
    Reverse — Same as A1 but without rules between paragraphs.
1910-20
A3 Face   — Same as A1 and A2.
    Reverse — Same as A2 except German text has but three lines.
1912-20
A4 Face   — Name of country in bold face type; letters 2 mm. to 2½ mm. high.
    Reverse — Same as A3.
1922-25
A5 Face   — French words "le mois d'émission écoulé, deux mois encore".
    Reverse — As A3 and A4 but overprinted with new contract in red; last line of red German text has five words.
1925-26   Watermarked
"50c Union Postale Universelle 50c".
A6 Face   — Same as A5.
    Reverse — Four paragraphs of five lines each.
1926-29
A7 Face   — French words "il est valable pendent un délai de six mois".
    Reverse — As A6 but overprinted with new contract in red; last line of red German text has two words.
1926-29   Watermarked
"40c Union Postale Universelle 40c".
A8 Face   — Design redrawn. Without lines in hemispheres.
    Reverse — Four paragraphs of four lines each.

Type B — Face.

1931-35   Wmkd. Double-lined "UPU"
B1 Face   — French words "d'une lettre simple".
    Reverse — Four paragraphs of three lines each.
1935-36
B2 Face   — French words "d'une lettre ordinaire de port simple".
    Reverse — Last line of German text contains two words.
1936-37
B3 Face   — Same as B2.
    Reverse — Last line of German text contains one word.
1937-40
B4 Face   — Same as B2 and B3. "Any Country of the Union."
    Reverse — German text is in German Gothic type.
1945
B5 Face   — "Any Country of the Universal Postal Union."
    Reverse — Each paragraph reads "Universal Postal Union."
Type B5 exists without central printing on face.
1950
B6 Face   — Same as B5.
    Reverse — Five paragraphs (English, Arabic, Chinese, Spanish, Russian).
1954
B7 Face   — Same as B5.
    Reverse — Six paragraphs (German, English, Arabic, Chinese, Spanish, Russian.)

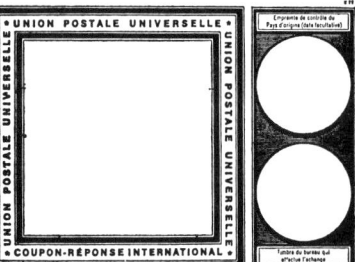

Type C — Face

INTERNATIONAL REPLY COUPONS

1968
- **C1** Face — French words "d'une lettre ordinaire de port simple".
  Reverse— Six paragraphs (German, English, Arabic, Chinese, Spanish, Russian).

1971
- **C2** Face —French words "d'une lettre ordinaire du premier échelon de poids."
  Reverse—Six paragraphs (German, English, Arabic, Chinese, Spanish, Russian).

Foreign coupons, but not U.S., of type C1 are known with large double-lined "UPU" watermark, as on type B coupons.

Type D — Face

1975
- **D1** Face French words "d'une lettre ordinaire, expédiée à l'étranger par voie de surface."
  Reverse—Six paragraphs (German, English, Arabic, Chinese, Spanish, Russian).

REPLY COUPONS ISSUED FOR THE UNITED STATES.

1907
1	A1	6c slate green & gray green	8.00
		(2-line English paragraph on face. Rules between paragraphs on reverse.)	
2	A2	6c slate green & gray green	1.25
		(Rules omitted on reverse.)	

1912
3	A4	6c slate green & gray green	85
		(3-line English paragraph on face.)	

1922
4	A5	11c slate green & gray green, name 81½ mm. long	2.25
	a.	Name 88½ mm. long	2.25
		(5-line English paragraph on face. Red overprint on reverse.)	

1925-26
5	A6	11c slate green & gray green	4.50
		(5-line English paragraph on face. No overprint on reverse.)	
6	A6	9c slate green & gray green	5.00

1926
7	A7	9c slate green & gray green	4.00
		(4-line English paragraph on face. Red overprint on reverse.)	
8	A8	9c slate green & gray green	60
		(Without lines in hemispheres.)	

1935
9	B2	9c blue & yellow	50
		(On reverse, last line of German text contains two words.)	

1936
10	B3	9c blue and yellow	45
		(On reverse, last line of German text contains one word.)	

1937
11	B4	9c blue & yellow	45
		(On reverse, German text in German Gothic type.)	

1945
12	B5	9c blue & yellow	45
		(On face, "Universal Postal Union" replaces "Union")	

1948
13	B5	11c blue & yellow	35
		(On face, "Universal Postal Union" replaces "Union")	

1950
14	B6	11c blue & yellow	30
		(On reverse, text in English, Arabic, Chinese, Spanish, Russian)	

1954
15	B7	13c blue & yellow	35
		(On reverse, text in German, English, Arabic, Chinese, Spanish, Russian.)	

No. 15 Surcharged in Various Manners.

1959
16	B7	15c on 13c blue & yellow	45

Individual post offices were instructed to surcharge the 13c coupon, resulting in many types of surcharge in various inks. For example, "REVALUED 15 CENTS," reading vertically; "15," etc.

1959
17	B7	15c blue & yellow	35

1964
18	B7	15c blue & yellow	30
		On face, box at lower left: "Empreinte de contrôle/du Pays d'origine/(date facultative)" replaces "Timbre du/Bureau/d'Emission"	
	a.	Reverse printing 60mm. deep instead of 65mm. (smaller Arabic characters)	30

1969
19	C1	15c blue & yellow	30

1971
20	C2	22c blue & yellow	45

No. 20 Surcharged in Various Manners.

1974
21	C2	26c on 22c blue & yellow	55
		See note after No. 16.	

1975
22	D1	26c blue & yellow	55

No. 22 Surcharged in Various Manners

1976
23	D1	42c on 26c blue & yellow	85
		See note after No. 16.	

1976
24	D1	42c blue & yellow	85

POST OFFICE SEALS

Official Seals begin to appear in 1872. They do not express any value, having no franking power.

The first seal issued was designed to prevent tampering with registered letters while in transit. It was intended to be affixed over the juncture of the flaps of the large official envelopes in which registered mail letters were enclosed and was so used exclusively. Beginning in 1877, official seals were used to repair damaged letters or to close those received by the Post Office unsealed.

POS1

National Bank Note Co.

Typographed from a steel plate.

Two or more plates: 9 subjects (3x3), 30 subjects (3x10).

White Wove Paper.

1872			**Perf. 12.**	**Unwmkd.**	
OX1	POS1	green		12.00	2.50
		On cover			20.00
		Block of four		75.00	
		a. Yellow green, pelure paper		30.00	
		b. Printed on both sides		250.00	
		c. Double impression			
		d. Imperf., pair		500.00	
		e. Horizontally laid paper			

Special Printing.

American Bank Note Co.

Plate of 30 subjects (5x6).

Soft Porous Paper

1880 (?)			**Perf. 12.**	
OX2	POS1	bluish green		425.00

POS2

("Post Obitum" in background.)

National Bank Note Co.

Engraved.

Plate of 100 subjects (10x10)

Silk Paper

1877			**Perf. 12.**		
OX3	POS2	brown		17.50	12.50
		Block of four		200.00	
		On cover			200.00

No. OX3 was intended for use in the Dead Letter Office.

POS3

American Bank Note Co.

Engraved.

Plate of 100 subjects (10x10)

bearing imprint of American Bank Note Co.

Also plates of 50 subjects with or without imprint.

1879			**Perf. 12.**		
OX4	POS3	brown		50	25
		a. dark brown		3.00	5.00
		b. yellow brown		1.00	50
		c. red brown		50	25
		Block of four		5.00	
		On cover			50.00
		Margin block with imprint		20.00	

A so-called "special printing" exists in deep brown on hard white paper.

POST OFFICE SEALS

POS4

Typographed.

Without words in lower label.

Outer frame line at top and left is thick and heavy.

Plate of 42 subjects (7x6).

Thin to Thick Paper

1888-99 *Imperf.*

OX6	POS4	light brown	75	
		a. yellow brown	75	
		b. chocolate, thin paper	5.00	
		Block of four	3.00	
		c. Toned paper		

No. OX6 was not regularly used.

Thin to Thick Paper
Perf. 12.

OX7	POS4	bister brown	20	15
		a. light brown	20	15
		b. chocolate	20	15
		c. gray brown	20	15
		d. dark brown	20	15
		e. rose brown	20	15
		Block of four	1.50	
		On cover		20.00
		f. Imperf. vertically, pair	7.50	—
		g. Imperf. horizontally, pair	7.50	—
		h. Vertical pair, imperf. between	5.00	—
		i. Double impression		
		j. Toned paper		

1892 *Rouletted 5½*

OX8	POS4	light brown	7.50	7.50
		a. brown	7.50	7.50
		Block of four	35.00	
		On cover		50.00

1895 (?) *Hyphen Hole Perf. 7*

OX9	POS4	gray brown	2.75	2.25
		Block of four	15.00	
		On cover		35.00

POS5

Scott Album Supplement Schedule

January
U.S. Commemorative
Plate Blocks
Regular & Air Plate Blocks
U.N. Singles & Postal
Stationery
U.N. Imprint Blocks
National Hingeless

March
Austria
France
Germany

April
Great Britain
British Europe
Channel Islands
Ireland
Monaco & Fr. Andorra
Korea
Israel Singles
Israel Tabs

May
Switzerland
Liechtenstein
Greece
Scandinavia &
Finland

June
Japan
Portugal
Spain & Sp. Andorra
Italy
San Marino
Vatican City

July
Belgium
Netherlands
Luxembourg
U.S.S.R.
Czechoslovakia
Poland
Hungary

August
Australia & Dep.
New Zealand
New Zealand Dep.
Mexico
Br. America Vol. 1
Br. America Vol. 2

November
National
Minuteman
American
Canada
Master Canada
International

December
U.S. Booklet Panes
U.S. Commemorative
Singles
U.S. Blocks of 4
U.S. Postal Stationery
U.S. Postal Cards

Scott Publishing Company
P.O. Box 828
Sidney, OH 45365

All supplements are available from your local dealer or direct from Scott.

POST OFFICE SEALS

Plate of 143 (11x13).

Outer frame line at top and left is thin. Otherwise similar to POS4.

1900-05   Perf. 12.   Lithographed.

OX10	POS5	red brown ('03)	20 20
		Block of four, red brown	1.00
		On cover, red brown	10.00
	a.	gray brown ('01)	1.50 1.50
	b.	yellow brown ('01)	80 80
	c.	dark brown ('02)	90 85
	d.	orange brown ('04)	60 60
	e.	Imperf., (pair), red brown	1.50
	f.	Imperf. vertically (pair)	3.50 —
	g.	Imperf. horizontally (pair)	5.00
	h.	Horiz. or vert. pair, imperf. btwn.	5.00

Design similar to POS5 but smaller. Issued in panes of 10 and 20.

1907   Perf. 12.   Typographed

OX11	POS5	**blue**	10 10
	a.	dark blue	10 10
	b.	violet blue	10 10
		Block of four	40
		On cover	5.00
	c.	Imperf., (pair)	1.00 —
	d.	Imperf. horizontally (pair)	2.00 —
	e.	Imperf. vertically (pair)	2.00 —
	f.	Horiz. or vert. pair, imperf. between	5.00
	h.	Tête bêche pair, perf.	—
	i.	Tête bêche pair, imperf.	20.00
	j.	Tête bêche pair, imperf. between	35.00
	k.	Double impression, imperf., (pair)	25.00
	l.	Double impression, tête bêche pair	35.00
	m.	Wmkd. Seal of U.S. in sheet	1.35 1.35
	n.	Wmkd. "Rolleston Mills" in sheet	1.35 1.35
	p.	Vert. pair with horiz. gutter btwn.	20.00

1912   Rouletted 6½.

OX12	POS5	**blue**	75 75
		Block of four	3.25
		On cover	15.00
	a.	Wmkd. Seal of U.S. in sheet	2.00 1.50
	b.	Wmkd. "Rolleston Mills" in sheet	2.00 1.50

1913   Perf. 12 x Rouletted 6½.

OX13	POS5	**blue**	2.00 2.00
		Block of four	12.00
		On cover	15.00
	a.	Rouletted 6½ x Perf. 12	4.00 4.00
		Block of four	17.50
	b.	Wmkd. Seal of U.S. in sheet	2.50 2.25
	c.	As "a" and "b"	4.50 4.50

1916   Perf. 12.

OX14	POS5	**black**, *pink*	45 65
		Block of four	1.85
		On cover	15.00
	a.	Imperf. horizontally, pair	2.50

1917   Perf. 12.

OX15	POS5	**black**	15 25
	a.	gray black	15 25
		Block of four	60
		On cover	15.00
	b.	Imperf. horizontally, (pair)	5.00
	c.	Vertical pair, imperf. between	10.00
	d.	Horizontal pair, imperf. between	3.50
	e.	Imperf. vertically, (pair)	5.00
	f.	Wmkd. Seal of U.S. in sheet	—
	g.	Imperf., pair	15.00

POS6

Quartermaster General's Office
Issued in sheets of 10.

1919   Perf. 12

OX16	POS6	indigo	75.00
		Block of four	300.00

Rouletted 7.

OX17	POS6	indigo	—

POS7

Issued in panes of 10, 16 or 20.

1919   Perf. 8½, 9, 12, 12½ and Compound

OX18	POS7	**black**	5 5
	a.	gray black	5 5
		Block of four	25
		On cover	2.50
	b.	Imperf., pair	2.00 1.50
	c.	Horiz. pair, imperf. vert.	1.00
	d.	Vert. pair, imperf. horiz.	1.00
	e.	Horiz. or vert. pair, imperf. btwn.	2.00
	g.	Wmkd. Seal of U.S. in sheet	1.00 1.00
	h.	Wmkd. letters	3.00 —

Hyphen Hole Perf. 9½xImperf.
Issued in vertical panes of 5.
Design width: 37½mm.

OX19	POS7	**black**	20 20
		Pane of 5	1.25
		On cover	1.50
	a.	Vert. pair, imperf. between	2.00
	b.	Imperf., pane of 5	5.00

Tab inscribed, "16-56164-1 GPO"

Design width: 38½mm.
Issued in vertical panes of 5.

1970 (?)   Hyphen Hole Perf. 9½xImperf.

OX19C	POS7	**black**	20 20
		Pane of 5	1.75
		On cover	3.00
	d.	Vert. pair, imperf. btwn	4.00
	e.	Imperf., pane of 5	7.50

Tab inscribed, "c43-16-56164-1 GPO"

POS8

Rouletted 6½, 8½ or 9½ x Imperf.,
Hyphen Hole Perf. 7 x Imperf.
Perf. 2½ x Imperf.

1972   Issued in vertical panes of 5   Lithographed

OX20	POS8	**black**	20 20
		Pane of 5	1.25
		On cover	2.00
	a.	Imperf., pair	2.00

Tab inscribed, "LABEL 21, JULY 1971"

TYPESET SEALS.

Little is known of the history and origin, but it is believed that they were privately made for sale to postmasters. Many are extremely rare. Unquestioned varieties are listed.

"U. S. POST OFFICE DEPARTMENT" in capital letters.

TSS1
Imperf.

OX25 TSS1 black 125.00 125.00

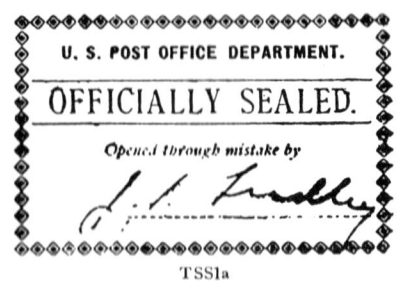

TSS1a
Imperf.

OX25A TSS1a black 150.00
"OFFICALLY"

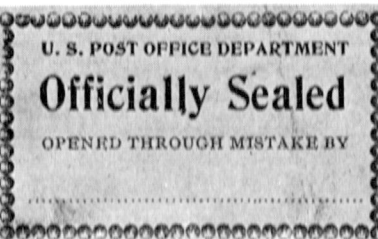

TSS2
Imperf.

OX26 TSS2 black

"U.S. Post Office Department" with initial capitals.

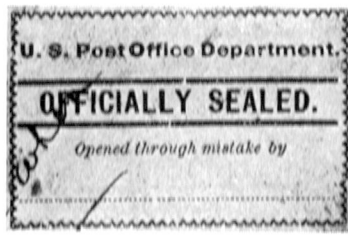

TSS3
Imperf.

OX27 TSS3 black, *pink*

TSS4
Imperf.

OX28 TSS4 black 125.00

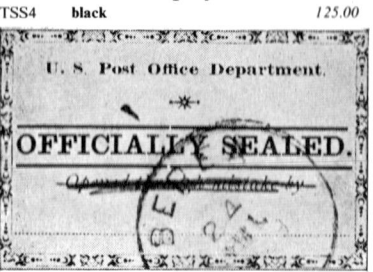

TSS4a
Imperf.

OX28A TSS4a black

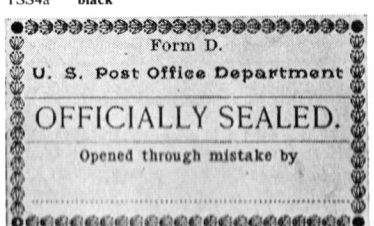

TSS5
Rouletted 9½ horizontally.

OX29 TSS5 black 150.00

TSS6
Printed in panes of four, two tête bêche pairs.
Rouletted 11½, 12½, 16½ in black at top & side

OX30 TSS6 black 30.00 30.00
              Tête bêche pair 70.00
              Sheet of four 150.00

TSS7

POST OFFICE SEALS

Solid lines above and below "OFFICIALLY SEALED"
Printed in panes of four, two tête bêche pairs.
Rouletted 12½, 16½ in black between.

OX31	TSS7	black	150.00	125.00
		Tête bêche pair		
		Sheet of four		

TSS8

Dotted lines above and below "OFFICIALLY SEALED"
Printed in panes of four.
Rouletted, 11½, 12½ or 16½ in black.

OX32	TSS8	black, *pink*	150.00
OX33	"	black	50
		a. Tête bêche pair	1.25
		b. Tête bêche sheet of four	3.00
		c. Period after "OFFICIALLY"	85
		d. As "c" in pair	1.70
		e. As "c" in tête bêche pair	2.00
		f. Tête bêche sheet of four, one stamp with period	4.00
		g. As "c", printed in blue	

"U. S. Postoffice Dept."

[image of TSS9 seal: U. S. Postoffice Dept. OFFICIALLY SEALED Opened through mistake by]

TSS9
Imperf.

OX34	TSS9	black or blue	125.00

[image of TSS10 seal: U. S. Postoffice Dept. OFFICIALLY SEALED Opened through mistake by]

TSS10
Imperf.

OX35	TSS10	blue	

[image of TSS11 seal: U. S. Postoffice Dept. OFFICIALLY SEALED Opened through mistake by]

TSS11

Imperf.

OX36	TSS11	black	
		blue	

"United States Post Office".

TSS12
Imperf.

OX37	TSS12	blue	

[image of TSS13 seal: U. S. Postoffice. Officially Sealed. Opened by Mistake by]

TSS13
Imperf.

OX38	TSS13	dark blue	30.00	30.00
		On cover		
		a. Printed on both sides	325.00	
		b. 2mm. btwn. "y" & "S", no period after "d"	85.00	
OX39	"	black	100.00	

TSS14
Imperf.

OX40	TSS14	black, *light green*	

[image of TSS15 seal: U. S. Postoffice PETALUMA, CAL. Officially Sealed Opened by Mistake by]

TSS15
Imperf.

OX41	TSS15	black, *blue*	

POST OFFICE SEALS

U. S. POST OFFICE,
NORTHFIELD, MASS.
OFFICIALLY SEALED.
OPENED THROUGH MISTAKE BY

TSS16
Imperf.

OX42　TSS16　black

TSS17
Imperf.

OX43　TSS17　black

U. S. Post Office Department.
Ipswich, Mass.
OFFICIALLY SEALED.
Opened through mistake by

TSS18

Imperf.
OX44　TSS18　black

POST OFFICE DEPARTMENT
Officially Sealed
Berkeley, Cal.

TSS19
Imperf.

OX45　TSS19　black
　a. Top line 4mm. high

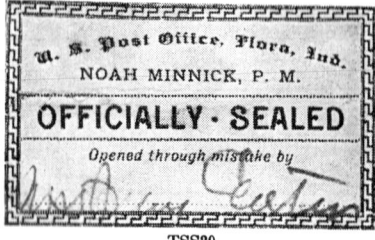

TSS20
Imperf.

OX46　TSS20　black

U. S. POST OFFICE, BERWICK, PA.
Opened through mistake, Aug 18 by
D. C. McHenry
OFFICIALLY SEALED

TSS21
Imperf.

OX47　TSS21　black, *dark brown red*

CHRISTMAS SEALS

Issued by the American National Red Cross (1907–1919), the National Tuberculosis Association (1920–1967), the National Tuberculosis and Respiratory Disease Association (1968–1972) and the American Lung Association (1973–   ).

While the Christmas Seal is not a postage stamp, it has long been associated with the postal service because of its use on letters and packages.

Einar Holboell, an employee of the Danish Post Office, created the Christmas Seal. He believed that seal sales could raise money for charity. The post offices of Denmark, Iceland and Sweden began to sell such seals in the 1904 Christmas season. In the United States, Christmas Seals were first issued in 1907 under the guidance of Emily P. Bissell, following the suggestion of Jacob Riis, social service worker.

Until 1975, all seals (except those of 1907 and 1908 type I) were issued in sheets of 100. The grilled gum (1908) has small square depressions like a waffle. The broken gum (1922), devised to prevent paper curling, consists of depressed lines in the gum, ½mm. apart, forming squares. The vertical and horizontal broken gum (1922, 1923, 1925, 1927–1932) forms diamonds. The perf. 12.00 (1917–1919, 1923, 1925, 1931) has two larger and wider-spaced holes between every 11 smaller holes.

Prices are for seals with original gum.

SEALS ISSUED AND SOLD BY THE DELAWARE CHAPTER OF THE AMERICAN NATIONAL RED CROSS.

CS1 (Type II)

Both types designed by Miss Emily P. Bissell.
Nearly $4,000.00 worth of seals were sold, $3,000.00 cleared.

1907			*Perf. 14*		**Red**
WX1	CS1	Type I. Inscribed "Merry Christmas" only			12.00
WX2	"	Type II. Inscribed "Merry Christmas" and "Happy New Year"			10.00

Types I and II. Lithographed by Theo. Leonhardt & Son, Philadelphia, Pa. The first seals were sold December 7, 1907, in Wilmington, Del. Both types were issued in sheets of 228 seals, 19 horizontal by 12 vertical. Type II was issued to extend the sale of seals until New Year's Day, 1908.
Counterfeits of both types exist (perf. 12).

SEALS ISSUED AND SOLD BY THE AMERICAN NATIONAL RED CROSS

CS2 (Type II)
Designed by Howard Pyle.
Realized from sales $135,000.00.

1908			*Perf. 12, 14.*		**Red and Green**
WX3	CS2	Type I. Frame lines with square corners. Small "C" in "Christmas." Perf. 14.			
		Smooth gum			25.00
		a. Perf. 12. Smooth gum			25.00
		c. Perf. 14. Grilled gum			35.00
		d. Perf. 12. Grilled gum			25.00
		e. Perf. 14. Booklet pane of six. Smooth gum			225.00
		f. Perf. 14. Booklet pane of six. Grilled gum			300.00
		g. Perf. 14. Booklet pane of three. Smooth gum			150.00

WX4	CS2	Type II. Perf. 12. Frame lines have rounded corners. Large "C" in "Christmas", and leaves veined			20.00
		a. Booklet pane of six			100.00
		b. Booklet pane of three			100.00

Type I. Lithographed by Theo. Leonhardt & Son. Sheets of 250 seals, 14 horizontal by 18 vertical, with the first space in the ninth and eighteenth rows left blank.
Type II. Lithographed by the American Bank Note Co., New York, N. Y. in sheets of 100 seals, 10 horizontal by 10 vertical.
Booklet panes have straight edges on three sides and perforated on left side where there is a stub, except No. WX4b which is a vertical strip of three with stub at top. The panes of six were made up in books of 24 and 48 seals and sold for 25c and 50c, and panes of three in books of 9 seals and sold for 10c. The grilled gum has small square depressions like on a waffle.

CS3
Designed by Carl Wingate.
Realized from sales $250,000.00.

1909		*Perf. 12*		**Red and Green**
WX5	CS3	One type only		50

Lithographed by The Strobridge Lithographing Company, Cincinnati, Ohio. Seals with a round punched hole of 3½ mm. are printers' samples.

CS4
Designed by Mrs. Guion Thompson.
Realized from sales $300,000.00.

1910		*Perf. 12*		**Red and Green**
WX6	CS4	One type only		8.00

Lithographed by The Strobridge Lithographing Co.

CHRISTMAS SEALS 759

SEALS ISSUED BY THE AMERICAN NATIONAL RED CROSS BUT SOLD BY THE NATIONAL ASSOCIATION FOR THE STUDY AND PREVENTION OF TUBERCULOSIS.

"The Old Home Among the Cedars"
CS5 (Type II)

Designed by Anton Rudert under directions of F. D. Millet.
Realized from sales $320,000.00.

1911   *Perf. 12.*   Red and Green

WX7   CS5   Type I. Diameter of circle 22 mm. Solid end in house   30.00
WX8   "   Type II. Same circle but thinner. Lined end to house   45.00

COIL STAMP.
Perf. 8½ Vertically.

WX9   CS5   Type III. Diameter of circle 20 mm. Lined end to house   40.00

All three types were typographed by Eureka Specialty Printing Co., Scranton, Pa. Type I has name and address of printer and union label in red in top margin. Type II has union label only in green on left margin.

CS6   CS7 (Type I)
Designed by John H. Zeh.   Designed by C. J. Budd.
Realized from sales $402,256.00.   Realized from sales $449,505.00.

1912   *Perf. 12*   Red, Green & Black

WX10   CS6   One type only   7.50
Lithographed by The Strobridge Lithographing Co.

1913   *Perf. 12*   Red and Green

WX11   CS7   Type I. With Poinsettia flowers and green circles around red crosses at either side   500.00
WX12   "   Type II. The Poinsettia flowers have been removed   5.00
WX13   "   Type III. The Poinsettia flowers and green circles have been removed   6.50
Lithographed by American Bank Note Co.

CS8   CS9
Designed by Benjamin S. Nash.   Designed by Benjamin S. Nash.
Realized from sales $555,854.00.   Realized from sales $760,000.00.

1914   *Perf. 12*   Red, Green & Black

WX15   CS8   One type only   7.50
Lithographed by The Strobridge Lithographing Co.

1915   Red, Green & Black

WX16   CS9   One type only. Perf. 12½   4.50
       a. Perf. 12   25.00
Lithographed by Andrew B. Graham Co., Washington, D. C.

CS10   CS11
Designed by T. M. Cleland.   Designed by T. M. Cleland.
Realized from sales $1,040,810.00.   Realized from sales $1,815,110.00.

1916   Red and Green

WX18   CS10   One type only. Perf. 12   2.50
       a. Perf. 12x12½   2.50
       b. Perf. 12½x12   7.50
       c. Perf. 12x12½   7.50
Lithographed by the Strobridge Lithographing Co.

Seals of 1917-21 are on coated paper.

1917   Red and Green

WX19   CS11   One type only, perf. 12   30
       a. Perf. 12½   7.50
       b. Perf. 12x12.00   35
       c. Perf. 12x12½   7.50

Typographed by Eureka Specialty Printing Co. The Perf. 12.00 has two larger and wider spaced holes between every eleven smaller holes. Sheets come with straight edged margins on all four sides also with perforated margins at either right or left. Perforated margins have the union label imprint in green.

SEALS ISSUED BY THE AMERICAN NATIONAL RED CROSS AND DISTRIBUTED BY THE NATIONAL TUBERCULOSIS ASSOCIATION

CS12
Designed by Charles A. Winter.

These seals were issued but not sold. They were given to members and others in lots of 10, the National Tuberculosis Association being subsidized by a gift of $2,500,000 from the American National Red Cross.

1918   Red, Green and Brown

WX21   CS12   Type I. "American Red Cross" 15 mm. long. Heavy circles between date. Perf. 11½x12.00   3.50
       a. Perf. 12   3.50
       b. Perf. 12.00   Booklet pane of ten   9.00
       c. Perf. 12x12.00   " " "   2.00
       d. Perf. 12   " " "   2.00
       e. Perf. 12.00x12   " " "   50.00

WX22   "   Type II. "American Red Cross" 15½ mm. long. Periods between date. Booklet pane of ten. Perf. 12½xRoulette 9½   2.00
       a. Perf. 12½   Booklet pane of ten   2.00
       b. Perf. 12½x12   " " "   —
       d. Perf. 12½xRoulette 12½   " " "   12.50
       e. Perf. 12½xRoulette 9½   " " "   12.50
       f. Perf. 12½   " " "   —
       h. Roulette 9½xPerf. 12½   " " "   12.50
       i. Roulette 9½xPerf. 12½ and Roulette 9½   " " "   60.00
       j. Perf. 12½x12½   " " "   —
       k. Perf. 12½x12½ and 12   " " "   —
       l. Roulette 9½xPerf. 12½   " " "   —
       m. Perf. 12½   " " "   —
       n. Perf. 12½, stub at bottom   " " "   35.00

Type I. Typographed by Eureka Specialty Printing Co. Type II. Lithographed by Strobridge Lithographing Co.

Nos. WX21–WX21a are from sheet of 100, no straight edges.

Type I. Booklet panes are of 10 seals, 2 horizontal by 5 vertical and normally have straight edges on all four sides. They were cut from the sheets of 100 and can be plated by certain flaws which occur on both. Sheets have union label imprint on top margin in brown.

Type II. Booklet panes are the same but normally have a perforated margin at top and stub attached. These too can be plated by flaws. One or both vertical sides are rouletted on Number WX22e; perforated on Numbers WX22f and WX22h. Number WX22i is rouletted 12½ on left perforatd 12½ on right. Numbers WX22j, WX22k and WX22l are booklet panes of 10 seals arranged 5 x 2. Number WX22m has a perforated margin at left.

The seal with "American Red Cross" 17¼ mm. long is believed to be an essay.

CS13 (Type II)
Designed by Ernest Hamlin Baker.
Realized from sales $3,872,534.00.

1919 **Ultramarine, Red and Green**

WX24 CS13 Type I. Plume at right side of Santa's cap. Perf. 12 — 20
a. Perf. 12x12.00 — 25
b. Perf. 12½x12 — 20
c. Perf. 12½x12.00 — 2.00

WX25 " Type II. No plume but a white dot in center of band on Santa's cap. Perf. 12½ — 25

This is the first time the double barred cross, the emblem of the National Tuberculosis Association, appeared in the design of the seals. It is also the last time the red cross emblem of the American National Red Cross was used on seals.

Type I. Typographed by Eureka Specialty Printing Co., and has union label on margin at left in dark blue. Type II lithographed by The Strobridge Lithographing Co.

SEALS ISSUED AND SOLD BY THE NATIONAL TUBERCULOSIS ASSOCIATION.

CS14
Designed by Ernest Hamlin Baker.
Realized from sales $3,667,834.00.

CS15
Designed by George V. Curtis.
Realized from sales $3,520,303.00

1920 **Ultramarine, Red and Green**

WX26 CS14 Type I. Size of seal 18x22 mm. Perf. 12x12½ — 35
a. Perf. 12 — 35
b. Perf. 12½x12 — 7.50
c. Perf. 12½x12½ — 5.00

WX27 " Type II. Size of seal 18½x23½ mm. Letters larger and numerals heavier than Type I. Perf. 12½ — 30

Type I typographed by Eureka Specialty Printing Co., and has union label imprint and rings on margin at left in dark blue. Type II lithographed and offset printing by The Strobridge Lithographing Co.

1921 **Ultramarine, Red and Green**

WX28 CS15 Type I. The dots in the shading of the chimney and faces are arranged in diagonal lines. The dots on chimney are separate except between the two top rows of bricks where they are a solid mass. Perf. 12½ — 35

WX29 " Type II. The dots in the shading of the chimney and faces are arranged in horizontal lines. Perf. 12½ — 35

WX29A " Type III. The same as Type I except the red dots on chimney are mostly joined and form lines. The dots between the two top rows of bricks are not a solid mass. Perf. 12 — 35

Type I typographed by Eureka Specialty Printing Co. Type II offset printing by The Strobridge Lithographing Co. Type III typographed by Zeese-Wilkinson Company Inc., Long Island City, N. Y.

CS16
Designed by T. M. Cleland.
Realized from sales $3,857,086.00.

CS17
Designed by Rudolph Ruzicka.
Realized from sales $4,259,660.00.

1922 **Pale Ultramarine, Red and Yellow**

WX30 CS16 One type only. Perf. 12½, broken gum — 35
a. Perf. 12, broken gum — 2.00
b. Perf. 12x12½, broken gum — 5.00
c. Perf. 12, smooth gum — 2.00
d. Perf. 12½, vertical broken gum — 5.00

Typographed by Eureka Specialty Printing Co.
The broken gum on this issue, which was devised to prevent curling of paper, consists of depressed lines in the gum ½ mm. apart, forming squares, or vertical broken gum forming diamonds.

1923 **Green and Red**

WX31 CS17 One type only. Perf. 12½. Vertical broken gum — 15
a. Perf. 12 — Horizontal broken gum — 2.50
b. Perf. 12x12.00 — Vertical broken gum — 2.50
c. Perf. 12½x12 — " " " — 5.00
d. Perf. 12 — " " " — 1.00
e. Perf. 12.00x12 — " " " — 2.50

Typographed by Eureka Specialty Printing Co.
The broken gum on this and issues following printed by the Eureka Co. consists of very fine depressed lines forming diamonds. The brown color in seals is due to the overlapping of the two colors.

CS18
Designed by George V. Curtis.
Realized from sales $4,479,656.00.

CS19 (Type II)
Designed by Robert G. Eberhard.
Realized from sales $4,937,786.00

1924 **Red, Ultramarine and Yellow**

WX32 CS18 One type only — 10

Offset printing by The Strobridge Lithographing Co., Edwards & Deutsch Lithographing Co., Chicago, Ill., and The United States Printing & Lithograph Co., Brooklyn, N. Y.

1925 **Green, Red and Pale Green**

WX35 CS19 Type I. Red lines at each side of "1925" do not join red tablet below. Perf. 12½ Vertical broken gum — 10
a. Perf. 12x12, vertical broken gum — 2.50
b. Perf. 12x12½ " " " — 35
c. Perf. 12.00x12½ " " " — —

WX36 " Type II. Red lines, as in Type I, join red tablet below. Perf. 12½ — 10

WX37 " Type III. Same as Type I but shorter rays around flames and "ea" of "Health" smaller. Perf. 12½ — 50

Type I typographed by Eureka Specialty Printing Co. Type II offset printing by Edwards & Deutsch Lithographing Co. Type III lithographed by Gugler Lithographing Co., Milwaukee, Wis.

CS20
Designed by George V. Curtis.
Realized from sales $5,121,872.00.

CS21
Designed by John W. Evans.
Realized from sales $5,419,959.00.

1926 *Perf. 12½* **Black, Red, Blue and Yellow**

WX38 CS20 One type only — 10

Offset printing by Edwards & Deutsch Lithographing Co., and The United States Printing & Lithograph Co.

Printers' marks on sheets: E. & D. has a red dot at upper right on seal No. 91 on some sheets. U. S. P. & L. has a black dot at upper left on seal No. 56 on some sheets.

CHRISTMAS SEALS

1927 — Red, Ultramarine, Green and Black

WX39	CS21	One type only. Perf. 12. Horizontal broken gum	10
		a. Perf. 12. Smooth gum. (See also No. WX 43)	1.00
WX40	"	Perf. 12½. No dot as on No. WX41	10
WX41	"	Perf. 12½. This seal has one larger red dot in background 1mm. above right post of dashboard on sleigh	10
WX42	"	"Bonne Santé" added to design under reindeer and sleigh. For French Canadians. Perf. 12	50
WX43	"	Same as WX39a but body of sleigh a myrtle green instead of green. For English Canadians. Perf. 12	50

All seals of 1927 are offset printing. Nos. WX39 and WX39a by Eureka Specialty Printing Co. No. WX40 by Edwards & Deutsch Lithographing Co. No. WX41 by The United States Printing & Lithograph Co. Nos. WX42 and WX43 by Canadian Bank Note Co., Ottawa, Ont. Canada.

Printers' marks on sheets: Eureka has no mark but can be identified by the Perf. 12. E. & D. has red dot to left of knee of first reindeer on seal No. 92. U. S. P. & Lithe. Co. has two red dots in white gutter, one at lower left of seal No. 46 (and sometimes No. 41) and the other at upper right of seal No. 55. The perforations often strike out one of these dots.

The Gallant Ship "Argosy"
CS22

Designed by John W. Evans.
Realized from sales $5,465,738.00.

CS23

Designed by George V. Curtis.
Realized from sales $5,546,147.00.

1928 — Black, Blue, Red, Orange and Green
Perf. 12½.

WX44	CS22	Type I. Shading on sails broken. Dots in flag regular. Vertical broken gum	10
WX45	"	Type II. Shading on sails broken. Dots in flag spotty	10
WX46	"	Type III. Shading on sails unbroken. Dots in flag regular	10
WX47	"	Type IV. Inscribed "Bonne Année 1929." For French Canadians	35
WX48	"	Type V. Same as Type II but green in water, and black lines of ship heavier and deeper color. For English Canadians	35

All seals of 1928 are offset printing. Type I by Eureka Specialty Printing Co., Type II by The Strobridge Lithographing Co., Type III by Edwards & Deutsch Lithographing Co., and Types IV and V by The Copp Clark Co., Ltd., Toronto, Ont., Canada.

Printers' marks on sheets: Type I comes with and without a blue dash above seal No. 10, also with a blue and a black dash. Type II has two blue dashes below seal No. 100. Type III has red dot in crest of first wave on seal No. 92.

1929 — Blue, Red, Yellow and Black

WX49	CS23	One type only. Perf. 12½. Vertical broken gum	10
		a. Perf. 12. Vertical broken gum	50
		b. Perf. 12½x12. Vertical broken gum	75
WX50	"	Perf. 12½. Smooth gum	10
WX53	"	Inscribed "Bonne Sante 1929" for French Canadians. Perf. 12½	35
		a. Perf. 14x12½	
WX54	"	Inscribed "Christmas Greetings 1929" for English Canadians. Perf. 12½	35

All seals of 1929 are offset printing. Nos. WX49 to WX49b by Eureka Specialty Printing Co. No. WX50 by Edwards & Deutsch Lithographing Co., The United States Printing and Lithograph Co., and R. R. Heywood Co., Inc., New York, N. Y. Nos. WX53 and WX54 by the Copp Clark Co., Ltd.

Printers' marks on sheets: Eureka is without mark but identified by broken gum. E. & D. has a black dot in lower left corner of seal No. 92. U. S. P. & L. Co. has blue dot above bell on seal No. 56. Heywood has a blue dot at lower right corner of seal No. 100.

CS24

Designed by Ernest Hamlin Baker, and redrawn by John W. Evans.
Realized from sales $5,309,352.00.

CS25

Designed by John W. Evans.
Realized from sales $4,526,189.00.

1930 — Green, Red, Gray and Black

WX55	CS24	One type only. Perf. 12½. Vertical broken gum	10
		a. Perf. 12. Vertical broken gum	50
		b. Perf. 12.00x12. " " "	25
		c. Perf. 12½x12. " " "	2.50
		d. Perf. 12. Blkt. pane of 10, horiz. broken gum	50
WX56	"	Perf. 12½. Smooth gum	10
WX59	"	Inscribed "Bonne Santé," on red border of seal, for French Canadians. Perf. 12½	25
WX60	"	Inscribed "Merry Christmas," on red border of seal, for English Canadians. Perf. 12½	25

All seals of 1930 are offset printing. Nos. WX55 to WX55d by Eureka Specialty Printing Co. No. WX56 by The Strobridge Lithographing Co., Edwards & Deutsch Lithographing Co. and The United States Printing & Lithograph Co. Nos. WX59 and WX60 by the Copp Clark Co., Ltd.

Printers' marks on sheets: Eureka has a dot between the left foot and middle of "M" of "Merry" on seal No. 1. Strobridge has two dashes below "ALL" on seal No. 100. E. & D. printed on Nashua paper has dot on coat just under elbow on seal No. 92, and on Gummed Products Co. paper has the dot on seals Nos. 91 and 92. U. S. P. & Litho. Co. has a dash which joins tree to top frame line just under "MA" of "Christmas" on seal No. 55.

The plate for booklet panes was made up from the left half of the regular plate and can be plated by certain flaws which occur on both.

1931 — Green, Black, Red and Cream

WX61	CS25	One type only. Perf. 12½. Horizontal broken gum (see foot note)	50
WX62	"	Perf. 12½. Horizontal broken gum	5
		a. Perf. 12x12½. Horizontal broken gum	35
		b. Perf. 12.00x12½. Horizontal broken gum	2.50
		c. Perf. 12 " " "	1.00
		g. Perf. 12. Vertical broken gum. Booklet pane of 10 seals	50
		h. Perf. 12x12.00. Vertical broken gum. Booklet pane of 10 seals	50
WX63	"	Perf. 12½. Smooth gum	5

All seals of 1931 are offset printing. Nos. WX61 to WX62h by Eureka Specialty Printing Co. No. WX63 by the Strobridge Lithographing Co. No. WX61 has green dash across inner green frame line at bottom center on each seal in sheet except those in first and last vertical rows and the two rows at bottom. This dash is omitted on all other numbers.

Printers' marks on sheets: Eureka has none. Strobridge has the usual two dashes under seal No. 100.

The plate for booklet panes was made up from transfers of sixty seals—twelve horizontal by five vertical. The six panes of the transfer can be plated by minor flaws.

CS26

Designed by Edward F. Volkmann.
Realized from sales $3,470,637.00.

CS27

Designed by Hans Axel Walleen.
Realized from sales $3,429,311.00.

1932 **Red, Ultramarine, Blue, Green and Yellow**

WX64	CS26	One type only. Perf. 12½x12¾	5
		a. Perf. 12½x12¾. Vertical broken gum	40
WX65	"	Perf. 12	5
WX66	"	Perf. 12½	5
WX67	"	Perf. 12½	5

All seals of 1932 are offset printing. No. WX64 by Eureka Specialty Printing Co. No. WX65 by Edwards & Deutsch Lithographing Co. No. WX66 by The United States Printing & Lithograph Co. No. WX67 by Columbian Bank Note Co., Chicago, Ill. Nos. WX64, WX66 and WX67 have a little red spur on bottom inner frame line of each seal, at left corner. Nos. WX65 and WX66 come without the spur.

Printers' marks on sheets: Eureka has a red dash, in each corner of the sheet, which joins the red border to the red inner frame line. E. & D. has a blue dot in snow at lower left on seal No. 91. U.S.P. & L. Co. has a blue dot on top of post on seal No. 56. Columbian Bank Note Co. has small "C" in lower part of girl's coat on seal No. 82.

1933 **Red, Black, Green and Yellow**

WX68	CS27	One type only. Perf. 12	5
WX69	"	Perf. 12½	5

All seals of 1933 are offset printing. No. WX68 by Eureka Specialty Printing Co. No. WX69 by The Strobridge Lithographing Co., The United States Printing & Lithograph Co., and the Columbian Bank Note Co.

Printers' marks on sheets; Eureka has rope joining elbow of figure to left on seals Nos. 11, 20, 91 and 100. Strobridge has the usual two dashes under seal No. 100. U. S. P. & L. Co. has green dot on tail of "s" of "Greetings" on seal No. 55. Columbian has white "c" on margin, under cross, on seal No. 93.

CS28

Designed by Herman D. Giesen.
Realized from sales $3,701,344.00.

CS29

Designed by Ernest Hamlin Baker.
Realized from sales $3,946,498.00.

1934 **Carmine, Ultramarine, Green, Blue and Yellow**

WX72	CS28	One type only. Perf. 12½x12¼	5
WX73	"	Perf. 12½. (see footnote)	5
WX74	"	Perf. 12½. " "	5
WX75	"	Perf. 12½. " "	5

All seals of 1934 are offset printing. No. WX72 by Eureka Specialty Printing Co., No. WX73 by The Strobridge Lithographing Co., No. WX74 by Edwards & Deutsch Lithographing Co. and No. WX75 by The United States Printing & Lithograph Co.

Cutting of blue plate for the under color: Nos. WX72, WX73 (early printing) and WX74 have lettering and date cut slightly larger than ultramarine color. No. WX73 (later printing) has square cutting around letters and date, like top part of letter "T". No. WX75 has cutting around letters and date cut slightly larger.

Printers' marks on sheets. Eureka has five stars to right of cross on seal No. 10. Strobridge has two blue dashes in lower left corner of seal No. 91 or same dashes in lower right corner of seal No. 100. E. & D. has a red dot in lower left corner of seal No. 99. U. S. P. & L. Co. has five stars to left of cross on seal No. 56.

Great Britain issued seals of this design which can be distinguished by the thinner and whiter paper. Sheets have perforated margins on all four sides but without any lettering on bottom margin. The perforation is 12½.

1935 **Blue, Carmine, Red Brown and Green**

WX76	CS29	One type only. Perf. 12½x12¼	5
WX77	"	Perf. 12½	5

All seals of 1935 are offset printing. No. WX76 by Eureka Specialty Printing Co., No. WX77 by The Strobridge Lithographing Co., The United States Printing & Lithograph Co. and Columbian Bank Note Co.

Eureka recut their blue plate and eliminated the faint blue shading around cross, girl's head and at both sides of the upper part of post. U. S. P. & L. Co. eliminated the two brown spurs which pointed to the base of cross, in all four corners of the sheet.

Printers' marks on sheets: Eureka has an extra vertical line of shading on girl's skirt on seal No. 60. Strobridge has two brown dashes in lower right corner of position No. 100 but sheets from an early printing are without this mark. U. S. P. & L. Co. has a blue dot under post on seal No. 55. Columbian has a blue "c" under post on seal No. 99.

The four corner seals in each sheet carry slogans: Seal 1, "Help Fight Tuberculosis." Seal 10, "Protect Your Home from Tuberculosis." Seal 91, "Tuberculosis Is Preventable." Seal 100, "Tuberculosis Is Curable."

Printers' marks appear on seal 56 on sheets of 100 unless otherwise noted:

- E Eureka Specialty Printing Co.
- S Strobridge Lithographing Co. (1930–1958).
- S Specialty Printers of America (1975–).
- D Edwards & Deutsch Lithographing Co.
- U United States Printing & Lithographing Co.
- F Fleming-Potter Co., Inc.
- W Western Lithograph Co.
- B Berlin Lithographing Co. (1956–1969); I. S. Berlin Press (1970–1976); Barton-Cotton (1977–).
- R Bradford-Robinson Printing Co.
- N Sale-Niagara, Inc.

Printers of Canadian seals, unmarked:

Arthurs-Jones Lithographing, Toronto (1943–1949).
Rolph, Clarke and Stone, Toronto (1950–1955).

Seals from 1936 onward are printed by offset.

Seals with tropical gum (dull), starting in 1966, were used in Puerto Rico.

CS30

Designed by Walter I. Sasse.
Realized from sales $4,522,269.00.

CS31

Designed by A. Robert Nelson.
Realized from sales $4,985,697.00.

1936 **Gray, Red, Green and Yellow**

Pair

WX80	CS30	Perf. 12½x12, red & grn. backgrounds (E)	5
WX81	"	Perf. 12½, red & grn. backgrounds (S,D,U)	5

Seals with red background and green cap-band alternate with seals showing green background and red cap-band. The four corner seals, positions 1, 10, 91 and 100, carry the same slogans as those of 1935.

Two of the three Strobridge printings show vertical green dashes in margin below seal 100, besides "S" on seal 56.

1937 **Blue, Red, Black and Yellow**

WX88	CS31	Perf. 12x12½ (E)	5
WX89	"	Perf. 12½ (S,D,U)	5

Four seals in each sheet, positions 23, 28, 73 and 78, carry slogans: "Health for all," "Protect your home," "Preventable" and "Curable."

The "U" printer's mark of United States Printing & Lithographing Co. appears on seal 55. It is omitted on some sheets.

CS32

Designed by Lloyd Coe.
Realized from sales $5,239,526.00.

CS33

Designed by Rockwell Kent.
Realized from sales $5,593,399.00.

1938 **Red, Brown, Green and Black**

WX92	CS32	Perf. 12½x12 (E)	5
WX93	CS32	Perf. 12½ (S,D,U)	5
		a. Miniature sheet, imperf.	2.50

The corner seals of each sheet bear portraits of Rene T. H. Laennec, Robert Koch, Edward Livingston Trudeau and Einar Holböll.

No. WX93a contains the four corner seals, with the regular seal in the center. Inscriptions in black include slogans and "They made landmarks in the fight against tuberculosis," with brief statements on the contributions of Laennec, Koch, Trudeau and Holböll. Size of sheet: 140x86mm. It sold for 25 cents.

CHRISTMAS SEALS

1939		**Red, Ultramarine and Pale Red**	
WX96	CS33	Perf. 12½x12 (E)	5
		a. Booklet pane of 20, Perf. 12	35
WX97	"	Perf. 12½ (S,D,U)	5

The four center seals in each sheet, positions 45, 46, 55 and 56, carry slogans: "Health to All," "Protect Your Home," "Tuberculosis Preventable Curable" and "Holiday Greetings."

CS34
Designed by Felix L. Martini.
Realized from sales $6,305,979.00.

CS35
Designed by Stevan Dohanos.
Realized from sales $7,530,496.00.

1940		**Blue, Ultramarine, Red and Yellow**	
WX100	CS34	Perf. 12½x12 (E)	5
WX101	"	Perf. 12½x13 (E)	5
WX103	"	Perf. 12½ (S,D,U)	5

Three seals in each sheet—positions 23, 32 and 34—carry the slogan "Protect Us from Tuberculosis." Each slogan seal shows one of the three children separately.

1941		**Blue, Black, Red and Yellow**	
WX104	CS35	Perf. 12½x12 (E)	5
WX105	"	Perf. 12½ (S,D,U)	5

"S" and "U" printers' marks exist on same sheet.

CS36
Designed by Dale Nichols.
Realized from sales $9,390,117.00.

CS37
Designed by André Dugo.
Realized from U. S. sales $12,521,494.00.

1942		**Yellow, Blue, Red and Black**	
WX108	CS36	Perf. 12x12½ (E)	5
WX109	"	Perf. 12½ (S,D,U)	5
1943		**Blue, Red, Buff and Black Pair**	
WX112	CS37	Perf. 12½x12 (E)	5
WX113	"	Perf. 12½ (S,D,U)	5
WX116	"	"Joyeux Noel" replaces "Greetings 1943" and "1943" added on curtain. For French Canadians. Perf. 12½	10
WX117	"	Same as WX113 but darker colors. For English Canadians and Great Britain. Perf. 12½	10

On alternate seals, the vertical frame colors (blue and red) are transposed and the horizontal frame colors (buff and black) are transposed.

CS38
Designed by Spence Wildey.
Realized from U. S. sales $14,966,227.00.

CS39
Designed by Park Phipps.
Realized from U. S. sales $15,638,755.00.

1944		**Gray, Blue, Red and Yellow**	
WX118	CS38	Perf. 12½x12 (E)	5
WX119	"	Perf. 12½ (S,D,U)	5
WX122	"	"Joyeux Noel" replaces "Merry Christmas" and "U S A" omitted. For French Canadians. Perf. 12½	10
WX123	"	Same as WX119 but "U S A" omitted. For English Canadians. Perf. 12½	10
1945		**Blue, Red, Black and Yellow**	
		"USA" at Lower Right Corner.	
WX124	CS39	Perf. 12½x12 (E)	5
WX125	"	Perf. 12½ (S,D,U)	5
WX128	"	"Bonne Santé" replaces "Greetings" and "USA" omitted. For French Canadians. Perf. 12½	10
WX129	"	Same as WX125 but "USA" omitted. For English Canadians. Perf. 12½	10

CS40
Designed by Mary Louise Estes and Lloyd Coe.
Realized from U. S. sales $17,075,608.44.

CS41
Designed by Raymond H. Lufkin.
Realized from U. S. sales $18,665,523.00.

1946		**Blue, Black, Red and Olive**	
		"USA" at Left of Red Cross.	
WX130	CS40	Perf. 12½x12 (E)	5
WX131	"	Perf. 12½ (S,D,U)	5
WX132	"	"Bonne Santé" replaces "Greetings" and "U S A" omitted. For French Canadians. Perf. 12½	10
WX133	"	Same as WX131 but "USA" omitted. For English Canadians and Great Britain. Perf. 12½	10
		a. Same, overprinted "NEWFOUNDLAND"	1.25
WX134	"	"Bermuda" replaces seven stars and "U S A" omitted. For Bermuda. Perf. 12½x12 (E)	25

Printers' marks are on seal 86.
The four center seals (45, 46, 55, 56) of Nos. WX130 and WX131 bear portraits of Jacob Riis, Emily P. Bissell, E. A. Van Valkenburg and Leigh Mitchell Hodges.

1947		**Red, Blue, Green and Brown**	
WX135	CS41	Perf. 12x12½ (E)	5
WX136	"	Perf. 12½ (S,D,U)	5
WX137	"	"Bonne Santé" replaces "Merry Christmas" and "U S A" omitted. For French Canadians. Perf. 12½	5
WX138	"	Same as WX136 but "U S A" omitted. For English Canadians and Great Britain. Perf. 12½	5
WX139	"	"BERMUDA" overprinted in red on WX138. For Bermuda. Perf. 12½	20

The "U" printer's mark of United States Printing & Lithographing Co. appears on seal 46.

CS42
Designed by Jean Barry Bart.
Realized from U. S. sales $20,153,834.47.

CS43
Designed by Herbert Meyers.
Realized from U. S. sales $20,926,794.15.

1948		**Blue, Red, Light Blue and Yellow**	
WX140	CS42	Perf. 12x12½ (E)	5
WX141	"	Perf. 12½ (S,D,U)	5
WX142	"	"Bonne Santé" replaces "Merry Christmas", date in white and "USA" omitted. For French Canadians. Perf. 12½	5

764 CHRISTMAS SEALS

WX143	"	Same as WX141 but date in white and "U S A" omitted. For English Canadians, Great Britain and Newfoundland. Perf. 12½	5
WX144	"	"BERMUDA" overprinted in black on WX143. Perf. 12½	20

1949   Green, Light Blue, Red and Ultramarine

WX145	CS43	Perf. 12x12½ (E)	5
WX146	"	Perf. 12½ (S,D,U)	5
WX147	"	"Bonne Santé" replaces "Greetings" and "U S A" omitted. For French Canadians. Perf. 12½	5
WX148	"	Same as WX146 but "U S A" omitted. For English Canadians, Great Britain and Newfoundland. Perf. 12½	5
WX149	"	"BERMUDA" replaces "USA" on WX145. For Bermuda. Perf. 12x12½ (E)	15

CS44
Designed by André Dugo.
Realized from U. S. sales $20,981,540.77.

CS45
Designed by Robert K. Stephens.
Realized from U. S. sales $21,717,953.09.

1950   Red, Green, Orange and Black

WX150	CS44	Perf. 12½x12 (E)	5
WX151	"	Perf. 12½ (S,D,U,F)	5
WX152	"	"Bonne Santé" replaces "Greetings" and "USA" omitted. For French Canadians. Perf. 12½	5
WX153	"	Same as WX151 but "USA" omitted. For English Canadians and Great Britain. Perf 12½	5
WX154	"	Same as WX150 but "BERMUDA" in larger letters replaces "USA" at bottom (E)	15

1951   Blue Green, Red, Flesh and Black

WX155	CS45	Perf. 12½x12 (E)	5
WX156	"	Perf. 12½ (S,D,U,F)	5
WX157	"	Same as WX156 but "U. S. A." omitted. For English Canadians. Perf. 12½.	5
WX158	"	"BERMUDA" replaces "USA" on WX155. For Bermuda. Perf 12½x12 (E)	15

CS46
Designed by Tom Darling.
Realized from U. S. sales $23,238,148.12.

CS47
Designed by Elmer Jacobs and E. Willis Jones.
Realized from U. S. sales $23,889,044.50.

1952   Green, Yellow, Red and Black

WX159	CS46	Perf. 12½x12 (E)	5
WX160	"	Perf. 12½ (S,D,U,F)	5
WX161	"	"CANADA" replaces "Christmas Greetings." Copyright mark and "USA" eliminated. Perf. 12½	5
WX162	"	"BERMUDA" in vertical lettering at right. "USA" eliminated. Perf. 12½x12 (E)	15
WX163	"	Overprinted "Ryukyus" (in Japanese characters) in black. Perf. 12½x12, 12½ (U)	1.50

1953   Gold, Red, Green and Black

WX164	CS47	Perf. 13 (E)	5
WX165	"	Perf. 12½ (S,D,U,F)	5
WX166	"	"CANADA" replaces "Greetings." Copyright mark, "NTA" and "USA" eliminated. Perf. 12½	5
WX167	"	"BERMUDA" replaces "NTA" and "USA." Perf. 13 (E)	15

CS48
Designed by Jorgen Hansen.
Realized from U. S. sales $24,670,202.85.

1954   Yellow, Black, Green and Red
Block of Four

WX168	CS48	Perf. 13 (E)	10
WX169	"	Perf. 12½ (S,U,F,W)	10
WX170	"	Perf. 11 (D)	10
WX171	"	CANADA, perf. 12½	20
WX172	"	BERMUDA, perf. 13 (E)	1.00

CS49
Designed by Miss Jean Simpson.
Realized from U. S. sales $25,780,365.96.

1955   Ultramarine, Olive Green, Red and Blue
Pair

WX173	CS49	Perf. 13 (E)	5
WX174	"	Perf. 12½ (S,U,F,W)	5
WX175	"	Perf. 11 (D)	5
WX176	"	CANADA, perf. 10½	10
WX177	"	BERMUDA, perf. 13 (E)	30

CS50
Designed by Heidi Brandt.
Realized from U. S. sales $26,310,491.

CHRISTMAS SEALS

1956 Dull Yellow, Red, Green and Black
Block of Four

WX178	CS50	Perf. 12½x12 (E)	10
WX179	"	Perf. 12½ (E,S,U,F,W)	10
WX180	"	Perf. 11 (D,B)	10
WX181	"	"Canada," perf. 11, pair	10
WX182	"	BERMUDA, perf. 12½	75
WX183	"	"Puerto Rico," perf. 12½	1.25

CS51
Designed by Clinton Bradley.
Realized from U. S. sales $25,959,998.51.

1957 Dark Green, Light Green, Red and Yellow
Block of Four

WX184	CS51	Perf. 13 (E)	10
WX185	"	Perf. 12½ (S,U,F,W,R)	10
WX186	"	Perf. 11 (D,B)	10
WX187	"	Perf. 10½x11 (D)	10
WX188	"	Perf. 10½ (D)	10
WX189	"	"Bermuda," perf. 13, pair	30
WX190	"	"Puerto Rico," perf. 13	1.25

CS52
Designed by Alfred Guerra.
Realized from U.S. sales $25,955,390.47

1958 Red, Green, Yellow and Black
Pair

WX191	CS52	Perf. 13 (E)	5
WX192	"	Perf. 12½ (S,U,F,W,R)	5
WX193	"	Perf. 10½x11 (B,D)	5
WX194	"	Perf. 11 (B,D)	5
WX195	"	"Bermuda," perf. 13	30
WX196	"	"Puerto Rico," perf. 13	60

CS53
Designed by Katherine Rowe.
Realized from U.S. sales $26,740,906.16.

1959 Crimson, Green, Bister & Black
Pair

WX197	CS53	Perf. 13 (E)	5
WX198	"	Perf. 12½ (F,R,W)	5
		a. Horiz. pair, imperf. btwn. (D)	1.50
WX199	"	Perf. 10½x11 (B)	5
WX200	"	Perf. 11 (B,D)	5
WX201	"	Perf. 10½ (B)	5
WX202	"	"Bermuda," perf. 13	30
WX203	"	"Puerto Rico," perf. 13	60

Edwards & Deutsch Lithographing Co. omitted every other vertical row of perforation on a number of sheets which were widely distributed as an experiment. No. WX198a is from one of these sheets.

CS54
Designed by Philip Richard Costigan.
Realized from U.S. sales $26,259,030.37.

1960 Red, Bistre, Green & Black
Block of Four

WX204	CS54	Perf. 12½ (E,F,R,W)	10
WX205	"	Perf. 12½x12 (E)	10
WX206	"	Perf. 11x10½ (B)	10
WX207	"	Perf. 11 (D)	10
WX208	"	"Bermuda," perf. 12½	75

Puerto Rico used No. WX204 (E).

CS55
Designed by Heidi Brandt.
Realized from U.S. sales $26,529,517.20.

1961 Dark Blue, Yellow, Green and Red
Block of Four

WX209	CS55	Perf. 12½ (E,F,R,W)	10
WX209A	"	Perf. 12½x12 (E)	10
WX210	"	Perf. 11x10½ (B)	10
WX211	"	Perf. 11 (D)	10
WX212	"	"Bermuda," perf. 12½	75

Puerto Rico used No. WX209 (E).

CS56
Designed by Paul Dohanos
Realized from U.S. sales $27,429,202.18.

CHRISTMAS SEALS

1962   **Emerald, Red, Prussian Blue & Yellow**
Block of Four

WX213	CS56	Perf. 12½ (F,R,W)	10
WX214	"	Perf. 13 (E)	10
WX215	"	Perf. 10½x11 (B)	10
WX216	"	Perf. 11 (D,B)	10
WX217	"	"Bermuda," perf. 13	75

Puerto Rico used No. WX214.

CS57

Designed by Judith Campbell Plussi.
Realized from U.S. sales $27,411,806.

1963   **Bright Ultra., Yel., Red, Green, Orange & Black**
Block of Four

| WX218 | CS57 | Perf. 12½ (E,F,R,W) | 10 |
| WX219 | " | Perf. 11 (B,D) | 10 |

Puerto Rico used No. WX218 (E).

CS58

Designed by Gaetano di Palma
Realized from U.S. sales $28,784,043.

1964   **Bister, Red, Emerald & Black**
Block of Four

| WX220 | CS58 | Perf. 12½ (E,F,R,W) | 10 |
| WX221 | " | Perf. 11 (B,D) | 10 |

Puerto Rico used No. WX221 (B).

CS59

Designed by Frede Salomonsen.
Realized from U.S. sales $29,721,878.

1965   **Blue, Red, Yellow, Green & Black**
Block of Four

WX222	CS59	Perf. 12½ (F,W)	10
WX223	"	Perf. 11 (B,D)	10
WX224	"	Perf. 13 (E)	10

Puerto Rico used No. WX223 (B).

CS60

Designed by Heidi Brandt.
Realized from U.S. sales $30,776,586.

1966   **Yellow Green, Black, Red & Yellow**
Block of Eight

WX225	CS60	Perf. 12½ (E,F,W)	25
WX226	"	Perf. 10½x11 (B)	25
WX227	"	Perf. 11 (D)	25

Blocks of four seals with yellow green and white backgrounds alternate in sheet in checkerboard style.
Puerto Rico used No. WX226.

Holiday Train
CS61

Designed by L. Gerald Snyder.
Realized from U.S. sales $31,876,773.

The seals come in 10 designs showing a train filled with Christmas gifts and symbols. The direction of the train is reversed in alternating rows as are the inscriptions "Christmas 1967" and "Greetings 1967". The illustration shows first two seals of top row. Each listing stands for two horizontal rows of 10 seals.

1967   **Red, Green, Black, Blue & Yellow**

Block of 20 (10x2)

WX228	CS61	Perf. 13 (E)	30
WX229	"	Perf. 12½ (F,W)	30
WX230	"	Perf. 10½ (B)	30
WX231	"	Perf. 11 (D)	30
WX232	"	Perf. 11x10½ (B)	30

Puerto Rico used No. WX229 (F).

CHRISTMAS SEALS

SEALS ISSUED BY NATIONAL TUBERCULOSIS AND RESPIRATORY DISEASE ASSOCIATION

CS62
Designed by William Eisele.
Realized from U.S. sales $33,059,107.

1968   Bluish Green, Yellow, Blue, Black & Red
Block of Four

WX233	CS62	Perf. 13 (E)	10
WX234	"	Perf. 10½x11 (B)	10
WX234A	"	Perf. 10½ (B)	10
WX235	"	Perf. 11 (D)	10
WX236	"	Perf. 12½ (F,W)	10

Blocks of four seals with bluish green and yellow backgrounds alternate in sheet in checkerboard style.
Puerto Rico used No. WX236 (F).

CS63
Designed by Bernice Kochan.
Realized from U.S. sales $34,437,591.

1969   Blue Grn., Verm., Emerald, Magenta & Black
Block of Four

WX237	CS63	Perf. 13 (E)	10
WX238	"	Perf. 12½ (F,W)	10
WX239	"	Perf. 10½x11 (B)	10
WX240	"	Perf. 11 (B)	10

Puerto Rico used No. WX238 (F).

CS64
Designed by L. Gerald Snyder.
Realized from U.S. sales $36,237,977.

Sheets of 100 show different design for each seal, Christmas symbols, toys, decorated windows; inscribed alternately "Christmas 1970" and "Greetings 1970." The illustration shows 6 seals from the center of the sheet.

1970   Ultramarine, Black, Red, Yellow & Olive
Sheet of 100 (10x10)

WX242	CS64	Perf. 12½ (E,F,W)	1.00
WX243	"	Perf. 11 (B)	1.00
WX244	"	Perf. 11x10½ (B)	1.00

Puerto Rico used No. WX242 (F).

CS65
Designed by James Clarke.
Realized from U.S. sales $36,120,000.

1971   Lilac Rose, Yellow, Green & Blue
Block of Eight (2x4)

| WX245 | CS65 | Perf. 12½ (E,F) | 20 |
| WX246 | " | Perf. 11 (B) | 20 |

The four illustrated seals each come in a second design arrangement: cross at left, inscriptions transposed, and reversed bugler, candle and tree ornaments. Each sheet of 100 has six horizontal rows of seals as shown and four rows with second designs.
Puerto Rico used No. WX245 (F).
Eureka printings are found with large "E", small "E" and without "E".

CS66
Designed by Linda Layman.
Realized from U.S. sales $38,000,557.

The seals come in 10 designs showing various holiday scenes with decorated country and city houses, carolers, Christmas trees and snowman. Inscribed alternately "1972 Christmas" and "Greetings 1972." Illustration shows seals from center of row.

1972   Bright Blue, Red, Green, Yellow & Black
Strip of 10

| WX247 | CS66 | Perf. 13 (E) | 30 |

Blue, Red, Green, Yellow & Black

| WX248 | CS66 | Perf. 12½ (F) | 30 |

Ultramarine, Red, Green, Yellow & Black

| WX249 | CS66 | Perf. 11 (B) | 30 |

Seal 100 has designer's name.
Puerto Rico used No. WX248.

CHRISTMAS SEALS

SEALS ISSUED BY AMERICAN LUNG ASSOCIATION

CS67

Designed by Cheri Johnson.
Realized from U.S. sales $36,902,439.

The seals are in 12 designs representing "The 12 Days of Christmas." Inscribed alternately "Christmas 1973" and "Greetings 1973." Illustration shows block from center of top two rows.

1973 Multicolored
Block of 12

WX250	CS67	Perf. 12½ (F), 18x22mm.		35
	a.	Size 16½x20½mm. (E)		35
WX251	"	Perf. 11 (B,W)		35

Seal 100 has designer's name.
Puerto Rico used No. WX250 (F).

CS68

Designed by Rubidoux.
Realized from U.S. sales $37,761,745.

1974 Green, Black, Red, Yellow & Blue
Block of Four

WX252	CS68	Perf. 12½ (E,F)		10
WX253	"	Perf. 11 (B)		10

Seal 99 has designer's name.
Puerto Rico used No. WX252 (F).

CS69

Children's paintings of holiday scenes. Different design for each seal, inscribed with name of state or territory. Paintings by elementary school children were selected in a nationwide campaign ending in January, 1974.
Realized from U.S. contributions $34,710,107.

1975 Multicolored
Sheet of 54 (6x9)

WX254	CS69	Perf. 12½ (S,F)		75
WX255	"	Perf. 11 (B)		75

Printers' marks are on seal 28 (New Mexico). Specialty Printers' seals (S) carry union labels: "Scranton 4", "Scranton 7", "E. Stroudsburg".
Puerto Rico used No. WX254 (F).

CS70

Continuous village picture covers sheet with Christmas activities and Santa crossing the sky with sleigh and reindeer. No inscription on 34 seals. Others inscribed "Christmas 1976", "Greetings 1976", and (on 9 bottom-row seals) "American Lung Association". Illustration shows seals 11–12, 20–21.
Realized from U.S. contributions $36,489,207.

1976 Multicolored
Sheet of 54 (9x6)

WX256	CS70	Perf. 12½ (F,N)		75
WX257	"	Perf. 11 (B)		75
WX258	"	Perf. 13 (S)		75

Printers' marks (N, B, S) on seal 32 and (F) on seal 23.
Puerto Rico used No. WX256 (F).

CHRISTMAS SEALS

Beginning in 1979 there is no longer one national issue. Additional designs are issued on a limited basis as test seals to determine the designs to be used the following year.

CS71

Children's paintings of holiday scenes. Different design for each seal, inscribed with name of state or territory.
Realized from U.S. contributions $37,583,883.

1977 Multicolored
Sheet of 54 (6x9)

WX259	CS71	Perf. 12½ (F)	75
WX260	"	Perf. 11 (B)	75
WX261	"	Perf. 13 (S)	75

Printers' marks on seal 28 (Georgia).
Puerto Rico used No. WX259.

CS72

Children's paintings of holiday scenes. Different design for each seal, inscribed with name of state or territory.
Realized from U.S. contributions $37,621,466.

1978 Multicolored
Sheet of 54 (6x9)

WX262	CS72	Perf. 12½ (F)	75
WX263	"	Perf. 11 (B)	75
WX264	"	Perf. 13 (S)	75

Printers' marks on seal 29 (New Hampshire).
Puerto Rico used No. WX262.

Type of 1978 Inscribed 1979

Children's paintings of holiday scenes. Different design for each seal, inscribed with name of state or territory.

1979 Multicolored
Sheet of 54 (6x9)

WX265	CS72	Perf. 12½ (F)	75
WX266	"	Perf. 11 (B)	75
WX267	"	Perf. 13 (S)	75

Printer's marks on seal 22 (Virgin Islands). Puerto Rico used No. WX265.

CONFEDERATE STATES

PROVISIONAL ISSUES

These stamps and envelopes were issued by individual postmasters generally during the interim between June 1, 1861, when the use of United States stamps stopped in the Confederacy, and Oct. 16, 1861, when the first Confederate Government stamps were issued. They were occasionally issued at later periods, especially in Texas, when regular issues of Government stamps were unavailable.

Canceling stamps of the post offices were often used to produce envelopes, some of which were supplied in advance by private citizens. These envelopes and other stationery therefore may be found in a wide variety of papers, colors, sizes and shapes, including patriotic and semi-official types. It is often difficult to determine whether the impression made by the canceling stamp indicates provisional usage or merely postage paid at the time the letter was deposited in the post office. Occasionally the same mark was used for both purposes.

The *press-printed* provisional envelopes are in a different category. They were produced in quantity, using envelopes procured in advance by the postmaster, such as those of Charleston, Lynchburg, Memphis, etc. *The press-printed envelopes are listed and priced on all known papers.*

The *handstamped* provisional envelopes are listed and priced according to type and variety of handstamp, but not according to paper. Many exist on such a variety of papers that they defy accurate, complete listing. The value of a handstamped provisional envelope is determined *primarily* by the clarity of the markings and its overall condition and attractiveness, rather than the type of paper. *All handstamped provisional envelopes, when used, should also show the postmark of the town of issue.*

Most handstamps are impressed at top right, although they exist from some towns in other positions.

Many illustrations in this section are reduced in size.

Prices for envelopes are for entires.

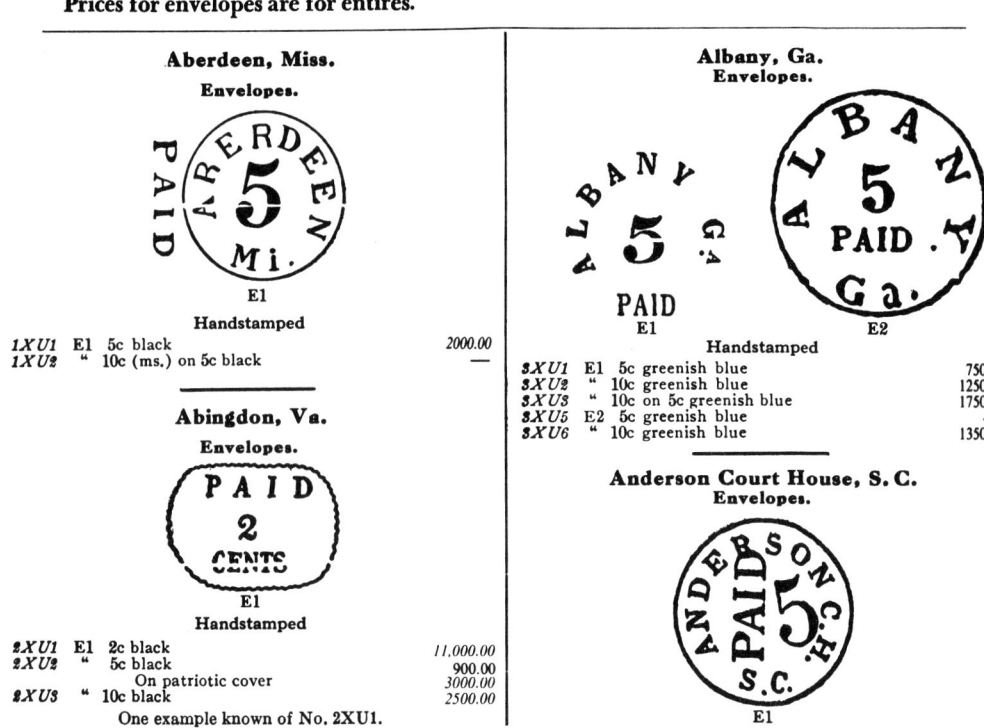

Aberdeen, Miss.
Envelopes.

E1
Handstamped

1XU1	E1	5c black	2000.00
1XU2	"	10c (ms.) on 5c black	—

Abingdon, Va.
Envelopes.

E1
Handstamped

2XU1	E1	2c black	11,000.00
2XU2	"	5c black	900.00
		On patriotic cover	3000.00
2XU3	"	10c black	2500.00

One example known of No. 2XU1.

Albany, Ga.
Envelopes.

PAID
E1   E2
Handstamped

3XU1	E1	5c greenish blue	750.00
3XU2	"	10c greenish blue	1250.00
3XU3	"	10c on 5c greenish blue	1750.00
3XU5	E2	5c greenish blue	—
3XU6	"	10c greenish blue	1350.00

Anderson Court House, S. C.
Envelopes.

E1

CONFEDERATE STATES

4XU1	E1	5c black		1000.00
4XU2	"	10c (ms.) black	700.00	3000.00

Athens, Ga.

A1 (type 1) A1 (type II)

Printed from woodcuts of two types. Pairs, both horizontal and vertical, always show one of each type.

5X1	A1	5c purple (shades)	750.00	800.00
		Pair	—	1750.00
		On cover		2000.00
		Pair on cover		3250.00
		Strip of four on cover (horiz.)		10,000.00
	a.	Tête bêche pair (vertical)		4000.00
		Tête bêche pair on cover		7500.00
5X2	"	5c red	—	2500.00
		On cover		8000.00
		Pair on cover		—

CANCELLATIONS.
Black grid | Black "Paid"
Black town

Atlanta, Ga.
Envelopes.

E1 E2

Handstamped

6XU1	E1	5c red		2000.00
6XU2	"	5c black	150.00	750.00
		On patriotic cover		4000.00
		On U. S. envelope No. U28		—
6XU3	"	10c on 5c black		1500.00
6XU4	E2	2c black		3500.00
6XU5	"	5c black		800.00
		On patriotic cover		2250.00
6XU6	"	10c black		700.00
6XU7	"	10c on 5c black		2500.00

E3

Handstamped

6XU8	E3	5c black		3250.00
6XU9	"	10c black ("10" upright)		2250.00

Augusta, Ga.
Envelope.

E1

7XU1	E1	5c black		—
		Provisional status questioned.		

Austin, Miss.
Envelope.

E1

Typographed. Impressed at top right.

8XU1	E1	5c red, *amber*		14,500.00
		Cancellation is black "Paid".		
		One example known.		

Austin, Texas.
Envelope

E1

Handstamped

9XU1	E1	10c black		1350.00

Cut squares of No. 9XU1 are known as adhesives on cover.

Autaugaville, Ala.
Envelopes.

E1 E2

Handstamped

10XU1	E1	5c black		8000.00
10XU2	E2	5c black		5000.00

Baton Rouge, La.

A1 A2

Typeset. Ten varieties of each.

11X1	A1	2c green	5000.00	3500.00
		On cover		10,000.00
	a.	"McCormick"	8000.00	7500.00
	a.	On cover		12,000.00
11X2	A2	5c green & carmine		
		(Maltese cross border)	1100.00	800.00
		On cover		3000.00
		Strip of three		4000.00
		Strip of five		8500.00
		Used in New Orleans, on cover		8000.00
	a.	"McCormick"	—	2000.00
	a.	On cover		6500.00

A3 A4

11X3	A3	5c green & car. (crisscross border)		3000.00	1750.00
		On cover			6250.00
		a. "McCormick"			3250.00
11X4	A4	10c blue			15,000.00
		On cover			32,500.00

Cancellation on Nos. 11X1–11X4: black town.

Beaumont, Texas.

A1   A2

Typeset.
Several varieties of each.

12X1	A1	10c black, *yellow*		—	4500.00
		On cover			8000.00
12X2	"	10c black, *pink*		—	4000.00
		On cover			6500.00
12X3	A2	10c black, *yellow*, on cover			35,000.00

Cancellations: black pen; black town.
One example known of No. 12X3.

Bridgeville, Ala.

A1

Handstamped in black within red pen-ruled squares.

13X1	A1	5c black & red, pair on cover		20,000.00

Cancellation is black pen.

Canton, Miss.
Envelopes.

E1

"P" in star is initial of Postmaster William Priestly.
Handstamped

14XU1	E1	5c black		1850.00
14XU2	"	10c (ms.) on 5c black		3500.00

Chapel Hill, N. C.
Envelope.

E1
Handstamped

15XU1	E1	5c black		1750.00
		On patriotic cover		4500.00

Charleston, S. C.

A1
Lithographed

16X1	A1	5c blue		500.00	500.00
		Pair		1500.00	1200.00
		On cover			1350.00
		On patriotic cover			5000.00
		Pair, on cover			5000.00

Cancellation: black town (two types).

Envelopes.

E1   E2

Typographed from Woodcut.

16XU1	E1	5c blue, *white*		300.00	1000.00
16XU2	"	5c blue, *amber*		300.00	1000.00
16XU3	"	5c blue, *orange*		300.00	1000.00
16XU4	"	5c blue, *buff*		300.00	1000.00
16XU5	"	5c blue, *blue*		300.00	1000.00
16XU6	E2	10c blue, *orange*			16,500.00

One example known of No. 16XU6.
Handstamped.

16XU7	E2	10c black		3000.00

Chattanooga, Tenn.
Envelopes.

E1
Handstamped

17XU2	E1	5c black		1750.00
17XU3	"	5c on 2c black		—

Christiansburg, Va.
Envelopes.

E1
Typeset. Impressed at top right

99XU1	E1	5c black, *blue*		1250.00
99XU2	"	5c blue, *white*		1250.00
99XU3	"	5c black, *orange*		1250.00
99XU4	"	5c green on U. S. envelope No. U27		
99XU5	"	10c black, *blue*		4500.00

CONFEDERATE STATES

Columbia, S. C.
Envelopes.

E1   E2

Handstamped

18XU1	E1	5c blue	135.00	750.00
18XU2	"	5c black	235.00	750.00
18XU3	"	10c on 5c blue	—	

Three types of "PAID", one in circle.

			1000.00	
18XU4	E2	5c blue (seal on front)		900.00
		a. Seal on back		1400.00
18XU5	"	10c blue (seal on back)		

Circular Seal similar to E2, 27 mm. diameter.

18XU6	E2	5c blue (seal on back)	1000.00

Columbia, Tenn.
Envelope.

E1

Handstamped

113XU1	E1	5c red	2250.00

Columbus, Ga.
Envelopes.

E1

Handstamped

19XU1	E1	5c blue	1000.00
19XU2	"	10c red	2500.00

Courtland, Ala.
Envelopes.

E1

Provisional status of No. 103XU1 questioned.

Handstamped from Woodcut

103XU1	E1	5c black	—	
103XU2	"	5c red		10,000.00

Dalton, Ga.
Envelopes.

E1

Handstamped

20XU1	E1	5c black	500.00
20XU2	"	10c black	700.00
20XU3	"	10c (ms.) on 5c black	1000.00

Danville, Va.

A1

Typeset, two varieties known.

Wove Paper

21X1	A1	5c red	5500.00
		Cut to shape	4000.00
		On cover	15,000.00
		On cover, cut to shape	6000.00

Laid Paper

21X2	A1	5c red	6500.00
		On cover, cut to shape	10,000.00

Cancellation: black town.

Envelopes

E1

E2   E3

Typographed.

Two types; "SOUTHERN" in straight or curved line. Impressed (usually) at top left.

21XU1	E1	5c black, *white*	5500.00
21XU2	"	5c black, *amber*	5500.00
21XU3	"	5c black, *dark buff*	4750.00

Handstamped.

21XU4	E2	10c black	1250.00
21XU5	"	10c blue	1250.00
21XU6	E3	10c black	1400.00

Types E2 and E3 both exist on one cover.

Demopolis, Ala.
Envelopes.

E1
Handstamped. Signature in ms.

22XU1	E1	5c black ("Jno. Y. Hall")	1250.00
22XU2	"	5c black ("J. Y. Hall")	1250.00
22XU3	"	5c (ms.) black ("J. Y. Hall")	1000.00

Eatonton, Ga.
Envelopes.

E1
Handstamped

| 23XU1 | E1 | 5c black | 3000.00 |
| 23XU2 | " | 5c+5c black | 1250.00 |

Emory, Va.

PAID

A1

Handstamped on margins of sheets of U.S. 1c stamps, 1857 issue. Also known with "5" above "PAID."

Perforated 15 on three sides.

| 24X1 | A1 | 5c blue | —— | 4000.00 |
| | | On cover | | 6000.00 |

Cancellation: blue town.

Envelopes

E1   E2
Handstamped

| 24XU1 | E1 | 5c blue | 1000.00 |
| 24XU2 | E2 | 10c blue | 2000.00 |

Fincastle, Va.
Envelope.

```
FINCASTLE
    10
   PAID
```

E1
Typeset. Impressed at top right.

| 104XU1 | E1 | 10c black | 15,000.00 |

One example known.

Franklin, N. C.
Envelope.

E1
Typographed. Impressed at top right.

| 25XU1 | E1 | 5c blue, *buff* | 30,000.00 |

The one known envelope shows black circular Franklin postmark with manuscript date.

Fredericksburg, Va.

```
* * * * * * * *
* FREDERICKSB'G. *
*                *
*   R T THOM    *
*                *
*       19       *
* POST OFFICE, VA. *
* * * * * * * *
```

A1
Typeset.
Sheets of 20, two panes of 10 varieties each.
Thin bluish paper.

26X1	A1	5c blue, *bluish*	200.00	600.00
		Block of four	950.00	
		On cover		2000.00
		Pair on cover		7000.00
26X2	"	10c red, *bluish*	650.00	
		Brown red, *bluish*	650.00	
		Block of four	—	

Cancellation: black town.

Gainesville, Ala.
Envelopes.

E1   E2
Handstamped

| 27XU1 | E1 | 5c black | 1500.00 |
| 27XU2 | E2 | 10c ("01") black | 7500.00 |

Postmark spells town name "Gainsville".

Galveston, Tex.
Envelopes.

E1
Handstamped

| 98XU1 | E1 | 5c black | 500.00 | 2000.00 |
| 98XU2 | " | 10c black | | 2250.00 |

E2

CONFEDERATE STATES

		Handstamped			
98XU3	E2	10c black		550.00	1000.00
98XU4	"	20c black			3500.00

Georgetown, S. C.
Envelope.

E1   Control

Handstamped

28XU1	E1	5c black		750.00

Goliad, Texas.

A1   A2

Typeset.

29X1	A1	5c black		5000.00
29X2	"	5c *gray*		4500.00
29X3	"	5c *rose*		5000.00
		On cover		8000.00
29X4	"	10c black		5000.00
29X5	"	10c *rose*		5000.00
		On cover		7500.00
		On patriotic cover		

Type A1 stamps are signed "Clarke-P.M." vertically in black.

29X6	A2	5c *gray*		5000.00
		Pair		
		On cover		7250.00
		a. "GOILAD"		5500.00
		Pair, left stamp the error		15,000.00
29X7	"	10c *gray*		5000.00
		On cover		7500.00
		a. "GOILAD"		5500.00
		a. On cover		8500.00
29X8	"	5c *dark blue*		6000.00
		On cover		8000.00
29X9	"	10c *dark blue*		6500.00
		On cover		

Cancellations in black: pen, town, "Paid"

Gonzales, Texas.

Colman & Law were booksellers when John B. Law (of the firm) was appointed Postmaster. The firm used a small lithographed label on the front or inside of books they sold. One variety was used, as listed.

A1

Lithographed on colored glazed paper.

30X1	A1	(5c) gold, *dark blue*		7500.00
		Pair on cover		15,000.00

Cancellation: black town. No. 30X1 must bear double-circle town cancel as validating control. All items of type A1 without this control are book labels. The control was applied to the labels in the sheet before their sale as stamps. When used, the stamps bear the additional Gonzales double-circle postmark.

Similar labels in gold on garnet and on black paper are known on cover. Some authorities believe Postmaster Law sold them for use as 10c stamps.

Greensboro, Ala.
Envelopes.

E1   E2

Handstamped

31XU1	E1	5c black	1000.00
31XU2	"	10c black	1000.00
31XU3	E2	10c black	1250.00

Greensboro, N. C.
Envelope.

E1

Handstamped

32XU1	E1	10c red	1500.00

Greenville, Ala.

   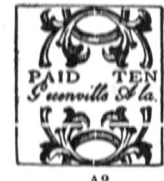

A1   A2

Typeset.
Two varieties of each.
On pinkish surface-colored glazed paper.
Type I—"Greenville, Ala." in Roman type.
Type II—"Greenville, Ala." in script type.

33X1	A1	5c red & blue, type I	4500.00	
		a. Type II	4500.00	
		On cover, type I or II		18,000.00
33X2	A2	10c red & blue, type II	5000.00	
		On cover, type II		20,000.00

Greenville Court House, S. C.
Envelopes.

PAID 5

E1   Control

Handstamped.   Several types.

34XU1	E1	5c black	800.00
34XU2	"	10c black	900.00
34XU3	"	20c (ms.) on 10c black	1000.00

Envelopes usually bear the black control on the back.

CONFEDERATE STATES

Greenwood Depot, Va.

A1

"PAID" Handstamped; Value and Signature ms.
Laid Paper.

35X1   A1   10c black, *gray blue*   4500.00   —
         On cover   16,000.00
Cancellation: black town.

Griffin, Ga.
Envelope

E1

Handstamped

102XU1   E1   5c black   1350.00

Grove Hill, Ala.

A1

Handstamped woodcut.

36X1   A1   5c black, on cover   35,000.00

Cancellations: black town, magenta pen.

Hallettsville, Texas.

A1

Handstamped. Ruled Letter Paper.

37X1   A1   10c black, *gray blue*, on cover   15,000.00
         Cancellation: black ms. One example known.

Hamburgh, S. C.
Envelope

E1

Handstamped

112XU1   E1   5c black   1000.00
      On cover with No. 16X1 (forwarded)   —

Helena, Texas.

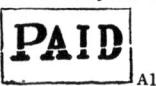
A1

Typeset.
Several varieties.

38X1   A1   5c black, *buff*   7500.00   5000.00
38X2   "   10c black, *gray*   5000.00
On 10c "Helena" is in upper and lower case italics.
Cancellation: black town.

Hillsboro, N. C.

A1

Handstamped.

39X1   A1   5c black, on cover   15,000.00
Cancellation: black town.

Houston, Texas.
Envelopes.

E1

Handstamped.

40XU1   E1   5c red   600.00
         On patriotic cover   1000.00
40XU2   "   10c red   1000.00
40XU3   "   10c black   750.00
40XU4   "   5c+10c red   1500.00
40XU5   "   10c+10c red   1500.00
40XU6   "   10c (ms.) on 5c red   3000.00
Nos. 40XU2–40XU5 show "TEX" instead of "TXS".

Huntsville, Texas.
Envelope.

E1   Control

Handstamped

92XU1   E1   5c black   1350.00
No. 92XU1 exists with "5" outside or within control circle.

Independence, Texas.

A1

		Handstamped.		
41X1	A1	10c *buff*		3250.00
		On cover		8000.00
41X2	"	10c *dull rose*		3500.00
		On cover		8500.00
		With small "10" and "Pd" in manuscript.		
41X3	A1	10c *buff*, cut to shape	4000.00	10,000.00
		On cover		

Cancellation: black town ("INDEPENDANCE").

Iuka, Miss.
Envelope.

I-U-KA
PAID 5 CTS
E1
Typeset

42XU1	E1	5c black		2000.00
		On patriotic cover		3500.00

Jackson, Miss.
Envelopes.

E1
Handstamped
Two types of numeral.

43XU1	E1	5c black		500.00
		On patriotic cover		3000.00
43XU2	"	10c black		2750.00
43XU3	"	10c on 5c black		1350.00
43XU4	"	10c on 5c blue		1350.00

The 5c also exists on a lettersheet.

Jacksonville, Ala.
Envelope.

E1
Handstamped

110XU1	E1	5c black	—	1500.00

Jetersville, Va.

A1
Typeset ("5"); ms. ("AHA.")
Laid Paper.

44X1	A1	5c black		7000.00
		Vert. pair on cover, uncanceled		16,000.00

Initials are those of Postmaster A. H. Atwood.
Cancellation: black town.

Jonesboro, Tenn.
Envelopes.

E1

Handstamped

45XU1	E1	5c black		4000.00
45XU2	"	5c dark blue		4250.00

Kingston, Ga.
Envelopes.

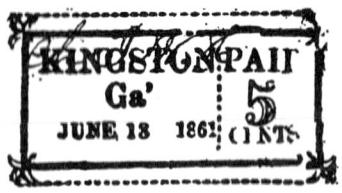

		E1	E2	E4

E3

Typo. (E1–E3); Handstamped (E4)

46XU1	E1	5c black		800.00
46XU2	E2	5c black	—	1500.00
46XU3	"	5c black, *amber*		1500.00
46XU4	E3	5c black	—	
46XU5	E4	5c black		5000.00

Knoxville, Tenn.

A1
Woodcut.
Grayish Laid Paper.

47X1	A1	5c brick red	1000.00	550.00
		Horizontal pair	3000.00	1300.00
		Vertical pair	2500.00	
		Vertical strip of three	5000.00	
		On cover		3500.00
		Pair on cover		7500.00
47X2	"	5c carmine	1500.00	1000.00
		Vertical strip of three		3500.00
		On cover		8500.00
		Pair on cover		
47X3	"	10c green	4500.00	6000.00
		On cover		17,500.00

CANCELLATIONS.

Black town | Black pen or pencil
Black bars |

The 5c has been reprinted in red, brown and chocolate on white and bluish wove and laid paper.

Envelopes.

E1   E2

Typographed

47XU1	E1	5c blue, *white*	500.00	1500.00
47XU2	"	5c blue, *orange*	500.00	1500.00
47XU3	"	10c red, *white* (cut to shape)		1000.00
47XU4	"	10c red, *orange* (cut to shape)		1000.00

Handstamped

47XU5	E2	5c black	500.00	2000.00
		On patriotic cover		3000.00
47XU6	"	10c on 5c black		35,000.00

Type E2 exists with "5" above or below "PAID".

La Grange, Texas.
Envelopes.

E1
Handstamped

48XU1	E1	5c black	—	1250.00
48XU2	"	10c black		1500.00

Lake City, Florida.
Envelope.

E1   Control
Handstamped

96XU1   E1   10c black   3500.00

Envelopes have black circle control mark, or printed name of E. R. Ives, postmaster, on face or back.

Laurens Court House, S.C.
Envelope

E1
Handstamped

116XU1   E1   5c black   —

Lenoir, N. C.

A1
Handstamped from woodcut.
White wove paper with cross-ruled orange lines.

49X1	A1	5c blue & orange	3250.00	3000.00
		Pair		—
		On cover		10,000.00

CANCELLATIONS

Blue town | Blue "Paid" in
Black pen | circle

Envelopes.

E1
Handstamped

49XU1	A1	5c black	
49XU2	"	10c (5c+5c) blue	—
49XU3	E1	5c blue	3500.00
49XU4	"	5c black	900.00

Lexington, Miss.
Envelopes.

E1
Handstamped

50XU1	E1	5c black	3000.00
50XU2	"	10c black	4000.00

Liberty, Va.

PAID
5cts.
A1

Typeset
Laid Paper

74X1   A1   5c black   10,000.00

No. 74X1 is on cover and uncanceled.
A cover with Salem, Va., postmark is known.

Livingston, Ala.

A1
Lithographed

51X1	A1	5c blue		7000.00
		On cover		30,000.00
		Pair on cover		—

Cancellation: black town.

Lynchburg, Va.

A1
Stereotype from Woodcut.

52X1	A1	5c blue (shades)	500.00	650.00
		Pair		1800.00
		On cover		5000.00
		Pair on cover		8000.00

Cancellations: black town, blue town.

Envelopes.

E1 **PAID.**
Typographed.
Impressed at top right or left.

52XU1	E1	5c black, *white*		1500.00
52XU2	"	5c black, *amber*	650.00	1500.00
52XU3	"	5c black, *buff*		1500.00
52XU4	"	5c black, *brown*	900.00	1500.00
		On patriotic cover		—

Macon, Ga.

A1   A2   A3

A4
Typeset. Wove Paper.
Several varieties of type A1, 10 of A

53X1	A1	5c *light blue green* (shades)	800.00	600.00
		On cover		3500.00
		Pair on cover		8000.00
53X3	A2	5c *yellow*	2250.00	750.00
		On cover		4000.00
		On patriotic cover		8000.00
		Pair on cover		6000.00
53X4	A3	5c *yellow* (shades)	2250.00	1000.00
		On cover		3500.00
		Pair on cover		8000.00
		a. Vertical tête bêche pair		12,000.00
53X5	A4	2c *gray green*		6500.00
		On cover		15,000.00

Laid Paper

53X6	A2	5c yellow	3000.00	3500.00
		On cover		6000.00
53X7	A3	5c yellow	6000.00	
		On cover		9000.00
53X8	A1	5c *light blue green*	1750.00	2000.00
		On cover		3750.00

Cancellations: black town, black "PAID" (2 types).

Envelope

E1

Handstamped
Two types: PAID over 5, 5 over PAID

53XU1	E1	5c black	250.00	500.00

Marietta, Ga.
Envelopes.

   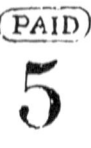
E1   E2

Handstamped
Two types of "PAID" and numerals.

54XU1	E1	5c black		400.00
54XU2	E2	10c on 5c black E1		1200.00
54XU3	"	10c black		750.00
54XU4	"	5c black		450.00

Marion, Va.

A1
Typeset frame, with handstamped numeral in center.

55X1	A1	5c black		5000.00
		On cover		8000.00
55X2	"	10c black	16,500.00	8000.00
		On cover		12,000.00

Bluish Laid Paper

55X3	A1	5c black		—

Cancellations: black town, black "PAID".
The 2c, 3c, 15c and 20c are believed to be bogus.

Memphis, Tenn.

A1   A2

Stereotype from woodcut.
Plate of 50 (5x10) for the 2c. The stereotypes for the 5c stamps were set in 5 vertical rows of 8, with at least 2 rows set sideways to the right (see Thomas H. Pratt's monograph, "The Postmaster's Provisionals of Memphis").

56X1	A1	2c blue (shades)	75.00	750.00
		Block of four	500.00	
		On cover		7500.00
		Cracked plate (16, 17, 18)	125.00	750.00

The "cracking off" (breaking off) of the plate at right edge caused incomplete printing of stamps in positions 5, 10, 15, 20, and 50. Poor make-ready also caused incomplete printing in position 50.

56X2	A2	5c red (shades)	150.00	200.00
		Pair	350.00	500.00
		Block of four	800.00	
		On cover		1000.00
		Pair on cover		2250.00
		Strip of four on cover		7000.00
		On patriotic cover		4000.00
		a. Tête bêche pair		1500.00
		Tête bêche pair on cover		10,000.00
		b. Pair, one sideways	750.00	
		c. Pelure paper		—

Cancellation on Nos. 56X1–56X2: black town.

CONFEDERATE STATES

Envelopes.
Typographed

56XU1	A2	5c red, *white*	2500.00
56XU2	"	5c red, *amber*	2500.00
		With No. 1	5000.00
56XU3	"	5c red, *orange*	2750.00
		On patriotic cover	4000.00

Micanopy, Fla.
Envelope.

E1
Handstamped

105XU1	E1	5c black	10,000.00
		One example known.	

Milledgeville, Ga.
Envelopes.

E1
Handstamped

57XU1	E1	5c black	300.00
57XU2	"	5c blue	400.00
57XU3	"	10c on 5c black	850.00

E2   E3

57XU4	E2	10c black	225.00	750.00
57XU5	E3	10c black		750.00

Mobile, Ala.

A1
Lithographed.

58X1	A1	2c black	1250.00	700.00
		Pair		1500.00
		On cover		2500.00
		Pair on cover		4000.00
		Three singles on one cover		5000.00
		Five copies on one cover		17,500.00
58X2	"	5c blue	250.00	150.00
		Pair	600.00	400.00
		On cover		750.00
		Pair on cover		1500.00
		Strip of three on cover		4000.00
		Strip of four on cover		5000.00
		Strip of five on cover		—

Cancellations: black town, express company.

Montgomery, Ala.
Envelopes.

E1
Handstamped

59XU1	E1	5c red		1000.00
59XU2	"	5c blue	400.00	1200.00
59XU3	"	10c red		1000.00
59XU4	"	10c blue		1250.00
59XU5	"	10c black		1000.00
59XU6	"	10c on 5c red		2000.00

The 10c design is larger than the 5c.

E2   E3

59XU7	E2	2c red		—
59XU7A	"	2c blue		3000.00
59XU8	"	5c black		1000.00
59XU9	E3	10c black		1500.00
59XU10	"	10c red		1500.00

Mt. Lebanon, La.

A1
Woodcut, Design Reversed

60X1	A1	5c red brown, on cover	50,000.00

Cancellation black pen. One example known.

Nashville, Tenn.

A1   A2
Typeset (5 varieties of 3c)

61X1	A1	3c carmine		125.00
		Horizontal strip of five		750.00

No. 61X1 was not placed in use.
Stereotype from Woodcut.
Gray Blue Ribbed Paper.

61X2	A2	5c carmine (shades)	700.00	400.00
		Pair		1000.00
		On cover		1750.00
		On patriotic cover		4500.00
		Pair on cover		6000.00
		On cover with U. S. 3c 1857 (express)		5000.00
		a. Vertical tête bêche pair		2000.00
61X3	"	5c brick red	700.00	400.00
		On cover		1500.00
		On patriotic cover		5000.00
		Pair on cover		4500.00
		On U. S. envelope No. U26		—
		On U.S. #U27 with #26 (express)		26,000.00

61X4	A2	5c gray (shades)	700.00	500.00	62X5	A2	5c yel brn, *off-white, Dec. 3, 1861*	90.00	200.00
		On cover		2000.00			Pair	200.00	450.00
		Pair on cover		5000.00			Block of four	600.00	
61X5	"	5c violet brown	600.00	400.00			On cover		425.00
		Block of four	—				On patriotic cover		2500.00
		On cover		1750.00			Pair on cover		1000.00
		On patriotic cover		—			Strip of 5 on cover		—
		Pair on cover		4500.00	62X6	"	5c red	—	7500.00
		a. Vertical tête bêche pair	4000.00	5000.00	62X7	"	5c red, *bluish*		10,000.00
		Vert. tête bêche pair on cover		—					
61X6	"	10c green	3000.00	2250.00					

CANCELLATIONS on Nos. 62X3 - 62X5.

Black town (single or double circle New Orleans)	Black "Paid" Express Company Packet boat,
Red town (double circle New Orleans)	cover "STEAM" "Southn Letter
Town other than New Orleans	Unpaid" on cover with
Postmaster's handstamp	U.S. No. 26

61X6 10c green
On cover
On cover with U.S. 3c 1857   10,000.00
On cover with No. 61X2   12,000.00

CANCELLATIONS on Nos. 61X2 to 61X5.

Blue "Paid"	Blue express
Blue "Postage Paid"	company
Blue town	Black express
Blue numeral "5"	company
Blue numeral "10"	

Envelopes.

E1
Handstamped

61XU1	E1	5c blue		900.00
		On patriotic envelope		1750.00
61XU2	"	5c+10c blue		1500.00

Envelopes.

J.L.RIDDELL, P.M
PD 5 CTS
N O.P.O

E1
Handstamped

62XU1	E1	5c black		3500.00
62XU2	"	10c black		5000.00
		"J. L. RIDDELL, P. M." omitted		
62XU3	E1	2c black		7500.00

New Orleans, La.

 A1    A2

Stereotype from Woodcut.   Plate of 40.

62X1	A1	2c blue, *July 14, 1861*	100.00	400.00
		Pair	400.00	900.00
		Block of four	4000.00	
		On cover		3000.00
		On patriotic cover		7500.00
		Pair on cover		7500.00
		Three singles on one cover		8500.00
		Strip of five on cover		17,500.00
		On U. S. envelope No. U27		—
		a. Printed on both sides		—
62X2	"	2c red (shades), *Jan. 6, 1862*	100.00	650.00
		Pair	250.00	
		Block of four	1200.00	
		On cover		16,000.00
62X3	A2	5c brown, *white, June 12, 1861*	200.00	125.00
		Pair	425.00	275.00
		Block of four	1000.00	
		On cover		375.00
		On patriotic cover		3000.00
		Pair on cover		750.00
		Strip of 5 on cover		5000.00
		On cover with U.S. No. 30A		
		a. Printed on both sides		1000.00
		b. 5c ocher, *June 18, 1861*	500.00	350.00
		Pair		1000.00
		On cover		1000.00
		On patriotic cover		5000.00
		Pair on cover		2500.00
62X4	"	5c red brown, *bluish, Aug. 22, 1861*	220.00	95.00
		Pair	475.00	195.00
		Horizontal strip of 6		2000.00
		Block of four		1250.00
		On cover		300.00
		On patriotic cover		3500.00
		Pair on cover		850.00
		Block of four on cover		5000.00
		On cover with No. 1		4000.00
		a. Printed on both sides		1050.00

New Smyrna, Fla.

A1
Handstamped.
On white paper with blue ruled lines.

63X1	A1	10c ("O1") on 5c black		25,000.00

One example known. It is uncanceled on a postmarked patriotic cover.

Oakway, S.C.

A1
Handstamped

115X1	A1	5c black, on cover	—	12,000.00

Pensacola, Fla.

Envelopes.

E1

Handstamped

106XU1	E1	5c black	4000.00
106XU2	"	10c (ms.) on 5c black	4250.00

Petersburg, Va.

A1
Typeset.
Ten varieties.
Thick white paper

65X1	A1	5c red	600.00	400.00
		Pair	1500.00	1000.00
		Block of four	4500.00	
		On cover		1500.00
		On patriotic cover		—
		Pair on cover		5500.00
		On cover with General Issue stamp No. 1		7500.00

Cancellation: blue town.

Pittsylvania Court House, Va.

A1
Typeset.
Wove Paper.

66X1	A1	5c dull red	6000.00	5000.00
		Cut to shape		3000.00
		On cover		20,000.00
		On cover, cut to shape		10,000.00
		On patriotic cover, cut to shape		14,000.00

Laid Paper.

66X2	A1	5c dull red		6500.00
		Cut to shape		3500.00
		On cover		20,000.00
		On cover, cut to shape		10,000.00

Cancellation: black town.

Pleasant Shade, Va.

A1
Typeset.
Five varieties.

67X1	A1	5c blue	2500.00	4500.00
		On cover		15,000.00
		Pair on cover		35,000.00
		Pair	5500.00	
		Block of six	25,000.00	

Cancellation: blue town.

Port Lavaca, Tex.

A1
Typeset.

107X1	A1	10c black	17,500.00

One example known. It is uncanceled on a postmarked cover.

Raleigh, N. C.
Envelopes.

Handstamped

68XU1	E1	5c red	425.00
		On patriotic cover	2500.00
		On U.S. envelope No. U10	1500.00
68XU2	"	5c blue	1000.00

Rheatown, Tenn.

A1
Typeset.
Three varieties.

69X1	A1	5c red	2000.00	2750.00
		On cover		8500.00
		Pair	5000.00	
		Pen cancellation		2000.00

Cancellations: red town or black pen.

Richmond, Texas.
Envelopes or Letter Sheets.

E1
Handstamped

70XU1	E1	5c red	2500.00
70XU2	"	10c red	2500.00
70XU3	"	10c on 5c red	5000.00
70XU4	"	15c (ms.) on 10c red	—

Ringgold, Ga.
Envelope.

E1

CONFEDERATE STATES

Handstamped

71XU1　E1　5c blue black　　　4000.00

Rutherfordton, N. C.

A1

Handstamped; "Paid 5cts" in ms.

72X1　A1　5c black, cut round　　—

No. 72X1 is on cover and uncanceled.

Salem, N. C.
Envelopes.

E1　　　　　　E2

Handstamped

73XU1	E1	5c black	750.00
73XU2	"	10c black	850.00
73XU3	E2	5c black	750.00
73XU4	"	10c on 5c black	1600.00

Reprints exist on various papers. They either lack the "Paid" and value or have them counterfeited.

Salem, Va.

See No. 74X1 under Liberty, Va.

Salisbury, N. C.
Envelope.

SALISBURY,
N. C.
POSTAGE

FIVE CENTS
P. M.

E1

Typographed. Impressed at top left

75XU1　E1　5c black, *greenish*　　　5000.00

One example known. Part of envelope is torn away, leaving part of design missing. Illustration E1 partly suppositional.

San Antonio, Texas.
Envelopes.

E1

E2　　　　　Control

Handstamped

76XU1	E1	10c black	275.00	1100.00
76XU2	E2	10c black		1250.00

Black circle control mark is on front or back.

Savannah, Ga.
Envelopes.

E1　　　　　　Control

PAID 10

E2

Handstamped

101XU1	E1	5c black	300.00
101XU2	E2	5c black	450.00
101XU3	E1	10c black	500.00
101XU4	E2	10c black	500.00
101XU5	E1	10c on 5c black	1500.00
101XU6	E2	20c on 5c black	3000.00

Envelopes must have octagonal control mark.

Selma, Ala.
Envelopes.

E1

Handstamped; Signature in ms.

77XU1	E1	5c black	1500.00
77XU2	"	10c black	2500.00
77XU3	"	10c on 5c black	3000.00

Signature is that of Postmaster William H. Eagar.

Sparta, Ga.
Envelopes.

E1

Handstamped

93XU1	E1	5c red	—	750.00
93XU2	"	10c red		1000.00

Spartanburg, S. C.

A1   A2

Handstamped on Ruled or Plain Wove Paper.

78X1	A1	5c black	2500.00
		On cover	12,500.00
		Pair on cover	—
		On patriotic cover	15,000.00
		a. "5" omitted (on cover)	—
78X2	A2	5c black, *bluish*	3000.00
		On cover	12,500.00
78X3	"	5c black, *brown*	3000.00
		On cover	15,000.00

Most examples of Nos. 78X1–78X3 are cut round. Cut square examples are worth much more.
Cancellations: black "PAID", black town.

Statesville, N. C.
Envelopes.

E1
Handstamped

79XU1	E1	5c black	135.00	700.00
79XU2	"	10c on 5c black		1500.00

Sumter, S. C.
Envelopes.

E1
Handstamped

80XU1	E1	5c black	160.00	
80XU2	"	10c black	100.00	
80XU3	"	10c on 5c black		175.00
80XU4	"	2c (ms.) on 10c black		800.00

Used examples of Nos. 80XU1–80XU2 are indistinguishable from handstamped "Paid" covers.

Talbotton, Ga.
Envelopes.

E1
Handstamped

94XU1	E1	5c black		750.00
		On U.S. envelope No. U27		—
94XU2	"	10c black		500.00
94XU3	"	10c on 5c black		1000.00

Tellico Plains, Tenn.

A1
Typeset. Settings of two 5c and one 10c.
Laid Paper.

81X1	A1	5c red	800.00
		On cover	—
81X2	"	10c red	1500.00
		Se-tenant with 5c	2500.00
		Strip of three (5c+5c+10c)	3500.00

Cancellation: black pen.

Thomasville, Ga.
Envelopes.

E1   Control
Handstamped

82XU1	E1	5c black	1000.00

E2

82XU2	E2	5c black	900.00

Tullahoma, Tenn.
Envelope.

E1   Control
Handstamped

111XU1	E1	10c black	3000.00

Tuscaloosa, Ala.
Envelopes.

PAID

5

E1
Handstamped

83XU1	E1	5c black	250.00	—
83XU2	"	10c black	250.00	—

Used examples of Nos. 83XU1–83XU2 are indistinguishable from handstamped "Paid" covers. Some authorities question the use of E1 to produce provisional envelopes.

CONFEDERATE STATES

Tuscumbia, Ala.
Envelopes.

E1
Handstamped

84XU1	E1	5c black		550.00
		On patriotic cover		—
84XU2	"	5c red		650.00
84XU3	"	10c black		1100.00

See also U.S. Postmasters' Provisional No. 12XU1.

Union City, Tenn.

E1

The use of E1 to produce provisional envelopes is doubtful.

Uniontown, Ala.

A1

Typeset in settings of four (2 x 2).
Four varieties of each value.
Laid Paper.

86X1	A1	2c dark blue, *gray blue*	95000.00	—
86X2	"	2c dark blue, *white*	5500.00	
		Block of four	30,000.00	
86X3	"	5c green, *gray blue*	2750.00	2000.00
		Pair	—	
		On cover		6500.00
86X4	"	5c green, *white*	2750.00	2000.00
		On cover		6500.00
		Pair on cover		18,500.00
86X5	"	10c red, *gray blue*	8000.00	5000.00
		On cover		22,500.00

Two examples known of No. 86X1, both on cover (drop letters), one uncanceled and one pen canceled.
Cancellation on Nos. 86X3–86X5: black town.

Unionville, S. C.

A1

Handstamped in two impressions.
Paper with Blue Ruled Lines.

87X1	A1	5c black, *grayish*, on cover	14,500.00
		Pair on patriotic cover	32,500.00

Cancellation: black town.

Valdosta, Ga.
Envelope.

E1   Control
Handstamped

100XU1	E1	10c black	800.00

The black circle control is usually on back of envelope.

Victoria, Texas.

A1

Typeset.
Surface colored paper.

88X1	A1	5c red brown, *green*	4000.00	
88X2	"	10c red brown, *green*	4000.00	—
		On cover		4500.00
88X3	"	10c red brown, *green* ("10" in bold face type), pelure paper	5500.00	17,500.00 5250.00

Walterborough, S. C.
Envelopes.

E1
Typeset.

108XU1	E1	10c black, *buff*	2000.00
108XU2	"	10c carmine	4000.00

Warrenton, Ga.
Envelopes.

E1

786   CONFEDERATE STATES

Handstamped

89XU1 E1 5c black   1250.00
89XU2 "   10c (ms.) on 5c black   1000.00

Washington, Ga.
Envelope

PAID 10

E1
Handstamped

117XU1 E1 10c black   1500.00
Envelopes must have black circle control on front or back.

Weatherford, Tex.
Envelopes.

E1
Woodcut with "PAID" inserted in type.
Handstamped

109XU1 E1 5c black   2000.00
109XU2 "   5c+5c black   16,000.00

Winnsborough, S. C.
Envelopes.

PAID
5
E1   Control
Handstamped

97XU1 E1 5c black   1000.00
97XU2 "   10c black   1000.00
Envelopes must have black circle control on front or back.

Wytheville, Va.
Envelope.

E1   Control
Handstamped

114XU1 E1 5c black   900.00

Addenda

Carolina City, N.C.
Envelope

E1
Handstamped

118XU1 E1   5c black

Colaparchee, Ga.
Envelope

E1   Control
Handstamped

119XU1 E1   5c black

CONFEDERATE STATES

Forsyth, Ga.

Envelope

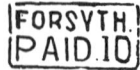

E1
Handstamped

| 120XU1 | E1 | 10c black | 450.00 |

Limestone Springs, S.C.

5

A1
Handstamped

| 121X1 | A1 | 5c | black, on cover | 4000.00 |
| | | | pair on cover | 7500.00 |

Stamps are round, square or rectangular. Covers are not postmarked.

For later additions, listed out of numerical sequence, see—

#74X1, **Liberty, Va.**
#92XU1, **Huntsville, Tex.**
#93XU1, **Sparta, Ga.**
#94XU1, **Talbotton, Ga.**
#96XU1, **Lake City, Fla.**
#97XU1, **Winnsborough, S. C.**
#98XU1, **Galveston, Tex.**
#99XU1, **Christiansburg, Va.**
#100XU1, **Valdosta, Ga.**
#101XU1, **Savannah, Ga.**
#102XU1, **Griffin, Ga.**
#103XU1, **Courtland, Ala.**
#104XU1, **Fincastle, Va.**
#105XU1, **Micanopy, Fla.**

#106XU1, **Pensacola, Fla.**
#107X1, **Port Lavaca, Tex.**
#108XU1, **Walterborough, S. C.**
#109XU1, **Weatherford, Tex.**
#110XU1, **Jacksonville, Ala.**
#111XU1, **Tullahoma, Tenn.**
#112XU1, **Hamburgh, S. C.**
#113XU1, **Columbia, Tenn.**
#114XU1, **Wytheville, Va.**
#115X1, **Oakway, S. C.**
#116XU1, **Laurens Court House, S. C.**
#117XU1, **Washington, Ga.**

Further additions
following Wytheville

#118XU1, Carolina City, N.C.
#119XU1, Colaparchee, Ga.
#120XU1, Forsyth, Ga.
#121XU1, Limestone Springs, S.C.

NEW EDITION! The DIETZ **NEW EDITION!**
CONFEDERATE STATES CATALOG & HANDBOOK

The product of three years' intensive work with the assistance of more than 100 collectors and institutions. Large new selections have been added and the contents completely reorganized. Earlier entries have been revised, expanded, supplemented, prices updated.
Int'l Gold Medal Ameripex '86.
Regular Edition $75 ppd., Deluxe Edition $125 ppd.
BOGG & LAURENCE PUBLISHING CO. Inc.
Phone: (305) 866-3600
1007 Kane Concourse, Bay Harbor Islands, FL 33154
Toll Free 1-800-345-5595   MasterCard, VISA

We'll buy it.

If you've just discovered an old family correspondence from the Confederacy, we'll buy it.

It's not that we're interested in what great-great-grandfather Randall wrote to his new bride, but that as dealers we're interested in the envelopes with those unfamiliar stamps and strange markings. And because they may be worth a lot of money to collectors of Confederate States postal history, they may be worth a lot of money to us and to you. Actually, we are interested in what Randall wrote, for having an envelope with the contents makes that envelope more desirable to a collector. That means more for you.

For heaven's sake! Don't burn them.

No stamps on the envelopes? Just markings? Or labels? Don't be disappointed. They might well be Postmaster Provisionals or Hand-Stamped Paids. They're often more valuable than letters with regular Confederate issue stamps. Or, alas, they may simply be nothing, worthless. But let an expert decide.

We know Confederates probably better than anything else.

We at John W. Kaufmann Inc. are collectors and, at the same time, professional stamp dealers. Our love of the stamps and postal history of the Confederacy goes back many years. As collectors, one of us, "Trish" Kaufmann, is the editor of the leading publication devoted to Confederate States stamps. Has been for Seventeen years. And as collectors, we've exhibited our personal collections and been honored with gold medals. As professionals, we buy and sell these fascinating stamps and covers to collectors throughout the world. Over the years, almost every known rarity — and some hitherto unknown — has passed through our hands. Sometimes it has come from lucky "finds" such as you may have just made. All this is important to you only to establish our credentials, for we want you to send your "find" to us for our buying offer.

You'll get a fair price when you sell to us.

Our offers often are higher than sellers expect. That's because we know what collectors want, we know the current state of the market, and because we can recognize a valuable sleeper if it's among the material sent us. Many dealers like you can confirm this. In fact, over 90% of the offers we make are accepted on the spot by collectors and non-collectors who have Confederate material to sell.

Both our interests and resources are broad. Consequently we'll buy "finds" as small as $100 in value to as high as $1,000,000. Even higher.

Write us or phone us.

Describe your "find". We'll tell you how to send it to us for our offer, fully insured by Lloyd's of London. We might even be able to tell you what you have and what it's worth, while you're on the phone. It could very easily be big enough and valuable enough to warrant our coming to you to examine and make our offer in person. Then we could both thank Randall and his bride.

Patricia A. Kaufmann
John W. Kaufmann

John W. Kaufmann, Inc.

Call toll-free
800-424-9519

1333 H Street N.W.
Washington, D.C. 20005-4707
202-898-1800

CONFEDERATE STATES

GENERAL ISSUES

For explanations of various terms used see the notes at the end of these listings.

Jefferson Davis
A1

1861   Lithographed   Imperf.
Soft Porous Paper.

All 5c Lithographs were printed by Hoyer & Ludwig, of Richmond, Va.

Stones A or B—First stones used. Earliest dated cancellation October 16, 1861. Plating not completed hence size of sheets unknown. These stones had imprints. Stamps from Stones A or B are nearly all in the olive green shade. Sharp, clear impressions. Distinctive marks are few and minute.

Stone 1—Earliest dated cancellation October 23, 1861. Plating completed. Sheet consists of four groups of fifty varieties arranged in two panes of one hundred each without imprint. The first small printing was in olive green and later small printings appeared in light and dark green; the typical shade, however, is an intermediate shade of bright green. The impressions are clear though not as sharp as those from Stones A or B. Distinctive marks are discernible.

Stone 2—Earliest dated cancellation December 2, 1861. Plating completed. Sheet consists of four groups of fifty varieties arranged in two panes of one hundred each without imprint. All shades other than olive green are known from this stone, the commonest being a dull green. Poor impressions. Many noticeable distinctive marks.

UNUSED.

			Stones A or B	Stone 1	Stone 2
1	A1	5c green		200.00	175.00
		bright green		175.00	175.00
		dull green		175.00	175.00
		a. 5c light green		175.00	180.00
		b. 5c dark green		180.00	190.00
		c. 5c olive green	200.00	190.00	
		Pair	550.00	450.00	450.00
		Block of four	1300.00	1000.00	1000.00

USED.

1	A1	5c green		125.00	125.00
		bright green		125.00	125.00
		dull green		125.00	125.00
		a. 5c light green		125.00	125.00
		b. 5c dark green		135.00	135.00
		c. 5c olive green	150.00	150.00	
		On cover	225.00	175.00	175.00
		Single on cover (overpaid drop letter)			275.00
		On wallpaper cover			500.00
		On prisoner's cover			—
		On prisoner's cover with U. S. #65			—
		On prisoner's cover with U. S. #U34			—
		On patriotic cover	1200.00	1100.00	1100.00
		Pair	350.00	275.00	275.00
		Pair on cover	400.00	335.00	285.00
		Block of four	900.00	750.00	750.00
		Horiz. pair, vert. gutter between			—

CANCELLATIONS.

	Stones A or B	Stone 1	Stone 2
Blue town	+ 10.00	+ 10.00	+ 10.00
Red town	+110.00	+ 80.00	+ 80.00
Green town		+175.00	+150.00
Orange town			+100.00
Texas town		+ 35.00	+ 35.00
Arkansas town		+ 90.00	+ 90.00
Florida town		+110.00	+110.00
Kentucky town		+200.00	+200.00
October, 1861, year date	+ 50.00	+ 40.00	
Blue gridiron	+ 5.00	+ 5.00	+ 5.00
Red gridiron		+ 50.00	+ 50.00
Blue concentric	+ 5.00	+ 5.00	+ 5.00
Star or flowers			+100.00
Numeral	+ 60.00	+ 50.00	+ 50.00
" Paid "	+ 50.00	+ 50.00	+ 50.00
" Steam "	+150.00		
" Steamboat "		+150.00	+150.00
Express Company	+400.00	+350.00	+350.00
Railroad		+300.00	+300.00

VARIETIES.

	Unused	Used
White curl back of head (S A or B)	225.00	175.00
Imprint (S A or B)	450.00	350.00
Acid flaw (S 1)	225.00	135.00
Arrow between panes (S 1)	350.00	235.00
Flaw on "at" of "States" (38 S 1)	235.00	175.00
Spur on upper left scroll (21 S 2)	235.00	175.00
Bottom scrolls doubled (re-entry 50 S 2)	325.00	235.00
Side margin copy showing initials (41 S 2 or 50 S 2)	650.00	450.00
Misplaced transfer (S 2)	425.00	625.00
Rouletted unofficially	—	325.00

Thomas Jefferson
A2

1861-62   Lithographed
Soft Porous Paper

Hoyer & Ludwig—First stone used. Earliest dated cancellation November 8, 1861. Sheet believed to consist of four groups of fifty varieties each arranged in two panes of one hundred each with imprint at bottom of each pane. Two different imprints are known. Hoyer & Ludwig printings are always in a uniform shade of dark blue. Impressions are clear and distinct, especially so in the early printings. Plating marks are distinct.

J. T. Paterson & Co.—Earliest dated cancellation July 25, 1862. Sheet consists of four groups of fifty varieties each arranged in two panes of one hundred each with imprint at bottom of each pane. Two different imprints are known and at least one pane is known without an imprint. Wide range of shades. Impressions are less clear than those from the Hoyer & Ludwig stone. Paterson stamps show small vertical colored dash below the lowest point of the upper left triangle.

Stone "Y"—Supposedly made by J. T. Paterson & Co., as it shows the distinctive mark of that firm. Plating not completed hence size of sheet unknown. No imprint found. Color is either a light milky blue or a greenish blue. Impressions are very poor and have a blurred appearance. Stone Y stamps invariably show a large flaw back of the head as well as small vertical colored dash beneath the upper left triangle.

CONFEDERATE STATES

UNUSED.

	Hoyer	Paterson	Stone Y
2 A2 **10c blue**		225.00	
a. 10c light blue		225.00	
light milky blue			
b. 10c dark blue	275.00	250.00	
c. 10c indigo	—		
e. 10c greenish blue			300.00
Pair	600.00	575.00	1000.00
Block of four	1500.00	1350.00	
Horiz. pair, gutter btwn.		750.00	

USED.

2 A2 **10c blue**		175.00	
a. 10c light blue		175.00	
light milky blue			200.00
b. 10c dark blue	200.00	160.00	
c. 10c indigo	—		
e. 10c greenish blue			225.00
On cover	375.00	225.00	375.00
On wallpaper cover	700.00	650.00	
On patriotic cover	1500.00	1350.00	1750.00
On prisoner's cover with U. S. #65	—	—	
Pair	575.00	500.00	
Pair on cover	1200.00	800.00	
Strip of 3 on cover	3500.00	—	
Block of four			1850.00

CANCELLATIONS.

	Hoyer	Paterson	Stone Y
Blue town	+30.00	+10.00	+10.00
Red town	+75.00	+75.00	+100.00
Green town		+200.00	+300.00
Violet town		—	
Texas town	+125.00	+125.00	+125.00
Arkansas town	+275.00	+275.00	+275.00
Florida town	+325.00	+325.00	—
Kentucky town	+400.00		
Nov., 1861, year date	+300.00		
July, 1862, year date		+300.00	
Straight line town	+500.00	+500.00	+500.00
Blue gridiron	+10.00	+10.00	+10.00
Red gridiron	+50.00	+50.00	+50.00
Blue concentric	+10.00	+10.00	+10.00
Numeral	+75.00	+80.00	+100.00
" Paid "	+50.00	+75.00	+100.00
Star or flower		+150.00	
Railroad	+350.00	+350.00	
Express Company	+300.00	+300.00	

VARIETIES.

	Unused	Used
Malformed "T" of "TEN" (No. 4 Hoyer)	325.00	250.00
"G" and "E" of "POSTAGE" joined (No. 10 Hoyer)	325.00	250.00
Circular flaw, upper left star (No. 11 Hoyer)	325.00	
Third spiked ornament at right, white (No. 45 Hoyer)	325.00	250.00
Hoyer & Ludwig imprint	500.00	550.00
d. Printed on both sides (Hoyer)	—	
d. Printed on both sides (Pat.)	—	
Malformed "O" of "POSTAGE" (No. 25 Pat.)	275.00	225.00
J. T. Paterson & Co. imprint	550.00	850.00

Andrew Jackson
A3

1862 (March)   Soft Porous Paper.
Lithographed.

Sheet consists of four groups of fifty varieties arranged in two panes of 100 each.

One stone only was used. Date of issue, probably March, 1862. Printed by Hoyer & Ludwig, of Richmond, Va. Issued to prepay drop letter and circular rates. Strips of five used to prepay regular 10c rate, which was changed from 5c on July 1, 1862. Earliest known cancellation, March 21, 1862.

	Unused	Used
3 A3 **2c green**	500.00	625.00
light green	500.00	625.00
dark green	550.00	625.00
dull yellow green	550.00	
On cover		—
Pair on cover (double circular rate)		4000.00
Strip of five on cover		8000.00
On patriotic cover		10,000.00
Pair	—	
Block of four	1200.00	1500.00
Block of five	2750.00	3250.00
a. 2c bright yellow green	1500.00	2000.00
a. On cover		—
a. Strip of five on cover		—
Diagonal half used as 1c with unsevered pair, on cover	—	—
Horiz. pair, vert. gutter between		
Mark between stamps (between Nos. 4 and 5)	1200.00	1600.00
Mark above upper right corner (No. 30)	600.00	750.00
Mark above upper left corner (No. 31)	600.00	750.00
Acid flaw	575.00	700.00

CANCELLATIONS.

Blue town	+500.00	Blue gridiron	+250.00
Red town	+800.00	" Paid "	—
Arkansas town	—	Express Company	—
Texas town	+1250.00	Railroad	+3000.00

1862   Soft Porous Paper.
Lithographed.

Stone 2—First stone used for printing in blue. Plating is the same as Stone 2 in green. Earliest dated cancellation Feb. 28, 1862. Printings from Stone 2 are found in all shades of blue. Rough, coarse impressions are typical of printings from Stone 2.

Stone 3—A new stone used for printings in blue only. Earliest dated cancellation April 10, 1862. Sheet consists of four groups of fifty varieties each arranged in two panes of one hundred each without imprint. Impressions are clear and sharp, often having a proof-like appearance, especially in the deep blue printing. Plating marks, while not so large as on Stone 2 are distinct and clearly defined.

UNUSED.

	Stone 2	Stone 3
4 A1 **5c blue**	100.00	
light blue	105.00	
a. 5c dark blue	150.00	125.00
b. 5c light milky blue	125.00	150.00
Pair	250.00	325.00
Block of four	575.00	775.00
Horiz. pair, wide gutter between	725.00	—
Vert. pair, narrow gutter between	—	

USED.

4 A1 **5c blue**	100.00	
light blue	100.00	
a. 5c dark blue	150.00	125.00
b. 5c light milky blue	125.00	135.00
On cover	225.00	250.00
Single on cover (overpaid drop letter)	300.00	
Pair on cover	325.00	375.00
On wallpaper cover	600.00	
On patriotic cover	1250.00	1500.00
On prisoner's cover	2000.00	
On prisoner's cover with U. S. #65	—	
Pair	200.00	350.00
Block of four	1400.00	1500.00
Horiz. pair, wide gutter btwn.		

CANCELLATIONS.

	Stone 2	Stone 3
Blue town	+20.00	+40.00

CONFEDERATE STATES

Red town	+ 75.00	+ 75.00
Texas town	+300.00	+300.00
Arkansas town	+325.00	+325.00
Florida town	+200.00	
Straight line town	+300.00	+325.00
Blue gridiron	+ 10.00	+ 10.00
Red gridiron	+ 65.00	
Star or Flowers	+100.00	+100.00
Numeral	+ 85.00	
Railroad		
"Paid"	+ 25.00	+ 50.00
"Steamboat"	+400.00	
Express Company	+250.00	
"Way"		

VARIETIES.	Unused	Used
Spur on upper left scroll (21 S 2)	140.00	115.00
Thin hard paper (S 2)		110.00
Tops of "C" and "E" of "cents" joined by flaw (33 S 3)	175.00	175.00
"Flying bird" above lower left corner ornament (19 S 3)	150.00	150.00

1862 (March) Soft Porous Paper.
Lithographed.

Settings of fifty varieties repeated.
Printed by Hoyer & Ludwig, of Richmond, Va. One stone used, being the same as that used for the Hoyer & Ludwig 10c value in blue. Color change occured probably in March, 1862.
There are many shades of this stamp. The carmine is a very dark, bright color and should not be confused with the deeper shade of rose.
Earliest known cancellation, March 10, 1862. The earliest date of usage of the carmine shade is May 1, 1862.

			Unused	Used
5	A2	10c rose	800.00	500.00
		dull rose	800.00	500.00
		brown rose	1100.00	650.00
		deep rose	850.00	550.00
		carmine rose	1050.00	600.00
		On cover		825.00
		On wallpaper cover		2000.00
		On patriotic cover		2500.00
		On prisoner's cover		5500.00
		On prisoner's cover with U. S. #65		
		Pair	2250.00	2000.00
		Strip of three		4000.00
		Block of four	9000.00	7500.00
a.		10c carmine		1000.00
a.		On cover		3000.00
		Malformed "T" of "TEN" (No. 4	1050.00	600.00
		"G" and "E" of "POSTAGE" joined (No. 10)	1050.00	600.00
		Circ. flaw, upper left star (No. 11)	1050.00	600.00
		Third spiked ornament at right, white (No. 45)	1050.00	600.00
		Scratched stone (occurring on Nos 40, 39, 49 and 48, one pane)	1150.00	700.00
		Imprint		1250.00
		Horiz. pair, vert. gutter between		
		Side margin copy, initials (No. 41)		1750.00

CANCELLATIONS.

Blue town	+ 50.00	April, 1862,	
Red town	+100.00	year date	
Green town	+350.00	Blue gridiron	+ 50.00
Texas town	+150.00	Black concentric	+ 50.00
Arkansas town	—	Blue concentric	+ 50.00
Straight line		"Paid"	
town	+500.00	Railroad	
		Express Company	

Jefferson Davis
A4

1862 (April) Hard Medium Paper.

Typographed by De La Rue & Co. in London, England.

Plate of 400 in four panes of 100 each. No imprint.

No. 6 represents London printings from De La Rue & Co., a number of sheets being sent over by blockade runners. Fine clear impressions. The gum is light and evenly distributed. Exact date of issue unknown. Earliest known cancellation, April 16, 1862.

6	A4	5c light blue	10.00	12.00
		Single on cover used before July 1, 1862		150.00
		Single on cover (overpaid drop letter)		350.00
		Single on patriotic cover used before July 1, 1862		1000.00
		Single on prisoner's cover used before July 1, 1862		—
		On wallpaper cover		400.00
		On patriotic cover		1000.00
		On prisoner's cover		1250.00
		On prisoner's cover with U. S. #65		1250.00
		Pair	22.00	35.00
		Pair on cover		75.00
		Block of four	55.00	250.00
		Block of four on cover		1000.00

CANCELLATIONS.

Blue town	+ 2.00	Blue gridiron	+ 2.00
Red town	+ 45.00	Red gridiron	+ 35.00
Green town	+ 75.00		
Texas town	+ 65.00	Blue concentric	+ 2.00
Arkansas town	+ 85.00	Express Company	+350.00
Straight line		Railroad	+250.00
town	+150.00	"Paid"	+ 50.00

1862 (August) Typographed.
Thin to Thick Paper.

Plate of 400 in four panes of 100 each. No imprint.

Locally printed by Archer & Daly of Richmond, Va., from plates made in London, England, by De La Rue & Co. Printed on both imported English and local papers. Earliest known cancellation, August 15, 1862.

No. 7 shows coarser impressions than No. 6, and the color is duller and often blurred. Gum is light or dark and unevenly distributed.

7	A4	5c blue	12.00	14.00
	a.	5c deep blue	12.00	14.00
		Single on cover (overpaid drop lette		300.00
		On wallpaper cover		350.00
		On patriotic cover		800.00
		On prisoner's cover		1000.00
		On prisoner's cover with U. S. #65		—
		Pair	25.00	32.00
		Pair on cover		100.00
		Block of four	60.00	250.00
		Block of four on cover		800.00
		Light on cover (Trans-Miss. rate)		—
		White tie (U.R. 30)	140.00	150.00
		White tie on cover		375.00
		De La Rue paper (thin)	20.00	25.00
		White tie, De La Rue paper	195.00	240.00
		Thick paper	15.00	18.00
		Horiz. pair, vert. gutter between	200.00	
	b.	Printed on both sides	1000.00	700.00

CANCELLATIONS.

Blue town	+ 2.00	Blue gridiron	+ 2.00
Red town	+ 60.00	Red gridiron	+ 60.00
Brown town	+ 30.00		
Violet town	+110.00		
Green town	+125.00	Blue concentric	+ 2.00
Texas town	+ 90.00	Railroad	+250.00
Arkansas town	+110.00	Express Company	+400.00
Florida town	+140.00	Design (stars, etc.	+ 75.00
Straight line		"Paid"	+ 50.00
town	+140.00		

The unissued 10c type A4 was privately printed in various colors for philatelic purposes. (See note below No. 14.) Price, each 50 cents.

Counterfeits of the 10c exist.

CONFEDERATE STATES

Andrew Jackson
A5

1863 (April)   Soft Porous Paper.

Line Engraved.

Sheet of 200 (two panes of 100 each).

One plate. Printed by Archer & Daly of Richmond, Va. Earliest known cancellation, Apr. 21, 1863. Issued to prepay drop letter and circular rates. Strips of five used to prepay regular 10c rate.

8	A5	2c brown red	50.00	225.00
	a.	2c pale red	60.00	250.00
		Single on cover		1300.00
		On prisoner's cover		3000.00
		On prisoner's cover with U.S. #65		4000.00
		Pair	110.00	500.00
		Pair on cover		3000.00
		On wallpaper cover		
		Block of four	250.00	—
		Block of five		—
		Strip of five on cover		5500.00
		Strip of five on wallpaper cover		—
		Strip of ten on cover		13,000.00
		Double transfer	125.00	275.00
		Horiz. pair, vert. gutter between	275.00	

CANCELLATIONS.

Blue town	+ 35.00	Blue gridiron	+ 35.00
Red town	+225.00	Black numeral	—
Army of Tenn.	—	Railroad	+325.00

Jefferson Davis
"TEN CENTS"
A6

1863, Apr.   Soft Porous Paper

Line Engraved.

One plate of 200 subjects all of which were probably recut as every copy examined to date shows distinct recutting. Plating not completed.

Printed by Archer & Daly of Richmond, Va. First printings in milky blue. First issued in April, 1863. Earliest known cancellation, April 23, 1863.

9	A6	10c blue	750.00	550.00
	a.	10c milky blue (first printing)	700.00	575.00
	b.	10c gray blue	750.00	550.00
		On cover		1150.00
		On wallpaper cover		3000.00
		On patriotic cover		3500.00
		On prisoner's cover		425.00
		On prisoner's cover with U.S. #65		—
		Pair	1550.00	2000.00
		Pair on cover		3000.00
		Block of four	3500.00	
		Four stamps on one cover (Trans-Mississippi rate)		13,500.00
		Curved lines outside the labels at top and bottom are broken in the middle (No. 63R)	650.00	650.00
		Double transfer	850.00	850.00
		Damaged plate	900.00	900.00

CANCELLATIONS.

Blue town	+ 25.00	Black gridiron	+ 25.00
Red town	+150.00	Blue gridiron	+ 50.00
Green town	+600.00	Red gridiron	+200.00
Violet town	—	Railroad	+400.00
Straight line town	+500.00	Circle of wedges	+1000.00
		Pen	400.00
April, 1863, year date	—		

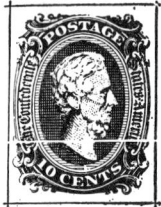

Frame Line
"10 CENTS"
(Illustration actual size)
A6a

1863, Apr.   Soft Porous Paper.

Line Engraved.
Printed by Archer & Daly ot Richmond, Va.

One copper plate of 100 subjects, all but one of which were recut. First issued in April, 1863. Earliest known use April 19, 1863.

Stamp design same as Die A (No. 11).

Prices are for copies showing parts of lines on at least two of the four sides. Copies showing lines on three or four sides sell for more.

10	A6a	10c blue	3000.00	1500.00
	a.	10c milky blue	3250.00	1750.00
	b.	10c greenish blue	3000.00	1500.00
	c.	10c dark blue	3000.00	1500.00
		On cover		2500.00
		On wallpaper cover		4500.00
		On patriotic cover		6000.00
		On prisoner's cover		7000.00
		On prisoner's cover with U.S. #65		—
		Pair	7000.00	5500.00
		Pair on cover		7000.00
		Block of four	15,000.00	
		Strip of four	17,000.00	
		Strip of seven	28,500.	
		Double transfer (No. 74)	3250.00	1750.00

CANCELLATIONS.

Blue town	+100.00	Blue gridiron	+100.00
Red town	+500.00	Pen	1100.00
Straight line town	+750.00		
April, 1863, year date	—		

CONFEDERATE STATES

No Frame Line
"10 CENTS"
A7 (Die A)
1863-64   Thick or Thin Paper
Line Engraved.

There are many slight differences between A7 (Die A) and A8 (Die B), the most noticeable being the additional line outside the ornaments at the four corners of A8 (Die B).

Stamps were first printed by Archer & Daly, of Richmond, Va. In 1864 the plates were transferred to the firm of Keatinge & Ball in Columbia, S. C., who made further printings from them. Two plates, each with two panes of 100, numbered 1 and 2. First state shows numbers only, later states show various styles of Archer & Daly imprints, and latest show Keatinge & Ball imprints. Archer & Daly stamps show uniformly clear impressions and a good quality of gum evenly distributed (Earliest known cancellation, April 21, 1863); Keatinge & Ball stamps generally show filled in impressions in a deep blue, and the gum is brown and unevenly distributed. (Earliest known cancellation, Nov. 7, 1864). The so-called laid paper is probably due to thick streaky gum. (These notes also apply to No. 12.)

11	A7	**10c blue**		10.00	15.00
	a.	10c milky blue		25.00	30.00
	b.	10c dark blue		10.00	15.00
	c.	10c greenish blue		10.00	15.00
	d.	10c green		35.00	45.00
		deep blue, Keatinge & Ball ('64)		15.00	30.00
		On cover			65.00
		Single on cover (overpaid drop letter)			225.00
		On wallpaper cover			400.00
		On patriotic cover			750.00
		On prisoner's cover			600.00
		On prisoner's cover with U. S. #65			1100.00
		On cover, dp. blue (K. & B.) ('64)			125.00
		On prisoner's cover (K. & B.) with U. S. #65 ('64)			—
		Pair		22.00	35.00
		Pair on cover			200.00
		Block of four		50.00	325.00
		Strip of four on cover (Trans-Mississippi rate)			4500.00
		Margin block of 12, Archer & Daly impt. & P #			325.00
		Margin block of 12, Keatinge & Ball impt. & P #			300.00
		Double transfer		60.00	75.00
		Horiz. pair, vert. gutter between		100.00	
	e.	Perforated		150.00	165.00
	e.	On cover			450.00
	e.	On wallpaper cover			—
	e.	Block of four			650.00

CANCELLATIONS.

Blue town	+ 5.00	April, 1863	
Red town	+ 35.00	year date	+75.00
Brown town	+60.00	"FREE"	+250.00
Green town	+110.00	Blue gridiron	+5.00
Violet town	+85.00	Black concentric	
Texas town	+60.00	circles	+20.00
Arkansas town	+125.00	Crossroads"	+150.00
Florida town	+200.00	"Paid"	+100.00
Straight line town	+350.00	Numeral	+100.00
Army of		Railroad	+175.00
Tenn.	+300.00	Steamboat	+1500.00

Jefferson Davis
A8 (Die B)
1863-64   Thick or Thin Paper
Line Engraved.

Plates bore Nos. 3 and 4, otherwise notes on No. 11 apply.
Earliest known cancellation May 1, 1863.

12	A8	**10c blue**		11.00	16.00
	a.	10c milky blue		25.00	30.00
	b.	10c light blue		11.00	16.00
	c.	10c greenish blue		11.00	16.00
	d.	10c dark blue		11.00	16.00
	e.	10c green		35.00	45.00
		deep blue, Keatinge & Ball ('64)		15.00	30.00
		On cover			70.00
		Single on cover (overpaid drop letter)			225.00
		On wallpaper cover			400.00
		On patriotic cover			750.00
		On prisoner's cover			600.00
		On prisoner's cover with U. S. #65			1000.00
		On cover, dp. blue (K. & B.) ('64)			125.00
		Pair		23.00	35.00
		Pair on cover			225.00
		Block of four		50.00	325.00
		Strip of four on cover (Trans-Mississippi rate)			4500.00
		Margin block of 12, Archer & Daly impt. & P #		350.00	
		Margin block of 12, Keatinge & Ball impt. & P #		300.00	
		Double transfer		60.00	75.00
		Horiz. pair, vert. gutter between		100.00	
	f.	Perforated		150.00	165.00
	f.	On cover			500.00
	f.	Block of four		675.00	

CANCELLATIONS.

Blue town	+ 5.00	Army of Tenn.	+350.00
Red town	+ 35.00	May, 1863, year date	+ 60.00
Brown town	+ 60.00		
Green town	+120.00	Blue gridiron	+ 5.00
Violet town	+ 85.00	Black concentric	
Texas town	+125.00	circles	+ 15.00
Arkansas town	+150.00	Railroad	+175.00
Florida town	+200.00		
Straight line town	+350.00		

George Washington
A9

1863 (June 1)
Line Engraved by Archer & Daly.

One plate which consisted of two panes of 100 each. First printings were from plates with imprint in Old English type under each pane, which was later removed. Printed on paper of varying thickness and in many shades of green. This stamp was also used as currency. Earliest known cancellation, June 1, 1863. Forged cancellations exist.

13	A9	20c green	40.00	200.00
	a.	20c yellow green	40.00	200.00
	b.	20c dark green	50.00	225.00
		On cover		950.00
		On wallpaper cover		1500.00
		On prisoner's cover		4000.00
		On prisoner's cover with U. S. #65		5000.00
		Pair	85.00	500.00
		Pair on cover (Trans-Mississippi rate)		6000.00
		Block of four	190.00	2000.00
		Strip of four with imprint	400.00	
	c.	Diagonal half used as 10c on cover		4000.00
	c.	On prisoner's cover		—
	d.	Horizontal half used as 10c on cover		4500.00
		Double transfer, 20 doubled (24L and 35R)	110.00	—
		Horiz. pair, vert. gutter between	250.00	
		"20" on forehead	1750.00	—

CANCELLATIONS.

Blue town	+ 50.00	Railroad	—
Red town	+200.00	Pen	125.00
Violet town	—		
Texas town	+100.00		

John C. Calhoun
A10

1862
Typographed by De La Rue & Co., London, England.

14	A10	1c orange	125.00	
	a.	1c deep orange	150.00	
		Pair	275.00	
		Block of four	600.00	

This stamp was never put in use.

Upon orders from the Confederate Government, De La Rue & Co. of London, England, prepared Two Cents and Ten Cents typographed plates by altering the One Cent (No. 14) and the Five Cents (Nos. 6-7) designs previously made by them. Stamps were never officially printed from these plates although privately made prints exist in various colors.

Explanatory Notes

The following notes by Lawrence L. Shenfield explain the various routes, rates and usages of the general issue Confederate stamps.

"Across the Lines"
Letters Carried by Private Express Companies

Express Company Handstamps
Used on "Across the Lines" Letters

About two months after the outbreak of the Civil War, in June, 1861, postal service between North and South and vice versa was carried on largely by Adams Express Company, and the American Letter Express Company. Northern terminus for the traffic was Louisville, Ky.; Southern terminus was Nashville, Tenn. Letters for transmission were delivered to any office of the express company, together with a fee, usually 20c or 25c per ½ ounce to cover carriage. The express company messengers carried letters across the lines and delivered them to their office on the other side, where they were deposited in the Government mail for transmission to addressees, postage paid out of the fee charged. Letters from North to South, always enclosed in 3c U. S. envelopes, usually bear the handstamp of the Louisville office of the express company, and in addition the postmark and "Paid 5" of Nashville, Tenn., indicating its acceptance for delivery at the Nashville Post Office. Letters from South to North sometimes bear the origin postmark of a Southern post office, but more often merely the handstamp of the Louisville express company office applied as the letters cleared through Louisville. In addition, they bear the 3c 1857 U. S. adhesive stamp, cancelled with the postmark and grid of Louisville, Ky., where they went into the Government mail for delivery. Some across-the-lines letters show the handstamp of various express company offices, according to the particular routing the letters followed. On August 26, 1861, the traffic ceased by order of the U. S. Post Office Dept. (Prices are for full covers bearing the usual Louisville, Ky., or Nashville, Tenn., handstamps of the express company. Unusual express office markings are rarer and worth more.)

North to South 3c U. S. Envelope, Adams Exp. Co. Louisville, Ky., handstamp..................	1250.00
North to South 3c U.S. Envelope, American Letter Express Co., Ky., handstamp..................	2000.00
South to North 3c 1857, Adams Exp. Co., Louisville, Ky., handstamp..................	1500.00
South to North 3c 1857, American Letter Exp. Co., Nashville, Tenn., handstamp..................	2500.00
South to North 3c 1861, Adams Exp. Co., Louisville, Ky., handstamp..................	3500.00

Blockade-Run Letters from Europe to the Confederate States

Charleston "STEAM-SHIP" in Oval Handstamp

As the Federal Fleet gradually extended its blockade of the Confederate States coastal regions, the South was forced to resort to blockade runners to carry letters to and from outside ports. These letters were all private-ship letters and never bore a foreign stamp if from Europe, nor a Confederate stamp if to Europe. The usual route from Europe was via a West Indies port, Nassau, Bahamas; Hamilton, Bermuda, or Havana, into the Southern ports of Wilmington, N. C. and Charleston, S. C. More rarely such letters came in to Savannah, Mobile and New Orleans. Letters from Europe are the only ones which are surely identified by their markings. They bore either the postmark of Wilmington, N. C., straightline "SHIP" and "12", "22", "32", etc., in manuscript; or the postmark of Charleston, S. C., "STEAMSHIP" in oval, and "12", "22", "32", etc., in manuscript. Very rarely Charleston used a straightline "SHIP" instead of "STEAMSHIP" in oval. All such letters were postage due; the single letter rate of 12c being made up of 2c for the private ship captain plus 10c for the regular single letter Confederate States rate. Over-weight letters were 22c (due), 32c, 42c, etc. A few examples are known on which Confederate General Issue stamps were used, usually as payment for forwarding postage. Covers with such stamps, or with the higher rate markings, 22, 32, etc., are worth more.

(Prices are for full covers in fine condition)

Charleston, S.C "6"	2000.00
Charleston, S. C., postmark, "STEAMSHIP," and "12" in ms.	2000.00
Charleston, S. C., postmark, "SHIP," and "12" in ms.	1500.00
Wilmington, N. C., postmark, "SHIP," and "12" in ms.	2500.00
Savannah, Ga., postmark "SHIP," and "7" in ms. (*)	4000.00
New Orleans, La. postmark "SHIP" and "10" in ms.	5000.00

(* 7c rate; 5c postage before July 1, 1862, plus 2c for ship captain.)

Express Company Mail in the Confederacy

Southern Express Company Handstamps

Shortly after the outbreak of war in 1861, the Adams Express Company divisions operating in the South were forced to suspend operations and turned their Southern lines over to a new company organized under the title Southern Express Company. This express did the bulk of the express business in the Confederacy despite the continued opposition of the Post Office Dept. of the C.S.A. and the ravages of the contending armies upon railroads. Other companies operating in the Confederacy were: South Western Express Co. (New Orleans), Pioneer Express Company, White's Southern Express (only one example known) and some local expresses of limited operation. The first three used handstamps of various designs usually bearing the city name of the office. Postal regulation necessitated the payment of regular Confederate postal rates on letters carried by express companies, express charges being paid in addition. Important letters, particularly money letters, were entrusted to these express companies as well as goods and wares of all kinds. The express rates charged for letters are not known; probably they varied depending upon the difficulty and risk of transmittal. Covers bearing stamps and express company handstamps are very rare.

Prisoner-of-War and Flag-of-Truce Letters

Prison Censor Handstamps

By agreement between the United States and the Confederate States, military prisoners and imprisoned civilians of both sides were permitted to send censored letters to their respective countries. Such letters, if from North to South, usually bore a U. S. 1861 adhesive, postmarked at a city near the prison, to pay the postage to the exchange ground near Old Point Comfort, Va.; and a 10c Confederate stamp, cancelled at Richmond, Va. (or "due" handstamp) to pay the Confederate postage to destination. If from South to North, letters usually bore a 10c Confederate stamp cancelled at a Southern city (or "paid" handstamp) and a U. S. 3c 1861 adhesive (or "due 3" marking) and the postmark of Old Point Comfort, Va. In addition, prison censor markings, handstamped or manuscript, the name and rank of the soldier, and "Flag of Truce, via Fortress Monroe" in manuscript usually appear on these covers. Federal prison censor handstamps of various designs are known from these prisons:

Camp Chase, Columbus, O.
David's Island, Pelham, N. Y.
Fort Delaware, Delaware City, Del.
Camp Douglas, Chicago, Ill.
Elmira Prison, Elmira, N. Y.
Johnson's Island, Sandusky, O.
Fort McHenry, Baltimore, Md.
Camp Morton, Indianapolis, Ind.
Fort Oglethorpe, Macon, Ga.
Old Capitol Prison, Washington, D. C.
Point Lookout Prison, Point Lookout, Md.
Fort Pulaski, Savannah, Ga.
Rock Island Prison, Rock Island, Ill.
Ship Island, New Orleans, La.
West's Hospital, Baltimore, Md.
U.S. General Hospital, Gettysburg, Pa.

Several other Federal prisons used manuscript censor markings.

Southern prison censor markings are always in manuscript, and do not identify the prison. The principal Southern prisons were at Richmond and Danville, Va.; Andersonville and Savannah, Ga.; Charleston, Columbia and Florence, S. C.; Salisbury, N. C.; Hempstead and Tyler, Tex.

Civilians residing in both the North and the South were also, under exceptional circumstances, permitted to send Flag of Truce letters across the lines. Such covers bore no censor marking nor prison markings, but were always endorsed "via Flag of Truce".

Prices will be found under various individual stamps for "on prisoner's cover" and are for the larger prisons. Prisoners' letters from the smaller prisons are much rarer. Only a very small percentage of prisoners' covers bore both a U. S. stamp and a Confederate stamp.

The "SOUTHERN LETTER UNPAID" Marking On Northbound Letters of Confederate Origin

DUE 3

SOUTH^N LETTER UNPAID.

By mid-May, 1861, correspondence between the North and South was difficult. In the South, postmasters were resigning and closing their accounts with Washington as the Confederacy prepared to organize its own postal system by June 1. From that date on, town marks and "paid" handstamps (and later postmasters' provisional stamps) were used in all post offices of the seceded states. The three most important Southern cities for clearing mail to the North were Memphis, Nashville and Richmond. The Richmond-Washington route was closed in April; Memphis was closed by June 1st, and mail attempting to cross the lines at these points generally ended up at the dead letter office. However, at Louisville, Kentucky, mail from the South via Nashville continued to arrive in June, July and August. On June 24, 1861, the Post Office Department advised the Louisville post office, "You will forward letters from the South for the Loyal States as unpaid, after removing postage stamps, but foreign letters in which prepayment is compulsory must come to the Dead Letter Office." However, Louisville avoided the task of "removing postage stamps," and instead prepared the "Southern Letter Unpaid" handstamp and special "due 3" markers for use. These markings were applied in the greenish-blue color of the Louisville office to letters of Southern origin that had accumulated, in addition to the usual town mark and grid of Louisville. The letters were delivered in the North or abroad as unpaid. Probably Louisville continued to forward such unpaid mail until about July 15. The marking is very rare. Other Southern mail was forwarded from Louisville as late as Aug. 27.

For listings see under U. S. 1857-61 issue, Nos. 26, 35-38. Prices shown there are generally for this marking on off-cover stamps. Complete covers bearing stamps showing the full marking are valued form $7,500 upward depending upon the stamps, other postal markings and unusual usages. Fraudulent covers exist.

Trans-Mississippi Express Mail — the 40c Rate

From the fall of New Orleans on April 24, 1862, the entire reach of the Mississippi River was threatened by the Federal fleets. Late in 1862 the Confederacy experienced difficulty in maintaining regular mail routes trans-Mississippi to the Western states. Private express companies began to carry some mail, but by early 1863 when the Meridian-Jackson-Vicksburg-Shreveport route was seriously menaced, the Post Office Department of the Confederate States was forced to inaugurate an express mail service by contracting with a private company the name of which remains undisclosed. The eastern termini were at Meridian and Brandon, Miss.; the western at Shreveport and Alexandria, La. Letters, usually endorsed "via Meridian (or Brandon)" if going West; "via Shreveport (or Alexandria)" if going East were deposited in any Confederate post office. The rate was 40c per ½ ounce or less. Such Trans-Mississippi Express Mail upon arrival at a terminus was carried by couriers in a devious route across the Mississippi and returned to the regular mails at the nearest terminus on the other side of the river. The precise date of the beginning of the Trans-Mississippi service is not known. The earliest date of use so far seen is November 2, 1863 and the latest use February 9, 1865. These covers can be identified by the written endorsement of the route, but particularly by the rate since many bore no route endorsements.

Strips of four of 10c engraved stamps, pairs of the 20c stamp and various combinations of 10c stamps and the 5c London or Local prints are known; also handstamped Paid 40c marking. No identifying handstamps were used, merely the postmark of the office which received the letter originally. Prices for Trans-Mississippi Express covers will be found under various stamps of the General Issues.

A 50c Preferred Mail Express rate, announced in April, 1863, preceded the Trans-Mississippi Express Mail 40c rate. Covers have been reported.

Packet and Steamboat Covers and Markings

Letters carried on Confederate packets operating on coastal routes or up and down the inland waterways were usually handstamped with the name of the packet or marked STEAM or STEAMBOAT. Either United States stamps of the 1857 issue or stamped envelopes of the 1853 or 1860 issues have been found so used, as well as Confederate Postmasters' Provisional and General Issue stamps. Some specially designed pictorial or imprinted packet boat covers also exist. All are scarce and command prices from $500 upward for handstamped United States envelopes and from $1,000 up for covers bearing Confederate stamps.

TABLE OF SECESSION

States in Order of Secession	Ordinance of Secession Passed	Admitted to Confederacy	Period for Use of U. S. Stamps As Independent State	Total to May 31, 1861*
South Carolina	Dec. 20, 1860	Feb. 4, 1861	1 mo. 15 days	5 mo. 11 days
Mississippi	Jan. 9, 1861	Feb. 4, 1861	26 days	4 mo. 22 days
Florida	Jan. 10, 1861	Feb. 4, 1861	25 days	4 mo. 21 days
Alabama	Jan. 11, 1861	Feb. 4, 1861	24 days	4 mo. 20 days
Georgia	Jan. 18, 1861	Feb. 4, 1861	17 days	4 mo. 13 days
Louisiana	Jan. 26, 1861	Feb. 4, 1861	9 days	4 mo. 5 days
Texas	Feb. 1, 1861†	Mar. 6, 1861	1 mo. 6 days	4 mo. 0 days
Virginia	April 17, 1861	May 7, 1861	20 days	1 mo. 14 days
Arkansas	May 6, 1861	May 18, 1861	12 days	25 days
North Carolina	May 20, 1861	May 27, 1861	7 days	11 days
Tennessee	June 8, 1861	July 2, 1861	0 *	0 *

* The use of United States stamps in the seceded States was prohibited after May 31, 1861.
† Ordinance of Secession adopted. Popular vote to secede Feb. 23, effective March 2, 1861.

Secession data by courtesy of August Dietz, Sr.

CONFEDERATE STATES

OFFICIAL ENVELOPES

The Confederate postal laws did not provide the franking privilege for any mail except official correspondence of the Post Office Department. Such letters could be sent free only when enclosed in officially imprinted envelopes individually signed by the official using them. These envelopes were prepared and issued for Post Office Department use.

The imprints were on United States envelopes of 1853-61 issue, and also on commercial envelopes of various sizes and colors. When officially signed and mailed, they were postmarked, usually at Richmond, Va., with printed or handstamped "FREE". Envelopes are occasionally found unused and unsigned, and more rarely, signed but unused. When such official envelopes were used on other than official Post Office Department business, Confederate stamps were used.

Semi-official envelopes also exist bearing imprints of other government departments, offices, armies, states, etc. Regular postage was required to carry such envelopes through the mails.

CONFEDERATE STATES OF AMERICA,
POST OFFICE DEPARTMENT,
OFFICIAL BUSINESS.
John H Reagan
POSTMASTER GENERAL

Confederate States of America,
POST OFFICE DEPARTMENT,
OFFICIAL BUSINESS
John B A Dimitry
Act. CHIEF CLERK P. O. DEPARTMENT

Typical Imprints of Official Envelopes of the Post Office Department.
(Many variations of type, style and wording exist.)

Office	Signature
Postmaster General	John H. Reagan
Chief of the Contract Bureau	H. St. Geo. Offutt
Chief of the Appointment Bureau	B. N. Clements
Chief of the Finance Bureau	Jno. L. Harrell
" " " "	J. L. Lancaster
" " " "	A. Dimitry
Dead Letter Office	A. Dimitry
" " "	Jno. L. Harrell
Chief Clerk, P. O. Department	B. Fuller
Chief Clerk	W. D. Miller
Auditor's Office	W. W. Lester
" "	B. Baker
" "	J. W. Robertson
First Auditor's Office, Treasury Department	J. W. Robertson
" " " " "	B. Baker
Third Auditor's Office	A. Moise
" " "	I. W. M. Harris
Agency, Post Office Dept. Trans-Miss.	Jas. H. Starr

THOMAS DELA RUE & CO.
All Die Struck PROOFS
PARTIAL & COMPLETE

WANTED
IMMEDIATE PAYMENT UPON RECEIPT
FRANKLIN FREEMAN
222 St. Paul Street, Suite 3204
Baltimore, Maryland 21202
ALSO POSTAL DOCUMENTS

19th Century COUNTER-FEITS
and CATALOGUE ILLUSTRATIONS

PROOFS

		DIE		PLATE
		(1) Glazed card	*(1a)* Wove paper	*(5)* Wove paper
1861				
1P	5c green			
2P	10c blue			*1500.00*
2TC	10c black (stone y)			*1500.00*
				3000.00
1862				
6P	5c light blue	1000.00		
6P	5c dark blue		1000.00	
6P	5c gray blue			600.00
6TC	5c black	650.00		
6TC	5c pink	1000.00		—
7P	5c carmine			850.00
1863				
8TC	2c black		1000.00	
9TC	10c black		1200.00	
11TC	10c black		900.00	
13P	20c green		900.00	
13TC	20c red brown		800.00	
1862				
14P	1c orange	700.00		
14TC	1c black	700.00		
14TC	1c light yellow brown			600.00

Essay Die Proofs.

In working up the final dies, proofs of incomplete designs in various stages were made. Usually dated in typeset lines, they are very rare. Others, of the 10c (No. 12) and the 20c (No. 13) were proofs made as essays from the dies. They are deeply engraved and printed in deep shades of the issued colors, but show only small differences from the stamps as finally issued. All are very rare.

Specimen Overprints.

The De La Rue typographed 5c and 1c are known with "SPECIMEN" overprinted diagonally, also horizontally for 1c.

Counterfeits.

In 1935 a set of 12 lithographed imitations, later known as the "Springfield facsimiles," appeared in plate form. They are in approximately normal colors on yellowish soft wove paper of modern manufacture.

CANAL ZONE

The Canal Zone, a strip of territory with an area of about 552 square miles following generally the line of the Canal, was under the jurisdiction of the United States, 1904–1979.

The Canal organization underwent two distinct and fundamental changes. The construction of the Canal and the general administration of civil affairs were performed by the Isthmian Canal Commission under the provisions of the Spooner Act. This was supplanted in April, 1914, by the Panama Canal Act which established the organization known as The Panama Canal. This was an independent Government Agency which included both the operation and maintenance of the waterway and civil government in the Canal Zone. Most of the quasi-business enterprises relating to the Canal operation were conducted by the Panama Railroad, an adjunct of the Panama Canal.

A basic change in the mode of operations took effect July 1, 1951, under provisions of Public Law 841 of the 81st Congress. This in effect transferred the canal operations to the Panama Railroad Co., which had been made a federal government corporation in 1948, and changed its name to the Panama Canal Co. Simultaneously the civil government functions of The Panama Canal, including the postal service, were renamed the Canal Zone Government. The organization therefore consisted of two units—the Panama Canal Co. and Canal Zone Government—headed by an individual who was president of the company and governor of the Canal Zone. His appointment as governor was made by the President of the United States, subject to confirmation by the Senate, and he was ex-officio president of the company.

The Canal Zone Government functioned as an independent government agency, and was under direct supervision of the President of the United States who delegated this authority to the Secretary of the Army.

The Panama Canal is 50 miles long from deep water in the Atlantic to deep water in the Pacific. Its runs from northwest to southeast with the Atlantic entrance being 33.5 miles north and 27 miles west of the Pacific entrance. The airline distance between the two entrances is 43 miles. It requires about eight hours for an average ship to transit the Canal. Transportation between the Atlantic and Pacific sides of the Isthmus is available by railway or highway.

The U.S. Canal Zone Postal Service began operating June 24, 1904, when nine post offices were opened in connection with the construction of the Panama Canal. It ceased Sept. 30, 1979, and the Panama Postal Service took over.

Numbers in parentheses indicate quantity issued.

100 CENTAVOS=1 PESO   100 CENTESIMOS=1 BALBOA   100 CENTS=1 DOLLAR

Map of Panama
A1

1904, June 24   Perf. 12   Unwmkd.

Violet to violet blue Handstamp on Panama Nos. 72, 72a-72c, 78, 79.

On the 2c "PANAMA" is normally 13mm. long. On the 5c and 10c it measures about 15mm.
On the 2c, "PANAMA" reads up on the upper half of the sheet and down on the lower half. On the 5c and 10c, "PANAMA" reads up at left and down at right on each stamp.
On the 2c only, varieties exist with inverted "V" for "A", accent on "A", inverted "N", etc., in "PANAMA."

1 A1 2c rose, both "PANAMA" reading up or down (*600*)		400.00	375.00
Single on cover			800.00
Strip of three on cover			1500.00
Block of four		1850.00	1850.00
a. "CANAL ZONE" inverted (*100*)		750.00	750.00
b. "CANAL ZONE" double		2000.00	2000.00
c. "CANAL ZONE" double, both inverted		4000.00	
d. "PANAMA" reading down and up (*5#*)		525.00	525.00
e. As "d," "CANAL ZONE" invtd.		3500.00	3500.00
f. Vert. pair, "PANAMA" reading up on top 2c, down on other		1250.00	1250.00
"PANAMA" 15mm. long (*60*)		475.00	475.00
"P NAMA"		475.00	475.00
2 A1 5c blue (*7800*)		250.00	200.00
On cover			400.00
First day cover			2500.00
Block of four		1300.00	1300.00
a. "CANAL ZONE" inverted		500.00	500.00
b. "CANAL ZONE" double		900.00	900.00
c. Pair, one without "CANAL ZONE" overprint		2250.00	2250.00
d. "CANAL ZONE" overprint diagonal, reading down to right		450.00	450.00
Left "PANAMA" 2¼mm. below bar (*156*)		400.00	400.00
Colon between right "PANAMA" and bar (*156*)		350.00	350.00
3 " 10c yellow (*4946*)		325.00	300.00
On cover			500.00
First day cover			2500.00
Block of four		1600.00	1600.00
a. "CANAL ZONE" inverted (*100*)		500.00	500.00
b. "CANAL ZONE" double			3000.00
c. Pair, one without "CANAL ZONE" overprint		2750.00	2750.00
Left "PANAMA" 2¼mm. below bar (*100*)		500.00	500.00
Colon between right "PANAMA" and bar (*100*)		425.00	425.00

Cancellations consist of town and/or bars in magenta or black, or a mixture of both colors.

Nos. 1-3 were withdrawn July 17, 1904.

Forgeries of the "Canal Zone" overprint and cancellations are numerous.

CANAL ZONE

United States Nos. 300, 319, 304, 306 and 307 Overprinted in Black

CANAL ZONE **PANAMA**

1904, July 18   Wmkd. USPS (191)

4	A115	1c blue green (43,738)	25.00 22.50
		green	25.00 22.50
		On cover	60.00
		Block of four	110.00 110.00
		Margin strip of three, Impt. & P #	120.00
		Margin block of six, Impt. & P #	800.00
5	A129	2c carmine (68,414)	22.50 20.00
		On cover	60.00
		Block of four	100.00 100.00
		Margin strip of three, Impt. & P #	100.00
		Margin block of six, Impt. & P #	800.00
	a.	2c scarlet	27.50 22.50
6	A119	5c blue (20,858)	90.00 70.00
		On cover	125.00
		Block of four	425.00 375.00
		Margin strip of three, Impt. & P #	450.00
		Margin block of six, Impt. & P #	1650.00
7	A121	8c violet black (7932)	150.00 130.00
		On cover	225.00
		Block of four	700.00 700.00
		Margin strip of three, Impt. & P #	700.00 700.00
		Margin block of six, Impt. & P #	2000.00
8	A122	10c pale red brown (7856)	160.00 130.00
		On cover	225.00
		Block of four	700.00 700.00
		Margin strip of three, Impt. & P #	750.00 700.00
		Margin block of six, Impt. & P #	2500.00 1650.00

Nos. 4 to 8 frequently show minor broken letters. Cancellations consist of circular town and/or bars in black, blue or magenta.

A2

CANAL ZONE
Regular Type

A3

CANAL ZONE
Antique Type

The Canal Zone overprint on stamps Nos. 9–15 and 18–20 was made with a plate which had six different stages, each with its peculiar faults and errors of which there was generally only one in each sheet. Stage 1: broken CA--L, broken L, A-L spaced, on Nos. 9, 10, 12-15. Stage 2: broken L, Z, N, E, on Nos. 9, 10, 12-14. Stage 3: same as 2 with additional antique ZONE, on Nos. 9, 11-14, 18. Stage 4: same as 3 with additional antique CANAL on Nos. 9, 12, 13. Stage 5: broken E and letters L, Z, N, and words CANAL and ZONE in antique type on Nos. 12-14, 19, 20. Stage 6: same as 5 except for additional antique Z on stamp which had antique L, on No. 12. The Panama overprints can be distinguished by the different shades of the red overprint, the width of the bar, and the word PANAMA. No. 11 has two different Panama overprints; No. 12 has six; No. 13 five; No. 14 two; and Nos. 15, 18-20, one each. In the "8cts" surcharge of Nos. 14 and 15, there are three varieties of the figure "8". The bar is sometimes misplaced so that it appears on the bottom of the stamp instead of the top.

1904-06   Black Overprint on Stamps of Panama.   Unwmkd

9	A2	1c green (319,800) Dec. 12, 1904	2.25 1.75
		On cover	5.00
		Block of four	10.00 9.00
	a.	"CANAL" in antique type (500)	125.00 125.00
	b.	"ZONE" in antique type (1500)	75.00 75.00
	c.	Inverted overprint	— 2000.00
	d.	Double overprint	1200.00 800.00
		Spaced "A L" in "CANAL" (700)	100.00 100.00
		"ON" of "ZONE" dropped	250.00 250.00
10	A2	2c rose (367,500) Dec. 12, 1904	4.50 2.50
		On cover	6.00
		Block of four	22.50 15.00
	a.	Inverted overprint	250.00 250.00
	b.	"L" of "CANAL" sideways	1000.00 1000.00
		Spaced "A L" of "CANAL" (1700)	85.00 85.00
		"ON" of "ZONE" dropped	225.00 225.00

"PANAMA" (15mm. long) reading up at left, down at right.
Overprint "CANAL ZONE" in Black, "PANAMA" and Bar in Red.

11	A3	2c rose (150,000) Dec. 9, 1905	6.00 4.00
		On cover	8.50
		Block of four	30.00 22.50
	a.	"ZONE" in antique type (1500)	100.00 100.00
	b.	"PANAMA" overprint inverted, bar at bottom (200)	300.00 300.00
		Inverted "M" in "PANAMA" (3,000)	60.00 60.00
		"PANAMA" 16mm. long (3000)	60.00 60.00
12	"	5c blue (400,000) Dec. 12, 1904	8.00 3.75
		On cover	10.00
		Block of four	40.00 20.00
	a.	"CANAL" in antique type (2750)	75.00 75.00
	b.	"ZONE" in antique type (2950)	75.00 75.00
	c.	"CANAL ZONE" double (200)	500.00 500.00
	d.	"PANAMA" double (120)	600.00 600.00
	e.	"PANAMA" inverted, bar at bottom	800.00 800.00
		Spaced "A L" in "CANAL" (300)	75.00 75.00
		"PAMAMA" reading up (2800)	60.00 60.00
		"PAMAMA" reading down (400)	175.00 175.00
		"PAMAMA" 16mm. long (1800)	50.00 50.00
		Inverted "M" in "PANAMA" (1800)	50.00 50.00
		Right "PANAMA" 5mm. below bar (600)	75.00 75.00
		"PANAM"	70.00 70.00
		"PANAAM" at right	600.00 600.00
		"PAN MA"	75.00 75.00
		"ANAMA"	80.00 80.00
13	"	10c yellow (64,900) Dec. 12, 1904	18.50 12.00
		On cover	25.00
		Block of four	90.00 65.00
	a.	"CANAL" in antique type (200)	175.00 175.00
	b.	"ZONE" in antique type (400)	150.00 150.00
	c.	"PANAMA" ovpt. double (80)	550.00 550.00
		Spaced "A L" in "CANAL" (200)	125.00 125.00
		"PANAMA" 16mm. long (400)	80.00 80.00
		"PAMAMA" reading down (200)	125.00 125.00
		Invtd. "M" in "PANAMA" (400)	100.00 100.00
		Right "PANAMA" 5mm. below bar (398)	100.00 100.00
		Left "PANAMA" touches bar (400)	100.00 100.00
	d.	"PANAMA" overprint in red brown (5000)	22.50 22.50
		"PANAMA" ovpt. in org. red	25.00 25.00

With Additional Surcharge in Red

8 cts
a

There are three varieties of "8" in the surcharge on Nos. 14-15.

14	A3	8c on 50c bistre brown (27,900) Dec. 12, 1904	30.00 20.00
		On cover	35.00
		Block of four	135.00 105.00
	a.	"ZONE" in antique type (25)	650.00 600.00
	b.	"CANAL ZONE" inverted (200)	300.00 300.00
		Spaced "A L" in "CANAL" (194)	110.00 110.00
		Right "PANAMA" 5mm. below bar (438)	110.00 110.00
	c.	"PANAMA" overprint in rose brown (6000)	37.50 37.50
	d.	As "c", "CANAL" in antique type (10)	1350.00
	e.	As "c", "ZONE" in antique type (10)	1350.00
	f.	As "c", "8cts" double (30)	550.00
	g.	As "c", "8" omitted	3500.00

Nos. 11-14 are overprinted or surcharged on Panama Nos. 77, 77e, 78, 78c, 78d, 78f, 78g, 78h, 79, 79c, 79e, 79g and 81 respectively.

CANAL ZONE

801

Panama No. 74a, 74b Overprinted "CANAL ZONE" in Regular Type in Black and Surcharged Type "a" in Red.
Both "PANAMA" (13mm. long) Reading Up.

15	A3 (a)	8c on 50c bistre brown (500)		2250.00	2250.00
		Dec. 12, 1904			6000.00
		On cover			
		Block of four		9500.00	9500.00
	a.	"PANAMA" reading down and up (10)		3000.00	3000.00
		"PANAMA" 15mm. long (50)		2500.00	2500.00
		"P NAMA"		2750.00	
		Spaced "A L" in "CANAL" (5)		3000.00	

Map of Panama
A4

Panama Nos. 19 and 21 Surcharged in Black:

a

b

c

d

e

f

1906

There were three printings of each denomination, differing principally in the relative position of the various parts of the surcharges. Varieties occur with inverted "v" for the final "a" in "Panama", "CA" spaced, "ZO" spaced, "2c" spaced, accents in various positions, and with bars shifted so that two bars appear on top or bottom of the stamp (either with or without the corresponding bar on top or bottom) and sometimes with only one bar at top or bottom.

16	A4 1c on 20c violet, type a (100,000) March		1.60	1.20
	On cover			3.00
	Block of four		7.00	6.00
	a. 1c on 20c violet, type b (100,000) May		1.60	1.20
	On cover			3.00
	Block of four		7.00	6.00
	b. 1c on 20c violet, type c (300,000) Sept.		1.25	1.20
	On cover			3.00
	Block of four		6.50	6.00
	Spaced C-A		12.50	
17	A4 2c on 1p lake, type d (200,000) Mar.		2.25	1.75
	On cover			5.00
	Block of four		10.00	9.00
	a. 2c on 1p lake, type e (200,000) May		2.25	1.75
	On cover			5.00
	Block of four		10.00	9.00
	b. 2c on 1p lake, type f (50,000) Sept.		20.00	20.00
	On cover			25.00
	Block of four		85.00	85.00

Panama Nos. 74, 74a and 74b Overprinted "CANAL ZONE" in Regular Type in Black and Surcharged in Red

8 cts.   8 cts
      b   c

1905-06
Both "PANAMA" Reading Up.

18	A3 (b) 8c on 50c bis. brown (17,500) Nov. 1905		65.00	65.00
	On cover			90.00
	Block of four		275.00	275.00
	a. "ZONE" in antique type (175)		175.00	175.00
	b. "PANAMA" reading down and up (350)		100.00	100.00
	"PANAMA" 15mm. long (1750)		80.00	80.00
	"P NAMA"		100.00	100.00
19	" (c) 8c on 50c bistre brown (19,000) April 23, 1906		65.00	60.00
	On cover			90.00
	Block of four		275.00	275.00
	a. "CANAL" in antique type (190)		150.00	150.00
	b. "ZONE" in antique type (190)		150.00	150.00
	c. "8 cts" double		1000.00	1000.00
	d. "PANAMA" reading down and up (380)		90.00	90.00
	"PANAMA" 15mm. long (1900)		65.00	65.00
	"P NAMA"		70.00	

Panama No. 81 Overprinted "CANAL ZONE" in Regular Type in Black and Surcharged in Red Type "c" plus Period.
"Panama" reading up and down.

20	A3 (c) 8c on 50c bis. brown (19,600) Sept. 1906		50.00	40.00
	On cover			60.00
	Block of four		200.00	160.00
	a. "CANAL" in antique type (196)		150.00	150.00
	b. "ZONE" in antique type (196)		150.00	150.00
	c. "8 cts" omitted (50)		600.00	600.00
	d. "8 cts" double		1250.00	
	"PAMANA" reading up (392)		75.00	75.00

Nos. 14 and 18-20 exist without CANAL ZONE overprint but were not regularly issued. Forgeries of the overprint varieties of Nos. 9-15 and 18-20 are known.

Vasco Núñez de   Fernández de
Balboa—A5   Córdoba—A6

Justo Arosemena   Manuel J. Hurtado   José de Obaldía
     A7   A8   A9

Engraved by Hamilton Bank Note Co. Overprinted in black by Isthmian Canal Commission Press.

1906-07   Perf. 12   Unwmkd.
Overprint Reading Up.

21	A6 2c red & black (50,000) Oct. 29, 1906		30.00	25.00
	On cover			35.00
	Block of four		150.00	135.00
	a. "CANAL" only		4250.00	

Overprint Reading Down.

22	A5 1c green & black (2,000,000) Jan. 14, 1907		2.25	1.25
	dull green & black		2.25	1.25
	On cover			3.00
	Block of four		10.00	6.00
	a. Horiz. pair, imperf. btwn. (50)		900.00	900.00
	b. Vert. pair, imperf. btwn. (20)		1400.00	1400.00
	c. Vert. pair, imperf. horiz. (20)		1400.00	1400.00
	d. Inverted overprint reading up (100)		250.00	250.00
	e. Double overprint (300)		225.00	225.00
	f. Double overprint, one inverted		1000.00	1000.00
	g. Invtd. center, ovpt. reading up		2250.00	2250.00
	"ANA" for "CANAL" (1000)		60.00	60.00
	"CAN L" for "CANAL"		75.00	75.00
	"ONE" for "ZONE" (3000)		50.00	50.00

CANAL ZONE

23	A6	2c red & black (*2,370,000*) *Nov. 25, 1906*		2.75	1.25
		scarlet & black, *1907*		2.75	1.25
		On cover			2.25
		Block of four		12.00	7.00
		a. Horizontal pair, imperf. between (*20*)		900.00	900.00
		b. Vertical pair, one without overprint		1400.00	1400.00
		c. Double overprint (*100*)		400.00	400.00
		d. Double overprint, one diagonal		500.00	500.00
		e. Double overprint, one diagonal in pair with normal		1200.00	
		f. 2c carmine red & black, *Sept. 9, 1907*		5.00	2.75
		g. As "f", inverted center and overprint reading up			5000.00
		h. As "d," one "ZONE CANAL"		2000.00	
		i. "CANAL" double		2500.00	
		"CAN L" for "CANAL"		45.00	
24	A7	5c ultramarine & black (*1,390,000*) *Dec. 1906*		7.25	2.75
		light ultramarine & black		7.25	2.75
		blue & black, *Sept. 16, 1907*		7.25	2.75
		dark blue & black		7.25	2.75
		On cover			6.00
		Block of four		35.00	20.00
		a. 5c dull blue & black		7.25	2.75
		b. 5c light blue & black		6.00	2.25
		c. Double overprint (*200*)		350.00	250.00
		d. "CANAL" only (*10*)		1750.00	
		e. "ZONE CANAL"		2750.00	
		"CAN L" for "CANAL"		60.00	
25	A8	8c purple & black (*170,000*) *Dec. 1906*		25.00	10.00
		On cover			27.50
		Block of four		105.00	50.00
		a. Horizontal pair, imperf. between and at left margin (*34*)		600.00	600.00
26	A9	10c violet & black (*250,000*) *Dec. 1906*		25.00	8.00
		On cover			30.00
		Block of four		120.00	50.00
		a. Dbl. ovpt., one reading up (*10*)		1750.00	
		b. Overprint reading up		2000.00	

The early printings of this series were issued on soft, thick, porous-textured paper, while later printings of all except No. 25 appear on hard, thin, smooth-textured paper. Normal spacing of the early printings is 7¼ mm. between the words; later printings, 6¾ mm. Nos. 22 and 26 exist imperf. between stamp and sheet margin. Nos. 22-25 occur with "CA" of "CANAL" spaced ½ mm. further apart on position No. 50 of the setting.

Córdoba
A11

Arosemena
A12

Hurtado
A13

José de Obaldía
A14

Engraved by American Bank Note Co.
1909 Overprint Reading Down.

27	A11	2c vermilion & black (*500,000*) *May 11,*		16.00	7.50
		On cover			12.00
		First day cover			400.00
		Block of four		75.00	40.00
		a. Horizontal pair, one without overprint		2000.00	
		b. Vert. pair, one without ovpt.		2100.00	
28	A12	5c deep blue & black (*200,000*) *May 28, 1909*		62.50	14.00
		On cover			25.00
		Block of four		265.00	75.00
29	A13	8c violet & black (*50,000*) *May 25, 1909*		55.00	12.50
		On cover			40.00
		Block of four		240.00	85.00
30	A14	10c violet & black (*100,000*) *Jan. 19, 1909*		55.00	15.00
		On cover			45.00
		Block of four		240.00	100.00
		a. Horizontal pair, one without overprint		3000.00	
		b. Vertical pair, one without overprint		3500.00	

Nos. 27-30 occur with "CA" spaced (position 50).

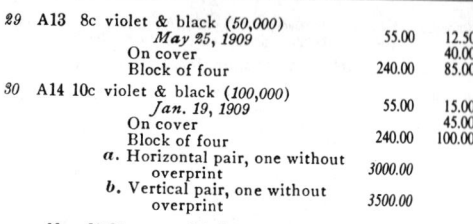

Vasco Núñez de Balboa
A15

Engraved, Printed and Overprinted by
American Bank Note Co.

Black Overprint Reading Up.

Type I

Type I Overprint: "C" with serifs both top and bottom. "L," "Z" and "E" with slanting serifs.

Illustrations of Types I to V are considerably enlarged and do not show actual spacing between lines of overprint.

1909-10

31	A15	1c dark green & black (*4,000,000*) *Nov. 8, 1909*		3.25	1.75
		On cover			2.50
		Block of four		15.00	9.00
		a. Inverted center and overprint reading down			11,000.00
		b. "CANAL" only		600.00	
		c. Booklet pane of 6 handmade, perf. margins		550.00	
32	A11	2c vermilion & black, (*4,000,000*) *Nov. 8, 1909*		4.00	1.75
		On cover			2.50
		Block of four		17.50	8.50
		a. Vert. pair, imperf. horiz.		500.00	500.00
		b. "CANAL" double		—	
		c. Bklt. pane of 6 handmade, perf. margins		700.00	
33	A12	5c deep blue & black, (*2,000,000*) *Nov. 8, 1909*		13.00	4.50
		On cover			8.00
		Block of four		65.00	25.00
		a. Double overprint (*200*)		250.00	250.00
34	A13	8c violet & blk., (*200,000*) *Mar. 18, 19*		9.50	5.00
		On cover			10.00
		Block of four		45.00	25.00
		a. Vertical pair, one without overprint (*10*)		1750.00	
35	A14	10c vio. & blk., (*100,000*) *Nov. 8, 1909*		60.00	22.50
		On cover			35.00
		Block of four		265.00	100.00

Normal spacing between words of overprint on No. 31 is 10 mm and on Nos. 32 to 35, 8½ mm. Minor spacing variations are known.

A16

A17

CANAL ZONE

1911

36	A16	10c on 13c gray (476,700) Jan. 14, 1911		5.00	2.00
		On cover			5.00
		Block of four		24.00	11.00
		a. "10 cts" inverted		275.00	225.00
		b. "10 cts" omitted		250.00	—

The "10 cts" surcharge was applied by the Isthmian Canal Commission Press after the overprinted stamps were received from the American Bank Note Co.

Many of the stamps offered as No. 36b are merely No. 36 from which the surcharge has been removed with chemicals.

1914

37	A17	10c gray (200,000) Jan. 6, 1914		50.00	12.00
		On cover			22.50
		Block of four		225.00	55.00

Type II

Type II Overprint: "C" with serifs at top only. "L" and "E" with vertical serifs. Inner oval of "O" tilts to left.

1912-16

38	A15	1c green & black (3,000,000) July 1913		12.00	2.75
		On cover			5.00
		Block of four		50.00	18.00
		a. Vertical pair, one without overprint		1100.00	1100.00
		b. Booklet pane of six, imperf. margins (120,000)		525.00	
		c. Booklet pane of 6 handmade, perf. margins		900.00	
39	A11	2c vermilion & black (7,500,000) Dec. 1912		7.00	1.25
		orange vermilion & black, 1916		7.00	1.25
		On cover			3.50
		Block of four		35.00	7.00
		a. Horizontal pair, one without overprint		600.00	
		b. "CANAL" only		850.00	850.00
		c. Booklet pane of 6, imperf. margins (194,868)		500.00	
		d. Overprint reading down		150.00	
		e. As "d" inverted center		650.00	650.00
		f. As "e" booklet pane of 6 handmade, perf. margins		5000.00	
		g. As "c," handmade, perf. margins		850.00	
40	A12	5c deep blue & black (2,300,000) Dec. 1912		22.50	2.50
		On cover			9.00
		Block of four		100.00	12.00
		a. With Cordoba portrait of 2c			6500.00
41	A14	10c violet & black (200,000) Feb. 1916		50.00	10.00
		On cover			25.00
		Block of four		250.00	55.00

Normal spacing between words of overprint on the first printing of Nos. 38-40 is 8½mm. and on the second printing 9¼mm. The spacing of the single printing of No. 41 and the imperf. margin booklet panes printing of Nos. 38 and 39 is 7¾mm. Minor spacing variations are known.

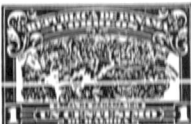

Map of Panama Canal
A18

Balboa Taking Possession of the Pacific Ocean
A19

Gatun Locks
A20

Culebra Cut
A21

Engraved, Printed and Overprinted by American Bank Note Co.

1915, Mar. 1 — Blue Overprint, Type II.

42	A18	1c dark green & black (100,000)		8.25	5.00
		On cover			7.00
		Block of four		35.00	22.50
		First day cover			150.00
43	A19	2c carmine & black (100,000)		10.00	5.50
		vermilion & black		10.00	5.50
		On cover			8.00
		First day cover			150.00
		Block of four		42.50	25.00
44	A20	5c blue & black (100,000)		9.50	5.00
		On cover			12.00
		Block of four		42.50	25.00
		First day cover			150.00
45	A21	10c orange & black (50,000)		20.00	12.50
		On cover			20.00
		Block of four		90.00	60.00
		First day cover			150.00

Normal spacing between words of overprint is 9¼mm. on all four values except position No. 61 which is 10mm.

Type III

Type III Overprint: Similar to Type I but letters appear thinner, particularly the lower bar of "L," "Z" and "E." Impressions are often light, rough and irregular.

Engraved and Printed by American Bank Note Co.

Black overprint reading up applied by Panama Canal Press, Mount Hope, C. Z.

1915-20

46	A15	1c green & black, Dec. 1915		200.00	120.00
		light green & black, 1920		225.00	175.00
		On cover			175.00
		Block of four		950.00	575.00
		a. Overprint reading down (200)		300.00	
		b. Double overprint (180)		325.00	
		c. "ZONE" double (2)		3000.00	
		d. Double overprint, one reads "ZONE CANAL" (18)		900.00	
		e. "CANAL" double		600.00	
47	A11	2c orange vermilion & black, Aug. 1920		2500.00	110.00
		On cover			350.00
		Block of four		12,000.00	600.00
48	A12	5c deep blue & black, Dec. 1915		700.00	200.00
		On cover			500.00
		Block of four		3000.00	900.00

Normal spacing between words of overprint on Nos. 46-48 is 9¼mm. This should not be confused with an abnormal 9½mm. spacing of the 2c and 5c values of type I, which are fairly common in singles, particularly used. Blocks of the abnormal spacing are rare.

S. S. "Panama" in Culebra Cut
A22   A23

S. S. "Cristobal" in Gatun Locks
A24

Engraved, Printed and Overprinted by American Bank Note Co.

1917, Jan. Blue Overprint, Type II.

49	A22	12c purple & black (314,914)		20.00	7.00
		On cover			15.00
		Block of four		90.00	30.00
50	A23	15c bright blue & black		50.00	30.00
		On cover			50.00
		Block of four		225.00	130.00
51	A24	24c yellow brown & black		50.00	15.00
		On cover			30.00
		Block of four		225.00	70.00

Normal spacing between words of overprint is 11¼ mm.

CANAL ZONE

Type IV

Type IV Overprint: "C" thick at bottom, "E" with center bar same length as top and bottom bars.

Engraved, Printed and Overprinted by American Bank Note Co.

1918-20 Black Overprint, Reading Up

52	A15	1c green & black (2,000,000) Jan. 1918		32.50	6.00
		On cover			10.00
		Block of four		140.00	30.00
		a. Overprint reading down		110.00	
		b. Booklet pane of 6 (60,000)		600.00	
		c. Booklet pane of 6, left vertical row of 3 without overprint		2250.00	
		d. Booklet pane of 6, right vertical row of 3, with double overprint		2250.00	
		e. Pair, one without overprint		850.00	
53	A11	2c vermilion & black (2,000,000) Nov. 1918		130.00	6.50
		On cover			10.00
		Block of four		575.00	35.00
		a. Overprint reading down		120.00	120.00
		b. Horiz. pair, one without ovpt.		850.00	
		c. Booklet pane of 6 (34,000)		700.00	
		d. Booklet pane of 6, left vertical row of 3, without overprint		2250.00	
54	A12	5c dp. blue & black (500,000) Apr. 1920		225.00	35.00
		On cover			100.00
		Block of four		950.00	165.00

Normal spacing between words of overprint on Nos. 52 and 53 is 9¼mm. On No. 54 and the booklet printings of Nos. 52 and 53, the normal spacing is 9mm. Minor spacing varieties are known.

CANAL ZONE

Type V

Type V Overprint: Smaller block type 1¾mm. high. "A" with flat top.

1920-21 Black Overprint, Reading Up.

55	A15	1c light green & black, Apr. 1921		22.50	4.50
		On cover			7.00
		Block of four		95.00	20.00
		a. Overprint reading down		140.00	140.00
		b. Horiz. pair, one without ovpt.		600.00	
		c. "CANAL" double		1100.00	
		d. "ZONE" only		2250.00	—
		e. Booklet pane of 6		2750.00	
		f. Vert. pair, one without ovpt.		2000.00	

56	A11	2c orange vermilion & black, Sept. 1920		8.00	3.00
		On cover			4.00
		Block of four		35.00	14.00
		a. Double overprint (100)		350.00	
		b. Double overprint, one reading down (100)		350.00	
		c. Horizontal pair, one without overprint		650.00	
		d. Vertical pair, one without overprint		1250.00	
		e. "CANAL" double		700.00	
		f. "ZONE" double		750.00	
		g. Booklet pane of 6		850.00	
		h. "CANAL" only		3000.00	
57	A12	5c dp. blue & black, Apr. 1921		300.00	42.50
		On cover			125.00
		Block of four		1300.00	185.00
		a. Horizontal pair, one without overprint (20)		1200.00	

Normal spacing between words of overprint on Nos. 55-57 is 9½mm. On booklet printings of Nos. 55 and 56 the normal spacing is 9¼mm.

Drydock at Balboa
A25

U. S. S. "Nereus" in Pedro Miguel Locks
A26

1920, Sept. Black Overprint Type V.

58	A25	50c orange & black		325.00	190.00
		On cover			325.00
		Block of four		1500.00	1000.00
59	A26	1b dark violet & black (23,014)		165.00	65.00
		On cover			150.00
		Block of four		750.00	300.00

José Vallarino
A27

"Land Gate"
A28

Bolívar's Tribute
A29

Municipal Building in 1821 and 1921
A30

Statue of Balboa
A31

Tomás Herrera
A32

José de Fábrega
A33

CANAL ZONE

Engraved, Printed and Overprinted by American Bank Note Co.

Type V overprint in black, reading up, on all values except the 5c which is overprinted with larger type in red.

1921, Nov. 13

60	A27	1c green		3.50	1.50
		On cover			2.50
		Block of four		17.00	7.00
		a. "CANAL" double		1100.00	
		b. Booklet pane of six		750.00	
61	A28	2c carmine		2.50	1.40
		On cover			2.50
		Block of four		11.00	6.00
		a. Invtd. overprint, reading down	135.00	135.00
		b. Double overprint		600.00	
		c. Vertical pair, one without overprint		3000.00	
		d. "CANAL" double		1500.00	
		e. "ZONE" only		3000.00	
		f. Booklet pane of six		1200.00	
62	A29	5c blue (R)		9.00	3.50
		On cover			6.00
		Block of four		40.00	20.00
		a. Overprint reading down (R)	60.00	
63	A30	10c violet		17.50	7.50
		On cover			15.00
		Block of four		80.00	35.00
		a. Invtd. overprint, reading down	90.00	
64	A31	15c light blue		55.00	15.00
		On cover			30.00
		Block of four		250.00	75.00
65	A32	24c black brown		65.00	25.00
		On cover			50.00
		Block of four		300.00	150.00
66	A33	50c black		135.00	95.00
		On cover			200.00
		Block of four		625.00	450.00

Experts question the status of the 5c with a small type V overprint in red or black.

1924, Jan. 28

Engraved and printed by the American Bank Note Co. Type III overprint in black, reading up, applied by the Panama Canal Press, Mount Hope, C. Z.

67	A27	1c green		475.00	200.00
		On cover			300.00
		Block of four		2000.00	1500.00
		a. "ZONE CANAL" reading down	750.00	
		b. "ZONE" only, reading down	1500.00	

Arms of Panama
A34

1924, Feb.

68	A34	1c dark green		12.50	4.00
		On cover			6.00
		Block of four		55.00	18.00
69	"	2c carmine		10.00	3.50
		carmine rose		10.00	3.50
		On cover			5.00
		Block of four		42.50	15.00

The following were prepared for use, but not issued.

A34	5c dark blue (600)	200.00	
	Block of four	800.00	
"	10c dark violet (600)	200.00	
	Block of four	800.00	
"	12c olive green (600)	200.00	
	Block of four	800.00	
"	15c ultramarine (600)	200.00	
	Block of four	800.00	
"	24c yellow brown (600)	200.00	
	Block of four	800.00	
A34	50c orange (600)	200.00	
	Block of four	800.00	
"	1b black (600)	200.00	
	Block of four	800.00	

The 5c to 1b values were prepared for use but never issued due to abrogation of the Taft Agreement which required the Canal Zone to use overprinted Panama stamps. Six hundred of each denomination were not destroyed, as they were forwarded to the Director General of Posts of Panama for transmission to the U. P. U. which then required about 400 sets.

All Panama stamps overprinted "CANAL ZONE" were withdrawn from sale June 30, 1924, and were no longer valid for postage after Aug. 31, 1924.

CANAL ZONE

United States Nos. 551 to 554, 557, 562, 564 to 566, 569, 570 and 571 Overprinted in Red or Black

Printed and Overprinted by the U. S. Bureau of Engraving and Printing.

Type A.
Letters "A" with Flat Tops.

1924-25   *Perf. 11.*   Unwmkd.

70	A154	½c olive brown (R) (399,500) *Apr. 15, 1925*	80	80
		On cover			1.25
		Block of four		3.50	3.50
		Margin block of six, P #	20.00	
71	A155	1c deep green (1,985,000) *July 1, 1924*	1.50	50
		On cover			75
		Block of four		6.50	2.25
		Margin block of six, P #	35.00	
		a. Inverted overprint	450.00	450.00
		b. "ZONE" inverted	300.00	300.00
		c. "CANAL" only (20)	900.00	
		d. "ZONE CANAL" (180)	250.00	
		e. Booklet pane of six (43,152)	125.00	
72	A156	1½c yellow brown (180,599) *Apr. 15, 192*	2.25	1.25
		brown		2.25	1.25
		On cover			2.50
		Block of four		9.50	7.00
		Margin block of six, P #	35.00	
73	A157	2c carmine (2,975,000) *July 1, 1924*	8.50	1.50
		On cover			2.00
		Block of four		35.00	7.00
		Margin block of six, P #	250.00	
		a. Booklet pane of six (140,000)	150.00	
74	A160	5c dark blue (500,000) *July 1, 1924*	20.00	8.50
		On cover			12.50
		Block of four		85.00	37.50
		Margin block of six, P #	375.00	
75	A165	10c orange (60,000) *July 1, 1924*	45.00	20.00
		On cover			35.00
		Block of four		185.00	90.00
		Margin block of six, P #	850.00	
76	A167	12c brown violet (80,000) *July 1, 1924*	40.00	22.50
		On cover			35.00
		Block of four		165.00	100.00
		Margin block of six, P #	600.00	
		a. "ZONE" inverted	3000.00	2000.00
77	A168	14c dark blue (100,000) *June 27, 1925*	22.50	15.00
		On cover			27.50
		Block of four		95.00	65.00
		Margin block of six, P #	400.00	
78	A169	15c gray (55,000) *July 1, 1924*	55.00	30.00
		On cover			60.00
		Block of four		240.00	135.00
		Margin block of six, P #	750.00	
79	A172	30c olive brown (40,000) *July 1, 1924*	30.00	20.00
		On cover			40.00
		Block of four		130.00	90.00
		Margin block of six, P #	550.00	
80	A173	50c lilac (25,000) *July 1, 1924*	65.00	40.00
		On cover			80.00
		Block of four		275.00	175.00
		Margin block of six, P #	1750.00	

CANAL ZONE

81 A174 $1 violet brown *(10,000) July 1, 1924*   325.00   165.00
    On cover   300.00
    Block of four   1400.00   700.00
    Margin block of four, arrow,
        top or bottom   1500.00
    Margin block of six, P ‡   3500.00

Normal spacing between words of the overprint is 9¼mm. Minor spacing variations are known. The overprint of the early printings used on all values of this series except No. 77 is a sharp, clear impression. The overprint of the late printings, used only on Nos. 70, 71, 73, 76, 77, 78 and 80 is heavy and smudged, with many of the letters, particularly the "A" practically filled.

Booklet panes Nos. 71e, 73a, 84d, 97b, 101a, 106a and 117a were made from 360 subject plates. The handmade booklet panes Nos. 102a, 115c and a provisional lot of 117b were made from Post Office sheets from regular 400-subject plates.

United States Nos. 554, 555, 557, 562, 564 to 567, 569, 570, 571s and 623 Overprinted in Red or Black	**CANAL** **ZONE**

Type B.
Letters "A" with Sharp Pointed Tops.

1925–28   *Perf. 11*

84 A157 2c carmine *(1,110,000) May*   1926   35.00   8.50
    On cover   10.00
    Block of four   150.00   40.00
    Margin block of six, P ‡   450.00
    Margin block of 6, P ‡ & large
      5 point star, side only   800.00
    a. "CANAL" only *(20)*   800.00
    b. "ZONE CANAL" *(180)*   300.00
    c. Horizontal pair, one without
      overprint   1750.00
    d. Booklet pane of six *(82,000)*   175.00

85 A158 3c violet *(199,200) June 27, 1925*   4.25   2.00
    On cover   3.25
    Block of four   17.50   9.00
    Margin block of six, P ‡   160.00
    a. "ZONE ZONE"   500.00   500.00

86 A160 5c dark blue *(1,343,147) Jan. 7, 1926*   4.00   2.00
    On cover   2.50
    Block of four   18.00   9.00
    Margin block of six, P ‡   175.00
    a. "ZONE ZONE" (LR18)   850.00
    b. "CANAL" inverted (LR7)   850.00
    c. Inverted overprint *(80)*   425.00
    d. Horizontal pair, one without
      overprint   3000.00
    e. Overprinted "ZONE CANAL"
      (90)   325.00
    f. "ZONE" only *(10)*   1750.00
    g. Vertical pair, one without
      overprint, other overprint
      inverted *(10)*   1750.00
    h. "CANAL" only   1750.00
    Double transfer (15571 U. L. 86)   50.00   50.00

87 A165 10c orange *(99,510) Aug., 1925*   40.00   10.00
    On cover   15.00
    Block of four   180.00   60.00
    Margin block of six, P ‡   600.00
    a. "ZONE ZONE" (LR18)   3250.00
    b. "ZONE" only   3500.00

88 A167 12c brown violet *(58,062) Feb., 1926*
                                                30.00   15.00
    On cover   30.00
    Block of four   130.00   70.00
    Margin block of six, P ‡   450.00
    a. "ZONE ZONE" (LR18)   3250.00

89 A168 14c dark blue *(55,700) Dec., 1928*   22.50   18.00
    On cover   30.00
    Block of four   100.00   80.00
    Margin block of six, P ‡   400.00

90 A169 15c gray *(204,138) Jan., 1926*   7.75   2.75
    On cover   6.00
    Block of four   32.50   13.00
    Margin block of six, P ‡   250.00
    Margin block of 6, P ‡ & large
      5 point star, side only   —
    a. "ZONE ZONE" (LR18)   3500.00
    b. "ZONE" only   3500.00

91 A187 17c black (R) *(199,500) Apr. 5, 1926*   4.25   2.00
    On cover   5.00
    Block of four   19.00   9.00
    Margin block of six, P ‡   200.00
    a. "ZONE" only *(20)*   900.00
    b. "CANAL" only   1100.00
    c. "ZONE CANAL" *(270)*   200.00

92 A170 20c carmine rose *(259,807) Apr. 5, 1926*   8.50   4.25
    On cover   8.50
    Block of four   35.00   18.50
    Margin block of six, P ‡   300.00
    a. "CANAL" inverted (UR48)   3500.00
    b. "ZONE" inverted (LL76)   3500.00
    c. "ZONE CANAL" (LL91)   3500.00

93 A172 30c olive brown *(154,700) Dec., 1926*   7.00   3.75
    On cover   7.00
    Block of four   30.00   18.50
    Margin block of six, P ‡   350.00

94 A173 50c lilac *(13,533) July, 1928*   300.00   130.00
    On cover   250.00
    Block of four   1300.00   625.00
    Margin block of six, P ‡   3250.00

95 A174 $1 violet brown *(20,000) Apr., 1926*   135.00   45.00
    On cover   110.00
    Block of four   575.00   225.00
    Margin block of four, arrow,
      top or bottom   625.00
    Margin block of six, P ‡   1750.00

Nos. 85-88, 90 and 93-95 exist with wrong-font "CANAL" and "ZONE". Positions are: Nos. 85-88 and 90, UL51 (CANAL) and UL82 (ZONE); Nos. 93-95, U51 (CANAL) and U82 (ZONE).

**Overprint Type B on
United States Sesquicentennial Stamp No. 627**

1926

96 A188 2c carmine rose *(300,000) July 6, 1926*   4.50   3.50
    On cover   4.50
    Block of four   20.00   15.00
    Margin block of six, P ‡   115.00

On this stamp there is a space of 5mm. instead of 9 mm. between the two words of the overprint.

The authorized date, July 4, fell on a Sunday with the next day also a holiday, so No. 96 was not regularly issued until July 6. But the postmaster sold some copies and canceled some covers on July 4 for a few favored collectors.

**Overprint in Black Type B on
United States Nos. 583, 584 and 591.**

1926-27   **Rotary Press Printings**   *Perf. 10*

97 A157 2c carmine *(1,290,000) Dec., 1926*   55.00   10.00
    On cover   15.00
    Block of four   225.00   45.00
    Margin block of four, P ‡   400.00
    a. Pair, one without overprint *(10)*   1750.00
    b. Booklet pane of six *(58,000)*   650.00
    c. "CANAL" only *(10)*   1300.00
    d. "ZONE" only   2250.00

98	A158	3c violet (*239,600*) *May 9, 1927*	8.50	4.00
		On cover		7.00
		Block of four	35.00	17.50
		Margin block of four, P #	135.00	
99	A165	10c orange (*128,400*) *May 9, 1927*	14.00	6.50
		On cover		12.50
		Block of four	60.00	30.00
		Margin block of four, P #	200.00	

Overprint in Black Type B on
United States Nos. 632, 634 (type I), 635, 637 and 642
Rotary Press Printings.

1927-31   Perf. 11x10½

100	A155	1c green (*434,892*) *June 28, 1927*	2.00	1.50
		On cover		2.25
		Block of four	8.50	7.00
		Margin block of four, P #	22.50	
		a. Vertical pair, one without overprint (*10*)	1750.00	
101	A157	2c carmine (*1,628,195*) *June 28, 1927*	2.25	80
		On cover		1.25
		Block of four	10.00	4.00
		Margin block of four, P #	25.00	
		a. Booklet pane of six (*82,198*)	175.00	
102	A158	3c violet (*1,250,000*) *Feb.*, *1931*	4.50	1.75
		On cover		3.00
		Block of four	24.00	8.00
		Margin block of four, P #	110.00	
		a. Booklet pane of six, handmade, perf. margins	2500.00	
103	A160	5c dark blue (*60,000*) *Dec. 13, 1927*	22.50	11.50
		On cover		17.50
		Block of four	95.00	50.00
		Margin block of four, P #	200.00	
104	A165	10c orange (*119,800*) *July, 1930*	20.00	8.00
		On cover		16.00
		Block of four	85.00	37.50
		Margin block of four, P #	200.00	

Maj. Gen. Harry Foote Hodges
A38

Lt Col. David Du Bose Gaillard
A39

Maj. Gen. William Luther Sibert
A40

Jackson Smith
A41

Maj. Gen. William Crawford Gorgas
A35

Maj. Gen. George Washington Goethals
A36

Rear Admiral Harry Harwood Rousseau
A42

Col. Sydney Bacon Williamson
A43

Gaillard Cut
A37

Joseph Clay Styles Blackburn
A44

Flat Plate Printing.

Printed by the U. S. Bureau of Engraving and Printing.
Plates of 400 subjects (except 5c), issued in panes of 100. The 5c was printed from plate of 200 subjects, issued in panes of 50. The 400-subject sheets were originally cut by knife into Post Office panes of 100, but beginning in 1948 they were separated by perforations to eliminate straight edges.

CANAL ZONE

1928–40   Perf. 11.   Unwmkd.

105	A35	1c yel grn *(22,392,147) Oct. 3, 1928*	10	8
		green	10	8
		First day cover		10.00
		Margin block of six, P ♯	75	—
106	A36	2c carmine *(7,191,600) Oct. 1, 1928*	20	10
		First day cover		10.00
		Margin block of six, P ♯	2.50	—
		a. Booklet pane of six *(284,640)*	15.00	6.00
107	A37	5c blue *(4,187,028) June 25, 1929*	1.50	60
		First day cover		6.00
		Margin block of six, P ♯	14.00	—
108	A38	10c org *(4,559,788) Jan. 11, 1932*	30	15
		First day cover		6.00
		Margin block of six, P ♯	6.00	—
109	A39	12c violet brown *(844,635) July 1, 1929*	1.00	60
		brown violet	1.00	60
		First day cover		10.00
		Margin block of six, P ♯	12.00	—
110	A40	14c blue *(406,131) Sept. 27, 1937*	1.10	85
		First day cover		6.50
		Margin block of six, P ♯	13.00	—
111	A41	15c gray *(3,356,500) Jan. 11, 1932*	50	35
		gray black	50	35
		First day cover		10.00
		Margin block of six, P ♯	8.00	—
112	A42	20c ol brn *(3,619,080) Jan. 11, 1932*	75	20
		First day cover		10.00
		Margin block of six, P ♯	8.00	—
113	A43	30c brn blk *(2,376,491) Apr. 15, 1940*	1.00	70
		First day cover		10.00
		Margin block of six, P ♯	11.00	—
114	A44	50c lilac, *July 1, 1929*	2.00	65
		rose lilac	2.00	65
		First day cover		10.00
		Margin block of six, P ♯	17.50	—

Coils are listed as Nos. 160–161.

Wet and Dry Printings

Canal Zone stamps printed by both the "wet" and "dry" process are Nos. 105, 108–109, 111–114, 117, 138–140, C21–C24, C26, J25, J27. Starting with Nos. 147 and C27, the Bureau of Engraving and Printing used the "dry" method exclusively.

See note on Wet and Dry Printings following U.S. No. 1029. Dry printings usually sell at a premium.

CANAL ZONE
United States Nos. 720 and 695 Overprinted

Type B.

Rotary Press Printing.

1933, Jan. 14   Perf. 11x10½

115	A226	3c deep violet *(3,150,000)*	3.00	25
		First day cover		7.50
		Margin block of four, P ♯	22.50	—
		b. "CANAL" only	3,000.	
		c. Booklet pane of six, handmade, perf. margins	325.00	—
116	A168	14c dark blue *(104,800)*	6.50	2.75
		First day cover		25.00
		Margin block of four, P ♯	50.00	—
		a. "ZONE CANAL"		
		(16)	1100.00	

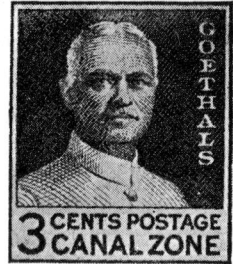

Maj. Gen. George Washington Goethals
A45

Issued in commemoration of the twentieth anniversary of the opening of the Panama Canal.

Flat Plate Printing.

1934, Aug. 15   Perf. 11   Unwmkd.

117	A45	3c deep violet	10	6
		red violet	10	6
		First day cover		1.00
		Margin block of six, P ♯	2.00	—
		a. Booklet pane of six	45.00	20.00
		b. As "a," handmade, perf. margins	225.00	—
		Coil is listed as No. 153.		

United States Nos. 803 and 805 Overprinted in Black   **CANAL ZONE**

Rotary Press Printing.

1939, Sept. 1   Perf. 11x10½   Unwmkd.

118	A275	½c red orange, *(1,030,000)*	15	10
		First day cover		75
		Margin block of four, P ♯	3.00	—
119	A277	1½c bistre brown *(935,000)*	20	20
		brown	20	20
		First day cover		75
		Margin block of four, P ♯	3.50	—

Balboa—Before
A46

Balboa—After
A47

CANAL ZONE

Gaillard Cut—Before
A48

Gaillard Cut—After
A49

Bas Obispo—Before
A50

Bas Obispo—After
A51

Gatun Locks—Before
A52

Gatun Locks—After
A53

Canal Channel—Before
A54

Canal Channel—After
A55

CANAL ZONE

Gamboa—Before
A56

Gamboa—After
A57

Pedro Miguel Locks—Before
A58

Pedro Miguel Locks—After
A59

Gatun Spillway—Before
A60

Gatun Spillway—After
A61

Issued in commemoration of the 25th anniversary of the opening of the Panama Canal.

Withdrawn Feb. 28, 1941; remainders burned Apr. 12, 1941.

Flat Plate Printing

1939, Aug. 15   Perf. 11   Unwmkd.

120	A46	1c yellow green (*1,019,482*)	40	30
		First day cover		1.00
		Margin block of six, P #	10.00	
121	A47	2c rose carmine (*227,065*)	50	35
		First day cover		1.00
		Margin block of six, P #	11.00	
122	A48	3c purple (*2,523,735*)	40	15
		First day cover		1.00
		Margin block of six, P #	10.00	
123	A49	5c dark blue (*460,213*)	1.00	90
		First day cover		2.50
		Margin block of six, P #	17.50	
124	A40	6c red orange (*68,290*)	2.25	1.35
		First day cover		5.00
		Margin block of six, P #	35.00	
125	A51	7c black (*71,235*)	2.25	1.35
		First day cover		5.00
		Margin block of six, P #	35.00	
126	A52	8c green (*41,576*)	3.25	2.00
		First day cover		5.00
		Margin block of six, P #	45.00	
127	A53	10c ultramarine (*83,571*)	3.25	1.75
		First day cover		5.00
		Margin block of six, P #	45.00	
128	A54	11c blue green (*34,010*)	7.50	5.00
		First day cover		10.00
		Margin block of six, P #	110.00	
129	A55	12c brown carmine (*66,735*)	6.00	4.50
		First day cover		10.00
		Margin block of six, P #	85.00	
130	A56	14c dark violet (*37,365*)	6.75	4.00
		First day cover		10.00
		Margin block of six, P #	100.00	

CANAL ZONE 811

131	A57	15c olive green (105,058)	11.00	3.75
		First day cover		10.00
		Margin block of six, P #	110.00	
132	A58	18c rose pink (39,255)	9.00	6.00
		First day cover		10.00
		Margin block of six, P #	100.00	
133	A59	20c brown (100,244)	13.00	3.00
		First day cover		10.00
		Margin block of six, P #	125.00	
134	A60	25c orange (34,283)	20.00	9.00
		First day cover		20.00
		Margin block of six, P #	225.00	
135	A61	50c violet brown (91,576)	22.50	3.50
		First day cover		25.00
		Margin block of six, P #	250.00	

Maj. Gen. George W. Davis
A62

Gov. Charles E. Magoon
A63

Theodore Roosevelt
A64

John F. Stevens
A65

John F. Wallace
A66

1946–49		Perf. 11		Unwmkd.
		Size: 19x22mm.		
136	A62	½c bright red (1,020,000) Aug. 16, 1948	35	15
		First day cover		1.25
		Margin block of six, P #	3.00	
137	A63	1½c chocolate (603,600) Aug. 16, 1948	35	15
		First day cover		1.25
		Margin block of six, P #	3.00	
138	A64	2c rose car (6,951,755) Oct. 27, 1949	10	5
		First day cover		50
		Margin block of six, P #	60	
139	A65	5c deep blue, April 25, 1946	40	10
		First day cover		1.00
		Margin block of six, P #	4.00	
140	A66	25c yellow green (1,520,000) Aug. 16, 1948	2.00	1.00
		First day cover		3.50
		Margin block of six, P #	18.00	

See Nos. 155, 162, 164.

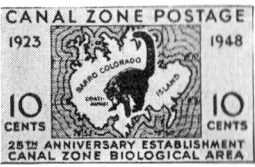

Map of Biological Area and Coati-mundi
A67

Issued to commemorate the 25th anniversary of the establishment of the **Canal Zone Biological Area** on Barro Colorado Island.

Withdrawn Mar. 30, 1951, and remainders destroyed April 10, 1951.

1948, Apr. 17		Perf. 11		Unwmkd.
141	A67	10c black (521,200)	1.75	1.35
		First day cover		2.00
		Margin block of six, P #	12.50	

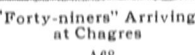

"Forty-niners" Arriving at Chagres
A68

Journeying in "Bungo" to Las Cruces
A69

Las Cruces Trail to Panama
A70

Departure for San Francisco
A71

Issued to commemorate the centenary of the California Gold Rush.

Stocks on hand were processed for destruction on Aug. 11, 1952 and destroyed Aug. 13, 1952.

1949, June 1		Perf. 11		Unwmkd.
142	A68	3c blue (500,000)	85	15
		First day cover		1.00
		Margin block of six, P #	7.50	
143	A69	6c violet (481,000)	90	45
		First day cover		1.00
		Margin block of six, P #	10.00	
144	A70	12c bright blue green (230,000)	2.50	1.40
		First day cover		1.75
		Margin block of six, P #	21.00	

812 CANAL ZONE

145	A71	18c deep red lilac (240,200)	3.25	2.00
		First day cover		3.00
		Margin block of six, P ♯	27.50	--

Workers in Culebra Cut
A72

Issued to commemorate the contribution of West Indian laborers in the construction of the Panama Canal. Entire issue sold, none withdrawn and destroyed.

1951, Aug. 15   **Perf. 11**   **Unwmkd.**

146	A72	10c carmine (480,000)	4.00	1.65
		First day cover		2.50
		Margin block of six, P ♯	32.50	

Early Railroad Scene
A73

Issued to commemorate the centenary of the completion of the Panama Railroad and the first transcontinental railroad trip in the Americas.

1955, Jan. 28   **Perf. 11**   **Unwmkd.**

147	A73	3c violet (994,000)	1.10	50
		First day cover		65
		Margin block of six, P ♯	9.00	

Gorgas Hospital and Ancon Hill
A74

Issued to commemorate the 75th anniversary of Gorgas Hospital.

1957, Nov. 17   **Perf. 11**   **Unwmkd.**

148	A74	3c dull blue green (1,010,000)	60	35
		Light blue green paper	60	35
		First day cover		50
		Margin block of four, P ♯	5.00	--

S. S. Ancon—A75
Engraved

1958, Aug. 30   **Perf. 11**   **Unwmkd.**

149	A75	4c greenish blue (1,749,700)	45	25
		First day cover		50
		Margin block of four, P ♯	3.50	--

Roosevelt Medal and Canal Zone Map
A76

Issued to commemorate the centenary of the birth of Theodore Roosevelt (1858–1919).

1958, Nov. 15   **Perf. 11**   **Unwmkd.**

150	A76	4c brown (1,060,000)	60	30
		First day cover		60
		Margin block of four, P♯	4.00	--

Boy Scout Badge
A77

Issued to commemorate the 50th anniversary of the Boy Scouts of America.

Giori Press Printing

1960, Feb. 8   **Perf. 11**   **Unwmkd.**

151	A77	4c dark blue, red & bistre (654,933)	75	40
		First day cover		70
		Margin block of four, P♯	5.00	--

CANAL ZONE
Unwatermarked
1906-07

Scott 22

Scott 23

Scott 24

Scott 25

1909

Scott 27

Scott 28

Scott 29

Scott 30

COLLECT THE SCOTT WAY .... WITH SCOTT'S

U.S. POSSESSIONS ALBUM

FEATURING:

- Spaces for all major variety stamps of Canal Zone, Cuba (U.S. Administration issues), Danish West Indies, Guam, Hawaii, and Philippines (U.S. Administration issues).
- Each stamp pictured or described and arranged in order by Scott number.
- A handsome, sturdy binder is standard with this album - not tacked on at an extra cost.
- Chemically neutralized paper protects your stamps for generations.
- Paper just the right thickness to make collecting a pleasure.

- No need to purchase yearly supplements. U.S. Trust Territories issues covered separately in the Scott U.S. Trust Territories Album.

$34⁹⁵ Album through 1978

AVAILABLE NOW AT
YOUR LOCAL DEALER
OR DIRECT FROM:

SCOTT

P.O. BOX 828, SIDNEY, OH 45365

814 CANAL ZONE

Administration Building, Balboa Heights
A78
Engraved

1960, Nov. 1   **Perf. 11**   Unwmkd.
152 A78 4c rose lilac *(2,486,725)*   20   12
          First day cover   65
          Margin block of four, P#   1.00 —

Coil Stamps
Types of 1934, 1960 and 1946.
1960-62 **Perf. 10 Vertically** Unwmkd.
153 A45 3c dp vio *(3,743,959)* Nov. 1, 1960   15   12
          First day cover   75
          Pair   30   20
          Joint line pair   75   30

Perf. 10 Horizontally
154 A78 4c dull ros lil *(2,776,273)* Nov. 1, 1960 20 12
          First day cover   75
          Pair   40   25
          Joint line pair   1.00   50

Perf. 10 Vertically
155 A65 5c dp bl *(3,288,264)* Feb. 10, 1962   30   20
          First day cover   75
          Pair   60   50
          Joint line pair   1.10   75

Girl Scout Badge and Camp at Gatun Lake
A79
Issued to commemorate the 50th anniversary of the Girl Scouts.

Giori Press Printing
1962, Mar. 12   **Perf. 11**   Unwmkd.
156 A79 4c blue, dark green & bistre *(640,000)*   40   30
          First day cover *(83,717)*   90
          Margin block of four, P#   4.00 —

Thatcher Ferry Bridge and Map of Western Hemisphere
A80
Issued to commemorate the opening of the Thatcher Ferry Bridge, spanning the Panama Canal.

Giori Press Printing
1962, Oct. 12   **Perf. 11**   Unwmkd.
157 A80 4c black & silver *(775,000)*   35   25
          First day cover *(65,853)*   90
          Margin block of 4, two P#   4.00 —
          a. Silver (bridge) omitted *(50)* 10,000.00
          a. Margin block of 4, black P# only —

Goethals Memorial,   Fort San Lorenzo
Balboa
A81   A82
1968-71   Giori Press Printing   **Perf. 11**
158 A81 6c green & ultra. *(1,890,000)* Mar. 15, 1968   40   30
          First day cover   50
          Margin block of 4, P#   2.50 —
159 A82 8c slate green, blue, dark brown & ocher
          (3,460,000) July 14, 1971   45   25
          First day cover   50
          Margin block of 4, P#   3.00 —

Coil Stamps
Types of 1928, 1932 and 1948
Engraved
1975, Feb. 14   **Perf. 10 Vertically**   Unwmkd.
160 A35 1c green *(1,090,958)*   20   10
          First day cover   35
          Pair   40   20
          Joint line pair   1.00   35
161 A38 10c orange *(590,658)*   85   25
          First day cover   50
          Pair   1.70 50
          Joint line pair   4.00 1.00
162 A66 25c yellow green *(129,831)*   4.00 1.00
          First day cover   1.50
          Pair   8.00 2.00
          Joint line pair   20.00 6.00

Dredge Cascadas
A83
1976   Giori Press Printing   **Perf. 11**
163 A83 13c multi *(3,653,950)* Feb. 23   40   20
          First day cover   75
          Margin block of 4, P#   2.00 —
          a. Bklt pane of 4 *(1,032,400)* Apr. 19   3.00 —

Stevens Type of 1946
Rotary Press Printing
1977   Size: 19x22½mm.   **Perf. 11x10½**
164 A65 5c deep blue *(1,009,612)*   60   25
          Margin block of 4, P#   3.00 —
          No. 164 exists tagged.

Towing Locomotive,
Ship in Lock, by
Alwyn Sprague
A84
1978, Oct. 25   Engraved   **Perf. 11**
165 A84 15c dp grn & bl grn *(2,921,083)*   40   20
          First day cover *(81,405)*   75
          Margin block of 4, P#   2.00 —

CANAL ZONE

AIR POST STAMPS.
AIR MAIL

Regular Issue
of 1928
Surcharged
in Dark Blue

25 CENTS 25

Flat Plate Printing.

1929–31   Perf. 11   Unwmkd.

15 (I)   **15** (II)

Type I.—Flag of "5" pointing up.
Type II.—Flag of "5" curved.

C1	A35	15c on 1c green, type I, *Apr. 1, 1929*	10.00	6.50
		First day cover		25.00
		Block of four	42.50	30.00
		Margin block of six, P ♯	175.00	85.00
C2	"	15c on 1c yellow green, type II, *Mar. 1931*	135.00	85.00
		On cover		100.00
		Block of four	575.00	375.00
		Margin block of six, P ♯	1350.00	750.00
C3	A36	25c on 2c carmine (*223,880*) *Jan. 11, 1929*	3.50	1.75
		First day cover		17.50
		Block of four	15.00	7.50
		Margin block of six, P ♯	90.00	25.00

AIR MAIL

Nos. 114 and 106
Surcharged
in Black

≡10c

1929, Dec. 31

C4	A44	10c on 50c lilac (*116,666*)	10.00	9.00
		First day cover		25.00
		Block of four	42.50	40.00
		Margin block of six, P ♯	150.00	65.00
C5	A36	20c on 2c carmine (*638,395*)	7.00	2.00
		First day cover		20.00
		Block of four	29.00	8.00
		Margin block of six, P ♯	120.00	55.00
	a.	Dropped "2" in surch. (*7,000*)	85.00	60.00

Gaillard Cut
AP1

Printed by the U. S. Bureau of Engraving and Printing
Plates of 200 subjects, issued in panes of 50.

1931–49   Perf. 11   Unwmkd.

C6	AP1	4c red violet (*585,000*) *Jan. 3, 1949*	75	60
		First day cover		2.00
		Margin block of six, P ♯	5.00	4.50
C7	"	5c yellow green (*9,988,800*) *Nov. 18, 1931*	50	10
		green	50	10
		First day cover		10.00
		Margin block of six, P ♯	4.00	2.00
C8	"	6c yellow brown (*9,440,000*) *Feb. 15, 1946*	70	10
		First day cover		2.00
		Margin block of six, P ♯	6.00	2.00
C9	"	10c orange (*5,140,000*) *Nov. 18, 1931*	85	10
		First day cover		10.00
		Margin block of six, P ♯	10.00	3.00
C10	AP1	15c blue (*11,961,500*) *Nov. 18, 1931*	1.00	25
		pale blue	1.00	25
		First day cover		10.00
		Margin block of six, P ♯	10.00	3.00
C11	"	20c red violet (*3,214,600*) *Nov. 18, 1931*	2.00	25
		deep violet	2.00	25
		First day cover		20.00
		Margin block of six, P ♯	15.00	3.00
C12	"	30c rose lake (*1,150,000*) *July 15, 1941*	3.00	1.00
		dull rose	3.00	1.00
		First day cover		22.50
		Margin block of six, P ♯	27.50	9.00
C13	"	40c yellow (*826,100*) *Nov. 18, 1931*	3.00	1.00
		lemon	3.00	1.00
		First day cover		30.00
		Margin block of six, P ♯	30.00	10.00
C14	"	$1 black (*406,000*) *Nov. 18, 1931*	10.00	2.25
		First day cover		50.00
		Margin block of six, P ♯	80.00	20.00

Douglas Plane over Sosa Hill—AP2

Planes and Map of Central America
AP3

Pan American Clipper and Scene near Fort Amador
AP4

Pan American Clipper at Cristobal Harbor
AP5

CANAL ZONE

Pan American Clipper over Gaillard Cut
AP6

Pan American Clipper Landing
AP7

Issued in commemoration of the 10th anniversary of Air Mail service and the 25th anniversary of the opening of the Panama Canal.

Withdrawn February 28, 1941 and remainders burned April 12, 1941.

Flat Plate Printing.

1939, July 15 Perf. 11. Unwmkd.

C15	AP2	5c greenish black *(86,576)*	3.75	3.25
		black	10.00	10.00
		First day cover		5.00
		Margin block of six, P ‡	30.00	20.00
C16	AP3	10c dull violet *(117,644)*	3.75	3.00
		First day cover		5.00
		Margin block of six, P ‡	40.00	17.50
C17	AP4	15c light brown *(883,742)*	4.00	1.25
		First day cover		3.00
		Margin block of six, P ‡	45.00	15.00
C18	AP5	25c blue *(82,126)*	17.50	11.00
		First day cover		17.50
		Margin block of six, P ‡	150.00	90.00
C19	AP6	30c rose carmine *(121,382)*	12.50	8.00
		First day cover		15.00
		Margin block of six, P ‡	110.00	60.00
C20	AP7	$1 green *(40,051)*	42.50	35.00
		First day cover		50.00
		Margin block of six, P ‡	325.00	240.00

Globe and Wing
AP8

Flat Plate Printing.

1951, July 16 Perf. 11. Unwmkd.

C21	AP8	4c red violet *(1,315,000)*	80	30
		Margin block of six, P ‡	7.50	—
C22	"	6c brown *(22,657,625)*	65	25
		Margin block of six, P ‡	7.00	—
C23	"	10c red orange *(1,049,130)*	1.10	40
		Margin block of six, P ‡	11.00	—
C24	"	21c blue *(1,460,000)*	9.50	3.50
		Margin block of six, P ‡	75.00	—
C25	AP8	31c cerise *(375,000)*	9.00	3.25
		Margin block of six, P ‡	90.00	—
		a. Horiz. pair, imperf. vert. *(98)*	600.00	—
C26	"	80c gray black *(827,696)*	6.50	1.25
		Margin block of six, P ‡	50.00	—

Nos. C21-C24 and C26 are found in both "wet" and "dry" printings. (See note after No. 114.)

Type of 1951.
Flat Plate Printing.

1958, Aug. 16 Perf. 11 Unwmkd.

C27	AP8	5c yellow green *(899,923)*	1.50	50
		First day cover *(2,176)*		1.50
		Margin block of four, P‡	8.00	
C28	"	7c olive *(9,381,797)*	1.40	40
		First day cover *(2,815)*		1.25
		Margin block of four, P‡	7.00	
C29	"	15c brown violet *(359,923)*	6.00	1.50
		First day cover *(2,040)*		2.50
		Margin block of four, P‡	40.00	
C30	"	25c orange yellow *(600,000)*	13.00	2.00
		First day cover *(2,115)*		4.50
		Margin block of four, P‡	85.00	
C31	"	35c dark blue *(283,032)*	11.50	2.00
		First day cover *(1,868)*		6.00
		Margin block of four, P‡	60.00	

Emblem of U.S. Army Caribbean School
AP9

Issued to honor the U.S. Army Caribbean School for Latin America at Fort Gulick.

Giori Press Printing.

1961, Nov. 21 Perf. 11 Unwmkd.

C32	AP9	15c red & blue *(560,000)*	2.00	1.25
		First day cover *(25,949)*		1.75
		Margin block of four, P ⚹	15.00	—

Malaria Eradication Emblem and Mosquito
AP10

Issued for the World Health Organization drive to eradicate malaria.

Giori Press Printing

1962, Sept. 24 Perf. 11 Unwmkd.

C33	AP10	7c yellow & black *(862,349)*	75	50
		First day cover *(44,433)*		95
		Margin block of four, P ⚹	4.50	—

Globe-Wing Type of 1951

1963, Jan. 7 Rotary Press Printing Perf. 10½x11

C34	AP8	8c carmine *(5,054,727)*	75	30
		First day cover *(19,128)*		90
		Margin block of four, P ⚹	6.00	—

CANAL ZONE 817

Alliance for Progress Emblem—AP11

Issued to commemorate the second anniversary of the Alliance for Progress, which aims to stimulate economic growth and raise living standards in Latin America.

Giori Press Printing

1963, Aug. 17   **Perf. 11**   Unwmkd.
C35   AP11   15c gray, grn. & dk. ultra. *(405,000)*   1.50   1.00
           First day cover *(29,594)*   1.50
           Margin block of four, P#   15.00

Jet over Cristobal
AP12

Issued to commemorate the 50th anniversary of the Panama Canal.

Designs: 8c, Gatun Locks. 15c, Madden Dam. 20c, Gaillard Cut. 30c, Miraflores Locks. 80c, Balboa.

Giori Press Printing

1964, Aug. 15   **Perf. 11**   Unwmkd.
C36   AP12   6c green & black *(257,193)*   55   35
           Margin block of four, P#   3.50
C37   "   8c rose red & black *(3,024,283)*   65   35
           Margin block of four, P#   4.00
C38   "   15c blue & black *(472,666)*   1.50   50
           Margin block of four, P#   8.50
C39   "   20c rose lilac & black *(599,784)*   2.50   85
           Margin block of four, P#   11.00
C40   "   30c reddish brown & black *(204,524)*   3.75   2.00
           Margin block of four, P#   17.00
C41   "   80c olive bister & black *(186,809)*   6.50   3.00
           Margin block of four, P#   27.50

Canal Zone Seal and Jet Plane
AP13

Giori Press Printing

1965, July 15   **Perf. 11**   Unwmkd.
C42   AP13   6c green & black *(548,850)*   45   20
           Margin block of four, P#   3.00
C43   "   8c rose red & black *(8,557,700)*   35   10
           Margin block of four, P#   3.25
C44   "   15c blue & black *(2,385,000)*   45   20
           Margin block of four, P#   3.00

C45   AP13   20c lilac & black *(2,290,699)*   75   30
           Margin block of four, P#   3.75
C46   "   30c redsh brn & blk *(2,332,255)*   1.00   35
           Margin block of four, P#   5.00
C47   "   80c bister & black *(1,456,596)*   3.25   90
           Margin block of four, P#   15.00

1968-76
C48   AP13   10c dull orange & black *(10,055,000)*
           Mar. 15, 1968   35   15
           Margin block of 4, P#   1.75
           a. Bklt. pane of 4 *(713,390)* Feb. 18, 1970   4.25
C49   "   11c ol & blk *(3,335,000)* Sept. 24, 1971   40   18
           Margin block of 4. P#   1.75
           a. Bklt. pane of 4 *(1,277,760)* Sept. 24, 1971   3.50
C50   "   13c emerald & black *(1,865,000)*
           Feb. 11, 1974   1.10   30
           First day cover   55
           Margin block of 4, P#   5.00
           a. Booklet pane of 4 *(619,200)*
           Feb. 11, 1974   5.00
C51   "   22c vio & blk *(363,720)* May 10, 1976   1.25   35
           Margin block of four, P#   8.00
C52   "   "25c pale yel. grn. & blk. *(1,640,441)* Mar. 15, 1968   1.10   35
           Margin block of four, P#   7.00
C53   "   35c sal & blk *(573,822)* May 10, 1976   2.00   50
           Margin block of four, P#   9.00

AIR POST OFFICIAL STAMPS.
(See note above No. O1)

Air Post Stamps of 1931-41   **OFFICIAL**
Overprinted in Black   **PANAMA CANAL**
Two types of overprint.

Type I.   "PANAMA CANAL" 19-20mm. long.

1941-42   **Perf. 11**   Unwmkd.
CO1   AP1   5c yel. green *(42,754)* Mar. 31, 1941   4.25   1.50
           green   4.25   1.50
           On cover   40.00
           Block of four   18.50   6.00
CO2   "   10c orange *(49,723)*   "   9.00   2.00
           On cover   30.00
           Block of four   40.00   9.00
CO3   "   15c blue *(56,898)*   "   11.00   2.75
           On cover   25.00
           Block of four   47.50   25.00
CO4   "   20c red violet *(22,107)*   "   14.00   4.50
           deep violet   14.00   4.50
           On cover   100.00
           Block of four   60.00   22.50
CO5   "   30c rose lake *(22,100)* June, 4, 1942   17.50   4.50
           dull rose   17.50   4.50
           On cover   40.00
           Block of four   75.00   20.00
CO6   "   40c yellow *(22,875)* Mar. 31, 1941   20.00   7.00
           lemon yellow   20.00   7.00
           On cover   50.00
           Block of four   85.00   35.00
CO7   " $1 black *(29,525)*   "   27.50   10.00
           On cover   125.00
           Block of four   115.00   45.00

Overprint varieties occur on Nos. CO1-CO7 and CO14: "O" of "OFFICIAL" over "N" of "PANAMA" (entire third row). "O" of "OFFICIAL" broken at top (position 31). "O" of "OFFICIAL" over second "A" of "PANAMA" (position 45). First "F" of "OFFICIAL" over second "A" of "PANAMA" (position 50).

1941, Sept. 22
Type II.   "PANAMA CANAL" 17mm. long.
CO8   AP1   5c yellow green *(?,000)*   200.00
           On cover   400.00
           Block of four   850.00
CO9   "   10c orange *(?,000)*   250.00
           On cover   350.00
           Block of four   1100.00
CO10   "   20c red violet *(?,000)*   200.00
           On cover
           Block of four   850.00
CO11   "   30c rose lake *(5,000)*   60.00
           On cover   125.00
           Block of four   250.00
CO12   "   40c yellow *(?,000)*   200.00
           On cover   400.00
           Block of four   850.00

1947, Nov.
Type I.   "PANAMA CANAL" 19-20mm. long.
CO14   AP1   6c yellow brown *(33,450)*   11.00   3.50
           On cover   50.00
           Block of four   50.00   15.00
           a. Inverted overprint *(50)*   1100.00

POSTAGE DUE STAMPS.

Prior to 1914, many of the postal issues were handstamped "Postage Due" and used as postage due stamps.

Postage Due Stamps
of the United States
Nos. J45a, J46a, and J49a
Overprinted in Black

CANAL ZONE

Wmkd. USPS (190)

1914, Mar.   **Perf. 12**

J1	D2	1c rose carmine (*23,533*)		65.00	17.00
		On cover			100.00
		Block of four (2 mm. spacing)		275.00	80.00
		Block of four (3 mm. spacing)		285.00	90.00
		Margin block of six, imprint, star and P ‡		500.00	125.00
J2	"	2c rose carmine (*32,312*)		200.00	50.00
		On cover			120.00
		Block of four		850.00	225.00
		Margin block of six, P ‡		1500.00	400.00
J3	"	10c rose carmine (*92,493*)		600.00	50.00
		On cover			250.00
		Block of four (2 mm. spacing)		2650.00	225.00
		Block of four (3 mm. spacing)		2650.00	225.00
		Margin block of six, imprint, star and P ‡		*5000.00*	—

Many examples of Nos. J1–J3 show one or more letters of the overprint out of alignment, principally the "E".

Statue of Columbus   San Geronimo Castle Gate, Portobelo   Pedro J. Sosa
D2   (See footnote)
                        D1   D3

1915, March   **Perf. 12**   **Unwmkd.**

Blue Overprint, Type II, on Postage Due Stamps of Panama.

J4	D1	1c olive brown (*50,000*)		10.00	4.25
		On cover			50.00
		Block of four		42.50	20.00
J5	D2	2c olive brown (*50,000*)		125.00	22.50
		On cover			75.00
		Block of four		525.00	100.00
J6	D3	10c olive brown (*200,000*)		35.00	11.00
		On cover			70.00
		Block of four		150.00	50.00

Type D1 was intended to show a gate of San Lorenzo Castle, Chagres, and is so labeled. By error the stamp actually shows the main gate of San Geronimo Castle, Portobelo.

Experts believe that examples of the 1c with overprint type V, reading up or down, are bogus.

Surcharged in Red   CANAL 2 ZONE

1915, Nov.   **Perf. 12**   **Unwmkd.**

J7	D1	1c on 1c olive brown (*60,614*)		100.00	20.00
		On cover			75.00
		Block of four		425.00	90.00
J8	D2	2c on 2c olive brown		25.00	7.50
		On cover			60.00
		Block of four		105.00	35.00
J9	D3	10c on 10c olive brown (*175,548*)		22.50	4.50
		On cover			45.00
		Block of four		100.00	22.50

One of the printings of No. J9 shows wider spacing between "1" and "0". Both spacings occur on the same sheet.

                 Capitol, Panama
D4   D5

1919, Dec. Surcharged in Carmine at Mount Hope.

J10	D4	2c on 2c olive brown		27.50	11.00
		On cover			60.00
		Block of four		120.00	50.00
J11	D5	4c on 4c olive brown (*35,695*)		35.00	15.00
		On cover			75.00
		Block of four		150.00	65.00
		a. "ZONE" omitted		3000.00	
		b. "4" omitted		2500.00	

United States
Postage Due Stamps
Nos. J61, J62b and J65b
Overprinted

CANAL ZONE POSTAGE DUE

Type A.
Letters "A" with Flat Tops.

1924, July 1   **Perf. 11**

J12	D2	1c carmine rose (*10,000*)		130.00	30.00
		On cover			60.00
		Block of four		550.00	130.00
		Margin block of six, P ‡		1200.00	225.00
J13	"	2c deep claret (*25,000*)		70.00	12.50
		On cover			60.00
		Block of four		300.00	55.00
		Margin block of six, P ‡		600.00	175.00
J14	"	10c deep claret (*30,000*)		300.00	50.00
		On cover			150.00
		Block of four (2 mm. spacing)		1300.00	225.00
		Block of four (3 mm. spacing)		1300.00	225.00
		Margin block of six, imprint, star and P ‡		2500.00	450.00

United States Nos. 552, 554 and 562
Overprinted Type A
and Additionally
Overprinted at Mount Hope
in Red or Blue

POSTAGE DUE

1925, Feb.   **Perf. 11**

J15	A155	1c deep green (R) (*15,000*)		90.00	17.50
		On cover			40.00
		Block of four		375.00	75.00
		Margin block of 6, P ‡		600.00	300.00
J16	A157	2c carmine (Bl) (*21,335*)		25.00	7.00
		On cover			25.00
		Block of four		110.00	30.00
		Margin block of 6, P ‡		200.00	120.00
J17	A165	10c orange (R) (*39,819*)		50.00	11.00
		On cover			40.00
		Block of four		225.00	47.50
		Margin block of 6, P ‡		400.00	100.00
		a. "POSTAGE DUE" double		400.00	
		b. "E" of "POSTAGE" omitted		350.00	
		c. As "b," double		*2500.00*	

Overprinted
Type B.

1925, June 24

Letters "A" with Sharp Pointed Tops.

On United States Postage Due Stamps Nos. J61, J62, J65 and J65a.

J18	D2	1c carmine rose (*80,000*)		9.00	3.00
		On cover			20.00
		Block of four		40.00	15.00
		Margin block of 6, P ‡		85.00	30.00
		a. "ZONE ZONE" (LR18)		1400.00	
J19	"	2c carmine rose (*146,430*)		20.00	5.00
		On cover			20.00
		Block of four		85.00	21.00
		Margin block of 6, P ✻		185.00	85.00
		a. "ZONE ZONE" (LR18)		1400.00	

J20	D2	10c carmine rose *(153,980)*		130.00	20.00
		On cover			75.00
		Block of four, 2 mm. spacing		525.00	85.00
		Block of four, 3 mm. spacing		550.00	90.00
		Margin block of 6, imprint, star and P #		1000.00	250.00
	a.	Vert. pair, one without ovpt. *(10)*		1750.00	
		Margin block of 6, imprint, Star and P #			
	b.	10c rose red		165.00	70.00
		On cover			110.00
	c.	Double overprint		325.00	

Nos. J18–J20 exist with wrong font "CANAL" (UL51) and "ZONE" (UL82).

Regular Issue of 1928-29 Surcharged

POSTAGE DUE

10

1929-30

J21	A37	1c on 5c blue *(35,990) Mar. 20, 1930*		2.50	1.75
		On cover			15.00
		Margin block of 6, P#		25.00	12.00
	a.	"POSTAGE DUE" omitted (5)		2250.00	
J22	"	2c on 5c blue *(40,207) Oct. 18, 1930*		4.50	2.50
		On cover			15.00
		Margin block of 6, P#		40.00	20.00
J23	"	5c on 5c blue *(35,464) Dec. 1, 1930*		4.50	2.75
		On cover			15.00
		Margin block of 6, P#		45.00	22.50
J24	"	10c on 5c blue *(90,504) Dec. 16, 1929*		4.00	2.75
		On cover			15.00
		Margin block of 6, P#		45.00	22.50

On No. J23 the three short horizontal bars in the lower corners of the surcharge are omitted.

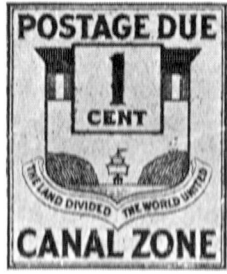

Canal Zone Seal
D6

Printed by the U. S. Bureau of Engraving and Printing. Plates of 400 subjects, issued in panes of 100.

1932-41 Flat Plate Printing

J25	D6	1c claret *(378,300) Jan. 2, 1932*		10	10
		red violet		20	10
		Margin block of 6, P#		3.00	75
J26	"	2c claret *(413,800) Jan. 2, 1932*		15	10
		Margin block of 6, P#		4.00	1.00
J27	"	5c claret *Jan. 2, 1932*		35	20
		red violet		60	20
		Margin block of 6, P#		6.00	2.00
J28	"	10c claret *(400,600) Jan. 2, 1932*		1.40	1.25
		Margin block of 6, P#		15.00	10.00
J29	"	15c claret *Apr. 21, 1941*		1.10	90
		Margin block of 6, P#		12.00	7.50

The 1c and 5c are found in both "wet" and "dry" printings. (See note after No. 114). The dry printings are in red violet.

OFFICIAL STAMPS.

Beginning in March, 1915, stamps for use on official mail were identified by a large "P" perforated through each stamp. These were replaced by overprinted issues in 1941. The use of official stamps was discontinued December 31, 1951. During their currency, they were not for sale in mint condition and were sold to the public only when cancelled with a parcel post rotary canceller reading "Balboa Heights, Canal Zone" between two wavy lines. After having been withdrawn from use, mint stamps (except Nos. O3, O8 and CO8-CO12) were made available to the public at face value for three months beginning Jan. 2, 1952. Prices for used stamps are for cancelled-to-order specimens, postally used copies being worth more. Sheet margins were removed to facilitate overprinting and plate numbers are, therefore, unknown.

Regular Issues of 1928-34 Overprinted in Black
by the Panama Canal Press, Mount Hope, C. Z.

OFFICIAL   OFFICIAL
PANAMA   PANAMA CANAL
CANAL
Type 1   Type 2

Type 1 —"PANAMA" 10 mm. long.
" 1A—"PANAMA" 9 mm. long.
" 2 —"PANAMA CANAL" 19½ mm. long.

1941, Mar. 31 *Perf. 11.* Unwmkd.

O1	A35	1c yellow green, type 1 *(87,198)*	2.00	35
		On cover		35.00
O2	A45	3c deep violet, type 1 *(34,958)*	3.75	70
		On cover		25.00
O3	A37	5c blue, type 2, *(19,105)*	—	35.00
		On cover		100.00
O4	A38	10c orange, type 1 *(18,776)*	5.75	1.75
		On cover		50.00
O5	A41	15c gray black, type 1 *(16,888)*	11.00	2.00
		gray		2.00
		On cover		50.00
O6	A42	20c olive brown, type 1 *(20,264)*	12.00	2.50
		On cover		60.00
O7	A44	50c lilac, type 1 *(19,175)*	45.00	7.50
		rose lilac		7.50
		On cover		125.00
O8	"	50c rose lilac, type 1A *(1000)*		650.00

No. O3 exists with "O" directly over "N" of "PANAMA."

1947, Feb. No. 139 Overprinted in Black

O9	A65	5c deep blue, type 1 *(21,639)*	7.50	3.00
		On cover		60.00

POST OFFICE SEALS

POS1

Issued in sheets of 8 without gum, imperforate margins.

Typographed.

1907   *Perf. 11½*   Unwmkd.

OX1	POS1	blue		40.00
		Block of four		175.00
	a.	Wmkd. seal of U. S. in sheet		55.00

No. OX1 clichés are spaced 3½ mm. apart.

1910

OX2	POS1	ultramarine		70.00
	a.	Wmkd. "Rolleston Mills" in sheet		90.00
	b.	Wmkd. U.S. Seal in sheet		225.00
		Block of four, clichés ½mm apart		325.00
		Block of four, clichés 1½mm apart horiz., 4mm vert.		800.00

CANAL ZONE

POS2

Printed by the Panama Canal Press, Mount Hope, C. Z. Issued in sheets of 25, without gum, imperforate margins.

1917, Sept. 22   *Rouletted 6 horizontally in color of seal, vertically without color.*

OX3	POS2	dark blue	4.00	—
		Block of four	17.50	
		a. Wmkd. double lined letters in sheet ("Sylvania")	30.00	

1946   *Rouletted 6, without color.*

Issued in sheets of 20, without gum, imperforate margins.

OX4	POS2	slate blue	7.00	
		Block of four	30.00	

POS3

Typographed by the Panama Canal Press
Issued in sheets of 32, without gum, imperforate margins except at top. Size: 46x27mm.

Seal Diameter: 13mm.

1954, Mar. 8   **Perf. 12½**   Unwmkd.

OX5	POS3	black *(16,000)*	5.00	—
		a. Wmkd. Seal of U. S. in sheet	20.00	—

Seal Diameter: 11½mm.

1961–74   Rouletted 5

OX6	POS3	black, *July 1, 1974*	2.50	—
		a. Perf. 12½, *May 16, 1961 (48,000)*	2.50	—
		b. Wmkd. Seal of U.S. in sheet, perf. 12½	6.00	
		c. Double impression, perf. 12½	65.00	

ENVELOPES.

Prices for cut squares are for copies with fine margins on all sides. Prices for unused entires are for those without printed or manuscript address. A "full corner" includes back and side flaps and commands a premium.

Vasco Núñez de Balboa
E1

Fernandez de Córdoba
E2

Envelopes of Panama Lithographed and Overprinted by American Bank Note Co.

1916, April 24   On White Paper.

U1	E1	1c green & black	15.00	10.00
		Entire	110.00	60.00
		a. Head and overprint only	—	—
		Entire	1500.00	1500.00
		b. Frame only	—	—
		Entire	2000.00	2000.00

U2	E2	2c carmine & black	12.50	5.00
		Entire	90.00	45.00
		a. 2c red & black	12.50	5.00
		Entire	85.00	45.00
		b. Head and overprint only	—	—
		Entire	1400.00	1200.00
		c. Frame only (red)	—	—
		Entire	1400.00	1200.00
		d. Frame double (carmine)	—	—
		Entire	2000.00	1750.00

José Vallarino
E3

"The Land Gate"
E4

1921, Nov. 13   On White Paper.

U3	E3	1c green	140.00	100.00
		Entire	1000.00	450.00
U4	E4	2c red	35.00	20.00
		Entire	240.00	120.00

Arms of Panama
E5

Typographed and embossed by American Bank Note Co. with "CANAL ZONE" in color of stamp.

1923, Dec. 15   On White Paper

U5	E5	2c carmine	55.00	32.50
		Entire	200.00	125.00

U. S. Nos. U420 and U429
Overprinted in Black by
Bureau of Engraving and Printing,
Washington, D. C.

CANAL ZONE

1924, July 1

U6	U92	1c green *(50,000)*	5.00	3.00
		Entire	40.00	22.50
U7	U93	2c carmine *(100,000)*	5.00	3.00
		Entire	40.00	22.50

Seal of Canal Zone
E6

CANAL ZONE

Printed by the Panama Canal Press,
Mount Hope, C. Z.

1924, Oct. On White Paper.
U8	E6	1c green *(205,000)*	2.00	1.00
		Entire	35.00	17.50
U9	"	2c carmine *(1,997,658)*	75	40
		Entire	30.00	9.00

Gorgas
E7

Goethals
E8

Typographed and Embossed by International
Envelope Corp., Dayton, O.

1932, April 8
U10	E7	1c green *(1,300,000)*	15	10
		Entire	2.75	1.00
U11	E8	2c carmine *(400,250)*	25	15
		Entire	3.50	1.50

No. U9 Surcharged in Violet by
Panama Canal Press, Mount Hope,
C. Z. Numerals 3 mm. high   **3 3**

1932, July 20
U12	E6	3c on 2c carmine *(20,000)*	17.50	7.50
		Entire	275.00	120.00

No. U11 Surcharged in Violet,
Numerals 5 mm. high   **3 3**

1932, July 20
U13	E8	3c on 2c carmine *(320,000)*	2.00	1.00
		Entire	25.00	14.00

1934, Jan. 17   Numerals with Serifs
U14	E6	3c on 2c carmine (Numerals 4mm. high) *(8,000)*	115.00	60.00
		Entire	600.00	500.00
U15	E8	3c on 2c carmine (Numerals 5mm. high) *(23,000)*	25.00	15.00
		Entire	300.00	135.00

Typographed and Embossed by International
Envelope Corp., Dayton, O.

1934, June 18
U16	E8	3c purple *(2,450,000)*	15	10
		Entire	1.10	55

1958, Nov. 1
U17	E8	4c blue *(596,725)*	20	15
		Entire	1.25	50

Surcharged at Left of Stamp in Ultra. as No. UX13

1969, Apr. 28
U18	E8	4c+1c blue *(93,850)*	15	10
		Entire	1.25	95
U19	"	4c+2c blue *(23,125)*	50	30
		Entire	2.50	1.50

Ship
Passing
through
Gaillard
Cut
E9

Typographed and Embossed by United States Envelope
Co., Williamsburg, Pa.

1971, Nov. 17
U20	E9	8c emerald *(121,500)*	25	12
		Entire	75	35

Surcharged at Left of Stamp in Emerald as No. UX13

1974, Mar. 2
U21	E9	8c+2c emerald	30	15
		Entire	1.00	35

1976, Feb. 23
U22	E9	13c violet *(638,350)*	35	20
		Entire	75	40

Surcharged at Left of Stamp in Violet as No. UX13

1978, July 5
U23	E9	13c+2c violet *(245,041)*	35	20
		Entire	75	40

AIR POST ENVELOPES.

No. U9 Overprinted with Horizontal Blue and Red
Bars Across Entire Face.

Overprinted by Panama Canal Press, Mount Hope, C.Z.
Boxed inscription in lower left with nine lines of instructions.
Additional adhesives required for air post rate.

1928, May 21
UC1	E6	2c red, entire *(15,000)*	120.00	60.00
		First day cancel		80.00

No. U9 with Similar Overprint
of Blue and Red Bars, and "VIA AIR MAIL" in Blue,
Centered, no box.

1929
UC2	E6	2c red, entire *(10,000)* Jan. 11, 1929	160.00	60.00
	a.	Inscription at left *(60,200)* Feb. 6, 1929	75.00	25.00

DC-4 Skymaster—UC3

Typographed and Embossed by International
Envelope Corp., Dayton, O.

1949, Jan. 3
UC3	UC1	6c blue *(4,400,000)*	25	15
		Entire	3.75	1.50
		Entire, 1st day cancel		2.00

1958, Nov. 1
UC4	UC1	7c carmine *(1,000,000)*	25	15
		Entire	4.00	1.00
		Entire, 1st day cancel		1.50

CANAL ZONE

No. U16 Surcharged at Left of Stamp and Imprinted "VIA AIR MAIL" in Dark Blue

Surcharged by Panama Canal Press, Mount Hope, C.Z.

1963, June 22
UC5 E8 3c+5c purple (105,000)   75   35
  Entire   8.50 4.00
  a. Double surcharge   600.00

Jet Liner and Tail Assembly—UC2
Typographed and Embossed by International Envelope Corp., Dayton, O.

1964, Jan. 6
UC6 UC2 8c deep carmine (800,000)   35   20
  Entire   1.75 1.25

No. U17 Surcharged at Left of Stamp as No. UC5 and Imprinted "VIA AIR MAIL" in Vermilion
Surcharged by Canal Zone Press, La Boca, C.Z.

1965, Oct. 15
UC7 E8 4c+4c blue (100,000)   50   25
  Entire   4.00 2.75

Jet Liner and Tail Assembly UC3
Typographed and Embossed by United States Envelope Co., Williamsburg, Pa.

1966, Feb. 25 (?)
UC8 UC3 8c carmine (224,000)   50   35
  Entire   3.50 1.75

No. UC8 Surcharged at Left of Stamp as No. UX13 in Vermilion
Surcharged by Canal Zone Press, La Boca, C.Z.

1968, Jan. 18
UC9 UC3 8c+2c carmine (376,000)   40   25
  Entire   2.75 1.10

No. UC7 with Additional Surcharge at Left of Stamp as No. UX13 and Imprinted "VIA AIR MAIL" in Vermilion
Surcharged by Canal Zone Press, La Boca, C.Z.

1968, Feb. 12
UC10 E8 4c+4c+2c blue (224,150)   60   40
  Entire   2.25 1.50

Type of 1966
Typographed and Embossed by United States Envelope Co., Williamsburg, Pa.

1969, Apr. 1   Luminescent Ink
UC11 UC3 10c ultramarine (448,000)   60   30
  Entire   3.50 1.40

No. U17 Surcharged at Left of Stamp as Nos. UC5 and UX13, and Imprinted "VIA AIR MAIL" in Vermilion

1971, May 17
UC12 E8 4c+5c+2c blue (55,775)   60   30
  Entire   3.00 2.25

No. UC11 Surcharged in Ultra. at Left of Stamp as No. UX13

1971, May 17   Luminescent Ink
UC13 UC3 10c+1c ultramarine (152,000)   45   30
  Entire   3.25 1.25

Type of 1966
Typographed and Embossed by United States Envelope Co., Williamsburg, Pa.

1971, Nov. 17
UC14 UC3 11c rose red (553,000)   30   15
  Entire   1.00   60
  a. 11c carmine, tagged   30   15
  Entire   1.00   60

Surcharged at Left of Stamp in Rose Red as No. UX13

1974, Mar. 2
UC15 UC3 11c+2c carmine, tagged (387,000)   35   20
  Entire   1.50   80
  a. 11c+2c rose red, untagged   35   20
  Entire   2.00   80

No. U21 with Additional Surcharge in Vermilion at Left of Stamp as No. UX 13 and Imprinted "VIA AIR MAIL" in Vermilion

1975, May 3
UC16 E9 8c+2c+3c emerald (75,000)   50   25
  Entire   1.25 1.00

REGISTRATION ENVELOPES

RE1
Panama Registration Envelope surcharged by Panama Canal Press, Mount Hope, C.Z.

1918, Oct.   8mm. btwn. CANAL & ZONE
UF1 RE1 10c on 5c black & red, *cream* (10,000), entire   1500.00 1250.00
  a. 9¼ mm. btwn. CANAL & ZONE (25,000), entire ('19)   1250.00 1000.00

Stamped envelopes inscribed "Diez Centesimos," surcharged with numerals "5" and with solid blocks printed over "Canal Zone," were issued by the Republic of Panama after being rejected by the Canal Zone. Parts of "Canal Zone" are often legible under the surcharge blocks. These envelopes exist without surcharge.

POSTAL CARDS.
Prices are for Entires.

Map of Panama
PC1
Panama Card Lithographed by American Bank Note Co., revalued and surcharged in black by the Isthmian Canal Commission.

1907, Feb. 9   On White.
UX1 PC1 1c on 2c carmine,
  "CANAL" 15 mm. (50,000)   35.00 25.00
  a. Double surcharge   1300.00 1300.00
  b. Double surcharge, one reading down   2500.00
  c. Triple surcharge, one reading down   2500.00
  d. "CANAL" 13 mm. (10,000)   225.00 175.00
  e. As "d," double surch.   2500.00

CANAL ZONE

Balboa
PC2

Panama card lithographed by Hamilton Bank Note Co. Overprinted in black by Isthmian Canal Commission.

At least six types of overprint, reading down.

1908, March 3
UX2　PC2　1c green & black,
　　　　　"CANAL" 13 mm. (*295,000*)　160.00　75.00
　　　　　a. Double overprint　1500.00　1500.00
　　　　　b. Triple overprint　1750.00　—
　　　　　c. Period after "ZONE"
　　　　　　　(*40,000*)　175.00　125.00
　　　　　d. "CANAL" 15 mm. (*30,000*)　170.00　110.00
　　　　　e. "ZONE CANAL",
　　　　　　　reading up　　　　　2750.00

　　　　　　　Balboa
PC3　　　　　　　PC4

Lithographed by Hamilton Bank Note Co.
Overprinted in Black by Panama Canal Press,
Mount Hope. C. Z.

1910, Nov. 10
UX3　PC3　1c green & black (*40,000*)　175.00　100.00
　　　　　a. Double overprint　　　　　2750.00

This card, with overprint reading up, is actually the fourth of seven settings of UX2.

Lithographed and Overprinted by American Bank Note Co.
1913, March 27
UX4　PC4　1c green & black (*634,000*)　150.00　60.00

Design of Canal Zone Envelopes.
Overprinted in black by the American Bank Note Co.
1921-24
UX5　E3　1c green, *Oct. 1921*　1100.00　700.00

Typographed and embossed by American Bank Note Co. with "CANAL ZONE" in color of stamp.
UX6　E5　1c green, *Jan. 1924*　1000.00　700.00

U. S. No. UX27　　　　**CANAL**
Overprinted by
U. S. Gov't. Printing Office
at Washington, D. C.　　**ZONE**

1924, July 1
UX7　PC17　1c green on buff (*Jefferson*) (*50,000*)　85.00　40.00

Design of Canal Zone Envelope.
Printed by Panama Canal Press.
1925, Jan.
UX8　E6　1c green on buff (*85,000*)　85.00　40.00
　　　　a. Background only　　　2000.00

U.S. No. UX27 Overprinted　　**CANAL**

1925, May　　　　　　　　　　**ZONE**
UX9　PC17　1c green on buff (*Jefferson*) (*850,000*)　8.50　2.50

U.S. No. UX27 Overprinted　　**CANAL**

1935, Oct.　　　　　　　　**ZONE**
UX10　PC17　1c green on buff (*Jefferson*)
　　　　　(*2,900,000*)　　1.50　60
　　　　a. Double overprint　2250.00

1952, May 1　Same on U.S. No. UX38
UX11　PC22　2c carmine rose on buff (*Franklin*)
　　　　　(*800,000*)　　1.75　75

Ship in Lock
PC5
Printed by Bureau of Engraving & Printing,
Washington, D.C.
1958, Nov. 1
UX12　PC5　3c dark blue on buff (*335,116*)　1.50　75

No. UX12 Surcharged at Left
of Stamp in Green by Panama
Canal Press, Mount Hope, C.Z.

1963, July 27
UX13　PC5　3c+1c dark blue on buff (*78,000*)　4.00　3.00

Ship Passing through
Panama Canal
PC6
Printed by Panama Canal Press, Mount Hope, C.Z.
1964, Dec. 1
UX14　PC6　4c violet blue on buff (*74,800*)　3.50　2.50

Ship in Lock (Tow car at right redrawn)
PC7
Printed by Bureau of Engraving & Printing,
Washington, D.C.
1965, Aug. 12
UX15　PC7　4c emerald on white (*95,500*)　1.00　65

No. UX15 Surcharged at Left of Stamp in Green as No. UX13
by Canal Zone Press, La Boca, C.Z.
1968, Feb. 12
UX16　PC7　4c+1c emerald on white (*94,775*)　1.00　65

Ship-in-Lock Type of 1965
1969, Apr. 1
UX17 PC7 5c light ultra. on white *(63,000)* 90 50

No. UX17 Surcharged at Left of Stamp in Light Ultramarine as No. UX13
1971, May 24
UX18 PC7 5c+1c light ultra. on white *(100,500)* 80 40

Ship-in-Lock Type of 1965
Printed by Bureau of Engraving & Printing, Washington, D.C.
1974, Feb. 11
UX19 PC7 8c brown on white *(90, 895)* 65 40

No. UX19 Surcharged at left of Stamp in Brown as No. UX13
1976, June 1
UX20 PC7 8c+1c brown on white *(60,249)* 50 40

No. UX19 Surcharged at Left of Stamp in Brown as No. UX13
1978, July 5
UX21 PC7 8c+2c brown on white *(74,847)* 60 40

AIR POST POSTAL CARDS

Plane, Flag and Map—APC1
Printed by Bureau of Engraving & Printing, Washington, D.C.
1958, Nov. 1
UXC1 APC1 5c blue & carmine rose on white *(104,957)* 3.50 3.00

No. UXC1 Surcharged at Left of Stamp in Green as No. UX13 by Panama Canal Press, Mount Hope, C.Z.
1963, July 27
UXC2 APC1 5c+1c blue & carmine rose on white *(48,000)* 9.50 6.00
    a. Inverted surcharge 1400.00

No. UX15 Surcharged at Left of Stamp as No. UX13 and Imprinted "AIR MAIL" in Vermilion
1965, Aug. 18
UXC3 PC7 4c+2c emerald on white *(41,700)* 4.00 3.00

No. UX15 Surcharged at Left of Stamp as No. UC5 and Imprinted "AIR MAIL" in Vermilion by Canal Zone Press, La Boca, C.Z.
1968, Feb. 12
UXC4 PC7 4c+4c emerald on white *(60,100)* 2.75 1.50

No. UX17 Surcharged at Left of Stamp as No. UC5 and Imprinted "AIR MAIL" in Vermilion
1971, May 24
UXC5 PC7 5c+4c light ultramarine on white *(68,000)* 75 50

PROOFS

	DIE	
	(1) Large	*(2)* Small

1928–40
106TC	2c black	700.00	
113P	30c brown black		600.00

1934
117P	3c deep violet	350.00	

1939
120P	1c yellow green		600.00
121P	2c rose carmine		600.00
122P	3c purple	700.00	600.00
123P	5c dark blue	700.00	600.00
124P	6c red orange		600.00
125P	7c black		600.00
126P	8c green		600.00
127P	10c ultramarine		600.00
128P	11c blue green	700.00	600.00
129P	12c brown carmine	700.00	600.00
130P	14c dark violet		600.00
131P	15c olive green		600.00
132P	18c rose pink		600.00
133P	20c brown	700.00	600.00
134P	25c orange	700.00	600.00
135P	50c violet brown	700.00	600.00

1946–48
136P	½c bright red	700.00	
137P	1½c chocolate	700.00	
139P	5c deep blue	700.00	
140P	25c yellow green	700.00	
141P	10c black	700.00	

1949
142P	3c blue	700.00	
143P	6c violet	700.00	
144P	12c bright blue green	700.00	
145P	18c deep red lilac	700.00	

1931–49 Air Post
C6P	4c red violet	800.00	
C7P	5c light green	800.00	
C8P	6c yellow brown	800.00	
C13P	40c yellow	800.00	

1939
C15P	5c greenish black		700.00
C15TC	5c scarlet		
C16P	10c dull violet	800.00	700.00
C17P	15c light brown		700.00
C18P	25c blue		700.00
C19P	30c rose carmine	800.00	700.00
C20P	$1 green		700.00

1951
C21P	4c red violet	800.00	

The Small Die proofs listed are on soft yellowish wove paper.

CANAL ZONE
WE STOCK ONE COUNTRY AND DO IT WELL
 From sea to shining sea

Mint - Used
Singles - Sets

Stationery - Errors - Varieties - Covers - First Days
Sheets - Booklets - Booklet Panes - Packets
Comprehensive Pricelist Free. 22¢ SASE Appreciated

WE ALSO BUY

BRUCE L. HECHT
P.O. Box 132, Dept. SS, Albertson, NY 11507
(516) 741-3696   Members: ASDA, APS, CZSG, BIA.

825

CUBA

AFTER the U. S. battleship "Maine" was destroyed in Havana harbor with a loss of 266 lives in February, 1898, the United States demanded the withdrawal of Spanish troops from Cuba. The Spanish-American War followed. By the peace treaty of Dec. 10, 1898, Spain relinquished Cuba to the United States in trust for its inhabitants. On Jan. 1, 1899, Spanish authority was succeeded by U. S. military rule which lasted until May 20, 1902, when Cuba, as a republic, assumed self-government.

The listings in this catalogue cover the U. S. Administration issue of 1899, the Republic's 1899-1902 issues under U. S. military rule and the Puerto Principe issue of provincial provisionals.

100 CENTS = 1 DOLLAR.

Puerto Principe Issue.

In December, 1898, Puerto Principe, a provincial capital now called Camagüey, ran short of 1c, 2c, 3c, 5c and 10c stamps. The Postmaster ordered Cuban stamps to be surcharged on Dec. 19, 1898.

The surcharging was done to horizontal strips of five stamps, so vertical pairs and blocks do not exist. Five types are found in each setting, and five printings were made. Counterfeits are plentiful.

First Printing.

Black Surcharge, 17½ mm. high.

HABILITADO	HABILITADO	HABILITADO	ñABILITADO	HABILITAΓO
2	**2**	**2**	**2**	**2**
cents.	**cents.**	**cents.**	**cents.**	**cents.**
Position 1	Position 2	Position 3	Position 4	Position 5

Position 1—No serif at right of "t".
" 2—Thin numeral except on 1c on 1m No. 176.
" 3—Broken right foot of "n".
" 4—Up-stroke of "t" broken.
" 5—Broken "DO".

This printing consisted of the following stamps:

176	1c on 1m orange brown, Pos. 1, 2, 3, 4 and 5
178	2c on 2m orange brown, Pos. 1, 3, 4 and 5
179	2c on 2m orange brown, Pos. 2
180	3c on 3m orange brown, Pos. 1, 3, 4 and 5
181	3c on 3m orange brown, Pos. 2
188	5c on 5m orange brown, Pos. 1, 3, 4 and 5
189	5c on 5m orange brown, Pos. 2

Surcharge measures 17½ mm. high and is roughly printed in dull black ink.

Second Printing.

Black Surcharge, 17½ mm. high.

This printing was from the same setting as used for the first printing, but the impression is much clearer and the ink quite shiny.

The printing consisted of the following stamps:

179F	3c on 2m orange brown, Pos. 1, 3, 4 and 5
179G	3c on 2m orange brown, Pos. 2
182	5c on 1m orange brown, Pos. 1, 3, 4 and 5

183	5c on 1m orange brown, Pos. 2
184	5c on 2m orange brown, Pos. 1, 3, 4 and 5
185	5c on 2m orange brown, Pos. 2
186	5c on 3m orange brown, Pos. 1, 3, 4 and 5
187	5c on 3m orange brown, Pos. 2
188	5c on 5m orange brown, Pos. 1, 3, 4 and 5
189	5c on 5m orange brown, Pos. 2
190	5c on ½m blue green, Pos. 1, 3, 4 and 5
191	5c on ½m blue green, Pos. 2

Third Printing.

Red Surcharge, 20 mm. high.

The same setting as for the first and second was used for the third printing. The 10c denomination first appeared in this printing and position 2 of that value has numerals same as on positions 1, 3, 4 and 5, while position 4 has broken "1" in "10".

The printing consisted of the following stamps:

196	3c on 1c black violet, Pos. 1, 3, 4 and 5
197	3c on 1c black violet, Pos. 2
198	5c on 1c black violet, Pos. 1, 3, 4 and 5
199	5c on 1c black violet, Pos. 2
200	10c on 1c black violet, Pos. 1, 2, 3 and 5
200a	10c on 1c black violet, Pos. 4

Fourth Printing.

Black Surcharge, 19½ mm. high.

The same type as before but spaced between so that the surcharge is 2 mm. taller. Clear impression, shiny ink.

HABILITADO	HABILITADO	HABILITADO	HABILITADO	HABILITADO
1	**1**	**1**	**1**	**1**
cents.	cents.	cents.	cents.	cents.
Position 1	Position 2	Position 3	Position 4	Position 5

Position 1—No serif at right of "t".
" 2—Broken "1" on No. 177.
" 2—Thin numerals on 5c stamps.
" 3—Broken right foot of "n".
" 4—Up-stroke of "t" broken.
" 4—Thin numeral on 3c stamps.
" 5—Broken "DO".

This printing consisted of the following stamps:

177   1c on 1m orange brown, Pos. 1, 3, 4 and 5
177a   1c on 1m orange brown, Pos. 2

179B   3c on 1m orange brown, Pos. 1, 2, 3 and 5
179D   3c on 1m orange brown, Pos. 4
183B   5c on 1m orange brown, Pos. 1, 3, 4 and 5
189C   5c on 5m orange brown, Pos. 1, 3, 4 and 5
192   5c on ½m blue green, Pos. 1, 3, 4 and 5
193   5c on ½m blue green, Pos. 2

Fifth Printing.

Black Surcharge, 19½ mm. high.

HABILITADO	HABILITADO	HABILITADO	HABILITADO	HABILITADO
3	**3**	**3**	**3**	**3**
cents.	cents.	eents.	cents.	cents.
Position 1	Position 2	Position 3	Position 4	Position 5

Position 1—Nick in bottom of "e" and lower serif of "s".
" 2—Normal surcharge.
" 3—"eents".
" 4—Thin numeral.
" 5—Nick in upper part of right stroke of "n".

This printing consisted of the following stamps:

201	3c on 1m blue green, Pos. 1, 2 and 5
201b	3c on 1m blue green, Pos. 3
202	3c on 1m blue green, Pos. 4
203	3c on 2m blue green, Pos. 1, 2 and 5
203a	3c on 2m blue green, Pos. 3
204	3c on 2m blue green, Pos. 4
205	3c on 3m blue green, Pos. 1, 2 and 5
205b	3c on 3m blue green, Pos. 3
206	3c on 3m blue green, Pos. 4
211	5c on 1m blue green, Pos. 1, 2 and 5
211a	5c on 1m blue green, Pos. 3
212	5c on 1m blue green, Pos. 4
213	5c on 2m blue green, Pos. 1, 2 and 5
213a	5c on 2m blue green, Pos. 3
214	5c on 2m blue green, Pos. 4
215	5c on 3m blue green, Pos. 1, 2 and 5
215a	5c on 3m blue green, Pos. 3
216	5c on 3m blue green, Pos. 4
217	5c on 4m blue green, Pos. 1, 2 and 5
217a	5c on 4m blue green, Pos. 3
218	5c on 4m blue green, Pos. 4
219	5c on 8m blue green, Pos. 1, 2 and 5
219b	5c on 8m blue green, Pos. 3
220	5c on 8m blue green, Pos. 4

Counterfeits exist of all Puerto Principe surcharges. Illustrations have been altered to discourage further counterfeiting.

1898-99   Puerto Principe Issue.

Regular Issues of Cuba of 1896 and 1898 Surcharged: Numerals in ( ) after color indicate printings.

Black Surcharge on Nos. 156-158, 160

HABILITADO

1

cent.

176	(a)	1 cent on 1m orange brown (1)	55.00	37.50

HABILITADO

1

cents.

177	(b)	1 cents on 1m orange brown (4)	45.00	30.00
		a. Broken figure "1"	75.00	60.00
		b. Inverted surcharge		200.00
		d. Same as "a" inverted		250.00

HABILITADO

2

cents.

178	(c)	2c on 2m orange brown (1)	22.50	15.00
		a. Inverted surcharge	250.00	50.00

CUBA

HABILITADO 2 cents.
d

179	(d)	2c on 2m orange brown (1)	40.00	25.00
		a. Inverted surcharge	350.00	100.00

HABILITADO 3 cents.
k

179B	(k)	3c on 1m orange brown (4)	375.00	150.00
		c. Double surcharge	1500.00	750.00

HABILITADO 3 cents.
l

179D	(l)	3c on 1m orange brown (4)	1500.00	600.00
		e. Double surcharge		

HABILITADO 3 cents.
e

179F	(e)	3c on 2m orange brown (2)		2000.00

HABILITADO 3 cents.
f

179G	(f)	3c on 2m orange brown (2)	—	2500.00
180	(e)	3c on 3m orange brown (1)	27.50	22.50
		a. Inverted surcharge		100.00
181	(f)	3c on 3m orange brown (1)	75.00	50.00
		a. Inverted surcharge		300.00

HABILITADO 5 cents.
g

182	(g)	5c on 1m orange brown (2)	700.00	175.00
		a. Inverted surcharge		500.00

HABILITADO 5 cents.
h

183	(h)	5c on 1m orange brown (2)	1500.00	400.00
		a. Inverted surcharge		700.00

HABILITADO 5 cents.
i

184	(g)	5c on 2m orange brown (2)	750.00	200.00
185	(h)	5c on 2m orange brown (2)	1500.00	400.00
186	(g)	5c on 3m orange brown (2)		165.00
		a. Inverted surcharge		700.00
187	(h)	5c on 3m orange brown (2)		400.00
		a. Inverted surcharge		1000.00
188	(g)	5c on 5m orange brown (1) (2)	70.00	55.00
		a. Inverted surcharge	400.00	175.00
		b. Double surcharge		
189	(h)	5c on 5m orange brown (1) (2)	350.00	225.00
		a. Inverted surcharge		400.00
		b. Double surcharge		
189C	(i)	5c on 5m orange brown (4)		4000.00

Black Surcharge on No. P25

190	(g)	5c on ½m blue green (2)	250.00	75.00
		a. Inverted surcharge	500.00	150.00
		b. Pair, one without surcharge		450.00
191	(h)	5c on ½m blue green (2)	300.00	90.00
		a. Inverted surcharge		200.00
192	(i)	5c on ½m blue green (4)	550.00	200.00
		a. Double surcharge, one diagonal		3000.00

HABILITADO 5 cents.
j

193	(j)	5c on ½m blue green (4)	700.00	300.00

Red Surcharge on No. 161

196	(k)	3c on 1c black violet (3)	60.00	25.00
		a. Inverted surcharge		200.00
197	(l)	3c on 1c black violet (3)	125.00	45.00
		a. Inverted surcharge		300.00
198	(i)	5c on 1c black violet (3)	20.00	20.00
		a. Inverted surcharge		100.00
		b. Vertical surcharge		2000.00
		c. Double surcharge	400.00	600.00
		d. Double inverted surcharge		
199	(j)	5c on 1c black violet (3)	50.00	40.00
		a. Inverted surcharge		250.00
		b. Vertical surcharge		2000.00
		c. Double surcharge	1000.00	600.00

HABILITADO 10 cents.
m

200	(m)	10c on 1c black violet (3)	20.00	50.00
		a. Broken figure "1"	40.00	100.00

Black Surcharge on Nos. P26–P30

201	(k)	3c on 1m blue green (5)	300.00	200.00
		a. Inverted surcharge		400.00
		b. "EENTS"	550.00	400.00
		c. Same as "b", inverted		850.00
202	(l)	3c on 1m blue green (5)	500.00	400.00
		a. Inverted surcharge		850.00
203	(k)	3c on 2m blue green (5)	850.00	250.00
		a. "EENTS"	1200.00	450.00
		b. Inverted surcharge		600.00
		c. Same as "a", inverted		750.00

CUBA

204	(l)	3c on 2m blue green (5)	1000.00	450.00
		a. Inverted surcharge		750.00
205	(k)	3c on 3m blue green (5)	900.00	250.00
		a. Inverted surcharge		500.00
		b. "EENTS"	1200.00	375.00
		c. Same as "b", inverted		700.00
206	(l)	3c on 3m blue green (5)	1200.00	375.00
		a. Inverted surcharge		700.00
211	(i)	5c on 1m blue green (5)		1400.00
		a. "EENTS"	—	2000.00
212	(j)	5c on 1m blue green (5)		2000.00
213	(i)	5c on 2m blue green (5)		1250.00
		a. "EENTS"	—	1750.00
214	(j)	5c on 2m blue green (5)		1750.00
215	(i)	5c on 3m blue green (5)		500.00
		a. "EENTS"		900.00
216	(j)	5c on 3m blue green (5)	—	900.00
217	(i)	5c on 4m blue green (5)	2000.00	500.00
		a. "EENTS"	2500.00	1200.00
		b. Inverted surcharge		900.00
		c. Same as "a", inverted		1400.00
218	(j)	5c on 4m blue green (5)		1100.00
		a. Inverted surcharge		1400.00
219	(i)	5c on 8m blue green (5)	2500.00	1000.00
		a. Inverted surcharge		1500.00
		b. "EENTS"	—	2000.00
		c. Same as "b", inverted		2500.00
220	(j)	5c on 8m blue green (5)		2000.00
		a. Inverted surcharge		2500.00

Puerto Principe pairs, strips and stamps properly canceled on cover are scarce and command high premiums.

CUBA

United States Stamps Nos. 279a, 267, 279B, 268, 281a, 282C and 283a

Surcharged in Black

1 c. de PESO.

Wmkd. USPS (191)

1899   *Perf. 12*

221	A87	1c on 1c yellow green	4.25	60
		On cover		4.00
		Block of four	20.00	6.00
		Margin strip of 3, Impt. & P ‡	50.00	
		Margin block of 6, Impt. & P ‡	225.00	
222	A88	2c on 2c carmine, type III	4.25	50
		On cover		4.00
		Block of four	20.00	6.00
		Margin strip of 3, Impt. & P ‡	50.00	
		Margin block of 6, Impt. & P ‡	300.00	
		a. 2c on 2c red, type III	5.00	40
		b. "CUPA"	120.00	120.00
		c. Inverted surcharge	2750.00	2750.00
		"CUBA" at bottom	300.00	
223	"	2½c on 2c red, type III	3.00	60
		On cover		4.00
		Block of four	15.00	6.00
		Margin strip of 3, Impt. & P ‡	50.00	
		Margin block of 6, Impt. & P ‡	225.00	
		a. 2½ on 2c carmine, type III	3.50	2.00

The 2½c was sold and used as a 2c stamp.

224	A89	3c on 3c purple	8.50	1.25
		On cover		12.00
		Block of four	40.00	17.50
		Margin strip of 3, Impt. & P ‡	85.00	
		Margin block of 6, Impt. & P ‡	475.00	
		a. Period between "B" and "A"	27.50	27.50
		Two types of surcharge		
		I "3" directly over "P"		
		II "3" to left over "P"		

225	A91	5c on 5c blue	8.50	1.25
		On cover		20.00
		Block of four	40.00	15.00
		Margin strip of 3, Impt. & P ‡	125.00	
		Margin block of 6, Impt. & P ‡	550.00	
		a. "CUPA"	60.00	50.00
		"CUBA" at bottom	—	—
226	A94	10c on 10c brown, type I	22.50	8.00
		On cover		50.00
		Block of four	90.00	50.00
		Margin strip of 3, Impt. & P ‡	250.00	
		Margin block of 6, Impt. & P ‡	1000.00	
		b. "CUBA" omitted	2500.00	2500.00
		"CUBA" at bottom	225.00	225.00
226A	"	10c on 10c brown, type II	4500.00	
		Block of four	—	

No. 226A exists only in the special printing.

Special Printing.

In 1899 one sheet each of Nos. 221 to 225, 226A; E1 (three sheets), and J1 to J4 (two sheets each) were specially printed for display at the Paris Exposition. All but a few copies, however, were later destroyed. Nearly all copies remaining bear impression of handstamp reading "Special Surcharge" on the back. Price: Nos. 221-225, J1-J4, each $250; No. E1, $400.

Issues of the Republic under U. S. Military Rule.

Statue of Columbus
A20

Royal Palms
A21

Allegory, "Cuba"
A22

Ocean Liner
A23

Cane Field
A24

Printed by the U. S. Bureau of Engraving and Printing.

1899   Wmkd. US-C (191C)

Perf. 12.

227	A20	1c yellow green	3.00	15
		On cover		2.00
		Block of four	12.50	1.50
		Margin block of 10, Impt. & P ‡, type VII	225.00	—
228	A21	2c carmine	3.00	15
		On cover		2.00
		Block of four	12.50	1.50
		Margin block of 10, Impt. & P type VII	175.00	—
		a. 2c scarlet	3.00	15
		b. Booklet pane of six	1750.00	
229	A22	3c purple	3.00	25
		On cover		4.00
		Block of four	12.50	4.00
		Margin block of 10, Impt. & P type VII	250.00	—

CUBA

230	A23	5c blue	4.50	30
		On cover		4.00
		Block of four	20.00	4.00
		Margin block of 10, Impt. & P #, type VII	550.00	—
231	A24	10c brown	10.00	75
		On cover		6.50
		Block of four	45.00	8.00
		Margin block of 10, Impt. & P#, type VII	800.00	—

Re-engraved.

The re-engraved stamps issued by the Republic of Cuba in 1905-07 may be distinguished from the Issue of 1899 as follows:

Nos. 227 to 231 are watermarked U S—C

The re-engraved stamps are unwatermarked.

No. 227   Re-engraved.

No. 228   Re-engraved.

No. 230   Re-engraved.

No. 231   Re-engraved.

1c: The ends of the label inscribed "Centavo" are rounded instead of square.

2c: The foliate ornaments, inside the oval disks bearing the numerals of value, have been removed.

5c: Two lines forming a right angle have been added in the upper corners of the label bearing the word "Cuba".

10c: A small ball has been added to each of the square ends of the label bearing the word "Cuba".

SPECIAL DELIVERY STAMPS.

Issued under Administration of the United States.

CUBA.

Special Delivery Stamp of the United States
No. E5 Surcharged in Red   **10c. de PESO.**

1899   Wmkd. USPS (191)   Perf. 12

E1	SD3	10c on 10c blue	100.00	80.00
		On cover		450.00
		Block of four	450.00	
		Margin block of four, arrow	500.00	
		Margin strip of 3, Impt. & P #	900.00	
		Margin block of 6, Impt. & P #	4500.00	
		a. No period after "CUBA"	350.00	350.00

Issue of the Republic under U. S. Military Rule.

Special Delivery Messenger
SD2

Printed by the U. S. Bureau of Engraving and Printing

1899   Wmkd. US–C (191C)

Inscribed: "Immediata".

E2	SD2	10c orange	45.00	12.00
		On cover		60.00
		Block of four	200.00	—
		Margin strip of 3, Impt. & P #, type VII	300.00	
		Margin block of 6, Impt. & P #, type VII	800.00	

Re-engraved.

In 1902 the Republic of Cuba issued a stamp of design SD2 re-engraved with word correctly spelled "Inmediata." The corrected die was made in 1899 (See No. E3P). It was printed by the U.S. Bureau of Engraving and Printing.

POSTAGE DUE STAMPS.

Issued under Administration of the United States.

Postage Due Stamps of the United States Nos. J38, J39, J41 and J42 Surcharged in Black Like Regular Issue of Same Date.

Wmkd. USPS (191)

1899   Perf. 12

J1	D2	1c on 1c deep claret	22.50	3.50
		Block of four	95.00	30.00
		Margin block of 6, Impt. & P#	650.00	
J2	"	2c on 2c deep claret	20.00	3.50
		Block of four	90.00	30.00
		Margin block of 6, Impt. & P#	650.00	
		a. Inverted surcharge		2000.00
J3	"	5c on 5c deep claret	22.50	3.50
		Block of four	95.00	30.00
		Margin block of 6, Impt. & P#	600.00	
		a. "CUPA"	175.00	160.00
J4	"	10c on 10c deep claret	20.00	1.25
		Block of four	90.00	12.50
		Margin block of 6, Impt. & P#	750.00	

ENVELOPES.

Prices are for Cut Squares.

U. S. Envelopes of 1887–99 Surcharged

CUBA.   **CUBA.**

1c. DE PESO.   **2c. DE PESO.**
a   *b*

1899

U1	U77	(a)	1c on 1c green on buff (No. U354)	2.50	3.50
			Entire	15.00	20.00
U2	"	(")	1c on 1c green on blue (No. U355)	2.50	2.75
			Entire	6.00	8.00
			a. Double surch., entire	2000.00	

830   CUBA

U3	U71 (b)	2c on 2c green on white (No. U311)		1.00	1.00
		Entire		3.50	4.50
		a. Double surch., entire		1750.00	1750.00
U4	" (")	2c on 2c green on amber (No. U312)		1.75	1.75
		Entire		6.00	7.50
		a. Double surch., entire		1750.00	
U5	" (a)	2c on 2c green on buff (No. U313)		10.00	8.50
		Entire		60.00	60.00
U6	U79 (")	2c on 2c carmine on amber (No. U363)		10.00	10.00
		Entire		60.00	60.00
U7	" (")	2c on 2c carmine on buff (No. U364)		17.50	17.50
		Entire		85.00	95.00
U8	" (")	2c on 2c carmine on blue (No. U365)		1.75	1.75
		Entire		9.00	10.00
		a. Double surch., entire			1750.00

In addition to the envelopes listed above, several others are known but were not regularly issued. They are:

1c on 1c green on white
1c on 1c green on manila
2c on 2c carmine on white
2c on 2c carmine on oriental buff
2c on 2c carmine on blue
4c on 4c brown on white
5c on 5c blue on white

Issue of the Republic under U. S. Military Rule.

Columbus
E1

Similar envelopes without watermark on white and amber papers, were issued by the Republic after Military Rule ended in 1902.

1899   Wmkd. "US POD '99" in Monogram.

U9	E1	1c green on white		50	50
		Entire		1.75	1.75
U10	"	1c green on amber		50	50
		Entire		1.75	1.75
U11	"	1c green on buff		12.00	9.00
		Entire		60.00	30.00
U12	"	1c green on blue		17.50	12.50
		Entire		60.00	30.00
U13	"	2c carmine on white		50	40
		Entire		1.50	1.25
U14	"	2c carmine on amber		40	40
		Entire		1.50	1.25
U15	"	2c carmine on buff		7.00	6.00
		Entire		25.00	15.00
U16	"	2c carmine on blue		17.50	15.00
		Entire		60.00	30.00
U17	"	5c blue on white		60	50
		Entire		2.50	1.00
U18	"	5c blue on amber		2.50	1.75
		Entire		8.50	5.00

WRAPPERS.

Issue of the Republic under U. S. Military Rule.

1899

W1	E1	1c green on manila		1.50	3.50
		Entire		11.00	35.00
W2	"	2c carmine on manila		5.00	7.00
		Entire		22.50	35.00

POSTAL CARDS.

Prices are for Entires.

U. S. Postal Cards of 1897–98 Surcharged

CUBA. 1c. de Peso.

UX1	PC8	1c on 1c black on buff, *Jefferson* (No. UX14) (1,000,000)		17.50	20.00
		a. No period after "1c"		50.00	50.00
		b. No period after "Peso"		40.00	
UX2	PC3	2c on 2c black on buff, *Liberty* (No. UX16) (583,000)		17.50	20.00
		a. No period after "Peso"		50.00	50.00
		b. Double surcharge		850.00	

In 1904 the Republic of Cuba revalued remaining stocks of No. UX2 by means of a perforated numeral "1".

PROOFS.

		DIE	
1899		(1) Large	(2) Small
227P	1c yellow green	225.00	150.00
227TC	1c blue green	400.00	
227TC	1c black	400.00	
228P	2c carmine	225.00	150.00
228TC	2c black	400.00	
229P	3c purple	225.00	150.00
229TC	3c black	400.00	
230P	5c blue	225.00	150.00
230TC	5c black	400.00	
231P	10c brown	225.00	150.00
231TC	10c gray	400.00	
231TC	10c black	400.00	
1902		**Special Delivery.**	
E2TC	10c blue	500.00	
E3P	10c orange	350.00	250.00

SPECIMEN STAMPS.

Overprinted Type E in black   **Specimen.**

1899		
221SE	1c on 1c yellow green	175.00
222SE	2c on 2c carmine	175.00
223SE	2½c on 2c orange red	175.00
224SE	3c on 3c purple	175.00
225SE	5c on 5c blue	175.00
226SE	10c on 10c brown, type I	175.00
226A-SE	10c on 10c brown, type II	2500.00
1899		
227SE	1c yellow green	300.00
228SE	2c carmine	300.00
229SE	3c purple	300.00
230SE	5c blue	300.00
231SE	10c brown	300.00
1899	**Special Delivery.**	
E1SE	10c on 10c blue	350.00
E2SE	10c orange	500.00
1899	**Postage Due.**	
J1SE	1c on 1c deep claret	250.00
J2SE	2c on 2c deep claret	250.00
J3SE	5c on 5c deep claret	250.00
J4SE	10c on 10c deep claret	250.00

"Specimen" overprint known on all stamps of the Special Printing.

DANISH WEST INDIES

**WANT LISTS FILLED.
SEND SASE FOR COMPLETE LIST.
APPROVALS BY ARRANGEMENT.**

COLLECTOR'S DESK
P.O. Box 1490, New Brunswick, NJ 08903

DANISH WEST INDIES

FORMERLY a Danish colony, these islands were purchased by the United States in 1917 and have since been known as the U.S. Virgin Islands. They lie east of Puerto Rico, have an area of 132 square miles and had a population of 27,086 in 1911. The capital is Charlotte Amalie (also called St. Thomas). Stamps of Danish West Indies were replaced by those of the United States in 1917.

100 CENTS = 1 DOLLAR   100 BIT = 1 FRANC (1905)

Coat of Arms
A1

Wmk. 111

Typographed.

1856   Wmkd. Small Crown. (111)   Imperf.
Yellowish Paper.
Yellow Wavy-line Burelage, UL to LR

1	A1	3c dark carmine, brown gum	200.00	200.00
		On cover		2250.00
		Block of four	1500.00	
		a. 3c dark carmine, yellow gum	250.00	250.00
		a. On cover		2750.00
		a. Block of four	4000.00	
		b. 3c carmine, white gum	2,000.00	

1981, carmine, back-printed across two stamps ("Reprint by Dansk Post og Telegrafmuseum 1978"), price, pair, $7.

1866   White Paper
Yellow Wavy-line Burelage UR to LL

2	A1	3c rose	75.00	70.00
		On cover		2250.00
		Block of four	375.00	850.00
		Rouletted 4½ privately	400.00	200.00
		On cover, rouletted 4½		2250.00
		Rouletted 9	400.00	200.00

No. 2 reprints, unwatermarked: 1930, carmine, price $120. 1942, rose carmine, back-printed across each row ("Nytryk 1942 G.A. Hagemann Danmark og Dansk Vestindiens Frimaerker Bind 2"), price $60.

1872   Perf. 12½

3	A1	3c rose	150.00	170.00
		On cover		4000.00
		Block of four	1000.00	

1873   Without Burelage.

4	A1	4c dull blue	275.00	350.00
		On cover		7000.00
		Block of four	1600.00	
		a. Imperf., pair	950.00	1200.00
		b. Horiz. pair, imperf. vert.	750.00	900.00

The 1930 reprint of No. 4 is ultramarine, unwatermarked and imperf., price $120.
The 1942 4c reprint is blue, unwatermarked, imperf. and has printing on back (see note below No. 2), price $60.

Numeral of Value
A2

NORMAL FRAME   INVERTED FRAME

The arabesques in the corners have a main stem and a branch. When the frame is in normal position, in the upper left corner the branch leaves the main stem half way between two little leaflets. In the lower right corner the branch starts at the foot of the second leaflet. When the frame is inverted the corner designs are, of course, transposed.

Wmk. 112

1874–79   Wmkd. Crown. (112)   Perf. 14x13½
Printings on White Wove Paper, Varying from Thin to Thick.

1c.   Nine printings
3c.   Eight printings
4c.   Two printings
5c.   Six printings
7c.   Two printings
10c. Seven printings
12c. Two printings
14c. One printing
50c. Two printings

Prices for inverted frames, covers and blocks are for the cheapest variety.

5	A2	1c green & brown red	25.00	22.50
		On cover		175.00
		Block of four	125.00	
		a. 1c green & rose lilac	37.50	30.00
		b. 1c green & red violet	37.50	30.00
		c. 1c green & violet	80.00	80.00
		green & claret	25.00	22.50
		e. Inverted frame	25.00	22.50

No. 5 exists with "b" surcharge, "10 CENTS 1895." See note below No. 15.

6	A2	3c blue & carmine	27.50	17.00
		On cover		120.00
		Block of four	140.00	
		Dull blue & rose	27.50	17.00
		Dull blue & red	27.50	17.00
		Blue & lake	27.50	17.00
		d. Imperf., pair	600.00	
		e. Inverted frame	27.50	16.00
		White "wedge" flaw	50.00	40.00

7	"	4c brown & dull blue	20.00	20.00
		On cover		140.00
		Block of four	100.00	
		Brown & bright blue	20.00	20.00
		b. 4c brown & ultramarine	225.00	160.00
		c. Diagonal half used as 2c on cover	750.00	225.00
		d. Inverted frame		550.00

831

DANISH WEST INDIES

8	A2	5c green & gray		32.50	20.00
		On cover			200.00
		Block of four		165.00	—
		Green & dark gray		32.50	20.00
		b. Inverted frame		32.50	20.00
9	"	7c lilac & orange		30.00	70.00
		On cover			900.00
		Block of four		150.00	—
		a. 7c lilac & yellow		70.00	80.00
		b. Inverted frame		60.00	90.00
10	"	10c blue & brown		32.50	20.00
		On cover			150.00
		Block of four		165.00	—
		Blue & black brown		32.50	20.00
		b. Period between "t" & "s" of "cents"		45.00	32.50
		c. Inverted frame		30.00	20.00
11	"	12c red lilac & yellow green		35.00	42.50
		On cover			750.00
		Block of four		175.00	—
		a. 12c lilac & deep green		80.00	65.00
12	"	14c lilac & green		625.00	750.00
		On cover			8500.00
		Block of four		4250.00	
		a. Inverted frame		†700.00	2,250.00
13	"	50c violet		120.00	140.00
		On cover			1800.00
		Block of four		600.00	—
		a. 50c gray violet		150.00	170.00

Issue dates: 1c, 3c, 4c, 14c, 7c, 1874; 5c, 10c, 1876; 12c, 1877; 50c, 1879. Colors of major numbers are generally those of the least expensive of two or more shades, and do not indicate the shade of the first printing.

Nos. 9 and 13 Surcharged in Black:

1 CENT
1887
a

14	A2 (a)	1c on 7c lilac & orange		75.00	100.00
		On cover			1200.00
		Block of four		450.00	—
		a. 1c on 7c lilac & yellow		120.00	140.00
		b. Double surcharge		250.00	300.00
		c. Inverted frame		110.00	120.00

10 CENTS
1895
b

15	A2 (b)	10c on 50c violet		30.00	40.00
		On cover			270.00
		Block of four		150.00	—

The "b" surcharge also exists on No. 5, with "10" found in two sizes. These are essays.

1896-1901
Perf. 13

16	A2	1c green & red violet ('98)		13.00	13.00
		On cover			135.00
		Block of four		65.00	—
		a. Normal frame		300.00	300.00
17	"	3c blue & lake ('98)		13.00	13.00
		On cover			135.00
		Block of four		65.00	—
		a. Normal frame		260.00	260.00
		White "wedge" flaw		50.00	50.00
18	"	4c bistre & dull blue ('01)		13.00	13.00
		On cover			135.00
		Block of four		65.00	—
		a. Diagonal half used as 2c on cover			40.00
		b. Inverted frame		60.00	60.00
		b. On cover			175.00
		As "a" and "b" on cover			200.00
19	"	5c green & gray		42.50	37.50
		On cover			325.00
		Block of four		225.00	—
		a. Normal frame		600.00	600.00
20	"	10c blue & brown ('01)		85.00	100.00
		On cover			1500.00
		Block of four		450.00	—
		a. Inverted frame		900.00	1400.00
		b. Period between "t" and "s" of "cents"		100.00	120.00

Two printings each of Nos. 18-19.

Arms
A5

1900

21	A5	1c light green		2.50	2.50
		On cover			52.50
		Block of four		11.00	12.50
22	"	5c light blue		15.00	15.00
		On cover			225.00
		Block of four		65.00	—

Nos. 6, 17 and 20 Surcharged in Black

2 CENTS
1902
c

1902			Perf. 14x13½		
23	A2	2c on 3c blue & carmine		450.00	500.00
		Block of four		2250.00	
		a. "2" in date with straight tail		475.00	525.00
		b. Normal frame		1250.00	—

Perf. 13

24	A2	2c on 3c blue & lake		10.00	12.00
		On cover			125.00
		Block of four		40.00	—
		a. "2" in date with straight tail		11.00	13.00
		b. Dated "1901"		400.00	450.00
		c. Normal frame		225.00	275.00
		d. Dark green surcharge		1400.00	
		e. As "d." & "a."		1500.00	
		f. As "d." & "c."			
		White "wedge" flaw		50.00	50.00
25	"	8c on 10c blue & brown		25.00	35.00
		On cover			200.00
		Block of four		100.00	—
		a. "2" with straight tail		27.50	37.50
		b. On No. 20b		35.00	45.00
		c. Inverted frame		325.00	350.00

Nos. 17 and 20 Surcharged in Black

8 Cents
1902
d

Perf. 13

27	A2	2c on 3c blue & lake		12.50	17.50
		On cover			200.00
		Block of four		50.00	—
		a. Normal frame		275.00	300.00
		White "wedge" flaw		52.50	52.50
28	"	8c on 10c blue & brown		11.00	11.00
		On cover			150.00
		Block of four		45.00	—
		a. On No. 20b		18.00	18.00
		b. Inverted frame		275.00	275.00

Wmk. 113

1903   Wmkd. Crown. (113)

29	A5	2c carmine		13.00	13.00
		On cover			125.00
		Block of four		52.50	—
30	"	8c brown		27.50	32.50
		On cover			325.00
		Block of four		120.00	—

King Christian IX
A8

DANISH WEST INDIES

1905 Typographed Perf. 12½

31	A8	5b green		7.50	4.00
		On cover			60.00
		Block of four		35.00	
32	"	10b red		7.50	4.00
		On cover			60.00
		Block of four		35.00	
33	"	20b green & blue		15.00	15.00
		On cover			160.00
		Block of four		65.00	
34	"	25b ultramarine		15.00	15.00
		On cover			120.00
		Block of four		65.00	
35	"	40b red & gray		12.50	12.50
		On cover			160.00
		Block of four		60.00	
36	"	50b yellow & gray		12.50	15.00
		On cover			225.00
		Block of four		60.00	

St. Thomas Harbor
A9
Frame Typographed, Center Engraved.

1905 Perf. 12 Wmkd. Two Crowns. (113)

37	A9	1fr green & blue		20.00	30.00
		On cover			275.00
		Block of four		85.00	
38	"	2fr orange red & brown		42.50	60.00
		On cover			425.00
		Block of four		180.00	
39	"	5fr yellow & brown		110.00	250.00
		On cover			550.00
		Block of four		475.00	

Nos. 18, 22 and 30
Surcharged in Black

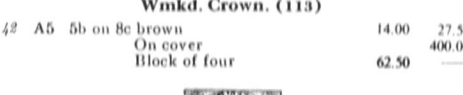

1905 Perf. 13 Wmkd. Crown. (112)

40	A2	5b on 4c bistre & dull blue		22.50	45.00
		On cover			400.00
		Block of four		100.00	
		a. Inverted frame		42.50	60.00
41	A5	5b on 5c light blue		14.00	27.50
		On cover			400.00
		Block of four		62.50	

Wmkd. Crown. (113)

42	A5	5b on 8c brown		14.00	27.50
		On cover			400.00
		Block of four		62.50	

King Frederik VIII
A10
Frame Typographed, Center Engraved.

1908 Perf. 13. Wmk. 113

43	A10	5b green		2.50	1.30
		On cover			40.00
		Block of four		12.50	
44	"	10b red		2.50	1.30
		On cover			45.00
		Block of four		12.50	
45	"	15b violet & brown		5.00	5.00
		On cover			90.00
		Block of four		25.00	
46	"	20b green & blue		37.50	20.00
		On cover			150.00
		Block of four		160.00	

47	A10	25b blue & dark blue		3.25	2.00
		On cover			40.00
		Block of four		14.00	
48	"	30b claret & slate		62.50	37.50
		On cover			300.00
		Block of four		275.00	160.00
49	"	40b vermilion & gray		6.50	8.00
		On cover			200.00
		Block of four		27.50	
50	"	50b yellow & brown		7.00	10.00
		On cover			200.00
		Block of four		30.00	

King Christian X
A11

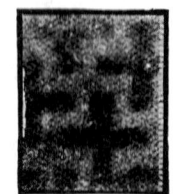
Wmk. 114

Frame Typographed, Center Engraved.
1915-17 Wmkd. Multiple Crosses. (114)
Perf. 14 x 14½.

51	A11	5b yellow green		3.00	6.00
		On cover			55.00
		Block of four		14.00	
52	"	10b red		3.00	52.50
		On cover			175.00
		Block of four		14.00	
53	"	15b lilac & red brown		3.00	52.50
		On cover			175.00
		Block of four		14.00	
54	"	20b green & blue		3.00	52.50
		On cover			250.00
		Block of four		14.00	
55	"	25b blue & dark blue		3.00	12.00
		On cover			85.00
		Block of four		14.00	
56	"	30b claret & black		3.00	52.50
		On cover			250.00
		Block of four		14.00	
57	"	40b orange & black		3.00	52.50
		On cover			250.00
		Block of four		14.00	
58	"	50b yellow & brown		3.00	52.50
		On cover			250.00
		Block of four		14.00	

Forged and favor cancellations exist.

POSTAGE DUE STAMPS.

Royal Cipher
"Christian Rex"
D1

Numeral
of Value
D2

Lithographed.

1902 Perf. 11½. Unwmkd.

J1	D1	1c dark blue		8.00	14.00
		Block of four		35.00	
J2	"	4c dark blue		12.50	17.50
		Block of four		55.00	
J3	"	6c dark blue		32.50	52.50
		Block of four		150.00	
J4	"	10c dark blue		25.00	35.00
		Block of four		110.00	

There are five types of each value. On the 4c they may be distinguished by differences in the figure "4"; on the other values differences are minute.

Used prices of Nos. J1-J8 are for canceled copies. Uncanceled examples without gum have probably been used. Price 60% of unused.
Excellent counterfeits of Nos. J1 to J4 exist.

DANISH WEST INDIES

1905-13			Perf. 13	
J5	D2	5b red & gray	6.50	8.00
		Block of four	30.00	—
J6	"	20b red & gray	14.00	20.00
		Block of four	60.00	—
J7	"	30b red & gray	8.50	13.00
		Block of four	37.50	—
J8	"	50b red & gray	12.50	18.00
		Block of four	55.00	—
		a. Perf. 14x14½ ('13)	20.00	80.00
		a. Block of four	100.00	
		b. Perf. 11½	275.00	

Nos. J5–J8 are known imperforate but were not regularly issued. Excellent counterfeits exist.

ENVELOPES.

E1

1877-78		On White Paper		
U1	E1	2c light blue ('78)	6.50	18.00
		Entire	25.00	80.00
		a. 2c ultramarine	20.00	100.00
		Entire	75.00	475.00
U2	"	3c orange	5.00	15.00
		Entire	20.00	65.00
		a. 3c red orange	5.00	15.00
		Entire	20.00	65.00

Three different Crown watermarks are found on entires of No. U1, four on entires of No. U2. Envelope watermarks do not show on cut squares.

POSTAL CARDS.

Prices are for entire cards.

Designs of Adhesive Stamps.

"BREV-KORT" at top.

1877		Inscription in Three Lines.		
UX1	A2	6c violet	25.00	275.00
1878-85		Inscription in Four Lines.		
UX2	A2	2c light blue (*8,800*)	25.00	50.00
UX3	"	3c carmine rose (*17,700*)	25.00	50.00
1888		Inscription in Five Lines.		
UX4	A2	2c light blue (*30,500*)	7.00	30.00
UX5	"	3c red (*26,500*)	10.00	40.00

Card UX5 Locally Surcharged with type "c"
but with date "1901."

1901				
UX6	A2	1c on 3c red (*2,000*)	60.00	175.00

1902
Card UX4 Locally Surcharged with type "c".

UX7	A2	1c on 2c light blue (*3,000*)	50.00	135.00

Card UX5 Surcharged similar to type "c"
but heavy letters.

1902				
UX8	A2	1c on 3c red (*7,175*)	10.00	55.00
1903				
UX9	A5	1c light green (*10,000*)	12.50	50.00
UX10	"	2c carmine (*10,000*)	18.00	110.00
1905				
UX11	A8	5b green (*16,000*)	12.00	30.00
UX12	"	10b red (*14,000*)	13.00	70.00
1907-08		Unwatermarked.		
UX13	A10	5b green ('08) (*30,750*)	13.00	30.00
UX14	"	10b red (*19,750*)	18.00	50.00
1913		Watermarked Wood-grain.		
UX15	A10	5b green (*10,000*)	150.00	300.00
UX16	"	10b red (*10,000*)	175.00	500.00
1915-16		Watermarked Wood-grain.		
UX17	A11	5b yellow green (*8,200*)	110.00	275.00
UX18	"	10b red ('16) (*2,000*)	185.00	550.00

PAID REPLY POSTAL CARDS.

Designs similar to Nos. UX2 and UX3
with added inscriptions in Danish and French:
Message Card—Four lines at lower left.
Reply Card—Fifth line centered, "Svar. Réponse."

1883				
UY1	A2	2c+2c light blue, unsevered (*2,600*)	30.00	125.00
		m. Message card, detached	10.00	50.00
		r. Reply card, detached	10.00	50.00
UY2	"	3c+3c carmine rose, unsevered	25.00	70.00
		m. Message card, detached	8.00	25.00
		r. Reply card, detached	8.00	25.00

Designs similar to Nos. UX4 and UX5
with added inscription in fifth line, centered in French:
Message Card—"Carte postale avec réponse payée."
Reply Card—"Carte postale-réponse."

1888-98				
UY3	A2	2c+2c light blue, unsevered (*26,000*)	18.50	100.00
		m. Message card, detached	6.00	35.00
		r. Reply card, detached	6.00	35.00
UY4	"	3c+3c carmine rose, unsevered (*5,000*)	30.00	85.00
		m. Message card, detached	10.00	30.00
		r. Reply card, detached	10.00	30.00

No. UY4 Locally Surcharged with type "c"
but with date "1901."

1902				
UY5	A2	1c on 3c+1c on 3c carmine rose, unsevered (*1,000*)	55.00	175.00
		m. Message card, detached	17.50	65.00
		r. Reply card, detached	17.50	65.00

No. UY4 Surcharged in Copenhagen with type
similar to "c" but heavy letters:

UY6	A2	1c on 3c+1c on 3c carmine rose, unsevered (*975*)	70.00	225.00
		m. Message card, detached	22.50	80.00
		r. Reply card, detached	22.50	80.00

Designs similar to Nos. UX9 and UX10
with added inscriptions in Danish and English.

1903				
UY7	A5	1c+1c light green, unsevered (*5,000*)	30.00	90.00
		m. Message card, detached	10.00	32.50
		r. Reply card, detached	10.00	32.50
UY8	"	2c+2c carmine, unsevered (*5,000*)	70.00	225.00
		m. Message card, detached	22.50	80.00
		r. Reply card, detached	22.50	80.00

Designs similar to Nos. UX11 and UX12
with added inscriptions.

1905				
UY9	A8	5b+5b green, unsevered (*5,000*)	30.00	70.00
		m. Message card, detached	10.00	25.00
		r. Reply card, detached	10.00	25.00
UY10	"	10b+10b red, unsevered (*4,000*)	50.00	100.00
		m. Message card	15.00	35.00
		r. Reply card, detached	15.00	35.00

Designs similar to Nos. UX13, UX14 and UX15
with added inscriptions.

1908		Unwatermarked.		
UY11	A10	5b+5b green, unsevered (*7,150*)	50.00	100.00
		m. Message card, detached	15.00	35.00
		r. Reply card, detached	15.00	35.00
UY12	"	10b+10b red, unsevered (*6,750*)	50.00	110.00
		m. Message card, detached	15.00	40.00
		r. Reply card, detached	15.00	40.00
1913		Watermarked Wood-grain		
UY13	A10	5b+5b green, unsevered (*5,000*)	800.00	
		m. Message card, detached		400.00
		r. Reply card, detached		400.00

The 10b + 10b red type A10 with wood-grain watermark was authorized and possibly printed, but no example is known.

GUAM

A FORMER Spanish island possession in the Pacific Ocean, one of the Mariana group, about 1,450 miles east of the Philippines. Captured June 20, 1898, and ceded to the United States by treaty after the Spanish-American War. Stamps overprinted "Guam" were used while the post office was under the jurisdiction of the Navy Department from July 7, 1899, until March 29, 1901, when a Postal Agent was appointed by the Post Office Department and the postal service passed under that Department's control. From this date on Guam was supplied with regular United States postage stamps, although the overprints remained in use for several more years. Population 9,000 (est. 1899).

100 CENTS=1 DOLLAR

United States Nos. 279, 267, 279c, 268, 280a, 281a, 282, 272, 282C, 283a, 284, 275, 275a, 276 and 276A

Overprinted **GUAM**

Wmkd. Double-lined USPS (191)

1899 *Perf. 12*

Black Overprint.

1	A87	1c deep green (*25,000*)		27.50	35.00
		On cover			200.00
		Block of four		125.00	200.00
		Margin strip of 3, Impt. & P ‡		140.00	
		Margin block of 6, Impt. & P ‡		450.00	
		a. Inverted overprint		—	
2	A88	2c carmine, type III (*105,000*)		25.00	35.00
		On cover			200.00
		Block of four		120.00	200.00
		Margin strip of 3, Impt. & P ‡		120.00	
		Margin block of 6, Impt. & P ‡		400.00	
		a. 2c rose carmine, type III		30.00	40.00
3	A89	3c purple (*5000*)		125.00	175.00
		On cover			400.00
		Block of four		550.00	850.00
		Margin strip of 3, Impt. & P ‡		550.00	
		Margin block of 6, Impt. & P ‡		1600.00	
4	A90	4c lilac brown (*5000*)		125.00	175.00
		On cover			450.00
		Block of four		550.00	850.00
		Margin strip of 3, Impt. & P ‡		550.00	
		Margin block of 6, Impt. & P ‡		1600.00	
		Extra frame line at top (Plate 793 R62)		—	
5	A91	5c blue (*20,000*)		35.00	45.00
		On cover			200.00
		Block of four		150.00	250.00
		Margin strip of 3, Impt. & P ‡		160.00	
		Margin block of 6, Impt. & P ‡		700.00	
6	A92	6c lake (*5000*)		125.00	175.00
		On cover			450.00
		Block of four		550.00	800.00
		Margin strip of 3, Impt. & P ‡		500.00	
		Margin block of 6, Impt. & P ‡		1600.00	
7	A93	8c violet brown (*5000*)		125.00	175.00
		On cover			450.00
		Block of four		550.00	850.00
		Margin strip of 3, Impt. & P ‡		550.00	
		Margin block of 6, Impt. & P ‡		1600.00	
8	A94	10c brown, type I (*10,000*)		55.00	70.00
		On cover			275.00
		Block of four		250.00	350.00
		Margin strip of 3, Impt. & P ‡		275.00	
		Margin block of 6, Impt. & P ‡		950.00	
9	"	10c brown, type II		5000.00	
10	A95	15c olive green (*5000*)		135.00	175.00
		On cover			900.00
		Block of four		600.00	900.00
		Margin strip of 3, Impt. & P ‡		600.00	
		Margin block of 6, Impt. & P ‡		2100.00	
11	A96	50c orange (*4000*)		250.00	350.00
		On cover			1250.00
		Block of four		1150.00	1750.00
		Margin strip of 3, Impt. & P ‡		1150.00	
		Margin block of 6, Impt. & P ‡		4000.00	
		a. 50c red orange		300.00	

Red Overprint.

12	A97	$1 black, type I (*3000*)		400.00	550.00
		On cover			2000.00
		Block of four		1850.00	2500.00
		Margin strip of 3, Impt. & P ‡		1850.00	
		Margin block of 6, Impt. & P ‡		7000.00	
13	"	$1 black, type II		3000.00	
		Block of four			

No. 13 exists only in the special printing.

Special Printing

In 1899 a special printing of all values Nos. 1 to 8, 10, 11, 12, and E1, was made for display at the Paris Exposition. Price: Nos. 1-8, 10, each $350; Nos. 11, E1, each $400; No. 12, $650.

Counterfeits of overprint exist.

SPECIAL DELIVERY STAMP.

Special Delivery Stamp of the United States No. E5

Overprinted diagonally in Red **GUAM**

Wmkd. Double-lined USPS (191)

1899 *Perf. 12.*

E1	SD3	10c blue (*5000*)		150.00	200.00
		On cover			600.00
		Block of four		650.00	
		Margin block of four, arrow		700.00	
		Margin strip of 3, Impt. & P ‡		750.00	
		Margin block of 6, Impt. & P ‡		4000.00	
		Dots in curved frame above messenger (Pl. 882)		275.00	

Counterfeits of overprint exist.

The special stamps for Guam were replaced by the regular issues of the United States.

GUAM GUARD MAIL.
LOCAL POSTAL SERVICE.

Inaugurated April 8, 1930, by Commander Willis W. Bradley, Jr., U.S.N., Governor of Guam, for the conveyance of mail between Agaña and the other smaller towns.

Philippines Nos. 290b and 291 Overprinted **GUAM GUARD MAIL**

1930, April 8 *Perf. 11* Unwmkd.

M1	A40	2c green (*2000*)		400.00	350.00
		On cover			500.00
		Block of four		1700.00	
M2	"	4c carmine (*3000*)		350.00	300.00
		On cover			500.00
		Block of four		1500.00	

Counterfeits of overprint exist.

Seal of Guam
A1

GUAM

1930, July   *Perf. 12*   Unwmkd.
Without Gum.

M3	A1	1c red & black	125.00	150.00
		On cover		300.00
		Block of four	550.00	
M4	"	2c black & red	125.00	150.00
		On cover		525.00
		Block of four	550.00	

Copies are often found showing parts of watermark "Cleveland Bond".

Philippines
Nos. 290b, 290 and 291
Overprinted in Black

GUAM GUARD MAIL

1930, August 10   *Perf. 11.*   Unwmkd.

M5	A40	2c green (20,000)	4.00	4.50
		On cover		75.00
		Block of four	17.50	
	a.	2c yellow green	3.75	4.00
M6	"	4c carmine (80,000)	75	2.75
		On cover		75.00
		Block of four	3.25	

Same Overprint in Red on Philippines
Nos. 290b, 291, 292, 293a, and 294

1930, December

M7	A40	2c green (50,000)	1.25	1.25
		On cover		50.00
		Block of four	5.25	
	a.	GRAUD (No. 63 in sheet) (500)	375.00	
	b.	MIAL (No. 84 in sheet) (500)	375.00	

M8	A40	4c carmine (50,000)	1.25	1.25
		On cover		50.00
		Block of four	5.25	
M9	"	6c deep violet (25,000)	3.50	4.00
		On cover		60.00
		Block of four	15.00	
M10	"	8c orange brown (25,000)	3.50	4.00
		On cover		60.00
		Block of four	15.00	
M11	"	10c deep blue (25,000)	3.50	4.00
		On cover		60.00
		Block of four	15.00	

The local postal service was discontinued April 8th, 1931, and replaced by the service of the United States Post Office Department.

SPECIMEN STAMPS.

1899   Overprinted Type E in Violet   *Specimen.*

1S	1c deep green	250.00
2S	2c carmine	250.00
3S	3c purple	250.00
4S	4c lilac brown	250.00
5S	5c blue	250.00
6S	6c lake	250.00
7S	8c violet brown	250.00
8S	10c brown, type I	250.00
10S	15c olive green	250.00
11S	50c orange	250.00
12S	$1 black, type I	500.00
13S	$1 black, type II	—

1899   **Special Delivery.**

E1S	10c blue	500.00

HAWAII
(hä·wī'ē)

UNTIL 1893, Hawaii was an independent kingdom. From 1893-1898 it was a republic. At the request of the inhabitants, Hawaii was annexed to the United States in 1898. Hawaiian stamps remained in use through June 13, 1900, and were replaced by U.S. stamps on June 14. In 1959 Hawaii became the 50th State of the Union. Hawaii consists of about 20 islands in the Pacific, about 2,000 miles southwest of San Francisco. The area is 6,434 square miles and the population was estimated at 150,000 in 1899. Honolulu is the capital.

100 CENTS = 1 DOLLAR.

Prices of early Hawaii stamps vary according to condition. Quotations for Nos. 5–18 are for fine copies. Very fine to superb specimens sell at much higher prices, and inferior or poor copies sell at reduced prices, depending on the condition of the individual specimen.

A1   A2   A3
        Typeset.
1851-52   *Imperf.*   Unwmkd.
       Pelure Paper.

1	A1	2c blue	350,000.00	250,000.00
		On cover		300,000.00
2	"	5c blue	35,000.00	15,000.00
		On cover		25,000.00
3	A2	13c blue	17,500.00	9000.00
		On cover		15,000.00
4	A3	13c blue	45,000.00	21,000.00
		On cover		27,500.00

Nos. 1-4 are known as the "Missionaries." Two varieties of each. Nos. 1-4, off cover, are almost invariably damaged.

King Kamehameha III
A4   A5
Printed in Sheets of 20 (4x5).
1853   Thick White Wove Paper   Engraved

5	A4	5c blue	650.00	450.00
		On cover		2250.00
		On cover with U. S. #17		12,000.00
		Line through "Honolulu"		
		(No. 2 in sheet)	1350.00	900.00
6	A5	13c dark red	325.00	350.00
		On cover		2500.00
		On cover with U.S. #17		7500.00
		On cover with #5 and U.S. #17		
		Pair	950.00	1200.00
		Block of four	2400.00	

A6
1857

7	A6	5c on 13c dark red	4500.00	5500.00
		On cover		10,000.00
		On cover with pair U. S. #7 and		
		U. S. #15		—
		On cover with U. S. #14		15,000.00
		On cover with U. S. #17		15,000.00

1857   Thin White Wove Paper

8	A4	5c blue	250.00	250.00
		On cover		1250.00
		On cover with U. S. #15 and #7		—
		On cover with U. S. #17		5000.00
		On cover with U. S. #26		—
		On cover with U. S. #36		5000.00
		On cover with U. S. #69		5500.00
		On cover with U. S. #76		—
		Pair	650.00	—
	a.	Double impression	2000.00	—
		Line through "Honolulu"		
		(No. 2 in sheet)	700.00	

1861   Thin Bluish Wove Paper.

9	A4	5c blue	110.00	110.00
		On cover		850.00
		On cover with U. S. #36		—
		On cover with U. S. #65 and #73		3500.00
		On cover with U. S. #68		4250.00
		On cover with U. S. #76		—
		Block of four	700.00	
	a.	Double impression		—
		Line through "Honolulu"		
		(No. 2 in sheet)	325.00	325.00

RE-ISSUE
1868   Ordinary White Wove Paper.

10	A4	5c blue		25.00
		Block of four		125.00
		Line through "Honolulu"		
		(No. 2 in sheet)		40.00
11	A5	13c dull rose		225.00
		Block of four		1100.00

Remainders of Nos. 10 and 11 were overprinted "SPECIMEN." See Nos. 108-118b.
Nos. 10 and 11 were never placed in use but copies (both with and without overprint) were sold at face value at the Honolulu post office.

REPRINTS (Official Imitations) 1889

5c. Originals have two small dots near the left side of the square in the upper right corner. These dots are missing in the reprints.
13c. The bottom of the 3 of 13 in the upper left corner is flattened in the originals and rounded in the reprints. The "t" of "Cts" on the left side is as tall as the "C" in the reprints, but shorter in the originals.

10R	A4	5c blue		50.00
11R	A5	13c orange red		200.00

On August 19, 1892, the remaining supply of reprints was overprinted in black "REPRINT." The reprints (both with and without overprint) were sold at face value. Quantities sold (including overprints) were 5c—3634 and 13c—1696. See Nos. 10R-S and 11R-S.

A7   Numerals of Value   A9
         A8

1859-62   Typeset from settings of 10 varieties.

12	A7	1c light blue, *bluish white*	2750.00	3000.00
		Pair		6250.00
	a.	"1 Ce" omitted	—	

HAWAII

13	A7	2c light blue, *bluish white*	2250.00	1250.00
		On cover		3500.00
		Block of four	10,000.00	
		a. 2c dark blue, *grayish white*	—	
		b. Comma after "Cents"	—	
14	"	2c black, *greenish blue* ('62)	3250.00	1250.00
		On cover		4000.00
		a. "2-Cents."	—	

1863

15	A7	1c black, *grayish*	225.00	275.00
		On cover		—
		Block of four	1100.00	
		a. Tête bêche pair	3500.00	
		b. "NTER"	—	
16	"	2c black, *grayish*	375.00	325.00
		On cover		2500.00
		Pair	—	
		a. "2" at top of rectangle	1800.00	1800.00
		b. Printed on both sides	—	
		c. "NTER"	1400.00	1400.00
		d. 2c black, *grayish white*	375.00	325.00
		e. Period omitted after "Cents"	—	
		f. Double impression	—	
		g. "tage."	—	
17	"	2c dark blue, *bluish*	3500.00	1600.00
		On cover		5000.00
		Pair	7500.00	
18	"	2c black, *blue gray*	700.00	1100.00
		On cover		4000.00
		Pair		3000.00
		Thick paper	—	

1864–65

19	A7	1c black	275.00	425.00
		Pair	650.00	
		Block of four	1500.00	
20	"	2c black	325.00	425.00
		On cover		1250.00
		Pair	800.00	
		Block of four	2250.00	
21	A8	5c blue, *blue* ('65)	275.00	275.00
		On cover with U. S. # 65		—
		On cover with U. S. # 76		5000.00
		Block of four	1400.00	
		a. Tête bêche pair	4500.00	
		b. 5c black, *grayish white*	—	
22	A9	5c blue, *blue* ('65)	225.00	250.00
		On cover		1100.00
		On cover with U. S. # 76		4500.00
		On cover with U. S. #63 and 76	—	
		Block of four	1100.00	
		a. Tête bêche pair	3500.00	
		b. 5c blue, *grayish white*	—	

1864

		Laid Paper		
23	A7	1c black	150.00	500.00
		On cover with U. S. # 76		—
		Block of four	675.00	
		a. "HA" instead of "HAWAIIAN"	1500.00	
		b. Tête bêche pair	3500.00	
24	"	2c black	150.00	500.00
		Block of four	750.00	
		a. "NTER"	700.00	
		b. "S" of "POSTAGE" omitted	700.00	
		c. Tête bêche pair	3500.00	

A10

King Kamehameha IV
A11

1865
Wove Paper

25	A10	1c dark blue	150.00	
		Block of four	750.00	
		Double impression	—	
		With inverted impression of No. 21 on face	—	
26	"	2c dark blue	125.00	
		Block of four	600.00	

Nos. 12 to 26 were typeset and were printed in sheets of 50 (5 settings of 10 varieties each). The sheets were cut into panes of 25 (5x5) before distribution to the post offices.

1861–63
Lithographed
Horizontally Laid Paper.

27	A11	2c pale rose	175.00	110.00
		On cover		550.00
		Pair	—	
		a. 2c carmine rose ('63)	600.00	500.00

Vertically Laid Paper.

28	A11	2c pale rose	175.00	110.00
		On cover		500.00
		Block of four	800.00	750.00
		a. 2c carmine rose ('63)	135.00	135.00
		a. Block of four	650.00	

1869
Engraved
Thin Wove Paper.

29	A11	2c red	50.00	—
		Block of four	250.00	

No. 29 is a re-issue. It was not issued for postal purposes although cancelled copies are known. It was sold only at the Honolulu post office, at first without overprint and later with overprint "CANCELLED." See No. 29S.

See note following No. 51.

Princess Victoria Kamamalu
A12

King Kamehameha IV
A13

King Kamehameha V
A14

Kamehameha V
A15

Mataio Kekuanaoa
A16

1864–71
Wove Paper   Perf. 12

30	A12	1c purple ('71)	7.50	6.00
		a. 1c violet	7.50	6.00
		On cover		125.00
		Block of four	40.00	
31	A13	2c rose vermilion	11.00	7.00
		a. 2c vermilion	11.00	7.00
		On cover		125.00
		On cover with U. S. #76		250.00
		Block of four	55.00	50.00
		b. Half used as 1c on cover	—	
32	A14	5c blue ('66)	50.00	19.00
		On cover		125.00
		On cover with any U. S. issues of 1861–67		1250.00
		On cover with U. S. #116		1500.00
		Block of four	225.00	100.00
33	A15	6c green ('71)	17.50	6.00
		a. 6c yellow green	17.50	6.00
		On cover		125.00
		On cover with U. S. #179		500.00
		Block of four	95.00	
34	A16	18c dull rose ('71)	85.00	14.00
		On cover		300.00
		Block of four	375.00	
		Without gum	17.50	
		Block of four without gum	85.00	

Half of No. 31 was used with a 5c stamp to make up the 6-cent rate to the United States.

No. 32 has traces of rectangular frame lines surrounding the design. Nos. 39 and 52C have no such frame lines.

King David Kalakaua
A17

Prince William Pitt Leleiohoku
A18

HAWAII

1875

35	A17	2c brown		6.00	2.25
		On cover			30.00
		Block of four		30.00	30.00
36	A18	12c black		40.00	20.00
		On cover			250.00
		Block of four		200.00	—

Princess Likelike
(Mrs. Archibald Cleghorn)
A19

King David Kalakaua
A20

Queen Kapiolani
A21

Statue of King Kamehameha I
A22

King William Lunalilo
A23

Queen Emma Kaleleonalani
A24

1882

37	A19	1c blue		4.00	6.00
		On cover			32.50
		Block of four		22.50	35.00
38	A17	2c lilac rose		90.00	30.00
		On cover			150.00
		Block of four		450.00	
		a. Half used as 1c on cover			1250.00
39	A14	5c ultramarine		12.00	2.25
		On cover			27.50
		Block of four		60.00	42.50
		a. Vert. pair, imperf. horiz.		3500.00	
40	A20	10c black		22.50	15.00
		On cover			125.00
		Block of four		100.00	100.00
41	A21	15c red brown		40.00	22.50
		On cover			175.00
		Block of four		200.00	175.00

1883-86

42	A19	1c green		2.25	1.50
		On cover			25.00
		Block of four		11.00	11.00
43	A17	2c rose ('86)		3.50	.75
		On cover			25.00
		Block of four		17.50	10.00
44	A20	10c red brown ('84)		17.50	7.00
		On cover			110.00
		Block of four		85.00	65.00
45	"	10c vermilion		20.00	12.50
		On cover			125.00
		Block of four		100.00	75.00
46	A18	12c red lilac		60.00	30.00
		On cover			300.00
		Block of four		300.00	200.00
47	A22	25c dark violet		85.00	42.50
		On cover			300.00
		Block of four		400.00	275.00
48	A23	50c red		135.00	75.00
		On cover			500.00
		Block of four		700.00	
49	A24	$1 rose red		200.00	85.00
		On cover			600.00
		Block of four		950.00	
		Maltese cross cancellation			25.00

Reproduction and Reprint
Yellowish Wove Paper.

1886-89 *Imperf.* Engraved

50	A11	2c orange vermilion		150.00	
		Block of four		750.00	

51	A11	2c carmine ('89)		25.00	
		Block of four		110.00	

In 1885 the Postmaster General wished to have on sale complete sets of Hawaii's portrait stamps, but was unable to find either the stone from which Nos. 27 and 28, or the plate from which No. 29 was printed. He therefore sent a copy of No. 29 to the American Bank Note Company, with an order to engrave a new plate like it and print 10,000 stamps therefrom, of which 5000 were overprinted "SPECIMEN" in blue.

The original No. 29 was printed in sheets of fifteen (5x3), but the plate of these "Official Imitations" was made up of fifty stamps (10x5). Later, in 1887, the original die for No. 29 was discovered, and, after retouching, a new plate was made and 37,500 stamps were printed (No. 51). These, like the originals, were printed in sheets of fifteen. They were delivered during 1889 and 1890. In 1892 all remaining unsold in the Post Office were overprinted "Reprint".

No. 29 is red in color, and printed on very thin white wove paper. No. 50 is orange vermilion in color, on medium, white to buff paper. In No. 50 the vertical line on the left side of the portrait touches the horizontal line over the label "Elua Keneta", while in the other two varieties, Nos. 29 and 51, it does not touch the horizontal line by half a millimeter. In No. 51 there are three parallel lines on the left side of the King's nose, while in No. 29 and No. 50 there are no such lines. No. 51 is carmine in color and printed on thick, yellowish to buff, wove paper.

It is claimed that both Nos. 50 and 51 were available for postage, although not made to fill a postal requirement. They exist with favor cancellation. See Nos. 50S–51S.

Queen Liliuokalani
A25

1890-91 *Perf. 12*

52	A25	2c dull violet, *Nov. 8, 1891*		6.50	1.25
		On cover			25.00
		Block of four		27.50	9.00
		a. Vert. pair, imperf. horiz.		2750.00	
52C	A14	5c deep indigo		110.00	75.00
		On cover			275.00
		Block of four		475.00	

Provisional GOVT. 1893

Stamps of 1864-1891
Overprinted in Red

1893

53	A12	1c purple		4.00	3.50
		On cover			35.00
		Block of four		20.00	20.00
		a. "189" instead of "1893"		200.00	
		b. No period after "GOVT"		35.00	
		c. Double overprint		300.00	
54	A19	1c blue		4.00	5.00
		On cover			35.00
		Block of four		20.00	30.00
		a. Double overprint		175.00	
		b. No period after "GOVT"		35.00	
55	"	1c green		1.50	2.00
		On cover			25.00
		Block of four		7.50	11.00
		a. Pair, one without overprint		1000.00	
		b. Double overprint		400.00	150.00
56	A17	2c brown		5.00	10.00
		On cover			60.00
		Block of four		25.00	70.00
		a. No period after "GOVT"		75.00	
		b. Double overprint		—	
57	A25	2c dull violet		1.50	1.25
		On cover			25.00
		Block of four		6.50	6.50
		a. Inverted overprint		900.00	900.00
		b. Double overprint		300.00	200.00
		c. "18 3" instead of "1893"		100.00	70.00
58	A14	5c deep indigo		9.00	15.00
		On cover			100.00
		Block of four		45.00	85.00
		a. No period after "GOVT"		85.00	
		b. Double overprint		1250.00	

840   HAWAII

59	A14	5c ultramarine	5.00	2.50
		On cover		40.00
		Block of four	25.00	20.00
		a. Inverted overprint	850.00	650.00
		b. Double overprint	1100.00	
60	A15	6c green	10.00	15.00
		On cover		135.00
		Block of four	50.00	85.00
		a. Double overprint	650.00	
61	A20	10c black	7.00	8.00
		On cover		125.00
		Block of four	35.00	45.00
		a. Double overprint	800.00	600.00
61B	"	10c red brown	16,500.00	17,500.00
		Block of four		
		Strip of five, plate imprint	—	
62	A18	12c black	7.50	10.00
		On cover		125.00
		Block of four	40.00	65.00
		a. Double overprint	700.00	
63	"	12c red lilac	125.00	150.00
		On cover		450.00
		Block of four	750.00	900.00
64	A22	25c dark violet	20.00	20.00
		On cover		175.00
		Block of four	100.00	100.00
		a. No period after "GOVT"	165.00	
		b. Double overprint	1000.00	

Same Overprint in Black

65	A13	2c rose vermilion	50.00	50.00
		On cover		250.00
		Block of four	250.00	250.00
		a. No period after "GOVT"	175.00	150.00
66	A17	2c rose	1.25	1.75
		On cover		25.00
		Block of four	6.50	8.50
		a. Double overprint	1100.00	
		b. No period after "GOVT"	35.00	25.00
66C	A15	6c green	16,500.00	—
		On cover	—	
		Block of four	—	
67	A20	10c vermilion	11.00	17.50
		On cover		125.00
		Block of four	60.00	100.00
		a. Double overprint	1100.00	
68	"	10c red brown	6.00	9.00
		On cover		100.00
		Block of four	30.00	55.00
		a. Double overprint	—	
69	A18	12c red lilac	225.00	250.00
		On cover		900.00
		Block of four	1000.00	1200.00
70	A21	15c red brown	17.50	25.00
		On cover		185.00
		Block of four	95.00	125.00
		a. Double overprint	600.00	
71	A16	18c dull rose	22.50	30.00
		On cover		225.00
		Block of four	110.00	150.00
		a. Double overprint	175.00	
		b. Pair, one without overprint	850.00	
		c. No period after "GOVT"	100.00	100.00
72	A23	50c red	55.00	75.00
		On cover		600.00
		Block of four	250.00	400.00
		a. Double overprint	650.00	
		b. No period after "GOVT"	225.00	
73	A24	$1 rose red	100.00	130.00
		On cover		750.00
		Block of four	450.00	700.00
		a. No period after "GOVT"	350.00	450.00

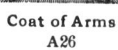

Coat of Arms   View of Honolulu
A26   A27

Statue of King   Star
Kamehameha I   and Palms
A28   A29

S. S. "Arawa"
A30

President Sanford   Statue of King
Ballard Dole   Kamehameha I
A31   A32

1894

74	A26	1c yellow	1.85	1.25
		On cover		25.00
75	A27	2c brown	2.00	60
		On cover		25.00
		Block of four	9.00	7.00
		"Flying goose" flaw (48 LR II)	275.00	250.00
		Double transfer		
76	A28	5c rose lake	3.75	1.50
		On cover		25.00
		Block of four	18.50	15.00
77	A29	10c yellow green	5.00	4.50
		On cover		45.00
		Block of four	25.00	25.00
78	A30	12c blue	10.00	10.00
		On cover		125.00
		Block of four	45.00	—
79	A31	25c deep blue	10.00	10.00
		On cover		100.00

Numerous double transfers exist on Nos. 75 and 81.

1899

80	A26	1c dark green	1.50	1.25
		On cover		25.00
		Block of four	7.00	7.00
81	A27	2c rose	1.35	1.00
		On cover		20.00
		Double transfer	—	—
		a. 2c salmon	1.50	1.25
		b. Vert. pair, imperf. horiz.	2250.00	
		"Flying goose" flaw (48 LR II)	275.00	250.00
82	A32	5c blue	5.00	3.00
		On cover		25.00
		Block of four	25.00	20.00

OFFICIAL STAMPS.

Lorrin Andrews Thurston
O1
Engraved.

1896   *Perf. 12*   Unwmkd.

O1	O1	2c green	27.50	17.50
		On cover		200.00
		Block of four	120.00	

HAWAII 841

O2	O1	5c black brown	27.50	17.50
		On cover		200.00
		Block of four	120.00	
O3	"	6c deep ultramarine	27.50	17.50
		On cover		200.00
		Block of four	120.00	
O4	"	10c bright rose	27.50	17.50
		On cover		200.00
		Block of four	120.00	
O5	"	12c orange	27.50	17.50
		On cover		200.00
		Block of four	120.00	
O6	"	25c gray violet	27.50	17.50
		On cover		200.00
		Block of four	120.00	

ENVELOPES.

All printed by American Bank Note Co., N.Y.

View of Honolulu Harbor
E1

Envelopes of White Paper, Outside and Inside.

1884

U1	E1	1c light green (*109,000*)	1.50	1.50
		Entire	6.00	15.00
		a. 1c green (*10,000*)	2.00	2.00
		Entire	17.50	27.50
U2	"	2c carmine (*386,000 including U2a, U2b*)	1.50	1.50
		Entire	6.00	17.50
		a. 2c red	1.50	1.50
		Entire	6.00	17.50
		b. 2c rose	1.50	1.50
		Entire	6.00	17.50
		c. 2c pale pink (*5,000*)	6.00	6.00
		Entire	35.00	60.00
U3	"	4c red (*18,000*)	9.00	11.00
		Entire	45.00	65.00
U4	"	5c blue (*90,775*)	5.00	5.00
		Entire	15.00	30.00
U5	"	10c black (*3,500 plus*)	17.50	15.00
		Entire	75.00	100.00

Envelopes White Outside, Blue Inside.

U6	E1	2c rose	125.00	125.00
		Entire	550.00	750.00
U7	"	4c red	125.00	125.00
		Entire	500.00	
U8	"	5c blue	125.00	125.00
		Entire	500.00	600.00
U9	"	10c black	285.00	285.00
		Entire	700.00	

Nos. U1, U2, U4 & U5 Overprinted Locally,
"Provisional Government 1893" in Red or Black

1893

U10	E1	1c light green (R) (*16,000*)	2.50	3.00
		Entire	7.50	20.00
		a. Double overprint		
		Entire	900.00	
U11	"	2c carmine (Bk) (*37,000*)	1.25	1.50
		Entire	6.00	15.00
		a. Double overprint		
		Entire	600.00	
		b. Double overprint, one inverted entire	800.00	
U12	"	5c blue (R) (*34,891*)	2.50	3.00
		Entire	12.00	15.00
		a. Double overprint, entire	550.00	
U13	E1	10c black (R) (*17,707 incl. No. U14*)	7.00	9.00
		Entire	25.00	75.00
		a. Double overprint, entire	800.00	600.00
		Envelope U9 with same overprint.		
U14	E1	10c black (R)	175.00	—
		Entire	550.00	—

SPECIAL DELIVERY ENVELOPE.
Price is for Entire.

Envelope U5 with added inscription
"Special Despatch Letter" etc. in red at top left corner

1885

UE1	E1	10c black, white inside (*2,000*)	250.00

Envelope UE1 was prepared for use but never issued for postal purposes. Favor cancellations exist.

POSTAL CARDS.
All printed by American Bank Note Co., N.Y.
Prices are for Entires.

Queen Liliuokalani
PC1

View of Diamond Head
PC2

Royal Emblems
PC3

			Engraved	
1882-92				
UX1	PC1	1c red on buff (*125,000*)	45.00	60.00
UX2	PC2	2c black on white (*45,000*)	70.00	80.00
		a. Lithographed ('92)	150.00	
UX3	PC3	3c blue green on white (*21,426*)	100.00	110.00

HAWAII

1889			Lithographed	
UX4	PC1	1c red on flesh (*171,240*)	40.00	50.00

Cards **UX4, UX2a** and **UX3** overprinted locally "Provisional Government 1893" in red or black.

1893

UX5	PC1	1c red on flesh (Bk) (*28,760*)	55.00	80.00
		a. Double overprint	1500.00	
UX6	PC2	2c black on white (R) (*10,000*)	75.00	90.00
UX7	PC3	3c blue green on white (R) (*8,574*)	100.00	110.00
		a. Double ovpt.	1000.00	

Iolani Palace
PC4

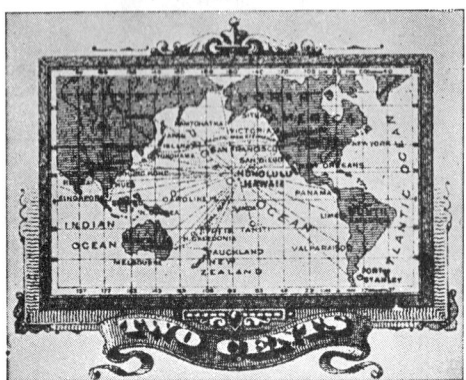

Map of Pacific Ocean, Mercator's Projection
PC5

1894-97			Lithographed	
		Border Frame 131½x72½mm.		
UX8	PC4	1c red on flesh (*100,000*)	30.00	37.50
		a. Border frame 132½x74mm. ('97) (*200,000*)	27.50	37.50
UX9	PC5	2c green on white (*60,000*)	60.00	75.00
		a. Border frame 132½x74mm. ('97) (*190,000*)	55.00	75.00

PAID REPLY POSTAL CARDS.

Double cards, same designs as postal cards with added inscriptions on reply cards.

1883			Lithographed	
UY1	PC1	1c+1c purple on buff, unsevered (*5,000*)	250.00	300.00
		m. Message card, detached	30.00	40.00
		r. Reply card, detached	30.00	40.00
UY2	PC2	2c+2c dark blue on white, unsevered (*5,000*)	300.00	375.00
		m. Message card, detached	55.00	65.00
		r. Reply card, detached	55.00	65.00
1889				
UY3	PC1	1c+1c gray violet on flesh, unsevered (*5,000*)	250.00	300.00
		m. Message card, detached	30.00	40.00
		r. Reply card, detached	30.00	40.00
UY4	PC2	2c+2c sapphire on white, unsevered (*5,000*)	250.00	300.00
		m. Message card, detached	30.00	40.00
		r. Reply card, detached	30.00	40.00

REVENUE STAMPS

R1   R2

R3

R4   R5   R6

Printed by the American Bank Note Co.

Sheets of 70.

Engraved

1877		*Rouletted 8*		Unwmkd.
R1	R1	25c green (*160,000*)	7.50	7.50
R2	R2	50c yellow orange (*190,000*)	7.50	7.50
R3	R3	$1 black (*580,000*)	12.50	5.00
		a. $1 gray	12.50	5.00

Denominations Typographed

R4	R4	$5 vermilion & violet blue (*21,000*)	25.00	25.00
R5	R5	$10 reddish brown & green (*14,000*)	50.00	25.00
R6	R6	$50 slate blue & carmine (*3,500*)	250.00	250.00

HAWAII

REPUBLIC OF TWENTY CENTS HAWAII

No. R1 Surcharged in Black or Gold

TWENTY CENTS
a

TWENTY CENTS
b

1893-94

R7	R1	(a) 20c on 25c green	10.00	10.00
		a. Inverted surcharge	110.00	110.00
R8	"	(b) 20c on 25c green (G)	30.00	30.00
		a. Double surcharge		
		b. Double surch., one black—	—	

R7

Kamehameha I
R8

Sheets of 50. Lithographed Perf. 14

1894

R9	R7	20c red (10,000)	125.00	125.00
		a. Imperf. (25,000)	125.00	125.00
R10	"	25c violet brown	175.00	175.00
		a. Imperf.	175.00	175.00

Printed by the American Bank Note Co.
Sheets of 100.

1897 Engraved Perf. 12

R11	R8	$1 dark blue (60,000)	7.00	4.00

No. R6 Inscribed "Territory of Hawaii"

1901 Engraved Rouletted 8

R12	R6	$50 slate blue & carmine (7,000)	37.50	—

Types of 1877
Printed by the American Bank Note Co.
Sheets of 70

1910-13 Engraved Perf. 12

R13	R2	50c yellow orange ('13) (70,000)	12.50	—
R14	R3	$1 black ('13) (35,000)	15.00	—
R15	R4	$5 vermilion & violet blue (14,000)	27.50	—
R16	R5	$10 reddish brown & green (14,000)	27.50	—

PROOFS.

		LARGE DIE (1)	PLATE (3) India
1853			
5TC	5c black on wove		
6TC	13c black on wove		
1868			
10TC	5c orange red	600.00	
11TC	13c orange red	600.00	400.00
1861-63			
27TC	2c black		550.00
1864-71			
30P	1c purple	550.00	125.00
	Block of four		550.00
31P	2c rose vermilion	550.00	125.00
	Block of four		
32P	5c blue	550.00	125.00
32TC	5c black	550.00	
"	5c dark red		150.00
"	5c orange red		150.00
"	5c orange		150.00
32TC	5c red brown		150.00
"	5c green		150.00
"	Block of four	—	
"	5c dark violet		150.00
33P	6c green	550.00	125.00
34P	18c dull rose	550.00	125.00
	Block of four		125.00
34TC	18c orange red	550.00	550.00
34TC	18c dark orange	550.00	
1875			
35P	2c brown	550.00	125.00
	Block of four		550.00
35TC	2c black	550.00	
36P	12c black	550.00	125.00
36TC	12c violet blue	550.00	
1882			
37P	1c blue		125.00
	Block of four		550.00
37TC	1c black	550.00	
39P	5c ultramarine	475.00	125.00
40P	10c black	475.00	125.00
	Block of four		475.00
41P	15c red brown		125.00
1883-86			
42P	1c green		75.00
			325.00
43P	2c rose		100.00
	Block of four		400.00
47P	25c dark violet	450.00	100.00
48P	50c red	450.00	100.00
49P	$1 rose red		100.00
	Block of four		400.00
49TC	$1 black		150.00
49TC	$1 orange red	450.00	
1886-89			
50P	2c orange vermilion	550.00	125.00
51P	2c carmine	550.00	
1890-91			
52P	2c dull violet	475.00	100.00
52C-P	5c deep indigo		100.00
1894			
74P	1c yellow	450.00	100.00
75P	2c brown	450.00	100.00
75TC	2c dark green	550.00	
76P	5c rose lake	500.00	100.00
77P	10c yellow green	500.00	100.00
	Block of four		400.00
78P	12c blue	500.00	125.00
79P	25c deep blue	500.00	100.00
1899			
82P	5c blue		150.00
1896	Official.		
O1P	2c green	300.00	100.00
O2P	5c black brown	300.00	100.00
O3P	6c deep ultramarine	300.00	100.00
O4P	10c bright rose	300.00	100.00
	Block of four		—
O4TC	10c black	300.00	
O5P	12c orange	300.00	100.00
O5TC	12c black	300.00	
O6P	25c gray violet	300.00	100.00
O6TC	25c black	300.00	

SPECIMEN STAMPS.

1868 Overprinted SPECIMEN. in Black or Red

10S	5c blue (R)	20.00
	Line through "Honolulu"	45.00
11Sa	13c dull rose	20.00

Overprinted SPECIMEN. in Black

11Sb	13c dull rose	50.00
	Dbl. ovpt., one as #11Sa, one as #11Sb	1000.00
	Period omitted	80.00

1889 Overprinted REPRINT in Black

10R-S	5c blue	45.00
11R-S	13c orange red	80.00

1869 Overprinted CANCELLED. in Black

29S	2c red	50.00

1886 Overprinted SPECIMEN. in Blue

50S	2c orange vermilion	60.00

1889 Overprinted REPRINT in Black

51S	2c carmine	25.00

MARSHALL ISLANDS

A group of 32 atolls and more than 867 reefs in the west Pacific Ocean, about 2,500 miles southeast of Tokyo. The islands, comprised of two major chains, the Ralik chain in the west, and the Ratak chain in the east, were annexed by Germany in 1885. Stamps issued under German Dominion (Nos. 1-27) are listed in Vol. III of the Scott Standard Postage Stamp Catalogue. Japan seized the islands in 1914. They were taken by the U.S. in World War II and became part of the U.S. Trust Territory of the Pacific in 1947. By agreement with the U.S. Postal Service, the islands began issuing their own stamps in 1984, with the U.S.P.S. continuing to carry the mail to and from the islands. Islands and atolls include Kwajalein, Jaluit and Majuro, site of the government headquarters. Land area: 70 sq. mi. Population: 31,042 (1980).

100 CENTS = 1 DOLLAR

Inauguration of Postal Service — A5

1984, May 2		Lithographed	Perf 14 x 13½	
31	A5	20c Outrigger canoe	40	40
32	A5	20c Fishnet	40	40
33	A5	20c Bavigational stick chart	40	40
34	A5	20c Islet	40	40
		a. Block of 4, #31-34	1.60	1.60

Maps and Navigational Instruments—A6

1984-85		Lithographed	Perf. 15 x 14	
35	A6	1c Mill Atoll, Astrolabe, *June 12*	5	5
36	A6	3c Likiep, Azimuth Compass, *June 12*	6	6
37	A6	5c Ebon, 16th Century Compass, *June 12*	10	10
38	A6	10c Jaluit, Anchor Buoys, *June 12*	20	20
39	A6	13c Ailinginae, nocturnal, *Dec. 19*	26	26
		a. Booklet pane of 10	2.60	2.60
40	A6	14c Wotho Atoll, navigational stick chart, *June 5, 1985*	28	28
		a. Booklet pane of 10	2.80	2.80
41	A6	20c Kwajalein and Ebeye, stick chart, *Dec. 19*	40	40
		a. Booklet pane of 10	4.00	4.00
		b. Booklet pane of 10 (5 #39, 5 #41)	3.30	3.30
42	A6	22c Enewetak, 18th century lodestone, storage case, *June 5, 1985*	44	44
		a. Blkt. pane of 10	4.40	4.40
		b. Blkt. pane of 5 each, 14c, 22c	3.60	3.60
43	A6	28c Ailinglaplap, printed compass, *Dec. 19*	56	56
44	A6	30c Majuro, Wapeepe Navigational stick chart, *June 12*	60	60
45	A6	33c Namu, stick chart, *June 5, 1985*	66	66
46	A6	37c Rongelap, quadrant, *Dec. 19*	74	74
47	A6	39c Taka, map compass, 16 century sea chart	78	78
48	A6	44c Ujelang, chronograph, *June 5, 1985*	88	88
49	A6	50c Maloelap and Aur, nocturlabe, *June 5, 1985*	1.00	1.00
49A	A6	$1 Arno, 16th Century Sector Compass	2.00	2.00
		Booklet stamps perforated on 3 sides.		

See Nos. 107-108.

No. 7—A7

Depicted stamps issued under German Dominion, Philatelic Salon, 19th U.P.U. Congress, Hamburg, June 19-26.

1984, June 19		Lithographed	Perf. 14½ x 15	
50	A7	40c shown	80	80
51	A7	40c No. 13	80	80
52	A7	40c No. 4	80	80
53	A7	40c No. 25	80	80
		a. Block of 4, #50-53	3.20	3.20

Dolphins — A8

1984, Sept. 5		Lithographed	Perf. 14	
54	A8	20c Delphinius delphis	40	40
55	A8	20c Grampus griseus	40	40
56	A8	20c Stenella attenuata	40	40
57	A8	20c Tursiops truncatus	40	40
		a. Block of 4, #54-57	1.60	1.60

MARSHALL ISLANDS

Christmas 1984 — A9

Design: The three kings following the star to Bethlehem.

1984, Nov. 7		**Lithographed**		*Perf. 14*	
58		Strip of 4		1.60	1.60
a.-d.	A9	20c Any single		40	40

Printed in sheets of 16, strips in continuous design; background inscribed with text from the Marshallese New Testament.

Marshallese Constitution, 5th Anniv. — A10

Historic political figures, period sailing vessels, flags of the Marshalls and: No. 59, World War II Germany. No. 60, U.S. No. 61, Japan. No. 62, United Nations.

1984, Dec. 19		**Lithographed**		*Perf. 14*	
59	A10	20c Island chief		40	40
60	A10	20c Pres. Amata Kabua		40	40
61	A10	20c U.S. Fleet Adm. Nimitz		40	40
62	A10	20c Sec.-Gen. Trygve H. Lie		40	40
		a. Block of 4, #59-62		1.60	1.60

Audubon Birth Bicentenary — A11

Illustrations by artist/naturalist J.J. Audubon (1785-1852).

1985, Feb. 15		**Lithographed**		*Perf. 14*	
63	A11	22c Forked-tailed petrel		44	44
64	A11	22c Pectoral sandpiper		44	44
		a. Pair, #63-64		90	90

See Nos. C1-C2.

Sea Shells — A12

1985, Apr. 17		**Lithographed**		*Perf. 14*	
65	A12	22c Vymatium lotorium		44	44
66	A12	22c Chicoreus cornucervi		44	44
67	A12	22c Strombus aurisdanae		44	44
68	A12	22c Turbo marmoratus		44	44
69	A12	22c Chicoreus palmarosae		44	44
		a. Strip of 5, #65-69		2.20	2.20

See Nos. 119-123.

Decade for Women — A13

Marshallese women and: No. 70, Native drum. No. 71, Palm branches. No. 72, Pounding stone. No. 73, Ak bird.

1985, June 5		**Lithographed**		*Perf. 14*	
70	A13	22c multi		44	44
71	A13	22c multi		44	44
72	A13	22c multi		44	44
73	A13	22c multi		44	44
		a. Block of 4, #70-73		1.80	1.80

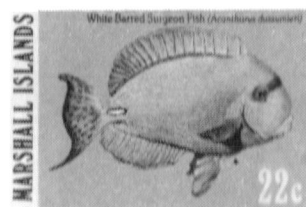

Reef and Lagoon Fish — A14

1985, July 15		**Lithographed**		*Perf. 14*	
74	A14	22c Acanthurus dussumieri		44	44
75	A14	22c Adioryx caudimaculatus		44	44
76	A14	22c Ostracion meleacaris		44	44
77	A14	22c Chaetodon ephippium		44	44
		a. Block of 4, #74-77		1.80	1.80

Intl. Youth Year — A15

IYY and Alele Nautical Museum emblems and: No. 78, Marshallese youths and Peace Corps volunteers playing basketball. No. 79, Legend-teller reciting oral history, girl listening to recording. No. 80, Islander explaining navigational stick charts. No. 81, Jabwa stick dance.

1985, Aug. 31		Lithographed	Perf. 14	
78	A15	22c multi	44	44
79	A15	22c multi	44	44
80	A15	22c multi	44	44
81	A15	22c multi	44	44
		a. Block of 4, #78-81	1.80	1.80

1856 American Board of Commissions Stock Certificate for Foreign Missions — A16

Missionary ship Morning Star I: 22c, Launch, Jothan Stetson Shipyard, Chelsea, MA, Aug. 7, 1857. 33c, First voyage, Honolulu to the Marshalls, 1857. 44c, Marshall islanders pulling Morning Star I into Ebon Lagoon, 1857.

1985, Oct. 21		Litho.	Perf. 14	
82	A16	14c multi	28	28
83	A16	22c multi	44	44
84	A16	33c multi	66	66
85	A16	44c multi	88	88

Christmas 1985.

U.S. Space Shuttle, Astro Telescope, Halley's Comet — A17

Comet tail and research spacecraft: No. 87, Planet A Space Probe, Japan. No. 88, Giotto spacecraft, European Space Agency. No. 89, INTERCOSMOS Project Vega spacecraft, Russia, France, etc. No. 90, U.S. naval tracking ship, NASA observational aircraft, cameo portrait of Sir Edmond Halley (1656-1742), astronomer. Se-tenant in continuous design.

1985, Nov. 21				
86	A17	22c multi	44	44
87	A17	22c multi	44	44
88	A17	22c multi	44	44
89	A17	22c multi	44	44
90	A17	22c multi	44	44
		a. Strip of 5, #86-90	2.25	2.25

Medicinal Plants — A18

1985, Dec. 31		Litho.	Perf. 14	
91	A18	22c Sida fallax	44	44
92	A18	22c Scaevola frutescens	44	44
93	A18	22c Guettarda speciosa	44	44
94	A18	22c Cassytha filiformis	44	44
		a. Block of 4, #91-94	1.80	1.80

Maps Type of 1984

1986, Mar. 7			Perf. 15x14	
107	A6	$2 Wotje and Erikub, terrestrial globe, 1571	4.00	4.00
108	A6	$5 Bikini, Stick chart	10.00	10.00

Marine Invertebrates — A19

1986, Mar. 31		Litho.	Perf. 14½x14	
110	A19	14c Triton's trumpet	28	28
111	A19	14c Giant clam	28	28
112	A19	14c Small giant clam	28	28
113	A19	14c Coconut crab	28	28
		a. Block of 4, #110-113	1.15	1.15

Souvenir Sheet

AMERIPEX '86, Chicago, May 22-June 1 — A20

1986, May 22		Litho.	Perf. 14	
114	A20	$1 Douglas C-54 Globester	2.00	2.00

1st Around-the-world scheduled flight, 40th anniv. No. 114 has multicolored margin continuing the design and picturing US Air Transport Command Base, Kwajalein Atoll and souvenir card. Size: 89x63mm.

See Nos. C3-C6.

MARSHALL ISLANDS

Operation Crossroads, Atomic Bomb Tests 40th Anniv. — A21

Designs: No. 115, King Juda, Bikinians sailing tibinal canoe. No. 116, USS Sumner, amphibious DUKW, advance landing. No. 117, Evacuating Bikinians. No. 118, Land reclamation, 1986.

1986, July 1		Litho.		Perf. 14	
115	A21	22c multi		44	44
116	A21	22c multi		44	44
117	A21	22c multi		44	44
118	A21	22c multi		44	44
		a. Block of 4, #115-118		1.80	1.80

See No. C7.

Seashells Type of 1985

1986, Aug. 1		Litho.		Perf. 14	
119	A12	22c Ramose murex		44	44
120	A12	22c Orange spider		44	44
121	A12	22c Red-mouth frog shell		44	44
122	A12	22c Laciniate conch		44	44
123	A12	22c Giant frog shell		44	44
		a. Strip of 5, #119-123		2.20	2.20

Game Fish — A22

1986, Sept. 10		Litho.			
124	A22	22c Blue marlin		44	44
125	A22	22c Wahoo		44	44
126	A22	22c Dolphin fish		44	44
127	A22	22c Yellowfin tuna		44	44
		a. Block of 4, #124-127		1.80	1.80

AIR POST STAMPS

Audubon Type of 1985

1985, Feb. 15		Lithographed		Perf. 14	
C1	A11	44c Booby gannet, vert.		88	88
C2	A11	44c Esquimaux curlew, vert.		88	88
		a. Pair #C1-C2		1.80	1.80

AMERIPEX Type of 1986

Designs: No. C3, Consolidated PBY-5A Catalina Amphibian. No. C4, Grumman SA-16 Albatross. No. C5, McDonnell Douglas DC-6B Super Cloudmaster. No. C6, Boeing 727-100.

1986, May 22		Litho.		Perf. 14	
C3	A20	44c multi		88	88
C4	A20	44c multi		88	88
C5	A20	44c multi		88	88
C6	A20	44c multi		88	88
		a. Block of 4, #C3-C6		3.60	3.60

Operation Crossroads Type of 1986
Souvenir Sheet

1986, July 1		Litho.		Perf. 14	
C7	A21	44c USS Saratoga		88	88

No. C7 has multicolored margin inscribed "Baker Day Atomic Bomb Test, 25 July 1946," and picturing mushroom cloud. Size: 106x72mm.

MICRONESIA, FEDERATED STATES OF

A group of more than 600 islands in the west Pacific Ocean, north of the equator. These islands, also known as the Caroline Islands, were bought by Germany from Spain in 1899. Caroline Islands stamps issued as a German colony are listed in Vol. II of the Scott Standard Postage Stamp Catalogue. The islands were seized by Japan in 1914. They were taken by the U.S. in World War II and became part of the U.S. Trust Territory of the Pacific in 1947. By agreement with the U. S. Postal Service, the islands began issuing their own stamps in 1984, with the U.S.P.S. continuing to carry the mail to and from the islands. Yap, Truk, Pohnpei and Kosrae are the four states of Micronesia. All but Kosrae are island groups. Kolonia, on Pohnpei, is the seat of government. Land area: 271 sq. mi. Population: 73,755 (1980).

100 CENTS = 1 DOLLAR

Map of State of Yap—A1

Postal Service inauguration.

1984, July 12		Lithographed	Perf. 14	
1	A1	20c shown	40	40
2	A1	20c Truk	40	40
3	A1	20c Pohnpei	40	40
4	A1	20c Kosrae	40	40
		a. Block of 4, #1-4	1.60	1.60

Fernandez de Quiros
A2

Men's House, Yap
A3

Designs: 1c, 19c, Pedro Fernandez de Quiros, Spanish explorer, discovered Pohnpei, 1595. 2c, 20c, Louis Duperrey, French explorer. 3c, 30c, Fyedor Lutke, Russian explorer. 4c, 37c, Dumont d'Urville. 10c, Sleeping Lady Hill, Kosrae. 13c, Lidduduhriap Waterfall, Pohnpei. 17c, Tonachau Peak, Truk. 50c, Devil Mask, Truk. $1, Sokeh's Rock, Pohnpei. $2, Canoes, Kosrae. $5, Stone Money, Yap.

1984, July 12		Lithographed	Perf. 13½ x 13	
5	A2	1c Prussian blue	5	5
6	A2	2c deep claret	5	5
7	A2	3c dark blue	6	6
8	A2	4c green	8	8
9	A3	5c yellow brown	10	10
10	A3	10c dark violet	20	20
11	A3	13c dark blue	26	26
12	A3	17c brown lake	34	34
13	A2	19c dark violet	38	38
14	A2	20c olive green	40	40
15	A2	30c rose lake	60	60
16	A2	37c deep violet	75	75
17	A3	50c brown	1.00	1.00
18	A3	$1 olive	2.00	2.00
19	A3	$2 Prussian blue	4.00	4.00
20	A3	$5 brown lake	10.00	10.00

Ausipex '84 — A4

1984, Sept. 21		Lithographed	Perf. 13½	
21	A4	20c Truk Post Office	40	40

See Nos. C4-C6.

Christmas '84 — A5

Child's drawing.

1984, Dec. 20		Lithographed	Perf. 13½	
22	A5	20c Child in straw manger	40	40

See Nos. C7-C9.

Ships — A6

1985, Aug. 19		Lithographed	Perf. 13½	
23	A6	22c U.S.S. Jamestown	44	44

See Nos. C10-C12.

Christmas 1985—A7

1985, Oct. 15		Litho.	Perf. 13½	
24	A7	22c Lelu Protestant Church, Kosrae	44	44

See Nos. C13-C14.

Audubon Birth Bicentenary—A8

1985, Oct. 30   ***Perf. 14½***

25	A8	22c Noddy tern	44	44
26	A8	22c Turnstone	44	44
27	A8	22c Golden plover	44	44
28	A8	22c Black-bellied plover	44	44
		a.Block of 4, #25-28	1.80	1.80

See No. C15.

Tall Ship Senyavin—A9   Natl. Seal—A10

1985-86   **Litho.**   ***Perf. 13½x13***

| 34 | A9 | 22c brt. blue green ('86) | 44 | 44 |
| 42 | A10 | $10 brt. ultra | 20.00 | 20.00 |

Issue dates: 22c, Apr. 14. $10, Oct. 15.

Intl. Peace Year—A17

1986, May 16

| 46 | A17 | 22c multi | 44 | 44 |

Nos. 1-4 Surcharged.

1986, May 19   **Litho.**   ***Perf. 14***

48	A1	22c on 20c No. 1	44	44
49	A1	22c on 20c No. 2	44	44
50	A1	22c on 20c No. 3	44	44
51	A1	22c on 20c No. 4	44	44
		a.Block of 4, #48-51	1.80	1.80

AMERIPEX '86—A18

Bully Hayes (1829-1877), Bucaneer.

1986, May 22

| 52 | A18 | 22c At ships helm | 44 | 44 |

See Nos. C21-C25.

Nan Madol Ruins, Pohnpei—A16

1985, Dec.   **Litho.**   ***Perf. 13½***

| 45 | A16 | 22c Land of the Sacred Masonry | 44 | 44 |

See Nos. C16-C18.

MICRONESIA

AIR POST STAMPS

Boeing 727, 1968—AP1

1984, July 12		Lithographed		Perf. 13½	
C1	AP1	28c shown		56	56
C2	AP1	35c SA-16 Albatross, 1960		70	70
C3	AP1	40c PBY-5A Catalina, 1951		80	80

Auxipex Type of 1984

1984, Sept. 21		Lithographed		Perf. 13½	
C4	A4	28c Caroline Islds. No. 4		56	56
C5	A4	35c No. 7		70	70
C6	A4	40c No. 19		80	80

Christmas Type of 1984
Children's drawings.

1984, Dec. 20		Lithographed		Perf. 13½	
C7	A5	28c Illustrated Christmas text		56	56
C8	A5	35c Decorated palm tree		70	70
C9	A5	40c Feast preparation		80	80

Ships Type of 1985

1985, Aug. 19		Lithographed		Perf. 13½	
C10	A6	33c L'Astrolabe		66	66
C11	A6	39c La Coquille		78	78
C12	A6	44c Shenandoah		88	88

Christmas Type of 1985

1985, Oct. 15		Litho.		Perf. 13½	
C13	A7	33c Dublon Protestant Church		66	66
C14	A7	44c Pohnpei Catholic Church		88	88

Audubon Type of 1985

1985, Oct. 31				Perf. 14½	
C15	A8	44c Sooty tern		88	88

Ruins Type of 1985

1985, Dec.		Litho.		Perf. 13½	
C16	A16	33c Nan Tauas inner courtyard		66	66
C17	A16	39c Outer wall		78	78
C18	A16	44c Tomb		88	88

Halley's Comet—AP2

1986, May 16					
C19	AP2	44c dk blue, blue & black		88	88

Return of Nauruans from Truk, 40th Anniv.—AP3

1986, May 16					
C20	AP3	44c Ship in port		88	88

AMERIPEX '86 Type of 1986
Bully Hayes (1829-1877), bucaneer.

1986, May 22					
C21	A18	33c Hawaii No. 5		66	66
C22	A18	39c Sinking of the Leonora, Kosrae		78	78
C23	A18	44c Hayes escapes capture		88	88
C24	A18	75c Biography, by Louis Becke		1.50	1.50

Souvenir Sheet

C25	A18	$1 Hayes ransoming chief		2.00	2.00

No. C25 has multicolored inscribed margin continuing the design and picturing cancellation and exhibition emblem. Size: 128x71mm.

ENVELOPES

National Flag—U1

1984, July 12				Lithographed	
U1	U1	20c blk, gray & bl, entire		50	50

PALAU

A group of about 100 islands and islets forming part of the western Caroline Islands in the west Pacific Ocean, 1,000 miles southeast of Manila. Part of the U.S. Trust Territory of the Pacific established in 1947, Palau became a republic in 1981. By agreement with the U.S. Postal Service, Palau began issuing its own stamps in 1983 with the U.S.P.S. continuing to carry the mail to and from Palau. Islands include Babelthuap, Angaur, Eli Malk, Peleliu, Urukthapel and Koror, site of government headquarters. Area: 179 sq. mi. Population: 16,000 (est. 1983).

100 CENTS = 1 DOLLAR

U.S. stamps remained in use for the first year.

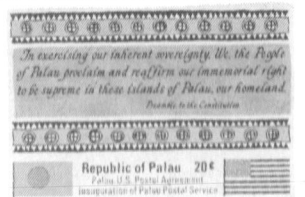

Inauguration of Postal Service
A1

1983, Mar. 10   **Litho.**   *Perf. 14*

1	A1	20c Constitution preamble	50	50
2	A1	20c Hunters	50	50
3	A1	20c Fish	50	50
4	A1	20c Preamble, diff.	50	50
		a. Block of 4, #1-4	2.00	2.00

14A	A3	28c Chambered Nautilus	56	56
16	A3	30c Dappled Sea Cucumber	60	60
17	A3	37c Sea Urchin	74	74
20	A3	50c Starfish	1.00	1.00
21	A3	$1 Squid	2.00	2.00

Booklet stamps perforate on three sides.

See Nos. 75-85.

A2

1983, Mar. 16   *Perf. 15*

5	A2	20c Palau fruit dove	40	40
6	A2	20c Palau morningbird	40	40
7	A2	20c Giant white-eye	40	40
8	A2	20c Palau fantail	40	40
		a. Block of 4, #5-8	1.60	1.60

A4

1983, Sept. 21   *Perf. 14*

24	A4	20c Humpback whale	40	40
25	A4	20c Blue whale	40	40
26	A4	20c Fin whale	40	40
27	A4	20c Great sperm whale	40	40
		a. Souvenir sheet of 4, #24-27	1.60	1.60

A3

1983   **Lithographed**   *Perf 13½ x 14*

9	A3	1c Sea Fan	5	5
10	A3	3c Map Cowrie	6	6
11	A3	5c Jellyfish	10	10
12	A3	10c Hawksbill Turtle	20	20
13	A3	13c Giant Clam	26	26
		a. Booklet pane of 10	2.60	2.60
		b. Booklet pane of 10, (5, #13, 5 #14)	3.30	3.30
14	A3	20c Parrotfish	40	40
		b. Booklet pane of 10	4.00	4.00

A5

Christmas 1983
Paintings by Charlie Gibbons, 1971

1983, Oct.   **Lithographed**   *Perf. 14½*

28	A5	20c First Child Ceremony	40	40
29	A5	20c Spearfishing from Red Canoe	40	40
30	A5	20c Traditional Feast at the Bai	40	40
31	A5	20c Taro Gardening	40	40
32	A5	20c Spearfishing at New Moon	40	40
		a. Strip of 5, #28-32	2.00	2.00

PALAU

A6

A7

Bicentennial of Capt. Henry Wilson's Voyage

1983, Dec. 14		Lithographed	Perf. 14 x 15	
33	A6	20c Capt. Henry Wilson	40	40
34	A7	20c Approaching Pelew	40	40
35	A7	20c Englishmans's Camp on Ulong	40	40
36	A6	20c Prince Lee Boo	40	40
37	A6	20c King Abba Thulle	40	40
38	A7	20c Mooring in Koror	40	40
39	A7	20c Village Scene of Pelew Islands	40	40
40	A6	20c Ludee	40	40
		a. Block of 8, #33-40	3.20	3.20

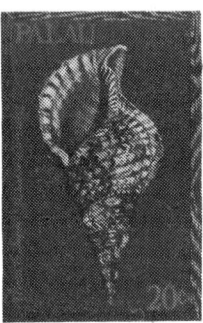

Local Seashells—A8

Shell paintings (dorsal and ventral) by Deborah Dudley Max.

1984, Mar. 15		Lithographed	Perf. 14	
41	A8	20c Triton Trumpet, Dorsal	40	40
42	A8	20c Horned Helmet, Dorsal	40	40
43	A8	20c Giant Clam, Dorsal	40	40
44	A8	20c Laciniate Conch, Dorsal	40	40
45	A8	20c Royal Cloak Scallop, Dorsal	40	40
46	A8	20c Triton Trumpet, Ventral	40	40
47	A8	20c Horned Helmet, Ventral	40	40
48	A8	20c Giant Clam, Ventral	40	40
49	A8	20c Laciniate Conch, Ventral	40	40
50	A8	20c Royal Cloak Scallop, Ventral	40	40
		a. Block of 10, #41-50	4.00	4.00

Explorer Ships—A9

1984, June 19		Lithographed	Perf. 14	
51	A9	40c Oroolong, 1783	80	80
52	A9	40c Duff, 1797	80	80
53	A9	40c Peiho, 1908	80	80
54	A9	40c Albatross, 1885	80	80
		a. Block of 4, #51-54	3.20	3.20

Traditional Fishing Techniques — A10

1984, Sept. 6		Lithographed	Perf. 14	
55	A10	20c Spearfishing	40	40
56	A10	20c Kite fishing	40	40
57	A10	20c Underwater spearfishing	40	40
58	A10	20c Net Fishing	40	40
		a. Block of 4, #55-58	1.60	1.60

Christmas 1984 — A11

Flowers used in Ngasech, or childbearing, ceremony.

1984, Dec. 5		Lithographed	Perf. 14	
59	A11	20c Eugenia malaccensis	40	40
60	A11	20c Ipomoea littoralis	40	40
61	A11	20c Curcuma domestica	40	40
62	A11	20c Plumeria obtusa	40	40
		a. Block of 4, #59-62	1.60	1.60

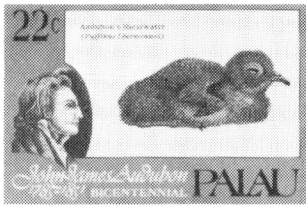

Audubon Birth Bicentenary — A12

Illustrations by artist/naturalist J.J. Audubon of shearwater ducks.

1985, Feb. 6		Lithographed	Perf. 14	
63	A12	22c Chick	44	44
64	A12	22c Head of an adult	44	44
65	A12	22c Adult in flight	44	44
66	A12	22c Floating in water	44	44
		a. Block of 4, #63-66	1.80	1.80

See No. C5.

PALAU

Shipbuilding — A13

1985, Mar. 27		Lithographed	Perf. 14	
67	A13	22c Cargo canoe (barotong)	44	44
68	A13	22c War canoe (kabekl)	44	44
69	A13	22c Bamboo raft (olechutel)	44	44
70	A13	22c Racing canoe (kaeb)	44	44
		a. Block of 4, #67-70	1.80	1.80

Marine Life Type of 1983

1985, June 11		Lithographed	Perf. 14½ x 14	
75	A3	14c Trumpet triton	28	28
		a. Booklet pane of 10	2.80	2.80
76	A3	22c Bumphead parrotfish	44	44
		a. Booklet pane of 10	4.40	4.40
		b. Booklet pane of 10 (5 #75, 5 #76)	3.60	3.60
77	A3	25c Soft coral, damsel fish	50	50
79	A3	33c Sea anemone, clownfish	66	66
80	A3	39c Green sea turtle	78	78
81	A3	44c Pacific sailfish	88	88

Booklet stamps are perforate on three sides.

Marine Life Type of 1983

1985, Mar. 31		Litho.	Perf. 15x14	
85	A3	$10 Spinner dolphins	20.00	20.00

Intl. Youth Year — A14

IYY emblem and children of all nationalities joined in a circle.

1985, July 15		Lithographed	Perf. 14	
86	A14	44c multi	88	88
87	A14	44c multi	88	88
88	A14	44c multi	88	88
89	A14	44c multi	88	88
		a. Block of 4	3.55	3.55

Nos. 86-89 printed in a continuous design.

Christmas 1985 — A15

Island mothers and children.

1985, Oct. 21		Litho.	Perf. 14	
90	A15	14c multi	28	28
91	A15	22c multi	44	44
92	A15	33c multi	66	66
93	A15	44c multi	88	88

Souvenir Sheet

Pan American Airways Martin M-130
China Clipper — A16

1985, Nov. 21		Litho.	Perf. 14	
94	A16	$1 multi	2.00	2.00

1st Trans-Pacific Mail Flight, Nov. 22, 1935. No. 94 has multicolored decorative margin continuing the design and picturing the S.S. North Haven support ship at sea, the flight map and China Clipper logo. Size: 96x70mm.

See Nos. C10-C13.

Return of Halley's Comet — A17

Fictitious local sightings.

1985, Dec. 21		Litho.	Perf. 14	
95	A17	44c Kaeb canoe, 1758	88	88
96	A17	44c U.S.S. Vincennes, 1835	88	88
97	A17	44c S.M.S. Scharnhorst, 1910	88	88
98	A17	44c Yacht, 1966	88	88
		a. Block of 4, #95-98	3.75	3.75

Songbirds — A18

PALAU

			1986, Feb. 24	Litho.		*Perf. 14*
99	A18	44c	Mangrove flycatcher		88	88
100	A18	44c	Cardinal honeyeater		88	88
101	A18	44c	Blue-faced parrotfinch		88	88
102	A18	44c	Dusky and bridled white-eyes		88	88
			a.Block of 4, #99-102		3.75	3.75

World of Sea and Reef—A19

	1986, May 22	Litho.	*Perf. 15x14*	
103		Sheet of 40	11.25	
		a.A19 14c, any single	28	28

AMERIPEX '86, Chicago, May 22-June 1

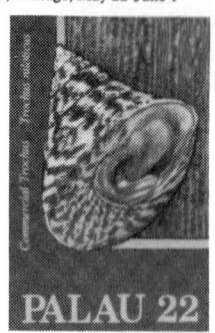

Seashells—A20

			1986, Aug. 1	Litho.	*Perf. 14*	
104	A20	22c	Commercial trochus		44	44
105	A20	22c	Marble cone		44	44
106	A20	22c	Fluted giant clam		44	44
107	A20	22c	Bullmouth helmet		44	44
108	A20	22c	Golden cowrie		44	44
			a.Strip of 5, #104-108		2.20	2.20

Intl. Peace Year—A21

			1986, Sept. 19	Litho.		
109	A21	22c	Decaying soldier's helmet		44	44
110	A21	22c	Underwater plane wreckage		44	44
111	A21	22c	Palauan woman playing guitar		44	44
112	A21	22c	Airai vista		44	44
			a.Block of 4, #109-112		1.76	1.76

PALAU
1985

John J. Audubon Birth Bicentenary

Scott 63

Scott 64

Scott 65

Scott 66

COLLECT THE SCOTT WAY... WITH SCOTT'S

U.S. TRUST TERRITORIES

FEATURING:
- Spaces for all U.S. Trust Territory stamps including Micronesia, Marshall Islands and Palau. Provides spaces for Booklet Panes also!
- Each stamp pictured or described and arranged in order by Scott number.
- Chemically neutralized paper protects your stamps for generations.
- Paper just the right thickness to make collecting a pleasure.
- Yearly supplement available.

PAGES ONLY $7.95

(Album through 1985)

AVAILABLE NOW AT YOUR LOCAL DEALER OR DIRECT FROM:

P.O. BOX 828,
SIDNEY, OH 45365

AIR POST STAMPS

Birds—AP1

1984, June 12   **Lithographed**   *Perf. 14*

C1	AP1	40c White-tailed Tropicbird	80	80
C2	AP1	40c Fairy Tern	80	80
C3	AP1	40c Black Noddy	80	80
C4	AP1	40c Black-naped Tern	80	80
		a. Block of 4, #C1-C4	3.20	3.20

Audubon Type of 1985

1985, Feb. 6   **Lithographed**   *Perf. 14*

C5	A12	44c Shearwater duck, webbed feet trait	88	88

Palau-Germany Political, Economic & Cultural Exchange Cent. — AP2

Germany Nos. 40, 65, Caroline Islands Nos. 19, 13 and: No. C6, German flag-raising at Palau, 1885. No. C7, Early German trading post in Angaur. No. C8, Abai architecture recorded by Prof. Frau Kramer (1908-1910). No. C9, S.M.S. Cormoran.

1985, Sept. 19   **Lithographed**   *Perf. 14x13½*

C6	AP2	44c multi	88	88
C7	AP2	44c multi	88	88
C8	AP2	44c multi	88	88
C9	AP2	44c multi	88	88
		a. Block of 4, #C6-C9	3.55	3.55

Trans-Pacific Airmail Anniv. Type of 1985

Aircraft: No. C10, 1951 Trans-Ocean Airways PBY-5A Catalina Amphibian. No. C11, 1968 Air Micronesia DC-6B Super Cloudmaster. No. C12, 1960 Trust Territory Airline SA-16 Albatross. No. C13, 1967 Pan American Douglas DC-4.

1985, Nov. 21   **Litho.**   *Perf. 14*

C10	A16	44c multi	88	88
C11	A16	44c multi	88	88
C12	A16	44c multi	88	88
C13	A16	44c multi	88	88
		a. Block of 4, #C10-C13	3.75	3.75

Haruo I. Remeliik (1933-1985), 1st President—AP3

Designs: No. C14, Presidential seal, excerpt from 1st inaugural address. No. C15, War canoe, address excerpt, diff. No. C16, Remeliik, US Pres. Reagan, excerpt from Reagan's speech, Pacific Basin Conference, Guam, 1984.

1986, June 30   **Litho.**   *Perf. 14*

C14	AP3	44c multi	88	88
C15	AP3	44c multi	88	88
C16	AP3	44c multi	88	88
		a. Strip of 3, #C14-C16	2.65	2.65

Intl. Peace Year, Statue of Liberty Cent.—AP4

1986, Sept. 19   **Litho.**

C17	AP4	44c multi		88	88

ENVELOPES

Marine Life Type of 1983

1985, Feb. 14   **Lithographed**

U1	A3	22c Parrotfish, entire	55	55

Paintings Type of 1983
without Inscription for Christmas

1985, Feb. 14   **Lithographed**

U2	A5	22c Spear Fishing from Red Canoe, entire	55	55

AIR LETTER SHEETS

Bird Type of 1983
Letter sheet for foreign postage.

1985, Feb. 14   **Lithographed**

UC1	A2	36c multi, entire	72	72

Designs of Nos. C1-C4 (without inscriptions) and text on reverse folding area.

POSTAL CARDS

Marine Life Type of 1983

1985, Feb. 14   **Lithographed**

UX1	A3	14c Giant Clam	28	28

PHILIPPINES

Issued under U.S. Administration.

Following the American occupation of the Philippines, May 1, 1898, after Admiral Dewey's fleet entered Manila Bay, an order was issued by the U. S. Postmaster General (No. 201, May 24, 1898) establishing postal facilities with rates similar to the domestic rates.

Military postal stations were established as branch post offices, each such station being placed within the jurisdiction of the nearest regular post office. Supplies were issued to these military stations through the regular post office of which they were branches.

Several post office clerks were sent to the Philippines and the San Francisco post office was made the nearest regular office for the early Philippine mail and the postmarks of the period point out this fact.

U. S. stamps overprinted "PHILIPPINES" were placed on sale in Manila June 30, 1899. Regular U. S. stamps had been in use from early March, and at the Manila post office Spanish stamps were also acceptable.

The first regular post office was established at Cavite on July 30, 1898, as a branch of the San Francisco post office. The first cancellation was a dated handstamp with "PHILIPPINE STATION" and "SAN FRANCISCO, CAL."

On May 1, 1899, the entire Philippine postal service was separated from San Francisco and numerous varieties of postmarks resulted. Many of the early used stamps show postmarks and cancellations of the Military Station, Camp or R. P. O. types, together with "Killers" of the types employed in the U. S. at the time.

The Philippines became a commonwealth of the United States on November 15, 1935, the High Commissioner of the United States taking office on the same day. The official name of the government was "Commonwealth of the Philippines" as provided by Article 17 of the Constitution. Upon the final and complete withdrawal of sovereignty of the United States and the proclamation of Philippine independence on July 4, 1946, the Commonwealth of the Philippines became the "Republic of the Philippines."

Numbers in parenthesis indicate quantities issued.

Authority for dates of issue, stamps from 1899 to 1911, and quantities issued — "The Postal Issues of the Philippines," by F. L. Palmer (New York, 1912).

100 CENTS=1 DOLLAR   100 CENTAVOS=1 PESO (1906)

Regular Issues of the United States Overprinted in Black

PHILIPPINES

Printed and overprinted by the U. S. Bureau of Engraving and Printing.

1899, June 30   Perf. 12.   Unwmkd.

On U. S. Stamp No. 260.

212	A96 50c orange		425.00	250.00
	On cover			
	Block of four		2000.00	
	Margin strip of 3, Impt. & P #		2000.00	
	Margin block of 6, Impt. & P #		6000.00	

On U. S. Stamps

Nos. 279a, 279d, 267, 268, 281a, 282C, 283, 284, 275 and 275a.

Wmkd. Double-lined USPS (191)

213	A87 1c yellow green (5,500,000)		1.75	.90
	On cover			9.00
	Block of four		17.00	6.00
	Margin strip of 3, Impt. & P #		30.00	
	Margin block of 6, Impt. & P #		200.00	
214	A88 2c orange red, type III (6,970,000)		1.75	.60
	On cover			7.50
	Block of four		7.50	5.00
	Margin strip of 3, Impt. & P #		22.50	
	Margin block of 6, Impt. & P #		150.00	
	a. 2c carmine, type III		2.50	1.00
	b. Booklet pane of six ('00)		325.00	175.00
215	A89 3c purple (673,814)		6.50	1.75
	On cover			30.00
	Block of four		30.00	20.00
	Margin strip of 3, Impt. & P #		65.00	
	Margin block of 6, Impt. & P #		500.00	
216	A91 5c blue (1,700,000)		6.50	1.50
	On cover			22.50
	Block of four		30.00	15.00
	Margin strip of 3, Impt. & P #		60.00	
	Margin block of 6, Impt. & P #		425.00	
	a. Inverted overprint		425.00	2750.00
217	A94 10c brown, type I (750,000)*		20.00	5.00
	On cover			65.00
	Block of four		100.00	65.00
	Margin strip of 3, Impt. & P #		100.00	
	Margin block of 6, Impt. & P #		700.00	

(*Quantity includes Nos. 217, 217A)

217A	" 10c orange brown, type II		250.00	50.00
	On cover			210.00
	Block of four		1100.00	350.00
	Margin strip of 3, Impt. & P #		1100.00	
	Margin block of 6, Impt. & P #		3000.00	
218	A95 15c olive green (200,000)		35.00	8.75
	On cover			150.00
	Block of four		160.00	100.00
	Margin strip of 3, Impt. & P #		160.00	
	Margin block of 6, Impt. & P #		650.00	
	a. 15c light olive green		40.00	12.50
219	A96 50c orange (50,000)*		125.00	50.00
	On cover			225.00
	Block of four		550.00	300.00
	Margin strip of 3, Impt. & P #		550.00	
	Margin block of 6, Impt. & P #		1500.00	
	a. 50c red orange		200.00	

(*Quantity includes Nos. 212, 219, 219a)

Special Printing.

In 1899 a special printing of Nos. 213 to 217, 218, 219 and J1 to J5 was made for display at the Paris Exposition. All but a few copies were destroyed. Most of the existing copies bear the handstamp "Special Surcharge" on the back. Price each $350.00

Regular Issue.

1901, Aug. 30   Same Overprint in Black.

On U. S. Stamps Nos. 280b, 282 and 272.

220	A90 4c orange brown (404,907)		22.50	6.00
	On cover			65.00
	Block of four		100.00	65.00
	Margin strip of 3, Impt. & P #		100.00	
	Margin block of 6, Impt. & P #		600.00	
221	A92 6c lake (223,468)		27.50	8.00
	On cover			90.00
	Block of four		125.00	75.00
	Margin strip of 3, Impt. & P #		125.00	
	Margin block of 6, Impt. & P #		800.00	
222	A93 8c violet brown (248,000)		30.00	8.00
	On cover			65.00
	Block of four		135.00	80.00
	Margin strip of 3, Impt. & P #		135.00	
	Margin block of 6, Impt. & P #		900.00	

PHILIPPINES

Same Overprint in Red.
On U. S. Stamps Nos. 276, 276A, 277a and 278.

223	A97	$1 black, type I (*3,000*)*		475.00	275.00
		On cover			800.00
		Block of four		2250.00	
		Margin strip of 3, Impt. & P ‡		2250.00	
		Margin block of 6, Impt. & P ‡			
		Horiz. pair, types I & II		4000.00	
		*(Quantity includes Nos. 223, 223A)			
223A	"	$1 black, type II		2750.00	1350.00
		On cover			
		Block of four		12,000.00	
		Margin strip of 3, Impt. & P ‡			
		one stamp No. 223		*11,000.00*	
		Margin block of 6, Impt. & P ‡,			
		two stamps No. 223			
224	A98	$2 dark blue (*1800*)		700.00	350.00
		On cover			2250.00
		Block of four		3250.00	
		Margin strip of 3, Impt. & P ‡		3250.00	
		Margin block of 6, Impt. & P ※			
225	A99	$5 dark green (*782*)		1650.00	1100.00
		On cover			2000.00
		Block of four		7500.00	
		Margin strip of 3, Impt. & P ‡		7500.00	
		Margin block of 6, Impt. & P ※			

Special Printing.

Special printings exist of Nos. 227, 221, 223-225, made from defaced plates. These were made for display at the St. Louis Exposition. All but a few copies were destroyed. Most of the existing copies have the handstamp "Special Printing" on the back. Price: Nos. 227, 221, each $400; No. 223, $850; No. 224, $1,200; No. 225, $2,000.

Regular Issue.
1903-04 Same Overprint in Black.
On U. S. Stamps Nos. 300 to 310 and shades.

226	A115	1c blue green (*9,631,172*)		4.50	50
		On cover			10.00
		Block of four		20.00	3.00
		Margin strip of 3, Impt. & P ‡		22.50	
		Margin block of 6, Impt. & P ‡		175.00	
227	A116	2c carmine (*850,000*)		7.50	1.75
		On cover			12.50
		Block of four		32.50	10.00
		Margin strip of 3, Impt. & P ‡		35.00	
		Margin block of 6, Impt. & P ‡		250.00	
228	A117	3c bright violet (*14,500*)		75.00	15.00
		On cover			75.00
		Margin strip of 3, Impt. & P ‡		325.00	100.00
		Margin block of 6, Impt. & P ‡		325.00	
				950.00	
229	A118	4c brown (*13,000*)		80.00	25.00
		On cover			50.00
		Block of four		350.00	125.00
		Margin strip of 3, Impt. & P ‡		350.00	
		Margin block of 6, Impt. & P ‡		1000.00	
		a. 4c orange brown		80.00	20.00
230	A119	5c blue (*1,211,844*)		12.00	1.25
		On cover			7.00
		Block of four		50.00	25.00
		Margin strip of 3, Impt. & P ‡		50.00	
		Margin block of 6, Impt. & P ‡		325.00	
231	A120	6c brownish lake (*11,500*)		75.00	20.00
		On cover			70.00
		Block of four		350.00	175.00
		Margin strip of 3, Impt. & P ‡		350.00	
		Margin block of 6, Impt. & P ‡		1000.00	
232	A121	8c violet black (*49,033*)		40.00	15.00
		On cover			75.00
		Block of four		200.00	120.00
		Margin strip of 3, Impt. & P ‡		200.00	
		Margin block of 6, Impt. & P ‡		950.00	
233	A122	10c pale red brown (*300,179*)		22.50	3.50
		On cover			20.00
		Block of four		100.00	30.00
		Margin strip of 3, Impt. & P ‡		100.00	
		Margin block of 6, Impt. & P ‡		750.00	
		a. 10c red brown		27.50	5.00
		b. Pair, one without overprint			1350.00
234	A123	13c purple black (*91,341*)		35.00	17.50
		a. 13c brown violet		35.00	17.50
		On cover			70.00
		Block of four		175.00	100.00
		Margin strip of 3, Impt. & P ‡		175.00	
		Margin block of 6, Impt. & P ※		1000.00	

235	A124	15c olive green (*183,965*)		60.00	13.00
		On cover			125.00
		Block of four		275.00	85.00
		Margin strip of 3, Impt. & P ‡		275.00	
		Margin block of 6, Impt. & P ‡		1100.00	
236	A125	50c orange (*57,641*)		175.00	55.00
		On cover			350.00
		Block of four		800.00	400.00
		Margin strip of 3, Impt. & P ‡		800.00	
		Margin block of 6, Impt. & P ‡		3750.00	

Same Overprint in Red.
On U. S. Stamps Nos. 311, 312 and 313.

237	A126	$1 black (*5617*)		625.00	300.00
		On cover			600.00
		Block of four		2750.00	1850.00
		Margin strip of 3, Impt. & P ‡		2750.00	
		Margin block of 6, Impt. & P ‡			
238	A127	$2 dark blue (*695*)		1850.00	1100.00
		Block of four		8500.00	
		Margin strip of 3, Impt. & P ‡		8500.00	
		Margin block of 6, Impt. & P ‡		14,000.00	
239	A128	$5 dark green (*746*)		2250.00	1350.00
		Block of four		10,000.00	
		Margin strip of 3, Impt. & P ‡		10,000.00	
		Margin block of 6, Impt. & P ‡			

Same Overprint in Black.
On U. S. Stamp No. 319.

240	A129	2c carmine (*862,245*)		5.50	2.50
		On cover			3.50
		Block of four		24.00	12.50
		Margin strip of 3, Impt. & P ‡		40.00	
		Margin block of 6, Impt. & P ‡		250.00	
		a. Booklet pane of six		1200.00	
		b. scarlet		6.50	2.75

Dates of issue:—
Sept. 20, 1903. Nos. 226, 227, 236.
Jan. 4, 1904. Nos. 230, 234, 235, 237.
Nov. 1, 1904. Nos. 228, 229, 231, 232, 233, 238, 239, 240.

Nos. 212 to 240 became obsolete on Sept. 8, 1906, the remainders being destroyed.

Special Printing.

Two sets of special printings exist of the 1903-04 issue. The first consists of Nos. 226, 230, 234, 235, 236, 237 and 240. These were made for display at the St. Louis Exposition. All but a few copies were destroyed. Most of the existing copies have the handstamp "Special Surcharge" on the back. Price: No. 237, $750; others $400; J6; J7, $450.

In 1907 the entire set Nos. 226, 228 to 240, J1 to J7 were specially printed for the Bureau of Insular Affairs on very white paper. They are difficult to distinguish from the ordinary stamps except the Special Delivery stamp which is on U. S. No. E6 (see Philippines No. E2A). Price: No. 237, $750; No. 238, $1500; No 239, $2000; others, $750

Regular Issue.

José Rizal   Arms of City of Manila
A40   A41

Printed by the
U. S. Bureau of Engraving and Printing.

Plates of 400 subjects in four panes of 100 each.

Booklet panes Nos. 240a, 241b, 242b, 261a, 262b, 276a, 277a, 285a, 286a, 290c, 291b and 292c were made from plates of 180 subjects. No. 214b came from plates of 360 subjects.

Wmkd. Double-lined PIPS (191)

1906, Sept. 8   *Perf.* 12

241	A40	2c deep green, (*51,125,010*)		30	6
		Block of four		1.25	30
		a. 2c yellow green ('10)		50	6
		Double transfer			50.00
		b. Booklet pane of six		200.00	

PHILIPPINES

242	A40	4c carmine (*McKinley*) (14,150,030)	40	6
		Block of four	1.75	25
		a. 4c carmine lake ('10)	75	6
		b. Booklet pane of six	200.00	
243	"	6c violet (*Fernando Magellan*) (1,980,000)	1.25	15
		Block of four	5.50	70
244	"	8c brown (*Miguel Lopez de Legaspi*) (770,000)	2.25	75
		Block of four	10.00	5.00
245	"	10c blue (*Gen. Henry W. Lawton*) (5,550,000)	1.65	10
		Dark blue	1.65	10
		Block of four	7.00	45
246	"	12c brown lake (*Lincoln*) (670,000)	5.00	2.25
		Block of four	23.00	15.00
247	"	16c violet black (*Adm. William T. Sampson*) (1,300,000)	3.25	25
		Block of four	13.50	1.75
248	"	20c orange brown (*Washington*) (2,100,000)	3.75	40
		Block of four	17.00	2.50
249	"	26c violet brown (*Francisco Carriedo*) (480,000)	6.00	2.50
		Block of four	27.50	16.00
250	"	30c olive green (*Franklin*) (1,256,900)	4.50	1.60
		Block of four	19.00	8.50
251	A41	1p orange (200,000)	25.00	11.00
		Block of four	105.00	60.00
252	"	2p black (100,000)	35.00	1.50
		Block of four	150.00	12.50
253	"	4p dark blue (10,000)	100.00	17.50
		Block of four	450.00	85.00
254	"	10p dark green (6,000)	200.00	85.00
		Block of four	950.00	400.00

1909-13   Change of Colors

255	A40	12c red orange (300,000)	8.00	3.00
		Block of four	37.50	14.00
256	"	16c olive green (500,000)	2.00	50
		Block of four	9.00	2.25
257	"	20c yellow (800,000)	7.50	1.50
		Block of four	32.50	9.00
258	"	26c blue green	1.50	80
		Block of four	6.50	4.50
259	"	30c ultramarine (600,000)	10.00	4.00
		Block of four	45.00	22.50
260	A41	1p pale violet (100,000)	30.00	6.00
		Block of four	150.00	40.00
260A	"	2p violet brown (50,000)	80.00	3.00
		Block of four	375.00	20.00

Wmkd. Single-lined PIPS (190)

1911-13   Perf. 12

261	A40	2c green	60	10
		Block of four	2.75	50
		a. Booklet pane of six	175.00	
262	"	4c carmine lake	3.00	12
		Block of four	13.00	55
		a. 4c carmine		
		b. Booklet pane of six	175.00	
263	"	6c deep violet	1.75	10
		Block of four	8.00	45
264	"	8c brown	8.00	50
		Block of four	35.00	2.25
265	"	10c blue	3.00	10
		Block of four	14.00	50
266	"	12c orange	2.00	50
		Block of four	9.00	2.50
267	"	16c olive green	2.25	20
		Pale olive green	2.25	20
		Block of four	10.00	1.00
268	"	20c yellow	2.00	15
		Block of four	8.50	65
		a. 20c orange	2.00	15
269	"	26c blue green	2.75	30
		Block of four	11.00	1.50
270	"	30c ultramarine	3.25	50
		Block of four	15.00	2.75
271	A41	1p pale violet	20.00	50
		Block of four	85.00	3.00
272	"	2p violet brown	25.00	1.00
		Block of four	110.00	5.50
273	"	4p deep blue	650.00	60.00
		Block of four	3000.00	325.00
274	"	10p deep green	200.00	22.50
		Block of four	950.00	110.00

1914

275	A40	30c gray	10.00	65
		Block of four	45.00	3.75

1914-23   Perf. 10

276	A40	2c green	1.50	12
		Block of four	6.25	55
		a. Booklet pane of six	185.00	
277	"	4c carmine	1.50	15
		Block of four	6.25	65
		a. Booklet pane of six	185.00	
278	"	6c light violet	30.00	12.50
		Block of four	130.00	75.00
		a. 6c deep violet	32.50	7.00
279	"	8c brown	30.00	10.00
		Block of four	130.00	60.00
280	"	10c dark blue	20.00	25
		Block of four	85.00	1.25
281	"	16c olive green	67.50	5.00
		Block of four	280.00	30.00
282	"	20c orange	17.50	1.00
		Block of four	75.00	6.00
283	"	30c gray	45.00	3.50
		Block of four	190.00	20.00
284	A41	1p pale violet	100.00	4.00
		Block of four	425.00	22.50

1918-26   Perf. 11.

285	A40	2c green	20.00	5.00
		Block of four	85.00	22.50
		a. Booklet pane of six	600.00	
286	"	4c carmine	27.50	3.00
		Block of four	125.00	15.00
		a. Booklet pane of six	600.00	
287	"	6c deep violet	37.50	2.00
		Block of four	150.00	10.00
287A	"	8c light brown	225.00	40.00
		Block of four	925.00	250.00
288	"	10c dark blue	50.00	1.75
		Block of four	210.00	10.00
289	"	16c olive green	100.00	8.00
		Block of four	425.00	35.00
289A	"	20c orange	55.00	10.00
		Block of four	235.00	50.00
289C	"	30c gray	50.00	17.50
		Block of four	210.00	85.00
289D	A41	1p pale violet	60.00	15.00
		Block of four	250.00	85.00

1917-25   Perf. 11   Unwmkd.

290	A40	2c yellow green	10	5
		Block of four	45	20
		a. 2c dark green	12	5
		Green	15	5
		Double transfer	—	—
		b. Vert. pair, imperf. horiz.		
		c. Horiz. pair, imperf. between	1100.00	
		d. Vertical pair, imperf. btwn.	1750.00	
		e. Booklet pane of six	20.00	
291	"	4c carmine	10	5
		Block of four	45	25
		a. 4c light rose	25	5
		b. Booklet pane of six	17.50	
292	"	6c deep violet	30	8
		Block of four	1.25	45
		a. 6c lilac	40	8
		b. 6c red violet	40	10
		c. Booklet pane of six	200.00	
293	"	8c yellow brown	20	12
		Block of four	90	50
		a. 8c orange brown	20	12
294	"	10c deep blue	20	8
		Block of four	85	35
295	"	12c red orange	40	15
		Block of four	1.75	75
296	"	16c light olive green	50.00	25
		Block of four	250.00	95
		a. 16c olive bistre	50.00	50
297	"	20c orange yellow	35	10
		Block of four	1.50	45
298	"	26c green	55	65
		Block of four	2.50	2.75
		a. 26c blue green	70	40
299	"	30c gray	50	10
		Block of four	2.20	50
		Dark gray	50	10

PHILIPPINES

300	A41	1p pale violet	27.50	1.25
		Block of four	115.00	5.50
		a. 1p red lilac	27.50	1.25
		b. 1p pale rose lilac	27.50	1.50
301	"	2p violet brown	25.00	75
		Block of four	105.00	3.50
302	"	4p blue	18.50	50
		Block of four	80.00	2.25
		a. 4p dark blue	18.50	50

1923–26

303	A40	16c olive bistre (*Adm. George Dewey*)	75	20
		Block of four	3.25	90
		a. 16c olive green	1.35	20
304	A41	10p deep green ('26)	60.00	8.00
		Block of four	250.00	35.00

Legislative Palace Issue

Issued to commemorate the opening of the Legislative Palace.

Legislative Palace
A42

Printed by the Philippine Bureau of Printing.

1926, Dec. 20   *Perf. 12.*   Unwmkd.

319	A42	2c green & black (*502,550*)	50	30
		First day cover		5.00
		Block of four	3.50	1.50
		a. Horiz. pair, imperf. between	275.00	
		b. Vert. pair, imperf. between	425.00	
320	"	4c carmine & black (*304,400*)	50	40
		First day cover		5.00
		Block of four	2.25	1.75
		a. Horiz. pair, imperf. between	275.00	
		b. Vert. pair, imperf. between	350.00	
321	"	16c olive green & black (*203,750*)	1.00	85
		First day cover		15.00
		Block of four	5.00	4.00
		a. Horiz. pair, imperf. between	325.00	
		b. Vert. pair, imperf. between	425.00	
		c. Double impression of center	550.00	
322	"	18c light brown & black (*103,950*)	1.25	75
		First day cover		15.00
		Block of four	5.50	3.50
		a. Double impression of center (*150*)	550.00	
		b. Vertical pair, imperf. between	425.00	
323	"	20c orange & black (*103,450*)	1.75	1.25
		Block of four	7.50	6.00
		a. 20c orange & brown (*100*)	400.00	—
		b. Imperf., (pair), orange & black (*50*)	450.00	450.00
		c. Imperf., (pair), orange & brown (*100*)	375.00	
		d. Vert. pair, imperf. between	425.00	
324	"	24c gray & black (*103,350*)	1.50	1.00
		Block of four	6.50	4.50
		a. Vert. pair, imperf. between	425.00	
325	"	1p rose lilac & black (*11,050*)	70.00	35.00
		Block of four	300.00	200.00
		a. Vert. pair, imperf. between	475.00	
		First day cover, # 319-325		125.00

Coil Stamp.
Rizal Type of 1906.

Printed by the U. S. Bureau of Engraving and Printing.

1928   *Perf. 11 Vertically.*   Unwmkd.

326	A40	2c green	8.50	8.50
		Pair	18.50	21.50
		Line pair	60.00	

Types of 1906–1923
1925–31   **Imperf.**   **Unwmkd.**

Two issues of imperforate stamps were made, in 1925 and in 1931. They differ in shade.

340	A40	2c yellow green ('31)	12	12
		Block of four	50	50
		green	50	
341	"	4c carmine rose ('31)	20	20
		Block of four	80	80
		carmine	60	
342	"	6c violet ('31)	2.00	2.00
		Block of four	8.50	8.50
		deep violet	5.00	
343	"	8c brown ('31)	1.75	1.75
		Block of four	7.50	7.50
		yellow brown	5.00	
344	"	10c blue ('31)	2.00	2.00
		Block of four	8.00	8.00
		deep blue	8.50	
345	"	12c deep orange ('31)	3.00	3.00
		Block of four	12.50	12.50
		red orange	8.50	
346	"	16c olive green (*Dewey*) ('31)	2.25	2.25
		Block of four	9.50	9.50
		bister green	8.50	
347	"	20c orange yellow ('31)	2.25	2.25
		Block of four	9.50	9.50
		yellow	8.50	
348	"	26c green ('31)	2.25	2.25
		Block of four	9.50	9.50
		blue green	8.50	
349	"	30c light gray ('31)	2.50	2.50
		Block of four	10.50	10.50
		gray	8.50	
350	A41	1p light violet ('31)	8.00	8.00
		Block of four	33.00	33.00
		violet	35.00	
351	"	2p brown violet ('31)	20.00	20.00
		Block of four	85.00	85.00
		violet brown	85.00	
352	"	4p blue ('31)	60.00	60.00
		Block of four	250.00	
		deep blue (*200*)	300.00	
353	"	10p green ('31)	175.00	175.00
		Block of four	725.00	
		deep green (*200*)	375.00	

Mount Mayon, Luzon
A43

Post Office, Manila
A44

PHILIPPINES

Pier No. 7, Manila Bay
A45

Vernal Falls, Yosemite Park, California
(See Footnote)
A46

Rice Planting
A47

Rice Terraces
A48

Baguio Zigzag
A49

1932, May 3		Perf. 11.	Unwmkd.	
354	A43	2c yellow green	75	35
		First day cover		3.00
		Block of four	3.25	1.50
355	A44	4c rose carmine	50	35
		First day cover		3.00
		Block of four	2.25	1.75
356	A45	12c orange	75	75
		First day cover		10.00
		Block of four	3.50	3.25
357	A46	18c red orange	25.00	12.50
		First day cover		20.00
		Block of four	100.00	50.00
358	A47	20c yellow	1.00	80
		First day cover		10.00
		Block of four	4.00	3.50
359	A48	24c deep violet	1.50	1.00
		First day cover		10.00
		Block of four	6.00	5.50
360	A49	32c olive brown	1.50	1.15
		First day cover		10.00
		Block of four	6.50	5.00
		First day cover, #354-360		75.00

The 18c vignette was intended to show Pagsanjan Falls in Laguna, central Luzon, and is so labeled. Through error the stamp pictures Vernal Falls in Yosemite National Park, California.

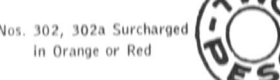

Nos. 302, 302a Surcharged in Orange or Red

1932				
368	A41	1p on 4p blue (O)	2.50	50
		On cover		70
		Block of four	10.00	2.50
		a. 1p on 4p dark blue (O)	3.50	1.50
369	"	2p on 4p dark blue (R)	4.50	1.00
		On cover		1.25
		Block of four	17.00	4.50
		a. 2p on 4p blue (R)	4.50	1.00

Far Eastern Championship.

Issued in commemoration of the Tenth Far Eastern Championship Games.

Baseball Players
A50

PHILIPPINES

Tennis Player
A51

José Rizal
A53

Woman and Carabao
A54

Basketball Players
A52

La Filipina
A55

Printed by the Philippine Bureau of Printing.

1934, April 14   **Perf. 11½**   **Unwmkd.**

380	A50	2c yellow brown	20	20
		brown	20	20
		First day cover		1.50
		"T" of "Eastern" malformed	2.50	2.00
381	A51	6c ultramarine	40	35
		pale ultramarine	40	35
		First day cover		2.50
		a. Vertical pair, imperf. between	800.00	
382	A52	16c violet brown	90	90
		dark violet	90	90
		First day cover		3.50
		a. Imperf. horizontally, pair	800.00	

Pearl Fishing
A56

PHILIPPINES

Fort Santiago—A57

Salt Spring—A58

Magellan's Landing, 1521—A59

"Juan de la Cruz"
A60

Rice Terraces—A61

Miguel Lopez de Legaspi and Chief Sikatuna
Signing "Blood Compact," 1565
A62

Barasoain Church, Malolos
A63

Battle of Manila Bay, 1898
A64

Montalban Gorge
A65

864   PHILIPPINES

George Washington
A66

Printed by U. S. Bureau of Engraving and Printing.
1935, Feb. 15   Perf. 11.   Unwmkd.

383	A53	2c rose	5	5
		First day cover		75
384	A54	4c yellow green	5	5
		Light yellow green	8	5
		First day cover		75
385	A55	6c dark brown	9	6
		First day cover		75
386	A56	8c violet	12	12
		First day cover		2.50
387	A57	10c rose carmine	25	20
		First day cover		2.50
388	A58	12c black	18	15
		First day cover		2.50
389	A59	16c dark blue	18	12
		First day cover		2.50
390	A60	20c light olive green	25	6
		First day cover		3.50
391	A61	26c indigo	35	35
		First day cover		4.50
392	A62	30c orange red	35	35
		First day cover		4.50
393	A63	1p red orange & black	2.50	1.85
		First day cover		12.50
394	A64	2p bister brown & black	5.00	1.75
		First day cover		20.00
395	A65	4p blue & black	5.00	3.75
		First day cover		30.00
396	A66	5p green & black	10.00	2.25
		First day cover		40.00

Issues of the Commonwealth
Commonwealth Inauguration Issue
Issued to commemorate the inauguration of the Philippine Commonwealth, Nov. 15, 1935.

"The Temples of Human Progress"
A67

1935, Nov. 15   Perf. 11   Unwmkd.

397	A67	2c carmine rose	15	10
		First day cover		1.00
398	"	6c deep violet	20	15
		First day cover		1.00
399	A67	16c blue	30	20
		First day cover		1.50
400	"	36c yellow green	50	45
		First day cover		2.00
401	"	50c brown	80	80
		First day cover		3.00

José Rizal Issue.
Issued to commemorate the 75th anniversary of the birth of José Rizal (1861–1896), national hero of the Filipinos.

José Rizal
A68

Printed by the Philippine Bureau of Printing.
1936, June 19   Perf. 12   Unwmkd.

402	A68	2c yellow brown	10	10
		light yellow brown	10	10
		First day cover		75
403	"	6c slate blue	15	10
		light slate green	15	10
		First day cover		1.50
		a. Imperf. vertically, pair	800.00	
404	"	36c red brown	75	70
		light red brown	75	70
		First day cover		3.50

PHILIPPINES

Commonwealth Anniversary Issue.

Issued in commemoration of the first anniversary of the Commonwealth.

President Manuel L. Quezon
A69

Printed by U. S. Bureau of Engraving and Printing.

1936, Nov. 15		Perf. 11.		Unwmkd.	
408	A69	2c orange brown		6	6
		First day cover			75
409	"	6c yellow green		12	10
		First day cover			1.25
410	"	12c ultramarine		18	15
		First day cover			2.25

Stamps of 1935 Overprinted in Black:

COMMON-WEALTH	COMMONWEALTH
a	b

1936-37			Perf. 11		Unwmkd.	
411	A53	(a)	2c rose, *Dec. 28, 1936*		6	5
			First day cover			50.00
			a. Bklt. pane of 6, *Jan. 15 1937*		5.00	1.00
			a. First day cover			60.00
412	A54	(b)	4c yellow green, *Mar. 29, 1937*		75	40
			On cover			50
413	A55	(a)	6c dark brown, *Oct. 7, 1936*		25	10
			On cover			12
414	A56	(b)	8c violet, *Mar. 29, 1937*		35	30
			On cover			35
415	A57	(")	10c rose carmine, *Dec. 28, 1936*		20	6
			First day cover			50.00
			a. "COMMONWEALT"			
416	A58	(")	12c black, *Mar. 29, 1937*		20	8
			On cover			10
417	A59	(")	16c dark blue, *Oct. 7, 1936*		25	20
			On cover			25
418	A60	(a)	20c lt. olive green, *Mar. 29, 1937*		75	50
			On cover			55
419	A61	(b)	26c indigo, *Mar. 29, 1937*		65	45
			On cover			55
420	A62	(")	30c orange red, *Dec. 28, 1936*		30	15
			First day cover			50.00
421	A63	(")	1p red org. & blk., *Oct. 7, 1936*		1.00	30
			On cover			50
422	A64	(")	2p bis. brn. & blk., *Mar. 29, 1937*		7.00	3.00
			On cover			4.00
423	A65	(")	4p blue & blk., *Mar. 29, 1937*		25.00	4.00
			On cover			5.00
424	A66	(")	5p green & blk., *Mar. 29, 1937*		2.50	1.65
			On cover			2.00

Eucharistic Congress Issue.

Issued to commemorate the 33rd International Eucharistic Congress held at Manila, Feb. 3-7, 1937.

Map, Symbolical of the Eucharistic Congress Spreading Light of Christianity
A70

FLAT PLATE PRINTING.

Plates of 256 subjects in four panes of 64 each.

1937, Feb. 3		Perf. 11.		Unwmkd.	
425	A70	2c yellow green		10	6
		First day cover			75
426	"	6c light brown		18	10
		First day cover			75
427	"	12c sapphire		20	10
		First day cover			1.25
428	"	20c deep orange		35	15
		First day cover			1.50
429	"	36c deep violet		60	50
		First day cover			2.00
430	"	50c carmine		70	35
		First day cover			3.00

Arms of City of Manila
A71

1937, Aug. 27		Perf. 11		Unwmkd.	
431	A71	10p gray		6.50	3.00
432	"	20p henna brown		3.50	2.00

Nos. 431-432 exist on one first day cover. Price $75.

Stamps of 1935 Overprinted in Black:

COMMON-WEALTH	COMMONWEALTH
(a)	(b)

1938-40			Perf. 11		Unwmkd.	
433	A53	(a)	2c rose ('39)		8	5
			a. Booklet pane of six		5.00	1.00
			b. "WEALTH COMMON-"		3000.00	—
			c. Hyphen omitted			
434	A54	(b)	4c yellow green ('40)		60	50
435	A55	(a)	6c dark brown, *May 12, 1939*		8	8
			First day cover			50.00
			a. 6c golden brown		15	8
436	A56	(b)	8c violet ('39)		10	10
			a. "COMMONWEALT"		85.00	
437	A57	(")	10c rose carmine, *May 12, 1939*		10	6
438	A58	(")	12c black ('40)		10	9
439	A59	(")	16c dark blue		18	10
440	A60	(")	20c light olive green ('39)		20	10
441	A61	(b)	26c indigo ('40)		30	30
442	A62	(")	30c orange red *May 23, 1939*		1.60	85
443	A63	(")	1p red org. & blk., *Aug. 29, 1938*		60	25
			First day cover			60.00
444	A64	(")	2p bister brown & black ('39)		4.00	1.00

PHILIPPINES

445	A65 (b)	4p blue & black ('40)		65.00	65.00
446	A66 (")	5p green & black ('40)		7.00	4.00

The overprint (b) measures 18¼x1¾ mm.

No. 433b occurs in booklet pane, No. 433a, position 5; all copies are straight-edged, left and bottom.

First Foreign Trade Week Issue.
Nos. 384, 298a and 432 Surcharged in Red, Violet or Black:

(a)

(b)

(c)

1939, July 5

449	A54 (a)	2c on 4c yellow green (R)		10	8
		First day cover			2.00
450	A40 (b)	6c on 26c blue green (V)		20	20
		First day cover			3.00
		a. 6c on 26c green		1.00	45
451	A71 (c)	50c on 20p henna brown (Bk)		1.25	1.25
		First day cover			7.50

Commonwealth 4th Anniversary Issue

Nos. 452–460 were issued to commemorate the fourth anniversary of the Commonwealth.

Triumphal Arch—A72

Printed by U. S. Bureau of Engraving and Printing.

1939, Nov. 15   *Perf. 11*   Unwmkd.

452	A72	2c yellow green		10	8
		First day cover			1.00
453	"	6c carmine		15	10
		First day cover			1.00
454	"	12c bright blue		25	10
		First day cover			2.00

Malacañan Palace—A73

1939, Nov. 15   *Perf. 11.*   Unwmkd.

455	A73	2c green		10	6
		First day cover			1.00
456	"	6c orange		15	10
		First day cover			1.00
457	"	12c carmine		25	8
		First day cover			2.00

President Quezon Taking Oath of Office
A74

1940, Feb. 8   *Perf. 11.*   Unwmkd.

458	A74	2c dark orange		10	8
		First day cover			1.00
459	"	6c dark green		15	12
		First day cover			1.00
460	"	12c purple		30	15
		First day cover			2.00

José Rizal
A75

ROTARY PRESS PRINTING.
Size: 19x22½mm.

1941, April 14   *Perf. 11x10½*   Unwmkd.

461	A75	2c apple green		5	5
		First day cover			1.00
		Margin block of 4, P #		1.50	

FLAT PLATE PRINTING.
Size: 18¾x22 mm.

1941–43   *Perf. 11*   Unwmkd.

462	A75	2c apple green		12	6
		a. 2c pale apple green ('41)		25	6
		b. Booklet pane of six (apple green)	1.50	1.50
		c. Booklet pane of six			
		(pale apple green) ('41)	4.00	3.50

This stamp was issued only in booklet panes and all copies have one or two straight edges.

Further printings were made in 1942 and 1943 in different shades from the first supply of stamps sent to the islands.

Stamps of 1935–41
Handstamped in Violet

VICTORY

1944   *Perf. 11, 11x10½.*   Unwmkd.

463	A53	2c rose (On 411), *Dec. 3*		225.00	125.00
		a. Booklet pane of six		1850.00	
463B	"	2c rose (On 433), *Dec. 14*		1450.00	1450.00
464	A75	2c apple green (On 461), *Nov. 8*	2.50	2.50
		On cover			5.00
465	A54	4c yellow green (On 384), *Nov. 8*	25.00	25.00
		On cover			
466	A55	6c dark brown (On 385), *Dec. 14*	1250.00	750.00
		On cover			

PHILIPPINES

467	A69	6c yellow green (On 409), *Dec. 3*	100.00	85.00
		On cover		
468	A55	6c dark brown (On 413), *Dec. 28*	500.00	300.00
469	A72	6c carmine (On 453), *Dec. 14*	125.00	100.00
		On cover		
470	A73	6c orange (On 456), *Dec. 14*	450.00	300.00
471	A74	6c dark green (On 459), *Nov. 8*	150.00	90.00
		On cover		
472	A56	8c violet (On 436), *Nov. 8*	12.50	15.00
		On cover		
473	A57	10c carmine rose (On 415), *Nov. 8*	100.00	60.00
		On cover		
474	"	10c carmine rose (On 437), *Nov. 8*	125.00	80.00
		On cover		
475	A69	12c ultramarine (On 410), *Dec. 3*	275.00	110.00
476	A72	12c bright blue (On 454), *Dec. 14*	3250.00	1400.00
		On cover		
477	A74	12c purple (On 460), *Nov. 8*	150.00	100.00
		On cover		
478	A59	16c dark blue (On 389), *Dec. 3*	600.00	
479	"	16c dark blue (On 417), *Nov. 8*	300.00	120.00
480	"	16c dark blue (On 439), *Nov. 8*	120.00	100.00
481	A60	20c light olive green (On 440), *Nov. 8*	27.50	27.50
		On cover		
482	A62	30c orange red (On 420), *Dec. 3*	175.00	125.00
		On cover		
483	"	30c orange red (On 442), *Dec. 3*	250.00	135.00
		On cover		
484	A63	1p red orange & black (On 443) *Dec. 3*	7000.00	4500.00
		On cover		

No. 463 comes only from the booklet pane. All copies have one or two straight edges.

Types of 1935-37 Overprinted

VICTORY **VICTORY** *VICTORY*
c

COMMONWEALTH **COMMONWEALTH**
a *b*
1945   *Perf. 11*   Unwmkd.

485	A53 (*a*)	2c rose, *Jan. 19*	10	6
		First day cover		4.00
486	A54 (*b*)	4c yellow green, *Jan. 19*	12	8
		First day cover		4.00
487	A55 (*a*)	6c golden brown, *Jan. 19*	15	10
		First day cover		4.00
488	A56 (*b*)	8c violet, *Jan. 19*	20	18
		First day cover		4.50
489	A57 (")	10c rose carmine, *Jan. 19*	20	15
		First day cover		4.50
490	A58 (")	12c black, *Jan. 19*	30	18
		First day cover		5.00
491	A59 (")	16c dark blue, *Jan. 19*	40	15
		First day cover		6.00
492	A60 (*a*)	20c light olive green, *Jan. 19*	45	12
		First day cover		6.50
493	A62 (*b*)	30c orange red, *May 1*	60	50
		First day cover		4.00
494	A63 (")	1p red orange & black, *Jan. 19*	1.75	40
		First day cover		10.00
495	A71 (*c*)	10p gray, *May 1*	60.00	20.00
		First day cover		30.00
496	" (")	20p henna brown, *May 1*	50.00	22.50
		First day cover		40.00

José Rizal—A76

ROTARY PRESS PRINTING.
1946, May 28   *Perf. 11x10½*   Unwmkd.
497	A76	2c sepia	10	6
		Margin block of 4, P#	75	

Later issues, released by the Philippine Republic on July 4, 1946, and thereafter, are listed in Scott's Standard Postage Stamp Catalogue, Vol. IV.

AIR POST STAMPS.
Madrid-Manila Flight Issue.

Issued to commemorate the flight of Spanish aviators Gallarza and Loriga from Madrid to Manila.

Regular Issue of 1917-26
Overprinted in Red or Violet
by the Philippine Bureau of Printing

1926, May 13   *Perf. 11*   Unwmkd.
C1	A40	2c green (R) (*10,000*)	5.00	4.00
		First day cover		35.00
		Block of four	22.50	20.00
C2	"	4c carmine (V) (*9,000*)	6.50	4.50
		First day cover		35.00
		Block of four	27.50	21.00
		a. Inverted overprint (*100*)	1200.00	
C3	"	6c lilac (R) (*5,000*)	35.00	12.00
		First day cover		50.00
		Block of four	150.00	
C4	"	8c orange brown (V) (*5,000*)	35.00	12.00
		First day cover		50.00
		Block of four	150.00	
C5	"	10c deep blue (R) (*5,000*)	35.00	12.00
		First day cover		50.00
		Block of four	125.00	
C6	"	12c red orange (V) (*4,000*)	40.00	17.50
		First day cover		50.00
		Block of four	175.00	
C7	"	16c light olive green (*Sampson*) (V) (*500*)	1350.00	1000.00
		Block of four		
C8	"	16c olive bistre (*Sampson*) (R) (*100*)	2000.00	1650.00
C9	"	16c olive green (*Dewey*) (V) (*4,000*)	40.00	17.50
		First day cover		50.00
		Block of four	175.00	
C10	"	20c orange yellow (V) (*4,000*)	40.00	17.50
		First day cover		50.00
		Block of four	175.00	
C11	"	26c blue green (V) (*4,000*)	40.00	17.50
		First day cover		50.00
		Block of four	175.00	
C12	"	30c gray (V) (*4,000*)	40.00	17.50
		First day cover		50.00
		Block of four	175.00	
C13	A41	2p violet brown (R) (*900*)	350.00	250.00
		On cover		325.00
		Block of four	—	
C14	"	4p dark blue (R) (*700*)	600.00	350.00
		On cover		425.00
		Block of four	—	
C15	"	10p deep green (V) (*500*)	900.00	600.00
		On cover		750.00
		Block of four	—	

Same Overprint on No. 269.
Wmkd. Single-lined PIPS (*190*)
Perf. 12.
C16	A40	26c blue green (V) (*100*)	2000.00	
		Block of four		

Same Overprint on No. 284.
Perf. 10.
C17	A41	1p pale violet (V) (*2,000*)	120.00	85.00
		On cover		100.00
		First day cover		140.00
		Block of four	525.00	

Overprintings of Nos. C1-C6, C9-C15 and C17 were made from two plates. Position No. 89 of the first printing shows broken left blade of propeller.

PHILIPPINES

London-Orient Flight Issue.

Issued Nov. 9, 1928, to celebrate the arrival of a British squadron of hydroplanes.

Regular Issue of 1917-25
Overprinted in Red

				Unwmkd.	
1928, Nov. 9		Perf. 11.			
C18	A40	2c green (101,200)		60	40
		First day cover			10.00
C19	"	4c carmine (50,500)		60	50
		First day cover			12.00
C20	"	6c violet (12,600)		2.25	1.75
		On cover			2.00
C21	"	8c orange brown (10,000)		2.50	2.25
		On cover			2.75
C22	"	10c deep blue (10,000)		2.50	2.25
		On cover			2.75
C23	"	12c red orange (8,000)		3.50	3.00
		On cover			4.00
C24	"	16c olive green (No. 303a) (12,600)		2.75	2.25
		On cover			3.00
C25	"	20c orange yellow (8,000)		3.50	3.00
		On cover			3.75
C26	"	26c blue green (7,000)		10.00	7.50
		On cover			10.00
C27	"	30c gray (7,000)		10.00	7.50
		On cover			10.00

Same Overprint on No. 271.
Wmkd. Single-lined PIPS (190)
Perf. 12.

C28	A41	1p pale violet (6,000)		35.00	35.00
		On cover			40.00

Von Gronau Issue.

Issued in commemoration of the visit of Capt. Wolfgang von Gronau's airplane on its round-the-world flight.

Nos. 354-360 Overprinted by the Philippine Bureau of Printing

				Unwmkd.	
1932, Sept. 27		Perf. 11.			
C29	A43	2c yellow green (100,000)		45	45
		First day cover			3.00
C30	A44	4c rose carmine (80,000)		50	50
		First day cover			3.00
C31	A45	12c orange (55,000)		80	80
		On cover			1.00
C32	A46	18c red orange (30,000)		4.00	4.00
		On cover			4.75
C33	A47	20c yellow (30,000)		2.25	2.25
		On cover			2.50
C34	A48	24c deep violet (30,000)		2.25	2.25
		On cover			2.75
C35	A49	32c olive brown (30,000)		2.25	2.25
		On cover			2.50
		First day cover, #C29–C35			50.00

Rein Issue.

Commemorating the flight from Madrid to Manila of the Spanish aviator Fernando Rein y Loring.

1933, April 11

Regular Issue of 1917-25
Overprinted in Black

C36	A40	2c green (95,000)	45	45
		First day cover		2.50
C37	"	4c carmine (75,000)	50	50
		First day cover		
C38	"	6c deep violet (65,000)	80	80
		First day cover		4.50
C39	"	8c orange brown (35,000)	1.75	1.65
C40	"	10c dark blue (35,000)	1.50	1.25
C41	"	12c orange (35,000)	1.25	1.25
C42	"	16c olive green (Dewey) (35,000)	1.25	1.25
C43	"	20c yellow (35,000)	1.25	1.25
C44	"	26c green (35,000)	1.50	1.50
		a. 26c blue green	2.50	2.50
C45	"	30c gray (30,000)	2.00	1.85
		First day cover, #C36–C45		50.00

No. 290b Overprinted
by the Philippine Bureau of Printing

			Unwmkd.	
1933, May 26		Perf. 11		
C46	A40	2c green	65	50

Regular Issue of 1932
Overprinted

C47	A44	4c rose carmine	10	8
C48	A45	12c orange	50	18
C49	A47	20c yellow	50	30
C50	A48	24c deep violet	50	35
C51	A49	32c olive brown	75	45
		First day cover, #C46–C51		50.00

Transpacific Issue.

Issued to commemorate the China Clipper flight from Manila to San Francisco, Dec. 2-5, 1935.

Nos. 387, 392
Overprinted in Gold

			Unwmkd.	
1935, Dec. 2		Perf. 11		
C52	A57	10c rose carmine (500,000)	25	25
		First day cover		3.00
C53	A62	30c orange red (350,000)	50	50
		First day cover		5.00

Manila-Madrid Flight Issue

Issued to commemorate the Manila-Madrid flight by aviators Antonio Arnaiz and Juan Calvo.

Nos. 291, 295, 298a, 298
Surcharged in Various Colors
by Philippine Bureau of Printing

1936, Sept. 6				
C54	A40	2c on 4c carmine (Bl) (2,000,000)	8	6
		First day cover		1.50
C55	"	6c on 12c red orange (V) (500,000)	15	12
		First day cover		5.00
C56	"	16c on 26c blue green (Bk) (300,000)	30	30
		First day cover		7.50
		a. 16c on 26c green	1.50	1.00

PHILIPPINES

Air Mail Exhibition Issue

Issued to commemorate the first Air Mail Exhibition, held Feb. 17–19, 1939.

Nos. 298a, 298, 431
Surcharged in Black or Red
by Philippine Bureau of Printing

1939, Feb. 17

C57	A40	8c on 26c blue green (Bk) *(200,000)*	1.00	55
		First day cover		5.00
	a.	8c on 26c green (Bk)	2.00	75
C58	A71	1p on 10p gray (R) *(30,000)*	3.00	2.50
		First day cover		12.50

Moro Vinta and Clipper—AP1

Printed by the U. S. Bureau of Engraving and Printing.

1941, June 30   *Perf. 11.*   Unwmkd.

C59	AP1	8c carmine	1.10	70
		First day cover		2.50
C60	"	20c ultramarine	1.40	55
		First day cover		3.00
C61	"	60c blue green	2.00	1.00
		First day cover		4.50
C62	"	1p sepia	1.00	65
		First day cover		3.50

No. C47 Handstamped
in Violet   **VICTORY**

1944, Dec. 3   *Perf. 11*   Unwmkd.

C63	A44	4c rose carmine	1650.00	1000.00
		On cover		

SPECIAL DELIVERY STAMPS.

U.S. No. E5
Overprinted in Red **PHILIPPINES**
a

Printed by U.S. Bureau of Engraving & Printing
Wmkd. Double-lined USPS (191)

1901, Oct. 15   *Perf. 12.*

E1	SD3	10c dark blue *(15,000)*	110.00	125.00
		On cover		350.00
		Block of four	475.00	
		Margin strip of 3, Impt. & P #	750.00	
		Margin block of 6, Impt. & P #	3250.00	
		Dots in curved frame above messenger (Pl. 882)	135.00	

Special Delivery Messenger—SD2

Wmkd. Double-lined PIPS (191)

1906, Sept. 8   *Perf. 12.*

E2	SD2	20c deep ultramarine *(40,000)*	30.00	8.00
		On cover		17.50
		Block of four	125.00	
	b.	20c pale ultramarine	30.00	10.00

SPECIAL PRINTING.

U.S. No. E6 Overprinted Type "a" in Red

1907   Wmkd. Double-lined USPS (191)
Perf. 12.

E2A	SD4	10c ultramarine	1500.00	
		Block of four	7000.00	
		Margin block of 6, Impt. & P #	—	

This stamp was part of the set specially printed for the Bureau of Insular Affairs in 1907. See note following No. 240.

Wmkd. Single-lined PIPS (190)

1911, April   *Perf. 12.*

E3	SD2	20c deep ultramarine *(90,000)*	20.00	2.00
		On cover		15.00
		Block of four	85.00	

1916   *Perf. 10.*

E4	SD2	20c deep ultramarine	165.00	40.00
		On cover		80.00
		Block of four	700.00	
		pale ultramarine	—	

Early in 1919 the supply of Special Delivery stamps in the Manila area was exhausted. A Government decree permitted the use of regular issue postage stamps for payment of the special delivery fee when so noted on the cover. This usage was permitted until the new supply of Special Delivery stamps arrived.

1919   *Perf. 11.*   Unwmkd.

E5	SD2	20c ultramarine	60	25
		On cover		35
		Block of four	2.50	
	a.	20c pale blue	1.00	25
	b.	20c dull violet	60	25

Type of 1906 Issue.

1925–31   *Imperf.*   Unwmkd.

E6	SD2	20c dull violet ('31)	20.00	25.00
		violet blue	25.00	30.00
		On cover		30.00
		Block of four	85.00	

Type of 1919
Overprinted in Black   **COMMONWEALTH**

1939, April 27   *Perf. 11*   Unwmkd.

E7	SD2	20c blue violet	30	30
		First day cover		50.00

Nos. E5b and E7
Handstamped in Violet   **VICTORY**

1944   *Perf. 11.*   Unwmkd.

E8	SD2	20c dull violet (On E5b)	350.00	250.00
E9	"	20c blue violet (On E7)	200.00	165.00
		On cover		—

Type SD2 Overprinted "VICTORY" As No. 486.

1945, May 1   *Perf. 11*   Unwmkd.

E10	SD2	20c blue violet	85	85
		First day cover		15.00
	a.	"IC" close together	3.50	3.50

SPECIAL DELIVERY OFFICIAL STAMP

Type of 1906 Issue Overprinted   **O. B.**

1931   *Perf. 11*   Unwmkd.

EO1	SD2	20c dull violet	85	65
	a.	No period after "B"	25.00	20.00
	b.	Double overprint	—	

POSTAGE DUE STAMPS.

U.S. Nos. J38–J44
Overprinted in Black

Printed by the
U. S. Bureau of Engraving and Printing.
Wmkd. Double-lined USPS (191)

1899, Aug. 16 Perf. 12.

J1	D2	1c deep claret *(340,892)*		5.00	2.00
		On Cover			35.00
		Margin block of 6, Impt. & P#	500.00		
J2	"	2c deep claret *(306,983)*		5.00	1.75
		On cover			40.00
		Margin block of 6, Impt. & P#	500.00		
J3	"	5c deep claret *(34,565)*		11.00	3.75
		On cover			50.00
		Margin block of 6, Impt. & P#	750.00		
J4	"	10c deep claret *(15,848)*		15.00	7.00
		On cover			60.00
		Margin block of 6, Impt. & P#	850.00		
J5	"	50c deep claret *(6,168)*		165.00	100.00
		On cover			—
		Margin block of 6, Impt. & P#	3000.00		

No. J1 was used to pay regular postage Sept. 5th to 19th, 1902.

1901, Aug. 31

J6	D2	3c deep claret *(14,885)*		15.00	10.00
		On cover			50.00
		Margin block of 6, Impt. & P#	850.00		
J7	"	30c deep claret *(2,140)*		225.00	100.00
		On cover			—
		Margin block of 6, Impt. & P#	3500.00		

Post Office Clerk
D3

1928, Aug. 21 Perf. 11 Unwmkd.

J8	D3	4c brown red		15	15
J9	"	6c	"	15	15
J10	"	8c	"	15	15
J11	"	10c	"	20	20
J12	"	12c	"	20	20
J13	"	16c	"	25	25
J14	"	20c	"	20	20

No. J8
Surcharged in Blue   **3 CVOS. 3**

1937, July 29 Perf. 11 Unwmkd.

J15	D3	3c on 4c brown red		25	15
		First day cover			50.00

Nos. J8 to J14
Handstamped in Violet   **VICTORY**

1944, Dec. 3 Perf. 11 Unwmkd.

J16	D3	4c brown red		120.00	—
J17	"	6c	"	85.00	—
J18	"	8c	"	90.00	—
J19	"	10c	"	85.00	—
J20	"	12c	"	85.00	—
J21	"	16c	"	90.00	—
J22	"	20c	"	90.00	—

OFFICIAL STAMPS.
Official Handstamped Overprints.

"Officers purchasing stamps for government business may, if they so desire, surcharge them with the letters 'O. B.' either in writing with black ink or by rubber stamps but in such a manner as not to obliterate the stamp that postmasters will be unable to determine whether the stamps have been previously used." C. M. Cotterman, Director of Posts, December 26, 1905.

Beginning with January 1, 1906, all branches of the Insular Government, used postage stamps to prepay postage instead of franking them as before. Some officials used manuscript, some utilized the typewriting machines but by far the larger number provided themselves with rubber stamps. The majority of these read "O. B." but other forms were: "OFFICIAL BUSINESS" or "OFFICIAL MAIL" in two lines, with variations on many of these.

These "O. B." overprints are known on U. S. 1899-1901 stamps; on 1903-06 stamps in red and blue; on 1906 stamps in red, blue, black, yellow and green.

"O. B." overprints were also made on the centavo and peso stamps of the Philippines, per order of May 25, 1907.

Beginning in 1926 the stamps were overprinted and issued by the Government, but some post offices continued to handstamp "O.B."

During the Japanese occupation period 1942-45, the same system of handstamped official overprints prevailed, but the handstamp usually consisted of "K. P.", initials of the Tagalog words, "Kagamitang Pampamahalaan" (Official Business), and the two Japanese characters used in the printed overprint on Nos. NO1 to NO4.

Legislative Palace Issue of 1926

Overprinted in Red   **OFFICIAL**

Printed and overprinted by the
Philippine Bureau of Printing.

1926, Dec. 20 Perf. 12 Unwmkd.

O1	A42	2c green & black *(90,500)*	2.50	1.75
		On cover		3.00
		Block of four	10.50	7.25
O2	"	4c carmine & black *(90,450)*	2.50	1.60
		On cover		3.00
		First day cover		15.00
		Block of four	10.00	7.00
		a. Vertical pair, imperf. between	375.00	
O3	"	18c light brown & black *(70,000)*	7.00	6.00
		On cover		10.00
		Block of four	35.00	30.00
O4	"	20c orange & black *(70,250)*	6.00	2.00
		On cover		3.00
		Block of four	30.00	10.00
		First day cover, #O1–O4		75.00

Regular Issue of 1917-25 Overprinted   **O. B.**

Printed and overprinted by the
U. S. Bureau of Engraving and Printing.

1931 Perf. 11 Unwmkd.

O5	A40	2c green	6	5
		a. No period after "B"	10.00	5.00
		b. No period after "O"		
O6	"	4c carmine	8	5
		a. No period after "B"	10.00	5.00
O7	"	6c deep violet	10	8
O8	"	8c yellow brown	10	8
O9	"	10c deep blue	40	12
O10	"	12c red orange	25	15
		a. No period after "B"	30.00	
O11	"	16c light olive green *(Dewey)*	25	10
		a. 16c olive bistre	1.50	30
O12	"	20c orange yellow	30	10
		a. No period after "B"	15.00	15.00
O13	"	26c green	45	45
		a. 26c blue green	1.25	1.00
O14	"	30c gray	40	35

Regular Issue of 1935 Overprinted in Black   **O. B.**

1935 Perf. 11 Unwmkd.

O15	A53	2c rose	6	5
		a. No period after "B"	10.00	5.00
O16	A54	4c yellow green	6	5
		a. No period after "B"	10.00	7.50
O17	A55	6c dark brown	10	6
		a. No period after "B"	17.50	17.50

PHILIPPINES

O18	A56	8c violet	12	12
O19	A57	10c rose carmine	15	6
O20	A58	12c black	20	15
O21	A59	16c dark blue	20	15
O22	A60	20c light olive green	20	15
O23	A61	26c indigo	40	35
O24	A62	30c orange red	45	40

Nos. 411 and 418
with Additional Overprint in Black **O. B.**

1937-38   *Perf. 11.*   Unwmkd.

O25	A53	2c rose, *Apr. 10, 1937*	8	5
		First day cover		75.00
		a. No period after "B"	6.50	3.50
O26	A60	20c light olive green, *Apr. 26, 1938*	1.00	75

Regular Issue of 1935 Overprinted in Black:

O. B.   **O. B.**

COMMON-WEALTH   **COMMONWEALTH**
(a)   (b)

1938-40   *Perf. 11.*   Unwmkd.

O27	A53	(a)	2c rose	8	5
			a. Hyphen omitted	17.50	15.00
			b. No period after "B"	20.00	15.00
O28	A54	(b)	4c yellow green	10	8
O29	A55	(a)	6c dark brown	15	6
O30	A56	(b)	8c violet	15	10
O31	A57	(")	10c rose carmine	17	10
			a. No period after "O"	25.00	25.00
O32	A58	(")	12c black	18	18
O33	A59	(")	16c dark blue	25	12
O34	A60	(a)	20c light olive green ('40)	35	35
O35	A61	(b)	26c indigo	45	45
O36	A62	(")	30c orange red	40	40

No. 461
Overprinted in Black   **O. B.**
(c)

ROTARY PRESS PRINTING.

1941, April 14   *Perf. 11x10½*   Unwmkd.

O37	A75	2c apple green	6	6
		First day cover		5.00
		Margin block of four, P #	35	

Nos. O27, O37, O16, O29,
O31, O22 and O26
Handstamped in Violet **VICTORY**

1944   *Perf. 11, 11x10½.*   Unwmkd.

O38	A53	2c rose (On O27)	130.00	85.00
O39	A75	2c apple green (On O37)	5.00	3.00
		On cover		10.00
		Block of four	25.00	
O40	A54	4c yellow green (On O16)	25.00	20.00
		Block of four	125.00	
O40A	A55	6c dark brown (On O29)	3000.00	—
O41	A57	10c rose carmine (On O31)	100.00	
		Block of four	400.00	
O42	A60	20c light olive green (On O22)	3500.00	
O43	"	20c light olive green (On O26)	1400.00	

No. 497 Overprinted Type "c" in Black.

1946, June 19   *Perf. 11x10½*   Unwmkd.

O44	A76	2c sepia	6	5
		Margin block of 4, P #	40	

POST OFFICE SEALS.

POS1

Lithographed.

1906   *Perf. 12.*   Unwmkd.

OX1	POS1	light brown	35.00	—

Wmkd. "P I R S" in Double-lined Capitals.

1907   *Perf. 12.*

OX2	POS1	light brown	60.00	—

Hyphen-hole Perf. 7.

OX3	POS1	orange brown	30.00	—

1911   *Hyphen-hole Perf. 7.*

OX4	POS1	yellow brown	25.00	—
OX5	"	olive bistre	55.00	—
		a. Unwatermarked	—	
OX6	"	yellow	60.00	—

1913   *Hyphen-hole Perf. 7*   Unwmkd.

OX7	POS1	lemon yellow	1.25	1.25

Perf. 12.

OX8	POS1	yellow	—	—

Wmkd. "U S P S" in Single-lined Capitals.

Hyphen-hole Perf. 7.

OX9	POS1	yellow	60.00	30.00

1934   *Rouletted.*   Unwmkd.

OX10	POS1	dark blue	1.25	1.25

POS2

OX11	POS2	dark blue	1.00	1.00

POS3

1938   *Hyphen-hole Perf. 7*

OX12	POS3	dark blue	8.50	3.50
		a. Perforated 12		

PHILIPPINES

ENVELOPES.

U. S. Envelopes of 1899 Issue — PHILIPPINES.
Overprinted below stamp
in color of the stamp, except where noted.

1899–1900

Note: Many envelopes for which there was no obvious need were issued in small quantities. Anyone residing in the Islands could, by depositing with his postmaster the required amount, order any envelopes in quantities of 500, or multiples thereof, provided it was on the schedule of U. S. envelopes. Such special orders are indicated by an asterisk.

U 1	U77	1c green on white (No. U352) (370,000)	1.25	1.25
		Entire	5.00	6.00
U 2	"	1c green on amber (No. U353) (1,000*)	11.00	12.00
		Entire	40.00	37.50
U 3	"	1c green on amber (No. U353) red overprint (500*)	19.00	20.00
		Entire	55.00	50.00
U 4	"	1c green on oriental buff (No. U354) (1,000*)	13.50	12.50
		Entire	30.00	30.00
U 5	"	1c green on oriental buff (No. U354) red overprint (500*)	32.50	35.00
		Entire	70.00	70.00
U 6	"	1c green on blue (No. U355) (1,000*)	7.00	8.00
		Entire	22.50	25.00
U 7	"	1c green on blue (No. U355) red overprint (500*)	16.50	15.00
		Entire	60.00	55.00
U 8	U79	2c carmine on white (No. U362) (1,180,000)	1.25	1.25
		Entire	3.50	2.50
U 9	"	2c carmine on amber (No. U363) (21,000)	4.00	3.50
		Entire	12.50	10.00
U10	"	2c carmine on oriental buff (No. U364) (10,000)	4.00	3.50
		Entire	12.50	10.00
U11	"	2c carmine on blue (No. U365) (10,000)	6.00	6.00
		Entire	12.50	12.50
U12	U81	4c brown on amber (No. U372), Die 1 (500*)	35.00	35.00
		Entire	100.00	95.00
		a. Double overprint		
		Entire	2000.00	
U13	U83	4c brown on white (No. U374), Die 3 (10,500)	7.00	7.00
		Entire	30.00	30.00
U14	"	4c brown on amber (No. U375), Die 3 ((500*))	45.00	45.00
		Entire	140.00	110.00
U15	U84	5c blue on white (No. U377) (20,000)	6.00	6.00
		Entire	12.50	12.50
U16	"	5c blue on amber (No. U378) (500*)	27.50	30.00
		Entire	85.00	100.00

1903 Same Overprint on U.S. issue of 1903.

U17	U85	1c green on white (No. U379) (300,000)	1.25	1.00
		Entire	3.50	3.50
U18	"	1c green on amber (No. U380) (1,000*)	12.00	12.00
		Entire	22.50	25.00
U19	"	1c green on oriental buff (No. U381) (1,000*)	12.00	12.00
		Entire	22.50	27.50
U20	"	1c green on blue (No. U382) (1,500*)	10.00	11.00
		Entire	22.50	27.50
U21	"	1c green on manila (No. U383) (500*)	16.00	17.50
		Entire	40.00	45.00
U22	U86	2c carmine on white (No. U385) (150,500)	4.00	3.00
		Entire	6.00	6.00
U23	"	2c carmine on amber (No. U386) (500*)	16.00	10.00
		Entire	40.00	35.00
U24	"	2c carmine on oriental buff (No. U387) (500*)	16.00	22.50
		Entire	40.00	
U25	"	2c carmine on blue (No. U388) (500'	16.00	15.00
		Entire	40.00	
U26	U87	4c chocolate on amber (No. U391) (500*)	45.00	55.00
		Entire	125.00	150.00
		a. Double overprint, entire	2000.00	
U27	U88	5c blue on amber (No. U394) (500*)	45.00	—
		Entire	125.00	125.00

1906 Same Overprint on Re-cut U. S. issue of 1904.

U28	U89	2c carmine on white (No. U395)	35.00	25.00
		Entire	130.00	110.00
U29	"	2c carmine on oriental buff (No. U397)	65.00	125.00
		Entire	200.00	225.00

Rizal
E1

1908

U30	E1	2c green on white	20	10
		Entire	1.00	1.00
U31	"	2c green on amber	4.00	2.00
		Entire	10.00	8.00
U32	"	2c green on oriental buff	5.00	3.00
		Entire	10.00	10.00
U33	"	2c green on blue	5.00	3.00
		Entire	10.00	10.00
U34	"	2c green on manila (500)	7.00	—
		Entire	17.50	25.00
U35	"	4c carmine on white, *McKinley*	20	20
		Entire	1.00	1.00
U36	"	4c carmine on amber	4.00	2.50
		Entire	10.00	8.00
U37	"	4c carmine on oriental buff	5.00	2.50
		Entire	10.00	12.50
U38	"	4c carmine on blue	4.50	2.00
		Entire	10.00	10.00
U39	"	4c carmine on manila (500)	10.00	—
		Entire	20.00	35.00

Rizal
E2

1927, April 5

U40	E2	2c green on white	12.00	10.00
		Entire	30.00	30.00
		Entire, 1st day cancel		50.00

PHILIPPINES

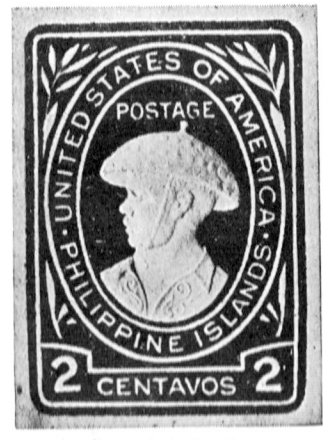

"Juan de la Cruz"
E3

1935, June 19

U41	E3	2c carmine on white	15	10
		Entire	60	50
U42	"	4c olive green on white	25	25
		Entire	1.00	1.25

Nos. U30, U35, U41 and U42 **VICTORY**
Handstamped in Violet

1944

U42A	E1	2c green on white (On U30), Entire	—	
U43	E3	2c carmine on white (On U41)	17.50	12.50
		Entire	35.00	50.00
U44	E1	4c carmine on white, *McKinley* (On U35)		
		Entire	700.00	700.00
U45	E3	4c olive green on white (On U42)	75.00	80.00
		Entire	120.00	130.00

WRAPPERS.

U. S. Wrappers
Overprinted in Color PHILIPPINES.
of Stamp

1901

W1	U77	1c green on manila (No. W357) (*320,000*)	85	85
		Entire	3.00	3.50

1905

W2	U85	1c green on manila (No. W384)	8.00	8.00
		Entire	17.50	17.50
		a. Double overprint, entire	2000.00	
W3	U86	2c carmine on manila (No. W389)	9.00	10.00
		Entire	20.00	20.00

1908 Design of Philippine Envelopes.

W4	E1	2c green on manila	90	90
		Entire	6.00	6.00

POSTAL CARDS.

Prices are for Entires.

U. S. Cards
Overprinted in Black below PHILIPPINES.
Stamp *a*

1900, February

UX1	(*a*)	1c black (Jefferson) (UX14) (*100,000*)	15.00	12.00
		a. Without period	40.00	
UX2	(")	2c black (Liberty) (UX16) (*20,000*)	35.00	20.00

PHILIPPINES
1903, Sept. 15 *b*

UX3	(*b*)	1c black (McKinley) (UX18)	1350.00	1100.00
UX4	(")	2c black (Liberty) (UX16)	750.00	600.00

PHILIPPINES.
c
1903, Nov. 10

UX5	(*c*)	1c black (McKinley) (UX18)	60.00	35.00
UX6	(")	2c black (Liberty) (UX16)	70.00	60.00

PHILIPPINES
d
1906

UX7	(*d*)	1c black (McKinley) (UX18)	325.00	325.00
UX8	(")	2c black (Liberty) (UX16)	1750.00	1350.00

1907 Designs same as postage issue of 1906.

UX9	A40	2c black on buff (Rizal)	10.00	7.50
UX10	"	4c black on buff (McKinley)	25.00	20.00

1911 Color changes

UX11	A40	2c blue on light blue (Rizal)	7.50	7.50
		a. 2c blue on white	22.50	20.00
UX12	"	4c blue on light blue (McKinley)	25.00	20.00

An impression of No. UX11 exists on the back of a U. S. No. UX21.

1915

UX13	A40	2c green on buff (Rizal)	3.25	2.25
UX14	"	2c yellow green on amber	2.25	1.25
UX15	"	4c green on buff (McKinley)	18.00	13.50

1935 Design of postage issue of 1935.

UX16	A53	2c red on pale buff (Rizal)	2.75	1.75

No. UX16
Overprinted at left of Stamp **COMMONWEALTH**

1938

UX17	A53	2c red on pale buff	2.75	1.50

COMMONWEALTH

UX18	A53	2c red on pale buff	50.00	40.00

COMMONWEALTH

UX19	A53	2c red on pale buff	4.00	4.00

Nos. UX13, UX18 and UX19 **VICTORY**
Handstamped in Violet

1944

UX20	A40	2c green on buff, *Rizal* (On UX13)	150.00	150.00
UX21	A53	2c red on pale buff (On UX18)	500.00	—
UX22	"	2c red on pale buff (On UX19)	250.00	—

Overprinted in Black at left **VICTORY**
1945, Jan. 19

UX23	A76	2c gray brown on pale buff	1.25	50
		First day cancel		3.00
		a. "IC" of "Victory" very close	5.00	3.00

This card was not issued without overprint.

PAID REPLY POSTAL CARDS.

U. S. Paid Reply Cards of 1892-93 issues
overprinted with type "a" in blue

1900, Feb.

UY1		2c+2c blue on white, unsevered (*5,000*)	150.00	150.00
		m. PM2, Message card, detached	20.00	25.00
		r. PR2, Reply card, detached	20.00	25.00

1903 Overprinted type "c" in black

UY2		1c+1c black on buff, unsevered (*20,000*)	150.00	175.00
		m. PM1, Message card, detached	20.00	25.00
		r. PR1, Reply card, detached	20.00	25.00
UY3		2c+2c blue on white, unsevered (*20,000*)	350.00	
		m. PM2, Message card, detached	50.00	50.00
		r. PR2, Reply card, detached	50.00	50.00

OFFICIAL CARDS.

Overprinted **O. B.** at Left of Stamp

1925 On postal card No. UX13

UZ1	A40	2c green on buff (Rizal)	30.00	27.50

874   PHILIPPINES

1935		On postal card No. UX16.		
UZ2	A53	2c red on pale buff	12.00	15.00

Overprinted **O. B.** at Left of Stamp.

1938		On postal card No. UX19.		
UZ3	A53	2c red on pale buff	13.50	15.00

Overprinted **O. B.** Below Stamp.

1941		Design of postage issue of 1941.		
UZ4	A75	2c light green on pale buff	125.00	150.00
		This card was not issued without overprint.		

Postal Card No. UX19

Overprinted **O. B.** at Left of Stamp.

1941				
UZ5	A53	2c red on pale buff	20.00	20.00

OCCUPATION STAMPS.
Issued Under Japanese Occupation.

Nos. 461, 438 and 439 Overprinted with Bars in Black.

1942-43		*Perf. 11x10½, 11.*	Unwmkd.	
N1	A75	2c apple green, *March 4, 1942*	6	6
		Margin block of 4, P#	30	
		a. Pair, one without overprint		
N2	A58	12c black, *April 30, 1943*	15	15
N3	A59	16c dark blue, *March 4, 1942*	4.50	3.50

Nos. 435a, 435, 442, 443, and 423 Surcharged in Black

1942-43			*Perf. 11*	
N4	A55 (a)	5(c) on 6c golden brown		
		Sept. 1, 1942	10	10
		First day cover		1.50
		a. Top bar shorter and thinner	20	20
		b. 5(c) on 6c dark brown	20	20
		c. As "b", top bar shorter and thinner	20	20

N5	A62 (b)	16(c) on 30c orange red,		
		Jan. 11, 1943	20	20
		First day cover		1.75
N6	A63 (c)	50c on 1p red orange & black,		
		April 30, 1943	60	60
		a. Double surcharge		250.00
N7	A65 (d)	1p on 4p blue & black,		
		April 30, 1943	67.50	52.50
		Inverted "S" in "PESO"; position 4	80.00	80.00

On Nos. N4 and N4b, the top bar measures 1½ x 22½ mm. On Nos. N4a and N4c, the top bar measures 1 x 21 mm. and the "5" is smaller and thinner.

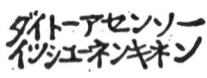

1942, May 18

N8	A54	2(c) on 4c yellow green	2.50	2.00
		First day cover		4.00

Issued to commemorate Japan's capture of Bataan and Corregidor. The American-Filipino forces finally surrendered May 7, 1942. No. N8 exists with "R" for "B" in BATAAN.

No. 384 Surcharged in Black

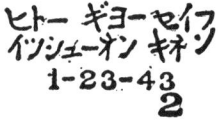

1942, Dec. 8

N9	A54	5(c) on 4c yellow green	45	30
		First day cover		1.50

Issued to commemorate the first anniversary of the "Greater East Asia War".

Nos. C59 and C62 Surcharged in Black

1943, Jan. 23

N10	AP1	2(c) on 8c carmine	20	20
N11	"	5c on 1p sepia	40	40
		First day cover, # N10-N11		2.00

Issued to commemorate the first anniversary of the Philippine Executive Commission.

Nipa Hut	Rice Planting	Mt. Mayon and Mt. Fuji
OS1	OS2	OS3

PHILIPPINES 875

Moro Vinta
OS4

Wmk. 257

José Rizal
OS7

Rev. José Burgos
OS8

Apolinario Mabini
OS9

Lithographed.

			Perf. 12	Unwmkd.	
1944, Feb. 17					
N32	OS7	5c blue		22	22
		a. Imperf.		22	22
N33	OS8	12c carmine		12	12
		a. Imperf.		12	12
N34	OS9	17c deep orange		16	16
		First day cover, #N32–N34			1.50
		a. Imperf.		16	16
		First day cover, #N32a–N34a, Apr. 17			2.25

Engr.; Typo. (2c, 6c, 25c)

		Perf. 13.	Wmk. 257	
1943-44				
N12	OS1	1c deep orange, June 7, 1943	5	5
N13	OS2	2c bright green, Apr. 1, 1943	5	5
N14	OS1	4c slate green, June 7, 1943	5	5
N15	OS3	5c orange brown, Apr. 1, 1943	8	8
N16	OS2	6c red, July 14, 1943	6	6
N17	OS3	10c blue green, July 14, 1943	75	75
N18	OS4	12c steel blue, July 14, 1943	6	6
N19	"	16c dark brown, July 14, 1943	85	85
N20	OS1	20c rose violet, Aug. 16, 1943	15	15
N21	OS3	21c violet, Aug. 16, 1943	6	5
N22	OS2	25c pale brown, Aug. 16, 1943	18	15
N23	OS3	1p deep carmine, June 7, 1943	1.75	1.50
N24	OS4	2p dull violet, Sept. 16, 1943		7.50
		First day cover	6.00	5.00
N25	"	5p dark olive, Apr. 10, 1944		7.50
		First day cover		

Nos. C60 and C61 Surcharged in Black

		Perf. 11.	Unwmkd.	
1944, May 7				
N35	AP1	5(c) on 20c ultramarine	50	50
N36	"	12(c) on 60c blue green	1.00	1.00
		First day cover, #N35–N36		3.00

Issued to commemorate the second anniversary of the fall of Bataan and Corregidor.

Map of Manila Bay Showing Bataan and Corregidor
OS5

		Photogravure.	Unwmkd.	
1943, May 7				
N26	OS5	2c carmine red	12	12
N27	"	5c bright green	18	18
		Colorless dot after left "5"	1.50	
		First day cover, #N26–N27		2.00

Issued to commemorate the first anniversary of the fall of Bataan and Corregidor.

No. 440 Surcharged in Black

		Engraved	Perf. 11	
1943, June 20				
N28	A60	12(c) on 20c light olive green	25	20
		First day cover		1.75
		a. Double surcharge		

Issued to commemorate the 350th anniversary of the printing press in the Philippines. "Limbagan" is Tagalog for "printing press."

José P. Laurel
OS10

Lithographed.
Without Gum.

		Imperf.	Unwmkd.	
1945, Jan. 12				
N37	OS10	5c dull violet brown	7	6
N38	"	7c blue green	10	8
N39	"	20c chalky blue	15	12
		First day cover, #N37–N39		1.00

Issued belatedly on Jan. 12, 1945, to commemorate the first anniversary of the puppet Philippine Republic, Oct. 14, 1944. "S" stands for "sentimos."

The special cancellers prepared for use on Oct. 14, 1944, were employed on "First Day" covers Jan. 12, 1945.

OCCUPATION SEMI-POSTAL STAMPS.

Rizal Monument, Filipina and Philippine Flag
OS6

Woman, Farming and Cannery
OSP1

		Photogravure.		
1943, Oct. 14		Perf. 12.	Unwmkd.	
N29	OS6	5c light blue	10	10
		a. Imperf.	12	12
N30	"	12c orange	14	14
		a. Imperf.	16	16
N31	"	17c rose pink	16	16
		First day cover, #N29–N31		1.25
		a. Imperf.	22	22
		First day cover, #N29a–N31a		1.25

Issued to commemorate the "Independence of the Philippines." Japan granted "independence" Oct. 14, 1943, when the puppet republic was founded. The imperforate stamps were issued without gum.

Lithographed.

			Perf. 12.	Unwmkd.	
1942, Nov. 12					
NB1	OSP1	2c+1c pale violet		15	15
NB2	"	5c+1c bright green		10	10
NB3	"	16c+2c orange		12.00	10.00
		First day cover, #NB1–NB3			17.50

Issued to promote the campaign to produce and conserve food. The surtax aided the Red Cross.

PHILIPPINES

Souvenir Sheet.

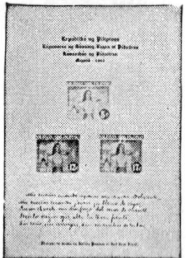

OSP2

	1943, Oct. 14		Without Gum.		Imperf.
NB4	OSP2	Sheet of three		35.00	2.00
		First day cover, Manila			5.00

Issued to commemorate the "Independence of the Philippines."
No. NB4 contains one each of Nos. N29a–N31a. Marginal inscription is from Rizal's "Last Farewell". Size: 127x177 mm. Sold for 2.50p.

Nos. N18, N20 and N21
Surcharged in Black

BAHA 1943 +21

	1943, Dec. 8		Perf. 13.		Wmk. 257
NB5	OS4	12c+21(c) steel blue		15	15
NB6	OS1	20c+36(c) rose violet		12	12
NB7	OS3	21c+40(c) violet		15	15
		First day cover, ✻ NB5–NB7			1.75

The surtax was for the benefit of victims of a Luzon flood. "Baha" is Tagalog for "flood."

Souvenir Sheet

OSP3
Lithographed

	1944, Feb. 9		Imperf.		Unwmkd.
		Without Gum.			
NB8	OSP3	Sheet of three		2.00	2.50
		First day cover			5.00

No. NB8 contains one each of Nos. N32a–N34a.
The sheet sold for 1p, the surtax going to a fund for the care of heroes' monuments. Size: 101x143mm. No. NB8 exists with 5c inverted.

OCCUPATION POSTAGE DUE STAMP.

No. J15 Overprinted with Bar in Blue.

	1942, Oct. 14		Perf. 11.		Unwmkd.
NJ1	D3	3c on 4c brown red		22.50	10.00
		First day cover			25.00
		Double bar			—

On copies of No. J15, two lines were drawn in India ink with a ruling pen across "United States of America" by employees of the Short Paid Section of the Manila Post Office to make a provisional 3c postage due stamp which was used from Sept. 1, 1942 (when the letter rate was raised from 2c to 5c) until Oct. 14 when No. NJ1 went on sale. Price on cover, $150.

OCCUPATION OFFICIAL STAMPS.

Nos. 461, 413, 435, 435a and 442
Overprinted or Surcharged in Black with Bars and 公用 (K. P.)

	1943–44		Perf. 11x10½, 11		Unwmkd.
NO1	A75	2c apple green, *April 7, 1943*		8	8
		Margin block of 4, P ✻		40	
		a. Double overprint			
NO2	A55	5(c) on 6c dark brown (On No. 413), *June 26, 1944*		20.00	20.00
		First day cover			45.00
NO3	"	5(c) on 6c golden brown (On No. 435a), *April 7, 1943*		15	15
		a. Narrower spacing between bars		20	20
		b. 5(c) on 6c dark brown (On No. 435)		15	12
		c. As "b", narrower spacing between bars		20	20
NO4	A62	16(c) on 30c orange red, *April 7, 1943*		45	45
		a. Wider spacing between bars		45	45
		First day cover (✻ NO1, NO3–NO4)			50.00

On Nos. NO3 and NO3b the bar deleting "United States of America" is 9¾ to 10 mm. above the bar deleting "Common". On Nos. NO3a and NO3c, the spacing is 8 to 8½ mm.
On No. NO4, the center bar is 19 mm. long, 3½ mm. below the top bar and 6mm. above the Japanese characters. On No. NO4a, the center bar is 20½ mm. long, 9 mm. below the top bar and 1 mm. above the Japanese characters.
"K. P." stands for Kagamitang Pampamahalaan, "Official Business" in Tagalog.

Nos. 435 and 435a
Surcharged in Black

	1944, Aug. 28		Perf. 11		Unwmkd.
NO5	A55	(5c) on 6c golden brown		10	10
		a. 5(c) on 6c dark brown		10	10

Nos. O34 and C62
Overprinted in Black

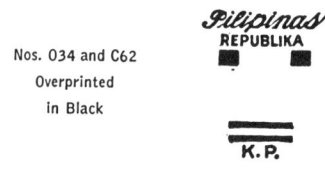

NO6	A60	(*a*) 20c light olive green	35	35
NO7	AP1	(*b*) 1p sepia	1.00	1.00
		First day cover, ✻ NO5–NO7		3.00

OCCUPATION ENVELOPES.

No. U41
Surcharged in Black

1943, April 1
NU1 E3 5c on 2c carmine on white   20   20
             Entire   1.00 1.00
             Entire, 1st day cancel   3.50

No. U41
Surcharged in Black

1944, Feb. 17
NU2 E3 5c on 2c carmine on white   20   20
             Entire   1.00 1.00
             Entire, 1st day cancel   3.50
             a. Inverted surcharge   —
             b. Double surcharge   —
             c. Both 5's missing   —

OCCUPATION POSTAL CARDS.
Prices are for entire cards.
Nos. UX19 and UZ4 Overprinted with Bars in Black

1942
NUX1 A53 2c red on pale buff,
                  March 4, 1942   6.00   3.00
                  First day cancel   100.00
                  a. Vertical obliteration bars
                       reversed   200.00
NUX2 A75 2c light green on pale buff,
                  Dec. 12, 1942   3.00   2.25
                  First day cancel   7.50

Rice Planting
A77

1943, May 17
NUX3 A77 2c green   75   1.00
                   First day cancel, Manila   2.00

OCCUPATION OFFICIAL CARDS
Nos. UX19, UX17 and UX18 Overprinted in Black
with Bars and   △ 🏣
                                                (K. P.)

1943-44
NUZ1 A53 2c red on pale buff,
                  Apr. 7, 1943   3.00   2.00
                  First day cancel   100.00
                  a. On No. UX17   —   —
                  b. On No. UX18   —   —

No. NUX3
Overprinted in Black

REPUBLIKA
NG PILIPINAS
(K. P.)

NUZ2 A77 2c green, *Aug. 28, 1944*   75   50
                  First day cancel   2.00
                  a. Double overprint

Filipino Revolutionary Government Issues.

The Filipino Republic was instituted by Gen. Emilio Aguinaldo on June 23, 1899. At the same time he assumed the office of President. Aguinaldo dominated the greater part of the island of Luzon and some of the smaller islands until late in 1899. He was taken prisoner by United States Troops on March 23, 1901.

The devices composing the National Arms, adopted by the Filipino Revolutionary Government, are emblems of the Katipunan political secret society or of Katipunan origin. The letters "K K K" on these stamps are the initials of this society whose complete name is "Kataastaasang, Kagalang-galang Katipunan nang Manga Anak nang Bayan," meaning "Sovereign Worshipful Association of the Sons of the Country."

The regular postage and telegraph stamps were in use on Luzon as early as Nov. 10, 1898. Owing to the fact that stamps for the different purposes were not always available together with a lack of proper instructions, any of the adhesives were permitted to be used in the place of the other. Hence telegraph and revenue stamps were accepted for postage and postage stamps for revenue or telegraph charges. In addition to the regular postal emission, there are a number of provisional stamps, issues of local governments of islands and towns.

POSTAGE ISSUES.

Coat of Arms   Coat of Arms   Coat of Arms
      A1   A2   A3

1898-99   *Perf. 11½.*   Unwmkd.
V1 A1 2c red   11.00   9.00
           a. Double impression   300.00
V2 A2 2c red   6   40
           a. Imperf., pair   —
           b. Double impression   —
           c. Imperf. horizontally, pair   —   —
           d. Horiz. pair, imperf. between —
V3 A3 2c red   3.00

REGISTRATION STAMP.

RS1

VF1 RS1 8c green   18   2.00
            a. Imperf., pair   —
            b. Imperf. vertically, pair   —

NEWSPAPER STAMP

N1

VP1 N1 1m black   6
            a. Imperf., pair   15

PHILIPPINES

PROOFS.

		DIE (1) Large	DIE (2) Small	(2a)	PLATE (4) Glazed Card
1906					
241P	2c yellow green		225.00		400.00
242P	4c carmine lake	600.00	225.00		400.00
243P	6c violet	600.00	225.00		400.00
244P	8c brown	600.00	225.00		400.00
245P	10c dark blue		225.00		400.00
246P	12c brown lake		225.00		400.00
247P	16c violet black	600.00	225.00		400.00
248P	20c orange brown		225.00		400.00
249P	26c violet brown		225.00		400.00
250P	30c olive green		225.00		400.00
251P	1p orange		225.00		400.00
252P	2p black		225.00		400.00
253P	4p dark blue		225.00		400.00
254P	10p dark green		225.00		400.00
1909-13					
255P	12c red orange		225.00		400.00
256P	16c olive green		225.00		400.00
257P	20c yellow		225.00		400.00
258P	26c blue green		225.00		400.00
259P	30c ultramarine		225.00		400.00
260P	1p pale violet		225.00		400.00
260A-P	2p violet brown		225.00		400.00
275P	30c gray		225.00		400.00
1923					
303P	16c olive bistre	600.00			
303TC	16c olive green	600.00			
1926					
322P	18c light brown & black				
1932					
357P	18c red orange	600.00			
357TC	18c orange red	600.00			
1935					
383P	2c rose	600.00			
384P	4c yellow green	600.00			
385P	6c dark brown	600.00			
386P	8c violet	600.00			
387P	10c rose carmine	600.00			
388P	12c black	600.00			
389P	16c dark blue	600.00			
390P	20c light olive green	600.00			
391P	26c indigo	600.00			
392P	30c orange red	600.00			
393P	1p red orange & black	600.00			
394P	2p bistre brown & black	600.00			
395P	4p blue & black	600.00			
396P	5p green & black	600.00			
1936					
408P	2c orange brown	600.00			
408TC	2c yellow green	600.00			
1937					
425P	2c yellow green		300.00		
1939					
452P	2c yellow green		300.00		
453P	6c carmine		300.00		
454P	12c bright blue		300.00		
1939					
455P	2c green	500.00	300.00		
456P	6c orange		300.00		
457P	12c carmine		300.00		
1940					
458P	2c dark orange	500.00	300.00		
459P	6c dark green		300.00		
460P	12c purple		300.00		
1941					
461P	2c apple green		300.00		
1946					
497P	2c sepia	—			

AIR POST.

1941			
C59P	8c carmin		500.00
C60P	20c ultramarine		500.00
C61P	60c blue green		500.00
C62P	1p sepia		500.00

SPECIAL DELIVERY.

1906					
E2P	20c ultramarine	600.00	200.00	350.00	
E2TC	20c green		225.00		

POSTAGE DUE.

1899			
J1P	1c deep claret		500.00
J2P	2c "		"
J3P	5c "		"
J4P	10c "		"
J5P	50c "		"
1901			
J6P	3c deep claret		"
J7P	30c "		"

SPECIMEN STAMPS.

1899   Overprinted **Specimen** in Black.

Type E.

213S E	1c yellow green	150.00
214S E	2c orange red	150.00
215S E	3c purple	150.00
216S E	5c blue	150.00
217S E	10c brown, type 1	150.00
218S E	15c olive brown	150.00
219S E	50c orange	150.00

Special Printings (Paris 1899) with "Specimen" overprints exist. Price, each $350.

1917-25   Overprinted **Specimen** in Black.

Type R

290S R	2c green	40.00
291S R	4c carmine	40.00
292S R	6c deep violet	40.00
293S R	8c yellow brown	40.00
294S R	10c deep blue	40.00
295S R	12c red orange	40.00
297S R	20c orange yellow	40.00
298S R	26c green	40.00
299S R	30c gray	40.00
300S R	1p pale violet	40.00
301S R	2p violet brown	40.00
302S R	4p blue	40.00

1923-26

303S R	16c olive bistre	40.00
304S R	10p deep green	40.00

1926   Overprinted Type R in Red.

319S R	2c green & black	50.00
320S R	4c carmine & black	50.00
321S R	16c olive green & black	50.00
322S R	18c light brown & black	50.00
323S R	20c orange & black	50.00
324S R	24c gray & black	50.00
325S R	1p rose lilac & black	50.00

1926   Overprinted **Cancelled** in Red.

Type S.

319S S	2c green & black	50.00
320S S	4c carmine & black	50.00
321S S	16c olive green & black	50.00
322S S	18c light brown & black	50.00
323S S	20c orange & black	50.00
324S S	24c gray & black	50.00
325S S	1p rose lilac & black	50.00

Imperforate copies of this set, on glazed cards with centers in brown, are known with the "Cancelled" overprint.

Handstamped "SPECIMEN"
in Red Capitals, 13x3mm.

1925		
340S	2c green	30.00
341S	4c carmine	30.00
342S	6c deep violet	30.00
343S	8c yellow brown	30.00

PHILIPPINES

344S	10c deep blue	30.00
345S	12c red orange	30.00
346S	16c olive bistre	30.00
347S	20c yellow	30.00
348S	26c blue green	30.00
349S	30c gray	30.00
350S	1p violet	30.00
351S	2p violet brown	30.00
352S	4p deep blue	40.00
353S	10p deep green	50.00

Special Delivery.

1919   Overprinted Type R in Black.

E5S R	20c ultramarine	250.00

Handstamped "SPECIMEN" in Red Capitals, 13x3mm.

1925

E6aS	20c violet blue	250.00

Postage Due.

1899   Overprinted Type E in Black.

J1S	E	1c deep claret	150.00
J2S	E	2c "	150.00
J3S	E	5c "	150.00
J4S	E	10c "	150.00
J5S	E	50c "	150.00

Official.

1926   Overprinted Type R in Red.

O1S	R	2c green & black	45.00
O2S	R	4c carmine & black	45.00
O3S	R	18c light brown & black	45.00
O4S	R	20c orange & black	45.00

1926   Overprinted Type S in Red.

O1S	S	2c green & black	45.00
O2S	S	4c carmine & black	45.00
O3S	S	18c light brown & black	45.00
O4S	S	20c orange & black	45.00

PUERTO RICO
(Porto Rico)

United States troops landed at Guanica Bay, Puerto Rico, on July 25, 1898, and mail service between various points in Puerto Rico began soon after under the authority of General Wilson, acting governor of the conquered territory, who authorized a provisional service early in August, 1898. The first Military Postal Station was opened at La Playa de Ponce on August 3, 1898. Control of the island passed formally to the United States on October 18, 1898. Twenty-one military stations operating under the administration of the Military Postal Service, were authorized in Puerto Rico after the Spanish-American war. After the overprinted provisional issue of 1900, unoverprinted stamps of the United States replaced those of Puerto Rico.

Name changed to Puerto Rico by Act of Congress, approved May 17, 1932.

100 CENTS = 1 DOLLAR.

Provisional Issues.

Ponce Issue.

A11

1898		Imperf. Handstamped		Unwmkd.	
200	A11	5c violet, *yellowish*		6000.00	—

Dangerous counterfeits exist.

Coamo Issue.

A12

Types of "5":
  I. Curved flag. Pos. 2, 3, 4, 5.
  II. Flag turns down at right. Pos. 1, 9, 10.
  III. Fancy outlined "5". Pos. 6, 7.
  IV. Flag curls into ball at right. Pos. 8.

Typeset, setting of 10.

1898, August		Imperf.	Unwmkd.	
201	A12	5c black, Type I	425.00	425.00
		Type II	450.00	450.00
		Type III	475.00	475.00
		Type IV	500.00	500.00
		Pair	950.00	—
		Block of four	2200.00	
		Sheet of ten	6500.00	
		On cover		1250.00
		Pair on cover		

The stamps bear the control mark "F. Santiago" in violet. About 500 were issued.

Dangerous counterfeits exist.

Regular Issue.

Stamps of the United States
Nos. 279, 267, 281, 272 and 282C
Overprinted in Black
at 36° Angle

Wmkd. Double-lined U. S. P. S. (191)

1899				Perf. 12	
210	A87	1c yellow green		6.50	1.75
		On cover			20.00
		Block of four		30.00	15.00
		Margin strip of 3, Impt. & P #		50.00	
		Margin block of 6, Impt. & P #		200.00	
	a.	Overprint at 25° angle		9.00	2.50
		Pair, 36° and 25° angles		25.00	
		"PORTO RICU"		30.00	—

PUERTO RICO

211	A88	2c carmine, type III	6.00	1.50
		On cover		12.50
		Block of four	30.00	12.50
		Margin strip of 3, Impt. & P #	40.00	
		Margin block of 6, Impt. & P #	200.00	
		a. Overprint at 25° angle	7.50	2.00
		Pair, 36° and 25° angles	22.50	
		"PORTU RICO"	60.00	22.50
		"FORTO RICO"		
212	A91	5c blue	9.00	2.25
		On cover		35.00
		Block of four	42.50	20.00
		Margin strip of 3, Impt. & P #	75.00	
		Margin block of 6, Impt. & P #	300.00	
213	A93	8c violet brown	30.00	17.50
		On cover		125.00
		Block of four	150.00	90.00
		Margin strip of 3, Impt. & P #	250.00	
		Margin block of 6, Impt. & P #	1000.00	
		a. Overprint at 25° angle	37.50	20.00
		Pair, 36° and 25° angles	85.00	
		"FORTO RICO"		
		c. "PORTO RIC"	125.00	125.00
214	A94	10c brown, type I	21.00	6.00
		On cover		100.00
		Block of four	95.00	45.00
		Margin strip of 3, Impt. & P #		
		Margin block of 6, Impt. & P #	750.00	
		"FORTO RICO"	100.00	100.00

Misspellings of the overprint on Nos. 210-214 (PORTO RICU, PORTU RICO, FORTO RICO) are actually broken letters.

United States
Nos. 279, 267 and 279d
Overprinted in Black

1900

215	A87	1c yellow green	6.50	1.75
		On cover		17.50
		Block of four	30.00	12.50
		Margin strip of 3, Impt. & P #	35.00	
		Margin block of 6, Impt. & P #	150.00	
216	A88	2c carmine, type III	6.00	1.25
		On cover		15.00
		Block of four	26.00	9.00
		Margin strip of 3, Impt. & P #	35.00	
		Margin block of 6, Impt. & P #	135.00	
		a. 2c orange red, type III	6.50	1.25
		b. Inverted overprint		3500.00

Special Printing.

In 1899 one sheet each of Nos. 210-212 and 214, and two sheets each of Nos. 213, J1-J3 were specially overprinted "Porto Rico" for display at the Paris Exposition. Price, each $350. Later another special printing of Nos. 212-216, J1-J3 was made reading "Puerto Rico." Price, each $500.00.
Of both printings, all but a few copies were destroyed. Nearly all existing copies of Nos. 215-216 are handstamped "Special Surcharge" on the back.

AIR POST.

In 1938 a series of eight labels, two of which were surcharged, was offered to the public as "Semi-Official Air Post Stamps", the claim being that they had been authorized by the "Puerto Rican postal officials." These labels, printed by the Ever Ready Label Co. of New York, were a private issue of Aerovias Nacionales Puerto Rico, operating a passenger and air express service. Instead of having been authorized by the postal officials, they were at first forbidden but later tolerated by the Post Office Department at Washington.

In 1941 a further set of eight triangular labels was prepared and offered to collectors, and again the Post Office Department officials at Washington objected and forbade their use after September 16, 1941.

These labels represent only the charge for service rendered by a private enterprise for transporting matter outside the mails by plane. Their use did not and does not eliminate the payment of postage on letters carried by air express, which must in every instance be paid by United States postage stamps.

POSTAGE DUE STAMPS.

Postage Due Stamps of the United States
Nos. J38, J39 and J42
Overprinted in Black at 36° Angle

Wmkd. Double-lined USPS (191)

1899   **Perf. 12**

J1	D2	1c deep claret	22.00	8.00
		On cover		
		Block of four	100.00	75.00
		Margin strip of 3, Impt. & P #	150.00	
		Margin block of 6, Impt. & P #	600.00	
		a. Overprint at 25° angle	27.50	10.00
		Pair, 36° and 25° angles	80.00	
J2	"	2c deep claret	15.00	7.50
		On cover		
		Block of four	70.00	
		Margin strip of 3, Impt. & P #	150.00	
		Margin block of 6, Impt. & P #	600.00	
		a. Overprint at 25° angle	20.00	8.50
		Pair, 36° and 25° angles	50.00	
J3	"	10c deep claret	150.00	55.00
		Block of four	750.00	
		Margin strip of 3, Impt. & P #	800.00	
		Margin block of 6, Impt. & P #	3000.00	
		a. Overprint at 25° angle	185.00	65.00
		Pair, 36° and 25° angles	425.00	

ENVELOPES.

U. S. Envelopes of 1887 Issue   **PORTO RICO.**
Overprinted in Black

1899-1900   20mm. long.

Note: Some envelopes for which there was no obvious need were issued in small quantities. Anyone residing in Puerto Rico could, by depositing with his postmaster the required amount, order any envelope in quantities of 500, or multiples thereof, provided it was on the schedule of U. S. envelopes. Such special orders are indicated by an asterisk, i. e.—Nos. U15 and U18, and half the quantities of Nos. U16 and U17.

U1	U71	2c green on white (No. U311) (3,000)	8.00	12.50
		Entire	45.00	55.00
		a. Double overprint, entire		
U2	U74	5c blue on white (No. U330) (1,000)	12.00	15.00
		Entire	55.00	55.00
		a. Double overprint, entire		

U. S. Envelopes of 1899
Overprinted in color   **PORTO RICO.**
of the stamp
    21mm. long.

U3	U79	2c carmine on white (No. U362) (100,000)	1.25	2.50
		Entire	10.00	12.50
U4	U84	5c blue on white (No. U377) (10,000)	6.00	6.00
		Entire	17.50	32.50

Overprinted **PORTO RICO.** in Black.
    19mm. long.

U5	U77	1c green on blue (No. U355) (1,000)		600.00
		Entire		2000.00
U6	U79	2c carmine on amber (No. U363), Die 2 (500)	400.00	500.00
		Entire	1250.00	1500.00
U7	"	2c carmine on oriental buff (No. U364), Die 2 (500)		500.00
		Entire		1500.00
U8	U80	2c carmine on oriental buff (No. U369), Die 3 (500)		500.00
		Entire		1500.00
U9	U79	2c carmine on blue (No. U365), Die 2		
		Entire		3500.00
U10	U83	4c brown on white (No. U374), Die 3 (500)		200.00
		Entire		400.00 500.00

PUERTO RICO

U. S. Envelopes of 1899 Issue Overprinted PUERTO RICO.

23mm. long.

U11	U79	2c carmine on white (No. U362) red overprint (100,000)	1.75	1.75
		Entire	10.00	11.00
U12	"	2c carmine on oriental buff (No. U364), Die 2, black overprint (1,000)	— —	250.00
		Entire	1000.00	1100.00
U13	U80	2c carmine on oriental buff (No. U369), Die 3, black overprint (1,000)		250.00
		Entire		2000.00
U14	U84	5c blue on white (No. U377) blue overprint (10,000)	10.00	10.00
		Entire	45.00	55.00

Overprinted PUERTO RICO. **in Black.**

U15	U77	1c green on oriental buff (No. U354) (500*)	12.50	40.00
		Entire	75.00	80.00
U16	"	1c green on blue (No. U355) (1,000*)	15.00	40.00
		Entire	95.00	135.00
U17	U79	2c carmine on oriental buff (No. U364) (1,000*)	12.50	40.00
		Entire	95.00	135.00
U18	"	2c carmine on blue (No. U365) (500*)	12.50	40.00
		Entire	75.00	135.00

There were two settings of the overprint, with minor differences, which are found on Nos. U16 and U17.

WRAPPER.

U. S. Wrapper of 1899 Issue Overprinted in Green PORTO RICO.

21mm. long.

W1	U77	1c green on manila (No. W357) (15,000)	5.50	25.00
		Entire	17.50	90.00

POSTAL CARDS.
Prices are for Entires.

Imprinted PORTO RICO. below stamp.

1899-1900   U. S. Postal Card No. UX14

UX1	PC8	1c black on buff, imprint 21mm. long	140.00	150.00
	b.	Double imprint		2250.00

Imprinted PORTO RICO. below stamp.

UX1A	PC8	1c black on buff, imprint 20mm. long	900.00	1100.00

Imprinted PORTO RICO. below stamp.

UX2	PC8	1c black on buff, imprint 26mm. long	150.00	160.00

Imprinted PUERTO RICO. below stamp.

UX3	PC8	1c black on buff	150.00	160.00

SPECIMEN STAMPS.
Overprinted in black **Specimen.**

1899

210S	E	1c yellow green	200.00
211S	E	2c carmine	200.00
212S	E	5c blue	200.00
213S	E	8c violet brown	200.00
214S	E	10c brown	200.00

The Special Printing of Nos. 212-214 (5c, 8c, 10c) with "Puerto Rico" overprint received the "Specimen" overprint. Price about $300 each.

1899   **Postage Due.**

J1S	E	1c deep claret	200.00
J2S	E	2c deep claret	200.00
J3S	E	10c deep claret	200.00

REVENUE STAMPS

U.S. Revenue Stamps Nos. R163, R168-R169, R171 and Type of 1898 Surcharged in Black or Dark Blue

PORTO RICO
10 c.
Excise Revenue
a

PORTO RICO $1 EXCISE REVENUE
b

1901   Wmk. USIR (191R)

Hyphen-hole Roulette 7

R1	R15	(a)	1c on 1c pale blue (Bk)	8.00	6.00
R2	"	(")	10c on 10c dark brown	11.00	7.00
R3	"	(")	25c on 25c purple brown	13.00	8.00
R4	"	(")	50c on 50c slate violet	21.00	11.00
R5	R16	(b)	$1 on $1 pale greenish gray	40.00	16.00
R6	"	(")	$3 on $3 " "	65.00	21.00
R7	"	(")	$5 on $5 " "	75.00	27.50
R8	"	(")	$10 on $10 " "	110.00	45.00
R9	"	(")	$50 on $50 " "	275.00	110.00

Lines of 1c surcharge spaced farther apart; total depth of surcharge 15¾mm. instead of 11mm.

RECTIFIED SPIRITS STAMPS

U.S. Wine Stamps of 1933-34 Overprinted in Red or Carmine

RECTIFIED

SPIRITS

Offset Printing

1934   *Rouletted 7*   **Wmk. 191R**

Overprint Lines 14mm. Apart, Second Line 25mm. Long

RE1	RE5	2c green		7.50
RE2	"	3c "		40.00
RE3	"	4c "		9.00
RE4	"	5c "		7.50
RE5	"	6c "		9.00

Overprint Lines 21½mm. Apart, Second Line 23½mm. Long

RE6	RE2	50c green		17.50
RE7	"	60c "		15.00

Handstamped overprints are also found on U.S. Wine stamps of 1933-34.

U.S. Wine Stamps of 1933-34 Overprinted in Black

RECTIFIED   **RECTIFIED**

SPIRITS   **SPIRITS**
a   b

Offset Printing

1934   *Rouletted 7*   **Wmk. 191R**

RE8	RE5	(a)	1c green		15.00
RE9	"	(")	2c "		7.00
RE10	"	(")	3c "		37.50

RE11	RE5	(a) 5c green		7.00
RE12	"	(") 6c "		9.00
RE13	RE2	(b) 50c "		12.00
RE14	"	(") 60c "		9.00
RE15	"	(") 72c "		52.00
RE16	"	(") 80c "		27.50

RECTIFIED SPIRITS

U.S. Wine Stamps of 1933–34
Overprinted in Black

PUERTO RICO

Offset Printing

1934   *Rouletted 7*   Wmk. 191R

RE17	RE5	½c green	2.50
RE18	"	1c "	60
RE19	"	2c "	50
RE20	"	3c "	3.50
RE21	"	4c "	75
RE22	"	5c "	1.00
RE23	"	6c "	1.25
RE24	"	10c "	3.50
RE25	"	30c "	30.00

Overprint Lines 12½mm. Apart

RE26	RE2	36c green	6.00
RE27	"	40c "	5.00
RE28	"	50c "	2.50
RE29	"	60c "	50
		a. Inverted overprint	—
RE30	"	72c green	3.00
RE31	"	80c "	4.00
RE32	"	$1 "	7.50

George Sewall Boutwell
R1

Engraved; 8c & 58c Lithographed

1942–57   *Rouletted 7*   Wmk. 191

Without Gum

RE33	R1	½c carmine	3.00	1.00
RE34	"	1c sepia	7.50	3.50
RE35	"	2c bright yellow green	1.00	15
RE36	"	3c lilac	60.00	30.00
RE37	"	4c olive	2.00	50
RE38	"	5c orange	4.50	1.00
RE39	"	6c red brown	3.50	1.25
RE40	"	8c bright pink ('57)	6.00	3.00
RE41	"	10c bright purple	11.00	5.00
RE41A	"	30c vermilion	175.00	
RE42	"	36c dull yellow	150.00	60.00
RE43	"	40c deep claret	18.00	6.00
RE44	"	50c green	10.00	3.50
RE45	"	58c red orange	65.00	5.00
RE46	"	60c brown	1.25	15
RE47	"	62c black	3.00	70
RE48	"	72c blue	35.00	80
RE49	"	77½c olive gray	10.00	3.50
RE50	"	80c brownish black	12.00	5.00
RE51	"	$1 violet	75.00	20.00

The 30c is believed not to have been placed in use.

RYUKYU ISLANDS
(rē·ōō′kyōō)

LOCATION—Chain of 63 islands between Japan and Formosa, separating the East China Sea from the Pacific Ocean.
GOVT.—Semi-autonomous under United States administration.
AREA—848 sq. mi.
POP.—945,465 (1970).
CAPITAL—Naha, Okinawa.

The Ryukyus were part of Japan until American forces occupied them in 1945. The islands reverted to Japan May 15, 1972.

100 Sen = 1 Yen
100 Cents = 1 Dollar (1958).

Cycad
A1

Lily
A2

Sailing Ship
A3

Farmer
A4

Wmk. 257

1948-49   Typographed
              Perf. 13   Wmk. 257
              Second Printing

1	A1	5s magenta	1.75	1.75
2	A2	10s yel grn	5.00	4.00
3	A1	20s yel grn	3.50	3.00
4	A3	30s vermilion	2.00	2.00
5	A2	40s magenta	1.75	1.50
6	A3	50s ultra	3.50	3.50
7	A4	1y ultra	3.50	3.50

First Printing

1a	A1	5s magenta	3.00	3.50
2a	A2	10s yel grn	1.50	2.00
3a	A1	20s yel grn	1.50	2.00
4a	A3	30s vermilion	3.00	3.50
5a	A2	40s magenta	40.00	40.00
6a	A3	50s ultra	3.00	3.00
7a	A4	1y ultra	275.00	175.00
		First day covers.		
		#1a-7a each		300.00

First printing: thick yellow gum, dull colors, rough perforations, grayish paper. Second printing: white gum, sharp colors, cleancut perforations, white paper.

Issue dates: First printing, July 1, 1948: second printing, July 18, 1949.

Imprint Blocks of 10, Unused

1	18.00	5	20.00
1a	40.00	5a	500.00
2	60.00	6	50.00
2a	20.00	6a	40.00
3	40.00	7	50.00
3a	20.00	7a	3500.00
4	30.00		
4a	40.00		

Roof Tiles
A5

Ryukyu University
A6

Designs: 1y, Ryukyu girl. 2y, Shuri Castle. 3y, Guardian dragon. 4y, Two women. 5y, Sea shells.

Photogravure
Off-white Paper
1950, Jan. 21   Perf. 13x13½   Unwmkd.

8	A5	50s dk car rose	20	20
		First day cover		30.00
		Imprint block of 6	2.00	
	a.	White paper	50	50
		First day cover. Sept. 6, 1958		50.00
		Imprint block of 10	6.50	
9	A5	1y dp bl	3.50	1.50
		First day cover		30.00
		Imprint block of 6	20.00	
10	A5	2y rose vio	10.00	4.00
		First day cover		30.00
		Imprint block of 6	65.00	
11	A5	3y car rose	22.50	5.00
		First day cover		30.00
		Imprint block of 6	180.00	
12	A5	4y grnsh gray	12.00	4.00
		First day cover		30.00
		Imprint block of 6	80.00	
13	A5	5y bl grn	6.50	3.50
		First day cover		30.00
		Imprint block of 6	55.00	
		First day cover. #8-13		200.00

No. 8a has colorless gum and an 8-character imprint in the sheet margin. The original 1950 printing on off-white paper has yellowish gum and a 5-character imprint.

1951, Feb. 12   Perf. 13½x13

14	A6	3y red brn	45.00	20.00
		First day cover		70.00
		Imprint block of 6	375.00	

Opening of Ryukyu University, Feb. 12.

Pine Tree
A7

Ryukyu Islands
UNITED STATES ADMINISTRATION 1945-1972

½ PRICE SALE!

NEW SCOTT RYUKYU ALBUM AND BINDER.....	34.50
117 MINT ALL DIFFERENT RYUKYU STAMPS...	58.95
5 MINT RYUKYU SOUVENIR SHEETS CPLT......	30.00
TOTAL VALUE OF THE COMPLETE OFFER.......	123.45

● All Stamps Are Never Hinged Original Gum ● All Are Complete Sets - No Short Sets ● All Prices from Scott 1986 Catalogue ● Complete Sept. 1963 Thru Final Issue ● 80 Page Album in Green Specialty Binder ● All Postage and Insurance Paid By Us ● Orders Shipped Same Day Received.

A $123.45 VALUE
Only **$61.70**

JOHN B. HEAD
P.O. Box 7, Bethel, ME 04217
  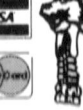

RYUKYUS HEADQUARTERS
More than just filling spaces.
Become involved in U.S. postal history.

RYUKYU ISLANDS
EXCELLENT STARTER KIT $20 PPD.
Includes $25.00 commemorative sets PLUS excellent ALBUM PAGES @ $15.90 . . . all at half price.

JOSEPH V. BUSH, INC.
BONITA, CALIF. 92002-0626
WW II Specialist dealer since 1945 . . . in-depth Allied Military Gov't. (A.M.G.); TRIESTE, PALAU

 Also members:
RPSS, USPPS, BIA, GPS

Specialists in
RYUKYUS
and JAPAN

SEND FOR 5 PAGE LIST
OF STAMPS, FDC's, etc.
Please include large self-addressed, stamped envelope.

SHULL SERVICE
P.O. Box 3432
Crofton, MD 21114
 Want lists serviced

1951, Feb. 19   *Perf. 13*

15	A7	3y dk grn	40.00	20.00
		First day cover		70.00
		Imprint block of 6	325.00	

Reforestation Week, Feb. 18-24.

Nos. 8 and 10 Surcharged in Black

改訂
＊
10圓
Type I

改訂
＊
10圓
Type II

改訂
＃
10圓
Type III

Three types of 10y surcharge:
    I. Narrow-spaced rules, "10" normal spacing.
    II. Wide-spaced rules, "10" normal spacing.
    III. Rules and "10" both wide-spaced.

1952   *Perf. 13x13½*

16	A5	10y on 50s dk car rose (II)	12.50	15.00
		Imprint block of 6	125.00	
		a. Type I	30.00	32.50
		Imprint block of 6	300.00	
		b. Type III	40.00	42.50
		Imprint block of 6	400.00	
17	A5	100y on 2y rose vio	1,750.	1,450.
		Imprint block of 6	14,500.	

These are two types of surcharge on No. 17.

Dove, Bean Sprout and Map
A8

Madanbashi Bridge
A9

1952, Apr. 1   *Perf. 13½x13*

18	A8	3y dp plum	85.00	30.00
		First day cover		90.00
		Imprint block of 10	1,300.	

Establishment of the Government of the Ryukyu Islands (GRI), April 1, 1952.

1952-53

Designs: 2y, Main Hall, Shuri Castle. 3y, Shruei Gate. 6y, Stone Gate, Soenji Temple, Naha. 10y, Benzaiten-do Temple. 30y, Sonohan Utaki (altar) at Shuri Castle. 50y, Tamaudun (royal mausoleum). Shuri. 100y, Stone Bridge, Hosho Pond, Enkaku Temple.

19	A9	1y red	30	30
		Imprint block of 10	4.00	
20	A9	2y green	40	50
		Imprint block of 10	5.50	
21	A9	3y aqua	50	45
		First day cover. #19-21		40.00
		Imprint block of 10	7.00	
22	A9	6y blue	2.50	3.00
		First day cover		30.00
		Imprint block of 10	35.00	
23	A9	10y crim rose	3.00	40
		First day cover		50.00
		Imprint block of 10	32.50	
24	A9	30y ol grn	12.00	5.50
		First day cover		90.00
		Imprint block of 10	150.00	
		a. lt ol grn ('58)	40.00	
		Imprint block of 10	600.00	
25	A9	50y rose vio	10.00	5.50
		First day cover		150.00
		Imprint block of 10	135.00	
26	A9	100y claret	12.50	3.50
		First day cover		250.00
		First day cover. #22-26		650.00
		Imprint block of 10	180.00	

Issue dates: 1y, 2y and 3y, Nov. 20, 1952. Others, Jan. 20, 1953.

Reception at Shuri Castle
A10

Perry and American Fleet
A11

1953, May 26   *Perf. 13½x13, 13x13½*

27	A10	3y dp mag	14.00	6.00
		Imprint block of 6	95.00	
28	A11	6y dl bl	1.50	1.50
		First day cover. #27-28		14.00
		Imprint block of 6	12.00	

Centenary of the arrival of Commodore Matthew Calbraith Perry at Naha, Okinawa.

Chofu Ota and Pencil-shaped Matrix
A12

Shigo Toma and Pen
A13

1953, Oct. 1   *Perf. 13½x13*

29	A12	4y yel brn	12.00	4.50
		First day cover		20.00
		Imprint block of 10	150.00	

Third Newspaper Week.

RYUKYU ISLANDS

1954, Oct. 1

30	A13	4y blue	14.00	6.00
		First day cover		25.00
		Imprint block of 10	170.00	

Fourth Newspaper Week.

Ryukyu Pottery
A14

Noguni Shrine and Sweet Potato Plant
A15

Designs: 15y, Lacquerware. 20y, Textile design.

1954-55   Photo.   *Perf. 13*

31	A14	4y brown	1.00	50
		First day cover		9.00
		Imprint block of 10	12.50	
32	A14	15y ver ('55)	3.25	2.00
		First day cover		15.00
		Imprint block of 10	40.00	
33	A14	20y yel org ('55)	2.50	2.00
		First day cover		15.00
		Imprint block of 10	32.50	
		First day cover, #32-33		40.00

1955, Nov. 26

34	A15	4y blue	14.00	6.00
		First day cover		25.00
		Imprint block of 10	170.00	

350th anniv. of the introduction of the sweet potato to the Ryukyu Islands.

Stylized Trees
A16

Willow Dance
A17

1956, Feb. 18   *Unwmkd.*

35	A16	4y bluish grn	12.00	5.00
		First day cover		22.50
		Imprint block of 6	95.00	

Arbor Week, Feb. 18-24.

1956, May 1   *Perf. 13*

Design: 8y, Straw hat dance. 14y, Dancer in warrior costume with fan.

36	A17	5y rose lil	1.00	60
		First day cover		10.00
		Imprint block of 10	14.00	
37	A17	8y vio bl	2.25	2.00
		First day cover		10.00
		Imprint block of 10	30.00	
38	A17	14y redsh brn	2.75	2.50
		First day cover		10.00
		First day cover, #36-38		35.00
		Imprint block of 10	30.00	

Telephone—A18

1956, June 8

39	A18	4y vio bl	17.50	6.00
		First day cover		15.00
		Imprint block of 6	125.00	

Establishment of dial telephone system.

Garland of Pine, Bamboo and Plum
A19

Map of Okinawa and Pencil Rocket
A20

1956, Dec. 1   *Perf. 13½x13*

40	A19	2y multi	2.00	90
		First day cover		4.00
		Imprint block of 10	25.00	

New Year, 1957.

1957, Oct. 1   Photo.   *Perf. 13½x13*

41	A20	4y dp vio bl	90	90
		First day cover		6.00
		Imprint block of 10	11.00	

7th annual Newspaper Week, Oct. 1-7.

Phoenix—A21

1957, Dec. 1   *Perf. 13*   *Unwmkd.*

42	A21	2y multi	20	20
		First day cover		2.00
		Imprint block of 10	3.50	

New Year, 1958.

RYUKYU ISLANDS

Ryukyu Stamps—A22

				Perf. 13½	
1958, July 1					
43	A22	4y multi		1.00	75
		First day cover			2.00
		Imprint block of 4		4.50	

10th anniv. of 1st Ryukyu stamps.

Yen Symbol and Dollar Sign A23

1958, Sept. 16   **Typographed**
Perf. 10, 10½, 11 & Compound
Without Gum.

44	A23	½c orange	60	60
		Imprint block of 6	3.50	
		Horiz. or vert. pair, imperf. btwn.	75.00	
		a. Imperf., pair	1,250.	
45	A23	1c yel grn	1.00	1.00
		Imprint block of 6	7.00	
		Horiz. pair, imperf. btwn.	100.00	
		Vert. pair, imperf. btwn.	90.00	
46	A23	2c dk bl	1.50	1.50
		Imprint block of 6	10.00	
		Horiz pair, imperf. btwn.	125.00	
		Vert. pair, imperf. btwn.	1,000.	
47	A23	3c dp car	1.00	1.00
		Imprint block of 6	7.00	
		Horiz. or vert. pair, imperf. btwn.	75.00	
48	A23	4c brt grn	1.25	1.25
		First day cover, #44-48		8.00
		Imprint block of 6	8.50	
		Horiz. pair, imperf. btwn.	500.00	
		Vert. pair, imperf. btwn.	100.00	
49	A23	5c orange	3.00	3.00
		Imprint block of 6	20.00	
		Horiz. pair, imperf. btwn.	100.00	
		Vert. pair, imperf. btwn.	300.00	
50	A23	10c aqua	5.00	5.00
		Imprint block of 6	35.00	
		Horiz. pair, imperf. btwn.	200.00	
		Vert. pair, imperf. btwn.	125.00	
51	A23	25c brt vio bl	7.00	7.00
		Imprint block of 6	50.00	
		Horiz. or vert. pair, imperf. btwn.	1,000.	
		a. Gummed paper ('61)	9.00	
		Imprint block of 6	85.00	
52	A23	50c gray	16.00	8.00
		Imprint block of 6	125.00	
		Horiz. pair, imperf. btwn.	1,000.	
		a. Gummed paper ('61)	12.00	
		First day cover, #51a-52a		20.00
		Imprint block of 6	90.00	
53	A23	$1 rose lil	12.50	3.00
		First day cover, #49-53		25.00
		First day cover, #44-53		40.00
		Imprint block of 6	90.00	
		Horiz. pair, imperf. btwn.	300.00	
		Vert. pair, imperf. btwn.	1,000.	

Printed locally. Perforation paper and shade varieties exist.

Gate of Courtesy—A24

				Perf. 13½	
1958, Oct. 15		**Photo.**			
54	A24	3c multi		1.50	1.00
		First day cover			2.00
		Imprint block of 4		6.50	

Restoration of Shureimon, Gate of Courtesy, on road leading to Shuri City.

Lion Dance   Trees and Mountains
A25   A26

			Perf. 13½	**Unwmkd.**	
1958, Dec. 10					
55	A25	1½c multi		20	20
		First day cover			1.75
		Imprint block of 6		2.25	

New Year, 1959.

1959, Apr. 30		**Litho.**		**Perf. 13½x13**	
56	A26	3c bl, yel grn, grn & red		1.00	50
		First day cover			2.00
		Imprint block of 6		8.00	
		a. Red omitted		—	

"Make the Ryukyus Green" movement.

Yonaguni Moth A27

				Perf. 13	
1959, July 23		**Photo.**			
57	A27	3c multi		1.50	50
		First day cover			2.00
		Imprint block of 6		9.50	

Meeting of the Japanese Biological Education Society in Okinawa.

RYUKYU ISLANDS

Hibiscus
A28

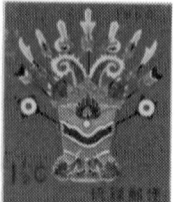
Toy (Yakaji)
A29

Designs: 3c, Fish (Moorish idol). 8c, Sea shell (Phalium bandatum). 13c, Butterfly (Kallinia Inachus Eucerca), denomination at left, butterfly going up. 17c, Jellyfish (Dactylometra pacifera Goette).

Inscribed: 琉球郵便

1959, Aug. 10   Perf. 13x13½

58	A28	½c multi		25	25
		Imprint block of 10		4.00	
59	A28	3c multi		1.25	50
		Imprint block of 10		15.00	
60	A28	8c lt ultra, blk & ocher		9.00	6.00
		Imprint block of 10		95.00	
61	A28	13c lt bl, gray & org		3.00	2.00
		Imprint block of 10		35.00	
62	A28	17c vio bl, red & yel		20.00	8.50
		First day cover, #58-62			25.00
		Imprint block of 10		225.00	

Four-character inscription measures 10x2 mm. on ½c; 12x3mm. on 3c, 8c; 8½x2 mm. on 13c, 17c. See also Nos. 76-80.

1959, Dec. 1   Lithographed

63	A29	1½c gold & multi		80	40
		First day cover			1.50
		Imprint block of 10		12.50	

New Year, 1960.

University Badge
A30

1960, May 22   Photo.   Perf. 13

64	A30	3c multi		1.10	55
		First day cover			1.50
		Imprint block of 6		8.50	

10th anniv. opening of Ryukyu University.

Dancer
A31

Designs: Various Ryukyu Dances.

1960, Nov. 1   Photo.   Perf. 13
Dark Gray Background

65	A31	1c yel, red & vio		1.50	75
		Imprint block of 10		20.00	
66	A31	2½c crim, bl & yel		2.50	1.00
		Imprint block of 10		30.00	
67	A31	5c dk bl, yel & red		1.00	75
		Imprint block of 10		12.50	
68	A31	10c dk bl, yel & red		1.00	90
		First day cover, #65-68			9.50
		Imprint block of 10		12.50	

See Nos. 81-87, 220.

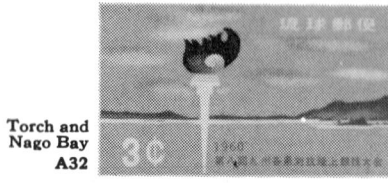
Torch and Nago Bay
A32

Runners at Starting Line
A33

1960, Nov. 8

72	A32	3c lt bl, grn & red		7.00	2.50
		First day cover			3.00
		Imprint block of 6		50.00	
73	A32	8c org & sl grn		1.00	1.00
		First day cover			3.00
		First day cover, #72-73			9.00
		Imprint block of 6		7.50	

8th Kyushu Inter-Prefectural Athletic Meet, Nago, Northern Okinawa, Nov. 6-7.

Little Egret and Rising Sun
A34

1960, Dec. 1   Perf. 13   Unwmkd.

74	A34	3c redsh brn		7.00	2.50
		First day cover			6.00
		Imprint block of 6		50.00	

National census.

Okinawa Bull Fight
A35

RYUKYU ISLANDS

1960, Dec. 10 — *Perf. 13½*

75	A35	1½c bis, dk bl & red brn	2.00	75
		First day cover		3.50
		Imprint block of 6	14.00	

New Year, 1961.

Type of 1959 With
Japanese Inscription Redrawn:

琉 球 郵 便

1960–61 — Photo. — *Perf. 13x13½*

76	A28	½c multi ('61)	40	40
		Imprint block of 10	5.00	
77	A28	3c multi ('61)	1.50	40
		First day cover		2.50
		Imprint block of 10	17.50	
78	A28	8c lt ultra, blk & ocher	1.50	60
		Imprint block of 10	17.50	
79	A28	13c bl, brn & red	2.00	1.00
		Imprint block of 10	22.50	
80	A28	17c vio bl, red & yel	10.00	6.00
		First day cover, #78-80		25.00
		Imprint block of 10	135.00	

Size of Japanese inscription on Nos. 78-80 is 10½x1½mm. On No. 79 the denomination is at right, butterfly going down.

Dancer Type of 1960 with
"RYUKYUS" Added.

1961–64 — *Perf. 13*

81	A31	1c multi	20	15
		First day cover		1.50
		Imprint block of 10	3.00	
82	A31	2½c multi ('62)	30	15
		Imprint block of 10	3.50	
83	A31	5c multi ('62)	40	40
		Imprint block of 10	4.50	
84	A31	10c multi ('62)	85	50
		First day cover, #82-84		3.00
		Imprint block of 10	11.00	
84A	A31	20c multi ('64)	2.00	1.50
		First day cover		3.50
		Imprint block of 10	25.00	
85	A31	25c multi ('62)	2.00	1.10
		First day cover		4.00
		Imprint block of 10	25.00	
86	A31	50c multi	4.50	80
		Imprint block of 10	50.00	
87	A31	$1 multi	6.00	20
		First day cover		45.00
		Imprint block of 10	70.00	

Pine
Tree
A36

1961, May 1 — Photo. — *Perf. 13*

88	A36	3c yel grn & red	2.00	1.25
		First day cover		2.50
		Imprint block of 6	15.00	

"Make the Ryukyus Green" movement.
40th anniv. of Naha.

Naha, Steamer and Sailboat
A37

1961, May 20

89	A37	3c aqua	2.50	1.25
		First day cover		2.50
		Imprint block of 6	18.50	

40th anniversary of Naha.

White Silver   Books and Bird
Temple   A39
A38

Typographed
1961, Oct. 1 — *Perf. 11* — Unwmkd.

90	A38	3c red brn	2.50	1.50
		First day cover		3.50
		Imprint block of 6	17.50	
		a. Horiz. pair, imperf. between	300.00	
		b. Vert. pair, imperf. between	350.00	

Merger of townships Takamine, Kanegushiku and Miwa with Itoman.

1961, Nov. 12 — Litho. — *Perf. 13*

91	A39	3c multi	1.75	1.25
		First day cover		2.50
		Imprint block of 6	14.50	

Book Week.

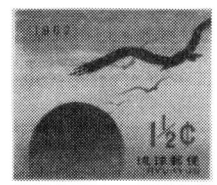 

Rising Sun and   Symbolic Steps,
Eagles   Trees and
A40   Government
                          Building
                            A41

1961, Dec. 10 — Photo. — *Perf. 13½*

92	A40	1½c gold, ver & blk	3.00	1.50
		First day cover		3.00
		Imprint block of 6	22.50	

New Year, 1962.

RYUKYU ISLANDS

1962, Apr. 1		Perf. 13½	Unwmkd.	

Design: 3c, Government Building.

93	A41	1½c multi	75	80
		Imprint block of 6	6.00	
94	A41	3c brt grn, red & gray	1.25	1.00
		First day cover, #93-94		3.00
		Imprint block of 6	9.00	

10th anniv. of the Government of the Ryukyu Islands (GRI).

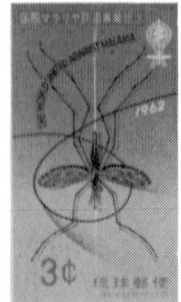

Anopheles
Hyrcanus
Sinensis
A42

Design: 8c, Malaria eradication emblem and Shurei gate.

1962, Apr. 7			Perf. 13½x13	
95	A42	3c multi	75	80
		Imprint block of 6	6.50	
96	A42	8c multi	1.50	1.00
		First day cover, #95-96		3.50
		Imprint block of 6	12.50	

World Health Organization drive to eradicate malaria.

Dolls and Toys
A43

Linden or
Sea Hibiscus
A44

1962, May 5		Litho.	Perf. 13½	
97	A43	3c red, blk, bl & buff	1.75	1.00
		First day cover		3.00
		Imprint block of 6	14.00	

Children's Day, 1962.

1962, June 1   Photogravure

Flowers: 3c, Indian coral tree. 8c, Iju (Schima liukiuensis Nakal). 13c, Touch-me-not (garden balsam). 17c, Shell flower (Alpinia speciosa).

98	A44	½c multi	10	10
		Imprint block of 10	1.50	
99	A44	3c multi	40	15
		Imprint block of 10	4.50	
100	A44	8c multi	50	40
		Imprint block of 10	6.00	
101	A44	13c multi	80	60
		Imprint block of 10	9.00	
102	A44	17c multi	1.20	90
		First day cover, #98-102		6.50
		Imprint block of 10	14.00	

See Nos. 107 and 114 for 1½c and 15c flower stamps.

Earthenware
A45

1962, July 5			Perf. 13½x13	
103	A45	3c multi	4.50	3.00
		First day cover		5.50
		Imprint block of 6	32.50	

Philatelic Week.

Japanese Fencing (Kendo)—A46

1962, July 25			Perf. 13	
104	A46	3c multi	5.00	3.50
		First day cover		5.50
		Imprint block of 6	37.50	

All-Japan Kendo Meeting in Okinawa, July 25, 1962.

Rabbit Playing
near Water,
Bingata Cloth
Design
A47

Young Man
and Woman,
Stone Relief
A48

1962, Dec. 10			Perf. 13x13½	
105	A47	1½c gold & multi	1.25	1.00
		First day cover		2.50
		Imprint block of 10	15.00	

New Year, 1963.

1963, Jan. 15		Photo.	Perf. 13½	
106	A48	3c gold, blk & bl	1.25	1.00
		First day cover		2.50
		Imprint block of 6	9.00	

 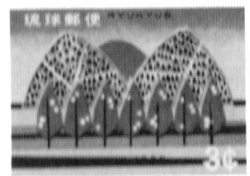

Gooseneck
Cactus
A49

Trees and
Wooded Hills
A50

RYUKYU ISLANDS

1963, Apr. 5   *Perf. 13x13½*

107	A49	1½c dk bl, grn, yel & pink	10	10
		First day cover		2.50
		Imprint block of 10	1.50	

1963, Mar. 25   *Perf. 13½x13*

108	A50	3c ultra, grn & red brn	1.25	1.25
		First day cover		2.50
		Imprint block of 6	9.00	

"Make the Ryukyus Green" movement.

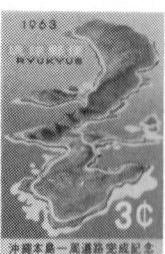

Map of Okinawa
A51

Hawks over Islands
A52

1963, Apr. 30   *Perf. 13½*   Unwmkd.

109	A51	3c multi	1.50	1.50
		First day cover		3.00
		Imprint block of 6	12.50	

Opening of the Round Road on Okinawa.

1963, May 10   Photogravure

110	A52	3c multi	1.25	1.25
		First day cover		2.50
		Imprint block of 6	12.50	

Bird Day, May 10.

Shioya Bridge
A53

1963, June 5

111	A53	3c multi	1.25	1.25
		First day cover		2.50
		Imprint block of 6	9.00	

Opening of Shioya Bridge over Shioya Bay.

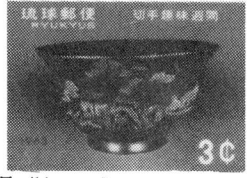

Tsuikin-wan Lacquerware Bowl
A54

1963, July 1   *Perf. 13½*   Unwmkd.

112	A54	3c multi	3.50	2.50
		First day cover		5.50
		Imprint block of 6	25.00	

Map of Far East and
JCI Emblem
A55

1963, Sept. 16   Photo.   *Perf. 13½*

113	A55	3c multi	1.10	60
		First day cover		2.50
		Imprint block of 6	8.50	

Meeting of the International Junior Chamber of Commerce (JCI), Naha, Okinawa, Sept. 16-19.

Mamaomoto
A56

Site of
Nakagusuku Castle
A57

1963, Oct. 15   *Perf. 13x13½*

114	A56	15c multi	1.25	50
		First day cover		2.50
		Imprint block of 10	15.00	

1963, Nov. 1   *Perf. 13½x13*

115	A57	3c multi	1.00	60
		First day cover		2.25
		Imprint block of 6	7.50	

Protection of national cultural treasures.

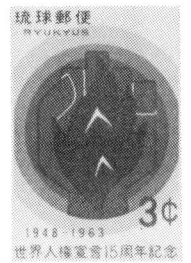

Flame
A58

Dragon (Bingata Pattern)
A59

1963, Dec. 10   *Perf. 13½*

116	A53	3c red, dk bl & yel	1.00	60
		First day cover		2.25
		Imprint block of 6	7.00	

15th anniv. of the Universal Declaration of Human Rights.

RYUKYU ISLANDS

1963, Dec. 10   **Photogravure**

117	A59	1½c multi	50	25
		First day cover		2.25
		Imprint block of 10	6.50	

New Year, 1964.

Carnation
A60

Pineapples and Sugar Cane
A61

1964, May 10   *Perf. 13½*

118	A60	3c bl, yel, blk & car	60	50
		First day cover		2.50
		Imprint block of 6	4.50	

Mothers Day.

1964, June 1

119	A61	3c multi	60	50
		First day cover		2.25
		Imprint block of 6	4.50	

Agricultural census.

Minsah Obi
(Sash Woven of Kapok)
A62

1964, July 1   *Perf. 13½*   Unwmkd.

120	A62	3c dp bl, rose pink & ocher	80	60
		First day cover		4.50
		Imprint block of 6	6.00	
	a.	dp bl, dp car & ocher	1.00	80
		First day cover		5.50
		Imprint block of 6	7.50	

Philatelic Week.

Girl Scout and Emblem
A63

1964, Aug. 31   **Photogravure**

121	A63	3c multi	40	30
		First day cover		2.25
		Imprint block of 6	3.00	

10th anniv. of Ryukyuan Girl Scouts.

Shuri Relay Station
A64

Parabolic Antenna and Map
A65

1964, Sept. 1   *Perf. 13½*   Unwmkd.
Black Overprint

122	A64	3c dp grn	1.00	1.00
		Imprint block of 6	8.00	
	a.	Figure "1" invtd.	35.00	35.00
123	A65	8c ultra	1.50	1.50
		First day cover, #122-123		9.50
		Imprint block of 6	11.00	

Opening of the Ryukyu Islands-Japan microwave system carrying telephone and telegraph messages. Nos. 122-123 not issued without overprint.

Gate of Courtesy, Olympic Torch and Emblem
A66

1964, Sept. 7   Photo.   *Perf. 13½x13*

124	A66	3c ultra, yel & red	40	30
		First day cover		2.50
		Imprint block of 6	2.75	

Relaying the Olympic torch on Okinawa en route to Tokyo.

"Naihanchi," Karate Stance
A67

893

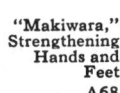

"Makiwara,"
Strengthening
Hands and
Feet
A68

"Kumite,"
Simulated
Combat
A69

1964-65			Photo.		Perf. 13½
125	A67	3c dl cl, yel & blk		80	50
		First day cover			2.50
		Imprint block of 6		5.50	
126	A68	3c yel & multi ('65)		60	50
		First day cover			2.50
		Imprint block of 6		4.50	
127	A69	3c gray, red & blk ('65)		60	50
		First day cover			2.50
		Imprint block of 6		4.50	

Karate, Ryukyuan self-defense sport.

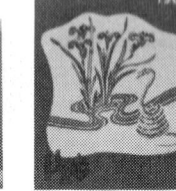

Miyara Dunchi
A70

Snake and
Iris (Bingata)
A71

1964, Nov. 1				Perf. 13½
128	A70	3c multi	50	40
		First day cover		2.25
		Imprint block of 6	3.50	

Protection of national cultural treasures. Miyara Dunchi was built as a residence by Miyara-pechin Toen in 1819.

1964, Dec. 10				Photo.
129	A71	1½c multi	25	20
		First day cover		2.25
		Imprint block of 10	4.00	

New Year, 1965.

Boy
Scouts
A72

1965, Feb. 6				Perf. 13½
130	A72	3c lt bl & multi	75	50
		First day cover		2.50
		Imprint block of 6	5.00	

10th anniv. of Ryukyuan Boy Scouts.

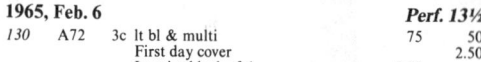

Main Stadium, Onoyama
A73

1965, July 1				Perf. 13x13½
131	A73	3c multi	30	25
		First day cover		2.00
		Imprint block of 6	3.00	

Inauguration of the main stadium of the Onoyama athletic facilities.

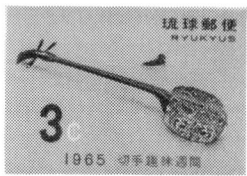

Samisen of King Shoko
A74

1965, July 1			Photo.		Perf. 13½
132	A74	3c buff & multi		50	40
		First day cover			2.50
		Imprint block of 6		4.00	

Philatelic Week.

Kin Power
Plant
A75

ICY Emblem,
Ryukyu Map
A76

1965, July 1				
133	A75	3c grn & multi	30	25
		First day cover		2.00
		Imprint block of 6	3.00	

Completion of Kin power plant.

1965, Aug. 24			Photo.		Perf. 13½
134	A76	3c multi		25	20
		First day cover			2.00
		Imprint block of 6		2.50	

20th anniv. of the United Nations and International Cooperation Year, 1964-65.

RYUKYU ISLANDS

Naha City Hall
A77

1965, Sept. 18		**Perf. 13½**		**Unwmkd.**
135	A77	3c bl & multi	25	20
		First day cover		2.00
		Imprint block of 6	2.50	

Completion of Naha City Hall.

Chinese Box Turtle
A78

Horse (Bingata)
A79

Turtles: No. 137, Hawksbill turtle (denomination at top, country name at bottom). No. 138, Asian terrapin (denomination and country name on top).

1965-66		**Photo.**		**Perf. 13½**
136	A78	3c gldn brn & multi	30	30
		First day cover		2.00
		Imprint block of 6	2.50	
137	A78	3c blk, yel & brn ('66)	30	30
		First day cover		2.00
		Imprint block of 6	2.50	
138	A78	3c gray & multi ('66)	30	30
		First day cover		2.00
		Imprint block of 6	2.50	

Issue dates: No. 136, Oct. 20, 1965. No. 137, Jan. 20, 1966. No. 138, Apr. 20, 1966.

1965, Dec. 10		**Photo.**		**Perf. 13½**
139	A79	1½c multi	10	10
		First day cover		2.00
		Imprint block of 10	2.00	
	a.	Gold omitted	1,000.	1,000.

New Year, 1966.

NATURE CONSERVATION ISSUE

Noguchi's Okinawa Woodpecker
A80

Sika Deer
A81

Design: No. 142, Dugong.

1966		**Photo.**		**Perf. 13½**
140	A80	3c bl grn & multi	25	25
		First day cover		2.00
		Imprint block of 6	2.00	
141	A81	3c bl, red, blk, brn & grn	30	30
		First day cover		2.00
		Imprint block of 6	2.25	
142	A81	3c bl, yel grn, blk & red	30	30
		First day cover		2.00
		Imprint block of 6	2.25	

Issue dates: No. 140, Feb. 15. No. 141, Mar. 15. No. 142, Apr. 20.

Ryukyu Bungalow Swallow
A82

1966, May 10		**Photo.**		**Perf. 13½**
143	A82	3c sky bl, blk & brn	20	20
		First day cover		2.00
		Imprint block of 6	1.75	

4th Bird Week, May 10-16.

Lilies and Ruins
A83

1966, June 23				**Perf. 13x13½**
144	A83	3c multi	20	20
		First day cover		2.00
		Imprint block of 6	1.50	

Memorial Day, end of the Battle of Okinawa, June 23, 1945.

University of the Ryukyus
A84

1966, July 1				
145	A84	3c multi	20	20
		First day cover		2.00
		Imprint block of 6	1.50	

Transfer of the University of the Ryukyus from U.S. authority to the Ryukyu Government.

RYUKYU ISLANDS

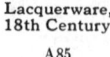

Lacquerware,
18th Century
A85

Tile-Roofed
House and
UNESCO Emblem
A86

Ram in Iris
Wreath
A89

Clown Fish
A90

1966, Aug. 1   *Perf. 13½*
146   A85   3c gray & multi   20   20
         First day cover   2.00
         Imprint block of 6   1.75

Philatelic Week.

1966, Sept. 20   **Photo.**   *Perf. 13½*
147   A86   3c multi   20   20
         First day cover   2.00
         Imprint block of 6   1.75

20th anniv. of the United Nations Educational, Scientific and Cultural Organization (UNESCO).

Government
Museum and
Dragon
Statue
A87

1966, Oct. 6
148   A87   3c multi   20   20
         First day cover   2.00
         Imprint block of 6   1.50

Completion of the GRI (Government of the Ryukyu Islands) Museum, Shuri.

Tomb of
Nakasone-
Tuimya
Genga, Ruler
of Miyako
A88

1966, Nov. 1   **Photo.**   *Perf. 13½*
149   A88   3c multi   20   20
         First day cover   2.00
         Imprint block of 6   1.50

Protection of national cultural treasures.

1966, Dec. 10   **Photo.**   *Perf. 13½*
150   A89   1½c dk bl & multi   10   10
         First day cover   2.00
         Imprint block of 10   1.75

New Year, 1967.

1966-67

Fish: No. 152, Young boxfish (white numeral at lower left). No. 153, Forceps fish (pale buff numeral at lower right). No. 154. Spotted triggerfish (orange numeral). No. 155. Saddleback butterflyfish (carmine numeral, lower left).

151   A90   3c org red & multi   25   20
152   A90   3c org yel & multi ('67)   25   20
153   A90   3c multi ('67)   35   30
154   A90   3c multi ('67)   35   30
155   A90   3c multi ('67)   40   30
         First day covers,
           #151-155 each   2.00
         Imprint block of 6,
           #151-155 each   2.50

Issue dates: No. 151, Dec. 20, 1966. No. 152, Jan. 10, 1967. No. 153, Apr. 10, 1967. No. 154, May 25, 1967. No. 155, June 10, 1967.

Tsuboya Urn
A91

Episcopal Miter
A92

1967, Apr. 20
156   A91   3c yel & multi   25   20
         First day cover   2.50
         Imprint block of 6   2.00

Philatelic Week, 1967.

1967-68   **Photo.**   *Perf. 13½*

Seashells: No. 158, Venus comb murex. No. 159, Chiragra spider. No. 160, Green truban. No. 161, Euprotomus bulla.

157   A92   3c lt grn & multi   30   25
         Imprint block of 6   2.25
158   A92   3c grnsh bl & multi   30   25
         Imprint block of 6   2.25
159   A92   3c emer & multi ('68)   40   30
         Imprint block of 6   3.00
160   A92   3c lt bl & multi ('68)   40   30
         Imprint block of 6   3.00
161   A92   3c brt bl & multi ('68)   70   50
         Imprint block of 6   5.50
         First day cover, each   2.00

Issue dates: 1967, No. 157, July 20. No. 158, Aug. 30, 1968. No. 159, Jan. 18. No. 160, Feb. 20. No. 161, June 5.

RYUKYU ISLANDS

Red-tiled Roofs and ITY Emblem
A93

1967, Sept. 11   Photo.   Perf. 13½

162	A93	3c multi		20	20
		First day cover			2.00
		Imprint block of 6		1.50	

International Tourist Year, 1967.

Mobile TB Clinic
A94

1967, Oct. 13   Photo.   Perf. 13½

163	A94	3c lil & multi		20	20
		First day cover			2.00
		Imprint block of 6		1.50	

15th anniv. of the Anti-Tuberculosis Society.

Hojo Bridge, Enkaku Temple, 1498
A95

1967, Nov. 1

164	A95	3c bl grn & multi		25	20
		First day cover			2.00
		Imprint block of 6		2.00	

Protection of national cultural treasures.

Monkey (Bingata)   TV Tower and Map
A96   A97

1967, Dec. 11   Photo.   Perf. 13½

165	A96	1½c sil & multi		15	15
		First day cover			2.00
		Imprint block of 10		2.50	

New Year, 1968.

1967, Dec. 22

166	A97	3c multi		30	20
		First day cover			2.00
		Imprint block of 6		2.25	

Opening of Miyako and Yaeyama television stations.

Dr. Kijin Nakachi and Helper   Pill Box (Inro)
A98   A99

1968, Mar. 15   Photo.   Perf. 13½

167	A98	3c multi		30	20
		First day cover			2.00
		Imprint block of 6		2.25	

120th anniv. of the first vaccination in the Ryukyu Islands, by Dr. Kijin Nakachi.

1968, Apr. 18

168	A99	3c gray & multi		50	45
		First day cover			2.50
		Imprint block of 6		4.00	

Philatelic Week, 1968.

Young Man, Library, Book and Map of Ryukyu Islands
A100

1968, May 13

169	A100	3c multi		40	35
		First day cover			2.00
		Imprint block of 6		3.00	

10th International Library Week.

Mailmen's Uniforms and Stamp of 1948—A101

1968, July 1   Photo.   Perf. 13x13½

170	A101	3c multi		40	35
		First day cover			2.00
		Imprint block of 6		3.00	

First Ryukyuan postage stamps, 20th anniv.

RYUKYU ISLANDS

Main Gate, Enkaku Temple
A102

Photogravure & Engraved

1968, July 15   *Perf. 13½*

171	A102	3c multi	40	35
		First day cover		2.00
		Imprint block of 6	3.00	

Restoration of the main gate Enkaku Temple, built 1492-1495, destroyed during World War II.

Old Man's Dance
A103

1968, Sept. 15   Photo.   *Perf. 13½*

172	A103	3c gold & multi	40	35
		First day cover		2.00
		Imprint block of 6	3.25	

Old People's Day.

Mictyris Longicarpus
A104

Crabs: No. 174, Uca dubia stimpson. No. 175, Baptozius vinosus. No. 176, Cardisoma carnifex. No. 177, Ocypode ceratophthalma pallas.

1968-69   Photo.   *Perf. 13½*

173	A104	3c bl, ocher & blk	60	50
		Imprint block of 6	5.00	
174	A104	3c lt bl grn & multi ('69)	70	50
		Imprint block of 6	5.50	
175	A104	3c lt grn & multi ('69)	70	50
		Imprint block of 6	5.50	
176	A104	3c lt ultra & multi ('69)	90	60
		Imprint block of 6	6.50	
177	A104	3c lt ultra & multi ('69)	90	60
		First day cover, each		2.50
		Imprint block of 6	6.50	

Issue dates: No. 173, Oct. 21, 1968. No. 174, Feb. 5, 1969. No. 175, Mar. 5, 1969. No. 177, June 2, 1969.

Saraswati Pavilion
A105

1968, Nov. 1   Photo.   *Perf. 13½*

178	A105	3c multi	40	30
		First day cover		2.00
		Imprint block of 6	3.25	

Restoration of the Sarawati Pavilion (in front of Enkaku Temple), destroyed during World War II.

Tennis Player   Cock and Iris (Bingata)
A106   A107

1968, Nov. 3   Photo.   *Perf. 13½*

179	A106	3c grn & multi	40	30
		First day cover		2.00
		Imprint block of 6	3.25	

35th All-Japan East-West Man's Soft-ball Tennis Tournament, Naha City, Nov. 23-24.

1968, Dec. 10

180	A107	1½c org & multi	15	15
		First day cover		2.00
		Imprint block of 10	2.00	

New Year, 1969.

Boxer   Ink Slab Screen
A108   A109

1969, Jan. 3

181	A108	3c gray & multi	40	35
		First day cover		2.00
		Imprint block of 6	3.00	

20th All-Japan Amateur Boxing Championships held at the University of the Ryukyus, Jan. 3-5.

RYUKYU ISLANDS

1969, Apr. 17		Photo.		Perf. 13½	
182	A109	3c sal, ind & red		50	35
		First day cover			2.50
		Imprint block of 6		3.50	

Philatelic Week, 1969.

Box Antennas and
Map of Radio Link
A110

Gate of Courtesy
and Emblems
A111

1969, July 1		Photo.		Perf. 13½	
183	A110	3c multi		25	20
		First day cover			2.00
		Imprint block of 6		2.00	

Opening of the UHF (radio) circuit system between Okinawa and the outlying Miyako-Yaeyama Islands.

1969, Aug. 1		Photo.		Perf. 13½	
184	A111	3c Prus. bl, gold & ver		25	20
		First day cover			2.00
		Imprint block of 6		2.00	

22nd All-Japan Formative Education Study Conference, Naha, Aug. 1-3.

FOLKLORE ISSUE

Tug of
War
Festival
A112

Hari Boat
Race
A113

Izaiho
Cere-
mony,
Kudaka
Island
A114

Mortar-
drum
Dance
A115

Sea God
Dance
A116

1969-70		Photo.		Perf. 13	
185	A112	3c multi		50	40
		Imprint block of 6		3.50	
186	A113	3c multi		60	40
		Imprint block of 6		4.00	
187	A114	3c multi		60	40
		Imprint block of 6		4.00	
188	A115	3c multi ('70)		90	60
		Imprint block of 6		6.50	
189	A116	3c multi ('70)		90	60
		First day cover, each			2.50
		Imprint block of 6		6.50	

Issue dates: No. 185, Aug. 1. No. 186, Sept. 5. No. 187, Oct. 3. No. 188, Jan. 20, 1970. No. 189, Feb. 27, 1970.

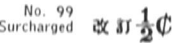

No. 99
Surcharged

1969, Oct. 15		Photo.		Perf. 13½	
190	A44	½c on 3c multi		30	30
		First day cover			3.00
		Imprint block of 10		4.00	

Nakamura-
ke
Farm
House,
Built
1713-51
A117

1969, Nov. 1		Photo.		Perf. 13½	
191	A117	3c multi		30	20
		First day cover			2.00
		Imprint block of 6		2.25	

Protection of national cultural treasures.

Statue of Kyuzo Toyama, Maps of
Hawaiian and Ryukyu Islands
A118

RYUKYU ISLANDS

1969, Dec. 5   Photo.   Perf. 13½

192   A118   3c lt ultra & multi   50   40
             First day cover   2.50
             Imprint block of 6   3.50
        a.   Without overprint   2,000.
        b.   Wide-spaced bars   600.00

70th anniv. of Ryukyu-Hawaii emigration Kyuzo Toyama leader.

The overprint "1969" at lower left and bars across "1970" at upper right was applied before No. 192 was issued.

Dog and Flowers (Bingata)
A119

Sake Flask Made from Coconut
A120

1969, Dec. 10

193   A119   1½c pink & multi   15   15
             First day cover   2.00
             Imprint block of 10   2.00

New Year, 1970.

1970, Apr. 15   Photo.   Perf. 13½

194   A120   3c multi   50   30
             First day cover   2.50
             Imprint block of 6   3.50

Philatelic Week, 1970.

CLASSIC OPERA ISSUE

"The Bell"
(Shushin Kaneiri)
A121

Child and Kidnapper
(Chu-nusudu)
A122

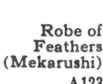

Robe of Feathers
(Mekarushi)
A123

Vengeance of Two Young Sons (Nidotichiuchi)
A124

The Virgin and the Dragon (Kokonomaki)
A125

1970   Photo.   Perf. 13½

195   A121   3c dl bl & multi   80   60
196   A122   3c lt bl & multi   80   60
197   A123   3c bluish grn & multi   80   60
198   A124   3c dl bl grn & multi   80   60
199   A125   3c multi   80   60
             First day cover, each   3.00
             Imprint block of 6, each 5.50

Souvenir Sheets

195a-199a Sheets of 4, each   6.00   7.00
             First day covers, each   10.00

Marginal decoration and inscription. Size: 93x102mm.

Underwater Observatory and Tropical Fish
A126

1970, May 22

200   A126   3c bl grn & multi   40   35
             First day cover   2.50
             Imprint block of 6   3.00

Completion of the underwater observatory of Busena-Misaki, Nago.

Noboru Jahana (1865-1908), Politician
A127

Map of Okinawa and People
A128

Portraits: No. 202, Saion Gushichan Bunjaku (1682-1761), statesman. No. 203, Choho Giwan (1823-1876), regent and poet.

1970-71			Engraved	Perf. 13½	
201	A127	3c	rose cl	80	50
			Imprint block of 6	5.00	
202	A127	3c	dl bl grn	1.25	90
			Imprint block of 6	10.00	
203	A127	3c	blk ('71)	80	50
			First day cover, each		2.50
			Imprint block of 6	5.00	

Issue dates: No. 201, Sept. 25, 1970. No. 202, Dec. 22, 1970. No. 203, Jan. 22, 1971.

1970, Oct. 1			Photogravure		
204	A128	3c	red & multi	25	20
			First day cover		2.00
			Imprint block of 6	2.00	

1970 census, Oct. 1, 1970.

Great Cycad of Une
A129

1970, Nov. 2			Photo.	Perf. 13½	
205	A129	3c	gold & multi	30	25
			First day cover		2.00
			Imprint block of 6	2.25	

Protection of national treasures.

Japanese Flag, Diet and Map of Ryukyus
A130

Wild Boar and Cherry Blossoms (Bingata)
A131

1970, Nov. 15			Photo.	Perf. 13½	
206	A130	3c	ultra & multi	1.00	80
			First day cover		2.50
			Imprint block of 6	7.50	

Citizens' participation in national administration to Japanese law of Apr. 24, 1970.

1970, Dec. 10

207	A131	1½c	multi	15	15
			First day cover		2.00
			Imprint block of 10	2.50	

New Year, 1971.

Low Hand Loom (Jibata)
A132

Farmer Wearing Palm Bark Raincoat and Kuba Leaf Hat
A133

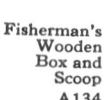 

Fisherman's Wooden Box and Scoop
A134

Designs: No. 209, Woman running a filature (reel). No. 211, Woman hulling rice with cylindrical "Shiri-ushi."

1971			Photo.	Perf. 13½	
208	A132	3c	lt bl & multi	40	35
			Imprint block of 6	3.00	
209	A132	3c	pale grn & multi	40	35
			Imprint block of 6	3.00	
210	A133	3c	lt bl & multi	50	40
			Imprint block of 6	3.25	
211	A132	3c	yel & multi	60	50
			Imprint block of 6	5.00	
212	A134	3c	gray & multi	50	40
			First day cover, each		2.50
			Imprint block of 6	3.90	

Issue dates: No. 208, Feb. 16. No. 209, Mar. 16. No. 210, Apr. 13. No. 211, May 20. No. 212, June 15.

Water Carrier (Taku)
A135

1971, Apr. 15			Photo.	Perf. 13½	
213	A135	3c	bl grn & multi	50	35
			First day cover		2.50
			Imprint block of 6	4.00	

Philatelic Week, 1971.

Old and New Naha, and City Emblem—A136

1971, May 20				Perf. 13	
214	A136	3c	ultra & multi	30	25
			First day cover		2.00
			Imprint block of 6	2.00	

50th anniv. of Naha as a municipality.

RYUKYU ISLANDS

Caesalpinia
Pulcherrima
A137

Design: 2c, Madder (Sandanka).

1971			Photo.	Perf. 13	
215	A137	2c gray & multi		15	10
216	A137	3c gray & multi		20	15
		First day cover, each			2.00
		Imprint block of 10, each		2.50	

Issue dates: 2c, Sept. 30; 3c, May 10.

GOVERNMENT PARK SERIES

View from
Mabuni Hill
A138

Mt. Arashi
from Haneji
Sea
A139

Yabuchi
Island
from
Yakena
Port
A140

1971-72					
217	A138	3c grn & multi		40	30
218	A139	3c bl & multi		40	30
219	A140	4c multi ('72)		50	30
		First day cover, each			2.50
		Imprint block of 6, each		3.00	

Issue dates: No. 217, July 30. No. 218, Aug. 30, 1971. No. 219, Jan. 20, 1972.

Dancer
A141

Deva King,
Torinji Temple
A142

1971, Nov. 1			Photo.	Perf. 13	
220	A141	4c Prus bl & multi		20	15
		First day cover			2.00
		Imprint block of 10		2.50	

1971, Dec. 1
221	A142	4c dp bl & multi		25	25
		First day cover			2.00
		Imprint block of 6		2.00	

Protection of national cultural treasures.

Rat and
Chrysanthemums
A143

Student
Nurse
A144

1971, Dec. 10
222	A143	2c brn org & multi		15	15
		First day cover			2.00
		Imprint block of 10		2.50	

New Year, 1972.

1971, Dec. 24
223	A144	4c lil & multi		35	25
		First day cover			2.00
		Imprint block of 6		2.50	

Nurses' training, 25th anniversary.

A145 A147

RYUKYU ISLANDS

Coral Reef
A146

1972   Photo.   Perf. 13

224	A145	5c brt bl & multi	60	40
225	A146	5c gray & multi	60	40
226	A147	5c ocher & multi	60	40
		First day cover, each		2.50
		Imprint block of 6, each	4.00	

Issue dates: No. 224, Apr. 14. No. 225, Mar. 30. No. 226, Mar. 21.

Dove, U.S. and Japanese Flags
A148

1972, Apr. 17   Photo.   Perf. 13

227	A148	5c brt bl & multi	1.00	75
		First day cover		3.00
		Imprint block of 6	7.50	

Antique Sake Pot (Yushibin)
A149

1972, Apr. 20

228	A149	5c ultra & multi	80	50
		First day cover		2.50
		Imprint block of 6	6.00	

Ryukyu stamps were replaced by those of Japan after May 15, 1972.

AIR POST STAMPS.

Dove and Map of Ryukyus
AP1

1950, Feb. 15   Photogravure   Perf. 13x13½   Unwmkd.

C1	AP1	8y brt bl	80.00	50.00
		Imprint block of 6	700.00	
C2	AP1	12y green	25.00	20.00
		Imprint block of 6	200.00	
C3	AP1	16y rose car	20.00	15.00
		Imprint block of 6	150.00	
		First day cover, each		35.00
		First day cover #C1-C3		175.00

Heavenly Maiden
AP2

1951-54

C4	AP2	13y blue	3.00	2.00
		First day cover		60.00
		Imprint block of 6, 5-character	250.00	
		Imprint block of 6, 8-character	50.00	
C5	AP2	18y green	4.00	3.00
		First day cover		60.00
		Imprint block of 6, 5-character	75.00	
		Imprint block of 6, 8-character	60.00	
C6	AP2	30y cerise	6.00	2.00
		First day cover		60.00
		First day cover, #C4-C6		250.00
		Imprint block of 6, 5-character	80.00	
		Imprint block of 6, 8-character	140.00	
C7	AP2	40y red vio ('54)	9.00	6.00
		First day cover		35.00
		Imprint block of 6	100.00	
C8	AP2	50y yel org ('54)	12.00	8.00
		First day cover		35.00
		First day cover, #C7-C8		100.00
		Imprint block of 6	120.00	

Heavenly Maiden Playing Flute
AP3

1957, Aug. 1   Engraved   Perf. 13½

C9	AP3	15y bl grn	5.00	3.00
		Imprint block of 6	40.00	
C10	AP3	20y rose car	8.00	4.50
		Imprint block of 6	60.00	
C11	AP3	35y yel grn	15.00	7.00
		Imprint block of 6	115.00	
C12	AP3	45y redsh brn	18.00	10.00
		Imprint block of 6	150.00	
C13	AP3	60y gray	24.00	12.00
		Imprint block of 6	230.00	
		First day cover, #C9-C13		70.00

On one printing of No. C10, position 49 shows an added spur on the right side of the second character from the left.

Same Surcharged in Brown Red or Light Ultramarine

1959, Dec. 20

C14	AP3	9c on 15y bl grn (BrR)	3.00	2.00
		Imprint block of 6	21.00	
		a. Inverted surch.	550.00	
		Imprint block of 6	4,000.	
C15	AP3	14c on 20y rose car (L.U)	4.00	3.00
		Imprint block of 6	27.50	
C16	AP3	19c on 35y yel grn (BrR)	8.00	5.00
		Imprint block of 6	52.50	
C17	AP3	27c on 45y redsh brn (L.U)	15.00	7.00
		Imprint block of 6	120.00	
C18	AP3	35c on 60y gray (BrR)	20.00	9.00
		Imprint block of 6	170.00	
		First day cover, #C14-C18		50.00

No. C15 is found with the variety described below No. C13.

RYUKYU ISLANDS

改訂

9¢

Nos. 31-33, 36 and 38 Surcharged in Black, Brown, Red, Blue or Green.

1960, Aug. 3   Photo.   *Perf. 13*

C19	A14	9c on 4y brn	3.50	2.00
		Imprint block of 10	45.00	
	a.	Invtd. surch.	10,000.	12,500.
C20	A17	14c on 5y rose lil (Br)	3.00	2.00
		Imprint block of 10	40.00	
C21	A14	19c on 15y ver (R)	2.00	1.50
		Imprint block of 10	30.00	
C22	A17	27c on 14y redsh brn (Bl)	7.00	4.00
		Imprint block of 10	90.00	
C23	A14	35c on 20y yel org (G)	8.00	5.50
		Imprint block of 10	100.00	
		First day cover, #C19-C23		40.00

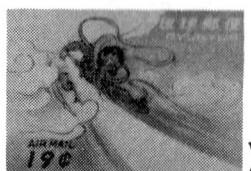

Wind God
AP4

Designs: 9c, Heavenly Maiden (as on AP2). 14c, Heavenly Maiden (as on AP3). 27c, Wind God at right. 35c, Heavenly Maiden over treetops.

1961, Sept. 21   *Perf. 13½*   Unwmkd.

C24	AP4	9c multi	45	20
		Imprint block of 6	3.50	
C25	AP4	14c multi	75	75
		Imprint block of 6	5.00	
C26	AP4	19c multi	80	75
		Imprint block of 6	6.00	
C27	AP4	27c multi	2.25	50
		Imprint block of 6	16.00	
C28	AP4	35c multi	1.75	1.00
		Imprint block of 6	13.00	
		First day cover, #C24-C28		60.00

AP5   AP6

1963, Aug. 28   *Perf. 13x13½*

C29	AP5	5½c multi	20	20
		Imprint block of 10	3.00	
C30	AP6	7c multi	25	30
		Imprint block of 10	3.50	
		First day cover, each		1.00
		First day cover, #C29-C30		2.50

SPECIAL DELIVERY STAMP

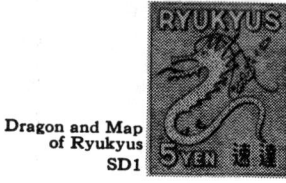

Dragon and Map
of Ryukyus
SD1

1950, Feb. 15   Photogravure
     Perf. 13x13½   Unwmkd.

E1	SD1	5y brt bl	30.00	17.50
		First day cover		100.00
		Imprint block of 6	275.00	

QUANTITIES ISSUED
Regular Postage and Commemorative Stamps

Cat. No.	Quantity	Cat. No.	Quantity	Cat. No.	Quantity
1	90,214	72	598,912	165	3,998,000
2	55,901	73	398,990	166-167, each	1,298,000
3	94,663	74	598,936	168	998,000
4	55,413	75	1,998,992	169-179, each	898,000
5	76,387	76	1,000,000	180	3,198,000
6	117,321	77	2,000,000	181-189, each	898,000
7	291,403	78	500,000	190	1,733,050
1a	61,000	79-80, each	400,000	191	898,000
2a-4a, each	181,000	81	12,599,000	192	864,960
5a	29,936	82	11,979,000	193	3,198,000
6a	99,300	83	6,850,000	194	898,000
7a	46,000	84	5,099,000	195-199, each	598,000
8	2,859,000	84A	1,699,000	195a-199a, each	124,500
8a	247,943	85	4,749,000	200-206, each	898,000
9	1,198,989	86	2,099,000	207	3,198,000
10	589,000	87	3,019,000	208-210, each	1,098,000
11	479,000	88	298,966	211-212, each	1,298,000
12	598,999	89	298,966	213	1,098,000
13	397,855	90	398,901	214	1,298,000
14	499,000	91	398,992	215-216, each	4,998,000
15	498,960	92	1,498,970	217	1,498,000
16	200,000	93	598,989	218-219, each	1,798,000
16a	200,000	94	398,998	220	2,998,000
16b	40,000	95	398,993	221	1,798,000
17	9,800	96	298,993	222	4,998,000
18	299,500	97	398,997	223	1,798,000
19	3,014,427	98	9,699,000	224-226, each	2,498,000
20	3,141,777	99	10,991,500	227	2,998,000
21	2,970,827	100	1,549,000	228	3,998,000
22	191,917	101	799,000		
23	1,118,617	102	1,299,000	**AIR POST STAMPS**	
24	276,218	103	398,995		
24a	ca. 1,300	104	298,892	C1-C3, each	198,000
25	231,717	105	1,598,949	C4	1,952,348
26	220,139	106	348,989	C5	331,360
27	398,993	107	10,099,000	C6	762,530
28	386,421	108	348,865	C7	76,166
29	498,854	109	348,937	C8	122,816
30	298,994	110	348,962	C9	708,319
31	4,768,413	111	348,974	C10	108,824
32	1,202,297	112	398,974	C11	164,147
33	500,059	113	398,911	C12	50,335
34	298,994	114	1,199,000	C13	69,092
35	199,000	115	398,948	C14	597,103
36	455,896	116	398,943	C15	77,951
37	160,518	117	1,698,912	C16	97,635
38	198,720	118	550,000	C17	98,353
39	198,199	119	549,000	C18	96,650
40	599,000	120	749,000	C19	1,033,900
41	598,075	121	799,000	C19a	100
42	1,198,179	122	389,000	C20	230,000
43	1,625,406	123	319,000	C21	185,000
44	994,880	124	1,999,000	C22	191,000
45	997,759	125-127, each	999,000	C23	190,000
46	996,759	128	799,000	C24	17,199,000
47	2,705,955	129	1,699,000	C25	1,999,000
48	997,542	130-131, each	799,000	C26	1,250,000
49	996,609	132	849,000	C27	3,499,000
50	996,928	133	799,000	C28	1,699,000
51	499,000	134	1,299,000	C29	1,199,00
52	249,000	135	1,099,000	C30	1,949,000
52a	78,415	136	1,299,000		
53	248,700	137-138, each	1,598,000	**SPECIAL DELIVERY STAMP**	
54	1,498,991	139	3,098,000		
55	2,498,897	140-142, each	1,598,000	E1	198,804
56	1,098,972	143-148, each	2,498,000		
57	998,918	149	2,298,000		
58	2,699,000	150	3,798,000		
59	2,499,000	151	2,298,000		
60	199,000	152-156, each	1,998,000		
61	499,000	157-158, each	1,698,000		
62	199,000	159-160, each	1,298,000		
63	1,498,931	161	898,000		
64	798,953	162	1,498,000		
65-68, each	999,000	163-164, each	1,298,000		

RYUKYU ISLANDS

Stamps of Japan Overprinted
by Postmasters
in Four Island Districts

Gen. Maresuke Nogi A84 — Admiral Heihachiro Togo A86 — Garambi Lighthouse, Taiwan A88 — Meiji Shrine, Tokyo A90 — Plane and Map of Japan A92 — Kasuga Shrine, Nara A93 — Mount Fuji and Cherry Blossoms A94

Horyu Temple, Nara A95 — Miyajima Torii, Itsukushima Shrine A96 — Golden Pavilion, Kyoto A97 — Great Budda, Kamakura A98 — Kamatari Fujiwara A99 — War Factory Girl A144 — Palms and Map of "Greater East Asia" A148

Aviator Saluting and Japanese Flag A150 — Torii of Yasukuni Shrine A151 — Mt. Fuji and Cherry Blossoms A152 — Torii of Miyajima A153 — Garambi Lighthouse, Taiwan—A154 — Coal Miners A163 — "Thunderstorm below Fuji," by Hokusai A167

PROVISIONAL ISSUES

Prices are for unused stamps. Used copies sell for considerably more, should be expertized and a. preferred on cover or document.

KUME ISLAND

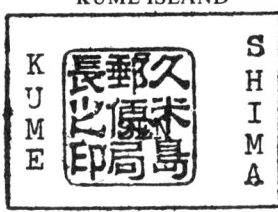

A1

Mimeographed
Seal Handstamped in Vermilion

1945, Oct. 1 Imperf. Ungummed Unwmkd.
1X1 A1 7s black, *cream (2,400)* 1200.00
   a. "7" & "SEN" one
      letter space to left 2500.00

Printed on legal-size U.S. military mimeograph paper and validated by the official seal of the Kume Island postmaster, Norifume Kikuzato. Valid until May 4, 1946.

Cancellations "20.10.1" (Oct. 1, 1945) or "20.10.6" (Oct. 6, 1945) are by favor. Copies on U.S. official bond paper, white and watermarked, were not issued.

AMAMI DISTRICT

Inspection Seal
("Ken," abbreviation
for *kensa zumi*,
inspected or examined;
five types)

Stamps of Japan 1937-46
Handstamped in Black, Blue, Purple,
Vermilion or Red

1947-48		Typo., Litho., Engr. Perf. 13, Imperf.	Wmk. 257
2X1	A82	½s purple, #257	800.00
2X2	A83	1s fawn, #258	
2X3	A144	1s orange brown, #325	1750.00
2X4	A84	2s crimson, #259	500.00
		a. 2s vermilion, #259c	
2X5	A84	2s rose red, imperf., #351	
2X6	A85	3s green, #260	1700.00
2X7	A84	3s brown, #329	
2X8	A161	3s rose carmine, imperf., #352	1800.00
2X9	A146	4s emerald, #330	650.00
2X10	A86	5s brown lake, #331	700.00
2X11	A162	5s green, imperf., #353	1500.00
2X12	A147	6s light ultramarine, #332	
2X13	A86	7s orange vermilion, #333	1250.00
2X14	A90	8s dark purple & pale violet, #265	1500.00
2X15	A148	10s crimson & dull rose, #334	500.00
2X16	A152	10s red orange, imperf., #355 (48)	2500.00
2X17	A93	14s rose lake & pale rose, #268	
2X18	A150	15s dull blue, #336	500.00
2X19	A151	17s gray violet, #337	1750.00
2X20	A94	20s ultramarine, #269	1750.00
2X21	A152	20s blue, #338	600.00
2X22	A152	20s ultramarine, imperf., #356 (48)	1750.00
2X23	A95	25s dark brown & pale brown, #270	900.00
2X24	A151	27s rose brown, #339	
2X25	A153	30s bluish green, #340	
2X26	A153	30s bright blue, imperf., #357	
2X27	A88	40s dull violet, #341	1750.00
2X28	A154	40s dark violet, #342	1750.00
2X29	A97	50s olive & pale olive, #272	
2X30	A163	50s dark brown, imperf., #358 (48)	
2X31	A164	1y deep olive green, imperf., #359	2500.00
2X32	A167	1y deep ultramarine, imperf., #364	
2X33	A99	5y deep gray green, #274	
2X34	A99	5y deep gray green, imperf., #360	

RYUKYU ISLANDS

MIYAKO DISTRICT

Personal Seal
of Postmaster
Jojin Tomiyama

Stamps of Japan 1937-46
Handstamped in Vermilion or Red

1946-47		Typo., Litho., Engr. Perf. 13	Wmk. 257
3X1	A144	1s orange brown, #325	175.00
3X2	A84	2s crimson, #259	125.00
		a. 2s vermilion #259c ('47)	150.00
3X3	A84	3s brown, #329	70.00
3X4	A86	4s dark green, #261	70.00
3X5	A86	5s brown lake, #331	550.00
3X6	A88	6s orange, #263	70.00
3X7	A90	8s dark purple & pale violet, #265	100.00
3X8	A148	10s crimson & dull rose, #334	70.00
3X9	A152	10s red orange, imperf., #355 ('47) (1,000)	120.00
3X10	A92	12s indigo, #267	70.00
3X11	A93	14s rose lake & pale rose, #268	70.00
3X12	A150	15s dull blue, #336	70.00
3X13	A151	17s gray violet, #337	70.00
3X14	A94	20s ultramarine, #269	—
3X15	A152	20s blue, #338	70.00
3X16	A152	20s ultramarine, imperf., #356 ('47)	175.00
3X17	A95	25s dark brown & pale brown, #270	70.00
3X18	A153	30s bluish green, #340	70.00
3X19	A88	40s dull violet, #341	250.00
3X20	A154	40s dark violet, #342	80.00
3X21	A97	50s olive & pale olive, #272	70.00
3X22	A163	50s dark brown, #358 ('47) (750)	200.00
3X23	A98	1y brown & pale brown, #273	—
3X24	A167	1y deep ultramarine, #364 ('47) (500)	1500.00

Nos. 3X22 and 3X24 have sewing machine perf.; No. 3X16 exists with that perf. also.

Nos. 3X1-3X2, 3X2a, 3X3-3X5, 3X8
Handstamp Surcharged
with 2 Japanese Characters

1946-47			
3X25	A144	1y on 1s orange brown	120.00
3X26	A84	1y on 2s crimson	2000.00
3X27	A84	1y on 3s brown ('47)	2000.00
3X28	A84	2y on 2s crimson	140.00
		a. 2y on 2s vermilion ('47)	140.00
3X29	A86	4y on 4s dark green	120.00
3X30	A86	5y on 5s brown lake	120.00
3X31	A148	10y on 10s crimson & dull rose	100.00

OKINAWA DISTRICT

Personal Seal
of Postmaster
Shiichi Hirata

 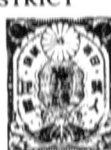

R1

Japan Nos. 355-356, 358, 364 Overprinted in Black

		Lithographed	
1947, Nov. 1		Imperf.	Wmk. 257
4X1	A152	10s red orange (13,997)	1200.00
4X2	A152	20s ultramarine (13,611)	500.00
4X3	A163	50s dark brown (6,276)	900.00
4X4	A167	1y deep ultramarine (1,947)	1750.00

On Revenue Stamp of Japan

| 4X5 | R1 | 30s brown (14,000) | 3500.00 |

No. 4X5 is on Japan's current 30s revenue stamp. The Hirata seal validated it for postal use.

Nos. 4X1-4X4 are known with rough sewing machine perforations, full or partial.

YAEYAMA DISTRICT

Personal Seal
of Postmaster
Kenpuku Miyara

Stamps of Japan 1937-46
Handstamped in Black

1948		Typo., Engr., Litho. Perf. 13	Wmk. 257
5X1	A86	4s dark green, #261	1200.00
5X2	A86	5s brown lake, #331	1200.00
5X3	A86	7s orange vermilion, #333	800.00
5X4	A148	10s crimson & dull rose, #334	5000.00
5X5	A94	20s ultramarine, #269	90.00
5X6	A96	30s peacock blue, #271	1000.00
5X7	A88	40s dull violet, #341	40.00
5X8	A97	50s olive & pale olive, #272	60.00
5X9	A163	50s dark brown, imperf., #358 (250)	1350.00
5X10	A99	5y deep gray green, #274	2000.00

Provisional postal stationery of the four districts also exists.

LETTER SHEETS

Typographed by Japan Printing Bureau. Stamp is in upper left corner.
Prices are for entires.

Stylized Deigo
Blossom
US1

Banyan Tree
US2

Designer: Shutaro Higa

1948-49				
U1	US1	50s vermilion, cream, July 18, 1949 (250,000)		50.00	75.00
		First day cancel			—
		a. Orange red, cream, July 1, 1948 (1,000)		550.00	—

Designer: Ken Yabu

1950, Jan. 21				
U2	US2	1y carmine red, cream (250,000)		45.00	60.00
		First day cancel			—

AIR LETTER SHEETS

DC-4 Skymaster and
Shurei Gate
UC1

UC2

RYUKYU ISLANDS

Designer: Chosho Ashitomi

"PAR AVION" (Bilingual) below Stamp

Litho. & Typo. by Japan Printing Bureau.

1952, Nov. 1
UC1 UC1 12y dull rose, *pale blue green (126,000)* 15.00 15.00
            First day cancel   75.00

Printed on tinted paper with colorless overall inscription, RYUKYU FOREIGN AIRMAIL, repeated in parallel vertical lines. Model: U.S. No. UC16.

Litho. & Typo. by Nippon Toppan K.K.
"AEROGRAMME" below Stamp

1955, Sept. 10
UC2 UC2 15y violet blue, *pale blue green*
            (200,000)   20.00 20.00
            First day cancel   75.00

No. UC2 surcharged in Red

a
"13" & "¢" aligned at bot.;
2 thick bars

b
"¢" raised;
2 thick bars

c
"13" & "¢" as in "a";
4 thin bars

d
"¢" raised;
4 thin bars

Printers: Type "a" Nakamura Printing Co "b" and "d," Okinawa Printing Co. "c," Sun Printing Co.

1958-60
UC3 UC2 13c on 15y type "a" *(60,000)*   20.00 20.00
            First Day Cancel   60.00
            a. Type "b" ('59) (E 10,000)   30.00 30.00
            b. Type "c" ('59) (E 2,000)   80.00 80.00
            c. Type "d" *Oct. 1, 1960 (E 3,000)* 250.00 250.00
            d. As "b," small "¢"   1000.00 —

No. UC3c has Nos. 55, 58 affixed to make the 15¢ rate.

UC3
Litho. by Japan Printing Bureau.

1959, Nov. 10
UC4 UC3 15c dark blue, *pale blue (560,000)* 4.00 3.50
            First day cancel   12.00

POSTAL CARDS

Nos. UX1-UX9 are typographed, others lithographed.
Printed by Japan Printing Bureau unless otherwise stated.
Quantities in parentheses; "E" means estimated. Prices are for entire cards.

Deigo Blossom Type

Designer: Shutaro Higa

1948, July 1
UX1 US1 10s dull red, *grayish tan (100,000)*   40.00 90.00

1949, July 1
UX2 US1 15s orange red, *gray (E 175,000)*   40.00 80.00
            First day cancel
            a. 15s vermilion, *tan*
            (E 50,000)   125.00 150.00

Banyan Tree Type

Designer: Ken Yabu

1950, Jan 21
UX3 US2 50s carmine red, *light tan (E 200,000)* 10.00 15.00
            First day cancel   90.00
            a. Grayish tan card (E 25,000)   42.50   80.00

Nos. UX2, UX2a Handstamp Surcharged in Vermilion

a   b
19-21 x 23-25mm   22-23 x 26-27mm

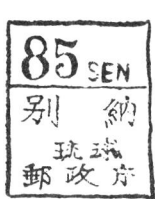 
c   d
20-21 x 24-24½mm   22-23½ x 25-26mm

1951
UX4 US1 (c) 15s + 85s on #UX2 *(E 35,000)*   100.00 100.00
            a. Type "c" on #UX2a *(E 5000)*   150.00 150.00
            b. Type "a" on #UX2 *(E39,000)*   75.00 100.00
            c. Type "a" on #UX2a   1000.00 ———
            d. Type "b" on #UX2   1000.00 1000.00
            e. Type "d" on #UX2 *(E 4,000)*   150.00 200.00
            f. Type "d" on #UX2a *(E 1,000)*   250.00 300.00

Type "a" exists on the 15s cherry blossom postal card of Japan.

RYUKYU ISLANDS

Crown, Leaf Ornaments

PC3	PC4
Naha die	Tokyo die
21 x 22mm	18½ x 19mm

Designer: Masayoshi Adaniya
Koshun Printing Co.

1952

UX5	PC3	1y	vermilion, tan, Feb. 8 (400,600)	40.00	40.00
UX6	PC4	1y	vermilion, off-white, Oct. 6 (1,295,000)	20.00	15.00
			a. Tan card, coarse (50,000)	35.00	25.00
			b. Tan card, smooth (16,000)	500.00	100.00

Naha die	Tokyo die
23x25½mm	22x24½mm
PC5	PC6

Naminoue Shrine

Designer: Gensei Agena

1953-57

UX7	PC5	2y	green, off-white (1,799,400)	40.00	20.00
			First day cancel, Dec. 2, 1953		100.00
			a. Printed both sides	500.00	
UX8	PC6	2y	green, off-white ('55) (2,799,400)	15.00	10.00
			a. Deep blue green ('56) (300,000)	30.00	20.00
			b. Yellow green ('57) (2,400,000)	10.00	5.00
			c. As "a," printed both sides	500.00	
			d. As "b," printed both sides	500.00	

Stylized Pine, Bamboo, Plum Blossoms
PC7

Designer: Koya Oshiro
Kotsura and Koshun Printing Companies
1956 New Year Card

1955, Dec. 1

UX9	PC7	2y	red, cream	90.00	45.00
			First day cancel		150.00

No. UX9 was printed on rough card (43,400) and smooth-finish card (356,600).

Sun	Temple Lion
PC8	PC9

Designer: Seikichi Tamanaha
Kobundo Printing Co.
1957 New Year Card

1956, Dec. 1

UX10	PC8	2y	brown carmine & yellow, off-white (600,000)	5.00	5.00
			First day cancel		15.00

Designer: Shin Isagawa
Fukuryu Printing Co.
1958 New Year Card

1957, Dec. 1

UX11	PC9	2y	lilac rose, off-white (1,000,000)	3.50	4.50
			First day cancel		6.00
			a. "1" omitted in right date	60.00	75.00
			b. Printed both sides	250.00	300.00

Nos. UX8, UX8a and UX8b "Revalued" in Red, Cherry or Pink by Three Naha Printeries.

 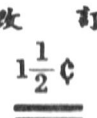 

a b c

1958-59

UX12	PC6	1½c on 2y green, type "a," Sept. 16 (600,000)	4.00	5.00
		First day cancel		15.00
		a. Shrine stamp omitted	750.00	1000.00
		b. Bar of ½ omitted, top of 2 broken	75.00	100.00
		c. Type "b," Nov. (1,000,000)	10.00	15.00
		d. Type "c" ('59) (200,000)	20.00	30.00
		e. Wrong font "e", type "c"	30.00	45.00
		f. "e" omitted, type "c"	1500.00	1500.00
		g. Double surcharge, type "c"	1000.00	
		h. Triple surcharge, type "c"	1500.00	

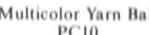

Multicolor Yarn Ball	Toy Pony
PC10	19½ x 23mm
	PC11

Designer: Masayoshi Adaniya
Kobundo Printing Co.
1959 New Year Card

RYUKYU ISLANDS

1958, Dec. 10

UX13 PC10 1½c black, red, yellow & gray blue,
off-white (1,514,000)   2.00   2.50
    First day cancel   3.00
    a. Black omitted   —

Designer: Seikichi Tamanaha
Kobundo Printing Co.

1959, June 20

UX14 PC11 1½c dark blue & brown *(1,140,000)*   2.00   2.50
    First day cancel   2.00
    a. Dark blue omitted   350.00

Toy Carp and Boy
PC12

Toy Pony
21 x 25mm
PC13

Designer: Masayoshi Adaniya
1960 New Year Card

1959, Dec. 1

UX15 PC12 1½c violet blue, red & black, *cream (2,000,000)*   1.50   2.50
    First day cancel   2.00

1959, Dec. 30

UX16 PC13 1½c gray violet & brown, *cream (3,500,000)*   3.00   75
    First day cancel   4.00

Household Altar
PC14

Coral Head
PC15

Designer: Shin Isagawa
1961 New Year Card

1960, Nov. 20

UX17 PC14 1½c gray, carmine, yellow & black,
off-white (2,647,591)   2.00   3.00
    First day cancel   2.50

Designer: Shinzan Yamada
Kidekuni Printing Co.

Summer Greeting Card

1961, July 5

UX18 PC15 1½c ultramarine & cerise, *off-white (264,900)*   3.00   5.00
    First day cancel   6.00

Tiger
PC16

Inscribed "RYUKYUS"
PC17

Designer: Shin Isagawa
1962 New Year Card

1961, Nov. 15

UX19 PC16 1½c ocher, black & red, *off-white (2,891,626)*   2.00   4.50
    First day cancel   2.50
    a. Red omitted   750.00
    b. Red inverted   500.00
    c. Red omitted on face, inverted
       on back   500.00
    d. Double impression of red, one
       inverted   500.00
    e. Double impression of ocher &
       black, red inverted   500.00
    f. Double impression of ocher &
       black, one inverted   500.00

Designer: Seikichi Tamanaha

1961-67

UX20 PC17 1½c gray violet & brown, *white ('67) (18,600,000)*   1.00   50
    a. Off-white card ('66) *(4,000,000)*   1.50   75
    b. Cream card, Dec. 23
       (12,500,000)   1.00   50
    First day cancel   2.00

Ie Island
PC18

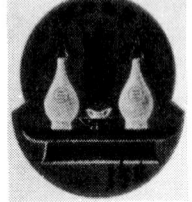
New Year Offerings
PC19

Designer: Shinzan Yamada
Sakai Printing Co.

Summer Greeting Card

1962, July 10

UX21 PC18 1½c bright blue, yellow & brown,
off-white (221,500)   2.50   3.50
    First day cancel   4.50
    Square notch at left   35.00   45.00

Designer: Shin Isagawa
Sakai Printing Co.

1963 New Year Card; Precanceled

1962, Nov. 15

UX22 PC19 1½c olive brown, carmine & black
(3,000,000)   3.00   4.50
    First day cancel   3.50
    a. Yellow brown background   ——
    b. Brown ocher background   ——

Ryukyu Temple Dog and Wine
Flask Silhouette
PC20

Water Strider
PC21

Designer: Shin Isagawa
International Postal Card

RYUKYU ISLANDS

1963, Feb. 15
UX23 PC20 5c vermilion, emerald & black, *pale yellow (150,000)*   2.00   3.50
    First day cancel   2.50
    a. Black & emerald omitted   450.00

Designer: Seikichi Tamanaha
Summer Greeting Card

1963, June 20
UX24 PC21 1½c Prussian green & black, *off-white (250,000)*   5.00   7.00
    First day cancel   4.00

Princess Doll   Bitter Melon Vine
PC22   PC23

Designer: Koya Oshiro
1964 New Year Card; Precanceled

1963, Nov. 15
UX25 PC22 1½c orange red, yellow & ultra., *off-white (3,200,000)*   3.00   3.50
    First day cancel   3.00

Designer: Shinzan Yamada
Summer Greeting Card

1964, June 20
UX26 PC23 1½c multicolored, *off-white (285,410)*   2.00   3.50
    First day cancel   2.75

Fighting Kite with Rider   Palm-leaf Fan
PC24   PC25

Designer: Koya Oshiro
1965 New Year Card; Precanceled

1964, Nov. 15
UX27 PC24 1½c multicolored, *off-white (4,876,618)*   2.00   2.50
    First day cancel   2.50

Designer: Koya Oshiro
Summer Greeting Card

1965, June 20
UX28 PC25 1½c multicolored, *off-white (340,604)*   2.50   3.50
    First day cancel   2.50

Toy Pony Rider   Fan Palm Dipper
PC26   PC27

Designer: Seikichi Tamanaha
1966 New Year Card; Precanceled

1965, Nov. 15
UX29 PC26 1½c multicolored, *off-white (5,224,622)*   2.00   2.50
    First day cancel   2.00
    a. Silver (background) omitted   250.00

Designer: Seikichi Tamanaha
Summer Greeting Card

1966, June 20
UX30 PC27 1½c multicolored, *off-white (339,880)*   2.50   3.50
    First day cancel   2.00

Toy Dove   Cycad Insect Cage
PC28   and
                     Praying Mantis
                     PC29

Designer: Seikichi Tamanaha
1967 New Year Card; Precanceled

1966, Nov. 15
UX31 PC28 1½c multicolored, *off-white (5,500,000)*   2.00   2.50
    First day cancel   2.50
    a. Silver (background) omitted   500.00
    b. Gray blue & green omitted   750.00

Designer: Shin Isagawa
Summer Greeting Card

1967, June 20
UX32 PC29 1½c multicolored, *off-white (350,000)*   2.50   3.50
    First day cancel   2.50

Paper Doll Royalty   Pandanus Drupe
PC30   PC31

Designer: Shin Isagawa
1968 New Year Card; Precanceled

1967, Nov. 15
UX33 PC30 1½c multicolored, *off-white (6,200,000)*   1.50   2.50
    First day cancel   2.50
    a. Gold omitted   500.00

Designer: Seikan Omine
Summer Greeting Card

1968, June 20
UX34 PC31 1½c multicolored, *off-white (350,000)*   2.00   3.50
    First day cancel   2.50

RYUKYU ISLANDS

Toy Lion
PC32

Ryukyu Trading Ship
PC33

Designer: Teruyoshi Kinjo
1969 New Year Card; Precanceled

1968, Nov. 15
UX35 PC32 1½c multicolored, *off-white (7,000,000)*   1.50   2.50
         First day cancel   2.00

Designer: Seikichi Tamanaha
Summer Greeting Card

1969, June 20
UX36 PC33 1½c multicolored, *(349,800)*   2.00   3.50
         First day cancel   2.50

Toy Devil Mask
PC34   Ripe Litchis
              PC35

Designer: Teruyoshi Kinjo
1970 New Year Card; Precanceled

1969, Nov. 15
UX37 PC34 1½c multicolored *(7,200,000)*   1.25   2.50
         First day cancel   2.00

Designer: Kensei Miyagi
Summer Greetng Card   1.50

1970, June 20
UX38 PC35 1½c multicolored *(400,000)*   2.00   3.50
         First day cancel   2.00

Thread-winding
Implements for Dance
PC36

Ripe Guavas
PC37

Designer: Yoshinori Arakai
1971 New Year Card; Precanceled

1970, Nov. 16
UX39 PC36 1½c multicolored *(7,500,000)*   1.50   2.50
         First day cancel   1.50

Designer: Kensei Miyagi
Summer Greeting Card

1971, July 10
UX40 PC37 1½c multicolored *(400,000)*   2.00   3.50
         First day cancel   2.00

Pony Type of 1961
Zip Code Boxes in Vermilion

1971, July 10
UX41 PC17 1½c gray violet & brown *(3,000,000)*   2.00   5.00
         First day cancel   2.50

No. UX1 Surcharged below Stamp in Vermilion

改訂2¢

"Revalued 2¢" applied by Nakamura Printing Co.

1971, Sept. 1
UX42 PC17 2c on 1½c gray violet & brown
                (1,699,569)   1.50   3.00
         First day cancel   3.00
         a. Inverted surcharge   500.00
         b. Double surcharge   500.00
         c. Surcharge on back   500.00
         d. Surcharge on back, inverted   500.00

Tasseled Castanets
PC38

Designer: Yoshinori Arakaki
Zip Code Boxes in Vermilion
1972 New Year Card; Precanceled

1971, Nov. 15
UX43 PC38 2c multicolored *(8,000,000)*   1.50   2.50
         First day cancel   2.00

Type of 1961
Zip Code Boxes in Vermilion

1971, Dec. 15
UX44 PC17 2c gray violet & brown *(3,500,000)*   2.00   2.50
         First day cancel   2.50

PAID REPLY POSTAL CARDS

Sold as two attached cards, one for message, one for reply. The listings are of unsevered cards except Nos. UY4-UY6.

往信   返信
Message   Reply

1948, July 1
UY1   US1   10s+10s dull red, *grayish tan (1,000)*   1200.00   ——
                m. Message card   350.00   ——
                r. Reply card   350.00   ——

1949, July 18
UY2   US1   15s+15s vermilion, *tan (E 150,000)*   30.00   ——
                First day cancel
                a. Gray card *(E 75,000)*   75.00   ——
                m. Message card   7.50   ——
                r. Reply card   7.50   ——

RYUKYU ISLANDS

1950, Jan. 21

UY3 US2 50s+ 50s carmine red, *gray cream*
(E 130,000) 40.00 —
First day cancel —
a. Message card, double impression — —
b. Light tan card (E 96,000) 10.00 —
m. Message card 3.00 —
r. Reply card 3.00 —

No. UY2a Handstamp Surcharged in Vermilion

1951

UY4 US1 1y (15s + 85s) message, type "b" (E 3750) 350.00 350.00
a. Reply, type "b" (E 3750) 350.00 350.00
b. Message, type "a" (E 1500) 600.00 —
c. Reply, type "a" (E 1500) 600.00 —
d. Message, type "d" (E 2250) 500.00 —
e. Reply, type "d" (E 2250) 500.00 —
f. Message, UY2, type "a" (E 250) 150.00 225.00
g. Reply, UY2, type "a" (E 250) 150.00 225.00
h. Message, UY2, type "b" (E 1500) 275.00 275.00
i. Reply, UY2, type "b" (E 1500) 275.00 275.00
j. Message, UY2, type "d" (E 250) 150.00 250.00
k. Reply, UY2, type "d" (E 250) 150.00 250.00

e

f

g

h

Typographed Surcharge in Vermilion

UY5 US1 1y (15s + 85s) message, type "f" (E 20,000) 125.00 125.00
a. Reply, type "f" (E 20,000) 125.00 125.00
b. Message, type "e" (E 12,500) 225.00 225.00
c. Reply, type "e" (E 12,500) 225.00 225.00
d. Message, type "g" (E 500) 1000.00 1000.00
e. Reply, type "g" (E 500) 1000.00 1000.00
f. Message, UY2, type "e" (E 15,000) 125.00 125.00
g. Reply, UY2, type "e" (E 15,000) 125.00 125.00
h. Message, UY2, type "f" (E 9,000) 125.00 125.00
i. Reply, UY2, type "f" (E 9,000) 125.00 125.00
j. Message, UY2, type "g" (E 500) 1000.00 1000.00
k. Reply, UY2, type "g" (E 500) 1000.00 1000.00

Nos. UY4-UY5 were also issued as unsevered cards.

Typographed Surcharge Type "h" in Vermilion on No. UY3

UY6 US2 1y (50s + 50s) message (E 35,000) 100.00 150.00
a. Reply (E 35,000) 100.00 150.00
b. Message, UY3b (E 10,000) 75.00 150.00
c. Reply, UY3b (E 10,000) 75.00 150.00

Smooth or Coarse Card

1952, Feb. 8

UY7 PC3 1y + 1y vermilion, *gray tan* (60,000) 75.00 —
First day cancel 250.00
m. Message card 20.00 50.00
r. Reply card 20.00 50.00

1953

UY8 PC4 1y + 1y vermilion, *tan* (22,900) 30.00 —
First day cancel —
a. Off-white card (13,800) 35.00 —
m. Message card 10.00 25.00
r. Reply card 10.00 35.00

Off-white or Light Cream Card

1953, Dec. 2

UY9 PC5 2y + 2y green (50,000) 50.00 —
First day cancel 100.00
m. Message card 15.00 25.00
r. Reply card 15.00 35.00

1955, May

UY10 PC6 2y + 2y green, *off-white* (280,000) 10.00 —
a. Reply card blank 500.00
m. Message card 3.50 15.00
r. Reply card 3.50 20.00

No. UY10 Surcharged in Red

1958, Sept. 16

UY11 PC6 1½c on 2y, 1½c on 2y (95,000) 10.00 —
First day cancel 40.00
a. Surcharge on reply card only 500.00 —
b. Surcharge on message card only 500.00 —
c. Reply card double surcharge 750.00 —
d. Reply card stamp omitted
(surcharge only) 1000.00 —
m. Message card 3.00 15.00
r. Reply card 3.00 25.00

Surcharge varieties include: "1" omitted; wrong font "2".

PONY TYPES

1959, June 20

UY12 PC11 1½c + 1½c dark blue & brown (366,000) 4.00 —
First day cancel 6.00
m. Message card 1.00 5.00
r. Reply card 1.00 5.00

1960, Mar. 10

UY13 PC13 1½c + 1½c gray violet & brown,
(150,000) 5.00 —
First day cancel 7.00
m. Message card 1.00 5.00
r. Reply card 1.00 5.00

INTERNATIONAL TYPE

1963, Feb. 15

UY14 PC20 5c + 5c vermilion, emerald & black,
pale yellow (70,000) 2.00 —
First day cancel 4.50
m. Message card 50 5.00
r. Reply card 50 5.00

PONY ("RYUKYUS" TYPE)

1963-69

UY15 PC17 1½c + 1½c gray violet & brown,
cream Mar. 15, (800,000) 2.00 —
First day cancel 3.50
a. Off-white card, *Mar. 13, 1967*
(100,000) 3.50 —
b. White card, Nov. 22, 1969
(700,000) 2.00 —
m. Message card detached 50 5.00
r. Reply card detached 50 5.00

No. UY14 Surcharged below Stamp
in Vermilion

1971, Sept. 1

UY16 PC17 2c on 1½c + 2c on 1½c gray violet &
brown (80,000) 2.50 —
First day cancel 3.50
m. Message card 1.00 5.00
r. Reply card 1.00 5.00

PONY ("RYUKYUS") TYPE

Zip Code Boxes in Vermilion

1971, Nov. 1

UY17 PC17 2c + 2c gray violet & brown (150,000) 2.50 —
First day cancel 4.00
m. Message card 1.00 5.00
r. Reply card 1.00 5.00

REVENUE STAMPS

Upon its establishment Apr. 1, 1952, the government of the Ryukyu Islands assumed responsibility for the issuing and the profit from revenue stamps. The various series served indiscriminately as evidence of payment of the required fees for various legal, realty and general commercial transactions.

1 yen
R1

3   5   10   50

100   500   1000

Litho. by Japan Printing Bureau.
Designer: Eizo Yonamine

1952, July 15		Perf. 13x13½	Wmk. 257	
R1	R1	1y brown	5.00	2.50
R2	"	3y carmine	10.00	2.50
R3	"	5y green	15.00	5.00
R4	"	10y blue	20.00	10.00
R5	"	50y purple	30.00	10.00
R6	"	100y yellow brown	45.00	20.00

1954, Apr. 16				
R7	R1	500y dark green	100.00	60.00
R8	"	1,000y carmine	150.00	100.00

"Cent" "Dollar"
Denomination Vertical

Litho. by Kobundo Printing Co., Naha.
Perf. 10, 10½, 11 and combinations.

1958, Sept. 16		*Without Gum*	Unwmkd.	
R9	R1	1c red brown	10.00	10.00
		a. Horiz. pair, imperf. btwn.	250.00	
R10	"	3c red	15.00	15.00
		a. Horiz. pair, imperf. btwn.	175.00	
R11	"	5c green	25.00	20.00
R12	"	10c blue	40.00	30.00
		a. Horiz. pair, imperf. btwn.	300.00	
R13	"	50c purple	70.00	40.00
R14	"	$1 sepia	100.00	50.00
R15	"	$5 dark green	250.00	90.00
R16	"	$10 carmine	350.00	125.00

R2

R3

R4

Litho. by Japan Printing Bureau.

1959-69		Perf. 13x13½	Wmk. 257	
R17	R2	1c brown	2.00	1.50
R18	"	3c red	2.50	1.50
R19	"	5c purple	4.00	3.00
R20	"	10c green	7.50	4.50
R21	"	20c sepia ('69)	30.00	10.00
R22	"	30c light olive ('69)	40.00	15.00
R23	"	50c blue	10.00	8.50
		Engraved		
R24	R3	$1 olive	15.00	12.50
R25	"	$2 vermilion ('69)	80.00	25.00
R26	"	$3 purple ('69)	100.00	30.00
R27	"	$5 orange	60.00	35.00
R28	"	$10 dark green	120.00	60.00
R29	R4	$20 carmine ('69)	400.00	200.00
R30	"	$30 blue ('69)	600.00	300.00
R31	"	$50 black ('69)	1000.00	—

PROVISIONAL ISSUES
MIYAKO

Stamps of Japan 1938-42
Handstamped in Black or Red

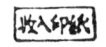

Typo., Litho., Engr.

1948		Perf. 13	Wmk. 257	
2XR1	A84	3s brown, #329	75.00	—
2XR2	A86	5s brown lake, #331	75.00	—
2XR3	A152	20s blue, #338 (R)	50.00	—
2XR4	A95	25s dark brown & pale brown, #270 (R)	50.00	—
		a. Black overprint	500.00	—
2XR5	A96	30s peacock blue, #271 (R)	50.00	—
2XR6	A154	40s dark violet, #342 (R)	50.00	—
2XR7	A97	50s olive & pale olive, #272 (R)	135.00	—

RYUKYU ISLANDS

"SPECIMEN" STAMPS

Regular stamps and postal cards of 1958-65 overprinted with three cursive syllabics *mi-ho-n* ("specimen").

Two trial color proofs, Nos. 46TC and 48TC, received vermilion mihon overprints in a different cursive type (100 each).

Type A

1961-64   Overprinted in Black or Red

91S	3c multi *(1,000)*	200.00
118S	3c multi *(1,000)*	500.00
119S	3c multi *(1,100)*	450.00

Type B みほん

1964-65   Overprinted in Red or Black

120aS	3c dp bl, dp car & ocher (R) *(1,500)*	200.00
121S	3c multi (R) *(1,500)*	150.00
124S	3c ultra, yel & red (R) *(5,000)*	40.00
125S	3s dl cl, yel & blk *(1,500)*	75.00
126S	3c yel & multi *(2,000)*	60.00
127S	3c gray, red & blk *(2,000)*	60.00
128S	3c multi *(1,500)*	75.00
129S	1½c multi (R) *(1,500)*	60.00
130S	3c lt bl & multi (R) *(1,500)*	125.00
131S	3c multi (R) *(1,500)*	60.00
132S	3c buff & multi *(2,000)*	60.00
133S	3c grn & multi (R) *(2,000)*	50.00
134S	3c multi *(2,000)*	50.00
135S	3c bl & multi *(2,000)*	50.00
136S	3c gldn brn & multi *(2,000)*	50.00
139S	1½c multi (R) *(2,500)*	45.00

Postal Cards

1964-65   Overprinted Type A or B in Black or Red

UX26S	A	1½c multi *(1,000)*	500.00
UX27S	B	1½c multi *(1,000)*	350.00
UX28S	A	1½c multi *(1,000)*	300.00
UX29S	A	1½c multi *(1,100)*	250.00

UNEMPLOYMENT INSURANCE STAMPS

These stamps, when affixed in an official booklet and canceled, certified a one-day contract for a day laborer. They were available to employers at certain post offices on various islands.

RQ1
Dove

RQ2
Shield

Lithographed in Naha
1961, Jan. 10   Without Gum   Unwmkd.

RQ1	RQ1	2c pale red	350.00	—
RQ2	RQ2	4c violet	15.00	15.00

Redrawn
Lithographed by Japan Printing Bureau
1966, Feb.   *Perf. 13x13½*   Unwmkd.

RQ3	RQ1	2c pale violet	—	—
RQ4	RQ2	4c violet	15.00	15.00

Redrawn stamps have bolder numerals and inscriptions, and fewer, stronger lines of shading in background.

RQ3
Cycad

Lithographed by Japan Printing Bureau
1968, Apr. 19   *Perf. 13x13½*   Wmk. 257

RQ5	RQ3	8c brown	15.00	15.00

Nos. RQ3-RQ4 Surcharged
with New Values and 2 Bars

1967-72

RQ6	RQ1	8c on 2c pale red	25.00	20.00
RQ7	RQ2	8c on 4c violet ('72)	15.00	15.00
RQ8	RQ2	12c on 4c violet ('71)	15.00	15.00

PROOFS AND TRIAL COLOR PROOFS

1948   Salmon Paper

1aP	5s magenta	———
2aP	10s yellow green	———
3aP	20s yellor green	———
5aP	40s magenta	———
6aP	50s ultramarine	———
7aP	1y ultramarine	———

Sheets of the second printing, Nos. 1-7, were overprinted in Tokyo with a swirl-pattern of blue or red dots. These essays sell for about $400 each.

1950   Soft White Paper

8P	50s dark carmine rose	600.00
9P	1y deep blue	"
10P	2y rose violet	"
11P	3y carmine rose	"
12P	4y greenish gray	"
12TC	4y olive	"
13P	5y blue green	"

1951

14P	3y red brown	800.00

1953

27P	3y deep magenta	———
28P	6y dull blue	———

1958

46TC	2c black	500.00
48TC	4c black	"

AIR POST

1950

C1P	8y bright blue	900.00
C2P	12y green	"
C3P	16y rose carmine	"

1951

C6P	30y cerise	800.00

SPECIAL DELIVERY

1950

E1P	5y bright blue	700.00

An official proof folder contains one each of Nos. 8P-13P, 12TC, C1P-C3P and E1P.

UNITED NATIONS

UNITED NATIONS stamps are used on U.N. official mail sent from U.N. Headquarters in New York City, or from the U.N. European Office in Geneva, Switzerland, to points throughout the world. They may be used on private correspondence sent through the U.N. post offices, and are valid only at the two U.N. post offices.

Through agreements between the U.N. and the United States Post Office Department, and between the U.N. and the Swiss P.T.T., U.N. mail is carried by the U.S. and Swiss postal systems.

The U.N. stamps issued for use in Geneva are listed in a separate section at the end of the other U.N. issues. They are denominated in centimes and francs, and are valid only in Geneva. The U.N. stamps issued for use in New York, denominated in cents and dollars, are valid only in New York. Mail bearing Nos. 170-174 provides an exception, as it was carried by the Canadian postal system.

See Switzerland official stamp listings in Scott's Standard Postage Stamp Catalogue, Volume IV, for stamps issued by the Swiss Government for official use of the U.N. European Office.

The 1962 U.N. Temporary Executive Authority overprints on stamps of Netherlands New Guinea are listed under West Irian in Scott's Standard Catalogue, Volume IV.

Blocks of four generally sell for four times the single stamp price.

Peoples of the World
A1

U. N. Headquarters Building
A2

"Peace, Justice, Security"
A3

U. N. Flag
A4

U. N. International Children's Emergency Fund
A5

World Unity
A6

Engraved and Photogravure.

Printed by Thomas De La Rue & Co., Ltd., London (1c, 3c, 10c, 15c, 20c, 25c), and Joh. Enschedé and Sons, Haarlem, Netherlands (1½c, 2c, 5c, 50c, $1). The 3c, 15c and 25c have frame engraved, center photogravure; other denominations are engraved. Panes of 50. Designed by O. C. Meronti (A1), Leon Helguera (A2), J. F. Doeve (A3), Ole Hamann (A4), S. L. Hartz (5c) and Hubert Woyty-Wimmer (20c).

1951   *Perf. 13x12½, 12½x13*   **Unwmkd.**

1	A1	1c magenta, *Oct. 24, 1951 (8,000,000)*	5	5
		First day cover		50
		Margin block of 4, UN seal	25	25
2	A2	1½c blue green, *Oct. 24, 1951 (7,450,000)*	5	5
		First day cover		50
		Margin block of 4, UN seal	25	25
		Precanceled *(361,700)*		30.00
3	A3	2c purple, *Nov. 16, 1951 (8,470,000)*	8	5
		First day cover		50
		Margin block of 4, UN seal	40	40
4	A4	3c magenta & blue, *Oct. 24, 1951 (8,250,000)*	8	6
		First day cover		50
		Margin block of 4, UN seal	40	40
5	A5	5c blue, *Oct. 24, 1951 (6,000,000)*	15	12
		First day cover		75
		Margin block of 4, UN seal	75	60
6	A1	10c chocolate, *Nov. 16, 1951 (2,600,000)*	50	30
		First day cover		1.50
		Margin block of 4, UN seal	2.50	1.50
7	A4	15c violet & blue, *Nov. 16, 1951 (2,300,000)*	60	40
		First day cover		2.25
		Margin block of 4, UN seal	3.50	2.00
8	A6	20c dark brown, *Nov. 16, 1951 (2,100,000)*	2.00	1.25
		First day cover		3.00
		Margin block of 4, UN seal	9.50	5.50
9	A4	25c olive gray & blue, *Oct. 24, 1951 (2,100,000)*	1.50	1.25
		First day cover		4.00
		Margin block of 4, UN seal	7.00	6.00
10	A2	50c indigo, *Nov. 16, 1951 (1,500,000)*	16.00	11.00
		First day cover		16.00
		Margin block of 4, UN seal	70.00	55.00
11	A3	$1 red, *Oct. 24, 1951 (2,012,500)*	5.00	3.00
		First day cover		17.50
		Margin block of 4, UN seal	25.00	15.00

First day covers of Nos. 1-11 and C1-4 total 1,113,216.

The various printings of Nos. 1-11 vary in sheet marginal perforation. Some were perforated through left or right margins, or both; some through all margins.

Sheets of this issue carry a marginal inscription consisting of the UN seal and "First UN / Issue 1951." This inscription appears four times on each sheet. The listing "Margin block of 4, UN seal" or "Margin block of 4, inscription" in this and following issues refers to a corner block.

Sheets of the 1½c, 2c, 50c and $1 have a cut-out of different shape in one margin. The printer trimmed this off entirely on most of the 1½c third printing, and partially on the 1½c fourth printing and $1 fifth and sixth printings.

For 30c in type A1 and 10fr in type A3, see U.N. Offices in Geneva Nos. 4 and 14.

Forgeries of the 1½c precancel exist.

Veterans' War Memorial Building, San Francisco
A7

UNITED NATIONS 917

Issued to mark the 7th anniversary of the signing of the United Nations Charter.

Engraved and printed by the American Bank Note Co., New York. Panes of 50. Designed by Jean Van Noten.

1952, Oct. 24   *Perf. 12.*

12	A7	5c blue *(1,274,670)*	1.20	60
		First day cover *(160,117)*		1.50
		Margin block of 4, inscription	6.25	3.00

Globe and Encircled Flame
A8

Issued to commemorate the 4th anniversary of the adoption of the Universal Declaration of Human Rights.

Engraved and printed by Thomas De La Rue & Co., Ltd., London. Panes of 50. Designed by Hubert Woyty-Wimmer.

1952, Dec. 10   *Perf. 13½x14*

13	A8	3c deep green *(1,554,312)*	40	30
		First day cover		75
		Margin block of 4, inscription	2.00	1.50
14	"	5c blue *(1,126,371)*	2.00	60
		First day cover		1.50
		First day cover, #13-14		2.00
		Margin block of 4, inscription	9.50	2.75

First day covers of Nos. 13 and 14 total 299,309.

Refugee Family
A9

Issued to publicize "Protection for Refugees."

Engraved and printed by Thomas De La Rue & Co., Ltd., London. Panes of 50. Designed by Olav Mathiesen.

1953, April 24   *Perf. 12½x13*

15	A9	3c dark red brown & rose brown *(1,299,793)*	75	30
		First day cover		70
		Margin block of 4, inscription	3.50	1.50
16	"	5c indigo & blue *(969,224)*	3.75	1.50
		First day cover		2.50
		First day cover, #15-16		3.00
		Margin block of 4, inscription	17.00	7.00

First day covers of Nos. 15 and 16 total 234,082.

Envelope, U. N. Emblem and Map
A10

Issued to honor the Universal Postal Union.

Engraved and printed by Thomas De La Rue & Co., Ltd., London. Panes of 50. Designed by Hubert Woyty-Wimmer.

1953, June 12   *Perf. 13*

7	A10	3c black brown *(1,259,689)*	1.00	35
		First day cover		75
		Margin block of 4, inscription	4.50	1.75

18	A10	5c dark blue *(907,312)*	5.00	2.00
		First day cover		2.75
		First day cover, #17-18		3.25
		Margin block of 4, inscription	22.50	9.00

First day covers of Nos. 17 and 18 total 231,627.

Plate number ("1A" or "1B") in color of stamp appears below 47th stamp of sheet.

Gearwheels and U. N. Emblem
A11

Issued to publicize United Nations activities in the field of technical assistance.

Engraved and printed by Thomas De La Rue & Co. Ltd. London. Panes of 50. Designed by Olav Mathiesen.

1953, Oct. 24   *Perf. 13x12½*

19	A11	3c dark gray *(1,184,348)*	40	35
		First day cover		75
		Margin block of 4, inscription	2.00	1.75
20	"	5c dark green *(968,182)*	3.50	90
		First day cover		1.25
		First day cover, #19-20		1.75
		Margin block of 4, inscription	16.00	4.00

First day covers of Nos. 19 and 20 total 229,211.

Hands Reaching Toward Flame
A12

Issued to publicize Human Rights Day.

Engraved and printed by Thomas De La Rue & Co., Ltd., London. Panes of 50. Designed by León Helguera.

1953, Dec. 10   *Perf. 12½x13*

21	A12	3c bright blue *(1,456,928)*	75	35
		First day cover		75
		Margin block of 4, inscription	3.50	1.75
22	"	5c rose red *(983,831)*	5.00	90
		First day cover		1.50
		First day cover, #21-22		2.00
		Margin block of 4, inscription	23.00	4.00

First day covers of Nos. 21 and 22 total 265,186.

Ear of Wheat
A13

Issued to honor the Food and Agriculture Organization.

Engraved and printed by Thomas De La Rue & Co., Ltd., London. Panes of 50. Designed by Dirk Van Gelder.

1954, Feb. 11   *Perf. 12½x13*

23	A13	3c dark green & yellow *(1,250,000)*	2.00	30
		First day cover		75
		Margin block of 4, inscription	9.00	1.50

918 UNITED NATIONS

24	A13	8c indigo & yellow *(949,718)*	3.75	1.40
		First day cover		2.00
		First day cover, #23-24		2.50
		Margin block of 4, inscription	17.00	6.50

First day covers of Nos. 23 and 24 total 272,312.

U. N. Emblem and Anvil Inscribed "ILO"
A14
Design: 8c, inscribed "OIT."
Issued to honor the International Labor Organization.
Engraved and printed by Thomas De La Rue & Co., Ltd., London. Panes of 50. Designed by José Renau.

1954, May 10   *Perf. 12½x13*

25	A14	3c brown *(1,085,651)*	50	40
		First day cover		75
		Margin block of 4, inscription	2.25	1.75
26	"	8c magenta *(903,561)*	7.50	1.90
		First day cover, #25-26		3.00
		Margin block of 4, inscription	35.00	8.50

First day covers of Nos. 25 and 26 total 252,796.

U. N. European Office, Geneva
A15
Issued on the occasion of United Nations Day.
Engraved and printed by Thomas De La Rue & Co., Ltd., London. Panes of 50. Designed by Earl W. Purdy.

1954, Oct. 25   *Perf. 14*

27	A15	3c dark blue violet *(1,000,000)*	10.00	2.25
		First day cover		3.00
		Margin block of 4, inscription	45.00	10.50
28	"	8c red *(1,000,000)*	75	75
		First day cover		90
		First day cover, #27-28		3.75
		Margin block of 4, inscription	4.50	3.25

First day covers of Nos. 27 and 28 total 233,544.

Mother and Child
A16

Issued to publicize Human Rights Day.
Engraved and printed by Thomas De La Rue & Co., Ltd. London. Panes of 50. Designed by Leonard C. Mitchell.

1954, Dec. 10   *Perf. 14*

29	A16	3c red orange *(1,000,000)*	25.00	5.50
		First day cover		7.50
		Margin block of 4, inscription	115.00	24.00
30	"	8c olive green *(1,000,000)*	1.00	1.00
		First day cover		1.35
		First day cover, #29-30		8.75
		Margin block of 4, inscription	5.00	5.00

First day covers of Nos. 29 and 30 total 276,333.

Symbol of Flight
A17
Design: 8c, inscribed "OACI."
Issued to honor the International Civil Aviation Organization.
Engraved and printed by Waterlow & Sons, Ltd., London. Panes of 50. Designed by Angel Medina Medina.

1955, Feb. 9   *Perf. 13½x14*

31	A17	3c blue *(1,000,000)*	10.00	90
		First day cover		1.50
		Margin block of 4, inscription	45.00	4.00
32	"	8c rose carmine *(1,000,000)*	3.00	1.35
		First day cover		2.75
		First day cover, #31-32		4.00
		Margin block of 4, inscription	13.00	6.25

First day covers of Nos. 31 and 32 total 237,131.

UNESCO Emblem
A18

Issued to honor the U. N. Educational, Scientific and Cultural Organization.
Engraved and printed by Waterlow & Sons, Ltd., London. Panes of 50. Designed by George Hamori.

1955, May 11   *Perf. 13½x14*

33	A18	3c lilac rose *(1,000,000)*	4.00	90
		First day cover		1.50
		Margin block of 4, inscription	18.00	4.00
34	"	8c light blue *(1,000,000)*	50	50
		First day cover		75
		First day cover, #33-34		2.00
		Margin block of 4, inscription	2.50	2.50

First day covers of Nos. 33 and 34 total 255,326.

United Nations Charter
A19

Design: 4c, Spanish inscription. 8c, French inscription.

Issued to commemorate the 10th anniversary of the United Nations.

Engraved and printed by Waterlow & Sons, Ltd., London. Panes of 50. Designed by Claude Bottiau.

1955, Oct. 24			Perf. 13½x14	
35	A19	3c deep plum *(1,000,000)*	11.00	1.85
		First day cover		2.25
		Margin block of 4, inscription	49.00	8.00
36	"	4c dull green *(1,000,000)*	30	30
		First day cover		1.30
		Margin block of 4, inscription	1.40	1.30
37	"	8c bluish black *(1,000,000)*	50	50
		First day cover		75
		First day cover, #35-37		3.25
		Margin block of 4, inscription	2.25	2.25

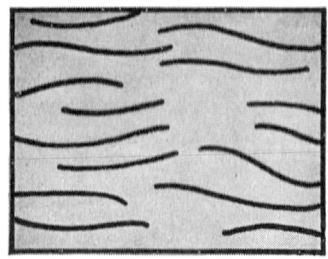

Wmk. 309
Souvenir Sheet

1955, Oct. 24		*Imperf.*	Wmkd. Wavy Lines (309)	
38	A19	Sheet of three *(250,000)*	325.00	90.00
		a. 3c deep plum	25.00	12.00
		b. 4c dull green	25.00	12.00
		c. 8c bluish black	25.00	12.00
		Sheet with retouch on 8c	325.00	90.00
		First day cover		110.00

No. 38 measures 108x83mm., contains one each of Nos. 35-37 and has marginal inscriptions in deep plum.

Two printings were made of No. 38. The first (200,000) may be distinguished by the broken line of background shading on the 8c. It leaves a small white spot below the left leg of the "n" of "Unies." For the second printing (50,000), the broken line was retouched, eliminating the white spot. The 4c was also retouched.

First day covers of Nos. 35-38 total 455,791.

Copies of No. 38 are known with the 4c and 8c stamps misaligned.

Hand Holding Torch
A20

Issued in honor of Human Rights Day.

Engraved and printed by Waterlow & Sons, Ltd., London. Panes of 50. Designed by Hubert Woyty-Wimmer.

1955, Dec. 9			Perf. 14x13½	Unwmkd.
39	A20	3c ultramarine *(1,250,000)*	25	25
		First day cover		75
		Margin block of 4, inscription	1.25	1.25
40	"	8c green *(1,000,000)*	3.25	1.00
		First day cover		1.50
		First day cover, #39-40		2.00
		Margin block of 4, inscription	15.00	4.50

First day covers of Nos. 39 and 40 total 298,038.

Symbols of Telecommunication
A21

Design: 8c, inscribed "UIT."

Issued in honor of the International Telecommunication Union.

Engraved and printed by Thomas De La Rue & Co., Ltd., London. Panes of 50. Designed by Hubert Woyty-Wimmer.

1956, Feb. 17			Perf. 14	
41	A21	3c turquoise blue *(1,000,000)*	1.00	35
		First day cover		75
		Margin block of 4, inscription	4.50	1.50
42	"	8c deep carmine *(1,000,000)*	2.50	90
		First day cover		1.50
		First day cover, #41-42		2.25
		Margin block of 4, inscription	11.00	4.00

Plate number ("1A" or "1B") in color of stamp appears below 47th stamp of sheet.

Globe and Caduceus—A22

Design: 8c, inscribed "OMS."

Issued in honor of the World Health Organization.

Engraved and printed by Thomas De La Rue & Co., Ltd., London. Panes of 50. Designed by Olav Mathiesen.

1956, April 6			Perf. 14	
43	A22	3c bright greenish blue *(1,250,000)*	20	20
		First day cover		75
		Margin block of 4, inscription	1.00	1.00
44	"	8c golden brown *(1,000,000)*	3.25	1.00
		First day cover		2.00
		First day cover, #43-44		2.25
		Margin block of 4, inscription	14.00	4.50

First day covers of Nos. 43 and 44 total 260,853.

General Assembly—A23

Design: 8c, French inscription.

Issued to commemorate United Nations Day.

Engraved and printed by Thomas De La Rue & Co., Ltd., London. Panes of 50. Designed by Kurt Plowitz.

1956, Oct. 24			Perf. 14	
45	A23	3c dark blue *(2,000,000)*	6	5
		First day cover		30
		Margin block of 4, inscription	30	25

UNITED NATIONS

46	A23	8c gray olive *(1,500,000)*	15	12
		First day cover		75
		First day cover, #45-46		75
		Margin block of 4, inscription	75	60

First day covers of Nos. 45 and 46 total 303,560.

Flame and Globe
A24

Issued to publicize Human Rights Day

Engraved and printed by Thomas De La Rue & Co., Ltd., London. Panes of 50. Designed by Rashid-ud Din.

1956, Dec. 10 — *Perf. 14*

47	A24	3c plum *(5,000,000)*	6	5
		First day cover		25
		Margin block of 4, inscription	30	25
48	"	8c dark blue *(4,000,000)*	16	12
		First day cover		45
		First day cover, #47-48		55
		Margin block of 4, inscription	80	60

First day covers of Nos. 47 and 48 total 416,120.

Weather Balloon
A25

Design: 8c, Agency name in French.

Issued to honor the World Meteorological Organization.

Engraved and printed by Thomas De La Rue & Co., Ltd., London. Panes of 50. Designed by A. L. Pollock.

1957, Jan. 28 — *Perf. 14*

49	A25	3c violet blue *(5,000,000)*	6	5
		First day cover		25
		Margin block of 4, inscription	30	25
50	"	8c dark carmine rose *(3,448,985)*	16	12
		First day cover		45
		First day cover, # 49-50		55
		Margin block of 4, inscription	80	60

First day covers of Nos. 49 and 50 total 376,110.

Badge of U. N. Emergency Force
A26

Issued in honor of the U. N. Emergency Force.

Engraved and printed by Thomas De La Rue & Co., Ltd., London. Panes of 50. Designed by Ole Hamann.

1957, April 8 — *Perf. 14x12½*

51	A26	3c light blue *(4,000,000)*	6	5
		First day cover		25
		Margin block of 4, inscription	30	25
52	"	8c rose carmine *(3,000,000)*	16	12
		First day cover		45
		First day cover, #51-52		55
		Margin block of 4, inscription	80	60

First day covers of Nos. 51 and 52 total 461,772.

Nos. 51-52 Re-engraved.

1957, April, May — *Perf. 14x12½*

53	A26	3c blue *(2,736,206)*	10	10
		Margin block of 4, inscription	50	50
54	"	8c rose carmine *(1,000,000)*	40	30
		Margin block of 4, inscription	2.00	1.50

On Nos. 53-54 the background within and around the circles is shaded lightly, giving a halo effect. The lettering is more distinct with a line around each letter.

U. N. Emblem and Globe
A27

Design: 8c, French inscription.

Issued to honor the Security Council.

Engraved and printed by Thomas De La Rue & Co., Ltd., London. Panes of 50. Designed by Rashid-ud Din.

1957, Oct. 24 — *Perf. 12½x13*

55	A27	3c orange brown *(3,674,968)*	6	5
		First day cover		25
		Margin block of 4, inscription	30	25
56	"	8c dark blue green *(2,885,938)*	16	12
		First day cover		45
		First day cover, #55-56		55
		Margin block of 4, inscription	80	60

First day covers of Nos. 55 and 56 total 460,627.

Flaming Torch
A28

Issued in honor of Human Rights Day.

Engraved and printed by Thomas De La Rue & Co., Ltd., London. Panes of 50. Designed by Olav Mathiesen.

1957, Dec. 10 — *Perf. 14*

57	A28	3c red brown *(3,368,405)*	6	5
		First day cover		25
		Margin block of 4, inscription	30	25
58	"	8c black *(2,717,310)*	16	12
		First day cover		45
		First day cover, #57-58		55
		Margin block of 4, inscription	80	60

First day covers of Nos. 57 and 58 total 553,669.

UNITED NATIONS

U. N. Emblem Shedding Light on Atom
A29

Design: 8c, French inscription.

Issued in honor of the International Atomic Energy Agency.

Engraved and printed by the American Bank Note Co., New York. Panes of 50. Designed by Robert Perrot.

1958, Feb. 10   *Perf. 12*

59	A29	3c olive *(3,663,305)*	6	5
		First day cover		25
		Margin block of 4, inscription	30	25
60	"	8c blue *(3,043,622)*	16	12
		First day cover		45
		First day cover, #59-60		55
		Margin block of 4, inscription	80	60

First day covers of Nos. 59 and 60 total 504,832.

Central Hall, Westminster
A30

Design: 8c, French inscription.

Central Hall, Westminster, London, was the site of the first session of the United Nations General Assembly, 1946.

Engraved and printed by the American Bank Note Co., New York. Panes of 50. Designed by Olav Mathiesen.

1958, April 14   *Perf. 12*

61	A30	3c violet blue *(3,353,716)*	6	5
		First day cover		25
		Margin block of 4, inscription	30	25
62	"	8c rose claret *(2,836,747)*	16	12
		First day cover		45
		First day cover, #61-62		55
		Margin block of 4, inscription	80	60

First day covers of Nos. 61 and 62 total 449,401.

U. N. Seal
A31

Engraved and printed by Bradbury, Wilkinson & Co., Ltd., England. Panes of 50. Designed by Herbert M. Sanborn.

1958, Oct. 24   *Perf. 13½x14*

63	A31	4c red orange *(9,000,000)*	8	6
		First day cover		30
		Margin block of 4, inscription	40	30

1958, June 2   *Perf. 13x14*

64	A31	8c bright blue *(5,000,000)*	16	12
		First day cover *(219,422)*		50
		Margin block of 4, inscription	80	60
		Margin block of 4, Bradbury, Wilkinson imprint	5.00	1.00

Gearwheels
A32

Design: 8c, French inscription.

Issued to honor the Economic and Social Council.

Engraved and printed by the American Bank Note Co., New York. Panes of 50. Designed by Ole Hamann.

1958, Oct. 24   *Perf. 12*   Unwmkd.

65	A32	4c dark blue green *(2,556,784)*	8	6
		First day cover		30
		Margin block of 4, inscription	40	30
66	"	8c vermilion *(2,175,117)*	16	12
		First day cover		50
		First day cover, #65-66		65
		Margin block of 4, inscription	80	60

First day covers of Nos. 63, 65 and 66 total 626,236.

Hands Upholding Globe
A33

Issued for Human Rights Day and to commemorate the tenth anniversary of the signing of the Universal Declaration of Human Rights.

Engraved and printed by the American Bank Note Co., New York. Panes of 50. Designed by Leonard C. Mitchell.

1958, Dec. 10   *Perf. 12*   Unwmkd.

67	A33	4c yellow green *(2,644,340)*	8	6
		First day cover		30
		Margin block of 4, inscription	40	30
68	"	8c red brown *(2,216,838)*	16	12
		First day cover		50
		First day cover, #67-68		65
		Margin block of 4, inscription	80	60

First day covers of Nos. 67 and 68 total 618,124.

New York City Building, Flushing Meadows
A34

Design: 8c, French inscription.

New York City Building at Flushing Meadows, New York, was the site of many General Assembly meetings, 1946-50.

Engraved and printed by Canadian Bank Note Company, Ltd., Ottawa. Panes of 50. Designed by Robert Perrot.

1959, March 30			Perf. 12		Unwmkd.	
69	A34	4c	light lilac rose (2,035,011)		8	6
			First day cover			35
			Margin block of 4, inscription		40	30
70	"	8c	aquamarine (1,627,281)		16	12
			First day cover			50
			First day cover, #69-70			70
			Margin block of 4, inscription		80	70

First day covers of Nos. 69 and 70 total 440,955.

U. N. Emblem and Symbols of Agriculture, Industry and Trade
A35

Issued to honor the Economic Commission for Europe.

Engraved and printed by Canadian Bank Note Company, Ltd., Ottawa. Panes of 50. Designed by Ole Hamann.

1959, May 18			Perf. 12		Unwmkd.	
71	A35	4c	blue (1,743,502)		15	10
			First day cover			40
			Margin block of 4, inscription		75	50
72	"	8c	red orange (1,482,898)		30	20
			First day cover			60
			First day cover, #71-72			90
			Margin block of 4, inscription		1.50	90

First day covers of Nos. 71 and 72 total 433,549.

Figure Adapted from Rodin's "Age of Bronze"
A36

Design: 8c, French inscription.

Issued to honor the Trusteeship Council.

Engraved and printed by Canadian Bank Note Co., Ltd., Ottawa. Panes of 50. Designed by León Helguera; lettering by Ole Hamann.

1959, Oct. 23			Perf. 12.		Unwmkd.	
73	A36	4c	bright red (1,929,677)		8	6
			First day cover			30
			Margin block of 4, inscription		40	30
74	"	8c	dark olive green (1,587,647)		16	12
			First day cover			50
			First day cover, #73-74			65
			Margin block of 4, inscription		80	60

First day covers of Nos. 73 and 74 total 466,053.

World Refugee Year Emblem
A37

Design: 8c, French inscription.

Issued to publicize World Refugee Year, July 1, 1959 – June 30, 1960.

Engraved and printed by Canadian Bank Note Co., Ltd., Ottawa. Panes of 50. Designed by Olav Mathiesen.

1959, Dec. 10			Perf. 12		Unwmkd.	
75	A37	4c	olive & red (2,168,963)		8	6
			First day cover			30
			Margin block of 4, inscription		40	30
76	"	8c	olive & bright greenish blue (1,843,886)		16	12
			First day cover			50
			First day cover, #75-76			65
			Margin block of 4, inscription		80	60

First day covers of Nos. 75 and 76 total 502,262.

Chaillot Palace, Paris
A38

Design: 8c, French inscription.

Chaillot Palace in Paris was the site of General Assembly meetings in 1948 and 1951.

Engraved and printed by Thomas De La Rue & Co., Ltd., London. Panes of 50. Designed by Hubert Woyty-Wimmer.

1960, Feb. 29			Perf. 14		Unwmkd.	
77	A38	4c	rose lilac & blue (2,276,678)		8	6
			First day cover			30
			Margin block of 4, inscription		40	30
78	"	8c	dull green & brown (1,930,869)		16	12
			First day cover			50
			First day cover, #77-78			65
			Margin block of 4, inscription		80	60

First day covers of Nos. 77 and 78 total 446,815.

Map of Far East and Steel Beam
A39

Design: 8c, French inscription.

Issued to honor the Economic Commission for Asia and the Far East (ECAFE).

Printed by the Government Printing Bureau, Tokyo. Panes of 50. Designed by Hubert Woyty-Wimmer.

Photogravure

1960, Apr. 11			Perf. 13x13½		Unwmkd.	
79	A39	4c	deep claret, blue green & dull yellow (2,195,945)		8	6
			First day cover			30
			Margin block of 4, inscription		40	30
80	"	8c	olive green, blue & rose (1,897,902)		16	12
			First day cover			50
			First day cover, #79-80			65
			Margin block of 4, inscription		80	60

First day covers of Nos. 79 and 80 total 415,127.

UNITED NATIONS

Tree, FAO and U.N. Emblems
A40

Design: 8c, French inscription.

Issued to commemorate the Fifth World Forestry Congress, Seattle, Washington, Aug. 29–Sept. 10.

Printed by the Government Printing Bureau, Tokyo. Panes of 50. Designed by Ole Hamann.

Photogravure

1960, Aug. 29		Perf. 13½	Unwmkd.	
81	A40	4c dark blue, green & orange *(2,188,293)*	8	6
		First day cover		30
		Margin block of 4, inscription	40	30
	a.	Imperf., pair		
82	"	8c yellow green, black & orange *(1,837,778)*	16	12
		First day cover		50
		First day cover, #81-82		65
		Margin block of 4, inscription	80	60

First day covers of Nos. 81 and 82 total 434,129.

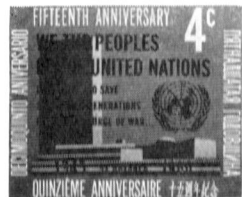

U.N. Headquarters and Preamble to U.N. Charter
A41

Design: 8c, French inscription.

Issued to commemorate the 15th anniversary of the United Nations.

Engraved and printed by the British American Bank Note Co., Ltd., Ottawa, Canada. Panes of 50. Designed by Robert Perrot.

1960, Oct. 24		Perf. 11	Unwmkd.	
83	A41	4c blue *(2,631,593)*	8	6
		First day cover		30
		Margin block of 4, inscription	40	30
84	"	8c gray *(2,278,022)*	16	12
		First day cover		50
		First day cover, #83-84		65
		Margin block of 4, inscription	80	60

Souvenir Sheet
Imperf.

85	A41	Sheet of two *(1,000,000)*	5.00	3.00
	a.	4c blue	1.00	.50
	b.	8c gray	1.00	.50
		First day cover *(256,699)*		3.75

No. 85 contains one each of Nos. 83-84. Dark gray marginal inscription. Size: 92x71mm. Broken "I" and "V" flaws occur in "ANNIVERSARY" in marginal inscription. Copies are known with the two stamps misaligned.

Block and Tackle
A42

Design: 8c, French inscription.

Issued to honor the International Bank for Reconstruction and Development.

Printed by the Government Printing Bureau, Tokyo. Panes of 50. Designed by Angel Medina Medina.

Photogravure

1960, Dec. 9		Perf. 13½x13	Unwmkd.	
86	A42	4c multicolored *(2,286,117)*	8	6
		First day cover		30
		Margin block of 4, inscription	40	30
87	"	8c multicolored *(1,882,019)*	16	12
		First day cover		50
		First day cover, #86-87		65
		Margin block of 4, inscription	80	60
	a.	Imperf., pair		

First day covers of Nos. 86 and 87 total 559,708.
No. 86 exists imperf.

Scales of Justice from Raphael's Stanze
A43

Design: 8c, French inscription.

Issued to honor the International Court of Justice.

Printed by the Government Printing Bureau, Tokyo, Japan. Panes of 50. Designed by Kurt Plowitz.

Photogravure

1961, Feb. 13		Perf. 13½x13	Unwmkd.	
88	A43	4c yellow, orange brown & black *(2,234,588)*	8	6
		First day cover		30
		Margin block of 4, inscription	40	30
89	"	8c yellow, green & black *(2,023,968)*	16	12
		First day cover		50
		First day cover, #88-89		65
		Margin block of 4, inscription	80	60

First day covers of Nos. 88 and 89 total 447,467.
Nos. 88-89 exist imperf.

Seal of International Monetary Fund
A44

Design: 7c, French inscription.

Issued to honor the International Monetary Fund.

Printed by the Government Printing Bureau, Tokyo, Japan. Panes of 50. Designed by Roy E. Carlson and Hordur Karlsson, Iceland.

Photogravure

1961, Apr. 17		Perf. 13x13½	Unwmkd.	
90	A44	4c bright bluish green *(2,305,010)*	8	6
		First day cover		30
		Margin block of 4, inscription	40	30
91	"	7c terra cotta & yellow *(2,147,201)*	14	10
		First day cover		50
		First day cover, #90-91		65
		Margin block of 4, inscription	70	50

First day covers of Nos. 90 and 91 total 448,729.

UNITED NATIONS

Abstract Group of Flags
A45

Printed by Courvoisier S.A., La Chaux-de-Fonds, Switzerland. Panes of 50. Designed by Herbert M. Sanborn.

Photogravure
1961, June 5   **Perf. 11½**   Unwmkd.
92   A45   30c multicolored *(3,370,000)*   60   30
    First day cover *(182,949)*   70
    Margin block of 4, inscription   2.75   1.50

See U.N. Offices in Geneva No. 10.

Cogwheel and Map of Latin America
A46

Design: 11c, Spanish inscription.

Issued to honor the Economic Commission for Latin America.

Printed by the Government Printing Bureau, Tokyo. Panes of 50. Designed by Robert Perrot.

Photogravure
1961, Sept. 18   **Perf. 13½**   Unwmkd.
93   A46   4c blue, red & citron *(2,037,912)*   15   10
    First day cover   30
    Margin block of 4, inscription   75   50
94   "   11c green, lilac & org. vermilion *(1,835,097)*   45   20
    First day cover   80
    First day cover, #93-94   1.00
    Margin block of 4, inscription   2.25   90

First day covers of Nos. 93 and 94 total 435,820.

Africa House, Addis Ababa, and Map
A47

Design: 11c, English inscription.

Issued to honor the Economic Commission for Africa.

Printed by Courvoisier S.A., La Chaux-de-Fonds, Switzerland. Panes of 50. Designed by Robert Perrot.

Photogravure
1961, Oct. 24   **Perf. 11½**   Unwmkd.
95   A47   4c ultramarine, orange, yellow & brown
    (2,044,842)   8   6
    First day cover   30
    Margin block of 4, inscription   40   30
96   "   11c emerald, orange, yellow & brown
    (1,790,894)   22   18
    First day cover   80
    First day cover, #95-96   1.00
    Margin block of 4, inscription   1.10   80

First day covers of Nos. 95 and 96 total 435,131.

Mother Bird Feeding Young and UNICEF Seal
A48

Designs: 3c, Spanish inscription. 13c, French inscription.

Issued to commemorate the 15th anniversary of the United Nations Children's Fund.

Printed by Courvoisier S.A., La Chaux-de-Fonds, Switzerland. Panes of 50. Designed by Minoru Hisano.

Photogravure
1961, Dec. 4   **Perf. 11½**   Unwmkd.
97   A48   3c brown, gold, orange & yellow *(2,867,456)*   6   5
    First day cover   30
    Margin block of 4, inscription   30   25
98   "   4c brown, gold, blue & emerald *(2,735,899)*   8   6
    First day cover   30
    Margin block of 4, inscription   40   30
99   "   13c dp. grn., gold, purple & pink *(1,951,715)*   26   20
    First day cover   1.20
    First day cover, #97-99   1.60
    Margin block of 4, inscription   1.25   90

First day covers of Nos. 97-99 total 752,979.

Family and Symbolic Buildings
A49

Design: 7c, inscribed "Services Collectifs".

Issued to publicize the U.N. program for housing and urban development, and in connection with the expert committee meeting at U.N. headquarters, Feb. 7-21.

Printed by Harrison and Sons, Ltd., London, England. Panes of 50. Designed by Olav Mathiesen.

Photogravure
1962, Feb. 28   **Perf. 14½x14**   Unwmkd.
Central design multicolored.
100   A49   4c bright blue *(2,204,190)*   8   6
    First day cover   30
    Margin block of 4, inscription   40   30
    a. Black omitted   550.00
    b. Yellow omitted   400.00
    c. Brown omitted   225.00
101   "   7c orange brown *(1,845,821)*   14   10
    First day cover   50
    First day cover, #100-101   70
    Margin block of 4, inscription   70   50
    a. Red omitted   400.00

First day covers of Nos. 100-101 total 466,178.

"The World Against Malaria"
A50

UNITED NATIONS

Issued in honor of the World Health Organization and to call attention to the international campaign to eradicate malaria from the world.

Printed by Harrison and Sons, Ltd., London, England. Panes of 50. Designed by Rashid-ud Din.

Photogravure
1962, March 30   *Perf. 14x14½*   Unwmkd.

Word frame in gray.

102	A50	4c orange, yellow, brown, green & black *(2,047,000)*	10	8
		First day cover		30
		Margin block of 4, inscription	50	40
103	"	11c green, yellow, brown & indigo *(1,683,766)*	30	20
		First day cover		70
		First day cover, #102-103		90
		Margin block of 4, inscription	1.50	90

First day covers of Nos. 102-103 total 522,450.

"Peace"
A51

U.N. Flag
A52

Hands Combining "UN" and Globe
A53

U.N. Emblem over Globe
A54

Printed by Harrison & Sons, Ltd., London, England (1c, 3c and 11c), and by Canadian Bank Note Co., Ltd., Ottawa (5c). Panes of 50. Designed by Kurt Plowitz (1c), Ole Hamann (3c), Renato Ferrini (5c) and Olav Mathiesen (11c).

Photogravure; Engraved (5c)
1962, May 25   *Perf. 14x14½*   Unwmkd.

104	A51	1c vermilion, blue, blk. & gray *(5,000,000)*	5	5
		First day cover		35
		Margin block of 4, inscription	25	25
105	A52	3c light green, Prussian blue, yellow & gray *(5,000,000)*	6	5
		First day cover		30
		Margin block of 4, inscription	30	25

Perf. 12

106	A53	5c dark carmine rose *(4,000,000)*	20	10
		First day cover		45
		Margin block of 4, inscription	1.00	45

Perf. 12½

107	A54	11c dark & light blue & gold *(4,400,000)*	22	18
		First day cover		70
		First day cover, #104-107		1.25
		Margin block of 4, inscription	1.00	85

First day covers of Nos. 104-107 total 738,985.
Size of 5c, No. 106: 36½x23½ mm. See also No. 167.
See U.N. Offices in Geneva Nos. 2 and 6.

Flag at Half-mast and U.N. Headquarters
A55

Issued on the first anniversary of the death of Dag Hammarskjold, Secretary General of the United Nations 1953-61, in memory of those who died in the service of the United Nations.

Printed by Courvoisier S. A., La Chaux-de-Fonds, Switzerland. Panes of 50. Designed by Ole Hamann.

Photogravure
1962, Sept. 17   *Perf. 11½*   Unwmkd.

108	A55	5c black, light blue & blue *(2,195,707)*	30	15
		First day cover		35
		Margin block of 4, inscription	1.40	70
109	"	15c black, gray olive & blue *(1,155,047)*	1.10	45
		First day cover		90
		First day cover, #108-109		1.15
		Margin block of 4, inscription	5.25	2.00

First day covers of Nos. 108-109 total 513,963.

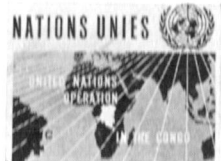

World Map Showing Congo
A56

Design: 11c inscribed "Operation des Nations Unies au Congo."

Issued to commemorate the United Nations Operation in the Congo.

Printed by Courvoisier S. A., La Chaux-de-Fonds, Switzerland. Panes of 50. Designed by George Hamori.

Photogravure
1962, Oct. 24   *Perf. 11½*   Unwmkd.

110	A56	4c olive, orange, blk. & yellow *(1,477,938)*	25	15
		First day cover		30
		Margin block of 4, inscription	1.15	70
111	"	11c bl. grn., orge., blk. & yel. *(1,171,255)*	1.00	40
		First day cover		80
		First day cover, #110-111		1.00
		Margin block of 4, inscription	4.75	2.00

First day covers of Nos. 110-111 total 460,675.

UNITED NATIONS

Globe in Universe and Palm Frond
A57

Design: 4c, English inscription.

Issued to honor the Committee on Peaceful Uses of Outer Space.

Printed by Bradbury, Wilkinson and Co., Ltd., England. Panes of 50. Designed by Kurt Plowitz.

Engraved

1962, Dec. 3			Perf. 14x13½	Unwmkd.	
112	A57	4c violet blue, *(2,263,876)*		8	6
		First day cover			30
		Margin block of 4, inscription		40	30
113	"	11c rose claret *(1,681,584)*		22	18
		First day cover			70
		First day cover, #112-113			80
		Margin block of 4, inscription		1.00	1.00

First day covers of Nos. 112-113 total 529,780.

Development Decade Emblem
A58

Design: 11c, French inscription.

Issued to publicize the U.N. Development Decade and to commemorate the U.N. Conference on the Application of Science and Technology for the Benefit of the Less Developed Areas, Geneva, Feb. 4–20.

Printed by Courvoisier S. A., La Chaux-de-Fonds, Switzerland. Panes of 50. Designed by Rashid-ud Din.

Photogravure

1963, Feb. 4			Perf. 11½	Unwmkd.	
114	A58	5c pale grn., maroon, dk. bl. & Prussian blue *(1,802,406)*		15	10
		First day cover			35
		Margin block of 4, inscription		75	50
115	"	11c yel., maroon, dk. bl. & Prussian blue *(1,530,190)*		35	20
		First day cover			70
		First day cover, #114-115			1.00
		Margin block of 4, inscription		1.60	90

First day covers of Nos. 114-115 total 460,877.

Stalks of Wheat
A59

Design: 11c, French inscription.

Issued for the "Freedom from Hunger" campaign of the Food and Agriculture Organization.

Printed by Courvoisier S. A., La Chaux-de-Fonds, Switzerland. Panes of 50. Designed by Ole Hamann.

Photogravure

1963, March 22			Perf. 11½	Unwmkd.	
116	A59	5c vermilion, green & yellow *(1,666,178)*		15	10
		First day cover			35
		Margin block of 4, inscription		75	50
117	"	11c verm., deep claret & yel. *(1,563,023)*		35	20
		First day cover			70
		First day cover, #116-117			1.00
		Margin block of 4, inscription		1.60	90

First day covers of Nos. 116-117 total 461,868.

Bridge over Map of New Guinea
A60

Issued to commemorate the first anniversary of the United Nations Temporary Executive Authority (UNTEA) in West New Guinea (West Irian).

Printed by Courvoisier S.A., La Chaux-de-Fonds, Switzerland. Panes of 50. Designed by Henry Bencsath.

Photogravure

1963, Oct. 1			Perf. 11½	Unwmkd.	
118	A60	25c blue, green & gray *(1,427,747)*		85	50
		First day cover *(222,280)*			1.20
		Margin block of 4, inscription		4.00	2.25

General Assembly Building, New York
A61

Design: 11c, French inscription.

Since October 1955 all sessions of the General Assembly have been held in the General Assembly Hall, U.N. Headquarters, N.Y.

Printed by the Government Printing Bureau, Tokyo. Panes of 50. Designed by Kurt Plowitz.

Photogravure

1963, Nov. 4			Perf. 13	Unwmkd.	
119	A61	5c vio. bl., bl., yel. grn. & red *(1,892,539)*		15	
		First day cover			
		Margin block of 4, inscription		75	
120	"	11c grn., yel. grn., bl., yel. & red *(1,435,079)*		35	
		First day cover			
		First day cover, #119-120			1.0
		Margin block of 4, inscription		1.60	9

First day covers of Nos. 119-120 total 410,306.

Flame
A62

UNITED NATIONS

927

Design: 11c inscribed "15e Anniversaire."
Issued to commemorate the 15th anniversary of the signing of the Universal Declaration of Human Rights.
Printed by the Government Printing Bureau, Tokyo. Panes of 50. Designed by Rashid-ud Din.

Photogravure
1963, Dec. 10   **Perf. 13**   **Unwmkd.**

121	A62	5c green, gold, red & yellow *(2,208,008)*	15	10
		First day cover		35
		Margin block of 4, inscription	75	50
122	"	11c carm., gold, blue & yellow *(1,501,125)*	35	20
		First day cover		70
		First day cover, #121-122		1.00
		Margin block of 4, inscription	1.60	90

First day covers of Nos. 121-122 total 567,907.

Ships at Sea and IMCO Emblem
A63

Design: 11c, inscribed "OMCI."
Issued to honor the Intergovernmental Maritime Consultative Organization.
Printed by Courvoisier S.A., La Chaux-de-Fonds, Switzerland. Panes of 50. Designed by Henry Bencsath; emblem by Olav Mathiesen.

Photogravure
1964, Jan. 13   **Perf. 11½**   **Unwmkd.**

123	A63	5c blue, olive, ocher & yellow *(1,805,750)*	15	10
		First day cover		35
		Margin block of 4, inscription	75	50
124	"	11c dark blue, dark green, emerald & yellow *(1,583,848)*	35	20
		First day cover		70
		First day cover, #123-124		1.00
		Margin block of 4, inscription	1.60	90

First day covers of Nos. 123-124 total 442,696.

World Map, Sinusoidal Projection   U.N. Emblem
A64   A65

Three Men United Before Globe   Stylized Globe and Weather Vane
A66   A67

Printed by Thomas De La Rue & Co., Ltd., London (2c) and Courvoisier S.A., La Chaux-de-Fonds, Switzerland (7c, 10c and 50c). Panes of 50.
Designed by Ole Hamann (2c), George Hamori (7c, 10c) and Hatim El Mekki (50c).

Photogravure
1964-71   **Perf. 14**   **Unwmkd.**

125	A64	2c light & dark blue, orange & yellow green *(3,800,000)*	5	5
		First day cover		25
		Margin block of 4, inscription	30	30
		a. Perf. 13x13½, Feb. 24, 1971 *(1,500,000)*	6	6

Perf. 11½

126	A65	7c dark blue, orange brown & black *(2,700,000)*	14	10
		First day cover		45
		Margin block of 4, inscription	70	50
127	A66	10c blue green, olive green & black *(3,200,000)*	20	15
		First day cover		70
		First day cover, #125-127		1.00
		Margin block of 4, inscription	1.00	70
128	A67	50c multicolored *(2,520,000)*	1.00	75
		First day cover *(210,713)*		2.00
		Margin block of 4, inscription	4.75	3.50

Issue dates: 50c, Mar. 6; 2c, 7c and 10c, May 29, 1964.
First day covers of 2c, 7c and 10c total 524,073.
See U.N. Offices in Geneva Nos. 3 and 12.

Arrows Showing Global Flow of Trade
A68

Design: 5c, English inscription.
Issued to commemorate the U.N. Conference on Trade and Development, Geneva, March 23–June 15.
Printed by Thomas De La Rue & Co., Ltd., London. Panes of 50. Designed by Herbert M. Sanborn and Ole Hamann.

Photogravure
1964, June 15   **Perf. 13**   **Unwmkd.**

129	A68	5c black, red & yellow *(1,791,211)*	15	10
		First day cover		35
		Margin block of 4, inscription	75	50
130	"	11c black, olive & yellow *(1,529,526)*	35	20
		First day cover		70
		First day cover, #129-130		1.00
		Margin block of 4, inscription	1.60	90

First day covers of Nos. 129-130 total 422,358.

Poppy Capsule and Reaching Hands
A69

Design: 11c, inscribed "Echec au Stupéfiants."
Issued to honor international efforts and achievements in the control of narcotics.
Printed by the Canadian Bank Note Co., Ottawa. Panes of 50. Designed by Kurt Plowitz.

Engraved
1964, Sept. 21   **Perf. 12**   **Unwmkd.**

131	69	5c rose red & black *(1,508,999)*	15	10
		First day cover		35
		Margin block of 4, inscription	90	50
132	"	11c emerald & black *(1,340,691)*	45	20
		First day cover		70
		First day cover, #131-132		1.00
		Margin block of 4, inscription	2.00	90

First day covers of Nos. 131-132 total 445,274.

UNITED NATIONS

Padlocked Atomic Blast
A70

Issued to commemorate the signing of the nuclear test ban treaty pledging an end to nuclear explosions in the atmosphere, outer space and under water.

Printed by Artia, Prague, Czechoslovakia. Panes of 50. Designed by Ole Hamann.

Photogravure and Engraved

1964, Oct. 23		Perf. 11x11½		Unwmkd.	
133	A70	5c dark red & dark brown *(2,422,789)*		10	8
		First day cover *(298,652)*			30
		Margin block of 4, inscription		50	40

Education for Progress
A71

Design: 11c, French inscription.

Issued to publicize the UNESCO world campaign for universal literacy and for free compulsory primary education.

Printed by Courvoisier, S. A., La Chaux-de-Fonds, Switzerland. Panes of 50. Designed by Kurt Plowitz.

Photogravure

1964, Dec. 7		Perf. 12½		Unwmkd.	
134	A71	4c org. red, bister, grn. & blue *(2,375,181)*		8	6
		First day cover			30
		Margin block of 4, inscription		40	30
135	"	5c bister, red, dk. & lt. blue *(2,496,877)*		10	8
		First day cover			35
		Margin block of 4, inscription		50	40
136	"	11c green, lt. blue, blk. & rose *(1,773,645)*		22	18
		First day cover			60
		First day cover, #134-136			1.00
		Margin block of 4, inscription		1.10	90

First day covers of Nos. 134-136 total 727,875.

Progress Chart of Special Fund, Key and Globe
A72

Design: 11c, French inscription.

Issued to publicize the Special Fund program to speed economic growth and social advancement in low-income countries.

Printed by the Government Printing Bureau, Tokyo. Panes of 50. Designed by Rashid-ud Din, Pakistan.

Photogravure

1965, Jan. 25		Perf. 13½x13		Unwmkd.	
137	A72	5c dull bl., dk. bl., yel. & red *(1,949,274)*		10	8
		First day cover			30
		Margin block of 4, inscription		50	40

138	A72	11c yel. grn., dk. bl., yel. & red *(1,690,908)*		22	18
		First day cover			70
		First day cover, #137-138			80
		Margin block of 4, inscription		1.10	90
	a.	Black omitted (U.N. emblem on key)			

First day covers of Nos. 137-138 total 490,608.

U.N. Emblem, Stylized Leaves and View of Cyprus
A73

Design: 11c, French inscription.

Issued to honor the United Nations Peace-keeping Force on Cyprus.

Printed by Courvoisier S.A., Switzerland. Panes of 50. Designed by George Hamori, Australia.

Photogravure

1965, March 4		Perf. 11½		Unwmkd.	
139	A73	5c orange, olive & black *(1,887,042)*		10	8
		First day cover			30
		Margin block of 4, inscription		50	40
140	"	11c yellow green, bl. grn. & blk. *(1,691,767)*		22	18
		First day cover			70
		First day cover, #139-140			90
		Margin block of 4, inscription		1.10	80

First day covers of Nos. 139-140 total 438,059.

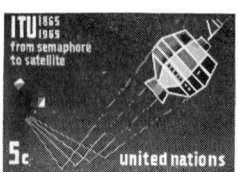

"From Semaphore to Satellite"
A74

Design: 11c, French inscription.

Issued to commemorate the centenary of the International Telecommunication Union.

Printed by Courvoisier S.A., Switzerland. Panes of 50. Designed by Kurt Plowitz, United States.

Photogravure

1965, May 17		Perf. 11½		Unwmkd.	
141	A74	5c aquamarine, orange, blue & purple *(2,432,407)*		10	8
		First day cover			35
		Margin block of 4, inscription		50	40
142	"	11c light violet, red orange, bister & bright green *(1,731,070)*		22	18
		First day cover			70
		First day cover, #141-142			90
		Margin block of 4, inscription		1.10	80

First day covers of Nos. 141-142 total 434,393.

ICY Emblem
A75

UNITED NATIONS 929

Design: 15c, French inscription.
Issued to commemorate the 20th anniversary of the United Nations and International Cooperation Year.
Printed by Bradbury, Wilkinson and Co., Ltd., England. Panes of 50. Designed by Olav Mathiesen, Denmark.

Engraved
1965, June 26   **Perf. 14x13½**   **Unwmkd.**

143	A75	5c dark blue *(2,282,452)*	10	8
		First day cover		35
		Margin block of 4, inscription	50	40
144	"	15c lilac rose *(1,993,562)*	30	20
		First day cover		75
		First day cover, #143-144		1.00
		Margin block of 4, inscription	1.35	90

Souvenir Sheet
145	A75	Sheet of two *(1,928,366)*	60	50
		First day cover		1.25

No. 145 contains one each of Nos. 143-144 with dark blue and ocher marginal inscription, ocher edging. Size: 92x70 mm.
First day covers of Nos. 143-145 total: New York, 748,876; San Francisco, 301,435.

"Peace"
A76

Opening Words,
U.N. Charter
A77

U.N. Headquarters
and Emblem
A78

U.N. Emblem
A79

U.N. Emblem Encircled
A80

Printed by Government Printing Bureau, Tokyo (1c); Government Printing Office, Austria (15c, 20c); Government Printing Office (Bundesdruckerei), Berlin (25c), and Courvoisier S.A., Switzerland ($1). Panes of 50.
Designed by Kurt Plowitz, U.S. (1c); Olav S. Mathiesen, Denmark (15c); Vergniaud Pierre-Noel, U.S. (20c); Rashid-ud Din, Pakistan (25c), and Ole Hamann, Denmark ($1).

Photogravure
1965-66   **Perf. 13½x13**   **Unwmkd.**

146	A76	1c vermilion, blue, blk. & gray *(7,000,000)*	5	5
		First day cover		20
		Margin block of 4, inscription	20	20

Perf. 14
147	A77	15c olive bister, dull yellow, black & deep claret *(2,500,000)*	30	25
		First day cover		75
		Margin block of 4, inscription	1.50	1.15

Perf. 12
148	A78	20c dk. blue, bl., red & yel. *(3,000,000)*	50	30
		First day cover		80
		First day cover, #147-148		1.25
		Margin block of 4, inscription	2.25	1.35
	a.	Yellow omitted		

Lithographed and Embossed
Perf. 14
149	A79	25c light & dark blue *(3,200,000)*	90	45
		First day cover		1.00
		First day cover, #146, 149		1.15
		Margin block of 4, inscription	4.50	2.00
		Margin block of 6, "Bundesdruckerei Berlin" imprint and inscription	35.00	

Photogravure
Perf. 11½
150	A80	$1 aquamarine & sapphire *(2,570,000)*	2.00	1.50
		First day cover *(181,510)*		2.50
		Margin block of 4, inscription	9.00	7.00

Issue dates: 1c and 25c, Sept. 20, 1965; 15c and 20c, Oct. 25, 1965; $1, Mar. 25, 1966.
First day covers of Nos. 146 and 149 total 443,964. Those of Nos. 147-148 total 457,596.

The 25c has the marginal inscription (U.N. emblem and "1965") in two sizes: 1st printing (with Bundesdruckerei imprint), 6mm. in diameter; 2nd printing, 8mm. In 1st printing, "halo" of U.N. emblem is larger, overlapping "25c."
See U.N. Offices in Geneva Nos. 5, 9 and 11.

Fields and People
A81

Design: 11c, French inscription.
Issued to emphasize the importance of the world's population growth and its problems and to call attention to population trends and development.
Printed by Government Printing Office, Austria. Panes of 50. Designed by Olav S. Mathiesen, Denmark.

Photogravure
1965, Nov. 29   **Perf. 12**   **Unwmkd.**

151	A81	4c multicolored *(1,966,033)*	8	6
		First day cover		30
		Margin block of 4, inscription	40	30
152	"	5c multicolored *(2,298,731)*	10	8
		First day cover		30
		Margin block of 4, inscription	50	40
153	"	11c multicolored *(1,557,589)*	22	18
		First day cover		50
		First day cover, #151-153		90
		Margin block of 4, inscription	1.10	80

First day covers of Nos. 151-153 total 710,507.

Globe and Flags
of U.N. Members
A82

UNITED NATIONS

Design: 15c, French inscription.
Issued to honor the World Federation of United Nations Associations.
Printed by Courvoisier S.A., Switzerland. Panes of 50. Designed by Olav S. Mathiesen, Denmark.

		Photogravure		
1966, Jan. 31		Perf. 11½		Unwmkd.
154	A82	5c multicolored (2,462,215)	10	8
		First day cover		30
		Margin bock of 4, inscription	50	40
155	"	15c multicolored (1,643,661)	30	25
		First day cover		70
		First day cover, #154-155		90
		Margin block of 4, inscription	1.35	1.10

First day covers of Nos. 154-155 total 474,154.

WHO Headquarters, Geneva
A83
Design: 11c, French inscription.
Issued to commemorate the opening of the World Health Organization Headquarters, Geneva.
Printed by Courvoisier, S.A., Switzerland. Panes of 50. Designed by Rashid-ud Din.

		Granite Paper		
1966, May 26		Photogravure	Perf. 12½x12	
156	A83	5c light & dark blue, orange, green & bister (2,079,893)	10	8
		First day cover		30
		Margin block of 4, inscription	50	40
157	"	11c orange, light & dark blue, green & bister (1,879,879)	22	18
		First day cover		50
		First day cover, #156-157		75
		Margin block of 4, inscription	1.10	80

First day covers of Nos. 156-157 total 466,171.

Coffee
A84
Design: 11c, Spanish inscription.
Issued to commemorate the International Coffee Agreement of 1962.
Printed by the Government Printing Bureau, Tokyo. Panes of 50. Designed by Rashid-ud Din, Pakistan.

		Photogravure	Perf. 13½x13	
1966, Sept. 19				
158	A84	5c orange, light blue, green, red & dark brown (2,020,308)	10	8
		First day cover		30
		Margin block of 4, inscription	50	40
159	"	11c light blue, yellow, green, red & dark brown (1,888,682)	22	18
		First day cover		40
		First day cover, #158-159		65
		Margin block of 4, inscription	1.10	80

First day covers of Nos. 158-159 total 435,886.

United Nations Observer
A85

Issued to honor the Peace Keeping United Nation Observers.
Printed by Courvoisier, S.A. Panes of 50. Designed by Ole S. Hamann.

		Granite Paper		
1966, Oct. 24		Photogravure	Perf. 11½	
160	A85	15c steel blue, org., blk. & grn. (1,889,809)	30	25
		First day cover (255,326)		40
		Margin block of 4, inscription	1.35	1.10

Children of Various Races
A86
Designs: 5c, Children riding in locomotive and tender. 11c, Children in open railroad car playing medical team (French inscription).
Issued to commemorate the 20th anniversary of the United Nations Children's Fund (UNICEF).
Printed by Thomas De La Rue & Co., Ltd. Panes of 50. Designed by Kurt Plowitz.

		Lithographed	Perf. 13x13½	
1966, Nov. 28				
161	A86	4c pink & multicolored (2,334,989)	8	6
		First day cover		25
		Margin block of 4, inscription	40	30
162	"	5c pale green & multicolored (2,746,941)	10	8
		First day cover		30
		Margin block of 4, inscription	50	40
		a. Yellow omitted		
163	"	11c light ultramarine & multicolored (2,123,841)	22	18
		First day cover		50
		First day cover, #161-163		90
		Margin block of 4, inscription	1.10	80
		a. Imperf. pair		
		b. Dark blue omitted		

First day covers of Nos. 161-163 total 987,271.

Hand Rolling up Sleeve and Chart Showing Progress
A87
Design: 11c, French inscription.
United Nations Development Program.
Printed by Courvoisier, S.A. Panes of 50. Designed by Olav S. Mathiesen.

		Photogravure	Perf. 12½	
1967, Jan. 23				
164	A87	5c grn., yel., pur. & org. (2,204,679)	10	8
		First day cover		30
		Margin block of 4, inscription	50	40
165	"	11c bl., choc., lt. grn. & org. (1,946,159)	22	20
		First day cover		40
		First day cover, #164-165		60
		Margin block of 4, inscription	1.10	80

First day covers of Nos. 164-165 total 406,011.

Type of 1962 and

U.N. Headquarters, New York, and World Map
A88

UNITED NATIONS 931

Printed by Courvoisier, S.A. Panes of 50. Designed by Jozsef Vertel, Hungary (1½c); Renato Ferrini, Italy (5c).

1967		Photogravure		*Perf. 11½*	
166	A88	1½c ultra., black, orange & ocher *(4,000,000)*		5	5
		First day cover *(199,751)*			25
		Margin block of 4, inscription		25	25

Size: 33x23mm.

167	A53	5c red brn., brn. & org. yel *(5,500,000)*	10	8
		First day cover *(212,544)*		35
		Margin block of 4, inscription	50	40

Issue dates: 1½c, March 17; 5c, Jan. 23.
For 5c of type A88, see U.N. Offices in Geneva No. 1.

Fireworks
A89

Design: 11c, French inscription.

Issued to honor all nations which gained independence since 1945.

Printed by Harrison & Sons, Ltd. Panes of 50. Designed by Rashid-ud Din.

1967, March 17		Photogravure		*Perf. 14x14½*	
168	A89	5c dark blue & multi. *(2,445,955)*		10	8
		First day cover			30
		Margin block of 4, inscription		50	40
169	"	11c brown lake & multi. *(2,011,004)*		22	18
		First day cover			50
		First day cover, #168-169			60
		Margin block of 4, inscription		1.10	90

First day covers of Nos. 168-169 total 390,499.

"Peace"   U.N. Pavilion, EXPO '67
A90   A91

Designs: 5c, Justice. 10c, Fraternity. 15c, Truth.

Issued to commemorate EXPO '67, International Exhibition, Montreal, Apr. 28–Oct. 27, 1967.

Under special agreement with the Canadian Government Nos. 170-174 were valid for postage only on mail posted at the U.N. pavilion during the Fair. The denominations are expressed in Canadian currency.

Printed by British American Bank Note Co., Ltd., Ottawa. The 8c was designed by Olav S. Mathiesen after a photograph by Michael Drummond. The others were adapted by Ole S. Hamann from reliefs by Ernest Cormier on doors of General Assembly Hall, presented to U.N. by Canada.

1967, Apr. 28		Engraved & Lithographed		*Perf. 11*	
170	A90	4c red & red brown *(2,464,813)*		10	10
		First day cover			30
		Margin block of 4, inscription		50	50
171	"	5c blue & red brown *(2,177,073)*		15	15
		First day cover			35
		Margin block of 4, inscription		70	70

		Lithographed			
172	A91	8c multicolored *(2,285,440)*		20	20
		First day cover			45
		Margin block of 4, inscription		1.00	1.00

		Engraved and Lithographed			
173	A90	10c green & red brown *(1,955,352)*		20	20
		First day cover			1.30
		Margin block of 4, inscription		90	90
174	"	15c dark brown & red brown *(1,899,185)*		30	30
		First day cover			1.65
		First day cover, #170-174			3.75
		Margin block of 4, inscription		1.35	1.35

First day covers of Nos. 170-174 total 901,625.

Luggage Tags and U.N. Emblem
A92

Issued to publicize International Tourist Year, 1967. Printed by Government Printing Office, Berlin. Panes of 50. Designed by David Dewhurst.

1967, June 19		Lithographed		*Perf. 14*	
175	A92	5c reddish brown & multi. *(2,593,782)*		10	8
		First day cover			30
		Margin block of 4, inscription		50	40
176	"	15c ultramarine & multi. *(1,940,457)*		30	25
		First day cover			75
		First day cover, #175-176			90
		Margin block of 4, inscription		1.50	1.10

First day covers of Nos. 175-176 total 382,886.

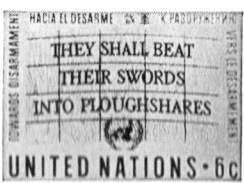

Quotation from Isaiah 2:4
A93

Design: 13c, French inscription.

Issued to publicize the U.N. General Assembly's resolutions on general and complete disarmament and for suspension of nuclear and thermonuclear tests.

Printed by Heraclio Fournier S.A., Spain. Panes of 50. Designed by Ole Hamann.

1967, Oct. 24		Photogravure		*Perf. 14*	
177	A93	6c ultra., yel., gray & brown *(2,462,277)*		12	8
		First day cover			35
		Margin block of 4, inscription		60	40
178	"	13c magenta, yel., gray & brown *(2,055,541)*	26	20
		First day cover			50
		First day cover, #177-178			75
		Margin block of 4, inscription		1.30	90

First day covers of Nos. 177-178 total 403,414.

**Art at U.N. Issue
Miniature Sheet**

Stained Glass Memorial Window by Marc Chagall, at U.N. Headquarters
A94

UNITED NATIONS

"The Kiss of Peace" by Marc Chagall
A95

Printed by Joh. Enschedé and Sons, Netherlands. No. 180 issued in panes of 50. Design adapted by Ole Hamann from photograph by Hans Lippmann.

1967, Nov. 17		Lithographed	Rouletted 9	
179	A94	Sheet of six (3,178,656)	75	60
		First day cover		1.75
	a.	6c multi, 41x46mm.	12	8
	b.	6c multi., 24x46mm.	12	8
	c.	6c multi., 41½x33½mm.	12	8
	d.	6c multi., 36x33½mm.	12	8
	e.	6c multi., 29x33½mm.	12	8
	f.	6c multi., 41½x47mm.	12	8
		Perf. 13x13½		
180	A95	6c multicolored (3,438,497)	12	8
		First day cover		30
		Margin block of 4, inscription	60	50

No. 179 is divisible into six 6c stamps, each rouletted on 3 sides, imperf. on fourth side. Size: 124x80mm. On Nos. 179a–179c, "United Nations·6c" appears at top; on Nos. 179d–179f, at bottom. No. 179f includes name "Marc Chagall."

First day covers of Nos. 179–180 total 617,225.

Globe and Major U.N. Organs
A96

Design: 13c, French inscriptions.
Issued to honor the United Nations Secretariat.
Printed by Courvoisier, S. A., Switzerland. Panes of 50. Designed by Rashid-ud Din.

1968, Jan. 16		Photogravure	Perf. 11½	
181	A96	6c multicolored (2,772,965)	12	8
		First day cover		35
		Margin block of 4, inscription	60	45
182	"	13c multicolored (2,461,992)	26	20
		First day cover		50
		First day cover, #181-182		75
		Margin block of 4, inscription	1.15	90

First day covers of Nos. 181–182 total 411,119.

Art at U.N. Issue

Statue by Henrik Starcke
A97

The 6c is part of the "Art at the U.N." series. The 75c belongs to the regular definitive series. The teakwood Starcke statue, which stands in the Trusteeship Council Chamber, represents mankind's search for freedom and happiness.

Printed by Courvoisier, S.A., Switzerland Panes of 50.

1968, March 1		Photogravure	Perf. 11½	
183	A97	6c blue & multicolored (2,537,320)	12	10
		First day cover		35
		Margin block of 4, inscription	60	50
184	"	75c rose lake & multicolored (2,300,000)	4.00	2.00
		First day cover		6.00
		First day cover, #183-184		6.50
		Margin block of 4, inscription	18.00	9.00

First day covers of Nos. 183–184 total 413,286.
No. 183 exists imperforate.
For 3fr in type A97, see U.N. Offices in Geneva No. 13.

Factories and Chart
A98

Design: 13c, French inscription ("ONUDI," etc.).
Issued to publicize the U.N. Industrial Development Organization.
Printed by Canadian Bank Note Co., Ltd., Ottawa. Panes of 50. Designed by Ole Hamann.

1968, Apr. 18		Lithographed	Perf. 12	
185	A98	6c greenish blue, lt. greenish blue, black & dull claret (2,439,656)	12	8
		First day cover		35
		Margin block of 4, inscription	60	40
186	"	13c dull red brown, lt. red brown, black & ultra. (2,192,453)	26	20
		First day cover		50
		First day cover, #185-186		75
		Margin block of 4, inscription	1.15	90

First day covers of Nos. 185–186 total 396,447.

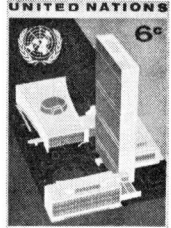

U.N. Headquarters
A99

Printed by Aspioti Elka-Chrome Mines, Ltd., Athens. Panes of 50. Designed by Olav S. Mathiesen.

1968, May 31		Lithographed	Perf. 12x13½	
187	A99	6c green, blue, black & gray (4,000,000)	12	10
		First day cover (241,179)		35
		Margin block of 4, inscription	60	40

Radarscope and Globe
A100

UNITED NATIONS

933

Design: 20c, French inscription.
Issued to publicize World Weather Watch, a new weather system directed by the World Meteorological Organization.
Printed by the Government Printing Bureau, Tokyo. Designed by George A. Gundersen and George Fanais, Canada.

1968, Sept. 19	Photogravure	Perf. 13x13½		
188	A100	6c grn., blk., ocher, red & bl. (2,245,078)	12	10
		First day cover		35
		Margin block of 4, inscription	60	50
189	"	20c lilac, blk., ocher, red & bl. (2,069,966)	40	30
		First day cover		80
		First day cover, #188-189		1.00
		Margin block of 4, inscription	2.00	1.65

First day covers of Nos. 188-189 total 620,510.

U.N. Building, Santiago, Chile
A103

Design: 15c, Spanish inscription.
The U.N. Building in Santiago, Chile, is the seat of the U.N. Economic Commission for Latin America and of the Latin American Institute for Economic and Social Planning.
Printed by Government Printing Office, Berlin. Panes of 50. Design by Ole Hamann, adapted from a photograph.

1969, March 14	Lithographed	Perf. 14		
194	A103	6c light blue, violet blue & light green (2,543,992)	12	10
		First day cover		35
		Margin block of 4, inscription	60	50
195	"	15c pink, cream & red brown (2,030,733)	30	25
		First day cover		55
		First day cover, #194-195		85
		Margin block of 4, inscription	1.35	1.10

First day covers of Nos. 194-195 total 398,227.

Human Rights Flame
A101

Design: 13c, French inscription.
Issued for International Human Rights Year, 1968.
Printed by Harrison & Sons, Ltd., England. Designed by Robert Perrot, France.

1968, Nov. 22	Photo.; Foil Embossed	Perf. 12½		
190	A101	6c brt. bl., dp. ultra. & gold (2,394,235)	15	10
		First day cover		75
		Margin block of 4, inscription	75	50
191	"	13c rose red, dk. red & gold (2,284,838)	25	20
		First day cover		60
		First day cover, #190-191		1.20
		Margin block of 4, inscription	1.25	90

First day covers of Nos. 190-191 total 519,012.

"UN" and U.N. Emblem
A104

Printed by Government Printing Bureau, Tokyo. Panes of 50. Designed by Leszek Holdanowicz and Marek Freudenreich, Poland.

1969, March 14	Photogravure	Perf. 13½		
196	A104	13c brt. blue, black & gold (4,000,000)*	26	20
		First day cover		50
		Margin block of 4, inscription	1.30	90

* Initial printing order.
For 70c in type A104, see U.N. Offices in Geneva No. 7.

Books and U.N. Emblem
A102

Design: 13c, French inscription in center, denomination panel at bottom.
Issued to publicize the United Nations Institute for Training and Research (UNITAR).
Printed by the Government Printing Bureau, Tokyo. Panes of 50. Designed by Olav S. Mathiesen.

1969, Feb. 10	Lithographed	Perf. 13½		
192	A102	6c yellow green & multicolored (2,436,559)	12	10
		First day cover		35
		Margin block of 4, inscription	60	50
193	"	13c bluish lilac & multicolored (1,935,151)	25	20
		First day cover		60
		First day cover, #192-193		85
		Margin block of 4, inscription	1.25	90

First day covers of Nos. 192-193 total 439,606.

U.N. Emblem and Scales of Justice
A105

Design: 13c, French inscripition.
Issued to publicize the 20th anniversary session of the U.N. International Law Commission.
Printed by Courvoisier S.A., Switzerland. Panes of 50. Designed by Robert Perrot, France.

Granite Paper

1969, Apr. 21	Photogravure	Perf. 11½		
197	A105	6c brt. green, ultra. & gold (2,501,492)	12	10
		First day cover		35
		Margin block of 4, inscription	70	55
198	"	13c crimson, lilac & gold (1,966,994)	26	20
		First day cover		50
		First day cover, #197-198		80
		Margin block of 4, inscription	1.15	90

First day covers of Nos. 197-198 total 439,324.

UNITED NATIONS

Allegory of Labor, Emblems of U.N. and ILO
A106

Design: 20c, French inscription.

Printed by Government Printing Bureau, Tokyo. Panes of 50. Designed by Nejat M. Gur, Turkey.

Issued to publicize "Labor and Development" and to commemorate the 50th anniversary of the International Labor Organization.

1969, June 5		Photogravure		Perf. 13	
199	A106	6c blue, dp. blue, yel. & gold (2,078,381)	12	10
		First day cover		35
		Margin block of 4, inscription	60	50
200	"	20c orange vermilion, magenta, yellow & gold (1,751,100)	40	30
		First day cover		80
		First day cover, #199-200		1.00
		Margin block of 4, inscription	1.85	1.35

First day covers of Nos. 199-200 total 514,155.

Art at U.N. Issue

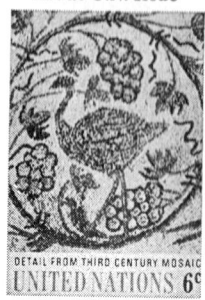

Ostrich, Tunisian Mosaic, 3rd Century
A107

Design: 13c, Pheasant; French inscription.

The mosaic "The Four Seasons and the Genius of the Year" was found at Haidra, Tunisia. It is now at the Delegates' North Lounge, U.N. Headquarters, New York.

Printed by Heraclio Fournier, S. A., Spain. Panes of 50. Designed by Olav S. Mathiesen.

1969, Nov. 21		Photogravure		Perf. 14	
201	A107	6c blue & mulicolored (2,280,702)	12	10
		First day cover		35
		Margin block of 4, inscription	60	50
202	"	13c red & multicolored (1,918,554)	26	20
		First day cover		60
		First day cover, #201-202		85
		Margin block of 4, inscription	1.15	90

First day covers of Nos. 201-202 total 612,981.

Art at U.N. Issue

Peace Bell, Gift of Japanese
A108

Design: 25c, French inscription.

The Peace Bell was a gift of the people of Japan in 1954, cast from donated coins and metals. It is housed in a Japanese cypress structure at U.N. Headquarters, New York.

Printed by Government Printing Bureau, Tokyo. Panes of 50. Designed by Ole Hamann.

1970, Mar. 13		Photogravure		Perf. 13½x13	
203	A108	6c violet blue & multi (2,604,253)	12	10
		First day cover		35
		Margin block of 4, inscription	60	50
204	"	25c claret & multi. (2,090,185)	50	40
		First day cover		1.00
		First day cover, #203-204		1.25
		Margin block of 4, inscription	2.25	1.75

First day covers of Nos. 203-204 total 502,384.

Mekong River, Power Lines and Map of Mekong Delta
A109

Design: 13c, French inscription.

Issued to publicize the Lower Mekong Basin Development project under U.N. auspices.

Printed by Heraclio Fournier, S.A., Spain. Panes of 50. Designed by Ole Hamann.

1970, Mar. 13				Perf. 14	
205	A109	6c dark blue & multi. (2,207,309)	12	10
		First day cover		35
		Margin block of 4, inscription	60	50
206	"	13c deep plum & multi. (1,889,023)	26	20
		First day cover		60
		First day cover, #205-206		85
		Margin block of 4, inscription	1.15	90

First day covers of Nos. 205-206 total 522,218.

"Fight Cancer"
A110

Design: 13c, French inscription.

Issued to publicize the fight against cancer in connection with the 10th International Cancer Congress of the International Union Against Cancer, Houston, Texas, May 22-29.

Printed by Government Printing Office, Berlin. Panes of 50. Designed by Leonard Mitchell.

1970, May 22		Lithographed		Perf. 14	
207	A110	6c blue & black (2,157,742)	12	10
		First day cover		35
		Margin block of 4, inscription	60	50
208	"	13c olive & black (1,824,714)	26	20
		First day cover		60
		First day cover, #207-208		85
		Margin block of 4, inscription	1.15	90

First day covers of Nos. 207-208 total 444,449.

U.N. Emblem and Olive Branch
A111

U.N. Emblem
A112

UNITED NATIONS 935

Design: 13c, French inscription.

Issued to commemorate the 25th anniversary of the United Nations. First day covers were postmarked at U.N. Headquarters, New York, and at San Francisco.

Printed by Courvoisier, S.A., Switzerland. Designed by Ole Hamann and Olav S. Mathiesen (souvenir sheet).

1970, June 26		Photogravure			Perf. 11½	
209	A111	6c red, gold, dk. & lt. blue *(2,365,229)*		12	10	
		First day cover			45	
		Margin block of 4, inscription		60	50	
210	"	13c dk. blue, gold, green & red *(1,861,613)*		26	20	
		First day cover			60	
		Margin block of 4, inscription		1.15	90	
		Perf. 12½				
211	A112	25c dark blue, gold & lt. blue *(1,844,669)*		50	40	
		First day cover			1.10	
		First day cover, #209-211			2.00	
		Margin block of 4, inscription		2.25	1.75	
		Souvenir Sheet				
		Imperf.				
212		Sheet of 3 *(1,923,639)*		90	70	
		a. A111 6c red, gold & multicolored		12	10	
		b. " 13c vio. blue, gold & multi.		26	20	
		c. A112 25c vio. blue, gold & lt. blue		50	35	
		First day cover			1.50	

No. 212 contains 3 imperf. stamps, gold border and violet blue marginal inscription. Size: 9 4½ x 78mm.

First day covers of Nos. 209-212 total: New York, 846,389; San Francisco, 471,100.

Scales, Olive Branch and Symbol of Progress
A113

Design: 13c, French inscription.

Issued to publicize "Peace, Justice and Progress" in connection with the 25th anniversary of the United Nations.

Printed by Government Printing Bureau, Tokyo. Panes of 50. Designed by Ole Hamann.

1970, Nov. 20		Photogravure			Perf. 13½	
213	A113	6c gold & multicolored *(1,921,441)*		12	10	
		First day cover			35	
		Margin block of 4, inscription		60	50	
214		13c silver & multicolored *(1,663,669)*		26	20	
		First day cover			60	
		First day cover, #213-214			85	
		Margin block of 4, inscription		1.15	90	

First day covers of Nos. 213-214 total 521,419.

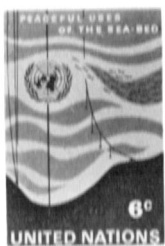

Sea Bed, School of Fish and Underwater Research
A114

Issued to publicize peaceful uses of the sea bed.

Printed by Setelipaino, Finland. Panes of 50. Designed by Pentti Rahikainen, Finland.

1971, Jan. 25		Photogravure and Engraved			Perf. 13	
215	A114	6c blue & multicolored *(2,354,179)*		12	10	
		First day cover *(405,554)*			35	
		Margin block of 4, inscription		60	50	

See U.N. Offices in Geneva No. 15.

Refugees, Sculpture by Kaare K. Nygaard—A115
International support for refugees.

Printed by Joh. Enschedé and Sons, Netherlands. Panes of 50. Designed by Dr. Kaare K. Nygaard and Martin J. Weber.

1971, Mar. 2		Lithographed			Perf. 13x12½	
216	A115	6c brown, ocher & black *(2,247,232)*		12	10	
		First day cover			35	
		Margin block of 4, inscription		60	50	
217	"	13c ultra., greenish blue & black *(1,890,048)*		26	20	
		First day cover			60	
		First day cover, #216-217			85	
		Margin block of 4, inscription		1.15	90	

First day covers of Nos. 216-217 total 564,785.
See U.N. Offices in Geneva No. 16.

Wheat and Globe
A116

Publicizing the U.N. World Food Program.

Printed by Heraclio Fournier, S.A., Spain. Panes of 50. Designed by Olav S. Mathiesen.

1971, Apr. 13		Photogravure			Perf. 14	
218	A116	13c red & multicolored *(1,968,542)*		26	20	
		First day cover			60	
		Margin block of 4, inscription		1.15	90	

See U.N. Offices in Geneva No. 17.

U. P. U. Headquarters, Bern
A117

Opening of new Universal Postal Union Headquarters, Bern.

Printed by Courvoisier, S.A. Panes of 50. Designed by Olav S. Mathiesen.

1971, May 28		Photogravure			Perf. 11½	
219	A117	20c brown orange & multi. *(1,857,841)*		40	30	
		First day cover *(375,119)*			80	
		Margin block of 4, inscription		1.85	1.35	

See U.N. Offices in Geneva No. 18.

"Eliminate Racial Discrimination"
A118   A119

International Year Against Racial Discrimination.
Printed by Government Printing Bureau, Tokyo. Panes of 50. Designers: Daniel Gonzague (8c); Ole Hamann (13c).

1971, Sept. 21		Photogravure		Perf. 13½	
220	A118	8c yellow green & multi. *(2,324,349)*		16	12
		First day cover			32
		Margin block of 4, inscription		80	55
221	A119	13c blue & multicolored *(1,852,093)*		26	20
		First day cover			60
		First day cover, #220-221			85
		Margin block of 4, inscription		1.15	90

First day covers of Nos. 220–221 total 461,103.
See U.N. Offices in Geneva Nos. 19–20.

U.N. Headquarters, New York—A120

U.N. Emblem and Symbolic Flags—A121
No. 222 printed by Heraclio Fournier, S.A., Spain. No. 223 printed by Government Printing Bureau, Tokyo. Panes of 50. Designers: O. S. Mathiesen (8c); Robert Perrot (60c).

1971, Oct. 22		Photogravure		Perf. 13½	
222	A120	8c violet blue & multi. *(5,300,000)**		16	12
		First day cover			35
		Margin block of 4, inscription		80	55
			Perf. 13		
223	A121	60c ultramarine & multi. *(3,500,000)**		1.20	90
		First day cover			2.40
		First day cover, #222-223			2.50
		Margin block of 4, inscription		5.00	3.50

First day covers of Nos. 222–223 total 336,013.
*Printing orders to Apr. 1982.

Maia, by Pablo Picasso
A122

To publicize the U.N. International School.
Printed by Courvoisier, S.A. Panes of 50. Designed by Ole Hamann.

1971, Nov. 19		Photogravure		Perf. 11½	
224	A122	8c olive & multicolored *(2,668,214)*		20	15
		First day cover			35
		Margin block of 4, inscription		1.00	70
225	"	21c ultra. & multicolored *(2,040,754)*		60	40
		First day cover			80
		First day cover, #224-225			1.00
		Margin block of 4, inscription		2.75	1.75

First day covers of Nos. 224–225 total 579,594.
See U.N. Offices in Geneva No. 21.

Letter Changing Hands
A123

Printed by Bundesdruckerei, Berlin. Panes of 50. Designed by Olav S. Mathiesen.

1972, Jan. 5		Lithographed		Perf. 14	
226	A123	95c carmine & multi *(4,500,000)**		1.90	1.50
		First day cover *(188,193)*			3.50
		Margin block of 4, inscription		8.00	6.00

"No More Nuclear Weapons"
A124

To promote non-proliferation of nuclear weapons.
Printed by Heraclio Fournier, S. A., Spain. Panes of 50. Designed by Arne Johnson, Norway.

1972, Feb. 14		Photogravure		Perf. 13½x14	
227	A124	8c dull rose, black, blue & gray *(2,311,515)*		16	12
		First day cover *(268,789)*			40
		Margin block of 4, inscription		70	55

See U.N. Offices in Geneva No. 23.

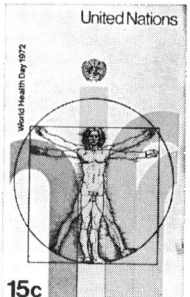

Proportions of Man, by Leonardo da Vinci
A125

World Health Day, Apr. 7.
Printed by Setelipaino, Finland. Panes of 50. Designed by George Hamori.

1972, Apr. 7		Litho. & Engr.		Perf. 13x13½	
228	A125	15c black & multicolored *(1,788,962)*		30	25
		First day cover *(322,724)*			55
		Margin block of 4, inscription		1.35	1.20

See U.N. Offices in Geneva No. 24.

"Human Environment"
A126

U.N. Conference on Human Evironment, Stockholm, June 5–16, 1972.
Printed by Joh. Enschedé and Sons, Netherlands. Panes of 50. Designed by Robert Perrot.

1972, June 5		Litho. & Embossed		Perf. 12½x14	
229	A126	8c red, buff, green & blue *(2,124,604)*		16	12
		First day cover			35
		Margin block of 4, inscription		70	55

UNITED NATIONS

230	A126	15c bl. green, buff, green & bl. *(1,589,943)*	30	25
		First day cover		55
		First day cover, #229-230		80
		Margin block of 4, inscription	1.35	1.10

First day covers of Nos. 229-230 total 437,222.
See U.N. Offices in Geneva Nos. 25-26.

"Europe" and U.N. Emblem
A127

Economic Commission for Europe, 25th anniversary.
Printed by Government Printing Bureau, Tokyo. Panes of 50. Designed by Angel Medina Medina.

1972, Sept. 11 Lithographed *Perf. 13x13½*

231	A127	21c yellow brown & multi *(1,748,675)*	50	40
		First day cover *(271,128)*		80
		Margin block of 4, inscription	2.25	1.75

See U.N. Offices in Geneva No. 27.

Art at U.N. Issue

The Five Continents
by José Maria Sert
A128

Design shows part of ceiling mural of the Council Hall, Palais des Nations, Geneva. It depicts the five continents joining in space.
Printed by Courvoisier, S. A. Panes of 50. Designed by Ole Hamann.

1972, Nov. 17 Photogravure *Perf. 12x12½*

232	A128	8c gold, brn. & golden brn. *(2,573,478)*	16	12
		First day cover		35
		Margin block of 4, inscription	70	55
233	"	15c gold, blue green & brown *(1,768,432)*	30	25
		First day cover		55
		First day cover, #232-233		80
		Margin block of 4, inscription	1.35	1.10

First day covers of Nos. 232-233 total 589,817.
See U.N. Offices in Geneva Nos. 28-29.

Olive Branch and
Broken Sword
A129

Disarmament Decade, 1970-79.
Printed by Ajans-Turk, Turkey. Panes of 50. Designed by Kurt Plowitz.

1973, Mar. 9 Lithographed *Perf. 13½x13*

234	A129	8c blue & multi *(2,272,716)*	16	12
		First day cover		35
		Margin block of 4, inscription	1.00	70
235	"	15c lilac rose & multi *(1,643,712)*	40	30
		First day cover		55
		First day cover, #234-235		80
		Margin block of 4, inscription	1.85	1.35

First day covers of Nos. 234-235 total 548,336.
See U.N. Offices in Geneva Nos. 30-31.

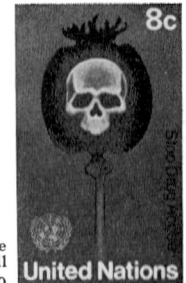

Poppy Capsule
and Skull
A130

Fight against drug abuse.
Printed by Heraclio Fournier, S.A., Spain. Panes of 50. Designed by George Hamori.

1973, Apr. 13 Photogravure *Perf. 13½*

236	A130	8c dp. orange & multi. *(1,846,780)*	20	15
		First day cover		35
		Margin block of 4, inscription	1.00	70
237	"	15c pink & multi. *(1,466,806)*	40	30
		First day cover		55
		First day cover, #236-237		80
		Margin block of 4, inscription	1.85	1.35

First day covers of Nos. 236-237 total 394,468.
See U.N. Offices in Geneva No. 32.

Honeycomb
A131

5th anniversary of the United Nations Volunteer Program.
Printed by Heraclio Fournier, S.A., Spain. Panes of 50. Designed by Courvoisier, S.A.

1973, May 25 Photogravure *Perf. 14*

238	A131	8c olive bister & multi. *(1,868,176)*	20	15
		First day cover		35
		Margin block of 4, inscription	90	70
239	"	21c gray blue & multi. *(1,530,114)*	50	40
		First day cover		80
		First day cover, #238-239		1.00
		Margin block of 4, inscription	2.25	1.75

First day covers of Nos. 238-239 total 396,517.
See U.N. Offices in Geneva No. 33.

Map of Africa with Namibia—A132

To publicize Namibia (South-West Africa) for which the U.N. General Assembly ended the mandate of South Africa and established the U.N. Council for Namibia to administer the territory until independence.
Printed by Heraclio Fournier, S.A., Spain. Panes of 50. Designed by George Hamori.

1973, Oct. 1 Photogravure *Perf. 14*

240	A132	8c emerald & multi. *(1,775,260)*	20	15
		First day cover		35
		Margin block of 4, inscription	1.00	70
241	"	15c bright rose & multi. *(1,687,782)*	40	30
		First day cover		55
		First day cover, #240-241		80
		Margin block of 4, inscription	1.85	1.35

First day covers of Nos. 240-241 total 385,292.
See U.N. Offices in Geneva No. 34.

UNITED NATIONS

U.N. Emblem and Human Rights Flame—A133

25th anniversary of the adoption and proclamation of the Universal Declaration of Human Rights.
Printed by Government Printing Bureau, Tokyo. Panes of 50. Designed by Alfred Guerra.

1973. Nov. 16		Photogravure		Perf. 13½	
242	A133	8c dp. carmine & multi. (2,026,245)		20	15
		First day cover			35
		Margin block of 4, inscription		1.00	70
243	"	21c bl. green & multi. (1,558,201)		50	40
		First day cover			80
		First day cover, #242-243			1.00
		Margin block of 4, inscription		2.25	1.75

First day covers of Nos. 242-243 total 398,511.
See U.N. Offices in Geneva Nos. 35-36.

ILO Headquarters, Geneva—A134

New Headquarters of International Labor Organization.
Printed by Heraclio Fournier, S.A., Spain. Panes of 50. Designed by Henry Bencsath.

1974, Jan. 11		Photogravure		Perf. 14	
244	A134	10c ultra. & multi. (1,734,423)		35	20
		First day cover			40
		Margin block of 4, inscription		1.50	90
245	"	21c blue green & multi. (1,264,447)		90	60
		First day cover			90
		First day cover, #244-245			1.10
		Margin block of 4, inscription		4.00	2.75

First day covers of Nos. 244-245 total 282,284.
See U.N. Offices in Geneva Nos. 37-38.

UPU Emblem and Post Horn Encircling Globe—A135
Centenary of Universal Postal Union.

Printed by Ashton-Potter Ltd., Canada. Panes of 50. Designed by Arne Johnson.

1974, Mar. 22		Lithographed		Perf. 12½	
246	A135	10c gold & multicolored (2,104,919)		20	15
		First day cover (342,774)			40
		Margin block of 4, inscription		90	65

See U.N. Offices in Geneva Nos. 39-40.

Art at U.N. Issue

Peace Mural, by Candido Portinari
A136

The mural, a gift of Brazil, is in the Delegates' Lobby, General Assembly Building.
Printed by Heraclio Fournier, S.A., Spain. Panes of 50. Design adapted by Ole Hamann.

1974, May 6		Photogravure		Perf. 14	
247	A136	10c gold & multi. (1,769,342)		25	20
		First day cover			40
		Margin block of 4, inscription		1.10	90
248	"	18c ultramarine & multi. (1,477,500)		45	35
		First day cover			70
		First day cover, #247-248			1.00
		Margin block of 4, inscription		2.00	1.50

First day covers of Nos. 247-248 total 271,440.
See U.N. Offices in Geneva Nos. 41-42.

Dove and U.N. Emblem
A137

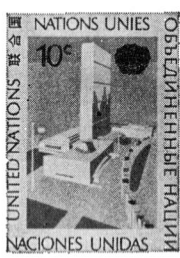

U.N. Headquarters
A138

Globe, U.N. Emblem, Flags
A139

Printed by Heraclio Fournier, S.A., Spain. Panes of 50.
Designed by Nejut M. Gur (2c); Olav S. Mathiesen (10c); Henry Bencsath (18c).

1974, June 10		Photogravure		Perf. 14	
249	A137	2c dark & light blue (5,000,000)*		5	5
		First day cover			30
		Margin block of 4, inscription		20	20
250	A138	10c multicolored (4,000,000)*		20	15
		First day cover			40
		Margin block of 4, inscription		80	75
251	A139	18c multicolored (2,300,000)*		36	25
		First day cover			70
		First day cover, #249-251			1.00
		Margin block of 4, inscription		1.40	1.25

Printing orders to Sept. 1981.
First day covers of Nos. 249-251 total 307,402.

Children of the World
A140

World Population Year

Printed by Heraclio Fournier, S.A., Spain. Panes of 50. Designed by Henry Bencsath.

1974, Oct. 18		Photogravure		Perf. 14	
252	A140	10c light blue & multi. (1,762,595)		25	20
		First day cover			35
		Margin block of 4, inscription		1.25	85

UNITED NATIONS 939

253	A140	18c lilac & multi. (*1,321,574*)	55	35
		First day cover		70
		First day cover, #252-253		1.00
		Margin block of 4, inscription	2.40	1.50

First day covers of Nos. 253–254 total 354,306.
See U.N. Offices in Geneva Nos. 43–44.

Law of the Sea
A141

Declaration of U.N. General Assembly that the sea bed is common heritage of mankind, reserved for peaceful purposes.
Printed by Heraclio Fournier, S.A., Spain. Panes of 50. Designed by Asher Kalderon.

1974, Nov. 22   Photogravure   *Perf. 14*

254	A141	10c green & multicolored (*1,621,574*)	30	25
		First day cover		40
		Margin block of 4, inscription	1.25	85
255	"	26c orange red & multicolored (*1,293,084*)	65	50
		First day cover		1.00
		First day cover, #254-255		1.25
		Margin block of 4, inscription	3.00	2.25

First day covers of Nos. 254–255 total 280,686.
See U.N. Offices in Geneva No. 45.

Satellite and Globe
A142

Peaceful uses (meteorology, industry, fishing, communications) of outer space.
Printed by Setelipaino, Finland. Panes of 50. Designed by Henry Bencsath.

1975, March 14   Lithographed   *Perf. 13*

256	A142	10c multicolored (*1,681,115*)	25	20
		First day cover		35
		Margin block of 4, inscription	1.25	85
257	"	26c multicolored (*1,463,130*)	65	50
		First day cover		1.00
		First day cover, #256-257		1.25
		Margin block of 4, inscription	3.00	2.25

First day covers of Nos. 256–257 total 330,316.
See U.N. Offices in Geneva Nos. 46–47.

Equality Between Men and Women
A143

International Women's Year

Printed by Questa Colour Security Printers, Ltd., England. Panes of 50. Designed by Asher Kalderon and Esther Kurti.

1975, May 9   Lithographed   *Perf. 15*

258	A143	10c multicolored (*1,402,542*)	25	20
		First day cover		35
		Margin block of 4, inscription	1.10	90
259	"	18c multicolored (*1,182,321*)	55	35
		First day cover		70
		First day cover, #258-259		1.00
		Margin block of 4, inscription	2.40	1.50

First day covers of Nos. 258–259 total 285,466.
See U.N. Offices in Geneva Nos. 48–49.

U.N. Flag and "XXX"
A144

30th anniversary of the United Nations.
Printed by Ashton-Potter, Ltd., Canada. Panes of 50. Stamps designed by Asher Calderon, sheets by Olav S. Mathiesen.

1975, June 26   Lithographed   *Perf. 13*

260	A144	10c olive bister & multi. (*1,904,545*)	20	15
		First day cover		35
		Margin block of 4, inscription	90	65
261	"	26c purple & multicolored (*1,547,766*)	50	40
		First day cover		1.00
		First day cover, #260-261		1.25
		Margin block of 4, inscription	2.25	1.75

Souvenir Sheet
Imperf.

262	A144	Sheet of 2 (1,196,578)	1.00	85
	a.	10c olive bister & multicolored	20	18
	b.	26c purple & multicolored	52	50
		First day cover		1.75

No. 262 has blue and bister margin with inscription and U.N. emblem. Size: 92x70mm.
First day covers of Nos. 260–262 total: New York 477,912; San Francisco 237,159.
See Offices in Geneva Nos. 50–52.

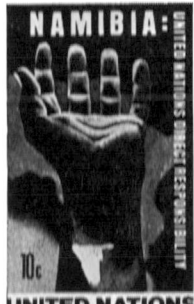

Hand Reaching up over
Map of Africa and Namibia
A145

"Namibia-United Nations direct responsibility." See note after No. 241.

Printed by Heraclio Fournier S.A., Spain. Panes of 50. Designed by Henry Bencsath.

1975, Sept. 22   Photogravure   *Perf. 13½*

263	A145	10c multicolored (*1,354,374*)	25	20
		First day cover		35
		Margin block of 4, inscription	1.25	90
264	"	18c multicolored (*1,243,157*)	40	35
		First day cover		70
		First day cover, #263-264		1.00
		Margin block of 4, inscription	1.80	1.60

First day covers of Nos. 263–264 total 281,031.
See U.N. Offices in Geneva Nos. 53–54.

UNITED NATIONS

Wild Rose Growing from Barbed Wire
A146

United Nations Peace-keeping Operations

Printed by Setelipaino, Finland. Panes of 50. Designed by Mrs. Eeva Oivo.

1975, Nov. 21		Engraved	Perf. 12½	
265	A146	13c ultramarine (*1,628,039*)	30	25
		First day cover		45
		Margin block of 4, inscription	1.50	1.10
266	"	26c rose carmine (*1,195,580*)	65	50
		First day cover		90
		First day cover, #265-266		1.15
		Margin block of 4, inscription	3.00	2.20

First day covers of Nos. 265-266 total 303,711.
See U.N. Offices in Geneva Nos. 55-56.

Symbolic Flags Forming Dove
A147

U.N. Emblem
A149

People of All Races—A148

United Nations Flag—A150

Dove and Rainbow
A151

Printed by Ashton-Potter, Ltd., Canada (3c, 4c, 30c, 50c), and Questa Colour Security Printers, Ltd., England (9c). Panes of 50.
Designed by Waldemar Andrzesewski (3c); Arne Johnson (4c); George Hamori (9c, 30c); Arthur Congdon (50c).

1976		Lithographed	Perf. 13x13½, 13½x13	
267	A147	3c multicolored (*4,000,000*)*	6	5
		First day cover		30
		Margin block of 4, inscription	30	
268	A148	4c multicolored (*4,000,000*)*	8	6
		First day cover		30
		Margin block of 4, inscription	40	
		Photogravure	Perf. 14	
269	A149	9c multicolored (*3,270,000*)	18	15
		First day cover		40
		Margin block of 4, inscription	90	
		Lithographed	Perf. 13x13½	
270	A150	30c blue, emerald & black (*2,500,000*)*	60	45
		First day cover		1.00
		Margin block of 4, inscription	2.50	
271	A151	50c yellow green & multicolored (*2,000,000*)*	1.00	75
		First day cover		2.00
		Margin block of 4, inscription	4.10	

* Initial printing order.
Issue dates: 3c, 4c, 30c, 50c, Jan. 6; 9c, Nov. 19.
First day covers of Nos. 267-268, 270-271 total 355,165.
See U.N. Offices in Vienna No. 8.

Interlocking Bands and U.N. Emblem
A152

World Federation of United Nations Associations.

Printed by Heraclio Fournier, S.A., Spain. Panes of 50. Designed by George Hamori.

1976, March 12		Photogravure	Perf. 14	
272	A152	13c blue, green & black (*1,331,556*)	40	25
		First day cover		45
		Margin block of 4, inscription	1.75	
273	"	26c green & multi. (*1,050,145*)	75	50
		First day cover		90
		First day cover, #272-273		1.15
		Margin block of 4, inscription	3.75	

First day covers of Nos. 272-273 total 300,775.
See U.N. Offices in Geneva No. 57.

Cargo, Globe and Graph
A153

U.N. Conference on Trade and Development (UNCTAD), Nairobi, Kenya, May 1976.

Printed by Courvoisier, S.A. Panes of 50. Designed by Henry Bencsath.

1976, Apr. 23		Photogravure	Perf. 11½	
274	A153	13c dp. magenta & multi. (*1,317,900*)	40	25
		First day cover		45
		Margin block of 4, inscription	1.75	

UNITED NATIONS

275	A153	31c dull blue & multi. (*1,216,959*)		85	60
		First day cover			1.00
		First day cover, #274-275			1.25
		Margin block of 4, inscription		4.00	

First day covers of Nos. 274-275 total 234,657.
See U.N. Offices in Geneva No. 58.

Houses Around Globe
A154

Habitat, U.N. Conference on Human Settlements, Vancouver, Canada, May 31–June 11.
Printed by Heraclio Fournier, S.A., Spain. Panes of 50. Designed by Eliezer Weishoff.

1976, May 28		Photogravure		*Perf. 14*	
276	A154	13c red brn. & multi (*1,346,589*)		40	25
		First day cover			45
		Margin block of 4, inscription		1.75	
277	"	25c green & multicolored (*1,057,924*)		70	50
		First day cover			85
		First day cover, #276-277			1.10
		Margin block of 4, inscription		3.25	

First day covers of Nos. 276-277 total 232,754.
See U.N. Offices in Geneva Nos. 59-60.

Magnifying Glass,
Sheet of Stamps,
U.N. Emblem
A155

United Nations Postal Administration, 25th anniversary.
Printed by Courvoisier, S.A. Panes of 20 (5x4). Designed by Henry Bencsath.

1976, Oct. 8		Photogravure		*Perf. 11½*	
278	A155	13c blue & multicolored (*1,996,309*)		40	30
		First day cover			1.25
		Margin block of 6, inscription		2.60	
279	"	31c green & multicolored (*1,767,465*)		6.50	3.00
		First day cover			7.00
		First day cover, #278-279			8.00
		Margin block of 6, inscription		40.00	

First day covers of Nos. 278-279 total 366,784.
Upper margin blocks are inscribed "XXV ANNIVERSARY"; lower margin blocks "UNITED NATIONS POSTAL ADMINISTRATIONS." See U.N. Offices in Geneva Nos. 61-62.

Grain
A156

World Food Council.
Printed by Questa Colour Security Printers, Ltd., England. Panes of 50. Designed by Eliezer Weishoff.

1976, Nov. 19		Lithographed		*Perf. 14½*	
280	A156	13c multicolored (*1,515,573*)		30	25
		First day cover (366,556)			45
		Margin block of 4, inscription		1.35	

See U.N. Offices in Geneva No. 63.

WIPO Headquarters,
Geneva
A157

World Intellectual Property Organization (WIPO).
Printed by Heraclio Fournier, S. A., Spain. Panes of 50. Designed by Eliezer Weishoff.

1977, Mar. 11		Photogravure		*Perf. 14*	
281	A157	13c citron & multi. (*1,330,272*)		40	30
		First day cover			45
		Margin block of 4, inscription		2.00	
282	"	31c brt. green & multi. (*1,115,406*)		90	75
		First day cover			1.00
		First day cover, #281-282			1.25
		Margin block of 4, inscription		4.50	

First day covers of Nos. 281-282 total 364,184.
See U.N. Offices in Geneva No. 64.

Drops of Water Falling
into Funnel
A158

U.N. Water Conference, Mar del Plata, Argentina, Mar. 14–25.
Printed by Government Printing Bureau, Tokyo. Panes of 50. Designed by Elio Tomei.

1977, Apr. 22		Photogravure		*Perf. 13½x13*	
283	A158	13c yellow & multi. (*1,317,536*)		40	30
		First day cover			45
		Margin block of 4, inscription		2.00	
284	"	25c salmon & multi. (*1,077,424*)		75	55
		First day cover			85
		First day cover, #283-284			1.10
		Margin block of 4, inscription		3.75	

First day covers of Nos. 283-284 total 321,585.
See U.N. Offices in Geneva Nos. 65-66.

Burning Fuse Severed
A159

U.N. Security Council.
Printed by Heraclio Fournier, S.A., Spain. Panes of 50. Designed by Witold Janowski and Marek Freudenreich.

1977, May 27		Photogravure		*Perf. 14*	
285	A159	13c purple & multi (*1,321,527*)		40	30
		First day cover			50
		Margin block of 4, inscription		2.00	

UNITED NATIONS

286	A159	31c dark blue & multi. (1,137,195)		90	75
		First day cover			1.00
		First day cover, #285-286			1.25
		Margin block of 4, inscription		4.50	

First day covers of Nos. 285-286 total 309,610.
See U.N. Offices in Geneva Nos. 67-68.

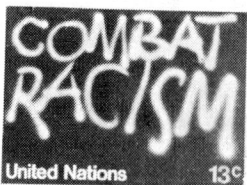

"Combat Racism"
A160

Fight against racial discrimination.

Printed by Setelipaino, Finland. Panes of 50. Designed by Bruno K. Wiese.

1977, Sept. 19		Lithographed		Perf. 13½x13	
287	A160	13c black & yellow (1,195,739)		40	30
		First day cover			50
		Margin block of 4, inscription		2.00	
288	"	25c black & vermilion (1,074,639)		75	55
		First day cover			85
		First day cover, #287-288			1.10
		Margin block of 4, inscription		3.75	

First day covers of Nos. 287-288 total 356,193.
See U.N. Offices in Geneva Nos. 60-70.

Atom, Grain, Fruit
and Factory
A161

Peaceful uses of atomic energy.

Printed by Heraclio Fournier, S.A., Spain. Panes of 50. Designed by Henry Bencsath.

1977, Nov. 18		Photogravure		Perf. 14	
289	A161	13c yel. bister & multi. (1,316,473)		40	30
		First day cover			50
		Margin block of 4, inscription		2.00	
290	"	18c dull green & multi. (1,072,246)		55	40
		First day cover			75
		First day cover, #289-290			1.50
		Margin block of 4, inscription		2.75	

First day covers of Nos. 289-290 total 325,348.
See U.N. Offices in Geneva Nos. 71-72.

Opening Words
of U.N. Charter
A162

"Live Together
in Peace"
A163

People of the World
A164

Printed by Questa Colour Security Printers, United Kingdom. Panes of 50. Designed by Salahattin Kanidic (1c); Elio Tomei (25c); Paula Schmidt ($1).

1978, Jan. 27		Lithographed		Perf. 14½	
291	A162	1c gold, brown & red (4,800,000)*		5	5
		First day cover			30
		Margin block of 4, inscription		20	
292	A163	25c multicolored (3,000,000)*		50	25
		First day cover			90
		Margin block of 4, inscription		2.10	
293	A164	$1 multicolored (2,500,000)*		2.00	1.00
		First day cover			3.00
		Margin block of 4, inscription		8.10	

*Initial printing order.
First day covers of Nos. 291-293 total 264,782.
See U.N. Offices in Geneva No. 73.

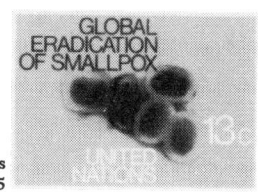

Smallpox Virus
A165

Global eradication of smallpox.

Printed by Courvoisier, S.A. Panes of 50. Designed by Herbert Auchli.

1978, Mar. 31		Photogravure		Perf. 12x11½	
294	A165	13c rose & black (1,188,239)		40	30
		First day cover			50
		Margin block of 4, inscription		1.75	
295	"	31c blue & black (1,058,688)		90	70
		First day cover			1.00
		First day cover, #294-295			1.25
		Margin block of 4, inscription		4.50	

First day covers of Nos. 294-295 total 306,626.
See U.N. Offices in Geneva Nos. 74-75.

Open Handcuff
A166

Liberation, justice and cooperation for Namibia.

Printed by Government Printing Office, Austria. Panes of 50. Designed by Cafiro Tomei.

1978, May 5		Photogravure		Perf. 12	
296	A166	13c multicolored (1,203,079)		35	25
		First day cover			50
		Margin block of 4, inscription		1.75	
297	"	18c multicolored (1,066,738)		45	35
		First day cover			75
		First day cover, #296-297			1.10
		Margin block of 4, inscription		2.25	

First day covers of Nos. 296-297 total 324,471.
See U.N. Offices in Geneva No. 76.

UNITED NATIONS

Multicolored Bands and Clouds
A167

International Civil Aviation Organization for "Safety in the Air."
Printed by Heraclio Fournier, S.A., Spain. Panes of 50. Designed by Cemalettin Mutver.

1978, June 12		Photogravure		*Perf. 14*	
298	A167	13c multicolored (*1,295,617*)		35	25
		First day cover			50
		Margin block of 4, inscription		1.60	
299	"	25c multicolored (*1,101,256*)		60	50
		First day cover			90
		First day cover, #298-299			1.25
		Margin block of 4, inscription		2.75	

First day covers of Nos. 298-299 total 329,995.
See U.N. Offices in Geneva Nos. 77-78.

General Assembly
A168

Printed by Government Printing Bureau, Tokyo. Panes of 50. Designed by Jozsef Vertel.

1978, Sept. 15		Photogravure		*Perf. 13½*	
300	A168	13c multicolored (*1,093,005*)		35	25
		First day cover			50
		Margin block of 4, inscription		1.60	
301	"	18c multicolored (*1,065,934*)		45	35
		First day cover			75
		First day cover, #300-301			1.10
		Margin block of 4, inscription		2.00	

See U.N. Offices in Geneva Nos. 79-80.

Hemispheres as Cogwheels
A169

Technical Cooperation Among Developing Countries Conference, Buenos Aires, Argentina, Sept. 1978.
Printed by Heraclio Fournier, S.A., Spain. Panes of 50. Designed by Simon Keter and David Pesach.

1978, Nov. 17		Photogravure		*Perf. 14*	
302	A169	13c multicolored (*1,251,272*)		35	25
		First day cover			50
		Margin block of 4, inscription		1.75	
303	"	31c multicolored (*1,185,213*)		75	60
		First day cover			1.00
		First day cover, #302-303			1.25
		Margin block of 4, inscription		3.50	

See U.N. Offices in Geneva No. 81.

Hand Holding Olive Branch
A170

Various Races Tree
A171

Globe, Dove with Olive Branch
A172

Birds and Globe
A173

Printed by Heraclio Fournier, S.A., Spain. Panes of 50.
Designed by Raymon Müller (5c); Alrun Fricke (14c); Eliezer Weishoff (15c); Young Sun Hahn (20c).

1979, Jan. 19		Photogravure		*Perf. 14*	
304	A170	5c multicolored (*3,000,000*)*		10	5
		First day cover			50
		Margin block of 4, inscription		50	
305	A171	14c multicolored (*3,000,000*)*		28	14
		First day cover			50
		Margin block of 4, inscription		1.15	
306	A172	15c multicolored (*3,000,000*)*		30	15
		First day cover			50
		Margin block of 4, inscription		1.25	
307	A173	20c multicolored (*3,000,000*)*		40	20
		First day cover			75
		First day cover, #304-307			1.75
		Margin block of 4, inscription		1.65	

* Initial printing order.

UNDRO Against Fire and Water
A174

Office of the U.N. Disaster Relief Coordinator (UNDRO).
Printed by Heraclio Fournier, S.A., Spain. Panes of 50. Designed by Gidon Sagi.

1979, Mar. 9		Photogravure		*Perf. 14*	
308	A174	15c multicolored (*1,448,600*)		40	30
		First day cover			50
		Margin block of 4, inscription		1.75	
309	"	20c multicolored (*1,126,295*)		50	40
		First day cover			75
		First day cover, #308-309			1.10
		Margin block of 4, inscription		2.25	

See U.N. Offices in Geneva Nos. 82-83.

UNITED NATIONS

Child and IYC Emblem
A175
International Year of the Child.

Printed by Heraclio Fournier, S.A., Spain. Panes of 20 (5x4). Designed by Helena Matuszewska (15c) and Krystyna Tarkowska-Gruszecka (31c).

1979, May 4		Photogravure	Perf. 14	
310	A175 15c	multicolored (2,290,329)	55	45
		First day cover		75
		Margin block of 4, inscription	2.50	
311	"	31c multicolored (2,192,136)	1.10	90
		First day cover		1.50
		First day cover, #310-311		2.25
		Margin block of 4, inscription	5.00	—

See U.N. Offices in Geneva Nos. 84–85.

Map of Namibia,
Olive Branch
A176
For a free and independent Namibia.

Printed by Ashton-Potter Ltd., Canada. Panes of 50. Designed by Eliezer Weishoff.

1979, Oct. 5		Lithographed	Perf. 13½	
312	A176 15c	multicolored (1,800,000)	35	25
		First day cover		50
		Margin block of 4, inscription	1.65	
313	"	31c multicolored (1,500,000)	75	60
		First day cover		1.00
		First day cover, #312-313		1.25
		Margin block of 4, inscription	3.50	—

See U.N. Offices in Geneva No. 86.

Scales and
Sword of Justice
A177

International Court of Justice, The Hague, Netherlands
Printed by Setelipaino, Finland. Panes of 50. Designed by Henning Simon.

1979, Nov. 9		Lithographed	Perf. 13x13½	
314	A177 15c	multicolored (1,244,972)	35	30
		First day cover		50
		Margin block of 4, inscription	1.60	
315	"	20c multicolored (1,084,483)	50	40
		First day cover		75
		First day cover, #314-315		1.10
		Margin block of 4, inscription	2.25	—

See U.N. Offices in Geneva Nos. 87–88.

Graph of
Economic Trends   Key
A178   A179

New International Economic Order.
Printed by Questa Colour Security Printers, United Kingdom. Panes of 50. Designed by Cemalettin Mutver (15c), George Hamori (31c).

1980, Jan. 11		Lithographed	Perf. 15x14½	
316	A178 15c	multicolored (1,163,801)	35	30
		First day cover		50
		Margin block of 4, inscription	1.65	
317	A179 31c	multicolored (1,103,560)	75	60
		First day cover		1.15
		First day cover, #316-317		1.25
		Margin block of 4, inscription	3.50	—

See U.N. Offices in Geneva No. 89; Vienna No. 7.

Women's Year Emblem—A180
United Nations Decade for Women.

Printed by Questa Colour Security Printers, United Kingdom. Panes of 50. Designed by Susanne Rottenfusser.

1980, Mar. 7		Lithographed	Perf. 14½×15	
318	A180 15c	multicolored (1,409,350)	35	30
		First day cover		50
		Margin block of 4, inscription	1.65	
319	A180 20c	multicolored (1,182,016)	50	40
		First day cover		70
		First day cover, #318-319		1.00
		Margin block of 4, inscription	2.25	—

See U.N. Offices in Geneva Nos. 90-91; Vienna Nos. 9-10.

UNITED NATIONS

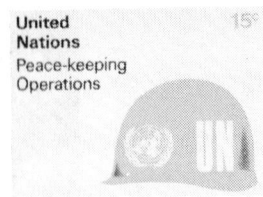

U.N. Emblem and "UN" on Helmet
A181

Arrows and U.N. Emblem
A182

United Nations Peace-keeping Operations.

Printed by Joh. Enschede en Zonen, Netherlands. Panes of 50. Designed by Bruno K. Wiese (15c), James Gardiner (31c).

1980, May 16		Lithographed		Perf. 14x13	
320	A181	15c blue & black *(1,245,521)*		35	30
		First day cover			50
		Margin block of 4, inscription		1.65	
321	A182	31c multicolored *(1,191,009)*		75	60
		First day cover			1.15
		First day cover, #320-321			1.25
		Margin block of 4, inscription		3.50	

See U.N. Offices in Geneva No. 92, Offices in Vienna No. 11.

"35" and Flags
A183

Globe and Laurel
A184

35th Anniversary of the United Nations.

Printed by Ashton-Potter Ltd, Canada. Pane of 50. Designed by Cemalettin Matver (15c), Mian Mohammad Saeed (31c).

1980, June 26		Lithographed		Perf. 13x13½	
322	A183	15c multicolored *(1,554,514)*		30	25
		First day cover			50
		Margin block of 4, inscription		1.50	
323	A184	31c multicolored *(1,389,606)*		75	50
		First day cover			1.15
		First day cover, #322-323			1.25
		Margin block of 4, inscription		3.50	

Souvenir Sheet
Imperf.

324	Sheet of 2 *(1,215,505)*	1.00	
	a. A183 15c multicolored	30	
	b. A184 31c multicolored	65	
	First day cover	1.25	

No. 324 has multicolored margin with inscription and U.N. emblem. Size: 92x73mm. See Offices in Geneva Nos. 93-95; Offices in Vienna Nos. 12-14.

Flag of Turkey—A185

Printed by Courvoisier, S.A., Switzerland. Sheets of 16. Designed by Ole Hamann.

Issued in 4 sheets of 16. Each sheet contains 4 blocks of 4 (Nos. 325-328, 329-332, 333-336, 337-340). A se-tenant block of 4 designs centers each sheet.

1980, Sept. 26		Lithographed		Perf. 12	
325	A185	15c shown *3,490,725)*		30	25
326	A185	15c Luxembourg *(3,490,725)*		30	25
327	A185	15c Fiji *(3,490,725)*		30	25
328	A185	15c Viet Nam *(3,490,725)*		30	25
329	A185	15c Guinea *(3,442,633)*		30	25
330	A185	15c Surinam *(3,442,633)*		30	25
331	A185	15c Bangladesh *(3,442,633)*		30	25
332	A185	15c Mali *(3,442,633)*		30	25
333	A185	15c Jugoslavia *(3,416,292)*		30	25
334	A185	15c France *(3,416,292)*		30	25
335	A185	15c Venezuela *(3,416,292)*		30	25
336	A185	15c El Salvador *(3,416,292)*		30	25
337	A185	15c Madagascar *(3,442,497)*		30	25
338	A185	15c Cameroon *(3,442,497)*		30	25
339	A185	15c Rwanda *(3,442,497)*		30	25
340	A185	15c Hungary *(3,442,497)*		30	25
		First day covers of Nos. 325-340 @			50

Symbols of Progress—A187

Printed by Ashton-Potter Ltd., Canada. Panes of 50. Designed by Eliezer Weishoff (15¢), Dietman Kowall (20¢).

1980, Nov. 21			Lithographed		Perf. 13½×13	
341	A186	15c	multicolored *(1,192,165)*		35	25
			First day cover			50
			Margin block of 4, inscription		1.65	
342	A187	20c	multicolored *(1,011,382)*		50	40
			First day cover			70
			Margin block of 4, inscription		2.25	

See offices in Geneva Nos. 96-97; offices in Vienna No. 15-16.

Inalienable Rights of the Palestinian People—A188

Printed by Courvoisier S.A., Switzerland. Sheets of 50. Designed by David Dewhurst.

1981, Jan. 30			Photogravure		Perf. 12×11½	
343	A188	15c	multicolored *(1,900,000)*		40	30
			First day cover			50
			Margin block of 4, inscription		1.85	

See offices in Geneva No. 98; offices in Vienna No. 17.

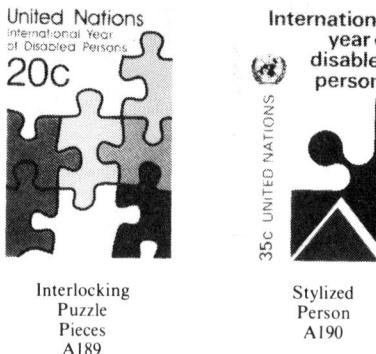

Interlocking Puzzle Pieces A189

Stylized Person A190

International Year of the Disabled.

Printed by Heraclio Fournier S.A., Spain. Panes of 50. Designed by Sophia Van Heeswijk (20c) and G.P. Van der Hyde (35c).

1981, Mar. 6			Photogravure		Perf. 14	
344	A189	20c	multicolored *(1,900,000)*		50	40
			First day cover			70
			Margin block of 4, inscription		2.25	
345	A190	35c	black & orange *(1,600,000)*		85	70
			First day cover			1.20
			First day cover, #344-345			1.50
			Margin block of 4, inscription		4.00	

See Offices in Geneva Nos. 99-100; Offices in Vienna Nos. 18-19.

Desislava and Sebastocrator Kaloyan, Bulgarian Mural, 1259, Boyana Church, Sofia—A191

Art at U.N. Issue
Printed by Courvoisier. Panes of 50. Designed by Ole Hamann.

1981, Apr. 15			Photogravure		Perf. 11½	
			Granite Paper			
346	A191	20c	multi *(1,900,000)*		50	40
			First day cover			70
			Margin block of 4, inscription		2.25	
347	A191	31c	multi *(1,600,000)*		75	60
			First day cover			1.15
			First day cover, #346-347			2.00
			Margin block of 4, inscription		3.50	

See U.N. Offices in Geneva No. 101; Offices in Vienna No. 20.

Solar Energy—A192

Conference Emblem
A193

Conference on New and Renewable Sources of Energy, Nairobi, Aug. 10-21.

Printed by Setelipaino, Finland. Panes of 50. Designed by Ulrike Dreyer (20c); Robert Perrot (40c).

1981, May 29			Lithographed		Perf. 13	
348	A192	20c	multi *(1,900,000)*		50	40
			First day cover			70
			Margin block of 4, inscription		2.25	
349	A193	40c	multi *(1,600,000)*		1.00	80
			First day cover			1.25
			First day cover, #348-349			2.25
			Margin block of 4, inscription		4.50	

See U.N. Offices in Geneva No. 102; Offices in Vienna No. 21.

UNITED NATIONS

Flag Type of 1980

Printed by Courvoisier, S.A., Switzerland. Sheets of 16.
Designed by Ole Hamann.

Issued in 4 sheets of 16. Each sheet contains 4 blocks of four (Nos. 350-353, 354-357, 358-361, 362-365). A se-tenant block of 4 designs centers each sheet.

1981, Sept.25 Lithographed

350	A185	20c	Djibouti	40	30
351	A185	20c	Sri Lanka	40	30
352	A185	20c	Bolivia	40	30
353	A185	20c	Equatorial Guinea	40	30
354	A185	20c	Malta	40	30
355	A185	20c	Czechoslovakia	40	30
356	A185	20c	Thailand	40	30
357	A185	20c	Trinidad & Tobago	40	30
358	A185	20c	Ukrainian SSR	40	30
359	A185	20c	Kuwait	40	30
360	A185	20c	Sudan	40	30
361	A185	20c	Egypt	40	30
362	A185	20c	US	40	30
363	A185	20c	Singapore	40	30
364	A185	20c	Panama	40	30
365	A185	20c	Costa Rica	40	30
		First day covers of Nos. 350-365 @			75

Seedling and Tree Cross-section—A194

"10" and Symbols of Progress—A195
United Nations Volunteers Program, 10th anniv.
Printed by Walsall Security Printers, Ltd., United Kingdom. Pane of 50.
Designed by Gabriele Nussgen (18c),
Angel Medina Medina (28c).

1981, Nov. 13 Litho.

366	A194	18c multi *(1,900,000)*	45	30
		First day cover		70
		Margin block of 4, inscription	2.00	
367	A195	28c multi *(1,600,000)*	70	45
		First day cover		1.00
		First day cover, #366-367		1.25
		Margin block of 4, inscription	3.00	

See Offices in Geneva Nos. 103-104; Offices in Vienna Nos. 22-23.

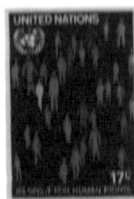

Respect for
Human Rights
A196

Independence of Colonial
Countries and People
A197

Second Disarmament Decade—A198
Printed by Courvoisier, S.A., Switzerland. Sheets of 50.
Designed by Rolf Christianson (17c); George Hamori (28c); Marek Kwiatkowski (40c).

PHOTOGRAVURE

1982, Jan. 22 *Perf. 11½x12*

368	A196	17c multicolored *(3,000,000)*	35	15
		First day cover		55
		Margin block of 4, inscription	1.45	
369	A197	28c multicolored *(3,000,000)*	56	25
		First day cover		1.00
		Margin block of 4, inscription	2.30	
370	A198	40c multicolored *(3,000,000)*	80	40
		First day cover		1.50
		First day cover, #368-370		1.75
		Margin block of 4, inscription	3.25	

Sun and Hand
Holding
Seedling
A199

Sun, Plant
Land and
Water
A200

10th Anniversary of United Nations Environment Program.
Printed by Joh. Enschede En Zonen, Netherlands. Panes of 50.
Designed by Philine Hartert (20c); Peer-Ulrich Bremer (40c).

1982, Mar. 19 Lithographed *Perf. 13½x13*

371	A199	20c multicolored *(1,900,000)*	50	35
		First day cover		75
		Margin block of 4, inscription	2.25	
372	A200	40c multicolored *(1,600,000)*	1.00	70
		First day cover		1.50
		First day cover, #371-372		1.75
		Margin block of 4, inscription	4.50	

See Offices in Geneva Nos. 107-108; Offices in Vienna Nos. 25-26.

U.N. Emblem and Olive Branch in Outer Space—A201

Exploration and Peaceful Uses of Outer Space.
Printed By Enschede. Panes of 50. Designed by Wiktor C. Nerwinski.

UNITED NATIONS

1982, June 11		Lithographed	Perf. 13x13½	
373	A201 20c	multicolored (1,900,000)	50	35
		First day cover		75
		Margin block of 4, inscription	2.25	

See Offices in Geneva Nos. 109-110; Offices in Vienna No. 27.

Flag Type of 1980

Printed by Courvoisier. Sheets of 16.
Designed by Ole Hamann.

Issued in 4 sheets of 16. Each sheet contains 4 blocks of four (Nos. 374-377, 378-381, 383-385, 386-389). A se-tenant block of 4 designs centers each sheet.

1982, Sept. 24		Lithographed	Perf. 12	
374	A185 20c	Austria	40	25
375	A185 20c	Malaysia	40	25
376	A185 20c	Seychelles	40	25
377	A185 20c	Ireland	40	25
378	A185 20c	Mozambique	40	25
379	A185 20c	Albania	40	25
380	A185 20c	Dominica	40	25
381	A185 20c	Solomon Islands	40	25
382	A185 20c	Philippines	40	25
383	A185 20c	Swaziland	40	25
384	A185 20c	Nicaragua	40	25
385	A185 20c	Burma	40	25
386	A185 20c	Cape Verde	40	25
387	A185 20c	Guyana	40	25
388	A185 20c	Belgium	40	25
389	A185 20c	Nigeria	40	25
		First day cover, #374-389		75

Printing order 5,000,000 each.

A202
Conservation and Protection of Nature
Printed by Fournier. Sheets of 50.
Designed by Hamori

1982, Nov. 19		Photogravure	Perf. 14	
390	A202 20c	Leaf	50	35
		First day cover		75
		margin block of 4, inscription	2.25	
391	A202 28c	Butterfly	70	45
		First day cover		1.00
		Margin block of f, inscription	3.00	

See Office in Geneva Nos. 111-112, Offices in Vienna Nos. 28-29.

A203

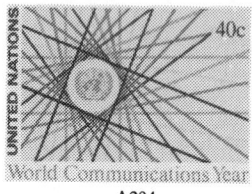

A204

World Communications Year
Printed by Walsal. Panes of 50. Designed by Hanns Lohrer (A203) and Lorena Berengo (A204).

1983, Jan. 28		Lithography	Perf. 13	
392	A203	20c multi (1,700,000)	40	20
		First Day Cover		75
		Margin block of 4, inscription	2.00	
393	A204	40c multi (1,400,000)	80	40
		First Day Cover		1.50
		First Day Cover, Nos. 392-393		1.75
		Margin block of 4, inscription	4.00	

See Offices in Geneva No. 113, Offices in Vienna No. 30.

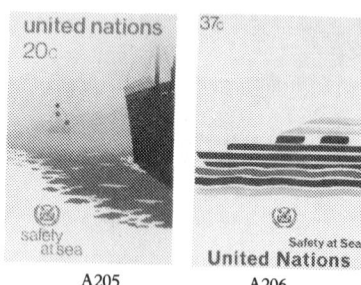

A205 A206

Safety at Sea

Printed by Questa. Panes of 50. Designed by Jean-Marie Lenfant (A205), Ari Ron (A206).

1983, Mar. 18		Lithographed	Perf. 14½	
394	A205	20c multi (1,700,000)	40	20
		First Day Cover		75
		Margin block of 4, inscription	2.00	
395	A206	37c multi (1,400,000)	75	38
		First Day Cover		1.50
		First Day Cover, Nos. 394-395		1.75
		Margin block of 4, inscription	3.75	

See Offices in Geneva Nos. 114-115, Offices in Vienna Nos. 31-32.

A207
World Food Program

Printed by Government Printers Bureau, Japan. Designed by Marek Kwiatskoski.

1983, Apr. 22		Engraved	Perf. 13½	
396	A207	20c multi (1,700,000)	40	20
		First Day Cover		75
		Margin block of 4, inscription	2.00	

See Office in Geneva Nos. 116, Offices in Vienna Nos. 33-34.

UNITED NATIONS

 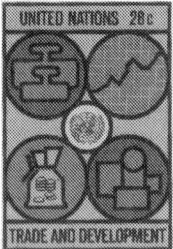

A208　　　　　A209

UN Conference on Trade and Development

Printed by Carl Uberreuter Druck and Vergal M. Salzer, Austria. Panes of 50. Designed by Dietmar Braklow (A208), Gabriel Genz (A209).

1983, June 6		Lithographed	Perf. 14	
397	A208	20c multi (1,500,000)	40	20
		First Day Cover		75
		Margin block of 4, inscription	2.00	
398	A209	37c multi (1,400,000)	80	40
		First Day Cover		1.00
		First Day Cover, Nos. 397-398		1.25
		Margin block of 4, inscription	3.75	

See Offices in Geneva Nos. 117-118, Offices in Vienna Nos. 35-36.

Flag Type of 1980

Printed by Courvoisier. Sheets of 16. Designed by Ole Hamann. Issued in 4 sheets of 16. Each sheet contains 4 blocks of four (Nos. 399-402, 403-406, 407-410, 411-414). A se-tenant block of 4 designs centers each sheet.

1983, Sept. 23		Photogravure	Perf. 12	
399	A185	20c Great Britain	40	20
400	A185	20c Barbados	40	20
401	A185	20c Nepal	40	20
402	A185	20c Israel	40	20
403	A185	20c Malawi	40	20
404	A185	20c Byelorussian SSR	40	20
405	A185	20c Jamaica	40	20
406	A185	20c Kenya	40	20
407	A185	20c People's Republic of China	40	20
408	A185	20c Peru	40	20
409	A185	20c Bulgaria	40	20
410	A185	20c Canada	40	20
411	A185	20c Somalia	40	20
412	A185	20c Senegal	40	20
413	A185	20c Brazil	40	20
414	A185	20c Sweden	40	20
		First Day Cover, #399-414 each		75
Print order 4,000,000 each.				

Window Right　　　Peace Treaty with Nature
A210　　　　　　　A211

35th Anniversary of the Universal Declaration of Human Rights

Printed by Government Printing Office, Austria. Designed by Friedensreich Hundertwasser, Austria. Panes of 16 (4x4).

1983, Dec. 9		Photo. & Engraved	Perf. 13½	
415	A210	20c multi	40	20
		First Day Cover		75
416	A211	40c multi	80	40
		First Day Cover		1.50
		First Day Cover, Nos. 392-393		1.75

See Offices in Geneva Nos. 119-120; Vienna Nos. 37-38.

International Conference on Population—A212

Printed by Bundesdruckerei, Federal Republic of Germany. Panes of 50. Designed by Marina Langer-Rosa and Helmut Langer, Federal Republic of Germany.

1984, Feb. 3		Lithographed	Perf. 14	
417	A212	20c multi	40	20
		First Day Cover		75
		Margin block of 4, inscription	2.00	
418	A212	40c multi	80	40
		First Day Cover		1.50
		First Day Cover, Nos. 417-418		1.75
		Margin block of 4, inscription	4.00	

See Offices in Geneva No. 121; Vienna No. 39.

Tractor Plowing—A213

Rice Paddy—A214

World Food Day, Oct. 16

Printed by Walsall Security Printers, Ltd., United Kingdom. Panes of 50. Designed by Adth Vanooijen, Netherlands.

1984, Mar. 15		Lithographed	Perf. 14½	
419	A213	20c multi	40	20
		First Day Cover		75
		Margin block of 4, inscription	2.00	
420	A214	40c multi	80	40
		First Day Cover		1.50
		First Day Cover, Nos. 419-420		1.75
		Margin block of 4, inscription	4.00	

See Offices in Geneva Nos. 122-123; Vienna Nos. 40-41.

950 UNITED NATIONS

Grand Canyon—A215

Ancient City of Polonnaruwa, Sri Lanka—A216

World Heritage

Printed by Harrison and Sons, United Kingdom. Panes of 50. Designs adapted by Rocco J. Callari, U.S., and Thomas Lee, China.

1984, Apr. 18		Lithographed	Perf. 14	
421	A215	20c multi	40	20
		First Day Cover		75
		Margin block of 4, inscription	2.00	—
422	A216	50c multi	1.00	50
		First Day Cover		1.75
		First Day Cover, Nos. 421-422		2.00
		Margin block of 4, inscription	5.00	—

See Offices in Geneva Nos. 124-125; Vienna Nos. 42-43.

A217 A218

Future for Refugees

Printed by Courvoisier. Panes of 50. Designed by Hans Erni, Switzerland.

1984, May 29		Photogravure	Perf. 11½	
423	A217	20c multi	40	20
		First Day Cover		75
		Margin block of 4, inscription	2.00	—
424	A218	50c multi	1.00	50
		First Day Cover		1.75
		First Day Cover, Nos. 423-424		2.00
		Margin block of 4, inscription	5.00	—

See Offices in Geneva Nos. 126-127; Vienna Nos. 44-45.

Flag Type of 1980

Printed by Courvoisier. Sheets of 16. Designed by Ole Hamann. Issued in 4 sheets of 16. Each sheet contains 4 blocks of four (Nos. 425-428, 429-432, 433-436, 437-440). A se-tenant block of 4 designs centers each sheet.

1984, Sept. 21		Photogravure	Perf. 12	
425	A185	20c Burundi	40	20
426	A185	20c Pakistan	40	20
427	A185	20c Benin	40	20
428	A185	20c Italy	40	20
429	A185	20c Tanzania	40	20
430	A185	20c United Arab Emirates	40	20
431	A185	20c Ecuador	40	20
432	A185	20c Bahamas	40	20
433	A185	20c Poland	40	20
434	A185	20c Papua New Guinea	40	20
435	A185	20c Uruguay	40	20
436	A185	20c Chile	40	20
437	A185	20c Paraguay	40	20
438	A185	20c Bhutan	40	20
439	A185	20c Central African Republic	40	20
440	A185	20c Australia	40	20
		First Day Cover, each		75

International Youth Year — A219

Printed by Waddingtons Ltd., United Kingdom. Panes of 50. Designed by Ramon Mueller, Federal Republic of Germany.

1984, Nov. 15		Lithographed	Perf 13½	
441	A219	20c multi (1,400,000)*	40	20
		First day cover		75
		Margin block of 4, inscription	2.00	—
442	A219	35c multi (1,400,000)*	70	35
		First day cover		1.25
		First day cover, Nos. 441-442		1.50
		Margin block of 4, inscription	3.50	—

See offices in Geneva, No. 128; Office in Vienna, Nos. 46-47.

*Initial print order.

ILO Turin Center — A220

Printed by the Government Printing Bureau, Japan. Panes of 50. Engraved by Mamoru Iwakuni and Hiroshi Ozaki, Japan.

1985, Feb. 1		Engraved	Perf. 13½	
443	A220	23c Turin Center emblem (1,400,000)*	46	24
		First day cover		85
		Margin block of 4, inscription	2.30	—

See Office in Geneva, Nos. 129-130; Office in Vienna, No. 48.

*Initial print order.

UNITED NATIONS

U.N. University — A221

Printed by Helio Courvoiser, Switzerland. Panes of 50. Designed by Moshe Pereg, Israel, and Hinedi Geluda, Brazil.

1985, Mar. 15			Photogravure		Perf. 13½	
444	A221	50c	Farmer plowing, discussion group *(1,400,000)**		1.00	50
			First day cover			2.00
			Margin block of 4, inscription		5.00	—

See Office in Geneva, Nos. 131-132; Office in Vienna, No. 49

*Initial print order.

People's of the World United
A222

Painting U.N. Emblem
A223

Printed by Carl Ueberreuter Druck and Verlag M. Salzer, Austria. Panes of 50. Designed by Fritz Henry Oerter, Federal Republic of Germany (22c), and Rimondi Rino, Italy ($3).

1985, May 10			Lithographed		Perf. 14	
445	A222	22c	multi *(2,000,000)**		44	22
			First day cover			80
			Margin block of 4, inscription		2.20	—
446	A223	$3	multi *(2,000,000)**		6.00	3.00
			First day cover			11.00
			First day cover, Nos. 445-446			11.50
			Margin block of 4, inscription		30.00	—

See Office in Geneva, Nos. 133-134; Office in Vienna, Nos. 50-51.

*Initial print order.

The Corner, 1947
A224

Alvaro Raking Hay, 1953
A225

U.N. 40th anniversary. Oil paintings (details) by American artist Andrew Wyeth (b. 1917). Printed by Helio Courvoisier, Switzerland. Panes of 50. Designed by Rocco J. Callari, U.S., and Thomas Lee, China (#449).

1985, June 26			Photogravure	Perf. 12 x 11½	
447	A224	22c	multi *(1,400,000)**	44	22
			First day cover		80
			Margin block of 4, inscription	2.20	—
448	A225	45c	multi *(1,400,000)**	90	45
			First day cover		1.60
			First day cover, Nos. 447-448		1.90
			Margin block of 4, inscription	4.50	—

Souvenir Sheet
Imperf.

449	Sheet of 2 *(1,400,000)*	1.35	1.35
	a. A224 22c multi	44	
	b. A225 45c multi	90	
	First day cover		2.50

No. 449 has multicolored margin containing inscription and U.N. emblem. Size: 75 x 83 mm. See Office in Geneva, Nos. 135-137; Office in Vienna, Nos. 52-54.

Flag Type of 1980

Printed by Helio Courvoisier, Switzerland. Designed by Ole Hamann. Issued in panes of 16; each contains 4 blocks of four (Nos. 450-453, 454-457, 458-461, 462-465). A se-tenant block of 4 designs is at the center of each sheet.

1985, Sept. 20			Photogravure	Perf. 12	
450	A185	22c	Grenada	44	22
451	A185	22c	Federal Republic of Germany	44	22
452	A185	22c	Saudi Arabia	44	22
453	A185	22c	Mexico	44	22
454	A185	22c	Uganda	44	22
455	A185	22c	St. Thomas & Prince	44	22
456	A185	22c	USSR	44	22
457	A185	22c	India	44	22
458	A185	22c	Liberia	44	22
459	A185	22c	Mauritius	44	22
460	A185	22c	Chad	44	22
461	A185	22c	Dominican Republic	44	22
462	A185	22c	Sultanate of Oman	44	22
463	A185	22c	Ghana	44	22
464	A185	22c	Sierra Leone	44	22
465	A185	22c	Finland	44	22
			First day covers, Nos. 450-465 @		80

Print order 2,500,000 each.

UNICEF Child Survival Campaign — A226

Printed by the Government Printing Bureau, Japan. Panes of 50. Designed by Mel Harris, United Kingdom (#466) and Dipok Deyi, India (#467).

1985, Nov. 22			Photo, & Engr.	Perf. 13½	
466	A226	22c	Asian Toddler *(1,200,000)*	44	22
			First day cover		80
			Margin block of 4, inscription	2.20	—
467	A226	33c	Breastfeeding *(1,200,000)*	66	32
			First day cover		1.15
			First day cover, Nos. 466-467		1.50
			Margin block of 4, inscription	3.30	—

See Office in Geneva, Nos. 138-139; Office in Vienna, Nos. 55-56.

UNITED NATIONS

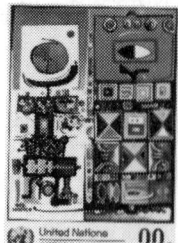

Africa in Crisis—A227

Printed by Helio Courvoisier, Switzerland. Panes of 50. Designed by Wosene Kosrof, Ethiopia.

1986, Jan. 31		Photo.	Perf. 11½x12	
468	A227	22c multi *(1,200,000)**	44	22
		First day cover		80
		Margin block of 4, inscription	2.20	—

Campaign against hunger. See Offices in Geneva, No. 140; Vienna, No. 57.

Water Resources—A228

Printed by the Government Printing Bureau, Japan. Panes of 40, 2 blocks of 4 horizontal and 5 blocks of 4 vertical. Designed by Thomas Lee, China.

1986, Mar. 14		Photo.	Perf. 13½	
469	A228	22c Dam *(1,600,000)**	44	22
		First day cover		80
470	A228	22c Irrigation *(1,600,000)**	44	22
		First day cover		80
471	A228	22c Hygiene *(1,600,000)**	44	22
		First day cover		80
472	A228	22c Well *(1,600,000)**	44	22
		First day cover		80
		First day cover, #469-472		2.25
		Margin block of 4, #469-472, inscription	2.20	—
		a. Block of 4, #469-472	1.80	88

U.N. Development Program. Nos. 469-472 printed se-tenant in a continuous design. See Offices in Geneva, Nos. 141-144; Vienna, Nos. 58-61.

Human Rights Stamp of 1954—A229

Stamp collecting: 44c, Engraver. Printed by the Swedish Post Office, Sweden. Panes of 50. Designed by Czeslaw Slania and Ingalill Axelsson, Sweden.

1986, May 22		Engraved	Perf. 12½	
473	A229	22c dk vio & brt bl *(1,200,000)**	44	22
		First day cover		80
		Margin block of 4, inscription	2.20	—
474	A229	44c brn & emer grn *(1,200,000)**	88	44
		First day cover		1.25
		First day cover, #473-474		1.75
		Margin block of 4, inscription	4.40	—

See Offices in Geneva, Nos. 146-147; Vienna, Nos. 62-63.

Bird's Nest in Tree—A230   Peace in Seven Languages—A231

Printed by the Government Printing Bureau, Japan. Panes of 50. Designed by Akira Iriguchi, Japan (#475), and Henryk Chylinski, Poland (#476).

1986, June 20		Photo. & Embossed	Perf. 13½	
475	A230	22c multi *(1,200,000)**	44	22
		First day cover		80
		Margin block of 4, inscription	2.20	—
476	A231	33c multi *(1,200,000)**	66	32
		First day cover		1.05
		First day cover, #475-476		1.50
		Margin block of 4, inscription	3.30	—

International Peace Year. See Offices in Geneva, Nos. 148-149; Vienna, Nos. 64-65.

Flag Type of 1980

Printed by Helio Courvoisier, Switzerland. Designed by Ole Hamman. Issued in panes of 16; each contains 4 blocks of four (Nos. 477-480, 481-484, 485-488, 489-492). A se-tenant block of 4 designs is at the center of each sheet.

1986, Sept. 19		Photo.		Perf.
477	A185	22c New Zealand	44	22
478	A185	22c Lao PDR	44	22
479	A185	22c Burkina Faso	44	22
480	A185	22c Gambia	44	22
481	A185	22c Maldives	44	22
482	A185	22c Ethiopia	44	22
483	A185	22c Jordan	44	22
484	A185	22c Zambia	44	22
485	A185	22c Iceland	44	22
486	A185	22c Antigua & Barbuda	44	22
487	A185	22c Angola	44	22
488	A185	22c Botswana	44	22
489	A185	22c Romania	44	22
490	A185	22c Togo	44	22
491	A185	22c Mauritania	44	22
492	A185	22c Colombia	44	22
		First day covers, Nos. 477-492 @		80

Print order 2,500,000 each.
*Initial print order.

Souvenir Sheet

World Federation of U.N. Associations, 40th Anniversary—A232

Printed by Johann Enschede and Sons, Netherlands. Designed by Rocco J. Callari, U.S.

Designs: 22c, Mother Earth, by Edna Hibel, U.S. 33c, Watercolor by Salvador Dali (b. 1904) Spain. 39c, New Dawn, by Dong Kingman, U.S. 44c, Watercolor by Chaim Gross, U.S.

1986, Nov. 14	Litho.		Perf.
493	Sheet of 4 *(1,800,000)**	2.80	2.80
	a. A232 22c multi	44	22
	b. A232 33c multi	66	33
	c. A232 39c multi	78	39
	d. A232 44c multi	88	44
	First day cover		3.25

See Offices in Geneva, No. 150; Vienna, No. 66. No. 493 has inscribed margin picturing U.N. and WFUNA emblems. Size:

UNITED NATIONS
1985

Flags

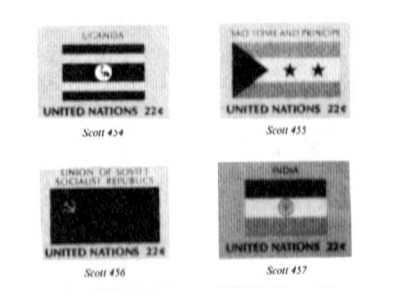

COLLECT THE SCOTT WAY...
WITH SCOTT'S TWO U.N. ALBUMS

U.N. IMPRINT BLOCKS ($59.95)

U.N. SINGLES
AND
POSTAL STATIONERY ($52.95)

FEATURING:

- Spaces for all United Nations stamps, including New York, Vienna and Geneva issues.
- Each stamp pictured or described and arranged in order by Scott number.
- A handsome, sturdy binder is standard with this album - not tacked on at an extra cost.
- Chemically neutralized paper protects your stamps for generations.

- Paper just the right thickness to make collecting a pleasure.
- Yearly supplement available.

Both albums through 1985

AVAILABLE NOW AT
YOUR LOCAL DEALER
OR DIRECT FROM:

P.O. BOX 828, SIDNEY, OH 45365

AIR POST STAMPS

Plane and Gull—AP1

Swallows and U.N. Emblem—AP2

Engraved and printed by Thomas De La Rue & Co., Ltd., London. Panes of 50. Designed by Ole Hamann (AP1) and Olav Mathiesen (AP2).

1951, Dec. 14   *Perf. 14*   Unwmkd.

C1	AP1	6c henna brown *(2,500,000)*	15	15
		First day cover		1.25
		Margin block of 4, inscription	75	75
C2	"	10c bright blue green *(2,750,000)*	35	35
		First day cover		1.50
		Margin block of 4, inscription	1.60	1.50
C3	AP2	15c deep ultramarine *(3,250,000)*	1.00	50
		Prussian blue	150.00	
		First day cover		2.25
		Margin block of 4, inscription	4.50	2.25
C4	"	25c gray black *(2,250,000)*	4.50	3.00
		First day cover		7.00
		First day cover, #C1-C4		9.00
		Margin block of 4, inscription	22.50	14.00

First day covers of Nos. 1-11 and C1-C4 total 1,113,216. Early printings of Nos. C1-C4 have wide, imperforate sheet margins on three sides. Later printings were perforated through all margins.

Nos. C1, C3 and C4 exist imperforate.

Airplane Wing and Globe
AP3

Engraved and printed by Thomas De La Rue & Co., Ltd., London. Panes of 50. Designed by W. W. Wind.

1957, May 27   *Perf. 12½x14*

C5	AP3	4c maroon *(5,000,000)*	8	6
		First day cover *(282,933)*		35
		Margin block of 4, inscription	35	25

Type of 1957 and

U. N. Flag and Plane—AP4

Engraved and printed by Waterlow & Sons, Ltd., London. Panes of 50. Designed by W. W. Wind (5c) and Olav Mathiesen (7c).

1959, Feb. 9   *Perf. 12½x13½*   Unwmkd.

C6	AP3	5c rose red *(4,000,000)*	10	8
		First day cover		40
		Margin block of 4, inscription	50	40

Perf. 13½x14

C7	AP4	7c ultramarine *(4,000,000)*	14	10
		First day cover		50
		First day cover, #C6-C7		75
		Margin block of 4, inscription	65	45

First day covers of Nos. C6 and C7 total 413,556.

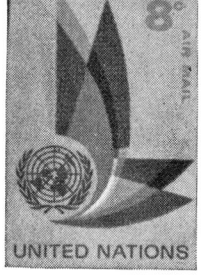

Outer Space
AP5

U.N. Emblem   Bird of Laurel Leaves
AP6   AP7

Printed by Courvoisier S.A., La Chaux-de-Fonds, Switzerland. Panes of 50. Designed by Claude Bottiau (6c), George Hamori (8c) and Kurt Plowitz (13c).

Photogravure

1963, June 17   *Perf. 11½*   Unwmkd.

C8	AP5	6c black, blue & yellow green *(4,000,000)*	12	10
		First day cover		35
		Margin block of 4, inscription	60	50
C9	AP6	8c yellow, olive green & red *(4,000,000)*	16	12
		First day cover		40
		Margin block of 4, inscription	80	55

Perf. 12½x12

C10	AP7	13c ultra., aquamarine, gray & carmine *(2,700,000)*	25	20
		First day cover		60
		First day cover, #C8-C10		1.00
		Margin block of 4, inscription	1.15	90

First day covers of Nos. C8-C10 total 535,824.

"Flight Across the Globe"   Jet Plane and Envelope
AP8   AP9

Printed by the Austrian Government Printing Office, Vienna, Austria. Panes of 50. Designed by Ole Hamann (15c) and George Hamori (25c).

UNITED NATIONS

Photogravure
1964, May 1   *Perf. 11½x12, 12x00½*   Unwmkd.

C11	AP8	15c violet, buff, gray & pale green *(3,000,000)*	40	30
		First day cover		75
		Margin block of 4, inscription	1.85	1.30
		a. Gray omitted		
C12	AP9	25c yellow, orange, gray, blue & red *(2,000,000)*	1.50	60
		First day cover		1.20
		First day cover, #C11-C12		1.75
		Margin block of 4, inscription	6.75	2.75

First day covers of Nos. C11–C12 total 353,696.
For 75c in type AP8, see U.N. Offices in Geneva No. 8.
Nos. C11–C12 exist imperforate.

Jet Plane and U.N. Emblem
AP10

Printed by Setelipaino, Finland. Panes of 50. Designed by Ole Hamann.

1968, Apr. 18   Lithographed   *Perf. 13*

C13	AP10	20c multicolored *(3,000,000)*	40	35
		First day cover *(225,378)*		1.00
		Margin block of 4, inscription	1.85	1.50

Wings, Envelopes and U.N. Emblem
AP11

Printed by Setelipaino, Finland. Panes of 50. Designed by Olav S. Mathiesen.

1969, Apr. 21   Lithographed   *Perf. 13*

C14	AP11	10c orange vermilion, orange, yellow & black *(4,000,000)*	25	20
		First day cover *(132,686)*		40
		Margin block of 4, inscription	1.15	90

U.N. Emblem and Stylized Wing
AP12

Birds in Flight
AP13

Clouds
AP14

"UN" and Plane
AP15

Printed by Government Printing Bureau, Japan (9c); Heraclio Fournier, S. A., Spain (11c, 17c); Setelipaino, Finland (21c). Panes of 50. Designed by Lyell L. Dolan (9c), Arne Johnson (11c), British American Bank Note Co. (17c) and Asher Kalderon (21c).

1972, May 1   Litho. & Engr.   *Perf. 13x13½*

C15	AP12	9c lt. blue, dk. red & vio. blue *(3,000,000)**	18	15
		First day cover		40
		Margin block of 4, inscription	90	70

Photogravure   *Perf. 14x13½*

C16	AP13	11c blue & multicolored *(3,000,000)**	22	15
		First day cover		50
		Margin block of 4, inscription	1.10	70

Perf. 13½x14

C17	AP14	17c yellow, red & orange *(3,000,000)**	34	25
		First day cover		75
		Margin block of 4, inscription	1.60	1.25

Perf. 13

C18	AP15	21c silver & multi. *(3,500,000)**	42	35
		First day cover		90
		First day cover, #C15-C18		1.85
		Margin block of 4, inscription	2.05	1.65

*Printing orders to Nov. 1979.
First day covers of Nos. C15–C18 total 553,535.

Globe and Jet
AP16

Pathways Radiating from UN Emblem
AP17

Bird in Flight, UN Headquarters
AP18

Printed by Setelipaino, Finland. Panes of 50. Designed by George Hamori (13c), Shamir Bros. (18c) and Olav S. Mathiesen (26c).

1974, Sept. 16   Litho.   *Perf. 13, 12½x13 (18c)*

C19	AP16	13c multicolored *(2,500,000)**	26	22
		First day cover		70
		Margin block of 4, inscription	1.10	1.00
C20	AP17	18c gray olive & multicolored *(2,000,000)**	36	30
		First day cover		1.15
		Margin block of 4, inscription	1.50	1.35
C21	AP18	26c blue & multi. *(2,000,000)**	52	45
		First day cover		1.00
		First day cover, #C19-C21		1.75
		Margin block of 4, inscription	2.35	2.25

* Initial printing order.
First day covers of Nos. C19–C21 total 309,610.

UNITED NATIONS

Winged Airmail Letter
AP19

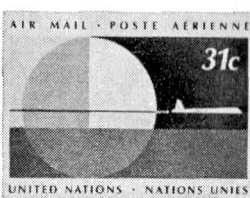

Symbolic Globe and Plane
AP20

Printed by Heraclio Fournier, S.A. Panes of 50. Designed by Eliezer Weishoff (25c) and Alan L. Pollock (31c).

			1977, June 27	Photogravure	Perf. 14
C22	AP19	25c	greenish blue & multi. (2,000,000)*	50	25
			First day cover		85
			Margin block of 4, inscription	2.50	—
C23	AP20	31c	magenta (2,000,000)*	62	30
			First day cover		1.00
			Margin block of 4, inscription	3.10	—

* Initial printing order.
First day covers of Nos. C22–C23 total 209,060.

ENVELOPES

Emblem of United Nations
E1

Printed by the International Envelope Corp., Dayton, Ohio. Die engraved by the American Bank Note Co., New York.

			1953, Sept. 15		Embossed
U1	E1	3c	blue, entire (555,000)	75	25
			Entire, first day cancel (102,278)		1.25

Printed by International Envelope Corp., Dayton, O.

			1958, Sept. 22		Embossed
U2	E1	4c	ultramarine, entire (1,000,000)	45	25
			Entire, first day cancel (213,621)		30

Stylized Globe and Weather Vane
E2

Printed by United States Envelope Co., Springfield, Mass. Designed by Hatim El Mekki.

			1963, Apr. 26		Lithographed	
U3	E2	5c	multicolored entire (1,115,888)		15	10
			Entire, first day cancel (165,188)			40

Printed by Setelipaino, Finland.

			1969, Jan. 8		Lithographed	
U4	E2	6c	black, bl., magenta & dull yel., entire (850,000)		25	20
			Entire, first day cancel (152,593)			40

Headquarters Type of Regular Issue, 1968
Printed by Eureka Co., a division of Litton Industries.

			1973, Jan. 12		Lithographed	
U5	A99	8c	sepia, blue & olive, entire (700,000)		20	15
			Entire, first day cancel (145,510)			50

Headquarters Type of Regular Issue, 1974
Printed by United States Envelope Co., Springfield, Mass.

			1975, Jan. 10		Lithographed		
U6	A138	10c	blue, olive bister & multi., entire (525,000)*30			20	
			Entire, first day cancel (122,000)			60	

* Initial printing order.

Bouquet of Ribbons — E3

Printed by Carl Ueberreuter Druck and Verlag M. Salzer, Austria. Designed by George Hamori, Australia.

			1985, May 10		Lithographed	
U7	E3	22c	multi, entire (250,000)*		50	25
			Entire, first day cancel			80

*Initial print order.

UNITED NATIONS

AIR POST ENVELOPES AND AIR LETTER SHEETS
Letter Sheet.
Type of Air Post Stamp of 1951.
Printed by Dennison & Sons, Long Island City, N. Y.

1952, Aug. 29   Lithographed

UC1	AP2	10c blue, *bluish (187,000)*, inscribed "Air Letter" at left, entire	32.50	3.50
		Entire, first day cancel *(57,274)*		5.50

Designed by C. Mutver.

Letter Sheet
1954-58   Lithographed

UC2	AP2	10c royal blue, *bluish*, inscribed "Air Letter" and "Aerogramme" at left, entire, *Sept. 14, 1954 (207,000)*	8.50	1.50
		Entire, first day cancel		
	a.	No white border ('58) *(148,800)*	5.50	1.00

No. UC2 was printed with a narrow white border (½ to 1mm. wide) surrounding the stamp. On No. UC2a, this border has been partly or entirely eliminated.

U. N. Flag and Plane—UC1
(U. N. Emblem Embossed)

Printed by International Envelope Corp., Dayton, O.
Die engraved by American Bank Note Co., New York.

1959, Sept. 21   Embossed

UC3	UC1	7c blue, entire *(550,000)*	2.75	75
		Entire, first day cancel *(172,107)*		1.00

Letter Sheet.
Type of Air Post Stamp of 1959.
Printed by Thomas De La Rue & Co., Ltd., London.

1960, Jan. 18   Lithographed

UC4	AP4	10c ultramarine, *bluish*, entire *(405,000)*	65	25
		Entire, first day cancel *(122,425)*		50

Printed on protective tinted paper containing colorless inscription "United Nations" in the five official languages of the U.N.

958 UNITED NATIONS

Letter Sheet.
Type of Air Post Stamp of 1951.
Inscribed "Correo Aereo" instead of "Poste Aerienne".
Printed by Thomas De La Rue & Co., Ltd., London.

1961-65 Lithographed

UC5	AP1	11c ultramarine, *bluish*, entire, June 26, 1961 *(550,000)*	25	20
		Entire, first day cancel *(128,557)*		50
	a.	11c dark blue, *green* entire, July 16, 1965 *(419,000)*	1.00	25

Printed on protective tinted paper containing colorless inscription "United Nations" in the five official languages of the U.N.

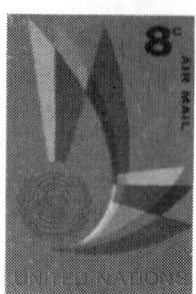

U.N. Emblem
UC2

Printed by United States Envelope Co., Springfield, Mass. Designed by George Hamori.

1963, Apr. 26 Lithographed

UC6	UC2	8c multicolored, entire *(880,000)*	25	15
		Entire, first day cancel *(165,208)*		40

Letter Sheet.

U.N. Emblem and Stylized Plane
UC3

Printed by Setelipaino, Finland. Designed by Robert Perrot.

1968, May 31 Lithographed

UC7	UC3	13c violet blue & light blue, entire *(750,000)*	30	23
		Entire, first day cancel *(106,700)*		65

Type of 1963
Printed by Setelipaino, Finland.

1969, Jan. 8 Lithographed

UC8	UC2	10c pink, Prussian blue, orange & sepia, entire *(750,000)*	30	20
		Entire, first day cancel *(153,472)*		50

Letter Sheet

U.N. Emblem, "UN," Globe and Plane—UC4

Printed by Joh. Enschedé and Sons. Designed by Edmondo Calivis, Egypt. Sheet surface printed in greenish blue.

1972, Oct. 16 Lithographed

UC9	UC4	15c violet blue & greenish blue, entire *(500,000)*	35	12
		Entire, first day cancel *(85,500)*		65

Bird Type of Air Post Stamp, 1972
Printed by Eureka Co., a division of Litton Industries.

1973, Jan. 12 Lithographed

UC10	AP13	11c blue & multicolored, entire *(700,000)*	25	20
		Entire, first day cancel *(134,500)*		45

Globe and Jet Air Post Type of 1974.
Printed by United States Envelope Co., Springfield, Mass.

1975, Jan. 10 Lithographed

UC11	AP16	13c blue & multicolored, entire *(525,000)**	30	25
		Entire, first day cancel *(122,500)*		50

* Initial printing order.

Letter Sheet
Headquarters Type of Regular Issue, 1971
Printed by Joh. Enschede and Sons, Netherlands.

1975, Jan. 10 Photogravure

UC12	A120	18c blue & multi., entire *(400,000)*	45	20
		Entire, first day cancel *(70,500)*		60

Letter Sheet

"UN" Emblem and Birds
UC5

Printed by Joh. Enschedé and Sons. Designed by Angel Medina Medina.

1977, June 27 Lithographed

UC13	UC5	22c multicolored, entire *(400,000)*	44	25
		Entire, first day cancel *(70,000)*		80

Paper Airplane—UC6
Printed by Joh. Enschede and Sons.
Designed by Margaret-Ann Champion.

1982, Apr. 28 Lithographed

UC14	UC6	30c black, *pale green*, entire *(400,000)**	60	35
		Entire, first day cancel		60

*Initial printing order.

UNITED NATIONS

POSTAL CARDS
Prices are for entire cards.
Type of Postage Issue of 1951.
Printed by Dennison & Sons, Long Island City, N. Y.

1952, July 18					Lithographed
UX1	A2	2c	blue, *buff (899,415)*	20	15
			First day cancel *(116,023)*		45

Printed by British American Bank Note Co., Ltd., Ottawa, Canada.

1958, Sept. 22					Lithographed
UX2	A2	3c	gray olive, *buff (575,000)*	40	15
			First day cancel *(145,557)*		20

World Map, Sinusoidal Projection
PC1

Printed by Eureka Specialty Printing Co., Scranton, Pa.

1963, Apr. 26					Lithographed
UX3	PC1	4c	light blue, violet blue, orange & bright citron *(784,000)*	10	7
			First day cancel *(112,280)*		20
		a.	Bright citron omitted		

U.N. Emblem and Post Horn
PC2

Printed by Canadian Bank Note Co., Ltd., Ottawa. Designed by John Mason.

1969, Jan. 8					Lithographed
UX4	PC2	5c	blue & black *(500,000)*	10	5
			First day cancel *(95,975)*		25

"UN"
PC3

Printed by Government Printing Bureau, Tokyo. Designed by Asher Kalderon.

1973, Jan. 12					Lithographed
UX5	PC3	6c	gray & multicolored *(500,000)*	15	6
			First day cancel *(84,500)*		30

Type of 1973
Printed by Setelipaino, Finland.

1975, Jan. 10					Lithographed
UX6	PC3	8c	light green & multicolored *(450,000)*	20	8
			First day cancel *(72,500)*		35

U.N. Emblem
PC4

Printed by Setelipaino, Finland. Designed by George Hamori.

1977, June 27					Lithographed
UX7	PC4	9c	multicolored *(350,000)*	30	8
			First day cancel *(70,000)*		45

PC5

Printed by Courvoisier. Designed by Salahattin Kanidinc.

1982, Apr. 28			**Photogravure**		
UX8	PC5	13c	multicolored *(350,000)**	30	15
			First day cancel		30

*Initial printing order.

AIR POST POSTAL CARDS
Prices are for entire cards.
Type of Air Post Stamp of 1957.
Printed by British American Bank Note Co., Ltd., Ottawa.

1957, May 27					Lithographed
UXC1	AP3	4c	maroon, *buff (631,000)*	10	10
			First day cancel *(260,005)*		20

No. UXC1 Surcharged in Maroon at Left of Stamp

1959, June 5					Lithographed
UXC2	AP3	4c	¢1c maroon, *buff (1,119,000)*	40	15
			Cancel first day of public use, June 8, 1959		18.00
		a.	Double surcharge		
		b.	Inverted surcharge		

Type of Air Post Stamp, 1957.
Printed by Eureka Specialty Printing Co., Scranton, Pa.

1959, Sept. 21					Lithographed
UXC3	AP3	5c	crimson, *buff (500,000)*	1.75	30
			First day cancel *(119,479)*		50

Outer Space—APC1
Printed by Eureka Specialty Printing Co., Scranton, Pa.

1963, Apr. 26		Lithographed		
UXC4	APC1 6c black & blue *(350,000)*		25	10
	First day cancel *(109,236)*			45

APC2
Printed by Eureka-Carlisle Co., Scranton, Pa. Designed by Olav S. Mathiesen.

1966, June 9		Lithographed		
UXC5	APC2 11c dark red, rose, yellow & brown *(764,500)*		25	11
	First day cancel *(162,588)*			50

1968, May 31		Lithographed		
UXC6	APC2 13c dark green, bright green & yellow *(829,000)*		30	13
	First day cancel *(106,500)*			60

U.N. Emblem and Stylized Planes
APC3
Printed by Canadian Bank Note Co., Ltd., Ottawa.
Designed by Lawrence Kurtz.

1969, Jan. 8		Lithographed		
UXC7	APC3 8c gray, dull yellow, lt. blue, indigo & red *(500,000)*		25	8
	First day cancel *(94,037)*			40

Type of Air Post Stamp of 1972
Printed by Government Printing Bureau, Tokyo. Designed by L. L. Dolan.

1972, Oct. 16		Lithographed		
UXC8	AP12 9c org., red, gray & green *(500,000)*		25	9
	First day cancel *(85,600)*			45

Type of 1969
Printed by Government Printing Bureau, Tokyo.

1972, Oct. 16		Lithographed		
UXC9	APC3 15c lilac, lt. blue, pink & car. *(500,000)*		40	15
	First day cancel *(84,800)*			75

Types of Air Post Stamps, 1972–74.
Printed by Setelipaino, Finland.

1975, Jan. 10		Lithographed		
UXC10	AP14 11c greenish bl., blue & dark blue *(250,000)*		30	11
	First day cancel *(70,500)*			55
UXC11	AP17 18c gray & multicolored *(250,000)*		45	18
	First day cancel *(70,500)*			90

Flying Mailman—APC4
Printed by Courvoisier. Designed by Arieh Glaser.

1982, Apr. 28		Photogravure		
UXC12	APC4 28c multicolored *(350,000)**		60	30
	First day cancel			60

SOUVENIR CARDS

These cards were issued by the United Nations Postal Administration and were not valid for postage.

Each card bears reproductions of U.N. stamps and a statement by the Secretary-General in English.

1 World Health Day, Apr. 7, 1972. Card of 5: Nos. 43, 102, 156, 207 and 228 — 3.50
A second printing shows several minor differences.
2 Art on U.N. Stamps, Nov. 17, 1972. Card of 11: Nos. 170–171, 173–174, 180, 183, 201–203, 224 and 232. Nos. 201–202 form a simulated se-tenant pair — 1.50
3 Disarmament Decade, Mar. 9, 1973. Card of 5: Nos. 133, 147, 177, 227 and 234 — 1.50
4 Declaration of Human Rights, 25th Anniversary, Nov. 16, 1973. Card of 10: Nos. 13, 22, 29, 39, 47, 58, 68, 121, 190 and 242 — 5.50
5 Universal Postal Union centenary, Mar. 22, 1974. Card of 7: Nos. 17–18, 219 and 246; Offices in Geneva Nos. 18 and 39–40. — 3.00
6 World Population Year, Oct. 18, 1974. Card of 7: Nos. 151–153 and 252–253; Offices in Geneva Nos. 43–44. — 24.00
7 Peaceful Uses of Outer Space, Mar. 14, 1975. Card of 6: Nos. 112–113 and 256–257; Offices in Geneva Nos. 46–47. — 5.50
8 U.N. Peace-Keeping Operations, Nov. 21, 1975. Card of 9: Nos. 52, 111, 118, 139, 160 and 265–266; Offices in Geneva Nos. 55–56. — 7.50
9 World Federation of United Nations Associations, Mar. 12, 1976. Card of 5: Nos. 154–155 and 272–273; Offices in Geneva No. 57. — 11.00
10 World Food Council, Nov. 19, 1976. Card of 6: Nos. 116–117, 218 and 280; Offices in Geneva Nos. 17 and 63. — 4.00
11 World Intellectual Property Organization (WIPO), Mar. 11, 1977. Card of 15: Nos. 17, 23, 25, 31, 33, 41, 43, 49, 59, 86, 90, 123 and 281–282; Offices in Geneva No. 64. — 2.75
12 Combat Racism, Sept. 19, 1977. Card of 8: Nos. 220–221 and 287–288; Offices in Geneva Nos. 19–20 and 69–70. — 2.75
13 Namibia, May 5, 1978. Card of 10: Nos. 240–241, 263–264, 296–297; Offices in Geneva Nos. 34, 53–54, 76. — 2.75
14 International Civil Aviation Organization, June 12, 1978. Card of 6: Nos. 31–32 and 298–299; Offices in Geneva Nos. 77–78. — 2.75
15 International Year of the Child, May 4, 1979. Card of 9: Nos. 5, 97, 161–163, 310–311; Offices in Geneva Nos. 84–85. — 2.25
16 International Court of Justice, Nov. 9, 1979. Card of 6: Nos. 88–89, 314–315; Offices in Geneva Nos. 87–88. — 2.75
17 UN Decade for Women, Mar. 7, 1980. Card of 4: Nos. 258, 318; Offices in Geneva No. 90; Offices in Vienna No. 9. — 25.00
18 Economic and Social Council, Nov. 7, 1980. Card of 8; Nos. 65–66, 341–342; Offices in Geneva Nos. 96–97; Offices in Vienna Nos. 15–16. — 2.75
19 International Year of Disabled Persons, Mar. 6, 1981. Card of 6; Nos. 344–345; Offices in Geneva Nos. 99–100; Offices in Vienna Nos. 18–19. — 2.75
20 New and Renewable Sources of Energy, May 29, 1981. Card of 4; Nos. 348–349; Offices in Geneva No. 102; Offices in Vienna No. 21. — 2.75
21 Human Environment, Mar. 19, 1982. Card of 5: Nos. 230, 371; Offices In Geneva Nos. 26, 107; Offices in Vienna No. 25 — 2.75
22 Exploration and Peaceful Uses of Outer Space, June 11, 1982. Card of 7: Nos. 112, 256, 373; Offices in Geneva Nos. 46, 109–110; Offices in Vienna No. 27. — 2.75
23 Safety at Sea, Mar. 18, 1983. Card of 8: Nos. 123–124, 394–395. Office in Geneva Nos. 114–115. Office in Vienna Nos. 31–32. — 2.75
24 Trade and Development, June 6, 1983. Card of 11: Nos. 129–130, 274–275, 397–398. Office in Geneva Nos. 58, 117–118. Office in Vienna Nos. 31–32. — 2.75
25 International Conference on Population, Feb. 3, 1984. Card of 10: Nos. 151, 153, 252–253, 417–418. Office in Geneva Nos. 43–44, 121. Office in Vienna No. 39. — 2.75
26 International Youth Year, Nov. 15, 1984. Card of 5: Nos. 441–442. Office in Geneva No. 128. Office in Vienna Nos. 46–47. — 2.75
27 ILO-Turin Center, Feb. 1, 1985. Card of 8: Nos. 25, 200, 244, 443. Office in Geneva Nos. 37, 129–130. Office in Vienna No. 48. — 2.75
28 Child Survival Campaign, Nov. 22, 1985. Card of 6: Nos. 466–467; Office in Geneva, Nos. 138–139; Office in Vienna, Nos. 55–56 — 2.75
29 Stamp Collecting, May 22, 1986. Card of 5: Nos. 278, 473; Office in Geneva, Nos. 61, 147; Office in Vienna, No. 63 — 2.75
30 International Peace Year, June 20, 1986. Card of 6: Nos. 475–476; Office in Geneva, Nos. 148–149; Office in Vienna, Nos. 64–65 — 2.75

OFFICES IN GENEVA, SWITZERLAND

For use only on mail posted at the Palais des Nations (United Nations European Office), Geneva. Inscribed in French unless otherwise stated.

100 Centimes = 1 Franc
Types of United Nations Issues 1961–69 and

United Nations European Office, Geneva
A1

Printed by Setelipaino, Finland (5c, 70c, 80c, 90c, 2fr, 10fr), Courvoisier, S.A., Switzerland (10c, 20c, 30c, 50c, 60c, 3fr), Government Printing Office, Austria (75c) and Government Printing Office, Federal Republic of Germany (1fr). Panes of 50. 30c designed by Ole Hamann, others as before.
Designs: 5c, U.N. Headquarters, New York, and world map. 10c, U.N. flag. 20c, Three men united before globe. 50c, Opening words of U.N. Charter. 60c, U.N. emblem over globe. 70c, "U.N." and U.N. emblem. 75c, "Flight Across Globe." 80c, U.N. Headquarters and emblem. 90c, Abstract group of flags. 1fr, U.N. emblem. 2fr, Stylized globe and weather vane. 3fr, Statue by Henrik Starcke. 10fr, "Peace, Justice, Security."
The 20c, 80c and 90c are inscribed in French. The 75c and 10fr carry French inscription at top, English at bottom.

Perf. 13 (5c, 70c, 90c); Perf. 12½x12 (10c); Perf. 11½ (20c–60c, 3fr); Perf. 11½x12 (75c); Perf. 13½x14 (80c); Perf. 14 (1fr); Perf. 12x11½ (2fr); Perf. 12 (10fr)

		1969–70	Photogravure	Unwmkd.	
1	A88	5c pur. & multi., *Oct. 4, 1969 (3,300,000)**		5	5
		First day cover			30
		Margin block of 4, inscription		25	25
		a. Green omitted		250.00	
2	A52	10c salmon & multi., *Oct. 4, 1969 (4,300,000)**7			5
		First day cover			40
		Margin block of 4, inscription		35	25
3	A66	20c black & multi., *Oct. 4, 1969 (4,300,000)**14			10
		First day cover			50
		Margin block of 4, inscription		65	45
4	A1	30c dk. blue & multi., *Oct. 4, 1969 (3,000,000)*20			15
		First day cover			50
		Margin block of 4, inscription		90	65
5	A77	50c ultra., & multi., *Oct. 4, 1969 (3,000,000)**40			30
		First day cover			60
		Margin block of 4, inscription		1.75	1.30
6	A54	60c dk. brown, salmon & gold, *Apr. 17, 1970 (3,300,000)**		40	30
		First day cover			75
		Margin block of 4, inscription		1.75	1.30
7	A104	70c red, black & gold, *Sept. 22, 1970 (3,300,000)**		50	35
		Margin block of 4, inscription		2.25	1.50
8	AP8	75c carmine rose & multicolored, *Oct. 4, 1969 (3,300,000)**		55	40
		First day cover			75
		Margin block of 4, inscription		2.40	1.75
9	A78	80c blue green, red & yellow, *Sept. 22, 1970 (3,300,000)**		55	40
		First day cover			75
		Margin block of 4, inscription		2.50	1.75
10	A45	90c bl. & multi., *Sept. 22, 1970 (3,300,000)** 65			50
		First day cover			75
		Margin block of 4, inscription		2.75	2.25

Lithographed and Embossed

11	A79	1fr light & dark green, *Oct. 4, 1969 (3,000,000)*70			55
		First day cover			90
		Margin block of 4, inscription		3.00	2.40

Photogravure

12	A67	2fr bl. & multi., *Sept. 22, 1970 (3,000,000)**1.40			1.00
		First day cover			2.50
		Margin block of 4, inscription		6.00	4.25
13	A97	3fr olive & multi., *Oct. 4, 1969 (3,000,000)**2.00			1.50
		First day cover			3.00
		Margin block of 4, inscription		8.50	6.50

Engraved

14	A3	10fr dark blue, *Apr. 17, 1970 (2,250,000)**	7.00	5.00
		First day cover			11.00
		Margin block of 4, inscription		30.00	22.00

* Printing orders to Mar. 1978.
First day covers of Nos. 1–5, 8, 11, 13 total 607,578; of Nos. 6 and 14, 148,055; of Nos. 7, 9–10 and 12, 226,000.

Sea Bed Type of U.N.

	1971, Jan. 25	Photogravure and Engraved	Perf. 13	
15	A114	30c green & multicolored (*1,935,871*)	25	20
		First day cover (*152,590*)		50
		Margin block of 4, inscription	1.10	90

Refugee Type of U.N.

	1971, Mar. 12	Lithographed	Perf. 13x12½	
16	A115	50c dp. car., dp. org. & black (*1,820,114*)	40	30
		First day cover (*148,220*)		1.00
		Margin block of 4, inscription	2.25	1.75

World Food Program Type of U.N.

	1971, Apr. 13	Photogravure	Perf. 14	
17	A116	50c dark violet & multicolored (*1,824,170*)	50	35
		First day cover (*151,580*)		1.00
		Margin block of 4, inscription	2.25	1.50

UPU Headquarters Type of U.N.

	1971, May 28	Photogravure	Perf. 11½	
18	A117	75c green & multi. (*1,821,878*)	1.00	75
		First day cover (*140,679*)		1.50
		Margin block of 4, inscription	4.50	3.25

Eliminate Racial Discrimination Types of U.N.

Designed by Daniel Gonzague (30c) and Ole Hamann (50c).

	1971, Sept. 21	Photogravure	Perf. 13½	
19	A118	30c blue & multicolored (*1,838,474*)	30	25
		First day cover		65
		Margin block of 4, inscription	1.30	1.10
20	A119	50c yellow green & multi. (*1,804,126*)	50	40
		First day cover		90
		First day cover, #19-20		1.35
		Margin block of 4, inscription	2.25	1.75

First day covers of Nos. 19–20 total 308,420.

Picasso Type of U.N.

	1971, Nov. 19	Photogravure	Perf. 11½	
21	A122	1.10fr multicolored (*1,467,993*)	1.25	90
		First day cover (*195,215*)		1.75
		Margin block of 4, inscription	5.50	4.00

Palais des Nations, Geneva
A2

Printed by Courvoisier, S. A. Panes of 50. Designed by Ole Hamann.

	1972, Jan. 5	Photogravure	Perf. 11½	
22	A2	40c olive, blue, salmon & dark green (*3,500,000*)*	30	25
		First day cover (*152,300*)		40
		Margin block of 4, inscription	1.30	1.10

* Initial printing order.

Nuclear Weapons Type of U.N.

	1972, Feb. 14	Photogravure	Perf. 13½x14	
23	A124	40c yel. green, black, rose & gray (*1,567,305*)60		45
		First day cover (*151,350*)		1.25
		Margin block of 4, inscription	2.60	2.00

World Health Day Type of U.N.

	1972, Apr. 7	Litho. & Engr.	Perf. 13x13½	
24	A125	80c black & multicolored (*1,543,368*)	85	65
		First day cover (*192,600*)		1.50
		Margin block of 4, inscription	3.75	2.80

UNITED NATIONS

Human Environment Type of U.N.
1972, June 5   Litho. & Embossed   *Perf. 12½x14*
25	A126	40c olive, lemon, green & blue *(1,594,089)*	55	40
		First day cover		75
		Margin block of 4, inscription	2.40	1.75
26	"	80c ultra., pink, green & blue *(1,568,009)*	1.10	80
		First day cover		1.75
		First day cover, #25-26		3.50
		Margin block of 4, inscription	4.75	3.50

First day covers of Nos. 25-26 total 296,700.

Economic Commission for Europe Type of U.N.
1972, Sept. 11   Lithographed   *Perf. 13x13½*
27	A127	1.10fr red & multicolored *(1,604,082)*	1.50	1.10
		First day cover *(149,630)*		2.25
		Margin block of 4, inscription	6.50	4.75

Art at U.N. (Sert) Type of U.N.
1972, Nov. 17   Photogravure   *Perf. 12x12½*
28	A128	40c gold, red & brown *(1,932,428)*	55	40
		First day cover		80
		Margin block of 4, inscription	2.40	1.75
29	"	80c gold, brown & olive *(1,759,600)*	1.10	80
		First day cover		1.50
		First day cover, #28-29		2.25
		Margin block of 4, inscription	4.75	3.50

First day covers of Nos. 28-29 total 295,470.

Disarmament Decade Type of U.N.
1973, Mar. 9   Lithographed   *Perf. 13½x13*
30	A129	60c violet & multi. *(1,586,845)*	60	45
		First day cover		90
		Margin block of 4, inscription	2.60	2.00
31	"	1.10fr olive & multi. *(1,408,169)*	1.10	85
		First day cover		1.60
		First day cover, #30-31		2.00
		Margin block of 4, inscription	4.75	3.50

First day covers of Nos. 30-31 total 260,680.

Drug Abuse Type of U.N.
1973, Apr. 13   Photogravure   *Perf. 13½*
32	A130	60c blue & multicolored *(1,481,432)*	70	55
		First day cover *(144,760)*		1.00
		Margin block of 4, inscription	3.00	2.40

Volunteers Type of U.N.
1973, May 25   Photogravure   *Perf. 14*
33	A131	80c gray green & multi. *(1,443,519)*	90	70
		First day cover *(143,430)*		1.10
		Margin block of 4, inscription	4.00	3.00

Namibia Type of U.N.
1973, Oct. 1   Photogravure   *Perf. 13½*
34	A132	60c red & multi. *(1,673,898)*	70	55
		First day cover *(148,077)*		1.00
		Margin block of 4, inscription	3.00	2.40

Human Rights Type of U.N.
1973, Nov. 16   Photogravure   *Perf. 13½*
35	A133	40c ultramarine & multi. *(1,480,791)*	40	30
		First day cover		60
		Margin block of 4, inscription	1.75	1.30
36	"	80c olive & multi. *(1,343,349)*	80	60
		First day cover		1.00
		First day cover, #35-36		1.50
		Margin block of 4, inscription	3.50	2.60

First day covers of Nos. 35-36 total 438,260.

ILO Headquarters Type of U.N.
1974, Jan. 11   Photogravure   *Perf. 14*
37	A134	60c violet & multi. *(1,212,703)*	60	45
		First day cover		80
		Margin block of 4, inscription	2.60	2.00
38	"	80c brown & multi. *(1,229,851)*	80	60
		First day cover		1.10
		First day cover, #37-38		1.75
		Margin block of 4, inscription	3.50	2.60

First day covers of Nos. 37-38 total 240,660.

Centenary of UPU Type of U.N.
1974, Mar. 22   Lithographed   *Perf. 12½*
39	A135	30c gold & multicolored *(1,567,517)*	30	25
		First day cover		50
		Margin block of 4, inscription	1.30	1.10
40	A135	60c gold & multicolored *(1,430,839)*	60	45
		First day cover		75
		First day cover, #39-40		1.10
		Margin block of 4, inscription	2.60	2.00

First day covers of Nos. 39-40 total 231,840.

Art at U.N. (Portinari) Type of U.N.
1974, May 6   Photogravure   *Perf. 14*
41	A136	60c dark red & multicolored *(1,202,357)*	60	45
		First day cover		75
		Margin block of 4, inscription	2.60	2.00
42	"	1fr green & multicolored *(1,230,045)*	1.00	80
		First day cover		1.20
		First day cover, #41-42		1.80
		Margin block of 4, inscription	4.25	3.50

First day covers of Nos. 41-42 total 249,130.

World Population Year Type of U.N.
1974, Oct. 18   Photogravure   *Perf. 14*
43	A140	60c bright green & multi. *(1,292,954)*	60	45
		First day cover		75
		Margin block of 4, inscription	2.60	2.00
44	"	80c brown & multicolored *(1,221,288)*	80	60
		First day cover		1.00
		First day cover, #43-44		1.60
		Margin block of 4, inscription	3.50	2.60

First day covers of Nos. 43-44 total 189,597.

Law of the Sea Type of U.N.
1974, Nov. 22   Photogravure   *Perf. 14*
45	A141	1.30fr blue & multicolored *(1,266,270)*	1.25	1.00
		First day cover *(181,000)*		1.75
		Margin block of 4, inscription	5.50	4.25

Outer Space Type of U.N.
1975, Mar. 14   Lithographed   *Perf. 13*
46	A142	60c multicolored *(1,339,704)*	60	45
		First day cover		75
		Margin block of 4, inscription	2.60	2.00
47	"	90c multicolored *(1,383,888)*	90	70
		First day cover		1.00
		First day cover, #46-47		1.75
		Margin block of 4, inscription	4.00	3.00

First day covers of Nos. 46-47 total 250,400.

International Women's Year Type of U.N.
1975, May 9   Lithographed   *Perf. 15*
48	A143	60c multicolored *(1,176,080)*	60	45
		First day cover		75
		Margin block of 4, inscription	2.60	2.00
49	"	90c multicolored *(1,167,863)*	90	70
		First day cover		1.00
		First day cover, #48-49		1.75
		Margin block of 4, inscription	4.00	3.00

First day covers of Nos. 48-49 total 250,660.

30th Anniversary Type of U.N.
1975, June 26   Lithographed   *Perf. 13*
50	A144	60c green & multicolored *(1,442,075)*	50	40
		First day cover		75
		Margin block of 4, inscription	2.25	1.75
51	"	90c violet & multicolored *(1,612,411)*	75	60
		First day cover		1.00
		First day cover, #50-51		1.75
		Margin block of 4, inscription	3.25	2.60

Souvenir Sheet
Imperf.
52	A144	Sheet of 2, *(1,210,148)*	1.50	1.50
		a. 60c green & multicolored		40 40
		b. 90c violet & multicolored		60 60
		First day cover		2.25

No. 52 has blue and bister margin with inscription and U.N. emblem. Size: 92x70mm.
First day covers of Nos. 50-52 total 402,500.

Namibia Type of U.N.
1975, Sept. 22   Photogravure   *Perf. 13½*
53	A145	50c multicolored *(1,261,019)*	50	40
		First day cover		60
		Margin block of 4, inscription	2.25	1.75
54	"	1.30fr multicolored *(1,241,990)*	1.25	1.00
		First day cover		1.50
		First day cover, #53-54		2.00
		Margin block of 4, inscription	5.50	4.25

First day covers of Nos. 53-54 total 226,260.

Peace-keeping Operations Type of U.N.

1975, Nov. 21		Engraved	Perf. 12½	
55	A146	60c greenish blue (1,249,305)	60	45
		First day cover		75
		Margin block of 4, inscription	2.60	2.00
56	"	70c bright violet (1,249,935)	70	55
		First day cover		85
		First day cover, #55-56		1.50
		Margin block of 4, inscription	3.00	2.40

First day covers of Nos. 55-56 total 229,245.

WFUNA Type of U.N.

1976, Mar. 12		Photogravure	Perf. 14	
57	A152	90c multicolored (1,186,563)	90	65
		First day cover		1.00
		Margin block of 4, inscription	4.00	2.80

First day covers of No. 57 total 121,645.

UNCTAD Type of U.N.

1976, Apr. 23		Photogravure	Perf. 11½	
58	A153	1.10fr sepia & multicolored, (1,167,284)	1.10	80
		First day cover (107,030)		1.35
		Margin block of 4, inscription	4.75	—

Habitat Type of U.N.

1976, May 28		Photogravure	Perf. 14	
59	A154	40c dull blue & multi. (1,258,986)	40	30
		First day cover		1.00
		Margin block of 4, inscription	1.75	—
60	"	1.50fr violet & multi. (1,110,507)	1.50	1.10
		First day cover		1.75
		First day cover, #59-60		2.25
		Margin block of 4, inscription	6.50	—

First day covers of Nos. 59-60 total 242,530.

U.N. Emblem, Post Horn and Rainbow
A3

U.N. Postal Administration, 25th anniversary.

Printed by Courvoisier, S.A. Panes of 20 (5x4). Designed by Hector Viola.

1976, Oct. 8		Photogravure	Perf. 11½	
61	A3	80c tan & multicolored (1,794,009)	2.25	1.75
		First day cover		4.50
		Margin block of 6, inscription	14.50	—
62	"	1.10fr lt. green & multicolored (1,751,178)	6.00	3.50
		First day cover		6.00
		First day cover, #61-62		10.00
		Margin block of 6, inscription	37.50	—

Upper margin blocks are inscribed "XXVe ANNIVERSAIRE"; lower margin blocks "ADMINISTRATION POSTALE DES NATIONS UNIES."
First day covers of Nos. 61-62 total 152,450.

World Food Council Type of U.N.

1976, Nov. 19		Lithographed	Perf. 14½	
63	A156	70c multicolored (1,507,630)	70	55
		First day cover (170,540)		85
		Margin block of 4, inscription	3.00	—

WIPO Type of U.N.

1977, Mar. 11		Photogravure	Perf. 14	
64	A157	80c red & multi. (1,232,664)	80	60
		First day cover (212,470)		1.00
		Margin block of 4, inscription	3.00	—

Drop of Water and Globe
A4

U.N. Water Conference, Mar del Plata, Argentina, Mar. 14-25.

Printed by Government Printing Bureau, Tokyo. Panes of 50. Designed by Eliezer Weishoff.

1977, Apr. 22		Photogravure	Perf. 13½x13	
65	A4	80c ultramarine & multi. (1,146,650)	80	60
		First day cover		90
		Margin block of 4, inscription	3.50	—
66	"	1.10fr dark carmine & multi. (1,138,236)	1.10	85
		First day cover		1.25
		First day cover, #65-66		2.00
		Margin block of 4, inscription	4.75	—

First day covers of Nos. 65-66 total 289,836.

Hands Protecting U.N. Emblem
A5

U.N. Security Council.

Printed by Heraclio Fournier, S.A., Spain. Panes of 50. Designed by George Hamori.

1977, May 27		Photogravure	Perf. 11	
67	A5	80c blue & multi. (1,096,030)	80	65
		First day cover		90
		Margin block of 4, inscription	3.50	—
68	"	1.10fr emerald & multi. (1,075,925)	1.10	85
		First day cover		1.25
		First day cover, #67-68		2.00
		Margin block of 4, inscription	4.75	—

First day covers of Nos. 67-68 total 305,349.

Colors of Five Races Spun into One Firm Rope
A6

Fight against racial discrimination.

Printed by Setelipaino, Finland. Panes of 50. Designed by M. A. Munnawar.

1977, Sept. 19		Lithographed	Perf. 13½x13	
69	A6	40c multicolored (1,218,834)	40	30
		First day cover		50
		Margin block of 4, inscription	1.75	—
70	"	1.10fr multicolored (1,138,250)	1.10	85
		First day cover		1.25
		First day cover, #69-70		1.60
		Margin block of 4, inscription	4.75	—

First day covers of Nos. 69-70 total 308,722.

UNITED NATIONS

Atomic Energy Turning Partly into Olive Branch
A7

Peaceful uses of atomic energy.
Printed by Heraclio Fournier, S.A., Spain. Panes of 50. Designed by Witold Janowski and Marek Freudenreich.

1977, Nov. 18		Photogravure		Perf. 14	
71	A7	80c dark carmine & multi. *(1,147,787)*		80	60
		First day cover			90
		Margin block of 4, inscription		3.50	
72	"	1.10fr Prus. blue & multi. *(1,121,209)*		1.10	85
		First day cover			1.20
		First day cover, #71-72			2.00
		Margin block of 4, inscription		4.75	

First day covers of Nos. 71-72 total 298,075.

"Tree" of Doves
A8

Printed by Questa Colour Security Printers, United Kingdom. Panes of 50. Designed by M. Hioki.

1978, Jan. 27		Lithographed		Perf. 14½	
73	A8	35c multicolored *(3,000,000)**		25	20
		First day cover			50
		Margin block of 4, inscription		1.10	

*Initial printing order.

Globes with Smallpox Distribution
A9

Global eradication of smallpox.
Printed by Courvoisier, S.A. Panes of 50. Designed by Eliezer Weishoff.

1978, Mar. 31		Photogravure		Perf. 12x11½	
74	A9	80c yellow & multi. *(1,116,044)*		80	60
		First day cover			85
		Margin block of 4, inscription		3.50	
75	"	1.10fr lt. green & multi. *(1,109,946)*		1.10	85
		First day cover			1.20
		First day cover, #74-75			2.00
		Margin block of 4, inscription		4.75	

Namibia Type of U.N.

1978, May 5		Photogravure		Perf. 12	
76	A166	80c multicolored *(1,183,208)*		80	60
		First day cover			85
		Margin block of 4, inscription		3.50	

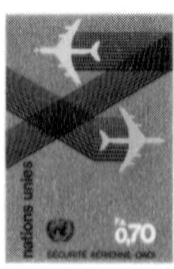

Jets and Flight Patterns
A10

International Civil Aviation Organization for "Safety in the Air."
Printed by Heraclio Fournier, S.A., Spain. Panes of 50. Designed by Tomas Savrda.

1978, June 12		Photogravure		Perf. 14	
77	A10	70c multicolored *(1,275,106)*		70	55
		First day cover			85
		Margin block of 4, inscription		3.00	
78	"	80c multicolored *(1,144,339)*		80	60
		First day cover			1.00
		First day cover, #77-78			1.60
		Margin block of 4, inscription		3.50	

General Assembly, Flags and Globe
A11

Printed by Government Printing Bureau, Tokyo. Panes of 50. Designed by Henry Bencsath.

1978, Sept. 15		Photogravure		Perf. 13½	
79	A11	70c multicolored *(1,204,441)*		70	55
		First day cover			85
		Margin block of 4, inscription		3.00	
80	"	1.10fr multicolored *(1,183,889)*		1.10	85
		First day cover			1.25
		First day cover, #79-80			2.00
		Margin block of 4, inscription		4.75	

Technical Cooperation Type of U.N.

1978, Nov. 17		Photogravure		Perf. 14	
81	A169	80c multicolored *(1,173,220)*		80	60
		First day cover			1.00
		Margin block of 4, inscription		4.50	

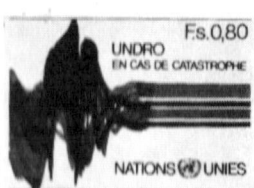

Seismograph Recording Earthquake
A12

Office of the U.N. Disaster Relief Coordinator (UNDRO).
Printed by Heraclio Fournier, S.A., Spain. Panes of 50. Designed by Michael Klutmann.

1979, Mar. 9		Photogravure		Perf. 14	
82	A12	80c multicolored *(1,183,155)*		80	60
		First day cover			1.00
		Margin block of 4, inscription		3.50	
83	"	1.50fr multicolored *(1,168,121)*		1.50	1.10
		First day cover			1.75
		First day cover, #82-83			2.50
		Margin block of 4, inscription		6.50	

966 UNITED NATIONS

Children and Rainbow
A13
International Year of the Child.

Printed by Heraclio Fournier, S.A., Spain. Panes of 20 (5x4). Designed by Arieh Glaser.

1979, May 4		Photogravure		Perf. 14	
84	A13	80c multicolored (2,251,623)		1.00	75
		First day cover			2.50
		Margin block of 4, inscription		4.50	—
85	"	1.10fr multicolored (2,220,463)		1.40	1.00
		First day cover			3.50
		First day cover, #84-85			5.50
		Margin block of 4, inscription		6.25	—

Namibia Type of U.N.

1979, Oct. 5		Lithographed	Perf. 13½	
86	A176	1.10fr multicolored (1,500,000)	1.10	85
		First day cover		1.25
		Margin block of 4, inscription	6.50	—

International Court of Justice, Scales
A14

International Court of Justice, The Hague, Netherlands
Printed by Setelipaino, Finland. Panes of 50. Designed by Kyohei Maeno.

1979, Nov. 9		Lithographed	Perf. 13x13½	
87	A14	80c multicolored (1,123,193)	80	60
		First day cover		1.00
		Margin block of 4, inscription	3.50	—
88	"	1.10fr multicolored (1,063,067)	1.10	85
		First day cover		1.25
		First day cover, #87-88		2.00
		Margin block of 4, inscription	4.75	—

New Economic Order Type of U.N.

1980, Jan. 11		Lithographed	Perf. 15x14½	
89	A179	80c multicolored (1,315,918)	80	60
		First day cover		1.00
		Margin block of 4, inscription	3.50	—

Women's Year Emblem—A15

United Nations Decade for Women.
Printed by Questa Colour Security Printers, United Kingdom. Panes of 50. Designed by M.A. Munnawar.

1980, Mar. 7		Lithographed	Perf. 14½×15	
90	A15	40c multicolored (1,265,221)	40	30
		First day cover	25	
		Margin block of 4, inscription	1.75	—
91	A15	70c multicolored (1,240,375)	70	55
		First day cover		85
		First day cover, #90-91		1.00
		Margin block of 4, inscription	3.00	—

Peace-keeping Operations Type of U.N.

1980, May 16		Lithographed	Perf. 14×13	
92	A181	1.10fr blue & green (1,335,391)	1.10	85
		First day cover		1.25
		Margin block of 4, inscription	4.75	—

35th Anniversary Type of U.N. and
Dove and "35"—A16

35th Anniversary of the United Nations.
Printed by Ashton-Potter Ltd., Canada. Panes of 50. Designed by Gidon Sagi (40c), Cemalattin Mutver (70c).

1980, June 26		Lithographed	Perf. 13×13½	
93	A16	40c blue green & black (1,462,005)	40	30
		First day cover		60
		Margin block of 4, inscription	1.75	—
94	A183	70c multicolored (1,444,639)	70	55
		First day cover		85
		First day cover, #93-94		1.00
		Margin block of 4, inscription	3.00	—

Souvenir Sheet
Imperf.

95	Sheet of 2 (1,235,200)	1.10	1.10
	a. A16 40c blue green & black	40	
	b. A183 70c multicolored	70	

No. 95 has multicolored margin with inscription and U.N. emblem. Size: 92x73mm.

ECOSOC Type of U.N. and

Family Climbing Line Graph—A17

Printed by Ashton-Potter Ltd., Canada. Panes of 50. Designed by Eliezer Weishoff (40¢), A. Medina Medina (70¢).

1980, Nov. 21			Lithographed	Perf. 13½×13	
96	A186	40c multicolored (986,435)		40	30
		First day cover			60
		Margin block of 4, inscription		1.75	
97	A17	70c multicolored (1,016,462)		70	55
		First day cover			85
		First day cover #96-97			1.00
		Margin block of 4, inscription		3.00	

Economic and Social Council (ECOSOC).

Palestinian Rights

Printed by Courvoisier S.A., Switzerland. Sheets of 50. Designed by David Dewhurst.

1981, Jan. 30		Photogravure	Perf. 12×11½	
98	A188	80c multicolored (1,900,000)	80	60
		First day cover		1.00
		Margin block of 4, inscription	5.00	

International Year of the Disabled.

Printed by Heraclio Fournier S.A., Spain. Panes of 50. Designed by G.P. Van der Hyde (40c) and Sophia van Heeswijk (1.50fr).

1981, Mar. 6		Photogravure	Perf. 14	
99	A190	40c black and blue (1,600,000)	40	30
		First day cover		60
		Margin block of 4, inscription	1.75	
100	A4	1.50fr black & red (1,600,000)	1.50	1.10
		First day cover		2.25
		First day cover, #99-100		2.50
		Margin block of 4, inscription	6.50	

Art Type of U.N.

1981, Apr. 15		Photogravure Granite Paper	Perf. 11½	
101	A191	80c multi (1,600,000)	80	60
		First day cover		1.25
		Margin block of 4, inscription	3.50	

Energy Type of 1981

1981, May 29		Lithographed	Perf. 13	
102	A192	1.10fr multi (1,600,000)	1.10	85
		First day cover		1.50
		Margin block of 4, inscription	4.75	

Volunteers Program Type and

Symbols of Science, Agriculture and Industry—A18
Printed by Walsall Security Printers, Ltd., United Kindgom. Pane of 50.
Designed by Gabriele Nussgen (40¢), Bernd Mirbach (70¢).

1981, Nov. 13			Litho.	
103	A194	40c multi (1,600,000)	40	30
		First day cover		60
		Margin block of 4, inscription	1.75	
104	A18	70c multi (1,600,000)	70	55
		First day cover		85
		First day cover, #103-104	1.00	
		Margin block of 4, inscription	3.00	

Fight against Apartheid A19

Flower of Flags A20

Printed by Courvoisier, S.A., Switzerland. Sheets of 50.
Designed by Tomas Savrda (30c); Dietmar Kowall (1fr).

PHOTOGRAVURE

1982, Jan. 22			Perf. 11½x12	
105	A19	30c multicolored (3,000,000)	20	10
		First day cover		50
		Margin block of 4, inscription	90	
106	A20	1fr multicolored (3,000,000)	70	35
		First day cover		1.25
		First day cover, #105-106		1.50
		Margin block of 4, inscription	3.00	

Human Environment Type of U.N. and

Sun and Leaves—A21

10th Anniversary of United Nations Environment Program.
Printed by Joh. Enschede en Zonen, Netherlands. Panes of 50.
Designed by Sybille Brunner (40c); Philine Hartert (1.20fr).

1982, Mar. 19			Lithographed	Perf. 13½x13	
107	A21	40c multicolored (1,600,000)		40	30
		First day cover			60
		Margin block of 4, inscription		1.75	
108	A199	1.20fr multicolored (1,600,000)		1.20	90
		First day cover			1.50
		First day cover, #107-108			1.75
		Margin block of 4, inscription		5.25	

UNITED NATIONS

Outer Space Type of U.N. and
Satellite, Applications of Space Technology—A22
Exploration and Peaceful Uses of Outer Space.
Printed by Enschede. Panes of 50. Designed by Wiktor C.
Nerwinski (80c) and George Hamori (1fr).

		1982, June 11	Lithographed	Perf. 13x13½	
109	A201	80c multicolored (1,600,000)		80	60
		First day cover			1.00
		Margin block of 4, inscription		3.50	
110	A22	1fr multicolored (1,600,000)		1.00	75
		First day cover			1.25
		First day cover, #109-110			1.50
		Margin block of 4, inscription		4.25	

Conservation & Protection of Nature

		1982, Nov. 19	Photogravure	Perf. 14	
111	A202	40c Reptile		40	30
		First day cover			60
		Margin block of 4, inscription		2.60	
112	A202	1.50fr Bird		1.50	1.10
		First day cover			1.85
		First day cover, #111-112			2.10
		Margin block of 4, inscription		6.50	

World Communications Year

		1983, Jan. 28	Lithographed	Perf. 13	
113	A204	1.20 multi (1,400,000)		1.60	1.15
		First Day Cover			1.50
		Margin block of 4, inscription		7.50	

Safety at Sea Type of UN and

A22

Designed by Valentin Wurnitsch (A22).

		1983, Mar. 28	Lithographed	Perf. 14½	
114	A205	40c multi (1,400,000)		50	38
		First Day Cover			60
		Margin block of 4, inscription		2.25	
115	A22	80c multi (1,400,000)		1.10	75
		First Day Cover			1.00
		First Day Cover, #114-115			1.25
		Margin block of 4, inscription		5.00	

World Food Program

		1983, Apr. 22	Engraved	Perf. 13½	
116	A207	1.50fr blue (1,400,000)		2.10	1.50
		First Day Cover			1.85
		Margin block of 4, inscription		9.50	

Trade Type of UN and

A23

Designed by Waldyslaw Brykczynski (A23).

		1983, June 6	Lithographed	Perf. 14	
117	A208	80c multi (1,400,000)		1.00	75
		First Day Cover			1.00
		Margin block of 4, inscription		4.50	
118	A23	1.10fr multi (1,400,000)		1.50	1.00
		First Day Cover			1.25
		First Day Cover, #117-118			1.50
		Margin block of 4, inscription		7.00	

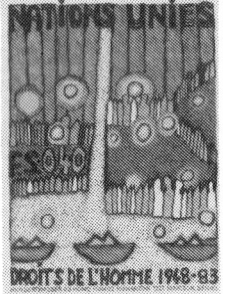
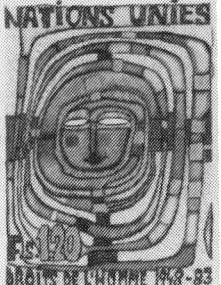

Homo Humus Humanitas—A25   Right to Create A26

35th Anniversary of the Universal Declaration of Human Rights

Printed by Government Printing Office, Austria. Designed by Friedensreich Hundertwasser, Austria. Panes of 16 (4x4).

		1983, Dec. 9	Photo. & Engraved	Perf. 13½	
119	A25	40c multi		50	38
		First Day Cover			60
120	A26	1.20fr multi		1.40	70
		First Day Cover			1.50
		First Day Cover, Nos. 119-120			1.75

International Conference on Population Type

Printed by Bundesdruckerei, Federal Republic of Germany. Panes of 50. Designed by Marina Langer-Rosa and Helmut Langer, Federal Republic of Germany.

		1984, Feb. 3	Lithographed	Perf. 14	
121	A212	1.20fr multi		1.40	70
		First Day Cover			1.50
		Margin block of 4, inscription		7.00	

UNITED NATIONS

Fishing—A27

Women Farm Workers, Africa—A28

World Food Day, Oct. 16

Printed by Walsall Security Printers, Ltd., United Kingdom. Panes of 50. Designed by Adth Vanooijen, Netherlands.

1984, Mar. 15		Lithographed	Perf. 14½	
122	A27	50c multi	50	25
		First Day Cover		65
		Margin block of 4, inscription	2.50	—
123	A28	80c multi	80	40
		First Day Cover		1.00
		First Day Cover, Nos. 122-123		1.40
		Margin block of 4, inscription	4.00	—

Valletta, Malta—A29

Los Glaciares National Park, Argentina—A30

World Heritage

Printed by Harrison and Sons, United Kingdom. Panes of 50. Designs adapted by Rocco J. Callari, U.S., and Thomas Lee, China.

1984, Apr. 18		Lithographed	Perf. 14	
124	A20	50c multi	50	25
		First Day Cover		65
		Margin block of 4, inscription	2.50	—
125	A30	70c multi	70	35
		First Day Cover		1.00
		First Day Cover, Nos. 124-125		1.40
		Margin block of 4, inscription	3.50	—

A31 A32

Future for Refugees

Printed by Courvoisier. Panes of 50. Designed by Hans Erni, Switzerland.

1984, May 29		Photogravure	Perf. 11½	
126	A31	35c multi	35	18
		First Day Cover		55
		Margin block of 4, inscription	1.75	—
127	A32	1.50fr multi	1.50	75
		First Day Cover		1.85
		First Day Cover, Nos. 126-127		2.10
		Margin block of 4, inscription	7.50	—

International Youth Year — A33

Printed by Waddingtons Ltd., United Kingdom. Panes of 50. Designed by Eliezer Weishoff, Israel.

1984, Nov. 15		Lithographed	Perf. 13½	
128	A33	1.20fr multi (1,300,000)*	90	45
		First day cover		1.20
		Margin block of 4, inscription	4.50	—

*Initial print order.

ILO Type of U.N. and

ILO Turin Center — A34

Printed by the Government Printing Bureau, Japan. Panes of 50. Engraved by Mamoru Iwakuni and Hiroshi Ozaki, Japan (#129) and adapted from photographs by Rocco J. Callari, U.S., and Thomas Lee, China (#130).

1985, Feb. 1		Engraved	Perf 13½	
129	A220	80c Turin Center emblem (1,300,000)*	60	30
		First day cover		80
		Margin block of 4, inscription	3.00	—
130	A34	1.20fr U Thant Pavilion (1,300,000)*	90	45
		First day cover		1.20
		First day cover, Nos. 129-130		1.70
		Margin block of 4, inscription	4.50	—

*Initial print order.

UNITED NATIONS

U.N. University Type

Printed by Helio Courvoisier, Switzerland. Panes of 50. Designed by Moshe Pereg, Israel, and Hinedi Geruda, Brazil.

		1985, Mar. 15	Photogravure	Perf 13½	
131	A221	50c	Pastoral scene, advanced communications *(1,300,000)**	40	20
			First day cover		50
			Margin block of 4, inscription	2.00	—
132	A221	80c	like #131 *(1,300,000)**	60	30
			First day cover		80
			First day cover, Nos. 131-132		1.05
			Margin block of 4, inscription	3.00	—

*Initial print order.

Flying Postman
A35

Interlocked Peace Doves
A36

Printed by Carl Ueberreuter Druck and Verlag M. Salzer, Austria. Panes of 50. Designed by Arieh Glaser, Israel ($133), and Carol Sliwka, Poland (#134).

		1985, May 10	Lithographed	Perf 14	
133	A35	20c	multi *(2,000,000)**	16	8
			First day cover		20
			Margin block of 4, inscription	80	—
134	A36	1.20fr	multi *(2,000,000)**	1.00	50
			First day cover		1.30
			First day cover, Nos. 133-134		1.40
			Margin block of 4, inscription	5.00	—

*Initial print order.

40th Anniversary Type

U.N. 40th anniversary. Oil paintings (details) by American artist Andrew Wyeth (b. 1917). Printed by Helio Courvoisier, Switzerland. Panes of 50. Designed by Rocco J. Callari, U.S., and Thomas Lee, China (#137).

		1985, June 26	Photogravure	Perf. 12 x 11½	
135	A224	50c	multi *(1,400,000)**	40	20
			First day cover		50
			Margin block of 4, inscription	2.00	—
136	A225	70c	multi *(1,400,000)**	56	28
			First day cover		70
			First day cover, Nos. 135-136		95
			Margin block of 4, inscription	2.80	—

Souvenir Sheet

			Imperf.		
137		Sheet of 2 *(1,400,000)*		96	96
		a. A224 50c	multi	40	
		b. A225 70c	multi	56	
		First day cover			1.25

No. 137 has multicolored margin containing inscription in French and U.N. emblem. Size: 75 x 83mm.

UNICEF Child Survival Campaign

Printed by the Government Printing Bureau, Japan. Panes of 50. Designed by Mel Harris, United Kingdom (#138) and Adth Vanooijen, Netherlands (#139).

		1985, Nov. 22	Photo. & Engr.	Perf 13½	
138	A226	50c	Three girls *(1,000,000)*	40	20
			First day cover		75
			Margin block of 4, inscription	2.00	—
139	A226	4fr	Infant drinking *(1,100,000)*	3.00	1.50
			First day cover		4.00
			First day cover, Nos. 138-139		4.25
			Margin block of 4, inscription	15.00	—

Africa in Crisis

Printed by Helio Courvoisier, Switzerland. Panes of 50. Designed by Alemayehou Gabremedhiu, Ethiopia.

		1986, Jan. 31	Photo.	Perf. 11½x12	
140	A227	1.40fr	Mother, hungry children *(1,100,000)**	1.25	62
			First day cover		1.60
			Margin block of 4, inscription	6.25	—

U.N. Development Program

Forestry. Printed by the Government Printing Bureau, Japan. Panes of 40, 2 blocks of 4 horizontal and 5 blocks of 4 vertical. Designed by Thomas Lee, China.

		1986, Mar. 14	Photo.	Perf. 13½	
141	A228	35c	Erosion control *(1,600,000)**	30	15
			First day cover		65
142	A228	35c	Logging *(1,600,000)**	30	15
			First day cover		65
143	A228	35c	Lumber transport *(1,600,000)**	30	15
			First day cover		65
144	A228	35c	Nursery *(1,600,000)**	30	15
			First day cover		65
			First day cover, #141-144		1.55
			Margin block of 4, #141-144, inscription	1.50	—
			a. Block of 4, #141-144	1.25	60

Nos. 141-144 printed se-tenant in a continuous design.

Dove and Sun—A37

Printed by Questa Color Security Printers, Ltd., United Kingdom. Panes of 50. Designed by Ramon Alcantara Rodriguez, Mexico.

		1986, Mar. 14	Lithographed	Perf. 15x14½	
145	A37	5c	multi *(2,000,000)**	5	5
			First day cover		65
			Margin block of 4, inscription	25	—

Stamp Collecting

Designs: 50c, U.N. Human Rights stamp. 80c, U.N. stamps. Printed by the Swedish Post Office, Sweden. Panes of 50. Designed by Czeslaw Slania and Ingalill Axelsson, Sweden.

		1986, May 22	Engraved	Perf. 12½	
146	A229	50c	dk grn & hen brn *(1,100,000)**	52	25
			First day cover		85
			Margin block of 4, inscription	2.60	—
147	A229	80c	dk grn & yel org *(1,100,000)**	85	42
			First day cover		1.20
			First day cover, #146-147		1.75
			Margin block of 4, inscription	4.25	—

UNITED NATIONS

Flags and Globe as Dove—A38

Peace in French—A39

International Peace Year. Printed by the Government Printing Bureau, Japan. Panes of 50. Designed by Renato Ferrini, Italy (#148), and Salahattin Kanidinc, US (#149).

1986, June 20		Photo. & Embossed	Perf. 13½	
148	A38	45c multi *(1,100,000)**	50	25
		First day cover		85
		Margin block of 4, inscription	2.50	—
149	A39	1.40fr multi *(1,100,000)**	1.60	80
		First day cover		2.00
		First day cover, #148-149		2.50
		Margin block of 4, inscription	8.00	—

*Initial print order.

WFUNA Anniversary Type of U.N. Souvenir Sheet

Printed by Johann Enschede and Sons, Netherlands. Designed by Rocco J. Callari, U.S.

Designs: 35c, Abstract by Benigno Gomez, Honduras. 45c, Abstract by Alexander Calder (1898-1976), U.S. 50c, Abstract by Joan Miro (b. 1893), Spain. 70c, Sextet with Dove, by Ole Hamann, Denmark.

1986, Nov. 14	Litho.		Perf.
150	Sheet of 4 *(1,800,000)**	2.45	2.45
	a. A232 35c multi	42	22
	b. A232 45c multi	55	28
	c. A232 50c multi	62	32
	d. A232 70c multi	85	42
	First day cover		2.85

No. 150 has inscribed margin picturing U.N. and WFUNA emblems. Size:

AIR LETTER SHEET
U.N. Type of 1968

Printed by Setelipaino, Finland. Designed by Robert Perrot.

1969, Oct. 4   Lithographed

UC1	UC3	65c ultra. & lt. blue, entire *(350,000)*	3.25	1.25
		Entire, first day cancel *(52,000)*		1.50

POSTAL CARDS
U.N. Type of 1969 and Type of Air Post Postal Card, 1966.

Printed by Courvoisier, S.A., Switzerland. Designed by John Mason (20c) and Olav S. Mathiesen (30c).

Wmkd. Post Horn, Swiss Cross, "S" or "Z"

1969, Oct. 4   Lithographed

UX1	PC2	20c olive green & black, *buff (415,000)*	70	20
		First day cancel *(51,500)*		50
UX2	APC2	30c violet blue, blue, light & dark green, *buff (275,000)*	1.10	25
		First day cancel *(49,000)*		75

No. UX2, although of type APC2, is not inscribed "Poste Aerienne" or "Air Mail."

U.N. Emblem
PC1

U.N. Emblem and Ribbons
PC2

Printed by Setelipaino, Finland. Designed by Veronique Crombez (40c) and Lieve Baeten (70c).

1977, June 27   Lithographed

UX3	PC1	40c multicolored *(300,000)**	40	16
		First day cancel		50
UX4	PC2	70c multicolored *(300,000)**	70	28
		First day cancel		85

* Initial printing order.

Emblem of the
United Nations
PC3

Peace Dove
PC4

Printed by Johann Enschede en Zonen, Netherlands. Designed by George Hamori, Australia (50c) and Ryszard Dudzicki, Poland (70c).

1985, May 10   Lithographed

UX5	PC3	50c multi *(300,000)**	42	22
		First day cancel		55
UX6	PC4	70c multi *(300,000)**	58	30
		First day cancel		75

*Initial print order.

UNITED NATIONS

OFFICES IN VIENNA, AUSTRIA

For use only on mail posted at Donaupark Vienna International Center for the United Nations and the Atomic Energy Agency.

Type of Geneva, 1978, U.N. Types of 1961–72 and

Donaupark, Vienna
A1

Aerial View
A2

Women's Year Emblem on World Map—A3

United Nations Decade for Women.

Printed by Questa Colour Security Printers, United Kingdom. Panes of 50. Designed by Gunnar Janssen.

1980, Mar. 7			Lithographed	Perf. 14½x15	
9	A3	4s	light green & dark green (1,569,080)	40	35
			First day cover		75
			Margin block of 4, inscription	1.75	
10	A3	6s	bister brown (1,556,016)	60	50
			First day cover		1.25
			First day cover, #9-10		1.50
			Margin block of 4, inscription	2.60	

Printed by Helio Courvoisier S.A., Switzerland. Panes of 50.
Designed by Henryk Chylinski (4s); Jozsef Vertel (6s).

1979, Aug. 24			Photo.	Perf. 11½	
1	A8	50g	multicolored (3,500,000)*	5	5
			First day cover		30
			Margin block of 4, inscription	25	
2	A52	1s	multicolored (3,500,000)*	8	8
			First day cover		45
			Margin block of 4, inscription	35	
3	A1	4s	multicolored (3,500,000)*	30	25
			First day cover		75
			Margin block of 4, inscription	1.30	
4	AP13	5s	multicolored (3,500,000)*	40	35
			First day cover		1.00
			Margin block of 4, inscription	1.75	
5	A2	6s	multicolored (3,500,000)*	50	45
			First day cover		1.25
			Margin block of 4, inscription	2.25	
6	A45	10s	multicolored (3,500,000)*	80	70
			First day cover		2.00
			Margin block of 4, inscription	4.75	

*Initial printing order.
No. 4 is not inscribed "Air Mail." No. 6 has no frame.

New Economic Order Type of U.N.

1980, Jan. 11			Lithographed	Perf. 15x14½	
7	A178	4s	multicolored (1,418,418)	1.50	1.35
			First day cover		2.00
			Margin block of 4, inscription	30.00	

Dove Type of U.N.

1980, Jan. 11			Lithographed	Perf. 14x13½	
8	A147	2.50s	multicolored (3,500,000)*	20	15
			First day cover		50
			Margin block of 4, inscription	1.25	

*Initial printing order.

Peace-keeping Operations Type of U.N.

1980, May 16			Lithographed	Perf. 14x13	
11	A182	6s	multicolored (1,719,852)	60	50
			First day cover		1.25
			Margin block of 4, inscription	2.60	

35th Anniversary Types of Geneva and U.N.

1980, June 26			Lithographed	Perf. 13x13½	
12	A16	4s	carmine rose & black (1,626,582)	40	35
			First day cover		75
			Margin block of 4, inscription	1.75	
13	A184	6s	multicolored (1,625,400)	60	50
			First day cover		1.25
			Margin block of 4, inscription	2.75	

Souvenir Sheet
Imperf.

14		Sheet of 2 (1,675,191)	1.00	1.00
	a.	A16 4s carmine rose & black	30	
	b.	A184 6s multicolored	45	

No. 14 has multicolored margin with inscription and U.N. emblem. Size: 92x73mm.

ECOSOC Types of U.N. and Geneva

Printed by Ashton-Potter Ltd., Canada. Panes of 50. Designed by Dietman Kowall (4s), Angel Medina Medina (6s).

1980, Nov. 21			Lithographed	Perf. 13½x13	
15	A187	4s	multicolored (1,811,218)	40	35
			First day cover		75
			Margin block of 4, inscription	1.75	
16	A17	6s	multicolored (1,258,420)	60	50
			First day cover		1.25
			First day cover #15-16		1.50
			Margin block of 4, inscription	2.60	

Economic and Social Council (ECOSOC).

UNITED NATIONS

Palestinian Rights Type of U.N.
Printed by Courvoisier S.A., Switzerland. Panes of 50.
Designed by David Dewhurst.

1981, Jan. 30		**Photogravure**		**Perf. 12x11½**	
17	A188	4s multicolored (2,100,00)		40	35
		First day cover			75
		Margin block of 4, inscription		1.75	—

Disabled Type of UN. and

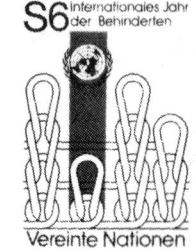

Interlocking Stitches—A4

International Year of the Disabled.
Printed by Heraclio Fournier S.A., Spain. Panes of 50.
Designed by Sophia van Heeswijk.

1981, Mar. 6		**Photogravure**		**Perf. 14**	
18	A189	4s multicolored (2,100,000)		40	35
		First day cover			75
		Margin block of 4, inscription		1.75	—
19	A4	6s black & orange (2,100,000)		60	50
		First day cover			1.25
		First day cover, #18-19			1.50
		Margin block of 4, inscription		2.60	—

Art Type of U.N.
1981, Apr. 15		**Photogravure**		**Perf. 11½**	
		Granite Paper			
20	A191	6s multi (2,100,000)		60	50
		First day cover			1.25
		Margin block of 4, inscription		2.60	—

Energy Type of U.N.
1981, May 29		**Lithographed**		**Perf. 13**	
21	A193	7.50s multi (2,100,000)		75	65
		First day cover			1.75
		Margin block of 4, inscription		3.25	—

Volunteers Program Types
1981, Nov. 13		**Litho.**			
22	A195	5s multi (2,100,000)		50	40
		First day cover			85
		Margin block of 4, inscription		2.25	—
23	A18	7s multi (2,100,000)		70	60
		First day cover			1.35
		First day cover, #22-23			2.50
		Margin block of 4, inscription		3.00	—

"For a Better World"—A5

Printed by Courvoisier, S.A., Switzerland. Sheets of 50.
Designed by Eliezer Weishoff.
PHOTOGRAVURE

1982, Jan. 22				**Perf. 11½x12**	
24	A5	3s multicolored (3,300,000)		25	20
		First day cover			75
		Margin block of 4, inscription		1.10	—

Human Environment Types of U.N.
10th Anniversary of United Nations Environment Program.
Printed by Joh. Enschede en Zonen, Netherlands. Panes of 50.
Designed by Peer-Ulrich Bremer (5s); Sybille Brunner (7s).

1982, Mar. 19		**Lithographed**		**Perf. 13½x13**	
25	A200	5s multicolored (2,100,000)		50	40
		First day cover			75
		Margin block of 4, inscription		2.25	—
26	A21	7s multicolored (2,100,000)		70	60
		First day cover			1.25
		First day cover, #25-26			1.50
		Margin block of 4, inscription		3.00	—

Outer Space Type of U.N.
Exploration and Peaceful Uses of Outer Space.
Printed by Enschede. Panes of 50. Designed by George Hamori

1982, June 11		**Lithographed**		**Perf. 13x13½**	
27	A22	5s multicolored (2,100,000)		50	40
		First day cover			75
		Margin block of 4, inscription		2.25	—

Conservation & Protection of Nature

1982, Nov. 16		**Photogravure**		**Perf. 14**	
28	A202	5s Fish		50	40
		First day cover			75
		Margin block of 4, inscription		2.25	—
29	A202	7s Animal		70	60
		First day cover			1.25
		Margin block of 4, inscription		3.00	—
		First Day Cover, #28-29			1.50

World Communications Year

1983, Jan. 28		**Litho**		**Perf. 13**	
30	A203	4s multi (2,100,000)		65	42
		First Day Cover			75
		Margin block of 4, inscription		3.25	—

Safety at Sea

1983, Mar. 18		**Lithographed**		**Perf. 14½**	
31	A22	4s multi (2,100,000)		65	42
		First Day Cover			75
		Margin block of 4, inscription		3.25	—
32	A206	6s multi (2,100,000)		95	62
		First Day Cover			1.25
		First Day Cover, Nos. 31-32			1.50
		Margin block of 4, inscription		4.75	—

World Food Program

		1983, Apr. 22	Engraved	Perf. 13½	
33	A207	5s green (2,100,000)		75	50
		First Day Cover			1.00
		Margin block of 4, inscription		3.75	
34	A207	7s brown (2,100,000)		1.05	70
		First Day Cover			1.35
		First Day Cover, #33-34			1.75
		Margin block of 4, inscription		5.25	

UN Conference on Trade and Development

		1983, June 6	Lithographed	Perf. 14	
35	A23	4s multi (2,100,000)		65	42
		First Day Cover			75
		Margin block of 4, inscription		3.25	
36	A209	8.50s multi (2,100,000)		1.40	1.00
		First Day Cover			1.50
		First Day Cover, Nos. 35-36			2.00
		Margin block of 4, inscription		7.00	

The Second Skin—A6

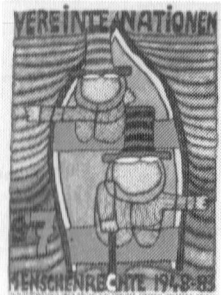
Right to Think—A7

35th Anniversary of the Universal Declaration of Human Rights

Printed by Government Printing Office, Austria. Designed by Friedensreich Hundertwasser, Austria. Panes of 16 (4x4).

		1983, Dec. 9	Photo. & Engraved	Perf. 13½	
37	A6	5s multi		75	50
		First Day Cover			1.00
38	A7	7s multi		1.05	70
		First Day Cover			1.35
		First Day Cover, Nos. 37-38			1.75

International Conference on Population Type

Printed by Bundesdruckerei, Federal Republic of Germany. Panes of 50. Designed by Marina Langer-Rosa and Helmut Langer, Federal Republic of Germany.

		1984, Feb. 3	Lithographed	Perf. 14	
39	A212	7s multi		70	50
		First Day Cover			1.00
		Margin block of 4, inscription		3.50	

Field Irrigation—A8

Pest Control—A9

World Food Day, Oct. 16

Printed by Walsall Security Printers, Ltd., United Kingdom. Panes of 50. Designed by Adth Vanooijen, Netherlands.

		1984, Mar. 15	Lithographed	Perf. 14½	
40	A8	4.50s multi		45	25
		First Day Cover			60
		Margin block of 4, inscription		2.25	
41	A9	6s multi		60	40
		First Day Cover			80
		First Day Cover, Nos. 40-41			1.20
		Margin block of 4, inscription		3.00	

Serengeti Park, Tanzania—A10

Ancient City of Shiban, People's Democratic Rep. of Yemen—A11

World Heritage

Printed by Harrison and Sons, United Kingdom. Panes of 50. Designs adapted by Rocco J. Callari, U.S., and Thomas Lee, China.

		1984, Mar. 15	Lithographed	Perf. 14	
42	A10	3.50s multi		35	25
		First Day Cover			50
		Margin block of 4, inscription		1.75	
43	A11	15s multi		1.50	90
		First Day Cover			1.80
		First Day Cover, Nos. 42-43			2.10
		Margin block of 4, inscription		7.50	

A12

A13

Future for Refugees

Printed by Courvoisier. Panes of 50. Designed by Hans Erni, Switzerland.

1984, Mar. 29			Photogravure	Perf. 11½	
44	A12	4.50s	multi	45	25
			First Day Cover		60
			Margin block of 4, inscription	2.75	—
45	A13	8.50s	multi	85	50
			First Day Cover		1.00
			First Day Cover, Nos. 44-45		1.30
			Margin block of 4, inscription	5.25	—

International Youth Year — A14

Printed by Waddingtons Ltd., United Kingdom. Panes of 50. Designed by Ruel A. Mayo, Phillipines.

1984, Nov. 15			Lithographed	Perf. 13½	
46	A14	3.50s	multi (1,700,000)*	32	20
			First day cover		45
			Margin block of 4, inscription	1.60	—
47	A14	6.50s	multi (1,700,000)*	60	40
			First day cover		80
			First day cover, Nos. 46-47		1.05
			Margin block of 4, inscription	3.00	—

*Initial print order.

ILO Type of Geneva

Printed by the Government Printing Bureau, Japan. Panes of 50. Adapted from photographs by Rocco J. Callari, U.S. and Thomas Lee, China.

1985, Feb. 1			Engraved	Perf. 13½	
48	A34	7.50s	U Thant Pavilion (1,700,000)*	68	45
			First day cover		90
			Margin block of 4, inscription	3.40	—

*Initial print order.

U.N. University Type

Printed by Helio Courvoisier, Switzerland. Panes of 50. Designed by Moshe Pereg, Israel, and Hinedi Geluda, Brazil.

1985, Mar. 15			Photogravure	Perf. 13½	
49	A221	8.50s	Rural scene, lab researchist (1,700,000)*	80	50
			First day cover		1.05
			Margin block of 4, inscription	4.00	—

*Initial print order.

Ship of Peace
A15

Shelter under U.N. Umbrella
A16

Printed by Carl Ueberreuter Druck and Verlag M. Salzer, Austria. Panes of 50. Designed by Ran Banda Mawilmada, Sri Lanka (4.50s), and Sophia van Heeswijk, Federal Republic of Germany (15s).

1985, May 10			Lithographed	Perf. 14	
50	A15	4.50s	multi (2,000,000)*	45	25
			First day cover		60
			Margin block of 4, inscription	2.25	—
51	A16	15s	multi (2,000,000)*	1.50	90
			First day cover		2.00
			First day cover, Nos. 50-51		2.75
			Margin block of 4, inscription	7.50	—

*Initial print order.

40th Anniversary Type

U.N. 40th anniversary. Oil paintings (details) by American artist Andrew Wyeth (b. 1917). Printed by Helio Courvoisier, Switzerland. Panes of 50. Designed by Rocco J. Callari, U.S., and Thomas Lee, China (#54).

1985, June 26			Photogravure	Perf. 12 x 11½	
52	A224	6.50s	multi (1,700,000)*	65	36
			First day cover		85
			Margin block of 4, inscription	3.25	—
53	A225	8.50s	multi (1,700,000)*	85	48
			First day cover		1.15
			First day cover, Nos. 52-53		1.60
			Margin block of 4, inscription	4.25	—

Souvenir Sheet

Imperf.

54			Sheet of 2 (1,700,000)*	1.50	1.50
			a. A224 6.50s multi	65	
			b. A225 8.50s multi	85	
			First day cover		2.00

No. 54 has multicolored margin containing inscription in German and U.N. emblem. Size: 75 x 83 mm.

UNICEF Child Survival Campaign

Printed by the Government Printing Bureau, Japan. Panes of 50. Designed by Mel Harris, United Kingdom (#55) and Vreni Wyss-Fischer, Switzerland (#56).

1985, Nov. 22			Photo. & Engr.	Perf. 13½	
55	A226	4s	Spoonfeeding children (1,500,000)	40	20
			First day cover		75
			Margin block of 4, inscription	2.00	—
56	A226	6s	Mother hugging infant (1,500,000)	60	30
			First day cover		1.05
			First day cover, Nos. 55-56		1.25
			Margin block of 4, inscription	3.00	—

Africa in Crisis

Printed by Helio Courvoisier, Switzerland. Panes of 50. Designed by Tesfaye Tessema, Ethiopia.

1986, Jan. 31			Photo.	Perf. 11½x12	
57	A227	8s	multi (1,500,000)*	90	45
			First day cover		1.25
			Margin block of 4, inscription	4.50	—

UNITED NATIONS

U.N. Development Program

Agriculture. Printed by the Government Printing Bureau, Japan. Panes of 40, 2 blocks of 4 horizontal and 5 blocks of 4 vertical. Designed by Thomas Lee, China.

1986, Mar. 14		Photo.	Perf. 13½	
58	A228	4.50s Developing crop strains *(1,800,000)* *	45	22
		First day cover		80
59	A228	4.50s Animal husbandry *(1,800,000)* *	45	22
		First day cover		80
60	A228	4.50s Technical instruction *(1,800,000)* *	45	22
		First day cover		80
61	A228	4.50s Nutrition education *(1,800,000)* *	45	22
		First day cover		80
		First day cover, #58-61		2.15
		Margin block of 4, #58-61, inscription	2.25	
		a.Block of 4, #58-61	1.80	88

Nos. 58-61 printed se-tenant in a continuous design.

Stamp Collecting

Designs: 3.50s, U.N. stamps. 6.50s, Engraver. Printed by the Swedish Post Office, Sweden. Panes of 50. Designed by Czeslaw Slania and Ingalill Axelsson, Sweden.

1986, May 22		Engraved	Perf. 12½	
62	A229	3.50s dk ultra & dk brn *(1,500,000)* *	45	22
		First day cover		80
		Margin block of 4, inscription	2.25	
63	A229	6.50s int bl & brt rose *(1,500,000)* *	80	40
		First day cover		1.15
		First day cover, #62-63		1.60
		Margin block of 4, inscription	4.00	—

Olive Branch, Rainbow, Earth—A17

International Peace Year. Printed by the Government Printing Bureau, Japan. Panes of 50. Designed by Milo Schor, Israel (#64), and Mohammad Sardar, Pakistan (#65).

1986, June 20		Photo. & Embossed	Perf. 13½	
64	A17	5s multi *(1,500,000)* *	65	32
		First day cover		1.00
		Margin block of 4, inscription	3.25	—
65	A17	6s Doves, U.N. emblem *(1,500,000)* *	80	40
		First day cover		1.15
		First day cover, #64-65		1.80
		Margin block of 4, inscription	4.00	—

*Initial print order.

WFUNA Anniversary Type of U.N. Souvenir Sheet

Printed by Johann Enschede and Sons, Netherlands. Designed by Rocco J. Callari, U.S.

Designs: 4s, White stallion by Elisabeth von Janota-Bzowski, Germany. 5s, Surrealistic landscape by Ernst Fuchs, Austria. 6s, Geometric abstract by Victor Vasarely (b. 1908), France. 7s, Mythological abstract by Wolfgang Hutter (b. 1928), Austria.

1986, Nov. 14	Litho.		Perf.
66	Sheet of 4 *(1,800,000)* *	3.15	3.15
	a. A232 4s multi	58	30
	b. A232 5s multi	72	35
	c. A232 6s multi	85	42
	d. A232 7s multi	1.00	50
	First day cover		3.55

No. 66 has inscribed margin picturing U.N. and WFUNA emblems. Size:

AIR LETTER SHEET

VLS1

Printed by Joh. Enschede and Sons. Designed by Ingrid Ousland.

1982, Apr. 28		Lithographed		
UC1	VLS1	9s multicolored, *light green*, entire (650,000)*	1.10	90
		First day cancel		1.25

*Initial printing order.

POSTAL CARDS

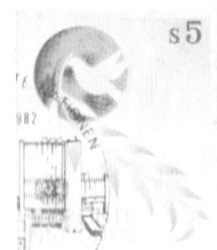

Olive Branch—VPC1   Bird Carrying Olive Branch—VPC2

Printed by Courvoisier. Designed by Rolf Christianson (3s), M.A. Munnawar (5s).

1982, Apr. 28		Photogravure		
UX1	VPC1	3s multicolored, *cream* (500,000)*	35	30
		First day cancel		40
UX2	VPC2	5s multicolored (500,000)*	60	50
		First day cancel		75

*Initial printing order.

Emblem of the United Nations — VPC3

Printed by Johann Enschede en Zonen, Netherlands. Designed by George Hamori, Australia.

1985, May 10		Lithographed		
UX3	VPC3	4s multi *(350,000)* *	40	22
		First day cancel		55

*Initial print order.

Scott's U.S. Minuteman Stamp Album!

FEATURES . . .

★ The famous Scott Catalogue identification number for every stamp.

★ Exciting stories of almost every stamp.

★ Attractive vinyl Binder.   ★ Supplemented annually.

"A must for every collector of United States postage stamps."

Available at your local dealer or direct from Scott Publishing Co.

Scott Publishing Company
P.O. Box 828, Sidney, OH 45365

NUMBER CHANGES
In Scott's 1987 U.S. Specialized Catalogue

No. in 1986 Cat.	No. in 1987 Cat.
UNITED STATES	
Envelopes	
U588a	deleted
Booklets	
BK140A	BK140B
Revenue Stamped Paper	
RN-A8a	deleted
RN-C16a	RN-C15
RN-K8a	deleted
RN-S3	deleted
Souvenir Cards	
100-102	101-103
MARSHALL ISLANDS	
39A-40A	40-42
41-42A	43-45
43-47	46-49A

READER SERVICE CARD ADVERTISER'S INDEX

The following is a listing of the Reader Service Card advertisers in this issue of the Scott 1987 U.S. Specialized Catalogue. For additional information about products or services use the handy Reader Service Card. If card is missing, write numbers on a postcard or letter, enclose your name, address, city, state, and zip and mail to...

SCOTT PUBLISHING CO., Readers Service Dept. 87-S, P.O. Box 828, Sidney, OH 45365

Reader
Service
Number

10 **DALE ENTERPRISES, INC.**
P.O. Box 539C
Emmaus, PA 18049
Free Comprehensive U.S.
and Pane Price List

35 **DANIEL F. KELLEHER CO., INC**
40 Broad St., Suite 830
Boston, Massachusetts 02109
FREE - Auction Information . . .
Buying or Selling

57 **JOHN A. FOX**
141 Tulip Avenue
Floral Park, NY 11001
Free Auction Catalogue

83 **SAM HOUSTON PHILATELICS**
14654 Memorial Drive
Houston, Texas 77079
Free Price Lists
and Auction Catalogues.

Reader
Service
Number

30 **J. RANDALL RARE STAMPS**
P.O. Box 56-1593
Miami, FL 33256-1593
FREE - Further Information
on Rare Classic U.S. Stamps

100 **SCOTT MOUNTS**
P.O. Box 828
Sidney, OH 45365
FREE Sample Package

91 **SCOTT STAMP MONTHLY and Catalogue Update**
P.O. Box 828
Sidney, OH 45365
Subscription information.

**READER SERVICE CARD
IS LOCATED IN THE BACK
OF THIS CATALOGUE**

SCOTT ADVERTISING

For information on advertising in future editions of the Scott Catalogues
or in the Scott Stamp Monthly and Catalogue Update

write or call. . .

Scott Publishing Co., Advertising Dept.
P.O. Box 828, Sidney, OH 45365 ● Phone 513-498-0802

Scott Catalogue Philatelic Marketplace

This "Yellow Pages" section of your Scott Catalogue contains advertisements to help you find what you need, when you need it ... conveniently.

AMERICAN STAMP DEALERS ASSOCIATION, INC.

5 Dakota Dr., Suite 102, Lake Success, NY 11042
Phone (516) 775-3600

When you make your move — look for the familiar ASDA symbol!

It took strategy to make the right moves in creating a code, that assures you of professional ethics!

ASDA DEALERS OFFER...

Honesty • Integrity • Dedication • Expertise • Hobby Builders • Reliability

MAKE YOUR MOVE NOW!
Look for the ASDA symbol before you buy or sell!

ACCESSORIES

Showgard® Mounts

The time proven hingeless method for protecting stamp values!

At Stamp Dealers everywhere
Sample on request from:
Vidiforms Company, Inc.
110 Brenner Drive, Congers, NY 10920 U.S.A.

AUCTIONS

DO YOU COLLECT U.S. OR WORLDWIDE STAMPS AND POSTAL HISTORY? ARE YOU A SPECIALIST?

AN INVITATION TO CONSIGN

Individual stamps, covers or collections for Public Auction or Private Treaty Sale.

WHAT IS A SCHIFF "ESPECIALLY FOR SPECIALISTS" AUCTION?

It's an auction designed with you in mind, whether you are a buyer or a seller of U.S. or Worldwide stamps.

Catalogs picked up at our office are complimentary.

WE ALSO PURCHASE OUTRIGHT!

Contact us first, describing your material. Include your address and phone numbers.

If you do not get our catalogs you are missing out! Send $8.50 ($12.50 overseas) for a year's subscription to catalogs and prices realized or send $1.50 for our next auction catalog and prices realized ($1.00 cat alogs only).

Especially For Specialists
Established 1947

Licensed and Bonded Auctioneers
JACQUES C. SCHIFF, JR., INC.
195 Main Street
Ridgefield Park, N.J. 07660
201-641-5566 (from NYC 662-2777)

AUCTIONS

Auction?

Collectors find treasures in our sales. Not just U.S. and Confederate States but countries, worldwide. Send $10.00 for 3rd class mailing or $20.00 for 1st, with your collecting interest, and receive the next 10 catalogs containing your countries. Want to sell at auction? See our ad on the inside front cover, then call 202-898-1800.

John W. Kaufmann, Inc.
1333 H Street N.W.,
Washington, D.C. 20005-4707

BUYING & SELLING

WE BUY....
Worldwide, British, U.S. Stamps,
Collections, Accumulations,
Dealer Stocks, etc.
Top Prices Paid! Prompt Payment!

WE SELL....
U.S., Worldwide - Choose from one of this areas largest stocks! Want lists filled upon request.

BREWART STAMPS
Visit our store - 2 blocks from Disneyland
401 W. Katella, Anaheim, California 92802
Mailing address: P.O. Box 8580   Ph. 714-533-0400

S·U·P·E·R·I·O·R

For 50 years, a leader in
BUYING — SELLING
U.S. & Worldwide Stamps & Covers
U.S., Foreign and Ancient Coinage
Franklin Mint
Currency and Antiquities
Wholesale / Retail — Auction / Private Treaty

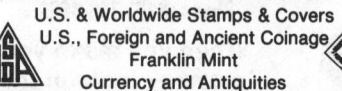

Superior Stamp & Coin Co., Inc.
ESTABLISHED 1930
9478 West Olympic Blvd., Beverly Hills, CA 90212-4236
Phone (213) 278-9740/203-9855
Toll Free: (800) 421-0754; in CA: (800) 874-3230

BUYING & SELLING

1,000 STAMPS $2.95
GUARANTEED WORTH OVER $30 AT STANDARD CATALOG PRICES!

Save These Valuable Postage Stamps *NOW* While They Last!

A great opportunity to increase the value of your present collection or to start a new one. Get 1,000 all-different stamps from over 55 countries: U.S.A., British Colonies, Europe, etc; Animals, Space, Olympics, spectacular Old and New Issues included — **Plus big Illustrated Collectors' Catalog — everything to enjoy the World's Most Rewarding Hobby!** Sold to you for only $2.95 for agreeing to look at other sensational stamps from our 10-Day Free Examination Stamps-On-Approval Service. You can return approval stamps with no obligation to buy and cancel Service anytime. But in any case, these 1,000 Stamps and Collectors' Catalog are yours to keep when sending $2.95 NOW!

MONEY BACK IF NOT DELIGHTED!
KENMORE,
Milford OT-452, New Hamp. 03055

WE WISH TO PURCHASE

Since 1923 we have been the purchaser of large holdings of U.S. & Foreign stamps, covers, coins, autographs and historic documents.

When you sell, you want top dollar. We are willing to make offers and will pay cash in currency or transfer of bank funds prior to the removal of any material purchased. We will fly anywhere immediately to view a substantial collection, dealers stock or accumulation. There is no fee involved.

WRITE - WIRE or CALL
1-800-645-3840
NYS Residents 516-354-1001

Our 437th Auction Sale
Now in Preparation.

Catalog Free on Request.

JOHN A. FOX
141 Tulip Avenue,
Floral Park, N.Y. 11001

Circle No. 57 on Reader Service Card

BUYING & SELLING

YES - WE STOCK U.S. MINT AND USED...

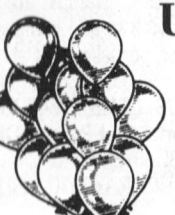

- Singles
- Plate Blocks
- B-O-B
- Booklets
- Possessions

WANT LISTS SOLICITED

RICHARD B. LEWIS
222 S. Easton Road, Glenside, PA 19038
Phone 215-886-1555

We're #1 in Customer Service!

POSTAL HISTORY

POSTAL HISTORY

EACH YEAR WE OFFER ABOUT 50,000 U.S.A. AND WORLDWIDE POSTAL HISTORY COVERS IN BOTH OUR PUBLIC AUCTION SALES AND NET CATALOGS. A SAMPLE CATALOG IS $2, FOREIGN CUSTOMERS AT $3 AND A FOREIGN SUBSCRIPTION IS $25 FOR A MINIMUM OF 10 CATALOGS PER YEAR.

WE WISH TO BUY:
Dealer Stocks, Collections, Individual Rarities, Original Correspondences, Archives, etc. In addition to Postal History we also buy Autographs, Documents, Baseball Cards, Valentines, etc.

KOVER KING, INC. Dept. S
24-16 Queens Plaza South, Long Island City, N.Y. 11101

STAMP STORES

OMEGA STAMP & COIN CO.
Brooklyn's Largest Buys & Sells U.S. & Foreign Coll.
1586 Flatbush Ave., Brooklyn, NY 11210.
718-859-5086

WHEN VISITING CENTRAL FLORIDA BE SURE TO STOP BY.

The Best Stamp/Postal History Inventory in Florida

Michael Rogers
WINTER PARK STAMP SHOP
(4 miles North of Orlando)
340 Park Ave. North,
Winter Park, FL 32789
305-628-1120
Mon. through Sat. 10-6

CZECHOSLOVAKIA

WANT LISTS FILLED
Svatik - Box 53
Ingleside, IL 60041-0053

PHILATELIC SERVICES

JAMES H. CRUM (APS, ASDA, ANS) (Est. 1929)
Thousands of Stamps plus Personal Helpful Advice
2720 E. Gage Ave., Huntington Park, CA 90255.
213-588-4467

PHILATELIC SOCIETIES

AMERICAN PHILATELIC SOCIETY
A Century of Service to 140,000 Stamp Collectors.
Dept. TZ, P.O. Box 8000, State College, PA 16803

UNITED STATES

U.S. EXPERIMENTALS

- Phosphor "Tagged"
- "Hibrite" Papers
- Demonstration Sets
- "Look" 3¢ Coil
- OCR Test Covers
- Testing Dummies
- First Day Covers

1909 Test Stamp $2.50

** "Un-tagged Bureau Precancels **

Professional Philatelist for over Fifty Years

ALFRED "Tag" BOERGER
Box 23822, Ft. Lauderdale, FL 33307

UNITED STATES

BELOW MARKET PRICES!!!
Used, Unused, Most Grades & Price Ranges
U.S.A.

Here is your opportunity to have the older and scarcer stamps of our country at low, reasonable prices. Issues prior to the year 1940 worth anywhere from 25¢ up to several hundred dollars each.

JUST SEND 22¢ POSTAGE for complete price list. Compare for PROOF OF LOWEST PRICES before ordering, and find out what you have missed until you discovered us!!!

LOWELL S. DONALD CO.
Box 728, Rutland, Vermont 05701

UNITED STATES

CLASSIC PHILATELIC GEMS

These and other Classic U.S. Stamps are IN STOCK at all times. If you wish to add items such as this to your collection or portfolio, you should write or phone, and let us know your areas of interest. OUR SPECIALTY: US GEMS, 1845-1869, 1893, 1898, Special Deliveries, and Postage Dues. QUALITY IS OUR ONLY BUSINESS!!!!!!
Members: APS #68359, USPCS RA#2070, ASDA

"Where The Finest
Collections Are Formed..."

J. Randall Rare Stamps
Phone 404-325-5514,
P.O. Box 56-1593
Miami, FL 33256-1593
Circle No. 30 on Reader Service Card

DISPLAY PAGES
Informative booklet with latest net prices and information on Souvenir Pages (Poster Bulletins). Complete listing of all Official, Unofficial and Stationery pages including all known paper, cancellation and printing variations.

LATEST EDITION $1.00 (refundable)

LESLIE ANDERSON
Box 9047   Coral Springs, FL 33075-9047

PLAN NOW TO FEATURE YOUR ADVERTISING MESSAGE IN THE SCOTT 1988 CATALOGUES

Call or write us and we'll place your name on our prospect list to receive full information, as soon as it is available, on advertising rates and copy deadlines.

Scott Publishing Company
P.O. Box 828, Sidney, OH 45365 • Ph. 513-498-0802

INVEST IN THE FUTURE OF YOUR BUSINESS!

ADVERTISERS
GO WITH THE LEADER ...
GROW WITH THE LEADER!

SCOTT STAMP MONTHLY and CATALOGUE UPDATE

If you're looking for new customers, developing a mailing list, building a stamp dealership or looking for new areas of business expansion ... put Scott Stamp Monthly to work for you! Call 513-498-0802 for information, or write for our return-mail response.

SCOTT PUBLISHING COMPANY
P.O. Box 828, Sidney, OH 45365